A DICTIONARY OF SURNAMES

A DICTIONARY OF SURNAMES

Patrick Hanks and Flavia Hodges

Special consultant for Jewish Names:

DAVID L. GOLD

Oxford New York

OXFORD UNIVERSITY PRESS

1988

Oxford University Press, Walton Street, Oxford OX2 6DP

Oxford New York Toronto
Delhi Bombay Calcutta Madras Karachi
Petaling Jaya Singapore Hong Kong Tokyo
Nairobi Dar es Salaam Cape Town
Melbourne Auckland

and associated companies in
Berlin Ibadan

Oxford is a trade mark of Oxford University Press

Published in the United States
by Oxford University Press, (USA)

British Library Cataloging in Publication Data

Hanks, Patrick
A dictionary of surnames.
1. European surnames
I. Title II. Hodges, Flavia
III. Gold, David L.
9.29.4'2'094

ISBN 0–19–211592–8

Library of Congress Cataloging-in-Publication Data

Hanks, Patrick.
A dictionary of surnames / Patrick Hanks and Flavia Hodges;
special consultant for Jewish names, David L. Gold.
Bibliography
1. Names, Personal—Dictionaries. I. Hodges, Flavia. II. Title.
CS2385.H27 988 929.4'2'0321—dc 19 88–21882

ISBN 0–19–211592–8

Printed in Great Britain by
Richard Clay Ltd
Bungay, Suffolk

INTRODUCTION

Scope of the Work

This dictionary is intended as a reference work for surname researchers, genealogists, family historians, local historians, social historians, historical linguists, comparative linguists, demographers, and other readers, in all parts of the world where European surnames are of interest. It contains entries for most major surnames of European origin, as well as for many rarer ones. For purposes of this dictionary, a surname is defined as a hereditary name borne by the members of a single family and handed down from father to son. Thus, surnames contrast with given names, which pick out individuals within the same family. There are of course unrelated families bearing the same surname, but it is nevertheless a characteristic of surnames that all members of a particular family normally have the same surname. There are also a few cases in which a surname is inherited from the mother, but again, the norm is patrilineal descent.

Surnames in the United States, Canada, Australia, and other English-speaking countries come from all parts of Continental Europe, as well as from Britain. Although the surnames of the British Isles are the primary focus of this dictionary, they are not its exclusive focus. On the world scene, British surnames constitute only a fraction of the surnames borne by English speakers.

European surnames are remarkably homogeneous. With few exceptions, the communities of Europe have similar social structures, similar social histories, and similar social attitudes. With the exception of Finnish, Estonian, Hungarian, Basque, and a few minor languages, the languages of Europe are cognate. In many parts of central and Western Europe, hereditary surnames began to become fixed at around the same time (i.e. from the 12th century onwards), and have developed and changed slowly over the years, down to the present day. Usually the earlier naming system supplanted or supplemented by a surname system was patronymic—that is, it was one in which the bearer of a particular given name was distinguished from other bearers of the same given name by identification of his father, and on occasion of his father's father, and even of a third, fourth, and fifth generation. In addition, the bearer of a given name was sometimes distinguished from others by reference to a locality—the one in which he lived or from which he originated. Both patronymics and local names have been major sources of surnames.

Absence of linguistic homogeneity in Europe has been no bar to cultural homogeneity. So, for example, even though the Hungarian language is unrelated to the languages which surround it, Hungarian culture (including Hungarian naming practice) has been strongly influenced by the surrounding cultures of central and Eastern Europe. In the far north of Europe, we can observe that Finnish surnames have social characteristics in common with other Scandinavian surnames—for example, late formation, and in many cases arbitrary or ornamental reasons for adoption. These are characteristics shared by many Ashkenazic surnames (the Jewish surnames of central and Eastern Europe), most of which are likewise of late formation: the continuing use of patronymics was one of the features marking out the Jewish communities as culturally distinct from their neighbours, until the intervention of bureaucracy in the eighteenth and nineteenth centuries forced the adoption of hereditary surnames.

Lexicographers are much concerned with inventorizing their subject, and we are no exception. We were determined to take an international view of surnames in the English-speaking world, but of course it would call for a work many times the size of the present one and far more resources than we had at our disposal to attempt to account for *every* known surname in the English-speaking world, let alone every surname in Europe. Selection was clearly called for: the question was, how to achieve a balanced selection on rational principles. The entries in some earlier surnames dictionaries seemed to us to have been more or less randomly selected, leaving many common surnames unexplained and unrecorded. The entries in the present work are selected on two separate but overlapping principles: frequency and informativeness. The surnames of all the countries of Europe, together with those found elsewhere in the English-speaking world, have been systematically sampled. Where we found a really common surname, we generally included an entry for it in the dictionary, even if we could say no more about it than that it exists in a particular country or region. But for the majority of common, everyday surnames, a great deal of information is available, and our task has been to evaluate and present sensibly rather than to originate. Our second principle, informativeness, meant that where we had reasonably reliable information available to us about a name, we decided to include it, even though the name itself might be quite rare. Many of these entries for less common names are based on information kindly supplied to us by one-name researchers and genealogists (see Acknowledgements). Thus, the dictionary consists of a mixture of common names, which are included whether or not their origin is known, and uncommon names about which useful information can be offered.

Reluctantly, it was decided not to attempt to deal with the comparatively recent advent of surnames derived from other naming traditions—in particular, those of India, Pakistan, China, and Japan—even though such names are found with ever-increasing frequency in English-speaking countries. Perhaps in a future edition it will be possible to tackle these names too, and show how different systems of nomenclature from different cultures have been transmuted into 20th-century surnames.

The form of each name selected for entry gave cause for thought. Eventually it was decided that it would be more useful to explain surnames in their original, European forms than to concentrate on the Anglicizations to which they have given rise. In the case of Russian, Belorussian, and Ukrainian, where questions of transliteration arise, we have as a general rule followed the transcriptions of Unbegaun, which approximate closely to the forms in which Russian surnames are normally Anglicized by emigrés themselves, and which are not overloaded with pedantic detail. In the case of those Jewish (Ashkenazic) surnames that are derived from Russian, the spellings cited are always those that are actually in use among English speakers, without any concern about issues of transliteration. Transliterations from Bulgarian are based on those of Holman and his colleagues, although some of the minor modifications that they have introduced into their transcription system reached us too late to influence this edition of the dictionary.

As a general rule, all the spellings of each name that are known to be in common use are listed in the dictionary, either as main entries or as variants or derivatives. There is an alphabetical index of names at the end of the work, and the reader is advised always to consult this first, since spelling variation may occur at the beginning of a name. Thus, for example, *Acket* is dealt with as a variant of *Hackett* and *Adar* as a variant of *Oder*.

The Origins of Surnames

Of the parameters mentioned above, the time plane shows greatest variation. It would be wrong to imply, as some writers do, that 'the surname period' in each culture had a fixed beginning and end. The acquisition of surnames in Europe during the past eight hundred years has been affected by many factors, including social class and social structure, naming practices in neighbouring cultures, and indigenous cultural tradition. On the whole, the richer and more powerful classes tended to acquire surnames earlier than the working classes and the poor, while surnames were quicker to catch on in urban areas than in more sparsely populated rural areas. These facts suggest that the origin of surnames is associated with the emergence of bureaucracies. As long as land tenure, military service, and fealty were matters of direct relationship between a lord and his vassals, the need did not arise for fixed distinguishing epithets to mark out one carl from another. But as societies became more complex, and as such matters as the management of tenure and in particular the collection of taxes were delegated to special functionaries, it became imperative to have a more complex system of nomenclature to distinguish one individual from another reliably and unambiguously.

Even after hereditary surnames were adopted, there was considerable variation. Hereditary surnames tended to coexist with more or less noticeable vestiges of patronymic systems. A child would know not only his surname, derived from his father, but also his lineage. Choice of the masculine possessive in the preceding sentence ('*his* father', '*his* lineage') is a reminder that in European cultures surnames have mostly been handed down from father to son, with women adopting the surname of the husband on marriage. The notion of free choice between adopting the mother's or the father's surname is a recent phenomenon, although it is now enshrined in the law in Denmark.

The bulk of European surnames in countries such as England and France were formed in the 13th and 14th centuries. The process started earlier and continued in some places into the 19th century, but the norm is that in the 11th century people did not have surnames, whereas by the 15th century they did.

In Ireland, surnames developed naturally out of a more ancient system of clan and sept names. These were themselves originally patronymic, but stretched back over a thousand years, so that by the 12th century a 'son of Murchadha' in Ireland could be many generations removed from the original bearer of the given name Murchadha. This system could in fact be regarded as an early version of a system of surnames. It was gradually incorporated into the system that was introduced into Ireland by the Normans and, later, the English. (In these circumstances it may seem somewhat surprising that Welsh surnames should be typically late in formation, in view of the fact that the neighbouring English have had surnames for some seven or eight centuries and that the surname tradition in the related Gaelic language goes back even further than it does in English. Explanation may be sought in differences of social organization between early Welsh and early Gaelic society.)

At the other end of the time scale lies Scandinavia, the region that has been the last to abandon patronymics in favour of hereditary surnames. Surnaming crept northwards from Germany through Denmark and into Norway (which was for much of its history administratively part of Denmark) in the 15th and 16th centuries. In Iceland, the traditional patronymic naming system has still not fully given way to hereditary surnames. Magnus Pálsson is Magnus the son of Pál, and his eldest son may well be called Pál Magnusson, preserving a traditional alternation that in some families goes back over a thousand years. His daughter would be called, for example, Gudrun Magnusdottir. Since this is a dictionary of surnames, not a study of naming practices, this is tantamount to saying that Icelandic names have no more place in this book than the names of the Arab world or Africa. The patronymic naming system still found in Iceland was common throughout Scandinavia until about two hundred years ago, and Swedish family histories still contain anecdotes about the incredulity and derision met by women who first called themselves Anna Andersson rather than Anna Andersdotter.

Over the centuries, most people in Europe have accepted their surname as a fact of life, as irrevocable as an act of God, however much the individual may dislike the name or even suffer ridicule as a result of unpleasant connotations associated with it. Sometimes these unpleasant connotations are of more recent origin than the surname. The surname *Daft*, for example, thrives in England, being characteristic of Leicestershire. The vocabulary word originally meant 'submissive', 'humble', or 'gentle', rather than 'stupid', and it is an open question with what force the nickname was applied at the time when it became established as a surname. What is undeniable is that generations of Dafts have borne the name uncomplainingly, if not proudly, undeterred by the taunts of schoolfellows and workmates. They have not sought to change the surname by deed poll, the mechanism in Britain for registering a change of surname. Mechanisms exist in most countries for official alteration of one's surname, but they are employed quite rarely in Europe. Alteration by personal choice is a much more common phenomenon in America, where each year many thousands of Americans choose to change their surname officially. A more common source of variation is in fact *involuntary* official change, in other words, clerical error.

Among the humbler classes of European society, and especially among illiterate people, individuals were willing to accept the mistakes of officials, clerks, and priests as officially bestowing a new version of their surname, just as they had meekly accepted the surname they were born with. In North America, the linguistic problems confronting immigration officials at Ellis Island in the 19th century were legendary as a prolific source of Anglicization. In the United States, according to Mencken, such processes of official and accidental change caused *Bauch* to become *Baugh*, *Micsza* to become *McShea*, *Siminowicz* to become *Simmons*, and so on. Many immigrants deliberately Anglicized or translated their surnames on arrival in the New World, so that *Mlynář* became *Miller*, and *Schwarz* became *Black*. These examples illustrate three of the main strands in Anglicization: phonetic assimilation to an unrelated name, phonetic assimilation to a cognate existing name or word, and straightforward translation of the vocabulary element, with no phonetic influences. A further feature is arbitrary adoption of an existing American name, with little or no apparent connection with the original name, as when *Chiariglione* became *Flynn* or when *Fischbein* became *Sullivan*. Mencken gives many examples: his chapter on proper names is still the most informative concise account of the Anglicization of surnames in America, though it is not always possible to check his sources, which are mostly anecdotal. In this dictionary, we have not attempted to deal systematically with the vast field of Anglicization, although it has been mentioned where the information was at hand.

Organization of Entries

The names in the dictionary are listed in 'nested' groups under a main entry. Where there are several names in a group, the choice of main entry is made on a variety of criteria such as comparative present-day frequency, historical priority, and etymological simplicity. Simple forms, that is, those having no overt diminutive, patronymic, or other morphemes, are usually preferred as main entries, and within each main entry the nested groups consist of variants, cognates in other languages, diminutives, patronymics, and so on, subdivided according to language. The spelling selected for the main entry is normally the one that is most common now as a surname. Other spellings of what is basically the same name are listed as variants. Preference has been given to English names when selecting a form for the main entry. Where there is no English name in a group, or where the English members of the group are comparatively rare, the main entry form is from one of the other languages of Europe, generally the one in which the name is most prominent.

In several cases, non-cognate equivalents, derived from words in other languages with similar meanings but of different derivation, are listed under an English heading. For example, at *Carpenter*, reference is made to German *Zimmermann*, Polish *Cieślak*, Russian *Plotnik*, and Hungarian *Ács*. This information is important because it sheds light on a frequent source of Anglicization among immigrants to English-speaking countries. It has not been possible to list these equivalents exhaustively, but they have been given for the main occupational names. Nicknames are more difficult, and require further study to elucidate the actual processes of Anglicization.

Each entry explains the linguistic origins of each surname, together with peculiarities of its history, current distribution, and other relevant facts. In many cases, more than one origin is postulated. There is a tendency for uncommon surnames to assimilate to more common ones, which partly underlies the phenomenon of multiple origin.

Selection of Entries

A little more should be said about how the entries were selected.

Preliminary studies had yielded some fascinating comparisons of the different surname forms in different languages derived from biblical personal names. In the absence of any other comparative dictionary, we decided to pursue the task systematically. Our first step was to survey the published literature on surnames throughout Europe, and to write some draft entries. We then spot-checked our draft text against an international survey of telephone directories. This was necessary because surnames study is a remarkably neglected field. There are some excellent studies of individual names, often from a genealogical rather than a linguistic point of view, and usually done by dedicated amateurs, few of whom have a linguistic training. Systematic surveys are rare. In few countries is there any substantial literature on surnames, and in some the names that have been researched are not necessarily those that are actually borne by large numbers of families. For an inventory of common surnames, the most convenient tool is the telephone directory. To establish an entry list, then, we first looked at the telephone directories of London, Edinburgh, Cardiff, Dublin, New York (Manhattan), Chicago, Cleveland Ohio, Los Angeles, Toronto, Vancouver, Sydney, and Melbourne, noting names with a frequency of over 50 subscribers. In the case of London, Edinburgh, Cardiff, and Dublin, we noted any name with a frequency of over 20 subscribers. For Britain, the 1978 issues were used; for other countries, 1980–2 issues. We were also fortunate in obtaining from British Telecom a listing of names with a frequency of over 174 subscribers in any one region, which provided a useful first check on frequent names outside the capital cities. This formed the basis of our list of items needing to be explained. Even given the weighting in favour of the British Isles, it was immediately clear that a large number of non-English names would call for explanation. Moreover, it is also well known that some ostensibly simple 'English' names such as *Begley* and *Terry* are not what they might appear to be.

For each country of Europe, then, we started by reviewing the existing literature on surnames. In so far as this proved adequate for our purposes, we drew on it to produce a summary of known facts about the common surnames in that country. Our initial spot-checks suggested that for Italy, Germany, and Russia there already exist adequate accounts of the common present-day surnames among those national and cultural groups. The work of de Felice on Italian surnames calls for special mention. It was supported by SEAT, the Italian telephone organization, and is computerized and systematic. The books which represent the fruits of his research are not only scholarly but also readable and well-informed. If every country in Europe possessed a study of its surnames as thorough as that of de Felice, the present work would be superfluous.

Unfortunately, the Italian case is the exception rather than the rule. In many of the countries of Europe, there is hardly any literature at all on surnames, and the information provided by what does exist is often very limited and sometimes of doubtful reliability. We therefore went on to compile an inventory of the common present-day surnames in French, Spanish, Catalan, Basque, Portuguese, Dutch, Danish, Swedish, Czech, and Polish, by examining the telephone directories for Paris, Madrid, Barcelona, Bilbao, Lisbon, Amsterdam, Copenhagen, Stockholm, Prague, and Łódź.

Next, we turned again to surnames in the British Isles, and decided to survey regional distribution in more detail. We took eight English regional directories for more detailed study: (from south-west to north) Plymouth (including Cornwall), Bristol, West Midlands, Nottingham, Norwich, Leeds, Preston (Lancs.), and Tyneside. To these we added the directories for Northern Ireland, and Ireland outside Dublin. Scotland was already represented by Edinburgh in the international survey. We knew that although individuals move around, surnames (statistically) are more stable. That is, more often than not the centre of greatest frequency of a surname is its place of origin, or is geographically very close by. At the very least, its distributional centre will normally be a place where the surname has been long established, and this fact alone is of importance to family historians. We wanted to study this aspect in more depth and, with this in mind, selected names with a frequency of greater than 20 listed subscribers in the regional directories mentioned above. We used our previous listings for London as a control. Our main interest in this part of our task was in the distribution of names that are, proportionally, more frequent outside London than in the capital.

Where a particular regional bias was evident, we tried to discover its centre of distribution by checking the name in question against directories for neighbouring regions to those actually surveyed, against earlier geographical studies such as that of Guppy, and indeed against the locations of early forms cited by Reaney and other writers. Where appropriate, we added brief comments on regional distribution, eliminated hypotheses that were incompatible with patterns of distribution, and began to seek explanations for names that were evidently habitational in form, but for which we had not found a source. In this latter task, Dr Margaret Gelling's encyclopedic knowledge of English placenames and of the work of the English Place-Name Society was invaluable: again and again she pointed out to us minor places, often as small as a farm, a field, or a lost hamlet, as probable sources of present-day surnames. An example is *Blakeway*, a surname found most commonly in the West Midlands and Shropshire. This is probably derived from Blakeway Farm near Much Wenlock, and is entered in the dictionary as such. In an ideal world, evidence from family-history research would always be available to confirm or disconfirm such hypotheses. We hope that people with such evidence for any name, evidence which will confirm, correct, or supplement the statements made in this dictionary, will write to the publisher.

Distribution of Surnames

In Britain and Continental Europe, few surnames are evenly distributed throughout the countries in which they occur. Some are characteristic of particular regions, while others are concentrated in quite small villages. Brett has shown how the surnames *Walker*, *Fuller*, and *Tucker* have a complementary distribution consequent on differences of the vocabulary word for this occupational term in the medieval cloth trade. He has also shown that even the commonest of English surnames, *Smith*, has interesting peculiarities of distribution. As an example of the distribution of less common surnames, we may mention *Hanks*. This is found randomly scattered in many different parts of England, but is concentrated in the village of Naunton in Gloucestershire, in which vicinity it has been established for some four hundred years.

Typical patterns of distribution may be illustrated by considering the case of Cornish surnames. Some Cornish surnames have migrated directly abroad, for example to the United States. Others have scattered more or less randomly throughout the rest of England. A few Cornish surnames which survive elsewhere have died out completely in Cornwall, but these are not and never have been common. The statistically interesting fact is that there are no large concentrations of Cornish surnames outside Cornwall that are not matched by even larger concentrations of Cornish surnames within Cornwall. Thus, there are 14 subscribers named *Tregear* in the London telephone directory; these are matched by 18 in Cornwall itself. A Tregear family history would perhaps tell us when the first Tregears moved to London and why. Given their comparative frequency in London, it is likely that the first move took place quite a long time ago—centuries ago rather than decades—and that most of the London Tregears are descended from a common ancestor. It is most unlikely that 14 separate Tregear families moved to London independently and recently.

Large cities such as London, Birmingham, Manchester, and Liverpool have had a distorting effect on the distribution of surnames, in that they attained their present size by attracting large numbers of immigrants from surrounding and even distant regions. However, a clustering of identical surnames in a particular place, even in a large city, indicates either that the surname is polygenetic (see below) or that it has been established there for a long time. The distribution patterns of monogenetic surnames, of which *Tregear* is almost certainly an example, are of particular interest. Surname distribution has been used as a basis for study of the genetic structure of human populations by geneticists such as Lasker. Lasker and his associates give distribution maps for a few selected English surnames, based on marriage records for the first quarter of 1975. They compare these statistics with Guppy's comments of 1890, and find that they correlate remarkably closely. Others have drawn distribution maps based on analysis of telephone directories: Brett has developed a computer program that will automatically draw such a map for any English surname from an input of telephone-directory data. Unfortunately, at present such data has to be collected from the directories clerically rather than automatically. Such maps are of the greatest interest to students of surnames. They can, for example, show where a surname is most strongly established and whether it has a single origin or multiple origin.

If the distribution pattern for Cornish surnames such as *Tregear* is skewed as stated here—and in fact the distribution of other names is even more skewed towards Cornwall, *Tregear* being exceptional in the high proportion of its bearers who are found in London—then why should we believe that, say, Yorkshire surnames or indeed Dutch or Czech surnames are any different? If a surname is common abroad, then it is probably even more common at home: the task is to find out where 'home' is. (Matters may be different in countries such as Poland and Germany, where the Second World War brought terrible upheavals and displacements of whole populations. Comparison of pre- and post-War distribution in these countries would no doubt shed light on the currents and cross-currents that were at work during resettlement in post-War Europe.)

In his study of West Yorkshire surnames, Redmonds shows how the surname *Armitage* originated in the parish of Almondbury, near Huddersfield, and spread out over the centuries from there. It is now widely distributed: there are, for example, nearly a hundred telephone subscribers in London called *Armitage*. Nevertheless, it is still a characteristically West Yorkshire surname, with ten times as many subscribers in Leeds and Bradford as in London.

If we now consider the case of a city such as Cleveland, Ohio, we find that the pattern of distribution of surnames in its telephone directory is rather different from those in any English regional directory. There are many thousands of different surnames in Cleveland, of an enormous variety of linguistic origins. (It is sometimes claimed that Cleveland is the most cosmopolitan city in the United States.) If we look at the common names in Cleveland, we find that the vast majority of them are of Anglo-Saxon etymology. This does not mean that the population of Cleveland is of predominantly Anglo-Saxon stock: rather, it means that processes of linguistic assimilation have been hard at work. The common surnames in Cleveland are almost certainly all polygenetic, and they are of a type that will have attracted assimilation from many non-Anglo-Saxon names. So, for example, *Adams*, which is the surname of nearly 700 subscribers in Cleveland, has probably assimilated many surnames from other linguistic stocks, based on the same biblical root. A glance at the surrounding columns of the telephone directory suggests the following candidates among others: *Adamcek*, *Adamcik*, *Adamczak*, *Adamczek*, *Adamczyk*, *Adamec*, *Adamek*, *Adamescu*, *Adametz*, *Adamic*, *Adamich*, *Adamik*, *Adamitis*, *Adamo*, *Adamonis*, *Adamopoulos*, *Adamos*, *Adamowski*, *Adamov*, *Adamovich*, *Adamovsky*, *Adamowicz*, *Adamski*, and *Adamus*. A really common surname such as *Brown* has surely assimilated many cases of German *Braun* and hundreds of surnames from other languages with similar meanings, as well as some, no doubt, that were totally unrelated.

Out of the 420,000 telephone subscribers in Cleveland, only 24 per cent have surnames with a frequency greater than 100, and there are only around 400 such surnames in Cleveland. By contrast, the telephone directory for Plymouth, England (which covers all of Cornwall as well as the city of Plymouth) is less than half the size, with 192,000 subscribers. There are some 640 surnames with a frequency greater than 50 (the equivalent of Cleveland's 100, given the difference in size of the two directories). These account for very nearly 40 per cent of the subscribers in Plymouth and Cornwall, and quite a large number of these common Cornish names are of monogenetic origin, such as *Polkinghorne* or *Trethowan*.

In spite of our efforts to associate local names with their places of origin, it must be acknowledged that this dictionary contains entries for some quite common surnames, apparently habitational in form, that remain unexplained. These stand as a challenge to future researchers.

The regional survey was more fruitful than we had dared to hope. Resources did not permit us to cover every directory in the British Isles, especially since the source material was not available in machine-readable form for computer processing, and so had to be collected clerically. The survey continues steadily, and already clerical work has been completed on directories for Colchester, Oxford, Canterbury, and Southampton: information from these directories will be incorporated into the survey, and will contribute to future editions of the dictionary. A more distant aim is to set up systematic computerized procedures for checking current distribution throughout the British Isles against distribution in earlier centuries. If this can be done systematically for Britain, no doubt it can be done for other places, and an even longer-term aim is to extend the survey to other countries, taking account where necessary of recent and not-so-recent political and other upheavals.

The Explanations

Armed with lists of common surnames and a growing understanding of their distribution, we went back to our draft texts and wrote many thousands of new entries. Generally, any name with a frequency of more than 50 subscribers in any of the directories surveyed was given an entry in our dictionary, even if its origin could be explained only tentatively, or indeed if nothing at all could be said about it beyond recording its existence in a particular community. We prefer to record the existence of a common surname, and admit that we do not know its origin, than to pretend that it does not exist. Perhaps such entries will serve as a stimulus to genealogists and one-name researchers. If so, future editions of the present work will be able to be more informative on these names.

In addition, many entries for less common names found in the surveys were included in the dictionary, but usually only where we felt able to give a reasonably reliable explanation or to state with some certainty that all reasonable efforts to discover an origin had been made and had proved fruitless. Accounts of the origins of many individual surnames, in the present state of our knowledge, contain an element of tentativeness; some are more tentative than others. We have not been afraid to speculate, using words like 'probably' and 'possibly', knowing that more detailed research may yet prove our speculation wrong. Surnames research is still in its infancy. Even though surnames are generally of much more recent origin than placenames, certainty is a rarer phenomenon in surnames studies. The student of placenames can, in cases of doubt, go to a place and inspect the lie of the land before deciding on the most probable elements of which the name is composed. But the surnames reseacher cannot go and inspect the original bearer of a surname to decide whether he was dark or fair (see *Blake*), or had a father called *Gerald* or *Gerard* (see *Garrett*).

The international survey prompted other decisions. In some cases the common present-day spelling of a surname was chosen as the main entry, in preference to a less common one preferred on etymological grounds by other authors. In other cases we did more research, in order to try to account for apparent discrepancies between present distribution and supposed origin. In other cases we consulted expert colleagues and advisers for further information; in still others we found we could do no more than record a doubt.

The sample surveys and checklists that form the basis of selection of entries for the present dictionary represent no more than a first modest step in the direction of what could be done. With computer technology, it would be comparatively simple to survey all the directories of a given country or region, and to define much more closely the centres of distribution of each surname. This would not, of course, yield any explanations; rather, it would give us some hard facts requiring explanation. One cannot claim that such-and-such a name is a Devonshire surname or a Kentish surname until one has surveyed all the other counties of the British Isles to ensure that it is not more frequent elsewhere.

After we had surveyed the telephone directories selected and compiled a checklist, our next priority was to provide some etymological explanations and to decide how to arrange the information. Our overall aim has been to group related entries together, and as far as possible to take a name back historically through all the vicissitudes of naming, borrowing, and renaming, until finally a vocabulary word is reached, and then to give some information about the meaning, origin, and cognates of that vocabulary word. Sometimes our journey is a short one, as in the case of the surname *Short*, which is derived from the English vocabulary word *short*, which means and has always meant 'short in stature'.

Often, however, the journey is long and fascinating. The huge clusters of common surnames in every language of Europe derived from biblical names and from the names of early Christian evangelists and saints take us back to Hebrew, Aramaic, Greek, and Latin, as well as to ancient Irish. Sometimes, we travel with early missionaries, and see how their influence has dominated the naming practices of other parts of Europe, as may easily be seen from a glance at such entries as *Coleman* 1, *Gall* 2, and *Vojtěch* and their lists of cognate and derivative surnames. In other cases, we reach back to and beyond the earliest records in Germanic languages, perceiving cognate relationships among forms not only in English, Dutch, and German, but also in non-Germanic languages such as French, Italian, and Spanish, and even Polish, Czech, and Hungarian for long-established European 'noble' names such as *Richard* and *William*.

Useful information was sometimes available from family-history research, but this generally peters out long before the researcher gets back to the actual point of origin of the surname. An ideal, but (alas) exceptional case is that of *Jewisson*, listed at *Julian*, where the original bearer, Juetta des Arches, of the eponymous personal name has actually been tentatively identified. Such cases are exceptional, and even so the identification cannot be more than tentative. More commonly, several dark and tantalizing centuries lie between the earliest recorded occurrences of a surname (or more precisely, of forms that can be tentatively identified with a modern surname) and the earliest bearers traced by family historians. For surname researchers, this remains a potentially fruitful area for exploration. In this book, genealogical notes are appended to some entries: these are no more than a first step in this direction, and no attempt has been made to be systematic. Many of the genealogical notes are derived from information kindly supplied by genealogists and one-name researchers (see Acknowledgements). Those whose chief interest is genealogy will no doubt consult some of the innumerable works of local and national genealogy or will join their local genealogical societies, or will start by consulting an international register such as the *Genealogical Research Directory* compiled and published each year by Keith A. Johnson and Malcolm R. Santy. The present work is not concerned primarily with genealogy or family history: it is a dictionary, and as such is concerned with surnames as a linguistic and cultural phenomenon.

Evidence and Interpretation

It is sometimes said that collection of the earliest forms is an essential component of the study of surnames. This is something of an overstatement. Surnames are generally of more recent origin than placenames. The great changes which English underwent in the Middle English period, long after most placenames were coined, has rendered the etymology of most English placenames opaque. Continental placenames show in some cases traces of a language that is no longer spoken in the region where they occur. By contrast, the etymology of many surnames is transparent, as in the case of such common surnames as *Wright*, *Miller*, *Baker*, and *Smith*. Only a little more knowledge is required to establish that *Webster* was an occupational name for a weaver, Middle English *webbe* being another word for a weaver, while *-ster* is a common agent noun suffix (it was originally feminine in meaning, but by the Middle English period was no more than a variant of *-er*). Similarly, *Baxter* is derived from the verb 'to bake', with the same suffix, and so is a doublet of *Baker*. In such cases, an account of the relative importance of these medieval occupations will shed more light on the surname than a collection of early spellings. In other cases, such as *Mallory*, only detailed family-history research can even hope to disentangle early members of this family from those bearing similar but unrelated surnames, and so tentatively identify the origin of the name.

Sometimes the older forms of a placename can help to identify the origin of a surname. So, for example, the surnames *Stopford*, *Stopforth*, *Stoppard*, and *Stopper* are all derived from *Stopford*, which is an older form of *Stockport* in Greater Manchester.

No special skill is called for to observe that the surname *Milton* is derived from a place called *Milton*. On the other hand, knowledge beyond the scope of the onomastician or the lexicographer is called for to say which of the thirty-odd places in Britain called Milton is the source of the surname for any particular present-day family. It is the task of the family historian to associate particular families with particular places. What the onomastician can observe is that the surname is and has long been widely distributed: many (if not all) of the places called *Milton* appear to have given rise to surnames. Occasionally it is possible to suggest that one rather than another placename is the source of the surname. Thus, although there are five places that are possible sources of the surname *Steventon*, the distribution pattern makes the one in Shropshire the best candidate.

Similar phenomena may be observed on the international scene. For example, it requires no more than a knowledge of the Polish or Czech languages to identify the surname *Ryba* with the vocabulary word *ryba* 'fish'. But to say whether a given family bears the Polish or the Czech surname is, again, a matter for the family historian. The dictionary can only note that both exist.

TYPOLOGY OF SURNAMES

Monogenetic and Polygenetic

How many different types of surname are there? One important distinction already mentioned is between *monogenetic* surnames and *polygenetic* surnames. Monogenetic surnames are those which have a single origin, often being derived from just one original bearer or family of bearers at one particular place and time. Most polygenetic surnames were coined independently in many different places. *Smith*, *Brown*, and *Newton* are classic examples of English polygenetic surnames.

It is not normally possible to identify the original bearer of a monogenetic surname, but it is sometimes possible to postulate that a name must be monogenetic on the basis of its distribution. Thus *Asquith* and *Auty*, the one a local name and the other from a Norse personal name, are both so strongly identified with West Yorkshire that the chances of their being monogenetic must be rated very high. However, whether present-day bearers of the surname *Asquith* are all descended from a single individual, or whether there are several lines stretching back to different individuals all from the village of *Askwith*, is another matter for family-history research rather than for a dictionary of surnames, and it may well be that, as in many questions arising about surnames, not enough evidence survives to give a definitive answer. However, it is also certainly the case that much evidence remains to be discovered and evaluated.

Classification by Type of Origin

Broadly, surnames are conventionally divided into a small number of types according to their origin. Cottle distinguishes just four broad types: those based on patronymics, those derived from local names, those from occupational names, and those from nicknames. We use a fuller classification, but Cottle's four types can be clearly seen underlying them.

Patronymic Surnames

The oldest and most pervasive type of surname is that derived from a given name. Two main strands in the origins of given names may be singled out: vernacular naming traditions and religious naming traditions. In vernacular naming traditions, names were originally composed of vocabulary elements in the local language, and no doubt bestowed for their auspicious connotations (e.g. *Raymond* is derived from elements meaning 'counsel' and 'protection'). In religious naming traditions, names were bestowed in honour of a cult figure. Leaving aside for the moment Jewish naming traditions, it is obvious that the most powerful religious influence on naming in Europe has been the Christian Church. There is hardly a country in Europe that does not have surnames derived from forms of *Peter*, *Paul*, and the other saints, apostles, and missionaries. It comes as something of a surprise, therefore, to note that in many countries, especially in northern Europe, baptismal names honouring Christian saints and biblical figures were a fairly recent introduction at the time when the bulk of surnames were taking shape. These Christian names were in competition with the older and better-established vernacular naming traditions, for example the Germanic names in use at the time of Charlemagne (742–814).

Surnames derived from ancient Germanic personal names have cognates in many languages. The court of Charlemagne was Christian and Latin-speaking, but the vernacular was the Frankish dialect of Old High German, and the personal names in use were Germanic and vernacular. These personal names were adopted in many parts of northwest Europe, especially among the ruling classes. They were in use among the Normans; hence, many common English and French names such as *Richard*, *Robert*, and

William (*Guillaume*) are of Germanic origin and have cognates in other European languages.

Some Germanic personal names such as *Siegfried* also have Slavonic derivatives, but on the whole the Slavs had their own inventory of personal names. In western Slavonic-speaking areas (in particular, in Poland and Czechoslovakia), native Slavonic names have given rise to surnames. In Russia, on the other hand, vernacular Slavonic names were proscribed as given names by the Orthodox Church in favour of those honouring Christian saints. For this reason, Russian patronymic surnames are mostly derived from saints' names rather than vernacular Slavonic names.

The most basic type of surname derived from a patronymic—that is, from a person's father's given name—simply presents the father's name as a distinguishing epithet placed either before (as in the case of Hungarian) or more usually after the bearer's own given name. Surnames of this type are found in almost all European languages, but in most of them they are rather, or considerably, less common than names formed with explicitly patronymic endings.

The range of affixes which have been utilized with a patronymic function is very wide. Some are prefixes (Gaelic *mac*, Welsh *ap*, *ab*, Norman French *fitz*, Italian *fi-*), but more are suffixes. These were for the most part originally adjectival or possessive in function (English *-s*, North German *-ing* and *-er*, Rumanian *-esco*, Russian *-ov*), or else result from a more or less reduced form of a phrase meaning 'son of' (English *-son*, Danish/Norwegian *-sen*, Swedish *-son*).

In such cases the surname was almost always originally patronymic in function, although the reference seems occasionally to have been to a grandfather or more distant relative, and in some early examples women are known to have acquired the given name of their husbands as a distinguishing epithet: it may be that some hereditary surnames are derived from this use.

In this category also belong surnames that are derived from shortened or familiar forms of given names, pet forms, and forms with diminutive suffixes. In the Middle Ages such forms were in common use, often almost to the exclusion of the official baptismal form, hence the frequency of such common English surnames as *Hobson* and *Dobson*, based on popular forms of the baptismal name *Robert*, or the equally common North and central European derivatives of *Hans*, a German pet form of *Johannes* John, or the great profusion of Italian surnames derivied from diminutive forms of given names.

Metronymic Surnames

Much less common than patronymics, with no more than a handful of surviving examples in the majority of European languages, are metronymics, derived from the name of the first bearer's mother. Since European society has been patriarchal throughout the historical period, it has naturally been the given name of the male head of the household that has been handed on as a distinguishing name to successive generations of sons (and daughters, until their marriage). The few exceptions (e.g. *Catling*, *Marguerite*, *Dyott*) seem to be derived from the names of women who were either widows for the greater part of their adult lives, or else heiresses in their own right. Because such instances are so rare in medieval records, it has been possible in a few cases to pinpoint the individual whose given name has been preserved in this way (see *Jewisson* at *Julian*).

However, Jewish naming practice differs from that of the rest of Europe in this respect, since metronymics are far from uncommon among Ashkenazim (see e.g. *Dvorkin*, *Sorkin*, *Rifkind*, *Reises*). There are several probable reasons for this, which cannot at present be ranked in importance due to the lack of statistical data: (a) before, during, and after the surname period, Ashkenazic Jews have frequently used nicknames, many of them consisting of a parent's given name plus Yiddish possessive *-s*; many of the nicknames containing the mother's given name presumably gave rise to metronymic family names; (b) in other cases, these nicknames consist of the spouse's given name plus Yiddish possessive *-s*, hence men could have taken these nicknames as family names; (c) it is probable that children of deserted mothers (or widows) took family names based on the mother's given name. In connection with (b), we may note a class of surnames which seems to exist only among Ashkenazic Jews (and no other Jews or non-Jews), indicating explicitly the husband of the woman named, for example *Esterman* ('Esther' + 'husband'). In other cases, we cannot tell whether Ashkenazic family names belong in this category or not: *Roseman(n)*, for instance, might be one of these names (cf. the Yiddish female given name *Royze* Rose) or it might be merely an ornamental name. *Perlman* is even more complicated: it could be one of these names (cf. the Yiddish female given name *Perl* Pearl); it might be an ornamental name; or it might indicate someone who dealt in pearls (though this last possibility is the least likely because the relative high frequency of the name clashes with the small number of Ashkenazic Jews who dealt in pearls).

Other Derivatives of Given Names

A few surnames in various languages illustrate some other relationship between the first bearer of the surname and the bearer of a given name incorporated in it: employment (e.g. *Bateman*), connection by marriage (e.g. *Watmough*), or residence in the same dwelling (e.g. *Anttila*).

Surnames from Kin Terms

A small group of surnames, but with representatives in most European languages, identifies the bearer by his family relationship (e.g. *Oade*, *Neame*, *Ayer*), presumably to some well-known local figure, simply by mentioning the kinship term.

Local Names

Surnames derived from placenames may be divided into two broad categories: *topographic* names and *habitation* names. These terms have been used throughout this work in preference to the traditional but vaguer term 'local name'. Topographic names are derived from general descriptive references to someone who lived near a physical feature such as an oak tree, a hill, a stream, or a church. Habitation names are derived from preexisting names denoting towns, villages, farmsteads, or other named habitations. Other classes of local names include those derived from the names of rivers, individual houses with signs on them, regions, and whole countries. As a general rule, the further someone had travelled from his place of origin, the broader the designation. Someone who stayed at home might be known by the name of his farm or locality in the parish; someone who moved to another town might be known by the name of his village; while someone who moved to another county could acquire the name of the county or region from which he originated.

Habitation Names

It is sometimes difficult, especially in the case of multiple-element names (in England usually a defining adjective plus a generic noun), to be precise about whether a surname is derived from an identifying topographic phrase such as '(at) the broad ford' or '(by) the red hill' or from an established placename such as *Bradford* or *Redhill*. It is also sometimes possible that what has been thought of as a topographic name is in fact a habitation name from some minor, unidentified place now lost.

Polish names ending in *-owski* have consistently been identified in this dictionary as habitation names, in spite of the fact that it has by no means always been possible to identify relevant places named with the base forms in *-ów* or *-owo*. Others may wish to pursue this task. Placenames with meanings such as 'oak-tree locality' or 'woody area' were clearly numerous in Poland. (In the case of Jewish surnames, the ending *-owski* does not normally indicate a habitation name, but has merely been borrowed as an appropriate surname ending to be attached to formations of several different classes. To some extent, this process was probably going on in Polish even earlier: much further research is needed on individual names before the threads can be properly disentangled in each case.)

Topographic Names

It has already been mentioned that topographic names are those that refer to physical features such as trees, forests, hills, streams, and marshes, as well as to man-made structures such as churches, city walls, and castles.

Surnames derived from the proper names of geographical features such as rivers have also been classed here as topographic rather than habitation names, since they refer to a geographic location rather than to a particular named settlement.

Some surnames that are ostensibly topographic, such as *Hall* and *Monkhouse*, are in fact occupational, for they originally denoted someone who was employed at such a place: for example, at a great house or monastery.

Regional and Ethnic Names

Another category of local surnames comprises those denoting origin in a particular region or country. These tended to be acquired when someone migrated a considerable distance from his original home, so that a specific habitation name would have been meaningless to his new neighbours, and he would be known simply as coming 'from the East', or 'from Devon', or 'from France'. Many of these names have the form of adjectives (e.g. *French*, *Dench*, *Walsh*); others are in the form of nouns denoting a person (e.g. *Fleming*, *Langlois*, *Moravec*). It is possible that in some cases these were originally nicknames bestowed in line with the imagined character traits associated with the inhabitants of the region or country concerned, rather than denoting actual nationality. Someone called 'French' may actually have been French, or he may have adopted sophisticated or even affected mannerisms and tastes popularly associated with French people and culture. In other cases, such names denoted some trading or other connection with a remote place, as is the case with some Ashkenazic Jewish surnames of this type.

House Names

Another category of local names is the 'house name', referring to a distinctive sign attached to mark out a house before the days of numbered streets and addresses. A number of early surnames have been documented as having this origin, and several old Jewish surnames are derived from the names of houses in the Jewish quarter of Frankfurt-am-Main, for example *Rothschild*. However, the importance of this category of surname has sometimes been exaggerated, and many names that have been so explained are in fact nicknames of uncertain significance, or, in the case of Jewish surnames, ornamental names.

Occupational Names

There are many types of surname that are explicitly occupational, in that they refer directly to the particular trade or occupation followed by the first bearer. Buried within this dictionary lies an inventory of the common trades of medieval Europe. These occupations can be divided into classes such as agricultural (e.g. *Sheppard*, *Bouvier*), manufacturing (e.g. *Smith*, *Glover*), retail (e.g. *Monger*, *Kuptsov*), and so on.

They can also be classified according to linguistic criteria. The most basic type of occupational name is represented by words straightforwardly denoting the activity involved, whether as a primary derivative of a verbal root (e.g. *Webb*, *Hunt*) or formed by means of an agent suffix attached to a verb (e.g. *Baker*, *Tissier*) or to a noun (e.g. *Potter*, *Stolarz*). Some occupational names are derived from a noun plus an agent noun from a verb (e.g. *Leadbetter*, *Belleter*, and the more lexicalized *Schuster* and *Stellmacher*).

Another type of surname refers to a calling by metonymy, naming the principal object associated with that activity, whether tool (e.g. *Pick*, *Nadel*) or product (e.g. *Fromage*, *Maslov*).

Particularly in the case of Ashkenazic Jewish surnames, occupational names may have attached to them the explicit suffix *-man(n)* (e.g. *Federman*, *Hirshman*). This is also occasionally the case with German (*-mann*) and English (*-man*) occupational names (e.g. *Habermann*, *Zimmermann*, *Milman*).

Another group is similar in form to one type of surname derived from nicknames (see below), but semantically it clearly belongs in the category of occupational names. Members of this group consist of a verb-stem plus a noun, describing the typical action and object involved in the trade of the person concerned, sometimes in a humorous way (e.g. *Catchpole* for a bailiff; *Knatchbull*, *Tueboeuf*, and *Mazzabue* for slaughterers).

In the Middle Ages, people, at least among the Christian population, did not pursue specialized occupations exclusively to the extent that we do today. Smiths, millers, and wrights were indeed specialists, but even they would normally have their own smallholding for growing crops and keeping a few animals. Other members of society who acquired occupational names would concentrate some but not all of their energies on the particular occupation.

Others were instead simply designated as the servant of some person of higher social status. This is the source, for example, of the English surnames *Maidment* and *Parsons*, and of many English surnames with *-man* added to a given name or even, in a few cases, to a surname. Many surnames ostensibly denoting high rank or descent from someone of high rank, such as *Abbott* and *Squire*, probably have this origin (see the section below on status names).

Surnames from Nicknames

Surnames having a derivation from nicknames form the broadest and most miscellaneous class of surnames. To a large extent this is a catch-all category, encompassing many different types of origin. The most typical classes refer adjectivally to the general physical aspect of the person concerned (e.g. *Blake*, *Hoch*, *Tolstoi*), or to his character (e.g. *Stern*, *Gentil*, *Smirnov*). Others point, with an adjective and noun, to some particular physical feature (e.g. *Whitehead*, *Białowąs*). Many nicknames refer unambiguously to some physical deformity (e.g. *Cripwell*, *Baube*), while others may be presumed to allude to it (e.g. *Hand*, *Daum*). Others probably make reference to a favoured article or style of clothing (e.g. *Boot*, *Cape*).

Many surnames derived from the names of animals and birds were originally nicknames, referring to appearance or character, from the attributes traditionally assigned to animals. In the Middle Ages anthropomorphic ideas were held about the characters of other living creatures, based more or less closely on their observed habits, and these associations were reflected and reinforced by large bodies of folk tales featuring animals behaving as humans. The nickname *Fox* (*Goupil*, *Lysenko*) would thus be given to a cunning person, *Lamb* to a gentle and inoffensive one. In other cases, surnames derived from words denoting animals are of anecdotal origin (see next paragraph).

Anecdotal Surnames

A large group of surnames derived from a particular kind of nickname arose as the result of some now irrecoverable incident or exploit that involved the bearer. In studies of modern nicknames borne by individuals within a community, this type is found to be common, but it is also apparent that the reason for the nickname, which may only ever have been known to a few people, is quickly forgotten, whereas the name itself may continue to have wide and enduring currency. It is fruitless to try to guess now at the events that lay behind the acquisition of nicknames such as *Death* and *Leggatt* in past centuries.

'Imperative' Surnames

Another group of anecdotal surnames consists of a small but disproportionately fascinating number of nicknames composed of a verb-stem plus a noun (e.g. *Shakespeare*, *Mazzalupo*). These apparently commemorate either a characteristic action (e.g. *Wagstaff*) or a particular incident (e.g. *Tiplady*). A further source of interest is that many of them may be obscene.

Seasonal Surnames

Also related to such 'incident' names are those names that refer to a season (e.g. *Winter*, *Lenz*), month (e.g. *May*, *Davout*), or day of the week (e.g. *Freitag*). It has been suggested that these names refer to the time of birth, baptism, or conversion. In the cases of more recently acquired surnames, in particular Jewish names, reference is sometimes to the time of official registration of the name. Certainly surnames derived from the names of various Christian festivals (e.g. *Christmas*, *Toussaint*, *Santoro*) seem to have been acquired in this way. But the seasonal names may also have referred to a 'frosty' or 'sunny' character, while the medieval day names may have referred to feudal service owed on a particular day of the week. No explanation offered for either Christian or Jewish names in this group has been proven conclusively.

Status Names

One group of surnames, dealt with by some writers as 'occupational names' and by others as 'nicknames', we have labelled as a separate category—status names. These for the most part denote a particular role in medieval society (e.g. *Bachelor*, *Franklin*, *Knight*, *Squire*). It must be remembered, though, that there are names that are ostensibly status names (e.g. *King*, *Prince*, *Duke*, *Earl*, *Bishop*), which are of comparatively exalted status, so that present-day bearers are most unlikely to be descended from a holder of the rank in question. In most cases the name was probably originally borne by a servant of the dignitary mentioned, in other cases it may have been given as an 'incident name' to someone who had acted such a role in a pageant or other festivities, or else mockingly to someone who behaved in a lordly manner. Jewish names of this type (e.g. *Kaiser*, *Graf*, *Herzog*) are probably all ornamental only.

Ornamental and Arbitrary Names

A category of surname not found in most European languages and apparently confined to communities where the adoption of surnames was late and enforced rather than organic, is the ornamental or arbitrary coinage. For further remarks on this class, see the sections on Swedish, Finnish, and Jewish surnames in the area-by-area survey below.

Variants, Diminutives, Augmentatives, and Pejoratives

Finally, brief mention must be made of the common classes of surnames that are derived from base forms of personal names and nicknames, and occasionally from occupational names. In this dictionary these are generally listed under the base form following an appropriate heading. Diminutives include surnames that are formed from vocabulary words with a hypocoristic suffix (e.g. Czech *Sedláček* 'little farmer', Italian *Scarsello* 'little miser') and those that are derived from pet forms of given names or nicknames (e.g. English *Jess* and *Jessel* from *Joseph*, *Russell* from *Rouse* 'red-head'). In addition, there are names that are explicitly patronymic in form, derived from pet forms of given names (e.g. English *Jesson* from *Jess*, *Robson* from a diminutive of *Robert*). As a general definition, a diminutive is a pet form, which has hypocoristic force. In practice, it has not always been possible to differentiate between a diminutive and a simple variant. The Flemish name *Gorick* is a case in point: it is a derivative of a Flemish form of the Greek name *Gēōrgios* 'George', but it is not clear from the available evidence whether it is hypocoristic. More often than not, however, diminutives are distinguished by specifically diminutive suffixes, of which Italian has a particularly rich and productive set. Russian and Polish are not far behind, while diminutives of one kind and another are also found in most other European languages. They are much rarer in Spanish surnames, which do not boast the wide variety of derivative forms found in most other European languages.

Augmentatives are much rarer. They mean 'big', whereas diminutives mean 'little'. Typical augmentative endings are Italian *-oni* and *-one*, and French *-at*. Czech *-ec* also has augmentative force.

The other class of derivative surname to be mentioned here is the pejorative, where an ending that originally had an insulting or derogatory force has been added to a word or given name to form a surname. Typical pejorative endings are Italian *-azzi* and *-acci* and French *-ard* and *-aud*.

SURVEY OF NATIONAL AND CULTURAL GROUPS OF SURNAMES

There follows a brief overview of the principal characteristics of surnames in each of the national or cultural groups mentioned in this dictionary.

Surnames in the British Isles

English

The earliest hereditary surnames in England are found shortly after the Norman Conquest, and are of Norman French origin rather than native English. The incoming Normans identified themselves by reference to the estates from which they came in northern

France. *Craker* or *Croaker* is from *Crèvecoeur* in Calvados, *Mandeville* probably from *Manneville* in Seine Maritime, *Haig* in part from *La Hague* in Manche. These Norman habitation names moved rapidly on with their bearers into Scotland and Ireland.

Others of the Norman invaders took names from the estates in England which they had newly acquired. It cannot, of course, be assumed that all present-day surnames derived from habitation names are associated with lordship of the manor of that place. Some are; some are not. It is for family historians to discover which are which. Some people bear the names of farms or hamlets where their ancestors once lived, farms or hamlets which in the mean time may have grown into substantial towns. Others acquired the name of a place because they had recently moved from there, and not because they had any rights over it.

The Normans also brought with them a store of characteristic personal names (e.g. *William*, *Robert*, *Richard*, *Hugh*), which soon more or less entirely replaced the traditional more varied repertoire of Old English personal names, at least among the upper and middle classes. A century or two later, given names of the principal saints of the Christian Church (e.g. *John*, *Paul*, *Peter*) began to be used. It is from these two types of given name that the majority of English patronymic surnames are derived, while relics of the Old English names are normally preserved without endings such as *-s* and *-son*, as if they were regarded as fossilized curiosities, often much altered in form (e.g. *Seawright*, *Wooldridge*). In Northern England and Norfolk, names owing their form to Anglo-Scandinavian influence may be found, especially in surnames derived from placenames.

English surnames of occupational origin likewise display a linguistic mixture: native terms such as *Harper* and *Weaver* coexist beside a wide range of Norman forms, some of which are familiar to us today as fully naturalized vocabulary words for these trades (e.g. *Cook*, *Butler*, *Carpenter*, *Taylor*), while others require a knowledge of Old French to interpret (e.g. *Arblaster*, *Frobisher*).

Nicknames, too, derive both from Norman originals (e.g. *Corbett*, *Mallory*) and much more frequently from native terms (e.g. *Long*, *Round*, *Thin*, *Black*, *Small*). In the North of England as well as in Scotland a few nicknames are also derived from Old Norse terms that survived into Middle English (e.g. *Bain*).

A large number of English surnames are monogenetic, and many of them are derived from habitation names. Where there are two or more habitations (farms, villages, or towns) bearing the same name, it is rarely possible to decide with certainty which of the places bearing the name are sources of the surname, although often the evidence from distribution is very suggestive.

Irish

Ireland was one of the first countries in which a system of hereditary surnames arose: they were known in Ireland long before the Norman invasions brought English-style surnames to the country. The Irish prefixes *Mac* ('son of') and *Ó* ('grandson or descendant of') gave rise at an early date to a set of fixed hereditary names in which the literal patronymic meaning was lost or obscured. *O'Neill*, for example, is known as a hereditary byname from the 4th century onwards.

These surnames originally signified membership of a clan, but with the passage of time, the clan system became less distinct, and surnames came to identify membership of what is called a 'sept': a group of people all living in the same locality, all bearing the same surname, but not necessarily descended from a common ancestor. Adoption of the name by people who did not otherwise have a surname and by dependents was not uncommon. Later, nicknames were in some cases to supersede the original clan names, giving rise to surnames like *Duff* 'Black'.

Considerable caution is called for in interpreting names in early Irish records. MacLysaght points out that, among the successors of St Patrick as bishops of Armagh, Torbac MacGormain (d. 812) and Diarmuid Ó Tighearnaigh were not members of the Gorman and O'Tierney families, but respectively son of a man whose baptismal name was Gorman and grandson of one called Tierney.

Just over one hundred years after the Norman Conquest of England, the first Normans arrived in Ireland. Richard de *Clare*, Second Earl of Pembroke (d. 1176), known as 'Strongbow', was invited to Ireland by Dermot MacMurrough, King of Leinster, whose daughter he married, to help him in his wars with his neighbours. He was accompanied by several retainers whose names, like his own, have become well established as surnames in Ireland, among them Maurice *Fitzgerald*, son of Gerald, steward of Pembroke Castle. The Normans established themselves in Leinster and paid homage to Henry II of England. Some of the Norman settlers acquired surnames derived from Irish. Thus, *de Bermingham* became *MacCorish* and *Nangle* became *Costello*. The process in these two cases was as follows. The Norman first name of *Piers de Bermingham* was Gaelicized as *Feoras*; his son was known as *Mac Fheorais* ('son of Piers'), which was later Anglicized phonetically as *MacCorish* (*fh* being silent in Irish). Likewise, the son of *Oisdealb de Nangle* was known as *Mac Oisdealbhaigh*, Anglicized as *Costello*.

In the latter part of the 16th century, another influx of settlers arrived under the patronage of Elizabeth I of England, and colonized the country beyond the 'Pale', the area around Dublin that was the only part firmly under English control. Typical of these was Richard *Boyle* (1566–1643), who gained control of Munster and was created Earl of Cork. The surname *Boyle* existed in Ireland before his arrival, and his original family name appears to have been *de Binville*. It is not clear how and when he acquired the distinctively Irish surname *Boyle*. His seven sons ensured that this surname would be well established in Ireland in the centuries to come. At the same time, groups of Presbyterian settlers were encouraged to migrate from Scotland to Ulster, thus establishing the distinctively Scots surnames of Protestant Ulster.

During the long centuries of English domination, Irish surnames were crudely Anglicized. The Irish Gaelic language was proscribed, and surnames were Anglicized phonetically or by translation. At its mildest, the prefixes *Mac* and *Ó* were abandoned, so that *Ó Manacháin* became *Monaghan* and *Mac an Fhailghigh* became *McNally* and then *Nally*. At worst, Irish surnames were distorted beyond all recognition. Thus, *Mac Giolla Eoin* 'son of the servant of Eoin' was transmuted into *Munday* by confusion of the last part of the name with Irish *Luain*, genitive of *Luan* Monday. *Ó Glasáin* became *Gleeson*, while *Ó Beaglaoich* became *Begley*. Only in recent years, since Irish independence in 1921, has a reversal set in, so that Irish people are now adopting Gaelicized forms of their names, even though they may not be able to speak Irish. Gaelicization of a surname has become a statement of national and political identity, so that some whose names are actually of Norman French or English origin nevertheless create Gaelic versions of them.

Irish surnames proper are never derived from placenames. The reverse is in fact the case. *Ballymahon* is a typical example of one of the many placenames derived from a surname: it is named as 'the townland of Mahon'.

In the 19th century, political repression and famine combined to force many Irish people to seek other countries in which to live. Large numbers emigrated to the United States, where strong emotional ties to Ireland are still preserved in many families, while others found themselves transported, willingly or otherwise, to Australia, often after having first tried to make a living in England. Irish surnames are now very widely dispersed, and are common in England as well as in Ireland, the United States, and Australia.

Scots

Scots surnames fall into two quite distinct linguistic groups: those of Gaelic origin and those of English origin. The Gaelic language was brought to Scotland from Ireland around the 5th century AD, displacing the British language (an early form of Welsh) previously spoken there as well as elsewhere. Gaelic was the main language of that part of Scotland not subject to English influence, a rather more extensive area than the present-day Highlands and Islands, where Gaelic is still spoken in places. It is from these northern and western area of Scotland that surnames of Gaelic origin, now almost universally Anglicized in form, have been disseminated around the world. Like their Irish kinsmen, Gaelic-speaking Scots were forced to seek emigration in large numbers by many factors: defeat and discrimination after the 1745 Rebellion, famine, and above all clearances of whole populations by rapacious landlords during the 19th century. There are now more Gaelic speakers in eastern Canada than in Scotland, and Scottish surnames are widely distributed throughout the English-speaking world. Scottish immigration has been a powerful factor in New Zealand, although many of the settlers there in fact came from the English-speaking rather than the Gaelic-speaking parts of Scotland.

The typical Gaelic-origin surname is patronymic in form, beginning with the element *Mac* 'son of'. This element is prefixed to Gaelic forms of given names derived both from traditional saints' names (e.g. *McShane*, *McFail*) and from the names of more particularly Celtic saints (e.g. *McKenzie*, *McMunn*). It is also quite often found attached to occupational names (e.g. *McNidder*, *McNucator*).

Scots surnames of English linguistic origin are often identical in form with surnames found in England itself. Nevertheless, many are shown to be predominantly Scottish in their distribution, for example *Fletcher* and *Robertson*. In some cases, specific features of northern rather than southern Middle English phonetic development are present, for example in *Braid* and *Laing*. In north-east Scotland, especially in coastal areas, Norse influence was strong, although this has had more influence on placenames than directly on surnames. Many Scots surnames from the north-east, the central lowlands, and the border country in the south of Scotland are habitation names from places in those areas. Some common habitation surnames in Scotland, however, which are now felt to be typically Scots (e.g. *Lindsay*, *Hamilton*) in fact derive from places in England and were taken there in the Middle Ages, in particular by retainers of Norman nobles who became involved in Scottish affairs. For example, after David, brother of King Alexander of Scotland, acquired the earldom of Huntingdon by marriage in the 12th century, several of his Norman English retainers moved north and founded important and influential Scottish families. The Norman influence on Scots names has been considerable. So, for example, *Sinclair*, an extremely common Scottish surname borne by the earls of Caithness, who were earlier also earls of Orkney, is of Norman origin, being derived from estates at Saint-Clair-l'Évêque in Calvados. Such names were often adopted by vassals and tenants of an overlord, which greatly contributed to their frequency.

Manx

The Manx language is closely related to Scots Gaelic, and its Gaelic surname forms are similar to those found in Scotland. In their present-day Anglicized forms, however, they differ in that the patronymic prefix *Mac-* has for the most part been reduced to an initial *C-*, *K-*, or *Q-*. This has the result that nearly 30 per cent of the surnames in the Manx telephone directory begin with these letters. Other typical Manx surnames are *Brew* (related to Gaelic *Brain*) and *Lewin* (a derivative of *William*).

Welsh

In former times, it was said that every true Welshman could recite his genealogy back through teens of generations, and strings of patronymics containing five or six elements were commonly used in official documents for the purpose of identifying individuals. Fixed hereditary surnames on the English (and general European) pattern began to be taken after the administrative union with England in the 16th century. At first, however, this development was confined to the classes who had dealings with English bureaucracy, and the adoption of surnames did not become general until the 18th century and after. This factor accounts for the currency in Wales of surnames derived from given names that were not common until long after the Middle Ages and which have given rise to few surnames in England (e.g. *Samuel*). These are often Old Testament names, associated as given names with the rise of Nonconformism and biblical fundamentalism, which were extremely powerful influences in Wales in the 18th and 19th centuries.

Welsh surnames, then, are for the most part derived from personal names. In some very common names, a vestige of the Welsh patronymic prefix *ap*, *ab* is still found preceding the name (as in *Price*, *Probert*; *Bowen*, *Beddoes*); in others the English suffix *-s* has been adopted (as in *Evans*, *Jones*, and *Williams*). Surnames of the habitation type (e.g. *Trevor*) and the nickname type (e.g. *Tegg*) are comparatively rare. The stock of Welsh surnames is not large, compared with that of other national and linguistic groups, so that even today some Welshmen are distinguished informally in their daily lives by the use of bynames, often associated with their occupation, as in 'Jones the Post'.

Cornish

Cornish naming practices are unfortunately poorly documented for the Middle Ages, but present-day Cornish surnames, somewhat surprisingly, do not follow the predominantly patronymic pattern of the other Celtic languages, including Welsh. This may be attributed to the greater influence of English bureaucracy and English naming practices in Cornwall than in Wales at the time when surnames came into use. The majority of Cornish names are habitation names (e.g. *Pengelly*, *Trevena*); some that appear to be topographic names may in fact derive from lost or unrecorded placenames. Other Cornish surnames are derived from medieval given names, but without the typical Celtic patronymic prefixes. One feature found in a few Cornish surnames derived from given names, and not elsewhere, is the suffix *-oe*, *-ow* (e.g. *Pascoe*, *Clemow*). This has been explained as deriving from the Cornish plural suffix *-ow*, used in a generalizing sense (cf. Italian *-i* and Manx *Qualtrough*). Occupational and nickname sources are distinctly rare in Cornwall.

Surnames of Breton Origin

There are a few common British surnames that are of Breton origin, for example *Harvey*, *Mingay*, and *Wymark*. These derive not directly from the Breton language, but rather from Breton personal names brought over by Breton followers of William the Conqueror. They are most common in East Anglia, which was the main area of settlement by Bretons after the Conquest (and consequently also the focus of the surnames *Brett* and *Britton*). See also the section on Breton names in France, below.

Huguenot Surnames

During the 17th century a characteristic group of surnames was brought to Britain, North America, and southern Africa by French Huguenot exiles. The Huguenots were French Protestants. In 1572 large numbers of them were massacred in Paris on the orders of the queen, Catherine de' Medici, and many of the survivors sought refuge in England and elsewhere. Although the Edict of Nantes (1598) officially guaranteed religious toleration, persecution continued, and when the Edict of Nantes was revoked by Louis XIV in 1685, intolerance became institutionalized: the trickle of emigration became a flood. Many migrated to England, while others joined groups of Dutch Protestants settling around the Cape of Good Hope. Others sailed across the Atlantic to establish themselves in North America. The French surnames which these migrants brought with them were only lightly Anglicized if at all, and remain to this day distinctive types of British, American, and South African surnames. See *Bosanquet* and *Garrick* for English Huguenot names, *Lanier* and *Marion* for American examples, and *Du Plessis* for a South African one.

Surnames in France

French

The earliest French hereditary surnames are found in the 12th century, at more or less the same time as they arose in England, but they are by no means common before the 13th century, and it was not until the 15th century that they stabilized to any great extent; before then a surname might be handed down for two or three generations, but then abandoned in favour of another.

Patronymics, occupational names, nicknames, and topographic names are all found in French. Habitation names are also found, but they are less common than in English, and are characteristically preceded by the possessive preposition *de*. Since possession of a habitational surname was normally associated with lordship over the estates of the place in question, the preposition *de* came to be regarded as a mark of aristocracy, and was later occasionally inserted in front of surnames that were not local at all.

In the south, many French surnames have come in from Italy over the centuries. The surnames of Corsica are almost all of Italian origin, for the island was a Genoese possession until the second half of the 18th century. In northern France, Germanic influence can often be detected, in particular in the surnames derived from Continental Germanic personal names, which often have English (Norman) cognates, and which were borne by the Franks, who were the dominant group in France from the time of Charlemagne onwards. In Alsace and Lorraine, surnames are often simply German, for these regions were for long German in language and culture.

Breton

Breton surnames fit in with the predominant Celtic pattern in being overwhelmingly patronymic in form. Many of them are recognizable by the prefix *ab* 'son of', cognate with Welsh *ap*, *ab* and more distantly with Irish and Scots Gaelic *Mac*, or by the Breton diminutive suffix *-ic*, *-ec*. There are also a fair number of occupational names (e.g. *Le Goff*) and names originating as nicknames (e.g. *Lefur*), as well as some topographic ones (e.g. *Penguern*). As a rule, Breton surnames have been Gallicized in spelling, but with the rise in Breton nationalism many bearers are reverting to traditional Breton forms.

Provençal

Provençal is the traditional language of southern France, more specifically of south-eastern France, which developed from the medieval *langue d'oc*. This is contrasted with the *langue d'oil* of the north, which became standard French. Provençal is linguistically close to Catalan, and the two languages often have similar surname forms (see e.g. at *Casa* and *Puy*). Provençal surnames have a number of features that distinguish them from standard French forms: for example, agent nouns typically end in *-er* or *-é* where standard French has *-ier*.

Gascon

Gascon is a dialect of *langue d'oc* spoken in Gascony, a region of south-west France. It has its own distinctive surnames, due largely to the distinctive phonetic features of the dialect, notably *h-* where other dialects have *f-* (see e.g. *Hau* at *Fage* and *Haure* at *Fèvre*). Gascony was named in Roman times from the Basques who lived there, but the Basque-speaking area has been much reduced over the centuries. Nevertheless, surnames of Basque origin are also found in Gascony: see the section on Basque surnames below.

Surnames in the Iberian Peninsula

Spanish

In Spain identifying patronymics are to be found from as early as the mid-9th century, but these changed with each generation, and hereditary surnames seem to have come in slightly later in Spain than in England and France. The characteristic patronymic suffix *-ez* is of uncertain, though much discussed, derivation. The most plausible supposition is that it derives from a Latin genitive: either *-ici* (denoting affiliation), genitive of the adjectival ending *-īcus*, used to form derivatives of personal names (e.g. *Lupici*), or *-ici*, *-aci*, from the genitive of certain given names (e.g. *Roderici*, *Didaci*).

The given names to which these patronymic suffixes attach are of multiple origin. As well as the names of the traditional major saints of the Christian Church (e.g. *Pérez*, *Martínez*), many of the most common Spanish surnames are derived from personal names of Germanic origin. For the most part these names are characteristically Hispanic, and are distinct from the Germanic personal names that lie behind many English, French, Italian, German, and Scandinavian surnames. They derive from the language of the Visigoths, who controlled Spain between the mid-5th and early 8th centuries. Visigothic is a member of the now extinct group of East Germanic languages, as opposed to the North Germanic of Scandinavia and the West Germanic of modern Germany, the Netherlands, and England. Visigothic personal name forms display various elements not paralleled in North and West Germanic names, for example *sind* 'path', *swinth* 'strong', and *funs* 'ready, prompt'. Common Spanish patronymic surnames derived from Visigothic personal names include *Álvarez*, *González*, and *Menéndez*. Others (e.g. *López*, *Sánchez*) are derived from typically Hispanic given names of the Middle Ages that are of ostensibly Romance etymology, though the details are problematic.

In the 8th century, Spain fell under control of the Moors, and this influence, which lasted into the 12th century, has also left its mark on Hispanic surnames. A few surnames (e.g. *Benavides*) are based directly on Arabic personal names and patronymic expressions, but the Arabic influence is more pervasively apparent indirectly, through its effect on placenames and vocabulary words. This may be seen both in habitation surnames (e.g. *Alcalá*, *Alcántara*) and in surnames derived from words denoting occupations (e.g. *Alcaide*, *Alcalde*) and nicknames (e.g. *Albarrán*). The majority of Spanish occupational and nickname surnames, however, are based on ordinary Spanish vocabulary words of Romance origin (e.g. *Herrero* 'smith' and *Redondo*, a cognate of English *Round*).

Several familiar Spanish surnames (e.g. *Mendoza*, *Loyola*) are in fact Hispanicized forms of Basque surnames; see below.

Catalan

Catalan is the language of north-east Spain and the Balearic islands. Its surnames share many of the characteristics of Spanish surnames, except that there is very little Arabic influence and the Germanic influence is Frankish (West Germanic) rather than Visigothic. There is often considerable overlapping with Provençal. Catalan names are nowadays quite widely distributed throughout the Iberian peninsula. They may often be recognized by their endings, such as *-é*, *-er* for Spanish *-ero* in the case of agent nouns and *-à* for Spanish *-án* in the case of words derived from Latin *-ānus*.

Basque

Basque is a non-Indo-European language spoken today in a small area of northern Spain and south-western France, but in the Middle Ages over a rather larger area. Basque is unusual among the languages in Europe in that surnames derived from given names are rare. The overwhelming majority of Basque surnames are topographic in form, combining a fairly small number of elements (e.g. *aran* 'valley', *mendi* 'hill', *etxe* 'house', *zabal* 'broad'). They originated as habitation names, referring to individual farmhouses, but it is now seldom possible to identify these, and the more common surnames must have had multiple origins. Basque surnames are found in both Spain and France, and often both Spanish and French spellings of a name (*Echegorri*, *Etchegorry*) are found alongside the accepted Basque orthography (*Etxegorri*).

Portuguese

Portuguese surnames share many of the features of Spanish surnames, in particular Arabic and Visigothic influence. A noticeable feature of Portuguese surnames is the class of religious names referring to festivals of the Church or attributes of the Virgin Mary. One respect in which Portuguese surnames differ from those of the rest of the Iberian peninsula is that some of them were adopted at a comparatively late date and honour saints who did not give rise to surnames in other languages. There are, for example, common surnames derived from given names honouring St Francis of Assisi (1181–1226; canonized 1228) and St Catherine of Siena (1347–80; canonized 1461). Portuguese surnames typically have the agent suffix *-eiro* where Spanish has *-ero*, and the patronymic suffix *-es* corresponding to Spanish *-ez*.

Italian Surnames

The origins of Italian surnames are not clear, and much work remains to be done on medieval Italian records. It seems that fixed bynames, in some cases at least hereditary, were in use in the Venetian Republic by the end of the 10th century. However, fixed hereditary surnames were comparatively slow to develop, and a comparatively flexible system of distinguishing bynames was long in use in many regions.

A characteristic of Italian surnames is the profusion of affective derivatives, overwhelmingly diminutive, but also augmentative and even pejorative, that have been coined from the base forms of given names. Other alterations in the form of a name may increase the opacity of its etymology: for example, the habit of creating aphetic derivatives by lopping off the first syllable. So, for example, this dictionary lists no less than 66 Italian diminutives of the given name *Iacopo* at *Jacob*, and a further 62 of its variant *Giacomo* at *James*. Some of these (e.g. *Gabotti*, *Cavozzi*; *Mizzi*, *Motto*) have no more than one or two letters in common with the base form from which they are derived. Surnames derived from given names are thus extremely common in Italian; nicknames are also common. Occupational names are rather less prolific, and topographic and habitational names are the least frequent of the major types. Habitation names are generally adjectival in form (e.g. *Genovese* 'Genoan', *Veneziano* 'Venetian'). Surnames formed from placenames standing on their own, unaltered in form, are for the most part characteristic of Italian Jews.

The typical Italian surname endings are *-i* and *-o*. The former is characteristic of northern Italy. It seems to have originally represented a masculine plural form, identifying the bearer as being 'one of' a certain family. It has now become a standard surname ending, taking over nouns which, on etymological grounds, might have been expected to have feminine inflections (e.g. *Stradivari*). The singular form, *-o*, is more typical of southern Italy.

The many dialects of Italian each have their distinctive features, many of which are reflected in surname forms. For example, the Venetian dialect tends to apocopate a final vowel. Some medieval Germanic given names were in use in Italian-speaking areas, especially in the north, and have given rise to surnames (e.g. *Rinaldo* from *Reginwald*, ultimately a cognate of English *Reynold*).

Also within the present-day borders of Italy are speakers of German and Slovene, whose surnames reflect their linguistic heritage.

Sardinian

Sardinian is very different from other forms of Italian; in fact, it is often considered to be a distinct language in its own right. Its surnames are formed in much the same way as Italian surnames, but they have distinctively Sardinian forms. For example, the diminutive ending *-eddu* in Sardinian corresponds to standard Italian *-ello*.

Surnames in German-Speaking Countries

The first hereditary surnames on German soil are found in the second half of the 12th century, slightly later than in England and France. However, it was not until the 16th century that they became stabilized—that is, virtually universal and fixed in form from one generation to the next. The practice of adopting hereditary surnames began in southern areas and gradually spread northward during the Middle Ages.

German surnames show a great deal of regional variation. The most obvious division is into High and Low German, which in this work are treated as separate languages in the same way as French and Provençal, Spanish and Catalan. One form of High German has become the standard modern German language, whereas Low German is linguistically closer to Dutch. Many German surnames may be recognized as belonging to one regional variety or another by their characteristic hypocoristic diminutive suffixes, for example Swiss and Alsatian *-lin*, *-li*, *-i*, Swabian *-len*, *-le*, Bavarian and Austrian *-l*. Among Low German dialects, that of the Rhineland is distinguished by its hypocoristics in *-gen* and *-ken*, that of Westphalia by its patronymics in *-ing* and (later) *-er*.

All the main types of surname are found in German-speaking areas. Names derived from occupations and from nicknames are particularly common (e.g. *Schuster* 'shoemaker', *Schwarz* 'black'). A number of these are also Jewish. Patronymic surnames are derived from vernacular Germanic given names much more often than from baptismal names honouring Christian saints. Regional and ethnic names are common (e.g. *Schwob* 'Swabian', *Unger* 'Hungarian'). Habitation names are less common than in some other languages. The German preposition *von* 'from' or 'of', used with habitation names, is taken as a mark of aristocracy: like French *de*, it originally denoted proprietorship of the village or estate named. The preposition *zu* 'at' also occurs, and is taken as a more emphatic mark of aristocracy, occurring generally with a title of nobility rather than a simple surname. Some members of the nobility affected the form *von und zu* with their titles.

In eastern Germany there was heavy influence both from and and on neighbouring Slavonic languages. Many Prussian surnames are actually of Slavonic origin, being derived from the language known as Wendish or Sorbian, which is now almost extinct, but was formerly widely spoken in the area from Berlin to Dresden. A characteristic Wendish surname ending is *-itz*. Slavonic forms of given names have also been encapsulated as German surnames (e.g. *Tess*, *Wenzel*, and *Schirach*, the last being a Wendish form of *George*). Hypocoristic forms in *-ke*, *-isch*, and *-usch* are similarly the result of Slavonic influence.

Surnames in the Low Countries

Dutch

The Dutch language is most closely related to Low German. Its surnames have been influenced by both German and French naming practices.

Prepositions and articles that were normally lost in other languages have survived as an integral part of some Dutch surnames. The preposition *van* 'of' is found especially with habitation names, but usually without the aristocratic connotations of French *de* and German *von*. *De* 'the' is found with nicknames (e.g. *Pieter de Haan* 'Peter the Cockerel') and sometimes with occupational names (e.g. *Jan de Bakker* 'John the Baker'). Both elements together occur in some topographic names (e.g. *Van den Berg* 'from the hill').

Fused forms are also found: for example, *Van der* 'from the' is found in some names collapsed as *Ver*. The preposition *tot*, corresponding to High German *zu*, is also found fused in the dialect forms *Ter*, *Tor*, *Ten*, and *Tom*. These are shared with Low German surnames from the Rhineland and Westphalia.

The classic Dutch patronymic suffix is *-sen* 'son' placed after a genitive *-s* inflection on the end of the given name. This has in many cases been reduced and the reductions have often been respelled, so that, for example, alongside *Hendriksen* we find *Hendrikse, Hendriksze, Hendriksz, Hendriks, Hendrikx*, and *Hendrix*.

The Dutch language has of course had a major influence on the surnames of South Africa (e.g. *Van de Merwe*), since the Afrikaner inhabitants of South Africa are mostly descended from Dutch settlers of the 17th century. Other linguistic origins of typically South African surnames include Frisian (e.g. *Botha*) and Huguenot French (e.g. *Du Plessis*).

Frisian

Frisian, the Germanic language that, historically, is most closely related to English, is spoken in the north-west Netherlands and on the islands off the North Sea coast of the Netherlands, Germany, and Denmark. It has its own characteristic surname forms, typical of which are the suffixes *-ma* 'man' (hypocoristic) and *-stra* '-ster' (agentive). So, for example, characteristic Frisian surnames are *Hendriksma* and *Dijkstra*.

Flemish

For long periods of history, the northern part of Belgium was administratively united with the Netherlands. The Flemish language, spoken in northern Belgium, is very closely related to Dutch, and its surnames are often identical or nearly identical to Dutch. The typical Flemish spelling of the patronymic derivative of the given name *Hendrik* is *Hendrickx*. There are other characteristic Flemish spellings, for example *-ae-* where Dutch has *-aa-*, so that Flemish *De Haese* corresponds to Dutch *De Haas*.

Walloon

Approximately half the population of Belgium is French-speaking and of largely French stock. Their surnames are thus in the main indistinguishable from those current in France itself, although some of them represent Gallicized forms of Flemish names.

Surnames in Scandinavia

Danish

The practice of adopting surnames spread to Denmark from North Germany during the late Middle Ages, but until the 19th century they were neither firmly fixed nor universal. They are for the most part patronymic, and a few common forms such as *Jansen* and *Andersen* are so overwhelmingly predominant that confusion is inevitable. For this reason, the Danish state has in recent years been encouraging the adoption of a wider range of surnames. These new surnames are often more or less arbitrarily adopted and tend to be composed of similar elements to Swedish ones. In other cases people are able to use the name of a farm once inhabited by their ancestors as a source of inspiration for the adoption of a new surname.

Norwegian

Norwegian surnames are to a large extent identical in form with Danish ones, and indeed until the language reform of the late 19th century, the official language of Norway was Danish, since Norway was administratively under Danish control. Norwegian was not so much a language as a collection of isolated dialects. Political independence prompted the development of an independent national Norwegian language, in addition to the many local dialects. However, the emergence of the national language had little effect on the development of surnames in Norway, which were formed in a similar way to Danish and Swedish surnames.

Swedish

In the 17th century, so-called 'soldiers' names' are found as the earliest kind of hereditary surnames in Sweden. These were names derived from vocabulary words, usually martial-sounding monosyllables such as *Rapp* 'prompt', *Rask* 'bold', *Spjut* 'lance', or occasionally names of animals and birds such as *Strutz* 'ostrich'. They were bestowed on soldiers for administrative purposes, and no doubt in some cases derived from pre-existing nicknames.

Most Swedes did not adopt hereditary surnames until a century or more later, and the patronymic system was still in active use in rural areas until late in the 19th century. Patronymics were replaced by hereditary surnames of two main kinds. The first kind may be described as frozen patronymics, as where *Andersson* or *Johansson* continued in use as the distinguishing family name, not merely of the son of a man called Anders or Johan, but by his grandchildren and great-grandchildren as well. The true test of hereditary surnames in the 19th century came when granddaughters as well as grandsons adopted such names, in lieu of the traditional patronymics for girls such as *Andersdotter* and *Johansdotter*. Those Swedish surnames that are extremely common all fall into this class, but it does not by any means constitute the most numerous class of Swedish surnames.

That honour is reserved for the arbitrary or ornamental coinages, derived mainly from vocabulary elements denoting natural phenomena and features of the landscape and seascape, words which denote aspects of the world which are held dear by Swedes of all classes and regions: names such as *Lund* 'grove', *Gren* 'branch', and *Sjö* 'sea'. Often, these names are indistinguishable from topographic names. In the absence of evidence from family history, it is impossible to know whether someone who adopted the surname *Öman* 'island man' chose it because he lived on an island or because he just liked the idea of islands.

Many typical Swedish ornamental names of this kind consist of two elements arbitrarily joined together, without consideration of logic or possibility: names such as *Sjögren* 'sea branch' or *Lundgren* 'grove twig'.

Finnish

Finnish is a non-Indo-European language, rather distantly related to Hungarian, and more closely to Estonian. Finland has always been culturally close to her Scandinavian neighbours, especially Sweden. Finland was under Swedish control during the Middle Ages, and there are many native speakers of Swedish within Finland's borders. Finnish surnames are similar to Swedish ones in typology, despite the difference in linguistic stock. Like Swedish names, they are to a large extent ornamental, taken from features of the natural landscape. Unlike Swedish ornamental names, Finnish ones are in general monothematic (i.e., they consist of only one element), but to the vocabulary word itself are often suffixed the genitive element *-nen* or the locative *-la*. A few common Finnish names, functionally patronymics and occupational names, are in form composed with an element that refers to residence in someone's house: the house of the bearer of a particular given name (e.g. *Anttila*, literally 'dweller in the house of Antti (Andrew)') or the follower of a particular trade (e.g. *Seppälä*, literally 'dweller in the blacksmith's house').

The Surnames of Eastern Europe outside Russia

Polish

In Poland, surnames may be patronymic, occupational, or local (both topographic and habitation) names, or nicknames.

The earliest Polish surnames were patronymic. The personal names from which they were derived are mainly Slavonic, but as the Middle Ages progressed, traditional Slavic given names began to give way to saints' names, mainly of Romance (Latin) origin, but in some cases even Irish (cf. *Gall*). German personal names were also occasionally adopted, and have given rise to some surnames, but on the whole there was much less intermingling and linguistic borrowing in Poland than in, say, Bohemia. Patronymic surnames in Polish may have an explicitly patronymic ending, *-owicz*, or they may have the agentive suffix *-ak*, which has a more general significance, that is, 'person associated with X', and is found also in occupational names. In this book those *-ak* names which come from a given name are listed as patronymics, while *-ak* names denoting an occupation or nickname are not. Polish surnames are also found that are identical in form to a given name, and these are of course of patronymic origin. A feature of Polish patronymics shared with those of most other Slavonic languages is the prevalence of diminutive and hypocoristic forms of the given names.

Broadly, surnames derived from Slavonic personal names are of early origin, and tend to be borne by aristocratic families. An exception is the group of names derived from forms of the name of the immensely popular Polish saint Stanisław, which has been borne by all classes of society throughout Polish history. Surnames derived from the names of saints tend to be associated with the urban classes rather than gentry or peasantry.

Perhaps the most common ending of Polish surnames is *-ski*. This is a standard adjective ending in the Polish language, cognate with English *-ish*. In surnames it originally indicated association with a place, but soon came to be regarded as equivalent to French *de* and German *von*, and so indicative of gentry status. In many but by no means all cases, the bearer was indeed lord of the estate or manor to which the name referred. Later, the suffix came to be used much more widely to form surnames, being attached indiscriminately to given names (as *Adamski*), nicknames, and occupational names (as *Bednarski*), as well as to habitation names. So, for example, *Baranowski* is probably a habitation name in origin, but it is also possible that it is merely an elaboration of a nickname, *Baran*, meaning 'ram'.

The *-ski* ending is still inflected as *-ska* for feminine bearers, but the traditional inflected forms of most other Polish surnames are now less widely used than they were formerly. Traditionally, there are distinct forms for male bearers of a name (e.g. *Lis*), married female bearers (e.g. *Lisowa*), and unmarried females (e.g. *Lisówna*).

The ending *-owski* is more closely identified with habitation names, *-ów* being a morpheme by which adjectives were derived from nouns, including personal names. In some cases, the derived adjective then became a proper noun itself, as a placename. Thus, *Adamowski* may be a habitation name from *Adamów* ('place named after someone called *Adam*'), a habitation name derived directly from the personal name (i.e. 'person from the place where Adam lives'), or simply a fanciful elaboration of the surname or the personal name *Adam*, adopted as a surname to suggest gentry status.

Surnames in Czechoslovakia

The modern state of Czechoslovakia comprises the medieval regions of Bohemia, Moravia, and Slovakia. The first two of these, where the language properly called Czech is spoken, were heavily subject to German cultural and linguistic influence from the Middle Ages onwards, being administratively a Crownland of Austria for much of the time until independence in 1918. This influence is reflected in the many Czech surnames derived from German, both from given names (e.g. *Kábrt*, a derivative of *Gebhardt*) and from vocabulary words (e.g. *Šnajdr*, a respelling of German *Schneider*, and the nickname *Krob* 'crude', which exists alongside a derivative of the Czech vocabulary word *Hrubý*, which is itself derived from the German word). Slovakia, the home of the closely related language known as Slovak, was under Hungarian control for most of the period from the 10th century until it was united with Czechoslovakia in 1918: it shares many surnames in common with Czech.

A noticeable feature of Czech phonology is that, like some other Slavonic languages, it has no /g/. Thus, the Czech equivalent of Polish *góra* 'mountain' is *hora*, and the Czech name corresponding to *Gregory* is *Řehoř*.

A large number of Czech surnames are of patronymic origin, but the language is unusual in that explicit patronymic morphemes are extremely rare. Given names are sometimes used as surnames without alteration in form, but more often a suffix is added. This may be hypocoristic, diminutive, augmentative, or indeed unclassifiable (being unique to surnames). Old Czech hypocoristic forms of given names sometimes altered the form of the original given name substantially (e.g. *Buzek* from *Budislav*), and some of these altered forms have been preserved as surnames.

Occupational names are quite common in Czech (e.g. *Suk* 'judge'), as are nicknames, especially those referring to some physical feature (e.g. *Kučera* 'curly', *Paleček* 'thumb'). Many of the most common Czech surnames have the diminutive ending *-ček*, which is often found attached to occupational names and nicknames. A type of characteristically Czech surname, not found in other languages, consists of those that are derived from past tense forms of verbs, ending in *-l* (e.g. *Doležal* 'he had a rest', *Dostál* 'he kept his word', *Navrátil* 'he came back'). These are mostly anecdotal or nickname surnames, referring to some lost incident or habit.

Czech surnames are fully inflected as nouns in the language. A distinction used to be made in form between the surnames of married and unmarried women, but this is no longer widely observed.

Hungarian

The Hungarian language is quite distinct from its Germanic and Slavonic neighbours, and is of Finno-Ugric rather than Indo-European origin—thus, it is related to Finnish. Nevertheless, the strongest cultural influence in historical times has been German, and the pattern of Hungarian surnames is similar to that found in Germany and Austria. Surnames of patronymic origin are mostly formed without an explicitly patronymic suffix, but some have the suffix *-fi* (from Hungarian *fia* 'son of', which is cognate with Finnish *poika* and thus an impeccably Finno-Ugric word and not, as sometimes claimed, derived from Latin *filius* 'son').

Hungarian surnames are placed before rather than after the given name. All the main types of surname are found in Hungarian: occupational names (e.g. *Eötvös* 'goldsmith', *Szabó* 'tailor', and the metonymic *Liszt* 'flour' for a baker or miller); nicknames (e.g. *Fekete* 'black', *Fehér* 'white', i.e. 'blond or pale-skinned'); and local names (both topographic, e.g. *Óváry* 'old castle', *Szigeti* 'island', and habitational, e.g. *Temesváry* 'of Temesvár'). A few surnames that are relatively common in Hungary are not in fact of Hungarian linguistic origin; they represent Magyarized forms of German and Slavonic names imported from neighbouring regions.

In a couple of cases, surnames in a wide area of central Europe, far beyond the frontiers of Hungary itself, were formed from Hungarian. One such is *Hajdú*, from a word which in Hungarian meant 'drover', and hence highwayman or armed mercenary. At the turn of the 16th–17th centuries, some 10,000 of these mercenaries were recruited by Prince István Bocskay. The Hungarian word spawned derivatives with much the same meaning, 'armed retainer', in German, Polish, Czech, and Croatian. All of these gave rise to surnames. Another example is *Kocsis* 'coachman', ultimately derived from the name of the village of *Kocs*, where the coach was invented in the 16th century: the new design of horse-drawn passenger transport, with its sprung chassis built for comfort and speed, spread rapidly all over Europe: indeed, it gave rise to the English word *coach* as well as to several central European surnames.

Many Hungarian surnames contain the final element *-y*, which is syllabic when it follows a vowel, but when it follows *g*, *l*, *n*, or *t* alters the phonetic quality of the preceding consonant to /d'/, /j/, /n'/, and /t'/ respectively. Thus the common surname *Nagy* 'big' is pronounced /nod'/. In the 19th century, surnames ending in *-y* came to be considered more aristocratic than those ending in *-i*—so that, for example, the novelist Jókay changed his name to *Jókai* in a fit of republican zeal. It has, however, been shown that the alternation between *-i* and *-y* depended on the whim of the clerk concerned, and had no connection with rank.

Rumanian

Rumanian is a Romance language, derived from Latin. It has, however, been greatly influenced in vocabulary by its Slavonic neighbours, as well as by Greek and Turkish.

Characteristic of Rumanian surnames are the patronymic suffixes *-esco* and *-escu*, which is attached to vocabulary words (e.g. *Alimanesco* 'the Swiss') as well as to given names (e.g. *Constantinesco*). Among Rumanian Jews, the Slavonic patronymic ending *-vich* (*-wicz* in Polish) is commonly found in the form *-vici*.

Several quite common Rumanian surnames are derived directly from vocabulary words. Examples are *Turcul* 'the Turk', which in Rumania is an ethnic name rather than a nickname, the occupational name *Ciobanu* 'shepherd', and the nickname *Ochila* 'eye'. Such names often contain the suffixed definite article *-l*.

Transylvania is administratively a region of present-day Rumania, but a large proportion of its population consists of Magyars, who of course have Hungarian surnames.

There are cases of Rumanianized spellings of these names, and there exist hybrid names such as *Farcasiu*, formed from Hungarian *farkas* 'wolf' with the Rumanian ending *-iu*.

Bulgarian

Bulgarian is a member of the South Slavonic group of languages, closely related to Old Church Slavonic, into which the Bible was translated by Saints Cyril and Methodius in the 9th century. Almost without exception Bulgarian surnames are patronyms, ending in *-ov* and *-ev*, derived from given names. From 1396 to 1878 Bulgaria was part of the Ottoman Empire, and the inevitable Turkish influence has produced a few distinctive Bulgarian surnames (e.g. *Aliyev*, from the Muslim personal name *Ali*, and *Hadzhev*, from the Muslim title *Al Hadj*, denoting someone who had made the pilgrimage to Mecca). However, these are not particularly common.

Surnames in Yugoslavia

Serbian and Croatian are so similar that for all practical purposes they may be regarded as the same language, with the exception that the former is written in the Cyrillic alphabet, the latter in the Roman. There are also a number of points of difference in vocabulary and usage.

The names recorded in this dictionary are described as Croatian forms, although they could also represent transliterations of Serbian forms. They characteristically end in the patronymic suffix *-ić*. Only the most common Croatian surnames are given, and we have not attempted in this edition to deal with the surnames of the other languages of Yugoslavia, such as Slovene and Macedonian.

Greek Surnames

The coverage of Greek surnames in this dictionary is strictly limited. Nevertheless, Greek forms will be found listed here among the cognates of certain surnames, especially those derived from New Testament personal names. Characteristic Greek surname endings include the patronymics *-opoulos* 'son of', which is derived from a modern Greek vocabulary word, and *-akis* and *-ides*, more traditional morphemes referring to descent.

Surnames in the Soviet Union

Russian

Russian surnames are almost exclusively patronymic (occasionally metronymic) in form, usually ending in *-ov* or *-ev* (when derived from nouns ending in a consonant) and in *-in* (from nouns ending in a vowel). These suffixes were originally possessive in function; compare the cognate Polish *-ów*, *-ew*, and *-in*.

Russian rivals Italian in the profusion of its pet forms and hypocoristic derivatives of given names. However, by no means all Russian surnames are derived from given names. Forms to which the patronymic suffix may be added include nicknames and occupational names. Habitation and topographic names are rare. Many common Russian surnames are polygenetic, and their literal meaning is clear, even though the reason for their adoption may not be.

It is a curious fact that some of the most widely known Russian surnames are in fact divergent from the usual pattern, exhibiting endings found with only very small numbers of surnames (e.g. *Tchaikovsky*, a habitation name on the Polish model; *Tolstoi*, derived directly from an adjective form; and *Zhivago*, a rare type of problematic origin, possibly preserving a case ending of Old Church Slavonic).

Ukrainian

Ukrainian surnames have much in common with Polish names in the way they are formed. For example, there are occupational names in Ukrainian (e.g. *Bondar*), without the patronymic ending that is almost obligatory in Russian. The common Ukrainian diminutive ending *-uk* corresponds to Polish *-ik*, which is also found in the Ukraine. The Ukraine was at various periods of its history under Polish rule, and is predominantly Catholic in religion rather than Orthodox. For this reason, there are some Ukrainian surnames derived from saints venerated in the Western rather than the Eastern Church. However, forms owing their origin to Russian influence are also found.

A typical Ukrainian surname ending is *-enko*, a diminutive suffix attached for the most part to given names, but also to nicknames and occupational names. This is also found with a few Belorussian names, but there it is probably a borrowing from Ukrainian rather than a truly Belorussian form.

Belorussian

The Belorussian language is similar to Ukrainian, and like the Ukraine its history is a mixture of Polish and Russian domination. The Polish patriot Kościuszko was actually born in Belorussia, and this fact illustrates the complex mixture of conflicting loyalties found in Belorussia. Its surnames show a mixture of features found in Polish names and those found in Russian. Thus, as in Polish, diminutive endings are common (a distinctive Belorussian ending is *-(y)onok*). There are also many patronymic surnames, formed both with *-ov*, as in Russian, and with *-ovich*, corresponding to Polish *-owicz*. Belorussian has a phonetic /h/ where Russian has /g/, so that, for example, the Belorussian equivalent of Russian *Grigorov* is *Hrihorovich*.

The Baltic States

Under this heading are comprised Estonia, Latvia, and Lithuania, all now part of the Soviet Union, but formerly independent. Latvian and Lithuanian are Baltic languages, distantly related to Slavonic. Estonian is Finno-Ugric, not Indo-European, and closely related to Finnish. Surnames coming from this part of the world may often be recognized by the characteristic endings *-aitis* (Lithuanian; Germanized *-eit*), *-ins* (Latvian), and *-ste* (Estonian; cognate with Finnish *-isto*).

Georgian

The Georgian language is Caucasian, not Indo-European. A few very common or very famous Georgian names are included here. Typical Georgian surname suffixes are the patronymics *-dze* and *-shvili*.

Turkic and Muslim Influences

The Tatar state established in the 13th century by Genghis Khan was subjugated by Russia in the mid-16th century. The language of its subjects was Turkic, the original Mongolian social element having been completely overwhelmed at an early period. Their religion was Islam, and many of the surnames from the Volga region derive from the personal names of this tradition: originally names of members of the Prophet's family (e.g. *Akhmatov*, *Khasanov*), names of Old Testament origin (e.g. *Ismailov*, *Musaev*), or epithets of Allah (e.g. *Azizov*, *Nuriev*).

Armenian

Armenian is an Indo-European language. The characteristic Armenian surname ending is the patronymic *-ian*, added to distinctively Armenian devotional names (e.g. *Garabedian*, *Khachaturian*) or much altered forms of the traditional Christian saints' names (e.g. *Bogosian*, *Petrosian*). Following a history of persecution in their native land, Armenians have spread to every part of Europe and the English-speaking world, where their surnames may now be found.

Jewish Family Names*

The Jewish surnames in this dictionary were obtained in the same way as other surnames in the book, with a great number of additions from the Jewish Family Name File of the Association for the Study of Jewish Languages. Within the compass of this File falls any family name borne by a Jew, whether or not it has also been borne by a non-Jew. For the File's purposes, *Jew* is defined as 'anyone who considers himself or herself a Jew'.

The explanations of Jewish family names were prepared by David L. Gold. First, a tentative explanation was drafted, which was then revised in the light of the information held in the Jewish Family Name File. The explanations given in 'standard' sources were also consulted. If these explanations differed from the draft, the two were weighed. In most cases, Dr Gold's original explanations are included here, since the alternate ones cannot be said to be more convincing. In a few instances the draft entries were modified. For many names, existing publications appear to agree on an explanation, whereas the explanation given in the present work appears to be a lone dissenter. Generally, this should not be taken as a majority versus a lone minority; the tendency of other sources to copy uncritically from one another, giving a superficial impression of agreement, should not be underestimated.

Because the dictionary is concerned mostly with European surnames, and because most European Jews of the last few hundred years have been Ashkenazim (Yiddish-speaking Jews and their descendants), most of the Jewish family names which it contains are Ashkenazic. Also, since the dictionary is written in English, it will naturally find its largest readership in English-speaking countries, where most Jews in recent times have been Ashkenazim. This double slant of the dictionary, then, explains the preponderance of Ashkenazic names, although some Sefardic ones are given too (Sefardim being the Jews of the Iberian Peninsula and their descendants). There are also a few Jewish family

* This section is based on an essay by David L. Gold, which appeared in the *Jewish Languge Review*, vol. 7, 1987.

names which are neither Ashkenazic nor Sefardic. Some of the Jewish family names in this dictionary are labelled merely *Jewish*. This means either that they are found among both Ashkenazim and Sefardim (and perhaps also among other Jewish groups), or that it has not been possible to determine their communal status.

This is the first general work which pays attention to the communal distribution of Jewish family names. In hundreds of instances, the classification has been taken beyond a simple division into *Ashkenazic* and *Sefardic*. *Western Ashkenazic* refers to speakers of Western Yiddish and their descendants; *Eastern Ashkenazic* refers to speakers of Eastern Yiddish and their descendants. The boundary between Western and Eastern Yiddish is more or less the 1939 German–Polish political boundary, with an imaginary extension southwards. Eastern Yiddish, in turn, is divided into North-eastern and Southern Yiddish; and Southern Yiddish is divided into Central and South-eastern Yiddish. For each of these linguistic divisions there is a corresponding communal division (North-eastern Ashkenazic, Southern Ashkenazic, etc.). For a succinct explanation of these distinctions, see the introduction to Marvin I. Herzog's *The Yiddish Language in Northern Poland: Its Geography and History* (The Hague: Mouton, 1965).

The label *Israeli* as used in this dictionary means that the name is a Jewish family name which arose in Israeli Hebrew—that is, in the last hundred years or so. Some of these names can be easily identified communally, but others cannot. For instance, *Harpaz* (literally 'mountain of pure gold') is clearly a translation of *Goldberg*, which is equally clearly an Ashkenazic family name. By contrast, *Gonen*, which means 'protector', cannot be further specified.

At times, the subclassification is based on non-Jewish linguistic criteria. Thus, the ending *-vici* points unmistakably to Rumanian orthographic influence, just as *-wicz* points to Polish orthographic influence (e.g. *Abramovici* and *Abramowicz* are therefore spelling variants of the same name). Many names show mixed spellings, like German–Polish *Honigsztein* (Polish *sz* occurring with German *ei*) and English–German *Fishbein* (English *sh* with German *ei*). In other instances, it is non-Jewish phonology which gives us the clue to the name's currency: since Russian has no /h/, it converts this sound in words from other languages into /g/ (Heinrich Heine is called *Gaynrikh Gayne* in Russian). An Ashkenazic name such as *Hirshfeld* thus becomes *Girshfeld* under Russian influence.

Jewish family names containing Yiddish- or German-origin elements are always Ashkenazic. Names containing Slavic-origin elements are almost always Eastern Ashkenazic (or are originally Eastern Ashkenazic but transplanted to Western Ashkenazic territory). Occasionally, however, they are not exclusively Ashkenazic. For example, *Abramov*, which contains the Russian-origin element *-ov*, is also found among the Jews of Bukhara, who are not Ashkenazic. This was one result of the absorption of the Emirate of Bukhara by the Russian Empire.

The Yiddish etymons in this dictionary have been romanized according to the Standardized Yiddish Romanization (a guide to which has appeared in the *Jewish Language Review*, vol. 5, 1985, pp. 96–103). The Hebrew etymons have been romanized according to the General-Purpose System of the American National Romanization of Hebrew (published by the American National Standards Institute).

A large class of Ashkenazic family names is described here as 'ornamental names'. These are sometimes called 'arbitrary names', but to call them arbitrary is to misrepresent their true character. No name is ever completely arbitrary. Rather, there are degrees of arbitrariness. Family names are either chosen or imposed. Many Jewish names were chosen, and recently enough for the circumstances of the choice to be known in family tradition. A butcher who chooses a name meaning 'butcher' is certainly not being arbitrary. If he chooses a name meaning 'gold mountain' he is being arbitrary from the occupational standpoint. However, since this name (e.g. *Goldberg*) has ornamental value in his culture, it is not an arbitrary choice from, shall we say, the poetic standpoint. 'Ornamental' is thus a more apposite label than 'arbitrary', and it corresponds to the probable motives of those who chose these names for themselves. They presumably said to themselves, 'Let's pick a nice-sounding name', not 'Let's pick an arbitrary name'.

The number of Ashkenazic family names which are purely ornamental is legion, and here a parallel suggests itself with Swedish, where the number of ornamental names is also large. In the Jewish religion to this day, as in traditional Swedish society, family names play no role whatsoever. People are—or were—known as 'X the son (or daughter) of Y' (or sometimes, in earlier Jewish history, as 'X the grandchild of Y'). When traditional Jews were forced to take family names by the local bureaucracy, it was an obligation imposed from outside traditional society, hence people often took it playfully and let their imaginations run wild by choosing names which either corresponded to nothing real in their world (like *Blumenthal* 'flower valley') or, even more surrealistically, corresponded to nothing in the world at all (like *Blumstein* and *Blumenstein* 'flower stone'). Much the same happened in Sweden, where playfully chosen compounds such as *Blomdahl* and *Lilje(n)ström* 'lily river' form the largest class of Swedish surnames after the frozen patronymics (see the section on Swedish above).

If students of Jewish family names have hitherto seldom even recognized the existence of the ornamental category, it goes without saying that no one has as yet attempted a typology of such names. At least some of the major subcategories are represented by names referring to flora, fauna, weather, climate, seasons, and colours. This is not to say that every Jewish family name so referring is necessarily an ornamental name. Thus, the Ashkenazic family name *Federman*, literally 'feather man', is clearly an occupational name, referring to someone who deals in feathers; and the Ashkenazic family name *Geller*, literally 'yellow one', refers to a redheaded person (not a blond, as has often been supposed; compare Yiddish *gel* 'yellow, redheaded' and *blond* 'blond').

Nor does this mean that every ornamental name is necessarily a surrealistic one. An ornamental name, as we have already noted, refers to nothing connected with its original bearer's life: those choosing or receiving the family name *Bieber* 'beaver', for example, did not raise beavers, trap them, sell their skins, look or dress like beavers, or have anything to do with beavers at all. They chose the name, or it was given to them because, somehow, words relating to the animal kingdom came to be used widely as ornamental names among Ashkenazim. None the less, the name does refer to something in the real world.

Another category of Ashkenazic ornamental names consists of hopeful names: *Morgenbesser* 'tomorrow [will be] better', *Leblang* 'live long', *Gutwetter* 'good weather',

Gutlohn 'good reward', *Lebenbaum* 'tree of life' (a translation of Yiddish *ets-hakhayim* and Hebrew *ets-hachayim*), *Trost* 'consolation', and so on.

Some Ashkenazic family names may be described as occupational-ornamental, for example *Gutfleisch* 'good meat', *Nagel* 'nail', and *Scher* 'scissors', taken by or given to a butcher, a carpenter, and a tailor respectively. Most of the surrealistic Jewish family names are purely ornamental, but some may be occupational-ornamental. How, for example, should we treat *Fischbaum* 'fish tree'? It is definitely surrealistic, but is it occupational-ornamental (did its first bearer have something to do with fish?) or purely ornamental? Good examples of the occupational-ornamental category are found at *Wechsler*, where the elaborations *Wexelbaum* 'exchange tree', *Wechselberg* 'exchange mountain', and *Wechselfisch* 'exchange fish' were probably all first adopted by or given to money changers.

Many occupational names among Ashkenazim are also common nouns in Yiddish or German, like *Schnayder* 'tailor' and *Stolyer* 'carpenter', whereas others are potentially but not actually common nouns, like *Fleyshman* and *Melman*, taken by or given to butchers and flour millers respectively.

No one alive today is old enough to remember the times when Jews took or were given family names (for most Ashkenazim this was the end of the 18th century or the beginning of the 19th), although many remember names being changed after immigration to other countries, such as the United States and Israel in recent years. In the absence of living witnesses or copious contemporary accounts of how names were acquired, we can in many cases only note the literal meaning of the name (and even this modest goal is often hard to attain, as the thousands of unanswered queries in the *Jewish Language Review* about the meaning of family names show). If the literal meaning of a name is not known, we can hardly say why it was taken or given. If its literal meaning is known, we may or may not be able to say why it was taken or given. At both of these stages in the examination of a name, there are degrees of certainty. Thus, it is perfectly clear that *Morgenbesser* literally means 'tomorrow [will be] better': compare German *Morgen*, Yiddish *morgn* 'tomorrow' and German *besser*, Yiddish *beser* 'better'. It is a reasonable assumption that the name expresses hope in a better future. However, we cannot be sure whether it expressed a person's habitual expectation, or whether it came in response to a specific set of circumstances (perhaps just before taking the name, the person had suffered a serious loss of some kind—this is unsubstantiated conjecture of a kind which must be avoided in a serious study of the origins of family names).

In some cases, behind the assumption of a family name is a now forgotten or unrecorded minor incident or some other extremely personal motive which is now irrecoverable. Occasionally, it is possible to determine the reasons why a particular family name was picked. For example, a man with the given names *Aren Hirsch* (so spelled) is known to have taken the family name *Arnholz* in Pomerania in 1812 (Arthur Kurzweil, *From Generation to Generation* (New York, 1980), p. 109). But it would be misleading to assert in a general work, on the basis of a single piece of evidence, that the surname *Arnholz* was always taken because of its phonetic similarity to the personal name *Aren* Aaron. For such generalizations to stand up, a statistical study on a much larger scale than anything that has been undertaken so far would be called for. It is by no means certain that sufficient evidence exists to make such studies possible in any but a few cases.

ACKNOWLEDGEMENTS

The study of a surname means many different things to many different people: it may be an exercise in family history or genealogy, drawing on family records and oral tradition as well as on old documents of many different origins. It may be an exercise in local history, studying the occurrence of a name in a particular region throughout the centuries, often with some reference to migrations to other parts of the world. Or it may be part of an exercise in the study of a particular community within a region: the Jewish communities of central Europe, for example, or expatriate Irish or Scottish communities. For others, the study of surnames is an exercise in philology: what are the linguistic origins of the surnames under scrutiny? What are their cognates in other dialects and other languages? What are their derivatives, and how were the derivatives formed? Still others study the statistics of surname distribution from a demographic point of view. What can surnames tell us about mobility of population or about human genetic structure?

No single author, or pair of authors, could hope to have expertise in all the many fields of knowledge required for a work of this scope. The ideal author would be a polyglot philologist, with expertise in the history of Celtic, Slavonic, and Finno-Ugric languages as well as in Germanic and Romance languages. Also needed would be a mastery of Hebrew and Aramaic, for explanations of names of biblical origin. He or she would have a detailed knowledge of the local history of every region of all the countries of Europe, and of every community within those regions, not to mention the United States, Canada, South America, Australia, New Zealand, and elsewhere. He or she would be a genealogist and a surveyor of family histories, with access to the innumerable family histories that have never been published, as well as to those that have actually appeared in print. Our ideal author would have a detailed knowledge of placenames, for the relationship between surnames and placenames is often deep and intricate. Statistics, too, is a prerequisite for surnames studies: for example, movements of population and generation need to be quantified, and the likelihood of single or multiple origin must be evaluated by studying statistically the historical and geographical distribution of the name.

Perhaps, with the development of computer technology, databases may in the not too distant future be built up containing most of these features: a vast repository of knowledge contributed by many authors. In the present state of our knowledge (and of available funds), we are still reliant on the harmless drudgery of the lexicographer. The lexicographer makes no claim to any of the attributes outlined above. Rather, he (or she) is a professional generalist, setting out to survey the field as objectively as possible from many different points of view. The number and variety of these points of view may go some way to explain why general works of good quality on surnames are so few and far between.

When we embarked on the present work, it was not our intention to carry out original research on individual surnames, but rather to survey the existing literature, summarizing systematically in dictionary form what is already known, and giving a balanced picture of surnames in Europe. However, as the work progressed, we found that, with a few honourable exceptions, our worst fears were confirmed: the existing literature tends to be skimpy to say the least, and often of doubtful reliability, while the coverage of present-day surnames tends to be selective to the point of eccentricity. For this reason, we were sometimes forced into more detailed research than we had intended, in order to preserve the balance of coverage. With the help of colleagues listed below, we have attempted not only to introduce a systematic pan-European perspective into the study of surnames, but also to advance understanding of many individual names, some of them of great frequency. We do not, of course, claim infallibility: in spite of all the efforts of colleagues and advisers, this dictionary no doubt contains mistakes and other shortcomings. For all of these, the authors accept sole responsibility.

We were singularly fortunate that such a large number of scholars from so many different disciplines agreed to read drafts of our dictionary entries, giving most generously of their time and making many valuable suggestions for additions and improvements. For example, Dr Gold wrote or rewrote the Jewish entries, contributing literally thousands of new explanations and classifications. Dr West did much the same for Iberian names, drawing on his extensive survey of Spanish, Portuguese, Catalan, and Basque surnames. Dr Gelling advised on English surnames derived from placenames, making many corrections and improvements and proposing a probable location of origin for some of the habitation names which baffled us. Professor de Bhaldraithe helped us pick our way through the mysteries of Irish philology, while Ian Fraser, Hywel Wyn Owen, and Oliver Padel made many helpful suggestions regarding Scottish, Welsh, and Cornish names. Mrs Ewa Radzimińska-Kaźmierczak checked frequencies in the Łódź telephone directory and supplied draft etymological information from Polish sources, while Dr Stone devoted a generous amount of his time to reading and commenting on a large number of the draft entries in Slavonic languages.

The full list of those who read part or all the text at various stages, in many cases more than once, correcting errors and suggesting additions and improvements, is as follows:

Professor Tomás de Bhaldraithe, Professor of Irish Dialectology, University College, Dublin.

Professor G. F. Cushing, Professor of Hungarian, School of Slavonic and Eastern European Studies, University of London.

Mr Ian A. Fraser, School of Scottish Studies, University of Edinburgh.

Dr Margaret Gelling, Reader: English Place Name Studies, University of Birmingham.

Dr David L. Gold, The Jewish Family Name File, Association for the Study of Jewish Languages, University of Haifa, Israel.

Mr M. J. de K. Holman, Department of Russian Studies, University of Leeds.

Dr Hywel Wyn Owen, Director, Clwyd Place-Name Council; Y Coleg Normal, Bangor, Wales.

Mr O. J. Padel, Institute of Cornish Studies (University of Exeter), Redruth, Cornwall.

Mrs Ewa Radzimińska-Kaźmierczak, Łódź Medical Academy, Łódź, Poland.

Dr Veronica Smart, Centre for Advanced Historical Studies, University of St Andrews, Scotland.

Dr G. C. Stone, Fellow of Hertford College, Oxford.

Mr C. J. Wells, Fellow and Tutor in Medieval German, St Edmund Hall, Oxford.

Dr Geoffrey West, Hispanic Section, The British Library.

Professor Morton Benson kindly lent us a list of Croatian surnames which he had prepared for another purpose, and from which we were able to take extracts. Many other scholars helped us with individual queries. Mr Tom Bonington of the Slavonic Cataloguing Section in Birmingham University Library helped us with Czech sources, while Mrs Ela Bullon did the same for Polish sources.

A word on our debt to the existing literature is also appropriate here. Our debt is considerable, but not uncritical. Surnames studies are sadly neglected in most of the countries of Europe; the number of reliable reference works is remarkably small. The reader will find on page li a bibliography of general works that were consulted. These are remarkable chiefly for their scarcity. In the case of Hispanic surnames, for example, little can be offered to the reader who wants further reading beyond a few short papers. In the British Isles, understanding of surnames was greatly advanced earlier this century by the work of Reaney, Black, and MacLysaght. Their publications, all grounded in studies of names preserved in ancient records, have been carefully studied, and for the most part their explanations have been accepted, in the absence of good evidence to the contrary. Nevertheless, for all their merits, these works have their shortcomings.

Reaney, for example, pays little attention to the single largest class of English surnames, namely habitation and topographic names; MacLysaght is highly selective; and Black is often silent on the subject of linguistic origins. Moreover, even though their work in each case is now decades old, it has, alas, rarely been followed up by a body of substantial detailed scholarship. Only the Department of Local History at Leicester University, with funds provided by the Marc Fitch Foundation, is seriously active in this field in the British Isles.

Occasionally, an exciting new study appears. Thus, in the case of Welsh surnames, an impressive work of scholarship by Dr T. J. Morgan, assisted by his son Dr Prys Morgan, was published in 1985. This was too late for their book to have more than a superficial effect on the present dictionary.

Among other honourable exceptions, the work of de Felice on Italian surnames is discussed in the Introduction to the present dictionary. Other especially valuable reference works include studies of German surnames by Gottschald and (more accessibly) Bahlow, and the study of Russian surnames, written in English, by Unbegaun. In 1983, Moldanová's excellent dictionary of Czech surnames was published in Prague. At this point the list of honourable exceptions begins to run out. Studies of particular names, good and bad, abound, but reliable general works are rare.

We were generously supported by many who kindly shared with us the fruits of their research into particular names. We would like to thank all those family historians, genealogists, and members of one-name societies who have written to us with information. Special thanks are due to Mr Derek Palgrave, chairman of the Guild of One-Name Studies, for his support and encouragement.

It has not been possible to include all the information received, but an attempt has been made to summarize genealogical and other information that may be of general interest, especially where this is not available in other published sources. The following people, in particular, contributed information about their own or other names. The entries to which they have contributed are printed in small capital letters. If the name discussed is a subentry in the dictionary, it is printed here in italics, along with the main entry in small capitals.

Mrs Hiley Addington (ADDINGTON); Mr C. M. Ainslie (AINSLIE); Mrs G. M. Alderson-Walker (*Alderson* at ALDER); Mr Derek John Allen (CODGBROOK); Prof. Samuel G. Armistead (ARMISTEAD); Mr H. J. Ash (PICKERDEN, ELBOROUGH); Mr and Mrs C. P. Baines (BAINES, also DENTON); Mrs Barbara Balch (DADSWELL); Dr L. H. Barfield (BARFIELD); Dr D. Barham (BARHAM—information also received from Mrs P. A. Howard); Mrs Charmian Barker (GUPPY); Mrs Elizabeth A. Barlow (QUALTROUGH); Mr J. D. Barnes (DENLEY); Mr Chris Barrett (UREN); Mr Clifford R. Baughen (BAUGHAN); Dr Alan M. Beattie (*Mewett* at MOËT); Mrs D. Beck (BUSS); Mr T. L. Beckham (BECKHAM); Mr Alan Ellison Bennett (BENNETT, also *Barnard* at BERNARD, *Ellison* at ELLIS, and SHALLCROSS); Prof. Morton Benson (BENSON 3); Mr Douglas K. Beresford (BERESFORD); Mr Alan Bevins (SIDNEY); Ms Polly Bird (GOLDRING); Mr H. R. Blackburn (AMBRIDGE); Prof. Haim Blanc (BLANC); Mr Anthony Russell Bleek (*Bleeke* at BLAKE); Mr F. Bluck (BLUCK); Mr Stewart James Boase (BOAS); Ms Mary Bodfish (BODFISH); Mr Stephen Boorne (*Boorne* at BOURNE); Mr Maurice J. Bowra (*Bowra* at BOWER); Mr Malcolm Boyes (BOYCE); Marion and Colin Brackpool (BRACKPOOL); Mr David Sidney Brown (*Krantzcke* at KRANZ); Miss Sue Brown (*Gorick* at GEORGE); Mr F. C. Brownhill (BROWNHILL); Mr Fred Wallis Brush (BRUSH); Mrs Katherine Grayson-Ashby Bullock (ASHBY); Mrs Sara A. Bunnett (BUNNETT); Mr David Bunter (BUNTER); Mr John W. Burden (BURDON); Mr K. Bushby (BUSHBY); Mr J. M. Butteriss (BUTTERISS); Mr J. H. Callow (CALLOW); Mr Leslie Campion (CAMPION); Miss Margaret Carlyon (CARLYON); Miss M. B. Carolan (*Amphlett* at FLEET); Mrs M. Catty (PITE); Mr Hugh Cave (CAVE); Mr Dudley John Cheke (*Cheke* at CHEEK); Mrs Ann V. Chiswell (CHISWELL, also WARNE); Mr Brian W. Christmas (CHRISTMAS); Mr Ron City (CITY, also

BROOKSBY, KELLO, and *Defries* at FRIES); Miss M. A. Clapp (CLAPP); Mrs V. F. Clasby (CLASBY, also MANDRY); Mr E. Roland Cleak (CLEAK); Mr C. J. Clemett (*Clemett* at CLEMENT); Mr Dick Clifford (CLIFFORD); Mr Stanley W. Clive (CLIVE); Mr David Cobb (COBB); the Revd H. W. Coffey (BRACKEN); Mr A. F. Cogswell (COXALL); Mrs Lynne Cowley (SCHROFF); Mr John Crawford (CRAWFORD, also CROWFOOT); Mr Richard A. Crimp (CRIMP); Mr H. Culling (CULLING); Mrs Hilda Davis (*Randon* at RAND, SHUGG); Mr Patrick Delaforce (*Delaforce* at FORCE); Mr Frank J. Denzey (DANSIE); Mr H. G. DeVille (DEVILLE); Mr Geoffrey Diss (DISS); Mrs Dorothy Dore (SPOTTISWOOD); Mr Edward Henry Dorrell (DARELL); Mr John Douch (*Douch(e)* at DUCE); Miss Phyl Drake (*Chaffin* at CHAFF); Mrs S. A. Drake-Feary (FEARY, also *Quay* at MCKAY); Herr Friedrich Dürrenmatt (DÜRRENMATT); Mrs Sarah Ricketts Dyson (RICKETTS); Mr E. C. Edwards (BATLEY, *Cane* at CHÊNE, *Dadd* at DODD, *Goozee* at GOOSEY, and *Southee* at SOUTHEY); Dr T. A. Edwards (EDWARDS, also CLEGG); Dr David E. Etheridge (*Etheridge* at EDRICH); Mr T. H. Failes (FAILES); Mr J. E. Fairfax (FAIRFAX); Mr Brian C. T. Faithfull (*Faithful(l)* at FAITH); Mr George F. Fallows (FALLOWS); Mr H. C. L. Fassnidge (FASSNIDGE); Mr Raymond Francis Fautley (FAUTLEY); Mr Robert Fenwick (FENWICK); Miss Mary Flower (FLOWER); Ms Jacqueline M. Freegard (FREEGARD); Mr P. Freeman (*Bernardes* at BERNARD); Mrs L. J. From (FROMM); Mr Paul Fursdon (FURSDON); Mr Royston Gambier (GAMBIER); Mr M. J. Gandy (GANDY); Mr W. S. Gilbert (GILBERT); Mr M. I. A. Goodbody (GOODBODY); Mr K. Goodey (GOODEY); Mr John P. Gordon (PREBBLE); Mr George A. Goulty (GOULTY); Prof. B. G. Gowenlock (GOWENLOCK); Mr and Mrs G. J. and J. A. E. Gracéy-Cox (HOGWOOD); Ms Mary D. Griffiths (PARLEY); Mr James T. Grinter (GRINTER); Mr Edward A. Grove (GROVE); Mr D. L. Gunn (GUNN); Mr Peter Donald Guyver (GUIVER); Mr Ian Haddrell (HATHERELL); Mr J. C. Halbrooks (HOLBROOK); Mr David Hall (PRENDERGAST); Mr D. W. Hamley (HAMBLY); Mr Michael A. Hansford (HANSFORD); Mr Hugh Richard Hards (HARDS); Mr Noel Harrower (HARROWER); Mr J. R. Hebden (HEBDEN, also EBDON); Mr John Heritage (HERITAGE); Mr John Hitchon (HITCHON); Mrs Joyce Hoad (ENOCK); Mr Wilf Hodgkinson (*Hodgkinson* at HODGE); Dr James D. Hodsdon (HODSDON, also HINDER); Mr Victor E. J. Holttum (HOLTUM); Cdr L. G. Hooke (HOOK); Mrs P. A. Howard (BARHAM—information also received from Dr D. Barham); M. Claude Hurel (*Hurel* at HURÉ, *Peverell* at PEPPER, *Costard* at CONSTANTINE); Mr E. Leslie Hyner (HYNER); Mr Arthur Richard Inch (*Inch* at INNES); Mr Kingsley James Ireland (CAVENETT); Mr Lytton Proom Jarman (PROOM); Mr Jess Arthur Jephcott (*Jephcott* at JEFFREY); Mr Ernest John Jewesson (*Jewesson* at JULIAN); Mr Walter Wesley Johnston (*Butson* at BUTT); Dr P. Kelvin (HACKWOOD); Mr Thomas H. F. Kidman (*Kidman* at KIDD); Miss Madeline R. Killick (KILLICK); Miss M. R. Killon (COMFORT, CORNFORD, and CORNFORTH); Mrs W. Berta Kivi (BICKNELL, BOLWELL, DEBANK, MILLIER, and *Inker* at INGER); Sir John Knill (KNILL); Mrs Hope Koontz (*Swainson* at SWAIN); Mr Basil La Bouchardière (*Bouchard* at BURKETT); Mrs Lynn B. Lane (HAMLETT); Ms Jean A. Larson (*Alborn* at ALBAN); Mr Jacob Lateiner (LATEINER, also FELDSCHER); Mr F. L. Leeson (LEES, LEIGH, and many other entries); Mr David James Leithead (LEITHEAD); Mr Philip E. Lloyd (SHOLL); Mr Douglas H. V. Lobb (LOBB); Mr Henry Longbottom (LONGBOTTOM, also FILDES, GUEST, SELLER); Mrs J. A. Longmire (LONGMIRE, also SOMERSCALES); the Revd Ian Lucraft (LUCRAFT); Mr and Mrs D. Lupton (LUPTON); Mr E. McDougall (*Cutlack* at GULLICK); Mr Alan A. Mallery (MALLORY—information also received from Mrs Sheila Mallory Smith); Mr J. D. Manley (MANLEY); Mr John K. Marfleet (MARFLEET); Lt. Col. Stanley N. Marker (MARKER); Mr Edward A. Martin (MARTIN); Mr Robert Thomas Buford Meteyard (MEATYARD); Mrs Margery G. Miller (MOMBRUN); Mr M. E. Millichamp (MILLICHAMP); Mr Roland D. Mirrington (MERITON); Col. L. F. Morling (MORLING); Mr Anthony Earle Newman (NEWMAN); Mrs L. B. Norman (*Powdrill* at PUTTERILL); Mr John Norrington (NORRINGTON); Mr A. C. Pagan (PAGAN); Mr Derek

A. Palgrave (PALGRAVE); Mrs Pamela Palgrave (SPILLING); Mr Eric V. Partington (PARTINGTON, also *Howkins* at HUGH); Mrs P. M. Pattinson (EAGLE, EAGLES); Mr A. G. Peake (PEAK); Mrs Ann Lisa Pearson (MORRELL); Mr George Pelling (PELLING); Mr Norman Penty (PENTY); Mr William A. Peplow (PEPLOW); Mr John W. Perrin (PERRIN); Mr Ron Phelps (*Phelps* at PHILIP); Mr and Mrs W. A. Philson (DUDER, also *Philson* and *Filson* at PHILIP); Mr B. Piercy (PERCY); Mr William Keith Plant (PLANT); Mr and Mrs J. Pockney (POCKNEY); Mr Albert Charles Polyblank (POLYBLANK); Mrs Ruth Pritchett (*Jobling* and *Joplin* at JOB); Mr J. E. Proudfoot (PROUDFOOT); Miss Thelma Constance Pruen (PRUEN); Capt. David Martin Pulvertaft (PULVERTAFT); Mr J. A. Rawes (*Rawes* at RAW); Mr Alan V. Reed (GLAISTER); Mrs Muriel Reson (COPLESTONE); Mrs Rita Restorick (RESTORICK); Mr C. F. Reynolds (*Phipson* at PHILIP); Mr W. E. Rounce (*Rounce* at ROUND, also CAWTHORN); Mr Alan V. Sabourin (*Sabourin* at SAVOUREUX); Mr A. Sandison (*Sandison* at SANDER); Mr John S. Sermon (SERMON); Mrs Betty Choyce Sheehan (CHOYCE); Mr H. F. Shipp (POPKISS); Mr Geoffrey Hubert Shipsides (SHIPSIDE, also CRIPWELL); Mr Brian O. Silverton (SILVERTON); Mrs Dorothy Simms (BRIDLE, BODLE); Mr G. R. Simpson (CURME); Mrs Mary Skipworth (SKIPWITH); Mr Eric Smith (EASY, BROXHOLME); Mr R. B. M. Smith (REFOY); Mrs Sheila Mallory Smith (MALLORY—information also received from Mr Alan A. Mallery); Mrs Thelma E. Smith (ROOTHAM); Mr B. Spaughton (SPAUGHTON); Mr F. W. Staples (*Staples* at STAPLE); Mrs Anne M. Storey (*Stiven* at STEPHEN); Mr W. Trevor Stott (STOTT); Mr J. Stumbke (STUMBKE); Lt. Col. I. S. Swinnerton (SWINNERTON); Mr J. C. C. Sworder (*Sworder* at SWORD); Mr C. Roger Tatler (TATLER); Mrs Aideen Taylor (PUGMIRE, BROCKWELL); Mr Michael R. Tedd (TEDD); Brig. C. R. Templer (*Templer* at TEMPLE); Mr Thomas Milton Tinney (TINNEY); Mr John S. Titford (TITFORD); Mr Peter J. Towey (DARLEY, *Featley* at FAIRCLOUGH, FREATHY, LANYON, *Neilder* at NADLER, ROSEMAN); Mr R. J. Tunnicliff (*Holah* at HOLE); Mr Colin Ulph (*Ulph* at WOLF); Mr T. F. Kenneth Ulyatt (*Ulyatt* at WOLFIT); Mr J. Waller (WALLER); Mr David J. Warnes (WARNES, also LITTLEPROUD); Mr Kelvin E. Warth (WARTH); Mrs B. R. Watson (CHITTENDEN, CROAKER, MUSGRAVE); Mr Monty Thomas Ousley Weddell (OUSLEY); Mrs B. M. Wells (TEARLE); Mr Alfred L. Wesson (*Wesson* at WESTON); Mr Peter M. Whitlock (WHITLOCK); Mr Hugh Whitworth (*Cuthbe* at CUTHBERT); Mrs Ruth Wilcock (*Towlard* at TOLLER); Mr Reginald Wildig (WILDIG); Mr E. A. Wildy (WILDY); Mr James Willerton (WILLERTON); Mrs Elaine I. Wiltshire (BURKIN); Dr Denis B. Woodfield (WOODFIELD); Mr Maurice G. Woodlock and Mr J. T. Woodlock (WOODLOCK); Mr Alan Raymond Worsfold (WORSFOLD); Mr Bill Wynne-Woodhouse (WOODHOUSE); Mr Edward R. Zenthon (ZENTHON).

Most of the original work for this dictionary was carried out in the Department of Language and Linguistics at the University of Essex. We would like to thank colleagues there for tolerating us and our periodic monopoly of the staff workroom in 1981–3, and in particular we wish to express our gratitude to Professor Yorick Wilks, who during his term as chairman of the department gave us unfailing support and encouragement. We would also like to thank the University Computing Service, Mr Charles Bowman, and Dr Alan Stanier, who gave us generous help and advice on computational aspects of the work and prepared validations and an index.

In its later stages, the work was transferred to the University of Birmingham. We would like to express our gratitude to Professor J. M. Sinclair, Professor of Modern English Language, for his support. We are also indebted to Mr Tim Lane, who gave us further help with computing, validation, indexing, and finalization.

Finally, it remains for us to thank two other colleagues at the University of Essex: Sandra Cardew, who carried out additional genealogical and biographical research, and Dilly Meyer, who organized the regional telephone-directory surveys.

P.W.H., F.M.H.

BIBLIOGRAPHY

Addison, William: *Understanding English Surnames* (London, 1978).
Álvarez, Grace de Jesús: *Topónimos en apellidos hispanos* (New York, 1968).
Álvarez-Altman, Grace, and Woods, Richard: *Spanish Surnames in the Southwestern United States* (Boston, 1978).
Asín Palacios, Miguel: *Contribución a la toponimia árabe de España* (2nd edn, Madrid, 1944).
Attwater, Donald: *The Penguin Dictionary of Saints* (Harmondsworth, 1965).
Bahlow, Hans: *Deutschlands geographische Namenwelt* (Frankfurt, 1965).
—— *Deutsches Namenlexikon* (Munich, 1967).
Barber, Henry: *British Family Names* (2nd edn, London, 1903).
Bardsley, C. W.: *A Dictionary of English and Welsh Surnames* (London, 1901).
Benedictine Monks of St Augustine's Abbey, Ramsgate: *The Book of Saints* (London, 1947).
Benson, Morton: *Dictionary of Russian Personal Names* (Philadelphia, 1964).
Black, George F.: *The Surnames of Scotland* (New York, 1962).
Brett, Donald: 'The Use of Telephone Directories in Surname Studies' in *The Local Historian*, vol. 16, 1985.
Bystroń, Jan Stanisław: *Nazwiska polskie* (2nd edn, Warsaw, 1936).
Carnoy, A.: *Origines des noms de famille en Belgique* (Louvain, 1953).
Cellard, Jacques: *Trésors des noms de familles* (Paris, 1983).
Cottle, Basil: *The Penguin Dictionary of Surnames* (Harmondsworth, 1978).
Dauzat, Albert: *Dictionnaire étymologique des noms de famille et prénoms de France* (Paris, 1951; rev. edn 1977).
—— and Rostaing, Charles: *Dictionnaire étymologique des noms de lieux en France* (Paris, 1963; rev. edn 1978).
de Felice, Emidio: *Dizionario dei cognomi italiani* (Milan, 1978).
—— *I cognomi italiani* (Bologna, 1981).
Díez Melcón, Gonzalo: *Apellidos castellano-leoneses* (Granada, 1957).
Dolan, J. R.: *English Ancestral Names* (New York, 1972).
Ekwall, Eilert: *The Concise Oxford Dictionary of English Place-Names* (4th edn, Oxford, 1960).
Feilitzen, Olof von: *The Pre-Conquest Personal Names of Domesday Book* (Uppsala, 1938).
Fekete, Antal: *Keresztneveink, Védöszentjeink* (Budapest, 1974).
Förstemann, Ernst: *Altdeutsches Namenbuch* (Bonn, 1916).
Fucilla, Joseph Guerin: *Our Italian Surnames* (Evanston, 1949).
—— 'Office and Occupational Names in Spain' in *Names*, vol. 24, 1976.
Godoy Alcántara, José: *Ensayo histórico etimológico filológico sobre los apellidos castellanos* (Madrid, 1871; repr. Barcelona, 1980).
Gottschald, Max: *Deutsche Namenkunde* (2nd edn Munich/Berlin, 1942; 4th edn 1971).
Guppy, Henry Brougham: *Homes of Family Names in Great Britain* (London, 1890).
Harrison, Henry: *Surnames of the United Kingdom* (London, 1912–18).
Hook, J. N.: *Family Names: How our Surnames came to America* (New York, 1982).
—— *Family Names: The Origins, Meanings and Mutations, and History of more than 2800 American Names* (New York, 1983).
Ilčev, Stefan: *Rečnik na ličnite i familni imena u Bulgarite* (Sofia, 1969).
Janowowa, W., *et al.*: *Słownik imion* (Warsaw, 1975).

Kaganoff, Benzion C.: *A Dictionary of Jewish Names and their History* (New York, 1977).
Kálmán, Béla: *The World of Names: A Study in Hungarian Onomatology* (Budapest, 1978).
Kelly, Patrick: *Irish Family Names* (Chicago, 1939).
Kluge, Friedrich: *Etymologisches Wörterbuch der deutschen Sprache* (17th–20th edns, ed. Walther Mitzka, Berlin, 1957–67).
Lasker, G. W.: *Surnames and Genetic Structure* (Cambridge, 1985).
Lebel, Paul: *Les Noms de personnes* (Paris, 1968).
Leeson, Francis: 'The History and Technique of Surname Distribution Studies' in *Family History*, vol. 3, 1965.
Maas, Herbert: *Von Abel bis Zwicknagel* (Munich, 1964).
Mac Giolla-Dhomnaigh, Padraig: *Some Ulster Surnames* (Dublin, 1975).
MacLysaght, Edward: *The Surnames of Ireland* (Dublin, 1969; 3rd edn 1978).
McKinley, Richard: *Norfolk and Suffolk Surnames in the Middle Ages* (London, 1975).
—— *The Surnames of Oxfordshire* (London, 1977).
—— *The Surnames of Lancashire* (London, 1981).
Mencken, H. L. (ed. Raven I. McDavid, Jr.): *The American Language* (New York, 1963).
Menéndez Pidal, Ramón: *Toponimia prerrománica hispana* (Madrid, 1952).
Michelena, Luis: *Apellidos vascos* (San Sebastián, 1953; 3rd edn 1978).
Moldanová, Dobrava: *Naše příjmení* (Prague, 1983).
Moll, Francesc de B.: *Els llinatges catalans* (Mallorca, 1982).
Moralejo Lasso, Abelardo: *Toponimia gallega y leonesa* (Santiago, 1977).
Moreu-Rey, Enric: *Renoms, motius, malnoms i noms de casa* (Barcelona, 1981).
Morgan, T. J., and Morgan, Prys: *Welsh Surnames* (Cardiff, 1985).
Morris, T. E.: *Welsh Surnames in the Border Counties of Wales* (London, 1932).
Nascentes, Antenor de Veras: *Dicionário etimológico da lingua portuguesa*, vol. 2 (Rio de Janeiro, 1952).
Padel, Oliver: *Cornish Place Name Elements* (English Place-Name Society, 1985).
Pawley White, G.: *A Handbook of Cornish Surnames* (Redruth, 2nd edn 1981).
Reaney, P. H.: *A Dictionary of British Surnames* (London, 2nd edn 1976).
Redmonds, George: *Yorkshire West Riding* (English Surname Series, 1) (London and Chichester, 1973).
Rosenthal, Eric: *South African Surnames* (Cape Town, 1965).
Smith, Elsdon C.: *New Dictionary of American Family Names* (New York, 1969; enlarged edn 1973).
Tengvik, G.: *Old English Bynames* (Uppsala, 1938).
Tibón, Gutierre: *Onomástica hispano-americana* (México, 1961).
Unbegaun, Boris Ottokar: *Russian Surnames* (Oxford, 1972).
Vasconcelos, José Leite de: *Antroponimia portuguesa* (Lisbon, 1928).
Vilkuna, Kustaa: *Etunimet* (Helsinki, 1977).
—— *et al.*: *Suomalainen nimikirja* (Helsinki, 1984).
Withycombe, E. G.: *The Oxford Dictionary of English Christian Names* (Oxford, 1945; 3rd edn 1977).
Woulfe, Patrick: *Sloinnte Gaedheal is Gall* (Dublin, 1974).

ABBREVIATIONS

Aberdeens.	Aberdeenshire
acc.	accusative
adj.	adjective
ANF	Anglo-Norman French
art.	article
aug.	augmentative
Ayrs.	Ayrshire
Banffs.	Banffshire
Beds.	Bedfordshire
Beloruss.	Belorussian
Berks.	Berkshire
Berwicks.	Berwickshire
Bret.	Breton
Brit.	British
Bucks.	Buckinghamshire
Bulg.	Bulgarian
Cambs.	Cambridgeshire
Cat.	Catalan
Celt.	Celtic
Ches.	Cheshire
Chron.	Chronicles
class.	classical
cogn.	cognate
Conn.	Connecticut (U.S.A.)
Corn.	Cornish
cpd	compound
Cumb.	Cumbria/Cumberland
Dan.	Danish/Daniel (context)
dat.	dative
def.	definite
Denbighs.	Denbighshire
Derbys.	Derbyshire
deriv.	derivative
dial.	dialect
dim.	diminutive
Du.	Dutch
Eng.	English
Exod.	Exodus
fem.	feminine
Finn.	Finnish
fl.	*floruit*, flourished
Flem.	Flemish
Flints.	Flintshire
Fr.	French
freq.	frequentative
Fris.	Frisian
Gael.	Gaelic
Gaul.	Gaulish
Gen.	Genesis
gen.	genitive
Ger.	German
Gk	Greek
Gloucs.	Gloucestershire
Gmc	Germanic
Hants	Hampshire
Hebr.	Hebrew
Herefords.	Herefordshire
Herts.	Hertfordshire
Hung.	Hungarian
Hunts.	Huntingdonshire
Ir.	Irish
It.	Italian
Jer.	Jeremiah
Josh.	Joshua
Judg.	Judges
Kincardines.	Kincardineshire
L	Latin
Lanarks.	Lanarkshire
Lancs.	Lancashire
Leics.	Leicestershire
LGk	Late Greek
Lincs.	Lincolnshire
lit.	literally
LL	Late Latin
masc.	masculine
Mass.	Massachusetts (U.S.A.)
Matt.	Matthew
MD	Maryland (U.S.A.)
MDu.	Middle Dutch

ABBREVIATIONS

ME	Middle English
med.	medieval
metr.	metronymic
MHG	Middle High German
MLG	Middle Low German
mod.	modern
n.	noun
Neh.	Nehemiah
neut.	neuter
nom.	nominative
Northants	Northamptonshire
Northumb.	Northumberland
Norw.	Norwegian
Notts.	Nottinghamshire
Num.	Numbers
O	Old (with various languages)
OBret.	Old Breton
OBulg.	Old Bulgarian
OCat.	Old Catalan
OCorn.	Old Cornish
OCzech	Old Czech
ODa.	Old Danish
OE	Old English
OED	*Oxford English Dictionary*
OF	Old French
OFris.	Old Frisian
OHG	Old High German
OIcel.	Old Icelandic
OIr.	Old Irish
OIt.	Old Italian
ON	Old Norse
ONF	Old Northern French
OProv.	Old Provençal
OSax.	Old Saxon
OSlav.	Old Slavonic
OSp.	Old Spanish
OSwed.	Old Swedish
OW	Old Welsh
Oxon.	Oxfordshire
part.	participle
patr.	patronymic
Pebbles.	Peebleshire
pej.	pejorative
Pembrokes.	Pembrokeshire
Perths.	Perthshire
pl.	plural
Pol.	Polish
Port.	Portuguese
pres.	present
Prov.	Provençal
Ps.	Psalm(s)
Renfrews.	Renfrewshire
Rev.	Revelation
Roxburghs.	Roxburghshire
Rum.	Rumanian
Russ.	Russian
Sam.	Samuel
Sc.	Scots
sc.	scilicet, namely
Shrops.	Shropshire
sing.	singular
Skt	Sanskrit
Slav.	Slavonic
Sp.	Spanish
Staffs.	Staffordshire
Stirlings.	Stirlingshire
Swed.	Swedish
Ukr.	Ukrainian
var.	variant
vocab.	vocabulary
W	West/Welsh (context)
Warwicks.	Warwickshire
Wigtons.	Wigtonshire
Wilts.	Wiltshire
Worcs.	Worcestershire
Yid.	Yiddish
Yorks.	Yorkshire
*	hypothetical form

A

Aalto Finnish: ornamental name from Finn. *aalto* wave. This is one of many Finn. surnames selected from vocab. words denoting natural phenomena of the landscape and sea at the time when surnames were being adopted in Sweden and Finland during the 18th and 19th cents.

Var.: **Aaltonen**.

Aaron Jewish: from the Hebr. given name *Aharon*, borne by the brother of Moses, who was the first high priest of the Israelites (Exod. 4: 14). The traditional derivation is from Hebr. *har-on* 'mountain of strength', but it is more probably of Egyptian origin, like MOSES, with a meaning no longer recoverable. In some countries *Aaron* was also a Gentile given name, and so not all occurrences of the surname and its derivs. are Jewish.

Vars.: **Aron** (esp. Fr.); **Agron(ski)** (Russ.); **Aharoni** (Israeli).

Patrs.: **A(a)rons, A(a)ronso(h)n** (Ashkenazic); **Aronov(ich), Aronoff, Aronow(icz), Arunowicz, Aronowitz, Aronovitz, Aronin** (E Ashkenazic); **Arnow(icz), Arnowitz** (from the E Yid. form *Arn*); **Ben-Aharon** (Israeli).

Patrs. (from dims.): **Areles** (Ashkenazic); **Arkow, Arkin** (E Ashkenazic).

Cpds: **Aronstam** ('stock of Aaron'); **Aronstein** ('rock of Aaron', ornamental elaboration).

Abajo Spanish: topographic name for someone who lived downhill or downstream from the main settlement, from Sp. *abajo* below (a development, not attested before the 15th cent., of OSp. *baxo*, from LL *bassus*; cf. BASS). Cf. ARRIBA.

Abascal Spanish (possibly of Basque origin; cf. ABASOLO): local name composed of the elements *abas* priest + *kale* street (cf. ABBÉ and CALLE).

Abasolo Basque: topographic name for someone who lived by or on a patch of land in the ownership of the church, from *abas* priest (a Romance borrowing; cf. ABBÉ) + *solo* meadow.

Abbé French: from OF *abe(t)*, *abed* priest, member of the clergy (see ABBOTT), perhaps a nickname for a sanctimonious person or an occupational name for someone employed in the household of a priest. The Scots cogn. **Abbie** in at least one case was an occupational name, borne by a family who provided hereditary lay abbots.

Vars.: **Labbé** (with fused def. art.); **Labbey** (Burgundy); **Labbez** (N France).

Cogns.: It.: **Ab(b)ate, Ab(b)ati, Ab(b)ado; Lab(b)ate; Ab(b)a, Lab(b)a** (N Italy; also a title of the master of a carnival). Sp., Cat.: **Abad**. Port.: **Abade, Abate**. Eng.: ABBOTT.

Dims.: It.: **Ab(b)atini, Ab(b)atelli, Ab(b)atucci; Labadini; Badini, Vatini**.

Patrs.: It.: **Dell'Ab(b)ate, Degli Ab(b)ati**.

Abbey English: topographic name for someone living by an abbey or occupational name for someone working in one, from ME *abbeye*, *abbaye* (OF *abeie*, LL *abbātia* abbey, priest's house, a deriv. of Gk *abbas*; see ABBOTT).

Vars.: **Abb(a)y, Abbe; Abdey, Abdie** (derived directly, not via OF, from the L term).

Cogns.: Fr.: **Ab(b)aye, Lab(b)aye, Delab(b)aye**. Prov.: **D'Ab(b)adie; Sabadie** (with the fused Gascon def. art. *sa*, from L *ipsa*). It.: **Badia**. Cat.: **Abadia(s); Badia**.

A New England family called Abbe *are descended from John Abbe (b. 1613), who emigrated from England to Salem, Mass., in 1635.*

Abbondi Italian: from the personal name *Abbondio* (L *Abundius*, from LL *abundus*, class. L *abundans*, copious, abundant (literally, 'overflowing')). This was the name of a 5th-cent. bishop, patron saint of Como. The surname is particularly common around Lake Como and in Ticino canton, Switzerland.

Vars.: **Abondi, Ab(b)ondio**.

Abbott English: occupational name for someone employed in the household of an abbot, or perhaps a nickname for a sanctimonious person thought to resemble an abbot, from ME *abbott*, OE *abbod*, reinforced by OF *abe(t)* priest; see ABBÉ. Both the OE and the OF term are from LL, Gk *abbas*, *abbatis* priest, from Aramaic *aba* father). The ostensible celibacy of the clergy makes it unlikely that the surname is an occupational one for a cleric, but cf. *Abbie* at ABBÉ.

Vars.: **Abbot, Abbet**.

Cogns.: Ger.: **Ab(b)t**.

Patrs.: Ir., Sc.: **McNab(b), McNabo, Monaboe** (Gael. **Mac an Aba(dh)**).

Abel 1. English, French, and Dano-Norwegian: from the Hebr. given name *Hevel*, which is of uncertain origin; the traditional derivation is from Hebr. *hevel* breath, vigour, used also in the figurative sense 'vanity', 'worthlessness'. This name was borne by the son of Adam who was murdered by his brother Cain (Gen. 4: 1–8), and was popular as a given name in Christendom during the Middle Ages, when there was a cult of suffering innocence which Abel represented.

2. German: dim. of ALBERT.

Vars. (of 1): Eng.: **Abell, Able**. Fr.: **Abeau**.

Cogn.: Hung.: **Ábel**.

Dims. (of 1): Eng.: **Ablett, Ablitt** (chiefly E Anglia); **Ablott; Hablot**.

Patrs. (from 1): Eng.: ABELSON. Dan., Norw.: **Abels**.

Patr. (from 1)(dim.): Eng.: **Abbs** (chiefly Norfolk).

Abella Catalan: 1. nickname for a small and active person, or metonymic occupational name for a bee-keeper, from Cat. *abella* bee (LL *apicula*, dim. of class. L *apis*).

2. habitation name from places so called in the provinces of Lérida and Barcelona. The name is of uncertain etymology, and may be akin to that of *Avella* in Italy, normally considered to be of Etruscan origin.

Vars. (of 2): **Abellan, Abellà**.

Cogn. (of 1): Prov.: **Abeille**.

Dims. (of 1): Prov.: **Abeilhé, Abeilhon, Abeilhou**.

Abelló Catalan: of uncertain origin. It may be akin to ABELLA, but is also possibly from the L personal name *Abellio*, gen. *Abelliōnis*, which seems to have originally denoted a god worshipped in the Pyrenean region in Roman times, and is of opaque etymology.

Abelson 1. English: patr. from the given name ABEL.
2. Jewish (Ashkenazic): patr. from *Abele*, a dim. of the Yid. given name *Abe*, from Aramaic *aba* father (cf. ABBOTT).

Vars. (of 1): **Ableson**. (Of 2): **Abeles**, **Abells**; **Abelov(itz)**, **Abelevitz**, **Abilowitz** (E Ashkenazic).

Abendroth German (nickname) and Jewish (Ashkenazic, ornamental name): from Ger. *Abendrot* sunset (OHG *ābintrōto*, from *ābint* evening + *rōt* red). As a Ger. nickname it may have been applied to a large man, in allusion to the giant *Abendrot*, the subject of several medieval folk tales. As a Jewish name it was chosen as an ornamental name; cf. MORGENSTERN.

Abensperg Austrian: habitation name from a place in Carinthia, so called from OHG *ābint* evening + *berg* hill, probably because the hill is to the W of the town and the sun sinks behind it in the evening.

Abercrombie Scots: habitation name from a place in Fife (earlier *Abarcrumbach*), so called from Brittonic *aber* confluence + a river name containing the element *crom* crooked + the local suffix *-ach*.

Var.: **Abercromby**.

This is the surname of a British military family which was prominent in the 18th cent.; its most famous member was killed at the battle of Aboukir Bay.

Åberg Swedish: ornamental name composed of the elements *å*, *aa* river + *berg* hill.

Var.: **Oberg** (an Anglicized spelling found in the U.S.).

Abernethy Scots: habitation name from a place near Perth, so called from Brittonic *aber* confluence + a river name possibly akin to Gael. *neithich* water sprite.

Var.: **Abernathy**.

The name is common in S Scotland and in Ireland, where it is especially common in Munster.

Abonville French: habitation name from a place in Eure-et-Loir, Normandy, so called from the Gmc personal name *Abbo* (of uncertain origin, perhaps akin to Gothic *aba* man) + OF *ville* settlement, village (see VILLE).

Vars.: **(D')Aboville**.

Abraham Jewish, English, French, German, Dutch, etc.: from the Hebr. personal name *Avraham*, borne by the first of the Jewish patriarchs, founder of the Jewish people (Gen. 11–25). The name is explained in Gen. 17: 5 as being derived from Hebr. *av hamon goyim* 'father of a multitude of nations'. It was commonly used as a given name among Christians in the Middle Ages, and has always been a popular Jewish given name.

Vars.: **Abram** (but for Eng. see also ADBURGHAM). Ger.: BRAHM. Jewish: **Abrahm**, **Abrahamer**; **Avra(h)am**, **Avra(h)m**, **Abramski**, **Abramsky** (E Ashkenazic); **Abra(ha)mi**, **Abrahamy**, **Avrahami**, **Avra(ha)my** (Israeli).

Cogns.: Hung.: **Ábrahám**. It.: **Abrami**, **Abriani**; **Br(i)amo** (aphetic forms).

Dims.: Jewish: **Abramcik**. Prov.: **Abramin**. It.: **Abramino**. Ukr., Beloruss.: **Abramchik**, **Avramchik**.

Patrs.: Eng.: **Abra(ha)ms(on)**. It.: **D'Abramo**. Ger.: **Abrami** (Latinized). Low Ger.: **Abra(h)ms**, **Abramsen**; **Brahms**. Flem., Du.: **Abrahams**; **Bra(h)ams**. Norw., Dan.: **Abrahamsen**, **Bramsen**. Swed.: **Abrahamsson**. Jewish: **Abra(ha)ms**; **Abrahamso(h)n**, **Abra(h)mson**, **Abramzon**, **Bramson**; **Abrah(a)mov**, **Abramov**, **Abra(ha)mof(f)**, **Abramow**, **Abrahamovitz**, **Abramowitz**, **Abra(ha)mowicz**, **Abramowitch**, **Abramovitz**, **Abramovicz**, **Abramovitch**, **Abramovic(h)**, **Abramowsky**, **Avra(ha)mov**, **Avrahamof(f)**, **Avramow**, **Avramovich**, **Avramovitz**, **Avramovsky** (E Ashkenazic); **Abra(h)movici** (Rum. spelling); **Abrahamian**, **Avra(ha)mian**, **Aprahamian** (among Iranian Jews). Russ.: **Abramov**, **Avramov**; **Ibraimov** (from *Ibrahim*, an Arabic form of the name used in Turkic (Moslem) areas). Ukr., Beloruss.: **Abramovich**. Pol.: **Abramowicz**. Croatian: **Abramović**, **Avramović**.

Patrs. (from dims.): Jewish: **Abrashkin**. Russ.: **Avrashkov**, **Avras(h)in**.

Abreu Portuguese: from the Gmc (Visigothic) personal name *Avredo*, probably composed of the elements *alb*, *alv* elf + *rēd* counsel (cf. ALFRED). The name was borne by a 7th-cent. Hispanic bishop.

Abry French: habitation name for someone living in a rudimentary dwelling, from OF *abri* shelter, refuge (from OF *abrier* to put under covers, keep dry, from L *apricāre* to dry in the sun).

Var.: **Abric**.

Absalom English: from the Hebr. personal name *Avshalom*, composed of the elements *av* father + *shalom* peace. This was the name of the third son of King David, who rebelled against him and was eventually killed, to the great grief of his father (2 Sam.: 15–18). The story was a favourite one in medieval England and elsewhere, and the given name was in use among Christians in spite of the omen. The actual circumstances in which Absalom met his death, with his long hair getting caught in a tree as he was fleeing in his chariot, led to the use of the name as a nickname for a man with a fine head of hair, and the surname may also have originated from this use.

Vars.: Eng.: **Absolom**, **Absolon**, **Aspelon**, **Asplen**, **Asplin(g)**; **Ashplant** (altered by folk etymology, as if from *ash* + *plant*).

Cogns.: Fr.: **Absalon**. Ger.: **Apsel**. Jewish: **Abshalom**, **Avs(c)halom**.

Patrs.: Gael.: MCAUSLAN. Russ.: **Avesalomov** (a clerical name adopted by priests). Jewish: **Abs(h)alomov**.

Abstreiter German: habitation name from a place in Bavaria called *Abstreit*, a metathesized deriv. of Late MHG *abtes* abbot's + *reut* clearing. Folk etymology, however, makes it appear to be derived from Ger. *abstreiten* to dispute, repudiate, deny.

Var.: **Absreuter** (*Absreuten* is the name of a place in Württemberg of the same origin).

Ace English: from the ONF given name *Ace*, *Asse*, which is from a Frankish personal name *A(t)zo*, a hypocoristic form of any of the various Gmc cpd names with a first element *adal* noble (see ADEL).

Var.: **Aze**.

Cogns.: Ger.: **Atz(e)**. It.: **Azzi**.

Dims.: Eng.: **As(t)let(t)**, **As(t)lin(g)**, **Ashlin**, ASHLING. Fr.: **Ascelin**, **Asselin(eau)**. It.: **Azzini**, **Azzol(in)i**.

Aug.: It.: **Azzoni**.

Patrs.: Ger.: **Atzen**. It.: **D'Azzi**.

Acedo Spanish: nickname for a brusque or stern person, from OSp. *açedo* harsh (LL *acētus* bitter, from *acētum* vinegar).

Aceituno Spanish: topographic name for someone who lived near an olive tree or in an olive grove, from Sp. *aceituno* olive tree (a deriv. of *aceite* (olive) oil, from Arabic *zait*).

Acero Spanish: nickname for an inflexible person, or metonymic occupational name for a maker of steel objects, from Sp. *acero* steel (LL *(ferrum) aciārium*, a deriv. of *acies* blade, point of a sword, from *acer* sharp, keen).

Acevedo Spanish: topographic name for someone who lived in a place overgrown with holly bushes, from a collective of OSp. *azevo* holly (L *acrifolium*; cf. GRIFFOUL).
Cogn.: Port.: **Azevedo.**

Acha Spanish form of Basque **Atxa**: topographic name for someone who lived near an outcrop of rock or a large boulder, from Basque *atx* rock, crag + the def. art. *-a*.

Achard English (Norman) and French: from the ANF personal name *Aschard*, a cogn. of ECKHARDT.
Vars.: Eng.: **Achert, Ashard, Hatchard**. Fr.: **Achart, Ac(c)ard, Acquard, Acquart.**
Cogns.: Prov.: **Aicard**. It.: **Accardi.**
Patr.: It.: **D'Accardo.**

Achatz German: from the L given name *Achātius*, probably a deriv. of *achātes* agate (of Gk origin). The name was borne by a 4th-cent. Byzantine saint, numbered among the '14 Holy Helpers' and honoured chiefly in Bavaria.
Vars.: **Agatz, Agotz.**

Achtermann Low German: habitation name for someone whose home was at the back of a settlement, from MLG *achter* behind (cogn. with Eng. *after*, which has been specialized in a temporal sense) + *mann* man.
Vars.: **Echtermann; Achterling, Echterling.**

Acker English, German, and Jewish (Ashkenazic): topographic name for someone who lived by a plot of cultivated land, from ME *acker* field (OE *æcer*) or from Ger. *Acker* field, agriculture (OHG *ackar*).
Vars.: Eng.: **Aker, A(c)kers, Acre(s), Akker(s), Akess.** Jewish: **Aker.**
Cogns.: Du.: **Ackere, Van der Akkere, Van Akkeren.** Fris.: **Akkeringa.** Dan.: **Agger.**
Cpds (ornamental): Swed.: **Åkerberg** ('field hill'); **Åkerblom** ('field flower'); **Åkerlind** ('field lime-tree'); **Åkerlund** ('field grove'); **Åkerstedt** ('field homestead'); **Åkerström** ('field river').

Ackerman 1. English and Jewish (Ashkenazic): topographic name, var. of ACKER.
2. English: status name under the feudal system for a bond tenant who was employed as a ploughman for a manor. On many manors there were separate tenements held by 'acremen' in return for ploughing service.
Vars.: **Akerman, Acreman.**
Cogns. (of 1): Ger.: **Ackermann.** Du.: **Akkerman.** Swed.: **Åkerman.**

Ackland English: 1. habitation name from *Acland* Barton in Landkey, Devon, earlier *Ackelane* (13th cent.), deriving from the OE personal name *Acca* + OE *lane* lane. Acca is probably a derivative of *āc* oak, with connotations of strength and reliability.
2. habitation name from any of various minor places so called from OE *āc* oak + *land* land.
3. habitation name from *Acklam* in Yorks., so called from OE *āc* oak + *lēum* dat. pl. of *lēah* wood, clearing.
Var.: **Acland.**

Ackroyd English: topographic name, most common in W Yorks., given originally to someone who lived in a clearing in an oak wood, from Northern ME *ake* oak (OE *āc*) + *royd* clearing (OE *rod*).
Vars.: **Acroyd, Ak(e)royd, Aykroyd, Akred, Ecroyd.**
A family bearing this name is descended from John de Aykerode, *who was constable of Wadsworth near Halifax in 1381.*

Acosta Spanish (probably of Portuguese origin): topographic name for someone who lived on a hillside or near the coast, from a misdivision of Port. *Da Costa* (see COSTE) into *(D')Acosta*.

Ács Hungarian: occupational name for a worker in wood, from *ács* carpenter.

Acton English: habitation name from one of the places so called in Shrops. and adjacent counties, most of which get their name from OE *āc* oak + *tūn* enclosure, settlement. A few may have a first element that represents the OE personal name *Acca* (see ACKLAND).
Two of the families bearing this name are of considerable historical importance. The Worcs. Actons, *who held lands at Wolverton Hall near Pershore from the 16th cent. onwards, are descended from Sir Roger Acton, captain of Ludlow Castle, who was executed for treason in 1414. The historian Lord Acton (1834–1902) came of a Roman Catholic Shrops. family, first recorded in the county with William* de Acton *in the reign of Edward III (1327–77). A branch of the latter family is established in Italy, founded by the brothers Joseph Acton (1737–1830) and John Francis Acton (1736–1811). Both served the King of Naples, and Joseph was created a Patrician of the Kingdom of Naples in 1802. His brother was both a government minister and a military commander.*

Adam English, French, Catalan, Italian, German, Flemish/Dutch, Polish, and Jewish (Ashkenazic): from the Hebr. personal name *Adam*, which was borne, according to Genesis, by the first man. It is of uncertain etymology; it is often said to be from Hebr. *adama* earth; cf. the Gk legend that Zeus fashioned the first human beings from earth. It was very popular as a given name among non-Jews throughout Europe in the Middle Ages.
Vars.: It.: **Adami; Dami** (an aphetic form). Pol.: **Adamski** (with the surname suffix *-ski*; see BARANOWSKI). Jewish: **Adamski, Adamsky** (E Ashkenazic).
Cogns.: Hung.: **Ádám.** Prov.: **Azam.** Sp.: **Adán.** Port.: **Adão.** Low Ger.: **Dehm.**
Dims.: Eng.: **Adnett, Adnitt; Ade; Ad(de)kin, Atkin; Ai(t)kin, Aitken** (chiefly Scots); **Ai(c)ken** (chiefly N Ireland); **Adcock** (esp. E Midlands), **Atcock, Hadcock; Ad(d)ie, Ad(d)(e)y, Adye; Haddy** (Devon and Cornwall). Fr.: **Adanet, Ad(e)net, Adné, Ad(e)not.** It.: **Adamini, Adamol(l)i; Dametti.** Low Ger.: **Dahmke.** Pol.: **Adamek; Adamczyk** (also Jewish). Czech: **Adamík, Adámek.** Ukr.: **Adamik.**
Augs.: Pol.: **Adamiec.** Czech: **Adamec.**
Patrs.: Eng.: **Ad(d)ams, Adhams; Adamson.** Welsh: **Abadam; Baddams.** Ir., Sc.: **McAdam** (Gael. **Mac Adaim**). Ir.: MEGAW. It.: **D'Adamo; D'Adda.** Sp.: **Adanez.** Dan., Norw.: **Adamsen.** Swed.: **Adamsson.** Pol.: **Adamowicz, Adamiak.** Jewish: **Adams; Adamov(itch), Adamovitz, Adamowitz, Adamovicz** (E Ashkenazic). Croatian: **Adam(ov)ić.** Beloruss.: **Adamovich.** Gk: **Adamou, Adamides.**
Patrs. (from dims.): Eng.: **Ades, Addess; Addis** (chiefly N Ireland); **Adkins, Hadkins, At(t)kins; Adcocks; Adeson, Addison; At(t)kinson; Ai(t)chison** (chiefly Scots); **A(t)cheson** (chiefly N Ireland). Sc.: **McAd(d)ie, McCad(d)ie, Ked(d)ie, Keddy, Kiddie, Kiddy** (Gael. **Mac Adaidh**). Pol.: **Adamkiewicz.**
'Servant of A. (dim.)': Eng.: **Addyman.**
Habitation names: Pol.: **Adamczewski.** Czech: **Adamovský.**
The Scottish architect and furniture designer Robert Adam *(1728–92) and his brother James (1730–94) were members of the landed gentry, with a family seat near Fife.*
The second president of the United States, John Adams *(1735–1826), and his son John Quincy Adams (1767–1848), who became the sixth president, were descended from Henry Adams, a yeoman farmer who had emigrated from Barton St David, Somerset, to Mass. in 1640.*
John Macadam *(1756–1836), the Scottish road builder, was born in Ayrshire, the son of a banker. His grandfather was Adam McGregor, a chief of the clan McGregor, whose descendants were known*

as McAdam rather than McGregor because the latter surname was proscribed a by Scottish Act of Parliament in April 1603.

Acheson *is the surname of an Ulster family established in Armagh c.1611 by Sir Archibald Acheson of Haddington, Scotland. The senior branch holds the title of Earl of Gosford in the Irish Peerage (cr. 1806); the family has also held a baronetcy in Scotland since 1628. One member, David Acheson, emigrated in 1788 to N America, where he founded a well-known American family.*

Adburgham English: habitation name from a place near Manchester (now *Abram*), named from the gen. case of the OE female personal name *Ēadburg* (composed of the elements *ēad* prosperity + *burh, burg* fort) + OE *hām* homestead.

Var.: **Abram** (chiefly common in Lancs., but may nevertheless also be derived from ABRAHAM).

Adderley English (W Midlands): habitation name from places in Staffs. and Shrops., both so called from OE personal names + OE *lēah* wood, clearing. The Staffs. Adderley contains *Ealdrēd* (see ALDRITT 2); the Shrops. placename contains a fem. personal name, perhaps *Ealdþryð*.

Addington English: habitation name from any of various places in Bucks., Kent, Northants, and Surrey, so called from OE *Eaddingtūn* or *Ǣddingtūn* 'settlement (OE *tūn*) associated with *Eadda* (or *Ǣddi*)'.

A well-known family of Addingtons, *which included Henry Addington, 1st Lord Sidmouth, Prime Minister of Great Britain in 1801–4, can be traced to the village of Pottersbury in Northants in the 14th cent.*

Adel 1. German: short form of any of the numerous Gmc cpd personal names with the first element *adal* noble; cf. e.g. ALBERT.

2. Jewish (Ashkenazic): ornamental name from Ger. *Adel* nobility; cf. EDEL.

Var. (of 2): **Adelman**.

Cogns. (of 1): Low Ger.: AHL. Fr.: **Ad(d)e**; **Ado(n)** (from the OF oblique case). Cat.: ADELL.

Dims. (of 1): Ger.: **Adde**. Low Ger.: **Adelmann**. Fris.: **Adema**.

Patrs. (from 1): Ger.: **Adelung**. Low Ger.: **Aden**. Fris.: **Adena**.

Cpds (ornamental): Jewish: **Adelbaum** ('noble tree'), **Adelsberg** ('noble hill'), **Adelsburg** ('noble city'), **Adelstein**, **Edelstein** ('precious stone').

Adell Catalan: 1. cogn. of ADEL 1.

2. from the L personal name *Atīlius*, an old Roman family name of uncertain origin.

Dim.: **Dalí**.

Adenauer German: habitation name from *Adenau*, a village in the Rhineland. The first element is a river name, *Adana*, of uncertain origin; the second is probably MHG *ou(we)* marshy ground (mod. Ger. *Aue*, cogn. with OE *ēg*; see NYE).

Adler German (nickname) and Jewish (Ashkenazic, ornamental name): from Ger. *Adler* eagle (MHG *adelar*, a cpd of *adal* noble (see ADEL 1) + *ar* eagle (var. of *arn*, cogn. with OE *(e)arn*; cf. EARNSHAW)). Nobility is an attribute of the eagle in most European cultures, it being considered king of the birds.

Vars.: Jewish: **Adlerman**; **Aldar** (Israeli).

Cogn.: Du.: **Adelaar**.

Cpds (probably ornamental coinages, but perhaps also habitation names from places so called): Jewish: **Adlerstein** ('eagle rock'), **Adlerberg** ('eagle hill').

Adlington English: habitation name from places so called in Ches. (*Edulvinton* in Domesday Book) and in Lancs. (*Adelventon*). Both get their names from OE *Ēadwulfingtūn*, 'settlement associated with *Ēadwulf*', a personal name composed of the elements *ēad* wealth, prosperity + *wulf* wolf.

Adolf German: from the Gmc personal name *Adalwulf*, composed of the elements *adal* noble + *wulf* wolf. This was a common given name until the Second World War and was, for example, a dynastic name in the noble houses of Holstein and Nassau.

Cogns.: Low Ger.: **A(h)lf**. It.: **Ad(in)olfi**.

Dims.: It.: **Adolfino**.

Patrs.: Low Ger.: **A(h)lfs**; **Adolfsen**. Swed.: **Adolfsson**.

Adorno Italian: from a medieval given name, meaning 'gifted' (L *adornātus*, past part. of *adornāre* to decorate, adorn), bestowed by fond parents as a good omen.

Dim.: **Adornetti**.

Adrados Spanish: habitation name from any of various places so called, for example in the provinces of Segovia and León. The placename is of uncertain derivation, possibly from LL *hederātus*, an adj. deriv. of class. L *hedera* ivy.

Adrian English, French, German, and Dano-Norwegian: from the L personal name *(H)adriānus*, originally an ethnic name referring to someone who came from the Adriatic Sea (L *Adria*, possibly akin to *ater* black). It was adopted as a cognomen by the emperor who was among other things responsible for the construction of Hadrian's Wall across the North of England. It was also borne by several minor saints, in particular an early martyr at Nicomedia (d. *c.*304) who is the patron saint of soldiers, butchers, and (in Flanders and Switzerland) smiths. There was also an English St Adrian (d. 710), born in N Africa; he was abbot of St Augustine's, Canterbury, and his cult enjoyed a brief vogue after the supposed discovery of his remains in 1091. Later, the name was adopted by several popes, including the only pope of English birth, Nicholas Breakspear, who reigned as Adrian IV (1154–9).

Var.: Fr.: **Adrien**.

Cogns.: Hung.: **Adorján**. It.: **Adriani**; **Ariani** (S Italy). Sp.: **Adrián**. Cat.: **Adrià**. Port.: **Adriano**, **Adrião**. Flem.: **A(d)riaen**. Du.: **A(d)riaan**.

Dims.: It.: **Arianello**, **Arianetto**.

Patrs.: Flem.: **Adriaens**. Du.: **Adriaans(z)**, **Adriaanse(n)**. Russ.: **Adrianov**.

Patr. (dim.): Russ.: **Adriyashev**.

Adshead English: habitation name from an unidentified place, probably in Lancs., the origin of which would be OE *Ǣddeshēafod* 'headland of *Ǣddi*' (cf. ADDINGTON).

Aelion Jewish (Sefardic): ornamental name from Hebr. *haelyon* 'the One on High', i.e. God.

Afanasyev Russian: patr. from the given name *Afanasi* (Gk *Athanasios* 'immortal', from *a-* not + *thanasios* mortal, a deriv. of *thanatos* death). The name owes its currency to the cult, especially popular in the Eastern Church, of St Athanasius (*c.*297–373), bishop of Alexandria, one of the most influential of the fathers of the Christian Church.

Var.: **Afanasov**.

Cogns. (patrs.): Ukr., Beloruss.: **Panasov**. Bulg.: **Athasov**. Croatian: **Atanasijević**, **Tanasijević**, **Tasić**. Rum.: **Tănăsescu**. Gk: **Athanasopoulos**.

Cogns. (not patrs.): Hung.: **Tanase**. Rum.: **Tănase**. Fr.: **Athanase**; **T(h)anase**. It.: **At(t)anasi(o)**, **Attana**; **Tanasi**. Sp.: **Atenio**.

Dims. (patrs.): Russ.: **Afonchikov, Afonyushkin, Afonichev, Afonchin; Fon(k)in, Funikov**. Croatian: **Atanacković, Tanasković**.

Dims. (not patrs.): Ukr., Beloruss.: **Panasik, Panchenko**.

Agace French: 1. nickname for someone supposedly resembling a magpie, such as a chattering or nagging person, from OF *agache*, *agasse* magpie (of Gmc origin; cf. OHG *agaza*).

2. cogn. of AGGIS.

Vars. (of 1): **Agasse, Lagasse; Agache, Lagache** (Normandy, Picardy); **Ageasse, Ajasse; Ayasse**.

Cogns. (of 1): It.: **Agazzi; Gazza**.

Dims. (of 1): Fr.: **Agassis, Agassiz** (Switzerland). It.: **Agazzini; Gazzini, Gazzola**.

Agapov Russian: patr. from the given name *Agap* (Gk *Agapios*, a deriv. of *agapē* spiritual love). This name was borne by various early saints, most notably one martyred at Caesarea in Palestine in AD 306.

Vars.: **Agapyev, Agapeev; Gapeev**.

Ågård Danish: habitation name from any of various minor places so called from the elements *å* river + *gård* enclosure, yard.

Var.: **Aagaard**.

Agate English: topographic name from someone who lived by a gate; the first syllable represents the fused ME preposition *a*, *o*, in origin a var. of the Eng. vocab. word *on*, reinforced by ANF *a* (L *ad*).

Agatestein Jewish (Ashkenazic): Anglicized form of an ornamental name composed of a Yid. element meaning 'agate' (cf. ACHATZ) + the ornamental suffix *-stein* stone.

Aggis English: from the medieval female given name *Agace*, a vernacular form of the name (L *Agatha*, Gk *Agathē*, from Gk *agathos* good) borne by a 3rd-cent. Sicilian martyr.

Vars.: **Agiss, Ag(g)as(s)**; HAGGIS.

Cogns.: Fr.: **Agathe**, AGACE. It.: **Agati**. Sp.: **Águeda, Gadea**. Ger.: **Agathe, Agethe; Eyth**. Pol.: **Agaciak**.

Dims.: Eng.: **Agget(t)**. It.: **Agatiello** (Naples); **Agatini**.

Aug.: It.: **Agatoni**.

Patrs.: Ger.: **Agethen; Eit(h)ner, Eidtner, Eythner**. Flem.: **Aegten, Achten**. It.: **D'Agata, Dell'Agata** (Sicily).

Agnew 1. English (Norman): nickname for a meek or pious person, from OF *agnel*, *agneau* lamb (LL *agnellus*, dim. of class. L *agnus*).

2. English (Norman): habitation name from *Agneaux* in La Manche, the etymology of which is uncertain; it was probably assimilated by folk etymology to Fr. *agneau* lamb from some unknown Gaul. original.

3. Irish: stressed on the second syllable, this is an Anglicized form of Gael. **Ó Gnímh** 'descendant of *Gníomh*', a byname meaning 'Action', 'Activity'. The Ó Gnímh family held the hereditary office of poet to a branch of the O'Neills and to the Macdonalds.

Cogns. (of 1): Fr.: **Agneau, Agnel; La(i)gneau, La(i)gnel**. It.: **Agnelli**.

Dims. (of 1): It.: **Agnellini, Agnellotti, Agnelutti**.

Patrs. (of 1): Fr.: **Delagneau**. It.: **D'Agn(i)ello**.

A Norman family from Agneaux *(see 2 above) settled in Scotland. In 1363 they were granted the hereditary post of sheriffs of Galloway by King David II.*

Agosti Italian: from the medieval given name *Agosto* (L *Augustus*, from *augere* to increase, become greater). Originally a title used by the Roman emperors after accession, the name was popular also among early Christians, who read into it the implication that the bearer had become greater by being baptized. The month of *August* was so called after the first Emperor Augustus, and occasionally the given name was bestowed because of some association with the month; cf. DAVOUT.

Var.: **Agusto**.

Cogns.: Fr.: **August(e)**. Port.: **Augusto**. Ger.: **Augst**.

Augs.: It.: **Agostoni, Agustoni**.

Patr.: Swed.: **Augustsson**.

Agricola German: Latinization of any of various names meaning 'farmer', esp. ACKERMAN and BAUER.

Aguado Spanish: topographic name, metonymic nickname, or metonymic occupational name, from Sp. *aguado* water, a deriv. of *agua* (L *aqua*). It may have denoted a water seller, an abstemious person who drank only water, or someone who lived by a spring. Cf. BOILEAU and DRINKWATER.

Agudo Spanish: nickname for a clever or witty person, from Sp. *agudo* sharp, astute (L *acūtus* sharp, past part. of *acuere* to sharpen).

Cogn.: Cat.: **Agut**.

Agüero Spanish: 1. habitation name from places so called in the provinces of Huesca and Santander. These probably get their name from LL (*vīcus*) *aquārius* well-watered (settlement).

2. from the given name or nickname *Agüero* '(good) omen' (L *augurium*), bestowed on a child in the hope that it would bring him luck.

Aguilar Spanish and Catalan: habitation name from any of numerous places so called, from L *aquilāre* haunt of eagles (a deriv. of *aquila*; see EAGLE). It is also found as a Jewish (Sefardic) name, in which case it is probably ornamental.

Var.: **Aguilera** (from L *aquilāria*).

Cogn.: Port.: **Aguiar**.

Aguiló Catalan: of uncertain origin, probably from the L personal name *Aquilo*, gen. *Aquilōnis*, 'North (wind)' (a deriv. of *aquila* EAGLE or *aqua* water).

Aguinaga Spanish form of Basque **Aginaga**: topographic name for someone who lived near a group of yew trees, from Basque *(h)agin* yew + the collective suffix *-aga*.

Aguirre Spanish form of Basque **Agirre**: topographic name for someone who lived in a prominent position in a village, from Basque *ager*, *agir* plainly visible, conspicuous. This is also used as the first element of a large number of topographic names referring to conspicuous geographical features, such as **Aguirrezabal(a)** 'conspicuous open space'.

It is also possible that this term (with the fused OF preposition *de*) is the origin of *Daguerre*, a place in the parish of Saint-Martin-de-Seignaux, Landes, which has given rise to the surname borne by the inventor of photography, Louis Jacques Mandé **Daguerre** (1789–1851).

Agulló Catalan: habitation name from a place near Àger, apparently so called from the L personal name *Aculeo*, gen. *Aculeōnis*, a deriv. of *aculeus* sting, point.

Agutter English: topographic name for someone living by a watercourse or drainage channel, from ME *a* (cf. AGATE) + *gutter* (ANF *goutiere*, LL *guttāria*, from *gutta* drop).

Ahern Irish: Anglicized form of Gael. **Ó hEachthighearna** 'descendant of *Eachthighearna*', a personal name composed of the elements *each* horse (see KEOGH) + *tighearna* master, lord (see TIERNEY). The name is most common in SW Ireland.

Vars.: **Ahe(a)rne**, HEARNE.

Ahl 1. German: nickname for a 'slippery' individual or metonymic occupational name for an eel fisher, from MHG, OHG *āl* eel.

2. Low German: cogn. of ADEL.

3. Swedish: ornamental name from Swed. *a(h)l* ALDER.

Vars. (of 3): **Ahlman**, **A(h)lsén**; **A(h)lenius** (Latinized).

Cpds (ornamental, from 3): Swed.: **Ahlberg** ('alder hill'); **Ahlbom** ('alder tree'); **Ahlborg** ('alder town'); **A(h)lfors** ('alder waterfall'); **A(h)lgren** ('alder branch'); **Ahlmark** ('alder territory'); **Ahlqvist** ('alder twig'); **Ahlstedt** ('alder homestead'); **Ahlström** ('alder river').

Ahonen Finnish: ornamental name from Finn. *aho* glade + the gen. suffix *-nen*, perhaps adopted in some cases as a topographic surname by someone who lived in a glade in the forest.

Ahrén Swedish: status name for a tenant farmer, from Swed. *arende* leasehold, tenancy.

Var.: **Arrhenius** (a Latinized form).

Åhs Swedish: ornamental name from Swed. *ås* ridge, perhaps in some cases adopted as a topographic surname by someone living on a ridge. This is one of the many surnames taken from words denoting features of the natural landscape when surnames were adopted in Sweden during the 18th and 19th cents.

Var.: **Åsell**.

Cpds: **Å(h)sberg** ('ridge hill'); **Åslund** ('ridge grove'); **Åstrand** ('ridge shore').

Aiello Italian: habitation name from any of the many places in S Italy so called, from LL *agellus*, dim. of L *ager* field.

Vars.: **D'Aiello**, **(D')Ajello**; **D'Azeglio** (Piedmont); **Gelli** (Tuscany); **Zelli** (Lombardy).

Aillier French: occupational name for a seller of garlic, OF *aillier* (L *alliārius*, a deriv. of *allium* garlic).

Cogns.: Eng. (Norman): **Ayler**. It.: **Aglieri**.

Ainger English (Norman) and French: from the Gmc personal name *Ansger*, composed of the elements *ans-* god + *ger*, *gar* spear.

Vars.: Eng.: **Ang(i)er**, **Angear**, **Aunger**. Fr.: **Anger**; **Anquier** (Normandy, Picardy); **Ansquer** (Brittany).

Ainscough English: habitation name from a lost place in Lancs. The second element of the name is clearly ON *skógr* wood; the first may be ON *einn* alone, solitary (a cogn. of OE *ān*, mod. E *one*), with the meaning 'wood standing alone'.

Var.: **Ainscow**.

Ainslie Scots: apparently a habitation name, from an unidentified place. The surname is found chiefly in the border regions of Scotland and Northumb. It may be that the placename source should be sought in this area, or the surname may have been brought in from elsewhere. If the name came from the South, it may derive from one of several places so named in the Midlands, such as *Ansley* in Warwicks. or *Annesley* in Notts. (The former is from OE *ānsetl* hermitage + *lēah* wood, clearing; the latter is apparently from the gen. case of a byname derived from OE *ān* solitary (see AINSCOUGH) + *lēah*.)

Vars.: **Ainsley**, **Aynsley** (more common south of the border); **Ainslee**.

Sir John Ainslie *is recorded as the keeper of Dolphinston Castle at Oxnam, near Jedburgh, in* c.*1275. The first known bearer of the name in Scotland is William* de Haneslei *or* de Anslee *of Glasgow, recorded at the beginning of the 13th cent.*

Ainsworth English: habitation name from a place near Manchester, so called from the gen. case of the OE personal name *Ægen* (a short form of the rare cpd names with the first element *ǣgen* own) + OE *worð* enclosure (see WORTH). The surname is most common in Lancs.

Airey English: habitation name from some minor place in N England named *Eyrará* 'gravel-bank stream', for example *Aira* Beck and *Aira* Force near Ullswater in Cumbria.

Var.: **Airy**.

Aïstov Russian: patr. from the nickname *Aïst* 'Stork', used for a tall thin man with long legs.

Akhmatov Russian: patr. of Turkic origin, from the Arabic given name *Ahmed*, *Ahmad* 'most praiseworthy one', borne by Muslims in honour of the son of the prophet Muhammad.

Cogns.: Pol.: **Achmatowicz**, **Achmetowicz**, **Achmeciewicz**.

Aksyonov Russian: patr. from the given name *Aksyon* (Gk *Auxentiós*, from *auxein* to increase, magnify). This name was borne by a 4th-cent. saint of Mopsuestia in Cilicia and a 5th-cent. Syrian hermit, both much revered in the Orthodox Church.

Vars.: **Aks(y)anov**, **A(v)ksentyev**, **Aksentsev**, **Aksentsov**, **Aksyutin**.

Cogn. (patr.): Croatian: **Aksentijević**.

Alabaster English: alteration (by folk etymology) of ANF *arblaster* crossbowman (OF *arbalestier*, LL *arcuballistārius*, from *arcuballista*, a cpd of *arcus* bow + *ballista* catapult, ballista). The term was not only an occupational name for a soldier trained to use one of these weapons, but also denoted a category of feudal tenant in sergeantry, originally, no doubt, one who provided armed service with a crossbow.

Vars.: **Arblaster**, **Albisser**.

Cogns.: Ger.: **Armbruster**, **Armbrüster**, **Armbriester**, **Arm(b)ster**. Low Ger.: **Armborster**, **Armburster**.

Aladerne Provençal: topographic name for someone living near a patch of buckthorn, OProv. *aladerne* (LL *alaterna*). In medieval France this shrub was regarded as a symbol of righteousness, and this fact suggests that in some cases the surname may have originally been a nickname for a righteous person.

Vars.: **Daladerne** (Roussillon); **Daladier** (Vaucluse).

Álamo Spanish: topographic name for someone who lived near a poplar tree or poplar grove, from Sp. *álamo* poplar (of uncertain etymology, probably from L (*populus*) *alba* white poplar, crossed with Celt. *elmos* poplar).

Collective: **Alameda**.

Alarcón Spanish: habitation name from places so called in the provinces of Cuenca and Córdoba, which are of uncertain etymology.

Cogn.: Cat.: **Alarcó**.

Alaric French: from a Gmc personal name composed of the elements *ala* all, entire + *rīc* power.

Vars.: **Alari**, **Alric**; **Hal(l)ary**; **Aury**, **Auric**.

Alauze French: nickname for a cheerful person, always singing, from OF *alauze* skylark (L *alauda*).

Cogn.: It.: **Allodi**.

Alayrac French: habitation name from *Alairac* in Aude, *Aleyrac* in Drôme, or *Alleyrac* in Haute-Loire, all apparently so called from the Gallo-Roman personal name *Alarius* (of uncertain origin) + the local suffix *-ācum*.
Var.: **D'Alayrac**.

Alba Spanish and Italian: habitation name from any of the numerous places so called. The meaning of the placename is unknown; the coincidence in form with L *alba* (fem.) white is probably no more than coincidental. It may be of Ligurian origin (compare *Alba Longa*, the name of the oldest Latin town).

Alban English, French, German, and Swedish: from the given name *Alban* (L *Albānus*, originally an ethnic name from the many places in Italy and elsewhere called ALBA). In England the given name was bestowed chiefly in honour of St Alban, the first British martyr (3rd or 4th cent.); it is now most common in E Anglia.
Vars.: Eng.: **Al(l)bon, Allbond, Allbone, Al(l)born**. Fr.: **Albain, Auba(i)n**. Ger.: **Albohn**.
Cogns.: It.: **Albano, Albani**. Cat.: **Albà**. Port.: **Albano**.
Dims.: Fr.: **Aubanel**. It.: **Albanelli**. Cat.: **Albanell**.

Albaret French: topographic name for someone who lived by a poplar grove, OF *albaret* (LL *albarētum*, collective of (*populus*) *alba* white poplar (see ÁLAMO), influenced by *arborētum*, a collective of *arbor* tree).
Vars.: **Albarède; Auvray**.
Cogns.: Cat.: **Albareda**. It.: **Alboreto**.

Albarracín Spanish: habitation name from a place in the province of Teruel, originally named as 'the land of *Razīn*', from the Arabic def. art. *al* + *barr* land + the personal name *Razīn*. During the 11th cent. this place constituted a small independent kingdom in Muslim Spain.

Albarrán Spanish: nickname for a newcomer to an area, from Sp. *albarrán* stranger (from the Arabic def. art. *al* + *barrani* foreign, a deriv. of *barr* land).

Albee English: habitation name from *Alby* in Norfolk or *Ailby* in Lincs., both of which are derived from the ON personal name *Ali* (a short form of the various cpd personal names with the first element *all* all) + ON *býr* farm, settlement.
Var.: **Alby**.

Alberdi Basque: topographic name, apparently from *arb(el)* slate + *erdi* centre, middle; the first element has undergone metathesis under the influence of the second.

Albert English, Low German, French, Catalan, and Hungarian: from a Gmc personal name (*Albrecht* in mod. Ger.), composed of the elements *adal* noble + *berht* bright, famous. This was one of the most common Gmc given names, and was borne by various medieval princes, military leaders, and great churchmen, notably St Albert of Prague (Czech name VOJTĚCH, Latin name *Adalbertus*), a Bohemian prince who died a martyr in 997 attempting to convert the Prussians to Christianity; St Albert the Great (?1193–1280), Aristotelian theologian and tutor of Thomas Aquinas; and Albert the Bear (1100–70), Margrave of Brandenburg.
Vars.: Eng.: **Al(l)bright** (altered by folk etymology); **Aubert** (Norman). Low Ger.: **Aber(t), Allebrach**. Fr.: **Auber(t), Aubé, Aubey**.
Cogns.: Ger.: **Albrecht; Brecht** (aphetic); **Obrecht, Obert** (Switzerland); **Olbricht, Ulbricht, Ulbrig** (Saxony, Silesia). Fris.: ALPERT. Flem.: **Albrecht, Aebracht, O(l)brecht**. Pol.: **Olbrycht, Olbrysz**. It.: **Al(i)berto, Al(i)berti, Aliperti; Liberti**. Sp.: **Alberto(s)**. Port.: **Alberto**.
Dims.: Fr.: **Aubertin, Auberty, Auberton; Aub(e)lin, Aub(e)let**. Prov.: **Alberty**. It.: **Albertini, Albert(in)elli, Albertol(l)i, Albertotti, Albertocci, Albertuzzi; Libertini, Libertucci**. Ger.: ABEL; **Ap(p)el** (Franconia; see also APPLE); **Opel** (Saxony); **Elbel, Etzel** (U.S. **Edsel**) (Bavaria); **Abe(r)le, Abe(r)li(n), Oberlin, Äbli** (Switzerland). Low Ger.: **Abb, Ab(b)eke**. Fris.: **Ab(b)ema**.
Aug.: It.: **Albertoni**.
Pej.: It.: **Albertazzi**.
Patrs.: Eng.: **Alberts**. Fr.: **D'Albert**. It.: **D'Alberti, De Albertis; De Liberto**. Ger.: **Alberding, Allerding, Albrink**. Low Ger.: **Albers**. Fris.: **Alpers**. Flem.: **Aebrechts, Olbrechts**. Du.: **Alberts, A(a)lbers**. Norw., Dan.: **Albrechtsen, Albertsen**. Pol.: **Olbrychtowicz**.
Patrs. (from dims.): Low Ger.: **Abbing, Ab(b)en; Ab(e)ken, Abeking**.

Albin English, French, and German (Austrian): from the given name *Albin*, (L *Albīnus*, a deriv. of *albus* white; cf. ALBAN). This was the name of several minor early Christian saints, including St Aubin, bishop of Angers (d. *c.*554). The popularity of the given name was also influenced, esp. in Austria, by the Gmc given name *Albuin*, composed of the elements *alb* elf + *win* friend. This was the name of the Lombard leader (d. 572) who made himself king of N Italy, and also of a bishop of Brixen (Bressanone) in S Tyrol who has been confused with St Aubin, mentioned above.
Vars.: Eng.: **Aubin, Obin**. Fr.: **Alby; Aubin, Auby**. Ger.: **Albien**.
Cogns.: It.: **Albi(o)ni; Albino**. Port.: **Albino**. Pol.: **Albiński**.
Dims.: Fr.: **Albinet, Aubinet, Aubineau**. It.: **Albinelli, Albinetti, Albinotti, Albinuzzi**.
Aug.: It.: **Albinoni**.
Patr.: Eng.: **Albinson**.
Habitation name: Pol.: **Albinowski**.

Albiol Catalan: habitation name from a place in Tarragona, so called from the L personal name *Albiōlus*, a dim. of *Albius* (from *albus* white).

Albuquerque Spanish: habitation name from *Alburquerque* in the province of Badajoz, so called from L *alba* white (fem.) + *quercus* oak. Although of Sp. origin, this surname is now much more common in Portugal.

Albutt English (W Midlands): from the Gmc personal name *Albodo*, composed of the elements *adal* noble + *bodo* messenger, which was introduced into England by the Normans.
Var.: **Allbutt**.

Alcaide Spanish: occupational name for the military governor of a castle or city, Sp. *alcaide* (from the Arabic def. art. *al* + *qā'id* captain, governor, a deriv. of *qāda* to lead). The word, first attested in the 11th cent., is still in use in Spain today.

Alcalá Spanish: habitation name from any of the numerous fortified villages named during the Moorish occupation of Spain with the Arabic def. art. *al* + *qalá* fortress, castle.

Alcalde Spanish: occupational name for a judge, OSp. *alcalde* (from the Arabic def. art. *al* + *qādī* judge, pres. part. of *qadā* to resolve, decide). In mod. Sp. the word means 'mayor', but this sense does not seem to have developed before the 15th cent., and is probably too late to be reflected in the surname.

Alcántara Spanish: habitation name from any of various places, for example in the provinces of Cáceres, Cadiz, and Valencia, so called from the Arabic def. art. *al* + *qántara* arch, bridge. The dim. **Alcantarilla** is still in use in Spain as a vocab. word.

Cogn.: Cat.: **Alcàntara**.

Alcaraz Spanish: habitation name from a place in the province of Albacete, so called from the Arabic def. art. *al* + *karaz* cherry tree.

Alcázar Spanish: habitation name from any of the numerous places, for example in the provinces of Ciudad Real, Cuenca, and Granada, so called from Sp. *alcázar* citadel, palace (from the Arabic def. art. *al* + *qasr* fortress, itself a borrowing of L *castrum*; cf. CASTRO).

Alcocer Spanish: habitation name from any of various places, for example in the provinces of Alicante and Guadalajara, so called from the Arabic def. art. *al* + *qusayr* small palace (a dim. of *qasr*; cf. ALCÁZAR).

Alcock English: from a dim., with ME *-cok* (see COCK 1), of various given names beginning with *Al-*, notably *Alan* (see ALLEN), ALBAN, ALBERT, and ALEXANDER.

Vars.: **Allcock, Alecock, Aucock, Awcock, Alcoe,** ALCOTT.

Patr.: **Al(l)cox**.

Alcolea Spanish: habitation name from any of the numerous places so called from the Arabic def. art. *al* + *qulay'a* fort.

Alcott English: 1. habitation name for someone living in an old cottage, from OE *(e)ald* old + *cot* cottage (see COATES).

2. var. of ALCOCK, in some cases the result of deliberate alteration because of the obscene connotations that could, from the 18th cent., be read into that name.

Vars.: **Allcott, Allcoat, Aucott, Aucutt**.

Louisa May Alcott *(1832–88), author of* Little Women *(1869), was the daughter of Amos Alcott (1799–1888), who had changed the family name from* Alcox. *The family could trace their descent back to an ancestor named* Alcocke *who had emigrated from England to Mass. with Winthrop in 1629.*

Alday Spanish form of Basque **Aldai**: habitation name from a place in the province of Biscay, so called from Basque *alde* region, area + the suffix *-i*.

Aldea Spanish: habitation name from any of the numerous places so called from Sp. *aldea* village (from the Arabic def. art. *al* + *dái'a* village, countryside).

Aldecoa Basque: apparently a local name composed of the elements *alde* region, area (cf. ALDAY) + the gen. suffix *-ko* + the def. art. *-a*.

Alden English: 1. from the ME personal name *Aldine*, OE *Ealdwine*, composed of the elements *eald* old + *wine* friend.

2. var. of HALDANE.

Vars.: **Aldin(e), Auden, Olden**. (Of 1 only): ALWYN.

John Alden *(c.1599–1687) was one of the Pilgrim Fathers who sailed on the* Mayflower. *Many of his descendants were merchant seamen, among them James Alden (1810–77), who made two circumnavigations of the globe.*

There was a belief in the family of the poet W. H. Auden *(1907–73) that their surname was evidence of Icelandic descent, because of its similarity to the Icelandic personal name* Auðunn *(composed of the elements* auð *riches, prosperity +* unna *to love). There does not seem to be any linguistic or genealogical foundation for this belief.*

Alder English: 1. from one of two OE personal names, *Ealdhere* or *Æðelhere*, composed of the elements *eald* old or *æðel* noble + *here* army.

2. topographic name for someone living near an alder tree (OE *alor*).

Vars. (of 2): NALDER, ALDERMAN.

Cogns. (of 2): Ger.: **Erle(r)**. Swed.: AHL.

Patrs. (of 1): Eng.: **Alders, Alderson**.

The surname Alderson *is most common in Yorks. and in Co. Durham, and at least one group of modern bearers are descended from Thomas Alderson (d. 1633), a miller, of Barnard Castle, Co. Durham. The name is found in Bolton, Lancs., in the 13th cent.*

Alderman English: 1. title of office, from OE *ealdorman* elder. In Anglo-Saxon England an alderman was a functionary appointed by the king to administer justice in a shire, and to lead the local militia into battle when needed; in the later Middle Ages the term came to be used to denote the governor of a guild.

2. var. of ALDER 2.

Alderton English: habitation name from any of various places so called. Those in Suffolk and Shrops. (*Alretuna* in Domesday Book) get the name from OE *alra*, gen. pl. of *alor* alder + *tūn* enclosure, settlement (cf. ALLERTON). Those in Gloucs., Northants, and Wilts. (*Aldri(n)tone* in Domesday Book) derive from OE *Ealdheringtūn* 'settlement associated with *Ealdhere*' (cf. ALDER 1). The one in Essex contains a different personal name, perhaps the fem. name *Æðelwaru*, composed of the elements *æðel* noble + *waru* defence.

Aldobrandi Italian: 1. from a Gmc (Langobardic) personal name composed of the elements *ald* old + *brand* (flaming) sword.

2. in the Tuscan dialect, in which initial *I-* regularly became *A-*, it may represent a version of HILDEBRAND.

Vars.: **Aldovrandi**; **Aldrovandi** (Emilia); **Drovandi** (Liguria).

Dim.: **Aldobrandini**.

Aldous 1. English: from the ME fem. given name *Aldus*, a pet form of any of the numerous OE personal names (borne by both sexes) with a first element *(e)ald* old.

2. Scots: habitation name from a place in Strathclyde (Renfrewshire), named as OE *eald* old + *hūs* house. (The Gael. etymology that has been suggested, from *alld* burn + *fhuathais* goblin, spectre, is less than plausible.)

Vars. (of 1): **Aldus, Al(l)dis(s), Audis, Oldis**. (Of 2, or by folk etymology from 1): **Aldhouse**.

Cogns. (of 1): It.: **Aldi, Audi, Audo; Alda, Auda** (fem.).

Dims. (of 1): It.: **Aldini, Audin(ucc)i**.

The surname Aldous *is common in E Anglia: one family can trace their ancestry to a certain William Aldous (d. 1528) of Fressingfield, Suffolk. The name is first recorded in Fressingfield in 1327, and it is also recorded as the name of the rector of Wreningham, Norfolk, in 1393.*

In 1265 Roger, son of Reginald de Aldhous *resigned all claim to the lands of Aldous, Renfrews., held by himself and his father, and in 1284 his son John* de Aldhus *reaffirmed this renunciation in a court of the justiciar of Lothian.*

Aldritt English (chiefly Sussex): 1. from the ME personal name *Aldred*, which represents a coalescence of two OE personal names: *Ealdrǣd*, composed of the elements *eald* old + *rǣd* counsel, and *Æðelrǣd* (Ethelred), from *æðel* noble + *rǣd*.

2. topographic name for someone who lived by an alder grove, ME *aldrett*, a deriv. of ALDER.

Vars.: **Audritt, Aldred, Al(l)red; Eldrett, Eldritt, Eldred**.

Alexander English: from the given name *Alexander*, which in various spellings was popular in the Middle Ages throughout Europe. An aphetic form (see SANDER) was also common, while in Slav. languages most of the dims. are indistinguishable from those of Russ. *Aleksei*, Pol. *Olek* (see ALEXIS). The name *Alexander* is from Gk *Alexandros*, which probably originally meant 'defender of men', from Gk *alexein* to defend + *anēr*, gen. *andros*, man. This was a byname of Paris, son of King Priam of Troy, in Homer's *Iliad*, but its popularity in the Middle Ages was largely due to the Macedonian conqueror, Alexander the Great (356–323 BC)—or rather to the hero of the mythical versions of his exploits which gained currency in the 'Alexander Romances'. The name was also borne by various early Christian saints, including a patriarch of Alexandria (AD *c*.250–326), who was venerated for condemning the Arian heresy.

Vars.: **Elesander, Elshenar, Alshioner; Alastar** (Scotland; from *Alasdair*, the Gael. form of the given name).

Cogns.: Fr.: **Alexandre; Lissandre.** Sp.: **Alejandre, Alejandro.** Port.: **Alexandre.** It.: **Alessandri; Assandri** (Liguria); **Lissandri, Lisciandro, Lassandri.** Czech: **Olexa, Ksandr.**

Dims.: It.: **Alessandrelli, Alessandretti, Alessandrini, Alessandrucci; Lissandrini; Lisciardelli** (Sicily). Czech: **Lešek, Lexa.** Ukr.: **Olenchenko, Lenchenko.**

Augs.: It.: **Alessandrone.**

Patrs.: Sc., Ir.: **McAl(l)aster, McAl(l)ister, McAlester, McCallister** (Gael. **Mac Alastair**). Manx: **Callister.** It.: **D'Alessandro.** Rum.: **Alexandrescu.** Dan., Norw.: **Alexandersen.** Swed.: **Alexandersson.** Pol.: **Aleksandrowicz.** Russ.: **Aleksan(dr)ov.** Ukr., Beloruss.: **Aleksandrovich.** Bulg.: **Aleksandrov, Aleksandrev.** Croatian: **Aleksić.** Jewish (E Ashkenazic): **Aleksandrovich, Alexandrowicz.** Gk: **Alexandrou.**

Patrs. (from dims.): Ir.: **McElistrum, McElistrim** (Gael. **Mac Alastraim**; common in Co. Kerry). Russ.: **Aleksankov, Aleksankin; Aleksakhin, Aleksashin; Alenov, Alenin, Alyonov, Alen(n)ikov, Alenshev, Alentyev, Alenichev, Alenchikov, Olenov, Olenin, Olyonov, Olen(n)ikov, Olenichev, Olenchikov;** LENIN.

'Son of the wife of A.': Russ.: **Aleksandrikhin.**

A well-known Scottish family with the surname Alexander *included among their ancestors Sir William Alexander, court poet to King James VI of Scotland and I of England, who created him Earl of Stirling in 1633. Among his descendants were the Jacobite James Alexander, who fled from Scotland after the 1715 rebellion, and his son William Alexander (1726–83), a distinguished general in the American Revolution. The latter claimed the title of Earl of Stirling, but failed to prove his right to it, although he was known to the colonists as 'Lord Stirling'.*

Alexis French: from the given name *Alexis*, ultimately from Gk *alexios* helping, defending. The name owed its popularity in the Middle Ages to St Alexi(u)s, a shadowy figure about whom many legends grew up. The historical St Alexis appears to have been a religious figure venerated as a 'man of God' who lived in the 4th–5th cent. in Edessa (a centre of early Christianity in Syria). His cult was also popular in the Eastern Church, which accounts for the frequency of the Russ. given name *Aleks(e)i* (dim. *Alyosha*).

Cogns.: Sp.: **Alejo.** Port.: **Aleixo.** It.: **Ales(s)i(o), Alesci(o), Alecci.** Pol.: **Oleś, Olek, Olech.**

Dims.: Pol.: **Olczyk, Oleszczuk.** Beloruss.: **Alekseichik, Lyosik.**

Patrs.: It.: **D'Ales(s)io, D'Alesco.** Pol.: **Olech(n)owicz, Olkowicz; Oleksiak.** Beloruss.: **Aleksich.** Russ.: **Alekseev.** Georgian: **Aleksidze.**

Patrs. (from dims.): Pol.: **Oleszkiewicz; Ol(esz)czak.** Russ.: **Alekhov, Aleshkov, Aleshintsev, Alyokhin, Alyoshin, Aloshh(i)kin, Aloshechkin, Alyukin, Alyushin, Alyutin, Alesin, Olekhov, Olyosh(k)in, Oleshunin, Olyunin,** LYOKHIN.

Habitation name: Pol.: **Oleksiński.**

Alfaro Spanish: habitation name from a place in the province of Logroño, apparently so called from the Arabic def. art. *al* + OSp. *faro* beacon (from LL *farus*, Gk *pharos*).

Alfonso Spanish: from a Gmc personal name, *Adafuns* (composed of the elements *adal* noble + *funs* ready). This was especially popular among the Visigoths and Langobards, and was later taken by a number of kings of Spain.

Var.: **Alonso.**

Cogns.: Port.: **Afonso.** It.: **Al(f)onso, Al(f)onzo; Fonso, Fonzo; Anfossi, Anfus(s)o, Affuso, Alfuso.**

Dims.: It.: **Alfonsetti, Alfonsini.**

Augs.: It.: **Alfonsoni; Fonzone.**

Alford English: habitation name from any of various places so called, three in particular: one in Surrey (recorded as *Aldeford* in the 14th cent.), from OE *eald* old + *ford* FORD; one in Somerset (*Aldedeford* in Domesday Book), of which the first element, according to Ekwall, is the OE female personal name *Ealdgȳð*, composed of the elements *eald* old + *gȳð* battle; and one in Lincs. (*Alforde* in Domesday Book), of which the first element is probably either OE *alor* ALDER or *(e)alh* temple, shrine. There is also a place of the same name in the former county of Aberdeen (now part of Grampian region), which may lie behind some Scots examples of the surname.

Var.: **Allford.**

Alfred English: from the ME personal name *Alvred*, *Alured*, OE *Ælfrǣd*, composed of the elements *ælf* elf + *rǣd* counsel. This owed its popularity as a given name in England chiefly to the fame of the W Saxon king Alfred the Great (849–99), who defeated the Danes, keeping them out of Wessex, and whose court was a great centre of learning and culture. The Fr. form given below is derived from a Continental Gmc cogn.

Vars.: **Al(l)ured** (with vocalization of the consonant in the Latinized spelling *Alvredus*).

Cogns.: Fr.: **Aufrède.** Port.: **Alfredo.**

Patrs.: Eng.: **Alfreds, Alfredson.** Swed.: **Alfredsson.**

Alger English: from the ME personal name *Alger*, in which several names of different origins, both Continental Gmc (through the Normans) and OE, have fallen together. The final element of all of them is *gar*, *ger* spear (cf. GORE 1 and GARLICK). The first element is generally *alb* elf, but may also be *adal* noble or *ald* old. The Norman French forms have also absorbed OE cogns. beginning in *Ælf-* and *Æðel-*. In regions that were under Scandinavian influence the name is normally derived from the ON cogn. *Álfgeirr* 'elf spear'.

Vars.: **Algar, Auger; Elgar, Elger.**

Cogns.: Fr.: **Aug(i)er.** Prov.: **Aug(i)é.**

Dims.: Fr.: **Augereau, Augeron.**

Alguacil Spanish: occupational name for the governor of a region or for an officer of justice, Sp. *alguacil* (from the Arabic def. art. *al* + *wazir* vizier, official, originally 'porter').

Aliaga Spanish: topographic name for someone who lived on a patch of land overgrown with gorse, Sp. *aliaga*, *aulaga* (of uncertain, probably pre-Roman, origin). The surname is now most common in Catalonia, especially in the provinces of Valencia, Alicante, and Barcelona, but it seems to have originated in Aragon.

Alison Scots: 1. dim. or metr. from the ME female name *Alise*, *Alice* (from an ONF contracted form of Gmc *Adalhaidis* (*Adelaide*), composed of the elements *adal* noble + *haid* kind, sort).

2. patr. from the ME male name Ellis, or else from a short form of Allen or Alexander (cf. Alcock).

Var.: **Allison.**

Allard English (Norman) and French: from an OF personal name, *Adelard*, composed of the Gmc elements *adal* noble + *hard* hardy, brave, strong. The ANF form *Alard* has probably absorbed the OE names *Ælfheard* and *Æðelheard*

Vars.: Eng.: **Adlard, Allart, Aylard, Ellard, Ellert, Hallard; Hallet(t)** (mainly Somerset and Devon). Fr.: **Alard.**

Cogns.: Low Ger.: **Alhard, Ahlert, Allert.** Fris.: **Aaldert.**

Patrs.: Low Ger.: **Ahlers, Aller(t)s.**

Allardyce Scots: habitation name from *Allardice* in the former county of Kincardines. This is of uncertain origin (the first element is probably ME *aller* alder, OE *alor*). The traditional pronunciation of the name is /ˈɛərdɪs/.

Vars.: **Allardice, Allardes; Alderdice** (N Ireland); **Ardes.**

Alleaume French: from an OF version of the Gmc personal name *Adalhelm*, composed of the elements *adal* noble + *helm* protection, helmet.

Vars.: **Alliaume, Allem.**

Cogns.: Ger.: **Ahlhelm.** Fris.: **Alm.** Eng.: **Adlam.**

Allegri Italian: nickname from It. *allegro* quick, lively, cheerful (L *alacer*, gen. *alacris*), which was also used occasionally as a given name in the Middle Ages.

Cogns.: Fr.: **Allègre.** Cat., Sp., Port.: **Alegre.**

Dims.: It.: **Allegretti, Allegrini, Allegrucci.** Fr.: **Allégret.** Cat.: **Alegret.**

Aug.: It.: **Allegroni.**

Derivs. (from abstract nouns meaning 'cheerfulness'): It.: **Allegria; Allegrezza.** Cat., Port.: **Alegria.** Sp.: **Alegría.**

The family name of the Italian painter Correggio (1494–1534) was Allegri. *Correggio was the name of his birthplace, a small town near Modena.*

Allen 1. English and Scots: from a Celt. personal name of great antiquity and obscurity. In England the given name is now usually spelt *Alan*, the surname *Allen* or (esp. in Scotland) *Allan*. Various suggestions have been put forward regarding its origin; most probably it originally meant 'little rock' (Gael. *ailín*, dim. of *ail* rock). The present-day frequency of the surname in England and Ireland is accounted for by the popularity of the given name among Bret. followers of William the Conqueror, by whom it was imported first to Britain and then to Ireland. St *Alan(us)* was a 5th-cent. bishop of Quimper about whom nothing factual is known, but who was a cult figure in medieval Brittany. Another St *Al(l)an* was a Corn. or Bret. saint of the 6th cent., to whom a church in Cornwall is dedicated.

2. Low German, Danish, and Swedish (**Allén**): probably from a Gmc personal name rather than a borrowing from Breton. The most likely source would be *Alle*, a Low Ger. short form of any of various Gmc cpd personal names with the first element *adal* noble (cf. Adel).

Vars. (of 1): **Al(l)an, Alleyne, Allin(e).**

Cogns. (of 1): Fr.: **Al(l)a(i)n.**

Patrs. (from 1): Eng.: Allis; **Allenson, Allanson, Alli(n)son, Hallison; FitzAlan.** Sc.: **McAllan, McAline, McEllen, McElane, McKellan, McKellen** (Gael. **Mac Ailín, Mac Aileáin**).

'Descendant of A.': Ir.: **O'Hallyn, Hallin** (Gael. **Ó hAilín**).

Allenby English: habitation name from *Allonby* or *Ellonby*, both in Cumb. and both being late (post-Conquest) formations from the personal name *Alein*, from ANF *aguillon* goad, spur + Northern ME *by* farm, settlement (ON *býr*).

Allende Spanish: habitation name for someone who lived some distance from the main settlement, or whose home was beyond some particular landmark, from OSp. *allende* (from) yonder, beyond (a cpd of *allá* (L *illāc* there) + *ende* (L *inde* thence)).

Allerton English: habitation name from any of several places so called. Allerton on Merseyside, Chapel Allerton in W Yorks., and most of the others in W Yorks. are so called from OE *alra*, gen. pl. of *alor* alder + *tūn* enclosure, settlement; cf. Alderton. Chapel Allerton in Somerset (*Allwarditone* in Domesday Book) and Allerton Mauleverer in W Yorks. (*Alvertone* in Domesday Book) were originally named in OE as the settlements of *Ælfweard* 'elf guardian' and *Ælfhere* 'elf army' respectively.

Isaac Allerton *(?1586–1658) was one of the most influential of the Pilgrim Fathers. His descendants included Samuel Allerton (1828–1914), one of the founders of modern Chicago.*

Allis English: 1. contracted form of *Allins*, patr. of Allen.

2. from the ME, OF female given name *Alis*, a contracted form of the Gmc personal name *Adalhaid(is)*, composed of the elements *adal* noble + *haid* kind, sort. A modern revival of the uncontracted form is *Adelaide*. The given name *Alice* (*Alis*) and its dim. Alison were very popular throughout the Middle Ages. It was the name of the wife of the emperor Otto the Great, St Adelaide (or Alice; d. 999); it was also the name of the goose in medieval beast tales. It fell out of use in the 16th–17th cents., being revived again in the 19th.

Vars.: **Alliss, Alis, Hallis.** (Of 2 only): **Alise.**

Cogns. (of 2): Fr.: **Alice, Al(l)ix, Alliz, Allex, Allez, Al(l)ais, Allet; Adèle, Adeau.** Ger.: **Adelheid, Alheit, Aleth.**

Dims. (of 2): Eng.: **Allott, Allatt** (both chiefly common in Yorks.). Fr.: **Al(l)ine, Allot; Adeline.**

Metrs. (from 2): Flem.: **Al(is)en, Aeles; Leyten.** Ger.: **Al(i)scher, Altscher, Alschner.**

Alloway 1. English: from the OE personal name *Æðelwīg*, composed of the elements *æðel* noble + *wīg* battle.

2. Scots: habitation name from any of several places called *Alloway*, *Alloa*, or *Alva*, e.g. *Alloway* in the former county of Ayrshire. All are so named from Gael. *allmhagh* rocky plain.

Vars.: **Aloway, Al(l)(a)way, Elloway, Halloway, Hallaway.**

Cogn. (of 1): Cat.: **Allué.**

Allsop English (chiefly Midlands): habitation name from *Alsop* in Derbys., named in OE as *Ælleshop* 'valley (see Hope) of *Ælli*'.

Vars.: **Allsopp, Alsop(p), Allsep(p); Elsop, Elsip.**

Almagro Spanish: habitation name from a place in the province of Ciudad Real, so called from the Arabic def. art. *al* + *mágra* red clay.

Alman 1. English: ethnic name for someone from Germany, from ANF *aleman* German or *alemayne* Germany (LL *Alemannus* and *Alemannia*, from a Gmc tribal name, probably meaning simply 'all the men'). In some cases the reference may have been to the Norman region of *Allemagne*, to the south of Caen, which was probably so named from Gmc settlers there.

2. Jewish (Ashkenazic): surname taken by a widower, Hebr. *alman*.

Vars. (of 1): **Allman, Al(l)mann, Aliman, Allmen, Almon; Al(l)mand, Allamand, Allimant, Al(l)ment,** Almond (the excrescent dental was common after a final *-n*; cf. *Dayman* at Day).

Cogns. (of 1): Fr.: **Alleman(d), Allmann** (Alsace); **Al(l)aman** (Switzerland). Sp.: **Alemán.** Cat.: **Alemany, Alemañy.** Port.:

Alemão. It.: **Al(e)manno**, **Allemano**, **Al(l)amanno**; **La Manna**, **La Magna** (by false word division and folk etymology).
Dims. (of 1): Fr.: **Allemandet**, **Allemandou**.
Patr. (from 1): Rum.: **Alimanesco** (usually referring to people of Swiss origin).

Almazán Spanish: habitation name from a place in the province of Soria, so called from the Arabic def. art. *al* + *mazan* fortified (place).

Almazov Russian: patr. from the nickname *Almaz* 'Diamond', perhaps denoting a jeweller, or more likely bestowed as an affectionate indication of worth. The word derives from Gk *adamas* (from *a-* not + *damān* to conquer, i.e. 'the unconquerable', with reference to its hardness) via Arabic, where the first syllable was assimilated to the def. art. *al*.

Almeida Portuguese: habitation name from any of the numerous places, including a town in the province of Beira Baixa, so called from the Arabic def. art. *al* + *mâ'ida* plateau, (low) hill.

Almendro Spanish: topographic name for someone who lived near an almond tree or in an almond grove, from Sp. *almendro* almond (L *amygdalus*, from Gk; the first syllable has been assimilated to the form of the Arabic def. art. *al*). Cf. MANDEL. There are various places named with this word, for example in the province of Huelva, and they may also have contributed to the surname as habitation names.
Var.: **Almendros** (pl.; the name of a place in Cuenca).

Almirall Catalan: occupational name for a local dignitary, Cat. *almirall* (from Arabic *'amīr* ruler + *a'ālī* high, with later assimilation of the first syllable to the form of the Arabic def. art. *al*).

Almond English: 1. var. of ALMAN.
2. from the OE personal name *Æðelmund*, composed of the elements *æðel* noble + *mund* protection. There is no evidence of any connection with the almond nut or tree (cf. ALMENDRO).

Alós Catalan: habitation name from any of various places so called. The placename is of pre-Roman origin and unknown meaning.
Var.: **Alòs**.

Alov Russian: patr. from the nickname *Aly* 'Crimson', a word taken from some Turkic language. It seems unlikely that the nickname referred to complexion or hair colour; more probably, it indicated a predilection for dressing in flamboyant colours.

Alpert 1. Frisian: var. of ALBERT.
2. Jewish (Ashkenazic): of uncertain origin, probably a var. of HEILBRONN.
Vars.: **Alper**. (Of 2 only): **Halper**.

Alpin Scots and Irish: apparently from the ancient Celt. personal name *Alpin*, of unknown etymology, which was borne by Pictish kings.
Vars.: **Alpine**; **Elfin**.
Patrs.: Sc.: **Macalpin(e)** (Gael. **Mac Ailpín**).
'Descendant of A.': Ir.: **(O')Halpin**, **(O')Halpen**, **Halpen(n)y**, HALFPENNY (Gael. **Ó hAilpín**).

Alston English: 1. from the ME personal name *Alstan*, representing a coalescence of various OE personal names composed of the elements *æðel* noble, *ælf* elf, *(e)ald* old, or *(e)alh* shrine, temple + *stān* stone.
2. habitation name from any of various places called *Alston* (in Lancs., Devon, and Somerset) or *Alstone* (in Gloucs. and Staffs.). These are variously the settlements (OE *tūn*) of bearers of the OE personal names *Ælfwine* ('elf friend'), *Ælfsige* ('elf victory'), *Æðelnoð* ('noble daring'), and *Ælfrēd* ('elf counsel'). Alston in Cumb. is a ME placename, *Aldenstune*, from the ON personal name *Alden* (from *Halfdan*; see HALDANE) + *tune* settlement.
Vars.: **Alstone**, **Allston(e)**, EDLESTONE.

Altbüsser German: occupational name for a cobbler or shoemender, from MHG *alt* old (OHG *alt*) + an agent deriv. of *buessen* to mend, improve (OHG *buossan*).
Vars.: **Albeisser** (S Germany and Switzerland); **Albiez**.
Cogn.: Low Ger.: **Olböter**.

Altés Catalan: habitation name from a place in the province of Lérida, recorded in the 12th cent. in the form *Autés*. The name is of uncertain origin, according to Corominas from Basque *othaitz* 'full of gorse' (from *ote* gorse + the suffix of plurality *-i(t)z*).

Alton English: habitation name from any of various places so called. Those in Hants, Dorset, and Wilts. are at the sources of the rivers Wey, Piddle, and Avon respectively, and derive their names from OE *æwiell* spring, source + *tūn* enclosure, settlement. Alton in Derbys. and Alton Grange in Leics. seem to have had as their first element OE *(e)ald* old. Other examples derive from various OE personal names; one in Staffs. was the settlement of *Ælfa* (a short form of any of the various cpd personal names with the first element *ælf* elf), one in Wilts. belonged to *Ælla*, and one in Worcs., recorded as *Eanulfintun* in 1023, to *Ēanwulf* (from an element of obscure origin + OE *wulf* wolf).

Altschul Jewish (Ashkenazic): from Yid. *alt* old (MHG *alt*) + *shul* synagogue (MHG *schul* school); the reason for adoption of the surname is unclear.
Var.: **Altschul(l)er**, **Altshuler**.

Álvaro Spanish and Portuguese: from a Gmc (Visigothic) personal name, probably composed of the elements *all* all + *wēr* true.
Var.: Sp.: **Alvar**.
Patrs.: Sp.: **Álvarez**. Port.: **Álvares**, **Alves**.

Alvey English: from the ME given name *Alfwy*, OE *Ælfwīg*, composed of the elements *ælf* elf + *wīg* battle. The surname is most common in Notts.
Vars.: **Alvy**, **Allvey**; **Elphey**, **Elv(e)y**.

Alwyn English: from the ME personal names *Al(f)win*, *Elwin*, representing a coalescence of various OE personal names: *Ælfwine* (composed of the elements *ælf* elf + *wine* friend), *Æðelwine* ('noble friend'), and *Ealdwine* ('old friend'). In some cases it may even be from the female name *Ælfwynn*, composed of the elements *ælf* elf + *wynn* joy.
Vars.: **Ailwyn**, **A(y)lwen**, **A(y)lwin**, **Allwyn**; **Elwyn**, **Elwin**; **Alvin**, **Alven**; **Elvin** (chiefly Norfolk).

Amadei Italian: from the given name *Amadeo*, which was coined in the early Middle Ages from the elements *ama-* love + *Deo* God. This was the name of two 12th-cent. Burgundian nobles (father and son) who became Cistercian monks, and their fame may have contributed to the subsequent popularity of the given name.
Vars.: **Amade**, **Amadi**, **Amaddei**, **Amad(d)io**, **Amedei**; **Amod(d)eo**, **Amod(d)io**; **Mad(d)ei**.
Cogns.: Prov.: **Amadieu**, **Amédée**. Hung.: **Amade**, **Amadé**.
Dim.: It.: **Amadini**.

Amalfi Italian: habitation name from the seaport of this name on the rocky coast south of Naples.

Vars.: **Malfi; Malfitano, Amalfitano.**

Amand French and English: from the given name *Amand* (L *Amandus* 'Lovable', from *amāre* to love), which was borne by a number of early Christian churchmen (abbots and bishops) in France and elsewhere, including a 5th-cent. bishop of Bordeaux, and a 7th-cent. bishop of Maastricht known as 'the apostle of the Netherlands'.

Vars.: Eng.: **Aman(n), Amman.**

Amant French: from the given name *Amans* (L *Amans*, gen. *Amantis*, 'Loving', pres. part. of *amāre* to love), bestowed on children with reference to spiritual love. In some cases it may also have been a nickname for a philanderer, and the It. patr. forms may refer obliquely to birth out of wedlock (cf. AMOR).

Cogns.: Eng.: **Ament.** It.: **Amante, Amanti.**

Dim.: It.: **Amantino.**

Patrs.: It.: **D'Amante, Damanti.**

Amaral Portuguese: habitation name from any of the numerous minor places so called. They are of uncertain etymology, probably from Port. *amaral* a kind of black grape (from L *amārus* bitter); alternatively a connection has been suggested with a collective deriv. of Sp. *maro*, *amaro* cat-thyme (L *marum*, influenced by Sp. *amargo* bitter).

Amatore Italian: from a medieval given name (L *Amātor* 'Lover' (i.e. of God), from *amāre* to love). The personal name was borne by several early Christian saints, most famously a hermit in Roman Gaul who founded the shrine of Our Lady of Rocamadour in Provence, which was a popular place of pilgrimage in the Middle Ages. The Sp. cogn. *Amador* owed its popularity as a given name chiefly to a 9th-cent. saint martyred at Cordoba by the Moors, while in Portugal many churches are dedicated to a local saint of this name, of uncertain date. A Fr. cogn. is noticeably absent, probably suppressed because of the pej. connotations of the vocab. word *amateur*, with which it would have been identical in form.

Vars.: **Amatori, Amadore.**

Cogn.: Sp., Cat., Port.: **Amador.**

Dims.: It.: **Amadorucci, Amadoruzzi.**

Ambler English: 1. occupational name for an enameller, ANF *amayler* (OF *esmailler*, from OF *esmail* enamel, a word of Gmc origin akin to mod. Eng. *smelt*). The *-b-* is intrusive.

2. from ME *ambler* walker (via OF from L *ambulāre* to walk), of uncertain application. The term was used of the slowest gait of a horse or mule, and the surname may have been an occupational name for a stable-keeper or a nickname for a person with an ambling gait.

The surname Ambler *can be traced back in Yorks. and Lincs., via William Ambler, Mayor of Doncaster in 1717, to the reign of Edward I (1272–1307). It is still more common in Yorks. than elsewhere.*

Ambridge English: of uncertain origin, in form ostensibly a habitation name from some unidentified place so called. If this is correct, the second element is OE *brycg* BRIDGE; the first is obscure. However, the name is more likely to be an alteration by folk etymology of AMBROSE.

The earliest known occurrence of this surname is in 1640 at Addington, Bucks. From the early 18th cent. onwards it has been concentrated mainly in Beds. and London.

Ambrose English: from a medieval given name (L *Ambrosius*, from Gk *ambrosios* immortal), which owes its popularity largely to the fame of St Ambrose (*c.*340–97), one of the four 'Latin Fathers of the Church', who was the teacher of St Augustine.

Cogns.: Fr.: **Ambrois(e), Ambroix.** Prov.: **Ambrodi** (Gascony). It.: **Ambrosi(o), Ambrogi(o); Brosi(o), Brog(g)i(o)** (aphetic). Port.: **Ambrosio.** Ger.: **Ambros(ch), Bros(e).** Flem.: **Ambroes; Bro(o)se, Bröse; Brosius** (Latinized). Ger. (of Slav. origin): **Brosch, Prosch.** Czech: **Ambrož, Brož.** Pol.: **Mróz.** Hung.: **Ambrus.**

Dims.: Fr.: **Ambroisin, Ambresin; Brosset** (Belgium). It.: **Ambrosini, Ambrogini, Ambrosetti, Ambrogetti, Ambrosoli, Ambrogioli, Ambrogelli, Ambrogiotti; Brosini, Brog(g)ini, Brosetti, Brogetti, Brosoli, Brogelli, Brogiotti; Brusin** (Venetia). Ger.: **Brösel.** Low Ger.: **Broseke, Bröseke.** Flem.: **Broseman.** Ger. (of Slav. origin): **Bros(ch)ke, Broschek; Pros(ch)ke, Pros(ch)ek.** Czech: **Brožek.** Pol.: **Ambrozik; Jambrozek; Brożek.**

Augs.: It.: **Ambrosoni, Ambrogioni; Brogioni.**

Patrs.: Sc., Ir.: **McCambridge** (Gael. **Mac Ambróis**). It.: **D'Ambrosi(o), D'Ambrogi(o), De Ambrosi(s).** Flem.: **Brosenius** (Latinized). Pol.: **Ambrożewicz; Ambroziak.**

Patrs. (from dims.): Pol.: **Broszkiewicz; Jamrowicz.**

Amery English: from a Gmc personal name composed of the elements *amal* bravery, vigour + *rīc* power, introduced into England by the Normans. In OF the given name has a profusion of different forms (*Amalri(c)*, *Aumari(c)*, *Amauri*, *Emaurri*, *Haimeri*, *Ymeri*, etc.) and several of these are reflected in vars. of the surname.

Vars.: **Amory; Emery, Emory, Emary; Ember(r)y, Embr(e)y, Embur(e)y; Emeric(k); Im(b)ery, Im(b)rie, Imbrey, Imray** (Scotland and Northumb.); **Hemery, Hembr(e)y.**

Cogns.: Fr.: **Amaury, Aymery, Emery; Maury, Méry.** Prov.: **Amalric, Amaurich.** Port.: **Amaro.** Ger.: **Amelrich, Emelrich, Emmerich, Embrich.** Hung.: **Imre.**

Dims.: Ger.: **Emmel, Emmlein.** Low Ger.: **Ahmel(mann), Ehm(e)cke.**

Patr.: Eng.: **Emerson.**

Patrs. (from dim.): Low Ger.: **Ahmels; Ameling, Amelung, Ahmling.**

Amey English (Norman): from the OF given name *Amé* (L *Amātus* 'Beloved', past part. of *amāre* to love).

Vars.: **Amy, Amie.**

Cogns.: Fr.: **A(i)mé; Amez** (Switzerland). Prov., Cat.: **Amat.** Sp., Port.: **Amado.** It.: **Amato, Amati.**

Dims.: It.: **Amatucci, Amatulli.**

Patrs.: Eng.: AMIS. It.: **D'Amato.**

Amezaga Basque: topographic name for someone who lived by an oak tree or in an oak wood, from *ametz* oak + the local suffix *-aga*.

Amherst English: habitation name from *Amhurst* Hill in Pembury, Kent which is found as *Hemhurst* in 1250, and probably derives its name from OE *hem* boundary + *hyrst* wooded hill (see HURST).

Jeffrey Amherst *(1717–97), who served as a British general in N America, came of a Kentish family of landed gentry, members of which included many lawyers and clergymen.*

Amis English (Norman): from the OF given name or nickname *Amis* (oblique case *Ami*) 'Friend' (L *amīcus*, a deriv. of *amāre* to love).

Vars.: **Amiss, Am(i)es.**

Cogns.: Fr.: **Ami, Amy; Lamy.** It.: **Amico.**

Dims.: Fr.: **Ami(gu)et, Amiot, Amyot, Amiel**. It.: **Amicelli, Amicino, Amighini, Ami(gh)etti, Amigotti**. Cat.: **Amigó**.

Augs.: It.: **Amiconi, Ami(g)oni**.

Pej.: Fr.: **Amiard**.

Patrs.: Eng.: **Am(i)son**. It.: **D'Amico, D'Amici; De Amicis**.

Ami(e)s *is the name of a prominent E Anglian family with many branches.*

Ammann German: occupational name for an administrative official or head of a community owing allegiance to a feudal superior, from an assimilated form of *Amtmann* (MHG *ambet(man)*, from OHG *ampacht* retainer). The surname is most common in S Germany and Switzerland.

Var.: **Amann**.

Amo Spanish: occupational name or nickname from Sp. *amo* tutor, guardian, master (a masc. form of *ama* nurse, LL *amma*, probably in origin a nursery word).

Amond N English: from a Scandinavian personal name (OIcel. *Ogmundr*, OSwed. *Aghmund*, mod. Dan. *Amund*), composed of the Gmc elements *agi* awe (or possibly *ag* point; cf. ACHARD) + *mund* protection. See also HAMMOND.

Vars.: **Am(m)on**.

Patrs.: Eng.: **Ammonds**. Norw., Dan.: **Amundsen**.

Amor Spanish, French, and English: from the medieval nickname or given name *Amor* (L *amor* love), which was popular in Spain, Italy, and France, and introduced into England by the Normans. There was a St Amor, of obscure history and unknown date, whose relics were preserved and venerated at the village of St Amour in Burgundy. The Ger. forms owe their origin to an 8th-cent. evangelist who founded the monastery of *Amorbach* in Franconia and a 9th-cent. Belgian saint who was sometimes confused with him. It is also possible that in some cases the surname arose from a nickname for a lovable person or a philanderer, or for someone who had played the part of Love (personified) in a pageant or mystery play.

Vars.: Sp.: **Amores**. Fr., Eng.: **Amour**.

Cogn.: It.: **Amore**.

Dims.: It.: **Amor(i)elli, Amoretti, Amorini**.

Patrs. (often suggesting illegitimate origin): It.: **D(ell)'Amore**.

Amorim Portuguese: habitation name from places in the provinces of Oporto and Aveiro, so called from L *Amorīni (villa)* '(settlement) of *Amorīnus*', a deriv. of AMOR.

Amos 1. Jewish: from the Hebr. given name *Amos* 'Borne (by God)'. This was the name of a prophet of the 8th cent. BC, whose oracles are recorded in the Book of Amos.

2. English (SE England): probably a var. of AMIS. The given name *Amos* is not found among non-Jews before the Reformation, and so the English surname is unlikely to be derived from it.

Patr. (from 1): **Ben-Amos** (Israeli).

Amoureux French: nickname for a philanderer or an affectionate man, from OF *amoureux* loving, amorous (L *amorōsus*, a deriv. of *amor* love).

Var.: **Lamoureux** (with fused def. art.).

Cogns.: Prov.: **Amouroux, Lamouroux**. It.: **Amoroso, Amoruso, Amorese**. Cat.: **Amorós**.

Dims.: It.: **Amoroselli, Amorosini**.

Amschel Jewish (Ashkenazic): from the Yid. male given name *An(t)shl*, ultimately from L *angelus* angel.

Vars.: **Amszel** (a Polish spelling), AMSEL, **Anchel** (a Fr. spelling), ANCEL.

Patr.: **Antzilewitz** (E Ashkenazic).

Amsel 1. German: from MHG *amsel* blackbird (OHG *ams(a)la*), in various applications; a habitation name for someone who lived in a house with a sign bearing a picture of this bird, a metonymic occupational name for a bird catcher, or a nickname for someone thought to resemble a blackbird in some way.

2. Jewish: var. of AMSCHEL.

Amsler Jewish (Ashkenazic): habitation name from *Amsle*, Yid. name of *Namsłau* in Silesia.

Var.: **Amschler**.

Amsterdam, van Dutch (largely Jewish): habitation name from the city in N Holland, so called from being originally built round a dam on the river *Amstel*. Many Jews settled in Amsterdam after being expelled from Spain and Portugal in the late 16th cent., and they helped to make it a centre of the diamond-cutting trade. Before the First World War approximately 10 per cent of the population of Amsterdam was Jewish.

Vars.: Jewish: **Amsterdam(er); Amsterdamski** (E Ashkenazic).

Anacleto Portuguese: from a given name (Gk *Anaklētos* 'Invoked', a deriv. of *anakalein* to call on) supposedly borne by the third pope, also known as *Anenklētos* 'Irreproachable'.

Anaya Spanish form of Basque **Anaia**: from *anai* brother + the def. art. *-a*, which was used in the Middle Ages both as a byname and as a personal name.

Ancel 1. French: occupational name for a domestic servant, OF *ancel(e)* (L *ancilla* serving maid).

2. Jewish (Ashkenazic): var. of AMSCHEL.

Vars. (of 1): **Ancelle** (fem.); **Anceau(x), Anseau(x), Ansiau; Lancel**.

Dims. (of 1): **Ancel(l)in, Anselin, Ancel(l)et, Anselet, Ancelot, Anselot**.

Patr. (from 2): **Ancelevitch**.

Anderton English: habitation name from either of two places, in Ches. and Lancs., so called from the OE personal name *Ēanrēd* (composed of the elements *ēan*, of uncertain origin, + *rēd* counsel) + *tūn* enclosure, settlement.

Andrade Portuguese: of uncertain origin. There are various minor places so called, for example near Coimbra, Estremoz, Figueira da Foz, and Penafiel, but the placename is probably derived from the surname, rather than the other way about. The surname may derive from the Gk personal name *Andras* (a short form of various cpd names with the first element *anēr*, gen. *andros*, man) by way of the LL acc. form *Andradem*. The surname is also relatively common in Spain.

Andrew English: from the name (Gk *Andreas*, a deriv. of *andreios* manly, from *anēr*, gen. *andros*, man, male) by which the first of Jesus Christ's disciples is known, in various local forms, throughout Christendom. (It is presumably a Gk translation of a lost Aramaic name.) The disciple is the patron saint of Scotland, and there is a legend that his relics were brought to Scotland in the 4th cent. by a certain St Regulus. He is also the patron saint of Russia. The name was also popular in Eastern Europe (Czech *Ondřej*, Pol. *Andrzej*, *Jędrej*), and in Pol. there has been some confusion with derivs. of *Henryk* (see HENRY).

Var. (aphetic): DREW.

Cogns.: Gael.: **Aindrias, Aindriú**. Fr.: **André, Andreix; Andrey** (E France); **Andrez** (N France). Prov.: **Andreu, Andrieu(x); Landrieu; Drieu**. Cat.: **Andreu**. Sp.: **Andrés**.

Port.: **André**. It.: **Andrei, Andrea, Andri(a)**; **Dr(e)i**. Rum.: **Andrei**. Ger.: **Andre(a)s, Anders(ch), Enders**; **Endres, Entre(i)s** (Bavaria). Low Ger.: **Dreus, Drees**. Flem., Du.: **Andries**; **Dries, Drees**. Swed.: **Andre(e)**. Ger. (of Slav. origin): **Andrasch, Hantusch, Jendrusch**; **Wandrey, Fandrey**. Czech: **Andrejs, Andrys**; **Ondruš, Ondřich, Ondra, Ondrák, Vondra, Vondrák, Vondrys**. Pol.: **Andrzej**; **Jędrzej**; **Jendrys, Jędrys, Jędrych, Jędruch, Indruch, Jędras, Jędryka**. Hung.: **Andor, András(sy)**. Gk: **Andreas**.

Dims.: Eng.: **Dand(y), Dandie**; **Tandy** (W Midlands); **Tancock**. Fr.: **Andrin**; **Andrivel, Andriveaux, Andrivot**. It.: **Andr(e)elli, Andr(e)etti, Andr(e)ini, Andr(e)ol(l)i, Andriol(l)i, Andr(e)oletti, Andrioletti, Andreotti, Andreutti, Andreucci, Andreuzzi, Andriuzzi**; **Andino**; **Dreini, Dreossi, Drioli, Driussi, Driuzzi, Driutti**. Ger.: **Anderl, Enderl(e), Enderlein**; **Enterl(e), Enterlein** (Bavaria). Ger. (of Slav. origin): **Andrich, Andrick, Angrick**; **Androck, Angrock**; **Andrag, Antrag, Antrack**; **Handri(c)k, Handrek, Handro(c)k**; **Gandrich**; **Wandrach, Wandrack, Wandrich**; **Vondrach**; **Fandrich**; **Wanderschek, Wondraschek**. Czech: **Andrýsek, Andrík**; **Ondráček, Ondrášek, Ondr(o)ušek, Ondřiček, Vondráček, Von(dr)ášek, Vondruška**. Pol.: **Jędrzejczyk, Jędraszczyk, Jędraszek, Jędrasik, Jędrysik**. Ukr.: **Andryushchenko, Andrichuk, Andrichak, Andrusyak**. Beloruss.: **Androsik, Andreichik**.

Augs.: Fr.: **Andrat**. It.: **Andreone, Andrioni**; **Dreoni**.

Pejs.: Fr.: **Andraud, Andrault**. It.: **Andreacci(o), Andreazzi**; **Dreassi**.

Patrs.: Eng.: **Andrew(e)s, Andress, Andriss**; **Anderson, Enderson**. Sc.: **McAndrew**; **Kendrew** (now common in W Yorks.). It.: **D'Andrea, De Andreis**. Ger.: **Anderer**; **Andresser, Endresser** (Austria). Low Ger.: **Drees(s)en, Driessen**; **Drewing**. Flem.: **Driesen**. Du.: **Andriesse(n)**. Norw., Dan.: **Andersen, Andresen, Andrea(s)sen**. Swed.: **Andersson, Andreasson**; **Andrén**. Pol.: **Jędrzejewicz, Jędrachowicz**; **Andrzejak, Andrysiak**; Russ.: **Andreev**. Lithuanian: **Andriulis**. Croatian: **Andr(ejev)ić**. Gk: **Andreou**.

Patrs. (from dims.): Gael.: **Mac Aindrín**. Eng.: **Dan(di)son**. Ger.: **Endler** (Bavaria). Pol.: **Jędrzejkiewicz, Jędrzaszkiewicz**; **Andrzejczak, Andryszczak, Jędrzejczak**. Russ.: **Andryushin, Andryunin, Andrusov**.

'Son of the servant of A.': Sc., Ir.: **Gillanders** (Gael. **Mac Gille Andrais** (Sc.), **Mac Giolla Aindréis** (Ir.)).

Habitation names: Pol.: **Andrzejewski, Andrzejowski, Jędrzéjewski, Jędrychowski**.

Andrewartha Cornish: habitation name from *Trewartha* in St Agnes parish (formerly called *Andrewartha*, from the def. art. *an* + *dre*, a mutated form of *tre* village + *wartha* higher).

Angel English and French: nickname from ME, OF *angel* angel (L *angelus*, from Gk *angelos* messenger; cf. ENGEL), denoting a person of angelic temperament or appearance, or one who had played the part of an angel in a mystery play or pageant. It was also occasionally used as a given name, especially on the Continent.

Vars.: Eng.: **Angell**. Fr.: **Ange(au)**.

Cogns.: It.: **Angelo** (chiefly southern); **Agnolo** (chiefly northern). Sp.: **Ángel** (also an ornamental Sefardic name). Port.: **Ângelo** (from the L given name *Angelus*); **Anjos** (in allusion to the Marian title *Nossa Senhora dos Anjos* Our Lady of the Angels). Rum.: **Anghel**. Czech: **Anděl**. Hung.: **Angyal**.

Dims.: Fr.: **Angelet, Angelot, Angelin**. It.: **Angelini, Angiolini**; **Angeletti, Angioletti, Agnoletti**; **Angelotti, Angiolotti**; **Angelozzi, Agnolozzi**; **Angelillo, Angiolillo**; **Angioli, Angiuli**.

Augs.: It.: **Angioni, Angheloni, Agnoloni**.

Patrs.: It.: **D'Angelo, De Angelis**; **D'Agnolo, Dell'Agnol**. Russ.: **Angelov** (adopted by priests). Croatian: **Andjelić**. Gk: **Angelopoulos**.

Patr. (from a dim.): Croatian: **Andjelković**.

Thomas Angell, *who emigrated to New England in 1631 and was one of the founders of Boston, is the ancestor of many Americans named* Angel.

Anglade Provençal: topographic name for someone who lived on a remote nook of land, from OProv. *anglade* corner, recess (LL *ang(u)lāta*, a deriv. of *angulus*; see ANGLE).

Cogn.: Cat.: **Anglada**.

Angle English: topographic name for someone who lived on an odd corner of land, from ME, OF *angle* (L *angulus* angle, corner).

Var.: NANGLE.

Cogn.: Sp.: **Ángulo**.

Anguera Catalan: topographic name for someone who lived on the banks of the river *Anguera*, in the province of Tarragona. The name is of uncertain etymology, perhaps related to L *angustiae* narrows, strait, gorge (from *angustus* narrow).

Angus Scots and Irish: from the Gael. personal name *Aonghus*, composed of the elements *aon* one + *ghus* choice. It was borne by a famous but shadowy 8th-cent. Pictish king, said to be the son of Daghda, the chief god of the Irish, and Boann, who gave her name to the river Boyne. This king gave his name to the county (now part of Tayside) called *Angus*, and many Scots have received it as a given name in his honour. Some examples of the surname may also be regional names from this source.

Vars.: INNES; **Nish**. See also MCGUINNESS, HENNESSY, and MCNEICE.

Angwin 1. English (Norman): regional name from OF *angevin* man from *Anjou*, a province of France which was ruled by a count as an independent territory from the 10th cent. until it became a property of the English Crown for fifty years at the end of the 12th cent.

2. Cornish: nickname for someone with fair hair or a pale complexion, from Corn. *an* def. art. + *gwyn* white, fair.

Aniceto Portuguese: from a medieval given name (L *Anicētus*, Gk *Anikētos* 'Invincible', the name of a 2nd-cent. pope).

Anne English: 1. var. of HANNA.

2. habitation name from *Ann* in Hants, which is so called from an old stream name, probably a Brit. cogn. of W *on* ash tree.

Sir William de Anne, *constable of Tickhill Castle in S Yorks. in 1315, was the ancestor of several landed and titled families, including the Annes of Burghwallis, the Charltons of Great Canfield, and the Barons Heneage.*

Annis English: from a ME vernacular form of the female given name *Agnes* (ultimately from Gk *hagnos* pure, chaste, but early associated by folk etymology with L *agnus* lamb, a symbol of Christ). The name was borne by an early Christian saint, a twelve-year-old Roman girl who was martyred for her Christian belief in the time of Diocletian.

Vars.: **Agnes(s)**; **Anness, Annas**.

Cogns.: Fr.: **Agnes**. Sp.: **Inés**. Port.: **Inês**. Ger.: **Agnete**. Low Ger.: **Neese, Nehse**. Flem.: **Nees**. It.: **Agnesi, Anese**; **Lagnese**.

Dims.: Eng.: **Annott, Annatt**; **Annett** (chiefly N Ireland). It.: **Agnesetti, Agnesini**.

Metrs.: Eng.: **Annison**. It.: **D'Agnese**. Ger.: **Agneter**. Low Ger.: **Agnesen, Ne(e)sen**. Flem.: **Agneesen(s), Niesen**.

Metr. (from a dim.): Eng.: **Annets**.

Anouilh S French: said by Dauzat to be from a Roussillonese dial. term meaning 'slowworm', and hence a nickname for a lethargic or sluggish person.

Ansell English (chiefly E Anglia): from a Gmc personal name composed of the elements *ans-* god + *helm* protection, helmet. This was a distinctively Langobardic name, and was common in Italy. Among its bearers were several famous medieval churchmen. It was brought to France and England by St Anselm (*c.*1033–1109), known as the father of Scholasticism. He was born in Aosta, joined the Benedictine order at Bec in Normandy, and in 1093 became archbishop of Canterbury.

Vars.: **Anshell, Ansill, Hansel(l), Hansill, Hancell.**

Cogns.: Fr.: **Anselme, Anseaume, Ansiaume, Anserme.** It.: **Anselmi, Anzelmi; Selmi.** Port.: **Anselmo.** Ger.: **Anselm, Ansalm.**

Dims.: Eng.: **Anslyn.** Fr.: **Ansermet.** It.: **Anselmini; Selmini.** Ger.: **Ansle, Ansli, Ensle, Ensli(n), Esslin.** Low Ger.: **Anselmann.**

Anslow English: habitation name from a place in Staffs., so called from the OE female name *Ēanswīð* + *lēah* wood, clearing.

Anstey English: habitation name from any of the dozen places in England called *Anstey* or *Ansty*, from OE *ānstiga*, a cpd of *ān* one + *stīg* path, used of a short stretch of road forking at both ends. The surname is found principally in Somerset and the W Country.

Vars.: **Anstie, Ansty.**

Anstice English: from the ME male given name *Ansta(y)se* (L *Anastasius*, from Gk *anastasis* resurrection) or the fem. *Anastasie* (L *Anastasia*).

Vars.: **Anstis(s), Ansteys.**

Cogns.: Fr.: **Anasta(i)se, Anastay.** It.: **Anastasi(o); Nastasi, Nastagi, Nasti; Stasi(o), Stassi** (S Italy). Ger.: **Anstett.** Port.: **Anastácio.** Rum.: **Nastase.**

Dim.: It.: **Stassino.**

Patrs.: It.: **D'Anastasio.** Flem., Du.: **Stassen** (see also STACE). Croatian: **Anastasijević; Nastić.** Gk: **Anastasiou.**

Anstruther Scottish: habitation name from a place in Fife, which is sometimes said to get its name from Gael. *an* the + *sruthar* stream, but which is more probably derived from ON *engi* meadow + an unattested word **struðr*, which would be a cogn. of OE *strōd* marshy land overgrown with brushwood. The pronunciation is usually /ˈænstrə/ or /ˈeɪnstrə/.

The lands of Anstruther were held in the 12th cent. by William de Candela, a member of the Norman family of Malherbe; he derived his title from the lands of Candel in Dorset, which he also held. His grandson Henry was the first to assume the name de Ainestrother. *The French barons* **Anstrude** *were descended from David Anstruther, an officer of the Scots Guard of France.*

Anthony English: from the given name so spelled, which, with its cogns. and derivs., is one of the commonest European given names. It is derived from L *Antōnius*, an ancient Roman family name of unknown etymology. The most famous member of the family was the soldier and triumvir Mark Antony (*Marcus Antonius*, *c.*83–30 BC). The spelling with *-h-*, which first appears in Eng. in the 16th cent. and in Fr. (*Anthoine*) at about the same time, is due to the erroneous belief that the name derives from Gk *anthos* flower.

The popularity of the given name in Christendom is largely due to the cult of the Egyptian hermit St Antony (AD 251–356), who in his old age gathered a community of hermits around him, and for that reason is regarded by some as the founder of monasticism. It was further increased by the fame of St Antony of Padua (1195–1231), who has always enjoyed a great popular cult, and is believed to help people find lost things.

Aphetic forms of the given name are common in most European languages (Eng. *Tony*, Fr. *Toine*, It. *Tonio*, Low Ger. *Thon*, etc.), and these have given rise to their own sets of surnames (see TONEY).

Vars.: **Antony, Ant(h)oney.**

Cogns.: Fr.: **Ant(h)oin(e).** Sp.: **Antón, Antonio; Antona** (a fem. form). Port.: **António, Antão.** It.: **Antoni(o), Antuoni.** Ger.: **Ant(h)on.** Ger. (of Slav. origin): **Antosch, Antusch.** Pol.: **Antecki** (with the surname suffix *-ski*; see BARANOWSKI). Czech: **Anton, Antoň, Antonín; Antoš.** Hung.: **Antal.**

Dims.: Fr.: **Antoinet.** It.: **Antonell(in)i, Antognelli, Anton(i)etti, Antognetti, Anton(i)utti, Antonucci, Antoniotti, Antognozzi, Antonioli, Antognoli.** Pol.: **Antonczyk, Antosik, Antoszczyk; Jadczyk.** Ukr.: **Anton(ch)ik, Antuk.**

Augs.: Fr.: **Anto(i)nat, Antonas.** It.: **Antonioni, Antognoni.**

Pejs.: It.: **Antonacci, Anton(i)azzi, Antognazzi.**

Patrs.: Sp.: **Antúnez.** Port.: **Antunes.** It.: **D'Antoni(o), D'Antuoni, De Antoni, Di Antonio, Degli Antoni.** Rum.: **Antonescu.** Low Ger.: **Anth(oni)es.** Flem.: **Antoons.** Dan., Norw.: **Ant(h)onsen.** Swed.: **Antonsson.** Russ.: **Antonov** (popular form); **Antonyev** (learned form). Ukr.: **Antonich.** Croatian: **Antonijević, Antonović, Antić.** Pol.: **Antonowicz, Antoniewicz; Antoniak.** Hung.: **Antalffy.** Gk: **Antoniou, Antonopoulos, Antoniades.**

Patrs. (from dims.): Russ.: **Anton(n)ikov; Antoshin, Antushev, Antyshev, Antyukhin.** Pol.: **Antczak; Jadczak.**

Habitation name: Pol.: **Antoniewski, Antoszewski, Antowski.**

Antipov Russian: patr. from the given name *Antip* (Gk *Antipas*, a short form of *Antipatēr*, from the elements *anti* equal to, like + *patēr* father). It was adopted as a baptismal name in the Eastern Church in honour of St Antipas of Pergamum, first bishop of that city, who was martyred in about AD 90, and who is referred to in the book of Revelation (2: 13) as the 'faithful witness'.

Vars.: **Antipyev, Antipin.**

Antonini Italian: 1. dim. of ANTHONY.

2. from the L personal name *Antōnīnus*, a deriv. of *Antōnius* (see ANTHONY), which was borne by several Roman emperors, starting with Antoninus Pius (AD 138–61), and by various early saints, including a 2nd-cent. converted executioner of Christians.

Vars.: **Antognini, Antongini.**

Cogns.: Fr.: **Antonin.** Prov.: **Antoni, Antony.** Sp.: **Antolín.** Cat.: **Antolí.**

Antrobus English: habitation name from a place in Ches., recorded in Domesday Book as *Entrebus*, apparently from the ON personal name *Eindriði*, *Andriði* (which is of doubtful etymology) + ON *buski* shrub, bush, thicket.

Anttila Finnish: topographic name for someone who lived at the house of a bearer of the given name *Antti* (Finnish equivalent of ANDREW), with the local suffix *-la*.

Antuñano Basque: habitation name from some minor place so called, from L *Antōniānus* (*fundus*) '(farm, estate) of *Antōnius*'; see ANTHONY.

Aparicio Spanish: from a given name bestowed on children born on the Feast of the Epiphany (6 January), from Sp. *aparición* appearance, manifestation (LL *apparitio*, gen. *apparitiōnis*, from *appārēre* to come into view).

Var.: **París.**

Cogns.: Cat.: **Aparici, París.** Port.: **Aparício.**

Apple English: from ME *appel* (OE *æppel*) apple, acquired as a surname in any of various senses. It may originally have been used as a topographic name for someone living by a prominent apple tree or apple orchard; a metonymic occupational name for a grower or seller of apples; or a nickname for someone supposed to resemble an apple in some way, e.g. in having bright red cheeks. The economic importance in medieval N Europe of apples, as a fruit which could be grown in a cold climate and would keep for use throughout the winter, is hard to appreciate in these days of easy imports of southern fruits.

Cogns.: Ger.: **Apfel(mann)**, **Apfler**. Du.: **Appel(man)**. Jewish: (Ashkenazic, largely ornamental): **Apfel**, **Appel**; **Ep(p)el** (from Yid. *epl*); **Appelman(n)**, **Epelman**; **Appleman** (Anglicized).

Cpds: Swed. (ornamental): **Appelberg** ('apple hill'), **Appelgren** ('apple branch'), **Appelkvist** ('apple twig'). Ger.: **Apfelbaum** ('apple tree'). Low Ger.: **Appel(bohm)**. Du.: **Appelboom**. Jewish: **Ap(p)elbaum**, **Applebaum**, **Ap(p)elbo(i)m**, **Epelbaum** ('apple tree', ornamental or topographic); **Apfelberg**, **Appelberg** ('apple hill', ornamental); **Ap(p)elblat** ('apple leaf', ornamental); **Apeloig** ('apple eye', ornamental, with Yid. *oyg*); **Apfelschnitt** ('apple slice'. ornamental).

Appleby N English: habitation name from any of various places, for example in Leics., Lincs. (Humberside), and Cumb., so called from ON *apall* APPLE + *býr* farm, settlement.

Vars.: **Applebey**, **Applebe(e)**, **Apelbe**.

Applegarth N English and Scots: topographic name for someone who lived by an apple orchard, Northern ME *applegarth* (from ON *apall* APPLE + *garðr* enclosure, orchard), or habitation name from a place so named, for example in Cumb. and N and E Yorks., as well as in the former county of Dumfries.

Vars.: **Applegath**, **Applegate**. See also APPLEYARD.

Applethwaite English: habitation name from one of the places in Cumb. so called, from ON *apall* APPLE + *þveit* meadow (see THWAITE).

Vars.: **Applewh(a)ite**, **Ablewhite**.

Appleton English: habitation name from any of the many places, for example in Ches., Oxon., and N Yorks., so called from OE *æppeltūn* orchard (a cpd of *æppel* APPLE + *tūn* enclosure, settlement).

Var.: **Napleton** (from OE *æt þǣm æppeltūne* 'at the orchard', ME *atten Appleton*).

Appleyard N English: topographic name for someone who lived by an apple orchard, ME *appleyard* (from OE *æppel* APPLE + *geard* enclosure, orchard; an Anglicized form of APPLEGARTH, replacing the native APPLETON) or at a place so named, of which the most significant source of surnames is in W Yorks.

Apps English: from ME *apse*, OE *æps*, *æspe* aspen, usually no doubt a topographic name for someone who lived near an aspen tree, but occasionally perhaps a nickname for a timorous person, with reference to the trembling leaves of the tree.

Vars.: **Aps**, **Happs**; **Apsey** (Somerset); **Aspey** (Lancs.; metathesized); **Asp**; **Epps**, **Hesp(e)**.

Cogns.: Ger.: **Asp(er)**. Swed.: **Asp**.

Cpd: Swed.: **Asplund** ('aspen grove').

Members of a Somerset family called Apsey *can trace their ancestry to Thomas* de Apse, *who held lands in the county in the reign of Edward II (1307–27).*

April English: from the month of April (OF *avril*, L *aprīlis* (*mensis*), apparently a deriv. of *aperīre* to open, with reference to the opening of buds and flowers in the spring). This was used as a given name for someone born, baptized, or officially registered in April, or having some other connection with the month.

Vars.: **Avril**, **Averill**. See also EVERILL.

Cogns.: Fr.: **Avril**. Prov.: **Abri(a)l**, **Avrial**. Sp., Cat.: **Abril**. Ger.: **April**, **Ab(e)rell**.

Dim.: Fr.: **Avrillon**.

Apt Jewish (E Ashkenazic): habitation name from *Apt*, Yid. name of *Opatów* in the province of Kielce, Poland, so called from Pol. *opactwo* abbey.

Vars.: **Apter(man)**; **Opatowski**, **Opatowsky**, **Opatovsky** (from the Pol. name of the town).

Aragón Spanish: ethnic name from *Aragón* in NE Spain, which was an independent kingdom from 1035 to the 14th cent. There are various speculations about the etymology of the name, but the true origin is probably irrecoverable. The royal house of *Aragón* was descended from Ramiro I of Aragon (reigned 1035–63), illegitimate son of Sancho III of Navarre.

Vars.: **Aragonés**, **Aragoneses**.

Cogns.: Cat.: **Aragonès**. Port.: **Aragão**. Fr.: **Ar(r)agon**, **Aragou**; **Dar(r)agon**. It.: **Aragona**, **Aragone**; **Ragona**, **Ragone** (aphetic forms resulting from the misdivision of forms such as **Daragona**); **Aragonese**, **Ragonese**.

Aramburu Spanish form of Basque **Aranburu**: topographic name for someone who lived at the upper end of a valley or in the principal settlement in a valley, from Basque *aran* valley (see ARANA) + *buru* head, summit.

Var.: **Arampuru** (Fr.).

Arana Basque: topographic name for someone who lived in a valley, from *aran* valley + the def. art. *-a*.

Var.: **Aran** (Fr.).

Aranda Spanish: habitation name from any of various places, for example in the provinces of Burgos and Saragossa. The placename may be from L *aranda* arable land (from the gerundive of *arāre* to plough), or from the Celt. elements *are-randa* near, next to the frontier, or from a deriv. of Basque *aran* valley (cf. ARANA).

Aranguren Basque: topographic name for someone who lived at the end of a valley, from Basque *aran* valley (see ARANA) + *guren* edge, border. There are places named with these elements in the provinces of Biscay and Navarre, and these may also be partial sources of the surname.

Araújo Portuguese: habitation name from any of various minor places so called, for example in Coimbra, Elvas, Estremoz, Lisbon, Moncorvo, Monsão, Serpa, Setúbal, and Villa Verde. The surname is also relatively common in Spain in the form **Araujo**.

Arbatov Russian: habitation name from an area of Moscow called the *Arbat*, with the addition of the usual surname ending *-ov* (formally a patr.). The origin of the placename is not clear. It is traditionally said to be derived from *arba* cart, but this is probably the result of folk etymology; it is more probably taken from some word in a Turkic language (cf. Khirgiz *yrabat* large building).

Arbós Catalan: topographic name for someone who lived by a strawberry tree or arbutus, Cat. *arboç* (LL *arbuteus*, from class. L *arbutus*, apparently a deriv. of *arbor* tree). In part it may derive from a place in the province of Tarragona called *L'Arbós*, from this word.

Arbuckle Scots: habitation name from a place in the parish of Airdrie, in the former county of Lanarks., so called from Gael. *àrd an buachaille* 'height of the shepherd'.

Vars.: **Arnbuckle; Ironbuckle** (by English folk etymology).

The first known bearer of the name is John Arnbuckle, *who is recorded in 1499 as a witness at Irvine.*

Arbus Jewish (E Ashkenazic): of uncertain origin, probably connected either with Yid. *arbes* pea or with Russ. *arbuz* watermelon (see ARBUZOV).

Vars.: **Arbuss, Arbuz, Arbusman.**

Arbuthnot Scots: habitation name from *Arbuthnott*, south of Aberdeen, earlier *Aberbuthnot*. The place is so called from Brittonic *aber* confluence + a stream name (*Buadhnat* in Gael.) from a dim. of *bothen* virtuous; that is, it was regarded as a holy stream with the power to heal wounds or sickness.

Var.: **Arbuthnott.**

The first known bearer of the name is Hugh de Aberbothenoth, *who held the lands in question during the 12th cent.*

Arbuzov Russian: patr. from the nickname *Arbuz* 'Watermelon' (ultimately from Persian *khärbuze* melon), perhaps referring to a grower or enthusiastic eater of the fruit. The word was also used as a term of endearment.

Arcas Spanish: 1. occupational name for a cabinet-maker, from the vocab. word *arca* chest, coffer (from L *arcēre* to shut in, enclose).

2. nickname for a broad-chested individual, from the same word applied to the part of the body in a sense development paralleled by Eng. *chest*.

3. topographic name from the same word used in any of various senses. In Galicia it was used of a dolmen, in Astorga of a millstone, from the supposedly box-like appearance of these objects.

Cogns. (of 1): It.: **Arcaro, Arcari** (occupational names, also denoting a public treasurer); **Arca** (S Italy). Fr.: **Ar(r)heur** (occupational name; Brittany); **Larher, Lar(r)eur, Lar(r)our; Narrour** (with the fused Bret. def. art. *an*). Prov.: **Archa**. Eng.: ARKWRIGHT.

Arce Spanish: 1. topographic name for someone who lived by a prominent maple tree, Sp. *arce* (metathesized from L *acer*, gen. *aceris*).

2. habitation name from places in the provinces of Santander and Navarre, whose names represent a Castilianized spelling of Basque *artze* stony place (from *arri* stone + the suffix of abundance *-tz(e)*).

Archdale English and Irish: ostensibly a habitation name from ME *arch* (of a bridge; see ARCO) + *dale* valley (see DALE). However, no place with this name exists, and the surname is more likely to be a garbling of some Gaelic or possibly Scandinavian original.

Family tradition among Irish bearers of this name has it that they are of Danish origin and that the second element of the name represents Dan. dal *valley. If the family is indeed of Scandinavian origin, this would explain some of the difficulties regarding the surname. Viking settlements were plentiful in Ireland in the Middle Ages, but the inhabitants used personal names and patronymics rather than surnames: surnames are of very late origin in Scandinavian languages. It is, however, possible that this surname may be an Anglicized garbling of some Norse personal name, or else of a local name representing an earlier family tradition about the location of origin.*

Archer English and French: occupational name for a bowman, from ME *archere*, OF *arch(i)er* (L *arc(u)ārius*, from *arcus* bow; see ARCO).

Vars.: Fr.: **Archier**, LARCHER; **Arquier** (Normandy, Picardy).

Cogns.: Prov.: **Arquier, Larquier**. Sp.: **Arquero**. Cat.: **Arquer, Arqué(s)**. It.: **Arc(i)eri.**

Archibald English and Scots: from a Norman given name, recorded in the form *Archambault*, composed of the Gmc elements *ercan* precious + *bald* bold, daring. The surname is chiefly common in Scotland, where it had been used as an Anglicized form of GILLESPIE, for reasons that are unclear.

Vars.: **Archibould, Archbo(u)ld, Archbald, Archbell, Archbutt.** Fr.: **Archimb(e)aud, Archambault.** Du.: **Arkenbout.**

The name is most common in Scotland, esp. around Edinburgh, whence it spread to Ulster and to Canada; it is the surname of a leading Nova Scotia family, taken there by four brothers who emigrated from Londonderry in 1750–62.

Arco Italian and Spanish: 1. metonymic occupational name for a bowman or a maker of bows, from It., Sp. *arco* bow (L *arcus*); cf. ARCHER.

2. topographic name for someone who lived by the arch of a bridge or aqueduct, from the same word used in an architectural sense.

Vars.: It.: **Archi, D(ell)'Arco.** Sp.: **Arcos.**

Cogns. (of 2): Fr.: **Darche, Desarches.** Prov.: **Desargues.**

Dims.: It.: **Archetto, Archetti, Archini, Arcucci.** Fr.: **Arquet, Arquin.**

Augs.: It.: **Arcone, Arconi.**

Arden English: regional name from the Forest of *Arden* in Warwicks. or from *Arden* in N Yorks. Both placenames are probably linguistically identical with the forest of the *Ardennes* in France and Belgium, and are derived from a Celtic word meaning 'high'.

The Arden *family who held the estate of Longcroft near Yoxall, Staffs., from 1569 to the end of the 19th cent. are one of the very few English families that can trace their ancestry back to before the Norman Conquest. They are descended from an Anglo-Saxon nobleman called Ælfwine, who was sheriff of Warwicks. in the mid-11th cent. His son, Thurkill de Warwick, also known as Thurkill* de Arden, *so ingratiated himself with the Norman conquerors that he held more lands, as Domesday Book shows, than any other non-Norman Englishman.*

Ardley English: habitation name from any of several places. *Ardley* in Oxon. and *Ardeley* in Herts. are so called from an OE personal name, *Eardwulf* (composed of the elements *eard* native land + *wulf* wolf) or a short form, *Earda*, + *lēah* wood, clearing. *Eardley* End in Staffs. is from OE *eard* dwelling place + *lēah*; *Ardleigh* in Essex may have the same origin, or it may have *erð* ploughed land as a first element.

Vars.: **Ardleigh; Eardley** (Staffs).

Ardouin French: from a Gmc personal name, *Hardwin*, composed of the elements *hard* hardy, brave, strong + *win* friend.

Vars.: **Hardo(u)in.**

Cogns.: It.: **Ardo(u)ini, Ard(ov)ini.**

Ardura Spanish: nickname, apparently for a careworn individual, from Sp. *ardura* difficulty, trouble, anxiety (LL *ardūra*, from *arduus* steep, difficult).

Arellano Spanish: habitation name from a place in the province of Navarre, so called from LL *Aurēliānus* (*fundus*) '(farm, estate) of *Aurēlius*', a personal name possibly derived from L *aurum* gold.

Arenas Spanish: habitation name from any of the numerous places so called, from the pl. (collective) form of Sp. *arena* sand (L *(h)arēna*).

Cogns.: It.: **Arena, Areni** (Sicily, Calabria, Naples).

Dims.: Sp.: **Arenillas.** It.: **Arenella, Aren(i)ello.**

Ares Spanish: of uncertain etymology. It is generally assumed to derive from a medieval personal name that is probably of Gmc origin.

Aresti Basque: topographic name for someone who lived by an oak wood, from *areitz* oak tree + the suffix of abundance *-di* (*-ti* after a sibilant).

Arévalo Spanish: habitation name from places in the provinces of Ávila and Soria. The placename is of uncertain etymology, possibly from Celt. *are-valon* 'near, next to the wall, fence'.

Argemí Catalan: from the Gmc (Gothic) personal name *Argimir*, composed of the elements *harjis* army + *meri*, *mari* famous.

Argent 1. French and English (Norman): from OF *argent* silver (L *argentum*). This was probably most commonly a nickname for someone with silvery grey hair, but it may also have been originally an occupational name for a worker in the metal or a topographic name for someone who lived near a silver mine. There are several French towns and villages called *Argent* (e.g. in Cher) because silver was mined there, and the surname may also derive from any of these.

2. French: habitation name from either of the places, in Aude and Basses-Alpes, called *Argens*, from the LL personal name *Argenteus* or *Argentius* 'Silvery'.

Vars.: Eng.: **Hargent, Largent**.

Cogn.: It.: **Argenti**.

Argenti *is the name of a family of Italian origin, with branches in Greece, France, and England, as well as Genoa and elsewhere in Italy. Members of the family were leaders of the Greeks in their War of Independence against the Turks, and later in the 19th cent. a branch settled in England.*

Argüello Spanish: habitation name from any of various minor places so called, from OSp. *arboleo* well-wooded (LL *arboleus*, for class. L *arboreus*, a deriv. of *arbor* tree).

Argyle Scots: regional name from *Argyll*, a district in SW Scotland, so called from Gael. *oirthir Ghaidheal* 'coast of the Gaels'.

Arias Spanish and Jewish (Sefardic): of uncertain origin. The Spanish name has been explained as a patronymic, either from the medieval personal name ARES, which is probably of Gmc origin, or else from a medieval personal name *Aria* or *Arius*, which is probably of Romance origin.

Cogn.: Port.: **Aires**.

Ariñó Catalan: topographic name for someone who lived by a sloe tree, Cat. *aranyó* (of Celt. origin).

Ariza Spanish: habitation name from a place in the province of Saragossa, so called from an Arabic term for a possession or holding.

Arkhipov Russian: patr. from the given name *Arkhip* (Gk *Arkhippos*, composed of the elements *arkh-* rule + *hippos* horse). The name was borne by a 1st-cent. companion of St Paul, traditionally regarded as the first bishop of Colossae.

Var.: **Arkhipyev**.

Arkle English: from the ON personal name *Arnkell*, composed of the elements *arn* eagle + *ketil* cauldron, helmet, or helmeted warrior. The surname is found chiefly in N England, where Scandinavian influence was strongest, and is most common in Northumb.

Vars.: **Arkley; Arkill, Arkell** (the two latter are now chiefly W Midlands).

Arkwright English: occupational name for a maker of chests, from ME, OF *arc* chest, ark (see ARCAS) + ME *wrytte* maker, craftsman (see WRIGHT). The surname is most common in Lancs.

Vars.: **Atrick; Hartwright, Hartrick, Hattrick**.

Cogn.: Du.: **Van Ark**.

Arlott English: nickname from ME, OF *(h)arlot*, *herlot* vagabond, rascal (of obscure origin). The vocab. word also denoted an itinerant entertainer, also a male servant, so it may in some instances have been originally an occupational name. The sense referring to a woman of easy sexual availability is not recorded before the 15th cent., and is unlikely to have contributed to the surname.

Var.: **Arlot**.

Cogns.: Fr.: **Harlot**. Prov.: **Arlot**.

Patr.: Prov.: **Darlot**.

Armengol Catalan: from a Gmc personal name composed of the element *ermin* (see ARMIN) + the tribal name *Gaut* (see JOCELYN).

Var.: **Armengou**.

Cogns.: Prov.: **Armengaud, Armengault**.

Armer English: occupational name for a maker of arms, ANF *armer* (OF *armier*, L *armārius*, a deriv. of *arma* arms).

Var.: **Larmer** (with fused ANF def. art.). See also ARMOUR.

Cogn.: Sp.: **Armero**.

Armetriding English: habitation name from *Armetridding*, a minor place in the parish of Leyland, Lancs., so called from ME *ermit*, *armit* hermit + *rid(d)ing* clearing.

Var.: **Armetrading**.

Armin English and French: from the ME, OF given name *Armin*, *Ermin*, derived from the Gmc element *ermin*. This seems to have been the name, of unknown etymology, of an ancient Gmc god, but in later times it was also used in various cpd names with the meaning 'whole', 'entire' (cf. ARMENGOL and MENÉNDEZ). For the change of *Er-* to *Ar-*, cf. MARCHANT.

Var.: **Ermin**.

Dim.: Fr.: **Arminot**.

Patrs.: Eng.: **Arminson, Arm(i)son; Armes** (Norfolk).

Armistead 1. English: topographic name for someone who lived by a hermit's cell, from ME *(h)ermite* hermit (see ARMITAGE) + *stede* place (see STEAD 1).

2. Anglicized form of **Darmstädter**, a habitation name from *Darmstadt* in Hesse, W Germany.

Var. (of 1): **Armstead**.

Armitage English: topographic name for someone who lived by a hermitage (ME, OF *(h)ermitage*, a deriv. of OF *(h)ermite* hermit, LL *erēmita*, Gk *erēmītēs*, from *erēmos* solitary), or habitation name from some place so named.

Vars.: **Armytage, Hermitage**.

Redmonds has shown that most if not all bearers of the surname Armitage *and* Armytage *can be traced back to a family living at* Hermitage *Bridge in Almondbury, near Huddersfield, in the 13th cent.; the name is still most common in Yorks. It was first taken to N America by Enoch Armitage (b. 1677) of Wooldale, Yorks.; other members of the family followed.*

Armour English and Scots: metonymic occupational name for a maker of arms and armour, from ME, OF *armure* (LL *armātūra*, a deriv. of *arma* arms), used of offensive weapons as well as defensive clothing. The ending of the vocab. word and surname has been assimilated to the agent suffix *-o(u)r*, and there has been some confusion with ARMER.

Vars.: **Armor; Larmo(u)r** (with fused ANF def. art.).

Armstrong N English and S Scots: nickname from ME *arm* + *strong*, i.e. with strong arms.

Var.: **Strongitharm**.

The first known bearer of the name is Adam Armstrong, *who was pardoned at Carlisle in 1235 for causing the death of another man.*

Arnold English: 1. from a Norman personal name composed of the Gmc elements *arn* eagle + *wald* rule.

2. habitation name from one of the two places, in Notts. and Humberside, named with the OE elements *earn* eagle + *halh* nook, hollow (see HALE 1). The name of both places has been assimilated to the given name from earlier *Ernehale*, *Arnhale*.

3. Jewish (Ashkenazic): of uncertain origin.

Vars. (of 1): **Arnhold, Arnould, Arnout, Arnoll, Arnald, Arnaud, Arnall, Arnell, Arnull,** ARNOTT, **Arnatt, Arnull; Harnott, Harnett, Hornet(t)**.

Cogns. (of 1): Fr.: **Arnou(l)d, Arnoult, Arnaud, Arnau(l)t, Arrault**; ERNAUD. Prov.: **Arnal**. Cat.: **Arnal, Arnau**. Sp.: **Arnaldo**. It.: **Arnaldo, Arnaldi, Arnaudi; Arnoldi** (N Italy); **Arn(a)o** (Sicily). Ger.: **Ar(nh)old(t); Arl(e)t** (Silesia). Low Ger.: **Arnold, A(h)rend, Arndt**. Flem., Du.: **Arent**. Norw., Dan.: **Ar(e)ndt**. Hung.: **Arnold**. See also AARON.

Dims. (of 1): Fr.: **Arnaudet, Arnaudin, Arnaudon, Arnaudot**. Prov.: **Arnaldy, Arnaudy; Arnauduc** (Gascony). Ger.: **Arni, Erni, Ärnli** (Switzerland). Low Ger.: **Arn(ec)ke, Ernke**.

Patrs. (from 1): Eng.: **Arnison, Arn(a)son**. Basque: **Arnáiz, Arnáez**. Low Ger.: **Arnhol(t)z, Ar(n)tz(en), Ahrens, Ahrendsen**. Flem.: **Arents**. Du.: **Aren(d)s; Arendse(n), Aartsen**. Norw., Dan.: **Arndtsen**.

The Victorian poet and essayist Matthew Arnold *(1822–88) and his father Thomas Arnold (1795–1842), famous as the headmaster of Rugby School, traced their ancestry back to fishermen in Lowestoft, Suffolk, in the time of Henry VII.*

Arnott 1. English.: var. of ARNOLD.

2. Scots: habitation name from *Arnot* near Kinross, probably so called from Gael. *ornacht* barley.

Var.: **Arnot**.

Arnou French: from the Gmc personal name *Arnwulf*, composed of the elements *arn* eagle + *wulf* wolf.

Vars.: **Arnoux, Arnoul(f)**.

Aróstegui Spanish form of Basque **Arostegi** or **Aroztegi**: habitation name for someone who lived near a house occupied by the village smith or carpenter, from Basque *arotz* smith, carpenter + the suffix *-tegi* house of.

Arranz Spanish: of unclear etymology. It is seemingly derived from a personal name, since the same element occurs also in the cpd surnames **Antoranz, Estebaranz**, and **Gilarranz**. The unusual final consonantal combination *-nz* is found also in the surnames *Herranz* (see FERNANDO) and *Sanz* (see SANCHO).

Arregui Spanish form of Basque **Arregi**: topographic name for someone who lived in a stony place, from Basque *arri* stone + the local suffix *-egi*, or for someone who lived by a rocky incline, from *arri* stone + *egi* slope.

Arriba Spanish: topographic name for someone who lived uphill or upstream from the main settlement, from Sp. *arriba* above, upstream (from LL *ad* at, towards + *ripa* riverbank). Compare ABAJO. There are various places, for example in the provinces of Lugo and Navarre, named with this word, and the surname may also be a habitation name from any of these.

Var.: **Arribas**.

Arriero Spanish: occupational name for a driver of mules and other pack animals, Sp. *arriero* (from *arrear* to drive animals, a deriv. of the interjection *(h)arre*, found also in Prov. and It. dialects, used to urge animals on).

Arrieta Basque: topographic name for someone who lived on a patch of stony soil, from *arri* stone + the collective suffix *-eta*. There are several places so named, for example in the provinces of Álava, Biscay, and Navarre, and they may all have contributed to the surname.

Var.: **Arriola** (with a local suffix).

Arrington English: 1. var. of HARRINGTON.

2. habitation name from a place in Cambs., so called from OE *Earningatūn* 'settlement (OE *tūn*) of the people of *Earn(a)*', a byname meaning 'Eagle'.

Arrizabalaga Basque: topographic name for someone who lived near a patch of open stony ground, from *arri* stone + *zabal* broad, wide + the local suffix *-aga*.

Arrowsmith English: occupational name for a maker of iron arrowheads, from OE *arwe* arrow + *smið* SMITH. The surname is most common in N England and the Midlands.

Vars.: **Arsmith, Harrowsmith, Harrismith**.

Arroyo Spanish: topographic name for someone who lived near a stream or irrigation channel, from Sp. *arroyo* watercourse (of pre-Roman origin).

Cogns.: Prov.: **Arrouy, Larrouy**.

Arrufat Catalan: nickname for someone with a wizened or wrinkled face or a habitually dishevelled appearance, from the past. part. of *arrufar* to crease, crumple (of uncertain origin).

Arscott English: habitation name from a place in Shrops., first recorded in the 13th cent. in the form *Ardescot(e)*. The first element probably represents a shortened form of the gen. case of a cpd OE personal name such as *Æðelrǣd* ('noble counsel') or *Ēadrǣd* ('prosperity counsel'); the second is OE *cot* hut, cottage (see COATES).

Arsenyev Russian: patr. from the given name *Arseni* (Gk *Arsenios* 'virile, masculine'). This was the name of several minor early Christian saints, but owes its currency mainly to St Arsenius the Great (d. *c*.449), who was tutor to the sons of the Emperor Theodosius, Honorius and Arcadius, who divided the Roman Empire between them.

Cogns.: Croatian: **Arsenijević, Arsenović, Arsić**.

Artaud French: from the Gmc personal name *Hartwald*, composed of the elements *hard* hardy, brave, strong + *wald* rule.

Vars.: **Arthaud, Arthault; Hartaud**.

Cogns.: Ger.: **Hartelt, Härtelt, Eztelt, Erd(t)elt**.

Arteaga Basque: topographic name for someone who lived by a holm oak, from *arte* holm oak + the local suffix *-aga*. There are several places in the province of Biscay named with these elements, all of which may have contributed to the surname.

Arteche Spanish form of Basque **Artetxe**: topographic name for someone who lived in a house on a patch of empty land, from Basque *arte* (intervening) space, middle + *etxe* house.

Arthur English and French: from the Celt. personal name *Arthur*, which is of obscure and disputed etymology; it may possibly be derived from some early cogn. of Gael. *art*, W *arth* bear (cf. CARTON). It has been continuously in use as a given name in Britain since the early Middle Ages, owing its popularity to the legendary exploits of King Arthur and his Round Table, which gave rise to a prolific literature in many W European languages, starting with Welsh. Virtually nothing is known of the historical figure who lies behind the legends beyond the fact that he was probably a Brit. leader in the 6th cent. who fought victorious battles against the Saxon invaders. The name has absorbed the Scandinavian name *Arnðórr*, which comes from *arn* eagle + *Þorr* the name of the god of thunder.

Vars.: Fr.: **Art(h)us, Arthuys**.

Cogns.: It.: **Arturo, Artus(i)o, Artusi**. Port.: **Artur**.

Dims.: Fr.: **T(h)urel, T(h)ureau, T(h)uret, T(h)urin, T(h)uron, T(h)urot**. It.: **Artusino**.

Patrs.: Eng.: **Arthurs** (chiefly N Ireland). Sc., Ir.: **McArthur, McArtair, McAirter, McCa(i)rtair, McCarter** (Gael. **Mac Artair**). Manx: CARTER.

One of the most distinguished families in Australia is descended from John MacArthur *(1767–1834), founder of the Australian wool and wine industries and one of the men who introduced the merino sheep to Australia from S Africa. He was born at Stoke Damerel, near Plymouth, England, the son of a linen draper who originally came from Argyllshire, Scotland.*

Artiga Catalan: topographic name for someone who lived on a patch of land newly broken up, Cat. *artiga* (of uncertain, possibly Celt. origin). There are places in the provinces of Biscay and Barcelona named with the pl. form of this word, and both may have contributed to the surname.

Vars.: **Artigas, Artigues**.

Cogns.: Prov.: **Artige, Artigue(s), Lartigue**.

Arundel English: 1. habitation name from a place in W Sussex, seat of the Duke of Norfolk, which perhaps gets its name from OE *hārhune* hoarhound (from *hār* grey + *hūne* an earlier name of the same plant, of obscure origin) + *dell* valley.

2. nickname (Norman) for someone supposedly resembling a swallow in some way, from OF *arondel*, dim. of *arond* swallow (L *hirundo*, confused with *(h)arundo* reed).

Vars.: **Ar(u)ndell, Ar(r)undale, Arrandale**.

Cogns. (of 2): Fr.: **Arondel, Arondeau; Irondelle; Lhirondel, L(h)irondelle** (with fused def. art.). It.: **Arondello; Rondello** (an aphetic form).

Arvidsson Swedish: patr. from the popular Nordic given name *Arvid*, composed of the elements represented by ON *are* eagle + *víð* wide.

Cogn.: Norw., Dan.: **Arvedsen**.

Arzt German and Jewish (Ashkenazic): occupational name for a physician, Ger. *Arzt* (MHG *arzet*, OHG *arzāt*, derived via LL *arciāter* from Gk *archiatros* chief physician, a cpd of *arch-* chief, principal + *iatros* physician). This word became the usual OHG term for a physician during the Carolingian period, gradually supplanting the earlier Gmc word (represented by MHG *lāchener*; cf. LEACH 1).

Var.: Jewish: **Arct** (Pol. spelling).

Cogn.: Du.: **Arts**.

Asbury English: habitation name of uncertain origin; the place from which it is derived has not been identified. The second element is clearly OE *burh* fortified town (see BURKE); the first may be ASH, EAST, or the OE personal name *Æsc* 'Spear'. The name is chiefly common in the W Midlands.

Ascensão Portuguese: from a given name bestowed on someone born on the Feast of the Ascension of Christ (LL *ascensio*, gen. *ascensiōnis*, for class. L *ascensus*).

Cogns.: Sp.: **Asensio, Asenjo** (from a given name, L *Ascensius*, a deriv. of *ascensus*). Cat.: **Ascensi**.

Ascham English: habitation name from any of several places called *Askham*. Those in Notts. and N Yorks. get the name from OE *æsc* ASH + *hām* homestead, while the one in Cumb. is from OE *æscum*, the dat. pl. of *æsc*, originally used after a preposition.

Vars.: **Ask(h)am**.

Ascot English: habitation name from places in Berks. and Oxon., so called from OE *ēast* EAST + *cot* hut, cottage (see COATES).

Var.: **Ascott**.

Ash 1. English: topographic name for someone who lived near a prominent ash tree, OE *æsc* ash, or habitation name from some minor place so named.

2. Jewish (Ashkenazic): acronym from Yid. *AltSHul* (see ALTSCHUL) or *AyznSHtot* (see EISENSTADT).

Vars. (of 1): **Ashe** (now chiefly Irish); **Asch(e), Aish, Aysh, Esh**; ASHMAN, ASHER; DASH, NASH, RASH, TASH. (Of 2): **Asch**.

Cogns. (of 1): Ger.: **Escher**. Flem., Du.: **Van Es(ch), Van (der) Essen; Veresse, Veress(ch)en, Verest; Van Nes, Van der Rest** (the result of misdivision). Swed.: **Ask**.

Cpd (of 1): Swed.: **Asklund** ('ash grove').

Ashall English: probably a habitation name from an unidentified place so called, from OE *æsc* ASH + *hall* HALL or *halh* nook, recess (see HALE 1). The surname is most common in Lancs.

Ashburnham English: habitation name from the village of *Ashburnham* in Sussex, which gets its name from the local stream, the *Ashburn* (from OE *æsc* ASH + *burna* stream; see BOURNE) + OE *hām* homestead.

Var.: **Esburnham**.

The earliest record of this habitation name used as a surname is of Reginald de Oseburnham *in 1166.*

Ashby English: habitation name from any of the numerous places so called from ON *askr* ASH + *býr* farm, settlement. It is possible that in some cases the first element is the ON personal name *Aski*, a short form of the various cpd personal names with the first element *ask-* ash, spear (spear shafts were generally made of ash wood).

Vars.: **Ashbey, Ashbee; Asby**.

One large group of Ashbys *traces its ancestry back to William* de Ashby *(1240–99), who held the manor of Ashby Magna in Leics.*

Ashcroft English: habitation name from any of various places so called from OE *æsc* ASH + *croft* paddock, enclosure (see CROFT).

Var.: **Ascroft**.

The surname and its var. are now found chiefly in Lancs., but the location of the place that gave rise to them has not been satisfactorily identified.

Ashdown English: regional name from either of two places: the *Ashdown* Forest in E Sussex, and *Ashdown*, which was until the 18th cent. the name of the Berkshire Downs. It is impossible to say whether the first part of these names is the tree-name *æsc* ASH or a personal name identical in form, from *æsc* in the sense 'spear'.

Ashenden English: topographic name for someone who lived by a valley in which ash trees grew, from OE *æscen* ashen (a deriv. of *æsc* ASH) + *denu* valley (see DEAN), or from a place named with these words, such as *Ashington* in Northumb.

Asher 1. English: topographic name, a var. of ASH.

2. Jewish: from the Hebr. given name *Asher* 'Blessed'.

Vars. (of 2): **Ascher; Asser** (among Sefardic Jews in Holland); **Asheri, Ashery** (Israeli; formed with the Hebr. suffix *-i*). See also OSHER and USHER.

Patrs. (from 2): **As(c)herov, Asheroff, Asherovi(t)ch** (E Ashkenazic).

Ashfield English (W Midlands): habitation name from any of several places so called, for example in Shrops. The placename is from OE *æsc* ASH + *feld* pasture, open country (see FIELD).

Ashford English: habitation name from any of several places so called. Those in Devon, Derbys., Essex, Shrops., and Surrey get their name from OE *æsc* ASH + *ford* FORD. One in Kent, however, is a collapsed form of *æsc-scēat-ford*, the middle element being OE *scēat* copse (see SKEAT). One in Middlesex is first recorded in 969 in the form *Ecelesford*, where the first element perhaps represents the gen. case of an OE personal name **Eccel*, dim. of *Ecca*, a short form of any of the OE personal names containing the first element *ecg* edge (of a sword).

Ashkenazi Jewish: name for an Ashkenazic (Yiddish-speaking) Jew who had settled in an area where non-Ashkenazic Jews were in the majority. *Ashkenaz* is a biblical placename (Gen. 10: 3, Jer. 51: 27), etymologically related to Gk *Skythia* Scythia. However, since the 9th cent. AD, if not earlier, it has been applied to Germany, probably because of its phonological similarity to Ger. *Sachsen* Saxony.

Vars.: **Ashkenazy, Ashkenasi, Ashkenasy, Ashkinazi, Ashkinazy, Ashkynazi, Ashkanazy, Aszkenazy, Aszkinazy, Askenazi, Askenazy, Askenasi, Askenasy, Askinazi, Askinazy, Aski(e)nasy, Askanazi; Ashkenaz, Ashkenas, Ashkinas, Ashkinos, Aszkenas, Askenas(e), Askinas; Eskenazi** (reflecting a Sefardic pronunciation); **Ashkinadze** (with the ending changed to resemble the Georgian patr. suffix *-adze*); **Schinasi** (an It. form).

Ashkettle English: from the ON personal name *Ásketill*, composed of the elements *óss*, *áss* god + *ketill* kettle, sacrificial cauldron.

Vars.: **Askel, Haskel(l), Ax(t)ell; Astell, Astill** (see also ASTLE); **Ankettle, Anketell, Ankill, Antill, Antell** (Norman).

Cogns.: Fr. (Norman): **Anquetil**. Swed.: **Antell, Axell**.

Dims.: Eng.: **Askin, Ashken, Haskin(g), Astin, Hastin; Ankin, Antin**. Fr. (Norman): **Anquetin, Lanquetin, Lanctin**.

Patrs.: Sc., Ir.: **McAsgill, McAskill, McCaskell, McCaskil(l), McKaskil(l)** (Gael. **Mac Asgaill**). Manx: **Castell, Caistel**. Low Ger.: **Eschels, Eschelsen**. Norw., Dan.: **Axelsen**. Swed.: **Axelsson**.

Patrs. (from dims.): Eng.: **Askins, Haskin(g)s, Astins, Hastins**. Sc., Ir.: **McAskie, McCaskie** (Gael. **Mac Ascaidh**).

Ashley English: habitation name from any of the numerous places in S and Midland England so called, from OE *æsc* ASH + *lēah* wood, clearing.

Ashling 1. from a Norman given name, a dim. of ACE.

2. habitation name from the villages of E and W Ashling in Sussex, probably so called from OE *Æscelingas* 'people of *Æscel*' (a hypocoristic deriv. of the personal name *Æsc*; see ASHDOWN).

The name de Asling *is found in Sussex at the beginning of the 13th cent.*

Ashman English: 1. topographic name, a var. of ASH.

2. from the ME given name *Asheman*, OE *Æscmann*, probably originally a byname from *æscman* seaman, pirate (a cpd of OE *æsc* (boat made of) ash + *mann* man). There is no evidence that the OE word *æscmann* survived into ME, but if it did this surname could also have been an occupational name for a seaman. Nor is there any evidence that *æscmann* was an occupational name for a spearman, even though this is inherently plausible since *æsc* was also used in OE to mean 'spear'.

Ashmole English: of unknown origin. It may represent a lost habitation name, derived perhaps from an OE personal name *Æschelm* (composed of the elements *æsc* ash, spear + *helm* protection, helmet) + *holh* hollow, depression.

Ashmore English: habitation name from any of several minor places, so called from OE *æsc* ASH + *mōr* marsh, fen (see MOORE 1). In the case of *Ashmore* in Dorset, however, the early forms suggest that the second element is probably OE *mere* lake or *(ge)mære* boundary.

Ashton English: habitation name from any of the numerous places so called, esp. *Ashton* under Lyne near Manchester. Most get the name from OE *æsc* ASH + *tūn* enclosure, settlement, but a few have been assimilated to this form from different sources. One in Devon was originally named as the settlement of *Æschere*, an OE personal name composed of the elements *æsc* ash, spear + *here* army; one in Herts. was the settlement of *Ælli* and one in Northants represents the OE dat. pl. *æscum*, originally used after a preposition.

The surname Ashton *is particularly common in Lancs., where there are at least three places so called. A family who preserve the old spelling* **Assheton** *came into possession of their estates at Ashton under Lyne as long ago as 1115, on the marriage of Orm, son of Ailward.*

Ashurst English: habitation name from any of various places, so called from OE *æsc* ASH + *hyrst* wooded hill (see HURST). The most significant of these are in Kent and Sussex, but the surname is found chiefly in Lancs., where it probably derives from *Ashurst* Beacon, near Wigan.

A family bearing the name de Ashurst *held land at Ashurst in Lancs. in the 13th cent., and the surname is still common in SE Lancs.*

Ashwell English: habitation name from any of various places, for example in Essex, Herts., and Leics., so called from OE *æsc* ASH + *well(a)* spring, stream (see WELL).

Ashwood English: topographic name for somebody who lived by an ash wood, or habitation name from a minor place so called, from OE *æsc* ASH + *wudu* WOOD.

Ashworth English: habitation name from any of various places, in Lancs. and elsewhere, so called from OE *æsc* ASH + *worð* enclosure (see WORTH). The surname is still especially common in Lancs.

Askew N English: habitation name from a place, such as *Aiskew* in N Yorks., named with the ON elements *eiki* OAK + *skógr* wood (see SHAW). The surname is found in ME as *Akeskeugh*.

Vars.: **Aiskew, Aschew, A(y)scough, Askey, Haskew, Haskey**.

This is the name of an old-established Cumb. family descended from Sir Hugh Askew, *who received the lands of the convent of Seaton during the dissolution of the monasteries in 1542.*

Aspden English: habitation name from a minor place in Lancs., between Accrington and Blackburn, so called from OE *æspe* aspen + *denu* valley.

Aspinall English (S Lancs. and W Yorks.): habitation name from *Aspinwall* or *Asmall*, a minor place in the parish of Ormskirk, Lancs., so called from OE *æspen* of the aspen, trembling poplar + *wæll(a)* spring, stream (see WALL 2 and WELL). According to McKinley, there may have been some confusion with the earlier surname *Aspin-*

halgh (which has a second element from OE *halh* nook, recess; see HALE 1).

Vars.: **Aspinal, Aspinell, Aspinwall, Haspineall, Asmall.**

Asquith English (Yorks): habitation name from *Askwith* in N Yorks., so called from ON *ask* ASH + *viðr* WOOD.

Var.: **Askwith.**

Astle English: 1. var. of ASTLEY 1.

2. habitation name from a place in Ches., so called from OE *(e)ast* EAST + *hyll* HILL.

Vars.: **Astles; Astell, Astill** (chiefly Notts.; see also ASHKETTLE).

Astley English: habitation name from a place in Warwicks., so called from OE *(ē)ast* EAST + *lēah* wood, clearing. There are several other places in W and NW England of this name, but the surname is particularly associated with the one in Warwicks. See also ASTLE.

The Astley *family of Warwicks. trace their descent from Andrew* de Astley, *who received the title Lord Astley in 1295.*

Aston English: 1. habitation name from any of a large number of places. Most are so called from OE *(ē)ast* EAST + *tūn* enclosure, settlement, but in a few cases the first element is from OE *æsc* ash (cf. ASHTON).

2. from some OE personal name such as *Æðelstān*, and so a var. of EDLESTONE or ALSTON 1.

3. topographic name for someone who lived by a conspicuous STONE, with fusion of the ME preposition *at*.

Astor Provençal: nickname for someone with a fancied resemblance to a bird of prey, from OProv. *astur* goshawk (LL *auceptor*, from class. L *accipiter* hawk, crossed with *auceps* fowler, from *avis* bird + *capere* to catch).

Cogns.: It.: **Astori, Asturi.**

Dim.: It.: **Astorini.**

The prominent and wealthy Anglo-American Astor *family was founded by John Jacob Astor I (1763–1848). He emigrated to America from Walldorf in Germany in 1784 and became a successful and wealthy fur trader. He was the son of a butcher. Successive generations increased their wealth, and they built the Waldorf-Astoria Hotel in New York. The great-grandson of John Jacob I, William Waldorf Astor (1848–1919), moved to England in 1890, becoming an influential newspaper proprietor, and taking British citizenship in 1899. In 1917 he was created Viscount Astor of Hever. His son, the 2nd Viscount (1879–1952), married Nancy Shaw (née Langhorne) (1879–1964), daughter of a Virginia planter. She became the first woman to sit in the British House of Commons as an MP.*

Astruc Provençal (also Jewish): from the medieval given name *Astruc*, a deriv. of L *astrum* star, bestowed in the sense 'born under a lucky star', 'fortunate', 'blessed'.

Vars.: Fr.: **Astrug, Stroux.** Jewish (Ashkenazic): **Stroic(h), Stroo(c)k, Stra(c)k.**

Asunción Spanish: nickname for someone born on 15 August, the Feast of the Assumption (OSp. *asumpción*, LL *assumptio*, gen. *assumptiōnis*, from *assumere* to take up). It may also reflect a given name bestowed with reference to the Marian title *Nuestra Señora de la Asunción* 'Our Lady of the Assumption'.

Cogn.: Port.: **Assunção.**

Atherton English: habitation name from a place near Manchester, so called from the OE personal name *Æðelhere* (composed of the elements *æðel* noble + *here* army) + *tūn* enclosure, settlement.

Athey English: topographic name for someone who lived by an enclosure, from ME *at* at (OE *æt*) + *hay*, *hey* enclosure (see HAY 1).

Vars.: **Athy, Atty.**

Athill English: topographic name for someone who lived by a hill, from ME *at* + HILL.

Vars.: **Atthill; Athell; At(t)rill, Attrell** (from ME *atter hill*; cf. RYE (1 and 2)).

Athol Scots: habitation name from the district of *Athol* in Glen Garry, seat of the Dukes of Atholl, recorded in the 8th cent. as *Athfhoithle*. Watson interprets this as meaning 'new Ireland', from Gael. *ath* new, re- + the personal name *Fhotla* or *Fodla*, of uncertain origin, borne by one of the seven sons of the legendary king Cruithne and eponymous for Ireland.

The first known bearer of the surname is Adam de Athetle, *who rendered homage at Perth in 1291.*

Atlas Jewish (Ashkenazic): 1. ornamental name from Ger. *Atlas*, Pol. *atłas* satin (ultimately from an Arabic word meaning 'smooth'), and possibly also a metonymic occupational name for a maker or seller of articles made of satin.

2. acrostic name from Hebr. *Ach Tov Leyisrael Sela* 'truly, God is good to Israel', the opening words of Psalm 73.

Vars.: **Atlasz** (Hung. spelling); **Atlasman; Atlasovitch, Atlasovitz, Atlasovicz, Atlasowich** (patr. in form, but there is no Jewish given name *Atlas*); **Atlasberg** ('satin hill', an ornamental name).

Attenborough English: habitation name for someone who lived 'at the manor house', from ME *atten* at the (cf. NYE) + *burh* manor house (see BERRY 1 and BURY).

Vars.: **Attenbrough, Attenb(ur)ow, Attenbarrow.**

Attoe English: topographic name for someone who lived by a hill or ridge, from ME *at* + *hoe* (cf. HOE and HUFF).

Vars.: **Atto, At(t)howe.**

Attwell English: topographic name for someone who lived by a spring or stream, from ME *at* + WELL.

Vars.: **At(te)well, Attawell, Twell(s); At(t)will, Atte(r)will, Attiwill; At(t)wool, Attwooll.**

Attwood English: topographic name for someone who lived by a wood, from ME *at* + WOOD.

Var.: **Atwood.**

Aubrey English: from the ME, OF given name *Aubri*, derived from the Gmc personal name *Alberic*, composed of the elements *alb* elf + *rīc* power. Some of the vars. listed below probably absorbed OE *Ælfrīc* (composed of the elements *ælf* elf + *rīc* kingdom). They seem also to have absorbed the much rarer female name *Albreda*, composed of the Gmc elements *alb* + *rēd* counsel (cf. ALFRED). Both *Alberic* and *Albreda* were introduced into England by the Normans.

Vars.: **Aubr(a)y, Aubery, Aubury, Obray; Alfr(e)y, Affery, Avery, Avory.**

Cogns.: Fr.: **Aubry, Auvray, Auf(f)ray, Aufroy, Aufroix.** Prov.: **Albéric, Albaric, Alfaric.** Cat.: **Alberic(h).** It.: **Alb(e)rici, Alberig(h)i, Albrigi(o), Albrisi(o), Albriz(z)i.** Ger.: **Albrich.**

Dims.: Fr.: **Aubriet, Aubryet, Aubriot.**

Patrs.: Eng.: **Averies.** Low Ger.: **Alverichs.**

Auchinleck Scots: habitation name from places in the former counties of Ayrs. or Angus called *Auchinleck* or (in a contracted form) *Affleck*, from Gael. *achadh na leac* 'field of the flat stones', i.e. tombstones.

Var.: **Affleck.**

The first known bearer of the name is Richard of Auchinlec, *recorded in 1263 as a juror on an inquest held before the sheriff of Lanark.*

Audley English: habitation name from a place in Staffs., so called from the OE female name *Ealdgȳð* (composed of the elements *eald* old + *gȳð* battle) + OE *lēah* wood, clearing.

Audsley English: habitation name from an unidentified place (probably in Yorks., where the surname is most common), so called from the gen. case of an OE personal name with the first element *(e)ald* old + OE *lēah* wood, clearing.

Auerbach Jewish (Ashkenazic): habitation name from any of several places in S Germany so called, usually taken as being from *Aurochs* (a kind of wild bull, now extinct) + *bach* stream.

Vars.: **Auerbacher**; **O(h)rbach** (associated by folk etymology with Ger. *Ohr* ear); **Awerbach**, **Averbach**, **Aberbach**, **Averback**, **Aberback**, **Awerbuch**, **Averb(o)uch**, **Aberbuch**; **Averbuj** (a Sp. spelling).

Aumonier French: nickname for a beggar, from an agent deriv. of OF *aumone* alms (ultimately from Gk *eleēmosynē* mercy; the word acquired a concrete monetary sense in LL).

Var.: **Laumonier** (with fused def. art.).

Aurrecoechea Spanish form of Basque **Aurrekoetxea**: habitation name for someone who lived in a house situated in front of its fellows, from Basque *aurre* front + the gen. particle *ko* + *etxe* house + the def. art. *-a*.

Austerlitz German and Jewish: habitation name from a town in Moravia, called *Austerlitz* in Ger. (*Slavkov* in Czech). In 1805 this was the site of a battle in which Napoleon defeated the armies of Austria and Russia.

The original surname of the American dancer and actor Fred **Astaire** *was Austerlitz. He was born in Nebraska in 1899.*

Austin English and French: from the ME, OF given name *Austin*, the vernacular form of L *Augustīnus* (a deriv. of *Augustus*; see AGOSTI). This was an extremely common given name in every part of W Europe during the Middle Ages, owing its popularity chiefly to St Augustine of Hippo (354–430), whose influence on Christianity is generally considered to be second only to that of St Paul. Various religious orders came to be formed following rules named in his honour, including the 'Austin canons', established in the 11th cent., and the 'Austin friars', a mendicant order dating from the 13th cent. The popularity of the name in England was further increased by the fact that it was borne by St Augustine of Canterbury (d. *c*.605), an It. Benedictine monk known as 'the Apostle of the English', who brought Christianity to England in 597 and founded the see of Canterbury.

Vars.: Eng.: **Austen, Auston**; **Augustin(e)** (a learned form). Fr.: **Augustin** (a learned form); **Gustin**; **Aoustin**; **Autin, Outin**.

Cogns.: It.: **Agostini**. Sp.: **Agustín**. Cat.: **Agustí**. Port.: **Agostinho**. Ger.: **Augstein, Auxten**. Flem.: **Austen, Ostin**. Pol.: **Augustyn**. Hung.: **Ágoston**.

Dims.: It.: **Augustinello, Agostinetti**. Low Ger.: **Stienke**. Flem.: **Tienke** (see also MARTIN).

Aug.: It.: **Agostinone**.

Patrs.: Eng.: **Austins**. Gael.: COSTAIN. It.: **De Agostini, Dell' Agostino**. Low Ger.: **Stienes, Stinnes, Stienen**. Pol.: **August(yn)owicz, Augustyniak**.

Patr. (from a dim.): Flem.: **Tienken**.

Habitation names: Pol.: **Augustowski, Gustowski, Augustyński**.

The novelist Jane Austen *(1775–1817) was the daughter of a clergyman who came of a Kentish family with ancestors who were clothiers in the Middle Ages.*

Auty English (Yorks): from the ON personal name *Auti*, a short form of the various cpd personal names with the first element *auð* riches, prosperity (cf. OADE).

Var.: **Alty**.

Aveyard English: habitation name from some minor place, presumably in Yorks., where the surname is most common. The second element is clearly OE *geard* enclosure; the first is probably a personal name such as OE *Afa*, of uncertain origin.

Avigdor Jewish: from a given name. This originated in the Hebr. phrase *avi-Gedor* 'father of Gedor', which occurs in 1 Chron. 4: 4, 18, and was used as a given name under the influence of VICTOR.

Vars.: **Vigdor, Wigdor, Figdor** (aphetic forms); **Vigder, Wigder** (Yid. forms).

Dims.: **Vigdorchik, Wigdorchik, Wigdorczik** (E Ashkenazic).

Patrs.: **D'Avigdor**; **Vigderson** (Ashkenazic); **Vigdorovitch, Vigderovitsch, Vigdorowitz, Vigdorowicz, Wigdorowicz** (E Ashkenazic).

Avila Spanish: habitation name from the city and province so called. The former is extremely ancient, reputedly founded by the Phoenicians, and its name, first found in the L forms *Avela* and *Abulia*, is of quite uncertain meaning.

Vars.: **Dávila, Avilés**.

Avis English: from the ME, OF given name *Avice* (L *Avitius* (fem. *Avitia*), of uncertain origin, perhaps an adaptation of a Gmc or Celt. name).

Patr.: **Avison**.

Avnet Jewish (Ashkenazic): name assumed by a member of the priestly caste, from Yid., Hebr. *avnet* girdle worn by priests.

Avogadro N Italian: regional var. of the occupational term *avocato* adviser, counsellor (L *advocātus*, past part. of *advocāre* to call on). In the Middle Ages the term was not restricted to lawyers but was applied to various functionaries and officials (cf. VOGT).

Vars.: **Avogaro, Avvocato**.

Cogn.: Jewish (E Ashkenazic): **Advokat** ('lawyer').

Avoine French: metonymic occupational name for a grower or seller of oats, from OF *avoine* oats (L *avēna*).

Vars.: **Avenne**; **Lavoin(n)e**, **Lavenne** (with fused def. art.); **Davei(s)ne**, **D(el)avenne** (with fused preposition *de*); **Avenier, Lavenier** (agent nouns).

Cogn.: Eng. (Norman): **Avner**.

Dims.: Fr.: **Avenel, Avenet, Avenol**.

Awdrey English: from the ME female given name *Aldreda*, recorded in Domesday Book, apparently from OE *Æðelþrȳð*, composed of the elements *æðel* noble + *þrȳð* strength. This was fairly common from the earliest times, and its popularity was increased in the Christian era by the fame of St Etheldreda (d. 679), queen of Northumbria and founder of the convent at Ely.

Vars.: **Audrey, Awdry**.

Ayckbourn N English: habitation name from a place, not now identifiable, deriving its name from ON *eiki* OAK + OE *burna* stream (see BOURNE).

Ayer 1. English: nickname for a man who was well known to be the heir to a title or fortune, from ME *eir*, *eyr* heir (OF *(h)eir*, from L *hērēs*).

2. Scots: habitation name from the city of *Ayr* in SW Scotland, so called from ON *eyrr* tongue of land, gravelly bank.

Vars.: **Ayr(e)**, **Air**. (Of 1 only): **Eyer**, **Eyre**, **Hayer**, **Heyer**.

Patrs. (of 1): **Ayers**, **Ayres**, **Ayris**, **E(a)yr(e)s**, **Eyers**.

One of several families bearing the surname Eyre *traces its descent from Humphrey* le Heyr *of Bromham, Wilts., who was one of the crusaders who accompanied Richard I to the Holy Land in the 12th cent.*

Edward Eyre (1815–1901), the Australian explorer after whom Lake Eyre was named, and who later in life became governor of New Zealand and then of Jamaica, was born in Hornsea, Yorks., where his father was vicar. He emigrated to Australia at the age of 17.

Ayliff English: 1. from the ME female given name *Ayleve*, *Aylgive*, OE *Æðelgifu*, composed of the elements *æðel* noble + *gifu* gift, which was borne by a daughter of King Alfred the Great, who became abbess of Shaftesbury.

2. from the ON byname *Eilífr*, which is composed of the elements *ei* always + *lífr* life.

Vars.: **Ayliffe**, **Ellif(f)**.

Ayling English: from the OE word *æðeling* prince, a deriv. of *æðel* noble. This word was commonly used as a byname among Anglo-Saxons before and after the Norman Conquest, and was in use for a time as a personal name. The surname derives from this use rather than from a nickname; still less does it denote descent from noble Anglo-Saxon blood.

Vars.: **Aylen**, **Aylin**.

Aylmer 1. English: from the ME given name *Ailmar*, OE *Æðelmǣr*, composed of the elements *æðel* noble + *mǣr* famous, which was reinforced after the Conquest by the introduction of OF *Ailmer*, from a Continental cogn.

2. Scots: apparently a habitation name. Emmed *de Ailmer* and Roger *de Almere* are recorded in Selkirk in 1296. The latter individual is recorded also as *de Aylemer* and *de Alnmer*, but the place from which he derived his name has not been identified. The *de* may be purely honorific, and the origin as in 1.

Vars.: **Ailmer**, **Aylmore**. (Of 1 only): **Elmer**, **Elmar**; **Aymer**, **Aimer**, **Amar**.

Cogns.: Prov.: **Adhémar**, **Azéma(r)**, **Adima**. It.: **Aimar**, **A(y)mar** (Piedmont, Lombardy); **Aumari**, **Ameri(o)** (Tuscany); **Altimari**, **Altomari** (altered by folk etymology, as if from It. *alto* high + *mare* sea); **Mari** (aphetic). Ger.: **Ad(e)mar**. Low Ger.: **Almer**.

Patrs.: Eng.: **Elmers**, **Aimers**. It.: **D'Ameri(o)**, **Damero**. Low Ger.: **Al(l)mers**.

Aylmer *is the name of an Irish family established in Kildare in the 14th cent. or before. John Aylmer was living at Lyons, Co. Kildare, in c.1360, but the name is first recorded in Ireland almost a century earlier.*

Aylward English: from a common Gmc personal name, found in OE as *Æðelweard*, composed of the elements *adal* noble + *ward* guard.

Vars.: **Ailward**, **Allward**; **Aluard**.

Cogns.: Low Ger.: **Ahlwardt**, **Allward**; see also ALLARD. Fr.: **Allo(u)ard**, **Alluard**.

Ayo Spanish: 1. apparently a name for someone who was the guardian of an orphan in a community, from Sp. *ayo* tutor, guardian, a masc. form of *aya* nurse (L *avia* grandmother).

2. The surname is common in Bilbao in the Basque country, and it is possible that it was adopted as a Castilian form of the Basque surname **Aia** or **Aya**, a topographic name from Basque *ai* slope + the def. art. *-a*.

Ayuso Spanish: topographic name for someone who lived in the lower part of a settlement, from Sp. *ayuso* (down) below (LL *ad* at + *jūsum*, *jōsum*, from class. L *deorsum* downwards).

Azcárate Spanish form of Basque **Azkarate**: topographic name for someone who lived by a pass between high rocks, from Basque *aitz*, *atx* rock, crag + *gara* high + *ate* pass, defile.

Azcona Spanish form of Basque **Azkona**: nickname for someone who resembled a badger in some way, from Basque *azkon* badger + the def. art. *-a*.

Azcorra Spanish form of Basque **Azkorra**: nickname from the adj. *azkor* forgetful + the def. art. *-a*. The adj. also has the meaning 'lively, animated' in the dialect of Biscay and 'shy, unsociable' in the Guipúzcoa dialect; either of these senses could also have contributed to the origin of the surname.

Azcue Spanish form of Basque **Azkue**: topographic name for someone who lived near a rock or crag, from Basque *aitz*, *atx* rock, crag + the local suffix *-qu(n)e*.

Aznar Spanish: from a medieval given name, L *Asinārius*. This is probably composed of the Gmc elements *ans* god + *hari*, *heri* army, but to have been altered as the result of folk etymological association with an agent deriv. of L *asinus* ass, donkey.

B

Baamonde Spanish (of Galician origin): habitation name from a place in the province of Lugo, so called from L *Badamundi (fundus)* '(farm) of *Badamundus*', a Gmc personal name composed of the elements *bad* (cf. BADE) + *mund* protection.

Vars.: **Bahamonde, Vaamonde.**

Baas Low German and Dutch: nickname or occupational name from MLG *baas* master, overseer, boss.

Var.: **Baasch.**

Babb English (chiefly Devon): Reaney suggests that this is from the medieval female given name *Babb*, a pet form of *Barbara* (see BARBARY), or a nickname meaning 'baby', from ME *bab(e)*. However, a more probable source is the OE personal name *Babba*, found in several placenames, including *Babbacombe* in Devon and BABINGTON in Somerset. This is of uncertain origin, perhaps a nursery name from a child's babbling.

Dims.: **Bab(b)itt, Babet, Babot, Babcock.**

Patr.: **Babbs.**

Babel 1. Jewish (Ashkenazic): surname chosen as a symbol of exile, from Hebr. *Bavel* Babylon (from the Assyrian elements *bāb* gate + *ilu* god). The Jewish people were held in captivity in Babylon from 597 to about 538 BC.

2. French: from a medieval given name bestowed in honour of St *Babylas*, a 3rd-cent. Christian patriarch of Antioch. His name is of uncertain origin; it is conceivably an ethnic name ultimately derived from the city of Babylon.

Var. (of 1): **Bavel; Babli, Bably, Bavli, Bavly, Bawli, Bawly** (Israeli habitation names). (Of 2): **Babeau.**

Dims. (of 2): **Bab(e)let, Bab(e)lon, Bab(e)lin.**

Patrs. (from 2): Russ.: **Vavilov, Vavilin; Avilov, Avilin.**

Baber English: surname common in Somerset, for which no satisfactory etymology has been proposed.

Babeuf French: occupational nickname for a slaughterman, from OF *bat(tre)* to hit, strike (LL *battuere*; cf. BATAILLE) + *boef, buef* bull (L *bōs*, gen. *bovis*).

Babin Russian: metr. or patr. from *Baba* 'Grandmother', 'Old Woman' (originally a nursery word), either meaning son of an old woman or a nickname denoting a fussy old man.

Cogns.: Ukr.: **Babich.** Pol.: **Babicz, Babski.** Czech: **Babič, Babický; Babka, Babák.** Croatian: **Bab(ov)ić.** Hung.: **Babics, Babits.** Rum.: **Baba.** Jewish (E Ashkenazic): **Babicz, Babitch.**

Dims.: Russ.: **Bab(ush)kin, Babukhin** (patrs.). Ukr.: **Babenko.**

Habitation name: Pol.: **Babiński.**

Babington English: habitation name from a place so called in Somerset or from *Bavington* in Northumb. Both are named from OE *Babbingtūn* 'settlement (OE *tūn*) associated with *Babba*' (see BABB). The latter was the original home of the family of the historian Thomas Babington Macaulay (1800–59).

Bacchus 1. English: var. of BACKHOUSE.

2. French: nickname for a heavy drinker, from *Bacchus*, the Greek and Roman god of wine, whose cult and name are probably of Oriental origin.

Cogn. (of 2): Flem.: **Baccus.**

Bach 1. German and English: topographic name for someone who lived by a stream, from MHG *bach* or ME *bache* (OHG *bah*; OE *bæce, bece*).

2. German and Low German: occupational name for a BAKER.

3. Polish and Czech: dim. of SEBASTIAN.

4. Jewish (Ashkenazic): acronymic surname from the initial letters of the Hebr. phrase *ben chayim* 'son of life'; cf. HYAM.

5. Catalan: topographic name for someone who lived in a sunless spot, from an aphetic form of Cat. *obac* dark, shady (L *opācus*).

Vars. (of 1): Eng.: **Bache** (chiefly W Midlands); **Batch, Ba(i)sh;** BACK. Ger.: **Bacher, Bachmann; Pach(er), Pachmann** (Bavaria). Low Ger.: BECK, **Becker, Beckmann, Bee(c)ke(r), Becken; Torbeck, Terbeck.** Flem.: **Bee(c)k, Beckx, Verbeke, Van der Beken.** Du.: **Beek, Van (der) Beek, Verbeek, Terbeek, Beekman.** (Of 4): **Bacher, Bachman(n).** (Of 5): Cat.: **Bachs, Ubach.**

Dims. (of 3): Pol.: **Baszek, Baszniak.** Czech: **Bašek.**

Patr. (from a dim. of 3): Pol.: **Baszkiewicz.**

Habitation name (from 3): Pol.: **Bachański.**

Bacharach Jewish (Ashkenazic): habitation name from a town on the Rhine near Koblenz, recorded in the earliest L documents as *Bacaraca*. The placename seems to be the same as that of *Baccarat* in the Vosges and is of Celt. origin but unknown meaning.

Vars.: **Bach(e)rach, Bach(e)rich, Bacherig.**

Bachelor English: status name for a young knight or novice at arms, ME, OF *bacheler* (med. L *baccalārius*, of unknown origin). The word had already been extended to mean '(young) unmarried man' by the 14th cent., but it is unlikely that many bearers of the surname derive it from the word in that sense.

Vars.: **Batchel(l)or, Ba(t)chel(l)er, Batcheldor, Batchelder, Backler.**

Cogns.: Fr.: **Bachelier.** Cat.: **Bachiller.** It.: **Baccel(l)ieri, Bac(c)i(g)lieri.** Czech: **Bakalář.**

Dims.: Fr.: **Bachelet, Bachelin, Bachelot.**

Pej.: Fr.: **Bachelard.**

Bachofen German: habitation or occupational name, ostensibly meaning 'bake-oven' and therefore perhaps denoting a baker. The second element is probably MHG *ofen* oven (OHG *ovan*), but the var. **Bachof** suggests that the name could in fact be a habitation name from MHG *bach* stream (see BACH 1) + the dat. pl. case (originally used after a preposition) of MHG *hof* court (see HOFER).

Vars.: **Backof(en).**

Back 1. English: nickname for someone with a hunched back or some other noticeable peculiarity of the back or spine, from ME *bakke* back (OE *bæc*).

2. topographic name for someone who lived on a hill or ridge (from the same OE word as in 1), or at the rear of a

settlement (this last sense being the meaning of the Scand. cogn).

3. English: from the OE personal name *Bacca*, which was still in use in the 12th cent. It is of uncertain origin, but may have been a byname in the same sense as 1.

4. English: nickname from ME *bakke* bat (apparently of Scand. origin), from some fancied resemblance to the animal.

5. Swedish: cogn. of BANKS.

Vars. (of 2): **Backer**, **Backman** (topographic names, most common in N England). (Of 5): **Backman**.

Cogn. (of 1 and 2): Dan., Norw.: **Bak**.

Patrs. (from 3): Eng.: **Backs**, **Bax**.

Backhouse English: habitation name for someone who lived at a bakery, or occupational name for someone employed in one, from OE *bǣchūs* bakehouse (from *bacan* to bake + *hūs* house).

Vars.: **Bakehouse**, **Backouse**, **Backus**, BACCHUS.

Cogns.: Ger.: **Backhaus**. Low Ger.: **Backhus**, **Back(e)s**, **Bax**. Du.: **Bakhuizen**, **Bakhuijsen**, **Bakhuysen**.

Bacon 1. English: metonymic occupational name for a preparer and seller of cured pork, from ME, OF *bacun*, *bacon* bacon, ham (of Gmc origin, akin to BACK 1).

2. English: from the Gmc personal name *Bac(c)o*, *Bahho*, from the root *bag-* to fight. The name was relatively common among the Normans in the form *Bacus*, of which the oblique case was *Bacon*.

3. Jewish (Ashkenazic): origin unknown.

Var. (of 2): BAGGE.

Cogns. (of 1): Fr.: **Baconnier**. Ger.: **Backner**. (Of 2): Fr.: **Baque**. Norw., Dan., Swed.: **Bagge**.

Dims. (of 2): Eng.: **Baggett**, **Bag(g)ot(t)**, **Bagehot**. Fr.: **Baqu(e)lin**.

Patrs. (from 2): Eng.: **Bagges**. Dan.: **Baggesen**.

An English family by the name of Bagot *trace their descent from a certain* Bagod, *recorded in Domesday Book as holding land near Bramshall, Staffs. By the 12th cent. the family name was also found at* Bagot's Bromley *in the same county*.

Badanes Jewish (E Ashkenazic): metr. from the Yid. female given name *Badane* (from Czech *Bohdana*, a fem. form of *Bohdan*; see BOGDANOV).

Vars.: **Bodanis**, **Bodanoff**; **Bodankin** (from a dim. form).

Badaud 1. French: from a Gmc personal name composed of the elements *badu* battle + *wald* rule.

2. Provençal: nickname for a stupid or naïve individual, an open-mouthed idiot, from OProv. *badar* to open (LL *batāre*; cf. BADIER) + the pej. suffix *au(l)d*.

Var.: **Badault**.

Dims. (of 2): Prov.: **Bad(i)ou**, **Badoc(he)**, **Badolle**.

Baddeley English: habitation name from a place in Staffs., the OE name of which was *Baddinglēah*, i.e. 'wood or clearing (OE *lēah*) associated with *Badda*' (see BADE).

Bade English: probably from a ME survival of the OE personal name *Bad(d)a*, which is of uncertain origin, perhaps a short form of the various cpd names with the first element *beadu* battle.

Dims.: **Badcock** (chiefly Devon); **Badcoe**.

Bader 1. German and Jewish (Ashkenazic): occupational name for an attendant in a public bath house, from an agent deriv. of Ger. *Bad* bath (MHG *bat*, OHG *bad*). In former times, such attendants undertook a variety of functions, including blood-letting and hair-cutting.

2. Provençal: var. of BADIER.

Vars. (of 1): **Bäder**, **Beder**; **Peder**.

Badger English (W Midlands): 1. habitation name from a place in Shrops., probably so called from the OE personal name *Bæcg* (a deriv. of *Bacga*, attested but of uncertain origin) + OE *ofer* ridge.

2. occupational name for a maker of bags (see BAGGE 1) or for a pedlar who carried his wares about with him in a bag. It is unlikely that the surname has anything to do with the animal (see BROCK 2), which was not known by this name until the 16th cent.

Cogns. (of 2): Norw., Dan.: **Bag(g)er**.

Patr. (from 2): **Badgers**.

Badham English: habitation name from some minor place (probably in the W Midlands, where the surname is commonest), so called from the OE personal name *Bēada* (a short form of the various cpd names with the first element *beadu* battle) + OE *hām* homestead. Reaney, however, derives it from *Abadam*, a Welsh patr. of ADAM.

Badier Provençal: occupational name for a janitor, from OProv. *badar* to open (cf. BADAUD 2).

Vars.: BADER, **Badé**; **Badaire**.

Badman English: in spite of appearances, this is probably not a nickname for a reprobate, but an occupational name for the servant of someone called *Badd* or BATT.

Badner Jewish: of uncertain origin, possibly a var. of *Bodner* (see BÜTTNER), or a habitation name from any of various places in Germany called *Baden* 'Baths'.

Baena Spanish: habitation name from a place in the province of Córdoba, so called from L *Badiāna* (*villa*) 'settlement of *Badius*', a byname meaning 'Reddish' (see BAY).

Baeta Portuguese: metonymic occupational name for a maker or seller of baize and flannelette, or a nickname for a habitual wearer of the material, Port. *baeta* (OF *bayette*, a dim. of BAY, from its normal colour).

Baeza Spanish: habitation name from a place in the province of Jaén, apparently so called from L *Vīvātia* (*villa*) 'settlement of *Vīvātius*'.

Bagge English: 1. metonymic occupational name for a maker of bags and sacks of various kinds, including wallets and purses, from ME *bagge* bag (of uncertain origin).

2. from the Gmc personal name *Bac(c)o*, *Bahho*; see BACON 1.

Vars.: **Bagg**, **Bage**.

Bagiński Polish: topographic name from *bagno* marsh + *-ski* suffix of local surnames (see BARANOWSKI).

Var.: **Bagieński**.

Bagley English: habitation name from any of the places so called, mainly in Berks., Shrops., Somerset, and W Yorks. These get their names either from the OE personal name *Bacga* (cf. BADGER) + OE *lēah* wood, clearing or from an OE word for a 'bag-shaped' animal + *lēah*.

Vars.: **Baguley** (a place in Ches.), **Bagguley**; **Baggaley**, **Baggal-l(a)y**, **Baggarley**.

Bagnall English: habitation name from a place in Staffs., so called from the OE personal name *Badeca*, *Baduca* (from a short form of the various cpd names with the first element *beadu* battle) + OE *halh* nook, recess (see HALE) or *holt* wood (see HOLT).

Vars.: **Bagnell**, **Bagenal**, **Bagnold**.

An Irish family by the name of Bagenal *can be traced to Sir Nicholas Bagenal (d. 1586), who fled from England* c.1539, *after he had killed a man in a brawl. He was later pardoned, and his descen-*

dants rose to prominence, mainly through marriage into some of Ireland's leading families. They gave their name to Bagenalstown *in Co. Carlow.*

Bagratian Armenian: patr. from the personal name *Bagratuni*. In AD 806 Ashot Bagratuni 'the Carnivorous' was chosen as Prince of Armenia, and he established a line of Bagratid emperors, who ruled the country until the 11th cent. Prince Pyotr Ivanovich Bagration (1765–1812), a distinguished Russian general at the time of the Napoleonic Wars, was descended from this line.

Vars.: **Bagration, Bagradian.**

Bagshaw English: habitation name from a place in Derbys. The first element of the placename is probably the OE personal name *Bacga* (cf. BADGER), the second is OE *sceaga* wood, copse.

Var.: **Bagshawe.**

A family by the name of Bagshawe *are associated with Wormhill and Ford Hall near Hucklow in Derbys. They can be traced back to a certain William Bagshawe, lord of the manor of Hucklow in 1662.*

Baião Portuguese: habitation name from a place in the region of Oporto, so called from L *Radiānus* (*fundus*) 'farm, estate of *Badius*' (cf. BAENA).

Baibakov Russian: patr. from the nickname *Baibak* 'Steppe-Marmot' (of Turkic origin). The animal was reputedly sluggish, and so the nickname was frequently used for a lazy person.

Bailey English: 1. occupational name for a steward or official (or occasionally perhaps an ironic nickname for an officious person), from ME *bail(l)i* (OF *baillis*, oblique case *bailif*, from LL *bāiulīvus*, a deriv. of *bāiulus* carrier, porter). The word survives in Scotland as *bailie*, the title of a municipal magistrate, and elsewhere as *bailiff*, which in England denotes an officer who serves writs and summonses and ensures that court orders are carried out.

2. topographic name for someone who lived in a district by the outermost wall of a castle, ME *bail(l)y*, *baile* (apparently from OF *bail(le)* enclosure, a deriv. of *bailer* to enclose, of unknown origin). The situation is complicated by the fact that this name, originally denoting a particular part of a castle, sometimes became a placename in its own right: some bearers of the name undoubtedly derive it from the Old Bailey in London, which formed part of the early medieval outer wall of the city.

3. habitation name from *Bailey* in Lancs., so called from OE *bēg* berry + *lēah* wood, clearing. Examples of the name derived from this source occur in the surrounding area from the 13th cent.

Vars.: **Baillie** (chiefly Scots); **Bailie** (chiefly N Irish); **Baily, Bayl(e)y, Baylay.** (Of 1 only): **Bail(l)if(f), Bayliff(e), Baylis(s), Bayless, Bailess.** (Of 2 only): **Bail(e)(s), Bale(s), Bayl(e)(s).**

Cogns. (of 1): Fr.: **Bailly, Bailli(f), Lebailly, Lebaillif; Bally** (Switzerland). It.: **Bagli(v)o; Bailo** (from L *bāiulus*). Sp.: **Baile.** Cat.: **Batllé.** (Of 2): Fr.: **Bail(l)(e), Lebail, Bayle, Beyle.**

Dims. (of 1): Fr.: **Baillivet.** (Of 2): Fr.: **Bail(l)et, Baylet, Beylet, Baillot, Baylot, Beylot.** Prov.: **Bailloux, Bailloud.** It.: **Baglietti, Baglini.**

Augs. (of 1): It.: **Baglione, Bailone.**

Pejs. (of 1): Fr.: **Baillaud.** It.: **Bagliardi.**

Bain 1. Scots: nickname for a fair-haired person, from Gael. *bàn* white, fair.

2. N English: nickname meaning 'bone', probably bestowed on an exceptionally tall, lean man, from OE *bān* bone. In Northern ME *-ā-* was preserved, whereas in Southern dialects (which later became standard), it was changed to *-ō-*.

3. N English: nickname for a hospitable person, from Northern ME *beyn*, *bayn* welcoming, friendly (ON *beinn* straight, direct).

4. English and French: metonymic occupational name for an attendant at a public bath house (cf. BADER 1), from ME, OF *baine* bath (L *balnea*, originally a neut. pl., later treated as fem. sing.).

Vars.: **Baine, Bayne.** (Of 1 only): **Bawn, Baun.**

Cogns. (of 2): Ger.: **Bein, Beyn** ('leg'). Flem., Du.: **Been(en).** Jewish (Ashkenazic): **Bain** (from Yid. *beyn* bone; reason for adoption as a surname unknown). (Of 4): It.: **Bagni, Bagnesi.** Sp.: **Baños; Bañares, Bañales.**

Dims. (of 4): It.: **Bagnu(o)lo, Bagnoli.** Sp.: **Banuelos.**

Augs. (of 4): It.: **Bagnone.** Sp.: **Bañón.**

Pej. (of 4): It.: **Bagnacci.**

Bainbridge English: habitation name from a place in N Yorks., so called from the river *Bain* on which it stands (which is from ON *beinn* straight; cf. BAIN 3) + OE *brycg* BRIDGE.

Baines 1. Scots and N English: nickname meaning 'bones' (cf. BAIN 2).

2. Welsh: patr. (*ab Einws*), from the given name *Einws*, a dim. of *Ennion* 'Anvil'.

Vars.: **Baynes, Bains, Banes.**

Many present-day English bearers of the names Baines *and* Baynes *are descended from Robert Baines, who was born c.1587 in Ipswich, Suffolk. It is not known whether he was of Scots or Welsh origin.*

Bairnsfather N English and Scots: nickname for the father or alleged father of an illegitimate child, from the gen. case of Northern ME *bairn* child (see BARNES 2) + *father* (OE *fæder*, reinforced by ON *faðir*). It has also been suggested that the name is a remodelling by folk etymology of the ON personal name *Barnvarðr*, composed of the elements *barn* warrior, hero + *varðr* guard.

Vars.: **Ba(r)n(s)father.**

Bairstow English: habitation name from *Bairstow* in W Yorks., probably so called from OE *beger* berry + *stōw* place. The surname is still most common in Yorks.

Vars.: **Barstow, Ba(i)stow.**

Bąk Polish: probably a nickname for an irritating individual, from Pol. *bąk* horsefly (also meaning 'bittern').

Dim.: **Bączyk.**

Cogn. (patr.): Croatian: **Bakić.**

Habitation name: Pol.: **Bąkowski.**

Baker English: occupational name, from ME *bakere*, OE *bæcere*, a deriv. of *bacan* to bake. It may have been used for someone whose special task in the kitchen of a great house or castle was the baking of bread, but since most humbler households did their own baking in the Middle Ages, it may also have referred to the owner of a communal oven used by the whole village. The right to be in charge of this and exact money or loaves in return for its use was in many parts of the country a hereditary feudal privilege; cf. MILLER. Less often the surname may have been acquired by someone noted for baking particularly fine bread or by a baker of pottery or bricks.

Vars.: Eng.: **Baiker, Bacher; Baxter** (originally a fem. form; common esp. in E Anglia).

Cogns.: Ger.: **Bäcker**, **Becker**, **Beckermann**. Flem., Du.: **Bakker**, **De Ba(e)cker**, **De Becker**, **Bakmann**. Jewish (Ashkenazic): **Be(c)ker(man)**. See also BECK.

Patr.: Flem, Du.: **Beckers**.

Equivs. (not cogn.): Fr.: BOULANGER, FOURNIER. Ger.: PFISTER. Pol.: KOŁACZ, PIEKARSKI. Russ.: KHLEBNIKOV. Hung.: LISZT.

Bakewell English: habitation name from the town in Derbys., so called from the OE personal name *Badeca*, *Baduca* (from a short form of the various cpd personal names with the first element *beadu* battle) + OE *well(a)* spring, stream (see WELL).

Baklanov Russian: patr. from the nickname *Baklan* 'Cormorant', presumably denoting a rapacious or greedy person (cf. the mod. Eng. use of the term *gannet*).

Bakunin Russian: patr. from the nickname *Bakuna*, a deriv. of *bakat* to chatter, gossip; cf. BALAKIREV.

Var.: **Bakulin**.

Bal French: 1. nickname, a deriv. of OF *baller* to move, shake, dance (LL *ballāre*, from Gk *ballein* to throw). The original meaning of the surname is by no means clear, as the verb had a wide variety of uses in OF. The most plausible of the many possible origins are that it was given in some cases to a musician, in others to a good dancer.

2. from the Gmc personal name *Ballo*, which is of uncertain origin and meaning, but may represent an assimilated form of *Baldo*, a short form of various personal names containing the element *bald* bold.

Vars. (of 1): **Bal(l)and** (from the pres. part.), **Bal(l)a(n)dier** (an agent deriv. of the last).

Cogn. (of 1): Prov.: **Ballaire** (an agent deriv.).

Dims.: **Bal(l)et**, **Bal(l)ot**, **Bal(l)on**. Prov.: **Bal(l)ou**.

Balaam English: habitation name from *Baylham* in Suffolk, recorded in Domesday Book as *Beleham*, and apparently deriving its name from OE ***bēgel*** bend + *hām* homestead or *hamm* water meadow. The spelling has been affected by folk etymological association with the biblical character who was converted to the Israelite cause by his talking ass (Num. 22–3).

Var.: **Ballaam**.

Balaguer Catalan: habitation name from a place in the province of Lérida, of uncertain etymology. It is possibly a deriv. of the regional term *bàlec* broom (perhaps of Celt. origin).

Var.: **Balagué**.

Balakirev Russian: patr. from the nickname *Balakir* 'Chatterer', a deriv. of *bal(irov)at* to chatter (of imitative origin; cf BAKUNIN). This is also the root of the name of the musical instrument the *balalaika*.

Balañá Catalan: habitation name from *Balenyà* in the province of Barcelona. The placename is of uncertain origin, but may be from LL *Valēniāna* (*villa*) 'settlement of *Valēnius*', a personal name probably related to VALENTE.

Balcells Catalan: topographic name from the pl. form of a dim. of Cat. *balç* precipice (L *balteus* belt; the transferred sense apparently derives from the notion of the cliffs encircling the mountain).

Var.: **Balsells**.

Balch English: 1. from ME *balch*, *belch* balk, beam (OE *bælc*, *balca*). This is either a habitation name for someone who lived in a house with a roof-beam rather than in a simple hut (cf. BELCHEM), or a nickname for a man built like a tree trunk, i.e. one of stocky, heavy build.

2. nickname from ME *balche*, *belche* swelling (OE *bælc(e)*). This was probably chiefly given in the sense 'swelling pride', 'overweaning arrogance', but it can also mean 'eructation', 'belch' and may therefore in some cases have been acquired by a man given to belching.

Vars.: **Baulch**, **Belch**, **Belk**; **Boakes**; **Ba(u)lcher**, BELCHER.

Dim.: **Balchin**.

Balcombe English: habitation name from a place in Sussex, which is so called from OE *bealu* evil, calamity + *cumb* valley (see COOMBE).

Balderston English: habitation name from either of two places in Lancs. called *Balderston(e)*, deriving their names from the gen. case of the OE personal name *Bealdhere* (composed of the elements *beald* bold, brave + *here* army) + OE *tūn* enclosure, settlement. A place of the same name and etymology in the former county of W Lothian may be the source of some examples of the surname in Scotland.

Vars.: **Balderstone**, **Bo(u)lderstone**.

Baldock English: habitation name from a place in Herts., first so called in the 12th cent. by the Knights Templar, who held the manor there. It was named in commemoration of the city of *Baghdad*, known in ME, OF as *Baldac*; its Arabic etymology is said to be 'city of *Dat*', the personal name of a dervish.

Var.: **Baldick**.

Baldry English: from a Gmc personal name composed of the elements *bald* bold, brave + *rīc* power. This may have been present in OE in the form **Bealdrīc*, but it was reintroduced by the Normans as *Baldri*, *Baudri*, and it is from these forms that the surname is derived. The name is now found chiefly in E Anglia.

Vars.: **Baldrey**, **Baudr(e)y**; **Boldry**, **Boldero(e)**, **Boldra**, **Bowdery**; **Baldrick**, **Baudrick**.

Cogns.: Fr.: **Baudric**, **Baudry**, **Baudri**. Ger.: **Baldrich** (rare).

Patr.: Flem.: **Bouderickx**.

Baldwin 1. English: from a Gmc personal name composed of the elements *bald* bold, brave + *wine* friend, which was extremely popular among the Normans and in Flanders in the early Middle Ages. It was the given name of the Crusader who in 1100 became the first Christian king of Jerusalem, and of four more Crusader kings of Jerusalem. It was also borne by Baldwin, Count of Flanders (1172–1205), leader of the Fourth Crusade, who became first Latin Emperor of Constantinople (1204).

2. Irish: surname adopted by bearers of the Gael. name **Ó Maolagáin** (see MILLIGAN), as a result of an association of the first element with Eng. *bald* hairless.

Cogns. (of 1): Fr.: **Baudouin**. It.: **Baldovino**, **Balduini**; **Baldoin** (Venetia); **Bauduin** (Naples, Piedmont). Sp.: **Valdovinos**. Ger.: **Baldewein**, **Ballwe(i)n**, **Bol(l)wahn**, **Bollwagen**. Flem., Du.: **Baudewijn**, **Bou(de)wijn**, **Bouwen**, **Bauwen**.

Patrs.: Low Ger.: **Bauwens**. Flem., Du.: **Baudewijns**, **Boudewijns**, **Bauwens**.

Balfe Irish: Anglicized form of Gael. *Balbh* 'Stammering', 'Dumb', itself probably a translation of a Norman family name of similar meaning (see for example BAUBE).

Patrs. (from dims.): **(O')Balivan** (Gael. **Ó Balbháin**).

Balfour 1. Scots: habitation name from any of several places in the Highlands, so called from Gael. *bail(e)* village, farm, house + *pùir*, gen. case of *pór* pasture, grass (lenited to *phùir* in certain contexts). The second element is akin to W *pawr* pasture. The principal family bearing this name derive it from lands in the parish of Markinch,

Fife. According to the traditional pronunciation the accent falls on the second syllable, but these days it is found more commonly on the first.

2. Jewish (Israeli): surname (and male given name) adopted in the 20th cent. in commemoration of the Balfour Declaration of 2 November 1917, in which the British foreign secretary Arthur James Balfour (1848–1930) pledged support for the establishment of a Jewish homeland in Palestine.

Balkwill English: habitation name from some minor place (probably in Devon, where the surname is most common), presumably so called from OE *balca* beam (see BALCH 1) + *wiell(a)* spring, stream (see WELL). The reference is probably to a place where a tree trunk had been placed across a stream as a primitive foot-bridge.

Ball English: 1. nickname for a short, fat person, from ME *bal(le)* ball (ON *böllr*). In some cases it may have referred to a bald man, from the same word used in the sense of a (round) hairless patch on the skull; mod. Eng. *bald* is from ME *ballede*, from *bal(le)* + *-ede*, i.e., 'having a *balle*'.

2. topographic name for someone who lived on or by a knoll or rounded hill, from the same ME word, *bal(le)*, used in this sense.

3. from the ON personal name *Balle*, apparently derived from *bal* torture, pain (see also BAL 2).

Vars. (of 1): **Balle**; **Bald** (Scots). (Of 2): **Baller**.

Cogn. (of 3): Dan.: **Balle**.

Pej. (of 1): Eng.: **Ballard** (a nickname).

Patrs. (from 3): Eng.: **Balls**. Dan.: **Balling**.

Ballantyne Scots: apparently a habitation name from *Bellenden* in the former counties of Roxburghs and Selkirk, probably so called from Gael. *baile an deadhain* farmstead of the dean.

Vars.: **Ballantine**, **Ballintyne**, **Ballintine**; **Ballentine**, **Ballendine** (N Ireland).

Ballaster English: occupational name for a maker of crossbows or a soldier armed with a crossbow, from an agent deriv. of ME, OF *baleste* crossbow (L *ballista* (military) catapult, ultimately from Gk *ballein* to throw; cf. BAL 1). During the Middle Ages the Sp. and Port. cogns. came to be used as the title of a minister who slept in a room adjoining his master's, originally as a kind of bodyguard, and also of various other court officials involved in royal ceremonial.

Vars.: **Bal(le)ster**, **Ballister**.

Cogns.: Fr.: **Balestier**. Prov.: **Balestra**. It.: **Bal(l)estr(i)eri**; **Balistreri** (Sicily); **Balestra**, **Ballista**. Sp.: **Ballestero(s)**; **Ballesta**. Cat.: **Ballester**, **Ballesté**; **Ballesta**. Port.: **Besteiro**.

Dims.: It.: **Balestrelli**, **Balestrini**.

Pejs.: It.: **Balestrazzi**, **Balestracci**, **Balestrassi**.

Balliol English and Scots (Norman): habitation name from *Bailleul*-en-Vimeu in Picardy, or from one of the numerous other places called *Bailleul* in N France, all of which are probably named from a deriv. of OF *baille* fortification; see BAILEY 2.

Var.: **Baliol**.

The Norman Bernard de Baliol *was granted extensive tracts of land in Scotland by David I (1084–1153).*

Balme 1. Provençal: topographic name for someone who lived by a cave, OProv. *baume* (of Celt. origin), or habitation name from one of the various minor places named with this word.

2. French: metonymic occupational name for a seller of perfumes and spices, from OF *balme* ointment; see BALMER 1.

Vars. (of 1): **Balma**, **Baume**, **Barme**; **Balmadier**, **Baum(ad)ier**.

Dim. (of 1): **Balmette**.

Aug. (of 1): **Baumat**.

Balmer 1. English: occupational name for a seller of spices and perfumes, from an agent deriv. of ME, OF *basme*, *balme*, *ba(u)me* balm, ointment (L *balsamum* aromatic resin, from Gk, and probably ultimately of Oriental origin). There is insufficient evidence to justify the speculation that the term meant an embalmer.

2. German: habitation name from one of the places in Switzerland and Baden called *Balm*, which almost certainly get their names from a Celt. word meaning 'cave', as in BALME 1.

Cogns. (of 1): Fr.: BALME. Ger.: **Balsam**.

Balogh Hungarian: nickname for a left-handed person, from *balog* left, left-handed, clumsy.

Var.: **Balog** (common in the U.S.).

Balser 1. German: var. of BALTHASAR.

2. Jewish (E Ashkenazic): habitation name, an altered form of *Belzer*, native or inhabitant of a town called *Belz*, of which there are two: one in the Ukraine and the other in Galicia.

Balthasar German and French: from the Babylonian personal names *Balthazar* and *Belshazzar*, which were originally distinct but by medieval times had come to be regarded as vars. of a single name. The first is from Aramaic *Balshatzar*, Babylonian *Baal tas-assar* 'may Baal preserve his life', the second from Babylonian *Baal sharuzzur* 'may Baal protect the king'. The second of these was borne by the Chaldean king for whom Daniel interpreted the writing on the wall (Dan. 5); the main reason for the popularity of the first in medieval Italy and Germany was that, according to legend, it was the name of one of the three Magi from the East who attended Christ's birth. His supposed relics were venerated at first in Milan, but after 1164 in Cologne, where they had been taken by Rainald of Dassel.

Vars.: Ger.: **Bal(t)zer**, BALSER; **Ba(l)thas**, **Baltus**, **Baldus**, **Baltes**, **Baldes**, **Bal(t)z**, **Bals**. Fr.: **Balthasard**, **Balthazar(d)**.

Cogns.: Prov.: **Bautesar**. It.: **Baldassari**, **Baldessari**, **Baldissari**, **Baldisseri**; **Balsari**, **Balzari**, **Bauzaro**, **Baussaro**; **Saro**, **Sarri**. Sp.: **Baltasar**. Port.: **Baltasar**, **Baltazar**. Pol.: **Balcar**, **Balcer(ski)**. Czech: **Balcar**; **Baláč**, **Baláš**, **Baláž**, **Balák**. Hung.: **Boldizsár**.

Dims.: Ger.: **Balzel**; **Balzl** (Bavaria); **Bälzle** (Swabia); **Balzli** (Switzerland). Pol.: **Balcerek**. Czech: **Balcárek**, **Balek**, **Balík**. It.: **Baldasserini**, **Baldisserotto**; **Balzarini**, **Balzarotti**; **Saretti**, **Serett(in)i**, **Sarotti**, **Serotti**.

Augs.: It.: **Baldasseroni**, **Seroni**.

Patrs.: Norw., Dan.: **Baltzersen**. Pol.: **Balcewicz**. Armenian: **Bogdass(ar)ian**, **Bogdikian**.

Balzac French: of uncertain origin, perhaps from a Basque nickname *baltsa* 'the black one', with the spelling altered by association with the common placename element *-ac* (from the Gallo-Roman local suffix *-ācum*).

Bamber English: habitation name from *Bamber* Bridge in Lancs., originally '*Bimme*'s bridge', from a ME personal name of uncertain origin.

Bamberger Jewish (Ashkenazic): habitation name from the city of *Bamberg* in Bavaria (formerly in Upper Franconia). Between 1007 and 1702 it was the capital of a powerful ecclesiastical state, and in the 15th cent. the bishops of Bamberg were raised to princely rank.

Var.: **Vámbéry** (Magyarized form, borne by Hungarian Jews).

Bambrough English: habitation name from the town of *Bamburgh* in Northumb., which is mentioned in the form *Bebbanburg* by the Venerable Bede, according to whom it was called after a certain queen *Bebbe* + OE *burh* fort. The surname is still most common in Northumb.

Bamford English: habitation name from any of various places (the two main ones being in Derbys. and Lancs.) so called from OE *bēam* tree, plank + *ford* FORD, i.e. a ford that could be crossed by means of a tree trunk or plank bridge by those who wished to keep their feet dry.

Vars.: **Bampford**, **Bam(p)forth**; **Balmforth** (with intrusive *-l-*).

Bampfylde English: habitation name from *Bampfylde* Lodge in Poltimore, Devon, recorded in 1306 as *Benefeld*, 'open land where beans are grown'. See BANFIELD.

Bampfylde is the family name of the Barons Poltimore, who held the manor of Poltimore in Devon in the reign of Edward I (1272–1307). They also held the manor of Weston Bampfylde, Somerset, from 1199.

Bampton English: habitation name from any of various places so called. Those in Cumb. and Oxon. are so called from OE *bēam* tree, plank + *tūn* enclosure, settlement, although the exact sense of the cpd is not clear. A further example in Devon represents a contracted form of OE *bæðhǣmatūn* 'settlement of the dwellers by a bath, hot spring'.

Banbury English: habitation name from the town in Oxon., so called from an OE personal name *Ban(n)a* (apparently a byname meaning 'Felon', 'Murderer') + OE *burh* fort.

Bancroft English: habitation name from any of various minor places so called, from OE *bēan* beans (a collective sing.) + *croft* paddock, smallholding (see CROFT).

Var.: **Bencroft** (a place in Northants).

Band German and Jewish (Ashkenazic): metonymic occupational name for someone who made the wooden hoops with which wooden barrels were fastened together, from Ger. *Band* hoop, band (MHG *bant*, OHG *band*, a deriv. of *bindan* to bind; cf. BINDER).

Vars.: Ger.: **Bandt**, **Bande**. Jewish: **Bandman(n)**, **Bandelman**, **Bandler**, **Bandner**.

Dims.: Ger.: **Bandel**, **Bandle**. Jewish: **Bandel**.

Banfield English: habitation name from an unidentified place, evidently so called from OE *bēan* beans (collective sing.) + *feld* field, land converted to arable use. The place may well be identical with Bampfylde Lodge in Devon (see BAMPFYLDE).

Var.: **Benfield**.

Bang Danish: nickname for a timid person, from Dan. *bang* fearful, nervous (from the ON prefix *bí* + *angr* grief, sorrow).

Banham English: habitation name from a place in Norfolk, so called from OE *bēan* beans (a collective sing.) + *hām* homestead. The surname is still much more common in Norfolk than elsewhere.

Bankhead English: topographic name for someone who lived at the top of a bank or hill; see BANKS 1. The name is now found mainly in N Ireland, where it is probably a habitation name of Scots origin. There are several minor places in Scotland so called, but the most likely source of the surname is one on the border between the parishes of Kilmarnock and Dreghorn in the former county of Ayrs. (now part of Strathclyde region).

Bańkowski Polish: of uncertain origin, probably a deriv. of *bańka* meaning 'bulging vessel', used as a nickname for a fat man. *Bańka* is not actually attested in this meaning, but the related word *bania* is.

Cogn. (patr.): Croatian: **Banković**.

Banks 1. English and Scots: topographic name for someone who lived on the slope of a hillside or by a riverbank, from Northern ME *bank(e)* (of Scand. origin; cf. ON *bakke*). The final *-s* may occasionally represent a plural form, but it is most commonly an arbitrary addition made after the main period of surname formation, perhaps under the influence of patr. forms with a possessive *-s*.

2. Irish: Anglicized form of Gael. **Ó Bruacháin** 'descendant of *Bruachán*', a byname for a large-bellied person. The Eng. form was chosen because of a mistaken association of the Gael. name with *bruach* boundary.

Vars. (of 1): **Bankes**, **Bangs**; **Banker**. (Of 2): **O'Bro(g)han**.

Cogns. (of 1): Ger.: **Bank(e)**. Du.: **Bank**. Norw., Dan.: **Banke**. Swed.: BACK.

Cpds (ornamental, from a cogn. of 1): Swed.: **Backlund** ('bank grove'); **Backström** ('bank river').

Bannan Irish: Anglicized form of Gael. **Ó Banáin**, 'descendant of *Banán*', a personal name representing a dim. of *ban* white.

Vars.: **O'Bannan**, **(O')Bannion**, **(O')Bynnan**, **(O')Banane**, **Banan**, **Bannon**, **Banin**, **Banim**.

Bannerman Scots: occupational name for a standard bearer, from ANF *banere* flag, ensign (OF *baniere*, LL *bandāria*, a deriv. of *bandum*, of Gmc origin) + ME *man* (OE *mann*).

Cogns.: Eng.: **Banner** (Midlands). Port.: **Bandeira(s)**.

Patr.: Du.: **Baanders**.

There is a tradition that the Scottish family called Bannerman *once held the hereditary office of banner-bearer to the King of Scotland. Since the Earl of Dundee held this office from 1298, this would make the Bannermans very early holders of the privilege if there is any truth in the tradition. A certain Donald Bannerman held the office of physician to King David II of Scotland (1329–71).*

Bannister English: metonymic occupational name for a basket weaver, from ANF *banastre* basket (the result of a LL cross between Gaul. *benna* and Gk *kanastron*). The word is not used of a stair rail before the 17th cent., too late to have given rise to a surname.

Vars.: **Banister**, **Bannester**.

A Lancs. family of this name are descended from a certain Richard Banester, *who held lands in Ches. and Shrops. in the early 12th cent. His son Robert was dispossessed by the Welsh, and was granted lands in Makerfield in compensation.*

Banwell English: habitation name from a place in Somerset, so called from the OE byname *Ban(n)a* (see BANBURY) + OE *well(a)* stream.

Banyard English: metathesized form of a Gmc personal name introduced by the Normans in the form *Baynard*. The first element is of uncertain origin, but may be akin to ON *beinn* straight (cf. BAIN 3); the second is *hard* brave, hardy, strong, a common element in Gmc names.

Vars.: **Bunyard**, **Baynard**.

Baptiste French: from a medieval given name, derived from the distinguishing epithet of St John the Baptist, who baptized people, including Christ Himself, in the river Jordan (Mark 1: 9), and was later beheaded by Herod. The name is from L *Baptista* (Gk *baptistēs*, a deriv. of *baptein* to dip, wash).

Var.: **Batisse**.

Cogns.: Prov.: **Bautiste**. It.: **Bat(t)ista, Bat(t)istio; Titta**. Sp.: **Bautista**. Cat.: **Batista**. Port.: **Baptista**. Eng.: **Baptist(e)**. Scot.: **Baptie**.

Dims.: It.: **Bat(t)istelli, Bat(t)istetti, Bat(t)istini, Bat(t)istuzzi, Bat(t)istucci, Bat(t)istotti**.

Augs.: It.: **Bat(t)istoni, Tittoni**.

Patrs.: It.: **Di Bat(t)ista**.

Barabino Italian: nickname for a ruffian, from a dim. of the Aramaic personal name *Bar-abas* 'son of *Aba*', a byname meaning 'father'. This was the name borne by the thief whose life was demanded by the crowd in Jerusalem in preference to that of Jesus (Matt. 27: 15–21). The surname is especially common in Liguria, in and around Genoa.

Baragwanath Cornish: metonymic occupational name for a baker of fancy loaves, from Corn. *bara* bread + *gwaneth* wheat, or a nickname for someone who would eat only wheat bread; everyday loaves were made of coarser rye or barley. Cf. WHITBREAD.

Var.: **Baragwaneth**.

Barahona Spanish: habitation name from places in the provinces of Segovia and Soria, of uncertain etymology (the first element possibly LL *vara* fence; cf. BARAJAS).

Barajas Spanish: habitation name from places in the provinces of Cuenca and Madrid; the latter is now the site of an international airport. The placename is of uncertain origin, but may be from LL *varālia* fencing, a deriv. of *vara* fence (of Celt. origin).

Baranda Spanish: habitation name from a place in the province of Burgos. Many different explanations of the origin of the placename have been offered, but none is convincing and the etymology remains uncertain.

Cogns.: Port.: **Varanda(s)**.

Baranov Russian: patr. from the nickname *Baran* 'Ram', which was given either to a forceful or lusty man or else to a shepherd.

Cogns.: Ukr.: **Baran** (nickname). Pol.: **Baran(ski)** (nicknames); **Baranowicz** (patr.). Jewish (E Ashkenazic): **Baran**, BARON (ornamental names); **Baranovich, Baranovitz, Baranowitz** (patrs. in form, but possibly also habitation names from *Baranowicze*, formerly in Poland, now part of the Soviet Union). Hung.: **Bárány** ('lamb').

Dims.: Beloruss.: **Baranchik**. Pol.: **Baraniek**. Czech: **Béránek**. Jewish: **Baranchuk**.

Baranowski Polish and Jewish (E Ashkenazic): habitation name from a place named with Pol. *baran* ram, + the possessive suffix *-ów* (a common placename element), with the addition of the suffix of surnames *-ski* (a standard adj. ending in Polish, cognate with Eng. *-ish*). In surnames *-ski* originally indicated association with a place, but soon came to be regarded as equivalent to Fr. *de* or Ger. *von*, and so indicative of gentry status. In many but by no means all cases, the bearer was indeed lord of the estate or manor to which the name referred. Later, the suffix came to be used much more widely to form surnames, being attached indiscriminately to given names (as *Adamski*), nicknames, and occupational names (as *Bednarski*), as well as to habitation names. Baranowski is therefore probably a habitation name in origin, but in some cases it may be no more than an elaboration of a nickname, *Baran*, meaning 'Ram' (see BARANOV).

The suffix *-ski* is also found as an ending of Russ. surnames, but these are generally of Pol. origin or formed under Pol. influence. The Czech cogn. suffix *-ský* is very much less common, and tends to be more strictly associated with habitation names. *-ski* is also found as a suffix of E Ashkenazic Jewish surnames. By the time most Jews on Polish territory were acquiring family names, in the late 18th and early 19th cents., it was already very widely used as a general surname suffix. In Jewish surnames, therefore, it is found attached to several different kinds of stems, including some of non-Slavic origin, as in the E Ashkenazic surname *Kohansky* (see COHEN). In English-speaking countries, most Jews bearing surnames with this suffix spell it *-sky*.

Vars.: Jewish: **Baranovski, Baranovsky**.

Barbary 1. English: from the female given name *Barbara*, which was borne by an enormously popular but almost certainly non-existent saint, who according to legend was imprisoned in a tower and later put to death by her own father for refusing to recant her Christian beliefs. The name comes from a fem. form of L *barbarus*, Gk *barbaros* foreign(er) (originally an onomatopoeic word formed in imitation of the unintelligible babbling of non-Greeks).

2. Provençal: from a dim. of OProv. *barbare* foreigner, barbarian; see above. In particular it came to be used for a Moor or *Berber* from the *Barbary* Coast in N Africa, and hence was applied to a man of swarthy appearance or uncouth habits.

Vars. (of 1): Eng.: **Barbara; Barbery** (Cornwall). (Of 2): Prov.: **Barbarin, Barbarou(x)**.

Cogns. (of 1): It.: **Barbara; Varvara, Varveri** (S Italy). Port.: **Bárbara**.

Dims. (of 1): Eng.: BABB. It. **Barbarelli, Barbarino, Barbarotto, Barbarulo**.

Pejs. (of 1): It.: **Barbarac(c)i**.

Metrs. (from 1): Russ.: **Varvarin; Varvarinski** (clerical).

Metrs. (from 1 (dim.)): Russ.: **Varvarkin, Varyushin**.

Barbe French: 1. nickname for someone with a beard, OF *barbe* (L *barba*).

2. from a pet form of the given name *Barbara*; see BARBARY.

Vars. (of 1): **Barbé, Barbu(t); Alabarbe**.

Cogns. (of 1): Prov.: **Barba**. It.: **Barba; Barbato, Barbuto; Barboso**. Sp.: **Barba; Barbado, Barbudo**. Cat.: **Barba**. Port.: **Barbas; Barbudo**. Rum.: **Barbu**.

Dims. (of 1): Fr.: **Barbet, Barbin, Barby, Barbot, Barbon**. It.: **Barbella, Barb(ol)ini, Barbetti, Barbucci, Barbuzzi**. Sp.: **Barbadillo**.

Augs. (of 1): Fr.: **Barbas, Barb(u)at**. It.: **Barbone**.

Pej. (of 1): It.: **Barbacci**.

Patr. (from 1): Rum.: **Barbulesco**.

Barber 1. English: occupational name for a barber (ANF *barber*, OF *barbier*, from LL *barbārius*, a deriv. of *barba* beard; see BARBE 1), who in the Middle Ages was a person who not only cut hair and shaved beards, but also practised surgery and pulled teeth.

2. Jewish (Ashkenazic): of uncertain origin. Since the name is found in areas where English influence is highly unlikely, it cannot always, if ever, be an Anglicization of some semantically equivalent Jewish surname. Possibly it is an acronymic surname from Hebr. *bar-* 'son of ...', with a male given name beginning with *B-* (cf. BROCK).

Var. (of 1): **Barbour** (Scots and N Irish).

Cogns. (of 1): Fr.: **Barbier, Barbié, Barbieux**. It.: **Barb(i)eri**. Sp.: **Barbero**. Cat.: **Barber**. Port.: **Barbeiro**. Hung.: **Borbély**.

Dims. (of 1): Fr.: **Barbereau, Barberet, Barberon, Barberot.** It.: **Barberini, Barbarolli.**

Patrs. From 1): It.: **De Barb(i)eri, De Barberis.** Du.: **Barbiers.**

Barberton *is the name of a S African family, whose surname was* Barber *until Frederick Barber founded the town of Barberton in 1884; some members of the family kept the original name. They were originally from Derbys., where they were foresters in the 13th cent.; they include Richard* le Barbur, *who was involved in a lawsuit in 1283, and Thomas* Barbur, *a surgeon at the Battle of Agincourt (1415).*

Barberà Catalan: habitation name from a place in the province of Tarragona, so called from LL *Barbariānum* 'place of *Barbarius*', a deriv. of *Barbarus* (see BARBARY).

Vars.: **Barbarà, Barberàn.**

Barbosa Portuguese: topographic name for someone who lived on a piece of land overgrown with leafy vegetation, from LL *barbōsa (terra)* 'bearded' land (cf. BARBE 1).

Barceló Catalan: habitation name from *Barcelona*, the principal city of Catalonia. The placename is of uncertain, certainly pre-Roman, origin. The settlement was established by the Carthaginians, and according to tradition it was named from the Carthaginian ruling house of *Barca*; the L form was *Barcino, Barcilo*.

Bárcena Spanish: habitation name from any of various places, for example in the provinces of Biscay, Burgos, León, Oviedo, Palencia, and Santander, so called from a pre-Roman topographical element **bargina*, descriptive of an area of cultivated land.

Vars.: **Bárcenas; Barcina** (a place in Burgos).

Dim.: **Barcenilla** (places in Burgos, Palencia, and Santander).

Barclay English and Scots: habitation name from *Berkeley* in Gloucs., or possibly in a few cases from another place similarly named, e.g. *Berkely* in Somerset. The placename is derived from OE *be(o)rc* BIRCH + *lēah* wood, clearing. For the change of *-er-* to *-ar-* in ME, cf. MARCHANT. The surname is particularly common in Scotland, whither it was brought by a Berkeley from Gloucs. in the 12th cent.; Walter *de Berchelai* or *Berkelai* was Chamberlain of Scotland in 1165.

Vars.: **Berk(e)ley; Barkley** (N Ireland).

Barclays *Bank was founded by John Barclay (1728–87) of Cambridge Heath in London. He was a grandson of Robert Barclay of Urie in Kincardine (b. 1648), and ultimately a descendant of the Norman Walter* de Berkeley *of Gartley, who, according to family tradition, was the son of a certain Roger de Berkeley mentioned in Domesday Book as the holder of Berkeley Castle in Gloucs.*

The Russian general Prince Mikhail Barclay de Tolly (1761–1818) was ultimately of Scottish descent; a branch of the family had settled in Mecklenburg and Livonia.

Barco Spanish: 1. metonymic occupational name for a boatman or ferryman, from Sp. *barco* boat (L *barca*).

2. habitation name from any of various places, for example in the provinces of Avila and Orense, called *(El) Barco*. These are of uncertain etymology, possibly from the Celt. element *berg, barg* height, eminence. The name could also be related to the N Italian dial. term *barco* haystack, hayloft (possibly of pre-Roman origin). In this case the name may have been given originally to a hill shaped like a haystack.

Var. (of 1): **Barquero.**

Barcroft English: habitation name from a place so called from OE *bere* barley + *croft* paddock, smallholding. For the change of *-er-* to *-ar-* in ME, cf. MARCHANT.

This is the name of an Irish family established in Ireland by William Barcroft *(1612–96), who settled in King's County. They can be traced to the parish of Barcroft, Lancs., in the reign of Henry III (1216–72).*

Bard 1. Scots: occupational name from Gael. *bàrd* poet, minstrel, singer.

2. Scots: perhaps a habitation name, to judge from the earliest forms—Henry *de Barde* and Richard *de Baard*—but no suitable place has been identified, and *de* occasionally occurs, either by analogy or by mistake, for *le*.

3. French: from the Gmc personal name *Bardo*, a short form of any of the rare cpd names with the first element *bard*, perhaps from *barta* axe.

4. French: habitation name from any of the several minor places called *Bar(d)*, from the Gaul. element *barro* height, hill (cf. BARR 3).

5. French: metonymic occupational name for someone who used a handcart or barrow in his work, from OF *bard* barrow (of uncertain origin, possibly akin to a Gmc element meaning 'carry, bear'). Dims. of this vocab. word were also used to denote beasts of burden, and so the surname may have originated as an occupational name for a driver of pack animals or as a nickname for an overworked servant.

6. French: from OF *bart* mud, clay (LL *barrum*, apparently of Celt. origin), in which case it is either a topographic name for someone living in a muddy area or an occupational name for a builder or bricklayer.

7. Jewish (Ashkenazic): possibly an acronymic surname from Hebr. *bar-* 'son of...', with a male given name beginning with *D-*, such as *David* (cf. BROCK). However, it is more likely to be a nickname for someone with a luxurious beard, from a blend of Ger. *Bart* and Yid. *bord*, both meaning 'beard'.

Vars.: **Bar(t).** (Of 3 only): **Bardon** (oblique case).

Cogns. (of 3): It.: **Bardi, Pardi.** (Of 4): Cat.: **Bas** (the name of several minor places in the province of Gerona). (Of 6): Sp.: BARROS, BARRERA; **Barroso** ('muddy'; also a nickname for a man with a ruddy complexion, from the reddish colour of potter's clay). Port.: **Barr(eir)os, Barroso.**

Dims. (of 3): Fr.: **Bardonneau, Bardonnet.** It.: **Bardell(in)i, Bardetti, Bardotti, Barducci; Pardelli, Pardini, Parducci** (Liguria). (Of 5): **Bardet, Bardot, Bardy, Bardinet, Bardinot, Bardineau, Bardinon.**

Augs. (of 3): It.: **Bard(i)oni.**

Pejs. (of 3): It.: **Bardacci, Bardazzi.**

Patrs. (from 1): Sc.: **Baird** (Gael. **Mac an Baird**). Ir.: **McAward, McWard, Quard, Ward** (Gael. **Mac an Bhaird**).

Collectives (of 6): Port.: **Barreto, Barradas.**

Barde Provençal: metonymic occupational name for someone who made and sold spades, or used them in his work, from OProv. *barda* spade (which probably derives from It., and ultimately from Arabic *barda'a*).

Barden English: habitation name from places in N and W Yorks., so called from OE *bere* barley (or the derived adj. *beren*) + *denu* valley (see DEAN 1).

Bardsley English: habitation name from a place in Lancs., so called from the gen. case of the OE personal name *Beornrēd* (composed of the elements *beorn* young warrior + *rǣd* counsel, advice) + OE *lēah* wood, clearing. There may have been some confusion with BEARDSLEY.

Bardwell English: habitation name from a place in Suffolk, so called from the OE byname *Bearda* (a deriv. of *beard* BEARD; cf. BEARDSLEY) + OE *well(a)* spring, stream (see WELL). An alternative possibility is that the first element may be from a dissimilated form of OE *bre(o)rd* brim, bank.

Vars.: **Beardwell, Bardell.**

Bärenreiter German: habitation name from the village of *Bernreut* in Bavaria, so called from MHG *brennen* to burn + *reut* clearing, i.e. a clearing made by burning trees. The name has been assimilated by folk etymology to Ger. 'bear rider' (from *Bär* bear + *reiten* to ride), which is a name given to the star Alkor in the Great Bear constellation.

Vars.: **Bernreut(h), Bernreith.**

Barfield English: 1. habitation name, probably from *Bardfield* in Essex, so called from OE *byrde* riverbank + *feld* cultivated land; the name is still most common in N Essex.

2. topographic name for someone who lived by an area where barley was cultivated, from ME *berefeld*.

The earliest recorded bearer of the name is Walter de Bardfield, *who received a grant of land in Bardfield itself* c.*1175. Genealogically, a line has been traced from the present day to Samuel Barfield (or Barfold), who was living in Ixworth, Suffolk, in about 1650.*

Barfoot English: nickname for someone who was in the habit of going about his business unshod, from OE *bær* bare, naked + *fōt* foot. It may have referred to a peasant unable to afford even the simplest type of footwear, or to someone who went barefoot as a religious penance. Black, however, is convinced that as a Scots surname it is 'doubtless of local origin'.

Var.: **Barefoot.**

Cogns.: Ger.: **Barfuss.** Low Ger.: **Barfoth, Barfaut.** Dan.: **Barfo(e)d.**

Bargalló Catalan: topographic name for someone who lived by a fan palm or palmetto, a tropical plant that grows on the Mediterranean coast and on the Balearic islands. The word has been derived from L *barba Jovis* 'Jupiter's beard', but is far more likely to come from Mozarabic *(a)bregalyon*, ultimately from LL *africānio*, gen. *africāniōnis*, a deriv. of *Africa*, the original home of the plant.

Barge English and French: metonymic occupational name for a boatman or mariner, from ME, OF *barge* boat, barge (L *barca*).

Vars.: Eng.: **Bargeman.** Fr.: **Barque.**

Dims.: Fr.: **Bargeton, Barjon, Barjou, Barjot.**

Barham English: habitation name from any of the various places so called. Most, for example those in Cambs. and Suffolk, are so called from OE *beorg* hill (see BERG) + *hām* homestead. The one in Kent, however, gets its first element from the OE byname *Biora, Beora* (a deriv. of *bera* BEAR).

Vars.: **Bareham, Barhams, Barhem(s), Barhims.**

A family of this name trace their descent from the Norman barons FitzUrse. When Reginald FitzUrse fled to Ireland after the murder of Thomas Becket in 1170, his estate at Barham, Kent, came into the hands of another branch of the family, which took its name from it. The first known bearer of the surname is Warine de Berham, *recorded in Kent in 1203; Richard de Berham, sheriff of Kent in 1390–91, may well have been a descendant. The surname is still largely confined to the Home Counties and E Anglia.*

Baril French: metonymic occupational name for a cooper, or a nickname for a rotund man, from OF *baril* barrel (of uncertain origin, perhaps a deriv. of *bar(r)e* bar; cf. BARR 1, 2).

Vars.: **Barial, Barral, Barrau(d), Barrau(l)t, Bar(r)aux; Barill(i)er, Barralier, Barrailler** (occupational names).

Cogns.: Eng.: **Barrell** (see also BARWELL). It.: **Bar(r)ile, Barilli; Labarile** (S Italy); **Baril(l)aro.** Sp.: **Barril; Barrilero.** Flem.: **Bareel.**

Dims.: Fr.: **Bar(il)let, Bar(il)lot, Bar(r)illon, Barlon.** It.: **Bar(i)letti, Bariglietti, Barletta, Barilini, Barilotti, Barilucci.**

Augs: It.: **Barilone, Bariglione.**

Barish Jewish (Ashkenazic): acronymic surname from a Hebrew-Aramaic patr. phrase *Bar Rabi SHelomo, SHemuel, SHimon, SHimshon*, etc., i.e. 'son of (rabbi) SALOMON, SAMUEL, SIMON, SAMSON', or some other male given name beginning with SH-. Cf. BROCK.

Vars.: **B(a)rasch, Barash, Brosch, Brisch.**

Barker English: 1. occupational name for a tanner of leather, from ME *bark(en)* to tan (from the *bark* of a tree, which was used in the process; the word is of Scand. origin, and is probably cogn. with OE *be(o)rc*, a byform of *bi(e)rce* BIRCH).

2. occupational name for a shepherd, ANF *bercher* (LL *berbicārius*, from *berbex*, gen. *berbicis*, ram). With the change of *-ar-* to *-er-* in ME, this became indistinguishable from the preceding name.

Cogns. (of 2): Fr.: **Berger, Bergey** (E France), **Berget** (N France). Prov.: **Berg(u)ier.**

Dims. (of 2): Fr.: **Bergeret, Bergerot, Bergeron, Berger(onn)eau.** Prov.: **Bergerioux.**

Barley English: 1. habitation name from any of various places so called. Those in Lancs. and W Yorks. get the name from OE *bār* wild boar or *bær* barley + *lēah* wood, clearing. A place of the same name in Herts. has as its first element the OE byname *Be(o)ra* (from *bera* BEAR).

2. metonymic occupational name for a grower or seller of barley, from OE *bærlic*, originally an adj. deriv. of *bær* barley (a byform of *bere*; cf. BARCROFT and BARDEN).

Vars.: **Barlee.** (Of 2 only): **Barleyman.**

Barlow English: habitation name from any of several places so called, esp. those in Lancs. and W Yorks. The former gets its name from OE *bere* barley + *hlāw* hill; the latter probably has as its first element the derived adj. *beren* or the cpd *bere-ærn* barn. There is also a place of this name in Derbys., so called from OE *bār* boar or *bær* barley + *lēah* wood, clearing, and one in Shrops., which is from *bær* barley + *lēah*.

Barnaby English: 1. from the ME vernacular form of the given name *Barnabas*, borne by the companion of St Paul (Acts 4: 36). This is of Aramaic origin, from *Bar-nabia* 'son of *Nabia*', a personal name perhaps meaning 'confession'.

2. habitation name from a place in N Yorks., so called from the OE personal name *Beornwald* (composed of the elements *beorn* young warrior + *wald* rule) + ON *býr* settlement.

Vars.: **Barnabe(e), Barneby.**

Cogns (of 1): Fr.: **Barnabé; Bernabé** (the *-er-* being the result of hypercorrection). Prov.: **Barnaba.** It.: **Barnabe(i), Barnaba, Barnobi, Bernabe, Bernab(e)o, Bernaba.** Sp.: **Bernabé.** Cat.: **Bernabeu.** Hung.: **Barna.**

Dims. (of 1): It.: **Barna, Barn(in)i, Barnabucci.**

Barnes 1. English: topographic name or occupational name for someone who lived or worked at a barn, from the gen. case or pl. of ME *barn* barn, granary (OE *bern*, originally a cpd of *bere* barley + *ærn* house, building). The placename *Barnes* (on the Surrey bank of the Thames in W London) has the same origin, and some bearers may be members of families hailing from there.

2. English: name borne by the son or servant of a *barne*, a term used in the early Middle Ages for a member of the upper classes, although its precise meaning is not clear (it derives from OE *beorn*/ON *barn* young warrior, akin to the Gmc element *ber(an)* BEAR). Barne was also occasionally used as a given name (from an OE/ON byname), and some examples of the surname may derive from this use.

3. Irish: Anglicized form of Gael. **Ó Bearáin** 'descendant of *Bearán*', a byname meaning 'Spear'.

4. Jewish: probably a var. of PARNES.

Vars. (of 1 and 2): **Barne, Barns**. (Of 3): BARRINGTON. (Of 4): **Barness**.

Barnet English: 1. habitation name from any of the numerous places, for example in N London, so called from OE *bærnet* place cleared by burning (a deriv. of *bærnan* to burn, set light to).

2. from a medieval given name, a var. of BERNARD or cogn. of BERAUD.

Var.: **Barnett**.

Barnfield English: habitation name from some minor place (probably in the W Midlands, where the name is commonest) so called, probably from OE *bern* barn (see BARNES 1) + *feld* pasture, open country (see FIELD).

Barnsley English: habitation name from any of the several places so called, notably one in W Yorks. (from the gen. case of the OE byname *Beorn* 'Warrior' + OE *lēah* wood, clearing) and one in Gloucs. (from the gen. case of the OE personal name *Beornmōd* ('warrior spirit') + *lēah*). The surname is common in the Birmingham area as well as in W Yorks.

Barnum English: 1. habitation name from one of the various places, for example in Norfolk, Suffolk, and W Sussex, called *Barnham*. They are probably all so called from the OE byname *Beorn(a)* (see BARNES 2) + OE *hām* homestead.

2. topographic or occupational name for someone who lived or worked at a group of barns, from the dat. pl. of OE *bern* (see BARNES 1).

Var. (of 1): **Barnham**.

Barnwell English: habitation name from a place so called; there is one in Cambs. and another in Northants. The former derives its name from OE *beorna* warriors' + *well(a)* stream; the latter from OE *byrgen* burial mound, barrow + *well(a)*.

Var.: **Barnewall**.

An Irish family named Barnewall *can be traced back to Sir Michael* de Berneval *or* Barneval *who took part in Strongbow's expedition in 1172. He first held land in Berehavan, Cork, before the main landing in Leinster. The name has been Gaelicized as* **de Bearnabhal**.

Baron 1. English and French: from the title of nobility, ME, OF *baron, barun* (of Gmc origin; cf. BARNES 2). As a surname it is unlikely to be a status name denoting a person of rank. The great baronial families of Europe had distinctive surnames of their own. However, 'baron' in Scotland denoted a member of a class of minor landowners who had a certain degree of jurisdiction over the local populace, and the title was also awarded to certain freemen of the cities of London and York and of the Cinque Ports; either of these uses might be the source of a surname. Far more commonly, however, the surname is derived from an OF personal name *Baro* (oblique case *Baron*), or else referred to service in a baronial household or was acquired as a nickname by a peasant who had ideas above his station.

2. Irish: Anglicized form of Gael. *Ó Bearáin*; see BARNES.

3. Jewish: of uncertain origin, possibly a var. of *Baran* (see BARANOV), or from the Hebrew-Aramaic patr. phrase *bar-Aharon* 'son of AARON', or an ornamental name meaning 'baron'. In Israel the surname is often interpreted, by folk etymology, as being from *Bar-On* 'Son of Strength'.

Var. (of 1 and 2): **Barron**.

Cogns. (of 1): Prov.: **Barou(x)**. It.: **Barone, Baronio, Var(r)one, Varune**. Sp.: **Barón**. Cat.: **Baró**. Flem., Du.: **Baroen**.

Dims. (of 1): Fr.: **Baronnet**. It.: **Barontini, Baroncini, Baroncelli**.

Barr 1. Scots and N Irish: habitation name from any of the many places in SW Scotland that get their names from Gael. *barr* height, hill, or from a Brit. cognate.

2. English: topographic name for someone who lived by a gateway or barrier, from ME, OF *barre* bar, obstruction (of obscure origin, possibly akin to the Celt. element *barr* height and therefore cogn. with 1).

3. English (Norman): habitation name from *Barre*-en-Ouche in Eure or *Barre*-de-Semilly in Manche. These places derive their names from the same word as in 2.

4. English: metonymic occupational name for a maker of bars, or nickname for a tall, thin man, from special applications of the ME, OF word *barre*.

5. English: habitation name from any of various places, as for example Great *Barr* in the W Midlands, named with the Celt. element *barro* height, hill (cf. BRYAN). This is also the origin of various Fr. placenames, as for example *Barre* in Lozère (cf. BARD 4).

6. Irish: see BARRY 6.

Cogns. (of 2 and 3): Fr.: **Barre, Labarre, Delabarre, Desbarres**; **Barrée, Labarrée** (Anglicized **Labarree**, the name of a wealthy New England family). Prov.: **Barada**. Du.: **Baars** (see also BASS 2); **(Van) Baaren, Van der Baaren, Van Baren**.

Dims. (of 2 and 3): Fr.: **Barret, Barrel(le), Bar(r)eau, Barrelet, Barrot**. Prov.: **Baradel, Baradeau**. Sp.: **Bar(r)ella**.

Augs. (of 2 and 3): Prov.: **Baradas, Baradat**.

Barraclough English (mainly Yorks.): habitation name from *Barrowclough* near Halifax in W Yorks., so called from OE *bearu* grove (see BARROW 1) + *clōh* ravine (see CLOUGH).

Vars: **Barrowclough**; **Barrowcliff(e)** (Notts.); **Barnaclough, Berecloth, Berrycloth**.

Barragán Spanish: 1. nickname for a strong or brave man, from Sp. *barragán* young man, warrior (of uncertain origin, probably a deriv. of a Gmc element; cf. BARNES 2).

2. metonymic occupational name for a maker or seller of a kind of material, Sp. *barragán* (from Arabic *barrakân*).

Barranco Spanish: habitation name from any of various minor places, for example in the province of Alicante, named with the topographical term *barranco* ravine, gorge (of pre-Roman origin).

Barré French: from the past part. of OF *barrer*, a deriv. of *barre* bar (see BARR 2). Both verb and noun had a large number of senses in OF and it is not certain what the original meaning of the name was. It may sometimes have been a topographic name for a person who lived in a place that was naturally cut off or particularly well fortified, but in most cases it was more probably a nickname meaning 'striped', referring to a habitual wearer of striped clothing or possibly to someone with a noticeable birthmark. In the Middle Ages the term was applied to the Carmelite Friars, who wore habits striped in black, yellow, and white, but in view of the celibacy of the clergy it is unlikely that this is the origin of many instances of the name, unless as a nickname for someone supposedly resembling a Carmelite in some way.

Barrena Basque: topographic name for someone who lived in a dip or hollow or at the bottom of a slope, from *barren* lowest point + the def. art. *-a*.

Barrenechea Spanish form of Basque **Barrenetxea**: topographic name for someone who lived in a house in a dip or hollow or at the bottom of a slope, from Basque *barren* lowest point + *etxe* house + the def. art. *-a*.

Barrera Spanish: 1. topographic name for someone who lived near a gate or fence, from Sp. *barrera* barrier (a deriv. of BARR 2).

2. topographic name for someone who lived by a clay-pit, Sp. *barrera*, *barrero* (a deriv. of *barro* mud, clay; cf. BARROS 1 and BARD 6).

Cogn.: Port.: **Barreira.**

Barrett English: 1. from a Gmc personal name introduced into England by the Normans; see BERNARD and BERAUD.

2. nickname for a quarrelsome or deceitful person, from ME *bar(r)et(t)e*, *bar(r)at* trouble, strife, deception, cheating (OF *barat* commerce, dealings, a deriv. of *barater* to barter, haggle, LL *prattāre*, from Gk *prattein* to do, practise). It is possible that the original sense of *barat* survived unrecorded into ME as a word for a market trader; the It. cogns. have this sense.

3. nickname or metonymic occupational name from OF *barette* cap, bonnet (LL *birrum* hood, cowl, of Celt. origin).

Vars.: **Barret, Barrat(t), Barritt.**

Cogns. (of 2): Fr.: **Bara(t), Baratte; Baratier.** It.: **Barat(ta); Barat(i)eri.** Port.: **Barata.**

Dims. (of 2): Fr.: **Baratin, Baraton, Barateau.** Prov.: **Baratoux.** It.: **Barattini, Barattucci.**

Aug. (of 2): **Barattoni.**

Barriga Spanish: nickname for someone with a large belly, from Sp. *barriga* belly, paunch. The word may be BARIL, and may originally have had the same sense, but this is not evidenced in the Middle Ages and is unlikely to lie behind the surname.

Barrington 1. English: habitation name from any of several places of this name. The one in Gloucs. is so called from OE *Beorningtūn* 'settlement (OE *tūn*) associated with *Beorn*' (see BARNES 2); the one in Somerset was probably named as the 'settlement associated with **Bāra*'; the one in Cambs. gets its first element from the gen. case of the personal name **Bāra*.

2. Irish: Anglicized form of Gael. *Ó Bearáin*; see BARNES 3.

Barrio Spanish: topographic name for someone who lived on the outskirts of a town, from Sp. *barrio* outlying region (Arabic *barr* suburb, dependent village).

Var.: **Barrios.**

Barros Spanish: 1. topographic name for someone who lived on a patch of muddy land or clay soil; cf. BARD 6.

2. nickname for someone with a birthmark or a spotty complexion, from Sp. *barro* spot, mark (LL *varus*).

Barrow English: 1. topographic name for someone who lived by a grove, OE *bearo*, *bearu* (dat. *bear(o)we*, *bearuwe*), or habitation name from any of the numerous places named with this word, in Ches., Derbys., Gloucs., Lancs., Leics., Lincs., Shrops., Suffolk, and Somerset.

2. topographic name for someone who lived by a hill or burial mound, OE *beorg* (dat. *beorge*, ME *berwe*, *barwe*; cf. BERG), or habitation name from either of the places named with this word, near Leicester and in Somerset.

3. habitation name from *Barrow* in Furness, Cumb., which gets its name from Celt. *barro-*, here meaning 'promontory'.

Vars.: (of 1 and 2): **Barrows, Barrass; Berrow** (W Midlands). (Of 2 only): **Bar(u)gh, Barff** (pronounced /bɑːf/; cf. *Barff* Hill in E Yorks. and *Barugh* in N Yorks.).

Barry 1. English and French: topographic name from ANF *barri* rampart, later a suburb outside the rampart of a town (a word of uncertain origin, perhaps a technical term derived from Sp. BARRIO).

2. Scots: habitation name from any of various places, esp. one in the former county of Angus, probably so called from Gael. *borrach* rough grassy hill.

3. Welsh: patr. from HARRY, the medieval Eng. vernacular form of HENRY, preceded by W *ap* 'son of'.

4. Welsh: habitation name from any of various places so called from W *barr* summit.

5. Irish: Anglicized form of Gael. **Ó Beargha** 'descendant of *Beargh*', a byname meaning 'Robber'.

6. Irish: Anglicized form of Gael. **Ó Báire** 'descendant of *Báire*', a short form of various personal names.

Vars. (of 1): Fr.: **Barri, Dubarry.** (Of 2): Sc.: **Barrie.**

Dims. (of 1): Fr.: **Barriol, Barrion.**

Barski Polish: 1. from *barć* wild honey bees' nest + *-ski* suffix of local surnames (see BARANOWSKI). It is therefore either a topographic name or an occupational name for a forester officially empowered to collect wild honey.

2. from a much reduced form of the given name *Bartłomiej* BARTHOLOMEW + *-ski*.

Barsukov Russian: patr. from the nickname *Barsuk* 'Badger' (of Turkic origin).

Cogn.: Jewish (E Ashkenazic): **Barsuk** (ornamental).

Barthe French: topographic name for someone who lived on a piece of land overgrown with bushes or scrub, OF *barthe* (apparently of Gaul. origin).

Vars.: **Barte, Labart(h)e; Barthès.**

Dims.: **Bart(h)et.**

Augs.: **Bart(h)as.**

Bartholomew 1. English: from a medieval given name, which is from the Aramaic patr. *bar-Talmay* 'son of *Talmay*', a given name meaning 'having many furrows', i.e. rich in land. As a given name in Christian Europe, it derived its popularity from the apostle St Bartholomew (Matt. 10: 3), the patron saint of tanners, vintners, and butlers, about whom virtually nothing is known.

2. Irish: Anglicized form of *Mac Pharthaláin*; see MCFARLANE.

Var.: **Bartlam** (Midlands).

Cogns.: Fr.: **Bart(h)él(e)my; Bert(h)él(e)my** (hypercorrected). Prov.: **Bart(h)olomicu, Bartomieu, Bert(h)omieu, Bourt(h)oumieux; Bert(h)ouloume, Bourt(h)ouloume; Bert(h)omé, Bert(h)omier.** It.: **Bartolo(m)meo; Bortolomei** (Venetia, Emilia); **Tolomei, Tom(m)e(i)** (Tuscany; see also THOMAS); **Tolomio** (Venetia); **Meo.** Sp.: **Bartolomé.** Cat.: **Bartomeu, Bertomeu.** Port.: **Bartolomeu.** Ger.: **Bart(h)olomä(us).** Low Ger.: **Barthelme(s); Meus, Meb(i)(u)s, Möbius, Miebes.** Flem., Du.: **Bartolomivis; Mewe, Mewis, Mee(u)s, Meys, Mebes.** Ger. (of Slav. origin): **Bartosch.** Czech: **Bárta, Barták, Bartoš, Bartoň.** Pol.: **Bartłomiej; Bartosz.** Hung.: **Bàrta(l).**

Dims.: Eng.: **Bartlet(t), Bartleet; Bart(le); Barty, Bartie;** BATE; BATT. Fr.: **Bert(h)elémot; Bart(h)ol(in), Bert(h)olin;**

Bart(h)el(et), Bert(h)el(et); Bart(h)ot, Bert(h)ot, Bart(h)od. It.: **Bartolomeotti, Bartolomucci; Bartol(in)i, Bartal(in)i, Bartoletti, Bartaletti, Bartolozzi, Bartalucci; Bartelli, Bartocci, Bartozzi; Vartoli** (Calabria); **Bortol(i), Bartul, Bortoletti, Bortolotti, Bortolozzi, Bortolini, Bortolutti, Bortoluzzi, Bortolussi** (Venetia); **Tolomelli, Tolumello; Tolotti, Tolossi, Tolussi.** Ger.: **Bart(h)(el), Bartl** (see also BEARD). Du., Flem.: **Ba(e)rt; Bartolijn, Bartoleyn.** Ger. (of Slav. origin): **Bartke, Bartek; Bach(ur)a, Bachnik.** Czech: **Bartošek, Bartušek, Bartůnek.** Pol.: **Bartłomiejczyk, Bartoszek, Bartosik.** Hung.: **Bartók, Bertók.**

Augs.: Fr.: **Bart(h)olat.** It.: **Bartolomeoni; Bartaloni, Bortoloni; Toloni.**

Pejs.: It.: **Bartolomeazzi, Bartolacci, Bortolazzi, Meazzi, Miazzi.**

Patrs.: It.: **Di Bartolom(m)eo; Di Meo, (De) Meis.** Pol.: **Bartoszewicz; Bartosiak.** Russ.: **Varfolomeev, Varfalameev; Vachrameev, Bachrameev, Achrameev, Achromov; Folomeev, Falameev.** Lithuanian: **Baltrushaitis.**

Patrs. (from dims.): Eng.: **Barson.** It.: **Di Bartoli.** Ger.: **Bart(h)els.** Low Ger.: **Bar(t)z(en).** Du., Flem.: **Ba(e)rts, Bartens; Mees(s)en(s), Meuwissen.** Russ.: **Vakhrushev, Vakhrushkov, Vakhrushin, Bakhrush(k)in; Vakh(l)ov, Vakh(o)nin; Folomin, Folomkin, Folonin; Cholomin, Chalonin.** Beloruss.: **Bartoshevich, Butrimovich.** Pol.: **Bartkiewicz; Bartłomieczak, Bartczak.** Croatian: **Bartolić.**

Habitation names: Pol.: **Bartoszewski, Bartos(z)iński; Bar(sz)czewski, Barczyński; Bartkowiak.**

Bartley English: habitation name from a place in Hants so called, or from *Bartley* Green in the W Midlands, both of which derive their name from OE *be(o)rc* birch + *lēah* wood, clearing; cf. BARCLAY.

Barton 1. English: habitation name from any of the numerous places so called from OE *bere* or *bær* barley + *tūn* enclosure, settlement, i.e. an outlying grange. Cf. BARWICK.

2. U.S.: Anglicization of Czech *Bartoň*, a form of BARTHOLOMEW.

Var. (of 1): **Barten.**

Baruch Jewish: from the Hebr. male given name *Baruch* 'blessed', 'fortunate'. This was borne by a disciple of Jeremiah, who is the supposed author of one of the books of the Apocrypha.

Var.: **Barukh.**

Patrs.: **Baruchso(h)n; Boruchson** (from Yid. *Borekh*); **Boro(k)hov, Borochov, Boru(c)hov, Borochovski, Borochowski, Borochovi(t)ch, Borochovitz, Borohovich** (E Ashkenazic).

Barwell English: habitation name from a place in Leics., so called from OE *bār* wild boar + *well(a)* spring, stream (see WELL).

Barwick English: habitation name from any of various places, chiefly in Norfolk, Somerset, and W Yorks., so called from OE *bere* barley + *wīc* outlying farm, i.e. a granary lying some distance away from the main village. Cf. BARTON.

Vars.: **Barrick, Berwick, Berrick, Borwick.**

Baryła Polish: from Pol. *barył* barrel, applied either as a metonymic occupational name for a cooper or as a nickname for a fat man.

Var.: **Barylski** (with surname suffix *-ski*; see BARANOWSKI).

Baryshnikov Russian: patr. from the nickname *Baryshnik* 'Lucky man' (a deriv. of *barysh* profit, gain).

Basch Jewish: acronymic surname from the Hebr. patr. phrases *Ben SHelomo*, *SHemuel*, *SHimon*, or *SHimshon*. See BARISH; see also BROCK.

Basham English: habitation name of uncertain origin. It may be from places in Norfolk and Suffolk called *Barsham*, from the gen. case of the OE byname *Bār* 'wild boar' + OE *hām* homestead.

Vars.: **Bassham, Barsham.**

Bashford English (W Midlands): habitation name from one of the several places called *Basford*, esp. the one in Staffs. There are others in Ches. and Notts. All are named from a personal name + OE *ford* FORD. The first element in the Staffs. place is *Beorcol*, in the Notts. place *Basa*, and in the Ches. place probably ON *Barkr*.

Vars.: **Bas(s)ford.**

Basil English and French: from a medieval given name spelled thus, ultimately from Gk *Basileios* 'Royal', the name borne by a 4th-cent. bishop of Caesarea in Cappadocia, regarded as one of the four Fathers of the Eastern Church; he wrote important theological works and established a rule for religious orders of monks. In some cases the surname also comes from the fem. form of the given name, ME, OF *Basil(l)(i)e*. St Basilla (d. AD 304) was a Roman maiden who according to legend chose death rather than marry a pagan. Various other saints are also known under these and cogn. names; the popularity of *Vasili* as a Russ. given name is largely due to the fact that this was the Church name of St Vladimir (956–1015), Prince of Kiev, who was chiefly responsible for the introduction of Christianity to Russia.

Vars.: Eng.: **Bassil(l), Bazell(e); Baz(e)ley, Basel(e)y** (from the fem. form). Fr.: **Bazil(l)e.**

Cogns.: Prov.: **Basire.** It.: **Basile, Basili(o), Baseli(o), Base(ll)i; Baseggio, Beggi(o)** (Venetia); **Vasile** (Sicily). Port.: **Basílio.** Rum.: **Vasile, Vasiliu.** Pol.: **Wasiel.** Hung.: **Vászoly.**

Dims.: Fr.: BAZIN, **Basin, Basillon.** Prov.: **Barizeret.** It.: **Basilotta; Basezzi; Beggini.** Low Ger.: **Bäseke, Beseke.** Pol.: **Wasielczyk.** Ukr.: **Vas(s)il(ch)enko, Vashchenko, Vasilik, Vasilechko.** Beloruss.: **Bazylets, Vasilchenko, Vasilyonok.**

Aug.: It.: **Basilone.**

Patrs.: Russ.: **Vasilyev(ski), Vasil(man)ov.** Ukr.: **Vasilevich.** Beloruss.: **Bazilev, Basilevich, Vasilevich.** Bulg.: **Vasiliev.** Croatian: **Vasil(jev)ić, Vasić, Vasović.** Pol.: **Wasi(e)lewicz, Wasiela.** Rum.: **Vasiescu.** Georgian: **Bassilashvili.** Armenian: **Vassilian.**

Patrs. (from dims.): Pol.: **Wasylkiewicz.** Russ.: **Vasilishchev, Vasil(chi)kov, Vasiltsov; Vasenkov, Vasi(sh)chev, Vasentsov, Vasyaev, Vasyukhichev, Vasyukhnov, Vasyuchov, Vasyukov, Vasyun(k)in, Vasyu(sh)khin, Vasyunichev, Vasyut(k)in, Vasyutochkin, Vasyutichev; Vaskov, Vasnetsov, Vasnev, Vasechkin, Vasenin, Vasyagin, Vasyanin, Vasyatkin, Vas(k)in.**

Habitation name: Pol.: **Wasi(e)lewski, Bazylewski.**

Baskerville English (Norman): habitation name from *Boscherville* in Eure, Normandy, so called from ONF *boschet* copse, thicket (a dim. of BOIS) + *ville* settlement, town (see VILLE). The name is now found chiefly in Devon.

Vars.: **Baskwell, Baskerful, Baskerfield, Basketfield, Basterfield, Pasterfield, Pesterfield.**

Baskin Jewish (E Ashkenazic): metr. from the Yid. female given name *Basye*, from Hebr. *Batya* 'daughter of God'; cf. PESHIN.

Var.: **Baskind** (for the excrescent *-d*, see SÜSSKIND).

Bass 1. English: nickname for a short man, from ME, OF *bas(se)* low, short (L *bassus* thickset, i.e. wide as opposed to tall, itself used as a family name in the Republican period). In the later Middle Ages the word was also used metaphorically to mean 'of humble origin', but apparently without contemptuous overtones, and in some cases this may have given rise to the surname.

2. English: nickname for a person supposedly resembling a fish or metonymic occupational name for a fish-seller, from *bass* the fish, OE *bæs*.

3. Scots: habitation name from a place in the former county of Aberdeen (now part of Grampian region), apparently so called from Gael. *bathais* forehead, front. Andrew *de Bas* is recorded as a juror in 1206.

4. Jewish (Ashkenazic): of unknown origin.

Vars.: **Ba(i)se, Basse.**

Cogns. (of 1): Fr.: **Bas, Lebas.** It.: **(Li) Bassi, (Lo) Basso** (Naples); **(Lo) Bascio, Lovascio** (S Italy, Liguria). Sp.: **Bajo.** Du.: **(De) Bas.** (Of 2): Du.: **Baars** (see also BARR).

Dims. (of 1): Eng.: **Basset(t).** Fr.: **Basset, Bassot.** It.: **Bassini, Bassetti, Bassotti, Bassoli, Bassolino.**

Aug. (of 1): It.: **Bassone.**

Patrs. (from 1): It.: **(De) Bassis.**

Bastable English (W Midlands): of uncertain origin; possibly, as Reaney suggests, a habitation name from *Barnstaple* in Devon or *Barstable* Hall in Essex, both from OE *beard* + *stapol* post, and so meaning 'bearded post', apparently referring to a post with something resembling a beard attached to it. However, the traceable distribution of the name casts doubt on Reaney's suggestion.

Bastard English and French: nickname for an illegitimate child, ME, OF *bastard* (of uncertain origin, probably a pej. from *bast* pack saddle (L *bastum*), i.e. a child conceived on a makeshift couch rather than in the marriage bed). The surname was formerly far more common than now, when the vocab. word *bastard* has become a general term of abuse, so that many former bearers of it have changed their names.

Vars.: Fr. **(Le) Bâtard.**

Cogns.: It.: **Bastardo.** Ger.: **Bastard, Basthart.** Flem.: **Bastaerd.**

Dims.: Fr.: **Bastardeau, Bâtardeau; Bastardon.**

Bastard *is the name of a Devon family established at Kitley near Yealmpton since the late 17th cent.*

Basterra Basque: topographic name for someone who lived by a boundary, or on the edge of a settlement or the corner of a street, from *bazter* border, edge, corner + the def. art. *-a*.

Basterrechea Spanish form of Basque **Basterretxea**: topographic name for someone who lived in a house by a boundary or on a corner, from Basque *bazter* border, edge, corner + *etxe* house + the def. art. *-a*.

Bastide Provençal: habitation name from OProv. *bastide* building (LL *bastīta*, fem. sing. or neut. pl. past part. of *bastīre* to build, of Gmc origin). The term was used in particular of a number of small fortified villages that were established in the 13th and 14th cents. and inhabited by free citizens.

Vars.: **(La) Bastie, (La) Bâtie, Labastida.**

Cogns.: Cat.: **Bastida, Sabastida.**

Dim.: Prov.: **Bastidon.**

Bataille French: nickname for a combative person, or topographic name for someone who lived at a place remembered as the site of a military engagement, from OF *bat(t)aille* battle (a fem. noun from the LL neut. pl. *battālia* military exercises, a deriv. of *batt(u)ere* to beat, strike, probably of Gmc origin).

Vars.: **Battaille; Bat(t)aill(i)er** (an agent noun).

Cogns.: Eng.: BATTLE. It.: **Battaglia; Battaia** (Lombardy); **Battaglieri** (an agent noun). Sp.: **Battala.** Cat.: **Battala; Battaler.** Port.: **Batalha.**

Dims.: Fr.: **Bat(t)aillon.** It.: **Batta(gl)ini, Battai(gl)ioli.**

Augs.: It.: **Battai(gl)ioni.**

Pejs.: Fr.: **Bat(t)aillard.**

Bate English and Scots: 1. from the ME given name *Bat(t)e*, a pet form of BARTHOLOMEW.

2. metonymic occupational name for a boatman, from OE *bāt* boat; for the Northern ME retention of *-ā-*, cf. ROPER.

Vars. (of 2): **Boatte; Boater** (see also BOWATER); **Boatman, Bottman.**

Dims. (of 1): **Batey** (Northumb.); **Batie** (Scots); BEATTY.

Cogns. (of 2): Du.: BOOT. Fris.: **Bootsma(n).**

Patrs. (from 1): **Bates; Bateson, Baitson, Beatson; Bason.**

'Servant of B. (1)': **Bateman.**

Bath English: habitation name from the town in Somerset, site of sumptuous, but in the Middle Ages ruined, Roman baths. The place is named from OE *bæð* bath. In some cases the surname may have originated as a metonymic occupational name for an attendant at a public bath house; cf. BADER 1 and BAIN 4.

Bathgate Scots: habitation name from a town in W Lothian, recorded *c.*1160 as *Batchet*, and probably derived from Brittonic *bat* boar + *cēd* wood.

Var.: **Baggat.**

Thomas de Bathket *was an archer in Edinburgh Castle in 1312.*

Bathurst English: habitation name from a place in the parish of Warbleton, Sussex, so called from the OE personal name *Bada* (a short form of the various cpd names with the first element *beadu* battle) + OE *hyrst* wooded hill (see HURST).

Batley English: habitation name from a place in W Yorks., so called from the OE personal name *Bata* (see BATT 2) + OE *lēah* wood, clearing.

In 1379 there were at least three householders of this name in Batley, where it is still a common surname. It is now also fairly common in E Anglia, as a result of migration in connection with the textile trade. In New Zealand it is borne by several people of Maori and Pakeha stock, as a result of intermarriage with descendants of Robert Thompson Batley, *who migrated there in 1863.*

Batsford English: habitation name from a place in Gloucs., so called from the gen. case of the OE personal name *Bæcci* (of uncertain origin) + OE *ōra* shore, slope. In some cases it may come from the much smaller place of the same name in the parish of Warbleton, Sussex, where the first element would seem to be a personal name, *Bætel*, and the second OE *ford* FORD. There has undoubtedly been some confusion with BATTISFORD.

Batt 1. English: like BATE, a deriv. of the ME given name *Batte*, a pet form of BARTHOLOMEW.

2. English: possibly from a ME survival of an OE personal name or byname *Bata*, of uncertain origin and meaning, but perhaps akin to *batt* cudgel and so, as a byname, given to a thickset man or a belligerent one.

3. English: topographic name, of uncertain meaning. That it is a topographic name seems clear from examples such as Walter *atte Batte* (Somerset 1327), but the term in question is in doubt. A connection has been suggested with OE *bāt* boat, but this would normally give ME *bote* in S England and *bate* in N England (cf. BATE 2). The surname is most common in Sussex.

4. German: from a medieval given name (L *Beātus* 'Blessed'), bestowed in honour of the apostle who was

reputed to have brought Christianity to Switzerland and S Germany.

Dims. (of 1 and 2): Eng.: **Battin(g)**, **Batten**, **Bat(t)on**; **Batty(e)** (chiefly Yorks.); **Battie** (chiefly Scots); **Baty** (Northumb.); **Batcock**. (Of 4): Low Ger.: **Battmann**.

Cogn. (of 3): Du.: **De Baat** ('profit', 'benefit').

Patrs. (from 1 and 2): Eng.: **Batts**; **Batson**, **Batt(e)son**.

'Servant of B. (1 and 2)': Eng.: **Batman**, BADMAN.

Battersby English: habitation name from a place in N Yorks., so called from the gen. case of the ON personal name *Boðvarr* (composed of the elements *boð* messenger + *var* guard) + ON *býr* settlement.

Battisford English: habitation name from a place in Suffolk, recorded in Domesday Book as *Beteforda* and *Betesfort*, from (the gen. case of) the OE personal name *Bætti* or *Betti* (of uncertain origin) + OE *ford* FORD. See also BATSFORD.

Battle English: habitation name from a place named as having been the site of a battle, e.g. *Battle* in Sussex, site of the Battle of Hastings.

Var.: **Battell**. Cf. BATAILLE.

Battu French: 1. nickname for a mistreated servant, from OF *battu*, past part. of *battre* to beat, strike (LL *bat-t(u)ere*; see BATAILLE).

2. topographic name for someone living by a beaten track, from the same word as in 1.

Vars: **Batu**, **Bat(t)ut**.

Baube French: nickname for someone with a speech defect, from OF *baube* stuttering, stammering (L *balbus*, itself used as a Roman family name).

Var.: **Baubier**.

Cogns.: Prov.: **Balb**, **Balp**.

Dims.: Fr.: **Baubet**, **Baubot**; **Bauberon**. Prov.: **Balbet**.

Pejs.: Fr.: **Baubault**, **Baubard**. Prov.: **Balbaud**.

Bauch German: nickname for a greedy or fat person, from Ger. *Bauch* belly, paunch (MHG *būch*, OHG *būh*).

Cogns.: Low Ger.: **Bu(u)(c)k**. Dan.: **Buck**.

Dim.: Ger.: **Bäuchle**, **Beuchel**.

Bauche French: topographic name for someone who lived on a patch of clay soil, or possibly denoting a house built of wattle and daub, from OF *bauche* clay (of Gaul. origin).

Dims.: **B(e)auchet**.

Baud French: 1. from the Gmc personal name *Baldo*, a short form of the various cpd names with the first element *bald* bold.

2. nickname for a lively person, from OF *baud* joyful, abandoned (of Gmc origin—see above—but with an altered sense).

Vars.: **Baude**, **Bault**.

Cogns. (of 1): It.: **Baldi**, **Baudi**. Ger.: **Balde**, BOLD, **Boldt**, **Bolte**, **Bölte**, **Bolle**. Low Ger.: **Bael(de)**, **Baal**, **Bahl**, **Bohl**. Eng.: **Ba(u)ld**, BOLD, BOLT.

Dims. (of 1): Fr.: BAUDEL, **Baud(in)et**, **Baudon**, **Baudin(ot)**; **Baudesson**, **Bod(es)son**, **Baudichon**, **Bodechon**; **Baudic** (Brittany). Prov.: **Baudou(x)**, **Baudy**. It.: **Baldin(ott)i**, **Baldelli**, **Baldetti**, **Balducci**, **Baldocci**; **Baudino**, **Baudinelli**, **Bauduc-c(i)o**. Eng.: **Bawcock**, **Bawcutt**, **Baucutt**; **Bowcock**, **Bo(o)-cock** (Yorks. and Lancs.); **Bowcutt**. Low Ger.: **Böldeke**, **Bö(h)lke**, **Ba(h)lke**; **Bohlje**; **Bo(h)lmann**, **Bahlmann**, **Bolz-mann**. Fris.: **Bolesma**, **Baack**, **Baake**, **Backe**.

Augs. (of 1): It.: **Baldoni**, **Baudone**.

Pejs. (of 1): It.: **Baldazzi**, **Baldassi**, **Baldacchi**, **Baldacco**; **Baudacci**, **Baudassi**, **Baudasso**.

Patr. (from 1): It.: **Di Baudi**. Sp.: **Val(a)déz**. Port.: **Valdes**. Eng.: **Balding**, **Bo(u)lding**, **Boulting**. Ger.: **Baldung**, **Bölting**. Low Ger.: **Bahls**, **Bo(h)l(en)s**, **Bolzen**, **Bo(h)lsen**, **Boolsen**, **Böhling**. Flem., Du.: **Baudts**, **Bouts**.

Patrs. (from 1) (dim.): Fris.: **Backen**.

Baudel French: 1. dim. of BAUD 1.

2. nickname for a stubborn or stupid person or occupational name for a pack driver, from OF *baudel* mule, donkey, pack animal (of uncertain origin, perhaps the same as in 1).

Vars.: **Baudeau**. (of 2 only) **Baudelier** (an agent noun).

Dims.: **Baudelot**; **Baudeloche**, **Baudeloque**.

Baudelaire French: of uncertain origin. It may be a Prov. cogn. of *Baudelier* (see BAUDEL), but more probably it is from OF *badelaire* cutlass (of unknown origin), and so a metonymic occupational name for a maker of these weapons or a nickname for a swordsman or armed robber.

Var.: **Bazelaire**.

Baudier French: from a Gmc personal name composed of the elements *bald* bold, brave + *hari*, *heri* army or *gar*, *ger* spear.

Var.: **Baudié**.

Cogn.: Eng.: **Balder** (partly from a native OE cogn.).

Dims.: Fr.: **Baudereau**, **Baud(e)ron**, **Baudrin**.

Bauer German and Jewish (Ashkenazic): status name for a peasant or nickname meaning 'neighbour, fellow citizen', from Ger. *Bauer*, MHG *(ge)būr* (OHG *gibūro*). The MHG word denoted an occupier of a *būr*, a small dwelling or building (cf. OE *būr*, mod. Eng. *bower*). This word later fell together with MHG *būwære* (OHG *būāri*), an agent noun from OHG *būan* to cultivate, later also (at first in Low Ger. dialects) to build. The Ger. surname thus had two possible senses: 'peasant' and 'neighbour, fellow citizen'. The precise meaning of the Jewish surname, which is of later formation, is unclear.

Vars.: Ger.: **Pauer** (Bavaria, Austria); **Gebühr**; **Baumann**. Jewish: **Bauman(n)**.

Cogns.: Low Ger.: **Bur(mann)**, **Bü(h)rmann**, **Bu(h)mann**; **Bouwer**. Fris.: **Boerma**, **Boe(r)sma**; **Bouma(n)**. Du.: **(De) Boer**, **Boere**, **Boerman** ('peasant'); **Buur(man)** ('neighbour'); **Bouwer**, **Bou(w)man**, **Bouwmeester** ('builder'). Dan.: **Bohr**. Hung.: **Pór**.

Dims.: Ger.: **Bäuerle**, **Beuerle**.

Patrs.: Low Ger.: **Bührs**, **Bu(h)rs**. Du.: **Boer(man)s**, **Boering**; **Boumans**.

Baugh Welsh: nickname for a small or short man, from W *bach* little.

Baughan 1. Welsh: dim. of BAUGH, from W *bychan*, hypocoristic form of *bach* little.

2. English: of uncertain origin. The earliest home of the surname seems to have been in Great Rollright in Oxon.; it may well be that all present-day bearers descend from a single family in this area, possibly of Welsh immigrants.

Vars.: **Baugh(e)n**, **Baugham**, **Baffin**, **Boffin**. (Of 1 only): VAUGHAN.

Cogn. (of 1): Corn.: BEAN.

Baum 1. German: topographic name for someone who lived by a tree that was particularly noticeable in some respect, from Ger. *Baum* tree (MHG, OHG *boum*), or else a nickname for a particularly tall person.

2. Jewish (Ashkenazic): possibly a topographic name as in 1, or an ornamental name from Ger. *Baum* tree, or a short form of any of the many ornamental surnames con-

taining this word as a final element, for example *Feigenbaum* (see FEIGE) and *Mandelbaum* (see MANDEL).

Vars. (of 1): **Baumer(t)**, **Bäum(l)er**.

Cogns. (of 1): Low Ger.: **Boom**; **Van den Boom**. Du.: **(Ten) Boom**, **Verboom**; **Van den Boom**.

Baumgarten German and Jewish (Ashkenazic): topographic or occupational name for someone who owned or lived by an orchard or was employed in one, from Ger. *Baumgarten* orchard, MHG *boumgarte* (a cpd of OHG *boum* tree + *garto* enclosure). There are also several villages named with this word, and so in some cases the surname may have originated as a habitation name from one of these.

Vars: Ger.: **Baumgart(e)**; **Baumgartner**. Jewish: **Baumgart**, **Baumgard**; **Baumgartner**.

Cogns.: Low Ger.: **Bohmgahren**; **Bo(n)gar(d)t**, **Bo(n)gartz** (Rhineland). Flem.: **Bongaerts**, **Bogaert(s)**, **Van den Bogaert**. Du.: **Boo(m)gard**, **Bo(o)gaart**, **Bogaard**, **Bo(o)gert**, **Bongers**, **(Van den) Boga(a)rde**.

Baverstock English: habitation name from a place in Wilts., which is so called from the gen. case of the OE personal name *Babba* (of uncertain origin, possibly a nursery name) + OE *stoc* farm (see STOKE).

Baxendale English (Lancs.): habitation name, probably from *Baxenden* near Accrington. This means 'bakestone valley', from OE *bæcstān* bakestone (a flat stone on which bread was baked) + *denu* valley. ME *dale* was sometimes substituted for OE *denu* in northern placenames.

Bay English and French: nickname for someone with chestnut or auburn hair, from ME, OF *bay*, *bai* reddish-brown (L *badius*, used originally of horses).

Var.: Fr.: **Bai**.

Cogns.: Sp.: **Bayo**. Du.: **Baaij**, **Bay**.

Dims.: Fr.: **Bayet**. Prov.: **Bayol**, **Bajol(et)**, **Bayoux**.

Pej.: Fr.: BAYARD.

Patrs.: Eng.: **Bay(e)s**.

Bayard English and French: 1. nickname for a reckless person, from ME, OF *baiard*, *baiart* foolhardy (the name—a deriv. of *baie* reddish-brown (see BAY)—of the magnificent but reckless horse given to Renaud by Charlemagne, according to numerous medieval romances).

2. metonymic occupational name for a carrier, from ME, OF *baiard*, *baiart* hand barrow, open cart (apparently a deriv. of OF *baier* to open; cf. BADAUD 2 and BADIER).

Vars.: Fr.: **Baiard**, **Bayart**, **Bajard**.

Baybutt English (Lancs.): of uncertain origin, possibly from *Baitebuk*, an occupational nickname for a goatherd, composed of the elements *baite(n)* to feed (ON *beita*, causative of *bíta* to bite) + *buk* BUCK, which is found in Lancs. in the 14th cent.

Bayer German and Jewish (Ashkenazic): regional name for someone from from *Bavaria*, Ger. *Bayern*. This region of S Germany derives its name from that of the Celt. tribe of the *Boii* who once inhabited this area as well as Bohemia (cf. BÖHM); in the 6th cent. AD they were displaced by a Gmc people, a branch of the Marcomanni, who took the name *Boioarii* or *Baiuoarii*.

Vars: **Baier**, **Beier**, **Beyer**.

Cogns.: Fr.: **Ba(i)vier**, **Baivy**; **Baiwir** (Belgium). Du., Flem.: **Baijer(man)**.

Dims.: Ger.: **Bayerle(in)**, **Beierle(in)**. Fr.: **Baverel**; **Baverey** (E France); **Baverez** (N and NE France).

Bayfield English: habitation name from a place in Norfolk, so called from the OE personal name *Bǣga* (of uncertain origin) + OE *feld* pasture, open country.

Bayford English: habitation name from a place in Herts., so called from the OE personal name *Bǣga* (cf. BAYFIELD) + OE *ford* FORD.

Bazin 1. French: dim. of BASIL.

2. French: metonymic occupational name for a maker or seller of *bombasin*, a kind of cheap cotton cloth. The word was popularly supposed to be a cpd of *bon* good + *basin*, and so lost its imagined first element, but in fact it comes whole from LL *bombacīnum*, a deriv. of Gk *bombyx* silk(worm).

3. Jewish: of unknown origin.

Vars. (of 1 and 2): **Bazy**. (Of 3): **Bazini**.

Dims. (of 1 and 2): **Bazinet**, **Bazenet**.

Beadle English: occupational name for a medieval court official, from ME *bedele* (OE *bydel*, reinforced by OF *bedel*). The word is of Gmc origin, and akin to OE *bēodan* to bid, command and OHG *bodo* messenger (see BOTHA). In the Middle Ages a beadle in England and France was a junior official of a court of justice, responsible for acting as an usher in a court, carrying the mace in processions in front of a justice, delivering official notices, making proclamations (as a sort of town crier), and so on. By Shakespeare's day a beadle was a sort of village constable, appointed by the parish to keep order.

Vars.: **Beadel(l)**, **Be(e)dle**; **Beddall**, **Bed(d)ell**; **Biddle**, **Biddell**; **Buddle**, **Buddell**.

Cogns.: Fr.: **Bedel**, **Bedé**, **Bedeau**. Ger.: **Büttel**; **Bittel** (Württemberg, Swabia). Flem.: **Pedel**.

Patrs.: Eng.: **Beadles**, **Biddles**, **Buddles**.

Beake English (Somerset): probably a nickname for someone with a prominent nose, from ME *beke* beak of a bird (OF *bec*, LL *beccus*, of Gaul. origin). Although this word is not recorded in the transferred sense 'human nose' until Florio (1598), it was probably in colloquial use somewhat earlier. Cf. BECK 2 and BECKETT 1.

Beal English: 1. Norman nickname for a handsome man, from OF *bel* fair, lovely (see BEAU).

2. habitation name from places so called in Northumb. and W Yorks. The former of these (*Behil* in early records) comes from OE *bēo* bee + *hyll* HILL; the latter (*Begale* in Domesday Book) is from OE *bēag* ring (or a derived personal name **Beaga*) + *halh* nook, recess (see HALE 1).

Vars.: **Beal(l)e**, **Beel**.

Patrs. (from 1): **Beal(l)(e)s**, **Beels**, **Beal(e)son**.

Béal French: topographic name for someone who lived by a millrace, from the Lyonnaise dial. term *béal*, *bezale*, *bedale* (of Gaul. origin).

Vars.: **Bezal**, **Bezault**, **Bedal**, **Bedau**, **Betau**; **Biez**, **Bié**, **(Du) Bief**.

Beamish English and Irish (Norman): habitation name from *Beaumais*-sur-Dire in Calvados, Normandy, or *Beaumetz* in Somme and Pas-de-Calais; in the last *département* there are three different places of the same name, distinguished as Beaumetz-lès-Aire, Beaumetz-lès-Cambrai, and Beaumetz-lès-Loges. These are from OF *beu* fair, lovely (see BEAU) + *més* dwelling (cf. MAS). Beamish in Co. Durham is a Norman Fr. placename of the same origin, first mentioned in the 13th cent.; it is possible that a few bearers take their name from this place.

Vars.: **Beam(e)s**, **Beamiss**.

Bean 1. English: metonymic occupational name for a grower or seller of beans, from OE *bēan* beans (a collective sing.). Occasionally it may also have been a nickname for a man regarded as of little importance.

2. English: nickname for a pleasant person, from ME *bēne* friendly, amiable (of unknown origin, with apparently no connection with BAIN 3 or BON).

3. Scots: Anglicized form of the Gael. personal name *Beathán*, a dim. of *be(a)tha* life.

Cogns. (of 1): Du.: BOON. Fris.: **Boonstra**. (Of 3): Ir.: **Behan**.

Dim. (of 1): Du.: **Boontje**.

Patrs. (from 3): Scot.: **McBean, McBain, McBayne** (Gael. **Mac Beathain**); **McVain** (Gael. **Mac Bheathain**).

Beanland English (Yorks.): habitation name from an unidentified place named as the place where beans were grown, from OE *bēan* (see BEAN 1) + *land* land, both of which are common formative elements in Eng. place-names.

Bear English: 1. from the ME nickname *Bere* 'Bear' (OE *bera*, which is also found as a byname), or possibly from a personal name derived from a short form of the various Gmc cpd names with this first element (cf. e.g. BERNARD). The bear has generally been regarded with a mixture of fear and amusement, due to its strength and unpredictable temper on the one hand and its clumsy gait on the other. Both these qualities are no doubt reflected in the nickname. Throughout the Middle Ages the bear was a familiar figure in popular entertainments such as bear baiting and dancing bears.

2. habitation name, var. of BEER 1.

Cogns. (of 1): Ger. (and Jewish (Ashkenazic), from the Yid. male given name *Ber*): **Baer, Bä(h)r**. Low Ger.: BEER. Flem., Du.: **De Beer** (also Jewish). Norw., Dan.: **Bjørn**. Swed.: **Björn**. Fr.: **B(é)ron** (from the OF oblique case of the Gmc personal name *Bero*).

Dims. (of 1): Ger.: **Beerli** (Switzerland). Fr.: **Béronneau**. It.: **Barell(in)i, Barett(in)o, Barini, Barotti, Barocci, Barutti, Barucci, Baruzzi, Barusso**.

Patrs. (from 1): Low Ger.: **Ba(h)ring, Be(h)ring; Bö(h)rnsen**. Du.: **Beers**. Dan., Norw.: **Bjørnsen**. Swed.: **Björnsson**. Jewish: **Berso(h)n, Berzon**.

Patrs. (from dims. of 1): Jewish (E Ashkenazic): **Berkovich, Berkowicz, Berkovitz**.

The Hants Baring *family are descended from an 18th-cent. John Baring of Devon, who was of Low Ger. origin, being the son of the minister of a Lutheran church in Bremen.*

Beard English: 1. nickname for a wearer of a beard (ME, OE *beard*). To be clean-shaven was the norm in non-Jewish communities in NW Europe from the 12th to the 16th cent., the crucial period for surname formation. There is placename and other evidence that this word was used as a byname in the OE period, when beards were the norm; in this period the byname would have referred to a large or noticeable beard.

2. habitation name from a place in Derbys., which derives its name by dissimilation from OE *brerd* brim, bank.

Cogns. (of 1): Ger.: **Bart(h)**. Low Ger.: **Baartman**. Flem., Du.: **Baart(man)**. Russ.: BORODIN.

Patrs. (from 1): **Beards** (W Midlands).

Beardmore English: apparently a habitation name from some lost place (probably in Staffs., where the surname is overwhelmingly common), so called from the OE byname *Beard* 'BEARD' + OE *mōr* marsh, fen (see MOORE 1). A less plausible possibility is that it originally referred to a relative (see MAW 2) of someone with the byname *Beard*.

Var.: **Bearsmore**.

Beardsley English: habitation name, from an unidentified place (probably in Notts., where the surname is overwhelmingly common), apparently so called from the gen. case of the OE byname *Beard* 'BEARD' + OE *lēah* wood, clearing.

Beardsworth English (Lancs.): habitation name, from *Beardsworth*, the former name of *Beardwood* in Lancs., which was so called from the gen. case of the OE byname *Beard* 'BEARD' + OE *worð* homestead (see WORTH).

Var.: **Beardwood** (from the later name of the same place).

Bearman English: occupational name for a keeper of a dancing bear or one who kept bears for baiting; see BEAR 1. See also BERMAN 1.

Beasley English: habitation name from *Beesley* in Lancs., perhaps a cpd of OE *bēos* bent grass + OE *lēah* wood, clearing. The name is now common in the W Midlands and elsewhere, as well as in Lancs.

Vars.: **Beazley, Beesley, Beazleigh, Beisley**.

Beaton English and Scots: 1. Norman habitation name from *Béthune* in Pas-de-Calais, Picardy, recorded in the 8th cent. in the L form *Bitunia*, probably an adj. (with *villa* understood; see VILLE) derived from the oblique form of a Gmc personal name *Betto*, a hypocoristic formation (cf. BETTENCOURT).

2. from the medieval given name *Be(a)ton*, apparently a dim. from a short form of BÉATRICE and (in Scotland) of BARTHOLOMEW.

Vars.: **Beeton, Beaten, Betton**. (Of 1 only): **Batti(g)ne** (the name of an ancient Hants and Sussex family).

Cogn. (of 1): Fr.: **Béthune**.

The name Beaton *is now most common in Scotland, where Robert* de Betunia *is recorded in the late 12th cent. The family held land in Angus (now part of Tayside region) and Fife, where the surname is still most common. A branch of the family settled in Skye in the mid-16th cent. and served as physicians for several generations. The surname form* **Bethune** *is still found in Scotland.*

Béatrice French: from a medieval female given name borne in honour of a 4th-cent. saint, martyred together with her brothers Simplicius and Faustinus. Her name was originally *Viātrix* 'Traveller' (a fem. form of *viātor*, from *via* way; the name was adopted by early Christians in reference to the journey through life, and Christ's description of Himself as 'the way, the life, and the truth'); it was later altered as a result of folk etymological association with L *bēatus* blessed.

Vars.: **Béatrix, Biétrix**.

Cogns.: Flem., Du.: **Beatrijs, Beltrijs**.

Dims.: Fr.: **Biétron, Beltrine**. Eng.: BEATON.

Metrs. (from dims.): Flem.: **Behets, Baeten**.

Beatty 1. Scots and N Irish: from the given name *B(e)atie*, a dim. from a short form of BARTHOLOMEW; cf. BATE 1.

2. Irish: Anglicized form of the Gael. occupational term *biadhtach* hospitaller; cf. MCVITIE.

Vars. (of 1): **Beattey, Beat(e)y, Beattie**.

Beau French: nickname for a handsome man (perhaps also ironically for an ugly one), from OF *beu, bel* fair, lovely (LL *bellus*). Fr. and It. forms such as *Labelle* and *La Bella* were in part ironical nicknames for an effeminate man. Without the article, they are more likely to represent a metronymic; the fem. form of the adj. was in common use as a medieval female given name.

Vars.: **Lebeau, (Le) Bel, Lebbel(l)**; **Labelle**; **Belle**.

Cogns.: Prov.: **Labère**. Eng.: BEAL, BELL. Flem.: **De Bel**. It.: **Belli, Bello**; **(La) Bella, Belle**; **Lobello, Lubello, Lubelli** (S Italy). Sp.: **Bello**. Port.: **Belo**.

Dims.: Fr.: **Bel(l)et, Bel(l)on, Bel(l)ot, Beluchot**. It.: **Bellini, Bellino, Bellel(l)i, Bellett(in)i, Bellotti, Bellozzi, Bellocci, Bellutti, Belluzzi, Bellucci(o), Belloli**. Cat.: **Belló**.

Augs.: Fr.: **Bellat**. It.: **Belloni**.

Pejs.: It.: **Bellacci, Bellazzi**.

Patrs.: Fr.: **Aubel**. Eng.: **Bewson**. It.: **Di Bello, Del Bello, De Bei, De Belli(s)**; **Belleschi, Belluschi**.

Patr. (from a dim.): Flem.: **Belleken**.

Metr.: It.: **Della Bella**.

Beauchamp English (Norman) and French: habitation name from any of several places in France, for example in the *départements* of Manche and Somme, that get their names from OF *beu*, *bel* fair, lovely (see BEAU) + *champ(s)* field, plain (see CHAMP). In Eng. the surname is generally pronounced /ˈbiːtʃəm/.

Vars.: Eng.: **Beacham(p), Beecham**; **Beacom** (N Irish); **Belchamp**, BELCHEM.

There were two families of this name which were prominent in the 13th and 14th cents. in England. One was established in Somerset, the other in Warwicks., and there is no apparent connection between them.

Beauclerk English (Norman): nickname meaning 'fair clerk', used either of a handsome priest or of one who wrote with a fair hand, from OF *beu*, *bel* fair, lovely (see BEAU) + *clerc* clerk, cleric (see CLARK).

This is the family name of the Dukes of St Albans. They are descended from Charles Beauclerk *(1670–1726), a natural son of Charles II and Nell Gwyn, who was created Duke in 1684.*

Beaufort English (Norman) and French: habitation name from various places in France, for example in the *départements* of Nord, Somme, and Pas-de-Calais, so called from OF *beu*, *bel* fair, lovely (see BEAU) + *fort* fortress, stronghold (see FORT 1).

Var.: **Belfort**.

A powerful English family of this name originated with the bastard children of John of Gaunt and Catherine Swinford, who were legitimized by Act of Parliament. Their name was derived from their father's castle, Beaufort, in Champagne. Henry Beaufort *(c.1374–1447) became a cardinal and papal legate, and was very influential as a statesman in the reign of Edward V; his brother Thomas (d. 1427) became Duke of Exeter; and a third brother, John (d. 1407), became Earl of Somerset. The latter's granddaughter, Margaret Beaufort (1443–1509) married Edmund Tudor, half-brother of Henry VI, and was the mother of Henry VII. She was a great patroness, endowing Christ's and St John's colleges at Cambridge.*

The English admiral Sir Francis Beaufort (1774–1857), who devised the Beaufort scale, used for measuring wind velocity, was the grandson of a French Huguenot refugee, Daniel de Beaufort, *who became pastor of a church in Spitalfields, London.*

Beaulieu French: habitation name from any of the extremely numerous places in France named from OF *beu*, *bel* fair, lovely (see BEAU) + *lieu* place, location (L *locus*). The name is occasionally also found in England; it is then either a Norman name from one of the French places just mentioned or derives from an English placename of the same origin, *Beaulieu* (pronounced /ˈbjuːlɪ/) in Hants, seat of the Montagu family.

Var.: **Beaulieux**.

Cogns.: Eng.: **Bewley**. Prov.: **Belloc**. Cat.: **Belloch**.

Hilaire Belloc *(1870–1953), the English essayist, wit, and writer of children's verses, was born in Paris; his forebears came from Nantes, but from the form of the name were presumably ultimately of Provençal origin.*

Beaumarchais French: habitation name from any of several places named from OF *beu*, *bel* fair, lovely (see BEAU) + *marchais* marsh, swamp (a word of Gaul. origin). This is the name of several villages in N France, for example in the parishes of Pleudihen (Côtes-du-Nord), Cintray (Eure), Cloyes (Eure-et-Loir), Autrèche (Indre-et-Loire), Othis (Seine-et-Marne), and Bretignolles (Vendée).

Vars.: **Beaumarchaix, Beaumarcheix**.

The French dramatist Pierre Caron de Beaumarchais *(1732–99) was the son of a Parisian watchmaker named Caron. He took the surname by which he is now generally known from a small country property in Brie, which belonged to his first wife.*

Beaumont 1. English (Norman) and French: habitation name from any of the five places in Normandy or several others elsewhere in France so named. The placename comes from OF *beu*, *bel* fair, lovely (see BEAU) + *mont* hill (see MONT). There are also places in England so named under Norman influence (in Cumb., Lancs., and Essex, the last of which changed its name in the 11th cent. from *Fulepet* 'foul pit' to *Bealmont* 'beautiful hill'); these may also have given rise to surnames. The surname is now widespread throughout England, but most common in Yorks.

2. Welsh: Anglicized form of a patr. from the given name EDMOND.

Vars. (of 1): Eng.: **Beamont, Beamond, Bea(u)ment, Bea(u)mant, Beamand, Bem(m)and**; **Beauman**, BEEMAN; **Belmont**.

Cogns.: Sp. and Jewish (Sefardic): **Belmonte**. Cat.: **Belmunt**.

Robert de Beaumont *(d. 1118) was one of those who fought alongside William the Conqueror in the Norman invasion of England in 1066. He took his name from an estate owned by his grandfather at Beaumont-le-Roger in Normandy. William rewarded him with large grants of land in Warwicks., and his brother was given custody of Warwick Castle.*

Most English bearers of the surname, however, are descended from Henry de Beaumont (d. 1340), who came to England from France as a soldier, serving Edward I, II, and III of England, and acquiring the earldom of Buchan in Scotland by marriage. He was descended from Count Engelbert of Brienne (fl. 950) and is himself the ancestor of the Baronets Beaumont of Cole Orton, Leics.

Belmonte *is the name of a Sefardic Jewish family in Germany, who originated in the city of Belmonte in Portugal, and reached Germany via the Spanish Netherlands.*

Beauregard French: 1. habitation name from any of various places, for example in Ain, Dordogne, Drôme, Lot, and Puy-de-Dôme, so called from OF *beu*, *bel* fair, lovely (see BEAU) + *regard* aspect, outlook (a deriv. of *regarder* to look at, watch, from *g(u)arder* to watch, guard; see WARD 1), with reference to their handsome site; cf. BEAVER 1.

2. nickname for someone of a pleasant appearance, from the same elements as above.

Beaurepaire French: habitation name from any of various places, for example in Isère, Nord, Oise, Saône-et-Loire, Seine-Maritime, and Vendée, so called from OF *beu*, *bel* fair, lovely (see BEAU) + *repaire* retreat (a deriv. of *repair(i)er* to retreat, LL *repatriāre* return to one's country, from *patria* native land).

Beaver English: 1. Norman habitation name from any of several places in France called *Beauvoir*, for example in Manche, Somme, and Seine-Maritime, or from *Belvoir* in Leics. All of these get their names from OF *beu*, *bel* fair, lovely (see BEAU) + *veïr*, *voir* to see (L *vidēre*), i.e. a place with a fine view.

2. nickname from ME *bevere*, OE *beofor* beaver, possibly referring to a hard worker, or from some other fancied resemblance to the animal.

Vars.: **Beever(s)** (Yorks.); **Biever, Be(e)vor, Bevar, Bevir**. (Of 1 only): **Belvoir; Belvedere**.

Cogns. (of 1): Fr.: **Beauvoir; Beauvois** (from the L past part. *visum*); **B(i)euvo, Biavo**. Prov.: **Belvezer; Betbeder, Begbeder** (Gascony). Cat.: **Bellver, Vallvé**. (Of 2): Ger.: **Beber(t), Bi(e)ber**. Jewish (Ashkenazic, ornamental): **Bi(e)ber, Biberman; Bi(e)berfeld, Biberstein**. Low Ger.: **Bewer**. Flem., Du.: **(De) Bever**.

Beavis English (Norman): 1. nickname from OF *bel fi(l)z*, a term of affectionate address, from *beu*, *bel* fair, lovely (see BEAU) + *filz*, *fi(t)z* son (L *filius*). The mod. Fr. sense 'son-in-law' is not attested before 1468, and only gradually ousted *filiâtre* (LL *filiaster*), so that it is not likely that this sense lies behind any examples of the surname.

2. habitation name from *Beauvais* in Oise (which derives its name from that of the Gaul. tribe recorded in L sources as the *Bellovaci*), or from various other places in N France called *Beauvois* (LL *bellum visum* lovely sight; cf. BEAVER 1).

Vars.: **Be(a)ves, Be(e)vis(s), Bovis**.

Cogn. (of 1): Fr.: **Beaufils**.

Bebbington English: habitation name from *Bebington* in Ches., so called from OE *Bebbingtūn* 'settlement (OE *tūn*) associated with Bebbe', a personal name borne by both men and women and of uncertain origin, perhaps a nursery word.

Becerra Spanish: nickname, probably for a high-spirited individual, from Sp. *becerra* young cow, heifer (of uncertain origin, perhaps akin to L *ibex*, gen. *ibicis*, chamois, mountain goat, an equally high-spirited creature). It may also have been a metonymic occupational name for a cowherd.

Vars.: **Becerro; Becerril** (an adj. deriv.).

Cogn.: Port.: **Bezarra**.

Becher 1. German: metonymic occupational name for a turner of wooden vessels, from Ger. *Becher* cup, mug (MHG *becher*, OHG *behhari*, L *bicārium*, from Gk *bikos* pot, pitcher).

2. German: occupational name for someone who worked with pitch, for example in making vessels watertight, from an agent deriv. of MHG *bech*, *pech* pitch (cf. PECHER 1).

3. Jewish (Ashkenazic): of uncertain origin, perhaps derived as in 1 or 2 above.

4. English: topographic name, var. of BEECH.

Cogns. (of 2): Dan.: **Bekker, Becker**; BEK, **Beck, Bech**.

Bechor Jewish (Sefardic): from the Judezmo male given name *Bexor* (from Hebr. *Bechor* 'First-born'), given to a first-born son. The Jewish surnames **Bechar** and **Behar** may be related to *Bechor*, but this is not certain.

Bechstein German: probably a topographic name for someone who lived near an outcrop of pitchstone, a smooth shiny black type of quartz, MHG *pechstein*.

Var.: **Pechstein**.

Beck 1. English: topographic name for someone who lived beside a stream, from Northern ME *bekke* stream (ON *bekkr*).

2. English (Norman): habitation name from any of the various places in N France, for example *Bec* Hellouin in Eure, which get their name from ONF *bec*, from the same ON root as in 1.

3. English: var. of BEAKE.

4. English: metonymic occupational name for a maker, seller, or user of a mattock or pickaxe, OE *becca*. In some cases the name may represent a survival of an OE byname derived from this word; cf. BECKFORD and BECKHAM.

5. German and Jewish (Ashkenazic): occupational surname, cogn. of BAKER, from Ger. dial. *Beck*, W Yid. *bek*, both meaning 'baker'. Some Jewish bearers of the name claim that it is an acronym of Hebr. *ben-kedoshim* 'son of martyrs', i.e. a name taken by one whose parents had been martyred for being Jews.

6. Low German: cogn. of BACH.

Vars. (of 1): **Becke, Beckman**. (Of 5): Ger.: **Becke, Baeck; Böck** (Bavaria); **Beckmann**. Jewish: BEK, **Be(c)kman**.

Cogns. (of 1 and 3): Fr.: **Bec(q), Becque, Lebec(q)**. (Of 1 only): Swed.: **Bäck(man)**. Fr.: **Debec, Dubec, Delbec(q)**. (Of 3 only): Fr.: **Béché, Béc(h)u** ('beaked').

Dims. (of 3): Eng.: BECKETT. Fr.: **Béchet, Bécher(eau), Bécherel(le); Becquet, Béquet, Becquereau, Becquerel; Béchillon; Becquelin**.

Pejs. (of 3): Fr.: **Béc(h)ard**.

Patr. (from 3): Eng.: **Bexon** (Notts.).

Cpds (ornamental, from a cogn. 1): Swed.: **Bäcklund** ('stream grove'); **Bäckström** ('stream river', a tautological formation).

Beckett English: 1. dim. of BECK 3 or, more rarely, of BECK 1.

2. habitation name from places so called in Berks. and Devon; the former is named from OE *bēo* bee + *cot* cottage, shelter (see COATES); the latter has as its first element the OE personal name *Bicca* (apparently from *becca* pickaxe, mattock; see BECK 4).

Var.: **Becket**.

Beckford English: habitation name from a place in Gloucs., so called from the OE byname *Becca* (see BECK 4) + OE *ford* FORD.

Beckham English: habitation name from a place in Norfolk, so called from the OE byname *Becca* (see BECK 4) + OE *hām* homestead.

The first known bearer of the surname is Sir Roger de Beckham, *recorded at W Beckham in 1379*.

Beckles English: habitation name from *Beccles* in Norfolk, which Ekwall derives from OE *bec(e)*, *bæce* stream + *lǣs* meadow.

Beckley English: habitation name from any of the various places, in Kent, Oxon., and Sussex, so called from the OE byname *Becca* (see BECK 4) + OE *lēah* wood, clearing.

Beckwith English: habitation name from a place in W Yorks., so called from OE *bēc(e)* BEECH + ON *viðr* WOOD (replacing the cogn. OE *widu*, *wudu*).

Most if not all present-day bearers of the surname are probably descended from a certain William Beckwith *who held the manor of Beckwith in 1364. In the U.S. the name also occurs in the elaborated form* **de la Beckwith**.

Beddow Welsh: from the personal name *Bedo*, a dim. form of *Meredydd*; see MEREDITH.

Vars.: **Beddoe, Bedo; Eddow** (a back-formation, as if from a patr. with the prefix *ap*).

Patrs.: **Beddow(e)s, Beddoes, Beddis, Eddowes, Edess**.

Bedford English: habitation name from the county town of Beds., or a smaller place of the same name in Lancs. Both are so called from the OE personal name *Bēda* (apparently a deriv. of *bēd* prayer) + OE *ford* FORD. The name is now very common in Yorks. as well as Beds.

Bedingfeld English: habitation name from a place in Suffolk, so called from OE *Bēdingafeld* 'FIELD of the people of *Bēda*' (cf. BEDFORD).

This is the name of a family of E Anglian origin; they took their name from lands at Bedingfeld, Suffolk. Peter de Bedingfeld *gave property to Snape Priory in the 12th cent.*

Bednarz Polish and Jewish (E Ashkenazic): occupational name for a cooper, Pol. *bednarz*.

Vars.: **Bednarski** (with surname suffix *-ski*; see BARANOWSKI); **Bednarsh** (U.S.). Jewish: **Bednarsky**.

Cogns.: Czech: **Bednář**; **Bečvář**. Ger.: BÜTTNER. Ukr.: BONDAR.

Dims.: Pol.: **Bednarek**, **Bednarczyk**. Czech: **Bednařík**.

Patr.: Pol.: **Bednarowicz**.

Bednyakov Russian: patr. from the nickname *Bednyak* 'Pauper' (a deriv. of *bedny* poor).

Bedwell English: habitation name from any of various minor places, e.g. in Herts., named with the OE elements *byde(n)* tub + *well(a)* spring, stream (see WELL).

Vars.: **Bid(d)well** (from *Bidwell* in Herts.); **Bidewell**.

Bedwinek Polish: dim. of Pol. *bedwin* pedlar, a borrowing via Ger. of OF *beduin* wanderer, nomad (a word picked up by Crusaders from Arabic *badāwi* (sing. *badwi*) Bedouins, desert dwellers, a deriv. of *badw* desert).

Bedworth English (W Midlands): habitation name from a place in Warwicks., so called from the OE personal name *Bēda* (cf. BEDFORD) + OE *worð* homestead (see WORTH).

Bee English: probably a nickname for an energetic or active person, from the insect, ME *be*, OE *bēo*, which has long been taken as the type of a busy worker. Cf. BEEMAN 2.

Cogns.: Ger.: **Bie(n)**. Du.: **De Bij**, **Van der Bij**.

Beeby English: habitation name from a place in Leics., so called from OE *bēo* bee + ON *býr* settlement, village.

Beech English: 1. topographic name for someone who lived by a stream, ME *beche* (OE *bece*, a byform of *bæce*; cf. BACH 1).

2. topographic name for someone who lived by a beech tree or beech wood, from ME *beche* beech tree (OE *bēce*). For Continental cogns., see at BUCH and BUKOWSKI.

Vars.: **Beach**, **Beecher**, BECHER, **Beech(a)man**.

Beechey English: habitation name from some minor place named as an enclosure by a beech wood, from ME *beche* beech (see BEECH 2) + *heie*, *haie* enclosure (see HAY 1).

Beecroft English: habitation name from some minor place named as the place where bees were kept, from OE *bēo* bee + *croft* paddock, smallholding.

Beeman English: 1. var. of BEAUMONT.

2. occupational name for a beekeeper, from OE *bēo* bee + *mann* man.

Vars.: **Be(a)man**.

Cogns. (of 2): Ger.: **Bie(ne)mann**.

Beer 1. English (W Country): habitation name from any of the forty or so places in SW England called *Beer(e)* and *Bear(e)*. Most of these derive their names from the W Saxon dat. case, *beara*, of OE *bearu* grove, wood (the standard OE dat. *bearwe* being preserved in BARROW). Some may be from OE *bǣr* swine pasture.

2. Low German: cogn. of BEAR.

Vars. (of 1): **Be(e)re**, **Beare**, BEAR; **Abear(e)** (with fusion of the preposition *at*).

Beeston English: habitation name from any of the various places so called. Most of them, for example those in Beds., Norfolk, Notts., and W Yorks., get the name from OE *bēos* rough grass + *tūn* enclosure, settlement. However, the one in Ches. probably gets it from OE *byge* trade, commerce + *stān* stone, meaning 'rock where a market was held'. A few other *Beestons* have different derivations.

Var.: **Beaston**.

Beetham English: habitation name from a place in Cumbria (formerly N Lancs.), recorded in Domesday Book as *Biedun*, the origin of which, according to Ekwall, is the dat. pl. of ON *bióðr* table, in the transferred sense 'flat land'. The surname is still most common in Lancs.

Var.: **Betham**.

The earliest known bearer of this surname is Ralph de Betham, *lord of the manor at Beetham, whose name is found as a witness on a charter of 1190.*

Beethoven Low German, Flemish, and Dutch: habitation name from some minor place named as the yard used for the cultivation of root crops, from MLG, MDu. *bete* beet + *hoven* dat. pl. (originally used after a preposition such as *van* of) of MLG, MDu. *hov* yard, court (cf. HOFER).

Begg Scots and N Irish: nickname or byname for a small man, from Gael. *beag* small.

Var.: BIGG.

Patrs.: **Beggs** (chiefly N Irish), **Biggs**.

'Descendant of the small man': Ir.: **Beggan**, **Beggin** (Gael. **Ó Beagáin**).

Begley Irish: Anglicized form of Gael. **Ó Beaglaoich** 'descendant of *Beaglaoch*', a personal name composed of the elements *beag* small + *laoch* hero.

Bègue French: nickname for someone afflicted with a stammer, a deriv. of OF *beguer* to stammer (from MLG *beggen* to chatter). In the 12th cent. in Liège a priest called *Lambert le Begue* (Lambert the Stammerer) founded a Christian sisterhood whose members followed an austere rule of life; they came to be known as the *Béguines*. A century later an order of lay brothers modelled on this sisterhood was founded in Flanders, called the *Beghards*. Both these orders have contributed to the Fr. vars. of this surname, doubtless as a result of some fancied resemblance to the religious, rather than by way of direct descent.

Vars.: **Lebègue**; **Bég(o)uin**, **Bégin**, **Béguen**; **Bég(h)ard** (pej. in form, though not necessarily in meaning).

Cogns. (from the brotherhood): Ger.: **Beckhard(t)**.

Dims.: Fr.: **Bégon**, **Béguet**, **Bégot**.

Behan Irish: Anglicized form of Gael. **Ó Beachain** 'descendant of *Beachán*', a personal name from a dim. of *beach* bee.

Behenna Cornish: of unknown origin. It is first found, in the form *Behennow*, in 1525.

Beilin Jewish (E Ashkenazic): metr. from the Yid. female given name *Beyle* (from the Czech given name *Běla*, which a blend of Czech *běl* white (cf. Pol. BIAŁAS) and L or It. *bella* beautiful), with the Slav. suffix *-in*.

Vars.: **Belin**, **Bailin** (E Ashkenazic); **Beiles**, **Beilis(s)** (Ashkenazic, with the Yid. possessive *-s* ending); **Beli(n)son** (Ashkenazic).

Bejarano Spanish and Jewish (Sefardic): habitation name for someone from the town of *Béjar* in the province of Salamanca. The placename is of pre-Roman origin and unknown meaning; the original form seems to have been *Bigerra*.

Vars.: Jewish: **Bejerano**, **Bidjerano**.

Bek 1. Polish: nickname for a stupid person or one with a bleating voice, from Pol. *bek* baa.

2. Jewish (Ashkenazic): generally a var. of BECK 5, but in some cases the derivation may be the same as that of the Pol. name in 1 above.

3. Danish: var. of *Bekker*; see BECHER.

Belchem English: 1. var. of BEAUCHAMP.

2. habitation name from a group of villages in Essex now called *Belchamp*. This name has been altered so that it appears to be derived from OF *bel* fair, lovely (see BEAU) + *champ(s)* field (see CHAMP), but in fact the ME name was *Balc-ham*, from OE *bælc*, *balca* roof beam + *hām* homestead, i.e. homestead with a prominent roof beam.

Vars.: **Belcham**, **Bel(l)sham**.

Belcher English: 1. (Norman) nickname from OF *beu*, *bel* fair, lovely + *chere* face, countenance (LL *cara*, from Gk *kara* head). Although it originally meant 'face', the word *chere* later came to mean also 'demeanour', 'disposition' (hence Eng. *cheer*), and the nickname may thus also have denoted a person of pleasant, cheerful disposition. There has been some confusion with BOWSER.

2. var. of BALCH.

Vars. (of 1): **Belshaw**, **Be(a)ushaw**, **Bewshaw**, **Bewshea**, **Beuscher**, **Beushire**, **Bowsher**.

Cogn. (of 1): Fr.: **Belchère**.

Jonathan Belcher *(1682–1757) was governor of Massachusetts Colony (1729/30–1741) and was one of the founders of Princeton University. He was a wealthy merchant, having inherited a substantial fortune from his father, Andrew Belcher (d. 1717). The family were established in America by another Andrew Belcher, a tavern keeper who had arrived from England in 1654. They could be traced back to the latter's grandfather, a weaver from Wilts.*

Belgrave English: habitation name from a place in Leics., recorded in Domesday Book as *Merdegrave*. The original name derived from OE *mearð* marten + *grāf* grove, but after the Norman Conquest the first element was taken to be OF *merde* dung, filth (L *merda*), and changed to OF *beu*, *bel* fair, lovely, to remove the unpleasant association. A mid-12th-cent. writer refers to the place as *Merthegrave, nunc* (now) *Belegrava*.

A family bearing the name Belgrave *were first recorded with William Belgrave (1638–1703), at N Kilworth, near Rugby, where their descendants can still be found.*

Belham English (Norman): nickname from OF *beu*, *bel* fair, lovely (see BEAU) + *homme* man (L *homo*).

Vars.: **Bell(h)am**.

Cogns.: Fr.: **Belhomme**. It.: **Bell(u)omo**, **Begliuomini**.

Bélier French: nickname from OF *belier* ram (MDu. *belhamel* belled sheep, i.e. the leader of the flock). The nickname no doubt refers in many cases to sexual prowess, but since *belier* also means 'battering ram', it may sometimes have been applied to a man of powerful build.

Dims.: **Béliot**, **Belin**, **Belisson**.

Pejs.: **Béliard**, **Beillard**.

Belkin 1. Russian: patr. from the nickname *Belka* 'Squirrel' (a deriv. of *bely* white, referring to the animal's white stomach).

2. Jewish (E Ashkenazic): metr. from *Beylke*, pet form of the Yid. female given name *Beyle* (see BEILIN), with the Slav. suffix *-in*. In some cases the Jewish name may have the same derivation as the Russian name in 1 above.

Vars.: (of 2): **Belkind** (for the excrescent *-d*, see SÜSSKIND); **Belkis** (with the Yid. possessive ending *-s*).

Bell 1. English: from the ME, OE vocab. word *belle* bell, in various applications; most probably a metonymic occupational name for a bellringer or bellfounder, or a habitation name for someone living 'at the bell' (as attested by 14th-cent. forms such as *John atte Belle*). This indicates either residence by an actual bell (e.g. a town's bell in a belltower, centrally placed to summon meetings, sound the alarm, etc.) or 'at the sign of the bell', i.e. a house or inn sign. However, surnames derived from house and inn signs are rare in English.

2. English and Scots: from the medieval given name *Bel*. As a man's name this is from OF *beu*, *bel* handsome (see BEAU), which was also used as a nickname. As a female name it represents a short form of *Isobel*, a form of *Elizabeth*.

3. Scots: Anglicized form of Gael. **Mac Giolla Mhaoil** 'son of the servant of the devotee'; see MULLEN 1.

4. Jewish (Ashkenazic): Anglicization of one or more like-sounding Jewish surnames.

Vars. (of 1): **Beller**, **Bel(l)man**. (Of 3): **(Mc)Gilveil**.

Bellamy Irish (Norman) and French: literal or ironic nickname meaning 'fine friend', from OF *beu*, *bel* fair, handsome (see BEAU) + *ami* friend (L *amīcus*).

Var.: Fr.: **Belami**.

Bellay French: habitation name from any of the numerous places that derive their names from LL *betullētum* birch grove (a deriv. of *betullus* birch; see BOUL).

Vars.: **Du Bellay**, **Belloy**.

Bellew English (Norman): habitation name from any of the various places in N France named with the OF elements *beu*, *bel* lovely (see BEAU) + *ewe* water (L *aqua*).

Cogns.: Fr.: **Belleau**. Prov.: **Belaigue**, **Belaygue**.

An Irish family of this name trace their descent from an early settler, Adam de Bella Aqua, *who was living in 1210. They have given their name to* Bellewstown *in Co. Louth and* Mountbellew *in Co. Galway.*

Bellhouse English: habitation name for someone who lived by a belltower; see BELL 1. The surname is largely confined to Yorks.

Var.: **Bellas**.

Bellido Spanish: nickname for a handsome person, from Sp. *bellido* beautiful, handsome (LL *bellitus*, perhaps the result of a cross between *bellus* (see BEAU) and the term of endearment *mellitus* 'honey'). Bellido was also used in the Middle Ages as a given name, and this may lie behind some examples of the surname.

Bellingham English: habitation name from places in Kent and Northumb. The former is so called from OE *Beringhām* 'homestead (OE *hām*) associated with *Be(o)ra*', a byname meaning 'BEAR'; the latter seems to have been originally named as the 'homestead of the dwellers at the bell', from OE *belle* used in a transferred sense of a bell-shaped hill.

An Irish family of this name trace their descent from William de Bellingham, *who was sheriff of Tynedale, Northumb., in 1279. They were established in Ireland by Robert Bellingham, who settled in Co. Longford in 1611. They gave their name to* Castlebellingham *in Co. Louth.*

Bellwood English: apparently a habitation name from a place named with OE *wudu* WOOD as second element. This may be *Belwood* in Lincs. (of which the first element is obscure), but the surname is most common in Yorks. and identification cannot be made with any certainty.

Belton 1. English: habitation name from any of various places so called, for example in Leics., Lincs., and Suffolk.

The first element, *bel*, is of uncertain origin; the second is OE *tūn* enclosure, settlement.

2. Irish: see WELDON.

Benavente Spanish: habitation name from places in the provinces of Badajoz, Huesca, and Zamora, so called from L *Beneventum*. The L placename seems to mean 'welcome' (from *bene* well + *ventum*, past part. of *venīre* to come), but this is probably a folk etymological distortion of an earlier name.

Cogn.: Cat.: **Benavent** (a place in Lérida).

Benavides Spanish: patr. from the common medieval given name *Ben Avid*, of Arabic origin, from *ibn Abd* 'son of the servant (of God)'.

Benbow English: occupational nickname for an archer, from ME *bend(en)* to bend (OE *bendan*) + *bowe* bow (OE *boga*).

Bench English (W Midlands): of uncertain origin. It is perhaps a topographic name for someone who lived by a bank or raised piece of ground, ME *benche* (from OE *benc* bench). However, this transferred sense of the word is not well attested, and some other sense of the word may be in question; perhaps one who sat on a bench in a hall, i.e. a retainer.

Bengoa Basque: topographic name for someone who lived at the lower end of a village, from *be(e)ngo* furthest down + the def. art. *-a*.

Bengoechea Spanish form of Basque **Bengoetxea**: habitation name from a house situated at the lower end of a village, from *be(e)ngo* furthest down + *etxe* house + the def. art. *-a*.

Benham 1. English: habitation name from a group of villages in Berks., so called from the OE personal name **Benna* (of uncertain origin) + OE *hamm* river-meadow.

2. Scots: habitation name from *Benholm* in the former county of Angus (now part of Tayside region) in which the final element is Northern ME *holm* island, dry land in a fen (see HOLME).

Benjamin Jewish, English, and French: from the Hebr. male given name *Binyamin* 'Son of the South'. In the Book of Genesis, it is treated as meaning 'Son of the Right Hand'. The two senses are connected, since in Hebr. the south is thought of as the right-hand side of a person who is facing east. Benjamin was the youngest and favourite son of Jacob and supposed progenitor of one of the twelve tribes of Israel (Gen. 35: 16–18; 42: 4). It is also a rare Eng. and Fr. surname, for although the given name was not common among Gentiles in the Middle Ages, its use was sanctioned by virtue of having been borne by a saint martyred in Persia in about AD 424. In some cases in medieval Europe it was also applied as a byname or nickname to the youngest (and beloved) son of a large family; this is the sense of the mod. Fr. vocab. word *benjamin*.

Vars.: Jewish: **Benyamin, Binyamin**; **Benjamini, Benjaminy, Benyamini, Binyamini, Biniamini** (Israeli, with the Hebr. ending *-i*).

Cogns.: Fr.: **Jamin** (an aphetic form). It.: **Beniamini, Bignami(ni), Biamini**. Hung.: **Benjámin**.

Dims.: Fr.: (aphetic); **Jaminet, Jaminot**.

Patrs.: Jewish: **Benjaminov, Benjaminowitsch, Benyaminov, Binyaminov(ich), Biniaminovitz**. Beloruss.: **Benyaminov**. Du.: **Benjamins, Benjamens**.

Patrs. (from the Russ. dim. *Velya*): Russ.: **Velyashev, Velyushin, Velekhov, Velikhov, Velyugin**.

Benn English (chiefly Yorks.): from the ME given name *Benne*, which is in part a short form of *Benedict* (see BENNETT), in part a form of the ON personal name *Bjorn* 'Bearcub, Warrior'.

Dims.: **Benney** (Devon and Cornwall); **Bennie** (Scots).

Patrs.: **Benn(i)s**, BENSON.

Patr. (from a dim.): Sc.: **Benzies** (pronounced /'bɛnjɪz/).

Bennett English: from the medieval given name *Benedict* (L *Benedictus* 'Blessed'). This owed its popularity in the Middle Ages chiefly to St Benedict (*c*.480–550), who founded the Benedictine order of monks at Monte Cassino and wrote a monastic rule that formed a model for all subsequent rules. No doubt the meaning of the L word also contributed to its popularity as a given name, especially in Romance countries. In the 12th cent. the L form of the name is found in England alongside versions derived from the OF form *Beneit*, *Benoit*, which was common among the Normans.

Vars.: **Bennet**; **Benedict, Ben(ne)dick** (Sc.).

Cogns.: Fr.: **Bénédi(c)t(e), Bénet, Beneix**; **Bené** (E France); **Benez** (N France); **Benech** (Brittany). Prov.: **Bénéze(i)t, Bénézit, Bénazet**. It.: **Ben(e)detti, Benditti**; **Venditti, Nitto** (S Italy). Sp.: **Benedi(c)to, Benito, Beneyto**. Cat.: **Benet**. Port.: **Bento**. Ger. (of Slav. origin): **Bendig, Bindig, Benditt**. Czech: **Benedikt**; **Beneš, Benda**. Pol.: **Banach, Banaś**. Jewish (Ashkenazic): **Beinisch, Banis(c)h, Beniesh** (from the Yid. male given name *Beynish*, from Czech *Beneš*); **Benda**. Hung.: **Benedek**.

Dims.: Eng.: BENN. Corn.: **Bennetto**. Fr.: **Beneteau, Benoîton**. It.: **Bene(de)ttini, Benet(t)elli, Benet(t)ollo, Benini**. Ger.: **Ben(t)z** (see also **Berthold**). Low Ger.: **Bente, Benn(e), Behn(e), Bein(e), Beyn(e)**; **Behn(e)(c)ke, Bein(c)ke, Beynke, Benck**. Fris.: **Be(n)tje, Be(n)tke**. Du.: **Betjeman**. Dan.: **Bennike**. Czech: **Bendík**. Pol.: **Banasik, Banaszczyk**. Lithuanian: **Benduhn**. Hung.: **Bede, Benkö**.

Patrs.: Eng.: **Bennet(t)s** (chiefly Devon and Cornwall). It.: **De Benedetti**; **De Benedictis, De Beneditti** (S Italy). Sp.: **Benítez**. Flem., Du.: BENTINCK. Low Ger.: **Bendix(en), Bentsen, Bentzen**. Norw., Dan.: **Ben(g)tsen, Bend(t)sen, Bennedsen, Bentzen, Ben(g)tson**. Swed.: **Benediktsson, Bengtsson**. Russ.: **Venediktov**; **Vedeniktov, Vedentyev, Vedenisov, Vedeneev, Videneev, Vidineev** (metathesized versions, in part associated by folk etymology with Russ. *videt* to see). Beloruss.: **Benediktovich**. Pol.: **Benedyktowicz**. Jewish (E Ashkenazic): **Beinosovitch**.

Patrs. (from dims.): Sp.: **Benítez**. Low Ger.: **Benes, Bennen**; **Behn(e)(c)ken, Bein(c)ken, Beynken**. Fris.: **Be(n)tje(n)s, Benning, Benninck, Behning, Behninck, Beining, Beininck**. Du.: **Beentjes, Bennink**. Pol.: **Banaszkiewicz**; **Banasiak**. Jewish (E Ashkenazic): **Banishevitz**. Russ.: **Vedeshkin, Vedyashkin, Vedekhov, Vedikhov, Vedekhin, Vedyaev, Vedyasov, Vedishchev, Vedenyakin, Vedenyapin, Vidyapin, Vedenichev**. Beloruss.: **Beneshevich, Banasevich**.

Habitation name (from a dim.): Pol.: **Banaszewski**.

The English surname Bennett *was particularly common in parishes on the Derbys./Ches. border in the 18th cent.*

Benson 1. English: patr. from the medieval given name *Benne* (see BENN).

2. English: habitation name from a place in Oxon., so called from OE *Benesingtūn* 'settlement (OE *tūn*) associated with *Banesa*', a personal name of obscure origin, perhaps a deriv. of *Bana* 'slayer'.

3. Jewish (E Ashkenazic): shortened form of **Besenson**, which is of uncertain origin.

Var.: **Benn(i)son**.

Benstead English: habitation name from any of various places, such as *Banstead* in Surrey (*Benestede* in Domesday

Book), named with the OE elements *bēan* beans (a collective sing.) + *stede* place.

Var.: **Bensted**.

Bent English: topographic name for someone who lived on a patch of land with bent grass, rushes, or reeds (OE *beonet*, a collective sing.) growing on it.

Benthall English: habitation name from a place in Shrops., so called from OE *beonet* bent grass + *halh* nook, recess (see HALE 1).

Vars.: **Bentall, Bendall, Bendell, Bendle.**

A family of this name have been living at Benthall near Broseley, Shrops., from the 12th cent. to the present. Anfrid de Benthall *signed a charter in 1120 and his descendant Philip* de Benedhal *claimed land in Benthall in 1255. Benthall Hall was rebuilt in 1535, but passed out of the hands of the family in the first half of the 18th cent. with the extinction of the direct male line. John Benthall (d. c.1590), a member of another branch of the family, married the daughter of a clothier from Halstead, Essex, and established a branch of the family in that county. A descendant, Frank* Bentall *(1843–1923), began his working life in his father's shop in Maldon, but in 1867 moved to Kingston upon Thames, Surrey, and opened a small draper's shop which later turned into a large department store. Another branch of the same family migrated from Essex to Devon. In 1843 they changed the spelling of their name back to Benthall, and in 1934 Mrs. Clementina Benthall repurchased the ancestral estate in Shrops.*

Bentham English: habitation name from any of various places, for example in W Yorks., so called from OE *beonet* bent grass (see BENT) + *hām* homestead.

Bentinck English and Dutch: patr. (formed with the Gmc suffix *-ing*) from the Du. given name *Bent*, a contracted form of *Benedict* (cf. BENNETT).

Var.: **Benting**.

Bentinck *is the surname of an ancient and powerful Dutch and English noble family. They have been associated with a place of this name near Deventer in Holland, but it is more probable that the place took its name from the family than vice versa. The family originated in the Palatinate, and came to the Netherlands during the 14th cent. Three hundred years later, William Bentinck (1649–1709) was a close adviser of William of Orange, and was largely instrumental in securing the European support necessary for the latter's accession, as William III, to the throne of England in 1688. He was rewarded with the earldom of Portland, and in 1716 his son was created Duke of Portland. The 3rd Duke (1738–1809) married a Cavendish and took the surname Cavendish-Bentinck.*

Bentley English: habitation name from any of various places, the chief of which are in Derbys., Essex, Hants, Shrops., Staffs., Suffolk, Warwicks., Worcs., and E and W Yorks., so called from OE *beonet* bent grass (see BENT) + *lēah* wood, clearing.

Benton English: habitation name, apparently from a pair of villages in Northumb., so called from OE *bēan* beans (a collective sing.) or *beonet* bent grass (see BENT) + *tūn* enclosure, settlement. However, the name is now most frequent in the W Midlands, so it may be that a place of the same name in that area should be sought as its origin.

Benveniste Italian and Jewish (non-Ashkenazic): nickname from the expression *benveniste* 'welcome' (L *bene venistis* you have arrived well; cf. BENVENUTI).

Vars.: Jewish: **Benvenisti, Benvenisty, Benvenishte, Benveneste.**

Benvenuti Italian: from the medieval given name *Benvenuto* 'Welcome' (from OIt. *bene* well + *venuto* arrived, past part. of *venire* to come, arrive). Generally it was applied to a long-awaited and much-desired child.

Vars.: **Benvegnu; Venut(t)i; Nuti, Gnuti, Gnudi.**

Dims.: **Venutelli, Vignudelli, Begnudelli, Vignodolli, Vignudini; Nutini.**

Beraud French: from the Gmc personal name *Ber(n)-wald*, composed of the elements *ber(n)* bear + *wald* rule. There has been some confusion between this name and the more common BERNARD; see BARRETT.

Vars.: **Béraud, Berau(l)t, Bérault, Braud, Brault; Bernaud, Barnaud.**

Cogns.: Prov.: **Béral, Bérau.** It.: **Beraldi, Beraudi; Veraldi, Veralli.** Cat.: **Bernal.** Ger.: **Berwald** (altered by folk etymology as if from Ger. *Bär* bear + *Wald* forest); **Be(e)r(h)old, Bärold, Bierhold; Börold** (Bavaria).

Dims.: Fr.: **Braudel, Braudey.** It.: **Beraldini.**

Berdyaev Russian: from the Tatar nickname *Berdi* 'he has given' (from *bermak* to give), with assimilation to the normal Russ. patr. ending *-ev*. The name was originally borne by a Tatar noble family; the Russianized form was adopted with the loss of Tatar independence in the 16th cent.

Vars.: **Berdiev, Berdyev.**

Beresford English: habitation name from a place in the parish of Alstonfield, N Staffs., so called from the gen. case of the OE byname *Beofor* 'Beaver' + OE *ford* FORD.

Vars.: **Berresford, Ber(r)isford.**

The first recorded bearer of the surname is John de Beveresford *who held the manor of Beresford* c.*1220–41. All present-day Beresfords seem to be descended from Thomas Beresford, who fought at Agincourt in 1415 and fathered sixteen sons and five daughters. There is an Irish branch which includes the Marquesses of Waterford.*

Bereznikov Russian: patr. from the topographic term *Bereznik* 'dweller by birch trees' (from *beryoza* birch; cogn. with Pol. *brzoza* birch tree, *brzezina* birch forest). The word is ultimately cogn. with Eng. BIRCH and probably also with *bright*, the reference originally being to the distinctive white bark of the tree.

Vars.: **Berezin, Berezov.**

Cogns.: Pol.: **Brzezicki.** Czech: **Březa, Bříza, Březina.** Jewish (E Ashkenazic, mostly ornamental names, but in some cases possibly topographic or habitation names): **Berez(a), Brzoza, Berezin, B(e)rezni(a)k, Breza(c)k; Brezner** (with Yid. or Ger. suffix *-er* of nouns denoting humans); **Berezov(ski), Berezovsky, Berezowski, Berezowsky, Brazovsky, Brzozowski; Berezowicz, Berezovitz; Brezenoff, B(e)rezinski, Brzezinski; Berenicky, Breznitz, Brezny.**

Dims.: Ukr.: **Berezko.** Beloruss.: **Beryozkin** (patr.). Pol.: **Brzózka.**

Habitation names: Pol.: **Brzeziński** (from places called *Brzezie* and *Brzeziny*); **Brzozowski.**

Berg 1. German and Swedish: topographic name for someone who lived on or by a hill or mountain (OHG *berg*, ON *bjarg*). As a Swedish surname it is often an ornamental name, one of the many formed by more or less arbitrary selection of vocab. words referring to natural phenomena.

2. Jewish (Ashkenazic): possibly a topographic name as in 1, or an ornamental name from Ger. *Berg* or Yid. *berg* hill, or a short form of any of the many ornamental surnames containing this word as a final element, for example *Schönberg* (see SCHÖN) and *Goldberg* (see GOLD).

Vars. (of 1): Ger.: **Berger, Bergmann.** Swed.: **Bergman, Bergén, Berg(l)in.**

Cogns. (of 1): Low Ger.: **Barg(mann).** Fris.: **Bergsma.** Du.: **Van den Berg(h), Van (den) Berge, (Van) Bergen, Ten Berge, Berger, Bergman.** Dan.: **B(j)erg, Bergman.**

Cpds (of 1, ornamental): Swed.: **Berg(en)dahl** ('hill valley'); **Berggren** ('hill branch'); **Bergholm** ('hill island'); **Berglind** ('hill lime'); **Berglöf** ('hill leaf'); **Berglund** ('hill grove'); **Bergqvist** ('hill twig'); **Bergstedt** ('hill homestead'); **Bergsten** ('hill stone'); **Bergstrand** ('hill shore'); **Bergström** ('hill river'); **Bergvall** ('hill slope').

Berge French: 1. topographic name for someone who lived on a steep bank, from OF *berge* bank (apparently of Gaul. origin).

2. hypercorrected var. of BARGE.

Var. (of 1): **Delbergue**.

Dims. (of 1): **Bergeau, Bergeon**.

Bergin 1. Irish: Anglicized form of Gael. **Ó Beirgin** or **Ó Meirgin**, a shortened version of **Ó hAimheirgin** 'descendant of *Aimheirgin*', a common personal name in early Irish mythology and historical tales, perhaps composed of the elements *amhra* wonderful + *gin* birth.

2. Swedish: var. of BERG.

Vars. (of 1): **Berrigan; Mergin**.

Beringer English (Norman): from the OF given name *Berenger*. This is in origin a Gmc personal name, composed of the elements *ber(n)* bear + *ger, gar* spear, and owed its popularity in part to the fact that it was the name of one of the characters in the Charlemagne romances.

Vars.: **Berringer, Bellinger, Bel(l)enger; Ballinger** (chiefly W Midlands); **Bell(h)anger** (altered by folk etymology); **Ben(n-in)ger**.

Cogns.: Fr.: **Béranger, Béreng(i)er, B(é)renguier, B(é)renguié, Bringuier**. It.: **Beringh(i)eri, Bering(h)eli, Berengari(o), Bel(l)ing(h)(i)eri, Berlingh(i)eri**. Cat.: **Berling(u)er**. Ger.: **Be(h)ringer**.

Berkhout Dutch: topographic name for someone who lived by a birch wood, from MDu. *berke* BIRCH + *holt* wood (see HOLT).

Berkutov Russian: patr. from the nickname *Berkut* 'Golden Eagle' (a borrowing from a Turkic language).

Berle French: apparently from OF *berle* water parsnip, an aquatic plant (of Celt. origin, cf. W *berur*, Gael. *biorar* watercress). The reasons why this word should have given rise to a surname are not clear; perhaps it was an occupational name for a grower of the plant.

Var.: **Berlier** (which has the form of an occupational name).

Dims.: **Berl(i)et, Berlot, Berlioz**.

Berlin Jewish (Ashkenazic) and German: habitation name from the city of *Berlin*, former capital of Germany, now of the German Democratic Republic. This city takes its name from a Wendish word meaning 'river rake', a scaffold of beams built over a river to prevent logs from jamming; the river in question is the Spree. Folk etymology, however, has put a bear into the arms of the city, as if the name were derived from *Bärlin*, a dim. of *Bär* bear. The German name is also found in the Hamburg area, where it may be derived from the village of the same name, but uncertain etymology, in Holstein.

Vars.: **Berliner; Berlinski, Berlinsky** (E Ashkenazic).

Berman 1. English: occupational name for a porter, ME *berman* (OE *bærmann*, from *beran* to carry + *mann* man).

2. English: possibly from a ME given name, *Ber(e)man*, which may be derived from OE *Beornmund*, composed of the elements *beorn* young man, warrior + *mund* protection.

3. Anglicized form of BERMANN (1–3).

4. Jewish (Ashkenazic): var. of BERMANN 4.

Cogns. (of 1): Fr.: **Bermond, Brémond, Brémont**. Sp.: **Bermudo**. Du.: **Bermon(d)**.

Patr. (from 1): Sp.: **Bermúdez**.

Bermann 1. German: occupational name for someone exhibiting a bear; see BEARMAN.

2. German: occupational name for a swineherd, from MHG, OHG *bēr* boar + *man* man.

3. Low German: pet form of any of the various medieval given names derived from Gmc cpd names with the first element *ber(n)* bear (cf., e.g., BERNARD and BERAUD).

4. Jewish (Ashkenazic): either an elaboration of the Yid. male given name *Ber* 'Bear' or else an ornamental name referring to the bear.

Vars. (of 1): **Permann** (Bavaria). (Of 2): **Behrmann, Bahrmann, Baarmann**. (Of 4): BERMAN: **Behrman(n)**.

Bermejo Spanish: nickname for a man with red hair or a ruddy complexion, from Sp. *bermejo* red, ruddy (LL *vermiculus*, from *vermis* worm, since a red dye was obtained from the bodies of worms).

Bernard English, French, Polish, and Czech: from the Gmc given name *Bernhard*, composed of the elements *ber(n)* bear + *hard* brave, hardy, strong. This was brought to England by the Normans, reinforcing OE *Beornheard*. The popularity of the given name among the Normans in the centuries immediately following the Conquest was greatly increased by virtue of its having been borne by St Bernard of Clairvaux (*c.*1090–1153), founder and abbot of the Cistercian monastery at Clairvaux, and in Holland and N Germany it vied with ARNOLD as the most popular given name during the 13th and 14th cents. Another sanctified bearer of the name was St Bernard of Menthon (923–1008), founder of Alpine hospices and patron saint of mountaineers, whose cult accounts for the frequency of the name in Alpine regions.

Vars.: Eng.: **Barnard**. Fr.: **Barnard, Bénard; Besnard** (hypercorrected); **Benard** (Belg.). Pol.: **Biernat, Biernacki, Bernadzki**. Czech: **Ber(n), Berán**.

Cogns.: Prov.: **Bernat**. It.: **Bern(ard)i**, NARDO. Sp.: **Bernardo(s), Bernaldo**. Cat.: **Bernat**. Port.: **Bernardo**. Ger.: **Bernhard(t), Bernhart; Berard(t)**. Low Ger.: **Berndt, Behrend**. Flem., Du.: **Bern(h)ard, Barnhart, Be(e)rnaert, Beer(n)t**. Dan.: **Bernt(h)**. Hung.: **Bernát(h)**.

Dims.: Eng.: BARNET. Fr.: **Bernardeau, Bénardeau, Besnardeau; Berna(r)det** (fem. **Berna(r)dette**), **Bernadé, Bernet** (fem. **Bernette**), **Berney; Berna(r)dot** (fem. **Berna(r)dotte**), **Bernot; Bernardin, Bernardy, Berna(r)don, Berna(r)dou(x), Bernon; Bernol(l)et, Nollet, Nolleau, Nolot, Nolin**. It.: **Bern(ard)ini, Bernard(in)elli, Bern(ard)otti, Bernetti, Bernocchi, Bernucci, Bernuzzi**. Sp., Port.: **Bernardino**. Ger.: **Betz** (see also BERTHOLD); **Berni, Bernli(n)** (Switzerland). Czech: **Bernášek; Beránek, Berka**.

Augs.: Fr.: **Bernat**. It.: **Bernardoni, Nardoni**.

Patrs.: Sp.: **Bernárdez, Bernáldez**. Port.: **Bernardes**. It.: **Di Bernardo, De Bernardi(s); Bernardeschi**. Low Ger.: **Baren(d)ts(en), Behren(d)s(en), Ber(e)ns; Bernhardi** (Latinized). Du.: **Behrens, Berends(en), Berndsen, Baren(d)s, Barense(n)**. Dan., Norw.: **Bern(d)tssen**. Swed.: **Bernhardsson, Bern(d)tsson**. Pol.: **Biernatowicz, Bernakiewicz; Bernaciak**.

The English surname Barnard *has been particularly common in Sussex from the 17th cent. onwards.*

The Irish philanthropist Dr Thomas Barnardo *(1845–1905), who founded the orphanages which still bear his name, was born in Dublin, the son of a furrier who came originally from Hamburg. The family were of Spanish origin; they became Protestants, and in the 18th cent. moved to Hamburg to escape religious persecution.*

A Scots family by the name of Bernardes *can trace their descent back to a certain John Bernardes Corea (b. 1778), who married the daughter of Robert Dunbar. According to family tradition he was descended from a sailor in the Spanish Armada who was shipwrecked on the coast of Scotland in 1588.*

Berner 1. English: from the Norman given name *Bernier*, which is of Gmc origin, being composed of the elements *ber(n)* bear + *hari*, *heri* army.

2. English: occupational name for a burner of lime or charcoal, from OE *beornan* to burn. This may also have occasionally denoted someone who baked bricks or distilled spirits, or who carried out some other manufacturing process involving burning.

3. English: occupational name for a keeper of hounds, from ONF *bern(i)er*, *brenier* (a deriv. of *bren*, *bran* bran (of Gaul. origin), on which the dogs were fed).

4. English: habitation name or topographic name, a var. of BARNES 1 or BOURNE.

5. Jewish (Ashkenazic): of unknown origin.

Var. (of 2 and 3): BRENNER.

Cogns. (of 1): Fr.: **Bernier, Bénier**; **Besnier** (hypercorrected).

Dims. (of 1): Fr.: **Berneret** (fem. **Bernerette**); **Berneron, Bernerin, Bernelin**.

Patr. (from 1): Eng.: **Berners**.

Bernstein 1. Jewish (Ashkenazic): ornamental name from Ger. *Bernstein* amber (from MLG *bernen* to burn + *stēn* stone; i.e. it was thought to be created by burning, although it is in fact fossilized pine resin).

2. German: habitation name from a place so called, of which there is one in Bavaria and another in what used to be E Prussia (now the town of *Pełczyce* in NW Poland; see PEŁCZYŃSKI). Both of these probably get their Ger. names from the notion of a 'burnt stone', for example in brick making, rather than from 'amber'.

Vars. (of 1): Jewish: **Bernshtein, Berens(h)tein**; **Bernstejn, Berensztejn** (Pol. spellings); **Bor(e)nstein, Bor(e)nshtein, Bor(e)nshtain, Borenstain**; **Bor(e)nsztein** (mixed Pol.-Ger. spellings); BURNS, BURSTIN.

Berrocal Spanish: topographic name for someone who lived on a patch of stony ground, Sp. *berrocal* (a deriv. of *berrueco* rock, crag, a word of uncertain, probably Celt., origin).

Berry 1. English: topographic name or habitation name, a var. of BURY.

2. Irish (Galway and Mayo): Anglicized form of Gael. *Ó Beargha*; see BARRY 6.

3. French: regional name for someone from *Berry*, a former province of central France, so called from L *Boiriācum*, apparently a deriv. of a Gaul. personal name, *Boirius* or *Barius*.

Vars. (of 3): Fr.: **Berrier, Berryer, Berruer, Berrue(i)x**.

Bert French, English, and (rarely) German: from the Gmc personal name *Berto*, a short form of the various cpd personal names with the first element *berht* bright, famous (cf. e.g. BERTHIER, BERTHOLD, BERTOLF, and BERTRAM). See also BURT.

Cogn.: It.: **Berti**.

Dims.: N Eng.: **Bertie**. Fr.: **Berton** (also from the oblique case), **Bert(h)oneau, Bertet, Bert(h)elin, Bert(h)elot, Bertil(l)on, Bert(h)ilet**. It.: **Bert(or)elli, Bertin(ett)i, Bertinotti**; **Bertuc-c(ell)i, Bertuccini, Bertuccioli**; **Bertozzi, Bertuzzi, Bertoc-c(h)(in)i**; **Pertini, Pertotti** (N Italy). Cat.: **Bert(h)elin, Bertolin**. Ger.: **Bert(h)el**; **Bertl** (Franconia). Low Ger.: **Beth(k)e, Bethmann**.

Aug.: It.: **Bertoni**.

Pejs.: It.: **Bertacco, Bertacchi**.

Patrs.: It.: **Bertenghi, Bertinghi**.

Patrs. (from dims.): Ger.: **Bert(h)els, Berlitz**.

Berthier French: from the Gmc personal name *Berther*, composed of the elements *berht* bright, famous + *heri*, *hari* army.

Var.: **Bertier**.

Cogns.: It.: **Bert(i)ero**.

Dims.: Fr.: **Bert(h)eron, Bertron**. Prov.: **Bert(h)erou(x), Bertrou**. It.: **Bertarini**.

Berthold German: from the Gmc personal name *Bertwald*, composed of the elements *berht* bright, famous + *wald* rule.

Vars.: **Berchthold, Bergdolt** (Bavaria); **Perthold** (Austria); **Bächtold, Bechtold** (Switzerland).

Cogns.: Low Ger.: **Bart(h)old**. Fr.: **Bert(h)ault, Bert(h)aud, Bert(h)aux**; **Bertoud**. It.: **Bertol(d)i, Bertoll(i)o, Bertogli(o)**; **Bertalti**; **Pertoldi** (Friuli).

Dims.: Ger.: **Ben(t)z** (Bavaria, Austria; see also BENNETT); **Betz** (see also BERNARD). Fr.: **Bert(h)audet, Bet(h)audé**. It.: **Bertoletti, Bertolini, Bertolucci, Bertoluzzi**.

Patrs.: Low Ger.: **Bart(h)els**; **Bartholdy** (Latinized). Swed.: **Bertilsson**.

Bertolf German: from the Gmc personal name *Bertolf*, composed of the elements *berht* bright, famous + *wolf* wolf.

Vars.: **Bertleff**; **Bechtolf, Bechtloff** (Switzerland).

Cogns.: Fr.: **Bertou(l)**; **Berthou(x)**. Eng.: **Bardolph**.

Dims.: Fr.: **Bert(h)o(u)let, Bert(h)ollet**.

Aug.: Fr.: **Bert(h)olat**.

Bertram English, French, and German: from the Gmc personal name *Bertram*, composed of the elements *berht* bright, famous + *hrabn* raven. The raven was the bird of Odin, king of the gods, in Gmc mythology. The given name was common in France throughout the Middle Ages, where its popularity was increased by the fame of the troubadour Bertrand de Born (?1140-?1214). The spelling *Bertrand* is Fr., coined by folk etymology under the influence of the pres. part. ending *-and*, *-ant*. The name was brought to England by the Normans in the forms *Bertran(d)*, *Bertram*, and *Bartram*.

Vars.: Eng.: **Bartram, Bart(t)rum**; **Ba(t)tram, Batterham, Borthram, Buttrum, Bertrand**. Fr.: **Bertran(d), Bétran**. Low Ger.: **Berterman** (Schleswig).

Cogns.: Prov.: **Beltram, Beltran(d)**. It.: **Bertrami, Beltrami, Bertrandi, Beltran(d)i**. Sp.: **Beltrán**. Cat.: **Bertran, Beltran**. Low Ger.: **Bartram**. Hung.: **Bertalan**.

Dims.: Fr.: **Bertran(d)et, Bertrandot, Bertrandeau, Bertrandon**. Prov.: **Bertaneu**. It.: **Beltramelli, Beltrametti, Beltramini**; **Bertamini**.

Patrs.: Low Ger.: **Tra(h)ms**.

Berzal Spanish: topographic name for someone who lived by a cabbage patch, Sp. *berzal* (a deriv. of *berza* cabbage, from LL *viridia* cabbage, 'greens', neut. pl. of *viridis* green).

Bès Provençal: topographic name for someone who lived by a birch tree or in a birch wood, from OProv. *bès* birch (LL *bettius*, of Gaul. origin).

Vars.: **Bex, Bez**; **Besse**.

Dims.: **Besseau, Besset, Bessey**; **Bezou(t)**.

Collectives: **Bessière(s), Besseire, Besseyre, Bessède**.

Besançon French: habitation name from the town in the *département* of Doubs, which apparently gets its name from a Celtiberian element *ves* mountain + suffix *-unt*, with a further (L) suffix *-io* (gen. *-iōnis*). In folk etymology there has been some association with OF *bison* the (European) bison, which animal appears in the arms of the city.

Var.: **Bezançon**.

Besant English: from ME *besant*, the name of a gold coin (via OF from L (*nummus*) *byzantius*, so called because it was first minted at Byzantium). The surname arose as a metonymic occupational name for a coiner or else a nickname for a man rich in cash. A certain Lefwin Besant is recorded in London in 1168 as a moneyer.
Vars.: **Bessant, Bessent, Bez(z)ant.**

Bessell English or Welsh: of uncertain origin, possibly a var. of BISSELL. The name apparently occurs in the placename *Bessels Leigh*, in Berks., the manor of which was held by Petrus *Besyles* in 1412.

Bessemer English: 1. occupational name for a maker of brooms, from an agent deriv. of ME *besem* broom (OE *bes(e)ma*).
2. altered form of Fr. *Bassemer*; see below.
Cogn. (of 1): Ger.: **Besemer.**
Sir Henry Bessemer *(1813–98), inventor of the Bessemer converter, came of a family of Huguenot origin, whose original surname is given as* **Bassemer**. *This is of uncertain origin: derivation as a topographic name, from Fr.* basse *(fem.) low +* mer *sea, seems implausible.*

Besser German: occupational name for a collector of fines, from an agent deriv. of MHG *buoz(e)* fine, reparation (OHG *buoz(a)*).
Var.: **Besserer.**

Besson Provençal: nickname for one of a pair of twins, from OProv. *besson* twin (a deriv. of OF, L *bis* twice).
Var.: **Bessou.**
Cogn.: It.: **Bessoni** (Piedmont).
Dims.: Prov.: **Bessonet, Bessoneau.**
Aug.: Prov.: **Bessonat.**
Pej.: Prov.: **Bessonaud.**

Best 1. English and French: from ME, OF *beste* animal, beast (L *bestia*). This was applied as a surname in two ways: as a metonymic occupational name for someone who looked after beasts—i.e. a herdsman—and as a nickname for someone thought to resemble an animal—i.e. a violent, uncouth, or stupid man. It is unlikely that the name is derived from *best*, OE *betst*, superlative of *good*.
2. German: topographic name for someone who lived by the river *Beste*, a tributary of the Trave, or habitation name from any of various villages called *Besten*, said by Bahlow to be named from a MLG word for poor soil.
3. German: short form of SEBASTIAN.
Vars.: **Beste.** (Of 1 only): Eng.: **Bester, Bestar, Best(i)man** (in the sense 'herdsman'). Fr.: **Best(e)au(x), Bétiau** (in the sense 'brutal', from OF *best(i)al*). Port.: **Bicha.**
Dims. (of 1): Fr.: **Bestel(le).** (Of 3): Ger.: **Bestel.**
Best *was a common name in Worcs. from the early 15th cent. One family can be traced back to Edward Best (d. 1628/9), a yeoman from Old Swinford, whose descendants included nailers and clothiers and, after the Industrial Revolution, a firm of Birmingham lamp-makers founded by Robert Best (b. 1843).*

Beswick English: habitation name from places in Lancs. and N Yorks., the second element of which is clearly OE *wic* outlying (dairy) farm (see WICK). The first element of the Lancs. name may be an OE personal name *Bēac*; that of the Yorks. name is possibly *Besi*.
Var.: **Bestwick.**

Bethell 1. English: from a medieval dim. of *Beth*, short form of the female name *Elizabeth* (cf. BELL 2 and LILLY).
2. Welsh: patr. (*ab Ithel*) from the given name *Ithael* 'bountiful lord'; cf. IDLE and JEKYLL.
Vars. (of 2): **Bithell** (now chiefly Lancs.); **Bythell**, BISSELL; see also BESSELL.

Bett English: from a medieval given name, a short form of *Bartholomew*, *Beatrice*, or *Elizabeth*.
Patrs./Metrs.: **Bett(i)s(on), Bettenson.**

Bettencourt French: habitation name from any of various places so called, with minor variations in spelling, of which the main one is in Somme. They get their name from a Gmc personal name *Betto* (of uncertain origin, probably an assimilated form of *Berto*; see BERT) + OF *court* farm(yard) (see COURT 1). The name is now very frequent in Portugal, where it first occurs in the 14th cent.
Var.: **Betancourt.**

Betteridge English: from the OE personal name *Beadurīc*, composed of the elements *beadu* battle + *rīc* power.
Vars.: **Bettridge, Betteriss, Bat(t)rick, Badrick, Badrock.**

Bevan Welsh: patr. from EVAN, with fused patr. prefix *ap*, *ab*.
Vars.: **Bevans**, BEVIN.

Beveridge English and Scots: probably from ME *beverage* drink (OF *bevrage*, from *beivre* to drink, L *bibere*). The term was used in particular of a drink bought by a purchaser to seal a bargain, and the surname may have been acquired as a nickname in this context. Reaney adduces evidence to suggest that the nickname may have been bestowed on a man who made a practice of getting free drinks by entering into bargains which he did not keep. The name is more common in Scotland than in England.
Vars.: **Bavridge; Berridge** (Midlands).

Beverley English: habitation name from a place in E Yorks. (now Humberside), the name of which contains OE *beofor* beaver, combined with a second element that may mean 'stream'.
Var.: **Beverly.**

Bevin 1. English (Norman): nickname for a wine drinker, from OF *bei(vre)*, *boi(vre)* to drink (L *bībere*) + *vin* wine (L *vīnum*).
2. Welsh: var. of BEVAN, patr. from EVAN.
Vars.: (of 1): **Beavin, Bivin, Bivan.**
Cogns. (of 1): Fr.: **Boi(s)(le)vin.** Prov.: **Beuvin.** It.: **Bevivino.**
Dim. (of 1): Fr.: **Boivinet.**
Patrs. (probably mostly of 1): Eng.: **Be(a)vins, Bevens, Bivins, Bivens, Bivans, Beavans, Bavens, Bavins, Beevens.**

Bevington English (SW Midlands): habitation name from one of the places so called, in Warwicks. and Gloucs. The placename means 'Bēofa's settlement', from the OE personal name *Bēofa* + OE *tūn* settlement.

Bewes 1. English (Norman): habitation name from *Bayeux* in Calvados, which gets its name from being the seat of a Gaul. tribe recorded in L sources as the *Ba(d)iocasses*.
2. Welsh: patr. from the given name HUGH, with the addition of the Welsh prefix *ab*, *ap*, and (tautologically) the Eng. suffix *-s*.
Vars.: BEWS. (Of 2 only): **Bew, Bugh**; PUGH.
Cogn. (of 1): Fr. **Bayeux.**
Bewes *is the name of a Cornish family; Richard Bewes was MP for Liskeard in 1384.*

Bewick English: habitation name from a place in Northumb., so called from OE *bēo* bee + *wīc* outlying farm; apparently originally a station for the production of honey. There is another place of the same name in N Yorks.
Vars.: **Bewicke, Bowick; Buick** (N Ireland).

Bezděk Czech: apparently from the adverb *bezděky* involuntarily, unintentionally. The application as a surname is not clear, but it may be a nickname from some lost anecdote. On the other hand there are several placenames in Bohemia formed with this element, and although the surname is not a habitation name in form, it may nevertheless be derived from one of these. Moldanová cites a certain Jan *Bezděcký* from *Bezděčí Hora*, recorded in 1576.

Bezobrazov Russian: patr. from the nickname *Bezobrazny* 'Ugly', from *bez* without + *obraz* shape, form, beauty.

Bezuidenhout Dutch: topographic name from MDu. *bezuiden* on the south side (from *zuid* south) + *hout* forest (see HOLT).

Białas Polish: nickname or byname for a fair-haired person, from Pol. *biał-* white, fair, blond + *-as* masc. suffix.

Var.: **Biela**.

Cogns.: Ukr.: **Bily**, **Bilan**. Czech: **Bíl(ý)**; **Bélohlávek** ('white-haired').

Dims.: Pol.: **Białasik**, **Białczyk**, **Białek**. Czech: **Bělík**, **Bílek**. Ukr.: **Bilko**. Beloruss.: **Belyak**. Jewish (E Ashkenazic): **Bialik**, **Bielak**; **Bialovchik**.

Patrs.: Pol.: **Białasiewicz**, **Bilewicz**, **Bielak**. Croatian: **B(i)jelić**, **Belić**. Russ.: **Belyaev**. Beloruss.: **Belov** (Anglicized **Beloff**). Jewish: **Bialovitch**, **Bialovitz**, **Bialowitz**, **Bialowice**.

Patrs. (from dims.): Polish: **Biłczak**. Russ.: **Belyanchikov**. Jewish: **Bialkovitz**, **Bialkovits**, **Bilkowitz**.

Habitation names: Pol.: **Białasiński**, **Białkowski**.

Biale Jewish (E Ashkenazic): habitation name from any of various places in E Europe named in Yid. as *Byale*, from a Slav. element meaning 'white' (cf. BIAŁAS, BIELSKI).

Vars.: **Biali**, **Bialy**, **Bialo**; **Bialer**, **Bieler**.

Bialistock Jewish (E Ashkenazic): habitation name from the Polish city of *Białystok*, which is so named from Pol. *biały* white + *stok* hillside.

Vars.: **Bialistocki**, **Bialistotzki**, **Bialistotzky**, **Bialystocky**, **Bialostocki**, **Bialostocky**, **Bialostotzky**, **Bialostotsky**, **Bialostozki**, **Bialostatzki**, **Bielostocki**.

Białobrzeski Polish: habitation name from the city of *Białobrzegi*, which is so named from Pol. *biało-* white + *brzeg* shore, riverbank.

Białoskórski Polish: from *białoskóra* white leather, probably an occupational name for a leather worker.

Białowąs Polish: nickname for someone with a white moustache, from Pol. *biało-* white + *wąs* moustache.

Biard French: from the Gmc personal name *Bighard*, composed of the elements *big*, of uncertain meaning + *hard* brave, hardy, strong.

Vars.: **Bihard**, **Bicard**, **Bigard**.

Cogn.: Ger.: **Bickhardt**.

Dims.: Fr.: **Biardeau**, **Biardot**.

Bibby English: from the medieval female given name *Bibbe*, a dim. of *Isabel* (see HIBBS). In this form the surname is most common in Lancs.

Var.: **Bibb** (chiefly W Midlands).

A family named Bibby, *which possessed a freehold at Ribchester during the 14th cent., are descended from Richard Bibby, living in the late 13th cent., who was the son of a woman named* Bibbi.

Bichet French: from OF *bichet* measure for grain (a word related to mod. Eng. *beaker* and *pitcher*; all derive ultimately from Gk *bīkos*, a type of vase). The surname was probably first applied as a metonymic occupational name for an official corn-measurer or perhaps a maker of such measures.

Bick 1. English: of uncertain origin, perhaps from the OE personal name *Bicca* (cf. BECKETT 2).

2. Jewish (E Ashkenazic): German or English spelling of E Yid. *bik*, Pol. *byk*, or Russ. *byk*, all meaning 'ox' or 'bull'. This may be one of the many Jewish ornamental names taken from the animal kingdom, or it may represent an unflattering nickname bestowed by a non-Jewish government official, or it may be taken from a nickname.

Vars. (of 2): **Byk**; **Bykoff**; **Bikovski**, **Bikovsky**, **Bykovski**.

Cogns. (of 2): Pol.: **Byk**. Czech: **Býk**.

Dims. (of 2): Jewish: **Bickel**. Czech: **Býček**.

Habitation name (related to 2): Pol.: **Bykowski**.

Bicker English: 1. occupational name for a beekeeper, ME *bīker* (OE *bēocere*). Bees were important in medieval England because their honey provided the only means of sweetening food, and was also useful in preserving.

2. habitation name from a place in Lincs., so called from ON *býr* farm, settlement + *kjarr* wet ground, brushwood (see KERR).

Var.: **Bikker**.

Patr. (from 1): **Bickers**.

Bickerdike English: habitation name from some place (probably in Yorks., where the surname is commonest), perhaps meaning 'disputed ditch', from ME *biker* to quarrel (of unknown origin) + *dik* dyke, ditch (ON *díki*, OE *dīc*).

Bickerstaff English: habitation name from a minor place in the parish of Ormskirk, Lancs. so called from OE *bēocere* beekeeper (see BICKER 1) + *stæð* landing place.

Vars.: **Bickerstaffe**, **Biggerstaff**, **Bick(er)steth**.

The surname first appears, in the form de Bikerstad, *in records of land grants at the end of the 12th cent.*

Bickerton English: habitation name from any of the various places (for example in Ches., Northumb., and W Yorks.) so called from OE *bēocere* beekeeper (see BICKER 1) + *tūn* enclosure, settlement. The name is common in Staffs.

Bickford English: habitation name from a place so named from the OE personal name *Bicca* (cf. BECKETT 2) + OE *ford* FORD. There is one such place in Staffs., but the surname is more common in Devon, where it is derived from *Bickford* Town in Plympton St Mary parish.

Bickley English: habitation name from one of the places called *Bickley* in Worcs., Ches., or Kent or *Bickleigh* in Devon, all of which are possibly so called from an OE personal name *Bicca* (cf. BECKETT 2) + OE *lēah* wood, clearing. The first element could alternatively be a word meaning 'bee's nest'.

Var.: **Bickle** (chiefly Devon).

Bicknell English: habitation name from *Bickenhall* in Somerset, so called from the OE personal name *Bicca* (cf. BECKETT 2) + OE *hyll* HILL or *h(e)all* HALL.

Vars.: **Bignell**, **Bignall**, **Bignold**.

The earliest known bearer of the surname is a certain John Bickonyll *of Woolvington Manor, whose sons William and John became respectively Chancellor of Canterbury and MP for Shaftesbury in the mid-15th cent. They are probably descended from John de Paveley, a nobleman of Norman descent who held Bickenhall in the 13th cent., and was sometimes referred to as John* de Bykenhull. *The name was taken to America by Zachary* Bicknell, *who emigrated from Barrington, Somerset, to Weymouth, Mass., in 1635.*

Biddlecombe English: habitation name from *Bittiscombe* in Somerset, which is recorded in 1180 in the form *Biteles-*

cumba, and apparently comes from the OE personal name **Bitel*, a deriv. of the attested name *Bita* (of unknown origin) + OE *cumb* valley (see COOMBE).

Biddulph English (Midlands): habitation name from a place in Staffs., recorded as *Bidolf* in Domesday Book. This gets its name from OE *bī* beside + **dylf* digging (a putative deriv. of *delfan* to dig), i.e. a mine or quarry.

Biedermann 1. German: nickname from Ger. *Biedermann* honest man, a cpd of MHG *biderbe* honourable (OHG *biderbi*) + *mann* man (OHG *man*). Associated with it is the surname **Biedermeier** (see MAYER), adopted in 1853 by a group of German humorists as the name of a fictitious writer, Gottlob Biedermeier, satirized as an unimaginative bourgeois philistine. The name came to be used to refer to the stolid style of furnishing and decoration that was popular in mid-19th-cent. Germany.

2. Jewish (Ashkenazic): surname adopted because of its honorific meaning, from mod. Ger. *bieder* honest, upright + *-mann*.

Vars. (of 2): **Bi(e)der(man)**.

Bielski Polish and Jewish (Ashkenazic): 1. habitation name from any of the many places in E Europe whose name incorporates the Slav. element *byel-* white (mod. Pol. *biały*; cf. BIAŁAS) + the surname suffix *-ski* (see BARANOWSKI).

2. nickname for a fair-haired person, var. of BIAŁAS. See also BIALE.

Vars.: Pol.: **Bielecki, Białecki**; **Bieliński, Bielawski**; **Bilski** (E Pol. and Ukr.). Jewish: **Bilski, Bialski**; **Bielecki, Bielicki, Biletzki, Bialecky**; **Bi(e)linski, Bi(e)linsky, Bielensky, Bialinski**.

Bien Jewish (Ashkenazic): ornamental name from Yid. *bin* bee, Ger. *Biene*, or metonymic occupational name for a beekeeper.

Vars.: **Bin, Biener, Binman**.

Cpds: **Binenbaum** ('bee tree'); **Binenfeld** ('bee field'); **Binenkopf** ('bee head', an unflattering name probably assigned by a non-Jewish government official); **Bi(e)nstein** ('bee stone').

Bienstock Jewish (Ashkenazic): name taken by a beekeeper, from Yid. *binshtok* beehive.

Vars.: **Bins(h)to(c)k**; **Bi(e)nenstock, Binens(h)tok** (from mod. Ger. *Bienenstock*).

Bier German and Jewish (Ashkenazic): metonymic occupational name for a brewer of beer, mod. Ger. *Bier*, Yid. *bir* (MHG *bier*, OHG *bior*, from LL *biber*, a deriv. of *bibere* to drink).

Vars.: Ger.: **Biermann**. Jewish: **Bierman(n)**.

Bigaud French: from the Gmc personal name *Bigwald*, composed of the elements *big* (see BIARD) + *wald* rule.

Vars.: **Bigau(l)t**.

Cogn.: Eng.: **Bigwood**.

Bigg 1. English (chiefly Birmingham): nickname from ME *bigge* large, strong, stout (apparently of ON origin). In the case of Laurentia *atte Bigge* (Somerset 1327), however, the name appears to be local; if so, the meaning is not certain, but there may be some connection with BIGGIN.

2. Scots and N Irish: var. of BEGG.

Biggin English: habitation name from any of the various places in England named from Northern ME *bigging* building (from ON). This word came to denote especially an outbuilding, and is still used in and around Northumb. and Cumb.

Vars.: **Biggin(g)s**.

Bignon French: apparently a dim. of OF *bigne* bruise, swelling (of unknown origin). The term was used in the Middle Ages as a nickname for someone who held his head on one side; the connection may be that this was perceived as the result of a beating. See also BUNYAN.

Aug.: **Bignat**.

Pejs.: **Bignau(l)d**.

Bigot French: originally a contemptuous nickname, of unknown origin, applied to the Normans by the French. The sense 'excessively religious individual' did not arise until the 15th cent., after the general period of surname formation. Roger *Bigod* was one of William the Conqueror's chief advisers.

Dim.: **Bigotteau**.

Bilbao Basque: habitation name from the city in the province of Biscay, which was founded in the 13th cent. on the site of an ancient settlement. The placename is of uncertain origin; it probably contains the element *ibai* river.

Biles English: topographic name for someone who lived on a promontory or elevation, from OE *bil(e)*, literally the bill or beak of a bird, but also used in a transferred sense.

Var.: **Byles**.

Bill 1. English and German: from a Gmc personal name, either a short form of cpd names such as BILLARD and BILLAUD, or else a byname *Bill(a)*, from OE *bil* sword, halberd (or a Continental cogn.). *Bill* was not used as a short form of WILLIAM during the Middle Ages.

2. English: metonymic occupational name for a maker of pruning hooks and similar implements, from ME *bill* (from OE *bil* sword, with the meaning shifted to a more peaceful agricultural application).

Var. (of 2): **Biller**.

Cogns. (of 1): Dan.: **Bille**. (Of 2): Ger.: **Beil(schmidt)**. Du.: **(Van der) Bijl** ('axe', 'hatchet'). Fris.: **Bijlsma**.

Patrs. (from 1): Eng.: **Bill(e)s, Billson, Billing(s)**. Ger.: **Billung**.

Billard French: from the Gmc personal name *Bilhard*, composed of the elements *bil* sword + *hard* brave, hardy, strong. The spelling has been influenced by OF *bille* piece of wood, stick (cf. BILLET 2).

Var.: **Bilard**.

Dim.: **Billardon**.

Patr.: Ger.: **Bilharz**.

Billaud French: from the Gmc personal name *Bilwald*, composed of the elements *bil* sword + *wald* rule, with the spelling influenced by *bille*, as in BILLARD.

Vars.: **Billau(l)t**.

Dims.: **Billaudet, Billaudel**.

Billet French: 1. aphetic var. of *Robillet*, itself a dim. of ROBERT.

2. metonymic occupational name for a carpenter, from a dim. of OF *bille* piece of wood, stick (of Gaul. origin).

3. metonymic occupational name for a secretary, from a dim. of OF *bulle* letter (L *bulla* round object, seal, applied to the seal on papal missives and so to the documents themselves). However, this sense of *billet* did not become established until the 15th cent., rather late for surname formation.

Cogn.: Eng.: **Billett**.

Billingham English: habitation name from a place so called. The surname is found chiefly in the NW Midlands (Staffs.), but the only place of this name recorded by

Ekwall is in Co. Durham, deriving its name from OE *Billingahām* 'homestead (OE *hām*) of the people of *Billa*' (see BILL 1). The distribution of this name, together with evidence from other names (for example the two following) suggests that it may be derived from a lost place in Staffs. or nearby.

Billingsley English: habitation name from a place so called in Shrops., which derives from OE *Billingeslēah*, probably 'clearing (OE *lēah*) near a sword-shaped hill' (see BILL).

Billington English: habitation name from places in Lancs. and Staffs. (and possibly Beds.). The first of these is first recorded in 1196 as *Billinduna* 'sword-shaped hill' (see BILL), the second in Domesday Book as *Belintone* 'settlement (OE *tūn*) of *Billa*'. The place in Lancs. is apparently the most important source of the surname, which to this day is found in large numbers in Preston and Liverpool.

Billon French: 1. aphetic var. of *Robillon*, itself a dim. of ROBERT.

2. metonymic occupational name for a coiner, from OF *billon* ingot of precious metal. This word is actually a specialized application of a dim. of *bille* stick; see BILLET 2. In S France it may be a metonymic occupational name for an assayer of weights and measures, from OProv. *bilhon* weight.

3. habitation name from *Billom* in Puy-de-Dôme, earlier *Billomaco*. This is of obscure etymology; it may be from a Gaul. personal name *Billios* or a doubtfully attested word *bilio* sacred tree + the Gaul. placename element *magos* plain.

Var.: **Billion**.

Billsborough English: habitation name from *Bilsborrow* in Lancs., near Preston, so called from the gen. case of the OE personal name *Bill* (see BILL 1) + OE *burh* fortified manor (see BURY).

Var.: **Bilsborrow**.

Bilt Low German: topographic name for someone who lived on a hillock or mound, MLG *bilte*, *bulte*.

Cogns.: Du.: **(Van der) Bilt**, **Van der Belt**, **Van der Beld**.

Bilton English: habitation name from places in Northumb. and Yorks., so called from the OE personal name *Billa* (see BILL 1) + OE *tūn* enclosure, settlement. There is a Bilton in Warwicks., of which the first element is probably OE *beolone* henbane, but this place does not seem to have yielded any surviving surnames.

Binchy Irish: of uncertain origin, apparently introduced to Ireland from England in the 17th cent.; there may be some connection with BINKS, or it may ultimately derive from a Norman habitation name. The Ir. surname is almost exclusively confined to Co. Cork, and has been Gaelicized as **Binnse**.

Binder German and Jewish (Ashkenazic): one of the many occupational names for a cooper or barrel maker, from Ger. *Binder*, an agent deriv. of *binden* to bind (OHG *bintan*). Less often the same word is used to denote a book binder. The surname is found principally in S Germany and Switzerland; see also BÖTTCHER, BÜTTNER, and SCHÄFFLER.

Var.: Jewish: **Binderman**.

Cpds: Ger. **Büddenbinder** (with *Büdde*, *Bütte* cask, wine flask); **Fassbinder** (with *Fass* barrel). Jewish: **Fassbinder**; **Buchbinder** ('book binder', Anglicized **Bookbinder**); **Einbinder** (from Yid. *aynbinder* book binder).

Bines Jewish (Ashkenazic): metr. from the Yid. female given name *Bine* (from Yid. *bin* bee, used as a translation of the Hebr. female given name *Devora* 'Deborah', the literal meaning of which is 'bee'; cf. DVORIN). However, *Bine* is often folk-etymologized as being from the Hebr. noun *bina* understanding.

Var. (E Ashkenazic): **Binovitch**.

Metr. (from a dim.): **Binkin** (from the dim. female given name *Binke*).

Bing 1. English: of uncertain origin. The most plausible suggestion is that it derives from an unattested OE clan name **Binningas*, a deriv. of the attested *Binna* (see BINN).

2. Jewish (Ashkenazic): habitation name from *Bing*, Yid. name of the Ger. town of *Bingen* in the Rhineland.

Vars. (of 1): **Byng**; **Binning**.

The Byng *family, of Wrotham in Kent, produced two English admirals. George Byng (1666–1733), who captured Gibraltar in 1704 and destroyed the Spanish fleet, was made Viscount Torrington in 1721. His son, John Byng, failed to lift the French siege of Minorca in 1756 and in consequence was executed for neglect of duty, amid a storm of controversy.*

Bingham English: habitation name from a place in Notts., so called from OE *Binningas* descendants of *Binna* (see BING 1) or an OE word cogn. with ON *bingr* stall, manger + OE *hām* homestead.

The Bingham *family of Melcombe Bingham in Dorset can trace their descent back to Robert* de Bingham, *recorded in 1273, who almost certainly came from Bingham in Notts. His descendants included the Earls of Lucan. A branch of the family was established in Ireland, where they gave their name to* Binghamstown *in Co. Mayo. Sir Richard Bingham (c.1528–99) was Marshal of Ireland. Charles Bingham (1735–99) was created earl in 1795. The 3rd Lord Lucan, George Bingham (1800–88), was commander of the cavalry at Balaclava. The surname is still common in Notts. as well as in Ireland.*

Binks N English: topographic name for someone living at a *bink*, a northern dial. term for a flat raised bank of earth or a shelf of flat stone suitable for sitting on. The word is a northern form of mod. Eng. *bench*.

Var.: **Binch** (Notts.).

Binn English: 1. from a ME given name, *Binne*, OE *Binna* (of uncertain origin).

2. topographic name for someone who lived by an open manger or stall or in a hollow place so named, from OE *binn* manger, bin. It may also have been a metonymic occupational name for a maker of mangers.

Patrs. (from 1): **Binns** (chiefly Yorks.); **Bim(p)son** (Lancs.).

Binney 1. English: topographic name for someone who lived on land surrounded by a bend in a river, from OE *binnan ēa* 'within the river'.

2. Scots: habitation name from *Binney* or *Binniehill* near Falkirk, so called from Gael. *beinn* hill + the local suffix *-ach*.

Var. (of 2): **Binnie**.

Birch English: topographic name for someone who lived by a birch tree or in a birch wood, from OE *birce* birch.

Vars.: **Burch**, **Byrch**; **Birk(s)**, **Burk** (northern forms).

Cogns.: Ger.: **Birch(n)er**; **Birck(mann)**, **Birkner**; **Pirch**, **Pirch(n)er**, **Pirk**, **Pirk(n)er** (Bavaria, Austria). Low Ger.: **Ba(a)rk**; **Berke(mann)**. Flem.: **Van den Berck**, **Berckman**. Du.: **(De) Berk**, **Van den Berk**, **Berkman**. Dan.: **Birk**, **Birch**; **Bork**, **Borch**. Swed.: **Björk(e)**, **Björkén**, **Björkman**, **Björling**. Jewish (Ashkenazic, either ornamental or topographic): **Berkner**, **Berkman(n)**; **Pirkner**.

Dim.: Ger.: **Birkle**, **Bürcklin**; **Pirkl**.

Cpds (ornamental): Swed.: **Björklund** ('birch grove'); **Björkqvist** ('birch twig'). Jewish: **Berkenblit** ('birch blossom'); **Birkenfeld, Berkenfeld** ('birch field'); **Birchental, Birkental** ('birch valley').

Birchall English: habitation name from a lost place in the parish of Eccles, Lancs., possibly so called from OE *birce* BIRCH + *hall* HALL or *halh* nook, recess (see HALE 1), or else from OE **bircel* group of birches.

Var.: **Burchall**.

Bircham English: habitation name from a group of villages in Norfolk, so called from OE *brǣc* land newly broken up for cultivation + *hām* homestead.

Bird 1. English: from ME *bird*, *brid* nestling, young bird (OE *bridd*), applied as a nickname or perhaps occasionally as a metonymic occupational name for a bird catcher. The metathesized form is first found in the Northumb. dial. of ME, but the surname is more common in the Midlands and South. It may possibly also be derived from ME *burde* maiden, girl, applied as a mocking nickname.

2. Irish: see HENEGHAN.

3. Jewish: trans. of various Ashkenazic surnames meaning 'Bird', as for example VOGEL.

Vars. (of 1): **Byrd, Burd; Bride** (but see also KILBRIDE).

Dim. (of 1): **Burdekin**.

Birdsall English: habitation name from a place in N Yorks., near Malton, so called from the gen. case of the OE byname *Bridd* 'BIRD' + OE *halh* nook, recess (see HALE 1). The surname is still largely confined to Yorks.

Birkbeck English: habitation name from a minor place named after the river in Cumb. on which it stands. This derives its name from ON *birki* BIRCH + *bekkr* stream (see BECK 1).

Var.: **Birbeck**.

Birkby English: habitation name from one of the places in N and W Yorks. so called, originally known as *Bretteby* 'settlement (ON *býr*) of the Britons', later assimilated to Northern ME *birke* BIRCH. The surname is still largely confined to Yorks.

Birkdale English: habitation name from a place in Lancs., so called from ON *birki* BIRCH + *dalr* valley (see DALE).

Var.: **Brickdale**.

A family by the name of Brickdale *came originally from Birkdale near Southport in Lancs. One of their earliest ancestors was Ralph Brickdale, who was recorded there in 1298. Another was John Brickdale, sheriff of Chester in 1513.*

Birkett N English: topographic name for someone who lived by a grove of birch trees, from OE *bircett*, *byrcett*, a deriv. of *birce* BIRCH. There has been some confusion with BURKETT.

Vars.: **Birchett, Burchett** (S Eng. forms); **Brickett** (a metathesized form).

Birmingham English: habitation name from the city in the W Midlands. In Domesday Book the name is already found as *Bermingeham*, but it seems likely that it was originally *Beornmundingahām* 'homestead (OE *hām*) of the people of *Beornmund*', a personal name composed of the elements *beorn* young man, warrior + *mund* protection.

Var.: **Bermingham** (this spelling now found chiefly in Ireland).

The Bermingham *family held the Irish barony of Athenry from the 13th to the 20th cent. Robert* de Bermyngcham *was apparently the first of the family to settle in Ireland, and his name is found on a number of important charters between 1175 and 1179. They were also known as* Mac Fheorais ((**Mc**)**Corish**) *after their ancestor Piers de Bermyngeham, the father of Robert.*

Birnbaum German and Jewish (Ashkenazic): topographic name for someone who lived by a pear tree, from Ger. *Birnbaum* pear tree, from Ger. *Birn(e)* pear (MHG *bir*) + *Baum* tree (MHG *boum*). As a Jewish name, it is largely ornamental.

Vars.: Ger.: **Bi(e)rbaum; Pirpamer** (Austria, Tyrol). Jewish (Ashkenazic, largely ornamental): **Birn, Bir(en)baum, Bir(e)nboim, Birnboym, Birnboum, Berebaum, Barenbaum, Barenboim** (also in part from the sign of house no. 187 in the Jewish quarter of Frankfurt-am-Main, and the name of a place outside Poznań).

Cogns.: Low Ger.: **Beerbohm, Behrbohm**. Flem., Du.: **(Van den) Peereboom**.

Cpds (ornamental): Jewish: **Bir(e)nbach** ('pear stream'); **Bir(e)nberg, Bernberg** ('pear hill'); **Birenblat** ('pear leaf'); **Ber(e)nblum** ('pear flower'); **Bir(e)ndorf** ('pear village'); **Birnfeld, Ber(e)nfeld** ('pear field'); **Birnholz, Berenhol(t)z, Berenholl(t)z, Birenholc, Berenholc, Barenhol(t)z, Barnholz** ('pear wood'); **Birnstein** ('pear stone'); **Birnstock** ('pear trunk'); **Bir(e)nzweig, Birenzwaig, Birencwaig, Birencwajg, Birencvaig, Birencweig** ('pear twig').

Birnie Scots: habitation name from a place in the former county of Morays. (now part of Grampian region), recorded in the 13th cent. as *Brennach*, probably from Gael. *braonach* damp place.

Var.: **Birney**.

James de Brennath *was recorded at Elgin in 1261.*

Biró Hungarian: occupational name for a judge, Hung. *bíró*.

Var.: **Bíró**.

Biron 1. French: habitation name from any of the places so called, in Charente-Maritime, Dordogne, and Basses-Pyrénées. The L form of the name is *Biriācum*, apparently from a Gaul. personal name *Birius* (of unknown origin) + the local suffix *-ācum*.

2. English: var. of BYRON.

Birtwistle English (Lancs.): habitation name from a now depopulated hamlet near Padiham, Lancs., so called from ME *bird* young bird, nestling (OE *bridd*; see BIRD) + *twissel* fork (i.e. stream-junction; OE *twisla*).

Vars.: **Birtwhistle, Bertwistle, Burtwistle; Birdwhistell**.

Bishop English: from ME *biscop*, OE *bisc(e)op*, which comes via L from Gk *episkopos* overseer (from *epi* on, over + *skopein* to look). The Gk word was adopted early in the Christian era as a title for an overseer of a local community of Christians, and has yielded cogns. in every European language: Fr. *évêque*, It. *vescovo*, Sp. *obispo*, Russ. *yepiskop*, Ger. *Bischof*, etc. The word came to be applied as a surname for a variety of reasons, among them service in the household of a bishop, supposed resemblance in bearing or appearance to a bishop, and selection as the 'boy bishop' on St Nicholas's Day.

Var.: **Bisp** (Bristol).

Cogns.: Fr.: **Evesque, Évêque; Levesque, Levecque, Lévêque; Vesque, Vèque; Lescop** (Brittany). Prov.: **Avesque, Besque**. It.: **(L')Episcop(i)o; Vesc(ov)o, Viscovi; Veschi, Visco, Vischi, Bisco** (S Italy, esp. Campania); **Pisc(op)o, Vispo** (S Italy, esp. Campania and Apulia). Sp.: **Obispo**. Port.: **Bispo**. Ger.: **Bischof(f); Pischof(f)** (Austria). Flem.: **(De) Bi(s)schop**. Czech.: **Biskup**. Pol.: **Biskup(ski)**.

Dims.: Fr.: **Evéquot** (Switzerland). Prov.: **Piscot**. It.: **Vescovini; Piscop(i)ello, Piscotti, Pisculli**. Czech.: **Biskupek**.

Pejs.: Fr.: **Véquaud, Vécard**.

Patrs.: Ir.: **McAnaspie** (Gael. **Mac an Easpuig**). Fr.: **Alévêque**. Pol.: **Biskupiak**. Russ.: **Yepiskopov**.

Bishton English (W Midlands): habitation name from any of the various places in Staffs., Shrops., etc., so called. All of them derive their names from OE *Biscopestūn* 'manor (OE *tūn* settlement) of the bishop'.

Bismarck German: habitation name from the place near Altmark in Magdeburg, recorded *c.*1200 in the form *Biscopesmark*, from its situation on the boundary (see MARK 2) of a bishopric.

Bispham English (Lancs.): habitation name from one of two places in Lancs, so called from OE *Biscopeshām* 'manor (OE *hām* homestead) of the bishop'.

Biss English: nickname for someone with an unhealthy complexion or who habitually dressed in particularly drab garments, from ME, OF *bis* dingy, murky (of Gmc origin).

Cogns.: It.: **Bis(c)io, Bisi, Big(g)io.**

Dims.: Eng.: **Bisset(t)** (Scots); BISSELL. Fr.: **Biset, Bizet, Bisot, Bizot.** It.: **Bisetti, Biselli, Bisini.**

Pejs.: Fr.: **Bisard, Bizard.**

Henricus Byset *witnessed a charter granted by King William the Lion at the end of the 11th cent.; he was an English nobleman who followed William to Scotland on his release from imprisonment in England. His son, John Byset, was granted extensive land in the North.*

Bissell 1. English: metonymic occupational name for a corn merchant or factor, one who measured corn, from ME *buyscel, busshell, bysshell* bushel, measure of corn (OF *boissel, buissel*, of Gaul. origin). The name may also have been applied to a maker of vessels designed to hold or measure out a bushel.

2. English: dim. of BISS.

3. Welsh: var. of BETHELL; cf. BESSELL.

Vars. (of 1): **Bissill, Bishell; Bushell, Bushill, Bussel; Boshell, Bossel.**

Cogns. (of 1): Fr.: **Boissel, Boisseau; Boisselier** (maker of vessels holding a bushel).

Dim. (of 1): Fr.: **Boisselet.**

Aug. (of 1): Fr.: **Boisselat.**

Pejs. (of 1): Fr.: **Bois(s)ard.**

Blache S French: topographic name for someone who lived by an oak grove, originating in the SE Fr. dial. word *blache* oak plantation (said to be of Gaulish origin), originally a plantation of young trees of any kind.

Vars.: Prov.: **Blach(i)er, Blachère.**

Dim.: Prov.: **Blachon.**

Aug.: Prov.: **Blacas.**

Black 1. English and Scots: from ME *blak(e)* black (OE *blæc, blac*), a nickname given from the earliest times to a swarthy or dark-haired man. The nickname may have been given for other reasons too: Tengvik records the case (1080) of a certain *Wlfricus Niger* (Wulfric the Black), who received the nickname after blackening his face with charcoal to go undetected at night among his enemies.

2. English and Scots: from OE *blāc* pale, fair, i.e. precisely the opposite meaning to 1, and a var. of BLAKE 2. *Blake* and *Black* are found more or less interchangeably in many surnames and placename elements.

3. English: var. of BLANC as a Norman name. The pronunciation of the nasalized vowel gave considerable difficulty to Eng. speakers, and its quality was often ignored.

4. Scots and Irish: trans. of various names from Gael. *dubh* black; see DUFF.

5. Jewish: trans. of various names meaning 'black', for example SCHWARZ.

Vars.: **Blacke;** BLEACH; **Blackman, Blackmon, Blakeman; Blagg.**

Dims.: BLACKETT, BLACKIE.

Blackall English: habitation name from any of various minor places so called from OE *blæc* BLACK, dark + *hall* hall, manor (see HALL) or *halh* nook, recess (see HALE 1).

Vars.: **Blackhall** (chiefly Scots); **Blackale.**

Blackburn English: habitation name from any of various places, but especially the one in Lancs., so called from OE *blæc* BLACK, dark + *burna* stream (see BOURNE). The surname is mainly found in N England; the second element, *burna*, is characteristically northern.

Vars.: **Blackburne, Blackbourn(e).**

Blacker English: occupational name for a bleacher of textiles, from ME *blāken* to bleach or whiten, from OE *blāc* white, pale (see BLAKE 2). The name might also plausibly be derived as an agent noun from *blæc* BLACK, but it is not clear to what occupation or activity this would refer.

Var.: BLEACHER.

Cogns.: Ger.: **Bleicher(t).** Low Ger.: **Bleecker.** Flem., Du.: **(De) Bleeker.**

Blackett English: 1. dim. of BLACK.

2. nickname for a person with dark hair, or topographic name for someone who lived by a dark headland, from ME *blak(e)* BLACK + *heved* head (OE *hēafod*).

Blackford English: habitation name from any of various places, e.g. in Somerset, so called from OE *blæc* BLACK, dark + *ford* FORD.

Blackham English: habitation name from some place so called, presumably deriving its name from OE *blæc* BLACK (or the OE personal name *Blaca*) + *hām* homestead. Reaney associates the name with *Blakenham* in Suffolk, but at the present day the name is found mainly in the W Midlands.

Blackhurst English: habitation name from some minor place so called, possibly in Lancs., where the surname is chiefly found. This would be derived from OE *blæc* BLACK, dark + *hyrst* wooded hill (see HURST).

Blackie Scots: 1. dim. of BLACK.

2. nickname for a person with beautiful dark eyes or one who was reputed to have the power of casting the evil eye on someone, from ME *blak(e)* BLACK + *ie* eye (OE *ē(a)ge*).

Vars.: **Blaikie; Blakey** (Northumb.).

Blackledge English: habitation name from *Blacklache* near Leyland, Lancs., so called from OE *blæc* BLACK, dark + *læc(e)* boggy stream.

Blacklock N English: nickname for someone with dark hair, ME *blakelok*, from OE *blæc* BLACK, dark + *locc* (lock of) hair. Reaney comments that although *blake* might mean either 'dark' or 'fair' (see BLAKE), the meaning 'dark hair' is the most probable since this name contrasts with WHITLOCK.

Blackmore English: habitation name from any of various places so called from OE *blæc* BLACK, dark + *mōr* moor, marsh (see MOORE 1) or *mere* lake (see DELAMARE). The former is the second element of *Blackmore* in Essex, Wilts., and Worcs., as well as *Blackmoor* in Dorset; the latter is the second element of *Blackmore* in Herts. and *Blackmoor* in Hants, the early forms of which are *Blachemere, Blakemere*.

Vars.: **Blackmoor, Blakemore.**

Blackshaw English: habitation name from a place in W Yorks., so called from OE *blæc* BLACK, dark + *sceaga* copse, thicket (see SHAW).

Blackwell English: habitation name from any of various places, for example in Cumb., Derbys., Co. Durham, Warwicks., and Worcs., named from OE *blæc* BLACK, dark + *wæll(a)*, *well(a)* spring, stream (see WALL 2 and WELL).

Var.: **Blackwall**.

Lands at Blackwall in Derbys. have been held by the same family, bearing this surname, since before 1414.

Blackwood English and Scots: habitation name from various places, for example in Yorks., Dumfries, and Strathclyde, so called from OE *blæc* BLACK, dark + *wudu* WOOD.

Blades English: 1. metonymic occupational name for a cutler, from the pl. or gen. sing. of ME *blade* cutting edge, sword (OE *blæd*).

2. habitation name from a place of uncertain location and etymology. Its status as a habitation name is deduced from early forms cited by Reaney, such as Alan *de Bladis* (Leics. 1230), Hugh *de Bladis* (Staffs. 1258), and William *de Blades* (Yorks. 1301).

Vars.: **Blaydes**. (Of 1 only): **Blade(r)**; **Bladesmith** (see SMITH).

An English family called Blaydes *claim descent from Drago de Bewere, a Danish nobleman who settled at a place called Blades in N England around 1016; he obtained extensive land grants, recorded in Domesday Book. The name became* Burseblades *(Bewere's Blades) by a compounding of the name of the founder and of the estate; Sir Philip de Burseblades fought at Poitiers. In the 16th cent. the surname was shortened to* Blaides *or* Blaydes.

Blagoveshchenski Russian: from *blagoveshchenie* (Feast of the) Annunciation, the Christian festival on 25 March in commemoration of the annunciation to the Virgin Mary of the impending birth of Christ, from *blago-* good (cf. BLÁHA) + *veshchenie* announcement, a calque of Gk *euangelismos*, from *eu-* good + *angelismos* announcement. The word came to be used as a surname in two ways; as a habitation name from various places in Russia called *Blagoveshchensk* on account of having a church dedicated to the Annunciation, but more commonly as a byname adopted by Orthodox priests in honour of this festival.

Bláha Czech: 1. nickname for a good man, from the vocab. word *blahý* good (now meaning 'happy, fortunate').

2. short form of one of the Czech personal names, principally *Blahoslav* and *Blahomil*, that contain *blaho-* good as a first element.

3. altered short from of the Czech given name *Blažej* BLAISE.

Vars.: **Blahák**, **Blahuta**, **Blaheň**.

Dims.: **Blaháček**, **Blahušek**.

Patr. (cogn. of 2): Croatian: **Blagojević**.

Blain Scots: 1. Anglicized form of the Gael. personal name *Bláán*, a dim. of *blá* yellow. This was the name of an early Celt. saint.

2. (also N English) nickname for a person suffering from boils, from ME *blain* blister, pustule (OE *blegen*).

Var.: **Blaine**.

Patr. (from 1): **McBlain**.

Blair Scots and N Irish: habitation name from one of the numerous places so called, from Gael. *blár* (gen. *bláir*) plain, field, esp. a battlefield.

Blaise French: from the medieval given name *Blaise* (L *Blasius*). This is an old Roman family name, orig. a byname for someone with some defect, either of speech or gait (cf. L *blaesus* stammering and Gk *blaisos* bow-legged). It was borne by a Christian saint martyred in Armenia in 316, whose cult achieved wide popularity, in particular as the patron saint of carders by virtue of the fact that he was 'carded' to death, i.e. his flesh was scraped off in small pieces with metal combs.

Var.: **Blais**.

Cogns.: Prov.: **Blasi**, **Blazi**. It.: **Blasi(o)**, **Blase**; **Blas**, **Biasi(o)** (Venetia); **Biag(g)i** (Tuscany). Sp.: **Blas**. Cat.: **Blasi**, **Blay**. Port.: **Brás**. Ger.: **Blasius**; BLOSS, **Blöss**, **Blöse**, **Bless**. Low Ger.: **Bla(a)s(e)**, **Blaasch**. Flem.: **Blaes**. Hung.: **Balázs**, **Balassa**, **Balassi**.

Dims.: Fr.: **Blaison**, **Blaisot**; **Blazin**, **Bla(i)zot**. It.: **Blasini**, **Biasini**, **Biagini**, **Blasetti**, **Biasetti**, **Biag(g)etti**, **Biag(g)elli**, **Biasioli**, **Biag(g)ioli**, **Biasotti**, **Biag(g)iotti**. Ger.: **Blasl**; **Bläsli**, **Blesli** (Switzerland). Low Ger.: **Bläsgen**, **Bläske**. Ger. (of Slav. origin): **Blaschek**, **Blaschke**, **Plaschke**, **Bluschke**, **Bloschke**. Czech: **Blažek** (from the Czech form of the given name, *Blažej*), BLÁHA. Pol.: **Błaszczyk**; **Błasik**, **Błażek** (from the Pol. form of the given name, *Błażej*). Ukr.: **Vlasyuk**; **Vlasenko** (also Beloruss.).

Augs.: It.: **Blasoni**, **Biasioni**, **Biag(g)ioni**.

Patrs.: It.: **De Blase**, **De Blasi(o)**, **De Blasiis**; **De Biasi(o)**, **Di Biasi(o)**; **De Biag(g)i**, **Di Biagio**. Ger.: **Bläsing**, **Blesing**; **Plessing**. Russ.: **Vlasov**, **Vlasyev**, **Vlasin**. Beloruss.: **Blazhevich**. Pol.: **Błażewicz**; **Błasiak**. Croatian: **Blaž(ev)ič**.

Patrs. (from dims.): Russ.: **Vlasenkov**. Pol.: **Błaszkiewicz**; **Błaszczak**.

Habitation names: Pol.: **Błaż(ej)ewski**, **Błażyński**; **Błaszczyński** (from a dim.).

Blake 1. English: var. of BLACK 1, meaning 'swarthy' or 'dark-haired', from a byform of the OE adj. *blæc*, *blac* black, with change of vowel length.

2. English: nickname from OE *blāc* wan, pale, white, fair. In ME the two words *blac* and *blāc*, with opposite meanings, fell together as ME *blake*. In the absence of independent evidence as to whether the person referred to was dark or fair, it is now impossible to tell which sense was originally meant.

3. Irish: Anglicized form of Gael. **Ó Bláthmhaic** 'descendant of *Bláthmhac*', a personal name from *bláth* flower, blossom, fame, prosperity + *mac* son. In part, however, the Irish name is derived from OE *blæc* dark, swarthy, as in 1 above. Many bearers are descended from Richard Caddell, nicknamed *le blac*, sheriff of Connaught in the early 14th cent. The Eng. name has been Gaelicized **de Bláca**.

Vars. (of 1 and 2): **Blaik** (Scots and N Eng.). (Of 3): **Blowick**.

Cogns. (of 2): Ger.: **Bleich** ('pale'). Low Ger., Du.: **Blee(c)k**, **Bleeke**.

The Low Ger. or Du. name Bleeke *was introduced to England by a waterman recorded at Gravesend, Kent, in 1653. Before that, however, the name John* Bleke *is recorded at Haddenham, near Ely, in 1585; his name may be derived from Eng.* bleak *pale (first attested in the 16th cent., but probably much older, as it is from ON* bleikr*, a cogn. of OE* blāc*). The spellings* **Bleek**, **Bleak**, *and* **Bleeck(e)** *are all found in England at the present day.*

Blakeley English and Scots: habitation name from some place called *Blakeley* or *Blackley* (e.g. in Greater Manchester, but probably also somewhere in Scotland), from OE *blæc* BLACK, dark + *lēah* wood, clearing.

Vars.: **Blackley** (Scots); **Blakely** (N Ireland).

Blakeway English (W Midlands): habitation name, probably from *Blakeway* Farm near Much Wenlock, Shrops. The placename is derived from OE *blæc* BLACK, dark + *weg* road, path, way.

Blamire N English: of uncertain origin, possibly a habitation name from a place named with the ON elements *blár* dark + *myrr* swamp, marsh. The place *Blamires* in W Yorks probably takes its name from the surname rather than vice versa.

Vars.: **Blaymire, Blamore, Blamires**.

Blanc 1. French: nickname for a man with white or fair hair or a pale complexion, from OF *blanc* white (of Gmc origin, cf. OHG *blanc* bright, shining, white, beautiful).

2. Jewish (Ashkenazic): probably an ornamental name from mod. Ger. *blank* bright, shiny.

Vars. (of 1): **Leblanc**; **Blanche**, **Blanque** (fem. forms; also a female given name). (Of 2): **Blank, Blank(i)er**.

Cogns.: Eng.: **Blank**, BLACK. It.: **Bianco, Bianchi**; **Lo Bianco**. Sp.: **Blanco**; **Blanca** (fem.). Cat.: **Blanc(h)**. Port.: **Branco**. Ger.: **Blan(c)k**. Flem., Du.: **Blank, De Blanke**.

Dims.: Fr.: **Blanchet(eau), Blanch(et)on, Blanchonnet, Blanchot**. Prov.: **Blanquet, Blancot, Blanqui**. It.: **Bianchetti, Bianchin(ott)i, Biancucci, Biancol(in)i, Biancotti**.

Aug.: It.: **Bianconi**.

Pej.: Fr.: BLANCHARD.

Patrs.: Eng.: **Blanks**. It.: **De Bianchi, Del Bianco**. Rum.: **Balanesco**.

Blanchard French and English: 1. pej. of BLANC.

2. from a Gmc personal name composed of the elements *blanc* shining, white, beautiful + *hard* brave, hardy, strong.

Var.: Fr.: **Blancard**.

Cogns. (of 2): Ger.: **Blankhart**. Low Ger., Flem.: **Blanckaert, Blanquaert**. It.: **Bianc(i)ardi**.

Patrs. (from 2): Low Ger.: **Blanka(e)rts, Blankertz**.

Blanchflower English: nickname from OF *blanche* (fem.) white (see BLANC) + *flour* FLOWER. Presumably the nickname was originally given ironically to a man of effeminate appearance.

Var.: **Branchflower**.

Bland English: habitation name from a place so called in W Yorks., the etymology of which is uncertain. Possibly it is from OE *(ge)bland* storm, commotion (from *blandan* to blend, mingle), with reference to its exposed situation. The mod. Eng. adjective *bland* did not come into English (from Latin) until the 15th cent., and is therefore unlikely to have given rise to surnames.

Blandford English: habitation name from *Blandford* Forum and other places called *Blandford* in Dorset (*Bleneford* in Domesday Book). The etymology of this is uncertain; Ekwall derives it from OE *blǣgna ford* ford of the gudgeons, from the gen. pl. of *blǣge* gudgeon.

Blaney Irish (of Welsh origin): topographic name from W *blaenau*, pl. of *blaen* point, tip, end, i.e. uplands, or remote region, or upper reaches of a river.

The first recorded bearer of this name is a certain Ieuan Blaenau, *who appears as Evan* Blayney *in a list of burgesses of Welshpool in 1406. The family claim descent from Brockwel Ysgythrog* (fl. 550), *the prince of Powys whose grandson was killed leading the Welsh attack on Chester* (c. 613). *Edward, 1st Lord Blayney, went to Ireland with the Earl of Essex in 1598; he was knighted in 1603 and elevated to the peerage of Ireland as Lord Blayney, Baron of Monaghan, Co. Monaghan. The Welsh line died out in 1795 with Arthur Blayney of Gregynog, Montgomeryshire.*

Blanton Ostensibly an Eng. habitation name, but no satisfactory origin has been proposed. There are several bearers in Los Angeles; the name may well represent an Anglicized form of a foreign original.

Blatchford English (chiefly Devon): habitation name from *Blatchford* in Sourton, Devon, which is probably derived from the OE personal name *Blæcca* + OE *ford* FORD.

Blatherwick English (E Midlands): habitation name from *Blatherwycke* in Northants. The second element of the placename is clearly OE *wīc* outlying settlement (see WICK); the first, Ekwall suggests, may be 'a worn-down form of OE *blæcþorn*' blackthorn.

Blatt Jewish (Ashkenazic): from Ger. *Blatt*, Yid. *blat* leaf, normally a shortened form of one of the cpds with this second element, adopted as ornamental surnames in the 18th and 19th cents.

Vars.: **Blat**; **Bleterman** (from Yid. *bleter* or Ger. *Blätter*, both meaning 'leaves').

Cogns.: Swed.: **Blad(h)**.

Blau German: from Ger. *blau* blue (MHG *bla*, OHG *blāo*), a nickname with various senses — a person who habitually wore blue clothes, a person with blue eyes, a sickly or pale person, a person with a bluish complexion resulting from poor circulation, etc.

2. Jewish (Ashkenazic): ornamental name, one of the many such Ashkenazic surnames taken from names of colours.

Vars.: Ger.: **Blauer(t)** (Bavaria); **Plab(st)** (Bavaria, Austria). Jewish: **Blauer**.

Cogns.: Flem.: **(De) Blauw, Blauwaert**. Du.: **Bla(a)uw**. Fr.: **Bleu, Lebleu**; **Blauf** (Auvergne). Prov., Cat.: **Blau**. Eng.: **Blue** (generally a fairly recent Anglicization of Ger. *Blau* or Fr. *Bleu*).

Dim.: Eng.: BLEWETT.

Cpds (ornamental unless otherwise stated): Jewish: **Blaufarb** ('blue colour'); **Blaufeder** ('blue feather'); **Blaufeld** ('blue field'); **Blaugrund** ('blue ground'); **Blaukopf** ('blue head'); **Blauschild** ('blue shield', topographic name from a house marked with a blue shield); BLAUSTEIN; **Blauweiss** ('blue white', a reference to the blue and white colours of the prayer shawl, which was to become the model for the flag of the State of Israel); **Blauzwirn** ('blue thread').

Blaustein Jewish (Ashkenazic): ornamental name from Ger. *blau* blue (MHG *blā*) + *Stein* stone, i.e. lapis lazuli.

Vars.: **Blausztein, Blausztain**; **Blus(h)tein, Blusztein, Blusztejn, Blusztain, Bluehstein, Bloustein, Bloustine, Bluvstein, Blovstein, Blowstein** (in part from the Yid. cogn. *bloyshteyn*); **Bluestein** (partly Anglicized); **Bluestone** (fully Anglicized).

Bleach English: var. of BLAKE 2, from the W Saxon form of OE *blǣc*, *blāc*, in which the final palatal consonant /c/ was affricated to /tʃ/ rather than retracted to velar /k/ as in other dialects.

Var.: **Blatch**.

Bleacher English: occupational name for someone who was responsible for bleaching newly woven cloth; cf. BLACKER and BLEACH.

Var.: **Blatcher**.

Bleasby English: habitation name from one of the places in Lincs. and Notts. so called from the ON byname *Blesi* (from *blesi* blaze, white spot) + ON *býr* settlement, village.

Bleasdale English (Cumb. and Lancs.): habitation name from a place in the Lake District, so called from the ON byname *Blesi* (cf. BLEASBY), or from the same word used in the sense of a white spot on a hillside, + ON *dalr* valley.

Vars.: **Blaisdale, Blaisdell**.

Blech German and Jewish (Ashkenazic): generally a metonymic occupational name from Ger. *Blech* tin, Yid. *blekh*

(MHG *blech* sheet metal, OHG *bleh*), denoting a worker in tin or other metal. The Ger. word also acquired the sense 'cheap rubbish', and it is therefore possible that the Ger. surname was sometimes bestowed as a derogatory nickname.

Vars.: Ger.: **Blech(n)er**, **Blechler**; **Blechschmidt** (see SMITH). Jewish: **Blechmann** (U.S. **Blechman**); **Blacher** (reflecting a central Yid. pronunciation of Yid. *blekher* tinsmith).

Bledsoe English: habitation name from *Bledisloe* in Gloucs., recorded in Domesday Book as *Bliteslav*, and apparently derived from OE *Blīðeshlāw* 'hill (see LAW 2) of *Blīð*', a byname meaning 'cheerful' (see BLIGH 1).

Blei Jewish (Ashkenazic): ornamental name from Ger. *Blei*, Yid. *blay* lead.

Vars.: **Bleiman(n)**; **Blajman** (Pol. spelling).

Cpds: **Bleiberg** ('lead hill', ornamental name); **Bleifeder** (apparently from Ger. *Bleifeder* lead pencil, unless the elements are to be interpreted literally as 'lead feather', in which case the reasons for its adoption as a surname are unknown); **Blajwajs** (Pol. spelling, apparently from Ger. *Bleiweiss* 'white lead, ceruse', reason for adoption unknown).

Blenkinsopp English: habitation name from a place in Northumb., of obscure etymology. A certain John *Blenkynson* is recorded in 1553 as a freeman of the city of York, and this suggests that there may have been a ME given name *Blenkyn* (perhaps from OE **Blenca*). The place-name may consist of the gen. case of this + ME, OE *hop* valley (see HOPE).

Var.: **Blenkinsop**.

This is the surname of a family established in Yorks. since the 14th cent., who trace their descent from Richard Blenkinsoppe, *grandson of a certain Ranulfus who held the manor of Blenkinsopp in 1240.*

Blennerhasset English: habitation name from a place in Cumb., so called from an old Brit. name composed of the elements *blaen* hill, top + *dre* farm, settlement, with the addition of a later ON name composed of the elements *hey* hay + *sætr* shieling, shelter.

Members of a family of this name represented Carlisle in Parliament continuously from the reign of Richard II to that of James I. Alan de Blenerhayset *was mayor of the city in 1382. They became established in Co. Kerry, Ireland, in the 17th cent.*

Blériot French: nickname meaning 'badger' or metonymic occupational name for a badger hunter, from OF *bleriot*, *blereau* badger (of Celt. origin, related to OF *bler* having a white blaze on the forehead, Gael. *blar*).

Vars.: **Bléreau, Blériau**.

Blessed English: nickname for a fortunate individual, from ME *(i)blescede*, *blissed* blessed (from OE *blētsian* to bless). The word also appears to have been in use in the Middle Ages as a female given name, and some cases of the surname may be derived from this.

Vars.: **Blissett, Blest**.

Blevin Welsh: from the given name *Ble(i)ddyn*, originally a byname meaning 'Wolf Cub', from *blaidd* wolf + the dim. suffix *-yn*. *Blaidd* was often used in Medieval Welsh as a term for a hero, and sometimes for a cruel man or for an enemy who feigned friendship.

Var.: **Blethyn**.

Patrs.: **Blevins**; **Ple(a)vin(s)**, **Pleven**, **Pleaden** (the last 3 from *ap Blethyn* son of Blethyn).

Blewett English: nickname for a habitual wearer of blue clothes or for someone with blue eyes, from ME *bluet* blue woollen cloth or *bleuet* cornflower. Both are from OF *bleuet*, dim. of *bleu* blue (of Gmc origin; see BLAU). The surname is now common chiefly in Devon and Cornwall.

Vars.: **Blewitt**, **Bl(o)uet**.

Cogns.: Fr.: **Balu(h)et**. Flem.: **Blauwet**.

Blick 1. English: var. of BLUCK.

2. Jewish (Ashkenazic): of uncertain origin; possibly from Yid. *blik* look, and based on some now irrecoverable anecdote.

Bligh 1. English: nickname for a cheerful person, from OE *blīðe* merry, cheerful.

2. Irish: Anglicized from of **Ó Blighe** 'descendant of *Blighe*', a personal name probably derived from the ON byname *Blígr* (from *blígja* to gaze).

3. Cornish: nickname from Corn. *blyth* wolf (cf. BLEVIN).

Vars.: **Bly(e)**; BLYTHE. (Of 3 only): **Blight**.

Cogns. (of 1): Ger.: **Blied(e)**.

The English naval officer William Bligh *(1754–1817), the captain of HMS* Bounty *in the South Pacific in 1789 when the crew mutinied and set him adrift in a small boat, was born in Plymouth into a Cornish family who had settled there in 1681. One of his ancestors was commissioner for the dissolution of the monasteries under Henry VIII; four others were mayors of Bodmin between 1505 and 1588.*

Bligh is also the family name of the Earls of Darnley. John Bligh (1683–1728), son of Thomas Bligh, MP for Meath, was given the title in 1725, having married in 1713 a descendant of the extinct Stuart earls of Darnley.

Blinov Russian: patr. apparently derived from the nickname *Blin*, from *blin* a type of pancake (ultimately connected with *molot* to mill or grind; cf. MOLOTOV). It is not clear what significance the nickname had, unless it was an occupational name.

Bliss 1. English: nickname for a cheerful individual, from ME *blisse* joy, OE *blīðs*; cf. BLIGH 1.

2. English (Norman): habitation name from the village of *Blay* in Calvados, recorded in 1077 in the form *Bleis* and of unknown origin. The village of *Stoke Bliss* in Worcs. was named after a Norman family *de Blez*, recorded several times in the county from the 13th cent.

3. Welsh: patr. from ELLIS.

4. Jewish: of unknown origin.

5. U.S.: Anglicized form of Ger. **Blitz(er)** lightning (MHG *blicze*), presumably a nickname for a fast mover.

Var. (of 2): **Blay**.

Cogn. (of 5): Swed.: **Blixt**.

Block 1. German: from Ger. *Block* block of wood, stocks (MHG *bloch*, OHG *bloh*). The surname apparently originated as a nickname for a large, lumpish man, or perhaps as a nickname for a persistent lawbreaker who found himself often in the stocks.

2. Jewish: Anglicized form of *Bloch* (see VLACH).

Vars. (of 1): **Blockmann**. (Of 2): **Blok**.

Cogns. (of 1): Du.: **Blo(c)k**. See also BLOGG.

Dim. (of 1): Ger.: **Blöcklin**.

Blokhin Russian: patr. from the nickname *Blokha* 'Flea', used for a small and light person, or else for someone who was infested with fleas.

Dim.: Ukr.: **Bloshchenko**.

Błonski Polish: topographic name for someone living by a meadow, from OPol. *błonie* meadow + *-ski* suffix of local surnames.

Blood 1. English: apparently from OE *blōd* blood, but with what significance is not clear. In ME the word was in use as a metonymic occupational term for a physician, i.e. one who let blood, and also as an affectionate term of address for a blood relative.

2. Welsh: of uncertain origin, possibly a patr. (with prefix *ap*, *ab*) from the given name LLOYD.

Bloom 1. Jewish (Ashkenazic): Anglicized spelling of BLUM.

2. English: metonymic occupational name for an iron worker, from ME *blome* ingot of iron (OE *blōma*). The mod. Eng. word *bloom* flower came into Eng. from ON in the 13th cent., but probably did not give rise to any surnames.

Vars. (of 2): Eng.: **Blo(o)mer**, **Blumer**.

Bloomfield 1. Jewish (Ashkenazic): Anglicized form of Yid. *Blumfeld* (see BLUM).

2. English (Norman): habitation name from *Blonville*-sur-Mer in Calvados. The first element is probably an ON personal name; the second is OF *ville* settlement (see VILLE).

Vars.: **Blom(e)field**.

Bloomingdale Jewish (Ashkenazic): Anglicized form of Ger. *Blument(h)al* or Du. *Bloemendaal*, both of which are ornamental names composed of elements meaning 'flower valley'; cf. BLUM and DALE.

Bloss German: 1. nickname for a simple person, from MHG *blōz* simple, straightforward (MLG *bloot*; cf. mod. Ger. *bloss* only).

2. nickname for a pale person, from Ger. *blass* pale, wan (MHG *blas* weak, insignificant).

3. cogn. of Fr. BLAISE.

Var. (of 2 and 3): **Blass**.

Cogns. (of 1): Flem., Low Ger.: **Bloot**. (Of 2): Jewish (Ashkenazic): **Blas(s)** (from Yid. *blas* or mod. Ger. *blass* pale).

Blower 1. English: from ME *blōwere* (OE *blāwere*, a deriv. of *blāwan* to blow; for the change in the vowel, cf. ROPER). The name was applied chiefly to someone who operated a bellows, either as a blacksmith's assistant or to provide wind for a church organ. In other cases it was applied to someone who blew a horn, i.e. a huntsman or a player of the musical instrument.

2. Welsh: patr. (with prefix *ap*, *ab*) from the given name *Llywerch*; see FLOWER.

Vars.: **Blow**; **Bloor(e)** (Midlands).

Patrs. (from 1): **Blowers** (E Anglia); **Blow(e)s**.

Bloxham English: habitation name from *Bloxham* in Oxon. and *Bloxholm* in Lincs., both of which are recorded in Domesday Book as *Blockesham*, apparently from an unrecorded OE byname **Blocc* (presumably referring to a large, ungainly fellow; cf. BLOCK 1) + OE *hām* homestead.

Vars.: **Bloxam**; **Bloxsom(e)**.

Blücher German: from a place of this name, of Slav. origin, near Boizenburg on the Elbe.

The Prussian general Gebhard Leberecht von Blücher, *Prince of Wahlstadt (1742–1819), was born at Rostock in Mecklenburg into a Prussian junker family, who could trace their ancestry back to Ulrich von Blücher, recorded in 1214.*

Bluck English: of unknown origin; possibly a var. of BLACK, BLAKE, or BLOGG, with alteration of the vowel.

Var.: BLICK.

The name is largely confined to the Midlands, and seems to have originated in SW Shrops. It is first found at Wistanstow, Shrops., in the 13th cent. in the form Blyke. *By the mid-15th cent. it had taken the form* Bluck, *with occasional variations such as* Blooke *and* Blowke.

Blum Jewish (Ashkenazic): ornamental name from Yid. *blum* flower (Ger. *Blume*).

Vars.: **Blume**, **Bluhm**, BLOOM.

Cogns.: Flem., Du.: **Bloem(en)**, **Blom**. Swed.: **Blom(me)**, **Blommén**.

Dims.: Jewish: **Blü(h)mke**.

Cpds (ornamental): Jewish: **Blum(en)berg**, **Blumberger** ('flower hill'; partly Anglicized as **Bloomberg**); **Blumenfarb** ('flower colour'); **Blum(en)feld(t)** (Anglicized as BLOOMFIELD and **Blumenfield**); **Blumenfrucht** ('flower fruit'); **Blumenkopf** ('flower head'); **Blumenkran(t)z**, **Blumenkranc** ('flower garland'; the second form is a Pol. spelling); **Blumenkrohn** ('flower crown'); **Blumrosen** ('flower roses'); **Blum(en)stein**, **Blumensztajn** ('flower stone'; the second form is a Pol. spelling); **Blument(h)al** ('flower valley'; see BLOOMINGDALE); **Blumenzweig** ('flower twig'). Swed.: **Blomberg** ('flower hill'); **Blomdahl** ('flower valley'); **Blomgren** ('flower branch'); **Blomqvist** ('flower twig'); **Blomstedt** ('flower homestead'); **Blomstrand** ('flower shore'); **Blomström** ('flower river').

Blumensohn Jewish (Ashkenazic): metr. from the Yidd. female given name *Blume* 'Flower'.

Vars.: **Bloomenson**; **Blumovitz** (E Ashkenazic); **Blumkin(d)** (from the dim. given name *Blumke*; for the excrescent *-d*, see SÜSSKIND), **Blumkine**.

Blunden English: of uncertain origin, perhaps a nickname for someone with grizzled hair, from OE *blonden-*, *blandan-feax* (a cpd of *blandan* to mix, blend + *feax* hair).

Blunt English: 1. nickname for someone with fair hair or a light complexion, from ANF *blunt* blond (OF *blund*, *blond*, of Gmc origin, perhaps akin to BLUNDEN).

2. nickname for a stupid person, from ME *blunt*, *blont* dull (prob. from OE *blinnan* to stop, cease or ON *blundr* sleepy, dozing).

Vars.: **Blund**, **Blount**.

Cogns. (of 1): Fr.: **(Le) Blond(e)**. It.: **Biondi**, **Blondi**, **Blundo**, **Blundo**, **Blunno**, **Biundo**, **Biunno**; **Brundu** (Sardinian). Flem.: **De Blond**.

Dims. (of 1): Eng.: **Blundell** (chiefly Lancs.). Fr.: **Blondel**, **Blond(el)eau**, **Blondiau(x)**, **Blondot**, **Blondet**, **Blondin**, **Blondy**, **Blondeix**. It.: **Biondell(in)i**, **Blondell(in)i**, **Biondetti**.

A family by the name of Blundell *have held lands at Ince Blundell in S Lancs. since the 13th cent.*

Bluntschli Swiss: nickname in the Alemannic dialect of German for a fat man, from MHG *blunsen* to swell up.

Vars.: **Pluntsch**, **Plunz** (also Bavarian).

Blüthner German: occupational name for a flower seller (cf. Silesian dialect *Blütnerei* flower shop), from Ger. *Blüte* bloom, flower head (MHG, OHG *bluot*).

Cogns.: Jewish (Ashkenazic): **Blutner**; **Blut(h)**, **Blutman**; **Blitt**.

Cpds (ornamental): **Blutreich** ('blossom-rich'); **Blut(h)stein**, **Blitstein** ('blossom stone').

Blythe English: 1. var. of BLIGH.

2. habitation name from any of several places, esp. the one in Northumb., named from OE *blīðe* merry, cheerful, probably on account of their pleasant situation, or from a nearby river, which would have been so named by reason of its merry chattering sound.

Vars.: **Blyth**, **Blyde**.

Boada Catalan: of uncertain origin, probably a habitation name from some place named from med. L *bouada* a measure of land equivalent to the amount that a team of oxen could plough in a day (from L *bōs*, gen. *bovis*, ox), or else from med. L *buada* silo, underground grain store (probably from L *volvita* vault).

Boarder English: 1. topographic name for someone who lived in a plank-built cottage, from OE *bord* board, plank of wood.

2. topographic name for someone who lived at the edge of a village or by some other boundary, from ME *border* (OF *bordure* edge, ultimately cogn. with OE *bord*, by way of the sense 'side of a ship').

Vars. (of 1): **Boardman** (chiefly Lancs.); **Bord(i)er**; **Board**, **Boord**.

Cogns. (of 1): Prov.: **Borde**, **Bourda**, **(De) Laborde**, **Lasbordas**; **Bo(u)rd(el)ier**. Cat.: **Borda(s)**, **Laborda**.

Dims. (of 1): Prov.: **Bourdet**, **Bordey**; **Lebo(u)rdais**; **Bo(u)rdillon**, **Bo(u)rdillot**, **Bo(u)rdel(le)**, **Bourdelin**. Cat.: **Bordils**, **Bordiu**.

Augs. (of 1): Fr.: **Bo(u)rdas(se)**.

Boas Jewish and English: from the Hebr. male given name *Boaz* (of uncertain etymology), which, in the Bible, was borne by Ruth's rich kinsman who later became her husband. Boaz was occasionally used as a given name by Christians in Britain, and this seems to have given rise to a surname, which in the 18th cent. is found as far apart as St Ives in Cornwall and Dundee in Scotland.

Vars.: Jewish (Ashkenazic): **Boaz**, **Boazi** (with the Hebr. suffix *-i*). Eng. (Cornwall): **Boase**, **Boays**.

Patr.: Jewish (Ashkenazic): **Boasson**.

Boast English: nickname for a boastful man, from ME *bōst* bragging, vainglory (of uncertain origin; cf. Bos).

Var.: **Boost**.

Bobo 1. Spanish: nickname for a sufferer from a speech defect, from Sp. *bobo* stammering (L *balbus*, which was also a Roman family name).

2. Jewish: of unknown origin.

Bobrov 1. Russian: patr. from the nickname *Bobr* 'Beaver'. The Russ. and the Eng. words are probably both ultimately cogn. with the Eng. vocab. word *brown*, referring to the brown colouring of the animal.

2. Jewish (E Ashkenazic): ornamental name from Russ. *bobr* beaver, one of the many Jewish ornamental names taken from words for animals.

Vars.: Jewish: **Bobroff**; **Bobrovsky**, **Bobrow(sky)**; **Bobrovitz(ki)**; **Bober(man)**.

Habitation name: Pol.: **Bobrowski**.

Bocca Italian: nickname for a talkative or indiscreet person, an orator, or a person with a large or deformed mouth, from It. *bocca* mouth (L *bucca* cheek).

Vars.: **Bocchi**; **Bucchi**, **Bucco**, **Bucca** (S Italy).

Dims.: It.: **Bocchetta**, **Bocchini**, **Boccucci**, **Boccuzzi**, **Boccotti**, **Buccello**, **Buccolini**.

Aug.: It.: **Boccone**.

Pejs.: It.: **Boccacci(o)**, **Boccaccia**.

Boccanegra Italian: nickname from *bocca* mouth (see Bocca) + *negra* (fem.) black (see Noir), referring to a foul-mouthed or abusive person.

Cogn.: Sp.: **Bocanegra**.

Boček Czech: 1. nickname for an illegitimate child, from the vocab. word *boček*, dim. of *bok* side.

2. from a dim. of the OSlav. personal name *Bok*, which is apparently from *bok* side, and may well have denoted illegitimacy as in 1 above.

Var.: **Bočko**.

Cogn.: Pol.: Boczek.

Bocheński Polish: occupational nickname for a baker, from Pol. *bochen* loaf + *-ski* suffix of surnames (see Baranowski).

Bocian 1. Polish: nickname for a tall, gangling individual, from Pol. *bocian* stork.

2. Jewish (E Ashkenazic): ornamental name from Pol. *bocian* stork.

Cogn.: Czech: **Bohdal**.

Habitation name: Pol.: **Bocianowski**.

Böckler German: occupational name for a shield-bearer, from an agent deriv. of MHG *buckel* shield (boss) (LL *buccula*, dim. of *bucca* (distended) cheek, mouth; see Bocca).

Cogn.: Eng.: **Buckler** (see also Buckle).

Boczek Polish: apparently from Pol. *boczek* side, which also means 'bacon'. The application of this word as a surname is not clear; unlike the Czech cogn. Boček, the Pol. word does not mean 'illegitimate'. However, the surname is common in Silesia, and may perhaps be the result of influence from across the Czech border. Alternatively, it could be a metonymic occupational name for a supplier of bacon.

Habitation name: Pol. and Jewish (E Ashkenazic): **Boczkowski**.

Bodas Spanish: nickname from *bodas* wedding (L *vōta* (marriage) vows, pl. of *vōtum*, from *vōvēre* to vow). The reasons for its adoption as a surname are probably anecdotal.

Boddington English: habitation name from either of the places so called in Gloucs. and Northants. The former is recorded in Domesday Book as *Botin(g)ton* 'settlement (OE *tūn*) associated with *Bōta*' (see Bott), the latter as *Botendone* 'hill (OE *dūn*) of *Bōta*'.

Bodfish English: of uncertain origin; possibly from ME *butte* flounder, flatfish + *fissche* fish, given either as a nickname or as an occupational name for a fishmonger.

Var.: **Botfish**.

The earliest known bearer of the name is Joane Botfishe *(d. 1523) of Sittingbourne, Kent, but she left no descendants. All present-day bearers of the name seem to be descended from John Botfish of Whetstone, Leics., whose will of 1534 mentions 5 sons and 3 daughters. By the late 18th cent. the name had spread to Northants and Oxon., and is now most common in the W Midlands. It was taken to America by a certain Robert Botfish, who was sworn in as a freeman of Lynn, Mass., in 1635, and was probably born at Braunstone, Leics., in 1602.*

Bodley English: habitation name, possibly from *Budleigh* in Devon (*Bodelie* in Domesday Book), so called from OE *budda* beetle (or the same word used as a byname) + *lēah* wood, clearing. However, the surname is more common in the W Midlands than in Devon, and it may be that a Midland origin should be sought.

Vars.: **Bodleigh**, **Budleigh**.

Bodner 1. German: topographic name for someone who dwelt in a valley bottom, from a deriv. of Ger. *Boden* floor, bottom (MHG *bodem*, OHG *bodam*).

2. Jewish (Ashkenazic): occupational name for a cooper, from Yid. *bodner* cooper; see Büttner, Bondar.

Vars. (of 1): **Bothner**; **Bodmer** (esp. from *Bodmen* in Switzerland near Zurich).

Bodros Hungarian: nickname for a man with curly hair, from Hung. *bodros* curly, frizzy.

Body English: 1. nickname from ME *body*, OE *bodig* body, trunk, presumably denoting a corpulent individual. In ME the word was also used in the sense 'individual', 'person'; cf. Goodbody.

2. occupational name for a messenger, ME *bode* (OE *boda*; cf. Botha), with the spelling altered to preserve a

disyllabic pronunciation. This development can be clearly traced in Sussex.

Vars.: **Boddy, Bod(d)ie, Bodey.**

The spelling Body *is found chiefly in N England;* Boddy *is more common in the W Country.*

Boeuf French: 1. nickname for a powerfully built man, from OF *boeuf* bull (L *bōs*, gen. *bovis*). In some cases it may have been originally a metonymic occupational name for a herdsman; cf. BOUVIER.

Vars.: **Leboeuf; Boey, Boez.**

Cogns.: Eng.: **Boff, Leboff.** Sp.: **Buey.** Prov., Cat.: **B(i)ou, Buou.** It.: **Bove, B(u)o; (Lo) Bue, (La) Bua; Boe, Boi** (Sardinia); **Lo Voi** (Sicily).

Dims.: Fr.: **Bouvel(et), Bouv(el)ot, Bouvon, Bou(v)et.** It.: **Bo(v)elli, Bo(v)etto, Bovino, Bovoli; Buini; Voiello** (Sicily, Campania).

Patrs.: It.: **Dal Bo, Del Bue.**

Bofill Catalan: nickname from the elements *bo* good + *fill* son; cf. BEAVIS. It seems also to have been used as a given name in the early Middle Ages (the Latinized form *Bonofilio* appearing in Cat. territory in the 10th cent.), and this may also be a partial source of the surname.

Bogatov Russian: patr. from the nickname *Bogaty* 'Rich' (of disputed etymology, perhaps akin to *Bog* God, in the sense of being favoured by God; cf. L *divus* divine, *dives* rich).

Cogns.: Pol.: **Bogacki.** Czech: **Boháč, Bohata.** Rum.: **Bogat(as).** Jewish (E Ashkenazic, probably a nickname for a rich man): **Bogatch.**

Dim.: Czech: **Boháček.**

Bogdanov Russian, Bulgarian, Croatian, and Jewish (E Ashkenazic): patr. from the Slav. personal name *Bogdan* (fem. *Bogdana*), composed of the elements *Bog* God + *dan* gift. It was not a Christian name sanctioned by the Orthodox Church, but was common as a familiar vernacular name, usually representing an equivalent of the baptismal *Feodor* (Gk *Theodoros* 'gift of God'; see TUDOR) or *Feodot* (Gk *Theodotos* 'given by God'). Among the Orthodox it was sometimes used to denote an illegitimate child or foundling. The Jewish surname represents an adoption of one of the Slav. form.

Vars.: Croatian: **Bogdanović.** Jewish: **Bogdanski, Bogdanowitch.**

Cogns. (patrs.): Ukr.: **Bohdanovich.** Beloruss.: **Bahdanovich.** Pol.: **Bogdanowicz.**

Cogns. (not patrs.): Ger. (of Slav. origin): **Bogda(h)n; Bugda(h)n.** Pol.: **Bogdański.** Hung.: **Bogdán.**

Dims. (not patrs.): Ukr.: **Bohdanchik, Bohdanets.**

Boggis English: probably a nickname from ME *boggish* boastful, haughty (of unknown origin, perhaps akin to the Gmc elements *bag* and *bug*, with the literal meaning 'swollen', 'puffed up'). The name (in the forms *Boge(y)s, Boga(y)s*) is found in the 12th cent. in Yorks. and E Anglia, and also around Bordeaux, which had trading links with E Anglia.

Vars.: **Bogg(er)s.**

Bogie Scots: habitation name from a place in Fife, first recorded as *Bolgyne*. The mod. Gael. name is *Srath* (valley) *Bhalgaidgh*. The origin of the placename is uncertain. Watson suggests a connection with Gael. *bolg* bag, sack, in the sense 'bag-shaped pool'.

Bogle Scots and N Irish: nickname for a person of frightening appearance, from older Scots *bogill* hobgoblin, bogy (of uncertain origin, probably Gael.).

Bogusławski Polish: from the given name *Bogusław* (composed of the Slav. elements *Bog* God + *slav* glory) + *-ski* suffix of surnames (see BARANOWSKI).

Cogns.: Czech: **Bohuslav.** Jewish (E Ashkenazic, adoptions of the non-Jewish surname): **Bogoslawski, Bogoslavski, Bogouslavsky.**

Dims.: Pol.: **Bogus(z), Bogucki.** Czech: **Boušek, Bouška** (from the Czech dim. personal name *Bohuša*).

Patrs.: Croatian: **Bogosavljević.** Jewish (E Ashkenazic, adoptions of the non-Jewish surname): **Bogoslawicz, Bogoslavitz.**

Böhm German: ethnic name for a native or inhabitant of Bohemia (the Czech part of Czechoslavakia), from *Böhmen* Ger. name of Bohemia (MHG *Böheim, Bēheim*). This derives its name from the tribal name *Baii* + *heim* homeland; the *Baii* were a tribe, probably Celtic, who inhabited the region in the 1st cent. AD and were gradually displaced by Slav. settlers up to the 5th cent. The same tribe also gave their name to *Bavaria* (see BAYER). Bohemia was an independent Slav. kingdom from the 7th cent. to 1526, when it fell to the Habsburgs. In 1627 it was formally declared a Habsburg Crown Land. It did not gain independence until 1918, after the defeat of Austria-Hungary in the First World War.

Vars.: **Böhme, Boehm(e); Behm, Beha(i)m; Böhmig, Böhmisch; Bömak.**

Cogns.: Jewish (Ashkenazic): **Böhme; Bohm(er); Beem(er); Paim** (from Yid. *Peyem* Bohemia); **Paymer, Peimer** (from Yid. *Peyemer* native or inhabitant of Bohemia). Low Ger.: **Böhmer, Bohm.**

Boieldieu French: nickname for someone who made frequent use of the OF oath *boyau Dieu* 'God's bowels' (from *bo(i)el* entrails, LL *botellus* + *Dieu* God; see DIOS). The surname is most common in the Rouen area.

Boileau French: nickname for a teetotaller, from OF *boi(re)* to drink (L *bibere*) + the def. art. *l'* (L *illa* that) + *eau* water (L *aqua*). Cf. DRINKWATER.

Var.: **Boilleau.**

Cogns.: Prov.: **Boi(s)lève.** It.: **Bevi(l)acqua, Bevacqua.**

A family called Boileau *are descended from Étienne Boileau, governor of Paris under Louis IX in 1255. A number of them later became Huguenots, and so exiles; Charles Boileau (1673–1733) was a military commander of the forces under Marlborough, and his sons settled in Dublin.*

Bois French: topographic name for someone living or working in a wood, from OF *bois* wood (LL *bosci*, pl. of *boscus* shrub, undergrowth, of Gmc origin; cf. OHG *busc*, Ger. *Busch*, Eng. *bush*). See also BUSH and BOISSIER.

Vars.: **Dubois, Desbois;** Bos, **Bost, Dubos(t)** (central France).

Cogns.: Eng.: BOYCE. Prov.: **Bosc, Bos(c)q, Delbos(cq), Dubos(cq).** Sp.: **Bosque.** Cat.: **Bosc(h), Bosqué, Boscos, Boscâ.** It.: **(Del) Bosco, Boschi, Busco.**

Dims.: Fr.: **Boisot, Boisin, Bo(u)squet, Boschet, Boschot.** It.: **Boschini, Boschetti, Boschetto, Boschello, Boschini, Boscolo.** Cat.: **Busquet(s).**

Boissier French: occupational name for a forester and, subsequently, for a carpenter or joiner, an OF agent noun from *bois* wood (see BOIS).

Var. (in the sense 'forester'): **Bosquier** (Normandy).

Cogns. (chiefly in the sense 'forester'): Eng.: **Bos(c)her, Boshere, Boshier, Busher.** Prov.: **Bousquier; Bouscatier, Bouscayre.** Sp.: **Bosquero.** Cat.: **Bosquer.** It.: **Boscaro, Boscari, Bosch(i)ero, Boschier(i).**

Dims.: Fr.: **Boissereau.** Prov.: **Bouscarel, Bouscayrol.** It.: **Boscarello, Bosca(r)ino, Busca(r)ino; Boscariolo, Boscaroli; Boscherini.**

Boissy French: habitation name from any of numerous places so called in N and NW France. These in Roman times were called *Bucciācum* or *Buxeācum* and get their names either from a Gallo-Roman personal name *Buccius*, *Buttius* (of obscure origin) + the local suffix *-ācum*, or from L *buxus* box (the shrub; see Box) + *-ācum*.
Var.: **Bussy**.

Boiteux French: nickname for someone with a limp, OF *boisteux*, from *boiste* box (L *buxus*, Gk *pyxis* container, from *pyxos* box wood, of which boxes used to be made). The nickname arose because the limp was thought to be caused by the leg fitting incorrectly into the 'box' of the pelvis.
Vars.: **Boiteau, Boitel**.

Bolam English (mainly Northumb.): habitation name from *Bolam* in Northumb. or Co. Durham, or from *Bolham* in Notts. These placenames could derive from the dat. pl. (*bolum*) of either of two unattested OE words, **bola* tree-trunk (cf. ON *bolr*, mod. Eng. *bole*) or **bol* rounded hill (cf. MLG *bolle* round object).

Boland 1. English: habitation name from any of various places such as *Bowland* in Lancs. and W Yorks., *Bowlands* in E Yorks., and *Bolland* in Devon. All of them are probably named with OE *boga* bow (in the sense of a bend in a river) + *land* land.
2. Irish: Anglicized form of Gael. **Ó Beólláin** 'descendant of *Beóllán*', an old Ir. name of uncertain origin.
Vars.: **Bolland(s), Bowland(s)**.

Bolaños Spanish: habitation name from any of various places, for example in the provinces of Valladolid and Ciudad Real, so called from the pl. of Sp. *bolaño* boulder.

Bold 1. English: nickname from ME *bold* courageous, daring (OE *b(e)ald*, cogn. with OHG *bald*). In some cases it may derive from an OE personal name; see BAUD 1.
2. English: habitation name for someone who lived or worked at a particular house, from OE *bold*, the typical W Midland and NW form of OE *bōðl*, *bōtl* dwelling house, hall.
3. English: habitation name for someone from *Bold* in Lancs., which gets its name from OE *bold* dwelling, as in 2 above. The surname is especially frequent in Lancs.
4. German: cogn. of BAUD.
Vars. (of 1–3): **Bou(l)d**, BOLT. (Of 2 only): BOOTLE, BOODLE.

Bolesławski Polish: from the given name *Bolesław* (composed of the Slav. elements *bole* greater + *slav* glory) + *-ski* suffix of surnames (see BARANOWSKI).
Cogns.: Jewish (E Ashkenazic, adoptions of the non-Jewish surname): **Boleslawski, Boleslavski, Boleslavsky**.
Dims.: Pol.: **Bolek**. Czech: **Boleček**.

Bolger 1. English: occupational name for a leather worker, from ME, OF *boulgier*, agent deriv. of OF *boulge* leather bag, wallet (ME *bulge*, LL *bulga*, a word probably of Gaul. origin).
2. Irish: Anglicized form of Gael. **Ó Bolguidhir** 'descendant of *Bolgodhar*', a personal name composed of the elements *bolg* belly + *odhar* yellow, sallow.
Vars.: **B(o)ulger, Bolgar, Boulsher**.

Bolingbroke English: habitation name from a place in Lincs., recorded in Domesday Book as *Bolinbroc*, from OE *Bulingbrōc* 'brook associated with *Bul(l)a*' (see BULL).
The first Lancastrian king of England, Henry IV (1367–1413), son of John of Gaunt and grandson of Edward III, was born at Bolingbroke Castle, Lincs., for which he was surnamed 'Bolingbroke'. He came to the throne in 1399 after deposing Richard II.

Bolitho Cornish: habitation name from one of two places in Cornwall, so called from Cornish *bos*, *bod* dwelling + a personal name of uncertain form.
The Bolitho *family have been influential in the affairs of Cornwall for many centuries. The family apparently comes from Bolitho in Crowan, where the name is first recorded in 1545. The earliest known record of the surname is in Penryn in 1524.*

Bolívar Spanish form of Basque **Bolibar**: habitation name from a place in the province of Biscay, so called from Basque *bolu* mill + *ibar* meadow, riverbank.

Bolognese Italian: habitation name for someone from the city of *Bologna* in N Italy. In early classical times this was an independent Tuscan town called *Felsina*, but was renamed *Bonōnia* (perhaps a deriv. of *bonus* good; see BON) when it became a Roman colony in 190 BC. See also BULLEN.
Var.: **Bologna**.

Bolshakov Russian: patr. from the nickname or familiar name *Bolshak* 'Big One', from *bolshoi* big (see BOLSHOV). This was often used as a familiar name to distinguish between two sons bearing the same given name. It was also a nickname for a large man. Compare MENSHIKOV.

Bolshov Russian: patr. from the adj. *bolshoi* big, normally referring simply to physical size (cf. BOLSHAKOV).

Bolt English (chiefly W Country): 1. occupational name for a bolter or sifter of flour, from the ME verb *bo(u)lt* (OF *beluter*, of Gmc origin).
2. from ME *bolt* bolt, bar (OE *bolt* arrow; cf. the *bolt* shot from a crossbow). In part this may have originated as a nickname or byname for a short but powerfully built person (cf. ON *Boltr* in the same sense), in part as a metonymic occupational name for a maker of bolts.
3. var. of BOLD.
Vars.: **Boult, Bo(u)lter**.

Boltflower English: occupational nickname for a miller or sifter of flour, from ME *boult* to sift (see BOLT 1) + *flour*, *flower* flour (see FLOWER).
Vars.: **Boultflower, Bo(u)tflower, Bough(t)flower**.

Bolton English: habitation name from any of the numerous places in N England, esp. the one in Lancs., so called from OE *bōðl* dwelling, house (see BOLD 2) + *tūn* enclosure, settlement.
Var.: **Boulton**.

Boltwood English: habitation name from an unidentified minor place, so called from the OE byname *Bolt* (see BOLT 2) + *wudu* WOOD.

Bolwell English (W Country): of uncertain origin, perhaps a habitation name from an unidentified place named with the OE elements *bol* trunk, plank + *well(a)* spring, stream, i.e. the site of a primitive bridge. On the other hand, it may be an Anglicized form of the Norman habitation name *de Bolville*, which is recorded in Somerset in the 13th cent.

Boman Swedish: topographic name for someone who lived on an outlying homestead, from Swed. *bo* dwelling, farm (ON *bú*) + *man* man (ON *maðr*). In some cases this may have been arbitrarily adopted as an ornamental name by people who had no connection with any outlying farm or homestead.
Vars.: **Bohman; Bo(h)lin**.
Cpds (ornamental): **Boberg** ('farm hill'); **Bogren** ('farm branch'); **Bolinder** ('dweller by the farm lime tree'); **Boqvist** ('farm twig'); **Boström** ('farm river').

Bompard Provençal: nickname meaning 'good companion', from OProv. *bon* good (see Bon) + *par* equal, fellow (see Pear 2).

Bon French: 1. generally an approbatory (or ironic) nickname, from OF *bon* good (L *bonus*).

2. occasionally from the L personal name *Bonus* (likewise meaning 'Good'), which was borne by a minor 3rd-cent. Christian saint, martyred at Rome with eleven companions under the Emperor Vespasian. It was adopted as a given name partly in his honour and partly because of the transparently well-omened meaning.

Vars.: **Lebon**; **Bonne, Labonne** (fem.).

Cogns.: Eng.: Bone; Boon. Sp.: **Bueno**. It.: **Bono**; **Buono** (S Italy); **Bon** (Venetia); **Lo B(u)ono**.

Dims.: Fr.: **Bon(n)in, Bonnineau, Bon(n)ot**, Bonnet. Prov.: **Bounin, Bouniol**. Port.: **Bonito** (in the sense 'pretty'). It.: **Bonelli, Boniello, Bonini, Bonucci, Bonuccello, Bonioli, Bon(i)otti**; **Bonito, Boniello** (S Italy); **Bonutti** (Venetia).

Augs.: Fr.: **Bonnat**. It.: **Bononi**.

Pejs.: Fr.: **Bon(n)ard, Bonnaud**. Prov.: **Bounaud**. It.: **Bonacci(o), Bonazzi, Bonassi**; see also Fibonacci.

Patrs.: It.: **De Bono, Di B(u)ono, De Boni(s), Del B(u)ono**; **De Vuono** (S Italy).

Bonaccorso Italian: from a medieval given name, composed of the elements *bono* good (see Bon) + *accorso* aid (LL *accursus*, from *adcurrere* to aid, lit. run up); cf. Bonaiuto.

Vars.: **Bonacorso, Bonac(c)orsi, Bonac(c)urso**; **Accorso, Accorsi, Accurs(i)o**; **Corso, Corsi**.

Dims.: **Corsini, Corsell(in)i, Corsello, Corsetti**.

Patrs.: **D'Accorso, D'Accurs(i)o, Del Corso**.

Bonagente Italian: nickname for someone who came from a well-respected family, perhaps someone suspected of being the illegitimate offspring of a noble house; from *bona* (fem.) good (see Bon) + *gente* family (L *gens*, gen. *gentis*).

Bonaiuto Italian: from a given name that was relatively frequent in the Middle Ages. Composed of the elements *bono* good (see Bon) + *aiuto* help, aid (LL *adiutus*, from *adiuvāre* to help), it was bestowed in the hope that the son so named would grow up to be a support to the family.

Bonally Scots (now rare): of uncertain origin. According to Black, it is from a placename, *Bonaly* near Edinburgh or *Banaley* (now lost) in Fife, which are of obscure origin. According to Reaney, it is more probably from *bonaillie*, a catch phrase used with a toast drunk on parting, from OF *bon* good (see Bon) + *aller* to go (from L *ambulāre* to walk), in which case it would have arisen as a nickname for one who made frequent use of this expression.

Vars.: **Bonallo, Bon(n)ella, Bonello**.

Bonaparte Italian: from It. *bona* (fem.) good (see Bon) + *parte* part, portion, place, party (L *pars*, gen. *partis*). The origin of application of this expression as a surname is uncertain, but it is claimed that it arose in the politics of early medieval Florence, where one party on the governing council described itself as the 'good party' (*buona parte*). The name has also been adopted as a Jewish surname.

Var.: **Buonaparte**.

The family of the French Emperor Napoleon Bonaparte *(1769–1821) had originally settled on the island of Corsica from Tuscany in 1512. They were landowners, proud of their noble Italian background, and they claimed descent from a 10th-cent. count of Pistoia.*

Bonar 1. English and Scots: nickname from ME *boner(e)*, *bonour* gentle, courteous, handsome (OF *bonnaire*, from the phrase *de bon(ne) aire* of good bearing or appearance, from which also comes mod. Eng. *debonair*).

2. Irish (Donegal): trans. of Gael. **Ó Cnáimhsighe** 'descendant of *Cnáimhseach*', a byname meaning 'Midwife'. The word seems to be a deriv. of *cnámh* bone (with the fem. ending *-seach*), but if so the reason for this is not clear.

Vars.: **Bonnar, Bon(n)er**.

Cogns. (of 1): Fr.: **Bonnaire**. It.: **Bonaro**.

Dim. (of 1): It.: **Bonarelli**.

Bonchrétien French: nickname for a notably pious individual, or ironically for a notorious reprobate, from OF *bon* good (see Bon) + *chrétien* Christian.

Var.: **Bonchrestien**.

Cogn.: It.: **Buoncristiano**.

Bond English: status name for a peasant farmer or husbandman, ME *bonde* (OE *bonda*, *bunda*, reinforced by ON *bónde*, *bóndi*). The ON word was also in use as a personal name, and this has given rise to other Eng. and Scandinavian surnames alongside those originating as status names. The status of the peasant farmer fluctuated considerably during the Middle Ages; moreover, the underlying Gmc word is of disputed origin and meaning. *OED* connects it with OE *būan* to dwell, via the pres. part. *būende* dweller. However, it is more likely that the word is ultimately akin to *bindan* to bind: the Proto-Gmc word **bonda* probably signified a member of a band or tribe bound together by loyalty to their chief. Among Gmc peoples who settled to an agricultural life, the term came to signify a farmer holding lands from, and bound by loyalty to, a lord; from this developed the sense of a free landholder as opposed to a serf. In England after the Norman Conquest the word sank in status and became associated with the notion of bound servitude, whereas in Scandinavia *bonde* means simply 'farmer', with no such derogatory overtones.

Vars.: **Bonde, Bound**; **Bound(e)y**; **Bund(e)y**.

Cogns.: Norw., Dan.: **Bonde, Bonne** ('farmer'). Low Ger.: **Bunde**.

Patrs.: Eng.: **Bo(u)nds**. Norw., Dan.: **Bondesen, Bonnesen**.

A number of English bearers of this name come from a Dorset family traceable back to Robert Bond *of Hache Beauchamp, whose name is found on records dating from 1431. The surname is, however, extremely common in N as well as S England, and several genealogically separate origins are probable.*

Bondar Ukrainian: occupational name for a cooper, Ukr. *bondar*, metathesized cogn. of Pol. Bednarz, Ger. Büttner.

Cogns.: Jewish (E Ashkenazic): **Bonder(man)**; **Bonderow, Bonderoff, Bonderefsky** (all from E Yid. *bonder*, which is from the Ukr. word).

Patrs.: Belorussian: **Bondarovich**. Jewish: **Bonderow, Bonderoff, Bonderefsky**.

Bondiou Provençal: nickname from OProv. *bon* good (see Bon) + *diou* God (L *deus*), presumably denoting a frequent user of this oath.

Var.: **Bondivenne**.

Bone English: 1. nickname, of Norman origin, meaning 'good', from OF *bon* good (see Bon).

2. nickname for a thin, bony individual; see Bain 2.

Vars. (of 1): **Bonn, Bunn**; Boon.

Bonehill English: habitation name from a place in Staffs. (*Bolenhull* in early records), probably so called from the gen. case of OE *bula* bull(ock) (or the same word used as a personal name) + OE *hyll* Hill.

Bonenfant French: nickname, probably slightly mocking in tone, from *bon* good (see Bon) + *enfant* child (see Infante).

Cogn.: It.: **Bonfante**.

Bonfield English (Norman): habitation name, altered by folk etymology, from any one of three places in Normandy called *Bonneville*, from OF *bonne* (fem.) good (see Bon) + *ville* settlement (see Ville).

Var.: **Bondfield**.

Cogn.: Fr.: **Bonville**.

This was one of the earliest Norman names to be taken to Ireland, where it was Gaelicized as **de Buinnbhíol**.

Bongars French: nickname for a trusted servant, from *bon* good (see Bon) + *gars* servant, lad (see Gars).

Var.: **Bongard**.

Cogn.: It.: **Bongarzoni**.

Bonham English: 1. generally an alteration of OF *bon homme* (L *bonus homo*). This had two senses relevant to surname formation; partly it had the literal meaning 'good man', and partly it came to mean 'peasant farmer'.

2. habitation name from an unidentified place, of which the second element is OE *hām* homestead, or possibly *hamm* water meadow, while the first may be a personal name (OE *Buna*), of unknown etymology.

Cogns. (of 1): Fr.: **Bonhomme**. It.: Bonomo. Jewish (Ashkenazic): **Bunim** (from the Yid. male given name *Bunem*, which is derived ultimately from the OF phrase *bon homme*); **Bunomovitz**, **Bunimovitz** (patrs.).

Dims. (of 1): Fr.: **Bonhommet**, **Bonzoumet**.

Bonheur French: from OF *bonne* (fem.) good (see Bon) + *heure* moment, time (from L *hōra* hour), probably a given name for a child whose birth was felt to be a happy or lucky moment, e.g. one born to parents long childless. The mod. Fr. sense 'happiness' is a more recent development, and is unlikely to underlie any instances of the surname.

Var.: **Bonheure**.

Bonhoff German: habitation name from a place near Siegburg in Westphalia or from any of several other minor localities in the same area. The second element is OHG *hof* court, yard (see Hofer); the first is of unknown origin (Bahlow regards it as one of many pre-Gmc terms denoting a marshy locality, but it is equally plausibly a personal name, perhaps cognate with OE *Buna* (cf. Bonham 2)).

Vars.: **Bonhöffer**; **Bohnhoff**.

Boniface English and French: from the medieval given name *Boniface* (L *Bonifatius*, from *bonum* good + *fātum* fate, destiny). In LL *-ti-* and *-ci-* came to be pronounced identically; the name was thus often respelled *Bonifacius* and assigned the meaning 'doer of good deeds', derived by folk etymology from L *facere* to do. Bonifatius was the name of the Roman military governor of N Africa in 422–32, who was a friend of St Augustine, and it was also borne by various early Christian saints, notably St Boniface (*c*.675–754), who was born in Devon and martyred in Friesland after evangelical work among Ger. tribes. It was also adopted by nine popes. The given name was always more popular in Italy (in its various cogn. forms; see below) than elsewhere; the original sense 'well fated' remained transparent in It., so the name was often bestowed there for the sake of the good omen.

Vars.: Eng.: **Bonniface**, **Bonifas**.

Cogns.: It.: **Bonifaci(o)**, **Bonifacci**, **Bonifazio**, **Bonifati**, **Bonfatti**, **Bonfà**; **Facci(o)**, **Faz(z)i(o)**, **Fassi(o)** (aphetic forms). Port.: **Bonifácio**. Flem., Du.: **Bonefaas**, **Faas**, **Faes**.

Dims.: It.: **Bonifacino**; **Fazzini**, **Fazzioli**, **Fazzuoli**, **Fassini**, **Fassioli**, **Fac(c)ini**, **Faccioli**, **Facciotti**. Hung.: **Bónis**.

Augs.: It.: **Fassone**, **Faccione**.

Patrs.: It.: **De Fazio**, **Di Fazio**, **De Facci**. Du.: **Faasen**.

Bonilla Spanish: habitation name from places in the provinces of Ávila and Cuenca, so called from LL *balnella*, pl. of *balnellum*, a dim. of class. L *balneum* bath (cf. Bain 4).

Bonjour French: nickname from OF *bon* good (see Bon) + *jorn*, *jour* day (LL *diurnum*, a deriv. of class. L *diēs*), presumably denoting someone who made frequent use of this salutation. The It. and Sp. cogns. were also occasionally used as given names in the Middle Ages, bestowed on a child as an expression of the parent's satisfaction at the birth, or for the sake of a good omen.

Cogns.: It.: **B(u)ongiorno**. Sp.: **Buendía**. Cat.: **Bondia**.

Bonnefoi French: nickname from Fr. *bonne* (fem.) good (see Bon) + *foi* faith (L *fidēs*), presumably denoting someone who made frequent use of this oath.

Cogn.: It.: **Bonafede**.

Bonnet French: 1. nickname from a dim. of Bon.

2. from the L personal name *Bonītus*, a deriv. of *bonus* good (see Bon). This name was borne by a 7th-cent. saint from the Auvergne, in whose honour it enjoyed considerable popularity there and elsewhere in France throughout the Middle Ages.

3. metonymic occupational name for a milliner, or nickname for a wearer of unusual headgear, from OF *bon(n)et* bonnet, hat. This word is found in med. L as *abonnis*, but is of unknown origin.

Vars. (chiefly of 2): **Bonet**; **Bon(n)ay**, **Bon(n)ey** (E France); **Bon(n)ex** (central France); **Bon(n)ez** (N France).

Cogns.: Eng.: **Bon(n)et(t)**. Cat.: **Bonet**. It.: **Bonetti**.

Dims.: Fr. (chiefly of 2): **Bonnet(a)in**, **Bonneteau**, **Bonneton**, **Bonnetot**.

Pej. (of 3): Fr.: **Bonnetaud**.

Patr. (from 2): Fr.: **Dubonnet**.

Bonnevie French: nickname for someone who enjoyed life, a glutton or womanizer or simply someone who enjoyed prosperity, from OF *bonne* (fem.) good (see Bon) + *vi(th)e* life (L *vīta*). In some cases the It. and Port. cogns. may derive from a given name bestowed on a child for the sake of the good omen.

Cogns.: It.: **Bonavita**. Port.: **Boavida**.

Bonney English (chiefly Lancs.): nickname for a handsome person, esp. a large or well-built one, from N dial. *bonnie* fine, beautiful (still a common Scots word; apparently a dim. of OF *bon* good, although the development is not clear).

Bonnington English: habitation name from any of various places of this name in Kent, Northumb., and Scotland, from OE *Buningtūn* 'settlement (OE *tūn*) associated with *Buna*'; cf. Bonham 2.

Bonomo Italian: 1. nickname meaning 'good man', a cogn. of Bonham 1.

2. occupational name for various elected officials, for example in 12th-cent. Florence, who bore this title.

Dims.: **Bonomelli**, **Bonometti**, **Bonomini**, **Bonomolo**.

Aug.: **Bonomone**.

Bonser English: nickname from OF *bon sire* good sir, given either to a fine gentleman (perhaps ironically), or to someone who made frequent use of this term of address. The surname is now found chiefly in Notts.

Bontemps French: nickname for a person of cheerful disposition, from OF *bon* good (see Bon) + *temps* weather (L *tempus* time, season). Cf. Merryweather.

Vars.: **Bontant, Bomptan**.

Cogns.: It.: **B(u)ontempo**.

Dim.: It.: **Bontempelli**.

Bonthuys Dutch: from residence in a brightly coloured or in a half-timbered house. MDu. *bont*, MLG *bunt* means either 'black-and-white', 'piebald', or 'gaily coloured'. MHG *bunt* means 'black-and-white' or 'grey-and-white' and is applied particularly to furs; the regular MHG word for 'brightly coloured' is *vēch*. The most plausible explanation for the origin for the name is therefore 'one living in a black-and-white house'.

Bonvoisin French: nickname for a neighbourly person, from OF *bon* good (see Bon) + *voisin* neighbour (L *vīcīnus*, a deriv. of *vīcus* neighbourhood, village).

Cogns.: It.: **Bonvicino**; **Bommicino** (Calabria).

Boodle English: topographic name for someone who lived or worked at a particular large house, from OE *bōðl*, *bōtl* dwelling house, hall, or habitation name for someone who came from a place named with this element, such as *Buddle* in Fordingbridge, Hants, *Buddle* in Niton, Isle of Wight, or *Buddle* Oak in Halse, Somerset.

Vars.: **Buddle**; **Buttle**; **Bodle**, **Boydell** (Sussex, probably from *Bodle* Street near Hailsham); Bootle, Bold.

Booker English: 1. occupational name for someone concerned with books, generally as a scribe or binder, from ME *boker*, OE *bōcere*, agent deriv. of *bōc* book.

2. occupational name for a bleacher of cloth, from ME *bouken* to bleach, steep in lye (from MLG, MDu. *būken*). See also Bowker 2.

Boon 1. English (Norman): var. of Bone 1.

2. English (Norman): habitation name from *Bohon* in La Manche, of obscure etymology.

3. Dutch: cogn. of Bean 1.

Vars. (of 1 and 2): **Boone** (the more common U.S. spelling); **Bown(e)**. (Of 2 only): **Bohun**.

The legendary American frontiersman Daniel Boone *(1734–1820) was born in Reading, Pennsylvania, into a Quaker family. His grandfather was a weaver who had emigrated from Exeter in England to Philadelphia in 1717, and his father was a cattle breeder.*

Boosey 1. English: topographic name for someone who lived by a cattle stall, and so in effect an occupational name for a cowherd, from ME *bōs(e)* cattle stall (from OE *bōsig*, reinforced by the cogn. MLG *bōs*).

2. Scots: habitation name from *Balhousie* in Fife, earlier *Balwolsy*, probably from Gael. *baile a'choille* farmstead of the wood.

Vars.: **Boosie, Bousie**.

Boot 1. English: metonymic occupational name for a maker or seller of boots, from ME, OF *bote* (of unknown origin).

2. Dutch: cogn. of Bate 2.

Var. (of 1): **Boote**.

Cogns. (of 1): Fr.: **Botte**. It.: **Botta**. Sp.: Botas.

The surname is common in the Nottingham area, where perhaps its most famous bearer was Jesse Boot *(1850–1931), founder of the chain of chemists' shops.*

Booth N English: topographic name for someone who lived in a small hut or bothy (ME *bōth(e)*), esp. a cowman or shepherd. The word is of Scandinavian origin (cf. ODa. *bōth*, OIcel. *búð*), and was used to denote various kinds of temporary shelter, typically a cowshed or a herdsman's hut. The surname is still today more common in N England, where Scandinavian influence was more marked, and in Scotland, where the word was borrowed into Gael. as *both(an)*.

Vars.: **Boothe**; **Boothman**.

Cogns.: Swed.: **Bodén, Bodin**.

Boothby English: habitation name from a group of villages in Lincs., so called from Northern ME *bōth(e)* hut, shed (see Booth) + *by* farm, settlement (ON *býr*).

Boothroyd English: habitation name from a place in W Yorks., so called from Northern ME *bōth(e)* hut, shed (see Booth) + *royd* clearing (see Rhodes).

Bootle English: habitation name from places in Lancs. and Cumb., so called from OE *bōtl* dwelling, large house (see Boodle, Bold 2).

Bordeaux French: habitation name from the city in Gironde, apparently so called from Old Aquitanian roots of obscure significance, *burd* and *gala*.

Borden English: habitation name from a place in Kent, perhaps so called from OE *bār* boar + *denn* (swine) pasture. Alternatively the first element may be OE *bord* board (cf. Boarder 1) or a Gmc element meaning 'elevation', 'hill' (cf. Boreham).

Boreham English: habitation name from any of three places so called, in Essex, Herts., and Sussex. The surname is most common in Essex. In each case early forms point clearly to an OE first element ***bor**, which is not independently attested, but may be akin to OHG *bor* upper chamber and OE *borlice* excellently, with some such sense as 'elevation', 'hill'. The second element is OE *hām* homestead.

Borges Catalan and Portuguese: habitation name from a place in the province of Tarragona, N Spain, of uncertain etymology. It may represent a pl. form of Borja, or else it may be of pre-Roman origin, cogn. with the Fr. placename *Bourges*.

Borgne French: nickname for a person with only one eye or with a squint, from OF *borgne* squinting, of unknown origin.

Vars.: **Borne, Lebor(g)ne**.

Dims.: **Bor(g)net, Bor(g)not** (E France). Prov.: **Borgn(i)ol**.

Pej.: **Bornard** (E France).

Borisov Russian: patr. from the common given name *Boris*. The etymology of this is uncertain. It may be a shortening of an OSlav. personal name, *Boroslav*, from *bor* struggle, conflict + *slav* glory, but more probably it is an alteration of the OBulg. personal name *Bogoris*, borne by the King of the Bulgars (sometimes known as Boris) who was converted to Christianity in 864. This is a byname from Turkic *bogori* small. *Boris* is one of the very few names of non-Byzantine origin admitted as a baptismal name in the Orthodox Church, largely because of the popular cult of St Boris (d. 1010), patron saint of Moscow (whose baptismal name was Roman). The surname has also occasionally been adopted by Jews.

Var.: **Borisovich**.

Cogns. (patrs.): Beloruss.: **Barysevich**. Pol.: **Borys(i)ewicz**. Ukr.: **Borishchenko, Borisyak**. Croatian: **Borisavljević**.

Cogns. (not patrs.): Ger. (of Slav. origin): **Borsch(k)e, Porsch(k)e; Borzig, Porzig, Borzik, Borsig; Bursian**.

Dims. (patrs.): Russ.: **Borin, Bori(sh)chev**.

Borja Spanish: habitation name from a place in the province of Saragossa, so called from Arabic *borǧ*, *borj* tower.

The powerful and notorious Borgia *family in Renaissance Rome was of Spanish origin. Rodrigo* Borja *(1431–1503), born in Játiva, Spain, became Pope as Alexander VI. He was an able politician and administrator, but he is remembered more for his irreligious worldliness. Among his four children by his mistress Vannozza Catanei were Cesare Borgia (1475–1507), and Lucrezia (1480–1519). Cesare was a brilliant but unscrupulous soldier and politician, who was made a cardinal at the age of 17 and implicated in the murders of his elder brother and his sister's husband, among others. Lucrezia was rumoured to have been a poisoner and to have had incestuous relations with her father and her brother, but she led a conventional life after her marriage to her third husband, Alfonso d'Este, Duke of Ferrara, in 1501, and became a patron of the arts and sciences.*

Borkowski Polish and Jewish (E Ashkenazic): habitation name from any of several places called *Borków* (so named from Pol. *bór* pine forest + *-ek* dim. suffix + *-ów* possessive suffix forming placenames), with the addition of the suffix of local surnames *-ski* (see BARANOWSKI).

Var.: **Borek**.

Borland Scots: habitation name from any of several places called *Bor(e)land* or *Bordland*, which get their names from ME or OE *bord* board, table + *land* land, i.e. land which supplied the lord's table, in other words 'home farm'.

Var.: **Boreland**.

Borley English: habitation name from *Borley* in Essex or *Boreley* in Worcs., both so called from OE *bār* (wild) boar (cf. BORDEN) + *lēah* wood, clearing.

Var.: **Boreley**.

Borodin Russian: patr. from the nickname *Boroda* 'BEARD' (the two words are ultimately cogn.). In E Europe cleanshavenness was in fashion from the 12th to 16th cents., except among Jews, so bearded men stood out as exceptional. Among Jewish men, on the other hand, beards were the norm, and someone who was beardles stood out, hence the E Ashkenazic surname **Bezborodko** 'Beardless'.

Cogns. (patrs.): Pol.: **Brodewicz, Brodniewicz**. Croatian: **Bradič**.

Cogns. (not patrs.): Beloruss.: **Boroda**. Pol.: **Broda, Brodecki**, BRODSKI. Czech: **Brada, Bradáč, Bradatý**. Jewish: **Bord(a), Boroda**.

Dims. (patrs.): Russ.: **Borodulin, Baradulin**. Beloruss.: **Baradzeya**.

Boronat Catalan: from a dissimilated form of the medieval given name *Bonanat* (L *bonā* (*horā*) *nātus* born in a good hour; cf. BONHEUR), bestowed on a child as a good omen. It may also in part have been a nickname for a lucky individual.

Borowski Polish and Jewish (E Ashkenazic): habitation name from a place named from Pol. *bór* pine forest + *-ów* possessive suffix, with the adition of *-ski* suffix of local surnames (see BARANOWSKI). The Pol. word *borowik* means 'forest mushroom', and in some cases surnames of this group may derive from it. In the case of Jewish instances of these surnames, the origin is generally ornamental.

Vars.: Pol.: **Borowicki, Borowiński**; **Borecki, Borucki**; **Burski**; **Borowiec, Borowicz** (patr. in form). Jewish: **Borovski, Borovsky, Borowsky**. See also BORKOWSKI.

Cogn.: Czech: **Borský**.

Cogn. (patr.): Croatian: **Borić**.

Borrego Spanish: nickname for a simpleton or a gentle person, or metonymic occupational name for a shepherd, from Sp. *borrego* lamb (LL *burrēcus*, a deriv. of *burra* lambswool).

Var.: **Borreguero** (an agent deriv.).

Cogn.: Port.: **Borrêgo**.

Borromeo Italian: nickname for a pious person who had made the pilgrimage to Rome, or an amiable man who bore the given name *Romeo*, from *bono* good (see BON) + *Romeo* ROMAN.

Var.: **Borromei**.

Borthwick Scots: habitation name from a place near Hawick in S Scotland, where a family of this name held Borthwick Castle since the 14th cent. The placename comes from OE *bord* board, table + *wīc* outlying village, dairy farm (see WICK). For the sense, compare BORLAND.

Bos French: 1. var. of BOIS.

2. from a Gmc personal name, *Boso*, derived from an element meaning 'audacious'; cf. MHG *boese*, MLG *bōse* reckless, daring (mod. Ger. *böse* naughty).

Vars. (of 2, from the oblique case of the Gmc word): **Boson, Bo(u)zon**.

Cogns. (of 2): It.: **B(u)osi(o), Bose**.

Dims. (of 2): Fr.: **Bosonnet, Bozounet**. It.: **Boselli, Bosetti, Bosin(ell)i, Bosotti, Bosutti**.

Aug. (of 2): It.: **Bosone**.

Bosanquet 1. Cornish: habitation name from *Bosanketh*, so called from Corn. *bos*, *bod* dwelling + a personal name of uncertain form.

2. English, of Huguenot origin: nickname for a short person, from the S French dial. term *bouzanquet* dwarf.

The name is said to have been brought to England in 1685 by Jean and David Bosanquet, *Huguenot refugees from Lunel in Languedoc. However, the surname* Bosancoth *is recorded in Cornwall as early as 1525. Many Huguenot settlers established themselves in Cornwall, and it seems likely that two originally distinct surnames have here fallen together.*

Boscawen Cornish: habitation name from any of three places, two near St Buryan and the other near Helston, so called from Corn. *bos*, *bod* dwelling + *scawen* elder tree (cf. Bret. *scaven*, W *ysgawen*).

Hugh Boscawen *(c.1680–1734) was created Baron of Boscawen Rose and Viscount Falmouth in 1720 in recognition of the support that he had given to George II as MP for various Cornish constituencies. His father, Edward Boscawen (d. 1685) was MP for Truro for twenty years; his mother was a sister of the Earl of Godolphin. He himself married a niece of John Churchill, 1st Duke of Marlborough, and his son, Edward Boscawen (1711–61), was a British admiral. A later descendant, Edward Boscawen (1787–1841), was created Earl Falmouth at the time of the coronation of George IV.*

Bossard French: 1. from a Gmc personal name composed of the elements *bos* audacious (see BOS 2) + *hard* hardy, brave.

2. nickname for a hunchback, from OF *bosse* hump, hunched back (of unknown origin) + the pej. suffix *-ard*.

Cogns.: Prov.: **Boussard**. (Of 1 only): Ger.: **Bosshardt**. Flem.: **Bossaert**.

Dim.: Prov.: **Boussardon**.

Bossut French: nickname for a hunchback, from OF *bossu* hunchbacked (a deriv. of *bosse* lump, hump; cf. BOSSARD 2).

Vars.: **Bossé, Bosseux; Bosse**.

Cogns.: Eng.: **Boss**. Flem.: **Bossuyt**.

Dim.: Fr.: **Bosuet**.

Aug.: Fr.: **Bossuat**.

Bostock English: habitation name from *Bostock* in Ches. (*Botestoch* in Domesday Book), so called from the OE personal name *Bōta* (see BOTT) + OE *stoc* place (see STOKE).

Many bearers of this name are members of a single family, who claim descent from a certain Sir Gilbert of Bostock, *living in the 12th cent. His great-great-grandson fought at the Battle of Evesham in 1265. There are branches of the family in Northants and Notts. as well as Ches. and Lancs.*

Boston English: habitation name from the place in Lincs., the name of which means 'Bōtwulf's stone'. This has been considered to refer to St Botulf, and to be the site of the monastery that he built in the 7th cent., but it is more likely that the Bōtwulf of the placename was an ordinary landowner, and that the association with the saint was a later development because of the name.

Boswell English and Scots (Norman): habitation name from *Beuzeville* in Seine Maritime, which gets its name from OF *Beuze* (a personal name probably of Gmc origin; cf. Bos 2) + *ville* settlement (see VILLE). The final element has been altered as a result of association with the common placename ending *-well* 'spring', 'stream'.

Var.: **Boswall**.

Scots bearers of this name may trace their ancestry to a Norman, Roger de Bosvil, *who held lands in Fife in the 13th cent. The most famous of his descendants is James* Boswell *(1740–95), biographer of Dr Johnson. His father, Alexander Boswell, Lord Auchinleck, was a judge.*

Bosworth English: habitation name from Market *Bosworth* in Leics., so called from an OE personal name *Bōsa* (cf. Bos 2) + OE *worð* enclosure (see WORTH). Husbands Bosworth is a different name in origin (*Baresworde* in Domesday Book), from OE *bār* boar + *worð*.

Botas Spanish: 1. metonymic occupational name for a maker of leather bottles for wine, or a maker of wine casks, called *botas* in OSp. (from LL *but(t)is*; see also BÜTTNER and BUTLER).

2. metonymic occupational name for a maker of boots, or nickname for a wearer of boots, at a time when the majority of the population had more primitive footwear. The vocab. word for all of these was *botas*, which is of uncertain origin; it has been suggested that it is the same word as in 1, since both boots and bottles were normally made of leather, but it is more probably of separate origin.

Var.: **Boto**.

Dim.: **Botija**.

Bote Spanish: 1. metonymic occupational name for a potter, from Sp. *bote* vase, pot (of unknown origin, perhaps akin to Eng. *pot*; see POTTER).

2. nickname for a forceful or pugnacious individual, from Sp. *bote* blow, thrust (a deriv. of *botar* to hit, strike, apparently of Gmc origin and cogn. with mod. Eng. *beat*, OE *bēatan*).

Botelho Portuguese: metonymic occupational name for a gatherer of kelp or seaweed, Port. *botelho*.

Botha Frisian: from an OFris. personal name *Botho* 'Messenger' (OHG *Boto*, *Bodo*, from Gmc **buð* to announce). See also BOTT and BOUDON.

Cogns.: Low Ger.: **Both(e)**, **Ba(a)de**, **Bahde**. Du.: **Bode**.

Dims.: Fris.: **Botje**, **Botma**. Low Ger.: **Bodeke**, **Badeke**.

Patrs.: Low Ger.: **Bo(h)den**, **Baden(ius)**, **Bading**.

Botha *is a very common Afrikaner name in S Africa, where it has been established since 1672. The name is, of course, of Dutch-Frisian origin, but it has also assimilated a French Huguenot name,* Boudier, *which was brought to S Africa in 1776.*

Bothwell Scots and N Irish: habitation name from a place in the former county of Lanarks. (now part of Strathclyde region), so called from ME *bōth(e)* (see BOOTH) + *well(a)* spring, stream (see WELL).

Bott English: apparently from an OE personal name, of uncertain form and origin. It may be a cogn. of BOTHA, or it may be akin to BUTT. Forms such as Walter *le botte* (Oxon. 1279) seem to point to a nickname, perhaps from OF *bot* but, cask, or the homonymous *bot* toad; cf. BOTTRELL.

Patr.: **Botting**.

Böttcher German: one of several occupational names for a cooper, Ger. *Böttcher*, from MHG *botecher*, *bötticher*, *bütticher*, an agent deriv. of *botige*, *butche* wine barrel (OHG *potega*, *poteche*, via L *apotēca* from Gk *apothēkē* wine cellar, store room). Böttcher was the term regularly used for a cooper in N and E Germany. See also BINDER, BÜTTNER, and SCHÄFFLER.

Vars.: **Bötticher**, **Böttger**, **Bötjer**, **Bittcher**.

Cogns.: Low Ger.: **Bödeker**, **Böcker**, **Bädeke(r)**, **Bäker**. Fris.: **Bätjer**. Sp.: **Bodega**.

Bottom N English: topographic name for someone who lived in a broad valley, from OE *botm* valley bottom.

Vars.: **Bottoms**, **Bottams**, **Botham**.

Cogn.: Ger.: BODNER.

Cpds: Eng.: HIGGINBOTTOM; LONGBOTTOM; SHUFFLEBOTTOM; SIDEBOTTOM; WINTERBOTTOM.

Bottomley English (Yorks. and Lancs.): habitation name from a place in W Yorks., so called from OE *botm* broad valley (see BOTTOM) + *lēah* wood, clearing.

Bottrell English (Norman): probably a habitation name from *Les Bottereaux* in Eure, Normandy, apparently so named from being infested with toads. The placename is recorded in the late 12th cent. in the L form *Boterelli*, from a dim. of OF *bot* toad (of Gmc origin, perhaps akin to a root meaning 'to swell, puff up'; cf. BUTT 1). It has also been suggested that the name originated as a Norman nickname, from ONF *bottereau* toad, or as an occupational name for a worker in a buttery, ME *butterer*.

Vars.: **Botterell**, **Bott(e)rill**; **Butteriss**.

The manor of Boscastle in Cornwall was held in 1302 by William de Botereus, *whose family probably came originally from Les Bottereaux in Normandy.*

Boudet 1. French: dim. of BOUDON.

2. Provençal: aphetic form of Prov. *néboudet* great-nephew, dim. of *nébout* nephew (L *nepos*, gen. *nepōtis*, nephew, grandson).

Boudin French: 1. dim. of BOUDON.

2. metonymic occupational name for a maker of black pudding and sausages, or nickname for a rotund individual, from OF *boudin* black pudding (cogn. with ME *poding* pudding, LG *pudden* sausage, probably from a Gmc root meaning 'to bulge'; cf. BOTT, BOTTRELL, and BUTT 1).

Vars.: **Boudy**, **Bo(u)in**. (Of 2 only): **Boudinier** (an agent noun).

Dims.: Fr.: **Bo(ud)ineau**, **Boudinot**.

Boudon French: from the OF oblique case of the Gmc personal name *Bodo* 'Messenger', 'Herald' (see BOTHA).

Var.: BOUTON.

Dims.: BOUDET, BOUDIN, **Boudot**, **Boudeau**.

Bouffard French: nickname for a glutton, a pej. from OF *bouffer* to stuff oneself, earlier to puff out the cheeks (a word probably of imitative origin).

Vars.: **Boufard**, **Bouffaud**.

Bough (pronounced /bɒf/ or /baʊ/): 1. English and Irish: var. of Bow.

2. English: from a Norman form of OF *boeuf* bull. See Boeuf.

Boughton English: habitation name from any of the numerous places so called. Those in Cambs. (formerly Hunts.). Lincs., Norfolk, Northants, and Notts. get their first element from the OE byname *Bucca* (see Buck 1); those in Ches. and Kent get the name from OE *bōc* beech (a byform of *bēce*; see Beech 2) + *tūn* enclosure, settlement.

Bouille French: 1. topographic name for someone who lived by a marsh, OF *bouille* (a deriv. of *boue* mud, of Celt. origin).

2. topographic name for someone who lived by a birch grove, from the OF dial. term *bouille* (from LL *betul(l)ia*, a deriv. of *bettius* birch; cf. Boul 1 and Bès).

Var.: **Delbouille.**

Dims.: **Bouillet(te), Bouillé, Bouillot, Bouillon.**

Aug.: **Bouillat.**

Pej.: **Bouillard.**

Boul French: 1. topographic name for someone who lived by a birch tree, OF *boul* (LL *bettulus*, a dim. of *bettius*; see Bès). The mod. Fr. term *bouleau* is a further dim. of this.

2. nickname for a short, rotund man, from OF *boule* ball (L *bulla*; cf. Billet 3).

Vars.: **Boul(l)e.**

Dims.: **Boul(l)et, Bouley, Boulez, Bouleau, Boul(l)ot.**

Collectives (of 1): **(Du) Boulay, (Du) Bouloy, Boulais, Boulois**; Bouille.

Boulanger French: occupational name for a baker, originally the man responsible for dividing the dough into *boules* (balls). The name is comparatively late in origin (12th cent.) and replaced the older Fournier only in N France.

Boultby English: habitation name from a place presumably so called from the ON personal name *Boltr* (see Bolt 2) + ON *býr* settlement. There is a *Boltby* in N Yorks. However, the surname is more common in the E Midlands.

Bourbon French: habitation name from a village in Allier, site of the (now ruined) castle of *Bourbon*, or from another place so called, e.g. one in Saône-et-Loire. The placename is of uncertain origin, according to Dauzat derived from a 'Celt. and pre-Celt.' element **borb-* describing a well or hot spring. Many bearers of the surname claim a connection with the former Fr. royal family, but the name is also derived from residence in these villages and from the *Bourbonnais*, a former province in central France around Bourbon in Allier.

Vars.: **Bourbonnais, Bourbonneux.** Sp.: **Borbón.**

The house of Bourbon, *which provided generations of monarchs of France and Spain and other European royalty, takes its name from the castle of Bourbon in Allier, which was held by Adhémar, a 9th-cent. noble. His descendant Beatrice, heiress of Bourbon, married Robert of Clermont, 6th son of King Louis IX of France, in 1272, and these two are considered founders of the royal house. Robert's son Louis was created Duke of Bourbon in 1327. By the 16th cent. they had added much of S France, the dukedom of Vendôme, and the kingdom of Navarre to their fiefs, and in 1589 a Bourbon succeeded to the throne of France as Henry IV. His grandson, Louis XIV, called 'the Sun King', reigned from 1643 to 1715, presiding over a golden age of French literature and art and attempting to establish French supremacy in Europe. The Bourbons ruled France until the Revolution in 1793 and again from 1815 to 1848. The present claimants to the French throne are descended from Louis XIV's brother, Philippe, Duke of Orléans. The Bourbons acquired the Spanish throne in 1700, when a grandson of Louis XIV succeeded as Philip V; they ruled until 1931 and were restored, in the person of King Juan Carlos, in 1975. The Bourbon kings of the Two Sicilies (i.e. Sicily and Naples), 1759–1861, and Bourbon dukes of Parma, 1748–1860, were descended from the Spanish branch of the family.*

Boure French: nickname for someone who habitually dressed in brown, or metonymic occupational name for a worker in the wool trade, from OF *b(o)ure*, a type of coarse reddish-brown woollen cloth with long hairs (LL *burra* coarse untreated wool).

Var.: **Bure.**

Cogn.: Sp.: **Boras.**

Bourgoin French: regional name for someone from Burgundy (OF *Bourgogne*), a region of E France having Dijon as its centre. The area was invaded by the *Burgundii*, a Gmc tribe from whom it takes its name, in AD *c*.480. The duchy of Burgundy, created in 877 by Charles II, King of the West Franks, was extremely powerful in the later Middle Ages, esp. under Philip the Bold (1342–1404; duke from 1363).

Vars.: **Bourgouin, Bergoin; Bourgogne, Bergogne; Bourguignon, Bergo(u)gnon, Bergougnan, Bergougnou(x).**

Cogns.: It.: **Borgogni.** Eng.: **Burgoin(e), Burgoyne, Burgon; Burgin** (chiefly Scotland).

Bourne English: topographic name for someone who lived beside a stream, e.g. Richard *atte Bourne* (Sussex 1327), or habitation name from a place named from being beside a stream. The OE word *burna*, *burne* spring, stream, was replaced as the general word for a stream in S dialects by OE *brōc* (see Brook) and came to be restricted in meaning to a stream flowing only intermittently, esp. in winter (cf. Winterborne). A large area of Kent by the Little Stow river was once called *Bourn*, but this is unlikely to be the origin for most bearers of the surname, which is established in the W Midlands and Staffs. rather than the South-East.

Vars.: **Bourn, Burn(e)**; Burns; **Born(e)** (see also Borgne), **Boorne; Burner, Bo(u)rner.** See also Brown.

Cogns.: Flem.: **Born(man), Vanderborn(e).** Du.: **Van den Borne, Van den Borre.** Low Ger.: **Born, Börne(r), Bor(ne)mann.** Ger.: **Brunner, Brünner; Prunner** (Bavaria); **Brunnemann.** Swed.: **Brunn.**

Cpd (ornamental): Swed.: **Brunnberg** ('well hill').

All bearers of the surname Boorne *now living in the British Isles apparently descend from Thomas Boorne (1755–1840) of Deptford, Kent.*

Bourrel French: 1. from a dim. of Boure. The word had many senses in OF, among them 'cushion', 'harness', 'collar', 'crest', and 'headdress'; the surname could have been used for a maker, seller, or habitual wearer of any of these.

2. occupational name for a judicial torturer, OF *bourreau*, from *bourrer* to maltreat, torture, lit. to card wool, a deriv. of Boure. It may also be an occupational name for a wool carder, but the corresponding vocab. word in OF does not seem to be recorded in this sense.

Vars.: **Bourreau, Bor(r)el.**

Cogns.: Eng.: **Burrel(l), Borrel(l), Birrell.** It.: **Bor(r)elli.**

Burrell *has been the name of a Sussex family since the 12th cent. They were among the three or four leading ironmasters of the county when that trade was at its most prosperous, and from these Burrell ironmasters are descended the families at Knepp Castle, W Grinstead, and Ockenden House, Cuckfield.*

Boursier French: occupational name for a maker of purses and leather wallets, from an agent deriv. of OF *bourse* purse (LL *bursa*, whence also OE *purs*; see PURSER.
Vars.: **Bourcier**; **Bourse**.
Cogn.: Du.: **Beurs**.
Dims.: **Bourseret**, **Bourseron**, **Bourserot**, **Boursereau**; **Bourset**, **Boursin**, **Bours(ill)on**; **Bourzec** (Brittany).

Bousfield English: habitation name from a hamlet of this name near Orton in Cumb. The surname was first recorded there as *Busfeld* in 1342. The first element may be from ON *buskr* bush, shrub, or it may represent a reduced form of the gen. case of some ON or OE personal name; the second is probably OE *feld* pasture, open country.

Bouton French: 1. var. of BOUDON.
2. nickname for someone with a prominent wart, carbuncle, or boil, from OF *bo(u)ton* knob, lump, excrescence (from *bo(u)ter* to thrust or strike; cf. BUTLIN).
3. metonymic occupational name for a maker or seller of buttons, from OF *bo(u)ton*, the same word as in 2, specialized to mean 'button'.
Vars. (of 3): **Bouton(n)ier**.
Cogns. (of 3): Eng.: **Button**, **Botten**; **Butner**.
Dims.: Fr.: **Boutonnet**, **Boutonneau**.

Bouverie French: topographic name for someone who lived by a cowshed or occupational name for someone who worked in one, from OF *boverie* stable for oxen (LL *bovāria*; cf. BOUVIER).
Vars.: **Boverie**, **Bovary**, **Bouv(e)ry**.

Bouvier French: occupational name for a herdsman, OF *bouvier* (LL *bovārius*, a deriv. of *bōs*, gen. *bovis*, ox; cf. BOEUF).
Var.: **Bovier**.
Cogns.: Prov.: **Bo(u)yer**, **Boyé**, **Boué**. Cat.: **Bover**, **Bové**, **Bober**, **Bobé**, **Boyer**, **Boyé**. Sp.: **Boyero**, **Bu(ey)ero**. Port.: **Boieiro**.
Dims.: Fr.: **Bouv(e)ret**, **Bouv(e)ron**.

Bovill English (Norman): habitation name from *Bouville* in Seine Maritime, recorded in 1212 as *Bovilla*, apparently from a Gmc personal name *Bolo* (of uncertain origin) + L *villa* settlement (see VILLE), or less probably from either of two places named *Beuville* in Calvados, so called from the Gmc personal name *Bodo* (see BOTHA and BOUDON) + *ville*.
Vars.: **Boville**, **Bovell**.

Bovingdon English: habitation name from a place in Herts., so called from the OE phrase *būfan dūne* on, upon the hill (see DOWN 1). The surname may also have arisen as a topographic name from the same phrase used independently. There has probably also been some confusion with BOVINGTON.
Vars.: BOWDEN, **Bowton**, **Bufton**.

Bovington English: habitation name from a place in Dorset, so called from OE *Bōfingtūn* 'settlement (OE *tūn*) associated with *Bōfa*', a personal name of uncertain origin. There is also likely to have been confusion with BOVINGDON, and it may also be a topographic name for someone living 'above the (main) settlement', OE *būfan tūne*.

Bow 1. English: metonymic occupational name for a maker or seller of bows, from ME *bow* (OE *boga*, from *būgan* to bend). Before the invention of gunpowder, the bow was an important long-range weapon for shooting game as well as in warfare. *Boga* is also found as a personal name in OE, and it is possible that this survived into ME and so may lie behind the surname.
2. English: topographic name for someone living near a bridge, e.g. Richard *atte Bowe*, *boga* having acquired the sense 'arch', 'vault', 'span (of a bridge)' from a supposed resemblance of the arch to a drawn bow.
3. Irish: Anglicized form of Gael. **Ó Buadhaigh** 'descendant of *Buadhach*', a personal name meaning 'Victorious'. (The Brit. name *Boudicca* or *Boadicea*, borne by the Queen of the Iceni who in AD 62 led a revolt against the Roman occupation of her country, is a cogn.)
Vars.: **Bowe** (chiefly Irish), BOWES; BOUGH.
Cogns. (of 1): Ger.: **Bogner**, **Bög(n)er**, **Bögler**; **Pogner**, **Bögl(e)** (Bavaria).

Bowater English: topographic name for someone who lived on a bank above an expanse of water, from ME *buven* above (OE *būfan*) + *water* (OE *wæter*); cf. the much less common **Bowbrick** 'above the BROOK'. The surname is most common in Staffs.
Vars.: **Bo(e)ter**; **Boater** (see also BATE).

Bowcott English: habitation name from some minor place (probably in Worcs., where the surname is most common), perhaps so called from OE *boga* arched bridge (see BOW 2) + *cot* cottage, dwelling (see COATES).

Bowden 1. English: habitation name from a place so called. The places called *Bowden* in Devon and Derbys., and *Bowdon* in Ches., get their names from OE *boga* Bow + *dūn* hill (see DOWN 1), i.e. hill shaped like a bow; one in Leics. (*Bugedone* in Domesday Book) comes, according to Ekwall, from the OE personal name *Būga* (masc.) or *Bucge* (fem.) + *dūn*. There are also Scots places of this name, and it is possible that these derive from Gael. *both an duin* 'house on the hill', but there are comparatively few bearers of the surname *Bowden* north of the Border. The surname is found most frequently in Lancs. and in the W Country; in Devon and Cornwall there has been some confusion with the Norman given name BALDWIN.
2. English: topographic name for someone who lived at the top of a hill, from the OE phrase *būfan dūne* above the hill; cf. BOWATER and see also BOVINGDON.
3. Irish: Anglicized form of Gael. **Ó Buadáin** 'descendant of *Buadán*', an OIr. personal name cogn. with *Buadach* (see BOW 3).
Vars.: **Bowdon**, **Bawdon**.

Bowditch English: habitation name, possibly from OE *boga* bow + *dīc* ditch, i.e. a bow-shaped water channel. There is a place of this name in Devon, however, which is derived from the OE phrase *būfan dīce* above the ditch; cf. BOWATER.
Var.: **Bowdidge**.
The surname Bowditch *is well known in New England. Nathaniel Bowditch (1773–1838), author of* The Practical Navigator *(1772), a standard work which went through more than sixty editions, was born in Salem, Mass., the son of a shipmaster. The family can be traced back, via a clothier who settled in New England in 1671, to Thorncombe in Devon in the early 16th cent.*

Bowell 1. English (Norman): habitation name from *Bouelles* in Seine Maritime, so called from ONF *boelle* enclosure, dwelling (of Gmc origin; cf. BOMAN and BOWER 1).
2. Welsh: patr. from the given name HOWELL, with fusion of the patr. element *ap*, *ab*.
Vars.: **Bowells**, **Bowle(s)** (but see also BOWLER).

Bowen 1. Welsh: patr. from the given name Owen, with fusion of the patr. element *ap*, *ab*.

2. Irish: Anglicized form of Gael. **Ó Buadhacháin** 'descendant of *Buadachán*', a dim. of *Buadach* (see Bow 3).

Vars. (of 2): **Boohan, Bohane, (O')Boug(h)an, (O')Boghan.**

A Welsh family called Bowen *trace their ancestry to Llewelyn* ap Owen, *living in Pembrokes. in 1364. One of his sons was recorded with the surname Bowen in 1424.*

Bower English: 1. topographic name for someone who lived in a small cottage or occupational name for a house servant (cf. Chambers), from OE *būr* bower, cottage, inner room (cf. Bauer).

2. habitation name from places in Essex and Somerset named *Bower(s)*, from the OE word mentioned in 1 above.

3. var. of Bow (1 and 2).

Vars. (of 1 and 2): **Bowers, Bour; Bow(e)rer, Bo(o)rer, Boarer, Bowra(h); Bowerman, Bo(o)rman; Bow(e)ring.**

Cogns. (of 1): Du.: **Van Bu(u)ren, Van den Bueren.**

Bearers of the surname Bowra *are descended from Thomas Bowra (b. 1654 at Grinstead, Sussex; d. 1690), surgeon, who moved to Sevenoaks, Kent, in 1682. This spelling was in use in E Grinstead from the early 17th cent.*

Martin Van Buren *(1782–1862), President of the U.S.A. (1837–41) and one of the founders of the Democratic Party, was born in Old Kinderhook, New York, the descendant of a certain Cornelius Van Buren who settled in America in 1631.*

Bowes 1. N English: habitation name from *Bowes* (formerly in N Yorks., now in Co. Durham), or from some other place so called, the name being derived from ME *boges* arches of a bridge (see Bow 2).

2. Irish: Anglicized form of Gael. *Ó Buadhaigh*; see Bow 3.

Bowie Irish and Scots: nickname from Gael. *buidhe* yellow, fair-haired.

Bowker English (chiefly Manchester): 1. var. of Butcher.

2. occupational name for someone whose job was to steep cotton or linen in alkali before bleaching it, from an agent deriv. of ME *bouken* to wash (from MDu.; cf. Booker 2).

Bowler English (chiefly Notts.): nickname for a heavy drinker (ME *boller*, from OE *bolla* bowl, drinking vessel + the agent suffix *-er*), or occupational name for a maker or seller of bowls. Medieval bowls were made of wood as well as of earthenware.

Vars.: **Bo(a)ler, Bowller; Bowle(s), Boule(s); Boal** (N Ireland).

Bowley English: habitation name from a place so called from OE *bula* Bull (perhaps a byname) + *lēah* wood, clearing. There is one such in Herefords. near Leominster, but the surname is most common in Notts.

Bowman English: 1. occupational name for an archer, from OE *boga* bow + *mann* man. This name seems to be generally distinguished from Bowyer, which denoted a maker or seller of the articles. It is possible that in some cases the surname referred originally to someone who untangled wool with a bow. This process seems to have originated in Italy, but became quite common in England in the 13th cent. The vibrating string of a bow was worked into a pile of tangled wool, where its rapid vibrations separated the fibres, while still leaving them sufficiently entwined to produce a fine, soft yarn when spun.

2. in America, sometimes an Anglicized form of Ger. and Du. *Baumann* (see Bauer).

Vars. (of 1): **Boman; Beauman** (see also Beaumont).

Cogn. (of 1): Flem., Du.: **Boogman.**

Bowser English (Norman): nickname from the term of address *beu sire* fine sir. The nickname would have been acquired by someone who used the phrase very frequently.

Vars.: **Beausire, Bellsyer, Belshire,** Belcher.

Cogn.: Fr. **Belsire.**

Bowyer English: occupational name for a maker or seller of bows (see Bow 1), rather than an archer (cf. Bowman 1).

Box English: from ME, OE *box* box tree (L *buxus*, from Gk *pyxos*), in any of a number of possible applications. It may have been a topographic name for someone who lived by a box thicket, or a habitation name from one of the places called *Box*, in Gloucs., Herts., and Wilts. Box wood is very hard and because of this it was used to make a variety of tools; the name may therefore also have been a metonymic occupational name for a worker in the wood. In some cases it may even have been a nickname for a person with pale or yellow skin, for example as the result of jaundice, with reference to the colour of box wood.

Var.: **Boxer.**

Cogns.: Fr.: **B(o)uis, Bouix, Dub(o)uis, Buisse.** Cat.: **Boix.** Ger.: Buchs.

Dims.: Fr.: Buisson; **Bouzic, Bouzit** (Brittany). Cat.: **Buxó.**

Collective: Fr.: **Bussière.**

Boxall English: habitation name from a lost hamlet near Kirford, Sussex, called *Boxholte*, from OE *box* Box + *holt* wood (see Holt). The surname has been found in the surrounding area since the 14th cent.

Vars.: **Boxhall, Boxell.**

Boyce 1. English: topographic name for someone who lived by a wood, from OF *bois* wood (see Bois).

2. English: patr. from the ME nickname *boy* lad, servant (a word of disputed origin, probably from a MLG form of OSax. *bodo* messenger, servant (see Botha), the dental being regularly lost between vowels). In some cases it may derive from an OE personal name **Boia* or a Continental Gmc cogn. of this, both being of uncertain origin. Examples such as Aluuinus *Boi* (Domesday Book) and Ivo *le Boye* (Lincs. 1232) support the view that it was a byname or even an occupational name; examples such as *Stephanus filius Boie* (Northumb. 1202) suggest that it was in use as a personal name in the ME period, while the placename *Boyland* in Norfolk is evidence for its use as an OE personal name.

3. Irish: Anglicized form of Gael. *Ó Buadhaigh*; see Bow 3.

Vars. (of 1 and 2): **Boy(e)s** (chiefly Yorks.); **Boice, Boise, Boyse.** (Of 2 only): **Boyson.**

Boycott English: habitation name from places in Bucks., Worcs., and Shrops., so called from the OE personal name **Boia* (see Boye) + OE *cot* shelter, cottage (see Coates).

The Eng. word boycott *derives from Captain C. C.* Boycott *(1832–97), son of a Norfolk clergyman, who was land agent on the estates of the Earl of Erne in Co. Mayo, Ireland, when disaffected tenants withheld their rents and refused to deal with him in an attempt to get the rents reduced.*

Boyd Scots and Irish: of uncertain origin, perhaps from the island of Bute in the Firth of Clyde, Gael. *Bód* (gen. case *Bóid*).

Vars.: **Boyde, Boyda.**

The first known bearers of the name are Robertus de Boyd *and Alan* de Bodha, *recorded in Irvine and Dumfries respectively in the early 13th cent. Black comments that the name was very common in Edinburgh in the 17th cent. One of the most successful early settlers in Australia was Benjamin* Boyd (c.*1796–1851*), *who was born in London, the son of a Scottish merchant from Wigtownshire. He went to Australia in 1841 and founded Boydtown in New South Wales, which, however, failed to fulfil his expectation that it would become a great seaport.*

Boye Low German and Danish: from a Gmc personal name, **Boio* or *Bogo*, of uncertain origin. It may represent a var. of BOTHA, with the regular Low Ger. loss of the dental between vowels, but a cogn. name appears to have existed in OE (see BOYCE, BOYCOTT and BOYTON), where this feature does not occur. *Boje* is still in use as a given name in Friesland. See also SAINTE-BEUVE.

Vars.: **Boje**, **Boie**. Low Ger.: **Böhe**. Dan.: **Bøje**.

Cogns.: It.: **Bov(i)o**, **Bovi** (see also BOEUF).

Dims.: Low Ger.: **Boyk(e)**. Eng.: **Boykin**.

Patrs.: Low Ger.: **Boysen**, **Boyens**, **Bojens**, **Boeing**. Dan.: **Boysen**, **Boisen**, **Boj(e)sen**, **Boesen**. Eng.: BOYCE.

Boyle 1. Irish: Anglicized form of Gael. **Ó Baoighill** 'descendant of *Baoigheall*', a personal name of uncertain meaning, perhaps from *baoth* rash + *geall* pledge.

2. Irish (Norman): apparently an altered form of *Binville*; see below.

3. Scots (Norman): habitation name from *Boyville* near Caen, so called from the Gmc personal name **Boio* (see BOYE) + OF *ville* settlement (see VILLE).

Vars.: **Boyles**, **Bole**. (Of 1 only): **O'Boyle**.

One of the most famous, influential, and extensive of Anglo-Irish families is descended from Richard Boyle, *a Jacobean adventurer from Kent, who acquired lands in Cork, Waterford, and Tipperary in 1604. His earliest known ancestor was Humphry* de Binville, *Norman lord of a manor near Ledbury, Herefords., in the 11th cent.*

Boyton English: habitation name from any of various places, for example in Cornwall, Essex, Suffolk, and Wilts., so called from the OE personal name **Boia* (see BOYCE 2) + OE *tūn* enclosure, settlement.

Brabazon English (Norman): ostensibly an ethnic name, from ONF *brabançon*, for a native of *Brabant* (see BRABHAM), but by the 13th cent., if not before, an occupational name for a mercenary, specifically a member of one of the more or less independent marauding bands of mercenaries, noted for their lawlessness and cruelty, who originated in Brabant but in the course of time accepted recruits from almost anywhere.

Var.: **Brobson**.

Cogns.: Fr.: **Brabançon**, **Brabanchon**, **Barbanchon**.

A distinguished Anglo-Irish family called Brabazon, *Earls of Meath since 1627, claim descent from a certain Jacques* le Brabazon, *who was in the service of William the Conqueror in 1066. They held lands in Leics. and Surrey before becoming established in Ireland; Sir William Brabazon was appointed Receiver General in 1534.*

Brabham English: altered form (by association with habitation names ending in *-ham*) of an ethnic name for someone from the duchy of *Brabant*, in what is now Belgium and the S Netherlands. See also BRABAZON.

Vars.: **Brab(b)an(t)**, **Brab(b)en**, **Brab(b)in**, **Brab(b)on**, **Brab(b)yn**; **Brab(i)ner**, **Brebner**; BREMNER.

Cogns.: Ger.: **Braban(d)t(er)**, **Braband(er)**. Flem.: **De Brabandere**. Fr.: **Brabant**, **Brébant**, **Braibant**.

Brace English: 1. metonymic occupational name for a maker or seller of armour, specifically armour designed to protect the upper arms, ME *brace* (from OF *brace* the (two) arms, L *bracchia*, pl. of *bracchium* arm).

2. metonymic occupational name for a maker of breeches, or nickname meaning 'Breeches', from OE *brēc*.

Var.: **Brass** (Northumb.).

Bracegirdle English (Lancs.): metonymic occupational name for a maker of belts for holding up the breeches, from OE *brēc* breeches (see BRACE 2) + *gyrdel* belt, girdle.

Bracewell N English: habitation name from a place in W Yorks., so called from the gen. case of the ON personal name *Breiðr* 'Broad' (which possibly replaced earlier OE *Brægd* 'Trick') + OE *well(a)* spring, stream (see WELL).

Brach English: 1. topographic name for someone who lived by any of the various pieces of land that were named from the time when they were first cultivated, from OE *brǣc* newly cultivated land (a deriv. of *brecan* to break, i.e land broken by the plough); cf. Ger. *Brachland* land ploughed and then left to lie fallow, Du. *braak* (adj.) fallow.

2. var. of BRACK.

Vars. (of 1): **Bre(a)ch**, **Britch**; **Bra(t)cher**, **Bre(a)cher**, **Britcher**.

Cogns. (of 1): Ger.: **Brachner**, **Brachmann**. Fris.: **Braaksma**. Flem.: **Van Brach**. Du.: **(Van den) Braak**, **Braakman**.

Brack German and English: metonymic occupational name for a master of hunting dogs or nickname for one thought to resemble a hunting dog, MHG *bracke* (OHG *bracho*). The cognate ME word was derived via OF *brachez* (pl. of *brachet*, dim. of **brache*), the sing. form being re-created by back-formation from the OF pl.

Vars.: Ger.: **Prack** (Bavaria). Eng.: BRACH; **Brackner**.

Cogns.: Fr.: **Brac(q)**, **Braque**; **Braconnier**, **Braquennier**. It.: **Bracco**, **Bracchi**; **Braccaro**.

Dims.: Ger.: **Präckl** (Bavaria). Eng.: **Bracket**, **Brachet**. Fr.: **Brachet**, **Braquet**; **Braconnet**, **Braconnot**.

Bracken Irish: Anglicized form of Gael. **Ó Breacáin** 'descendant of *Breacán*', a personal name from a dim. of *breac* speckled, spotted. This name was borne by a 6th-cent. saint who lived at Ballyconnel, Co. Cavan, and was famous as a healer; in his honour is named St Bricin's Military Hospital, Dublin.

Vars.: **(O')Brackan**, **(O')Breckan**.

Brackenridge Scots: habitation name from *Brackenrig* in the former county of Lanarks. (now part of Strathclyde region), probably so called from Northern ME *braken* bracken (ON *brækni*) + *rigg* ridge (ON *hryggr*).

Vars.: **Breckenridge**, **Brekonridge**.

Brackley English: habitation name from a place in Northants, so called from the OE personal name *Bracc(a)* (perhaps akin to BRACK) + OE *lēah* wood, clearing.

Brackpool English: apparently a habitation name from an unidentified place. *Brapool* Barn in Patcham, Sussex, has been suggested, but this may derive from the surname rather than vice versa. The first element is probably the OE personal name *Bracca* (although it is tempting to link it with MDu. *brac*, the source of Mod. Eng. *brackish*); the second is fairly clearly OE *pōl* pool, pond.

The surname is first found in 1265 in manorial records relating to E Sussex. Some if not all modern bearers are descended from the John Brackpole *who was living at Buxted in Sussex* c.*1510*.

Bradbrook English: habitation name from some minor place so called from OE *brād* broad + *brōc* stream.

Vars.: **Braybrook(e)** (from a place in Northants, in which the first element is from ON *breiðr* broad, a cogn. of *brād*).

Bradbury English: habitation name from one of the minor places so called, in several counties, all first recorded fairly late. The etymology is generally OE *brād* broad + *burh* fort (see BURY), but *Bradbury* in Co. Durham is recorded in OE as *Brydbyrig*, the first element probably being OE *bred* board. This is probably also the first element in *Bradbury*, Ches.

Vars: **Bradber(r)y**.

Braddock English: topographic name for someone living by a notable broad oak, from OE *brād* broad + *āc* oak, or habitation name from a minor place so named. The only modern village with this name is *Braddock* in Cornwall (*Brodehoc* in Domesday Book, later *Brethok*, *Brothok*), the name of which is probably of Celt. origin; it is unlikely to be the source of the surname. The Eng. phrase was certainly used in forming placenames, e.g. Hatfield *Broad Oak* in Essex.

Braddon English: habitation name from the *Braddons*, a range of heights in S Devon, on the north side of Torquay, so called from OE *brād* broad + *dūn* hill.

Braden Irish: Anglicized form of Gael. **Ó Bradáin** 'descendant of *Bradán*', a personal name meaning 'Salmon'.

Vars.: **Braiden, (O')Bradane, (O')Bradden**, SALMON, FISHER.

Bradfield English: habitation name from any of the places so called in Berks., Devon, Essex, Suffolk, S Yorks., and elsewhere, from OE *brād* broad + *feld* pasture, open country (see FIELD).

Var.: **Broadfield** (places in Herefords. and Herts.).

Bradford English: habitation name from any of the many places, large and small, so called; in particular the city in W Yorks, which was originally a wool town. There are others in Derbys., Devon, Dorset, Greater Manchester, Norfolk, Somerset, and elsewhere. They all take their names from OE *brād* broad + *ford* FORD.

Vars.: **Bradforth, Braidford**.

William Bradford *(1589–1657) was one of the Pilgrim Fathers who emigrated to America on the* Mayflower *and was a member of the first exploratory expedition (1621). He was the son of a yeoman farmer, born in Austerfield in S Yorks.*

Bradley 1. English and Scots: habitation name from one of the many places so called, from OE *brād* broad + *lēah* wood, clearing. Places named with these elements are found in every part of England and also in Scotland.

2. Irish: Anglicized form of Gael. *Ó Brolcháin*; see BROLLY.

Vars. (of 1): **Bradly, Bratl(e)y, Bradlaugh, Broad(e)ly**.

The English astronomer James Bradley *(1693–1762) was born in Gloucs. into a family that can be traced back to Bradley Castle near Wolsingham in Co. Durham.*

Bradman English: nickname from OE *brād* broad (in this case, well built) + *mann* man. See also BROAD.

Var.: **Braidman**.

Bradshaw English: habitation name from one of the places so named, from OE *brād* broad + *sceaga* thicket (see SHAW). There are places so called in Lancs., W Yorks., and elsewhere. The surname is widely distributed, but most frequent in Lancs.

Vars.: **Brayshaw** (chiefly W Yorks.); **Brashaw, Brayshay**.

Bradstreet English: topographic name for someone living by a Roman road or other great highway, from OE *brād* broad + *strǣt* highway (see STREET).

Bradwell English: habitation name from a place so called, of which there are examples in Bucks., Derbys., Essex, Somerset, Suffolk, and elsewhere. The name is from OE *brād* broad + *well(a)* spring, stream (see WELL).

Brady 1. Irish: Anglicized form of Gael. **Ó Brádaigh** 'descendant of *Brádach*', a byname the meaning of which is not clear. It is unlikely to be connected with Gael. *bradach* thieving, dishonest, which has a short first vowel.

2. English: nickname for a person with large or wide-set eyes, from OE *brād* broad + *eage* eye.

3. English: habitation name from some place known as 'broad island', from OE *brād* broad + *ēg* island.

4. English: topographic name for someone who lived by a broad enclosure, from OE *brād* broad + *(ge)hæg* enclosure (see HAY 1).

Vars.: **Bradey, Bradie, Bready**. (Of 1 only): **O'Brady**. (Of 2–4): **Broady, Broadie**.

Dims. (of 1): **O'Bradaghan; (O')Braddigan, (O')Brodigan, Bradekin, Bradican** (Gael. **Ó Bradacháin**).

A line of the GRADY *family changed their name to* O'Brady *(for reasons that are not clear) when its leader, Donogh, was knighted by Henry VIII. Donogh's son Hugh was the first Protestant bishop of Meath.*

Braga Portuguese: habitation name from a city in N Portugal, so called from L *Bracāria*, a deriv. of the Celt. tribal name *Bracari*. This is apparently from *bracae* trousers, leggings, breeches (cf. BRACE 2), but it may alternatively derive from Celt. *berg*, *barg* height, eminence.

Bragg English: nickname for a cheerful or lively person, from ME *bragge* lively, gay, active (of unknown origin).

The English scientists Sir William Bragg *(1862–1942) and his son, Sir Lawrence Bragg (1890–1971), who shared the Nobel prize for physics in 1915, came of a Cumbrian family from near Wigton, whose members had been farmers and seamen for generations.*

Brahm 1. German and Jewish: aphetic var. of ABRAHAM.

2. German: topographic name for someone who lived by a bramble thicket, from MHG *brāme* blackberry, bramble (OHG *brāmo*).

Var. (of 1): Jewish: **Braham**.

Cogn.: Du.: **Braam**.

Patr. (from 1): **Brahms**.

Braille French: of uncertain origin. It is possibly from the OF verb *brailler* to squabble (LL *bragulāre*, apparently of Celt. origin), and hence a nickname for a quarrelsome individual, or alternatively it may be a metonymic occupational name for a winnower, from the OF dial. term *braile* harvest.

Brailsford English: habitation name from a place in Derbys., so called from OE **brægels*, a metathesized form of *bærgels*, itself a byform of *byrgels* tumulus, barrow + *ford* FORD. The name is still found chiefly in the E Midlands, esp. in Nottingham.

Vars.: **Brel(lis)ford**.

Brain Irish and Scots: Anglicized form of Gael. **Mac an Bhreitheamhan** 'son of the judge', from *breitheamh* judge (see BREW 2).

Vars.: **Braine, Brayne, Brohoon**.

Patrs.: **McBrayne, McBrehon, McBrohoon, McVrehoune, McEbrehowne, McEvrehune, McAbreham, McAbrahams**.

Braines Jewish (Ashkenazic): metr. from the Yid. female given name *Brayne*, a back-formation from *Brayndl*, itself a dim. of Yid. *broyn* brown.

Vars.: **Breines; Brainin** (E Ashkenazic).

Braithwaite N English: habitation name from any of the places in Cumb. and Yorks. named from ON *breiðr* broad + *þveit* clearing (see THWAITE).

Var.: **Braithwait**.

Brake English: topographic name for someone who lived by a clump of bushes or by a patch of bracken. *Brake* thicket and *brake* bracken were homonyms in ME. The first is from OE *bracu*; the second is by folk etymology from northern ME *braken* (from ON *brakni*), *-en* being taken as a pl. ending. After the words had fallen together, their senses also became confused.

Bramall English: habitation name from one of the places, in Ches. and Sheffield, named as a sheltered spot with broom (gorse) growing in it, from OE *brōm* broom + *halh* nook, recess (see HALE 1). There may also have been some confusion with BRAMWELL.

Vars.: **Brammall**, **Bramhall**, **Bramah**, **Brammer**, **Bramble**, **Brummell**.

Bramley English: habitation name from any of various places (in Derbys., Hants, Surrey, Yorks., and elsewhere), so called from OE *brōm* broom, gorse + *lēah* clearing, wood. The surname is found chiefly in Yorks., Notts., and Derbys.

Var.: BROMLEY.

Brampton English: habitation name from any of the various places, found in every part of England, so called from OE *brōm* broom, gorse + *tūn* enclosure, settlement.

Bramwell English: habitation name from one or more unidentified minor places, so called from OE *brōm* broom, gorse + *well(a)* spring, stream (see WELL). The surname is distributed fairly evenly throughout England. See also BRAMALL.

Branch English: from ME, OF *branche* branch (LL *branca* foot, paw), the application of which as a surname is not clear. In America it has been adopted as a translation of any of the numerous Swed. surnames containing the element *gren* branch, and likewise of Finn. HAARLA.

Cogns.: Fr.: **Branche**, **Branque**. Prov.: **Branca(s)**. Rum.: **Brancusi**.

Dims.: Fr.: **Branchet**, **Branquet**.

Brand 1. English, French, and German: from the Gmc (esp. Langobardic) personal name *Brando*, a short form of the various cpd personal names containing the element *brand* sword (a deriv. of *brinnan* to flash), of which the best known is HILDEBRAND. There is placename evidence for **Brant(a)* as an OE personal name, and in ME and ONF it is found as *Brand*, but was probably introduced to both from Norse; *Brandr* is a common ON personal name.

2. German: topographic name for someone who lived in an area that had been cleared by fire, MHG *brant* (from *brennen* to burn, causative of *brinnen*).

Vars. (of 1): Eng.: **Braund** (Devon); **Brant** (W Midlands). Fr.: BRANDON. (Of 1 and 2): Ger.: **Bran(d)t** (also Jewish).

Cogns. (of 1): It.: **Brando**, **Brandi**; **Branno**, **Branni**; **Prando**, **Prandi** (N Italy). (Of 2): Eng.: BRENT. Fris.: **Brandsma**.

Dims. (of 1): Ger.: **Brandel**, **Brändel**, **Brändle**, **Brantl**; **Brendel** (also Jewish); **Prantl** (Bavaria); **Brändli** (Switzerland). Low Ger.: **Brendeke**, **Brenneke**. Fris.: **Brandsma**. Fr.: **Brandin**. It.: **Brand(ol)ini**, **Brandino**; **Prandin(i)** (N Italy).

Augs. (of 1): It.: **Brandoni**, **Brandone**; **Prandoni**, **Prantoni** (N Italy).

Pejs. (of 1): It.: **Brandacci**, **Brandassi**.

Patrs. (from 1): Eng.: **Braunds**; **Branson**, **Bransom**; **Bramson** (see also ABRAHAM); BRANSTON. Ger.: **Brand(t)s**, **Brandes**. Du.: **Brands(en)**.

Brandejs Czech: habitation name from the town of *Brandýs*, on the Labe (Elbe) some 20 km. north of Prague, called *Brandeis* in German.

Cogns.: Jewish (Ashkenazic): **Brande(i)s**.

Brandon 1. English: habitation name from any of various places so called, found in Co. Durham, Northumb., Norfolk, Suffolk, Warwicks., and elsewhere. Most of these get the name from OE *brōm* broom, gorse + *dūn* hill. One in Lincs., however, may be named from the river *Brant*, on which it stands, whose name is derived by Ekwall from OE *brant* steep, presumably with reference to its steep banks.

2. French: var. of BRAND, from the OF oblique case of the name.

Brangwyn English or Welsh: perhaps from the W female given name *Branwen* (composed of the elements *bran* raven + *gwen* fair). Brangwain is the name of Isolde's companion in the Tristan legend; Branwen, daughter of Llyr, was a legendary Welsh heroine.

Var.: **Brangwin**.

Braniff Irish: Anglicized form of Gael. **Ó Branduibh** 'descendant of *Brandubh*', a personal name composed of the elements *bran* raven + *dubh* black.

Brannick Irish: Anglicized form of the Gael. ethnic name or nickname *Breathnach* Briton (*Breithneach* in Donegal and Ulster).

Vars.: **Bran(n)agh**, **Brennach**, **Brawnick**.

Brannigan Irish: Anglicized form of Gael. **Ó Branagáin** 'descendant of *Branagán*', a personal name from a dim. of *bran* raven (cf. BYRNE).

Vars.: **O'Brannigan**, **(O')Branigan**, **(O')Branagan**, **Brankin**.

Branston English: 1. habitation name from any of various places, such as *Branston* in Leics., Lincs., and Staffs., *Braunston* in Leics. and Northants, *Brandeston* in Suffolk, or *Brandiston* in Norfolk, all of which get their name from the gen. case of the OE personal name **Brant* (see BRAND 1) + OE *tūn* enclosure, settlement.

2. altered form of *Branson*; see BRAND 1.

Brash Scots: probably a nickname for an impetuous person, from the N Eng. dial. term *brasche* rash, impetuous (associated with *brasche* assault, attack, a word of imitative origin).

Brasher English: 1. occupational name, of Norman origin, for a brewer, from OF *brasser* to brew (LL *braciāre*, a deriv. of *braces* malt, of Gaul. origin).

2. occupational name for a worker in brass, from OE *bræsian* to cast in brass (a deriv. of *bræs* brass).

Vars. (of 1): **Braisher**, **Bracer**, **Brasseur**. (Of 2): **Brasier**, **Bra(i)zier**.

Cogns. (of 1): Fr.: **(Le) Brasseur**.

Brassington English: habitation name from a place in Derbys., which Ekwall suggests is derived from OE *Brantstīgtūn* 'enclosure (*tūn*) by the steep (*brant*) path (*stīg*)'. *Brandsigingtūn* 'settlement associated with **Brandsige*' is more likely. *Brandsige*, composed of the elements *brand* sword + *sige* victory, is not attested as an OE personal name, but seems plausible.

Bratt English (W Midlands): of uncertain origin, possibly a nickname for an unruly child, or somebody who behaved like one, though this sense of *brat* is not recorded by *OED* before the 16th cent. Alternatively, it may be derived from the older word *brat(te)* apron, pinafore (of Celt. origin), as a nickname for someone who habitually wore one.

Braunschweig German and Jewish (Ashkenazic): habitation name from the city in Saxony known in Eng. as *Brunswick*. This derives its name from the gen. case of the Gmc personal name *Bruno* (see BROWN), borne by the Duke of Saxony who founded the city in 861 + OHG *wīch* dwelling place (see WICK).

Cogns.: Eng.: **Brunswick**. Fr.: **Brunschvieg**.

Braunstein Jewish (Ashkenazic): ornamental surname, composed of the Ger. elements *braun* Brown + *stein* Stone.

Vars.: **Brons(h)tein, Bronstien; Brons(z)tejn** (Pol. spelling); **Brownstein** (partly Anglicized); **Brownstone** (fully Anglicized).

Bravo Spanish and Portuguese: nickname for a cruel or fierce-tempered man, from Sp., Port. *bravo* fierce, violent (probably from L *barbarus* barbarian, ruffian; cf. Barbary). The sense 'courageous', 'brave' did not emerge until the 16th cent., and is therefore too late to be reflected in the surname.

Cogn.: Flem.: **De Brave.**

Dim.: It.: **Bravetti.**

Pej.: Fr.: **Bravard.**

Braxton English: habitation name from an unidentified place, so called from the gen. case of the OE personal name *Bracc* (cf. Brackley) + OE *tūn* enclosure, settlement.

Bray English: habitation name from places in Berks. and Devon. The former is probably so called from OF *bray* marsh (cf. Briard), the latter from the Corn. element *bre* hill.

Brazil Irish: Anglicized form of Gael. **Ó Breasail** 'descendant of *Breasal*', a byname meaning 'Strife'. The accent is on the first syllable.

Vars.: **Brassill, (O')Breassell.**

Dims.: **(O')Breslane, Breslin** (Gael. **Ó Breisle(á)in**).

Breakspear English: nickname for a successful warrior or participant in a joust, from ME *brek(en)* to break (OE *brecan*) + *sper(e)* spear (OE *spere*).

Var.: **Brakspear.**

Adrian IV, the only Englishman to become Pope (1154–9), was born Nicholas Breakspear *in Langley, near St Albans, and spent much of his early life in monasteries in France. His father was reputedly a poor peasant who later became a monk.*

Breakwell English: apparently a habitation name from some unidentified minor place (probably in the W Midlands, where the surname is commonest). The etymology is unclear. The second element is almost certainly OE *well(a)* spring, stream (see Well), but the first cannot be established without placename evidence.

Var.: **Breakell** (Lancs.).

Bream English: 1. habitation name from *Braham* or *Bramham* in E Yorks., both of which derive their name from OE *brōm* broom, gorse + *hām* homestead.

2. habitation name from *Brantham* in Suffolk, so called from the OE personal name *Brant* (see Brand 1) + *hām* homestead.

3. nickname for a fierce or energetic person, from ME *brem(e)*, *brim(me)* fierce, vigorous (apparently from OE *brēme* famous, noble, although the semantic development is unclear).

Vars. (of 1): **Braham(e), Bra(i)me, Brayham; Bramham.** (Of 2): **Brantham.** (Of 3): **Breem,** Brim.

Brear English (Yorks.): 1. topographic name for someone who lived by a briar patch, ME *brere* (OE *brǣr*, *brēr*).

2. nickname for a prickly, difficult individual, from the same word as in 1, applied in a transferred sense.

Var.: **Brier(s), Bryer(s), Briar(s).**

Breddy English (Bristol): of uncertain origin, possibly a habitation name from Long or Little *Bredy* in Dorset, so called from their situation on the river *Bride*, which apparently bears a Brit. name akin to W *brydio* to boil.

Breed English: habitation name from any of various minor places, e.g. *Brede* in Sussex, named with OE *brǣdu* breadth, broad place (a deriv. of *brād* broad).

Vars.: **Bre(e)de, Breeds; Breeder.**

Breedon English: habitation name from *Breedon* in Leics. or *Bredon* in S Worcs., which are so called from the Brit. term *bre* hill + the tautologous OE addition *dūn* (see Down).

Var.: **Bredon.**

Breen Irish: Anglicized form of Gael. **Ó Braion** 'descendant of *Braon*', a byname meaning 'Moisture', 'Drop'.

Vars.: **O'Breen, O'Brean; O'Bruen; Brewin** (Liverpool).

Breeze 1. English: nickname for an irritating person, from ME *breeze* gadfly (OE *brēosa*).

2. Welsh: patr. from Rhys.

Var.: **Breese.**

Bregman Jewish (Ashkenazic): topographic name for someone who lived near a river or stream, from E Yid. *breg* shore, bank, coast (from Pol. *brzeg*) + *-man*.

Breit German: nickname for a stout or fat person, from Ger. *breit* Broad.

Var.: **Breitmann.**

Cogns.: Jewish (Ashkenazic): **Breitman, Braitman, Brajtman** (from Ger. *breit* broad + *Mann* man, or Yid. *breyt* + *man*).

Cpds: Jewish: **Breitbart, Braitbart, Breitbard, Brajtbard** ('broad beard', a nickname); **Breitholz** ('broad wood', ornamental name); **Breitstein** ('broad stone', ornamental or topographic name).

Brejcha Czech: of uncertain origin, perhaps an altered form of the OCzech personal name *Brixí*, or a topographic name for someone who lived by a ford (from Czech dial. *brejchat se* to wade, ford a stream).

Bremner Scots: regional name for someone from *Brabant* in the Low Countries, from earlier Scots *Brebner*, *Brabanare*, native or inhabitant of Brabant (see Brabham).

Vars.: **Brimner, Brymner.**

Brenchley English: habitation name from a place in Kent, so called from an OE personal name *Brœnci* (of uncertain history) + OE *lēah* wood, clearing.

Brennan Irish: Anglicized form of Gael. **Ó Braonáin** 'descendant of *Braonán*', a personal name from a dim. of *braon* moisture, drop; cf. Breen.

Vars.: **O'Brennan, (O')Brenane, (O')Brinan(e), Brannan;** Brennand.

Brennand English (Lancs.): according to Reaney a nickname for someone whose hand had been scarred by burning, as a punishment or in trial by ordeal rather than by accident, from ME *brent* burnt (past part. of *brennen* to burn) + *hand* hand; this is clearly the meaning in the case of Matilda *Brendhand*, recorded in Cambs. in 1295. Reaney ascribes the origin of forms such as *Brenhand* (N Yorks. 1229) to a nickname for the official who carried out the harsh punishment. Independent evidence for the existence of an official so named is not, however, forthcoming. The mod. surname may be no more than a var. of Brennan.

Vars.: **Burnand.**

Brenner 1. German and Jewish (Ashkenazic): from Ger. *Brenner*, literally 'burner', an agent deriv. of Ger. *brennen* to burn, in various applications. Often it is an occupational name for a distiller of spirits. In the case of the non-Jewish surname, it may also refer to a charcoal burner or to someone who cleared forests by burning.

2. English: metathesized var. of BERNER.

Vars.: Jewish: **Brener, Brenman**.

Brent English: 1. topographic name for someone who lived by a piece of ground that had been cleared by fire, from ME *brent*, past part. of *brennen* to burn.

2. habitation name from one of the places in Devon and Somerset so called from OE *brant* steep, or from an earlier Celt. (Brit.) word meaning 'hill', 'high place'.

3. byname or nickname for a criminal who had been branded; cf. Henry *Brendcheke* ('burned cheek'), recorded in Northumb. in 1279.

Vars.: **Brend, Brunt**. (Of 1 only): **Brind** (a place in Humberside).

Cogn. (of 1): Ger.: BRAND.

Brentnall English: of uncertain origin, possibly a habitation name from some place (probably in Notts., where the surname is most common) so called from the gen. case of the OE personal name **Branta* (see BRAND 1) + *halh* nook, recess (see HALE 1).

Brenton English (Devon): habitation name from *Brenton* near Exminster, probably named in OE as *Brȳningtūn* 'settlement (OE *tūn*) associated with *Brȳni*' (see BRYNING), and therefore identical with BRINGTON.

Brereton English: habitation name from places so called in Ches. and Staffs. The former gets its name from OE *brǣr*, *brēr* briar (see BREAR) + *tūn* enclosure, settlement; the latter originally had as its final element OE *dūn* hill (see DOWN 1).

Breslau Jewish (Ashkenazic): from the Ger. name, *Breslau*, of the city of *Wrocław* in Poland (see WROCŁAWSKI), which for a long time was part of Germany.

Vars.: **Bres(s)lauer; Breslaw(ski), Breslav(ski); Breslow; Bres(s)ler** (from the Yid. name of the city, *Bresle*).

Bressington English (chiefly Bristol): habitation name from an unidentified place so called, probably originally *Brīosingtūn* 'settlement (OE *tūn*) associated with *Brīosa*', a byname meaning 'Gadfly' (see BREEZE 1).

Bretécher French: occupational name for a maker of a kind of wooden fortification, or topographic name for a dweller by such a fortification, from OF *bretesche*, med. L *britisca*, which also means 'British'. The connection, if any, between these two meanings is not clear.

Var.: **Labretesche**.

Bretherick English: habitation name from some minor place (probably in Yorks., where the surname is most common) so called from ON *brœðr* or OE *breðra* (see BRETHERTON) + OE *wīc* village, outlying farm (see WICK).

Bretherton English: habitation name from *Bretherton* in Lancs., which gets its name from ON *brœðr* (gen. sing.) of the brother or OE *breðra* (gen. pl.) of the brothers + OE *tūn* enclosure, settlement. The surname is still most common in Lancs.

Brett English and French: ethnic name for a Breton, from OF *bret* (oblique case *breton*). The Bretons were Celt.-speakers driven from SW England to NW France in the 6th cent. AD by Anglo-Saxon invaders; some of them reinvaded England in the 11th cent. as part of the army of William the Conqueror. In France and among Normans, Bretons had a reputation for stupidity, and in some cases this name and its vars. and cogns. may have originated as derogatory nicknames. The Eng. surname is most common in E Anglia, where many Bretons settled after the Conquest. In Scotland it may also denote a member of one of the Celt.-speaking peoples of Strathclyde, who were known as *Bryttas* or *Brettas* well into the 13th cent.

Vars.: Eng.: **Britt; Breton** (Scotland), BRETTON, BRITTAIN. Fr.: **Bret, Lebret; Breton, Lebreton; Bretonnier, Bretegnier; Bretagne, Bretange**.

Cogns.: Ir.: **Breathnach** (given originally to Welshmen who arrived in the wake of the Anglo-Norman invasion or later; Anglicized *Welsh* and *Walsh(e)* (see WALLACE)). It.: **Bretoni**. Port.: **Bretanha**. Flem., Du.: **Britt**.

Dims.: Eng.: **Brettell, Brettle, Brittle** (W Midlands). Fr.: **Bretel, Breteau, Brethiot, Brétillon; Breton(n)el** (see BRUDENELL), **Bretonneau**.

Pej.: Fr.: **Bretaud**.

Patrs.: Fr.: **Aubreton, Laubreton**. Sc.: **McBratney, McBratnie** (Gael. **Mac an Bhreatnaich**, an old Galloway surname).

Bretton English: 1. var. of BRETT, from the OF oblique case.

2. habitation name from Monk and West *Bretton* in W Yorks., or *Bretton* in Derbys. These are so called either from OE *brēc* broken (i.e. newly cultivated) land (cf. BRACH 1) + *tūn* enclosure, settlement or from *Brettatūn* 'settlement of Britons'. The surname is most common in the area around Barnsley, and also in Leeds.

Breuil French: topographic name from OF *breuil* marshy woodland (LL *brogilum*, of Gaul. origin). In Fr. the term later came to mean 'enclosed woodland' and then 'cleared woodland', and both these senses may also be reflected in the surname.

Vars.: **Breuilh, Bruel, Bre(i)l; Dubreuil, Dubrule**.

Dims.: **Breu(il)let, Breuillon, Breuillot**.

Aug.: **Breuillat**.

Pejs.: **Breuillaud, Breuillard**.

Brew 1. Irish: Anglicized form of Gael. **Ó Brughadha** 'descendant of *Brughaidh*', a byname meaning 'Farmer'.

2. Manx: Anglicized form of the Gael. occupational term *breitheamh* judge; see BRAIN.

Patr. (from 2): **McBreive**.

Brewer English: 1. occupational name for a brewer of beer or ale, from OE *brēowan* to brew. The name in this form is found chiefly in the W Country.

2. Norman habitation name, a var. of Fr. BRUYÈRE, from a place in Calvados.

Vars. (of 1): **Brewster**, BRUSTER (the *-ster* suffix originally denoted fem. gender, but by the 13th cent. the term was used indiscriminately for male and female brewers).

Cogns. (of 1): Ger.: **Breuer, Bräuer, Breier, Breyer, Breger** (all from MHG *briuwer*); **Breu, Brei** (from MHG *briuwe* brewer); **Preu(er)** (Bavaria); **Prey(er)** (Austria). Low Ger.: **Bruwer, Bruyer, Brauer; Braumann, Breymann, Brauermann**. Flem., Du.: **(De) Brouwer** (U.S. **Brower**). Jewish: **Breuer** (W Ashkenazic).

Patrs. (from 1): Low Ger.: **Brauers, Breuers**. Flem., Du.: **Brouwers, Broyers**.

Equivs. (not cogn.): Pol.: PIWOWARSKI. Czech: PATOČKA.

The Mayflower *pilgrim William* Brewster *(1567–1644) was the son of the bailiff of the manor of Scrooby, Notts., home of one of the earliest Puritan congregations.*

Brewis English (chiefly Northumb.): 1. Norman habitation name from *Briouse* in Orne, which probably gets its name from a Gaul. word meaning 'muddy'; cf. BREUIL.

2. occupational name for someone who worked in a brewery, from ME *brewhus* (a cpd of OE *brēow(an)* to brew + *hūs* house, building).

Brezhnev Russian: of uncertain origin. It is perhaps from the Ukr. nickname *Berezhny* 'Careful', 'Cautious', with the additon of the Russ. patr. ending, or a contracted form of the topographic name BEREZNIKOV.

Briard French: habitation name for someone from any of several places called *Brie*, of varied origins. In most cases the name comes from Gaul. *briga* height, hill (cf. BRYAN), but the places so called in Aisne and Ille-et-Villaine get their names from OF *brai* mud (of Gaul. origin). Brie in the *département* of Somme probably represents Gaul. *briva* bridge.

Vars.: **Briaud, Briault; Brie, Debrie.**

Bric French: 1. derogatory nickname from OF *bric* foolish, idle (of unknown origin).

2. metonymic occupational name for a bird catcher, from OF *bric*, *brit*, *bret* snare (from Gmc *bredan* to snare).

Vars.: **Bri(cq), Bry.**

Dim.: **Bricon.**

Pejs.: **Bricard, Bricaud, Bricault.**

Brice* 1. English and French: from a personal name, probably of Celt. origin (Latinized as *Britius*), which was borne by a 5th-cent. saint who succeeded St Martin as bishop of Tours. It consequently had a certain currency in France in the early Middle Ages and in England after the Norman Conquest.

2. Jewish (Ashkenazic): Anglicization of **Briess**, a Jewish family name of unknown origin.

Vars.: Eng.: **Bryce** (chiefly Scots). Fr.: **Bris(se), Brés, Brix.**

Cogns.: Cat.: **Bris.** Ger.: **Britt, Brix, Bricks.** Dan.: **Brix.**

Dims.: Fr.: **Bresset, Bresson, Bressot; Brisset, Brisson(neau), Brissot.** Ger.: **Brixle.**

Pejs.: Fr.: **Brissaud, Brissard.**

Patrs.: Eng.: **Bryceson,** BRYSON.

Bridge English: topographic name for someone who lived near a bridge or metonymic occupational name for a bridge keeper, from ME *brigge*, OE *brycg* bridge, cogn. with MHG *brucke*, OHG *brucca*. Building and maintaining bridges was one of the three main feudal obligations, along with bearing arms and maintaining fortifications. The cost of building a bridge was often defrayed by charging a toll, the surname thus being acquired by the toll gatherer. The form *Bridge* (without the *-s*) is most common in Lancs. The *-s* in the form *Bridges* generally represents the gen. case, but may occasionally be a pl.; in some cases this name denoted someone from the Flem. city of *Bruges* (*Brugge*), meaning 'bridges', which had extensive trading links with England in the Middle Ages.

The Ger. cogns. generally have the same meaning as the Eng.; in addition, there are several Ger. villages called *Brügge(n)* and the Low Ger. surname in some cases indicates origin from one of these. The word *Brückner* denoted a road maker as well as a bridge builder.

Vars.: **Bridge(n)s; Brigg(s)** (N English and Scots, from ON *bryggja*); BURGE; **Bridger; Bridg(e)man; Brigman.**

Cogns.: Ger.: **Bruck(mann), Brück(mann); Bruck(n)er; Brückner** (E Germany); **Prückner** (Austria). Low Ger.: **Brüg(ge)(mann), Brügger; Anderbrügge, Toderbrügge, Terbrüggen** ('at the bridge(s)'). Flem.: **Van Bruggen** (i.e. 'from Bruges'); **Verbrugghen.** Du.: **Van (der) Brug, Vanbrugh, Van der Brugge, Van Bruggen, Verbrugge(n), Terbrugge, Tenbrug, Brug(ge)man.** Fris.: **Brugsma.** Jewish (Ashkenazic): **Bruck(man), Bruckner; Brik** (from Yid. *brik* bridge); **Brickman(n), Brickner** (altered by folk etymology in English-speaking countries, as if derived from Eng. *brick*).

Cpds: Jewish (ornamental elaborations): **Bruckstein** ('bridge stone'); **Bruckent(h)al** ('bridge valley').

The surname Briggs *is found chiefly in W Yorks. A family of gentry so called have held lands at Keighley in W Yorks continuously for 500 years. The mathematician Henry Briggs (1561–1631), who invented logarithms, was born in Halifax.*

The family of the Austrian composer Anton Bruckner *(1824–96) was of peasant stock, and had lived on the same lands near Linz (in a house by a bridge, from which they took their name) since the early 15th cent.*

The great English architect and dramatist Sir John Vanbrugh *(1664–1726), designer of Blenheim Palace, was born in Chester into a family of Flemish origin. His grandfather, Gillis* van Brugg, *was a Protestant merchant who had settled in England to escape Spanish rule in the Low Countries.*

Bridgewater English: habitation name from *Bridgwater* in Somerset (or possibly from some other place with a prominent bridge); the water which the bridge at Bridgwater crosses is the river Parrett, but the placename actually derives from *Brigewaltier*, i.e. 'Walter's bridge', after Walter de Dowai, the 12th-cent. owner. The surname has become common in Birmingham.

Var.: **Bridgwater.**

Bridle English: 1. metonymic occupational name for a maker of bridles for horses, from OE *brīdel* bridle.

2. habitation name from some minor place called *Brid(e)well*, e.g. *Bridwell* in Uffculme, Devon, or *Bridewell* Springs in Westbury, Wilts. These two get the name from OE *brȳd* 'bride' + *well(a)* spring (perhaps a spring associated with a fertility cult). There may be other places so called with different derivations, e.g. from OE *bridd* nestling, young bird (see BIRD) or from St *Bride* (see KILBRIDE). There has probably also been some confusion with BRIGHTWELL.

Vars.: **Bridel(l).** (Of 2 only): **Bridewell.**

Brierley English: habitation name from any of the places called *Brierl(e)y*, in the W Midlands, W and S Yorks., and elsewhere, all of which get their names from OE *brǣr* briar + *lēah* clearing.

Vars.: **Brierly, Brearley, Briarl(e)y.**

The spelling Brierley *is found most frequently in Lancs., while* Brearley *is more common in Yorks.*

Brigden N English: of uncertain origin, possibly a habitation name from some lost place named with OE *brycg* BRIDGE + *denu* valley.

Bright English: 1. from a ME nickname or given name, meaning 'bright', 'fair', 'pretty', from OE *beorht* bright, shining.

2. from a short form of any of several OE personal names of which *beorht* was the first element, such as *Beorhthelm* 'bright helmet'; cf. BERT.

Var.: **Brightman.**

A family called Bright *trace their ancestry back to Henry Bright (d. 1626), master of the King's School, Worcester. His descendants became wealthy bankers in Bristol and include Richard Bright (1789–1858), one of the leading physicians of the 19th cent., who gave his name to Bright's disease, which he was the first to diagnose.*

Brighton English: habitation name from *Breighton* in Humberside on the river Derwent. This place gets its name from OE *brycg* BRIDGE + *tūn* enclosure, settlement. The surname is unlikely to derive from *Brighton* in Sussex, which was known as *Brighthelmestone* until the end of the 18th cent.

Var.: **Brighten.**

Brightwell English: habitation name from any of various places, for example in Berks., Oxon., and Suffolk, so called from OE *beorht* bright, clear + *well(a)* spring, stream. See also BRIDLE.

Brill 1. Low German and Dutch: habitation name from a place in E Friesland, of uncertain etymology. It may be akin to the fish name *brill*.

2. Jewish (Ashkenazic): acronymic surname from Hebr. *bar-* 'son of ...', with a male given name beginning with *L-*. Cf. BROCK.

Vars. (of 1): Du.: **Brilleman**. (Of 2): **Bril**.

Brillant Jewish (Ashkenazic): ornamental name from Ger. *Brillant* diamond of the finest cut (from Fr. *brillant*, pres. part. of *briller* to shine, glitter), or from the Pol. cogn. *brylant*, which has the same meaning, or from the Yid. cogn. *brilyant* which has a more general meaning, 'diamond, jewel'. Cf. DIAMOND and JAGLOM.

Vars.: **Brilant**, **Bril(l)iant**; **Berland** (metathesized, and with excrescent *-d* under the influence of Yid. *land* or Ger. *Land* country).

Dim.: Jewish (E Ashkenazic): **Berlanczyk**.

Brim 1. English: var of BREAM 3.

2. Jewish (Ashkenazic): of unknown origin, possibly an acronymic surname from Hebr. *bar-* 'son of ...', with a male given name beginning with *M-*. Cf. BROCK.

Var. (of 1): **Brimm**.

Brindle English: habitation name from a place in Lancs., so called from OE *burna* stream (see BOURNE) + *hyll* HILL. The surname is still largely restricted to Lancs.

Brindley English (chiefly Ches., Staffs., and S Lancs.): habitation name from a place in Ches., so called from OE *berned* burnt (see BRENT 1) + *lēah* wood, clearing.

Brington English: habitation name from places in Cambs. (formerly Hunts.) and Northants, so called from OE *Brȳningtūn* 'settlement (OE *tūn*) associated with *Brȳni*' (see BRYNING).

Brink 1. Low German, Dutch, and Danish: topographic name for someone who lived by a pasture, from MLG *brinc* meadow, pasture, esp. a raised meadow in low-lying marshland.

2. Jewish (Ashkenazic): of unknown origin, possibly an acronymic surname from Hebr. *bar-* 'son of...', with a male given name beginning with *K-*. Cf. BROCK.

Vars. (of 1): Low Ger.: **Brinck**, **Brinken**; **Brin(c)kmann**; **Tenbrin(c)k**, **Tombrin(c)k** (Germanized **Zumbrink**); **Beimbrinke**. Du.: **(Ten) Brink**, **Van de(n) Brin(c)k**, **Brin(c)kman**. Dan.: **Brinck**, **Brinch**. (Of 2): **Brinkmann**.

Cogns. (of 1): Fris.: **Brinkema**, **Brinksma**, **Brinkstra**.

Brinkley English: habitation name from a place in Cambs., apparently so called from the OE personal name *Brynca* (of uncertain origin) + OE *lēah* wood, clearing.

Brinton English: habitation name from a place so called, perhaps the one in Norfolk, which has the same origin as BRINGTON.

Brion French: habitation name from any of several places so called. Most of them apparently derive from the Gaul. element *briga* height, hill (cf. BRYAN) + the suffix *-o(n)*. A few are more plausibly derived from Gaul. *berria* plain, with the same suffix. The Sp. placename (examples in the provinces of Logroño and La Coruña) and surname **Briones** is of similar origin.

Brisard French: nickname for a clumsy person, from OF *bris(er)* to break (of Celt. origin) + the pej. suffix *-ard*.

Brisbane English: nickname from OF *bris(er)* to break + OE *bān* bone. The sense of this hybrid name is not entirely clear; it may have been used for someone crippled by a broken bone or, more probably, for a violent man who broke other people's bones.

Briscoe N English: habitation name from any of various places so called. *Briscoe* in Cumb. is so called from ON *Bretaskógr* 'wood of the (Strathclyde) Britons' (cf. BRETT), whereas *Brisco* in Cumb. and *Briscoe* in N Yorks. are so called from ON *birki* BIRCH + *skógr*.

Vars.: **Brisco**, **Briskey**; **Brisker** (see also BRISK).

Brisk Jewish (E Ashkenazic): habitation name from *Brisk*, the Yid. name of two Polish cities (Brześć Litewski, now Brest Litovsk in the Soviet Union, and Brześć Kujawski). See also BRZESKI.

Vars.: **Brisker** (from Yid. *Brisker* native or inhabitant of Brisk); **Briskman**, **Briskin**.

Bristow English: habitation name from the city of *Bristol*, so called from OE *brycg* BRIDGE + *stōw* assembly place. The final *-l* of the modern form is due to a regional pronunciation.

Vars.: **Bristowe**, **Bristo(e)**, **Brister**.

Brito Portuguese: habitation name from a place in the province of Minho, or from any of the numerous other minor places with the same name, which is of uncertain origin.

Brittain English: 1. national or ethnic name for a Briton or Breton; see BRETT.

2. surname adopted by recent immigrants to Britain as a token of their new patriotism.

Vars.: **Brittan**; **Britton** (very common around Bristol); **Britten**, **Brittin** (Northants); **Brittner**, **Britnor**, **Bruttner**.

Broad English: nickname for a stout or fat person, from ME *brode*, OE *brād*. The surname **Brading** (i.e. 'son of Broad') suggests that OE **Brāda* and ME *Brade* may have been in use as personal names. For the Northern ME retention of *-ā*, cf. ROPER.

Vars.: **Brade**; **Braid** (Scots); BRADMAN.

Cogn.: Ger.: BREIT.

Broadbent N English: habitation name from a minor place in Lancs., near Oldham, so called from OE *brād* BROAD + *beonet* bent grass (see BENT).

Broadhead English (Yorks.): nickname for someone with a wide forehead or large head, from ME *brōd* BROAD + *heved* head (OE *hēafod*).

Broadhurst English: habitation name from a minor place so called, perhaps *Broadhurst* Manor Farm in Horsted Keynes, Sussex. The placename is from OE *brād* BROAD + *hyrst* wooded hill (see HURST).

Broc French: 1. nickname, probably for a person with a prickly temperament, from OF *broc* point, spur (of Gaul. origin). The word has many other meanings—a pointed weapon for stabbing, a deer's antler, a needle, a spit, a jug with a pointed handle, spiny vegetation, etc.—and any or all of these senses may also have contributed to the surname, which may also have been originally an occupational or topographic name.

2. nickname meaning 'badger', from Bret. *broc'h* (see BROCK 2).

Vars. (of 1): **Broche**, **Bro(c)que**; **Broch(i)er**, **Broquier** (these last being occupational names for makers of pointed objects of some kind).

Cogns. (of 1): Prov.: **Broca(s)**.

Dims. (of 1): Fr.: **Brochet**, **Bro(c)quet**, **Brochon**, **Brochot**.

Pejs. (of 1): Fr.: **Broc(h)ard**, **Broc(h)art**.

Brock 1. English and Low Ger.: var. and cogn. of BROOK.
2. English: nickname for a person supposedly resembling a badger, ME *broc(k)* (OE *brocc*, of Celt. origin; cf. Welsh *broch*, Corn. *brogh*, Ir. *bruic*). In the Middle Ages badgers were regarded as unpleasant creatures.
3. Jewish (Ashkenazic): probably an acronymic surname from Hebr. *bar-* 'son of...', with a male given name beginning with *K-*. Many Jewish surnames beginning with *Br-* and *Bar-* are probably of acronymic origin, but without detailed evidence from family histories it is impossible to specify the given name from which each is derived.

Vars. (of 1): Eng.: **Brockman**. Low Ger.: **Bröcker, Brockmann, Tombrock**. (Of 3): **Brok, Brockman(n)**; **Brockmon**.

Cogns. (of 2): Ir.: **Ó Bruic**.

Dim. (of 2): Scot: **Brockie**.

Brockhole English: habitation name from an unidentified minor place named from ME *broc(k)* badger (see BROCK 2) + *hole* hole, hollow (see HOLE). See also BROCKWELL.

The Lancs. family called Brockhole *take their name from* Brockholes *near Preston; they are descended from Roger* de Brochol (fl. *1260*), *who with his descendants held the manor there until 1396*.

Brocklebank English: habitation name from a place in Cumb., near Wigton, apparently so called from a bank of earth that was a favourite haunt of badgers; cf. BROCKHOLE and BANKS.

Brocklehurst English (Lancs.): habitation name from a place near Accrington, apparently so called from a wooded hill that was a favourite haunt of badgers; cf. BROCKHOLE and HURST.

Brocklesby English (Lancs.): habitation name from a place in Lincs., so called from the ON byname *Bróklauss* 'Breechless' + ON *býr* farm, settlement.

Brockwell English: probably a var. of BROCKHOLE. OE *Brocchol* is known to have developed into *Brockwell* in at least one instance, in Derbys. Both Brockwell Park in London and Brockwell Farm in Bucks. are of comparatively recent origin, probably deriving their names from the surname rather than vice versa.

Brodie 1. Scots: habitation name from *Brodie* Castle on the coast between Nairn and Forres. The placename is probably from Gael. *brothach* muddy place rather than *bruthach* steep place.
2. Jewish (E Ashkenazic): Anglicized spelling of *Brodi*; see BRODSKI.

The senior branch of the Scots Brodie *family are still established at Brodie Castle. Early family records were destroyed by fire in 1645; according to tradition, they are descended from Malcolm, Thane of Brodie* (fl. *1285*).

Brodski 1. Jewish (Ashkenazic) and Polish: habitation name from *Brod* in Moravia or *Brody* in the Ukraine, which were important centres of Jewish life up to the time of Hitler. Both places get their names from the Slav. element *brod* ford, Pol. *bród*.
2. Polish: nickname for a bearded man, a cogn. of BORODIN.

Vars. (of 1): Jewish: **Brodsky**; **Broda, Brodi, Brody**, BRODIE; **Broida, Broide, Broido**; **Braude** (W. Ashkenazic); **Brode(r)**, **Brod(t)**, **Brodman**. (Of 1 and 2): Pol.: **Brodowski, Brodziński**.

Patrs. (from 1): Jewish: **Broderson, Broderzon**.

Brogan Irish: Anglicized form of Gael. **Ó Brógáin** 'descendant of *Brógán*', a personal name apparently derived from a dim. of *bróg* shoe.

Vars.: **O'Brognan(e)**.

Brogden English (Yorks.): habitation name from *Brogden* in W Yorks., so called from OE *brōc* BROOK + *denu* valley (see DEAN 1).

Brolin Swedish: topographic name for someone who lived by a bridge, from Swed. *bro* bridge + the local suffix *-lin*.

Vars.: **Brohlin**; **Broman**.

Cpds (ornamental): **Broberg** ('bridge hill'); **Broström** ('bridge river').

Brolly Irish: Anglicized form of Gael. **Ó Brólaigh** 'descendant of *Brolach*', a personal name possibly derived from *brollach* breast.

Var.: **Brawley**.

Dims.: **(O')Brollaghan**, BRADLEY (Gael. **Ó Brolcháin**).

Bromage English: habitation name from any of the various places called *Bromwich* (West Bromwich, Castle Bromwich, Little Bromwich) in the W Midlands, to which area the surname and its vars. are still largely confined. The placename is from OE *brōm* broom, gorse + *wīc* dairy farm (see WICK).

Vars.: **Bromwich, Bromidge, Brommage**.

Bromberg Jewish (Ashkenazic): from the Ger. name of the city of *Bydgoszcz* in Poland, from *Brom(beere)* bramble (OHG *brāma*) + *berg* hill.

Var.: **Bromberger**.

Bromley English: habitation name from any of the many places called *Bromley* in Essex, Herts., Kent, Greater London, Greater Manchester, Staffs., and elsewhere. All are probably named with OE *brōm* broom + *lēah* wood, clearing.

Vars.: **Bromiley, Bromilow**, BRAMLEY.

Broms Swedish: nickname for an irritating person, from *broms* gadfly, horsefly; cf. BREEZE 1.

Bronfman Jewish (Ashkenazic): occupational name for a distiller, from Yid. *bronfn* brandy (cf. Ger. *Brantwein*) + *man* man.

Vars.: **Bronfmann**; **Bronfin**; **Brandwein(man)**, **Brandwain(man)**, **Brandwin**; **Brandweinhendler** ('brandy seller').

Broniewski Polish: habitation name from a place named with a short form of various cpd Slav. personal names with the first element *broń* weapon, armour, protection, such as *Bronisław* (lit. 'weapon (i.e. defender) of glory'), with the addition of the surname suffix *-ski* (see BARANOWSKI).

Dims.: **Bronisz** (directly from the given name); **Broniszewski** (habitation name).

Bronowski Polish and Jewish (E Ashkenazic): of uncertain origin, apparently a habitation name from some place called *Bronów* or *Bronowo*, perhaps named with the same element as BRONIEWSKI.

Bronson English: patr. from the nickname BROWN. In Lancs. it may sometimes derive from the surname BROWN; formation of surnames ending in *-son* from existing surnames was a relatively common phenomenon in NW England.

Vars. (of 1): **Brownson, Brunson**.

Brook English: topographic name for someone who lived by a brook or stream, from OE *brōc* brook or, by extension, water meadow. 'Water meadow' or 'marsh' is the regular meaning of the Low Ger. cogn. *brook* (Du. *broek*; Ger. *Bruch*, OHG *bruoh*). The Eng. spelling *Brooke* preserves a trace of the OE dat. sing. case, originally used after a preposition (e.g. 'at the brook'), and forms in *-(e)s* preserve a gen. (i.e. 'of the brook'). Both nom. and dat. sing. forms are widely distributed throughout England, but especially common in W and S Yorks.; the gen. var. *Brook(e)s*, on the other hand, has a much more even distribution. Brooks is also borne by Ashkenazic Jews, presumably as an Anglicization of one or more like-sounding Jewish surnames.

Vars.: **Brooke**, **Brook(e)s**, **Broke**, BROCK, **Bruck**; **Brooker**, **Brucker**; **Brookman**; **Brooking** (Devon).

Cogns.: Ger.: **Bruch(mann)**; **Brücher**. Low Ger.: **Brook(mann)**, BROCK. Du., Flem.: **Broek**, **Ten Broek(e)**; **Van den Broek(e)**, **Broekman**. Fris.: **Brookstra**, **Broekstra**, **Broekema**.

Some modern bearers of this name, who preserve the spelling Broke, *are descended from Sir Richard Broke (d. 1529) of Broke Hall in Suffolk, who was Chief Baron of the Exchequer to Henry VIII in 1526.*

English bearers of the name Brockman *can trace their ancestry to a certain John Brockman who was granted lands in Kent by Richard II.*

Brookfield English: habitation name from a minor place (probably in Lancs., where the surname is commonest) so called, from OE *brōc* BROOK + *feld* pasture, open country (see FIELD).

Brooksbank English (Yorks.): habitation name from a minor place named from ME *brokes*, gen. of *broke* BROOK + *bank* bank (see BANKS). There are places with this name in Bradfield and Agbrigg, W Yorks.

Brooksby English: habitation name from a place in Leics., recorded in Domesday Book as *Brochesbi*. This may contain a Scandinavian personal name *Brók* + ON *býr* farm, settlement, but it is also possible that the first element is OE *brōc* BROOK, or its Dan. cogn.

Var.: **Bruxby**.

The first known bearer of the name was Geraldus de Brooksby, *who became a freeman of Leicester in 1208. A family of this name, probably descended from him, grew prosperous and wealthy in the wool trade and married into many of the noble families of England.*

Broom English: habitation name from a place named *Broom(e)* or *Brome*, from OE *brōm* broom, gorse. There are such places in Beds., Co. Durham, Norfolk, Shrops., Suffolk, Worcs., and elsewhere.

Vars.: **Bro(o)me**.

Broomfield English: habitation name from one of the places named from OE *brōm* broom, gorse + *feld* open country, e.g. *Broomfield* in Essex, Kent, and Somerset, or *Bromfield* in Cumb. and Shrops. The name is now most common in Lancs.

Var.: **Bromfield**.

Broomhall English: habitation name from a place so called, probably the one in Ches., which takes its name from OE *brōm* broom, gorse + *halh* nook, hollow—i.e. 'hollow with gorse growing in it'; cf. BRAMALL.

Broomhead English (chiefly S Yorks.): habitation name from *Broomhead* Hall, near Penistone, so called from OE *brōmig* overgrown with broom + *hēafod* headland.

Brophy Irish: Anglicized form of Gael. **Ó Bróithe** 'descendant of *Brōth*', a personal name or byname of unknown origin.

Var.: **Broy**.

Brosnahan Irish: Anglicized form of Gael. **Ó Brosnacháin** 'descendant of *Brosnachán*', a personal name derived from *Brosne*, a town and river in Co. Kerry.

Var.: **Brosnan**.

Brosse French: topographic name for someone who lived in a scrubby area of country, from OF *broce* brushwood, scrub (LL *bruscia*). Occasionally it may be a metonymic occupational name for a brush maker, from the same OF word in the transferred sense 'brush'.

Vars.: **Brouss**, **Brosses**, **Labro(u)sse**, **De(la)bro(u)sse**; **Brossier** (an occupational name).

Cogn.: Eng.: BRUSH.

Dims.: Fr.: **Brousset**, **Broussot**, **Brousseau**, **Brouss(el)oux**; **Brosset** (see also AMBROSE); **Brossollet**, **Brossolette**.

Pejs.: Fr.: **Bro(u)ssard**.

Brother 1. English: from a byname occasionally used for a younger son, i.e. the brother (OE *brōðor*) of someone important, or for a guild member, esp. a fellow guild member (*brother* being used in this sense in ME).

2. English and Irish: from the cogn. ON *Bróðir*, which was in use as a personal name, originally for a younger son. In Ireland **Ó Bruadair** (Anglicized as **Brothers**) is an ancient Donegal sept name: it has also been derived, probably wrongly, from Gael. *bruadar* dream, reverie.

Cogns.: Ger.: **Bruder**. Low Ger.: **Broder**. Flem., Du.: **Den Broeder**, **Broere**. Jewish (Ashkenazic): **Bruder(man)** (reasons for adoption as a surname not clear).

Dim.: Fris.: **Broersma**.

Patrs.: Low Ger.: **Broders(en)**; **Bröers**. Flem., Du.: **Broeders**; **Broeren**, **Broerse(n)**. Dan.: **Brodersen**. Jewish: **Bruderso(h)n** (reasons for adoption as a surname not clear). Croatian: **Bradić**.

Patr. (from a dim.): Du.: **Broertjes**.

Brotherstone Scots: habitation name from a place so called in Midlothian, or from another in Berwicks. The Midlothian place is first recorded in 1153 as *Brothirstanys*, and is either from the ON personal name *Bróðir* 'Brother' + the pl. of OE *stān* stone, or means 'twin stones'.

Var.: **Brotherston**.

Brouard French: nickname for a poor man or a miser, one who could or would only eat gruel, from OF *breu*, *brou* broth, thin soup, gruel (of Gmc origin; cf. Ger. *Brühe*) + the pej. suffix *-ard*.

Dim.: **Brouardel**.

Brough English: habitation name from any of the various places, of which there are several in Yorks. and Derbys. as well as elsewhere, so called from OE *burh* fortress (see also BERRY, BURY, and BURKE). In most cases these are the sites of Roman fortifications. The name is widely distributed, but most common in Staffs. The pronunciation is usually /brʌf/.

Vars.: **Brugh**, **Bruff**.

Brougham English: habitation name from *Brougham* in Cumb., so called from OE *burh* fortress (see BURKE) + *hām* homestead. The pronunciation is /bru:m/.

The type of four-wheeled horse-drawn carriage known as a brougham *was named after Henry, Lord Brougham (1778–1868). He was descended from a certain Henry Brougham, who had bought the manor of Brougham in 1726.*

Broughton English: habitation name from any of the many places in all parts of England so called. The first element is variously OE *brōc* BROOK, *burh* fortress (see BURKE), or *beorg* hill, mound (see BARROW); the second is in all cases OE *tūn* enclosure, settlement.

A family of this name trace their ancestry to John Broughton, *who held the manor of Broughton in Staffs. in the 15th cent.*

Brown English: generally a nickname, ME *brun*, *le brun*, from OE *brūn* or OF *brun* (both of Gmc origin; cf. OHG *brūn*), referring to the colour of the hair, complexion, or clothing. It may occasionally be from a personal name, OE *Brūn* or ON *Brúni*, with the same origin. *Brun-* was also a

Gmc name-forming element; some instances of OE *Brūn* may therefore be short forms of cpd names such as *Brungar*, *Brunwine*, etc. The Ger. cogns. are associated with the much more common Continental personal name *Bruno*, which was borne by the Dukes of Saxony, among others, from the 10th cent. or before. It was also the name of several medieval German and Italian saints, including the founder of the Carthusian order (1030–1101), who was born in Cologne.

Brown also occurs as an Anglicization of the Jewish names listed below, including compounds, and of names in other langs. meaning 'Brown'.

Vars.: **Browne, Broun(e)**.

Cogns.: Ger.: **Braun**. Low Ger.: **Bru(h)n**. Flem.: **De Bruyn(e), Bruineman, Bruinen; Bryn**. Du.: **(De) Bruin(e), De Bruijn(e), Bruyn(e)**. Dan., Norw., Swed.: **Bru(h)n, Bruun, Brunn**. Jewish (Ashkenazic): **Braun(er); Broinlich** (from Yid. *broynlekh* brownish). Fr.: **Lebrun**. It.: **Bruno, Bruni**. Cat.: **Bru(n); Bruna** (fem.). Port.: **Bruno**.

Dims.: Eng.: **Brunet, Brownett, Burnet(t), Burnell**. Ger.: **Bräunle(in), Breinl(ein); Praundl(in)** (Bavaria). Low Ger.: **Bru(h)nke, Brü(h)nicke; Brüntje**. Fris.: **Bruinsma**. Fr.: **Brunet(on), Brunel, Bruneau, Brunon, Brunot; Brugnot** (Switzerland). It.: **Brunetti, Brunelli, Brunini, Brunotti**. Cat.: **Brunet**.

Aug.: It.: **Brunone**.

Patrs: Eng.: BRONSON. Ger.: **Brauns**. Low Ger. **Bru(h)ns(en)**. Fris.: **Bruins**. Flem.: **Br(u)yns**. Du.: **Bruns**. Fr.: **Aubrun**. Rum.: **Brunesco**.

Patrs. (from dims.): Low Ger.: **Brüntjen**. Du.: **Bruyntjes**. It.: **Brunelleschi**.

Cpds (ornamental): Jewish: **Braunfeld** ('brown field', Anglicized as **Brownfield**); **Braunroth** ('brownish red'); **Braunstein** ('brown stone', Anglicized as **Brownstein**); **Braunthal** ('brown valley').

Brown *is one of the most common surnames in the English-speaking world, with, for example, some 5000 listings in the London Telephone Directory and over 2500 in Manhattan. The var.* Browne *is also common in all parts of Britain and Ireland; in Galway it is borne by descendants of a 12th-cent. Norman invader called* le Brun, *and has in part been Gaelicized as* **de Brún**.

Brownhill 1. English: habitation name from any of various places, for example in Yorks., Ches., and Staffs., so called from OE *brūn* BROWN + *hyll* HILL.

2. Jewish: Anglicization of some unidentified Jewish surname.

Vars.: **Brownell, Brownill, Brownhall**.

Present-day bearers of this surname are probably all descended from a single family, which can be traced to Brownhill near Sale in Ches. in the late 13th cent. The name is still most common in Ches. and the neighbouring counties of Lancs., Derbys., and Yorks. A branch of the family was established in Scotland in the early 14th cent.

Browning English: from the ME and OE personal name *Brūning*, originally a patr. from the byname *Brūn* (see BROWN).

Var.: **Brunning**.

Cogns.: Ger.: **Brauning**. Low Ger.: **Brüning**. Du.: **Bruning**. Dan.: **Breuning**.

Patrs.: Eng.: **Brownings**. Ger.: **Brünings**. Flem.: **Bruyninckx**. Fris.: **Bruninga**.

The poet Robert Browning *(1812–89) came of a family that had been settled in Dorset for 500 years.*

Brownridge English: habitation name from an unidentified place so called from OE *brūn* brown + *hrycg* ridge. The surname is commonest in Yorks., but the placename *Brownrigg* is common in Cumb.; two of the places so called are earlier recorded as *Brownridge*.

Broxholme English: habitation name from a place in Lincs., recorded already in this form in Domesday Book, from the gen. case of ODan. *brōk* marsh + ON *holmr* island, dry land in a fen (see HOLME 2). The surname is still largely confined to Lincs., with smaller concentrations in the nearby areas of Derbys., Notts., and S Yorks.

Bruce Scots and English (Norman): habitation name from a place in Normandy, whose identification has been much disputed. Traditionally it is derived from *Brix* near Cherbourg, but *Le Brus* in Calvados and *Briouze* in Orne have also been proposed as candidates. If the last is correct, the name is identical with BREWIS 1.

Several Norman knights bearing the name de Bruce *or* de Bru(i)s *accompanied William the Conqueror in 1066. They received grants of land mainly in N England and were among the leading Normans to settle in Scotland in the 12th cent. One of them, Robert de Bruis, was granted lands in Yorks. and held the castle and manor of Skelton and Hertness in the bishopric of Durham. He married Isabel, niece of King William the Lion (1143–1214), a direct descendant of the Celt. chiefs of Galway. Their son Robert (1210–95) was one of the claimants to the Scottish throne in 1290, but it went to John de Baliol, who enjoyed the support of Edward I of England. However, Edward caused great resentment by treating Scotland as an English fiefdom. In defiance of the English, Robert 'the Bruce' (1274–1329), grandson of the 1290 claimant, was crowned king of Scotland in 1306, and consolidated Scottish independence when he defeated the English forces of Edward II at Bannockburn (1314). Robert's brother Edward was crowned king of Ireland (1315), but was killed in 1318. The many eminent Scottish families bearing this name may well all be descended from the 12th-cent. Norman baron. It is the family name of, among others, the earls of Elgin.*

Brudenell English (Norman): ethnic name for a Breton, or nickname, probably with derogatory overtones, meaning 'little Breton', from ONF *Bretonnel*, dim. of *Bret* Breton (see BRETT). Among the followers of William the Conqueror were many Bretons, ancestors of the bearers of this name among them.

Brudenell *is the family name of the earls of Cardigan. They have been associated with Aynhoe in Bucks. since at least the 14th cent. The name is found in a land deed of 1366, and at that time was used more or less interchangeably with the Fr. forms* Bretonel *and* Bretenell.

Brühl 1. German: topographic name for someone who lived by a water meadow, MHG *brüel* (OHG *bruil*, a cogn. of Fr. BREUIL).

2. German and Jewish (Ashkenazic): habitation name from the town of *Brühl* in Germany.

Vars. (of 1): **Breuel**. (Of 2): **Brühler**.

Cogns. (of 1): Low Ger.: **Brögel(mann), Briel, Breil(mann); Tombreul** (Westphalia). Flem., Du.: **Breul(s), Van der Brule, Broghel, Breughel, Van Breugel, Van Breukelen**. Pol.: **Bryl(a)**.

Brûlé French: topographic name for someone living in a place cleared for use by burning, from OF *brusle* burnt, past part. of *brusler* to burn (probably a blend of LL *ustulāre* (OF *usler*) with a Gmc verb **brōjan*). Some instances of the name may derive from the same word used with reference to disfigurement by burning, either accidentally or as a medieval ordeal or punishment (cf. BRENT 3).

Vars.: **Bruley, Buslé**.

Dims.: **Brulot, Brul(l)on, Brulin**.

Pej.: **Brulard**.

Brunton N English and Scots: habitation name from either of two places in Northumb. so called from OE *burna* stream (see BOURNE) + *tūn* enclosure, settlement.

Brush English: of uncertain origin. It may be a nickname for someone thought to resemble a brush (ME *brusche*, from OF *brosse*; see BROSSE) or a metonymic occupational name for a brush maker. It could also be from a related word, *brusche* cut wood, branches lopped off trees (OF *brousse*, cogn. with *brosse*), as a metonymic occupational name for a forester or woodcutter.

Var.: **Brusch**.

The earliest known mention of the surname is Richard Brusshe, *recorded at Reading in 1493. It is now found mainly in W England (Gloucs., Worcs., and Herefords.) as well as in London.*

Bruster English: 1. var. of *Brewster* (see BREWER).

2. occupational name for an embroiderer or embroideress, ME *broudestere* (from OF *brouder* to embroider, of Gmc origin). The suffix *-ster(e)* was originally feminine, but by the ME period was being used interchangeably for both men and women in words like *Brewster* (see BREWER) and *Baxter* (see BAKER), and in some regions such as E Anglia was the standard occupational suffix for men as well as women. However, there is no evidence that men did very much embroidery.

Var.: **Broster**.

Bruton English: habitation name from a place so called in Somerset, 'settlement (OE *tūn*) on the river *Brue*'. The river name is derived from a Brit. element cogn. with W *bryw* brisk, vigorous.

Var.: **Brueton**.

Bruyère French: topographic name for someone who lived in a place where heather grew, from OF *bruyere* heather (LL *brucāria*, from Gaul. **bruko*), or habitation name from one of the places in France (e.g. in Calvados) deriving their names from this word.

Vars.: **Labruyère, Delabruyère**; **Bruère**; **Brug(i)ère, Brug(i)er**; **Brière, Brierre, Delabrierre**.

Cogns.: Eng.: BREWER. Cat.: **Bruguera**.

Dims.: **Brugerolle(s), Brugeron**.

Bryan English: from the Celt. personal name *Brian*, which apparently contains the element *bre-* hill, probably with the transferred sense 'eminence'. Breton bearers of this name were among the Normans who invaded England in 1066, and they went on to invade and settle in Ireland in the 12th cent., where the name mingled with a native Irish version of it, borne in particular by one of the greatest of Irish septs, descendants of Brian Boru, who rose to the high kingship of Ireland in 1002. This native Ir. name had also been borrowed by Vikings, who introduced it independently in NW England before the Norman Conquest.

Vars.: **Brian, Brien**; **Bryant, Briant** (with excrescent *-t*).

Cogns.: Fr.: **Briand, Briant, Briend**.

Dim.: Fr.: **Briandet**.

Patrs.: Ir. **Bryans** (N Ireland); **McBrien** (Gael. **Mac Briain**).

'Descendant of B.': Ir.: **O'Brien** (one of the commonest surnames in Ireland), **O'Brian, O'Bryan** (Gael. **Ó Briain**).

The American poet William Cullen Bryant *(1794–1878) came of a New England family, being descended from Stephen Bryant, who had settled in Plymouth Colony in 1632.*

Bryning English: from a ME, OE personal name, *Bryning*, a patr. from the OE personal name *Brȳni* (from OE *bryne* fire, flame). The latter is found as a placename element; cf. e.g. BRINGTON.

Bryson 1. English: patr. from the given name BRICE.

2. Irish: Anglicized form of Gael. **Ó Briosáin**, an altered version of *Ó Muirgheasáin* (see MORRISSEY).

Brzeski Polish: 1. habitation name from the town of *Brzeg*, which gets its name from Pol. *brzeg* shore, bank, coast.

2. habitation name from one of the towns named *Brześć* (cogn. with Pol. *brzost* elm; see also BRISK).

Bubb English: of uncertain origin, possibly from an OE personal name, *Bubba*; this is attested in placenames, but there is no evidence of its survival into the ME period. The surname may also be from an unrelated nursery word, i.e. a nickname meaning 'baby', but there is no evidence of a ME vocab. word with *-u-* with this meaning.

Bube German: nickname meaning 'boy', MHG *buobe* (originally a nursery word). The word was also used to denote a menial servant.

Var.: **Bueb**.

Dims.: **Bübelin**; **Buberl** (Bavaria).

Buch German: topographic name for someone who lived by a beech tree or beech wood, Ger. *Buche* (MHG *buohe*; cf. BEECH).

Vars.: **Bucher(t), Büch(n)er, Buchmann, Büchmann**; **Puchner** (Bavaria).

Cogns.: Low Ger.: **Bookman, Böckmann, Böcking**. Fris.: **Beukema**. Flem., Du.: **Beuker, Van den Beuken**. Dan., Norw.: **Bøgh**. Jewish (Ashkenazic, topographic or ornamental): **Buchner, Bochner**.

Cpds: Jewish (topographic or ornamental): **Buchhol(t)z** ('beech wood'; also a Ger. habitation name); **Buchwald** ('beech forest').

Buchan Scots: regional name from any of various districts so called, principally that north of Aberdeen, although there is an obsolete barony of *Buchquane* in Strathore, Fife, a settlement called *Buchan* in Kirkcudbright, and a hill so called near Minnigaff in Dumfries and Galloway. There may be others. The derivation is probably from a Brit. word meaning 'cow' (cf. W *buwch*), or from the cogn. Gael. *baogh* cow + the dim. suffix *-an*.

The earliest known bearers of the name are Ricardus de Buchan, *who was clerk of the bishopric of Aberdeen c.1207–8, and William de Buchan, who held land in Aberdeen in 1281.*

Buchanan Scots: habitation name from a place near Loch Lomond, so called from Gael. *buth* house + *chanain* of the canon.

The placename Buchanan *was taken as a surname in the 13th cent. by Gilbrid McAuslan, head of a cadet branch of the clan McAuslan. One of his descendants was James Buchanan (1791–1868), 15th President of the U.S. (1857–61), who was born in Pennsylvania, the son of a successful land speculator.*

Buchs German: topographic name for someone who lived by a box thicket, Ger. *Buchs* (MHG *buhs*; cf. Box).

Vars.: **Buchsbaum, Bux(baum)**; **Puxbaum** (Austria).

Cogns.: Low Ger.: **Busboom**. Jewish (Ashkenazic; ornamental): **Buchs(en)baum, Buks(en)baum, Buxbaum, Boks(en)baum, Boksenboum, Boxenbaum; Buchsenboim, Bu(c)ksboim, Boxboim** (second element from Yid. *boym* tree); **Bukszpan** (Pol. spelling); **Bu(c)kspan, Bookspan** (Anglicized).

Buck 1. English: nickname for a man with some fancied resemblance to a he-goat (OE *bucc(a)*). OE *Bucca* is found as a personal name, as is ON *Bukkr, Bukki*. Names such as *Walter le Buk* (Somerset 1243) seem to be nicknames, but it is not clear what quality was alluded to: lechery, sturdiness, or something else.

2. English: topographic name for someone who lived near a prominent beech tree, as *Peter atte Buk* (Suffolk 1327), from OE *bōc* BEECH.

3. German: from a given name, a short form of *Burkhardt* (see BURKETT).

4. Low German and Danish: cogn. of BAUCH.

Cogns. (of 1): Ger.: **Bock**. Fris.: **Bokma**. Flem.: **De Bo(e)ck**. Du.: **Bok, De Bock**. Fr.: **Bouc, Lebouc(q)**.

Dims. (of 1): Ger.: **Böcklin**. Fr.: **Bo(c)quet, Bouquet, Bo(c)-quel**.

Buckingham English: habitation name from the town of this name, or perhaps in some cases from the county of which it was the county town. The placename comes from OE *Buccingahamm* 'water meadow (OE *hamm*) of the people of *Bucc(a)*' (see BUCK 1).

Buckland English: habitation name from any of the many places so called in S England (nine in Devon alone), which get their names from OE *bōc* book + *land* land, i.e. land held by right of a written charter, as opposed to *folcland*, land held by right of custom.

Buckle English: 1. metonymic occupational name for a maker of buckles, from ME *bokel* buckle (OF *bocle*, from L *buccula* cheek strap of a helmet, dim. of *bucca* cheek).

2. metonymic occupational name for a maker of shields; see BÖCKLER.

Vars.: **Buckell, Buckler; Buckles**.

Buckley 1. English: habitation name from any of the minor places so called, most of which are from OE *bucc(a)* he-goat (see BUCK 1) + *lēah* clearing, wood. Several instances of *Buckley* and *Buckleigh* in Devon derive from *boga* Bow + *clif* cliff, however. It is also possible that in some cases the surname derives from the contracted local pronunciation of *Bulkeley*, Ches., so called from OE *bulluc* bullock + *lēah*.

2. Irish: Anglicized form of Gael. **Ó Buachalla** 'descendant of *Buachaill*', a byname meaning 'Cowherd' or 'Servant'.

Vars. (of 1): **Buckleigh**. (Of 2): **O'Boughelly, (O')Buhilly**.

Buckman English: 1. occupational name for a goatherd, ME *bukkeman*, from OE *bucca* he-goat (see BUCK 1) + *mann* man.

2. occupational name for a scholar or scribe, ME *bocman*, from OE *bōc* book + *mann* man.

3. possibly also a habitation name representing a contracted pronunciation of BUCKINGHAM; cf. *Deadman* from DEBENHAM.

Buckmaster English: ostensibly an occupational name meaning 'master of the goats', but in fact a habitation name from *Buckminster* in Leics., which gets its name from the OE byname *Bucc(a)* (see BUCK 1) + OE *mynster* monastery (L *monastērium*).

Var.: **Buckminster**.

Bucknell English: habitation name from places called *Bucknell* in Oxon. and Shrops. or *Bucknall* in Lincs. and Somerset. The first element in all these is the OE byname *Bucc(a)* (see BUCK 1); the second element is *hyll* HILL in the first two, *healh* nook, hollow (see HALE 1) in the latter two.

Var.: **Bucknall**.

Budd English: from an OE byname, *Budde*, which was applied to a thickset or plump person, for reasons that are now obscure. By the ME period it had become a common personal name, with derivs. showing hypocoristic suffixes, *Budecok* and *Budekin*. Reaney, however, derives the name from OE *budda* beetle.

Dim.: **Budcock**.

Patrs.: **Budds; Budding**.

Buddenbrock German: habitation name from a place in Westphalia, so called from a MLG personal name *Budde* (probably cognate with OE *Budde*; see BUDD) + MLG *brock* water meadow, marsh (see BROOK).

Vars.: **Buddenbrook(s)**.

Budge 1. English: nickname from ANF *buge* mouth (LL *bucca*; see BOCCA), applied either to someone with a large or misshapen mouth or to someone who made excessive use of his mouth, i.e. a garrulous or indiscreet person or a glutton. The word is also recorded in ME in the sense 'victuals supplied for retainers on a military campaign', and the surname may therefore also have arisen as a metonymic occupational name for a medieval quartermaster.

2. Welsh: var. of BEWES.

3. Scots: surname found in Caithness and Orkney, of uncertain origin.

Vars. (of 1): **Bouch, Buche**.

Budgen English: nickname from the ANF phrase *bon Jean* 'good JOHN'.

Var.: **Budgeon**.

Cogns.: Fr.: **Bonjean** (most common in E France). It.: **B(u)ongiovanni, Bongi(o)anni, Bonjovi**.

Dims.: It.: **Bong(in)i, Bongino**.

Bugg English: 1. from the ON byname *Buggi* 'Fat man'.

2. nickname for an uncouth or weird man, from ME *bugge* hobgoblin, scarecrow (perhaps from W *bwg* ghost); cf. BOGLE.

Buhl German: 1. nickname for a relative (i.e. a member of an important family who was not the head of it), from MHG *buole* kinsman (OHG *buolo*, also used as a personal name).

2. nickname for a lover or the (illegitimate) child of a lover, from the same word in the later sense 'paramour', 'lover', 'mistress'.

Var.: **Buhle**.

Bühler German: topographic name for someone who lived on a hillside, from Ger. *Büh(e)l* hill (Swiss, Austrian, and S German dialects; OHG *buhil*), or habitation name from a place so called, e.g. *Bühl* in Baden.

Vars.: **Büh(e)l, Bühlmann, Biehlmann; Ambühl, Ambihl, Abbühl, Zumbühl, Zumbichl** (chiefly Swiss, with assimilated preposition); **Biehler, Biegler, Bichler, Bichl, Biegel** (chiefly Bavarian); **Pichl(er), Pigler, Piller, Pillmann** (chiefly Austrian); **Büchler, Büchelmann** (but see also BEECH).

Buisson French: topographic name for someone who lived in an area of scrub land or by a prominent clump of bushes, from OF *buisson* bush, scrub (a dim. of *bois* wood; see BOIS and also BUSH).

Vars.: **Dubuisson; Boisson; Bisson** (Normandy).

Cogn.: Prov.: **Bouisson, Bouissou**.

Dims.: Fr.: **Buissonnet, Boissonet**.

Collective: Fr. **Buissonnière**.

Buitrago Spanish: habitation name from places in the provinces of Madrid and Soria, so called from the LL personal name *Vulturius* (a deriv. of *vultur* vulture) + the local suffix *-ācum*.

Bukowski Polish and Jewish (E Ashkenazic): topographic name for someone who lived in a beech wood or by a beech tree, Pol. *buk* (see BEECH 2). Jewish instances of this group of names are generally, if not always, ornamental.

Vars.: Pol.: **Buczkowski, Bukowiecki; Buczyński**. Jewish: **Bukowsky, Bukovski; Bukovitz**.

Cogns.: Czech: **Bukovský**. Bulg.: **Bukov**. Ger. (of Slav. origin): **Bukowitz** (patr. in form).

Dims.: Pol.: **Buczek, Buczak**. Jewish: **Buczko**.

Bulgakov Russian: patr. from the nickname *Bulgak* 'Restless', 'Troublesome' (of Turkic origin).
Var.: **Bulganin**.

Bull English: nickname for a large, aggressive, bull-like man, from ME *bul(l)e*, *bol(l)e*. Occasionally, the name may denote a keeper of a bull (cf. BULMAN), while the form *Simon atte Bole* (London 1377) suggests that in addition this may be derived from a house or inn sign. *Bula* is not attested as an OE word except by the existence of placenames such as BULMER and *Bulwick* (see BULLICK), where it may in some cases represent a personal name. Nevertheless the vocab. word may well have been in use long before it occurs in surviving records: the deriv. *bulluca* BULLOCK is attested in OE. The fact that it gave rise to surnames that are of mainly S English distribution suggests that in the ME period it was established in S England as a vocab. word, and makes it unlikely that it is a Norse borrowing.
Vars.: **Bulle**; **Bool(e)**.
Cogns.: Flem., Du.: **(De) Bul**.
Dims.: Eng.: BULLOCK; **Bullcock**.

Bullen English: habitation name from the French Channel port of *Boulogne*, recorded in L sources both as *Gessoriācum* and as *Bonōnia*. The latter name is clearly the source of the modern placename. It is ostensibly a deriv. of L *bonus* good (cf. BOLOGNESE), but may in fact come from a Gaul. element **bona* foundation. Boulogne has long been a major trading port between England and France.
Vars.: **Bulleyn**, **Bullon**, **Bullin**, **Bullan(t)**, **Bullent**; **Boullen**, **Boullin**; **Bollen**, **Boleyn**.

Buller 1. English: occupational name for a scribe or copyist, from an agent deriv. of ME, OF *bulle* letter, document (cf. BILLET 3).
2. English (Norman): habitation name from a place in Normandy that has not been identified. If it is *Bouillé*, and so identical with BULLEY 1, the *-er(s)* may have arisen by analogy with other Norman placenames in *-ière(s)*; cf. e.g. FERRERS and VILLIERS.
3. German: nickname for a man with a loud voice, from an agent deriv. of MHG *bullen* to roar (of imitative origin).
Vars. (of 1): Eng.: **Bullar**. (Of 2): Eng.: **Bullers**.
Cogn. (of 1): Fr.: **Bullier**.
The name **Bowdler** *appears to be an altered form of this name (sense 2). The manor of* Hope Bowdler *in Shrops. was held by Robert* de Bullers *in 1201; throughout the 13th cent. it is referred to as* Hope Bulers *or* Hope Bolers. *Thomas Bowdler (1754–1825), notorious for his expurgated edition of Shakespeare, was born near Bath, but his family took their name from this place.*

Bulley English: 1. Norman habitation name from any of the several places in Normandy called *Bouillé* or *Bully*, from a Gaul. personal name of uncertain form and meaning + the local suffix *-ācum*.
2. habitation name from *Bulleigh* in Devon or *Bulley* in Gloucs., both of which get their names from OE *bula* BULL (perhaps a byname) + *lēah* wood, clearing.
Var.: **Bully**.

Bullick English: habitation name, perhaps from *Bolwick* in Norfolk or *Bulwick* in Northants, which are so called from OE *bula* BULL (perhaps a byname) + *wīc* outlying settlement (see WICK). The surname is now found mainly in N Ireland.

Bullock English: nickname for an exuberant young man, from ME *bullok* bullock, referring to a young steer rather than a castrated one (OE *bulluca*, dim. of *bula* BULL).

Bulman English (chiefly Northumb.): occupational name for the keeper of a bull, from ME *bule* BULL + *man* man.
Var.: **Bullman**.

Bulmer English: habitation name from a place in Essex, recorded in Domesday Book as *Bulenemera*, from OE *bulena*, gen. pl. of *bula* BULL + *mere* lake (cf. DELAMARE).

Bulstrode English: habitation name from a place in Bucks., so called from OE *burh* fortress, town + *strōd* brushwood, or from one in Herts., which is from OE *bula* BULL + *strōd*.

Bumpas English: nickname, of Norman origin, for someone who was a swift walker, from OF *bon* good (see BON) + *pas* pace (L *passus*). It may also have been a local name, with the second element used in the sense 'passageway'. Cf. MALPAS.
Cogns.: Fr.: **Bompas**, **Bonpas**.

Bunbury English: habitation name from *Bunbury* near Nantwich, Ches., so called from the OE personal name *Buna* (of uncertain origin) + OE *burh* fortress.
The ancestry of bearers of this name can be traced to Henry de Boneberi, *who held the manor of Bunbury in the 12th cent.*

Bunch English: nickname for a hunchback, from ME *bunche* hump, swelling (of unknown origin).
Var.: **Bunche**.

Buncombe English: habitation name from an unidentified place, probably named as a valley with reeds growing in it, from OE *bune* reed + *cumb* valley (see COOMBE).
Var.: **Bunkum**.

Bunin 1. Jewish (E Ashkenazic): metr. from a southern Yid. pronunciation of the Yid. female given name *Bone*, from It. *Bona* 'Good' (see BON), with the addition of the Slav. suffix *-in*.
2. Russian: patr. from the nickname *Buna* (from *bunet* to drone), referring to a haughty or boring person.
Vars. (of 1): **Bunis**; **Bones**, **Bonis** (from a NE Yid. pronunciation);
Metr. (from a dim. of 1): **Bunkin** (from the S Yid. dim. given name *Bunke*).
Cogn. (of 2): Pol.: **Bujnowicz** (patr.).

Bunker English: nickname, of Norman origin, for a reliable or good-hearted person, from OF *bon* good (see BON) + *cuer* heart (L *cor*; cf. COEUR).
Cogns.: Fr.: **Boncoeur**. It.: **Boncore**.

Bunnett English: of uncertain origin, probably a var. of *Bonnett*; see BONNET. This form is recorded in Suffolk in the early years of the 17th cent.
Var.: **Bunnyt**.

Bunney English (now chiefly Devon): of uncertain origin, possibly a nickname, as Reaney suggests, for someone having a prominent lump or swelling, from ME *bunny* swelling, bunion (see BUNYAN). It is also possibly a topographic name from the SW Eng. dial. word *bunny* ravine.

Bunter S English: occupational name for a sifter of flour, from an agent deriv. of ME *bont(en)*, *bunt(en)* to sieve, sift (of uncertain origin, possibly akin to BOLT 1).

Bunting English: nickname from the bird so called. The word is attested from at least the 13th cent., and may be the first element in the placename *Buntingford*, recorded a century earlier. It is of unknown origin; it is possibly a deriv. of a Gmc element meaning 'short and thick', cf. BUNZ.
Vars.: **Buntin(e)**, **Bunten**, **Bunton**, **Buntain**, **Bontein**, **Bontine**.

Bunyan English: nickname for someone disfigured by a lump or hump, from a dim. of OF *bugne* swelling, protuberance. The term *bugnon* was also applied to a kind of puffed-up fruit tart, and so the surname may also have been a metonymic occupational name for a baker of these.

Vars.: **Bunyon, Bunnion.**

Most, if not all, bearers of this name, including John Bunyan *(1628–88), author of* The Pilgrim's Progress, *are members of a single family, originating from Ampthill in Beds., where the name is recorded as early as 1199 and recurs as* Bui(g)non, Buniun, *etc. throughout the 13th cent. The etymology from ANF* bon *good + the given name* Jean *(see* BUDGEN*) is now generally disregarded.*

Bunz German: nickname for a fat man, from the Alemannic (Swiss) dialect word *bunz* little barrel (perhaps ultimately from L *punctio* stamp, i.e. a barrel stamped with a seal of approval).

Dims.: **Bünzli** (Switzerland). Jewish (Ashkenazic): **Bunzel.**

Buonarroti Italian: from the medieval (chiefly Tuscan) given name *Buonarroto*, composed of the elements *buona* (fem.) good (see BON) + *arrota* gain, increase (from the verb *arrogare*, L *adrogāre* to appropriate, acquire). The name was used to denote a child whose birth provided a welcome addition to the family.

Buonsangue Italian: nickname for an illegitimate child suspected of being of noble parentage, from OIt. *buon(o)* good (see BON) + *sangue* blood (L *sanguis*).

Burbage English: habitation name from places in Wilts., Derbys., and Leics., so called from OE *burh* fort (see BURKE) + *bæc* hill, ridge (see BACK 1).

Vars.: **Burbidge.**

Burchfield English: habitation name from some minor place named with the OE elements *birce* BIRCH + *feld* pasture, open country (see FIELD).

Burda Czech: 1. nickname for a large, loutish fellow, Czech *burda*.

2. dim. of BURIAN.

Var.: **Burdák.**

Burdon English (chiefly W Country): 1. Norman, from the OF personal name *Burdo* (oblique case *Burdon*), probably of Gmc origin, but uncertain meaning.

2. nickname for a pilgrim or one who carried a pilgrim's staff (ME, OF *bourdon*, of uncertain origin, probably from LL *burdo*, gen. *burdōnis*, mule, pack animal, with later extension to mean 'support').

3. habitation name from places in W Yorks and Co. Durham, so called from OE *burh* fortress (see BURKE) + *dūn* hill (see DOWN 1). Another Burdon in Co. Durham means 'valley with a byre', from *bȳre* byre + *denu* valley.

Var.: **Burden.**

Burford English: habitation name from places in Oxon. and Shrops., so called from OE *burh* fortress (see BURKE) + *ford* FORD.

Burge English (chiefly Somerset and Dorset): 1. var. of BRIDGE, OE *brycg*, with metathesis of *u* and *r*, as exemplified in several placenames of this origin in various parts of S England.

2. var. of BURKE.

Burgemeister German: status name for the mayor or chief magistrate of a town, from Ger. *Bürgemeister*, a cpd of MHG *burc* town (see BURKE) + *meister* MASTER.

Cogn.: Du.: **Burgemeester.**

Burger German, Dutch/Flemish, and English: status name for a freeman of a town, esp. one who was a member of its governing council, a deriv. of MHG *burc*, ME *burg* (fortified) town (see BURKE). There is a difficulty with the Eng. name, in that it is found occasionally as a surname from the 13th cent. onwards, but is not recorded as a vocab. word until the 16th cent., when it was apparently borrowed from Ger. The usual Eng. term was the OF word *burgeis* BURGESS. This name also occurs as a Jewish surname, but the reasons for its adoption are uncertain.

Vars.: Ger.: **Bürger.** Flem., Du.: **De Burg(h)er; Borger.** Eng.: **Burgher, Burker.** Jewish: **Burg(mann).**

Cogns.: Low Ger.: **Borger, Börger.** Hung.: **Polgár.**

Patrs.: Low Ger.: **Borgers; Bürgers** (Rhineland). Du., Flem.: **Burgers, Borgers.**

Burgess English: from ME *burge(i)s*, OF *burgeis* inhabitant and (usually) freeman of a (fortified) town (see BURKE), esp. one with municipal rights and duties. Burgesses generally had tenure of land or buildings from a landlord by *burgage* (L *burgāgium*). In medieval England burgage involved the payment of a fixed money rent (as opposed to payment in kind); in Scotland it involved payment in service, guarding the town. The *-eis* ending is from L *-ēnsis* (mod. Eng. *-ese* as in *Chinese*). Compare BURGER.

Vars.: **Burges, Burgis(s).**

Cogns.: Fr.: **Bourgès, Bourgey, Bourgeix, Bourgeois, Bourjois, Bourzeix.** It.: **Borghese, Borgesio; Burgisi** (Sicily; often a tenant farmer, by extension of the sense of *burgāgium*). Cat.: **Burquès.**

Dims.: It.: **Borghesetti, Borghesini.**

One of the most influential families in Italy in the early 17th cent. was called Borghese*: it came originally from Sienna, and the first member to arrive in Rome was Marcantonio Borghese (1504–74). His son Camillo (1552–1621) brought wealth and power to the family and increased that of the papacy, culminating in his election as Pope Paul V in 1605. A later member of this family was Camillo Borghese (1775–1832), who was one of Napoleon's generals and who married the latter's sister Pauline.*

Burian Czech: from an OSlav. personal name, which appears to derive originally from the Russ. or Pol. word *bury* grizzly (a borrowing from Turkish, *bur* chestnut, applied to horses; not found in Czech as a vocab. word) + *Jan* JOHN.

Dims.: **Buriánek, Burýšek; Bureš,** BURDA.

Burke English: topographic name from ME *burc*, *burk* fort, from OE *burh* or (via OF) OHG *burg*, the common Gmc word for a fortification. In the Middle Ages any sizeable habitation had to be fortified, but in England the term *burc* came to be specialized to denote the site of a prehistoric hill fort, while its doublet *burig*, *borough* denoted a fortified manor house or fortified town (see BURY).

Vars.: **Bourke; Burgh** (the name of places in Cumb., W Yorks., Lincs., and Norfolk, as well as Suffolk), **De Burgh;** BROUGH, BURGE.

Cogns.: Ger.: BURGER. Low Ger.: **Tomborg** (with fused preposition and article). Flem.: **Van den Borcht, Van den Burcht.** Du.: **Van den Burg(h), Verburg.** Dan.: **Borg(en).** Swed.: **Borg(h).** Fr.: **Bourg, Lebourg, Dubourg, Delbourg.** It.: **(Del) Borgo, Borghi, Burgo, Dal Borgo.** Sp.: **Burgos** (habitation name from the ancient city in Old Castile).

Dims.: Fr.: **Bourgel, Bourget, Bourgey, Bourquet; Dubourquet.** It.: **Borghetti, Borghini, Borgotti.**

Augs.: Fr.: **Bourg(e)at, Bourgeas.** It.: **Borgoni.**

Pej.: It.: **Borgazzo.**

Cpd (ornamental): Swed.: **Borgström** ('town river').

The name in the form Burke *owes its great frequency as an Irish surname to William FitzAdelm* de Burgo, *a Norman knight from* Burgh *in Suffolk, who invaded Ireland with Henry II in 1171 and received the earldom of Ulster, along with grants of large tracts of land in Connacht. His descendants quickly associated themselves with the native population, Gaelicizing their name as* **de Búrca**, *and within a century they had become the most powerful family in Ireland. In more recent centuries they have included Edmund Burke (1729–97), the celebrated orator and political theorist, who was born in Dublin, where his father was an attorney, and Robert O'Hara Burke (1820–61), who with W. J. Wills was first to cross Australia from north to south (though they died on the return journey).*

Burkett English: from an OE personal name, *Burgheard*, composed of the elements *burh, burg* fort (see BURKE) + *heard* hardy, brave, strong. The name was reintroduced into ME by the Normans in the forms *Bou(r)chart, Bocard*; hence many of the variants. In the form *Burkhard* it was a very popular medieval Ger. name. There has been considerable confusion between this Eng. surname and BIRKETT.

Vars.: **Burkitt, Burkart, Borkett, Bockett, Buckett; Burchett, Burchatt, Burchard, Butchard, Budgett.**

Cogns.: Ger.: **Burghard(t), Bur(c)khard(t), Burkert, Burchard(t), Burchert.** Low Ger.: **Borchard(t), Borchert, Borgert, Borghard(t).** Flem.: **Burkart, Bourchaert.** Fr.: **Bourcard, Bourcart; Bou(r)chard.** It.: **Boccardi, Bocc(h)iardi, Broccardi.**

Dims.: Ger.: BUCK, **Bürk(el); Birkle** (Württemberg); **Bürkli, Busse, Bosse** (S Germany, Switzerland).

Patrs.: Low Ger.: **Borchers; Borcherding.**

The French name Bouchard *is first recorded in Haute Savoie in the early 18th cent. A certain Jean-Antoine Bouchard went from there to Pondicherry in India in 1757, and in about 1788 he or his son Maurice changed their family name to* **La Bouchardière**, *and the family became well established in British India. There does not seem to be any direct connection with either of the places called* La Bouchardière *in Normandy.*

Burkin 1. English: habitation name from the parish of *Birkin* in W Yorks., so called from OE *bircen* birch grove (originally an adj. deriv. of *birce* BIRCH).

2. Jewish (Ashkenazic): of unknown origin.

Var. (of 1): **Birkin.**

The first recorded holder of the English surname seems to be a certain John de Birkin *who held lands in Yorks. in the time of King John, but the name is also found further afield at an early date. The form* Burkin *is now more common in Kent, Surrey, and London, whereas* Birkin *is largely confined to Yorks., Notts., and Derbys.*

Burkinshaw English (Yorks.): habitation name from *Birkenshaw* near Wakefield in W Yorks., so called from OE *bircen*, an adj. deriv. of *birce* BIRCH + *sceaga* copse (see SHAW).

Vars.: **Birkenshaw, Burtenshaw, Birtenshaw, Brigginshaw, Bro(c)kenshaw.**

Burkman English: from ME *burghman, borughman* (OE *burhmann*) inhabitant of a (fortified) town (see BURKE), esp. one holding land or buildings by *burgage* (see BURGESS).

Vars.: **Burman; Borro(w)man, Barrowman, Barryman.**

Cogns.: Ger.: **Burgmann.** Low Ger.: **Borgmann.**

Burley English: habitation name from any of various places, for example in Derbys., Leics., Shrops., and W Yorks., so called from OE *burh* fort (see BURY) + *lēah* wood, clearing.

Var.: **Burleigh.**

Burling English: apparently an OE patr. in *-ing* from a personal name that has not been certainly identified, possibly a dim. of *Burgheard* (see BURKETT), **Byrgla* (suggested by Ekwall as underlying *Birlingham* in Worcs.), or **Bærla* (from OE *bār* boar, suggested by Ekwall as underlying *Birling* in Kent and *Barling* in Essex).

Vars.: **Birling, Barling.**

Burney 1. English (Norman): habitation name from *Bernay* in Eure, Normandy, so called from a Gaul. personal name *Brenno* (cf. BRYAN) + the local suffix *-ācum*, or from *Berney* in Norfolk, which apparently gets its name from Ralph *de Bernai* (Domesday Book), a Norman who received grants of land there.

2. Irish: Anglicized form of the personal name *Biorna*, a Gael. form of ON *Bjarni* (from *björn* bearcub, warrior; cf. BARNES 2).

Vars. (of 1): **Berney, Burnie.**

Patrs. (from 2): **McBurney, McBirney** (Gael. **Mac Biorna**).

Burnham English: habitation name from any of several places so called. Those in Bucks. (Burnham Beeches), Norfolk (various villages), and Essex (Burnham-on-Crouch) get the name from OE *burna* stream (see BOURNE) + *hām* homestead. In the case of Burnham-on-Sea in Somerset, however, the second element is OE *hamm* water meadow. Burnham in Lincs. is so called from *brunnum*, dat. pl. of ON *brunnr* spring, originally used after a preposition, i.e. '(at) the springs'.

Burnley English (Lancs. and Yorks.): habitation name from *Burnley* in Lancs., so called from OE *burna* stream (see BOURNE) + *lēah* wood, clearing.

Burns 1. Scots and N English: topographic name for someone who lived by a stream or streams, from the ME nom. pl. or gen. sing. of *burn* (see BOURNE).

2. Scots: topographic name or habitation name from the ME elements *burn* stream + *house* house.

3. Irish: Anglicized form of Gael. *Ó Broin*; see BYRNE.

4. Jewish (Ashkenazic): Anglicized and shortened form of BERNSTEIN.

Vars. (of 2): **Burnhouse, Burness.**

The ancestors of the Scots poet Robert Burns *(1759–96) were Campbells from Burnhouse in Taynuilt, by Loch Etive. They migrated first to Forfar, where they were known as Campbells of* Burness. *In April 1786 Robert and his brother decided to adopt the spelling* Burns *as a surname.*

Burnside Scots and N Irish: topographic name for someone living beside a burn or stream or habitation name from one of the places so called, of which the most significant is near Dalry, in the former county of Ayrs.

Burr English: of uncertain origin. Reaney explains this as a nickname for a person who is difficult to shake off, from ME *bur(r)* bur (seed-head that sticks to clothing). There is a problem with this explanation, in that *Burre* occurs as a surname or byname as early as 1185, whereas the vocab. word is not recorded by *OED* until the 14th cent. Reaney says, 'This sense may well be older'. The surname could be a var. of BURKE, but the loss of the final consonant would be hard to explain. Another possibility is derivation from OE *būr* small dwelling or building (mod. Eng. *bower*; cf. Ger. BAUER), but there are phonological difficulties here too.

The American statesman Aaron Burr *(1756–1836), whose votes as a presidential candidate tied with Jefferson's in 1800, was the son of a clergyman and academic, president of Princeton. On his mother's side he was descended from the Puritan preacher Jonathan Edwards; on his father's from Jehu Burr, who emigrated from England with Winthrop in 1630.*

Burrett English: 1. from the ME given name *Burret*, OE *Burgrǣd*, composed of the elements *burh*, *burg* fortress, stronghold + *rǣd* counsel.

2. nickname for someone with thick and dishevelled hair, from ME *b(o)urre* coarse woollen cloth (cf. BOURE) + *heved* head (OE *hēafod*).

Vars.: **Borrett, Boret, Borritt.**

Burridge English: 1. habitation name from any of three places in Devon so called from OE *burh* fort (see BURKE) + *hrycg* ridge.

2. from the ME given name *Burrich*, OE *Burgrīc*, composed of the elements *burh*, *burg* fortress, stronghold + *rīc* power.

Var.: **Burrage.**

Burrows English: topographic name (with locative gen. *-s*) for someone who lived by a hill or tumulus (OE *beorg*, a cogn. of OHG *berg* hill, mountain; see BERG). However, the name has become inextricably confused with derivs. of OE *burh* fort (see BURKE and BURY). (Reaney suggests a further derivation from OE *būr* BOWER + *hūs* house.)

Vars.: **Burrowes, Burrough(e)s, Burris; Burrow** (Yorks. and Lancs.); **Burrough; Borrow(s).**

Burstin Jewish (E Ashkenazic): from Yid. *burshtin* amber, which is from Pol. *bursztyn*, which in turn is from Ger. *Bernstein* (see BERNSTEIN).

Vars.: Jewish: **Burshtin, Burshtyn, Burs(z)tyn; Burs(h)tein, Burs(h)tain, Burszt(e)in, Bursztejn** (showing infulence of Ger. *-stein*); **Bursten, Bourstin** (Anglicized).

Burt English (common in SW England): probably a var. of BERT, from the OE byform *Byrht* of *Be(o)rht*.

Var.: **Birt.**

Burton English: habitation name from a placename that is very common in Midland and Northern England. The derivation is generally from OE *burh* fort (see BURKE) + *tūn* enclosure, settlement.

Vars.: **Bo(u)rton.**

A Shrops. family of this name came originally from Burton near Much Wenlock. They have held lands near Shrewsbury since the time of Edward IV. Richard Burton (1821–90), the explorer and orientalist, was a member of a cadet branch.

Bury English: habitation name or topographic name, ultimately from the dat. case, *byrig*, of OE *burh* fortified place (see BURKE), originally used after a preposition (e.g. Richard *atte Bery*). As inflections were lost in ME, derivs. of the OE dat. replaced the OE nom., the word taking forms such as *biri*, *berie*, and *burie*. In ME this word acquired two different senses, both of which have given rise to surnames. In late OE and early ME it denoted a fortified manor house, and the surname was used for someone who lived near a manor house or as an occupational name for someone employed in a manor house. The word also came to denote a fortified town, and is therefore a habitation name from any of various places so named. From this sense developed the mod. Eng. word *borough*. The surname *Bury* is especially common in Lancs., where it is no doubt mainly if not exclusively a habitation name from the town of this name, but may also be from various other, less important, places similarly named.

Vars.: BERRY; **Berryman, Berriman** (chiefly Devon); **At(ter)-bury, Atberry** (with fused preposition; cf. ATTENBOROUGH).

Burzyński Polish: habitation name from a place called *Burzyn*, which apparently gets its name from Pol. *burza* tempest, storm.

Busby English: habitation name from a place in N Yorks., recorded in Domesday Book as *Buschebi*, from ON *buski* bush, shrub (see BUSH) + *býr* homestead, village, or from some other place so called. The surname is now most common in the W Midlands.

Bush 1. English: topographic name for someone who lived by a thicket of bushes, from ME *bush(e)* bush (probably from ON *buski*, or an unrecorded OE *busc*). The surname may also be from ON *Buski* used as an personal name.

2. Jewish (Ashkenazic): Anglicized form of Ger. *Busch*, which was adopted by some Jews in allusion to the story of the burning bush from which God spoke to Moses (Exod. 3: 2–4).

Vars.: Eng.: **Bish, Bysh, Bysshe** (from a hypothetical OE word **(ge)bysce* bushy area, thicket).

Cogns.: Ger.: **Busch, Büscher.** Low Ger.: **Bosch(e), Bösch, Boschmann; Zumbusch** (Rhineland: 'at the bush'). Du., Flem.: **Bosch** (a common topographic name, meaning 'wood' rather than 'bush', also found in placenames, such as *'s Hertogenbosch* (*Bois-le-Duc*)); **Van den Bos(ch), (Van) Bosse, Tenbosch; Bosman** ('forester'). Fris.: **Bosma, Bosk(er).** Dan., Norw.: **Bus(c)k.**

Dims.: Low Ger.: **Büschgen, Böschgen.**

The Dutch painter Hieronymus Bosch *(?1450–1516) was born Jerome van Aaken. He took the name by which he is now known from the city of 's Hertogenbosch, where he was born. His family came originally from Aachen (now in Germany).*

The English surname **Busk** *is not of English origin: the family of this name whose ancestry has been traced is descended from Jacob Hans* Busck *(d. 1755), a wool merchant from Gothenburg, who settled in England in 1712.*

Bushby English: habitation name from a place so called, or a var. of BUSBY. There is a *Bushby* in the parish of Thurnby, Leics., named from the ON personal name *Butr* (see BUTT 1) + ON *býr* homestead, village. Derivation has also been proposed from *Bushbury* in Staffs., recorded in Domesday Book as *Biscopesberie*, i.e. the manor (see BURY) of the BISHOP. However, neither of these Midland origins is supported by the early distribution of the surname, which is Northern; it is first recorded in Cumb. From the 16th cent. it has been found in three main groups: in Cumb., Northumb., and N Yorks; in Beds.; and in Sussex.

Var.: **Bushbye.**

The earliest known bearer of this surname is John Bushbye *of Bothel Hall, Cumb. (b. 1525). Most if not all bearers in the area of Ampthill, Beds., are descended from a single family, which had settled there by the early 16th cent. A third group has been centred on Steyning in Sussex since the same period.*

Buss English: metonymic occupational name for a cooper or else a nickname for a rotund, fat man, from ME, OF *busse* cask, barrel (of unknown origin). The word was also used in ME of a type of ship, and the surname may perhaps have been given to someone who sailed in one. The byname seems to occur already in Domesday Book, where a Siward *Buss*, and a John and Richard *Buss* are recorded at Brasted in Kent.

Var.: **Busse.**

Cogns.: Du.: **Bui(j)s(man), Buysman, Buijzer, Buyzer.**

Sir John Buss of Lincoln emigrated to Flanders in the Middle Ages. It seems probable that Miss Frances Buss (1827–94), the pioneering headmistress of the North London Collegiate School for Girls, whose family came from Holland, was a descendant of his.

Bussey English: Norman habitation name from any of several places in Normandy: *Boucé* in Orne, from which came Robert *de Buci* mentioned in Domesday Book, *Boucey* (Manche), or *Bucy*-le-Long (Aisne). All of these places get their names from a L personal name *Buccius* (presumably a deriv. of *bucca* mouth; cf. BOCCA) + the local suffix *-ācum*.

Bustamante Spanish: habitation name from a lost place, so called from LL *bustum Amantii* 'pasture (see BUSTO) of *Amantius*', a personal name derived from LL *Amans*, gen. *Amantis*, 'Loving'.

Busto Spanish: habitation name from any of various minor places in W Spain, so called from LL *bustum* pasture for oxen or bullocks (a deriv. of *bos* ox, gen. *bovis*; cf. BOEUF and BOUVIER).

Var.: **Bustos**.

Dim.: **Bustillos**.

Butcher English: occupational name for a butcher or slaughterer, ME *bo(u)cher* (OF *bouchier*, a deriv. of *bouc* ram; cf. BUCK 1).

Vars.: **Bucher, Bou(t)cher**; BOWKER, **Boucker**.

Cogns.: Fr. (also with the transferred sense 'executioner'): **Bouch(i)er, Bouché; Bouchez** (N France); **Bouchey** (E France). Prov.: **Bouquier**. Cat.: **Boquer**. It.: **Beccaro, Beccari, Beccai(o); Boccieri; Buccieri** (Calabria); **Beccheri; Beghe** (Piedmont).

Dims.: Fr.: **Bouchereau, Boucherot, Boucheron**. It.: **Becherini**.

Aug.: It.: **Becheroni**.

Patr.: It.: **Del Beccaro**.

Equivs. (not cogn.): Sp.: CARNICERO. Ger.: METZGER. Pol.: RZEŹNIK. Russ.: MYASNIKOV.

Butler English and Irish: occupational name for a wine steward, usually the chief servant of a medieval household, from ANF *butuiller* (OF *bouteillier*, L *buticulārius*, from *buticula* bottle, dim. of *but(t)is* cask; cf. BOTAS). In the large households of royalty and the most powerful nobility, the title frequently denoted an officer of high rank and responsibility, only nominally concerned with the supply of wine. The name has also been adopted as a Jewish surname, for reasons that are not clear.

Vars.: **Botler** (though this may also be derived from ME *boteler* maker of (leather) bottles, from ME *botel*, OF *bouteille*); **Bottle, Bottell, Buttle**.

Cogns.: Fr.: **Bouteill(i)er, Boutillier**. Sp. (in the sense 'bottle maker'): **Botlero; Botella**.

Many Irish bearers of this name may trace their ancestry to Theobald FitzWalter, who accompanied Henry II to Ireland in 1170 and who in 1177 was created 'Chief Butler' (i.e. overlord) of Ireland by the king. His direct descendants include the earls and dukes of Ormonde. The dukedom was acquired after James Butler *(1610–88), the 12th Earl, a staunch supporter of Charles I during the Civil War, had negotiated the restoration of Charles II in 1660. He was succeeded by his grandson, also called James (1665–1745), who was a staunch Protestant and supporter of William of Orange in 1685. He served as Lord Lieutenant of Ireland and became Commander-in-Chief of the British army. However, after the death of Queen Anne he opposed the accession of George I and took part in a Jacobite rising (1715), after which he spent the rest of his life in exile.*

Butlin English: apparently from ME *Butevilain* (recorded in Norfolk in 1130 and elsewhere), which is either a compounded byname, 'BUTT the peasant', or a nickname meaning 'strike the peasant', from ANF *but(er)* to strike (of Gmc origin) + *vilain* peasant, bondsman (see VILLAIN). The surname is now found chiefly in the E Midlands.

Butt English: 1. from a ME personal name, *But(t)*, of unknown origin, perhaps originally a nickname meaning 'short and stumpy', and akin to late ME *butt* thick end, stump, buttock (of Gmc origin). ME *but(te)* was also a vocab. word denoting various types of salt fish, originally a fish with a blunt head. The surname may sometimes have been acquired by a seller of salt fish.

2. topographic name for someone who lived near a place used for archery practice, from ME *but* mark for archery, target, goal (from OF *but* aim, target; of unknown origin).

Patrs. (from 1): **Butts; Butson** (common in Devon and Cornwall from the 17th cent. onwards); **Butting**.

Butter English: 1. nickname for someone with some fancied resemblance to a bittern, perhaps in the booming quality of the voice, from ME, OF *butor* bittern (of obscure etymology).

2. metonymic occupational name for a dairyman or seller of butter, from OE *butere* butter (from L *būtyrum*, Gk *boutyron*, a cpd of *bous* cow + *tyron* cheese).

Var. (of 2): **Butterman**.

Cogns. (of 1): Fr.: **Butor**. (Of 2): Jewish (Ashkenazic): **Put(t)er(man)** (from NE Yid. *puter*); **Piterman** (from S Yid. *piter*).

Patr. (from 1): Eng.: BUTTERS.

Butterfield English: topographic name, common in the Bradford and Leeds area, for someone who lived by a pasture for cattle or at a dairy farm, or habitation name from a place so called (of which there is one in W Yorks.), from OE *butere* butter (see BUTTER 2) + *feld* pasture, open country (see FIELD).

Butteriss English: 1. var. of BOTTRELL (according to Reaney).

2. occupational name for a servant working in a wine cellar, ANF *boterie* (LL *botāria*, a deriv. of *bota* cask), with the ME gen. ending *-s*.

Vars.: **Buttriss, Buttress, Buttrice**, BUTTERS, **Buttrey**.

A family who moved from Northants. to Leics. in the 18th cent. appear to have changed their name from Buttrey *to* Buttress, *but the reason for this is not known.*

Butters English: 1. patr. from BUTTER 1.

2. var. of BUTTERISS.

Butterworth English (Lancs. and Yorks.): habitation name from places in Lancs. (near Rochdale) and in W Yorks. Both are so called from OE *butere* butter (see BUTTER 2) + *worð* enclosure (see WORTH). The surname is recorded from an early date in each of these two places; it probably arose independently in each.

Büttner German: one of several occupational names for a cooper or barrel-maker, Ger. *Büttner*, agent deriv. of MHG *būte(n)* cask, wine barrel (OHG *butin*, prob. via LL from Gk *butinē* chamber pot; cf. BOTAS and BUTLER). This name is more common in eastern German-speaking regions. The vocab. word was taken into Czech (as *bednář*), Pol. (as *bednarz*), and Ukr. (in the metathesized form *bondar*). See also BINDER, BÖTTCHER, SCHÄFFLER.

Vars.: **Bittner; Pittner** (Bavaria). Low Ger.: **Budde**.

Cogns.: Jewish (Ashkenazic): **Bit(t)ner**; BODNER. Pol.: BEDNARZ. Ukr.: BONDAR. Hung.: BODNÁR.

Buxtehude German: habitation name from a town so called SW of Hamburg, which apparently gets its name (earlier *Bucstede*) from a Gmc personal name, *Bucc* (see BUCK 1) + MLG *stede* homestead, place (see STEAD 1).

The name is chiefly famous as that of the composer and organist Dietrich Buxtehude *(1637–1707), who was born in Holstein, but whose family came from this place in the early 16th cent.*

Buxton English: 1. habitation name from *Buxton* in Derbys., which in ME was called *Buchestanes, Bucstones* (i.e. 'bowing stones', from ME *b(o)ugen*, OE *būgan* to bow + *stanes* stones). It probably gets its name from logan stones in the vicinity. (Logan stones are boulders so poised that they rocked at a touch.)

2. less commonly, a habitation name from *Buxton* in Norfolk, which gets its name from the gen. case of the OE personal name *Bucc* (see BUCK 1) + OE *tūn* settlement, enclosure.

Vars.: **Buckston(e)**.

Buzek Czech: from a dim. of the Czech personal name *Budislav*, composed of the elements *budi-* to awaken, inspire + *slav* glory, or of any other personal name containing *budi-* as the first element.

Vars.: **Bouzek, Bušek; B(o)uda, Budek, Budík, Budil**.

Byatt English: topographic name for someone who lived near a gate, from ME *by* by, beside (OE *bī*) + *yat(e)* gate (OE *geat*).

Bye English: topographic name for someone who lived near a bend in a river, from OE *byge* bend (a deriv. of *būgan*; cf. BUXTON 1).

Vars.: **By, Buy(e)**.

Byers N English and Scots: topographic name for someone who lived by a cattleshed, ME, OE *bȳre*, or habitation name from a place so named, e.g. *Byers* Green in Co. Durham or *Byres* near Edinburgh.

Vars.: **Byres, Biers**.

Byfield English: 1. habitation name from a place, for example in Northants, so called from OE *byge* bend (see BYE) + *feld* pasture, open country.

2. topographic name for somone who lived near a patch of open land, from ME *by* by, beside (OE *bī*) + *fe(i)ld(e)* open country.

Byford English: 1. habitation name from a place so named from OE *byge* bend (see BYE) + *ford* FORD. There is one such on the Wye near Hereford.

2. topographic name for someone who lived by a ford, from ME *by* by, beside (OE *bī*) + *ford*. The surname is found chiefly in Essex.

Bygrave English: topographic name for someone whose home was by a (defensive) ditch or dike, from ME *by* by, beside (OE *bī*) + *grave* ditch (OE **grafa*, a deriv. of *grafan* to dig), or a habitation name from *Bygrave* in Herts.

Vars.: **Bygraves, Bigrave(s)**.

Byrne Irish: Anglicized form of Gael. **Ó Broin** 'descendant of *Bran*', a personal name probably from *bran* raven. Bran was the name of a son of the King of Leinster, who died at Cologne in 1052.

Vars.: **O'Byrne, (O')Be(i)rne, Byrnes**, BURNS.

Byron English: from OE *bȳrum* 'at the cattle sheds', dat. pl. of *bȳre* byre, and thus a topographic name for one living at such a place or occupational name for one employed there, a cowman. This name and its vars. *Biron* and *Biram*, have occasionally been adopted as Jewish surnames, presumably as Anglicizations of Jewish names that cannot now be identified.

Vars.: **Biron, Byran, Byrom, Byram, Biram**.

The title of Baron Byron *was granted to John Byron (?1600–52), one of Charles I's officers in the Civil War. The family had been given its seat, at Newstead Abbey in Notts., by Henry VIII after the dissolution of the monasteries. The most famous member of the family is George Gordon Noel Byron, 6th Baron Byron (1788–1824), the poet. He inherited the title unexpectedly at the age of ten from his great-uncle, who had lived as a recluse at Newstead after killing his cousin in a scuffle: he was known as 'The Wicked Lord Byron'. The poet's grandfather, John Byron (1723–86), achieved fame as an admiral, nicknamed 'Foul Weather Jack': he wrote an account of his shipwreck on the shores of Patagonia, which was widely read in its day.*

Bytheway English: topographic name for one whose home was beside a main highway, from the ME phrase *bi the weie*. The surname is found mainly in the W Midlands.

Bywater 1. English: topographic name for someone living by a lake or river, from ME *by* by, beside (OE *bī*) + *water* water (OE *wæter*).

2. Irish: translation of *Ó Sruthāin* (see STROHANE).

Var.: **Bywaters**.

C

Cabaço Portuguese: nickname for a fat man or a heavy drinker, from Port. *cabaço* gourd (cogn. with Sp. *calabaza*, of uncertain, probably pre-Roman, origin).

Cabane Provençal: topographic name for someone who lived in a rough or temporary dwelling, from OProv. *cabane* hut, cabin (LL *capanna*, apparently of Celt. or Gmc origin). There are a number of places in France named with this word (and its vars. and derivs.), and the surname may also be a habitation name from any of these.
Vars.: **Caban(ne)**; **Chaban(n)e(s)** (Limoges, Auvergne); **Chavan(n)e(s)** (Poitou); **Cabanès, Cabanais**; **Cabanié, Chabanier, Chebanier**.
Cogns.: It.: **Cavan(n)a, Cavan(n)i**. Sp.: **Cabaña(s)**. Cat.: **Cabana(s), Cabanes**. Port.: **Cabana**.
Dims.: Prov.: **Cabanel, Chavanel, Chavaneau**; **Chabanet, Chabaneix**; **Cabanot**; **C(h)abanon, Chavenon**. Sp.: **Cabanillas, Cavanillas**.
Augs.: Prov.: **Chabanas, Chabanat**.

Cabello Spanish: nickname for a man with a particularly luxuriant growth of hair (or perhaps ironically for a bald man), from Sp. *cabello* hair (L *capillus*, a collective noun).
Var.: **Cabellos**.

Cabestany Catalan: topographic name for someone who lived at the head of a lake, from Cat. *cap* head, top (see Cap) + *estany* lake, pond. There is a place named with these elements in Rousillon, S France, which may be a partial source of the surname.
Var.: **Cavestany**.

Cabeza Spanish: habitation name from any of the numerous minor places so called from LL *capitia* head (a deriv. of class. L *caput*; cf. Cap), a frequent term for a small hill. In some case it may also have been a nickname for someone with a large or deformed head.
Vars.: **Cabezas**; **Cabezudo** (a nickname).
Cogn.: Port.: **Cabeça**.
Dim.: Sp.: **Cabezuelo**.
Aug.: Sp.: **Cabezón**.

Cable English: metonymic occupational name for a maker of rope, especially the type of stout rope used in maritime applications, from ANF *cable* cable (LL *capulum* halter, of Arabic origin, but associated by folk etymology with L *capere* to take, seize).
Var.: **Cabel**.

Cabot French: nickname for someone with a large head, or metonymic occupational name for a fisherman, from OF *cabot* miller's thumb, *Cottus gobio* (OProv. *cabotz*, from LL *capōceus*, a deriv. of *caput* head; cf. Cap).
Cogn.: It.: **Caboto**.
Dim.: Fr.: **Cabotin**.

Cabrera Spanish: habitation name from any of various minor places so called from LL *caprāria* 'place of goats' (a deriv. of *caper* goat; cf. Cheever).

Cáceres Spanish: habitation name from a city in W Spain, whose name apparently derives, via Arabic *Al-Cazires*, from L *castra Cereris* 'town of *Ceres*', the Roman goddess of agricultural prosperity, who had a temple there.

Cadbury English: habitation name from places in Somerset and Devon, so called from the OE personal name *Cada* (see Cade 1) + OE *burh* fortress, town (see Bury), here referring to prehistoric hill-forts.

Caddock 1. Welsh: from the OW personal name *Cadoc*, which is possibly a dim. of the Celt. element reflected in W *cad* battle (cf. Cadell), or else a pet form of *Cadfael*.
2. English: nickname for a frail or infirm person or a sufferer from epilepsy, from ME, OF *caduc* (LL *cadūcus*, a deriv. of *cadere* to fall).
Var. (of 1): **Caddick** (chiefly W Midlands).
Dims. (of 1): **Cadwgan, Cadogan**; Duggan.
The Earls Cadogan *are said to be descended from the ancient princes of Wales, including* Cadwgan (*d. 1112*). *They were later found in Somerset, and became established in Ireland when William Cadogan (1601–61) was appointed governor of Trim*, *Co. Meath*.

Cade English: 1. from a ME given name, *Cade*, a survival of the OE personal name or byname *Cada*, which is apparently from a Gmc root meaning 'lump', 'swelling'; it may have been applied to a fat person.
2. metonymic occupational name for a cooper, from ME, OF *cade* cask, barrel (of Gmc origin, probably akin to the root mentioned in 1).
3. nickname for a gentle or inoffensive person, from ME *cade* domestic animal, pet (of unknown origin).
Var.: **Cadd**.
'Servant of C.': **Cadman**.

Cadel Provençal: 1. nickname for a playful person, from OProv. *cadel* puppy (L *catulus*).
2. status name for a chieftain or village elder, OProv. *capdel* (LL *capitelum*, a dim. of *caput*; see Cap).

Cadell British: from an OW personal name derived from the Celt. element reflected in W *cad* battle. The surname is found in Scotland and Ireland, and also in Wales where the given name was popular in the Middle Ages as a result of the fame of Cadell ab Urien, a 7th-cent. saint who founded the chapel of Llangadell 'church of Cadell', in Glamorgan.
Vars.: **Caddel(l), Cattell, Cadle**.

Cadena Catalan and Spanish: metonymic occupational name for a maker of chains, or perhaps for a gaoler, from Sp. *cadena* chain (L *catēna*). The sing. *Cadena* is rare as a surname in Castile, but frequent in Catalonia; the pl. **Cadenas** occurs in both regions but is more frequent in the former.

Cadillac French: habitation name from a place in Gironde, so called from the Gallo-Roman personal name *Catilius* (probably a Latinized form of a Celt. deriv. of the element *cad* battle; cf. Cadell) + the local suffix *-ācum*.
Vars.: **Cadilhac**; **Cadilhon, Cadilhou** ('man from C.').

Cadiou 1. Provençal: nickname from a favourite oath, OProv. *cap* head (see Cap) + *Diou* God (L *deus*).
2. N French: from a Bret. personal name, a dim. formation from the Celt. element *cad* battle (cf. Cadell).
Vars.: **Cadioux, Cadio(t)**. (Of 1 only): **Cadéo, Cadieu**.

Cadwallader Welsh: from a given name composed of the elements *cad* battle + *gwaladr* leader.

Cage English: metonymic occupational name for a maker and seller of small cages for animals or birds, or a keeper of the large public cage in which petty criminals were confined for short periods of imprisonment. The name is from ME, OF *cage* cage, enclosure (L *cavea* container, cave, from *cavus* hollow; cf. CAVE 1).

Vars.: **Cadge; Ca(i)ger.**

Dims.: Fr.: **Cajet, Cajot, Cajel(ot).** Prov.: **Caujol(le).**

Cagney Irish: Anglicized form of Gael. **Ó Caingnigh** 'descendant of *Caingneach*', a personal name meaning 'Pleader', or a byname for a contentious person.

Cahill Irish: Anglicized form of Gael. **Ó Cathail** 'descendant of *Cathal*', a personal name composed of the proto-Celt. elements *cad* battle + *valos* powerful, mighty.

Var.: **O'Cahill.**

Cail French: 1. nickname for a timid or stupid person, or metonymic occupational name for a catcher of quails, from OF *caille* quail (L *quaccula*; cf. QUAIL 1).

2. in Normandy and Picardy, normally a topographic name for someone who lived on a patch of stony soil, from ONF *cail(ou)* pebble, stone (of Celt. origin).

3. in S France, a metonymic occupational name for a dairy worker, from OProv. *cail* curds (L *coagulum*, from *coagulāre* to congeal).

Vars.: **Caill.** (Of 1 only): **Lacaille.** (Of 2 and 3): **Caillier.** (Of 3 only): **Couaillier.**

Dims. (of 1): **Caillette.** (Of 2): **Cailloux, Caillouet; Chaillou(x), Chaillouet, Chaillot, Chaillet.** (Of 3): **Calhau; Caill(i)ot, Caill(e)aux, Cailleteau, Cailleton, Caillotin; Couaillet.**

Augs.: Fr.: **Caill(i)at.**

Pej.: Fr.: **Caillard.**

Cain English: 1. nickname for a tall, thin man, from ME, OF *cane* cane, reed (L *canna*). It is also possibly a topographic name for someone who lived in a damp area overgrown with reeds, or a metonymic occupational name for someone who gathered reeds, which were widely used in the Middle Ages as a floor covering and for weaving small baskets.

2. Norman habitation name from the town of *Caen* in Calvados, Normandy, named with the Gaul. elements *catu* battle + *magos* field, plain.

3. Manx: var. of COYNE 2 and 3.

Vars.: **Ca(i)ne, Kain(e), Ka(y)ne**; see also KEYNES.

Cogns. (of 1): Sp.: **Caña(s), Cañero.** Port.: **Canas.** (Of 2): Fr.: **Caen, Ducaen.**

Dims. (of 1): Cat.: **Cañellas.** Port.: **Canelas.**

Collectives (of 1): Fr.: CANET. Sp.: **Cañada(s), Cañete, Cañizares.**

Caird Scots: occupational name from Gael. *ceard* craftsman, tinker.

Patrs.: **McNecaird, McNokerd, McNakard** (Gael. **Mac na Ceardadh**).

Cairnduff Scots and N Irish: habitation name from a minor place named as the 'black cairn', from Gael. *carn* (see CAIRNS) + *dubh* black (see DUFF). Most examples probably derive from the lands of *Carnduff* in the old lordship of Avondale.

Var.: **Carnduff.**

Cairns Scots: topographic name for someone who lived by a cairn, i.e. a pile of stones raised as a boundary marker or a memorial, from Gael. *carn* cairn. The surname comes mainly, if not exclusively, from lands in the parish of Mid-Calder, Lothian.

Vars.: **Carn(e)s**, CARNE.

This is the name of an ancient Scottish family, holding the title Earl Cairns. *An ancestor, William* de Carnys, *was granted two baronies by David II in 1363.*

Cakebread English: metonymic occupational name for a baker who specialized in fancy breads, from ME *cake* flat loaf made from fine flour (ON *kaka*) + *bread* bread (OE *brēad*).

Calabria Italian: regional name for someone from the region of this name in SW Italy. The surname and its vars. may also in part have been originally nicknames, for in the Trentine dialect the Calabrians are a byword for craft and guile, in the Abruzzi for high living, and in Naples for coarse boorishness.

Vars.: **Calabri, Calabro; Calabresi, Calabrese.**

Cogn.: Jewish (Sefardic): **Kalavrez.**

Calado Portuguese: nickname for a silent or reserved person, from Port. *calado*, past part. of *calar* to be silent (LL *callāre*, from Gk).

Calatayud Spanish: habitation name from a place in the province of Saragossa, so called from Arabic *qala(t)* fortress, castle (see ALCALÁ) + the personal name *Ayub* (an Arabic form of JOB).

Caldas Portuguese: habitation name from any of various minor places so called, from Port. *caldas*, fem. pl. form of *caldo* hot (L *calidus*, from *calēre* to be hot). Some word such as *fontes* springs or *águas* waters has been lost.

Calder 1. Scots: habitation name from any of the various places called *Calder*, *Caldor*, or *Cawdor*. Calder in Thurso is recorded in the early 13th cent. in the form *Kalfadal* and gets its name from ON *kalf* calf + *dalr* valley. The others are of more problematic origin; they seem to derive from river names, perhaps the same as in 2 below, or from ON *kaldr* cold (cf. CALDICOTT), or from Gael. *call* hazel + *dobhar* water.

2. English: habitation name from *Calder* in Cumb., named from the river on which it stands. This is probably a Brit. name, from ancestors of W *caled* hard, harsh, violent + *dwfr* water, stream.

Vars.: **Caulder, Cau(l)dor, Caldor.**

The earliest known bearer of the name in Scotland is Hugh de Kaldouer, *who witnessed various charters in the late 12th cent.*

Calderon English, French, and Jewish (Sefardic): metonymic occupational name for a tinker or maker of large cooking vessels, from OF *cauderon* cauldron (L *caldārium* hot bath).

Vars.: Eng.: **Cauldron, Cowdron, Coldron.** Fr.: **Chaudron, Codron.** Jewish: **Kalderon.**

Cogns.: Sp.: **Calderón; Caldero, Caldera.** Port.: **Caldeira.** Prov.: **Caldairou(x), Caldayrou(x), Caldeyroux.** It.: **Calderone, Calterone, Caldroni; Caldaro.**

Dims.: Fr.: **Chaudret, Chaudrelle; Jodrellec** (Brittany). It.: **Calderonello.**

Calderwood Scots: habitation name from a place in the former county of Lanarks. (now part of Strathclyde region), so called from the river name CALDER + ME *wood* WOOD.

The first known bearer of the name is Isabele de Calrewode *of Lanarks., who rendered homage to Edward II of England in 1296.*

Caldicott English: habitation name from any of the numerous places (in Beds., Berks., Cambs., Ches., Northants, Warwicks., and elsewhere), mostly spelled *Caldecote*, which get their names from OE *c(e)ald* cold + *cot* cottage, dwelling (see COATES). It has been suggested that the OE expression *calde cot* denoted an unattended shelter for wayfarers, although in fact some places with this name were of considerable status by 1086, when they appear in Domesday Book. The surname is most common in the W Midlands. Some examples of the contracted forms listed below may come from *Calcutt* in Wilts., *Collacott(s)* in Devon, or a lost *Calcot* in Berks., in all of which the first element apparently comes from the OE personal name *Cola* (see COLE 2) or the vocab. word *col* (char)coal, in which case the meaning would be something like 'coal-shed'.

Vars.: **Caldicot, Caldecot(t), Caldecourt, Callicot, Cal(l)cott, Calcut(t), Caulcutt, Caulkett, Cawcutt, Corcut, Corkett, Corkitt, Coldicott, Colicot, Collacot(t), Collecott, Collicutt, Colcot(t), Colcut(t), Colkett, Colocott, Chaldcott, Chalcot.**

Caldwell English, Scots, and N Irish: habitation name from any of several places in England and Scotland, variously spelled, that get their names from OE *c(e)ald* cold + *well(a)* spring, stream (see WELL). Caldwell in N Yorks. is one major source of the surname; Caldwell in the former county of Renfrews. in Scotland (now part of Strathclyde region) another.

Vars.: **Calwell, Cau(l)dwell, Caudell, Caudle, Cawdell; Cowdell; Cadwell, Cardwell, Cou(l)dwell, Chadwell, Cholwell.**

Calendri Italian: nickname from the lark, OIt. *calendra* (L *calendula*). The bird was noted for its fine voice and early rising, but was also widely believed to be very stupid, so that in a number of cases the nickname may have denoted a vague or credulous man (cf. ALAUZE).

Var.: **Calendra.**

Cogn.: Prov.: **Calandre.**

Dims.: It.: **Calandrino, Calandrini.** Prov.: **Calandreau, Calendreau.**

Pej.: Prov.: **Calandraud.**

Calero Spanish: occupational name for a quarryman or a lime-burner, Sp. *calero*, an agent deriv. of *cal* lime, chalk (L *calx*; cf. CHAUSSÉE).

Cogn.: Port.: **Caeiro.**

Calf English: from the ON personal name *Kalfr*, originally a byname meaning 'Calf', or possibly from OE *calf*, Anglian form of *cealf* calf, used either as a nickname or as a metonymic occupational name for someone who was responsible for tending calves.

Var.: **Callf.**

Cogns.: Ger.: **Kalb; Kälberer, Kelberer.** Low Ger., Flem., Du.: **Kalf.** Jewish (Ashkenazic): **Kalb; Kelberman** (reasons for adoption as a surname uncertain).

Dims.: Ger.: **Kälble, Kelble** (Swabian).

Calladine English (Notts.): of unknown origin. It is conceivably a var. of CARWARDINE.

Callaghan Irish: Anglicized form of Gael. **Ó Ceallacháin** 'descendant of *Ceallachán*', a dim. of the personal name *Ceallach* 'Contention', 'Strife'. This name was borne by a 10th-cent. king of Munster, from whom many present-day bearers of the surname claim descent.

Vars.: **O'Calla(g)han, Callahan, Calligan, (O')Kelaghan, Kealahan.**

Callan 1. Irish: Anglicized form of Gael. **Ó Cathaláin** 'descendant of *Cathalán*', a personal name representing a dim. of *Cathal*; see CAHILL.

2. Scots: Anglicized form of Gael. **Mac Ailin**, patr. from an old Gael. personal name derived from *ail* rock; cf. ALLEN.

Vars.: **Callen, Callin.** (Of 1 only): **Cahalan(e).** (Of 2 only): **McCallan.**

Callander 1. English: occupational name for a person who gave a smooth finish to freshly woven cloth by passing it between heavy rollers to compress the weave. The Eng. term for such a worker, *calander*, is from OF *calandrier*, *calandreur*, from the verb *calandrer*. The origin of this verb is by no means certain, but it seems likely that it comes from LL **colendrāre*, a deriv. of **colendra* roller (Gk *kylindros*, from *kylindesthai* to roll; the fem. gender of the L word could have arisen by confusion with *columna* column).

2. Scots: habitation name from either of two places so called, near Falkirk and Perth. The original form and meaning of both placenames is unclear, but it is certain that they were once distinct, later falling together through the accident of having the same lords—the Livingstones, Earls of Linlithgow.

Vars.: **Cal(l)endar, Callender.**

The first known bearer of the name in Scotland is Alwyn de Calyntyr, *who witnessed a document* c.*1248 and was probably related to the Earls of Lennox.*

Calle Spanish: topographic name for someone who lived beside a narrow path or a cattle track, Sp. *calle* (L *callis*). In mod. Sp. this is the normal word for a street, but at the time when surnames were being formed it referred to something rather more modest.

Var.: **Calles.**

Dims.: **Calleja(s), Callejo.**

Callegaro Italian: occupational name for a maker of footwear and leggings, from an agent deriv. of It. *callega* shoe (L *caliga* military boot).

Vars.: **Callegari, Calegari; Cal(l)igari, Calgari, Cal(li)garo, Cal(l)iari, Cagliari, Calligher, Callegher** (Venetia); **Galliga(r)i** (Tuscany); **Cal(l)(i)eri, Caliero, Callero, Caglieri, Cagliero** (NW Italy).

Dims.: **Callegarin(i), Cagliarotti, Caglierotti, Callierotti.**

Patrs.: **Cal(le)garis, Caligaris, Caglieris.**

Callot French: metonymic occupational name for a hatter, or nickname for a man given to wearing unusual headgear, from OF *callot*, a dim. of OF *cale* hat, head-dress (a word for which various more or less fanciful etymologies have been suggested).

Vars.: **Calot, Cal(l)et, Calon.**

Callow 1. English: habitation name from any of several places so called, esp. in Derbys. Most get their names from OE *calu* bare, bald (i.e. bald-topped hill), often with the addition of *hlāw* hill. In some cases, e.g. the places by Wirksworth and by Hathersage, Derbys., the etymology is OE *cald* cold + *hlāw*. Calow by Chesterfield is from *calu* + *healh* nook (see HALE).

2. English: of uncertain origin, introduced into England via Sussex from Bordeaux in the mid-13th cent., and subsequently established in Norfolk. It may be a var. of CALLOWAY, but could equally well be from the Dutch or Flemish nickname *de Caluwe* 'the bald one' (see KAHL), which could have been taken to Bordeaux by Dutch or Flemish traders.

3. Manx: Anglicized form of Gael. **Mac Caolaidhe**, a patr. from the personal name *Caoladhe*, a deriv. of *caol* slender, comely.

Vars.: **Callowe, Calow(e), Caloe.** (Of 3 only): CAYLEY.

The name is most common in Derbys., with smaller concentrations in Devon and Worcs. There is also a Norfolk family of this name, whose earliest recorded ancestor is Nicholas de Kalewe (*1286*), *who appears to have come there via Sussex from Bordeaux*.

Calloway English (Norman): habitation name from *Caillouet*-Orgeville in Eure, so called from a collective of ONF *cail(ou)* pebble (see CAIL 2).

Vars.: **Callaway, Calway, Kellaway, Kel(le)way.**

Calnan Irish: Anglicized form of Gael. **Ó Callanáin** 'descendant of *Callanán*', a personal name of uncertain origin.

Vars.: **Callanan, Callinan.**

Calver English: habitation name from *Calver* in Derbys., so called from OE *c(e)alf* CALF + *ofer* ridge. There may have been some confusion with CALVERT and absorption by CARVER.

Calverley English: habitation name from *Calverley* in W Yorks., so called from OE *c(e)alfra*, gen. pl. of *c(e)alf* CALF + *lēah* wood, clearing; or from *Calverleigh* in Devon, so called from OE *calu(w)* bare, bald (see CALLOW 1) + *wudu* wood + *lēah*.

Calvert English: occupational name for a tender of cattle, from ME *calfhirde*, from OE (Anglian) *calf* CALF + *hierde* herdsman (see HEARD). The surname is now most common in N and NE England and in N Ireland.

Vars.: **Calverd, Calvard.**

Camacho Spanish: of uncertain origin. The surname seems to have originated in Andalusia and is now also very common in Portugal. It was probably originally a nickname for a lame or bowlegged person, and is probably akin to the Celt. element *camb-* bent (cf. CAMPBELL).

Camber English: occupational name from an agent deriv. of OE *camb* comb, referring perhaps to a maker or seller of combs, or to someone who used them in disentangling wool or flax. This was an alternative process to carding, and caused the wool fibres to lie more or less parallel to one another, so that the cloth produced had a hard, smooth finish without nap.

Vars.: **Cammer**; **Com(b)er** (see also COOMBE); **Lecomber**; **Camb**; **Kember**; **Kempster** (in origin a fem. form).

Cogns.: Ger.: **Kammer, Kämm(l)er, Kemm(l)er** (see also CHAMBERS). Jewish (Ashkenazic): **Kemelman** (occupational, from Yid. *keml* comb).

Camden English: of uncertain origin, possibly a habitation name from Chipping *Campden* and Broad *Campden* in Gloucs., although the loss of the *-p-* is not easily explained. These derive their names from OE *campas* enclosure (from L *campus* plain) + *denu* valley (see DEAN 1).

Var.: **Cambden.**

Camel 1. English and French: nickname from the animal, ANF *came(i)l* (L *camēlus*, from Gk *kamēlos*, ultimately of Semitic origin; cf. Hebr. *gamal*). The surname may originally have denoted a clumsy or ill-tempered person. It may also be a house name for someone who lived at a house with a sign depicting a camel.

2. English: from an assimilated pronunciation of CAMPBELL.

Vars.: **Cam(m)ell.**

Cogns. (of 1): Port.: **Camelo.** Ger.: **Kam(m)el.**

Cpds (ornamental, perhaps associated with the clothing trade): Jewish (Ashkenazic): **Kamelgarn** ('mohair', literally 'camel yarn'); **Kamelhar, Kamelhor** ('camlet' (a type of fabric), lit. 'camel hair'); **Kamelhorn** ('camel horn', ornamental).

Cameron Scots: 1. as a Highland clan name it represents a nickname from Gael. *cam* crooked, bent + *sròn* nose.

2. in the Lowlands it is normally a habitation name from any of various places so called, all of which show early forms such as *Cambrun*, and seem to be named from Gael. *cam* crooked, bent + *brun* hill (cf. BRYAN).

Camilo Portuguese: from the medieval given name *Camilo* (L *Camillus*, a Roman family name of Etruscan origin).

Camões Portuguese: habitation name for someone from *Camós* in Galicia, which is of uncertain etymology.

Var.: **Camoens.**

Camoys English (Norman): nickname from ME, ONF *cammus, camois* snub-nosed (OF *camus*, of obscure origin). Some early forms, such as Stephen *de Cameis* (Northants 1200) and Matillis *de Camois* (Surrey 1205) point to origin as a habitation name, but derivation from *Campeaux* in Calvados, Normandy, which has been proposed, is far from certain. The *de* in these instances may be purely honorific.

Vars.: **Cammis(h), Camis, Cam(o)us, Keemish, Kemmis.**

Cogns.: Fr.: **Camus, Lecamus.** It.: **Camus(ci)o, Camozzi.**

Dims.: Fr.: **Camuset, Camuzet, Camuseau, Camuzeau.** It.: **Camozzini.**

Augs.: Fr.: **Camus(s)at, Camuzat.**

Pej.: Fr.: **Camard.**

A family by the name of Kemmis *can be traced to Ralph* de Kammeys, *who was granted lands by the Earl of Pembroke in 1246*.

Campbell Scots: nickname from Gael. *cam* crooked, bent + *beul* mouth. This nickname was first borne by Gillespie Ó Duibhne, who lived at the beginning of the 13th cent. and was the founder of the clan Campbell. The surname was often rendered in L documents as *de bello campo* 'of the fair field', which led to the name sometimes being retranslated into Norman French as BEAUCHAMP.

Vars.: **Cambell, Camble**; see also CAMEL.

Campion English (Norman) and French: 1. occupational name for a professional champion, esp. as an agent employed to represent one of the parties in a trial by combat, a method of settling disputes current in the Middle Ages. The word comes from ANF *campion, campiun* (LL *campio*, gen. *campiōnis*, a deriv. of *campus* plain, field of battle).

2. habitation name from *Compiègne* in Oise, Picardy, so called from L *compendium* shortcut, abridgement (a deriv. of *compendere* to weigh together).

Var. (of 1): **Champion.**

Cogn. (of 1): It.: **Campione.**

Dim. (of 1): Fr.: **Championnet.**

A family of this name in Witham, Essex, are descended from Nicole de Campion, *who accompanied Robert II, Duke of Normandy, on the First Crusade (1096–99). One member of this family was Edmund* Campion (*1540–81*), *the English Jesuit who was executed for treason and is now venerated as a saint by Roman Catholics*.

Campling English: metonymic occupational name for a maker or seller of camel-hair cloth, or perhaps a nickname for a wearer, from ANF *camelin* (L *camēlīnus*, a deriv. of *camēlus* CAMEL).

Var.: **Camplin.**

Cogns.: Fr.: **Camelin.** It.: **Camellini.**

Canavan Irish: Anglicized form of Gael. **Ó Ceanndubháin** 'descendant of *Ceanndubhán*', a byname meaning 'little black-headed one', from *ceann* head + *dubh* black + the dim. suffix *-án*.

Vars.: **Cannavan, Kinavan, O'Can(n)avan, O'Cannovane, O'Kennavain.** See also WHITEHEAD.

Candelario Spanish: nickname from the Catholic feast of the Purification of the Virgin, given perhaps to someone born on this day of the year (2 February) or having some other association with it. The name derives from L *candela* candle (cf. CHANDLER), since on this day candles were blessed by a priest and then lit to invoke the protection of the Virgin Mary (cf. the English word for this feast day, *Candlemas*).

Cogns.: It.: **Candeloro, Candiloro** (from L *(festa) candelorum* 'feast of candles').

Cândido Portuguese: nickname for someone with white hair, from Port. *cândido* (shining) white (L *candidus*, a deriv. of *candēre* to be white). In Port. the word also came to mean 'innocent', 'simple', and the surname may in many cases originally have had this sense.

Canet 1. French: metonymic occupational name for a maker or seller of jugs, from OF *canet* jug, pitcher (apparently a dim. of *canne* reed, and not related to OE *canna* can).

2. French: nickname from a dim. of OF *can* duck (of uncertain, possibly imitative, origin).

3. Provençal and Catalan: habitation name from any of various places so called. Most seem to get their names from L *can(n)ētum*, a collective of *canna* reed (cf. CAIN 1), but in a few cases the name may go back to a pre-Roman element *kan-* height, hill.

Canham English: habitation name representing a contracted form of *Cavenham*, Suffolk, so called from the gen. case of the OE byname *Cāfa* 'Bold', 'Active' (cf. CAVENDISH) + OE *hām* homestead.

Cann English: habitation name from a place in Dorset, so called from OE *canna* can, used in a transferred sense of a deep valley. Alternatively, it may be a topographic name from the same word used elsewhere in SW England.

Var.: **Canner**.

Canning 1. English: habitation name from a place in Wilts. called *Cannings*, apparently from OE *Caningas* 'people of *Cana*', a byname of uncertain origin.

2. Irish: var. of CANNON 2.

Cannon 1. English: nickname from ME *canun* canon, a clergyman living with others in a clergy house (ONF *canonie*, *canoine* (from LL *canōnicus*, a deriv. of *canōn* rule, discipline, from Gk *kanōn* rule, measure), which completely absorbed the OE form *canonic* from the same L source). Most early bearers of the name were serfs who perhaps gained the name from a certain dignity of bearing, or as the result of a now irrecoverable anecdote.

2. Irish: Anglicized form of Gael. **Ó Canáin** 'descendant of *Canán*', a personal name derived from *cana* wolf-cub.

3. Manx and Irish: Anglicized form of Gael. **Mac Canannáin** 'son of *Canannán*', a personal name of uncertain origin, perhaps a double dim. of *cana*.

Vars. (of 1): **Canon, Cannan, Canaan**; CHANNON. (Of 2): **(O')Cannan, O'Cannon**, CANNING. (Of 3): **McCanon**.

Cogns. (of 1): Fr.: **Canon(n)e; Chanoine**. Prov.: **Canourge, Canonge**. It.: **Canonico, Canonici, Canonaco**. Sp.: **Calonge**.

Patr. (from 1): Eng.: **Cannons**.

Caño Spanish: topographic name for someone who lived near an underground passage or cave, Sp. *caño* (of uncertain origin; probably derived from L *canna* reed (cf. CAIN 1), although the semantic development is not clear).

Cant English and Scots: metonymic occupational name for a singer in a chantry, or nickname for a person who sang a lot, from ONF *cant* song (OF *chant*; cf. CHANSON).

Vars.: **Caunt** (chiefly E Midlands); **Chant; C(h)anter, Cantor** (see also KANTOR).

Dims.: **Canty, Cantie** (Scotland).

A family by the name of Cant, *who held land at Masterton, near Dunfermline, are descended from Flemish cloth merchants of the 15th cent. The German philosopher Immanuel* **Kant** *(1724–1804) was the grandson of a Scots immigrant to Königsberg, where he lived all his life.*

Cantalejo Spanish: habitation name from a place in the province of Segovia, so called from Sp. *cantal* rocky place (see CANTO) + the dim. or pej. suffix *-ejo*.

Cantarero Spanish: occupational name for a potter, Sp. *cantarero*, an agent deriv. of *cántaro* jug, pitcher (LL *cantarus*, from Gk *kanthēros*).

Cantellow English (Norman): habitation name from any of a number of places in Normandy, such as *Canteleu* in Seine-Maritime or *Canteloup* in Calvados, so called from ONF *cante(r)* to sing (L *cantāre*, freq. of *canere*) + *lou*, *leu* wolf (L *lupus*) or the fem. *loup* (L *lupa*; cf. LOVE 2). These appear originally to have been grimly humorous names denoting settlements where the wolves could be heard howling in the uncleared woods around the settlement; cf. CHANTERAINE.

Vars.: **Cantel(l)o, Cantlow**.

Cogns.: Fr.: **Cantelue, Canteloup, Canteloube; Chantalou(p), Chantelouve**. It.: **Cantalupo**.

Canto Spanish and Portuguese: 1. topographic name for someone who lived on a patch of stony ground or near a quarry, or metonymic occupational name for a quarryman or mason, from Sp., Port. *canto* stone (of uncertain, probably pre-Roman, origin).

2. topographic name for someone who lived on the corner of a street, Sp., Port. *canto* (L *cantus*, rim, edge (of a wheel)).

Vars.: **Cantos**. (Of 1 only): **Cantera** (habitation name); **Cantero** (occupational name).

Cogn. (of 2): Cat.: CANTÓ.

Cantó Catalan: 1. topographic name for someone who lived on the corner of a street, a cogn. of CANTO 2.

2. from a medieval given name of uncertain origin; it appears in the L form *Cantonus* in early Hispanic inscriptions.

Cantwell English: apparently a habitation name from an unidentified place, perhaps so called from the OE personal name **Cant(a)* + *well(a)* spring, stream (see WELL). The surname is fairly common in Ireland as well as England.

Var.: **Cantle**.

Cap Provençal: nickname for a person with something distinctive about his head, from OProv. *cap* head (L *caput*). The word was often used in the metaphorical sense 'chief', 'principal', and the surname may also have denoted a leader or a village elder. In some cases it may also be a topographic name from the same word used in the sense of a promontory or headland.

Cogns.: Fr.: **Chef, Ché**. It.: **Capo** (Venetia, Naples); **Caputo, Caputi** (S Italy). Sp.: **Cabo**.

Augs.: It.: **Capone, Caponi** (S Italy, esp. Naples; see also CAPON).

Pejs.: Fr.: **Capard, Capart**. It.: **Capasso, Capaccio**.

Caparròs Catalan: nickname for a person with a small head or limited intellect, from Cat. *cap* head (see CAP) + *arròs* (grain of) rice.

Capdevielle Provençal: topographic name for someone who lived at the top of a village, from OProv. *cap* head (see

CAP) + *de* of (L *de* from) + *vi(e)lle* village, settlement (see VILLE).

Vars.: **Capdeville, Chefdeville, Chédeville, Chavialle, Duchefdelaville.**

Cogn.: Cat.: **Capdevila.**

Capitaine French: status name from OF *capitaine* captain (LL *capitāneus* head, chief, principal, from *caput* head; cf. CAP). This title was used in various senses, for example of the master of a boat and as an official rank in the army.

Vars.: **Capita(i)n, Capitand, Capiten, Cabiten.**

Cogns.: Sp.: **Capitán.** It.: **Capitani; Capitanio, Capitaneo** (Venetia); **Cattaneo** (Liguria); **Cattanei** (Lombardy); **Cattano, Catta(g)ni** (Emilia). Du.: **Kaptei(j)n, Kapteyn.** Hung.: **Kapitán(y).**

Dims.: It.: **Capitanelli, Capitanucci; Capitanin** (Venetia).

Capon English and French: nickname from ME, OE *capun* capon, castrated cock (L *capo*, gen. *capōnis*), referring to a cuckold, or else a metonymic occupational name for someone who was engaged in raising poultry.

Vars.: **Cappon.** Fr. only: **Chap(p)on; Capou.**

Cogns.: It.: **Cap(p)one, Cap(p)oni** (see also CAP); **Cabo(n)i** (S Sardinia). Ger.: **Kapaun, Kappuhn; Kaphahn** (the product of folk etymology; see HAHN). Flem., Du.: **Cap(p)oen, Capuyn.**

Dims.: Fr.: **Chap(p)oneau, Chap(p)onet.**

Patrs.: Flem., Du.: **Cap(p)oens, Capuyns.**

Capper English: occupational name for a maker of caps and hats, or nickname for a wearer of some kind of noticeable headgear, from an agent deriv. of ME *cappe* cap, headgear (OE *cæp*, reinforced by ONF *cape*; cf. CHAPE).

Vars.: **Capp, Cape.**

Patrs.: **Capps, Capes.**

Capron English (Norman) and French: nickname for someone who wore a particularly distinctive head-dress, from ONF *caprun*, a dim. of *cape* (cf. CHAPE).

Vars.: Fr.: **Caperon, Chap(e)ron; Capronnier** (occupational name for a maker of headgear).

An English family by the name of Capron *trace their descent from William* Caperun, *who held lands at Shutlanger, Northants, in the 13th cent. In 1531 Thomas* Caprun *married into the Fitzhugh family, and his descendants adopted the surname* Fitzhugh.

Capstick English (Lancs. and Yorks.): apparently an occupational nickname for a woodcutter, from OF *coupe(r)* to cut (from *coup* cut, blow, LL *colaphus* blow, punch, from Gk) + ME *stikke* (OE *sticca*) stick or *stake* (OE *staca*) pin, stake. Cf. TALBOYS.

Vars.: **Capstack, Capstake, Copestake, Copestick.**

Carballo Spanish: topographic name for someone who lived by a conspicuous oak tree or in an oak wood, from the dial. term *carvallo* oak. This is also the name of several villages in Galicia and Asturias, and so the surname may also be a habitation name from any of these.

Vars.: **Caraballo, Carbajo.**

Cogn.: Port.: **Carvalho.**

Collectives: Sp.: **Car(a)bajal, Car(a)vajal(es); Carballedo, Carballeda.** Port.: **Carvalhal; Carvalheira.**

Carberry 1. Scots: habitation name from a place in the parish of Inveresk, Lothian, first recorded in the form *Crebarrin*, from Gael. *craobh* tree + *barran* hedge.

2. Irish: Anglicized form of Gael. **Ó Cairbre** and **Mac Cairbre** 'descendant' and 'son of *Cairbre*', a byname perhaps meaning 'Charioteer'.

Vars. (of 2): **Carb(e)ry.**

Carbonell English (Norman), French, and Catalan: nickname for a man with dark hair or swarthy complexion, from a dim. of ANF, OF, OCat. *carbon* charcoal (L *carbo*, gen. *carbōnis*).

Vars.: Eng.: **Charbonell, Shrapnel.** Fr.: **Carbon(n)el, Carboneau; Charbonel, Charbonneau(x); Cherbonneau** (a hypercorrected form); **Charbonnet.** Cat.: **Carbó.**

Cogns.: It.: **Carbone; Carbonelli; Carbonetti, Carbonin(i).**

Carceller Catalan: occupational name for a gaoler (LL *carcellārius*, a deriv. of *carcer* gaol).

Carcopino Italian: habitation name from a place in Sarrola, Corsica, apparently so called from *carcare* to load (LL *carricāre*, from *carricus* waggon; cf. CARRIER) + *pino* pine tree (L *pīnus*), although the exact meaning of this compound is not clear. The surname is also relatively common in France.

Card English: metonymic occupational name for someone who carded wool, from ME, OF *card(e)* instrument for untangling wool (OProv. *carda*, a deriv. of *cardar* to card, from L *cārere*, an ultimate cogn. of Eng. *shear*, crossed with *card(e)* thistle; cf. CARDING).

Vars.: **Carde; Carder.**

Cárdenas Spanish: habitation name from places in the provinces of Almería and Logroño, so called from the fem. pl. form of Sp. *cárdeno* blue or blueish purple (LL *cardinus*, from *carduus* thistle; cf. CARDING). Presumably the noun *tierras* 'lands' is to be understood, and the reference is to land covered with bluish plants, e.g. thistles themselves or vines.

Cardew Cornish and English: habitation name from places so called in the parishes of Trevalga and Warbstow, Cornwall, and in Cumb. All are of Celt. origin, from the elements *ker* fort (cf. W *caer*) + *du* dark, black.

Vars.: **Carthew** (from places in the parishes of St Issey, St Austell, Wendron, and Madron, Cornwall, which show a mutated form (*dhu*) of the adj.), **Cardy.**

Cardinal English and French: nickname from ME, OF *cardinal* cardinal, the church dignitary (L *cardinālis*, originally an adj. meaning 'crucial', 'vital', from *cardo*, gen. *cardinis*, door-hinge). The surname could perhaps also have denoted a servant who worked in a cardinal's household, but far more often it was bestowed on someone who habitually dressed in red or who had played the part of a cardinal in a pageant, or on one who acted in a lordly and patronizing manner, like a prince of the Church.

Vars.: Eng.: **Cardinall, Cardnell,** CARNELL. Fr.: **Cardinau(x), Cardenal.**

Cogns.: It.: **Cardinali, Cardinale.** Sp.: **Cardenal.** Port.: **Cardeal.** Ger.: **Kardinal.** Flem.: **Kardinael.**

Dim.: It.: **Cardinaletti.**

Patr.: Du.: **Cardinaels.**

Carding English: topographic name for someone who lived on a patch of land overgrown with thistles, from ONF *cardon* thistle (a dim. of *carde*, from L *carduus*). It may also have been an occupational name for someone involved in the carding of wool, originally carried out with thistles and teasels; perhaps also a nickname for a prickly and unapproachable person.

Vars.: **Carden** (see also CARWARDINE), **Cardon.**

Cogns.: Fr.: **Chard(r)on, Lechardon; Cardon** (Normandy, Picardy). Prov.: **Cardou(x).** It.: **Cardone, Cardoni.** Port.: **Cardo; Cardoso** (habitation name); **Cardoeiro, Cardante** (occupational names).

Dims.: Fr.: **Chardon(n)et, Chardonnot, Chardenot, Chardon(n)el, Chardon(n)eau.**

Collectives: Fr.: **Chardonnay, Chardonnière.**

Cardona Catalan: habitation name from a place in the province of Barcelona. Its name dates from the pre-Roman period and probably has the same origin as that of *Cortona* in Italy, but the meaning is unknown.

Careaga Spanish form of Basque **Kareaga**: topographic name for someone who lived on a patch of chalk soil, from Basque *kare* chalk, limestone + the local suffix *-aga*.

Carew Welsh: habitation name from any of various minor places in Wales, so called from W *caer* fort + *rhiw* hill, slope, or just possibly from *caerau*, pl. of *caer* fort. It is also possible that the surname in some cases may derive from the cogn. Corn. *kerrow* (pl. of *ker*), which occurs seven times as a placename in Cornwall.

Var.: CAREY.

A Welsh family of this name trace their descent from William Fitzgerald (d. 1173), son of Gerald Fitzwalter. William's maternal grandfather was Tudor Mawr, Prince of S Wales, and from him the family inherited the castle of Carru *or* Carew *near Pembroke, from which they took their name. A sizeable branch of the family is established in Ireland.*

Carey 1. Welsh and Cornish: var. of CAREW.

2. English: habitation name from one of the minor places in Devon and Somerset so called from their situation on a river of this name, apparently from the Celt. root *car-* love, liking (cf. CRADDOCK), and meaning perhaps 'pleasant stream'. The same element is probably also to be seen in the Fr. river names *Cher* and *Chiers*, as well as the *Car* in Wales.

3. English (Norman): habitation name from the manor of *Carrey*, near Lisieux, Normandy, of uncertain etymology.

4. Irish: Anglicized form of Gael. **Ó Ciardha** 'descendant of *Ciardha*', a personal name derived from *ciar* dark, black.

Vars.: **Cary(e)**. (Of 4 only): **Keary, Keery**.

Carey *is the name of a family established for centuries in the parish of St Martin, Guernsey. Their earliest traceable ancestor was Jean* Careye, *who lived at St Martin in 1393, but the surname, in the form* Caree, *was recorded there in 1288. This is probably the Norman name (see 3 above).*

The Carey family who held the estate of Anthony in Cornwall throughout the Middle Ages seem to have received their name as a var. of CAREW.

Cargill Scots: habitation name from a place near Stanley on the Tay, apparently originally named as 'fort of the pledge', from ancient Brit. cogns. of OW *kaer* fort (cf. CARDEW) + *geall*, gen. *gill*, pledge, wager, tryst. The placename thus apparently commemorates some otherwise forgotten incident.

The first known bearer of the name is Walter de Kergyl, *who witnessed a document in 1260.*

Caritat Provençal: nickname for a kindly person, from OProv. *caritat* love, kindness, charity (L *cāritās*, gen. *cāritātis*, from *cārus* dear, beloved, a distant cogn. of the Celt. element mentioned in CAREY 2 above).

Cogn.: It.: **Caritato**.

Carless English (chiefly W Midlands): nickname for a carefree person, from OE *carlēas* (a cpd of *caru* grief, care + *lēas* free from, without).

Vars.: **Careless**; **Corless** (Lancs.); **Curless**.

Carlin 1. Irish (now also common in Scotland): Anglicized form of Gael. **Ó Cearbhalláin** 'descendant of *Cearbhallán*', a dim of the personal name *Cearbhall*; see CARROLL.

2. Jewish (E Ashkenazic): Anglicized spelling of KARLIN.

3. French: dim. of CHARLES.

Vars. (of 1): **Carolan**, CARLTON, CHARLTON.

Carlisle English: habitation name from the city in Cumb., in whose name Brit. *ker* fort (cf. CARDEW) has been compounded with the Romano-British name of the settlement, *Luguvalium*. The surname is now very common in N Ireland.

Vars.: **Carlile, Carlill, Carlyle**.

Carlton 1. English: habitation name from any of various places so called, from ON *karl* common man, peasant + OE *tūn* settlement; cf. CHARLTON 1. The places with *C-* rather than *Ch-* are in areas of Scandinavian settlement, mostly in N England.

2. Irish: var. of CARLIN 1.

Var.: **Carleton**.

Carlyon Cornish: habitation name from any of three places in Cornwall so called, in St Minver and Kea parishes. The first element is Brit. *ker* fort; the second could represent the plural of Corn. *legh* slab.

It has not been possible to trace bearers of this surname back genealogically beyond the 16th cent., when it was found almost exclusively within a small district of Cornwall. It is still found chiefly in Cornwall. The placename is found in 13th and 14th cent. records.

Carman 1. English: from an ON personal name *Kar(l)-maðr* (acc. *Kar(l)mann*), composed of the elements *karl* male, man (cf. CHARLES) + *maðr* man, person.

2. English and Flemish: occupational name for a carter, from ANF, MLG *car* cart (LL *carrus*; cf. CARRIER) + ME, MLG *man* man.

Var. (of 2): Flem.: **Carreman**.

Cogns. (of 2): Sp.: **Carro**.

Patr. (from 2): Flem.: **Carmans**.

Carmichael Scots: habitation name from *Carmichael* in the former county of Lanarks. (now part of Strathclyde region), from Brit. *ker* fort (cf. CARDEW) + the personal name MICHAEL.

Carmo Portuguese: from the medieval given name *Carmo*, from the Marian title *Maria do Carmo* 'Mary of Mt Carmel'. The epithet refers to a mountain range in the Holy Land extending southward from Haifa, and probably derived from Hebr. *kerem-el* God's vineyard. The range came to be inhabited by hermits in the early Christian centuries, and at the time of the Crusades they grew in number, becoming the order of Carmelite friars. The cult of Our Lady of Mt Carmel, their patron, was instituted in the 14th cent.

Related name: Jewish: **Karmeli** (Israeli, with the Hebr. ending *-i*).

Carmody Irish: Anglicized form of Gael. **Ó Cearmada** 'descendant of *Cearmaid*', a personal name of uncertain origin.

Carmona Spanish (now also very common in Portugal): habitation name from places in the provinces of Santander and (more famously) Seville. The placename is of pre-Roman origin and uncertain meaning.

Carne 1. Cornish: cogn. of CAIRNS.

2. French: Norman and Picard form of CHARME.

Vars. (of 2): **Carme, Ducarne, Ducarme**.

Carné French: nickname for a thin man or alternatively for a fat one. The surname derives from the OF past part. of the verb *charner* (Norman, Picard, and Prov. *carner*), from *c(h)ar* flesh, meat (L *caro*, gen. *carnis*). The verb was used in a variety of contradictory senses, as for example to strip flesh from the bone or to feed animals with meat, and it is from this that the ambiguity of the nickname arises.

Vars.: **Carnu(s)**, **Charnu(t)**.

Carnegie Scots: habitation name from a place near Carmyllie in the former county of Angus (now part of Tayside region), so called from Gael. *cathair an eige* fort at the gap or nick.

Var.: **Carnegy**.

The principal family of this name acquired the lands in question c.1340; previously they had been known as de Balinhard.

Carnell English: 1. apparently an occupational name for a crossbowman who specialized in fighting from the battlements of castles, from ANF *carnel* battlement, embrasure (a metathesized form of *crenel*, LL *crenellus*, a dim. of *crēna* notch; for the change of *-er-* to *-ar-* cf. MARCHANT).

2. contracted form of CARBONELL or CARDINAL.

Vars.: **Carnall**. (Of 1 only): **Crenel(l)**.

Carnero Spanish: nickname for a forceful or lusty person, or metonymic occupational name for a keeper of rams, from Sp. *carnero* ram (a deriv. of *carne* meat, flesh (cf. CARNÉ), since the animal was reared for its meat rather than its wool).

Cogns.: Cat.: **Carnier**. Port.: **Carneiro**.

Carnevali Italian: nickname from It. *carnevale* festival (from *carnelevare* fast, lit. removal of meat, from L *caro*, gen. *carnis*, meat (cf. CARNÉ) + *levāre* to lift, remove; it was the normal practice to have a riotous carnival before a period of solemn fast such as Lent, and this gradually acquired a greater significance than the fast itself and usurped the meaning of the word). The nickname may have denoted someone born at the time of a carnival, or someone of a particularly festive spirit. In mod. It. a *carnevale* is normally a fat, awkward, stupid fellow, but in the Bolognese dialect it is used less unkindly of a corpulent and jovial person.

Vars.: **Carnevale**, **Carnavale**, **Carnovali**, **Carnovale**; **Carlevari**, **Carlvaro**, **Carleveri** (N Italy); **Carlavara** (Venetia).

Dims.: **Carnevalini**, **Carlevarini**, **Carlevarino**.

Carney Irish: Anglicized form of Gael. **Ó Catharnaigh** 'descendant of *Catharnach*', a byname meaning 'Warlike'.

Vars.: **(O')Caherny**, **O'Carney**.

Many present-day bearers of these names descend from Tadhg Ó Catharnaigh, *who was killed in battle in 1084. He was nicknamed* An Sionnach *'The Fox', and for this reason the surname has also been Anglicized as* Fox.

Carnicero Spanish: occupational name for a butcher, Sp. *carnicero* (LL *carnicārius*, an agent deriv. of *carniceus*, itself an adj. deriv. of *caro*, gen. *carnis*, meat, flesh; cf. CARNÉ).

Cogns.: Cat.: **Carnicer**. Port.: **Carniceiro**.

Caro Italian and Spanish: nickname from It., Sp. *caro* dear, beloved (L *carus*).

Vars.: It.: **Cari**; **Li Cari** (S Italy).

Dims.: It.: **Carello**, **Carelli**; **Carillo** (S Italy); **Caretti**; **Carino**, **Carini**; **Carucci(o)**, **Carrocci**; **Carricchio** (S Italy); **Carollo**, **Carullo**, **Carulli** (S Italy); **Carotti**.

Augs.: It.: **Caroni**, **Carone**. Sp.: **Carazo**.

Patrs.: It.: **De Caro**, **Di Caro** (S Italy).

Caron French: from a personal name of Gaul. origin, represented in L records in the form *Caraunus* and probably derived from the Celt. element *car* to love (cf. CAREY 2 and CRADDOCK). This name was borne by a 5th-cent. Bret. saint who lived at Chartres and was murdered by robbers; his legend led to its widespread use as a given name during the Middle Ages.

Var.: **Chéron**.

Dims.: **Caronet**; **Cheronnet**, **Cheroneau**.

Carpenter English: occupational name for a worker in wood, ANF *carpentier* (LL *carpentārius* cartwright, from *carpentum* cart, a word of Gaul. origin related to *carrum*; cf. CARRIER).

Cogns.: Fr.: **Carpentier**, **Carpentié**; **Charpentier**, **Charpantier**; **Lec(h)arpentier**. It.: **Carpentieri**, **Carpentiere**, **Carpentiero**, **Carpint(i)eri**, **Carpintiero**. Sp.: **Carpintero**. Port.: **Carpinteiro**.

Dims.: Fr.: **Charpent(e)reau**.

Equivs. (not cogn.): French: CHAPUIS; BOISSIER. Ger.: ZIMMERMANN. Polish: CIEŚLAK (q.v. for other Slav. words). Russ.: PLOTNIK. Hung.: ÁCS.

Carpio 1. Spanish: habitation name from any of the various minor places in the area of Salamanca named with the regional term *carpio* hill (of uncertain origin).

2. Italian: nickname for someone thought to resemble a carp in some way, from It. *carpio(ne)* carp (of Gmc origin; cf. KARPOV 2).

Carr 1. N English and Scots: var. of KERR.

2. Irish: Anglicized form of Gael. **Ó Carra** 'descendant of *Carra*', a byname meaning 'Spear'.

3. Irish: Anglicized form of Gael. **Mac Giolla Chathair** 'son of the servant of *Cathar*', a personal name derived from *cath* battle.

Carrasco Spanish and Portuguese: topographic name for someone who lived by a holm-oak or in a wood of the trees, from Sp. *carrasco*, *carrasca* (from L *cerrus*, itself apparently representing a pre-Roman word native to the peninsula).

Dims.: **Carrasquillo**, **Carrasquilla**. Cat.: **Carrascó**.

Collective: Sp.: **Carrascal**.

Cogn. (collective): It.: **Cereto**, **Cereti**.

Carré French: nickname for a squat, thickset man, from OF *carré* square (L *quadrātus*, past part. of *quadrāre* to form a square, from *quadr-* four).

Vars.: **Carrey**, **Carrez**; **Le Carré**.

Cogn.: Sp.: **Cuadrado**.

Carrier English and French: occupational name for someone who transported goods, from ME, OF *car(r)ier* (LL *carrārius*, a deriv. of *carrum* cart, waggon, of Gaul. origin; cf. CARMAN, CARTER, and also CARPENTER).

Vars.: Eng.: **Carryer**. Fr.: **Carrié**, **Carriez**, **Quarrier**, **Charrier**, **Chareour**; **Carrec** (Brittany).

Cogns.: Prov.: **Carrer**. It.: **Carraro**, **Carrari**, **Carr(i)ero**, **Carr(i)eri**, **Carriere**; **Carr(i)er** (Venetia); **Carrai** (Tuscany). Sp.: **Carrero**. Port.: **Carreiro**.

Dims.: It.: **Carraretto**, **Carrarini**, **Carraroli**.

Carrière French: topographic name for someone who lived on a fairly major thoroughfare, originally a road passable by vehicles as well as pedestrians (from LL *carrāria* (*via*), a deriv. of *carrum* cart; cf. CARRIER).

Vars.: **Carrère**, **Charrière**, **Charraire**, **Charrayre**, **Charreyre**.

Cogns.: Sp.: **Carrera(s)**. Port.: **Carreira(s)**.

Dim.: Fr.: **Charreyron**.

Carrillo Spanish: nickname for a person with some peculiarity of the cheek or jaw, Sp. *carrillo*. The word is attested since the 13th cent., but its etymology is uncertain. It appears to be a dim. of *carro* cart, wagon, and it has been suggested that the reference is to the movements of the jaw in chewing. The surname may also have denoted originally a bold or shameless person; for the semantic development cf. CHEEK.

Cogn.: Port.: **Carrilho**.

Carrington English and Scots: habitation name from any of the places so called, in Ches., Lincs., and Lothian. The one in Lincs. is probably 'settlement (OE *tūn*) of *Cora*'s people'; those in Ches. and Lothian seem to be 'settlement associated with *Cāra*'.

Carrión Spanish: habitation name from any of the various places, for example in the provinces of Ciudad Real, Palencia, Seville, and Valladolid, so called.

Cogn.: Cat.: **Carrió**.

Carrizo Spanish: topographic name for someone who lived on a patch of ground thickly grown with reeds, from Sp. *carrizo* rush, sedge (LL *cariceum*, in origin an adj. deriv. of class. L *carex*, gen. *caricis*). In some cases it may alternatively represent a nickname for a tall, thin person.

Cogn.: Port.: **Carriço**.

Collective: Sp.: **Carracedo**.

Carroll Irish: Anglicized form of the Gael. personal name *Cearbhall*. This is of uncertain origin, perhaps originally a byname for a butcher or a fierce warrior, from *cearbh* hacking.

Vars.: **Carrol**, CARVILL.

Patrs.: **McCarroll**, **McCarvill**, **McKarrill** (Gael. **Mac Cearbhaill**).

'Descendant of C.': **O'Carro(wi)ll**, **O'Carvill**, **O'Carwell** (Gael. **Ó Cearbhaill**).

Carruthers Scots: habitation name from a place near Ecclefechan in Dumfries, locally pronounced /'krɪdɛrz/. The name is first recorded in 1334 in the form *Carrothres*, and then more clearly in *c.*1350 as *Caer Ruther*, and derives from Brit. *ker* fort (cf. CARDEW) + a personal name probably composed of elements meaning 'red' + 'king', 'ruler'.

Vars.: **Car(r)others**; **Crothers** (see also CROWTHER); **Carradice**, **Carrodus**, **Cardis**, **Cardus**, **Crowdace**, **Cruddace**, **Cruddas**, **Caruth**.

In the 13th cent. a family of this name held the hereditary stewardship of Annandale under the Bruces.

Carslake English: apparently a habitation name from a lost place, perhaps named from OE *cærse* (water)cress + *lacu* stream (see LAKE). For the semantics, cf. CRESWELL.

Vars.: **Caslake**, **Karslake**, **Ke(r)slake**.

Carson Scots: of uncertain origin, probably a habitation name. The surname is now prominent in N Ireland.

Vars.: **Corson**, **Corsan** (see also CURZON).

This was the surname of an ancient Galloway family, of which the direct line died out in the late 15th cent. Carsons *were provosts of Dumfries for several generations, and were also prominent in the local affairs of Kirkcudbrightshire. The first known bearer of the name is Sir Robert* de Acarson *or* de Carsan, *who witnessed a charter* c.*1270*.

Carstairs Scots: habitation name from a place in the former county of Lanarks., recorded in 1170 in the form *Casteltarres* and apparently named from ME *castel* CASTLE + a personal name *Tarra*, of uncertain origin.

Carter 1. English: occupational name for a transporter of goods, from ME *carter*, from ANF *car(e)tier*, a deriv. of OF *caret*, dim. of *car* cart (LL *carrum*, cf. CARRIER). The OF word coalesced with an earlier ME word *cart(e)* cart, which is from either ON *kartr* or OE *cræt*, both of which, like the LL word, were probably originally derived from Celtic).

2. Manx: var. of *McArthur*; see Arthur.

Var.: **Charter**.

Cogns.: Fr.: **Carret(i)er**, **Cartier**; **Charretier**, **Chart(i)er**; **Chareter**, **Charater**. Prov.: **Car(ra)tier**, **Carratié**. Sp.: **Carretero**.

Dims.: Fr.: **Cart(e)ron**, **Cart(e)ret**.

Cartledge English: habitation name from a place in Derbys., so called from ON *kartr* rocky ground + OE *læcc* boggy stream.

Var.: **Cartlidge**.

Cartmell English (Cumb. and Lancs.): habitation name from *Cartmel* in Cumb. (formerly N Lancs.), the site of a famous priory, inland from Cartmel Sands. The place-name is derived from ON *kartr* rocky ground + *melr* sandbank.

Var.: **Cartmill**.

Cartwright English: occupational name for a maker of carts, from ME *cart* (apparently a metathesized form of OE *cræt*, or a borrowing of the cogn. ON *kartr*; cf. CARTER) + WRIGHT. The surname is attested from the late 13th cent., although the vocab. word does not occur before the 15th cent.

Var.: **Kortwright**.

Carus English: habitation name from a dwelling named as the 'house on wet ground' or 'house by the brushwood', from ME *kerr* wet ground or brushwood (ON *kjarr*; see KERR) + *h(o)us* house (OE *hūs*).

Vars.: **Carass**, **Carras**, **Caress**, **Car(r)iss**.

Caruso Italian: nickname from It. *caruso* close-cropped. This word was also used in the more general sense 'boy', 'lad', since in the Middle Ages young men of fashion sometimes wore their hair much shorter than was the prevailing style (cf. TOUS). In the Girgenti area of Sicily the term was an occupational one for a worker in the sulphur pits, since such workers apparently were required to wear their hair short.

Vars.: **Carusi(o)**, **Carosi(o)**.

Dims.: **Carusello**, **Caruselli**, **Caros(i)ello**, **Caroselli**.

Augs.: **Carusone**, **Carosoni**.

Carver English: 1. occupational name for a carver of wood or a sculptor of stone, from an agent deriv. of ME *kerve(n)* to cut, carve (OE *ceorfan*).

2. occupational name for a ploughman, ANF *caruier* (LL *carrucārius*, a deriv. of *carruca* cart, plough—a word from the same group as *carrum* and *carpentum*, cf. CARRIER and CARPENTER; in Ger. the word has been borrowed in a different sense, see KARCH).

Carvill 1. English and Irish (Norman): habitation name from places in Calvados and Seine-Maritime called *Carville*, from the Scandinavian personal name *Kare* + OF VILLE settlement.

2. Irish: var. of CARROLL.

Vars.: **Carville**, **Carvell**.

Carwardine English: habitation name from *Carden* in Ches., which is recorded in the mid-13th cent. in the form *Kawrdin* and in the early 14th as *Cawardyn*; it is probably named from OE *carr* rock + *worðign* enclosure (see WORTHY).

Var.: **Carden** (see also CARDING).

Carden is the name of an Irish family, known originally as (de) Cawarden *or* de Kawrdin. *They became established in Tipperary in the late 17th cent. They trace their descent from Sir John* de Cawarden (*b*. c.*1375*).

Casa Italian and Spanish: habitation name from It., Sp. *casa* house (L *casa* hut, cottage, cabin). It perhaps originally denoted the occupier of the most distinguished house in the village.

Vars.: It.: CASE, **Caso**; **Ca** (N Italy); **Della Casa, Dalla Casa, Dalla C(h)a, Da C(h)a, Dacca**. Sp.: **Casas**; **Casero** ('tenant').

Cogns.: Prov.: CASE, **Caze, Cha(i)se, Chaize, Ch(i)èze, Lacase, Lacaze, Lachaize, Lachèze, Sacaze, Decaze, Descazes**. Cat.: **Casas, Cases, Lacasa**.

Dims.: It.: **Casella, Casello, Caselli**; **Casel** (Venetia); **Casi(e)llo, Casol(l)a** (Naples); **Casetta, Caset(ti)**; **Casina, Casine, Casino, Casini**; **Casotti**. Prov.: **C(h)azelle(s), Chézelle(s), C(h)azot(te), C(h)azet(te), Casin, Cazin**. Sp.: **Casillas**. Cat.: **Casellas**.

Augs.: It.: **Casone, Casoni** (Lombardy); **Cason** (Venetia).

Pejs.: It.: **Casacc(h)ia, Casacci(o), Casassa, Casazza**.

Casado Spanish: nickname for a married man, the head of his own household, from Sp. *casado*, past part. of *casar* to marry (a deriv. of CASA house).

Casale Italian: topographic name for someone who lived in a hut or small cottage, OIt. *casale* (LL *casāle*, a deriv. of CASA house), or habitation name from any of the various places named with this word, most notably a town in Piedmont.

Vars.: **Casal(i)**; **Casalaro, Casalari**.

Cogns.: Prov.: **Cazal, Caz(e)aux**; **Chazal, Chazaux** (Massif Central); **Chezel**; **Ducazeau(x)**. Sp., Port.: **Casal, Casar(es)**. Cat.: **Casals**.

Dims.: It.: **Casaletto, Casaletti**; **Casalin(i), Casalino** (Venetia); **Casagli(a)** (Tuscany). Prov.: **Cazalet, Cazalin**.

Augs.: It. **Casalone, Casaloni**.

Casanova Italian, Spanish, and Catalan: habitation name for someone who lived in a newly built house, from Romance derivs. of L *casa* house (see CASA) + *nova* (fem.) new.

Vars.: It.: **Canova**. Sp.: **Casanueva**. Cat.: **Casanovas, Cànovas**.

Cogns.: Prov.: **Caseneuve, Cazenove, Cazenave**.

Casaubon Provençal: habitation name for someone who lived in an impressive or well-built house, from OProv. *casal* cottage (see CASALE) + BON good.

Var.: **Cazaubon**.

Case 1. English: metonymic occupational name for a maker of boxes or chests, from ANF *cas(s)e* case, container (L *capsa*, a deriv. of *capere* to hold, contain).

2. Provençal: cogn. of CASA.

3. Italian: metonymic occupational name for a maker or seller of cheese; see CHEESEMAN.

Vars. (of 1): **Cash**, CASHMAN.

Cogns. (of 1): Du.: **Kas**. Jewish (Ashkenazic): **Cassirer, Kassi(e)rer** (presumably an occupational name translating Hebr. *gabay*, Yid. *gabe*; see GABBAI).

Casement Manx: Anglicized form of Gael. *Mac Easmuinn*; see OSMOND.

Sir Roger Casement (*1864–1916*) *was a British diplomat and Irish nationalist who was hanged by the British for treason as a result of his efforts to enlist German support for Irish independence during World War I. He was born into an Ulster Protestant family in Ballymena, the son of an army officer whose ancestors had emigrated from the Isle of Man in the 18th cent.*

Casey Irish: Anglicized form of Gael. **Ó Cathasaigh** 'descendant of *Cathasach*', a byname meaning 'Vigilant' or 'Noisy'.

Var.: **O'Casey**.

Cashman 1. English: var. of CASE.

2. Irish: Anglicized form of Gael. *Ó Ciosáin*; see KISSANE.

3. Jewish (Ashkenazic): of unknown origin.

Var. (of 3): **Kashman**.

Cashmore English: apparently a habitation name from *Cashmoor* in Dorset, which is probably so called from OE *cærse* cress + *mōr* fen, marsh (see MOORE 1). The surname is now most frequent in Birmingham.

Cass English: from the medieval female given name *Cass*, a short form of *Cassandra*. This was the name (of uncertain, possibly non-Gk, origin) of an ill-fated Trojan prophetess of classical legend, condemned to foretell the future but never be believed; her story was well known and widely popular in medieval England.

Dim.: **Cassie** (Scotland).

Metr.: **Casson** (N England).

Cassagne Provençal: topographic name for someone who lived by an oak tree or in an oak wood, from OProv. *cassagne* oak (LL *cassanea* (*arbor*), a deriv. of *cassanos*; see CASSE 1).

Vars.: **Cassaigne, Cassan, Chassa(i)gne, Chasseigne, Chassa(i)ng, Chassin, Chassan(t)**; **Lac(h)assagne**.

Dims.: **C(h)assagnol, Cassagnou, Cassagnau, Cassignol**.

Aug.: **Chassinat**.

Collective: **Cassagnade**.

Cassard French: apparently a nickname for a clumsy person, from OF *casse(r)* to break, smash (L *quassāre* to shake violently, freq. of *quatere* to shake), with the addition of the pej. suffix *-ard*.

Var.: **Cassart**.

Casse French: 1. topographic name for someone who lived by an oak tree or in an oak wood, from OF *casse* oak (LL *cassanos*, of Celt. origin; cf. CASSAGNE).

2. metonymic occupational name for a maker of ladles, from OF *casse* ladle (OProv. *cassa*, LL *cattia*, from Gk *kyathion*, dim. of *kyathos* cup).

Vars. (of 1): **Cassé, Casses**; **Delcasse, Delcassé, Ducasse**.

Dims. (of 1): **Cassin, Casset**. It.: **Cassini**.

Cassegrain French: apparently an occupational nickname for a miller, from OF *casse(r)* to break (see CASSARD) + *grain* grain, corn (L *grānum*).

Cassidy Irish: Anglicized form of Gael. **Ó Caiside** 'descendant of *Caiside*', a byname from *cas* curly(-headed).

Vars.: **Cassedy, Kassidy, Casserl(e)y**; **O'Cassidy, O'Cahsedy**.

Castan French: topographic name for someone who lived by a (horse-)chestnut tree, OF *castan(h)* (L *castanea*, from Gk). The surname may also perhaps have been originally a nickname for someone of chestnut or auburn colouring.

Vars.: **C(h)astaing, Chastan(g), Chastand, Chat(a)in**; **C(h)astagnier, Châtai(g)nier, Chatenier, Castanié, Castagné**.

Cogns.: Eng.: **Chaston**. It.: **Casta(g)na, Castagno**; **Castangia** (Sardinia); **Castagnaro, Castagneri**. Sp.: **Castaño(s)**. Cat.: **Castanyer, Castañer, Castañé**. Port.: **Castanho**. Ger.: **Kestenbaum**. Czech: **Kaštánek**.

Dims.: Fr.: **Casta(i)gnet, C(h)astanet, Chastenet, Châtenet, Chataignon, Châtaignoux, Chataigneaux**. It.: **Castagnetta, Castagnetto, Catagnetti, Castagnotto; Castagnoli** (Liguria).

Augs.: It.: **Castagnone**. Sp.: **Castañón**.

Pej.: It.: **Castagnasso**.

Collectives: Fr.: **Châtenay**. It.: **Castagneto**. Sp.: **Castañeda**. Port.: **Catanheira**.

Castejón Spanish: habitation name from any of the numerous places so called, from LL *castellio*, gen. *castel-liōnis*, fortified town or village (a deriv. of *castellum*; see CASTLE).

Castel-Branco Portuguese: habitation name from a place so called, from Port. *castelo* CASTLE + *branco* white (see BLANC).

Var.: **Castelo-Branco**.

Castellan English (Norman): occupational name for the governor or constable of a castle, or the warder of a prison, from ANF *castelain* (L *castellānus*, a deriv. of *castellum* CASTLE).

Vars.: **Castellain, Castelein, Castling, Chatelain**.

Cogns.: Fr.: **Chastel(l)ain, Châtelain; Ca(s)telain** (Normandy, Picardy). Prov.: **Castelan, Castelin**. It.: **Castellan(i), Castellano**. Sp.: **Castellano(s)**. Cat.: **Castellà**. Port.: **Castelhano, Castelão**. Flem., Du.: **Casteleyn, Castelijn**.

Castelnau Provençal: topographic name for someone living by a castle of relatively recent construction at the time when the surname was formed, from OProv. *castel* CASTLE + *nau* new (L *novus*), or habitation name from a place so named.

Cogns.: Fr.: **Châteauneuf**. It.: **Castelnuovo** (also Jewish); **Castelnovo, Castelnovi**.

Castelvieil Provençal: topographic name for someone who lived by an ancient castle, from OProv. *castel* CASTLE + *vieil* old, or habitation name from a place so named.

Cogns.: Fr.: **Châteauvieux**. Cat.: **Castellví**. It.: **Castelvecchi(o), Castelvetro, Castelvetri**.

Castille French: regional name for someone from *Castille*, the Fr. name of Sp. *Castilla*. An independent kingdom between the 10th and 15th cents., it formed the largest power in the Iberian peninsula. The name derives from the many castles in the region.

Cogns.: Sp.: **Castilla**. Port.: **Castela**. It.: **(Del) Castiglio; Castiglione, Castiglioni**.

Castle English: topographic name from ANF *castel* castle, fortified building or set of buildings, especially the residence of a feudal lord (LL *castellum*, a dim. of *castrum* fort; see CASTRO). The name would also have denoted a servant who lived and worked at such a place. The LL word was used occasionally (as, for example, in the Vulgate translation of the Bible) in the sense 'village', 'settlement', and this use had already been borrowed into OE, but was almost entirely restricted to scriptural contexts, and died out in the face of the competing sense introduced from France.

Vars.: **Castles, Castell(s); Cassel(l)(s)** (perhaps largely from the place in the *département* of Nord so named); **Kestle, Kestell** (Cornwall); **Castleman**.

Cogns.: Fr.: **C(h)astel, Chasteau, Châtel, Château; Duchasteau, Duchâteau, Duchâtel**. Prov.: **Castel, Ducastel, Delcastel**. It.: **Castello, Castelli; Castiello** (Naples); **Del Castello**. Sp.: **Castillo(s)**. Cat.: **Castel(l), Castels**. Port.: **Castelo, Castilho**. Jewish (Sefardic): **Castel, Kastel**. Ger.: **Kassel** (the name of a city in Hesse). Flem., Du.: **Van (de) Castele, Van Cassel**.

Dims.: Fr.: **Castelot, Châtelot, Châtelet**. Prov.: **Castillon, Castillou; Casterot, Casterou** (Gascony). It.: **Castelletti, Castelletto, Castellini, Castellino, Castellucci(o), Castelluzzi, Castelluzzo, Castellotti, Castellotto**. Sp.: **Castillejo**. Cat.: **Castellet**.

Augs.: It.: **Castellone** (Lombardy). Sp.: **Castillón**.

Pejs.: It.: **Castellacci(o), Castellazzi, Castellazzo**.

Castro Italian, Spanish, Portuguese, and Jewish (Sefardic): topographic name for someone living by a castle or walled town, from It., Sp., Port. *castro* (L *castrum* legionary camp), or habitation name from a place named with this element.

Vars.: It.: **Castri, Lo Cast(r)o, Licastri, De Castri(s)**.

Dim.: Sp.: **Castrillo**.

Catalán Spanish: regional name for someone from Catalonia (Sp. *Cataluña*), apparently so called from a pre-Roman tribal name, which is of unknown origin and meaning.

Cogns.: Cat.: **Català**. Port.: **Catalão**. Prov.: **Cat(h)ala(n); Catalogne**. It.: **Catalano, Catalan(i), Catelani**. Jewish (Sefardic): **Katalan; Kataloni** (with Hebr. or Arabic suffix *-i*).

Dim.: It.: **Catalanotti**.

Catchpole English (chiefly E Anglia): occupational name for a bailiff, originally one empowered to seize poultry and other livestock in case of default on debts or taxes. The name comes from ANF *cachepol*, a cpd of *cache(r)* to chase, pursue (OF *chace(r)*, L *captāre* to snatch at, freq. of *capere* to take, seize) + *pol* fowl (L *pullus* young animal or bird; cf. PULLEN).

Vars.: **Catchpo(o)l, Catchpoole, Catchpoule**.

Cater English: occupational name for the buyer of provisions for a large household, from an aphetic form of ANF *acatour* (LL *acceptātor*, agent deriv. of *acceptāre* to accept, freq. of *accipere* to receive). Mod. Eng. *caterer* results from the addition of a second agent suffix to the word.

Vars.: **Cator; Chater, Chaytor**.

Cates English: apparently a patr. from the ON byname *Káti* (from *káti* boy). (*Kate* was not in use as a short form of *Catherine* during the Middle Ages.)

Var.: **Kates**.

Catesby English: habitation name from a place in Northants, so called from the common ON byname *Káti* (see CATES) + ON *býr* settlement, village.

Probably all bearers of this name are descended from William Catesby, *a 14th-cent. landowner of Coventry in Warwicks. His descendant William Catesby was Richard III's chief minister, executed in 1485 by Henry VII, while another descendant, Robert Catesby, was an associate of Guy Fawkes and was executed in 1605. The present family are descended via Sir John Catesby (d. 1486), a judge.*

Cathcart Scots: habitation name from a place near Glasgow, the second element of which clearly refers to the river *Cart*, on which it stands. This river name is extremely ancient, probably of pre-Celtic origin; Nicolaisen connects it with IE *kov-* hard, stony. The first element ostensibly commorates a battle (Brit. *cad* or Gael. *cath*; cf. CADELL). However, the earliest recorded spelling of the placename is *Kerkert* (1158), which suggests derivation from Brit. *ker* fort (cf. CARDEW).

The first known bearer of the name is Reginaldus de Cathekert, *who came to Scotland with Walter Fitzalan, ancestor of the house of Stewart, and may have been of Breton origin.*

Catlin English: from the medieval female given name *Cat(e)lin(e)*, ANF form of *Catherine*. This is of obscure origin and etymology, being first attested in the form *Aika-*

terina but later affected by folk etymological associations with Gk *katharos* pure. It was borne by numerous early Christian saints, and was popular throughout the Middle Ages.

Vars.: **Cattlin, Catling**.

Cogns.: Fr.: **Cat(h)elin(e), Cat(h)erin(e)**. It.: **Caterina, Caterino, Caterini, Cattarin(i)**. Sp.: **Catalina**. Cat.: **Catarinea**. Port.: **Catarino**. Ger.: **Kathrein(er)** (probably a habitation names from a place named in honour of a St Katherine). Flem: **Catriene, Cathelyn**. Russ.: **Yekaterinski** (a form adopted by Orthodox priests).

Dims.: Eng.: CATT, CATTON, CATON, **Catten; Cattell** (chiefly W Midlands). Fr.: **Cathelineau, Catherinet; Cat(he)ron, Cat(he)rou(x); Cat(h)elet, Cat(h)elon, Cat(h)elot; Cat(h)eau, Cat(h)et, Cat(t)in, Catineau**, CATON, **Catillon**. It.: **Cat(t)era, Cattaruccia, Cataruzza, Cataruzzi, Cattarossi, Cattarulla; Cat(t)a, Cat(t)e, Cattini, Cattozzo, Cattuzza**. Ger.: **Triene**. Flem.: **Kate, Trine**. Ukr.: **Katerinyuk**.

Augs.: Fr.: **Cathelat, Catenat, Catinat**.

Pejs.: Fr.: **Catheraud, Catinaud**.

Metrs.: Russ.: **Yekaterinin, Katerinin, Katerinov**. Ukr.: **Katerinich**.

Metrs. (from dims.): Ger.: **Trienen, Treinen**. Russ.: **Katynin, Katyush(k)in**. Ukr.: **Katrin, Katr(ev)ich**.

Caton 1. English: habitation name from places in Derbys. and Lancs. The former is probably so called from the OE personal name or byname *Cada* (see CADE 1) + OE *tūn* enclosure, settlement; the latter derives its first element from the ON byname *Káti* (see CATES).

2. English and French: dim. of CATLIN.

Dims. (of 2): Fr.: **Cat(t)onnet, Catonné, Catenot, Cathenod**.

Catt English: 1. nickname from the animal, ME, OE *catte* cat, reinforced by ONF *cat* (OHG *kazza*; LL *cattus* is probably from this, rather than vice versa). The word is found in similar forms in most European languages from very early times (e.g. Gael. *cath*, Slav. *kotu*). Domestic cats were unknown in Europe in classical times, where weasels fulfilled many of their functions, for example in hunting rodents. When they were introduced into S Europe, apparently in the 1st cent. AD, they were known to the Romans by the Gk name *ailouros* 'wavy tail'. They seem to have come from Egypt, where they were regarded as sacred animals.

2. from a medieval female given name, a short form of CATLIN.

Vars.: **Chatt, Katte**.

Cogns. (of 1): Fr.: **Lechat**. Prov.: **Lecat**. It.: **(Lo) Gatto** (S Italy); **Gatti** (Liguria, Lombardy); **Jatta** (Tarento). Sp.: **Gato**. Ger.: **Kater**; see also KATZ. Low Ger.: **Katte**. Flem., Du.: **De Cat, (De) Kat**. Czech: **Kot(t), Kotal, Kotas; Kocour**. Pol.: **Kot, Kotecki; Kociński**.

Dims. (of 1): It.: **Gattin(ell)i, Gattullo**. Czech: **Kot'átko; Kotík, Kotek; Kocourek**. Pol., Jewish (E Ashkenazic): **Kotek**.

Aug. (of 1): It.: **Gattone**.

Patrs. (from 1): Flem., Du.: **Cats, Kats**. Pol.: **Kotowicz, Kotkiewicz** (from the dim.). Russ., Bulg.: **Kotev**.

Habitation names: Pol., Jewish (E Ashkenazic): **Kotowski** (in some cases no doubt from the city of *Kotovsk*, now in the Ukraine); **Kotkowski; Kociszewski**.

Catterall English: habitation name from a place in Lancs., of uncertain etymology, perhaps from the gen. case of ON *kottr* cat + *hali* tail, referring to a long, thin piece of land. The surname is common in Lancs., and almost unknown elsewhere.

Vars.: **Cattrall, Catt(e)rell, Catterill, Catt(e)roll, Cath(e)rall**.

Cattermole English: of uncertain origin. It is confined mainly to E Anglia and London, and may be a Low German importation.

Var.: **Cattermoul**.

Catton English: 1. habitation name from any of the various places so called, for example in Derbys., Norfolk, and N Yorks., all apparently from an OE byname *Catta* 'Cat' (see CATT 1) or ON *Káti* 'Boy' (see CATES) + OE *tūn* enclosure, settlement.

2. dim. of CATLIN.

Caughey Irish: (pronounced /'kahi/) 1. Anglicized form of Gael. **Mac Eachaidh**, patr. from the byname *Eachaidh* 'Horseman' (a deriv. of *each* horse; cf. KEOGH).

2. Anglicized form of Gael. *Ó Maolchathaigh*; see MULCAHY.

Vars. (of 1): **McCaughey, McCah(e)y, McGaughey, McGaughie, McGauhy, McGuggy, McGah(e)y, Megahey, (Mc)Gaffey**.

Caulfield English: apparently a habitation name from an unidentified minor place, perhaps so called from OE *c(e)ald* cold + *feld* pasture, open country (see FIELD).

Var.: **Cauldfield**.

Caumont French: habitation name from any of various places called *C(h)aumont*, for the most part clearly so named from OF *c(h)auf* bald, bare (see CHAFF) + *mont* hill (see MONT). In a few cases the first element may originally have been Gaul. *calm* plateau (see CHAUME 1).

Vars.: **Chaumont, Chomont**.

Causey English (Norman): topographic name for someone who lived by a causeway, ME *caucey* (from ONF *cauciée*; see CHAUSSÉE); the ending of the vocab. word was in time assimilated by folk etymology to ME *way* (OE *weg* path).

Var.: **Cawsey**.

Cavalcanti Italian: occupational nickname for a horseman or knight, from It. *cavalcante*, pres. part. of *cavalcar* to ride on horseback (LL *caballicāre*, from *caballus* horse; cf. CAVALLO and CHEVALIER).

Cavallo Italian: metonymic occupational name for a man in charge of horses, perhaps also a nickname for someone supposedly resembling a horse, from It. *cavallo* horse (LL *caballus*).

Vars.: **Cavalli(o)**.

Cogns.: Fr.: **Cheval, Chevau(x); Queval, Quéval** (Normandy). Prov.: **Caval; Chavau(x)** (Massif Central). Sp.: **Caballo**.

Dims.: It.: **Cavallin(i), Cavallino, Cavaletti, Cavaletto, Cavalotti, Cavalotto, Cavallucci(o), Cavaluzzi**. Fr.: **Chevaleau, Cheval(l)et, Chevalley, Chevalin, Chevalon**.

Aug.: It.: **Cavallone**.

Pejs.: It.: **Caval(l)acci**. Fr.: **Cheval(l)ard**.

Cave 1. English: habitation name from a place in Humberside, apparently so called from a river name derived from OE *cāf* swift.

2. English (Norman): var. of CHAFF.

3. French: metonymic occupational name for someone employed in or in charge of the wine cellars of a great house, from OF *cave* cave, cellar (L *cavea*, a derivative of *cavus* hollow; see also CAGE).

4. French: topographic name for someone who lived in or near a cave, from the same word as in 3 in an older sense.

Vars. (of 1 and 2): **Kave**. (Of 3 and 4): **Lacave; Cavier**.

Cogns. (of 3 and 4): It.: **Cava; Cavari**. Sp.: **Cueva(s), Coba(s)**.

Dims. (of 3 and 4): Fr.: **Cavel, Caveau, Cavin, Cavy**.

Sir Alexander de Cave *(b. 1262) was among the knights summoned to serve against the Scots in 1296–7. In 1311 he became keeper of the Templars' lands in York. The name has had many subsequent distinguished bearers. One not-so-distinguished bearer was Captain George Cave, privateer, of Kingston-upon-Hull, recorded in 1594.*

Cavendish English: habitation name from a place in Suffolk, so called from an OE byname *Cāfna* 'Bold', 'Daring' + OE *edisc* enclosed pasture.

Var.: **Candish** (a contracted form).

The Cavendish *family, who hold the dukedom of Devonshire, first gained influence at court through Sir William Cavendish (?1505–57), a Suffolk gentleman. His descendant William Cavendish (1640–1707) was created 1st Duke of Devonshire in 1694 for services to William III. Among his other descendants were William Cavendish, 1st Duke of Newcastle (1592–1676), a poet and patron of Dryden and Hobbes, and Henry Cavendish (1731–1810), the scientist.*

Cavenett English: of uncertain origin, probably from a Fr. nickname for a bald man, from a double dim. (*-in* + *-et*) of *cave* (see CHAFF).

The name is not, as far as is known, recorded in England before 1579, when Henry Cavnit *was apprenticed as an armourer in London. It is possible that his family had moved to England in the first wave of Huguenot immigration after the St Bartholomew's Day Massacre of 1572. In 1840 the name was taken to Australia by John* Cavenett *(also known as* Cavinet *and* Cavernett*) and all present-day bearers in that country seem to be descended from him.*

Cavero Spanish: 1. in Aragon and Navarre, a status name for a knight, or nickname meaning 'knight'. The word is either a deriv. of *cabo* head, chief (see CAP) or else a contracted form of *cabellero* (see CHEVALIER).

2. in the province of Álava, an occupational name for a digger of ditches, from an agent deriv. of *cavar* to dig, excavate (L *cavāre*, from *cavus* hollow; cf. CAVE 3).

Cavill English: habitation name from *Cavil(le)* in E Yorks. The placename is from OE *cā* jackdaw (see COE) + *feld* pasture, open country (see FIELD).

Cawood English (Yorks. and Lancs.): habitation name from places in N Yorks. and Lancs., both so called from OE *cā* jackdaw (see COE) + *wudu* WOOD.

Cawston English: habitation name from places in Norfolk and Warwicks., so called from the gen. case of the ON byname *Kalfr* 'Calf' + OE *tūn* enclosure, settlement.

Var.: **Causton**.

Cawthorn English: habitation name from *Cawthorn* in N Yorks. or *Cawthorne* in W Yorks., both so called from OE *c(e)ald* cold + *þorn* thorn bush.

Var.: **Cawthorne**.

One line of a family of the name Cawthorn *has been traced back to the late 17th cent. The present-day centres of distribution are in Yorks., S and W Cambs., and Lincs.*

Caxton English: habitation name from a place in Cambs., so called from the gen. case of the ON byname *Kakkr* (apparently a deriv. of *kokkr* lump) + OE *tūn* enclosure, settlement.

Cayley 1. English (Norman): habitation name from places in Eure and Seine-Maritime called *Cailly*, from a Gallo-Roman personal name *Callius* + the local suffix *-ācum*.

2. English: habitation name from a minor place in the parish of Winwick, Lancs., so called from OE *cā* jackdaw (see COE) + *lēah* wood, clearing.

3. Manx: Anglicized form of Gael. *Mac Caolaidhe*; see CALLOW.

Vars.: **Cal(l)ey, Callie, Ka(y)ley**.

Cogn. (of 1): Fr.: **Cailly**.

William de Caley *is recorded as the holder of lands at Heacham, Norfolk, in the early 12th cent.*

Cea Spanish: habitation name from places in the provinces of León and Orense. The placename is first found in the form *Cegia*, and it is probably related to CEJA 2.

Cebolla Spanish: 1. metonymic occupational name for a grower or seller of onions, from Sp. *cebolla* onion (from LL *cēpulla*, dim. of class. L *cēpa*; the Ger. name ZWIEBEL is a cogn.).

2. habitation name from a place in the province of Valencia, originally named with the Arabic element *jubayla* small hill (which underlies the placename *Gibraltar*), but altered by folk etymology to *Cebolla* 'onion'.

Var. (of 1): **Cebollas, Cebollero**.

Cogn. (of 1): It.: **Cipolla**.

Cebrián Spanish: from the medieval given name *Cebrián* (L *Cypriānus*, originally an ethnic name for an inhabitant of *Cyprus*, Gk *Kypros*). The name was borne by a 3rd-cent. bishop of Carthage, and by another saint, probably legendary, whose cult was suppressed by the Holy See in 1969.

Vars.: **Cipran(o)**.

Cogns.: Cat.: **Cebrià**. Port.: **Cipriano**.

Čech Czech: name meaning 'Czech', used in particular to distinguish a native or inhabitant of Bohemia (Czech *Čechy*) from Slovaks, Moravians, and other ethnic groups. The word itself is of unknown but vigorously disputed etymology.

Cogns.: Ger.: **Tschech(e), Tschäche**. Pol.: **Czech, Echt** (see below). Hung.: **Cseh**.

Patrs.: Pol.: **Czechowicz**. Russ.: **Chekhov**.

Habitation name: Pol., Jewish (Ashkenazic): **Czechowski**.

Bystroń records that the Pol. surname Echt *(meaning 'real', 'true' in mod. Ger.) was derived by deliberate alteration from* Czech*, with official permission, after a man called Czech had made an attempt on the life of Friedrich Wilhelm IV, King of Prussia.*

Cecil Welsh: from the OW personal name *Seisyllt*, apparently a mutilated form of the L name *Sextilius*, a deriv. of *Sextus* 'Sixth' (from *sex* six; cf. SIX). The spelling has, however, been modified as a result of folk etymological association with the L name *C(a)ecilius*, a deriv. of *caecus* blind.

Vars.: **Saycell, Seisill**.

The powerful English Cecil *family first came to prominence with William Cecil, Lord Burghley (1520–98), Elizabeth I's chief adviser for 40 years. They were originally minor Welsh gentry; their name is found in a variety of forms, including* Sitsylt, Ceyssel, *and* Sisseld. *David Cecil, grandfather of Lord Burghley, had espoused the cause of Henry Tudor, and came to court in London after the latter became king in 1485. The Elizabethan Lord Burghley's two sons both established noble houses; Thomas (1542–1623) became Earl of Exeter, and Robert (1563–1612) became Earl of Salisbury. The latter's descendants include the statesman Robert Cecil, 3rd Marquis of Salisbury (1830–1903), Lord David Cecil (b. 1902), the critic and biographer. Descendants of Thomas Cecil include David Brownlow Cecil, 6th Marquis of Exeter (b. 1905), who was an athlete and Olympic gold medallist in 1928.*

Ceder 1. Jewish (Ashkenazic): ornamental name from Yid. *tseder* cedar or Ger. *Zeder* (from L *cedrus*, from Gk).

2. Swedish: ornamental name from Swed. *ceder*, of the same origin as 1.

Vars.: Jewish: **Tseder**, **Zeder(baum)**; **Cederbaum**, **Cederboim** (Pol. spellings).

Cpds (ornamental): Swed.: **Cederberg** ('cedar hill'); **Cederblad** ('cedar leaf'); **Ced(er)gren** ('cedar branch'); **Cederholm** ('cedar island'); **Cederlund** ('cedar grove'); **Ced(er)löf**, **Ced(er)löv** ('cedar leaf'); **Cederquist** ('cedar twig'); **Cederstrand** ('cedar shore'); **Cederström** ('cedar river'); **Ced(er)wall** ('cedar pasture)'.

Cegielski Polish: topographic name for someone who lived by a brickworks, or occupational name for one who worked in one, from Pol. *cegielna* brickworks.

Var.: **Cegiełkowski**.

Cogn.: Czech: **Cihlář** (brickmaker).

Ceja Spanish: 1. nickname for someone particularly noted for his beetling brows, from Sp. *ceja* eyebrow (LL *cilium*, which in class. L meant 'eyelid', a deriv. of the root *cel-* hide, conceal).

2. topographic name for someone who lived on the brow of a hill, from the same word used in this transferred sense.

Celada Spanish: habitation name from any of various places, for example in the provinces of Burgos, Córdoba, Palencia, and Santander, so called from Sp. *celada* place of concealment (for hunters), ambuscade (LL *celāta*, a deriv. of *celāre* to hide, conceal).

Celaya Spanish form of Basque **Zelaia**: topographic name for someone who lived by a patch of pastureland, from Basque *zelai* field, meadow + the def. art. *-a*.

Var.: **Zelaya**.

Celle French: habitation name from any of the numerous places so called from having once been the site of a hermit's cell, OF *celle* (L *cella* (small) room, a deriv. of the root *cel-* hide, conceal). The Sp. cogn. *Cela* denoted a granary or storehouse, and the surname may have been acquired as a metonymic occupational name by an official responsible for receiving produce into the lord's granary. See also SELLER 3.

Var.: **Celles**.

Cogns.: It.: **Cella**, **Celli**; **Cella(r)i**, **Cellani**, **Cellesi**. Sp.: **Cela**.

Dims.: It.: **Celletti**, **Cellin(i)**, **Cellucci**, **Cellotto**.

Augs.: It.: **Cellon(i)**.

Centeno Spanish: metonymic occupational name for someone who grew or sold rye, or topographic name for someone who lived by a field given over to the cultivation of this crop, from Sp. *centeno* rye (LL *centēnum*, a deriv. of *centum* hundred, so called as the plant was supposed to be capable of producing a hundred grains on each stalk).

Cepeda Spanish: topographic name for somebody who lived on a patch of land that had been cleared of trees, leaving only stumps behind, from Sp. *cepeda*, a collective of *cepo* base of a tree trunk (from L *cippus* pillar).

Cerda Spanish: apparently a nickname for someone with a prominent tuft of hair, from Sp. *cerda* bristle, hair (LL *cirra*, for class. L *cirrus*; the form may have been influenced by the now obsolete *seda* bristle, L *saeta*). One of the sons of King Alfonso X (1221–84) was known as Fernando *de la Cerda*.

Cogn.: Port.: **Lacerda**.

Cerf 1. French: nickname from the stag, OF *cerf* (L *cervus*), given with reference to the presumed lustiness of the creature, or conversely to the horns supposed to be a sign of a cuckold (see HORN 4).

2. Jewish: surname adopted because of the connection of the deer with the Hebr. given name *Naftali*; cf. HIRSCH 2.

Var. (of 1): **Lecerf**.

Cogns. (of 1): It.: **Cervo**, **Cervi**. Sp.: **Ciervo**.

Dims. (of 1): Fr.: **Cerfon**. It.: **Cervini**.

Aug. (of 1): It.: **Cervoni**.

Cerisier French: topographic name for someone who lived near a cherry tree or who owned a cherry orchard, from OF *cerisier* cherry tree (LL *cerasārius*, a deriv. of *cerasus* cherry, from Gk).

Vars.: **Cérié**, **Serier(s)**, **Seriés**, **Serieys**, **Serieyx**.

Cogns.: Eng.: CHERRY. It.: **Ceresa**, **Ceresi**, **Cereso**; **Cerasa**, **Cerasi**, **Ceraso**; **Cirasa**, **Ciraso**; **Ceresero**. Sp.: **Cerezo**. Cat.: **Cerera**.

Dims.: It.: **Cersini**, **Ceresoli**, **Ceresolo**, **Ceras(u)ola**, **Cerasoli**, **Cerisola**.

Collectives: It.: **Cereseto**. Sp.: **Cereceda**.

Čermák Czech: nickname meaning literally 'redstart', the name of a common European songbird. The Czech word was also used as a euphemism for the devil, and this no doubt affected its use as a nickname.

Cerqueira Portuguese: habitation name from a place near Braga, so called from LL *quercāria* oak grove (a deriv. of *quercus* oak).

Cerro Spanish: topographic name for someone who lived on or by a hill or ridge, Sp. *cerro* (from L *cirrus* bristle, hair (cf. CERDA); the transfer of meaning seems to be due to the fact that the L word was used in particular of the hairs along the spinal ridge of an animal).

Dim.: **Cerrillo**.

Cervantes Spanish: of uncertain origin and meaning. Most probably it is a patr. from a medieval given name *Servanto*, arising as the result of a cross between L *serviens*, gen. *servientis*, 'servant (of the Lord)' and *servandus* 'he who shall be saved'. There seems to have been some further confusion in the spelling with Sp. *ciervo* stag (cf. CERF).

Cervera Spanish: habitation name from any of numerous places so called, from LL *cervāria* 'place of stags' (a deriv. of *cervus* stag; see CERF).

Dim.: Cat.: **Cerveró**.

Cesare Italian: from the given name *Cesare*, from the famous Roman family name *Caesar*. This was associated by folk etymology in classical times with L *caesaries* head of hair, but is in fact probably of Etruscan origin, perhaps ultimately a cogn. of CHARLES. After the spectacular success of Julius Caesar the name was adopted by his imperial successors, and eventually came to be taken as a generic title. As such it has been adopted into most European languages (see KAISER).

Vars.: **Cesaro**, **Cesar(i)**.

Cogns.: Fr.: **César(d)**, **Cézar(d)**. Port.: **César**.

Dims.: It.: **Cesarin(i)**, **Cesarelli**, **Cesarotti**.

Augs.: It.: **Cesaroni**, **Cesarone**.

Patrs.: It.: **De Cesare**, **Di Cesare**, **De Cesaris**.

Céspedes Spanish: topographic name for someone who lived on a patch of peat soil, from the pl. of Sp. *cesped* peat, turf (L *caespes*, gen. *caespitis*). In some cases it may originally have been a metonymic occupational name for someone who cut and sold turf.

Cézanne French: habitation name from a place in Upper Piémont, apparently so called from the L personal name *Caetius* + the local suffix *-ānum*.

Chacón Spanish: of uncertain meaning. It may have been a nickname for a noisy, jolly person, from a word of imitative origin. The element *chac-* is used in other Sp. words descriptive of the noise of musical instruments or of convulsive laughter, as for example *chacota* and *chacona*.

Chadwick English: habitation name from any of various places so called, in Lancs., Warwicks., and two in Worcs. One of the latter and the one in Warwicks. are named as being the dairy farm (OE *wīc*, see WICK) of *Ceadel*. The other Worcs. place and the one in Lancs. are named as '*Ceadda's* dairy farm'. *Ceadda* is the name of an Anglo-Saxon bishop, St Chad.

Vars.: **Chadwyck, Chaddock, Chattock; Shadwick, Shaddick, Shaddock, Shattock.**

Chaff English (Norman): nickname for a bald man, from OF *chauf* bald (L *calvus*; cf. CALLOW). *Calvus* was a Roman family name, originally a byname, and was still occasionally used as a given name in Italy in the Middle Ages, so that in some cases the It. cogns. may derive from this source.

Vars.: **Chaffe, Chave; Caff,** CAVE (from Norman forms).

Cogns.: Fr.: **Chalve, Charve, Chauve; Calve.** It.: **Calvo, Calvi** (Liguria, Lombardy). Sp.: **Calvo,** COBO. Port.: **Calv(ã)o.**

Dims.: Eng.: **Chaffin, Chafen, Chauvin; Cavell.** Fr.: **Chalvet, Chauvet, Cho(u)vet, Charvet; Chauveau, Choveau, Chauvel(et), Chovel, Chauvelin, Chauvelon, Chauvelot; Chalvin, Chauvin(eau), Chauvenet, Cho(u)vin, Chevin, Charvin; Chalvon, Chalv(e)ron, Chauvon, Chauv(e)ron, Chauvillon.** It.: **Calvino, Calvini, Calvelli, Calvello, Calv(i)etti, Calvillo.** Cat.: **Calvet, Calvó.**

Aug.: Fr.: **Chauvat.**

Pej.: Fr.: **Chauvard.**

All present-day English bearers of the name Chaffin *are apparently descended from John Chaffin (d. 1658), a blacksmith of Bruton, Somerset. The surname is now much more common in America than in England. The var.* Chafyn *seems to have become extinct in the early 19th cent.; it was once borne by a group of landowning families with branches in Chettle and Folk (Dorset), Zeals (Wilts.), and Salisbury (Wilts.), who can be traced back to Warminster in the 15th cent.*

Chagas Portuguese: religious byname from the pl. form of Port. *chaga* wound (L *plāga* blow), with reference to the wounds of Christ.

Chait Jewish (Ashkenazic): occupational name for a tailor, Yid. *khayet* (from Hebr. *chayat*). In Anglophone countries the name is often given the spelling pronunciation /tʃeɪt/, as opposed to the original /ˈxajət/.

Vars: **Khait, Khaet; Chayat, Chajat** (from the Hebr. form; the latter is a Pol. spelling); **Hayat, Hyat(t)** (see also HIGHET).

Dims.: **Chaitchik, Chajczyk, Chajczuk** (E Ashkenazic).

Patrs.: **Chaitin, Chaitow(itz), Khaitovich** (E Ashkenazic).

Chalk English: topographic name for someone who lived on a patch of chalk soil, or habitation name from any of the various places named from OE *cealc(e)* chalk, as for example *Chalk* in Kent or *Chalke* in Wilts.

Vars.: **Chalke, Chaulk; Chalker, Cawker, Kalker** (in part occupational names from OE *(ge)cealcian* to chalk, whitewash).

Chalkley English: habitation name from an unidentified place (probably in S England, where the surname is commonest and where chalk hills abound), apparently so called from OE *cealc* chalk + *lēah* wood, clearing.

Challamel French: probably a metonymic occupational name for a gatherer of reeds or a thatcher, from a dim. of OF *c(h)al(l)ame* reed (L *calamus*).

Vars.: **C(h)alamel(le), Charameau, Chalamet, Chalumeau, Charamon.**

Challenor English: occupational name for a maker or seller of blankets, from an agent deriv. of ME *chaloun* blanket, coverlet. The articles were named from being first and most notably produced in the town of *Châlons*-sur-Marne, so called from having been the seat of a Gaul. tribe recorded in L sources as *Catalauni*.

Vars.: **Challen(d)er, Challinor, Chal(l)oner, Chawner, Channer; Challen(s), Challin.**

Challis English (Norman): habitation name from *Eschalles* in Pas-de-Calais, which gets its name from the pl. form of OF *eschelle* ladder (L *scala*).

Vars.: **Challiss, Chal(l)ice, Challace, Challes.**

Chalmers Scots: var. of CHAMBERS. The *-l-* was originally an orthographic device to indicate the length of the vowel after assimilation of *-mb-* to *-m(m)-*.

Chaloupek Czech: status name for a poor farmer living in a cottage (Czech *chalupa*), esp. one with very little land attached to it. A *chalupník* had even less land than a smallholder (ZAHRADNÍK).

Var.: **Chal(o)upník.**

Habitation names: **Chalupa, Chaloupka.**

Chamberlain English: occupational name from ANF *c(h)ambrelain, cambrelanc, cambrelen(c)* chamberlain (of Gmc origin, cf. OHG *kemerlinc*, from *kamer, chamara* chamber, room (L *camera*; see CHAMBERS) + the suffix *-(l)ing*). This was originally the name of an official in charge of the private chambers of his master, later a title of high rank (for similar increases in dignity, see BUTLER, MARSHALL, SCHENKE, SENESCHAL, and STEWART). The Italian cogn. *camerlengo* was used of the manager of a pontifical court.

Vars.: **Chamberlaine, Chamberlayne, Chamberlen, Chamberlin, Champerlen.**

Cogns.: Fr.: **C(h)amberlin, Cambreleng, Chambellan(d), Chamberland.** It.: **Camerlengo, Camerlenghi, Camerlingo, Camerlinghi, Ciambellani, Ciamberlini.** Ger.: **Käm(m)erling.** Flem.: **Camerlynk.**

Chambers English: occupational name for someone who was employed in the private living quarters of his master, rather than in the public halls of the manor. The name represents a gen. or pl. form of ME, OF *cha(u)mbre* chamber, room (L *camera*), and is synonymous in origin with CHAMBERLAIN, but as that office rose in the social scale, this term remained reserved for more humble servants of the bedchamber.

Var: CHALMERS.

Cogns.: Fr.: **C(h)ambre, Lac(h)ambre, De(la)chambre; Chambrier.** Prov.: **Delcambre; Crambe(s), Lacrambe** (Gascony). It.: **Camera.** Sp.: **Cámara; Camarero.** Cat.: **Cambra, Lacambra.** Port.: **Câmara; Câmarão.** Ger.: **Kammer(er), Käm(m)erer** (see also CAMBER). Flem.: **Camerman.** Pol.: **Kamer(ski).** Jewish (Ashkenazic): **Kammer(man)** (reason for adoption unknown).

Dims.: Fr.: **Cambron, Cambran(d), Cambrin, Cambret(te), Cambrillon.** It.: **Camerino.** Sp.: **Camarillo.** Port.: **Camarin(h)o.**

Aug.: Fr.: **Chambras.**

Chamizo Spanish: 1. topographic name for someone who lived in a thatched cottage, Sp. *chamizo* (from *chamiza* dried straw, of Galician/Port. origin, from *chama* flame, L *flamma*).

2. nickname for someone with dark hair or a swarthy complexion, from *chamizo* soot, half-burned wood (likewise from *chama* flame).

Chamorro Spanish: nickname for a clean-shaven or closely cropped man. The word is first attested in the mid-14th cent. and is of unknown origin, possibly a survival of a pre-Roman word with cogns. in Basque. In the Middle Ages it was applied as an ethnic nickname to the Portuguese, who wore their hair short in contrast with the Castilian custom of allowing it to attain its natural length.

Champ French: topographic name for someone who lived in or near a field or expanse of open country, or else in the countryside as opposed to a town, from OF *champ* field, open land (L *campus* plain, expanse of flat land).

Vars: **Camp** (Normandy, Picardy); **C(h)amps**; **Dec(h)amp**, **Delcamp**, **Duc(h)amp**, **Desc(h)amps**, **Decamps**; **Auchamp**.

Cogns: It.: **Campi** (N Italy); **Campo** (S Italy); **Campus** (S Sardinia); **Campari** (N Italy); **Campai** (Tuscany); **Camper** (Venetia); **Campieri**; **Campeggi** (Emilia); **Campese**, **Campesi**, **Campise**, **Campisi** (S Italy, Venetia). Sp.: **Campo(s)**. Cat.: **Camp(s)**. Port.: **Campos**. Low Ger.: **Kamp(mann)**, **Kammann**; **Kamper**, **Kämper**, **Kemper** (see also KEMP); **Ingenkamp**. Fris.: **Kampstra**. Du.: **Van (den) Camp**, **Van den Kamp**, **Van Campen**, **Van Kampen**. Flem.: **Camps**, **Van (de) Kamp**.

Dims.: Fr.: **Champeau(x)**, **Champel**, **Champon(net)**, **Champot**, **Champet**, **Champeix**. It.: **Campetti**, **Campolo**, **Campoli**, **Campino**. Sp.: **Campillo**.

Augs.: It.: **Campone**, **Camponi**.

Pejs.: It.: **Campacci(o)**, **Campasso**, **Campassi**, **Campazzo**, **Campazzi**.

Champney English: regional name for someone from *Champagne* in France, from ANF *champeneis*, a deriv. of OF *Champagne* (L *Campānia*, from *campus* plain, flat land; see CHAMP). This is also the name of various villages in France, and in a few cases the Fr. cogns. may derive from one of these. Rarely the name may also have referred in general terms to a dweller in the countryside rather than a town.

Vars.: **Champneys** (usually pronounced /'tʃæni:z/); **Champness**, **Champniss**; **Champain**.

Cogns.: Fr.: **Champenois**, **Champonnois**; **C(h)ampagne**, **Champaigne**.

Champouillon French: apparently a habitation name from some minor place so called from OF CHAMP field + *pouillon* bug (a dim. of *pou* flea, L *pūlex*).

Var.: **Champollion**.

Chance English: nickname for an inveterate gambler, or perhaps for someone who had survived an accident by a remarkable piece of luck, from ANF *chea(u)nce* (good) fortune (a deriv. of *cheoir* to fall (out), L *cadere*).

Vars.: **C(h)aunce**.

Chancellor English and Scots: occupational name for a secretary or administrative official, from ANF *c(h)ancelier* (LL *cancellārius* usher of a law court, from *cancelli* lattice, grating dividing the court officials from the general public). The King's Chancellor was one of the highest officials in the land, but the term was also used to describe the holder of a variety of offices in the medieval world, such as the secretary or record keeper in a minor manorial household. In some cases, however, the name is found referring to people in very humble circumstances, including serfs, who are unlikely to have been chancellors or descended from chancellors, in any sense of the word. This suggests origin as a nickname.

Var.: **Cancellor**.

Cogns.: Fr.: **C(h)ancelier**. It.: **Cancellario**, **Cancellieri**. Ger. and Jewish (Ashkenazic): **Kanzler** (reason for adoption as a Jewish name unknown).

A Scots family called Chancellor *were in vassalage to the Lord of Somerville before 1432, and possessed Shieldhill and Quothquhan for centuries.*

Chandler English: occupational name for a maker and seller of candles, ME *cha(u)ndeler* (OF *chandelier*, LL *candēlārius*, a deriv. of *candēla* candle, from *candēre* to be bright). While a medieval chandler no doubt made and sold other articles beside candles, the extended sense of mod. Eng. *chandler* does not occur until the 16th cent. The name may also, more rarely, have denoted someone who was responsible for the lighting arrangements in a large house, or else one who owed rent in the form of wax or candles.

Var.: **Chantler**.

Cogns.: Fr.: **C(h)andelier**, **Candeliez**. It.: **Candelari**, **Candelaro**, **Candelieri**. Sp.: **Candela(s)**. Cat.: **Can(d)ela**. Port.: **Candeias**. Ger.: **Schandel**.

Channon English (chiefly W Country): var. of CANNON 1, taken from the central French form *chanun*, as opposed to the Norman *canun*.

Chanson French: 1. nickname for a man with a fine voice or fond of singing at his work, from OF *chanson* song (LL *cantio*, gen. *cantiōnis* singing, song, a deriv. of *cantāre* to sing, replacing class. L *cantus*; cf. CANT).

2. occupational name for a cup-bearer, from an aphetic form of OF *échanson*, a word of Gmc origin (see SCHENKE).

Chanteraine French: habitation name from a place in the Vosges, so called from OF *chante(r)* to sing (L *cantāre*, freq. of *canere*) + *raine* frog (L *rāna*), a humorous name for a marshy locality where the frogs could be heard croaking.

Vars.: **Chantraine**, **Chantreine**, **Chanterenne**.

Chapaev Russian: patr. from a nickname derived from either of two homonymous verbs *chapat* to snatch, seize and *chapat* to swing, waver (both are of uncertain, but apparently distinct, origin).

Chape French: from OF *chape* hooded cloak, cape, hood, or hat (LL *cappa*, *cāpa*, perhaps a deriv. of *caput* head; see CAP), applied as a metonymic occupational name for a maker of either cloaks or hats, or as a nickname for a habitual wearer of a distinctive cloak or hat. The two L byforms, *cappa* and *cāpa*, were borrowed into OE as *cæppe* and *cāp* respectively, becoming mod. Eng. *cap* and *cope* (see CAPPER and COPE), with later semantic differentiation. Mod. Eng. *cape* could in part represent a N English development of OE *cāp* (cf. ROPER), but more probably it was reintroduced, with yet another distinction in meaning, from Provence in the 16th cent.

Vars.: **Chappe**; **Cape** (Normandy, Picardy); **Chapu(t)** (nicknames); **Chapier**, **Caper(s)** (occupational names).

Cogns.: It.: **Cappa** ('cape'), **Cappe**; **Capparo** (occupational). Ger.: **Kappe**; **Käppner**, **Keppner** (occupational). Pol.: **Kapelusz**.

Dims.: Fr.: **Chapet**, **Chapé**, **C(h)apez**, **Chapey**; **Chapel(et)**, **Chapeau**, **C(h)aplot**, **Chapleteau**; **Capelon**, **Capot**; **Chapel(l)ier** (occupational). It.: **Cappini** ('small cape'); **Cappell(in)i** ('hat'), **Capp(i)ello**, **Cappilli**, **Cap(p)elletti**, **Cappellut(t)i**, **Cap(p)ellozzi**; **Capelli**, **Capèllo** (S Italy; see also CABELLO); **Cap(p)ellaro**, **Cap(p)pellari**, **Cappell(i)eri** (occupational); **Cappuza** ('hood'), **Cap(p)ucc(in)i**; **Copozzi** (Emilia); **Capucciaro** (occupational); COPPOLA. Sp.: **Capote** ('cape'); **Capellero** ('hat'; occupational). Cat.: **Capel(l)**; **Capeller**, **Capellé**. Ger.: **Käppel(e)** ('cape'), **Keppel**; **Kep(p)ler** (occupational). Bulg.: **Shápka**. Jewish: **Keppel**, **Kep(p)ler** (Ashkenazic, occupational for a cloak maker); **Kapelushnik** (E Ashkenazic, occupational for a hat maker).

Chaplin 1. English and French: occupational name for a clergyman, or perhaps for the servant of one, from ME, OF *chapelain* chantry priest, a priest endowed to sing mass daily on behalf of the souls of the dead (LL *capellānus*, a deriv. of *capella*; see CHAPPELL).

2. Russian: patr. from the nickname *Chaplya* 'Heron', 'Stork' (Pol. *czapla*), referring to a man with long, thin legs or perhaps one who was shy and easily frightened.

Vars. (of 1): Eng.: **Chaplain, Chapling, Chaperlin(g), Cap(e)len, Cap(e)lin, Capeling**. Fr.: **Chapel(a)in, Chaplain; Cap(el)ain, Capelan, Capéran; Lechapelain, Lecap(e)lain**. See also KAPLAN. (Of 2): Russ.: **Tsaplin**.

Cogns. (of 1): Sp.: **Capellán**. Cat.: **Capellà**. (Of 2): Ukr.: **Chapla**. Pol.: **Czapla; Czapski**. Czech: **Cáp**.

Dims. (of 2): Pol.: **Czapnik**. Czech: **Čapek**.

Habitation names (from 2): Pol.: **Czapliński, Czaplicki**.

Chapman English: occupational name for a merchant or trader, ME *chapman*, OE *cēapmann*, a cpd of *cēap* barter, bagain, price, property + *mann* man.

Vars.: **Chipman** (from W Saxon *cȳp(e)mann*); **Chapper, Chipper, Cheeper** (from the OE verb *cē(a)pan, cȳpan*); COPEMAN.

Cogns.: Ger.: **Kauf(f)mann; Kaf(e)mann** (Bavaria, Austria); **Käufer; Kauf; Käufler** ('dealer in second-hand goods'), **Kaifler, Käufel, Kaifel**. Low Ger.: **Kop(p)mann; Köper**. Du.: **Koopman**. Flem.: **Coopman, De Copman**. Jewish (Ashkenazic): **Kauf(er), Käufer, Kauf(f)man(n); Koifman, Koyfman, Kojfman** (from a Yid. pronunciation).

Patrs.: Du.: **Koo(p)mans**. Flem.: **Coo(p)mans**. Finn.: **Kauppinen**.

Chappell English: topographic name for someone who lived close to a chapel, or occupational name for someone employed in one. The name comes from ME, OF *chapel(l)e* chapel (LL *capella*, originally a dim. of *cāpa* hood, cloak (see CHAPE), but later transferred to the sense 'chapel', 'sanctuary', with reference to the shrine at Tours where the cloak of St MARTIN was preserved as a relic).

Vars: **Chappel(le), Chapell; Chapple** (W Country); **Cap(p)el(l), Capelle** (from Norman forms); **Capewell** (chiefly Midlands).

Cogns.: Fr.: **C(h)apelle, Capell**. Prov.: **Capela**. It.: **Cappella, Cappelle**. Sp.: **Capilla**. Cat.: **Capella**. Port.: **Capela**. Du.: **Capel, Van (de) Keppel**. Flem.: **Van de Capelle**.

Capel *is the family name of the present Earl of Essex. His forebears rose to prominence with Sir William Capell, who was Lord Mayor of London in 1503.*

Van Keppel *is the name of a Dutch family who held the lordship of Keppel in Guelderland. Their earliest recorded ancestor was Walter van Keppel, living in 1179. A branch of the family was established in England when Arnold van Keppel (1669–1718) accompanied William of Orange, who created him Earl of Albermarle.*

Chapuis French: occupational name for a carpenter or joiner, a deriv. of OF *chapuiser* to cut, trim (LL *cappulāre*, of uncertain origin).

Vars.: **C(h)apus**.

Dims.: **Chapu(i)set, Chapuzet, Chapu(i)sot, Chapuzot, Chapuiseau**.

Aug.: **Chapuisat**.

Charles 1. French, Welsh, and English: from the Gmc personal name *Carl* 'Man' (which was Latinized as *Carolus*). In France the given name was popular from an early date, due to the fame of the Emperor *Charlemagne* (?742–814; Latin name *Carolus Magnus*, i.e. Charles the Great). The OF form *Charles* was briefly introduced to England by the Normans, but was rare during the main period of surname formation. It was introduced more successfully to Scotland in the 16th cent. by the Stuarts, who had strong ties with France, and was brought by them to England in the 17th cent. Its frequency as a Welsh surname is attributable to the late date of Welsh surname formation. The Ger. cogn., *Karl*, is rare or unknown as a surname, probably because the given name was not in use among the general population in German-speaking countries in the Middle Ages, but was restricted to the nobility. OE *Ceorl* 'peasant' is also found as a byname, but the resulting ME form, *Charl*, with a patr. in *-s*, if it existed at all, would have been absorbed by the French form introduced by the Normans. English vars. pronounced with initial /k-/ for the most part reflect the cogn. ON personal name *Karl*, *Karli*.

2. English: patr. from an occupational name or status name for a peasant farmer, ME *charl*, *cherl*, OE *ceorl* peasant (see CHARLTON).

Vars: Eng.: **Carl(e), Karl(e)**. (Of 1 only): Fr.: **Charle; Charlon** (oblique case); **Carle** (Normandy, Picardy); **Chasle(s)** (Beauce).

Cogns.: It.: **Carlo; Caroli** (Emilia); **Carlesi, Carlisi, Carlesso** (Venetia). Sp.: **Carlos**. Cat.: **Carles**. Low Ger.: **Ke(h)rl, Keerl**. Flem., Du.: **Carl**. Jewish (Ashkenazic): **Karl**. Czech: **Karel, Kareš**. Hung.: **Károly** (also borne by Hungarian Jews); **Karolyi**.

Dims. (of 1): Fr.: **C(h)arlet, Charley, Charlin, Charlon, Charlo(t)**; CARLIN. It.: **Carletti, Carletto, Carlin(i), Carlin(o), Carlucci(o), Carluzzi, Carlotti, Carlotto, Carlozzi**. Czech: **Karlík, Karlíček**. Pol.: **Karolczyk**.

Augs. (of 1): It.: **Carlon(i), Carlone**.

Patrs. (from 1): Eng.: **Charleston** (with intrusive *-t-*, cf. JOHNSTON 2; the various places called *Charleston* are all of too recent origin to have given rise to surnames). Sc.: **McCarlish** (Gael. **Mac Carlais**). It.: **De Carlo, De Carli, Di Carlo, De Caroli(s)**. Flem., Du.: **Carlens**. Dan., Norw.: **Karlsen, Carlsen**. Swed.: **Karlsson, Carlsson**. Pol.: **Karłowicz; Karolak, Karolczak**.

Habitation names (from 1): Pol.: **Karolewski, Karłowski**. Czech: **Karlovský**.

Charlesworth English: habitation name from a place in Derbys., recorded in Domesday Book as *Cheuenesuurde* and in the 13th cent. as *Chauelisworth*. The name apparently comes from the gen. case of an OE byname derived from *ceafl* jaw + OE *worð* enclosure (see WORTH), but the first element has suffered from late folk etymological association with the given name CHARLES.

Charlier French: occupational name for a cartwright, from OF *charrelier*, a deriv. of *charrel* cart (dim. of *char*, LL *carrum*; cf. CARRIER).

Var.: **Carlier** (Norman, Picard).

Charlton 1. English: habitation name from any of the numerous places so called in every part of England, from OE *Ceorlatūn* 'settlement (OE *tūn*) of the peasants'. OE *ceorl* denoted originally a free peasant of the lowest rank, later (but probably already before the Norman conquest) a tenant in pure villeinage, a serf or bondsman.

2. Irish: var. of CARLIN 1.

Vars.: **Charleton**, CHORLTON, CARLTON.

Charme French: topographic name for someone who lived by a conspicuous hornbeam (witch elm) or group of such trees, from OF *charme* (L *carpīnus*).

Vars.: **Charmes, Charne**, CARNE; **Decharme, Ducharme, Ducharne**.

Cogns.: Prov.: **Carpe, Ducarpe**. It.: **Carp(in)i, Carpino, Carpano, Carpine, Carpene**.

Dims.: Fr.: **Charmet, Charmey**. It.: **Carpinelli, Carpanelli, Carpenetti, Carpanini**.

Aug.: It.: **Carpanoni**.

Collectives: Fr.: **C(h)armoy, Charmay, Carnoy, Charpenay**. It.: **Carpineto, Carpineti, Carpaneto, Carpeneto, Carpeneti**.

Charnley English (Lancs.): apparently a habitation name from an unidentified place so called, possibly from the same element as in CHARNOCK with the addition of OE *lēah* wood, clearing.

Charnock English (Lancs.): habitation name from *Charnock* Richard or Heath *Charnock* in S Lancs., so called from a Brit. deriv. of a placename element cogn. with W *carn* stone (see CAIRNS).

Charrette French: from OF *char(r)ette* cart, a dim. of *char(re)* (LL *carrum* (neut.) and *carra* (fem., originally neut. pl.), of Celt. origin). This may have been acquired as a metonymic occupational name for a user or maker of carts (see CARTER, CARTWRIGHT), or perhaps as a nickname for someone who owned a wheeled vehicle in an area where asses or mules were the usual means of transport.

Vars.: **C(h)arette**.

Cogn.: It.: **Caretto**.

Charron French: metonymic occupational name for a maker of carts, from OF *charron* cart (L *carro*, gen. *carrōnis*, a deriv. of *carrum* cart; cf. CARMAN).

Vars.: **Carron** (Normandy; see also CARON); **Charrondier, Charrandier** (with added agent suffix).

Chart English: habitation name from any of various places named with OE *ce(a)rt* rough heathland, as for example *Chart* in Kent and Surrey or *Churt* in Surrey, or possibly a topographic name from the same word used independently.

Var.: **Chard** (a place in Somerset).

Charteris 1. Scots and English: Norman habitation name from the Fr. town of *Chartres*, so called from having been the seat of a Gaul. tribe whose name is recorded in L sources in the form *Carnutes*.

2. English: habitation name from *Chatteris* in Cambs., which is of uncertain etymology, possibly the 'ridge (OE *hrycg*) of *Ceatta*', a personal name of uncertain origin (cf. CHATFIELD).

Vars. (of 1): **Charters, Chatres**. (Of 2): **Chatter(i)s**.

Cogn. (of 1): Fr.: **Chartres**.

A family of the name Charteris *can be traced to Thomas, clerk to the King of Scotland in* c.*1277–82, who became Chancellor of Scotland in* c.*1288. Other members of this family include Walter* de Carnato, *who gave churches to the Abbot of Kelso* c.*1180, and Andrew* de Charteris, *who paid homage to Edward I in 1295.*

Chartres *is the name of an Irish family descended from two brothers, William and Alexander Chartres. They were Huguenot soldiers who were granted lands in Westmeath and Cavan between 1661 and 1665.*

Chase English: apparently a metonymic occupational name for a huntsman, or rather a nickname for an exceptionally skilled huntsman, from ME *chase* hunt (OF *chasse*, from *chasser* to hunt, chase, L *captāre*; cf. CATCHPOLE).

Var.: **Chace**.

Cogns.: Fr.: **Chasseur**. Port.: **Caçador**.

Chateaubriand French: habitation name from a place in Loire-Inférieure, so named from being the seat (OF *chasteau*; see CASTLE) of a Bret. proprietor bearing a personal name meaning 'Eminence' (see BRYAN).

The French writer and politician François, Vicomte de Chateaubriand *(1768–1848), was from an ancient Bret. family. He was descended from Baron Brien, who fought with William the Conqueror at Hastings and from whose keep at* Chateaubriant *the family took its name.*

Châtelier French: habitation name any of the numerous places named from OF *chastelier* small castle, minor fort (L *castellāre*, a deriv. of *castellum* castle; cf. CASALE from CASA and VILLIERS from VILLE).

Vars.: **Chatellier, Duchâtelier, Duchatellier**.

Cogns.: Prov.: **Cayla, Ducayla**. It.: **Castel(l)ari, Castel(l)aro**.

Dims.: It.: **Castel(l)arin(i)**.

Chatfield English: habitation name from an unidentified place, apparently so called from the OE personal name *Ceatta* (probably a var. of *Catta*; see CATT 1) + OE *feld* pasture, open country (see FIELD).

Chatham English: habitation name from the place so called in Kent (or possibly from *Chatham* Green in Essex). These places appear in Domesday Book as *Ceteham* and *Cetham* respectively, and Ekwall derives the first part from a Brit. element *ceto-* forest (cf. W *coed*); the second is OE *hām* homestead. See also CHEETHAM.

Chattaway English: habitation name from an unidentified place (probably in the W Midlands, where the surname is commonest), apparently so called from the OE personal name *Ceatta* (cf. CHATFIELD) + OE *weg* path, way.

Chatterley English: habitation name from a place in Staffs., so called from a first element *chader-* (probably a Brit. word meaning 'chair', used of a commanding hill; cf. CHATTERTON) + OE *lēah* wood, clearing.

Chatterton English: habitation name from *Chadderton* in Lancs., which was recorded in 1224 in the form *Chaterton*. The first element may preserve a Brit. term which became W *cadair* chair, used in placenames to denote a commanding hill; the second is OE *tūn* enclosure, settlement.

Var.: **Chaderton**.

Chatto Scots: habitation name from a place in the former county of Roxburghs. (now part of Borders region), of uncertain, possibly Gael., etymology. The surname is now rare in SE Scotland.

The first known bearer of the name is William de Chetue, *who witnessed a charter at the beginning of the 13th cent.*

Chaucer English: occupational name for a maker of leggings; see CHAUSSE.

Vars.: **Chauser; Causer** (W Midlands).

Chaume French: 1. topographic name for someone who lived on a high treeless plateau, from the OF dial. term *chaume* plateau (of apparently Gaul. origin).

2. topographic name for someone who lived by a patch of fallow land, from OF *chaume* hay stubble (L *calamus* reed; cf. CHALLAMEL).

Vars.: **Chaulme(s); Lachaume; Delachaume; Chaumier, Chaumié**.

Cogns.: Prov.: **Calme, Cam, Can; Lecalm(e), Lacam, Lacan**.

Dims.: Fr.: **Chaumel, Chomel, Chaumet(te), Chomet(te), Chaumeix, Chaumeil, Chaumot, Chaumillon, Chaumeton**. Prov.: **Calmette, Calmel(s)**.

Aug.: Fr.: **Chaumat**.

Chausse French: metonymic occupational name for a maker of shoes or leggings, or nickname for a wearer of distinctive ones, from OF *chausse* footwear or leggings (LL *calcia*, for class. L *calceus* sandal, shoe, a deriv. of *calx*, gen. *calcis*, heel). In medieval Europe this term was used very widely, and denoted boots, shoes, leggings, leg armour, gaiters, hose, breeches, pantaloons, and so on; its modern descendants include Fr. *chaussures* shoes and *chaussettes* socks.

Vars.: **Cauce** (Normandy, Picardy); **Chaussier** (occupational); **Chaussé** (nickname).

Cogns.: Prov.: **Chaussaire, Chossaire** (occupational); **Chaussat** (nickname). Eng.: CHAUCER. It.: **Calza, Calzo; Calzola(r)i** (occupational).

Dims.: Fr.: **Chausson; Chaussec, Chossec** (Brittany). It.: **Calzetta, Calzette, Calzetti.**

Pej.: Fr.: **Chausard.**

Chaussée French: topographic name for someone who lived by a paved road, Fr. *chaussée*, a relatively rare feature of the medieval countryside. *Chaussée* is from L (*via*) *calciāta* 'limed (way)', from *calx* chalk, limestone, gen. *calcis*. This word has also named a number of Fr. villages, and the surname may be a habitation name from one of these.

Vars.: **Lachaussée, Delachaussée; Cauchie, Cauchy, Delcauchie** (Normandy, Picardy).

Cogns.: Prov.: **Caussade, Lacaussade.** Eng.: CAUSEY. Sp.: **Calzada.** Port.: **Calçada.**

Chaves Portuguese: habitation name from a place in the province of Tras-os-Montes, so called from L (*aquis*) *Flaviis*, the abl. case, originally used after a preposition, of *aquae Flaviae* 'waters of *Flavius*'. The place was the site of sulphurous springs with supposedly health-giving properties, around which a settlement was founded in the 1st cent. AD by the Emperor Vespasian.

Chazan Jewish (Ashkenazic): occupational name for a cantor in a synagogue, Hebr. *chazan*.

Vars.: **Chasan, Haz(z)an, Khazan, Kazan; Chason** (reflecting an Ashkenazic pronunciation of the Hebr. word); **Chazen, Chasen, Chasin** (reflecting Yid. *khazn*).

Patrs.: **Chazanow, Chazanoff, Chasanoff, Chas(i)noff; Khazanov(ich), Kazanov(ich), Kazanowitz, K(h)azanovski** (E Ashkenazic); **Chasins** (with Yid. possessive *-s*).

Cheadle English: habitation name from *Cheadle* in Ches. and Staffs. Ekwall explains the name as being from the Brit. element *ceto-* wood, with the tautologous addition of OE *lēah* wood, clearing (cf. CHETWODE).

Var.: **Chettle.**

Cheater English: occupational name for an escheator, the official in charge of supervising the reversion of property to the feudal lord in the absence of legal heirs. The name comes from ME *chetour*, an aphetic form of ANF *eschetour* (a deriv. of *eschete* lot, from *eschoir* to fall to the lot of, L *excadere* to fall out; cf. CHANCE); the opportunities for dubious dealing implicit in the post led to the later sense of the verb *cheat*.

Var.: **Chetter.**

Checkley English: habitation name from any of the places so called, in Ches., Herefords., and Staffs. The last two are probably '*Ceacca*'s clearing (OE *lēah*)'; the Ches. name is '*Ceaddica*'s clearing', from a deriv. of the same personal name.

Cheek English: nickname for someone with some deformity or scar in the region of the cheek or jawbone, ME *cheeke* (OE *cē(a)ce*).

Vars.: **Che(e)ke, Cheak(e).**

A family called Cheke *trace their descent in unbroken line to Richard Cheke, who in the reign of Richard II held the manor of Motteston on the Isle of Wight. A later member was Sir John Cheke (1514–57), who was Professor of Greek at Cambridge and owned Pyrgo Park at Havering-atte-Bower, Essex, as well as property in Clare, Suffolk, and Spalding, Lincs. The surname is fairly well established in Essex, Hants, the Isle of Wight, and the W Country, but rare elsewhere.*

Cheesbrough English: probably a habitation name from an unidentified place, apparently so called from OE *cis* gravel + *burh* fortress, town. A place in Northumb., now *Cheeseburn*, is recorded in 1286 as *Cheseburgh*; a place now called *Chirbury* in Hodnet parish, Shrops., is spelled *Ches(e)bury* in 1291–5. Either of these may be the source of this surname, which, however, is now found most commonly in Yorks.

Cheeseman English: occupational name for a maker or seller of cheese, from OE *cȳse*, *cēse* cheese (L *cāseus*) + *mann* man.

Vars.: **Cheesman, Ches(e)man, Cheasman, Chi(e)sman, Chessman, Chismon; Cheese, Chiese; Cheese(w)right, Che(e)swright, Chesswright, Cherrett, Cherritt** (see WRIGHT).

Cogns.: Ger.: **Käsmann; Käser,** KESER; **Käs(e).** Low Ger.: **Kaas(man), Keesman, Keese.** Flem.: **Caesman.** Du.: **Kaes, Kaas(kooper).** Jewish (S Ashkenazic): **Keizman, Keyzman.** Fr.: **C(h)asier, Chazier, Chesier, Chezier; Chazerand.** It.: **Casari, Casaro, Caser(i), Casieri, Casiero;** CASE. Port.: **Queyeiro, Queyos.**

Dims.: Fr.: **Chazereau.** It.: **Casarin(i), Casarino, Casaroli, Casiroli, Casaril(e).**

Patrs.: Flem.: **Caesmans.** Du.: **Kaesmans, Kaesmakers.**

Cheetham English: habitation name from a place in Lancs., apparently so called from the Brit. element *ceto-* wood + OE *hām* homestead; cf. CHATHAM.

Vars.: **Cheatham.**

Cheever English: nickname for a stubborn person, or metonymic occupational name for a goatherd, from ANF *chivere*, *chevre* goat (L *capra* nanny goat).

Cogns.: Fr. **Chèvre, Lachèvre; Quièvre, Laquièvre** (Normandy); **Chevrier, Chevreux, Quevreux, Quiévreux** (occupational). Prov.: **Cabre, Cabré; Chabre(s), Chabri** (Massif Central); **Crabe, Crave** (Gascony); **C(h)abrier, C(h)abrié** (occupational). It.: **Capra, Crapa, Capro; Cavra, Crava** (N Italy); **Chiabra** (Liguria); **Cabras** (Sardinia); **Capraro, Caprari, Cravari, Craveri, Cravero, Chiabrero, Cibrario** (occupational). Sp.: **Cabrer(iz)o** (occupational). Cat.: **Cabrer, Cabré** (occupational). Port.: **Cabreiro** (occupational).

Dims.: Fr.: **Chevrel, Chevreau, Chevret, Chevrey, Cheuret, Chevr(et)ot, Chevrill(on).** Prov.: **Crabet(te), Crabot; Cabiron, Cabrit.** Eng.: **Cheverell, Cheverall, Cheverill, Chiv(e)rall, Chiverell.** It.: **Caprin(i), Caprino, Capretti, Capr(i)otti, Capruzzi, La Capruccia; Cavrini, Cavrotti, Cavrulli, Cavaretta; Cravetti, Cravetta, Cravino, Cravin(i), Cravotta, Craviotto; Crapulli.** Port.: **Cabrita.**

Aug.: It.: **Caproni.**

Patrs.: Eng.: **Che(e)vers; Chivers.**

The name of the Irish family now known as Chevers *has taken many forms, including* Che(e)ver(s) *and* Ch(i)evre. *It can be traced to Gosfred* Chievre, *a Norman nobleman living in 1100, whose son William* Chevre *received land in Wexford when he took part in Strongbow's invasion of Ireland in 1172.*

Chegwin Cornish: habitation name from the elements *chy* house + *gwyn* white (see GWYN).

Var.: **Chegwyn.**

Chemin French: topographic name for someone who lived near a thoroughfare, from OF *chemin* path, way (LL *camminus*, of apparently Celt. origin).

Vars.: **Duchemin; Quemin, Quémin, Duquemin** (Normandy).

Cogns.: Prov.: **Cami(n)**, **Camy**; **Chamin** (Massif Central); **Ducami(n)**, **Ducamy**. It.: **Delcamino**. Sp.: **Camino**; **Caminero**. Cat.: **Camí**.

Dims.: Fr.: **Cheminel**, **Chemineau**. Prov.: **Caminel**.

Chenal French: topographic name for someone who lived near an irrigation channel, from OF *chenal* channel, pipe (LL *canālis*, a deriv. of *canna* reed; cf. CAIN 1).

Vars.: **Chenau(d)**, **Chenault**, **Chenaux**; **Lachenal**, **Lachenaud**, **Delachenal**.

Cogns.: Prov.: **Canal**, **Canau(d)**, **Canault**, **Lacanal**, **Lacanau**; **Chanal**, **Chanau(lt)** (Massif Central). It.: **Canele**, **Caneli**; **Da Canal(e)** (Venetia). Sp.: **Canal(es)**. Cat.: **Canal(s)**.

Dims.: It.: **Canaletto**, **Canalini**.

Chêne French: topographic name for someone who lived near a conspicuous oak tree, or in an oak forest, from OF *chesne* oak (LL *caxinus*, a var. of *cassanus* (see CASSE 1 and CASSAGNE), influenced by *fraxinus* ash). The surname may perhaps occasionally also have been a nickname for a man with a 'heart of oak'.

Vars.: **Chesne**, **Cha(i)gne**; **Lechêne**, **Lechesne**; **Dechêne**, **Dechesne**; **Duchêne**, **Duchesne**; **Chénier**, **Chesnier**. See also QUÊNE.

Cogns.: Eng.: **(Du) Cane**; **Cheyne** (now found chiefly in Scotland; usually pronounced /'tʃeɪnɪ/).

Dims.: Fr.: **Chénel**, **Chesnel**, **Chéneau**, **Chesneau**, **Chénet**, **Chesnet**, **Chesné**, **Chénot**, **Chesnot**, **Chênelot**; **Chagneaux**, **Chagnon**, **Chagnoux**, **Chagnot**, **Chagnol**.

Collectives: Fr.: **Chênai(s)**, **Chesnais**, **Che(s)nay**, **Chênois**, **Chênoy**, **Chesnoy**, **Duchenois**, **Duchenoy**, **Chénière(s)**, **Chesnière**. Eng.: **Che(y)ney**, **Cha(i)ney**, **Cheenay**, **Chesnay**, **Chesnoy** (from various places in France so named); **Chenery**, **Chin(n)ery** (Suffolk).

The first known bearer of the name Cheyne *or* Chesne *in Scotland is William* de Chesne, *who witnessed a charter c.1200.*

The English family by the name of Du Cane *are descended from the Rev. Thomas Roger Du Cane, prebendary of Ely Cathedral and vicar of East Tuddenham, Norfolk, in the early 18th cent. He was the son of Abraham* Du Quesne, *second son of the Huguenot Marquis du Quesne (1610–88). Abraham was a lieutenant in the French navy, who came to England after the revocation of the Edict of Nantes in 1685.*

Chenevier French: occupational name for a cultivator of hemp, from an agent deriv. of OF *cheneve* (L *cannabis*, from Gk; said to be ultimately from Scythian). The tough fibres found in the stem of this plant were long used in the manufacture of ropes and canvas.

Var.: **Chennevier**.

Cogns.: It.: **Caneparo**, **Canepari** (Liguria); **Canaparo**, **Canapa(r)i** (central Italy); **Canevaro**, **Canevari** (N Italy). Sp.: **Cañamero**.

Chenoweth Cornish: habitation name from the elements *chy* house + *noweth* new.

Var.: **Chynoweth**.

Chenu French: nickname for an old man or someone with prematurely white hair, from OF *chenu* white-haired (LL *cānūtus*, for class. L *cānus*). The word also acquired the sense 'prudent', 'judicious', through association with the wisdom and experience of old age.

Var.: **Quenu** (Normandy).

Cogns.: Prov.: **Canu(t)**, **Lecanu(t)**; **Chenut**; **Chanu(t)** (Massif Central). It.: **Canuto**, **Canuti**, **Canudo**, **Canudi**; **Cani**. Sp.: **Cano**. Cat.: **Canut**.

Dims.: Fr.: **Chenu(d)eau**, **Chenuet**, **Chenuil**; **Chanudet**. Prov.: **Canu(d)et**, **(Le) Canuel**.

Cheptel French: topographic name for someone who lived near an enclosure for livestock, from OF *cheptel* pen, fold (L *capitālia*, a deriv. of *caput*, gen. *capitis*, head (of cattle)), or occupational name for someone who worked in such an enclosure, tending the animals.

Vars.: **Chétel**, **Cheteau**; **Cheftel** (Normandy); **Chatal** (Brittany). Prov.: **Captal**; **Chaptal**, **Chateau** (Massif Central).

Cherntsov Russian: patr. from the occupational term (or nickname) *chernets* monk (a deriv. of *cherny* black; see CHERNYAKOV).

Vars.: **Chentsov**, **Cheltzov**.

Chernyakov Russian: patr. from the nickname *Chernyak* 'Black(-haired)' or 'Dark(-skinned) one' (from *cherny* black; Pol. *czarny*, Czech *černý*).

Vars.: **Chernakov**, **Chernyakin**, **Chernyagin**, **Chernigin**, **Chern(ya)ev**, **Chernyshyov**, **Chernishev**, **Chernukhin**, **Chernyatin**, **Chernavin**; **Chernov**; **Chernyshevski** (a clergy name formed by the addition of the suffix *-ski* to an existing surname).

Cogns. (not patrs.): Beloruss.: **Chernyak**. Ukr.: **Chorny**. Pol.: **Czerniak**, **Czernicki**, **Czarn(i)ecki**. Czech: **Černík**, **Černý**, **Černický**. Croatian: **Crn(č)ić**, **Crnko**. Ger. (of Slav. origin): **Scharnach**, **Schornach**, **Schornack**, **Schornich**, **Schörnich**, **Schornig**, **Scherni(n)g**, **Tscherna(c)k**, **Tscherning**, **Tscharnach**, **Tschornig**; **Tscherne**, **Tscherny**, **Tschorn**, **Tschörner**. Jewish (E Ashkenazic): **Cherny**, **Czerny**, **Czerno**, **Czarny**, **Charn(e)y**, **Charni**, **Tcharni**, **Chorny**, **Chorni**, **Tshorni**; **Cherni(a)k**, **Czerni(a)k**, **Tsherniak**, **Charniak**, **Charnyak**; **Charnietzky**, **Czernocki**, **Tchernatzki**, **Czarnecki**.

Dims.: Beloruss.: **Chernyonok**. Ukr.: **Chernenko**. Pol.: **Czernik**, **Czernek**. Ger. (of Slav. origin): **Scharnke**, **Tscharnke**, **Tschernke**, **Zarn(c)ke**, **Zörneke**.

Patrs.: Jewish: **Tshernichov**, **Tshernichow**; **Chernichowsky**, **Tchernichovsky**, **Czernichowski**. Croatian: **Crnković**.

Metrs.: Jewish (from the E Yid. female given name *Tsharne* or *Tsherne*): **Charnes**, **Czernas**, **Czernin**, **Chernov**, **Czernov**; **Czerninski**, **Czarninski**, **Chernovsky**, **Czerniawski**.

Metrs. (from a dim.): Jewish: **Charnylas**, **Czarnylas**, **Czernilov**; **Czarnolewski**.

Cpds: Jewish: **Chernobelski**, **Czernobilski** ('black-white'); **Charnobroda**, **Czarnobroda** ('black beard'); **Czarnoczapka** ('black cap'); **Chernomorski**, **Chernomorsky** (from the Black Sea, Russ. *Chernoe More*, with the addition of the general surname ending *-ski*). Czech: **Černohlávek** ('black-haired man').

Cherrington English: habitation name from any of various places called *Cherington* or *Cherrington*. *Cherrington* in Shrops. may mean 'settlement by a river bend', but others (*Cherington* in Gloucs. and *Cherrington* in Warwicks.) are 'church settlement', from OE *cyrice* church + *tūn* settlement. Places called *Cheriton* in Devon, Hants., Kent, and Somerset also have this last etymology.

Vars.: **Charrington**; **Cheriton**.

Cherry English: topographic name for someone who lived by a cherry tree, or metonymic occupational name for a grower and seller of cherries, from ME *cheri(e)* (a back-formation from ANF *cherise* (see CERISIER), taken as a pl.).

Vars.: **Cherrie**; **Cherryman**, **Cherriman**.

Cheseldine English: apparently a habitation name from an unidentified place in Lincs., perhaps so called from OE *ceosel* gravel + *denu* valley (see DEAN 1).

Cheshire English: regional name for someone from the county of Cheshire in NW England, the name of which is recorded in Domesday Book as *Cestrescire*, a cpd of the county town CHESTER + OE *scīr* district, division.

Vars.: **Chesshire**, **Chesshyre**, **Cheshir**, **Chesher**, **Chesser**, **Chessor**.

Chester English: habitation name from the county town of CHESHIRE, or from any of the various smaller places so called from OE *ceaster* Roman fort (L *castra* legionary camp).

Vars.: **Chaster**, **Chesters**.

Chesterton English: habitation name from any of the various places, for example in Cambs., Gloucs., Oxon., Staffs., and Warwicks., so called from OE *ceaster* Roman fort (see CHESTER) + *tūn* enclosure, settlement.

Var.: **Kesterton** (chiefly W Midlands).

Chestworth English: habitation name from an unidentified place. The name is now most common in Lancs., but it is a late arrival there and the place in question should probably be sought elsewhere. The second element of the placename is presumably OE *worð* enclosure (see WORTH); the first may be a personal name.

Chetwode English: habitation name from a place in Bucks., so called from the Brit. element *ceto-* wood, with the tautological addition of OE *wudu* (see WOOD) when the old name was no longer understood. Cf. CHEADLE.

Var.: **Chetwood**.

A family of this name can be traced to Chetwode in Bucks., where Sir John Chetwode, *apparently an ancestor, was living* c.*1100*.

Chetwynd English: habitation name from a place in Shrops., so called from the OE personal name *Ceatta* (see CHATFIELD) + OE *(ge)wind* winding ascent.

Var.: **Chatwin**.

Adam de Chetwynd *is recorded as lord of the manor of Chetwynd in 1180*.

Chevalier French: from OF *chevalier* knight (lit. horseman, rider, LL *caballārius*, a deriv. of *caballus* horse; cf. CAVALLO). In the Middle Ages only men of comparative wealth were able to afford the upkeep of a riding horse. It is likely that in the majority of cases the surname was originally a nickname, or an occupational name for a knight's servant, rather than a status name, for most men of the knightly class belonged to noble families which had more specific surnames derived from their estates.

Vars.: **Chaval(l)ier**; **Lecheval(l)ier**.

Cogns.: Prov.: **Caval(l)ier**, **Caval(l)ié**. It.: **Caval(l)iere**, **Caval(l)ieri**, **Caval(l)iero**, **Cavalleri**, **Cavallero**, **Cavallar(o)**. Sp.: **Caballero**. Cat.: **Caballer**, **Caballé**. Port.: **Caval(h)eiro**.

Dims.: Fr.: **Chevallereau**, **Chevalleret**.

Chevreuil French: nickname from OF *chevreuil* roebuck (L *caprĭōlus*, a deriv. of *caper* goat; cf. CHEEVER), or else a metonymic occupational name for a worker in buckskin.

Vars.: **Chevreul**; **Chevrol(l)ier** (occupational).

Cogns.: Prov.: **Cabr(i)ol**; **Chabrol(le)**, **Chabroux** (Massif Central); **Cabrioler**, **Cabriolé** (occupational). It.: **Caprioli**, **Capriolo**.

Dims.: Fr.: **Chevrolet**. Prov.: **Chabroullet** (Massif Central).

Aug.: Fr.: **Chevrollat**.

Chew English: 1. habitation name from a place in Somerset, so called from a Brit. river name perhaps cogn. with W *cyw* young animal or bird, chicken.

2. habitation name from places in W Yorks. or in the parish of Billington, Lancs., so called from OE *cēo* fish gill, used in the transferred sense of a ravine, in a similar way to ON *gil* (see GILL 2).

3. nickname for a talkative or thievish person, from OE *cēo* chough, a bird closely related to the crow and the jackdaw.

Var.: **Chue**.

Chicharro Spanish: nickname for a chirpy individual, from OSp. *chicarro* cricket, cicada (L *cicāda*).

Chichester English: habitation name from the city in Sussex, apparently so called from the OE personal name *Cissa* + OE *ceaster* Roman fort (see CHESTER). *Cissa* is attested as the name of a historical person, but it is of uncertain etymology.

A family bearing the name Chichester *trace their descent from Richard* de Cicester, *who was granted lands in Sussex by King John. They later became prominent in Ireland, and hold the titles of Marquesses and Earls of Donegal in the Irish peerage*.

Chick English: 1. metonymic occupational name for someone who bred poultry for the table, from ME *chike* (a shortened form of *chiken*, OE *cīcen* young fowl). In some cases it may have been a nickname from the same word used as a term of endearment.

2. var. of CHEEK.

Var. (of 1): **Chicken**.

Chico Spanish: nickname for a small man, or for the younger of two bearers of the same given name, from Sp. *chico* small, young (of uncertain origin, perhaps from L *ciccum* trifle).

Aug.: **Chicote**.

Chidgley English (Bristol): habitation name from a place called *Chidgley* in W Somerset. The first element of this is probably from an OE personal name of uncertain form and meaning; the second is OE *lēah* wood, clearing.

Chilcott English: habitation name from a place in Somerset, so called from the OE personal name *Cēola* (a short form of various cpd names with a first element *cēol* ship) + OE *cot* cottage, dwelling (see COATES).

Child English: 1. nickname from ME *child*, OE *cild* child, infant, in various possible applications. The word is found in OE as a byname, and in ME as a widely used affectionate term of address. It was also used as a term of status for a young man of noble birth, although the exact meaning is not clear; in the 13th and 14th cents. it was a technical term used of a young noble awaiting elevation to the knighthood. In other cases it may have been applied as a byname to a youth considerably younger than his brothers or to one who was a minor on the death of his father.

2. possibly a topographic name from OE *cielde* spring (water), a rare word apparently derived from *c(e)ald* cold.

Vars.: **Childe**, **Cheeld**, **Chill**.

Patrs. (from 1): **Childs**, **Chil(l)es**.

Childers English: apparently a habitation name from some lost place named *Childerhouse*, from OE *cildra*, gen. pl. of *cild* CHILD + *hūs* house. This may have referred to some form of orphanage perhaps run by a religious order, or perhaps the first element is to be understood in its later sense as a term of status (cf. CHILTON).

Vars.: **Childerhouse**, **Childress**.

Chilton English: habitation name from any of the various places so called, for example in Berks., Bucks., Co. Durham, Hants, Kent, Shrops., Somerset, Suffolk and Wilts. The overwhelming majority are shown by early forms to derive from OE *cild* CHILD + *tūn* enclosure, settlement; cf. CHILDERS. One place of this name in Somerset gets its first element from OE *cealc* chalk, limestone, and one on the Isle of Wight from the personal name *Cēola* (see CHILCOTT).

Chilver English: probably from a ME survival of the OE personal name *Cēolfrið*, composed of the elements *cēol* ship + *frið* peace.

Patr.: **Chilvers**.

Chinn English: nickname for someone with a prominent chin or else for someone notably clean-shaven, from OE *cin* chin.

Chippendale English (chiefly Lancs.): habitation name from *Chippingdale* in Lancs. near Clitheroe, so called from OE *cīeping* commerce, market (town) (cf. CHAPMAN) + ME *dale* valley (see DALE).
Vars.: **Chippindale, Chippindall.**

Chipperfield English: habitation name from a place in SW Herts., near Watford, so called from OE *cēapere* merchant (see CHAPMAN) + *feld* pasture, open country (see FIELD), i.e. probably an open space where markets were held.

Chirac French: habitation name from any of the various places, for example in Charente, Corrèze, and Lozère, so called from the Gallo-Roman personal name *Carius* (a deriv. of the Celt. root *car-* love; cf. CRADDOCK) + the local suffix *-ācum*.

Chisholm Scots: habitation name from *Chisholme* near Hawick in S Scotland, which derives its name from OE *cȳse*, *cēse* cheese (L *cāseus*; cf. CHEESEMAN) + *holm* piece of dry land in a fen (see HOLME 2) and refers to a waterside meadow good for dairy farming and hence for producing cheeses.
Vars.: **Chisholme, Chisolm.**
The first known bearer of the name is John de Chesehelme, *mentioned in a bull of Pope Alexander IV in 1254. By the middle of the 14th cent. bearers of the name had migrated to the Highlands, particularly around Strathglass, and the name acquired the Gaelic form* Siosal.

Chisnall English: habitation name from *Chisnall* Hall in Lancs., in which *Chisnall* is probably derived from an OE adj. **cisen* gravelly, from *cis* gravel + *halh* nook, hollow.

Chiswell English (chiefly Devon): apparently a habitation name from an unidentified minor place. The surname is recorded in the parish of Langford, Devon, in 1244, and again in 1332. There is an area in the parish of Ugborough, Devon, known as Inner and Outer *Chissels*, but this probably derives from the surname rather than vice versa. If it is a habitation name, the placename probably derives either from OE *cis* gravel or from the OE personal name *Cissa* (cf. CHICHESTER) + OE *well(a)* spring, stream (see WELL). The surname also became established in W Leics. in the early 17th cent.

Chittenden English: habitation name from a place in Kent, possibly so called from the gen. case of an OE personal name *Citta* (perhaps a byname derived from *cīð* shoot, sprout) + OE *denn* swine pasture.

Chitty English: 1. nickname from ME *chitte* pup, cub, young of an animal (apparently related to OE *cīð* shoot, sprout; cf. CHITTENDEN).
2. habitation name from a place so called in the parish of Chislet, Kent, or possibly from the manor of *Chiltley* in the parish of Bramshott, Hants, apparently so called from a Brit. hill name **celt* + OE *lēah* wood, clearing.
Vars.: **Chittey(e), Chittie.**
Dim. (of 1): **Chittock** (chiefly Suffolk).
The surname Chitty *is largely confined to a relatively small area in S England. Throughout most of the 17th cent. it was the commonest surname in the parish of Godalming, Surrey (where it was first found in 1371), and it was also well represented in nearby Aldershot, Farnham, Guildford, and Worplesdon.*

Chiva Catalan: habitation name from *Chiva* de Morella in the province of Castellón. In early records the placename is spelled *Xiva*; it is of uncertain, probably Mozarabic, origin.

Chmielewski Polish: habitation name from any of various places deriving their names from Pol. *chmiel* hops + *-ew* suffix of placenames, with the addition of *-ski* suffix of local surnames (see BARANOWSKI).
Vars.: **Chmielecki, Chmieliński, Chmielnicki; Chmielowiec; Chmiel(a)** (probably a metonymic nickname for a drunkard).
Cogns.: Ukr.: **Khmelnytsky** (from *Khmelnyk* in the Ukraine). Czech: **Chmelař, Chmelík, Chmel(a)** (occupational names for a grower of hops); **Chmelenský** (habitation name).
Dim.: Czech: **Chmelíček.**

Chodakowski Polish: occupational name for a clog maker, in form a habitation name from Pol. *chodak* clog + *-ów* possessive suffix, with the addition of *-ski*, suffix of surnames (see BARANOWSKI).

Chodosh Jewish (Ashkenazic): nickname for a newcomer to a place (cf. NOVÁK and NEWMAN), from an Ashkenazic pronunciation of Hebr. *chadash* new.
Var.: **Chadash** (Israeli).

Choice English: probably a var. of JOYCE. There is a family tradition among bearers of the name that it means 'chosen', from ME, OF *chois* (of Gmc origin). In the Middle Ages the word was used both for an 'act of choosing' and a 'thing chosen', and as an adj. with the meaning 'chosen', 'select', 'favoured'. It is conceivable that this word could have given rise to a nickname, but in the absence of evidence to support this derivation, the question must remain open: the derivation may be merely the result of folk etymology.
Vars.: **Choyce, Choise, Choyse.**

Choiseul French: habitation name from a place in Haute-Marne, so called from a L personal name *Causius* + the Gaul. element *ialo* clearing, field.

Chojnacki Polish: topographic name for someone who lived among pine trees, from Pol. *choina* fir tree + *-ak* personal suffix, with the addition of *-ski*, suffix of local surnames (see BARANOWSKI).
Var.: **Chojnowski.**

Cholewiński Polish: occupational name for a boot-maker, in form a habitation name from Pol. *cholewa* upper part of a boot + *-in* possessive suffix, with the addition of *-ski*, suffix of surnames (see BARANOWSKI).
Var.: **Cholewicki.**

Cholmondeley English: habitation name from a place in Ches., so called from the OE personal name *Cēolmund* (composed of the elements *cēol* ship + *mund* protection) + OE *lēah* wood, clearing. The surname is normally pronounced /'tʃʌmlɪ/.
Vars.: **Cholmeley, Chumley, Chumbly, Chambly.**

Chomsky Jewish (E Ashkenazic): habitation name from the town of *Chomsk*, with the addition of the Pol. local suffix *-ski* (see BARANOWSKI). The town was situated in the medieval Grand Duchy of Lithuania, but has successively fallen under the control of Poland and Russia. In America the name is normally pronounced /'tʃɑːmskiː/.
Var.: **Chomski.**

Chopin French and English: 1. nickname for a heavy drinker, from OF *chopine*, a (large) liquid measure (from MLG *schōpen* ladle), from which the derived verb *chopiner* has the sense 'tipple', 'drink'. Less plausibly, but more respectably, the surname may have been acquired as a metonymic occupational name for a maker of ladles or vessels used in the casting of metal, which were also called *chopines*.

2. nickname for a pugnacious person, from OF *chopin* violent blow (in form a dim. of *chop* blow, L *colpus*, from Gk *kolaphus*; cf. CAPSTICK).

Vars.: Fr.: **Chopy, Ch(o)upin**. Eng.: **Choppin(g), Choppen**.

Cogns. (of 1): Ger.: **Schuffenhauer** (see HAUER); **Schüffner**. Low Ger.: **Schopp(e), Schoop; Schop(p)enhauer, Schuppenhauer, Schüppenhauer**.

Dims.: Fr.: **Chopinel, Chopinet**.

The Polish composer and pianist Frédéric Chopin *(1810–49) spent most of his career in France, although he was born near Warsaw. His father, who was born in Marainville in the Vosges region, where his family were vineyard owners, went to Poland to make his fortune at the age of 16, and became tutor to an aristocratic Polish family, marrying a poor relative of his employers and cutting himself and his children off completely from his family in France.*

Choque French: 1. habitation name from *Chocques* in Pas-de-Calais, so called from a Picard dial. form of OF *souches* tree stumps (left in a patch of cleared land); see SUCH.

2. nickname for a clumsy person, from a deriv. of OF *chocqu(i)er* to crash into (of Gmc origin, probably ultimately an imitative formation).

3. nickname for a tippler, from Norman dial. *choque* toast, act of clinking glasses together, a sense development of the word given in 2.

Vars.: **Chocque, Choc(q)**.

Dims. (of 2 and 3): **Choqu(en)et, Choqueneau**.

Pej. (of 2 and 3): **Choquard**.

Chorley English: habitation name from any of various places, for example in Ches., Herts., Lancs., Shrops., and Staffs., so called from OE *ceorla*, gen. pl. of *ceorl* churl, peasant (cf. CHORLTON) + *lēah* wood, clearing.

Chorlton English: habitation name from any of the various places, in Ches., Lancs., and Staffs., so called from OE *ceorla*, gen. pl. of *ceorl* churl, peasant + *tūn* enclosure, settlement; see CHARLTON. Chorlton cum Hardy in Lancs., however, gets its first element from the OE personal name *Cēolfrið* (a cpd of *cēol* ship + *frið* peace).

Var.: **Cholton**.

Chouan French: nickname for a raucous person, from OF *chouan* screech-owl (a word of imitative origin, perhaps taken from Gaul., and later altered by folk etymology to the form *chat-huant* howling cat).

Vars.: **Chua(n)t, Cahu**.

Dims.: **Ch(o)uet(te), Cah(o)uet** (later the name of the brown owl, but the terms were of more general meaning in the Middle Ages).

Pejs.: **Ch(o)u(an)ard**.

Christian English and French: from the OF given name *Christian* (L *Chrīstiānus* 'follower of *Christ*', L *Chrīstus*, Gk *Khrīstos*, a deriv. of *krīein* to anoint, calqued on Hebr. *mashiach* Messiah). This male given name was introduced into England following the Norman conquest, especially by Bret. settlers. It was also used in the same form as a female name, and in some cases the surname may be metronymic in origin.

Vars.: Eng.: **Christin(e)**. Fr.: **Crestien, Chrétien, Christin(e), Christiné, Christiane, C(h)resti(a)n**.

Cogns.: Prov.: **C(h)restin, Crétin**. It.: **Cristi(a)ni, Cristi(a)no, Cristi(a)na** (in the Tarentine and Sicilian dialects *cristiano* is a complementary term for a clever, judicious person). Low Ger.: **Kri(e)sten, Ki(r)sten, Kirstan; Kirstein, Kir(s)chstein** (see also KIRSCH), **Kürsten, Korsten, Ke(r)sten, Ka(r)sten, Carsten** (all of these ending in *-en* may also be patrs. derived from short forms). Fris.: **Cassen**. Flem.: **Christaen**. Du.: **Korstiaan, Karsten, Kersten**. Ger. (of Slav. origin): **Krischan, Kittan**. Czech: **Kříž**.

Dims.: Eng.: **Christie, Christ(e)y** (chiefly Scots and N Irish). Fr.: **Christinet, Crétinon, Crétinot**. Low Ger.: **Crist, Ki(r)st, Korst, Ke(r)st, Ka(r)st, Kirst(e)gen**. Ger. (of Slav. origin): **Krisch(e), Krischke, Kitschold, Kitschelt**. Czech: **Křížek; Křist'ál, Krýsl**.

Aug.: Fr.: **Chrétinat**.

Patrs.: Low Ger.: **Kirstens, Kerstens, Ka(r)stens, Carstens; Christensen, Carstensen, Kastensen**. Fris.: **Cassens**. Flem.: **Christiaens, Korstinens**. Du.: **Carstens, Kars(ten)sen**. Norw., Dan.: **Christiansen, Kristiansen, Christensen, Kristensen**. Swed.: **Christiansson, Kristiansson, Christensson, Kristensson, Kristersson**. Russ.: **Krestyan(in)ov** (largely from the sense 'peasant', 'farmer', 'worker on the land', borne by the word *khrestyanin* since the 14th cent.); **Khristinin** (metr.). Beloruss.: **Khrishtanovich**.

Patrs. (from dims.): Eng.: **Christison** (Scots). Ger.: **Christ(al)ler, Kristeller**. Low Ger.: **Kisting, Ke(r)sting, Kasting; Kürstgens, Corstgens, Körschkes, Köschges, Kerstgens**. Russ.: **Khristin**. Ukr.: **Khristin, Khristich**. Ger. (of Slav. origin): **Kitscher, Kitzer**. Croatian: **Hristić**. Gk: **Christou**.

Christian *is the surname of a family first recorded in the Isle of Man with John* McCrystyn *(b. ?1368). His many descendants included Fletcher Christian (1764-?93), who led the mutiny on HMS* Bounty *in 1787.*

Christmas English: nickname for someone born on Christmas Day, or who had some other particular association with that time of year, from OE *Crīstesmæsse* mass, festival of Christ.

Var.: **Chrismas**.

This surname seems to have originated in E Anglia and has been common in Colchester from a relatively early period. Other concentrations are all in S England: in Devon, Dorset, Kent, Hants, Surrey, and Sussex. One family can be traced in Co. Waterford, Ireland, between 1622 and the end of the 19th cent.

Christopher English: from a medieval given name which ostensibly means 'Bearer of Christ' (L *Chrīstopherus*, Gk *Khrīstophoros*, from *Khrīstos* Christ (cf. CHRISTIAN) + *pher-*, *phor-* carry). This was borne by a rather obscure 3rd-cent. martyred saint. His name was relatively common among early Christians, who desired to bear Christ metaphorically with them in their daily lives, but it was later explained by a wholly legendary story in which he carried the infant Christ across a ford and so became the patron saint of travellers. In this guise he was enormously popular in the Middle Ages, and many inns providing accommodation for travellers were named with this sign; in some instances the surname may have derived originally from residence at or association with an inn.

Vars.: **Stoffer, Stopher** (aphetic forms).

Cogns.: Fr.: **Christofor, Christauffour, Christofol, Christoph(l)e, Christof(l)e, Christoffe**. Prov.: **C(h)ristol, C(h)ristou**. It.: **Cristofori, Cristoforo, Cristoferi; Cristofolo, Toffolo, Tofful, Fol(l)i, Cristofano, Tof(f)ano, Foffano** (Venetia); **Cristofaro, Cristofari, Cristofalo, Toffalo** (S Italy). Sp.: **Cristóbal**. Cat.: **Cristòfor, Cristòfol**. Port.: **Cristóvão**. Rum.: **Cristofor**. Ger.: **Christoffer; Stoffer, Stoffel, Stöffel, Toffel, Töffel**. Czech: **Krištof, Kryštof**. Pol.: **Kr(z)ysztof**. Hung.: **Kristóf**.

Dims.: Eng.: **Kit(t)**, KIDD; **Kitto(w)** (Cornwall). Fr.: **Christon**. It.: **Cristoforetti, Cristofolini, Toff(ol)etto, Fol(l)etti; Cristofolini, Toffolini, Folini; Cristofanini, Tof(f)anini; Tof(f)anelli**. Czech: **Krištůfek**. Pol.: **Krys(z)ka, Krystek; Krysztowczyk**. Rum.: **Cristea**.

Augs.: It.: **Toffoloni, Toffaloni**.

Patrs.: Eng.: **Christophers(on)**. It.: **De Cristoforo, De Cristofalo** (S Italy). Ger.: **Stoffler, Toffler**. Low Ger.: **Stoffers(en)**.

Flem., Du.: **Christoffels, Stoffels**. Dan., Norw.: **Christophersen, Cristoffersen, Kristoffersen**. Swed.: **Kristoffersson**. Russ.: **Khristoforov**. Beloruss.: **Khrishtafovich**. Pol.: **Krysztofowicz**; **Kr(z)ysztofiak**. Bulg.: **Khristoforov**. Lithuanian: **Krishtopaitis**. Gk: **Christoforou**.

Patrs. (from dims.): Eng.: **Kitts, Kitson**. Rum.: **Cristescu**. Russ.: **Khristyukhin**. Pol.: **Kryszkiewicz**; **Krysiak**. Gk: **Christofides**.

Chruściel Polish: nickname from Pol. *chruściel* corncrake, a bird with speckled plumage and reddish wings inhabiting fields and meadows. The Pol. word is ultimately derived from Slav. *chrust-* to rustle, and so is cogn. with Russ. *khrushch* may beetle (see KHRUSHCHEV).

Habitation name: **Chruścielewski**.

Chrzanowski Polish: habitation name from a place named from Pol. *chrzan* horseradish (cogn. with Czech *křen*) + *-ów* possessive suffix, with the addition of *-ski*, suffix of local surnames (see BARANOWSKI).

Cogns.: Czech: **Křen** (apparently a nickname meaning 'horseradish', acquired perhaps by someone with a stinging tongue). Russ.: **Khrenov** (patr. in form).

Dim.: Czech: **Křenek**.

Chubb English (chiefly W Country): nickname from the fish, *Leuciscus cephalus*, ME *chubbe* (of unknown origin). The fish is notable for its short, fat shape and sluggish habits. The word is well attested in ME as a description of an indolent, stupid, or physically awkward person, and this is probably the origin of mod. Eng. *chubby*, although the vocab. word has lost any pejorative overtones.

Chudzik Polish: nickname for a thin man, from Pol. *chudy* thin.

Church English: topographic surname for someone who lived near a church. The vocab. word comes from OE *cyrice* (LGk *kyrikon*, for earlier *kyriakon* (*dōma*) (house) of the Lord, from *kyrios* lord; cf. KIRILOV).

Vars.: **Churcher, Churchman**. See also KIRK.

Churchill English: habitation name from any of various places, for example in Devon, Oxon., Somerset, and Worcs., so called from OE *cyrice* CHURCH + *hyll* HILL. In some cases (e.g. in Oxon. and Devon) the placenames may originally have contained as their first element the Brit. name *crūc* hill, but if so this was altered early on as the result of folk etymology.

The British statesman Sir Winston Spencer Churchill *(1875–1965) was born at Blenheim Palace. It had been built by the nation for his forebear John Churchill (1650–1722), 1st Duke of Marlborough, hero of the 18th-cent. wars against France. The 1st Duke's father was a lawyer from Dorset, a supporter of the King in the Civil War. The line continued through the Duke's daughter, who married Lord Spencer, and the 4th Duke received permission to add Churchill to his own name of Spencer in the reign of George III.*

Churchyard English: topographic name for someone who lived by a churchyard, or metonymic occupational name for someone who was employed to look after one, from ME CHURCH + *yard* enclosure (OE *geard*).

Var.: **Churchard**.

Cogns.: Dan.: **Ki(e)rkegaard, Kirkegård**.

Churm English (Yorks.): probably a nickname for a noisy person or a chatterbox, from ME *churme*, *chirme* hubbub, birdsong (OE *cierm* noise).

Ciardo Italian: from a medieval given name, an aphetic form of RICHARD.

Var.: **Ciardi**.

Dims.: **Ciardelli, Ciard(i)ello, Ciardetti, Ciardini, Ciardulli, Ciardullo**; **Ciardin** (Venetia). Fr.: **C(h)ardin(eau), Chardy, Chardel, C(h)ardot, C(h)ardon, C(h)ardet, Cardinet**.

Augs.: It.: **Ciardon(e)** (Venetia).

Cichy Polish: nickname for a quiet person, from Pol. *cichy* quiet, calm (cf. TIKHONOV).

Vars.: **Cichoń**; **Cichosz, Cichocki, Cichecki**.

Cogn.: Czech: **Tichý**.

Dims.: Pol.: **Cichończyk**. Czech: **Ticháček**.

Patr.: Pol.: **Cichowicz**.

Cid Spanish and Portuguese: from a medieval given name, of uncertain origin and meaning. It occurs in L documents of the Middle Ages in the form *Citi*, and is apparently distinct from the honorific title *Cid* (from Arabic *sayyid* lord) borne by Christian overlords with Moslem vassals.

Cieślak Polish: occupational name for a carpenter, from Pol. *cieśla* carpenter (cogn. with Russ. *teslo* adze) + the redundant agent suffix *-ak*.

Vars.: **Cieśla**; **Ciesielski** (with surname suffix *-ski*; see BARANOWSKI).

Cogns.: Jewish (E Ashkenazic): **Cieslar**. Czech: **Tesař**. Ukr.: **Tesler**.

Dims.: Pol.: **Cieślik**. Czech: **Tesařik, Tesárek**. Ukr.: **Teslenko**. Beloruss.: **Teslyuk**.

Patr.: Pol.: **Cieślewicz**.

Cifaro S Italian (esp. Campania and Apulia): nickname from the S It. dial. term *cifaro*, *cifero* devil, demon (an aphetic form of the personal name ascribed to the fallen angel, L *Lūcifer* 'bearer of light', from *lux*, gen. *lūcis*, light + *ferre* to bear, bring). The first syllable was lost because it it was understood as the regional form, *lu*, of the def. art.

Vars.: **Cefaro, Cifero**.

Dims.: **Cifariello, Cefariello, Cifarelli**.

Cifuentes Spanish: habitation name from any of various places, for example in the provinces of León and Guadalajara, so called from Sp. *cien* hundred (L *centum*) + *fuentes* springs (L *fontes*; see FONT). The places were so named because of the abundance of natural springs in the area.

Čihák Czech: 1. occupational name for a fowler, Czech *čihăr*, from the verb *čihat* to lie in wait.

2. occupational name for a blacksmith, from the vocab. word *čihák*, which denoted one of the implements used by blacksmiths.

Ciobanu Rumanian (partly Jewish): occupational name for a shepherd, from *cioban* shepherd (a borrowing of Turkish *çoban*), with the addition of the def. art. *-u*.

Var.: **Cioban**.

Circuit English (Beds.): a rare surname, apparently a late respelling, under the influence of folk etymology, of a name representing the local pronunciation of *Southcott* in the parish of Linslade, Bucks. (near the Beds. border).

Vars.: **Sircutt, Sirkett, Surcutt, Surcot, Surcoate, Cercott**.

Cisneros Spanish: habitation name from a place in the province of Palencia, originally named with a deriv. of Sp. *cisne* swan (via OF from L *cycnus*, Gk *kyknos*).

Ciszewski Polish: habitation name from a place called *Ciszew* (from Pol. *cisza* silence (cf. CICHY) + *-ew* possessive suffix), with the addition of *-ski*, suffix of local surnames (see BARANOWSKI).

Citroen Dutch and Flemish: metonymic occupational name for a grower or seller of lemons, or perhaps a nickname for a sharp and disagreeable person (cf. CRABBE), from MDu. *citroen* lemon (OF *citron*, from L *citrus* lemon tree).

Cogns.: Jewish (E Ashkenazic, mainly ornamental): **Citron, Cytron, Zitron(enbaum)**; **Citrin(baum), Cytryn(baum), Zitrin(baum), Zitrinboim** (all with Ger. *Baum* or Yid. *boym* tree); **Cytrinik, Zitroniak** (from Yid. *tsitrin*). Fr.: **Citron**.

Patrs.: Jewish: **Citronowicz, Cytrynowicz, Cytrynowitz**.

City English: of uncertain origin. The earliest form that looks as though it might belong here is William *Citti* of Highclere, Hants, recorded in the 13th cent., but this may well be a form of CHITTY. All present-day non-Jewish bearers of the name seem to belong to a single line, which can be traced back to the early 17th cent. and has always been confined to the London area. It is possible that the original bearer was an immigrant (possibly a Huguenot) who adopted this name on moving to the City of London. The name is also sometimes borne by Jews, in which case its origin is unknown.

Ciurana Catalan: habitation name from a place in the province of Gerona, earlier called *Siverana*. The name is from L *Severiāna (villa)* 'estate (see VILLE) of *Severus*'; cf. SÉVERIN.

Clachar Scots: occupational name for a stonemason, Gael. *clachair*, an agent deriv. of *clach* stone.

Var.: **Clacher**.

Patr.: **McClacher**.

Clack English: from an OE personal name or byname *Clacc*, or the cogn. ON *Klakkr*. The name is of uncertain origin; it may have been an imitative formation given originally to a chatterer, or it may have described a lumpish person (cf. CLAUGHTON).

Claffey Irish: Anglicized form of Gael. **Mac Fhlaithimh**, patr. from the personal name *Flaitheamh* 'Prince'.

Vars.: **Claffy; McClave**.

Clamp English: of uncertain origin, probably from the vocab. word denoting an iron band for binding things together (a borrowing from Du., first attested in the 15th cent). This may have been used as a nickname for someone with a 'vice-like' grip, or more plausibly a metonymic occupational name for a smith who specialized in making clamps.

Clancy Irish: Anglicized form of Gael. **Mac Fhlannchaidh**, patr. from the personal name *Flannchadh*, which is derived from *flann* red; cf. FLYNN.

Var.: **Glancy**.

Clapham English: habitation name from any of various places, for example in Beds., Surrey, Sussex, and W Yorks., so called from OE **clop* lump, hillock (cf. CLAPP) + *hām* homestead.

Clapp English (chiefly Bristol): nickname for a large and ungainly person, ME *cloppe*, *le clop*, from OE **clop* lump, hillock.

Vars.: **Clap, Clappe**.

Patrs.: **Clapson** (Sussex); **Clappison** (Yorks).

The surname Clappe *is found in Devon in the Subsidy Roll for 1332, with three occurrences.*

Clare 1. Irish and English: habitation name from *Clare* in Suffolk, apparently so called from a Brit. river name which may have had the meaning 'bright', 'gentle', or 'warm'.

2. English: habitation name from *Clare* in Oxon., so called from OE *clǣg* clay + *ōra* slope.

3. English: from the ME, OF female given name *Cla(i)re* (L *Clāra*, from *clārus* famous), which achieved a moderate popularity, greater on the Continent than in England, through the fame of St Clare of Assisi. See also SINCLAIR.

3. English: occupational name for a worker in clay, for example someone expert in building in wattle and daub, from a ME deriv. of OE *clǣg* clay, with the agent suffix *-er*.

Vars.: **Claire, Clear(e), Clere**.

Cogns. (of 3; the apparently masc. forms are probably altered forms for male bearers of the surname, but it is just possible that some derive from the much rarer equivalent male given name): Fr.: **Clair(e), Clère, Clar, Cler**. It.: **Chiara, Chiari, Chiaro; Clari, Claro** (Venetia, Friuli). Port.: **Clara, Claro**. Ger.: KLAR.

Dims. (of 3): Fr.: **Cla(i)ret, Cléret, Clarey, Cla(i)rin, Clérin, Cla(i)rot, Clér(i)ot, Claron**. It.: **Chiarelli, Chiarella; Chiariello** (Campania); **Chiarini, Chiarotti, Chiarulli, Chiarutti; Claretti, Clarini, Clarotti**.

Aug. (of 3): It.: **Chiaroni**.

Metrs. (from 3): It.: **De Chiara, Di Chiara**.

The surname Clare *is common in Ireland, where in general bearers are members of a family originally from Clare in Suffolk. The earliest Norman invader of Ireland, Richard, 2nd Earl of Pembroke (d. 1176), known as 'Strongbow' bore the family name* de Clare.

Clarges English: occupational name for the servant of a clergyman, from *clargies*, gen. case of ME *clergie* the clergy, a clergyman (from OF *clergie*, a deriv. of *clerc*, see CLARK; for the change of *-er- to -ar-* cf. MARCHANT). In a few cases, the surname may have been acquired by the son of a clergyman in minor orders.

Var.: **Clargis**.

Cogns.: Fr.: **Clergé, Clercy** (also referring to the clergyman himself); **Clergier** (with the addition of the OF agent suffix).

Claridge English: 1. from the ME, OF female given name *Clarice* (L *Clāritia* 'Fame', 'Brightness', a deriv. of *clārus* famous, bright; cf. CLARE 1).

2. habitation name from *Clearhedge* Wood in Sussex, which is of obscure etymology; the second element is presumably OE *hecg* hedge, the first is unidentified.

Vars.: **Clarage**. (Of 1 only): **Claris**.

Cogns. (of 1): Fr.: **Clarice, Clariss(e), Clérisse**. It.: **Chiarizia, Clarizia**.

Dim. (of 1): Fr.: **Clarisseau**.

Clark English: occupational name for a scribe or secretary, or for a member of a minor religious order. Originally the word *clerc* denoted a member of a religious order, from OE *cler(e)c* priest, reinforced by OF *clerc* (both from LL *clēricus*, from Gk *klērikos*, a deriv. of *klēros* inheritance, legacy, with reference to the priestly tribe of Levites (see LEVI) 'whose inheritance was the Lord'). For the regular change of *-er- to -ar-* see MARCHANT. Clergy in minor orders were permitted to marry and so found families; thus the surname could become established. In the Middle Ages it was virtually only members of religious orders who learned to read and write, so that the term *clerk* came also to be used of any literate man. In many cases the surname may have referred originally to a professional secretary.

Vars.: **Clarke, Clerk(e)**.

Cogns.: Fr.: **Clerc(q), Leclerc(q), Lecler(t), Leclair; Cloarec, Cloerec** (Brittany). Prov.: **Clergue**. It.: **Ch(i)erici, Clerici; Chierego** (Venetia). Flem., Du.: **Clerc, De Cler(c)k, De Cler(c)q, (De) Klerk**.

Dims.: Fr.: **Clergeau, Clergeot, Clerjot, Clergeon, Clerget**. It.: **Chiericetti, Clericetti**.

Patrs.: Eng.: **Clar(k)son; Clarkstone** (Notts.). Fr.: **Auclerc, Duclerc, Duclert**. Du.: **Clerkx, Cler(c)x**. Flem.: **Cler(c)(k)x**.

Equivs. (not cogn.): See at SCRIBE.

Clasby English: apparently a habitation name from an unidentified place, probably in N England and perhaps so called from a Scandinavian form of NICHOLAS (see KLAUS) + Northern ME *by* settlement (ON *býr*).
Vars.: **Clasbey, Clasbye, Clasbie, Clasbery, Clasbury.**
A family of this name was established in Ringwood, Hants, from the late 16th cent. onwards.

Clatworthy English: habitation name from a place in Somerset, so called from OE *clāte* burdock + *worðig* enclosure (see WORTHY 1).
Var.: **Clotworthy.**

Claude French: from a medieval given name (L *Claudius*, a Roman family name derived from *claudus* lame) which was popular as a result of having been borne by a 7th-cent. saint, bishop of Besançon.
Vars.: **Claud, Claux,** CLOT.
Cogns: Port.: **Cláudio.** Ger.: **Klaudius, Clodius.** Flem.: **Cloot.** Czech: **Kloud(a).**
Dims.: Fr.: **Claudel, Claudet, Claudin, Claudon, Claudot; Glodeau; Clodic** (Brittany). Port.: **Claudino.**
Patrs.: Flem.: **Cloots, Clotten(s).**

Claughton English (chiefly Yorks.): habitation name from a place so called, of which there are two in Lancs. and one in Ches. Ekwall derives the name from ON *klakkr* lump (i.e. lump-shaped hill, but cf. CLACK) + OE *tūn* enclosure, settlement.

Clavero Spanish: occupational name for someone who had charge of keys, a chatelain or treasurer or a ceremonial official, from an agent deriv. of OSp. *clave* key (L *clavis*).
Var.: **Llavero.**
Cogns.: Cat.: **Claver.** Prov.: **Clavier, Clavié.**
Dims.: Prov.: **Clavereau, Clavareau.**

Claxton English: habitation name from any of the various places, for example in Co. Durham, Norfolk, and N Yorks., so called from the gen. case of the OE personal name *Clacc* or ON *Klakkr* (see CLACK) + OE *tūn* enclosure, settlement.

Clay English: topographic name for someone who lived in an area of clay soil, or occupational name for a worker in a claypit, from OE *clǣg* clay.
Vars.: **Claye; Clayman;** CLARE.
Cogns.: Low Ger.: **Zumkleg.** Flem.: **Van der Cleie, Vercleyen.** Du.: **Kley, Kleij, Van der Klei.**

Claydon English: habitation name from any of the various places, for example in Suffolk, Bucks., and Oxon., so called from OE *clǣg* CLAY + *dūn* hill (see DOWN 1).
Var.: **Clayden.**

Clayton English: habitation name from any of the various places, for example in Lancs., Staffs., Sussex, and W Yorks., so called from OE *clǣg* clay + *tūn* enclosure, settlement.

Cleak English: of uncertain origin. The first possible instance is William *Cleike* (Yorks 1176), but this may well be a mistake for *Clerke*. In subsequent records the name is concentrated in Devon, and seems to have been originally a habitation name connected with a piece of land in the parish of Ermington near Plymouth, first recorded in 1278 as *Clekeland(e)*, and still known as *Clickland*; the surnames John *de Clakelond* and Robert *Cleaklond* occur within this parish in 1332 and 1337 respectively. The placename may be from OE *cleaca* stepping stone, boundary stone (of Celt. origin; cf. CLACHAR) + *land* territory.
Vars.: **Cleake, Cleek(e), Cleke, Cleik(e), Cleeick, Clake, Click.** See also CLACK.

Cleary Irish: occupational name for a clerk, from Gael. *cléireach* (from LL *clēricus*; cf. CLARK).
Var.: **Clery.**
Patrs.: **McCleary, McCleery, McC(h)lery, McAle(a)ry, McAlary, McLeary, McLeery** (Gael. **Mac Cléirich**).
'Descendant of the clerk': **O'Cle(a)ry** (Gael. **Ó Cléirigh**).
'Descendant of the clerk (dim.)': **O'Clearkane, O'Clercan, Clerihan, Clerkan, Clerkin, Clarkins** (Gael. **Ó Cléireacháin, Ó Cléirchín**).

Cleaver English: 1. occupational name for a butcher or someone who split wood into planks by the use of wedges, from OE *clēofan* to split, cut.
2. var. of CLIVE.
Vars.: **Cleever; Clover.**

Clee English: 1. habitation name from *Clee* or *Cleobury* in Shrops., which are of uncertain etymology, probably from an ancient Brit. hill-name. Ekwall comments that derivation of this from OE *clǣg* CLAY seems unlikely, since the Clee Hills are noted for their hard rock.
2. topographic name from OE *clawu*, *cléo* claw, cloven hoof, used in the sense of a fork in a river or road.

Cleeve English: habitation name or topographic name, a var. of CLIVE, found chiefly in Gloucs. and Somerset. There are places of this name in Gloucs., Somerset, and Worcs.
Vars.: **Cleeves; Cleve** (name of a place in Herefords.).

Clegg 1. English (chiefly Lancs. and Yorks.): habitation name from a place in Lancs., so called from ON *kleggi* haystack, originally the name of a nearby hill.
2. Manx: Anglicized form of Gael. **Mac Liaigh** 'son of the physician', from *mac* son + *liaigh* physician (cf. LEACH 1).
Var. (of 2): **Clague.**
There is evidence that the Manx name Clague *has been assimilated to* Clegg *in comparatively recent times. A certain Paul Clague moved in the 1860s from the Isle of Man to Liverpool, where the Eng. name Clegg was common, and in 1875 his daughter married as Elizabeth Clegg.*

Cleghorn Scots: habitation name from either of two minor places of this name in the former county of Lanarks., now part of Strathclyde region.

Cleland 1. Irish: Anglicized form of Gael. *Mac Giolla Fhaoláin*; see WHELAN.
2. habitation name from *Clelland* near Motherwell, probably so called from OE *clǣg* CLAY + *land* land.
Var.: **Clelland.**

Clement 1. English and Dutch: from a ME, OF male given name (L *Clēmens* 'Merciful', gen. *Clēmentis*) which achieved popularity firstly through having been borne by an early saint who was a disciple of St Paul, and later because it was selected as a symbolic name by a number of early popes. There has also been considerable confusion with the originally distinct male given name *Clemence* (in part a female given name, from L *Clēmentia* 'Mercy', an abstract noun derived from the adj.; in part a masc. name from L *Clēmentius*, a later deriv. of *Clēmens*).
2. Cornish: habitation name from the parish of St *Clement*, near Truro.
Vars.: Eng.: **Clemett, Clemitt.**
Cogns. (of 1): Fr.: **Clément; Clémence.** It.: **Clemente, Clementi; Chim(i)enti, Chiumenti, Chiommienti** (S Italy); **Cle-**

menzi, Clemenzo, Clemenza. Sp., Port.: **Clemente**. Cat.: **Climent**. Ger.: **Klement, Klem(m)t, Klim(p)t**. Low Ger.: **Kleeman, Kliemann** (see also KLEE). Flem.: **Clemens, Clem(m)en**. Ger. (of Slav. origin): **Kliemt, Klam(m)t, Klambt, Klämbt, Klampt**. Pol.: **Klimas, Klimecki**. Czech: **Kliment, Klement, Kment, Klimt**. Hung.: **Kelemen**.

Dims. (of 1): Eng.: **Clem(m)**; **Clemmey, Climie** (largely Scots); **Clem(m)o(w), Climo, Clymo, Clyma, Clymer** (Cornish). Fr.: **Clémentel, Clémentet, Clemendet, Clemendot, Clémot; Clemenceau, Clemencet, Clemençon, Clemenson, Clemanceau, Clemançon**. It.: **Clementini, Clementucci**. Low Ger.: **Kliemchen, Kliemke**. Ger. (of Slav. origin): **Klem(p)ke, Klim(p)ke, Klampke, Klim(m)ek, Klima, Kli(m)sch, Klich(e), Klimschak**. Pol.: **Klimek; Klich(e)**. Czech: **Klíma, Klimeš**. Beloruss.: **Klimentyonok, Klimuk**. Ukr.: **Klimko, Klimchuk, Klimus**.

Patrs. (from 1): Eng.: **Clements, Clemon(t)s; Clemetts; Clem(m)ens, Clem(m)ans, Clemence, Climance, Clemas, Climas; Cleme(n)tson, Cleminson, Climenson, Clemerson**. It. **De Clemente, Di Clemente**. Ger.: **Klemen(t)z, Klemz**. Dan.: **Clem(m)ensen**. Russ.: **Klimentov, Klimentyev**. Beloruss., Ukr.: **Klimontovich**. Pol.: **Klemensiewicz**. Croatian: **Klemenčić**.

Patrs. (from dims. of 1): Eng.: **Clem(p)son, Climpson**. Low Ger.: **Klem(p)s**. Ger. (of Slav. origin): **Klicher**. Russ.: **Klim(k)ov, Klim(och)kin, Klimushev, Klishin**. Beloruss.: **Klimkovich, Klimashevich**. Ukr.: **Klim(k)ovich**. Pol.: **Klimowicz, Klimkiewicz; Klimczak**. Finn.: **Miettinen**.

Habitation names (cogn. with 1): Pol.: **Klimaszewski, Klim(k)owski**.

All known present-day bearers of the name Clemett *descend from a single Devon family. The first known bearer of the name, which seems to be in origin a Corn. form, is Thomas* Clemet, *who was married in 1558 at Brixham, Devon. John* Clemott *is recorded in Landulph, near Saltash, Cornwall, in 1544.*

Clerihew Scots (chiefly Aberdeen): of uncertain origin, not recorded before the 17th cent.

Clermont French: habitation name from any of the various places so called, from OF *clair, cler* bright, clear (cf. CLARE 1) + *mont* hill (see MONT), i.e. a hill that could be seen a long way off.

Cogn.: Cat.: **Claramunt** (a place in the province of Lérida).

Cléry French: habitation name from any of the various places so called from the Gallo-Roman personal name *Clārius* (a deriv. of *Clārus*; see CLARE 1) + the local suffix *-ācum*.

Cleveland English: regional name from the district around Middlesbrough, so called from OE *clif* cliff (see CLIVE) + *land* land.

Cleverley English: probably a habitation name from *Cleveley* in Lancs., with intrusive *-r-* under the influence of the vocabulary word *cleverly*. The place gets its name from OE *clif* cliff (see CLIVE) + *lēah* wood, clearing.

Vars.: **Cleverly, Cleveley**.

Clewer English (W Midlands): habitation name, probably from either of the two places, in Berks. and Somerset, so called from the OE tribal name *Clifware* dwellers on the hill or slope, from OE *clif* slope (see CLIVE) + *ware* inhabitants.

Clifford English: habitation name from any of the various places, for example in Devon, Gloucs., Herefords., and W Yorks., so called from OE *clif* slope (see CLIVE) + *ford* FORD.

Var.: **Clifforth**.

A family of this name trace their descent from Walter de Clifford, *eldest son of Richard FitzPons, living in the reign of Henry II (1154–89). He adopted the surname from Clifford Castle near Hay-on-Wye, which he acquired on his marriage to the daughter of Ralph de Toeni. Titles later held by his descendants include the barony of Westmorland and the earldom of Cumberland, the latter dying out through the lack of a male heir on the death in 1643 of Henry, the 5th Earl. The present Lord Clifford of Chudleigh descends directly from Walter de Clifford in the male line; the hereditary title was acquired by Thomas Clifford (1630–73), a leading minister of Charles II. The present Clifford family of Frampton-on-Severn descends through the female line, but deliberately resumed the name in 1801 and again in 1943.*

Clift English: topographic name for someone who lived by a crevice in rock, ME *clift* cleft, past part. of *cleave, cleeve* to split (OE *cleofian*).

Var.: **Cleft**.

Clifton English: habitation name from any of the numerous places in all parts of England so called, from OE *clif* slope (see CLIVE) + *tūn* enclosure, settlement.

Clinch English: 1. habitation name from a place in Wilts., so called from OE **clenc* lump, hill. The same term seems also to have been used of a patch of dry raised ground in fenland surroundings, and the surname may be of topographic origin, from this sense.

2. occupational name for a maker or fixer of bolts and rivets, from a deriv. of ME *clench(en)* to fix firmly (OE *clencian*).

Vars.: **Clench**. (Of 2 only): **Clink(er)** (N England).

Clinton English: habitation name, either from *Glympton* in Oxon., named as 'settlement on the river *Glyme*', or from *Glinton* in Northants, recorded in 1060 as *Clinton* (from an unrecorded OE element akin to MLG *glinde* enclosure, fence + OE *tūn* enclosure, settlement).

A family of this name, who have been earls of Lincoln and dukes of Newcastle, was founded by Geoffrey de Clinton *(fl. 1130), who held lands at Glympton, Oxon. He was Chamberlain and Treasurer to Henry I (1100–35).*

Cliquet French: apparently a nickname from OF *cliquet*, the sound of a bell (an imitative formation). This may in effect have been an occupational name for a bellringer or for a wandering pedlar who rang a handbell to advise people of his approach, much like the modern rag-and-bone merchant or ice-cream salesman.

Vars.: **Cliquot, Cloquet(te)**.

Clitheroe English: habitation name from a place in Lancs., perhaps from ON *kliðra* song-thrush + *haugr* hill. The first element may alternatively be an OE word, *clȳder* loose stones.

Vars.: **Clitherow, Cleatherow, Cluderay**.

Clive English: habitation name from a place named from OE *clif* slope, bank, cliff, or topographic name from the same word used independently. The OE word was used not only in the sense of mod. Eng. *cliff* but also of much gentler slopes and frequently also of a riverbank. The surname in the form *Clive* reflects the dat. case of the OE word, originally used after a preposition; the var. in *-s* preserves the OE gen. ending. *Clive* is most common in Ches. and Shrops., and it probably derives principally from the places so called in those two counties.

Vars.: **Clives, Clyve, Cliff(e); Cleave(s)** (chiefly Devon); CLEEVE.

The names Clive *and* Cliffe *are particularly associated with the manors of Huxley and Styche. Stephen* de Cliffe, *recorded in 1189, is an early ancestor. In about 1750 George* Clive *settled in Birmingham, and was the ancestor of a prolific family of gunmakers.*

Clohessy Irish: Anglicized form of Gael. **Ó Clochasaigh** 'descendant of *Clochasach*', a personal name apparently derived from *cloch* stone (cf. CLACHAR).

Close English: 1. topographic name for someone who lived by an enclosure of some sort, such as (in towns) a courtyard set back from the main street or (in country districts) a farmyard, from ME *clos(e)* (OF *clos*, from LL *clausum*, past part. of *claudere* to close, shut).
2. nickname for a reserved or secretive person, from ME *clos(e)* secret.
Vars.: **Cluse, Closs**; CLOWES; **Clowser.**
Cogns. (of 1): Fr.: **Clos**; CLOT; **Cloux** (see also CLOUD); **Duclos, Duclot, Ducloux; Clo(u)sier, Clo(u)zier.** Prov.: **Claus, Claux, Duclaux, Clauzier, Clauzié.** Cat.: **Clos(a), Closas; Saclosa.**
Dims. (of 1): Fr.: **Clo(u)sel, Clusel, Clo(u)seau, Clo(u)zel, Cl(a)uzel, Clo(u)zeau, Cluzeau(x), Closset, Closson, Clauzet, Clauzin, Ducl(o)uzeau, Desclo(u)zeaux.**

Clot 1. French: var. of CLAUDE.
2. French: var. of *Clos* (see CLOSE).
3. Catalan: topographic name for someone who lived by a pit or hollow, from the dial. term *clot*, used of a depression in the ground (apparently of pre-Roman origin).
Dim. (of 3): **Clotet.**

Clothier English (now mainly Bristol): occupational name for a maker or seller of cloth and clothes, from ME *cloth* (OE *clāð*) + the agent suffix -*(i)er*.
Var.: **Clother.**

Cloud 1. English: topographic name for someone who lived near an outcrop or hill, from OE *clūd* rock (only later used of the formations in the sky).
2. French: from the Gmc personal name *Hlodald*, composed of the elements *hlōd* fame + *wald* rule, which was borne by a saint and bishop of the 6th cent.
Vars. (of 1): **Cloude.** (Of 2): **Clou(x)** (see also CLOSE).
Dims. (of 2): **Clouet; Closon** (Belgium).

Clough English: topographic name for someone who lived near a precipitous slope, from OE *clōh* ravine.
Vars.: **Cleugh, Cluff; Cloke** (Devon); **Clow, Clew, Clue**; CLOWES, **Clew(e)s** (W Midlands; from the gen. case).

Clout English: metonymic occupational name for a repairer of clothes, shoes, or household utensils, or a nickname for a wearer of much-mended clothes, from ME *clut* patch (OE *clūt*).
Vars.: **Cloutt, Clouter, Cloutman.**

Clowes English: 1. var. of CLOUGH (pronounced /klaʊz/).
2. var. of CLOSE (pronounced /kləʊz/).

Clune Irish: Anglicized form of Gael. **Mac Glúin**, patr. from the personal name *Glún*. This is either a byname meaning 'Knee', or else a short form of various OIr. cpd names such as *Glúnfhionn* 'Fair-kneed' or *Glúncoramhn* 'Iron-kneed'.
Vars.: **McClo(o)ne.**

Clutterbuck English: of unknown origin, possibly an Anglicized garbling of a Du. name.
This is the name of a family who were prominent in Gloucs. life for many generations, providing mayors for the city of Gloucester in 1545 and 1646. They are said to have come from the Low Countries, but nothing definite is known about the origins of them or their name, which is still found in Gloucs. today.

Clyde Scots and N Irish: apparently a topographic name for someone who lived on the banks of the river *Clyde* (Gael. *Cluaidh*, probably of pre-Celtic origin), which flows through Glasgow.

Clyne 1. Scots: habitation name from any of various places so called, from Gael. *claon* slope.
2. Jewish (Ashkenazic): Anglicized spelling of KLEIN.

Clynes 1. Scots: var. of CLYNE 1.
2. English: habitation name from *Claines*, just north of Worcester, recorded as *Cl(e)ynes* in the 13th cent. It is by the river Severn, and gets its name from OE *clǣg* CLAY + *næss* ness, point of land.

Coad English (Devon): probably a metonymic occupational name for a cobbler's assistant, from ME *cōde* cobbler's wax. Alternatively, it may possibly be a topographic name from OCorn. *cuit* wood.
Var.: **Code.**

Coakley Irish: Anglicized form of Gael. **Mac Caochlaoich**, patr. from *Caochlaoch*, a personal name composed of the elements *caoch* blind + *laoch* warrior, hero.
This surname is largely confined to Cork.

Coates 1. English: topographic name for someone who lived in a relatively humble dwelling, from the gen. sing. or nom. pl. case of ME *cote, cott* shelter, cottage (OE *cot*). Cf. COTTER 1.
2. English: habitation name from any of the numerous English places named with this word, esp. *Coates* in Cambs. and *Cotes* in Leics.
3. Scots: var. of COUTTS.
Vars.: **Cotes, Coat(t)s, Cottis; Co(a)te** (from the dat. sing.); **Co(a)tman; Dallicoat, Dallicote, Delicate** (with fused ANF preposition and article).
Cogns.: Low Ger.: **Koth(e), Kathman.** Du.: **Ten Kate, Ten Cate.**

Cobb English: 1. from the ME byname or personal name *Cobbe, Cobba*, or the cogn. ON *Kobbi*, both of which are probably from an element meaning 'lump', used to denote a large man.
2. aphetic form of JACOB.
Vars.: **Cobbe, Cob.**
The name Cobb *is especially common in Dorset and E Anglia, though widely distributed throughout S England. One present-day Oxon. family are descended from Sir Francis Cobb (c.1606–71), a royalist officer in Oxford, who came from Burnham, Norfolk.*

Cobbold English (chiefly E Anglia): from the ME personal name *Cutebald, Cubald*, OE *Cūðbeald*, composed of the elements *cūð* famous, well-known + *beald* bold, brave.
Vars.: **Cobbald, Cobbett.**

Cobden English: habitation name from either of two places, in Derbys. and Devon, so called from the OE personal name *Cobba* (see COBB 1) + OE *dūn* hill (see DOWN 1).

Cobham English: habitation name from a place so called, probably one of those in Kent, Surrey, or Sussex, although the surname is now more common in Lancs. The place-names derive from the OE personal name *Cobba* (see COBB 1) + OE *hām* homestead, except for the one in Surrey, which was originally *Coveham* and so probably derives from the OE personal name *Cofa* + *hām*.

Cobley English: habitation name from either of two places in Devon called *Cobley*, from the OE personal name *Cobba* (see COBB 1) + OE *lēah* wood, clearing.
Var.: **Cobleigh.**

Cobo 1. Spanish: popular form of the medieval nickname *Calvo* 'Bald' (L *calvus*; see CHAFF).

2. Spanish: habitation name from any of various minor places. They may have been so called from the same word as in 1, referring to a bare and treeless appearance, or alternatively the placename may be from LL *cova* hollow (of Gmc origin; cf. Cove).

3. Italian: aphetic short form of *Giacobo*; see Jacob.

Vars. (of 1 and 2): **Covo**. (Of 2 only): **Cobos** (the name of places in the provinces of Palencia and Segovia).

Dim.: Sp.: **Covillo**.

Cochrane Scots: habitation name from lands in the parish of Paisley, near Glasgow. The placename is of uncertain origin, perhaps from a Brit. cogn. of W *coch* red (cf. Gough 2), although this etymology is not supported by the earliest recorded spelling, *Coueran*.

Vars.: **Cochran, Cochren, Colqueran**.

Cochrane *is the family name of the Earls of Dundonald, assumed by Sir William Blair, 1st Earl, on his marriage into the ancient Scottish family of Cochrane. The 10th Earl of Dundonald, Thomas Cochrane (1775–1860), was imprisoned for fraud and on his release went to Chile, where he took part in the liberation of the country from Spanish rule. He later served in Brazil, and he also served as a commander of the Greek navy.*

Cock English: 1. nickname from the bird, ME *cok*, OE *cocc*, given for a variety of possible reasons. Applied to a young lad who strutted proudly like a cock, it soon became a generic term for a youth and was attached with hypocoristic force to the short forms of many medieval given names (e.g. Alcock, *Hancock*, *Hiscock*, *Mycock*). The nickname may also have referred to a natural leader, or an early riser, or a lusty or aggressive individual. The surname may also occasionally derive from the cock used as a house sign.

2. from the ME byname *le Cok*, OE *Cocca*, derived from the word given in 1 above or from the homonymous *cocc* hillock, clump, lump, and so denoting a fat and awkward man. This name is not independently attested, but appears to lie behind a number of placenames and (probably) the medieval given name *Cock*, which was still in use in the late 13th cent.

Cogns. (of 1): Fr.: **Coq, Lecoc(q)**.

Dims. (of 1): Eng.: **Cocklin(g)**; **Cock(e)rell, Cock(e)rill, Cockarill**. Fr.: **Co(c)quet, Coc(que)teau, Coquot, Coquel(et), Coquelin, Coclet, Coclin, Cochet, Cochey, Cochez, Cocheteau, Cochin(eau), Cochy**.

Patrs.: Eng.: **Cocks**, Cox; **Coxon, Coxen**; **Cocking**. Fr.: **Aucoc**.

Cockayne English: nickname for an idle dreamer, from ME *cokayne* cloud-cuckooland, an imaginary paradise (OF (*pays de*) *cocaigne*, from MLG *kōkenje*, a dim. of *kōke* cake, since in this land the very houses were supposed to be made of cake).

A family of this name, long established at Ashbourne, Derbys., trace their descent from John Cockayne, *who lived c.1150.*

Cockburn Scots and Northumbrian: habitation name from a place in the former county of Berwicks. (now part of Borders region) so called from OE *cocc* cock (or the byname *Cocca*; see Cock 2) + *burna* stream (see Bourne). The surname is normally pronounced /'koubʌrn/ (in S England /'kəubɜ:n/), apparently to veil the imagined indelicacy of the first syllable.

Var.: **Coburn**.

Cockcroft English (Yorks. and Lancs.): habitation name from an unidentified place named as an enclosure where poultry were raised, from OE *cocc* Cock + *croft* paddock, smallholding (see Croft).

Var.: **Cockroft**.

Cockell English: from ME, OF *cokille* shell (derived via L from Gk *konkhylion*, a dim. of *konkhē* shellfish). The name could be a metonymic occupational name for a gatherer and seller of shellfish, or it could be a nickname for someone who had been on a pilgrimage to Santiago (cf. Kumsteller) and wore a cockle badge in commemoration. The word was also applied in the Middle Ages to a type of woman's head-dress that somewhat resembled the mollusc in form, and so the surname may also have arisen as a metonymic occupational name for a milliner who produced such items.

Vars.: **Cockill, Cockle**.

Cogn.: Fr.: **Coquille**.

Dim.: Fr.: **Coquillon**.

Cocker English: 1. nickname for a bellicose person, from ME *cock* to fight, wrangle (a deriv. of OE *cocc* cock; cf. Cock 1).

2. occupational name for someone who was particularly skilled in building haystacks, from ME *cock* heap of hay (of ON origin, or from OE **cocc* mound, hill; cf. Cock 2).

Cockerham English: habitation name from a place in Lancs., so called from the river *Cocker* (a Brit. name apparently derived from an element **kukro* winding; cf. OIr. *cúcar* crooked, awkward) + OE *hām* homestead. The surname is now most common in this form in the Leeds area; in the var. **Cockram** around Bristol.

Codd 1. English: metonymic occupational name for a maker of purses and bags, from OE *cod* bag.

2. English: metonymic nickname for a man noted for his apparent sexual prowess, from *cod*(*piece*), the garment worn in Tudor times prominently over the male genitals.

3. English: metonymic occupational nickname for a fishmonger, from ME *cod*, the fish (of uncertain origin, perhaps a transferred use of 1).

4. Irish: var. of Cody.

Var. (of 1–3): **Codman**.

Dim. (of 1–3): Codlin.

Codgbrook English: habitation name from *Cottesbrook* in Northants, so called from the gen. case of the OE personal name **Cott* + OE *brōc* stream (see Brook).

Var.: **Cotsbrooke**.

The earliest known bearer of this name is Ralphe de Cotesbroke *(1308); an Adam* de Cotesbrok *was MP for Northampton in the 1320s and mayor of Northampton in 1340. All modern bearers are probably descended from a certain John* Cotsbrooke *whose marriage is recorded in 1684; the spelling* Codgbrook *was first used in recording the birth of his son William in 1685.*

Codina Catalan: topographic name for someone who lived on a piece of stony land that could be worked only with difficulty, Cat. *codina* (LL *cotīna*, a deriv. of *cotis* stone).

Codlin English: 1. double dim. of Codd.

2. nickname for a brave man, or ironically for an exceptionally timorous one, from OF *ceur de lion* 'lion heart' (cf. Coeur).

Vars.: **Codling** (Yorks.); **Quodling, Quadling** (Norfolk, Suffolk); **Girling, Gurling** (Suffolk, Essex, Norfolk).

Codrington English: habitation name from a place in Gloucs., so called from OE *Cūðeringatūn* 'settlement (OE *tūn*) associated with *Cūðhere*', a personal name composed of the elements *cūð* famous, well-known + *here* army.

Cody Irish: 1. Anglicized form of Gael. **Ó Cuidighthigh** 'descendant of *Cuidightheach*', a byname for a helpful person.

2. Anglicized form of Gael. **Mac Óda** 'son of *Óda*', a personal name of uncertain origin. This name was taken by a family in Kilkenny formerly known as *Archdeacon*.

Vars. (of 1): **Coady**; **O'Codihie**, **O'Kuddyhy**, **O'Cuddie**, **Cud(d)ihy**, **Cuddehy**, **Quiddihy**.

Coe English: nickname from the jackdaw, from a S English var. of KAY (for the change of *-ā-* to *-ō-* cf. ROPER). The surname is chiefly found in Essex and Suffolk.

Var.: **Coo**.

Coeur French: nickname from OF *ceur* heart (L *cor*), given originally to a stout-hearted man, or ironically to a faint-hearted one. In some cases it may have been originally a house name for someone living at the sign of the sacred heart.

Vars.: **Cor**; **Lecour**.

Dim.: **Coeuret**.

Coffey Irish: Anglicized form of Gael. **Ó Cobhthaigh** 'descendant of *Cobhthach*', a byname meaning 'Victorious'.

Vars.: **O'Coffey**, **O'Coffie**, **O'Cohey**, **Coffee**, **Cow(h)ey**, **Cowhiy**.

Coffin French and English: metonymic occupational name for a basket maker, from OF *cof(f)in* basket (LL *cophīnus*, from Gk). Mod. Eng. *coffin* represents a specialized development of this word, not attested before the 16th cent. See also KYFFIN.

Vars.: Fr.: **Couffin**, **Co(u)fin**; **Coffinier**. Eng.: **Ca(u)ffin** (Sussex).

Dims.: Fr.: **Co(u)ffinel**, **Coffineau**, **Co(u)ffinet**.

This is an ancient Devon name: Sir Elias Coffin *held lands in the county in the reign of King John (1199–1216). The direct line became extinct with Richard Coffin in 1766, when his estates were inherited by his nephews. Their descendants reassumed the surname Coffin in 1797. A branch of the family was established in America by Tristram* Coffyn *(1605–81), who founded the colony of Nantucket. He emigrated in 1642 and is probably the ancestor of all American bearers of the name.*

Cogan 1. Irish (of Welsh origin): habitation name from a parish near Cardiff, which may have been named with a W word meaning 'bowl', 'depression'. There is evidence of a family named *de Cogan* in the 12th cent., and by the 13th cent. the name was also associated with Somerset, Devon, Co. Limerick, and Co. Cork.

2. Irish: Anglicized form of Gael. **Mac Cogadháin** 'son of *Cogadhán*', a dim. from a reduced form of the personal name *Cúchogaidh* 'Hound of War'.

3. Jewish (E Ashkenazic): var. of COHEN.

Vars. (of 2): **Coogan**; **Coggan**, **Coggin(s)**; **Gogan**, **Goggin**.

Coghill Scots: apparently an Anglicized form of Dan. **Køgel**; cf. KUGEL.

A family of this name can be traced to David Coghill *(d. c.1790). However, they are said to be descended from a Danish family called* Køgel*, who settled at Papa Stour in the Shetlands.*

Cohen 1. Jewish: from Hebr. *kohen* priest. Priests are traditionally regarded as members of a hereditary caste descended from Aaron, brother of Moses. Not all Jews bearing the name *Cohen* belong to the priestly caste: when many Jews were being forced to join the Russian Army for 25 years, a number changed their surnames to *Cohen* because members of the clergy were exempt from service. See also KAPLAN.

2. Irish (Galway): Anglicized form of Gael. *Ó Cadhain*; see COYNE.

Vars.: **Cohan**, **Coen**, **Cohn**. (Of 1 only): **Koh(e)n**, **Cahan**, **Cah(e)n**, **Kah(e)n**, **Cohane**, **Kahan(e)**; **Cohani**, **Cahani**, **Cahany**, **Kahany** (with the Hebr. suffix *-i*); **Cahana**, **Kahana** (from Jewish Aramaic *kahana* the priest); **Cohener**, **Kohener**, **Kohaner**, **Kah(a)ner**; **Cohansky**, **Cahansky**, **Cahansky**, **Kahansky**; COGAN, **Kogen**, **Kogan**, **Cagan**, **Kagan** (under Russ. influence, since the Russ. language has no /h/). Hung.: **Kún**.

Patrs. (from 1): **Kohanoff**, **Kahanov**, **Kahanoff**, **Cahanov**, **Cahanoff**, **Kahanow(ich)**, **Kahanowicz**, **Kahanowitz**, **Kahanovitz**, **Kahanovi(t)ch**, **Cahanovitz**, **Cahanovitch**; **Kaganov(ich)**, **Kaganoff**, **Kaganovic**, **Caganovitz**, **Kaganovski**, **Kaganowski** (E Ashkenazic); **Bar-Cohen**, **Barkan**, **Barcan** (with the Jewish Aramaic prefix *bar-* son of).

Coimbra Portuguese: habitation name from a place in the province of Beira, first recorded in the form *Colimbria*, from Celt. *Conimbriga*, apparently a cpd of *con* height (cf. CONAN 1) + *briga* hill, fortress (cf. BRYAN).

Coker English: habitation name from a group of villages in Somerset, so called from a Brit. river name meaning 'crooked'; cf. COCKERHAM.

Colaço Portuguese: nickname for a foundling who was brought up by foster-parents together with their own children, from Port. *colaço* foster brother (LL *collact(ān)eus*, from *con-* with, together + *lac*, gen. *lactis*, milk; the term originally referred to an infant wet-nursed together with a woman's own child).

Colbeck N English: habitation name from any of various minor places, such as *Caldbeck* in Cumb., named with the ON elements *kaldr* cold + *bekkr* stream; cf. CALDWELL and COLBOURNE.

Vars.: **Colebeck**, **Coulbeck**, **Caldbeck**.

Colbourne English: habitation name from a place possibly so named with the OE elements *cōl* cool + *burna* stream (see BOURNE). One such place is *Colburn* near Catterick in N Yorks., but the surname is now most frequent in Birmingham.

Vars.: **Colbourn**, **Colborn(e)**, **Colburn(e)**.

Colby English: habitation name from places in Norfolk and Cumb., so called from the ON personal name *Koli* (a byname for a swarthy person, from *kol* (char)coal; see COLE 2) + ON *býr* settlement.

Colclough English: habitation name from *Cowclough* in the parish of Whitworth, Lancs., recorded in the 13th cent. as *Colleclogh*, probably from the OE byname *Cola* (see COLE 2) + OE *clōh* ravine (see CLOUGH).

Var.: **Coleclough**.

Coldham English: habitation name from a place in Cambs., so called from OE *c(e)ald* cold + *hām* homestead.

Cole 1. English: from a ME pet form of NICHOLAS; cf. COLL 1.

2. English: from a ME personal name derived from the OE byname *Cola* (from *col* (char)coal, presumably denoting someone of swarthy appearance), or the cogn. ON *Koli*.

3. Scots and Irish: Anglicized form of Gael. **Mac Gille Chomhghaill** (Sc.), **Mac Giolla Chomhghaill** (Ir.) 'son of the servant of (St) *Comhghall*', a personal name, of uncertain origin, borne by an early Ir. saint.

Vars.: **Coull** (Scots). (Of 3 only): **McCole**, **McCool(e)** (see also MCDOUGALL); **Coyle**, **Gilhool**.

Patrs. (from 1): **Co(a)les**, **Coules**, **Cowles**; **Coleson**, **Coulson**, **Cowlson**.

An Irish family by the name of Cole *were established in Fermanagh by Sir William Cole (1576–1653). He was the first Provost of Enniskillen, and his descendants became Earls of Enniskillen. The family are thought to have originated in Devon and Cornwall, where the name occurs in an 11th-cent. deed.*

Coleman 1. Irish and English: from the OIr. personal name *Colmán*, earlier *Columbán*, a dim. of *Colum(b)* (L *Columba* 'Dove'; see COLOMB). This was the name of an Ir. missionary to Europe, generally known as St *Columban* (*c*.540–615), who founded the monastery of Bobbio in N Italy in 614. With his companion St GALL, he enjoyed a considerable cult throughout central Europe, so that forms of his name were adopted as given names in It. (*Colombano*), Fr. (*Colombain*), Czech (*Kolman*), and Hung. (*Kálmán*). From all of these surnames are derived. In Irish and English, the name of this saint is identical with dims. of the name of the 6th-cent. missionary now generally known as St *Columba* (521–97), who converted the Picts to Christianity, and who was known in Scandinavian languages as *Kalman*.

2. Irish: Anglicized form of Gael. **Ó Clumháin** 'descendant of *Clumhán*', a personal name of uncertain origin.

3. English: occupational name for a burner of charcoal or a gatherer of coal, ME *coleman*, from OE *col* (char)coal + *mann* man; cf. COLLIER.

4. English: occupational name for the servant of a man named COLE.

5. Jewish (Ashkenazic): Anglicized form of any of the names given at KALMAN.

Vars. (of 1–4): **Colman, Coll(e)man, Coulman.** (Of 1 only): Scots: **Callum, Cullum.**

Cogns. (of 1): Fr.: **Colomba(i)n.** It.: **Columban(i).** Czech: **Kolman.** Hung.: **Kálmán.** Ger.: **Kohlmann** (altered by folk etymology to look like a deriv. of Ger. *Kohl* cabbage + *man*).

Patrs. (from 1): Ir.: **McCalman, McCalmon(t)** (Gael. **Mac Colmáin, Mac Calmáin**).

'Descendant of C. 1': Ir.: **O'Coleman** (Gael. **Ó Colmáin**).

Colenso Cornish: habitation name from a place in the parish of St Hilary, which is of unknown etymology.

Coleridge English: habitation name from two places in Devon so called, from OE *col* (char)coal + *hrycg* ridge.

Coley English (W Midlands): nickname for a swarthy person, from OE *colig* dark, black (a deriv. of *col* (char)coal; cf. COLE 2).

Vars.: **Colley, Collie.**

Coll 1. English: from an aphetic pet form of NICHOLAS. Forms of this name in which the first syllable is lost are found in several European languages. Forms spelled with an initial *K*- are listed at KLAUS.

2. Irish: var. of COLE 3.

3. Irish: Anglicized form of the Gael. personal name *Colla*, which was borne by a warrior in Celt. mythology; it is of uncertain etymology.

4. Catalan: topographic name for someone who lived by a hill or mountain pass, Cat. *coll* (L *collis* hill).

Vars. (of 1–3): **Colle.**

Cogns. (of 1): Fr.: **Colle.** It.: **Cola(o), Coli; Cullo, Culle** (Sicily). Du.: **Colle.** Flem.: **Col(le), Colla.** (Of 4): Prov.: **Col.**

Dims. (of 1): Eng.: **Col(l)in,** COLLING, **Collen; Collett; Colcock; Colkin.** Fr.: **Col(l)et, Col(l)in(et), Col(l)inot, Coli(g)non, Coll(en)ot, Coleçon, Col(le)son, Collechon; Collec, Colleu(c)** (Brittany). It.: **Colino, Colini, Colelli, Colotti, Colozzi, Colucci(o), Colaucci, Colluc(i)ello, Col(a)ussi, Colusso, Colauzzi, Colichio, Cullicchi.** Du.: **Collet, Colijn, Kolijn.** Flem.: **Collin, Colson.** (Of 4): Cat.: **Collell.**

Pejs. (of 1): Eng.: **Collard.** Fr.: **Col(l)ard.** It.: **Collazzo.**

Patrs. (from 1): Eng.: **Colls, Colson.** It.: **De Cola, Di Cola.** Du.: **Cols, Colen.**

Collado Spanish: topographic name for someone who lived by a hill or mountain pass, Sp. *collado* (LL *collātum*, a deriv. of class. L *collis* hill; see COLL 4).

Cogn.: Prov.: **Colade.**

Dim.: Prov.: **Coladon.**

Colleran Irish: Anglicized form of Gael. **Ó Callaráin** 'descendant of *Callarán*', which is probably a dim. of the byname *Callaire* 'Cryer'.

Collier English: occupational name for a burner of charcoal or a gatherer or seller of coal, from ME *cole* (char)coal (see COLE 2 and COLEMAN 3) + the agent suffix -*(i)er*.

Vars.: **Collye(a)r, Colyer, Colliar(d), Colleer.**

Cogns.: Ger.: **Köhler, Köller; Kohler, Koller** (Bavaria). Low Ger.: **Kähler.** Jewish (Ashkenazic): **Kohl(er); Kohlmann; Koilman** (from Yid. *koyl* coal); **Kohlenbrenner** ('coal burner'); **Kohl(en)berg** ('coal hill', ornamental elaboration).

Equiv. (not cogn.): Czech: UHLÍŘ.

Colling English: 1. from the ON personal name *Kollungr*, a deriv. of *Koli*, or from an OE cogn., *Colling*, a deriv. of *Cola*; see COLE 2.

2. dim. of COLL, a pet form of NICHOLAS.

Vars.: **Collinge, Co(w)ling.**

Patr.: **Collings.**

Collingwood English: habitation name, probably from *Callingwood* in Staffs., although the surname is now more common on Tyneside. The origin of the placename is from a wood whose ownership was disputed (from ME, OF *chalenge* dispute, challenge, L *calumnia* wrong, injury).

Vars.: **Collinwood, Collingworth.**

Collins 1. English: patr. from ME *Col(l)in*, a dim. of COLL, itself a pet form of NICHOLAS.

2. Irish: Anglicized form of Gael. *Ó Coileáin* and *Mac Coileáin*; see CULLEN 3.

Vars.: **Collyns, Collis; Colli(n)son.**

Colmenar Spanish: habitation name from any of the numerous minor places named with this word, a deriv. of Sp. *colmena* beehive (of uncertain origin, perhaps preserving a pre-Roman term derived from the Celt. element *kolmos* straw, a material of which such constructions were commonly made).

Vars.: **Colmenares** (pl.); **Colmenero** (occupational name for a beekeeper).

Dim.: **Colmenarejo.**

Colomb French: 1. metonymic occupational name for a keeper of doves, from OF *colomb* dove (L *columbus*), or a nickname for a person of a mild and gentle disposition.

2. from a given name of the same origin. The name in its Latin forms *Columbus* and *Columba* was popular among early Christians because the dove was considered to be the symbol of the Holy Spirit. See also COLEMAN 1.

Vars.: **Collomb, Collomp, Col(l)om, Col(l)on; Colombier.**

Cogns.: Prov.: **Coulomb(e), Couloumbe, Coul(l)omp, Coul(l)on; Colomer, Colom(i)ès.** It.: **Colombo, Colomi, Colomba, Columbo; Colombari, Columberi.** Sp.: **Colomo; Colón** (a Castilianized form of It. *Colombo*, adopted by the explorer). Cat.: **Colom(a); Colomer, Colomé.**

Dims.: Fr.: **Co(u)lombet, Co(u)lombel, Co(u)lombeau, Co(u)lombot; Colomic** (Brittany). It.: **Colombetti, Colombetta; Colombin(i)** (in Milan this was the surname regularly used for the foundlings taken into the orphanage of St Catherine there).

Augs.: Fr.: **Co(u)lombat.**

Pej.: It.: **Colombazzi.**

Colquhoun Scots: habitation name from a place in the former county of Aberdeens. (now part of Grampian region), first recorded in the form *Colqhoun* in 1246. The name appears to derive from Gael. *còil, cùil* nook, corner, or *coill(e)* wood + *cumhann* narrow. The regular pronunciation is /kə'hu:n/.

Vars.: **Colhoun** (N Ireland), **Calhoun** (U.S.).

Colquhoun *is the name of a Scottish family descended from Umfridus de Kilpatrick, who acquired the lands of Colquhoun in the reign of Alexander II (1214–49). Several Swedish families with names such as* **Cahun(d)**, **Caun**, **Gaun**, **Gahn**, *and* **Kharun** *descend from Walter Colquhoun, a 16th-cent. cannon founder.*

Colston English: 1. from a ME given name, *Colstan*, which is probably from ON *Kolsteinn*, composed of the elements *kol* charcoal + *steinn* stone.

2. habitation name from *Colston* (Basset) in Notts., or the nearby *Carcolson*, both of which seem to have originally been named as the settlement (OE *tūn*) of a bearer of the ON name *Kolr*. The first syllable of *Carcolson* was originally the defining prefix *kirk* church.

3. habitation name from *Coulston* in Warwicks., so called from the gen. case of an OE personal name *Cufel* (dim. of *Cufa*) + OE *tūn* enclosure, settlement.

Var.: **Coulston**.

Colt English: 1. metonymic occupational name for someone who looked after asses and horses, from ME, OE *colt* young ass, later also young horse, colt. In N England *colt* was the generic word for working horses and asses. See also COULTHARD.

2. nickname for an obstinate or frisky person, from the same word.

Vars.: **Coult**; **Colter**; **Coltman**.

Colton English: habitation name from any of various places so called. Examples in Norfolk and W Yorks. are from the OE personal name *Cola* (or the cogn. ON *Koli*; see COLE 2) + OE *tūn* enclosure, settlement. Another in Somerset has as its first element the personal name *Cūla* (of uncertain origin); one in Lancs. has a river name apparently derived from a Brit. word for the hazel; and one in Staffs. may be from OE *colt* COLT.

Colville English and Scots (Norman): habitation name from *Colleville* in Seine-Maritime, so called from the Scandinavian personal name *Koli* (see COLE 2) + OF *ville* settlement, village (see VILLE).

Var.: **Colvill**.

A family of this name trace their descent from Philip de Colville, *who in the 12th cent. held lands in Roxburghs.*

Colwell English: habitation name from places in Northumb. and Devon. The former is so called from OE *col* (char)coal or *cōl* cool + *well(a)* spring, stream (see WELL); the latter has as its first element a Brit. river name, *Coly*, apparently meaning 'narrow'.

Var.: **Colwill**.

Comerford 1. English: habitation name from *Comberford* in Staffs., so called from the OE personal name *Cumbra* (originally an ethnic name for a British Celt), or from the gen. pl., meaning 'of the British' + OE *ford* FORD.

2. Irish: Anglicized form of Gael. **Mac Cumascaigh** 'son of *Cumascach*', a byname derived from *cumascach* mixer, confuser.

Vars.: **Cummerford**. (Of 2 only): **(Mc)Cumisky**, **(Mc)Cumesky**, **(Mc)Comisky**, **Cumiskey**, **Cumeskey**, **Commiskey**, **Cumish**, **Comisk**.

Comfort English (Kent): 1. nickname or given name from ME *cumfort* (OF *confort* strengthening, succour, from LL *confortāre* to strengthen).

2. habitation name from a lost place, possibly *Comports* near Birling in Kent or *Compworthy* near Oxted in Surrey.

Var.: **Comport**.

Comley English: nickname for a handsome man, from ME *cumelich* fair, lovely (from OE *(be)cuman* to befit + the adj. suffix *-līc*).

Compagnon French: nickname for a good neighbour or amiable fellow-worker, from the oblique case of OF *compain* companion, fellow (LL *compānio*, gen. *compāniōnis*, mess-mate, from *con-* together, with + *panis* bread).

Vars.: **Compain(g)**, **Compin**, **Cop(a)in**, **Coppin** (from the nom. case).

Cogns.: It.: **Compagni**, **Compagno**; **Pagni** (Tuscany).

Dims.: Fr.: **Copinet**, **Copinot**, **Copigneau**. It.: **Compagnini**, **Compagnino**, **Compagnucci**; **Pagnin(i)**, **Pagnotti**, **Pagnussi**, **Pagnut(ti)**.

Augs.: It.: **Compagnoni**, **Compagnone**; **Pagnoni**.

Companys Catalan: from the abstract noun 'company' (cf. COMPAGNON). The name may have referred to one of the members of a nobleman's retinue, or it may derive from a rare medieval given name bestowed on a child in recognition of the companionship he brings to his relatives.

Compton English: habitation name from any of the numerous places throughout England so called from OE *cumb* short, straight valley (see COOMBE) + *tūn* enclosure, settlement.

Var.: **Cumpton**.

Comrie Scots: habitation name from any of various places called *Comrie*, for example in Fife and in the former county of Perths. All are so called from Gael. *comarach*, from *comar* confluence, river-fork, + the local suffix *-ach*.

Conan 1. English: from an OBret. personal name, derived from an element meaning 'high', 'mighty', which was introduced into England by followers of William the Conqueror and subsequently into Ireland, where it still has some currency as a given name.

2. Scots: habitation name from a place in the former county of Kincardines. (now part of Grampian region). The placename is of uncertain origin, possibly from early Celt. **Conona* 'hound stream'.

Vars.: **Conen**, **Conant**.

Conaty Irish: Anglicized form of Gael. **Ó Connachtaigh** 'descendant of *Connachtach*', a byname for someone from the province of Connaught.

Dim.: **Conaughton**.

Concannon Irish: Anglicized form of Gael. **Ó Concheanainn** 'descendant of *Cúcheanann*', a personal name composed of the elements *cú* hound, dog + *ceann* head + *fionn* fair, white. Bearers of this surname claim descent from a single 10th-cent. ancestor.

Conceição Portuguese: from a medieval female given name (from LL *conceptio*, gen. *conceptiōnis*, conception, a deriv. of *concipere* to conceive), alluding to the Immaculate Conception of the Virgin Mary.

Cogn.: Sp. **Concepción**.

Conche French: 1. topographic name for someone who lived in or near a hollow or depression in the land, from OF *conche* basin (L *concha* shell, from Gk *konkhē* shellfish; cf. COCKELL), or habitation name from any of the places in France which get their names from this word, as for example *Conques* in Aude and Aveyron.

2. occasionally, perhaps, a metonymic occupational name for a maker or seller of wooden basins or other vessels, which were also named with the word *conche*.

Var.: **Conches**.

Cogns.: It.: **Conca**. Sp.: **Cuenca**; **Concha** (the name of places in the provinces of Biscay, Guadalajara, and Santander).

Dims.: Fr.: **Conchon, Conquet**.

Condamine French: habitation name from a place so called from OF *condumine* condominium, (land held in) joint ownership (LL *condominium*, originally an abstract noun, from *con-* together, with + *dominus* lord, master). Later, by a different interpretation of the compound, the term came to denote land included directly within the feudal lord's own residence and so exempt from taxation.

Vars.: **Condamin, Contamin(e), Condemine, Condomine**.

Condell Irish: of uncertain, presumably English, origin. It may be a habitation name from *Cundall* in N Yorks, which is of uncertain etymology; or from the group of Dorset villages called *Caundle*, apparently from a Brit. hill-name of uncertain form and meaning.

Condom French: habitation name from a place in Aveyron, so called from the Gaul. personal name *Condus* + the Gaul. element *magos* field, plain.

Condon Irish: Anglicized form of Gael. *Condún*, itself a Gaelicized form of the Anglo-Norman habitation name *de Caunteton*. This seems to have been imported from Wales, but probably derives ultimately from *Caunton* in Notts., so called from the OE personal name *Calunōð* (composed of the elements *calu* bald + *nōð* daring) + OE *tūn* enclosure, settlement.

Var.: **Congdon** (Devon).

Condy English: topographic name for someone who lived by a water channel, ME, OF *cond(u)it* (LL *conductus*, a deriv. of *conducere* to lead).

Vars.: **Condie** (chiefly Scotland); **Cundy** (chiefly Devon).

Conesa Catalan: habitation name from a place in the province of Tarragona. The placename is of uncertain origin, and has been explained in terms of various Arabic and pre-Roman elements, as well as more than one Romance source.

Coney English: nickname meaning 'rabbit' or metonymic occupational name for a dealer in rabbits, from ME *cony* (a back-formation from *conies*, from OF *conis*, pl. of *conil*, from L *cuniculus*).

Vars.: **Cony, Conie**; **Conning** (from the ONF form *coning*).

Cogns.: Prov.: **Conil**. It.: **Coniglio**; **Conigliaro** (an occupational name). Sp.: **Conejo**; **Coello** (W Spain); **Conejero**. Cat.: **Conill, Cunill, Cuní**; **Cunillé**. Port.: **Coelho**. Flem., Du.: **Konijn**.

Dims.: Prov.: **Conillon**. Sp.: **Conejillo**.

Aug.: It.: **Coniglione**.

Congreve English: habitation name from a place in Staffs., so called from OE *cumb* short valley (see COOMBE) + *grǣfe* grove, brushwood, thicket.

Vars.: **Congr(e)ave**.

A family of this name trace their descent from Simon de Congreve *who was living in 1327. They were long established at Stretton, Staffs. Later members of the family included the dramatist William Congreve (1670–1729).*

Conn Irish: short form of any of the names listed under CONNELL, CONNOLLY, CONNOR, and CONROY.

Connell Irish: Anglicized form of Gael. **Ó Conaill** 'descendant of *Conall*', a personal name of uncertain origin, possibly composed of the elements *con* (from *cú* hound) + *gal* valour. The name was popularized by the fame of a 7th-cent. Irish saint, abbot of Inis Caoil.

Vars.: **O'Connell, Gunning**.

Conner English: occupational name for an inspector of weights and measures, from ME *connere*, *cunnere* inspector, an agent derviv. of *cun(nen)* to examine, test (OE *cunnian*, from *cunnan* to know).

Connolly Irish: Anglicized form of Gael. **Ó Conghalaigh** 'descendant of *Conghalach*', a byname meaning 'Valiant'.

Vars.: **O'Connolly, (O')Connally, Connelly, Conneely, Conally, O'Conely, Conley**.

Connor Irish: Anglicized form of Gael. **Ó Conchobhair** 'descendant of *Conchobhar*', a personal name apparently composed of the elements *cú* hound, dog + *cobhar* desiring. Many present-day bearers of the surname claim descent from a 10th-cent. king of Connaught of this name. In Irish legend, Conchobhar was a king of Ulster who adopted the youthful Cuchulain.

Vars.: **O'Connor, Connors**.

Conroy Irish: Anglicized form of Gael. **Ó Conaire** 'descendant of *Conaire*', a byname meaning 'Keeper of the Hound' (an agent deriv. of *cú* hound, dog).

Vars.: **Con(ner)ry**.

Dims.: **O'Conoran, O'Coneran, Conran, Condron, Condrin** (Gael. **Ó Conaráin**).

Constable English: occupational name for the law-enforcement officer of a parish, ME, OF *conestable*, *cunestable* (LL *comes stabuli* officer (see COUNT) of the stable). The title was also borne by various other officials during the Middle Ages, including the chief officer of the household (and army) of a medieval ruler, and this may in some cases be the source of the surname.

Constance English and French: 1. from the medieval female given name *Constance* (L *Constantia*, originally a fem. form of *Constantius* (see CONSTANT), but later taken as the abstract noun *constantia* steadfastness).

2. habitation name from *Coutances* in La Manche, Normandy, which was given its L name of *Constantia* (see above) in honour of the Roman emperor Constantius Chlorus, who was responsible for fortifying the settlement in AD 305–6.

Vars.: Eng.: **Custance**. Fr.: **Coutance**.

Cogn. (of 1): It.: **Costanza**.

Dims. (of 1): Eng.: **Cust, Cuss(e)**; **Cussen, Cusson** (see also COUSIN and CUTHBERT).

Metr. (from 1): Eng.: **Custerson**.

Metrs. (from 1) (dims.): Eng.: **Cussons, Cussens**.

Constant French: from a medieval given name (L *Constans*, gen. *Constantis*, 'Steadfast', 'Faithful', pres. part. of *constāre* to stand fast, be consistent) borne by an 8th-cent. Irish martyr. This surname has also absorbed examples of the name *Constantius*, a deriv. of *Constans*, borne by a 2nd-cent. martyr, bishop of Perugia.

Vars.: **Constans, Coutans, Contant, Coutant**.

Cogns.: It.: **Co(n)stanti**; **Costanzo, Costanzi**; **Tanzi, Tansi** (aphetic forms).

Dims.: Prov.: **Constensoux, Coutanceau, Coutanson**. It.: **Tanzilli, Tanzillo, Tanzini, Tansini**.

Aug.: It.: **Tanzoni**.

Patrs.: It.: **De Costanzo, Di Costanzo**.

Constantine 1. English: from a medieval given name (L *Constantīnus*, a deriv. of *Constans*; see CONSTANT). The name was popular in Continental Europe, and to a lesser extent in England, as having been borne by the first Christian ruler of the Roman Empire, Constantine the Great (?280–337), in whose honour Byzantium was renamed Constantinople.

2. Norman habitation name or regional name from *Cotentin* (*Coutances*) in La Manche; see CONSTANT 2.

Vars.: **Cossentine, Consterdine, Considine**, COSTAIN.

Cogns. (of 1): Fr.: **Co(n)statin**. Prov.: **Constanty, Costanti**. It.: **Co(n)stantino**. Port.: **Constantino**. Rum.: **Constantin, Constandin**. Pol.: **Konstancin**; **Kostecki, Kostański**. (Of 2): Fr.: **Cotentin**.

Dims. (of 1): Eng.: COSTE. Rum.: **Costache, Tinu, Dinu**. Ger.: **Kost**. Czech: **Kostka**. Pol.: **Kostko, Kostiuk, Kościuk, Kościuszko** (of Beloruss. origin). Ukr.: **Kostenko, Kostashchuk, Kostyura**. Hung.: **Koszta, Kosztka**.

Pej. (from 1 or 2): Fr.: **Costard**.

Patrs. (from 1): Russ., Bulg.: **Konstantinov**. Pol.: **Konstantynowicz**. Croatian: **Konstantinović**. Rum.: **Constantinesco**. Gk: **Constantinou, Constantinides**.

Patrs. (from 1) (dim.): Eng.: **Costin(g)s, Costons**. Russ.: **Kostin, Kostikov, Kostyushin, Kostyunin**. Beloruss.: **Katusov**. Pol.: **Kostkiewicz**. Croatian: **Kondić, Konjević, Konjović**; **Kostić**.

Constantine *is the name of an Anglo-Norman family said to be descended from a certain Radulf, who is recorded as holder of land in Shrops. in Domesday Book. Walter* de Constantiis *(d. 1207) was Vice Chancellor of England in 1173, and as archbishop of Rouen he was present at the coronation of Richard I. Bearers of the name are frequently recorded in Norman and English records between 918 and 1206.*

The Polish patriot Tadeusz Kościuszko *(1746–1817), who fought on the Colonists' side in the American Revolution in 1776–84, and who led Polish resistance to the partitioning of Poland in 1794, was born into an aristocratic family at Mereczowszczyna in what is now Belorussia.*

Contreras Spanish: habitation name from a place in the province of Burgos. The placename is derived from LL *contrāria* surrounding area, region (from the prep. *contra* opposite, against, hard by).

Cogn.: Port.: **Contreiras**.

Converse English: nickname for a Jew converted to Christianity, or more often an occupational name for someone converted to the religious way of life, a lay member of a convent. The name comes from ME, OF *convers* convert (L *conversus*, past part. of *convertere* to turn, change).

Cogns.: Fr.: **Convers, Convert**.

Convery Irish: Anglicized form of Gael. **Mac Ainmhire** 'son of *Ainmhire*', a byname meaning 'Fierceness'.

Conway 1. Welsh: habitation name from *Conwy*, the fortified town on the coast of N Wales, itself named from the river on which it stands. This is of Brit. origin, perhaps from a word meaning 'reedy'.

2. Scots: habitation name from *Conway* in the parish of Beauly, recorded *c.*1215 as *Coneway* and in 1291 as *Convathe*. It probably gets its name from Gael. *coinmheadh* billet, free quarters, being so named as the district in which the local lord's household troops were billeted.

3. Irish: Anglicized form of various Gael. names, such as *Mac Conmidhe* (see McNAMEE), **Mac Connmhaigh** ('son of *Connmhach*', a personal name derived from *condmach* head-smashing; also Anglicized as **Conoo**), and **Ó Conbhuide** ('descendant of *Conbhuidhe*', a personal name composed of the elements *cú* hound, dog + *buidhe* yellow).

Var. (of 1): **Conwy**.

Cook 1. English: occupational name for a cook, a seller of cooked meats, or a keeper of an eating house, from OE *cōc* (L *coquus*). There has been some confusion with COCK.

2. Jewish (Ashkenazic): in part an Anglicization of the Jewish surnames given below, in part an Anglicization of the Jewish surname **Kuk**, which is of unknown origin; it is sometimes Anglicized as **Kook**.

Vars.: **Cooke, Coke**.

Cogns.: Ger.: KOCH. Low Ger.: **Ko(o)(c)k, Kaa(c)k**. Du.: **Cok, Kok, De Cock, De Kock**. Flem.: **De Cock, De Kok(er)**. Swed.: **Cock, Kock**. Pol.: **Kucharski** (from the vocab. word *kucharz* cook, from MHG *koch* + *-arz* Pol. suffix of agent nouns); **Kuchciak**. Czech: **Kuchař, Kuchta**. Beloruss.: **Kukhar**. It.: **C(u)oco, Coci, C(u)ogo, Cuoghi, Lo Cuoco**. Jewish: **Koch, Kochman(n)**.

Dims.: Pol.: **Kucharczyk, Kucharek**. Ukr.: **Kukharenko**. It.: **Cuocolo, Cocuccio, Cogolo**.

Aug.: It.: **Cogoni**.

Patrs.: Eng: **Cookson, Cuckson, Cux(s)on**; Cox. Low Ger.: **Kocks, Kox**. Beloruss.: **Kukharov**. It.: **Del Coco**.

'Servant of the c.': Eng.: **Cookman, Cockman**.

Equiv. (not cogn.): Russ.: POVAROV.

Cooksey English (chiefly W Midlands): habitation name from a place in Worcs., so called from the gen. case of the OE personal name *Cucu* (perhaps a byname from OE *cwicu* lively) + OE *ēg* island.

Coole Irish: 1. Anglicized form of Gael. **Mac Cumhaill** 'son of *Cumhall*', a byname meaning 'Champion'.

2. Anglicized form of Gael. *Mac Dhubhghaill*; see DOUGALL.

Vars.: **Cooil**; **Coolson, Coulson** (see also COLE).

Cooling English: 1. var. of CULLING.

2. habitation name from a place in Kent, originally so called from the OE tribal name *Cūlingas* 'people of *Cūl(a)*'; see CULLING. The pronunciation is normally /'kʊlɪŋ/, sometimes /'ku:lɪŋ/.

Coombe English: habitation name from any of various places named with OE *cumb* (apparently of Celt. origin) denoting a short, straight valley, or else a topographic name from ME *combe* used independently in the same sense. There are a large number of places in England, mostly spelled *Combe*, named with this word. The vars. in *-e* for the most part derive from the OE dat. case, those in *-(e)s* from the gen.

Vars.: **Co(u)mbe, Coom, Co(o)mb(e)s, Co(o)mber** (see also CAMBER).

Cogns.: Fr.: **Com(b)e, Coume(s)**; **Lacombe, Lacom(m)e**; **Lecombe** (NW France); **Delacombe, Descombes**; **Combier**. Prov.: **Lascombes**. Cat.: **Coma(s)**.

Dims.: Fr.: **Com(b)eau, Combelle(s), Combin, Combet(te), Co(u)met, Combot, Comboul, Coumoul**. Cat.: **Comella(s)**.

Augs.: Fr.: **Combas, Coumas, Coumat**.

The surnames Coombes *(the most common form)*, Coombs, *and* Coombe *are now most common in W England, while* Combe *is found mainly in Scotland.*

Cooney Irish: Anglicized form of Gael. **Ó Cuana** 'descendant of *Cuana*', a personal name derived from *cuanna* elegant, comely.

Vars.: **O'Cooney, Cowney, Cunnea**.

Dims.: **(O')Coonaghan, Counihan, Coonihan, Coonan** (Gael. **Ó Cuanacháin**).

Cooper 1. English: occupational name for a maker and repairer of wooden vessels such as barrels, tubs, buckets, casks, and vats, ME *couper*, *cowper* (apparently from MLG *kūper*, a deriv. of *kūp* tub, container, which was borrowed independently into Eng. as *coop*). The prevalence of the surname, its cogns., and equivalents bears witness to the fact that this was one of the chief specialist trades in the Middle Ages throughout Europe.

2. Jewish (Ashkenazic): Anglicized form of *Kupfer* and *Kupper*; see COPPER.

Vars. (of 1): COPPER, COUPAR, **Cupper**; **Kooper**; **Coop(e)**, **Coupe** (Yorks. and Lancs.). (Of 2): **Cooperman**.

Cogns. (of 1): Ger.: KIEFER. Low Ger.: **Küp(p)er**. Fris.: **Kupker**. Flem.: **(De) Cuyper(e)**; **Cuyp**. Du.: **Kui(j)per**, **(De) Kuyper**.

Patrs. (from 1): Low Ger.: **Küp(p)ers**. Du., Flem.: **Kui(j)pers**, **Kuypers**, **Cuijpers**, **Cuypers**.

Equivs. (not cogns.): Fr.: CUVIER, TONNELLIER. Ger.: BÖTTCHER, BÜTTNER, KIEFER, SCHÄFFLER. Ger. and Jewish (Ashkenazic): BODNER, BINDER. Pol. and Jewish (E Ashkenazic): BEDNARZ. Ukr.: BONDAR. Hung.: KÁDÁR.

Coote English: nickname for a bald or stupid man, from ME *co(o)te* coot (apparently from MLG). The bird was regarded as bald because of the large white patch, an extension of the bill, on its head. It is less easy to say how it acquired the reputation for stupidity.

Var.: **Coot**.

Patrs.: **Coot(e)s**.

Cope English (common in the Midlands and Lancs.): metonymic occupational name for someone who made cloaks or capes, or nickname for someone who wore a distinctive one, from ME *cāpe* (OE *cāp*, reinforced by the cogn. ON *kápa*; both are from LL, see CHAPE). For the change of *-ā-* to *-ō-*, cf. ROPER.

Copeland English and Scots: habitation name from *Copeland* in Cumb. or *Coupland* in Northumb., both so called from ON *kaupland* bought land, a feature worthy of note during the early Middle Ages, when land was rarely sold, but rather held by feudal tenure and handed down from one generation to the next.

Vars.: **Co(u)pland**, **Coopland**, **Cowpland**.

The surname is found in Orkney from the mid-15th cent.

Copeman English: occupational name for a merchant or trader, ME *copman*, from ON *kaupmaðr* (cogn. with OE *cēapman*; see CHAPMAN). *Kaupmaðr* is also found as a personal name in England, and this use may lie behind some cases of the surname.

Vars.: **Copman**, **Coopman**, **Coupman**.

Coplestone English: habitation name from *Copplestone* in the parish of Colebrooke, Devon, so called from the OE element *copel*, of uncertain meaning, possibly 'peaked', + *stān* STONE.

Vars.: **Copleston**, **Copplestone**.

The earliest known bearer of the name is Richard de Copleston, *recorded in Lincoln in 1200, but said to have come from Devon. The* Coplestone *family were powerful landowners in the West Country from the 15th to the 19th cents.*

Copley English (Yorks.): habitation name from any of various places, for example in Co. Durham, Staffs., and Yorks., so called from the OE personal name *Coppa* (apparently a byname for a tall man) or from *copp* hill-top (see COPP) + *lēah* wood, clearing.

Copp English: 1. topographic name for someone who lived on the top of a hill, from ME *coppe*, OE *copp* summit (a transferred sense of *copp* head, bowl, cogn. with mod. Eng. *cup*, MHG and mod. Ger. *Kopf*, and Pol. *kopa* hill).

2. nickname for someone with a large or deformed head, from ME *cop(p)* head (the same word as in 1).

Cogns.: Du.: **Kop**. Low Ger.: **Kopp**. (Of 1 only): Pol.: **Kopiec**.

Dim. (of 1): Pol.: **Kopka**.

Pejs. (of 2): Eng: **Copp(e)ard**.

Copper English: 1. var. of COOPER 1, from ME *copere*, found from the 12th cent. alongside *cupere*.

2. metonymic occupational name for a worker in copper, OE *coper* (L *(aes) Cyprium* Cyprian bronze).

Cogns. (of 2): Ger.: **Kupfer(mann)**, **Kupper**. Low Ger.: **Kopper(mann)**. Flem.: **Coper(man)**. Du.: **Koper**. Jewish (Ashkenazic): **Kupfer**, **Kupferman(n)** (from Ger. *Kupfer*; **Kup(p)er(man)** (from a W or NE Yid. pronunciation of Yid. *koper*); **Kip(p)er**, **Kiperman** (from a S Yid. pronunciation of Yid. *koper*).

Cpds (ornamental): Jewish: **Kuperbaum**, **Kuperboim**, **Kiperbaum** ('copper tree'); **Kupferberg**, **Kup(p)erberg** ('copper hill'; *Kupferberg* also exists as a Ger. vocab. word meaning 'copper mine', but this is probably not relevant to any of the Jewish surnames); **Kuperfish** ('copper fish'); **Kup(p)ermintz** ('copper coin'), **Kupferminc** (Pol. spelling); **Kuperschlak** ('copper blow'); **Kupferstein**, **Kupers(h)tein**, **Kupperstein** ('copper stone'); **Kupfersto(c)k**, **Kuperstock** ('copper staff'); **Kup(f)erwasser** ('copper water').

Coppersmith 1. English: occupational name for a SMITH who worked in COPPER.

2. Jewish (Ashkenazic): Anglicization of any of the Jewish surnames listed below.

Cogns. (of 1): **Kupferschmi(e)dt**, **Kup(f)ershmid(t)**, **Kup(p)erschmidt**, **Kupershmit**.

Copping English: 1. dim. of JACOB.

2. topographic name for someone who lived on the top of a hill, from an OE deriv. of *copp* summit (see COPP 1).

Vars. (of 1): **Coppin**, **Coppen**. (Of 2): **Coppinger**.

Coppola S Italian: from the Neapolitan dial. term *coppola*, denoting a type of beret characteristic of the region (cf. CHAPE); either a nickname for a habitual wearer of a beret, or a metonymic occupational name for a maker of such berets.

Var.: **Coppolaro** (occupational name).

Dims.: **Coppolelli**, **Coppoletta**, **Coppoletti**, **Coppolino**.

Aug.: **Coppolone**.

Copsey English (Suffolk): from the ON personal name *Kupsi*. This is of uncertain origin, but is recorded in Domesday Book as *Copsi* and seems to have been used as a fairly frequent given name in the early Middle Ages.

Corbeil French: metonymic occupational name for a maker and seller of baskets, from OF *corbeil(le)* basket (LL *corbicula*, a dim. of *corbis* basket). It may also be a habitation name from any of the various places named with this word because of a depression in the ground.

Vars.: **(Le) Corbeiller**, **Corbeillier**.

Cogns.: Ger.: **Korf(f)**; **Körber**, **Kerber**.

Corbett English (Norman; esp. common in the W Midlands): nickname meaning 'Little Crow', from ANF *corbet*, a dim. of *corb*; cf. CUERVO.

Vars.: **Corbet**, **Corbitt**.

Cogns.: Fr.: **Corbet**. It.: **Corbetti**, **Corv(i)etto**; **Crovetti**, **Crovetto** (Lombardy).

Corbet(t) *is the name of an ancient Shrops. family descended from a Norman baron, Hugh* Corbet *or* Corbeau, *living in 1040. He came to England with his son Robert and settled in Shrops. His descendant Sir Richard Corbet was granted land near Shrewsbury in 1223, at a place now known as Moreton Corbet. The name was taken from Shrops. to Scotland in the first quarter of the 12th cent.*

Corby 1. English: habitation name from any of various places in N England. Those in Lincs. and Northants are so called from the ON personal name *Kori* (see CORY) + ON *býr* farm, settlement, whereas the one in Cumb. has as its first element the OIr. personal name *Corc*.
2. French: dim. of *corb* crow (see CUERVO).
Var. (of 1): **Corbie**.

Corday French: habitation name from any of various places, in Orne, Boucé, and Montrée, so called from the Gallo-Roman personal name *Cordus* ('Young'; cf. CORDERO) + the local suffix *-ācum*.

Corde French: metonymic occupational name for a maker of cord or string, or nickname for a habitual wearer of decorative ties and ribbons, from OF *corde* string (L *c(h)orda*, from Gk *khordē*).
Vars.: **Cordier, Cordié, Lecordier** (occupational names).
Cogns.: Eng.: **Coard, Cord(e)s; Cord(i)er**. Sp.: **Cuerda**.
Dims.: Fr.: **Cordet, Cordey, Cordeix; Cordel(le), Cordelet(te)**; CORDONNIER. Eng.: **Cordell, Cordall, Cordle**.

Cordero Spanish: metonymic occupational name for a shepherd, or nickname meaning 'lamb', from Sp. *cordero* young lamb (L *cordārius*, a deriv. of *cordus* young, new).
Cogn.: Port.: **Cordeiro**.

Corderoy English: nickname for a proud man, from OF *cuer de roi* king's heart. There is no connection with the name of the fabric, which is not recorded before the 18th cent.
Vars.: **Cord(e)rey, Cordurey, Corde(a)ry, Cordray**.

Córdoba Spanish: habitation name from the city in S Spain, of extremely ancient foundation and uncertain etymology.
Vars.: **Córdova; Cordobés, Cordovés**.
Cogns.: Jewish (Sefardic): **Kordova(ni), Kurdvani**.

Cordonnier French: 1. occupational name for a maker or seller of cord or ribbon, from an agent deriv. of OF *cordon*, a dim. of CORDE.
2. occupational name for a worker in fine Spanish kid leather, OF *cordoan* (so named from being originally produced at CÓRDOBA).
Vars. (of 1): **Cordon, Cordoux**. (Of 2): **Cordouën, Cordouant**.
Cogns. (of 1): Sp.: **Cordón**. (Of 2): Eng.: **Cordner** (now found chiefly in N Ireland); **Cordon, Corden, Cordwin, Cordwent**. Ger.: **Kordewan**.

Cordwell English: habitation name from a minor place in the parish of Holmsfield, Derbys. The placename is of uncertain origin; the second element is probably OE *well(a)* spring, stream (see WELL).

Corfield English (W Midlands): habitation name from a place so called by the river *Corve* in Shrops. This gets its name from the river name (which is from OE *corf* cutting) + OE *feld* pasture, open country (see FIELD).

Cork English: metonymic occupational name for a supplier of red or purple dye, ME *cork* (of Celt. origin; cf. CORKERY), or for someone who used it in dying cloth.
Vars.: **Corck, Corke; Corker**.

Corkery Irish: Anglicized form of Gael. **Ó Corcra** 'descendant of *Corcra*', a personal name derived from *corcair* purple (ultimately cogn. with L *purpur*).
Var.: **Corkerry**.
Dims.: **O'Corcrane, O'Corkerane, O'Corkran, Corcoran, Cork(e)ran** (Gael. **Ó Corcráin**); **(O')Corkan, Corken, Corkin** (Gael. **Ó Corcain**).

Corlett Manx: Anglicized form of Gael. **Mac Thorliot**, patr. from a personal name of ON origin, composed of the divine name *Þórr* + *ljóðr* people.

Corley 1. English: habitation name from a place in Warwicks., recorded in Domesday Book as *Cornelie*, apparently from OE *corna*, a metathesized form of *crona*, gen. pl. of *cron*, *cran* CRANE + *lēah* wood, clearing.
2. Irish: var. of CURLEY.

Cormack Scots: Anglicized form of the Gael. personal name *Cormac*, composed of the elements *corb* raven + *mac* son.
Var.: **Cormick**.
Dim.: **Cormican**.
Patrs.: **McCormack, McCormick** (Gael. **Mac Cormaic**).

Cormier French: topographic name for someone who lived near a sorb or service tree, OF *cormier* (from *corme*, the name of the fruit for which the tree was cultivated, apparently of Gaul. origin).
Dims.: **Cormieau(d), Cormillot, Cormoul**.

Cornall English (Lancs.): apparently a habitation name from a lost place in Lancs., perhaps so called from OE *corn* corn, grain or *corn*, a metathesized form of *cron*, *cran* CRANE + *hall* HALL or *halh* nook, recess (see HALE 1).

Corne French: nickname for a cuckold (see HORN 4), or metonymic occupational name for a hornblower or worker in horn, from OF *corne* horn (LL *corna*, originally a contraction of *cornua*, pl. of *cornu*, but later treated as a fem. sing.).
Vars.: **Lacorne; Cornu(t), Cournu, Lecornu, Co(u)rné**.
Dims.: Fr.: **Cornet(te), Cournet, Corney, Cornez; Cornu(d)et, Cornuel, Cornuchet; Cornec, Cornic** (Brittany). Eng.: **Cornet(t)**. Du.: **Cornet**.
Aug.: Fr.: **Cornat**.
Pejs.: Fr.: **Cornard, Cornaud, Cornuau**. Flem.: **Co(o)rnaert**.

Corneille French: 1. from a given name (L *Cornēlius*, an old Roman family name, probably derived from *cornu* horn; cf. CORNE), which was borne by a 3rd-cent. Christian saint and pope. The cathedral of St Cornelius at Aachen was a centre of pilgrimage, and the given name was especially popular in this area in the Middle Ages.
2. nickname for a prattling person, from OF *corneille* crow (LL *cornicula*, a dim. of *cornix* raven).
Vars. (of 1): **Cornély; Cornil, Quernel** (Belgium). (Of 2): **Corn(e)il, Cornille**.
Cogns. (of 1): Low Ger.: **Corne(h)l, Cornill, Kornel; Nelius, Nehl, Nell(e)**. Flem., Du.: **Cornelis; Nelis**. Swed.: CORNELL; **Cornelius** (Latinized). Czech: **Kornel**. Pol.: **Kornacki**. Sp.: **Cornejo** (see also CORNIER).
Dims. (of 1): Beloruss.: **Korneichik**. Ukr.: **Korneichuk**. Pol.: **Korneluk**. Czech: **Kornalík, Kornoušek; Korous, Koreš, Korejs, Kureš**; KORDA. (Of 2): Fr.: **Cornilleau, Cornelleau, Cornillot**.
Patrs. (from 1): Low Ger.: **Cornels, Cornils; Neles, Nellen, Nilles; Nehls(en), Neels**. Du., Flem.: **Cornelisse(n), Nelissen**. Dan.: **Corneliussen**. Russ.: **Kornilov, Kornilyev; Korneev**.
Patrs. (from 1) (dim.): Low Ger.: **Corneljes; Neljes, Nellies, Nilges**. Russ.: **Kornyakov, Kornyshev**.

Cornell 1. English (U.S.): Anglicization of any of the many Continental European surnames derived from the L given name *Cornelius*; see CORNEILLE 1.
2. Swedish: vernacular form of *Cornelius*.
3. English: var. of CORNWELL.
4. English: var. of CORNHILL.

Corney English: habitation name from places in Cumb. and Herts., so called from OE *corn* corn, grain or *corn*, a metathesized form of *cron*, *cran* CRANE + *ēg* island. It seems possible, from the distribution of early forms, that it may also derive from a lost place in Lancs.

Cornford English (Sussex, Kent, and Surrey): habitation name from any of several minor place in SE England, named with OE *corn* corn + *ford* FORD. There appears also to have been some confusion with COMFORT.

Cornforth English: habitation name from *Cornforth* in Co. Durham, so called from OE *corn*, a metathesized form of *cron*, *cran* CRANE + *ford* FORD.

Var.: **Cornfoot**.

Cornhill English: 1. habitation name from *Cornhill* in Northumb., so called from OE *corn*, a metathesized form of *cron*, *cran* CRANE + *halh* nook, recess (see HALE 1).

2. English: habitation name from *Cornhill* in London, a medieval grain exchange, so called from OE *corn* corn, grain + *hyll* HILL, or from any other place elsewhere similarly named.

Var.: CORNELL.

Cornier French: 1. occupational name for a hornblower; see CORNE.

2. habitation name for someone who lived on the corner of two streets in a town, from OF *cornier* corner (a deriv. of *corne* horn; see CORNE).

3. topographic name for someone who lived by a dogwood tree, OF *cornier* (L *cornārius*).

Var. (of 3): **Cornoueil**.

Cogns. (of 1 and 2): Eng.: **Corner**, **Cornah**. (Of 3): Sp.: **Cornejo** (see also CORNEILLE).

Cornish English: regional name for someone from the county of Cornwall, from OE *cornisc* Cornish (from *Corn-* (see CORNWELL 1) + the adj. suffix *-isc*). Not surprisingly, the surname is most common in adjacent Devon, but it is also well established as far afield as Colchester and Preston.

Vars.: **Corn(e)s** (from OF *corneis*).

Cornwell English (now most common in London and Lancs.): 1. regional name from the county of *Cornwall*, so called from the OE tribal name *Cornwealas*. This is from *Kernow*, the native name that the Cornish used to denote themselves (of uncertain etymology, perhaps connected with a Celt. element meaning 'horn', 'headland'), compounded with OE *wealas* strangers, foreigners (see WALLACE), the term used by the Anglo-Saxons for British-speaking people.

2. habitation name from *Cornwell* in Oxon., so called from OE *corn*, a metathesized form of *cron*, *cran* CRANE + *well(a)* spring, stream (see WELL).

Vars. (of 1): **Cornwall**; **Curnow** (from the native Cornish word); CORNISH.

Coromina Catalan: topographic name for someone who lived on a patch of land not subject to irrigation, Cat. *coromina* (a cogn. of CONDAMINE, although the semantic development is not clear).

Vars.: **Corominas**, **Coromines**, **Colomines**.

Corona Spanish and Italian: from Sp., It. *corona* crown (L *corōna* garland, chaplet, diadem), perhaps a house name for someone who lived in a house with this sign or a nickname for someone who had a tonsure in fulfilment of a religious vow.

Vars.: Sp.: **Coronas**; **Coronado**.

Cogns.: Fr.: **Couronne**. Ger.: **Kron(e)**. Flem., Du.: **(Van der) Kroon**. Dan., Norw.: **Crone**. Swed.: **Kron**, **Kroon**. Jewish (S Ashkenazic, ornamental): **Kroin** (from Yid. *kroyn* crown, **Krojn** (Pol. spelling).

Dim.: Jewish **Kroinik**.

Pej.: Fr.: **Couronnaud**.

Cpds (ornamental): Swed.: **Kronberg** ('crown hill'); **Cronholm** ('crown island'); **Kronquist**, **Cronquist** ('crown twig'); **Cronstedt** ('crown homestead'); **Cronström** ('crown river'); **Cronvall**, **Cronwall** ('crown slope'). Jewish: **Kron(en)berg**, **Kronnberg**, **Kronenberger** ('crown hill'); **Kronenblat** ('crown leaf'); **Kronfeld**, **Kron(n)enfeld** ('crown field'); **Krongold** ('crown gold'); **Krongrad** ('crown city'); **Kronkopf**, **Kronkop(p)** ('crown head'); **Kronstein** ('crown stone'); **Kronent(h)al** ('crown valley').

Corot French: topographic name for someone who lived at a corner or angle of land, from a dim. of OF *cor* corner (L *cornu* horn, cf. CORNIER and CORNE).

Corr Irish: Anglicized form of Gael. **Ó Corra** 'descendant of *Corra*', a personal name from *corr* spear, pointed object.

Dims.: **Corrigan**, **O'Corrigane**, **(O')Currigan**, **Corragan**, (Gael. **Ó Corragáin**).

Corral Spanish: topographic name for someone who lived near an enclosure for livestock, Sp. *corral*. This word, which has entered mod. Eng. as a result of contact in the New World, is found in Spain as early as the 11th cent. and is of uncertain etymology, perhaps from a L deriv., **currāle*, of *currus* chariot, as being a run for vehicles. There are numerous places named with this word, in both the sing. and pl. forms, and to a large extent the surname is a habitation name from these.

Var.: **Corrales**.

Correa Spanish: possibly from Sp. *correa* leather strap, belt, rein, shoelace (L *corrigia* fastening, from *corrigere* to straighten, order, correct). The surname could have arisen as a metonymic occupational name for a maker or seller of any of these articles, or as a nickname for a strong or patient person.

Var.: **Correas**.

Cogn.: Port.: **Correia**.

Corredor Spanish: occupational name for a messenger, or nickname for a swift runner, from Sp. *corredor* runner (LL *curritor*, for class. L *cursor*, a deriv. of *currere* to run).

Corrie Scots: habitation name from places in Arran, Dumfries, and elsewhere, so called from Gael. *coire* cauldron, applied to a circular hanging valley on a mountain. See also CURRY.

Var.: **Corry**.

An Irish family by the name of Corry *are said to have originated in Dumfries, Scotland. They settled in Turnagardy, near Newtownards, in the reign of James I.*

Cortada Catalan: topographic or occupational name from Cat. *cortada* court, residence, a deriv. of *cort*; see COURT 1.

Cogn.: Prov.: **Courtade**.

Dims.: Cat.: **Cortadellas**. Prov.: **Courtadon**.

Cortázar Spanish form of Basque **Kortazar**: topographic name for someone living by an old stable or farmyard, from the Basque elements *korta* stable, cowshed, (farm)yard (a Romance borrowing; see COURT 1) + *za(h)ar*, *zar* old.

Côrte-Real Portuguese: metonymic occupational name for someone who was employed at a royal court, from Port. *côrte* COURT + *real* royal (L *rēgālis*, a deriv. of *rex*, gen. *rēgis*, king).

Cory 1. English: from the ON personal name *Kori*, which is well attested both in Scandinavia and England, but of uncertain meaning.

2. Irish: Anglicized form of Gael. **Ó Comhraidhe** 'descendant of *Comhraidhe*', a personal name of uncertain meaning.

Vars.: **Corey**. (Of 2 only): **O'Corry, O'Corrie,** CURRY; WEIR.

Coryton English: habitation name from a place in Devon, so called from a Brit. river name (see CURRY 1) + OE *tūn* enclosure, settlement.

A family of this name, established for centuries in Cornwall, trace their descent from Jeffrie Coryton, *living* c.*1242*.

Cosby English: habitation name from a place in Leics., so called perhaps from an OE personal name *Cossa* + ON *býr* farm, settlement.

Cosgrove 1. English: habitation name from a place in Northants, so called from OE *Cōfesgrāf* 'grove, thicket (OE *grāf*; see GROVE) of **Cōf*', an otherwise unattested personal name.

2. Irish: Anglicized form of Gael. **Ó Coscraigh** 'descendant of *Coscrach*', a byname meaning 'Victorious', 'Triumphant' (from *coscur* victory, triumph).

Vars.: **Cosgrave**. (Of 2 only): **Cosgreave, Cosgrive, Cosgriff, Cosgry, O'Cosgra, (O')Cosker(r)y, Cuskery**.

Dims. (of 2): **Coskeran, Cuskern** (Gael. **Ó Coscracháin**).

Costain 1. Scots and Irish: Anglicized form of Gael. **Mac Austain** 'son of AUSTIN'.

2. English: var. of CONSTANTINE.

Vars. (of 2): **Costin, Coste(a)n**.

Coste 1. French: topographic name for someone who lived on a slope or riverbank, less often on the coast, from OF *coste* (L *costa* rib, side, flank, also used in a transferred topographical sense). There are several places in France named with this word, and the surname may also be a habitation name from any of these.

2. English: short form of CONSTANTINE.

Vars. (of 1): **Côte; Lacoste; Delacoste, Delacôte**.

Cogns. (of 1): Prov.: **Costa, Costes**. It.: **(Della) Costa, Costi; Da(lla) Costa** (Venetia). Sp.: **Cuesta**. Cat.: **Costa(s)**. Port.: **Costa**.

Dims. (of 1): Fr.: **Costel(le), Cot(t)el, Co(us)teau, Cotteaux, Co(u)ston, Coustet; Costiou** (Brittany). Prov.: **Costil(he), Coustille, Costy, Cot(t)y**. Sp.: **Costilla**.

Aug. (of 1): Fr.: **Coutas**.

Costello Irish: said to be an Anglicized form of Gael. **Mac Oisdealbhaigh** 'son of *Oisdealbhach*', a personal name composed of the elements *os* deer, fawn + *dealbhadh* in the form of, resembling. However, the main family of this name are of Norman origin, and the name may therefore in fact be a deriv. of COSTE.

Vars.: **McCostalaighe, McCosdalowe, (Mc)Costelloe, Costellow, Costily, Costley**.

Coster 1. English: metonymic occupational name for a grower or seller of *costards*, a popular variety of large apples, so called from their prominent ribs; cf. COSTE.

2. Dutch: cogn. of KÜSTER.

Cot 1. French: aphetic form of a dim. of any of several given names containing the sound /k/ at the beginning of the second syllable, e.g. *Jacquot* (see JACK) or *Nicot* (see NICHOLAS).

2. Catalan: topographic name for someone who lived by a boundary stone, Cat. *cot* (L *cote* stone), or habitation name from one of the numerous places named with this word.

Var. (of 2): Cat.: **Cots**.

Dims. (of 1): Fr.: **Co(u)tet, Cotin(eau), Coutinet, Co(u)ton, Couthon, Coutou(t), Cotot, Coutisson**.

Pej. (of 1): Fr.: **Cotard**.

Cotte French: metonymic occupational name for a maker of chain mail, from OF *cot(t)e* coat of mail (of Gmc origin). It is unlikely to have been a nickname for a wearer of a coat of mail, since only the richest classes, who already had distinguished family names of their own, could afford to be so well protected in a garment which required many hours of skilled labour to construct. It may perhaps have been used as a nickname for a hard and unfeeling person.

Vars.: **Lacotte; Cotté, Cottu**.

Dims.: Fr.: **Cottet, Cottez, Cottey, Cottin(eau)**, COTTON, **Cottenet, Cott(en)ot**.

Pej.: Fr.: **Cottard**.

Cotter 1. English: from ME *cotter*, a technical term of status in the feudal system for a serf or bond tenant who held a cottage by service rather than rent, from OE *cot* cottage, hut (see COATES) + *-er* agent suffix.

2. Irish: Anglicized form of Gael **Mac Oitir** 'son of *Oitir*', a personal name borrowed from ON *Óttarr*, composed of the elements *ótti* fear, dread + *herr* army.

Vars. (of 1): **Cottier; Cotman**.

Cogns. (of 1): Low Ger.: **Kotter, Kother, Kötter, Köther, Kather, Käther**.

Dims. (of 1): Eng.: **Cotterel(l), Cottrell, Cott(e)rill, Cotherill** (all chiefly Midlands). Fr.: **Cott(e)rel(l), Cott(e)reau, Cottarel**.

An Irish family by the name of Cotter *has been established in Cork for generations. They are said to be of Danish origin, although the surname clearly is not. William* Cottyr *(b.* c.*1498) was recorded at Innesmore, Co. Cork in the early 16th cent.*

Cottle English: 1. metonymic occupational name for a maker of chain-mail, from an ANF dim. of COTTE.

2. metonymic occupational name for a cutler, from OF *co(u)tel*, *co(u)teau* knife (LL *cultellus*, a dim. of *culter* ploughshare).

Vars.: **Cottel(l), Cuttell, Cuttill, Cuttles**; CUTLER.

Cotton 1. English: habitation name from any of numerous places throughout England so called from the dat. pl. of OE *cot* cottage, dwelling (see COATES).

2. French: dim. of COTTE.

Vars. (of 1): **Coton, Cottom, Cottem, Cottam**.

Couch 1. Cornish: probably a nickname for a red-haired man, from *cough* red; cf. GOUGH 2. The normal pronunciation of this name is /ku:tʃ/.

2. English: metonymic occupational name for a maker of beds or bedding, or perhaps a nickname for a lazy man, from ME, OF *couche* bed (a deriv. of OF *coucher* to lay down, L *collocāre* to place).

Vars. (of 1): **Cooch, Cough**. (Of 2): **Couche; Coucher, Coucha, Cowcha; Couchman**.

Coudert Provençal: topographic name for someone who lived by a grassy patch, Prov. *coudert* (LL *cotericum*, apparently of Gaul. origin). There are various places in SW France named with this word, and the surname may also be a habitation name from any of these.

Vars.: **Couder(c)**.

Coufal Czech: nickname derived from a dial. form of the verb *couvat* to retreat or go backwards, perhaps applied to a timid or cowardly person.

Coughlan Irish: Anglicized form of Gael. **Ó Cochláin** 'descendant of *Cochlán*', a byname derived from *cochal* cloak, hood.

Vars.: **O'Coghla(i)ne, Coughlin, Coghlan, Coglin, Coughan**.

Couillet French: nickname for a good companion, from OF *couillet*, dim. of *couille* testicle (from L *colea*, a neut. pl. later treated as a fem. sing.).

Vars.: **Couillette, Couilleau, Couillot, Couillon.**

Pejs.: **Co(u)illau(d), Co(u)illard.**

Coulange French: habitation name from any of the various places that derive their names from LL *colōnica* (*terra*) land cultivated by a 'colonist', a technical term of the feudal system for a peasant labourer who was free in body but bound to the land he worked.

Vars.: **Coulanges, Coulonge(s), Col(l)ange, Col(l)onge, Collongues; Coulangeon.**

Coulet French: 1. aphetic form of *Nicoulet*, a dim. of NICHOLAS.

2. topographic name for someone who lived on or near a hill, from a dim. of OF *co(u)l* (L *collis*; see COLL 4). There are various places in Aveyron and SE France named with this word, and the surname may be a habitation name from any of these.

3. metonymic occupational name for a maker or seller of neckbands, or nickname for a wearer of one, from OF *collet*, *coulet* neckband, kerchief, a dim. of *co(u)l* neck (LL *collum*).

Coultas English (Yorks.): habitation name or occupational name for someone who lived or worked at a stables, from early mod. Eng. *coulthus*, a cpd of *co(u)lt* COLT + *hus* HOUSE.

Coulter Scots and N Irish: habitation name from places in the former counties of Lanarks. and Aberdeens., so called from Gael. *cùl tir* back land.

Vars.: **Coultar, Culter.**

The first known bearer of the name is Richard 'of Culter', who was sheriff of Lanark in 1226.

Coulthard N English and Scots: occupational name for someone who looked after asses or working horses, ME *colthart*, *coltehird*, from OE *colt* ass, young horse (see COLT) + *hierde* herdsman (see HEARD).

Vars.: **Coulthart, Colthard, Colt(h)art, Coltherd, Colthert.**

Coulthurst English (Lancs.): apparently a habitation name from an unidentified place so called from OE *colt* ass, young horse (see COLT) + *hyrst* wooded hill (see HURST). *Colthurst* in W Yorks takes its name from a family so called, rather than vice versa.

Coulton English (Lancs.): habitation name from *Coulton* in N Yorks., perhaps so called from OE *colt* ass, young horse (see COLT) + *tūn* enclosure, settlement.

Counsel English: 1. nickname for a wise or thoughtful man, from ANF *counseil* consultation, deliberation, also counsel, advice (L *consilium*, from *consulere* to consult).

2. some of the forms were probably influenced by the similar meaning of ANF *councile* council, assembly (L *concilium* assembly, from the archaic verb *concalere* to call together, summon), and it may also have been an occupational name for a member of a royal council or, more probably, a manorial council.

Vars: **Co(u)nsell, Councel(l), Council.**

Cogns. (of 1): Fr.: **Cons(e)il.** It.: **Consigli(o); Consiglieri, Consigliere.** Sp.: **Consejo; Consejero.** Port.: **Conselheiro.** (Of 2): It.: **Conci(g)lieri.**

Count English: nickname from the Norman title of rank, OF *conte*, *cunte* (L *comes*, gen. *comitis*, companion, from *com-* together, with + *īre* to go).

Vars.: **Conte; Lecount.**

Cogns.: Fr.: **Comte, Conte; Lecomte.** Prov.: **Conde, Leconde.** It.: **Conte, Conti, Comti; Cont** (Venetia); **Cunto, Cunti** (Naples); **Lo Conte, Li Conti** (S Italy). Sp.: **Conde(s).** Cat.: **Conte, Compte.** Port.: **Conde.**

Dims.: Fr.: **Comtet.** Prov.: **Condet.** It.: **Contini** (also Jewish); **Contin(o), Continelli, Contuzzi; Contiello** (Naples); **Contինoli** (Emilia). Port.: **Condinho.**

Patr.: It.: **Del Conte** (Tuscany).

Patr. (from a dim.): It.: **Di Contino.**

Coupar Scots: 1. habitation name from *Cupar* in Fife, which is probably of Pictish origin, with an unknown meaning. There are several other places similarly named, for example *Cuper* Angus and *Cupar* Maculty (now Couttie), but these do not seem to have given rise to surnames.

2. var. of COOPER.

Vars.: **Couper, Cowper.**

The first known bearer of the name in Scotland is Salomone de Cupir, *who witnessed a charter in 1245; between the 13th and 15th cents. it was much more common in Fife than elsewhere.*

Courage English and French: nickname from OF *corage*, *curage* courage, stout-heartedness (a deriv. of *cuer* heart, L *cor*), which was occasionally used in ME as an adj., normally with reference to bodily corpulence. Reaney suggests an alternative derivation from *Cowridge* End in Beds., but it is doubtful what evidence there is to support this.

Dims.: Fr.: **Courageot, Courajot.**

Courbe French: topographic name for someone who lived near a bend in a road or river, from OF *courbe* bend (from the verb *courber* to bend, L *curvāre*). There are a number of minor places throughout France named with this word, and the surname may be a habitation name from one of these. It may also sometimes have been a nickname for a man with a stooping gait.

Dims.: **Courbet, Courbin, Courbon, Courbot.**

Aug.: **Courbat.**

Pej.: **Courbaud.**

Courcelles French: habitation name from the various places that derive their names from LL *corticella* (a dim. of *co(ho)rs*; see COURT 1), probably resulting from the division between heirs of an originally larger estate.

Vars.: **Coursel(le), Courseaux, Courcelle.**

Court 1. English and French: occupational name or habitation name from OF, ME *court(e)*, *curt* court (L *cohors*, gen. *cohortis*, yard, enclosure). This word was used primarily with reference to the residence of the lord of a manor, and the surname is usually an occupational name for someone employed at a manorial court.

2. English: nickname from OF, ME *curt* short, small (L *curtus* curtailed, truncated, cut short, broken off).

Vars.: Eng.: **Corte, Curt.** (Of 1 only): Eng.: **A'Court** (with ANF preposition); **Courtman.** See also COURTIER. Fr.: **Cour; Lacour(t), Laco(u)rte; De(la)cour(t).**

Cogns. (of 1): It.: **Corte, Corti; La Corte** (Sicily); **Della Corte, Dalla Corte.** Cat.: **Cort(s).** (Of 2): Fr.: **Lecourt.** It.: **(Lo)-Curto, Curti.** Cat.: **Curt.** Port.: **Curto.** Rum.: **Skurtul.** Ger.: **Kur(t)z(e)** (Latinized as **Curtius**). Low Ger.: **Kort(e)** (see also KONRAD). Du.: **Korte, De Kort.**

Dims. (of 1): It.: **Cortella, Cortello, Cortell(ett)i, Cortellino, Cort(ell)ini; Corticelli** (Bologna). Sp.: **Cortina(s), Cortijo.** Cat.: **Cortina(s).** (Of 2): Cat.: **Curtó.** See also CURTIN and CURZON.

Pej. (of 2): Fr.: **Courtauld.**

Patrs. (from 2): Eng.: **Courts.** Fr.: **Aucourt.** It.: **De Curti(s), Di Curti.** Low Ger.: **Ko(h)rts.** Flem.: **Corten(s).**

Courtenay 1. English (Norman): habitation name from *Courtenay* in Loiret or Gâtinais, both named from a Gallo-

Roman landlord *Curtenus* (a deriv. of L *curtus* short; cf. COURT 2) + the local suffix *-ācum*.

2. English (Norman): nickname for someone with a snub nose, from OF *c(o)urt* short (see COURT 2) + *nes* nose (L *nāsus*).

3. Irish: Anglicized form of Gael. **Ó Curnáin** 'descendant of *Curnán*', an OIr. personal name of uncertain origin.

Vars.: **Courtney, Cort(e)ney, Cortnay.**

An Anglo-Norman family associated with W England can be traced back to Courtenay, near Sens in N France, which was fortified by Athon, Sire de Courtenay, around 1010. Renaud de Courtenay *fled from France to England c.1150, and acquired lands in Devon by marriage. He was a nephew of the crusader Joscelin de Courtenay (d. 1131) and uncle of the Peter de Courtenay (d. 1218) who in 1216 was elected Emperor of Constantinople. They hold the title Earls of Devon in direct descent from Hugh de Courtenay, who married Margaret de Bohun, granddaughter of King Edward I, in 1325; his title was recognized in 1335.*

Courtier 1. French and English: occupational name for a judge, less often also for a servant employed at the court or residence of a lord, from OF *courtier*, an agent deriv. of *court* (see COURT 1). OF *court* came to be used of a court of law, as local justice was dispensed originally by the lord of the manor. Later he was assisted by advisers, to whom he eventually delegated responsibility entirely for most practical purposes. The surname is unlikely ever to have been acquired by a courtier in the sense of one who frequented a royal court, for those in this position were always of at least knightly class and already held distinctive surnames from their estates.

2. French: habitation name from places called *Courtier* in Seine-et-Marne and Basses-Alpes, or *Courtié* in Tarn, all of which get their names from LL *co(ho)rtiāre*, a deriv. of *co(ho)rs* court.

Var. (of 1): Eng.: **Curter.**

Courtil French: topographic name for someone who lived by a walled kitchen garden attached to a farm or manor, OF *courtil* walled garden (a deriv. of *court*; see COURT 1). The surname may also have been an occupational name for someone who was employed in a kitchen garden.

Vars.: **Courtille; Courtil(l)ier.**

Dims.: **Courtillet, Courtillon, Courtillol(e)s.**

Courvoisier French: occupational name for a shoemaker, OF *corvisier* (from LL *cordovesārius*, from *Cordove(n)sis*, an adj. deriv. of CÓRDOBA; see CORDONNIER 2).

Vars.: **Corvisier, Corvisy; Crouvoisier, Crouvisier, Crouvezier, Cravoisier; Corbisier, Corbusier, Lecorbusier** (Belgium).

Cousin English and French: 1. nickname from ME, OF *co(u)sin, cusin* (L *consobrīnus*), which in the Middle Ages, as in Shakespearean English, had the general meaning 'relative', 'kinsman'. The surname would thus have denoted a person related in some way to a prominent figure in the neighbourhood. In some cases it may also have been a nickname for someone who used the term 'cousin' frequently as a familiar term of address. The old slang word *cozen* 'cheat', perhaps derives from the medieval confidence trickster's use of the word *cousin* as a term of address to invoke a spurious familiarity. The patrs. constitute the most frequent forms of this name.

Vars: Eng.: **Cousen, Cosin; Cussen, Cusson, Cuzen** (see also CONSTANCE and CUTHBERT); **Cushing, Cushion, Cushe(o)n.**

Cogns.: Prov.: **Cousi, Couzi, Couzy.** It.: **Cugini.** Flem., Du.: **Cousyn, Couzyn.**

Dims.: Fr.: **Cousinet, Couzinet, Cousiney, Cousinot, Couzineau, Cous(in)ou.**

Patrs.: Eng.: **Cousins, Co(u)sens, Co(u)zens, Cosyns, Cossins, Cossons, Cozins, Cus(s)ins, Cuzons, Cussens, Cussons.**

Couto Portuguese: topographic name for someone who lived by an enclosed pasture, Port. *couto* (LL *cautum*, from the past part. of *cavēre* to make safe, secure).

Dim.: **Coutinho.**

Coutts Scots: habitation name from *Cults* in the former county of Aberdeens. (now part of Grampian region), so called from Gael. *coillte* woods, with the later addition of the Eng. pl. *-s*.

The earliest known bearer of the name is Richard de Cotis, *recorded as a landowner in Elgin in 1343. The principal family of this name received the earldom of Mar by a crown charter in 1433, which also bestowed the lands of Ochtercoul or Auchtercoul on William Coutts, his brother Alexander, their cousin John, and his brother Alexander. A branch of the family settled in Montrose at the end of the 16th cent. and the founder of Coutts Bank was a descendant of this line.*

Couturier French: 1. occupational name for a tailor, from an agent deriv. of OF *cousture* seam (L *consutūra*, from *(con)suere* to sew (together)).

2. occupational name for a holder of a smallholding, from an agent deriv. of OF *couture* small plot, kitchen garden (LL *cultūra*, in class. L used in the abstract sense 'cultivation', 'agriculture', from *colere* to till, tend).

Vars.: **Couturié, Couturieux, Cou(r)durier, Courdurié; Couture, Coudure.** (Of 1 only): **Cousturier, Cousture.**

Couvert French: topographic name for someone who lived in a shady spot sheltered by trees, from OF *co(u)vert* covered (L *coopertum*, past part. of *cooperire*; cf. COUVREUR). There are villages in Calvados, Manche, Lot, and Haute-Loire that get their name from this word, and the surname may also be a habitation name from any of these.

Couvreur French: occupational name for a roofer, from OF *co(u)vreur*, an agent deriv. of *co(u)vrir* to cover (L *cooperire*, cf. COUVERT). Roofing materials in the Middle Ages might be tiles (cf. TILER), slates (cf. SLATER), or thatch (cf. THATCHER), depending on the regional availability of suitable materials.

Vars.: **Couvreux; Couvrant** (pres. part.).

Cogn.: Eng.: **Cover** (see also CUVIER).

Cove English: topographic name for someone who lived near a bay or inlet on the coast or an embayment in a river, OE *cofa*. There are places with this name in Devon, Hants, and Suffolk, and the surname may be a habitation name from one of these.

Coveney English: habitation name from a place in Cambs., so called from the gen. case of OE *cofa* (see COVE; the place is in former fenland, where there may have been a bay on a lake or waterway) or of a personal name *Cōfa* (of uncertain origin) + OE *ēg* island. The surname is now established in Ireland as well as in E Anglia.

Coventry English: habitation name from the city in the W Midlands, which is probably so called from the gen. case of the OE personal name *Cōfa* (cf. COVENEY) + OE *trēow* tree.

Coverdale English: habitation name from the place so called in N Yorks, in the valley (ME *dale*) of the river *Cover* (a Brit. name perhaps containing the element which has given W *cau* hollow).

Covington 1. Scots: habitation name from *Covinton* in the former county of Lanarks., first recorded in the late

12th cent. in the L form *Villa Colbani*, and twenty years later as *Colbaynistun*. By 1434 it had been collapsed to *Cowantoun*, and at the end of the 15th cent. it first appears in the form *Covingtoun*. It is nevertheless clearly named with the personal name *Colban* (see COLEMAN 1) + OE *tūn* enclosure, settlement; the proprietor in question was a follower of David, Prince of Cumbria, in about 1120.

2. English: habitation name from a place in Hunts. (now Cambs.), so called from OE *Cōfingtūn* 'Cōfa's settlement'.

Cowan Scots: 1. common Lowland surname of uncertain origin. None of the explanations put forward is very convincing. The name is not recorded before the middle of the 16th cent. (James *Cowhen*, Berwicks. 1560).

2. Highland surname of Gael. origin; see EWAN.

Var.: **Cowen**.

Coward English: occupational name for a tender of cattle, ME *cowherde*, OE *cūhyrde*, from *cū* cow + *hierde* herdsman (see HEARD). (The surname has nothing to do with mod. Eng. *coward*, which is from OF *cuard*, app. a pej. from *coue* tail (L *cauda*) with ref. to an animal with its tail between its legs.)

Var.: **Cowherd** (a rare surname, apparently the result of a conscious respelling by a bearer anxious to avoid association with mod. Eng. *coward*).

Cogns.: Low Ger.: **Ko(h)hardt**, **Koherde**, **Kuhardt**, **Kuhert**. Flem., Du.: **Coeheert**.

Cowburn English (Lancs.): habitation name from *Cowburgh*, a minor place in the parish of Kirkham, Lancs. The medieval spellings of the placename indicate uncertainty about whether the final element is OE *burna* stream (see BOURNE) or *burh* fort (see BURKE). The first element is *cū* cow.

Cowden English and Scots: habitation name from any of at least three places so called. One in Northumb. occurs in 1286 as *Colden* and is derived from OE *col* (char)coal + *denu* valley (see DEAN 1); that in E Yorks. occurs in Domesday Book as *Coledun* and is from OE *col* + *dūn* hill (see DOWN 1); while one in Kent occurs in 1160 as *Cudena* and is from OE *cū* cow + *denn* pasture. The last does not appear to have yielded any surnames; the surname is more or less restricted to N England, and is also found in N Ireland, where it may be of Scots origin, from places so called near Dollar and near Dalkieth, Lothian.

Cowdrey English (Norman): habitation name from *Coudrai* in Seine-Maritime or *Coudray* in Eure, or *Cowdray* in Sussex, which seems to have been named after one of these two. All are named from OF *coudraie* hazel copse (a collective of *coudre* hazel tree, LL *colurus*, a metathesized form of class. L *corylus*, from Gk).

Vars: **Cowdr(a)y**, **Cowd(e)roy**, **Cowdery**, **Coudray**.

Cogns.: Fr.: **Coudray**, **Coudrais**, **Coudroy**; **Ducoudray**, **Ducoudré**.

Cowell English: habitation name from places in Lancs. and Gloucs. called *Cowhill*, from OE *cū* cow + *hyll* hill.

Cowie Scots: habitation name from any of several places of this name, esp. one near Stirling, probably so called from Gael. *colldha*, adj. from *coll* hazel.

Var.: **Coey**.

The first known bearer of the name is Herbert de Cowy, *who witnessed a charter by Nicholas de Dumfries in 1394*.

Cowley 1. English: habitation name from any of the various places so called. One in Gloucs. is named from OE *cū* cow + *lēah* wood, clearing; two in Derbys. get their first element from OE *col* (char)coal; and one near London has it from OE *cofa* recess, bay (see COVE) or the personal name *Cōfa* (cf. COVENEY and COVENTRY). The largest group, however, with examples in Bucks., Devon, Oxon., and Staffs., were apparently named as the wood or clearing of *Cufa*; however, in view of the number of places named with this element, it is possible that it conceals a topographical term as well as a personal name.

2. Irish and Manx: aphetic form of *Macaulay*; see OLIFF.

Var. (of 2): **Kewley**.

Cox 1. English: patr. from the ME hypocoristic suffix *-coke* (with genitive *-s*), which was attached freely to almost any given name to create a pet form (see COCK).

2. Flemish: patr. from the occupational term *cok* COOK.

Coxall English: habitation name from *Coggeshall* in Essex, so called from the gen. case of the OE personal name *Cogg* (of uncertain origin) + OE *halh* recess (see HALE 1).

Vars.: **Coggeshall**, **Coxwell**, **Cogswell**.

The first recorded bearer of the name is Sir Thomas Coggeshall, *who was living at Coggeshall in 1149. In the 13th and 14th cents. various bearers of the name served as sheriffs of Essex and Herts. The name was taken to America in 1632 by John Coggeshall, who became first governor of Rhode Island, and in 1635 by John* Cogswell. *In 1887 a descendant, Daniel Cogswell, founded Cogswell College, San Francisco.*

Coy English: nickname for a quiet and unassuming person, from ME, OF *coi*, *quei* calm, quiet (L *quiētus*).

Coyle Irish: 1. from the Gael. personal name *Cathmhaol*, composed of the elements *cath* battle + *maol* chief.

2. Anglicized form of Gael. *Mac Giolla Chomhghaill*; see COLE.

3. Anglicized form of Gael. *Mac Dhubhghaill*; see COOLE and DOUGALL.

Coyne 1. English: metonymic occupational name for a minter of money, or nickname for a miser, from ME *coin* piece of money (earlier of the die used to stamp money, from L *cuneus* wedge).

2. Irish: Anglicized form of Gael. **Ó Cúáin** 'descendant of *Cúán*', a byname from a dim. of *cú* hound, dog.

3. Irish: Anglicized form of Gael. **Ó Cadhain** 'descendant of *Cadhan*', a byname from *cadhan* barnacle goose.

Vars. (of 1): **Conyer** (occupational). (Of 2): **O'Coyne**, **O'Cuayn**, **(O')Quane**, **Quaine**, **Cain**. (Of 3): **O'Coyne**, **(O')Kine**, **Kyne**, CAIN, COHEN; **Barnacle**.

Patr. (from 1): **Conyers**.

Crabbe English and Scots: 1. nickname for someone with a peculiar gait, from ME *crabbe*, OE *crabba* crab (the crustacean).

2. topographic name for someone who lived by a crab-apple tree, from ME *crabbe* (apparently of ON origin). It may also have been a nickname for a cantankerous person, a sense which developed primarily from this word, with reference to the sourness of the fruit, but may also have been influenced by the awkward-seeming locomotion of the crustacean.

Vars.: **Crab(b)**. (Of 2 only): **Crabtree**.

Cogns. (of 1): Ger.: **Krebs**. Low Ger.: **Kreft**, **Kräft**, **Kräwt**, **Krabbe**. Dan.: **Krabbe**. Jewish (Ashkenazic): **Krebs** (probably one of the unflattering names assigned to Jews by non-Jewish government officials in 18th- and 19th-cent. central Europe).

As a Scots surname Crabbe *is probably of Flemish origin. Edward II of England complained to the Count of Flanders about the activities of the engineer John Crabbe in designing engines for the Scots at the siege of Berwick in 1319 and received the reply that he had already been banished for murder. Robert I of Scotland made him large grants of land, and his family were prominent in the affairs of Aberdeen during the succeeding centuries.*

Cracknell English: habitation name from either of two places in N Yorks, one called *Crakehall* and the other *Crakehill*, both from ON *kráka* crow (or OE *craca* crake) + OE *halh* recess (see HALE 1). The surname is now more common in E Anglia than in Yorks.
Vars.: **Cracknall, Crackel.**

Craddock Welsh: from the OW personal name which gives mod. W *Caradog* 'Amiable' (from the Celt. root *car* love; cf. CAREY). A Brit. bearer of this or a cogn. name is recorded in the L form *Cara(c)tacus* and remembered for his leadership of a revolt against the Roman occupation in the 1st cent. AD.
Vars.: **Cradduck, Cradock, Cradick.**
Cogns.: Bret.: **Caradec, Carado(t), Caradeau.**

Craig Scots: topographic name for someone who lived near a steep or precipitous rock, from Gael. *creag*, a word that has been borrowed in ME *crag(g)*.
Vars.: **Craik** (a place in the former county of Aberdeens., now part of Grampian region); **Carrick** (a district in the former county of Ayrs., now part of Strathclyde region); **Craigie** (from the Gael. locative case); **Cragg(s)** (from ME forms).

Crane English: nickname from the bird, OE *cran(uc)*, *cron(uc)*, *corn(uc)* (a term which included the HERON until the introduction of a separate word for the latter in the 14th cent.), probably denoting a tall, thin man with long legs.
Var.: CRANK.
Cogns.: Ger.: **Kran(i)ch, Krohn.** Low Ger.: **Krahn.** Du.: **Kraan.** Flem.: **De Craen.**
Dims.: Ger.: **Kränkel, Krenkel.** Low Ger.: KRANKE.

Cranfield English: habitation name from a place in Beds., so called from OE *cran(uc)* CRANE + *feld* pasture, open country (see FIELD).

Crank English (chiefly Lancs.): 1. nickname for a cheerful, boisterous, or cocky person, from ME *cranke* lively, lusty, vigorous.
2. var. of CRANE.
Var.: **Cronk.**

Crankshaw English: habitation name from *Cranshaw* in Lancs., so called from OE *cran(uc)* CRANE + *sceaga* grove, thicket (see SHAW).
Vars.: **Cranshaw, Cron(k)shaw, Crenshaw.**

Cranmer English: habitation name, probably from *Cranmore* in Somerset, so called from OE *cran(uc)* CRANE + *mere* lake, pool (see DELAMARE).

Cranston Scots: habitation name from a place, probably *Cranstoun* Riddel near Dalkeith, so called from the gen. case of the OE byname *Cran* 'CRANE' + OE *tūn* enclosure, settlement.
Vars.: **Cranstone, Cranstoun.**

Crathorne English: habitation name, probably from *Crathorne* in N Yorks., although the surname is now more or less restricted to the W Midlands. The Yorks. place is of uncertain etymology; Ekwall suggests that it may be from OE *craca* crake (cf. CRACKNELL) + *þorn* thorn bush.
Var.: **Craythorne.**

Craven English: regional name from the district of W Yorks. so called, which is probably from a Brit. word, the ancestor of W *craf* garlic. There is probably no connection with ME *cravant* cowardly, feeble, which is of uncertain origin.

Cravo Portuguese: 1. metonymic occupational name for someone who made and sold nails, especially those used in horseshoes, from Port. *cravo* nail (L *clāvus*).
2. topographic name for someone who lived by a spot where pinks grew, from Port. *cravo* pink, carnation (a transferred use of the same word, from the shape of the bud).
Var. (of 1): **Craveiro** (an agent deriv.).
Cogns. (of 1): Fr.: **Clout(r)ier.**
Dims. (of 1): Fr.: **Cloutot; Clavel, Claveau** (central France).

Crawford 1. English, Irish, and Scots: habitation name from any of the various places, for example in Dorset and Lancs., England, and Strathclyde, Scotland, so called from OE *crāwa* CROW + *ford* FORD.
2. English: var. of CROWFOOT.
Vars.: **Crauford, Crawfurd, Craufurd, Crawforth.**

Crawshaw English: habitation name from *Crawshaw* Booth in Lancs., so called from OE *crāwa* CROW + *sceaga* grove, thicket (see SHAW).
Vars.: **Crashaw, Crawshay, Croshaw, Crowsher.**

Cray Irish: Anglicized form of Gael **Ó Craoibhe** 'descendant of *Craobhach*', a byname meaning 'Curly(-headed)' or 'Prolific' (from *craobh* branch, bough).
Vars.: **O'Crevy, Creev(e)y, Creavagh; Creagh.**
Dims.: **O'Crevan, Creaven, Creavin** (Gael. **Ó Craobháin**).

Creamer 1. English: occupational name for a seller of dairy products, from an agent deriv. of ME, OF *creme* cream (LL *crāma*, apparently of Gaul. origin).
2. Scots and N Irish: occupational name for a pedlar, a cogn. of KRÄMER. Sir John Skene, in his *De verborum significatione* ('On the Meaning of Words', 1681), explains the term *pedder* as 'ane mechand or *cremer*, quha beris ane pack or *creame* upon his back'.
3. U.S.: Anglicization of KRÄMER.
Var. (of 2 and 3): **Cramer.**

Crease English: nickname from ME *crease* fine, elegant (OE *crēas*). There is probably no connection with mod. Eng. *crease*, which is first attested in the 16th cent., from earlier *crest* (cf. CRESTE).
Vars.: **Crees(e); Creasey** (chiefly Suffolk).

Creedon Irish: Anglicized form of Gael. **Ó Críodáin** and **Mac Críodáin** 'descendant' and 'son of *Críodán*', an OIr. personal name of uncertain origin (the ending is dim. in form).

Creggan Irish: Anglicized form of Gael. **Ó Croidheagáin** 'descendant of *Croidheagán*', a personal name from a dim. of *croidhe* heart, used as a term of endearment.
Vars.: **O'Cridigan, O'Crigan(e), O'Criane, Creddon, Creeghan, Cre(i)gan, Cre(h)an, Creane, Cree.**

Creighton Scots: habitation name from *Crichton*, 15 miles south-east of Edinburgh, first recorded *c.*1145 in the form *Crechtune*, in 1250 as *Krektun*, and in 1367 as *Creigchton*. The name is probably an early hybrid cpd of Gael. *crioch* border, boundary + ME *tune* farm, settlement (OE *tūn*).
Vars.: **C(h)richton, Crichten, Crighton.**

A Scots family by the name of Crichton, *also found as* Creighton *and* Creichtoun, *can be traced to William* de Crichton *in 1240. His son, Thomas de Crichton (d.* c.*1300), swore an oath of loyalty to Edward I of England in 1296. Members of this family have been Earls of Dumfries, Marquesses of Bute, and Earls of Erne; a branch of the family was established in Ireland before 1616 by two brothers, Abraham and James Crichton.*

Cremin Irish: Anglicized form of Gael. **Ó Croimín** 'descendant of *Croimín*', a byname from a dim. of *crom* bent, crooked; cf. CROME.

Crépy French: habitation name from places in Aisne, Oise, and Pas-de-Calais, all so called from their Gallo-Roman landlord *Crispius* (a deriv. of *Crispus*; see CRISP), with the addition of the local suffix *-ācum*.

Crès Provençal: topographic name for someone who lived on a patch of stony ground, from OProv. *cres*, *gres* (of uncertain etymology).

Var.: **Ducrès**.

Dims.: **Cresset, Cressin, Cressy, Cressot, Cresseau(x), Cresson**.

Crescent French: from a given name (L *Crescens*, gen. *Crecentis*, 'Growing (sc. in virtue)', pres. part. of *crescere* to grow, increase) borne by an early Christian saint martyred in Galatia under the Roman emperor Trajan.

Vars.: **Cressent, Cressan(t)**.

Creste French: topographic name for someone who lived near the crest of a hill, OF *creste* (LL *crista*), or habitation name from any of the numerous places named with this word. It may also in part have been originally a nickname for an arrogant individual, from the same word used with reference to the cock's comb (cf. OF *crester* to strut).

Vars.: **Crète; Cresté, Crété, Cretté** (nicknames).

Cogn.: Prov.: **Cresta**.

Dims.: Fr.: **Cretet, Créteau(x)**.

Aug.: Fr.: **Crétat**.

Creswell English: habitation name from any of the various places in England that get their names from OE *cærse* (water)cress + *well(a)* spring, stream (see WELL), as for example in Derbys., Notts., and Staffs.

Vars.: **Cresswell; Carswell** (from a place in Berks.); **Caswell** (from places in Dorset, Northants, and Somerset), **Casswell, Casewell; Craswall** (from a place in Herefords.), **Cras(s)well, Caswall, Caswill; Cressall, Cressel, Criswell, Crissel; Kerswell** (from places in Devon and Worcs.), **Kerswill; Crassweller**.

Creux French: topographic name for someone who lived by a hollow in the ground, OF *creus(e)* (apparently of Gaul. origin).

Vars.: **Cr(e)use, Creuze; Lecreux, Ducreux**.

Cogns.: Prov.: **Cros(e), Croz(e), Crozes; Ducros, Delcros**. Cat.: **Cros**.

Dims.: **Creuzet, Cr(e)uset, Creusot, Creuzot**. Prov.: **Croset, Cro(u)zet, Crozel**; see also CROSS.

Aug.: Prov.: **Crozat**.

Crew English: habitation name from *Crewe* in Ches., so called from OW *criu* weir (mod. W *cryw* weir, ford). This seems to have denoted a wickerwork fence that was stretched across the river Dee to catch fish. The town of *Crewe* near Edinburgh was probably named after this place by settlers from Ches., and may also be a partial source of the surname.

Var.: **Crewe**.

Criado Spanish: nickname for a foster child, from the past part. of Sp. *criar* to raise, bring up (L *creāre* to create, form). In medieval Spain it was a frequent practice for the offspring of a nobleman's vassals to be brought up at his court, and the name may well in some cases have originally been used as a title of honour for one of these.

Cribbin Irish: Anglicized form of Gael. **Mac Roibín**, a patr. from the ANF given name *Robin*, dim. of ROBERT.

Vars.: **Cribbins, Crebbin; Gribbin, Gribben, Gribbon** (Ulster).

Crible French: metonymic occupational name for a maker or seller of sieves, from OF *crible* sieve (LL *cribellum*, a dim. of class. L *cribrum*).

Vars.: **Crevel, Creveau, Cruvel; Cribellier, Crib(l)ier, Crivelier, Crevelier, Cruvel(h)ier, Cruveilh(i)er**.

Cogn.: It.: **Crivelli**.

Crich English: habitation name from the place so called in Derbys., which apparently gets its name from a Brit. element **crūc* hill. The pronunciation is normally /kraitʃ/.

Var.: **Crick** (a place in Northants).

Crimond Scots: habitation name from one of the places in Scotland called *Crimond*, probably the one near Peterhead in the former county of Aberdeens., now part of Grampian region. The place is first recorded in 1250 in the form *Creymund*, and is named with the Gael. elements *creachann* bare summit + *monadh* hill.

Crimp English: of uncertain origin, possibly a nickname for a cripple or hunchback, from an unattested blend of ME *cripel* (cf. CRIPWELL) and *crome* (cf. CROME 1). The earliest known bearers are Richard *Crempe*, Richard *Crempa*, and William *Crempa*, all of whom are recorded in S Devon in 1332, and the surname has been almost entirely confined to this locality ever since.

Cripwell English: nickname for a cripple, from ME *cripel*, *crepel*, *crupel* (OE *crypel*, a deriv. of *crēopan* to creep). The spelling may have been consciously altered to the form of a habitation name to avoid unpleasant associations.

Cogns.: Ger.: **Krüppel, Krupp**.

The earliest known bearer of the name in England is Thomas Crepel, *who was born in 1575 at Clifton, Notts. His son Richard* Criple *or* Cripwell *was born in 1602 at Bunney, Notts. It is found slightly earlier in Scotland, where Katherine* Cripple *is recorded at Dunkeld in 1514 and Ellen* Crippill *at Aberdeen in 1517.*

The German dynasty of munitions manufacturers by the name of Krupp *has been established in the Ruhr town of Essen since Arndt Krupp (d. 1624) settled there and bought land from people fleeing from the plague.*

Crisp English: 1. nickname for a man with curly hair, from ME *crisp*, OE *crisp*, *cryps* (L *crispus*), reinforced in ME by an OF word also from L *crispus*.

2. short form of CRISPIN.

Vars.: **Crispe, Chrisp; Crip(p)s, Crippes** (metathesized forms).

Cogns. (of 1): Fr.: **Cresp**. It.: **Crispo, Crispi, Crespo, Crespi**. Sp., Port.: **Crespo**. Ger.: **Krisp; Kr(a)uspe** (crossed with KRAUS).

Dims. (of 1): Fr.: **Crespet, Crespel, Crespon, Crespoul, Crispoul, Crépet, Crépey, Crépon**.

Crispin English and French: 1. from the ME, OF given name *Crispin* (L *Crispīnus*, a family name derived from *crispus* curly-haired; see CRISP). This name was especially popular in France in the early Middle Ages, having been borne by a saint who was martyred at Soissons in AD *c.*285 along with a companion, *Crispiniānus* (whose name is a further deriv. of the same word).

2. dim. of CRISP.

Vars.: Eng.: **Chrispin, Crip(p)in, Crippen, Crepin**. Fr.: **Cre(s)pin, Crépin, Crespi, Crespy**.

Cogns. (of 1): It.: **Crespino, Crespini**. Cat.: **Crespí**. Port.: **Crispim**. Ger.: **Krischpin**. Low Ger.: **Krispien**.

Cristal Scots: from a Sc. pet form of the given name CHRISTOPHER.

Vars.: **C(h)rystal(l), Crystol, Kristall**.

Patr.: **McCrystal**.

Croaker English (Norman): habitation name from any of the various places in Normandy, most notably in Calvados,

Oise, and Nord, called *Crèvecoeur* 'heartbreak' (from OF *creve(r)* to break, destroy, die (L *crepāre* to rattle) + *ceur* heart (L *cor*)), a reference to the infertility and unproductiveness of the land.

Vars.: **Crawcour**, **Craker**, Crocker, **Cre(e)gor**.

Cogn.: Fr.: **Crèvecoeur**.

A Norman baronial family called Crevequer *followed William the Conqueror to England and held Leeds Castle in Kent from the 11th to the 13th cents., later establishing branches in other parts of England. A branch bearing the name* Creuker *held land in Derbys. from about 1346 to 1601. All modern bearers of the surname* Craker *are probably descended from a certain Thomas Craker, who held land in Ombersley, Worcs., in 1484.*

Croasdale English (Lancs.): habitation name from *Crossdale* in Cumb., so called from the gen. pl. of ON *kross* Cross + *dalr* valley.

Vars.: **Cros(s)dale**.

Crocker English (chiefly W Country): 1. var. of Croaker.

2. occupational name for a potter, from an agent deriv. of ME *crock* pot (OE *croc(ca)*).

Crockett 1. English and Scots (Galloway): nickname for someone who affected a particular hairstyle, from ME *croket* large curl (ONF *croquet*, dim. of *croque* curl, hook, OF *croche*; see Crook).

2. Scots: Anglicized form of Gael. **Mac Riocaird** 'son of Richard'.

Vars.: **Croket**, **Crockatt**.

Crockford English: habitation name from *Crockford* Bridge in the parish of Chertsey, Surrey. The placename is of uncertain origin; the first element may be OE *croc(ca)* pot, used of a hollow in the ground or of a place where potsherds were found, the second is OE *ford* Ford.

Croft English: topographic name for someone who lived by an arable enclosure, normally adjoining a house, OE *croft*. There are several places in England named with this word, and the surname may equally be a habitation name from any of them. *Croft* in Leics. is so called from OE *cræft* craft, skill, also used in the concrete sense of a machine, engine, or mill.

Vars.: **Crofts**, **Craft(s)**, **Cruft(s)**; **Crofter**.

One family of this name trace their descent from Bernard de Croft, *recorded in Domesday Book as the holder of lands at* Croft *near Hereford, from which the surname was derived.*

Crofton English: habitation name from any of the various places so called, for example in Cumb., Hants, Kent, Lincs., Wilts., and W Yorks. Most of these are so called from OE *croft* paddock, smallholding (see Croft) + *tūn* enclosure, settlement, but the one in Kent probably has as its first element OE *cropp* swelling, mound (cf. Cropper), and that in Lincs. OE *croh* saffron (L *crocus*, from Gk).

An Irish family called Crofton *were established in Ireland by John Crofton (d. 1610), who held high office under Elizabeth I and acquired vast estates when he accompanied Sir Henry Sidney, Lord Deputy, into Ireland in 1565.*

Crombie Scots: habitation name from a place in the former county of Aberdeens. (now part of Grampian region), so called from Gael. *crom(b)* crooked or the Brit. cogn. of this word, ancestor of W *crwm*.

Vars.: **Cromie** (chiefly N Ireland); **Crumbie**, **Crummie**, **Crum-m(e)y**, **Crummay**.

Crome English: 1. nickname for a cripple or hunchback, from ME *crome*, OE *crumb* bent, crooked, stooping.

2. metonymic occupational name for a maker, seller, or user of hooks, from ME *crome*, *cromb* hook, crook (from OE *crùmb* bent, reinforced by an OF borrowing from a Gmc cogn.).

3. habitation name from *Croom* in E Yorks., so called from OE *crōhum*, dat. pl. (used originally after a preposition) of *crōh* narrow valley (a cogn. of ON *krá* corner, bend, and related to the words mentioned in 1 and 2 above).

4. habitation name from *Croome* in Worcs., so called from an old Brit. river name ultimately cogn. with the other words mentioned here; cf. W *crwm* crooked, winding.

Vars.: **Croom(e)**. (Of 1 only): **Cromb**, **Crumb**; **Crump** (chiefly W Midlands), **Cramp**, Crimp.

Cogns. (of 1): Ger.: **Krump(p)**. Du.: **Krom**. Flem.: **De Crom**, **Crommelinck**.

Dim. (of 1): Ger.: **Krüm(m)el**, **Krimmel**. Low Ger.: **Krimpke**.

Patr. (from 1): Flem.: **Crommen**.

Crompton English: habitation name from *Crompton* in Lancs., so called from OE *crumb* bent, crooked (see Crome 1) + *tūn* enclosure, settlement, i.e. a settlement by a bend in a river or road.

Vars.: **Crumpton** (chiefly W Midlands), **Crampton**.

Cromwell English: habitation name from places in Notts. and W Yorks., so called from OE *crumb* bent, crooked (see Crome 1) + *well(a)* spring, stream (see Well).

Cronin Irish: Anglicized form of Gael. **Ó Cróinín** 'descendant of *Cróinín*', a byname from a dim. of *crón* swarthy.

Var.: **Crone**.

Crook English: 1. from the ON byname *Krókr* 'Crook', 'Bend', originally no doubt bestowed on a cripple or hunchback or a devious schemer, but in early medieval England used as a personal name.

2. topographic name for someone who lived by a bend in a river or road, or metonymic occupational name for a maker, seller, or user of hooks, from ON *krókr* borrowed into ME as a vocabulary word.

Vars.: **Crooke**, **Krook**. (Of 1 only): **Croke** (Ireland). (Of 2 only): **Crooker**.

Cogns. (of 2): Fr.: **Croc(he)**, **Croque**; **Lecroc(q)**; **Ducroc(q)**. Swed.: **Krook**.

Dims.: Fr.: **Crochet**, **Crochot**, **Crochon**.

Pej.: Fr.: **Crochard**.

Patrs. (from 1): Eng.: **Crook(e)s**, **Crookson**.

Cropper English (chiefly Lancs.): occupational name for a picker of fruit or vegetables or a reaper of corn, from an agent deriv. of ME *crop(en)* to pick, pluck (a deriv. of *crop* produce, OE *cropp* swelling, head of a plant). The word was used also of the polling of cattle and the name may therefore have been given to someone who did this.

Var.: **Crapper**.

Crosby 1. English and Scots: habitation name from any of various places in N England and S Scotland that get their names from ON *kross* Cross + *býr* farm, settlement.

2. Irish: var. of Cross 2 (see below).

Vars.: **Crosbie**, **Crossby**.

The name of the Irish family of Crosbie *is ultimately derived from providing the chief bards to the O'Mores, Chiefs of Leix* (crosán *means 'bard', 'poet'). Pádraic* Mac Crosáin *or* Mac An-Chrosáin *took the name Patrick Crosbie c.1583.*

Cross 1. English: topographic name for someone who lived near a stone cross set up by the roadside or in a marketplace, from ON *kross* (via Gael. from L *crux*, gen. *crūcis*), which in ME quickly and comprehensively displaced the OE form *crūc* (see CROUCH). In a few cases the surname may have been given originally to someone who lived by a crossroads, but this sense of the word seems to have been a comparatively late development. In other cases, the surname (and its European cogns.) may have denoted one who carried the cross in processions of the Christian Church, but in Eng. at least the usual word for this sense was CROZIER.

2. Irish: Anglicized form of Gael. **Mac an Chrosáin**, a patr. from *crosán* reciter of satirical verse, satirist (originally a cross-bearer in a religious procession; see also CROSBY).

Vars.: **Crosse**. (Of 1 only): **Crossman** (chiefly Somerset). (Of 2 only): **Crossey**, **Crossin**, **(Mc)Crossan**, **McEcrossan**, **McAncrossane**.

Cogns. (of 1): Corn.: **Grose**. Fr.: **Croix**, **Lacroix**, **De(la)croix**, **Descroix**. Prov.: **Croux**; **Lacroux**, **Lacrouts**, **Lacroutz**; **Delacroux**. It.: **(Della) Croce**, **Croci**, **Cruce**; **La Croce** (S Italy); **Crose**, **Crosio** (N Italy). Sp.: **Cruz**, **Cruces**. Cat.: **Creus**. Port.: **Cruz**. Ger.: **Kreu(t)z(er)**; **Kreuziger** ('pilgrim'). Du.: **(Van der) Krui(j)s**, **Van (der) Kruys**. Flem.: **Vercruysse**, **Crutzen**. Pol.: **Krzyżaniak**. Beloruss.: **Kryzhov**.

Dims. (of 1): It.: **Crocetti**, **Crucetti**, **Crucitti**, **Crosetto**, **Crosetti**.

Habitation names: Pol.: **Krzyż(an)owski**.

Crossfield English (Yorks.): apparently a habitation name from an unidentified place so called, from ME CROSS + *fe(i)ld(e)* open country, FIELD.

Var.: **Crosfield**.

Crossland English (chiefly W Yorks.): habitation name from a place in the parish of Almondbury, W Yorks., so called from ME CROSS + *land* land.

Vars.: **Cros(se)land**.

Crossley English: habitation name from either of two places in W Yorks. named from ME CROSS + LEE clearing, pasture.

Crossthwaite N English: habitation name from any of several places in NW England that derive their names from ME CROSS + THWAITE clearing.

Vars.: **Crosthwaite**, **Crosswaite**.

Crosston English: habitation name from *Croston* near Leyland in Lancs., which gets its name from ME CROSS + *tune*, *tone* enclosure, settlement.

Crotty Irish: Anglicized form of Gael. **Ó Crotaigh** 'descendant of *Crotach*', a byname for a hunchback.

Crouch English: topographic name for someone who lived by a CROSS, from ME *crouch*, OE *crūc*, a word that was replaced in ME by the ON form *cross*.

Vars.: **Crotch**, **Crutch**; **Croucher**, **Crouchman**.

Crow 1. English: nickname from the bird, ME *crowe*, OE *crāwa*.

2. Irish (Munster): Anglicized form of Gael. *Mac Conchradha*; see MCENROE.

3. Irish: translation of any of various Gael. names derived from *fiach* raven, crow; see FEE.

Vars.: **Crowe** (very common in Ireland); **Craw**.

Cogns. (of 1): Ger.: **Krah(e)**, **Kroh(e)**, **Kräh(e)**, **Krehe**, **Krach**, **Kra(y)**. Low Ger.: **Krey**, **Krei**. Flem.: **Craey**. Du.: **Kraaij**, **Kraay**. Dan.: **Krag(h)**.

Crowell English: habitation name from a place in Oxon., so called from OE *crāwa* CROW + *well(a)* spring, stream (see WELL).

Crowfoot English: nickname for someone with splayed feet, or with a foot deformed in some other way.

The name is first found in Cheshire in the 16th cent. In many cases it has been absorbed by CRAWFORD.

Crowhurst English: habitation name from places in Surrey and Sussex. The former gets its name from OE *crāwa* CROW + *hyrst* wooded hill (see HURST); the latter originally had as its first element OE *crōh* narrow valley (see CROME 3).

Var.: **Crowest**.

Crowle English: according to Reaney, this is a habitation name from places in Lincs. and Worcs. The Lincs. place is named from a river (now no longer extant, due to draining) called *Crull* 'winding'; the Worcs. placename is a cpd of OE *croh* saffron or *crōh* bend + *lēah* wood, clearing. However, the surname is more commonly found in Devon and Cornwall than anywhere else. There is no plausible derivation in the Corn. language. The surname is possibly a var. of *Croll* (see KROLL), as Reaney alternatively suggests.

Crowley 1. English: habitation name from any of various places so called from OE *crāwe* CROW + *lēah* wood, clearing.

2. Irish: Anglicized form of Gael. **Ó Cruadhlaoich** 'descendant of *Cruadhlaoch*', a personal name composed of the elements *cruadh* hardy + *laoch* hero.

Vars. (of 1): **Crawley**. (Of 2): **O'Cro(w)l(e)y**, **Crol(l)y**, **Crolla**.

Crowther English: occupational name for a player on the *crowd*, ME *crouth*, *croude*, a type of popular medieval stringed instrument (W *crwth*).

Vars.: **Crowder**, **Crother**, **Crewther**.

Patrs.: **Crothers** (see also CARRUTHERS); MCWHIRTER.

Croxford English: habitation name from an unidentified minor place, apparently so called from the gen. case of the ON byname *Krókr* (see CROOK 1) + OE *ford* FORD.

Crozier English and French: occupational name for one who carried a cross or a bishop's crook in ecclesiastical processions, from ME, OF *croisier* (originally an agent deriv. of OF *crois* CROSS, but later associated also with *croce* CROOK).

Vars.: Eng.: **Cros(i)er**. Fr.: **Croisier**, **Croizier**.

Cogns.: Prov.: **Crousier**, **Crouzier**, **Crousié**.

Crudgington English: habitation name from a place in Shrops., earlier *Crugelton*, apparently from the Brit. element **crūc* hill (see CRICH) + the explanatory OE *hyll* hill + OE *tūn* enclosure, settlement.

Cruikshank Scots: nickname for a man with a crooked leg or legs, from older Scots *cruik* hook, bend (ME *crook*, ON *krókr*; see CROOK 2) + *shank* leg(-bone) (OE *sceanca*). Black, however, suggests that it is a local name from the river *Cruik* in the former county of Kincardine (now part of Grampian region) + *shank* used in the sense of a 'projecting point of a hill joining it to the plain'.

Vars.: **Cruikshanks**; **Cruickshank(s)**, **Crookshank(s)**.

Cruise English: 1. nickname from ME *cr(o)us(e)* bold, fierce (apparently from MLG, cogn. with KRAUS).

2. Norman habitation name from a place in France, perhaps *Cruys*-Straëte in Nord, apparently so called from Gaul. **crodiu* hard.

Vars.: **Cr(o)use**, **Crew(e)s**, **Cruwys**.

Crummock English: topographic name for someone who lived near a twisted oak tree, from OE *crumb* crooked, bent (see CROME 1) + *āc* OAK. There is no connection with

Crummock Water in Cumbria, the name of which is of Brit. origin.

Vars.: **Crummack, Cromack.**

Cogn.: Flem.: **Cromeeke.**

Crutchley English (W Midlands): apparently a habitation name from an unidentified place so called from OE *crūc* cross (see CROUCH) or Brit. **crūc* hill (see CRICH) + OE *lēah* wood, clearing.

Var.: **Critchley.**

Cryer English: occupational name for a town crier, one whose job was to make public announcements in a loud voice, from ME, OF *criere* (a deriv. of OF *crier* to cry aloud, L *quirītāre*).

Cudmore English (E Anglia): apparently a habitation name from an unidentified place so called, probably from the OE personal name *Cūða* (a short form of the various cpd names with a first element *cūð* famous, well known) + OE *mōr* marsh, fen (see MOORE).

Var.: **Cutmore.**

Cuerden English: habitation name from a place in Lancs., which according to Ekwall gets its name from Brit. **cerden*, W *cerddin* ash tree.

Cuervo Spanish: nickname for a man with strikingly glossy black hair, or for one with a raucous voice, from Sp. *cuervo* raven, rook (L *corvus*).

Cogns.: It.: **C(u)orvo, Corvi, Corbo, Corbi; Crovo, Crovi** (central and W Italy); **Crobu** (Sardinia); **Coropi, Corobi** (Calabria). Prov.: **Gorb.**

Dims.: Fr.: **Corbeau, Corbel, Corb(e)let, Corbin,** CORBY. Eng. (Norman): CORBETT. It.: **Corvini, Corvino, Corbell(in)i, Corbini, Corbucci; Crovelli** (Lombardy).

Cueto Spanish: habitation name from any of various places, for example in the provinces of Biscay, León, Oviedo, and Santander, named with the Sp. topographical term *cueto* crag, hill (of uncertain, probably pre-Roman, origin).

Cuff 1. English: metonymic occupational name for a maker and seller of gloves or nickname for a wearer of particularly fine gloves, from ME *cuffe* glove (of uncertain origin; attested in this sense from the 14th cent., with the modern meaning first in the 16th cent.).

2. Irish: Anglicized form of Gael. **Mac Dhuibh**, a var. of *Mac Duibh* 'son of the black one'; see DUFF.

3. Irish: approximate translation of Gael. *Ó Doirnín*; see DORNAN.

4. Cornish: nickname from Corn. *cuf* dear, kind.

Var.: **Cuffe.**

Cugat Catalan: from the medieval given name *Cugat* (L *Cucuphas*, gen. *Cucuphatis*, apparently of Carthaginian derivation). The name was borne by a 3rd-cent. African saint who was martyred at Barcelona.

Cuisine French: metonymic occupational name for someone employed in the kitchens of a great house or monastery, from OF *cuisine* kitchen (LL *coquīna*, from *coquere* to cook; cf. COOK).

Vars.: **Cu(i)sin(ier).**

Cogns.: Prov.: **Cuisinaire.** Eng.: KITCHEN.

Culebras Spanish: habitation name from a place in the province of Cuenca, so called from the pl. form of Sp. *culebra* snake (L *colubra*), apparently because snakes were frequently encountered there.

Cullen 1. Scots: habitation name from a place in the former county of Banffs. (now part of Grampian region), so called from Gael. *cùilan*, a dim. of *còil*, *cùil* nook, recess.

2. Irish: Anglicized form of Gael. **Ó Cuilinn** 'descendant of *Cuileann*', a byname meaning 'Holly'.

3. Irish: Anglicized form of Gael. **Ó Coileáin** 'descendant of *Coileán*', a byname meaning 'Puppy', 'Young Dog'.

4. English: habitation name from the Rhineland city of *Cologne* (OF form of MHG *Köln*, named from L *colōnia* colony).

5. English: var. of CULLING.

Vars.: **Cullin, Cullon.** (Of 3): **O'Collaine, (O')Collan, Cullane, Culhane,** COLLINS.

Cogns. (of 4): Ger.: **Köllen, Kölling, Köll(mann), Kölsch, Köllner.** Du.: **Van Keulen.**

Dims. (of 2): **Cullinan(e).**

Culling English: from a medieval given name, originally an OE patr. from the personal names *Cūl(a)* or *Cēola*. The former may be from a Gmc root *kūl* meaning 'swollen'; the latter is a short form of various cpd names with the first element *cēol* ship.

Vars.: **Cull;** COOLING, CULLEN.

The two main homes of the surname are Norfolk and Devon. In the former county the first known bearer of the name is recorded at Forncett St Peter in 1404 as Ricardus Cullyng. *A note in the parish register of Woodlands, Devon, records the death in 1509 of William* Culling *the ninth, which would take the line back to the late 13th cent.*

Cullingworth English (Yorks.): habitation name from a place in W Yorks., originally named in OE as the 'enclosure (see WORTH) of the people of *Cūla*' (see COOLING).

Cully Irish: Anglicized form of Gael. **Ó Colla** 'descendant of *Colla*', an OIr. personal name of uncertain origin.

Culpepper English: occupational name for a herbalist or spicer, from ME *cull(en)* to pluck, pick (OF *coillir*, from L *colligere* to collect, gather) + *peper* (OE *piper*; see PEPPER).

Vars.: **Cul(l)peper.**

The earliest recorded bearer of this surname is Sir Thomas de Colepeper, *who served as a member of a jury in the reign of King John.*

Culshaw English (Lancs.): habitation name from *Cowlishaw* near Oldham, Lancs. The placename is recorded as *Cowleshagh* in 1422 and *Colleshawe* in 1558; it is probably from ME *colly* dark, black (OE *colig*, from *col* (char)coal) + SHAW copse.

Var.: **Cowlishaw.**

Culver English: metonymic occupational name for a keeper of doves, or nickname for someone bearing some fancied resemblance to a dove, such as mildness of temper, from OE *culfre* dove (LL *columbula*, a dim. of *columba*; see COLOMB).

Cpd: **Culverhouse** ('dovehouse', topographic).

Cumberbatch English: habitation name from *Comberbatch* in N Ches., so called from the OE personal name *Cumbra* (originally a byname meaning 'Cumbrian') or the gen. pl. of *Cumbre* 'Britons' + OE *bæce* stream (see BACH 1).

Var.: **Cumberpatch.**

Cumming English, Scots, and Irish (Norman): from a Bret. personal name derived from the element *cam* bent, crooked (cf. CAMERON and CAMPBELL). This was relatively frequent in Norfolk, Lincs., and Yorks. in the 12th and 13th cents. as a result of Bret. immigration. The Sc. and

Ir. families bearing this name and its vars. are apparently all descended ultimately from a companion of William the Conqueror who came from the area of Rouen, where Bret. influence was strong. According to another theory it is a habitation name from *Comines* near Lille, but there is no evidence in favour of this and no early forms with prepositions have been found.

Vars: **Cuming**, **Cum(m)ine**, **Cummin**, **Commin**, **Comyn**, **Commane**, **Cummane**, **Cowman**.

Patrs.: Eng.: **Cum(m)in(g)s**, **Com(m)ings**; **Cummins**, **Com(m)ins** (mainly Irish); **Commons**. Gael.: **Mac Coimín**.

'Descendant of C.': Ir.: **O'Co(w)mane**, **O'Comman**, **O'Cumyn** (Gael. **Ó Coimín**, **Ó Cuimín**, **Ó Comáin**).

Cunard English: from the OE personal name *Cyneheard*, composed of the elements *cyne* royal, kingly + *heard* hardy, brave, strong.

Cunha Portuguese: habitation name from any of the numerous places so called. The placename is of uncertain origin; a common early form is *Cuin(h)a*.

Cunliffe English: habitation name from a place in Lancs., near Rishton, recorded in 1246 as *Kunteclive*, from OE *cunte* cunt + *clif* slope (see CLIVE), i.e. 'slope with a slit or crack in it'.

Var.: **Cunnliffe**.

Cunningham 1. Scots: habitation name from a place near Kilmarnock, first recorded in 1153 in the form *Cunegan*, a Brit. name of uncertain origin. The spelling in *-ham*, first recorded in 1180, represents an assimilation to the Eng. placename element *-ham*.

2. Irish: Anglicized form of **Ó Cuinneagáin** 'descendant of *Cuinneagán*', a personal name from a dim. of the OIr. personal name *Conn* 'Leader', 'Chief'.

Vars.: **Cuningham(e)**, **Cunninghame**, **Coningham**, **Conyngham**. (Of 2 only): **Conag(h)an**, **Cunnigan**, **Cunihan**, **Cunnahan**; **Kennigan**, **Kinnegan**, **Kin(a)ghan**, **Kinnighan**, **Kinahan**.

A Scots family of this name trace their ancestry back to Wernebald, a vassal of Hugh de Morville, who obtained the manor of Cunningham from his feudal superior in the early 12th cent.

Cunnington English: habitation name from either of two places in Cambs. (one formerly in Hunts.) called *Conington*, from ON *kunung* king, chieftain (probably replacing earlier OE *cyning*) + OE *tūn* enclosure, settlement.

Curd English: metonymic occupational name for a seller of dairy products, from ME *crud(de)*, *curd(de)* curd (cheese) (of uncertain, possibly Celt., origin).

Curley Irish: Anglicized form of Gael. *Mac Toirdhealbhaigh*; see MCTERRELLY.

Vars.: **(Mc)Corley**, **McCurlye**, **Kirley**, **(Mc)Kerley**, **McKerlie**, **McKyrrelly**; **McGorley**.

Curme English: of unknown origin, perhaps a topographic name from early mod. Eng. *corm(e)* service fruit (OF *corme*; cf. CORMIER), attested in the 16th cent.

Vars.: **Cur(ru)m**, **Curr(o)m**.

The earliest known bearer of a name resembling Curme *is recorded in 1591 at Maiden Newton, Dorset, as John* Corrm.

Curran Irish: Anglicized from of Gael. **Ó Corraidhín** 'descendant of *Corraidhín*', a personal name from a dim. of *corradh* spear; cf. CORR.

Vars.: **Corran**, **(O')Corrin**, **O'Corren**, **O'Corhane**, **O'Curran(e)**, **O'Currine**, **O'Carran**, **Curreen**.

Curry 1. English: habitation name from one of the places in Somerset so called from the river *Curry*, on which they stand, the name of which is of unknown origin.

2. Scots: habitation name from *Currie* in the former county of Midlothian, now part of Lothian region, first attested in this form in 1230. It is apparently from Gael. *curraigh*, dat. of *currach* wet plain, marsh.

3. Scots: habitation name from *Corrie* in the former county of Dumfries; see CORRIE.

4. Irish: Anglicized form of Gael. *Ó Comhraidhe*; see CORY 2.

5. Irish: Anglicized form of Gael. *Ó Corra*; see CORR.

6. Cornish: habitation name from a place in the parish of Boyton, so called from Corn. *cor* corner + *e(g)y* place.

Vars.: **Currey**, **Currie**.

Curtin 1. English: dim. of COURT.

2. Irish and Scots: Anglicized form of Gael. **Mac Cruitín** 'son of *Cruitín*', a byname for a hunchback.

Vars. (of 2): **McCrutten**, **McCruttan**, **(Mc)Curtain**, **Curtayne**.

Curtis English: 1. nickname for a refined person, sometimes no doubt given ironically, from OF, ME *curteis*, *co(u)rtois* refined, accomplished (a deriv. of OF *court*, see COURT 1).

2. nickname for a short person or one who wore short stockings, from ME *curt* short (see COURT 2) + *hose* leggings (OE *hosa*). Compare SHORTHOUSE. This nickname was borne by William the Conqueror's son Robert, but it is not clear whether it has given rise to any surnames.

Var.: **Curtiss**.

Cogns. (of 1): Fr.: **Courtois**. Prov.: **Court(h)ès**. It.: **Cortesi**, **Cortese**. Sp.: **Cortés**. Cat.: **Cortès**. (Of 2): Ger.: **Korthase**.

Dim. (of 1): It.: **Cortesini**.

Curwen 1. Scots: habitation name from *Colvend* in the former county of Kirkcudbright, now part of Dumfries and Galloway region. It has been suggested that the placename probably derives from Gael. *cùl a'beinn* at the back of the hill.

2. Manx: aphetic form of Gael. *Mac Eireamháin*; see IRVING.

Vars. (of 1): **Culwen**. (Of 2): **Curwin**, **Kermeen**.

Curzon English (Norman): 1. dim. of COURT.

2. habitation name from Notre-Dame-de-Courson in Calvados, Normandy, so called from the Gallo-Roman personal name *Curtius* (from *curtus* short; see COURT 2) + the local suffix *-o*, gen. *-ōnis*.

Vars.: **Curson**, **Corson** (see also CARSON).

Cusack Irish (Norman): habitation name from *Cussac* in Guienne, so called from the Gallo-Roman personal name *Cūcius* or *Cussius* + the local suffix *-ācum*. The surname more or less died out in England, but is quite common in Ireland, where it was taken at the time of the Anglo-Norman invasion and has been Gaelicized as **de Cíosóg**.

Cusker Irish: Anglicized form of Gael. **Ó Coscair** 'descendant of *Coscar*', a personal name from *coscur* victory.

Vars.: **O'Coskirr**, **(O')Cosker**, **Coscor**.

Custódio Portuguese: from a religious byname, chosen to invoke the protection of a guardian angel, Port. *anjo custódio* (LL *angelus custōdius*, from *custos*, gen. *custōdis*, guardian, keeper).

Cusworth English: habitation name from a place in W Yorks., so called from the OE personal name *Cūðsa* (apparently a short form of a name composed of the elements *cūð* famous, well known + *sige* victory) + OE *worð* enclosure (see WORTH).

Var.: **Cushworth**.

Cuthbert English: from the ME given name *Cudbert*, OE *Cuðbeorht*, composed of the elements *cūð* famous, well known + *beorht* bright, famous. The name was borne by a 7th-cent. saint, bishop of Hexham and later of Lindisfarne, and remained popular because of his cult throughout the Middle Ages, especially in N England and the lowlands of Scotland.

Vars.: **Cudbird, Cutbirth.**

Dims.: **Cuthbe, Cudby, Cudd(y), Cutt; Cussen, Cusson** (see also CONSTANCE and COUSIN).

Patrs.: Eng.: **Cuthbertson.** Sc.: **McCoubr(e)y, McCoubrie, McCaubrey** (Gael. **Mac Cúthbhréith**).

Patrs. (from dims.): Eng.: **Cutts, Cutting; Cussens, Cussons.**

The dim. Cuthbe *is rare and apparently confined to a small area on the Suffolk-Essex border. It first occurs in this form in the early 19th cent.; a century earlier the forms* Cuthbert, Cutbee, *and* Cutbie *are all used of the same person.*

Cutler 1. English: occupational name for a maker of knives, from an agent deriv. of ME, OF *co(u)tel, co(u)teau* knife (LL *cultellus*, a dim. of *culter* ploughshare; cf. COTTLE).

2. Jewish (E Ashkenazic): Anglicization of *Kotler* (see KESSEL).

Var. (of 1): **Cuttelar.**

Cuvier French: occupational name for a maker of barrels and tubs, from an agent deriv. of OF *cuve* vat, tub (LL *cūpa*, of Gmc origin; cf. COOPER).

Cogns.: Eng. (Norman): **Cover** (see also COUVREUR). Sp.: **Cubero; Cubas, Cubo.** Low Ger.: **Küver, Köver.**

Dims.: Sp.: **Cubillo.** Cat.: **Cubells.**

Patr.: Flem.: **Cuyvers.**

Czajkowski Polish: habitation name from a place named with Pol. *czajka* lapwing (cogn. with Russ. *chaika* seagull) + *-ów* possessive suffix, used in forming placenames, with the addition of the surname suffix *-ski* (cf. BARANOWSKI).

Var.: **Czajka** (probably a nickname).

Cogns.: Russ.: **Chaikovski, Tchaikovsky.** Czech: **Čejka.**

The spelling Tchaikovsky, *by which the Russ. composer is generally known, is a Fr. romanization of the Cyrillic spelling. Unbegaun cites this name as an example of a Russ. name of Pol. or Ukr. origin, with the* -ski *suffix suggestive of social prestige, since Pol. bearers of names ending in* -ski *were often masters rather than merely inhabitants of the places named.*

Czerwiński Polish: nickname for someone with red hair or a reddish complexion, from Pol. *czerwień* red + *-ski* suffix of surnames (see BARANOWSKI).

Var.: **Czerwieński.**

Cogn.: Czech: **Červeny.**

Dims.: Czech: **Červenka, Červinka.**

Czupryniak Polish: nickname for a man with a thick head of hair, from Pol. *czupryna* head of hair + *-iak* suffix of animate (human) nouns.

Var.: **Czupryński.**

Czyż Polish and Jewish (E Ashkenazic): nickname or, in the case of the Jewish name, ornamental name, from Pol. *czyż(yk)* greenfinch.

Var.: Pol.: **Czyżo.**

Cogn.: Czech: **Čížek.**

Habitation names: Pol.: **Czyżewski; Czyżykowski.**

D

Dąbrowski Polish: habitation name from any of various places called Dąbrowa, from Pol. *dąbrowa* oak grove (from *dąb* oak, pl. *dęby*; see DUBNIKOV), with the addition of *-ski*, suffix of local surnames (see BARANOWSKI).

Cogns.: Russ.: **Dubrovsky** (from the placename *Dubrova*). Czech: **Doubrava**. Jewish (E Ashkenazic, either ornamental or habitation names): **Dombrovski**, **Dombrovsky**, **Dombrowski**, **Dombrowsky**; **Dubrovsky**; **Dembrover** (habitation name).

Dach 1. German: habitation name from any of the places, in various parts of Germany, so called from MHG *tāhe*, *dāhe* marsh (OHG *dāha*).

2. Jewish (Ashkenazic): of uncertain origin, probably from mod. Ger. *Dach* or Yid. *dakh* roof.

Vars. (of 1): **Dacher**, **Dachmann**. (Of 2): **Dachner** ('roofer', occupational name).

Dacheux French: 1. occupational name for a nailsmith, from a var. spelling of OF *dacheur*, an agent deriv. of *dache* nail (of uncertain origin; cf. DAGG).

2. habitation name, with fused preposition *de*, from *Acheux* in Somme, so called from LL *apiōsum* patch of smallage or wild celery (a deriv. of *apium* parsley, celery; the word *smallage* was itself originally a cpd of the adj. *small* + ME, OF *ache*).

Dachs 1. German: nickname for someone who resembled a badger in some way, for example in nocturnal habits or in having a streak of white hair among black, from Ger. *Dachs* badger (MHG, OHG *dahs*).

2. Jewish (Ashkenazic): from Ger. *Dachs* badger, adopted either as an ornamental name or acquired as a nickname, with the same origins as in 1.

Vars.: Jewish: **Taks** (from Yid. *taks* badger), **Tax** (Anglicized spelling).

Cogn.: Flem., Du.: **Das**. See also TASSO 2.

Dack English: apparently from an OE personal name or byname *Dæcca* (of uncertain origin), which may have survived into the Middle English period as a given name. The surname is found mainly in Norfolk.

Patr.: **Dax**.

Dacre English: habitation name from a place in Cumb. that gets its name from the river on which it stands. This is apparently of Brit. origin, and may originally have meant 'trickling'. The surname is now most common in the Leeds area.

The first known bearer of the surname is William de Dakyr *or* Dakre, *who was sheriff of Cumberland in 1278.*

Dadswell English: habitation name from *Dowdeswell* in Gloucs., first recorded in the 8th cent. as *Dogodeswyllan*, from the gen. case of the OE personal name *Dogod* (see DOWDING) + OE *w(i)ell(a)* spring, stream (see WELL).

Var.: **Dowdeswell**.

The first known bearer of the surname is Robert Doudeswell, *b. c.1560, who came from Gloucs. and settled c.1588 in Sussex, where he established a family still in existence. The surname is now far more common in Sussex, Kent, and the London area than in Gloucs.*

Daft English: nickname for a meek person rather than a stupid one, from ME *daffte* mild, gentle, meek (OE *gedæfte*). The surname survives in the E Midlands in spite of the unfavourable connotations that were acquired by the vocab. word in the 15th cent.

Dagg English: metonymic occupational name for a maker or seller of daggers, or nickname for someone who carried one, from OF *dague* dagger (of uncertain origin). ME **Dagger** is a later development of the same word; Fr. **Daguier** is an agent noun derived from it, meaning 'dagger maker'.

Dims.: Eng.: **Daggett**. Fr.: **Dagon(et)**, **Dagonneau**, **Dagot**, **Daguin(ot)**, **Dagu(en)et**, **Dagueneau**.

Daimler German: occupational name for a judicial torturer (who applied the thumbscrew), or else a nickname for a cruel person, from an agent deriv. of MHG *diumeln* to torture (a deriv. of *dūme* thumb; see DAUM).

Vars.: **Deimler**, **Däumler**.

Dain English: 1. nickname for a worthy and honourable citizen, or for a haughty and self-important one, from ME *d(e)igne*, *deyn(e)*, *dain(e)* worthy, fitting (OF *digne*, from L *dignus*).

2. var. of DEAN.

3. var. of DENCH.

Vars.: **Daine**, **Dayne**, **Dyne**.

Patrs.: **Daines**, **Daynes**, **Deyns**, **Dines**.

Daintith English: affectionate nickname or term of address, from ME *deinteth* pleasure, titbit (OF *deintiet*, from L *dignitas*, gen. *dignitātis*, worth, value, a deriv. of *dignus* worthy; cf. DAIN 1). The word was also used as an adj. in the later form *deinte* (OF *deint(i)é*) in the sense 'fine', 'handsome', 'pleasant'. The surname is especially common in Lancs.

Vars.: **Dainteth**, **Dentith**; **Dainty**, **Denty**.

Daintry English: habitation name from *Daventry* in Northants, of which the normal local pronunciation is (or was) /deɪntrɪ/. The place is probably named from the gen. case of an OE personal name or byname *Dafa* (perhaps related to *(ge)dafan* fitting, appropriate) + OE *trēow* tree.

Vars.: **Daintree**, **Daintrey**, **Daventry**.

Dalby English: habitation name from any of various places so called from ON *dalr* valley (see DALE) + *býr* farm, settlement. The surname is common in Yorks., and it probably derives mainly from *Dalby* in N Yorks., but similarly named places in Leics. and Lincs. are also possible sources.

Dale English: topographic name for someone who lived in a valley, ME *dale* (OE *dæl*, reinforced in N England by the cogn. ON *dalr*), or habitation name from any of the numerous minor places named with this word.

Vars.: **Daile**, **Dales**; **Deal** (from the Kentish form *del*, and the name of a place in Kent).

Cogns.: Ger.: **T(h)al**, **Thal(l)er**, **Thalmann**. Low Ger.: **Dahl(er)**, **Dal(l)mann**; **Tendahl** (Rhineland). Flem.: **Dael**, **Van den Dael(e)**, **Van Dale(n)**, **Daleman**. Du.: **(Van) Dael**, **Van (der) Daal**, **Van Da(a)len**, **Daelman**, **Daalman**. Dan.: **Dahl**, **Dall**. Swed.: **Dahl(én)**, **Dahlin**, **Dahlman**.

Cpds (ornamental): Swed.: **Dahlbäck** ('valley stream'); **Dahlberg** ('valley hill'); **Dahlbom** ('valley tree'); **Dahlborg** ('valley town'); **Dahlgren** ('valley branch'); **Dahlquist** ('valley twig'); **Dahlstedt** ('valley homestead'); **Dahlstrand** ('valley shore'); **Dahlström** ('valley river').

Dalgetty Scots: habitation name from a place near Dunfermline, which, according to Watson, derives its name from Gael. *dealg* prickle. There are also lands of the same name in the former county of Aberdeens. (now part of Grampian region) that belonged to a family so called, but it is not clear whether the family took the name from the land or vice versa.

Var.: **Dalgety**.

Dalgleish Scots: habitation name from a place near Selkirk, first recorded in 1383 in the form *Dalglas*, from Gael. *dail* field + *glas* green (cf. GLASS 2), perhaps taken over from Brit. *dollas*, with the same meaning.

Vars.: **Dalgli(e)sh, Dalgleas, Dagless, Daglish**.

Dalhousie Scots: habitation name from a place near Edinburgh, of uncertain etymology. It is recorded *c.*1235 in the form *Dalwussy*, in 1298 as *Dalw(u)lsy*, and in 1461 as *Dalwosie*. It has been suggested that the name originally meant 'field of slander', from Gael. *dail* field + *thuaileais*, gen. of *thuaileas* slander.

Dalkeith Scots: habitation name from a place near Edinburgh, the etymology of which is probably Brit. *dol* meadow + *cēd* wood.

Dallas 1. Scots: habitation name from a place near Forres, probably so called from Brit. *dol* meadow (Gael. *dail*) + *gwas* dwelling.

2. English: topographic name or name from OE *dæl* valley (see DALE) + *hūs* house, either directly or by way of some placename with this origin, as for example *Dalehouse* in N Yorks.

Var. (of 1): **Dall**.

The lands of Dolays *Mykel were granted to the Englishman Willelmus de Rypeley in the 12th cent.*

Dallaway English (W Midlands): of uncertain origin. It is possibly a Norman habitation name, with fused preposition *de*, from *Alluyes* in Eure-et-Loire. This placename is recorded in the 6th cent. in the L form *Avallocium*, apparently a deriv. of the Gaul. element *aballo* apple.

Var.: **Dallow**.

Dalmas French: from a medieval given name (L *Dalmatius*, originally an ethnic name for someone from *Dalmatia* in modern Yugoslavia; the name may be of Illyrian origin and akin to S Albanian *delme* sheep). The name was borne by a 3rd-cent. bishop of Pavia and a 6th-cent. bishop of Rodez, both of whom were popularly venerated in the Middle Ages.

Vars.: **Damas; Dalmais, Dalmay; Da(l)mace** (learned forms).

Cogns.: Cat.: **Dalmau; Dalmases** (a pluralized form). It.: **Dalmasso** (more common in Nice than in Italy itself).

Dalrymple Scots: habitation name from a place in the former county of Ayrs. (now part of Strathclyde region), said to be so called from Gael. *dail chruim puill* field of the crooked stream.

The barony of Dalrymple *was jointly held in 1371 by Malcolm and Hew* de Dalrympill. *The Dalrymple family who held the earldom of Stair can be traced directly to William* de Dalrymple, *probably a descendant of one of these men, who in 1429 acquired the estate of Stair in Kyle, Ayrs. In the muster rolls of the Scots Guards in France, the name appears as* de Romple.

Dalton English: 1. habitation name from any of the various places, for example in Cumb., Co. Durham, Lancs., Northumb., and Yorks., so called from OE *dæl* valley (see DALE) + *tūn* enclosure, settlement.

2. Norman habitation name, with fused preposition *de*, from *Autun* in Seine-et-Loire, whose modern name derives from the L form *Augustodunum*. This is a cpd of the imperial name *Augustus* + the Gaul. element *dūn* hill, fort (cf. DOWN 1).

Vars.: **Daulton, Daughton, Da(w)ton**. (Of 2 only): **Dautun, D'A(l)ton**.

Daltry English (Norman): habitation name, with fused preposition *de*, from *Hauterive* in Orne, so called from OF *haute rive* high bank (L *alta rīpa*).

Vars.: **Dawtr(e)y, Daughtr(e)y, Daughtery, Da(u)ltrey, Dealtry, Doughtery, Dowtry; Ha(w)try**.

Daly Irish: Anglicized form of Gael. **Ó Dálaigh** 'descendant of *Dálach*', a personal name from *dál* (mod. *dáil*) meeting, assembly.

Vars.: **O'Daly, Daley, Dail(e)y, Dall(e)y**.

An Irish family of this name claim to be descended from Dálach, *tenth in descent from Niall of the Nine Hostages.*

Dalziel Scots: habitation name from a place in the Clyde valley, recorded in 1200 in the forms *Dalyell, Daliel* and in 1352 as *Daleel*, apparently from Gael. *dail* field + *g(h)eal* white. The *z* in the spelling is not really a /z/ at all; it represents ME ȝ (cf. MENZIES), and the pronunciation, regardless of spelling, was normally /di:ˈɛl/ or /daɪˈɛl/, sometimes /dælˈjɛl/. Black quotes an 'old Galloway rhyme': 'Deil (devil) and Da'yell begins with yae letter; Deil's no gude and Da'yell's nae better'. Nowadays /dælˈzi:l/ and /dælˈzɛl/ are also heard.

Vars.: **Dalyell, Dalyiel; Dalzell** (the latter now being most common in Ireland).

The first known bearer of the name is Hugh de Dalyhel, *who was sheriff of Lanark in 1288 and probably a son of the feudal baron of Dalziel.*

Dam Dutch: topographic name for someone who lived by a dike, esp. one built to keep out the sea, MLG *dam* (the source of the mod. Eng. word *dam*). A homonymous Du. word denotes the game of draughts (from the same source as DAME), but the surname is not likely to be connected with this.

Vars.: **Dam(m)en; Van Dam** (partly Jewish), **Van Damme, Opdam, Damman, Dammer**.

Cogns.: Low Ger.: **Tendam** (N Rhineland). Fris.: **Damstra**. Dan.: **Dam(m)**.

Dame English and French: from OF *dame* lady (L *domina* mistress), originally a nickname for a foppish man or a title of respect for a widow. It may also have been an occupational name for someone in the service of a lady.

Var.: Fr.: **Danne**.

Cogns.: It.: **Donna**. Sp.: DUEÑAS. Port.: **Damas**.

Metrs.: Eng.: **Damson**. It.: **Dalle Donne** (Emilia); **Delle Donne** (Campania).

Dampier English (Norman): habitation name from any of various places in Normandy named *Dampierre*, in honour of St Peter. The first element, *Dam-* or *Don*, is an OF title of respect (from L *dominus* lord), prefixed particularly to the names of saints.

Var.: **Damper**.

Cogn.: Fr.: **Dampierre**.

Damyon English: from the medieval given name *Damian* (L *Damiānus*, from a Gk name probably derived from that of the goddess *Damia*, which is probably akin to Gk *damān* to tame, subdue, kill). Damian was the name borne by a famous early Christian saint who was martyred in Cilicia in AD 303 under the emperor Domitian, together with his brother Cosmas. In some accounts the brothers were said to be doctors, and together they were regarded as the patrons of physicians and apothecaries. A later St Damian lived in the 7th–8th cents. and was bishop of Pavia; he may have had some influence on the popularity of the given name in Italy.

Var.: **Damon**.

Cogns: Fr.: **Damien**; **Damian** (also Jewish, of uncertain origin). It.: **Damiano**, **Damian(i)**. Ger.: **Damian**. Ger. (of Slav. origin): **Domian**, **Dohmjan**. Hung.: **Demény**, **Demjén**, **Domján**.

Dims.: Beloruss.: **Demyanok**, **Demeshko**. Ukr.: **Demyanchuk**, **Demyanets**, **Demchenko**.

Patrs.: Ger.: **Damiani** (Latinized). Flem., Du.: **Damiaens**. Russ.: **Demyanov**. Bulg.: **Damyanov**. Croatian: **Damjanović**.

Patrs. (from dims.): Flem.: **Dams**. Russ.: **Dem(a)kov**, **Demykin**, **Dyom(k)in**, **Dyomyshev**, **Dyomichev**, **Dyomshin**, **Dyominov**, **Dyoshin** (see also DEMIDOV). Ukr.: **Demchinyat**.

Danby English: habitation name from any of several places called *Danby* in N Yorks., originally named in ON as *Danebýr* 'settlement of the Danes', and so cogn. with DENBY.

Dando English (Norman): habitation name, with fused preposition *de*, from *Aunou* in Orne, Normandy, which gets its name from OF *aunaie* alder grove (see DELANEY).

Var.: **Daddow**.

The name is chiefly common in Somerset, whither it was brought in the 13th cent. by a Norman called Dando, *who gave his name to the village of Compton Dando.*

Daňek Czech: 1. dim. of DANIEL or of any of the Slav. cpd personal names containing the element *dan-* gift, as for example *Danomír*, *Danoslav*, and BOGDANOV.

2. nickname from the vocab. word *daňek* buck, fallow deer.

Cogns. (of 1): Ger. (of Slav. origin): **Dänecke**, **Dähnick(e)**, **Dahnke**.

Patrs. (from 1): Ger.: **Däniken**. Croatian: **Daničić**.

Dangerfield English (Norman): habitation name, with fused preposition *de*, from any of the various places in Normandy called *Angerville*, from the ON personal name *Ásgeirr* (from *ás* god + *geirr* spear) + OF *ville* settlement, village. The English surname is now found chiefly in the W Midlands.

Daniel English, French, Portuguese, German, Polish, and Jewish: from the Hebr. male given name *Daniel* 'God is my judge', borne by a major prophet in the Bible. The major factor influencing the popularity of the given name (and hence the frequency of the surname) was undoubtedly the dramatic story in the Book of Daniel, recounting the prophet's steadfast adherence to his religious faith in spite of pressure and persecution from the Mesopotamian kings in whose court he served: Nebuchadnezzar (who went mad) and Belshazzar (at whose feast Daniel interpreted the mysterious message of doom that appeared on the wall, being thrown to the lions for his pains). The name was also borne by a 2nd-cent. Christian martyr and by a 9th-cent. hermit, the legend of whose life was popular among Christians during the Middle Ages; these had a minor additional influence on the adoption of the Christian name. Among Orthodox Christians in E Europe the name was also popular as being that of a 4th-cent. Persian martyr, who was venerated in the Orthodox Church. See also DONALD.

Vars.: Eng.: **Daniell**; **Danniel(l)**, **Danell**, **Dannel**, **Dennell**; **Denial** (with the accent on the first syllable). Fr.: **Deniel**, **Daniau**, **Deniau(d)**. Ger.: **Dan(i)gel**, **Dangl**, **Dannöhl**, **Dan(n)ehl**, **Danneil**. Jewish: **Daniel(l)i**, **Daniely** (with the Hebr. suffix *-i*); **Danielski**, **Danielsky** (E Ashkenazic).

Cogns.: Prov.: **Danis**, **Dany**. It.: **Daniel(l)i**, **Daniele**, **Dan(i)ello**, **Danielli**. Czech: **Danihel**, **Daňhel**. Hung.: **Dániel**.

Dims.: Fr.: **Danelet**, **Daniellot**; **Daniélou** (Brittany). It.: **Danelutti**, **Dan(i)elut** (Venetia); **Dani** (Tuscany). Flem.: **Daen**, **Danick**. Beloruss.: **Danilenko**, **Danilchik**. Ukr.: **Dan(il)chenko**, **Danilyuk**, **Danilchik**, **Danilyak**, **Dakhno**. Czech: DAŇEK, **Danihelka**. Hung.: **Dankó**. Jewish (E Ashkenazic): **Danielczyk**.

Patrs.: Eng.: **Daniel(l)s**, **Danels**. It.: **Danielis**. Low Ger.: **Daniels(en)**. Flem., Du.: **Daniels**. Dan.: **Danielsen**. Swed.: **Danielsson**. Ashkenazic: **Daniels**, **Danielso(h)n**. Russ.: **Danilov**, **Danilin**. Beloruss.: **Danilevich**. Ukr.: **Danilovich**. Pol.: **Danilewicz**, **Daniłowicz**. Croatian: **Danilović**. Jewish (E Ashkenazic): **Dani(e)lovitch**. Armenian: **Danielian**.

Patrs. (from dims.): Eng.: **Danson** (chiefly Lancs.; see also ANDREW); **Danks** (chiefly Birmingham). Flem.: **Daens**, **Daenen**. Russ.: **Dankov**, **Danshin**, **Dashkov**, **Dakhov**. Ukr.: **Danovich**, **Dashkovich**. Pol.: **Danielkiewicz**, **Daszkiewicz**. Bulg.: **Danilchev**, **Danev**.

'Son of the wife of D.': Ukr.: **Danilishin**.

A family by the name of Daniell *trace their descent from Robert* Danyers, *who was involved in transactions concerning land in Lymm, Ches., in the reign of Henry III (1216–72). The name is not recorded as* Danyell *until the early 15th cent. and the form* Danyers *may well be of different origin, although it is not clear what this could be.*

Dankmar German: from a Gmc personal name composed of the elements *þank* thought + *mari*, *meri* famous, renowned.

Cogns.: Low Ger.: **Dammert**. It.: **Tammaro**.

Dims.: Low Ger.: **T(h)amm**, **Tamme**, **Tan(c)k**, **Tamcke**.

Patr.: Low Ger.: **Dammers**.

Patrs. (from dims.): Low Ger.: **Tammen**, **Tam(m)s**, **Thams(en)**. Fris.: **Tamminga**.

Dansie English (Norman): habitation name, with fused preposition *de*, from *Anizy* in Calvados, recorded in 1155 in the form *Anisie*. The placename is probably derived from the Gallo-Roman personal name *Anitius* (of uncertain origin) + the local suffix *-ācum*.

Vars.: **Dansey**, **Danc(e)y**, **Dauncey**; **Densey**, **Densie**, **Denzey**; **Dinzey** (W Indies).

After the Norman Conquest the manor of Chacombe, Northants, was given by William to Sir Hugh d'Anisy. *A descendant, Robert* Densey, *made a number of land gifts to the priory there in the 14th cent.*

Dantas Portuguese: topographic name, with fused preposition *de*, for someone who lived near a group of prehistoric standing stones, from the pl. form of OPort. *anta* dolmen (L *anta* pillar, pilaster).

Danton French: habitation name, with fused preposition *de*, from places in Isère and Haute-Savoie called *Anthon*. The placename is probably from an unrecorded Gaul. personal name rather than from a version of ANTHONY.

Danvers English (Norman): habitation name, with fused preposition *de*, from *Anvers*, the French form of the name of the Belgian town of Antwerp (Flem. *Antwerpen*, which gets its name from MDu. *an de werfen* at the wharf).

Danzig Jewish (Ashkenazic): local name from the Ger. form of *Gdańsk*, name of the major Baltic port that is now in Poland. The wide distribution and frequency of the name suggests that it may in many cases have been acquired by merchants who had visited the city or who regularly traded with it, as well as those who were actually born there.

Vars.: **Dantzig**, **Danzik**, **Dancyg**; **Danz(i)ger**, **Dancig(i)er**, **Dancyg(i)er**; **Dancigerkron** (an ornamental elaboration; cf. CORONA); **Danz** (from *Dants*, the Yid. name of the city); **Van Dantzig** (Du.); **G(e)danski**, **G(e)dansky** (from the Pol. name of the city). Forms with *-c-* show Pol. influence on the spelling.

Darby 1. English: habitation name from *Derby*, the county town of Derbys., and perhaps occasionally from the much smaller town of West *Derby* in Lancs. Both of these get their name from ON *djúr* deer (a cogn. of OE *dēor*; see DEAR 2) + *býr* farm, settlement. The usual spelling of the surname represents the pronunciation of both town and surname.

2. Irish: Anglicized form of Gael. *Ó Duibhdhiormaigh*; see DORMER.

3. Irish: Anglicized form of Gael. *Ó Diarmada*; see DERMOTT.

Vars.: **Darbey**, **Derby**.

Darbyshire English: 1. regional name from the hundred of West Derby in Lancs., which was often referred to in the Middle Ages as *Derbyshire*, from the name of the town + ME *schire* region, administrative district. The surname is still chiefly common in Lancs.

2. regional name from the county of Derbyshire, centred on the city of *Derby* (see DARBY).

Vars.: **Darbishire**, **Derbyshire**.

Darcy 1. English (Norman): habitation name, with fused preposition *de*, from *Arcy* in La Manche, so called from a Gaul. personal name (which, it has been suggested, may be akin to the Indo-European root *ars-* bear) + the local suffix *-ācum*.

2. Irish: Anglicized form of **Ó Dorchaidhe** 'descendant of the dark one', from *dorcha* dark, gloomy. This has fallen together with the Norman surname, which is certainly attested in Ireland, having been introduced there by Sir William D'Arcy (see below) and Sir John D'Arcy, who was appointed Chief Justiciar of Ireland in the 14th cent.

Vars.: **Darcey**, **D'Arcy**. (Of 2 only): **O'Dor(o)ghie**, **O'Dorchie**, **(O')Dorcey**, **Darky**.

Cogns. (of 1): Fr.: **Arcy**, **D'Arcy**, **Darcey**, **Darcet**.

A Norman de Arci *or* D'Arcy *was recorded in Domesday Book as lord of over 30 manors in Lincs. An Irish branch of the family was established in the 1360s in Co. Meath by Sir William D'Arcy (b. 1330). However, lands in Ireland had previously been granted to the family by Edward III because of their services at Crécy (1346).*

Dard French: from OF *dard* spur (of Gmc origin), and so probably in most cases a metonymic occupational name for a maker or seller of spurs, more rarely perhaps a nickname for a hasty or irritating individual. See also DARDE.

Darde French: from OF *darde* arrow (a byform of DARD; cf. Eng. DART 2), and so probably in most cases a metonymic occupational name for a maker of arrows or a bowman, more rarely perhaps a nickname for a swift runner.

Dims.: **Dardel(et)**, **Dardelin**, **Dardet**. Prov.: **Dardol**. (All of these could also derive from DARD.)

Darell English (Norman): habitation name, with fused prepositon *de*, from *Airel* in La Manche, Normandy, so called from LL *areālis*, open space, courtyard (an originally adj. deriv. of *area* threshing floor).

Vars.: **Darrell**; **Dorrell** (chiefly Worcs.).

Cogns.: Fr.: **Darel**, **Dareau**.

A family of this name trace their descent from William Darell, *who was living at Sesay, Yorks., in the reign of King John (1199–1216).*

Dargan Irish: Anglicized form of Gael. **Ó Deargáin** 'descendant of *Deargán*', a byname from a dim. of *dearg* red.

Var.: DORGAN.

Dark English: nickname for someone with dark hair or a dark complexion, from ME *darke*, OE *deorc* dark. The surname is most frequently found in the W Country.

Vars.: **Darke**, **Durk**.

Patr.: **Darkes**.

Darley English: habitation name from either of two places in Derbys., so called from OE *dēor* beast, deer (see DEAR 2) + *lēah* wood, clearing.

Darling English: from ME *derling*, OE *dēorling* darling, beloved one, a deriv. of *dēor* dear, beloved (see DEAR 1). This was quite a common OE byname, which remained current as a given name into the 14th cent. The surname probably derives at least in part from this use, probably in part also from a ME nickname. The surname is common in Scotland and also occurs in Ireland. In these areas it may represent a translation of FARQUHAR.

Vars.: **Dearling**, **Dorling**; **Dyrling** (from the OE byform *dyrling*).

Darlington English: habitation name from a place in Co. Durham, recorded in *c.*1009 as *Dearthingtun*, from OE *Dēornōðingtūn* 'settlement (OE *tūn*) associated with *Dēornōð*', a personal name composed of the elements *dēor* dear + *nōð* daring.

Darras French: habitation name, with fused preposition *de*, from various places called *Arras*. The one in Pas-de-Calais gets its name, in much reduced form, from having once been the seat of the Gaul. tribe of the *Atrebates*; that in Hautes-Pyrénées is named with the Basque elements *harr* stone + *ast* rocky peak; a further example in Ardèche is of impenetrable etymology.

Var.: **Daras**.

Darroch Scots: 1. habitation name from a place near Falkirk, in the former county of Stirlings., said to be so called from Gael. *darach* oak wood, a deriv. of *dara* oak.

2. from the Gael. personal name *Darach*, a deriv. of *dara* in the sense 'stout-hearted'; cf. ROBUSTI.

Vars.: **Darrach**, **Darragh**, **Darrow**.

Dart English: 1. topographic name for someone living beside the river *Dart* in Devon, which apparently gets its name from a Brit. term meaning 'oak', and is thus a cogn. of DARWIN 2.

2. metonymic occupational name for a maker of arrows, from ME *dart* (OF *darde*; see DARDE).

Darvill English: probably a Norman habitation name, with fused preposition *de*, from *Arville* in Seine-et-Marne, which is so called from the Gmc personal name *Ara* 'Eagle' + OF *ville* settlement, village.

Var.: **Darvell**.

Darwin 1. English: apparently from the OE personal name *Dēorwine*, composed of the elements *dēor* dear + *wine* friend. This name is attested in the 10th cent., but it was apparently not common; nevertheless it may have survived long enough to become a ME given name and so given rise to the surname.

2. English: habitation name from *Darwen* in Lancs., named from the river *Derwent* on which it stands. This seems to be a Brit. name derived from a word meaning 'oak' (cf. W *dâr* oak; see also DARROCH and DART 1).

3. Jewish: of unknown origin.

Var. (of 2): **Darwen**.

Dash English: topographic name for someone who lived near an ash tree, or habitation name from a place named with the OE word *æsc* (see ASH). The ANF preposition *de* of, from, has become fused to the name.

Dashwood English: topographic name for someone living in an ash wood, or habitation name for someone who came from a place called ASHWOOD. The ANF preposition *de* of, from, has become fused to the name.

Daubeney English (Norman): habitation name, with fused preposition *de*, from any of the various places in N France named with the Gallo-Roman personal name *Albinius* (a deriv. of *albus* white; cf. ALBAN and ALBIN) + the local suffix *-ācum*.

Vars.: **Daubeny, Daubney, Dabney, Dobney, D'Aubney**.

The name of the principal English Daubeney *family is derived from lands at* Aubigny *or* Aubigné, *Brittany, acquired in 1040. The family are descended from Eystein Glunold of Romsdal, Norway, who accompanied his nephew, Rollo, to France, where the latter became Duke of Normandy. Bearers of the name served as soldiers in France and Wales, including Sir Helié (or Elis)* D'Aubeney *(d. 1305), who served Edward I.*

Dauchez French: habitation name, with fused preposition *de*, from *Auchel* in Pas-de-Calais. The name is a dim. of that of the nearby *Auchy*, of which it was once a minor dependency. The name *Auchy* itself derives from the Gallo-Roman personal name *Alcius* (of uncertain origin) + the local suffix *-ācum*.

Daudet French: 1. from OF vernacular pronunciations, such as /dosde/, /dozde/, of the L phrase *Deus dedit* 'God has given', which was occasionally used as a given name in the Middle Ages; cf. DIEUDONNÉ and DONAT.

2. in Gascony it represents a local form of OProv. *doncel* young knight, squire (LL *dom(i)nicellus*, a dim. of *dominus* master).

Var. (of 1): **Daudé**.

Daum German and Jewish (Ashkenazic): nickname from Ger. *Daum* thumb (MHG *dūme*, OHG *thūmo*, a cogn. of OE *þūma*). This would have been acquired either by someone with a deformed or missing thumb, or by a very small person (cf. the folk tale of 'Tom Thumb').

Var.: Ger.: **Daumann**.

Cogns.: Low Ger.: **Duhm(e)**. Flem.: **Duym**. Du.: **Duim**.

Daumier Provençal: status name for a farmer who held his land by virtue of contributing a tithe of its produce to the landlord, OProv. *desmier*, *deumier* (a deriv. of *desme* tithe, L *decima (pars)* tenth).

Dim.: **Daumet**.

Pej.: **Daumard**.

Dauphin French: from a medieval given name (L *Delphīnus*, from *delphis* dolphin). This name was borne by a 4th-cent. saint who was bishop of Bordeaux, and from the early 12th cent. it was in use as a hereditary given name in the family of the counts of Albon, so that it soon came to be used as a title, and led to their territory being known as the *Dauphiné*. When it became part of the Kingdom of France in 1349, the title of *dauphin* thereafter denoted the heir apparent to the throne, and it is possible that in some cases this is the origin of the surname, as a nickname in the sense of 'prince'. The Italian cogns. may derive directly from a nickname for someone supposedly resembling a dolphin in some way.

Vars.: **Delphin, Delphy, Dalfin, Dalphy**.

Cogns.: It.: **Delfini, Delfino; Dalfini, Dalfino** (S Italy); **Dolfini, Dolfino** (Venetia).

Dim.: It.: **Dalfinelli**.

Pej.: Fr.: **Dauffard**.

Daval French: topographic name, with fused preposition *de*, for someone who lived downstream from the main settlement, from OF *aval* downstream (L *ad vallem* towards the valley, opposed to *ad montem* (OF *amont*) towards the hill, upstream).

Vars.: **Davau(x), Davault, Daveau**.

Davenport 1. English: habitation name from a place in Ches., so called from a Brit. river name (apparently a cogn. of MW *dafnu* to drop, trickle) + OE *port* market town.

2. Irish: Anglicized form of Gael. **Ó Donndubhartaigh** 'descendant of *Donndubhartach*', a personal name composed of the elements *donn* brown + *dubh* black + *artach* nobleman.

A Ches. family called Davenport *have been associated for centuries with the area around Macclesfield. They claim descent from Vivian* de Davenport *(d. c.1257). The family seat is still Capesthorne Hall, near Macclesfield.*

David Welsh, Scots, English, French, Portuguese, Czech, and Jewish: from the Hebr. male given name *David* 'Beloved'. The given name has been perennially popular among Jews, in honour of the biblical king of this name, the greatest of the early kings of Israel. His prominence, and the vivid narrative of his life contained in the First Book of Samuel, led to adoption of the given name on a limited scale among Christians throughout Europe in the Middle Ages. The friendship of David and Jonathan (1 Sam. 18: 1–4) was proverbial, adding significance to the name. Its popularity was increased in Britain firstly by virtue of its being the name of the patron saint of Wales (about whom very little is known: he was probably a 6th-cent. monk and bishop) and secondly because it was borne by two kings of Scotland (David I, reigned 1124–53, and David II, 1329–71). Its popularity in Russia is largely due to the fact that this was the church name adopted by St Gleb (d. 1015), one of the two sons of Vladimir, duke of Muscovy, who were martyred for their Christian zeal.

Vars.: Eng.: **Daud, Doud**. Ir.: **Davitt, Devitt; Daid, Dade; Taaffe**. Welsh: **Dewi** (an early form); **Dafydd** (a later form), **Daffey, Taffie, Taffee**. Fr.: **Davy**. Jewish: **David(a)i, Davidy** (with the Hebr. ending *-i*); **Davidman, Dawid(man)**.

Cogns.: It.: **David(d)e, David(d)i, Davitti**. Pol.: **Dawid**. Hung.: **Dávid**.

Dims.: Eng.: DAW, DAY. Sc., Ir.: DAVIE. Fr.: **Davet, Davin(et); Davidou** (Brittany). Prov.: **Davion, Daviot, Davioud**. Beloruss.: **Davydzenko**. Ukr.: **Davydenko**. Czech: **Davídek**.

Patrs.: Eng., Sc.: **Davids, Davidge, Davage; Davi(e)s, Davys; Dav(id)son, Davis(s)on**. Ir.: **McDavitt, McDevitt, McCavitt, McKevitt** (Gael. **Mac Daibhéid**); **McDaid, McDade, McCaet**. Sc.: **McDavid**. Rum.: **Davidescu**. Low Ger.: **Davidsen**. Du.: **Davids**. Dan.: **Davidsen**. Swed.: **Davidsson**. Jewish (Ashkenazic): **Davids; Davidso(h)n, Dawidsohn, Davidzon; Davidov(e), Davidof(f), Davidow; Davidowitz, Davidovitz, Davidovits, Davidovic(h), Davidovitch, Davidovics, Davidovicz, Davidowich, Dawidowitz, Dawidowi(ts)ch; Dawidowicz** (Pol. spelling); **Davidovici** (Rumanian spelling); **Davidovsky, Davidowsky, Dawidowsky, Davidofski** (E Ashkenazic; all sometimes Anglicized as *Davis*); **Davidesco, Davidescu** (among Rumanian Jews). Russ.: **Davidov, Davydov; Daudov** (from an Arabic form used in (Muslim) Turkic areas). Beloruss.: **Davidovich**. Pol.: **Dawidowicz**. Croatian: **Davidović, Daviǒ**. Lithuanian: **Dovidaitis, Dovydėnas**. Armenian: **Davidian**. Georgian: **Davitashvili**.

Patrs. (from dims.): Russ.: **Davydkov, Davydochkin, Davydychev**. Jewish: **Tewelson, Tevelov** (from Yid. *Tevele*).

An Irish family by the name of Taaffe *are first recorded in Co. Louth in the 13th cent.; they are said to be of Welsh origin, and to have arrived in Ireland with Strongbow in 1172. In the 17th cent. they held the earldom of Carlingford, which was bestowed as a reward for the family's support of the Stuarts. After the failure of the Stuart cause, branches of the family were established in Europe and rose to high office in Austria. Nicholas Taaffe (d. 1769) served in the Imperial army and was created a count of the Holy Roman Empire in 1758. A later Count Taaffe was Prime Minister of Austria-Hungary, 1879–93.*

Davie 1. Scots and Irish: dim. of DAVID.
2. English: var. of WAY (see below).

A family whose name is now found as Davie *originated from* Wey *or* Way *near Torrington, Devon. Their earliest recorded ancestor was William* de Wy *or* de la Wey, *living in the reign of Henry II (1154–89). The name later occurred as* de Vye *and* de Vie.

Davout French: nickname, originally *d'Avout*, for someone who was born in the month of August (OF *auoust*, from L (*mensis*) *Augustus*, from the name of the first Roman emperor), or who owed a feudal obligation to help with the harvest in that month.
Vars.: **Daou(s)t, Davous(t), Davoud; Laoust.**

Daw English: 1. pet form of DAVID.
2. nickname from the (jack)daw, ME *dawe*, a bird noted for its sleek black colour, raucous voice, and thievish nature, any of which characteristics could readily have given rise to a nickname. The word is probably derived from an unattested OE cogn. of OHG *tāha*.
3. Irish: Anglicized form of Gael. **Ó Deághaidh**, 'descendant of *Deághadh*', a personal name of uncertain etymology. It may be composed of the elements *deagh-* good + *ádh* luck, fate, and some such association seems to lie behind its Anglicization as GOODWIN.
Vars. (of 1–3): **Dawe**, Dow. (Of 3 only): **Ó Diaghaidh, O'Dea(y), O'Daa, O'Dawe, O'Daye, Dea**, DAY, DEE.
Dim. (of 1): **Dawkin.**
Patrs. (from 1): **Daw(e)s, Dawson.**
Patrs. (from 1) (dim.): **Dawkins, Dawkes, Daukes.**

Dawber English (chiefly Lancs.): occupational name for a builder using wattle and daub, from an agent deriv. of the ME verb *daube(n)* to coat with a layer of plaster, from OF *dauber*, L *dēalbāre* to coat with whitewash.

Day 1. English: pet form of DAVID.
2. English: from the ME given name *Day(e)* or *Dey(e)*, OE *Dæi*, apparently from OE *dæg* day, perhaps a short form of OE personal names such as *Dægberht* and *Dægmund*.
3. Irish: Anglicized form of Gael. *Ó Deághaidh*; see DAW.
Vars.: **Daye, Dey; D'Eye** (apparently no more than an orthographical affectation intended to make the name look French).
Dims. (of 1 and 2): **Daykin** (chiefly E Midlands); **Dakin.**
Patrs. (from 1 and 2): **Deyes; Dayson, Deason.**
'Servant of D. 1/2': **Dayman**, DIAMOND.

Dayan Jewish: occupational name from Hebrew *dayan* rabbinic judge.
Patrs.: **Ben-Dayan, Bar-Dayan.**

Deakin English: occupational name for a deacon, or perhaps more probably for his servant. In ME two forms coalesced: *deakne*, from OE, and *diacne*, from OF. Both are ultimately from LL *diaconus*, from Gk *diakonos* servant.
Vars.: **Deacon, Deakan.**
Cogns.: It.: **Diacono; (Lo) Iacono, (Lo) Jacono** (S Italy); **Zago, Zaghi** (Venetia). Beloruss.: **Dzyak.** Hung.: **Deák.**
Dims.: It.: **Diagonetti; Zaghetto, Zaghetti, Zaghino, Zaghini, Zagotto, Zagotti** (Venetia). Ukr.: **Dyachenko.**
Patrs.: Eng.: **Deakins.** It.: **Dello Iacono, Dello Jacono.** Rum.: **Diaconescu.** Russ.: **Dyakonov.**

Dean English: 1. topographic name from ME *dene* valley (OE *denu*), or habitation name from a place named with this word.
2. nickname for someone thought to resemble a dean, an ecclesiastical official who was the head of a chapter of canons in a cathedral, or perhaps more probably an occupational name for a servant of a dean. The ME word *deen* is a borrowing of OF *d(e)ien*, from L *decanus* (originally a leader of ten men, from *decem* ten).
Vars.: **Deen; Dane** (see also DENCH); DAIN. (Of 1 only): **Deane** (in so far as the final *-e* is a survival of the OE dat. case, and not merely a spelling var.); **Deaner, Denner;** DENMAN; **Adeane, Atherden, A'Deane.**
Cogns. (of 2): Fr.: **Doyen, Ledoyen.** Prov.: **Dega(n), Degas.** It.: **Degani; Degano** (S Italy); **Deganu** (Sicily); **Degan** (Venetia); **De Gan** (a misdivision). Ger.: **Dechan(d)t** (the title being used in the Middle Ages for various civil functionaries as well as the clerical office). Flem., Du.: **De Deken.** Hung.: **Dkány.**
Dims. (of 2): It.: **Deganut(ti).**
Patrs. (from 2): Eng.: **Deans** (chiefly Scot.); **Danes; Denson, Densum.** It.: **Dal Degan.** Flem., Du.: **Dekens.**
'Descendant of the D. 2': Ir.: **O'D(y)eane** (Gael. **Ó Déaghain**).

Dear English: 1. from the ME personal name *Dere*, OE *Dēora*, in part a short form of various cpd names with the first element *dēor* dear, in part a byname meaning 'Beloved'.
2. nickname from ME *dere*, OE *dēor* wild animal, or from the adj. of the same form, meaning 'wild', 'fierce'. By the ME period the adj. was falling out of use, and the noun was beginning to be restricted to the sense of mod. Eng. *deer*, so that this may be the sense of the surname in some cases.
Vars.: **D(c)are, Deer(e); Dearman, Dorman, Durman.**
Cogns. (of 1): Jewish (Ashkenazic, ornamental): **Teuer** (from Ger. *teuer*); **Tayer, Taier, Tajer** (from Yid. *tayer*; the last is a Pol. spelling); **Teuerstein, Teyerstein** ('dear' + 'stone'). (Of 2): Ger.: **Thier, Dier.** Flem.: **De Diere.** Fris.: **Duursma.** Dan.: **Dyhr.**
Patrs. (from 1): Eng.: **Dearing, De(e)ring, Doring; Deares; Dearson, Dairson.** Dan.: **Dyhring.**

Dearden English (Lancs.): habitation name from a place near Edenfield, so called from OE *dēor* beast, deer (see DEAR 2) + *denu* valley (see DEAN 1).
Vars.: **Durden, Duerden.**

Deasy Irish: Anglicized form of Gael. **Déiseach**, a nickname for a member of the vassal community known as the *Déis*, a term of uncertain meaning and origin.
Var.: **Deacy.**

Death English: 1. nickname from ME *de(e)th* death, OE *dēað*, which might have been acquired by someone who had played the part of the personified figure of Death in a pageant or play, or else one who was habitually gloomy or sickly.
2. metonymic occupational name for a gatherer or seller of kindling, from ME *dethe* fuel, tinder (OE *dȳð*).
3. supposedly a habitation name, with fused preposition *de*, from *Ath* in Belgium. However, modern spellings that divide the name into two elements may be no more than attempts to avoid the unpleasant associations of the vocab. word, and the derivation may in fact be as in 1.
Vars.: **Deeth, Dearth, D'Eath, D'Aeth, De Ath.**
Cogn. (of 1): Ger.: TOTH.

Deathridge English (chiefly W Midlands): of uncertain origin. According to Reaney, it is derived from ME *dethe-wright*, which is an occupational name for one who chopped up wood into tinder, from ME *dethe* tinder (see DEATH 2) + *wryht* maker (see WRIGHT).

Var.: **Detheridge**.

Debank English: Huguenot importation of unknown origin, perhaps a topographic name (with preposition *de*) from F *banc* bench, bank, possibly referring to a terrace on a hillside.

Var.: **Debanc, Debanks**.

This was a common Huguenot name in the 17th and 18th cents. The earliest known bearers in England are three people called Thomas Debanck *of Hartshorne, Derbys. (father, son, and grandson, from 1611); Nathaniel* Debanke *of Martock, Somerset (1655); and Joseph Debanke, a weaver in London (1656).*

Debbage English: habitation name from *Debach* in Suffolk, which derives its name from the OE river name *Dēopa* 'Deep' + OE *bæc* ridge. The surname is largely confined to E Anglia.

Debenham English: habitation name from a place in Suffolk, probably so called from the gen. case of the OE river name *Dēopa* (see DEBBAGE) + OE *hām* homestead.

Vars.: **Debnam, De(a)dman**.

Debrie French: habitation name, with fused preposition *de*, from *Brie* in Seine-et-Marne, apparently so called from the Gaul. element *briga* hill (cf. BRYAN).

Var.: **Debray**.

Debussy French: habitation name, with fused preposition *de*, from various places called *Bussy*. The placename has two possible origins. On the one hand it may be from a Gallo-Roman personal name *Buccius* (perhaps a deriv. of LL *bucca* mouth, cf. BOCCA) + the local suffix *-ācum*. On the other hand it may also be from LL *buxācum* grove of box trees (see BOX), with perhaps some confusion with *bus*, a regional form of OF *bois* wood (see BUSH).

Decaux French: habitation name, with fused preposition *de*, from various places called *Caux*. These seem to derive their name from two distinct sources: on the one hand from L *cavus* hollow, and on the other more distantly from a pre-Roman element *kal*, which probably meant 'rock' or 'stone'.

Déchaux French: nickname for someone in the habit of going barefoot, whether an ascetic or a poor man who could not afford footwear, from OF *deschaux* barefoot (LL *discalceus*, for class. L *discalceātus*, from the privative prefix *dis-* + a deriv. of *calceus* sandal, shoe).

Decker 1. German: occupational name for a thatcher or for a maker of blankets or matting, from an agent deriv. of MHG *decke* covering (from MHG, OHG *decken* to cover), a word which was normally used to refer to roofs, but sometimes also to other sorts of covering; mod. Ger. *Decke* still has the twin senses 'ceiling' and 'blanket'. See also THATCHER.

2. English: var. of DITCH.

Vars. (of 1): **Deckert; Döcker** (Bavaria); **Deckwer(th), Deckwarth** (see WRIGHT).

Cogns. (of 1): Low Ger., Du.: **Dekker**. Flem.: **De Decker**. Pol.: **Dekownik** (the vocab. word having been borrowed from MHG).

Patrs. (from 1): Low Ger.: **Deckers**. Du.: **Dekkers, Deckers**.

Decourcey English (Norman): habitation name, with fused preposition *de*, from any of various places in Normandy called *Courcy*, from the Gallo-Roman personal name *Curtius* (a deriv. of *curtus* short; cf. COURT 2) + the local suffix *-ācum*.

Vars.: **De Courcy, (De) Coursey**.

This is the name of an Irish family which can be traced back to Patrick de Courcy, *who was appointed justiciar of Ireland in 1221 and died at some date before 1261.*

Dee 1. Welsh: nickname for a swarthy person, from W *du* dark, black; cf. DUFF.

2. Irish: var. of DAW 3.

3. English and Scots: topographic name for someone living on the banks of the river *Dee* in Ches. or one of the same name in Scotland. The origin of both of these is a Brit. word meaning 'sacred'.

Deegan Irish: Anglicized form of Gael. **Ó Duibhginn** 'descendant of *Dubhceann*', a byname from *dubh* black + *ceann* head.

Vars.: **Deegin, D(u)igan, Deighan, Deehan, Dig(g)in**; DUFFIN.

Dims.: **O'Duigenain, Duignan, D(u)ignam, Di(e)gnan, Dignen** (Gael. **Ó Duibhgeannáin**).

Deeley English (common in the Birmingham area): of unknown origin, possibly a var. of DALY.

Deery Irish: 1. Anglicized form of Gael. **Ó Daighre** 'descendant of *Daighre*', a byname meaning 'Fiery'.

2. var. of DWYER.

Degenschein Jewish (Ashkenazic): ornamental name meaning 'sword shine', from Ger. *Degen* sword, rapier + *Schein* shine.

Vars.: **Degenszejn, Degenszajn** (E Ashkenazic, Pol. spellings).

Deighton English (chiefly Yorks.): habitation name from one of several places in Yorks. so called from OE *dīc* ditch, dyke + *tūn* enclosure, settlement. See also DITTON.

Vars.: **Dighton, Dightham**.

Deinhard German: from a Gmc personal name composed of the elements *degen* warrior, hero + *hard* hardy, brave, strong.

Vars.: **Degenhard, Deinhardt; Dönhardt** (Bavaria); **Deinert, Dennert**.

Cogns.: Low Ger.: **Dehnhardt, Dähnhard(t), Dehnert, Dahnert, Thienert**.

Dims.: Ger.: **Dein(lein), Dennerlein, Theinel(t); Deindl** (Bavaria); **Thiendl, Dienl** (Austria). Low Ger.: **Dehn, Denecke, Dehn(e)cke, Denicke, Dänecke**.

Patrs. (from dims.): Low Ger.: **Dehning, Dehns**.

Delahunty Irish: Anglicized form of Gael. **Ó Dulchaointigh** 'descendant of *Dulchaointeach*', a byname composed of the elements *dul* satirist + *caointeach* plaintive.

Vars.: **Ó Dulchonta; Delahunt, Dolohunty, Dulanty, Dulinty**.

Delaitre French: topographic name, with fused preposition and article *del*, for someone who lived near a churchyard or cemetery, OF *aitre* (L *atrium* courtyard).

Vars.: **Delaite, Delatte; Delattre** (see also DELÂTRE).

Delamare English and French: habitation name, with fused preposition *de*, from one of the places in Normandy called *La Mare*, from ONF *la* the + *mare* pool, pond (ON *marr*). In England the surname was later understood as ANF *de la* of the + ME *mere* pool (OE *mere*, a cogn. of the ON word) or *more* moor (OE *mōr*; see MOORE 1).

Vars.: Eng.: **Delamar, Delamere, Delamore, Dallamore, Dallimore, Dillamore, Dol(l)amore, Dolle(y)more, Dollimore, Dollymore**. Fr.: **Delamarre; Demare, Démare; Lamar(r)e, Lamard; Mare**.

Delaney 1. English (Norman): habitation name, with fused preposition and article *del*, from any of various minor places in Normandy so called from OF *aunaie* alder grove (L *alnētum*, collective of *alnus* alder).

2. Irish: Anglicized form, influenced by the Norman name, of Gael. **Ó Dubhshláine** 'descendant of *Dubhshláine*', a personal name composed of the elements *dubh* black (cf. DUFF) + *slán* challenge, defiance.

Vars.: **Delany, Delaun(e)y, Deleaney**. (Of 1 only): **Dawney, Dawnay, Dauney, Daunay**; DANDO. (Of 2 only): **O'Dowlaney, O'Dulaney**. See also DOLAN.

Cogns. (of 1): Fr.: **Delaunay, Delauney, Delaunoy, Delaunois; Launay, Launoy, Launois; Aunay, Auneau.**

The Dawnay *family who hold the title Viscount Downe trace their descent from Sir Nicholas* Daunay, *who was summoned to Parliament in the 14th cent.*

Delâtre French: topographic name, with fused preposition and article *del*, for someone who lived by a paved area, or occupational name for someone who tended the hearth in a manor hall, from OF *astre* hearth (LL *astricum*, from Gk *ostrakon* tile).

Vars.: **Dela(i)stre, Delestre; Delattre** (see also DELAITRE).

Delgado Spanish and Portuguese: nickname for a thin person, from Sp., Port. *delgado* slender (L *dēlicātus* dainty, exquisite, a deriv. of *dēliciae* delight, joy, from *dēlicere* to lure, seduce). It is also possible that the etymological meaning persisted as a pej. nickname.

Dim.: **Delgadillo.**

Dell English: topographic name for someone who lived in a small valley, from ME, OE *dell* dell, valley.

Vars.: **Deller, Dellar,** DELMAN.

Delman 1. English: var. of DELL.

2. Jewish (Ashkenazic): of unknown origin.

Var. (of 1): **Delleman.**

Dembitzer Jewish (Ashkenazic): habitation name, Yid. *Dembitser*, for a native or inhabitant of *Dembits*, Yid. name of *Dębica*, a town in SE Poland, which derives its name from Pol. *dęby* oaks, pl. of *dąb* oak (cf. DĄBROWSKI, DUBNIKOV).

Demidov Russian: patr. from the given name *Demid* (earlier *Diomid*, from Gk *Diomēdēs*, composed of the elements *Zeus*, gen. *Dios*, the principle Indo-European god, whose name is akin to the word meaning 'day' + *mēd-* counsel, deliberation). The name was borne by a 3rd-cent. Christian saint martyred in Bithynia under Diocletian.

Dims.: Beloruss.: **Demidyonok.** Ukr.: **Demidas.** See also DAMYON for several forms which may derive from either name.

Dempsey Irish: Anglicized form of Gael. **Ó Díomasaigh** and **Mac Díomasaigh** 'descendant' and 'son of *Díomasach*', a byname meaning 'Proud', 'Haughty', from *díomas* pride. The name was occasionally Anglicized as **Proudman** (see PROUD).

Vars.: **Dempsy; O'Dempsey; McGimpsey.**

Dempster Scots, Manx, and English: occupational name for a judge or arbiter of minor disputes, from OE *dēm(e)stre*, a deriv. of *dēmian* to judge, pronounce judgement. Although this was originally a fem. form of the masc. *dēmere*, by the ME period the suffix *-stre* had lost its fem. force, and the term was used of both sexes (cf. *Baxter* at BAKER, and *Webster* at WEBB). The surname is not common in England, where the term was early replaced by ANF JUDGE, but relatively frequent in Scotland, where until 1747 every laird of a barony could have certain offences within his territory tried by his *dempster*, and on the Isle of Man, where *deemsters* also played an important part in the administration of justice.

Vars.: **De(e)mer, Deamer** (from OE *dēmere*, see above); **Deem, Deam, Dome** (from the OE root word, *dēma*, *dōma*, which likewise meant arbiter or judge); **De(e)ming** (from OE *dēmung* judgement, act of judging).

Patr.: **Demers.**

Denby English: habitation name from places in Derbys. and W Yorks. This placename has the same origin as DANBY, but the ON first element has been replaced by the cogn. OE *Dene*.

Vars.: **Denb(e)igh.**

Dench English: ethnic name for someone from Denmark, from ME *den(s)ch* Danish (OE *denisc*). The Danes probably originally gained their name from a proto-Gmc cogn. of OE *denu* valley (see DEAN 1), with reference to their inhabitation of a low-lying area. There were many Danes in England in the Middle Ages, not only the long-established settlers in the Danelaw region, but also more recent immigrants.

Vars.: **Dentch, Dennish; Dence, Denns** (N English, Scots); **Danais, Dennys,** DENNIS (from ME/OF *danais*); **Dane** (see also DEAN).

Vars.: Fr.: **Danay(s), Danois, Daney, Dané.** Prov.: **Danès.** It.: **Da(i)nese, Da(i)nesi; Danise, Danisi** (S Italy). Ger.: **Dähn(e), Dehn(e).** Flem., Du.: **Deen.**

Pej.: Fr.: **Danard.**

Dennys *is the name of a family that was established for centuries in Devon. It was first recorded there with Robert* le Daneis, *who held various manors, and who witnessed a charter in 1133.*

Dengler German: occupational name for a knife-sharpener, Ger. *Dengler*, from MHG *tengelen* to sharpen instruments (such as large knives, sickles, and scythes), originally by carefully angled hammer blows (from OHG *tangol* hammer).

Vars.: **Teng(e)ler, Tengel(mann).**

Denham English: habitation name from any of various places so called. One in Bucks. (near Uxbridge) and two in Suffolk get the name from OE *denu* valley (see DEAN 1) + *hām* homestead; another in Bucks. (near Quainton) was originally named in OE as *Duningdūn* 'hill (OE *dūn*; see DOWN 1) associated with *Dunna*', a byname meaning 'Brown' (see DUNN 2).

Denholm 1. Scots: habitation name from a place in S Scotland near Hawick, so called from OE *denu* valley (see DEAN 1) + *holm* piece of dry land in a fen (see HOLME 2).

2. English: habitation name from *Denholme* in W Yorks, so called from OE *denum*, dat. pl. of *denu* valley.

Var.: **Denholme.**

Denley English: apparently a habitation name, perhaps from an unidentified minor place so called from OE *denu* valley + *lēah* wood, clearing.

Var.: **Denly.**

The name is not common and is found mainly in Devon, Gloucs., and the Home Counties. A genealogy has been traced to James Denley *of Kempsford, Gloucs. (1678). John Denley of Maidstone, Kent, was burnt at the stake in 1555. The earliest known bearer is a certain Thomas* de Denley *(Oxford 1279), who probably came from* Delly *in Hailey, near Witney, Oxon., which is recorded as* Denleghe *in 1316.*

Denman 1. English (chiefly E Midlands): topographic name for someone who lived in a valley; see DEAN 1.

2. Jewish (Ashkenazic): of unknown origin.

An English family of this name trace their descent from William Denman, *who lived in the reign of Richard II (1377–99).*

Dennery French: habitation name, with fused preposition *de*, from either of two places, in Seine-et-Oise and Moselle, called *Ennery*, from the Gmc personal name *Hunheri* (composed of the elements *hūn* bear-cub + *heri*, *hari* army) + the local suffix *-ācum*.

Dennington English: habitation name from a place in Suffolk, recorded in Domesday Book as *Dingifetuna*, from the OE female personal name *Denegifu* (composed of the elements *Dene* Dane + *gifu* gift) + OE *tūn* enclosure, settlement.

Dennis 1. English: from the medieval given name *Den(n)is* (L *Dionysius*, Gk *Dionysios* '(follower) of *Dionysos*', an eastern god introduced to the classical pantheon at a relatively late date and bearing a name of probably Semitic origin). The name was borne by various early saints, including St Denis, the martyred 3rd-cent. bishop of Paris who became the patron of France; the popularity of the name in England from the 12th cent. onwards seems to have been largely due to Fr. influence. The fem. form *Dionysia* (in the vernacular likewise *Den(n)is*) is also found, and some examples of the surname may represent a metronymic form.

2. English: var. of DENCH.

3. Irish: Anglicized var. of DONOHUE.

Vars. (of 1): Eng.: **Den(n)iss, Denis(s), Dennes(s), Dinnis.**

Cogns. (of 1): Fr.: **Denis, Deny(s).** It.: **Dionis(i)o, Dionis(i), Doniso, Donisi, Denisi; D'Onisi, D'Onise** (by misdivision). Port.: **Dinis; Dionísio** (a learned form). Ger.: **Denis.** Low Ger.: **Denys, Dinnies, Dins(e).** Pol.: **Denys.** Czech: **Diviš, Divín(a).** Hung.: **Dénes, Dienes, Gyenes.**

Dims. (of 1): Eng.: **Denn(e), Din(n),** DENNY, **Dennet(t);** DYE; TENNEY. Fr.: **Deniset, Denizet, Denisot, Denizot, Deniseau, Denison; Niset, Nizet, Nisot, Nizot; Donizeau.** It.: **D(i)onisetti, D(i)onisetto.** Ger.: **Niess, Niesel, Nissle.** Low Ger.: **Nies(e), Nys, Niesgen, Nüss(gen); Nisius** (Latinized). Flem.: **Nys.** Du.: **Nijs.** Czech: **Divíšek.** Pol.: **Dziwisz.** Beloruss.: **D(z)enisenya.** Ukr.: **Denisyuk.**

Pejs.: Fr.: **Denisard, Nisard, Nizard.**

Patrs.: Eng.: **Den(n)ison.** Dan.: **Dinesen.** Fr.: **Audenis.** It.: **Addionisio, Addionizio.** Russ.: **Denisov, Denisyev.** Beloruss.: **Denisevich.** Ukr.: **Denisovich.**

Patrs. (from dims.): Eng.: **Dennitts.** Low Ger.: **Dinjes, Dinniges; Niessen, Neissen, Nüssen; Niesing, Neising.** Flem.: **Nyssen(s), Nisen.** Du.: **Nijssen, Niessen, Niezen.** Russ.: **Denyakin, Denyukhin, Denyagin.** Beloruss.: **D(z)eniskevich.**

Denniston Scots: habitation name from *Danzielstoun* in the former county of Renfrews. (now part of Strathclyde region), so called from the gen. case of the given name DANIEL + ME *toun*, *tone* settlement (OE *tūn*).

Robert Denniestoun, *who was admitted as a freeman of the Incorporation of Goldsmiths of Edinburgh in 1547, was known also as* Danielston.

Denny 1. English and Scots: dim. of DENNIS.

2. English: habitation name from a place in Cambs., apparently so called from OE *Dene* Dane + *ēg* island.

3. Scots: habitation name from a town in the former county of Stirlings.

4. Irish: Anglicized form of Gael. **Ó Duibhne** 'descendant of *Duibhne*', a byname meaning 'Ill-tempered', 'Disagreeable'.

Vars.: **Denney.** (Of 3 only): **Deen(e)y.**

Dent English: 1. habitation name from places in Cumb. and W Yorks., so called from a Brit. hill name cogn. with OIr. *dinn*, *dind* hill.

2. nickname from OF *dent* tooth (L *dens*, gen. *dentis*), bestowed on someone with some deficiency or peculiarity of dentition, or of a gluttonous or avaricious nature.

Cogns. (of 2): Fr.: **Dentu, Ledentu; (Le) Dantec** (Brittany).

Denton English and Scots: habitation name from any of the numerous places so called. The vast majority, including those in Cambs., Cumb., Dumfries, Co. Durham, Kent, Lancs., Lincs., Norfolk, Northumb., Oxon., Sussex, and W Yorks., get the name from OE *denu* valley (see DEAN 1) + *tūn* enclosure, settlement. An isolated example in Northants appears in Domesday Book as *Dodintone* 'settlement associated with *Dodda*'; see DODD.

A family of Scandinavian origin came via Ireland to Cumbria, where they settled in Nether Denton, and had acquired the surname de Denton *by about 1169.*

Denyer English: nickname for a poor or insignificant man, from the name of a very small medieval coin, ME, OF *denier* (L *dēnārius*, a deriv. of *decem* ten, since the Roman coin was worth ten asses).

Dermott Irish: Anglicized form of the Gael. personal name *Difharmait*, composed of the separative prefix *di-* + *farmat* envy, and apparently meaning 'free from envy'. This name was borne in Celtic legend by the lover of Gráinne, and in historical times by Diarmaid Mac Murchadha, the 12th-cent. King of Leinster whose appeal to the English for support led directly to the Anglo-Norman invasion of Ireland.

Patrs.: Ir.: **McDermot(t), McDermit, McDermid, McDerment.** Sc.: **Mac Diarmid, McDiarmond, McDairmid, McDairmond, McD(e)armid, McDe(a)rmont, McDerm(a)id, McDermand.** Manx: **Kermode, Cormode.**

'Descendant of D.': Ir.: **Dermody, Darmody,** DARBY (Gael. **Ó Diarmada**).

Derrick English: from the given name *Derrick*, now more commonly spelled *Derek*, earlier *Dederick*. This given name was introduced into England in the 15th cent., from Du. *Diederick*, *Dirck*; see TERRY. As a surname it is now most common in Somerset.

Cogns.: Ger.: **Diet(e)rich, Dittrich; Dietreich** (Austria). Low Ger.: **D(i)ederich, Dierck; Dörk** (N Rhineland). Fris.: **Derk.**

Dims.: Ger.: **Dieterle, Deitel, Dietle(in), Diet(h), Dietz(e), Die(t)sch; Dietschi** (Switzerland). Low Ger.: **D(i)ede; Dietmann, Dittman, Diehm; Dedeke; Die(h)l, Diehlmann, Dihl, Dilmann, Dehl** (Latinized **Delius**).

Patrs.: Low Ger.: **D(i)ericks, Dier(c)ks, Dirks, Dörks; Diedericksen, D(i)erksen, Dörk(s)en; Derering, Dierking.** Fris.: **Derksen.** Flem.: **Dier(i)ckx, Dierix, Dirks.** Du.: **Diedericks, Dirks(en), Derks(en).** Norw., Dan.: **Dideriks, Didriksen.**

Patrs. (from dims.): Ger.: **Dietler, Detels.** Low Ger.: **Didden(s); Dedeking, Dedekind, De(e)ken; D(i)ehls, De(h)lsen, Dehling.** Fris.: **Dietjen, Dekena.** Flem.: **Diets, Didden.**

The English composer Frederick Delius *(1862–1934) was of German descent. He was born in Bradford, Yorks., where his family was in the wool trade. Both his parents were born in Bielefeld, Germany, and his father became a naturalized British subject in 1850.*

Desborough English: 1. habitation name from a place in Bucks., so called from OE *dwostle* pennyroyal, an aromatic plant formerly much used in herbal cures + *beorg* hill.

2. habitation name from a place in Northants, which was originally named in OE as *Dēoresburh* 'fort (OE *burh*; see BURKE) of *Dēor*' (see DEAR 1).

Descartes French: habitation name, with fused preposition *de*, from places in the parishes of Rochecorbon and Sanzay in Indre-et-Loire called *Les Cartes*.

Desmond Irish: Anglicized form of Gael. **Ó Deasmhumhnaigh** 'descendant of the man from S Munster', from *deas* south + *Mumhain* Munster, so called from *Mumhu*, the name (of uncertain origin) of an ancient king of the region. The surname has passed into common use as a given name, not only in Ireland. Cf. ORMOND.
Vars.: **O'Dassuny, O'Dasshowne, O'Desmonde, O'Deason.**

Destombes French: topographic name, with fused preposition and article *des*, for someone who lived by a graveyard, perhaps also an occupational name for a grave digger, from the pl. form of OF *tombe* tomb, grave (LL *tumba* burial mound, from Gk *tymbos*).
Vars.: **Detombes, Destombe.**

Deutsch 1. German: ethnic name given in areas of mixed population to inhabitants speaking a Gmc rather than Slav. language, from Ger. *Deutsch* German (MHG *tiu(t)sch*, OHG *diutisk*, from *diot*, *deot*, people, race, from a Gmc root **þeudō-*).
2. Jewish (Ashkenazic): regional name for someone who had come from a German-speaking area to another part of Europe.
Vars.: **Deutscher.** (Of 1 only): **Deusch, Dutsch, Dutz; Deutschmann; Deutschländer.** (Of 2 only): **Deutschman; Deit(s)ch(man), Dayczman** (from Yid. *daytsh*), **Deichman** (see also DITCH); **Taitz, Teitz(man)** (from the NE Yid. dial. var. *tayts*).
Cogns.: It.: TEDESCO. Hung.: TÓTH.
Dims.: Ger.: **Dutschke, Dutzke.**

Devane Irish: 1. Anglicized form of Gael. **Ó Damháin** 'descendant of *Damhán*', a byname meaning 'Fawn' (a dim. of *damh* ox).
2. Anglicized form of **Ó Dubháin** 'descendant of *Dubhán*', a byname from a dim. of *dubh* black. There has been considerable confusion with DEVANEY.
Vars. (of 1): **Ó Daimhín; Davin(e)**, DEVIN. (Of 2): **O'Doy(a)ne, O'Do(w)ane, O'Downe, (O')Duan(e), Doane, Doone, Dune, Dewan**, DUFFIN; **Kidney** (the result of association with the homonymous *dubhán* kidney).

Devaney Irish: Anglicized form of Gael. **Ó Duibheannaigh** 'descendant of *Duibheannach*', a personal name of uncertain origin; the first element is *dubh* black, the second may be *eanach* marshy place. The surname has become inextricably confused with DEVANE.
Vars.: **Devany, Devenny.**

Deventer Dutch: 1. habitation name from a place in the province of Overijssel, recorded in 772 in the form *Daventre*. According to Bahlow the name is from prehistoric elements meaning 'marshy place'.
2. occupational name, with fused def. article, for a hawker or pedlar, from an agent deriv. of MDu. *venten* to sell (L *vendere*).
Vars. (of 1): **Van Deventer.** (Of 2): **Venter.**
Cogn. (of 2): Eng.: **Vender.**

Devereux English (Norman): habitation name, with fused preposition *de*, from *Evreux* in Eure, Normandy; see EVEREST.
Vars.: **Dever(e)aux, Devereu, Deveroux, Deverose.**
The name is common in Ireland, where it was first taken at the time of the Anglo-Norman invasion. One branch of the family became the most powerful Norman settlers in Wexford. It was also the family name of the Earls of Essex, who at the time of Elizabeth I had much to do with Ireland. Walter Devereux, *1st Earl of Essex (1541–76) attempted to colonize part of Ulster; his son Robert, the flamboyant 2nd Earl (1567–1601), was briefly lord lieutenant of Ireland in 1599, and encouraged English colonization.*

Devèze French: topographic name for a dweller by an enclosure to which access was forbidden, as for example a park or forest belonging to the lord of the manor, or occupational name for a guardian of such land. The word derives from L *dēfensa*, past part. of *dēfendere* to ward off, prohibit.
Var.: **Ladevèze** (with fused definite article *la*).

Deville 1. English: Norman habitation name from *Déville* in Seine-Maritime, probably so called from L *dei villa* 'settlement of (i.e. under the protection of) God'. This name was early interpreted as a prepositional phrase *de ville* or *de val* and applied to dwellers in a town or valley (see VILLE and VALE; and for a similar misapplication cf. DELAMARE).
2. English: nickname from ME *devyle*, OE *dēofol* devil (L *diabolus*, from Gk *diabolos* slanderer, enemy), referring to a mischievous youth or perhaps to someone who had acted the role of the Devil in a pageant or mystery play. Most of the modern variations in spelling and pronunciation are no more than attempts to disguise the unpleasant connotations of the word (cf., e.g., DEATH for similar processes).
3. French: var. of VILLE, with fused preposition *de*.
Vars.: **De Ville.** (Of 1 and 2 only): **Devill, Deaville, Deyville, D(e)avall, Devall, Divall, Divell, Davell, Davoll.**
Cogns. (of 2): Ger.: **Teuf(f)el, Teifel; Toifel** (Bavaria); **Deubel** (Swabia); **Deufel, Deifel, Deibel.** Low Ger.: **Düwel, Düvel.**
Robert de Daiville *held land in Yorks. and Notts.* c.*1120. A descendant, John* Deyville, *was a supporter of Simon de Montfort. He was the member for Notts. and Derbys. in the first English Parliament, and became the leader of the barons after de Montfort's death at Evesham in 1265. Another member of the same family, Goscelin Deyville, supported the Duke of Lancaster in the Wars of the Roses and was hanged, drawn, and quartered at York after the defeat of the Lancastrians at Boroughbridge in 1322. Henry* Davell *was the last abbot of Whitby at the time of the Dissolution of the Monasteries.*

Devin 1. English and French: nickname, of literal or ironic application, from ME, OF *devin*, *divin* excellent, perfect (L *dīvīnus* divine, god-like, a deriv. of *dīvus*, byform of *deus* god).
2. Russian: metronymic from *deva* girl, normally a designation of an illegitimate child. Sometimes it may be a patronymic from a nickname for an effeminate man.
3. Irish: var. of DEVANE.
Vars. (of 1): **Devine, Devinn, Deavin, Divine.**
Dims. (of 2): Russ.: **Dev(och)kin, Devushkin** (metrs.).

Devlin Irish and Scots: Anglicized form of Gael. **Ó Dobh(a)iléin** 'descendant of *Dobhailéan*', a personal name of uncertain origin, probably from a dim. of *dobhail* unlucky, unfortunate.
Vars.: **Ó Doibhlin; O'Devlin.**

Devonshire English: regional name for someone from the county of *Devon*. This was originally an ancient Brit. tribal name, OE *Defnas* men of Devon, L *Dumnonii*, perhaps meaning 'worshippers of the god *Dumnōnos*'.
Vars.: **Devonish, Devenish; Devon.**

Devoy Irish: Anglicized form of Gael. **Ó Dubhuidhe** 'descendant of *Dubhuidhe*', a personal name probably derived from *dubh* dark, black + *buidhe* sallow.
Vars.: **(O')Deev(e)y, Devey.**

Dewar Scots: 1. occupational name for a custodian of holy relics (which was normally a hereditary office), from Gael. *deoradh* pilgrim, stranger.

2. habitation name from a place near Dalkeith, of uncertain etymology. It may derive from the same word as in 1, from having once been the resting place of some relic, or it may be from Gael. *dubh* black, dark (see DUFF) + *ard* height, or from Brit. cogns. of W *du* black, dark + *ar* ploughed land.

There are two Scottish families which derive the same surname from different sources (see above). Members of the first were from the 13th cent. hereditary guardians of the relics of St Fillan. Another family originated in the parish of Dewar, Midlothian, where Thomas and Piers de Deware *rendered homage in 1296.*

Dewey English: of uncertain origin. It may be a Norman habitation name, from *Douai* in Nord, so called from the Gaul. personal name *Dous* (of uncertain meaning) + the local suffix *-ācum*.

Dewhurst English: habitation name from a place in Lancs., apparently so called from the adj. *dewy* + ME *hyrst* wooded hill (see HURST).

Vars.: **Dewhirst, Jewhurst.**

Diamond 1. English: var. of *Dayman*; see DAY. Forms with the excrescent dental are not found before the 17th cent., and are in part the result of folk etymology.

2. Jewish (Ashkenazic): Anglicized form of various Jewish surnames derived from mod. Ger. *Diamant*, *Demant*, or Yid. *dime(n)t*, all of which go back to MHG *dīemant* diamond (OF *diamant*, via L from Gk *adamas*, gen. *adamantos*, 'unconquerable', a reference to the hardness of the stone). The name is mostly ornamental, one of the many Ashkenazic surnames based on mineral names, though in some cases (esp. those vars. ending in *-man*) it may have been taken by jewellers. Cf. BRILLANT and JAGLOM.

Vars.: **Diamand, Diamant.** (Of 1 only): **Dayment, D(a)ymond, Dimond, Dimont, Dymont, Dyment.** (Of 2 only): **Diamont, Di(e)mant, Diament, Diment, Demant, Dymant; Dimet(man); Dymetman** (Pol. spelling).

Cpds (of 2): **Diamantstein, Diamandstein, Dimantstein, Diamontstein, Dime(n)tstein, Dyme(n)tsztain, Dymantsztain** ('diamond stone'); **Dimetbarg** ('diamond hill').

Dibb English: topographic name for someone living in a hollow, ME *dybbe*. The surname is most common in Yorks., where a number of minor placenames are formed from it.

Var.: **Dibbs.**

Dibden English: habitation name from a place in Hants, so called from OE *dēop* deep + *denu* valley (see DEAN 1).

Dichter 1. German: ostensibly an occupational name for a minstrel or poet, Ger. *Dichter*, from MHG *tichten* to compose, write (L *dictāre* recite, dictate, frequentative of *dīcere* to say).

2. Jewish (Ashkenazic): of uncertain origin. It is probably a nickname from Ger. *Dichter* poet, but could also be an inflected form of Ger. *dicht* thick. In neither case is the reason for the adoption of the word as a surname clear.

Var.: Jewish: **Dychterman** (E Ashkenazic, Pol. spelling).

Dick 1. Scots and English: pet form of RICHARD. Although found in every part of Britain, the form *Dick* is especially common in Scotland.

2. German and Jewish (Ashkenazic): nickname for a stout, thickset man, from Ger. *dick*, Yid. *dik* (MHG *dic(ke)*, OHG *dicki*, *dichi*).

3. German: topographic name for someone who lived by a thicket or patch of thickly grown undergrowth, from MHG *dicke*, a special use of *dic(ke)* thick (cf. Ger. *Dickicht* thicket).

Vars. (of 1): **Dicke;** DIGG. (Of 2): Jewish: **Dickman(n), Dik(er)man, Dickerman; Dykierman** (Pol. spelling). (Of 2 and 3): **Dicke.** See also DICKER.

Cogns. (of 2): Eng.: **Thick(e).** Flem.: **(De) Dick.** Du.: **Dik.**

Dims. (of 1): Eng.: **Dicken** (chiefly W Midlands), **Dickin, Diggen, Diggon, Dig(g)an; Dickie** (chiefly Scotland and N Ireland), **Dickey** (N Ireland), DIXIE (Scotland).

Patrs. (from 1): Eng.: **Dicks, Dix; Dickson** (chiefly Scotland and N Ireland); **Dixon** (chiefly N England and the Midlands); **Dixson.** (From 2): Eng.: **Thicks.** Flem.: **Dikken.** Du.: **Dikkes.**

Patrs. (from 1) (dims.): **Dickin(g)s, Dickens, Dickons, Diggin(g)s, Diggens, Digance; Dicketts; Dickels; Dickinson** (chiefly N England and the Midlands), **Dickison, Dickenson** (chiefly Midlands), **Dicke(r)son, Dickason.**

'Servant of D. 1': **Dickman; Digman** (see also DITCH).

Cpds (of 2): Jewish: **Dikfeld** ('thick field'); **Dickhoff** ('thick farm'); **Dickstein, Diks(h)tein, Diksztejn, Dickenstein** ('thick stone'; *Diksztejn* is a Pol. spelling). All of these compounds are semantically odd, and it is not clear how they were acquired as surnames.

Dicker 1. English: occupational name for a digger of ditches, or topographic name for someone living by a ditch or dyke; see DITCH.

2. English: regional name from an area of E Sussex, near Hellingly, called 'the *Dicker*', from ME *dyker* unit of ten (L *decuria*, from *decem* ten); the reason for the place being so named is not clear. It has been suggested that the reference is to a bundle of iron rods, in which sense *dicras* appears in Domesday Book. Such a bundle could have been the rent for property in this iron-working area. Surname forms such as *atte dicker* occur in the surrounding region in the 13th and 14th cents.

3. German and Jewish (Ashkenazic): inflected form of DICK 2.

Var. (of 3): **Dickert.**

Didier French: from a medieval given name (L *Dēsīderius*, a deriv. of *dēsīderium* desire, longing, given either to a longed-for child, or in expression of the Christian's spiritual longing for God). The name was borne by a 3rd-cent. bishop of Langres and a 6th-cent. bishop of Vienne in the Dauphiné, both of whom were locally venerated as saints.

Var.: **Dizier.**

Cogns.: It.: **Desideri(o).** Hung.: **Dezsö.**

Dims.: Fr.: **Didion, Did(i)ot, Dideron, Did(e)rot, Didelot, Didelet.**

Patrs.: Hung.: **Dessewffy, Dezsöffi.**

Diego Spanish: from the medieval given name *Diego*, *Diago*, which is of uncertain origin. It was early taken to be an aphetic form of SANTIAGO (cf. Port. *Tiago*), and is commonly taken by English speakers as being a form of JAMES, but this is no more than folk etymology. It is found in the Middle Ages in the L forms *Didacus* and *Didagus*, which Meyer-Lübke derived from Gk *didakhē* doctrine, teaching, but in view of the fact that it is unknown outside the Iberian Peninsula it may possibly have a pre-Roman origin.

Var.: **Diago.**

Cogn.: Port.: **Diogo.**

Patrs.: **Diéguez, Díez; Díaz.** Port.: **Dias.**

Diesel S German: from a given name, an aphetic diminutive form of *Mathies*; see MATTHEW.

Rudolf Diesel *(1858–1913) was a German engineer whose name has been given to the internal-combustion engine of which he was the inventor. He was born in Paris, where his Bavarian Lutheran parents had settled.*

Dietmar German: from a Gmc personal name composed of the elements ***þeudō-** people, race (OHG *diot*, *deot*) + *meri*, *mari* famous.
Vars.: **Dittmar, Dittmer, Diemar, Diemer**; **Dittmai(e)r, Dittmeyr** (the result of folk etymological association with MAYER).
Cogn.: Low Ger.: **Dettmer**.
Dims.: Ger.: **Diem, Thieme**. Low Ger.: **Dittmann**; TIMM.
Patrs.: Ger.: **Dittmers**. Low Ger.: **Dettmers**.

Dieudonné French: from a medieval given name (OF *Dieudonné* 'God-given', from L *deus* god + *dōnātus* given; cf. DAUDET and DONAT).
Vars: **Déodat, Deudat, Dêat, Diat, Diet, Diez, Dief** (all from the L form *Deodatus*).
Cogns.: Prov.: **Dioudonnat**. It.: **Deodato, Deodati**; **Diodato** (Naples); **Diodati** (Tuscany).

Dieulafoy French: nickname for someone who frequently employed this oath, OF *Dieu* God (L *deus*) + *la foy* (the) faith (L *(illa) fides*).
Cogn.: Prov.: **Dieulafé**.

Digby English: habitation name from *Digby* in Lincs., so called from OE *dīc* dyke (see DITCH) + ON *býr* farm, settlement.

Digg English: 1. var. of DICK 1.
2. nickname from some fancied resemblance to a duck, ME *digge* (of uncertain relation to OE *duce*; cf. DUCKETT).
Vars. (of 2): **Duck, Doke**.
Dim.: **Diggle**.
Patrs.: **Digges**. (From 2 only): **Duckes, Dooks**.
Patr. (from a dim.): **Diggles**.

Dillon 1. English and French: from the Gmc personal name *Dillo* (of uncertain origin, perhaps a byname from the root *dīl* destroy), introduced into England by the Normans. The surname derives from the OF oblique case of the name, ending in *-n*.
2. English: habitation name from *Dilwyn* near Hereford, recorded in 1138 as *Dilun*, probably from OE *dīglum*, dat. pl. case (originally used after a preposition) of *dīgol*, *digle* recess, retreat.
3. Irish (Norman): altered form of *de Leon*; see LYON and also further below.
4. Irish: Anglicized form of Gael. **Ó Duilleáin** 'descendant of *Duilleán*', a personal name of uncertain origin, probably a var. of *Dallán*, originally a byname meaning 'Blind man'.
5. Jewish: Anglicized form of **Dilon**, an Ashkenazic surname of uncertain origin, perhaps an altered form of Sefardic *de León*; see LYON.
Var. (of 3): **Dillane**.
Patr. (from 1) (dim.): **Dilks** (chiefly E Midlands).
An Irish family named Dillon *trace their descent from Sir Henry* de Leon, *who was a member of a noble Breton family. In 1185 he accompanied the Earl of Morton, later King John, into Ireland, and was granted large estates at Longford and Westmeath. His son used the surname* Dylon. *A number of members of this family were Jacobites who served in European armies in the 18th cent. They included Arthur Dillon (1750–94), a French Jacobin general, who was guillotined during the French Revolution.*

Dilworth English: habitation name from a place in Lancs. so called from OE *dile*, *dyle* dill (a medicinal herb) + *worð* enclosure (see WORTH).

Dimbleby English: habitation name from *Dembleby* in Lincs., which probably gets its name from an unattested ON antecedent of Northern ME *dimble* ravine with a watercourse in it (cf. mod. Norw. *dembel* pool) + ON *býr* farm, settlement.
Vars.: **Dimblebee, Dimbledee**.

Dineen Irish: Anglicized form of Gael. **Ó Duinnín** 'descendant of *Duinnín*', a byname from a dim. of *donn* brown, dark (see DUNN).
Vars.: **Dinneen, Dinan, Dunnion**; DUNNING, **Denning**; **O'Dunneen, O'Dunnion**).

Dines Jewish (Ashkenazic): metr. from the Yid. female given name *Dine* (from the Hebr. name *Dina* Dinah, which appears in Gen. 30: 21) + the Yid. possessive suffix *-s*.
Vars.: **Diness, Dinnis**; **Dineso(h)n, Dinzon**; **Dinin, Dinovitz, Dinowitz** (E Ashkenazic).

Dingle English: habitation name for someone living in a small wooded dell or hollow, ME *dingle* (of uncertain origin, perhaps akin to *dimble*; cf. DIMBLEBY). There is a district of Liverpool called *Dingle*.

Dingott Jewish (Ashkenazic): ornamental name composed of Yid. *din(en)* to serve + *got* God, or perhaps of the verb in the imperative, with the sense 'serve God!'

Dinsdale English: habitation name from a settlement on both sides of the river Tees, so partly in Co. Durham and partly in N Yorks. The name is from OE *Dīctūneshalh* 'nook, recess (OE *halh*; see HALE 1) belonging to DEIGHTON'.

Dion French: habitation name from any of various places called *Dion(s)* and *Dionne*, all apparently derived from a Gaul. element *divon-* (sacred) spring (cf. DEE 3).
Var.: **Dionne**.
Dim.: **Dion(n)et**.

Dios Spanish: nickname from Sp. *Dios* God (L *Deus*). The name seems to have been given either respectfully or mockingly to a notably pious person; in the later Middle Ages it may also have been used as a given name in honour of St John of God (Port. *João de Deus*, 1495–1550).
Cogn.: Port.: **Deus**.

Disley English: habitation name from a place so called in Ches., the origin of which is uncertain. Early forms were *Distislegh* and *Distelee*. The second element is clearly OE *lēah* wood, clearing; the first is obscure. Ekwall comments that the forms suggest a personal name, but no suitable candidate has been found.

Disney English (Norman): habitation name, with fused preposition *de*, from *Isigny* in Calvados, so called from the Gallo-Roman personal name *Isinius* (a Latinized form of Gaul. *Isina*) + the local suffix *-ācum*.

Diss English: habitation name from *Diss* in Suffolk, which gets its name from a Norman pronunciation of ME *diche*, OE *dīc* ditch, dyke; see DITCH.
This name was firmly established in E Anglia by the beginning of the 14th cent. From about 1550 to 1800 it is found mainly in N Essex, between Colchester and Haverhill.

Distel 1. German, Low German, Dutch, and Flemish: topographic name for someone who lived by a patch of ground overgrown with thistles, or perhaps a nickname for a 'prickly' person, from Ger. *Distel* thistle (MHG, MLG, MDu. *distel*; cf. OHG *distil(a)*, OE *ðistel*).
2. Jewish (Ashkenazic): probably in most cases an unflattering name bestowed on Jews by non-Jewish government officials in 18th- and 19th-cent. central Europe.

Vars.: Ger.: **Diestel**, **Distler**, **Di(e)stelmann**. Jewish: **Distelman**; **Distelfeld**.

Ditch English: topographic name for someone who lived by a ditch or dyke, ME *diche*, *dike*, OE *dīc* dyke, earthwork. The medieval dyke was larger and more prominent than the modern ditch, and was usually constructed for purposes of defence rather than drainage. Mod. Eng. *ditch* represents the regular development of the nominative of the OE word; *dyke* may be from OE oblique cases, reinforced by ON *díki*.

Vars.: **Deetch**; **Dike(s)**, **Dyke(s)**; **Deek(e)s**, **Deakes**, **Deex**; DISS; **Ditcher**, **Deetcher**, DICKER, DECKER, **Deeker**; **Dickman**, **Digman** (see also DICK).

Cogns.: Low Ger.: **Dieck(mann)**, **Zumdieck**; **Tendyck** (N Rhineland); **Tomdieck** (Westphalia). Fris.: **Deickstra**, **Dijkstra**, **Dykstra**; **Dijkema**, **Dykema**; **Opdyck**. Flem.: **Van Dy(c)k**, **Dykman**. Du.: **Van Dij(c)k**, **Van Dy(c)k**, **Van Dijken**, **Van Dyken**; **Dijkman**, **Dykman**.

Ditchburn English: habitation name from a place in Northumb., so called from OE *dīc* DITCH, dyke + *burna* stream (see BOURNE).

Ditchfield English (Lancs.): habitation name from a hamlet near Widnes, so called from OE *dīc* DITCH, dyke + *feld* pasture, open country (see FIELD).

Ditton English: 1. habitation name from any of the numerous places so called, from OE *dīc* DITCH, dyke + *tūn* enclosure, settlement.

2. from *Ditton* in Shrops., a var. of DODDINGTON.

Var.: DEIGHTON.

Diver 1. Irish: var. of DWYER.

2. English, of uncertain origin: possibly from the vocab. word *diver*, an agent deriv. of ME *dive* dip, plunge (OE *dȳfan*), but if so the application is obscure. It may be a nickname for someone compared to a diving bird (cf. DUCKER).

3. Jewish: of unknown origin.

Patr. (from 2): **Divers**.

Dives French and English (Norman): habitation name from places in Calvados and Oise, both of which get their names from the river *Dive* on which they stand. The name is of Gaul. origin and meant 'sacred' (cf. DEE 3 and DION).

Var.: Fr.: **Dive**.

Dixie English: 1. generally a dim. of DICK 1.

2. according to Reaney and Dauzat, a nickname for a chorister, from L *dixi* I have spoken, the first word of the 39th Psalm.

Vars.: **Dixey**, **Dixcee**, **Dixcey**, **Dicksee**.

Cogn. (of 2): Fr.: **Dixi**.

Dmitriev Russian: patr. from the given name *Dmitri*, from Gk *Dēmētrios* '(follower) of *Dēmētēr*', the goddess of fertility, whose name derives from an obscure element *dē*, sometimes taken as a Doric equivalent of Attic *gē* earth + *mētēr* mother. This ostensibly pagan name was in fact borne by several early Christian martyrs, and its popularity in E Europe is largely due to the fame of a 4th-cent. saint executed under Diocletian.

Vars.: **Dimitriev** (from an earlier unsyncopated form); **Dmitrievski** (a clerical elaboration).

Cogns. (patrs.): Beloruss.: **Zmitrovich**. Croatian: **Dimitrijević**, **Dmitrović**; **Mitrović**. Bulg.: **Dimitrov**. Pol.: **Dymidowicz**. Rum.: **Dimitresco**, **Dumitrescu**. Gk: **Demetriou**, **Demetriades**.

Cogns. (not patrs.): Czech: **Demet(e)r**, **Dmych**. Rum.: **Dimitrie**, **Dumitru**. Hung.: **Demeter**, **Dömötör**. It.: **Mitro**; **De Mitri(s)** (ostensibly a patr., but actually the result of misdivision).

Dims. (patrs.): Russ.: **Mit(k)in**, **Mitkov**, **Mityakov**, **Mityukov**, **Mityashev**, **Mityashin**, **Mityush(k)in**, **Mitykhin**, **Mityanin**, **Mit(r)yaev**, **Mitasov**, **Mitusov**, **Mityagin**, **Mityurev**, **Mitrikov**, **Mitrukov**, **Mitrosh(k)in**, **Mitroshinov**, **Mitrikhin**, **Michurin** (see also MITROFANOV). Beloruss.: **Mitskevich**. Pol.: **Demkowicz**; **Mickiewicz** (of Beloruss. origin). Croatian: **Dimić**, **Mitić**.

Dims. (not patrs.): Beloruss: **Dmiterko**, **Zmitruk**, **Zmitrichenko**. Ukr.: **Dmiterko**, **Dmitruk**, **Dmitri(ch)enko**. Pol.: **Dmytryk**, **Demko**; **Mićka**. Czech: **Demčák**, **Demčík**, **Dmíšek**. Hung.: **Deme**, **Döme**.

Habitation names: Pol.: **Demitrowski**, **Demkowski**.

Dobb English: from the medieval given name *Dobbe*, a pet form of ROBERT. The surname is esp. common in N England and the Midlands.

Var.: **Dobbe**.

Dims.: **Dob(b)ie**, **Dob(b)y**, **Dobey** (chiefly Scotland); DOBKIN; **Dobbin(g)**, **Dobbyn**, **Dobing** (chiefly N Ireland); **Dabinett**.

Patrs.: **Dobbs**, **Dab(b)s**; **Dobson**, **Dopson**, **Dabson**.

Patrs. (from dims.): **Dobbin(g)s**; **Dob(b)inson**, **Dobbison**, **Dobieson**.

Dobbin *is the name of an Irish family who were prominent in the affairs of Carrickfergus from 1400, when Peter* Dobyn *was constable of the castle. They provided a number of sheriffs and mayors of the city, and one of them was mayor of Waterford in 1460.*

Dobel 1. English (Norman): nickname from OF *doubel* twin (lit. 'double', from LL *duplus*, class. L *duplex*, from *du(o)* two + *plek-*, a root meaning 'fold'). See also BESSON and JUMEAU.

2. German: var. of TOBEL.

Vars. (of 1): **Do(u)bell**, **Do(u)ble**, **Doubble**. (Of 2): **Dobelmann**, **Dobler**.

Dobkin 1. English: dim. of DOBB.

2. Jewish (E Ashkenazic): dim. of DOBRIN.

Dobrin Jewish (E Ashkenazic): metr. from the Yid. female given name *Dobre* 'Good'; cf. DOBRYNIN.

Dims.: DOBKIN, **Dopkin** (from the Yid. dim. given name *Dobe*, a pet form of *Dobe*, var. of *Dobre*).

Dobronravov Russian: patr. from the nickname *Dobronravy* 'Pleasant', 'Well-mannered' (a cpd of *dobry* good (cf. DOBRYNIN) + *nrav* manner).

Dobrovolski Russian: compound surname meaning 'good will', composed of the elements *dobry* good (cf. DOBRYNIN) + *volya* will + the (orig. Pol.) suffix of surnames *-ski* (see BARANOWSKI). According to Unbegaun, the Russ. name is a made-up surname of the type assumed by Orthodox priests. Bystroń indicates that the Pol. cogn. is either from villages named *Dobrowole* or *Dobrawola* or from nicknames denoting peasants who had been freed from serfdom. In Czech, on the other hand, Moldanová says that the name was bestowed as a nickname on one who voluntarily accepted serfdom.

Cogns.: Pol.: **Dobrowolski**. Czech: **Dobrovolný**.

Dobrovský Czech: 1. habitation name from a place called *Dobrovice*, named with the element *dobrý* good.

2. var. of DOBRÝ.

Dobrý Czech: nickname for a good man, from Czech *dobrý* good.

Var.: DOBROVSKÝ.

Cogns.: Pol.: **Dobroń**, **Dobroniak**. Rum.: **Dobre**.

Patrs.: Croatian: **Dobrić**. Rum.: **Dobrescu**.

Dobrynin Russian: patr. from the given name *Dobryna*, a short form of the various Slav. personal names with a first element *dobr-* good, kind. Such names, which had originated in a pagan culture and not been made respectable by any saint, were frowned upon by the Orthodox Church and not accepted as baptismal names, but nevertheless they were relatively common as unofficial names among the peasantry.

Cogns.: Bulg.: **Dobrovich(ev)**, **Dobrovev** (patrs.).

Dim.: Russ.: **Dobryshin** (patr.).

Dobrzyński Polish: habitation name from a place called *Dobrzyń*, named with the element *dobrzy* good.

Dočekal Czech: nickname of uncertain application, from Czech *dočekat* to wait long enough (composed of the perfective prefix *do-* + *čekat* to wait). It may have signified a person who had lived to a great age.

Var.: **Dočkal**.

Docker English: habitation name from places in Lancs. and Cumb. so called from ON *dokk* hollow, valley + *erg* shieling or dairy building (of Celt. origin). The name is now found chiefly in the W Midlands.

Dockray 1. English: habitation name from any of several places so called, of which there are four in Cumb. The probable origin is ON *dokk* hollow, valley + *vrá* isolated place; the first element may, however, be OE *docce* dock (the plant).

2. Irish: Anglicized form of Gael. **Ó Dochraidh** 'descendant of *Dochrach*', a variant of *Dochartach*; see DOHERTY.

Vars.: **Dockeray**, **Dock(e)ry**, **Docwra(y)**.

Dodd 1. English: from the ME personal name *Dodde*, *Dudde*, OE *Dodda*, *Dudda*, which remained in fairly widespread and frequent use in England until the 14th cent. It seems to have been originally a byname, but the meaning is not clear; it may come from a Gmc root used to describe something round and lumpish—hence a short, plump man.

2. Irish: var. of DUDDY.

Vars.: **Dod**; **Dadd** (Kent).

Cogns. (of 1): Fr.: **Dode**; **Dodon**, **Do(n)**. It.: **Tozzi**.

Dims. (of 1): Eng.: **Dodell**, **Duddell**, **Duddle**. Fr.: **Dodet**, **Dodin(et)**; **Do(u)in**. It.: **Tozzetti**, **Tozzini**.

Aug. (of 1): It.: **Tozzoni**.

Patrs. (from 1): Eng.: **Dod(d)s**, **Dadds**; **Dodson**, **Dotson**, **Dudson**; **Dodding**.

'Servant of D. 1': Eng.: **Dodman**, **Dudman**.

The Dod *family of Edge, near Malpas, Ches., have held lands there since the late 12th cent.; Cadogan Dod made a grant of land there in c.1180, and a direct line has been traced back to the 14th cent.*

Doddington English: habitation name from any of the numerous places called *Dod(d)ington*, found in every part of England. The placename generally means 'settlement (OE *tūn*) associated with *Dodda*' (see DODD 1). This placename has taken the forms *Detton* and *Ditton* in Shrops.

Var.: DITTON.

Dodge English (N England): 1. from the ME given name *Dogge*, a pet form of ROGER.

2. possibly also a nickname from ME *dogge* dog (OE *docga*, *dogga*).

Vars.: **Doi(d)ge** (SW England).

Dims.: **Dodgin**, **Dodgeo(o)n**.

Patrs.: **Dodgs(h)on**, **Dodgshun**.

Dodsworth English: habitation name from *Dodworth* in W Yorks. (*Dodeswrde* in Domesday Book), which gets its name from the OE personal name *Dodd(a)* (see DODD 1) + OE *worð* enclosure.

Doe English: 1. nickname for a mild and gentle man, from ME *do* doe (OE *dā*; for the change in the vowel cf. ROPER).

2. habitation name, with fused preposition *de*, from *Eu* in Seine-Maritime, whose name either represents a dramatic reduction of Latin *Augusta* '(city of) Augustus' (cf. DALTON 2), or else derives from the Gmc element *auwa* water-meadow, island.

Doggett English: 1. nickname, probably with abusive connotations, from a dim. of ME *dogge* dog (OE *docga*).

2. nickname from ME *dogge* dog + *heved* head (OE *heafod*).

Var.: **Dockett**.

Doherty Irish and Scots: Anglicized form of Gael. **Ó Dochartaigh** 'descendant of *Dochartach*', a byname meaning 'Unlucky' or 'Hurtful'.

Vars.: **O'Doherty**, **(O')Do(u)gherty**, **Dougharty**, **Doghartie**; **Dogerty**, **Daugherty**; **Dockerty**; **Doggart**; **Docherty**, **Docharty** (Scots).

Dohnal Czech: nickname from the verb *dohnat* to drive up to or reach a particular point. The application as a surname is uncertain; it may have been given to someone who 'arrived' in a village as opposed to being born there.

Doig Scots: Anglicized form of Gael. **Mac Gille Doig** 'son of the servant of *Dog*', an aphetic form of the personal name *Cadog*; see CADDOCK 1.

Vars.: **Doag**, **Doeg**; **Doak** (N Ireland).

Dolan Irish: 1. Anglicized form of Gael. **Ó Dubhshláin** 'descendant of *Dubhshlán*', a personal name composed of the elements *dubh* dark, black + *slán* challenge, defiance.

2. Anglicized form of Gael. *Ó Dobhailéin*; see DEVLIN.

Vars. (of 1): **O'Do(w)lane**, **Dowlan**, **Dowlin**, DOWLING. See also DELANEY.

Dolé French: nickname for a troubled or anxious person, from OF *dolé*, past part. of *doler*, to rue, regret (L *dolēre* to hurt, *dolet* it is a matter of regret, lit. it hurts).

Var.: **Dollé**.

Cogns.: Prov.: **Dol(l)at**.

Dolejš Czech: topographic name for someone living in the lower part of a village, or on the ground floor of a multistorey building divided into apartments, from Czech *dolejší* lower down, downstairs. Compare HOŘEJŠ.

Var.: **Dolejší**.

Dim.: **Dolejšek**.

Doležal Czech: nickname for a lazy or idle person, from the verb *doležat* to have rested up to the present time or long enough (composed of the perfective prefix *do-* + *ležat* to lie down, rest).

Var.: **Doležel**.

Dolgopolov Russ.: according to Unbegaun, this is a nickname for someone who habitually wore long skirts, from Russ. *dolgi* long (see DOLGOV 1) + *pola* skirt. However, the Jewish name *Dolgopolski* means 'long field' rather than 'long skirt'; see POLAŃSKI.

Dolgov Russian: 1. patr. from the nickname *Dolgi* 'Long', 'Tall'.

2. patr. from the nickname *Dolg* 'Debt', 'Duty', acquired perhaps by someone who owed a particular feudal obligation.

Cogns. (of 1, not patrs.): Pol.: **Długosz**. Czech: **Dlouhý**. Jewish (E Ashkenazic): **Dlug**, **Dlugacz**, **Dlugatch**, **Dlugatz**.

Cogns. (of 1, patrs.): Jewish (E Ashkenazic): **Dolgin**, **Dlugin**, **Dlugovitzky**.

Habitation name (from 1): Pol.: **Długoszewski**.

Doliński Polish: topographic name for someone living in a valley, from Pol. *dolina* valley + *-ski* suffix of local surnames (see Baranowski).

Dolittle English: nickname for a lazy man, from ME *do* (OE *dōn*) + *little* (OE *lytel*).

Var.: **Doolittle**.

Dolk Swedish: nickname from Swed *dolk* dagger. This is one of the 'soldiers' names', adopted on military service in the days before surnames came into use in Swedish (i.e. before the 18th cent.), and later retained in civilian life and handed down to descendants as a surname.

Dölker German (chiefly Württemberg): of uncertain origin. It may be a nickname for a stammerer or someone with a speech impediment, from MHG *tolken* to mutter, mumble. Alternatively it may be an occupational name for a translator or interpreter, MHG *tolke*, which is derived from the same verb in the more common sense 'speak'.

Doll English: nickname for a foolish individual, from ME *dolle* dull, foolish (OE *dol*). The byform **dyl(le)* gave rise to ME *dil(le)*, *dul(le)*, mod. Eng. *dull*.

Vars.: **Dol(l)man** (chiefly Midlands).

Dolomieu French: habitation name from a place in the Dauphiné, recorded in the 7th cent. as *Doloimeiacum*, apparently from an otherwise unrecorded Gaul. personal name + the local suffix *-ācum*.

Domagała Polish: nickname for a selfish or demanding person, from Pol. *domagać* demand.

Var.: **Domagalski** (with surname suffix *-ski*; see Baranowski).

Domański Polish: from a deriv. of the OPol. given name *Domarad*, which is composed of the elements *doma* home + *rad* glad, and according to Kupis does not mean 'glad to be at home', but rather 'glad to welcome a guest into one's home'. The (originally local) suffix of surnames *-ski* has been added (see Baranowski).

Domecq Provençal: topographic name from a Gascon form of OF *demaine* (feudal) estate, land belonging to the lord (LL *dominicum*, a deriv. of *dominus* lord, master; cf. Dominique).

Var.: **Domec**.

Dominique French: from a medieval given name (L *Dominicus* of the Lord, from *dominus* lord, master; cf. Domecq). It was borne by a Sp. saint (1170–1221) who founded the Dominican order of monks and whose fame gave an added boost to the popularity of the name, already well established because of its symbolic value.

Vars.: **Demange** (Lorraine); **Domange, Domenge** (Bordeaux); **Demanche, Dimanche** (Paris); **Demo(n)ge** (Burgundy); **Doumic** (Brittany).

Cogns.: Prov.: **Do(u)merc, Domerq, Dom(m)erque, Doumerque; Doumer** (Auvergne); **Do(u)menc, Domengue** (Gascony); **Mengue, Mergue** (aphetic forms). It.: **Domenico, Domenici, Dominico, Domin(ic)i, Dominighi, Domico; Dumini** (Venetia); **Menico, Menichi, Me(c)co, Me(c)chi; Mingo, Minghi** (Emilia); **Minico, Minichi** (Campania); **Men(e)go, Men(e)ghi, Menoghi, Minigo** (N Italy); **Menco, Menc(h)i** (S Italy); **Minchi, Mecchi, Micco, Meni**. Sp.: **Domingo**. Cat.: **Domènech**. Port.: **Domingos**. Ger. (of Slav. origin): **Domnick**. Czech: **Dominik, Dominka, Dominec; Mink**. Pol.: **Dominik, Domański**. Hung.: **Domo(n)kos**.

Dims.: Fr.: **Domenget, Monget, Mouget; Demangel, Mougel; Demangeon, Mangeon; Demangeot, Demongeot, Demo(u)geot, Mangeot, Manjot, Mongeot, Mougeot; Demangin, Demougin, Manjin, Mongin, Mougin, Mangenet, Mangeney, Ma(n)ginot, Mangenot, Mo(n)genot, Mougenel**. It.: **Dom(en)ichelli, Domin(ich)elli; Menichelli, Menichi(e)llo, Minichiello, Min(ich)elli, Men(e)ghelli, Meneghello, Minghelli; Domin(ich)etti, Domeneghetti, Domenichetti; Men(i)chetti, Men(i)chetto, Meneghetto, Men(e)ghetti, Minghetti; Domenichini, Dominichini, Domeneghini; Men(i)chini, Men(i)chino, Men(c)ini, Men(e)ghini, Meneghino, Mengheni, Minichini, Minichino, Minghini, Menini; Domenicucci; Men(i)cucci, Men(e)gucci, Min(i)cucci, Min(i)gucci; Menc(i)otti, Men(g)otti, Mi(n)cotti, Min(g)otti; Menicocci, Minocchi, Minicozzi, Min(g)ozzi, Men(g)ozzi, Mengossi, Mecocci, Mecozzi, Mecucci, Mecuzzi, Mecozzi; Cocci, Cozzi, Gozz(in)i, Gozzoli; Meneguzzi, Meniguzzi, Minguzzi, Minucci**. Pol.: **Domiczek**. Czech: **Domek, Dománek**.

Augs.: Fr.: **Demangeat**. It.: **Domenicone; Me(ni)coni, Miniconi, Menegone, Micone, Mingone, Men(c)oni, Men(g)oni**.

Pejs.: Fr.: **Demageard; Menjaud; Mongeaud**. It.: **Dominicacci, Dominigazzo; Men(i)cacci, Menegazzo, Mingazzi, Men(eg)azzi, Mecacci; Men(e)gazzi; Mengardo, Mengardi, Mingardo, Mingardi**.

Patrs.: It.: **De Domenico, De Domenicis, De Dominici(s), Di Domenico; De Minico; Menis**. Sp.: **Domínguez**. Port.: **Domingues**. Pol.: **Dominiak**.

Habitation name: Pol.: **Miniszewki**.

Donald Scots and Irish: from a Gael. personal name, *Domhnall*, composed of the Celt. elements *dubno-* world + *val-* might, rule.

Vars.: **Donnell, Doull, Doole**; Daniel.

Patrs.: **Donaldson**; McDonald, McConnell.

'Descendant of D.': **O'Donnell, O'Donill, O'Daniel** (Gael. **Ó Domhnaill**).

'Descendant of D. (dim.)': **(O')Donnellan, (O')Donel(l)an, (O')Donlan, (O')Donlon** (Gael. **Ó Domhnalláin**).

Donat English, French, and German: from a medieval given name (L *Dōnātus*, past part. of *dōnāre*, freq. of *dare* to give). The name was much favoured by early Christians, either because the birth of a child was seen as a gift from God (cf. Daudet and Dieudonné), or else because the child was in turn dedicated to God. The name was borne by various early saints, among them a 4th-cent. Italian bishop martyred in *c.*350 under Julian the Apostate, a 6th-cent. hermit of Sisteron, and a 7th-cent. bishop of Besançon, all of whom contributed to the popularity of the given name in the Middle Ages, which was not checked by the heresy of a 4th-cent. Carthaginian bishop who also bore it. Another bearer was a 4th-cent. grammarian and commentator on Virgil, widely respected in the Middle Ages as a figure of great learning.

Vars.: Eng.: **Donnet(t); Donnay; Doney** (Devon and Cornwall). Fr.: **Donnat; Donné, Donnet, Donney**. Ger.: **Donath, Donet**.

Cogns.: It.: **Donato, Donati; Dona** (Venetia). Czech: **Donát**. Hung.: **Donáth**.

Dims.: It.: **Donatelli; Donatiello** (Naples); **Donatini; Donadini** (Venetia).

Augs.: It.: **Donatoni; Donadon(i)** (Venetia).

Patrs.: Ger.: **Donaty** (alteration of *Donāti*, gen. of *Donātus*). Flem.: **Dons**. It.: **De Donato, Di Donato** (S Italy); **De Dona** (Venetia).

Donegan Irish: Anglicized form of Gael. **Ó Donnagáin** 'descendant of *Donnagán*', a personal name from a dim. of *donn* brown, dark (see Dunn 1).

Vars.: **Dunnigan, Doonican, Dunegain(e)**, Duncan; **O'Donegan, O'Donegaine, O'Dungan**.

Donker Dutch: nickname for someone with dark hair or a dark complexion, from MDu. *donker*, *donkel* dark (cf. mod. Ger. *dunkel*).

Cogns.: Low Ger.: **Dun(c)ker, Dunckel(mann)**. Jewish (Ashkenazic): **Tunkel** (W and NE Yid.); **Tinkel(mann)** (S Yid.).
Patr.: Du.: **Donkers**.

Donnelly Irish: Anglicized form of Gael. **Ó Donnghaile** 'descendant of *Donnghal*', a personal name composed of the elements *donn* brown (see DUNN 1) + *gal* valour. It is claimed that most bearers of this surname descend from Donnghal O'Neill, 17th in descent from Niall of the Nine Hostages.
Vars.: **Donneely, O'Donnelly**.

Donner 1. German: nickname for a man with a fierce or blustery temperament, from Ger. *Donner* thunder (MHG *doner*, OHG *thonar*).
2. Jewish (Ashkenazic): from Ger. *Donner* thunder, one of the many ornamental names derived from vocab. items referring to natural phenomena.
Vars. (of 1): **Donnerer, Donder(er), Daunderer, Dundrer**.

Donohue Irish: Anglicized form of Gael. **O Donnchadha** 'descendant of *Donnchadh*', a personal name composed of the elements *donn* brown (see DUNN 1) + *cath* battle.
Vars.: **O'Donohue, O'Donog(h)ue, O'Donohoe, O'Donochowe; O'Donaghie, O'Dunaghy; Donoghue, Dona(g)hue, Donohoe, Donaghoe; Donaghie, Donagh(e)y, Denaghy, Dennehy; Donachie** (Scots); DENNIS.

Donoso Spanish: nickname for a hospitable person, from OSp. *donoso* generous (L *dōnōsus* generous, liberal, a deriv. of *dōnum* gift). The adj. later developed the sense 'witty', 'amusing', and in some cases this may be the meaning of the surname.

Donovan Irish: Anglicized form of Gael. **Ó Donndubháin** 'descendant of *Donndubhán*', a personal name composed of the elements *donn* brown (see DUNN 1) + *dubh* black (see DUFF) + the dim. suffix *-án*.
Vars.: **Donavan, Donavin; O'Donovan**.

Doolan Irish: Anglicized form of Gael. **Ó Dubhlainn** 'descendant of *Dubhfhlann*', a personal name composed of the elements *dubh* black (see DUFF) + *flann* blood-coloured, red.
Vars.: **O'Doolan, Doolen, Doolin**.

Dooley Irish: Anglicized form of Gael. **Ó Dubhlaoich** 'descendant of *Dubhlaoch*', a personal name composed of the elements *dubh* black (see DUFF) + *laoch* champion, hero.
Vars.: **Dooly, O'Dooley, (O')Dowley**.

Doppler German: nickname for a gambler or occupational name for a maker of dice, from an agent deriv. of MHG *dopel(stein)* die (see also TOBEL).
Vars.: **Töppler; Doppelstein, Dobbelstein**.
Cogns.: Low Ger.: **Däbel(er); Dabelstein, Dabelsteen**.

Doran 1. Irish: Anglicized form of Gael. **Ó Deoradháin** 'descendant of *Deoradhán*', a byname representing a dim. of *deoradh* pilgrim, stranger, exile (cf. DEWAR 1).
2. English: var. of DURANT.
Vars.: **Dorran**. (Of 1 only): **Dorrian, O'D(e)oran**.

Dore 1. English: habitation name from either of two places, one in Derbys. and the other near Hereford. The former gets its name from OE *dor* door, used of a pass between hills; the latter from a Brit. river name of the same origin as DOVER 1.
2. Irish: Anglicized form of Gael. **Ó Doghair** 'descendant of *Doghar*', a byname meaning 'Sadness'.

Doré French: nickname from OF *doré* golden (past part. of *dorer* to gild, LL *dēaurāre*, from *aurum* gold), denoting either a goldsmith or someone with bright golden hair.
Cogns.: Prov.: **Dorat, Daurat**. Eng. (Norman): **Doree, Dorey**. Sp.: **Dorado**. Port.: **Dourado**.

Dores Portuguese: 1. nickname for a person oppressed with troubles and anxieties, from the pl. form of Port. *dor* pain, grief (L *dolor*; cf. DOLÉ).
2. from a medieval female given name, bestowed in allusion to the Marian title *Nossa Senhora das Dores* Our Lady of the Sorrows.

Dorgan Irish: 1. Anglicized form of Gael. **Ó Dorcháin** 'descendant of *Dorchán*', a byname representing a dim. of *dorcha* black, gloomy.
2. var. of DARGAN.

Dorival French: habitation name, with fused preposition *de*, from any of the places in Charente, Seine-Maritime, and Somme called *Orival*, from L *aurea* golden (i.e. lovely; cf. DORÉ) + *vallis* valley (see VALE). There are also other places throughout France with the same origin but different modern spellings, and these may have contributed to the surname.
Var.: **Dorval**.

Dormer 1. English (Norman): nickname for a lazy man or a sleepyhead, from OF *dormeor* sleeper, sluggard (L *dormītor*, from *dormīre* to sleep).
2. English: apparently a habitation name in view of the early forms with *de* (see below), but no suitable place of origin has been identified, nor is it clear whether it should be sought in Bucks. or N France. The *de* may be purely honorific.
3. Irish: Anglicized form of Gael. **Ó Díorma**, a shortened form of **Ó Duibhdhíormaigh** 'descendant of *Duibhdhíormach*', a personal name composed of the elements *dubh* black + *díormach* trooper.
Var. (of 3): DARBY.
The Dormer *family who hold the title Baron Dormer are of Bucks. origin. They trace their descent from Richard* de Doremere, *who held land at W Wycombe in 1244.*

Dornan Irish: Anglicized form of Gael. **Ó Doirnáin** 'descendant of *Doirnín*', a byname representing a dim. of *dorn* fist.
Vars.: **Durnin** (Gael. **Ó Doirnín**).

Dorofeev Russian: patr. from the male given name *Dorofei* (Gk *Dōrotheos*, composed of the elements *dōron* gift + *theos* God; the same elements in the reverse order make up the name THÉODORE). The name was borne by several early saints, including a 4th-cent. bishop of Tyre much venerated in the Orthodox Church.
Var.: **Dorofanov**.
Dims.: Russ.: **Dorofankin, Dorosh(a)ev, Dor(k)in, Donov**. Beloruss.: **Doroshkevich**. Ukr.: **Dorosh(en)ko; Doroshevich**.
Habitation name: Pol.: **Doroszewski**.

Dorrington English: habitation name from any of several places so called. One in Lincs. and one in Shrops. (near Woore) get the name from OE *Dēoringtūn* 'settlement (OE *tūn*) associated with *Dēor(a)*' (see DEAR 1); another in Shrops. (near Condover) was earlier *Dodintone*, identical with DODDINGTON.

Dorsett English: regional name from the county of *Dorset*, so called from OE *Dorn*, an early name of Dorchester (of Brit. origin, from *durn* fist, probably referring to fist-sized pebbles) + *sǣte* dwellers.
Vars.: **Dorset, Dossett**.

Dorsey English (Norman): habitation name, with fused preposition *de*, from *Orsay* in Seine-et-Orne, recorded in the 13th cent. as *Orceiacum*, from the L personal name *Orcius* + the local suffix *-ācum*.

Dostál Czech: nickname for a reliable, trustworthy person, from Czech *dostát* (*slovu*) to keep, abide by (one's word).
Cogn. (patr.): Croatian: **Dostanić**.

Dostoevski Russian: habitation name from a village called *Dostoevo*, situated in the Pinsk-Pripet marshes on the border between Poland and the Ukraine.
The writer Fyodor Dostoevski (*1821–81*) *was from a family of Lithuanian origin. The village of Dostoevo was one of a number granted to an ancestor, a boyar called Daniel Irtishevich, in 1506 by the Prince of Pinsk. In the mid-17th cent. a branch of the family moved to the Ukraine.*

Douet French: 1. topographic name for someone who lived near a stream or irrigation channel, OF *doit* (L *ductus*, from *ducere* to lead, convey).
2. dim. of the Gmc personal name *Dodo*(*n*) (see DODD 1).
Vars. (of 1): **Douit, Douis, Douy; Dudoit, Dudouet, Dudouit, Dudouyt, Dudoy; Desdouets, Desdouits, Desdoights.**
Dim.: **Douetteau.**

Dougall Scots and Irish: from the Gael. personal name *Dubhgall*, composed of the elements *dubh* black (see DUFF) + *gall* stranger (see GALL 1). This was used as a byname for Scandinavians, in particular to distinguish the darker-haired Danes from fair-haired Norwegians.
Vars.: **Dougal, Dougill, Dugall, Dugald; Dowell, Dowall, Doyle.**
Patr.: MCDOUGALL.
'Descendant of D.': Ir.: **O'Douill, O'Dowilly, O'Doyle** (Gael. **Ó Dubhghaill**).
Most bearers of patr. forms of this name are descended from members of a Scots clan related to the McDonalds, founded by Somhairle, Thane of Argyle (d. 1163). Several members of the clan moved to Ireland in the 14th cent., settling at first in the north-west of the country.

Doughty English: nickname for a powerful or brave man, esp. a champion jouster, from ME *doughty*, OE *dohtig*, *dyhtig* valiant, strong.
Vars.: **Douty, Dowty, Dufty.**

Douglas Scots: habitation name from any of the various places so called from their situation on a river named with the Gael. elements *dubh* dark, black (see DUFF) + *glais* stream (a deriv. of *glas* blue; cf. GLASS 2). There are several localities in Scotland and Ireland so named, but the one from which the surname is derived in most if not all cases is 20 miles south of Glasgow, the original stronghold of the Douglas family and their retainers. The traditional pronunciation of the name is /'du:gləs/, but now /'dʌgləs/ is more common.
Var.: **Douglass.**
This is the name of one of the most famous and powerful families in Scottish history, Earls of Douglas and later Earls of Angus. The first known bearer of the name is William de Duglas, *recorded at the end of the 12th cent.*

Douillet French: 1. habitation name from places in Sarthe and Orne, of obscure etymology, perhaps from a personal name.
2. nickname from OF *douillet* delicate, tender, a dim. of *doux* sweet, soft (see DUCE).
Var. (of 2): **Douillot.**
Pej. (of 2): **Douillard.**

Dove 1. English: nickname for a mild and gentle person, or metonymic occupational name for a keeper of doves, from ME *dove*, OE *dūfe* dove (or perhaps occasionally from the ON cogn. *dúfa*). The OE word was used as a given name for either sex in the early ME period, and the surname at least in part derives from this use.
2. Irish: translation of *Mac Calmáin* (see COLEMAN 1).
3. Scots: var. of DUFF.
4. Low German: nickname for a deaf man; see TAUBER 3.
Cogns. (of 1): See TAUBE.

Dover 1. English: habitation name from the port in Kent, so called from the river on which it stands, a Brit. name from the word which became W *dwfr* water.
2. Low German: habitation name from *Doveren* in the Rhineland, of uncertain etymology but perhaps with a Celt. origin and so related ultimately to 1.
3. Jewish: of unknown origin.
Var. (of 2): Ger.: **Dovermann.**

Dow 1. English: var. of DAW.
2. Scots: var. of DUFF.
Var.: **Dowe.**
Patr. (from 1): **Dowson** (see also DUCE).
'Servant of D. 1': **Dowman.**

Dowding English: patr. from an OE personal name, *Dogod* (apparently a deriv. of *dugan* to avail, be of use). The surname is chiefly found in Gloucs. and Somerset.
Var.: **Dowden.**

Dowler English: occupational name for a maker of dowels and similar objects, from an agent deriv. of ME *dowle* dowel (headless peg, bolt) (cf. MLG *dövel*).

Dowling 1. English: nickname for a stupid person, ME *dolling*, a deriv. of OE *dol* dull, stupid; see DOLL.
2. Irish: var. of DOLAN 1.
Vars. (of 1): **Dolling, Dilling.**

Down English: 1. topographic name from OE *dūn* down, low hill, a common element in placenames. The word is of Celt. origin and was taken into OE from Brit. The surname is chiefly found in SW England.
2. var. of DUNN.
Vars.: **Downe; Downer; Downman, Dunman.**

Downie Irish and Scots: 1. Anglicized form of Gael. **Ó Dúnadhaigh** 'descendant of *Dúnadhach*', a personal name meaning 'fortress-holder' (from *dún* fortress, fortified hill; see DOWN 1).
2. var. of MOLONEY.
3. habitation name from the Scots barony of *Downie* or *Duny* in the parish of Monikie in the former county of Angus (now part of Tayside region), so called from Gael. *dùn* hill (cf. DOWN 1) + the local suffix *-ach*.
Vars.: **Downey, Duny.**

Doyley English (Norman): habitation name, with fused preposition *de*, from any of several places in Calvados called *Ouilly*, from the Gallo-Roman personal name *Ollius* (of uncertain etymology) + the local suffix *-ācum*.
Vars.: **Dol(l)ey, Dul(e)y; Olley, Ollie** (Norfolk).

Dozier French: topographic name, with fused preposition *de*, for someone who lived near a willow tree or willow grove, from OF *osier* willow (of Gaul. origin).
Vars.: **D'Hozier; Lhozier, Losier** (with fused definite article); **Osier.**

Dráb Czech: occupational name from Czech *dráb*, which originally meant footsoldier, but also came to denote a servant or retainer, esp. an overseer of workers on an estate.

Dims.: **Drábe(če)k**.

Drabble English: of uncertain origin, perhaps from a dim. of the OE personal name *Drabba*. This too is of uncertain etymology; it may be akin to mod. Eng. *drab* sloven, a word that is first recorded in writing in the 16th cent. but, like many slang terms, may have been in spoken use much earlier.

Drage English: metonymic occupational name for a confectioner, or perhaps a nickname from a term of endearment, from ME *drag(i)e* sweetmeet, sugar-coated spice (OF *dragie*, *dragee*, ultimately from Gk *tragēmata* spices, condiments).

Var.: **Dredge**.

Dragon 1. French and English: nickname or occupational name for someone who carried a standard in battle or else in a pageant or procession, from ME, OF *dragon* snake, monster (L *draco*, gen. *dracōnis*, from Gk *drakōn*, ultimately from *derkesthai* to flash). This word was applied in LL to military standards in the form of a windsock and hence resembling a snake.

2. French: cogn. of Drake 1.

3. Jewish: of unknown origin.

Var.: Jewish: **Dragoner**.

Cogns.: Prov.: **Drago**, **Draco**. It.: **Drago**, **Draghi**.

Dims.: Fr.: **Draconet**, **Drahonnet**. It.: **Draghetto**, **Draghetti**, **Dragotto**, **Dragotti**.

Drake English: 1. from the OE byname *Draca* 'Snake' or 'Dragon', ME *Drake*, or sometimes from the cogn. ON *Draki*. Both are common bynames and, less frequently, given names. Both the OE and the ON forms are from L *draco* snake, monster (see Dragon).

2. nickname for someone with some fancied resemblance to a duck, from ME *drake* male duck (from MLG *andrake*; cf. mod. Ger. *Enterich*).

Cogns. (of 1): Fr.: Dragon. (Of 1 and 2): Low Ger.: **Draa(c)k**, **Dracke**.

Patr.: Eng.: **Drakes**.

Drane 1. English: nickname for a lazy man, from ME *drane* drone, male honey bee, long taken as a symbol of idleness (OE *drān*).

2. Irish: Anglicized form of Gael. **Ó Dreain** 'descendant of *Drean*', a byname meaning 'Wren'.

3. Irish: Anglicized form of Gael. *Ó Druacháin*; see Drohan.

Var.: **Drain**.

Dransfield English: habitation name, perhaps from *Dransfield* Hill in Mirfield, W Yorks., which contains the OE gen. of *drān* drone (see Drane 1) + *feld* pasture, open country. *Drān* may be a byname in this instance. The surname is mainly found in Yorks.

Draper English: occupational name for a maker and seller of woollen cloth, ANF *draper* (a deriv. of *drap* cloth, possibly of Gaul. origin).

Vars.: **Drapper**, **Drapier**; **Drape**.

Cogns.: Fr.: **Drap(p)ier**; **Drapy**, **Drapeau**. Sp.: **Trapero** (a seller of second-hand clothes, rag-and-bone man).

Dim.: Fr.: **Draperon**.

Draycott English: habitation name from any of the numerous places in England so called, from OE *dræg* drag, portage, slipway, or sledge (a place where boats were dragged across land or where loads had to be dragged uphill or on sledges across wet ground, from *dragan* to draw, drag) + *cot* cottage (see Coates).

Drayton English: habitation name from any of the very numerous places in England so called from OE *dræg* (see Draycott) + *tūn* enclosure, settlement.

Drechsler German and Jewish (Ashkenazic): occupational name for a turner, Ger. *Drechsler* (MHG *dreseler* or *dræselære*, OHG *drāslāri*, formed by the addition of a superfluous agent suffix to *drāsil* turner, a primary deriv. of *drāen* to turn, spin). A turner would be responsible for making small objects not just from wood, but also from bone, ivory, and amber, all of which were widely used in the Middle Ages for their decorative value.

Vars.: **Dressler**, **Drexler**. Ger. only: **Drössler** (E Franconia, Thuringia); **Traxler**, **Draxler** (Bavaria, Austria). Jewish only: **Dres(s)ler** (see also Thrussell); **Draksler**.

Cogn.: Flem.: **De Dresseler**.

Dreier 1. German and Jewish (Ashkenazic): nickname derived from Ger. *drei* three, MHG *drī(e)*, with the addition of the suffix *-er*. This was the name of a medieval coin worth three Hellers, and it is possible that the Ger. surname may have been derived from this word. More probably, the nickname is derived from some other connection with the number three, too anecdotal to be even guessed at now.

2. Low German: occupational name for a turner of wood or bone, from an agent deriv. of MLG *draeyen* to turn, spin (cf. Drechsler).

Vars.: **Dreyer**. (Of 2 only): Low Ger.: **Dreigher**, **Dreger**; **Dreher** (Württemburg).

Cogns. (of 2): Du.: **Dra(a)ijer**, **Dra(a)yer**. Fris.: **Draaisma**. Dan.: **Drejer**. Jewish: **Dreher**.

Drennan Irish: Anglicized form of Gael. **Ó Draighneáin** 'descendant of *Draighneán*', a byname from a dim. of *draighean* blackthorn.

Vars.: **Dr(e)inan**, **Drinnan**, **Drynan**; Thornton.

Drescher German and Jewish (Ashkenazic): occupational name for a thresher, Ger. *Drescher*, Yid. *dresher*, agent derivs. of MHG *dreschen*, Yid. *dresh(e)n* to thresh (OHG *dreskan*).

Vars.: **Dreschner**. Ger.: **Draschner**; **Trescher**, **Tröscher**, **Trösch(e)**. Jewish: **Dresher**.

Cogns.: Low Ger.: **Dröscher**, **Dö(r)scher**. Du.: **Dorsman**. Eng.: **Thresher**, **Thrasher**.

Drew 1. English: aphetic var. of Andrew.

2. English (Norman): from the Gmc personal name *Drogo*, which is of uncertain etymology; it is possibly akin to OSax. *(gi)drog* ghost, phantom, or with a stem meaning 'to bear, carry' (OHG *tragan*). Whatever its origin, the name was borne by one of the sons of Charlemagne, and the name was subsequently popular throughout France in the forms *Dreus*, *Drues* (oblique case *Dreu*, *Dr(i)u*), whence it was introduced to England by the Normans. Drogo de Monte Acuto (as his name appears in its Latinized form) was a companion of William the Conqueror and founder of the Montagu family, among whom the given name *Drogo* was revived in the 19th cent.

3. English (Norman): nickname from OF *dru* favourite, lover (originally an adj., apparently from a Gaul. word meaning 'strong', 'vigorous', 'lively', but influenced by the sense of the OHG element *trūt*, *drūt* dear, beloved).

4. English (Norman): habitation name from any of various places in France called *Dreux*, from the Gaul. tribal name *Durocasses* (of obscure etymology).

5. English (Norman): habitation name, with fused preposition *de*, from any of the numerous places in France that get their names from OF *rieux* streams (see RIEU).

6. Irish: Anglicized form of Gael. **Mac an Druaidh** and **Ó Druaidh** 'son' and 'descendant of the druid'. The word for these ancient Celt. priests is of uncertain origin, possibly akin to Gael. *derb* sure, true or *dara* oak.

Vars.: **Drewe, Dru; Druce, Drewes, Dreux** (the final sibilant representing the Eng. possessive case of 1 or 2, the OF nom. case of 2, or an alternative pronunciation of 4 or 5).

Cogns. (of 2): Fr.: **Dr(o)uon, Dron, Drompt** (from a later form of the oblique case); **Droz.** (Of 3): Fr.: **Dru(t), Ledru.**

Dims. (of 2): Eng.: **Drewett, Drewitt, Druett, Druitt, Drouet; Drewell.** Fr.: **Drou(h)et, Druot, Drou(h)in, Droin, Drouineau; Derouin, Derouet; Droniou** (Brittany).

Dreyfuss Jewish (W Ashkenazic): habitation name from the town of *Trier* on the Moselle, known in Fr. as *Trèves*; both the Fr. and Ger. names come from L *Augusta Treverorum* 'city of Augustus among the *Treveri*', a Celt. tribal name of uncertain etymology. The form of the surname has been altered by folk etymological association with mod. Ger. *Dreifuss* tripod.

Vars.: **Dre(y)fus, Dreifus(s), Trefus, Treves, Trevis, Trives, Trivis, Trivus, Trivas, Tribus, Trève(s); Trivier.**

Cogns.: It.: **Treves, Trevis.** Ger., Dan.: **Trier.** Flem., Du.: **Van Trier.**

Driburg Low German: habitation name from *Driburg* near Höxter in N Rhineland-Westphalia, so called from MLG *tō der Iburg* 'at the Iburg'. This is an old Saxon fortress nearby, which was captured in 775 by Charlemagne; its name is of uncertain origin. The second element is clearly OSax. *burg* fortress (see BURKE), but the first is opaque; according to Bahlow it preserves an ancient name of the settlement.

Driesch Low German: topographic name from the dial. word *drēsch* land used as pasture rather than for the cultivation of crops. There are several minor places of this name in the Rhineland, and the surname may also be a habitation name from any of these.

Var.: **Drieschmann.**

Cogn.: Flem., Du.: **Van den Driesch.**

Driffield English: habitation name from places in Gloucs. and E Yorks., both so called from ME *drit*, *dirt* mud, manure (ON *drit*) + *feld* pasture, open country (see FIELD).

Var.: **Driffel.**

Dring English: from ON *drengr* young man, but with more than one possible interpretation. It may reflect the personal name (originally a byname) of this form, which had some currency in the most Scandinavian-influenced areas of medieval England. Alternatively it may reflect the ME borrowing of the vocab. word in the sense 'servant', later a technical term of the feudal system of Northumb. for a free tenant who held land by military and agricultural service, sometimes paying rent as well or in commutation.

Var.: **Dreng.**

Drinkwater English: nickname from ME *drink* (OE *drincan*) + *water* (OE *wæter*). In the Middle Ages weak ale was the universal beverage among the poorer classes, and so cheap as to be drunk like water, whereas water itself was only doubtfully potable. The surname was perhaps a joking nickname given to a pauper or miser allegedly unable or unwilling to afford beer, or may have been given in irony to an innkeeper or a noted tippler. The suggestion that some bearers may have been diabetics with voracious unnatural thirsts is interesting but unconvincing. (See also BOILEAU.)

Cogn.: Flem., Du.: **Waterdrinker.**

Driscoll Irish: Anglicized form of Gael. **Ó hEidirsceóil** 'descendant of the messenger', from *eidirsceól* go-between, intermediary, news bearer (a cpd of *eidir* between + *sceól* story, news). Most bearers of this surname claim descent from a single 10th-cent. ancestor.

Vars.: **O'Driscoll, O'Driscole, O'Hederscoll, O'Hidirscoll.**

Driver English: occupational name for a driver of horses or oxen attached to a cart or plough, or of loose cattle, from a ME agent deriv. of OE *drīfan* to drive.

Cogns.: Ger.: **Treiber.** Low Ger.: **Driewer.** Jewish (Ashkenazic): **Treiber, Treibman** (occupational name for someone who floated lumber down a river; cf. SCHWEMMER).

Equivs. (not cogn.): Pol.: WOŹNIAK.

Drobný Czech: nickname for a small person, from Czech *drobný* small.

Var.: **Drobník, Drobek.**

Cogns.: Pol.: **Drobnik.** Croatian: **Drobnjak.**

Drohan Irish: Anglicized form of Gael. **Ó Druacháin** 'descendant of *Druachán*', a byname representing a dim. of *druach* wise man.

Vars.: **Drohane, Droohan, Drohun,** DRANE.

Droop English: nickname from ME *drup* dejected, sad, gloomy (from ON, akin to OE *dropian* to drop).

Droste Low German: occupational name for a steward or head servant, MLG *drotsete* (a cogn. of MHG *truhsæze*, from OHG *truhtsazzo*). The term derives from the elements *truht* body of servants + *sizzen* to sit, in the sense of 'preside'. The term was also used as a title in various different contexts.

Cogns.: Flem.: **Drossate, Drossaerd.** Du.: **Drossart, Drost.**

Drouilly French: habitation name from a place in Marne, so called from the Gallo-Roman personal name *Drull(i)us* (of uncertain etymology) + the local suffix *-ācum*.

Drożdż Polish: nickname from Pol. *drozd* thrush.

Cogn.: Czech: **Drozd(a).**

Habitation name: Pol.: **Drozdowski.**

Drucker Jewish (Ashkenazic): occupational name for a printer, from Ger. *Drucker* or Yid. *druker* printer (agent derivs. of Ger. *drucken*, Yid. *drukn* to print, derived from a Mainz dial. var. of *drücken* to press. Printing was first developed in Mainz in the 15th cent.).

Vars.: **Druck; Druker; Driker** (S Yid. var. of *Druker*); **Druckier** (Pol. spelling); **Druckmann, Drukman(n).**

Drummond Scots: habitation name from any of the various places, as for example *Drymen* near Stirling, that get their names from Gael. *dromainn*, a deriv. of *druim* ridge.

The first known bearer of the name is Gilbert de Drummyn, *chaplain to Alwyn, Earl of Levenax, who witnessed a charter by that earl c.1199. The principal family of this name are apparently descended from a Hungarian nobleman, Maurice, who in 1068 accompanied Edgar Atheling and his sister Margaret to Scotland, where she married King Malcolm III. The* Drummonds *made alliances with the nobility and royalty of Scotland, including Annabella Drummond (?1350–1402), who married Robert III and was the mother of James I. The 18th-cent. Drummonds were Jacobites and were raised to the titular dukedom of Perth by the exiled James II. They still hold the earldom of Perth.*

Drummy Irish: Anglicized form of Gael. **Ó Droma** 'descendant of *Droma*', a personal name of uncertain origin; it may be from *druim* back (cf. DRUMMOND), and have been given originally to someone with a deformed back.

Vars.: **Dromey, Drumm.**

Drury English (Norman) and French: 1. nickname from OF *druerie* love, friendship (a deriv. of *dru* lover, friend; see DREW 3). In ME the word also had the concrete meanings 'love affair', 'love token', 'sweetheart'.

2. from a Gmc personal name composed of the elements *triuwa* truth, trust + *rīc* power.

Vars.: Eng.: **Drew(e)ry, Druery.**

Dryden English: habitation name from an unidentified place, probably in Cumb. or Northumb., where the name is still common, and so called from OE *drȳge* dry + *denu* valley (see DEAN 1).

The poet John Dryden *(1631–1700) was born in Northants, but his forebears had moved there from Cumb. in the 16th cent.*

Drysdale Scots: habitation name from *Dryfesdale* near Dumfries, so called from the river *Dryfe* + OE *dæl* valley (see DALE).

The surname is common in Fife, where it was taken in the 16th cent. by three brothers Douglas who had fled from Dryfesdale after killing several men in a dispute over territorial rights and who adopted the name of their former home as a surname.

Drzewiecki Polish: 1. habitation name from a village called *Drzewce* (named with Pol. *drzewa* trees) + *-ski* suffix of local surnames (see BARANOWSKI), or topographic name for someone living among trees, from *drzewa* used independently.

2. nickname for a stiff or upright person, from Pol. *drzewiec* lance + *-ski* general surname suffix (see BARANOWSKI).

Dubnikov Russian: patr. from the nickname *Dubnik* 'Oak-man' (a deriv. of *dub* oak, cogn. with Czech *dub*, Pol. *dęb*), with ref. to personal strength or to location of residence.

Vars.: **Dubin, Dubov(oi).**

Cogns.: Bulg.: **De(u)bov.** Pol.: **Dembiak.** Czech: **Dub(ský), D(o)ubec, Doubek.** Jewish (E Ashkenazic, ornamental): **Domb(e), Dombek, Demb(a), Dembe, Dembo, Demby, Dembak, Dembin.**

Dims.: Pol.: **Dąbek.** Czech: **Dubček, Dubík.**

Patrs.: Jewish: **Dembowitz, Dembovitz, Dembovich.**

Collective: Russ.: **Dubrovin.**

Habitation names: Pol.: **Dębowski, Dembowski, Dębicki, Dębecki, Dembiński; Dąbkowski;** DĄBROWSKI. Jewish (E Ashkenazic): **Dombovsky, Dembinsk, Dembinsky, Dembski, Dembowsky.**

Duce English: nickname from ME *douce*, *dowce* sweet, pleasant (OF *dolz*, *dous*, from L *dulcis*). This was also in occasional use as a female given name in the Middle Ages, and some examples may derive from this.

Vars.: **Douce, Dowse; Douch(e).**

Cogns.: Fr.: **Douce, Ledoux; Douche** (Normandy, Picardy). It.: **Dolci; (Lo) Dolce** (Sicily).

Dims.: Eng.: **Doucet, Dowsett, Dowcett.** Fr.: **Doucet, Doucin(el); Dousset, Doussot, Doussin(et), Doussain(t), Doussinel(le); Douchet, Douchez, Douchin.** It.: **Dolcetti, Dolcetta, Dolcini, Dolcino, Dolciotti.**

Pejs.: Fr.: **Doussard, Douss(in)aud.**

Metrs.: Eng.: **Dowson** (see also Dow). Jewish (Ashkenazic): **Tol(t)zis** (from the Yid. female given name *Toltse*), **Tolces** (Pol. spelling), **Dolcis, Tolciss.**

The first known bearer of the name Douche *is a certain William Douche, recorded in 1349 in a document of Merton College, Oxford, as one of 'the boyes that were of the founder's kin'.*

Duchier French: occupational name for a tavern-keeper, from an aphetic form of OF *conduchier* (LL *condūcārius*, a deriv. of *condūcere* to conduct, manage).

Vars.: **Ducher, Duché; Conduché.**

Dim.: **Ducheron.**

Duckenfield English: habitation name from *Dukinfield* in Manchester, probably so called from OE *dūcena feld* pasture of the ducks; cf. DIGG 2 and FIELD.

Ducker 1. English (E Anglia): nickname from an agent deriv. of ME *douke(n)* to dive, plunge (apparently of native origin and akin to *duck* (the bird); cf. DIGG 2 and DUCKETT 1).

2. Jewish (Ashkenazic): of unknown origin.

Duckett English: 1. nickname from a dim. of ME *douke*, *duk(ke)* duck (OE *duce*; cf. DIGG 2).

2. nickname from ME *douke*, *duk(ke)* duck + *heved* head (OE *hēafod*).

3. nickname from OF *ducquet* owl (a dim. of *duc* guide, leader; see DUKE 1).

4. from a ME dim. of the OE personal name or byname *Ducca*, of uncertain origin.

5. from a ME dim. of the given name DUKE.

Vars.: **Ducket, Duckit(t).**

Duckworth English (chiefly Lancs.): habitation name from *Duckworth* Fold, in the borough of Bury, Lancs., which presumably derives its name from the OE personal name *Ducca* (see DUCKETT 4) + *worð* enclosure (see WORTH).

Ducost French: topographic name, with fused preposition and article *du*, from OF *cost* hill (a masc. var. of COSTE, specialized in this sense).

Var.: **Ducos.**

Ducrot French: topographic name, with fused preposition and article *du*, from OF *crot* cave, grotto (a masc. var. of the regional term *crote*, LL *crupta*, from Gk *kryptos* hidden, secret).

Duda Polish, Ukrainian, and Czech: metonymic nickname for a player on the bagpipes, from the Slav. word *duda* bagpipe.

Var.: Czech: **Dudák.**

Cogns.: Beloruss.: **Dudar** (occupational). Jewish (Ashkenazic): **Dudnik, Dudman; Dudel(sak), Dudelzak** (from Ger. *Dudelsack* bagpipes). Hung.: **Dudás.**

Dim.: Pol.: **Dudaczyk.**

Patrs.: Russ.: **Dudin.** Beloruss.: **Dudarov, Dudorov.** Croatian: **Dudić.** Jewish: **Dudovitz** (E Ashkenazic).

Patrs. (from dims.): Russ.: **Dud(ysh)kin.**

Duddy Irish: Anglicized form of Gael. **Ó Dubhda** 'descendant of *Dubhda*', a byname derived from *dubh* dark, black (see DUFF). The surname is very common in Co. Kerry.

Vars.: **Doody, (O')Dowd,** DODD.

Dude Low German: from the Gmc personal name *Dudo*, of uncertain etymology. In some cases at least it is apparently a pet form of the compound name *Liudolf* (composed of the elements *leud* people + *wolf* wolf); in the 12th cent. Otto I's son Liudolf was known also as both *Ludo* and *Dudo*. In other cases it may have been originally a byname (cf. DODD 1).

Vars.: **Dü(d)e, Dode.**

Patrs.: **Dud(d)en, Doden.**

Dudek Polish and Czech: nickname from the vocab. word *dudek* hoopoe. In Pol. the word also means 'simpleton' and this no doubt contributed to the surname, but in Czech no such meaning is attested, and the surname may have originated as a nickname with reference to some other attribute of the bird, such as its repetitive call or its bright plumage.

Vars.: Pol.: **Dudka**. Czech: **Dedek, Dydek**.

Cogns.: Ukr.: **Dudko**. Jewish (E Ashkenazic, ornamental): **Dudke**.

Patrs.: Pol.: **Dudkiewicz, Dutkiewicz**. Jewish (presumably adoptions and alterations of the Pol. surname as ornamental names): **Dudkiewicz, Dudkewi(t)z, Dudkewich, Dudkevich, Dudkevi(t)z**.

Habitation name: Pol.: **Dutkowski**.

Duder English: of uncertain origin, perhaps a var. of Welsh *Tudor*; see THÉODORE.

The earliest known bearer of the name is Maud Duder, *widow of John, recorded in Somerset in 1545. The surname has always been largely confined to the W Country, particularly Devon. Most present-day English bearers of the name seem to descend from Samuel* Duder *(b. 1775) of Kingskerswell, Devon. The name was taken to Newfoundland by his brother Thomas (b. 1787), to New Zealand by his nephew Thomas (b. 1806), and to Brazil by a grandson (c.1865).*

Dudgeon English and Scots: of uncertain origin, but possibly an occupational name for a turner or cutler. The word *dudgeon* (of unknown origin) denoted the wood (probably boxwood; cf. BOX) used in the handles of knives and daggers in the Middle Ages. Black explains it as a patr. from DODGE, but this seems unlikely.

Dudley English: habitation name from the town in the W Midlands so called from the OE personal name *Dudda* (see DODD 1) + OE *lēah* wood, clearing.

Dueñas Spanish: occupational name for someone who was employed in the quarters of the female members of a noble family, from Sp. *dueñas* ladies (a cogn. of DAME). In a few cases it may have been originally a habitation name, from places in Palencia and Teruel called *(Las) Dueñas*, perhaps of folkloric origin.

Cogn.: Jewish (Sefardic): **Duenias** (reason for adoption unknown).

Duff Scots and Irish: Anglicized form of Gael. *dubh* dark, black. This word was widely used as a nickname or byname (for a swarthy man or man of dark temperament) and as a personal name. See also DEVANE, DUDDY, DUFFY, and DUGGAN.

Vars.: Dow, DOVE.

Cogns.: Welsh: DEE. Corn.: **Dew**. Bret.: **(Le) Duigo**.

Patr.: Sc., Ir.: **McDuff**.

Duffield English: habitation name from places in Derbys. and E Yorks., so called from ON *dúfa* DOVE (perhaps a byname) + OE *feld* pasture, open country (see FIELD).

Vars.: **Duffell, Duffill**.

Duffin 1. English: from the ON personal name *Dólgfinnr*, composed of the elements *dólgr* wound, scar + *Finnr* Finn.

2. Irish: var. of DEEGAN and DEVANE 2.

Var. (of 1): **Dolphin** (chiefly W Midlands). See also DAUPHIN.

Duffy 1. Irish: Anglicized form of Gael. **Ó Dubhthaigh** 'descendant of *Dubhthach*', a byname derived from *dubh* black (see DUFF). This name was borne by a 6th-cent. saint who was archbishop of Armagh.

2. Scots and Irish: Anglicized form of Gael. **Mac Dhuibhshíthe** 'son of *Dubhshíth*', a personal name composed of the elements *dubh* black (see DUFF) + *síth* peace.

Vars.: **Duffey, Duffie, Dowey, Dowie, Do(v)ey, Duthy, Duthie**. (Of 1 only): **O'Duff(e)y, O'Duffie, O'Duhie, O'Duhig, O'Dowey**. (Of 2 only): **McDuffie, McFee, McFie, McPhee, McPhie, MacAfee, McAffer, Maccaffie, McCaffer, McCov(v)ie, McGuffie, Machaffie, Mehaffy, McHaffie, McHaffy**.

'Son of the servant of D. 1': **McGildowie, McIldowie, Dowie, Doey, Duthy** (Gael. **Mac Giolla Dubhthaigh**).

Duflocq French: of uncertain origin. It probably derives from OF *floc* tuft (L *floccus*). This may be a nickname for someone with a distinctive tuft or quiff of hair, but in view of the fact that it is invariably found with a fused preposition-cum-article *du*, it is more probable that it is a topographic name for someone who lived by a tuft or tump of raised ground.

Vars.: **Duflo(s), Duflot**.

Dugdale English: habitation name from a place so called, probably the hamlet near Uttoxeter, Staffs., now known as *Dagdale*, from the OE personal name or byname *Ducca* (see DUCKETT 4) + OE *dæl* or ON *dalr* valley (see DALE). The surname is now found chiefly in Lancs.

Duggan 1. Scots and Irish: Anglicized form of Gael. **Ó Dubhagáin** 'descendant of *Dubhagán*', a byname representing a double dim. of *dubh* black, dark (see DUFF).

2. Welsh: Anglicized aphetic form of the personal name *Cadwgan, Cadogan* (see CADDOCK 1).

Vars. (of 1): **O'Dooghaine, O'Dowgaine, O'Duggan, O'Doogan, (O')Dugan, Duggon, Duggen, Dougan, Doohan**.

Patr. (from 2): **Duggins**.

Dugmore English (chiefly W Midlands): of uncertain origin, probably a habitation name from some unidentified place so called from the OE personal name or byname *Ducca* (see DUCKETT 4) + OE *mōr* moor, marsh (see MOORE 1).

Duguid Scots: probably a nickname for a well-intentioned person or do-gooder, from Northern ME *du* do (OE *dōn*) + *gu(i)d* good (OE *gōd*).

The earliest known bearer of the name is John Dogude *or* Dugude, *who was bailie of Perth in 1379 and went to Prussia in the king's service in 1382. The name has always been most common in the area of Aberdeen.*

Duin Dutch: topographic name for someone who lived by a sand dune, MDu. *dūne* (a cogn. of DOWN 1).

Vars.: **Van Duijn, Van Duyn, Van Duinen**.

Duke English: 1. nickname for someone who gave himself airs and graces, from ME *duk(e)* duke (OF *duc*, from L *dux*, gen. *dūcis*, leader, a deriv. of *dūcere* to lead), or else an occupational name for a servant employed in a ducal household.

2. possibly also from the given name *Duke*, a short form of *Marmaduke*, a given name of Ir. origin, said to be from Ir. *mael Maedoc* 'devotee (*mael*) of *Maedoc*', a given name of uncertain origin, borne by various early Ir. saints, in particular a 6th-cent. abbot of Clonmore and a 7th-cent. bishop of Ferns.

Cogns. (of 1): Fr.: **Duc, Leduc**. It.: **Duc(a), Duchi; Lo Duca** (Sicily). Sp., Port.: **Duque**. Cat.: **Duch**. Jewish (Ashkenazic): **Dukas** (from mod. Hebr., an ornamental adoption of the vocab. word).

Dims. (of 1): **Duchet, Du(c)quet, Duchez, Duchey, Duchon** (all of these may be in part nicknames from the owl, called the 'little guide' in French folklore because of its ability to find its way around in the dark; cf. DUCKETT). It.: **Duchini**.

Patrs.: Eng.: **Dukes**. (From 1 only): Fr.: **Auduc**. It.: **Del Duca** (Naples).

Dumville English (Norman): habitation name from *Donville* in Calvados, so called from the Gmc personal name

Dono (of uncertain meaning) or *Dodo* (see DODD 1 and DUDE) + OF *ville* settlement, village (see VILLE).
Vars.: **Dunville, Domvil(l)e; Dunfield.**

Dunant French: topographic name, with fused preposition-cum-article *du*, from OF *nant* stream (of Gaul. origin).
Var.: **Dunan.**

Dunbar Scots: habitation name from a town on the North Sea coast near Edinburgh, so called from Gael. *dùn* fort + *barr* top, summit (cf. BARR 1).
The name of this family is derived from lands granted to Gospatrick (?1040–?75) by King Malcolm III of Scotland. They later acquired the earldoms of Dunbar and of March, but in 1434 were deprived of both by James I of Scotland, who felt that they had become too powerful.

Duncan Scots and Irish: 1. Anglicized form of Gael. *Duinnchinn*, a byname composed of the elements *donn* dark, brown (see DUNN 1) + *ceann* head.
2. var. of DONEGAN.
Patrs. (from 1): **Duncanson, Dunkinson.**

Duncombe English: probably a var. of DUNCAN rather than a habitation name, even though the first element could be OE *dūn* hill (see DOWN 1) and the second OE *cumb* valley (see COOMBE).

Dundas Scots: habitation name from the place so called near Edinburgh, which gets its name from Gael. *dùn* hill (cf. DOWN 1) + *deas* south. The traditional pronunciation is /dən'das/.
This is the name of a Scottish family descended from Gospatrick, Earl of March (d. 1139). His grandson, Helias de Dundas, *was the first to bear the surname, derived from lands in W Lothian. The family later acquired the titles Viscount Melville and Marquess of Zetland.*

Dunderdale English (Lancs. and Yorks.): local name from the district called *Dunnerdale* in Cumb. along the river *Duddon*, which appears in the 12th cent. as *Dudun*, *Dudena*, and *Duthen* (of unexplained origin). The surname is composed of this river name + ME *dale* DALE.

Dunford English: habitation name from *Dunford* Bridge, a hamlet near Penistone, W Yorks., so called from the river *Don* (a Brit. name, possibly meaning 'river') + OE *ford* FORD, or from *Dunford* House in Methley, W Yorks., which is named in OE as '*Dunn's* ford' (see DUNN 2).

Dung Low German: topographic name for someone who lived on a piece of raised dry land in marshy surroundings, or habitation name from any of the various places named with the dial. term for such a patch of land, MLG *dung*.
Vars.: **Dungs, Düngen, Dunk, Donk; Dunkmann; Von der Dunk.**
Cogns.: Du.: **Van Dongen, Van Donks.**

Dunham English (chiefly Norfolk): habitation name from any of several places so called, of which there is one in Norfolk. Most get the name from OE *dūn* hill (see DOWN 1) + *hām* homestead; one in Ches. originally had as its first element the OE personal name *Dunna* (see DUNN 2). A place in Lincs. now known as *Dunholme* appears in Domesday Book as *Duneham* and this too may be a partial source of the surname; in this case again the first element is probably from a personal name.

Dunin Russian: 1. metr. from the female given name *Dunya*, a dim. of *Avdotya* (Gk *Eudokia* 'of good repute', cf. YEVDOKIMOV). The name was borne by a Samaritan penitent who was beheaded under Trajan.
2. patr. from the nickname *Dyna* (ORuss. *Dunya*) 'Watermelon', given perhaps to a cultivator of this crop or to a person with a large head (cf. ARBUZOV).
Cogn.: Croatian: **Dunić.**
Dim.: Russ.: **Dunkin.**

Dunkley English: of uncertain origin, possibly a habitation name from *Dinckley* in Lancs., recorded in 1246 as *Dunkythele* and *Dinkedelay*. The placename is probably named with an old Brit. name, composed of elements meaning 'fort' + 'wood', with the addition of OE *lēah* wood, clearing. The surname is now most common in Northampton.

Dunleavy Irish: Anglicized form of Gael. **Ó Duinnshléibhe** and **Mac Duinnshléibhe** 'descendant' and 'son of *Duinnsliabh*', a personal name composed of the elements *donn* brown + *sliabh* mountain.
Vars.: **O'Dunleavy, (O')Donleavy, Dunle(e)vy, Dunlavy,** DUNLOP; **McAnle(a)vy, McAleavy, McEnleavy, McEnlevie, McEnle(i)ve, McLeavy,** MCLAY, **Killeavy; Dunlea, Dullea, Delea, Delee, Delay; O'Downlay; McAlea, McConloy, McColley, McClew; Leavy.** See also LIVINGSTONE.

Dunlop 1. Scots: habitation name from a place near Kilmarnock, so called from Gael. *dùn* fort + *lápach* muddy. The traditional pronunciation places the stress on the second syllable, although nowadays it is usually placed on the first.
2. Irish: Anglicized form of DUNLEAVY.
3. Irish: Anglicized form of **Ó Lapáin (O'Lappin)** 'descendant of *Lapán*', a byname from *lápán* mire, dirt, used figuratively of a poor man.
Var.: **Dunlap** (U.S.).

Dunn 1. Scots and Irish: from Gael. *Donn*, a byname for a person with dark hair or a swarthy complexion, from Gael. *donn* dark, brown.
2. English: nickname for a man with dark hair or a swarthy complexion, from ME, OE *dunn* dark-coloured. In part it may also derive from an unrecorded ME survival of the OE byname *Dunn(a)* 'Dark'.
3. Scots: habitation name from *Dun* in the former county of Angus (now part of Tayside region), from Gael. *dùn* fort. Adam *de Dun* was elected to the deanery of Moray in 1255 and William *de Dun*, perhaps a relative, was dean there in 1268.
Vars.: **Dun(ne), Don, Donn(e),** DOWN.
Cogn. (of 1): Welsh: **Dwynn.**
Dims. (of 1): Ir.: DONOVAN, DONEGAN, DINEEN; **Donnan** (chiefly N Ireland). (Of 2): Eng.: **Dunnet(t).**
Patrs. (from 2): Eng.: **Down(e)s; Downing,** DUNNING.
'Descendant of D. 1': Ir.: **O'Dunn(e)** (from Gael. **Ó Duinn, Ó Doinn**).
'Son of the servant of D. 1': Ir.: **McIldoon, McEldoon,** GUNN (from Gael. **Mac Giolla Dhuinn**).

Dunning 1. English: patr. from DUNN 2.
2. Scots: habitation name from a place in the former county of Perths., recorded in 1200 as *Dunine* and later as *Dunyn*, from Gael. *dùnan*, a dim. of *dùn* fort.
3. Irish: var. of DINEEN.
The principal Scots family of this name are descended from Anechol, thane of Dunning, who flourished at the end of the 12th cent., and who was succeeded by his son, Gillemichel de Dunin.

Dunsford English: habitation name from *Dunsford* in Devon or *Dunsforth* in W Yorks., both so called from the gen. case of the OE byname DUNN + OE *ford* FORD.

Dunstable English: habitation name from a place in Beds., so called from the OE byname *Dunn(a)* (see DUNN 2) + OE *stapol* post, pillar.

Dunstall English: habitation name from places so called in Lincs. and Staffs., which have the same origin as TUNSTALL.

Dunstan English: 1. from a ME given name *Dunstan*, composed of the OE elements *dunn* dark, brown (see DUNN 2) + *stān* stone. This name was borne by a 10th-cent. archbishop of Canterbury who was later canonized.

2. habitation name from *Dunstone* in Devon, so called from OE *Dunstānestūn* 'settlement of *Dunstan*' (as in 1). The surname is still chiefly common in Devon, but there are places in other parts of the country with similar names but different etymologies (e.g. *Dunstan* in Northumb., *Dunston* in Lincs., Norfolk, Staffs., and Derbys.), which may possibly have contributed to the surname.

Dunster English: habitation name from a place in Somerset, which derives its name from the gen. case of the OE byname *Dunn(a)* (see DUNN 2) + OE *torr* rocky peak (of Celt. origin).

Dunton English: habitation name from any of various places so called. Most (e.g. those in Essex, Leics., Norfolk, and Warwicks.) get the name from OE *dūn* hill (see DOWN 1) + *tūn* enclosure, settlement. One in Beds. is probably named as *Dunningtūn* 'settlement (OE *tūn*) associated with *Dunna*' (see DUNN 2). One in Bucks probably has as its first element the OE personal name *Dudda* (see DODD).

Var.: **Downton** (there are places spelled thus in Shrops., Herefords., and Wilts.)

Dunwoodie Scots: habitation name from *Dinwoodie* near Dumfries, of uncertain etymology. It is first recorded in 1296 in the form *Dinwithie*, *Dunwythye* (then later 1482 *Donwethy*; 1503 *Dunwedy*; 1578 *Dumwiddie*) and is probably named with Brit. words that are ancestors of W *din* forest + *gwydd* shrubs, bushes.

Vars.: **Din(s)woodie, Dinwiddie**.

The first known bearers of the name are Sir Alan de Dunwidi, *who was seneschal of Annandale in the first quarter of the 13th cent., and Adam* de Dunwidie *or* de Dunwudhi, *who is recorded in several documents of the same period.*

Durant English (Norman) and French: from OF *durant* enduring (pres. part. of *durer* to endure, last, L *dūrāre*, from *dūrus* hard, firm; cf. DURO). This was fairly frequently used in the Middle Ages as a given name in the sense 'Steadfast', and seems also to have been a nickname with the meaning 'obstinate'.

Vars.: Eng.: **Durrant, Dur(r)an(d), Dorant**; DORAN. Fr.: **Durand, Dirand**.

Cogns.: It.: **Durante, Duranti**; **Durando** (Piedmont, Liguria); **Dante** (Tuscany); **Danti** (Venetia). Sp.: **Durán**. Cat.: **Duran(y)**. Port.: **Durão**.

Dims.: Fr.: **Durandeau, Durandet, Durandin, Duranteau, Durantel, Durantet, Durant(h)on, Duranseau**. It.: **D(ur)antini**.

Patrs.: Eng.: **Durrans, Durrance, Dorrins, Dorrance**. Port.: **Durães**.

Durcan Irish: Anglicized form of Gael. **Mac Duarcáin** 'son of *Duarcán*', a byname representing a dim. of *duairc* surly.

Vars.: **Durkan, Durkin**.

Dureau French: 1. nickname from a dim. of OF *dur* hard(y) (see DURO).

2. patr., originally *(fils) d'hureau*, from the nickname *hureau* scallywag, a dim. of *huré* shock-headed (see HURÉ).

Vars. (of 1): **Durel, Duret**.

Cogns. (of 1): Eng. (Norman): **Durrel(l)**.

Dürer German: 1. occupational name for a janitor, Ger. *T(h)ürer*, from MHG *tür* door.

2. In the case of the artist Albrecht Dürer (1471–1528), it has a habitational origin. His grandfather was a Hungarian from *Ajtós* (near Gyula, 46 miles from Nagyvárad, now Oradea in Rumania), so called from Hung. *ajtó* door (cf. DORE 1). The artist's father accordingly adopted the Germanized form *Türer* or *Dürer*, together with a coat of arms showing an open door.

Durham English: habitation name from the city in NE England, so called from OE *dūn* hill (see DOWN 1) + ON *holmr* island (see HOLME 2).

Var.: **Durram**.

Durie Scots: habitation name from a place in Fife, so called from Gael. *dobhar* stream + the local suffix *-ach*.

The first known bearer of the name is Duncan de Durry, *who witnessed a charter by Malise, Earl of Strathearn, in the latter part of the 13th cent.*

Düring German: regional name for someone from *Thuringia*. The region is named from its former occupation by the Gmc tribe of the *T(h)uringii*, displaced in the 6th cent. AD. This tribal name has been tentatively connected with the element *tur-* to dare (cf. ON *ðora*). The surname is especially common in Silesia, Saxony, and Bohemia as a result of the Ger. expansion eastwards during the early Middle Ages.

Vars.: **During, Dühri(n)g, Dürich, Dörich, Dierich**.

Cogns.: Low Ger.: **Dö(h)ring**.

Durkheim Jewish (W Ashkenazic): habitation name from *Turkheim* in Alsace, *Dürkheim* on the Isanach in the Palatinate, or *Türkheim* on the Neckar in Württemberg. All of these seem to be named from a Gmc byname *Turinc* 'Thuringian' (see DÜRING) + OHG *heim* homestead.

Vars.: **Durkheimer, Turkheim(er)**.

Duro Italian, Spanish, and Portuguese: nickname for a tough or unyielding man, from It., Sp., Port. *duro* hard, tough (L *dūrus*). The word had both the approving sense 'steadfast', 'enduring' (cf. DURANT) and the less favourable sense 'stubborn', 'obstinate', 'cruel'; the nickname may have been bestowed with either motivation.

Var.: It.: **Duri**.

Cogns.: Fr.: **Dur, Ledur**.

Dims.: It.: **Durin(i)** (Venetia). Fr.: DUREAU.

Dürrenmatt Swiss: habitational name from a place so named as the 'barren meadow', from MHG *dürre* barren, infertile (OHG *durri*) + *matte* meadow (a Swabian and Alemannic dial. term, from OHG *matta*; cf. MEAD 1), with the adj. preserving the weak dat. ending originally used after a preposition and def. article.

Dursley English: habitation name from *Dursley* in Gloucs., which is recorded in Domesday Book as *Dersilege*, from the OE personal name *Dēorsige* (composed of the elements *dēor* dear + *sige* victory) + *lēah* wood, clearing.

Durtnell English: habitation name from *Dorkinghole*, a lost settlement near Penshurst, Kent. The final element of this placename is *holh* (see HOLE); the first could be a derivative of OE *deorc* DARK.

A family of this name can be traced back to the 12th cent. through a large number of changes in the form of the name. Ralph de Darkinhole *was born* c.*1190, and in succeeding centuries his descendants were known variously as* Dirkinghole, Darknall, Derkinghale, Dartnall, Darknoll, Dartnoll, *and finally* Durtnell.

Duruflé French: apparently a habitation name, with fused preposition and (surprisingly) def. art., i.e. *du* rather than *de*, from places in Côtes-du-Nord and Saint-Doran called *Ruflet*.

Dušek Czech: from a dim. of the Slav. personal name *Duchoslav*, composed of the elements *duch* spirit + *slav* glory.

Vars.: **Dušák, Duch(ek), Duchoň, Duchaň, Ducháček**.

Dutetre French: topographic name, with fused preposition-cum-article *du*, from OF *tetre* mound, hillock (from LL *termes* (gen. *termitis*) boundary, a re-formation of class. L *termen* (gen. *terminis*) on the pattern of *limes* (gen. *limitis*), a word of similar meaning; the change of sense probably reflects the use of small mounds as clearly identifiable boundaries).

Vars.: **Dutartre, Duteutre**.

Dutton English: habitation name from places so called, esp. those in Ches. and Lancs., which get their names from the OE personal name *Dudd(a)* (see DODD 1) + OE *tūn* enclosure, settlement.

There is a family of this name who have been established at Dutton, Ches., since the 11th cent. An ancestor, Odard, was recorded there in Domesday Book; his grandson, Hugh de Dutton, *was lord of the manor in the reign of Henry II (1154–89).*

Duxbury English: habitation name from a place in Lancs., recorded in the early 13th cent. as *D(e)ukesbiri*, from the gen. case of the OE personal name *Deowuc* or *Duc(c)* (both of uncertain etymology; cf. DUCKETT 4) + OE *burh* fort (see BURKE).

Var.: **Duxberry**.

Dvořák Czech: status name for a man who worked at a manor house rather than on the land, from Czech *dvůr* manor, court (cf. Pol. *dwór*). In Moravia the word denoted a freeholder, subject only to the king. This is the fourth most common surname in Czechoslovakia.

Cogns.: Pol.: **Dworak** (also Jewish (E Ashkenazic); **Dwornik**.

Dims.: Czech: **Dvoraček**. Pol.: **Dworczak, Dworczyk**.

Habitation names: Czech: **Dvorský** (from places called *Dvůr* or *Dvory*). Pol.: **Dworakowski; Dworzyński**.

Dvorin Jewish (E Ashkenazic): metr. from the Yid. female given name *Dvoyre* (from the Hebr. name *Devorah*, lit. 'Bee', whence Eng. *Deborah*) + the Slav. suffix *-in*. The name *Devorah* was borne in the Bible by Rebecca's nurse (Gen. 35: 8) and by a prophetess and judge (Judges 4: 4). The popularity of the Yid. name is due largely to the latter.

Vars.: **Dvoirin** (SE Ashkenazic); **Dvojres** (with Yid. possessive *-s*); **Dvossis** (from *Dvosye*, a by-form of the given name).

Metrs. (from a dim.): **Dvorkin, Dworkin, Dworkis** (from the dim. given name *Dvorke*); **D(e)voskin, Dwoskin** (from the dim. given name *Dvoske*).

Dwyer Irish: Anglicized form of Gael. **Ó Du(i)bhuidhir** 'descendant of *Du(i)bhuidhir*', a personal name composed of the elements *dubh* dark, black (cf. DUFF) + *odhar* sallow, tawny.

Vars.: **O'Dwyer, O'Du(v)ire, Dwire, Dwyr**, DIVER, **Dever, (O')Deere**, DEERY, DYER.

Dye English: from a pet form of the medieval female given name DENNIS. The surname is most common in Norfolk, but found also in Yorks.

Dims.: **Dyet(t), Dyott**.

Metrs.: **Dyson** (chiefly Yorks.); **Dyason, Dyerson** (see also DYER); TYSON.

Dyer 1. English: occupational name for a dyer of cloth, ME *dyer* (from OE *dēag* dye; the verb is a back-formation from the agent noun).

2. Irish: var. of DWYER.

Vars.: **Dyster, Dexter** (originally these were fem. forms, but from an early period they are used also of men).

Patrs.: **Dyers; Dyerson** (see also DYE).

Dymock English: habitation name from a place in Gloucs., perhaps so called from a Brit. word akin to W *tymoch* pigsty (a cpd of *ty* house + *moch* pigs), but more probably from *din* fort + *moch* pigs.

Vars.: **Dymick, Dymo(c)ke, Dim(m)ock, Dimmack, Dimmick**.

The Dymoke *family have held the hereditary position of King's Champion for thirty-four generations. The office is attached to the lordship of the manor of Scrivelsby, Lincs., which was part of the dowry of Margaret de Ludlow on her marriage to Sir John Dymoke (d. 1381) around 1373.*

Dymowski Polish: habitation name from a place called *Dymów* (from Pol. *dym* smoke + the possessive suffix *-ów*, often used in forming placenames) + *-ski* suffix of local surnames (see BARANOWSKI), or perhaps a nickname from *dym* used independently, for example with reference to someone whose home was noticeably smoky.

Vars.: **Dymecki, Dymkowski**.

Dim. (a nickname, meaning 'Smoky'): **Dymek**.

Dysart Scots: habitation name from any of various places, for example those near Fife and Montrose, so called from Gael. *dìseart* hermit's cell, church (from L *dēsertum* desert, waste, solitary spot).

Dzięciełowski Polish: habitation name from a place called *Dzięciłów* (named with Pol. *dzięcioł* woodpecker + *-ów* possessive suffix, often used in forming placenames) + *-ski* suffix of local surnames (see BARANOWSKI).

Cogn.: Russ.: **Dyatlov**.

Dziedzic Polish: status name from Pol. *dziedzic* landowner, squire.

Var.: **Dziedziczak**.

Dzięgielewski Polish: habitation name from a place called *Dzięgielew* (named with Pol. *dzięgiel* angelica, from a Slav. root *dyag-* be strong) + *-ski* suffix of local surnames (see BARANOWSKI).

Cogns.: Russ.: **Dyagilev, Diaghilev**.

Dzierżyński Polish: habitation name from a place named with Pol. *dzierżawa* leasehold + *-yń* placename suffix, with the addition of the suffix of local surnames *-ski* (see BARANOWSKI). In some cases this may have been in effect a status name for a leaseholder.

Vars.: **Dzierżawski, Dzierżawa**.

Dzikowski Polish: habitation name from a place called *Dzików* (from Pol. *dzik* wild boar + *-ów* possessive suffix, often used in forming placenames) + *-ski* suffix of local surnames (see BARANOWSKI).

Dzugashvili Georgian (partly Jewish): said by Unbegaun to be from an unflattering nickname in the Ossetic language, derived from *dzuka* dross + the patronymic suffix *-shvili*.

E

Eade English: 1. from *Eda*, a ME short form of the female given name *Edith* (OE *Ēadgȳð* 'prosperity battle').

2. from a ME short form of ADAM, common esp. in Scotland and N England.

Vars.: **Ead, Ede.**

Dims.: **Eacock**; **Eady, Eadie** (chiefly Scots); **Eakin** (chiefly Irish; see also HIGGINS).

Patrs./metrs.: **Ead(e)s, Edes**; **Ed(e)son, Ed(d)ison**; **Eason** (see also MCKAY); **E(a)sson.**

Patrs./metrs. (from dims.): **Edkins, E(a)kins.**

Eagle English (mainly E Anglia): 1. nickname for a lordly, impressive, or sharp-eyed man, from the word denoting the bird, ME *egle*, from OF *aigle* (L *aquila*, replacing OE *earn*; cf. EARLY 1 and EARNSHAW).

2. habitation name from a place in Lincs., so called from ON *eik* oak + OE *lēah* wood, clearing; cf. OAKLEY.

3. Norman habitation name from *Laigle* in Orne, Normandy, whose name apparently means 'the eagle', although the reasons for this origin are not clear. The recorded forms may represent the result of the operation of early folk etymology on some unknown original. Matilda *de Aquila* is recorded in 1129 as the widow of Robert Mowbray, Earl of Northumberland.

Var.: **Egle.**

Cogns. (of 1): Fr.: **Aigle, Laigle.** It.: **Aquila, Aquili.** Sp.: AGUILAR.

Dims. (of 1): Eng.: **Eaglen, Eagling** (Norfolk). It.: **Aquilini, Aquilotti.**

Augs. (of 1): It.: **Aquiloni, Aquilone.**

Patrs. (from 1): Eng.: EAGLES. It.: **D(ell)'Aquila.**

Eagles English: 1. patr. from the nickname EAGLE.

2. Anglicized form of Fr. **Eglise**, a topographic name for someone who lived near a church (OF *eclise*, from L *ecclēsia*; cf. ECCLES).

Var.: **Eglese.**

This surname is most common in Gloucs. and Warwicks. A certain Solomon Eagles, *who was a Quaker musician in London in the second half of the 17th cent., was also known as* ECCLES *and may well have been of Huguenot origin. The Bristol family of this name are probably descended from a certain William Eagles, admitted burgess in 1630. As Bristol traders, they also acquired estates in Carolina, whence the name became established in North America.*

Eame English: from ME *eme* (maternal) uncle (OE *ēam*), a name presumably given originally to a man who acted as guardian to a niece or a young nephew after the death of the father.

Vars.: **Heam, Heme.**

Cogns.: Ger.: **Oheim, Öheim(b)**; **Ehe(i)m, Eham** (Bavaria); **Eha** (Swabia). Low Ger.: **Ohm(e), Öhm(e).** Flem., Du.: **Ohm, Oom.**

Dims.: Low Ger.: **Öhmke, Öhmichen.**

Patrs.: Eng.: **Eames, Heams, Hemes.** Low Ger.: **Ohms(en), Öhms.** Flem., Du.: **Ooms, Oomen.**

Earl English: originally, like most of the English names derived from the ranks of nobility, either a nickname or an occupational name for a servant employed in a noble household. The vocab. word is a native one, from OE *eorl* nobleman, and in the Middle Ages was often used as an equivalent of the Norman COUNT.

Vars.: **Earle, Hearl(e),** HARLE, **Hurle, Hurll.**

Cogn.: Swed.: **Jarl.**

Patrs.: Eng.: **Earles, Hurles.**

Early 1. English: habitation name from any of various places, such as *Earley* in Berks., *Earnley* in W Sussex, and *Arley* in Ches., Lancs., Warwicks., and Worcs., that derive their names from OE *earn* eagle + *lēah* wood, clearing.

2. English: nickname from OE *eorlīc* manly, noble (a deriv. of *eorl*; see EARL).

3. Irish: translation of Gael. *Ó Mocháin* (see MOHAN) and other related surnames, as for example *Ó Mochóir*, *Ó Mochóirghe*, and *Ó Maoil-Mhochóirghe*.

Vars.: **Earley, Erleigh, Erl(e)y.**

Earnshaw English: habitation name from a place in Lancs., so called from the gen. case of an OE personal name *Earn* 'Eagle' + OE *halh* nook (see HALE).

Earwaker English: from the ME given name *Erewaker*, OE *Eoforwacer*, composed of the elements *eofor* wild boar (cf. EVERARD) + *wacor* watchful, vigilant.

Vars.: **Earwicker, Erricker.**

East English: topographic name for someone who lived in the eastern part of a town or settlement, or outside it to the east, or regional name for one who had migrated westwards (and hence was regarded as coming from the east; cf. WEST, NORTH, NORRIS, SOUTH, SOUTHAM).

Vars.: **Eastes,** EASTER, EASTMAN.

Cogns.: Ger.: **Ost.** Low Ger.: **O(h)st, Öst, (Van) Oest, Van der Osten, Östing.** Flem., Du.: **Oost, Van Oost(en).** Swed.: **Öst(h), Östlin(g).**

Cpds (mostly arbitrary or ornamental coinages, rather than genuine topographic names): Swed.: **Östberg** ('east hill'); **Östlind** ('east lime'); **Östlund** ('east grove'). Jewish (Ashkenazic): **Ostberg** ('east hill'), **Ostfeld** ('east field'), **Ostwald** ('east wood'), **Ostwind** ('east wind').

Easter English: 1. topographic name for someone living to the east of a main settlement, from ME *easter* eastern (OE *ēasterra*, in form a comparative of *ēast*; see EAST).

2. habitation name from a group of villages in Essex, so called from OE *eowestre* sheepfold.

3. nickname for someone who had some connection with the festival of Easter, such as being born or baptized at that time (OE *ēastre*, perhaps from the name of a pagan festival connected with the dawn).

Var. (of 1): **Easterling** (with the Gmc suffix *-ling*).

Cogns. (of 1): Ger.: **Österer, Östermann.** Low Ger.: **Oster(mann), Osterling**; **Auster(mann), Austerling** (Westphalia). Flem., Du.: **Ossterling.** Swed.: **Öster(man).** (Of 1 or 3): Jewish (Ashkenazic, either from Ger. *Ost* east or *Oster* easter; reasons for adoption not clear): **Oster(er)**; **Osterman(n)**; **Ostern** ('Easter'). (Of 3 only): Ger.: **Oster.**

Dims. (of 1): Ger.: **Österle, Österl(e)in.**

Cpds (of cogns. of 1): Swed. (mainly ornamental rather than topographic): **Österberg** ('eastern hill'); **Östergren** ('eastern branch'); **Österholm** ('eastern island'); **Österlund** ('eastern grove'). Jewish (topographic or regional): **Ostersetzer** ('eastern setter'); **Osterweil** ('eastern settlement').

Easterbrook English: topographic name for someone who lived by a brook to the east of a main settlement, from ME *easter* eastern (see EASTER 1) + *brook* stream (see BROOK).

Vars.: **East(a)brook, Esterbrook.**

Eastham English: habitation name, now chiefly common in Lancs., from any of various places so called from OE *ēast* EAST + *hām* homestead or *hamm* water-meadow. There are places so named in Ches., Somerset, and Worcs., the first of which seems to have contributed most to the surname.

Eastman English: 1. topographic name, a var. of EAST.

2. from the OE personal name *Ēastmund*, composed of the elements *ēast* grace (or *ēast* east) + *mund* protection. The name survived the Norman Conquest, although it was never very frequent, and is attested in the 13th and 14th cents. in the forms *Estmund* and *Es(t)mond*.

Vars. (of 2): **Eastment, Astman, Esmond(e).**

Cogn. (of 1): Low Ger., Swed.: **Östman.**

Easton English and Scots: 1. habitation name from any of the numerous places so called. Most are from OE *ēast* EAST + *tūn* enclosure, settlement; examples in Devon and the Isle of Wight get their names from the OE phrase *be ēastan tūne* '(place) to the east of the settlement'. Another in Devon gets its first element from the gen. case of the OE personal name *Ælfrīc* (composed of the elements *ælf* elf + *rīc* power) or *Aðelrīc* (composed of the elements *aðel* noble + *rīc* power). One in Essex is from OE *ēg* island + *stān(as)* stone(s). Finally *Easton Neston* in Northants gets its name from OE *Ēadstānestūn* 'settlement of *Ēadstān*', a personal name composed of the elements *ēad* prosperity, riches + *stān* stone.

Eastwood English: habitation name from any of various places so called. Most, such as the one in Essex, get the name from OE *ēast* EAST + *wudu* WOOD, but an example in Notts. originally had as its final element ON *ðveit* meadow (see THWAITE).

Easy English: of uncertain origin, perhaps a nickname for a carefree person, from ME *aisy* at ease, untroubled (OF *aisié*, past part. of *aiser* to put at ease, from *aise* ease, a deriv. of L *adiacens* adjacent, to hand, convenient). The surname is found mainly in Cambs., E Suffolk, and the London area.

Vars.: **Easey; Heas(e)y.**

Eaton English: habitation name from any of the numerous places so called from OE *ēa* river or *ēg* island, low-lying land + *tūn* enclosure, settlement.

Var.: **Eyton.**

At least one Eyton *family derive their name from an estate in Shrops. which they have held since the 12th cent. Robert* de Eyton *is recorded in transactions with Shrewsbury Abbey in the reign of Henry II (1154–70).*

Eatwell English: habitation name from *Etwall* in Derbys., so called from a short form of some OE cpd name with a first element *Ēad-* prosperity (cf., e.g., EDMOND) + OE *well(a)* spring, stream (see WELL).

Ebdon English (E Devon and Somerset): habitation name from a hamlet in NE Somerset, near Weston-super-Mare, of uncertain etymology.

Var.: **Ebden.** See also HEBDEN.

Ebner 1. German: topographic name for someone who lived on a piece of flat ground or a plateau, from MHG *eben(e)* flat, smooth (OHG *eban*), with *-er* suffix of human agents.

2. German: occupational name for an arbiter or judge, MHG *ebenære* (from the same word, in the sense 'fair', 'equitable').

3. Jewish (Ashkenazic): of uncertain meaning, possibly of the same origin as 1 or 2.

Eccles Scots and English: habitation name from places near Berwick, Dumfries, Manchester, and elsewhere, all so called from the Brit. word that lies behind W *eglwys* church (from L *ecclesia*, Gk *ekklēsia* gathering, assembly, a deriv. of *ekkalein* to summon, call out). Such places would have been the sites of notable pre-Anglo-Saxon churches or Christian communities.

Var.: **Ecles.**

Eccleston English: habitation name from any of several places so called in Ches. and Lancs., which get their names from an ancient Brit. word meaning 'church' (see ECCLES) + OE *tūn* enclosure, settlement.

Echave Spanish form of Basque **Etxabe**: topographic name for someone who lived on the ground floor of a house, from the Basque elements *etxe* house + *be(e)* bottom, lower part.

Var.: **Echabe.**

Echeandía Spanish form of Basque **Etxeandia**: topographic name for someone who lived in a large house, from the Basque elements *etxe* house + *andi* large + the def. art. *-a*.

Echeverría Spanish form of Basque **Etxeberria**: topographic or habitation name from the Basque elements *etxe* house + *berri* new + the def. art *-a*. This is the origin of the name of a village near Pamplona, now called *Javier*, the birthplace of St Francisco de Jassu XAVIER (1506–52), missionary to East Asia and founder of the Society of Jesus.

Vars.: **Echeberría, Echevarría, Echebarría; Echéberri, Echébarri, Echévarri, Echávarri, Echarri; Chávarri, Chavarría.**

Eck 1. German and Jewish (Ashkenazic): topographic name for someone living at a corner, Ger. *Eck(e)*, Yid. *ek* (MHG *ecke*, *egge*, OHG *ecka*, *egga*). This could have been the corner of two streets in a town or, in the case of the Ger. name, the corner of a field or area of land.

2. German: short form of any of the various Gmc cpd personal names with a first element *agi(n)*, *agil* edge, point (of a weapon, akin to the word in 1 above); cf., e.g., ECKHARDT, EGGEBRECHT, and EGILOFF.

3. Swedish: cogn. of OAK.

Vars. (of 1 and 2): **Ecke, Egg(e).** (Of 1 only): Ger.: **Ecker, Egger.** Jewish: **E(c)ker, Ekler, Eckmann, E(c)kerman; E(c)kerling** (with the Gmc suffix *-ling*); **E(c)khaus, Ekhause, Ekhaizer, Eckheizer, Ekhajzer** ('dweller in the corner house'; the last form is a Pol. spelling). (Of 2 only): Ger.: **Ege; Egi** (Switzerland).

Dims. (of 2): **Öckl** (Bavaria); **Eggle** (Swabia); **Eg(g)li** (Switzerland). Low Ger.: **Eckmann.** It.: **Aghini.**

Patrs. (from 2): Ger.: **Eck(e)s, Egges.** Low Ger.: **Eggen(s), Egges, Egging.** Fris.: **Eggena.** Du.: **Egging, Eggink.**

Eckersley English (Lancs.): habitation name from a lost place in the parish of Leigh, near Wigan, apparently so called from the gen. case of the OE personal name *Ecgheard* (see ECKHARDT) or *Ecghere* + OE *lēah* wood, clearing.

Eckhardt German: from a Gmc personal name composed of the elements *agi(n)* edge, point + *hard* hardy, brave, strong. The OE cogn. *Ecgheard*, attested in various placenames such as ECKERSLEY and EGERTON, does not seem to have survived the Norman Conquest in sufficient strength to have given rise to a surname.

Vars.: **Eck(e)hard**, **Eckart**, **Eckert**; **Einhart**, **Einert**. Low Ger.: **Eggehart**; **Eggert** (see also EGGEBRECHT); **Ehnert**. Fris.: **Edzart**, **Edzard**. Du.: **Egger**.

Patrs.: Low Ger.: **Eggers**; **Eggerding**, **Eierding** (Westphalia). Du.: **Eggers**.

Eckstein German and Jewish (Ashkenazic): nickname or ornamental name from Ger. *Eckstein* cornerstone, Yid. *ekshteyn* (from OHG *ecka* corner + *stein* stone), given perhaps to a trusty, reliable person.

Vars.: Jewish: **Ekstein**, **Ekstien**; **Eksztajn** (Pol. spelling).

Cogn.: Low Ger.: **Eksteen**.

Eddington English: 1. habitation name from a place in Berks., *Eddevetone* in Domesday Book, named from the OE female personal name *Ēadgifu* (composed of the elements *ēad* prosperity, wealth + *gifu* gift) + OE *tūn* enclosure, settlement.

2. var. of EDINGTON.

Eddy English (W Country): from the ME given name *Edwy*, OE *Ēadwīg*, composed of the elements *ēad* prosperity, fortune + *wīg* war.

Var.: **Eddie**.

Edel 1. German: from Ger., MHG *edel* noble (OHG *edili*, a deriv. of *adel* nobility). In the Middle Ages this was a term applied to the lowest order of free citizen, ranking below the nobility and knightly class, but above the masses of the servile population.

2. Jewish (Ashkenazic): from the Yid. female given name *Eydl* 'Noble'.

3. Jewish (Ashkenazic): ornamental name from mod. Ger. *edel* or Yid. *eydl* noble, splendid, fine. See also ADEL 3.

Vars. (of 1): **Edelmann**, **Ed(e)ler**. (Of 3): **Edelman(n)**, **Eidelman**; **Eidler**, **Aidler**; **E(i)delheit**, **Edelheid** ('nobleness').

Metrs. (from 2): **Eidels**, **Edelso(h)n**, **Eidelson**; **Aides(s)** (from the back-formation *Eyde*, which has also given the surname **Eida**).

Cpds: Jewish (ornamental, from 3): **E(i)delbaum**, **Edelboum** ('noble tree'); **Eidelberg**, **Edelsberg**, **Aidelsberg** ('noble hill'); **Edelsburg** ('noble town'); **Eidelkind** ('noble child'); **E(i)delstein** ('precious stone', 'jewel').

Eden 1. English: from the ME given name *Edun*, OE *Ēadhūn*, composed of the elements *ēad* prosperity, wealth + *hūn* bear-cub.

2. English: habitation name from Castle *Eden* or *Eden* Burn in Co. Durham, both of which derive from a Brit. river name perhaps meaning 'water', recorded by the Greek geographer Ptolemy in the 2nd cent. AD in the form *Ituna*.

3. Frisian: patr. from the given name *Ede* (see OADE).

4. Jewish: ornamental name referring to the garden of Eden; cf. LUSTGARTEN.

Vars. (of 1): **Eaden**, **E(a)don**.

Patr. (from 1): **Edens**.

A family of the name Eden *have held lands at Windleston Hall, by Eden Burn in Co. Durham, since at least the 15th cent.; they acquired a baronetcy in 1672. Their most prominent member has been Sir Anthony Eden (1897–1977), who was Foreign Secretary (1935–38, 1940–45, and 1951–55) and Prime Minister (1955–57), and who was later created Lord Avon.*

Eder 1. German: topographic name for someone who lived on a patch of bare, uncultivated land, from Ger. *öd* empty, bare (MHG *(o)ed(e)*, OHG *ōdi*) + *-er* suffix of human nouns. It may also be a habitation name from any of the numerous places named with this element.

2. Jewish: of uncertain origin, possibly from Hebr. *eder* herd, flock, or (if Ashkenazic) possibly derived as in 1.

Vars. (of 1): **Ederer**, **Öder(er)**.

Cogns. (of 1): Du.: **Van Ede**, **Van E(e)den**.

Edgar 1. English: from the OE personal name *Ēadgār*, composed of the elements *ēad* prosperity, fortune + *gār* spear. The name is found in ME in various forms, e.g. *Edgar*, *Adger*, *Agar*.

2. Jewish: of unknown origin, possibly an Anglicization of one or more like-sounding Jewish names.

Vars. (of 1): **Eagar**, **Eag(g)er**, **Eg(g)ar**, **Egarr**, **Eg(g)er**, **Edger**, **Adger**; **Agar**, **Ager**; **Adair**; **Odge(a)r**, **Og(i)er** (from the Continental Gmc cogn., introduced into England by the Normans). (Of 2): **Agar**.

Cogns. (of 1): Fr.: **Edgar(d)**; **Odier**, **Audier**, **Aut(h)ier**; **Augier**, **Og(i)er**, **Ougier**, **Ogé**. It.: **Ugg(i)eri**, **Ucciero**, **Ogg(i)eri**, **Oggero** (N Italy); **Ogier** (Venetia); **Ugge** (Lombardy); **Auggieri**, **Auggiero**, **Aug(i)eri**, **Aug(i)ero** (S Italy).

Patrs. (from 1): Eng.: **Edgars**, **Eagers**, **Eggars**, **Agars**; **Odgers**.

Edge English: topographic name, esp. in Lancs. and the W Midlands, for someone who lived on or by a hillside or ridge, from OE *ecg* edge (cf. ECK).

Edgeley English: habitation name from places in Ches. and Shrops., so called from OE *edisc* enclosed pasture + *lēah* wood, clearing.

Var.: **Edgley**.

Edgeworth English: habitation name from places in Gloucs. and Lancs., so called from OE *ecg* hillside, ridge (see EDGE) + *worð* enclosure (see WORTH).

Var.: **Edgworth**.

Edgington English (W Midlands): apparently a habitation name, of uncertain origin. It may be from a lost place, so called as the 'settlement (OE *tūn*) associated with *Ecgi*', a short form of the various cpd names with the first element *ecg* edge, point (of a weapon). Alternatively, it may be a corruption of *Erdington*, a place in the W Midlands that derives its name from the OE personal name *Ēanrēd* + OE *tūn* enclosure, settlement.

Edington N English and Scots: habitation name from any of various places so called, esp. one in Northumb. originally named in OE as *Idingtūn* 'settlement (OE *tūn*) associated with *Ida*'; see IDE. The place of the same name in Somerset, which may not have contributed to the surname, appears in Domesday Book as *Eduuintone*, from the OE personal name *Ēadwine* (see EDWIN) or *Ēadwynn* (a female personal name composed of the elements *ēad* prosperity, wealth + *wynn* joy) + OE *tūn* enclosure, settlement.

Var.: EDDINGTON.

Edlestone 1. English: from the OE personal name *Æðelstān*, composed of the elements *æðel* noble + *stān* stone.

2. Jewish (Ashkenazic): Anglicized form of *Edelstein* (see EDEL).

Vars. (of 1): ALSTON, ASTON.

Edmead English: nickname for a humble or self-effacing person, from ME *edmede* humble, OE *ēadmēde*, a cpd of *ēaðe* easy, gently + *mōd* mind.

Vars. (of 1): **Edmed**, **Edmett**, **Edmott**.

Patrs.: **E(a)dmead(e)s**.

Edmond English and French: from the ME given name *Edmund* (OE *Ēadmund*, composed of the elements *ēad* prosperity, fortune + *mund* protection. In medieval

England and France the name was often bestowed in honour of the E Anglian King St Edmund the Martyr (d. 869), who was killed by pagan Danish invaders, and about whom many legends grew up.

Vars.: Eng.: **Edmund**. Fr.: **Edmont, Émon(d), Émont**.

Dims.: Fr.: **Émonet, Émonot**; MONET, **Monot**.

Patrs.: Eng.: **Edmon(d)s, Edmunds; Edmon(d)son, Edmundson, Edmenson, Edminson**. Welsh: **Bedmond** (with the patr. prefix *ap*; sometimes altered to BEAUMONT). Sc.: MCKEEMAN.

Edrich English: from the ME given name *Edrich, Ederick*, OE *Ēadrīc*, composed of the elements *ēad* prosperity, fortune + *rīc* power.

Vars.: **Edridge; Etheridge** (an altered form current since the beginning of the 17th cent., developed from the late 16th-cent. forms *Et(t)riche, Et(t)ridge*).

Edward English: from the ME given name *Edward*, OE *Ēadward*, composed of the elements *ēad* prosperity, fortune + *w(e)ard* guard. Although apparently of exclusively OE origin, the given name also became popular on the Continent, perhaps as a result of the fame of the two canonized kings of England, Edward the Martyr (962–79) and Edward the Confessor (1004–66). They certainly contributed largely to its great popularity in England.

Var.: **Edwarde**.

Cogns.: Fr.: **Edouard**. Prov.: **Edard**. Sp.: **Duarte**. Cat.: **Duart**. Port.: **Eduardo**. Fris.: **Edert**.

Patrs.: Eng.: **Edward(e)s; Edwardson**. W: **Bedward, Beddard**. Dan., Norw.: **Edvardsen**. Swed.: **Edvardsson**.

The surname Edwards *is very common in Wales, where surnames were fixed at a relatively late date. For example, the name was assumed in the late 15th cent. by John Edwards, the son of John* ap Edward hên *'son of Old Edward'*.

Edwin English: from the ME given name *Edwine*, OE *Ēadwine*, composed of the elements *ēad* prosperity, fortune + *wine* friend.

Vars.: **Edwing, Edwyn**.

Cogn.: Ger.: **Ettwein**.

Patr.: Swed.: **Edvinsson**.

Efron Jewish: ornamental name, taken from the biblical placename *Efron*, a mountain mentioned in Josh. 15: 9 and a Benjaminite city mentioned in 2 Chron. 13: 19.

Vars.: **Ephron, Evron; Efroni, Efron(n)y, Ephrony, Evroni** (with the Hebr. suffix *-i*).

Egerton English: habitation name from places in Kent and Ches. The former is so called from OE *Ecgheardingtūn* 'settlement (OE *tūn*) associated with *Ecgheard*' (see ECKHARDT); the second, which is the main source of the surname, is more likely to have been named as the 'settlement of *Ecghere*' (in which the second element is OE *here* army).

Vars.: **Eggerton, Edgerton**.

Bearers of this name, including the Duke of Sutherland and the Earl of Wilton, are descended from David, Sheriff of Chester in the reign of Henry III (1216–72). His son, Philip, was the first in the family to be known by the surname, derived from lands in Ches. which he acquired from Urian de Egerton.

Eggebrecht German: from a Gmc personal name composed of the elements *agi(l)* edge, point (of a weapon) + *berht* bright, famous. The Eng. cogn. *Egbert* is not found as a surname, in spite of the fame of King Egbert of Wessex.

Vars.: **Ebbrecht, Ebrech(t), Ehebrecht, Eckebrecht, Eckbrett; Ehlebracht, Eilebrecht, E(i)lbracht, El(e)brecht**.

Cogns.: Low Ger.: **Egbert; Eggert** (see also ECKHARDT); **Eb(b)ert** (see also EVERARD); **Eppert; E(i)lbert**.

Dims.: Fris.: **Ebbe(ke), Ebke(ma), Epp(mann)**.

Patrs.: Ger.: **Eckenbrecher**. Low Ger.: **Ebbers, Eppers; Elbers, Elbertz, Elberding** (N Rhineland). Du.: **Egberts, Ebbers**.

Patrs. (from dims.): Low Ger.: **Eppen(s), Epping, Eppink**. Fris.: **Ebben, Eb(be)sen, Ebbing(a), Ebbena, Ebeling**.

Eggleston English: habitation name from a place in Co. Durham so called, or from *Egglestone* in N Yorks, both of which are named from the gen. case of the OE personal name *Ecgwulf* (see EGILOFF) + OE *tūn* enclosure, settlement.

Vars.: **Egleston, Egglestone**.

Eggleton English: habitation name from a place near Hereford, named in OE as the settlement (OE *tūn*) associated with *Ecgwulf* (see EGILOFF) or *Ecgel* (a derivative of the various cpd names with the first element *ecg*; cf. EDGINGTON).

Egido Spanish: topographic name for someone who lived by a patch of common land, situated at the edge of a village, OSp. *exido* (L *exitus* exit, way out, a deriv. of *exīre* to go out).

Var.: **Ejido**.

Egiloff German: from a Gmc personal name composed of the elements *agi(l)* edge, point (of a weapon) + *wolf* wolf, cogn. with OE *Ecgwulf*. This was the name of several Lombard kings (ancestors of the Bavarian ducal line of the *Agilolfinger*), who introduced the name to Italy.

Vars.: **Egelolf, Egloff, Eckloff; Egleha(a)f** (Franconia); **Eginolf, Egenolf(f), Egenlauf, Einolf** (with a first element *agin*, a different extension of the same stem).

Cogns.: It.: **Aghinolfi; Aiolfi, Ajolfi** (Lombardy).

Patr.: Swed.: **Elofsson**.

Eguía Spanish form of Basque **Egia**: topographic name for someone who lived on a mountain ridge, from Basque *egi* ridge, slope + the def. art. *-a*.

Egúsquiza Spanish form of Basque **Eguskiza**: topographic name for someone who lived in a spot that caught the sun, from *eguzki* sun + the suffix of abundance *-tza*.

Ehlert Low German: from a medieval given name, composed of the Gmc elements *agil* edge, point (of a weapon) + *hard* brave, hardy, strong or *ward* guard.

Vars.: **Ehler, Eiler(t)**.

Dims.: **Ehlermann, Eildermann**.

Patrs.: **Ehlers, Eilers; Ehlerding, Eilerding** (Westphalia). Fris.: **Eil(der)ts**. Dan.: **Ehlers, Eiler(t)sen**.

Ehmann 1. German: nickname for someone under feudal obligations of some particular kind, from MHG *ē* law, contract (OHG *ēwa*) + *mann* man (OHG *man*).

2. Jewish: (Ashkenazic): nickname from mod. Ger. *Ehemann* husband (the word *Ehe* having progressively become restricted to the marriage contract and then to the state of matrimony itself). At one time in the Austrian Empire, only one son in a Jewish family was officially permitted to marry and start a family of his own: this may have been a surname adopted by such a person.

Var.: **Ehemann**.

Ehn Swedish: ornamental name from Swed. *en* juniper. This is one of the many names derived from words denoting natural features, which were used to form Swed. surnames in the 19th cent.

Cpds (ornamental): **E(h)nlund(h)** ('juniper grove'); **E(h)nqvist** ('juniper twig'); **E(h)nström** ('juniper river').

Ehrlich German and Jewish (Ashkenazic): nickname or ornamental name from Ger. *ehrlich* honourable, honest, or

Yid. *erlekh* honest, virtuous (MHG *ērlich* respected, honoured, from OHG *ēra* honour).
Vars.: Jewish: **Erlich(man)**.
Patr.: Jewish: **Erlichson**.
Cpd (ornamental): Jewish: **Erlichgerecht** ('honest and fair').

Ehrmann Jewish (Ashkenazic): ornamental name from mod. Ger. *Ehre* honour + *Mann* man.
Vars.: **Ehre, Ehrenmann**.
Cpds (ornamental): **E(h)renberg** ('honour hill'); **Ehrenfeld** ('honour field'); **E(h)renfried** ('honour peace'); **Ehrenfreund** ('honour friend'); **Ehrenhalt** ('honour support'); **Ehrenhaus** ('honour house'); **Ehrenkranz** ('honour garland'); **Ernlib** ('honour love'); **Ehrenpreis** ('honour praise'); **E(h)renreich** ('rich in honour'); **Ehrenstein, Ernstein** ('honour stone'), **Ehrent(h)al, Erental** ('honour valley'), **Ernwert** ('honourable, respectable'); **Ehrenwort** ('word of honour'); **Ehrenzweig** ('honour twig').

Eichhorn 1. German: nickname from Ger. *Eichhorn* squirrel (now replaced as a vocab. word by its dim. *Eichhörnchen*). The vocab. word is from OHG *eihhurno*, a cpd of *eih* oak + *urno*, from the ancient Gmc and Indo-European name of the animal, which was later wrongly associated with *hurno* horn.
2. Jewish (Ashkenazic): ornamental name from the vocab. word as in 1.

Eiffel German and French: regional name for someone from the district bounded by the mid-Rhine, Moselle, and Ardennes known as the *Eifel*. The first record of the place-name occurs AD *c*.800 in the L form *in pago Aflense*, *E(i)flense*. According to Bahlow the term is of pre-Gmc origin.
Vars.: **Eif(f)ler**.

Eigner 1. German: status name originally denoting a smallholder who held his land outright, rather than by rent or feudal obligation. In the Middle Ages this was sufficiently rare to be worthy of remark and was normally a special privilege granted in recognition of some exceptional service. The vocab. word is from MHG *aigen* own (OHG *eigan*), with the addition of the suffix *-er*, denoting human nouns.
2. Jewish (Ashkenazic): from Ger. *Eigner* owner, presumably adopted as an indication of property-owning status.
Var.: **Aigner** (Bavaria).

Einhorn 1. German: nickname from Ger. *Einhorn* unicorn (MHG *einhorn*, OHG *einhurno*, a cpd of *ein* one + *hurno* horn). This may also be a house name, from a house sign depicting the fabulous animal.
2. Jewish (Ashkenazic): ornamental name from Ger. *Einhorn* unicorn.
Var. (of 2): **Ainhorn**.

Einold German: from a medieval given name, composed of the Gmc elements *agin* edge, point (of a weapon) + *wald* rule.
Cogns.: Fr.: **E(y)nault, Aynauld, Eynaud, Enaux**.
Patr.: Dan.: **Enevoldsen**.

Einsiedel German: from MHG *einsidel* solitary settler, hermit, monk (OHG *einsidilio*, a cpd of *ein* one, alone + *sedal* seat, settlement, inspired by L *monachus*; see MONK). The surname may in some cases have referred to an actual hermit, or by extension to a dweller in an isolated situation or an unsociable individual, but more often it is simply a habitation name from places in Bavaria, Austria, and Switzerland called *Einsiedeln*, from having once been the site chosen by hermits (cf. ARMITAGE; and Ger. *München* from MHG (*zu den*) *münichen* 'at the (place of the) monks'). The famous monastery of this name in Switzerland was founded by a hermit named Meinrad in 830.

Einstein 1. German: habitation name from various places named with a MHG deriv. of *einsteinen* to enclose, surround with stone. In the unsettled social climate of the Middle Ages even relatively minor settlements were commonly surrounded with stone walls as a defence against attack.
2. Jewish (Ashkenazic): adoption of the Ger. name, or else an ornamental name, one of the many ending in *-stein*.
Var. (of 2): **Ainstein**.

Eisen German and Jewish (Ashkenazic): metonymic occupational name for an ironworker or smith, or an ironmonger, from Ger. *Eisen* iron (MHG *īsen*, OHG *īsan*). It may also have been used as a nickname, with reference to the strength and hardness of iron or to its colour, while as a Jewish name it was also adopted as an ornamental name from mod. Ger. *Eisen* iron or the Yid. cogn. *ayzn*.
Vars.: Ger.: **Eis(en)mann, Eiser(mann), Eisler, Eisner**. Jewish: **Aizen, Ajzen, Aizin; Eisenman, Ajsenman, Aizenman, Ajzenman, Aizner, Ajzner** (occupational names).
Cogn.: Du.: **IJzer**.
Cpds (mainly ornamental): Jewish: **Eisenbach** ('iron stream'); **Eisenbaum, Eisenboum, Aizenbaum, Ajzenbaum** ('iron tree'); **Eisenberg(er), Aisenberg, Ajsenberg, Aizenberg, Ajzenberg, Ajzinberg** ('iron hill'); **Eisenfarb** ('iron colour'); **Eisenfeld, Aizenfeld** ('iron field'); **Eisenfish, Ajzenfisz** ('iron fish'); **Eisenhardt, Aizengart** ('iron hard'); **Eisenkeit** ('iron chain'); **Eisenkraft** ('iron strength'); **Ajzenkranz** ('iron wreath'); **Eisenpresser** ('iron presser', presumably an occupational name for a blacksmith); **Eisenreich** ('iron rich'); **Eisens(c)her** ('iron scissors or shears'); **Eisenschmidt** ('iron smith', an occupational name); **Eisenschreiber** ('iron writer'; reason for adoption unknown); **Aizenstark** ('strong as iron'); **Eisenstein, Aizenstein, Aizenshtain, Ajzensztein** ('iron stone'); **Eisent(h)al, Aizental, Ajzental** ('iron valley'); **Eisenzweig** ('iron twig').

Eisenbein German: nickname from MHG *īsen* iron (see EISEN) + *bein* leg (OHG *bein*), denoting someone who had an artificial leg made of metal (cf. PETTIFER), or perhaps a metal-worker who manufactured greaves and leg-armour.

Eisengrein German: from a Gmc personal name composed of the elements *īsan* iron + *grīm* mask. This is the name born by the wolf in the popular medieval cycle of beast tales, in part in reference to the iron-grey colour of the animal (cf. FARRANT 1), in part a memory of the older association of the wolf with Odin (cf. GRIME). The surname may represent a nickname given in jesting allusion to this. It is found principally in Baden-Württemberg.

Eisenhandler Jewish (Ashkenazic): occupational name for an ironmonger, from Ger. *Eisenhändler* ironmonger, from *Eisen* iron + *Händler* dealer.
Var.: **Eisenhendler**.

Eisenhauer German: occupational name for a worker in iron, from MHG *īsen* iron (see EISEN) + *houwære*, a deriv. of *houwen* to cut, chop, hew (OHG *houwan*).
Vars.: **Haueis(en)**.
Cogns.: Du.: **Eisenhouwer** (U.S. **Eisenhower**).

Eisenstadt Jewish (Ashkenazic): habitation name from a town formerly in Hungary, now in Austria, known in Yid. as *Ayznshtot* 'Iron City'. See also ASH 2.
Vars.: **Aizens(h)tat, Ajzensta(d)t, Ajzensztad**.

Eitel German: nickname from MHG *ītel* only, purely, simply (OHG *ītal*, a cogn. of IDLE 3). In the days before surnames had begun to make their mark, bearers of common given names would often have a second given name as a distinguishing feature; someone who did not have such a second given name could be distinguished by this fact in itself, as for example *ītel Hans* (just Hans) as against *Hans Joachim*. The meaning 'vain', 'conceited' is comparatively late and has probably not contributed to the surname.

Vars.: **Eytel, Eydel.**

Eke English (E Anglia): habitation name from *Eyke* in Suffolk, named from ON *eik* oak.

Elborough English: habitation name, probably from a minor place in the parish of Hutton, near Weston-super-Mare in Somerset. It gets its name from the OE personal name *Ella* + OE *bearu* grove.

Vars.: **Elbro(w), Elbra.**

The first known bearer of the name is William Elborough, *recorded in Cambs. in 1617. The first known occurrences of the form* Elbro *are in Wilts. in 1790 and Somerset in 1816.*

Elder English: distinguishing nickname bestowed on the elder (OE *ealdra*, comp. of *eald* OLD) of two bearers of the same given name. At first sight it might be thought to be a topographic name from the tree (OE *ellern*, with later dissimilation), but this origin does not seem to be supported by any evidence from early forms with prepositions.

Cogn.: Jewish (Ashkenazic): **Elter(mann)** ('elder (man)'; reasons for adoption as a surname unclear).

Elend German: from MHG *ellende* banished, miserable, luckless (OHG *elilenti*, from *ali* other, foreign + *land* land), apparently used more often as a nickname than as a descriptive term of literal application.

Vars.: **Ellend, Ehlend.**

Cogn.: Jewish (Ashkenazic): **Elent** (from Yid. *elent* lonely or mod. Ger. *elend* miserable).

Elford English: habitation name from a place so called from the OE personal name *Ella* (see ELLINGTON) + *ford* FORD, or from OE *alor*, *elre* alder tree + *ford*. There is a place of this name in Staffs. and another in Northumb., but the surname is now chiefly common in Devon.

Elizalde Basque: topographic name for someone who lived by a church, from *eleiza* church (a Romance borrowing; cf. ECCLES) + the suffix *-alde* by. This also occurs as the name of a village in N Spain, from which the surname may in part be derived.

Var.: **Elejalde** (a common placename).

Elizondo Basque: topographic name for someone who lived near a church, from *eleiza* church (cf. ELIZALDE) + the suffix *-ondo* near, beside. This also occurs as a placename in Navarre, from which the surname may alternatively be derived as a habitation name.

Elkin 1. English: dim. of *Elias*; see ELLIS.

2. Jewish (E Ashkenazic): metr. from the Yid. female given name *Elke* + the Slav. suffix *-in*.

Patr. (from 1): **Elkins.**

Elkington English: habitation name from a place so called, probably N and S *Elkington* in Lincs., which are named from an OE personal name, possibly *Ēa(n)lāc* + OE *tūn* enclosure, settlement. *Elkington* in Northants did not acquire the name until 1617, before which it was *Eltington* or *Elteton*.

Ellen English: from the normal medieval vernacular form of the given name *Helen* (Gk *Helenē*, of uncertain origin, perhaps akin to *helanē* torch). This was the name of the mother of Constantine the Great, credited with finding the True Cross; according to legend she was of British origin, and the name was consequently popular in England during the Middle Ages.

Vars.: **Elen, El(l)in, Elleyne, Hel(l)en, Hellin.**

Metrs.: **Ellens, Ellin(g)s, Hellens.**

Eller 1. German: habitation name from places in the N Rhine and Moselle areas, so called from an old stream-name *Elera*, *Alira*, possibly of Celt. origin.

2. Low German: topographic name for someone who lived by an alder tree, from MLG *elre*, *alre* alder (cf. OHG *elira*; the mod. Ger. form *Erle* is from the metathesized *erila*).

3. Jewish (E Ashkenazic): var. of HELLER, reflecting varieties of Yid. in which there is no /h/.

4. Italian: Venetian form of the given name HILARY.

Var. (of 1–3): **Ellermann.**

Cogns. (of 2): Pol.: OLSZEWSKI. Jewish (Ashkenazic, ornamental): **Erlbaum** (with Ger. *Baum* tree).

Ellingham English: habitation name from places in Hants, Northumb., and Norfolk. The first of these is so called from OE *Ēdlingahām* 'homestead (OE *hām*) of the people of *Ēdla*', a personal name derived from a short form of the various cpd names with a first element *ēad* prosperity, fortune; the others may have the same origin or incorporate the personal name *Ella* (see ELLINGTON).

Ellington English: habitation name from places in Cambs., Kent, Northumb., and N Yorks.; most are so called from OE *Ellingtūn* 'settlement (OE *tūn*) associated with *Ella*', a short form of the various cpd names with a first element *ælf* elf, but the one in Kent has its first element from the OE byname *Ealda* OLD.

Var.: **Elington.**

Elliott 1. English: dim. of ELLIS.

2. English and Scots: from a ME given name, *Elyat*, *Elyt*. This represents at least two OE personal names which have fallen together: the male name *Aðelgēat* (composed of the elements *aðel* noble + *Gēat*, a tribal name; see JOCELYN), and the female personal name *Aðelgȳð* (composed of the elements *aðel* noble + *gȳð* battle). The ME name seems also to have absorbed various other given names of OE or Continental Gmc origin, as for example OE *Ælfweald*; see ELLWOOD and see also below.

3. Scots: Anglicized form of the originally distinct Gael. surname **Elloch, Eloth**, a topographic name from Gael. *eileach* dam, mound, bank.

Vars.: **Elliot, Eliot(t)** (these different spellings have been adopted by different families as a distinguishing feature.)

A major family spelling their name Eliot *is found in the Border region of Scotland. They can be traced to Robert* Elwald *(d. 1497) of Redheugh, Roxburghs., who was squire to the Earl of Angus.*

Andrew Eliot, *a shoemaker of East Coker, Somerset, who emigrated to Boston, Mass., in 1670, was the founder of a distinguished American family which included the poet T. S. Eliot (1888–1965), who was born in St Louis, Missouri.*

However, the earliest Eliot *recorded in North America was John Eliot (1604–90), a Puritan missionary known as the 'Indian Apostle', who was born in Herts. and sailed to Boston in 1631. He then settled in Roxbury, Mass. His father was a yeoman who owned a considerable amount of land, some in Essex, and claimed Norman descent.*

Ellis English: from the medieval given name *Elis*, the normal vernacular form of *Elijah* (Gk *Elias*, from Hebr. *Eliyahu* 'Jehovah is God'). This name was borne by a biblical prophet, but its popularity among Christians in the

Middle Ages was a result of its adoption by various early saints, as for example a 7th-cent. bishop of Syracuse and a 9th-cent. Sp. martyr. In Wales this surname seems to have absorbed forms derived from the W personal name *Elisedd*, a deriv. of *elus* kindly, benevolent.

Vars.: **Elliss, Elis, Ellice, Eles, Elys, Heelis, Hel(l)is, Elias.**

Cogns.: Fr.: **Élie, Hélie, Élias.** It.: **Elia(s).** Sp.: **Elías.** Cat.: **Elias.** Port.: **Elias.** Ger.: **Elias, Elies, Leyes.** Du.: **Elias.** Czech: **Eliáš.** Pol.: **Eliasz.** Hung.: **Ill(y)és.** Jewish: **Elijah, Elias, El(i)yahu, Eli(j)ahu.**

Dims.: Eng.: ELLIOTT; ELKIN; **Elcock, Hellcat, Hillcoat.** Fr.: **Éliet, Éliez, Élion; Al(l)iot; Héliet, Héliot, Hélin.** Ukr.: **Ilyenko, Ilchenko, Ilchuk.**

Patrs.: Eng.: **Ellis(s)on, Elliston.** Welsh: **Bellis(s),** BLISS. It.: **D'Elia(s).** Rum.: **Eliesco.** Low Ger.: **Eliassen, Ellissen.** Dan., Norw.: **Eliasen.** Swed.: **Eliasson.** Pol.: **Ilewicz.** Russ.: **Ilyin; Ilmanov** (from an expanded form); **Ilyinski** (a name adopted by Orthodox priests); **Ilyasov** (from an Arabic form used in the (Muslim) Turkic regions). Armenian: **Helian.** Georgian: **Iashvili.**

Patrs. (from dims.): Eng.: ELSON. Russ.: **Ilyushkin, Ilyukhov, Ilyunin, Ilyasov, Ilyuchyov, Ilyinykh.** Beloruss.: **Yelyashev, Yeliashev.**

'Son of the daughter of E.': Russ.: **Ilyinichnin.**

Ellison *was a common name in SW Lancs., esp. Liverpool, in the 18th–19th cents.; many bearers were workers in base metals.*

Ellwood English: 1. habitation name from a place in Gloucs., which is probably named from OE *ellern* elder tree + *wudu* WOOD.

2. from the OE personal name *Ælfweald*, composed of the elements *ælf* elf + *weald* rule.

Vars.: **Elwood, Allwood.**

Elm English: topographic name for someone who lived near an elm tree or in an elm grove, from ME, OE *elm* elm.

Vars.: **Elm(e)s; Nelm(e)s** (from ME *atten elms*).

Cogns.: Swed.: **Almén.** Cat.: **Olm, Om(s), Homs.**

Cpds (ornamental): Swed.: **Almberg** ('elm hill'); **Almgren** ('elm branch'); **Almqvist** ('elm twig'); **Almroth** ('elm clearing'); **Almstedt** ('elm homestead'); **Almström** ('elm river').

Elman 1. Jewish (E Ashkenazic): var. of *Hellmann* (see HELLER), reflecting varieties of Yid. in which there is no /h/.

2. English: occupational name for a seller of oil, from ME *ele* oil + *man* man; cf. ULMAN 2.

Vars. (of 2): **Elliman, Ellerman.**

Elmhirst English: habitation name from one of several places in W Yorks. so called from OE *elm* ELM + *hyrst* wooded hill (see HURST).

Var.: **Elmhurst** (the name of places in Somerset and Staffs.).

The Elmhirst *family of Yorks. derive their name from lands in the county which they have held for centuries. Their earliest known ancestor, Robert of Elmhirst (?1300–?50), was a serf on these same lands.*

Elmore English: habitation name from a place in Gloucs., so called from OE *elm* elm + *ofer* ridge.

Elorduy Spanish form of Basque **Elordui**: topographic name for someone who lived by a piece of land overgrown with brambles, from Basque *elor* bramble + the suffix of abundance *-dui*.

Var.: **Elorza** (with a different suffix of the same meaning).

Elorriaga Basque: topographic name for someone who lived by a thorn-bush, from Basque *elorri* hawthorn + the local suffix *-aga*.

Eloy French: from the medieval given name *Eloy* (L *Ēligius*, a deriv. of *ēligere* to choose, elect) made popular by a 6th-cent. saint who came to be venerated as the patron of smiths and horses.

Vars.: **Eloi,** LEY.

Cogns.: Ger.: **El(l)oy, El(l)ey; Gloy, Gley; Loy, Ley(h).**

Elphick English: from the ME given name *Elfegh*, *Alfeg*, OE *Ælfhēah*, composed of the elements *ælf* elf + *hēah* high. The name was sometimes bestowed in honour of St *Alphege* (954–1012), archbishop of Canterbury, who was stoned to death by the Danes, and came to be revered as a martyr.

Vars.: **Elphicke, Elfick, Elvidge, Alphege.**

Elphinston Scots: habitation name from a place in the former county of Midlothian, first recorded in the mid-13th cent. in the form *Elfinstun*; in spite of the superficial approximation to Eng. 'elfin stone', it is likely that the first element is a Gael. personal name altered by folk etymology; cf. ALPIN.

Var.: **Elphinstone.**

Elsässer German and Jewish (Ashkenazic): regional name for someone from Alsace (Ger. *Elsass*, Yid. *Elzes*), with the suffix *-er* indicatign a native or inhabitant of a place. The name of the region (first attested in L documents in the form *Alisatia*) has traditionally been derived from OHG *ali* other, foreign + *saz* seat, possession, but Bahlow traces the first element back to a river name *Ill* or *Ell*.

Vars.: Jewish: **Elzesser, Elzas.**

Elsey English: from the ME given name *El(f)si*, OE *Ælfsige*, composed of the elements *ælf* elf + *sige* victory.

Vars.: **Elsie, Elsy, Elcy.**

Elson 1. English: habitation name from places in Hants and Shrops. The former is so called from the OE personal name *Æðelswīð* (composed of the elements *æðel* noble + *swīð* strong) + OE *tūn* enclosure, settlement; the latter from the gen. case of the OE personal name *Elli* (see ELLINGTON) + OE *tūn* settlement or *dūn* hill (see DOWN 1).

2. English: patr. from ELLIS.

3. Jewish (Ashkenazic): patr. from the Yid. male given name *Elye*, from Hebr. *Eliyahu* Elijah (see ELLIS).

Var.: **Ellson.**

Elston English: habitation name from any of various places so called. One in Lancs. gets the name from the OE female personal name *Æðelsige* (composed of the elements *aðel* noble + *sige* victory) + OE *tūn* enclosure, settlement; one in Notts. originally had as its first element the gen. case of the ON byname *Eilífr* 'Everlasting'; one in Wilts. was so named from *Elias* (see ELLIS) Giffard, holder of the manor in the 12th cent.

Elsworth English: habitation name from a place in Cambs., so called from the gen. case of the OE personal name *Elli* (see ELLINGTON) + OE *worð* enclosure (see WORTH).

Var.: **Ellsworth.**

Elton English: habitation name from any of the various places so called. For the most part they derive from the OE personal name *Ella* or *Elli* (see ELLINGTON) + OE *tūn* enclosure, settlement. One in Berks., however, gets its first element from the OE female personal name *Æðelflǣd* (composed of the elements *æðel* noble + *flǣd* beauty. One in Cambs. has its first element from the personal name *Æðelhēah* (composed of the elements *æðel* noble + *hēah* high). Finally, the place of this name in Co. Durham probably gets its first element from OE *ǣl* eel.

Eltringham English: habitation name from a village in Northumb., so called from OE *Ælfheringahām* 'homestead (OE *hām*) of the people of *Ælfhere*'; the *t* was inserted for the sake of euphony after the name had been collapsed in pronunciation. The surname is still largely restricted to the Newcastle area.

Elvira Spanish: from the medieval female given name *Elvira*. This is of Gmc origin, probably composed of the elements *gail* happy, content (cf. GALE 1), or perhaps *adel* noble (cf. EDEL), + *wēr* true.

Elwell English: habitation name from a place apparently so called from OE *hǣl* omen + *well(a)* spring, stream; the reference is presumably to pagan river worship. This is the origin of a place of this name in Dorset. Two minor places in Devon are probably 'elder-tree spring', from OE *ellern* elder tree + *well(a)*. The surname is now found chiefly in the W Midlands; cf. also HALLIWELL.

Elwes English: from the OF female given name *Eloïse*, introduced into England by the Normans; it is composed of the Gmc elements *heil* hale, sound, healthy + *widi(s)* wide.

Var.: **Elwess**.

Ely English: habitation name from the cathedral city on an island in the fens N of Cambridge. It is so called from OE *ǣl* eel + *gē* district.

Vars.: **Eley, Eal(e)y, Eely**.

Embleton English: habitation name from any of various places so called. One in Northumb. is probably from the OE personal name *Æmele* + *dūn* hill; one in Co. Durham was earlier *Elmedene*, from OE *elm* ELM + *denu* valley. Embleton in Cumb. is probably from the personal name *Eanbald* + OE *tūn* enclosure, settlement.

Émilien French: from a personal name (L *Aemiliānus*, a deriv. of *Aemilius*, a Roman family name perhaps derived from *aemulus* rival) borne by various early saints, and hence widely used as a given name in the Middle Ages.

Vars.: **Émilian, Émilion; Mil(l)ien, Milian, Mil(l)ion** (aphetic forms).

Cogns.: It.: **Emiliani, Emiliano; Mil(l)iani; Miani** (Venetia); **Miano** (S Italy). Sp.: **Millán, Milián**. Cat.: **Millà**. Beloruss.: **Yemelyan**.

Patr.: Russ: **Yemelyanov**.

Patrs. (from dims.): Russ.: **Yemelyanchikov, Yemyashev**.

Emmanuel 1. Jewish: from the Hebr. given name *Imanuel* 'God is with us'.

2. French: from the same name used in the Middle Ages by Christians in honour of a minor 3rd-cent. martyr.

Vars. (of 1): **Emanuel(i), Manuely** (with the Hebr. ending *-i*). (Of 2): Fr.: **Manuel, Manueau, Manuaud**.

Cogns. (of 2): It.: **Em(m)anuele, Emmanueli, Emanuel(l)i, Manuele, Manuello, Manuel(l)i, Manoelli**. Sp., Port.: **Manuel**.

Patrs. (from 1): Jewish: **Emanuelov; Manes, Manis** (Ashkenazic, from the Yid. male given name *Mane*), **Manin** (E Ashkenazic, with the Slavic possessive suffix *-in*). (From 2): It.: **D'Emanuele**. Swed.: **Emanulsson**. Bulg.: **Manolov**.

Emmett English: from a ME dim. of the female given name *Emma*, introduced into England by the Normans, among whom it was extremely popular. The name is of Gmc origin, originally apparently a hypocoristic form of women's names with a first element *ermin* entire.

Vars.: **Em(m)et, Emmott, Emmitt, Emmatt, Hemmett; Emeline, Emlyn, Emblin(g), Emblem**.

Cogn.: Du.: **Emmelot**.

Metrs.: Eng.: **Emms; Emmison, Em(p)son, Hemson**.

Empereur French: nickname from OF *empereor* emperor (L *imperātor*, originally meaning 'general', 'commander', from the verb *imperāre* to rule, order). The name may have been acquired by someone with an imperious manner, or who had acted the part of an emperor in a pageant, or presided at some festival, or who had won the title by being the champion in a contest.

Var.: **Lempereur** (with fused def. art.).

Cogns.: It.: **Imperatore** (S Italy, esp. Campania); **Imperadore** (Venetia).

Fem. forms: Fr.: **Lemprière** (with fused def. art.). It.: **Imperatrice**.

Emslie Scots: habitation name largely confined to the Aberdeen region. It is probably of Eng. origin, from a place called *Elmley*, named with the OE elements *elm* ELM + *lēah* wood, clearing, with an intrusive *-s-*. There are places so called in Kent and Worcs.

Vars.: **Elmslie, Elmsl(e)y**.

The first known bearer of the name in Scotland is Robert de Elmleghe *or* de Elmely *of Aberdeens., who rendered homage in 1296. The first example of the intrusive* -s- *occurs in the early 14th cent. with William* de Elmysley *(Aberdeen 1333).*

Encabo Spanish: from OSp. *en* in, at (L *in*) + *cabo* head (see CAP). The precise meaning of the surname is not clear. OSp. *cabo* had various figurative and transferred meanings, the anatomical sense being normally represented by CABEZA, and so the name may have originally denoted a leader or overseer who was placed at the head of a group of workers, or it may be a topographic name for someone who lived at the upper end of a settlement.

Encarnación Spanish: religious byname, or nickname for someone who was born on Christmas Day, celebrated as the feast of the Incarnation of Christ (L *incarnātio*, from *incarnāre* to make flesh, a deriv. of *caro*, gen. *carnis*, flesh).

Cogn.: Port.: **Encarnação**.

Encina Spanish: topographic name for someone who lived by a holm oak, Sp. *encina* (OSp. *leçina*, LL *īlicīna*, a deriv. of class. L *īlex*, gen. *īlicis*).

Var.: **Encinas** (the name of various places, for example in the provinces of Salamanca, Valladolid, and Segovia).

Cogn.: Cat.: **Alsina**.

Collective: Sp.: **Encinar**.

Ende German: topographic name for someone living at the end of a settlement or street, from MHG *ende* (OHG *enti*).

Vars.: **Endemann; Amend(e), Mende**.

Cogns.: Flem.: **Van den Eynde, Van den Hende**. Du.: **Ent, Van der Ende**.

Endecott English (Devon): topographic name for someone who lived 'at the end of the cottages', from ME, OE *ende* end + *cot* cottage. One locality so named is *Endicott* in Cadbury, Devon; another is now called *Youngcott*, in Milton Abbot.

Vars.: **Endicott, Endacott**.

John Endecott *(c.1588–1665), colonial governor of Massachusetts, from whom several American families are descended, was probably born in Chagford, Devon, and went to America in 1628 as one of six adventurers forming the 'New England Company for the Plantation of Massachusetts'. They went to Naumkeag, which was already settled by an offshoot of the Plymouth community, and the two groups agreed to combine and change the name to Salem at Endecott's suggestion. Little is known of his life before 1628, beyond the fact that his grandfather and mother were wealthy, but Endecott was disinherited, probably because of religious differences with his parents.*

Enderby English: habitation name from places in Leics. and Lincs., so called from the ON personal name *Eindriði* (composed of the elements *ein* one, sole + *ræði* ruler) + ON *býr* farm, settlement.

Var.: **Endersby**.

Endlich Jewish (Ashkenazic): from mod. Ger. *endlich* finally, at last; presumably a nickname based on some now irrecoverable incident.

Eng Swedish: ornamental name from Swed. *ång* meadow (ON *eng*), in some cases perhaps chosen as a topographic name by someone who lived beside a meadow. This is one of the many Swedish surnames that were coined in the 19th cent. from vocab. words denoting aspects of the countryside, and which were also used more or less arbitrarily to form compound surnames.

Vars.: **Engh, Engman**.

Cpds: **Engberg** ('meadow hill'); **Engblom** ('meadow flower'); **Engborg** ('meadow town'); **Engdahl** ('meadow valley'); **Engholm** ('meadow island'); **Englund** ('meadow grove'); **Engqvist** ('meadow twig'); **Engstrand** ('meadow shore'); **Engström, Ångström** ('meadow river'); **Engwall, Engvall** ('meadow slope').

Engel 1. German and Dutch: from a short form of various Gmc personal names (cf., e.g., ENGELBERT and ENGELHARD). A number of different elements have fallen together in *Engel-*, mainly *Angel* Angle and *Ingal*, extended form of *Ing*, name of a Gmc god or folk hero. The *Angles* were a Gmc tribe who invaded E and N Britain in the 5th–6th cents. and gave their name to *England* (OE *Englaland*). Cf. ENGLISH. Other elements present in *Engel-* are an extension of *Ang* 'Spike' and, in later names, the Christian *angel* (see below and at ANGEL).

2. German and Dutch: nickname for a remarkably good or kind person, from Ger. *Engel* angel (MHG *engel*, L *angelus*, from Gk *angelos* messenger). In some cases it may have originated as a house name, from a house bearing the sign of an angel. See also ANGEL.

3. Jewish (Ashkenazic): ornamental name from the Ger. vocab. word *Engel* angel (see 2).

Dims. (of 1): Low Ger.: **Engleke, Eng(e)lmann**. Fris.: **Engesma**.

Patrs. (from 1): Ger.: **Engels, Engler, Engling**. Flem.: **Engels, Ingels, Engelen**. Du.: **Engels**. (From 3): Jewish (E Ashkenazic): **Engelowitch**.

Patrs. (from dims. of 1): Low Ger.: **Engelken, Engelking**. (From 3): Jewish: **Engelchin** (altered form of the Ger. dim. vocab. word *Engelchen* 'little angel' under the influence of the Slavic possessive suffix *-in*).

Cpds (of 3): Jewish: **Engel(s)berg** ('angel('s) hill'); **Engel(s)man(n)** ('angel('s) man or husband'); **Engelmayer** ('angel steward'); **Engelrad** ('angel wheel'); **Engelsrath** ('angel's counsel'); **Engelstein** ('angel stone').

Engelbert English, French, and Low German: from a Gmc personal name composed of the elements *engel* (see ENGEL) + *berht* bright, famous. The widespread popularity of the name in France during the Middle Ages was largely a result of the fact that it had been borne by a son-in-law of Charlemagne; in the Rhineland it was more often given in memory of an early medieval martyr of this name, who had been bishop of Cologne (1216–25).

Vars.: Eng.: **Englebert**. Fr.: **Englebert, Englibert, Enjalbert, Enjeubert; Anglebert, Angilbert; Langlebert**. Low Ger.: **Engelbrett**.

Cogns.: Ger: **Engelbrecht**. Flem.: **Ingelbrecht**. Du.: **Engelbrecht, Engelbracht**.

Patrs.: Ger.: **Engelbrecher**. Low Ger.: **Engelbertz** (Rhineland).

Engelhard English, German, and Dutch: from a Gmc personal name composed of the elements *engel* (see ENGEL) + *hard* brave, hardy, strong. The personal name was introduced into England by the Normans.

Vars.: Ger.: **Engelhar(d)t**.

Cogns.: Low Ger.: **Englert**. Jewish (Ashkenazic): **Engelhar(d)t** (an adoption of the Ger. surname).

Patr.: Low Ger.: **Englerding**.

An English family now called **Engleheart** *originated in Schnellenstein, Silesia, where the name is first recorded in the 14th cent. They trace their descent from Francis* Englehart *who settled in England in 1722, when he was employed as a craftsman to work on the plaster ceilings at Hampton Court.*

Englefield English: habitation name from *Englefield* Green in Surrey, so called from the OE personal name *Ingweald* (composed of the elements *Ing*, a divine name (see ING) + *weald* rule) + OE *feld* pasture, open country; or from *Englefield* in Berks., which is named as the 'open land (OE *feld*) of the Angles' (see ENGEL 1).

English 1. English: from OE *Englisc*. The word had originally distinguished Angles (see ENGEL) from Saxons and other Gmc peoples in the Brit. Isles, but by the time surnames were being acquired it no longer had this meaning. Its frequency as an Eng. surname is somewhat surprising. It may have been commonly used in the early Middle Ages as a distinguishing epithet for an Anglo-Saxon in areas where the culture was not predominantly English—for example the Danelaw area, Scotland, and parts of Wales—or as a distinguishing name after 1066 for a non-Norman in the regions of most intensive Norman settlement. However, explicit evidence for these assumptions is lacking, and at the present day the surname is fairly evenly distributed throughout the country.

2. Irish: see GOLIGHTLY.

Vars. (of 1): **Inglis(h)** (Scotland); **Angliss, Angless, Anglish** (from OF *angleis*); **England**.

Cogns. (of 1): Fr.: **Anglais; Langlais, Lenglet, Lenglé, Langlois, Langloy; Linglay, Linglet** (Belgium); **Angloes** (Switzerland). Prov.: **Anglès**. It.: **Inglese**. Sp.: **Inglés**. Cat.: **Anglès**. Flem., Du.: **Engelander, Van Engeland**. Jewish (Ashkenazic): **Englisher; Engla(e)nder, Englender**.

Dims. (of 1): Fr.: **Lenglin(ey); Anglichaud**.

Pej. (of 1): Fr.: **Lenglard**.

Enock English: from the medieval given name *Enock* (Gk *Enōkh*, from Hebr. *Chanoch* 'Dedicated'). This was the name borne in the Bible by the eldest son of Cain (Gen. 4: 17) and by the father of Methuselah, who was said to have 'walked with God' (Gen. 5: 22). The surname is relatively common in Wales, but much rarer in England, where it is concentrated on the Warwicks./Oxon. border and probably has a unitary origin.

Var.: **Enoch** (mainly Welsh; a learned form apparently not recorded before the 18th cent.).

Cogns.: Jewish: **Hanoch; Hanochi** (with the Hebr. suffix *-i*).

Patrs.: Swed.: **Eno(c)ksson, Enochsson**. Jewish (E Ashkenazic): **Hanochov, Hanochow, Hanokhov**.

The earliest known bearer of the surname is the clerk John Enoc*, who witnessed a deed at Warmington, Wilts., in 1216. Robert Enoc is recorded in 1237 at Paulshot, Wilts. Other forms of the 13th and early 14th cents. are* En(n)ok, Enock, Ennocke, *and* Enhoke.

Enright Irish: Anglicized form of the Gael. byname *Indreachtach* 'Attacker'.

Ensor English: habitation name from *Edensor* in Derbys., which derives its name from the gen. case of the OE personal name *Eadhūn* (see EDEN 1) + OE *ofer* ridge.

Entwistle English: habitation name from the village of *Entwisle* in Lancs., so called from OE *henna* (water) hen or *ened* duck + *twisla* tongue of land in a river fork.

Vars.: **Entwisle, Entissle, Entwhistle.**

Eötvös Hungarian: occupational name for a goldsmith, Hung. *ötvös*. The surname retains an older spelling of the word.

Var.: **Ötvös.**

Épine French: topographic name for someone who lived by a prominent thorn-bush, OF *espine* (L *spina*), or in an area overgrown with such bushes. Occasionally the name may derive from the same word used in a transferred sense of the crest or ridge of a hill.

Vars.: **Lépine, Delépine.**

Cogns.: Prov.: **Espin(e), Espinas.** It.: **Spino, Spini; (La) Spina** (S Italy); **Spinas** (Sardinia). Sp.: **Espín, Espino(s), Espina.** Cat.: **Espí, Espina.** Port.: **Espinho, Espinha.**

Dims.: Fr.: **Espinel, Espinet.** It.: **Spinelli, Spin(i)ello, Spinella, Spinetti, Spinozzi.** Sp.: **Espínola.** Port.: **Espínola, Spínola.**

Aug.: Sp.: **Espinazo.**

Collectives: Fr.: **Espinay, Épinay, Épinoy, Lépinay.** Sp.: **Espinal, Espinar; Espinosa.** Cat.: **Espinós, Espinosa.** Port.: **Espinheira, Espinosa.**

Epstein German and Jewish (Ashkenazic): habitation name, perhaps from *Eppstein* in Bavaria, so called from OHG *ebur* wild boar + *stein* stone.

Vars.: Jewish: **Eppstein, Ebstein; Epsztejn, Epsztajn** (Pol. spellings).

Erasmus German: from the personal name (a Latinized form of Gk *erasmos* loved, a deriv. of *erān* to love) borne by a rather obscure early Christian saint who was numbered among the 'fourteen holy helpers' and regarded as the patron of turners and seamen. The fame of the great Humanist scholar Desiderius Erasmus of Rotterdam (?1466–1536) enhanced the popularity of the given name, but not in time to have much effect on the frequency of the surname.

Vars.: **Rasmus** (aphetic), **Asmus; Eras.**

Dims.: Ger.: **Rasem, Asam, Asum.** Low Ger.: **Rassmann, Assmann.** Flem., Du.: **Raes, Raskin.**

Patrs.: Ger.: **Erasmi** (Latinized); **Asmes(en).** Low Ger.: **Asmussen.** Dan., Norw.: **Rasmussen, Asmussen.**

Erhard German: from a Gmc personal name composed of the elements *ēra* honour (cf. EHRLICH) + *hard* brave, hardy, strong. This Ger. surname has also been adopted by Ashkenazic Jews.

Vars.: **Erhar(d)t.**

Cogn.: Fr.: **Erard.**

Erlanger German and Jewish (Ashkenazic): habitation name from *Erlangen* in Bavaria, which derives its name from an obscure element *er*, according to Bahlow a prehistoric word for water + the dial. term *wang* water meadow (cf. FEUCHTWANGER and FURTWANGER).

Ermgard German: from a Gmc female personal name composed of the elements *erm(en)* whole, entire + *gard* enclosure, garden.

Vars.: **Irm(in)gard, Armgardt, Harmgardt.**

Cogns.: Fr.: **Ermengard(e), Ermenjard; Mengard, Menjard, Minjard.**

Dims.: Fr.: **Mengardon, Mengarduque; Ermenjon; Menjon, Mingeon.**

Ernaud French: hypercorrected form of *Arnaud* (see ARNOLD). Since the pronunciation of *-er-* as *-ar-* in words like *personne* came to be regarded as vulgar, there was a tendency for names containing *-ar-* to receive a 'refined' pronunciation with *-er-*.

Vars.: **Ernau(l), Ernout.**

Ernst 1. German and Dutch: from the Gmc byname *Ernust* 'Seriousness', 'Firmness', or a nickname from MHG *ern(e)st* seriousness, battle.

2. Jewish (Ashkenazic): nickname from mod. Ger. *ernst* earnest, serious.

Vars. (of 1): **Ernest.** (Of 2): **Ernster** (an inflected form of the Ger. adjective).

Cogns.: Flem., Du.: **Ernstig** (a nickname). It.: **Nesti** (from the byname).

Patr.: Ger.: **Ernsting.**

Erpel Low German: 1. nickname from MLG *erpel* drake (apparently from the OSax. byname *Erpo* 'Dark'; cf. the dial. terms *gäret* (see GARRETT) and *gaber* (see GABRIEL) for the goose), or metonymic occupational name for someone responsible for tending ducks.

2. habitation name from a place in the Rhineland called *Erpel*, according to Bahlow a name of pre-Gmc origin.

Errington English: habitation name from a place in Northumb., so called from a Brit. river name apparently akin to W *arian* silvery, bright + OE *tūn* enclosure, settlement.

Erskine Scots: habitation name from a place on the south bank of the Clyde outside Glasgow, first recorded in 1225 in the form *Erskin*. Other early spellings vary (1227 *Yrskin*; 1262 *Ireskin*; 1300 *Harskin, Irschen*). The etymology is not clear: it may be from Celt. elements cogn. with W *ir* green + *esgyn* to ascend.

The Erskine *family hold some of the oldest titles in Scottish history, including the earldoms of Mar, Buchan, Kellie, and Rosslyn. An ancestor, Henry* de Erskyn, *is mentioned in a charter in the reign of Alexander II (1214–49).*

Escalada Spanish: habitation name from a place in the province of Burgos. The placename is probably a deriv. of *escala* ladder (see ESCHELLE), referring to a terraced slope.

Eschelle French: from OF *eschelle* ladder (L *scāla*, a deriv. of *scandere* to climb). This was probably a topographic name for a dweller by a terraced slope or in a house with an exterior staircase or ladder; perhaps also a metonymic occupational name for a maker or seller of ladders or a nickname for the unique possessor of one in a small village.

Vars.: **Échelle; Deschelle, Déchelle; Leschelle, Léchelle; Echal(l)ier, Echal(l)ié.**

Cogns.: Prov.: **Escale, Désesquelle.** It.: **(Della) Scala, Scali(a); Scalera.** Sp.: **Escala; Escalero, Escalera; Escalante.**

Dims.: Fr.: **Eschalette, Eschalotte; Déchelette.**

Escobar Spanish: topographic name for someone who lived in a place overgrown with broom (LL *scopāre*, from *scopa* broom), or habitation name from any of the numerous villages, for example in Murcia, Segovia, and León, named with this word.

Var.: **Escobedo.**

Escoda Catalan: metonymic occupational name for a stone mason, from OCat. *escoda* hammer used in dressing stone (of uncertain origin, perhaps from L *excūdere* to hammer into shape).

Escoffier Provençal: occupational name for a leather-worker or tanner, or for a slaughterman, from an agent deriv. of the OProv. verb *escofia*, used both of dressing leather and of slaughtering animals (from L *exconficere* to finish off).

Vars.: **Escofier, Escofié**.

Escorial Spanish: topographic name for someone who lived near a refuse tip or slag heap, OSp. *escorial* (LL *scoriāle*, a deriv. of *scoria* refuse, slag). This was also the name of several villages, including *El Escorial* near Madrid, the site of the royal palace and monastery built by Philip II (1527–98); the surname may be a habitation name from any of these.

Espada Spanish, Catalan, and Portuguese: metonymic occupational name for an armourer or a swordsman, from Sp., OCat., Port. *espada* sword (LL *spatha*, from Gk *spathē*, originally denoting a broad, two-edged sword without a point).

Vars.: Sp.: **Espadas**; **Espadero**. Cat.: **Espasa**; **Espadater, Espadaté**.

Cogns.: It.: **Spada**; **Spata** (S Italy); **Spadari, Spadaro, Spatari, Spataro**. Rum.: **Spătarul**.

Dims.: It.: **Spadelli, Spad(ol)ini, Spadotto, Spaduzza, Spatuzza, Spaduzzi, Spaducci**.

Augs.: It.: **Spadon(i), Spatoni**.

Pej.: It.: **Spadazzi**.

The Russian-born bacteriologist Élie Metchnikoff *(1845–1916), a colleague of Pasteur, was a direct descendant of the Rumanian nobleman Gheorghe Stefan* Spătarul, *who emigrated to Russia with Prince Demetrius Cantemir in 1711. His surname derived from a title at the court of Moldavia, and in Russia he translated it literally to become Yuri Stepanovich* Mechnik.

Esposito Italian: surname commonly denoting a foundling, meaning literally 'exposed' (L *expositus*, past part. of *expōnere* to place outside). At the present day this is the commonest surname in Naples.

Vars.: **Espos(u)to, Espos(t)i, Sposito**.

Cogn.: Sp.: **Expósito**.

Esquivel Spanish form of Basque **Aizkibel**: of uncertain origin, possibly a topographic name composed of the Basque elements *aitz* rock, crag + *gibel* rear, back.

Essart French: topographic name for someone who lived in a clearing, OF *essart* (LL *exsartum*, past part. of *exsarire* to weed out, grub up).

Vars.: **Essert** (hypercorrected); **Issart(e), Issert**; **Lessart, Lessard**; **Desessarts, Desessard**; **Essartier, Essertier**.

Dims.: **Essertel**; **Issartel, Issarteaux**.

Essex English: regional name for someone from the county of Essex, which is so called from OE *ēast* EAST + *Seaxe* Saxons. The surname is now particularly common in Birmingham.

Este Italian: habitation name from a place in Venetia, originally named in L as *Ateste*. The surname is common in Padua and Venice, and is that of a leading noble family.

Var.: **D'Este**.

Esterházy Hungarian (partly Jewish): from *szerhás* master roofer + *ház* house, the name of the family's original estate in Csallóköz (cf. Old Church Slavonic *strěcha* roof).

The family had many branches, one of which became particularly known for patronizing music in the 18th cent. Their descent can be traced from Benedict Esterhas *(d. 1552), whose grandson Miklós (Nikolaus) (1582–1645) established the family fortune through two advantageous marriages, being created a count in 1626. In 1687 his son Pál (Paul) (1635–1713) was created a prince by Emperor Leopold I. The composer Joseph Haydn was Kappelmeister to three generations of Prince Pál's descendants, and other branches of the family employed major composers including Mozart and Schubert.*

Estersohn Jewish (Ashkenazic): metr. from the Yid. female given name *Ester* Esther, from Hebr. *Ester*, the name borne in the Bible by a Jewish captive of the Persian King Ahasuerus. According to the biblical story, she became his favourite concubine and managed to save the Jews of Persia from the machinations of the royal counsellor Haman.

Vars.: **Esterson**; **Est(e)rin** (E Ashkenazic).

Dim.: **Esterkin** (E Ashkenazic).

Estival French: 1. topographic name for a dweller by a patch of summer pasture, OF *estival* (L *aestivāle*, a deriv. of *aestas* summer), or habitation name from one of the several villages named with this word.

2. metonymic occupational name for a maker of boots and shoes, from OF *estival* (summer) shoe, light boot (of the same origin as 1).

Vars.: **Estivau(x)**.

Cogn. (of 2): Ger.: STIEFEL.

Dim.: Fr.: **Estivalet**.

Etang French: topographic name for someone who lived near a pond or pool, OF *estang* (L *stagnum* standing water, a deriv. of *stāre* to stand).

Vars.: **Esta(i)ng**; **Destan, Destaing, Détang, Delétang**.

Dim.: **Estagnol**.

Etchells English: habitation name from any of various minor places in N England named with the OE term *ēcels* piece of land added to an estate (a deriv. of *ēcan* to increase).

Vars.: **Neachell** (from ME *atten eachel*); **Nechells** (now the name of a district of Birmingham).

Étourneau French: nickname for a sprightly person, or metonymic occupational name for a bird-catcher, from OF *estournel* starling (LL *sturnellus*, a dim. form of class. L *sturnus*).

Vars.: **Étournaud, Estourneau, Estournel, Létourneau**.

Cogns.: Rum.: **Stur(d)za**.

Eugène French: from the personal name (L *Eugenius*, from Gk *Eugenios* 'Well-born', 'Noble') borne by a 3rd-cent. bishop and martyr, who gave the given name some currency during the Middle Ages.

Euler German and Jewish (Ashkenazic): occupational name for a potter, most common in the Rhineland and Hesse, Ger. *Euler* (*MHG ūl(n)ære*, an agent deriv. of the dial. word *ūl*, *aul* pot, from L *olla*).

Vars.: Ger.: **Eulner**; **Aul(n)er**.

Eusébio Portuguese: from the personal name (Gk *Eusebios* 'Revered', from *eu-* good, well + *sebesthai* to honour, respect) borne by a large number of early saints, including a 5th-cent. friend of Jerome popularly credited with the foundation of the monastery of Guadalupe. A 4th-cent. bishop of Samosata in Syria who bore the same name is venerated in the Orthodox Church.

Dims.: Ukr.: **Ovsienko**. Pol.: **Owsik, Owsiejczyk**.

Patrs.: Russ.: **Yevseev, Yevsenov, Ovseev, Avseev**.

Patrs. (from dims.): Russ.: **Yevsikov, Yevsyunin, Yevsyutin**.

Evan 1. Welsh: from the given name *Ifan*, *Evan* JOHN.

2. Scots: var. of EWAN.

3. Jewish: of unknown origin.

Vars. (of 1): **Heavan, Heaven**.

Cogn. (of 1): Bret.: **Even**.

Patrs. (from 1): Welsh: **Evans, Evens, Evance**; **Ifans, Ivin(g)s**; **Avans**; **Heavans, Heavens**; BEVAN.

Eve English: from the rare medieval female given name *Eve*, *Eva* (from Hebr. *Chava*, of uncertain origin, perhaps originally meaning 'Serpent' or akin to *chaya* to live; cf. HYAM). This was, according to the Book of Genesis, the name of the first woman, and in some cases the name may have been acquired by someone (invariably a man) who had played the part in a drama dealing with the Creation. See also KHAVKE.

Var.: **Eva**.

Dims.: **Evett, Evatt, Evitt**.

Metrs.: **E(a)ves; Eve(r)son, Evason, Evison**.

Metrs. (from dims.): **Evetts, Evitts**.

Evelegh English: habitation name from a lost place in Broad Clyst, Devon, so called from OE *ifig* ivy + *lēah* wood, clearing.

A family of this name originated in the manor of Evelegh, Devon, recorded in Domesday Book as Ivelie. *Their descent can be traced directly from John* Evelegh (*b.* c.*1450*).

Evelyn English: from the ME, OF female given name *Aveline*, a double dim. of the Gmc personal name *Avo*, from the element *avi*, perhaps meaning 'desired, wished for'.

Vars.: **Aveline, Aveling**.

Metr.: Du.: **Eveleens**.

The diarist John Evelyn (*1620–1706*) *claimed to come of a family of Norman origin who had settled in Shrops. However, his earliest recorded ancestor was William* Avelyn *or* Evelyn (*d. 1476*), *who lived at Harrow, Middlesex*.

Everard English: from a Gmc personal name composed of the elements *eber* wild boar + *hard* brave, hardy, strong. The surname was at first found mainly in E Anglia (still one of the principal locations of the var. *Everett*), which was an area of heavy Norman and Breton settlement after the Conquest. This suggests that the personal name may be of Continental (Norman) origin, but it is also possible that it swallowed up an unattested OE cogn., **Eoforheard*.

Vars.: **Evered, Everid; Everett, Everitt, Everatt**.

Cogns.: Fr.: **E(u)vrard, Evras, Evrat, Ebrard, Levrard, Oeuvrard**. Ger.: **Eberhard(t), Eberhart; Ebhard** (Thuringia). Low Ger.: **Ebert** (see also EGGEBRECHT); **Evert, Ewert**. Flem.: **Everaert, Ever(t)**.

Dims.: Ger.: **Ebe, Ebi, Eby, Eble, Eb(er)lein; Eberle, Epple** (Swabia); **Eberl** (Bavaria). Low Ger.: **Ebermann, Evermann, Ewermann**.

Patrs.: Low Ger.: **Ebers, Evers, Ewers; Eber(t)z, Evertz, Effertz** (Rhineland); **Everding**. Flem.: **Everaerts, Evers; Everdey** (Latinized). Du.: **Ever(t)s**.

Patrs. (from dims.): Ger.: **Ebler, Everling**. Low Ger.: **Eveking**.

Everard *is the name of a Somerset family who trace their descent from Ranulph* FitzEverard, *who held lands at Luxborough in 1066. Another ancestor, Sir William* Evarard, *was sheriff of Somerset and Dorset in 1258*.

Everest English (Norman): habitation name from *Evreux* in Eure, Normandy, so called from having apparently been the capital of the *Eburovices*, a Gaul. tribe. This tribal name appears in turn to derive from the river name *Ebura* (now the *Eure*), which may perhaps be akin to a Celt. word for the yew tree (cf. IVE and YORK).

Vars.: **Everist, Everix, Everiss, Evreux, Everist**; DEVEREUX.

Everill English: from the OE female personal name *Eoforhild*, composed of the elements *eofor* wild boar + *hild* battle. The surname is chiefly found in the W Midlands.

Ewald Low German: from a Gmc personal name composed of the elements *ēo* law, custom, right (a rare element in personal names, found mostly in OSax.) + *wald* rule. This name was borne in the 7th cent. by two brothers (distinguished as 'Ewald the White' and 'Ewald the Black') who were missionaries in N Germany. They became the patron saints of Cologne and Westphalia, and so contributed to the popularity of the given name (and hence the eventual frequency of the surname) in these areas.

Vars.: **Ehwalt, Ewold**.

Patrs.: **Ewols(en)**.

Ewan Scots: Anglicized form of the Gael. personal name *Eògann*. This is now generally acknowledged to be a Gael. form of L *Eugenius* (see EUGÈNE), but it was formerly widely believed to be a form of JOHN, and attempts have also been made to derive it from a proto-Celt. name meaning 'born of the yew'.

Vars.: EWEN, **Ewin(g), Hewin, Yewen**, EVAN.

Patrs.: Sc.: **Ewens, Ewin(g)s, Hewins, Youens, Youings; Eunson; McEwan, McEwen, McEwing** (Gael. **Mac Eòghainn**). Ir.: **McKeo(w)n, McCune, McCown, McCone, McGeown, McGuone, Keown**, COWAN.

Ewart English and Scots: 1. from *Ewart*, a Norman form of the given name EDWARD.

2. occupational name for a shepherd, from ME *ewehirde*, from OE *eowu* ewe + *hierde* herdsman (see HEARD).

3. habitation name from a place in Northumb., so called from OE *ēa* river + *worð* enclosure; it is enclosed on three sides by the rivers Glen and Till.

Vars. (of 2): **Yeoward, Yeowart, Youat(t)**, HOWARD.

Ewart *is the surname of a Galloway family, who probably migrated there from Roxburghs. They came originally from Northumb. and are not found in Scotland before the late 16th cent.*

Ewen 1. Scots: var. of EWAN.

2. Jewish (Israeli): from Hebr. *even* stone, a translation of the surname *Stein* (see STONE) or any of its compounds.

Ewer English: occupational name for a transporter or server of water, ME *ewer* (ONF *evier*, OF *aiguier*, from L *aquārius*, a deriv. of *aqua* water). There has been considerable confusion with URE.

Vars.: **Lewer** (with fused ANF def. art.).

Patr.: **Ewers**.

Exley English: habitation name from a place in W Yorks., near Halifax, so called from a Brit. *ecclēsia* name meaning 'church' (see ECCLES) + OE *lēah* clearing, wood. The surname is still most common in W Yorks.

Ezekiel Jewish: from the Hebr. given name *Yechezkel* 'God will strengthen'.

Vars.: **Yechezkiel, Yechesk(i)el, Jecheskel; Jechezkieli, Yecheskely, Yecheskiely** (with the Hebr. suffix *-i*); **Heskel, Haskel(l), Ha(t)zkel** (Ashkenazic, from the Yid. forms *Kheskl*, *Khatskl*).

Patrs.: (Ashkenazic): **Haskelevic, Haskilewitz, Hazkelevitch, Hazkelevitz, Chaskelovic**. (E Ashkenazic): **Yecheskelov**.

Ezquerra Basque: nickname for a left-handed person, from *ezker* left(-handed) + the def. art. *-a*. This term has been taken into the other languages of the Iberian Peninsula (see also IZQUIERDO) in place of the Romance descendants of L *laevus* and *sinister*, since the left side was felt to be ill-omened and the words themselves consequently became taboo.

Var.: **Ezquerro**.

Cogn.: Cat.: **Esquerrà**.

F

Fabian 1. English, French, Polish, Austrian, and Venetian: from a given name (L *Fabiānus*, a deriv. of *Fabius*, a Roman family name perhaps derived from *faba* bean; cf. FAVIER). The given name achieved some popularity in the Middle Ages as having been borne by a 3rd-cent. pope and saint.

2. Jewish: adoption of the non-Jewish surname under the influence of the Yid. male given name *Fayvish* (see FAIVISH).

Vars.: Fr.: **Fabien**. Pol.: **Fabijan**, **Fabi(j)ański**, **Fabicki**; **Pabi(a)n**, **Pabiański**, **Pabich**. Ger.: **Fabigan**, **Pfabi(g)an**, **Fabion**; **Fobian**. It.: **Fabjan**; **Fabbiano**, **Fab(b)iani**.

Cogns.: Sp.: **Fabián**. Czech: **Fabián**. Hung.: **Fábiń**.

Dims.: Pol.: **Fabi(j)ańczyk**, **Pabi(j)ańczyk**, **Pabimak**. Ger.: **Fabel** (also Jewish); **Fabig**, **Fabisch**, **Fabianke**, **Fobianke**, **Fabianek** (of Slav. origin).

Patrs.: Pol.: **Fabi(j)anowicz**; **Pabisiak**.

Habitation name: Pol.: **Fabiszewski**.

Fabrikant Jewish (Ashkenazic): occupational name for a factory owner or manufacturer of any type of goods, from Russ. *fabrikant* manufacturer, Ger. *Fabrikant* (from L *fabricans*, gen. *fabricantis*, pres. part. of *fabricāre* to make, a deriv. of *faber*; see FÈVRE).

Vars.: **Fabricant**; **Fabrykant** (Pol. spelling).

Fabrizio Italian: from the medieval given name *Fabrizio* (L *Fabrīcius*, a Roman family name of unknown, possibly Etruscan, etymology). Already in the Roman period the name was associated by folk etymology with *faber* (see FÈVRE) and L forms of the name were extensively used in the late Middle Ages as equivalents of the various vernacular terms denoting craftsmen.

Vars.: **Fabrizi**, **Fab(b)rizzi**, **Fabrici**.

Cogns.: Ger.: **Fabrit(z)ius**. Dan.: **Fabricius**. Hung.: **Fabricius**, **Fabriczy**, **Fabritius**.

Fagan Irish: of uncertain origin. The Gael. form is **Ó Faodhagáin**, but a personal name **Faodhagán* is not known, and it may be a Gaelicized version of a surname of Norman origin.

A number of Irish bearers of this name are descended from Patrick Fagan, *who owned estates in Co. Meath in the 13th cent. According to tradition, his name was originally O'Hagan and he assumed the name Fagan at the command of King John, for reasons which are unclear.*

Fage 1. French: topographic name for someone who lived by a beech tree or beech wood, from OF *fage* beech (LL *fāgea* (*arbor*), a deriv. of class. L *fāgus*).

2. English: nickname for a flatterer, from ME *fage* coaxing, flattery, deception (of unknown origin).

Vars. (of 1): **Fages**, **Laf(f)age**; **Le Faou** (Brittany).

Cogns. (of 1): Prov.: **Fay(e)**, **Fey**, **Fau**, **Fou**; **Lafay(e)**, **Laffay**, **Lephay**; **Defau(x)**, **Deffou(x)**, **Dufay(s)**, **Dufau**, **Duffeau(x)**, **Desfaux**, **Desfoux** ; **Hau** (Gascony). It.: **Faggi(o)** (Tuscany, Emilia, Venetia); **Fazi** (Parma; see also BONIFACE); **Fago**, **Faga** (S Italy, Venetia); **Fo** (N Italy). Cat.: **Fages**. Port.: **Faia**.

Dims. (of 1): Fr.: **Faget(te)**, **Lafagette**, **Fageau**, **Fajon**. Prov.: **Fayet(te)**, **Lafayette**, **Fayol(le)**, **Fayot**, **Fayon**, **Fayel**, **Feyel**, **Feyeux**, **Fo(u)et**, **Dufayel**, **Dufayet**. It.: **Faggin(i)**, **Faggioli**, **Faggiola**, **Faggiotto**, **Fagotti**, **Fagotto**.

Augs. (of 1): It.: **Faggion(i)**, **Fag(i)one**.

Pejs. (of 1): Fr.: **Fajard**. Prov.: **Fayard**, **Dufayard**. Sp.: **Fajardo** (Galicia).

Collectives (of 1): It.: **Faet(t)o**, **Faeti**, **Faito** (S Italy); **Faedi**, **Faedo**, **Faeta**, **Fae** (N Italy); **Faceto** (Parma).

Fagg English (Kent): of uncertain origin, perhaps a var. of FAGE 2 or a nickname from either of two homonymous ME words *fagge*. One apparently denotes a fault in the weave of a piece of cloth, the other is the name of a type of fish; both are attested in OED in only single passages.

Vars.: **Fagge**; **Vagg**.

Patr.: **Vaggs**.

Fagot French: metonymic occupational name for a gatherer or seller of firewood, from OF *fagot* bundle of firewood (of uncertain origin, perhaps a distant cogn. of Gk *phakelos* bundle).

Vars.: **Faguet**, **Fagon**.

Faherty Irish: Anglicized form of Gael. **Ó Fathartaigh** 'descendant of *Fathartach*', a personal name (with a var. *Faghartach*) of unknown meaning.

Fahy Irish: Anglicized form of Gael. **Ó Fathaigh** 'descendant of *Fathach*', a personal name probably derived from *fothadh* base, foundation.

Vars.: **O'Fahy**, **O'Fa(u)ghy**, **O'Faye**, **Fahey**, **Faughy**, FAY, FOY; GREEN (a result of erroneous association with *faithche* lawn).

Faiertag Jewish (Ashkenazic): ornamental name from mod. Ger. *Feiertag* holiday.

Failes English (mainly Cambs.): of uncertain origin, possibly a cogn. of FAILLE 3, from ME *fail(l)e* default, or a var. of FALLAS.

Vars.: **Fails**, **Fales**.

It has not been possible to find occurrences of this name before the late 16th cent., when, in 1575, there is record of the marriage at Lenton, Notts., of a certain Agnes Failes.

Faille French: 1. metonymic occupational name for a maker or seller of a kind of silk material known in OF as *faille* (MHG *pfelle*, from L *palliōlum*, a type of light garment).

2. metonymic occupational name for a torch-bearer, from OF *faille* torch (LL *facilla*, a dim. of class. L *fax*, gen. *facis*).

3. nickname for an inept or luckless individual, from OF *faille* fault, failing, mistake (a deriv. of *faillir* to fail, miss, be wanting, L *fallere* to deceive, disappoint).

Cogn. (of 1): Ger.: **Pfell**.

Dims.: Fr.: **Faillon**, **Faillot**.

Fair English: nickname meaning 'beautiful', from OE *fæger* fair, lovely. The word was also occasionally used as a given name in the Middle Ages, and applied to both men and women.

Vars.: **Faire**, **Fayre**, **Fayer**, **Feyer**, **Phair**, **Phayre**.

Patrs.: **Fair(e)s**, **Fa(i)ers**, **F(a)yers**.

Cpds (ornamental): Swed.: **Fagerberg** ('lovely hill'); **Fagerlund** ('lovely grove'); **Fagerström** ('lovely river').

Fairbairn N English and Scots: probably a nickname from Northern ME *fair* lovely (see FAIR) + *bairn* child (see BARNES 2); cf. FAIRCHILD. Black, however, suggests that it is probably a var. of FREEBORN.

Patrs.: **Fairba(i)rns**.

Fairbank English: habitation name from any of various minor places so called. Most get their names from ME *fair* lovely (see FAIR) + *bank* bank, hill (see BANKS), but in some cases the first elements may derive from OE *fearn* FERN.

Var.: **Fairbanks**.

Fairbrother English: term of relationship, probably meaning 'brother of a FAIR person' or else referring to the better-looking of a pair of brothers. It is quite a common name, and may also in part be derived from *father's brother*, i.e. uncle; cf. EAME.

Vars.: **Far(e)brother, Fayerbrother**.

Fairburn 1. English: habitation name from *Fairburn* in Cleveland or *Fairbourne* in Kent, so called from OE *fearn* FERN + *burna* stream (see BOURNE).

2. Scots: habitation name from a place in the former county of Ross and Cromarty, now part of Highland region, originally named with the Gael. elements *far braoin* 'over the wet place', but later altered by folk etymology.

Vars.: **Fairbourn(e), Fairburne**.

Fairchild S English: nickname from ME *fair* lovely (see FAIR) + *child* CHILD; cf. FAIRBAIRN.

Fairclough English (Lancs.): topographical name from ME *fair* lovely (see FAIR) + *cloh* ravine (see CLOUGH), or habitation name from an unidentified place so called.

Vars.: **Faircloth, Fairtlough, Faircliff(e), Featley**.

All present-day bearers of these names seem to be descended from a common ancestor. The family held property around Ormskirk in the Middle Ages, and can be traced back to 1320.

In a short biography of Dr Daniel Featley (1582–1645) published in 1660, his nephew John Featley explains that 'His right name was Faireclough...but this then varied and altered from Faireclough to Faircley, then to Fateley and at length to Featley'.

Fairfax English: nickname for someone with beautiful long hair, from OE *fæger* lovely + *feax* hair, tresses. This was a common descriptive phrase in ME; the alliterative poem 'Sir Gawain and the Green Knight' refers to 'fair fanning fax' encircling the shoulders of the doughty warrior.

Fairgrieve Scots: of uncertain origin. It may be a combination of the nickname FAIR + the occupational name GRIEVE, but if so both parts may have been altered by folk etymology. Perhaps it is a habitation name, with unexplained variation in the vowel of the second element, from an unidentified place named with the OE elements *fōr* pig + *grāf* grove, i.e. a wood where pigs were fed on mast.

Vars.: **Forgrieve, Forgrave**.

The first known bearer of the name in something approaching its modern form seems to be Thomas Feirgrive, *recorded in 1658.*

Fairhead English (Norfolk): nickname from ME *fair* lovely (see FAIR) + *heved* head (OE *hēafod*) or *hood* hood (OE *hōd*).

Fairhurst English (Lancs.): habitation name from a hamlet near Parbold, not far from Wigan, so called from OE *fæger* lovely (see FAIR) + *hyrst* wooded hill (see HURST).

Var.: **Fairest**.

Fairlamb English (said by Reaney to be found in Manchester; also found in Newcastle): ostensibly a nickname from OE *fæger* lovely (see FAIR) + *lamb* LAMB, perhaps from frequent use of this affectionate form of address. More probably, however, it is a habitation name, altered by folk etymology, from *Farlam* in Cumb., so called from OE *fearn* FERN + the dat. pl. of *lēah* wood, clearing.

Vars.: **Farlam, Fairlem**.

Fairlie Scots: habitation name from a place on the Firth of Clyde, so called from OE *fæger* lovely (see FAIR) + *lēah* wood, clearing.

Vars.: **Fairley** (see also FARLEY); **Fairless** (Northumb.).

A Scots family acquired this surname when they were granted lands at Fairlie by Robert Bruce; their name is said to have been originally de Ros *(see* Ross*).*

Fairman 1. English: occupational name for the servant of a man named FAIR, or a nickname for a handsome man (see FAIR).

2. Jewish (Ashkenazic): presumably an Anglicization of one or more like-sounding Jewish surnames, notably *Feuerman* (see FEUER).

Vars.: **Fierman, Fayerman, Fireman**. See also FARMAN.

Fairweather English and Scots: nickname for a person with a sunny temperament; cf. MERRYWEATHER. According to a family tradition, a Scots family of Highland origin assumed this name on migrating southwards, in punning allusion to Job 37: 22, 'Fair weather cometh out of the north'.

Var.: **Fareweather**.

Faist German: nickname for a stout person, from MHG *veiz(e)t* fat, corpulent (OHG *feizit*), a word which was gradually replaced in all dialects of Ger. by the originally Low Ger. FETT or by the unrelated *dick* (cogn. with Eng. *thick*). The vocab. word *feist* survives in mod. Ger. meaning 'corpulent', and this lies behind Jewish cogn.

Vars.: **Feist, Feest, Fehst**.

Cogn.: Jewish (Ashkenazic): **Feist**.

Dims.: Ger.: **Faistle** (Swabia); **Faistl** (Bavaria).

Faith English: nickname for a trustworthy person, from ME *fe(i)th* faithfulness, loyalty (OF *feid*, *feit*, from L *fides*).

Vars.: **Faithful(l)** (from the adj.).

The earliest known bearer of the surname Faithful(l) *is a certain William* Feythful, *first recorded at Chichester in 1492, and in 1500/01 described as a burgess of the town. The wills of Hugo* Faythful *and Margaret* Faythfule *were registered in Hants in 1548.*

Faivish Jewish (Ashkenazic): from the Yid. male given name *Fayvish*, apparently from Gk *Phoebus*, the name of the sun god. This seems to have been used as a trans. equivalent of Hebr. *Shimshon* (see SAMSON). Alternatively, the Yid. name may derive from LL *Vivus* 'Living', used as a trans. equivalent of Hebr. *Chayim* (see HYAM).

Vars.: **Faibis(h), Faybish, Feibish, Feibus(c)h**.

Dims.: **Feivel, Feiwel, Feibel** (from the Yid. dim. given name *Fayvl*).

Patrs. (E Ashkenazic): **Faivisevitz, Faivuszevicz, Faivuschevitch, Fajwshewitz, Favshevitz, Feibischoff, Feibushewitz**.

Patrs. (from dims.): **Faivelson, Feivelson; Fajwlewicz, Fajwlewich, Feivlovitz, Feiwlowicz, Feiwlewicz, Feibelovitz** (E Ashkenazic).

Fajeraizen Jewish (E Ashkenazic): apparently an ornamental name taken by a blacksmith, from Yid. *fayer* fire + *ayzn* iron.

Falcon English: metonymic occupational name for a falconer (see FAULKNER), or nickname for someone thought to resemble a falcon, from ME, OF *faucon*, *falcun* falcon

(L *falco*, gen. *falcōnis*). In a few cases, it may also have been a metonymic occupational name for a man who worked the 16th-cent. piece of artillery named after the bird of prey.

Vars.: **Fa(u)con**. See also FAULKNER.

Cogns.: Fr.: **Faucon**; **Falc'hun** (Brittany). Prov.: **Falcon, Falcou**. It.: **Falcon(e), Falconi(o)**. Sp.: **Falcón, Halcón**. Cat.: **Falcó**. Port.: **Falcão**. Ger.: **Falk(e)**. Du.: **(Van der) Valk**. Dan., Norw., Swed.: **Fal(c)k, Falkman**. Jewish (Ashkenazic): **Falk, Valk** (in part ornamental; in part from the Yid. male given name *Falk* 'Falcon', which is associated with Yid. *Shue*, Hebr. *Yehoshua*, male given names cogn. with Eng. *Joshua*).

Dims.: Fr.: **Falcon(n)et, Fauconnet, Fauconneau**. It.: **Falconetto**.

Augs.: Fr.: **Falcon(n)at**.

Patrs.: Jewish (E Ashkenazic): **Falkoff, Falkov(sky), Falkovski, Falkowsky, Falkowicz, Falkowitz, Falkovitz, Falkovitch, Falkievich**.

Cpds: Jewish (Ashkenazic, ornamental): **Falkenberg** ('falcon hill'); **Falkenflik** (*-flik* is of unknown origin); **Falkenstein** ('falcon stone').

Equiv. (not cogn.): Czech: SOKOL.

Falkingham English (W Yorks.): apparently a habitation name from some place so called from OE *Falcingahām* 'homestead of the people of *Falca*' (a byname meaning 'Falcon'). This may be *Falkenham* in Suffolk, which appears in Domesday Book as *Faltenham*. It is of problematic etymology.

Fall English: topographic name for someone who lived by a clearing or a waterfall, ME *fall* (OE *(ge)feall*, a deriv. of *fealan* to fall).

Vars.: **Falle, Faul(l), Fawle**.

Fallas English (Norman): 1. habitation name from *Falaise* in Calvados, birthplace of William the Conqueror. The place is so called from ONF *faleise* cliff (of Gmc origin; cf. FALL).

2. topographic name for someone who lived by a cliff, from the ANF vocab. word.

Vars.: **Fall(i)s**. See also FAILES.

The name Fallas *is now found mainly in W Yorks., while* Fallis *and* Falls *are found chiefly in N Ireland.*

Fallon 1. English: var. of FULLER.

2. Irish: Anglicized form of Gael. **Ó Fallamhain** 'descendant of *Fallamhan*', a byname meaning 'Leader' (from *follamhnas* supremacy).

Vars.: **O'Fallon, O'Fallo(w)ne, Fal(l)oon**; **Hallon** (Gael. **Ó Fhallamhain**).

Fallow English: topographic name for someone who lived by a patch of fallow land, ME *falwe* (OE *fealh*). The word was used both of land left uncultivated for a time to recover its fertility and of land recently brought into cultivation.

2. nickname for someone with tawny hair, from ME *fallow* yellow, tawny (OE *fealu*, early confused with *fealh* as the colour was understood as being that of exposed soil).

Vars. (of 1): **Fallows** (also borne by Ashkenazic Jews as an Anglicization of one or more like-sounding Jewish surnames); **Fallowes**.

Cogn. (of 1): Ger.: **Falge**.

The earliest known bearer of the name is Robert del Falwiz, *who was given lands so named in the parish of Nether Alderley, Ches., by his brother Henry de Aldford in the late 12th cent. Robert and Henry were descended from Robert Bigot, a companion of William the Conqueror who had been granted extensive estates in Ches.*

Fane 1. English: nickname from ME *fein*, *fayn*, *fane* glad, well disposed (OE *fægen*). The word seems also to have been occasionally used as a given name in the Middle Ages, and in some instances the surname may derive from this.

2. Welsh: nickname from *fain* slender.

Vars.: **Fayne, Va(y)ne**.

Patrs.: **Faynes, Va(i)nes**.

A family by the name of Vane *trace their descent from John Vane or Fane (d. 1554). Another branch of the family, descended from the same man, spell their name* Fane*; they hold the earldom of Westmorland. Some Vanes were recorded in Kent in 1426, but a family tradition that they were originally from Monmouth cannot be confirmed.*

Fanner 1. English: occupational name for someone who winnowed corn or performed a similar process on crushed metalliferous rock, from an agent deriv. of ME *fan* fan, winnow (OE *fann*, from L *vannum*).

2. English: topographic name, a var. of FENN.

3. Jewish (Ashkenazic): presumably an Anglicization of one or more like-sounding Jewish surnames.

Vars.: **Vanner, Vannar**.

Fanon French: metonymic occupational name for a standard-bearer, from OF *fanon* flag (of Gmc origin, cf. GONFALONIERI). The word was also used by extension for a priest's maniple, and the surname may occasionally have been a nickname from this source.

Färber German and Jewish (Ashkenazic): occupational name for a dyer, Ger. *Färber*, an agent deriv. of MHG *varwe* colour (OHG *farawa*).

Vars.: **Ferber**. Jewish: **Farber** (in part from Yid. *farber*, in part an Eng. re-spelling of the Ger. word); **Farb(man)**; **Farbiarz, Farbiasz** (from Pol.): **Farbstein, Farbsztein** ('colour stone', an ornamental elaboration).

Cogns.: Low Ger.: **Ferver**. Flem., Du.: **De Verver**.

Patrs.: Low Ger.: **Fervers, Ferfers**. Jewish: **Farberso(h)n**; **Ferberov** (E Ashkenazic).

Fargo Perhaps Welsh, but of unknown origin and not recorded as a surname in Wales.

The name is said to have been taken from Wales to America in about 1670, and established in Connecticut. At this time, however, surnames were not generally in use in Wales. William Fargo *(1818–81), who, with Henry Wells, founded the Wells Fargo express company in 1844, was a member of this family, born in New York.*

Faria Portuguese: habitation name from a town in the province of Minho, apparently so called from the personal name *Farus*.

Var.: **Farias**.

Farine 1. French: metonymic occupational name for a miller or flour-merchant, from OF *farine* wheat flour (L *fārīna*, a deriv. of *fār* coarse grain, spelt). In some cases it may possibly have been originally a nickname for someone with a pale complexion.

2. Jewish: of unknown origin.

Vars. (of 1): **Far(i)nier** (agent derivs.).

Cogns. (of 1): It.: **Farina**; **Farini** (also Jewish); **Farinaro, Farinari**. Sp.: **Harina**. Port.: **Farinha**.

Dims. (of 1): Fr.: **Far(i)nel, Far(i)neau, Far(i)naux, Farinet, Farinez**. It.: **Farinelli, Farinel(l)a, Farinetti, Farinola, Farinotti**. b

Augs. (of 1): It.: **Farinone, Farinon(e)**.

Pejs. (of 1): It.: **Farinacci, Farinasso, Farinazzo**.

Farkas 1. Hungarian: nickname from *farkas* wolf.

2. Jewish (Ashkenazic): Hungarian trans. of the Yid. male given name *Volf* 'WOLF', or else an ornamental name.

Vars. (of 2): **Farkash** (Eng. spelling); **Farkache** (Fr. spelling).

Farley 1. English: habitation name from any of various places, for example in Berks., Derbys., Hants, and Staffs., so called from OE *fearn* FERN + *lēah* wood, clearing.

2. Irish: Anglicized form of Gael. *Ó Fearghaile*; see FARRELL.

Vars. (of 1): **Farleigh** (the name of places in Hants, Kent, Somerset, Surrey, and Wilts.); **Fairley** (the name of a place in Shrops.; see also FAIRLIE); **Fearnley** (a Yorks. surname).

Farman 1. English and French: from an ON personal name composed of the elements *fara* to go + *maðr* (acc. *mann*) man. There is also a Continental Gmc personal name *Faraman*, *Fareman* (which Förstemann derives from *fara* family), and this may be the origin of some instances of this surname.

2. English: occupational name for a pedlar or itinerant merchant, ME *far(e)man* (from an ON vocab. word composed of the same elements as above).

3. Jewish (Ashkenazic): of unknown origin, presumably a pseudo-Germanization of FORMAN.

Farmer English: occupational name from ME, OF *ferm(i)er* (LL *firmārius*). The term denoted in the first instance a tax-farmer, one who undertook the collection of taxes, revenues, and imposts, paying a fixed (L *firmus*) sum for the proceeds, and only secondarily someone who rented land for the purpose of cultivation; it was not applied to an owner of cultivated land before the 17th cent.

Vars.: **Farmar**, **Fermer**, **Fermor**.

Cogn.: Fr.: **Fermier** (rare).

Farmery English: occupational name for a worker at an infirmary, or topographic name for someone who lived by one, from an aphetic form of ME, OF *enfermerie* (LL *infirmāria*, a deriv. of *infirmus* weak, ill). In the Middle Ages an infirmary was generally part of a monastery.

Farndon English: habitation name from any of the various places, in Ches., Northants, and Notts., so called from OE *fearn* FERN + *dūn* hill (see DOWN 1).

Farnell English: habitation name from any of the many places, such as *Farnell* (Kent, Wilts.), *Farnhill* (W Yorks.), and *Fernhill* (Ches.), named from OE *fearn* FERN + *hyll* HILL. In a few cases it may also derive from Farnell in the former county of Angus, Scotland (now part of Tayside region). Duncan *de Ferneuel* witnessed various documents in Angus in the 13th cent., but the surname is not now common in Scotland.

Vars.: **Farnall**, **Farn(h)ill**, **Fearnall**.

Farnese Italian: habitation name from a minor place near lake Bolsena in central Italy, where the family held land and had established a castle by the 12th cent.

Var.: **Farnes**.

The Farnese *family rose to power with Alessandro Farnese (1468–1549), who became Pope Paul III, the pontiff who excommunicated Henry VIII and approved the decree establishing the Jesuits. For his family he separated the states of Parma and Piacenza from the papal possessions and granted them to Pierluigi Farnese, 1st Duke of Parma (1503–47), his illegitimate son. These lands remained in the family until 1731. The family also played an important role in the history of Spain. Alessandro Farnese, Duke of Parma (1545–92), was regent for Philip II in the Netherlands, and kept control over these rebellious possessions. Elizabeth Farnese (1692–1766), who was married to Philip V of Spain, helped to extend Spain's influence in Europe.*

Farnham English: habitation name from any of various places so called. Most, including those in Bucks., Dorset, Essex, Suffolk, Surrey, and W Yorks., get the name from OE *fearn* FERN + *hām* homestead or *hamm* water-meadow. One in Northumb. was originally named *Thirnum*, from the dat. pl. (originally used after a preposition) of OE *þyrne* thornbush, i.e. 'at the thornbushes'.

Farnworth English: habitation name from either of two places in Lancs. so called from OE *fearn* FERN + *worð* enclosure (see WORTH).

Vars.: **Farnsworth**, **Farnorth**.

Faro 1. Portuguese: habitation name from one of the places named with Port. *faro* beacon (L *pharos*, from Gk; the lighthouse built on the island of *Pharos* at Alexandria was one of the seven wonders of the ancient world), or topographic name for someone who lived near a beacon. Cf. ALFARO and HARO. Some of the places so called may instead derive their names from the Arabic personal name *Harun*.

2. English: var. of FARRAR.

Farquhar Scots: from the Gael. personal name *Fearchar*, derived from OCelt. elements meaning 'man' + 'dear', 'beloved'.

Vars.: **Farquar**, **Faraquhart**; **Faraker**, **Forker**; **Farragher**, **Far(a)gher** (Ir.).

Patrs.: **Farqu(h)arson**; **McFarqu(h)ar**, **McKer(i)char**, **McKer(i)cher**, **McKerricher**, **McKer(r)acher**, **McCaragher**, **McErchar** (Gael. **Mac Fearchair**).

As a clan or sept the Farquhars *are descended from Farquhar Macintosh, a grandson of the laird of Macintosh who came to Braemar before 1382.*

Farr English and Scots: nickname for a fierce or lusty man, or metonymic occupational name for an oxherd, from ME *farre* bull (OE *fearr*).

Farrant English: 1. nickname for a person with grey hair or for someone who used to dress in grey, from OF *ferrant* (iron-)grey (a deriv. of *fer* iron, L *ferrum*; cf. FERRO). For the change of *-er-* to *-ar-* cf. MARCHANT.

2. from the medieval given name *Fer(r)ant*, probably in origin an OF form of FERDINAND, but early associated with the colour term.

Vars.: **Ferran(d)**, **Farran(d)**, FARREN.

Cogns.: Fr.: **Ferrant**, **Ferrand**. It.: **Ferranti**, **Ferrante**, **Ferrandi**, **Ferrando**; **Afferrante** (Apulia). Sp.: **Herrán**, **Herranz**; **Ferrán**. Cat.: **Ferran**, **Farran**. Port.: **Ferrão**.

Dims.: It.: **Ferrantello**, **Ferrantelli**, **Ferrantini**, **Ferrantino**; **Ferrantin** (Venetia).

Patrs.: Eng.: **Farrants**, **Farrance**, **Ferrans**, **Ferens**, **Ference**. Sp.: **Herráez**, **Herráiz**. Port.: **Ferraz**.

Farrar English (in this spelling, most common in Yorks.): occupational name for a smith or worker in iron, from ME, OF *ferreor*, *ferour* (a deriv. of *fer* iron, L *ferrum*; see FERRO). Most forms show the change of *-er-* to *-ar-*, for which see MARCHANT.

Vars.: **Farrier** (Northumb.); FERRIER (Scots and N English); **Ferrer**, **Ferrar**, **Farrer**, **Farra(h)**, **Farrey**, **Farrow**, FARO; **Pharrow**, **Pharaoh** (alteration by folk etymology); **Varah**, **Var(e)y**, **Varrow**, **Vairow**.

Cogns.: Fr.: **Ferr(i)er**. Prov.: **Férier**, **Férié**. It.: **Ferraro**, **Ferrari**; **Ferrero** (Piedmont, Liguria); **Ferreri** (Sardinia); **Ferrario**; **Ferrai** (Tuscany); **Ferreli** (Sardinia); **Ferriero**, **Ferrieri**, **Ferrerio**; **Ferrer**, **Fer(r)e**, **Fare** (Lombardy). Sp.: **Herrero(s)**; **Ferrero**; **Ferreiro** (Galicia). Cat.: **Ferrer**, **Ferré(s)**, **Farrer**, **Farré(s)**. Port.: **Ferreiro**.

Dims.: It.: **Ferrarello**, **Ferraretto**, **Ferrarin(i)**, **Ferrarotti**. Cat.: **Ferre(i)ró**.

Augs.: It.: **Ferraron(e)**.

Pej.: It.: **Ferraraccio**.

Patrs.: It.: **De Ferrari(s)**.

Farràs Catalan: nickname for a iron-willed or inflexible person, from Cat. *farràs* (made of) iron (LL *ferrāceus*, a deriv. of *ferrum* iron; cf. FERRO).

Var.: **Farreny**.

Farrell Irish: Anglicized form of Gael. **Ó Fearghail** 'descendant of *Fearghal*', a personal name composed of the elements *fear* man + *gal* valour.

Vars.: **O'Farrell, O'Ferrall, Farrel, Ferrell**; **(O')Farrelly, O'-Ferrally**, FARLEY (Gael. **Ó Fearghaile** or **Ó Fearghailaigh**); **Frawley** (Gael. **Ó Freaghaile**, a metathesized form; see FRIEL).

Farren 1. English: from ME *farhyne*, which is either an occupational name for an oxherd, from OE *fearr* bull (see FARR) + *hīne* servant (see HINE), or a nickname from OE *fæger* handsome (see FAIR) + *hīne* servant.

2. English: var. of FARRANT.

3. Irish: Anglicized form of Gael. **Ó Faracháin** 'descendant of *Farachán*', a personal name perhaps derived from *forcha* bolt of thunder, lightning.

Vars.: **Farrin, Varran**.

Farrimond English (Lancs.): from a Norman personal name *Faramund*, composed of the Gmc elements *fara* family (see FARMAN 1) + *mund* protection. Alternatively, it may be from an unattested ON personal name **Farmundr*, composed of the elements *fara* to go + *mundr* protection.

Farrington English: habitation name from a place so called, of which there is one in Somerset. The name derives from OE *fearn* FERN + *tūn* enclosure, settlement.

Farthing English: 1. nickname denoting someone who paid this amount in rent, or given for some other anecdotal reason, from ME *farden*, *ferthing*, OE *feorðing* quarter of a penny (a deriv. of *fēower* four).

2. topographic name for someone who lived on a division of land known by this name, from being the fourth part of a larger area.

3. from the ON personal name *Farþegn*, composed of the elements *fara* to go + *þegn* warrior, hero.

Fass German and Jewish (Ashkenazic): metonymic occupational name for a maker or seller of casks and tubs, or nickname for someone as rotund as a barrel. The Ger. name is from MHG, OHG *faz* vat, the Jewish name from mod. Ger. *Fass* or Yid. *fas* cask.

Vars.: **Fäss(l)er, Fessler** (agent derivs.).

Fassbinder German and Jewish (Ashkenazic): occupational name for a cooper, Ger. *Fassbinder*, from MHG *faz* cask, tub (see FASS) + *binden* to join, construct (OHG *bindan*). This is the term used for the craft in N Germany; for surnames derived from terms used in other German-speaking regions, see BÖTTCHER, BÜTTNER, and SCHÄFFLER.

Var.: Ger.: **Fassbender**.

Fassnidge English (Bucks): habitation name from a lost place, *Fastendich* near W Wycombe in Bucks., named with the OE elements *fæsten* stronghold + *dīc* ditch.

Var.: **Fastnedge**.

Fastolf English: from the ON personal name *Fastúlfr*, composed of the elements *fast* secure, strong + *úlfr* wolf.

Faucheur French: occupational name for a mower or reaper or for a maker or seller of scythes, from an agent deriv. of OF *fauche* scythe (LL *falca*, for class. L *falx*, gen. *falcis*).

Vars.: **Faucheux**; **Lefaucheur, Lefaucheux**; **Fauquer, Fauquex, Lefauquer, Lefauquex** (Normandy, Picardy).

Cogn.: It.: **Falciatori**.

Faughnan Irish: Anglicized form of Gael. **Ó Fachtnáin** 'descendant of *Fachtnán*', a personal name representing a dim. of *Fachtna*, an ancient name of unknown origin.

Faulkes English: from the Norman given name *Fau(l)ques* (oblique case *Fau(l)que*), originally a Gmc byname meaning 'FALCON'.

Vars.: **Fawlks, Fa(w)kes, Faux**; **Falkous, Falk(h)us, Falcus** (Northumb.); **Fa(w)ke**.

Cogns.: It.: **Falco, Falchi**.

Dims.: It.: **Falchetti, Falchini, Falcucci**.

Patrs.: It.: **De Falco, Di Falco**.

Faulkner English and Scots: occupational name for someone who kept falcons for the use of the lord of the manor (a common feudal service), or for someone who operated the siege gun known as a *falcon*.

Vars.: **Falconer, Falconar, Faulkener, Falk(i)ner, Faulknor**.

Cogns.: Fr.: **Fau(l)connier**. Prov.: **Falconnier**. It.: **Falconieri**. Ger.: **Fal(c)kner, Felkner**. Flem.: **De Valkener**.

The family of the American novelist William Faulkner *(1897–1962), who was born in New Albany, Mississippi, was descended from Scottish settlers from Inverness called* Falconer. *Their name was altered in America to* Faulkner *and then to* Falkner. *The novelist added the* u *again himself.*

Faust 1. German and Jewish (Ashkenazic): presumably a nickname for a strong or pugnacious person or for someone with a club hand or other deformity of the hand, from Ger. *Faust* fist (MHG, OHG *fūst*).

2. German: from a personal name (L *Faustus* 'Fortunate', 'Lucky', a deriv. of *favēre* to favour), which was borne by a few relatively insignificant early Christian martyrs. *Fausto* is quite common today as an It. given name, but was not so used until after the Renaissance, hence the absence of It. surnames from this source.

Cogns. (of 1): Low Ger.: **Fust**. Flem., Du.: **De Vuyst**. Eng.: **Fust, Fist**.

Dims.: Ger.: **Fäustlein**; **Fäustel, Feistel**; **Feistle** (Swabia).

Patrs. (from 2): Russ.: **Faustov, Favstov, Chaustov**.

Patr. (from 2) (dim.): Russ.: **Faustsev**.

Faustino Portuguese: from a medieval given name (L *Faustīnus*, a deriv. of *Faustus*; see FAUST 2), borne in honour of various early saints, including a 2nd-cent. martyr of Lombardy and a 4th-cent. bishop of Brescia, supposedly his descendant.

Fautley English: of uncertain origin. It is possibly an alteration, influenced by the numerous habitation names in *-ley* (from OE *lēah* wood, clearing), of an unidentified Fr. surname introduced by Huguenot settlers.

Vars.: **Fautly, Faultley**.

A certain Thomas Fawltey *had a daughter Margaret baptized at St Clement's Church, Hastings, in 1595, but he is probably unconnected with this family. The earliest Huguenot record in England of the name is the baptism in 1712 of Jean-Baptiste* Fauletie.

Fauvel French: 1. nickname for someone with a dusky complexion, from a dim. of OF *fauve* tawny (of Gmc origin; cf. FALLOW 2).

2. nickname for a devious or hypocritical person. The word came to have this sense as a result of being borne by the cunning horse in a popular medieval cycle of beast tales (cf. REYNARD), and was reinforced by associations with OF *favel* story, tale (LL *fabella*, for class. L *fabula*).

Var.: **Fauveau**.

Cogns: Eng.: **Favel(l), Favill**.

Favard Provençal: nickname from the wild pigeon, OProv. *favart*, a pej. deriv. of *fave* bean (cf. FAVIER). The birds feed greedily on this diet and are responsible for large losses among crops; the nickname presumably denoted similarly gluttonous and destructive individuals.

Var.: **Favart.**

Dims.: **Favardel, Favardon, Favardin.**

Favier French: occupational name for a grower or seller of beans, OF *favier* (LL *fabārius*, a deriv. of *faba* bean).

Cogns.: It.: **Favaro, Favari.**

Dims.: Fr.: **Fav(e)reau.**

Fawcett English: habitation name from *Fawcett* in Cumb. or *Facit* in Lancs., both so called from OE *fāg*, *fāh* (brightly) coloured, variegated, flowery + *sīde* slope. *Forcett* in N Yorks. is named from OE *ford* FORD + *(ge)sete* house, settlement, and this may also be a partial source of the surname, which is common esp. in N England.

Vars.: **Fawcitt, Faws(s)ett, Faucett, Fausset(t), Fasset, Fosset, Fossit(t).**

Fay 1. English: nickname for a person believed to have supernatural qualities, from ME, OF *faie* fairy (LL *fāta* fate, destiny, originally neut. pl., but later taken as fem. sing.).

2. English: nickname for a trustworthy person, from ME, OF *fei* loyalty, trust, a later form of *feit*, *feid*; cf. FAITH.

3. English (Norman) and French: habitation name from any of the various places in France named with OF *faie* beech; see FAGE.

4. Irish: var. of FAHY and FEE.

Vars.: **Faye, Fey.**

Fayerman 1. Jewish (Ashkenazic): a deriv. of Yid. *fayer* fire (see FEUER).

2. English: var. of FAIRMAN.

Vars. (of 1): **Faierman; Fayer, Faier; Fajer(man)** (Pol. spelling).

Fazakerley English (Lancs.): habitation name from a minor place in the parish of Walton on the Hill near Liverpool, so called from OE *fæs* border, fringe + *æcer* field, ploughed land + *lēah* wood, clearing.

Vars.: **Fazackerly, Phizackerl(e)y** (pseudo-learned spelling, in imitation of Gk words beginning with *Ph-*).

Many modern bearers of these names are descended from a certain Henry de Fazakerley, *recorded in 1276*.

Fear English: 1. nickname for a sociable person, from ME *fe(a)re* comrade, companion (OE *(ge)fēra*).

2. nickname for a proud or haughty person, from ME *fere* proud (OF *fier*, L *ferus* wild, savage).

Vars.: **Feare, Phear.**

Patr.: **Fears.**

Fearnside English (Yorks.) and Scots (Aberdeens.): probably a habitation name from one or more unidentified places, apparently so called from OE *fearn* FERN + *sīde* slope, hillside.

Fearon English (Norman): occupational name for a blacksmith or worker in iron, from OF *ferron* blacksmith (L *ferro*, gen. *ferrōnis*, a deriv. of *ferrum* iron; cf. FERRO).

Cogns.: Fr.: **Ferron(ier), Fernier.**

Dims.: Fr.: **Fer(ro)net, Fernez, Fer(ro)nel.**

Feary English (mostly Lincs.): of uncertain origin, perhaps a habitation name from an unidentified place named with the OE elements *fearr* bull or *fearn* fern + *(ge)hæg* enclosure or *ēg* low-lying land.

Vars.: **Fearey, Fery, Farey, Fairy.**

The first known bearer of the name is John Feary *or* Farey, *who lived at Denford, Lincs., in the later part of the 17th cent.*

Feather English: 1. metonymic occupational name for a trader in feathers and down or a maker of quilts, or possibly also of pens, from ME *fether*, OE *feðer* feather. Feathermongers are recorded from the 13th cent. onwards.

2. nickname for a very light person or perhaps a person of no account, from the same word as in 1.

Vars.: **Fed(d)er.**

Cogns. (of 1): Ger.: **Feder(er), Fiederer; Federmann.** Du.: **Vedder; De Veer,** VEERMAN. Jewish (Ashkenazic): **Feder(er), Federman(n).**

Dim. (of 1): Ger.: **Federle.**

Cpds (ornamental): Jewish: **Federbus(c)h** ('feather bush'); **Federgrün, Federgrin** ('feather green', partly Anglicized as **Federgreen**); **Federschneider** ('feather cutter').

Featherstone N English: habitation name from places in Staffs., W Yorks., and Northumb. (but see also FEATHERSTONEHAUGH), which are so called from OE *feðerstān* tetralith, a prehistoric structure consisting of three upright stones capped with a headstone (from OE *fe(o)ðer-* four + *stān* stone).

Vars.: **Fe(a)therston.**

Featherstonehaugh English: habitation name from a place in Northumb. now called FEATHERSTONE, but originally containing the extra element ME *halgh*, OE *halh* nook, recess (see HALE 1). The name is normally pronounced /ˈfænʃɔː/.

Vars.: **Fe(a)therstonhaugh; Fanshaw(e).**

Fedotov Russian: patr. from the given name *Fedot* (Gk *Theodotos* 'God-given', a less common equivalent of *Theodoros* 'God-gift'; see TUDOR). This name was borne by several early Christian saints, among them 4th-cent. bishops of Cyreneia and Laodicea.

Var.: **Fedotyev.**

'Son of the wife of F.': **Fedotikhin.**

Fee Irish: Anglicized form of Gael. **Ó Fiaich** 'descendant of *Fiach*', a byname meaning 'Raven'.

Vars.: FAY, FOY; **O'Fee, O'Fay.**

Dims.: **O'Fighane, (O')Feehan, Fe(g)han, Fegan, Fe(h)ane** (Gael. **Ó Fiacháin**).

Feely Irish: 1. Anglicized form of Gael. **Ó Fáilbhe** 'descendant of *Fáilbhe*', a byname meaning 'Lively'.

2. Anglicized form of Gael. **Ó Fithcheallaigh** 'descendant of *Fithcheallach*', a byname meaning 'Chess-player'.

Vars.: **Feeley, Feal(e)y.** (Of 1 only): **O'Falv(e)y, O'Falvie, O'Falie, Falvey.** (Of 2 only): **O'Fihily, O'Fihillie, O'Fielly, Fihelly, Fe(e)hely, Feehily.**

Feeney Irish: 1. Anglicized form of Gael. **Ó Fiannaidhe** 'descendant of *Fiannaidhe*', a byname meaning 'Warrior', 'Champion' (from *fian* army).

2. Anglicized form of Gael. **Ó Fidhne** 'descendant of *Fidhne*', a personal name apparently derived from *fidh* tree, wood.

Var.: **O'Feeney.**

Fehér Hungarian and Jewish (Ashkenazic): nickname for a fair-skinned or blond-haired person, from Hung. *fehér* white.

Var.: **Fejér.**

Feicht German: topographic name for someone who lived by a conspicuous pine tree or in a pine forest, from MHG *viehte* pine (OHG *fiohta*), mod. Ger. *Fichte* spruce. The vowel of the first syllable underwent a variety of changes in different dialects.

Vars.: **Ficht(e)**, **Feucht**; **F(e)icht(n)er**, **Feuchtner**, **Füchter**.

Feige 1. German: topographic name for someone who lived by a fig tree, or metonymic occupational name for a grower or seller of figs, from Ger. *Feige* fig, MHG *vīge* (OHG *fīga*, from L *ficus*).

2. Jewish (Ashkenazic): from the Yid. female given name *Feyge*, a back-formation from *Feygl* (see FEIGEL), as if this contained the dim. suffix *-l*.

Cogns. (of 1): Jewish (Ashkenazic, ornamental): **Feig**, **Faig**; **Feigenbaum**, **Feigenboim**, **Faigenbaum**, **Faigenboum**, **Fajgenbaum** ('fig tree'); **Feigman** (occupational). Flem.: **Vyghen**. Du.: **Vijg(enboom)**. Eng.: **Figg(e)**. Fr.: **Figuier**. Prov.: **Figuière**, **Figuère(s)**. Sp.: **Higuera(s)**, **Figuera(s)**. Cat.: **Figuera(s)**. Port.: **Figueira(s)**.

Dims. (of 1): Prov.: **Figa(i)rol**. Sp.: **Figueroa** (Galicia). Cat.: **Figuerola**.

Collectives (of 1): Prov.: **Figadère**. Sp.: **Figueredo**. Port.: **Figueiredo**.

Metrs. (from 2): Jewish: **Feiges**, **Feigenson**; **Feigin**, **Fejgin**, **Faigin** (E Ashkenazic); **Fagin** (an Anglicized spelling).

Cpds (of 1, ornamental): Jewish: **Feigenberg**, **Faigenberg** ('fig hill'); **Feigenblat(t)**, **Faigenblat**, **Fajgenblat** ('fig leaf').

Feigel Jewish (Ashkenazic): from the Yid. female given name *Feygl* (from Yid. *foygl* bird (cf. VOGEL and FOWLE), a translation of the Hebr. name *Tsipora* (Eng. *Zipporah*) 'Bird', borne by the wife of Moses).

Metrs.: **Feigelso(h)n**; **Fogelson** (Germanized); **Feig(e)lewitz**, **Feiglin** (E Ashkenazic).

Feighery Irish: Anglicized form of Gael. **Ó Fiachra** 'descendant of *Fiachra*', a personal name of uncertain origin, probably a deriv. of *fiach* raven (cf. FEE).

Feijoo Spanish (Galicia): metonymic occupational name for a grower or seller of kidney beans, or perhaps a nickname for a small person, from the dial. term *feixó* kidney bean (LL *phaseōlus*).

Fein 1. German: nickname from MHG *fīn* fine, splendid (a cogn. of FIN).

2. Jewish (Ashkenazic): ornamental name from mod. Ger. *fein*, Yid. *fayn* fine, excellent.

Vars.: Ger.: **Feine**, **Feiner(t)**, **Feinmann**. Jewish: **Fajn(er)**, **Feiner**, **Feinman**.

Cogns.: Low Ger.: **Fie(h)n**.

Dim.: Ger.: **Feinle**.

Cpds (ornamental): Jewish: **Feinberg** ('fine hill'); **Feinblatt** ('fine leaf'); **Feinbrun** ('fine fountain'); **Feinbus(c)h** ('fine bush'); **Feinburg** ('fine town'); **Feindeitsch** ('fine German'); **Feingang** ('fine gait'); **Feingold**, **Fajngold** ('fine gold'); **Feinholz**, **Fajnhol(t)z** ('fine wood'); **Feinkind** ('fine child'); **Feinkoch** ('fine cook', or from Yid. *faynkukhn* omelette); **Feinmesser** ('fine knife'); **Feinsilber**, **Fajnzylber** ('fine silver'); **Feinstein** ('fine stone'); **Feintuch**, **Fajntuch** ('fine cloth'); **Feinwachs** ('fine wax'); **Feinzak** ('fine sack').

Feinschreiber Jewish (Ashkenazic): occupational name for a scribe who specialized in preparing Torah scrolls, phylacteries, and mezuzot, from mod. Ger. *fein* fine + *Schreiber* writer.

Feio Portuguese: nickname for an ugly person, from Port. *feio* repugnant (L *foedus* foul, shameful).

Feito Spanish: nickname from the past part. *feito* (L *factus*) of OSp. *fer* to make, do (L *facere*). The word was used of a grown man as opposed to a child, and it is probably in this sense that the surname arose, to designate an adult as opposed to a minor with the same given name.

Fekete Hungarian: nickname for a dark-haired or swarthy person, from Hung. *fekete* black.

Felber 1. German: topographic name for someone who lived by a conspicuous willow tree or a group of such trees, from MHG *velwe* willow (presumably from an unrecorded OHG cognate of OE *welig*). The vocab. word has now been entirely supplanted by WEIDE 1. Both words ultimately derive from a root meaning 'bent', 'twisted', and refer to the useful suppleness of willow twigs. Some examples may derive from places called *Felben*, from the dat. pl. of the word (originally used after a preposition).

2. Jewish (Ashkenazic): ornamental name, from the tree.

Vars. (of 2): **Felbert**, **Felberbaum**.

Feldner 1. German: from MHG *veldener*, a technical term of the feudal system for a vassal or bondsman. The word is a deriv. of OHG *feld* FIELD.

2. Jewish: ornamental extension of *Feld*; see FIELD.

Var.: **Fellner** (see also FELL 2).

Feldscher Jewish (Ashkenazic): occupational name for an old-time barber-surgeon, who not only cut hair but also pulled teeth, let blood, and applied other remedies. The vocab. word is from Yid. or Russ. *feldsher* (from Ger. *Feldscher* army surgeon, from *Feld* field + *Scher(er)* agent noun from *scheren* to shave, cut). Probably no later than the 20th cent., the occupations of barber and 'barefoot doctor' became separate, but this was probably after the surname had been acquired.

Feliciano Italian, Spanish, and Portuguese: from a medieval given name (L *Fēlīciānus*, a deriv. of FELIX). The name was borne by a number of early saints, most notably a 3rd-cent. bishop of Foligno and apostle of Umbria.

Cogn.: Pol.: **Felicjan**.

Patr.: Pol.: **Felicjaniak**.

Feliński Polish: habitation name from a place called *Felin*.

Var.: **Felińczak**.

The surname Feliński *was given in 1603 by Zygmunt III of Poland to one Marek Siedor for his part in taking the fortress of* Felin *in Livonia.*

Felix 1. English and German: from a medieval given name (L *Fēlix*, gen. *Fēlīcis*, 'Lucky', 'Fortunate'). This was a relatively common Roman family name, apparently first adopted as a nickname by Sulla. It was very popular among early Christians, and was borne by a large number of early saints.

2. Jewish: presumably an adoption of the non-Jewish surname.

Vars.: Eng.: **Felice**, **Fillis**.

Cogns.: Fr.: **Félix**. Prov.: **Féli**. It.: **Felice**, **Felici**, **Filice**; **Felis(e)** (Venetia). Sp.: **Félix**, **Feliz**. Cat.: **Fèlix**, **Feliu**. Pol.: **Feliks**, **Peliks**.

Dims.: It.: **Felicetti**, **Felicini**, **Felicioli**, **Feliciotti**. Fr.: **Félizon**, **F(é)lizot**, **Félissot**, **F(é)lizet**. Pol.: **Felczyk**.

Aug.: It.: **Felicioni**.

Patrs.: It.: **De(l) Felice**, **De Felici**, **Di Felice**. Port.: **Felices**. Pol.: **Feli(k)siak**, **Pelisiak**. Jewish (Ashkenazic): **Felickson**.

Habitation name (from a dim.): Pol.: **Felczykowski**.

Fell 1. English (chiefly Northern): topographic name for someone who lived by an area of high ground or by a prominent crag, from Northern ME *fell* high ground, rock, crag (ON *fjall*).

2. English and Jewish (Ashkenazic): metonymic occupational name for a furrier, from ME, OE *fell* or from Ger. *Fell*, Yid. *fel* (MHG *vel*), all of which words mean 'skin,

hide, or pelt'. Yid. *fel* refers to untanned hide, in contrast to *pelts* tanned hide (see PILCHER).

Vars.: Eng.: **Fells**; **Feller**, **Fella**. (Of 2 only): Jewish: **Fel(l)ner**, **Fel(l)man**; **Felhandler** (with mod. Ger. *Händler* dealer or Yid. *hendler*).

Cogns. (of 1): Ger.: **Fels(mann)**, **Feltz(mann)**, **Felser**, **Felz(n)er**. Swed.: **Fjell(man)**; **Fjellander** (a humanistic form, with the final element from Gk *anēr*, gen. *andros* man). (Of 2): Ger.: **Fell(er)er**, **Fell(er)mann**, **Fellner** (see also FELDNER). Swed.: **Fälman**.

Cpds (of 1): Swed.: **Fjellstedt** ('hill homestead'); **Fjellström**, **Fjällström** ('hill stream').

Fellow English: from ME *felagh*, *felaw*, late OE *fēolaga* partner, shareholder (ON *félagi*, from *fé* fee, money + *legja* to lay (down)). In ME the term was used in the general sense of a companion or comrade, and the surname thus probably denoted a (fellow) member of a trade guild (cf. FEAR 1).

Patrs.: **Fellow(e)s** (but see also FIELDHOUSE).

Felsted English: habitation name from a place in Essex, so called from OE *feld* pasture, open country (see FIELD) + *stede* homestead (see STEAD 1).

Var.: **Felstead**.

Feltham English: habitation name from places SW of London and in Somerset. The former is so called from OE *feld* pasture, open country + *hām* homestead; the latter from OE *filiðe* hay + *hamm* water meadow.

Felton English: habitation name from any of various places so called. Most of them, including those in Herefords., Shrops., and Somerset (Winford), get the name from OE *feld* pasture, open country (see FIELD) + *tūn* enclosure, settlement. Another place of the same name in Somerset, also known as Whitchurch, has its first element from OE *filiðe* hay. *Felton* Hill in Northumb. gets it from the OE personal name *Fygla* (a deriv. of *fugol* bird; cf. FOWLE). The surname is now found most frequently in the W Midlands of England, though it is also common in the United States.

Femister English and Scots: occupational name for a senior herdsman, from ME *fee* cattle (OE *fēoh*) + *master* MASTER.

Vars.: **Fimister**, **Phemister**, **Phimister**, **Whimster**; **Feam(a)ster**, **Feemster**, **Feimster** (U.S.).

Fenaghty Irish: Anglicized form of Gael. **Ó Fionnachta** (often now written **Ó Fiannachta**) 'descendant of *Fionnachta*', a personal name composed of the elements *fionn* fair, white + *sneachta* snow.

Vars.: **Finnerty**, FENTON.

Fenck German: metonymic occupational name for a cultivator of millet or panic grass (MHG *ven(i)ch*, from L *pānicum*), or a topographic name for someone who lived by a patch of land where the crop was grown. There seems also to have been some confusion with MHG *fenich*, a byform of *fēnichel*, mod. Ger. *Fenchel* fennel (see FENNELL).

Var.: **Fenech**.

Fenier French: occupational name for a hay merchant, OF *fe(i)nier* (L *f(a)enārius*, from *faenum* hay).

Vars.: **Fenié**, **Fanier**.

Cogns.: Prov.: **Fenayre**. Eng: **Feiner**, **Fainer** (rare).

Dims.: Fr.: **Feneron**. Prov.: **Fenayrol**, **Fenayroux**.

Fenlon 1. Irish: Anglicized form of Gael. **Ó Fionnaláin** 'descendant of *Fionnalán*', a personal name from a dim. of *fionn* fair, white (see FINN 1).

2. English (Huguenot): habitation name from *Fénelon* in the Dordogne, which is of uncertain etymology.

Var. (of 1): **Fenelon**.

Cogn. (of 2): Fr.: **Fénelon**.

Fenn English: topographic name for someone who lived in a low-lying marshy area, from OE *fenn* marsh, bog. The forms with the voiced initial consonant (*V-*) are characteristic of SW dialects of ME. The forms with *Fa-* may represent OE *fænn*, the East Saxon form of *fenn*.

Vars.: **Fann**; **Venn**, **Vann(e)**, **Vance**; **Avann**; **Fenning**, **Fanning**; **Venning** (W Country); **Fenner**, FANNER.

Cogns.: Low Ger.: **Fenn**; **Intveen**; **Terveen** (N Rhineland). Fris.: **Feenstra**, **Veenstra**; **Venema**. Flem.: **Van de Ven**, **Van den Vinne**, **Venneman**. Du.: **Van den Ven**, **Van (den) Veen**, **Veenman**.

Fanning *is the name of a family once closely associated with Limerick in Ireland. The name is first found there when Richard Fanning obtained lands at Bunratty* c.*1220*.

Fennell 1. English: metonymic occupational name for a grower or seller of fennel (OE *finugle*, *fenol*, from LL *fenuculum*, dim. of *f(a)enum* hay). Fennel was widely used in the Middle Ages as a seasoning. The surname may also have been a topographic name for someone who lived near a patch where the herb was grown, or a nickname for a particularly enthusiastic user of it.

2. Irish: Anglicized form of Gael. **Ó Fionnghail** 'descendant of *Fionnghal*', a personal name composed of the elements *fionn* fair, white + *gal* valour.

Vars.: **Fennel**. (Of 1 only): **Funnell**, **Fonnell** (forms developed in E Sussex in the 16th and 17th cents.). (Of 2 only): **Fennelly** (Gael. **Ó Fionnghaile** or **Ó Fionnghalaigh**).

Cogns. (of 1): Ger.: **Fenchel**. Low Ger.: **Fen(ne)kohl**, **Vennekohl**, **Vennekold**, **Fönekold**. It.: **Finocchi(o)**, **Fenocchio**; **Fenoglio** (Piedmont); **Finocchiaro** (Sicily). Sp.: **Hinojo**. Cat.: **Fenoll(er)**, **Fenellosa**.

Dims. (of 1): It.: **Finoccietti**; **Fenoglietto** (Piedmont).

Fennessy Irish: Anglicized form of Gael. **Ó Fionnghusa** 'descendant of *Fionnghus*', a personal name composed of the elements *fionn* fair, white + *gus* vigour, force.

Fenster German and Jewish (Ashkenazic): metonymic occupational name for a maker of windows, from Ger. *Fenster* window (MHG *venster*, from L *fenestra*). Medieval windows were often just holes in the wall; indeed, the Eng. word *window* derives from ON *vindauga* 'wind eye'. Later they were filled with a frame containing thin layers of translucent horn, and eventually glass, normally only in small pieces leaded together. In the case of the Ger. name, the derivation is in some cases from a habitation name from any of various minor places so called from being in a gap in a range of hills or a clearing in a wood; it may also have been a topographic name for someone who lived in a house remarkable for its windows.

Vars: Ger.: **Fensterer**, **Fenstermann**. Jewish (Ashkenazic): **Fenstermacher** ('window maker').

Cogns.: Fr.: **Fenêtre**, **Delafenestre**.

Fentiman English: occupational name for a servant or retainer of a family called FENTON.

Var.: **Fenteman**.

The formation of a surname denoting a servant from another surname of local (habitation) origin is unusual in English; most servants' names are based on the given name of the original master. All modern bearers of this surname seem to derive from a single source, a servant or steward of the Fenton *family that held land around 1379 in Swillington, W Yorks., a few miles from Church* Fenton.

Fenton 1. English: habitation name from any of various places, in Lincs., Northumb., Staffs., and S Yorks., so called from OE *fenn* marsh, fen (see FENN) + *tūn* enclosure, settlement.

2. Irish: Anglicized form of Gael. *Ó Fionnachta*; see FENAGHTY.

3. Jewish (Ashkenazic): Anglicized form of various like-sounding names, for example *Finkelstein* (see FUNKE).

Var. (of 1): **Venton** (W Country).

Fenwick N English and Scots: habitation name from either of two places in Northumb. or from one in W Yorks., all of which are so called from OE *fenn* marsh, fen (see FENN) + *wīc* dairy farm, outlying village (see WICK). There is also a place in the former county of Ayrs., Scotland (now part of Strathclyde region) which has the same name and origin. This last is the source of at least some early examples of the surname: Nicholaus *Fynwyk* was provost of Ayr in 1313, and Reginald *de Fynwyk* or *Fynvyk* appears as bailie and alderman of the same burgh in 1387 and 1401. The name is usually pronounced /ˈfɛnɪk/.

Vars.: **Fennick, Finnick, Vinnick; Fenix, Ph(o)enix; Fenwich** (Scots).

The earliest known bearer of the name is Robert de Fenwick, *who was living in the late 12th cent. at Fenwick in Northumb. The name is still very much more common in Northumb. than elsewhere, but it spread right down the east coast of England, from the Moray Firth to E Anglia, quite early on, and can now be found as far afield as Glasgow and Wales.*

Fenyvesi Hungarian: topographic name for someone who lived in or near a pine forest, Hung. *fenyves* (from *fenyö* pine tree).

Vars.: **Fenyves** (also Jewish (Ashkenazic) ornamental name); **Fenyvessy**.

Feo Italian: from a given name, an aphetic short form of *Maffeo*; see MATTHEW.

Var.: **Fei**.

Dim.: **Feoli**.

Féral French: nickname for a man of a cruel disposition or scruffy and uncouth appearance, from OF *féral* wild, bestial (L *ferālis*, from *fera* wild animal).

Ferdinand German and French: from a Spanish (Visigothic) personal name composed of the elements *farð* journey, expedition (or a metathesized form of *frið* peace) + *nanð* daring, brave. The surname is of comparatively recent origin in German-speaking countries and in France, for the given name was not introduced from Spain until the late 15th cent. It was brought to Austria by the Habsburg dynasty, among whom it was a hereditary name, and from Austria it spread to France. The Iberian cogns. given below are of more ancient origin and more frequently found today, since the name was much favoured in the royal house of Castile. It owes its popularity in large measure to King Ferdinand III of Castile and León (1198–1252), who recaptured large areas of Spain from the Moors and was later canonized.

Var.: Fr.: **Fernant**; see also FARRANT.

Cogns.: Sp.: **Hernando, Hernán, Hernanz; Fernando, Fernán**. Port.: **Fernando, Fernão, Ferrão**.

Patrs.: Sp.: **Hernández, Hernáez, Hernáiz; Fernández, Ferrández; Ferrándiz** (Aragon). Port.: **Fernandes, Fernandez**.

Fereday Irish: Anglicized form of Gael. **Ó Fearadaigh** 'descendant of *Fearadach*', a personal name apparently composed of old Celt. elements meaning 'man' + 'wood'.

Var.: **Faraday**.

Fergus Scots and Irish: from the Gael. personal name *Fearghus*, composed of the elements *fear* man + *gus* vigour, force. This was the name of an early Irish mythological figure, a valiant warrior, and also of the grandfather of St Columba.

Vars.: **Ferris, Farris** (chiefly N Ireland).

Dim.: **Fergie** (Sc.).

Patrs.: **Fergu(s)son, Fergyson**.

'Descendant of F.': **O'Fearguise, O'Fergus, O'Ferris, O'Farris** (Gael. **Ó Fearghuis**); **O'Farrisa, Farrissy** (Gael. **Ó Fearghusa**).

Some Irish bearers of this name claim descent from Fergus, *Prince of Galloway (d. 1161), although documentary evidence is missing. Of all the forms and derivatives of this name,* Ferguson *is by far the most common.*

Fern 1. English: topographic name for someone who lived in a place where there was an abundance of ferns, from OE *fearn* fern (a collective noun). The forms with voiced initial consonant (*V*-) represent south-western ME developments (cf. FENN).

2. Jewish: of unknown origin.

Vars. (of 1): **Fearn, Fa(i)rn, Feirn; Fe(a)rne; Ferns, Farnes; Vern(e), Varn(e)s**.

Fernie Scots: habitation name from an estate in Fife, near Cupar, so called from Gael. *fearnach* place of alders, alder wood (from *fearna* alder + the local suffix *-ach*).

Var.: **Fairnie**.

The earliest known bearer of the name is William de Ferny, *who was juror on an inquest in Fife in 1390.*

Ferragut Provençal and Catalan: nickname for a good swordsman, or metonymic occupational name for a master cutler, from OProv., Cat. *ferro* iron (L *ferrum*) + *agut* sharp (L *acūtus*).

Vars.: Prov.: **Farragut, Ferragu(s)**.

Ferrers English (Norman): habitation name from any of various places in Normandy called *Ferrières* 'iron workings' (L *ferrāriae*, a deriv. of *ferrum* iron; cf. FERRO).

Cogns.: Fr.: **Ferrière(s)**. It.: **Ferre(r)a** (NW Italy, Liguria); **Ferrara** (S Italy); **Ferrarese, Ferraresi** (Lombardy, Emilia). Sp.: **Herrera, Ferrera(s); Ferreira** (Galicia). Cat.: **Farrera(s), Farreres, Ferrera, Ferreres**. Port.: **Ferreira**.

This is the name of a great Norman family who held the earldom of Derby from 1138 to 1266. Many present-day descendants of this family still bear the name, although the direct male line died out in the Middle Ages, and the senior cadet branch in 1884.

Ferrier English (chiefly N) and Scots: 1. var. of FARRAR.

2. var. of FERRY.

Ferro 1. Italian and Portuguese: metonymic occupational name for someone who worked in iron (L *ferrum*; cf. FARRAR and FEARON), or nickname from the colour or hardness of iron (cf. FARRANT 1 and FARRÀS).

2. Jewish: of unknown origin.

Vars. (of 1): It.: **Ferri; Fierro** (Campania).

Cogns. (of 1): Sp.: **Hierro, Fierro**. Fr.: **Fer, Dufer**.

Dims. (of 1): It.: **Ferrett(in)i, Ferrett(in)o, Ferrin(i), Ferrino, Ferrucci, Ferruzzi, Ferrulli, Ferrotti, Ferroli; Ferrillo, Ferrulli** (S Italy).

Augs. (of 1): It.: **Ferron(i), Ferrone**. Fr.: **Ferras**.

Ferry 1. English: metonymic occupational name for a ferryman, or topographic name for someone who lived by a ferry crossing on a river. ME *feri* ferry is from ON *ferja* ferry, ultimately cogn. with the OE verb *ferian* to carry.

2. Irish: Anglicized form of Gael. **Ó Fearadhaigh** 'descendant of *Fearadhach*', a personal name of uncertain origin, probably an adj. deriv. of *fear* man.

Vars. (of 1): **Ferrey, Ferrie; Ferriman, Ferryman**; FERRIER.

Cogn. (of 1): Du.: VEERMAN.

Fertig German and Jewish (Ashkenazic): nickname from Ger. *fertig* ready, prepared (MHG *vertec*, OHG *fertīg*, a deriv. of *vart* journey, expedition, and so meaning originally 'ready for an expedition').

Var.: Ger.: **Förtig** (Bavaria).

Fett Low German: nickname for a fat man, from MLG *vett* fat (cf. OFris. *fett, fatt*, OE *fǣt(t)*).

Cogns.: Jewish (Ashkenazic, from mod. Ger. *fett*, Yid. *fet*): **Fettman, Fetter(mann)**.

Patr.: Low Ger.: **Fetting**.

Feuchtwanger German and Jewish (Ashkenazic): habitation name from *Feuchtwangen* in Franconia, so called from MHG *viuhte* damp (OHG *fūht(i)*) or the dial. term *feuchte* pine, spruce + *wang* meadow, grassland.

Feuer 1. German: metonymic occupational name for a stoker in a smithy or public baths, or nickname for someone with red hair or a fiery temper, from Ger. *Feuer* fire (MHG *viur*, OHG *fuir*).

2. Jewish (Ashkenazic): nickname or ornamental name from mod. Ger. *Feuer* fire. Kaganoff suggests that this is a name often given to or adopted by members of the priestly caste (cf. the Jewish folk belief, found as early as the Talmud, that Kohanim (see COHEN) have a violent temper), but there seems to be no evidence to support this suggestion.

Vars. (of 1): **Feurer, Feirer; Feuerman(n)**.

Dims. (of 1): **Feuerlein, Feierle**.

Feuerbach German: habitation name from a place near Stuttgart, according to Bahlow so called from a prehistoric term for a marsh + OHG *bah* stream (see BACH 1).

Feuerstein 1. German: metonymic occupational name for a seller of flints, or topographic name for someone who lived near an outcrop of flint, from Ger. *Feuerstein* flint (from MHG *viur* fire (see FEUER) + *stein* STONE).

2. Jewish (Ashkenazic): ornamental cpd of the elements FEUER fire + *stein* stone, or ornamental name from the Ger. vocab. word *Feuerstein* flint.

Vars. (of 2): **Faierstein, Fayerstein; Firestein** (partly Anglicized); **Firestone** (fully Anglicized).

Feverel English: from a ME form of the name of the month of *February* (L *(mensis) februārius*, perhaps a deriv. of *febris* fever, sickness), perhaps originating as a nickname for someone born or found in this bitter month, or for someone who was of a frosty character.

Vars.: **Feave(a)ryear, Feveyear, Fevyer; Febry** (chiefly Bristol).

Cogn.: Fr.: **Février**.

Fèvre French: occupational name for an iron-worker or smith, OF *fevre* (L *faber* craftsman).

Vars.: **Febvre** (the *-b-* having been introduced by hypercorrection under the influence of the L word); **Feu(b)re** (Brittany); **Fèbre** (Poitou); **Faivre** (Lorraine); **Lefe(b)vre, Lefébure, Lefeu(v)re, Lefeubre; Faber(t)** (from the L form often used in medieval documents).

Cogns.: Prov.: **Fabre, Favre, Faur(e); Fauré; Haur(e)** (Gascony). Eng.: **Fe(a)ver, Feaviour, Lefe(a)ver, Lefe(u)vre** (from ANF forms); **Faber** (from the L form). It.: **Fav(e)ri, Fab(b)ri**; FRAU (Sardinia). Cat.: **Fabre, Fabra, Faura**. Ger., Du., Dan.: **Faber** (a humanistic translation of *Schmidt* or some other cogn. of SMITH).

Dims.: Fr.: **Faivret, Févret, Fevret; Febreau; Févrichaud**. Prov.: **Favret; Favreau, Favrel, Faurel; Fabron, Favr(ich)on, Fauron, Faurou; Fabry, Faury; Haurillon** (Gascony). It.: **Fav(a)retti, Fab(b)retti, Fab(r)etto, Fab(b)rini, Favruzzi, Fab(b)rucci, Favaroli; Favret(in), Frabet, Fav(a)rin, Fabbrin** (Venetia); **Frabbetti** (Emilia).

Augs.: It.: **Favarone, Fabbroni, Frab(b)oni; Fav(a)ron** (Venetia).

Patrs.: Prov.: **Dufaure, Aufau(v)re**. Eng.: **Fe(a)vers**. It.: **Dal Fabbro, Del Fabbro**.

Fewtrell English (W Midlands): of uncertain origin, perhaps from a dim. of the ME occupational term *vewter* keeper of greyhounds (ANF *veutrier*, an agent deriv. of *veutre* greyhound, of Gaul. origin).

Feydit French: nickname from the past part. of OF *faidir* to banish, outlaw (a deriv. of *faide* feud, vengeance, of Gmc origin).

Var.: **Faydit**.

Dims.: **Feydel, Feydeau, Faydel**.

Fiala Czech: very common surname, derived from the vocab. word *fial(k)a* violet (the flower). This may have given rise to a surname in various possible ways: as a nickname for a shy, delicate person; as a topographic name for someone who lived where violets grew or, in a town, at a house distinguished with the sign of a bunch of violets; or simply as an ornamental name.

Dims.: **Fialka; Fialek** (altered to masc. form).

Cogn.: Pol.: FIJAŁKOWSKI.

Fialho Portuguese: nickname for a thin person, from Port. *fialho* fine thread (a deriv. of *fio* thread, L *filum*; cf. FILER 2). The nickname is attested in this sense from the 16th cent. and may well have occurred earlier.

Fibonacci Italian: patr. from the nickname *Bonnacci*, a pej. of *bono* 'good' (see BON), denoting an excessively pious or a hypocritical person. The first syllable derives from a scribal abbreviation of the L term *filius* son.

Fiche French: topographic name for someone who lived by a stake planted in the ground as a boundary or signpost, from OF *fiche* stake (a deriv. of *ficher* to fix, plant, L *figere*).

Cogn.: Eng.: FITCH.

Dims.: Fr.: **Fichet, Fichot; Fiqu(en)et** (Normandy).

Fiddes Scots: apparently a habitation name from a place a few miles south of Aberdeen, first recorded in the forms *Futhes* (1240) and *Fothes* (1390), probably from Gael. *fiodhais* wood-place, wood-stance. There is another place of the same name (with similar early forms) in the former county of Kincardine, and this may also have given rise to some examples of the surname.

The first recorded bearers of the name are Edmund de Fotheis *and his son Alwin, who witnessed two charters at the beginning of the 13th cent.*

Fiddy English (Norman): nickname meaning 'son of God', bestowed on an illegitimate child, esp. the illegitimate child of a priest, from ANF *fi(t)z* son (L *filius*) + *Deu* God (L *Deus*).

Vars.: **Fido(e)**.

Fieback German: topographic name for someone who lived by a drovers' road, MHG *vihewec*, from *vehe, vihe, vich* cattle (OHG *feho, fihu*) + *wec* way, path (OHG *weg*).

The surname originated chiefly in Saxony, Silesia, and Bohemia.

Vars.: **Fiebeck, Fiebig, Fiebich, Viebig; Fiebiger.**

Fiedler German and Jewish (Ashkenazic): occupational name for a professional player on the fiddle, or nickname for a skilled amateur, from Ger. *Fiedler*, Yid. *fidler* (MHG *videlære*). The instrument (OHG *fidula*) gets its name from LL *vītula*, a deriv. of *vītulāri* to celebrate.

Cogns.: Eng.: **Fid(d)ler**, VIDLER.

Field 1. English: topographic name for someone who lived on land which had been cleared of forest, but not brought into cultivation, from OE *feld* pasture, open country (opposed on the one hand to *æcer* cultivated soil, enclosed land (see ACKER) and on the other to *weald* wooded land, uncleared forest; see WALD).

2. Jewish (Ashkenazic): Anglicized and shortened form of any of the Jewish surnames given below.

Vars.: Eng. **Feild**; **Fields** (from the OE gen. case); **Fielden, Feilden** (from the OE dat. pl. case); **Velden** (S England); **Fielder**; **Fielding, Feilding**; **At(t)field**; **Delafield.**

Cogns.: Ger.: **Feld, Felder(er), Feldmann.** Fris.: **Veldstra.** Flem.: **Van de(r) Velde, Van Velden.** Du.: **Veld, Van den Veldt, Van den Velde(n), Veldman, Veltman.** Jewish: **Feld(er), Feldman(n).**

Cpds (ornamental unless otherwise stated): Jewish: **Feldbau** ('agriculture', perhaps occupational for a farmer); **Feldbaum** ('field tree'); **Feldberg(er)** ('field hill'); **Feldblum** ('field flower'); **Feldbrin** ('field well', perhaps topographic); **Feldfisher** ('rural fisherman', nickname or occupational name); **Feldharker** ('field smallholder', occupational); **Feldhammer** ('field hammer'); **Feldheim** ('field home'); **Feldhorn** ('field horn'); **Feldhuhn** ('partridge'); **Feldklein** ('field little'); **Feldmark** ('field boundary', perhaps topographic); **Feldmes(s)er** ('field knife' or 'field measurer', occupational name for a surveyor); **Feldmus** ('field-mouse'); **Feldstein** (field stone); **Feldstern** ('field star').

An English family by the name of Feilding, *also found as* Fieldeng *and* Fyilding, *trace their descent from Geoffrey Feilding, who fought under Henry III (1216–72). They hold the earldoms of Denbigh and Desmond, and a branch of the family included the novelist Henry* Fielding *(1707–54). The given name Rudolph became popular in the family because of a claimed relationship to the Habsburgs, for which there is no documentary foundation.*

Fieldhouse English (chiefly W Midlands and N England): topographic name for someone who lived in a house (OE *hūs*) in open pasture land (see FIELD). Reaney draws attention to the form *de Felhouse* (Staffs. 1332), and suggests that this may have become *Fellowes* (see FELLOW).

Fiennes English (Norman): habitation name from a place in Pas-de-Calais, recorded in the 11th cent. as *Filnes* and *Finles*. The earliest form of all is *Flidmum* (9th cent.), possibly akin to a Gmc word meaning 'plain' (cf. FILDES). The surname is normally pronounced /faɪnz/.

Vars.: **Fienes, Fynes.**

Fiévet French: status name for a feudal tenant who held land in return for service, from a dim. of OF *fief* land held in this way (of Gmc origin).

Var.: **Fievez.**

Figgis English: nickname for a trustworthy or reliable person, from a Norman form of OF *ficheis*.

Var.: **Figgess.**

Fijałkowski Polish: habitation name from a place named with OPol. *fijałek*, *fijałka* violet (mod. Pol. *fiołek*) + *-ów* possessive suffix often used in forming placenames, with the addition of *-ski*, suffix of local surnames (see BARANOWSKI).

Cogn.: Czech: FIALA.

Filatov Russian: patr. from the given name *Filat*, a vernacular form of Gk *Theophylaktos*, composed of the elements *theos* God + *phylakt-* guard, protect. This was the name of a 9th-cent. bishop of Nicomedia, who is venerated in the Orthodox Church.

Vars.: **Feofilaktov, Filakhtov, Filatyev.**

Filby English: habitation name from a place in Norfolk, so called from the ON personal name *Fili* (of uncertain origin) + ON *býr* farm, settlement.

Vars.: **Filbey, Filbee, Philb(e)y.**

In the summer of 1981 the village of Filby in Norfolk was the scene of a gathering of more than 100 people from all over the world who bear this surname and claim descent from a Norman, Richard de Filby.

Fildes English and Scots (Aberdeen): regional name from a district in Lancs. called The *Fylde*, from OE *(ge)filde* plain.

Var.: **Fyldes.**

Filer English: 1. occupational name for a maker or user of a file (the abrading tool), from an agent deriv. of ME *file* file (OE *fīl*).

2. occupational name for a spinner, from an agent deriv. of ME, OF *fil* thread (L *filum*).

Cogn. (of 1): Ger. and Jewish (Ashkenazic): **Feiler.**

Filkins English: 1. patr. from the medieval given name *Filkin*, a dim. from a short form of PHILIP.

2. habitation name from a place in Oxon. so called, whose name is probably a tribal deriv. of the OE personal name *Filica* (of uncertain origin). Surname forms such as *de Filking(es)* are found in the surrounding area from the 12th and 13th cents.

Fillery English: nickname from ANF *fi(t)z le rei* son of the king. This may have been a nickname bestowed on an illegitimate son of a monarch, but more probably it was either a humorous allusion to a bastard of unknown parentage who claimed an illustrious father or else was bestowed on a man who gave himself airs, acting as if he were of royal blood.

Vars.: **Fillary, Fildrey**; FITZROY.

A Sussex family called Fillery *claim to be descended from an illegitimate son of King John (1167–1216), but evidence in support of this tradition is lacking.*

Fillingham English: habitation name from a place in Lincs., so called from OE *Fyglingahām* 'homestead (OE *hām*) of the people of *Fygla*', a personal name from OE *fugol* bird (see FELTON, FOWLE).

The surname Fillingham *is still found in Lincs., but is now more common in Lancs.*

Fillon French: nickname for the youngest son in a family, from a dim. of OF *fils* son (L *filius*).

Var.: **Fillion.**

Cogn.: Prov.: **Filhon** (Gascony).

Filzer German: occupational name for a maker or seller of felt, MHG, OHG *filz*, with the addition of *-er* suffix denoting agent nouns.

Var.: **Filz.**

Cogns.: Eng.: **Felt(er).** Low Ger.: **Filt(er), Vilder, Fild.** Jewish (Ashkenazic): **Filtser, Filz; Filc(man)** (Pol. spelling).

Fin 1. French: nickname for a clever or elegant man, from OF *fin* fine, delicate, skilled, cunning (originally a noun from L *finis* end, extremity, boundary, later used also as an adj. in the sense 'ultimate', 'excellent').

2. Jewish (Ashkenazic): of unknown origin.

Cogns.: Eng.: **Fine**. Ger.: FEIN.

Dims.: Fr.: **Finet, Finel, Finot**.

Finch English: nickname from ME *finch* finch (OE *finc*). In the Middle Ages this bird had a reputation for stupidity. It may perhaps also in part represent a metonymic occupational name for someone who caught finches and sold them as songsters or for the cooking pot. The surname is found in all parts of Britain, but is most common in Lancs. See also FINK.

Fincham English: habitation name from a place in Norfolk, so called from OE *finc* finch + *hām* homestead.

Findlater Scots: habitation name from a place in the former county of Banffs. (now part of Grampian region) so called from Gael. *fionn* white (see FINN) + *leitir* hillside.

Vars.: **Finlater, Finlator**.

The first known bearer of the name is Galfridus de Fynleter, *who was juror on an inquest held at Banff in 1342*.

Findling German and Jewish (Ashkenazic): nickname for a foundling, Ger. *Findling*, MHG *vindelīn* (a deriv. of OHG *findan* to find).

Var.: Ger.: **Findl** (Bavaria).

Finer English: occupational name for a refiner of gold and other metals, from ME *fine(n)* to refine, purify (a deriv. of *fine* fine, pure; see FIN).

Var.: **Finar**.

Finger English, German, and Jewish (Ashkenazic): nickname from ME, MHG, Yid. *finger*, mod. Ger. *Finger* (OE *finger*, OHG *fingar*). The name may originally have denoted a man who had some peculiarity of the fingers, such as possessing supernumerary ones or having lost one or more of them in an accident or fight, or it may have been acquired as the result of some irrecoverable anecdote.

Vars.: Jewish: **Fingerman**; **Fingherman** (Rumanian spelling); **Fingerreich** ('finger rich', possibly a nickname for a person with an extra finger); **Fingeryk** (probably from a Yid. adj. deriv.).

Fingerhut Jewish (Ashkenazic): name bestowed on or taken by a tailor, from mod. Ger. *Fingerhut*, Yid. *fingerhut* thimble (lit. 'finger hat'). The vocab. word also means 'foxglove', but this sense is not relevant to the surname.

Fink German, Jewish (Ashkenazic), and English: nickname (or in the case of the Jewish name, ornamental name) meaning 'Finch', variously from Ger. *Fink* or Yid. *fink* (MHG *vinke*, OHG *finc(h)o*), and Northern ME *fink* (an unpalatalized var. of FINCH).

Vars.: Ger.: **Finker**. Jewish: **Finkman, Finkler**. Eng.: **Vin(c)k**.

Cogns.: Flem., Du.: **(De) Vin(c)k, Vinke**.

Dims.: Ger.: **Finkel, Finkle** (but see also FUNKE).

Finlay Scots: from the Gael. personal name *Fionnlagh*, composed of the elements *fionn* white, fair (see FINN) + *laoch* warrior, hero, which seems to have been reinforced by an ON personal name composed of the elements *finn* Finn + *leikr* play.

Vars.: **Findlay, Fin(d)ley, Fin(d)low**.

Patrs.: **Finlayson, Finla(i)son**; MCKINLEY.

Finn 1. Irish: Anglicized form of the Gael. byname *Fionn* 'White'.

2. English: from the ON personal name *Finnr* Finn, used both as a byname and as a short form of various cpd names with this first element.

3. Jewish (Ashkenazic): of unknown origin. A connection with Finland seems unlikely.

Vars. (of 1 and 2): **Finne, Fynn, Phin(n)**.

Patrs. (from 1): Ir.: MCGINN. (From 2): Dan.: **Finsen**.

Patrs. (from 1) (dim.): Ir.: **McKynnan, Kinnan** (Gael. **Mac Fhionnáin**).

'Descendant of F. 1': Ir.: **O'Fi(o)nn, O'Finne** (Gael. **Ó Finn**).

'Descendant of F. 1 (dim.)': Ir.: **O'Finane, O'Fenane, O'Fanane, Fain(n)an, Fin(n)an, Fannon, Fannin** (Gael. **Ó Fionnáin**); **O'Finegane, O'Fenegane, Fin(n)igan, Fin(n)egan, Fenegan, Fanagan, Finucane** (Gael. **Ó Fionnagáin**).

'Son of the servant of F. 1': Ir.: **McAleenan** (Gael. **Mac Giolla Fhionnain**); MCALINDEN; MCCLINTOCK.

Finnemore English: nickname from OF *fin* fine, splendid (see FIN) + *amour* love (L *amor*).

Vars.: **Fen(n)emore, Fenimore**.

Finney English: habitation name from one of several places in Ches., so called probably from OE *fīnig* heap, esp. of wood.

Var.: **Finnie**.

Finster German and Jewish (Ashkenazic): nickname from Ger. *finster* dark, gloomy, or Yid. *fintster* (MHG *vinster*, OHG *finstar*, *finstrēr*, a byform of *dinstar*). The name may have referred to a person's habitual character or it may have been acquired as a result of some now irrecoverable anecdote.

Var.: Ger.: **Finsterer**.

Dims.: Ger.: **Finsterlin, Finsterle**.

Cpd: Jewish: **Finsterbush** ('dark bush').

Firbank English: habitation name from a place in Cumb., so called from ME *firth* woodland (see FIRTH) + *banke* slope (see BANKS).

Var.: **Furbank**.

Fireman 1. Jewish (Ashkenazic): trans. of FAYERMAN and *Feuerman* (see FEUER).

2. English: var. of FAIRMAN.

Firkin English (W Midlands): metonymic occupational name for a maker of casks and barrels, or nickname for a stout man or a heavy drinker, from ME *fer(de)kyn* small cask (apparently from a MDu. dim. of *vierde* fourth (part); as a measure of capacity a 'firkin' was reckoned as a quarter of a 'barrel').

Patr.: **Firkins**.

Firmin English and French: from the medieval given name *Firmin* (L *Firmīnus*, a deriv. of *firmus* firm, resolute). This name was borne by several early saints, including two bishops of Amiens of the 2nd and 3rd cents.

Vars.: Eng.: **Firman, Furman** (see also FÜHRER). Fr.: **Fermin, Frémin**.

Cogns.: Sp.: **Fermín**. Port.: **Firmino**.

Firth 1. English and Scots: topographic name from OE *firhðe*, *(ge)fyrhðe* woodland or scrub on the edge of a forest.

2. Welsh: topographic name from W *ffrith*, *ffridd* barren land, mountain pasture (a borrowing of the OE word in 1).

Vars.: **Frith, Frid(d), Fryd, Freeth, Freed(er), Vreede; Frift, Thrift; Fright; Freak(er), Fre(a)ke; Firk(s)**.

Fischbein 1. German: metonymic occupational name for a seller of whalebone, from MHG *(wal)visch* whale + *bein* bone. This elastic bony substance obtained from the upper jaw of whales was much in demand before the development of plastics, and its scarcity made it expensive.

2. Jewish (Ashkenazic): in some cases this name may be occupational, as in 1, but since its high frequency is out of proportion to the small number of Ashkenazic Jews who may have sold whalebone, it is in most cases probably to be interpreted as being composed of Ger. *Fisch* FISH + *Bein* bone or leg. If so, it is one of the unflattering surnames imposed by non-Jewish government officials in central Europe when surnames became compulsory, because of its ridiculous connotations.

Vars. (of 2): **Fishb(e)in**, **Fishbain**.

Cogn. (of 1): Du.: **Visbeen**.

Fish 1. English: metonymic occupational name for a catcher or seller of fish (cf. FISHER 1) or nickname for someone bearing some supposed resemblance to a fish, from ME *fische*, *fish*, OE *fisc* fish.

2. Jewish (Ashkenazic): from mod. Ger. *Fisch* or Yid. *fish*, selected either for the same reasons as in 1, or because of its associations with the Hebr. given names *Yona* Jonah and *Efraym* Ephraim. Jonah, in the book of the Bible that bears his name, was swallowed up by a 'great fish'. Ephraim became associated with the fish because he was blessed by his father Jacob (Gen. 48: 16) with the words *veyidgu larov* 'Let them grow into a multitude', the verb *yidgu* containing the root letters of Hebr. *dag* fish.

Vars.: Eng.: **Fishe**, **Fysh**; FISK. Jewish: **Fisch**, **Fisz**; **Fischman(n)**.

Cogns.: Ger.: **Fisch(mann)**. Flem., Du.: **(De) Vis(ch)**.

Equivs. (not cogn.): It. and other Romance names: PESCE. Pol. and other Slav. names: RYBA.

Dims.: Ger.: **Fisch(e)l**, **Fischlin**. Jewish: **Fis(c)h(e)l**, **Fiszel** (from the Yid. male given name *Fishl*, lit. 'Little Fish'); **Fis(c)hlein** (from the Ger. dim. vocab. word).

Patrs. (in form only, lit. 'son of the fish'): Jewish: **Fischsohn**, **Fishson**; **Fis(c)hov**, **Fishof**, **Fiszow** (E Ashkenazic).

Patrs. (from the Yid. male given name *Fishl*): Jewish: **Fis(c)helson**, **Fishelzon**, **Fishlsin**; **Fishelov**; **Fischelovitch**, **Fischelovitz**, **Fischelewitz**, **Fish(e)levitz**, **Fishlovitz**, **Fiszelewicz**.

Patrs. (from the dim. male given name *Fishke*): Jewish: **Fishkov**; **Fishkin(d)** (for the excrescent *-d*, see *Süsskind*); **Fishkinhorn** (apparently an ornamental elaboration of the preceding, with the Ger. element *Horn* horn).

Cpds: Jewish: **Fischauf** ('fish pile'; the second element being mod. Ger. *Hauf* pile); **Fis(c)hbach** ('fish stream'); **Fishbaum** ('fish tree'); **Fish(el)berg** ('fish hill'; *-el-* is dim.: 'little fish hill'); **Fishburger** ('fish citizen'); **Fishfeder** ('fish feather'); **Fis(c)hgrund** ('fish bottom'); **Fischhof(er)**, **Fisherhofer**, **Fiszhof** ('fish courtyard'; *-er* is a residential suffix); **Fischleiber** ('fish bellies'); **Fishstein** ('fish stone'); **Fisht(h)al** ('fish valley'); **Fischzang** (second element of uncertain origin).

Fisher 1. English: occupational name for a fisherman, ME *fischer*, OE *fiscere*, a deriv. of *fiscian* to catch fish. The name has also been used in Ireland as a loose equivalent of BRADEN.

2. English: topographic name for someone who lived near a fish weir on a river, from ME *fisch* fish (OE *fisc*) + *gere* weir, apparatus (ON *gervi*).

3. Jewish (Ashkenazic): occupational name for a fisherman, mod. Ger. *Fischer*, Yid. *fisher*.

Vars. (of 1): **Fishman**. (Of 3): **Fischer**; **Fiszer** (Pol. spelling); **Visser** (from Dutch); **Fis(c)hler**; **Fishner** (partly Anglicized); **Fisherman** (fully Anglicized); **Fis(c)hfanger** ('fish catcher').

Cogns. (of 1): Ger.: **Fischer**. Low Ger.: **Fisser**, **Visser**, **Wisser**. Flem., Du.: **(De) Viss(ch)er**. Pol. (from Ger.): **Fiszer**. Czech (from Ger.): **Fišer(a)**. Dan., Norw.: **Fisker**.

Equivs. (not cogn.): Fr. and other Romance names: PÊCHEUR. Pol. and other Slav. names: RYBAK. Hung.: HALÁSZ.

Patrs. (from 1): Ger.: **Fischers**. Low Ger.: **Vissers**. (From 3) Jewish: **Fisherovich** (E Ashkenazic).

Fishwick English (Lancs.): habitation name from a place in Lancs., so called from OE *fisc* FISH + *wīc* outlying farm (see WICK).

Fisk English (E Anglia): metonymic occupational name for a fisherman or fishseller, or nickname for someone supposedly resembling a fish in some way, from ON *fiskr* fish (cogn. with OE *fisc*; see FISH).

Var.: **Fiske**.

Fisk *is found in Norfolk as a personal name in Domesday Book, and the surname in this form is still restricted largely to that county.*

Fitch English: although the origins of this surname have been much discussed, no very satisfactory conclusion has been reached. Early forms do not seem to occur with prepositions, so it is not likely to be a habitation name. Reaney rejects the old explanation that it is a nickname derived from early mod. Eng. *fitch* polecat, on the grounds that this word is not found in this form until the 16th cent., whereas the byname or surname *Fitchet* is found as early as the 12th cent. He opts instead for the solution that the name is from OF *fiche* (see FICHE), but with the sense 'iron point', and so a metonymic occupational name for a workman who used an iron-pointed implement.

Vars.: **Fidge**; **Fitcher** (an agent deriv.); **Fick**, **Feak(e)s**, **Feek(s)** (from a Norman form).

Dims.: **Fitchet(t)**, **Fidget**, **Fickett**; **Fitchell**; **Fitchen**, **Ficken**, **Fickin(s)**.

Bearers of this name are probably ultimately all of one stock, most being descended from Richard Fitch *(d. 1494) of Steeple Bumpstead in Essex. The name has been traced further back, to Cotton in Suffolk in 1240.*

Fitt English (chiefly Norfolk): nickname for a polite and amiable person, from ME *fit* proper, suited (of uncertain origin).

Fitter 1. English: apparently an occupational name for one who prepared things or made them ready. However, the word *fitter* in the sense of a workman appears only in the 19th cent., and the verb to *fit* is not recorded in a relevant sense until the 16th cent. Reaney draws attention to the NE Eng. dial. sense of *fitter* meaning 'coal broker' (although this is not recorded until the 17th cent.). We are either dealing with a very late surname (in which case Reaney's Geoffrey and Hugh *le Fittere* of 1195 and 1231 remain unexplained), or much earlier evidence must be found for the vocab. word.

2. Jewish (Ashkenazic): occupational name for a furrier, from a S Yid. pronunciation of Yid. *futer* fur, furcoat.

Var. (of 2): **Fiter(man)**.

Fitton English (chiefly Lancs.): 1. nickname from ME *fitten* lying, deceit (of unknown origin).

2. possibly also a habitation name from *Fitton* Hall in Cambs., which probably gets its name from ON *fit* grassland on the bank of a river + OE *tūn* enclosure, settlement.

Fitzclarence English: this was the surname assumed by George Fitzclarence, Earl of Munster (1794–1842), one of the ten illegitimate children of the Duke of Clarence, later William IV, and Mrs Jordan, one of the leading actresses of the day. He formed his surname by adding the ANF prefix *fitz-* (see FITZGERALD) to his father's title, a revival of one created in 1362 for a son of Edward III, who had married the heiress of CLARE in Suffolk and was given the L title *dux Claresis* or *dux Clareciae*.

Fitzgerald Irish (Norman): ANF patr. from the given name *Gerald*; see GARRETT. The name was formed by the addition of the ANF prefix *fi(t)z* son of (L *filius*) to the given name. The Gaelicized form **Mac Gearailt** is common in the Gael.-speaking areas of W Kerry.

This is the name of an ancient and powerful Irish family. The head of the main branch, the Duke of Leinster, is the premier peer of Ireland. A branch of the family also hold the title Knight of Glin, which they have held since at least 1299. The family seat, Glin Castle in Limerick, was built c.1260. The family can be traced to an English landowner, Walther FitzOther, who was a keeper of Windsor Forest before 1100. His son Gerald was constable of Pembroke Castle, and it was the latter's son who went to Ireland and established the Irish family. Maurice Fitzgerald *fought for the King of Leinster, who had lost his territory in 1168, and also assisted in Strongbow's invasion of Ireland in 1172. A branch of the family was established in France, where it became prominent under the name* **Giraldin**.

Fitzgibbon Irish (Norman): ANF patr. (cf. FITZGERALD) from a dim. of the medieval given name *Gibb*, itself a short form of GILBERT.

Fitzhenry English and Irish (Norman): ANF patr. (cf. FITZGERALD) from the given name HENRY.

Vars.: **Fitzharry**, **Feeharry** (Irish); **Feehally** (Liverpool).

Fitzhugh English (Norman): ANF patr. (cf. FITZGERALD) from the given name HUGH.

Vars.: **Fitzhugues**; **Fitchew**, **Fit(c)hie**, **Fithye**.

Fitzmaurice Irish (Norman): ANF patr. (cf. FITZGERALD) from the given name *Maurice*; see MORRIS 1.

The Irish family of Fitzmaurice *share a common Norman ancestry with the Fitzgeralds. They can be traced to Thomas Fitzmaurice, whose elder brother Gerald was the ancestor of the Dukes of Leinster; their father was Maurice Fitzgerald (d. 1176). The Fitzmaurice line holds the title Marquess of Lansdowne.*

Fitzpatrick Irish: occasionally this may be a genuine ANF patr. (cf. FITZGERALD) from the given name PATRICK, but more often it has been adopted as an Anglicized form of Gael. *Mac Giolla Pádraig*; see KILPATRICK.

Fitzroy English: the surname (from ANF *fi(t)z roy* son of the king; cf. FILLERY) bestowed by Charles II on Henry Fitzroy (1663–90), his illegitimate son by the Duchess of Cleveland. He was created Duke of Grafton in 1675 and was a soldier; he fought under Marlborough and was fatally wounded at the siege of Cork. His descendants include Robert Fitzroy (1805–65), commander of the *Beagle*, the ship in which Darwin made his voyage to S America.

Fitzsimmons Irish (Norman): ANF patr. (cf. FITZGERALD) from the given name SIMON. The name is also found in the Gaelicized form **Mac Síomóin**.

Vars.: **Fitzsimon(s)**, **Fitzsymon(s)**, **Fitzsymonds**.

Flack 1. English: of unknown origin. The surname is found mostly in Cambs., and so is unlikely to be a var. of FLAGG. It may be akin to the dial. term *flack* to flap about, and so have denoted a scruffily dressed individual.

2. Low German: topographic name apparently derived from a lost word referring to stagnant water.

Vars.: **Flacke**. (Of 2 only): **Flackmann**.

Flagg English: habitation name from places such as *Flagg* in Derbys. and *Flags* in Notts., so called from OE *flage* or ON *flaga* slab, or from ON *flag* turf, sod. The meaning 'standard-bearer' is almost certainly excluded, for the word *flag* in this sense first appears (of unknown provenance) in the 16th cent.

Flaherty Irish: Anglicized form of Gael. **Ó Flaithbheartaigh** 'descendant of *Flaithbheartach*', a byname meaning 'Generous', 'Hospitable' (from *flaith(eamh)* prince, ruler + *beartach* acting, behaving).

Vars.: **O'Fla(g)herty**, **Flagherty**, **Flaverty**, **Flarity**.

Flamstead English: habitation name from a place in Herts., so called from OE *flēamstede* sanctuary, refuge (a cpd of *flēam* flight + *stede* place, site (see STEAD)).

Vars.: **Flamsteed**, **Flamstede**.

Flanagan Irish: Anglicized form of Gael. **Ó Flannagáin** 'descendant of *Flannagán*', a personal name derived from a dim. of the element *flann* red(dish), ruddy.

Vars.: **Flanaghan**, **Flannagan**, **Flannigan**.

Flannery Irish: Anglicized form of Gael. **Ó Flannghaile** 'descendant of *Flannghal*', a personal name composed of the elements *flann* red(dish), ruddy + *gal* valour.

Vars.: **O'Flannylla**, **O'Flannelly**, **Flannally**.

Flaschner 1. German: occupational name for a maker of flasks and bottles, from an agent deriv. of MHG *vlasche* bottle (OHG *flasca*). For the ordinary households of the Middle Ages bottles were made more often from leather than glass, but also sometimes from wood and metal.

2. Jewish (Ashkenazic): of uncertain origin: possibly as in 1, or possibly an occupational name for a tinsmith, mod. Ger. *Flaschner*.

Vars. (of 1): **Fleschner**; **Pflöschner** (Bavaria); **Flasch(e)**. (Of 2): **Flashner**, **Fleshner**; **Fleschler** ('bottle maker').

Flash 1. English: topographic name from ME *flasshe* pool, marsh. This is thought to be from ODan *flask* swamp, swampy grassland, shallow water, with *-sh* for *-sk* perhaps due to influence from the synonymous Fr. *flache* (from L *flaccus* soft).

2. Jewish (Ashkenazic): of uncertain origin, possibly akin to FLASCHNER 2.

Vars.: **Flasher**, **Flashman**.

Cogn. (of 1): Fr.: **Flache**.

Dims. (of 1): Fr.: **Flachet**, **Flachot**.

Aug. (of 1): Fr.: **Flachat**.

Pej. (of 1): Fr.: **Flachard**.

Flatt English (chiefly E Anglia): topographic name for someone who lived on a flat, a patch of level or low-lying ground (ON *flat*, *flǫt*).

Var.: **Flatman** (also E Anglian).

Flavell English: surname common in the Midlands. *Flavell* was the Normanized form of *Flyford*, Worcs., from OE *ford* with an obscure first element.

Flavien French: from the given name (L *Flāviānus*, a deriv. of *Flāvius*, a Roman family name from *flavus* golden, tawny). This was made popular by two minor saints of the fourth and fifth cents.

Cogns.: Prov. and Jewish: **Flavian** (reason for adoption as a Jewish surname unknown). It.: **Flaviano**.

Flavin Irish: Anglicized form of Gael. **Ó Flaithimhín** and **Ó Flaitheamháin** 'descendant of *Flaithimhín*' and 'of *Flaitheamhán*'. Both personal names are from dims. of *flaith(eamh)* prince, ruler.

Flax English (E Anglia) and Jewish (Ashkenazic): metonymic occupational name for someone who grew, sold, or treated flax for weaving into linen cloth, from ME *flax* (OE *fleax*) or Ger. *Flachs* (OHG *flahs*).

Vars.: **Flaxman**. Eng.: **Flexman**, **Flexer**. Jewish: **Fla(c)ks**, **Flachs(er)**, **Flaxer**, **Flakser**, **Flaksman**, **Fleksman**.

Cogns.: Ger.: **Flachs(mann)**; **Flächsner** (U.S. **Flexner**). Low Ger.: **Flass(mann)**. Du.: **Vlasman**.

Fleck German and Jewish (Ashkenazic): from Ger. *Fleck* patch, spot, Yid. *flek* (MHG *vlec(ke)*), of uncertain application. Bahlow suggests various possible reasons for its adoption as a surname, among them the possibility that it is a metonymic occupational name for a user of patches in repairing shoes, clothes, or utensils, or a habitation name from a place named with this word. In some parts of Germany the word denoted a type of round, flat loaf; the surname could perhaps have been a metonymic name acquired by a baker of such loaves. The reasons for the adoption of this word as a Jewish surname are unknown.

Vars.: Ger.: **Fleck(n)er**. Jewish: **Flek, Fleckman**.

Cogns.: Low Ger.: **Vleck**. Du.: **Vlek**.

Fleet English: 1. habitation name from one of the places so called, in Dorset, Hants, Kent, and Lincs., or from Holt *Fleet* on the river Severn in Worcs., all named with OE *flēot* stream, estuary, creek. It may also be a topographic name from the same word used independently.

2. nickname for a swift runner, from ME *flete* fleet, rapid (apparently from OE *flēotan* to float, glide rapidly, and so ultimately akin to 1).

Var. (of 1): **Amphlet(t)** (Worcs.; with fused ME preposition *an* on).

Cogns. (of 1): Fris.: **Fleetjer, Vlietstra**. Flem., Du.: **Van (de) Vliet, Vervliet, Vlietman**.

The earliest known reference to the surname Amphlett *is the will of the widow Agnes* Anfleete *of Ombersley, Worcs., who died in 1373. Property in this area remained in the family until the 19th cent.*

Fleetwood English: apparently a habitation name from an unidentified place named with OE *flēot* stream, estuary (see Fleet 1) + *wudu* Wood. The town of this name in Lancs. got its name in the 19th cent. from its founder, Sir Peter Hesketh Fleetwood, and is not the source of the surname.

Fleming English: ethnic name for someone from Flanders. In the Middle Ages there was considerable commercial intercourse between England and the Netherlands, particularly in the wool trade, and many Flemish weavers and dyers settled in England. The word reflects an ANF form of OF *flamenc*, from the stem *flam-* + the Gmc suffix *-ing*. The surname is also common in south and east Scotland and in Ireland, where it is sometimes found in the Gaelicized form **Pléimeann**.

Vars.: **Flemming, Flemyng, Fleeming, Fleeman, Flamank, Flament, Flement, Le Fleming; Flanders, Flinders**.

Cogns.: Fr.: **Flammang, Flamenc(k), Flaman(d), Flam(m)ant, Flamen(t); Flandre, Flandrois**. It.: **Fiammenghi**. Ger.: **Flaming, Flemmi(n)g, Flähming, Flehmig; Flemisch; Flander**. Du.: **Vlaming, (De) Vlaminck, Vleminck; (Van) Vlaanderen**. Jewish (Ashkenazic): **Fleming(er)**.

Dim.: Ger.: **Flehmke**.

Pej.: Fr.: **Flamard**.

Patrs.: Eng.: **Flemons**. Flem.: **Vleminckx**. Du.: **Fleminks**.

Fleming *is a common surname in the Furness district (formerly part of Lancs., now in Cumb.), where it can be traced to Michael* le Fleming, *who held lands there in the early 12th cent.*

Flesher English: occupational name for a butcher. In part it is from ME *flescher*, an agent deriv. of OE *flǣsc* flesh, meat; in part a contracted form of ME *fleschewere*, OE *flǣschēawere*, in which the second element is an agent noun from *hēawan* to hew, cut (cf. Hauer).

Cogns.: Ger.: **Fleisch(n)er, Fleischmann; Fleissner** (E Germany); **Fleischhauer; Fleischhack(er)** (S Germany). Flem., Du.: **(De) Vlees(ch)auwer, (De) Vlees(ch)ouwer, (De) Vlesave**. Jewish (Ashkenazic): **Fleisch; Fleis(c)her, Flescher, Flaisher; Flajszer** (Pol. spelling); **Fleis(c)hner, Fleshner; Fleischman(n), Fleschmann; Fleis(c)hhacker** ('meat cutter').

Fletcher English: occupational name for an arrowsmith, ME, OF *flech(i)er* (from OF *fleche* arrow, of Gmc origin; cf. Flower 3).

Cogns.: Fr.: **Fléch(i)er; Flèche**.

Flett Scots: apparently a habitation name originating in the Orkneys, from a place in the parish of Delting, Shetland, so called from an ON term denoting a strip of arable land or pasture. On the other hand it may be from the ON byname *Fljótr* 'Swift', 'Speedy' (cf. Fleet 2). The surname is now most common around Aberdeen.

Fleury French and English (Norman): 1. from the medieval given name *Fleuri* (L *Flōrius*, a deriv. of the Roman family name *Flōrus*, from *flōs*, gen. *flōris*, flower; see Flower 1). This name was borne by a 3rd-cent. saint martyred in Nicomedia under Decius. There seems to have been some confusion with a Gmc personal name composed of the elements *hlōd* fame + *rīc* power.

2. habitation name from any of the various places in N France which get their names from the Gallo-Roman personal name *Florus* (see above, and Flower 1) + the local suffix *-ācum*.

3. nickname from OF *fluri* flowered, variegated (a deriv. of *flur* Flower). This could have denoted someone who dressed in an extravagant mixture of colours or perhaps had a blotchy complexion.

Vars.: Fr.: **Flury**. Eng.: **Flury, Flor(e)y**.

Cogns. (of 1): Prov.: **Flo(u)ry**. It.: **Florio**. Rum.: **Florea**.

Dims. (of 1): Fr.: **Fleuriot**. Prov.: **Flouriot**. It.: **Florino**.

Patrs. (from 1): It.: **De Florio**. Rum.: **Florescu**.

Flewitt English (E Midlands): from the Norman personal name *Flodhard*, composed of the Gmc elements *hlōd* fame + *hard* brave, hardy. The initial *F-* is explained by difficulty experienced by the Normans with the Gmc aspirate (cf. *Flobert* at Robert).

Vars.: **Flewett, Flowitt**.

Cogn.: Fr.: **Floutard**.

Flink Jewish (Ashkenazic) and Swedish: nickname from mod. Ger., Yid., Swed. *flink* quick, agile, nimble. As a Swed. name this is one of the group of 'soldiers' names', monosyllabic names adopted (before surnames came into general use in Sweden) by peasants serving in the army, and later transmitted to their descendants. These were the first Swedish surnames.

Vars.: Jewish: **Flinker** (an inflected form, used before a male given name). Swed.: **Flinck**.

Flint 1. English: topographic name for someone who lived near a notable outcrop of flint (OE *flint*), or nickname for a hard-hearted individual.

2. Welsh: habitation name from the town of *Flint* in Clwyd, which gave its name to the old county of Flints.

3. Jewish: of unknown origin, possibly in some cases a translation of Feuerstein.

Cogns.: Ger.: **Flins(ch)**. Dan.: **Flindt**.

Flockhart Scots: of uncertain origin, probably a metathesized form of Folkard.

Var.: **Flucker**.

Flockton English: habitation name from a place in W Yorks., near Wakefield, so called from the ON personal name *Flóki* (see Flook) + OE *tūn* enclosure, settlement.

Flood 1. English: topographic name for someone who lived by a small stream or an intermittent spring (OE *flōd(e)*, from *flōwan* to flow).

2. Welsh: var. of LLOYD.

3. Irish: translation of various names correctly or erroneously associated with Gael. *tuile* flood; see TOOLE.

Vars.: **Floud, Fludd, Flude.**

Cogns. (of 1): Swed.: **Flodén, Flodin.**

Cpds (of cogns. of 1, ornamental): Swed.: **Flodquist** ('stream twig'); **Flodström** ('stream river').

Flook English: from the ON personal name *Flóki*, originally a byname meaning 'Outspoken', 'Enterprising'.

Var.: **Fluck.**

Patr.: **Flux.**

Florence English and French: 1. from the medieval given name *Florence*, used by both sexes (L *Flōrentius* (masc.) and *Flōrentia* (fem.), derivs. of *Flōrens*; see FLORENT). Both names were borne by several early Christian martyrs, but in the Middle Ages the masc. name was far more common.

2. local name for someone from *Florence* in Italy, originally named in L as *Flōrentia*.

Vars.: Fr.: **Florance, Fleurance.**

Cogns. (of 1): Cat.: **Florensa** (fem.). Port.: **Florêncio** (masc.). (Of 2): It.: **Firenze**; **Fiorentino, Fiorentin(i)** (see also FLORENTIN). Jewish: **Florenz**; **Fiorentino.**

Florent French: from a medieval given name (L *Flōrens*, gen. *Flōrentis*, pres. part. of *flōrēre* to flourish, bloom, from *flōs*, gen. *flōris*, FLOWER). The name was borne by a number of early saints, amongst them bishops of Cahors in the 4th cent. AD, Orange in the 6th, and Strasbourg in the 7th.

Vars.: **Florant, Fleurent, Fleurant.**

Cogn.: Prov.: **Flourens.**

Florentin French (also borne by Sefardic Jews): from a medieval given name (L *Flōrentīnus*, a deriv. of *Flōrens*; see FLORENT). This name was borne by a 6th-cent. saint who was abbot of Arles.

Cogn.: Prov.: **Florenty.**

Flórez Spanish: patr. from the medieval given name *Floro*. This derives in part from the L name *Flōrus* (see FLOWER 1), but has also absorbed the Gmc name *Froila*, a deriv. of the element *fro* lord, master.

Var.: **Flores** (also borne by Sefardic Jews).

Floriano Italian: from a medieval given name (L *Flōriānus*, a further deriv. of *Flōrius*; see FLEURY) borne by a 3rd-cent. saint who was drowned in Noricum during the persecutions of Christians under Diocletian and became the patron of Upper Austria, widely invoked as a protector from the danger of fires.

Vars.: It.: **Florian(i), Floreano, Florean(i).**

Cogns.: Pol.: **Florian, Florjan.** Czech: **Florián.** Hung.: **Flórián.**

Dims.: Pol.: **Florczyk**; **Florek.** Hung.: **Flóris, Fóris.**

Patrs.: It.: **De Florian.** Pol.: **Florianowicz**; **Florysiak.** Croatian: **Florjanić.**

Patr. (from a dim.): Pol.: **Florczak.**

Habitation name (from a dim.): Pol.: **Florkowski.**

Flotow German: habitation name from a place on the Weser called *Vlotho* (earlier *Vlotuwe*, from a cogn. of FLOOD) or another in Mecklenburg, near Penzlin, called *Flotow*, which is of Slav. origin.

Var.: **Floto.**

Flower 1. English: nickname from ME *flo(u)r* flower, blossom (OF *flur*, from L *flōs*, gen. *flōris*). This was a conventional term of endearment in medieval romantic poetry, and as early as the thirteenth cent. it is also regularly found as a female given name. The Romance cogns. derive from the L personal names *Flōrus* (borne by a saint active in the Auvergne during the 4th or 5th cents.) and *Flōra* (borne by a 9th-cent. Sp. martyr) as well as formations in the vernacular.

2. English: metonymic occupational name for a miller or flour merchant, or perhaps a nickname for a pasty-faced person, from ME *flo(u)r* flour. This is in origin the same word as in 1, with the transferred sense 'flower, pick of the meal'. Although the two words are now felt to be accidental homophones, they were not distinguished in spelling before the 18th cent.

3. English: occupational name for an arrowsmith, from an agent deriv. of ME *flō* arrow (OE *flā*). For the change of *-ā- to -ō-*, cf. ROPER.

4. Welsh: Anglicized form of the W personal name *Llywerch*.

Cogns. (of 1): Fr.: **Fleur.** Prov.: **Flo(i)re.** It.: **Floro, Flori, Fior(i), (La) Fiore, Fiora.** Sp.: **Flor(es).** Swed.: **Florén, Florin.** Beloruss., Ukr.: **Frol.** (Of 4): Corn.: **Lower, Lawer.**

Dims. (of 1): Fr.: **Fleurel(le), Fleureau, Fleuret(te), Fleuron, Fleurot.** Prov.: **Florel(le), Flouret(te).** It.: **Fiorell(in)i, Fiorell(in)o, Fiorella**; **Fiorillo, Fioriglio** (S Italy); **Fiorini, Fioretti, Fioretto, Fiorit(t)o, Fiorotto, Fiorucci, Fioruzzi.** Ger.: **Flörl.** Low Ger.: **Flor(ic)ke.**

Augs. (of 1): It.: **Fiorone, Fioroni.**

Patrs. (from 1): Eng.: **Flowers.** It.: **Dal Fiore** (Venetia); **Dalla Fior** (Trentino); **Di Fiore** (Sicily); **Floris** (Sardinia). Sp.: FLÓREZ. Low Ger.: **Flöring.** Flem.: **Fleurinck.** Russ.: **Florov, Frolov(ski), Florin.** (From 4): Welsh: BLOWER.

Patrs. (from 1) (dim.): Russ.: **Frolkov, Frolkin, Frolochkin.**

The Eng. surname Flower *is first found in Wilts. in the form* de Flore. *It is now common mainly in Somerset and Bristol.*

Flynn Irish: Anglicized form of Gael. **Ó Floinn** 'descendant of *Flann*', a byname meaning 'Red(dish)', 'Ruddy'.

Vars.: **O'Floin(g)e, O'Flynn, (O')Flinn.** See also LYNN.

Foch French: habitation name from a place in Ariège, Gascony, of obscure, probably Gaul., etymology.

Var.: **Foix** (representing the original Gascon pronunciation, /fɥa/; now common in Catalonia).

Fodor Hungarian and Jewish (Ashkenazic): nickname for a person with curly hair, from Hung. *fodor* curl.

Fogarty Irish: Anglicized form of the Gael. personal name *Fógartach*, from *fógartha* banished, outlawed.

Vars.: **Foggarty, Fogaty, Fogerty.**

Patrs.: **Gogarty, Go(g)erty** (Gael. **Mac Fhógartaigh**).

'Descendant of F.': **O'Fogarty, O'Fogerty** (Gael. **Ó Fógartaigh**); **O'Hogertie, Hogerty, Hogart(y),** HOWARD (Gael. **Ó Fhógartaigh**).

Fogg English: from ME *fogge* grass left to grow after the hay has been cut, long grass in a water meadow (probably of ON origin), applied either as a topographic name to someone who lived by an area of such grass or as a metonymic occupational name to someone who grazed cattle on it in the winter. The vocab. word is still in use as a dial. term in Craven, Yorks., and in E Lancs. Mod. Eng. *fog* thick mist, first attested in the 16th cent., is perhaps a back-formation from the deriv. *foggy*, which developed the sense 'marshy', 'murky'. It is unlikely to be the source of any surnames.

Cogns.: Dan.: **Fog(h).**

Foggin English (Northumb.): of uncertain origin, perhaps from a ME given name, a dim. of the various Norman and Scandinavian personal names with the first element *folk* people (see FOULKES).
Var.: **Foggon**.

Fokin Russian: patr. from the given name *Foka* (Gk *Phōkas*, from *phōkē* seal). This name was borne by several early saints venerated in the Orthodox Church, among them a 2nd-cent. bishop of Sinope (on the Black Sea) who was martyred under Trajan, a 4th-cent. gardener of the same place who was martyred under Diocletian, and a 4th-cent. martyr of Antioch who was suffocated in a bath.
Vars.: **Fokinov**, **Fokanov**.

Fold English: topographic name for someone who lived near a pen for animals, or occupational name for someone who worked in one, from ME *fold* pen, enclosure (OE *falod*, *fald*).
Vars.: **Fould**; **Fo(u)ld(e)s**, **Fowlds**; **Folder**; **Faulds**, **Faulder** (Scots); **Atherfold** ('at the fold').

Földes Hungarian and Jewish (Ashkenazic): occupational name for a farmer, a deriv. of *föld* earth, soil.
Var.: Hung.: **Földesi**.

Foley Irish: 1. Anglicized form of Gael. **Ó Foghladha** 'descendant of *Foghlaidh*', a byname meaning 'Pirate', 'Marauder'.
2. Anglicized form of Gael. *Mac Searraigh* (see MCSHARRY), chosen because of its phonetic approximation to Eng. *foal*.
Vars. (of 1): **O'Folowe**, **O'Foley**.
Dim. (of 1): **Folan**.

Foljambe English: nickname for someone with a withered or crippled leg, from OF *fol* foolish, useless (see FOLL) + *jambe* leg (see GAMBE).
Var.: **Fulljames**.

Folkard English (Norfolk): from the ME given name *Folc(h)ard*, a Norman name of Gmc origin, composed of the elements *folk* people + *hard* hardy, brave, strong.
Var.: **Folkart**.
Cogns.: Fr.: **Fouc(h)ard**, **Foucart**. Low Ger.: **Volkert**, **Vollert**, **Follert**. Pol.: **Folkierski** (from the Ger. given name).
Patrs.: Eng.: **Folkerts**. Low Ger.: **Volkerts**, **Folkerts**.

Foll English: nickname for a foolish or eccentric person, from OF *fol* mad, stupid (LL *follis*, originally a noun denoting any of various objects filled with air, but later transferred to vain and empty-headed notions).
Dims.: Eng.: **Follet(t)**, **Follit(t)**.

Follows English (W Midlands): of uncertain origin; perhaps a late var. of FALLOWS or *Fellows* (see FELLOW), which have themselves been considerably confused.
Var.: **Follis**.

Fonaryov Russian: patr. from the nickname *Fonar* 'Lamp', 'Lantern' (LGk *phanarion*, a dim. of class. Gk *phanos*, from *phainein* to show, reveal). The reasons for the acquisition of the nickname are not altogether clear; they were probably anecdotal and so are now lost irrecoverably.

Fonseca Spanish and Portuguese: topographic name for someone who lived by a spring that dried up during the summer months, from Romance descendants of L *fons* spring, well (see FONT) + *sicca* (fem.) dry.
Cogn.: Prov.: **Fonsèque**.

Font Provençal and Catalan: topographic name for someone living near a spring or well, OProv. *font* (L *fons*, gen. *fontis*).
Vars.: Prov.: **Hont** (Gascony); **Lafon(t)**, **Lafond**; **Defont**, **Defond**; **Delafon(t)**. Cat.: **Fon(t)s**, **Safont**.
Cogns.: Sp.: **Fuente(s)**, **Lafuente**. Port.: **Fonte(s)**.
Dims.: Prov.: **Fontel(le)**, **Fontin**. Cat.: **Fontelles**.

Fontaine N and central French: topographic name for someone who lived near a spring or well, OF *fontane* (LL *fontāna*, a deriv. of class. L *fons*; see FONT, and cf. MONT and MONTAGNE).
Vars.: **Fonteyne**; **Lafontaine**; **De(la)fontaine**, **Desfontaines**; **Fontanier**, **Fontenier**.
Cogns.: Prov.: **Fontane(s)**, **La Fontant**. Eng.: **Fountain(e)**. It.: **Fontana**, **Fontani**; **Fontanari**, **Fontanesi**. Sp., Cat.: **Fontana**. Ger.: **Fontane**. Du.: **Fontijn**, **Fontyn**, **Fontein**.
Dims.: Fr.: **Fontanet**, **Fontenet**; **Fontanel**, **Fontenel(le)**, **Fonteneau**. Prov.: **Fontenille**, **Fontenieu**. It.: **Fontanella**, **Fontanelli**; **Fontanino**, **Fontanin(i)**; **Fontanot(ti)**. Sp.: **Fontanillas**. Cat.: **Fontanella(s)**.
Pej.: It.: **Fontanazzi**.
Collectives: Fr.: **Fontenay**, **Fontenoy**. Cat.: **Fontanet**, **Fontanals**.

Foody Irish: Anglicized form of Gael. **Ó Fuada**, 'descendant of *Fuada*', a personal name from *fuad* haste.
Vars.: **O'Foody**, **O'Foodie**, **O'Foedy**; **Foudy**, **Foddy**; SPEED, SWIFT, RUSH.

Foot English (chiefly Devon): nickname for someone with some peculiarity or deformity of the foot, from ME *fot*, OE *fōt*, or in some cases from the cogn. ON byname *Fótr*. Early examples with prepositions, which would support its origin as a topographic name for someone who lived at the foot of a hill, have not been found.
Var.: **Foote** (chiefly Somerset).
Cogns.: Ger.: **Fuss**. Low Ger.: **Foth**, **Vo(o)th**. Du.: **(Van der) Voet**.
Dims.: Eng.: **Footitt** (Notts.). Ger.: **Füssel**; **Füssle** (Swabia); **Füssli** (Switzerland).

Foran Irish: Anglicized form of Gael. **Ó Fuar(th)áin** 'descendant of *Fuar(th)án*', a personal name derived from *fuar* cold.
Var.: **O'Foran**.

Forbes 1. Scots (now also found in Ireland): habitation name from a place near Aberdeen, so called from Gael. *forba* field, district + the local suffix *-ais*. The placename is pronounced in two syllables, with the stress on the second, and the surname until recently reflected this. Today, however, it is generally a monosyllable.
2. Irish: Anglicized form of Gael. **Mac Fearbhisigh**, patr. from the personal name *Firbhsigh*, composed of Celt. elements meaning 'man' + 'prosperity'. A family of this name in Connacht was famous for its traditional historians.
Forbes *is the name of a family who hold the premier barony in the Scottish peerage, as well as the Irish title Earl of Granard. The lands from which the surname is derived were granted in a charter to Duncan* de Forbes *by Alexander III around 1271. The Irish branch of the family originated with Sir Arthur Forbes, who settled in Co. Longford in 1620.*

Force French: topographic name for someone who lived by a fortress or stronghold, OF *force* (LL *fortia*, a deriv. of *fortis* strong; see FORT). There are several places named with this word (for example in Aude, and baronial lands in the Dordogne), and it may also be a habitation name from any of these.
Var.: **Delaforce**.
Cogns.: Eng. (Norman): **Delforce**, **Dullforce**. It.: **Sforza**.

The name Delaforce *occurs in France as early as the 10th cent., and was brought to England at the time of the Norman Conquest. There seems to have been some confusion with* Fosse, *as in the case of Sir Hugo* de (la) Force *or* Fosse, *who went on the First Crusade in 1096. The title Earl of Albemarle was first bestowed on William* de Force *in 1190, but this line died out with the 4th earl in 1300.*

Forcher German and Jewish (Ashkenazic): topographic name for someone who lived by a conspicuous pine tree or in a coniferous forest, from Ger. *Föhre* pine, MHG *vorhe*.

Vars.: Ger.: **Forchert, Forchner**.

Forchheimer Jewish (W Ashkenazic): apparently a habitation name from an unidentified place called *Forchheim* or *Vorchheim*.

Var.: **Vorchheimer**.

Ford 1. English: topographic name for someone who lived near a ford, OE *ford*, or habitation name from one of the many places named with this word.

2. Irish: Anglicized form of various Gael. names, for example *Mac Giolla na Naomh* (see Gildernew), *Mac Conshámha* (see Kinneavy), and *Ó Fuar(th)áin* (see Foran).

3. Jewish: Anglicization of one or more like-sounding Jewish surnames.

Vars. (of 1): **Foord, Foard, Forth; Forder** (chiefly E Anglia). (Of 1 and 2): **Forde** (very common in Ireland).

Cogns. (of 1): Ger.: **Furt, Forth; Furt(n)er, Fürther, Furterer, Fürterer, Förther, Fortner; Forthmann**. Low Ger.: **Fuhr, Fohr(mann); Tomfo(h)r, Tomforde, Tomfort** (Westphalia); **Tervoooren** (N Rhineland); **Beimfohr; Anderfur**. Flem., Du.: **Van der Voort, Vervoort, Voortman**.

Fordham English: habitation name from any of the places in Cambs., Essex, and Norfolk so called, from OE *ford* Ford + *hām* homestead.

Fordyce Scots: habitation name from a place near Banff, so called from Gael. *forba* field (cf. Forbes) + *deas* south.

Forell German: metonymic occupational name for a trout fisher, or nickname for a person bearing some supposed resemblance to a trout, Ger. *Forelle* trout (MHG *forhel*, *forhen*; OHG *forhana*).

Var.: **Forel**.

Forgan 1. Scots: habitation name from a place in Fife, formerly known as *Forgrund*, perhaps from OE *fōr* pig + *grund* ground.

2. Irish: Anglicized form of Gael. *Ó Mhurcháin*; see Morgan.

Forge English and French: topographic name for someone who lived near a forge or smithy, ME, OF *forge* (from L *fabrĭca* workshop, a deriv. of *faber* workman; cf. Fèvre). The surname is thus in most cases an indirect designation for a Smith or his assistants and servants.

Vars.: Fr.: **Forgue, Farge(s); Laforge, Laforgue; De(la)-forge, Desforges; Fargier**.

Cogns.: Prov.: **Fargue(s), Laf(f)argue**. Sp.: **Fragua(s)**. Cat.: **Fàbrega(s), Fargas**.

Dims.: Fr.: **Forgette, Fargette; Fargeon, Farjon, Forjonnel**.

Aug.: Fr.: **Farjat**.

Forman 1. English: occupational name for a keeper of swine, ME *foreman*, from OE *fōr* hog, pig + *mann* man.

2. English: status name for a leader or spokesman for a group, from OE *fore* before, in front + *mann* man. The word is attested in this sense from the 15th cent., but is not used specifically of the leader of a gang of workers before the late 16th cent.

3. Czech and Jewish (Ashkenazic): occupational name for a driver of a horse-drawn vehicle, from Czech *forman* driver (derived, like Pol. and Yid. *furman*, from Ger. *Fuhrmann*; see Führer).

Vars. (of 1 and 2): **Foreman**. (Of 3): Jewish: **Formanski, Formansky, Furmanski, Furmansky; Fu(h)rman(n)**.

Cogns. (of 3): Pol.: **Furmański, Furmaniak**.

Dims. (of 3): Czech: **Formánek**. Pol.: **Furmańczyk, Furmanek**. Jewish: **Formanek, Furmanek**.

Patr. (of 3): Jewish: **Furmanov**.

Formby English: habitation name from the place on Merseyside, so called from ON *forn* old (or perhaps a byname *Forni* with this meaning) + *býr* farm, settlement.

Forrest English: topographic name for someone who lived in or near a royal forest, or occupational name for a keeper or worker in one. ME *forest* was not, as today, a near-synonym of Wood, but referred specifically to large areas of woodland reserved by law for the purposes of hunting by the king and his nobles; the same applied to the European cogns., both Gmc and Romance. The Eng. word is from OF *forest*, LL *forestis* (*silva*), apparently a deriv. of *foris* outside; the reference was probably originally to woods lying outside a dwelling. On the other hand MHG *for(e)st* has been held to be a deriv. of OHG *foraha* fir (see Forcher), with the addition of a collective suffix.

Vars.: **Forest; For(r)ester, Forrestor, Forrestier** (see also Forster and Foster).

Cogns.: Fr.: **Forest, Forêt; Laforest, Laforêt; De(la)forest, Delaforêt; Forestier**. Prov.: **Fourest(ier), Forastier, Forast(i)é**. Cat.: **Forés, Forest**. Ger.: **Forst**, Forster. Low Ger.: **Vorster**. Flem.: **(Van de) Vorst; Voster, Vaster, De Veuster**. Du.: **Van Voorst, Van den Vorst**. Czech (from Ger.): **Foršt, Fořt**.

Dim.: Fr.: **Forichon**.

Forester *is the name of a Shrops. family who once held custody of part of the Wrekin forest. One of the earliest bearers of the name was Hugh Forester, who witnessed a document in 1187. His son, who was living in 1200, was known as Robert* de Wellington the Forester.

Fors Swedish: ornamental name from Swed. *fors* waterfall (ON *fors*), or perhaps in some cases a topographic name adopted by someone who lived by a waterfall. This is one of the many Swedish surnames taken more or less arbitrarily in the 19th cent. from vocab. words referring to natural phenomena, and compounded with other such elements more or less arbitrarily to make compound surnames.

Vars.: **Forss(én), Fors(s)ell, Forselius, Forslin(g), Forsman**.

Cogns.: Dan.: **Foss**. N English: **Forse** (topographic).

Cpds (ornamental): Swed.: **Forsberg** ('waterfall hill'); **Forsgren** ('waterfall branch'); **Forslund** ('waterfall grove'); **Forsström** ('waterfall river').

Forshaw English (Lancs.): habitation name from a lost place in the parish of Prescot, Lancs. It is first recorded in 1315 as *Fourocshagh* 'Four Oak Wood' (for the last element see Shaw), and by 1446 had become *Fauroshaw*.

Forster 1. English and German: topographic name for someone who lived by a forest, or occupational name for someone employed in one; see Forrest.

2. English (Norman): occupational name for a maker or user of scissors, from OF *forcetier* (a deriv. of *forcettes*, dim. of *forces* clipping shears, L *forfices*).

3. English (Norman): occupational name for a worker in wood, from a metathesized var. of OF *fust(r)ier* (a deriv. of *fustre* block of wood, L *fustis*).

4. Jewish (Ashkenazic): ornamental name from Ger. *Forst* forest.

Vars. (of 1): Ger.: **Förster**, **Ferster**, **Forstner**. (Of 3): **Fewster**, **Foister**, **Foyster**, **Fuster**; see also FOSTER.

Cogns. (of 3): Cat.: **Fuster**, **Fusté**.

Forsyth Scots: from an Anglicized form of the Gael. personal name *Fearsithe*, composed of the elements *fear* man + *sithe* peace. Some early forms with prepositions, as for example William *de Fersith* (Edinburgh 1365), seem to point to an alternative origin as a habitation name, but no placename of suitable form has yet been discovered.

Var.: **Forsythe** (chiefly N Ireland).

Fort English and French: 1. nickname from OF *fort* strong, brave (L *fortis*). In some cases it may be from the rare L personal name of the same origin borne by an obscure saint whose cult was popular during the Middle Ages in S and SW France.

2. topographic name for someone who lived near a fortress or stronghold, or occupational name for someone employed in one; cf. FORTIER 1.

Vars.: Eng.: **Forte**. Fr.: **Lefort**.

Cogns. (of 1): It.: **Forte**, **Forti**; **Lo Forto** (Sicily). Sp.: **Fuerte(s)**. Cat.: **Fort**. Port.: **Forte(s)**.

Dims. (of 1): Fr.: **Fortet**, **Forton**, **Fortin**, **Fo(u)rteau**. Prov.: **Fo(u)rtoul**, **Fortoly**. It.: **Fortino**, **Fortin(i)**, **Fortuzzi**.

Patrs. (from 1): It.: **Fortis**. Sp.: **Ortiz**.

Fortescue English (Norman): nickname for a valiant warrior, from OF *fort* strong, brave (see FORT 1) + *escu* shield (L *scutum*; cf. SQUIRE).

Vars.: **Fortesquieu**, **Foskew**.

There is a tradition that the English family of this name are descended from a notably strong Norman warrior who carried a massively heavy shield in the service of William of Normandy at Hastings. The family who hold the title Earl Fortescue *are associated with the town of Modbury, Devon; they appear to be a branch of the Norman family. Radulfus* Fortescu *is recorded in 1086 as holding lands at Modbury.*

Fortgang Jewish (Ashkenazic): presumably from Ger. *Fortgang* continuation; the reason for its adoption or bestowal are unknown (cf. the rarer Ashkenazic surname **Mitgang**).

Fortier French: 1. occupational name for someone employed at a fortress or castle, from a deriv. of OF *fort* stronghold (from the adj. *fort* strong; see FORT).

2. occupational name for a worker in wood or metal who made use of a drill, OF *foret* (from *forer* to drill, pierce, L *forāre*).

Var.: **Fourtier**.

Fortnum English (Norman): nickname for a man with more brawn than brain, from OF *fort* strong (see FORT 1) + *anon*, dim. of *asne* donkey (L *asinus*).

Var.: **Fortnam**.

Fortunato Italian and Portuguese: from a medieval given name (L *Fortūnātus*, a deriv. of *fortūna*; see FORTUNE 1). The L name was fashionable among early Christians, chosen with reference to their joy in the faith. It was borne by a large number of early saints, which further increased its popularity as a given name in the Middle Ages.

Vars.: It.: **Fortunat(i)**.

Cogns.: Fr.: **Fortuné**. Prov.: **Fortunat**.

Fortune 1. English: nickname for a gambler, from ME, OF *fortune* chance, luck (L *fortūna*); cf. CHANCE and HASARD. In some cases it may derive from the rare medieval given name *Fortune* (L *Fortūnius*).

2. Scots: habitation name from a place in Lothian, apparently so called from OE *fōr* hog, pig + *tūn* settlement, enclosure; John *de Fortun* was servant to the abbot of Kelso *c.*1200.

Cogns. (of 1): Cat.: **Fortuny**. Port.: **Fortuna**. It.: **Fortuna**, **Fortuni(o)**, **Fortugno**.

Forward English: occupational name for a keeper of swine, from OE *fōr* hog, pig (cf. FORMAN 1) + *weard* guardian (see WARD 1).

Var.: **Forwood**.

Fosdyke English: habitation name from a place in Lincs., so called from the gen. case of the OE byname *Fōt* 'Foot' (or the ON cogn. *Fótr*; see FOOT) + OE *dīc* ditch, dyke (see DITCH).

Vars.: **Forsdyke**, **Forsdike**, **Forsdick**; **Frosdick** (Norfolk).

Foskett English: habitation name from any of various places, such as *Foscott* (Bucks., Oxon.), *Foscote* (Northants, Wilts.), *Foxcott* (Hants), *Foxcote* (Gloucs., Warwicks.), so called from OE *fox* Fox + *cot* shelter, burrow (see COATES).

Fosse English and French: habitation name from some place named with OE *foss* ditch, OF *fosse* (both from L *fossa*, a deriv. of *fodīre* to dig, excavate). In Eng. the term did not survive as a vocab. word into the period when surnames were acquired, and the surname must therefore normally either be an importation from French or refer to any of the various minor places named *Foss(e)*, either from being near the Roman *Fosse* Way, itself named in the OE period from the ditch running alongside it, or from the river *Foss* in Yorks.

Vars.: Eng.: **Foss**; **Vos(s)**. Fr.: **Lafosse**, **Delafosse**.

Cogns.: Prov.: **Fousse**. It.: **Fossa** (Liguria); **Fosso** (Campania); **Fossi** (Tuscany).

Dims.: Fr.: **Fosset**, **Fossé**, **Fossez**, **Fossey**, **Dufosset**, **Dufossés**, **Desfossés**. Prov.: **Foussé**.

Augs.: Fr.: **Fossat**. Prov.: **Foussat**.

Foster 1. English: simplified var. of FORSTER, in any of its senses.

2. English: nickname from ME *foster* foster parent (OE *fōstre*, a deriv. of OE *fōstrian* to nourish, rear, from *fōster* food).

3. Jewish: of unknown origin, perhaps an Anglicization of one or more like-sounding Jewish surnames, such as FORSTER.

One of the families called Foster, *known as* Forester *or* Forster *until the 17th cent., once held the position of hereditary Master of the Game and Chief Forester to the Bishop of Durham. Their first recorded ancestor was a certain Adam de Bucton in the 13th cent.; his grandson (b. 1237) was known as Gilbert de Bucton alias Gilbert Forester.*

Fothergill English: habitation name from a place in Cumb. or some other place similarly named (e.g. in W Yorks.), from ON *fóðr* fodder, forage + *gil* steep valley, ravine (see GILL 2).

Fotheringham Scots: habitation name from *Fothringham* near Forfar, which seems to have been named after *Fotheringhay* in Northants, which was held in the 12th cent. by the royal family of Scotland as part of the honour of Huntingdon. The Northants place appears in Domesday Book as *Fodringeia*, apparently from OE *fōdring* grazing (a deriv. of *fōdor* fodder) + *ēg* island, low-lying land. In the case of the Scots place, the final element has early been replaced by *-hām* homestead.

Var.: **Fothringham**.

Foucault French: from a Gmc personal name composed of the elements *folk* people + *wald* rule.
Vars.: **Foucau(l)d, Foucaut.**

Fougère French: topographic name for someone who lived in a place densely grown with ferns, from OF *foug(i)ere* fern, bracken (from LL *filicāria*, a deriv. of class. L *filix*, gen. *filicis*, fern).
Vars.: **Fouchère; Feug(i)ère** (NW France); **Feuchère** (NE France); **Feuquières** (Picardy); **Faug(i)ère** (Puy-de-Dôme).
Cogns.: Prov.: **Fouquière, Falquière.** Cat.: **Falguera(s).**
Dim.: Fr.: **Fougeron.**
Aug.: Fr.: **Fougerat.**

Fouine French: 1. metonymic occupational name for a maker or user of pitchforks, from OF *foisne* (L *fuscīna* three-pronged fork; cf. FOURCHE).
2. nickname for a crafty or sly individual, from OF *faïne* weasel, marten (L *fāgīna* (sc. *mustēla* weasel), a deriv. of *fāgus* beech tree (see FAGE), apparently the favourite haunt of the animals).
Vars.: **Fouin, Foin(e), Foing.**
Dims.: **Fo(u)ineau.** (Of 1 only): **Foisneau.**
Aug.: **Fouinat.**
Pej.: **Foinard.**

Foulkes English: from a Norman given name, a short form of the various Gmc names with the first element *folk* people. See also VOLK.
Vars.: **Folk(e)s, Fulk(e)s; Fook(e)s, Fou(k)x, Fo(a)kes, Fowkes; Fewkes** (chiefly E Midlands); **Volk(e)s, Vokes; Folk(e), Fulk(e), Fuke, Volk(e), Voak** (from the oblique case).
Cogns.: Fr.: **Foulcque(s), Fou(c)que(s).** It.: **Folc(i)o, Folchi, Fulco.** Cat.: **Folc(h).**
Dims.: Fr.: FOUQUET, **Fouqué, Fouchet; Fouqueau.** It.: **Folchetti, Folc(h)ini, Fulcoli.**
Aug.: It.: **Fulconi.**
Patrs.: Eng.: **Folkson, Foxon, Foxen.** It.: **Di Folca.**

Fouquet French: 1. dim. of FOULKES.
2. nickname for someone who in some way resembled a squirrel, OF *fouquet* (originally from the given name, but later understood as a dim. of *fou*, *fol* mad; cf. FOLL).

Fourche French: 1. metonymic occupational name for a maker or user of forked instruments, from OF *fourche* (L *furca* two-pronged fork; cf. FOUINE).
2. topographic name for someone who lived by a fork in a road or river, from the same word used in this sense.
Var.: **Fourquier** (Normandy).
Cogns.: It.: **Forca.** (Of 2 only): Prov.: **Fourcade, Lafourcade; Hourcade** (Gascony). Cat.: **Forcada.**
Dims.: Fr.: **Fourquet.** It.: **Forcella, Forcell(in)i.** (Of 2 only): Cat.: **Forcadell.**
Aug.: It.: **Forcone.**

Fourish Irish: Anglicized form of Gael. **Ó Fuarisc(e)** 'descendant of *Fuarisc(e)*', a personal name perhaps derived from *fuar* cold (cf. FORAN).
Vars.: **Foorish, Furish; Whorisky, Horisky;** WATER (by association with *fuaran* well, spring).

Fournier French: occupational name for a baker, OF *fo(u)rnier* (LL *furnārius*, a deriv. of *furnus* oven). As a Fr. surname this is considerably more frequent than BOULANGER, the term which gradually replaced it as a vocab. word during the later Middle Ages.
Vars.: **Fournié; Lefournier, Lefournié.**
Cogns.: Eng.: **Furner.** It.: **Fornari, Fornar(i)o; Fornai** (Tuscany); **Fornero** (Piedmont); **Forner** (Venetia); **Furnari, Furneri.** Cat.: **Forner, Forné(s); Forn(s).**
Dims.: Fr.: **Fourneret.** Prov.: **Fourneyron.** It.: **Fornarini, Fornarino, Fornarotti.**
Patrs.: It.: **Fornaris, Forneris.**

Fourrier French: occupational name for a supplier of fodder, from an agent deriv. of OF *fourre* fodder (of Gmc origin).
Vars.: **Fourier, Fourié.**

Fowle English: nickname for someone who in some way resembled a bird, in part representing a ME continuation of the OE personal name *Fugol* 'Bird', originally a byname.
Vars.: **Fowell; Vowell; Fuggle.**
Cogn.: Ger. and Jewish (Ashkenazic): VOGEL.
Patrs.: **Fowl(e)s, Fowells; Vowel(l)s, Vowles, Vouls** (W Country); **Fuggles.**

Fowler English: occupational name for a bird-catcher (a common medieval occupation), ME *fogelere*, *foulere* (OE *fugelere*, a deriv. of *fugol* bird; cf. FOWLE).
Vars.: **Fugler; Vowler** (S England).
Cogns.: Ger.: **Vog(e)ler, Vög(e)ler.** Low Ger.: **Vageler.** Du.: **Vogelaar.** Jewish (Ashkenazic): **Vogler, Fogler.**
Equivs. (not cogn.): Czech: PTÁČNÍK, ČIHÁK.

Fox 1. English: nickname from the animal, ME, OE *fox*. It may have denoted a cunning individual or been given to someone with red hair or for some other anecdotal reason; there is no evidence (in the shape of early forms with prepositions) to suggest that it was ever derived from a house sign. This relatively common and readily understood surname seems to have absorbed some early examples of less transparent surnames derived from the Gmc personal names mentioned at FAULKES and FOULKES.
2. Irish: translation of Gael. *Mac an tSionnaigh* 'Son of the fox'; see SHINNOCK. See also CARNEY.
3. Jewish (Ashkenazic): Anglicized form of the Jewish cogns. given below, often the result of a desire to avoid association with mod. Eng. *fucks*.
4. Low German: patr. from the given name *Fock*; see VOLK.
Vars. (of 1–3): **Foxe.** (Of 3): **Foxman, Fuchsman.**
Cogns. (of 1): Low Ger.: **Voss, Fochs.** Flem., Du.: **De Vos.** Ger.: **Fuchs.** Jewish: **Fuchs(man), Fu(c)ks, Fux(sman), Fuksman; Fiks(man)** (S Ashkenazic).
Dims. (of 1): Ger.: **Füchsel.** Low Ger.: **Vöske, Vössgen.** Jewish: **Fiksel** (from Yid. *fiksl*).
Patrs. (from 1): Low Ger.: **Vossen, Vossing.**

Foxall English (W Midlands): habitation name from some minor locality, probably the lost *Foxhale* near Claverley, Shrops., the name of which is derived from OE *fox* Fox + *halh* hollow, recess (see HALE 1). It is less likely that the surname is derived from *Foxhall* in Suffolk (earlier *Foxhole*), which gets its name from OE *fox* + *hol(h)* hollow, depression (see HOLE): the surname is not established in E Anglia.

Foxley English: habitation name from places in Norfolk, Northants, and Wilts., all of which are so called from OE *fox* Fox + *lēah* wood, clearing.

Foxton English (Yorks.): habitation name from any of the various places so called, of which the most likely source for the surname is the one in N Yorks., which is from OE *fox* Fox + *tūn* enclosure, settlement. The places so called in Co. Durham and Northumb. are from OE *fox* Fox + *denu* valley.

Foxwell English: apparently a habitation name from an unidentified place so called from OE *fox* Fox + *well(a)* spring, stream (see WELL).

Foy 1. French: nickname, from OF *foi* faith (L *fides*), either for a pious person or for someone who frequently used this term in oaths.

2. French: from the medieval female given name *Foy*, which is from *foi* faith, as above.

3. Irish: var. of FAHY and FEE.

Vars. (of 1): **Lafoy, Delafoy**.

Foyle English and Irish (Norman): topographic name for someone who lived near a pit or man-made hollow, from OF *fouille* pit (a deriv. of *fouillir* to dig up, excavate, LL *fodiculāre*, for class. L *fodīre*; cf. FOSSE). The pit in question could have been a limepit or claypit, or an excavation designed to receive refuse (cf. PITT). There are several minor places in England named with this word, and the surname may also be a habitation name derived from one of these rather than directly from the physical feature.

Fozzard English (chiefly W Yorks.): of unknown origin.

Var.: **Fozard**.

Fragonard French: nickname, given perhaps to a man with a livid complexion or a birthmark, from OF *frage*, *fraie* strawberry (LL *frāga*, originally a neut. pl. form, but later used as fem. sing.) + the dim. suffix *-on* + the pej. suffix *-ard*.

Fragoso Spanish and Portuguese: topographic name for someone who lived on a patch of rocky ground, from Sp., Port. *fragoso* rocky, uneven (LL *fragōsus*).

Var.: **Fraga** (the name of places in the provinces of Corunna and Huesca).

Frain English (Norman): topographic name for someone who lived near an ash tree or ash wood, from OF *fraisne*, *fresne* ash (L *fraxinus*).

Vars.: **(De) Fraine, Fra(y)ne, Frean, Freen, (De) Freyne**.

Cogns.: Fr.: **Fraisne, Fresne, Frêne, Frai(g)ne; Defresne, Dufresne, Defrêne, Dufrêne, Dufrenne, Dufraisne, Dufragne, Dufrègne**. Prov.: **Fraisse, Fra(y)sse, Fre(y)sse; Dufraisse**. Sp.: **Fresno**. Cat.: **Freixa(s), Freixes**. Port.: **Freixo**.

Dims.: Fr.: **Fresnel, Fresneau, Frénel, Fréneau, Fra(i)gneau; Fresnet, Fresneix**. Sp.: **Fresnillo**.

Collectives: Eng.: **Franey, Fre(e)ney**. Fr.: **Fresnay, Fresnoy, Frênay, Frênais, Frênoy, Dufresnoy**. Sp.: **Fresneda**.

Frame 1. Scots: of unknown origin. Black notes that 'several persons of this name are recorded in the Commissariot Records of Campsie and of Lanark', and it is now very common in Scotland, esp. around Glasgow. The earliest known instance of the name occurs in 1495.

2. Jewish: of unknown origin.

Frampton English: habitation name from any of various places so called, of which there are several in Gloucs. and one in Dorset. Most take the name from the river *Frome* (which is apparently from a Brit. word meaning 'fair', 'brisk') + OE *tūn* enclosure, settlement. One near Tewkesbury was originally named in OE as *Frēolingtūn* 'settlement associated with *Frēola*', a short form of any of the various cpd names with the first element *frēo* free. Frampton in Lincs. probably gets its name from the OE byname **Frameca* (a deriv. of *fram* valiant) + OE *tūn*.

Francis 1. English: from a very popular medieval given name (L *Franciscus*, introduced into England in the OF form *François*). This was originally an ethnic name meaning 'Frenchman'; most of the Romance cogns. are ambiguous between derivation from the ethnic name and the given name. The numerous dims., however, almost all belong to the given name, and in Eng. the ethnic name is normally represented by FRENCH. The given name owed much of its popularity during the Middle Ages to the fame of St Francis of Assisi (1181–1226), whose baptismal name was actually *Giovanni* (see JOHN) but who was nicknamed *Francisco* because his father was absent in France at the time of his birth.

2. Jewish: of uncertain origin, presumably an Anglicization of one or more like-sounding Jewish surnames or an adoption of the non-Jewish surname.

Vars.: Eng.: **Franc(i)es, Franses**. Jewish: **Frances**.

Cogns.: Fr.: **François, Français**. Prov.: **Francès**. It.: **Francesco, Franceschi, Francisco, Franseco, Cesco, Ceschi, Cisco**. Sp.: **Francisco** (from the given name); **Francés** (from the ethnic name). Cat.: **Francesc(h)** (from the given name); **Francès** (from the ethnic name). Port.: **Francisco** (from the given name); **França** (ethnic name). Ger.: **Fran(t)z**. Pol.: **Franc**. Czech: **Ferenc, Franc**. Hung.: **Ferenc(z), Ferenc(z)i, Ferenczy**. Jewish: **Fran(t)z; Franc** (among Pol. Jews); **Ferencz, Ferentz, Ferens** (among Hungarian Jews).

Dims.: Sc.: **Francie, Francey**. It.: **Francesch(i)elli, Ceschelli, Schellini; Franceschetti, Schetti, Schettini; Franceschini, Ceschini, Scini, Scinelli, Schinetti; Francescotti, Franciotti, Cescot(ti), Scotti, Scottini; Franceschelli, Francello, Francillo, Frangello; Franceschino, Fragino; Francescoccio, Francescozzi, Francescuccio, Francescuzzi; Francioli, Franzol(in)i, Zolini; Fransinelli; Francino, Cino, Cinelli; Franzini, Zini; Franzetto, Franzitti, Zetto; Franciotto, Ciotto, Giotto, Giottini; Franzotto, Zott(ol)i; Franzelini, Franzonello, Franzonetti; C(h)ecchi, Ch(i)eco, C(h)ecchetelli, Ceccoli, C(h)ec(c)ucci, Ceccuzzi; Cicco, Cicchetto, Chicchelli, Cicchillo, Cicchin(ell)i, Cicchitello, Ciccitti, Cicutto, Cic(c)olini, Ciccolo, Cicculi, Cicconetti, Cic(c)ott(in)i, Cicullo; Cicci, Cic(c)etti, Cicciotti; Chicco, Chicotti, Chiechio, Sciuscietto; Fraschetti, Fra(n)scini; Fresch(in)i; Zecchi, Zecchetti, Zecchin(i), Zechinelli** (Venetia). Ger.: **Fränzel, Frenz(e)l**. Low Ger.: **Franzke**. Du.: **Fransman**. Ger. (of Slav. origin): **Frensch(e), Fronzek**. Czech: **Franěk, Froněk**. Pol.: **Frączek**. Beloruss.: **Franchyonok**.

Augs.: It.: **Francesconi, Fransecone; Francione, Franscioni, Frascone, Frangione, Franchioni, Fransoni; Cescon(i)**.

Patrs.: It.: **De Francesco, Di Francesco, De Franceschi, De Francisci(s)** (Liguria). Low Ger.: **Frantzen, Franssen**. Fris.: **Fransema, Frankema**. Flem.: **Franssen, Cissen, Ceyssen**. Du.: **Fran(s)sen, Fran(t)zen**. Dan., Norw.: **Frantzen, Frandsen**. Swed.: **Fransson, Franzen**. Pol.: **Franciskiewicz; Ferencowicz** (from the Hung. form of the given name, *Ferenc*). Beloruss.: **Frantsev**. Jewish: **Franzewitch, Fransevich** (E Ashkenazic).

Patrs. (from dims. of 1): It.: **Di Frisco, Del Checolo**. Pol.: **Frankiewicz, Frąc(z)kiewicz; Frą(t)czak, Fron(t)czak; Franiak**.

Habitation name (from a dim.): Pol.: **Frankowski**.

Francombe English (chiefly Bristol): status name from the ANF feudal term *franchomme* free man (see FREE), composed of the elements *franc* free (see FRANK 2) + *homme* man (L *homo*). The spelling has been altered as the result of folk etymological association with the common Eng. placename endings *-combe* and *-ham*.

Vars.: **Frankcombe, Frank(c)om, Francom** (also Bristol); **Frankham**.

Frangipane Italian: nickname from It. *frangere* to break, divide (L *frangere*) + *pane* bread (L *panis*; cf. PAIN 2). A Roman family of this name supposedly acquired it because they distributed bread to the populace during a famine.

Vars.: **Fragapane, Fregapane**.

Frank 1. English: from the Norman given name *Franc*, in origin an ethnic name for a Frank, a member of the Gmc people who inhabited the lands around the river Rhine in

Roman times. In the 6th cent., under their leader Clovis I, the Franks established a substantial empire in central Europe, which later developed into the so-called Holy Roman Empire. Their most famous ruler was the Emperor Charlemagne (742–814). Their name is of uncertain ultimate etymology; it may be akin to a Gmc word meaning 'javelin', of which the OE form is *franca*.

2. English: nickname from ME, OF *franc* liberal, generous (earlier 'free', deriving from the fact that in Frankish Gaul only those of Frankish race enjoyed the status of free men).

3. German, Flemish/Dutch, Danish/Norwegian, Czech, Hungarian, and Jewish (Ashkenazic): ethnic or regional name for someone from *Franconia* (Ger. *Franken*), a region of SW Germany so called from its early settlement by the Franks.

Vars. (of 1 and 2): Eng.: **Francke.** (Of 3): Ger.: **Franke, Franck(e).** Flem., Du.: **Franke.** Dan., Norw.: **Franck.** Jewish: **Franken.**

Cogns. (of 1 and 2): Fr.: **Franc.** It.: **Franco, Franchi.** Sp.: **Franco(s).** Cat.: **Franch.** Port.: **Franco.** (Of 1 only): Fr.: **Francon** (from the OF oblique case). (Of 2 only): Fr.: **Lefranc.** Cat.: **Franquesa** ('frankness', 'sincerity'). Jewish (Sefardic): **Franko, Franco** (names given to Jews who were exempted from taxes because of services rendered to the King of Castile during the Christian re-conquest of the Iberian Peninsula).

Dims. (of 1 and 2): Fr.: **Franchet, Franquet, Franchineau, Francin(e), Françon, Francillon, Francou(l).** It.: **Franchelli, Franchetti, Franchitti, Franch(ol)ini, Francucci.** (Of 3): Ger.: **Fränk(e)l, Frenkel, Frankel, Fränkle.** Jewish: **Frank(e)l, Frenk(i)el.**

Augs. (of 1 and 2): It.: **Franconi, Francone.**

Patrs. (from 1): Eng.: **Franks.** It.: **De Franco, Di Franco, De Franchi(s)** (Liguria). (From 3): Ger.: **Franks.** Low Ger.: **Fran(c)ken; Frenking** (N Rhineland). Du.: **Franken.** Jewish: **Frankovits** (E Ashkenazic).

Cpds: Jewish (ornamental unless otherwise stated): **Frankenheim** ('Franconian home', perhaps also a habitation name from a place so called); **Frankenschein** ('Franconian light'); **Frankenstein** ('Franconian rock'); **Frankent(h)al, Frenkental** ('Franconian valley', perhaps also a habitation name from a place so called).

Frankland English: status name for someone who lived on a piece of land held without obligations of rent or service, from ANF *frank* free (see FRANK 2) + ME *land* land; cf. FREELAND.

Franklin English: status name from ME *frankelin* franklin, a technical term of the feudal system, from ANF *franc* free (see FRANK 2) + the Gmc suffix *-ling* (cf. CHAMBERLAIN). The status of the franklin varied somewhat according to time and place in medieval England; in general, he was a free man and a holder of fairly extensive areas of land, a gentleman ranked above the main body of minor freeholders, but below a knight or a member of the nobility. The surname is also borne by Jews, in which case it represents an Anglicization of one or more like-sounding Jewish surnames.

Vars.: **Francklin, Fran(c)klyn, Franklen, Frankling.**

The American statesman and scientist Benjamin Franklin *(1706–90) was of British descent. His father, a maker of soap and candles, had emigrated in about 1682 from Ecton, Northants, to Boston, where his son was born.*

Fraser Scots: of uncertain origin. The earliest recorded forms, of the mid-12th cent., are *de Fresel*, *de Friselle* and *de Freseliere*. These appear to be Norman, but there is no place in France with a name answering to them. It is possible, therefore, that they represent some Gael. name corrupted beyond recognition by an Anglo-Norman scribe. The Gael. form is **Friseal**, sometimes Anglicized to FRIZZELL. The surname *Fraser* is also borne by Jews, in which case it represents an Anglicization of one or more like-sounding Jewish surnames.

Vars.: **Frazer** (chiefly N Irish); **Frazier** (chiefly U.S.).

Most if not all bearers of this common Scots surname are ultimately connected with the Scottish family who hold the title Baron Lovat. Their origins are uncertain, the relevant records having been destroyed or lost in various stormy episodes in medieval Scottish history. As early as 1340 the lack of charters interfered with Hugh Fraser's claim to succeed his brother.

Frau 1. German: nickname from Ger. *Frau* lady, MHG *vrouwe* (OHG *frouwa*), given for the most part to an effeminate man. It may also have been an occupational name for a servant employed by a noblewoman or lady. In particular cases there may have been more idiosyncratic origins: for example, at the beginning of the 14th cent. the Minnesinger Heinrich von Meissen was nicknamed *Vrowenlob* 'Lady-praise', because he used the word *vrouwe* as a term of address rather than the more usual *wīp*.

2. Sardinian: cogn. of FÈVRE.

Fraunhofer German: local name indicating residence and service at a manor (see HOFER) held by a lady (see FRAU), presumably a rich widow. The surname is most common in Bavaria.

Var.: **Frau(e)nhof.**

Freathy Cornish: of uncertain origin, probably an altered form of *Friday* (see FREITAG). The farm of this name in St Johns parish near Antony in SE Cornwall is probably so called from the surname.

Vars.: **Freethy, Frethey.**

The earliest record of this name is in the Cornwall Military Survey of 1522, which mentions eight bearers, in various spellings including Friday.

Frebel German: nickname from MHG *vrebel*, *vrevel* bold, adventurous, daring (OHG *fravalī*, *frabarī*).

Var.: **Frevel.**

Frech German: nickname from MHG *vrech* eager, bold, brave (OHG *freh* wild, greedy); cf. mod. Ger. *frech* cheeky.

Var.: **Freche.**

Cogns.: Low Ger.: **Freck(e), Freckmann** (see also FREDERICK).

Frederick English: from a Gmc personal name composed of the elements *frid*, *fred* peace + *rīc* power, introduced into England by the Normans. The name was borne by a canonized 9th-cent. bishop of Utrecht, and was a hereditary name among the Hohenstaufen ruling family; hence its popularity in central Europe.

Cogns.: Fr.: **Frédéric, Fréry, Frary.** It.: **F(r)ederico, Fed(e)rici, Fedrizzi, Fed(e)rigo, Federig(h)i, Ferrighi, Frigo, Frighi; Fenderico** (Naples); **Ferdico** (W Sicily). Ger.: **Fried(e)rich.** Low Ger.: **Fred(e)rich, Fredderich.** Fris.: **Frerk.** Flem.: **Fredric(k), Vreurich.** Czech: **Fridrich.** Pol.: **Frydrych.** Jewish (E Ashkenazic): **Frydrych, Frydrich** (adoptions of the Pol. surname, or Pol. spellings of the Ger. surname).

Dims.: Fr.: **Fériot, Ferriot.** It.: **Frizz(ott)i** (Tuscany). Ger.: **Friede, Fried(e)l, Friedlein; Fritz(e), Fritzmann, Fritz(e)l, Fritzle** (Switzerland); FRIES; **Friesz, Freysz; Frickel, Frickle.** Low Ger.: **Frede(ke), Freke, Frick(e), Frickmann.** Fris.: **Fedde(rc)ke, Fedde(ma), Feck(e), Fick, Vick.** Flem.: FREER, **Frick.** Ger. (of Slav. origin): **Friedsch(e), Frit(z)sch(e).** Pol.: **Fryś, Fryszczyk.**

Augs.: It.: **Federzoni, Fedrigon(i), Frizzone.**

Pej.: Fr.: **Ferriaud.**

Patrs.: Eng.: **Fredericks.** Ger.: **Fried(e)richs; Friedreicher** (Austria). Low Ger.: **Fred(e)richs, Fr(i)ederichs(en).** Fris.:

Fre(e)r(i)cks, Fre(e)rks(en), Frerking. Flem.: **Frederi(ck)x, Fedrix**. Du.: **Fre(de)riks**. Norw., Dan.: **Frederiksen, Feddersen**. Swed.: **Fred(e)riksson, Freeri(c)ksson**. Pol.: **Frydrychowicz**.

Patrs. (from dims.): Ger.: **Fritzler, Fritschler**. Low Ger.: **Frede(r)king, Feking**. Fris.: **Feddinga, Fecken, Fekkena, Fitschen**. Pol.: **Fryszkiewicz**.

Habitation name: Pol.: **Frydrychowski**.

Free English (chiefly E Anglia): nickname or term of status from OE *frēo* free(-born), i.e. not a serf.

Vars.: **Freeman; Freebody** (see BODY); FRY.

Cogns.: Ger.: **Frei(er), Frey(er); Freimann, Freymann**. Low Ger.: **Frig(g)e, Frie(he), Freye; Friemann**. Swed.: **Frey, Frei; Freyman, Fr(e)iman**.

Freeborn English (now most common in N Ireland): term of status for someone who was born a free man (from OE *frēo* FREE + *boren* born), rather than a serf emancipated in later life; cf. FREEDMAN 1.

Vars.: **Freeborne, Freebern(e), Freeburn**.

Freedman 1. English (Yorks.): status name in the feudal system for a serf who had been freed.

2. Jewish (Ashkenazic): Anglicized form of *Friedmann* (see FRIED).

Freegard English (Wilts.): of uncertain origin, probably imported from Germany in the early 18th cent. It may be an Anglicized form of Ger. **Friedgar**, a rare surname from a Gmc personal name comprised of the elements *frid*, *fred* peace + *gar* spear.

Var.: **Freeguard**.

The first known bearer in England is Frances Frigard, *baptized on Christmas Eve 1721 at Bremhill, Wilts.*

Freeland English: status name for someone who lived on a piece of land held without obligations of rent or service, from OE *frēo* FREE + *land* land; cf. FRANKLAND.

Freer 1. English: nickname for a pious person or for someone employed at a monastery, from ME, OF *frere* friar, monk (L *frāter* brother).

2. Flemish: cogn. of FREDERICK.

Vars. (of 1): **Fre(e)ar, Frere, Frier, Fryer, Friar**.

Cogns. (of 1): Sp.: **Freire, Fraile**. Port.: **Freire**.

Patrs. (from 1): Eng.: **Frears(on), Frierson**.

Freestone English (chiefly E Anglia and E Midlands): from the OE personal name *Frēostān*, composed of the elements *frēo* free, noble, generous + *stān* stone.

Freidis Jewish (Ashkenazic): metr. from the Yid. female given name *Freyde* 'Joy'.

Vars.: **Fradis; Freidin, Fradin** (E Ashkenazic); **Freidlin; Fradlin, Freidkin, Fradkin, Fratkin** (from dims.).

Freiling German: status name for a freeman or for a serf who had been freed, from MHG *vrīlinc* freeman or freed man; cf. FREE.

Freitag German and Jewish (Ashkenazic): nickname from Ger. *Freitag* (MHG *vrītac* Friday, OHG *frīatag*, *frījetag*, a translation of LL *Veneris dies*; Freya was the pagan goddess of love, sometimes considered as equivalent to the Roman Venus. Her name is akin to OE *frīgan* to make love, and ultimately to FRIEND). The Ger. name may have denoted someone born on that day of the week or who performed his feudal service then, but the day was superstitiously considered unlucky throughout the Middle Ages, and it seems more likely that the name was given in allusion to habitual or outstanding bad luck or to a person considered ill-omened; it is found as a byname in this sense in OHG. This is by far the commonest of the surnames drawn from the days of the week, followed by SONNTAG 'Sunday', traditionally a day of good omen. See also MONDAY. Among Jews, it seems to have been one of the group of names denoting days of the week that were distributed at random by government officials.

Var.: **Freytag**.

Cogns.: Low Ger.: **Friedag, Frieday**. Flem., Du.: **Vrydagh**. Eng.: **Friday(e)** (not common; in part perhaps from the cogn. OE *friggandæg*, but more often a translation of the Ger. or Jewish name. See also FREATHY).

Freitas Portuguese: topographic name for someone who lived on a patch of stony ground, from Port. *(pedras) freitas* broken stones (LL *(petrae) fractae*, from the past part. of *frangere* to break, shatter; cf. FRAGOSO).

Var.: **de Freitas**.

Fremantle English (Norman): habitation name from any of the various minor places in France called *Fromentel*, from OF *froid* cold (L *frīgidus*) + *mantel* cloak, coat (LL *mantellum*), or from the place in Hants named in imitation of them. The placename seems to have originated as a sort of nickname for a forest, as providing some sort of inadequate cover for a poor man who could not afford a cloak of his own.

Var.: **Freemantle**.

Frémond French: from a Gmc personal name composed of the elements *frid*, *fred* peace (or *frija* free, noble, generous) + *mund* protection.

Vars.: **Frémon(t)**.

Dim.: **Frémeau**.

French English: ethnic name for someone from France, ME *frensche*. In some cases it may originally have been no more than a nickname for someone who adopted French airs.

Irish bearers of this name are said to be descended from Theophilus de Frensche, *a Norman baron who accompanied William the Conqueror, a branch of whose descendants settled in Wexford c.1300. Some of the same family settled in Roscommon c.1620, and this was the branch that produced Field Marshal Sir John* French *(1852–1925), commander-in-chief of the British Expeditionary Force in the First World War.*

Frescobaldi Italian: from a Gmc personal name composed of the elements *frisc* fresh, brisk + *bald* bold, daring.

Freshwater English: topographic name for someone who lived by a source of clear drinking water, from ME *fresch* fresh, not salty (OF *freis*, of Gmc origin; cf. FRESCOBALDI) + *water* water (OE *wæter*). There is a place of this name on the Isle of Wight, which may be a source of the surname.

Fretwell English: habitation name from a minor place in W Yorks., where the surname is commonest, apparently so called from OE *freht* augury + *well(a)* spring, stream (see WELL).

Freud German and Jewish (Ashkenazic): nickname for a person of a cheerful disposition, from Ger. *Freud(e)* joy (MHG *vröude*, *vreude*).

Vars.: Ger. only: **Freude(mann)**. Jewish only: **Freudman, Freudiger** (inflected form of Ger. *freudig* joyous, cheerful, used before a male given name).

Cogns.: Low Ger.: **Fröde**. Flem., Du.: **Vreugde**. Swed.: **Fröjd**.

Cpds (ornamental): Jewish: **Freudenberger** ('joy hill', with *-er* suffix indicating habitation); **Freudenfels** ('joy cliff'); **Freudenstein** ('joy stone'); **Freudent(h)al** ('joy valley').

Freville English (Norman): habitation name from *Fréville* in Seine-Maritime, so called from the Gmc personal name or byname *Friso* 'Frisian' + OF *ville* settlement (see VILLE).

Var.: **Freeville.**

Frew Scots: habitation name from the Fords of *Frew*, a fortified site on the river Forth, probably so called from a Brit. element **frwd* current, stream. This place was the lowest crossing-point on the river Forth, and so an important strategic location in the Middle Ages.

Frewin English: from the ME personal name *Frewine*, OE *Frēowine*, composed of the elements *frēo* free, noble, generous (or the rarer *frēa* lord, master) + *wine* friend.

Vars.: **Frewen, Frewing, Frowen, Frowing, Fruen, Fruin.**

Frías Spanish: habitation name from any of various places, for example in the provinces of Burgos and Teruel, so called from the fem. pl. form of the adj. *frío* cold (L *frīgidus*); a noun such as *aguas* waters or *fuentes* springs has been lost.

Cogn.: Port.: **Frias.**

Fricker English: of uncertain origin, perhaps an occupational name for a herald or crier, from the OE agent noun *fricca* with the addition of the ME agent suffix *-er*.

Fried 1. German: dim. of FREDERICK.

2. Jewish (Ashkenazic): from Yid. *frid* peace (cf. mod. Ger. *Friede*), which may sometimes have been chosen as a translation of the Hebr. given name *Shelomo*, whose root letters are the same as those of *shalom* peace (see SALOMON), but which in most cases is simply an ornamental name.

Vars. (of 2): **Frid, Freed; Fried(e)man(n), Fridman(n), Friedler, Friediger, Friedlich, Fridnik** (ornamental elaborations; the last is E Ashkenazic).

Cogns. (of 2): Du.: **(De) Vree, De Vré.** Swed.: **Frid(h), Fridell, Fridén.**

Cpds (of 2 or its cogns, ornamental except where otherwise stated): Jewish: **Fri(e)d(en)berg** ('peace hill'); **Friedfertig** ('ready for peace'); **Friedgut** ('peace good'); **Friedhaber** ('one who has peace'); **Friedheim** ('peace home'); **Friedhof** ('peace courtyard', or 'graveyard', in which case it could be a topographic name); FRIEDLAND; **Friedenreich** ('kingdom of peace'); **Fried(en)stein** ('peace stone'); **Friedent(h)al** ('peace valley'); **Fri(e)dwald** ('peace forest'). Swed.: **Fredberg** ('peace hill'); **Fredholm** ('peace island'); **Fredlund** ('peace grove').

Friedland German and Jewish (Ashkenazic): habitation name from any of various places bearing this name, for example in the former German territories of Prussia and Upper Silesia. Bahlow mentions a protected Jewish settlement of this name in Bohemia. As a Jewish name, it is probably in many cases simply an ornamental elaboration of FRIED.

Vars.: Jewish only: **Friedländer, Fri(e)dlander, Fridlender.**

Friel Irish (common in Donegal, and now also in Glasgow): from Gael. **Ó Frighil**, which is probably a metathesized variant of *Ó Fearghail* (see FARRELL).

Friend 1. English: nickname for a companionable person, from ME *frend* friend (OE *frēond*). In the Middle Ages the term was also used to denote a relative or kinsman, and the surname may also have been acquired by someone who belonged to the family of a more important figure in the community.

2. Jewish: (Ashkenazic): trans. of the Jewish cogns. given below.

Var. (of 1): **Frend.**

Cogns.: Ger. and Jewish (Ashkenazic): **Freund; Freundlich** ('friendly'); **Freundschaft** ('friendship'). Low Ger.: **Fründ(t), Fröndt; Frind** (N Rhineland). Flem., Du.: **Vriend, De Vrient.**

Dims.: Ger.: **Freundl** (Bavaria). Low Ger.: **Früngen.**

Patr.: Du.: **Vriens.**

Fries German, Jewish, and Swedish: 1. ethnic name for someone from *Frisia (Friesland)*. The name of this region is ancient and of uncertain etymology; the most plausible speculation derives it from an Indo-European root *prei-* to cut, with reference to the dykes necessary for the cultivation of low-lying land. There is archaeological evidence of the construction of ditches and dams along the southern shores of the North Sea from at least the time of Christ.

2. occupational name for a builder of dams and dykes. The word was used in this sense in various parts of Germany during the Middle Ages, and is probably a transferred use of the ethnic term, dyke building being a characteristic occupation of Frieslanders.

3. dim. of *Friedrich* (see FREDERICK).

Vars.: Ger.: **Friese, Freyse.** Swed.: **Fris, Frisell.** Jewish (Ashkenazic): **Friss, Friser, Frizner, Frieslander.**

Cogns. (of 1): Low Ger.: **Fre(e)se, Frehse.** Flem.: **De Vrees(e), De Fries, Vrieseman, Freseman, Frieslander.** Du.: **De Vries** (in part borne by Jews). Dan., Norw.: **Friis.**

Dims. (of 1): Low Ger.: **Frieseke.** Jewish: **Friesel.**

The names **Defriez, Defries,** *and* **Devries** *were introduced into England by Dutch immigrants during the 17th cent. One present-day family can trace their ancestry back as far as Joseph Defriez (c.1724–90), who was a customs officer in E London, as were his son and grandson. In Canada the Low Ger. name* **Fr(i)esen** *has been altered to* **Reson.**

Frisby English: habitation name from *Frisby* on the Wreake or *Frisby* by Gaulby, or another lost *Frisby* in Leics., all so called from ON *Frísir* Frisians (see FRIES 1) + *býr* farm, settlement.

Frisch 1. German: from a medieval given name, a pet form of FREDERICK.

2. Jewish (Ashkenazic): nickname from mod. Ger. *frisch*, Yid. *frish* fresh.

Vars. (of 1): **Frische, Frischmann.** (Of 2): **Frish, Fris(c)h(l)er; Fryszer** (Pol. spelling); **Fris(c)hling, Fris(c)hman(n); Fresco, Fresko** (among Sefardic Jews).

Cpds (of 2, ornamental): **Fris(c)hberg** ('fresh hill'); **Frishtag** ('fresh day', or possibly altered by folk etymology from Yid. *frishtik* breakfast; all Yid. days of the week end in *-tik*); **Frischwasser** ('fresh water').

Frizzell English (Norman; now most common in N Ireland): 1. nickname for someone who affected an ornate style of dress, from OF *frisel*, *fresel* decoration, ribbon, tassel, fringe (a dim. of *frese*, of Gmc origin).

2. Anglicized form of the Sc. Gael. version, *Friseal*, of the surname FRASER.

Fröbe German: habitation name of Slav. origin, from *vrba* willow, a common element in the placenames of Thuringia, Bohemia, and Silesia.

Vars.: **Fröba, Friebe(n); Fröb(n)er, Frieb(n)er.**

Cogns.: Jewish (Ashkenazic): **Frober** (habitational); see also VRBA.

Dims.: Ger.: **Fröbel, Friebel.**

Frobisher English: occupational name for a polisher of metal, in particular someone employed by an armourer to put the finishing touches to his work. The name is a metathesized form of OF *fo(u)rbisseor*, from *fourbir* to burnish, furbish (of Gmc origin).

Vars.: **Furber, Forber.**

Frodsham English (Lancs.): habitation name from a place near Runcorn in Ches., which gets its name from the gen. case of the OE byname *Frōd* (see FROUD) + OE *hām* homestead.

Var.: **Frodson**.

Froggatt English (S Yorks. and Midlands): habitation name from a place in Derbys., near Bakewell, which probably gets its name from OE *frogga* frog (perhaps a byname) + *cot* shelter, cottage (see COATES).

Var.: **Frogget**.

Fröhlich German: nickname for a person with a cheerful temperament, from Ger. *fröhlich* happy, cheerful (a deriv. of *froh* happy, OHG *frō*).

Var.: **Frölich**.

Cogns.: Jewish (Ashkenazic): **Fro(e)hlich, Froelich** (nicknames, from Ger. *fröhlich*); **Freilich(man)** (nicknames, from Yid. *freylekh*), **Freilach**. Low Ger.: **Fröleke, Fröhlck**. Du.: **Vrolijk**.

Patr. (from a dim.): Low Ger.: **Fröhlking**.

Froissant French: nickname for a strong but clumsy man, from the pres. part. of OF *froisser* to break, shatter (L *frustiāre*, from *frustrum* crumb, scrap).

Pejs.: **Fro(i)ssard, Froissart**.

Froment French: metonymic occupational name for a corn merchant, from OF *froment* corn, grain (L *frūmentum*).

Cogns.: It.: **Formento, Formenti** (Venetia, Lombardy); **Frumento** (Liguria).

Dims.: Fr.: **Fromenteau, Fro(u)mentin, Froumenty**. It.: **Formentin(i)**.

Augs.: Fr.: **Fromentas**. It.: **Formenton(e)**.

Fromm 1. German: nickname for an honourable man, from MHG *vrum*, *vrom* noble, honourable, trustworthy (from OHG *fruma* use, advantage).

2. Jewish (Ashkenazic): nickname for a pious man, from mod. Ger. *fromm* devout, pious (a later sense of the same word as in 1).

Vars.: Ger.: **Fromme(r), Frömmer, Frommann**. Jewish: **From, From(m)er(man); Frum, Frumer(man)** (from Yid. *frum*); **Frymer** (Pol.-based spelling of a S Yid. pronunciation); **Frumak** (from the Yid. pej. term *frumak* hypocrite).

Cogns.: Low Ger.: **Frohm(e), Frahm**. Flem., Du.: **(De) Vroom(e)**. Dan., Norw., Swed.: **Fro(h)m**.

Dims.: Ger.: **Frommel**. Low Ger.: **Frommke, Frö(h)mke, Frä(h)mke**. Jewish: **Fromel**.

Patr.: Low Ger.: **Frömming**.

Froome English: habitation name from any of various places so called from the rivers on which they stand, or simply a topographic name for someone living beside a river with this name, which is apparently cogn. with W *ffraw* fair, fine, brisk; cf. FRAMPTON.

Vars.: **Froom, Frome, Vroome**.

Frost English, German, and Danish: nickname for someone of an icy and unbending disposition or who had white hair or a white beard, from OE, OHG, ON *frost* frost (a deriv. of the verb 'to freeze').

Froud English: from the OE personal name *Frōd(a)*, originally a byname, or the cogn. ON *Fróði* 'Wise', 'Prudent'.

Vars.: **Fr(o)ude, Frowd(e), Frood**.

Cogns.: Fr.: **Frot; Frodon** (from the oblique case); **Fron** (a contraction of the preceding form). Fris.: **Fröde**.

Dim.: Fr.: **Frouin**.

Patrs.: Fris., Dan.: **Frödden, Früdden**.

Fruling Jewish (Ashkenazic): from mod. Ger. *Frühling* spring. It may be an ornamental name, or it may be one of the group of names referring to the seasons that were distributed at random by government officials; cf. HERBST, WINTER, and SUMMER. The Ger. vocab. word *Frühling* did not occur before the 15th cent., and has not given rise to any non-Jewish surnames; cf. LENZ 3.

Vars.: **Fruhling; Fri(e)ling** (from Yid. *friling* spring).

Frumin Jewish (E Ashkenazic): metr. from the Yid. female given name *Frume* (from *frum* pious; see FROMM 2) + the Slav. suffix *-in*.

Vars.: **Froumin** (Fr. spelling); **Frumson** (Ashkenazic).

Metr. (from the Yid. dim. female pesonal name *Frumke*): **Frumkin, Frumkis, Frumkes; Fromkin** (*-o-* under the influence of mod. Ger. *fromm*).

Frutos Spanish: 1. from a medieval given name (L *Fructus* 'Profit', 'Benefit'). The name was borne by an 8th-cent. hermit of Sepúlveda. Together with his brother Valentine and sister Engratia, who were killed by the Moors, he is regarded as the patron of Segovia.

2. metonymic occupational name for a grower or seller of fruit, Sp. *fruto(s)* (L *fructus*, the same word as in 1, used in this specific sense).

Cogns. (of 2): Fr.: **Fruit(ier)**. Prov.: **Frugier**. Jewish (Ashkenazic): **Frucht(er), Fruchtman(n)**.

Dims.: Prov.: **Fruchon, Fruchou**.

Pej.: Prov.: **Fruchard**.

Cpds (either ornamental or occupational): Jewish: **Frucht(en)-baum, Fruchtenboim** ('fruit tree'; the latter from Yid. *boym* tree); **Fruchtgarten** ('fruit garden'); **Fruchtlander** ('dweller on fruit land'); **Fruchtnis** ('fruit nut'); **Fruchtzweig** ('fruit twig').

Fry English (chiefly S and SW England): 1. var. of FREE, from the OE byform *frīg*.

2. nickname for a small person, from ME *fry* small person, child, offspring (ON *frió* seed).

Var.: **Frye**.

Fryazinov Russian: patr. from the ethnic name *fryazin* Frank, Western European, a borrowing, through Byzantine mediation, of the name of the Franks (see FRANK 1).

Füger German: occupational name for a steward or overseer, Ger. *Füger*, from an agent deriv. of MHG *vüegen* to arrange, dispose (OHG *fuogen*, a deriv. of *fuog* neat, smart).

Vars.: **Fug(e)ner, Fiegner, Fieger(t)**.

Fugger German: occupational name for a shearer of sheep or of cloth, or a maker and seller of shears, from an agent deriv. of MHG *fucke* shears.

Vars.: **Fucker(t), Fuckart**.

A Swabian family of this name grew immensely rich through banking and trade in the early 16th cent.; they became powerful and influential, and were notable patrons of the arts and sciences. They were established in Augsburg in 1368 by a master weaver, Johannes Fugger *(1348–1409). The main branch of the family is descended from Jakob Fugger I (d. 1469), whose three sons were all ennobled. His son Jacob II (1459–1525) extended the family's wealth and power by exploiting the new sea routes to India. He was created a count by the Emperor Maximilian I, to whom he made a loan of 10,000 golden guilders in return for the mortgage of the county of Kirchberg and the lordship of Weissenhorn. The family spread throughout Europe; the name is, for example, found as* **Fukier** *as late as 1944 in Warsaw.*

Führer German: occupational name for a carrier or carter, a driver of horse-drawn vehicles, from Ger. *Führer*, MHG *vüerer* (from MHG *vüeren* to lead, transport, OHG *fuoren*, a deriv. of *faran* to travel).

Vars.: Ger.: **Fürer; Führ; Fuhrmann**.

Cogns.: Low Ger.: **Vormann**. Du.: **Voerman**. Czech and Jewish: FORMAN.

Fulcher English (chiefly E Anglia): from a Gmc personal name composed of the elements *folk* people + *hari*, *heri* army, which was introduced into England by the Normans; isolated examples may derive from the cogn. OE *Folchere* or ON *Folkar*, but these names were far less common.

Vars.: **Fulger, Fo(u)lger; Fulker, Folker; Fulsher, Foulser; Fu(t)cher, Fu(d)ger; Fullagar, Fulleger.**

Cogns.: Fr.: **Fouch(i)er, Fouché, Fouquíe.** It.: **Folchieri, Folc(i)eri, Folgieri, Fulcieri, Fulg(i)eri, Furg(i)eri.** Ger.: **Volker, Völker.**

Dims.: Eng.: **Fudge** (chiefly Somerset); **Fuche, Fuge.** Fr.: **Fouchereau, Fouchareau; Fouquereau, Fouqueret, Foucreau, Foucret.**

Augs.: Fr.: **Fouquerat, Foucrat.**

Patrs.: Low Ger.: **Volkers, Völkers; Volkering, Völkering** (Westphalia).

Fulford English: habitation name from places in Devon, Somerset, Staffs., and E Yorks., all so called from OE *fūl* dirty, muddy + *ford* FORD.

A number of bearers of this name are descended from William de Fulford, *who held the manor of Great Fulford, near Exeter, in the reign of Richard I (1189–99). The family seat is still there.*

Fullbrook English: habitation name from places in Bucks., Oxon., and Warwicks. called *Fulbrook*, from OE *fūl* dirty, muddy + *brōc* stream (see BROOK).

Fuller English: occupational name for a dresser of cloth, OE *fullere* (from L *fullo*, with the addition of the Eng. agent suffix). The ME successor of this word had also been reinforced by OF *fouleor*, *foleur*, of similar origin. The work of the fuller was to scour and thicken the raw cloth by beating and trampling it in water. This surname is found mostly in SE England and E Anglia; see also TUCKER and WALKER.

Vars.: **Voller** (S England); **Fulloon,** FALLON (from OF *f(o)ulun*).

Cogns.: Fr.: **Foul(l)on, Lefoulon.** It.: **Folladore** (Milan). Ger.: **Fuller.** Flem.: **(De) Voller, Volder.**

Dim.: Fr.: **Foulonneau.**

Patr.: Eng.: **Vollers.**

Fullerton Scots and N Irish: habitation name from a place so called from OE *fuglere* bird-catcher (see FOWLER) + *tūn* enclosure, settlement. There is a place with this spelling in Hants, but the surname derives chiefly if not exclusively from *Fullerton* near Ayr or *Foulertoun* near Forfar, both in Scotland.

Vars.: **Fullarton, Foulerton.**

This is the name of a Scottish family who trace their descent from Allan de Fowlertoun, *recorded in 1240. There is a less secure claim to descent from Galfredus* Fullerton, *who was granted lands in Angus in the 14th cent. by Robert I and appointed by him to the position of hereditary royal fowler.*

Fullwood English (Midlands): habitation name from places in Notts. and Lancs. called *Fulwood*, from OE *fūl* dirty, muddy + *wudu* WOOD.

Var.: **Fulwood.**

Fulton Scots and N Irish: 1. contracted form of FULLERTON.

2. habitation name from a place in the former county of Roxburghs. (now part of Borders region), so called from OE *fugol* bird (see FOWLE) + *tūn* enclosure, settlement.

Funke German: nickname for a small, lively individual, from Ger. *Funke* spark (MHG *vunke*, OHG *funcho*).

Cogns.: Flem., Du.: **Fon(c)k, Vonck.** Norw., Dan.: **Funck.** Swed.: **Fun(c)k(e).** Jewish (Ashkenazic, ornamental): **Funk** (from Yid. *funk* spark); **Fink(i)el, Finkels, Finkelman** (from Yid. *finkl* sparkle).

Cpds (ornamental): Jewish: **Funkenstein** ('spark stone'); **Finkelberg** ('sparkle hill'); **Finkelbrand** ('sparkle torch'); **Finkelkraut** ('sparkle herb'); **Finkelstein, Fink(i)elstejn, Finkelstejn, Finkelsztain** ('sparkle stone').

Furet French: nickname for a vicious person, from OF *furet* ferret, a dim. of *fu(i)r* thief (L *fūr*).

Vars.: **Furon, Fureau.**

Furey Irish: Anglicized form of Gael. **Ó Fiúra**, earlier **Ó Furreidh**. The personal name lying behind these names is of uncertain form and meaning.

Var.: **Fury.**

Furlong English and Irish: apparently a topographic name from ME *furlong* length of a field (from OE *furh* furrow + *lang* long), the technical term for the block of strips owned by several different persons which formed the unit of cultivation in the medieval open-held system of farming. The surname is now chiefly common in Ireland.

Vars.: **Furlonge(r), Forlong.**

Furneaux English (Norman): habitation name from any of the places in N France named from OF *fournel*, a dim. of *four* oven (cf. FOURNIER).

Vars.: **Furnell, Fournel.**

Furness English: local name from the district on the S coast of Cumb. (formerly in Lancs.), earlier *Fuðarnes*, so called from the gen. case (*Fuðar*) of ON *Fuð* 'Rump', the name of the peninsula, formerly of an island opposite the southern part of this district + ON *nes* headland, nose.

Vars.: **Furniss, Furnass.**

Furnival English (Norman): habitation name from *Fournival* in Oise and *Fourneville* in Calvados, both first recorded in the form *Furnivilla*, from a Gallo-Roman personal name *Furnus* (of uncertain origin) or L *furnus* kiln (cf. FOURNIER and FURNEAUX) + OF *ville* settlement (see VILLE). The second element has been later replaced by OF *val* valley (see VALE).

Vars.: **Furnivall, Furnifall.**

Cogn.: Fr.: **Fournival.**

An English family by the name of Furnival *are said to have originated at* Fourneville *near Honfleur, Normandy. Among their earliest members was Gerard* de Furnivall, *who was at the siege of Acre in 1191 and was granted lands by King John in 1200.*

Fursdon English: habitation name from any of several minor places in Devon, so called from OE *fyrse* gorse + *dūn* hill (see DOWN).

Var.: **Fursdonne** (a 19th-cent. development).

The first known bearer of the name is Walter de Fursdon, *who held lands amounting to one-sixteenth of a knight's fee within the manor of Cadeleigh (now part of the parish of Cadbury) in 1279.*

Furse English (chiefly Devon): topographic name for someone who lived on a piece of land that was thickly grown with gorse, from OE *fyrse* gorse.

Vars.: **Furze(r); Furseman, Furzeman.**

Fürst 1. German: nickname for someone who gave himself princely airs or occupational name for someone who worked in the household of a prince, from Ger. *Fürst* (MHG *füerst* prince, OHG *furisto*, a cogn. of OE *fyrest* first, foremost).

2. Jewish (Ashkenazic): ornamental name from Ger. *Fürst* prince.

Vars. (of 2): **Furst**; **Firs(h)t**, **Firszt** (from Yid. *firsht* duke; *Firszt* is a Pol. spelling); **Firstenfeld** (an ornamental elaboration).

Dims.: Ger.: **Förstel**, **Ferstel**.

Fürstenberg German and Jewish (Ashkenazic): habitation name from a place in Swabia, so called from the gen. case of OHG *furisto* prince (see FÜRST) + *berg* hill.

Var. (Jewish): **Firstenberg**.

Furtwanger German: habitation name from *Furtwangen* in the Black Forest, so called from OHG *furt* FORD + *wang* water meadow (cf. FEUCHTWANGER).

Vars.: **Furtwängler**, **Fortwängler**.

Fusco Italian: nickname for someone with dark hair or a swarthy complexion, from It. *fusco* dark (L *fuscus*); in some cases it may be from a medieval given name derived from the Roman family name *Fuscus*, originally of the same meaning.

Vars.: **Fuschi**; **Fosco**, **Foschi**.

Dims.: **Fuschini**, **Fuscolo**, **Fuscoli**, **Fuschillo**; **Foschini**, **Foscolo**, **Foscoli**.

Augs.: **Fusconi**, **Fuscone**.

Fussell English (Bristol): of uncertain origin, perhaps a Norman metonymic occupational name for a spinner or a maker of spindles, from OF *fusel* spindle (LL *fusellus*, a dim. of class. L *fūsus*).

Fyfe Scots: regional name from the former kingdom of *Fife* in E Scotland, of obscure etymology. Tradition has it that the name is derived from an eponymous *Fib*, one of the seven sons of Cruithne, founding father of the Pictish race.

Vars.: **Fife**, **Fyffe**, **Phyffe**.

G

Gabaldón Spanish: habitation name from a place in the province of Cuenca, so called from the Gallo-Roman personal name *Gabalus* (of uncertain meaning) + the Celt. placename element *dūn* hill fort, settlement (see DOWN).

Gabarró Catalan: topographic name for someone who lived on a patch of land overgrown with brambles, from a dim. of OCat. *gavarra* bramble (of pre-Roman origin).

Var.: **Gavarró**.

Gabbai Jewish: occupational name, from Hebr. *gabay*, for a trustee or warden of a Jewish public institution, esp. a synagogue, or a manager of the affairs of a Chasidic rabbi.

Vars.: **Gabai, Gab(b)ay**.

Gabin 1. French: nickname for a man given to mockery and teasing, from a dim. of OF *gab* joke, teasing. The word is of uncertain etymology, but may be akin to ON *gabba* to mock, originally 'open the mouth wide' (cf. JABOUILLE).

2. Jewish (E Ashkenazic): patr. from the Yid. occupational term *gabe* synagogue treasurer (from Hebr. *gabay*; see GABBAI) + the Slav. suffix *-in*.

Vars. (of 1): **Gabet, Gabot**. (Of 2): **Gabbin; Gabovitch, Gabowicz; Gabison, Gabizon** (Ashkenazic).

Gable N English: of uncertain origin, perhaps a habitation name from one of the minor places named with ON *gafl* gable, applied to a triangular-shaped hill. The mountain called Great *Gable* in Cumb. is named in this way.

Var.: GABLER.

Gabler 1. German: occupational name for a maker and seller of forks, from an agent deriv. of Ger. *Gabel* fork (MHG *gabel(e)*, OHG *gabala*). The reference is to any of the various pieces of agricultural equipment denoted by this word, for example hay forks, shearlegs, etc. Table forks were not used in Germany for eating before the 16th cent.

2. German: topographic name for someone who lived near a fork in a road or river, from the same Ger. word in this transferred sense.

3. German: habitation name from a place called *Gabel* in Ger., in particular one in Bohemia, which derives its name from the Slav. element *jablo* apple tree (cf. JABŁOŃSKI).

4. English: occupational name for a tax collector or usurer, OF *gabelier*, *gableor* (a deriv. of *gable* tax, revenue, of Gmc origin).

5. English: var. of GABLE.

6. Jewish (Ashkenazic): of unknown origin, perhaps derived as in 1–3 above.

Vars. (of 1–3 and 6): **Gabel**. (Of 1 only): **Gäbler**.

Gabriel English, Scots (Aberdeen), French, German, Spanish, Portuguese, and Jewish: from the Hebr. personal name *Gavriel* 'God has given me strength'. This was borne by an archangel in the Bible (Dan. 8: 16 and 9: 21), who in the New Testament announced the impending birth of Jesus to the Virgin Mary (Luke 1: 26–38). It has been a comparatively popular given name in all parts of Europe, among both Christians and Jews, during the Middle Ages and since (cf. MICHAEL and RAPHAEL). In Russia its acceptability was improved by the fact that it was the official name of St Vsevolod (d. 1138).

Vars.: Ger.: **Gaber**. Jewish: **Gavriel; Gabrieli, Gabriely, Gavriel(l)i, Gavriel(l)y** (with the Hebr. suffix *-i*; **Gabrielski** (E Ashkenazic).

Cogns.: Prov.: **Gabrié**. It.: **Gab(b)riello, Gab(b)rielli** (N Italy); **Gabriele, Gabreli** (S Italy). Pol.: **Gabryel, Gabara, Gabryś, Gabrysz**. Czech: **Gabriel, Gabrich, Gabrys, Gabris, Gabriš; Kabrhel, Kába, Kabeš**. Hung.: **Gábor** (partly Jewish).

Dims.: Fr.: **Gabion**. Prov.: **Gab(r)y, Graby**. It.: **Gabriel(l)ini**. Ger.: **Gäberlein; Gaberl(e)** (S Germany). Ger. (of Slav. origin): **Gabrisch**. Czech: **Kabíček, Kabík**. Pol.: **Gabryjańczyk**. Ukr.: **Gavrilyuk, Gavril(ch)ik, Gavrilechko, Gavrilenko, Gavrys**. Beloruss.: **Gabrusyonok, Gavrilchik**.

Patrs.: Dan., Norw.: **Gabrielsen**. Swed.: **Gabrielsson**. Russ.: **Gavrilov, Gavrilin**. Pol.: **Gabriałowicz, Gabryłowicz**. Croatian: **Gavrilović, Gavrić**. Jewish: **Gabrielov, Gabrielow, Gabrieloff, Gabrilewicz, Gabrilovitz, Gawryelov**. Armenian: **Gabrielian, Kaprilian**.

Patrs. (from dims.): Russ.: **Gavrilichev; Gavrish(ch)ev, Gavrikov, Gavryutin; Gavshikov, Gaveshin, Gavurin; Gashkov; Gan(el)in, Ganyushkin, Ganichev**. Pol.: **Gabarkiewicz, Gabrysiewicz; Gabrysiak, Gawrysiak, Gawryszczak**.

Gache 1. Provençal: topographic name for someone who lived by a look-out spot, OProv. *gache* (a deriv. of *gachar* to watch, of Gmc origin), or habitation name from any of the various minor places named with this term.

2. French: metonymic occupational name for a sawyer, from OF *gache* saw (of uncertain origin).

3. French: nickname for a wasteful or destructive person, from OF *gaschier* to spoil, defile (originally 'stain', 'dye', from a cogn. of OHG *wascan* to wash).

Dims.: **Gachet, Gachlin, Gachenot, Gachon**.

Gadd English: occupational name for a driver of cattle or nickname for a persistent and irritating person, from ME *gad* goad, spike, sting (ON *gaddr*). In N England it may in part represent a survival into the ME period of the ON byname *Gaddr*; see GADSBY.

Gaddesden English: habitation name from a place in Herts., recorded in Domesday Book as *Gatesdene*, from the gen. case of the OE byname *Gǣte* 'Goat' + OE *denu* valley (see DEAN 1).

Vars.: **Gad(e)sden, Gadsdon**.

Gadsby English: habitation name from *Gaddesby* in Leics., recorded in Domesday Book as *Gadesbi*, from the gen. case of the ON byname *Gaddr* 'Sting' (see GADD), or from this word used of a spur of land + ON *býr* farm, settlement.

Var.: **Gatsby**.

Gaetano Italian: from a medieval given name, L *Caiētānus*, originally an ethnic name from *Caiēta* in Latium. According to legend the town was named after the elderly nurse of Aeneas, who died on that spot after fleeing with him from the ruins of Troy.

Vars.: **Gaetani; Tani**.

Cogns.: Sp.: **Gaitán**. Port.: **Caetano**.

Dims.: It.: **Tanini, Tanucci**.

Patr.: It.: **Di Gaetano**.

Gaffney Irish: Anglicized form of Gael. **Ó Gamhna** 'descendant of *Gamhain*', a byname meaning 'Calf'.

Vars.: **O'Gowney, O'Gooney, O'Gaeney.**

Dims.: **O'Gownane, O'Gownain, Goonan(e)** (Gael. **Ó Gamhnáin**).

Gagarin Russian: patr. from the nickname *Gagara* 'Diving-bird', presumably denoting a strong swimmer.

Gage English and French: 1. metonymic occupational name for an assayer, an official in charge of checking weights and measures, from ME, OF *ga(u)ge* measure (probably of Gmc origin).

2. metonymic occupational name for a moneylender or usurer, from ME, OF *gage* pledge, surety against which money was lent (an apparently unrelated word, also of Gmc origin).

Vars.: Eng.: **Gauge; Ga(i)ger.** Fr.: **Dugage.**

Dims.: Fr.: **Gaget, Gageot, Gagelin; Gagey** (Burgundy).

Gagern German: habitation name from a place near Rügen on the Baltic coast. The placename is recorded in 1290 as *Gawere*, and is of Slav. origin.

Gagneux French: occupational name for a farmer or cultivator, from a modified spelling of OF *gagneur*, an agent deriv. of *ga(i)gnier* to till, cultivate (of Gmc origin; cf. WEIDE 2).

Vars.: **Gagnie(u)r, Legagneur, Legagneux; Gaigneux** (Normandy); **Gaignoux** (Ille-et-Vilaine, W France).

Cogn.: Prov.: **Gagnaire.**

Dims.: Fr.: **Gagneron, Gagnerot; Gagnet, Gagnot, Gagneau.**

Patr.: Fr.: **Augagneux.**

Gago Spanish and Portuguese: nickname for a man afflicted with a stammer, from Sp., Port. *gago* stammering, stuttering (of imitative origin).

Gahan Irish: 1. Anglicized form of Gael. **Mag Eacháin**, patr. from the personal name *Eachán*, a dim. of *each* horse; cf. KEOGH.

2. Anglicized form of Gael. **Mac Gaoithín**, patr. from the personal name *Gaoithín*, a dim. of *gaoth* wind. This personal name may have been in origin a short form of *Maolghaoithe*, with the first element *maol* chief, leader.

Vars. (of 1): **Gagan, Guihan, Gaughan, Geghan, McGahan, Magahan, Magann.**

Gaillard English (Norman) and French: 1. from *Gailhard*, a Gmc personal name composed of the elements *gail* gay, joyous (see GALE 1) + *hard* hardy, brave, strong.

2. nickname for a forceful or boistrous person, from OF *gaile* cheerful (of Gmc origin; cf. GALE 1) + the pej. suffix *-ard*.

Vars.: Eng.: **Gall(i)ard, Gaylard, Gaylord.**

Cogns. (of 1): Prov.: **Ga(i)lhard.** It.: **Gagliardi; Guagliardo** (Sicily). Sp.: **Gallardo.** Cat.: **Gallart.**

Dims. (of 1): Fr.: **Gaillardet, Gaillardon; Gaillourdet.** It.: **Gagliardini, Gagliarducci.**

Aug. (of 1): It.: **Gagliardone.**

Gain English (Norman): nickname for a crafty or ingenious person, from an aphetic form of OF *engaine* ingenuity, trickery (L *ingenium* native wit, from *in-* in + *gen-* to be born). The word was also used in a concrete sense of a stratagem or device, particularly a trap.

Vars.: **Ga(i)ne, Gaines**; cf. JENNER, and see also INGHAM 2.

The Engaine *or* Ingaine *family were Northants tenants in Domesday Book, and were most probably of Norman origin. Colne Engaine in Essex is so called because it was acquired by Vital Engaine in 1219.*

Gainsborough English: habitation name from a place in Lincs., so called from the OE personal name *Gegn* (a short form of various cpd names with the first element *gægn* against) + *burh* fortress, town (see BURKE).

Gajda Polish: nickname or metonymic occupational name from Pol. *gajda* bagpipe (from Rumanian *gaidă*, from Turk. *gajda*). In Pol. this word also has the figurative meanings 'fat legs' or 'awkward person'.

Gajownik Polish: occupational or topographic name for a forester or woodman, Pol. *gajownik*, from Pol. *gaj* grove (cogn. with Czech *háj*; see HÁJEK) + *-ów* possessive suffix + *-nik* suffix of human agent nouns.

Var.: **Gajowiak.**

Patr.: Pol.: **Gajewicz.** Croatian: **Gajić.**

Habitation name: Pol.: **Gajewski.**

Gałązka Polish: nickname for a small or physically insignificant person, from Pol. *gałązka* twig.

Galbraith Scots: name for someone descended from a tribe of Britons living in Scotland, from Gael. *gall* stranger (see GALL) + *Bhreathnach* Briton (see BRETT). These were either survivors of the Brit. peoples who had been living in Scotland before the Gael. invasions from Ireland in the 7th cent., or they had perhaps migrated northwards at the time of the Anglo-Saxon invasions. In either case they never became fully integrated with their fellow Celts.

Var.: **Galbreath.**

This name is first recorded as a surname in the area of Lennox, near Dumbarton, in the 12th cent. This region was known as 'the kingdom of the Britons' and was not integrated into the rest of Scotland until 1124. The first recorded chief of the Galbraiths was Gilchrist 'the Briton', living in 1193.

Galceran Catalan: from the Gmc personal name *Gauzhramn*, composed of the tribal name *Gaut* (see JOCELYN) + *hramn* raven.

Var.: **Galcerà.**

Cogns.: Prov.: **Gauzeran, Gauceran, Gauceron.** Fr.: **J(o)userand.**

Galdós Spanish: of Basque origin but of uncertain meaning. The suffix *-os*, *-oz* occurs in many Basque surnames, particularly in the province of Navarre, and seems generally to have patr. force, but it is not certain whether that is the case here.

Gale English: 1. nickname for a cheerful or roisterous person, from ME *ga(i)le* jovial, rowdy (from OE *gāl* light, pleasant, merry, reinforced by OF *gail*, of cogn. Gmc origin).

2. from a Gmc personal name introduced into England by the Normans in the form *Gal(on)*. Two originally distinct names have fallen together in this form: one was a short form of cpd names with the first element *gail* cheerful (cf. GAILLARD), the other was a byname from the element *walh* stranger, foreigner.

3. metonymic occupational name for a jailer, topographic name for someone who lived near the local jail, or nickname for a jailbird, from ONF *gaiole* jail (LL *caveola*, a dim. of class. L *cavea* CAGE).

Vars.: **Gail, Gayle.** (Of 2 only): **Gallon** (chiefly Northumb.). (Of 3 only): **Ga(y)ler, Gaylor, Jailler.**

Cogns. (of 1): Fr.: **Gail.** Sp.: **Gala** (a noun meaning 'elegance', 'finery'). (Of 2): Fr.: **Gallon.** Ger.: **Gail, Geil.** (Of 3): Fr.: **Geolier, Géolier.**

Dims. (of 1): Fr.: **Gaillet, Gal(l)et, Ga(i)llé, Ga(i)llot, Gaillochet, Galichet, Galichon.**

Patrs. (from 2): Ger.: **Gailer, Geiler(t).**

Galera Spanish and Catalan: metonymic occupational name for a shipbuilder or a sailor, from Sp., Cat. *galera* galley (L *galea*, from Gk). The word originally denoted a particular type of ship built in Catalonia.

Galiana Spanish and Catalan: 1. from a medieval female given name, a fem. form of GALIANO.

2. topographic name for someone who lived by the *via Galliana* 'Gaulish path', the pilgrim route from France to the shrine of Santiago de Compostela. The word *galiana* later came to have the weakened sense 'cattle track', but this development is probably too late to lie behind any instances of the surname.

Galiano Spanish: from a medieval given name (LL *Galliānus*, a deriv. of *Gallius*, from *Gallus*; see GALL 2).

Cogn.: Cat.: **Galià**.

Galindo Spanish: from the medieval given name *Galindo*, of predominantly Aragonese origin and distribution, but of unknown etymology.

Patr.: **Galíndez**.

Gałka Polish: nickname from Pol. *gałka* knob, lump, probably denoting someone who was disfigured by a prominent carbuncle.

Patr.: **Gałkiewicz**.

Habitation name: **Gałkowski**.

Galkin Russian: patr. from the nickname *Galka* 'Jackdaw', denoting a thievish or talkative person.

Gall 1. British: nickname, of Celt. origin, meaning 'foreigner' or 'stranger' (ultimately akin to the Gmc forms mentioned at WALLACE). In the Highlands of Scotland the Gael. term *gall* was applied to people from the English-speaking lowlands and to Scandinavians; in Ireland the same term was applied to settlers who arrived from Wales and England in the wake of the Anglo-Norman invasion. The surname is also found at an early date in Lincs., where it apparently has a Breton origin, having been introduced by Breton followers of the Norman Conquerors.

2. French and German: from a given name (*Gallus* in L) which was widespread in Europe during the Middle Ages. Its popularity was due to the fame of a 7th-cent. Irish monk, St *Gall* (apparently from the L family name *Gallus*, originally a nickname from *gallus* cock, but later associated with the ethnic term *Gallus* Gaul, probably the same word as in 1). He established a Christian settlement to the S of Lake Constance, which became the monastery later known as St Gall. His given name was taken into Czech as *Havel* and into Pol. as *Gaweł*, the extra syllable being introduced by analogy with L *Paulus*, which yielded Czech *Pavel* and Pol. *Paweł*.

Vars. (of 1): Sc., Ir.: **Gaul(e)**, **Gaw**; GALT, GALLEY. Fr. (Bret.): **Le Gall**, **(Le) Galle**, **(Le) Gallo**.

Cogns.: (of 2): It., Sp.: **Gallo**. Czech: **Havel**, **Habel**, **Hála**; **Kála**, **Kalaš**, **Kališ**; **Kalous** (also means 'horn owl'). Pol.: **Gaweł**; **Gal(a)**; **Galicki**, **Gałecki**. Hung.: **Gálos**, **Gál(l)**.

Dims. (of 1): Fr. (Bret.): **(Le) Gallic**, **Galliou**. (Of 2): Low Ger.: **Gallmann**. Ger. (of Slav. origin): **Gallasch**, **Galuschke**. Czech: **Havlík**, **Havlíček**; **Hálek**, **Halík**; **Kalousek**. Pol.: **Gawlik**.

Patrs. (from 1): Sc., Ir.: **McIngill**, **McAgill**, **McEgill**, **Magill**, **McGill**, GILL (Gael. **Mac an Ghoill**). (From 2): Ger.: **Galler**. Pol.: **Galewicz**. Croatian: **Galić**. Hung.: **Gálffy**, **Gálfi**.

Habitation names (from 2): Pol.: **Galewski**, **Galiński**; **Gawłowski**, **Gawliński**.

Habitation names (from dims. of 2): Pol.: **Gawlikowski**, **Gałczyński**.

Gallagher Irish: Anglicized form of Gael. **Ó Gallchobhair** 'descendant of *Gallchobhar*', a personal name from the elements *gall* strange, foreign + *cabhair* help, support.

Vars.: **Gallacher** (Scot.); **Gallaher**, **Gallogher**, **Galliker**, **Gilliger**; **O'Gallagher**, **O'Galleghure**.

Galland French: nickname for a cheerful or high-spirited person, from the pres. part. of OF *galer* to be in good humour, enjoy oneself (of Gmc origin; see GALE 1 and GAILLARD). The meanings 'gallant', 'attentive to women' are further developments, which may lie behind some examples of the surname.

Vars.: **Galan(d)**, **Gal(l)ant**.

Cogns.: Eng.: **Gallant** (chiefly E Anglia). It.: **Galante**. Sp.: **Galán**. Pol.: **Galant**, **Galanciak**.

Dims.: Fr.: **Gallandon**, **Galandin**.

Gallego Spanish: regional name for someone from the region of *Galicia* in NW Spain, so called from L *Gallaecia*, a deriv. of the tribal name *Gallaeci*, *Callaeci*, of unknown origin. The E European region of *Galicia* was Latinized into an identical form when it became part of the Austro-Hungarian Empire in the late 18th cent.; before that it had been the duchy of *Galich* (Pol. *Halicz*).

Var.: **Gallegos**.

Cogns.: Port.: **Galego**. It.: **Gallico**.

Gallen Irish: Anglicized form of Gael. **Ó Galláin** 'descendant of *Gallán*', a personal name from a dim. of *gall* cock.

Galley 1. English: metonymic occupational name for a seaman, from ME *galy(e)* ship, barge (OF *galie*, of uncertain origin).

2. English: nickname for someone who had been on a pilgrimage to the Holy Land, from a contracted form of the placename *Galilee*.

3. Scots: var. of GALL 1, from the deriv. *gallda* or the collective form *gallaich*.

Vars.: **Gallie**, **Gally**, **Galey**. (Of 2 only): **Galilee**, **Gallally**.

Galligan Irish: Anglicized form of Gael. **Ó Gealagáin** 'descendant of *Gealagán*', a personal name from a double dim. of *geal* bright, white.

Gallimard French: of uncertain origin. Dauzat first supposed it to be a nickname from the stem found in mod. Fr. *galimafrée* hotch-potch, confused mass (perhaps from OF *galer* to enjoy oneself (see GALLAND) + *mafrer* to be gluttonous, from MLG *maffelen*) with the addition of a pej. suffix, but in his supplement he derives it from OF *galemart* ink-well, ink-stand.

Var.: **Galimard**.

Gallo Italian and Spanish: 1. nickname from the cock (L *gallus*), given originally to a person with some of the attributes associated with this bird, as for example a fine voice or sexual prowess.

2. from the medieval given name *Gallo*; see GALL 2.

Dims.: It.: **Gallelli**, **Galletti**, **Gallini**, **Gallucci(o)**, **Galluzzi**, **Gallussi**, **Gallozzi**, **Gall(in)otti**.

Augs.: It.: **Galloni**, **Gallone**.

Pejs.: It.: **Gallaccio**.

Gallop English: apparently a nickname for a rash or impetuous person, from mod. Eng. *gallop* run (ME *wallop*, from ONF *walop*, central OF *galop*, probably of imitative origin).

Vars.: **Gallup**, WALLOP.

Galloway Scots: regional name from the area so called in SW Scotland, whose name derives from Gael. *gall* foreigner + *Gaidhel* Gael. From the 8th cent. or before it was a province of Anglian Northumbria. Its Gaelic inhabitants were known as 'the foreign Gaels', who from the 9th cent. onwards tended to be allied with the Norsemen rather than with their fellow Gaels.

The earliest known bearers of the surname are Thomas de Galwethia, *Earl of Athol, who made a gift of lands to the Abbey of Newbolt c.1230, and Michael* de Galewath, *who witnessed a document at about the same time.*

The Irish surname **Galway** *is probably a var. of this, rather than a habitation name from the town of this name in S Connacht. During the Middle Ages Galways were wealthy merchants on the south coast of Ireland, but now the name is largely confined to Ulster.*

Galofre Catalan: from a Gmc personal name composed of the elements *wald* rule or *walh* stranger + *frid*, *fred* peace.

Cogns.: Prov.: **Gau(de)froy, Gaufré, Gaufre**. See also JEFFREY.

Dim.: Prov.: **Gaufreteau**.

Patr.: Prov.: **Gaufridy** (Latinized).

Galsworthy English: habitation name from a place in Devon, recorded in Domesday Book as *Galeshore*, probably from OE *gagol* sweet gale, bog myrtle + *ōra* slope. The second element has been assimilated to the commoner placename ending *-worthy* (see WORTHY 1). However, some examples may be from places in the parishes of Crowan and Gwennap, Cornwall, called *Goldsworthy*, allegedly from Corn. *gol* field + *erewy* fair, market, i.e. an open space where fairs were held.

Vars.: **Golsworthy, Galsery**.

Galt 1. English: nickname from the wild boar, ME *galte*, *gaute*, *gault* (ON *goltr*). Wild boars were common in the British Isles from the earliest times, and became extinct only with the clearing of the large tracts of forest which formerly covered the country; hunting them was a favourite pastime in the Middle Ages.

2. Scots: var. of GALL 1.

Vars. (of 1): **Gau(l)t, Gaught, Gaute, Gauld**.

Galton English: habitation name from a place in Dorset so called from OE *gafol* tribute + *tūn* enclosure, settlement, denoting an estate held by the payment of rent rather than by feudal gift.

Galván Spanish: from a medieval given name. This is in origin the L name *Galbānus* (a deriv. of the Roman family name *Galba*, of uncertain origin). However, it was used in a number of medieval romances as an equivalent of the Celt. name *Gawain* (see GAVIN), and it is probably this association that was mainly responsible for its popularity in the Middle Ages.

Var.: **Galbán**.

Cogn.: Port.: **Galvão**.

Galve Spanish: from the medieval given name *Galve* (Arabic *Ghālib*), which was borne by several Moorish chieftains in Spanish legends, notably the father-in-law of Almansur, the 10th-cent. vizier of Córdoba. In view of its associations it may also have been used as a nickname; cf. SALADIN.

Patr.: **Gálvez**.

The city of Galveston, *Texas, was so named in the 1830s after the Mexican viceroy Bernardo* de Gálvez.

Galvin 1. Irish: Anglicized form of Gael. **Ó Gealbháin** 'descendant of *Gealbhán*', a personal name from the elements *geal* bright + *bán* white.

2. French: nickname for a cheerful drunkard, from OF *galer* to enjoy oneself (see GALLAND), also used in a transitive sense with the meaning 'waste', 'consume' + *vin* wine (L *vīnum*).

Gama Portuguese: apparently a habitation name of Sp. origin, from a place in the province of Santander which is of uncertain etymology, perhaps akin to GAMO (cf. GAMERO 2).

Gamage English (Norman): habitation name from places called *Gamaches* in Eure and Somme, first recorded in the 8th cent. as *Gannapio* and *Gammapium* respectively. The placename is of uncertain etymology; one suggestion is that it was named with the Celt. elements *cam* bent, winding + *apia* water.

Vars.: **Gammage, Gammidge, Cam(m)idge**.

Cogn.: Fr.: **Gamache**.

Gambe French: nickname for a person with some peculiarity of the legs or gait, from the Norman-Picard and Prov. form of OF *jambe* (LL *gamba*, from Gk *kampē* bend, joint, knee).

Cogns.: It.: **Gamba, Gambi**.

Dims.: Fr.: **Gambet, Gambin, Gambon; C(h)ambin, C(h)ambet, Chambonnet, Chambonneau**. It.: **Gambin(o), Gambetta, Gambitta, Gambella, Gambuzza, Gambozza**.

Aug.: It.: **Gambone**.

Pejs.: It.: **Gambassi; Gambaccini** (dim.).

Gambier French and English (Huguenot): metonymic occupational name for an armourer specializing in the production of leg-pieces, from OF *gambier* greave (a deriv. of *gambe*, *jambe* leg; see GAMBE).

The earliest known bearer of this name was Guillaume Ganbier, *a 12th-cent. Norman baron. The name was brought to England by Huguenots in the 16th cent., and in recent years it has occasionally been spelled* **Gambia**, *apparently by erroneous association with the W African state.*

Gamble English: from the ON byname *Gamall* 'Old', which, surprisingly enough, was occasionally used in N England during the Middle Ages as a given name.

Vars.: **Gambell, Gammell, Gammil; Gemmell, Gemmill** (Scots).

Dims.: **Gam(b)lin(g), Gamlen, Gamlane**.

Patr.: **Gambles**.

Game English: nickname for a merry or sporty person, from ME *gamme* amusement, pastime (OE *gamen*).

Vars.: GAMMON, **Gam(m)an**.

Gamero Spanish: 1. occupational name for a keeper of deer or warden in a park where deer were bred for hunting, from an agent deriv. of GAMO.

2. habitation name from any of various minor places so called, from Sp. *gamero* 'place of deer'.

Cogn.: Port.: **Gameiro**.

Gammon English: 1. var. of GAME.

2. from ANF *gambon* ham, a dim. of GAMBE.

Vars.: **Gamon, Gammond**.

Gamo Spanish: nickname for a timid person or for a fast runner, from Sp. *gamo* fallow deer (LL *gammus*, of uncertain origin), or perhaps a metonymic occupational name for the warden of a deer park (see GAMERO).

Patr.: **Gámez**.

Gance French: of uncertain origin. It may be a spelling var. of *ganse* ribbon (Prov. *ganso* fastening, buckle, from Gk *kampsos* bent), and so a metonymic occupational name for a maker or seller of ribbons. However, this explanation is rendered doubtful, though not impossible, by the fact that the vocab. word is not attested until the very end of the 16th cent. Alternatively it may be a nickname from a

Norman-Picard form of OF *guenche* equivocation, deceit, a deriv. of *guenchir* to move awkwardly, proceed indirectly (of Gmc origin; cf. mod. Ger. *wanken* to hesitate, stumble).

Dims.: **Gancel**, **Ganson**.

Gander English: 1. metonymic occupational name for a keeper of geese, or nickname for someone supposedly resembling a gander, from ME *gander*, OE *gand(r)a* gander, male goose.

2. occupational name for a glover; see GAUNT 3.

Gandy English (Norman): of uncertain origin. The most plausible suggestion is that it is a nickname for someone who was in the habit of wearing gloves, from OF *ganté*, a deriv. of *gant* glove (see GAUNT 3) or an occupational name for a glove-maker, OF *gantier*. However, a certain Hugh *de Gandy* was High Sheriff of Devon in 1167; it is possible that his surname is a habitation name from some unidentified place in France or even from Ghent in Flanders (see GAUNT 1).

Vars.: **Gandey**; **Gandee** (apparently a 19th-cent. alteration).

Gange English (Norman): of uncertain origin. It may be a habitation name, perhaps from *Ganges* in S France. This is recorded in the 12th cent. as *Agange* and *Aganthicum*, perhaps from a deriv. of L *acanthus* bear's-foot. On the other hand, it may be from the ON personal name *Gangi*, a cogn. of OE *Gegn* (see GAINSBOROUGH).

A family of this name trace their descent from Ralph de Gangi, *recorded in 1165. The name was later found as* Gangus *and* Gangy.

Gannon Irish: Anglicized form of Gael. **Mag Fhionnán**, patr. from the given name *Fionnán*. This name, from a dim. of *fionn* white, fair, was borne by several early Ir. saints.

Ganter 1. German: occupational name for an official in charge of the legal auction of property confiscated in default of a fine; such a sale was known in MHG as a *gant* (from It. *incanto*, a deriv. of LL *inquantāre* to auction, from the phrase *In quantum?* 'To how much (is the price raised)?').

2. English: occupational name for a glover; see GAUNT 3.

Gapper English (Somerset): 1. nickname for someone whose mouth hung perpetually open, from an agent deriv. of ME *gappen* to gape (ON *gapa*).

2. topographic name for someone who lived by a gap in a chain of hills, from ME *gappe* (ON *gap*, a deriv. of the verb quoted above).

Somerset is not an area in which words of ON origin were usual in ME, and so if either of the above explanations is correct, the surname is likely to be an importation from further north.

Garabedian Armenian: patr. from the given name *Garabed* 'Precursor', the traditional epithet of John the Baptist in the Armenian Church.

Vars.: **Garabetian**, **Karapetian**.

Garand French: nickname for someone who had stood guarantor for the good behaviour or financial responsibility of a member of his family, from the pres. part. of OF *garer* to warrant, guarantee (of Gmc origin, akin to OHG *wār* true).

Var.: **Garant**.

Dims.: **Garandel**, **Garanton**.

Gárate Spanish form of Basque **Garate**: topographic name for someone who lived by a mountain pass, from Basque *gara* heights, summit + *ate* pass.

Garay Spanish form of Basque **Garai**: topographic name for someone who lived by a barn or in an elevated situation, from Basque *garai* barn or the homonymous adj. *garai* high (both of which derive from *gara* heights, summit).

Garber 1. English: occupational name for someone who bound wheat into sheaves, or who collected wheatsheaves owed in rent, from an agent deriv. of ME, OF *garbe* wheatsheaf (of uncertain origin).

2. Low German: cogn. of GARBETT or GERBER.

3. Jewish (Ashkenazic): var. of GERBER.

Var. (of 1): **Garbe**.

Cogns. (of 1): Fr.: **Gerbier**; **Gerbe**, **Girbe**.

Dims. (of 1): Fr.: **Gerberon**; **Gerbet**, **Girbet**, **Gerbeau(x)**, **Girbeau**.

Garbett English (chiefly W Midlands): from *Gerberht*, a Norman personal name composed of the Gmc elements *geri*, *gari* spear + *berht* bright, famous. Gerbert, archbishop of Rheims, became Pope as Silvester II at the beginning of the 12th cent. There has been some confusion with GARBUTT.

Cogns.: Fr.: **Gerbert**, **Gébert**. Ger.: **Gerbert**, **Gehrbrecht**, **Gehrbracht**, **Gerberich**. Low Ger.: **Garbrecht**, GARBER.

Patrs.: Ger.: **Gerberding**. Low Ger.: **Garberding**, **Garbers**.

Garbo Italian: 1. apparently a nickname from It. *garbo* graciousness, pleasing manners.

2. from the name of a street in Florence, the *via del Garbo*, which was populated mainly by workers in *lana del Garbo* wool from the Algarve in Portugal, *Garbo* being the It. name of the Algarve.

The famous medieval Florentine doctors Dino and Tommaso Garbo *are known to have taken their name from the via del Garbo in Florence.*

Garbutt English (Norman; now chiefly Cleveland and Tyneside): 1. from *Geribodo*, a Gmc personal name composed of the elements *geri*, *gari* spear + *bodo* messenger. The name was borne notably by a 7th-cent. saint, bishop of Bayeux; as a result of his fame the name was popular among the Normans and introduced by them into England.

2. from *Geribald*, a Gmc personal name composed of the elements *geri*, *gari* spear + *bald* bold, brave. This name owed its popularity largely to a 9th-cent. saint, bishop of Châlons-sur-Seine.

Cogns. (of 1): Ger.: **Gerbod**, **Gerboth**, **Gerpott**. Low Ger. **Garbade**. (Of 2): Fr.: **Gerbold**, **Gerboud**, **Gerbaud**, **Gerbault**, **Gerbaux**. Prov.: **Girbal**. It.: **Garibaldi** (Liguria); **Gariboldi** (Lombardy); **G(i)ribaldi** (Tuscany); **Gribaudo** (Piedmont); **Grippaldi**, **Grippaudo**, **Garimoldi**.

García Spanish: extremely common surname, from a medieval given name of uncertain origin. It is normally found in medieval records in the Latin form *Garsea*, and may well be of pre-Roman origin, perhaps akin to Basque *(h)artz* bear.

Vars.: **Garci**, **Garza**.

Cogn.: Port.: **Garcia**.

Patrs.: Sp., Cat.: **Garcés**.

Gardener English: occupational name from ME, ONF *gardin* garden (a dim. of *gard* enclosure, of Gmc origin; cf. GARTH). Reference is normally to a cultivator of edible produce in an orchard or kitchen garden, rather than to a tender of ornamental lawns and flower beds.

Vars.: **Gard(i)ner**, **Gardinor**, GARNER; **Gairdner** (Scots); **Garden**, **Gardyne**; **Jardin(e)**, **Jerde(i)n**, **Jerdan**, **Jerdon** (Scots and Northumb., from the central OF form).

Cogns.: Fr.: **Gardinier**, **Jard(in)ier**; **Gard(in)**, **Dugard(in)**, **Jard(in)**, **Dujardin**, **Desjardins**. It.: **Giardinaro**, **Giardinieri**; **Giardino**, **Giardini**; **Giardinu** (Sardinia); **Iardino** (Sicily). Port.: **Jardim**. Ger.: **Gärtner**, **Gartner**; **Gart(en)mann**. Low Ger.: **Gardner**. Jewish (Ashkenazic): **Gärtner**, **Gartner**.

Equivs. (occupational, not cogn.): Czech: ZAHRADNÍK. Pol.: OGRODOWSKI. Hung.: KERTÉSZ.

Garet French: 1. metonymic occupational name for a herdsman or topographic name for someone who lived by a covered shelter for animals, OF *garet* shelter, a deriv. of the verb *garer* to guard, protect, shelter (of Gmc origin). There are villages named with this word in Puy-de-Dôme and Allier, and the surname may also be a habitation name from one of them.

2. from a dim. of any of various Gmc personal names with the first element *geri*, *gari* spear or *ward* guard, protect, shelter.

Vars.: **Garel**, **Gareau**, **Gari(o)t**, **Gariou**.

Garfield 1. English: apparently a habitation name from an unidentified place, probably from a field-name referring to a triangular area (OE *gāra*; see GORE 1) left at the corner of an open field after rectangular furlongs had been laid out.

2. Jewish: Anglicization of one or more like-sounding Jewish surnames.

Garforth English (Yorks.): habitation name from a place in W Yorks., apparently so called from OE *gāra* triangular piece of ground (see GORE 1) + *ford* FORD.

Gargan Irish: Anglicized form of Gael. **Ó Geargáin** and **Mac Geargáin** 'descendant' and 'son of *Geargán*', a personal name from a dim. of *gearg* fierce.

Garland English: 1. metonymic occupational name for a maker of garlands or chaplets, perhaps also a local name from a house sign. The word is first attested in the 14th cent., from OF, and appears to be of Gmc origin.

2. habitation name from a minor place, probably *Garland* in Chulmleigh, Devon, named from OE *gāra* triangular piece of land (see GORE 1) + *land* land.

Var.: **Garlant**.

Garlick 1. English (chiefly Lancs.): metonymic occupational name for a grower or seller of garlic, ME *garlek*, OE *gārlēac* (a cpd of *gār* spear + *lēac* leek, named from the shape of its leaves). It may perhaps also have been a nickname for someone who ate a lot of garlic.

2. English (chiefly Lancs.): possibly also from a given name, an unrecorded survival into ME of the OE personal name *Gārlāc*, composed of the elements *gār* spear + *lāc* sport, play.

3. Jewish (E Ashkenazic): Anglicized form of Jewish *Garelik*; see GORELIK.

Vars. (of 1 and 2): **Garlic(ke)**.

Cogns. (of 2): Ger.: **Gerlach**, **Gerlich**, **Görlach**, **Görlich**, **Girlach**. Low Ger.: **Garlach**, **Garlich**.

Patrs. (from 2): Ger.: **Gerlacher**, **Gerlicher**, **Görlacher**.

Garmendia Basque: topographic name. The first element is unidentified, but the remainder is clearly *mendi* mountain + the def. art. *-a*.

Garner English: 1. topographic name for someone who lived near a barn or granary, or metonymic occupational name for someone in charge of the stores kept in a granary, from ANF *gerner* granary (OF *gernier*, from LL *grānārium*, a deriv. of *grānum* grain, corn; cf. GRANGER). For the change of *-er-* to *-ar-*, cf. MARCHANT.

2. var. of WARNER 1, from a central OF form.

3. contracted var. of GARDENER.

Vars. (of 1): **Garnier**, **Garnar**, **Gerner**.

Dim. (of 1 and 2): GARNETT.

Garnett English: 1. metonymic occupational name for a grower or seller of pomegranates, from a metathesized form of OF (*pome*) *grenate* (L *pōmum* fruit, apple + *grānātum* full of seeds, from *grānum* seed, grain). For the change of *-er-* to *-ar-*, cf. MARCHANT. The name of the red-coloured precious stone derives from the same source, comparison being originally made with the rich red of the inside of a pomegranate.

2. metonymic occupational name for a maker or fitter of hinges, from a dim. of OF *carne* hinge (L *cardo*, gen. *cardinis*).

3. dim. of GARNER, in either of its first two senses.

Var.: **Garnet**.

Cogns. (of 1): Sp.: GRANADO. Swed.: **Granat(h)**. Jewish (Ashkenazic, ornamental): **Granat**; **Granatov** (patr. in form); **Granatstein** ('pomegranate stone'); cf. MILGRIM.

Garnham English (Suffolk and N Essex): apparently a habitation name from some unidentified place, so called from the gen. case of the OE personal name *Gāra* (a short form of the various cpd names with the first element *gār* spear) + OE *hām* homestead.

Garnon 1. English: nickname for someone who wore a moustache, from ME, OF *gernon*, *grenon* moustache.

2. English and French: dim. of WARNER.

Vars. (of 1): **Garnons**, **Gernon**, **Grennan**.

Cogn. (of 1): Fr.: **Grenon**.

Garrett English (Norman): 1. from *Gerard*, a personal name introduced to Britain by the Normans, composed of the Gmc elements *geri*, *gari* spear + *hard* hardy, brave, strong.

2. from *Gerald*, a personal name introduced to Britain by the Normans, composed of the Gmc elements *geri*, *gari* spear + *wald* rule.

Vars.: **Garratt**, **Garrit**, **Garred**, **Garrad**, **Gerrett**, **Geratt**, **Gerred**, **Gerrad**, **Jarrett**, **Jarratt**, **Jarritt**, **Jar(r)ed**, **Jarad**, **Jerratt**, **Jereatt**, **Jerred**. (Of 1 only): **Gar(r)ard**; **Ger(r)ard** (chiefly Lancs.), **Jarrard**, **Jerrard**. (Of 2 only): **Garrould**, **Garrod**, **Gerald**, **Gerold**; **Jarro(l)d**; **Jarrott**, **Jerrold**.

Cogns. (of 1): Fr.: **Gérard**, **Girard**, **Guirard**. It.: **Gherardi**, **Ghirardi**, **Ghelardi**, **Ghilardi** (N Italy); **Gerardi**, **Ierardi**, **Gelardi**, **Gilardi**, **Girardi**. Ger.: **Gerhard(t)**, **Görhardt**, **Gehrt**. Low Ger.: **Gerri(e)t**, **Gi(e)rhard**, **Gi(e)rth**. Flem., Du.: **G(h)eer(h)aert**, **Gert**. Hung.: **Gellért**. (Of 2): Fr.: **Géraud**, **Gérault**, **Girau(l)d**, **Girau(l)t**, **Giraux**, **Guiraud**, **Girod**, **Giral**, **Gérald**. It.: **Gheraldi**, **Ghiraldi**, **Ghiroldi** (N Italy); **Geraldi**, **Geroldi** (Lombardy); **Giraldo**, **Ciraldo** (S Italy); **Giraud(o)** (Piedmont); **Giroldi** (Val d'Aosta). Sp.: **Giraldo**. Cat.: **Giralt**; **Guira(d)o**, **Guirau**, GRAU. Ger.: **Ger(h)old**. Low Ger.: **Gerrelt**, **Garrold**, **Jerrold**, **Jerrolt**, **Jarrelt**.

Dims. (of 1): Fr.: **Gérardet**, **Girardet**, **Girardey**, **Girardez**, **Gérardin**, **G(u)irardin**, **Girardy**, **Gérardot**, **Girardot**, **Gérardeaux**, **Girardeau**. It.: **Gherardelli**, **G(h)iriardelli**, **Gherardini**, **Girardin(i)**, **Ghelerdini**, **G(h)ilardini**, **Gherarducci**, **Ghelarducci**, **Girardetti**. Fris.: **Gerritsma**. Du.: **Geerling**. Ger. (of Slav. origin): **Gierek**, **Gierok**, **Gi(e)rke**, **Gierck(e)** (in part shared with GEORGE). Low Ger.: **Geertje**. (Of 2): Fr.: **Giraudeau**, **Giraudel**, **Giraudou(x)**, **Giraudot**, **Giraudy**, **Géraudel**, **Géraudy**, **Girodier**, **Girodin**, **Girodon**, **Giraldon**. It.: **Geraldini**, **Geroldini**.

Augs. (of 1): It.: **Ghelardoni**, **Gilardoni**, **Girardoni**, **Girardoni**. (Of 2): Fr.: **Giraudat**, **Girodias**.

Patrs.: Eng.: **Garretts**; **Garret(t)son**, **Garrison**; FITZGERALD. (From 1 only): It.: **Gherardesci**; **Gilardengo**, **Girardengo**.

Ger.: **Gerhartz**. Low Ger.: **Ge(e)rdts, Gehrts, Ge(h)rtz, Gerriets, Gerretz, Geertz, Gerdes, Jertz, Gi(e)raths, Gietz; Gerding; Gerritzen, Gerressen**. Du.: **Geer(i)ts, Gerrets; Gerritse(n), Gerretsen**. Dan.: **Ge(e)rtsen**. (From 2 only): Sp.: **Giráldez**. Port.: **Geraldes**. Ger.: **Gerholz**. Low Ger.: **Garral(t)s, Garrel(t)s, Gerrel(t)s, Gerlts, Gehrels**.

The English forms Garrod *and* Jarrold *are particularly common in E Anglia*.

Garrido Spanish and Portuguese: nickname from Sp., Port. *garrido* elegant, splendid, ostentatious, in origin apparently the past part. of *garrir* to talk, chatter (L *garrīre*). The word also formerly had the sense 'scandalous', 'wanton', and the surname may sometimes have been given with this meaning.

Garrote Spanish: nickname for a belligerent individual or metonymic occupational name for a crossbowman, from Sp. *garrote* stick, cudgel, also used of a wooden bolt fired from a crossbow and of the weapon itself (of uncertain, possibly Celt., origin).

Gars French: occupational name for a young servant, from OF *gars* boy, lad (apparently of Gmc origin).

Vars.: **Garçon, Garson** (from the oblique case).

Cogns.: Eng.: **Garson**. It.: **Garzoni**. Sp.: **Garzón** (apparently a nickname with pej. overtones, in part borne by Sefardic Jews in Morocco and their descendants).

Dims.: Fr.: **Garçonnet, Garçonnot, Garsonnin**. Prov.: **Garcin, Garcioux**. It.: **Garzonetti**.

Garside English (Lancs. and Yorks.): habitation name from *Gartside* or *Garside* in Oldham, Lancs., apparently so called from Northern ME *garth* enclosure (ON *garðr*) + *side* hill slope (OE *sīde*).

Var.: **Gartside**.

Garstang English: habitation name from a town in N Lancs., apparently so called from ON *geiri* triangular piece of land (cf. GORE 1) + *stang* pole. Ekwall sugggests that the original reference may have been to a boundary mark.

Garston English: habitation name from any of various places so called. Those in Hants and Herts. are named with the OE elements *gærs, græs* grass, grazing + *tūn* enclosure, referring to a paddock. This cpd probably survived into the Middle Ages as a vocab. word. A place of the same name in Lancs. has a different origin, from a metathesized form of OE *grēat* large + *stān* stone.

Garth N English: topographic name for someone who lived near an enclosure, normally a paddock or orchard, from Northern ME *garth* enclosed area, yard (from ON *garðr* enclosure).

Var.: **Gath**.

Garton English: habitation name from a place on the coast near Hull or another on the E Yorks. wolds. They both get their names from ON *garðr* enclosure (see GARTH) + OE *tūn* settlement, place.

Garvey Irish: Anglicized form of the Gael. personal name *Garbhith*, from *garbh* rough, cruel + a second element of uncertain origin, which has been associated with *bith* fate, (ill) fortune.

Var.: **Garvie** (Scots).

Patr.: Ir.: **MacGarvey** (Gael. **Mac Gairbh(e)ith**).

'Descendant of G.': Ir.: **O'Garvey, O'Garvie** (Gael. **Ó Gairbh(e)ith**).

Garvin Irish: Anglicized form of Gael. **Ó Gairbhín** 'descendant of *Gairbhín*', a personal name derived from *garbh* rough, cruel.

Vars.: **O'Garvin, O'Garven, Garavin, Garvan, Garwin; Girvin, Girvan, Girwin** (N Ireland).

Garwood English: habitation name from an unidentified minor place, probably so called from OE *gāra* triangular piece of land (see GORE 1) + *wudu* WOOD.

Gascoigne English: regional name for someone from the province of Gascony, OF *Gascogne*. The name of the region derives from that of the Basques, who are found close by and formerly extended into this region as well; they are first named in Roman sources as *Vascōnes*, but the original meaning of the name, derived from a root *eusk-* in the non-Indo-European language that they still speak today, is completely obscure. By the Middle Ages the Basques had been displaced from most of Gascony by speakers of Gascon (a dialect of Occitan, related to French), who were proverbial for their boastfulness.

Vars.: **Gascogne, Gascoyne, Gascon(e), Gasken, Gaskin(g)**.

Cogns.: Fr.: **Gascogne, Gasco(i)n, Gasq**. Prov.: **G(u)asch**. Cat.: **G(u)asch, Gascó**. Sp.: **Gascón**.

Dims.: Fr.: **G(ou)asquet, Gasquié, Gasquiel, Gascuel**.

Pej.: Fr.: **Gascard**.

Patr.: Eng.: **Gaskens**.

Gąsior Polish: nickname for a stupid person or metonymic occupational name for a keeper of geese, from Pol. *gąsior* gander; cf. GANDER and GOOSE.

Var.: **Gąsiorski** (with surname suffix *-ski*; see BARANOWSKI).

Dim.: **Gąsiorek**.

Patr.: **Gąsiorowicz**.

Patr. (from a dim.): Pol.: **Gąsiorkiewicz**.

Habitation name: **Gąsiorowski**.

Gaskell English (Lancs.): habitation name from *Gatesgill* in Cumb., so called from ON *geit* goat + *skáli* shelter (see SCHOLES).

Vars.: **Gaskill; Gaitskell, Gaitskill**.

Gass 1. German and Jewish (Ashkenazic): topographic name for someone who lived in a narrow lane or alley, Ger. *Gasse*, Yid. *gas* street (MHG *gazze*, OHG *gazza*, a cogn. of ON *gata* road; cf. GATE 1).

2. English: var. of WACE.

Vars. (of 1): Ger.: **Gass(n)er, Gäss(n)er, Gessner**. Jewish: **Gas, Gass(n)er; Gassmann**.

Gast 1. German and Jewish (Ashkenazic): cogn. of GUEST.

2. French: topographic name for someone who lived on a patch of waste land, OF *gast* (of Gmc origin (cf. WÜST), crossed with the ultimately cogn. L *vastum*).

Vars. (of 2): Fr.: **Dugas(t)**.

Cpd (of 1): Jewish: **Gastfreund** ('generous entertainer' or 'welcome guest').

Gaston French: from the OF oblique case of a Gmc personal name, originally probably a byname from *gasti* stranger, guest, host (cf. GUEST). The surname is also found in England and Ireland, where it is probably a Norman importation.

Cogn.: Prov.: **Gastou**.

Gate English (chiefly Northern): 1. topographic name for someone who lived by a main road or street, from Northern ME *gate* road, thoroughfare (ON *gata*; cf. GASS 1).

2. topographic name for someone who lived by a gate, from the sing. of GATES.

3. metonymic occupational name for a goatherd, or nickname for a stubborn or particularly smelly person, from ME *gayte* goat, OE *gāt*, or the cogn. ON *geit*. For the

Northern ME preservation of *-ā-*, in contrast to the Southern change to *-ō-*, cf. ROPER.

4. metonymic occupational name for a watchman, from a central OF form of ONF *waite*; see WAITE.

Vars.: **Gait(e)**, **Gaitt**. (Of 1 and 3): **Ga(i)ter**, **Gayter**, **Gaytor**. (Of 3 only): **Goate(r)**, **Goatman**.

Cogn. (of 1): Dan.: **Gade** ('street').

Gateacre English: habitation name from *Gatacre* in Shrops. or *Gateacre* in Lancs., named with the OE elements *gāt* goat + *acer* cultivated land (see ACKER).

The Gateacre *family of Gatacre Hall, Shrops., can be traced back to Stephen* de Gateacre, *who held the manor of this place in the 13th cent. Another branch of the family uses the spelling* **Gataker**.

Gatehouse English: habitation name for someone living in the house above the gates of a town or castle, ME *gatehus*.

Gately Irish: Anglicized form of Gael. **Mag Athlaoich**, patr. from the byname *Athlaoch* 'Ex-Warrior', composed of the elements *ath* former + *laoch* warrior, hero.

Gatenby English (Yorks.): habitation name from a place in N Yorks., said to be derived from an OIr. personal name *Gaithan* + ON *býr* farm, settlement.

Gates English: topographic name for someone who lived by the gates of a medieval town. The ME sing. *gate* is from the OE pl., *gatu*, of *geat* gate (see YATE). Since medieval gates were normally arranged in pairs, fastened in the centre, the OE pl. came to function as a sing., and a new ME pl. ending in *-s* was formed. In some cases the name may refer specifically to the Sussex place *Eastergate* (i.e. 'eastern gate'), known also as *Gates* in the 13th and 14th cents., when surnames were being acquired.

Gatterer German: topographic name for someone who lived by the wooden fence surrounding a small community, from Ger. *Gatter* wooden fence (MHG *gater*, from OHG *gataro*) + *-er* suffix denoting human nouns.

Vars.: **Gatter(mann)**.

Gatward English: 1. occupational name for a gatekeeper, from OE *gatu* GATES + *weard* guardian (see WARD 1).

2. occupational name for a goatherd, from OE *gāt* goat + *weard* guardian.

Gaughran Irish: Anglicized form of Gael. **Mag Eachráin**, patr. from the personal name *Eachrán*, of uncertain etymology, perhaps containing the element *each-* horse; cf. GAHAN 1.

Vars.: **McGa(ug)hran**, **McGawran**, **McGarran**, **Mageachrane**, **Magaher(a)n**.

Gaugin French: of uncertain origin. It may be a dim. form of OF *gauge*, a kind of nut, and so a topographic name for someone who lived by a nut-tree of this type, or a metonymic occupational name for a grower or seller of the nuts.

Vars.: **Gaugain**; **Gauge**; **Gaugier**.

Gaulle, de French: of uncertain origin. It is possibly a Gallicized form of Flem. *De Walle* 'the foreigner, Walloon' (cf. WALLIS). On the other hand, a tradition within the family of the statesman and soldier General Charles de Gaulle connects it with OF *gaule* pole (of Gmc origin). His earliest known ancestor, Richard de Gaulle, was granted land in Normandy in the 13th cent.

Gaumont French: of uncertain origin, probably from a Gmc personal name, *Walmund*, composed of the elements *wala* death in battle + *mund* protection. The second element was assimilated by folk etymology to MONT hill.

Var.: **Gaumond**.

Gaunt English: 1. local name from the town of *Ghent* in Flanders, from which many wool workers and other skilled craftsmen migrated to England in the early Middle Ages. The surname is found most commonly in W Yorks. around Leeds. The Flem. placename is first recorded in L documents as *Gandi* and *Gandavum*; it is apparently of Celt. origin, but of uncertain meaning.

2. nickname from ME *gaunt* thin, wasted, haggard (of uncertain, possibly Scandinavian, origin).

3. metonymic occupational name for a maker and seller of gloves, from OF *gant* glove (of Gmc origin).

Vars. (of 3): **Gant**; **Gaunter**, GANTER, GANDER.

Cogns. (of 1): Flem.: **De Gentenaer**. Du.: **Van G(h)ent**. Ger.: **Gent**, **Gend(t)**. Fr.: **Gant**, **Gand**, **Degant**, **Degand**, **Gantois**, **Gandois**. (Of 3): Fr.: **Gant**; **Gantier**. Cat.: **Guanter**.

Gavaldà Catalan: habitation name from *Gavaudan* in S France, which has the same origin as GABALDÓN.

Vars.: **Gavaldó**, **Gabaldà**.

Gavigan Irish: Anglicized form of Gael. **Mag Eachagáin**, patr. from the personal name *Eachagán*, a double dim. of *each* horse; cf. GAHAN 1.

Vars.: **Gavaghan**, **Gavecan**, **Gaffican**, **Gaffikin**, **Gahagan**, **McGaffigan**.

Gavilán Spanish: nickname for a hawklike person, from Sp. *gavilán* sparrowhawk (of Gmc origin, apparently a deriv. of *gabal* fork (cf. GABLER), referring to the talons of the bird). *Gavilán* was also used in the Middle Ages as a given name, perhaps in part preserving a Gmc byname, and this may also lie behind some examples of the surname.

Cogn.: Cat.: **Gavilà**.

Gavin English (now also common in Ireland): from a given name popular in the Middle Ages in the ME form *Gawayne* as well as the OF *Gauvin*. The name was introduced from Fr. versions of the Arthurian romances, where this name was borne by one of the knights of the Round Table, the brother of Galahad and Mordred and a nephew of Arthur. It is probably from an OW personal name composed of the elements *gwalch* hawk + *gwyn* white, influenced in part by Bret. forms.

Vars.: **Gaven**, **Gauv(a)in**, **Gawen**; **Gawn(e)** (see also GOUGH); **Wawn(e)**.

Cogns.: Fr.: **Gauv(a)in**, **Gauwain**. It.: **Gavino**, **Galvano**, **Galvani**. Sp.: GALVÁN. Ger.: **Gabain**.

Dims.: Fr.: **Gauvreau**, **Gauvrit**, **Gauvry**.

Patrs.: Eng.: **Gawenson**, **Ga(u)nson**.

Gawroński Polish: from Pol. *gawron* rook + *-ski* suffix of surnames (see BARANOWSKI), in various possible applications. It may be a nickname for an acquisitive or thievish person, or it may be a habitation name from a place called *Gawrony*.

Cogn. (dim.): Czech: **Havránek**.

Gawthorpe English (Yorks.): habitation name from any of several places in W Yorks. called *Gawthorpe* or *Gawthrop*, all of which derive their names from ON *gaukr* cuckoo + *þorp* enclosure (see THORPE).

Var.: **Gawthrop**.

Gay 1. English, French, and Catalan: nickname for a lighthearted or cheerful person; the adj. is of unknown origin, perhaps a borrowing of a Prov. cogn. of JAY.

2. English (Norman): habitation name from places in Normandy called *Gaye*, from an early proprietor bearing a Gmc personal name cogn. with WADE.

3. Catalan: from a medieval given name (L *Gaius*, of uncertain, possibly Etruscan, origin; cf. KAY 3).

4. Irish: see KILDEA.

Vars. (of 1 and 2): Eng.: **Gaye**. (Of 1 only): Fr.: **Gai, Leg(u)ay, Leguey**.

Cogn. (of 1): Sp.: **Gayo**.

Dims. (of 1): Fr.: **Gayet, Gayon, Gayot**.

Pejs. (of 1): Fr.: **Gayard, Gayaud**.

As an English surname, Gay *is found mainly in the south-west.*

Gaynor 1. Irish: Anglicized form of Gael. **Mag Fhionnbhairr** 'son of *Fionnbharr*', a personal name composed of the elements *fionn* fair, white + *barr* top, head.

2. Welsh: from the female given name *Gaenor* (a form of *Gwenhwyfar*; see JUNIPER 2).

3. Jewish: of unknown origin.

Vars. (of 1): **McGynnowar, Maginnoire, Magennure, Magenor**.

Gazeley English: habitation name from a place in Suffolk, so called from the gen. case of the OE personal name *Gǣgi* (apparently related to the verb *gǣgan* to turn aside) + OE *lēah* wood, clearing.

Geach English (Devon and Cornwall): nickname from ME *geche, ge(c)ke* fool, stupid person (of uncertain origin, but apparently with Gmc cogns.).

Var.: **Geake**.

Cogns.: Ger.: **Gack; Gagg** (Swabia). Low Ger.: **Geck, Gegg**.

Dims.: Ger.: **Gackl, Gäckle**.

Patrs.: Eng.: **Jeeks, Jecks, Jex**.

Geaney Irish: Anglicized form of Gael. **Mag Éanna**, patr. from the personal name *Éanna*, which is of unknown origin.

Geary 1. Irish: Anglicized form of Gael. **Ó Gadhra** 'descendant of *Gadhra*', a personal name derived from *gadhar* hound, mastiff.

2. English: from a Gmc personal name derived from *geri, gari* spear, a short form of the various cpd names with this first element (cf., e.g., GARBETT, GARBUTT, and GARRETT).

3. English: nickname for a wayward or capricious person, from ME *ge(a)ry* fickle, changeable, passionate (a deriv. of *gere* fit of passion, apparently a Scandinavian borrowing).

Vars. (of 1): **O'Geary, O'Geiry, O'Garey, (O')Garry, (O')Gara, Guiry, Gwyre**. (Of 2 and 3): **Gerr(e)y, Gerrie** (chiefly Devon). (Of 2 only): **Garey, Gar(r)y**; JARRY. (Of 3 only): **Gear(e), Geer(e); Ger(r)ish, Garrish** (chiefly Somerset).

Cogns. (of 2): Fr.: **Geron, Giron(d)** (from the oblique case); **Gier, G(i)é** (from the nom. case). Low Ger.: **Geer, Gehr(e)**.

Dims. (of 2): Fr.: **Gerin, Gérin, Ger(on)net, Gérondeau; Géricot, Géricault**. Ger.: **Gerle, Ge(h)rlein; Görl** (Bavaria); **Gerli** (Switzerland). Low Ger.: **Gere(c)ke, Gehricke, Gehrke, Garke, Gahr(mann), Ge(h)rmann, Giermann**. Fris.: **Jahrmann**, JARRE.

Patrs. (from 2): Eng.: **Gearing, Geering**. Ger.: **Ge(h)ring, Gerung; Gö(h)ring** (Bavaria). Low Ger.: **Geers, Geeren, Gerren(s), Ge(h)rs, Ge(h)ring, Jhering, Ge(h)righ, Gehrich**. Fris.: **Jarren, Jarr(e)s, Jarsen**.

Patrs. (from 2) (dims.): Ger.: **Gerler, Gerling; Görler, Görling** (Bavaria). Low Ger.: **Ger(c)ken(s), Garken, Gerking**.

Most present-day Irish bearers of the name Geary *and its vars. and derivs. are descended from a single 10th-cent. ancestor, a nephew of Eadhra, who founded the family of* O'HARA.

Gebhardt German: from a Gmc personal name composed of the elements *geb* gift + *hard* brave, hardy, strong. A saint of this name was bishop of Constance around the end of the 10th cent., and his popularity may have had an influence on the continued use of the given name into the Middle Ages.

Vars.: **Gebhard, Geber(t), Gebbert, Gabert, Göbhardt**.

Cogns.: Fr.: **Gibard**. Eng.: **Gibbard**, GIFFARD. Low Ger.: **Gävert, Gäwert, Gewert, Gevert, Geffert**. Czech: **Geb(e)rt, Kebert, Kábrt**.

Dims.: Ger.: **Geberl**. Low Ger.: **Gebb(e), Gebecke, Ge(e)ve, Geffe, Gibke, Giebecke**.

Patrs.: Ger.: **Geberding**. Low Ger.: **Geb(b)ers, Gewers, Gevers, Geffers**.

Patrs. (from dims.): Low Ger.: **Gebken, Gefken**.

Gębski Polish: nickname for a braggart or a foul-mouthed person, or else one with a big mouth in a literal sense, from Pol. *gęba* gob + *-ski* suffix of surnames (see BARANOWSKI).

Vars.: **Gębicki, Gembicki**.

Cogns.: Czech: **Huba, Hubál**.

Dims.: Czech: **Hubáček, Hubálek**.

Geddes Scots: habitation name from a place in the former county of Nairn, which apparently gets its name from a Gael. term for a mountain ridge.

Var.: **Geddis** (chiefly N Ireland).

Geddie Scots: of unknown origin.

The name is first recorded in 1394 at Arbroath, when John Gedy, *Abbot of Arbroath, played a large part in organizing the building of a harbour there.*

Gedge English (E Anglia): nickname from ME *gegge*, a term of abuse or contempt applied to a foolish or loose woman or an awkward or boorish man (of uncertain origin).

Gee English: although this is a common name, especially in N England, it is of very uncertain origin. Forms which certainly belong here are not found before the 16th cent. The existence of the patr. **Geeson** points to a given name, or, less probably, an occupational name or nickname, but this as not been identified.

Geest Low German and Dutch: topographic name for someone who lived in an area of barren sandy soil, MLG *gēst*.

Vars.: GEIST; **Vergeest, Bergeest, Borgeest**. Flem., Du.: **Van (der) Geest, Van Gheest, Geestman**. Fris.: **Geestra**.

Gefen Jewish (Israeli): ornamental name from Hebr. *gefen* vine, a Hebraicization usually of the various Ashkenazic surnames listed at WEIN.

Gegner German: topographic name for someone who lived not in the main settlement itself but in the surrounding countryside, from a deriv. of MHG *gegende* (OHG *gegenōti*, a deriv. of *gegin* opposite, against, based on LL *contrāta* region, country, from *contra* opposite, against).

Geier 1. German: nickname from a greedy or rapacious person, from Ger. *Geier* vulture (MHG, OHG *gīr*). Some early examples may be house names, from house signs depicting this bird, and some others may be habitation come from a place near Zwickau called *Geyer*, which is probably ultimately from the same word.

2. Jewish (Ashkenazic): occupational name from Yid. *geyer* pedlar (a deriv. of *geyn* to go) or in some cases perhaps an unflattering name from Ger. *Geier* vulture, as in 1, bestowed by non-Jewish government officials in central Europe at the time when surnames became compulsory.

Vars. (of 1): **Geyer, Gayer**. (Of 2): **Gajer** (Pol. spelling), **Geierman**.

Cogn. (of 1): Flem., Du.: **De Gier**.

Geiger German and Jewish (Ashkenazic): occupational name for a player on the fiddle, from Ger. *Geiger*, an agent deriv. of *Geige* violin, fiddle (MHG *gīge*, Late OHG *gīga*, of uncertain origin).

Geist 1. German: metonymic occupational name for a goatherd or nickname for a stubborn person, from S Ger. dial. *Geiss* goat (MHG, OHG *geiz*, a cogn. of OE *gāt* and ON *geit*; see GATE).

2. German: house name for someone who lived in a house marked by the sign of the Holy Spirit (normally depicted as a dove), from Ger. *Geist* spirit (MHG, OHG *geist*). Both *Geist* and *Heilgeist* occur as house signs in Frankfurt-am-Main in the mid-14th cent.

2. Low German: var. of GEEST.

Vars. (of 1): **Geiss(er)**, **Gaiss(er)**. (Of 2): **Geister(t)** (Silesia).

Cogn. (of 2): Du.: **De Geest**.

Geldart English: occupational name for a person responsible for looking after oxen and castrated horses, from ME *geld* sterile, barren (animal) (ON *geldr*) + *herd* herdsman (OE *hierde*; see HEARD).

Vars.: **Geldard**, **Gelder** (Yorks.).

Cogns.: Ger.: **Gel(t)zer**, **Gölzer** (from MHG *gelze* castrated swine).

Geles Jewish (Ashkenazic): metr. from the Yid. female given name *Gele* 'Blonde' (cf. GELLER 3).

Vars.: **Gelles(s)**, **Gel(l)is**; **Gelin** (E Ashkenazic).

Geller 1. Low German: habitation name from the N German town of *Geldern* or from the Du. province of *Gelderland*, earlier *Geler* and *Gelre*. Both places get their names from what may be an ancient element descriptive of marshland.

2. German: occupational name for a town crier, Ger. *Geller*, MHG *gellære* (from *gellen* to shout, yell, OHG *gellan*).

3. Jewish (Ashkenazic): nickname for a man with red hair, from the strong form of Yid. *gel* red-headed (MHG *gel* yellow, OHG *gelo*, gen. *gelwes*). There has been considerable confusion with Ger. *Gelb* yellow, since the meaning change from 'yellow' to 'red' took place only in Yiddish and only with reference to people's complexion or hair colouring.

4. Jewish (E Ashkenazic): nickname for a man with light hair or a sallow complexion, a var. of HELLER 3, originating under Russ. influence, since Russ. has no /h/ and alters /h/ in borrowed words to /g/.

Vars. (of 1): **Gellermann**, **Gelder(mann)**. (Of 2): **Gellert**, **Gehler(t)**. (Of 3): **Gelb(er)**. Jewish only: **Gelb(er)man(n)**, **Gelbert**, GILBERT. (Of 4): **Gel(l)**, **Geler**, **Gel(l)erman**, **Gel(l)man(n)**.

Cogns. (of 1): Du., Flem.: **(Van) Gelder**, **Van Gelderen**, **Gelderland**, **Gelderman**.

Patr. (from 3): Jewish: **Gelberson**.

Cpds. (of 3; mostly ornamental): Jewish: **Gelband** ('yellow ribbon'); **Gelbart**, **Gelbard**, **Gelbort**, **Gelbord** ('red beard' or 'yellow beard', a nickname); **Gelbaum** ('yellow tree'); **Gelbein** ('yellow leg'); **Gelberg** ('yellow hill'); **Gilblum** ('yellow flower'); **Gelbrun** ('yellow-brown' or 'yellow fountain'); **Gelfarb** ('yellow colour'); **Gelbfisch** ('yellow fish'); **Gelbgies(s)er**, **Gelbgiser** ('yellow pourer'; apparently occupational, but the occupation in question has not been identified); **Gelbhar** ('red hair' or 'yellow hair', a nickname); **Gelkop(f)** ('red head' or 'yellow head', a nickname); **Gelmond**, **Gelmont** ('yellow moon'); **Gel(b)stein**, **Gel(l)erstein** ('yellow stone'); **Gelbwachs** ('yellow wax').

Gendre French: nickname from OF *gendre* son-in-law (L *gener*), presumably often given with slightly mocking intent to someone who had bettered his lot by marrying the daughter of a rich or influential person.

Vars.: **Legendre**, **G(e)indre**, **Genre**.

Dims.: **Gendreau**, **Gendrot**, **Gendron**, **Gendrin**, **Gendry**.

Genès French: from a medieval given name (L *Genēsius*, from Gk *gnēsios* well-born, legitimate, from the root *gen-* to be born). This was the name of an early Christian martyr under Domitian, and later of a 7th-cent. bishop of Lyons, both of whom helped the name to enjoy a modest popularity. There has, however, been some confusion with GENEST.

Var.: **Geniès**.

Cogns.: Sp.: **Ginés**. Cat.: **Ginés**, **Genís**.

Genest French: topographic name for someone who lived by a patch of broom, OF *genest(e)* (LL *(planta) genesta*).

Vars.: **Genest(r)e**, **Gine(s)t**, **Gineste**, **Dugene(s)t**. See also GENÈS and GENET.

Cogns.: Sp.: **Iniesta**. Cat.: **Genestà**, **Ginestà**. Flem., Du.: **Van der G(h)eynst**.

Dims.: Fr.: **Gene(s)ton**. Prov.: **Genestou(x)**, **Ginestou(x)**.

Augs.: Prov.: **Genestat**, **Ginestat**.

Collectives: Fr.: **Gene(s)tay**.

Geoffrey **Plantagenet** *was so called from wearing in his cap a sprig of the broom plant. He was the elder son of Fulk V, Count of Anjou, son-in-law of Henry I of England, and father of Henry II (1133–89), the first Plantagenet King of England. His descendants ruled England until ousted by the House of Tudor at the end of the Wars of the Roses.*

Genet French: 1. var. of GENEST.

2. aphetic dim. of EUGÈNE.

3. nickname or metonymic occupational name from *genet*, a type of Sp. horse, a jennet. The word *genet* came into OF from Cat. *ginet*, itself a borrowing of Arabic *Zanātah*, the name of a Moorish people renowned for their horsemanship.

Genevois French: local name for someone from the Swiss city of *Geneva*, Fr. *Genève*. The name of the city is of uncertain etymology, but may be akin to L *janua* door, gateway (cf. *Genoa* at JANUARY 2).

Vars.: **Genevoix**, **Genevai**, **Genevay**; **Genève**.

Pej.: Fr.: **Genevard**.

Gentle English: nickname, sometimes perhaps ironic, from ME, OF *gent(il)* well-born, noble, courteous (L *gentilis*, from *gens* family, tribe, itself from the root *gen-* to be born).

Vars.: **Gentile**, **Jentle**; **Gent**, **Jent**; **Gentry**.

Cogns.: Fr.: **Genti(a)l**, **Genty**, **Legentil**; **Gent(e)**. It.: **Gentile**, **Gentili**; **Ientile** (Calabria, Sicily).

Dims.: Fr.: **Gentilleau**, **Gentizon**; **Gentet**, **Gent(h)on**, **Gentot**. It.: **Gentilini**, **Gentillotti**, **Gentillucci**.

Geoghegan Irish: Anglicized form of Gael. **Mag Eochagáin**, patr. from the personal name *Eochagán*, probably from a double dim. of *eachadhe* horseman; cf. CAUGHEY.

George English, French, and German: from a Gk personal name, *Gēōrgios* (from *gēōrgos* farmer, a cpd of *gē* earth, soil + *ergein* to work, till), which was in use in England before the Norman Conquest. Its popularity increased at the time of the Crusades, which brought greater contact with the Orthodox Church, in which there was a thriving cult of an obscure saint of this name, supposedly martyred at Nicomedia in AD 303, although the authenticity of his very existence is doubtful. In 1348 Edward III founded the Order of the Garter under the patronage of St George, and in 1415 his day was made a festival of the highest rank. By the end of the Middle Ages he had acquired an entirely unhistorical legend of dragon-slaying exploits, which caught the popular imagination throughout Europe, and was considered the patron saint of England.

Vars.: Fr.: **Georges**. Ger.: **Georg, Jörg, Gurg; Georgius** (Latinized).

Cogns.: Corn.: **Jory**, JURY. Prov.: **Jo(i)re, Jo(i)ris, Jori, Jor(r)y**. It.: **Giorgi(o), Giorio; I(u)orio, Iori, J(u)orio** (S Italy); **Giurio, Zorzi** (Venetia). Sp., Port.: **Jorge**. Cat.: **Jordi**. Rum.: **Gheorgh(i)e**. Fris.: **Jörck**. Flem.: **Joris**. Du.: **Jorg**. Low Ger.: **Gerg(e), Gergus**. Ger. (under Slav. influence): **Jerg; Gerasch, Gerratsch; Jerche, Jersch, Ju(h)rich, Jur(i)sch, Jerratsch, Jerok, Gerok, Jero(s)ch, Jeri(s)ch** (see also JEROME); **Hürch(e), Hur(i)ch, Hirche, Herche, Horche; Schirach, Schirak, Schirok, Schurig, Schuricht, Schiersch; Tschersich, Tschursch, Tschi(e)rsch, Tschirschky, Tschierse**. Czech (from the Czech form of the given name, *Jiří*): **Jiří, Jíra, Jírů, Jura; Jirsa, Jirka, Jirků; Jirák; Jiráň, Jiras, Jiruš, Jiruch; Jurča**. Pol. (from the Pol. form of the given name, *Jerzy*): **Jerzyk, Jerzak; Jurzyk, Jura, Jurasz**. Ukr.: **Gurko, Gurys**. Hung.: **György**.

Dims.: Fr.: **Georgel(in), Georgeau, George(o)t, Georgeon, Georger, Georgé**. Prov.: **Jorin, Joreau, Joriot, Jorioz, Joron, Joret, Jorez, Jorey**. It.: **Giorgetti, Giorgini, Giorielli, Gioretto; Iorillo, Iorizzo, Iorrizzi** (S Italy); **Giorgiutti, Giurin(i), Zorzet(ti), Zorzin(i), Zorzutti** (Venetia). Ger.: **Görg(e)l**. Low Ger.: **Görgen, Jürgen** (in which a patr. suffix *-en* added to the *-g* of the stem was later confused with the dim. ending *-gen*, *-chen*). Du.: **Jurgen**. Fris.: **Jörn, Jürn, Jurn**. Flem.: **Gorick** (also found in London); **Horick** (Enghien). Ger. (of Slav. origin): **Jerschke, Jerke, Jirzik, Jirek, Jirak, Jir(k)a, Jorczyk, Juhr(k)e, Jur(cz)ik, Jurick, Juschke, Juschka; Gör(c)ke, Göricke, Gork(e); Schuricke, Schuhrke; Tschi(e)rschke**. Czech: **Jiřík, Jiříček, Jiřička; Jiráček, Jirásek, Jurásek, Jiránek, Juránek, Jirousek, Jir(o)ušek, Jiroudek, Jiroutek, Jiroutka**. Pol.: **Jurek, Jurczyk**. Ukr.: **Yurchenko**. Hung.: **Gyurkó**.

Augs.: Fr. **Jorat** (Switzerland). It.: **Giorgioni, Giorgione; Zorz(en)oni** (Venetia).

Patrs.: Eng.: **Georgeson** (chiefly Northumb.). It.: **De Giorgi(s), De Giorgio, Di Giorgio, Di Iorio; Giorgeschi**. Rum. **G(h)eorg(h)escu**. Ger.: **Georges, Georgi, Gerger, Jerger**. Low Ger.: **Görger, Jörger; Görges, Jür(ge)s, Juris, Jürr(i)es**. Du.: **Jorissen**. Dan., Norw.: **Jørgesen**. Russ.: **Georgiev(ski)** (a form adopted by members of the Orthodox clergy, from the given-name form *Georgi*, preserved only in ecclesiastical contexts); **Yegorev** (from the ORuss. form of the name, *Yegor(g)i*, a metathesized form of *Georgi*); **Yegorov** (from a less formal version of this form with the final vowel lost); **Yuryev** (from the ORuss. vulgar form *Yur(i)*); **Yur(m)anov** (from extended forms of the popular version). Ukr., Beloruss.: **Yurevich**. Pol.: **Jurewicz; Jurczak**. Croatian: **Djor(djev)ić, Djurdj(ev)ić, Djur(ov)ić**. Bulg.: **Georgiev**. Lithuanian: **Jur(g)aitis**. Gk: **Georg(h)iou, Georgeou, Georgiades**. Hung.: **Györffy**.

Patrs. (from dims.): Ger.: **Görgler, Gergler**. Low Ger.: **Jörgensen, Jürgens(en)**. Du.: **Jurgens**. Dan.: **Jörgensen, Jurgensen, Jurgenson**. Russ.: **Yegorkov, Yegorkin, Yego(r)shin, Yegorchenkov; Yurasov, Yur(iv)tsev, Yurenev, Yurikov, Yurinov, Yuryaev, Yuryichev, Yur(k)ov, Yurlov, Yur(y)shev, Yur(en)in, Yuryatin, Yur(och)kin, Yurukhin, Yurygin; Yukhnev, Yukh(n)ov, Yush(ach)kov, Yushmanov, Yukh(n)in, Yukhtin, Yushankin, Yush(k)in**. Beloruss.: **Yurkevich, Yukhnevich**. Pol.: **Jerzykiewicz, Jurkiewicz**. Croatian: **Djurković, Djuričić, Djurišić, Jurišić**. Hung.: **Gyurkovics** (with Slav. ending).

'Son of the wife of G.': Ukr.: **Yurchishin**.

'Son of the daughter of G.': Russ.: **Yegorovnin**.

Habitation names: Pol. **Jurkowski, Jerzykowski**. Czech: **Jirkovský**.

Geraghty Irish: Anglicized form of Gael. **Mag Oireachtaigh** 'son of *Oireachtach*', a byname meaning 'Member of the Assembly'.

Vars.: **McGer(r)aghty, McGer(r)ity, McGarrity, (Mc)Gerety, Mageraghty, Geraty, Gerity, Ge(a)rty, Jerety**.

Most present-day bearers of the name Geraghty *descend from a single 11th-cent. ancestor, a member of the* CONNOR *family of Connaught, who had settled in Roscommon*.

Gerasimov Russian: patr. from the given name *Gerasim* (Gk *Gerasimos*, a deriv. of *geras* honour), which was borne by a 5th-cent. saint, venerated in the Eastern Church, who was chiefly famous for the devotion he is said to have inspired in a lion from whose paw he extracted a thorn.

Vars.: **Garasimov, Garaseev**.

Cogns.: Beloruss.: **Arasimovich** (patr.).

Dims.: Russ.: **Gerasov, Gerasyutin, Gereev, Geran(k)in, Geranichev, Gerakhov, Garshin, Gar(an)in, Garinov** (all patrs.). Ukr.: **Gerasimenko, Gerasimchuk, Garasimchuk**. Beloruss.: **Gerasimenya**.

Gerber German and Jewish (Ashkenazic): occupational name for a tanner, Ger. *Gerber* (MHG *gerwer*, OHG *(ledar)garawo* leather preparer, a deriv. of *garawen* to prepare, from *gar*, gen. *garawes*, ready, prepared).

Vars.: Ger.: **Gerb**. Jewish: GARBER (from Yid. *garber*).

Cogns.: Low Ger.: GARBER. Du.: **Gerver**. Beloruss.: **Garbar** (borrowed via Pol. from Ger.).

Dim.: Ger.: **Gerbl** (Bavaria).

Cpds: Ger.: ROTGERBER, WEISSGERBER.

German English: 1. ethnic name from OF *germain* German (L *Germānus*); this sometimes denoted an actual immigrant from Germany, but was also used to refer to a person who had trade or other connections with the country. The L word *Germānus* is of obscure and disputed origin; the most plausible of the etymologies that have been proposed is that the people were originally known as the 'Spear-men', with *geri*, *gari* spear as the first element. For a similar naming from a characteristic weapon, see FRANK.

2. from a ME and OF given name, *Germa(i)n*. This was popular in France, where it had been borne by a 5th-cent. saint, bishop of Auxerre, and achieved some currency in medieval England. It derives partly from the tribal name discussed above and partly from the L and OF homonym meaning '(full) brother, cousin' (originally an adj. meaning 'of the same stock', from L *germen* bud, shoot). In the Romance languages, esp. It., the popularity of the equivalent given name has been enhanced by association with the meaning 'brother (in God)', and in Sp. the cogn. surname is derived from the vocab. word meaning 'brother' rather than from a given name.

Vars.: **Germann, Germain(e), Germing; Jerman, Jermine, Jermyn(n); Jarma(i)n** (W Country).

Cogns. (of 2): Fr.: **Germain**. It.: **Germani, Germano**. Sp.: **Germán**. Rum.: **Gherman**. Hung.: **Germán**. Jewish (Ashkenazic): **G(h)erman** (adoptions of the non-Jewish surnames; see also HERMANN).

Dims. (of 2): Fr.: **Germaneau, Germineau, Germinet, Germiny**. It.: **Germanino, Germanini**. Hung.: **Gera**.

Patrs.: Eng.: **Jarmains**. It.: **De Germano** (S Italy).

Gershon Jewish: from the Hebr. male given name *Gershon*, *Gershom*, of uncertain etymology.

Vars.: **Gerson, Gershun, Gershom; Gershoni, Gershony, Gershuny** (with the Hebr. ending *-i*).

Patrs.: **G(h)ershensohn** (Ashkenazic); **Gershonov, Gerszonowicz, Gers(c)honowitz, Gershenowitz, Gershanovits** (E Ashkenazic).

Gesell German: from Ger. *Gesell* companion (MHG *geselle*, OHG *gisell(i)o*, a deriv. of *sal* hall, originally referring to someone who shared living accommodation). In the medieval trade guilds, this word acquired the specialized sense of 'journeyman', i.e. one who had completed his apprenticeship and was working in the workshop of a master craftsman; the surname may well be derived from this specialized sense, rather than being merely a nickname meaning 'companion' or 'friend'.

Vars.: **Gsell**, **Gsöll**.

Patr.: Jewish (E Ashkenazic): **Gesellewitz**.

Getty N Irish: Anglicized form of Gael. **Mag Eitigh**, patr. from the personal name *Eiteach*, which is largely confined to Derry but is of uncertain origin.

Gewirtz Jewish (Ashkenazic): metonymic occupational name for a spicer, from Yid. *gevirts* spice (MHG, OHG *(ge)würz* herb, plant, root; cf. WORT).

Vars.: **Gevirtz(er)**, **Gevirtzman**, **Gewir(t)zman(n)**; **Gewirzer**; **Gevertz(man)** (from the SE Yid. and a central Yid. form); **Gewirc**, **Geverc(man)** (Pol. spellings); **Gewu(e)rz**, **Gewurtz(man)** (from mod. Ger. *Gewürz*).

Ghini Italian: from the medieval given name *Ghino*, an aphetic form of *Aghino* (a short form of any of the various Gmc personal names with the first element *agi(n)* edge, point (of a weapon)), *Ughino* (a dim. of *Ugo*, see HUGH), or *Arrighino* (a dim. of *Arrigo*, see HENRY).

Dims.: **Ghinelli**, **Ghinello**, **Ghinetti**.

Pej.: **Ghinazzi**.

Gibb Scots and English: from the common medieval pet name *Gib*, a short form of the given name GILBERT.

Var.: **Gipp**.

Dims.: **Giblett**, **Giblin(g)**, GIBBON.

Patrs.: **Gibbs** (chiefly Midland, W, and SW England, though by no means rare elsewhere); **Gibbes**, **Gipps**, **Gypps**; **Gibson** (most common in Scotland, Northumb., and N Ireland); **Gibbeson**, **Gipson**, **Gypson**.

Gibbon English: 1. dim. of GIBB.

2. from the Gmc personal name *Gebwine*, composed of the elements *geba* gift + *wine* friend.

Vars.: **Gibben**, **Gibbin**, **Gubbin**.

Patrs. (from 1): **Gibbons**, **Gibbens**, **Gibbin(g)s**, **Gubbins**; FITZGIBBON. Ir.: **McGibbon**, **McCubbin(e)**, **McCubbing**, **McKibbin**, **McKibben**, **McKibbon** (Gael. **Mac Giobúin**).

Gibki Polish: nickname for a flexible person (physically or mentally), from Pol. *gibki* supple, pliable.

Gibney Irish: Anglicized form of Gael. **Ó Gibne** 'descendant of *Gibne*', a byname meaning 'Hound'.

Giddings English: habitation name from a group of villages near Huntingdon, called Great, Little, and Steeple *Gidding*, from OE *Gyddingas* 'people of *Gydda*', a personal name of uncertain origin.

Gide French: from the Gmc personal name *Gid(d)o*, of uncertain origin. It may represent a hypocoristic derivative of the various compound personal names containing the element *hild* battle.

Var.: **Gidon** (from the oblique case).

Dim.: **Gidel**.

Giffard English (Norman) and French: 1. cogn. of GEBHARDT.

2. nickname from OF *giffard* chubby-cheeked, bloated (a pej. of *giffel* jaw, cheek, of Gmc origin; cf. mod. Ger. *Kiefer* jaw).

Vars. (of 2): Eng.: GIFFORD, **Jefferd**, **Jefford**. Fr.: **Giffaut**.

Some, if not all, English bearers of the name Giffard *are descended from Osbern de Bol(e)bec, Sire de Longueville. He flourished* c.*975 and married into the family of Richard, Duke of Normandy (d. 960). His grandson Walter took part in the Norman invasion of 1066, receiving 107 lordships and manors in England as a reward for his support.*

Gifford English: 1. var. of GIFFARD 2.

2. habitation name from a place in Suffolk, now *Giffords Hall*. It was originally named in OE as *Gyddingford* 'ford (OE *ford*) associated with *Gydda*'; cf. GIDDINGS.

Gigot French: nickname for someone with peculiar legs, from a dim. of OF *gigue* leg, originally a type of small fiddle (of Gmc origin; cf. GEIGER) but applied to the legs because of a supposed similarity of shape.

Vars.: **Gigon**, **Giguet**, **Jiguet**.

Gilbert 1. English (Norman), French, and Low German: from *Gislebert*, a Norman personal name composed of the Gmc elements *gīsil* hostage, noble youth + *berht* bright, famous. This given name enjoyed considerable popularity in England during the Middle Ages, partly as a result of the fame of St Gilbert of Sempringham (1085–1189), the founder of the only native English monastic order. This at one time had over twenty houses, but became extinct on the Dissolution of the Monasteries.

2. Scots and Irish: Anglicized form of KILBRIDE.

3. Jewish (Ashkenazic): Anglicization of one or more like-sounding Jewish surnames.

Vars. (of 1): English: **Gilberd**, **Gilb(e)art**, **Gil(l)bard**, **Gilburt**, **Gilburd**, **Gilbird**, **Gelbert**; **Jelbert**, **Jelbart** (Devon and Cornwall). Fr.: **Gilibert**, **Gi(la)bert**. Low Ger.: **Giesebrecht**, **Gelbert**; **Schilbert** (Rhineland).

Cogns. (of 1): It.: **Giliberti**. Cat.: **Gilabert**, **Gelabert**; **Gisbert**, **Gispert**. Ger.: **Geis(s)elbrecht**, **Gelbrecht**, **Gilbrecht**, **Gilbracht**. Flem.: **Gyselbrecht**, **Ghillebaert**.

Dims. (of 1): Eng.: GIBB, GIBBON, GILBY. Fr.: **Gi(l)bertin**, **Gi(l)berton**, **Gilbon**, **Gilbain**. Ger.: **Geis(s)el**, **Geip(p)el**, **Geipelt**. Low Ger.: **Gies(el)**, **Gieselmann**, **Gissel**, **G(i)ese(cke)**, **Gesche**, **Gibbe**. Flem.: **Ghys**. Dan.: **Giese**.

Patrs. (from 1): Eng: **Gilbertson**. Low Ger.: **Gisbertz**, **Gilbertz**, **Gilber(t)s**. Flem.: **Gyselbrechts**. Du.: **Gijsbers**.

Patrs. (from 1) (dim.): Low Ger.: **Ges(ch)en** (Latinized **Gesenius**), **Giesges**, **Gibbels**, **Gibbens**. Flem.: **Ghys(el)en**. Du.: **Gijsen**, **Gijzen**.

The Devon family of Gilbert *can be traced to Geoffrey Gilbert (d. 1349), who represented Totnes in Parliament in 1326. His descendants included Sir Humphrey Gilbert (d. 1583), who discovered Newfoundland. The librettist W. S. Gilbert (1836–1911), author of the Savoy operas, also claimed to be a descendant. Another family called Gilbert have been established in Wigston Magna, Leics., since at least the 14th cent.*

Gilby English: 1. habitation name from a place in Lincs., so called from the ON personal name *Gilli*, which is abstracted from the various Ir. personal names containing Gael. *giolla* servant (i.e. of a particular saint) + ON *býr* farm, settlement.

2. dim. of GILBERT.

Var.: **Gilbey**.

Gilchrist Scots: from the Gael. personal name *Gille Críosd* 'servant of Christ'.

Vars.: **Gilcriest**, **Gillcrist**, **Gilgryst**.

Patrs.: **Gilkison**, **Gilk(e)s**; **McGilchrist**.

Gildernew Irish: Anglicized form of Gael. **Mac Giolla na Naomh** 'son of *Gilla na Naomh*', a personal name meaning 'servant of the saints'.

Vars.: **McAneave**; FORD.

Gildersleeve English: nickname for an ostentatious dresser, from the ME nickname *gyldenesleve* 'golden sleeve', from OE *gylden* golden (a deriv. of *gold* GOLD) + *slīf*, *slēf* sleeve.

Var.: **Gildersleve**.

Gilduff Irish: Anglicized form of Gael. **Mac Giolla Dhuibh** 'son of the blackhaired lad'.

Vars.: **McGil(le)duff, McGilleguff, McIlduff, McElduff, (Mc)Kilduff, Killduff; McIlghuie, McAhuie, H(o)uie.**

Giles 1. English: from a medieval given name of which the original form was L *Ægidius* (from Gk *aigidion* kid, young goat). This was the name of a 7th-cent. Provençal hermit, whose cult popularized the name in a variety of more or less mutilated forms: *Gidi* and *Gidy* in S France, *Gil(l)i* in the area of the Alpes-Maritimes, and *Gil(l)e* elsewhere. This last form was brought over to England by the Normans, but by the 12th cent. it was being confused with the Gmc names *Gisel*, a short form of GILBERT, and *Gilo*, which is from *Gail* (as in GAILLARD).

2. Irish: Anglicized form of Gael. *Ó Glasáin*; see GLEESAN.

Vars. (of 1): **Gyles, Jiles, Jellis(s).**

Cogns. (of 1): Fr.: **Gil(l)e; Gil(l)i, Gilly; Gilles, Gilis, Gélis; Gire, Giri, Giry; Gély, Gelly.** Prov.: **Gidy, Gidi.** It.: **Gil(l)i, Gillo, Gil(l)io, Gil(i); Zilli, Zill(i)o** (Venetia). Sp., Port.: **Gil.** Cat.: **Gil(i).** Ger.: **Ägidi, Egidy, Egyde; Giel(e), Gillig, Gilly, Gilg; Illig(e), Ilg.** Flem.: **Giele, Gillis.** Du.: GILL. Czech: **Jilý.** Hung.: **Egyed.**

Dims. (of 1): Eng: GILLETT. Fr.: **Gil(l)et, Gill(i)on, Gillot(te), Giloteau, Gilotin, Gilotot, Gillier, Gilliéron, Gillou(in), Gil(le)son.** It.: **Giletto, Gilioli; Zilioli, Zil(i)otti, Zilocchi** (Venetia). Low Ger.: **Gilgmann, Ilchmann, Ill(ich)mann.** Flem.: **Gil(le)quin.** Czech: **Jílek.**

Aug. (of 1): Fr.: **Giriat.**

Pejs. (of 1): Eng.: **Gillard, Jillard, Jellard.**

Patrs. (from 1): Eng.: **Gil(l)son** (see also GILL). Ger.: **Gilcher, Gilger, Gilles, Gielen, Gieles, Gieling; Ill(i)es, Ilgen.** Flem.: **Gielen, Gillen, Gillyns.**

Gilfillan Scots: from the Gael. personal name *Gille Fhaoláin* 'servant of (St) *Faolán*'; see WHELAN.

Vars.: **Gilfilland, Gillilan(d), Gellan(d); Kilfillan.**

Patrs.: See MCCLELLAN.

Gilfoil Irish: Anglicized form of Gael. **Mac Giolla Phóil**, patr. from the personal name *Giolla Phóil* 'servant of (St) PAUL'.

Vars.: **G(u)ilfoyle, Kilfoyle.**

Gilhool Irish: Anglicized form of Gael. *Mac Giolla Chomhghaill*; see COLE 3.

Vars.: **Gilhool(e)y; McGillecole, McGilleghole, McGillacoell.**

Gill 1. English: from a short form of the given names GILES, JULIAN, or WILLIAM. In theory the name would have a soft initial when derived from the first two of these, and a hard one when from *William* or from the other possibilities discussed below. However, there has doubtless been much confusion over the centuries, and the modern pronunciation can hardly be taken as a reliable guide to the origin.

2. N English: topographic name for someone who lived by a ravine or deep glen, ME *gil(l)* (ON *gil* gill of a fish, also used in a transferred sense of a ravine).

3. Scots and Irish: Anglicized form of Gael. **Mac Gille** (Sc.), **Mac Giolla** (Ir.), patrs. from an occupational name for a servant or a short form of the various personal names formed by attaching this element to the name of a saint. The ON personal name *Gilli* is probably of this origin (cf. GILBY 1), and may lie behind some examples of the name in N England.

4. Scots and Irish: Anglicized form of Gael. *Mac An Ghoill*; see GALL 1.

5. Dutch: cogn. of GILES.

6. Jewish (Israeli): ornamental name from Hebr. *gil* joy.

Gillespie Scots and Irish: Anglicized form of Gael. **Mac Gille Easbuig** (Sc.), **Mac Giolla Easbuig** (Ir.), patrs. from a byname meaning 'servant of the bishop'.

Vars: **McGillaspick; Gillesp(e)y, Gillaspy, Gilhespy, G(a)lasby, Aspig, Aspol,** ARCHIBALD.

Gillett English: 1. from a dim. of the given names GILES, JULIAN, or WILLIAM; see GILL 1.

2. topographic name for someone living at the top of a glen or ravine, from Northern ME *gil(l)* glen (see GILL 2) + *heved* head (OE *heafod*).

Vars. (of 1): **Gillet, Gill(i)att, Giliat, Gillyatt, Gil(l)iot, Gilyot(t); Gillot(t)** (chiefly S Yorks.); **Jillett, Jillitt, Jellett; Gillette** (a fem. form).

Gillibrand England (Lancs.): from a Norman personal name *Gillebrand*, composed of the Gmc elements *gīsil* hostage + *brand* sword.

Vars.: **Gillebrand, Gellibrand.**

Gillies Scots: from the Gael. personal name *Gilla Iosa* 'servant of Jesus'.

Vars.: **Gillis,** LEES.

Patrs.: **Gillison; McAleese, McAleece, McAlish, McL(e)ish, McLees, McLese, McLise** (also Ir., from Gael. **Mac Gille Iosa** (Sc.), **Mac Giolla Íosa** (Ir.)).

Gilling English: 1. var. of JULIAN.

2. habitation name from places in N Yorks., so called from OE *Gētlingas* or *Gȳðlingas* 'people of *Gētla*' or 'of *Gȳðla*'. The first of these personal names is from a short form of the various cpd names with the tribal name *Gēat* (see JOCELYN) as their first element; the second is from those with a first element *gȳð* battle.

Gillingham English: habitation name from places in Dorset, Norfolk, and Kent, so called from OE *Gȳðlingahām* 'homestead (OE *hām*) of the people of *Gȳðla*'; cf. GILLING 2.

Gillow English: habitation name from a place in Herefords., so called from W *cil* retreat + *llwch* pool.

Gilmartin Irish: Anglicized form of Gael. **Mac Giolla Mhartain**, patr. from the personal name *Giolla Mhartain* 'servant of (St) MARTIN'.

Var.: **Kilmartin.**

Gilmore 1. Scots and Irish: Anglicized form of Gael. **Mac Gille Mhoire** (Sc.), **Mac Giolla Mhuire** (Ir.), patrs. from personal names meaning 'servant of (the Virgin) Mary'.

2. English: habitation name from *Gillamoor* in N Yorks., so called from the nearby town of GILLING + OE *mōr* moor, marsh (see MOORE 1).

Vars. (of 1): **Gillmor(e), Gilmour, Gilmer, Kilmore; McGilmore, McGilmour, McGilmurry, McGillworry, McIlmurray, McElmurray;** MURRAY.

Gilpin Irish: Anglicized form of Gael. **Mac Giolla Fionn** 'son of the fair-haired lad'; cf. FINN 1.

Gilroy Irish: Anglicized form of Gael. **Mac Giolla Ruaidh** 'son of the red-haired lad'; cf. ROY 1.

Vars.: **McGillaro(w)e, McGil(la)roy, McKillroe, (Mc)Kilroy, (Mc)Ilroy, McElroy, McAlroy, McLeroy.**

Gimpel Jewish (Ashkenazic): 1. from the Yid. male given name *Gimpl*, a deriv. of the Ger. given name *Gumprecht* (cogn. of *Gundbert*; see GOMBERT).

2. ornamental name from mod. Ger. *Gimpel* bullfinch, or an unflattering surname from the same word in the sense 'dunce, dupe, simpleton', bestowed by anti-Semitic government officials in 18th- and 19th-cent. central Europe.

Vars.: **Gimpl**; **Gimbel** (W Ashkenazic).

Patrs. (of 1): **Gimp(e)levitch** (E Ashkenazic).

Gingell English (common in Bristol): of unknown origin.

Vars.: **Gingold**, **Gingle**.

Ginn 1. English: metonymic occupational name for a trapper, or nickname for a cunning person, from ME *gin* trick, contrivance, snare (an aphetic form of ME *engin*; see INGHAM 2).

2. Irish: Anglicized form of Gael. *Mag Fhinn*; see FINN 1.

Var.: **Gynn**.

Ginsberg Jewish (Ashkenazic): 1. habitation name from *Gunzberg* in Bavaria, so called from OHG *gen(e)st*, *gin(e)st* gorse (L *(planta) genesta*; see GENEST) + *berg* hill (see BERG).

2. habitation name from *Günzburg* in Swabia, which derives its name from the river *Günz* (in early L records *Guntia*, probably of Celt. origin) + OHG *burg* fortress, town.

3. possibly also a habitation name from *Gintsshprik*, the Yid. name of *Königsberg* ('King's hill') in E Prussia, now Kaliningrad in the Soviet Union.

Vars.: **Ginsberger**, **G(h)inzberg**, **Gunsberg(er)**, **Gunzberg**, **Ghinsberg**, **Gincberg**; **Gincbarg** (with Yid. *barg* hill); **Ginsburg**, **Ginsbo(u)rg**, **Ginzb(o)urg**, **Ghinzburg**; **Ginsburski**, **Ginsborski**, **Ginzburski**, **Ginzbursky**. Ginc- is a Pol. spelling; *Ghin-* is a Rumanian spelling; *-bourg* is a Fr. spelling.

Girdwood Scots (SE and central Scotland): habitation name from a place in the parish of Carnwath in the former county of Lanarks. (now part of Strathclyde region). The placename is of uncertain origin, possibly from ME *gerth*, *girth* band, hoop (ON *gjorð*) + *wode* WOOD.

Girona Catalan: habitation name from the town of *Gerona* (Cat. *Girona*) in N Spain. The placename is recorded in L sources in the form *Gerunda*, but it is of pre-Roman origin and unknown meaning.

Vars.: **Giró(n)**; **Gironès**.

Cogn.: Jewish (Sefardic): **Geron**.

Gissing English: habitation name from a place in Norfolk, so called from OE *Gyssingas* 'people of *Gyssa*' or 'of *Gyssi*', an OE or ON personal name representing a short form of the various cpd names with the first element *gīsil* hostage, noble youth (cf., e.g., GILBERT).

Gitter 1. German: topographic name for someone who lived by a gate or barrier, or metonymic occupational name for a janitor, from Ger. *Gitter* grid, grating (MHG *gitter* railing, bar, OHG *getiri*; cf. GATTERER).

2. German: habitation name from a place near Brunswick, which bears an ancient name of uncertain, probably Celt., origin.

3. Jewish (S Ashkenazic): cogn. of GOOD.

Var.: **Gitterman**.

Gitting Welsh: 1. from the W personal name *Gutyn*, *Guto*, a hypocoristic from of *Gruffydd* (see GRIFFITH).

2. possibly also a byname from W *cethin* dusky, swarthy.

Var.: **Gething**.

Patrs.: **Gethings**, **Gettens**, **Gettin(g)s**, **Gittens**, **Gittin(g)s**.

Givenchy French: habitation name from a place in Pas-de-Calais, Picardy, so called from the L personal name *Juventius* + the Gaul. local suffix *-ācum*.

Głąbski Polish: 1. topographic name for someone living in a low-lying spot or at the bottom of a valley, from Pol. *głąb* depth, bottom.

2. nickname for a stupid person, from Pol. *głąb* fool (lit., 'cabbage-stalk') + *-ski* suffix of surnames (see BARANOWSKI).

Vars.: **Głąb**; **Głębski**; **Glomski** (U.S. Anglicization).

Habitation names: **Głąbowski**, **Głębowski**; **Głąbicki**, **Głębocki**.

Glad English: 1. from a short form of the various OE personal names with a first element *glæd* shining, joyful; cf., e.g., GLADWIN.

2. nickname for a cheerful person, from ME *glad* merry, jolly (from the OE element given above).

Var. (of 2): **Gladman**.

Cogns. (of 2): Swed.: **Glad(h)**.

Patrs. (from 1): Eng.: **Glad(d)ing**; **Gladden** (E Anglia).

Gladstone 1. Scots: habitation name from a place near Biggar in the former county of Lanarks. (now part of Strathclyde region), apparently so called from the OE *gleoda* kite + *stān* stone.

2. Jewish (Ashkenazic): Anglicized form of **Glatshteyn**, an ornamental surname composed of the Yid. elements *glat* flat + *shteyn* stone.

Var. (of 1): **Gledstane**.

The first known bearer of the name is Herbert de Gledstan(e) *of the county of Lanark, who took the oath of fealty to Edward I in 1296. The British statesman William Ewart* Gladstone *(1809–98) was born in Liverpool, where his father was a merchant, but he was of pure Scots descent. His mother's family, named Robertson, were from the Highlands, while his father came from Lanarks.*

Gladwin English: from the late OE personal name *Glædwine*, composed of the elements *glæd* shining, joyful + *wine* friend.

Var.: **Gladwyn**.

Glaister Scots: of uncertain origin. The earliest recorded form of the name is *de Glasletter* (1254), which appears to be a habitation name composed of the Gael. elements *glas* green (see GLASS 2) + *leitir* hillside. Later forms such as *de Glacealester* (*c.*1256), *de Glassester* (1368), and *de Glacestre* (1374) seem to have been influenced by the common Eng. placename element *-cester* (OE *cæster* Roman fort). The forms *Glastre* and *Glastir* appear for the first time in the 15th cent.

Glantz Jewish (Ashkenazic): ornamental name from Ger. *Glanz* shine, radiance, Yid. *glants* (MHG, OHG *glanz*, a distant cogn. of GLAD).

Vars.: **Glanz(er)**, **Glantzmann**, **Glanzman**; **Glanzberg** (an ornamental elaboration with Ger. *Berg* hill).

Glanville English (chiefly Devon): 1. Norman habitation name from a place in Calvados, so called from a Gmc personal name of uncertain form and meaning + OF *ville* settlement (see VILLE).

2. habitation name from *Glanvill* Farm in Devon, *Clanville* in Somerset and Hants, or *Clanfield* in Hants, or from

some other place similarly named, all of which are so called from the OE elements *clǣn* clean (i.e. free of brambles and undergrowth) + *feld* pasture, open country (see FIELD).
Vars.: **Glanvill, Glan(d)field.**

Glascott 1. English: habitation name from *Glascote* in Warwicks., so called from OE *glæs* glass + *cot* hut, shelter; it was probably once a site inhabited by a glass blower.
2. Welsh: habitation name from *Glascoed* in the former county of Monmouths., so called from W *glas* grey, green + *coed* wood.
Vars.: **Glasscote, Glasscock.**

Glasgow 1. Scots: local name from the city on the Clyde (first recorded in 1116 as *Glasgu*), or from either of two minor places with the same name in the former county of Aberdeens. The etymology of the placename is much disputed; it is most probably from Brit. words that were the ancestors of W *glas* grey, green, blue + *cau* hollows.
2. Scots and Irish: var. of MCCLUSKEY.
Var. (of 1): **Glasscoe.**

Glass 1. English: metonymic occupational name for a glazier or glass blower, from OE *glæs* glass (akin to GLAD, referring originally to the bright shine of the material).
2. Irish and Scots: Anglicized form of any of various Gael. surnames derived from *glas* grey, green, blue; cf., e.g., MCGLASHAN.
3. Jewish (Ashkenazic): ornamental name from mod. Ger. *Glass* glass, or occupational name for a glazier or glass blower.
Vars. (of 1): **Glaze** (W Midlands); **Glassman; Glazier, Glazyer, Glaisher, Glaysher.** (Of 3): **Glas, Glas(s)er, Glasner, Glazer, Glas(s)man, Glaserman; Glozman** (NE Ashkenazic); **Gluz(er), Gluzman(n), Glusman** (S Ashkenazic); **Gle(j)zer.**
Cogns. (of 1): Ger.: **Glas(man), Glas(n)er, Gläs(en)er.** Flem., Du.: **(Van den) Glas; Glasius** (Latinized). Fris.: **Glastra.** (Of 2): Welsh: **Glace, Lace.** Corn.: **Glasson, Glazzon.**
Cpds (of 3, ornamental except where otherwise stated): **Gluzband** ('glass ribbon'); **Glas(s)berg, Gluzberg** ('glass hill'); **Glassgold** ('glass gold'); **Glassheib** ('pane of glass', perhaps also occupational); **Gluzschneider** ('glass cutter', occupational).
Equivs. (not cogn.): Eng., Fr.: VERRIER. Pol.: SZKLAR. Jewish (Ashkenazic): STECKLER.

Glatz 1. German and Jewish (Ashkenazic): nickname for a bald man, from Ger. *Glatze* baldness, MHG *gla(t)z* bald head, bald (a deriv. of MHG, OHG *glat* smooth, shiny, a cogn. of GLAD).
2. Jewish (Ashkenazic): habitation name from *Glatz*, Ger. name of *Kłodzko* in Lower Silesia.
Vars. (of 2): **Glatzer.**
Dim. (of 1): **Glätzel.**

Glazebrook English: habitation name from a place in Lancs., so called from the *Glaze Brook*, the stream on which it stands (a Brit. name, from a Brit. word that was the ancestor of W *glas* grey, green, blue; cf. GLASS 2) + OE *brōc* stream (see BROOK). The surname is also common in Devon, where it may have an independent origin from a similarly named place, now lost.
Var.: **Glassbrook.**

Glazurin Russian: patr. from the nickname *Glazura*, a deriv. of *glaza* eye, referring to someone with some noticeable peculiarity of the eyes.
Vars.: **Glazyrin, Glazov(oi), Glazeev, Glazachov, Glazatov, Glazunov.**

Gleave English (chiefly Lancs.): metonymic occupational name for a maker and seller of swords or nickname for an accomplished swordsman, from ME *gle(y)ve* sword (OF *gleive, glaive*, L *gladius*).
Vars.: **Glave, Gl(e)aves.**

Glebov Russian: patr. from the given name *Gleb*, which represents an early borrowing, at the time of the Viking settlement of Kiev, of an ON personal name composed of the elements *gúð* battle, combat + *leifr* love. It is one of the few given names of non-Gk origin officially accepted by the Orthodox church, largely as a result of the enormous popularity of St Gleb (d. AD 1010), who actually bore the Christian baptismal name of DAVID.

Gledhill English: habitation name from a place in W Yorks., so called from OE *gleoda* kite (see GLEED) + *hyll* HILL.
Vars.: **Gledall, Gleadell, Gleadle, Gladhill.**

Gleed S English: nickname from ME *glede* kite (OE *gleoda*), probably with reference to the bird's rapacious qualities.
Vars.: **Glede, Glide, Glyde.**

Gleesan Irish: Anglicized form of Gael. **Ó Glasáin** 'descendant of *Glasán*', a personal name from a dim of *glas* grey, green, blue.
Vars.: **Gleeson, Gleason; (O')Gleasan, O'Glesaine, O'Glassane;** GILES.

Glen 1. Scots: topographic name for someone who lived in a valley, Gael. *gleann*, or habitation name from a place named with this word, such as *Glen* near Peebles.
2. English: habitation name from a place in Leics. This bears a Brit. name, probably a cogn. of Gael. *gleann* valley.
3. Jewish (Ashkenazic): presumably an Anglicization of one or more like-sounding Jewish names.
Vars.: **Glenn.** (Of 1 only): GLYNN.

Glendinning Scots: habitation name from a place in the parish of Westerkirk, Dumfries, recorded in 1384 as *Glendonwyne*. It is apparently so called from Brit. ancestors of the W words *glyn* valley (see GLYNN) + *din* fort + *gwyn* fair, white (see GWYN).
Vars.: **Glenden(n)ing, Clendenning, Clendennen, Clindening.**

Glew English (Yorks.): nickname for a cautious, prudent, or wise man, from ME *glew* wise, prudent (OE *gleaw*).
Var.: **Glue.**

Glickin Jewish (E Ashkenazic): metr. from the Yid. female given name *Glike* (from Yid. *glik* luck; cf. GLÜCK) + the Slav. suffix *-in*.
Vars.: **Glikin, Glikovsky; Gli(c)kson, Gluekson** (Ashkenazic; the last form is partly Germanized, as if from Ger. *Glück* luck).

Gliddon English (Devon): apparently a habitation name from an unidentified place, possibly *Glidden* in Hants, which is named with the OE elements *glida* kite + *dūn* hill (see DOWN 1); cf. GLEDHILL.

Glock German: topographic name for someone who lived by the bell tower of a church, or house name from a house marked by the sign of the bell, from Ger. *Glocke* bell (MHG *glocke, glogge*, OHG *glocka*, apparently ultimately from a Celt. source). It could also be a metonymic occupational name for a sexton, who among other duties was responsible for ringing the church bell; *Glockner* is the usual term for a sexton in some parts of Germany (see also KIRCHNER, MESNER, and OPPERMANN).
Vars.: Ger.: **Glocke; Glock(n)er, Glöckner, Glöckler, Glogger.**

Cogns.: Low Ger.: **Klöckner**. Flem.: **Clocke**. Du.: **Klok(ke)**, **Klokman**. Fr.: **Cloche**.

Dims.: Ger.: **Glöckel**, **Glöckl(e)**, **Glockle**, **Glöggl** (S Germany and Austria).

Głogowski Polish and Jewish (E Ashkenazic): habitation name from any of various places named with Pol. *głóg* hawthorn + *-ów* possessive suffix, with the addition of the suffix of local surnames *-ski* (see BARANOWSKI). One such place is *Głogów* in W Poland, the Ger. name of which is *Glogau*.

Cogns.: Jewish (W Ashkenazic): **Glogau**, **Gloger**.

Glossop English: habitation name from a place in N Derbys., so called from the gen. case of the OE byname *Glott* (apparently akin to mod. Eng. *gloat*) + OE *hop* valley.

Gloster English: local name from *Gloucester*, the county town of Gloucs. The place originally bore the Brit. name *Glēvum* (apparently from a cogn. of W *gloyw* bright), to which was added the OE element *ceaster* Roman fort (L *castra* legionary camp).

Glover English: occupational name for a maker or seller of gloves, ME *glovere*, agent noun from OE *glōf* glove.

Głowacki Polish: nickname for a clever person or for someone literally with a big head, from Pol. *głowacz* clever person (from *głowa* head) + *-ski* suffix of surnames (see BARANOWSKI).

Var.: **Głowacz**.

Cogns.: Czech: **Hlaváč** (see also HLAVA).

Dim.: Czech: **Hlaváček**.

Habitation name: Pol.: **Głowiński**.

Glück 1. German: nickname for a individual considered fortunate, perhaps someone who had had a narrow escape, from Ger. *Glück* luck (MHG *g(e)lücke*, of uncertain origin, not attested before the late 12th cent.).

2. Jewish (Ashkenazic): ornamental name from mod. Ger. *Glück* luck (Yid. *glik*), or one expressing hope for good luck in the future.

Vars. (of 2): **Glu(e)ck**, **Gli(c)k**; **Gluckman(n)**, **Glueckman**, **Gluecksmann**, **Glucksman**, **Gli(c)k(s)man**; **Glucker**, **Glik(n)er**; **Gluecklich**, **Glicklich** (from the adj. *glücklich* (Ger.), Yid. *gliklekh*, both meaning 'lucky'); **Glucksam**, **Gliksam** (pseudo-German, with the adj. ending *-sam*).

Cogns. (of 1): Flem.: **Geluk**. Dan.: **Lykke**.

Cpds (of 2): **Gli(c)ksberg** ('luck hill'); **Glekfeld** ('luck field'); **Glueckselig** ('blissful', expressing hope for a blissful future condition); **Glueckstadt** ('luck city'); **Gluckstein**, **Gli(c)kstein**, **Gluckshtin** ('luck stone'); **Glueckstern** ('luck star').

Glynn 1. Cornish and Welsh: topographic name for someone who lived in a valley, Corn. *glin*, W *glyn*.

2. Scots: var. of GLEN 1.

Vars. (of 1): **Glynne**, **Glyn(e)**.

A number of bearers of the name Glynn *can be traced to the manor of Glynn near Bodmin, Cornwall, where Hubert* de Glin *was living in 1100.*

Gobbi Italian (chiefly Lombardy and Venetia): nickname for a hunchback, from the N Italian regional term *gobbo*.

Var.: **Gobbo**.

Dims.: **Gob(b)etti**, **Gobbetto**, **Gobbini**.

Patrs.: **De Gob(b)i(s)**.

Gobel French: metonymic occupational name for a maker or seller of goblets and tankards, from OF *gobel* drinking vessel, cup (of Celt. origin; cf. GOBET). The surname is also borne by Ashkenazic Jews, the reason(s) for its adoption being unknown.

Vars.: **Gobeau(x)**, **Goubel**, **Goubeau**; **Goublier**.

Dims.: **Gobelet**, **Gobelot**, **Gobelin**.

Gobet French: nickname for a proud or boastful man, from OF *gobet* haughty, vainglorious (apparently from Celt. *gob* mouth, cf. GOBEL).

Var.: **Goubet**.

Godbert English: from a medieval given name, *Godebert*, composed of the Gmc elements *gōd* good or *god*, *got* god + *berht* bright, famous. The name was popularized in England by the Normans, but probably absorbed an OE form **Godbeorht*. An Exeter moneyer named *Godbryt* is recorded in the reign of King Canute (1016–35).

Vars.: **Gobert**; **Godber** (E Midlands).

Cogns.: Fr.: **Gobert**, **Gobart**. Ger.: **Go(de)brecht**, **Godebert**, **Gobbert**, **Göbbert**.

Dims.: Fr.: **Gobin(ot)**. Ger.: **Gobbel**, **Goppel(t)**, **Göb(b)el**. See also GODBOLD.

Patrs. (from dims.): Ger.: **Göbbels**, **Göbler**.

Godbold English: from a Norman personal name, *Godebald*, composed of the Gmc elements *gōd* good or *god*, *got* god + *bald* bold, brave.

Vars.: **Godbolt**, **Godball**, **Goble**.

Goddard English (Norman) and French: from *Godhard*, a personal name composed of the Gmc elements *gōd* good or *god*, *got* god + *hard* hardy, brave, strong. The name was popular in Europe during the Middle Ages as a result of the fame of St Goddard, an 11th-cent. bishop of Hildesheim who founded a hospice on the pass from Switzerland to Italy that bears his name. This surname and the var. *Godard* are also borne by Ashkenazic Jews, presumably as an Anglicization of one or more like-sounding Jewish surnames.

Vars.: Eng.: **Godard**, **Godart**. Fr.: **Go(u)dard**, **Godar(t)**.

Cogns.: Ger.: GOTHARD, **Gotthard(t)**. Low Ger.: **Godehard**, **Goddert**, **Göddert**, **Göttert**, **Goh(e)rt**. Flem., Du.: **Goedhard**, **Goedhart**. Fris.: **Gord**, **Jordt**. Hung.: **Got(t)hárd**.

Patrs.: Low Ger.: **Göddertz**; **Gäderts** (N Rhineland).

Patrs. (from dims.): Low Ger.: **Gödden**, **Gudden**.

Godfrey English: from a Norman personal name, *Godefrei*, *Godefroi(s)*, composed of the Gmc elements *god*, *got* god + *fred*, *frid* peace. See also JEFFREY.

Vars.: **Godfray**, **Godfree**, **Godfer**, **Gotfrey**.

Cogns.: Fr.: **Godefroi**, **God(e)froy**, **God(e)frey**; **Godfroid** (assimilated by folk etymology to the word *froid* cold). It.: **Goffredo**; **Gioffredo** (Sicily, Piedmont, Liguria); **Giof(f)re**, **Giuffre**, **Giuffri**; **Loffreda**, **Loffredo**. Ger.: **Got(t)fried**, **Godfried**, **Gotfert**, **Göpfert**, **Göppert**, **Gepfert**, **Geppert**. Low Ger.: **Govert**, **Goffer**, **Goffarth**. Flem.: **Go(de)vaard**.

Dims.: Fr.: **Godfr(a)in**, **Goefrain(t)**.

Patrs.: Low Ger.: **Godeferding**, **Godtfring**; **Goverts**, **Jovers**. Du.: **Govers**. Dan.: **Gotfredsen**.

There is an Irish family of the name Godfrey *who originated in Romney, Kent. The first of them to settle in Ireland was Colonel John Godfrey, who was rewarded with lands in Kerry for his services in the 1641 rebellion.*

Godin French and English: from the Gmc personal name *Godino*, a dim. short form of the various cpd names with the first element *god*, *got* god (cf. e.g. GODBERT, GODBOLD, GODDARD, and GODFREY).

Vars.: Fr.: **Gohin**, **Go(u)in** (see also GWYN). Eng.: **Godden**.

Cogns.: Prov.: **Gody**. Sp.: **Godino**. Port.: **Godinho**.

Dims.: Fr.: **Godineau**, **Godinet**; **Gouineau**. Prov.: **Godinou(x)**.

Patr.: Sp.: **Godínez**.

Godley English: habitation name from *Godley* in Ches. or *Goodleigh* in Devon, both of which are so called from the OE byname *Gōda* 'Good' + OE *lēah* wood, clearing.

Vars.: **Godly**; **Goodl(e)y**; **Goodleigh** (a place in Devon).

Godolphin Cornish: habitation name from a place in the parish of Breage, which is of unknown etymology.

Godoy Spanish: habitation name from a place in Galicia. The origin of the placename is uncertain, but a connection has been suggested with the Goth. elements *guðs* god + *wīhs* saint.

Godson English: nickname for someone who was the godson (ME *godsune*) of an influential or powerful member of the community, from OE *god* god + *sunu* son. A master would sometimes bestow a special favour on a trusted servant by agreeing to stand godfather to his first child. There has also been some confusion with Goodson.

Godunov Russian: patr. from the nickname *Godun* (a deriv. of *goditsya* to idle, enjoy oneself), denoting a lazy and self-indulgent person.

Gofton English (Northumb.): habitation name from a minor place, perhaps *Gofton* in Simonburn, Northumb., earlier *Gofden*, from OE *denu* valley (see Dean 1), with an uncertain first element.

Gogh Low German: habitation name from any of the various minor places which get their names from an ancient Gmc element *goch*, *gog* marsh, bog, fen.

Var.: **Goch**.

Cogns.: Du.: **Van Gog(h)**.

Gogol Ukrainian and Jewish (E Ashkenazic): nickname or ornamental name from Ukr. *gogol* wild duck, denoting a hunter of the birds or acquired on account of some other association with them.

Cogn. (habitation name): Pol.: **Gogolewski**.

Goguin French: nickname for a person of easy-going temperament and large appetite, from a dim. of OF *gogue* enjoyment, relaxation, used in some areas also in the more concrete sense 'pudding'; the word is apparently of imitative origin.

Vars.: **Goguy**, **Goguel**.

Dims.: **Goguineau**, **Goguillon**.

Aug.: **Goguelat**.

Goicoechea Spanish form of Basque **Goikoetxea**: topographic name for someone who lived in a house situated on a hill or in the upper part of a village, from Basque *goiko* upper (a deriv. of *goi* top; cf. Goya) + *etxe* house + the def. art. *-a*.

Goiri Basque: topographic name for someone who lived near the top of a hill or the upper part of a village, from *goi* top (see Goya) + the suffix *-iri* near.

Goitia Basque: topographic name for someone who lived on the top floor of a house or at the top of a hill or in the upper part of a village, from *goiti* top part, attic (composed of *goi* top + the local suffix *-ti*) + the def. art. *-a*.

Golby English: apparently a habitation name from an unidentified place, the name of which could be derived from OE *golde* marigold (a deriv. of *gold* Gold) + ON *býr* farm, settlement. The surname is commonest in the W Midlands, but a placename formed with ON *býr* is not likely to occur in that area; the name is therefore either an alteration of some other name or an importation from further North. It could be a collapsed form of Goldsby or a mincing variant of Goodby.

Gold 1. English and German: metonymic occupational name for someone who worked in gold (OE, OHG *gold*)—a refiner, jeweller, or gilder.

2. English and German: nickname for someone with bright yellow hair, with reference to the colour of the metal.

3. English: from an OE personal name *Golda* (or the fem. *Golde*) which persisted into the Middle Ages as a given name. The name was in part a byname from *gold* gold, and in part a short form of the various cpd names with this first element.

4. Jewish (Ashkenazic): ornamental name from mod. Ger. *Gold*, Yid. *gold* gold. In the U.S. it is often a shortened form of any of the compounds listed below.

Vars. (of 1, 2, and 3): Eng: **Goold**, **Gould**. (Of 1 and 2): Eng.: **Goldman**. (Of 1 only): Eng.: **Gilder**. Ger.: **Göldner**, **Göllner**, **Geldner**, **Gellner**. (Of 2 only): Eng.: **Go(o)lden**, **Goulden**. (Of 4) Jewish: Golder, **Goldner**, **Goldman(n)**.

Patrs. (from 3): Eng.: **Golds**, Golding.

Cpds (of 4; ornamental unless otherwise stated): Jewish: **Goldbach** ('golden stream'); **Goldband** ('golden ribbon'); **Goldbaum**, **Goldboim** ('golden tree'); **Goldberg**, **Golde(r)nberg** ('golden hill'); **Goldberger** ('person from golden hill'); **Goldblat** ('golden leaf'); **Goldblum** ('golden flower', Anglicized as **Goldbloom**); **Goldbren(n)er** ('gold melter', occupational name for a goldsmith); **Goldbruch** ('gold quarry'); **Goldfaber** ('goldsmith', occupational: see Faber); **Goldfaden** ('golden thread'); **Gold(en)farb** ('golden colour'); **Goldfeder** ('golden feather'); **Goldfein**, **Goldfajn** ('fine as gold', Anglicized as **Goldfine**; *-fajn* is a Pol. spelling); **Gold(en)feld** ('golden field'); **Goldfinger** ('golden finger'); **Goldfis(c)h** ('golden fish'); **Goldfis(c)her**; **Goldflam** ('golden flame'); **Goldfleiss** ('golden assiduousness'); **Goldfracht** ('golden freight'); **Goldfri(e)d** ('golden peace'); **Goldfus** ('golden foot', Anglicized as **Goldfoot**); **Goldgart** ('golden garden'); **Goldgewicht** ('golden weight'); **Goldglass** ('golden glass'); **Goldgraber** ('gold digger'); **Goldgrub** ('gold mine'); **Goldhaber** ('possessor of gold' or 'golden oats'); **Goldham(m)er** ('golden hammer'); **Goldhand** ('golden hand'); **Goldhar** ('golden hair', perhaps taken by a blond person); **Goldhecht** ('golden pike'); **Goldhirs(c)h** ('golden deer'); **Goldenhol(t)z** ('golden wood'); **Goldenhorn** ('golden horn'); **Goldkind** ('golden child'); **Goldklang** ('golden sound'); **Goldkorn** ('golden rye'); **Goldkrantz**, **Goldkranc** ('golden wreath', *-kranc* is a Pol. spelling); **Goldlust** ('golden pleasure'); **Goldmacher** ('gold maker', occupational or nickname); **Goldmin(t)z**, **Goldminc** ('gold coin', *-minc* is a Pol. spelling); **Goldmund** ('golden mouth'); **Goldnadel** ('golden needle'); **Goldrat(h)** ('golden counsel'); **Goldreich** ('golden kingdom' or 'rich in gold'); Goldring; **Goldrosen** ('golden roses'); **Goldenrot** ('golden red'); **Goldsand** ('golden sand'); **Goldschein** ('golden shine'); **Goldschla(e)ger** ('gold beater', occupational); **Goldsobel** ('golden sable'); **Gold(en)stein** ('gold stone', Anglicized as Goldstone); **Goldstern** ('golden star'); **Goldstoff** ('golden fabric'); **Goldstrom** ('golden stream'); **Goldstuck** ('gold coin'); **Goldenthal** ('golden valley'); **Goldwasser**, **Goldvasser** ('golden water', Anglicized as **Goldwater**); **Goldwein** ('golden wine', Anglicized as Goldwin); **Goldwei(t)z** ('golden wheat'); **Goldwerger** (occupational, from Yid. *goldvarger* dealer in items made of gold); **Goldwirth** ('golden host'); **Goldworm** ('golden worm'); **Goldzimmer** ('golden room'); **Goldzweig** ('golden twig'). Of 2 (ornamental): Swed.: **Gullberg** ('gold hill'); **Gullström** ('gold river'); **Gyllenhammar** ('golden hammer'); **Gyllensten** ('golden stone').

Golde Jewish (Ashkenazic): from the Yid. female given name *Golde* 'Gold'.

Var.: **Golda**.

Metrs.: **Goldes**, **Goldis**; **Goldin** (E Ashkenazic).

Golder 1. English: from the OE personal name *Goldhere*, composed of the elements *gold* gold + *here* army.

2. English: habitation name from a place in Oxon., so called from OE *golde* marigold (a deriv. of *gold* GOLD) + *ōra* slope.

3. Jewish: var. of GOLD.

Goldfinch English: nickname from the bird, a cpd of OE *gold* GOLD + *finc* FINCH.

Goldie Scots: 1. dim. of GOLD.

2. nickname for a wall-eyed person with an unnatural pigmentation of one eye, from ME *gold* GOLD + *ie* eye (OE *eage*).

Vars.: **Gou(l)die, Gou(l)dy.** (Of 2 only): **Goldney.**

Golding 1. English: from the late OE personal name *Golding*, formally a patr. from *Golda* 'Gold' (see GOLD 3).

2. Jewish (Ashkenazic): habitation name from *Golding*, the Yid. name of the town of *Kuldīga* in Latvia.

Goldingay English (W Midlands): apparently a habitation name from an unidentified place. There is a field-name, *Goldenhays*, in Frodsham, Ches., which was *Goulding Hey* in 1684, from ME *golden* golden + *hey* enclosure (see HAY 1). This may once have been a habitation name, and could be the source of the surname.

Goldring 1. English, German, and Jewish (Ashkenazic): from the ME, Ger., or Yid. elements *gold* + *ring*. As an Eng. or Ger. surname it is most probably a nickname for someone who wore a gold ring. As a Jewish surname it is generally an ornamental name.

2. Scots: according to Black, a habitation name from the old 50-shilling lands of Goldring in the bailiary of Kylestewart.

The name is found in England as early as 1230, when Thomas Goldring *is recorded as holding property in Essex and Herts. The name was quite common in London, Sussex, and Hants from early times, and descendants of these bearers are now also well established in Canada. The first known bearer in Scotland is Thomas* of Goldringe, *who held land in Prestwick in 1511.*

Goldsby English: habitation name from *Goulceby* in Lincs., *Colchesbi* in Domesday Book. Ekwall states that the 'correct' form of the name is *Golkesby*, which would indicate derivation from the gen. case of a personal name **Golk* + ON *býr* farm, settlement. In view of the Domesday Book form, however, Ekwall's other suggestion, that the first element is from the attested ON byname *Kolkr*, seems more plausible.

Goldsmith English: occupational name for a worker in gold, a cpd of OE *gold* GOLD + *smið* SMITH. To a large extent it is an Anglicized form of Ger. or Jewish (Ashkenazic) **Goldschmid(t).**

Cogns.: Flem., Du.: **Goudsmit, Goudsmid, Goudsmet.**

Equivs. (not cogn.): Russ. and other Slav. names: ZOLOTARYOV. Jewish: ZOREF. Hung.: EÖTVÖS.

Goldspink English (E Anglia): nickname from the GOLDFINCH. ME *spink* was another name for the finch, probably of imitative origin and largely confined to the N English dialects.

Goldstone English: 1. Anglicized form of Jewish (Ashkenazic) *Goldstein*; see GOLD.

2. from the OE personal name *Goldstān*, composed of the elements *gold* gold + *stān* stone.

3. habitation name from a place in Shrops., so called from the gen. case of the OE personal name *Golda* (see GOLD 3) + OE *stān* stone; or from one in Kent, recorded in the early 13th cent. as *Goldstanestun* 'settlement (OE *tūn*) of *Goldstān*'.

Vars. (of 3): **Goldston, Gouldstone, Goulston(e), Gols(t)on, Guls(t)on.**

Goldthorpe English (Yorks.): habitation name from a place in W Yorks., so called from the OE personal name *Golda* 'GOLD' + OE *þorp* farm, village.

Goldwin 1. English: from the OE personal name *Goldwine*, composed of the elements *gold* gold + *wine* friend.

2. Jewish (Ashkenazic): Anglicized form of *Goldwein*, a cpd. of GOLD.

Var.: **Goldwyn.**

Golec Polish: nickname from Pol. *golec* (n. deriv. of the adj. *goły* naked) in various possible senses. The basic meaning is 'naked man' or 'hairless man'. It could therefore be a nickname for someone totally destitute, a naked wretch, which is certainly a meaning of the vocab. word. Equally, if not more plausibly, it could be a nickname for a bald or clean-shaven man.

Var.: **Golis.**

Cogns.: Czech: **Holec, Holík; Holá, Holan, Holas; Holý** (from the cogn. adj. *holý*, also meaning 'naked, bare, clean-shaven').

Dim.: Czech: **Holeček** (also used as a term of endearment, which may lie behind some cases of this surname).

Habitation names: Pol.: **Goliński, Golański.** Czech: **Holíček** (from a placename *Holicky*).

Golightly 1. English: nickname, given perhaps to a messenger, from ME *gō(n)* to go (OE *gān*) + *lihtly* lightly, swiftly (OE *lēoht(līc)*).

2. Scots: altered form of a surname of uncertain origin, possily an unidentified habitation name. The earliest known bearer is William *Galithli*, who witnessed a charter at the beginning of the 13th cent. Henry *Gellatly*, an illegitimate son of William the Lion, of whom little or nothing is known, was the grandfather of Patric *Galythly*, one of the pretenders to the crown of Scotland in 1291.

3. Irish: Anglicized form of Gael. **Mac an Ghallóglaigh** 'son of the gallowglass', Ir. *gallóglach*. A gallowglass was a mercenary retainer or auxiliary soldier (a cpd of *gall* foreigner (see GALL 1) + *óglach* youth, warrior).

Vars. (of 2): **Gallatly, Galletl(e)y, Gelatly, Gelletly.** (Of 3): **Goligher, Goligly, Golagley;** INGOLDSBY, ENGLISH.

Golubev Russian: patr. from the nickname *Golub* 'Dove' (cogn. with Pol. *gołąb* and ultimately with L *columba*; see COLOMB), denoting a mild-mannered or peace-loving man.

Var.: **Golubinski** (name adopted by members of the Orthodox clergy, with reference to the dove as a symbol of the Holy Spirit).

Cogns. (not patrs.): Ukr.: **Holub.** Pol.: **Gołąb.** Czech: **Holub(ec).** Slovene: **Golob.** Ger. (of Slav. origin): **Gollub.** Jewish (E Ashkenazic, ornamental): **Golomb, Golembo.** Hung.: **Galamb.**

Cogns. (patrs.): Beloruss.: **Holubovich.** Slovene: **Golobič.** Croatian: **Golub(ov)ić.** Jewish: **Golobov, Golo(u)bow, Golobovich, Golombovitz, Goloubowitz.**

Dims.: Pol.: **Gołąbik, Gołąbek.** Czech: **Holoubek.** Jewish: **Golombek, Golombik.**

Habitation names: Pol.: **Gołębiewski, Gołębiowski.** Jewish: **Golombursky, Golobiwsky, Golembiewski.**

Gombert French and Low German: from *Gundbert*, a Gmc personal name composed of the elements *gund* battle, strife + *berht* bright, famous. The name was relatively popular in both France and Germany during the Middle Ages, and was also adopted by Ashkenazic Jews (see also GIMPEL).

Vars.: Fr.: **Gombart.** Low Ger.: **Gumbert, Gumpert, Gummert, Gompert, Gommert.**

Cogns.: Ger.: **Gumbrecht, Gumprecht, Gombrich, Gumb(e)rich, Gumprich.** Jewish (Ashkenazic): **Gumpert.**

Patrs.: Low Ger., Du., Flem., and Jewish (Ashkenazic): **Gomper(t)z, Gumper(t)z, Gompers**.

Gomer English: from ME *Godmer*, a blend of two names, OE *Godmær* and ONF *Godmar*, both composed of the Gmc elements *gōd* good or *god* god + *meri*, *mari* famous.

Var.: **Gummer**.

Cogns.: Fr.: **God(e)mer**. Prov.: **Godemar**, **Godmard**. Cat.: **Gomar**, **Gomà**.

Patr.: Eng.: **Gummerson** (Yorks.).

Gomersall English (Yorks.): habitation name from *Gomersal* in W Yorks., so called from the gen. case of an assimilated form of the OE personal name *Gūðmær* (composed of the elements *gūð* battle + *mær* fame) + OE *halh* nook, recess (see Hale 1).

Gomme English: apparently from ME *gome*, OE *guma* man, and so perhaps a nickname or byname, although the exact significance is not clear.

Vars.: **Gomm**, **Goom**; **Gumm(e)**, **Gumb**.

Patrs.: Sp.: **Gómez**. Cat.: **Gomis**. Port.: **Gomes**.

Goncharov Russian: patr. from the occupational term *gonchar* potter, earlier *gornchar* (a deriv. of *gorn* pot).

Cogns.: Beloruss.: **Horshalyov** (patr.). Ukr.: **Honchar** (occupational). Czech: **Hrnčír**. Hung.: **Gerencsér**.

Gonfalonieri N Italian: occupational name for a standard-bearer, either in a military context or as the officer of a guild responsible for carrying the banner in religious processions. It was also a title borne by mayors of the Florentine republic, and by other magistrates designated more specifically as *gonfalonieri di giustizia* ('officers of justice'), *gonfalonieri della chiesa* ('officers of the church'), etc. The word is an agent noun derived from It. *gonfalone* standard, from OF *gonfalon* (of Gmc origin, a cpd of the elements *gund* battle + *fan* flag; cf. Vaandrager).

Var.: **Confalonieri**.

Gonzalo Spanish: from a Gmc personal name first recorded in the L form *Gundisalvus*. The first element is *gund* battle, strife; the second was perhaps originally *sal* hall, later influenced by L *salvus* safe.

Vars.: **Gonzalvo**, **Gozalo**.

Patrs.: Sp.: **Gonzál(v)ez**, **Gosálvez**. Port.: **Gonçaves**.

Good English: 1. nickname from ME *gode* good (OE *gōd*).

2. from a medieval given name, a survival of the OE personal name *Gōda*, which was in part a byname and in part a short form of various cpd names with the first element *gōd*.

Vars.: **Goode**, **G(o)ude**, **Gudd**. (Of 1 only): **Legood** (with fused ANF def. art., as often found in medieval records).

Cogns. (of 1): Ger.: **Gut(h)**, **Guthe**. Low Ger.: **Gode**, **Gude**. Du., Flem.: **Goed**, **De Goede**. Jewish (Ashkenazic): **Gut(t)er**; **Git(t)er** (S Ashkenazic). See also Gute and Goodman.

Patrs. (from 2): Eng.: **Gooding(e)**, **Goodings**; see also Goodson.

Goodall English (chiefly Yorks. and Notts.): 1. habitation name from a place in Yorks., either *Goodall* House, a lost place in Leven, E Yorks., or *Gowdall* in W Yorks., named from OE *golde* marigold + OE *halh* nook, recess (see Hale 1).

2. metonymic occupational nickname for a brewer or innkeeper, from ME *gode* Good + *ale* ale, malt liquor (OE *ealu*).

Vars. (of 1): **Goodhall**. (Of 2): **Gooda(y)le**.

Gooday English: 1. from the OE personal name *Gōddæg*, composed of the elements *gōd* good, auspicious + *dæg* day. There may also have been some confusion with Goodey.

2. nickname for someone who made frequent use of the greeting 'good day', cf. Gooden.

3. forms such as John *de Goday* (Staffs. 1327) suggest that it may occasionally be a habitation name, perhaps from some minor place named with the OE elements *gōd* good + *(ge)hæg* enclosure (see Hay 1). On the other hand, the *de* in these cases may be purely honorific, indicating gentry status.

Cogn.: Jewish (Ashkenazic): **Guttentag** ('good day'; reason for adoption unclear).

Goodbody English: nickname for a good person, from ME *gode* Good + *body* person, creature (OE *bodig*).

Vars.: **Goodboddy**, **Goodbaudy**.

The surname is comparatively common in Ireland, where the earliest known bearer was John Goodbody, *living in Co. Cavan in 1631. During the 18th and 19th cents. most members of the Irish family were Quakers. The earliest known bearer of the name is Richard* Godbodi, *recorded in Coventry, Warwicks., in 1221.*

Goodby English (W Midlands): nickname for someone who made frequent use of the expression 'God be with you', ME *God b'ye*, not necessarily as a farewell. The first syllable was altered under the influence of parallel expressions such as *good day* and *good even* (see Gooday 2 and Gooden), yielding the mod. E vocab. word *goodbye*.

Goodchap English: nickname for a trader who made frequent use of this cry, from ME *gode* Good + *ch(e)ap* bargain, barter (cf. Chapman). The mod. Eng. word *cheap* is a reduction of this phrase.

Var.: **Goodcheap**.

Cogn.: Du.: **Goedkoop**.

Goodchild English (mainly Southern): 1. from a ME given name, a survival of OE *Gōdcild*, composed of the elements *gōd* good + the late OE name-forming element *cild* Child. This name may also have been used in the ME period as a nickname for a good person.

2. nickname for someone who was the godchild of an important member of the community; cf. Godson and its confusion with Goodson.

Cogn.: Ger. and Jewish (Ashkenazic): **Gutkind**.

Gooden English: nickname from frequent use of the ME salutation *(God ye) gooden* 'good evening' (originally *God give you good even*).

Goodenough English: 1. nickname from ME *gode* Good + *enoh* enough (OE *genōh*). Reaney suggests that it was bestowed on one who was easily satisfied; it may also have been used with reference to one whose achievements were average, 'good enough' though not outstanding.

2. possibly also a nickname meaning 'good lad' or 'good servant', from ME *gode knave*, from OE *gōd* Good + *cnafa* boy, servant.

Vars.: **Goodanew**, **Goodnow**, **Goodner**.

It is said that the sons of the Russ. tsar Boris Godunov *settled in England and adopted the surname* Goodenough.

Gooder English: from a ME given name *Godere*, OE *Gōdhere*, composed of the elements *gōd* good + *here* army.

Vars.: **Goodere**, **Gooda**, **Gouda**.

Patr.: **Gooders**.

Goodey English: 1. from a ME female given name *Godeve*, OE *Gōdgifu*, composed of the elements *gōd* good or *god* god + *gifu* gift. This name has perhaps absorbed a less common name with the second element *gūð* battle.

2. nickname for a widow or an independent woman, from ME *goodwife* mistress of a house (from OE *gōd* good + *wīf* woman; cf. GOODMAN 1).

Vars.: **Goodee, Good(d)y, Goodiff, Goodeve,** GOODAY.

Metr.: **Goodison** (Northern).

Up to the mid-15th cent. the surname Goodey *seems to have been confined to NW Essex.*

Goodfellow English: nickname for a congenial companion, from ME *gode* GOOD + *felawe* FELLOW.

Goodfriend English: nickname for a reliable friend or neighbour, from ME *gode* GOOD + *frend* FRIEND.

Cogns.: Jewish (Ashkenazic): **Gut(t)freund.**

Goodhew English: 1. nickname for a trusted servant, from ME *gode* GOOD + *hewe* servant (a deriv. of OE *hīwan* retinue, household).

2. from an ON personal name, composed of the elements *guð* battle + *hugi* mind, spirit.

Vars.: **Goodhue, Goodhugh.**

Goodlad Scots (common in Orkney and Shetland): nickname for a trusted servant, from ME *gode* GOOD + *ladde* lad, servant (see LADD); cf. GOODHEW 1, GOODENOUGH 2, and GOODSWEN.

Vars.: **Goodlatt, Goodlet(t).**

Goodman English: 1. status name from ME *gode* GOOD + *man* man, in part from use as a term for the master of a household; cf. GOODEY 2. In Scotland the term was used of a landowner, however large his estate, who held his land not directly from the crown but from a feudal vassal of the king.

2. from a ME given name *Godeman*, OE *Gōdmann*, composed of the elements *gōd* good or *god* god + *mann* man.

3. from the OE personal name *Gūðmund*, composed of the elements *gūð* battle + *mund* protection, or the ON cogn. *Guðmundr*.

4. Jewish (Ashkenazic): Anglicization of any of the Jewish surnames given below.

Vars.: **Goudman; God(d)man.**

Cogns. (of 1): Ger.: **Gut(t)mann, Gutermann.** Low Ger.: **Gothmann, Godemann, Gudemann.** Jewish (Ashkenazic): **Gutman** (also used as a male given name, from which the surname may in some cases be derived), **Gutmann, Guttman(n); Gut(t)erman; Git(t)erman** (S Ashkenazic).

Patrs. (from 1): Flem., Du.: **Goemans.** (From 3): Swed.: **Gudmundsson.**

Goodrum English (mainly Norfolk): from the ON personal name *Guðormr*, composed of the elements *guð* battle + *ormr* snake, serpent.

Vars.: **Goodram, Gooderham, Guthrum.**

Goodsir English: 1. nickname for an elderly and venerable gentleman, from ME *goodsire* grandfather, a cpd of *gode* GOOD + *sir(e)*, a form of respect.

2. nickname for one who used the expression 'good sir' to excess as a term of address.

Goodson English (chiefly E Anglia and E Midlands): 1. nickname for a dutiful son, from ME *gode* GOOD + *sune* son.

2. from a ME survival of the OE personal name *Gōdsunu*, composed of the elements *gōd* good + *sunu* son. See also GODSON.

Cogn. (of 1): Jewish (Ashkenazic): **Guterson.**

Goodswen English (chiefly Norfolk): nickname for a trusted servant, from ME *gode* GOOD + *sweyn* servant (see SWAN 2).

Goodwill English (Yorks.): nickname for a friendly or amiable person, from ME *gode* GOOD + *will* desire (OE *willa*). The cpd is attested in the sense 'favourable disposition' since before the Norman Conquest.

Goodwin English: from the ME personal name *Godewyn*, OE *Gōdwine*, composed of the elements *gōd* good + *wine* friend.

Vars.: **Godwin, Godwyn.**

Goodyear English: from ME *gode* GOOD (OE *gōd*) + *year* year (OE *gear*), of uncertain application as a surname.

Vars.: **Goodyer, Goodier, Goudier, Goodger, Gudger.**

Cogn.: Ger.: **Gutjahr.**

Goose English (now chiefly E Anglia): nickname for a foolish person or metonymic occupational name for a breeder of geese, from OE *gōs* goose. In both Eng. and Low Ger. there has been some confusion with forms of JOYCE.

Var.: **Gooseman.**

Cogns.: Ger.: **Gans(er), Gan(t)z, Gansmann; Gansner, Gansler, Gänsler; Gonser** (Swabia). Low Ger.: **Gaus, Goos; Goosmann; Gauser.** Flem., Du.: **(De) Gans, Degoes.** Jewish (Ashkenazic): **Gan(t)z, Gandz, Gans, Ganc, Gens** (ornamental); **Gansler, Gensler; Genzman** (occupational). Czech: **Hous(k)a.** Pol.: GĄSIOR.

Dims.: Ger.: **Gansl, Genslein, Gänsli.** Low Ger.: **Gäusgen, Gösgen.** Jewish: **Ganzel, Gans(e)l, Genzel.**

Goosey English: 1. nickname from a place in Berks., so called from OE *gōs* GOOSE + *ēg* island.

2. nickname from OE *gōs* GOOSE + *ēage* eye.

Var.: **Goozee.**

American and Canadian bearers of the name Goozee *are descended from the Englishman William Ellinger Goozee (d. 1890), clerk and sexton to the parish of Ringwould, Kent, members of whose family have been established in the U.S. and Canada since 1883.*

Gordeev Russian: patr. from the given name *Gordei*, earlier *Gordi* (from Gk *Gordios*, a name of uncertain and probably non-Gk etymology, borne by the legendary king of Phrygia who tied the 'Gordian knot', which was untied only when Alexander the Great cut it through with his sword). It was also the name of a saint martyred under Diocletian in AD 304 and much venerated in the Orthodox Church.

Dim.: Ukr.: **Hordienko** (Russianized as **Gordienko**).

Gordo Spanish and Jewish (Sefardic): nickname for a fat man, from Sp. *gordo* fat (LL *gurdus*, of uncertain origin). The word is attested as a Sp. byname, though not as a hereditary surname, as early as the 11th cent.

Dim.: **Gordillo.**

Aug.: **Gordón.**

Gordon 1. Scots: habitation name from a place in the former county of Berwicks. (now part of Borders region), apparently so called from Brit. words that were ancestors of W *gor* spacious + *din* fort.

2. English (Norman): habitation name from *Gourdon* in Saône-et-Loire, so called from the Gallo-Roman personal name *Gordus* + the local suffix *-o, -ōnis*.

3. Irish: Anglicized form of Gael. **Mag Mhuirneacháin**, patr. from the personal name *Muirneachán*, a dim. of *muirneach* beloved.

4. French: nickname for a fat man, from a dim. of OF *gort, gord* fat (see GORDO).

5. Jewish (E Ashkenazic): probably a habitation name from the Beloruss. city of *Grodno* (Lithuanian *Gardinas*, whence the E Ashkenazic surnames **Gardin(ski)**). It goes

back at least to 1657. It was widespread among Jews in Poland by the end of the 17th cent., when two naturalized Polish noblemen, Henry and George Gordon, obtained legislation to prevent its continued adoption by Jews. Various suggestions, more or less fanciful, have been put forward as to its origin. Kaganoff believes it to be an 'Anglicized' form of Russ. *gorodin* townsman (from *gorod* town), but Anglicization was not a factor in E Europe in the 17th cent. There is a family tradition among some bearers that they are descended from a son of the Duke of Gordon who converted to Judaism in the 18th cent., but this would seem to be pure fantasy: the Jewish surname was in existence long before the 18th cent. Others claim descent from earlier Scottish converts, but the Jewish surname existed long before any non-Jew named Gordon converted to Judaism.

Vars. (of 1–4): **G(o)urdon**. (Of 3 only): **McGournaghan, McGounasan**. (Of 4 only): **Gordet, Gordin**. (Of 5): **Gordin**.

Patrs. (from 5): **Gordonoff, Gordonowitz**.

The first bearer of the name recorded in Scotland is Richer de Gordun, *who held the barony of Gordon in the mid-12th cent. Most modern bearers can trace their descent to Sir Adam* de Gordon *(d. 1333), a powerful statesman and soldier. There are reckoned to be 157 branches of the family, and titles they have held include Lord of Strathbogie, Duke of Gordon, Earl of Aboyne, and Earl and Marquess of Huntly. Members have included Lord George Gordon (1751–93), whose name was given to the anti-Catholic 'Gordon riots', and, through the female line, the poet Lord Byron.*

Gore 1. English: habitation name from any of the various places, for example in Kent and Wilts., so called from OE *gāra* triangular piece of land (a deriv. of *gār* spear, with reference to the triangular shape of a spearhead).

2. French: nickname for a gluttonous and idle individual, from OF *gore* sow (of allegedly imitative origin, reflecting the grunting of the animal).

Vars. (of 1): Eng.: **Gorer**, GORMAN. (Of 2): Fr.: **Lagore**.

Cogn. (of 1): Du.: **Vergeer**.

Dims. (of 2): Fr.: **Go(u)ret, Gor(r)on, Gorin, Go(u)ry, Gorel, Go(u)reau, Gorichon, Gori(ll)ot**.

Pej. (of 2): Fr.: **Goraud**.

Goreham English (Norfolk): apparently a habitation name from an unidentified place, so called from OE *gāra* triangular piece of land (see GORE 1) + *hām* homestead.

Var.: **Gorham**.

Gorelik Jewish (Ashkenazic): occupational name for a distiller, Yid. *gorelik* (from a Slav. verb meaning literally 'to burn'; cf. BRENNER 1).

Vars.: **Gorelick, G(o)ralni(c)k, Gorlnik; Gareli(c)k** (among Beloruss. Jews; Anglicized GARLICK); **Guralni(c)k** (among Ukr. Jews).

Goren Jewish (Ashkenazic): altered form of HORN 5 under Russ. influence, since Russ. has no /h/ and alters /h/ in borrowed words to /g/. In Israel the name has been reinterpreted by folk etymology as being from Hebr. *goren* threshing floor, which is in fact etymologically and semantically unrelated.

Var.: **Gorenn**.

Cpd: **Gorenstein** (alteration, under Russ. influence, of *Hornstein*; see cpds of HORN).

Gorfinkel Jewish (Ashkanzic): ornamental name or metonymic nickname meaning 'carbuncle', from Yid. *gorfinkl* or Ger. *Karfunkel* (MHG *carbunkel* jewel, diamond, from LL *carbunculus*, a deriv. of *carbo* glowing coal; cf. CARBONELL). The vocab. word denoted both a red precious or semi-precious stone, esp. a garnet or ruby cut into a rounded shape, or a large inflamed area of skin like a large boil.

Vars.: **Gorfunkel, Garfinkel, Gorfunkel, Garfunkel; Karfunkel** (from Ger. *Karfunkel*); **Karfunkiel** (Pol. spelling), **Gurfinkiel** (S Ashkenazic).

Cogn.: Flem.: **Carbonkel**.

Gorge English and French: topographic name for someone who lived by or in a deep valley, from ME, OF *gorge* gorge, ravine (from OF *gorge* throat, LL *gurga*, from class. L *gurges* whirlpool). There are various places in England and France named with this word, and the surname may be a habitation name from any of these.

Vars.: Eng.: **Gordge, Gorch, Gorges**.

Dims.: Fr.: **Gorgeau, Gorgeon, Gorgeot**.

A family by the name of Gorges *originated in the village of Gorges near Périers in Normandy, where Ralph* de Gorges *was living in the late 11th cent. A branch of the family was established in England when Thomas de Gorges lost his lands to the King of France. He became warden of Henry III's manor of Powerstock, Devon.*

Goring 1. English: habitation name from places in Oxon. and W Sussex, so called from OE *Gāringas* 'people of *Gāra*', a short form of the various cpd names with the first element *gār* spear. For the change of OE *-ā-* to Southern ME *-ō-*, cf. ROPER.

2. Jewish (Ashkenazic): of unknown origin.

Vars.: **Gorin**. (Of 1 only): **Gor(r)inge**.

Gorman 1. English: from the ME given name *Gormund*, OE *Gārmund*, composed of the elements *gār* spear + *mund* protection.

2. English: topographic name for someone who lived by or on a triangular patch of land; see GORE 1.

3. Irish: Anglicized form of Gael. **Mac Gormáin** and **Ó Gormáin** 'son' and 'descendant of *Gormán*', a personal name from a dim. of *gorm* blue.

4. Jewish (Ashkenazic): of unknown origin.

Vars. (of 1): **Garman, Garment**. (Of 3): **MacGorman, O'Gorman**.

Gormley Irish: Anglicized form of Gael. **Ó Gormghaile** 'descendant of *Gormghal*', a personal name from *gorm* noble + *gal* valour.

Vars.: **O'Gorm(e)ley, O'Gorumley, O'Grimley, Gormilly, Germly, Grumley**, GRIMLEY.

Gornall English (Lancs.): apparently a habitation name from a place so called, perhaps *Gornal(wood)* near Birmingham, which probably derives its name from OE *cweorn* mill + *halh* recess, hollow (see HALE 1).

Gorokhov Russian: patr. from the nickname *Gorokh* 'Pea', given perhaps to a market gardener or to a very small man.

Cogn.: Czech: **Hrach**.

Habitation names: Pol.: **Grochowski, Grochocki, Grochulski**. Czech: **Hráský, Hrachovec**. Jewish (E Ashkenazic): **Gorochov(ski), Gorohovski**.

Gorostiaga Basque: topographic name for someone who lived near a holly tree, from *gorosti* holly + the local suffix *-aga*.

Gorostiza Basque: topographic name for someone who lived in an area thickly grown with holly bushes, from *gorosti* holly + the suffix of abundance *-tza*.

Gorse 1. French: habitation name from any of various minor places, all of which are probably named from a Celt. word denoting a hawthorn hedge (cf. OIr. *garb* rough).

2. English: topographic name for someone who lived in an area overgrown with gorse bushes, from OE *gors(t)* gorse (apparently ultimately cogn. with 1).

Vars. (of 1): **Gorsse, Gorce, Lagorce.** (Of 2): **Gorst.**

Górski Polish and Jewish (E Ashkenazic): topographic name for someone who lived on a hillside or in a mountainous district, from Pol. *góra* mountain, hill + the surname suffix *-ski* (see BARANOWSKI). See also ZAGÓRSKI.

Vars.: Pol.: **Góral**; **Górny** (from the adj.); **Górak, Górczak, Górniak**; **Górniok** (Silesian); **Górnicki, Górecki.** Jewish: **Gorsky, Gurski, Gursky**; **Goretzki, Guretzky**; **Gora, Gura.**

Cogns.: Russ.: **Gornykh.** Beloruss.: **Horetski.** Ukr.: **Hirnyak.** Czech: **Hora, Horák, Horský.** Bulg.: **Goranov** (see also GREGORY).

Dims.: Pol.: **Gór(al)czyk.** Czech: **Horáček, Horálek.**

Habitation names: Pol.: **Górowski, Góralski.**

Gorton English: habitation name from a place in Lancs., so called from OE *gor* dirt + *tūn* enclosure, settlement.

Gosling English: 1. var., with hard initial, of JOCELYN.

2. nickname from ME *gosling* young goose (from OE *gōs* + the Gmc suffix *-ling* (cf., e.g., CHAMBERLAIN), partly in imitation of ON *gǿslingr* from *gás*).

Vars. (mainly of 1): **Gossling, Goseling, Gostling, Gos(se)lin, Gosland.**

Cogn. (of 1): Fr.: **Gosselin.**

Gosney English (Yorks.): of uncertain origin, probably a habitation name from some minor place deriving its name from the gen. case of the OE byname *Gōsa* 'GOOSE' + OE *ēg* island.

Gossage English: habitation name from the hamlet of *Gorsuch*, Lancs., earlier *Gosefordsich*, from OE *Gōsford* 'goose ford' + *sīc* small stream. *Gorsage Hall* is shown on the 19th-cent. Ordnance Survey map beside the road from Halsall to Scarisbrick.

Vars.: **Gorsuch, Gorstidge, Gostage.**

This name is first recorded as that of a manor near Ormskirk held by Walter de Gosefordsich *in the late 13th cent. The spelling* Gossage *is now much the most common, but in spite of its Lancs. origin the surname is largely confined to the W Midlands.*

Gossart 1. English: occupational name for a keeper of geese, ME *goseherde*, from OE *gōs* GOOSE + *hierde* herdsman, keeper (see HEARD).

2. French: pej. of GOSSE.

Vars. (of 1): **Gozzard, Gozzett.**

Gosse English (Norman), French, and Low German: from the OF given name *Gosse*, representing the Gmc personal name *Gozzo*, a short form of the various cpd names with the first element *gōd* good or *god, got* god.

Vars.: Eng.: **Goss** (chiefly W Country). Low Ger.: **Gösse.**

Cogn.: Ger.: **Goss.**

Dims.: Eng.: **Gosset(t).** Fr.: **Gosset, Gossin.**

Patrs.: Flem., Du.: **Goos(s)en(s).**

Gostellow English: habitation name from *Gorstella* in Ches., so called from OE *gors(t)* GORSE + *hyll* HILL + *hlāw* mound (see LAW 2).

Got Jewish (Ashkenazic): ornamental name from mod. Ger. *Gott* God, Yid. *got.*

Var.: GOTT.

Cpds.: **Gotajner** ('One God', an expression of monotheistic faith; Pol. spelling); **Gottdenker** ('thinker about God'); **Gott(es)diener, Got(t)esdiner** ('servant of God'); **Gottesdonner** ('God's thunder'); **Gottehrer** ('honourer of God'); **Gottesfeld** ('God's field'); **Gotsforcht** ('fear of God'); **Gotfreund** ('friend of God'); **Gotfri(e)d, Gotfryd, Gottfried** ('God's peace'; see also GODFREY); **Gottesgnade** ('grace of God'); **Gottheil, Gotshal** ('God's salvation'); **Got(t)helf, Got(t)hilf** ('God's help'); **Gotkind** ('child of God'); GOTTLIEB; **Gottesmann, Got(t)esman** ('God's man'); **Gottreich** ('kingdom of God'); GOTTSCHALK; **Gott(es)segen** ('God's blessing'); **Gottselig** ('blessed by God').

Gothard 1. English: occupational name for a keeper of goats, ME *gotherde*, from OE *gāt* goat (see GATE 3) + *hierde* herdsman, keeper (see HEARD).

2. German: cogn. of GODDARD.

Gott 1. English (Norman) and German: from a personal name, a short form of the various Gmc cpd names with the first element *gōd* good or *god, got* god.

2. Jewish (Ashkenazic): var. of GOT.

Vars. (of 1): Ger.: **Gotte, Godt, Göth(e).**

Cogns. (of 1): Low Ger.: **God(d)e, Gohde, Göde, Gad(d)e, Gäde, Gädt.** Fris.: **Jäde.**

Dims. (of 1): Ger.: **Gott(e)l, Gödel, Götz(e).** Low Ger.: **Gö(d)tke, Gödeke, Gädtke, Gädcke, Gäde(c)ke.** Fris.: **Jädecke.** Fr.: **Go(u)don, Godot, Godet, Godey.**

Patrs. (from 1): Eng.: **Gotts.** Low Ger.: **Goder, Göder(s), Gohde(n)s, Gödens, Gaden.** Fris.: **Goens.**

Patrs. (from dims. of 1): Ger.: **Göttler.** Low Ger.: **Göttgens, Göttjens, Gäthgens, Göcker, Göcks, Göcken, Göcking.**

Gottlieb 1. German: from a medieval given name, originally a Gmc personal name composed of the elements *god, got* god + *leoba* love.

2. Jewish (Ashkenazic): from the Yid. male given name *Gotlib*, derived from the Ger. name given above, or else an ornamental name from Yid. *got* God + *lib* love.

Vars. (of 2): **Gotlieb, Got(t)lib.**

Patrs. (from 2): **Gotlibowicz, Gotlibovski.**

Gottschalk 1. German: from a medieval given name composed of the MHG elements *got* God (OHG *got*) + *schalk* servant, court jester (OHG *scalc*; cf. MARSHALL and SENESCHAL).

2. Jewish (Ashkenazic): ornamental name composed of the Ger. elements *Gott* God + *Schalk* servant or jester.

Vars.: **Gottschall, Gottschald**; **Gutschalk** (also a nickname meaning 'good servant').

Cogns.: Low Ger., Flem., Du.: **Godschalk.** Ger. (under Slav. influence): **Gottschlich, Gottschling, Goslich, Gosselk, Schalck.**

Dims.: Ger.: **Göschel.** Low Ger.: **Gosch, Gösch(e).** Ger. (under Slav. influence): **Gutsch(mann), Gutsch(k)e.**

Patrs. (from dims.): Low Ger.: **Göschen.** Ger. (under Slav. influence): **Gutsch(l)er, Gutschner.**

Gough 1. English, of Celtic origin: occupational name for a smith, from Gael. *gobha*, Corn./Bret. *goff*. The surname is common in E Anglia, where it is probably of Bret. origin, introduced by followers of William the Conqueror.

2. Welsh: nickname for a red-haired person, from W *coch* red, showing the mutation of the initial consonant that occurs when the adj. is used attributively with a proper name.

Vars. (of 1): **Goff(e)**; **Gow** (Sc.); **Angove** (Corn.). (Of 2): **Gou(d)ge, Goodge, Gudge**; **Gutch, Gooch** (mainly E Anglia).

Cogns. (of 1): Bret.: **Le Goff.** (Of 2): Corn.: COUCH.

Dims. (of 1): Eng.: **Goffin, Gowen** (both chiefly E Anglia). Bret.: **Goffic, Govic, Go(u)ïc.**

Pej. (of 1): Eng.: **Goward** (E Anglia).

Patrs. (from 1): Sc.: **McGow(e)** (Gael. **Mac Gobha**). See also MCGOWAN.

Goujon French: nickname from the gudgeon, OF *gougon* (L *gōbio*, gen. *gōbionis*, a deriv. of *gōbius*, the name of a related fish). The fish is considered easy to catch, and so the nickname may have been used with reference to a greedy or credulous person.

Vars.: **Gougeon**, **Goujou**.

Cogns.: Eng.: **Gudgeon**, **Gudgin**.

Goulet French: nickname for a greedy or voracious man, from OF *goulet* gullet, a dim. of *goule* throat (L *gula*). It may also be in part a topographic name for someone who lived by a narrow pass or defile (cf. GORGE).

Var.: **Gouley**.

Goulty English: of unknown origin. No forms have been found before 1544, when Robert *Golty* was married at Debach, Suffolk. The name has always been a rare one, largely confined to Norfolk and Suffolk, and all bearers may well descend from a common ancestor.

Var.: **Golty**.

Goupil French: nickname for a cunning person, from OF *goupil* fox (LL *vulpiculus*, dim. of class. L *vulpes*, a distant cogn. of WOLF). This was replaced as a vocab. word during the Middle Ages by the modern form *renard*, originally the given name (of Gmc origin; cf. REYNARD) borne by the fox in the popular beast tales.

Vars.: **Goupy**, **Verpy**.

Dims.: **Goupillet**, **Goupillon**, **Guerpillon**.

Pej.: **Verpillat**.

Gourlay Scots: of uncertain origin, possibly a habitation name from some place in Normandy. According to Black it is 'probably from some place in England', but elsewhere he mentions a certain Aleyn GURNAY whose seal reads *S(igillum) Alani Gorley*.

Vars.: **Gourley** (chiefly N Ireland), **Gourlie**.

The first known bearer of the name in Scotland is Ingelramus de Gourlay, *who held land in Clydesdale and Lothian* c.*1174. His son, Hugh* de Gurley, *is recorded as possessing lands in Fife and Lothian.*

Gous French: nickname from OF *go(u)s* dog, cur (of uncertain origin), widely used as a term of abuse in the Middle Ages. Unlike the majority of surnames derived from offensive nicknames current at that time, this one has survived to the present day. This is no doubt because for some reason the vocab. word fell quickly out of use, so that the name was no longer understood as offensive, and there was no pressure to change it.

Dims.: **Goussin**, **Gousson**, **Gousset**.

Pejs.: **Goussard**, **Goussaud**.

Gouveia Portuguese: habitation name from any of various places so called, in particular a town in the province of Beira Baixa. The placename is first recorded in the L forms *Gaudela* and *Goudela*; it is of obscure origin.

Gouverneur French: occupational name for various sorts of minor administrative officials, from OF *gouverneur* manager, steward (L *gubernātor*, a deriv. of *gubernāri* to steer, control, itself an early borrowing from Gk).

Cogn.: Prov.: **Gouvernaire**.

Govan Scots: 1. occupational name from Gael. *gobhan*, a dim. of *gobha* smith; see GOUGH 1.

2. habitation name from a place near Glasgow, first recorded *c.*1134 as *Guven*. It is probably from Gael. *gudhbhan*, a dim. of *gudhbh* schoolhouse.

Christian, widow of Simon de Govane, *held lands in Govan in 1293.*

Gover 1. English: of uncertain origin. In part it seems to be a nickname from ME *go(n)* to go (OE *gān*) + *fair* lovely, quiet(ly) (see FAIR), but early examples such as Richard *le Gofiar* (Somerset 1327) point to its origin as an occupational name or perhaps a nickname, from an unknown element.

2. Jewish: of unknown origin.

Gowanlock Scots: of unknown origin, possibly a habitation name from some minor place that cannot now be identified. The name is first recorded in the Lowlands, (in Edinburgh in 1471, in the form *Gowanlok*), so an Eng. rather than a Gael. etymology should probably be sought.

Vars.: **Gowenlock** (the most common spelling in England); **Govenlock**; **Govinlock** (U.S., Canada).

Gower 1. English (Norman): regional name for someone from the district north of Paris known in OF as *Gohiere*.

2. English (Norman): habitation name from any of the various places in N France called *Gouy* (from the Gallo-Roman personal name *Gaudius* + the local suffix *-ācum*), with the addition of the ANF suffix *-er*.

3. English (Norman): from a Norman personal name, *Go(h)ier*, cogn. with the OE name mentioned at GOODER.

4. Welsh: from the peninsula in S Wales, whose W name is *Gŵyr*.

5. Jewish: var. of GOVER.

Vars.: **Gowar**, **Guwer**.

Cogn. (of 1 or 3): Fr.: **Gohier**.

Patr. (from 3): Eng.: **Gowers**.

Goya Spanish form of Basque **Goia**, **Goya**: topographic name for someone who lived at the top of a hill or the upper part of a settlement, from Basque *goi* top + the def. art. *-a*.

Graber 1. German: occupational name for a digger of graves or ditches, or an engraver of seals, from an agent deriv. of Ger. *graben* to dig, excavate (OHG *graban*).

2. Jewish (Ashkenazic): occupational name for a grave-digger, mod. Ger. *Gräber*.

Vars. (of 1): **Grabert**, **Grabner**; **Gräber**, **Grebert**. (Of 2): **Graberman**; **Greber** (from Yid. *greber*).

Cogns.: Pol.: **Grabarz**. Eng.: **Graver** (chiefly E Anglia).

Dim.: Pol.: **Grabarczyk**.

Grabowski Polish and Jewish (E Ashkenazic): habitation name from any of various places named with Pol. *grab* hornbeam, the wood of which was used for making yokes, with the addition of the surname suffix *-ski* (see BARANOWSKI). In some cases it may be an occupational name for a yoke-maker.

Vars.: Pol.: **Grab(ski)**. Jewish: **Grabovski**.

Cogn.: Ger. (of Slav. origin): **Grabau**.

Patr.: Pol.: **Grabowicz**.

Grace English: 1. nickname from ME, OF *grace* charm, pleasantness (L *grātia*).

2. from the female given name *Grace*, which was popular in the Middle Ages. This seems in the first instance to have been from a Gmc element *grīs* grey (see GRICE 1), but was soon associated by folk etymology with 1.

Cogns.: It.: **Grazia**, **Graz(z)i**. Sp.: **Gracia**. Cat.: **Gràcia**. Port.: **Graça**.

Dims.: It.: **Grazzini**, **Grazioli**, **Graziotti**.

Metrs.: It.: **Di Gratia**, **Delle Grazie**.

Graczyk Polish: nickname for a gambler or musician (or possibly an actor), Pol. *graczyk* player, dim. of *gracz*, agent noun from *grać* to play, in various senses: to play cards, to play a musical instrument, or to act.

Gradillas Spanish: topographic name for someone who lived at a place where a hillside had been shaped into terraces, Sp. *gradillas* (pl. of *gradilla*, dim. of *grada* step, a fem. var. of *grado*, from L *gradus* step, a deriv. of *gradi* to go, proceed).

Cogns.: Cat.: **Graell(s)**.

Grady Irish: Anglicized form of Gael. **Ó Gráda** 'descendant of *Gráda*', a byname meaning 'Noble'. The form **Mac Gráda** 'Son of *Gráda*' (Anglicized **McGrady**) is much rarer.

Vars.: **O'Grady, O'Grada**. See also BRADY.

Graf 1. German: status name from Ger. *Graf* count, magistrate (MHG *grāve*, *grābe*, OHG *grāv(i)o*), a title denoting various more or less aristocratic dignitaries and officials. In later times it became established as a title of nobility equivalent to the Romance COUNT. The vocab. word also denoted various minor local functionaries in different parts of Germany. In the Grand Duchy of Hesse, for example, it was used for the holder of the comparatively humble office of village headman (cf. MAYER, SCHULTZ, and VOGT). The surname could have originated from any of these senses.

2. Jewish (Ashkenazic): ornamental name selected, like HERZOG and other words denoting titles, because of their aristocratic connotations.

Vars. (of 1): **Grafe** (Rheinland); **Gräfe** (Westphalia); **Grauf** (Swabia); **Grebe** (Hesse). (Of 2): GRAFF, **Grafman**.

Cogns. (of 1): Low Ger.: **Greve, Grewe**. Flem.: **De Greef, De Graeve**. Du.: **De Graf(f)**. Dan.: **Greve**. Czech: **Hrabě**.

Dims. (of 1): Low Ger.: **Greveke**. Czech: **Hrabek**.

Patrs. (of 1): Low Ger.: **Greving, Grewing**. Flem.: **Schrevens**. Dan.: **Gravesen**.

Patr. (from a dim. of 1): Russ.: **Grafchikov**.

Graff 1. English: metonymic occupational name for a clerk or scribe, from ANF *grafe* quill, pen (a deriv. of *grafer* to write, LL *grafāre*, from Gk *graphein*).

2. Jewish (Ashkenazic): var. of GRAF.

Grafton English: habitation name from any of the numerous places so called from OE *grāf* grove + *tūn* enclosure, settlement.

Graham Scots: habitation name from *Grantham* in Lincs., recorded in Domesday Book as *Graham* (as well as *Grantham*, *Grandham*, and *Granham*). See also GRANTHAM.

Vars.: **Grahame, Graeme, Grayham, Greim**.

The surname Graham *is now most common in Scotland and Northern Ireland. It was taken to Scotland at the beginning of the 12th cent. by the Norman baron William* de Graham, *holder of the manor in Lincs., from whom many if not all modern bearers are probably descended.*

Grail French: 1. nickname for a thin man, from OF *grail* lean, slender (L *gracilis*).

2. nickname for a raucous or thievish person, from OF *grail* crow, jackdaw (L *graculus*, perhaps of imitative origin). This word has been retained to the present day in certain regional dialects, but in the standard language it has been replaced by CORNEILLE.

Var.: **Graille**.

Dims.: **Graillet, Grail(l)ot, Graillon, Gralhon, Grol(l)eau, Grollet**.

Gram Danish: nickname for an irascible person, from Dan. *gram* angry (ON *gramr*).

Grame 1. French: nickname for an unfortunate or careworn person, from OF *grame* trouble, anxiety (of apparently Gmc origin).

2. Provençal: topographic name for someone who lived on a patch of meadowland, from OProv. *grame* grass, pasture (L *gramen*).

Var.: **Gramme**.

Gran 1. Swedish: ornamental surname, from Swed. *gran* Norway spruce, adopted in the 19th cent. This belongs to the large class of ornamental surnames taken from natural features of the landscape.

2. Catalan: cogn. of GRANT 1.

Vars. (of 1): **Grann, Grahn**.

Cpds (of 1): **Granberg** ('spruce hill'); **Granholm** ('spruce island'); **Granlund** ('spruce grove'); **Granlöf** ('spruce leaf'); **Granquist** ('spruce twig'); **Granström** ('spruce river').

Granado Spanish: 1. metonymic occupational name for a grower or seller of pomegranates, from Sp. *granado* pomegranate (L *(pōmum) grānātum*; see GARNETT 1).

2. nickname for a (self-)important man, from Sp. *granado* famous, important, in origin the same word as in 1, but used as an adj. with this sense as a result of confusion with *grande* (see GRANT 1).

Granda Spanish: habitation name from any of various places in Asturias and Galicia named with the dial. term *granda* rocky plain, scrub-covered upland with poor soil (of pre-Roman origin). The surname is also borne by Jews, the reasons for its adoption being unknown.

Grandison English and Scots: habitation name from *Granson* on Lake Neuchâtel. The first known bearer of the surname is Rigaldus *de Grancione* (*fl.* 1040). The name was brought to Britain by Otes *de Grandison* (d. 1328) and his brother, sons of the Lord of Granson. They were among a group of Savoyards who settled in England after Henry III had married a granddaughter of the Count of Savoy.

Granet French: nickname for someone afflicted with pockmarks or similar blemishes, from OF *granet*, a dim. of *grain* grain (L *grānum*).

Vars.: **Granel, Grenot, Grenet(ton)**.

Cogn.: It.: **Granillo**.

Grange English and French: topographic name for someone who lived by a granary, ME, OF *grange* (L *grānica* granary, barn, from *grānum* grain, corn).

Vars.: Eng.: **Grainge**. Fr.: **Granche, Lagrange**.

Cogn.: Sp.: **Granja**.

Granger English and French: occupational name for a farm bailiff, responsible for overseeing the collection of the rent in kind into the barns and storehouses of the lord of the manor. This official had the ANF title *grainger* (OF *grangier*, from LL *grānicārius*, a deriv. of *grānica* granary; see GRANGE).

Vars.: Eng.: **Grainger**. Fr.: **Grangier, Grancher**.

Cogns.: Prov.: **Grang(i)é**.

Grant English and (now esp.) Scots: 1. Norman nickname from ANF *graund*, *graunt* tall, large (OF *grand*, *grant*, from L *grandis*), given either to a person of remarkable size, or else in a relative way to distinguish two bearers of the same given name, often representatives of different generations within the same family.

2. from a medieval given name, probably a survival into ME of the OE byname *Granta* (see GRANTHAM).

Vars. (of 1): **Grand** (E Anglia); **Le Grand**.

Cogns. (of 1): Fr.: **Grand, Legrand**. It.: **Grandi, Grande, Grando; Lo Grande** (Sicily). Sp.: **Grande**. Cat.: GRAN.

Dims. (of 1): Fr.: **Grandel, Grandeau, Grandet, Grandon, Grandot**. It.: **Grandin(ett)i, Grandotto**.

Augs. (of 1): It.: **Grandoni, Grandone**.

Patrs. (from 1): It.: **De Grandi, (De) Grandis, Del Grande**.

The name Grant *is found in Scotland from the mid-13th cent. Apparently it was brought to Scotland by a Norman family from Notts., and possibly also by others at around the same time.*

Grantham English: habitation name from *Grantham* in Lincs., of uncertain etymology. The final element is OE *hām* homestead; the first may be OE **grand* gravel or perhaps a personal name **Granta*, which probably originated as a byname meaning 'Snarler'. See also GRAHAM.

Grape Low German: metonymic occupational name for a maker of metal or earthenware vessels, from MLG *grope* pot (cf. POTTER, EULER, and TÖPFER).

Vars.: **Gra(a)p, Grope; Gropius** (Latinized); **Gräper, Gröp(p)er**.

Grapes English (E Anglia): of uncertain origin, perhaps a house name from a house bearing the sign of a bunch of grapes. The vocab. word is attested from the 13th cent. (at first in the cpd *wingrape*; cf. WEIN), and comes from OF *grape*, which is probably related to a Gmc element meaning 'hook', perhaps by way of the OF verb *graper* to gather.

Grass 1. English and German: topographic name for someone who lived on a patch of meadowland, from ME *gras* or Ger. *Grass* grass, pasture, grazing (OE *græs*, OHG *gras*).

2. English: nickname for a stout or corpulent person, from ANF *gras* fat (from L *crassus* (itself used as a family name), with the initial changed under the influence of *grossus*; see GROSS).

3. Scots: occupational name from Gael. *greusaiche* shoemaker (a deriv. of *gréas* handicraft). A certain John *Grasse* alias *Cordonar* is recorded in Scotland in 1539.

Vars. (of 1): Ger.: **Gras; Grassmann; Graser, Gräser**. (Of 3): **Grassick, Grassie, Gracie; Gracey** (N Ireland).

Cogns. (of 2): Fr.: **Gras, Legras**. It.: **Grassi; (Lo) Grasso** (S Italy). Cat.: **Gras**.

Dims. (of 2): Fr.: **Grasset, Grassot, Grassin, Grasson**. It.: **Grassell(in)i, Grassilli, Grasigli, Grassetti, Grassotti, Grassini**.

Patrs. (from 2): Fr.: **Augras**. It.: **De Grassi**.

Gratien French: from the given name (L *Grātiānus*, a deriv. of *grātus* welcome, pleasing) borne by an early saint who was martyred at Amiens during the reign of the Roman emperor Diocletian.

Cogns.: It.: **Graz(z)iani** (in part borne by Jews, the reasons for its adoption being unknown); **Graz(z)iano**. Cat.: **Gracià**.

Gratton English: habitation name from any of various places so called. *Gratton* in Derbys. is from OE *grēat* great + *tūn* enclosure, settlement. *Gratton* in High Bray, Devon, is probably 'great hill', from OE *grēat* + *dūn* (see DOWN). A number of minor places in Devon are from the dial. word *gratton*, *gratten* stubble-field.

Vars.: **Gratten, Grattan**.

Grau 1. German: cogn. of GRAY.

2. French: metonymic occupational name for a maker, seller, or user of agricultural hooks, from OF *grau* hook (apparently of Gmc origin). It may perhaps also be in part a nickname for a hunchback or a devious person; cf. CROOK.

3. Provençal: topographic name for someone who lived near a canal giving access to the sea, OProv. *grau* (L *gradus* step, from *gradi* to go; cf. GRADILLAS).

4. Catalan: from a contracted form of the common medieval given name *Guerau*, a popular form of *Gerald*; see GARRETT.

Var. (of 2 and 3): **Graux**.

Grave 1. English: occupational name from ME *greyve* steward (ON *greifi*, itself from Low Ger. *grēve*; see GRAF).

2. English: topographic name, a var. of GROVE.

3. French: topographic name for someone who lived on a patch of gravelly soil, from OF *grave* gravel (of Celt. origin).

4. Low German: cogn. of GRAF.

Var. (of 3): Fr.: **Gravier**.

Dims. (of 1): Eng.: **Graveling** (E Anglia; the suffix *-ling* probably has contemptuous overtones, suggesting petty officialdom). (Of 3): Fr.: **Gravel(le), Gravelin(e), Graveleau, Gravot**.

Patrs. (from 1): Eng.: **Graves; Graves(t)on, Grays(t)on; Grayshon** (Yorks.).

Graverend French: occupational name for a collector of taxes, OF *graverenc* (of uncertain origin).

Dims.: **Gravereau(x), Graveron**.

Gray 1. English: nickname for someone with grey hair or a grey beard, from OE *græg* grey. In Scotland and Ireland it has been used as a translation of various Gael. surnames derived from *riabhach* brindled, grey; see REAVEY.

2. English and Scots (Norman): habitation name from *Graye* in Calvados, so called from the Gallo-Roman personal name *Grātus* 'Welcome', 'Pleasing' + the local suffix *-ācum*.

Vars. (of 1): **Grey; Legrey** (with the ANF def. art.).

Cogns. (of 1): Ger.: GRAU, **Grauer(t), Graumann**. Low Ger.: **Grage, Grahe, Graw(e); Gra(h)mann, Gro(h)mann**. Jewish (Ashkenazic): **Grau(er); Groy** (from Yid. *groy*).

Patr. (from 1): Flem.: **Schraawen**.

Cpds.: Jewish: **Graubart, Graubard, Grobard, Grubard** ('grey beard', a nickname); **Grauberg** ('grey hill', ornamental); **Grauweis** ('grey-white'); **Grauzalc** ('grey salt', Pol. spelling).

A family by the name of Grey, *holders of the earldom of Stamford, can be traced to Henry* de Grey, *who was granted lands at Thurrock, Essex, by Richard I (1189–99). They once held great power, and Henry Grey, Duke of Suffolk (1517–54), married a granddaughter of Henry VII. Because of this he attempted to place his daughter, Lady Jane Grey (1537–54), on the throne, and for this, and his part in Wyatt's rebellion, both he and his daughter were beheaded.*

Another family of the same name originated in Northumb., where they held land at Wark-on-Tweed in 1398. Members include the Earls Grey, of whom the best known is probably Charles, 2nd Earl Grey (1764–1845), the prime minister under whom the 1832 Reform Bill was passed.

Grealey English (Norman): nickname for someone with a pock-marked face, from ONF *greslé* pitted, scarred (from *gresle* hailstone, of Gmc origin).

Vars.: **Grealy, Grealish, Greelish** (Ireland); **Greel(e)y, Gra(y)ley, Grelley; Gredley, Gridley**; GRESLEY.

Cogns.: Fr.: **Greslé, Grêlé**.

Dims.: Eng.: **Greslet**. Fr.: **Greslet, Greslon, Grel(l)on, Grelot**.

The holders of the manor of Manchester in the 12th to 14th cents. were members of the Greslet *family, of which junior branches are still found in Lancs.*

Greathead English: nickname for someone with a large head, from ME *great* large (OE *grēat*) + *heved* head (OE *hēafod*).

Greatrex English (Midlands): apparently a habitation name from some minor place named as *Great Rakes*, from

Northern ME *great* large (OE *grēat*) + *rake* path, track, used in Derbys. in a lead-mining sense 'vertical vein of ore'. In this sense *rake* became the name of several lead-mines, including *Greatrake* Mine in Carsington, which could be the source of the surname.

Var.: **Greatorex**.

Greave English: topographic name from OE *græfe* brushwood, thicket, or habitation name from a place named with this word (of which there is one in Lancs.). There has been some confusion with GRAVE and GRIEVE.

Vars.: **Greve, Greaves, Gre(e)ves**.

Greco Italian: ethnic name for a Greek, It. *Greco* (L *Graecus*, from *Graecia* Greece). In some cases it may have been merely a nickname for a crafty or guileful person, for these were the qualities traditionally attributed to the Greeks.

Vars.: **Grec(h)i, Greg(h)i, Grieco; Lo Greco** (S Italy).

Cogns.: Fr.: **Grec, Grieu(x)**. Flem., Du.: **De Griek**. Jewish (SE Sefardic): **Grego**.

Patr.: It.: **Del Greco**.

Green 1. English: one of the most common and widespread of Eng. surnames, either a nickname for someone who was fond of dressing in this colour (OE *grēne*) or who had played the part of the 'Green Man' in the May Day celebrations, or a topographic name for someone who lived near a village green, ME *grene* (a transferred use of the colour term).

2. Jewish (Ashkenazic): Anglicized form of **Grün** or **Grin**, presumably ornamental names from the mod. Ger. and Yid. words respectively, or short form of any of the cpds listed below.

3. Irish: translation of various Gael. surnames derived from *uaithne* (see HOONEY) and *glas* (see GLASS 2). See also FAHY.

4. Norwegian and Danish: cogn. of GREN.

Vars. (of 1): Eng.: **Gre(e)ne; Greening; Greenman, Greenmon**.

Cogns. (of 1): Ger.: **Grün(e), Gru(h)n**. Low Ger.: **Gröhn(e)**. Flem., Du.: **Groen**. Dan., Norw.: **Grøn**. Jewish (Ashkenazic): **Gru(e)n(er), Griner** (Anglicized as GREENER).

Cpds (ornamental): Jewish: **Grünbaum, Gru(e)nbaum, Gruenebaum, Grunebaum, Grinbaum, Grinbo(i)m**, ('green tree', partly Anglicized as **Greenbaum**, and **Greenbom**); **Grünberg, Gru(e)nberg(er), Grinberg** ('green hill', partly Anglicized as **Greenberg(er)**); **Grünblatt, Gruenblat, Grunblat(t), Grinblat(t)** ('green leaf', partly Anglicized as **Greenblat(t)**); **Grunfarb** ('green colour'); **Grinfas(s)** ('green barrel'); **Grünfeld, Gru(e)nfeld, Grinfeld** ('green field', partly Anglicized as **Greenfeld, Grinfield**; fully Anglicized as GREENFIELD); **Gringart(en)** ('green garden'); **Grunglas, Gringlas(s)** ('green glass', Anglicized as **Greenglass**); **Gruengras, Gringras(s)** ('green grass', Anglicized as GREENGRASS); **Grunhaus, Grinhaus, Greenhoiz** ('green house', Anglicized as GREENHOUSE); **Grünheim, Grinheim** ('green home'); **Grünhol(t)z, Grinholc** ('green wood', partly Anglicized as **Greenholtz**, fully Anglicized as GREENWOOD; *Grinholc* is a Pol. spelling); **Gru(e)nhut, Grinhut** ('green hat'); **Gru(e)nkraut, Grinkraut** ('green herb'); **Grinman** ('green man', Anglicized as **Greenman**); **Grunseid** ('green silk'); **Grünstein, Gru(e)nstein, Grinstein** ('green stone', partly Anglicized as **Greenstein, Greenstien**); **Grintuch** ('green cloth'); **Grün(e)wald, Gruen(e)wald, Grunwall, Grinwald, Grinvald** ('green forest', partly Anglicized as **Greenwald**); **Gru(e)nwurzel, Grinwurcel** ('green root'; *Grinwurcel* is a Pol. spelling); **Grunzweig** ('green twig', partly Anglicized as **Greenzweig**). Swed.: **Grönberg** ('green hill'); **Grönblad(h)** ('green leaf'); **Gröndahl** ('green valley'); **Grönlund** ('green grove'); **Grönkvist** ('green twig'); **Grönskog** ('green forest'); **Grönstedt** ('green homestead'); **Grönwall, Grönvall** ('green pasture').

Greenacre English (E Anglia): topographic name for someone who lived by a patch of luxuriantly fertile land, from OE *grēne* GREEN + *æcer* cultivated land (see ACKER).

Greenaway 1. English: topographic name for someone who lived by a grassy path, from OE *grēne* GREEN + *weg* path (see WAY).

2. Welsh: alteration of the W personal name *Goronwy*, perhaps originally a byname meaning 'Heron'.

Vars.: **Greenway**. (Of 2 only): **Grenow, Grono(w)**.

Greener 1. English: habitation name from *Greenhaugh* in Northumb., so called from OE *grēne* GREEN + *halh* nook, recess (see HALE 1). See also GREENHALGH.

2. Jewish (Ashkenazic): Anglicized form of *Griner*; see GREEN.

Greenfield 1. English: habitation name from any of the numerous minor places so called from OE *grēne* GREEN + *feld* pasture, open country (see FIELD).

2. English (Norman): habitation name from any of various places in Normandy called *Grainville*, from the Gmc personal name *Guarin* (see WARING) + OF *ville* settlement (see VILLE).

3. Jewish (Ashkenazic): Anglicized form of *Grünfeld* and its vars.; see cpds at GREEN.

Vars. (of 2): **Grenville, Grenfell, Granville** (all now chiefly found in Devon).

Cogns. (of 1): Du.: **Groen(e)veld**.

Greengrass English (E Anglia): apparently a topographic name for someone who lived at a spot where the grass was particularly lush and green, from OE *grēne* GREEN + *græs* GRASS.

Greenhalgh English (Lancs.): habitation name from either of two places in Lancs., both so called from OE *grēne* GREEN + *holh* hollow (see HOLE). See also GREENER.

Vars.: **Greenalf, Greenhall**, GREENHOUGH, **Grinaugh**.

Greenham English: habitation name from a place in Berks., so called from OE *grēne* GREEN + *hamm* water meadow or *hām* homestead.

Greenhill 1. English: habitation name from any of the various places in England so called, from OE *grēne* GREEN + *hyll* HILL.

2. Jewish (Ashkenazic): translation of *Grünberg* and its vars.; see cpds at GREEN.

Var. (of 1): **Grinnell**.

Greenhorn Scots: according to Black, a habitation name from an unidentified place, apparently named with the OE elements *grēne* GREEN + *hyrne* corner (see HEARN 2).

Var.: **Greenhorne**.

Greenhough English (Yorks.): 1. habitation name from either of two places, in N and W Yorks., called *Greenhow*, or from *Gerna* in the parish of Downham, Lancs., all of which are named with OE *grēne* GREEN + *hōh* mound (or the cogn. ON *haugr*; see HOE).

2. var. of GREENHALGH.

Var.: **Greenough** (Lancs.).

Greenhouse 1. English: topographic name for someone who lived in a house by a village green, from OE *grēne* GREEN + *hūs* house. The term was not used to denote a glasshouse for the cultivation of 'greens' or sensitive plants until the late 17th cent.

2. Jewish (Ashkenazic): Anglicized form of *Grünhaus* and its vars.; see cpds at GREEN.

Greenland English: topographic name for someone who lived near a patch of land left open as communal pasturage, from OE *grēne* GREEN + *land* land.

Greenslade English: topographic name for someone who lived near a fertile valley, from OE *grēne* GREEN + *slæd* valley, dell.

Greensmith English (chiefly E Midlands and Yorks.): occupational name or nickname for a coppersmith, from ME *grene* GREEN + SMITH, with reference to the characteristic colour of oxidized copper.

Greenwell English (Northumb.): topographic name for someone who lived by a stream among lush pastures, from OE *grēne* GREEN + *well(a)* spring, stream (see WELL), or habitation name from a minor place so named.

The main family of this name came originally from Greenwell, Wolsingham, Co. Durham, where they are recorded as owning land as early as 1183.

Greenwood 1. English: topographic name for someone who lived in a dense forest, from OE *grēne* GREEN + *wudu* WOOD.

2. Jewish (Ashkenazic): Anglicized form of *Grünholz* and its vars.; see cpds at GREEN.

Greep Cornish: either a nickname from Corn. *cryp* crest, comb, or a habitation name from *Pengreep* in the parish of Gwennap, so called from Corn. *pen* head, top, summit + *gryp*, a mutated form of *cryp* in the sense 'ridge'.

Greet English (now mainly Devon and Cornwall): 1. topographic name for someone who lived on a patch of gravelly soil or by a gravel pit, from ME *grēt* gravel (OE *grēot*), or an occupational name for a supplier of gravel or a worker in a gravel pit.

2. nickname for a large person, from ME *grēt* great (OE *grēat*).

Gregory English: from a given name that was popular throughout Christendom in the Middle Ages. The name is of Gk origin, *Grēgorios* being a deriv. of *grēgorein* to be awake or watchful, but at an early date the L form *Gregorius* was associated by folk etymology with *grex*, gen. *gregis*, flock, herd, under the influence of the Christian image of the good shepherd. The Gk name was borne in the early Christian cents. by two fathers of the Orthodox Church, St Gregory Nazianzene (*c*.325–90) and St Gregory of Nyssa (*c*.331–95), and later by sixteen popes, starting with Gregory the Great (*c*.540–604). It was also the name of a 3rd- and 4th-cent. apostle of Armenia.

Vars.: **Grigorey**; **Greg(g)or**; **Grigor** (Scots); GRIER.

Cogns.: Fr.: **Grégoire**, **Grigoire**, **Gregori**. It.: **Gregori(o)**, **Grigori(o)**, **Ghirigori**, **Gregoli**, **Gri(g)oli**, **Grigolli**; **Greg(u)ol** (NE Italy); **Gligori**, **Grivori** (Calabria); **Gori** (N Italy). Sp.: **Gregorio**. Cat.: **Gregori**. Port.: **Gregório**. Rum.: **Grigore**. Ger.: **Gregor**, **Gröger**, **Grieger**, **Grüger**; **Göreis**, **Gareis**, **Greyes**. Low Ger.: **Greger**; **Görr(i)es**, **Gör(e)s**. Flem.: **Goor**. Ger. (of Slav. origin): **Regorz**, **R(z)ehor(z)**, **Sehorsch**. Czech: **Řehoř**, **Říha**; **Záhoř**; **Gregor**, **Grégr**. Hung.: **Gergely**. Jewish (Ashkenazic): **Gregor** (an adoption of the non-Jewish surname).

Dims.: Eng.: **Greg(g)**, **Grigg**. Scots: **Greig**, **Grieg**. It.: **Gregoretti**, **Gregoletti**, **Grigoletti**, **Gregorini**, **Gregorutti**, **Gorghetto**; **Gergolet**, **Gregorin**, **Gregolin** (NE Italy); **Gorelli**, **Goretti**, **Gorini**, **Gorioli**, **Gorusso** (N Italy). Flem.: **Gregh**. Ger. (of Slav. origin): **Gresch(ke)**, **Reschke**, **Greschik**, **Grelka**, **Grelik**, **Grelak**. Czech: REHÁK; **Řehořek**; **Říhánek**, **Říhošek**. Pol.: **Gr(z)egorek**, **Grzegorzecki**, **Gr(z)egorczyk** (forms with *Gr*- rather than *Grz*- are not typically Polish, although they do occur among Poles); **Grzeszczyk**, **Grzelczyk**; **Grześ**; **Hrycek**, **Hryńczyk**. Ukr.: **Hritzko**, **Hrinchenko**, **Hrishchenko**. Beloruss.: **Hrishanok**. Hung.: **Gerö**.

Augs.: It.: **Grigolon** (NE Italy); **Goroni** (N Italy).

Pejs.: Fr. **Grigaut**. It.: **Gregorace**, **Gregoraci**, **Gligoraci** (Calabria); **Goracci** (N Italy).

Patrs.: Sc.: MCGREGOR. It.: **De Gregorio**, **Di Gregorio**, **De Gregoli**, **Grigoriis**. Rum.: **Grigorescu**. Low Ger.: **Greg(g)ersen**; **Gorriessen**, **Görrissen**. Dan., Norw.: **Gregersen**. Russ.: **Grigoryev**, **Grigorov**. Ukr.: **Hrihorovich**. Beloruss.: **Ryhorovich**. Pol.: **Grzegorzewicz**, **Gregorowicz**, **Grygor(ce)wicz**. Croatian: **Gligor(ijev)ić**. Bulg.: **Grigoriev**; **Goranov** (see also GÓRSKI). Georgian: **Grigolashvili**. Armenian: **Grigorian**, **Krikorian**. Gk: **Gregoriou**.

Patrs. (from dims.): Eng.: **Greg(g)s**, **Griggs**, **Gricks**, **Grix**; **Gregson**, **Grigson**. Russ.: **Grigor(ush)kin**, **Grenkov**, **Grinyov**, **Grin(nik)ov**, **Grin(ikh)in**, **Grinishin**, **Grinyakin**, **Grishaev**, **Grish(a)kov**, **Grishan(k)ov**, **Grishelyov**, **Grishenkov**, **Grishinov**, **Grishmanov**, **Grishukov**, **Grish(ak)in**, **Grishagin**, **Grishanin**, **Grishechkin**, **Grishukhin**, **Grishunin**, **Gritsaev**, **Gritskov**, **Gritsunov**, **Grichukhin**, **Grikhanov**. Ukr.: **Hritzkov**. Pol.: **Grzesiak**, **Grzeszczak**; **Grzelak**, **Grzelczak**; **Grzesiewicz**; **Hryckiewicz**, **Hryniewicz**, **Hryniewicki**, **Hryńcewicz**. Croatian: **Grgić**, **Grčić**.

'Son of the wife of G. (dim.)': Russ.: **Grinikhin**. Ukr.: **Hrin(ch)ishin**.

Habitation name: Pol.: **Grzegorzewski**.

Habitation names (from dims.): **Grzelewski**, **Gryglewski**, **Grześkowski**.

The Norwegian composer Edvard Grieg *(1843–1907) was born in Bergen, where his father was British consul. His paternal grandfather, Alexander Grieg (1739–1803) had settled there in 1779; he was the son of a certain John Grieg of Fraserburgh.*

Greif 1. German: house name from a house distinguished by the sign of a gryphon, Ger. *Greif* (MHG *grīf(e)*, OHG *grīf(o)*, from L *grӯphus*, Gk *gryps*, of Assyrian origin).

2. German: nickname for a grasping man, the gryphon in folk etymology having come to be associated with Ger. *greifen* to grasp, snatch (OHG *grīfan*; cf. GRIFFE).

3. Jewish (Ashkenazic): of uncertain origin, possibly related to 2 above.

4. N English and Scots: var. of GRIEVE.

Vars. (of 1): Ger.: **Greiff**. (Of 3): **Greifman**, **Greifner**.

Cogn. (of 1): Low Ger.: **Griep**.

Greitzer Jewish (Ashkenazic): from Yid. *graytser* kreuzer, the old Austro-Hungarian unit of currency. The reason(s) for the adoption of this word as a surname are not known. Cf. *Fenig* (at PENNY) and *Rubel* (at RUBLYOV).

Gren Swedish: ornamental surname from Swed. *gren* branch (ON *grein*). In some cases the name may have been chosen with some reference to the notion of the 'branches' making up a family 'tree', but it also falls into the category of words denoting natural features, which were drawn on heavily when Swedish surnames came to be formed wholesale in the 19th cent. The element *gren* was also widely used in forming compounds such as *Lindgren*.

Cogn.: Norw., Dan.: GREEN.

Gresham English: habitation name from a place in Norfolk, so called from OE *græs*, *gærs* grass(land), pasturage + *hām* homestead.

Gresley English: 1. habitation name from *Gresley* in Derbys. or *Greasley* in Notts., both of which get their name from OE *grēosn* gravel + *lēah* wood, clearing.

2. nickname from OF *greslé* pock-marked (see GREALEY).

Var.: **Greasley**.

Gresley is the name of a Derbys. family who have held lands in that county since the Norman Conquest. They have been traced to Nigel, son of Roger de Toeny, a kinsman of William the Conqueror.

Gretton English: habitation name from places, for example in Gloucs. and Shrops., so called from OE *grēot* gravel + *tūn* enclosure, settlement.
Vars.: **Gritton, Gritten.**

Greuze French: nickname for a touchy or hot-tempered individual, from OF *greüse* quarrel, dispute (of unknown origin).
Dim.: **Gruson.**
Pej.: **Greuzard.**

Greville English (Norman): habitation name from *Gréville* in La Manche, so called from a Gmc personal name *Creiz* + OF *ville* settlement (see VILLE).
Cogn.: Fr.: **Gréville.**
The Greville *family who hold the earldom of Warwick can be traced to John* Grevill, *who was living before 1327. His grandson William Greville made a loan to Richard II in 1397. His descendants included Fulke Greville (1554–1628), Elizabeth I's favourite, who was granted Warwick Castle.*

Grew English: nickname for a tall, scrawny person, from ME, OF *grue* crane (LL *grua*, for class. L *grus*).
Var.: **Grewe.**
Dims.: Eng.: **Grewcock, Growcock, Gro(o)cock; Gro(w)cott, Groucutt.** Fr.: **Gruet, Gruot.**

Gribov Russian: patr. from the nickname *Grib* 'Mushroom', given perhaps to a grower or an enthusiastic eater of mushrooms; cf. GRIBOEDOV.
Cogns.: Ukr.: **Hriban.** Pol.: **Grzyb.** Ger. (of Slav. origin): **Griebner.**
Dims.: Ukr.: **Hribko.** Pol.: **Grzybek.** Ger. (of Slav. origin): **Griebke, Greibke, Griebsch, Greibel.**
Habitation name: Pol.: **Grzybowski.**

Griboyedov Russian: patr. from the nickname *Griboyed*, composed of the elements *grib* mushroom + *yed-* to eat.

Grice English: 1. nickname for a grey-haired man, from ME *grice*, *gris* grey (OF *gris*, apparently of Gmc origin, and probably a distant cogn. of GRAY 1).

2. metonymic occupational name for a swineherd or nickname meaning 'pig', from ME *grice*, *grise* pig (ON *gríss*, probably akin to 1).
Vars.: **Grise, Griss, Le Grice, Le Grys.**
Cogns. (of 1): Fr.: **Gris, Legris, Legrix.** It.: **Grisi, Griggi.** Ger.: **Greis(e).** Low Ger.: **Griese.** Flem.: **De Gryse.** Du.: **De Grijse.**
Dims. (of 1): Eng.: **Grissin, Grisson, Grissom.** Fr.: **Grisel(in), Griseau, Grizeau, Gris(e)lain, Griset, Grisez, Grisot, Grison(net), Grizon.** It.: **Grisini.**
Aug. (of 1): It.: **Grisoni.**
Pejs. (of 1): Fr.: **Grisard, Grizard.**

Gridin Russian: patr. from the medieval given name *Gridya*, in origin a byname meaning 'Guard' (from ON *griði* companion, guard), but used as a dim. of *Gregory* from an early date.
Vars.: **Gridnin, Gridnev, Gridunov.**

Grier Scots: var. of GREGORY.
Var.: **Greer** (chiefly N Ireland).
Patrs.: **Grierson, Greerson.**
A Scottish family by the name of Grierson *claim descent from Gilbert, son of Malcolm MacGregor (d. 1374), 11th Lord of MacGregor. Gilbert was known as both MacGregor and Gregorson. In 1400 he was granted lands by the Earl of March in the name Grierson. The numerous N Irish bearers of the name* Greer *claim descent from this same Gilbert.*

Grieve Scots: occupational name for a steward or manager, ME *greve* (OE (Northumbrian) *græfa*; cf. REEVE and SHERIFF). This word was originally distinct from GRAVE 1, but some confusion has occurred as a result of the close similarity in both form and meaning.
Vars.: **Grief(f), Greef,** GREIF.
Patrs.: **Grieves, Grieveson, Greavison, Gre(e)son.**

Griffe French: nickname for a grasping or vicious person, or perhaps occasionally a more jocular name for a man with an artificial hand, from OF *griffe* claw (of Gmc origin).
Dim.: **Griffon.**
Pejs.: **Griffaut, Griffaud, Griffard.**

Griffin 1. Welsh: from a var. of GRIFFITH.

2. English: nickname for a fierce or dangerous person, from ME *griffin* gryphon; see GREIF.

3. Irish: Anglicized form of Gael. **Ó Gríobhtha** 'descendant of *Gríobhtha*', a personal name from *gríobh* gryphon (see GREIF).
Vars. (of 3): **O'Grighie, O'Greefa, (O')Griffy, Griffey, Greehy.**
Cogns. (of 2): Fr.: **Grip(p)on.** Du.: **Griffoen.**

Griffith Welsh: from the OW personal name *Gruffydd*, composed of the elements *griff*, of uncertain significance + *udd* chief, lord.
Var.: GRIFFIN.
Patrs.: **Griffi(th)s.**
Patrs. (from dims.): **Gittoes, Gittus.**

Griffoul Provençal: topographic name for someone who lived by a holly tree, OProv. *griffoul* (L *acrifolium*, from *acer*, gen. *acris*, sharp, pointed + *folium* leaf). See also ACEVEDO.
Vars.: **Agrifoul, Aigrefeuille, Greffu(e)lhe, Grifuel, Grifoul.**

Grignon French: 1. nickname for a proud or contemptuous person, from OF *grignier* to grit the teeth or curl the lips, gestures of fierce contempt. The verb is of Gmc origin and was originally probably an imitative formation suggestive of grunting through clenched teeth; cf. GRANT 2 and GRAHAM.

2. habitation name from any of the various places, for example in Côte-d'Or and Savoie, so called from the LL personal name *Granius*, *Crinius* + the local suffix *-o*, *-ōnis*.
Pej. (of 1): **Grignard.**

Grill 1. English: nickname for a fierce or cruel man, from ME *grill(e)* angry, vicious (from OE *gryllan* to rage, gnash the teeth; cf. GRIGNON 1).

2. German: nickname for a cheerful person, from Ger. *Grille* cricket (MHG *grille* cricket, OHG *grillo*, from LL *grillus*, Gk *gryllos*). The insect is widely supposed to be of a cheerful disposition, no doubt because of its habit of infesting hearths and warm places. The vocab. word is confined largely to S Germany and Austria, and it is in this region that the surname is most frequent.

3. German: habitation name from a place in Upper Bavaria, perhaps so called from MHG *grille* cricket.
Cogns. (of 2): Fr.: **Gril(le).** It.: **Grillo, Grilli; A(g)rillo** (Naples). Port.: **Grilo.**
Dims. (of 2): Fr.: **Grillet, Grillot, Grillon.** Prov.: **Grilhot.** It.: **Grilletti, Grilletto, Grillini; Arillotta.**
Augs. (of 2): It.: **Grilloni, Grillone.**
Pej. (of 2): Fr.: **Grillard.**
Patrs. (from 1): Eng.: **Grills, Grylls.**

Grimaud French: from *Grimwald*, a Gmc personal name composed of the elements *grīm* mask, helmet + *wald* rule.
Vars.: **Grimault, Grimal, Grimaux, Grémaud.**
Cogns.: It.: **Grimaldi, Grimaldo**; **Grimaudo** (NW Italy, Sicily); **Grimoldi** (Lombardy); **Grimaudi** (Emilia); **Grimod** (Val d'Aosta).

Grimble English: from a Norman personal name *Grimbald*, composed of the Gmc elements *grīm* mask, helmet + *bald* bold, brave.
Vars.: **Gribble, Gribbell; Grumble, Grumell.**
Cogns.: Fr.: **Gribaud, Gribaut.**

Grime English: from the ON personal name *Grímr* (a cogn. of OE *grīma* mask), which remained popular as a given name in the form *Grim* in Anglo-Scandinavian areas well into the 12th cent. It was a byname of Woden with the meaning 'masked person' or 'shape-changer', and may have been bestowed on male children in an attempt to secure the protection of the god. The Continental Gmc cogn. *grīm* was also used as a first element in cpd names (cf. GRIMAUD and GRIMBLE), with the original sense 'mask', 'helmet'. Some examples of the surname may derive from short forms of such names.
Cogns.: Ger.: **Greim.** Low Ger.: **Griem.**
Dims.: Ger.: **Greimel, Greimbl.**
Patrs.: Eng.: **Grimes, Grimson; Grimason** (N Ireland).

Grimley 1. English: habitation name from a place in Worcs., probably so called from an OE personal name, *Grīma* (see GRIME) + OE *lēah* wood, clearing.
2. Irish: var. of GORMLEY.

Grimm German: nickname for a dour and forbidding individual, from OHG *grimm* stern, severe.
Vars.: **Grimme**, GRIMMER.
Cogns.: Flem., Du.: **Grim.** Eng.: **Grim, Grimme**, GRIME.

Grimmer 1. English: from a Norman personal name *Grimier*, composed of the Gmc elements *grīm* mask, helmet + *heri, hari* army.
2. German: var. of GRIMM.
Var. (of 2): **Grimmert.**

Grimshaw English: habitation name from one of two places in Lancs., both so called from the ON personal name *Grímr* (see GRIME) or OE *grīma* ghost + OE *sceaga* copse (see SHAW).

Grimston English: habitation name from any of the various places in N and E England so called from the gen. case of the ON personal name *Grímr* (see GRIME) + OE *tūn* enclosure, settlement.
Var.: **Grimstone.**

Grimward English: from a Norman personal name *Grimward*, composed of the Gmc elements *grīm* mask, helmet + *ward* guardian.
Vars.: **Grimwade, Grimwood.**

Grinder English: occupational name for a grinder of corn, i.e. a miller, ME, OE *grindere*, an agent noun from OE *grindan* to grind. Less often it may have referred to someone who ground blades to keep their sharpness or who ground pigments, spices, and medicinal herbs to powder.

Grindley English: habitation name from any of various minor places, for example in Staffs., so called from OE *grēne* GREEN + *lēah* wood, clearing.
Vars.: **Grinley, Grinlay, Greenl(e)y, Greenlee.**

Grindrod English: habitation name from a minor place in the parish of Rochdale, Lancs., so called from OE *grēne* GREEN + *rod* clearing (see RHODES).
This name is first recorded in Rochdale in 1541 in the spelling Greneroade.

Grinter English: of uncertain origin. It is probably an occupational name for an official in charge of a granary, ANF *grenetier*, but it could also be a var. of GRINDER.
Var.: **Grint.**
The name Grinter *is fairly common in Dorset from the 16th to the 18th cents. It is recorded as* Grenter *in 1570 in that county.*

Grist English: of uncertain origin. It may be an occupational name for a miller, from the ME abstract noun *grist* grinding (OE *grist*, a deriv. of *grindan*; see GRINDER). The word was not used in the concrete sense of corn to be ground until the 15th cent.

Grivel French: nickname from the thrush, from a dim. of OF *grive* thrush, itself a fem. of *gri(e)u* Greek (see GRECO), for the birds were thought to spend the winter in Greece. One reason for the giving of the nickname could have been a 'pepper and salt' colouring of the hair, similar to the plumage on the breast of this bird; another was perhaps a propensity to inebriation, since it was a popular belief that the thrush became drunk on the grapes it stole.
Vars.: **Griveau, Grivet, Grivé, Grivot.**
Dim.: **Grivelet.**

Grob German and Jewish (Ashkenazic): nickname for a boorish individual, from Ger. and Yid. *grob* coarse, crude (MHG *g(e)rop*, OHG *g(e)rob*). As a Jewish name it may sometimes have denoted a fat man, since Yid. *grob* also means 'fat'.
Vars.: Ger.: **Grobe, Grobmann.** Jewish: **Grobman, Grober(man).**
Cogns.: Low Ger.: **Grow(e)**, GROVE; **Grovemann, Groffmann.** Czech: **Hrubý, Hrubec, Hrubeš, Hrubant; Krob.** Croatian: **Grubišić** (patr.).

Grobelaer Dutch: nickname for a disorderly person, or perhaps an occupational name of some sort, from an agent deriv. of MDu. *grobellen* to turn over, rummage, search.
Vars: **Grob(b)elaar; Grobler.**

Grodzki Polish: from Pol. *gród* castle, fortification (cogn. with Czech *hrad*, Russ. *grad*). Generally, no doubt, this was a topographic name for someone living in or beside a castle or beside the citadel of a fortified town. However, the adj. *grodzki* also occurs in the expression *sąd grodzki* meaning 'castle court', something like a magistrates' court or petty sessions; the surname may therefore also have denoted someone connected with such a court.
Vars.: **Grodziński, Grodzicki.**
Cogns.: Czech: **Hradský; Hradil**; RADECKY.
Dim.: Czech: **Hrádek.**

Grogan Irish: 1. Anglicized form of Gael. **Ó Grúgáin** 'descendant of *Grúgán*', a personal name from a dim. of *grúg* anger, fierceness.
2. Anglicized form of Gael. **Ó Gruagáin** 'descendant of *Gruagán*', a personal name from a dim. of *gruag* hair. The patr. form **Mac Gruagáin** (Anglicized **McGrogan**) is much rarer.
Vars.: **O'Grogaine, O'Growgane, Groggan, Groogan.**

Gromyko Ukrainian: nickname for a noisy or obstreperous person, from *grom* thunder, crashing, loud noise, perhaps also used with reference to someone who used the word *grom* frequently in an oath.
Vars.: **Gromeko; Gromykin** (assimilated to a Russ. patr. form).
Cogns.: Pol.: **Gromek.** Czech: **Hromas, Hromíř; Hromačík, Hromek** (dims.).

Groom English (common in E Anglia): occupational name for a servant or a shepherd, from ME *grōm(e)* boy, servant (of uncertain etymology), which in some places was specialized to mean 'shepherd'.

Var.: **Groome**.

Groombridge English: habitation name from a place in Kent, recorded in 1239 as *Gromenebregge* 'the BRIDGE of the GROOMS'.

Gross German, Jewish (Ashkenazic), and English: nickname for a big man, from Ger. *gross* large, thick, corpulent (MHG, OHG *grōz*, cogn. with OE *grēat* great, large; cf. GREET 2), or, in the case of the Eng. name, from ME, OF *gros* (LL *grossus*, of Gmc origin). The Eng. vocab. word did not develop the sense 'excessively fat' until the 16th cent. The Jewish name has been Hebraicized as **Gadol**, from Hebr. *gadol* large.

Vars. (of 1): Ger.: **Grosse, Groos, Grosser(t), Grossmann**. Jewish: **Gros, Gros(s)man, Grossmann, Grosser**; GROSZ. (Of 2): Eng.: **Groce**.

Cogns. (of 1): Low Ger.: **Grote, Groot(e), Groth(e)**. Flem., Du.: **(De) Groot(e); Grotius** (Latinized). (Of 2): Fr.: **Gros, Legros**. It.: **Grosso, Grossi; Ingrosso** (Campania, Apulia). Rum.: **Grossu**. Hung.: **Grósz**.

Dims. (of 2): Eng.: **Grosset**. Fr.: **Grosset, Grossin, Grosson**. Prov.: **Grousset, Groussin, Grousson, Groussot**. It.: **Grosetti**.

Pejs. (of 2): Fr.: **Grossard, Groussaud**.

Patrs. (from 1): Flem., Du.: **Grootaers, Grootmans**. (From 2): Fr.: **Augros**. It.: **Del Grosso** (Tuscany).

Cpds: Jewish: **Gros(s)baum, Grosboim** ('large tree'); **Gros(s)berg** ('large hill'); **Gros(s)feld** ('large field'); **Grosgluck, Grossglick** ('great good fortune'); **Gros(s)gold** ('large gold'); **Grosshaus** ('large house'); **Gros(s)kopf** ('large head', probably a nickname); **Grossvogel** ('large bird'); **Grosswasser** ('large water').

Grosvenor English (Norman): occupational name for a person who was in charge of the arrangements for hunting on a lord's estate, from ANF *gros* great, chief (see GROSS) + *veneo(u)r* hunter (L *venātor*, from *venāri* to hunt).

This is the name of one of the wealthiest families in Britain, which holds the title Duke of Westminster. They have been long established in Ches., with strong links with the city of Chester. One of the earliest recorded bearers of the name was Robert le Grosvenor *of Budworth, who was granted lands by the Earl of Chester in 1160. The family's fortunes were founded by Thomas* Grosvenor *(b. 1656), who in 1677 married an heiress, Mary Davies, whose inheritance included Ebury Farm, Middlesex. This now forms an area of central London that includes Grosvenor Square and Belgrave Square.*

Grosz Jewish (E Ashkenazic): 1. nickname, given probably in reference to some now irrecoverable event, from Pol. *grosz*, a coin of small value (MHG *gros(ch)*, med. L *(denārius) grossus* thick coin; cf. GROSS).

2. Hung. spelling of GROSS.

Cogn.: Russ. **Groshev** (patr.).

Grout English: metonymic occupational name for a dealer in coarse meal, OE *grūt*, ON *grautr* porridge.

Vars.: **Grut(e)**.

Grove 1. English: topographic name for someone who lived by a grove or thicket, OE *grāf*; for the change of *-ā-* to *-ō-*, cf. ROPER.

2.English (Huguenot): from the French surname **Le Grou(x)** or **Le Greux**, which is of uncertain origin. See below.

3. Low German: cogn. of GROB.

Vars. (of 1): **Groves, Grover**; GRAVE.

The surnames Grove *and* Groves *are common mainly in the W Midlands. A Huguenot family who acquired the name* Grove *are descended from a certain Isaac* Le Greux *or* Grou(x) *or his brother. They fled from Tours in France in the late 17th cent. and settled in Spitalfields, London. Their children were known as* Grou(x) *or* Grove*; their grandchildren also used the form* Grew*; but their great-grandchildren, born at the end of the 18th cent., were universally* Grove.

Grubb English: nickname for a small person, from ME *grub* midget (of uncertain origin).

Var.: **Grubbe**.

Gruber German and Jewish (Ashkenazic): topographic name for someone who lived in a depression or hollow, from Ger. *Grube* pit, hollow (MHG *gruobe* OHG *gruoba*, a deriv. of *graben* to dig; cf. GRABER) + *-er* suffix denoting habitation.

Vars.: **Grüb(n)er, Grübler**. Ger. only: **Griebler; Grub(e), Grüb**. Jewish only: **Grubner**.

Grudziński Polish: from Pol. *Gridzień* December, a surname bestowed on someone who was born or baptized or who registered a surname in that month.

Cogn.: Jewish (E Ashkenazic): **Grudzinsky** (perhaps acquired by someone who registered the surname in December).

Grundy English (chiefly Lancs.): probably a metathesized form of *Gondri*, *Gundric*, an OF personal name introduced to Britain by the Normans. It is composed of the Gmc elements *gund* battle + *rīc* power.

Vars.: **Gundr(e)y, Goundry**.

Grünspan Jewish (Ashkenazic): ornamental name from Ger. *Grünspan* verdigris (MHG *gruenspān*, which is a calque of med. L *viride hispanicum* 'Spanish green').

Vars.: **Gru(e)nspan; Grynszpan, Grinszpan, Grins(h)pan** (from Pol. *grynszpan*); **Grins(h)pon, Grinspoon** (from Yid. *grinshpon*); **Greenspan, Greenspon** (partly Anglicized forms); **Grinspanholz** (an elaboration, with Ger. *Holz* wood).

Grushin Russian: 1. metr. from the female given name *Grusha*, a pet form of *Agrafya*, from L *Agrippina* (a deriv. of *Agrippa*, a family name of obscure, possibly Etruscan, etymology). In W Europe the name is best known as having been borne by the mothers of the Roman emperors Caligula and Nero, neither of whom was a particularly exemplary character, but in the Orthodox Church it is held in high regard as the name of a 3rd-cent. saint martyred under Valerian.

2. patr. from the nickname *Grusha* 'Pear', given perhaps to a grower or seller of the fruit, or possibly to an individual thought to resemble a pear in some way.

Cogns. (of 2): Pol.: **Gruszka, Gruszecki; Gruszczak**. Czech: **Hruš(ka)**. Ger. (of Slav. origin): **Grusche, Krusch(e)**. Jewish (E Ashkenazic, ornamental): **Grushevski, Grushevsky**.

Dims. (of 2): Czech: **Hrušík**. Ger. (of Slav. origin): **Kruschke, Kruschka, Kruschel**. Jewish: **Grus(c)hka, Grushko; Gruszka, Gruszko; Grishka; Grus(c)hkewitz, Grushkewitch** (patrs. in form).

Habitation name: Pol.: **Gruszczyński**.

Grüter Low German: occupational name for a brewer, from MLG *gruten* to brew, a deriv. of *grut* groats (cf. GROUT), which were sometimes used instead of hops in beer making.

Cogns.: Flem., Du.: **De Gruyter, Grutter**.

Patrs.: Low Ger.: **Grüters, Gruiters**.

Gruzinov Russian: patr. from the ethnic name *gruzin* Georgian (from the Georgians' own name for themselves,

Gurz, of somewhat obscure, but presumably Caucasian, etymology).

Var.: **Gruzintsev**.

Cogn.: Armenian: **Gurgian** (patr.).

Grzywacz 1. Polish: nickname from Pol. *grzywacz* ring-necked dove.

2. Jewish (E Ashkenazic): ornamental name from Pol. *grzywacz* ring-necked dove, one of the many such Ashkenazic names taken from vocab. words denoting birds.

Habitation name: **Grzywaczewski**.

Gsänger S German: habitation name from any of the various minor places called *G(e)seng* or *Gesäng*, from OHG *(gi)seng* clearing (originally one made by burning the vegetation; a deriv. of *(bi)sengan* to burn, singe).

Gscheid S German: topographic name for someone who lived near a boundary, MHG *(ge)scheide* (OHG *(gi)s-ceida*, a deriv. of *sceidan* to divide, separate), or habitation name from one of the numerous minor places named with this word.

Vars.: **Gscheider, Gschaider**.

Guadalupe Spanish: habitation name from a place in the province of Cáceres, so called from Arabic *wad-el-ûbb* 'river of the wolf' or 'river with a curve'. The place is the site of a Hieronymite convent founded in the 14th cent., which possesses a famous image of the Virgin Mary. A shrine in Mexico has been given the same name, and Our Lady of Guadalupe is regarded as the patron saint of Mexico. Guadalupe has also come to be used as a female given name, but this is almost certainly too late to lie behind any examples of the surname.

Gual Catalan: 1. topographic name for someone who lived by a ford, Cat. *gual* (LL *vadāle*, a deriv. of class. L *vadum*). The initial consonant has been influenced by Gmc cogns.; cf. WADE.

2. from a medieval given name of Gmc origin, probably a form of *Waldo*, which is a short form of several cpd names containing the element *wald* rule.

Var. (of 1): GÜELL.

Guard English: occupational name from OF *garde* watch, protection (of Gmc origin; cf. WARD 1), also used later in the concrete sense of a watchman.

Var.: **Gard**.

Cogns. (mostly topographic names referring to a watchtower or vantage point): Fr.: **Garde(s)**. Prov.: **Lagarde**. Sp.: **Guardia**. Cat.: **Guàrdia**. It.: **Laguardia**; **Guardi** (also an aphetic form of the medieval given name *Dio(ti)guardi* 'God preserve (you)').

Dims.: Fr.: **Gardet, Gardey, Gardot**. Cat.: **Guardiola**. It.: **Guarducci**.

Gucci Italian: from a medieval given name, an aphetic form of a dim. of *Ugo* (see HUGH), *Arrigo* (see HENRY), or *Berlinghiero* (see BERINGER).

Vars.: **Guzzi, Guzzo**.

Dims.: **Guccini, Guzz(ol)ini, Guzzetti**.

Guedes Portuguese: patr. from the medieval given name *Guede, Gueda*. This is clearly of Gmc origin, but its meaning and derivation are uncertain. It may be akin to GUY.

Güell Catalan: 1. topographic name for someone who lived by a spring or well, Cat. *güell* (of Gmc origin; cf. WELL).

2. from a medieval given name of Gmc origin; perhaps from *Gudila*, a deriv. of the element *gūd* battle, or from *Wilia*, a short form of the various cpd names containing the element *will* will, desire.

3. var. of GUAL.

Guest English: nickname for a stranger or newcomer to a community, from ME *g(h)est* guest, visitor (from ON *gestr*, which has absorbed the cogn. OE *giest*).

Cogns.: Ger.: GAST. Du.: **De Gast**.

Dims.: Ger.: **Gastl** (Bavaria); **Gästle** (Swabia).

Guevara Basque: habitation name from a place in the province of Álava. The origin and meaning of the place-name are uncertain; it was recorded in the form *Gebala* by the geographer Ptolemy in the 2nd cent. AD.

Guggenheim Jewish (W Ashkenazic): habitation name from *Gugenheim* in Alsace or *Jugenheim* (earlier *Guggenheim*) near Bensheim. In both cases the second element is from OHG *heim* homestead, while the first is of obscure and disputed etymology.

Vars.: **Gugenheim, Guckenheim**; **Guggenheimer**; **Koukenheim** (a Fr. spelling).

Guichard French: from a Gmc personal name composed of the elements *wīg* war + *hard* brave, hardy, strong.

Cogns.: Ger.: **Weich(h)ard, Weichert, Weickert, Weigert**. Low Ger.: **Wiegard, Wieghardt, Wieger(t), Wigger(t), Wi(e)chert, Wickert, Wicher**. Fris.: **Wiart, Wiert**.

Dims.: Fr.: **Guichardet, Guichardon, Guichardot, Guichardin, Guichon, Guichot, Guichet(eau)**.

Patrs.: Low Ger.: **Wiegers, Wi(e)chers, Wiggers, Wickerts**; **Wicharz** (N Rhineland). Fris.: **Wiarda, Wyerda, Wiards**.

Guignard French: 1. nickname for someone with a squint, from OF *guign(ier)* to wink, squint, look askance (of Gmc origin; cf. OE *wincian* to wink) + the pej. suffix *-ard*.

2. from a Gmc personal name composed of the elements *win* friend + *hard* brave, hardy, strong.

Vars. (of 1): **Guignier, Guigneux**. (Of 2): **Guin(n)ard**.

Dims.: **Guignardeau, Guignet, Guignot, Guignon**.

Guijarro Spanish: nickname for a small man or topographic name for someone who lived on stony soil, from Sp. *guijarro* pebble (a pej. deriv. of *guija*, from LL *(petra) aquīlea* sharp stone, from class. L *acūleus* pointed, sharp).

Guillamon Catalan: from the Gmc personal name *Willimund*, composed of the elements *will* will, desire + *mund* protection.

Guimarães Portuguese: habitation name from any of various places, in particular a town in the province of Minho, so called from L *(villa) Vimaranis* 'estate of *Vimara*', a Gmc personal name probably composed of the elements *wīg* war + *marah* horse.

Guinan Irish: 1. Anglicized form of Gael. **Ó Cuinneáin** 'descendant of *Cuinneán*', a personal name from a dim. of *conn* chief.

2. Anglicized form of Gael. **Ó Cuineáin** 'descendant of *Cuineán*', a personal name from a dim. of *cana* whelp.

Var.: **Guinane**.

Guisado Spanish: nickname from OSp. *guisado* (well) prepared, (well) equipped (past part. of the verb *guisar*, LL *wīsāre*, from *wīsa* manner, way, of Gmc origin).

Guise English: regional name for someone from the district of France of this name, which is of unknown etymology.

A family of this name can be traced to Nicholas de Gyse, *who on his marriage in 1262 received the manor of Elmore, Gloucs. Bearers of the name are still found at Elmore, and it has spread to Birmingham and elsewhere.*

Guitart Catalan: from the Gmc personal name *Withard*, composed of the element *wit, wid* (see GUY 1) + *hard* hardy, brave, strong.

Cogns.: Fr.: **Guit(t)ard**; **Vitard** (Normandy).

Guiver English: of uncertain origin; perhaps from an OE personal name composed of the elements *wīg* war and *beorht* famous. However, the earliest known form that seems to belong here is Thomas *Gyva* (Bishops Stortford, Herts., 1489); this is more likely to be from a ME form of the OE female personal name *Gifu*, a short form of any of the various cpd names with a final element *gifu* gift.

Var.: **Guyver**.

All present-day bearers of the name are probably descended from Richard Gyver *(d. 1543) of Ugley in Essex.*

Gullick English: from the ME given name *Gullake, Gudloc*, OE *Gūðlāc*, composed of the elements *gūð* battle + *lāc* sport, play, reinforced by the ON cogn. *Gúðleikr*.

Vars.: **Gulick, Gillick**; **Goodlake, Goodluck**; **Cutlack, Cutlock** (Norfolk).

Cogns.: Ger.: **Gund(e)lach, Gundlack, Gundloch**.

Patr.: Eng.: **Gullickson**.

The names Cutlack *is recorded on the N Norfolk coast in 1415, and later in the 15th cent. is found quite commonly in Norwich and on the Isle of Ely, along with the var.* Cutlock.

Gulliver English: nickname for a greedy person, from OF *goulafre* glutton (of uncertain origin).

Vars.: **Gulliford, Galliford, Galliver**.

Gully English: nickname for a giant or large man, from ME *golias* giant, from the Hebr. personal name *Golyat* Goliath, which occurs in the Bible as the name of the champion of the Philistines, who stood 'six cubits and a span', but was defeated in single combat by the shepherd boy David (I Sam. 17), who killed him with a stone from his sling. The surname is unlikely to be a topographic name for a dweller by a water channel, as the vocab. word *gully* (from OF *goulet* neck of a bottle, a dim. of *goule* throat, L *gula*) is not attested in this sense until the 17th cent.

Vars.: **Golley, Gullyes**.

Gulyaev Russian: patr. from the nickname *Gulyai*, a deriv. of *gulyat* to walk, wander, formerly also 'revel', which is presumably the sense that lies behind the surname.

Gumbel English: from a Norman personal name *Gumbald*, composed of the Gmc elements *gund* battle + *bald* bold, brave.

Dim.: **Gumbley** (W Midlands).

Gunkel German: metonymic occupational name for a spinner or a maker of spindles, from Ger. *Kunkel* spindle, distaff (MHG *kunkel*, from LL *conicula*, dim. of *cōnus* cone, peg).

Vars.: **Kunkel, Künkel, Kinkel**; **Künkler**.

Gunn 1. English and Scots: from the ON personal name *Gunnr*, or the fem. form *Gunne*, short forms of the various cpd names with the first element *gunn* battle.

2. English: metonymic occupational name for someone who operated a siege engine or cannon, perhaps also a nickname for a forceful person, from ME *gunne, gonne* ballista, cannon (originally a humorous application of the female personal name).

3. Scots: Anglicized form of Gael. **Mac Gille Dhuinn** 'son of the servant of the brown one'; see DUNN 1.

Var. (of 1): **Gun**.

Dims. (of 1): **Gunnet(t)**.

Patrs. (from 1): **Gunns, Gunson**.

Gunnell English: from the ON female personal name *Gunnhildr*, ME *Gunnilla, Gunnild*, composed of the elements *gunn* battle + *hild* strife, contention. This was extremely popular in those parts of England that were under Norse influence in the Middle Ages.

Var.: **Cunnell**.

Gunner English: 1. from the ON female personal name *Gunvǫr*, composed of the elements *gunn* battle + *vǫr* the feminine form of *varr* defender.

2. occupational name for an operator of heavy artillery; see GUNN 2.

Gunter English: from the Norman personal name *Gunter* (OF *Gontier*), composed of the Gmc elements *gund* battle + *heri, hari* army.

Var.: **Gunther**.

Cogns.: Fr.: **Gontier**. Ger.: **Gunther**. Swed.: **Gunnar**.

Dims.: Ger.: **Gunz, Gün(t)zel, Günzl(ein), Günzelmann**.

Patrs.: Norw., Dan.: **Gundersen**. Swed.: **Gunnarsson**.

Patr. (from a dim.): Ger.: **Günzler**.

Gunton English (E Anglia): habitation name from either of two places, one in Norfolk and the other in Suffolk, so called from the ON personal name *Gunnr* or *Gunne* (see GUNN 1) + OE *tūn* enclosure, settlement.

Guppy English: habitation name from a place in Wootton Fitzpaine, Dorset, so called from the OE personal name *Guppa* (perhaps a short form of a cpd name composed of the elements *gūð* battle + *berht* bright, famous) + *(ge)hæg* enclosure. It is not a nickname from the tropical fish, since this was unknown in medieval England, and was in fact named in the 19th cent. in honour of R. J. L. Guppy, a clergyman in Trinidad who first presented specimens to the British Museum.

Vars.: **Guppey, Guppie**.

The earliest known bearer of the name is Nicholas de Gupehegh *(Somerset, 1253/4). Most if not all present-day bearers of the name seem to descend from a certain William* Guppy *of Chardstock, Devon, who in 1497 was fined forty shillings for his alleged part in the rebellion of Perkin Warbeck.*

Gurnay English (Norman): habitation name from *Gournay*(-en-Brai) in Seine-Maritime, so called from a Gallo-Roman personal name *Gordīnus* + the local suffix *-ācum*.

Var.: **Gurney**.

Gurton English: habitation name from *Girton* in Cambs. and Notts., which get their names from OE *grēot* grit, gravel (or the derived adjective *grēoten*) + *tūn* enclosure, settlement.

Vars.: **Girton, Girtin**.

Gusev Russian: patr. from the nickname *Gus* 'Goose', given perhaps to a foolish person, or occupational name for someone who raised geese. The fact that the Eng. and Russ. words sound practically identical is something of a coincidence, for, although the words are ultimately cogn., the rules of Slav. sound changes would lead us to expect a form like *zus* rather than *gus*; there may have been early influence on the Russ. word by Gmc forms. For the Pol. equivalent, see GĄSIOR.

Var.: **Gusakov**.

Cogns.: Czech: **Husák**. Jewish (Ashkenazic; reasons for adoption unknown): **Gusman, Hus(s)**; **Gusakov** (E Ashkenazic).

Dim.: Czech: **Húsek**.

Gustavsson Swedish: patr. from an ON personal name composed of the tribal name *Gaut* (see JOCELYN) + *staf* staff, cudgel.

Var.: **Gustafsson**.

Cogn.: Norw., Dan.: **Gustafsen**.

Gute Jewish (Ashkenazic): from the Yid. female given name *Gute* 'GOOD'.

Var.: **Gite** (from a S Yid. form).

Dim.: **Gittel** (from the Yid. dim. female given name *Gitl*).

Metrs. (from dims.): **Gittelson**; **Gitlin** (E Ashkenazic).

Guthrie 1. Scots: habitation name from a place near Forfar, Tayside, so called from Gael. *gaothair* windy place (a deriv. of *gaoth* wind) + the local suffix *-ach*.

2. Scots: Anglicized form of Gael. **Mag Uchtre** 'son of *Uchtre*', a personal name of uncertain origin, perhaps akin to *uchtlach* child.

3. Irish: Anglicized form of Gael. **Ó Flaithimh** 'descendant of *Flaitheamh*', a byname meaning 'Prince'. This Anglicized form seems to be the result of an erroneous association of the Gael. name with *laithigh* mud, and of mud with gutters.

Gutiérrez Spanish: patr. from the medieval given name *Gutierre*, from a Visigothic personal name of uncertain form and meaning, perhaps a cpd of the elements *gunþi* battle + *hairus* sword.

Guttenberg German and Jewish (Ashkenazic): habitation name from any of various places, for example in Bavaria, so called from the weak dat. case (originally used after a preposition and article) of OHG *guot* good + *berg* hill. The shortening of the vowel in the first syllable is a feature found in various dialects of German.

Vars.: **Gutenberg**. Jewish only: **Gutenberger**.

Gutteridge English: 1. from the ME given name *Goderiche*, OE *Gōdrīc*, composed of the elements *gōd* good + *rīc* power.

2. from the ME given name *Cuterich*, OE *Cūðric*, composed of the elements *cūð* famous, well known + *rīc* power.

Vars.: **Gut(t)ridge**. (Of 1 only): **Good(e)ridge, Godridge, Go(o)drich, Good(e)rick, Goodwright**. (Of 2 only): **Cutt(e)ridge, Cuttriss, Cutress**.

Guy 1. English: from a French form of the Gmc personal name *Wido*, of uncertain origin. It may be from the element reflected in OHG *witu*, OE *widu*, *wudu* wood, or else from that of OHG *wīt*, OE *wīd* wide. Whatever its origins, this name was popular among the Normans in the forms *Wi*, *Why* as well as in the rest of France in the form *Guy*; both versions are reflected in the Eng. vars.

2. English: occupational name for a guide, OF *gui* (a deriv. of *gui(d)er* to guide, of Gmc origin).

3. Jewish: of unknown origin.

Vars.: **G(u)ye, Why(e), Wye**; **Guyon, Wyon** (from the OF oblique case).

Cogns.: Fr.: **Guy**; **Guitte** (reborrowed from Gmc at a later date, when Fr. no longer suppressed dental consonants between vowels); **V(u)itte** (E France); **Guion, Guyon**; **Guit(t)on**; **V(u)itton**. It.: **Guido, Guidi**; **Ghio** (N Italy). Cat.: **Guiu**. Flem.: **Wyd**.

Dims.: Fr.: **Guiet, Guyet, Guiot, Guyot, Guyonnet, Guyonneau**; **Guit(t)et, Guitel, Guitonneau**; **Vit(t)et, Vuittet**. It.: **Guidelli, Guidetti, Guidini, Guiducci, Guiduzzi, Guidotti**; **Ghidelli, Ghidetti, Ghidini, Ghidoli, Ghi(d)otti, Ghiotto** (Lombardy, Emilia). Hung.: **Vida**.

Augs.: It.: **Guidone, Guidoni**; **Ghi(d)oni, Ghion(e)**.

Patrs.: Eng.: **Guys, Guyson**.

Guyler English (Nottingham): nickname for a deceitful or treacherous person, from an agent deriv. of ME *guylen* to deceive (a deriv. of *guyle* guile, from OF but of Gmc origin).

Guymer English (Norfolk): from the OF personal name *Guymer*, which was introduced to Britain by the Normans in the form *Wymer*. It is composed of the Gmc elements *wīg* war + *meri*, *mari* fame. The surname is therefore a doublet of WYMER 1, although this has also absorbed an OE form of the same underlying Gmc name.

Guyton English (Norfolk): habitation name from *Gayton* in Norfolk, probably so called from an OE personal name or stream-name **Gǣga* or **Gǣge* (presumably akin to *gǣgan* to turn aside) + OE *tūn* enclosure, settlement.

Guzek Polish: nickname for a man with a prominent carbuncle or wart, Pol. *guzek*, dim. of *guz* knob.

Vars.: **Guziak**; **Guz**.

Patr.: **Guzewicz**.

Habitation name: **Guzowski**.

Guzik Polish: 1. nickname for a small person, from Pol. *guzik* button, originally a dim. of *guz* knob.

Var.: **Guzicki**.

Guzmán Spanish: from a Visigothic personal name, apparently composed of the tribal name *Gaut* (see JOCELYN) + *man* man.

Cogn.: Port.: **Gusmão**. Jewish: **Guzman** (probably an adoption of the Spanish surname).

Gwiazda Polish: nickname meaning 'Star', Pol. *gwiazda*.

Habitation name: **Gwiazdowski**.

Gwinnett Welsh: regional name from the district in N(W) Wales called *Gwynedd*. The name first occurs in L documents in the form *Venedotia* 'Land of the *Vēnii*', a tribal name of uncertain, though presumably Celt., etymology.

Vars.: **Gwyneth, Gwioneth**.

Gwizdka Polish: nickname for someone noted for his cheerful whistling, from a deriv. of Pol. *gwizdać* to whistle.

Var.: **Gwizdała**.

Gwyn Welsh: nickname for a person with fair hair or a noticeably pale complexion, from W *gwyn* light, white, fair. This was also used as a personal name in the Middle Ages, and some early examples may reflect this.

Vars.: **Gwynn(e), Gwinn**; QUINN; WINN.

Cogns.: Bret.: **(Le) Guen, Gouin**.

Dims.: Bret.: **(Le) Guen(n)ec**.

Gzik Polish: nickname for an irritating person, from Pol. *gzik* gadfly.

H

Haar 1. German and Jewish (Ashkenazic): nickname for someone with a copious or noticeable head of hair, from Ger. *Haar* hair (MHG *hār*).

2. German: metonymic occupational name for someone who worked with raw flax in the production of linen, from Ger. *Haar* raw flax (a different word from that in 1, from MHG *har*, OHG *haro*).

3. Low German and Dutch: topographic name for someone who lived on a moor, from MLG *haar* marsh, moor.

Vars. (of 3): Low Ger., Du.: **Van der Haar**, **Verhaar(en)**, **Haaren**, **Ter Haar**.

Cogn. (of 1): Du.: **Haahr**.

Dim. (of 1): Ger.: **Härle**.

Haarla Finnish: ornamental name from *haara* branch + the local suffix *-la*; cf. Swed. GREN.

Habbert German: from a Gmc personal name composed of the elements *hadu* battle, strife + *berht* bright, famous.

Vars.: **Happert**, **Habbrecht**.

Cogns.: Low Ger.: **Hobbert**, **Hobbart**. Fr.: **Habert**.

Dims.: Ger.: **Happel**, HASS. Low Ger.: **Hadeke**. Fris.: **Habbe(ma)**, **Hobbe(ma)**, **Hapke**, **Hatje**. Du.: **Hobbema**. Fr.: **Hablet**, **Hablot**.

Patrs. (from dims.): Fris.: **Hab(be)s**, **Haps**; **Habben**, **Hobben**; **Habbing**, **Hobbing**.

The Dutch landscape artist Meindert Hobbema *(1638–1709) was born in Amsterdam and was a pupil and friend of van Ruisdael. His name was originally Meydertz; he received the byname Hobbema as a young man.*

Habenicht German: nickname for a poor man, from Ger. *Habenichts* have-not, a cpd formed from MHG *habe(n)* to have (OHG *habēn*) + *niht* nothing (OHG *niwiht*, *neowiht*).

Var.: **Habnit**.

Cogn.: Low Ger.: **Havenith**.

Haber German and Jewish (Ashkenazic): metonymic occupational name for a grower of or dealer in oats, from early mod. Ger. *Haber* oats (mod. Ger. *Hafer*; MHG *haber(e)*, OHG *habaro*). As a Jewish surname, it is in many cases ornamental.

Vars.: Ger.: **Hafer**; **Haberer**, **Häberer**; **Habermann**. Jewish: **Haberer**, **Haberman**; **Hober(man)** (from Yid. *hober*); HUBER; **Gaber(man)**, **Goberman** (under Russ. influence; see GOREN); **Aberman** (in regions where Yid. has no /h/).

Cogns.: Low Ger.: **Haver**. Flem., Du.: **Van Havre**, **Verhavaert**, **Ravert**.

Dims.: Ger.: **Haberl**, **Häberle(in)**, **Heberl**, **Heberle(in)**.

Cpds: Jewish: **Haberberg** ('oat hill'); **Haberkorn** ('oat grain', partly Anglicized as **Habercorn**); **Haberfeld** ('oat field', partly Anglicized as **Haberfield**); **Haberstaub**, **Habershtoub** ('oat dust').

Habersham English: metonymic occupational name for a maker of coats of chain mail, from ME, OF *haubergeon* mail jerkin, a dim. of *hauberc* coat of mail, a word of Gmc origin composed of elements meaning 'neck' (see HALS) and 'protection'. After coats of mail became obsolete and the word fell out of use, the name was altered by folk etymology to assume the appearance of a habitation name.

Vars.: **Habershon**, **Habberjam**, **Haversham**, **Havisham**; **Hab(b)eshaw**, **Hab(b)ishaw** (from the OF agent noun *haubergier*).

Habsburg German: habitation name from a castle in Aargau, built in the 11th cent. by Werner, Bishop of Strasburg, and named from the gen. case of MHG *habech* HAWK + *burg* fortress, stronghold.

Var.: **Hapsburg** (an Anglicized form).

The Habsburgs *are one of the great families of Europe, having worn the crown of the Holy Roman Empire (subsequently Austria and Austro-Hungary) from 1440 to 1918, with a brief interlude in 1806 caused by Napoleon's invasion of Austria. They also sat on the thrones of Spain, Hungary, Bohemia, and elsewhere at various periods.*

Hache 1. French: metonymic occupational name for a maker or user of axes, either for domestic and agricultural purposes or as weapons of war, from OF *hache* axe (of Gmc origin; cf. HACKER).

2. German: occupational name for a servant, from MHG *hache* lad, boy, servant.

3. Ger. (of Slav. origin): pet form of HANS.

Vars. (of 1): **Lahache**. (Of 3): **Hach**, **Hachnik**, **Hachnek**.

Dims. (of 1): **Hachet(te)**, **Hachin**, **Hachon**.

Hack 1. English: var. of HAKE 1.

2. Jewish (Ashkenazic): of unknown origin.

Hacker English (chiefly Somerset), German, and Jewish (Ashkenazic): occupational name for a butcher, or less often for a woodcutter, from an agent deriv. of ME *hack(en)*, Ger. *hacken* to chop, cut (OE *haccian*, OHG *hacchōn*). The Jewish surnames in this group may be from Yid. *heker* butcher, *holtsheker* woodcutter (Ger. *Holzhacker*), or *valdheker* lumberjack, or from Ger. *Hacker* woodchopper. Another possibility for Jewish forms spelled with *-e-* is that they are from Yid. *heker* retail or retailer (the exact meaning is unclear); akin to Ger. *Höker* street trader, pedlar (see HAKE).

Vars.: Ger.: **Häcker**, **Hecker** (see also HEDGE); HACKMANN. Jewish: **Haker**, **He(c)ker**, HACKMANN.

Dims.: Ger.: **Heckerle(in)**.

Hackett 1. English (chiefly W Midlands): dim. of the medieval given name *Hack*, *Hake*; see HAKE.

2. Scots: perhaps a habitation name from the lands of *Halkhead* in the former county of Renfrews. (now part of Strathclyde region), apparently so called from ME *hauk*, *halk* HAWK + *wode*, *wude* WOOD.

Vars. (of 1): **Haggett**, **Haggitt**, **Acket**. (Of 2): **Halket(t)**.

Patr. (from 1): **Acketts**.

An Irish family of this name were established in Ireland by William de Haket, *who accompanied King John and was granted estates in Tipperary in the early 13th cent. The form* Hackett *was first used by his descendants in the 16th cent.*

Hacking English: habitation name from a place in Lancs., of uncertain origin. Early forms appear with the definite article, and the name may represent an OE term for a fish weir, a deriv. of *hæcc* hatch or *haca* bolt.

Hackmann 1. German and Jewish (Ashkenazic): var. of HACKER.

2. Low German: var. of HAKE 2.

Var. (of 1): Jewish: **Hackman**.

Hackwood English: of uncertain origin. It is either an occupational nickname for a woodcutter, from ME *hack(en)* to cut, chop (see HACKER) + *wode* wood, or else a habitation name from some place such as *Hackwood* near Basingstoke, Hants, so called from OE **hacga* hawthorn (see HAW 1) + *wudu* WOOD.

During the Middle Ages the name was found in two main geographical regions. The first known bearer is Johanne Hackewude, *recorded at Bexhill, Sussex, in 1230, and the name subsequently became relatively common in the southern coastal counties, but the last modern descendants of this branch seem to have died out in the mid-19th cent. The second regional concentration is in the Midlands, where the first known bearers are William and John* Hackewode, *recorded in 1331 at Elford, Staffs. All present-day bearers of the name seem to be descended from a handful of ancestors living in the villages of Kingsley, Ipstones, and Cheddleton, Staffs., in the mid-17th cent.*

Hacon English: from the ON personal name *Hákon*, originally a byname meaning 'Handy', 'Useful'.

Patrs.: Dan., Norw.: **Håkonsen**. Swed.: **Håkonsson**.

Haddleton English: habitation name from a lost place near Bingley in W Yorks. called *Hathelton*, later *Halton* (*Hateltun* in Domesday Book). The placename is of uncertain origin; the final element is presumably OE *tūn* enclosure, settlement, but the first element is unidentified.

Haddock English, of uncertain origin. Three possibilities are discussed by Reaney: 1. metonymic occupational name for a fishmonger or nickname for someone supposedly resembling the fish, from ME *hadduc* haddock (of unknown origin).

2. from a medieval survival, with added initial *H-*, of an OE personal name *Ædduc*, a dim. of *Æddi*, itself a short form of various cpd names with the first element *ēad* prosperity, fortune.

3. habitation name from *Haydock* near Liverpool, perhaps so called from W *heiddog* barley farm, a deriv. of *haidd* barley, but more likely from OE *hæþ* HEATH + *hōc* HOOK.

Haddon 1. English: habitation name from any of the various places, in Derbys., Dorset, and Northants, so called from OE *hǣð* heathland, heather (see HEATH) + *dūn* hill (see DOWN 1).

2. Scots: var. of HALDANE 2.

Haddow Scots: habitation name from *Haddo* in the former county of Aberdeens. (now part of Grampian region), so called from ME *half* + Gael. *dabhach*, a land measure equivalent to four ploughgates.

The earliest known bearer of the name is Alanus de Haldawach, *who was excommunicated in 1382.*

Haden English (W Midlands): habitation name from *Haden* Hill near Dudley, which may get its name from OE *hǣð* HEATH + *dūn* hill (see DOWN 1).

Hader German and Jewish (Ashkenazic): 1. nickname for a quarrelsome person, from Ger. *Hader* discord, argument, quarrel (MHG *hader*; cf. the element *hadu* strife, contention, in Gmc personal names).

2. nickname for a scruffy person or metonymic occupational name for a trader in rags, from Ger. *Hader* tattered clothes, rags (MHG *hader*, OHG *hadara* skins for clothing).

Vars.: Ger.: **Haderer**, **Hadermann**. (Of 2 only): Ger.: **Hodermann**.

Dims.: Ger.: **Häderle**, **Haderlin**.

Hadley English (chiefly W Midlands): habitation name from a place so called near Telford in Shrops. or another near Droitwich, Worcs., or possibly from any of the places called *Hadleigh* in Suffolk, Essex, and elsewhere. Most of these get the name from OE *hǣð* heathland, heather (see HEATH) + *lēah* wood, clearing. However, the one in Worcs. appears to have as its first element the OE personal name *Hadda* (probably a short form of the various cpd names beginning with *heard* hardy, brave, strong).

Vars.: **Hadleigh** (rare as a surname); **Hadlee**. See also HEADLEY and HEATLEY.

Hadlow English: habitation name from a place in Kent. The second element of this is fairly certainly OE *hlāw* (see LAW 2 and LOW 1); the first may be OE *hāð* heathland, heather (a byform of *hǣð*; see HEATH) or perhaps *hēafod* head, chief.

Hafner German and Jewish (Ashkenazic): occupational name for a potter, from an agent deriv. of Ger. dial. *Hafen* pot, dish (MHG *hafen*, OHG *havan*). This is the normal term for the occupation in S Germany and Austria, and the Ger. surname is confined largely to this area. Other names referring to this occupation may be found at EULER, TÖPFER, and POTTER.

Vars.: **Haffner**, **Hef(f)ner**. Ger. only: **Häfner**.

Haft German and Jewish (Ashkenazic): metonymic occupational name for a maker and seller of various sorts of clamps and fastenings, from Ger. *Haft* clasp (MHG *haft*).

Vars.: **Hafter**. Ger.: **Haftmann**, **Haftenmacher**.

Dim.: Ger.: **Haftel**.

Hagan Irish: Anglicized form of Gael. **Ó hÁgáin** 'descendant of *Ógán*', a personal name from a dim. of *óg* young.

Vars.: **O'Hagan**; **Haggan** (N Ireland).

Hägg Swedish: ornamental name from *hägg* bird cherry (*Prunus padus*). This is one of the surnames drawn from the vocab. of nature and adopted more or less arbitrarily in the 19th cent.

Cpds: **Häggberg** ('cherry hill'); **Häggblad** ('cherry leaf'); **Häggblom** ('cherry flower'); **Hägglund** ('cherry grove'); **Häggmark** ('cherry land'); **Häggqvist** ('cherry twig'); **Häggström** ('cherry river').

Haggard English: 1. nickname from ME, OF *hagard* wild, untamed (of uncertain etymology, perhaps from a Gmc element meaning 'hedge'; cf. HAIG). The word was adopted into ME as a technical term in falconry to denote a hawk that had been captured and trained when already fully grown, rather than being reared in captivity, and the surname could therefore conceivably have developed as an occupational name for a falconer.

2. said to be an Anglicized form of Dan. ÅGÅRD; see below.

Vars. (of 1): **Haggar(t)**, **Hagard**, **Hagger**.

Cogn. (of 1): Fr.: **Agard**.

The English writer Sir H. Rider Haggard *(1856–1925) was born into the landed gentry in Norfolk. His family were descended from a Danish nobleman, Andrew* Ogard, *who came to England in the 15th cent. from the city of* Ågård *in Denmark.*

Haggis 1. Scots: habitation name from any of the numerous places in the Lowlands so called, apparently from Northern ME *hag* clearing (ON *hǫgg*, akin to HACHE 1 and HACKER) + *hous* house (OE *hūs*). There does not seem to be any direct connection with the vocab. word denoting the typical dish of the region, although this word is itself of uncertain origin.

2. English (Cambs.): var. of AGGIS.

Vars. (of 1): **Haggish, Haggas.**

The first known bearer of the name is Gilbert of Haggehouse, *a Scots merchant arrested at King's Lynn in 1394.*

Hague English: 1. var. of HAIG.

2. in a few cases perhaps, a local name from *The Hague* in the Netherlands, Du. *Den Haag*, from *haag* enclosure, a cogn. of ON *hagi*, OE *haga* (see HAIG).

Hahn 1. German: nickname for a proud or lusty person, from Ger. *Hahn* cock (MHG *hane*, OHG *hano*, of which the fem. *henin* is cogn. with OE *henn*, mod. Eng. *hen*). In some cases it may also have been a house name, from a house sign bearing a picture of a cock, or a metonymic occupational name for a chicken farmer.

2. Jewish (Ashkenazic): ornamental name from Ger. *Hahn* cock, one of the many Ashkenazic surnames based on vocab. words denoting birds or animals.

3. German: var. of HAIN 4 and 5.

Var. (of 1): **Hahner(t).**

Cogns. (of 1): Du., Flem.: **De Haan** (also among Dutch Jews).

Haig 1. Scots (Norman): habitation name from any of various places in N France named from ON *hagi* enclosure, a word with cogns. in most Gmc languages (cf. HAY).

2. English: topographic name for someone who lived by a hedged or fenced enclosure (OE *haga*), or habitation name from a place named with this word (or its ON cogn. *hagi*), esp. three places called *Haigh*, two in W Yorks. and the other near Manchester.

Var.: **Haigh** (chiefly Yorks.).

Cogns.: Ger.: **Hag(e), Häge; Hager, Häger; Hagemann, Heg(g)emann.** Low Ger.: **Haag.** Fris.: **Haagsma.** Flem.: **Van der Haeghe, Verhaeghe.** Du.: **Haag, Ha(a)gen, Verhagen, Hageman, Hagenaar.** Dan., Norw.: **Hagemann.** Swed.: **Hag(e)man.**

Dims.: Ger.: **Hägle, Hegel(e).**

Cpds: Swed.: **Hagberg** ('enclosure hill'); **Haglund** ('enclosure grove'); **Hagstedt** ('enclosure homestead'); **Hagstrand** ('enclosure shore'); **Hagström** ('enclosure river').

The Scottish Borders family of Haig *came originally from* La Hague *in Manche, Normandy. Their first ancestor in Scotland was Petrus* del Hage, *whose name appears on documents of the 1160s. The direct line died out in 1867 and the ancestral manor of Bemersyde passed into other hands, but in 1921 it was purchased by the nation and presented to Field Marshal Sir Douglas Haig (1861–1928), who had been created 1st Earl Haig in 1919.*

Hailes 1. Scots: habitation name from *Hailes* in Lothian, so called from the ME gen. or pl. form of *hall* HALL.

2. English: habitation name from *Hailes* in Gloucs., which is an old Brit. river name meaning 'polluted', from a word that is an ancestor of W *halog* dirty.

3. English: from the gen. or pl. form of OE *halh* nook, recess (see HALE 1).

Vars.: **Hails.** (Of 3 only): **Ha(y)les; Hallow(e)s; Hallas** (chiefly Yorks.); **Heal(e)s** (Wessex).

Hailwood English: habitation name from *Halewood* in Lancs., so called from OE *halh* nook, recess (see HALE 1) + *wudu* WOOD.

Hain 1. English: habitation name from any of various places named with ME *heghen*, a weak pl. of *hegh*, from OE *(ge)hæg* enclosure (see HAY 1). *Hayne* is a common minor placename in Devon.

2. English: from the ME given name *Hain*, *Heyne*. This is derived from the Gmc personal name *Hagano*, originally a byname meaning 'Hawthorn'. It is found in England before the Conquest, but was popularized by the Normans. In the Danelaw, it may be derived from ON *Hagni*, *Hǫgni*, a Scandinavianized version of the same name.

3. English: nickname for a wretched individual, from ME *hain(e)*, *heyne* wretch, niggard (OE *hēan*).

4. German: topographic name for someone who lived by a patch of enclosed pastureland, MHG *hagen* (OHG *hagan* hawthorn, hedge).

5. German: from a Gmc personal name, originally a byname from the same element as in 2 above.

6. Jewish (Ashkenazic): of unknown origin.

Vars. (of 1–3): **Haine, Hayn(e).** (of 4 and 5): **Hagen,** HAHN. (Of 4): **Haine, Hayn.**

Cogns. (of 2): Fr.: **Hainon, Hénon.**

Patrs. (from 2): Eng.: HAINES. Dan.: **Haagensen, Hågensen.**

A certain Isaac Hayne *(1745–81) was an American Revolutionary militia officer, executed by the British for breaking parole. He owned an ironworks and was manufacturing ammunition for the American forces when he was caught. His grandfather had emigrated from England to S Carolina in about 1700.*

Haines 1. English: patr. from the medieval given name HAIN 2.

2. English: habitation name from *Haynes* in Beds. This name first appears in Domesday Book as *Hagenes* and has been explained in several different ways, none of them very convincing.

3. Welsh: from the personal name *Einws*, a dim. of *Einion* (of uncertain origin, popularly associated with the vocab. word *einion* anvil).

Vars.: **Hayn(e)s, Hanes, Heynes.**

The first governor of Connecticut colony was John Haynes *(?1594–1653). Earlier he had been governor of Massachusetts. He had emigrated from Essex, England, where his father was lord of the manor of Copford Hall near Colchester.*

Hainsworth English (common in W Yorks.): 1. habitation name from *Hainworth* in W Yorks., so called from an Anglo-Scandinavian form of the Norse personal name *Hagni* or *Hǫgni* (see HAIN 2) + OE *worð* enclosure (see WORTH).

2. habitation name from AINSWORTH in Lancs., from the OE personal name *Ægen* + *worð* enclosure. Names such as *de Hayneswurth* and *de Heyneswurth* occur in the surrounding area in the 14th cent.

Hajdú Hungarian: from *hajtó* drover. Drovers were armed, and often became highwaymen and mercenaries. *Hajdú* acquired both meanings, but the surname is chiefly associated with the settlement of some 10,000 mercenaries in E Hungary by Prince István Bocskay as a reward for their support. Their towns, dating from 1605, still retain *Hajdú-* as a first element. The word was borrowed into Ger., Pol., and Czech to denote an armed retainer of a nobleman. In Pol. it also denoted a Hung. footsoldier in the Pol. army in the 16th cent. The name is also borne by Hungarian Jews, among whom it is either occupational ('drover') or an adoption of the Hung. name.

Cogns.: Ger.: **Haydu(k), Haiduk.** Pol.: **Hajduk.** Czech: **Hejduk, Hejda.**

Patrs.: Pol.: **Hajdukiewicz.** Croatian: **Hajduković.**

Hájek Czech: 1. topographic name for someone who lived in or near a thicket or grove, from Czech *hájek* thicket, from *háj* grove, or directly from *háj* grove, the dim. suffix *-ek* being added in forming the surname.

2. occupational name for a keeper of animals, especially one who looked after horses, from *hejno-* herd, flock.

Vars. (of 2): **Hajný, Hejný, Hejna**.

Cogns. (of 1): Pol.: **Gajek**, GAJOWNIK.

Hakala Finnish: ornamental or topographic name from *haka* pasture, paddock + the local suffix *-la*.

Hake 1. English: from the ON byname *Haki*, cogn. with HOOK, and given originally to someone with a hunched figure or a hooked nose.

2. Low German: occupational name for a pedlar or street trader, from MLG *höken* to carry things about (on one's back). The Eng. word *hawker* derives from a 16th-cent. borrowing of this term.

Vars. (of 1): HACK. (Of 2): **Haack, Hocke; Haker, Haacker, Höck(n)er, Heckner**; HACKMANN.

Cogns. (of 2): Du.: **Ha(a)k**.

Patr. (from 1): Eng.: **Hakes**.

Hakkarainen Finnish: patr. from the occupational term *hakkari* woodman, lumberjack (a borrowing of Swed. *hackar*, agent deriv. of *hacka* to chop; cogn. of HACKER).

Häkkinen Finnish: ornamental or topographic name from *häkki* pen, enclosure + the gen. suffix *-nen*.

Hałas Polish: nickname for a noisy person, from Pol. *hałas* noise.

Dim.: **Hałaszczyk**.

Halász Hungarian: occupational name for a fisherman, from *hal* fish + *-ász* occupational suffix.

Haldane Scots: 1. from the ON personal name *Halfdanr* or the Late OE Anglicized form of this, *Healfdene*, composed of the elements *healf* half + *Dene* Dane, originally a byname for someone of mixed parentage.

2. var. of HOWDEN 1.

Vars.: **Halden, Haldin, Hallding, Holdane**.

Halder German: topographic name for someone who lived high on a mountainside, from S Ger. *Halde* slope, hillside (MHG *halde*, OHG *halda*).

Vars.: **Halter, Haldner, Haldermann; Hald, Halt, Häld(e)**.

Hale English: 1. topographic name for someone who lived in a nook or hollow, from OE *hale*, dat. of *h(e)alh* nook, hollow, recess. In N England the word often has a specialized meaning, denoting a piece of flat alluvial land by the side of a river, originally one deposited in a bend; in the south-east it seems often to have referred to a patch of dry land in a fen. In some cases the surname may be a habitation name from any of the several places in England named with this fossilized inflected form, which would originally have been preceded by a preposition such as *at*.

2. from a ME given name derived from either of two OE bynames, **Hæle* 'Hero' or **Hægel*, which is probably akin to Gmc *Hagano* 'Hawthorn' (see HAIN 2).

Vars. (of 1): **Haile, Haill; Heal(e), Hele** (chiefly W Country); **Attale** (with fused ME preposition *at*); **Haugh, Hauff** (from the OE nom. case); HAILES (from the gen. sing. or nom. pl.).

Dim. (of 2): **Haylock**.

Haley English (chiefly W Yorks.): habitation name from any of various places named with the OE elements *hēg* hay + *lēah* wood, clearing.

Vars.: **Hayley, Hail(e)y, Haly**.

Halford English (chiefly Midlands): habitation name from any of various places so called. Most, for example that in Warwicks., get the name from OE *halh* nook, recess (see HALE 1) + *ford* FORD. One in Shrops. has as its first element ME, OE *hafocere* hawker (see HAWK).

Halfpenny 1. English: nickname from the coin. The first regular issues of round halfpence were made in the reign of Edward I. Before that, there had been sporadic issues, but the term was originally used to denote a silver penny that had been literally (and legally) cut in half to provide smaller change. The nickname may have been bestowed on a man worth very little or on one of small stature. In some instances, the origin may be anecdotal, connected for example with a requirement to pay a rent of a halfpenny.

2. Irish: Anglicized form of Gael. *Ó hAilpín*; see ALPIN.

Halicz Polish: habitation name from the town of *Halicz*, now in the Soviet Union.

Var.: **Halicki**.

Hall English, German, Danish/Norwegian, and Swedish: topographic name for someone who lived near a large house, or occupational name for someone employed at a hall or manor (OE *heall*, OHG *halla*, ON *holl*). Some cases may be habitation names from towns named with this word, in particular *Halle* in the south-west corner of East Germany.

Vars.: Eng.: **Halls; Hallman**. Ger.: **Halle(r)** (see also HELLER); **Hal(l)mann**. Swed.: **Hallén, Hallin, Hallman**.

Cogns.: Du.: **Hal, Van (der) Hall**. Fr.: **Lahalle, Delahalle**. Prov.: **Alle**.

Dims.: Fr.: **Hallet, Hallez**, HALLEY, **Hallé**.

Cpds (mostly ornamental): Swed.: **Hallberg** ('hall hill'); **Hallgren** ('hall branch'); **Hallqvist** ('hall twig'); **Hallström** ('hall river').

Hall *is one of the commonest and most widely distributed of English surnames, bearing witness to the importance of the hall as a feature of the medieval village.*

John Hall (b. 1584), an Englishman born in Kent who emigrated to New England in 1632, founded a notable American family, whose members have included Lyman Hall (1724–90), politician and one of the signatories of the Declaration of Independence, Asaph Hall (1829–1907), astronomer who discovered the two satellites of Mars, and Stanley Hall (1844–1924), pioneer in psychophysics.

Another John Hall emigrated to America in about 1652, settling in Massachusetts. His descendants include Charles M. Hall (1863–1914), who invented a process for the mass production of aluminium.

Häll Swedish: ornamental or topographic name from Swed. *häll* stone, rock (ON *hallr*).

Cpds (ornamental): **Hällgren** ('stone branch'); **Hällström** ('stone river').

Hallahan Irish: Anglicized form of Gael. **Ó hÁilleacháin** 'descendant of *Áilleachán*', a personal name from a dim. of *áille* beauty.

Vars.: **O'Halleghane, (O')Hallaghan, Hallihane, Halligan**.

Hallam English (chiefly S Yorks. and E Midlands): regional name from the district in S Yorks. around Sheffield and Ecclesfield so called, or habitation name from the town of this name in Derbys. The Derbys. name is from OE *halum*, dat. pl. of *halh* nook, recess (see HALE 1). The Yorks. district, sometimes called *Hallamshire*, is from *hallum*, dat. pl. of *hall* stone, rock (cf. HÄLL).

Var.: **Hallum**.

Halley 1. French: dim. from a cogn. of HALL.

2. N English and Scots: apparently a habitation name from an unidentified place, perhaps named with the OE elements *hall* HALL + *(ge)hæg* enclosure (see HAY 1).

Var.: **Hally**.

Halliday N English and Scots: from OE *hāligdæg* holy day, religious festival. The reasons why this word should have become a surname are not clear; perhaps it was used as a nickname for persons born at Christmas or Easter.

Vars.: **Haliday, Hallad(e)y, Halleday, Hol(l)iday, Holyday, Holladay.**

Hallinan Irish: Anglicized form of Gael. **Ó hÁilgheanáin** 'descendant of *Ailgheanán*', a dim. form of a personal name composed of old Celt. elements meaning 'mild person'.

Hallissey Irish: Anglicized form of Gael. **Ó hÁilgheasa** 'descendant of *Ailgheas*', a personal name meaning 'Desire'.

Halliwell N English (Lancs.) and Scots: habitation name from a place near Manchester, so called from OE *hālig* holy + *well(a)* well, spring, or from any of the numerous other places named with the same elements, such as *Holwell* in Dorset, Leics., Herts., and Oxon., *Halwill* and *Halwell* in Devon, and *Holywell* in Cambs., Cornwall, Clwyd, and Northumb. In medieval times many springs were dedicated to saints, but this usually represented no more than a Christian patina on an earlier pagan and animistic belief. See also HEILBRONN.

Vars.: **Hallawell, Hallewell, Hallowell; Helliwell; Holliwell, Hollowell.**

Halloran Irish: Anglicized form of Gael. **Ó hAllmhuráin** 'descendant of *Allmhurán*', a personal name from a dim. of *allmhurach* foreigner (from *all* beyond + *muir* sea).

Vars.: **O'Halowrane, O'Halloraine, O'Halloran, O'Hallaran, O'Halleran, O'Halleron, Holloran.**

Hallu French: habitation name from a place in Somme, apparently named with the Gmc elements *hasal* HAZEL + *ōdi* wasteland (see EDER).

Hallworth English: habitation name from either of two places in W Yorks. now called *Holdsworth*, both probably originally from an OE byname **Halda* 'Bent' + *worð* enclosure (see WORTH).

Vars.: **Hallsworth, Hol(d)sworth, Hou(l)dsworth, Holesworth.**

Halonen Finnish: ornamental or anecdotal name from *halko* log, firewood + the gen. suffix *-nen*. If the origin is anecdotal, the circumstances surrounding its adoption as a surname are no longer known.

Hals German and Dutch: from Ger. *Hals*, Du. *hals* neck. Generally this was a nickname for a man with a long neck or for a conspicuous sufferer from goitre (a common affliction in medieval times, esp. in Alpine regions).

Var.: Du.: **De Hals.**

Cogns.: Eng.: **Halse.** Fris.: **Halsema.**

Cpds: Jewish (Ashkenazic, reasons for adoption unknown): **Halsband** ('neckband'); **Halstuch** ('neckerchief').

The Dutch painter Franz Hals *(?1580–1666) came from a patrician family which was active in the affairs of Haarlem for over 300 years. The name is first found in the city annals in 1350.*

Halsall English (Lanc.): habitation name from a place in Lancs. (*Heleshale* in Domesday Book), probably so called from the gen. case of the OE personal name *Hœle* (see HALE 2) + OE *halh* nook, recess (see HALE 1).

Halsey English: probably a habitation name from an unidentified place in the London area, so called from OE *hals* neck of land, channel of water (cf. HALS) + *ēg* island.

Halstead English: habitation name from any of the various places bearing this name, for example in Essex (*Haltesteda* in Domesday Book), Kent, and Leics., all of which are probably so called from OE *(ge)heald* hut, temporary shelter + *stede* site. However, the name is now most frequently found in Lancs., where it is from High *Halstead* in Burnley, which is named as the 'site of a hall', from OE *h(e)all* hall + *stede* place.

Vars.: **Halsted, Alstead.**

Halton English: habitation name from any of the many places so called from OE *h(e)alh* nook, hollow (see HALE 1) + *tūn* enclosure, settlement.

A number of bearers of this name trace their descent from William de Halton, *who was living at Halton, Lancs., in 1346.*

Ham 1. English (W Country): topographic name for someone living on low-lying land by a stream; see HAMMER 1.

2. Scots: habitation name from a place in the former county of Caithness (now part of Highland region), so called from ON *hámi* homestead.

Hambly English (W Country): apparently from the ANF given name *Ham(b)lin*, a double dim. of HAMMOND 1.

Vars.: **Hambley, Haml(e)y; Ham(b)lin, Ham(b)lyn, Ham(b)ling, Hamblen; Hamelly** (Cornwall).

Both given name and surname have always been most common in Cornwall; bearers of the name Hamlin *were recorded in Domesday Book as holding 23 manors in Cornwall.*

A Devon family called Hamlyn *trace their descent from Richard Hamlyn, recorded at Larkbear, Devon, in 1219. Sir John* Hamelly *(b. c.1235) served as Sheriff of Cornwall in 1307.*

Hambro Low German and Danish: habitation name from some minor place apparently named with the Gmc elements *ham* water meadow (see HAMMER 1) + *bru* marsh, bog (see BREUIL).

The Hambro *merchant banking family are of Jewish-Danish origin, being descended from Calmer Joachim Hambro, a Copenhagen silk merchant in the late 18th cent. His son was Danish Court Councillor in London (1821); the bank was founded by his grandson Charles Joachim Hambro (1807–77).*

Hambrook English: habitation name from a place in Gloucs., so called from OE *hān* rock, stone + *brōc* stream.

Hamburg German and Jewish (Ashkenazic): habitation name from the great city at the mouth of the river Elbe, or from some other place so named, from the Gmc elements *ham* water meadow (see HAMMER 1) + *burg* fortress, town (see BURKE).

Vars.: **Hamburger.** Ger.: **Hamborg, Hamborch.** Jewish: **Gamb(o)urg** (under Russ. influence; see GOREN).

Hamel 1. German and Jewish (Ashkenazic): habitation name from the city of Hamlin, Ger. *Hameln*, Yid. *Haml*, where the river *Hamel* empties into the Weser. The name of the river probably derives from the Gmc element *ham* water meadow (see HAMMER 1).

2. Dutch: nickname or metonymic occupational name for a shepherd, from MDu. *hamel* wether, castrated ram.

3. French: topographic name for someone who lived and worked at an outlying farm dependent on the main village, OF *hamel* (a dim. from a Gmc element cogn. with OE *hām* homestead).

Vars. (of 1): Ger.: **Hamelmann.** Jewish: HAMMEL.

Cogn. (of 2): Ger.: HAMMEL.

Dims. (of 3): Fr.: **Hamelin, Hamelet, Hamelot.**

Hamer 1. English: habitation name from a place in Lancs., so called from OE *hamor* rock, crag.

2. Flemish, Dutch: metonymic occupational name for a maker of hammers or a user of a hammer, for example in a forge; a cogn. of HAMMER 2.

3. Jewish (Ashkenazic): var. of HAMMER 2.

Hamill 1. Scots (Norman): habitation name from *Haineville* or *Henneville* in Manche, so called from the Gmc personal name *Hagano* (see HAIN 2) + OF *ville* settlement (see VILLE).

2. English: nickname for a scarred or maimed person, from ME, OE *hamel* mutilated, crooked.

Vars.: **Hammill**, HAMMEL.

The first known bearer of the name in Scotland was a certain William, recorded variously as de Hameville *and* de He(y)neuile *at the end of the 12th cent. For long it was associated with Roughwood in Ayrs. It has now more or less died out in Scotland, but is common in N Ireland, where its bearers can trace their ancestry to Hugh* Hammill *of Roughwood, who went to Ireland with Montgomery of Ards.*

Hamilton Scots and N Irish: habitation name, ultimately not from the town of *Hamilton* near Glasgow (which is derived from the surname), but from what is now a deserted village in the parish of Barkby, Leics. This is so called from OE *hamel* scarred, mutilated, crooked (see HAMILL 2) + *dūn* hill (see DOWN 1). However, some bearers may derive their name from the town founded by the Hamiltons, rather than from being members of the Norman family mentioned below.

This name is borne by one of the most distinguished families of the Scottish nobility; they hold many titles, including the Marquessate and Dukedom of Hamilton, the Marquessate of Douglas, the Dukedom of Abercorn, and the Earldom of Haddington. They are descended from Walter FitzGilbert de Hameldone, *a Norman baron who gave his support to Robert the Bruce in the 13th cent. A member of this family was Sir William Hamilton (1730–1803), a British diplomat and archaeologist, whose wife, Lady Emma Hamilton (?1765–1815), became the mistress of Horatio Nelson. In the 16th cent. bearers of the name found their way to Russia, where they became naturalized; hence the Russ. forms* **Gamentov**, **Khamentov**, *and* **Khomutov** *(the last having been affected by folk etymological association with* khomut *horse collar). A branch of the family was established in Ireland by Sir Frederick Hamilton (d. 1646), who served in the Swedish army of Gustavus Adolphus. He later became governor of Ulster, and his descendants were created Viscounts Boyne. Another branch of the family was to be found in Denmark, where Henrik Albertsen Hamilton (1588–1648) was a noted Latin poet in his day.*

Hamlett English (Gloucs.): from a ME given name, a double dim. of HAMMOND 1.

Vars.: **Hamlet**, **Hamblet(t)**.

Hammel 1. English: var. of HAMILL 2.

2. Ger.: cogn. of HAMEL 2.

3. Jewish (Ashkenazic): var. of HAMEL 1.

Hammer 1. English and German: topographic name for someone who lived by a patch of flat, low-lying alluvial land beside a stream, OE *hamm*, OHG *ham*.

2. German and Jewish (Ashkenazic): metonymic occupational name for a maker or user of hammers, for example in a forge, or nickname for a forceful person, from Ger. *Hammer* hammer, Yid. *hamer* (MHG *hamer*, OHG *hamar* stone, hence hammer made of stone).

Vars. (of 1): Eng.: HAM, **Hamm(e)**. (Of 2): Ger.: **Hammermann**. Jewish: HAMER; **Hammerman**.

Cogns. (of 2): Flem., Du.: HAMER. Fris.: **Hamersma**. Swed.: **Hammar**, **Hamrén**, **Hamrin**.

Dims. (of 2): Ger.: **Hammerl**, **Hämmerle**.

Cpds (of 2): Jewish (Ashkenazic): **Hammerschlag** ('hammer blow'); **Ham(m)erschmidt** ('hammer smith'). Swed. (ornamental): **Hammarbäck** ('hammer stream'); **Hammarberg** ('hammer hill'); **Hammargren** ('hammer branch'); **Hammarlund** ('hammer grove'); **Hammarskjöld** ('hammer shield'); **Hammarstedt** ('hammer homestead'); **Hammarstrand** ('hammer shore'); **Hammarström** ('hammer river').

Hammerstein German and Jewish (Ashkenazic): habitation name from any of various places so called from OHG *hamar* rock, crag (cf. HAMER 1) + *stein* STONE. The Jewish surname is associated in particular with a town formerly in E Prussia (now Czarne in Poland), which once had a large Jewish population.

Var.: Jewish: **Hammerstone** (Anglicized by folk etymology, as if the first element meant 'hammer' rather than 'crag').

Hammerstein *is the name of a Hanoverian noble family, which according to family tradition originated in a small place of this name on the Rhine opposite Andernach. The most famous bearer of the name, however, is Oscar Hammerstein (1895–1960), the Jewish-American song writer. He was the grandson of Oscar Hammerstein (1848–1919), an operatic impresario who had made his fortune with a machine that rolled cigars.*

Hammerton English: habitation name from any of several places in W Yorks., now *Hamerton* or *Hammerton*, so called from OE *hamor* rock, crag (see HAMER 1) + *tūn* enclosure, settlement.

Hammond English: 1. from the Norman personal name *Hamo(n)* (from Gmc *Haimo*, a short form of the various cpd names with the first element *haim* home), with excrescent *-d*.

2. from the ON personal name *Hámundr*, composed of the elements *há* high + *mund* protection.

3. from the ON personal name *Ámundr*, composed of the elements *á* great-grandfather, ancestor + *mund* protection. This name seems to have been less common than *Hámundr*, and was widely confused with it.

Vars. (of 1): **Ham(m)on**, **Ha(i)me**. (Of 2): **Oman**, **Omond**.

Cogns. (of 1): Fr.: **Ha(i)mon**, **Hémon(d)**, **Aimon(d)**, **Aymon**. Ger.: **Haym**, **Heim**, **Heym**. It.: **Aimo(ni)**.

Dims. (of 1): Eng.: **Hamnet(t)**, HAMLETT, HAMBLY. Fr.: **Hamonet**, **Monet**, **Hamoneau**, **Hémon(n)ot**; **Hamonic**, **Aymonic**, **Mounic** (Brittany). It.: **Aim(on)ino**, **Aimetti**.

Patrs. (from 1): Eng.: **Ham(p)son**; **Ha(i)mes**, **Haymes**. Bret.: **Abhamon**. (From 3): Dan., Norw.: **Amundsen**.

Hampden English: habitation name from a place in Bucks., so called from OE *hamm* water meadow + *denu* valley.

John Hampden *(1594–1643), one of the leaders of the Parliamentarian opposition to Charles I in the period leading up to the English Civil War, was the son of William Hampden of Great Hampden in Bucks. He was one of twelve men granted rights to a large tract of land in N America by the Earl of Warwick in 1631. This land is now the State of Connecticut.*

Hampe German: from the MHG personal name *Hampo*, a short form of the cpd name *Hamprecht*, OHG *Hagenberht*, composed of the elements *hagano* hawthorn (cf. HAIN 2) + *berht* bright, famous.

Vars.: **Hempe**, **Hamprecht**, **Hemprecht**, **Hemprich**.

Dims.: **Hamp(e)l**, **Hemp(e)l**.

Hampshire English: 1. regional name from the S English county, which derives its name from HAMPTON (i.e. the port of Southampton) + OE *scīr* division, district.

2. regional name from the area of *Hallamshire* in S Yorks., so called from HALLAM + ME *schir* division, administrative region (OE *scīr*). The surname is most common in Yorks., where this second derivation is most likely to be the source.

Vars.: **Hamsher(e)**, **Hamshar**, **Ham(p)shaw**. (Of 2 only): **Halmshaw**.

Hampton English: habitation name from any of the numerous places so called, in all parts of England, including the cities of *Southampton* and *Northampton*. They all share the final OE element *tūn* enclosure, settlement, but the first is variously *hām* homestead, *hamm* water meadow, or *hēan*, weak dat. case, originally used after a preposition and article, of *hēah* high. It is generally impossible to distinguish between these possibilities in individual cases.

Hanauer German and Jewish (Ashkenazic): habitation name from the town of *Hanau* in Hesse, so called from OHG *hano* cock + *ouwa* low-lying land, island.

Var.: Jewish: **Hanau**.

Hanbury English: habitation name from *Hanbury* in Staffs. or Worcs., which get their name from the OE phrase *æt ðǣm hēan byrg* 'at the high fortress'. In some cases it may also be from *Handborough* in Oxon., which is apparently so called from the OE byname *Hagena* 'Hawthorn' (cf. HAIN 2) + OE *beorg* hill.

Vars.: **Handbury**, **Hambury**, **Hamburgh**.

Hance 1. English: patr. from HANN.

2. English: from a pl. form of HAND 1.

3. Scots: from a contracted form of ANGUS.

Hancock English: from a dim. of the ME given name HANN, with the hypocoristic suffix *-cock* (see COCK), which was commonly added to given names. This surname is also borne by Gypsies in Britain.

Var.: **Handcock**.

Patrs.: **Han(d)cocks**, **Hancox**.

Hand 1. English and German: nickname for someone with a deformed hand or who had lost one hand, from ME, OE *hand*, Ger. *Hand* (MHG, OHG *hant*), found in such appellations as *Liebhard mit der Hand* (Augsburg 1383). Cf. FINGER, FOOT, etc.

2. Irish: Anglicized form of Gael. *Ó Flaithimh*; see GUTHRIE. This Anglicized form is the result of an erroneous assocation of the Gael. name with *lámh* hand; cf. LAVIN.

Vars. (of 1): Eng.: **Hands** (chiefly W Midlands), HANCE.

Handford English: habitation name from any of various places, such as *Hanford* in Staffs. and *Handforth* in Ches., so called from OE *hana* cock (cf. HAHN 1), perhaps used as a byname + OE *ford* FORD. See also HANSFORD.

Vars.: **Han(na)ford**, **Han(d)forth**, **Hanfirth**.

Handler German and Jewish (Ashkenazic): occupational name for a merchant or dealer, Ger. *Händler*, an agent deriv. of MHG *handeln* to deal, trade (OHG *hantalōn* to undertake, manage, a deriv. of *hant* HAND).

Vars.: Jewish: **Handeles** (from Pol. *handełes* rag-and-bone man, street buyer of used clothes); **Handel(s)man**; **Gandler**, **Gendler(man)**, **Gandelman**, **Gendel(s)man**, **Gandelis** (under Russ. influence; see GOREN); **Andel(s)man** (in regions where Yid. has no /h/); **Hendel(man)**; **Hendlerski**, **Hendlersky**.

Handley 1. English: habitation name from any of various places, such as *Handley* in Ches., Derbys., and Dorset and *Hanley* in Staffs. and Worcs., so called from the weak dat. case (originally used after a preposition and article) of OE *hēah* high + OE *lēah* wood, clearing.

2. Irish: Anglicized form of Gael. **Ó hÁinle** 'descendant of *Áinle*', a personal name meaning 'Champion'.

Vars.: **Hanl(e)y**. (Of 2 only): **O'Hanl(e)y**, **O'Hanlee**.

Handschuh German and Jewish (Ashkenazic): metonymic occupational name for a glover, from Ger. *Handschuh* glove (MHG *hantschuoch*, a cpd of *hant* HAND + *schuoch* shoe, covering (OHG *scuoh*).

Vars.: **Handschu**. Ger. only: **Hanschuch**, **Hendeschuh**.

Dim.: Ger.: **Handschiegl**.

Handy English: of uncertain origin, perhaps a nickname meaning 'skilful with one's hands', although the vocab. word in this sense is not recorded until the 16th cent. It may alternatively be a var. of HENDY.

Handyside Scots: habitation name from a place in the former county of Berwicks (now part of Borders region), so called from ME *hanging* + *side*, i.e. probably a natural shelf on a hillside, but just possibly a place where executions were carried out.

Var.: **Handasyde**.

The first known bearer of the name is Richard de Hangganside, *who was lord of the place concerned at the end of the 14th cent.*

Hanham English: habitation name from a place in Gloucs., so called from OE *hānum*, dat. pl. of *hān* rock.

Hankin 1. English (chiefly Lancs.): from the ME given name *Hankin*, a dim. of HANN, with the addition of the hypocoristic suffix *-kin*, of Low Ger. origin.

2. Jewish (E Ashkenazic): metr. from *Khanke* (a pet form of the Yid. female given name *Khane*; see HANNA) + *-in* Slavic possessive suffix.

Var. (of 1): **Hanking**.

Patrs. (from 1): **Hankins(on)**.

Hanks English (Gloucs.): patr. from the ME given name *Hank*, a back formation from HANKIN (with the suffix taken to be *-in*, of OF origin).

Hanlon Irish: Anglicized form of Gael. **Ó hAnluain** 'descendant of *Anluan*', a personal name from the intensive prefix *an-* + *luan* light, radiance, or warrior.

Vars.: **O'Hanlon**, **O'Hanlo(w)ne**, **(O')Handlon**, **Hanlan**.

Hanmer Welsh: habitation name from a place in the former county of Flints. (now part of Clwyd), so called from the Gmc personal name *Hagena* borrowed into OE + *mere* lake, pond.

An early ancestor of the Welsh family of this name was Sir David Hanmer, *who was appointed a judge in the 14th cent. and whose daughter married the chieftain Owen Glendower (?1350-?1416), leader of a revolt against Henry IV's rule in Wales.*

Hann English: from the medieval given name *Han(n)*, which is usually a short form of *Johan* (see JOHN). In some cases, however, it may be from HENRY and even RANDOLPH (for the replacement of *R-* by *H-* in Gmc names introduced by the Normans, cf. HODGE from ROGER and HOBB from ROBERT).

Dims.: HANKIN, HANCOCK.

Patrs.: HANCE; **Hanson** (chiefly Midlands and N England), **Hansom**.

A family by the name of Hanson *were established in America by John Hanson, one of four brothers sent there by Queen Christina of Sweden in 1642. They were grandsons of an Englishman who had married into the Swedish royal family; he was descended from a certain Roger de Rastrick, who had lived in Yorks. in the 13th cent.*

Hanna 1. English: from the medieval female given name *Hannah* or *Anna* (from Hebr. *Chana* 'He (God) has favoured me (i.e. with a child)'). The name is borne in the Bible by the mother of Samuel (1 Sam. 1: 1–28), and there is a tradition (unsupported by biblical evidence) that it was the name of the mother of the Virgin Mary; this St Anne was a popular figure in the Middle Ages (cf. JOACHIM).

2. Scots: habitation name from an unidentified place; see below.

3. Irish: Anglicized form of Gael. **Ó hAnnaigh** 'descendant of *Annach*', a byname meaning 'Iniquity'.

Vars.: **Hannah**. (Of 2 only): **Hannay**.

Dims. (of 1): Jewish (Ashkenazic): **Khan(in)ke, Khanele**. (Of 2): **Hann(ig)an, (O')Hannon, Hanneen** (Gael. **Ó hAnn(ag)áin**).

Metrs. (from 1): Jewish: **Han(e)son, Hanis**; **Hanin, Chanin** (E Ashkenazic).

Metrs. (from dims. of 1): Jewish: **Hankes**, HANKIN, **Chankin, Haninkes, Chanlewicz, Chaneles** (all E Ashkenazic except the last; the underlying dim. female given names are respectively *Khanke*, *Khaninke*, and *Khanele*).

Gilbert de Hannethe *or* de Hahanith *was recorded in Wigtons. at the end of the 13th cent., and may have been an early bearer, if not the first, of a name that belongs at 2. John* of Hanna *is recorded as the master of a ship belonging to the King of Scotland in 1424.*

Hänninen Finnish: apparently an ornamental name from Finn. *hännys* tail, with the addition of the gen. suffix *-nen*.

Hannington English: habitation name from a place in Wilts., recorded in Domesday Book as *Hanindone*, apparently from the gen. case of the OE byname *Hana* 'Cock' (or the gen. pl., *hanena*, of the vocab. word; cf. HAHN 2) + OE *dūn* hill (see DOWN 1).

Hannover German and Jewish (Ashkenazic): habitation name from the city of *Hannover* in Lower Saxony, whose name is first recorded in the form *Honovere* and is probably composed of a Gmc element *hon*, perhaps meaning 'marsh' and akin to OE *hamm* (see HAMMER 1), + MLG *ōver* bank, shore.

Vars.: Ger.: **Hanover**. Jewish: **Hanower**.

Hanrahan Irish: Anglicized form of Gael. **Ó hAnradháin** 'descendant of *Anradhán*', a personal name from a dim. of *ánrad(h)* hero, warrior, champion, a title denoting the nobleman next in rank to the king in medieval Ireland. The title was also used to denote court poets of the second rank.

Vars.: **O'Hanrahan, O'Harragan, O'Horogan, O'Hor(i)gan, O'Howrane, (O')Hourihan, (O')Hourigan, Hourihan(e), Horrigan**, HORGAN, **Horkan**, HORAN, **Haran, Hawrane**.

Hanratty Irish: Anglicized form of Gael. **Ó hInreachtaigh** 'descendant of the lawyer'; see ENRIGHT.

Hans German: from a medieval given name, an aphetic form of *Johannes*; see JOHN. The surname is also borne by Ashkenazic Jews, presumably as an adoption of the Ger. surname. Aphetic forms of this name are also found in Slav. languages, and for convenience these are listed here as cogns.

Vars.: **Hanse**; **Honse** (Bavaria). Ger. (of Slav. origin): **Han(n)usch, Hanich, Han(t)sch, Hänisch, Haensch, Hasch(e)**, HACHE.

Cogns.: Czech: **Hanuš, Hanus**; **Hán, Hanák**. Pol.: **Hanusz**.

Dims.: Ger.: **Hans(e)l, Hänsel(in), Hensel, Hensolt**; **Ha(h)nel(t), Hand(e)l, Händel, Hendel, Henle**; **Hansi, Hänggi, Henggi** (Switzerland). Jewish: **Hansel, Hendl**. Low Ger.: **Hans(e)mann, Han(ne)mann, Hahnemann, Hens(e)mann, Hemmann**; **Hahn(e)(c)ke, Hanne(ke), Henne, Henne(c)ke**; **Hensgen**. Fris.: **Hannema**. Ger. (of Slav. origin): **Hansli(c)k, Hanik, Han(n)uschik, Han(t)schke, Haschke, Haschke**. Czech: **Hanousek**; **Hanz(e)l, Hanzal, Hanzlík, Hanzálek**; **Hánek**. Pol.: **Hanke**.

Patrs.: Low Ger.: **Hannessen, Han(s)sen, Hen(ne)ssen**; **Hansing, Hensing**. Flem., Du.: **Hansen, Hensen, Haesen**. Dan., Norw.: **Han(s)sen**. Swed.: **Hansson**. Pol.: **Hańczak**.

Patrs. (from dims.): Low Ger.: **Hanneken**. Ger. (of Slav. origin): **Henschler, Hachner**. Pol.: **Han(usz)kiewicz**.

Hansard English: metonymic occupational name for a cutler, from OF *hansard*, *hansart* cutlass, dagger (of Gmc origin, composed of elements meaning 'hand' (see HAND 1) and 'knife' (see SACHS)).

This is the name of a family who have held land in Surrey and Sussex from the late 12th cent. It has come to denote the official verbatim report of British parliamentary proceedings, first printed by Luke Hansard *(1752–1828), who had left Norwich for London with one guinea in his pocket and a training as a journeyman printer. He himself believed (probably wrongly) that his surname came from Ger.* Hanse *(OHG* hansa *company, band), as in the* Hanseatic *League, and that it was acquired by his ancestors through a connection with the E Anglian wool trade.*

Hansford English: habitation name from an unidentified place, perhaps *Ansford* in Somerset, which is recorded in Domesday Book as *Almundsford*, from the gen. case of the OE personal name *Ealhmund* (composed of the elements *ealh* temple + *mund* protection) + OE *ford* FORD.

Var.: **Handsford**.

The surname is most frequent in Dorset, where it has been traced back to 1525 in Loders.

Hanvey Irish: Anglicized form of Gael. **Ó hAinbhith** 'descendant of *Ainbhtheach*', a byname meaning 'Stormy'.

Harber English: metonymic occupational name for a keeper of a lodging house, from late OE *herebeorg* shelter, lodging (from *here* army + *beorg* shelter). For the change of *-er-* to *-ar-* in the first syllable, cf. MARCHANT.

Vars.: **Harbo(u)r, Arber, Harberer**; **Harbage, Herbage, Harbidge, Harbisher**.

Cogns.: Ger.: **Herberg(er), Herbrig, Herbrich**.

Harborne English (W Midlands): habitation name from a place in Birmingham, so called from OE *horu* dirt + *burna* stream (see BOURNE).

Var.: **Harbron** (Northumb.).

Harbottle English (Northumb.): habitation name from a place in the foothills of the Cheviots, so called from OE *hȳra* hireling (a deriv. of *hȳr* wages, reward) + *bōtl* dwelling. For the development of OE *-y-* in the first syllable to *-e-*, cf. HILL; for the subsequent change of *-er-* to *-ar-*, cf. MARCHANT.

Harcourt 1. English (Norman) and French: habitation name from places in Eure and Calvados, so called from OF *cour(t)* COURT with an obscure first element.

2. English: habitation name from either of two places in Shrops. The one near Cleobury Mortimer gets the name from OE *heafocere* HAWKER + *cot* hut, cottage (see COATES); the one near Wem has as its first element OE *hearpere* HARPER.

This is the name of a family of Norman origin with branches in France and England. Their name is derived from their lands in Normandy, held in 1024 by Turchetil, Sire de Harcourt. They also held lands in England, which were increased on the marriage of Sir Robert de Harcourt *(d. 1202), who acquired the manor of Stanton, Oxon. The family seat is still at Stanton Harcourt.*

Hard English: 1. from the OE personal name *Heard* or a Norman cogn. *Hard(on)*, both of which are of Gmc origin. This was normally an independent byname meaning 'Hardy', 'Brave', 'Strong', but it also seems to have been a short form of the various cpd names containing this as a first element.

2. nickname for a stern or severe man, from ME *hard* hard, inflexible.

3. topographic name for someone who lived on a patch of particularly hard ground or one that was difficult to farm. This origin is supported by forms with the preposition *de*

and article *le*, for example Gilbert *del Hard* (Lincs. 1232); see also HARDAKER.

Var. (of 3): **Harder**.

Cogns. (of 2): Flem.: **De Harde**. Swed.: **Hård**.

Dims. (of 1): Eng.: **Harkin**. Ger.: **Härtel**, **Hertel**, **Här(d)tle**, **Hertlein**; **Hörtle** (Bavaria); HERZ; **Hartisch** (E Germany).

Patrs. (from 1): HARDS; HARDING.

Patrs. (from 1) (dims.): Eng.: **Harkins**, **Harkiss**; **Harkess** (Scots).

Hardaker English (Yorks.): topographic name for someone who lived on a patch of poor, stony land, from ME *hard* hard, difficult + *aker* cultivated land (see ACKER), or habitation name from a minor place in Clapham, W Yorks., called *Hardacre*, which has this etymology.

Var.: **Hardacre** (Lancs.).

Hardcastle English (Yorks.): habitation name from *Hardcastle* Cross in W Yorks., near Hebden Bridge, so called from ME *hard* difficult, inaccessible, impregnable, or perhaps cheerless + *castel* castle, fortress, stronghold (see CASTLE).

Harden English: habitation name from *Harden* in W Yorks., which get its name from OE *hara* HARE + *denu* valley (see DEAN 1). Harden in Staffs., which originally had the same name as *Hawarden* in Clwyd (from OE *hēah* high + *worðign* enclosure) was probably not reduced to its modern form early enough to lie behind any examples of the surname.

Hardenberg German and Dutch: habitation name from any of various places, esp. one near Göttingen, so called from the weak dat. case (originally used after a preposition and article) of MLG *hard* difficult, inaccessible, impregnable + *berg* hill.

The real name of the German Romantic novelist 'Novalis' was Friedrich, Freiherr von Hardenberg *(1772–1801). He was a member of the Lower Saxon nobility and his family had an estate at Grossenrode, the name of which means 'great clearing'. From this his ancestors devised a Latin version of their name,* de Novalis *'of the clearing', which was adopted by the writer.*

Hardiman 1. English: nickname for a brave or foolhardy man, from ME *hardi* HARDY + *man* man.

2. Irish: Anglicized form of Gael. **Ó hArgadáin** 'descendant of *Argadán*', a personal name from a dim. of *argad* silver.

Var.: **Hardeman**. See also HARDMAN.

Hardin 1. French: cogn. of HARDING.

2. Jewish: of unknown origin.

Harding English: from the OE personal name *Hearding*, formally a patr. from HARD 1.

Var.: **Arding**.

Cogns.: Ger.: **Hartung**. Fr.: HARDIN, **Ardin**. It.: **Ardinghi**, **Ardenghi**.

Hardisty English: habitation name from a place in Yorks., in the parish of Fewston. The placename is recorded in 1379 as *Hardolfsty*, from the OE personal name *Heardwulf* (composed of the elements *heard* hardy, brave, strong + *wulf* wolf) + OE *stīg* path.

Var.: **Hardesty**.

Hardman English (chiefly Lancs.): 1. occupational name for a herdsman, a var. of *Herdman*; see HEARD. For the change of *-er-* to *-ar-*, cf. MARCHANT.

2. from the OE personal name *Heardmann*, composed of the elements *heard* hardy, brave, strong + *mann* man.

Hards English: 1. patr. from HARD 1.

2. habitation name from a place in Kent, near Canterbury, called *Hardres* (pronounced /hɑ:dz/), from a ME pl. form of OE **harað* wood (a cogn. of HARDT 1).

Vars.: **Hardes(s)**. (Of 2 only): **Hardres(s)**.

Hardstaff English (Notts.): of uncertain origin, possibly an obscene nickname for a man with a more or less permanent erection, from ME *hard* hard, firm + *staf* wooden pole, rod (OE *stæf*). Alternatively, it may be a habitation name from *Hardstoft* in Derbys., so called from the gen. case of the OE byname *Heorot* 'HART' + OE *toft* site, plot.

Hardt 1. German: topographic name for someone who lived by a range of wooded hills or by a drovers' road for cattle, both of which are meanings of MHG *hart* (OHG *hard*).

2. Low German: cogn. of HEARD.

3. Jewish (Ashkenazic): of unknown origin.

Vars. (of 1): **Har(t)z(er)**, **Harzmann**; **Hort(er)** (S Germany, Austria).

Cogns. (of 1): Low Ger.: **Haart**, **Terhardt**. Flem., Du.: **Van der Hart**, **Van Harten**.

Hardwick English: habitation name from any of various places, for example in Bucks., Cambs., Norfolk, Northants, Worcs., and W Yorks., so called from OE *heorde* herd, flock + *wīc* outlying farm (see WICK).

Vars.: **Hardwicke**, **Herdwick**.

Hardy English and French: nickname for a brave or foolhardy man, from OF, ME *hardi* bold, courageous (of Gmc origin; cf. HARD 1). The surname is also borne by Jews, but the reasons for its adoption are unknown.

Vars.: Eng.: **Hardey**; **Hardie** (Scotland). Fr.: **Hardi**.

Dim.: Fr.: **Hardion**.

Hare 1. English: nickname for a swift runner or a timorous person, from ME *hare* hare (OE *hara*).

2. Irish: Anglicized form of **Ó hAichir** 'descendant of *Aichear*', a personal name apparently derived from *aichear* fierce, sharp. See also O'HARA.

Vars. (of 2): **Hair** (Scotland), **Haire** (N Ireland); **O'Ha(i)re**, **O'Hagher**, **O'Hahir**, **O'Heare**, **(O')Hehir**.

Cogns. (of 1) Ger.: **Hase**. Low Ger.: **Haas(e)**. Flem.: **De Haese**. Du.: **De Haas**. Jewish (Ashkenazic, ornamental): **Haas**.

Harel 1. French: nickname for a boisterous or quarrelsome individual, from OF *harel* tumult, hue and cry (of Gmc origin, apparently an imitative formation).

2. Jewish (Israeli): ornamental surname from Hebr. *harel*, which is of disputed origin: it is either a cpd of *har* mountain + *el* God or a var. of *ariel*, which is a cpd of *ari* lion + *el* God. Harel is an epithet for the altar in the ancient Jewish temple in Jerusalem and, in mod. Hebrew, for Mount Sinai. Ariel is an epithet for Jerusalem and for the altar in the ancient Jewish temple.

Vars. (of 2): **Harell**, **Har-El**; **Hareli**, **Harely** (with Hebr. suffix *-i*).

Harford English: habitation name from places in Gloucs. and Devon. The former gets its name from OE *heorot* HART + *ford* FORD, the latter has as its first element OE *here* army.

Hargreaves English (Yorks. and Lancs.): habitation name from any of various places, for example in Ches., Northants, and Suffolk, called *Hargr(e)ave*, from OE *hār* grey (see HOARE 1) or *hara* HARE + *grāf* GROVE or *græfe* thicket. An additional source may be a piece of land in the parish of Standen, near Whalley, Lancs., recorded in 1323 as *Hargreves*.

Vars.: **Hargreves, Hargreave, Hargrave(s), Hargrove(s)**.

Harju Finnish: ornamental or topographic name from Finn. *harju* ridge, one of the numerous names adopted from the vocab. of the natural landscape in the 19th cent.

Harker English (Northumb.): 1. habitation name from either of two places in Cumb., or from one in the parish of Halsall, near Ormskirk, Lancs. The places in Cumb. are probably named from ME *hart* male deer (see HART 1) + *kerr* marshland (see CARR). The first element of the one in Lancs. is probably OE *hār* grey (see HOARE 1) or *hara* HARE.

2. nickname for an eavesdropper or busybody, from an agent deriv. of ME *herkien* to listen (OE **he(o)rcian*).

Harkness Scots: apparently a habitation name from an unidentified place, probably so called from the OE personal name *Hereca* (a deriv. of the various cpd names with the first element *here* army) + OE *næss* headland, cape.

Harland English: habitation name from any of various minor places (including perhaps some now lost) named from OE *hār* grey (see HOARE 1) or *hara* HARE + *land* land, patch of country. The surname is largely concentrated around Middlesbrough.

Var. (U.S.): **Harlan**.

George and Michael Harland *were Quakers who emigrated from Durham, England, to Ireland. George then went to Delaware in 1687 and became governor in 1695, while Michael went to Philadelphia. George Harland's descendants, who dropped the final* -d *from their name, included a number of prominent American politicians, in particular James* Harlan *(1820–99), who became a senator and Secretary of the Interior.*

Harle English: 1. habitation name from a place in Northumb., of whose name the second element is OE *lēah* wood, clearing. The first element may perhaps be an OE personal name **Herela*, a deriv. of the various cpd names with the first element *here* army.

2. var. of EARL.

Harley English: habitation name from places in Shrops. and W Yorks., so called from OE *hær* rock, heap of stones or *hara* HARE + *lēah* wood, clearing.

Harling English: from a Norman personal name, *Herluin* or *Arluin*, composed of the Gmc elements *erl* warrior + *wine* friend.

Vars.: **Harlin; Arling; Hurlin(g), Hurlen; Urlin(g), Urlwin**.

Harlow English: habitation name from any of various places so called. One in W Yorks. probably gets its name from OE *hær* rock, heap of stones + *hlāw* hill (see LAW 2 and LOW 1); those in Essex and Northumb. have *here* army as the first element, perhaps in the sense 'host', 'assembly'.

Harmer English: from the ME given name *Heremer*, OE *Heremær*, composed of the elements *here* army + *mǣr* fame.

Vars.: **Harmar, Hermer**.

Harmsworth English: habitation name from *Harmondsworth*, to the west of London, so called from the gen. case of the OE personal name *Heremund* (composed of the elements *here* army + *mund* protection) + OE *worð* enclosure (see WORTH).

Harney Irish: Anglicized form of Gael. **Ó hAthairne** 'descendant of *Athairne*', a personal name derived from *aithirne* calf, which was borne by a famous OIr. satirist.

Haro Spanish: habitation name from a place in the province of Logroño, so called from a N Castilian form of Sp. *faro* beacon; cf. FARO and ALFARO.

Harper English and Scots: occupational name for a player on the harp, from an agent deriv. of ME *harp* harp (OE *hearp*). The harper was one of the most important figures of a medieval baronial hall, especially in Scotland and N England, and the office of harper was sometimes hereditary. See also CROWTHER.

Vars.: **Harpour** (with the OF agent suffix *-our*); **Harpur** (chiefly N Ireland); **Harp**.

Cogns.: Fr.: **Harpin, Arpin, Larpin; Herpin, Herpeux** (hypercorrected forms). It.: **Arpino**.

Harpham English: habitation name from a place in Humberside near Bridlington, so called from OE *hearp* harp (possibly denoting a place where the harp was played, or else from the device called a 'harp', and shaped like one, which was used for purifying sea salt) + *hām* homestead.

Harradine English: habitation name from places in Beds. and Northants called *Harrowden*, from OE *h(e)arg* (pagan) temple (see HARROW) + *dūn* hill (see DOWN 1).

Vars.: **Harraden, Harridine**.

Harriman English: occupational name for a servant (see MANN) of someone who bore the given name HARRY.

Harrington 1. English: habitation name from places in Cumb., Lincs., and Northants. The first gets its name from OE *Hæferingtūn* 'settlement (OE *tūn*) associated with *Hæfer*', a byname meaning 'He-goat'; the second may have meant 'settlement on stony ground', from OE **hær* + the suffix *-ing*; the third may contain a word meaning 'heath'.

2. Irish: Anglicized form of Gael. **Ó hArrachtáin** 'descendant of *Arrachtán*', a personal name from a dim. of *arrachtach* mighty, powerful. See also HERAGHTY.

Vars. (of 1): **Harington**. (Of 2): **O'Haraghtane, O'Harrighton, O'Herraghton, Haroughton, Harraughton**.

Harington *is the name of a family derived from the place in Cumb. The earliest recorded bearer of the name was Robert* de Heverington *in the reign of Richard I (1189–99).*

Harris 1. English: patr. from the medieval given name HARRY.

2. Jewish: assumed as an Anglicized form of various like-sounding Jewish names.

Vars.: **Harrison**. (Of 1 only): **Harries** (chiefly Wales).

Both Harris *and* Harrison *are extremely common Eng. surnames; the former tends to be more common in the W Midlands and SW England, whereas the latter is commoner in N England.*

A large and influential American Harrison family are descended from Benjamin Harrison, who emigrated from England to Virginia in 1633 or 1634. Ancestors include another Benjamin Harrison (?1726–91), who was an activist in the American Revolution and a signatory of the Declaration of Independence. His son William Henry Harrison (1773–1841) and great-grandson Benjamin Harrison (1833–1901) both became president of the United States.

Harrod English: 1. from the OE personal name *Hereweald*, its ON cogn. *Haraldr*, or the Continental form *Herold* introduced to Britain by the Normans. These all go back to a Gmc personal name composed of the elements *heri*, *hari* army + *wald* rule, which is attested in Europe from an early date; the Roman historian Tacitus records a certain *Cariovalda*, chief of the Gmc tribe of the Batavi, as early as the 1st cent. AD.

2. occupational name for a herald, ME *herau(l)d* (OF *herau(l)t*, from a Gmc cpd of the same elements as above, used as a common noun). For the change of *-er-* to *-ar-*, cf. MARCHANT.

3. var. of Harwood.

4. var. of Herrod 1.

Vars. (of 1 and 2): **Harrold** (W Midlands), **Harroll; Har(r)ald, Harral(t), Harrel(l); Her(r)ald, Her(r)old, Herauld.**

Cogns. (of 1): Ger.: **Harold, Herold, Herholdt, Herl(e)t; Höhrold, Höreth** (Bavaria); **Heirold, H(e)ireth** (Austria). It.: **Airaldi; A(i)roldi, Araldi** (Lombardy); **Airaudo, Ariaudo** (Piedmont). (Of 2): Fr.: **Héraud, Hérault, Lhéraud, Lhérault.** Prov.: **Heral.**

Dim. (of 2): Fr.: **Héraudet.**

Patrs. (from 1): Ger.: **Herholz; Hörholz** (Bavaria). Swed.: **Haraldsson.** It.: **Da Rold, Da Rolt** (misdivided for *D'Arold*).

Harrop English: habitation name from any of several places in W Yorks., or from one in Ches., all of which are so called from OE *hara* Hare + *hop* valley (see Hope).

Vars.: **Harrap, Harrup.**

Harrow 1. English: habitation name from the place in NW London, which derives its name (*Herges* in Domesday Book) from OE *h(e)arg* (pagan) temple.

2. Scots: from various minor places of the same name and etymology.

Harrower Scots and English: occupational name for someone who harrowed cultivated land (perhaps someone who did this as a feudal service on manorial land), from an agent deriv. of ME *harwen* to rake (of Scandinavian origin).

Vars.: **Harrowar, Harroway.**

The first known Scots bearer of this surname was William Harrower, *who lived in Fife in the mid-14th cent.; he was also known as* Herwart. *Reaney records a Geoffrey* Harver *in Essex in 1255, and Geoffrey* le Harewere *in Suffolk in 1275.*

Harry English (chiefly Devon and Cornwall): from the medieval given name *Harry*, which was the usual vernacular form of Henry, with assimilation of the consonantal cluster and regular change of *-er-* to *-ar-* (cf. Marchant).

Harsch 1. German: nickname for a stern or severe man, from Ger. *harsch* harsh, stern (MLG *harsch*, from *harsten* to grow hard, firm; cf. Hard).

2. German: occupational name for a soldier, from MHG *harsch*, *harst* body of troops.

3. Jewish (Ashkenazic): var. of Hirsch, reflecting a central Yid. pronunciation.

Vars. (of 2): **Harscher, Harst(er).**

Hart 1. English: nickname meaning 'stag', ME *hert*, OE *heorot*, used for someone bearing some fancied resemblance to the animal. The OE word became *hurt* or *hort* in some dialects of ME, esp. western dialects, and these forms are reflected in the vars., but in the standard dialect it became *hert* and later *hart*.

2. Jewish (Ashkenazic): Anglicization of one or more like-sounding Jewish surnames.

3. Irish: Anglicized form of Gael. **Ó hAirt** 'descendant of *Art*', a byname meaning 'Bear', 'Hero' (cf. Arthur and Carton).

Vars. (of 1): **Heart; Hurt** (Notts.); **Hort.** (Of 3): **Harte, O'-Hart(e).**

Cogns. (of 1): Ger.: Hirsch. Low Ger.: **Hart(mann).** Flem.: **De Herdt.** Swed.: **Hiort(h), Hjort(h).**

Dims. (of 3): **(O')Hartigan** (Gael. **Ó hArtagáin**).

The American poet Bret Hart *(1836–1902) was of Jewish ancestry on his father's side. One of his forebears was Sir Balliol Brett, 1st Lord Esher, who settled in New York in 1700.*

Hartill English (W Midlands): habitation name, probably from one of the places called *Harthill*, from OE *heorot* Hart + *hyll* Hill. There are several places of this name, for example in Ches., Derbys., and W Yorks., but apparently none in the W Midlands. It is possible that the surname represents a truncated deriv. of *Hartlebury* in Worcs. This placename derives from the OE personal name *Heortla* + OE *burh* fort.

Vars.: **Hartle, Hartell.**

Hartland English (mainly W Midlands): apparently a habitation name from an unidentified place or region so named from OE *heorot* Hart + *land* land. Hartland in Devon was originally *Heorotēg*, from OE *heorot* + *ēg* island; the element *-land* is a later addition. The Devon place is unlikely to be the source of the surname.

Hartley English: habitation name from any of various places so called. Several, in particular those in Hants, Kent, and Devon, get their names from OE *heorot* Hart + *lēah* wood, clearing. One in Northumb. has as its second element OE *hlāw* hill, and one in Cumb. contains *clā* claw, in the sense of a tongue of land between two streams, with an uncertain first element. The surname is widely distributed, but most common in Yorks.

Var.: **Hartly.**

Hartnell English (W Country): of uncertain origin, perhaps a habitation name from an unidentified place, possibly named from the gen. case of the OE byname *Heorta* (from *heor(o)t* 'Hart') + OE *hyll* Hill or *h(e)alh* nook, recess (see Hale 1). If the source is *Hartnoll* in Marwood, Devon, the final element is OE *cnoll* hill (see Knoll 1).

Hartnett Irish: Anglicized form of Gael. **Ó hAirtnéada** 'descendant of *Airtnéad*', a personal name of uncertain origin. The first syllable is probably from *art* bear, hero; see Hart 3.

Hartshorn English: habitation name from *Hartshorne* in Derbys., so called from the gen. case of the OE byname *Heorot* 'Hart' + OE *horn* used of a horn-shaped hill (see Horn 3).

Var.: **Hartshorne.**

Hartwell English: habitation name from any of the various places, for example in Bucks., Northants, and Staffs., so called from OE *heorot* Hart + *well(a)* spring, stream (see Well).

Most early bearers of this name seem to get it from the place in Northants. The manor there was held by a family of this name from the early 12th cent. until the 17th cent.

Hartwig German: from a Gmc personal name composed of the elements *hard* hardy, brave, strong + *wīg* war.

Vars.: **Härtwig, Hertwig; Hartig; Hattwig, Hattwich.**

Cogns.: Low Ger.: **Hard(e)wig, Hardeweg.** Dan.: **Hartvig.**

Patrs.: Ger.: **Hartwiger.** Low Ger.: **Hartwigsen.** Dan.: **Hartvigsen.**

Harty Irish: Anglicized form of Gael. **Ó hA(tha)rtaigh** 'descendant of *Faghartach*', a byname for a noisy person.

Var.: **Hearty.**

Harvard English: from the OE personal name *Hereweard*, composed of the elements *here* army + *weard* guard, which was borne by an 11th-cent. thane of Lincs., leader of resistance to the advancing Normans. The ON cogn. *Hervarðr* was also common and, particularly in the Danelaw, it may in part lie behind the surname.

Vars.: **Harward, Hereward.**

John Harvard *(1607–38), who gave his name to Harvard College, was the son of a London butcher. He inherited considerable prop-*

erty, and emigrated to Massachusetts in 1637. On his death he bequeathed half his estate and the whole of his library to the newly founded college at Cambridge, Mass.

Harvey 1. English and Scots: from the Bret. personal name *Aeruiu* or *Haerviu*, composed of the elements *haer* battle, carnage + *vy* worthy, which was introduced into England by Bret. followers of William the Conqueror, for the most part in the Gallicized form *Hervé*. The surname is most common in Staffs., Cornwall and S Devon, and E Anglia. For the change of *-er-* to *-ar-*, cf. MARCHANT.

2. Irish: Anglicized form of Gael. **Ó hAirmheadhaigh** 'descendant of *Airmheadhach*', a personal name of uncertain origin. It seems to be a deriv. of *Airmheadh*, the name borne by a mythological physician.

Vars. (of 1): **Harvie** (Scots); **Hervey**; **Herve** (Jersey).

Cogns. (of 1): Fr.: **Herv(i)é**, **Hervieux**; **Hervo** (Brittany).

Dims. (of 1): Fr.: **Herv(ou)et**, **Hervochon**.

Patr. (from 1): Bret.: **Abhervé**.

Hervey *is the name of an English family whose influence greatly increased in the early 18th cent. due to their support of the Hanoverian succession. Their earliest recorded ancestor was John Hervey (b. c.1290) of Beds. The manor of Ickworth, where the family seat is located, was brought into the family on the marriage of Thomas Hervey of Thurleigh, Beds., in 1457. They became Earls of Bristol in 1714 and Marquesses of Bristol in 1826.*

Harwood English and Scots: habitation name from any of various places, for example in the Scottish Borders and in Lancs., Lothian, Northumb., and N Yorks., so called from OE *hār* grey (see HOARE 1) or *hara* HARE + *wudu* WOOD; cf. HARGREAVES and HARLEY.

Vars.: **Harewood** (places in Hants, Herefords., and W Yorks.); HARROD.

Hasard English and French: nickname for an inveterate gambler or a brave or foolhardy man prepared to run risks, from ME, OF *hasard* game of chance, later used metaphorically of other uncertain enterprises. The word derives from Arabic *az-zahr*, from *az*, assimilated form of the def. art. *al* + *zahr* die. It appears to have been picked up and brought back to Europe by Provençal crusaders.

Vars.: Eng.: **Haz(z)ard**; **Hassard** (N Ireland); **Hassett** (Ireland); **Assard**. Fr.: **Hazard**, **Hazart**.

Hašek Czech: 1. from a dim. given name, a shortened form of *Haštal* (L *Castulus*, from *castus* pure, chaste) with the dim. suffix *-ek*.

2. altered dim. of the given *Havel* (see GALL 2).

Vars.: **Haš**, **Háša**.

Haslam English: topographic name for someone who lived 'by the hazels', or habitation name from *Haslam* in Lancs., in both cases from OE *hæslum*, dat. pl. of *hæsel* HAZEL.

Vars.: **Haslum**, **Haslem**, **Haslen**, **Hesl(eh)am**; **Aslam**, **Aslum**, **Aslen**.

Hasling English: topographic name for someone who lived by a hazel copse, OE **hæsling* (a deriv. of *hæsel* HAZEL; see also HAZLETT).

Vars.: **Haslin**, **Heslin(g)**, **Hessling**.

Hass 1. German: from a pet form, *Hasso*, of the Gmc personal name *Hadubert* (see HABBERT), or of some other personal name containing *hadu* battle, strife as the first element.

2. German: nickname for a bitter and vicious man, from Ger. *Hass* hatred (MHG, OHG *haz*).

3. Jewish (Ashkenazic): of uncertain origin, perhaps from Ger. *Hass* hatred, imposed by a non-Jewish government official in central Europe at the time when surnames hbecame obligatory.

Var. (of 1): **Hasse**.

Hassall English: habitation name from a place in Ches., so called from the gen. case of the OE byname *Hætt* 'Hat' (or possibly from the OE vocab. word *hætse* witch) + OE *halh* nook, recess (see HALE 1).

Var.: **Hassell**.

Hasson 1. Scots and N Irish: assimilated form of a patr. from the medieval given name *Hal*, a pet form of HARRY.

2. Jewish (Sefardic): of unknown origin.

Var. (of 2): **Hason**.

Hastings English: 1. habitation name from the place in Sussex, near which the English failed to repel the Norman invasion. It is so called from OE *Hǣstingas* 'people of *Hǣsta*', a byname from *hǣst* violence, fury.

2. patr. from the comparatively rare Norman personal name *Hasten(c)*, *Hastang*. This appears to be of ON origin, composed of the elements *há* high + *steinn* stone.

Vars. (of 2): **Hasting**, **Hastain**.

Hastings *is the family name of the Earls of Huntingdon, granted the title in 1529. Their descent can be traced from Sir Henry* de Hastings *(d. 1268). The family once held great power; by marriage they were related to the kings of Scotland, and John, 1st Lord Hastings (1262–1312), was one of the claimants to the Scots throne in 1290.*

Hasty English: nickname for a brisk or impetuous person, from ME, OF *hasti* quick (a deriv. of OF *haste* swiftness, of Gmc origin; cf. HASTINGS 1).

Var.: **Hastie** (Scotland).

Haswell English (chiefly Northumb.): habitation name from *Haswell* in Co. Durham (or possibly from one elsewhere), so called from OE *hæsel* HAZEL + *well(a)* spring, stream (see WELL).

Hatch English: topographic name for someone who lived by a gate, OE *hæcce* (normally a gate marking the entrance to a forest or other enclosed piece of land, sometimes a floodgate or sluice-gate), or habitation name from one of the many places named with this word.

Var.: **Hatcher**.

Hatfield English: habitation name from any of the various places, for example in Essex, Herts., Notts., Herefords., Worcs., and E and W Yorks., so called from OE *hǣð* heathland, heather (see HEATH) + *feld* pasture, open country (see FIELD).

Vars.: **Hatfeild**, **Hatful(l)**; **Hadfield** (a place in Derbys.); HEATHFIELD.

Hathaway English: 1. topographic name for someone who lived by a path across a heath, from ME *hath* heath (OE *hǣð*) + *way* way (OE *weg*).

2. from an (apparently rare) OE female personal name, *Heaðuwīg*, composed of the elements *heaðu* strife, contention + *wīg* war, which has Continental cogns. such as Ger. *Hedwig* (OHG *Haduwig*). A St Hedwig lived in the 12th–13th cents.; she was the wife of Henry the Bearded, Duke of Silesia, and founded numerous charitable institutions as well as increasing German influence in Silesia.

Vars.: **Hathway**, **Hadaway**.

Cogns. (of 2): Ger.: **Hed(e)wig**, **Hadewig**.

Metrs. (from 2) (dims.): Ger.: **Hädscher**. Low Ger.: **Heeschen**.

Hatherell English: probably a habitation name from an unidentified place, possibly so called from OE *hægþorn* HAWTHORN + *hyll* HILL.

Vars.: **Hatherill**, **Hatherall**; **Haddrell**, **Had(d)rill**.

The name seems to have originated in N Wilts. or S Gloucs.; the first known bearer is Editha Hathrell, *who was baptized on 12 Jan. 1538 at Calne, Wilts. The form* Haddrell *is first found in the 18th cent., and is largely confined to Wilts., whereas* Hadrill *is now most common in the London area. The var.* Hadrill *was exported to Australia in 1830 by an emigrant from Calne.*

Hatherley English (Devon): habitation name from *Hatherleigh* in Devon, or possibly *Hatherley* in Gloucs., both of which get their names from OE *hægþorn* HAWTHORN + *lēah* wood, clearing.

Hatley English: habitation name from any of a group of places in Beds. and Cambs., so called from OE *hætt* hat (see HATT), probably the name of a hill + OE *lēah* wood, clearing.
Var.: **Hateley**.

Hatt English: metonymic occupational name for a hatter or nickname for someone noted for the hat or hats that he wore. The bynames *Hætt* and *Hætta* occurred already in the OE period; cf. HASSALL and HATLEY. Some early forms such as Thomas *del Hat* (Oxon. 1279) and Richard *atte Hatte* (Worcs. 1327) indicate that the word was used of a hill shaped like a hat, and in these cases the surname may be topographic in origin.
Var.: **Hatter**.

Hattersley English: habitation name from a place in Ches., of uncertain etymology, perhaps from the gen. case of OE *hēahdēor* deer, stag (a cpd of *hēah* high + *dēor* animal, deer, because the deer was the most prized of the game animals) + OE *lēah* wood, clearing.

Hatton 1. English: habitation name from any of the various places, for example in Ches., Derbys., Lincs., W London, Shrops., Staffs., and Warwicks., so called from OE *hǣð* heathland, heather (see HEATH) + *tūn* enclosure, settlement.

2. French: from the OF oblique case of the Gmc personal name *Hatto*, apparently a short form of the various cpd names with the first element *hadu* strife, contention; cf., e.g., HABBERT and HATHAWAY 2.
Var. (of 2): Fr.: **Haton**.
Dims. (of 2): Fr.: **Hatté, Hatin, Hatot**.

The centre of London's diamond trade is Hatton Garden, which was once an actual garden, granted by Elizabeth I to her favourite Sir Christopher Hatton *(1540–91), whose chief attraction was said to be his graceful dancing. He came of a family which claimed to be of Norman lineage.*

Hauer German and Jewish (Ashkenazic): occupational name for a butcher, a woodcutter, or a stonemason, Ger. *Hauer* (*Holzhauer*, *Steinhauer*), agent derivs. of *hauen* to chop, hack (MHG *houwen*, OHG *houwan*); cf. HACKER.
Var.: **Heuer**.
Cogns.: Eng.: **Hewer, Hewar**.

Haughey Irish: Anglicized form of Gael. **Ó hEachaidh** 'descendant of *Eachaidh*', a byname meaning 'Horseman', from *each* horse (see KEOGH). See also HOWEY and CAUGHEY.

Haughton English: habitation name from any of various places so called. Nearly all, including those in Ches., Co. Durham, Lancs., Northumb., Shrops., and Staffs., get the name from OE *halh* nook, recess (see HALE 1) + *tūn* enclosure, settlement; in the case of one in Notts., however, the first element is OE *hōh* spur of a hill (see HOUGHTON).

Hauptmann 1. German: status name for a headman, leader, or captain, Ger. *Hauptmann*, from MHG *houb(e)t*, *houpt* HEAD + *man* man. This word denoted any of various civil and military officials at different times and places. The first element represents the original Gmc word for 'head', but already during the Middle Ages it was being replaced in the literal sense by KOPF, so that today it is retained only in cpds, such as this, where it has the transferred sense 'chief', 'principal'.

2. Jewish (Ashkenazic): probably a name taken by or given to a rabbi, as the head of a Jewish community.
Vars.: Ger.: **Heuptmann, Heiptmann**. Jewish: **Hauptman**.
Cogn. (of 1): Low Ger.: **Hettmann**. Pol.: HETMAN.

Hauschild German: 1. topographic name for someone who lived in a house marked with a shield-shaped sign, from Ger. *Hausschild* house shield, from *Haus* house (MHG, OHG *hūs*) + *Schild* shield (MHG *schilt*, OHG *scilt*).

2. according to Bahlow, who quotes a line from Hans Sachs, it may also be from MHG ***Houwschilt**, nickname or byname for a ferocious soldier, from MHG *houw(en)* to chop, hack (see HAUER) + *schilt* shield.
Vars.: **Hauenschild, Haufschild**.

Haüy French: of uncertain origin. It is possible that it is a habitation name from *Havys* in the Ardennes, recorded in the 9th cent. as *Elaviacum*, from the Gaul. personal name *Elavus* + the local suffix -*(i)ācum*. It seems that after the loss of the initial *E*- the *l*- was taken for an elided form of the Fr. def. art. and so also dropped. The present form of the surname can be explained only as the result of a misreading of the written form of the placename.

Havekost Low German: habitation name from any of the various places, principally in Westphalia, so called from MLG *havek* HAWK + *horst* wooded hill (cf. HURST).
Vars.: **Havekoss, Havighorst**.

Havelock English: from the ME given name *Havelok*, from ON *Hafleikr*, composed of the elements *haf* sea + *leikr* sport, play. The name was popularized in England in the Middle Ages partly by the ME romance *Havelok the Dane*.

Havet French: metonymic occupational name for someone who used a pickaxe, OF *havet*, a dim. of *hef*, of Gmc origin), or for a manufacturer of pickaxes.
Vars.: **Havot, Havon**.

Haw English: 1. topographic name for someone who lived by an enclosure, OE *haga* (a byform of *(ge)hæg*; see HAIG and HAY 1), or habitation name from a place named with this word, such as *Haw* in Gloucs.

2. from a ME given name, a back-formation from HAWKIN.
Var.: **Hawe**.
Patrs. (from 2): HAWES, **Hawson**.

Hawdon English: habitation name from an unidentified minor place, probably in Northumb., apparently so called from OE *haga* enclosure (see HAW 1) + *dūn* hill (see DOWN 1).

Hawes English: 1.* patr. from HAW 2.

2. from a Norman female personal name, *Haueis*, from Gmc *Haduwidis*, composed of the elements *hadu* strife, contention + *widi* wide.
Var.: **Hawyes**.

Hawk English (Devon): 1. metonymic occupational name for a HAWKER or nickname for someone supposedly resembling a hawk in some way, e.g. a fierce or rapacious person or one with a large hooked nose, from ME *hau(l)k*, *haueke* hawk (OE *heafoc*). There was an OE personal name (originally a byname) *H(e)afoc* 'Hawk', which persisted into the early ME period as a given name and may therefore also be a source.

2. topographic name for someone who lived in an isolated nook, from ME *halke*, one of the forms taken by OE *halh*; see HALE 1.

Var.: **Hawke**.

Cogns. (of 1): Ger.: **Habich(t)**, **Häbich**, **Hebich**, **Habig**. Low Ger.: **Habeck**, **Häwicke**, **Hävecke**, **Häfke**. Dan., Norw.: **Hø(e)g(h)**. Swed.: **Hö(ö)k**.

Dims. (of 1): Eng.: **Hawkett**, **Hawkitt**; HAWKIN.

Patr. (from 1): Eng.: **Hawkes** (or a var. of 2).

Hawker English (now found chiefly in the SW Midlands down to Somerset): occupational name for someone who bred and trained hawks, ME *haueker* (an agent deriv. of HAWK). Hawking was a major medieval sport, and the provision and training of hawks for a feudal lord was a not uncommon obligation in lieu of rent. The right of any free man to keep hawks for his own use was conceded in Magna Charta.

Cogns.: Ger.: **Häbicher**. Low Ger.: **Habecker**, **Hebecker**, **Häwecker**.

Hawkesford English (W Midlands): habitation name from an unidentified place, apparently named with the gen. case of the OE personal name or byname *Heafoc* 'HAWK' + OE *ford* FORD.

Hawkeswood English (W Midlands): habitation name, probably from one of the two places in Shrops. called *Hawkswood*. The one in the parish of Hordley is named with the gen. case of the OE personal name or byname *Heafoc* 'HAWK' + OE *wudu* wood; the one in the parish of Sidbury is earlier *Hokkyswode*, with a first element apparently from the gen. case of an OE personal name *Hocc*.

Hawkin English: from the ME given name *Hawkin*, a dim. of HAWK with the ANF hypocoristic suffix *-in*, or of *Hal*, a pet form of HARRY, with the originally Low Ger. suffix *-kin*.

Vars.: HAWKING, **Hawken**.

Patrs.: **Hawkin(g)s**, **Hawkyns**.

The patr. Hawkins *is by far the most common of the forms of this name, being found most frequently in the W Country and W Midlands.*

Sir John Hawkyns *(1532–95) was a renowned English naval commander who was knighted for his services against the Spanish Armada in 1588. Until recent times the family still used the spelling* Hawkyns. *They had been established in Plymouth as far back as 1480, when a certain John Hawkyns held land there. They were originally a branch of a Kentish family from the village of* HAWKINGE, *but the name had early on become assimilated to the form of the more common patr.*

Hawking English: 1. var. of HAWKIN.

2. var. of HAWKINGE.

Hawkinge English: habitation name from a place in Kent, so called from OE *Hafocing* 'hawk place'; see HAWK 1.

Var.: HAWKING.

Hawkley English: habitation name from a place, for example one in Hants, so called from OE *heafoc* HAWK + *lēah* wood, clearing.

Hawkshaw English (Yorks.): habitation name from a place in W Yorks., which survives as a field-name, so called from OE *heafoc* HAWK + *sceaga* wood, copse (see SHAW).

Hawksworth English (chiefly Yorks.): habitation name from a place so called in W Yorks., derived from the OE personal name *Hafoc* 'HAWK' + OE *worð* enclosure (see WORTH). A place similarly named in Notts. may have the same origin, but if so, the early spellings such as *Houkeswurda* must be explained by postulating Scandinavian interference (from the Anglo-Scandinavian form of the personal name, *Hauk*).

Hawley English: habitation name from any of various places so called. One in Kent is, according to Ekwall, named with OE *hālig* holy + *lēah* wood, clearing, and would therefore have once been the site of a sacred grove. One in Hants has as its first element OE *h(e)all* hall, manor (see HALL), or the homonymous *h(e)all* rock, stone (see HÄLL). However, the surname is common mainly in S Yorks. and Notts., and may derive from a lost place called *Hawley* near Sheffield, which is from ON *haugr* mound + OE *lēah* clearing.

Haworth English (Yorks. and Lancs.): 1. habitation name from *Haworth* in W Yorks., which is so called from OE *haga* enclosure (see HAW 1; here perhaps with the sense 'hedge') + *worð* enclosure (see WORTH).

2. var. of HOWARTH.

Hawthorn English: topographic name for someone who lived by a bush or hedge of hawthorn (OE *haguþorn*, *hægþorn*, i.e. thorn used for making hedges and enclosures; cf. HAW 1 and HAY 1), or habitation name from a place named with this word, such as *Hawthorn* in Co. Durham.

Vars.: **Ha(w)thorne** (chiefly N Ireland).

Cogns.: Ger.: **Hagedorn**, **Haydorn**, **Heydorn**, **Heidorn**. Flem.: **Van Hagendoren**. Du.: **Hagedoorn**.

The American novelist Nathaniel Hawthorne *(1804–64) was a direct descendant of Major William* Hathorne, *one of the English Puritans who settled in Massachusetts in 1630, and whose son John Hathorne was one of the judges in the Salem witchcraft trials. The writer's father was a sea captain, as was his grandfather, the Revolutionary war hero Daniel Hathorne (1731–96). The spelling of the surname was altered by the novelist himself.*

Hawtin English: 1. nickname for a proud or disdainful person, from ME, OF *hautain* haughty (a deriv. of *haut* high, lofty, L *altus*).

2. occupational name for a servant employed in the manor of a feudal lord, from OE *h(e)all* HALL + *þegn* THANE.

Var.: **Hawtayne**.

Hay Scots and English: 1. topographic name for someone who lived by an enclosure, ME *hay(e)*, *heye* (OE *(ge)hæg*, which after the Norman Conquest became confused with OF *haye* hedge, a word of Gmc origin and ultimately cogn. with the OE word; cf. HEDGE), or habitation name from any of the various places named with this word, including *Les Hays* and *La Haye* in Normandy. The OF and ME word was used in particular to denote an enclosed forest; cf. HAYWOOD.

2. nickname for a tall man, from ME *hay*, *hey* tall, high (OE *hēah*).

3. from the medieval given name *Hay*, which represented in part the OE byname *Hēah* 'Tall', in part a short form of the various cpd names with the first element *hēah* high.

Vars.: **Haye**; **Hey(e)** (chiefly Yorks. and Lancs.). (Of 2 only): HIGH.

Cogns. (of 1): Fr.: **Hay(e)**, HAYES; **Lahaye** (with fused article); **De(la)haye**, **Deshayes** (with fused article and preposition).

Dims. (of 1): Fr.: **Hayet, Hayot, Hayon**. (Of 3): Eng.: **Haylet(t)**; HAYCOCK.

Patr. (from 3): Eng.: HAYES.

The surname Hay *is particularly common in Scotland, where it has been established since 1160. The principal family of the name are of Norman origin; they trace their descent from William* de la Haye, *who was Butler of Scotland in the reign of Malcolm IV (1153–65). They hold the titles Marquess of Tweeddale, Earl of Kinnoul, and Earl of Erroll. The Earl of Erroll also holds the hereditary office of Constable of Scotland, first bestowed on the family by Robert I in 1314.*

Haycock English (chiefly W Midlands): from a medieval given name, a dim. of HAY 3, formed with the ME hypocoristic suffix *-cock* (see COCK).

Vars.: **Heycock, Heacock**.

Patr.: **Hickox**.

Hayday English: nickname for someone having some particular connection with a festival of the Church, from OE *hēah* high + *dæg* day; cf. HALLIDAY.

Hayden 1. English: habitation name from any of various places called *Hayden* or *Haydon*. The three cases of *Haydon* in Northumb. are named from OE *hēg* hay + *denu* valley. Others, for example in Dorset, Herts., Somerset, and Wilts., get the name from OE *hēg* hay (or perhaps *hege* hedge or *(ge)hæg* enclosure) + *dūn* hill.

2. Irish: Anglicized form of Gael. **Ó hÉideáin** and **Ó hÉidín** 'descendant of *Éideán*' or 'of *Éidín*', personal names from a dim. of *éideadh* clothes, armour.

Vars.: **Haydon, Heydon**. (Of 2 only): **O'He(y)den, O'Headen, O'Headyne, O'Hedin, (O')Hedian, Haydin**.

Hayes 1. English: habitation name from any of various places, for example in Devon and Dorset, so called from the strong pl. of ME *hay* enclosure (see HAY 1).

2. English: habitation name from any of various places, for example in Kent, so called from OE *hǣs* brushwood.

3. Irish: Anglicized form of Gael. **Ó hAodha** 'descendant of *Aodh*', a personal name meaning 'Fire' (cf. McKAY).

3. English: patr. from HAY 3.

4. French: pl. cogn. of HAY 3.

Vars.: Eng.: **Hays; Hey(e)s** (Lancs.). (Of 3 only): **Atheis; Hayesman, Heas(e)man, Easman**.

Cogns. (of 3): Low Ger.: **Heese(mann), Van Heesen**. Du.: **Van He(e)s**.

Hayfield English (Midlands): habitation name from *Hayfield* in Derbys. or from some other minor place elsewhere having this name. The name is derived from OE *hēg* hay + *feld* pasture, open country (see FIELD).

Hayhoe English: topographic name for someone who lived on a high spur, from OE *hēah* high (see HAY 2) + *hōh* (see HOWE 1), or habitation name from a minor place named with these elements.

Vars.: **Hayhow, Heyhoe, Heyo, H(e)igho**.

Hayhurst English (Lancs.): habitation name from *Hay Hurst* in the parish of Ribchester, Lancs., so called from OE *hæg* enclosure (see HAY 1) or *hēg* hay + *hyrst* wooded hill (see HURST).

Hayler English: 1. occupational name for a haulier, from an agent deriv. of ME *halien* to haul, transport (OF *haler*, of Gmc origin).

2. topographic name for someone who lived in a nook or recess; see HALE 1.

Vars.: **Hayller, Haylor, Haler**.

Hayling 1. English: habitation name from a place in Hants, so called from OE *Hægelingas* 'people of *Hægel*'; see HALE 2.

2. Welsh: from the OW personal name *Heilyn*, originally a byname meaning 'Cup-bearer'.

Var. (of 2): **Helyn**.

Patrs. (from 2): **Paling, Pa(i)lin**, PELLING, **Ballin, Bolan** (W *ap Heilyn*).

Hayman English (W Country): 1. topographic name for a man who lived by an enclosure, from HAY 1 + *man*. The term was in many cases in effect a synonym for HAYWARD.

2. nickname for a tall man; see HAY 2.

3. occupational name for the servant of someone called HAY 3, with *man* in the sense 'servant'.

Var.: **Heyman**.

Hayton English (Northern): habitation name from any of various places, in Cumb., Notts., Shrops., and elsewhere, so called from OE *hēg* hay + *tūn* enclosure, settlement.

Hayward English: occupational name for an official who was responsible for protecting land or enclosed forest from damage by animals, poachers, or vandals, from ME *hay* enclosure (see HAY 1) + *ward* guardian (see WARD).

Vars.: **Heyward; Haward** (see also HOWARD).

Haywood English: habitation name from any of various places, for example in Herefords., Notts., Shrops., and Staffs., so called from ME *hay* enclosure (see HAY 1) + *wude* WOOD. It was a common practice in the Middle Ages for areas of woodland to be fenced off as hunting grounds for the nobility. This name may have been confused in some cases with HAYWARD and perhaps also with HOGWOOD.

Hazel English: topographic name for someone who lived near a hazel tree or grove, OE *hæsel*.

Vars.: **Hazell, Hasel(l), Haisell; Hessel(s), Heazel(l)** (from the cogn. ON *hesli*); HASLAM (from the OE dat. pl.); **Has(e)ler, Haselar, Heasler**.

Cogns.: Swed.: **Hassel, Hessel**.

Collectives: Eng.: HASLING, HAZLETT.

Cpds (ornamental): Swed.: **Hasselberg, Hesselberg** ('hazel hill'); **Hasselblad, Hesselblad** ('hazel leaf'); **Hasselgren, Hesselgren** ('hazel branch'); **Hasselqvist** ('hazel twig').

Hazelden English: habitation name from any of various places that get their names from OE *hæsel* (or the cogn. ON *hesli*) HAZEL + *denu* valley (see DEAN 1).

Vars.: **Haizelden, Hayzelden, Haiselden, Hayselden, Hasleden, Haselden, Hes(s)elden, Hesleden, Heseldin, Hazeldon; Ha(y)zeldene, Hazelde(a)ne, Haseldene; Haz(z)eldine, Haz(z)ledine** (Notts.); **Haseldine, Hazeltine, Haseltine, Hes(s)eltine**. See also HAZELTON.

Hazelgrave English (W Yorks.): habitation name from a minor place that gets its name from OE *hæsel* (or the cogn. ON *hesli*) HAZEL + *grāf* grove or *grǣfe* thicket. *Hazelgrove* in Rishworth and *Hezzlegreave* in Saddleworth, both W Yorks., have this origin.

Hazelton English: habitation name from either of two places so called in Gloucs. At least one and probably both of these derive their name from OE *hæsel* hazel + *denu* valley (see DEAN 1). It is possible that there are other minor places elsewhere of this name, in which the second element is OE *tūn* enclosure, settlement. There has been considerable confusion of this name with HAZELDEN.

Vars.: **Haselton, Heselton, Hastleton**.

Hazelwood English: habitation name from any of various places, for example in Derbys., Suffolk, and W Yorks., so called from OE *hæsel* (or the cogn. ON *hesli*) HAZEL + *wudu* WOOD.

Vars.: **Haz(z)lewood, Haselwood, Haslewood; Hes(s)elwood, He(a)slewood; Aizlewood.**

Hazlett English (now chiefly N Ireland): topographic name for someone who lived by a hazel copse, OE **hæslett* (a deriv. of *hæsel* HAZEL).

Vars.: **Hazlitt, Haslett, Haslitt, Hezlet(t), Heaslett.**

Head English (chiefly Kent): 1. nickname for someone with some peculiarity or disproportion of the head (ME *heved*, OE *heafod*).

2. topographic name for someone who lived on a hill or at the head of a stream or valley.

Var.: **Heed.**

Cogns.: Ger.: **Haupt, Haubt, Heubt, Haipt**; see also HAUPTMANN. Low Ger.: **Hoef(t), Höf(t), Hövet.** Flem., Du.: **(Van den) Hooft.**

Dims.: Ger.: **Häup(te)l, Heupl, Heppl.**

Patr. (from 1): Eng.: **Heads** (Northumb.).

Headford English (Bristol): habitation name from an unidentified minor place, apparently so called from OE *hēafod* HEAD or *hǣð* heathland, heather (see HEATH) + *ford* FORD.

Headley English: habitation name from any of various places, for example in Hants, Surrey, Worcs., and W Yorks., so called from OE *hǣð* heathland, heather (see HEATH) + *lēah* wood, clearing.

Var.: **Hedley** (places in Co. Durham and Northumb.). See also HADLEY and HEATLEY.

Heald English (Lancs. and Yorks.): topographic name for someone who lived on a hillside, from OE *hylde*, *hielde* slope.

Vars.: HELD, **Hield(s).**

Healey 1. English: habitation name from a place near Manchester, so called from OE *hēah* high (see HAY 2) + *lēah* wood, clearing. There are various other places in N England, for example in Northumb. and Yorks., with the same name and etymology, and it is possible that they may also have contributed to the surname.

2. Irish: Anglicized form of Gael. **Ó hÉilidhe** 'descendant of the claimant', from *éilidhe* claimant.

3. Irish: Anglicized form of Gael. **Ó hÉalaighthe** 'descendant of *Éalathach*', a personal name perhaps from *ealadhach* ingenious.

Vars.: **Healy, Heel(e)y.** (Of 2 and 3): **O'He(a)ly, O'Healie.** (Of 3 only): **O'Healihy.**

Among the Irish Jacobite exiles who settled in France after 1685 was Peter O'Hely, *whose descendants became the powerful family of* Hely d'Oissel, *with a seat at Oissel in Normandy.*

Heaney Irish: Anglicized form of Gael. **Ó hÉanna** 'descendant of *Éanna*', a very common personal name of uncertain meaning. It was borne by various early saints, most notably St Éanna of Aran.

Vars.: **(O')Heany, (O')Heney, Heeney.**

Heap English (chiefly Lancs.): habitation name from *Heap* Bridge in Lancs., or topographic name for someone who lived by a hill or heap, from OE *hēap* heap, mound, hill.

Vars.: **Heape, Heaps.**

Heard English (chiefly W Country): occupational name for a tender of animals, normally a cowherd or shepherd, from ME *he(a)rde* (OE *hi(e)rde*, akin to *heord* herd, flock).

Vars.: **Heardman; Herd** (chiefly Scots), **Herdman** (chiefly Northumb.), HARDMAN, **Hird** (Yorks.), **Hurd** (chiefly Midlands), **Hurdman** (W Midlands); **He(a)rder** (agent derivs. of ME *he(a)rden* to herd, tend animals).

Cogns.: Ger.: **Hirt(h); Hirter, Herter, Herder; Hörter** (Bavaria).

Dim.: Ger.: **Hirtel, Hirtle.**

Hearn 1. English: var. of HERON 1.

2. English: topographic name for someone who lived by a bend in a river or in a recess in a hill, both of which are meanings of ME *herne* (OE *hyrne*). It may also be a habitation name from any of the various places, such as *Herne* in Kent and *Hurn* in Dorset, which are named with the OE word. Its exact original sense and its etymology are not clear; it may be a deriv. of *horn* HORN.

3. English: habitation name from *Herne* in Beds., so called from the dat. pl. (originally used after a preposition) of OE *hær* stone.

4. Irish: see AHERN.

Vars. (of 2): **Hearne, Hern(e), Hurn(e), Harn; Hernaman, Herniman, Harniman, Horniman, Hurman.**

Heath English: topographic name for someone who lived on a heath (ME *hethe*, OE *hǣð*) or habitation name from any of the numerous places, for example in Beds., Derbys., Herefords., Shrops., and W Yorks., named with this word. The same word also denoted heather, the characteristic plant of heathland areas.

Vars.: **Heather, Heathman;** HOAD.

Cogns.: Ger.: **Heide, Heyde, Heid(t), Haid; Heider, Haid(l)er, Haidner; He(i)demann, Heydemann, Haidmann.** Low Ger.: **Heed(e), Heeder.** Fris.: **Heidema.** Flem.: **Heyd, Van Heden, Van Hee, Verheyden.** Du.: **Van der Heide, Van der Hejde, Van den Heyden, Heij(er), Hey(er), Verheij(en), Verhey(en), Heijman, Heyman.** Dan., Norw.: **He(d)e.** Swed.: **Hed(h), Heed, Hedén, Hedin, Hedman.**

Cpds (ornamental): Swed.: **Hed(en)berg** ('heath hill'), **Hedlund** ('heath grove'); **Hedqvist** ('heath twig'); **Hed(en)ström** ('heath river').

Heathcote English: habitation name from any of various places, for example in Derbys. and Warwicks., so called from OE *hǣð* heathland, heather (see HEATH) + *cot* cottage, dwelling (see COATES).

Vars.: **Heathcoat, Heathcott.**

Heathfield English: habitation name from any of various places, for example in Somerset and Sussex, so called from OE *hǣð* heathland, heather (see HEATH) + *feld* pasture, open country (see FIELD). Cf. HATFIELD.

Heatley N English and Scots: habitation name from various places so called, of which the most significant is in Ches. near Manchester. However, the surname is now found chiefly in Scotland, N Ireland, and Northumb. The placename is derived from OE *hǣð* HEATH + *lēah* wood, clearing.

Vars.: **Heatlie, Haitlie.** See also HEADLEY and HADLEY.

The surname is well established in Scotland, the earliest recorded bearer being William de Hatteley, *son of Sir Robert 'called de Hatteley', who held lands at Kelso in the early 13th cent.*

Heaton English (N England): habitation name from any of the numerous places, for example in Lancs., Northumb., and W Yorks., so called from OE *hēah* high + *tūn* enclosure, settlement. Cf. HAMPTON.

A landowning family of this name, originally from Heaton in the parish of Lonsdale, Lancs., can be traced to the 12th cent. Another landowning family bearing the name can be traced to Heaton-under-Horwich in Lancs. in the 13th cent.

Hebblethwaite English (Yorks.): habitation name from *Heblethwaite* in W Yorks., so called from the ME dial.

term *hebble* plank bridge (probably of Scand. origin) + Northern ME *thwaite* meadow (see THWAITE).

Vars.: **Hebblewaite**, **Hebblewhite**, **Hepplewhite**, **Ebblewhite**.

Hebden English (Yorks.): habitation name from a place in W Yorks., so called from OE *hēope* rose-hip + *denu* valley.

Vars.: **Hebdon**; **Hepden**; **Hepton**.

In 1120 the manor of Hebden was granted by Roger de Mowbray to Uctred de Hebden, *a descendant of Uctred, Earl of Northumberland (d. 1016). The lands descended in the Hebden family until the 15th cent., when they were divided between the families of Tempest and Dymoke as the result of the marriage of heiresses.*

Hecht 1. German: nickname for a rapacious and greedy person, from Ger. *Hecht* pike ((MHG *hech(e)t*, OHG *hechit*, *hachit*). It may also have been a metonymic occupational name for a catcher of this unattractive but edible fish.

2. Jewish (Ashkenazic): ornamental name from Ger. *Hecht* or Yid. *hekht* pike, one of the many Ashkenazic ornamental names taken from vocab. words denoting wildlife.

Vars.: Ger.: **Höcht** (Bavaria). Jewish: **Gecht** (under Russ. influence; see GOREN); **Hechtkopf** ('pike head', presumably one of the unflattering names assigned more or less at random by non-Jewish government officials in 18th- and 19th-cent. central Europe).

Cogn.: Low Ger.: **Heekt**.

Dims.: Ger.: **Hechtl**; **Höchtl** (Bavaria).

Hector Scots: Anglicized form of the Gael. personal name *Eachdonn*, composed of the elements *each* horse (cf. KEOGH) + *donn* brown (cf. DUNN). The name has been assimilated to that of one of the princes of Troy.

The surname is also found in Yorks., where it may derive directly from a rare medieval given name; according to medieval legend Britain *derived its name from being founded by* Brutus, *a Trojan exile, and so* Hector *was occasionally chosen as a given name.*

Hedegård Danish: habitation name from a placename formed with the elements *hede* HEATH (ON *heiðr*) + *gård* enclosure (ON *garðr*; see GARTH).

Vars.: **Hedegaard**, **Heegård**, **Heegaard**.

Hedge English: topographic name for someone who lived by a hedge, OE *hecg*.

Vars.: **Hedges**; **Hedger**; **Hedgeman**.

Cogns.: Ger.: **Heck**; **Höck**, **Högg** (Bavaria); **Hecker** (see also HACKER); **Heckmann**. Flem.: **Van Heghe**, **Verhegge**. Du.: **Hekman**, **Terheggen**. Dan.: **Hegner**. Fr.: **Hec(q)**.

Dim.: Fr.: **Hequet**.

Heffer English: metonymic occupational name for a cowherd, or perhaps a nickname for a cowlike person, from ME *heffre*, *heffour* young cow, heifer (OE *heahf(o)re*, *heafru*, of obscure derivation).

Var.: **Hefferman**.

Heffernan Irish: Anglicized form of Gael. **Ó hIfearnáin** 'descendant of *Ifearnán*', a personal name from a dim. of *ifreannach* demon (from *ifreann* hell).

Vars.: **O'Hifferane**, **(O')Hiffer(n)an**, **Heffernon**, **Hefferan**.

Hegarty Irish: Anglicized form of Gael. **Ó hÉigceartaigh** 'descendant of *Éigceartach*', a byname meaning 'Unjust'.

Vars.: **O'He(a)gertie**, **O'Hagirtie**, **(O')Hagerty**, **Hegerty**, **Haggarty**, **Haggerty**, **Higerty**.

Hegedüs Hungarian and Jewish (Ashkenazic): occupational name for a player on the fiddle (Hung. *hegedü*, of unknown origin).

Hehl Low German: 1. from a medieval given name, a short form of various Gmc personal names with the first element *heil* salvation, safety.

2. nickname for a secretive or reclusive person, or topographic name for someone who lived at a remote or concealed spot, from MLG *hēle* secret, concealed.

Var.: **Hehle**.

Dim. (of 1): **Hehlke**.

Patrs. (from 1): Low Ger.: **Hehler**. Dan., Norw.: **Heilsen**.

Heidegger German and Swiss: habitation name from *Heidegg* near Zurich or any of the various places in Germany called *Heideck*. All of them get their names from MHG *heide* HEATH + *egge*, *ecke* corner (see ECK).

Var.: **Heidecker**.

Heiden 1. German: nickname from Ger. *Heiden* heathen (MHG *heiden*, OHG *heidano*, apparently a deriv. of *heida* HEATH, modelled on L *pāgānus*; see PAIN 1). The nickname was sometimes used to refer to a Christian knight who had been on a Crusade to wrest the Holy Land from the Muslims.

2. Jewish (Ashkenazic): of unknown origin. The Ashkenazic surname **Heidenberg** is perhaps an ornamental elaboration.

Var.: **Haydn**.

Cogns.: Du.: **Heijden**, **Heyden**.

Heifetz Jewish (Ashkenazic): ornamental name from Hebr. *chefets* delight, pleasure.

Vars.: **Che(i)fetz**, **Hejfec**, **Hefetz**, **Hefets**; **Haifetz**, **Chaifetz**; **Keyfetz**.

Height English: topographic name for someone who lived at the top of a hill or on a piece of raised ground, from ME *heyt* summit, height (OE *hīehðu*, a deriv. of *hēah* high; cf. HAY 2).

Vars.: **Hight**, **Hite**; **Hayter**, **Haytor**.

Heikkilä Finnish: name borne by a member of a household headed by someone called *Heikki* (a pet form of HENRY). The surname is formed from the given name with the addition of the local suffix *-la*.

Heilbronn Jewish (Ashkenazic): habitation name from a town so called in Württemberg, where there was once a large Jewish community. The town gets its name from OHG *heil(ag)* holy + *brunno* spring, well; cf. HALLIWELL.

Vars.: **Heilbronner**; **Heilbron**, **Heilborn**, **Heilbrun(n)**, **Heilbruner**, **Heilprun**; **Heilpern**, **Halper(n)**, **Halpert**, **Helper(n)**, **Halp(e)rin**, **Helprin**, **Halprin**; **Galper(n)**, **Galperin**, **Gelperin** (under Russ. influence; see GOREN); **Alpron**, **Alper(n)**, ALPERT, **Elper(i)n** (in regions where Yid. has no /h/), **Alperson**, **Alperin**, **Alperovi(t)ch**, **Alperowich**, **Alperowicz**, **Alperovitz**, **Alperovitsh** (patrs.); **Alperstein** (an ornamental elaboration).

Heimbürge German: status name for a village headman, MHG *heimbürge*, a cpd of *heim* homestead, settlement (OHG *heim*) + *bürge* guardian (OHG *burigo*, from the verb *bor(a)gēn* to guard). This was the title regularly used for the office of village headman in Franconia; cf. GRAF, HOFFMANN, MAYER, SCHULTZ, and VOGT.

Vars.: **Heimbürger**, **Heimburger**, **Heimberger**.

Heister Low German: topographic name for someone who lived by a conspicuous beech tree, MLG *hēster*.

Var.: **Hester**.

Cogns.: Du.: **Heester**, **Hesterman**. Fr.: **Hêtre**, **Lehêtre** (although *hêtre* is now the standard word for the tree, this surname is rare and found only in Picardy; for the normal medieval equivalent, see FAGE). Eng.: **Hester**.

Dim.: Fr.: **Hêtreau**.

Collective: Fr.: **Hétroy**.

Held 1. German, Dutch, and Jewish (Ashkenazic): nickname from Ger. *Held* hero, or Du. or Yid. *held* (MHG, MDu. *held*). As a Jewish name, it is often ornamental.

2. English: var. of HEALD.

Vars. (of 1): Ger.: **Heldt, Heldmann**. Jewish: **Heldman**.

Cpds (of 1; ornamental): Jewish: **Heldenberg** ('hero's hill'); **Heldstein** ('hero stone'), **Geldstein** (the latter under Russ. influence; see GOREN).

Heller 1. German: nickname from the small medieval coin known as the *häller* or *heller* because it was first minted (in 1208) at the Swabian town of (*Schwäbisch*) *Hall*; cf. HALL.

2. Jewish (Ashkenazic): nickname for a person with fair hair or a light complexion, from an inflected form, used before a male given name, of Ger. *hell* light, bright, Yid. *hel* (MHG *hell*).

3. English: var. of HILL 1.

Vars. (of 2): **Hellerman, Heler(man), Hel(l)man; Hellerstein** ('bright stone', an ornamental elaboration). See also GELLER and ELLER. (Of 3): **Helle, Hellman**.

Hellier English: occupational name for a roofer (tiler or thatcher), from an agent deriv. of ME *hele(n)* to cover (OE *helian*).

Vars.: **Helliar, Hel(l)yer, Hilliar,** HILLIER, **Hillyar, Hil(l)yer**.

Hellings English: of uncertain origin, probably a habitation name. Reaney ascribes it to the village of *Healing* in Lincs. (of the same origin as HAYLING), but since the surname is now found mainly in Devon, it could equally well be a var. of HAYLING or of some other origin entirely.

Helm 1. English (chiefly Lancs.): topographic name for someone who lived or worked at a rough temporary shelter for animals, ME *helm* (ON *hialmr*, a cogn. of the OE and OHG words in 2 below).

2. English and German: metonymic occupational name for a maker of helmets, from ME, OE *helm*, Ger. *Helm* (MHG, OHG *helm*).

3. German: from a medieval given name, a short form of any of the various cpd names containing the element *helm* helmet; cf., e.g., HELMOLD, HELMUND, and WILLIAM.

Vars. (of 1): Eng.: **Helme** (Lancs.), **Helms**.

Dims. (of 3): Ger.: **Helmel, Helmle**. Low Ger.: **Helm(e)cke, Helmchen**.

Patr. (from 3): Low Ger.: **Helms(en)**.

Patrs. (from 3) (dim.): Low Ger.: **Helmker**.

Helmold German: from a Gmc personal name composed of the elements *helm* helmet + *mund* protection.

Vars.: **Helm(h)olt**.

Patrs.: **Helmhol(t)z**.

Helmund German: from a Gmc personal name composed of the elements *helm* helmet + *mund* protection.

Vars.: **Hellmund(t)**.

Cogn.: Low Ger.: **Helmont**.

Helps English (Southern): of uncertain origin, probably a patr. from an OE personal name **Help*, a short form of a cpd name with the first element *help* help, aid (e.g. *Helpric*, for which there is placename evidence). Alternatively, it may derive from the cogn. ON female personal name *Hialp*, which is attested.

Helsby English (Lancs.): habitation name from a place in Ches., recorded in Domesday Book as *Helesbe*, which gets its name from ON *hjallr* ledge, used of a ledge on a mountainside + *býr* farm, settlement.

Hemingway English (W Yorks.): apparently a habitation name from an unidentified minor place in W Yorks., probably in the parish of Halifax, to judge by the distribution of early occurrences of the surname. The placename is from the personal name HEMMING + ME *wey* way, path (OE *weg*).

Var.: **Hemmingway**.

Hemming English (chiefly W Midlands), Danish/Norwegian, and Swedish: from the ON personal name *Hemmingr*, originally a patr. from a short form of any of the various cpd personal names with a first element *heim* home.

Patrs.: Eng.: **Hemmings**. Fris.: **Hemminga**. Dan., Norw.: **Hemmingsen**. Swed.: **Hemmingsson**.

Hemphill N Irish, originally Scots: habitation name from a place near Galston in the former county of Ayrs. (now part of Strathclyde region), apparently so called from OE *henep* hemp + *hyll* HILL.

Var.: **Hempill**.

Hems English (W Midlands): regional name for someone who lived in the border country between England and Wales, or habitation name from *The Hem*, a village in Shrops., or *Hem* near Montgomery, all from OE *hemm* border (used in a much wider sense than mod. Eng. *hem*).

Hemsley English (chiefly Yorks. and Notts.): habitation name from either of two places in N Yorks. called *Helmsley*. The names are of different etymologies: the one near Rievaulx Abbey is from the OE personal name *Helm* + OE *lēah* wood, clearing, whereas Upper Helmsley, near York, is from the OE personal name *Hemele* + OE *ēg* island, and had the form *Hemelsey* up to at least the 14th cent.

Vars.: **Hemesley, Helmsley**.

Hemstock English (Notts.): habitation name from an unidentified minor place; the first element is probably from a personal name of uncertain original form, the second is OE *stoc* place (see STOCK).

Hemsworth English (Yorks.): habitation name from the town in W Yorks., recorded as *Hilmeuuord* and *Hamelesuurde* in Domesday Book. 'This can hardly be anything else than Hymel's *worð*', comments Ekwall, i.e. from the gen. case of the OE personal name *Hymel* (apparently from a short form of names such as *Hūnbeald* 'bear-cub bold' and *Hūnbeorht* 'bear-cub bright') + OE *worð* enclosure (see WORTH).

Hemus English: of uncertain origin, probably a topographic name for someone who lived in a house situated at a border of some sort, from ME *hem(m)* border (see HEMS) + *h(o)us* house (OE *hūs*).

Henderson Scots: patr. from *Hendry*, a chiefly Sc. var. of the given name HENRY; the intrusive *-d-* between *n* and *r* is found also in other languages. Several Scottish bearers of this name have ancestors whose name was *Henryson*.

Hendra Cornish: habitation name from any of various places so called from Corn. *hendre* winter homestead, the home farm of a people who practised transhumance, from *hen* old + *tre* homestead.

Hendy English (mainly W Country): nickname for a pleasant and affable man, from ME *hende* courteous, kind, gentle (OE *gehende* skilful, handy, a deriv. of *hand* hand).

Hendy was also sometimes used as a given name in the Middle Ages and some examples of the surname may derive from this rather than from the nickname.

Vars.: **Hendey, Henday**.

Patr.: **Hendisson**.

Heneghan Irish: Anglicized form of Gael. **Ó hEidhneacháin** 'descendant of *Eidhneachán*', a personal name of uncertain origin.

Vars.: **Henegan**; BIRD (the result of the association of the Gael. name with *éan* bird).

Hengst German: metonymic occupational name for someone who worked with horses, or nickname for a lustful man, from Ger. *Hengst* stallion (MHG *heng(e)st*, OHG *hengist*). In part it may also have been a house name, from the use of a picture of a horse as a house sign.

Var.: **Hengstmann**.

Cogns.: Low Ger.: **Hingst(mann)**. Du.: **Van der Hengst**. Eng.: **Hensman, Hinckesman**.

Hénin French: 1. habitation name from a place in Pas-de-Calais, so called from the Gmc byname *Henno* 'Cock' (see HAHN 1) + the local suffix *-īnum*.

2. metonymic occupational name for a maker or seller of the tall and elaborate head-dresses worn in the Middle Ages by fashionable ladies, known in OF as *hennins*. The word is apparently from MLG *henninck* cock, with reference to the similarity in appearance and function between these garments and the cock's comb.

Var.: **Hennin**.

Henley English: habitation name from any of the various places so called. Most, e.g. those in Oxon., Suffolk, and Warwicks., get the name from the weak dat. case (originally used after a preposition and article) of OE *hēah* high + OE *lēah* wood, clearing. Others, for example one near Ludlow in Shrops., have as their first element OE *henn* hen, wild bird. Others still, for example those in Somerset and Surrey, are ambiguous between the two possibilities.

Var.: **Henly**.

Henn English (chiefly W Midlands): 1. from the ME given name *Henn(e)*, a short form of HENRY.

2. nickname, perhaps for a fussy man, from ME *hen(n)* hen (OE *henn*, related to *hana* cock; cf. HAHN 1).

Dim. (of 1): **Henkin**.

Patr. (from 1): **Henson**.

Hennessy Irish: Anglicized form of Gael. **Ó hAonghusa** 'descendant of ANGUS'.

Vars.: **Hennessey, Heness(e)y, Hen(n)es(e)y, O'Hen(n)es(s)(e)y, O'Heanesey, Hench(e)y, Hinchy, Hinsey**.

The cognac Hennessy *is produced by a French family of Irish stock, founded by Richard Hennessy (b. 1720), an exile from Ballymacmoy in Co. Cork. His son James, although never formally naturalized as a French citizen, became a peer of France and married into the Martell family, also famous for its cognac.*

Henning Scots (most common around Hawick and Dumfries): of uncertain origin. The earliest known occurrence is around 1630.

Vars.: **Ha(i)n(n)ing**.

Henry 1. English and French: from a Gmc personal name composed of the elements *haim, heim* home + *rīc* power, introduced into England by the Normans in the form *Henri*. During the Middle Ages this name became enormously popular in England and was borne by eight kings, a record not equalled until the 20th cent. (when EDWARD caught up). Continental forms of the given name were equally popular (Ger. *Heinrich*, Fr. *Henri*, Czech *Jindřich*, etc.). In the period in which the majority of Eng. surnames were formed, a common vernacular form of the name was HARRY; official documents of the period normally used the Latinized form *Henricus*. Eng. *Henry* has absorbed an originally distinct Gmc personal name that had *hagan* hawthorn (cf. HAIN 2) as its first element, and there has also been considerable confusion with AMERY.

2. Irish: Anglicized form of Gael. **Ó hInnéirghe** 'descendant of *Innéirghe*', a byname meaning 'Abandonment', 'Elopement'.

Vars. (of 1): Eng.: **Henrey; Hendr(e)y, Hendrie** (Scotland); **Hendrick** (Ireland). Fr.: **Henri, Hendry, Hanry**. (Of 2): **O'Henery**.

Cogns. (of 1): Prov.: **Henric, Enric; Aimeric, Aymeric; Méric**. Cat.: **Enrich, Aymerich**. Sp.: **Enrique**. Port.: **Henrique**. It.: **Enrico, Errico, Endrici, Errichi, Enr(d)igo, Errigo, Endrighi, Arrigo, Arrighi; Americi, Amerighi** (N Italy, Tuscany). Ger.: **Hein(d)rich, Heinreich**. Low Ger.: **Hendrich, Hindrich, Hindrick**. Fris.: **Hinnerk**. Flem.: **Heindrick**. Du.: **Hendrik, Hinrich; Hemerijk**. Dan.: **Hammerich**. Ger. (of Slav. origin): **Jennrich, Jendrich, Jendricke, Jendrach, Jindrich, Jendrusch, Genn(e)rich, Gendrich, Gendricke**. Czech: **Jind(r)a, Jína, Jindrák, Jindřich; Henrych** (from the Ger. name).

Dims. (of 1): Eng.: HERRIOT, HENN, HAWKIN, HAW. Fr.: **Henri(qu)et, Henrion, Henr(i)ot, Hariot; Hémeret; Riquet** (see also RICHARD); **Mériguet, Mérigeau, Mérigot, Mérigon; Mériet, Mériel, Mériot**. It.: **Enrietto, Arrighetti, Arrighini, Errichelli, Errichiello, Arrichiello, Endrizzi, Endricci, Arrigucci**. Ger.: **Hein(e)(l), Heyn(e)(l), Heindl(e), Heinle(in), He(i)n(t)ze, Heinz(el), Heitz, Hin(t)z(e)**. Low Ger.: **Heine(c)ke, Heinicke, Heinke, Hen(c)ke, Henkmann, Hei(ne)mann, Heymann, Hehnke, Hennemann**. Fris.: **Herrema, Harrema**. Flem.: **Heine(man)**. Du.: **Heijne, Heyne, Henze, Heins(ius)**. Dan.: **Hein**. Ger. (of Slav. origin): **Hein(i)sch, Heint(z)sch, Heinschke, Hinsch(e), Hi(t)schke, Hitzschke, Hitzke, Heinig, Hönig, Hönack, Hönatsch, Hön(i)sch**. Czech: **Jind(r)áček**. Finn.: **Heino**. Hung.: **Jendrássik**.

Patrs. (from 1): Eng.: **Hen(e)ries**, HARRIS; **Henryson**, HENDERSON (Scotland); FITZHENRY (Ireland). Sc.: MCHENRY. Welsh: PARRY. Sp.: **Enríquez**. Port.: **Henriques, Enriques**. It.: **D'Enrico, D'Errico, D'Arrigo**. Ger.: **Heinritz(e)** (Hesse); **Heinrici** (Latinized). Low Ger.: **Hen(d)richs, Hendricks, Hinrichs(en)**. Fris.: **Hinners**. Flem.: **Hendricks, Hendri(ck)x, Hendriksen**. Du.: **Hendriks, Hendrix, Hendrikse(n)**. Dan., Norw.: **Hen(d)riksen, Henrichsen, Hinrichsen**. Swed.: **Henriksson, Henricsson**.

Patrs. (from 1) (dims.): Scots: HASSON. Ger.: **Heiner(t), Heinzler, Hentz(e)ler, Hen(t)zer, Hin(t)zer**. Low Ger.: **Hein(ek)en, Hein(ek)ing, Hein(s)sen, Henken(s), Henker, Hinken(s), Hinksen, Henner**. Du.: **Heijnen, Heynen**. Flem.: **Heyns, Heynen, Hens(mans)**. Ger. (of Slav. origin): **Hitscher; Henniger, Hänniger**. Finn.: **Heinonen, Heikkinen**.

Henshaw English: 1. habitation name from a place in Northumb., so called from the gen. case of the OE personal name *Heðīn* (from a short form of the rare cpd names with the first element *hǣð* heath) + OE *halh* nook, recess (see HALE 1).

2. habitation name from a place in the parish of Prestbury, Ches., and from a lost place in SE Lancs., both so called from ME *hen* hen + *shaw* wood. The name *de Henneshagh* occurs at Rochdale as early as 1325.

Vars.: **Henshall, Henshell, Hensher**.

Henton English: habitation name from a place so called, probably either *Henton* in Oxon., which is from the OE weak dat. case, originally used after a preposition and article, of *hēah* high (see HAY 2) + OE *tūn* enclosure, settlement, or *Henton* in Somerset, which is from OE *henn* hen (perhaps a byname; cf. HENN 2) + *tūn*. The surname, however, is now chiefly common in Notts.

Henty English (Sussex): according to Reaney this is a habitation name from *Antye* Farm in the parish of Wivelsfield, which gets its name from OE *hēan* (dat. of *hēah* high) + *tēag* enclosure.

Henwood Cornish: habitation name from a place in Linkinhorne parish, so called from OE *henn* hen + *wudu* wood. There is also a place of the same name (but different etymology) in Warwicks., but this does not seem to have given rise to any surnames.

Hepburn N English and Scots: habitation name from a place in Northumb., so called from OE *hēah* high + *byrgen* burial mound, tumulus. Some examples of the surname may derive from *Hebburn* in Co. Durham, which has the same origin, as does *Hebron* in Northumb.

Vars.: **Hebburn, Hebborn, Hebbourne**.

Hepple English (Northumb.): habitation name from a place in Northumb., so called from OE *hēope* rose-hip + *halh* nook, recess (see HALE 1).

Var.: **Heppell**.

Heptinstall English (Yorks.): habitation name from *Heptonstall* in W Yorks., which derives its name from HEBDEN + OE *stall* cattle-station (or simply 'place'), i.e. 'cattle-stall belonging to Hebden'.

Vars.: **Heptonstall, Heppenstall**.

Hepworth English: habitation name from places so called, of which there is one in Suffolk and another in W Yorks., deriving their name from OE *hēope* rose hip + *worð* enclosure (see WORTH). The surname is still largely confined to Yorks., so it seems that the latter place is by far the most likely source of the surname.

Var.: **Hipworth**.

Heraghty Irish: Anglicized form of Gael. **Ó hOireachtaigh** 'descendant of *Oireachtach*', a byname for a member of an assembly; cf. GERAGHTY.

Heras Spanish: habitation name from any of various places, for example in the provinces of Santander and Guadalajara, probably so called from the pl. of Sp. *era* threshing floor (L *ārea*). The initial *H-* is silent and in this case inorganic. According to an alternative theory, the place-name is derived from L *hedera* ivy.

Herbaud French: from a Gmc personal name composed of the elements *heri*, *hari* army + *bald* bold, brave.

Vars.: **Herbau(l)t, Herbaux; Harbaud, Harbaut, Harbaux; Arbaud**.

Cogns.: Eng.: **Harbot(t), Harbut(t), Harbud**. Ger.: **Herbold, Herpoldt**.

Herbert English, French, and German: from a Gmc personal name composed of the elements *heri*, *hari* army + *berht* bright, famous. This OF name, introduced to Britain by the Normans, reinforced the less common OE cogn. *Herebeorht*.

Vars.: Eng.: **Herbit; Hebbert, Heb(b)ard; Harbert, Harberd, Harbard, Harbird, Harbord**. Fr.: **Hébert, Herbet, Harbert**. Ger.: **Herbrecht, Herbricht**.

Cogn.: Low Ger.: **Harbert**.

Dims.: Eng.: **Hebb, Hipkin; Hercock, Hircock**. Fr.: **Hébertet, Hébertot, Herbreteau, Herb(el)et, Herb(el)in, Herb(el)ot, Harbelot, Harbulot**. Low Ger.: **Harr(e), Harck, Herck, Harich**.

Patrs.: Eng.: **Herbertson, Harbertson, Harburtson; FitzHerbert**. Ger.: **Her(i)bertz**. Low Ger.: **Harbers, Harberding, Harbring**.

Patrs. (from dims.): Eng.: **Herbi(n)son; Harbi(n)son** (chiefly N Ireland); **Hebson; Hipkins, Hipkiss**. Fris.: **Harbs**.

Herbert *is the name of a family originating on the Welsh borders, earlier recorded as* Herberd. *They are descended from Jenkin ap Adam of Monmouth, recorded in the reign of Edward III (1327–77), and hold the Earldoms of Pembroke, Montgomery, and Carnarvon. A later member of the family, William Herbert (1580–1630), 3rd Earl of Pembroke, gave his name to Pembroke College, Oxford, in 1624. He was a patron of Inigo Jones and Ben Jonson. Also from this family was the metaphysical poet George Herbert (1593–1633). A branch of the family was established in Ireland, descended from Thomas Herbert of Montgomery, a nephew of the first Earl of Pembroke. He settled in Ireland in 1656 and became High Sheriff of Co. Kerry in 1659. A family by the name of* Fitzherbert, *who hold the title Baron Stafford, trace their descent from William, son of Herbert, who was granted the manor of Norbury, Derbys., in 1125 and was the first to use the surname.*

Herbst German: nickname from MHG *herb(e)st*, which still bore the meaning of its Eng. cogn. *harvest* (of cereals or wine), whereas mod. Ger. *Herbst* has come to mean 'autumn', the time of year when the harvest takes place. The exact application of the nickname is not clear; perhaps it referred to a peasant who had certain obligations to his master at the time of the harvest, or it may have been acquired for some other anecdotal reason which is now lost.

2. Jewish (Ashkenazic): ornamental name from mod. Ger. *Herbst* autumn, perhaps reflecting the season when the name was first taken or given. In some cases, it seems to have been one of the group of names referring to the seasons that were distributed at random by government officials; cf. FRULING, WINTER, and SUMMER.

Vars.: Jewish: **Herbstman; Erbst** (in regions where Yid. has no /h/).

Cogns.: Low Ger.: **Harfst**. Flem., Du.: **Herfst**. Dan.: **Høst**.

Heredero Spanish: nickname for someone who had inherited or was known to be due to inherit property, from Sp. *heredero* heir (LL *hērēditārius*, a deriv. of class. L *hērēs*, gen. *hērēdis*; cf. AYER).

Heredia Spanish: habitation name from any of various places, for example in the province of Álava, so named from the pl. form of LL *hērēdium* hereditary estate (a deriv. of *hērēs*; cf. HEREDERO and AYER), i.e. one that could be passed on to the heirs of its tenant instead of reverting to the overlord.

Herfahrt German: occupational nickname for a soldier, from MHG *hervart* campaign, military expedition (from OHG *heri* army + *vart* journey).

Vars.: **Her(r)fart, Her(r)forth, Her(r)furth, Her(r)fert**.

Hérisson French: 1. nickname from OF *hérisson* hedgehog (LL *ēricio*, gen. *ēriciōnis*, for class. L *ēricius*). In the Middle Ages the animal was supposed to have a bad character, and the nickname may have been given in a generalized pej. sense, as well as from more obvious points of comparison, such as an unkempt appearance.

2. habitation name from places in Allier and Deux-Sèvres, apparently so called from the vocab. word mentioned above; the reference is presumably to some defensive system.

Var. (of 1): **Hérichon**.

Heritage English: status name for someone who held or occupied land inherited from an ancestor, rather than by feudal gift from an overlord, from ME, OF *(h)eritage* inherited property (LL *hēritagium*, from *hērēs* heir; cf. AYER).

Var.: **Heretage**.

The first known bearers of the name are John Heritage *of Oxon. and John* Erytage *of Hunts., both recorded in the Hundred Rolls for 1279. The name also occurs early in Warwicks., near the Oxon. border, and at least one present-day family of this name probably goes back to that source. All American bearers of the name seem to be descended from a single individual who emigrated from England in 1684.*

Herkes Scots: habitation name from *Harcarse* in the parish of Fogo, Berwicks. The placename is recorded in 1200 as *Harkarres* and in 1328 as *Harcarres*. It is of uncertain origin.

Vars.: **Harkes(s)** (SE Scotland); **Hercus, Harcus** (Orkney).

Herkommer German: habitation name from *Herkheim* in Bavaria. The assimilation to the form of an agent noun from *herkommen* to come forward (i.e. 'new arrival') has been brought about partly by phonetic change and partly by folk etymology.

Vars.: **Herk(he)imer**; **Horkheimer** (also Jewish (W Ashkenazic)).

Herlihy Irish: Anglicized form of Gael. **Ó hIarfhlatha** 'descendant of *Iarfhlaith*', a byname describing a feudal underlord.

Vars.: **O'Herlihy, O'H(i)erlehy, Herley,** HURLEY.

Hermann German: from a Gmc personal name composed of the elements *heri, hari* army + *man* man. This is undoubtedly of very ancient origin, and the 1st-cent. leader of the Cherusci recorded by the L historian Tacitus as *Arminius* has been claimed as the first known bearer, but there are phonetic problems with this interpretation, and his name may rather be a deriv. of the element *Irmen, Ermen*, the name of a god. The surname is also borne by Ashkenazic Jews, probably as an adoption of the Ger. surname.

Vars.: **Herrmann**; **Hörmann** (Bavaria); **Hiermann** (Austria); **Herman** (Jewish).

Cogns.: Low Ger.: **Harmen**. Flem., Du.: **Herman**. Fr.: **Herman, Harman(d), Harmant, Armand, Armant**. Eng. (Norman): **Herman, Harman(d), Harmant, He(a)rmon**; **Harmon** (Ireland). Pol.: **Herman**. Czech: **Heřman**. It.: **Arman(n)i, Arman(n)o, Erman(n)i, Erman(n)o** (N Italy); **Arman, Erman** (Venetia).

Dims.: Ger.: **Hermel** (see also HERMELIN), **Hermle, Her(r)l(e), Herlein**; **Hörl** (Bavaria); **Hierl** (Austria). Low Ger.: **Herm, Harm, Herm(ec)ke, Hermichen**. Ger. (under Slav. influence): HESS, **Hessel, Hetzel, Hetzold, He(t)schold**; **Hersch(el), Herschmann** (see also HIRSCH); **Men(t)zelmann**. Czech: **Heřmánek**. Fr.: **Armandin**. Eng.: **Harm**. It.: **Armanetti, Armanini, Armanino**.

Patrs.: Jewish (E Ashkenazic): **Hermanoff, Germanoff, Germanov(itz)**. Pol.: **Hermanowicz**. Russ.: **Germanov**. Low Ger.: **Hermans, Harmaning**. Du., Flem.: **Hermans(z), Hermanszoon**. Dan., Norw.: **Hermansen**. Swed.: **Hermansson**.

Patrs. (from dims.): Ger.: **Herrler, Her(r)ling**; **Hörring** (Bavaria). Low Ger.: **Herms(en), Harms(en)**. Flem.: **Hermes**. Du.: **Hermsen, Harms(en)**. Ger. (of Slav. origin): **Menzler**. Eng.: **Harms**. Finn.: **Manninen**.

Habitation name: Pol.: **Hermanowski**.

Hermelin Jewish (Ashkenazic): ornamental name from Ger. *Hermelin* ermine (MHG *hermelīn*, OHG *harmilī* weasel, a dim. of *harmo*; cf. OE *hearma*).

Vars.: **Harmel** (from Yid. *harml*), **Hermel(e)**; **Harmelin, Harmolin**.

Hermès Provençal: topographic name for someone who lived in a deserted spot or on a patch of waste land, from OProv. *erm* desert, waste (Gk *erēmia*, a deriv. of *erēmos* lonely, solitary) + the local suffix *-ès*. The name has, however, long been associated by folk etymology with that of the Gk god *Hermes*, the etymology of which is unknown.

Var.: **Hermier**.

Hermida Spanish: 1. cogn. of HERMITE.

2. habitation name from any of various places, for example in the provinces of Lugo, Orense, and Pontevedra, so called from OSp. *hermida* hermitage, shrine (a later development of the same word as in 1).

Hermite French: nickname from OF *hermite* hermit (Gk *erēmitēs*; cf. ARMITAGE), which was probably given at least as often to people living in isolated spots (cf. HERMÈS), or not on good terms with their neighbours, as to actual hermits.

Vars.: **Hermitte, Lhermit(t)e**.

Cogns.: Eng.: **Hermitte, Armit(t), Armett**. Sp.: HERMIDA.

Hermoso Spanish: nickname meaning 'fine', 'handsome' (L *formōsus*, from *forma* shape, form, beauty), given either in admiration or in mockery of a dandy.

Heron 1. English: nickname for a tall, thin person resembling a heron, ME *heiroun, heyron* (OF *hairon*, of Gmc origin).

2. Irish: Anglicized form of Gael. **Ó hEaráin** 'descendant of *Earán*', a personal name from a dim. of *earadh* fear, distrust.

3. Irish: Anglicized form of Gael. **Ó hUidhrín** 'descendant of *Uidhrín*', a personal name probably from a dim. of *odhar* dun-coloured, swarthy.

4. Irish: Anglicized form of Gael. **Mac Giolla Chiaráin** 'son of the servant of (St) *Ciarán*'; see KIERAN.

Vars. (of 1): **Herro(u)n, Hairon,** HEARN, **Leherne**. (Of 2): **O'Heron, O'Har(a)n, O'Harran(e), Her(r)an, Harran, Harron**. (Of 4): **McIlheron, McElharan**.

Cogns. (of 1): Fr.: **Héron, Hairon, Lehéron**. Prov.: **A(i)gron**.

Herr 1. German: nickname for someone who gave himself airs and behaved in a lordly manner, from Ger. *Herr* master, lord (MHG *herre*, OHG *herro*).

2. German: occupational name for someone in the service of the lord of the manor, likewise from Ger. *Herr*, MHG *herre*.

3. Jewish (Ashkenazic): of unknown origin, possibly originating as in 1 above.

Var.: Ger.: **Herre**.

Cogns.: Low Ger.: **Heer**. Flem., Du.: **De Heer, Heere**.

Dims.: Ger.: **Herrle(i)n**. Low Ger.: **Herrgen**.

Patrs.: Jewish: **Herrenson, Her(r)enzon**. Flem., Du.: **Heeren**.

Herrgott German: from Ger. *Herrgott* 'Lord God', a cpd of MHG *herre* lord (see HERR) + *got* God. The use of the surname reflects a robust attitude to blasphemy, but the circumstances under which it was acquired are not clear. It may in part be an occupational name for a producer or seller of crucifixes or religious paintings; alternatively, it may be a nickname, either for a frequent user of this expression as an oath, or for arrogant person who behaved 'like God Almighty'.

Vars.: **Hergot**; **Herg(e)t** (Franconia).

Herrick English: from the ON personal name *Eiríkr*, composed of the elements *eir* mercy, peace (a cogn. of OHG *ēra* honour; cf. EHRLICH) + *rík* power. The addition in English of an inorganic *H-* to names beginning with a vowel is a relatively common phenomenon; cf., e.g., HOSKIN and HUCK. It is possible that this name may have swallowed up a less common Gmc personal name with the first element *heri, hari* army. There seems also to have been some confusion with Henry.

Cogn.: Ger.: **Erich.**

Patrs.: Low Ger.: **Erichs(en).** Norw., Dan.: **Eriksen, Erichsen.** Swed.: **Eriksson, Ericsson.** Finn.: **Eerikäinen.**

The English poet Robert Herrick *(1591–1674) was from a prosperous family of goldsmiths, who had a long association with the city of Leicester. There is a family tradition was that they were of Scandinavian origin, descended from Eric the Forester, who settled in the city in the 11th cent. The initial aspirate came into the name in the late 16th cent.; the name of the poet's great-grandfather is recorded in the corporation books of the city of Leicester in 1511 as Thomas* Ericke.

Herring English: metonymic occupational name for a seller of the fish, ME *hering* (OE *hǣring, hēring*). In some cases it may have been a nickname in the sense of a trifle, something of little value, a meaning which is clearly apparent in medieval phrases and proverbial expressions such as 'to like neither herring nor barrel', i.e. not to like something at all.

Vars.: **Hering; Harenc** (from the OF word, which is itself of Gmc origin).

Cogns.: Ger.: **Hering; Höring** (Bavaria). Low Ger., Du.: **Haring.** Flem.: **Haerinck.** Jewish (Ashkenazic): **Hering** (either a metonymic occupational name for a fishmonger, or one of the several ornamental names taken from vocab. words referring to fish). Fr.: **Hareng, Haran(d), Harant, Harong; Harenger.**

Herrington English: habitation name from a place in Co. Durham, so called from OE *Heringtūn* 'settlement (OE *tūn*) associated with *Here*', a short form of the various cpd names with the first element *here* army.

Herriot 1. English and French: dim. (with the suffix *-ot*) of the medieval given name *Herry*, Harry (a var. of Henry).

2. Scots: habitation name from a place, e.g. *Heriot* to the south of Edinburgh, named with ME *heriot*, which denoted a piece of land restored to the feudal lord on the death of its tenant. The ME word is from OE *heregeatu*, a cpd of *here* army + *geatu* equipment, referring originally to military equipment that was restored to the lord on the death of a vassal.

Vars. (of 1): **Harriot.** (Of 2): **Heriot.**

Herrod English (chiefly Notts.): 1. nickname from the personal name *Herod* (Gk *Hērōdēs*, apparently derived from *hērōs* hero), borne by the king of Judea (d. AD 4) who at the time of the birth of Christ ordered that all male children in Bethlehem should be slaughtered (Matt. 2: 16–18). In medieval mystery plays Herod was portrayed as a blustering tyrant, and the name was therefore given to someone one who had played the part, or who had an overbearing temper.

2. var. of Harrod (1 or 2).

Var.: **Herod.**

Herz 1. German: from a Gmc personal name derived from a short form of the various cpd names with the first element *hard* hardy, brave, strong.

2. German: nickname for a stout-hearted or kind-hearted individual, from Ger. *Herz* heart (MHG *herze*, OHG *herza*).

3. Jewish (Ashkenazic): ornamental name from mod. Ger. *Herz* heart, Yid. *harts*.

4. Jewish (Ashkenazic): from the Yid. male given name *Herts*, which is from MHG *hir(t)z* deer, hart (see Hirsch).

Vars.: Ger.: **Hertz.** (Of 2 only): Ger.: **Herzen** (also a patr. of 1). (Of 3 and 4): **Herc** (Pol. spelling); **Gertz** (under Russ. influence; see Goren). (Of 3 only): **Herzer** (from the Yid. pl. *hertser* hearts); **Herzman(n), Hertzmann; Gartzman** (under Russ. influence).

Dims. (of 3): **Herzl, Her(t)zel.**

Cpds (of 3, mostly ornamental): **Harzbach** ('heart stream'); **Herzbaum** ('heart tree'); **Her(t)z(en)berg, Hercenberg, Herzberg(er)** ('(person from) heart hill'), **Gertzberg** (under Russ. influence); **Hertzburg** ('heart town'); **Herzfeld, Harzfeld** ('heart field'); **Hertzheim** ('heart home'); **Harzstark** ('heart-strong'); **Herz(en)stein** ('heart stone'); **Hercwolf** ('heart wolf'); **Herzweig** ('heart twig').

The SI unit of frequency is named after Heinrich Herz *(1857–94), a German physicist who was the first person to produce electromagnetic waves. His father was a lawyer from a wealthy Hanseatic Jewish family.*

The Russian philosopher Alexander Herzen *(1812–70) was given this surname because he was technically an illegitimate child, one born of the heart* (vom Herzen). *His father was Ivan Yakovlev, a Russian nobleman from a minor branch of the Romanovs, and he had married Alexander's mother only according to the Lutheran rite, which was not officially accepted.*

Herzhaft Jewish (Ashkenazic): nickname or ornamental name from the Ger. adj. *herzhaft* bold, courageous.

Var.: **Hertzhaft.**

Herzig Jewish (Ashkenazic): ornamental name from the Ger. adj. *herzig* delightful, charming.

Vars.: **Hertzig, Her(t)ziger.**

Herzlich Jewish (Ashkenazic): ornamental name from the Ger. adj. *herzlich* cordial, sincere.

Var.: **Hertzlich.**

Herzog 1. German: from the Ger. title of nobility *Herzog* duke (OHG *herizoho*, from *heri* army + *ziohan* to lead, a calque of the Byzantine title *stratēlatēs* general, commander, from Gk *stratos* army + *elaunein* to lead). The name is unlikely to refer to an actual duke himself; it is normally an occupational name for the servant of a duke or a nickname for one who put on the airs and graces of a duke.

2. Jewish (Ashkenazic): ornamental name; cf. Graf and Kaiser.

Vars.: Ger.: **Herzig.** Jewish: **Hertzog, Hercog, Hartzog; Gertzog** (under Russ. influence; see Goren).

Cogns.: Low Ger.: **Hartog, Hartoch.** Flem., Du.: **(De) Hertog(he).** Hung.: **Herc(z)eg(h).**

Patrs.: Flem., Du.: **Hertogs.** Jewish: **Hartogs, Hartogso(h)n** (from the Jewish Dutch male given name *Hartog* 'Duke').

Hesketh English (Lancs.): habitation name from places in Lancs. and N Yorks., so called from ON *hestr* horse, stallion (a cogn. of Hengst) + *skeið* racecourse. The ancient Scandinavians were fond of horse-racing and horse-fighting, and introduced both pastimes to England.

Vars.: **Heskett, Heskitt.**

A family of this name originating at Hesketh, Lancs., trace their descent from Sir William Hesketh, *who was living in the reign of Edward I (1272–1307).*

Heslop English (Northumb.): habitation name from an unidentified place in N England, so called from OE *hæsel* (or the cogn. ON *hesli*) Hazel + *hop* enclosed valley (see Hope).

Vars.: **Haslop, Has(e)lup, Heslep; Heslip, H(e)aslip** (N Ireland); **Hislop, Hyslop** (Scotland).

Hess 1. German and Jewish (Ashkenazic): regional name for someone from the state of *Hesse* (Ger. *Hessen*). The placename is first recorded as *Hassia* and probably derives from the *Chatti*, a Gmc tribe mentioned by the Roman historian Tacitus in the 1st cent. AD.

2. Ger. (of Slav. origin): dim. of HERMANN.

Var. (of 1): Ger.: **Hesse**.

Hession Irish: Anglicized form of Gael. **Ó hOisín** 'descendant of *Oisín*', a personal name from a dim. of *os* deer.

Hetherington English: habitation name from a place in Northumb., probably having the same origin as *Harrington* in Northants. (see HARRINGTON 1).

Vars.: **Heatherington, Etherington**.

Hetman Polish and Jewish (E Ashkenazic): from Pol. *hetman* military leader (from a var. of Ger. HAUPTMANN captain), an occupational name for a military officer or status name for the elected leader of a community, or else a nickname. As a Jewish name, the literal sense 'military leader' never applies.

Cogn. (dim.): Czech: **Hejtmánek**.

Hetterich German: from the Gmc personal name *Hadurīc*, composed of the elements *hadu* battle, strife + *rīc* rule. See also HEYDRICH.

Vars.: **Hed(d)erich**.

Heugh N English and Scots: habitation name from any of various places, for example in Co. Durham and Northumb., so called from OE *hōh* spur; see HOUGH, HUFF, HOE.

Heurtebise French: perhaps a topographic name for someone living in an exposed situation, buffeted by the north wind, from OF *hurte(r)* to collide, knock against + *bise* north wind (both these elements being of Gmc origin); cf. *Heurtevent* in Calvados. It is also possible that it may have been a humorous nickname for someone with a prominent nose.

Heuse French: metonymic occupational name for a maker or seller of boots and shoes or nickname for someone noted for footwear of an unusual design, from OF *heuse*, *ho(u)se* boot, shoe (of Gmc origin; cf. HOSIER).

Vars.: **Heuze; Heuzé, Heuzey, Houzé** (nicknames meaning 'shod'; cf. HUSSEY 3).

Dims.: **Houzet, Huzette, Houzel, Houzeaux**.

Pejs.: **H(o)uzard**.

Hevesy Hungarian: 1. habitation name from a place in Hungary called *Heves*.

2. nickname for a man of violent temper, from Hung. *heves* violent, vehement.

Var.: **Hevesi** (partly Jewish (Ashkenazic)).

Hewitt English: 1. from the medieval given name *Huet*, a dim. of HUGH.

2. topographic name for someone who lived in an newly made clearing in a wood, ME *hewett* (OE *hīewet*, a deriv. of *hēawan* to chop, cut, hew).

Vars.: **Hewit, Hewet(t), Hewat.** (Of 1 only) **Howet(t), Howat(t); Howitt** (Notts.); **Huet(t), Huitt**.

Patrs. (from 1): **Hewitson, Hewetson; Hewison** (Northumb.); **Howetson, Howatson; Hui(t)son, Huetson**.

Hewlett English (chiefly Worcs.): from the ME given name *Huwelet*, *Huwelot*, *Hughelot*, a double dim. of HUGH formed with the dim. suffixes *-el* + *-et* and *-ot*.

Vars.: **Hewlitt, Howlett, Hulett, Hullot**.

Heydrich German: from the medieval given name *Heidenreich*, ostensibly composed of the elements *heiden* heathen, infidel (see HEIDEN) + *reich* power, rule, but probably in origin a var. by folk etymology of HETTERICH. The name was extremely popular at the time of the Crusades, the sense 'power over the heathens' being attributed to it.

Vars.: **Heid(en)r(e)ich, Heydenrych, Hädrich**.

Dims.: **Heidel, Hiedle**. Low Ger.: **He(i)decke, Heydicke, Hädicke**.

Heywood English (chiefly Lancs.): habitation name from a place near Manchester, so called from OE *hēah* high (see HAY 2) + *wudu* WOOD. There is also a place in Wilts. so called, from OE *(ge)hæg* enclosure + *wudu* (cf. HAYWOOD), although this is probably not the source of the surname.

Heyworth English (Lancs.): habitation name from an unidentified place probably deriving its name from OE *hēah* high (see HAY 2) + *worð* enclosure (see WORTH).

Hibbert English: from the Norman personal name *Hil(de)bert*, composed of the Gmc elements *hild* battle, strife + *berht* bright, famous.

Vars.: **Hibberd, Hibbard, Hilbert, Ilbert**.

Cogns.: Fr.: **Hilbert, Ilbert**. Ger.: **Hildebrecht, Hilprecht, Hilpert**. Low Ger.: **Hilber(t)**. Ger. (of Slav. origin): **Hilbrich(t), Hilbrig**.

Dims.: Ger.: **Hilpl** (Bavaria, Austria). Fris.: **Hibbe, Hidde**.

Patrs.: Low Ger.: **Hilbers, Ibbers; Hilb(e)ring, Hilbrink** (Westphalia); **Hilbertz** (Rheineland).

Patrs. (from dims.): Eng.: HIBBS. Low Ger., Dan.: **Ibsen, Ipsen**. Fris.: **Hibben; Hibbing, Ibing**.

Hibbs English (chiefly Devon): 1. patr. from a dim. of HIBBERT.

2. metr. from the medieval female given name *Ibb*, a pet form of *Isabel(le)*; for the initial *H-*, cf. HERRICK. *Isabel* is by origin a var. of *Elizabeth*, a name which owed its popularity in medieval Europe to the fact that it was borne by John the Baptist's mother. The original form of the name was Hebr. *Elisheva* 'my God (is my) oath'; it appears thus in Exod. 6: 23 as the name of Aaron's wife. By NT times the second element had been altered to Hebr. *shabat* rest, Sabbath. The form *Isabella* originated in Spain, the initial syllable being detached because of its resemblance to the def. art. *el*, and the final one being assimilated to the characteristic Sp. fem. ending *-ella*. The name in this form was introduced into France in the 13th cent., being borne by a sister of St Louis who lived as a nun after declining marriage with the Holy Roman Emperor. Thence it was brought to England, where it achieved considerable popularity as an independent given name alongside the root form *Elizabeth*.

Vars.: **Ibbs, Ibson**.

Dims.: **Ibbot(t)s, Ebbet(t)s; Ibbotson, Ibbetson, Ibbe(r)son, Ibbison**.

Hick English: from the medieval given name *Hicke*, a pet form of RICHARD. The substitution of *H-* as the initial resulted from the inability of the English to cope with the velar Norman *R-*; cf. HOBB, HODGE, and also HANN.

Vars.: **Hitch; Ick(e)**.

Dims.: **Hickin(g)** (E Midlands), **Hicken** (W Midlands); **Hicklin**, HICKLING; **Higgett, Higgitt; Higgon; Hitchin(g), Hitchen, Hitch(e)on** (Lancs., esp. around Burnley); **Hitchcock, Hedgecock, Hitchcott, Hedgecote, Hitchcoe; Hickock; Hiscock, Hiscoke, Hiscott, Hiscutt, Hiskett**.

Patrs.: **Hick(e)s** (widely distributed, but most common in the W Country); **Higgs** (chiefly W Midland); **Hitches; Ickes; Hick(e)son, Hixon; Higson** (Lancs.); **Hi(t)chisson**.

Patrs. (from dims.): HIGGINS; **Hi(t)chens, Hitchin(g)s, Hitchcox, Hiscocks, Hiscox** (chiefly Bristol).

'Servant of H.': **Hickman**, **Hitchman** (chiefly W Midlands); **Higman** (chiefly Devon).

The earliest known bearer in Lancs. of the surname Hitchon *was Richard Hitchon, recorded in Burnley in 1534. Reaney records a certain John* Hitchun *in Oxon. in 1279.*

Hickey Irish: Anglicized form of Gael. **Ó hÍcidhe** 'descendant of *Ícidhe*', a byname meaning 'Doctor', 'Healer'.

Vars.: **O'Hickey, O'Hickee, Hickie, Hicky.**

A number of Irish bearers of the name claim descent from the hereditary physicians to the kings of Thomond.

Hickling English (Notts.): 1. habitation name from a place near Nottingham, so called from the OE tribal name *Hicelingas* 'people of *Hicel(a)*', a personal name or byname of unknown origin. There is also a place of this name and origin in Norfolk, which is another possible source of the surname.

2. dim. of HICK.

Hickmott English (chiefly Yorks. and Lancs.): from the ME given name HICK + ME *maugh, mough* relative (from ON *mágr* or OE *magu*). The exact nature of the relationship is not clear; the ME word meant 'relative by marriage', but was also used occasionally of a female blood relation.

Vars.: **Hitchmough, Hitchmouth.**

Hidalgo Spanish: from Sp. *hidalgo* nobleman (attested in this form since the 12th cent.), a contraction of the phrase *hijo de algo* 'son of something'. The expression *hijo de* (L *filius* son + *de* from, of) is used to indicate the abundant possession of a quality, probably influenced by similar Arabic phrases with *ibn*; *algo* (L *aliquid* something) is used in an elliptical manner to refer to riches or importance. As in the case of other surnames denoting high rank, the name does not normally refer to the nobleman himself, but is usually an occupational name for his servant or a nickname for someone who gave himself airs and graces.

Var.: **Fidalgo** (Aragon).

Cogn.: Port.: **Fidalgo.**

Hiedler S German and Austrian: topographic name for someone who lived by a spring which dried up periodically, from a deriv. of S Ger. dial. *Hi(e)del* intermittent spring.

Vars.: **Hidler** (see also HÜTTLER); **Hiedl.**

Hiess S German and Austrian: from a given name, an aphetic short form of *Mathies*; see MATTHEW.

Vars.: **Hies; Heiss, Haiss.**

Dims.: **Hi(e)sel, Heisel.**

Patr. (from a dim.): **Hiesler.**

Higginbottom English: habitation name from a place in Lancs. now known as *Oakenbottom*. The history of the placename is somewhat confused, but it is probably composed of the OE elements *ǣcen* oaken + *botme* broad valley. During the Middle Ages this name became successively *Eakenbottom* and *Ickenbottom*, the second element becoming associated with the dial. word *hicken* or *higgen* mountain ash.

Vars.: **Higginbotham, Higginbottam, Higenbotham, Higenbottam, Higinbothom, Higgenbottom, Heckingbottom, Heginbotham, Heginbottom, Hickinbottom, Hickenbotham.**

Higgins 1. English: patr. from the medieval given name *Higgin*, a dim. of HICK.

2. Irish: Anglicized form of Gael. **Ó hUiginn** 'descendant of *Uiginn*', a byname meaning 'Viking', 'Sea-rover' (from ON *víkingr*).

3. Irish: Anglicized form of Gael. **Ó hAodhagáin** 'descendant of *Aodhagán*', a personal name representing a double dim. of *Aodh* 'Fire' (cf. MCKAY).

Vars.: **Higgens.** (Of 1 only): **Higginson.** (Of 2 and 3): **O'Higgins.** (Of 3 only): **O'Higane, O'He(a)gane, O'Heaken, O'Huggin, He(e)gan, E(a)gan; Eakin** (see also EADE).

Francis Higginson *(1586–1630) was a Leics. Puritan who emigrated to New England in 1629 as first minister of the Massachusetts Bay Company. Most of his descendants were merchants, including his grandson Nathaniel, who returned to England in 1694. As an employee of the E India Company he became Lieutenant-General of India.*

The Irish adventurer Don Ambrosio O'Higgins *(1721–1801) rose to become Viceroy of Peru under the Spaniards, but his fame was exceeded by that of his son Bernardo O'Higgins (1780–1846), remembered today in S America as the 'Liberator of Chile', where O'Higgins province is named after him. Very little is known of their origins. Don Ambrosio claimed to have been born in Ballinary, Co. Sligo, and he was granted the Spanish title Barón de Vallenar, i.e. Baron Ballinary.*

High English (chiefly Northumb.): 1. nickname for a tall man, from ME *hegh, hie* high, tall (OE *hēah*; see also HAY 2).

2. topographic name for a dweller on a hilltop or high place, from the same word used in a topographical sense. This second use is supported by early forms such as Richard *atte High* (Sussex 1332).

Vars.: **Highe, Hie; Highman.**

Higham English (Lancs.): habitation name from one of the many places in England so called, of which the most plausible candidate for present-day bearers is that near Burnley. The placename is from OE *hēah* HIGH + *hām* homestead.

Var.: HYAM.

Highet Scots: habitation name, probably from *Highgate* in the former county of Ayrs. (now part of Strathclyde region), so called from OE *hēah* HIGH + *geat* GATE.

Vars.: **Hyett; Hyatt** (also Jewish, see CHAIT).

Highfield English: habitation name from any of the numerous minor places so called from OE *hēah* HIGH + *feld* pasture, open country (see FIELD).

Var.: **Heafield.**

Highton English (Lancs.): habitation name from a place named with the OE elements *hēah* HIGH + *tūn* enclosure, settlement, possibly *Hightown* in SW Lancs. or a similarly named place within the parish of Salford.

Hignett English (Lancs.): from a medieval given name, probably a double dim. of *Higg* (see HICK) formed with the suffixes *-on* + *-et*.

Hilary English: 1. from a medieval male given name (from L *Hilarius*, a deriv. of *hilaris* cheerful, glad, from Gk *hilaros* propitious, joyful). The L name was chosen by many early Christians to express their joy and hope of salvation, and was borne by several saints, including a 4th-cent. bishop of Poitiers noted for his vigorous resistance to the Arian heresy, and a 5th-cent. bishop of Arles. Largely due to veneration of the first of these, the name became popular in France in the forms *Hilari* and *Hilaire*, and was brought to England by the Norman conquerors.

2. from the much rarer female given name *Eulalie* (from L *Eulalia*, from Gk *eulalos* eloquent, lit. well-speaking, chosen by early Christians as a reference to the gift of tongues), likewise introduced into England by the Normans. A St Eulalia was crucified at Barcelona in the reign of the Emperor Diocletian and became the patron of that city. In

England the name underwent dissimilation of the sequence *-l-l-* to *-l-r-* and the unfamiliar initial vowel was also mutilated, so that eventually the name was considered as no more than a feminine form of *Hilary* (of which the initial aspirate was in any case variable).

Vars.: **Hillary, Hillery, Eller(a)y, Elray.**

Cogns. (of 1): Fr.: **Hil(l)aire,** Hillier, **Hélier, Al(l)aire.** Prov.: **Hilari.** It.: **Ilari(o); Ellero, Elleri,** Eller (Venetia). Port.: **Hilário.** Ger.: **Larius, Glari(s), Gläri, Gläre, Glori(us), Glöre.**

Dims. (of 1): Eng.: Hill. Fr.: **Hillairet, Hilleret, Hillairin, Hillerin, Hillaireau, Hillel, Hillion.** Ger.: **Lahr, Lähr; Glohr, Klohr, Klör.**

Pej. (of 1): Fr.: **Hillard.**

Patrs. (from 1): Sc.: **McKellar, MacKeller, McEllar, McEller** (Gael. **Mac Ealair**). Fr.: **Allilaire.**

Hildebrand English, French, and German: from a Gmc personal name composed of the elements *hild* battle + *brand* (flaming) sword, introduced into England by the Normans.

Vars.: Eng.: **Hilderbrand.** Fr.: **Hillebrand.** Ger.: **Hille(r)-brand, Hülle(r)brand, Hiltebrandt, Hildenbrand.**

Cogns.: Low Ger., Du.: **Hil(le)brand.**

Dims.: Eng.: Hill. Ger.: **Hild(t), Hilt, Hiltl(e); Hilty** (Switzerland); see also Brand. Low Ger.: Hill.

Patrs.: Ger.: **Hil(de)brands.** Low Ger.: **Hillebrenner.**

Hildesheim Jewish (WAshkenazic): habitation name from a place near Hanover, recorded in medieval documents in the form *Hildenesheim*. The placename is probably from the gen. case of a personal name derived from a short form of the various Gmc cpd names with a first element *hild* battle, strife + OHG *heim* homestead, but according to Bahlow the first element is a term for a moor or marsh preserved in some modern Fris. dialects.

Vars.: **Hildesheimer, Hillesheim.**

Hill 1. English: extremely common and widely distributed topographic name for someone who lived on or by a hill, OE *hyll*. The sound represented by OE *y* developed in various ways in the different dialects of ME: in N England and the E Midlands it became *i*, in SE England *e*, and in the W and central Midlands *u*. Traces of these regional differences may be found in the vars., in spite of the influence of the standard Eng. vocab. word.

2. English: from the medieval given name *Hill*, a short form of Hilary or of one of the Gmc cpd names with the first element *hild* battle, strife (cf., e.g., Hildebrand and Hilliard).

3. Low German: dim. of Hildebrand.

4. Jewish (Ashkenazic): Anglicized form of various like-sounding names.

Vars. (of 1): **Hell,** Hull; **Hille** (from the OE dat. sing. *hylle*); **Hillam** (from the OE dat. pl. *hyllum*; also the name of a place in W Yorks.); Hills; **Hiller,** Heller; **Hillman.** (Of 3): **Hille, Hil-l(e)mann, Hilmann.**

Cogns. (of 1): Ger.: **Hüg(g)el(mann); Hügler; Hiegel** (Alsace). Low Ger.: **Hübel, Hieb(e)l, Höbel, Hövel, Heuvel; Hübler, Hi(e)bler.** Flem.: **Van Hille, Van Hulle, Van den Heuvel, Heuvelman.** Du.: **Van Heuvel.** Jewish (Ashkenazic): **Hillman** (reason for adoption unknown).

Patrs. (from 3): Low Ger.: **Hillen, Hillemans.**

Hilliard English: from the Norman female personal name *Hildiarde, Hildegard*, composed of the Gmc elements *hild* battle, strife + *gard* fortress, stronghold.

Vars.: **Hilleard, Hillyard, Hildyard.**

Hillier 1. English: var. of Hellier.

2. French: cogn. of Hilary.

Hills English: 1. topographic name, a var. of Hill 1.

2. patr. from Hill 2.

Vars.: **Hillis** (N Ireland). (Of 2 only): **Hilson.**

Hilse German: topographic name for someone who lived by a holly tree, MHG *huls* (OHG *hulis*, cogn. with OE *hole(g)n*; cf. Holme 1).

Cogns.: Low Ger.: **Hüls(e), Hülss, Hülst; Hülster; Hülse-mann; Ophüls.** Flem., Du.: **Van (der) Hilst, Van (der) Hulst, Verhulst, Hilster, Hulsenboom, Hulsman.** Fr.: **Lehoux, Duhoux.**

Dims.: Fr.: **Houssel, Housset, Houssin.**

Collectives: Fr.: **Houssay(e), Houssais, Houssière.**

Hilton English: 1. habitation name from any of various places so called. Most, including those in Cambs. (formerly Hunts.), Cleveland, Derbys., and Shrops., get the name from OE *hyll* Hill + *tūn* enclosure, settlement. Others, including those in Cumb. and Dorset, have early forms in *Hel-* and probably have as their first element OE *hielde* slope (see Heald) or possibly *helde* tansy.

2. a few early examples such as Ralph *filius Hilton* (Yorks. 1219) point to occasional derivation from a given name, possibly a Norman name **Hildun*, composed of the Gmc elements *hild* battle, strife + *hūn* bear cub.

Var.: **Hylton.**

A family now bearing this name originated at Hetton *in Co. Durham (from OE* hēope *rosehip +* dūn *hill). The surname had already been assimilated to* Hilton *by the time of Robert* de Hilton *(d. c.1309).*

Hiltunen Finnish: patr. from the given name *Hiltu* (of Gmc origin, probably a deriv. of *hild* battle, strife), with the gen. suffix *-nen*.

Himmel 1. German: habitation name from any of various places named with MHG *himel* heaven, paradise (OHG *himil* heaven, sky), in reference to their pleasant situation and/or the fruitfulness of the soil.

2. Jewish (Ashkenazic): ornamental name from Ger. *Himmel* heaven, selected because of the pleasant associations of the word.

Vars.: Ger.: **Himml; Himm(e)ler; Himmelmann.** Jewish: **Himel(man); Himlich** ('heavenly').

Cogn.: Du.: **Hemelaar.**

Cpds (ornamental): Jewish: **Himmelbaum** ('heaven tree'); **Himelberg** ('heaven hill'); **Himmelblau** ('heaven blue'); **Him-(m)elbrand** ('sword of heaven'); **Himmelburg** ('heaven town'); **Him(m)elfarb** ('heavenly colour'); **Himmelreich** ('kingdom of heaven'); **Him(m)elschein** ('heavenly light', partly Anglicized as **Himelshine**); **Him(m)elstein** ('heaven stone'), **Himelsztajn** (Pol. spelling), **Gimelstein** (under Russ. influence; see Goren).

Hinchcliffe English: habitation name from a place in W Yorks., so called from OE *henge-clif* 'steep cliff'.

Vars.: **Hinchcliff, Hinchliff(e), Henchcliff(e), Hinchsliff.**

Hinckley English: habitation name from a place in Leics., so called from the OE byname *Hȳnca* (a derivative of *Hūn* 'Bear-cub') + OE *lēah* wood, clearing.

Vars.: **Hinkley, Hingley, Hinsley.**

Hind English: 1. nickname for a gentle or timid person, from ME, OE *hind* female deer.

2. var. of Hine; for the excrescent dental, cf. Diamond.

Vars.: **Hinde; Hynd** (Scots). (Of 2): **Hyndman** (N Ireland).

Patrs.: **Hinds, Hynds,** Hindes; **Hindson** (Northumb.).

Hindenburg German: habitation name from a place so called from the gen. case of the OHG byname *Hinta* 'Hind' + OHG *burg* fortress, stronghold.

Paul von Beneckendorff und von Hindenburg *(1847–1934), field marshal in the First World War and President of Germany*

(1925–34), was from a family which in the 18th cent. had united two noble houses, both of which traced their military history back to the 13th-cent. Teutonic Knights.

Hinder 1. German: topographic name for someone who lived at the back of a village or beyond the main settlement, from MHG *hinder* behind, beyond (OHG *hintaro*; mod. Ger. *hinter*); cf. Low Ger. ACHTERMANN.

2. English: probably a nickname from ME *hinder* crafty, treacherous, anxious, fretful (of uncertain origin).

Vars. (of 1): **Hinner, Hintner; Hinderer; Hindermann.**

The earliest known bearer of the Eng. name is William Hinder *(Gloucs. c.1264). The name probably had a single origin, near Cirencester, Gloucs. All present-day bearers are probably descended from a family living in Latton, Wilts., in the early 16th cent.*

Hindes 1. English: var. of *Hinds*, patr. from HIND.

2. Jewish (Ashkenazic): metr. from the Yid. female given name *Hinde* 'HIND'.

Vars. (of 2): **Hindin, Hinden** (E Ashkenazic); **Hindels** (from a dim.).

Hindle English: habitation name from a place in the parish of Whalley, Lancs., so called from OE *hind* female deer (see HIND 1) + *hyll* HILL.

Hindley English (Lancs.): habitation name from a place near Manchester, so called from OE *hind* female deer (see HIND 1) + *lēah* wood, clearing.

Var.: **Hindeley.**

Richard de Hindele *was a substantial landowner in Lancs. c.1210–40. It seems likely that many modern bearers of the name are descended from him.*

Hindmarsh English (Northumb.): habitation name from an unidentified place, probably so called from OE *hind* female deer (see HIND 1) + *mersc* MARSH.

Var.: **Hindmarch.**

Hine English: occupational name for a servant, from ME *hīne* lad, servant (originally a collective term for a body of servants, from OE *hīwan* (pl.) household).

Vars.: **Hyne,** HIND.

Patr.: HYNES.

Hingston English (Devon): habitation name from a place in Cornwall, apparently so called from the OE byname *Hengest* 'Stallion' (see HENGST) + OE *dūn* hill (see DOWN 1).

Hinks English (W Midlands): apparently a patr. from a medieval given name, perhaps a survival of OE *Hȳnci* or *Hȳnca* (cf. HINCKLEY).

Vars.: **Hin(k)son.**

Hinksey English: habitation name from a place on the Thames just outside Oxford, so called from the gen. case of the OE byname *Hengest* 'Stallion' (see HENGST) + OE *ēg* island, low-lying land.

Hinojosa Spanish: habitation name from any of the numerous places so called, from a deriv. of Sp. *hinoja* fennel (see FENNELL).

Hinton English: habitation name from any of the numerous places so called, which split more or less evenly into two groups with different etymologies. One set (with examples in Berks., Dorset, Gloucs., Hants, Herefords., Somerset, and Wilts.) gets the name from the OE weak dat. *hēan* (originally used after a preposition and article) of *hēah* high + OE *tūn* enclosure, settlement. The other (with examples in Cambs., Dorset, Gloucs., Herefords., Northants, Shrops., Somerset, Suffolk, and Wilts.) gets the first element from OE *hīwan* household, monastery (cf. HINE). The surname is fairly evenly distributed in S and Midland England.

Hipólito Spanish and Portuguese: from a medieval given name (Gk *Hippolytos*, composed of the elements *hippos* horse + *luein* to loose). This was the name of a figure in classical mythology who rejected the incestuous love of his stepmother Phaedra, but in the Middle Ages was more closely associated with various minor early Christian saints, especially a bishop of Oporto who was martyred by drowning in the 3rd cent.

Cogns.: Fr.: **Hippolyte** (rare). Eng.: **Pollit(t)** (Lancs.). It.: **Ippolito, Ippoliti; Polito, Politi** (Naples). Pol.: **Polit.**

Dims.: It.: **Politelli.** Ger.: **Polte; Pölt(l)** (S Germany).

Patrs.: Russ.: **Ippolitov, Politov.**

Patrs. (from dims.): Ger.: **Poltes.** Russ.: **Polyushkin, Polshin, Polykhov, Polyukhin, Polyusov, Polunin, Polutov.**

Hiron French and English (Norman): 1. nickname for a lively person, from OF *hirond*, *arond* swallow; see ARUNDEL.

2. nickname for a discontented individual, from a dim. of OF *hire* grumble, complaint (of unknown origin).

Vars. (of 1): Fr.: **Ironde, Liron(de); Aronde, Laronde.**

Patr.: Eng.: **Hirons** (chiefly Birmingham).

Hirsch 1. German: metonymic occupational name for a keeper of deer or nickname for someone who resembled a deer in some way, from Ger. *Hirsch*, MHG *hir(t)z* HART (OHG *hir(u)z*).

2. Jewish (Ashkenazic): from the Yid. male given name *Hirsh* 'Deer', which is common because of the association of the deer with the Hebr. given name *Naftali*, deriving from the blessing by Jacob of his sons (Gen. 49: 21), in which Naftali is referred to as 'a hind let loose'.

3. Jewish (Ashkenazic): ornamental name from Ger. *Hirsch* or Yid. *hirsh* deer, one of the many Ashkenazic surnames taken from vocab. words denoting wildlife.

Vars. (of 1): **Hirschmann, Hir(t)z.** (of 2 and 3): **Hirsh; Hirs(c)hman; Hers(c)h(man), Herschman(n); Girs(c)h, Gers(c)h, Gershman** (under Russ. influence; see GOREN); **Erszman** (in regions where Yid. has no /h/).

Dims. (of 1): **Hirschel, Hirschle; Hirtzel** (Switzerland). (Of 2 and 3): **Hirschel; Hers(c)hel** (see also HERMANN); **Hers(c)hko** (among Rumanian Jews).

Patrs. (from 2): **Hirshin, Hirschenson, Hers(h)enson, Hershinson; Hershenov, Hersc(h)owitz, Hersovich; Girshov(ich), Girshevich, Gershov, Gershevich** (under Russ. influence).

Patrs. (from a dim., *Hershke*, of 2): Jewish: **Hershkoff, Hers(c)hkowitz, Hershkovitz, Hers(h)covitz, Herscovitch, Herscowicz, Herscovics, Hers(h)kovits, Hershkovich, Herschkovic, Harshkowitch; Herschkovici, Herscovici** (among Rumanian Jews); **Girshkovich, Girshkevich, Gershkevich** (under Russ. influence).

Cpds (of 3, ornamental): Jewish: **Hirschenbach** ('deer stream'); **Hirschbein, Hers(c)hbein** ('deer leg'); HIRSCHBERG; **Hi(r)schenboim, Herschbaum, Hershenbaum, Herszenbaum** ('deer tree'); **Hershfang** ('deer claw'); **Hirs(c)hfeld, Hirsfeld, Hers(c)hfeld, Girshfeld, Gerschfeld** ('deer field', partly Anglicized as **Hirschfield**); **Hershfinger** ('deer finger'); **Hershfinkel** ('deer sparkle'); **Gerschenfus** ('deer's foot'); **Hershenhaus** ('deer house'); **Herszenhaut** ('deerskin'); **Hirsch(h)orn, Hers(hen)horn** ('deer horn'); **Hirschkop, Hershkopf, Hershcopf** ('deer head'); **Hirschkorn, Herschkorn** ('deer grain'; in this case the first element could be from Yid. *hirzh* millet, cf. HIRSEMANN); **Hirshprung** ('deer leap'); **Hirsch(en)stein, Girshtein, Girstejn** ('deer stone'); **Hershenstrauss** ('deer bouquet') **Hirscht(h)al** ('deer valley').

Hirschberg Jewish (Ashkenazic): 1. habitation name from any of several places in Germany, for example in Thuringia, North Rhine-Westphalia, or what is now *Jelenia Góra* in W Poland, all named with the elements HIRSCH deer + BERG hill.

2. ornamental name composed of the Ger. vocab. elements *Hirsch* deer + *Berg* hill.

Vars.: **Hirshberg**, **Hers(c)hberg**; **Hirschberger**, **Hars(c)hberger**, **Hars(c)hbarger**.

Hirsemann German: occupational name for a grower of or dealer in millet or panic grass, or topographic name for someone who lived by a patch of land devoted to this crop, from Ger. *Hirse* millet (MHG *hirs(e)*, OHG *hirsi*, *hirso*) + *Mann* man (OHG *man*).

Vars.: **Hiersemann**, **Hirs(ch)er**.

Cogn.: Low Ger.: **Herse**.

Hirvonen Finnish: patr. from the OFinn. personal name *Hirvo(i)*, from *hirvi* elk.

Hladík Czech: 1. nickname for a clean-shaven or bald man, from the Czech adj. *hladký* smooth + the dim. suffix *-ík*.

2. occupational name for a finisher or polisher of furniture, from a deriv. of the verb *hladit* to polish, burnish, from *hladký*; the word *hladík* is also a technical term in carpentry denoting a kind of rasp or plane.

Var. (of 1): **Hladký**.

Hlava Czech: nickname for someone with some peculiarity of the head, from Czech *hlava* head.

Var.: **Hlavatý** (from the adj. form).

Hloušek Czech: nickname for a deaf man, from Czech *hluchý* deaf + the dim. suffix *-ek*.

Vars.: **Hloužek**, **Hlouch(a)**.

Hoad English: topographic name for someone who lived on a heath, from ME *hōth* heath (OE *hāð*, a byform of *hǣð*; see HEATH). This form was restricted in the Middle Ages to SE England, and the surname is still largely confined to Kent and Sussex. In some cases it may be specifically a habitation name from the village of *Hoath* in Kent.

Vars.: **Hoath**, **Ho(a)ther**.

Hoadley English: habitation name from East or West *Hoathley* in Sussex, so called from OE *hāð* HEATH + *lēah* wood, clearing. Cf. HOAD.

Hoare English: 1. nickname for an old man or someone with prematurely grey hair, from ME *hore*, OE *hār* grey. For the change of OE *-ā-* to ME *-ō-*, cf. ROPER.

2. topographic name for someone who lived by a slope or shore, OE *ōra*; see ORR 3. For the inorganic *H-*, cf. HERRICK.

Vars.: **Hoar**, **Hore**.

Hoban Irish: Anglicized form of Gael. **Ó hÚbáin** 'descendant of *Úbán*', a personal name of unknown origin.

Hobb English: from the medieval given name *Hobb(e)*, a pet form of ROBERT. For the altered initial, cf. HICK and HODGE, also HANN. See also DOBB.

Vars.: **Hob**, **Hopp**.

Dims.: **Hobbin**; **Hoblin(g)**, **Hoblyn**; HOPKIN.

Patrs.: **Hobb(e)s**; **Hobbis(s)** (chiefly W Midlands); **Hobson** (most common in W Yorks.); **Hopson**.

Patr. (from a dim.): **Hobbins**.

Hobday English (W Midlands): from the given name HOBB + ME *day* servant, i.e. either 'Hobb the servant' or 'servant of Hobb'.

Var: **Hobdey**.

Hoch German and Jewish (Ashkenazic): nickname for a tall person, from Ger. *hoch* tall, Yid. *hoykh* (MHG *hōch*, OHG *hōh*, a cogn. of OE *hēah*; see HIGH and HAY).

Vars.: Ger.: **Hoher**, **Ho(c)hmann**, **Höhmann**. Jewish: **Hochman(n)**, **Hocherman**, **Hochner**; **Hojman** (a Spanish spelling); **Goichman** (under Russ. influence; see GOREN); **Heichman** (from NE Yid.).

Cogns.: Low Ger.: **Hoge**, **Höge**, **Ho(ge)mann**. Fris.: **Hoogma**. Flem., Du.: **De Hoog(he)**, **Hoogman**. Dan.: **Høj(er)**, **Høy(er)**, **Høier**. Swed.: **Hö(ö)g**, **Högen**, **Högman**.

Patrs.: Flem., Du.: **Hogens**. Jewish: **Hochmanovich** (E Ashkenazic).

Cpds: Jewish: **Hochbaum**, **Hochboim**, **Hochbojm** ('high tree', ornamental, or nickname for a tall person; the last of these is a Pol. spelling); **Hochberg(er)** ('(dweller on a) high hill', topographic); **Hochdorf** ('high village', topographic); **Hochfeld(er)** ('(dweller in a) high field', topographic); **Hochgeborn** ('high-born', ornamental); **Hochgelernter** ('highly learned', ornamental or a nickname); **Hochgraf** ('high Count', ornamental); **Hochhauser** ('dweller in a high house', topographic); **Hochrad** ('high wheel', ornamental); **Hochschild** ('high shield', ornamental); **Hochsinger** ('high singer', presumably occupational for a cantor); **Hochstadt(er)** ('dweller in a big city', topographic); **Hochstein** ('high rock', ornamental); **Hochstim** ('high voice', a nickname or ornamental var. of *Hochsinger*); **Hochteil** ('high part', topographic); **Hochwald** ('high forest', probably ornamental). Swed. (all ornamental): **Högberg** ('high hill'); **Höglund** ('high grove'); **Högström** ('high river').

Hoche French: nickname for a gambler, from a deriv. of OF *hochier* to shake (of Gmc origin), used especially of playing at dice.

Vars.: **Hochedé**, **Hochedel** ('shake the die').

Dims.: **Hochet**, **Hochon**.

Pej.: **Hochard**.

Hochzeit Jewish (Ashkenazic): presumably a surname taken by someone who was about to get married or who had just been married at the time when the surname was first registered, from Ger. *Hochzeit* wedding (from MHG *hōch(ge)zīt* festival, lit. 'high time').

Hockey English: apparently a habitation name from an unidentified place, probably in S England and named with the OE elements *hocc* mallow + *ēg* island, low-lying land.

Hockley English: habitation name from any of various places, for example in Essex and Warwicks. The former is so called from the OE personal name *Hocca* or the vocab. word *hocc* mallow + *lēah* wood, clearing; the latter from the personal name *Hucca* + *hlāw* hill (see LAW 2 and LOW 1).

Hodder English (chiefly W Country): occupational name for a maker or seller of hoods, from a ME agent deriv. of OE *hōd* HOOD.

Hoddinott Welsh: habitation name from *Hodnet* in Shrops., or any of various places called *Hoddnant* in Wales. The placename is from W *hawdd* pleasant, peaceful + *nant* valley, stream.

Vars.: **Hodinott**; **Hodnett** (now found chiefly in Ireland).

Hodek Czech: from a dim. form of the Czech given name *Hodislav*, composed of the elements *hodi-* be fit, suited + *slav* glory, splendour.

Vars.: **Hodač**, **Hodouš**; **Hoch**, **Hošek**, **Hocek**.

Double dims.: **Hodeček**, **Hodáček**, **Hodoušek**.

Hodes Jewish (Ashkenazic): from the Yid. female given name *Hodes* (Hebr. *Hadasa* 'Myrtle', Eng. *Hadassah*). This was a name of the heroine of the Book of Esther (2: 7), who is more familiarly known in Hebr. and Yid. as *Ester* (from the Babylonian divine name *Ishtar* Astarte).

Vars.: **Hodess, Hodas, Hodis, Hodus**; **Hodys** (a Pol. spelling); **Hudus** (reflecting a S Yid. pronunciation of the name).

Metrs.: **Hodesson, Hodison.**

Hodge English: 1. from the medieval given name *Hodge*, a pet form of ROGER. For the change of initial, cf. HICK and HOBB, also HANN.

2. nickname from ME *hodge* hog, which occurs as a dial. var. of *hogge*, for example in Ches. placenames; cf. DODGE 2.

Dims.: **Hodgin, Hodge(o)n; Hodgett; Hod(g)kin, Hotchkin, Hodskin.**

Patrs.: **Hodges; Hod(g)son, Hodgshon.**

Patrs. (from dims.): **Hodgins, Hodgens; Hodgetts** (common in the W Midlands); **Hodg(s)kins, Hodgki(e)ss, Hadgkiss, Hotchkins, Hotchkis(s); Hodg(e)kinson, Hodgkis(s)on, Hodgeskinson, Hodkinson.**

The name Hodgkinson *has always had two main areas of concentration; in W Lancs. around Preston, and in N Derbys. around Ashover. It appears in the Preston Guild Rolls in 1582 in the spelling* Hogekynson.

Hodsdon English: habitation name from *Hoddesdon* in Herts., which gets its name from the OE personal name *Hod* + OE *dūn* hill (see DOWN).

Vars.: **Hodsden, Hodgdon; Hoddesdon.**

The earliest known bearer of this name is Norman de Hoddesdon, *recorded in 1165–6. The surname was taken to America by Nicholas Hodsdon in about 1628. Probably all current U.S. bearers of the name are descended from him.*

Hoe English: topographic name for someone who lived by a spur of a hill, from the OE dat. case *hō* (originally used after a preposition) of *hōh* (see HUFF, HOUGH). In many cases the surname may be a habitation name from a minor place named with this element, for example one in Norfolk.

Vars.: Hoo, ATTOE.

Hofer S German: topographic name for someone who lived at a particular farmstead, from MHG, OHG *hof* settlement, farm, court + *-er* suffix denoting human nouns.

Vars.: **Hof(f)ert, Hofner, Höf(n)er, Höfler; Hoffer** (also Jewish; cf. HOFFMANN 3); **Imhof(f).**

Cogns.: Low Ger.: **Hoff; Tenhaeff** (Rhineland); **Tomhaeve** (Westphalia); **Zumhoff** (approximated to High Ger.). Fris.: **Hofstra, Havinga.** Flem.: **Van (den) Hove.** Du.: **Van't Hoff, Verhoeven.**

Hoffmann 1. German: nickname for a farmer who owned his own land as opposed to holding it by rent or feudal obligation, from Ger. *Hof*, MHG *hof* settlement, farm, court (see HOFER) + *mann* man.

2. E German: occupational name for the manager or steward of an estate, from the same elements as above. The surname, with this sense, was particularly common in Silesia.

3. Jewish (Ashkenazic): of uncertain origin; Kaganoff suggests that it was selected because of its association with Ger. *hoffen*, Yid. *hofn* to hope, and so expressive of hope for a better future and freedom from persecution. It is also possible that this is an occupational name, as in 2: many Jews in the Russ. Empire held managerial positions on non-Jewish estates.

Vars. (of 1): **Hofmann** (S Germany); **Hobemann** (Hesse). (Of 3): Jewish: **Hoffman, Hofman(n); Gof(f)man** (under Russ. influence; see GOREN); **Hof(f)er, Hof(f)ner, Gof(f)er** (clearly meaning 'hoper', the latter under Russ. influence); **Of(f)man,** OFFER (in regions where Yid. has no /h/).

Cogns. (of 1): Low Ger.: **Havemann, Hammann.**

Hoffnung Jewish (Ashkenazic): ornamental name from Ger. *Hoffnung* hope, which, like HOFFMANN, may well have been adopted as expressive of hope for a better future.

Vars.: **Hofnung; Hofen** (from the verb *hoffen* to hope); **Hof(f)enberg** ('hope hill', an ornamental elaboration); **Hoffmitz** ('hope cap', an ornamental elaboration).

Hoffschläger Low German: occupational name for a shoeing-smith, from an agent deriv. of MLG *huof* hoof (mod. Ger. *Huf*) + *sla(h)en* to strike, hammer (mod. Ger. *schlagen*). High Ger. equivs. for the same occupation are **Hufeisen** 'hoof iron' and **Hufnagel** 'hoof nail'.

Höflich German: nickname for a man of refined behaviour, from Ger. *höflich* polite, well-mannered, refined, MHG *hovelich* (an adj. deriv. of *hof* court (see HOFMEISTER), a calque on OF *courtois* (see CURTIS 1)). See also HÜBSCH.

Hofmeister German: occupational name for the chamberlain in a noble household or an official with similar functions in a religious house, Ger. *Hofmeister*, from MHG *hof* court, household (originally 'settlement' or 'farm'; see HOFER and HOFFMANN) + *meister* MASTER. This name is also borne by Ashkenazic Jews, the reason for its adoption as a Jewish surname being unclear.

Cogns.: Low Ger.: **Hoveme(i)ster, Haveme(i)ster, Homme(i)ster.**

Hofrichter German: 1. occupational name for a judge at a manor court, MHG *hoverichter* (cf. HOFER, HOFFMANN; also RICHTER).

2. nickname for a hunchback, from the strong form of MHG *hoverecht* hunchbacked (a cogn. of OE *hoferede*).

Var.: **Hoffrichter.**

Hogan Irish: Anglicized form of Gael. **Ó hÓgáin** 'descendant of *Ógán*', a personal name from a dim. of *óg* young. The family claims descent from an uncle of Brian Boru.

Vars.: **O'Hogan(e), O'Hogaine.**

Hogarth English (Northumb.) and Scots: probably a var. of HOGGARD, but possibly a habitation name from an unidentified place, the second element of whose name would be Northern ME GARTH enclosure.

Var.: **Hoggarth.**

Hogben English (Kent): nickname for someone with a crippled or deformed hip, from ME *huckbone* hip bone.

Var.: **Hogbin.**

Hogg 1. English (Northumb.) and Scots: metonymic occupational name for a swineherd, from ME *hog* pig (of uncertain origin). It may also occasionally have been a nickname—for a person supposedly resembling a pig in appearance rather than for a dirty person, since in the Middle Ages pigs were not felt to be especially unclean.

2. Scots and Irish: translation of Gael. *Mac an Bhanbh* 'son of the hog'.

Vars.: **Hogge; Hogger, Hoggar.**

Hoggard English: occupational name for a keeper of swine, from ME *hog* (see HOGG) + *herd*, *hard* herdsman (see HEARD).

Var.: **Hoggart.** See also HOGARTH.

Hogwood English and Scots (Borders): of uncertain origin, in form evidently a habitation name from a minor place named with ME *hog* (see HOGG) + *wode* WOOD, i.e. 'swine wood'. However, the name apparently alternates from an early date with forms such as *Haigwood*, and if so it may be a N var. of HAYWOOD, or perhaps even 'wood belonging to the HAIG family'.

Vars.: **Haig(h)wood**.

Hohenzollern German: habitation name from a place near Hechingen in Swabia, so called from MHG *hōchen*, weak dat. (originally used after a preposition and article) of *hōch* high (see HOCH) + the ancient placename *Zolorin*, of uncertain etymology.

The German princely family of this name can trace their ancestry back to Friedrich I, Count of Zollern (d. 1125). The names of Burchard and Wetzel of Zollern are recorded in 1001; they may well be early ancestors.

Holbeche English (Midlands): habitation name from *Holbeach* in Lincs., which derives its name from OE *hol* hollow, sunken + *bæc* back, ridge.

Holbein German: nickname for a bow-legged man, i.e. one with a gap between his knees, from MHG, OHG *hol* hollow + *bein* leg.

Var.: **Hohlbein**.

Holbrook English: habitation name from any of various places, for example in Derbys., Dorset, and Suffolk, so called from OE *hol* hollow, sunken + *brōc* stream (see BROOK). The name has probably absorbed the Du. **van Hoobroek**, found in London in the early 17th cent., and possibly a similar Low Ger. surname; several American bearers of the name in the 1880 census give their place of birth as Oldenburg or Hanover, Germany.

Vars.: **Holbrooke**, **Houlbrook(e)**, **Holdbrook**, **Holebrook**; **Holbrock**, **Ha(u)lbrook**, **Halbrooks**, **Albrook(s)** (U.S.).

This name was first taken to America by the brothers Thomas and John Holbrook, *who emigrated to Massachusetts in the 17th cent.; their line can be traced back to Dundry, Somerset, in the first half of the 16th cent. Other Eng. bearers who started early lines of descent in the New World are Joseph* Ho(u)lbrook *of Warrington, Lancs., who emigrated to Maryland as an indentured servant in the later 17th cent.; Randolph Holbrook, who was in Virginia in the 1720s but later returned to Nantwich, Ches.; and the Revd John Holbrook, who emigrated from Handbury, Staffs., to New Jersey c.1723. The spelling* Haulbrook *originated in Georgia in the 1870s, reflecting the Southern U.S. pronunciation of the name.*

Holcombe English: habitation name from any of various places, for example in Devon, Dorset, Gloucs., Lancs., Oxon., and Somerset, so called from OE *hol* hollow, sunken, deep + *cumb* valley (see COOMBE); cf. HOLDEN.

Vars.: **Holcom(b)**.

Holdcroft English: habitation name from *Holcroft* in Lancs., so called from OE *holh* hollow, depression + *croft* paddock, smallholding (see CROFT).

Vars.: **Ho(u)lcroft**, **Houldcroft**.

Holden English: habitation name from places in Lancs. and W Yorks., both so called from OE *hol* hollow, sunken, deep + *denu* valley (see DEAN 1); cf. HOLCOMBE.

Vars.: **Houlden**, **Howlden**, **Ho(u)ldin**, **Holding**.

Holder 1. German: topographic name for someone who lived by an elder tree, Ger. *Hol(un)der* (OHG *holuntar, holantar*).

2. Jewish (Ashkenazic): ornamental name from Ger. *Hol(un)der* elder tree.

3. English (chiefly W Midlands): occupational name for a tender of animals, from an agent deriv. of ME *hold(en)* to guard, keep (OE *h(e)aldan*). It is possible that this word was also used in the wider sense of a holder of land within the feudal system.

Vars. (of 1): **Holderer**; **Holdermann**; **Holderbaum**. (Of 3): **Houlder**.

Dims. (of 1): **Hölderl(e)in**, **Hölderle**.

Holderness English: regional name from the coastal district of E Yorks. (Humberside), the origin of which is probably ON *hǫldr*, a Danelaw rank of feudal nobility immediately below earl + *næs* nose, headland.

Var.: **Holness**.

Holdrup English: of uncertain origin, most probably a habitation name from a place (perhaps in Hants, where the surname seems to have originated) so called from OE *holh* hollow, depression + *þrop* village (see THORPE).

Var.: **Holdup**.

Hole English (Somerset and Devon): topographic name for someone who lived in or by a depression or low-lying spot, from OE *holh* hole, hollow, depression, akin to the adj. *hol* hollow, sunken, deep.

Vars.: **Houle**, HOYLE; **Hollow**; **Holer**, **Holah**; HOLMAN.

Cogns.: Ger.: **Hohl(er)**. Fris.: **Holla**. Flem., Du.: **Hol**, HOLMAN.

The surname Holah *seems to have originated in Yorks., where this spelling is first recorded in the early 18th cent.*

Holford English: habitation name from any of various places, for example in Somerset, so called from OE *hol* hollow, sunken, deep + *ford* FORD.

Vars.: **Houlford**, **Holdford**, **Holdforth**.

Holgado Spanish: from Sp. *holgado* idle (past part. of *holgar* to be idle, enjoy oneself, from LL *follicāre*). It may have been a nickname for an indolent or fun-loving person, or a topographic name for someone who lived on a patch of uncultivated land.

Var.: **Folgado** (Aragon).

Cogn.: Port.: **Folgado**.

Holgate English: habitation name from any of various places, for example in W Yorks., so called from OE *hol* hollow, sunken + ON *gata* road; cf. HOLLOWAY.

Holland 1. English: habitation name from any of the eight villages in various parts of England so called, from OE *hōh* ridge (see HOE) + *land* land.

2. English, German, Jewish (Ashkenazic), Flemish, and Dutch: regional name from *Holland*, a county of the Holy Roman Empire in the Netherlands (for which it has long been used in Eng. as a synonym). The name is generally assumed to be from MLG *hol* hollow, sunken + *land* land, but Bahlow prefers to see in the first syllable an ancient element descriptive of marshland.

3. Irish: Anglicized form of various Gael. surnames; cf. HOULIHAN, MULHOLLAND, and WHELAN.

Vars. (of 1): **Hollands**, **Howland**, **Hoyland**. (Of 2): **Holla(e)nder**, **Holand(er)**; **Goland**, **Golender** (under Russ. influence; see GOREN).

Cogns. (of 2): Fr.: **Hollande**. Hung.: **Hollenzer**.

This is the name of an important landowning family, traceable to Upholland in Lancs. in the 13th cent.

Hollier English and French: occupational name for a brothel-keeper, ME, OF *hol(l)ier* (a dissimilated var. of *horier*, agent noun from *hore*, *hure* whore, of Gmc origin). It may also have been used as an abusive nickname.

Vars.: Eng.: **Hollyer**, **Hullyer**; **Hollister** (originally a fem. form; cf. BAXTER).

Pej.: Fr.: **Hollard**.

Hollingsworth English: habitation name from places in Ches. and Lancs. called *Hollingworth*, from OE *hole(g)n* holly (see HOLME 1 and HOLLIS) + *worð* enclosure (see WORTH).

Var.: **Hollingworth.**

Hollington English: habitation name from any of various places, for example in Derbys., Staffs., and Sussex, so called from OE *hole(g)n* holly (see HOLME 1 and HOLLIS) + *tūn* enclosure, settlement.

Hollinshead English: habitation name from an unidentified place in Co. Durham, apparently called *Hollingside* or *Holmside*, from OE *hole(g)n* holly (see HOLME 1 and HOLLIS) + *sīde* side of a hill.

Vars.: **Hollingshead, Hollin(g)shed.**

Hollis English: topographic name for someone who lived by a group of holly trees, from ME *holi(n)s*, pl. of *holin*, *holi(e)* (OE *hole(g)n*; see HOLME 1).

Vars.: **Holliss, Holl(i)es; Holl(e)y; Hollins, Holling(s), Hollen(s)** (chiefly Yorks.).

Holloway English: habitation name from any of the numerous minor places so called, from OE *holh* hollow, sunken + *weg* way, path; cf. HOLGATE.

Vars.: **Holl(a)way, Holdaway, Holoway.**

Hollywood Irish: translation of Gael. **Ó Cuileannáin** 'descendant of *Cuileannán*', a personal name from a dim. of *cuileann* holly tree. See also QUILL.

Holman 1. English, Flemish, and Dutch: topographic name for a dweller in a hollow; see HOLE.

2. English: topographic name for a dweller by a holly tree or on an island, from ME *holm* (see HOLME) + *man*.

Vars.: Eng.: **Hollman, Ho(le)man.** Flem., Du.: **Holleman.**

Holme English and Scots: 1. topographic name for someone who lived by a holly tree, from ME *holm*, a divergent development of OE *hole(g)n*; the main development was towards mod. Eng. *holly* (see HOLLIS).

2. topographic name for someone who lived on an island, in particular a piece of slightly raised land lying in a fen or partly surrounded by streams, Northern ME *holm* (ON *holmr*), or habitation name from a place named with this element.

Vars.: **Holmes, Hulme(s); Home, Hume;** HOMER.

Cogns. (of 2): Swed.: **Holm(e), Holmén, Holmin, Holmer.** Dan.: **Holm(e), Holmen.** Ger.: **Holm.**

Cpds (of 2; mostly ornamental): Swed.: **Holmberg** ('island hill'); **Holmgren** ('island branch'); **Holmlund** ('island grove'); **Holmqvist** ('island twig'); **Holmstedt** ('island homestead'); **Holmsten** ('island stone'); **Holmstrand** ('island shore'); **Holmström** ('island river').

Oliver Wendell Holmes *(1809–94), author of* The Autocrat of the Breakfast Table, *and his son, also called Oliver Wendell Holmes (1841–1935), were descended from John Holmes, who emigrated from England to Massachusetts in 1686 and became a sawmill owner. Their other family name was from Evert Jansen Wendell, who had emigrated to Albany c.1640 from E Friesland.*

A Scottish family by the name of Home *(pronounced /hju:m/) have held the Earldom of Home since 1605. The 14th Earl, Sir Alex Douglas-Home (b. 1903), disclaimed his title in 1963 when he became Prime Minister. The name is derived from* Home *in the former county of Berwicks. (now part of Borders region); the addition of* Douglas *was made by the 12th Earl when he inherited the Douglas estate through his mother in 1877. One of their earliest recorded ancestors was Sir Thomas Home, living in 1385.*

Holopainen Finnish: patr. from the occupational term *holop* worker, servant.

Holroyd English: habitation name from any of various minor places in N England so called from OE *hol* hollow, sunken + *rod* clearing (see RHODES).

Vars.: **Holroyde, Holdroyd, Howroyd.**

Holst Low German, Dutch, and Danish: topographic name for someone who occupied a patch of woodland, from a reduced form of MLG *holtsäte*, a cpd of *holt* wood (see HOLT) + *säte* tenant (from *sitten* to sit). The province of *Holstein*, long disputed between Germany and Denmark, gets its name from the dat. pl. *holsten* of this word (originally used after a preposition); the final syllable has been erroneously altered, on the assumption that it is Low Ger. *sten* stone, which in High Ger. has the form *stein*.

Var.: **Holste.**

Holt English: topographic name for someone who lived in or by a wood or copse, ME, OE *holt*, or habitation name from one of the very many places named with this word. The surname is widely distributed, but rather more common in Lancs. than elsewhere.

Vars.: **Hoult; Holter.**

Cogns.: Ger.: **Hol(t)z(er), Hölz(l)er, Hölzner; Hol(t)zmann.** Low Ger.: **Hol(d)t; Holtmann, Holdmann; Hölting.** Fris.: **Houtsma.** Flem.: **Van Houtte, Van den Hout(e).** Du.: **Hout, Van Houten, Houtman.** Dan., Norw.: **Hol(d)t, Holten.** Swed.: **Hult.** Jewish (Ashkenazic, occupational for a woodcutter or someone who sold wood): **Hol(t)z(er), Holc(er), Holzner, Hol(t)zman(n), Holtsman, Holcman; Gol(t)z(er), Gol(t)zman** (under Russ. influence; see GOREN).

Dims.: Ger.: **Hölzl(e).** Low Ger.: **Höltje, Höltgen.**

Cpds (ornamental unless otherwise stated): Jewish: **Hol(t)zberg, Holcberg** ('wood hill'); **Holzblat, Holcblat** ('wood leaf'); **Holzdorf** ('wood village'); **Holzhendler** ('wood dealer', occupational); **Holzstein, Holcstein** ('wood stone').

Holtham English: habitation name from an unidentified place, presumably named from OE *holt* wood + *hām* homestead. Alternatively, it may be an altered form of HOLTUM.

Holton English: habitation name from any of the numerous places so called. The final syllable represents OE *tūn* enclosure, settlement. The first element has a wide variety of possible origins. In the case of three examples in Lincs. it is OE *hōh* spur of a hill (see HOUGH); for places in Oxon. and Somerset it is OE *halh* nook, recess (see HALE 1); for one in Dorset it may be OE *holh* hollow, depression (see HOLE) or *holt* wood, copse (see HOLT); for a further pair in Suffolk it may be *hola*, gen. pl. of *holh* hollow, but more probably a personal name *Hōla*.

Holtum 1. English (Kent): probably a habitation name from some minor place named with OE *holtum*, dat. pl. of *holt* wood (see HOLT).

2. Low German: habitation name from any of various places named with the MLG elements *holt* wood + *heim*, *hēm* homestead.

Var. (of 1): **Holttum.**

Most present-day bearers of these names in England seem to be descended from Richard Holttum *(d. 1779) of Shepherdswell, Kent.*

Holyoak English: 1. topographic name, from ME *holy* holy (OE *hālig*) + *oke* (OE *āc* oak), for someone who lived near an oak tree with religious associations. This would have been one which formed a marker on a parish boundary and which was a site for a reading from the Scriptures in the course of the annual ceremony of beating the bounds.

2. habitation name from the village of *Holy Oakes* in Leics., recorded in Domesday Book as *Haliach*, and no doubt deriving its name as above.

Vars.: **Holyoake, Hollyoak(e), Hollyhock.**

Holzapfel German: topographic name for someone who lived by a crab-apple tree or nickname for someone with a sour temperament, from Ger. *Holzapfel* crab-apple (literally 'wood-apple'; cf. HOLT and APPLE).

Cogn.: Low Ger.: **Holtappel.**

Homburg Jewish (Ashkenazic): habitation name from places in Hesse and Saarland, so called from the weak dat. case (originally used after a preposition and article) of OHG *hōh* high (see HOCH) + *burg* town, fortress (see BURKE).

Var.: **Homburger.**

Homer English (W Midlands): 1. occupational name for a maker of helmets, from the adopted OF term *he(a)umier* (from *he(a)ume* helmet, of Gmc origin; cf. HELM 2).

2. var. of HOLME.

Homewood English (Sussex): habitation name from any of various places of this name, in particular one in the parish of Perching recorded as *Homwood* in about 1280; there were others in Chailey and Forest Row. All are probably named from ME *home* homestead, manor (OE *hām*; for the vowel change, cf. ROPER) + *wode* WOOD.

Homola Czech: from the vocab. word *homole* cone, in various applications. In some cases it is a habitation name from a place deriving its name from being near a cone-shaped hill; in other cases it is a nickname for someone with a pointed or cone-shaped head.

Homolka Czech: nickname for a mild or soft person, from the vocab. word *homolka* (cone-shaped lump of) cream cheese, a dim. of *homole* cone (see HOMOLA).

Cogn.: Pol.: **Gomulka.**

Hone English: topographic name for someone who lived by a boundary stone or a prominent outcrop of rock, from ME *hōn* stone, rock (OE *hān*, cf. mod. Eng. *hone* whetstone; for the vowel change, cf. ROPER).

Vars.: **Hones, Honer.**

There are a number of Irish bearers of this name who claim that it is an altered form of the Welsh name Owen, *but this has not been substantiated. The surname has been established in Devon and Gloucs. since the 14th cent. One family in Ireland can be traced to Samuel* Hone, *who went to Ireland as a soldier in 1649 and settled in Dublin.*

Höne German: from the Gmc personal name *Huno*, a short form of the various cpd names with the first element *hūn* (cf., e.g., HUMBOLDT and HUMPHREY). The exact meaning of this element is disputed, but it may be cogn. with ON *húnn* bear cub.

Dims.: Low Ger.: **Hönemann, Hönecke, Hönk.**

Patr. (from a dim.): Low Ger.: **Hönks.**

Honegger German: habitation name from any of the various places (including one in Switzerland) that get their names from an uncertain first element + OHG *ecka*, *egga* corner, bend, nook (see ECK).

Var.: **Honecker.**

Honey English (chiefly W Country): metonymic occupational name for a gatherer or seller of honey, OE *hunig*, or nickname from the same word used as a term of endearment, a sense which was common in medieval England.

Vars.: **Hon(n)eyman.**

Cogns.: Ger.: **Honig(mann).** Du.: **Honing(h).** Jewish (Ashkenazic, occupational): **Honig(man); Honikman** (from Yid. *honik*).

Cpds (ornamental): Jewish: **Honigbaum** ('honey tree'); **Honig(s)berg** ('honey hill'); **Honigsfeld** ('honey field', Anglicized HONEYFIELD); **Honigstein** ('honey stone'); **Honigwachs** ('honey wax').

Honeyball English: from a given name of uncertain origin, perhaps a Gmc personal name composed of the elements *hūn* bear cub + *bald* bold, brave, or else an altered form of the female given name *Anabel*.

Vars.: **Honniball, Hunneyball, Hunnibal, Honneybell, Hunneybell, Hunnibell, Hunnable.**

Honeycombe English (W Country): 1. habitation name from *Honeycomb* in Cornwall, so called from OE *hunig* HONEY + *cumb* valley (see COOMBE).

2. nickname from ME *honeycomb*, used as a term of endearment, for example in Chaucer, in the same way as the simple HONEY.

Honeyfield 1. English (W Country): topographic name for someone who lived in an area of open land where honey was found or which was regarded as particularly pleasant, from OE *hunig* HONEY + *feld* pasture, open country (see FIELD), or habitation name from an unidentified place named with these elements.

2. Jewish (Ashkenazic): Anglicized form of *Honigsfeld*; see HONEY.

Honkanen Finnish: ornamental or topographic name from Finn. *honka* pine + the gen. suffix *-nen*.

Honoré French: from a medieval given name (L *Honorātus* 'Honoured'). The name was borne by a 5th-cent. bishop of Arles and a 6th-cent. bishop of Amiens, both of whom became popular minor saints and contributed to the frequency of the name in the Middle Ages.

Cogns.: Prov.: **Hon(n)orat.**

Hoo English (S England and E Anglia): topographic name for someone who lived on a spur of a hill, from the OE dat. case *hō* (originally used after a preposition) of *hōh* (see HOE). In many cases the surname may derive from minor places named with this word, such as *Hoo* in Kent and *Hooe* in Devon and Sussex.

Var.: **Hooe.**

Hood 1. English: metonymic occupational name for a maker of hoods or nickname for someone who wore a distinctive hood, from OE *hōd* hood (a cogn. of HUTH 1 and a distant cogn. of HATT). Some early examples with prepositions seem to be topographic names, referring to a place where there was a natural shelter or overhang, providing protection from the elements.

2. Irish: Anglicized form of Gael. **Mac hUid** 'son of *Ud*', a personal name of uncertain derivation.

Vars. (of 1): **Hodd(e); Hoods, Hodd(e)s** (local names). (Of 2): **Mahood.**

Hoogland Dutch: topographic name for someone who lived on a piece of raised land, from MDu. *hooch* high (see HOCH) + *land* land.

Hoogstraeten Dutch: topographic name for someone who lived on the principal thoroughfare of a town, from MDu. *hooch* high (see HOCH) + *strāte* STREET; the ending represents the remains of an inflected form following the loss of the preposition and article *van der* 'of the'.

Cogn.: Jewish (Ashkenazic): **Hochstrasser.**

Hook English: from ME *hoke*, OE *hōc* hook, in any of a variety of senses: 1. metonymic occupational name for someone who made and sold hooks as agricultural implements or employed them in his work.

2. topographic name for someone who lived by a 'hook' of land, i.e. the bend of a river or the spur of a hill.

3. nickname (in part a survival of an OE byname) for someone with a hunched back or a hooked nose. A similar ambiguity of interpretation presents itself in the case of CROOK.

4. Jewish (Ashkenazic): of unknown origin.

Vars.: **Hooke**; **Hooker** (from 1 or 2); **Hook(e)s** (from 2, or patrs. from 3); **Athoke** (from 2).

Cogns.: Ger.: **Hake** (occupational). Fris.: **Hoeksema**; **Hoekstra** (local). Flem.: **Van Hoeck** (local). Du.: **Van (den) Hoek** (local).

Many modern bearers of the name Hook *are descended from Eustace* de la Hooke, *who is recorded in Domesday Book as holding land at Hooke, near Southampton. A descendant, Florence* Hooke, *was a mistress of Henry II, and their offspring founded an Irish branch of the family, giving their name to Hooketown near Waterford.*

Hookway English (Devon): habitation name from a place near Crediton, probably so called because the road (OE *weg*) took a detour here around a spur of a hill or bend in a river (see HOOK 2).

Hooley English (N England): habitation name from places called *Hoole* in Ches. and Lancs. The former is so called from the OE dat. case *hole* of *holh* hollow, depression; the latter from ME *hule* hut, shelter (OE *hulu* husk, covering). In both cases the final *-e* is now silent in the placename, but has been retained in the surname, with consequent alteration in the spelling.

Vars.: **Whooley**, **Hoole**.

Hooney Irish: Anglicized form of Gael. **Ó hUaithnigh** 'descendant of *Uaithneach*', a personal name from *uaithne* green.

Vars.: **O'Honie**, **O'Howney**, **Houghney**; GREEN.

Dims.: **O'Hoonin**, **O'Hownyn**, **O'Honeen**, **O'Hunnyn**, **Ho(u)neen**, **Huneen**, **Oonin** (Gael. **Ó hUaithnín**).

Hooper English (widely distributed, but most common in Devon): occupational name for someone who fitted wooden or metal hoops on wooden casks and barrels, an agent deriv. of ME *hoop* hoop, band (a borrowing from MDu.).

Hopcroft English (E Midlands): habitation name from an unidentified place, probably named with the OE elements *hop* valley among hills (see HOPE) + *croft* paddock, smallholding (see CROFT).

Hope English and Scots: topographic name for someone who lived on a patch of enclosed land or in a small, enclosed valley, ME *hop(e)*, OE *hop*, or habitation name from a place named with this word, of which there are examples in Ches., Devon, Derbys., Herefords., Kent, Lancs., Shrops., Sussex, N Yorks, and Clwyd. The surname is most common in N England and Scotland.

Vars.: **Hopes**, **Hopping**.

Hope *is the name of a Scottish family whose ancestor John* de Hope *accompanied Queen Madelene de Valois, wife of James V, to Scotland in 1537. They hold the titles Earl of Hopetoun and Marquess of Linlithgow. The former is said to have been granted to the 1st Earl (in 1703), in recognition of his father's heroism in giving up his place in a lifeboat to the Duke of York during a shipwreck, as a result of which he died.*

Members of this family have included John Hope, 1st Marquess of Linlithgow (1860–1908), who was the first Governor-General of Australia (1900–2); and his son Victor, 8th Earl and 2nd Marquess (1887–1952), who was Viceroy and Governor-General of India (1936–43).

Höpfner German: occupational name for a grower of hops or dealer in hops, or occupational nickname for a brewer, from the use of hops in the manufacture of beer, from Ger. *Hopfen* hops (MHG *hopfe* OHG *hopfo*) + *-er* suffix of agent nouns.

Vars.: **Höpfer**, **Höptner**, **Heptner**, **Hep(p)ner**; **Hopf(n)er** (Bavaria); **Hopf**.

Cogns.: Jewish (Ashkenazic): **Hopfer**, **Hoffner**; **Hopman**. Low Ger.: **Höppner**; **Hoppe**. Du.: **Hopman**, **Van Hoppe**.

Dim.: Ger.: **Höpfli** (Switzerland).

Hopkin English: from a medieval given name, a dim. of HOBB, formed with the addition of the suffix *-kin* (of Low Ger. origin) and subsequent devoicing by assimilation.

Var.: **Hobkin**.

Patrs.: **Hopkins**, **Hopkinson**; **Hobkins**, **Hobkinson**.

Hopkirk Scots: habitation name from *Hopekirk* in the parish of Hawick, so called from Northern ME *hop(e)* valley among hills (see HOPE) + *kirk* church (see KIRK).

Var.: **Hobkirk**.

Hopton English: habitation name from any of various places, for example in Derbys., Herefords., Shrops., Staffs., Suffolk, and W Yorks., so called from OE *hop* valley among hills (see HOPE) + *tūn* enclosure, settlement.

Hopwood English: habitation name from a place in Lancs., so called from OE *hop* valley among hills (see HOPE) + *wudu* WOOD.

Horan Irish: 1. Anglicized form of Gael. **Ó hUghróin** 'descendant of *Ughrón*', a personal name from *ughrach* warlike.

2. Anglicized form of Gael. **Ó hOdhráin** 'descendant of *Odhrán*', a personal name (borne, according to legend, by St Patrick's charioteer) from *odhar* dun-coloured (cf. HERON 3).

3. var. of HANRAHAN.

Hörauf German: from a Gmc personal name, *Heriwulf*, composed of the elements *heri*, *hari* army + *wulf* wolf. The first syllable embodies a regular development of the vowel in the S German dialects, but the whole name has subsequently been altered by folk etymology to the imperative form of *aufhören* to cease, desist, i.e. as if it meant 'Stop it!'

Horcajada Spanish: habitation name from places in the provinces of Cuenca and Ávila, so called from a deriv. of HORCAJO.

Horcajo Spanish: habitation name from any of several places so called from Sp. *horcajo* fork (in a road or a river), a deriv. of *horca* fork (the implement; from L *furca*, cf. FOURCHE).

Hořejš Czech: topographic name for someone who lived in the upper part of a village or on an upper story of an apartment house, from Czech *hořejš* upper, higher, upstairs. Compare DOLEJŠ.

Var.: **Hořejší**.

Horgan Irish: 1. var. of HANRAHAN.

2. var. of MORGAN.

Horký Czech: nickname for a hot-tempered, choleric, or embittered individual, from Czech *horký* hot, bitter (cogn. with Pol. *gorzki* bitter).

Cogn.: Pol.: **Gorzki** ('bitter').

Dims.: Czech: **Horčík**, **Horčička**.

Patr.: Pol.: **Gorzkiewicz**.

Habitation name: Pol.: **Gorzkowski**.

Horlacher German: habitation name from *Horlach* in Bavaria or *Horlachen* in Württemberg, both so called from OHG *hor* mud, marsh (cf. HORTON) + *lahha* pool, pond (cf. LAKE); the latter place retains traces of an inflected ending.

Horley English: habitation name from places in Oxon. and Surrey, both so called from OE *horn* tongue of land, spur of a hill (see HORN 3) + *lēah* wood, clearing.

Horlock English: either a more explicit var. of HOARE 1 or else a nickname for someone with just a patch of grey in his hair, from OE *hār* grey + *locc* lock of hair.

Vars.: **Harlock**, **Horlick**.

Hormaeche Spanish form of Basque **Ormaetxe**: topographic name for someone who lived in a stone house, from Basque *orma* stone wall + *etxe* house.

Vars.: **Hormaechea**, **Ormaeche(a)**.

Horn English, German, and Danish/Norwegian: from OE, OHG, ON *horn* horn, in a variety of senses: 1. occupational name for someone who made small articles, such as combs, spoons, and window lights, out of horn. Horn was a commonly used material in the Middle Ages, when glass was for most people prohibitively expensive and plastics had, of course, not been invented.

2. metonymic occupational name for someone who played the musical instrument, which was made from the actual horn of an animal. This was used not only in recreation and entertainment but also as a signal.

3. topographic name for someone who lived by a horn-shaped spur of a hill or tongue of land in a bend of a river, or habitation name from any of the places named with this element (for example, one in Surrey on a spur of a hill and one in Leics. in a bend of a river).

4. nickname of uncertain application, perhaps referring to some feature of a person's physical appearance, or else used to refer to a cuckolded husband. The notion of the cuckold growing horns is attested from late antiquity and is found in most European languages; the best guess at its origin probably lies in the fact that when a cock was castrated the spurs and comb, outward symbols of its virility, were also removed; the spurs were sometimes grafted to the root of the comb, where they grew into 'horns' of up to several inches in length. This barbarous practice added to the variety of the sport in cock-fighting.

5. Jewish (Ashkenazic): presumably from Ger. *Horn* horn, adopted as a surname for reasons that are not clear. It may be purely ornamental, or it may refer to the ram's horn (Hebr. *shofar*) blown in the Synagogue during various ceremonies. The latter is probably the reference of the cpd **Hornblas(s)** 'horn blow'.

Vars.: Eng.: **Horne**; **Horner**, **Hornor**. Ger.: **Horner**, **Hörner**; **Horn(e)mann**, **Hormann**. (Of 3 only): Eng.: **Athorn(e)**. (Of 5): **Horen**, GOREN; **Horner**; **Hornik(er)** ('horn-like').

Cogns. (of 3): Du.: **Van (den) Ho(o)rn**.

Dims. (of 4): Ger.: **Hornlein**, **Hörnle**.

Cpds (mainly ornamental): Swed.: **Hörnfeldt** ('corner field'); **Hörnqvist** ('corner twig'). Jewish: **Hornfeld** ('hornfield'); **Hornreich** ('horn rich'); Hor(e)nstein ('horn stone'), **Hornsztajn** (Pol. spelling), **Or(e)nstein**, **Orensztein** (in regions where Yid. has no /h/); also *Gorenstein* (see at GOREN).

It is sometimes claimed that the Jack Horner *of the nursery rhyme was a historical figure, a steward to Richard Whitling, last abbot of Glastonbury. During Henry VIII's dissolution of the monasteries the abbot is said to have sent his steward with a gift for the king of a pie containing the deeds of some manor houses, one of which Horner extracted. Although this story does not appear in print before the 19th cent., it is true that a Thomas Horner took over the manor of Mells just after the dissolution, and his family have lived there to the present day.*

Hornby English (chiefly Lancs., but also found elsewhere): habitation name from any of various places in N England so called. Those in Lancs. and near Bedale in N Yorks. are from the ON personal name *Horni* 'HORN' + ON *býr* farm, settlement. One in the parish of Great Smeaton, N Yorks., is recorded in Domesday Book as *Horenbodebi* and probably has as its first element an ON personal name composed of the elements *horn* horn + *boði* messenger.

Horncastle English: habitation name from a place in Lincs., so called from OE *horn* tongue of land (see HORN 3) + *ceaster* (Roman) fort (see CHESTER). The town is situated between the rivers Bain and Waring.

Horník Czech: occupational name for a miner, Czech *horník* (from *hora* mountain (see GÓRSKI) + *-ník* suffix of agent nouns).

Dim.: **Horníček**.

Hornsby English: habitation name from a place in Cumb., so called from the gen. case of the ON byname *Ormr* 'Serpent' (see ORME 1) + ON *býr* farm, settlement. The form of the name seems to have been influenced by confusion with HORNBY.

Horowitz Jewish (Ashkenazic): habitation name from *Hořovice* in Bohemia, part of Czechoslovakia. The name is a deriv. of the Slav. element *gora* hill (see GÓRSKI).

Vars.: **Horovitz**, **Horwitz**, **H(a)urwitz**; **Gorwitz**, **Gurvitz**, **Gur(e)vich**, **Gurovich** (under Russ. influence; see GOREN); **Urwitz**, **Urevich** (from S Yid. dialects which have no /h/).

Horridge English: habitation name from *Horwich* in Lancs., so called from OE *hār* grey (see HOARE 1) + *wice* wych elm.

Var.: **Horwich**.

Horrocks English (chiefly Lancs.): habitation name from Great or Little *Horrocks* in Greater Manchester, so called from the pl. form. of the dial. term *hurrock* heaped-up pile of loose stones or rubbish (of uncertain origin).

Horsburgh Scots: habitation name from a place in the parish of Innerleithen in the former county of Peebles (now part of Borders region). The name is first recorded before the Conquest as OE *Horsabrōc* 'brook of the horses'.

The first known bearer of the name is Symon de Horsbroc, *recorded in the reign of Alexander II (1214–49).*

Horseford English: habitation name from any of various places, for example in Norfolk, so called (from OE *hors* horse + *ford* FORD) because they lay at fords that could only be crossed on horseback.

Vars.: **Horseforth** (from a place in W Yorks.), **Hosford** (now common in N Ireland).

Horsey English: habitation name from places in Norfolk, Somerset, and Sussex, so called from OE *hors* horse (perhaps a byname) + *ēg* island, low-lying land.

Horsfall English: habitation name from *Horsefall* in W Yorks., so called from OE *hors* horse (perhaps a byname) + *fall* clearing, place where the trees have been felled (from *fellan* to fell, causative of *feallan* to fall).

Horsfield English: either a var. of HORSFALL, or else a habitation name from an unidentified place named with the elements *hors* horse (perhaps a byname) + *feld* pasture, open country (see FIELD).

Horsley English: habitation name from any of various places, for example in Derbys., Gloucs., Northumb.,

Staffs., and Surrey, so called from OE *hors* horse + *lēah* wood, clearing. The reference is probably to a place where horses were put out to pasture.

Horsman English: occupational name for a stable worker, from OE *hors* horse (cf. Ross 4) + *mann* man. It is unlikely to have been a nickname for a skilled rider, for in the Middle Ages the maintenance and use of a horse was far beyond the means of the mass of common people.

Var.: **Horseman**.

Horton English: habitation name from any of the various places so called. The majority, with examples in at least fourteen counties, get the name from OE *horh* mud, slime + *tūn* enclosure, settlement. One in Gloucs. has a different origin, from OE *heorot* HART + *dūn* hill (see DOWN 1).

Horváth Hungarian (partly Jewish): name for a Croat, Hung. *Horváth* (from Slav. *Hrvat*), one of the Slavonic people who settled in what had been the Roman province of Pannonia in the 7th cent. AD, and who were therefore the southern neighbours of the Magyars when they settled in what is now Hungary in the 10th cent. From 1091 to 1526 Croatia was under Hungarian rule. As a Jewish name, this indicates provenance from Croatia.

Vars.: Hung.: **Horvát**. Jewish: **Horvat**.

Cogns.: Ger.: **Krawath, Krabat, Crobath**. Croatian: **H(o)rvat, Hrobat**. Czech: **Charvát**. It.: **Crovat(t)o, Croatto**.

Dim.: It.: **Croattini**.

Horwell English (Devon): habitation name from *Horwell* in Colebrook, Devon, which is named with the OE elements *horh* mud, slime + *well(a)* spring, stream (see WELL).

Horwood English: habitation name from places in Bucks. and Devon, the former being so called from OE *horh* mud, slime + *wudu* WOOD. The latter place shows early forms in *Har-* and probably has the same origin as HARWOOD.

Hoseason Scots. (Shetland): patr. from the given name *Hosea*. This was probably originally *Osie*, a dim. of OSWALD, but was later altered by association with the name of the biblical prophet *Hosea*.

Hosier English: occupational name for a maker of leggings, from an agent deriv. of ME *hose* (OE *hosa*). Hose was the regular name for garments worn on the legs until the 18th cent. Cf. HEUSE.

Hoskin English (Devon): from the ME given name *Osekin*, a dim. of the various personal names with an OE first element *ōs* god (cf., e.g., OSBORN, OSGOOD, and OSMOND), or its ON cogn. *ās*. For the inorganic initial *H-*, cf. HERRICK.

Vars: **Hoskyn, Hosken, Hosking** (all Devon).

Patrs.: **Hoskin(g)s, Hosky(n)s; Huskinson, Hoskis(s)on, Huskisson**.

Hostal French: from OF *hostel*, *hostal*, a house of some size and standing, in which it was possible to accommodate guests in separate rooms (LL *hospitāle*, from *hospes*, gen. *hospitis*, guest; cf. the mod. Fr. *hôtel de ville*). The word was probably used as an occupational name for someone who was employed as a servant in such a grand house, in the later Middle Ages perhaps also a keeper of a hotel as now understood (cf. OSTLER).

Vars.: **Host(e)aux, Hôtel; O(u)stal, O(u)stau; Lhostal, Loustal, Loustau** (with fused def. art.); **Dhôtel** (with fused preposition); **Delho(u)stal, Delhoustau** (with fused preposition and def. art.).

Dims.: **Oustalet, Oustalot; Loustalet, Loustalot**.

Hothersall English (Lancs.): habitation name from a place in Lancs., found in ME sources as *Hudereshal* and *Huddeshalh*. Ekwall proposes an etymology from an OE personal name **Huder* + OE *halh* nook, recess (see HALE 1).

Houard French: apparently an occupational name for a humble type of agricultural worker, from OF *houe* hoe (of Gmc origin) + the pej. suffix *-ard*. There has probably also been confusion with HUARD.

Houdard French: from a Gmc personal name composed of the elements *huld* friendly + *hard* hardy, brave, strong.

Var.: **Houdart**.

Dims.: **Houdin(et), Houdon, Houdot**.

Hougård Danish: habitation name from a placename composed of the elements *hov* court (cf. HOFER) + *gård* enclosure (cf. GARTH).

Vars.: **Hougaard, Hovgård, Hovgaard**.

Hough English: habitation name from any of various places, for example in Ches. and Derbys., so called from OE *hōh* spur of a hill (literally 'heel').

Var.: HUFF.

Houghton English: habitation name from any of the various places so called. The majority, with examples in at least fourteen counties, get the name from OE *hōh* ridge, spur (see HOUGH) + *tūn* enclosure, settlement; cf. HUTTON. *Haughton* in Notts. also has this origin, and may have contributed to the surname. A smaller group of *Houghtons*, with examples in Lancs. and W Yorks., have as their first element OE *halh* nook, recess (see HALE 1). In the case of isolated examples in Devon and E Yorks., the first elements appear to be OE personal names or bynames, of which the forms approximate to **Huhha* and **Hofa* respectively, but the meanings are unknown.

Houlihan Irish: Anglicized form of Gael. **Ó hUallacháin** 'descendant of *Uallachán*', a personal name from a dim. of *úallach* proud, arrogant.

Houliston Scots: habitation name from *Howlison* in the parish of Heriot, Lothian, apparently so called from the Norman personal name *Hulot* (a dim. of *H(e)ude*, from the Gmc element *hild* battle) + ME *toun* settlement (OE *tūn*).

The earliest known bearer of the name is Richard de Hulotistun, *recorded in 1296*.

House English: 1. from OE *hūs*. In the Middle Ages the majority of the population lived in cottages or huts rather than houses, and in most cases this name probably indicates someone who had some connection with the largest and most important building of the settlement, either a religious 'house' or simply the local 'great house'. In some cases it may indicate a 'householder', someone who owned his own dwelling as opposed to being a tenant.

2. a relatively modern respelling of HOWES.

Vars. (of 1): **Hoose; Houser; Hous(e)man; Household(er)**.

Cogns. (of 1): Ger.: **Hause; Haus(s)(n)er, Häusler, Heuser, Heis(l)er, Heiss(n)er, Heyseler; Hausmann**. Low Ger.: **Huse; Hüseler; Hus(e)mann, Hüs(e)mann, Hussmann**. Fris.: **Huisinga, Huizinga** (of which **Housego** is probably an Anglicized form). Flem., Du.: **Huis(e); Van Huis, Van Huizen; Hui(j)sman, Huysman**. Jewish (Ashkenazic): **Haus(n)er, Hauzer, Hausman(n), Hauzman**.

Dim.: Low Ger.: **Hüsgen**.

Patrs.: Flem., Du.: **Hui(j)smans, Huysmans**.

Housley English: habitation name from *Housley* Hall in Ecclesfield, W Yorks., a cpd of OE *hūs* (see HOUSE 1) with *lēah* wood, clearing.

Houston Scots: 1. habitation name from a place near Glasgow, so called from the gen. case of the medieval given name Hugh + ME *tune*, *toun* settlement, village (OE *tūn* enclosure, settlement). The landlord in question is a certain *Hugo* de Paduinan, who held the place *c.*1160.

2. Anglicized form of Gael. *Mac Uistean*; see McCutcheon.

Vars. (of 1): **Houstoun, Huston.**

In 1836 the newly founded town of Houston, *Texas, was named in honour of Sam Houston (1793–1836), soldier and statesman. His ancestors were Ulster Scots who had emigrated to Philadelphia in the 18th cent. As Commander in Chief of the Texan army he achieved Texan independence from Mexico by routing the army of Santa Ana.*

Hovorka Czech: nickname for a talkative person, Czech *hovorka*, from *hovor* talk, conversation.

Howard 1. English: from the Norman personal name *Huard*, *Heward*, composed of the Gmc elements *hug* heart, mind, spirit + *hard* hardy, brave, strong.

2. English: from the Anglo-Scandinavian personal name *Hāward*, composed of the ON elements *há* high + *varðr* guardian.

3. English: var. of Ewart.

4. Irish: see Fogarty.

Vars. (of 1): **Heward, Hewart, Huart.** (Of 2): **Haward.**

Cogn. (of 1): Fr.: Huard.

Patrs. (from 1): **Hewartson, Hewertson, Huartson, Huertson.**

The house of Howard, *the leading family of the English Roman Catholic nobility, was founded by Sir William Howard or Haward of Norfolk (d. 1308). They gained the title of Duke of Norfolk by marriage. The first Duke of Norfolk of the Howard line was created Earl Marshal of England by Richard III in 1483, and this office has been held by his succeeding male heirs to the present day. They also hold the Earldoms of Suffolk, Berks., Carlisle, and Effingham. Henry VIII's fifth queen, Catherine Howard (?1520–42), was a niece of Thomas Howard, 3rd Duke of Norfolk.*

Howarth English (Lancs.): habitation name from *Howarth* or *Haworth* in the parish of Rochdale, Lancs., apparently so called from OE *hōh* mound (see Hoe) + *worð* enclosure (see Worth). However, if the 13th-cent. form *Halwerdeword* refers to this place, the first element may instead represent a personal name such as OE *Hælweard* or ON *Hallvarðr*.

Vars.: **Howo(u)rth,** Haworth.

Howcroft English (Yorks. and Lancs.): habitation name from some place named as a smallholding (see Croft) on the spur of a hill (see Hoe), e.g. *Howcroft* in Rimington, W Yorks.

Howden 1. Scots: habitation name from a place so called near Kelso on the Eng. border. Early forms include *Hadden*, *Hauden*, and *Halden*; the placename is probably from OE *halh* nook, recess (see Hale 1) + *denu* valley (see Dean 1).

2. English: habitation name from a place in Humberside (formerly E Yorks.), so called from ON *hofuð* head (replacing OE *hēafod*) + OE *denu* valley (see Dean 1); the first element may have been used in the sense 'principal', 'top', or 'end'.

Vars. (of 1): **Hadden,** Haddon.

Howe English: topographic name for someone who lived by a small hill or a man-made mound or barrow, ME *how* (ON *haugr*), or habitation name from a place named with this word, such as *Howe* in Norfolk and W Yorks.

2. English: var. of Hugh.

3. Jewish (Ashkenazic): Anglicized form of one or more like-sounding Jewish surnames.

Vars. (of 1 and 2): **How;** Howes.

Howell 1. Welsh: from the personal name *Hywel* 'Eminent', popular since the Middle Ages in honour of the great 10th-cent. law-giving Welsh king.

2. English: habitation name from a place in Lincs., probably so called from the OE personal name *Huna* (a short form of the various cpd names with the first element *hūn* bear cub; cf. Höne) + OE *well(a)* spring, stream (see Well).

Vars.: **How(e)l.**

Patrs. (from 1): **Howel(l)s,** Powell, Bowell. See also McHale.

Howes English: 1. topographic name from the pl. of ME *how* barrow (see Howe 1).

2. patr. from Hugh.

Vars.: **Howse,** House.

Howey 1. N English and Scots: from a medieval given name, a dim. of Hugh.

2. Irish: Anglicized form of Gael. **Ó hEochaidh** 'descendant of *Eochaidh*', a var. of *Eachaidh*; see Haughey.

Vars. (of 1): **Howie.** (Of 2): **Hoey, Huey, Hoy; Houghy, O'Hohy, O'Huhy.**

Patrs. (from 1): **Howi(e)son.**

Howgate English (Yorks.): habitation name, probably from one of several minor places called *Howgate* in W Yorks., earlier *Holgate* (see Holgate). Alternatively, the surname may be from *Huggate* in Humberside, which is named as the 'road by the tumuli' (from ON *haugr* tumulus + *gata* road). This was recorded as *Howgate* in 1406.

Howick English: habitation name from places in Lancs. and Northumb. The former gets its name from OE *hōh* spur of a hill (see Hoe) or *hōc* Hook + *wīc* outlying farm (see Wick); the latter probably originally had as its first element OE *hēah* High, but was later influenced by *hōh*.

Hoyle English (Yorks. and Lancs.): topographic name, a var. of Hole reflecting a regional pronunciation.

Vars.: **Hoile; Hoyles, Hoiles.**

Hoyo Spanish: topographic name for someone who lived by a hollow or depression in the ground, Sp. *hoyo* (a byform of *hoya*, from L *fovea* pit).

Var.: **Hoyos** (also a nickname for someone scarred by pockmarks).

Hoz 1. Spanish: topographic name for someone who lived by a narrow pass, Sp. *hoz* (L *fauces* throat, used also in a transferred sense of a defile or gorge).

2. Spanish: metonymic occupational name for someone who made and sold sickles, or who used them in reaping, from Sp. *hoz* sickle (L *falx*, gen. *falcis*).

3. Jewish (Ashkenazic): ornamental name from Yid. *hoz* rabbit, one of the many Ashkenazic ornamental surnames taken from words for animals.

Hrabák Czech: nickname for a greedy or miserly person, from a deriv. of the verb *hrabat* to rake in, hoard.

Vars.: **Hrabáč.**

Dims.: **Hrabánek, Hrabáček.**

Hrb Czech: nickname for a hunchback, from Czech *hrb* hump.

Vars.: **Hrba, Hrbáč, Hrbatý.**

Dims.: **Hrbek, Hrbáček.**

Cogn. (patr.): Croatian: **Grbić.**

Hrdlička Czech: nickname meaning 'Turtledove', denoting someone with a mild, peaceable, or affectionate temperament, or metonymic occupational name for a keeper of doves, from Czech *hrdlička* dove.

Hrdý Czech: nickname for a brave, proud, or haughty man, from the Czech adj. *hrdý* (cogn. with Gmc *hard*; see HARD). This is also found as a first element in OCzech personal names such as *Hrděbor*, and this may in some cases account for the origin of the surname.

Var.: **Hrdina**.

Hron Czech: from an OCzech personal name of uncertain origin; Moldanová suggests that it may be an altered form of *Hroznata*, an OCzech name that is apparently an erroneous translation of *Methodius*, the name of the saint who accompanied St Cyril in bringing Christianity to the Slavs. The error arose because *Methodius* was taken as a deriv. of L *metus* fear and translated with a deriv. of Czech *hrozný* fearful, timid, whereas it is in fact from Gk *methodeia* craft, skill, method.

Vars.: **Hroch**, **Hroz**.

Dims.: **Hroník**, **Hroněk**.

Huard French: 1. cogn. of HOWARD 1.

2. nickname for a wise or vigilant person, from OF *huard* owl (a deriv. of *huer* to cry, howl, of imitative origin). There has probably also been some confusion with HOUARD.

Hubble English (W Midlands): from the Norman personal name *Hubald*, composed of the Gmc elements *hug* heart, mind, spirit + *bald* bold, brave.

Vars.: **Hubball**, **Hubbold**.

Cogns.: Fr.: **Hubaud**, **Hubau(l)t**.

Hubený Czech: nickname for a thin man, from Czech *hubený* thin.

Huber 1. German and Dutch: from MHG *huobe* (OHG *huoba*), a measure of land, varying in size at different periods and in different places, but always of considerable extent, appreciably larger than the holding of the average peasant. The surname usually denotes a holder or owner of this amount of land, who would have been a prosperous small farmer and probably one of the leading men of his village. However, it seems also to have been acquired sometimes by men of lower status who merely worked on such a holding in return for a wage, having no land of their own.

2. Jewish (Ashkenazic): from a S Yid. pronunciation of Yid. *hober* oats; see HABER.

Vars. (of 1): Ger.: **Hüb(n)er**; **Hüf(f)ner** (Franconia); **Hue(b)mer**, **Hiemer** (Bavaria, from *huebmeier*; see MAYER). In the U.S. the surname is often Anglicized as **Hoover**. (Of 2): **Hubner**, **Huberman**; **Guber(man)** (under Russ. influence; see GOREN); **Guberblit** ('oat blossom', an ornamental elaboration).

Patr. (from 1): Du.: **Hubers**.

Hubert English, French, and German: from a Gmc personal name composed of the elements *hug* heart, mind, spirit + *berht* bright, famous. The name was borne by an 8th-cent. bishop of Maastricht who was adopted as the patron of hunters, and helped to increase the popularity of the given name, especially in the Low Countries.

Vars.: Eng.: **Hubbert**, **Hubbart**, **Hubbard**, **Hobart** (this last form being especially common in E Anglia). Ger.: **Hübert**, **Hup(p)recht**.

Cogns.: Low Ger.: **Hubbert**, **Huppert**. Flem.: **Hu(y)brecht**.

Dims.: Fr.: **Huberdeau**; **Hubel**, **Hubeau**, **Hub(e)lot**, **Hub(e)lin**, **Hubelet**, **Hubin(et)**, **Huby**. Low Ger.: **Hubbe**, **Hübbe**, **Hup(j)e**, **Hübgen**, **Hüpgen**.

Patrs.: Ger.: **Hubbertz**, **Huppertz**. Low Ger.: **Hüb(b)ers**, **Huppers**. Flem.: **Huybrechts**.

Patrs. (from dims.): Low Ger.: **Hübgens**, **Hüpgens**, **Hübben**, **Hupen**. Flem.: **Huyben(s)**.

Hübsch German: nickname from Ger. *hübsch* polite, refined, agreeable (MHG *hübesch*, *hübisch*, *hōvesch*; cf. HÖFLICH). The present-day sense of the vocab. word, 'pretty', 'handsome', 'nice', is a comparatively recent development and is unlikely to have affected acquisition of the Ger. surname. However, it underlies all the Jewish cogns. listed below.

Vars.: **Hübscher**, **Hübschmann**.

Cogns.: Jewish (Ashkenazic): **Hubsch(man)**, **Hubs(c)her**; **Hibsh(er)**, **Hibshman(n)**; **Hips(c)h**, **Hipsher**, **Hipshman**. Forms with *-i-* have been affected phonologically but not semantically by Yid. *hipsh* considerable, sizeable.

Dim.: Ger.: **Hübschle**.

Huchet French: metonymic occupational name for a town-crier or herald, from OF *huchet*, a small horn used by such officials to secure the attention of the populace (a word of uncertain, possibly Gmc, origin).

Vars.: **Huchez**; **Huquet** (Normandy, Picardy); **Huchot** (with a different suffix); **Huchier**, **H(e)ucheux**, **Huqueux** (agent nouns).

Pej.: **Huchard**.

Huck English: from the medieval given name *Hucke*, perhaps from the OE personal name *Hucca* (see HUCKNALL) or *Ucca*, which may in some cases be a pet form of OE *Ūhtrǣd*; see UTTRIDGE. (For the inorganic initial *H-*, cf. HERRICK.) Later, however, this name fell completely out of use and the forms became inextricably confused with those of HUGH.

Vars.: **Hucke**, **Hug**.

Dims.: **Huckle**, **Huckel(l)**.

Patrs.: **Huck(e)s**.

'Servant of H.': **Hugman**.

Hucker English (Somerset): occupational name for a pedlar or other tradesman, from an agent deriv. of ME *hukken* to hawk, trade (cf. HAKE 2).

Huckfield English (Somerset): of uncertain origin, perhaps a habitation name from a place named with the OE personal name *Hucca* or *Ucca* (see HUCK) + OE *feld* pasture, open country (see FIELD). Alternatively, it may be a topographic name from some place where an open market was held, from ME *hukken* to hawk, trade (cf. HUCKER) + *fe(i)ld* open space.

Hucknall English (Notts.): habitation name from a place so called in Notts., which was once part of a larger district bearing this name (*Hochenale* in Domesday Book). It is derived from the gen. case of the OE personal name *Hucca* + OE *halh* nook, recess (see HALE 1).

Hudd English: from the popular medieval given name *Hudde*, which is of complex origin. It is usually explained as a pet form of HUGH, but there was a pre-existing OE personal name, *Hūda*, underlying placenames such as *Huddington*, Worcs. This personal name may well still have been in use at the time of the Norman Conquest. If so, it was absorbed by the Norman HUGH and its many dims. Reaney adduces evidence that *Hudde* was also regarded as a pet form of RICHARD.

Var.: **Hutt**.

Dims.: **Huddy** (Devon and Cornwall); **Huddle**.

Patrs.: **Hudson**, **Hutson**.

The surname Hudd *is now found mainly in the Bristol area. However, the given name was once common throughout England, and especially in Yorks. The patr.* Hudson *is very common and widely distributed, but is still most frequent in Yorks.*

Huddleston English: habitation name from a place in W Yorks., so called from the gen. case of the OE personal name **Hūdel* (a deriv. of *Hūda*; see HUDD) + OE *tūn* enclosure, settlement. There is a place of the same name in the parish of Westerkirk in the former county of Dumfries (now part of Dumfries and Galloway region), which seems to have been named from the Yorks. place and may in turn lie behind some examples of the surname in Scotland and N Ireland.

Vars.: **Huddlestone**; **Hiddleston(e)** (Scots).

This surname is of Yorks. origin, but is now most common in N Ireland, whither was brought from Scotland. The earliest known bearer in England is Sir John Hudleston, *who died before 1306; in Scotland it did not appear until 1534, when James* Hedilstone *is recorded as a dempster in the barony of Carnwath.*

Hudec Czech: occupational name for a fiddler, Czech *hudec*, from *housti* to play the fiddle.

Dims.: **Hudeček**, **H(o)udek**.

Huete Spanish: habitation name from a place in the province of Cuenca. The placename is first recorded in the L form *Opta*, but is of unknown origin.

Huff English: topographic name for someone who lived by a spur of a hill, OE *hōh* (literally, 'heel').

Vars.: HOUGH, HEUGH, **Hughf(f)**, **Houf(e)**, **Hoof(f)**; **Hoes**, **Hose** (from the pl. *hōs* spurs; *Hose* is also the name of a place in Leics., from which the surname may be derived).

Huffton English (Notts.): habitation name from some unidentified place, presumably named with the OE elements *hōh* ridge, spur (see HUFF) + *tūn* enclosure, settlement; it may well be a var. of HOUGHTON or HUTTON.

Hugh English: from the OF personal name *Hu(gh)e*, introduced to Britain by the Normans. This is in origin a short form of any of the various Gmc cpd names with the first element *hug* heart, mind, spirit (cf., e.g., HOWARD 1, HUBBLE, and HUBERT). It was a popular given name among the Normans in England, partly due to the fame of St Hugh of Lincoln (1140–1200), who was born in Burgundy and who established the first Carthusian monastery in England. The popularity of the European cogns. (Fr. *Hugues*, It. *Ugo*, etc.) perhaps owes more to St Hugh of Cluny (1024–1109). In Scotland and Ireland this name has been widely used as an equivalent of Celt. *Aodh* 'Fire' (see MCKAY).

Vars.: **Hugo** (Cornwall; probably a recent reintroduction from France); **Hew(e)**, HOWE.

Cogns.: Fr.: **Hugo**, **Hugues**, **Hue**; **Hu(g)on** (from the OF oblique case); **Gon** (an aphetic form). Prov.: **Huc**, **Uc**. It.: **Ugo**, **Ughi**. Ger.: **Hug(k)**; **Hüge** (Switzerland); **Haug(g)** (Bavaria); **Hauch** (Franconia). Flem.: **Huyg(h)e**. Ger. (of Slav. origin): **Hauck(e)**.

Dims.: Eng.: **Huget(t)**, HEWITT; **Huggin**, HUTCHIN; **Hug(g)on**; HEWLETT; **Hug(h)lin**, **Huelin**, **Hul(l)in**; **Howlin(g)** (Ireland); **Hewkin**, **Hu(c)kin**; HUDD; HULL; HOWEY. Fr.: **Hugon(n)et**, **Hugu(en)et**, **Huet**, **Higonnet**, **Higounet**, **Igo(u)net**, **Gon(n)et**, **Gounet**; **Hugonneau**, **Gon(n)eau**, **Gon(n)el**, **Gounel**; **Hug(on)ot**, **Huot**, **Gounot**, **Gounod**, **Got**; **Hugonin**, **Hugu(en)in**, **Gon(n)in**, **Gounin**, **Gouny**; **Husson**, **Huchon**, **Husset**; **Huonic** (Brittany). Cat.: **Huguet**. It.: **Ughelli**, **Ughetti**, **Ugoletti**, **Ughini**, **Ug(ol)otti**; **Ugolini** (Tuscany). Ger.: **Hügle**, **Hügli(n)**, **Heugel**, **Heugle**, **Heigl**, **Hegel**.

Augs.: It.: **Ugon(i)**.

Pejs.: Eng.: **Huggard**. Fr.: **Gon(n)ard**, **Gounard**.

Patrs.: Eng.: **Hugh(e)s**, **Huws**, **Hew(e)s**, HOWES; **Hughson**, **Hewson**; **Howson** (Yorks.); **Hooson** (Lancs.); FITZHUGH. Welsh: PUGH, BEWES. It.: **D'Ugo**. Ger.: **Hauger**. Flem., Du.: **Huygen(s)**.

Patrs. (from dims.): Eng.: **Hewlin(g)s**, **Howlings**, **Hullins**, **Hulance**; **Hukins**, **Hookins**; **Howkins** (Leicester area); **Huggins**, **Huggens**, **Huggons**.

The French Romantic novelist Victor Hugo *(1802–85) was the grandson of a carpenter born in Nancy. The name is common in this form in Lorraine. Hugo himself liked to claim descent from more illustrious forebears of this name, such as Pierre-Antoine Hugo (b. 1532), who was Privy Counsellor to the Grand Duke of Lorraine, and a Louis Hugo, who was a bishop.*

Christiaan Huygens *(1629–95), who first formulated the wave theory of light, was a member of a prominent Dutch family; his grandfather, father, and brother were all in the private service of the Dutch royal family. His father Constantin (1596–1687) was an equally distinguished 17th-cent. savant, knighted by James I in 1622 and still regarded as one of the greatest classical Dutch authors.*

Hühne German: nickname from Ger. *Hüne*, MHG *hiune* giant, monster, bogeyman, from MHG *Hiune* Hun (OHG *Hūni*), a word probably ultimately of Turkic origin.

Vars.: **Hühn**, **Hüne**; **Hihn**, **Hien**.

Hulbert English: from a ME given name *Holbert*, which according to Reaney is probably a survival of an unrecorded OE personal name **Holdbeorht*, composed of the Gmc elements *hold* friendly, gracious + *berht* bright, famous.

Vars.: **Holbert**, **Hulburd**, **Holberd**, **Holbird**.

Hull English: 1. var. of HILL 1.
2. pet form of HUGH.

Vars. (of 1): **Hull(e)s**; **Huller**; **Hullah** (Yorks.).

Patrs. (from 2): **Hull(e)s**, **Hulson**.

Hulse English: habitation name from a place in Ches., recorded in the mid-13th cent. in the forms *Holes*, *Holis*, and *Holys*. This probably represents a ME pl. of OE *holh* hollow, depression (see HOLE).

Hulton English: habitation name from places in Lancs. and Staffs., so called from OE *hyll* HILL + *tūn* enclosure, settlement; cf. HILTON.

A family of this name has been established at Hulton, near Bolton, Lancs., since the 12th cent., when Bleythin de Hulton *was mentioned in records of the reign of Henry II (1154–89).*

Humber English: habitation name from any of the various places so called from their situation on a stream with this name. *Humber* is a common prehistoric river name, of uncertain origin and meaning.

Humberstone English: habitation name from places in Lincs. and Leics. According to Ekwall, the former is so called from the river name HUMBER + OE *stān* stone, while the latter has as its first element the personal name *Hūnbeorht* (see HUMBERT).

Vars.: **Humberston**, **Humblestone**, **Humerstone**, **Hummerston(e)**.

Humbert German and French: from a Gmc personal name composed of the elements *hūn* bear cub + *berht* bright, famous. This was particularly popular in the Netherlands and N Germany during the Middle Ages as a result of the fame of a 7th-cent. St Humbert, who founded the abbey of Marolles in Flanders. A cogn. personal name seems to have existed in OE (see HUMBERSTONE), but did not survive to give rise to a modern surname.

Vars.: Ger.: **Humbrecht**, **Humprecht**, **Humpert**.

Cogns.: Fris.: **Hummer**, **Hommer**.

Dims.: Fr.: **Humberdot**, **Humb(e)lot**.

Patrs.: Ger.: **Humpertz**. Low Ger.: **Humperding**, **Humperdinck**. Fris.: **Hummers**, **Hommers**.

Humble English (Northumb.): nickname for a meek or lowly person, from ME, OF *(h)umble* (L *humilis* low(ly), mean, base, a deriv. of *humus* ground).

Humboldt German: from a Gmc personal name composed of the elements *hūn* bear cub + *bald* bold, brave. The name was relatively rare, and does not seem to have given rise to cogn. surnames in other European languages.

Var.: **Humbolt**.

Humm 1. English (Norman): nickname from OF *homme* man (L *homo*), normally representing an ANF translation of MANN.

2. Frisian: short form of HUMBERT and HUMBOLDT.

Vars. (of 1): **Hum**. (Of 2): **Homm**.

Patrs. (from 2): **Hummen, Hommen, Hommes**.

Hummel 1. German: dim. of HUMBERT and HUMBOLDT.

2. Low Ger.: nickname for a busy or bustling person, from MLG *hommel* bee (of imitative origin, cf. Eng. *humblebee*, now normally altered to the alliterative *bumblebee*). The surname may in some cases have been a metonymic occupational name for a beekeeper.

Vars.: **Hommel; Huml**.

Humphrey 1. English: from the OF personal name *Humfrey*, introduced to Britain by the Normans. This is composed of the Gmc elements *hūn* bear cub + *frid*, *fred* peace. It was borne by a 9th-cent. saint, bishop of Therouanne, who had a certain following in England among Norman settlers.

2. Irish: see OLIFF.

Vars.: **Humph(e)ry, Humfrey, Homfray**.

Cogn.: Ger.: **Humfrid**.

Patrs.: Eng.: **Humphr(e)ys, Humphries, Humphris(s), Humfress; Humphers(t)on**. Welsh: **Bo(u)mphrey, Bumphries**.

Hund German: metonymic occupational name for a keeper of dogs for hunting or other purposes, or derogatory nickname, from Ger. *Hund* dog (OHG *hunt*).

Var.: **Hundt**.

Cogns.: Flem.: **Hondt, Dehondt**.

Dim.: Low Ger.: **Hüngen**.

Patr. (from a dim.): Low Ger.: **Hüngens**.

Hunt English: occupational name for a hunter, OE *hunta* (a primary deriv. of *huntian* to hunt). The term was used not only of hunters on horseback of game such as stags and wild boars, which was in the Middle Ages a pursuit restricted to the ranks of the nobility, but also of much humbler bird catchers and poachers seeking food. The word seems also to have been used as an OE personal name (cf. HUNTINGTON and HUNTLEY) and to have survived into the Middle Ages as an occasional given name.

Vars.: **Hunte** (retaining a trace of the OE final vowel); **Hunter** (chiefly Scots; a ME secondary deriv. formed with the addition of the agent suffix *-er*).

Equiv.: Ger.: JÄGER.

Hunter *is the name of a Scottish family established at Hunterston in the former county of Ayrs. (now part of Strathclyde region), an estate which was granted to Norman* Huntar *in 1271. Earlier records were witnessed by Norman and William Huntar or* Venator *(a L translation) in 1116.*

Huntington English: habitation name from one of the places that get their names from the gen. pl. *huntena* of OE *hunta* hunter (see HUNT) + *tūn* enclosure, settlement or *dūn* hill (the forms in *-ton* and *-don* having become inextricably confused). In addition, a number of bearers of this name and its vars. can no doubt derive it from the more important town of *Huntingdon* in Cambs. (formerly a county town in its own right), which gets its name from the gen. case of OE *hunta* huntsman, perhaps used as a personal name + *dūn* hill.

Vars.: **Huntingdon, Huntinton**.

A powerful and prominent American family of this name was founded by Simon Huntington, *who himself never saw the New World, for he died in 1633 on the voyage to Boston, where his widow settled with her children. Their descendants include Jabez Huntington (1719–86), a wealthy W Indies trader, and Samuel Huntington (1731–96), who was one of the signatories of the Declaration of Independence.*

Collis Potter Huntington (1821–1900) was an American railway magnate whose ancestors had emigrated to America from England in the 17th cent. Beginning with little education or money, he made a huge fortune, some of which he left to his nephew, Henry Huntington (1850–1927), who used the money to establish the Huntington library and art gallery in California.

Huntley 1. English: habitation name from a place in Gloucs., so called from OE *hunta* hunter (perhaps a byname; see HUNT) + *lēah* wood, clearing.

2. Scots: habitation name from a lost place called *Huntlie* in the former county of Berwicks. (now part of Borders region), with the same etymology as in 1. *Huntly* near Aberdeen was named from the Borders place, but does not itself seem to have given rise to any surnames.

Var.: **Huntly**.

Hüpfer German: occupational name for a professional tumbler or acrobat at a fair, or nickname for a restless individual with plenty of energy, from Ger. *Hüpfer* 'hopper', 'jumper', an agent deriv of *hüpfen* to hop, skip, or jump (OHG *hupfen*, MLG *huppen*, a cogn. of OE *hoppian*, mod. Eng. *hop*).

Vars.: **Hupfer** (S German); **Hupf; Hupfauf** ('hop up').

Cogns.: Low Ger.: **Hupp, Hüp(p)er**. Eng.: **Hopper**.

Huré French: nickname for someone with an untidy head of shaggy hair, from the past part. of OF *hurer* to bristle, ruffle, stand on end (trans. and intrans.; of uncertain, possibly Gmc, origin).

Vars.: **Hurran, Hurren** (from the pres. part.).

Dims.: **Hurel, Hureau, Hurot, Huron**. Eng. (Norman): **Hurrell**.

Pej.: Fr.: **Hurard**.

Hurford English: habitation name from an unidentified place. The second part of the name is clearly OE *ford* FORD; the first is most probably OE *hyrne* corner, bend (see HEARN 2).

Hurley 1. English: habitation name from places in Berks. and Warwicks., so called from OE *hyrne* corner, bend (see HEARN 2) + *lēah* wood, clearing.

2. Irish: var. of HERLIHY.

Var.: **Hurly**.

Hurst English: topographic name for someone who lived on a wooded hill, OE *hyrst*, or habitation name from one of the various places named with this word, for example *Hurst* in Berks., Kent, Somerset, and Warwicks., or *Hirst* in Northumb. and W Yorks. For the divergent development of the vowel, cf. HILL 1.

Vars.: **He(a)rst; Hirst** (widespread, but most common in W Yorks.).

Cogns.: Ger.: **Hurst, Härst**. Low Ger.: **Horst(mann), Terhorst**. Flem., Du.: **Van der Horst, Horsten, Hors(t)man**.

Hurtado Spanish: nickname from the past part. of Sp. *hurtar* to rob, conceal (LL *furtāre*, from *furtum* theft, *fur* thief). The reference was probably to an illegitimate offspring, whose existence was concealed, or to a kidnapped child.

Cogn.: Port.: **Furtado**.

Husband English: occupational name for a peasant farmer, from ME *husband* tiller of the soil, husbandman. The term (late OE *hūsbonda*, ON *húsbóndi*, a cpd of *hús* HOUSE + *bóndi* BOND) originally described a man who was head of his own household, and this may have been the sense in some of the earliest examples of the surname.

Patrs.: **Husbands, Hosbons**.

Hussey 1. English (Norman): habitation name from *Houssaye* in Seine-Maritime, so called from a collective noun from OF *hous* holly (see HILSE).

2. English: nickname for a woman who was mistress of her own household, from ME *husewif* (a cpd of OE *hūs* HOUSE + *wīf* woman). No pej. sense is apparent in the word at least until the 17th cent.

3. English: nickname for someone noted for his boots, from OF *h(e)usé* 'booted' (see HEUSE), either because they were of an unusual design or because he was considered fortunate to have them at all at a time when most of the peasantry had to be content with leggings or sandals.

4. Irish: Anglicized form of Gael. **Ó hEodhusa** 'descendant of *Eodhus*', a personal name given in bardic families.

Vars.: **Hussy, Husey, Hosey; Hosie** (Scots). (Of 4 only): **O'-Hossy, O'Hoasy, O'Hosey**.

Members of an Irish family called Hussey *are descended from the hereditary bards to the Maguires of Fermanagh.*

Hustin French: nickname for a quarrelsome person, from OF *hustin* dispute, argument, commotion (of uncertain origin, perhaps from MLG *hutselen* to shake).

Var.: HUTIN.

Hutchin English and Scots: from the medieval given name *Huchin*, a dim. of HUGH.

Vars.: **Hutcheon** (chiefly Scots); **Hotchen, Houchen, Howchin**.

Patrs.: **Hutchin(g)s** (chiefly Devon and Somerset); **Hutchison, Hutche(r)son** (chiefly Scots); **Hutchin(g)son** (widespread, but most common in N England and N Ireland). See also MCCUTCHEON.

Anne Maybury Hutchinson *(1591–1643) became famous in the early history of the American settlers when she was banished from the Massachusetts Bay colony for her religious views. She was the daughter of an English preacher, and married to a wealthy merchant; they had emigrated in 1634. The family prospered in America, and her great-great-grandson Thomas Hutchinson (1711–80) became governor of Massachusetts.*

Hüter German: occupational name for a watchman or herdsman, from Ger. *Hüter* protector, agent deriv. of *hüten* to guard, watch over (OHG *huotan*; cf. HUTH 2).

Cogn.: Jewish: **Hit(t)er** ('protector', Yid. *hiter*, a deriv. of *hitn* to protect).

Huth German: 1. metonymic occupational name for a maker of hats or nickname for a wearer of distinctive hats, from Ger. *Hut(h)* hat (MHG, OHG *huot*; cf. the cogn. HOOD and related HATT; all these words are ultimately akin to OHG *huotan* to protect (see 2 below), since hats were regarded as being primarily for protection rather than ornamentation).

2. occupational name for a herdsman, MHG *huote* (a primary deriv. of *hüeten* to protect, OHG *huotan*); cf. HÜTER.

Vars.: **Hut(h)er, Hüter, Huthmann**.

Cogns. (of 1): Low Ger.: **Hoth, Hodt; Hodemacher**. Du.: **Hoe(d)t, (Van) den Hoed, Hoetmech**. Jewish (Ashkenazic): **Hut(t), Hutter(er), Hutner, Hutnik, Hut(t)man**.

Dims.: Ger.: **Hütel**. (Of 1 only): Low Ger.: **Hoetje**.

Hutin 1. French: nickname for a quarrelsome person, var. of HUSTIN.

2. Jewish (E Ashkenazic): habitation name from *Hotin*, the Rumanian name of *Khotin* in the Ukraine. Medial *-u-* indicates a S Yid. pronunciation.

Var. (of 2): **Hutiner**.

Dims. (of 1): **Hutinel, Hutineau, Hut(i)net**.

Hüttler German: agent deriv. of Ger. *Hüttl* little hut, dim. of MHG *hütte* hut (OHG *huttea*). This may have been a topographic name for someone who lived in a small hut, but in Bavaria it was an occupational name for a carpenter (i.e. 'builder of huts').

Vars.: **Hit(t)ler; Hidler** (see also HIEDL); **Hütter** (topographic only).

Hutton English and Scots: habitation name from any of the numerous places so called from OE *hōh* ridge, spur + *tūn* enclosure, settlement.

Vars.: **Houton; Hoghton** (a place in Lancs.). See also HOUGHTON and HUFFTON.

A landowning family by the name of Hutton *can be traced back to the 12th cent. at Hutton in Leyland Hundred, Lancs.*

Huxley English: habitation name from a place in Ches., which is probably so called from the gen. case of the OE personal name *Hucc* or from the OE vocab. word *husc, hux* insult, taunt + *lēah* wood, clearing.

Huyton English (Lancs.): habitation name from a place near Liverpool, so called from OE *hȳð* landing place + *tūn* enclosure, settlement.

Hyam 1. Jewish (Ashkenazic): from the Yid. male given name *Khayim* (from Hebr. *chayim* life).

2. English: var. of HIGHAM.

Vars. (of 1): **Hyman, Hay(e)m, Hai(e)m, Hayim, Hey(e)m, He(y)im; Chaim**.

Patrs. (from 1): **Hyams, Chaimso(h)n; Haimovich, Khaimovich** (E Ashkenazic).

Hyde English: 1. topographic name for someone living on (and farming) a place originally named as being a hide of land, OE *hī(gi)d*. This was quite a large amount, varying at different times and places between 60 and 120 acres, and seems from the etymology to have been originally fixed as the amount necessary to support one (extended) family (OE *hīgan, hīwan* household; cf. HIND).

2. var. of IDE, with inorganic initial *H-*; cf. HERRICK.

Var.: **Hide**.

Hyland 1. English: topographic name for someone who lived on a patch of high ground, from ME *hegh, hie* HIGH + *land* land (OE *land*); cf. HOOGLAND.

2. Irish: var. of WHEELAN.

Vars. (of 1): **Highland, Hylands**.

Hyner English (Suffolk): of uncertain origin, possibly an occupational name for a peasant or agricultural labourer, a var. of HINE, with the addition of the ME agent suffix *-er*.

Var.: **Hiner**.

The earliest known bearer of the name is Philip Hyner, *who was married on 25 July 1608 at Mildenhall, Suffolk. The name seems to have originated somewhere on the Cambs./Suffolk border.*

Hynes 1. Irish: Anglicized form of Gael. **Ó hEidhin** 'descendant of *Eidhin*', a personal name or byname of uncertain origin. It may be a deriv. of *eidhean* ivy, or it may represent an altered form of the placename *Aidhne*. The principal family of this name are descended from Guaire of Aidhne, King of Connacht. From the 7th cent. they provided chiefs of a territory in Galway for over a thousand years.

2. English: patr. from HINE.

Vars.: **Hines**. (Of 1 only): **O'Heyne**, **Heynes** (see also HAINES).

I

Ibarra Basque: habitation name from any of several places in the Basque country, so called from *ibar* meadow + the def. art. *-a*.

Ibarruri Basque: habitation name from a place in the province of Biscay, so called from *ibar* meadow + *uri* settlement, village.

Iddon English (Lancs.): from the ON female personal name *Idunn*, *Iðuna*, probably composed of the elements *iðja* to work, do, perform (cf. IDE) + *unna* to love. The name is often recorded in the L form *Idonea*, as a result of folk etymological association with the fem. form of L *idoneus* suitable.

Dim.: **Innett**.

Metrs.: **Iddins, Iddison; Ineson** (Yorks.).

Ide English and Low German: from the Gmc personal name *Ida* (from the element *id* to work, do, perform; cf. IDDON), which was used for both men and women. It was popular among the Normans and to some degree was taken up in England. It remained in favour until at least the mid-14th cent., but then died out, to be revived in the 19th cent., perhaps because it sounds like a L or Gk name. (In actual fact, the Gk name *Ida* is that of a mountain, not a woman.) There may also have been an OE male personal name from the same stem, and this could have contributed to the surname. There is a place called *Ide* (pronounced /i:d/) near Exeter in Devon; the etymology is obscure, perhaps from a river name; it does not seem to have given rise to a surname.

Vars.: Eng.: HYDE. Low Ger.: **Ihde**.

Cogn.: Ger.: **Itt**.

Dim.: Eng.: **Ikin**.

Patrs./Metrs.: Eng.: **I(de)son, Izon**. Ger.: **It(t)ensohn, Idtensohn**. Low Ger.: **I(h)den, Iding**.

Idle 1. English: habitation name from a place in W Yorks., perhaps named with a deriv. of OE *īdel* unused ground, patch of waste land.

2. English: nickname for a lazy person, from ME *idle* idle, indolent (OE *īdel*).

3. English: var. of ISLES.

4. Welsh: from the OW personal name *Ithel*; cf. JEKYLL.

Vars.: **Idel(l)**. (Of 4 only): **Ithell**.

Cogn. (of 2): Ger.: EITEL.

Igel German: nickname from Ger. *Igel* hedgehog (OHG *igil*), given perhaps to a prickly or unapproachable person. There is a place near Trier called *Igel*, but it does not seem to have contributed to the surname. The surname is also borne by Ashkenazic Jews, in which case it is probably one of the unflattering surnames bestowed on Jews by non-Jewish government officials in 18th- and 19th-cent. central Europe.

Cogn.: Flem.: **Deghel**.

Cpds (ornamental): Jewish: **Igelberg** ('hedgehog hill'); **Igelfeld** ('hedgehog field').

Ignace French: from a medieval given name (L *Egnatius*, a Roman family name of uncertain, probably Etruscan, etymology). The spelling *Ignatius* appeared in the early Christian era, partly due to folk etymological associations with L *ignis* fire. In this form the name was borne by an early bishop of Antioch who was martyred at Rome under Trajan. As a given name it was not common in the Middle Ages, and the surname is correspondingly infrequent. Its comparative popularity in Catholic countries today is due to the fame of St Ignatius Loyola (Iñigo Yáñez de Oñaz y Loyola, 1491–1556), founder of the Society of Jesus (Jesuits).

Cogns.: Sp.: **Iñigo**. Port.: **Inácio**. Ger.: **Igna(t)z; Na(a)tz**. Czech: **Hnát**. Hung.: **Ignác(z)**.

Dims.: Ukr.: **Hnatyuk, Hnatik**. Beloruss.: **Ihnazenya, Ihnatchik**. Czech: **Hnátek**.

Patrs.: Sp.: **Iñíguez**. Russ.: **Ignatov** (also Jewish (E Ashkenazic), an adoption of the Russ. surname); **Ignatyev**. Ukr.: **Hnatovich**. Pol.: **Ignatowicz, Nacewicz; Ignaczak**. Croatian: **Ignjatović**. Gk: **Ignatides**.

Patrs. (from dims.): Russ.: **Igna(sh)ev, Igoshin, Igonin**.

Habitation names: Pol.: **Ignatowski, Gnatowski**.

Ignoto Italian: nickname for a foundling or bastard, from It. *ignoto* unknown, unacknowledged, i.e. child of an unknown father or unacknowledged by its father (L *ignōtus*, from *in-* not + *(g)nōtus*, past part. of *(g)noscere* to know, acknowledge). The surname is especially common in Sicily.

Var.: **Ignoti**.

Igolkin Russian: patr. from the nickname *Igolka* 'Little Needle' (a dim. of *igla* needle), referring to a tall, thin person or someone with a spiteful tongue.

Cogn.: Pol.: **Igielski**.

Ikonnikov Russian: patr. from the occupational term *ikonnik* icon painter (a deriv. of *ikona* ikon, Gk *eikōn* image, from *eikein* to resemble). Icon painting was a common occupation in Orthodox Christian countries, especially Russia, where every church and every devout family possessed images of Christ, the Virgin Mary, and popular saints.

Illingworth English: habitation name from a place in W Yorks. near Halifax, so called from OE *Illingworð* 'enclosure (see WORTH) associated with *Illa*' (a personal name from a short form of the various cpd names with the first element *hild* battle, strife; cf. ILSLEY).

Ilsley English: habitation name from the villages of E and W *Ilsley* on the Berks. Downs, so called from the gen. case of the OE personal name *Hild* (a short form of any of the various cpd names with the first element *hild* battle, strife) + OE *lēah* wood, clearing.

Imber 1. English: habitation name from places in Surrey and Wilts. The former (also called *Ember*) gets the name from the OE personal name *Imma* (see IMM) + OE *worð* enclosure (see WORTH), the latter from the same personal name + OE *mere* lake, pond (see DELAMARE).

2. Jewish (Ashkenazic): var. of INGBER, from Yid. *imber* ginger.

Imbrogno Italian: nickname for a muddled or confused person, from a deriv. of It. *imbrogliare* to confuse, embroil (cf. BREUIL).

Imm English: from the ME given name *Imma*, *Emma*, a short form of any of various cpd Gmc personal names with the first element *irmin*, *ermen* whole, entire (apparently originally the name of a Gmc demigod). The most famous bearer of the name *Imma* in the OE period was the wife of King Canute, who had previously been married to Ethelred. In the early Middle Ages it was often used as a male personal name (cf. IMBER) as well as a female one, but later, under Norman influence, it came to be used almost exclusively for women, being taken as a short form of *Ermingard*.

Metrs.: **Im(m)s**.

Immer German: habitation name from a place in Austria, apparently so called from a river name of obscure origin; there is no connection with Ger. *immer* always.

Var.: **Immermann**.

Impey English: habitation name from any of various minor places named with the OE elements *imp* young tree, sapling + *(ge)hæg* or *haga* enclosure (see HAY 1 and HAIG).

Var.: **Impy**.

Ince English: habitation name from places in Lancs. and Ches., so called from a Brit. word corresponding to W *ynys* island, strip of land between two rivers (cf. INNES).

Inchausti Spanish form of Basque **Intxausti**: topographic name for someone who lived by a grove of walnut trees, from Basque *intxaur* walnut + *-ti*, suffix of abundance.

Var.: **Incháustegui**.

Inchbald English: from a Gmc personal name composed of the elements *Ingel*, *Engel* (see ENGEL 1) + *bald* brave, bold, which was introduced into England by the Normans in the form *Inge(l)bald*.

Infante Italian and Spanish: nickname for someone of childish (or childlike) disposition, from It., Sp. *infante* child (L *infans*, gen. *infantis*, from *in-* not + *fāri* to speak). This was also a title borne in medieval Spain by the eldest sons of noblemen before they inherited, and in particular by the son of the king of Castille, and so in Spain the surname may also have originated as a nickname for one of a lordly disposition or as an occupational name for a member of the household of an infante. The Fr. cogn. has the senses 'boy',' servant', and 'foot soldier'.

Vars.: It.: **Fante, Fanti; Fant** (Venetia). Sp.: **Infantes**.

Cogns.: Fr.: **Enfant, Lenfant**. Eng. (Norman): **Fa(u)nt, Vant**. Ger.: **Fend(t)**.

Dims.: It.: **Fantino, Fantin(ell)i, Fantocci, Fantozzi, Fantucci, Fantuzzi; Fancello, Fanciullo, Fanciulli** (Tuscany); **Infant(ol)ino** (Palermo). Fr.: **Enfantin, Fantin, Fanton**. Prov.: **Fanty, Fantou**. Ger.: **Fendel**.

Augs.: It.: **Fantone, Fanton(i)**.

Pejs.: It.: **Fantacci, Fantazzi**.

Patrs.: It.: **Del Fante** (N Italy); **De Fant** (Trentino). Eng.: **Fantes**.

Ing English: 1. from the OE personal name *Ing(a)*, a short form of any of several cpd names with the first element *ing*; cf. INGER 1, INGLE 1, and INGRAM 2. This element is of uncertain origin; it was the name of a minor Norse god associated with fertility, and may be from a Gmc root meaning 'swelling', 'protuberance'.

2. habitation name from a place in Essex, recorded in Domesday Book as *Inga* and *Ginga*, apparently from an OE tribal name **Gigingas* 'people of **Giga*', a personal name of uncertain etymology, but paralleled on the Continent.

Var.: **Inge**.

Patr. (from 1): **Ings**.

Ingber German and Jewish (Ashkenazic): metonymic occupational name for a spicer, from Ger. *Ingwer* ginger, MHG *ingeber*, *ingewer* (OHG *gingiber(o)*, from OF *gingebre*; the word is ultimately, like the spice, of Oriental origin).

Vars.: Jewish (Ashkenazic): **Ingbar, Ingberman; Ingberg** (altered under the influence of the many Jewish ornamental surnames ending in *-berg* hill); IMBER, **Inber, Imberman**.

Inger 1. English (Notts.): from the ON personal name *Ingvarr*, composed of the elements *ing* (see ING 1) + *varr* guard.

2. Jewish (Ashkenazic): probably from the NE Yid. pronunciation of Yid. *yinger* younger, a name taken by a younger son.

3. Jewish (Ashkenazic): perhaps also a var. of HUNGER 3.

Vars. (of 1): **Inker** (Somerset). (Of 2 and 3): **Ingerman**.

Cogns. (of 1): Low Ger. **Ingward, Ingwer**.

Patrs. (from 1): Eng.: **Inkerson**. Low Ger.: **Ingwers, Engwers, Ingwer(t)sen**.

Ingham English (chiefly Yorks. and Lancs.): 1. habitation name from any of several places so called, of which the largest are in Lincs., Norfolk, and Suffolk. The placename is from the OE personal name *Inga* (see ING 1) + OE *hām* homestead.

2. nickname for a crafty or ingenious person, from OF *engaine*; see GAIN.

Ingle English: 1. from the ON personal name *Ingialdr*, composed of the elements *ing* (see ING 1) + *gialdr* tribute. This name has become confused with the rarer *Ingólfr*, in which the second element is from *úlfr* wolf.

2. habitation name from *Ingol* in Lancs., so called from the OE personal name *Inga* (see ING 1) + OE *holh* hollow, depression.

Vars. (of 1): **Ingold, Ingall, Hingle**.

Patrs. (from 1): **Ingles(on)**.

Ingleby English: habitation name from one of the places, in N Yorks., Derbys., and Lincs., so called from ON *Englabýr* 'settlement (ON *býr*) of the English'.

Ingoldsby 1. English: habitation name from a place in Lincs., so called from the gen. case of the ON personal name *Ingjaldr* (see INGLE 1) + ON *býr* settlement, village.

2. Irish: see GOLIGHTLY.

Ingram English: 1. from a Gmc personal name composed of the ethnic name *Engil* (see ENGEL 1) + *hraban* raven, which was introduced into England by the Normans in the form *Eng(u)erran*.

2. from a Gmc personal name composed of the divine name *Ing* (see ING 1) + *hraban*. This was introduced into England by the Normans, and was reinforced by the ON cogn. *Ingrafn*.

Patr.: **Ingrams**.

Ingres French: of uncertain origin. It may be a nickname from OF *haingre* thin, scrawny (of Gmc origin, probably a cogn. of mod. Eng. *hungry*). The surname is found mostly in SE France.

Inkersall English: habitation name from a place in Derbys., recorded in the 13th cent. as *Hinkershil(l)* and

Hinkreshill. The final element is clearly OE *hyll* HILL; the first may be the ON personal name *Ingvarr* (see INGER) or an OE byname meaning 'Limper' (cf. HINCHCLIFFE and HINCKLEY). Ekwall suggests that it may represent a contracted version of OE *hīgna æcer* monks' field (cf. HINE and ACKER).

Vars.: **Ingersoll, Inkersole, Ingsole.**

Inman English: occupational name for a keeper of a lodging house, ME *innmann*, from OE *inn* abode, lodging + *mann* man. To this day there remains in English a technical distinction between an inn, where lodgings are available as well as alcoholic beverages, and a tavern, which offers only the latter.

Innes Scots: 1. habitation name from a barony in the former county of Moray (now part of Grampian region), so called from Gael. *inis* island, esp. in a river, or piece of land between two rivers.

2. var. of ANGUS.

Vars.: **Inness, Innis(s), Inns.**

Cogns. (of 1): Ir., Manx: **Ennis, Inch.** Corn.: **Ninnis** (with fused *an*, Corn. def. article); **Enys**; **Inch.** Bret.: **Inizan.**

The surname Innes *is particularly associated with the barony of Innes in Urquhart, Scotland, where the earliest known bearer is Walter* de Ineys, *living in 1226*.

The earliest known bearer of the name Inch *is Richard* Ynch, *recorded in 1406 at Lanowe (now St Kew) in NE Cornwall. An approximate contemporary is Sir William Inch, recorded as a parson on the Isle of Man in 1419*.

Innocenti Italian: nickname meaning 'innocent' (L *innocens*, from *in-* not + *nocens*, pres. part. of *nocēre* to hurt, harm) and often bestowed on a simpleton, following the Christian notion that simpletons, like children, were incapable of doing evil. The surname is found principally in Tuscany and neighbouring regions and is extremely common in Florence, where it was given as a surname to all foundlings received into the *Spedale degli Innocenti*, an orphanage established in the 15th cent. Occasionally the surname may derive from a given name, borne by a 4th-cent. bishop of Tortona, several popes from the 5th cent. onwards, and a 6th-cent. bishop of Le Mans.

Var.: **Nocenti** (an aphetic form).

Dims.: **Innocentini, Nocentini, Nocentino.** Hung.: **Inc(z)e.**

Inskip English: habitation name from a place in Lancs., the etymology of which is uncertain; the first element has been tentatively connected with W *ynys* island (cf. INCE) and the second with OE *cȳpe* osier basket (for catching fish).

Vars.: **Inskipp, Inskeep.**

Insley English (Midlands): habitation name from an unidentified place, of which the second element is most probably OE *lēah* wood, clearing; the first may be from the gen. case of the OE personal name *Ing* (see ING 1).

Instone English (W Midlands): habitation name from *Innerstone* in Worcs., so called from the gen. case of an OE personal name cogn. with ISNARD + OE *tūn* enclosure, settlement.

Inverarity Scots: habitation name from a place near Forfar, first recorded in 1250 as *Inuerarethin*. The first element is Gael. *inbhir* river-mouth, confluence; the second may be from a Brit. river name originally meaning 'slow'.

Irby English: habitation name from any of various places, in Lincs., Ches., and N Yorks., so called from ON *Írabýr* 'settlement of the Irish'; cf. IRETON.

Var.: **Ireby** (places in Cumb. and Lancs.).

Irby *is the family name of the Barons Boston, derived from Irby-in-Humber, Lincs*.

Iredale English: habitation name from a lost hamlet in Cumb., so called from ON *Íradalr* 'valley (see DALE) of the Irish'. The surname is recorded from the 16th cent.; until recently it was found almost exclusively in the surrounding area.

Var.: **Iredell.**

Ireland English and Scots: ethnic name for someone from *Ireland*, OE *Īraland*, so called from the gen. case of *Īras* Irishmen + *land* land, territory. The stem *Īr-* is taken from the Celt. name for Ireland, *Ériu*, earlier *Everiu*, of uncertain origin. The surname is especially common in Liverpool.

Var.: **Irish.**

Cogns.: Fr.: **Irois, Yrois, Hirois, Hyrois.**

Ireton English: habitation name from either of two places in Derbys. called *Ireton*, or one in N Yorks. called *Irton*, all from the gen. case of OE *Īras* Irishmen (see IRELAND) + OE *tūn* enclosure, settlement.

2. habitation name from *Irton* in Cumb., so called from the old river name *Irt*, of uncertain origin + OE *tūn* enclosure, settlement.

Var.: **Irton.**

Irigoyen Spanish, from Basque: habitation name from a place named as being a village on the top of a hill, from *iri* settlement, village + *goien* highest point, summit.

Irisov Russian: 1. patr. from the male given name *Iris*, a familiar form of *Irinei* or *Irinarkh*. The former is derived from Gk *Eirēnaios* 'Peaceful', a name borne by a 2nd-cent. bishop of Lyons; the latter comes from Gk *Eirēnarkhos* (composed of the elements *eirēnē* peace + *arkhē* beginning, rule).

2. surname adopted by Orthodox priests, from *iris* iris (the flower) (Gk *iris* (goddess of) the rainbow). The ending *-ov* was added to give the appearance of a surname of the usual Russ. patr. type.

Ironmonger English: occupational name for a trader in iron goods, ME *irenmongere*, from OE *īren* iron + *mangere* dealer, trader. Dealers in iron played an important role in the medieval economy, before the advent of cheap mass-production of steel.

Vars.: **Iremonger**; **Icemonger, Isemonger** (with the first element from the Kentish form *isern*); **Ernmonger, Yernmonger** (with the first element from the cogn. ON *earn, jarn*).

Cogn.: Ger.: **Eisenmenger** (see also EISEN).

Equiv.: Ukr.: ZALIZNYAK.

Irons English (Norman): habitation name from *Airaines* in Somme, so called from L *harēnas* (acc. case) sands. The form of the name has been altered as a result of folk etymology, associating the name with the metal.

Ironside 1. English: from ME *irenside* (a cpd of OE *īren* iron + *sīde* side), a nickname for an iron-clad warrior. The best-known bearer of this nickname (though not, of course, as a surname) was Edmund Ironside, who was briefly king of England in 1016.

2. Scots: habitation name from a place in the parish of New Deer in the former county of Aberdeens. This was probably originally named with the OE elements *earn* eagle + *sīde* side (of a hill).

Irrgang German: unflattering nickname for an impatient person or a foolish one, from MHG *irreganc* restless wandering or Ger. *Irrgang* blind alley (a cpd of MHG *irre* mad, aimless (OHG *irri*) + *ganc* going (OHG *gang*)).

Cogns.: Low Ger.: **Ergang**. Jewish (Ashkenazic): **Irgang** (apparently one of the unflattering names assigned to Jews by non-Jewish government officials in 18th- and 19th-cent. central Europe).

Irvine 1. Scots: habitation name from *Irvine* in Strathclyde, or from *Irving* in Dumfries and Galloway region. The two names have become confused and are impossible to disentangle. Both are derived from a Celt. river name probably composed of elements cogn. with W *ir*, *yr* green, fresh + *afon* water.

2. English: from the ME given name *Irwyn*, *Erwyn*, *Everwyn*, OE *Eoforwine*, composed of the elements *eofor* wild boar + *wine* friend.

3. Irish: Anglicized form of Gael. **Ó hEireamhóin** 'descendant of *Eireamhón*', a personal name of uncertain origin. See also CURWEN and HORAN.

Vars.: **Irvin, Ervin(e), Urvine; Irving, Erving**. (Of 2 only): **Irwin(e), Irwing, E(ve)rwin; Urwin** (Northumb.). (Of 3 only): **O'Hirwen**.

Cogns. (of 2): Ger.: **Eberwein; Erwin** (also borne by Jews, an adoption of the Ger. surname).

There are two major Scottish families called Irvine. *They share a common ancestor, Duncan, known as 'the first of* Eryvine'. *He was killed at the battle of Duncrub in 965. They are said to be of Irish origin, descended from Cineal Conaill, a member of the O'Neill clan.*

A branch of the Irvine family was re-established in Ireland, where they built Castle Irvine in Co. Fermanagh. Members of this family later went on to settle in America, including the brothers William (d. 1804), Andrew (d. 1789), and Matthew Irvine (d. 1827), who all served in the American Revolution. The forms Irwin *and* Irvine *are now as common in N Ireland as in Scotland.*

Isaac Jewish, French, and English: from the Hebr. male given name *Yitschak*, a deriv. of *tsachak* to laugh. This was the name of the son of Abraham (Gen. 21: 3); the traditional explanation of the name is that Abraham and Sarah laughed with joy at the birth of a son to them in their old age, but a more plausible explanation is that the name originally meant 'may God laugh', i.e. 'smile on him'. Like ABRAHAM, this name has always been immensely popular among Jews and was also widely used in medieval Europe among Christians. Hence it is the surname of many gentile families. In E Europe the given name was popular in both Orthodox (Russ., Ukr., and Bulg.) and Catholic (Pol. and Czech) Churches. The name was borne by a 5th-cent. father of the Armenian Church and by a Sp. saint martyred by the Moorish rulers of Cordoba in AD 851 on account of his polemics against Islam.

Vars.: Jewish: **Isac, Isa(a)k, Issac, Issak, Izac, Izak, Itshak, Itz(c)hak, Itzhai(e)k, I(t)zhayek, Izhak, Ishak, Izsak, Jzak, Yitshak, Yi(t)zhak, Yitzhok; Eisik, Eisig, Aizik, Aizic, Aysik, Ajsik** (from *Ayzik*, one of the Yid. forms of the given name); **Is(h)aki, Iz(c)haki, Izhaky, Yitschaky, Yitshaki, Yitzchaki, Yi(t)zhaki, Yitzhaky, J(i)zhaki, Itz(c)haki, Itz(c)haky** (with the Hebr. adj. suffix *-i*).

Cogns.: Du., Flem.: **Isacq, Izaac**. ung.: **Izsák**.

Dims.: Jewish (Ashkenazic): **Itzik, Itzig** (from the Yid. dim. *Itsik*). Fr.: **Haquin**. Russ.: **Izachik**. Ukr.: **Izachenko**.

Patrs.: Jewish: **Isaacs, Izaks; Isaacson, Isaaksohn, Is(s)acson, Isakson, I(t)zakson; Is(s)akov, Is(s)acov, Izakov, Izacov, Isakof(f), Issacof, Isacoff, Yitzhakov, Yitzhakof, Itschakov, Izhakov, Jzhakov, Izikov, Itzkov, Ickov, Iskow, Isakower, Izakowicz, Isakowitz, I(t)zakovitz, Izikovitz, Isakovitch, Itzkowicz, Itzkowitz, Itzkovi(t)ch, Itzkowitch, Itzcovich, Itskovitz, Itscovitz, Ickowicz, Ickowics, Ickovicz, Ickovitz, Ickovits, Ickovic, Iczkovitz, Iczkovits, Yitzkowitz, Yitzkovitz, Yitzkovicz, Izkovitch, Izkovicz, Izkovitz, Iskowitz, Iscowitz** (all E Ashkenazic); **Eisikowitz, Eisikowitch, Aizikovitch, Aizicovitch, Aizikowicz, Aizikovitz, Aiskowitz, Eiskovitsh** (E Ashkenazic, based on Yid. *Ayzik*); **I(t)zkovici, Ickovici** (Rumanian spellings); **Itzkovsky, Izkoveski; Itzkin**. Russ.: **Aizikov(ich)**. Bulg.: **Isakov**. Croatian: **Isaković**. Eng.: **Isaacs, Isa(a)cson**. Sc., Ir.: **McIsaac, McKis(s)ack**. Manx: **Kissack, Kissock**. Welsh: **Bissex**. Dan., Norw.: **Isaksen**. Swed.: **Isaksson, Isacsson**.

Patrs. (from dims.): Jewish (Ashkenazic): **Itzikson, Itzigsohn, Izygson, Icigson** (based on Yid. *Itsik*). Russ.: **Isachkov**. Pol.: **Iszczak**.

Isambert French: from a Gmc personal name in which the first element probably represents *īsan* iron, but could also be an extended form of *īs* ice; the second element is *berht* bright, famous.

Vars.: **Isembert, Isambard**.

Cogns.: Ger.: **Isbrecht**. Low Ger.: **Isbert; Eisenbart** (altered by folk etymology as if derived from 'iron beard').

Isasi Basque: of uncertain origin, partly due to the lack of distinction in Castilian spelling between the Basque sibilants *s* and *ts*. The name appears to come from *isasi* arum lily (a dialect word confined to the Biscay area), but it may also be from *isats* broom (the plant and the implement).

Isern Catalan: from a Gmc (probably Visigothic) personal name derived from the element *īsarn* iron.

Cogns.: Prov.: **Isarn, Izarn**.

Isherwood English (Lancs.): habitation name from a lost place in the parish of Bolton-le-Moors. The name is first found in Lancs. records in the 13th cent. and is still largely confined to that area.

Vars.: **Esherwood, Usherwood**.

The family of the novelist Christopher Isherwood *(1904–86) were landowners in Ches. since the 16th cent. One of his ancestors was president of the court which condemned Charles I to death.*

Isidore French: from a medieval given name (Gk *Isidōros*, from *Isis*, the name (of uncertain etymology) of an originally Egyptian goddess + *dōron* gift). The name has never been common among non-Jews in W Europe; in E Europe it has been more popular, as it was borne by three saints of the 3rd to 5th cents. much venerated in the Orthodox Church.

Vars: **Isidor**.

Cogns.: Sp., Port.: **Isid(o)ro**. Low Ger.: **Dörries, Dörges**. Pol.: **Sidor(ski)**.

Dims.: Pol.: **Izydorczyk; Sidorczyk**. Ukr.: **Sidorenko**. Beloruss.: **Sidorchik**.

Patrs.: Pol.: **Sidorowicz**. Russ.: **Sidorov, Sidorin**.

Patrs. (from dims.): Russ.: **Sidorkov, Sidorshin**.

'Son of the daughter of I.': Russ.: **Sidorovnin**.

Isles English: topographic or habitation name from ANF *isle*, *idle* island (OF *isel*, L *insula*). As this is a Norman French word, the island in question is more likely to have been in N France than anywhere in Britain.

Vars.: **Iles** (now found mainly in Gloucs.), **Illes; Eyles**; IDLE, LISLE.

Islip English: habitation name from places in Northants and Oxon. The former (*Islep* in Domesday Book) is so called from the Brit. river name *Ise*, which originally seems to have meant no more than 'water' + OE *slǣp* slipway, slippery place; the latter (*Ichteslep* in ME, *Gihtslepe* in OE) shares the same second element, but is preceded by a different river name, namely *Ight*, which is probably akin to W *iaith* language, perhaps with the sense 'Chattering'.

Isnard French: from a Gmc personal name composed of the elements *īsan* iron (or ice; cf. ISAMBERT) + *hard* brave, hardy, strong, which acquired some currency in medieval Europe as it was borne by a minor Bavarian saint of the 7th cent. and by a 13th-cent. Italian monk who founded the friary at Pavia.

Cogns.: Ger.: **Eisenhar(d)t**.

Israel Jewish: from the Hebr. male given name *Yisrael* 'Fighter of God', in the Bible a byname bestowed on Jacob after he had wrestled with the angel at the ford of Jabbok (Gen. 32: 24–8). See also ISRAELER.

Vars.: **Izrael**; **Yisrael**; **Israelski**; **Is(s)er** (Yid. form); **Srol** (NE Yid. aphetic form); **Srul** (S Yid. aphetic form).

Dim.: **Isserl**.

Patrs.: **Israels(on)**, **Israelov**, **Israelow**, **Israeloff**, **Isrelof(f)**; **Israelovi(t)ch**, **Israelevitch**, **Israelowicz**, **Israelewicz**, **Israelowitz**, **Israelovitz**, **Israelewitz**, **Israelevitz**; **Israelovici** (Rumanian spelling); **Israelashvili** (among Georgian Jews); **Disraeli** (among Italian Jews); **Srolov**, **Sroloff**, **Srulov**, **Srolovitz**, **Srulovich**, **Srulovitz**, **Srulowitz**, **Srulevich**, **Srulewitch**; **Srulovici** (a Rumanian spelling); **Isserso(h)n**, **Iserson**, **Isseroff**, **Iserovich**.

Patrs. (from dims.): **Srulikov**; **Is(s)erles**, **Iserlis**, **Isserlin**.

Israeler Jewish: name adopted with reference to the ancient Kingdom of Israel, destroyed by the Assyrians in 721 BC, or to the concept of Jewish nationhood, or, in modern times, to the state of Israel.

Vars.: **Izraeler**; **Israeli**, **Israely**, **Izraeli**, **Izraely**, **Izreeli**, **Isreeli**, **Yisraeli**, **Yisraely** (with the Hebr. adj suffix *-i*; also derivable from the given name ISRAEL); **Israelit(h)**, **Yisraelit** (with the Hebr. fem. adj. suffix *-it*, but not necessarily fem. in meaning).

Ittelson Jewish (Ashkenazic): metr. from the Yid. female given name *Itl*, a dim. of *Ite*, from the Yid. female given name *Yudes* (from Hebr. *Yehudit* Judith, 'Jewess').

Vars.: **Itelson**; **Itkin** (E Ashkenazic, based on *Itke*, an E yid. dim. of *Ite*).

Iturbe Basque: topographic name for someone who lived downstream from a spring, from *iturri* spring + the local suffix *-be*, meaning 'lower down'.

Ive English: from the Norman personal name *Ivo*, in origin a short form of any of the various Gmc cpd names with a first element *īv* (ON *ýr*, pl. *ifar*) yew, bow (a weapon generally made from the supple wood of the yew tree). This was a popular name in Normandy and Brittany, and was introduced into England at the time of the Conquest, perhaps reinforcing OE *Ifa*, *Iva*. There was a bishop of Chartres called St Ivo (d. 1115), and a 13th-cent. Bret. saint of this name came to be recognized as the patron of lawyers. St Ives in Cambs. gets its name from a church dedicated to a legendary Persian bishop who is said to have become a hermit there. The more famous *St Ives* in Cornwall is named from a 5th-cent. female Ir. saint more accurately known as *Ia*. Yet another *St Ives*, in Hants, did not originally commemorate a saint at all but is named from a deriv. of OE *īfig* ivy.

Var.: IVEY.

Cogns.: Fr.: **Yve(s)**; **Yvon**, **Yven**, **Iva(i)n** (from the oblique case). It.: **Ivi**; **Ivone**. Ger.: **Erbe**. Fris.: **Iwe**.

Dims.: Eng.: **Ivatt**. Fr.: **Yvelin**, **Ivelain**; **Ivonnet**, **Yvonnet**; **Yvonou**, **Yvenec** (Brittany).

Patrs.: **Ives**; **Iveson**, **Ivison**. Fr.: **Abivon** (Brittany). Ger.: **Iven(s)**, **Iwen**, **Iben(s)**.

Ivey English (Devon): 1. var. of IVE.

2. Norman habitation name from *Ivoy* in Cher, so called from OF *ivoie*, a collective from *if* yew tree (of Gmc or Celt. origin).

Vars.: **Ivy**, **Ivie**.

Ivolgin Russian: patr. from the nickname *Ivolga* 'Oriole', given perhaps in admiration for a fine singing voice or with some reference to the striking yellow and black plumage of the bird.

Ivor British: from the ON personal name *Ivarr*, of uncertain origin, probably from *īw* yew, bow (see IVE) + *herr* army. The given name was adopted at an early date by the Irish, Scots, and Welsh, much later and more rarely by the English. Many bearers of the modern surname are therefore of Celt. ancestry.

Patrs.: **Ivers(on)**. Sc., Ir.: **MacIvor**, **McIver**, **McEevor**, **McEever**, **McHeever**, **McCure**. Dan., Norw.: **Iversen**. Swed.: **Ivarsson**, **Iwarsson**. Fris.: **Ivers**, **Iwers**; **Ywersen**.

Ivory English (Norman): habitation name from *Ivry*-la-Bataille in Eure, so called from the Gallo-Roman personal name *Eburius* (a deriv. of L *ebur* ivory) + the local suffix *-ācum*.

Var.: **Ivery**.

Ivushkin Russian: 1. patr. from the given name *Ivushka*, a dim. of *Ivan*; see JOHN.

2. patr. from the nickname *Ivushka*, a dim. of *iva* willow (which has itself given rise to the surname **Ivin**), perhaps denoting a pliant individual or a topographic name for someone who lived by a willow tree.

Izaguirre Spanish form of Basque **Izagirre**, probably a var. of **Aizagirre**, topographic name for someone who lived in a place exposed to the wind, from Basque *aize* wind + *ager*, *agir* visible, exposed.

Izard 1. English and French: from a Gmc female personal name composed of the elements *īs* ice + *hild* battle, strife, introduced into England by the Normans in the forms *Iseu(l)t*, *Isolde*. The popularity of the various versions of the legend of Tristan and Isolde led to widespread use of the given name in the Middle Ages.

2. French: from *Ishard*, a Gmc male personal name composed of the elements *īs* ice + *hard* hardy, brave, strong; cf. ISNARD.

3. Provençal: nickname for an agile and sure-footed climber, from OProv. (*bouc*) *izar* mountain goat (apparently of pre-Roman origin).

Vars. (of 1): Eng.: **Izzard**, **Izzett**, **Izat(t)**, **Is(s)ard**, **Issett**, **Issit(t)**, **Isso(l)t**.

Cogns. (of 1): It.: **Isoldi**, **Isotti**; **Soldi**, **Sotti**. Ger.: **Eisold(e)**, **Eiselt**.

Izdebski Polish: topographic name for someone who lived in a small, isolated dwelling, from Pol. *izdebka* chamber, cell + *-ski* suffix of local surnames (see BARANOWSKI).

Izquierdo Spanish: nickname for a left-handed man, from Sp. *izquierdo* left (a word of pre-Roman origin, akin to Basque *ezker*).

J

Jabłoński Polish: topographic name for someone who lived by an apple tree or apple orchard, or occupational name for a grower or seller of apples, from Pol. *jabłoń* apple tree + *-ski* suffix of local surnames (see BARANOWSKI).

Var.: **Jabłonowski**.

Dims.: **Jabłkowski**; **Jabłonka**.

Cogns.: Russ.: **Yablokov**; **Yablochkov**, **Yablochkin** (dims.). Czech: **Jablon(ec)**. Ger. (of Slav. origin): **Jablonski**, **Gablonz**. Jewish (E Ashkenazic; not clear whether topographic, occupational, or merely ornamental): **Jablon(s)**, **Jablin**, **Yablon**, **Jabloner**, **Yabloner**, **Jablonsky**, **Yablonsky**, **Jablow**, **Yablokov**, **Yablokoff**.

Patr.: Pol.: **Jabłonowicz**.

Patr. (from a dim.): Pol.: **Jabłkiewicz**.

Jabouille French: nickname for a garrulous person, a deriv. of ONF *jaber* to jabber, chatter (apparently from ON and originally meaning 'to open the mouth wide').

Jacek Polish: from a dim. of the given name *Jacenty* (L *Hyacinthus*, Gk *Hyakinthos*). This was the name of a 3rd-cent. saint who was martyred together with his brother Protus. He enjoyed a certain cult in Portugal as well as in Poland. His name, which is almost certainly of pre-Gk origin, in classical times denoted a flower (not the modern hyacinth, but perhaps the martagon lily), and it was borne by a mythological character from whose blood the flower was supposed to have sprung up.

Cogn.: Port.: **Jacinto**.

Patrs.: Pol.: **Jackowicz**, **Jackiewicz**.

Habitation names: Pol.: **Jackowski**, **Jackowiak**; **Jaczewski**.

Jach 1. Polish, Czech, and German (esp. in Slav.-speaking regions): from the given name *Jach*, a dim. of various names beginning with *Ja-*, principally *Jan* (see JOHN), *Jakub* (see JACOB), and, in Pol., *Jacenty* (see JACEK).

2. Jewish (E Ashkenazic): of unknown origin; perhaps an adoption of the non-Jewish surname.

Vars. (of 1): Czech: **Jech**, **Jícha**; **Jač**; **Jaš**, **Ješ**. Ger.: **Jachmann**, **Jochmann**; **Jäch**, **Jach(i)sch**; **Jeche**, **Jecht**, **Jasche**, **Jäsche**, **Jesche**; **Jok(i)sch**, **Jokusch**. (Of 2): **Jachmann**.

Dims. (of 1): Pol.: **Jakowczyk**. Czech: **Jachek**, **Jacháček**; **Jaček**, **Jačka**; **Jašek**, **Jašík**, **Jaška**, **Ješek**. Ger.: **Jaschke**, **Jaschek**, **Jeschke**, **Jeschek**; **Jächel**, **Jächle**; **Jochel**, **Jöchel**; **Jäckl(e)in**, **Jackl**. (Of 2): **Jachel**.

Patrs. (from 1): Pol.: **Jachowicz**. Ger.: **Jachner**, **Jachler**, **Jackner**.

Jack 1. Scots and English: from the OF given name *Jacques*, the usual Fr. form of L *Jacōbus* JACOB.

2. Scots and English: from a pet form of JOHN, probably a borrowing of the Low Ger. and Du. pet forms *Jankin* and *Jackin*, which are from *Jan* (cf. JANE) + the dim. suffix *-kin*. (The loss of the nasal was a regular development in Low Ger.) In English, the ending came to be associated with the more familiar ANF dim. suffix *-in*, which was then omitted to yield *Jack* as a back-formation.

3. Jewish (Ashkenazic): Anglicization of one or more like-sounding Jewish surnames.

Vars. (of 1 and 2): Eng.: **Jake**, **Jagg**. (Of 1 only): Eng.: **Ja(c)ques** (usually pronounced /'dʒeɪkwɪz/); **Jaquith**.

Cogns. (of 1): Welsh: **Iago**. Corn.: **Jago(e)**, **Jeggo** (Anglicized as **Jacka**). Fr.: **Jacque(s)**. Prov.: **Jacq**. It.: **Gia(c)chi**; **Ia(c)chi**; **Zacchi**, **Zacco**. Sp.: **Yagüe**. Ger., Pol.: JACH.

Dims. (of 1): Eng.: **Jackett** (Cornwall); **Jacot**; **Jacklin(g)** (Notts.); **Je(a)cock**. Fr.: **Ja(c)quot**, **Jacot**, **Jaccoud**, **Jaccoux**, **Jac(qu)otin**, **Jac(qu)oton**, **Jac(qu)otet**, **Jac(qu)o(u)tot**; **Ja(c)quel(et)**, **Ja(c)quelot**, **Ja(c)quel(a)in**, **Ja(c)queau**; **Ja(c)quin(el)**, **Jacqui**, **Ja(c)quinet**, **Ja(c)quinot**, **Ja(c)quenet**, **Ja(c)quenot**, **Ja(c)quenod**, **Quinel**, **Quinet**, **Quinot**, **Quineau(x)**, **Quenel**, **Quenot**, **Queneau(x)**. It.: **Gia(c)chini**, **Iacchino**, **Zacchini**, **Giachinotti**; **Giacchello**, **Iachelli**, **Zachelli**; **Giachetti**, **Iachetti**, **Za(c)chetti**, **Ghetti**; **Iac(ch)ini**; **Iacol(l)o**, **Iacoletti**, **Giacoletti**, **Coletti**, **Iacolucci**; **Iaccello**; **Iacucci**, **Cucci**; **Iacuzzi(o)**, **Cuzzi**; **Giacozzi**, **Iacozzo**, **Cozz(in)i**, **Cozzolini**; **Iacotti**.

Augs. (of 1): It.: **Giac(c)one**, **Giac(c)oni**, **Iacone**, **Zaccone**, **Zacconi**, **Zagone**, **Coni**.

Pejs. (of 1): Fr.: **Ja(c)quard**. It.: **Iaccacci**, **Cacci**.

Patrs. (from 1): Eng.: **Jacks**, **Jaggs**, **Jakes**; **Jackson** (very common in all parts of the British Isles); **Jagson**.

Patrs. (from 1) (dims.): Eng.: **Jacketts**, **J(e)akin(g)s**, **Jacocks**, **Jacox**.

Jackman 1. English: occupational name for the servant of someone who bore the given name JACK.

2. English: Anglicized form of Fr. *Jacquème*; see JAMES.

3. Jewish (Ashkenazic): Anglicization of one or more like-sounding Jewish surnames.

Vars.: Eng.: **Jackaman**, **Jakeman**.

Jacob English, Jewish, and Portuguese: via L *Jacōbus* from the Hebr. given name *Yaakov*. In the Bible, this is the name of the younger twin brother of Esau (Gen. 25: 26), who took advantage of the latter's hunger and impetuousness to persuade him to part with his birthright 'for a mess of potage'. The name is traditionally interpreted as coming from Hebr. *akev* heel, and Jacob is said to have been born holding on to Esau's heel. In English *Jacob* and *James* are now regarded as quite distinct names, but they are of identical origin (see JAMES), and in most European languages the two names are not distinguished. For convenience, cognates containing *-m-* are listed at JAMES; cognates lacking the *-ob-* syllable are listed at JACK. The principal forms of the given name in other major European languages are French *Jacques* (see JACK); Italian *Giacobo*, *Giacopo*, and *Iacopo* (also *Giacomo*; see JAMES); Spanish *Jaime* (see JAMES) and DIEGO (which is in fact almost certainly of distinct origin but now generally taken as a form of *Jacob*); German *Jakob*; Polish *Jakub*; and Russian *Yakov*. Throughout Eastern Europe, Jewish forms of the name were extremely common, ranging from *Yaakov* through various derivs., including *Yankev* and *Jankl* (see JANKOFF). Aphetic versions of the given name, dropping the initial *Ja-*, were also once common in central Europe and in Italy, hence many of the derivs. listed below.

Vars.: Eng.: **Jacobb(e)**; **Je(a)cop** (Suffolk). Jewish: **Jakov**, **Yakob**, **Ya(a)kov**; **Jacobi**, **Jacoby** (with the Hebr. adj. suffix *-i*); JANKOFF.

Cogns.: It.: **Giacob(b)o**, **Giacubbo**, **Giacoppo**; **Iacobo**, **Iacopo**, **Iapico**, **Iacovo**, **Iacofo**; COBO, **Cop(p)o**. Ger.: **Jakob**. Flem., Du.: **Kobus**. Pol.: **Jakubski**; **Kobus**, **Kobiera**, **Kobierski**, **Kobierzycki**, **Kobierecki**; **Kubas**, **Kubis(z)**, **Kupis(z)**, **Kubacki**, **Kubicki**; **Kubera**. Czech: **Jakoub(eč)**;

Kubů, K(o)uba; **Kob(a)**, **Kobera**; **Kopa**, **Kopáč**, **Kopal**, **Kubal(a)**, **Kubát**, **Kubec**, **Kubeš**, **Kubín**, **Kubiš**, **Kubišta**; **Kupec** (see also KUPTSOV). Hung.: **Jakab**, **Kabos**.

Dims.: Eng.: COPPING. It.: **Giacobelli**, **Giacop(p)ello**, **Giacovelli**, **Iacobelli**, **Iacovelli**, **Iacoviello**, **Iaci(v)elli**, **Sciacovelli**, **Cobello**, **Cobelli**, **Copello**, **Copelli**, **Cov(i)ello**, **Co(v)elli**; **Giacob(b)ini**, **Giacopini**, **Iacobini**, **Iacopini**, **Iacovino**, **Iacovini**, **Coppini**, **Covino**, **Cubbino**, **Cubinelli**, **Govini**, **Gavini**, **Capin(ett)i**; **Giacopetti**, **Giacovetti**, **Iacobetto**, **Iacopetti**; **Giacobucci**, **Giacobuzzi**, **Iacobucci**, **Iacabucci**, **Iacopucci**, **Iacovucci**, **Iacovuzzi**, **Cubucci**; **Giacoppoli**, **Iacovolo**; **Iacovozzo**, **Copozio**, **Capozzi**; **Giacobillo**, **Billo**; **Covotti**, **Cabotto**, **Cavoto**, **Gabotti**, **Cavozzi**, **Gavozzi**, **Bottin(ell)i**, **Botticelli**; **Covolini**, **Cavolini**, **Bolino**, **Bollini**, **Bolletti**. Ger.: **Köbi**. Low Ger.: **Kob**, **Ko(o)p**, **Kopp(e)**, **Koepp(k)e**, **Köpke**, **Köbke**. Ger. (of Slav. origin): **Joppich**, **Jobke**, **Jopke** (chiefly Silesian); **Huba(ts)ch**, **Hupka** (Wendish); **Kopisch**, **Kob(i)sch**, **Kab(i)sch**, **K(a)ubisch**, **Kuba(ts)ch**, **Kupka**, **Kupke**, **Kubek**, **Kubik**, **Kuban**, **Kubin**; **Kosch(ke)**, **Koschek**, **Kusch(a)**, **Kusch(k)e**, **Kuschel**, **Kuscha(c)k** (see also NICHOLAS). Pol.: **Jakubczyk**; **Kubik**, **Kubiczek**, **Kubyszek**; **Kupka**, **Kupczyk**. Czech: **Jakoubek**, **Koubek**, **Kubík**, **Kubáček**, **Kubíček**, **Kubička**, **Kubečka**; **Kubalek**, **Kubelka**, **Kubánek**, **Kubásek**, **Kupka**; **Kopaček**. Hung.: **Jákó**, **Kubica**. Jewish: **Jekel**, **Yekel** (from the Yid. dim. *Yekl*); **Jok(e)l**, **Yokel**, **Yockelman** (from the Yid. dim. *Yokl*; **Jankel** (see JANKOFF).

Augs.: It.: **Giacoboni**, **Giacoponi**, **Iacoboni**, **Iacovone**, **Iacavone**.

Pejs.: It.: **Giacobazzi**, **Giacopazzi**, **Giacovazzo**, **Iacobacci**, **Iacobassi**, **Iacovazzi**, **Iacovacci(o)**.

Patrs.: Eng.: **Jacobs(on)**. Low Ger.: **Jakobs(en)**. Flem., Du.: **Jacobs(z)**, **Jacobsen**. Dan., Norw.: **Jacobsen**, **Jakobsen**. Swed.: **Jacobsson**, **Jakobsson**. Russ.: **Yakovlev** (from the archaic patr. **Yakovl**, so avoiding *-ovov*); **Yakubov**. Ukr.: **Yakovliv**, **Yakovich**. Beloruss.: **Yakubovich**. Pol.: **Jakubowicz**, **Jakucewicz**, **Kubasiewicz**; **Jakubiak**, **Kubiak**. Croatian: **Jakovljević**, **Jauković**; **Djaković**, **Djok(ov)ić**, **Djek(ov)ić**. Gk: **Iacovides**. Jewish: **Jacobs**, **Jacobso(h)n**, **Yakobso(h)n**; **Jacobskind** ('Jacob's child'); **Yakobov**, **Yakoboff**, **Yakubov**; **Jakubowski**, **Jakubowsky**, **Jakubovski**, **Yakubowski**, **Yakubovsky**; **Jacobovitch**, **Jacobowitz**, **Jacobowits**, **Jacobovitz**, **Jacobovits**; **Jakubowicz**, **Jakubowitz**, **Jakubovitz**, **Jakubovitch**, **Jakubovits**, **Jakubovicz**, **Jakubovics**, **Yakobovi(t)ch**, **Yakobovicz**, **Yakobovitz**, **Yakobowitz**, **Yakobowitch**, **Yakobowitsh**, **Yakubovitch**, **Yakubowitch**, **Yakubowicz**, **Yakubowitz**, **Yakubovitz**, **Yakubovics**; **Jakovlevitch**, **Jakovljevic**.

Patrs. (from dims.): Eng.: **Coppins**, **Coppens**. Low Ger.: **Kob(e)s**, **Kop(p)s**, **Köppen**, **Koppen(s)**. Flem.: **Cops**. Du.: **Coppens**, **Koppen**. Norw., Dan.: **Jep(pe)sen**, **Jessen**. Swed.: **Jepsson**. Pol.: **Jakubczak**, **Kubczak**. Croatian: **Jakšić**. Russ.: **Yashin**, **Yashaev**, **Yash(a)nov**, **Yashunin**; **Yakhnov**, **Yakhnin**; **Yakun(k)in**, **Yakuntzov**, **Yakun(n)ikov**, **Yakunchikov**, **Yakushev**, **Yakush(k)in**, **Yakutin** (these forms are now generally associated with *Yakov*, although in fact they come from an ORuss. given name derived from Scandinavian *Håkon*).

Habitation names: Pol.: **Jakubowski**, **Jakuszewski**.

Jaén Spanish: local name from a city so called in S Spain. The current form represents an alteration, under the influence of Arabic, of earlier *Gaén*, from L *Gaiēnum*, a deriv. of the personal name *Gaius* (see GAY 3).

Jäger German: occupational name for a huntsman, Ger. *Jäger*, agent deriv. of *jagen* to hunt (OHG *jagōn*). The surname has also been Latinized as **Venator**.

Vars.: **Jeger**; **Jager** (Austria).

Cogns.: Du.: **De Jager**, **Jagerman**. Dan.: **Jæger**. Jewish (Ashkenazic): **Jager(man)**, **Jeger**, **Y(a)eger** (it is not clear how the Jewish surnames were acquired, since Ashkenazic Jews were not hunters; perhaps they are simply adoptions of non-Jewish surnames). Russ.: **Yegerlev** (a patr. from *yeger*, borrowed from Ger. as a military term).

Jagger English: occupational name from a word meaning 'pedlar' in the Yorks. dialect, an agent deriv. of ME *jag* pack, load (of unknown origin). All or most present-day bearers of this surname are probably members of a single family, which originally came from Staniland in the parish of Halifax. During the 16th cent. it spread through the Calder valley, and thence to other parts of England.

Patr.: **Jaggers**.

Jagiełło Polish: surname from the princely house of *Jagiełło*, who derived it from Władysław *Jagiełło* (1348–1434), the Lithuanian founder of the dynasty. The Jagiełłos ruled the Kingdom of Poland and the Grand Duchy of Lithuania from 1386 to 1572. The surname in some cases may conceivably indicate genuine descent from a branch of this family, but more often it seems to have been adopted to suggest a connection with them, or in honour of the dynasty and the glorious period of Polish history that they represent.

Vars.: **Jagieła**; **Jagielski**.

Jaglom Jewish (E Ashkenazic): ornamental name from Hebr. *yahalom* diamond; cf. BRILLANT and DIAMOND. The change from *-h-* to *-g-* is due to Russ. influence.

Var.: **Yaglom**.

Jaillet French: topographic name for someone who lived on marshy land, from a dim. of OF *jaille* marsh, mud, now a regional term found mainly in W France. It may also perhaps have been a nickname with the sense 'muddy'; in the Jura the word is applied to a cow with dark patches on its side.

Var.: **Jaillon**.

Pej.: **Jaillard**.

James English: from a given name that has the same origin as JACOB but that is now felt to be a separate name in its own right. This is largely because in the Authorized Version of the Bible (1611) the form *James* is used in the New Testament as the name of two of Christ's apostles (James the brother of John and James the brother of Andrew), whereas in the Old Testament the brother of Esau is called *Jacob*. The form *James* comes from L *Jacōbus* via LL *Jac(o)mus*, which also gave rise to *Jaime*, the regular form of the name in Sp. (as opposed to the learned *Jacobo*). See also JACK and JACKMAN.

Cogns.: Fr.: **Jacquème**. Prov.: **Jayume**, **Jau(l)me(s)**, **Jamme(s)**. It.: **Gia(co)mo**, **Giacomi**, **Iacomo**, **Iacomi**, **Como**, **Comi**, **Cumo**. Sp.: **Jaime**. Cat.: **Jaume**.

Dims.: Fr.: **Jacquemot**, **Jacquemet**, **Ja(c)quemy**, **Ja(c)queminot**, **Ja(c)queminet**. Prov.: **Jaumet**, **Jam(m)et**, **Jamot**. It.: **Giacomello**, **Giacomelli**, **Giammelli**, **Iacomelli**, **Comello**, **Comelli**, **Comel(l)ini**, **Mello**; **Gia(co)metti**, **Giamitti**, **Iacometti**, **Iamitti**, **Cometto**, **Cometti**; **Giacomini**, **Iacomini**, **Comin(ell)o**, **Comin(ett)i**, **Cominotti**, **Cominoli**; **Giacomucci**, **Gia(co)muzzi**, **Giacomuzzo**, **Giamusso**, **Comucci**, **Comuzzo**, **Comusso**, **Mucci**, **Mucillo**, **Muccino**, **Muzz(in)i**, **Muzzillo**, **Muzzolo**, **Muzzullo**, **Musso**, **Mussett(in)i**, **Muselli**, **Mussilli**, **Mussotti**, MUSSOLINI; **Giacomozzo**, **Camosso**, **Mozz(in)i**, **Mozzetti**; **Comolli**, **Camolli**, **Comoletti**, **Camoletto**; **Comizzoli**, **Mizzi**; **Motto**, **Mottin(ell)i**.

Aug.: It.: **Giacomoni**.

Pejs.: Fr.: **Ja(c)quemar(d)**, **Jacmar(d)**. It.: **Giacomazzo**, **Giacomasso**, **Comazzo**, **Mazzo**.

Patrs.: Eng.: **Jameson**; **Jami(e)son** (chiefly Scot.); **Jemison**, **Jim(p)son**, **Gemson**, **Gimson** (the latter often pronounced with initial /g/). Sc.: **McKeamish**, **McJames** (Gael. **Mac Sheumais**). It.: **Di Giacomo**. Sp.: **Jaimez**.

Patr. (from a dim.): It.: **Di Giacomettino**.

Fitzjames *was the surname assumed by James Fitzjames (1670–1734), illegitimate son of James II of England and Arabella*

Churchill, sister of the Duke of Marlborough. He was created Duke of Berwick but was attainted after taking part in the siege of Londonderry. He then served as a soldier in Hungary and France, and was created Marshal of France. The family's European titles include the Fr. dukedom of Fitzjames and the Sp. dukedom of Alba.

Jane English (chiefly Devon and Cornwall): from the ME given name *Jan*, a var. of John. (As a given name, *Jane* was not specialized as a female form until the 17th cent.)

Vars.: **Jain(e), Jayne; Jean; Jenn(e), Genn.**

Dims.: **Janet, Jennett; Jankin.** See also Jenkin.

Patrs.: **Ja(y)nes, Jeynes; Jean(e)s, Jeens, Jeneson; Jan(ni)s, Janson; Jenns, Jenness, Jen(n)ison.**

Jankoff Jewish (E Ashkenazic): from the male Yid. given name *Yankev*, from Hebr. *Yaakov* (see Jacob).

Vars.: **Yankov, Yankow, Yankev, Yanko, Yanku; Yankovsky, Yankofsky.**

Dim.: **Jankel(l)** (from Yid. *Yankl*).

Patrs.: **Jankovi(t)ch, Jankovitz, Jankowitz; Jankowicz** (Pol. spelling); **Yankowitz, Yankovi(t)ch, Yankowi(t)ch, Yankovitsch, Yankovitz, Yankovits.**

Patrs. (from dims.): **Jankeloff, Yankelevsky; Jank(i)elewicz, Jankilewicz, Jankielowicz, Jankelewitz, Jankelevitz, Jankilevitz, Jankelovicz, Jankelovits, Jankelowitz, Jankolowitz, Jankolovits, Jankulovits, Janklowicz, Janklewitz, Yankelovi(t)ch, Yankelevitz, Yankelewich, Yankelovich, Yankelovitz, Yankelowitz, Yankielewicz, Yankilevi(t)ch.**

January English: 1. nickname or given name for someone born or baptized in January, or having some other particular connection with that month, which gets its name from L (*mensis*) *Januārius* '(month) of *Janus*'. Janus was the god of gateways and entrances (his name is akin to L *janua* door), and was represented as having two faces, one looking forward at what is to come, the other backward at what is past. In some cases the surname may reflect the L personal name *Januārius*, which was borne by a number of early Christian saints, most famously a 3rd-cent. bishop of Benevento who became the patron of Naples.

2. local name, altered by folk etymology, from *Genoa* in Liguria. The ME term for a Genoese was *Janaway*, a back-formation from *Janaways*, which was taken as a pl. but is in fact an Eng. spelling of OF *Genoveis*, It. *Genovese* Genoese. Genoa was one of the great seaports of the Mediterranean in medieval times, and merchants and master mariners from there were found in all the coastal and trading towns of Europe. The origin of the name of the city is uncertain. It has been associated with L *janua* door (see above), but is more probably of pre-Roman origin. In the Middle Ages the Genoese were regarded as clever individuals, and it is possible that the surname is sometimes a nickname with this sense.

Var.: (of 2): **Janaways.**

Cogns. (of 1): Fr.: **Janvier.** Cat.: **Janer, Jané; Giner, Giné.** Port.: **Januário, Janeiro.** It.: **Gennaro; Gennai** (Tuscany); **Zen(n)aro, Zennari, Zonari** (Venetia, Emilia); **Nari.** Ger.: Jenner. (Of 2): It.: **Geno(v)ese; Genova, Genua.**

Dims. (of 1): It.: **Gennarelli, Gennarino.**

Patr. (from 1): It.: **Di Gennaro.**

Jara Spanish: habitation name from places in the provinces of Alicante and Cádiz called *La Jara*, from OSp. *jara* wood, thicket (Arabic *šaʿra*). In some cases the surname may derive directly from the vocab. word, as a topographic name.

Jarosz Polish: from a short form of the given name *Jarosław* (composed of the elements *jaro-* young, robust + *-sław* glory; cogn. with Czech *Jaroslav*), or from some other given name in which *jaro-* forms the first element, or from a dial. form of the given name *Hieronim* Jerome. In some cases it may have originated as a nickname for a vigorous young man, from the adj. *jary*.

Vars.: **Jaros; Jarecki.**

Cogns.: Czech: **Jaroś, Jareš, Jarý.**

Dims.: Pol.: **Jaroszek, Jarosik, Jaraszek.** Czech: **Jarušek.**

Patrs.: Pol.: **Jarewicz, Jaruszewicz; Jaroszczak.** Croatian: **Jarić.**

Habitation names: Pol.: **Jaroszewski, Jaroszyński.**

Jarre 1. French: metonymic occupational name for a potter, from OF *jarre* earthenware vessel (OProv. *jarra*, from Arabic *jarrah,* a word brought back by the Crusaders, which has also given Eng. *jar*).

2. Frisian: cogn. of Geary 2.

Var. (of 1): **Jarrier.**

Dims. (of 1): **Jarret, Jarron.**

Jarry 1. English (Norfolk): var. of Geary 2.

2. Provençal: topographic name for someone who lived by an oak tree or oak grove, from OProv. *garric* (masc.) kermes oak or *garrique* (fem.) grove of such oaks.

Vars. (of 1): **Jear(e)y, Jary.** (Of 2): **Garric, Garrit; Jarrige, Lajarrige, Garrigue, Garrique.**

Cogns. (of 2): Cat.: **Garriga, Sagarriga.**

Dims. (of 2): Prov.: **Jarrijon, Garrigou, Garrioux.**

The English actor-manager David Garrick *(1717–79) was of Huguenot descent. His father was born in France, and his grandfather, David* de la Garrique, *left Bordeaux in 1685, changing the family name to* Garric.

Järvinen Finnish: ornamental name from Finn. *järvi* lake + the gen. suffix *-nen*, perhaps in some cases chosen as a topographic name by someone who lived by a lake.

Jarvis English: 1. from the Norman personal name *Gervase*, composed of the Gmc element *geri*, *gari* spear + a second element of uncertain meaning and original form. (For the change of *-er-* to *-ar-*, cf. Marchant.) The name had some currency throughout Europe in the Middle Ages, partly because it was borne by a saint who was martyred under the Roman Emperor Domitian; this saint became one of the patrons of Milan.

2. habitation name from *Jervaulx* in N Yorks., site of a famous Cistercian monastery, so called from an ANF form of the river name *Ure* (of Brit. origin; it may be cogn. with the Ger. *Isar*, and have some meaning such as 'strongly flowing') + ANF *vaulx* valley (see Vale).

Vars.: **Jervis.** (of 1 only): **Gervis, Gervase; Jarvie** (Scotland).

Cogns. (of 1): Fr.: **Gervais(e), Gervois, Gervex.** Sp.: **Hervás.** Ger.: **Gervas; Vas(ius).** Low Ger.: **Vaas, Faas** (see also Boniface).

Dims. (of 1): Fr.: **Gervaiseau, Gervot.** It.: **Gervasini, Gervasutti; Vasol(in)i, Vasolin** (Venetia). Port.: **Gervasinho.** Ger.: **Vaslin, Vassle; Fäsi(n)** (Switzerland).

Augs. (of 1): It.: **Gervasoni; Vason** (Venetia).

Patr. (from 1): Low Ger.: **Gervasing.**

Jarzębowski Polish: habitation name from a place named with Pol. *jarząb* service tree + *-ów* possessive suffix, with the addition of *-ski*, suffix of local surnames (see Baranowski).

Vars.: **Jarzębski; Jarząbek.**

Jasiński Polish: probably an elaboration of the given name *Jasiek*, a dim. of *Jan* John, or else a habitation name from some place named with this element.

Var.: **Jasieński.**

Cogns.: Jewish (E Ashkenazic, reasons for adoption unknown): **Jassen**, **Jassin**, **Jasyn**, **Jason**, **Jashunsky**, **Jassinowsky**, **Jashinovsky**.

Jastrow Jewish (Ashkenazic): habitation name from the town of *Jastrowic* in NE Poland (also called *Jastrów*), where there was a large Jewish community.

Var.: **Jastrov**.

Jaubert French: from a Gmc personal name of uncertain origin. The first element is probably the tribal name *Gaut* (see JOCELYN); the second is *berht* bright, famous.

Var.: **Gaubert** (Normandy, Picardy).

Cogns.: Prov.: **Jo(u)bert**. Eng. (Norman): **Jo(u)bert**, **Jubert**, **Goubert**.

Dims.: Prov.: **Joubertin**, **Jouberton**.

Jaune French: nickname for someone with a sallow skin, from OF *jaune* yellow (L *galbīnus* greenish-yellow, which was itself used as a family name in classical times; cogn. with Ger. *gelb* yellow; cf. GELLER).

Dims.: **Jauneau**, **Jaunet**.

Pejs.: **Jaunard**, **Jaunasse**.

Jáuregui Spanish form of Basque **Jauregi**: topographic name for someone who lived by a manor house, or occupational name for someone who was employed in one, from *jauregi* palace, manor house (a cpd of *jaur* lord + the local suffix *-egi*).

Javier Spanish: from a given name or religious byname bestowed in honour of St Francis *Xavier* (1506–52), Jesuit missionary to the Far East. He was a member of a noble family who took their name from the castle of *Javier* in Navarre, where he was born. The placename is of Basque origin; see ECHEVERRÍA.

Cogns.: Port.: **Xavier** (also used in Sp., where it is an archaic spelling).

Jaworski Polish: topographic name for someone who lived by a maple or sycamore tree, from Pol. *jawor* maple, sycamore + the surname suffix *-ski* (see BARANOWSKI).

Var.: **Jaworowski**.

Cogns.: Ukr.: **Yavorski**. Czech: **Javorský**, **Javůrek**. Bulg.: **Yavorov** (patr.). Ger. (of Slav. origin): **Jauer(t)**; **Jauerni(c)k**, **Jauernig**. Jewish (E Ashkenazic, probably ornamental): **Javor**, **Yavor**; **Jawerbaum** (with Ger. *Baum* tree). Hung.: **Jávor(ka)**.

Jay English and French: nickname from the vocab. word denoting the bird (ME, OF *jay(e)*, *gai*, LL *gaius*, from the personal name *Gaius*; cf. GAY 3), probably referring to an idle chatterer or a showy person, although the jay was also noted for its thieving habits.

Vars.: Fr.: **Geai(x)**, **Geay**, **Legeay**, **Lejay**.

Patrs.: Eng.: **Jay(e)s**.

Jayet French: of uncertain origin, perhaps a metonymic occupational name for a jeweller, from OF *jaiet* jade, which is derived, like It. *geada*, from Sp. (*piedra de*) *ijada* stone of the flanks (LL *īliata* for class. L *īlia*), so called because it was thought to offer a remedy against kidney stones.

Vars.: **Jayez**, **Jayot**; **Jahier** (agent noun).

Jeavon 1. English: distinguishing name from ANF *jovene* young; see JEUNE.

2. Welsh: from the given name *Ievan*, an earlier form of EVAN, the W version of JOHN.

Var.: **Jevon**.

Patrs.: **Je(a)vons**.

Jeeves English: metr. from *Geva*, a pet form of the medieval female given name *Genevieve*, introduced into England by the Normans. This is of obscure etymology, but may represent a reworking of a Gaul. name in which the first element meant 'people', the second 'woman'. It was very popular in France, where a 5th-cent. saint bearing it became patroness of Paris.

Vars.: **Jeves**, **Geaves**, **Geeves**.

Jeffrey English: from a Norman personal name that appears in ME as *Geffrey* and in OF as *Je(u)froi*. Some authorities regard this as no more than a palatalized form of GODFREY, but early forms such as *Galfridus* and *Gaufridus* point to a first element from Gmc *gala* to sing or *gawi* region, territory. It is possible that several originally distinct names have fallen together in the same form.

Vars.: **Jeff(e)ry**, **Jeffree**, **Jeffray**, **Jeffroy**, **Jaffrey**, **Jaffray**, **Geoffrey**, **Geoffroy**.

Cogns.: Fr.: **Geof(f)roy**, **Geffroy**, **Geoffré**, **Geoffre**, **Jeuffroy**, **Joffrey**, **Jof(f)re**; **Jaffré**, **Jaffrès**, **Jaffre** (Brittany). Prov.: **Gaufré**, **Gaufre** (see also GALOFRÉ); **Jauffret** (Massif Central, Lyons); **Jauf(f)red** (Savoy). Cat.: **Jofré**, **Jofre**.

Dims.: Eng.: **Jebb**, **Jepp(e)**, **Gebb**, **Gepp**, **Jeff(e)**; **Jef(f)cock**, **Jef(f)cott**, **Jephcott**, **Jef(f)cote**, **Jephcote**, **Jef(f)coat**. Fr.: **Geoffrion**, **Joufrion**, **Joffrin**; **Jaffrennou**, **Jaffrezic**, **Jaffrézo** (Brittany).

Patrs.: Eng.: **Jeff(e)ries**, **Jeff(e)ry(e)s**, **Jeffer(i)s**, **Jeffress**, **Geoffreys**; **Jefferson**.

Patrs. (from dims.): Eng.: **Jeff(e)s**; **Jebbs**, **Jepps**; **Jebson**, **Jibson**, **Jep(pe)son**, **Gepson**, **Jephson**.

Bearers of the name Jephcott *and other variants ending in* -t *are apparently all descended from John* Jefcott, *who died at Ansty in Warwicks in 1561. The Ansty parish registers contain several entries for the name* Jeffcock, *and the form in* -t *may be the result of deliberate alteration (cf.* ALCOTT*).*

George Jeffreys, *1st Baron Jeffreys of Wem (?1645–89), was an English judge whose harshness during the trials of those involved in Monmouth's Rebellion (1685) led to their being called the 'Bloody Assizes'. He was a member of an Oxon. family, who claimed descent from a Welsh prince who made a treaty with King Athelstan in 934.*

Jekyll English: of Breton or Cornish origin, from a Celt. personal name, OBret. *Iudicael*, composed of elements meaning 'lord' + 'generous', 'bountiful', which was borne by a 7th-cent. saint, a king of Brittany who abdicated and spent the last part of his life in a monastery. Forms of this name are found in medieval records not only in Devon and Cornwall, where they are of native origin, but also in E Anglia and even Yorks., whither they were imported by Bretons after the Norman Conquest. The vowel of the first syllable is traditionally long, but now often pronounced short.

Vars.: **Jeckell**, **Jockle**, **Jiggle**, **Giggle**; **Jewell**, **Juell**, **Joel(l)**, **Jowle**, **Joule**.

Cogns.: Fr.: **Jézéquel**, **Giquel(le)**, **Géquel**; **Juhel** (Brittany). Welsh: **Ithel**, IDLE.

Dims.: Eng.: **Jiggen**, **Jickling**, **Jugg**; **Jol(l)in**, **Jowling**, **Gollin**, **Jolland**, **Gollan(d)**.

Patrs.: Eng.: **Jeckells**, **Jickells**, **Jickles**, **Jockelson**; **Jewels**, **Joels**, **Joules**, **Jo(e)lson**. Welsh: BETHELL.

Patrs. (from dims.): Eng.: **Jiggins**, **Juggins**, **Jeggons**; **Jukes**, **Jewkes**, **Jouxson**; **Jollands**, **Gollins**.

Jelen 1. Czech: nickname from *jelen* stag, perhaps given with reference to the supposed sexual powers of the stag.

2. Jewish (E Ashkenazic): ornamental name from Czech *jelen* stag, also widely adopted as a translation of HIRSCH.

Vars.: Jewish: **Jel(l)in**, **Yel(l)en**, **Yel(l)in**, **Yel(l)on**, **Yalin**, **Yalon**; **Jelinsky**.

Cogn.: Pol. **Jeliński**.

Dims.: Czech: **Jelínek**. Jewish: **Jel(l)inek**, **Jelinak**, **Yel(l)inek**. Pol.: **Jelonek**, **Jelonka**.

Patrs.: Croatian: **Jelenić**. Jewish: **Jelinowicz, Yelinovitz; Yelinsohn**.

Jenkin English: from the ME given name *Jenkin*, a dim. of JOHN with the addition of the suffix *-kin* (of Low Ger. origin).

Vars.: **Jenken, Jinkin, Junkin**.

Patrs.: **Jenkins, Jinkins; Jenki(n)son, Jenkerson, Junki(n)son**.

Jenkins *is one of the most common names in England, but is also especially associated with Wales. The form* Jenkinson *is rather more common in Lancs. and S Yorks., while* Jenkin *is typically a Devon name.*

Jenks English: patr. from the ME given name *Jenk*, a back-formation from JENKIN with the removal of the supposed ANF dim. suffix *-in*.

Vars.: **Jencks, Jen(c)kes; Janks; Jinks** (W Midlands).

Jenner 1. English (chiefly Kent and Sussex): occupational name for a designer or engineer, from a ME aphetic form of OF *engineor* contriver (a deriv. of *engaigne* cunning, ingenuity, stratagem, device; cf. GAIN and INGHAM 2). Engineers in the Middle Ages were primarily designers and builders of military machines, although in peacetime they might turn their hands to architecture and other more pacific functions.

2. German: from the given name *Januārius*; see JANUARY 1. The Austrian dial. word for 'January' is *Jänner*, and so it is possible that in Austria this is one of the surnames acquired from words denoting months of the year, for example by converts who had been baptized in that month or people who were born or baptized in that month.

Vars. (of 1): **Jenoure, Genower, Genner, Ginner**.

Cogns. (of 1): It.: **Ingegneri, Ingigneri**.

Jennewein German: from the L personal name *Ingenuīnus* 'True-born', borne by a 7th-cent. saint, bishop of Brixen (now Bressanone) in the S Tyrol.

Vars.: **Gen(n)ewein, Gendebein**.

Jennings English: patr. from the ME given name *Janyn*, *Jenyn*, a dim. of JOHN.

Vars.: **Jannings, Jennins, Jennens**.

Jentel 1. French: dim. of *Jean* JOHN.

2. Jewish (Ashkenazic): from *Yentl*, a Yid. female given name (ultimately from L *gentilis* well-born, noble; see GENTLE).

Var. (of 2): **Yental**.

Jeremy English: from the medieval given name of the same form, which enjoyed a modest popularity among Christians as having been borne by the biblical prophet *Jeremiah* (Hebr. *Yirmeyahu* 'may God exalt him'), noted for his lamentations over the faithlessness of Israel.

Vars.: **Jerm(e)y** (Norfolk); **Jarm(e)y, Jarmay**.

Cogns.: Ger.: **Jeremias, Jeremies, Jermis; Jermas, Jermatz** (S Germany). Jewish: **Jeremiahu, Jirmyahu, Yermiahu, Yirmiyahu**.

Patrs.: Russ.: **Yeremeev, Yeryomin**. Croatian: **Jerem(ov)ić**. Jewish: **Yermus, Yarmus** (from the Yid. form *Yermye*).

Patrs. (from dims.): Russ.: **Yer(sh)in, Yerkin, Yerk(h)ov, Yerasov, Yerychov, Yeryushev, Yeryuchin**. Jewish: **Jermulowicz** (E Ashkenazic, from the Yid. dim. *Yermyele*).

Jerez Spanish: habitation name from places in the provinces of Badajoz and Cadiz, of unknown etymology. The former, now known in full as Jerez de los Caballeros, was the birthplace of the explorer Vasco Núñez de Balboa (*c.*1475–1519); the latter, Jerez de la Frontera, was an important centre for the manufacture of sherry (named in Eng. from the town) and brandy.

Jerome English: ostensibly from the medieval given name of the same spelling (OF *Jérôme*, from Gk *Hieronymos*, composed of the elements *hieros* sacred + *onyma* name), which achieved some popularity in France and elsewhere, being given in honour of St Jerome (?347–420), who created the Vulgate, the standard L version of the Bible, working partly from earlier L texts and partly from the original Hebr., Aramaic, and Gk. However, this was a rather rare given name in England in the Middle Ages; the comparative frequency of the surname is explained by the fact that it has also absorbed a Norman personal name, *Gerram*, composed of the Gmc elements *geri*, *gari* spear + *hraban* raven.

Vars.: **Jerrom(e), Jerram, Gerram, Jerran, Jaram**.

Cogns.: Fr.: **Jérôme, Gérôme, Girome, Giraume; Hieronimus** (learned form); **Onimus** (aphetic var.). It.: **Geronimi** (learned); **Girolami** (popular). Sp., Port.: **Jerónimo**. Ger.: **Hieronymus, Kronymus, Ronymus, Onimus, Ohnemus**. Flem., Du.: **Geeroom**. Czech: **Jarolím**.

Dims.: Ger.: **Grom(me)s, Grummes, Grolms, Grulms**. Czech: **Jarolímek**.

Patrs.: Eng.: **Jer(r)om(e)s, Jerrams, Jerrans**. Flem.: **Geerooms; Rooms**.

Jesionowski Polish: habitation name from a place named with Pol. *jesion* ash tree + *-ów* possessive suffix, with the addition of *-ski*, suffix of local surnames (see BARANOWSKI).

Dim.: Pol.: **Jesionek**.

Jesus Portuguese: from a medieval given name, taken in honour of Christ. The name *Jesus* is from a Gk form, *Iēsos*, of Hebr. *Yeshua*, a byform of *Yehoshua* (Eng. *Joshua*) 'may Jehovah help him'. In most of Christian Europe this name is felt to be too sacred to bestow on mortal children, but there have been no such inhibitions in Spanish- and Portuguese-speaking areas, where it is extremely popular.

Jeune French: from OF *jeuvene* young (L *iuvenis*), used to distinguish the younger of two bearers of the same given name within a community, who might be two brothers, father and son, or no relation at all to each other.

Var.: **Lejeune**.

Cogns.: Prov.: **Jouve(n)**. Cat.: **Jove**. Eng.: JEAVON. It.: **Giovine; Iovine, Iovene, Iovane** (Naples).

Dims.: Fr.: **Jeunet, Jeuneau; Jon(n)et, Jonneau; Jouvenel, Jouvenet, Jouvenot; Jouvel, Jouveau, Jouvet**. It.: **Giovinetti, Iovinelli**.

Pejs.: Fr.: **Jonnart**. It.: **Giovinazzo**.

Jeziorski Polish: topographic name for someone who lived by a lake, Pol. *jezioro*.

Vars.: **Jezierski, Jeziorny**.

Cogns.: Russ.: **Ozerov, Ozyornikov, Azyornikov** (patrs. in form). Jewish (E Ashkenazic): **Jezerski, Jezersky**.

Jimeno Spanish: from a medieval given name of uncertain origin. It has normally been assumed to be a form of SIMON, but this is disputed. The medieval form was *Ximenus*, which Menéndez Pidal derives from L **Siminius*.

Var.: **Gimeno**.

Patrs.: **Jiménez, Giménez; Ximénez** (archaic spelling).

Joachim French and German: from the Hebr. male given name *Yoyakim* 'God has granted (a son)', which occurs in the Bible (Neh. 12: 10) and was also borne, according to medieval legend, by the father of the Virgin Mary.

Vars.: Fr.: **Joaquin**. Ger.: **Jochum, Joche(i)m**.

Cogns.: Low Ger.: **Jochen**. Pol.: **Jachymski**. Port.: **Joaquim**. It.: **Gio(v)a(c)chini**.

Dim.: Pol.: **Jechimczyk**.

Patrs.: Ger.: **Joachimi** (Latinized). Low Ger.: **Joachimsen, Jochims(en), Jochens**. Dan.: **Jockumsen**. Russ.: **Akimov**. Pol.: **Jachimowicz, Joachimiak, Jachimczak**. Jewish: **Joachinsohn, Yoachimsohn; Jo(a)chimowicz, Jochimowich; Jakimowski, Jakimovski, Jakimovsky, Yakimov(ski), Yakimovsky** (all apparently from non-Jewish surnames).

Patrs. (from dims.): Russ.: **Akim(a)kin, Akimchev, Akimchin, Akimochkin, Akimushkin, Akimychev**.

'Son of the wife of J.': Russ.: **Akimikhin**. Ukr.: **Yakimishin**.

Job English: 1. from the personal name (Hebr. *Iyov*) borne by a biblical character, the central figure in the Book of Job, who was tormented by God and yet refused to forswear Him. The name has been variously interpreted as meaning 'Where is the (divine) father?' and 'Persecuted one'. It does not seem to have been used as a given name in the Middle Ages: the surname is probably a nickname for a wretched person or one tormented with boils (which was one of Job's afflictions).

2. nickname from OF *job*, *joppe* sorry wretch, fool (perhaps a transferred application of the name of the biblical character).

3. perhaps also a metonymic occupational name for a cooper, from ME *jubbe*, *jobbe* vessel containing four gallons (of unknown etymology). This could also have been a metonymic nickname for a heavy drinker or for a tubby person.

4. metonymic occupational name for a maker or seller (or nickname for a wearer) of the long woollen garment known in ME and OF as a *jube* or *jupe* (cf. mod. Fr. *jupe* skirt). This word ultimately derives from Arabic.

Vars.: **Jobe, Jope, Jupe; Jopp, Jubb, Jupp; Juby**. (Of 3 and 4): **Jobar, Jobber, Jubber**.

Cogns. (of 1): Hung.: **Jób**. (Of 4): It.: **Giubba; Gipa** (Piedmont).

Dims.: Eng.: **Jobin; Joblin(g) Joplin(g)** (Northumb.). Fr.: **Jobet, Jobey, Job(el)in, Jobineau, Jobot**. (Of 4 only): It.: **Giubbini**.

Patrs. (from 1): Eng.: **Jobes, Jobson, Jopson**.

Patrs. (from 1) (dims.): Eng.: **Jobbins**. Low Ger.: **Jöbken, Jöbgen, Jöbges**.

The surnames Jobling *and* Joplin *are found mainly in NE England. The earliest known bearer is Robert* Joplyn, *recorded as renting lands in S Northumberland in 1499*.

Jocelyn English: from an OF personal name of complex origin, imported into England in the forms *Goscelin, Gosselin, Joscelin*. The name was known in England before the Conquest, but was spread by the Normans, among whom it was very popular. For the most part it is from the Gmc personal name *Gauzelin*, a dim. from a short form of the various cpd names having as their first element the tribal name *Gaut* (apparently the same as OE *Gēatas*, the Scandinavian people to which Beowulf belonged, and also akin to the name of the *Goths*). However, the name also came to be considered as a dim. of OF *Josse*; see JOYCE.

Vars.: **Joscelyn(e), Josselyn, Joselin, Joslen, Joslin(g), Jos(e)land**, GOSLING.

Cogns.: Fr.: **Jo(u)sselin(e)**.

Jodar Catalan: of uncertain origin, possibly from an Arabic personal name *Ǧaudar* or a Gmc personal name composed of the tribal name *Gaut* (see JOCELYN) + *heri*, *hari* army.

John English: from the Hebr. name *Yochanan* 'Jehovah has favoured (me with a son)' or 'may Jehovah favour (this child)', which was adopted into L (via Gk) as *Johannēs*, and has enjoyed enormous popularity in Europe throughout the Christian era, being given in honour of St John the Baptist, precursor of Christ, and of St John the Evangelist, author of the fourth gospel, as well as others of the nearly one thousand saints of the name. Some of the principal forms of the given name in other European languages are W *Evan*, *Ioan*; Sc. *Ia(i)n*; Ir. *Séan*; Ger. *Johann*, *Hans*; Flem., Du. *Jan*; Fr. *Jean*; It. *Giovanni*, *Gianni*, *Vanni*; Sp. *Juan*; Port. *João*; Gk *Ioanni*; Czech *Jan*; Russ. *Ivan*. Polish has surnames both from the W Slav. forms *Jan(usz)* and from the E Slav. form *Iwan*.

There were a number of different forms of the name in ME, including *Jan(e)* (see JANE); *Jen* (see JENKIN); *Jon(e)* (see JONES); and *Han(n)* (see HANN). There were also various ME fem. versions of this name (e.g. *Joan*, *Jehan*), some of them indistinguishable from the masc. forms. The distinction on grounds of sex between *John* and *Joan* was not firmly established in English until the 17th cent. It was even later that *Jean* and *Jane* were specialized as specifically fem. names in English; bearers of these surnames and their derivs. are more likely to derive them from a male ancestor than a female.

Vars.: **Jon(e), Ion**; JANE.

Cogns.: Welsh: EVAN. Sc.: **Ia(i)n**. Ir.: SHANE. Fr.: **Je(h)an, Ja(h)an, Jo(u)(h)an; Jaouen** (Brittany). Prov.: **Jouen**. Sp.: **Juan; Ibán**. Cat.: **Joan**. Port.: **João**. It.: **Giovan(n)i; Gioani** (Piedmont, Liguria); **Gioan** (Venetia); **Ioan** (Friuli); **Gian(n)i, Cian(n)i, Ianni, Ianne, Ianno; Zan(n)i, Zoane, Zuan(n)** (Venetia); **Nan(n)i; Vanni**. Rum.: **Io(a)n**. Ger.: **Johann(es)**; HANS; **Jaggi, Jäggli** (Swiss). Low Ger.: **Jann, Jahn**. Flem., Du.: **Jan**. Dan.: **Jahn**. Pol.: **Janas, Janus(z); Janecki, Janicki; Jon; Iwański, Iwiński** (E Pol. or Ukr.). Czech: **Jan, Ján, Jano(u)š, Jano(u)ch, Janout; Janů; Janák, Janata, Janota, Janda, Jandera, Jandák; Janč, Janča(r); Janský, Jansa, Janda(č)**. Jewish: **Johanan; Jochanany** (with the Hebr. suffix *-i*).

Dims.: Eng.: JENKIN; JOHNCOCK; **Jo(h)nikin, Jo(h)nigan** (chiefly Irish); see also JACK. Fr.: **Jean(n)et, Joannet, Jouan(d)et, Jeandet, Jantet, Jentet, Jo(u)an(n)eton; J(e)an(n)in, Jo(u)an(n)in, Jo(u)an(n)y, Jan(n)y, Jeandin, Jentin, Jean(n)enet; Jean(n)ot, Jo(u)an(n)ot, Jeandot, Jantot, Janodet; Jean(n)on, Jeandon, Janton, Jenton; J(e)an(n)el, Jeandel, Jantel**, JENTEL, **Jean(n)eau, Jou(h)an(d)eau, Jeandeau, Jenteau; Jean(n)equin, Jannequin; Johanchon, Jean(n)esson, Jo(u)an(n)isson, Janisson; Jeandillou; Joan(n)ic** (Brittany). It.: **Gi(ov)an(n)elli, Giovannilli, Gian(i)ello, Gianilli, Cianelli, Ian(n)elli, Iannello, Ian(n)iello, Iannilli, Zan(n)elli, Zuanelli, Zuenelli, Van(n)elli, Nanelli; Gi(ov)an(n)etti, Giovanitti, Gioanetti, Gianeti, Gianettini, Ian(n)etti, Ianniti, Ianitti, Ianittello, Zan(n)etti, Zanetto, Zoanetti, Zanitti, Zanettini, Zanetello, Vannetti, Svanetti, Nannetti, Netti, Nitti; Gio(v)annini, Gian(n)ini, Gianinotti, Iannini, Zan(n)ini, Zaninelli, Van(n)ini, Svanini, Nannini, Ninn(ol)i, Ninotti; Gian(n)otti, Zan(n)otti, Zanotelli, Zanutto, Zanutti, Notti, Noto; Gian(n)ucci, Gianuzzi, Ianuccelli, Iannuzz(ell)i, Ianussi, Zanucioli, Zanussi, Vannucc(in)i, Vanucchi, Vannozzi, Nanuccio, Nannuzzi, Nozzol(in)i, Nucci(tell)i, Nuciotti, Nuzz(ett)i, Nussi; Gianolo, Gianolini, Gianullo, Gianulli, Zan(n)ol(l)i, Zaniolo, Zanolini, Zanoletti, Nol(l)i; Zanicchi, Zan(n)ichelli; Giovanizio, Ianizzi, Nannizzi**. Sp.: **Juanico**. Ger.: **Jä(h)ne(l), Jä(h)ndel, Jahn(d)el**. Low Ger.: **Johnke, Jönk(e), Jenne(mann)**. Fris.: **Jansema**. Ger. (of Slav. origin): JACH; **Jä(h)n(c)ke, Jä(h)n(i)sch, Ja(h)n(i)sch, Jä(h)nig, Janna(s)ch, Jan(n)uschek, Janoschek, Jen(i)(c)ke, Jent(z)sch; Gen(i)(c)ke, Gent(z)sch; Wa(h)n(c)ke, Wanka, Wan(j)ek, Wandtke; Nusch(k)e, Nuscha**. Pol.: **Janek, Janik, Janczyk, Janasik, Janusik, Janeczek, Jasi(a)k**; JACH; **Jończyk; Iwańczyk; Waszczyk**. Czech: **Janík, Jeník; Jančík, Janoušek, Janeček, Janáček, Janíček, Jeníček; Janatka, Jandl, Jand'ourek, Janků**; JACH. Ukr.: **Iv(ash)chenko, Ivan(en)ko, Ivanonko, Ivanushka, Ivasechko, Ivanets,**

Ivakhno, Ivanitsa. Beloruss.: **Yanshonok, Yanuk, Ivanets**. Hung.: **Jancsó, Jankó**.

Augs.: It.: **Gi(ov)annoni, Ian(n)oni, Iannone, Zan(n)oni, Vannoni, Nannoni, Noni**.

Pejs.: Fr.: **Jeannard, Jeannaud, J(o)anaud**. It.: **Giovan(n)azzi, Giovannacci, Giovan(n)ardi, Giannazzi, Gianazzo, Gian(n)assi, Gianasi, Iannazzi, Zuanazzi, Zanassi, Zanardi, Vannacci, Nacci, Nas(s)i**.

Patrs.: Eng.: **Johns**, JONES; **Johnson, Jo(i)nson, Joynson; Ions** (Northumb.). Sc.: **Ianson**; MCLEAN. See also JOHNSTON 2. Ir.: MALONE. Fr.: **A(u)jean, Ajam**. It.: **De Giovanni, De Zuani; Fig(l)iovanni; Gianneschi, Vaneschi**. Sp.: **Juanes, Yáñez, Ibáñez**. Rum.: **Ionesco, Ionescu**. Low Ger.: **J(oh)an(s)sen, Johanning; Ja(h)ns, Jan(t)z(en), Janning**. Flem.: **Jehaes, Jans, Jans(s)en(s)**. Du.: **Jans; Johansen, Janse(n), Janssen(s), Janzen**. Dan.: **Johann(e)sen, Johansen, Jo(h)nsen, J(o)ensen, Ja(h)nsen, Jantzen**. Swed.: **Johan(ne)sson, Jo(h)nsson, Jönsson, Jansson**. Russ.: **Ivanov, Yanov, Ivanaev, Ivantyev, Ivanilov, Ivanisov**. Pol.: **Januszewicz, Janowicz; Janiak, Janczak, Jaszczak, Jatczak; Iwanowicz**. Croatian: **Jovanović; Ivanović; Janić**. Bulg.: **Ivanov**. Jewish: **Johannes** (with possessive *-s*); **Johananov, Johananoff, Iohanof**. Albanian: **Jonuzi**. Gk: **Ioannou, Io(a)nnidis**. Armenian: **Ionnisian, Ohanessian, Ogan(es)ian, Ovanesian**.

Patrs. (from dims.): Fr.: **Aujouanet**. Low Ger.: **Johäntges, Jentge(n)s**. Fris.: **Joontjes**. Flem.: **Nijns**. Ger. (of Slav. origin): **Jä(h)ner, Jaher, Jeschner**. Pol.: **Janaszkiewicz, Jankiewicz, Januszkiewicz, Jaśkiewicz; Iwaszkiewicz, Waszkiewicz**. Croatian: **Ivić, Iv(an)ković, Ivančević; Jovašević, Jov(ič)ić, Jovićević, Jovović; Jocić, Jojić, Jončić; Janković, Jančić, Janjić, Janošević, Janjušević, Janićijević**. Russ.: **Ivankov, Ivan(n)ikov, Ivanch(ik)ov, Ivan(ch)enkov, Ivantsov, Ivan(i)chev, Ivanish(ch)ev, Ivanyukov, Ivanshintsev, Ivanusyev, Ivan(k)in, Ivanchin, Ivanikhin, Ivan(i)shin, Ivanyush(k)in, Ivanyutin; Ivachyov, Ivakhnov, Ivashev, Ivash(k)ov, Ivash(k)in, Ivashintsov, Ivash(in)nikov, Ivashnyov, Ivak(h)in, Ivashechkin, Ivasyushkin; Iv(o)shin**, IVUSHKIN; **Yanyshev, Yanshin(ov), Yanukhin, Yanyushkin, Yants(ur)ev; Van(k)in, Van(k)eev, Van(ni)kov, Vanshin, Vanshenkin, Vanshev, Vantsov, Vanchakov, Vanchikov, Vanichev, Vanichkov, Vanichkin, Vanyukov, Vanya(r)kin, Vanyush(k)in, Vanyash(k)in, Vanyukhin, Vanyutin, Vanyatin**.

'Son of the wife of J.': Ukr.: **Yankishin**.

'Servant of J.': Eng.: **Janman, Jenman**.

Habitation names: Pol.: **Janowski; Janaszewski, Janiszewski, Januszewski; Janczewski; Iwanicki, Iwanowski**. Czech: **Jan(k)ovský**.

Habitation names (from dims.): Pol.: **Jan(i)kowski, Waszczykowski**.

The Eng. forms John *and* Johns *are rather more common as surnames in Wales and the W Country than elsewhere. Neither is as common as* JONES. *The patr.* Johnson *is one of the most common of all Eng. surnames, with some 3,000 subscribers in the London telephone directory and many thousands more elsewhere.*

Johncock English: dim. of JOHN, with the ME suffix *-cock* (see COCK).

Vars.: **Joncock, Jo(h)ncook**.

Johnston 1. Scots: habitation name, deriving in most cases from the place so called in Annandale, in the former county of Dumfries. This is derived from the gen. case of the given name JOHN + ME *tone, toun* settlement (OE *tūn*). There are other places in Scotland so called, including the city of Perth, which used to be known as *St John's Toun*, and some of these may also be sources of the surname.

2. var. of *Johnson* (see JOHN), with intrusive *-t-*.

Var.: **Johnstone**.

As far as can be ascertained, most Scottish bearers of this surname are descendants of a certain John, probably a Norman baron from England, who held lands at Johnstone in Annandale from the Bruce family in the late 12th cent. His son Gilbert was the first to take the surname Johnstone *and their descendants later held the earldom of Annandale.*

Joiner English: occupational name for a maker of wooden furniture, ANF *joignour* (OF *joigneor*, from *joinre* to join, connect, L *iungere*).

Var.: **Joyner**.

Patr.: **Joiners**.

Equivs. (not cogn.): Fr.: BOISSIER, CHAPUIS. Ger.: SCHREINER; TISCHLER (also Jewish). Czech: TRUHLÁŘ. Pol. and Jewish (E Ashkenazic): STOLARSKI.

Jokinen Finnish: ornamental name from Finn. *joki* river + the gen. suffix *-nen*, perhaps sometimes chosen as a topographic name by someone who lived by a river.

Jolly English, Scots, and French: nickname for someone of a cheerful disposition, from ME, OF *joli(f)* merry, happy (apparently of Gmc origin, perhaps ultimately akin to ON *jol* (see YULE), the midwinter festival when everyone celebrated the end of the shortening of the days).

Vars.: Eng.: **Jolley, Jollie, Jollye; Jolliff(e), Juliffe**. Fr.: **Joly, Joli(f)**.

Dims.: Fr.: **Joli(v)et, Jolivel, Joliveau, Jolivot, Jolliot, Jolion, Jol(l)et, Jol(l)in**.

Jonas 1. English and French: from a medieval given name, which is ultimately from the Hebr. male given name *Yona*, lit. 'Dove'. In the book of the Bible which bears his name, Jonah was appointed by God to preach repentence to the city of Nineveh, but tried to flee instead to Tarshish. On the voyage to Tarshish, a great storm blew up, and Jonah was thrown overboard by his shipmates to appease God's wrath, swallowed by a 'great fish', and delivered by it on the shores of Nineveh. This story exercised a powerful hold on the popular imagination in medieval Europe, and the given name was a relatively common choice. The Hebr. name and its reflexes in other languages (for example Yid. *Yoyne*) have been popular Jewish given names for generations.

2. Jewish (Ashkenazic): Anglicized form of any of the Jewish surnames listed below, or a respelling of *Yonis* or some similar form with Yid. possessive *-s*.

Var.: **Jonah**.

Cogn.: Jewish: **Yona(h), Jona**. Czech: **Jonáš, Jonák**. Hung.: **Jónás**.

Patrs.: Dan., Norw.: **Jonasen**. Swed.: **Jonasson**. Jewish: **Yonis** (with Yid. possessive *-s*); **Yonovitz** (E Ashkenazic).

Jonchay French: habitation name from any of the various minor places so called from a collective of OF *jonc* rush, reed (L *iuncus*).

Vars.: **Jonchère, Joncière, Joncherie**.

Cogns.: Prov.: **Jonqu(i)ères**. Sp.: **Junquera**. Cat.: **Juncosa, Juncà**.

Jones 1. English and Welsh: patr. from the ME given name *Jon(e)* JOHN. The surname is especially common in Wales.

2. Jewish: Anglicized form of some like-sounding Jewish surname.

Vars.: Eng.: **Joynes, Joans**. See also patrs. of JOHN.

Jorba Catalan: habitation name from a place in the province of Barcelona in N Spain. The placename is of uncertain origin; it is probably pre-Roman.

Jordan 1. English, French, German, and Polish: from the baptismal name of the same spelling, which is taken from the name of the river *Jordan* (Hebr. *Yarden*, from *yarad* to go down, descend, i.e. to the Dead Sea). At the time of the Crusades it was common practice for crusaders and pilgrims to bring back flasks of water from the river, in which John the Baptist had baptized people, including Christ Himself, and to use it in the christening of their own children. Thus *Jordan* became quite a common given name, in commemoration of this.

2. Jewish: ornamental name taken directly from the name of the river.

Vars.: Eng.: **Jord(a)in, Jourdan, Jo(u)rdon, Juden**. Fr.: **Jordain, Jourda(i)n, Jourde; Joudren** (Brittany). Pol.: **Jordański**. Jewish: **Jarden(i), Yarden(i), Jardeny, Yardeny** (with the Hebr. suffix *-i*); **Yardinovsky**.

Cogns.: Prov.: **Jordi**. Cat.: **Jordà; Jordana** (a fem. form). Sp.: **Jordán**. Port.: **Jordão**. It.: **Giordano; Giorda(n), Zordan** (Venetia). Czech, Hung.: **Jordán**. Pol.: **Jordański**. Russ.: **Iordanski** (a name adopted by priests).

Dims.: Eng.: **Jurd, Judd**, JUDE. Fr.: **Jo(u)rdanet, Jo(u)rdaney, Jourdin(eau), Jourdon; Dan(n)et, Dan(n)ot, Danon**.

Patrs.: Eng.: **Jordens**. Low Ger.: **Jordans, Jördens**. Rum.: **Iordanesco**. Bulg.: **Jordanov**.

Patrs. (from dims.): Eng.: **Judson, Jutson, Jutsum(s); Justum, Justham** (metathesized forms); **Jetson**.

Joseph English, French, and Jewish: from the male given name (Hebr. *Yosef* 'may He (God) add (another son)'). In medieval Europe this name was borne frequently, but by no means exclusively, by Jews. In the Book of Genesis, Joseph is the favourite son of Jacob, who is sold into slavery by his brothers but rises to become a leading minister in Egypt (Gen. 37–50); in the New Testament Joseph is the husband of the Virgin Mary.

Vars.: Eng.: **Jessop, Jessup, Jessep** (representing the usual pronunciation of the name in the Middle Ages). Fr.: **José**. Jewish: **Josef(f); Josephi** (with the Hebr. suffix *-i*).

Cogns.: Sp., Port.: **José**. Ger.: **Josef**. Czech: **Josef**. Pol.: **Józef**. Hung.: **József**.

Dims.: Eng.: **Joe, Josey; Jess(e), Jessel, Jessett**. Ger.: **Jessel, Jossel**. Czech: **Joska, Jůza, Juzek**. Pol.: **Jóźwik, Juszczyk**. Ukr.: **Os(s)ipenko, Ishchenko**. Beloruss.: **Asipenko**. Hung.: **Józsa, Józsika, Szepe**.

Patrs.: Eng.: **Josephs(on)**. Ger.: **Josefs, Josefer; Josephi, Josephy** (Latinized). Dan., Norw.: **Josefsen, Josephsen**. Swed.: **Josefsson**. Russ.: **Osipov; Yesipov** (N Russia); **Yezafovich, Iozefovich** (chiefly Jewish); **Yusupov** (from an Arabic form of the given name, originating among Muslims). Lithuanian: **Jout(ap)aitis; Joutapavicius** (Latinized); **Josupeit, Josuweit** (Ger. spellings). Pol.: **Józefowicz; Józefczak, Józefiak**. Croatian: **Josifović, Josipović**. Jewish: **Josefso(h)n** (Ashkenazic); **Josephov, Josephoff, Josefowicz, Josefovic, Josifovitz, Josipovitz, Jos(of)ovitz, Josowitz, Josovich, Yosifov, Yosevitz** (E Ashkenazic). Armenian: **Ovasapian**.

Patrs. (from dims.): Eng.: **Jesson**. Russ.: **Yeskov, Yeskin, Yesenev, Yesinov, Yesichev, Yesenin, Yesinin, Ozintsev, Osichev** (see also OSININ). Ukr.: **Iskov**. Pol.: **Juszkiewicz; Juszczak, Jóźwiak, Jóźwicki**. Jewish: **Josselso(h)n, Joselson, Yoselson** (Ashkenazic); **Joselovitch, Joselevitch, Joselevitz, Josilevich, Josilowski, Yoseloff, Yos(s)elevitch, Ioselev(ich), Joslow, Joslin, Yoslow(itz), Yosko(witz), Joskowitz, Josskovi(t)z, Joskovitch, Joskowicz** (E Ashkenazic). Lithuanian: **Jozaitis**.

Jougleux French: occupational name for a jester or entertainer, OF *jougleor* (L *ioculātor*, from *ioculāri* to jest, sport, a deriv. of *iocus* joke, jest).

Cogns.: Eng.: **Juggler**. Prov.: **Jo(u)gla(r), Jouglas, Joucla**. Ger.: **Gaugler, Gauggele, Gaukele(r)**.

Jouvin French: from the L personal name *Iovīnus*, derived from *Iupiter* (gen. *Iovis*; cf. JULIO), the principal god of pagan Rome. It survived as a given name into the Middle Ages by virtue of having been borne by an obscure early saint whose cult achieved some popularity in W and N France.

Vars.: **Jovin, Jo(u)in, Jev(a)in**.

Dims.: **Jovi(g)net, Jovelin, Jovelet; Join(d)eau, Joinet; Jouon, Jouot, Jouet**.

Jover Catalan: occupational name for a maker of yokes, Cat. *jover* (L *iugārius*, an agent deriv. of *iugum* yoke). This word was apparently also used as an occupational name for an oxherd, hence the relative frequency of the surname.

Vars.: **Jové, Juvé; Jou**.

Jowett English (chiefly Yorks.): from the ME given name *Juwet*, *Jowet* (fem. *Juwette*, *Jowette*). These originated as dims. (with the ANF suffix *-et(te)*) of *Juwe*, *Jowe*, vars. of *Jull*, a short form of JULIAN, which were borne by both men and women.

Vars.: **Jowitt, Jewett, Jewitt, Juett**.

A certain Thomas, son of Jouette, *recorded in 1328 at Gristhorpe, near Filey, N Yorks., reappears in 1332 as Thomas* Jouetson.

Joy English: metonymic nickname for a person of a cheerful disposition, from ME, OF *joie*, *joye* (LL *gaudia*, for class. L *gaudium*). In some cases it may derive from a given name (normally borne by women) of this origin, which was in sporadic use during the Middle Ages.

Vars.: **Joye, Joie**.

Cogns.: Fr.: **Joie**. It.: **Gioia, Ioia, Lagioia**.

Dims.: Fr.: **Joyet**. It.: **Gioiella, Gioiello**.

Metrs.: Eng.: **Joyes** (see also JOYCE). It.: **De Gioia, Di Gioia**.

Joyce English and Irish: from the Bret. personal name *Iodoc*, a dim. of *iudh* lord, introduced by the Normans in the form *Josse*. Iodoc was the name of a Bret. prince and saint, the brother of *Iudicael* (see JEKYLL), whose fame helped to spread the name through France and, after the Norman Conquest, England as well. The name was occasionally borne also by women in the Middle Ages, but was predominantly a male name, by contrast with the present usage.

Vars.: **Joi(s)ce, Joss(e), Joass, Joce; Jose** (Devon and Cornwall); GOSSE, CHOICE.

Cogns.: Fr.: **Jo(u)(i)sse; Docq** (Belgium). Ger.: **Jost**, JUST; **Joos** (Switzerland); **Joas** (Bavaria); **Johst, Jaus** (Swabia). Flem., Du.: **Jooss, Jooste**.

Dims.: Fr.: **Jo(u)sset, Jo(u)sson, Jo(u)ssot, Jo(u)ssin, Joisson; Jos(se)quin** (Belgium); **Jossic** (Brittany). Ger.: **Jostel, Jöstel, Jüstel**.

Patrs.: Ger.: **Josten, Jostes, Jösting**. Flem., Du.: **Joosten**.

The name Joyce *is common in Ireland, where it was introduced in the 12th cent. by Normans from Wales; there is record of a certain Thomas* de Joise *marrying the daughter of the prince of Thomond. It has been Gaelicized as* **Seoighe** *and is especially common in Connemara.*

Jude 1. English and French: from the vernacular form of the Hebr. male given name *Yehuda* Judah (of unknown meaning), the name of Jacob's eldest son. This was not a popular name among Christians in medieval Europe, because of the associations it had with Judas Iscariot, the disciple who betrayed Christ for thirty pieces of silver. Among Jews, however, the Hebr. name and its reflexes in various Jewish languages (such as Yid. *Yude*) have been popular for generations, hence the many Jewish surnames given below.

2. French: name for a Jew, OF *jude* (L *Iudaeus*, Gk *Ioudaios*, from Hebr. *Yehudi* member of the tribe of *Judah*, the same word as in 1).

3. English: pet form of JORDAN.

Var. (of 1): **Judas** (from the learned form of the name).

Cogns. (of 1): Jewish: **Yuda, Yuditzki**. (Of 2): Eng.: **Jew** (see also JULIAN). Ger.: **Jud(t)**. Flem., Du.: **De Jode, Jut, Jeude**.

Dims. (of 1): Jewish: **Yudko, Judelman, Idel(man), Idelchek**.

Patrs. (from 1): Jewish: **Yudayov, Yudin, Judovitch, Judevitch, Judovitz, Judovits, Yudevitz, Yudovitz, Yudowitz, Yudowicz**.

Patrs. (from dims. of 1): Jewish: **Idels, Idelso(h)n; Judelevi(t)ch, Judelevitz, Judelewitz, Yudelevitz, Yudelewitz, Yudelovitz, Idelovitch, Idelovitz, Idelovici; Judkes, Judeikin, Yudeikin, Yudkin, Judkowski, Yudkowski, Judkiewicz, Judkewich, Judkevitz, Judkovicz, Yudkevitz, Yudiovitch**. Fr.: **Judet, Judon, Jud(l)in**. Ger.: **Jüdl**.

Judge 1. English: occupational name for an officer of justice or nickname for a solemn and authoritative person thought to behave like a judge, from ME, OF *juge* (L *iudex*, from *ius* law + *dīcere* to say), which replaced the OE term *dēma* (cf. DEMPSTER).

2. Irish: trans. of Gael. *breitheamhnach* judge (see BREW).

Cogns.: Fr.: **Juge**. It.: **Giudice, Iodice; Logiudice, Loiudice, Loiodice** (with fused article). Sp.: **Juez**.

Dims.: Fr.: **Juget, Jugeau, Jugelet**.

Patrs.: Eng.: **Judges**. It.: **Del Giudice**.

Juhász Hungarian: occupational name for a shepherd, from *juh* sheep + *-ász* occupational suffix.

Julian English (mainly Devon and Cornwall), French, and German: from a medieval given name (L *Iuliānus*, a deriv. of *Iulius*; see JÚLIO), which had been borne by a number of early saints. In ME the name was borne in the same form by women, whence the mod. girl's name *Gillian*.

Vars.: Eng.: **Julyan; Gillian, Gillion**, GILLING, **Gellion**. Fr.: **Jullian, Jul(l)ien, Joul(l)(a)in, Jeul(l)in**.

Cogns.: It.: **Giuliano; Iuliano** (S Italy); **Zulian(o), Zuian(i)** (Venetia). Sp.: **Julián, Illán**. Cat.: **Julià**.

Dims.: Eng.: **Jull, Joll(e)**, JOWETT; GILL, GILLETT; **Gell(e)** (E Midlands), **Jell(ey), Jellicoe; Jew** (see also JUDE). Fr.: **Juliot, Juillot, Juillet**. It.: **Giulianelli, Giulianini**.

Pejs.: Fr.: **Juliard, Juillard**.

Patrs./Metrs.: Eng.: **Julians, Jullens, Jullings, Jillions, Jillings, Jellings, Gillions, Gillings**. Russ.: **Ulyanov, Ulyan(i)chev**.

Patrs./Metrs. (from dims.): Eng.: **Jules, Jolles; Jellison, Jilson, Jew(i)son, Jewesson, Juson**. Russ.: **Ulyachin, Ulyankin, Ulyanishchev, Ulyash(k)ov**.

Contrary to popular belief, the surname Jewesson *does not point to Jewish ancestry. All present-day bearers of it seem to be descended from George Jewesson (d. 1794), a butcher of Maltby in N Yorks., both of whose parents were buried under the name of* Jewison. *The name is recorded in Yorks at Gristhorpe, near Filey, as early as 1332, and is derived from the fem. dim. given name* Jouet(te) *or* Juette. *This may be one of the rare surnames for which an original bearer of the given name from which it is derived can be identified: Juetta de Arches (d. c.1206) was a rich and powerful Norman heiress living at Thorpe Arch near York. She outlived her second husband by more than 30 years, which would explain why her offspring and descendants came to be identified by reference to her.*

The surname is also established in Canada. A family called Jewison *emigrated to Canada from Yorks. c.1803; a descendant is the film producer and director Norman Jewison.*

Júlio Portuguese: from a medieval given name (L *Julius*, a Roman family name of uncertain etymology, possibly an adj. deriv. of *Iuppiter*, gen. *Iovis*, the supreme god, whose name seems to be akin to words for 'sky', 'light', and 'day'). The name was borne in the Middle Ages in honour of various minor Christian saints, and was nearly as popular as its deriv. JULIAN.

Cogns.: Fr.: **Jule(s)**. Prov.: **Julhe(s)**. It.: **Giuli(o); Iuli** (S Italy), **Zuli** (Venetia).

Dims.: It.: **Giulietti, Giuliotti, Giuliuzzi; Zulin**.

Aug.: It.: **Giulioni**.

Patrs.: It.: **De Giuli, Di Giulio**. Dan.: **Juliussen**.

Jumeau French: nickname for a twin, OF *jumeau* (L *gemellus*). There are also various minor places of this name, so called from an anthropomorphic metaphor applied to a pair of rocks or other topographical features, and the surname may possibly be a habitation name from one of these.

Vars.: **Jumel, Gemeau(x), Gimel**.

Cogns.: It.: **Gemelli** (Lombardy, Calabria, Sicily); **Gemin(ian)i, Gemignani, Gimignani** (central and W Italy); **Iemolo, Iomelli; Zemelli** (Venetia, Emilia).

Dim.: Fr.: **Jumelet**.

Jun Czech: nickname for a lively young man, Czech *jurý* (ultimately cogn. with Fr. JEUNE and Eng. YOUNG).

Vars.: **Juna, Jůn(a)**.

Dim.: **Junek**.

Juniper English: 1. topographic name for someone who lived in a place overgrown with juniper bushes (L *jūniperus*, of obscure origin).

2. from the medieval female given name *Jennifer*, *Junifer*, from W *Gwenhwyfar*, a cpd of *gwen* fair, white + *(g)wyf* smooth, yielding + *fawr* large. This was the name of King Arthur's queen *Guinevere*. Until the 19th cent. the given name *Jennifer* was characteristically Cornish.

Var. (of 2): **Junifer**.

Cogns. (of 1): Fr.: **Genévrier**. Prov.: **Genébrier**. It.: **Ginevri, Cinefra**.

Dims. (of 2): Corn.: **Genn, Gynn**.

Jurado Spanish: occupational name for any of various officials who had to take an oath that they would perform their duty properly, from Sp. *jurado* sworn, past part. of *jurar* to swear (L *iurāre*).

Jury 1. English: habitation name from ME, OF *ju(ie)rie* Jewish quarter, most often denoting a non-Jew living in the Jewish quarter of a town, rather than a Jew. Most medieval English cities had their Jewish quarters, at least until King Edward I's attempted expulsion of the Jews from England in 1290. This did not succeed in expelling the Jews, but it did give a licence to persecution and so broke up many of the old Jewish quarters; as a name for a locality this word therefore originated well before the end of the 13th cent.

Var.: **Jewry**.

Cogn.: Sp.: **Juderías**.

Just 1. French, English, Catalan, Polish, Czech, and Danish: from a given name of the same spelling (L *Justus* 'Honourable', 'Upright', a deriv. of *ius* right, law; cf. JUDGE). There were several early saints of this name, among them a 4th-cent. bishop of Lyons and a 6th-cent. bishop of Urgell in Catalonia.

2. Jewish (NE Ashkenazic): from a Ger. or Pol. spelling of Yid. *yust* well-to-do; cf. MITTELMAN.

3. German: cogn. of JOYCE.

Vars. (of 1): Fr.: **Juste**, **Jut**, **Jux**. (Of 2): Jewish: **Yust**; **Yuster** (representing a Yid. inflected form); **Yustman**.

Cogns. (of 1): It.: **Giusto**. Sp.: **Justo**, **Yuste**. Port.: **Justo**.

Dims. (of 1): Fr.: **Jutel**, **Juteau**, **Jutot**.

Patrs. (from 1): Flem.: **Justens**. Dan.: **Justesen**.

Justice English: nickname for a fair-minded man, from ME, OF *justice* justice, equity (L *iustitia*, a deriv. of *iustus*; see JUST 1). It may well also have been an occupational name for a judge, for this metonymic use of the word is attested from as early as the 12th cent.

Var.: **Jestice**.

Justin French and English: from a medieval given name (L *Justinus*, a deriv. of *Justus*; see JUST 1). This name was borne by various early saints, including a 3rd-cent. Parisian martyr and the first archbishop of Tarbes.

Var.: Fr.: **Jutin**.

Cogns.: It.: **Giustini**. Port.: **Justino**. Pol.: **Justyn(a)**.

Dim.: Ukr.: **Ustimenko**.

Patrs.: Russ.: **Ustinov**, **Ustimov**, **Ustyanov**. Ukr.: **Ustimovich**.

Patrs. (from dims.): Russ.: **Ustin(n)ikov**, **Ustyukhin**.

K

Kabanov Russian: patr. from the nickname *Kaban* 'Wild Boar' (a borrowing from a Turkic language).

Cogns.: Jewish (E Ashkenazic): **Kaban(owitz)** (reason(s) for adoption unclear). Pol.: **Kabaciński**.

Kabat Polish: metonymic nickname for someone who habitually wore a jerkin or whose jerkin was particularly noticeable, from Pol. *kabat* jerkin.

Cogn.: Czech: **Kabát**.

Dim.: Czech: **Kabátek**.

Kabeláč Czech: metonymic nickname or occupational name from a deriv. of Czech *kabela* satchel, leather bag, applied to someone who habitually carried such a bag, i.e. a pedlar.

Var.: **Kabelka**.

Kachler German: occupational name for a potter, from an agent deriv. of MHG *kachel* pot, earthenware vessel (OHG *chachala*, from LL *caculus*, class. L *cacabus*, coming via Gk from a Semitic source). The surname is common in the Alemannic and Swabian regions, and the vocab. word is still current in Alsace, Switzerland, and the Tyrol. The mod. Ger. sense 'glazed tile' is a fairly recent development, and probably has not contributed to the surname. Cf. EULER, HAFNER, POTTER, and TÖPFER.

Var.: **Kächler**.

Kaczor 1. Polish: nickname for someone supposedly resembling a drake, from Pol. *kaczor* drake.

2. Jewish (E Ashkenazic): ornamental name from Pol. *kaczor* drake, one of many taken from vocab. words denoting birds and animals.

Cogns.: Czech: **Kačer**; **Kačena** ('duck').

Dims.: Pol.: **Kaczorek**. Czech: **Kačírek**.

Habitation name: Pol.: **Kaczorowski**.

Kádár Hungarian and Jewish (Ashkenazic): occupational name for a cooper, Hung. *kádár*.

Käfer German: nickname from Ger. *Käfer* bug, beetle (MHG *kever*, OHG *chevar*; cf. Eng. *cockchafer*).

Dims.: **Käferle(in)**.

Kafka 1. Czech: nickname from Czech *kavka* jackdaw (of imitative origin; Pol. *kawka*).

2. Jewish (Ashkenazic): ornamental name from Czech *kavka* jackdaw. According to Kaganov, this was sometimes selected as a Jewish surname because of its phonetic similarity to the Hebr. male given name *Yaakov* (see JACOB), but there does not seem to be any evidence to support this conjecture.

Var.: Czech: **Kavka**.

Cogns.: Pol.: **Kawka, Kawa**; **Kawecki**. Hung.: **Kaffka**.

Habitation names: Pol.: **Kawiński, Kawczyński**.

Kahl German: nickname for a bald man, from Ger. *kahl* bald (cogn. with OE *calu*, used of bare hilltops; see CALLOW 1).

Vars.: **Kahle, Kahler(t)**.

Cogns.: Low Ger.: **Kahl(e)mann**. Du., Flem.: **De Kale, Kaalman, (De) Caluwe, Caluwaert**.

Kahoun Czech: of uncertain origin, possibly an ironic nickname for a sluggish or oafish person, from a deriv. of the dial. word *káhat* to move, budge, stir oneself.

Kaiser 1. German: from Ger. *Kaiser* emperor (MHG *keiser*, OHG *keisar*), from the L imperial title *Caesar*, originally itself a family name (see CESARE). This is widely distributed as a Ger. surname, originating partly as a nickname, perhaps for someone who behaved in an imperious manner. It may also have referred to one who had played the part of an emperor in a pageant or play, and it is also recorded as a house name.

2. Jewish (Ashkenazic): ornamental name from Ger. *Kaiser* emperor, adopted like GRAF, HERZOG, etc., because of its aristocratic connotations.

Ger. *Kaiser* was the title borne by Holy Roman Emperors from Otto I (962) to Francis II (who relinquished the title in 1806). Later, it was borne by the ruler of Bismarck's united Germany (1871–1918). The Russ. word *tsar* was formally adopted as a title at his coronation in 1547 by Ivan the Terrible (1530–84), grand duke of Moscow. However, the word was well established in Russia long before this. Ivan's father, Vasily III (1479–1533) and grandfather, Ivan III (1440–1505), both considered themselves successors to the Byzantine Empire, and Ivan III had in fact married the niece of the last Byzantine emperor.

Vars.: Ger.: **Ke(i)ser, Kayser, Keyser**. Jewish (Ashkenazic): **Kaiserman, Keiser(man), Keizer**.

Cogns.: Eng.: **Cayzer, Kayser, Kayzer, Keyser, Keysor, Keyzor**. Flem., Du.: **(De) Keyser, Keijser, Keyzer, Kei(j)zer**. Czech: **Císař, Císarovský**. Hung.: **Császár**.

Patrs.: Low Ger.: **Keysers**. Russ.: **Tzaryov**. Croatian: **Cesarić**.

Patr. (from a dim.): Russ.: **Tzarkov**.

Kaland German: from MHG *kaland* first day of the month (from L *calendae* (*dies*) (pl.), a deriv. of the archaic verb *calere* to call, announce; in the early Roman calendar it was on this day each month that the dates of the other, movable, landmarks of the calendar were announced). In medieval Ger. guilds, meetings were normally held on the first day of the month, often accompanied by a good deal of revelry. Some guilds were known as *Kalands-Brüderschaften*. The surname probably denoted a member of such a guild, or someone who took a notable part in organizing the guild's meetings and revels.

Vars.: **Kahlandt**; **Kalander**.

Kaleta Polish: metonymic nickname for someone who habitually wore a leather purse, Pol. *kaleta*.

Kalinin Russian: patr. from the given name *Kalina*, a short form of *Kalinik* (from Gk *Kal(l)inik(i)os*, a cpd of the elements *kalos* fair, lovely or *kallos* beauty, loveliness + *nikē* victory). *Kallinikios* was a 3rd-cent. martyr venerated in the Orthodox Church.

Vars.: **Kal(l)inikov**; **Kalinnikov** (by association with agent nouns in *-nnik* from the common adj. ending *-nny*); **Lin(n)ikov**.

Cogn.: Ukr.: **Kalinovich**.

Dims.: Russ. (patrs.): **Kalinkin, Kalinkov, Kalinychev, Kalinichev, Kalitsev**; **Linkov**. Ukr.: **Kalenichenko**.

Kalinowski Polish and Jewish (E Ashkenazic): topographic name or ornamental name from Pol. *kalina* snowball tree, guelder rose (a species of viburnum), or habitation name from a place called *Kalinów*, which gets its name from these plants.

Vars.: Pol.: **Kaliński**. Jewish: **Kalinski**, **Kalinsky**, **Kalinov(sky)**, **Kalinoff**, **Kalina**.

Cogns.: Czech: **Kalina**, **Kalenský**.

Dims.: Pol.: **Kalinka**. Ger. (of Slav. origin): **Kalinke**.

Kalisz Polish and Jewish (E Ashkenazic): habitation name from the town of *Kalisz* in W central Poland, which probably derives its name from OPol. *kal* muddy place, slough (see KAŁUŻA).

Var.: **Kaliszewski**.

Dim.: **Kaliszek**.

Kalivoda Czech: 1. nickname for a troublemaker, from Czech *kalit* to stir + *voda* water.

2. habitation name from the town of *Kalivoda* near Nové Strašecí in central Bohemia.

Var.: **Kalvoda**.

Käll Swedish: ornamental name from Swed. *kjäll* spring, source (ON *kelda*), one of the many words for natural features that were used in the formation of Swed. surnames when these became obligatory during the 18th and 19th cents.

Vars.: **Källén**, **Kjäll(én)**, **Kjell(én)**, **Tjellén**, **Kjellin**; **K(j)ällman**, **Kjellman**; **Kjellander**, **Tjellander**.

Cpds: **K(j)ällberg**, **Kjellberg**, **Tjellberg** ('spring hill'); **K(j)ällgren**, **Kjellgren**, **Tjellgren** ('spring branch'); **K(j)ällqvist**, **Kjellqvist** ('spring twig'); **K(j)ällström**, **Kjellström**, **Tjellström** ('spring river').

Kallio Finnish: ornamental name from Finn. *kallio* rock, one of the many words for natural features that were used in the formation of Finn. surnames when these became obligatory during the 18th and 19th cents.

Kalman Jewish (Ashkenazic): from the Yid. male given name *Kalmen*, the everyday form of the Yid. male given name *Kloynemes* (from Hebr. *Kalonimos*, which is from Gk *kalos* fair, lovely, or *kallos* beauty, loveliness (see KALININ) + *onyma* name). The Hebr. given name is first recorded in the Talmud and has been used continuously since then. Among Hungarian Jews, Yid. *Kalmen* became confused in some cases with the Hung. male given name *Kálmán* (see COLEMAN 1).

Vars.: **Kallman**, **Kel(l)man**, **Kol(l)man**; **Klonymus**.

Patrs.: **Kalmanoff**, **Kalmenoff**, **Kalmanowicz**, **Kalmonowski**, **Kalmowitz** (E Ashkenazic); **Kalmans(on)**, **Kalmenson**, **Kalminson** (Ashkenazic).

Kałuża Polish: topographic name for someone who lived in a muddy or marshy spot, from Pol. *kałuża* puddle, from OPol. *kal* slough.

Vars.: **Kałużka**, **Kałużny**, **Kałużyński**.

Kálvaitis Lithuanian: patr. from the occupational term *kálvis* smith.

Kamiński Polish: 1. occupational name for a quarryman or stone-cutter, from Pol. *kamień* stone + *-ski* suffix of surnames.

2. habitation name from any of the several places named with the Pol. word *kamień* stone, e.g. *Kamieniec* in Lower Silesia, with the addition of the local surname suffix *-ski* (see BARANOWSKI).

Vars.: **Kamieński**; **Kamecki**. (Of 1 only): **Kaminiarz**, **Kamieniak**.

Cogns.: Czech: **Kaminský**, **Kamenský**, **Kamenický**. Jewish (E Ashkenazic): **Kaminski**, **Kaminsky**, **Kamionski**; **Kaminitz(er)**, **Kaminitzki**, **Kaminitzky**, **Kaminitski**, **Kaminitsky**, **Kamin(i)ecki**, **Kamenetzky**, **Kamenetski**, **Kamenetsky**, **Kami(on)ner**; **Kamenka**, **Kami(o)nka**, **Kaminker**; **Kaminkovski**, **Kaminovsky**. (Of 1 only): Czech: **Kamenář**, **Kameník**. Russ.: **Kamenshchikov** (patr.).

Kändler German and Jewish (Ashkenazic): occupational name for a wine steward or cup-bearer, or for a maker of jugs, from Ger. *Kändler*, an agent deriv. of Ger. *Kandel* jug (MHG *kandel*, *kannel*, a dim. of *kanne* can, pot); cf. KANNENGIESSER. The name is most common in Bavaria, Swabia, and E Franconia.

Vars.: **Kendler**; **Kandel** (metonymic).

Kania Polish: nickname for a fierce or powerful person, from Pol. *kania* kite, hawk.

Vars.: **Kani(e)cki**, **Kaniera**.

Cogn.: Hung.: **Kánya**.

Patr. (from a dim.): **Kankiewicz**.

Habitation name: **Kaniewski**.

Kaňka Czech: derogatory nickname of various possible origins. Czech *kaňka* means 'blot' or 'smudge', but it also means 'runt' or 'stunted gosling'. Alternatively, it may be derived from the verb *kanit*, which means variously 'to tattle or gossip', 'to slobber', or in the reflexive 'to flatter'.

Var.: **Kaňák**.

Kannengiesser German and Jewish (Ashkenazic): occupational name for a maker of metal vessels, from Ger. *Kannengiesser* lit. 'can pourer', i.e. a pewterer, one who poured metal alloy into a mould to make cans, from Ger. *Kanne* can, pot (see CANET) + *giessen* to pour, mould (OHG *giozan*). Ger. *Kannegiesser* is also an old slang word for an alehouse politician, and in some cases the name may be a nickname for such a person.

Vars.: **Kann(e)giesser**; **Kanner**.

Cogns.: Low Ger.: **Kanneg(i)eter**.

Kantor 1. German and Czech: occupational name for a master of music, choirmaster, or village schoolmaster, Ger. *Kantor* (from L *cantor*, a deriv. of *cantāre* to sing; cf. CANT).

2. Jewish (Ashkenazic): occupational name for a cantor (see CHAZAN), from Ger. *Kantor*, as in 1.

Vars.: Jewish: **Kanter(man)**; **Cantor**, **Canter** (Anglicized spellings).

Cogn.: Hung.: **Kántor**.

Patrs.: Jewish: **Kanters** (Ashkenazic); **Kantrow**, **Kantorovi(t)ch**, **Kantorowitch**, **Kantorowitsh**, **Kantorovitz**, **Kant(o)rowicz**, **Kant(o)rowitz**, **Cantrowitz**, **Kanterovich**, **Kantarovitch**, **Kantarovitz**, **Kantarowitch**, **Kantarowicz**, **Kantorovsky** (E Ashkenazic).

Kapf German: topographic name for someone who lived near a prominent hill, from MHG *kapfe* mountain peak, top of a hill (apparently from *kapfen* to look, watch, and so applied to a look-out hill or beacon). This word is still current in the Swabian dialect, and the surname is relatively common in Bavaria, Baden, and Württemberg.

Vars.: **Kapfer(er)**.

Kapitonov Russian: patr. from the given name *Kapiton* (L *Capito*, gen. *Capitōnis*, a Roman family name derived originally from *caput*, gen. *capitis*, head; cf. CABEZA and CAP). This name was borne by a 4th-cent. missionary bishop who preached in the Crimea and S Russia, and by another saint commemorated in the Gk martyrology, of whom nothing more than his name is known.

Cogn.: Croatian: **Kapetanović**.

Kaplan 1. German and Czech: occupational name for a curate, Ger. *Kaplan* (a cogn. of CHAPLIN 1), or nickname for someone resembling a clergyman.

2. Jewish (Ashkenazic): surname used as a translation of COHEN, from Ger. *Kaplan* or Pol. *kapłan* chaplain, curate. Not all Jews bearing this name belong to the priestly caste; at one time in the Russian Empire male Jews other than priests were required to join the Russian army for 25 years, and a number changed their surnames to *Kaplan* in the hope of gaining exemption from military service; cf. COHEN.

Vars.: Jewish: **Kaplanski, Kaplinsky, Kaplin(ski)**; **Caplan** (an Anglicized spelling); **Kaplanowicz** (patr.).

Cogn.: Flem., Du.: **Capelaan**.

Kapuściński Polish: habitation name from a place named from Pol. *kapuścisko* cabbage patch (see KAPUSTA) + *-in* possessive suffix, with the addition of *-ski*, suffix of local surnames (see BARANOWSKI).

Kapusta Polish and Jewish (E Ashkenazic): unflattering nickname, of uncertain application, from Pol. *kapusta* cabbage.

Var.: **Kapuściak**.

Karaś Polish and Jewish (Ashkenazic): nickname for someone supposedly resembling a carp, from Pol. *karaś* crucian carp or, in the case of the Jewish name, ornamental name from this word. The word is also found in 16th-cent. Polish with the meaning 'penis', and so the Pol. nickname may be of obscene origin.

Cogns.: Czech: **Karas, Karaus**. Jewish (Ashkenazic): **Karas**.

Dims.: Pol.: **Karasek**. Czech: **Karásek**.

Patrs.: Pol.: **Karasiewicz, Karaszewicz**.

Habitation name: Pol.: **Karasiński**.

Karban Czech: metonymic nickname for a gambler, from Czech *karban* gambling.

Karbowiak Polish: occupational name for a overseer, Pol. *karbowy*, from *karbować* to make notches, i.e. to keep records.

Vars.: **Karbownik, Karbowski**.

Karch German: metonymic occupational name for a carter, from MHG *karrech* two-wheeled cart (from L *carrūca*, a deriv. of *carrus*; cf. CARRIER).

Vars.: **Karcher, Kärcher, Kercher**.

Karczewski Polish and Jewish (Ashkenazic): habitation name from a place called *Karczew* (from Pol. *karcz* stump (cf. Czech KRČ) + *-ew* possessive suffix), with the addition of *-ski*, suffix of local surnames (see BARANOWSKI).

Kardos Hungarian and Jewish (Ashkenazic): occupational name for a swordsman, from Hung. *kard* sword, a borrowing from Turkish. The Jewish name is presumably an adoption of the Hung. one.

Karg 1. German: nickname from MHG *karc* crafty, cunning (OHG *karag* troubled, preoccupied; mod. Eng. *chary* derives from the cogn. OE *cearig*, a deriv. of *cear* care, worry; cf. CARLESS).

2. Jewish (Ashkenazic): nickname from Yid. *karg* miserly (a different sense development of the same word as in 1), or from mod. Ger. *karg* mean, miserly.

Vars.: **Karger**. Jewish: **Kargman**.

Dim.: Ger.: **Kärgel**.

Karjalainen Finnish: regional name for someone from Karelia, from Finn. *Karjala* Karelia + the locative suffix *-ainen*. Karelia was a region of Finland until 1940, when most of it became part of the Soviet Union.

Kärkkäinen Finnish: patr. from a nickname derived from Finn. *kärkkas* eager.

Karlin Jewish (E Ashkenazic): habitation name from a place of this name in Belorussia, near Pinsk, in which Jews formed a majority of the population up to the Second World War. A well-known Chasidic sect originated in Karlin and at one time it attracted so many followers that a (now obsolete) Russian word for 'Chasid' was *Karliner* (of Yid. origin). It is possible that at least some people taking this surname did so because they were members of this sect and not because they were born or lived in Karlin. There is also a Czech town called *Karlín*, but there is no evidence that any of these Ashkenazic surnames derive from it.

Vars.: **Karliner** (with the Yid. suffix *-er* meaning 'native or inhabitant of'); **Karlinski, Karlinsky** (with the Slav. adj. suffix *-ski*); CARLIN, **Carliner** (Anglicized forms).

Karmann German: 1. occupational name for a maker of baskets and other small containers, from MHG, OHG *kar* vessel + *-man(n)* man.

2. topographic name for someone who lived by a patch of land at the bottom of a valley used for pasture, from the Tyrolean dial. term *kar* (apparently a specialized use of the word given in 1) + *-mann*.

Vars.: **Kahr**; **Karer**.

Karpov Russian: 1. patr. from the given name *Karp* (from Gk *karpos* fruit, used with mystical connotations by early Christians). This was the name of a contemporary of St Paul, of whom nothing is known apart from a passing mention in one of the Epistles, but in the Orthodox Church he is believed to have been a bishop and is revered as a saint.

2. patr. from the nickname *Karp* 'Carp' (both the Russ. and Eng. words come from OHG *karpfo*, the latter via OF).

Var. (of 1): **Karpeev**.

Cogns. (of 2, not patrs.): Pol.: **Karp**. Czech: **Kapr, Kapras**. Ger.: **Karpf**. Low Ger., Flem., Du.: **Karpe**. Jewish (Ashkenazic ornamental names): **Karp(man), Karpf(en)**; **Carp** (an Anglicized spelling). Finn.: **Karppi, Karpio**. It.: CARPIO. Port.: **Carpes**.

Dims. (of 1): Beloruss.: **Karpenya, Karpets**. Ukr.: **Karpenko**. Pol.: **Karpik**. Czech: **Karpísek**. Jewish: **Karpel** (in part from the Yid. male given name *Karpl*, a dim. of Yid. *karp* carp).

Patrs. (from 2): Jewish: **Karpoff** (an adoption of the Russ. surname, perhaps under the influence of Yid. *karp* carp). Finn.: **Karpinen**.

Patrs. (from 1) (dims.): Russ.: **Karpushkin, Karputkin, Karpukhin, Karpyshev, Karpychev, Karpunichev, Kartsev**. Jewish: **Karpeles** (from *Karpele*, a dim. of the Yid. given name, + Yid. possessive *-s*).

Habitation name: Pol.: **Karpiński**.

Karski Polish: 1. nickname for a dwarf or for a person of stunted growth, from the Praslovian dial. word *kars* handicapped, stunted (cogn. with Russ. KRIVOV, Czech *krs* stunted).

2. nickname for a left-handed person, from Pol. dial. *karśniawy* left-handed (cogn. with Czech *krška* left-hander, from the same element as in 1). Left-handedness was regarded as a deficiency or deformity in many countries of Europe in earlier times.

Var. (of 2): **Karśnicki**.

Cogns. (of 1): Czech: **Krs**. (Of 2): Czech: **Krška, Kršák, Kršňák**.

Dims. (of 1): Czech: **Krsek**. (Of 2): Czech: **Kršek**.

Karwacki Polish: 1. nickname from a deriv. of Pol. dial. *karw* ox.

2. nickname for someone who habitually wore a waistcoat, from a deriv. of Pol. *karwatka* waistcoat.

Vars. (of 2): **Karwat, Karwatek.**

Habitation names (from 1): **Karwowski, Karwański.**

Kaspar German and Polish: from a given name which was especially popular in central Europe up to the 18th cent. Originally a Persian word meaning 'treasurer', it was ascribed by popular tradition in Europe to one of the three Magi. Their supposed remains were brought to Cologne from Constantinople in the 12th cent., and the name gained considerable popularity in Europe after this. See also BALTHASAR and MELCHIOR.

Vars.: Ger.: **Kasper, Kesper, Casper.** Pol.: **Kasparski, Kasper(ski), Kaszper; Sperski** (aphetic form).

Cogns.: Low Ger.: **Jaspar, Jasper, Jesper.** Flem.: **Jesper.** Eng. (Devon and Cornwall): **Jasper.** Czech: **Kašpar, Kasper.** Hung.: **Gáspár.** Fr.: **Gaspar(d); Jaspar** (NE France). It.: **Casperri, Gasperi, Gaspero, Gaspar(r)i, Gaspar(r)o, Gaspardo, Gaspardi, Gasbarri; Parri** (Tuscany). Port.: **Gaspar.**

Dims.: Pol.: **Kasparek, Kasperek; Kasprzyk, Kacprzyk, Kasprzycki; Kacperczyk; Kaszczyk.** Czech: **Kašpárek.** Fr.: **Gasperin, Gasparin, Gasparoux.** It.: **Gasperini, Gaspar(r)ini, Gaspardini, Gasbarrini, Gasperetti, Gaspar(in)etti, Gasperotti, Gasparotti, Gasparelli, Gasparoli; Sperelli, Sperotto** (Venetia); **Parelli, Par(r)ini, Parrucci** (Tuscany).

Augs.: It.: **Gasperoni, Gasparoni; Speroni** (Venetia).

Patrs.: Ger.: **Caspary** (also Jewish (Ashkenazic), adoption of the Ger. name). Low Ger.: **Jaspars, Jaspers, Kespers, Caspers; Jasparsen, Jaspersen, Jespersen.** Flem., Du.: **Jaspers, Jespers, Caspers.** Dan.: **Jespersen.** It.: **De Gasperi, De Gaspari, Gaspardis.** Pol.: **Kasprowicz, Kacprowicz; Kasprzak, Kacprzak; Przykowicz; Kasprowiak.** Beloruss.: **Kasperov(ich), Kasparov.**

Patrs. (from dims.): Pol.: **Kasparkiewicz, Kasprzykiewicz.**

Habitation name: Pol.: **Kasprowicki.**

Kastner German and Jewish (Ashkenazic): occupational name for a maker of boxes and chests, from Ger. *Kastner*, agent deriv. of *Kasten* chest (MHG *kaste* casket, OHG *kasto*). The Ger. word also denoted a treasurer or other official responsible for financial matters, i.e. one who had control of a money chest, and this may in some cases be the source of the surname.

Vars.: Ger.: **Kästner, Kestner; Köstner** (Bavaria).

Kaszuba Polish: ethnic name for a Kashubian, Pol. *Kaszuba*, a member of a Slav. people living in N Poland southwest and west of Gdańsk.

Var.: **Kaszubski.**

Cogn.: Czech: **Kašuba.**

Kataev Russian: patr. from the nickname *Katai* (from *katat* to roll, turn, spin), denoting a restless individual.

Katan Jewish (Sefardic): nickname from Hebr. *katan* small; cf. KLEIN.

Vars.: **Kattan, Cat(t)an.**

Katona Hungarian and Jewish (Ashkenazic): occupational name for a soldier, Hung. *katona*.

Katz Jewish (Ashkenazic): acronym from the Hebr. phrase *Kohen TSedek* priest of righteousness. The surname cannot be derived from Hebr. *katsin* rich man, since the Ashkenazic pronunciation of this word always has /o/ in the first syllable.

Vars.: **Katzman(n).**

Cpd (ornamental): **Katzenstein** (ostensibly Ger. 'cat stone').

Katzenellenbogen Jewish (Ashkenazic): habitation name from *Katzenelnbogen* in the Prussian province of Hesse-Nassau. The place is probably named from the Celt. tribal name *Chattimelibochi*, which is of unknown origin. However, it has been altered by folk etymology as if it meant 'cat's elbow'.

Vars.: **Katz(e)nelson** (sometimes assumed by bearers to be from KATZ, with the addition of *Nelson* (see NEIL) during or after the Napoleonic Wars in honour of the English admiral Lord Nelson, but this is no more than folk etymology).

The earliest known bearer of this name is Meir Ben Yitschak (c.1480–c.1565), Chief Rabbi of the Venetian Republic, who was born in Katzenellenbogen in Hesse-Nassau.

Katzev Jewish (Ashkenazic): occupational name for a butcher, Yid. *katsev* (from Hebr. *katsav*).

Vars.: **Katsevman; Katzeff, Katziff** (*-ff* reflecting a regional Yid. pronunciation); **Katzoff; Kacew** (Pol. spelling), **Kacev, Kaciff.**

Patrs. ('son of the butcher'; E Ashkenazic): **Katzowitz, Katzowitch, Kacowicz.**

Kavanagh Irish: Anglicized form of the Gael. personal name *Caomhánach* '(follower) of (St) *Caomhán*', a personal name from a dim. of *caomh* gentle, tender (cf. KEEFE) which was borne by no less than fifteen early Ir. saints.

Vars.: **Cavana(u)gh.**

Irish bearers of this name trace their descent from the ancient Kings of Leinster, including Dermot McMorrough (d. 1170).

Kay English: 1. occupational name for a maker of keys or for someone who held the (often largely ceremonial) office of key-bearer, from OE *cǣg* key.

2. topographic name for someone who lived by a wharf or was employed on one, from ME, OF *kay(e)* quay (apparently of Gaul. origin; cf. Bret. *cai* fence).

3. from a ME given name of Celt. origin (OW *Cai*, Corn. *Key*), borne by the boastful foster-brother of King Arthur. This name may be ultimately derived from the old Roman name *Gaius* (see GAY 3).

4. nickname from the jackdaw, Northern ME *kay* (ON *ká*, of imitative origin). See also COE.

5. nickname for a left-handed man, from the Dan. dial. term *kei* left, which was borrowed in the 13th cent. into the dialects of Lancs. and Ches., and survived in this area up to the 19th cent.

6. surname adopted by immigrants to an English-speaking country who originally bore any of various non-English surnames beginning with the letter *K*-.

Vars.: **Kaye, Keay, Key(e).** See also KEYES. (Of 2 only): **Atkey.**

Cogns. (of 3): Low Ger.: **Kai, Kay.** (Of 4): Flem.: **De Cae, De Cauw.**

Kazimierski Polish and Jewish (E Ashkenazic): habitation name from a town called *Kazimierz* (from the given name; see KAŹMIERCZAK) + *-ski* suffix of local surnames (see BARANOWSKI). Kazimierz to the NE of Cracow was founded in 1335 by King Casimir the Great (1310–70), and had a substantial Jewish population.

Vars.: Pol.: **Kazimierz, Kaźmierski.** Jewish (E Ashkenazic): **Kazimirski, Kazimi(e)rsky.**

Kaźmierczak Polish: from the Pol. given name *Kazimierz* Casimir (composed of the elements *kazić* to spoil, destroy + *mir* peace, i.e. destroyer of the enemy's peace) + the associative suffix *-czak*, which has patronymic force when used with given names. This name was much used by Pol. royalty, starting with Duke Casimir the Restorer (1015–58), who united the central Polish lands under the Holy Roman Empire. Casimir III, called Casimir the Great (1310–70), presided over a period of great peace and prosperity in Poland. A son of the 15th-cent. Casimir IV, himself called Casimir, became the patron saint of Poland and Lithuania; he spurned his father's ambitions for him to seize the Hungarian throne, and devoted himself instead to a religious life.

Var.: **Kazimierczak**.

Cogns.: Hung.: **Kázmér**. Fr.: **Casimir**. Port.: **Casimiro**.

Patrs.: Pol.: **Kazimierowicz**. Beloruss.: **Kazimirov**.

Patr. (from a dim.): Pol.: **Kazkiewicz**.

Keane 1. Irish: Anglicized form of Gael. **Ó Catháin** 'descendant of *Cathán*', a personal name from a dim. of *cath* battle.

2. English: var. of KEEN.

Vars.: **Kean**. (Of 1 only): **Kane** (see also CAIN), **Cahane**.

Kearney Irish: Anglicized form of Gael. **Ó Ceithearnaigh** 'descendant of *Ceithearnach*', a byname meaning 'Soldier'.

Var.: **O'Kearney**.

Kearns Irish: Anglicized form of Gael. **Ó Céirín** 'descendant of *Céirín*', a personal name from a dim. of *ciar* dark, black (cogn with the Slav. word *cherny*; cf. Russ. CHERNYAKOV).

Kearsley English (Lancs.): habitation name from a place near Manchester, which Ekwall etymologizes as being from OE *cærs*, *cræs* watercress + *hlāw* hill or *lēah* wood, clearing. There is another place of the same name but different etymology in Northumb., which does not seem to have contributed to the surname.

Keast Cornish: nickname for a fat man, from Corn. **kest* paunch (cf. W *cest* belly, also used as a medieval byname).

Keating 1. English: from the OE personal name *Cȳting*, originally a patr. from *Cȳta* 'KITE'.

2. Irish: var. of KEATY.

Keaty Irish: Anglicized form of Gael. **Ó Céatfhadha** 'descendant of *Céatfhaidh*', a byname from *céat(fhadh)ach* reasonable, urbane.

Vars.: **O'Keaty**; KEATING.

Keble English: nickname given either to a thick, heavy man or to a belligerent individual, from ME *kibble* cudgel (probably of native origin, although no OE forms are attested).

Vars.: **Keeble, Keable, Kebble, Keb(b)ell, Kibble, Kib(b)el**.

Kedge English: nickname from ME *kedge* brisk, lively, a dial. term confined to E Anglia, and probably of ON origin (cf. mod. Swed. *käck* bold, brisk).

Var.: **Ketch**.

Cogn.: Swed.: **Käck**.

Keech English: unflattering nickname for a fat, lumpish man, from ME *keech* lump of fat (of unknown origin).

Vars.: **Keetch, Kea(t)ch, Keitch**.

Keefe Irish: Anglicized form of Gael. **Ó Caoimh** 'descendant of *Caomh*', a byname meaning 'Gentle', 'Kind'.

Vars.: **Keeffe, O'Keefe, O'Keeve**.

Dims.: **(O')Ke(a)vane, Keevane, Kevans, Cavan**, CAVENDISH (Gael. **Ó Caomháin**).

Keegan Irish: 1. Anglicized form of Gael. **Mac Aodhagáin**, patr. from the personal name *Aodhagán*, a double dim. of *Aodh* 'Fire'; cf. MCKAY.

2. Anglicized form of Gael. **Mac Thadhgáin**, patr. from the personal name *Tadhgán*, a dim. of the byname *Tadhg* 'Poet'; cf. TIGHE.

Vars. (of 1): **McKeegan, McKeagan, McKiegan(e), McKeggan; McEgan, McEgaine, McHeagan**. (Of 2): **Kegan, Keggin(s)**.

Keeler English (SE England): occupational name for a boatman or boatbuilder, from ME *kele* ship, barge (a borrowing of MDu. *kiel* rather than a direct descendant of OE *cēol*).

Var.: **Keel**.

Keeley 1. Irish: Anglicized form of Gael. **Ó Caollaidhe** 'descendant of *Caollaidhe*', a personal name derived from *caol* slender, graceful.

2. English: var. of KEIGHLEY.

Vars. (of 1): **Keely, Keal(e)y; Queely, Queal(l)y**; KIELY.

Keeling English: of uncertain origin, perhaps from a medieval given name, originally an OE patr. from a short form of any of the various cpd personal names with the first element *cēol* keel, ship.

Keen 1. English: nickname from ME *kene* fierce, brave, proud (OE *cēne*).

2. English: from the ME given name *Kene*, a short form of any of the various OE personal names with the first element *cēne* (see above) or *cyne-* royal (from *cyning* chieftain, king, a deriv. of *cyn(n)* tribe, race, people).

3. Irish: var. of KEANE.

Var.: **Keene**.

Patr. (from 2): **Kenning**.

Keenlyside N English: habitation name from an unidentified minor place, apparently so called from the OE name *Cēna* (a byname meaning 'Keen', 'Bold' or a short form of various cpd personal names with this first element) + OE *lēah* wood, clearing + *sīde* hillside.

Keep English: occupational name for someone who was employed in the dungeon of a castle, ME *keep* (probably from the verb *keep(en)* to hold, defend, OE *cēpan*).

Keevil English: habitation name from a place in Wilts., recorded in Domesday Book as *Chivele*. It is probably so called either from an OE personal name *Cyfa* (related to *cufa*) or from the gen. pl. of OE *cȳf* tub, vessel + OE *lēah* wood. The second alternative would denote a wood which produced material used for making tubs.

Kehl German: 1. nickname for someone with some deformity of the throat or neck, perhaps goitre, which was common in the Alpine regions, from Ger. *Kehle* throat (MHG *kel*, OHG *kela*).

2. topographic name from the same word used in the sense of a narrow gorge or defile, or habitation name from one of the minor places named with this word.

Keighley English: habitation name from a place in W Yorks., recorded in Domesday Book as *Chichelai*, apparently from the OE name *Cyhha* (of uncertain origin) + OE *lēah* wood, clearing.

Vars.: **Keighly**; KEELEY; **K(e)ightley, K(e)itley, Keatley, Keetley, Kitlee; Cichle** (Wales).

Most bearers of this surname in its various spellings are descended from Sir Henry de Kygheley *or* Kighley, *who held the manor in 1305. His direct male line died out in the 16th cent., but by that time the surname was already spreading across Yorks. and into Derbys. and Notts. The Keighley estates came into the possession of the Cavendish family through the marriage in the early 17th cent. of a Keighley heiress to Sir William Cavendish of Hardwick.*

Keil German: nickname for a large and clumsy individual, from Ger. *Keil* wedge (MHG, OHG *kīl*); this use of the word is reflected in the proverb *auf einem grossen* KLOTZ *gehört ein grosser Keil* ('a great lump needs a great wedge'). Occasionally the surname may have been acquired as an occupational name by someone who made use of wedges, for example in splitting stone, or as a topographic name by someone who lived on a wedge-shaped piece of land. The surname is also borne by Ashkenazic Jews, but the reason(s) for its adoption are unkown.

Cogns.: Swed. (ornamental): **Ki(h)lén, Ki(h)lin.**

Cpds (ornamental): Swed.: **Ki(h)lberg** ('wedge hill'); **Ki(h)lgren** ('wedge branch'); **Ki(h)lström** ('wedge river').

Keith Scots: habitation name from a place so called between Huntly and Elgin. The placename is first recorded in 1187 as *Geth* and in *c.*1220 as *Keth*; it is probably from the Brit. element *cet* wood (cf. W *coed*).

This is the name of a family who have held the title Mariscal of Scotland since the 12th cent. They trace their descent from a certain Hervey, who in the 12th cent. owned the lands from which the name is derived. They have held the earldom of Kintore since 1677.

Kelleher Irish: Anglicized form of Gael. **Ó Céileachair** 'descendant of *Céileachar*', a byname meaning 'Uxorious'.

Var.: **Kelliher.**

Kellett English: habitation name from Nether and Over *Kellet* in N Lancs. near Lancaster, or *Kelleth* in Cumb., all of which derive their names from ON *kelda* spring (see KÄLL) + *hlíð* slope, hillside. The former is the usual source of the surname.

Vars.: **Kellet, Kellitt.**

Kellner 1. German: occupational name for a person in charge of the wine cellars in a great house or castle, MHG *kelnære* (OHG *kelnari*, agent deriv. of *kellari* cellar, from LL *cellārium*, a deriv. of *cella* small room, store-room, from *celāre* to hide; cogn. of Eng. SELLER 3). The mod. Ger. sense of *Kellner*, 'waiter', is a comparatively recent development. It has not influenced the Ger. surname, but may lie behind some cases of the Jewish name.

2. Jewish: probably a habitation name from *Keln*, the Yid. name of the city of *Cologne* (Ger. *Köln*).

Vars.: **Kelner.** (Of 1 only): **Keller(t), Kellar(t), Kel(l)ermann.**

Cogns. (of 1, in the sense 'waiter' or 'cellarman'): Jewish (Ashkenazic): **Kel(l)ner, Kel(l)er, Kellerman(n), Kelerman.**

Kello English: habitation name from *Kelloe* in Co. Durham, so called from OE *cealf* CALF + *hlāw* hill (see LAW 2 and LOW 1).

The Durham family of this name are descended from Thomas de Kelloe, *who lived in the early 13th cent. Richard Kello was bishop of Durham 1310–16.*

Kellogg 1. English: occupational nickname for a pork butcher, from ME *kellen, killen, kullen* to kill, slaughter (OE **cyllan*, a byform of *cwellan*) + *hog* hog, pig (see HOGG).

2. Irish: Anglicized form of Gael. *Ó Ceallaigh*; see KELLY 1.

3. Welsh: of uncertain origin, popularly associated with W *ceiliog* cock.

Var.: **Kellog.**

A certain Joseph Kellogg *emigrated from Great Leighs, Essex, to Connecticut in 1651. Among his descendants were Albert Kellogg (1813–87), an eminent botanist, son of a prosperous farming family, and William Kellogg (1830–1918), who became governor of Louisiana.*

Kellow Cornish: habitation name from a minor place so called, from Corn. *kellow*, pl. of *kelli* wood, grove (cf. KELLY 3).

Kelly 1. Irish: Anglicized form of Gael. **Ó Ceallaigh** 'descendant of *Ceallach*', originally a byname meaning 'Troublesome', 'Contentious', also said to mean 'Bright-headed'. There were several early Ir. saints who bore this name, and *Kelly* is now the most common of all Ir. surnames. The form **Mac Ceallaigh** 'son of *Ceallach*' (Anglicized **McKelly**, Ulster **Miskelly**) is much rarer.

2. Scots: habitation name from any of various places, such as *Kelly* near Arbroath, named with the Gael. element *coille* wood, grove.

3. English: habitation name from *Kelly* in Devon, named with a Corn. cogn. of 2 (cf. KELLO).

Vars. (of 1): **O'Kelly, Kelley,** KELLOGG, **Kelloch, Kellock.**

There has been a family of this name at Kelly in Devon since Martin de Kelly *was recorded there c.1100.*

Kelsall English: habitation name from a place in Ches., so called from the gen. case of the ME personal name *Kell* (ON *Kell* or *Ketill*) + ME *hale* nook, recess (OE *halh*).

Var.: **Kilshaw.**

Kelsey English: habitation name from a place in Lincs., so called from the gen. case of the OE personal name **Cēnel* (a deriv. of cpd names with the first element *cēne* fierce, brave; cf. KEEN) + OE *ēg* island, low-lying land.

Kelso Scots and N Irish: habitation name from a place so called on the river Tweed, perhaps from OE *cealc* CHALK + *hōh* ridge, spur.

Kemble 1. English: from the ME given name *Kimbel, Chimbel*, OE *Cynebeal(d)*, composed of the elements *cyne-* royal + *beald* bold, brave.

2. English: habitation name from a place in Gloucs., named from a Brit. word related to W *cyfyl* border.

3. Welsh: from a Celt. personal name composed of the elements *cyn* chief + *bel* war. This personal name was borne by an early Brit. chieftain whose name is recorded in a Latinized form as *Cunobelinus*; he provided the inspiration for Shakespeare's *Cymbeline*.

The English theatrical dynasty, the Kembles, *were members of a family of Wilts. origin. Another member of the family was Father John Kemble, a priest who was hanged in 1676 for his alleged part in the 'Popish Plot'.*

Kemény Hungarian and Jewish (Ashkenazic): nickname for a stern or severe person, from Hung. *kemény* hard.

Kemmelman Jewish (Ashkenazic): 1. occupational name for a maker or seller of combs, from Yid. *keml* comb (a dim. of *kam*) + *man* man.

2. possibly a nickname from Yid. *keml* CAMEL + *man*.

Var.: **Kemelman.**

Kemp English: occupational name for a champion at jousting or wrestling, ME *kempe* (a weakened sense of OE *cempa* warrior, champion, from *camp* battle, L *campus* plain, field (of battle); cf. CAMPION).

Vars.: **Kempe.**

Cogns.: Ger.: **Kampf, Kempf; Kömpf** (Bavaria); **Kempner** (also Jewish, presumably an adoption of the Ger. surname). Low Ger.: **Kempe.** Du.: **Kemper.**

Dims.: Ger.: **Kämpfl, Kempfle.**

Patrs.: Eng.: **Kempson.** Du.: **Kempers.** Finn.: **Kemppainen.**

Kempa Polish: topographic name for someone who lived on a small island or by an isolated clump of trees, from Pol. *kępa* islet; the same word is also applied to isolated clumps of trees and to tufts of grass.

Vars.: **Kępa; Kempski; Kępski.**

Cogn.: Jewish (E Ashkenazic): **Kempe** (from *kempe*, the Yid. reflex of the Pol. vocab. word); **Kempinski.**

Dim.: Pol.: **Kępka.**

Habitation names: Pol.: **Kempiński; Kępiński, Kępczyński.**

Kempton English: habitation name from *Kempton* in Shrops. or *Kempton* Park near London, recorded in Domesday Book as *Chenpitune* and *Chenetone* respectively. The former is so called from the OE byname *Cempa* 'Warrior' (see KEMP) + OE *tūn* enclosure, settlement; the latter from the OE personal name *Cēna* (see KEENLYSIDE) + *tūn*.

Kendall English: habitation name from *Kendale* in the parish of Driffield, Yorks., or *Kendal* in Cumb. The latter is so called from the Brit. river name KENT + OE *dæl* valley (see DALE); the former is from ON *kelda* spring + ON *dalr* or Late OE *dæl* valley. The surname is very widespread, with a large number of bearers now found as far away as Cornwall.

Vars.: **Kendal, Kendell, Kendle, Kindall, Kindell, Kindle.**

Kendrick 1. English: from the ME given name *Cenric*, *Kendrich*, OE *Cynerīc*, composed of the elements *cyne-* royal + *rīc* power.

2. Welsh: from the W personal name *Cyn(w)rig*, *Cynfrig*, possibly composed of the elements *cyn* chief + *(g)wr* man, hero + the suffix of quality *-ig*.

3. Scots: apocopated form of MCKENDRICK; see MCHENRY.

4. Irish: see ENRIGHT.

Vars. (of 1): **Kindrick, Ken(w)rick, Kerrick; Kerrich, Kerridge, Kerrage, Kirrage, Carriage, Courage** (E Anglia); **Kerry** (E Midlands).

Patr. (from 1): **Kerrison.**

Kennard English: from the ME given name, *Keneward*, OE *Cyneweard*, composed of the elements *cyne-* royal + *heard* hardy, brave, strong or *weard* guard.

Vars. (from the second possibility): **Kenward, Kenwood.**

Kennaway English: from the ME given name *Kenewi*, OE *Cynewīg* or *Cēnwīg*, composed of the elements *cyne-* royal or the rarer *cēne* keen, bold + *wīg* war.

Var.: **Kenway.**

Kenneally Irish: Anglicized form of Gael. **Ó Cionnfhaolaidh** 'descendant of *Cionnfhaoladh*', a personal name derived from *ceann* head + *faol* wolf.

Vars.: **(O')Kennelly, O'Kenneally, (O')Kin(n)eally, Kenne(a)ly.**

Kennedy 1. Irish: Anglicized form of Gael. **Ó Cinnéidigh** 'descendant of *Cinnéidigh*', a personal name derived from *ceann* head + *éidigh* armoured. The name thus meant literally 'helmeted head', but was apparently also a byname for someone with an ugly or deformed head, as in the case of the nephew of Brian Boru, who is claimed as an ancestor by many present-day Kennedys.

2. Jewish: Anglicized form of **Kenedi**, a surname found among Hungarian Jews, which is of unknown origin.

Vars. (of 1): **O'Kennedy, O'Kinedy.**

A Scottish family called Kennedy *claim descent from Duncan, Earl of Carrick (cr. 1228). He was the grandson of Fergus, Lord of Galloway (d. 1161). The family also hold the marquessate of Ailsa and the earldom of Cassillis.*

Kennett English: habitation name from a place in Wilts., so called from the river *Kennet*, on which it stands. This bears an old Brit. name of unknown origin.

Kenngott German: from a Gmc female personal name composed of the elements *kuni* race, people + *gund* battle. This name was popular in the Middle Ages as a result of the fame of St Kunigunde (d. 1039), wife of the Holy Roman Emperor Heinrich II, and also of a Bohemian queen of the same name, the wife of St Wenceslas. In later times the surname has been altered by folk etymology, associating it with Ger. *kennen* to know + *Gott* God.

Vars.: **Könngott, Kunigunde.**

Dims.: **Künne, Kinne.**

Metrs.: **Köngeter, Kingeter.**

Metrs. (from dims.): Ger.: **Kin(t)scher, Küntscher.**

Kenny 1. Scots: Anglicized form of the Gael. personal name *Cionaodha*, of uncertain origin, perhaps composed of the elements *cion* respect, affection + *Aodh*, the name of a pagan god of fire. The personal name thus probably means 'beloved of Aodh', but has also been interpreted as 'ardent love'.

2. Irish: Anglicized form of Gael. **Ó Coinnigh** 'descendant of *Coinneach*', an OIr. personal name borne, for example, by the 6th-cent. monk and saint who gave his name to the town of *Kilkenny* 'Church of Coinneach'.

Vars.: **Kenney, Kinn(e)y, Kinnie.**

Patrs. (from 1): **McKenny, McKinn(e)y, McKinnie, McKe(a)ney, McKenna, McKinna** (Gael. **Mac Cionaodha**).

Patr. (from 1) (dim.): **(Mc)Kennan** (Gael. **Mac Cionaodháin**).

'Descendant of K. 1': **O'Kenn(e)y, O'Kinn(e)y, (O')Kenna, O'Kinna, O'Kenaith** (Gael. **Ó Cionaodha**).

Kennan *is the name of an Irish family of Scottish origin. They are recorded in Dumfries and Kirkcudbright until the late 17th cent.; one of the first bearers recorded in Ireland was Andrew Kennan, who obtained lands in Co. Dublin in the 18th cent.*

Kent English: regional name from the county of *Kent*, which is of apparently Brit. origin, but uncertain etymology. It may mean 'coastal district', from the Celt. element *canto* (cf. W *cant* rim, border).

Vars.: **Kentish, Kintish.**

Kenton English: habitation name from any of various places so called, which have a number of different etymologies. One near London has the same origin as KEMPTON nearby; one in Northumb. has as its first element OE *cyne-* royal; one in Suffolk may have the same origin as either of the two preceding examples, or it may get its first element from the OE personal name *Cyna*, a short form of the various cpd names with the first element *cyne-* royal; one in Devon is so called from its situation on the river *Kenn*, which bears an old Brit. name of uncertain origin.

Kenworthy English: habitation name from a place in Ches., apparently so called from the OE personal name *Cyna* (see KENTON) or *Cēna* (see KEENLYSIDE) + OE *worðig* enclosure (see WORTHY).

Kenyeres Hungarian: occupational name for a bread-seller, from a deriv. of Hung. *kenyér* bread.

Kenyon English (Lancs.): habitation name from a place near Warrington, which is of uncertain etymology. There was formerly an ancient burial mound there and Ekwall has speculated that the name is a shortened form of a Brit. name composed of the elements *crūc* mound (see CRICH) + a personal name cogn. with Welsh *Einion* 'Anvil'.

The earliest known ancestor of bearers of this name was Jordan Kenyon, *lord of the manor of Kenyon in the 13th cent.*

Keogh Irish: Anglicized form of Gael. **Mac Eochaidh** 'son of *Eochaidh*', a personal name derived from *each* horse.

Vars.: **Keoghoe, (Mc)K(e)ough, (Mc)Kehoe, McKeogh(oe), McKeo, McGeogh, McEoghoe.** + Kough

Dims.: **Keohane, Keog(h)an** (Gael. **Mac Eocháin**); see also GAHAN and MCGUIGAN. Manx: **Quaggin, Weggin.**

Keppie Scots: habitation name from *Kippo* in Fife, so called from Gael. *ceap*, *cip* block, tree-stump, hillock + the local suffix *-ach*.
Var.: **Kippie**.

Kerfoot English (Lancs.): habitation name from an unidentified place, which perhaps derives its name from ME *kerr* wet ground (see KERR) + *fote* foot, bottom of a hill (cf. FOOT).
Vars.: **Kerfod, Kerfed**.

Kern German and Jewish (Ashkenazic): from Ger. *Kern* kernel, seed, pip, Yid. *kern* (MHG *kerne*, OHG *kerno*, related to KORN 1). The application as a surname is not clear: it could be a metonymic occupational name for a seller of shelled nuts or for a supplier of seeds, a nickname for a small person, or, in the case of the Jewish name, simply ornamental. See also KERNER.

Kernaghan Irish: Anglicized form of Gael. **Mac Thighearnacháin**, patr. from the personal name *Tighearnachán*, a dim. of *tighearnach* lord, master; cf. TIERNEY.
Var.: **Kernohan**. See also MCKIERNAN.

Kerner 1. German and Jewish (Ashkenazic): occupational var. of KERN, with agent suffix.
2. Low German: occupational name for a carter, from MLG *kerenere*, an agent deriv. of *kar(r)e* cart (cf. CARRIER).
Var. (of 1): Jewish: **Kernerman**.

Kerr Scots and N English: topographic name for someone who lived near a patch of wet ground overgrown with brushwood, Northern ME *kerr* (ON *kjarr*). The pronunciation /kɑ:(r)/ reflects the ME change of *-er-* to *-ar-* (cf. MARCHANT), seen in the var. spelling CARR. A legend grew up that the Kerrs were left-handed, from Gael. *cearr* wrong, left-handed.
Vars.: **Ke(i)r**.
Cogns.: Dan.: **Kjær, Kiær**.
Cpd (ornamental): Swed.: **Kärrström** ('marsh river').
Ker(r) *is the name of a Scottish family with many branches, among them the Marquesses of Lothian. One of their earliest recorded ancestors was John Kerr of Selkirk Forest, mentioned in a charter of 1357. Another branch of the family, using the spelling* Carr, *acquired the earldom of Somerset in 1613, when James I granted this title to his favourite Robert Carr (?1587–1645), to whom he had previously granted the confiscated lands of Sir Walter Raleigh at Sherborne.*

Kerrigan Irish: Anglicized form of Gael. **Ó Ciaragáin** 'descendant of *Ciaragán*', a byname from a double dim. of *ciar* dark, black (cf. KEARNS and CAREY).
Vars.: **Ker(i)gan, O'Kerrigane, O'Kierrigain**.

Kersey English: habitation name from a place in Suffolk, recorded in Domesday Book as *Careseia*, probably from OE *cærs* watercress + *ēg* island, low-lying land.

Kershaw English: habitation name from *Kirkshaw* in the parish of Rochdale, Lancs., so called from Northern ME *kirk* church (see KIRK) + *shaw* grove (see SHAW). There are two minor places in W Yorks. called *Kershaw*, which may be of the same origin and may also lie behind the surname, but on the other hand they may themselves derive from the surname.
Vars.: **Kersaw, Kirshaw**.

Kertész Hungarian (partly Jewish): occupational name for a gardener, Hung. *kertész*, from *kert* garden + *-ész* occupational suffix.

Keser 1. German: var. of KAISER.
2. German: cogn. of CHEESEMAN.
3. Low German: status name for someone who held the franchise in respect of a particular electoral procedure, from MLG *ke(e)sen* to chose; cf. KIESER.
Var. (of 3): **Keeser**.

Kessel German: metonymic occupational name for someone who made cooking vessels of various sizes from copper, from Ger. *Kessel* kettle, cauldron (MHG *kezzel*, OHG *kezzil*; cf. KETTLE).
Vars.: **Kessler; Kössler** (Bavaria).
Cogns.: Low Ger.: **Ket(t)el, Kettler**. Flem., Du.: **Van Kessel, Kesseler**. Ukr.: **Kotlyar(evski)**. Beloruss.: **Kotlyarov** (patr.), **Kotlyarchuk** (dim.). Jewish (Ashkenazic): **Kes(s)ler, Kettler, Kesselman; Kotl(i)ar, Kotlarski, Kotlarsky, Kotler, Cotler**, CUTLER.

Ketley English: habitation name from a place in Shrops., so called from OE *catta* (wild) cat (see CATT) + *lēah* wood, clearing.

Kett 1. English (Norfolk): var. of KITE.
2. Jewish (Ashkenazic): of unknown origin.

Kettle English: from the ON personal name *Ketill*, a short form of the various cpd names in *-ketill* cauldron (cf. ASHKETTLE and THIRKILL).
Vars.: **Kettel(l), Ketill, Kitell, Kittle; Kell** (Northumb.).
Patrs.: Eng.: **Kettles(s), Kells; Kettelson**. Norw., Dan.: **Ketels(en), Kjeldsen**. Swed.: **Kilsson**.

Kettlewell English: habitation name from a place in W Yorks., so called from OE *cetel* KETTLE, deep valley + *well(a)* spring, stream (see WELL).

Kettunen Finnish: patr. from the nickname *Kettu* 'Fox', with the addition of the gen. suffix *-nen*.

Kevern Cornish: habitation name from the parish of *St Keverne* on the Lizard peninsula. The patron of the parish is a rather shadowy figure, whose name is first recorded as *Achobran* in the 10th cent., probably identical with the Irish saint *Accobrán*.

Kew English: 1. occupational name for a cook, ANF *k(i)eu* (L *coquus*; see COOK).
2. Norman habitation name from *Caieu*, a lost town near Boulogne in N France.
3. habitation name from a place in Middlesex, now part of SW London, so called from OE *cǣg* key, projection + *hōh* ridge, slope.
Vars. (of 1): **Le Keux, Lequeux**. (Of 2): **Kehoe, Keyho(e)** (see also KEOGH).
John de Caiho *was one of the sheriffs of London in 1201–2, and may well be an ancestor of some bearers of this name.*

Keyes 1. English: var. of KAY.
2. English (Norman): habitation name from *Guise* in Aisne, Picardy, which is first recorded in the 12th cent. as *Gusia* and is of uncertain etymology.
3. Irish: Anglicized form of Gael. *Mac Aodha*; see MCKAY.
Vars.: **Kay(e)s, Ke(a)ys, Keeys**.
A number of English bearers of this name can be traced to the Norman family of Guiz *or* Gyse. *The name has taken various forms, including* Cays, Caius, Gyz, Kees, *and* Keyse. *It is now most common in Ireland.*

Keynes English (Norman): habitation name from *Cahaignes* in Eure or *Cahaynes* in Calvados, both apparently named from a Celt. element denoting the juniper bush.
Vars.: **Kaines, Cain(e)s**.

Keyworth English: habitation name from a place in Notts., recorded as *Caworde* in Domesday Book, of uncertain etymology. The second element is clearly OE *worð* enclosure (see WORTH); Ekwall suggests that the first element may be OE *cǣg* key, projection.

Khachaturian Armenian: patr. from the personal name *Khachatur* 'Cross-bearer'.

Khavke Jewish (E Ashkenazic): from *Khavke*, a pet form of the Yid. female given name *Khave* (from Hebr. *Chava* EVE).

Metrs.: **Khavkin, Chavkin, Havkin, Havken**; **Havlin** (based on *Khavele*, a different dim. of *Khave*).

Khlebnikov Russian: patr. from the occupational term *khlebnik* baker (from *khleb* bread, a borrowing from a Gmc cogn. of mod. Eng. *loaf*).

Cogns.: Pol. and Jewish (E Ashkenazic): **Chlebowski**.

Khrushchev Russian: patr. from the nickname *Khrushch* 'May Beetle'. This word is ultimately from *khrust-* to rustle, and so is cogn. with Pol. CHRUŚCIEL.

Var.: **Krushchyov**.

Cogns.: Pol.: **Chrząszcz**. Czech: **Chroust**.

Habitation name: Pol.: **Chrząszczyński**.

Kidd 1. English: nickname for a frisky person or metonymic occupational name for a goatherd, from ME *kid(e)* young goat (of uncertain origin, perhaps from ON *kith*).

2. English: metonymic occupational name for a seller of faggots, from ME *kidde* faggot (of unknown origin).

3. Scots: from a medieval given name, a var. of *Kit* (a pet form of CHRISTOPHER).

Vars.: **Kid(de)**, **Kyd(d)**; **Kidman** (occupational name from 1 or 2).

Patrs. (from 3): **Kydds, Kidson**.

The surname Kidman *is still found in Cambs., but since the 19th cent. it has been more common in Australia than anywhere in England. Many Australian bearers are related to Sir Sidney Kidman (1857–1935), born near Adelaide, S Australia, who was known as 'the cattle king' and was at one time the largest landowner in the British Empire (as it then was).*

Kiddle English: topographic name for someone who lived by a fish-weir, ME *kidel* (OF *cuidel*, *quidel*, of Bret. origin).

Var.: **Kiddell**.

Kiefer German: 1. occupational name in SW areas of Germany for a cooper, from an agent deriv. of Ger. dial. *Kief(e)*, Ger. *Kufe* barrel (MHG *kuofe*, OHG *kuofa*); a cogn. of Eng. COOPER.

2. topographic name for someone who lived in a pine forest or by an isolated pine tree, from Ger. *Kiefer* pine. This word, which is first attested in the early 15th cent., results from a combination of the terms *kien* and *forhe*, both meaning 'pine'; *kieboom* is still the normal Flem. and Du. term, and in large parts of Germany the word for the tree is *Föhre*. The surname is also borne by Ashkenazic Jews, among whom it is an ornamental name from the word for tree.

3. nickname for a glutton or messy eater, from an agent deriv. of MHG *kīfen* to chew (whence mod. Ger. *Kiefer* jaw).

4. nickname for a combative individual, from MHG *kiffen* to quarrel.

Var. (of 1): **Kiefner**; **Küf(l)er**, **Küf(f)ner**; **Kaufner** (Bavaria); **Kief**.

Cogns.: see at COOPER.

Kiełbasa Polish: metonymic occupational name or nickname from Pol. *kiełbasa* sausage, bestowed either on a seller of sausages or on someone with a fancied resemblance to a sausage.

Var.: **Kiełbasiak**.

Habitation name: **Kiełbasiński**.

Kiely Irish: 1. Anglicized form of **Ó Cadhla** 'descendant of *Cadhla*', a personal name meaning 'Beautiful'.

2. var. of KEELEY 1.

Kieran Irish: Anglicized form of the Gael. personal name *Ciarán* (a dim. of *ciar* dark, black), borne by a large number of early Ir. saints.

Patr.: **Kierans**.

Kiesel German: nickname, perhaps for someone with a bald head, or topographic name for someone who lived on a patch of gravelly land, from Ger. *Kiesel* pebble, also in a collective sense 'gravel' (MHG *kisel*, OHG *kisil*). There are several minor places named with this word, and the surname may also be a habitation name from any of them. See also KIESSLING 1.

Cogns.: Flem.: **De Kesel**. Jewish (Ashkenazic): **Ki(e)selstein**. See also KISELYOV.

Kieser German: occupational name for an official who tested the weights and measures in use in the public markets and checked foodstuffs on sale for possible adulteration. The MHG word *kieser* derives from *kiesen* to test (OHG *kiosan*, a cogn. of mod. Eng. *choose*; cf. KESER 3).

Kiesewetter German: of uncertain origin. It appears to be either from *kieseln* to hail (from MHG *kisel* pebble, gravel, hailstone; see KIESEL) + *wetter* weather, and so perhaps used for someone of a blustery temperament; or from MHG *kiesen* to test, watch (see KIESER) + *wetter*, and so perhaps denoting an amateur weather prophet. However, as neither of these explanations is particularly convincing, and the surname is found mainly in Saxony and Silesia, it is possible that it represents an alteration through folk etymology of some unidentified Slav. name.

Vars.: **Kisswetter, Küssewetter**.

Kiessling German: 1. topographic name for someone who lived in an area of gravelly soil, from MHG *kiselinc* gravel (a deriv. of OHG *kisil* pebble, gravel (see KIESEL), with the addition of the Gmc suffix *-ing*). There are various minor places named with this word, and the surname may also be a habitation name from any of these.

2. patr. from the OHG personal name *Gisilo*, a short form of any of the various cpd names with the first element *gīsil* hostage (cf., e.g., GILBERT).

Vars.: **Kiesling, Kies(s)lich, K(i)eserling**.

Kilbane Irish: Anglicized form of Gael. **Mac Giolla Bháin** 'son of the fair-haired lad' (cf. BAIN).

Kilbride 1. Irish and Scots: Anglicized form of Gael. **Mac Giolla Brighde** (Ir.) or **Mac Gille Bríghde** (Sc.) 'son of the servant of (St) Brigit'. The name *Brighid* is of uncertain origin, but may mean 'Exalted'; it probably originally denoted a pagan fire goddess, many of whose attributes have become attached to the historical figure of St Brigit of Kildare (452–523), founder of the first Irish convent.

2. Scots: habitation name from any of the various places with this name, from Gael. *cill Brighde* church (from L *cella* room, cell) of St Brigit.

Vars. (of 1): **McKillbride, (Mc)Gil(l)bride, McGillvrid(e), MacIlvride, MacIlvreed, McElvride, Micklebride, Mackelbreed**; **McBride, McBryde**; **Bridson, Brydson, Brigetson**; BRIDGE, GILBERT.

Kilburn English: habitation name from a place in N Yorks., or one in Derbys., both of which are of uncertain etymology, possibly so called from OE *cylen(e)* kiln (see KILNER) + *burna* stream (see BOURNE). The place of this name in London does not seem to have contributed to the surname.

Kilby English: habitation name from a place in Leics., recorded in Domesday Book as *Cilebi*. It was probably originally named with the OE elements *cild* CHILD + *tūn* enclosure, settlement (cf. CHILTON), the second element being later replaced by the equiv. ON *býr*.

Vars.: **Kilbey, Killby, Kilbuy**.

Kilcoyne Irish: Anglicized form of Gael. **Mac Giolla Chaoin** 'son of the servant of (St) *Caoin*', a personal name meaning 'Gentle'.

Kildare Irish: Anglicized form of Gael. **Mac Giolla Dhorcha** 'son of the dark-haired lad'.

Vars.: **Kildaire; McIlderry, McElderry**.

Kildea Irish: Anglicized form of Gael. **Mac Giolla Dhé** 'son of the servant of God', from *Dia* God. The name originated with a monastic family in Donegal in the 11th cent. and has always been more or less confined to NW Ireland.

Vars.: **Gildea**, GRAY.

Kilfeather Irish: Anglicized form of Gael. **Mac Giolla Pheadair** 'son of the servant of (St) PETER'.

Vars.: **Kilfedder, Gilfedder**.

Kilgour Scots: habitation name from a place in Fife, so called from Gael. *coille* wood + *gobhar, gabhar* goat.

Var.: **Kilgore**.

Killeen Irish: Anglicized form of the Gael. personal name *Cillín*, a dim. of *Ceallach* (see KELLY 1). The name was borne by various early Ir. saints, including the leader of a 7th-cent. mission to Franconia and Thuringia, hence the popularity of the given name *Kilian* in medieval central Europe, from which several surnames are derived.

Var.: **Killen**.

Cogns.: Ger.: **Kil(l)ian; Kilius, Kilgus; Kill**. Pol.: **Kiljan, Kiljański**. Czech: **Kilián**.

Killick SE English: of unknown origin (apparently not a habitation name, for none of the early forms appear with prepositions).

Var.: **Killik**.

The first known bearer of the name is John Kyllyk, *a vintner of London, whose will was proved in 1439. In it he directs that candles should be lit for him in the churches of Nutfield and Bletchingley, Surrey, which suggests that he may have originally come from that county. John Killick was parish constable of Bletchingley c.1450.*

Killigrew Cornish: habitation name from *Killigrew* in St Erme parish, which probably gets its name from Corn. *kelly* grove + *cnow* hazel trees or nuts.

The Killigrew *family of Falmouth, which built Arwenack House, was once one of the most powerful families in Cornwall. They are descended from Raphe Killigrew, who held lands at St Erme in the time of Henry III (1216–72).*

Killingbeck English (Yorks.): habitation name from a place in N Yorks., most probably from an ON personal name *Killing* + ON *bekkr* stream (see BECK).

Var.: **Killingback**.

Killington English: habitation name from a place in Cumb., so called from OE *Cyllingtūn* 'settlement (OE *tūn*) associated with *Cylla*', a personal name of uncertain origin.

Kilminster English (W Midlands): habitation name, probably from *Kidderminster* in Worcs. (recorded as *Kedeleministre* in 1155), which gets its name from the OE personal name *Cydela* (a dim. of *Cydda*) + OE *mynster* monastery church (L *monastērium*).

Kilner English: occupational name for a potter or limeburner, from an agent deriv. of OE *cylen(e)* kiln (LL *culīna* kitchen, a deriv. of *coquere* to cook).

Kilpatrick 1. Irish: Anglicized form of Gael. **Mac Giolla Phádraig** 'son of the servant of (St) PATRICK'.

2. Scots: habitation name from any of various places named in Gael. as *cill Padraig* 'church of (St) PATRICK'.

Kilvert English: apparently from an unattested ON personal name *Ketilfrǫðr, Ketilfrith*, Anglicized as *Cytelferð*. This is composed of the elements *ketil* cauldron (cf. KETTLE) + *frǫðr, friðr* peace.

Kilvington English: habitation name from one of the places so called: N and S *Kilvington* near Thirsk in N Yorks. or *Kilvington* in Notts. These are either 'settlement (OE *tūn*) associated with *Cynelāf*' or 'settlement associated with *Cynewulf*'. The OE personal names are from *cyne-* royal + *lāf* survivor or *wulf* wolf.

Kimber English: from the OE female personal name *Cyneburh*, composed of the elements *cyne-* royal + *burh* fortress, stronghold. This name was borne by a daughter of the 7th-cent. King Penda of Mercia, who, in spite of her father's staunch opposition to Christianity, was converted and founded an abbey, serving as its head. She was venerated as a saint in the Middle Ages, and children were named after her.

Var.: **Kimbrough**.

Kimberley English (chiefly W Midlands): habitation name from any of various places so called, from different OE personal names + OE *lēah* wood, clearing. *Kimberley* in Warwicks. is first recorded in 1311 in the form *Kynebaldeleye* 'wood of *Cynebald*' (see KEMBLE); *Kimberley* in Notts. is recorded in Domesday Book as *Chinemarelie* 'wood of *Cynemǣr*', a name composed of the elements *cyne-* royal + *mǣr* fame; *Kimberley* in Norfolk is recorded in Domesday Book as *Chineburlai* 'wood of *Cyneburh*' (see KIMBER).

Var.: **Kimberly**.

Kimpton English: habitation name from places in Hants and Herts., so called from the OE personal name *Cyma* (a short from of *Cynemǣr*; see KIMBERLEY) + OE *tūn* enclosure, settlement.

Kincaid Scots: habitation name from a place near Lennoxtown in Campsie Glen, north of Glasgow, which is first recorded in 1238 as *Kincaith* and in 1250 as *Kincathe*. The former spelling would suggest derivation from Gael. *ceann* head, top + *càithe* pass, whereas the latter would point to *cadha* quagmire as the second element.

Vars.: **Kincade, Kinkead, Kinkaid, Kinkade, Kincaidie**.

Kind German and Jewish (Ashkenazic): nickname for someone resembling a child, Ger. *Kind* (OHG *kind*). In some cases it may also be a shortening of cpd names ending in *-kind*, which is sometimes found as a patr. ending of Jewish surnames, by folk-etymological alteration of the ending *-kin*; see SÜSSKIND.

Var.: Ger.: **Kindt**.

Dims.: Ger.: **Kind(e)l**.

Kinder English: habitation name from a place in Derbys., the name of which is probably Brit., but of obscure etymology.

Kinderlehrer Jewish (Ashkenazic): occupational name for a teacher in a traditional Jewish elementary school (cf. KNELLER 2). The name is from Ger. *Kinder* children + LEHRER teacher, or the cogn. Yid. *kinder* + *lerer*.
Var.: **Kinderlerer**.

King English: nickname from ME *king*, OE *cyning* king (originally merely a tribal leader, from OE *cyn(n)* tribe, race + the Gmc suffix *-ing*). The word was already used as a byname before the Norman Conquest, and the nickname was common in the Middle Ages, being used to refer to someone who conducted himself in a kingly manner, or to one who had played the part of a king in a pageant, or to one who had won the title in some contest. In rare cases it may actually have referred to someone who had served in the king's household. The surname is also borne by Ashkenazic Jews, among whom it is presumably an Anglicization of KÖNIG or a related form.
Var.: Eng.: **Kinge**.
Dims.: Eng.: **King(g)ett**.
Patrs.: Eng.: **Kings(on)**.
'Servant of K.': Eng.: **Kingman**.

Kingdon English (Devon): habitation name from Higher *Kingdon* in Alverdiscott, Devon, or from *Kendon* in N Bovey, Devon. Both are from OE *cyning* KING + *dūn* hill.
Var.: **Kindon**.

Kingham English: habitation name from a place in Oxon., so called from OE *Cǣgingahām* 'homestead (OE *hām*) of the people of *Cǣga*', apparently a byname from *cǣg* key, peg.

Kinghorn Scots: habitation name from *Kinghorn* in Fife, *Kyngorn* in 1374, the spelling of which has been affected by folk etymology, but which gets its name from Gael. *ceann* head, height + *gronna* bog.
Var.: **Kinghorne**.

Kingsbury English: habitation name from any of several places, for example in NW London, Somerset, and Warwicks. The last mentioned is so called from OE *Cynesburh* 'stronghold (OE *burh*) of *Cyne*', a short form of any of the various cpd names with the first element *cyne-* royal. The others have as the first element OE *cyning* KING, chieftain.

Kingscote English: habitation name from a village near Tetbury, Gloucs., so called from the gen. case of OE *cyning* KING, chieftain + *cot* hut, shelter (see COATES).
Var.: **Kingscott**.
A family of this name has been recorded at Kingscote for over 800 years. The manor was acquired by a certain Nigel FitzArthur as a dowry on his marriage, and his son became known as Adam de Kingscote. *The latter's holding of the manor was confirmed in 1188, and the surname has been in continuous use ever since.*

Kingsley English: habitation name from any of the places, in Ches., Hants, and Staffs., so called from from OE *cyningeslēah* 'wood, clearing of the KING, chieftain'.

Kingston English: habitation name from any of the very numerous places in England called *Kingston* or *Kingstone*. Almost all of them, regardless of the distinction in spelling, were originally named in OE as *cyningestūn* 'settlement of the KING', i.e. royal manor. However, *Kingston* upon Soar in Notts. and *Kingstone* in Somerset are respectively 'royal stone' and 'king's stone', perhaps from some local monument.
Var.: **Kingstone**.

Kington English: habitation name from any of various places in Dorset, Herefords., Warwicks., Wilts., and Worcs. These derive their name either from OE *cyne-* royal or from OE *cyning* KING, chieftain + *tūn* settlement, enclosure, and are thus identical in meaning with KINGSTON, even though the possessive *-s* is missing.

Kingwell English (Devon): habitation name from a place in Somerset, probably so called from OE *cyning* KING, chieftain + *well(a)* spring, stream (see WELL).

Kinloch Scots: habitation name from any of various places that derive their names from Gael. *ceann* head(land) + *loch* loch. The most likely source of the surname is *Kinloch* at the head of Loch Rossie in Fife, where a certain John Kinloch is recorded in charters dating from *c.*1240.
Var.: **Kinlock**.

Kinnaird Scots: habitation name from a place so called on Tayside, which derives its name from Gael. *ceann* head + *aird* height, i.e. 'summit', 'peak'.
A certain Richard Kinnaird *was granted lands at this place by King William the Lion in the late 12th cent.*

Kinnear Scots: habitation name from *Kinneir* in Fife, first recorded at the beginning of the 13th cent. as *Kyner*, apparently from Gael. *ceann* head(land) + *iar* west.
Var.: **Kinneir**.

Kinneavy Irish: Anglicized form of Gael. **Mac Conshnámha** 'son of *Conshnámha*', a personal name composed of the elements *con* dog + *snámh* to swim.
Var.: **McKinnawe**. The name has also been 'translated' FORD, as if from Gael. *Mac an Átha* 'son of the ford'.

Kinneen Irish: Anglicized form of Gael. **Ó Coinín** 'descendant of *Coinín*', a personal name probably from a dim. of *cú*, gen. *con*, hound. As the result of confusion by association with Gael. *coinín* rabbit, the name has also been Anglicized as RABBITT, **Rabitte**, **Rabette**, etc.

Kinsella Irish: Anglicized form of Gael. **Ó Cinnsealaigh** 'descendant of *Cinnsealach*', a byname meaning 'Proud', 'Overbearing'.
Vars.: **O'Kynsillaghe**, **Kinshela**, **Kinsley**.

Kinsey English: from an OE personal name composed of the elements *cyne-* royal + *sige* victory.
Vars.: **Kincey**, **Kynsey**, **Kinzie**.

Kinsman English: from ME *kin(ne)sman* (a cpd of OE *cyn(n)* kin + *man* man), presumably used to refer to someone who was related to an important personage or influential family.

Kipling English: 1. habitation name from *Kiplin* in N Yorks., so called from OE *Cyppelingas* 'people of **Cyppel*', an OE personal name of uncertain origin and meaning.
2. habitation name from *Kipling Cotes* in E Yorks., probably named from OE *Cybbelingcot* 'cottage(s) associated with *Cybbel*', another OE personal name of unknown origin and meaning.
The English author Rudyard Kipling *was from a Yorks. family, who were mainly small farmers and craftsmen.*

Kirby English: habitation name from any of the numerous places in N England called *Kirby* or *Kirkby*, from ON *kirkja* church (see KIRK) + *býr* settlement.
Vars.: **Kerb(e)y**, **Kirkby**, **Kirkebye**.
Cogn.: Dan.: **Kirkeby**.

Kirchner German: occupational name for a church sexton, from MHG *kirchenære*, a deriv. of *kirche* church (see

Kirk). This is the regular term for the occupation in Thuringia; see also Küster, Mesner, and Oppermann. The surname is also borne by Ashkenazic Jews, in which use it presumably originally referred to a sexton in a synagogue.

Kirilov Russian and Bulgarian: patr. from the given name *Kiril* Cyril (Gk *Kyrilos*, from *kyrios* lord; cf. the L equivalent at Dominique). This was the name borne by a 9th-cent missionary to the Slavs who, together with his companion Methodius, first translated biblical and liturgical texts into Old Slavonic. No Slav. language had previously been written down, and so the two men devised their own system of transcription, based on the Gk alphabet, This remains the basis of the modern Cyrillic scripts. The given name was not in use in the West during the Middle Ages, and surnames derived from it are confined to E Europe.

Vars.: **Kirillov, Kiril(l)in, Kurilov, Kurilin; Kiryanov, Kuryanov, Kirsanov, Kursanov, Kirisov, Kurisov, Kirilichev.**

Cogns.: Ukr.: **Kurilas.**

Dims.: Russ.: **Kiril(li)tsev, Kirilochkin, Kuriltsev, Kurilchikov, Kurilyov, Kurylyov, Kurilkin, Kurylkin; Kirtsov, Kireev, Kirichev, Kirichkov, Kiryaev, Kiryunchev, Kirshov, Kir(yak)in, Kiryukhin, Kiryupin, Kiryush(k)in, Kiryutin, Kirkin, Kirsanin, Kirshin; Kurasov, Kurikov, Kurinov, Kurlov, Kurysev, Kuryshev, Kur(ikh)in, Kyryshkin, Kurshin** (all patrs.). Ukr.: **Kirilenko, Kireiko, Kirilyuk.** Beloruss.: **Kireenko.**

Kirk N English and Scots: topographic name for someone who lived near a church or metonymic occupational name for someone who was employed in one, from Northern ME *kirk* church (ON *kirkja*; see further at Church).

Vars.: **Kirke, Kerk, Kyrke; Kir(c)kman.**

Cogns.: Dan.: **Kirk.** Du.: **Kerk, Verkerk.** Low Ger.: **Kirk, Kerk.** Ger.: **Kirch.**

Kirkbride N English: habitation name from any of various places so named from having a church (see Kirk) dedicated to St Brigit (cf. Kilbride), of which there is one in Cumb. near Carlisle. Cf. Kirkpatrick.

Var.: **Kirkbright.**

Kirkham N English: habitation name from places in Lancs. and W Yorks., the name of which is a Scandinavianized form of OE *ciric-hām*, from *cirice* church + *hām* homestead.

Kirkland N English: topographic name for someone who lived on land belonging to the Church, from Northern ME Kirk church + *land* land (OE *land*). There are several villages named with these elements, for example in Cumb., and they may have contributed to the surname. Exceptionally, *Kirkland* in Lancs. has its second element from ON *lund* grove.

Kirkley English: habitation name from a place so called in Northumb., which ostensibly derives its name from ON *kirkja* church (see Kirk) + OE *lēah* wood, clearing. However, it is found as *Crekellawe* in early records; it is therefore derived from Brit. *crūc* hill (see Crich) + the tautologous OE *hlāw* hill (see Law 2 and Low 1).

Kirkpatrick Scots and N Irish: habitation name from any of various places so called from the dedication of their church (see Kirk) to St Patrick. The order of the elements is the result of Gael. influence.

Kirkup English (Northumb.): apparently a habitation name from an unidentified place, probably named with the Northern ME elements Kirk church + Hope valley.

Kirkwood Scots: habitation name from any of several places named as being a Wood belonging to the Church or situated by a church (see Kirk). There are places so called in the former counties of Ayrs., Dumfries, and Lanarks., any of which may have given rise to the surname.

Kirsch 1. German: topographic name for someone who lived near a cherry orchard or a wild cherry tree, from Ger. *Kirsch(baum)* cherry (tree) (MHG *kirse*, OHG *kirsa*). It may also have been a metonymic occupational name for a gatherer or seller of cherries or a nickname for a man with a ruddy complexion.

2. Jewish (Ashkenazic): ornamental name, one of the many taken from words for trees and other features of the natural world. The surname is from either the Ger. or the NE or W Yid. form of the word.

Vars. (of 1): Ger.: **Kirsche.** (Of 2): Jewish: **Kirsh** (Anglicized spelling), **Kirs(c)hman; Kirsz** (Pol. spelling); **Kersch** (from a S Yid. pronunciation, Anglicized **Kersh**), **Kers(c)hman; Karsch** (from a central Yid. pronunciation, Anglicized **Karsh**; also **Karshen, Karshon,** from the Yid. pl. *karshn*); **Kirshonovitz, Kirsenovitz** (patrs. in form).

Cpds (of 2): Jewish: **Kirs(c)h(en)baum, Kirszenbaum, Kirsh(en)bom, Kirshenboim, Kerschenbaum** ('cherry tree'); **Kirs(c)henberg, Kirszberg, Kirshberg** ('cherry hill'); **Kirschenblatt, Kirshenblat(t), Kershenblat** ('cherry leaf'); **Kirschblum, Kirs(h)blum** ('cherry flower'); **Kirs(c)henblut** ('cherry blood', from Ger. *Blut* blood, or 'cherry blossom', from Ger. *Blüte* blossom); **Kirshenfeld** ('cherry field'); **Kirschenhaut** ('cherry skin', perhaps a nickname for a man with a ruddy complexion); **Kirschholz, Kirsholz, Kirszholc** ('cherry wood'); **Kirschensaft** ('cherry juice'); **Kirschstein, Kirs(h)tein, Kirstain, Kerstein, Karschenstein** ('cherry stone'; see also Christian); **Kirshenzweig, Kirszenzweig** ('cherry twig').

Kirton N English: habitation name from any of various places, for example in Lincs., Notts., and Staffs., so called from OE *cirice* church, replaced by ON *kirkja* church (see Kirk), + OE *tūn* enclosure, settlement.

Kirwan Irish: Anglicized form of Gael. **Ó Ciardhubháin** 'descendant of *Ciardhubhán*', a personal name composed of the elements *ciar* dark + *dubh* black + the dim. suffix *-an*.

Vars.: **Kirwen, Kirwin, Kir(i)van, Kier(e)van; O'Kirwan, O'Kerevan, O'Kerrywane.**

Kiselyov Russian: patr. from the nickname *Kisel*, a type of blancmange containing the juice of various acid fruits such as cranberry. This derives its name from *kisly* sour; the nickname was perhaps used to refer to a person with an acid disposition.

Cogns.: Pol.: **Kisiel.** Ukr.: **Kisel** (borne by Ashkenazic Jews too; see also Kiesel).

Habitation names: Pol.: **Kisielewski, Kiślański.**

Kiss 1. Hungarian (partly Jewish): nickname from *kis* small. At least in the case of the Hung. name, this word was also used in contrast with Nagy as a distinguishing name for the younger of two bearers of the same first name, not necessarily one who was physically smaller.

2. English: metonymic occupational name for a maker of leg armour, normally of leather, from ANF *cuisse* thigh (piece) (L *coxa* thigh).

Vars. (of 1): **Kis**; U.S. **Kish, Kisch.** (Of 2): **Cuss(e)** (see also Constance); **Kisser, Kissa.**

Kissane Irish: Anglicized form of Gael. **Ó Ciosáin** 'descendant of *Ciosán*', a personal name perhaps derived from a dim. of *ceas* coracle.

Kissinger German and Jewish (W Ashkenazic): habitation name from *Kissingen* in Franconia or *Kissing* in Bavaria, both of which, according to Bahlow, are named with a lost element *kis(s)* denoting a marsh or swamp.

The American diplomat and academic Henry Kissinger (*b. 1923*) *was born in Germany into a middle-class Jewish family.*

Kitchen English: metonymic occupational name for a cook or someone who worked in a kitchen, from ME *kychene*, OE *cycen(e)* (L *cucīna*; cf. CUISINE).

Vars.: **Kitchin(g), Ketchen, Ketchin; Kitchener; Kitch(e)-man, Kitchin(g)man.**

Cogns.: Ger.: **Küch(en)meister.** Pol.: **Kuczyński.** Czech: **Kuchynka.**

Kite English (chiefly W Midlands): nickname for a fierce or rapacious person, from ME *kete* kite (the bird of prey; OE *cȳta*).

Vars.: **K(e)yte, Keight** (W Midlands); KETT; **Keet, Keat(e).**

Patrs.: **Kites, Ketts, Keat(e)s;** KEATING.

Kiteley English: apparently a habitation name from an unidentified place deriving its name from OE *cȳta* KITE + *lēah* wood, clearing. This may be identical with *Kitley* in Devon.

Klapper 1. German: nickname for a talkative person or gossip, from an agent deriv. of MHG *klappern* to chatter, rattle (an imitative formation).

2. E German: dial. var. of KLEPPER 1.

3. Jewish (Ashkenazic): of uncertain origin, possibly as in 1 above.

Vars. (of 1): **Klappert.** (Of 2 and 3): **Klapperman.**

Cogn.: Czech: **Klepáč** (from *klepat* to chatter, gossip).

Klar 1. German: metr. from the female given name *Klara*, *Clara* (see CLAIRE 1 and SINCLAIR).

2. Jewish (Ashkenazic): ornamental name from mod. Ger. *klar* clear.

Vars. (of 2): **Klahr, Klarman(n); Klor** (from Yid. *klor*); **Klurman** (from S. Yid. *klur*).

Cpds (of 2): **Klar(s)feld, Klorfeld** ('clear field'); **Klurglus** ('clear glass'); **Klarreich** ('clear rich').

Klaus 1. German: from the medieval given name *Klaus*, still popular in mod. Ger., which originated as an aphetic form of *Niklaus* NICHOLAS. There are, or have been, common aphetic pet forms of NICHOLAS in several European languages, for example Russ. *Kolya*, and many of these have given rise to surnames. Those beginning with *C-* are listed at COLL.

2. Jewish (W Ashkenazic): from Yid. *kloyz* small synagogue or house of study, especially one that is restricted to use by some occupational or social group. The surname was taken by a member of such a group. The vocab. word is related to Ger. *Kloster* monastery; see KLOSTERMANN.

Vars. (of 1): **Klais, Kleis,** KLEIST, **Kles(s), Klesse, Klus(s), Klöss, Klaffs; Clausius** (Latinized). (Of 2): **Klausner, Kloisner, Klousner.**

Cogns. (of 1): Low Ger.: **Klaas, Klaes, Klas(s).** Flem., Du.: **Claus.** Ger. (of Slav. origin): **Kollas, Kollach, Kolla(t)sch.** Pol.: **Kołak;** KOLASA. Czech: **Klos, Klouz; Kološ, Koleš, Kolín; Kuliš, Kulič.**

Dims. (of 1): Ger.: **Kleisel, Kleisle, Kles(e)l, Klessel, Klössel; Kläwi, Klewi** (Switzerland). Low Ger.: **Klassmann, Klessmann, Klossmann; Klag(g)e, Klageman, Klamman.** Ger. (of Slav. origin): **Kollaschek, Klossek, Klos(k)a.** Czech: **Kulík; Kulíček, Kulíšek.**

Patrs. (from 1): Ger.: **Klaiser, Kleiser, Klös(s)er, Kloser.** Low Ger.: **Klaus(s)en, Kla(e)sen, Claus(s)en, Cla(a)sen, Classen, Klasing.** Fris.: **Klazenenga.** Flem.: **Claesen, Claessens.** Du.: **Kla(a)sen, Klaassen, Claasens, Claesens.** Dan.: **Klausen, Clausen.** Swed.: **Kla(e)sson, Cla(e)sson.** Ger. (of Slav. origin): **Klausewitz, Clausewitz; Koscher.** Russ.: **Kolyagin, Kolin, Kolushev.** Croatian: **Kolaković.**

Patrs. (from dims. of 1): Ger.: **Klaves, Klebes** (Switzerland). Low Ger.: **Klösges, Klag(g)es.** Flem.: **Claeskens.**

Habitation names: Pol.: **Kołakowski, Kolczyński.** Czech: **Kolinský.**

Klayman Jewish (E Ashkenazic): possibly an occupational name for a maker of glue, from E Yid. *kley*, Pol. *klej*, or Russ. *klei* glue + *man* man.

Vars.: **Klaiman, Klajman, Kleiman.**

Klečák Czech: nickname for a lame man, from a deriv. of OCzech *klecavý* lame (cogn. with Pol. *kulawy*, mod. Czech *kulhavý*).

Var.: **Klečka.**

Cogn.: Pol.: **Kulawiak.**

Dims.: Pol.: **Kulawczyk, Kulawik.**

Habitation name: Pol.: **Kulawiński.**

Klee German: apparently from MHG *klē* clover (OHG *klēo*), possibly a topographic name for someone who lived near a field of clover, a nickname of uncertain application, or a metonymic occupational name for someone who grew clover to feed cattle.

Vars.: **Kle(e)man** (see also CLEMENT).

Cogns.: Du.: **Klaver, Van Klaveren.** Jewish (Ashkenazic): **Kleemann.**

Klein German, Dutch, and Jewish (Ashkenazic): nickname for a small man, from Ger., Du. *klein* small, Yid. *kleyn* (MHG, MDu. *kleine*, OHG *kleini*, OSax. *klēni*; cogn. with OE *clǣne* pure, mod. Eng. *clean*).

Vars.: Ger.: **Kleiner(t), Kleint; Klei(n)mann.** Du.: **Kle(i)ne, Kl(e)ijn, Kl(e)yn.** Jewish: **Kleiner, Klein(er)man; Klain(er), Klainman; Kline(r), Klyne, Cline,** CLYNE (Anglicized); see also KATAN.

Cogns.: Low Ger.: **Klehn, Kleen.** Flem.: **(De) Cleyne, (De) Cleene; Cleynaert; Cl(e)ynman.** Czech: **Klejna.**

Patrs.: Du.: **Kleynen, Kleynermans.** Flem.: **Clynmans.**

Cpds: Jewish (it is hard to tell which are ornamental, which anecdotal, based on some minor incident, and which descriptive or topographic): **Kleinbaum** ('small tree'); **Kleinberg(er)** ('(dweller by a) small hill'); **Kleinfeld** ('small field'); **Kleingrub** ('small pit', probably topographic); **Kleinhaus** ('small house', topographic); **Kleinhaut** ('small skin'); **Kleinholz** ('small wood'); **Kleinmintz, Kleinmuntz** ('small coin'); **Kleinpeltz** ('small pelt'); **Kleinplatz, Kleinplac** ('small place'); **Kleinsinger** ('small singer'); **Kleinstein** ('small stone', ornamental); **Kleinstub** ('small room'); **Kleinstern** ('small star', ornamental); **Kleinzweig** ('small twig', ornamental).

Kleinhändler Jewish (Ashkenazic): occupational name for a retail dealer, i.e. a shopkeeper rather than a merchant, mod. Ger. *Kleinhändler* (lit. 'small trader').

Var.: **Kleinhendler.**

Kleinlerer Jewish (Ashkenazic): occupational name for a teacher of the smallest children in a traditional Jewish elementary school, from Ger. *klein* or Yid. *kleyn* small + Ger. *Lehrer* or Yid. *lerer* teacher.

Kleinschmidt Jewish (Ashkenazic): occupational name for a maker of hand tools, mod. Ger. *Kleinschmidt* (lit. 'small smith').

Kleist 1. German and Jewish (Ashkenazic): of unknown origin, probably from a habitation name of Slav. etymology.

2. German: var. of KLAUS.

Klempner N German and Jewish (Ashkenazic): occupational name for a tinker or plumber, an agent deriv. of Ger. *klempern* to clamp, bolt, rivet (of Low Ger. origin, from *klampe* clamp, which gradually replaced High Ger. *klampfen*).

Vars.: **Klemperer** (Bavarian). Ger. only: **Klemper(t)**, **Klemptner**; **Klampfer(er)** (Bavaria).

Klepper 1. German: nickname for someone who was under a feudal obligation to provide horses for his lord, from MHG *klepper* horse provided in this way (said to be of imitative origin, from the sound of the hooves).

2. Jewish (Ashkenazic): of uncertain origin, perhaps a var. of KLAPPER 3.

Vars. (of 1): KLAPPER. (Of 2): **Kleper**.

Klika Czech: apparently from the vocab. word *klika* handle, knob, of uncertain application as a surname. It may be an obscene nickname, with the sense 'penis'.

Var.: **Klik** (altered to masc. gender).

Dim.: **Klička**.

Klincksieck French and German: habitation name from a place in Alsace, of uncertain origin; the first element is probably akin to MHG *klinge* mountain stream (see KLINGE); the second may be akin to MLG *siek* damp, marshy land.

Klinge German: 1. topographic name for someone who lived near a mountain stream, MHG *klinge* (OHG *klinga*, of apparently imitative origin). There are a large number of places named with this word, and the surname may also be a habitation name from any of them.

2. metonymic occupational name for a swordsmith, from MHG *klinge* sword (a later imitative deriv. from the verb *klingen* to ring, clatter).

Vars.: **Kling**, KLINGER, **Klingemann**.

Klinger 1. German: var. of KLINGE.

2. Jewish (Ashkenazic): of unknown origin.

Vars. (of 2): **Klingerman**, **Klingel**, **Kling(man)**; **Clingerman** (an Anglicized spelling). The surnames **Kling(en)stein**, **Klinghof(f)er**, **Klingweil**, and **Klingsberg** may have originated from the combination of this first element with common placename or surname suffixes.

Klonowski Polish: habitation name from a place called *Klonów* (from Pol. *klon* maple tree + *-ów* possessive suffix) + *-ski* suffix of local surnames (see BARANOWSKI).

Var.: **Klonowicz** (patr. in form, perhaps from *klon* used as a nickname; the 16th-cent. Pol. poet Klonowic called himself *Acernus* in Latin).

Klopstock German: occupational nickname from MLG *kloppen* to strike, beat (of imitative origin) + *stoc* (tree) stump (see STOCK). The exact meaning of the surname is not clear, since the second element had a variety of technical senses in the crafts of the Middle Ages. One possibility is that it refers to a cutler, who would have made use of a small anvil known by this name in the sharpening of scythes and other instruments which needed their blades honed. The surname is also borne by Ashkenazic Jews, but the reason for its adoption is not certian. It could well be an occupational name for a cutler, which was a not infrequent occupation among Ashkenazic Jews.

Kłos Polish: of uncertain origin, perhaps from Pol. *kłos* ear or spike of corn. This could have been a nickname for a small person or else a topographic name for someone living by a cornfield. It is unlikely to be an aphetic form of *Mikołaj* NICHOLAS, for *Kłos* is not recorded as a given name.

Habitation names: **Kłosiński**, **Kłosowski**.

Klostermann German: occupational name for a servant in a monastery or for a lay member of a monastic community, from Ger. *Kloster* monastery (MHG *klōster*, OHG *klōstar*, from LL *clōstrum* monastic cell, from class. L *claustrum* bolt, bar, from *claudere* to close) + *mann* man. The surname may also have denoted someone who farmed land belonging to a monastery and who paid rent in the form of provisions for the monks.

Cogns.: Du.: **Kloosterman**, **Van (den) Klooster**.

Klotz German and Jewish (Ashkenazic): nickname for a clumsy, awkward man, from Ger. *Klotz* lump, block, or Yid. *klots* (MHG, OHG *klotz*, cogn. with mod. Eng. *clot*, which is similarly used in a transferred sense to denote a stupid person).

Vars.: Ger.: **Klut(h)**. Jewish: **Klots**, **Klotzman(n)**.

Cogns.: Low Ger.: **Kloth**, **Kloot(h)**.

Dim.: Ger.: **Klötzel**.

Klouček Czech: nickname for a mischievous, impish person, from Czech *klouček* little boy, imp.

Klöver Low German: occupational name for someone whose job it was to split wood into planks, from MLG *klöven* to cleave, divide (cogn. with OE *clēofan*).

Vars.: **Klöwer**, **Klöber**; **Klüver**, **Klüwer** (also of a court official responsible for placing convicted criminals in the stocks, MLG *kluver*, from *kluven* a slit piece of wood used for this purpose).

Klucznik Polish: occupational or status name for an officer in a manorial or noble household. A *klucznik* was roughly equivalent to a butler; the word is derived from Pol. *klucz* key + *-nik* suffix of agent nouns.

Habitation name: **Kluczyński**.

Klug 1. German: nickname from Eastern MHG *klūc* wise, prudent, or from the Western byform *kluoc*, which had the sense 'noble', 'refined'; both forms probably go back to a single unattested OHG original.

2. Jewish (Ashkenazic): nickname from Ger. *klug* or Yid. *klug* clever, wise.

Vars.: Ger.: **Kluge(r)**; **Glauer(t)**, **Glauber**. Jewish: **Kluger**, **Klugman**; **Kli(e)ger**, **Kli(e)g(er)man** (from a S Yid. pronunication).

Cogns.: Low Ger.: **Klook**. Du., Flem.: **Kloek**. Eng.: GLEW.

Dims.: Ger.: **Klügel**, **Kliegel**.

Patr.: Low Ger.: **Klöcking**.

Kmieć Polish: status name for a peasant farmer who had his own land, Pol. *kmieć*.

Var.: **Kmieciak**.

Cogns: Ger. (of Slav. origin): **Kmetz**.

Dim.: Pol.: **Kmiecik**.

Kmoch Czech: from the vocab. word *kmotr* godfather, sponsor (from LL *comater* godmother, from *co-* joint, co- + *mater* mother; one of the earliest attested borrowings from Latin in a Slav. language).

Knaggs N English: topographic name for someone who lived by a geographical feature named with the ME word *knagg*, which had various senses, including a stunted dead branch or a jagged crag or outcrop of rock.

Knapp 1. English (chiefly W Country): habitation name from one of the places named with OE *cnæpp* hilltop, of which there are examples in Devon, Hants, and Sussex. It may also be a topographic name from the same word used independently.

2. German: status name for a servant or squire, Ger. *Knappe* (MHG *knappe* boy, lad, OHG *knappo*, a byform of *knabo*, cogn. with OE *cnapa* boy, servant). The surname is also borne by Ashkenazic Jews.

Vars. (of 1): **Knapper**, **Knap(p)man**. (Of 2): Ger.: **Knappe**, **Knab(b)e**.

Cogn. (of 2): Flem., Du.: **De Knaap**. Pol., Czech: **Knap**.

Dims. (of 2): Ger.: **Knäple**, **Knäble**, **Knable**. Pol.: **Knapik**.

Patrs. (from 2): Ger.: **Knabben**. Flem., Du.: **Kna(e)pen**.

Knapton English (Yorks.): habitation name from one of two places in Yorks., so called from OE *cnapa* boy, servant (perhaps used as a personal name) + *tūn* enclosure, settlement.

Knatchbull English: occupational nickname for a slaughterer and butcher, from ME *knatch(en)*, *knetch(en)* to fell, knock on the head (a byform of *knack(en)*, from Low Ger. or Du.) + *bull* BULL.

This is the name of a Kent family who hold the title Baron Brabourne. The first known bearer is Clement Nechebol, *who was living at Aloesbridge, Kent, in 1272. John* Knatchbull *held lands at Lympne in the 14th cent., and the family seat at Mersham was acquired by Richard Knatchbull in c.1485. The present family is certainly descended from William Knatchbull of Barham, who died in 1491.*

Knaus German: 1. nickname for a haughty person, from MHG *knūz* proud, contemptuous (no OHG form is recorded, but the word may nevertheless be akin to OE *cnēatian* to quarrel).

2. topographic name for someone living on a hillock, from *knaus* hillock in the Swabian and Alemannic dialects of German.

Dims.: **Knäusle**, **Kneisel**, **Kneiss(e)l**, **Kneussel**.

Kneebone English (Devon and Cornwall): of uncertain origin, perhaps in part a nickname for someone with knobbly knees, but probably also in part an alteration by folk etymology of a habitation name from *Carnebone* in the parish of Wendron, Cornwall. The placename is first recorded in 1298 as *Carnebwen*, from Corn. *carn* pile of rocks (cf. CAIRNS) + a second element of uncertain form and meaning.

Knef German: metonymic occupational name for a shoemaker, from MLG *knīf* (shoemaker's) knife (a cogn. of OE *cnīf*).

Vars.: **Knief**, **Kneif**, **Kneip(p)**, **Kniep(e)**, **Knieper**, **Kneib**.

Cogn.: Eng.: **Knife**.

Kneller 1. German: nickname for a raucous or disruptive person, from an agent deriv. of MHG *knellen* to make a noise, cause a rumpus. The mod. Ger. slang word *Kneller*, meaning 'poor-quality tobacco', is unlikely to be relevant to the surname.

2. Jewish (Ashkenazic): occupational name for a teacher in a traditional Jewish elementary school, Yid. *kneler*. Cf. KINDERLEHRER.

2. English: var. of KNILL.

Var. (of 2): **Kneler**.

Sir Godfrey Kneller *(?1646–1723), court painter through successive English reigns, was born in Lübeck, Germany.*

Knight English: status name from ME *knyghte* knight, OE *cniht* boy, youth, serving lad. This word was used as a personal name before the Norman Conquest, and the surname may in part reflect a survival of this. It is also possible that in a few cases it represents a survival of the OE sense into ME, as an occupational name for a domestic servant. In most cases, however, it clearly comes from the more exalted sense that the word achieved in the Middle Ages. In the feudal system introduced by the Normans the word was applied at first to a tenant bound to serve his lord as a mounted soldier. Hence it came to denote a man of some substance, since maintaining horses and armour was an expensive business. As feudal obligations became increasingly converted to monetary payments, the term lost its precise significance and came to denote an honourable estate conferred by the king on men of noble birth who had served him well. Knights in this last sense normally belonged to ancient noble families with distinguished family names of their own, so that the surname is more likely to have been applied to a servant in a knightly house or to someone who had played the part of a knight in a pageant or won the title in some contest of skill.

Vars.: **Knevet(t)**, **Knivit**, **Knivett**, **Knyvett**, **Nevet**, **Nevitt** (reflecting the ANF pronunciation).

Cogns.: Ger.: **Knecht** (in the sense 'servant', 'lad'). Du.: **De Kneght**. Jewish (Ashkenazic): **Knacht** (from a central Yid. pronunciation of Yid. *knekht* slave. Since Ashkenazic Jews were not slaves at the time when they took surnames, this is based either on a nickname or on some now irrecoverable minor event); **Knecht** (from mod. Ger. *Knecht* servant, menial, farmhand, or from Yid. *knekht* slave, in which case the foregoing remarks about *Knacht* apply here also).

Patr.: Eng.: **Knights** (chiefly Norfolk).

Knightley English: habitation name from any of various places, for example in Staffs., so called from OE *cnihtā*, gen. pl. of *cniht* servant, retainer + *lēah* wood, clearing.

Var.: **Knightly**.

Knighton English: habitation name from any of the numerous places named with OE *cnihta*, gen. pl. of *cniht* servant, retainer + *tūn* enclosure, settlement.

Vars.: **Knighten**, **Nighton**.

Knill English: topographic name for someone who lived on a hillock, from OE *cnyll*, a byform of *cnoll* (see KNOLL and KNOWLES).

Vars.: **Knyll**, **Knell**, **Knull**; KNELLER.

The surname Knill *was first adopted in the 13th cent. by Sir John* de Knill, *second Lord of Knill in Herefords., son of Sir John de Braose, first Lord of Knill.*

Knipe N Irish: habitation name from a place in the former county of Ayrs., Scotland, so called from Gael. *cnap* hill(ock) (akin to OE *cnæpp*; see KNAPP).

Kníže Czech: nickname meaning 'Prince', Czech *kníže* (ultimately cogn. with Ger. *Knecht* boy, young man, and with Eng. KNIGHT).

Dim.: **Kníček**.

Patr.: Croatian: **Knežević**.

Knobloch German: metonymic occupational name for a grower and seller of garlic, from a dissimilated form of MHG *klobelouch* (mod. Ger. *Knoblauch*). The word is a cpd of the elements *klob-* split (cf. KLÖVER) + *louch* leek.

Vars.: **Knoblich**, **Knoflach**; **Knopfloch** (Bavaria).

Cogns.: Jewish (Ashkenazic, occupational names, or perhaps among the unflattering names bestowed at random on Jews by non-Jewish government officials in central Europe in the 18th and 19th cents.): **Knoblauch**, **Knobeloch**, **Knoblich**; **Knobel** (from Yid. *knobl*); **Knobler** (clearly occupational); NOBLE.

Knochenhauer Low German: occupational name for a butcher, from MLG *knocke* bone + *houwen* to cut, chop (see HAUER).

Knoll English: 1. topographic name for someone who lived at the top of a hill, OE *cnoll*, or habitation name from one of the many places named with this word.

2. from an OE byname of the same origin, denoting a short, stout person.

Vars. (of 1): **Knowl(d)er, Knowlman**.

Knopf German and Jewish (Ashkenazic): metonymic occupational name for a maker of buttons, normally of horn, from Ger. *Knopf* button (MHG, OHG *knopf*, like other words in *kn-* originally descriptive of a swelling or lump). The Ger. surname may also be a nickname for a small, rotund man or a topographic name for someone who lived by a rounded hillock.

Vars. (all occupational): Ger.: **Knöpfler**; **Knöfler** (Bavaria). Jewish: **Knopfler**; **Knepler** (from Yid. *knepl* button); **Knop(f)-macher, Knopfelmacher** ('button maker').

Cogns.: Low Ger.: **Kno(o)p, Knopp**.

Dims.: Ger.: **Knöpfel, Knöpfle**; **Knöpfli** (Switzerland); **Knöf(f)el** (Bavaria). Jewish: **Knopl, Knep(p)el**. Low Ger.: **Knöpken**.

Knorr 1. German: metonymic nickname for a hunchback or someone with some other bodily protuberance, from MHG *knorre* lump, outgrowth (mod. Ger. *Knorren* knot in a piece of wood) The word is not attested in OHG but is presumably of native origin, belonging in the same group as other nouns beginning with *kn-*.)

2. German: topographic name for someone who lived by a small hill or mound, from the same word used in a transferred sense.

3. English: habitation name from *Knarr* Farm and Lake in Cambs., in which the element in question appears to be a cogn. of that in 2.

Vars.: Ger.: **Knorn, Knör(r)e**. (Of 2 only): Ger.: **Knauer(t), Knür** (from the byform *knür*).

Dims. (of 2): Ger.: **Knörndl**; **Knürle**.

Knotek Czech: from Czech *knotek* 'little knot or tangle' (from *knot* knot, tangle + the dim. suffix *-ek*), applied as a nickname either to someone with a tangle of hair or to a dwarf or person of stunted growth.

Knott 1. English: nickname for a lumpish, thickset person, from OE *cnotta* knot, lump, swelling (another member of the large group of Gmc words in *kn-* with related meanings).

2. English: topographic name for someone who lived by a hillock or projecting rock, from ME *knot* hillock (apparently from the same OE source as in 1).

3. English: from the ON personal name *Knútr*, originally a byname cogn. with 1. This given name became popular in England in the reign of the Danish king Canute (1016–35), and was still in regular use in the 13th cent.

4. Jewish (Ashkenazic): Anglicization of one or more like-sounding Jewish surnames.

Cogns. (of 1 and 2): Ger.: **Knot(h)(e), Knaut(h), Knode**. (Of 3): Dan., Norw., Swed.: **Knut(h)**.

Dims. (of 1 and 2): Ger.: **Knötel, Knödel**. Low Ger.: **Knödgen**.

Patrs. (from 3): Eng.: **Knotts(on)**. Dan., Norw.: **Knudsen**. Swed.: **Knutsson**. Finn.: **Nuutinen**.

Knowles English: 1. topographic name for someone who lived at the top of a hill, from a gen. or pl. form of ME *knol* (see KNOLL 1).

2. patr. from the same word used as a byname for a short, stout person (see KNOLL 2).

Vars.: **Knollys, Nowles**. (Of 2 only): **Knowlson**; **Knowling**.

Knox Scots, N English, and N Irish: topographic name for someone who lived on a hilltop, from a gen. or pl. form of OE *cnocc* round-topped hill, or habitation name from one of the places called *Knock* in Scotland and N England, in particular one in the former county of Renfrews. The surname is also borne by E Ashkenazic Jews as an Anglicization of one or more like-sounding Jewish surnames.

Vars.: **Knock(er)**.

Cogns.: Ger.: **Nock(e)** (Bavaria, Austria).

Dim.: Ger.: **Nöckl**.

A Scottish family bearing the name Knox *trace their descent from Adam, son of Uchtred, who was granted lands at Knock near Greenock in the 13th cent.*

Knuckey Cornish: probably a habitation name from *Kenneggy* in the parish of Breage, *Kenegie* in the parish of Gulval, or *Keneggy* in the parish of Kenwyn, all so called from Corn. ***keunegy*, pl. of *keunek* reed-bed, marsh.

Koblenz Jewish (Ashkenazic) and German: local name from the city of *Koblenz*, situated at the confluence of the Rhine and Mosel. It was founded in 9 BC as a Roman town with the L name of *Confluentes* (*fluvii*) 'confluent rivers', from which the modern name derives. The surname is to a large extent Jewish and has been carried into a number of European languages, where it has been variously spelled.

Vars.: Jewish: **Koblentz, Coblen(t)z**; **Koblenc** (a Pol. spelling); **Koblence, Coblence, Coblance, Caublance** (Fr. spellings); **Koblenzer** ('native or inhabitant of Koblenz').

Köbler German: topographic name for someone who lived in a crude or temporary hut, or occupational name for a keeper of animals, an agent deriv. of S Ger. dial. *Kobel* little hut, shelter, or stall (from MHG *kobe* stall, shelter; not attested in OHG, but probably akin to mod. Eng. *cover*).

Vars.: **Kobler** (also borne by Ashkenazic Jews); **Kobel(mann)**.

Kobyłecki Polish: habitation name from a place named from Pol. *kobyła* mare, with addition of the surname suffix *-ski* (see BARANOWSKI).

Vars.: **Kobyłański, Kobyliński**.

Cogn.: Czech: **Kobylak**.

Koch 1. German: occupational name for a cook, from Ger. *Koch* COOK (MHG *koch*, OHG *choc*, from L *coquus*).

2. Czech: altered form of any of several obsolete personal names beginning with *Ko-*, for example *Kocián*, *Kojata*, and *Kosmas*.

3. Jewish (Ashkenazic): of unknown origin.

Vars. (of 1): **Kocher, Kochmann**.

Dim. (of 1): **Köchle**.

Kochanek Polish: nickname from Pol. *kochanek* darling, dear (from *kochać* to love), used as a term of address. Prince Karol Stanisław Radziwiłł (1734–90) was generally known as 'Panie Kochanku' (vocative), presumably because he habitually addressed others in this way. In other cases, the word may have been applied as a nickname to a good-looking or amorous man.

Vars.: **Kochaniak, Kochański**.

Patr.: **Kochanowicz**.

Habitation name: **Kochanowski**.

Köchel German: habitation name from any of the numerous minor places in Bavaria and the Tyrol that get their names from *Köchel*, a dial. term, of uncertain etymology, said by Bahlow to denote an island of raised land surrounded by marsh.

Vars.: **Köchl(er)**.

Kochetov Russian: patr. from the ORuss. nickname *Kochet* 'Cock', a byform of *kokot*. Both words, which are of imitative origin, from the clucking of farmyard fowls, have been replaced in mod. Russ. by *petukh* (a deriv. of *pet* to sing).

Var.: **Kogutov**.

Cogns.: Ukr.: **Kohut, Kogutovski**. Czech: **Kohout; Kokeš**. Ger. (of Slav. origin): **Kokott**. Jewish (E Ashkenazic, ornamental): **Koh(o)ut; Kogut** (under Russ. influence); **Cogut** (Anglicized spelling).

Dims.: Pol.: **Kokoszko, Kokoszka**. Czech: **Kohoutek, Kokoška**. Ger. (of Slav. origin): **Kakosch, Kakuschke, Kokosch(k)a**. Jewish: **Kokotek, Kokutak**.

Kocsis Hungarian: occupational name for a coachman, from Hung. *kocsi* coach, which is from the placename *Kocs*, the village where in the 16th cent. coaches were were first made, with the addition of the adjectival ending *-i*. Mod. Eng. *coach* and Fr. *coche* are derived from this Hung. word, as well as Ger. *Kutsche* and Czech *kočí*.

Cogns.: Czech: **Kočí; Kočar**.

Dim.: Czech: **Kočarek**.

Koekemoer Low German and Dutch: habitation name from a place in Westphalia, which probably gets its name from elements meaning 'frog' + 'marsh', 'moor'.

Kofoed Danish: uncomplimentary nickname from the elements *ko* cow (ON *kýr*) + *fod* foot (ON *fótr*).

Vars.: **Koefoed, Kofod**.

Cogns.: Ger.: **Kuhfuss, Kühfuss**. Low Ger.: **Kofoth**.

Kofroň Czech: nickname for someone who talked about things that he did not really understand. The word is derived from the placename *Gafron* in Polish Silesia, whose inhabitants had such a reputation.

Var.: **Kofrň**.

Dim.: **Kofránek**.

Kogel 1. Low German: metonymic occupational name for a maker of hoods or nickname for a habitual wearer of a distinctive hood, from MLG *kogel* hood (LL *cuculla*).

2. S German: topographic name from the dial. word *kogel* mountain top.

3. Jewish (Ashkenazic): of unknown origin.

Vars. (of 1): **Kagel(mann); Kogler, Kögler, Kag(e)ler** (occupational names).

Kohl German: metonymic occupational name for a grower or seller of cabbages, from Ger. *Kohl* cabbage (OHG *chōlo, kōl(i)*, cogn. with L *caulis* stalk; cf. OF *chol* cabbage).

Var.: Swiss Ger.: **Köhl**.

Cogns.: Du.: **Kool(e)**. Fr.: **Chol, Chou(x); Chol(l)ier**.

Dims.: Fr.: **Chol(l)et, Chollez, Cholley, Cholé, Choulet, Choleau, Chol(a)in, Cholot, Choloux**.

Collective: Cat.: **Colet**.

Koivisto Finnish: ornamental or topographic name meaning 'birch wood', from Finn. *koivo* birch tree + the collective suffix *-isto*.

Kokkonen Finnish: patr. from the OFinn. personal name *Kokko*, a deriv. of the vocab. word *kotka* eagle.

Kołacz Polish: metonymic occupational name for a fancy baker, from Pol. *kołacz* a kind of sweet loaf in which the dough has been twisted into an ornamental shape. Loaves of this kind of bread were eaten especially at weddings.

Var.: **Kołacki**.

Cogns.: Jewish: **Kolatsch** (reason for adoption unknown).

Kolasa Polish: 1. metonymic occupational name for a coachman, from Pol. *kolasa* carriage.

2. perhaps also an aphetic derivative of *Mikołaj* Nicholas.

Habitation name: **Kolasiński**.

Kołodziej Polish: occupational name for a wheelwright, Pol. *kołodziej*, from *koło* wheel.

Var.: **Kołodziejski**.

Cogn.: Slovak: **Kolař; Kolařský**.

Dims.: Pol.: **Kołodziejczyk**. Czech: **Kolařík**.

Patr.: Pol.: **Kołodziejczak**.

Komarov Russian: patr. from the nickname *Komar* 'Gnat', 'Mosquito', originally given perhaps to a small and insignificant person or to an irritating one.

Cogns. (not patrs.): Pol.: **Komar**. Jewish (E Ashkenazic): **Komar; Komer** (from E Yid. *komer* mosquito).

Cogns. (patrs. in form): Jewish: **Komaroff, Komarow**.

Dim.: Czech: **Komárek**.

Komorowski Polish: habitation name for a cottager or tenant, from Pol. *komora* hut, cottage (cf. *komorne* rent), + *-ów* possessive suffix + *-ski* suffix of local surnames (see Baranowski).

Konarski Polish: 1. occupational name for a horse-breeder or for someone who worked with horses, i.e. a groom or ostler, Pol. *koniarz* (from *koń* horse) + the surname suffix *-ski* (see Baranowski).

2. habitation name from the town of *Konary* near Sandomierz, or from some other place similarly named. The placename is likewise derived from *koń* horse or *koniarz* groom.

Cogn. (of 1): Czech: **Koníř**.

Dims. (of 1): Czech: **Koňaŕík, Konárek**.

Habitation names: Pol.: **Konarowski, Konarzewski**.

Kondratyev Russian: patr. from the given name *Kondrati*. This is officially derived from Gk *Kodratos* (from L *Quadrātus*; see Carré), which was acceptable as a baptismal name in the eyes of the Orthodox Church because it was the name of several early saints. However, the *-n-* can only be explained by derivation from the Gmc name Konrad (Pol. *Kondrat*); there has clearly been some confusion between the two names. In the Russ. name, the final *-i* is an example of hypercorrection; it was added after the pattern of Gk names in *-ios*, which lost the vowel in the popular forms but retained it in a learned form.

Var.: **Kondratov**.

Dims.: **Kondrakov, Kondrushkin, Kondrashov, Kondryukhov, Kand(r)eev, Kondrichev** (all patrs.).

'Son of the wife of K. (dim.)': **Kondrashikhin**.

Konieczny Polish: from the Pol. adj. *konieczny* necessary, although the application is not clear. It may be a status name for someone with 'great expectations', from the expression *dziedzic konieczny* heir apparent.

Vars.: **Skon(i)eczny, Skonieczka, Skonieczko** (by mis-division).

Cogn.: Czech: **Konečný**.

König 1. German: cogn. of King.

2. Jewish (Ashkenazic): name chosen as a translation of the Yid. male given names *Meylekh* (from Hebr. *Melech* 'King') and *Elemeylekh* (from Hebr. *Elimelech* 'God is my king'), or an ornamental name, one of several such Ashkenazic surnames based on European titles of nobility or royalty (cf. Graf, Herzog, Fürst, and Kaiser).

Var.: Jewish: **Kinig** (from Yid. *kinig*).

Cogns.: Flem.: **(De) Conynck, Coninck**. Du.: **De Koning**.

Dim.: Jewish: **Kinigel** (alternatively this may be from Yid. *kinigl* rabbit; cf. Krolikov).

Patrs.: Flem.: **Conings, Conin(ck)x**. Du.: **Konings**. Jewish: **Kinigson**.

Cpds (ornamental elaborations): Jewish: **Kinigstein**; KÖNIGSBERG.

Königsberg 1. Jewish (Ashkenazic) and German: local name from the city of *Königsberg*, former capital of E Prussia, which gets its name from MHG *künigesberc* 'hill of the king', i.e. of King Ottokar II of Bohemia, who founded the city in 1255. It is now in the Soviet Union and called *Kaliningrad*.

2. Jewish (Ashkenazic): ornamental elaboration of KÖNIG.

Vars.: Jewish: **Konigsberger**; **Kin(i)gsberg**, GINSBERG.

Konopka Polish: nickname meaning 'linnet', perhaps denoting an individual noted for his cheerful singing.

Konovalov Russian: patr. from the occupational term *konoval* horse doctor (a cpd of *kon* horse + *valyat* to throw, i.e. castrate).

Cogn.: Ukr.: **Konovalets**.

Dims.: Beloruss.: **Konoval(ch)ik, Konovalyuk**.

Konrad German: from a Gmc personal name composed of the elements *kuoni* daring, brave + *rad* counsel, which has probably fallen together with an originally distinct name in which the first element was *kuni* race, people. The given name was extremely popular during the Middle Ages, being a hereditary name in several ruling families and also widely adopted by the people at large; the expression *Hinz und Kunz* (short forms of HENRY and Konrad) was the Ger. equivalent of 'every Tom, Dick, and Harry'. The surname is also borne by Ashkenazic Jews, presumably as an adoption of the Ger. surname.

Vars.: **Kunrad, Ku(h)nert**; **Kundert** (Switzerland); **Kuhnhardt** (with the second element altered to the more common *hard* hardy, brave, strong); **Keinrat** (altered by folk etymology to 'no counsel'); **Kuhnt, Kundt, Kurt(h)**.

Cogns.: Low Ger.: **Ko(h)nert**; **Kohrt, Kor(d)t**. Du.: **Koenraad**. Czech: **Kunrád, Konrád**. Pol.: **Kondrat**. Russ.: KONDRATYEV. It.: **Corradi, Corrado**; **Cunradi, Cunrado** (Tuscany); **Gurrado, Corr(a)o, Curr(a)o** (S Italy). Fr.: **Conrad, Conrath, Conré, Corré**; **Conrard, Conrart**. Hung.: **Konrád, Korlát**.

Dims.: Ger.: **Kuhn, Kühn(e), Kühn(d)el**; **Kiehne(lt), Kien(d)l, Kien(z)le, Kienlein** (Austria); **Kienle** (Swabia); **Kaindl, Kainz** (Tyrol); **Kunz(e), Künzel(mann), Kin(t)zel, Konzel(mann)**; **Kull(mann)**. Low Ger.: **Cohr**; **Keune(ke), Keunemann, Keuntje**; **Kö(h)n(e)(ke), Könneke, Künneke, Kö(h)n(e)mann**. Du.: **Koene, Keune**. Ger. (of Slav. origin): **Kuhnke, Kunisch**. Czech: **Kuna, Kuneš**; **Kunc** (from the Ger. pet form *Kunz*); **Kyncl** (from the Ger. pet form *Künzl*). Ukr.: **Kondratenko, Kondratyuk**. Beloruss.: **Kondratenya, Kondrachenko**. It.: **Corradetti, Corradini, Corradino**; **Corain(i)** (Venetia). Hung.: **Gunda**.

Patrs.: Ger.: **Kürten**. Low Ger.: **Konertz, Coners**; **Konerding, Conerding, Conring, Ko(h)rding, Körting**; **Kordes, Cordes**; **Cordsen, Corssen**. Flem.: **Coenraets**. Dan.: **Conradsen**. Pol.: **Kondratowicz**. Ukr., Beloruss.: **Kondratovich**. It.: **Corradengo** (Liguria); **Corradeschi** (Tuscany).

Patrs. (from dims.): Ger.: **Künzler, Kiezler**. Low Ger.: **Kohnen, Köhnen**; **Kohrs, Cohrs, Kohrsen, Köhring**. Du., Flem.: **Koenen, Keuning**. Ger. (of Slav. origin): **Kunat(h)**.

Kooy Dutch: topographic name for someone who lived by a pen or fold where animals were confined, MDu. *kooy*.

Vars.: **Kooyman, Kooi(j)(man), Van (der) Kooi**.

Cogn.: Fris.: **Kooistra**.

Kopczyński Polish: topographic or habitation name from Pol. *kopczyk* hillock, mound (from *kopa* hill; cogn. with Czech *kopec*), with the addition of *-ski*, suffix of local surnames (see BARANOWSKI).

Vars.: **Kopacki**; **Kopka**.

Cogns.: Czech: **Kopecký, Kopečka, Kopečný**.

Kopeć Polish: from OPol. *kopeć* smoke, soot, given perhaps as a nickname to a dirty or swarthy person or to someone who lived in a smoky place, or alternatively perhaps used as an occupational nickname for a chimneysweep.

Cogn.: Czech: **Kopta**.

Dim.: Czech: **Koptík**.

Koper Polish: topographic name from Pol. *koper* dill, fennel, or perhaps an occupational name for a grower or seller of dill or fennel.

Var.: **Koperski**.

Dim.: **Kopernik**.

Habitation name: **Koprowski**.

Kopf 1. German: metonymic occupational name for a maker or seller of cups or flasks, from MHG *kopf* flask (from LL *cuppa* cask; cf. COOPER).

2. German: metonymic nickname for someone with some noticeable peculiarity or deformity of the head, from Ger. *Kopf*, the same word as in 1, used in a transferred sense which during the Middle Ages gradually ousted the earlier word *Haupt* (see HEAD).

3. Jewish (Ashkenazic): from Ger. *Kopf* head, the reasons for its adoption being unclear, but probably as in 2.

Var. (of 3): **Kopman** (from Yid. *kop* head).

Cogns.: see COPP. See also JACOB.

Dims. (of 1 and 2): Ger.: **Köpfel, Köpfle, Köppel**.

Cpds (of 3): **Kopstein** ('head stone', presumably an ornamental elaboration); **Kopfstein** (either an ornamental elaboration or from Ger. *Kopfstein* cobblestone, and so perhaps an anecdotal surname based on some now irrecoverable minor incident).

Kopřiva Czech: from Czech *kopřiva* nettle, presumably either a topographic name or a nickname for a person with a prickly temperament.

Kořán Czech: metonymic occupational name for a herbalist or seller of herbs and spices, from S Czech dial. *kořán* root (cf. Czech *koření* (pl.) spices, Pol. *korzenie*).

Cogn.: Pol.: **Korzeniowski**.

Dim.: Czech: **Kořánek**.

Korb 1. German: metonymic occupational name for a basket-maker, from Ger. *Korb* basket (MHG *korb*, OHG *churp*, from L *corbis*; cf. CORBEIL).

2. German: metonymic occupational name for a pedlar who carried his goods around in a basket, from the same word as in 1.

3. Jewish (Ashkenazic): of uncertain origin, probably as in 1 and 2.

Vars.: Ger.: **Körb(l)er, Kerb(l)er, Kreber**. Jewish: **Korber**; **Korf(f), Korfman(n)**.

Cogns.: Low Ger.: **Korf(f)**; **Körfer, Körver**; **Korfmann**. Du.: **Korff, Korver, Corver**. Czech: **Korbelář**. (Of 1 only): Flem., Du.: **Korfmaker**.

Dims.: Ger.: **Körbel, Korbel**. Low Ger.: **Korfgen**.

Patrs.: Low Ger.: **Körfers**. (Of 1 only): Flem., Du.: **Korfmakers**.

Korda Czech: from a pet form of the OCzech given name *Kornel* Cornelius (see CORNEILLE 1).

Var.: **Kordač**.

Dim.: **Kordík**.

The film producer Sir Alexander Korda *(1893–1956) came of a Hungarian Jewish family, who were originally called* KELLNER. *He adapted his new surname from the Latin phrase* Sursum Corda *'Lift up your hearts', which he had taken in 1917 as a nom-de-plume. The surname* Korda *is also borne by Jews unrelated to Alexander Korda, in which case it is probably an adoption of the Czech surname.*

Korecky Czech and Jewish (Ashkenazic): apparently a topographic name for someone living by a watermill, from Czech *koreček* in the dial. sense 'overshot watermill', from Czech *korec* bucket, container.

Var.: **Koreček**.

Korhonen Finnish: patr. from the nickname *Korho* 'Deaf'. This is the fourth commonest Finn. surname, so presumably some metaphor is involved in the acquisition of the surname, as deafness is not a noticeably more common affliction in Finland than elsewhere.

Kořínek Czech: nickname for a man with a ruddy, healthy complexion, Czech *kořínek*.

Korn 1. German: metonymic occupational name for a factor or dealer in grain, from Ger. *Korn* grain (MHG, OHG *korn*).

2. Jewish (Ashkenazic): metonymic occupational name as in 1, or ornamental name from Ger. *Korn* grain, Yid. *korn*.

3. Czech: from a short form of the OCzech given name *Kornel* Cornelius (see CORNEILLE 1).

Vars. (of 1): **Körner, Kor(ne)mann**.

Dims. (of 1): **Körn(d)le**.

Cpds (of 2; ornamental except where otherwise stated): **Kornberg** ('grain hill'); **Kornblatt, Kornblitt** ('grain blossom'); **Kornblau** ('grain blue'); **Kornblum(e)** ('grain flower'); **Kornfein** ('fine as grain'); **Kornfeld** ('grain field', partly Anglicized as **Kornfield, Cornfeld**; fully Anglicized as **Cornfield**,); **Korngold** ('grain gold'); **Korngruen** ('grain green'); **Kornhaber** ('grain oats'); **Kornhauser** ('(owner of or worker in) a granary', occupational); **Kornhendler** ('grain merchant', occupational); **Kornmehl** ('grain flour', probably occupational for a grain merchant); **Kornreich** ('rich in grain'); **Kornstein** ('grain stone'); **Kornwasser** ('grain water'); **Kornweiss** ('grain white'); **Kornweitz** ('grain wheat'); **Kornzweig** ('grain twig').

Korostelyov Russian: patr. from the nickname *Korostel* 'Landrail' (allegedly of imitative origin).

Var.: **Korostylyov**.

Korotygin Russian: patr. from the nickname *Korotyga* 'Shorty', a deriv. of *korotky* short (ultimately cogn. with L *curtus*; see COURT 2).

Vars.: **Karatygin** (reflecting the actual pronunciation of the unstressed vowels); **Korotkikh** (gen. pl. of the adj.); **Korotky** (apparently nom. sing. of the adj., probably of Ukr. or Beloruss. origin).

Cogns.: Ukr.: **Korotich** (patr.); **Korotchenko** (dim.). Czech: **Krátký, Kratěna**. Jewish (Ashkenazic): **Korot(ky)**; **Korotkin** (patr.).

Korovnikov Russian: patr. from the occupational term *korovnik* cowherd (a deriv. of *korova* cow).

Korsakov Russian: patr. from the nickname *Korsak* 'Steppe Fox' (a word borrowed from a Turkic language).

Kos 1. Czech: nickname from Czech *kos* blackbird. Blackbirds had a reputation for being cunning and devious, even devilish, so the nickname would have been used to refer to a smart or unscrupulous person. The related adj. *kusý*, meaning 'bob-tailed', was likewise applied to the devil.

2. Jewish: of unknown origin. The explanation given in 1 may apply here, or the name may be from Hebr. *kos* (drinking) glass or Yid. *kos* goblet, cup. In the latter case, the surname is probably an anecdotal nickname based on some now irrecoverable minor incident, an assumption supported by the fact that the name is rare. The Ashkenazic surname **Kosman**, on the other hand, is more frequent, and this suggests that it is probably a metonymic occupational name referring to someone who made glasses or cups.

Vars. (of 1): **Kosa, Kus, Kůs**.

Cogn. (of 1): Pol.: **Kusiak**.

Dim. (of 1): Czech: **Kosík**.

Habitation name: Pol.: **Kosiński**.

Kościelski Polish: topographic name for someone who lived near a church, from Pol. *kościół* church, with the addition of *-ski*, suffix of local surnames (see BARANOWSKI).

Cogn.: Czech: **Zákostelecký** (lit. 'beyond the church').

Koskinen Finnish: ornamental name from Finn. *koski* waterfall, rapids + the gen. suffix *-nen*. This was one of the many words for natural features that were used in the formation of Finn. surnames when these became obligatory during the 18th and 19th cents.

Vars.: **Koski, Koskela**.

Kosmala Polish: nickname for a shaggy, unkempt individual, from a deriv. of Pol. *kosmaty* shaggy, hairy.

Var.: **Kosmalski**.

Košnář Czech: occupational name for a basket-maker, from Czech *koš* basket + *-(n)ář* suffix of occupational names.

Vars.: **Koš(n)ar**.

Kosorotov Russian: patr. from the nickname *Kosoroty* 'Wry-mouthed', a deriv. of *kosoi* twisted, awry + *rot* mouth.

Košt'ál Czech: apparently from Czech *kost'a* spike, perhaps a nickname for a person of tall and spiky appearance.

Var.: **Košt'ák**.

Dim.: **Košt'álek**.

Kostrzewa Polish: topographic name for someone who lived by a meadow, from Pol. *kostrzewa* meadow grass, fescue, from *kostra* spike (cogn. with Czech *kost'a* spike).

Var.: **Kostrzewski**.

Kosygin Russian: patr. from the nickname *Kosyga* 'Deformed', a deriv. of *kosoi* twisted, crippled, cross-eyed.

Kotliński Polish: topographic name for someone living in a dale, Pol. *kotlina*, with the addition of *-ski*, suffix of local surnames (see BARANOWSKI).

Var.: **Kotlicki**.

Kotrba Czech: metonymic nickname for someone with a noticeably large or deformed head, or possibly used as a nickname for a headstrong person, from Czech *kotrba* head, skull.

Var.: **Kotrbatý**.

Kotrč Czech: from the vocab. word *kotrč* stick (which had various specialized senses, including 'rudder on a raft'). According to Moldanová, this word was used as a nickname for a small person around Sušice in S Bohemia.

Var.: **Kotrc**.

Koudela Czech: apparently a metonymic occupational name for someone who unravelled old rope to make tow, from *koudel* oakum, tow, or else a nickname for someone with tow-coloured hair. According to Moldanová, however, in Olomouc this is a slang word for a blockhead, and so it may well be a derogatory nickname with this meaning.

Koutský Czech: topographic name for someone who lived on a corner (from Czech *kout* corner + *-ský* suffix of local surnames), or habitation name from one of the places named with this element. In some cases it also denoted the keeper of a corner shop, and so is an equiv. of Ger. WINCKEL.

Vars.: **Koucký, Kautský, Kaucký; Kout(ný); Koutník.**

Dims.: **Koutek, Koutecký.**

Kovanda Czech: nickname meaning 'trueborn', applied to a person of good breeding.

Kowalski Polish and Jewish (E Ashkenazic): occupational name for a blacksmith, Pol. *kowal* (from *kować, kuć* to forge, akin to ORuss. *kuzn* forged work; see KUZNETSOV), with the addition of *-ski*, suffix of surnames (see BARANOWSKI).

Vars.: **Kowal.** Jewish only: **Koval(ski), Kovalsky, Kowalsky; Kovel(man)** (from E Yid. *kovl* smith); **Kovac(s)** (among Hungarian Jews).

Cogns.: Ukr.: **Koval(ski)** (Russianized as **Kovalyov**); **Kovalevski.** Czech: **Kovář, Kováč, Koval.** Croatian: **Kovač.** Hung.: **Kovács, Kováts, Kovách** (Anglicized **Kofax**, which is also Jewish). Ger. (of Slav. origin): **Kowa(h)l, Kofahl.**

Dims.: Pol.: **Kowalczyk, Kowalik.** Ukr.: **Kovanko.** Beloruss.: **Kovalyonok, Kovalenya; Kovalchuk.** Czech: **Kovářík, Kovaříček.** Ger. (of Slav. origin): **Kowalke.**

Patrs.: Pol.: **Kowalewicz.** Beloruss.: **Kovalevich.** Croatian: **Kovač(ev)ić, Ković.** Jewish: **Kowaloff, Kowlowitz.**

Habitation names: Pol.: **Kowalewski, Kowalczyński, Kowaliński.**

Kozak Polish: 1. name for a *Cossack*, a member of a people descended from a group of runaway serfs who set up a semi-independent military republic in the Ukraine in the 15th and 16th cents. The Cossacks became noted for their military prowess.

2. var. of *Kozieł*; see KOZLOV.

3. Jewish (E Ashkenazic): presumably a nickname for a ruthless person, from Pol. *Kozak* as in 1, unless this is a spelling var. of KOZÁK (see also KOZLOV).

Patr.: Pol.: **Kozakiewicz.**

Kozák Czech: 1. occupational name for a goatherd, Czech *kozák*, or derogatory nickname from the vocab. word *koza* goat (cf. KOZLOV).

2. regional name from the district of *Kozácko* in S Bohemia.

Var. (of 1): **Koza.**

Kozlov Russian and Jewish (E Ashkenazic): patr. in form from the nickname *Kozyol* 'Goat', denoting a stubborn, lecherous, or malodorous man; also perhaps an occupational name for a goatherd. It is not clear how the Jewish surname was acquired.

Vars.: Russ.: **Kozin.** Jewish: **Koziol; Kozlovski, Kozlow(ski), Koslovsky, Koslofsky; Kozlovitz, Koslovitz; Kozloff, Koslow.**

Cogns.: Pol.: **Kozieł; Koziara, Koziarz** (occupational); **Koziarski.** Czech: **Kozel;** KOZÁK. Croatian: **Kozlović** (patr.).

Dims.: Czech: **Kozlík, Kozelka.**

Habitation name: Pol.: **Kozłowski.**

Kraft German, Danish, and Jewish (Ashkenazic): metonymic nickname for a strong man, from Ger. *Kraft* or Dan. *kraft* strength (OHG *kraft*). The Ger. and Dan. names possibly also derive from a late survival of the OHG byname *Chrafto* 'Strong' or its ON cogn. *Kraptr.*

Var.: Ger.: **Krafft.**

Cogn.: Low Ger.: **Kracht.**

Kraindels Jewish (Ashkenazic): metr. from the Yid. female given name *Kreyndl* (from a dim. of Yid. *kroyn* crown) + Yid. possessive *-s*.

Vars.: From the Yid. female given name *Kreyne* (a back-formation from *Kreyndl*): **Krainin, Kreinin, Krainovitz** (E Ashkenazic); **Krainis** (Ashkenazic); **Krajnis, Krejnis** (Pol. spellings). Germanized forms: **Kro(h)nson, Kronzon.**

Krajewski Polish: probably a topographic name for someone who lived on the edge of a parish or other administrative district, from Pol. *kraj* border area + *-ew* possessive suffix + *-ski* suffix of local surnames (see BARANOWSKI).

Cogns.: Czech: **Krajina; Krajný** (adjectival form); **Krajník** (with Czech *-ník* suffix denoting human agent nouns). Jewish (Ashkenazic): **Krajnik.**

Krakowiak Polish: local name for someone from the city of Cracow, Pol. *Kraków.*

Var.: **Krakowski** (also Jewish (E Ashkenazic)).

Cogn.: Ger. and Jewish (Ashkenazic): **Krakauer.**

Krämer German and Jewish (Ashkenazic): occupational name for a shopkeeper, from Ger. *Krämer* (Yid. *kremer*), an agent deriv. of MHG *krām* (OHG *crām*) trading post, tent. The Slav. cogns. listed below are derived from German.

Vars.: Ger.: **Kremer; Kromer, Krömer.** Jewish: **Kra(e)mer, Kramerman, Krammer, Kremer(man).** U.S.: **Creamer.**

Cogns.: Flem., Du.: **Cramer, Kremer, (De) Cre(e)mer.** Dan.: **Cramer.** Ukr., Beloruss.: **Kramar.** Czech: **Kramář.**

Dims.: Ukr.: **Kramarenko, Kramarchuk.**

Patrs.: Low Ger.: **Kramers.** Flem.: **Cre(e)mers.** Du.: **Kra(e)mers.** Beloruss.: **Kramarov.** Jewish: **Kremers, Kremerov.**

The Flemish cartographer Gerhard Kremer *(1512–94) preferred the Latinized form of his name, Gerardus* Mercator, *and it is from this that 'Mercator's projection' takes its name.*

Kranke 1. German: nickname from MHG *kranc(k)* thin, slight, weak (the word is not attested in OHG, but appears to be of native origin); towards the end of the surname-forming period the Ger. word *krank* acquired its modern sense 'ill' (replacing MHG *siech* sick) and in some cases the surname may refer to a chronic invalid or a hypochondriac. The word is akin to mod. Eng. *cringe* (from OE *cringan* to writhe, collapse from wounds).

2. Low Ger.: dim. of CRANE.

Var. (of 1): **Krankheit** (an abstract noun).

Cogn. (of 1): Du.: **Krankheid** (U.S. **Cronkite**).

The ancestors of the American Cronkite *family, one of whose members is the broadcaster Walter Cronkite (b. 1919), were Dutch merchants who settled in the 17th cent. in what is now New York, then the Dutch settlement of New Amsterdam.*

Kranz 1. German: metonymic occupational name for a maker of chaplets and wreaths or house name for someone who lived at a house distinguished by the sign of a garland, Ger. *Kranz* garland, wreath (MHG *kranz*, OHG *cranz*).

2. Jewish (Ashkenazic): ornamental name from Ger. *Kranz* or Yid. *krants* wreath, garland.

Vars.: **Krantz, Kranzler.** Ger.: **Kränzler; Kranzlbinder** (see BINDER). Jewish: **Krantzler; Kranc** (a Pol. spelling).

Dims.: Ger.: **Kränz(e)l, Kränzle, Krenzle.** Low Ger.: **Krantz(c)ke.**

Cpds: Jewish: **Kranzbaum** ('wreath tree'); **Kran(t)zberg, Krancberg** ('wreath hill'); **Krancenblum** ('wreath flower'); **Kranzdorf** ('wreath village').

The surname Krantzcke *was established in London at the end of the 18th cent., with Frederick Krantzcke (1779–1850), a tailor. The name has now died out in England.*

Krapf German: nickname for someone with a hooked nose or a hunched back, from MHG *krāp(f)e* hook (OHG *krāpfo*, akin to mod. Eng. *grapple*, which has come via OF from a Gmc source). The word was also applied to a type of crescent-shaped pastry, and the surname may thus also have been a metonymic occupational name for a baker.

Var.: **Krapp**.

Dims.: Ger. and Jewish (Ashkenazic): **Krapfl**, **Krappel** (reasons for adoption as a Jewish name unclear). Jewish only: **Krep(p)el** (from Yid. *krepl*, a kind of boiled dumpling; reasons for adoption unclear).

Krarup Danish: habitation name from a placename composed of the elements *krage* crow + *rup* settlement (see THORPE).

Krasilnikov Russian: patr. from the occupational term *krasilnik* dyer (from *krasit* to dye, a deriv. of *krasa* brightness, beauty, colour; cf. KRASNIKOV and NEKRASOV).

Var.: **Krasilshchikov**.

Krasnikov Russian: patr. from the nickname *Krasnik* 'Handsome One', from ORuss. *krasny* handsome, a deriv. of *krasa* brightness, beauty, colour; in mod. Russ., since the formation of the surname, the adj. has come to mean 'red', the meaning 'beautiful' being transferred to the byform *krasivy*.

Vars.: **Krasnov**, **Krasnykh**; **Krasavchikov**, **Krasukhin**.

Cogns.: Pol.: **Krasnowski**, **Krasoń**. Czech: **Krásný**, **Krása**. Ger. (of Slav. origin): **Krasner**. Jewish (E Ashkenazic): **Krasny**, **Krasno**, **Krasne**; **Krasnick**, **Kras(s)ner**; **Krasnicki**, **Krasnitzki**, **Krasnianski**, **Krasniansky**; **Krasnovsky**, **Krasnoff**, **Krasnow**, **Krasnove**.

Kraszewski Polish: topographic name for someone who lived in an area where the soil was reddish brown, e.g. containing sandstone, from Pol. *krasz* reddish-brown soil (cogn. with Russ. *krasny* red) + *-ew* possessive suffix + *-ski* suffix of local surnames (see BARANOWSKI).

Kratochvíl Czech and Jewish (Ashkenazic): nickname for an idle pleasure-seeker, from Czech *kratochvíl* pastime, amusement, entertainment.

Kraus German and Jewish (Ashkenazic): nickname for someone with curly hair, from Ger. *kraus* curly(-haired) (MHG *krūs*, not attested in OHG).

Vars.: Ger.: **Krause**, **Krauss**; **Kraushaar**, **Krauskopf**. Jewish: **Krauz(e)**, **Krause(r)**, **Krauzer**, **Krausz(man)**, **Krausman**, **Krauzman**; **Kraushar**, **Krauzhar**.

Cogns.: Low Ger.: **Kruse**, **Kruskopf**. Flem., Du.: **(De) Croes**, **Croese**, **Kroes(e)**, **Kroeze**. Dan.: **Kru(u)se**. Czech: **Krousa**, **Kroužil**, **Kro(u)til**.

Dims.: Ger.: KREISEL. Czech: **Kroužek**.

Kraut 1. German: metonymic occupational name for a market gardener or herbalist, from Ger. *Kraut* herb, plant (MHG, OHG *krūt*).

2. Jewish (Ashkenazic): ornamental or occupational-ornamental name from Ger. *Kraut* plant, herb.

Vars.: Ger.: **Krauth**. Jewish (occupational): **Krauter**, **Kreit(n)er**, **Kreitler**, **Kreitman**, **Krautman**.

Dim.: Ger.: **Kräutl**.

Cpds: Jewish (ornamental or occupational-ornamental): **Kraut(en)berg**, **Kreitenberger** ('(dweller on a) herb hill'); **Krautblatt** ('herb leaf'); **Krautheim(er)**, **Krauthamer** ('herb homestead(er)', the last reflecting a W Yid. form).

Krawiec Polish and Jewish (E Ashkenazic): occupational name for a tailor, Pol. *krawiec* (derived from OSlav. *kroit* to cut, a distant cogn. of Gk *krinein* to distinguish, judge, and L *cernere* to divide, discern, decide).

Vars.: Pol.: **Krawiecki**. Jewish: **Krav(i)etz**, **Krawetz**, **Kravitz**, **Kravits**, **Krawitz**, **Kravet**, **Kravett(e)**, **Krawet**, **Kravit(t)**, **Krawitt**, **Kravetsky**, **Kravetzky**, **Kravitsky**, **Krawi(e)cki**, **Krawiecky**, **Krawatsky**, **Crawetz**; **Croitoru**, **Kroitoru** (among Rumanian Jews).

Cogns.: Czech: **Krejčí(ř)**; **Krajčí(r)**, **Krajča** (E Moravian). Ger. (of Slav. origin): **Krawietz**. Rum.: **Krojtor**, **Kraitor**.

Dims.: Pol.: **Krawczyk**. Czech: **Krejčík**; **Krajíček**. Jewish: **Kravchuk**, **Krawchuk**, **Kravtshuk**, **Kravchook**, **Krawczuk**; **Krafchik**, **Kravchick**, **Kravtchik**, **Kravc(z)ich**, **Kravzik**, **Krawchick**; **Kravtchinsky**, **Krafchinsky**. Ukr., Beloruss.: **Kravchenko**.

Patrs.: Russ.: **Kravtsov**. Jewish: **Krawzow**.

Habitation name: Pol.: **Krawczyński**.

Krč Czech: nickname for a dwarf or someone of stunted growth, from Czech *krč* stump of a tree, block of wood, stunted tree.

Var.: **Krčál**.

Dim.: **Krček** (also a dim. of *krk* neck).

Kreisel 1. German: dim. of KRAUS.

2. German: nickname for a perpetually active and somewhat disorganized person, from Ger. *Kreisel* spinning top (MHG *kriusel*, dim. of *krūs* jug; the vowel of the mod. Ger. word has been influenced by association with *Kreis* circle).

3. Jewish (Ashkenazic): of uncertain origin, perhaps derived as in 1 and 2 above.

Var.: **Kreisler**.

Walter **Chrysler** *(1875–1940), founder of the famous American car firm, was born in Kansas to a Canadian father of German ancestry.*

Kretschmar German: occupational name for an innkeeper, from MHG *kretscham* inn. The word is of Slav. origin (cf. Czech *krčma* inn, *krčmář* innkeeper; Pol. *ka(r)czma*, *ka(r)czmarz*).

Vars.: **Kret(z)schmer**, **Kratschmer**; **Kretschmann**, **Kretschmeyer**.

Cogns.: Pol.: **Ka(r)czmar(ski)**. Czech: **Krčmář**, **Krčma**; **Kračmar**, **Kráčmer**, **Krečmar**, **Krečmer**. Jewish (mainly E Ashkenazic): **Krets(c)hmer**, **Kre(t)chmer**; **Kreitchman**; **Karczmar**, **Karczmer**, **Kar(ts)chmer**.

Dims.: Pol.: **Ka(r)czmarek** (*Kaczmarek* is also the name of a place in the Kujawy district near Sandomierz); **Ka(r)czmarczyk**. Czech: **Krčmarík**, **Kračmarík**.

Patr. (from a dim.): Pol.: **Kaczmarkiewicz**.

Krieger 1. German: occupational name for a mercenary soldier, Ger. *Krieger* warrior, soldier (MHG *kriegære*, possibly from LL *(miles) gregārius* common soldier, from *grex* herd, flock, crowd, gen. *gregis*).

2. German and Jewish (Ashkenazic): nickname for a quarrelsome person, Ger. *Krieger*, Yid. *kriger* (from MHG *kriec* quarrelsome, a derivative of *krieg* war, struggle).

Vars. (of 2): Jewish: **Kriger**; **Krigier** (Pol. spelling); **Kri(e)gman**, **Kri(e)gsman**.

Cogns.: Flem., Du.: **(De) Kri(j)ger**, **Krijgsman**. Dan.: **Kryger**.

Krivov Russian: patr. from the nickname *Krivoi* 'Defective', 'Deformed', 'Crippled', 'Crooked', or 'One-eyed'.

Var.: **Krivtzov**.

Cogns.: Pol.: **Krzywiec**, **Krzywicki**. Czech: **Křiva(n)**, **Křivak**, **Křivka**. Jewish (E Ashkenazic): **Krzywicki**; **Krywoshej**, **Krivoshei**; **Crivosei** (a Rumanian spelling).

Dims.: Ukr.: **Kriv(ch)enko**. Czech: **Křivánek**.

Habitation name: Pol.: **Krzywański**.

Król Polish: nickname from the vocab. word *król* king, presumably given to someone who gave himself regal airs. The vocab. word is derived from the personal name *Karol* CHARLES, for this was the name borne by the Frankish king and Holy Roman Emperor Charlemagne (L *Carolus Magnus*) (?742–814) and by several of his successors.

Var.: **Królak**.

Cogns.: Czech: **Král**; **Królak**. Hung.: **Király**. Ger. (of Slav. origin): **Kra(h)l**. Jewish (E Ashkenazic): **Krol**, KROLL.

Dims.: Pol.: KRÓLIK. Ukr.: **Korolenko**. Beloruss.: **Korolyonok**. Ger. (of Slav. origin): **Kralik**.

Patrs.: Pol.: **Królewicz**. Beloruss.: **Koralyov**. Russ.: **Korolyov**. Croatian: **Kraljević**, **Kragelić**. Hung.: **Királyfi**.

Królik Pol.: 1. nickname from the vocab. word *królik* rabbit. This is a dim. of KRÓL king, being an attempted calque on a Low Ger. dial. form *kuniklīn*, misanalysed as a dim. of *König*, but in fact from L *cunīculus* (see CONEY).

2. dim. of KRÓL.

Cogns.: Czech: **Králík**. Jewish (E Ashkenazic, ornamental): **Kroli(c)k**, **Kruli(c)k**; **Kroli(t)zki**, **Krolizky**, **Krulitzky**.

Dim.: Czech: **Kraliček**.

Patr.: Russ.: **Krolikov**.

Habitation name: Pol.: **Królikowski**.

Kroll 1. German: nickname for a man with curly hair, from MHG *krol* curly(-haired) (a deriv. of *krol(le)* curl; Eng. *curl* is a cogn., and the whole group is akin to KRAUS).

2. Jewish (E Ashkenazic): possibly as in 1, or alternatively perhaps a var. of Pol. KRÓL.

Cogns. (of 1): Low Ger.: **Krull**. Flem., Du.: **Krol**. Dan.: **Krøll**. Eng.: **Croll**, **Curl(e)**; see also CROWLE. Czech: **Krul(a)**, **Kruliš**.

Kronewitter German (Austria and Tyrol): habitation name from any of several minor places named with the MHG dial. term *kronewitt* juniper bush (a cpd of OHG *krano* crane + *witu* wood).

Vars.: **Kranewitter**, **Kronebitter**, **Kronenbitte**, **Kronenwetter**.

Kropaček Czech: from a dim. of the vocab. word *kropáč* sprinkler, dispenser of holy water. The application as a surname is not clear.

Kropotkin Russian: patr. from a nickname *Krapotka*, denoting an industrious or unsettled person (from *krapotat* to bustle, be busy).

The Moravian cogn. name **Krpata** has the opposite meaning, being from the Moravian dial. word *krpat* to work slowly, dawdle.

Var.: **Krapotkin**.

The anarchist revolutionary Prince Pyotr Kropotkin *(1842–1921) was said to have a better claim to the throne than the tsar he sought to overthrow; he was a direct descendant of the original ruling princes, the Rurik dynasty, of Scandinavian origin. It was his ancestor the Muscovite Prince Dmitri who received the nickname 'Krapotka', in the 15th cent.*

Krtil Czech: nickname from Czech *krt*, *krtek* mole, perhaps bestowed on an extremely short-sighted person or one thought to look like a mole.

Vars.: **Krt(ek)**.

Cogn.: Pol.: **Kret**.

Krüger 1. German: occupational name for a seller or maker of mugs, jugs, and pitchers, an agent deriv. of Ger. *Krug* jug, pitcher (MHG *kruoc*, OHG *kruog*). Medieval jugs and pitchers were made of leather and metals such as pewter, as well as of earthenware.

2. N German: occupational name for a tavern keeper, Ger. *Krüger*, an agent deriv. of *Krug* inn, tavern (MLG *krūch*, *krōch*, probably originally a different word from 1, with which it has subsequently fallen together).

Vars. (of 1 and 2): **Kröger**, **Kroger**, **Kruger**; **Krug**, **Kroge** (metonymic); **Krogmann**, **Krochmann**, **Krugmann**.

Cogns. (of 1): Pol.: **Krygier**. Jewish (Ashkenazic): **Krug(man)**, **Kruger**. (Of 2): Dan., Norw., Swed.: **Krog(h)**.

Dims. (of 1): Ger.: **Krügel**, **Krügle**.

Kruglov Russian: patr. from the nickname *Krugloi* 'Rotund' (from *krug* ring; the Eng. word *ring* is a distant cogn.).

Var.: **Kruglin**.

Cogn.: Jewish (E Ashkenazic): **Krugliakov**.

Kruk 1. Polish: nickname from Pol. *kruk* raven, denoting a person with black hair or perhaps one with a dark and gloomy temperament.

2. Jewish (E Ashkenazic): ornamental name from Pol. *kruk* raven, one of the many such Ashkenazic names taken from words denoting birds.

Habitation names: **Krukowski**; **Kruczkowski**.

Krupa Polish and German (of Slav. origin): metonymic occupational name for a dealer in grain, from a Slav. element represented by Pol. *krupa* grain.

Vars.: Pol.: **Krupski**. Ger.: **Kruppa**.

Cogns.: Czech: **Kroupa**, **Krupka**.

Dims.: Czech: **Krupička**. Ger. (of Slav. origin): **Krupke**.

Habitation name: Pol.: **Krupiński**.

Kruszyński Polish: of uncertain origin, perhaps either: 1. topographic name from OPol. *krusza* pear tree or *kruszyna* a kind of buckthorn (*Rhamnus frangula*) + *-ski* suffix of local surnames (see BARANOWSKI).

2. nickname from the vocab. word *krusza* meaning 'crumb, fragment', and so by extension 'small person'.

Var.: **Kruszyewski**.

Krůta Czech: derogatory nickname for an obstinate, stupid, or headstrong person, from Czech *krůta* turkey.

Vars.: **Kruták**, **Krutský**.

Krylov Russian: patr. from the nickname *Krylo* 'Wing' (from *(po)kryt* to cover), given perhaps to a protective or secretive person; it probably owes its surprising frequency to confusion with derivs. of *Cyril* (see KIRILOV).

Cogn.: Beloruss.: **Krylovich** (patr.).

Krzemiński Polish: habitation name from a place named with Pol. *krzemień* flint, with the addition of *-ski*, suffix of local surnames (see BARANOWSKI).

Vars.: **Krzemień(ski)**, **Krzemionka**, **Krzemieniewski**.

Cogn.: Czech: **Křemen**.

Krzeszewski Polish: habitation name from *Krzeszowice*, near Kraków, or from some other place similarly named. The placename is probably from Pol. *krzesz* the part of a pine which faces north, the wood of which is consequently noticeably more brittle.

Książek Polish: 1. nickname meaning 'little priest' or possibly patr. for an illegitimate son of a priest, from Pol. *ksiądz* priest + *-ek* dim. suffix.

2. nickname meaning 'little prince', from Pol. *książe* prince.

Kučera Czech: nickname for someone with curly hair, from Czech *kučera* curl. This is the eighth most common Czech surname. Other Czech surnames with the same meaning are *Kudrna* and *Kadeř* (see KUDRYAVTSEV).

Kuciński Polish: of uncertain origin, probably a nickname for a dwarf, Pol. dial. *kucin*, with the surname suffix *-ski* (see BARANOWSKI).

Kudravtsev Russian and Jewish (E Ashkenazic): patr. from the nickname *Kudravets* 'Curly', from *kudravy* curly-haired, cogn. with Pol. *kędzior* curl, Czech *kudrna*, *kadeř*.

Cogns.: Pol.: **Kędzior(a)**, **Kędzierski**, **Kędziak**; **Kudła**, **Kudlik**, **Kudelski**, **Kudliński**. Czech: **Kudrna**, **Kudrnáč**; **Kadeř**;

Kadeřábek, Kadeřávek ('curly-head'). Jewish (E Ashkenazic): **Kendzersky**; **Kudroff**; **Kudrowitz** (patr.).
Dim.: Beloruss.: **Kondzyereyonok**.

Kugel Jewish (Ashkenazic): unclear whether from Yid. *kugl* (of uncertain etymology) which denotes several different kinds of pudding, or from Ger. *Kugel* 'ball' (MHG *kugel(e)*), which has several derived meanings which might be relevant, or from both.
Vars.: **Kugelman(n)**; **Kugler**; **Kig(h)el** (from S Yid. pronunciations of *kigl*); **Kuglovitz** (in form a patr.).

Kuhl German: topographic name for someone who lived by a hollow or depression, MLG *kūle*, or habitation name from one of the numerous minor places in N Germany named with this word. The name has been altered by folk-etymological association with the High Ger. word *kuhl* cool (MHG *küele*).
Vars.: **Kühl(e)**, **Kühlen**; **Kuhl(e)mann**, **Kulemann**.
Cogns.: Low Ger.: **Zerkuhl**, **Zerkaulen**, **Zurkaulen** (Rhineland forms, with fused preposition and article, i.e. 'at the hollow'); **Torkuhl** (Westphalia, likewise with fused preposition and article).

Kujawa Polish: regional name from the district of *Kujawy*, on the left bank of the Vistula between Włocławek and Bydgoszcz.
Vars.: **Kujawski**, **Kujawiak**.

Kukla Czech: metonymic nickname from Czech *kukla* hood, probably bestowed on a habitual wearer of a hood.
Dim.: **Kuklík**.

Kukuła Polish: nickname meaning 'Cuckoo', or else a habitation name from a place named with this word.
Var.: **Kukulski**.

Kulesza Polish: from the Pol. word meaning 'millet gruel', probably a nickname for a weak or insipid person, rather than one who cooked gruel or who sold millet for gruel.
Habitation name: **Kulaszyński**.

Kulig Polish: 1. apparently a nickname from Pol. *kulig* sledge party, cavalcade on sledges, perhaps bestowed on someone who organized or took a prominent part in such a cavalcade.
2. var. of KULIK.
Patr.: **Kuligowicz**.
Habitation name: **Kuligowski**.

Kulik 1. Polish: nickname from Pol. *kulik* curlew, or else a habitation name from some place named with this word.
2. Jewish (E Ashkenazic): meaning and reasons for adoption as a surname not clear.
Vars.: **Kulka**. Pol.: **Kulon**; KULIG.
Patrs.: **Kulikiewicz**. Russ.: **Kulikov** (the Russ. word means 'snipe').
Habitation name: Pol.: **Kulikowski**.

Kümmel German and Jewish (Ashkenazic): metonymic occupational name for a seller of caraway seeds, from Ger. *Kümmel* caraway (MHG *kümmel*, OHG *kumil*, a byform of *kumin*, from L *cumīnum*; the word is ultimately, like the plant itself, of Oriental origin).
Vars.: **Kümmelmann**. Jewish only: **Kimmel**, **Kimel(mann)**, **Kim(m)elman** (from Yid. *kiml*); **Kummel** (Anglicized).
Cpds: Jewish (ornamental elaborations): **Kimelfeld** (partly Anglicized as **Kimmelfield**); **Kimelheim**.

Kumsteller German: from a byname for someone who had made the pilgrimage to the alleged tomb of St James the Greater at *Compostela* in Spain, a common penance. The placename is apparently from L *campus* field (see CHAMP) + *stella* star, but this may be no more than folk etymology.

Kuptsov Russian: patr. from the occupational term *kupets*, gen. *kuptsa*, merchant (from *kupit* to buy, a distant cogn. of CHAPMAN).
Cogns.: Ukr.: **Kupets**. Pol.: **Kupiec**, **Kupiecki**. Czech: **Kupec** (see also JACOB); **Kupča(k)**. Jewish (E Ashkenazic): **Kupetz**, **Kupets**, **Kubetz**, **Kupi(e)tz**, **Kupiec**.

Kurek Polish: nickname from Pol. *kurek*, dim. of *kur* cock.
Cogn.: Czech: **Kurka**.
Patrs.: Pol.: **Kurkiewicz**. Russ.: **Kuritsin** ('hen'). Jewish (E Ashkenazic): **Kuritsky**, **Kuritzky** (reasons for adoption as a surname not clear).
Habitation names: Pol.: **Kur(k)owski**; **Kurczewski** (from *kurcze* chicken).

Kurland Jewish (E Ashkenazic): regional name from Ger., Yid. *Kurland* Courland, which is now part of Latvia. The name of the region comes from the name of the *Kurs*, a Baltic people who, together with the Letts, inhabited this area, + OHG *land* land, territory.
Vars.: **Korland**, **Curland**; **Kurlander**, **Kurlender**, **Korlander** (with *-er* denoting a native or inhabitant); **Kurlandski**, **Kurlansky**, **Korlansky** (adjectival forms); **Kurliandschick**, **Kurliandcik** (dims.).

Kürner German: occupational name for a worker with a hand mill, an agent deriv. of MHG *kürn(e)* hand mill (OHG *quirn*, a cogn. of OE *cweorn* quern). The word and the object were gradually replaced from the 13th cent. by the more efficient apparatus operated by wind, water, or animals, which was named with the loan word *Mühle* (from L *molīna*; see MILL). For a while the vocab. word *Kürn* denoted a granary, before it disappeared completely: some examples of the surname may therefore be equivalents of GRANGER. It may also be a habitation name from *Kürn* in Bavaria or from some other minor place named with this word.
Var.: **Kirner**.

Kürschner German: occupational name for a furrier, Ger. *Kürschner* (MHG *kürsenære*, from *kürsen* fur garment, OHG *kursinna*, a borrowing from a Slav. language).
Vars.: **Kürssner**, **Ki(e)rschner**, **Körschner**.
Cogns.: Pol.: **Kuśnierz**. Ukr.: **Kushnir**. Jewish (Ashkenazic): **Kurshner** (from Ger., an Anglicized form); **Kus(c)hner**, **Kushnir** (from Pol. and Ukr.); **Kirs(c)hner**, **Kirsner**, **Kers(c)hner**, **Kersner** (from Yid. *kirzner* furrier or hatter; for the dial. variations, cf. KIRSCH).

Küster German: occupational name for a sexton or churchwarden, Ger. *Küster* (MHG *kuster*, OHG *kustor*, from LL *custor* guard, warden, from class. L *custos*). The umlaut of the modern form is due to association with other agent nouns in *-er* from OHG *-ari* (L *-ārius*).
Vars.: **Küstermann**, **Kustermann**. U.S.: **Custer**.
Cogns.: Low Ger.: **Köster**, **Kostermann**. Flem., Du.: **Kuster**, **Koster**, COSTER. Jewish: **Koster** (probably an occupational name for a synagogue beadle).
Patrs.: Ger.: **Küsters**. Low Ger.: **Kösters**, **Köstering**. Flem., Du.: **Kosters**, **Custers**.
The American general George Custer *(1839–76) was a descendant of a German officer from Hesse by the name of* Küster.

Kutuzov Russian: from a nickname in a Turkic language, *Qutuz* 'Rabid', 'Mad', which has been adapted to the normal pattern of Russ. surnames by the addition of the patr. suffix *-ov*.

Kuusi Finnish: ornamental name from Finn. *kuusi* fir tree, one of the many words for natural features that were used in the formation of Finn. surnames when these became obligatory during the 18th and 19th cents.
Var.: **Kuusinen**.

Kužel Czech: apparently from the vocab. word *kužel* head of a distaff. The application as a surname is unclear; it may have been a nickname for an effeminate man.

Var.: **Kužela**.

Dim.: **Kužilek**.

Kuzmin Russian: patr. from the given name *Kuzma* (Gk *Kosmas*, from *kosmos* order, arrangement, (ordered) universe). St Cosmas was martyred together with his brother Damian (see DAMYON) in Cilicia in the early 4th cent. AD, and came to be widely revered in the Eastern Church. The Russ. form of the given name has probably been altered by association with *kuznets* smith (see KUZNETSOV). The surname is also borne by Ashkenazic Jews, as an adoption of the Russian surname.

Vars.: **Kozmin, Kosmin**; **Kosminski** (a clerical name); **Kuzminsky** (Jewish).

Cogns. (patrs.): Ukr.: **Kuzmich**. Croatian: **Kuzmanović**.

Cogns. (not patrs.): Pol.: **Kuźmiński**. Hung.: **Kozma**. Fr.: **Cosme, Côme**. It.: **Cosma**; **Cos(i)mo, Cos(i)mi** (forms dating from the early 15th cent.); **Cosmano, Cosmani, Gusmani** (Venice; the last syllable is by association with *Damian*); **Cus(i)mano, Cusumano** (Sicily); **Coccimano**. Port.: **Cosmao**.

Dims. (patrs.): Russ.: **Kuz(k)in, Kuzyakin, Kuzemchikov, Kuzichkin, Kuzyutin, Kuzmishchev, Kuzishchin, Kuzminov, Kuzmichyov**.

Dims. (not patrs.): Ukr.: **Kuzik**. Beloruss.: **Kuzmyanko**. It.: **Cos(i)melli, Cos(i)mini, Cosmin, Gosmin, Gusmin** (all predominantly Venetian).

'Son of the wife of K.': Ukr.: **Kuzmishin**.

Kuznetsov Russian: patr. from the occupational term *kuznets* smith (from ORuss. *kuzn* forged work, from *kovat* to forge, ultimately a cogn. of OHG *houwan* to hew; cf. HAUER).

Cogns.: Jewish (E Ashkenazic): **Kuznitz, Kuznits, Kuznitzki, Kuznetzky, Kuznitsky, Kuznicki**. Pol.: **Kuzniak, Kuznicki**; KOWALSKI.

Dim.: Pol.: **Kuźnik**.

Kwapisz Polish: nickname for a busy person or one who was always in a hurry, from a deriv. of Pol. *kwapić* to rush, hasten, hurry.

Cogn.: Czech: **Kvapil**.

Patr.: Pol.: **Kwapisiewicz**.

Habitation name: Pol.: **Kwapiński**.

Kwaśniak Polish: nickname for a sour-faced individual, Pol. *kwaśniak*, from *kwaśny* sour, peevish, from *kwas* acid.

Habitation name: **Kwaśniewski**.

Kwiatek 1. Polish: from the given name *Kwiatek*, dim. of the vocab. word *kwiat* flower. This given name was generally regarded as a vernacular equivalent of *Florián* (L *Floriānus*; see FLORIANO), as was the Czech cogn. *Květoň*.

2. Polish: var. of KWIECIEŃ.

3. Jewish (E Ashkenazic): ornamental name from Pol. *kwiat* flower.

Vars.: Jewish: **Kwiat, Kviat**; **Kviatek**.

Cogns.: Czech: **Květ, Kv(i)ełon**.

Patr.: Russ.: **Tsvetkov(ski)** (apparently a surname adopted by Orthodox priests).

Kwiatkowski 1. Polish: habitation name from some place called *Kwiatków* (from Pol. KWIATEK + *-ów* possessive suffix) + *-ski* suffix of local surnames (see BARANOWSKI).

2. Jewish (E Ashkenazic): from the Pol. surname adopted as an ornamental name.

Vars. (of 1): **Kwiatosiński, Kwietniewski**. (Of 2): **Kviatkovsky**.

Kwiecień Polish and Jewish (E Ashkenazic): from the Pol. vocab. word *kwiecień* April, adopted by someone who was baptized in that month or, in the case of Jewish bearers, officially took the surname in that month. The cogn. Czech word, *květen*, means 'May'.

Var.: **Kwieciński**.

Kyffin Welsh: habitation name from any of various places named with W *cyffin* boundary, such as the hamlet of *Cyffin* in Powys and the parish of *Gyffin* in Gwynedd.

Vars.: **Caffyn**, COFFIN.

Kyle Scots and N Irish: 1. regional name from a district in the former county of Ayrs. in SW Scotland. This is so called from the name of the Brit. chieftains who ruled it in the 5th cent., the *Coel Hen*.

2. habitation name from any of the numerous Scot. places that are so called from Gael. *caol* narrows, strait.

L

Laakso Finnish: ornamental name from Finn. *laakso* valley, perhaps sometimes chosen as a topographic name by someone who lived in a valley.

Var.: **Laaksonen**.

Labitte French: topographic name, with fused def. art. *la*, for someone who lived by a boulder or roughly carved stone, probably some kind of memorial, OF *bite*. It may also be a habitation name from a minor place so named, and perhaps also an occupational name for a quarryman or a nickname for a lumpish individual.

Laborier French: occupational name for a worker of any sort, OF *laborier* (from *laborer* to work, toil, L *labōrāre*, from *labor* effort), but especially used of someone who worked the land, a farmer.

Var.: **Laborieux**.

Cogns.: Prov.: **Lauraire**. Cat.: **Llauradó**. Sp.: **Labrador**. Port.: **Lavrador**. It.: **Lavoratore**.

Lacey English and Irish (Norman): habitation name from *Lassy* in Calvados, so called from a Gaul. personal name *Lascius* (of uncertain meaning) + the local suffix *-ācum*. The surname is widespread, but is most common in Notts.

Vars.: **Lacy**, **Lassey**, **De Lac(e)y**; **Leacy** (Ireland, rare).

Two members of this family came to England with William the Conqueror. One of them, Ilbert de Lacy, *was the ancestor of John, 1st Earl of Lincoln, who in 1215 was involved in compelling King John to sign Magna Charta. The 3rd Earl, Henry (?1249–1311), was a close counsellor of Edward I and Edward II. His house in London gave its name to Lincoln's Inn, the law school, which now stands on the site.*

Another branch is descended from Ilbert's brother William, 1st Baron Lacy, reputed to have fought with the Norman forces at Hastings. His most renowned descendant was Hugh (d. 1186), 1st Lord of Meath, who in 1172 received the submission of Roderic, King of Connaught, on behalf of Henry II. From him many notable Irish soldiers claimed descent, among them Peter, Count Lacy (1678–1751), who was born at Limerick, where the name is still found. He fought for the Jacobite cause and in the service of France and Poland, eventually becoming military adviser to Peter the Great of Russia. His son Maurice Francis Lacy (1725–1801) was a field marshal in the Austrian army. Lacys were also active at this time in the service of Spain, including Don Luis Lacy, who fought in the Peninsular War.

Lach 1. Polish: name meaning 'Pole', from the Slav. word *Lach* Pole. According to legend, the northern Slav. nations were founded by three brothers called Rus, Lach, and Czech.

2. Polish: topographic name for a dalesman, from OPol. *lach* dalesman, originally the same word as in 1.

3. Czech and German (of Slav. origin): from a given name, a short form of the name *Ladislav*, *Vlasdislav*, composed of the elements *(v)ladi-* government + *slav* glory.

Vars. (of 2): Czech: **Lacha**, **Lachout**, **Laš**.

Dim. (of 2): Czech: **Laček**.

Patr. (from 1): Pol.: **Lachowicz**.

Habitation name (from 1): Pol.: **Lachowski**.

Lachlan Irish: from the Gael. personal name *Lochlann* 'Stranger', originally a byname applied to Viking settlers (from the name used for Scandinavia, a cpd of *loch* lake, fjord + *lann* land). Many Ir. bearers of the name claim descent from Lochlann, a 10th-cent. lord of Corcomroe, Co. Clare.

Vars.: **Lo(u)ghlan**, **Lo(u)ghlin**, **Lo(u)ghlen**, **La(u)ghlan**, **Laughlin**, **Laughland**, **Lafflin(g)**; LOFTUS (Connaught).

Patrs.: **Lackli(n)son**; MCLACHLAN.

'Descendant of L.': **O'Lo(u)ghlan**, **O'Lo(u)ghlin**, **O'Lo(u)ghlen**, **O'La(u)ghlan** (Gael. **Ó Lochlainn**).

Lachmann 1. German: topographic name for someone who lived by the boundary of a parish or other administrative unit, from MHG *lāche* boundary stone (OHG *lāh*, of uncertain origin).

2. German: topographic name for someone who lived near a pond or lake, MHG *lache* (OHG *lahha*, mod. Ger. *Lache* puddle; cogn. with OE *laca*, a byform of *lacu*; cf. LAKE).

3. S German: topographic name for someone who lived in or near a small wood or grove, from the Bavarian dial. term *la(i)ch* copse; cf. LEICHER 2.

4. German: occupational name for a physician; see LEACH 1.

5. German (of Slav. origin): cogn. of LACH 1 or 2.

6. Jewish (Ashkenazic): of uncertain origin. It has been suggested that the name was chosen as a translation of the given name ISAAC, which means 'to laugh'; if so the first element here would be mod. Ger. *lachen* or Yid. *lakhn*. Another suggestion is that there may be some connection with E Yid. *lakhman* rag (from Pol. *łachman*). Kaganoff mentions a suggestion that *Lachman* was the way non-Jews in Silesia pronounced the Hebr. given name *Nachman* 'Consolation'. This is questionable, not least because the Yid. form of *Nachman*, the form which people in Silesia would have actually been exposed to, is *Nachmen*, but the spelling var. ***Lachmen**, which one would predict if this hypothesis is correct, does not occur. In fact, none of these explanations is really satisfactory, and the origin may be as in 4 above.

Var. (of 6): **Lachman**.

Patr. (from 6): **Lachmanovici** (Rumanian spelling).

Lacina Czech: nickname from the Czech vocab. word *lacino* cheaply, apparently bestowed on someone who drove a hard bargain.

Lackenby English: habitation name from a place in N Yorks., of uncertain etymology. The second element is ON *býr* farm, settlement; the first may be the ON personal name *Lakkandi* 'the shouting one' or 'the slow-moving one'.

Ladbrooke English: habitation name, apparently from *Ladbro(o)ke* in Warwicks., although the surname is now more common in Norfolk than the Midlands. The second element is OE *brōc* BROOK. Early forms with *H-* suggest that the first element may be OE *hlot* lot, choice, decision, and Ekwall suggests that the meaning is therefore 'stream used for divining the future'.

Ladd English: occupational name for a servant, ME *ladde*. The word first appears in the 13th cent. and at first meant 'servant' or 'man of humble birth', the modern meaning of 'young man', 'boy' being a later shift. It is of uncertain origin, perhaps a Scandinavian borrowing, and possibly akin to the verb *lead*.

Patrs.: **Ladds**, **Ladson**.

Most American bearers of this name trace their ancestry to a certain Daniel Ladd, *who emigrated from London to Ipswich, Mass., in 1634.*

Ladefoged Danish: occupational name for an official who was responsible for collecting tithes of produce into the manorial stores, from Dan. *lade* barn (ON *hlaða*; cf. LATHAM) + *foged* overseer (ON *fógutr*, *fóguti*; cf. VOGT).

Ladler English and Scots: probably an occupational name for a maker of ladles, from an agent deriv. of ME *ladel*(*e*) (OE *hlædel*).

Vars.: **Laidler**; **Ladel(l)**.

Laffitte French: topographic name, with fused def. art. *la*, for someone who lived near a boundary marker driven firmly into the ground, OF *fitte* (LL *fixta* (*petra*) fixed stone, from the past part. of *figere* to fix, fasten; cf. FICHE).

Var.: **Laffite**.

Cogns.: Prov.: **Lahitte** (Gascony). Sp.: **Hita** (mostly, no doubt, from the name of a place in the province of Guadalajara).

Lage Portuguese: topographic name for someone who lived by a large flat rock or slab of stone, Port. *lage*, *laja* (of uncertain, possibly Celt., origin).

Var.: **Lages**.

Lager Swedish: ornamental name from Swed. *lager* laurel, bay; one of the many surnames derived from words denoting natural phenomena that were adopted and also used in forming compound surnames in Sweden in the 18th and 19th cents.

Vars.: **Lahger**, **Lagerman**.

Cpds: **Lagerbäch** ('laurel stream'); **Lagerberg** ('laurel hill'); **Lagerborg** ('laurel town'); **Lagercrantz**, **Lagerkran(t)z** ('laurel wreath'); **Lagerdahl** ('laurel valley'); **Lagerfel(d)t** ('laurel field'); **Lagerfors** ('laurel waterfall'); **Lagergre(e)(h)n** ('laurel branch'); **Lagerholm** ('laurel island'); **Lagerlöf** ('laurel leaf'); **Lagerlund** ('laurel grove'); **Lagerquist** ('laurel twig'); **Lagerstedt** ('laurel homestead'); **Lagerstrandt** ('laurel shore'); **Lagerström** ('laurel river'); **Lagerwall**, **Lagervall** ('laurel bank').

Laguna Spanish: topographic name for someone who lived by a pool or pond, Sp. *laguna* (L *lacūna* hollow, hole).

Var.: **Lagunas**.

Lahtinen Finnish: ornamental name from Finn. *lahti* bay, gulf, cove + the gen. suffix *-nen*.

Var.: **Lahti**.

Laidlaw Scots: of uncertain origin. According to Black, there is a family tradition that the name comes from LUDLOW in Shrops., England.

Vars.: **Laidler**, **Laidley**. See also LADLER.

This is a Border surname that has always been largely confined to the former county of Selkirk and the vales of Ettrick and Yarrow. The name is recorded in the Scottish borders as early as 1296, when William of Lodelawe *was accused of concealing a horse from the English.*

Laine Finnish: ornamental name from Finn. *laine* wave. This is one of the most common names among those that were derived from words denoting natural features when hereditary surnames were adopted in Finland in the 18th and 19th cents.

Laird Scots and N Irish: probably a status name for a landlord, from Northern ME *laverd*, N dial. var. of *lover*(*e*)*d* LORD.

The first known bearer of the name is Roger Lawird *or* Lauird *of Berwick, who in 1257 made an agreement with the Abbey of Kelso concerning some of his land.*

Laithwaite English: habitation name from either of two minor places, one in the parish of Amounderness, Lancs., the other near Prescot in Merseyside (formerly Lancs.). The former gets its name from ON *hlaða* barn (see LATHAM) + *þveit* meadow, piece of land (see THWAITE); in the case of the latter the first element is probably the ON personal name *Leikr*, a short form of the various cpd names containing the element *leikr* sport, play (cf. LAKER 2).

Laitinen Finnish: patr. from the given name *Laiti*, of Gmc origin but uncertain meaning.

Lake English (chiefly W Country): topographic name for someone who lived by a stream, OE *lacu*, or habitation name from a place named with this word, for example in Wilts. and Devon. The mod. Eng. vocab. word *lake* is only distantly related, if at all; it comes via OF from L *lacus*. This meaning, which ousted the native sense, came too late to be found as a placename element, but may lie behind some examples of the surname.

Vars.: **Lack**; **Lakes**; LAKER; **Lakeman**.

Cogns. (meaning 'lake'): Fr.: **Lac**; **Dulac** (with fused prep. and def. art.). Prov.: **Dellac**. Sp.: **Lago**. Ger.: **Lach(n)er** (see also LEICHER), LACHMANN. Low Ger.: **La(a)ck(mann)**, **Lackemann**. Flem., Du.: **Verlaeken**.

Dim.: Fr.: **Lacquet**.

Laker English: 1. topographic name, a var. of LAKE.

2. occupational name from Northern ME *leyker* actor, player (an agent deriv. of *leyk*(*en*) to sport, play, ON *leikja*).

Cogn. (of 2): Ger.: LEICHER.

Lakin 1. Jewish (E Ashkenazic): metr. from *Leyke*, a pet form of the Yid. female given name *Leye* (from the Hebr. female given name *Lea*, literally 'Gazelle' (or 'Weak', from which Eng. *Leah* is derived; see Gen. 29: 16) + the Slav. metr. suffix *-in*.

2. English: from a medieval given name, a dim. of LAWRENCE; cf. LAW 1 and LARKIN.

Vars. (of 1): **Laikin**, **Leikin**; **Leyeles** (Ashkenazic, based on *Leyele*, a different pet form of *Leye*).

Patr. (from 2): **Lakins**.

Lam Danish: 1. cogn. of LAMB (from ON *lamb*).

2. nickname for a lame man (from ON *lami*).

Lama Spanish: topographic name for someone who lived on a patch of marshland, Sp. *lama* (LL *lāma*).

Vars.: **Lamas**; **Llama(s)** (Asturias).

Cogns.: Port.: **Lam(eir)as**.

Lamb 1. English: nickname for a meek and inoffensive person or metonymic occupational name for a keeper of lambs, from ME, OE *lamb*. It may also have been a habitation name for someone who lived at a house distinguished by the sign of the paschal lamb, though surnames derived from house signs are less common in England than in Germany and central Europe.

2. English: short form of the given name LAMBERT.

3. Irish: Anglicized form of Gael. *Ó Luain*; see LANE 3.

Var.: **Lambe**.

Cogns. (of 1): Ger.: **Lamm**. Jewish (Ashkenazic, ornamental): **Lamm**. Dan.: LAM.

Dims. (of 1 and 2): Eng.: **Lambie**, **Lamby**, **Lammie**, **Lammey**; **Lam(b)kin**, **Lampkin**; **Lampin**, **Lampen**, **Lammin(g)**. (Of 1 only): Ger.: **Lämmel**, **Lemmel**, **Lammel**, **Lämmle**. Jewish (Ashkenazic): **Lemel** (from the Yid. male given name *Leml*, which is conventionally associated with the Yid. male given name *Osher*, see ASHER).

Patrs. (from 1 and 2): Eng.: **Lam(b)son, Lampson**. Flem., Du.: **Lammens**.

Patrs. (from 1 and 2) (dims.): Low Ger.: **Lammeling**. Flem., Du.: **Lammekins**. Jewish: **Lemelson**.

Lambert 1. English, French, and German: from a Gmc personal name composed of the elements *land* land, territory + *berht* bright, famous. A native OE name *Landbeorht* is attested, and seems to have survived the Norman Conquest, when it was massively reinforced by the Continental form imported by the Normans from France. The name gained yet wider currency in the Middle Ages with the immigration of weavers from Flanders, where St Lambert, bishop of Maastricht *c.*700, was a popular figure. In Italy the name was popular in the Middle Ages as a result of the fame of Lambert I and II, Dukes of Spoleto and Holy Roman Emperors.

2. English: occupational name for a shepherd, from OE *lamb* (see LAMB 1) + *hierd* (see HEARD).

Vars. (of 1): Eng.: **Lambart(h), Lambard, Lampert, Lamperd, Lampard, Lampart, Lammert, Lambrick**. Ger.: **Lamprecht, Lambrecht, Lambrich(t), Lammerich, Limprecht, Limprich(t)**.

Cogns. (of 1): Low Ger.: **Lampert, Lammert, Lempert, Limpert**. Flem., Du.: **Lambrecht, Lampaert**. It.: **Lamberti, Lamberto; Lamperti** (Lombardy).

Dims. (of 1): Eng.: LAMB. Ger.: **Lamp(e)l, Lämpl, Lemp(e)l, Lemppl**. Low Ger.: **Lamp(e), Lam(p)ke, Lamcke, Lempke, Lem(b)cke, Lembke, Lemm(e)**. Fr.: **Lamb(l)in, Lambinet, Lamb(l)ot, Lambotin**. It.: **Lambertini** (Emilia); **Lamba** (Naples).

Aug. (of 1): It.: **Lambertoni**.

Pej. (of 1): It.: **Lambertazzi**.

Patrs. (from 1): Eng.: **Lamberts(on)**. Ger.: **Lambrechts**. Low Ger.: **Lamberts, Lam(m)ers, Lemmers; Lambertsen; Lambertz, Lammertz, Lempertz, Lemmertz, Limpertz** (N Rhineland); **Lammer(d)ing** (Westphalia). Fris.: **Lammenga**. Flem., Du.: **Lambregts, Lammer(t)s, Lammertse**. It.: **Lambertenghi, Lamberteschi**.

Patrs. (from 1)(dims.): Low Ger.: **Lamps, Lamping; Lamcken, Lemmen**. Flem., Du.: **Lampens, Lemmen(s)**.

Lambart *is the family name of the Earls of Cavan. They were established in Ireland by Oliver Lambart (d. 1618), who accompanied the Earl of Essex and became governor of Connaught. Their earliest ancestors include John* Lambert *of Preston, named in 15th-cent. documents.*

Lambourne English: habitation name from *Lambourne* in Essex or *Lambourn* in Berks., both of which are probably so called from OE *lamb* LAMB + *burna* stream (see BOURNE), i.e. a place where lambs were washed. It is possible, but less likely, that the first element was OE *lām* loam, referring to rich clay soil in the area.

Vars.: **Lambourn, Lamborn(e), Lamburn(e)**.

Lambton English: habitation name from a place in Co. Durham, so called from OE *lamb* LAMB + *tūn* enclosure, settlement.

The Lambton *family take their name from the town in Co. Durham, where they can be traced from the 12th cent. Robert* de Lambton *(d. 1350) was feudal lord of Lambton Castle, which has remained the family seat into the 20th cent. John Lambton (1792–1840) was created Earl of Durham in 1833; he was known as 'radical Jack' for his advocacy of parliamentary reform, and became governor-general of Canada.*

Lamerton English: habitation name from a place in Devon, which derives its name from *Lumburn* Water on which it stands (see LAMBOURNE) + OE *tūn* enclosure, settlement.

Lamont Scots and N Irish: from the medieval given name *Lagman*, which is from ON *Logmaðr*, composed of the elements *log* law (from the verb *legja* to lay down) + *maðr*, gen. *manns*, man.

Vars.: **Lam(m)ond; Lawman**, LEMON.

Patrs.: **McLamon(t), McClemment, McClements, McClymond, McClymont** (Gael. **Mac Laomuinn**).

Lampet English: topographic name for someone who lived near a clay pit or loam pit (ME *lampit*) or occupational name for someone who worked in one. The ME word is from OE *lām* loam, clay + *pytt* pit, hollow (see PITT). The excavation of clay was an important occupation in the Middle Ages as it was widely used in the wattle-and-daub construction of houses, in which wicker hurdles were packed and coated with clay.

Vars.: **Lampitt, Lamputt**.

Lancaster English: habitation name from the city in NW England, so called from the river *Lune*, on which it stands, + OE *cæster* Roman fort (L *castra* legionary camp). The river name is probably Brit., perhaps cogn. with Gael. *slán* healthy, salubrious.

Vars.: **Lankester, Langcaster, Lon(g)caster, Lan(g)castle**.

This is the surname of one of the major landowning families in Lancs. from the 13th cent. (at one point descending through the female line).

Lance English: from the Gmc personal name *Lanzo*, originally a short form of various cpd names with the first element *land* land, territory (cf., e.g., LAMBERT 1) but later used as an independent name. It was introduced into England by the Normans, among whom it was a popular name with the ruling classes, perhaps partly as a result of association with OF *lance* lance, spear (see LANCIA).

Cogns.: Ger.: **Lan(t)z**, LENZ. It.: **Landi, Lando; Lanzi, Lanzo; Lanni, Lanno** (S Italy).

Dims.: Ger.: **Lanzl, Lendl**. Low Ger.: **Lendeke, Lenk(e)**. It.: **Landini, Landino; Lanzini; Lannino; Landucci, Landuzzi**.

Augs.: It.: **Landoni, Landone; Lanzoni, Lanzone**.

Lancia Italian: metonymic occupational name for an armourer or for a soldier who wielded the lance, It. *lancia* (L *lancea*).

Var.: **Lanza**.

Cogn.: Port.: **Lança**.

Dims.: It.: **Lancini, Lanciotti; Lanzetta, Lanzola**.

Aug.: It.: **Lancioni**.

Land English: 1. topographic name from OE *land* land, territory. This had various more specialized senses in the Middle Ages, and was used of the countryside as opposed to a town (as in the ME lyric *My lief is faren in londe*) and of an estate.

2. topographic name for someone who lived in a forest glade, from ME, OF *la(u)nde* (of apparently Gaul. origin; cf. Bret. *lann* heath), or habitation name from *Launde* in Leics., which is named with this word.

Var. (of 2): **Lawn**.

Cogns. (of 1): Ger.: **Land(t)**, LANDER, LANDMANN. Flem., Du.: **Van den Land**. Swed. (ornamental): **Land(h), Landell, Landelius, Landén, Landin**.

Cpds (of 1; ornamental): Swed.: **Landberg** ('land hill'); **Land(e)gren** ('land branch'); **Landquist** ('land twig'); **Landström** ('land river'). + Landford

Landa 1. Czech: from an aphetic form of the given name *Mikulanda*, a var. of *Mikuláš* (see NICHOLAS).

2. Jewish (Ashkenazic): presumably a representation of the Yid. placename *Lande* (see LANDER 2).

3. Basque: topographic name from the element *landa* field, plot of land. There is a place of this name in the province of Álava, and the surname may in fact be a habitation name from this place.

Var. (of 3): **Landeta** (with the addition of a suffix of abundance).

Lander 1. German: cogn. of LAND 1, used originally to denote either someone who was a native of the area in which he lived (in contrast to *Neumann*; see NEW) or someone who lived in the countryside as opposed to a town.

2. Jewish (Ashkenazic): habitation name derived from either of two places called *Landau* in German (from OHG *lant* land, territory + *auwa* damp valley), *Lande* in Yid. The one in the Palatinate was the home of many Jews in the Middle Ages, and when they were expelled in 1545 they moved mostly to Prague, where they adopted the name of the town from which they had come; the other was part of Alsace until the Vienna settlement of 1815 and has given rise to the high frequency of the name in France.

3. English: var. of LAVENDER.

Vars. (of 1): LANDMANN. (Of 2): **Lande**, LANDA, **Landau(er)**; **Landoj** (Pol. spelling); **Landow(ski)**.

Landmann 1. German: var. of LANDER 1.

2. Jewish (Ashkenazic): of uncertain origin, perhaps chosen for its phonetic similarity to Hebr. *lamdan* Talmudic scholar.

Vars. (of 1): Ger.: **Land(e)smann**. (Of 2): **Land(e)sman**, **Lansman**.

Cogn. (of 1): Flem., Du.: **Landman**.

Landseer English: topographic name for someone who lived near a border of some kind, ME *landschare*, from OE *land* land, territory + *scearu* boundary.

Lane 1. English: local name for someone who lived in a lane, ME, OE *lane*, originally a narrow way between fences or hedges, later used of any narrow pathway, including one between houses in a town.

2. Irish: Anglicized form of Gael. **Ó Laighin** 'descendant of *Laighean*', a byname meaning 'Spear', 'Javelin'.

3. Irish: Anglicized form of Gael. **Ó Luain** 'descendant of *Luan*', a byname meaning 'Warrior'.

4. Irish: Anglicized form of Gael. *Ó Liatháin*; see LEHANE.

5. French: metonymic occupational name for a worker in wool, from OF *la(i)ne* wool (L *lana*).

6. S French: Gascon cogn. of LAND 2.

Vars. (of 1): **Layne, Lain; Lanes; Loan, Lones**. (Of 2): **O'-La(y)ne, O'Loyne, (O')Leyne**, LEAN, LYON. See also LYNE.

Cogns. (of 1): Du.: **Laan, Verlaan**.

A certain William Lane *emigrated from England to Dorchester, Mass., in c.1635. He was the ancestor of a prominent New England family.*

Langan Irish: Anglicized form of Gael. **Ó Longáin** 'descendant of *Longán*', a personal name probably derived from *long* tall, or possibly from the homonymous *long* ship (and so originally a byname for a seafarer).

Vars.: **Langin, Longan, O'Langan(e), O'Longan(e)**, LONG.

Langdon English: habitation name from any of various places, for example in Devon, Dorset, Essex, Kent, and Warwicks., so called from OE *lang*, *long* LONG + *dūn* hill (see DOWN 1).

Var.: **Longdon** (the name of places in Shrops., Staffs., and Worcs.).

Langenscheidt German: habitation name from any of various minor places in N Germany, so called from the weak dat. case (originally used after a preposition and art.) of MHG *lang* LONG + *scheide* boundary (see SCHEIDT).

Var.: **Langenscheid**.

Langford English: habitation name from any of the numerous places so called from OE *lang*, *long* LONG + *ford* FORD.

Vars.: **Longford, Langsford**.

Langham English: habitation name from any of various places so called. Most, as for example those in Dorset, Norfolk, Leics. (formerly Rutland), and Suffolk, get the name from OE *lang*, *long* LONG + *hām* homestead, but one in Essex is recorded in Domesday Book as *Laingaham*, from OE *Lāwingahām* 'homestead of the people of **Lāwa*', and one in Lincs. originally had as its second element ME *holm* island (see HOLME 2).

Vars.: **Lanham; Longham** (a place in Norfolk, with the same etymology as *Langham* in Essex).

Langlands Scots and N English: habitation name from a property in the former county of Peebles, so called from OE *lang*, *long* LONG + *land* land, territory.

The principal family of this name were long known also as WILTON, *from the barony of Wilton in Roxburghs., of which they held half. The direct line became extinct in 1814.*

Langley English: 1. habitation name from any of the numerous places named with OE *lang*, *long* LONG + *lēah* wood, clearing.

2. from the ON female personal name *Langlíf*, composed of the elements *lang* long + *líf* life.

Var.: **Longley** (found chiefly in Notts. and S Yorks.).

Langnese Low German: nickname for someone with a long nose, from MLG *lang* LONG + *nese* nose.

Langridge English: topographic name for someone who lived on or by a long ridge, or habitation name from any of the various places named with the OE elements *lang*, *long* LONG + *hrycg* ridge, for example in Somerset.

Var.: **Longridge** (places in Lancs. and Staffs.).

Langston English: habitation name from any of various places, for example *Langstone* in Devon and Hants, named with OE *lang*, *long* LONG, tall + *stān* stone, i.e. a menhir. The surname is now most common in the W Midlands.

Langton English: habitation name from any of numerous places so called from OE *lang*, *long* LONG + *tūn* enclosure, settlement. Langton in Co. Durham, however, has the same origin as LANGDON.

Vars.: **Longton** (places in Lancs. and Staffs.); **Longtown** (places in Cumb. and Herefords.).

A family of this name can be traced to the mid-12th cent. in Langton, Lincs. The manor there was held by the Earl of Chester according to Domesday Book, and Osbert de Langton *gave tithes of '2 oxgangs and 1 toft' to the dean and chapter of Lincoln in 1196. The earliest known ancestor of the present Lincs. family was Thomas de Langton (d. 1283).*

Langtree English: habitation name from places in Devon, Oxon., and Lancs., so called from OE *lang*, *long* LONG, tall + *trēow* tree.

Lanier French: 1. occupational name for a worker involved in any of the stages of producing woollen cloth or a seller of the finished material, from an agent deriv. of OF *la(i)ne* wool (L *lana*; cf. LANE 5).

2. occupational name, with fused def. art., for a pack-driver, from OF *asne* donkey (L *asinus*).

Var. (of 2): **Lasnier**.

Cogns. (of 1): Eng.: **Lainer**, LEINER.

A number of French Huguenot refugees of this name settled in Virginia in the 18th cent. Among them was Thomas Lanier, *whose descendants include two of New York's leading bankers.*

Lansdown English: habitation name from a place in Somerset, *Lantesdune* in early records, probably so called from OE **langet* (see LANT) + *dūn* hill (see DOWN 1).

Lánský Czech: topographic name for someone living near open land or a cleared area of land, from a deriv. of OCzech *lán* open land, cleared area. It may also be a habitation name from any of several places called *Lány*, named with this element.

Cogn.: Jewish (Ashkenazic): **Lansky**.

Lant English (Northumb.): of uncertain origin, perhaps a habitation name from some place named with OE **langet* long strip of ground, long ridge (a deriv. of *lang* LONG).

Lanyon Cornish: habitation name from a place in Madron parish near Penzance, which gets its name from Corn. *lyn* pool + *yeyn* cold.

John de Linyeine *is recorded in 1244 as the plaintiff in a foot of fine.*

Lapid Jewish (Ashkenazic): of uncertain origin, probably from Hebr. *lapid* torch, lightning. The surname may have been adopted as an allusion to any of the numerous Hebr. given names referring to light, such as *Uri* and *Meir*.

Lapidus Jewish (Ashkenazic): of uncertain origin, possibly from the Hebr. given name *Lapidoth*, borne in the Bible by the husband of Deborah (Judg. 4: 4).

Vars.: **Lapiduss, Lapidos, Lapides; Lapidot(h)** (Israeli).

Łapiński Polish: of uncertain origin, perhaps a habitation name from some place named with Pol. *łapa* paw, or possibly a nickname from this word, denoting a clumsy person or one with ugly or deformed hands or feet.

Cogns.: Jewish (Ashkenazic): **Lapin(er), Lapinski, Lapinsky**.

Patr.: Russ.: **Lapin**.

Patr. (from a dim.): Russ. and Jewish (Ashkenazic): **Lapkin**.

Lappalainen Finnish: ethnic name for a Laplander, from Finn. *Lappala* Lapland + the locative suffix *-ainen*. The meaning of the tribal name *Lapp* is unknown; although the Laplanders now speak a language related to Finnish, it is likely that this was adopted at a comparatively late (although still prehistoric) date. They seem to have come originally from central Asia and to have been pushed into their extreme northerly situation by the migrations of the Finns, Goths, and Slavs.

Lapworth English: habitation name from a place in Warwicks., so called from the OE personal name **Hlappa* + OE *worð* enclosure (see WORTH).

Lara Spanish: habitation name from a place in the province of Burgos.

Laranjeira Portuguese: topographic name for someone who lived by an orange grove, Port. *laranjeira* (a deriv. of *laranja* orange, from Arabic and ultimately from Persian; cf. NARANJO).

Larcher 1. German: from Ger. *Lärche* larch (MHG *larche, lerche*, from LL *larix*, possibly of Celt. origin) + *-er* suffix denoting a human agent or inhabitant. The application is not clear: it may be a topographic name for someone living among larches, an occupational name for a woodman in a larch wood, or a nickname for one tall as a larch. The surname is also borne by Ashkenazic Jews, the reason(s) for its adoption also being unclear.

2. French: var. of ARCHER, with fused definite article.

Var. (of 1): **Lercher**.

Larder English: metonymic occupational name for a servant in charge of a larder or storeroom for provisions, from ANF *larder* (LL *lardārium*, a deriv. of *lar(i)dum* bacon fat).

Vars.: **Lard(i)ner**.

Large English and French: nickname (literal or ironic) meaning 'generous', from ME, OF *large* generous, free (L *largus* abundant). The Eng. word came to acquire its mod. sense only gradually during the Middle Ages; it is used to mean 'ample in quantity' in the 13th cent., and the sense 'broad' first occurs in the 14th. This use is probably too late for the surname to have originated as a nickname for a fat man.

Vars.: Eng.: **Lardge, Largman**. Fr.: **Lelarge**.

Dims.: Eng.: **Largey**. Fr.: **Largeau(lt), Larget(eau), Largeot**.

Lark English: 1. nickname for a merry person or an early riser, from ME *lavero(c)k, lark* (OE *lāwerce*; cogn. with MHG *lerche*). It was perhaps also a metonymic occupational name for someone who netted the birds and sold them for the cooking pot.

2. from a medieval given name, a byform of LAWRENCE, derived by back-formation from LARKIN.

Vars.: **Larke** (chiefly Norfolk). (Of 1 only): **Laverack, Laverick** (Northumb. and Yorks.).

Cogns. (of 1): Ger. and Jewish (Ashkenazic): **Lerch**. Low Ger.: **Lewark**. Dan., Norw.: **Lerche**.

'Servant of L. 2': Eng.: **Larkman** (E Anglia).

Larkin 1. English: from a medieval given name, a dim. of LAWRENCE, formed with the addition of the ME suffix *-kin* (of Low Ger. origin).

2. Irish: Anglicized form of Gael. **Ó Lorcáin** 'descendant of *Lorcán*', a personal name from a dim. of *lorc* fierce, cruel.

Vars.: **Larking, Lorkin(g)**.

Larnach Scots: regional name (with the suffix *-ach*) for someone from *Lorne* (Gael. *Latharn*), an area in the former county of Argyll, named from an ancient Scottish king bearing the byname *Loarn* 'Fox'.

Var.: **Larnack**.

Larner English: 1. occupational name for a scholar or schoolmaster, from ME *lern(en)* which meant both 'to learn' and 'to teach' (OE *leornian*). For the change of *-ar-* to *-er-*, cf. MARCHANT.

2. in the case of a Suffolk family who bore this surname by the 16th cent., ancestors are recorded in the forms *Lawney* (1381) and *de Lauuenay* (1327); this is therefore probably a var. of DELANEY.

Var. (of 1): LERNER.

Larrazabal Basque: topographic name for someone who lived by a large expanse of meadowland, from *larre* pasture, meadow + *zabal* broad, wide.

Larrea Basque: topographic name for someone who lived by a patch of meadowland, from *larre* pasture, meadow + the def. art. *-a*. This is also the name of places in the provinces of Álava and Biscay, which may have contributed to the surname.

Var.: **Larrinaga** (with the addition of a local suffix).

Lasa Basque: topographic name for someone who lived by a stream, from *lats* stream + the def. art. *-a*.

Lascelles English (Norman): habitation name from *Lacelle* in Orne, so called from OF *la* the + *celle* hermit's cell (L *cella* small room; cf. SELLER 3).

Var.: **Lessells.**

A number of bearers of this name found in the 12th and 13th cents. in N England have a common ancestor in Picot de Lascelles, *a vassal of the count of Brittany, living* c.1080. *Roger de Lascelles held land in Yorks. and Lincs. in 1130. A later member of the family was Edward* Lascelles *(1740–1820), created Earl of Harewood in 1812.*

Łaski Polish: topographic name from Pol. *łas*, *łaz* clearing in a forest (ultimately cogn. with OE *lēah*).

Var.: **Łasek.**

Cogns.: Jewish (Ashkenazic): **Lasky, Laske.**

Laskowski Polish and Jewish (E Ashkenazic): habitation name from a place called *Lasków* (Ger. *Laskau*), of which there is one in Lithuania and another in Galicia. They derive their name from Pol. *lasek*, dim. of *las*, *les* wood.

Vars.: Jewish: **Laskow, Laskov(ski), Laska(u)** (W Ashkenazic); **Lask(i)er, Laskar.**

Laso Spanish: nickname for a feeble or indolent person, from OSp. *laso* tired, weak(ened) (L *lassus*).

Lasoń Polish: occupational name for a woodman, from Pol. *las*, *les* wood, forest + *-oń* suffix indicating association or relationship.

Vars.: **Lasota, Lasocki.**

Patr.: **Laśkiewicz.**

Lassalle 1. French: local name or occupational name for someone who lived or worked at a manor house, from OF *sal(e)* hall (mod. Fr. *salle*; see also SALE 1), with fused def. art. *la*.

2. Jewish: Gallicized spelling of *Lossal*, from *Loslau*, the Ger. name of the town of *Wodisław Śląski* in Silesia.

Var. (of 1): **Lasalle.**

Ferdinand Lassalle *(1825–64), one of the founders of socialism, was the son of a Jewish merchant whose surname was* **Lossal**.

Last 1. English (E Anglia): metonymic occupational name for a cobbler, or perhaps for a maker of cobblers' lasts, from ME *last*, *lest* the wooden form in the shape of a foot used for making or repairing shoes (OE *lǣste* from *lāst* footprint).

2. German: metonymic occupational name for a porter, from Ger. *Last* burden, load (MHG *last*).

3. Jewish (Ashkenazic): of unknown origin, possibly from Ger. *Last* burden, load, in which case the origin is presumably as in 2.

Var. (of 1): **Laster.**

Cogns. (of 1): Ger.: **Leist, Leistenmacher, Leistenschneider.** Flem.: **Leestman, Van de Leest.**

Lastra Spanish: topographic name for someone who lived by a flat stone slab, probably a boundary marker of some kind, Sp. *lastra* (of uncertain origin; cf. DELÂTRE). There are numerous places in Spain named with this word, and they may also have contributed to the surname.

Var.: **Lastras.**

Łaszczewski Polish: habitation name from a place called *Łaszczew*, which is said by Rospond to have been named in the 16th cent. from a byname *Łaszcz* 'Robber', from Pol. *łaszczyć się* to covet (dial. to rob).

Latchford English: habitation name from any of various places, for example in Ches. and Oxon., so called from OE *lǣcc* stream (cf. LEACH 2) + *ford* FORD.

Vars.: **Lashford, Letchford.**

Lateiner Jewish (Ashkenazic): nickname for a learned man who owned books in Latin (Ger. *Lateiner* Latinist; cf. LATIMER).

In at least one case this surname was acquired by a family who for generations had had the role of village barber in Grzymalów in E Galicia, and whose original family name was FELDSCHER.

Latek Polish: apparently a nickname from Pol. *lato* summer + the dim. suffix *-ek*, perhaps denoting someone of a sunny disposition, or acquired for some anecdotal reason now lost. Cf. SUMMER.

Habitation name: **Latkowski.**

Latham English: habitation name from any of the various places in N England named with the dat. pl. form (used originally after a preposition) of ON *hlaða* barn, as for example *Latham* in W Yorks., *Lathom* in Lancs., and *Laytham* in E Yorks.

Vars.: **Laytham, Lathom, Lathem; Le(a)tham** (Scotland); **Leathem** (N Ireland); **Leed(h)am, Leedom.**

Latimer English: occupational name for a clerk or keeper of records in Latin, ANF *latinier*, *latim(m)ier*. Latin was the more or less universal language of official documents in the Middle Ages, displaced only gradually by the vernacular—ANF at first in England, and eventually English.

Vars.: **Lattimer, Latimore, Lat(t)ner, Laturner.**

Cogns.: Fr.: **Latinier, Latimier.** Jewish (Ashkenazic): LATEINER.

The name Latimer *is found in Yorks. from the 13th cent. Early bearers include William* le Latimer *(d. 1268) of Scampston, and his descendant Thomas* de Latimer *(b. ?1270), who was made a baron in 1299. Another family of this name is recorded in Billinges, Yorks., from the 12th cent. onwards.*

The manor of the town in Bucks. now known as Latimer *was acquired by a certain William Latimer in 1330. The place took its name from his family name; previously it had been known as* Isenhampstede.

Latter 1. English: occupational name for a worker in wood or nickname for a thin person, from an agent deriv. of ME *latt* thin narrow strip of wood (OE *lætt*).

2. Jewish: of uncertain origin.

Presumed vars. (of 2): **Latterman, Lattner.**

Latto Scots: according to Black, this is a habitation name from *Laithis* in the former county of Ayr, a minor place of uncertain etymology, which is apparently now lost.

Vars.: **Latta, Lattey, Lawtie,** LAWTY.

Lauder Scots and Northumb.: habitation name from *Lauder* in the former county of Berwicks., recorded in 1250 in the form *Lawedir*, in 1298 as *Loweder*, and in 1334 as *Lawadir*; the placename is apparently Brit., perhaps from a cogn. of Bret. *laour* trench, ditch.

Vars.: **Lawder, Lawt(h)er.**

Lauer 1. German: unflattering nickname from MHG *lūre* crafty or cunning person, cheat (apparently originally 'one with narrowed eyes'; the word is akin to mod. Ger. *Lauer* ambush and mod. Eng. *lower*).

2. German: occupational name for a tanner, MHG *lōwære*, from *lō* (gen. *lōwes*) tannin, which is extracted from the bark of trees (cf. BARKER 1).

3. German: habitation name from *Lauer* in Franconia, named from the stream on which it stands, in turn perhaps originally named with a Celt. word meaning 'turbulent'.

4. Jewish (Ashkenazic): of uncertain origin. Any or all of the explanations of the Ger. name are possible.

Var.: LAUR.

Läufer German: occupational name for a messenger, Ger. *Läufer* runner, an agent deriv. of *laufen* to run (MHG *loufen*, OHG *(h)louf(f)an*).

Cogns.: Jewish (Ashkenazic): **Laufer** (nickname meaning 'runner', or adoption of the Ger. surname). Low Ger.: **Löper**.

Laughton English: habitation name from any of the numerous places in England so called. Most of them, as for example those in Leics., Lincs. (near Gainsborough), Sussex, and W Yorks., are named with OE *lēac* leek + *tūn* enclosure. The cpd was also used in the extended sense of a herb garden and later of a kitchen garden. Laughton near Folkingham in Lincs., however, was probably named as *loc-tūn* enclosed farm (see LOCK 2).

Laukkanen Finnish: patr. from a nickname for a brisk and active person, from Finn. *laukka* to gallop, canter.

Laur 1. French: topographic name for someone who lived by a conspicuous laurel tree, OF *laur* (L *laurus*).

2. French: from a given name of the same etymology, borne by various minor early saints, including a hermit, a martyr, and an abbot.

3. German: var. of LAUER.

Vars. (of 1 and 2): **Laure**. (Of 1 only): **Laurier**.

Cogns. (of 1 and 2): It.: **Lauro, Lauri**. (Of 1 only): Port.: **Loureiro**.

Dims. (of 1 and 2): Fr.: **Laurel, Laureau, Laurot, Laur(a)in, Lorin**. It.: **Lauriello, Laurini, Laurino**.

Aug. (of 1 and 2): Fr.: **Lauras**.

Collective (of 1): Cat.: **Lloret**.

Patrs. (from 2): It.: **Di Lauro**. Russ.: **Lavrov**.

Lautrec French: habitation name from places in Tarn and Haute-Vienne, probably so called from the OProv. def. art. *le* + *autreg* privilege, concession (from *autrejar* to grant, concede, LL *auctōrizāre*), i.e. a community that enjoyed certain special rights.

Lavelle Irish: Anglicized form of Gael. **Ó Maoil Fhábhail** 'descendant of the devotee of (St) *Fábhal*', a personal name meaning 'Movement', 'Travel'.

Vars.: **Lavell**; **Mulfaul**.

Lavender English: occupational name for a washerman or launderer, ANF *lavend(i)er* (LL *lavandārius*, an agent deriv. of *lavanda* washing, things to be washed, from the gerundive of *lavāre* to wash). The term was applied especially to a worker in the wool industry who washed the raw wool or rinsed the cloth after fulling. There is no evidence for any direct connection with the word for the plant (ME, OF *lavendre*, LL *lavendula*), although the etymology of this word is obscure and it may have been named from the same root, in reference to the use of lavender oil in making soap or of dried heads of lavender in perfuming freshly washed clothes.

Vars.: **Launder**, LANDER.

Cogns.: Fr.: **Lavandier**. Ger.: **Lavator** (a Latinized form).

Laver 1. English: occupational name for a washerman, ANF *laver* (an agent deriv. of OF *laver* to wash, L *lavāre*; cf. LAVENDER).

2. S French: nickname for a rich man, from OProv. *aver* possessions, property (from the verb *aver* to have, possess, L *habēre*), with fused def. art. *le*. In SE France the word is used of a flock of sheep (the principal form of property in the area) and the surname may have been originally an occupational name for a shepherd.

Patrs. (from 1): Eng.: **Lavers** (chiefly Devon and Cornwall), **Lavis(s)** (chiefly W Country).

Laverty Irish (chiefly N Ireland): Anglicized form of Gael. **Ó Fhlaithbheartaigh** and **Mac Fhlaithbheartaigh** 'descendant' and 'son of *Flaithbheartach*', a personal name composed of the elements *flaith* prince, ruler + *beartach* doer of valiant deeds.

Vars.: **Lafferty**; **McLaverty**.

Lavery Irish (chiefly N Ireland): anglicized form of Gael. **Ó Labhradha** 'descendant of *Labraidh*', a byname meaning 'Spokesman'.

Var.: LOWRY.

Three branches of the sept are sometimes distinguished as **Baun-Lavery** *(from* bán *white),* **Roe-Lavery** *(from* rua *red) and* **Trin-Lavery** *(from* tréan *strong; see also* ARMSTRONG*).*

Lavin Irish: Anglicized form of Gael. **Ó Laimhín**, a reduced form of *Ó Flaithimhín* 'descendant of *Flaithimhín*', a personal name from a dim. of *flaith* prince, ruler.

Vars.: **Laffin, Laffan**; HAND (an erroneous translation, based on the assumption that the Gael. form is **Ó Láimhín*, from a dim. of *lámh* hand, arm).

Lavoisier French: unflattering nickname for a sly or cunning person, from OF *avoisié* crafty, with fused def. art. and respelling of the ending to coincide with the agent suffix. The word itself is a blend in OF of *voizié* evil, cunning (LL *vitiātus* and *avisé* clever, learned (LL *advisātus*).

Var.: **Levéziel** (Normandy).

Law English and Scots: 1. from a ME pet form of LAWRENCE.

2. topographic name for someone who lived near a hill, Northern ME *law* (from OE *hlāw* hill, burial mound).

Patrs. (from 1): **Law(e)s** (found chiefly in S England), **Lawson**.

Richard Law *emigrated from England to America in 1638, and in 1641 was one of the founders of Stamford, Conn.*

Lawford English: habitation name from a place so called, of which examples are to be found in Essex and Warwicks. These derive their name from the OE personal name **Lealla* (cogn. with the attested OHG *Lallo*, but of unkown meaning) + OE *ford* FORD.

Lawless English: nickname for an unbridled and licentious man, from ME *laghless*, *lawelas* (a cpd of late OE *lagu* law (from ON) + the native suffix *-l(ē)as* without, lacking). Reaney suggests additionally that this name may have referred to an outlaw (i.e. one from whom the protection of the law had been withdrawn), but this seems unlikely.

Lawley English (chiefly W Midlands): habitation name from a place in Shrops., so called from the OE personal name *Lāfa* (from *lāf* remnant, survivor) + OE *lēah* wood, clearing.

Lawlor Irish: Anglicized form of Gael. **Ó Leathlobhair** 'descendant of *Leathlobar*', a personal name composed of the elements *leath* half (i.e. 'somewhat', 'fairly') and *lobar* leprous, sick. The name seems to have been originally a byname for a man of unhealthy constitution.

Vars.: **(O')Lawler, (O')Lalo(u)r**.

Ławnicki Polish: occupational name for an assessor, Pol. *ławnik* (from *ława* bench), with the addition of the surname suffix *-ski* (see BARANOWSKI).

Var.: **Ławniczak**.

Lawrence English: from the ME and OF given name *Lorens*, *Laurence* (L *Laurentius* 'man from *Laurentum*', a town in Italy probably named from its laurels or bay trees). The name was borne by a saint who was martyred at Rome in the 3rd cent. AD; he enjoyed a considerable cult throughout Europe, with consequent popularity of the given name (Fr. *Laurent*, It., Sp. *Lorenzo*, Port. *Lourenço*, Ger. *Laurenz*; Czech *Vavřinec*, Pol. *Wawrzyniec* (assimilated to the Pol. vocab. word *wawrzyn* laurel)). The surname is also borne by Jews, among whom it is presumably an Anglicization of one or more like-sounding Ashkenazic surnames.

Vars.: **Lawrance, Laurence, Laurance, Laurens, Lorence, Lowrance.**

Cogns.: Fr.: **Laurent, Laurant, Laurand, Lorent, Lorant, Lorand, Laurens, Lorens, Lorans, Lorence.** It.: **Laurenti, Laurenzi, Lorenzi; Renzi, Renzo, Rensi; Nenci.** Sp.: **L(l)orente, Lorenzo.** Cat.: **Llorente, Llorens, Lorenz.** Port.: **Lourenço.** Ger.: **Laurent, Laurenz, Loren(t)z, Laveren(t)z, Leveren(t)z, Lewerenz, Lab(e)renz, Lafren(t)z, Lawrenz; Ren(t)z** (Bavaria; see also REYNARD). Low Ger.: LENZ, **Len(t)sch, Frentz, Lörtz, Lortz.** Flem.: **Lauren(s); Rens.** Du.: **Lourens.** Dan.: **La(h)rs, Las.** Ger. (of Slav. origin): **Lauri(s)ch; Wawer, Wabersich, Wabersinke.** Czech: **Vávra, Vavřín, Vavruš; Lorenc** (under Ger. influence). Pol.: **Wawrzyniec, Wawrzyński, Wawrzecki; Lorenc** (under Ger. influence). Hung.: **Lörinc(z), Lörincze.** Jewish (Ashkenazic): **Lorens, Lorenz, Lorinez, Wawer** (all adoptions of non-Jewish surnames).

Dims.: Eng.: **Lawrie, Laurie; Lawr(e)y** (Devon); LOWRY (N England and Scotland); LAW, LOW, LARKIN, LARK, LAKIN, **Larrie, Larrett.** Fr.: **Laurentin, Laurenty, Laurendin, Laurencin, Laurendeau, Laurenceau, Lorenceau, Laurencet, Laurençot, Lorensot, Laurençon, Laurenson.** It.: **Lorenzetti, Lorenzetto, Lorenzin(i), Lorenzut(ti); Laurito; Renzetti, Renzini; Renzulli, Renzullo; Nencetti, Nencini, Nenciol(in)i.** Sp.: **Laurentino.** Ger. (of Slav. origin): **Lorek, Loricke, Löhrke, Lorck.** Pol.: **Wawrzeńczyk, Wawrzonek, Wawrzyk; Wach.** Czech: **Vavřík, Vavřička, Vavruška.**

Augs.: It.: **Lorenzon(i); Renzoni; Nencioni.**

Patrs.: Eng.: **Lawrenson** (chiefly Lancs.; also adopted as a Jewish surname). Sc.: **Laurenson** (chiefly Orkney and Shetland); MCLAUREN. It.: **(De) Laurentis, De Laurenzis, De Lorenzis, De Lorenzo, Di Lorenzo; De Renzis.** Low Ger.: **Lorentzen, Lohrensen, Lornsen; Lörtzing, Lortzing.** Du.: **Rensen.** Norw., Dan.: **Lorentsen, Loren(t)zen, Lauritsen, Lauritzen, Lauridsen, Lau(e)(r)sen, Laugesen, Larsen, Lassen.** Swed.: **Lorentzson, Larsson.** Pol.: **Wawrzyniak, Wawrzyńczak; Lorentowicz** (from a Ger. form of the given name). Russ.: **Lavrenov, Lavrinov.** Croatian: **Lavrenčić.** Lithuanian: **Laurinaitis.** Latvian: **Labrencis.**

Patrs. (from dims.): Eng.: **Larson.** Pol.: **Wawrzkiewicz; Wachowicz, Wachowiec, Wachowiak; Wasiak, Waszak.** Russ.: **Lavrin, Lavrushin, Lavrukhin, Lavrishchev** (all also from the less common LAUR). Lithuanian: **Loreit, Lorat.**

Habitation name: Pol.: **Wachowski.**

'Servant of L. (dim.)': Eng.: **Lap(p)age** (see PAGE).

Lawrence *is the surname of a family of landowners in N Lancs. traceable from the early 14th cent.*

John Lawrence of Suffolk, England, settled in Watertown, Mass., in 1635. Six generations later his descendant Samuel (b. 1754) was one of the minutemen at Bunker Hill, and the surname is still frequent in New England.

Lawton English: habitation name, common in Lancs. and Yorks., from *Buglawton* or *Church Lawton* in Ches., so called from OE *hlāw* hill, burial mound (see LAW 2) + *tūn* enclosure, settlement.

Lawty 1. English: nickname for a trustworthy person, from ME *lawty* loyalty (OF *léauté*, L *lēgālitas*, a deriv. of *lēgālis*; see LEAL).

2. Scots: var. of LATTO.

Vars. (of 1): **Laity, Lewt(e)y, L(e)uty.**

Lax 1. German: metonymic occupational name for a salmon fisher or a seller of salmon and other delicacies, from Ger. *Lachs* salmon (MHG, OHG *lahs*, originally meaning 'leaping', 'playful'; cf. LAKER 2).

2. German: nickname for a lively person, from MHG *lahs* in the sense 'playful', 'leaping'.

3. Jewish (Ashkenazic): it is unclear to what extent this name is occupational, as in 1, and to what extent it is ornamental, one of the many Ashkenazic surnames taken from words denoting fish, birds, and animals.

Vars. (of 3): **Lachs, Lacks, Lass; Laxer, Lachser, Lakser; Laxman, Lachsman, Laksman.**

Cogn.: Low Ger.: **Lass.**

Laycock English (chiefly Yorks.): habitation name from *Laycock* in W Yorks. (or possibly from *Lacock* in Wilts.). Both are recorded in Domesday Book as *Lacoc* and seem to be named with OE **lacuc*, a dim. of *lacu* stream (see LAKE).

Var.: **Leacock.**

Layton English: habitation name from any of various places so called, e.g. in Lancs. (near Blackpool) and in N Yorks. The former gets its name from OE *lād* water-course (cf. LOADER 1) + *tūn* enclosure, settlement, the latter from OE *lēac* leek + *tūn* (cf. LAUGHTON, LEYTON, and LEIGHTON).

Lazar Jewish (Ashkenazic), German, and (rarely) English: from the Aramaic male given name *Lazar* (an aphetic form of the Hebr. male given name *Elazar*, composed of the elements *El* God + *azar* help, and meaning 'may God help him' or 'God has helped (i.e., by granting a son)'). In the New Testament, this was the name of the brother of Martha and Mary who was restored to life by Christ (John 11: 1–44). According to an ancient popular tradition, after the death of Christ he came to Provence with his two sisters and became the first bishop of Marseilles. As a Ger. or Eng. name it may in some cases be a nickname for a beggar or especially an outcast leper; this use arises from the biblical parable of Dives and Lazarus (Luke 16: 19–31).

Vars.: Jewish: **Laz(a)rus, Lazerus; Lozerus** (from Yid. *Lozer*). Ger.: **La(t)zarus, Lazer, Lasar, Laser, Leser, Löser.**

Cogns.: Fr.: **Lazare, Lazard, Lazart, Lazere.** It.: **Lazzari, Lazzaro; Lazzeri, Lazzero** (Tuscany). Sp., Port.: **Lázaro.** Rum.: **Lazăr.** Pol.: **Łazarski.** Hung.: **Lázár.**

Dims.: Jewish: **Lazaruk** (E Ashkenazic). Ukr.: **Lazarchuk.** It.: **Lazzarin(i), Lazzarino, Lazzerini, Lazzarelli, Lazzaretti, Lazzeretti, Lazzarotti, Lazzarotto, Lazzarutti.** Pol.: **Łazarczyk, Łazarek.**

Augs.: It.: **Lazzaroni, Lazzarone, Lazzeroni.**

Patrs.: Jewish: **Lazarson, Lazerson; Lazarin, Lazarow, Lazaroff, Lazarovitch, Lazarowicz, Lazarowics, Lazarowitz, Lazerowitz, Lazarovitz, Lazarofsky** (E Ashkenazic), **Lazarovici** (Rumanian spelling). Russ.: **Lazarev.** Pol.: **Łazarowicz.** Croatian: **Lazarević, Laz(ov)ić.** Bulg.: **Lazarov.** It.: **Di Lazzari** (Venetia). Armenian: **Azarian.**

Patr. (from a dim.): Pol.: **Laśkiewicz, Łaszkiewicz.**

Lazenby N English: habitation name from *Lazenby* in N Yorks. or *Lazonby* in Cumb., both so called from ON *leysing* freedman (also used as a byname and personal name) + *býr* farm, settlement.

Var.: **Lasenby.**

Leach English: 1. occupational name for a physician, OE *lǣce*. It may also have been a nickname for a demanding or bloodthirsty person, from the bloodsucking creature of the same name, although the metaphor lay originally in calling the animal 'healer' rather than the doctor 'bloodsucker'.

2. local name for someone who lived by a boggy stream, OE *læcc*, *læce* (related to *lacu* stream; see LAKE, LATCHFORD).

Vars. (of 1): **Leche**, **Lee(t)ch**, **Leitch**. (Of 2): **Latches**, **Letcher**.

Cogns. (of 1): Ger.: LACHMANN, **Lachner**.

Bearers of the surname Leche *can still be found in Carden, Ches. John Leche acquired land there through his marriage to the daughter of William de Carwarden of Carden in the 14th cent.*

Leadbetter English: occupational name for a worker in lead, ME *ledbetere*, agent noun from OE *lēad* lead + *bēatan* to beat, strike.

Vars.: **Ledbetter**, **Leadbeat(t)er**, **Lidbetter**, **Leadbitter**.

Leader English: 1. occupational name for someone who led a horse and cart conveying commodities from one place to another, ME *ledere*, agent noun from OE *lǣdan* to lead. The word may also sometimes have been used to denote a foreman or someone who led sport or dance, but the name certainly did not originate with *leader* in the modern sense 'civil or military commander'; this is a comparatively recent development.

2. occupational name for a worker in lead, an agent deriv. of OE *lēad* lead; cf. LEADBETTER.

Vars. (of 1): **Leeder** (Norfolk). (Of 2): **Ledder**.

Cogn. (of 1): Jewish (Ashkenazic): **Leiter** (see also LEITNER).

Leaf English: 1. from the OE personal names *Lēofa* (masc.) and *Lēofe* (fem.) 'Dear', 'Beloved'. These names were in part short forms of various cpd names with this first element (cf., e.g., LEWIN 1 and LEVERIDGE), in part independent affectionate bynames. See also LOVE.

2. topographic name for someone who lived in a densely foliated area, from ME *lēaf* leaf; a certain Robert *Intheleaves* is recorded in London in the 14th cent.

3. as an American surname it is normally a translation of BLATT 'leaf' or an Anglicized form of the Swed. ornamental cpds.

Vars.: **Leafe**, **Leefe**, **Lief**, **Leif**, **Life**, **Liff**.

Cogns. (of 2): Swed. (ornamental): **Lö(ö)f**, **Löv**.

Patrs. (from 1): Eng.: **Leaves**, **Leavis**.

Cpds (of 2; ornamental): Swed.: **Löfberg**, **Lövberg** ('leaf hill'); **Löfdahl**, **Lövdahl** ('leaf valley'); **Löfgren**, **Lövgren** ('leaf branch'); **Löfquist**, **Lövquist** ('leaf twig'); **Löfstedt**, **Lövstedt** ('leaf homestead'); **Löfstrand** ('leaf shore'); **Löfström** ('leaf river').

Leahy Irish: Anglicized form of Gael. **Ó Laochdha** 'descendant of *Laochdh*', a personal name derived from *laoch* hero.

Var.: **Lehigh**.

Leal Spanish and Portuguese: nickname for a loyal or trustworthy person, from Sp., Port. *leal* loyal, faithful to obligations (L *lēgālis*, from *lex*, gen. *lēgis*, law, obligation). Cf. LAWTY 1.

Cogns.: Eng. (Norman): **Leal(e)**, **Lealman**.

Lean 1. English (chiefly Devon): nickname for a thin or lean person, from ME *lene* lean, OE *hlǣne*.

2. Irish and Scots: abbreviated form of MCLEAN.

3. Irish: Anglicized form of Gael. *Ó Laighin*; see LANE 2.

4. Irish: Anglicized form of Gael. *Ó Liatháin*; see LEHANE.

Var.: **Leane**. (Of 3 and 4): **O'Leane**.

Leapman English: occupational name for a basket-maker, from OE *lēap* basket + *mann* man. The term *lepemakere* denoting a basket-maker occurs in ME.

Vars.: **Leaper**, **Leeper**, **Leiper**, **Laiper** (Scotland); LEPPER.

Lear English: 1. habitation name from any of various places in N France named with the Gmc element *lār* clearing.

2. habitation name from *Leire* in Leics., apparently so called from an old Brit. river name, which may be the base of the tribe-name *Ligore* found in LEICESTER.

Learmonth Scots: habitation name from a place in the former county of Berwicks., of uncertain etymology. The second element may be from Gael. *monadh* mountain, moor, but since the place is in the Lowlands, an Eng. (or Scandinavian) etymology should probably rather be sought.

Vars.: **Learmont**, **Learmond**, **Leirmonth**.

In the early 17th cent. a Scot by the name of George Learmont *served as a mercenary in the Polish army, but was captured by the Russians in 1613 and settled in Russia. His descendants include the novelist and poet Mikhail Yurievich* **Lermontov** *(1814–41).*

Learoyd English (Yorks.): apparently a habitation name from an unidentified place, perhaps named from OE *lēah* wood, pasture + *rod* clearing.

Leary Irish: Anglicized form of **Ó Laoghaire**, 'descendant of *Laoghaire*', a byname originally meaning 'Keeper of Calves', from *loagh* calf. This was the name of a 5th-cent. king of Ireland, after whom the port of *Dún Laoghaire* ('fort, citadel of Laoghaire') is named, and from whom many modern bearers of this name claim descent.

Var.: **O'Leary**.

Leask Scots: habitation name from a place, now called Pitlurg, in the parish of Slains, Aberdeen. The name is first recorded in 1380 in the form *Lask*, but its origin is not known.

Var.: **Leisk**.

Leather English (chiefly Lancs. and Yorks.): metonymic occupational name for a leatherworker or seller of leather goods, from ME *lether*, OE *leþer* leather.

Cogns.: Ger.: **Leder(er)**, **Ledermann**. Jewish (Ashkenazic): **Lederer**, **Lederman** (Anglicized **Leatherman**), **Lejderman** (a Pol. spelling representing a S Yid. pronunciation); **Lederhandler** (see HANDLER); **Lederkramer** (see KRÄMER).

Dim.: Ger.: **Lederle**.

Patr.: Eng.: **Leathers**.

Cpds (occupational-ornamental): Jewish: **Lederberg** ('leather hill'); **Lederfajn** ('leather fine', a Pol. spelling); **Ledereich**, **Lederaich** ('leather rich'); **Lederstein** ('leather stone').

Equiv. (not cogn.): Pol.: SKÓRA.

Leatherbarrow English (Lancs.): habitation name from *Latterbarrow* in Furness, probably so called from ON *látr* lair of a wild animal + OE *bearu* grove, wood.

Leathley English: habitation name from a place in W Yorks., which appears to derive its name from OE *hleoða*, dat. pl. of *hlið* slope + *lēah* wood, clearing.

Leavesley English (Midlands): habitation name from an unidentified place, apparently so called from the gen. case of some OE personal name with the first element *lēof* beloved (cf. LEAF 1) + OE *lēah* wood, clearing.

Lebedev Russian and Jewish (E Ashkenazic): patr. from the nickname *Lebed* 'Swan' (a distant cogn. of L *albus* white). The Jewish surnames are ornamental.

Vars.: Russ.: **Lebedinski** (a clergy name). Jewish: **Lebedoff**; **Lebed**, **Lebedinsky**; **Lebedkin** (from a dim.).

Cogns.: Beloruss.: **Lebyadzevich**, **Lebedevich** (patrs.). Pol.: **Łabęcki**, **Łabędzki**. Czech: **Lebeda**.

Lech Polish: from the Pol. given name *Lech*.

Łęcki Polish: topographic name from Pol. dial. *łęk* swamp, waterlogged ground, or from the related *łąka* meadow, with the addition of the surname suffix *-ski* (see BARANOWSKI).

Leckie Scots: habitation name from a place in the parish of Gargunnock, in the former county of Stirlings., so called from a deriv. of Gael. *leac* flagstone (i.e. 'place of flagstones').

Vars.: **Leck(e)y** (N Ireland).

Lecue Spanish form of Basque **Lekue**: topographic name for someone who lived at a particular spot outside the main village, from Basque *lek(h)u* place, spot + the local suffix *-ue* (from *(g)une* space, distance). Alternatively it may be a topographic name for someone who lived at a lower spot, in which case it is a var. of **Lekube**, containing the suffix *-be* lower down.

Leddy Irish: Anglicized form of Gael. **Ó Lideadha** 'descendant of *Lideadh*', a personal name of uncertain origin.

Var.: **Liddy**.

Ledesma Spanish: habitation name from places so called in the provinces of Logroño, Salamanca, and Soria. The placename probably derives from a superlative form of a Celt. adj. meaning 'broad', 'wide' (cf. LEITH).

Ledger English: 1. from a Gmc personal name composed of the elements *liut* people, tribe + *geri*, *gari* spear, introduced into England in the form *Legier* by Norman settlers. The name was borne by a 7th-cent. bishop of Autun, and although he was martyred for political rather than religious reasons his fame contributed to the popularity of the name in France; in Germany the name was connected with a different saint, an 8th-cent. bishop of Münster.

2. voiced var. of *Letcher* (see LEACH 2), in part a deliberate alteration to avoid unpleasant association with ANF *lecheor* lecher.

Var. (of 1): **Leger**. See also LEGARD and LEGGATT.

Cogns. (of 1): Fr.: **Lég(i)er, Laug(i)er, Laugé, Lig(i)er, Liget, Ligez**. Ger.: **Lüt(t)ger(t)**.

Dims. (of 1): Fr.: **Légeret, Légerot, Légeron, Ligereau, Ligerot, Ligeron**.

Patrs. (from 1): Ger.: **Lüdgering**. Flem.: **Luytgaeren(s)**.

Lee 1. English: topographic name for someone who lived near a meadow, pasture, or patch of arable land, ME *lee*, *lea* (from OE *lēa*, dat. case—originally used after a preposition—of *lēah* wood, clearing, a term with cogns. in many European languages; cf. LEICHER 2, LOO, LACHMANN 3, and ŁASKI).

2. English: habitation name from any of the many places names with OE *lēah* wood, clearing, as for example *Lee* in Bucks., Essex, Hants, Kent, and Shrops., and *Lea* in Ches., Derbys., Herefords., Lancs., Lincs., and Wilts.

3. Irish: Anglicized form of **Ó Laoidhigh** 'descendant of *Laoidheach*', a personal name derived from *laoidh* poem, song (originally a byname for a poet).

Vars. (of 1 and 2): **Lea**, LEIGH, LEES; **Lay(e)**, LEY, **Lye** (from the later OE dat. form, preserved in ME as *l(e)ye*; *Lye* is the name of a place in the W Midlands). (Of 1 only): **L(a)yman, Leyman**; **At(t)lee, Atley, Atlay, Attle** (with fused preposition); **Atherlee** (with fused preposition and article). (Of 3): **O'Lee, O'Loye, O'L(e)ye, O'Lie**.

Leeds English: habitation name from the city in W Yorks. The placename is of Brit. origin, appearing in Bede in the form *Loidis* 'People of the *Lāt*', an earlier name of the river Aire, meaning 'the violent one'. *Loidis* was a district name, only later restricted to the town.

Leek English: 1. topographic name for someone who lived by a stream, from ON *lækr* brook. There are also a number of places named with this word—such as *Leak* in N Yorks., *Leake* in Lincs. and Notts., *Leek* in Staffs., and *Leck* in Lancs.—and the surname may also be from any of these.

2. metonymic occupational name for a grower or seller of leeks, from OE *lēac*.

Vars.: **Leeke, Leak(e), Leck, Leeks, Leaker**. (Of 1 only): **Latch(es), Letch(er)**, LEACH (palatal forms in Southern dialects of ME).

Leeming English: 1. habitation name from either of two places so called in W Yorks. near Keighley and in N Yorks. near Northallerton. Both are so called from a river name, a deriv. of OE *lēoma* gleam, sparkle.

2. var. of LEMON (1 and 2).

Lees 1. English: topographic name from ME *lees* fields, arable land, pl. of *lee* (see LEE 1).

2. English: habitation name from any of the various places named with the nom. pl., *lēas*, of OE *lēah* wood, clearing. Examples of places so named are *Lees* near Ashton-under-Lyne and *Leece* near Barrow-in-Furness.

3. English: from the medieval female given name *Lece*, a contracted form of *Lettice* (see LETT).

4. Scots: aphetic form of GILLIES.

Vars.: **Leese, Leece**. (Of 4 only): **Leish(man)**.

Metrs. (from 3): **Leeson** (chiefly Northants.); **Leason, Lesson, Lisson**.

The surname Lees *is found mainly in SE Lancs, with a smaller concentration in S Staffs.*

The form Leceson *is found in widely different locations in the Middle Ages, but it seems likely that modern bearers of the surname* Leeson *descend from a common ancestor, originally from Packington, Leics. One branch of the family became earls of Milltown in the Irish peerage.*

Legard English (Yorks.): from the Continental Gmc female personal name *Liutgard* (borne by Charlemagne's wife), composed of the elements *liut* people, tribe + *gard* enclosure, which was introduced into England in this form by the Normans. In some cases it may be a var. of LEDGER 1, with an excrescent dental. See also LEGGATT.

Cogns.: Ger.: **Lauckhardt, Luckard, Leukart; Leickard, Leikart, Leichart, Leikert, Leichert** (Bavaria).

Legg English (chiefly W Country): 1. metonymic nickname for someone with some malformation or peculiarity of the leg(s), or just with particularly long ones, from ME *legg* (ON *leggr*, of obscure further etymology; in the OE period *fōt* (see FOOT) denoted both foot and leg).

2. var. of LEIGH.

Var.: **Legge**.

The Earls of Dartmouth, whose family name is Legge, *trace their descent from Thomas Legge, a wealthy Lord Mayor of London who in 1338 helped Edward III to finance a war against France. His wife is said to have been a daughter of the Earl of Warwick.*

Leggatt English: 1. occupational name for an ambassador or deputy, from ME, OF *legat* (L *lēgātus*, past part. of *lēgāre* to appoint, ordain, from *lex*, gen. *lēgis*, law, command). The name may have been given to an official elected to represent his village at the manor court.

2. from a medieval personal name, a var. of LEDGER 1 or LEGARD.

Vars. (mainly of 1): **Legatt, Legat(e), Leggate, Legget(t), Leggitt, Leggott, Legwood**.

Lehane Irish: Anglicized form of Gael. **Ó Liatháin** 'descendant of *Liathán*', a personal name from a dim. of *liath* grey.

Vars.: **O'Lehane**, **O'Lyhane**, **O'Leaghan**, **L(e)yhane**, **Leehan(e)**, **Lihane**, **Lyhan**, LANE, LEAN.

Lehmann 1. German: status name for a feudal tenant or vassal, MHG *lēheman*, *lēnman* (from *lēhen* loan(ed land) + *man* man). The tenant held land on loan for the duration of his life in return for rent or service, but was not free to transfer or divide it.

2. Jewish (Ashkenazic): of uncertain origin. According to Kaganoff it is normally an occupational name for a banker, pawnbroker, or usurer, from MHG *lēhenen* to lend, and was sometimes adopted as an equivalent of LEVI, apparently because of the coincidence of the first two letters. However, there are phonetic problems with the first of these explanations, while the second seems to be unsupported by any evidence.

Vars. (of 1): **Le(c)hner**, **Lohner**, **Löhner(t)**. (Of 2): **Lehman**.

Cogns. (of 1): Flem., Du.: **Le(e)man**, **De Lee(n)man**; **De Leener**.

Lehrer 1. Jewish (Ashkenazic): occupational name for a teacher in a traditional Jewish elementary school, from mod. Ger. *Lehrer*, Yid. *lerer* teacher; cf. KINDERLEHRER, KLEINLERER, and KNELLER 3.

2. German and, possibly in some cases, Jewish (Ashkenazic): topographic name for someone who lived in a marshy area. There are a number of minor places, mostly in S Germany, named with this element, and the surname may also come from any of them.

Vars. (of 2): **Lehr(mann)**.

Lehtinen Finnish: ornamental name from Finn. *lehti* leaf + the gen. suffix *-nen*. This is one of the many Finn. surnames taken in the 19th cent. from vocab. words denoting features of the natural landscape.

Lehtonen Finnish: ornamental name from Finn. *lehto* grove of trees + the gen. suffix *-nen*. This is one of the many Finn. surnames taken in the 19th cent. from vocab. words denoting features of the natural landscape.

Var.: **Lehto**.

Leib Jewish (Ashkenazic): from the Yid. male given name *Leyb* 'Lion'; cf. LÖWE 2.

Var.: **Leibush** (from Yid. **Leybish**, an extended form of the given name).

Dims.: **Leib(e)l** (from the Yid. dim. male given name *Leybl*).

Patrs.: **Leibso(h)n**; **Leibin**, **Leibov**, **Leibow**, **Leibowicz**, **Leibovi(t)ch**, **Leibowit(s)ch**, **Leibowitz**, **Leibowics**, **Leibovicz**, **Leibovitz**, **Leibovic** (E Ashkenazic), **Leibovici** (Rumanian spelling).

Patr.(from a dim.): **Leiblowicz**.

Leibnitz German: habitation name from one of the various places in Saxony and elsewhere called *Leubnitz* or *Leipnitz* (formerly *Lubenice*). The placename is of Slav. origin and the first element apparently refers to lime trees (cf. LIPPE and LIPSCHUTZ).

Var.: **Leibniz**.

Leicester English: habitation name from the county town of Leics., so called from the OE tribal name *Ligore* (itself adapted from a Brit. river name) + OE *cæster* Roman fort (L *castra* legionary camp). Cf. LEAR 2.

Vars.: **Leycester**; **Lessiter**, **Lissiter**, **Lassiter**, **Lasseter**.

Leicher German: 1. occupational name for a musician or singer, from an agent deriv. of MHG *leich* music, song (akin to ON *leika* to play, sport; see LAKER 2).

2. topographic name for someone who lived in a copse, from the dial. term *la(i)ch* (cf. LACHMANN 3).

Vars.: **Leichner** (also Jewish (Ashkenazic), having a similar origin to 1; presumably an occupational name for a cantor). (Of 2 only): **Laich(n)er**; **Lach(n)er** (see also LAKE).

Leigh English: habitation name from any of the numerous places (in at least sixteen counties)—but especially *Leigh* in Lancs.—so called from the nom. case of OE *lēah* wood, clearing (see LEE 1) or from *lēage*, a form of the dat. case of this word.

Vars.: **Legh**, LEGG.

The surname Leigh *is most common in Ches. and S Lancs. A Ches. family spelling the name* Legh *claim descent from Edward* de Lega, *who received large grants of land in the county in the 11th cent.*

Leighton English: habitation name from any of various places so called. Most, as for example those in Beds., Cambs., Ches., Lancs., and Shrops., get the name from OE *lēac* leek + *tūn* settlement; cf. LAUGHTON, LAYTON, and LEYTON.

A family of this name claim descent from Tihel de Lathune, *who witnessed various documents between 1155 and 1166. He took his name from the manor in Shrops. now known as Leighton. His grandson Sir Richard de Lathune was confirmed in possession of the manor around 1200.*

Leiner 1. English: cogn. of LANIER.

2. Jewish (W Ashkenazic): name taken by someone who was good at chanting the Pentateuch at public worship in the synagogue or who regularly did so, from W Yid. *layner* reader (a deriv. of the W Yid. verb *laynen* to read, which comes ultimately from L *legere* to read).

Leinonen Finnish: patr. from the OFinn. personal name *Leino*, originally a byname meaning 'Sad'.

Var.: **Leino**.

Leirer German: occupational name for a player on the lyre, from an agent deriv. of Ger. *Leier* lyre (MHG *līre*, OHG *līra*, from L *lȳra*, from Gk).

Var.: **Leyrer**.

Cogn.: Low Ger.: **Liermann**.

Leitão Portuguese: metonymic occupational name for a keeper of pigs, or nickname meaning 'Pig', from Port. *leitão* (suckling) pig (LL *lacto*, gen. *lactōnis*, a deriv. of *lac*, gen. *lactis*, milk; cf. LEITE).

Leite Portuguese: nickname for someone with a notably pale complexion, from Port. *leite* milk (LL *lacte*, for class. L *lac*, gen. *lactis*).

Leith Scots: habitation name from the port near Edinburgh, which takes its name from the river at whose mouth it stands. The river name is from Gael. *Lìte* meaning 'Wet'; compare W *llaith* damp, moist.

Leithead Scots: habitation name from lands in the parish of Kirknewton in the former county of Midlothian. The lands stand at the head of the river known as the Water of LEITH.

Var.: **Leithhead**, **Leathead**.

Leitner German and Jewish (Ashkenazic): topographic name for someone who lived on the side of a mountain or slope of a hill, from Ger. *Leite* slope (MHG *līte*, OHG *(h)līta*) + *-(n)er* suffix denoting a native or inhabitant of a place, also an agent noun. The Ger. surname is particularly common in Bavaria and Austria.

Vars.: **Laitner**; **Leiter** (see also LEADER). Ger. only: **Leuthner**.

Leiva Spanish: habitation name from places in the provinces of Logroño and Murcia. The placename is early recorded in the form *Libia*; it is of uncertain etymology.

Lelli Italian: aphetic form of a dim. from various medieval given names, as for example *Angelo* (see ANGEL) and *Gabriello* (see GABRIEL).

Patrs.: **De Lello, De Lellis.**

Lemon 1. English: from a ME given name *Lefman*, OE *Lēofman*, composed of the elements *lēof* dear, beloved + *mann* man.

2. English: nickname for a lover or sweetheart, from ME *lem(m)an*, originally a cpd of the same elements as in 1, but used of either sex. There is no connection with the citrus fruit (whose name is of Arabic origin); this could not be grown in the Eng. climate.

3. Scots and N Irish: var. of LAMONT.

Vars. (of 1 and 2): **Loveman, Lowman, Luffman, Leaman, Leamon, Le(e)man, Lemmon, Liman, Limon, L(e)aming,** LEEMING.

Lemos Portuguese: of uncertain meaning, coming originally from Galicia in W Spain. It is probably from the name recorded in L sources as *Lemavos*, apparently a deriv. of the Celt. element *lemos*, *limos* elm (cf. LENNOX and LIMA).

Lengyel Hungarian: ethnic name for a Pole, Hung. *lengyel*, of ORuss. origin.

Lenihan Irish: Anglicized form of Gael. **Ó Leanacháin** 'descendant of *Leanachán*', a personal name of uncertain origin (derivation from *léanach* sorrowful being phonologically impossible).

Vars.: **Lennihan, Lenehan, Len(n)ahan; O'Leneghan, (O')-Lenaghan.**

Lenin Russian: one of a group of patrs. from dims. of ALEXANDER. This particular form was chosen as a pseudonym by Vladimir Ilyich Ulanov (1870–1924), with reference to political disturbances among Siberian exiles on the river *Lena*.

Vars.: **Lenkin, Lenshin; Len(k)ov, Lentsov, Lennikov; Lelikov, Lelyakov, Lelyanov, Lelyakin, Lelyashin, Lelyukhin; Lelkin.**

Lennie Scots: habitation name from *Leny* in the parish of Callander in the former county of Perths., so called from Gael. *lèana* bog, marsh + the local suffix *-ach*.

Vars.: **Len(n)y.**

Lennon Irish: 1. Anglicized form of Gael. **Ó Leannáin** 'descendant of *Leannán*', a byname meaning 'Lover', 'Paramour', 'Concubine'.

2. Anglicized form of Gael. **Ó Lonáin** 'descendant of *Lonán*', a personal name from a dim. of *lon* blackbird.

Vars.: **(O')Len(n)an(e), (O')Lannan, Lan(n)on, Lannen, Lannin, Linnane,** LEONARD. (Of 2 only): **O'Lonan(e), O'Lonnan.**

Dims. (of 2): **O'Lonagan, O'Lonegan, O'Lanegane, O'Lannegan, (O')Lanigan, Lannigan** (Gael. **Ó Lonagáin**).

Lennox Scots and N Irish: habitation name from the district near Dumbarton, recorded in 1174 in the form *Leuenaichs*, in the following year as *Levenax*. Apparently it gets its name from Gael. *leamhan* elm + the local suffix *-ach*.

Var.: **Lenox.**

Lennox *is in part the surname of the descendants of the union between Charles II and Louise Renée de Kérouaille, Duchess of Portsmouth. Their natural son Charles Lennox (1672–1723) was made Duke of Lennox at the age of three, and Lennox came to be used as his surname; up to that time he had been known as* FITZROY. *He was also created Duke of Richmond, by which title he is probably better known. Through his mother's side he acquired the French title Duc d'Aubigny. His descendants were prominent in English public life down to the 19th cent.*

Lenthéric Provençal: from a dim. of a Gmc personal name *Lantier*, composed of the elements *land* land, territory + *hari*, *heri* army.

Lenton English: habitation name from one of the places so called, in Notts. and Lincs. The former derives its name from the river on which it stands, the *Leen* (an ancient Brit. name) + OE *tūn* settlement, enclosure. The latter, also known as *Lavington*, is probably from the OE personal name *Lēofa* (see LEAF 1) + *tūn*.

Lenz 1. Low German: contracted form of LAWRENCE.

2. German: cogn. of LANCE.

3. German: nickname from Ger. *Lenz* spring (MHG *lenze*, OHG *lenzo*, from *lang* LONG, since in this season the days grow longer). The name may have been bestowed on someone who was born in the spring or who owed rent or service at that time of year, or it may have denoted someone who was of a sunny and spring-like disposition. The vocab. word is now somewhat literary or archaic, having been replaced in mod. Ger. by *Frühling*.

4. Jewish (Ashkenazic): of uncertain origin. It may be one of the class of ornamental names adopted from words denoting the seasons (cf. SUMMER 1, WINTER 2, HERBST, and FRULING), or perhaps an adoption of the Ger. surname.

Cogns. (of 3): Flem.: **Lente.** Du.: **Van Lent.**

León Spanish: 1. cogn. of LYON (1 and 2).

2. habitation name from the city in NW Spain, so called from L *legio* legion, gen. *legiōnis*, a division of the Roman army. In Roman times the city was the garrison of the 7th legion, known as the *Legio Gemina*.

Leonard 1. English: from a Norman personal name composed of the Gmc elements *leo* lion (a late addition to the vocab. of name elements, from L) + *hard*, hardy, brave, strong. A saint of this name, who is supposed to have lived in the 6th cent., but about whom absolutely nothing is known except for a largely fictional life dating from half a millennium later, was popular throughout Europe in the early Middle Ages and was regarded as the patron of peasants and horses.

2. Irish: var. of LENNON.

3. Italian: in the U.S., an Anglicization of any of the It. names listed below.

Vars. (of 1): **Len(n)ard, Learnard, Learned.**

Cogns. (of 1): Fr.: **Lé(o)nard, Lénars, Liénard, Lévenard.** It.: **Leonardi, Leonardo; Leinardi, Leinardo** (Sardinia); **Lonardi, Lonardo** (central and S Italy); **Lunardi, Lunardo** (Lombardy, Liguria, Venetia); **Lenardi, Linardi, Linardo** (Venetia); for aphetic forms see NARDO. Cat.: **Lleonart.** Port.: **Leonardo.** Ger.: **Le(o)nhard(t), Le(o)nhart, Lienhard(t).** Low Ger.: **Lehnhard, Lehnert, Linnert.** Flem.: **Leendert.** Du.: **Leynaert.** Pol.: **Lenart.** Czech: **Linhart.** Hung.: **Lénárt.**

Dims. (of 1): It.: **Leonardelli, Leonardini, Le(o)narduzzi; Lunardelli.** Pol.: **Lenarczyk.** Czech: **Linek, Linka.**

Augs. (of 1): It.: **Lenardon(i), Lunardon(i), Linardon.**

Patrs. (from 1): It.: **De Leonardi(s), Di Leonardi.** Low Ger.: **Lennartz, Lehnertz, Lennerts, Linnartz.** Fris.: **Leenderts.** Flem.: **Leenerts, Linders.** Du.: **Leenders.** Swed.: **Lennartsson.** Pol.: **Lenartowicz.** Beloruss.: **Lenartovich.**

Leonidov Russian: patr. from the given name *Leonid* (Gk *Leōnidēs*, originally itself a patr. from the byname *Leōn* 'Lion'; cf. LYON 2). The name was borne by various early martyrs of whom little is known, but who are venerated in the Orthodox Church.

Var.: **Levanidov.**

Leontyev Russian: patr. from the given name *Leonti* (Gk *Leōntios*, from *leōn* lion, gen. *leontos*). The name was borne by a number of early Gk martyrs, and also by a 4th-cent. bishop of Caesarea in Cappadocia, all of whom contributed to the popularity of the name in E Europe.

Var.: **Levontyev**.

Leopold German: from a Gmc personal name composed of the elements *liut* people, tribe + *bold* bold, brave. The form of the first element has been affected by the influence of LEONARD. The surname is also borne by Ashkenazic Jews, in which case it is an adoption of the Ger. surname.

Vars.: **Leupold(t), Leipold(t), Leibold, Leipelt, Luitpold.**

Leppänen Finnish: ornamental name from Finn. *leppä* alder tree + the gen. suffix *-nen*. This is one of the many Finn. surnames taken in the 19th cent. from vocab. words denoting features of the natural landscape.

Leppard English (originating in E Sussex): from ME, OF *lepard* leopard, from LL *leopardus*, a cpd of *leo* lion + *pardus* panther), perhaps a nickname for a stealthy but violent man, or a house name for someone who lived in a house distinguished by the sign of a leopard.

Vars.: **Leopard, Lepperd, Lippard.**

Cogns.: It.: **Leopardo, Leopardi.** Cat.: **Llopart.** Ger.: **Lebart, Lebert.**

It is likely that the Eng. surname Leppard *originated with one family, in E Sussex.*

Lepper 1. German: occupational name from an agent deriv. of MHG *lappe* rag, cloth (OHG *lappa*), apparently denoting a cobbler who repaired footwear with rags rather than leather. Leather shoes in the Middle Ages were a luxury and many people either went barefoot or contented themselves with felt leggings which could easily be repaired with scraps of cloth.

2. English: var. of LEAPMAN.

Vars. (of 1): **Lepple, Läpple.**

Patr. (from 1): **Leppers.**

Lerner 1. German: occupational name for a pupil or apprentice, Ger. *Lerner*, an agent deriv. of *lernen* to learn (MHG, OHG *lernen*; cf. LARNER).

2. Jewish (Ashkenazic): from Yid. *lerner* student of the Talmud, an agent deriv. of *lernen* to study (the Talmud).

3. English: var. of LARNER.

Leskinen Finnish: metr. from Finn. *leski* widow.

Leslie Scots: habitation name from a barony in the former county of Aberdeens., which is first recorded *c.*1180 in the form *Lesslyn*. The placename is probably from Gael. *leas celyn* court, garden of hollies. Leslie in Fife is said to be named in imitation of this place; in some cases the surname may come from there.

Vars.: **Lesslie, Lesley.**

The Scottish family of Leslie, *who hold the earldom of Rothes, trace their ancestry to Malcolm, son of Bertolf, who was granted lands at Leslie in the 12th cent. As a surname it was first used by Norman* de Lescelin *in 1214. The family was closely associated with the Scottish royal house, and George Leslie was created Earl of Rothes in 1457. After this the family split into two branches. One of these, the Balquhains, were Roman Catholic supporters of Mary, Queen of Scots. Both branches produced many soldiers, including two who fought for the Swedish king Gustavus Adolphus in the 17th cent.*

Leśniak Polish: occupational name for a woodman or forester, Pol. *leśni(a)k* (from Pol. *les, las* wood, forest + the agent suffixes *-nik, -niak*).

Vars.: **Leśnik, Leśnicki, Lesiak.**

Cogns.: Ger. (of Slav. origin): **Lessnick, Lessing.** Jewish (Ashkenazic): **Less** (possibly ornamental; see WALD).

Dim.: Pol.: **Leśniczak.**

Patr.: Pol.: **Leśniewicz.**

Habitation names: Pol.: **Leśniewski, Leśnikowski.**

Lesseps Provençal: topographic name for someone who lived by a hedge, from OProv. *seps* hedge (L *saepes*), with fused def. art. *le*.

Leszczyński 1. Polish: topographic name for someone who lived by a hazel tree or in a hazel wood, from Pol. *leszczyna* hazel tree + *-ski* suffix of local surnames (see BARANOWSKI). It may also be in part a habitation name from a place named with these elements.

2. Jewish (E Ashkenazic): ornamental name from Pol. *leszczyna* hazel tree + *-ski*, one of the many Ashkenazic ornamental surnames taken from vocab. words denoting features of the natural world.

Cogn.: Czech: **Liška.**

Lethaby English: of uncertain origin, probably a habitation name from an unidentified place in N England, of which the second element is ON *býr* farm, settlement; the first has not been satisfactorily identified.

Lett English: from a medieval female given name, a short form of *Lettice* (L *Laetitia* 'Happiness', 'Gaiety'; see also LEES 2).

Dims.: **Lett(e)y.**

Metrs.: **Letts; Letson, Letsom.**

Leuthard German: from a Gmc personal name composed of the elements *liut* people, tribe + *hard* hardy, brave, strong.

Vars.: **Leutert, Leitert, Luithardt, Luthard(t).**

Cogns.: Fr.: **Liétard, Léautard, Liautard, Liotard, Leotard** (for the treatment of the first element, cf. LEOPOLD).

Leuther German: from a Gmc personal name composed of the elements *liut* people, tribe + *heri, hari* army.

Vars.: LUTHER, **Leither.**

Cogns.: Low Ger.: **Lü(d)er, Lühr.** Fr.: **Léauthier, Liautier, Liotier.**

Dims.: Low Ger.: **Lüthke, Lüt(h)ge, Lüt(t)gen, Lütje(n)** (possibly also from other, rarer Gmc names with *liut* as a first element).

Patrs.: Low Ger.: **Lüd(d)ers, Lüers, Lührs(en), Lü(e)rsen, Lühri(n)g.**

Patrs. (from dims.): Low Ger.: **Lütkens, Lüthgens, Lüttgens, Lütjens.**

Lever English: 1. Norman nickname for a fleet-footed or timid person, from OF *levre* hare (L *lepus*, gen. *leporis*). It may also have been a metonymic occupational name for a hunter of hares.

2. topographic name for someone who lived in a place thickly grown with rushes, from OE *lǣfer* rush, reed, iris. Great and Little *Lever* in Lancs. are named with this word (in a collective sense) and the surname may also be derived from them.

3. possibly also from an unrecorded ME survival of an OE personal name, *Lēofhere*, composed of the elements *lēof* dear, beloved + *here* army.

Var.: **Leaver.**

Cogns. (of 1): Fr.: **Lièvre, Lelièvre.** It.: **Lepri, Lepre; Lepori, Lepore** (S Italy); **Lever(i), Levere** (N Italy); **Legori** (Lombardy).

Dims. (of 1): Eng.: LEVERETT. It.: **Leporini, Leporino, Levorin(i), Levrini; Leprotti, Levrotto.**

Aug. (of 1): It.: **Leproni.**

Patrs. (from 3): Eng.: **Lievers; Leivers** (Notts. and Derbys.).

Leverett English: 1. dim. of LEVER 1.

2. from the ME given name *Lefred*, OE *Lēofrǣd*, composed of the elements *lēof* dear, beloved + *rǣd* counsel.

Var.: **Leveritt**.

Leveridge English: from the ME given name *Lefric*, OE *Lēofrīc*, composed of the elements *lēof* dear, beloved + *rīc* power.

Vars.: **Leverich, Leverick, Lefridge, Loveridge, Loveredge, Livery, Luffery**.

Leverton English: habitation name from any of several places so called. One in Berks. is so called from the OE female personal name *Lēofwaru* (composed of the elements *lēof* dear, beloved + *waru* care) + OE *tūn* enclosure, settlement; one in Lincs. has as its first element OE *lǣfer* rush, reed (see LEVER 2); and N and S *Leverton* in Notts. may contain a river name identical to that in LEAR 2.

Levett English: 1. Norman nickname from a dim. of ANF *leu* wolf; see LOW 3.

2. habitation name from any of the various places in Normandy called *Livet*. All are of obscure, presumably Gaul., etymology.

3. from the ME given name *Lefget*, OE *Lēofgēat*, composed of the elements *lēof* dear, beloved + the tribal name *Gēat* (see JOCELYN).

4. possibly also from an unrecorded ME survival of the OE female personal name *Lēofgȳð*, composed of the elements *lēof* dear, beloved + *gȳð* battle.

Vars.: **Levet, Livett, Livitt, Leavett, Le(a)vitt**.

Levi Jewish: from the Hebr. male given name *Levi* 'Joining', borne by a son of Jacob and Leah (Gen. 29: 34). Bearers of this given name or surname are Levites, members of the tribe of Levi, who form a hereditary caste who assist the *kohanim* (see COHEN).

Vars.: LEWI, LEVY, **Leve; Levit(e), Levitt, Lewit(t); Levit(t)an, Leviton; Lévi, Lévy, Lévit(t)e, Lévitan** (among French-speaking Jews); **Levie(t)** (among Dutch-speaking Jews); **Levinsky, Levit(an)sky** (E Ashkenazic); **Halevy, Halévi** (with the Hebr. def. art. *ha*).

Dims.: LEVICK, **Leivick** (E Ashkenazic).

Patrs.: **Levis**, LEWIS, **Levites, Levitas; Levison, Levinso(h)n, Levinsen, Levenson, Levenzon** (Ashkenazic); **Leviev**, LEWIN, **Levin(e), Leven(e), Le Vi(g)ne** (a pseudo-Gallicization of *Levin(e)*), **Levinski, Levinsky, Levinov, Levitin** (E Ashkenazic); **Levitov** (either from *Levi(t)* Levite + the Slav. patr. suffix *-in*, or from Hebr. *Levi* Levite + Hebr. *tov* good, i.e. 'good Levite').

Cpds (ornamental elaborations): **Levinberg, Levinthal, Levinstein** (see also LÖWE).

Levick 1. English: nickname from ANF *l'eveske* 'the BISHOP'.

2. English: from the ME given name *Lefeke*, OE *Lēofeca*, a deriv. of *Lēofa* (see LEAF 1).

3. Jewish (E Ashkenazic): from Yid. *Leyvik*, a dim. of the male given name *Leyvi*; see LEVI.

Vars. (of 1 and 2): **Livick, Livock, Leffeck**. (Of 1 only): **Veck, Vick** (by wrong division). (Of 3): **Leivik, Levak**.

Patrs. (from 2): **Lucking** (from OE *Lēofecing*). (From 3): **Levikson, Levakov**.

Levy 1. Jewish: var. of LEVI.

2. English: from the ME given name *Lefwi*, OE *Lēofwīg*, composed of the elements *lēof* dear, beloved + *wīg* war.

3. French: habitation name from *Lévy*(-Saint-Nom) in Seine-et-Oise, so called from the Gallo-Roman personal name *Laevius* (from L *laevus* left) + the local suffix *-ācum*. Members of a noble family originally from this place followed Simon de Montfort on the Albigensian crusade, and were granted an estate at Mirepoix in Arriège.

Vars. (of 1 and 2): **Leavy, Le(a)vey**. (Of 3): **Lévis**.

Lewandowski Polish: habitation name from an estate called *Lewandów* (probably named from the Pol. personal name *Lewanda*, or Beloruss. *Levon*, forms of *Leo* (see LYON 2) + *-ów* possessive suffix), with the addition of *-ski*, suffix of local surnames (see BARANOWSKI). A possible alternative derivation for the placename is from a var. of *lawenda* lavender.

Lewin 1. English: from the ME given name *Lefwine*, OE *Lēofwine*, composed of the elements *lēof* dear, beloved + *wine* friend. This was the name borne by an Eng. missionary who became the patron of Ghent, and the given name was consequently popular in the Low Countries during the Middle Ages.

2. Jewish (E Ashkenazic): patr. from LEVI.

3. Manx: Anglicized form of Gael. **Mac Giolla Guillin** 'son of the servant of WILLIAM'.

Vars. (of 1): **Lowin, Lowen**. (Of 3): **Gelling**.

Cogns. (of 1): Low Ger.: **Lewen, Leven**.

Patrs. (from 1): Eng.: **Lewins, Lewens, Livens**. Low Ger.: **Lewens, Levens**.

Lewis 1. English: from *Lowis*, *Lodowicus*, a Norman personal name composed of the Gmc elements *hlod* fame + *wīg* war. This was the name of the founder of the Frankish dynasty, recorded in L chronicles as *Ludovicus* and *Chlodovechus* (the latter form becoming OF *Clovis*, *Clouis*, *Louis*, the former developing into Ger. *Ludwig*). The name was popular throughout France in the Middle Ages and was introduced into England by the Normans. On the continent it was a hereditary name borne by many Fr. kings and by the Bavarian WITTELSBACHS.

2. Welsh: Anglicized form of LLYWELYN.

3. Scots: local name from the Hebridean island of *Lewis*. This seems to have been named with ON *hlóðr* silent, melancholy or *ljoð* song + *hús* house, but these rather fanciful forms may well represent the workings of folk etymology on some more ancient name.

4. Scots and Irish: Anglicized form of Gael. **Mac Lughaidh** 'son of *Lugaidh*'. This is one of the most common OIr. personal names. It is derived from *Lugh* 'Brightness', which was the name of a Celtic god. In Scotland the name was taken as a Gaelicized form of *Lewie*, a pet form of the given name *Lewis* (as in 1).

5. Jewish (Ashkenazic): patr. from LEVI or Anglicization of some like-sounding Jewish surname.

Vars. (of 1): **Louis, Lowis**. (Of 4): **(Mc)Cloy**.

Cogns. (of 1): Fr.: **Louis, Louy(s)**. It.: **Ludovico, Ludovici, Ludovisi, Lodovico, Lodovic(h)i, Lodovisi; Loisi, Luisi, Luis(o); Luigi; Alois(i), Alloisi, Al(l)ois(i)o, Aluis(i)o, Aluigi, Aloigi, Al(o)visi, Alvisio, Alvigi**. Sp.: **Luis**. Cat.: **Lluís**. Port.: **Luís**. Ger.: **Lud(e)wig, Lod(e)wig**. Low Ger.: **Lad(e)wig**. Flem.: **Luyck**. Du.: **Lodewijk**. Pol.: **Ludwicki**. Czech: **Ludvík**. Hung.: **Lajos**.

Dims. (of 1): Fr.: **Louiset, Louisot, Luizet, Louichon**. It.: **Lodovichetti, Luiselli, Luisetti**. Ger.: **Lude, Lutz(mann), Litzmann, Lutsch; Lotze** (Hesse); **Ludl** (Bavaria); **Lösel**. Low Ger.: **Lode(mann), Lade(mann), Lohde, Löhde, Lödeke; Lo(o)s, Lose(mann), Lossman, Loseke**.

Pej. (of 1): Fr.: **Luizard**.

Patrs. (from 1): Fr.: **Ludovici** (Latinized). It.: **D'Aloisio, D'Aluisio, D'Alisi, De Luisi, Di Luisi**. Fris.: **Luickinga**. Flem.: **Luyckx, Louckx, Loix**. Du.: **Lodewijks**. Dan.: **Ludvigsen**. Pol.: **Lud(wi)kiewicz; Ludwiczak, Ludwisiak**.

Patr. (from 1) (dim.): Low Ger.: **Löding**.

Lewkowicz 1. Polish: patr. from a dim. of the given name *Lew* 'Lion' (see Lvov and Lyon 2).

2. Polish: perhaps also a patr. from the nickname *Lewek* 'Left-handed', a dim. of Lewy 1.

3. Jewish (E Ashkenazic): patr. of uncertain origin, possibly as in 1 and 2.

Vars. (of 1): **Lwowicz** (not dim.). (Of 1 and 2): **Lewicki, Lewiński**. (Of 3): **Lewkowitz, Levkowitz, Lewkovitz, Levkovitz, Levkovits, Lefkovitz, Lefkowicz, Lefkowits, Lefkovits, Lefkovich**.

Lewy 1. Polish: nickname for a left-handed person, from Pol. *lewy* left.

2. Jewish (Ashkenazic): probably in most cases a var. of Levi, but possibly also derived as in 1.

Vars. (of 1): **Lewiak**. (Of 2): **Lewi**.

Cogn. (of 1): Czech: **Levý, Levák**.

Patr. (from 1): Pol.: Lewkowicz.

Ley 1. English: var. of Lee 1 and 2.

2. French and German: var. and cogn. of Eloy.

Leyburn English: habitation name from *Leyburn* in N Yorks. or *Leybourne* in Kent. The former is so called from the OE personal name **Lylla* (a byform of the attested *Lulla*) + OE *burna* stream (see Bourne). The latter probably has as its first element OE *hlīg*, a byform of *hlēow* shelter.

Vars.: **Leyborne, Laybo(u)rn, Leeburn, Lyburn, Labern**.

Bearers of this name have been found in Kent from the 12th cent. in the village of Leybourne. Philip de Leiburn *held land there in 1166. Roger* de Leybourne *(d. 1271) was a warden of the Cinque Ports and after a chequered career, including killing a man at a joust in 1252, became sheriff of Kent.*

Leyden Irish: Anglicized form of Gael. **Ó Loideáin** 'descendant of *Loideán*', a personal name of uncertain origin.

Vars.: **L(e)ydon**.

Leyland English (Lancs.): topographic name or habitation name from ME *layland*, OE *lǣgeland* land left lying uncultivated. This is the name of a place in Lancs., and the present-day distribution of the surname suggests that this place is the source for most bearers. Others may, however, get their name from the same word used in other parts of the country.

Var.: **Layland**.

Leyton English: 1. habitation name from *Leyton* in Essex, so called from the Brit. river name *Lea* (of uncertain etymology, perhaps from the Celt. element *lug-* light) + OE *tūn* enclosure, settlement.

2. var. of Layton or Leighton.

Lhoták Czech: topographic name from the vocab. word *lhota* village or habitation name from any of the many small places named with this word.

Vars.: **Lhota, Lhotský**.

Libby English (Devon): from a medieval female given name, a pet form of *Elizabeth*; see Hibbs 2.

Libes Jewish (Ashkenazic): metr. from the Yid. female given name *Libe*, from *lib* dear, beloved (cf. Lieb).

Vars.: **Li(e)bis; Libin, Libov(itz), Libovits, Libowicz** (E Ashkenazic), **Libovici** (Rumanian spelling).

Metr. (E Ashkenazic, from a dim., Yid. *Libke*): **Libkowicz**.

Lichfield English: 1. habitation name from the city in Staffs. The first element preserves a Brit. name recorded as *Letocetum* during the Romano-British period. This means 'grey wood', from words which are the ancestors of W *llŵyd* grey and *coed* wood. By the OE period this had been reduced to *Licced*, and the element *feld* pasture, open country (see Field) was added to describe a patch of cleared land within the ancient wood.

2. habitation name from *Litchfield* in Hants, recorded in Domesday Book as *Liveselle*. This is probably from OE *hlif* shelter + *scylf* shelf, ledge. The subsequent transformation of the placename may be the result of folk etymological association with OE *hlið, hlid* slope + *feld* open country.

Var.: **Litchfield**.

Licht 1. German: metonymic occupational name for a chandler, from Ger. *Licht* light, MHG *lieht* candle (MHG *lieht*, OHG *lioht*).

2. Jewish (Ashkenazic): occupational name as in 1, or else an ornamental name, perhaps chosen in some cases in allusion to one of the various male Hebr. given names referring to light, such as *Uri* and *Meir*.

3. Low German: cogn. of Light 2.

Vars. (of 1 and 2): **Licht(n)er, Lichtmann** (occupational). (Of 2): **Likht; Lichtig(er), Likhtiger, Likhtikman** (from Yid. *likhtik* bright (i.e. 'full of light')); **Licht(er)man, Lichtermann** (occupational).

Cpds (of 2; all ornamental): **Lichtbach** ('light stream'); **Lichtenbaum** ('light tree'); **Lichtenberg** ('light hill'); **Lichtblau** ('light blue'); **Lichtbrun** ('light brown'); **Lichtenfeld** ('light field'); **Lichtenholz** ('light wood'); **Lichtschein, Lichtszain** ('light shine'), **Lichtszajn** (Pol. spelling); **Licht(en)stein, Lichtensztein** ('light stone'; see also Liechtenstein); **Lichtenthal** ('light valley').

Lichtzer German: occupational name for a chandler or candle-maker, Ger. *Lichtzieher*, from MHG *lieht* candle (see Licht 1) + *zieher*, an agent deriv. of *ziehen* to draw, dip. Candles were made by repeatedly dipping the wicks into tubs of molten wax.

Cogn.: Jewish (Ashkenazic): **Lichtzieher**.

Liddell N English and Scots: habitation name from any of various places in Cumb. and the Scots Borders called *Liddel*, from the OE river name *Hlȳde* 'Loud' + OE *dæl* valley (see Dale).

Vars.: **Liddel, Lidell, Liddle, Liddall, Lydall**.

Liddiard English: habitation name from *Lydiard* in Wilts. or *Lydeard* in Somerset, both of which apparently preserve a Brit. name composed of W *garth* hill with an obscure first element.

Liddiatt English and Scots: topographic name from ME *lidyate* gate in a fence between ploughed land and meadow (OE *hlid-geat* swing-gate), or habitation name from one of the places named with this word, as for example *Lidgate* in Suffolk or *Lydiate* in Lancs.

Vars.: **Lidgate, Lydiate, Liggat(t); Liggett** (N Ireland); **Lidgett**.

Liddicoat English (Devon and Cornwall): habitation name from any of various places in E Cornwall now known as *Lidcott, Lydcott, Ludcott*, and *Lidcutt*. All get their names from OCorn. *luit* grey + *cuit* wood; cf. Lichfield 1.

Lidstone English: habitation name from a place in Devon, so called from the gen. case of the OE personal name *Lēofede* (a deriv. of *Lēofa*; see Leaf 1) + OE *tūn* enclosure, settlement.

Lieb 1. German and Jewish (Ashkenazic): nickname for a pleasant or agreeable person, from Ger. *lieb* or Yid. *lib* dear, beloved (MHG *lieb*, a cogn. of OE *lēof*; see Leaf 1).

2. German: from a medieval given name, a short form of the various cpd Gmc personal names with the first element *lieb*.

3. German (of Slav. origin): from a short form of the various cpd Slav. personal names with a first element *lubo-* love (ultimately cogn. with 1).

Vars. (of 1): **Liebe(r)**, **Lieb(er)mann**. Jewish only: **Lieb(er)-man**; **Liber**, **Liberman(n)**, **Libman**; **Li(e)blich** ('lovely'); **Li(e)bling** ('darling'); **Lib(e)st** ('dearest').

Cogn. (of 1): Low Ger.: **Levermann**.

Dims. (of 1): **Li(e)blein**. (Of 2): **Li(e)bi(n)g**, **Lieb(i)sch**.

Cpds (of 1): Jewish: **Liebfreund**, **Liberfreund** ('dear friend'); **Li(e)bermens(c)h**, **Liebermensz** ('dear person'); **Li(e)b-so(h)n**, **Li(e)berso(h)n** ('dear son'); **Libertal** ('dear valley').

Liechtenstein 1. Austrian: habitation name from a castle near Vienna. The noble family of this name trace their descent from Hugo of Liechtenstein, who lived in the early 12th cent. The tiny European principality of this name was created in 1719 when the Austrian family holding the barony of Schellenberg acquired the county of Vaduz, which is now the capital of the principality.

2. Jewish (Ashkenazic): ornamental cpd of LICHT light + STEIN stone.

Light English: 1. nickname for a happy, cheerful person, from ME *lyght*, OE *lēoht* light (not dark), bright, cheerful.

2. nickname for someone who was busy and active, from ME *lyght*, OE *līoht* light (not heavy), nimble, quick. The two words *lēoht* and *līoht* were originally distinct, but they were confused in Eng. from an early period.

3. nickname for a small person, from ME *lite*, OE *lȳt* LITTLE, influenced by *lyght* as in 1 and 2.

Vars.: **Lyte**; **Lightman**, **Lyteman**, **Lit(t)man**, **Lut(t)man**.

Cogns. (of 2): Ger.: **Leicht**. Low Ger.: LICHT. Flem., Du.: **De Lichte**. Dan.: **Leth**. (Of 3): Low Ger.: **Lütt**.

Dims. (of 2): Ger.: **Leichtl(e)**.

Lightbody Scots and N English: 1. nickname for a cheerful person or a busy and active one; cf. LIGHT (1 and 2) + BODY.

2. nickname for a small person, from ME *lite* little (see LIGHT 3) + BODY.

Lightfoot English (chiefly N England, esp. Liverpool): nickname for a fast runner, from ME *lyght* light, nimble, quick (OE *līoht*; cf. LIGHT 2) + *fote* foot (OE *fōt*; cf. FOOT).

Cogns.: Low Ger.: **Lichtfoth**. Flem., Du.: **Ligtvoet**.

Lightowler English (Yorks. and Lancs.): habitation name from the village of *Lightollers* in Lancs., so called from OE *lēoht*, *līht* light, bright (cf. LIGHT 1) + *aloras* alders (cf. OLLERENSHAW).

Vars.: **Lightowlers**, **Lightoller(s)**.

Lilburn English, Scots, and N Irish: habitation name from a village in Northumb., so called from the OE personal name *Lilla* (of uncertain origin, perhaps a nursery word; cf. LILLO) + OE *burna* stream (see BOURNE).

Lillicrop English (chiefly Devon): nickname for someone with very fair hair, from OE *lilie* lily (see LILLY 2) + *cropp* top, head (see CROPPER).

Var.: **Lillicrap**.

The village of Lillicrap *in Devon seems to be named from a 14th-cent. proprietor, Peter* Liliecrop, *who presumably had fair hair or was descended from a forebear noted for his fair hair. However, the traditional etymology, that it derives from ME* littel *little +* crop *harvest and denotes a place where the harvest was notoriously poor, is not impossible.*

Lillo Spanish: from a medieval given name recorded in the L forms *Lilus* and *Lilius*. It is of uncertain, probably Gmc (cf. LILBURN), origin and unknown meaning.

Lilly English: 1. from a dim. of the female given name *Elizabeth* (see HIBBS 2).

2. nickname for someone with very fair hair or skin, from ME, OE *lilie* lily (L *līlium*). The It. cogn. *Giglio* was used as a given name in the Middle Ages. In Eng. and other langs. there has also been some confusion with forms of GILES.

3. habitation name from *Lilley* in Herts. or in Berks. The Herts. place is named from OE *līn* flax + *lēah* wood, clearing (see LINDLEY 1). The Berks name is OE *Lillinglēah* 'wood associated with *Lilla*'.

Vars.: **Lil(l)ey**, **Lil(l)ie**, **Lely**; **Lill(e)yman**, **Lilliman**.

Cogns. (of 2): It.: **Gigli(o)**; **Ziglio**, **Zeggio** (Venetia). Swed. (ornamental): **Lilja**, **Lilje**, **Lille**. Jewish (Ashkenazic; ornamental): **Lilien**, **Lilian**.

Dims. (of 2): It.: **Giglietti**, **Giglietto**, **Gigliucci**, **Giglioli**, **Gigliotti**; **Zigliotto**, **Zigliotti**.

Aug. (of 2): It.: **Giglioni**.

Pej. (of 2): It.: **Zeggiato**.

Patrs. (from 2): Eng.: **Lillis** (now found chiefly in Ireland). It.: **De Giglio**.

Cpds (of 2; ornamental): Swed.: **Lilje(n)berg** ('lily hill'); **Liljeblad(h)** ('lily leaf'); **Lilje(n)dahl** ('lily valley'); **Liljegren** ('lily branch'); **Liljeqvist** ('lily twig'); **Liljero(o)s** ('lily rose'); **Liljestrand** ('lily shore'); **Lilje(n)ström** ('lily river'). Jewish: **Lilienberg** ('lily hill'); **Lilienblum** ('lily flower'); **Lilienfeld** ('lily field'); **Lilienstein** ('lily stone'); **Lilient(h)al** ('lily valley').

Lillywhite English: nickname for someone with very fair hair or complexion, who was 'as white as a lily'.

Var.: **Lilywhite**.

Lima Portuguese: apparently a topographic name for someone living on the banks of the river of this name (of pre-Roman origin, probably akin to a Celt. element meaning 'elm'; cf. LEMOS and LENNOX).

Linacre English: topographic name for someone who lived near a field where flax was grown for the manufacture of linen cloth, from OE *līn* flax + *æcer* (cultivated) field (see ACKER). In part the surname may derive directly from *Linacre* in Lancs. or Cambs., both of which get their names from this source.

Vars.: **Linaker**, **Lineker**, **Liniker**, **Linnecar**, **Lin(n)egar**.

Linares Spanish: habitation name from any of various places so called, from the pl. form of Sp. *linar* flax field (L *līnāre*, a deriv. of *līnum* flax).

Cogn.: Cat.: **Llinares**.

Lincoln English: habitation name from the city of *Lincoln*, so called from an original Brit. name *Lindo-* lake (cf. W *llyn*) + L *colōnia* settlement, colony. The town was an important administrative centre during the Roman occupation of Britain and in the Middle Ages it was a centre for the manufacture of cloth, including the famous 'Lincoln green'.

Var.: **Linkin**.

Abraham Lincoln *(1809–65), 16th President of the United States, was the son of an illiterate Virginia labourer, descended from a certain Samuel Lincoln, who had emigrated from England to Massachusetts in 1637.*

Linde German: topographic name for someone who lived by a conspicuous lime tree, Ger. *Linde* (MHG *linde*, OHG *linta*). There are several places, especially in N Germany, named with this word, and the name may also be a habitation name from any of these. The word was also used in a number of OHG women's given names, with the meaning 'Shield' or 'Spear' (shields and spears being made from the hard wood of the lime); it is possible that the surname in some cases is a deriv. of a short form of one of these. As a Jewish (Ashkenazic) name, it is ornamental, adopted from the vocab. word for the tree.

Vars.: **Linden, Lind(n)er, Linde(r)mann**. Ger. only: **Lingner**. Jewish only: **Lind, Lindeman, Lind(en)man** (possibly also topographic for a man who lived by a conspicuous lime tree).

Cogns.: Low Ger.: **Linne(mann), Terlinden**. Flem., Du.: **Linden, Van der Linde(n), Verlinde(n), Van Lint, Lindeman, Lindeboom**. Eng.: LINE. Dan.: **Lind(e), Lindeman, Linneman**. Swed.: **Lind(h)(e), Lindell, Lindén, Linder, Linné(r), Lindman**.

Dim.: Ger.: **Lindl**.

Cpds (ornamental): Jewish: **Lindenbaum** (also Ger.), **Lindenboim** ('lime tree'); **Lindenberg** ('lime hill'); **Lindenblat(t)** ('lime leaf'); **Lindenbluth** ('lime blossom'); **Lindenfeld** ('lime field'); **Lindenstrauss** ('lime bouquet'); **Lindwasser** ('lime water'). Swed.: **Lindbäck** ('lime stream'); **Lind(e)berg, Lindberg(h)** ('lime hill'); **Lindblad(h)** ('lime leaf'); **Lindblom** ('lime flower'); **Linbo(h)m** ('lime tree'); **Lind(e)borg** ('lime town'); **Linda(h)l** ('lime valley'); **Lindfors** ('lime waterfall'); **Lind(e)gren** ('lime branch'); **Lindholm** ('lime island'); **Lindelöf** ('lime leaf'), **Lindmark** ('lime land'); **Lindqvist** ('lime twig'); **Lindro(o)s** ('lime rose'); **Lind(e)rot(h)** ('lime root'); **Lindsjö** ('lime sea'); **Lindskog** ('lime copse'); **Lindstedt** ('lime homestead'); **Lindstrand** ('lime shore'); **Lindström** ('lime river'); **Lind(e)wall, Lind(e)vall** ('lime bank').

Lindegård Danish: topographic or habitation name composed of the elements *lind* lime tree + *gård* enclosure.

Var.: **Lindegaard**.

Lindhardt Danish: from an ON personal name composed of the elements *lind* lime, shield, spear + *harðr* hardy, brave, strong.

Lindley English: 1. habitation name from either of two places in W Yorks. called *Lindley*, or from *Linley* in Shrops. and Wilts., all so called from OE *līn* flax + *lēah* wood, clearing, with epenthetic *-d-*; cf. LILLY 3.

2. habitation name from the other *Lindley* in W Yorks. (near Otley), so called from OE *lind* lime tree (see LINDE and LINE 1) + *lēah* wood, clearing. Lindley in Leics. probably also has this origin, and is a further possible source of the surname.

Vars.: **Lin(g)ley**.

Lindop English (Yorks.): habitation name from an unidentified place, presumably named with the OE elements *lind* lime tree (see LINDE and LINE 1) + *hop* enclosed valley (see HOPE).

Lindsay 1. English and Scots: habitation name from *Lindsey* in Lincs. This is first found in the form *Lindissi*, apparently a deriv. of the Brit. name of LINCOLN. To this has later been added the OE element *ēg* island, since the place was virtually cut off by the surrounding fenland.

2. English: habitation name from *Lindsey* in Suffolk, named in OE as *Lelleseg* 'island of *Lelli*', a personal name representing a byform of **Lealla*, cogn. with the attested OHG *Lallo*.

3. Irish: Anglicized form of various Gael. surnames, as for example *Ó Loingsigh* (see LYNCH 1), *Mac Giolla Fhionntóg* (see FINN), and *Ó Floinn* (see FLYNN).

Vars.: **Linsey, Lincey**.

Members of the ancient Scottish family called Lindsay *have been prominent in Scottish public affairs for centuries. Their titles include Earls of Crawford, Earls of Balcarres, and Dukes of Montrose. Their earliest ancestor in Scotland was Sir Walter* de Lindissi, *a Norman noble from Lincs. Early in the 12th cent., David, younger brother of King Alexander I of Scotland, acquired the earldom of Huntingdon by marriage. As a result, several of his new retainers moved north to Scotland, among them Sir Walter, and settled in the Scottish Lowlands. See also* RAMSAY.

Lindsell English: habitation name from a place in Essex, so called from OE *lind* lime tree (see LINDE and LINE 1) + *(ge)sell* shelter, hut.

Line English: 1. topographic name for someone who lived by a lime tree, ME *lind, line* (OE *lind*, cf. LINDE; mod. Eng. *lime* is an ill-explained alteration of the second form).

2. from the medieval female given name *Line*, an aphetic form of *Cateline* (see CATLIN) and of various other names, such as *Emmeline* and *Adeline*, containing the ANF dim. suffix *-line* (originally a double dim., composed of the elements *-el* and *-in*).

Vars.: LYNE. (Of 1 only): **Lind(er), Lynde, Lynds**.

Metrs. (from 2): **Lines, Lynes**.

Linforth English: habitation name from Great and Little *Linford* in Bucks. or *Lynford* in Norfolk. The former may have OE *hlyn* maple as its first element; the latter is more likely to contain *līn* flax. The second element in each case is OE *ford* FORD.

Vars.: **Linford, Linfoot**.

Ling English (E Anglia): habitation name from *Lyng* in Norfolk, which Ekwall suggests may be derived from OE *hlinc* hillside.

Lingen English: habitation name from a place in Herefords., so called from an old Brit. stream-name, perhaps composed of words which became W *llyn* water + *cain* clear, beautiful. The spelling *Lingham* in Domesday Book reflects scribal assimilation to the common placename element *-ham* homestead.

In 1086 the manor of Lingen in Herefords. was held by a certain Turstin de Wigmore. His descendants took the name of the manor, and in 1305 one of them, Sir John de Lingen, *was knighted by Edward I.*

Lingwood English (E Anglia): habitation name from a place in Norfolk, so called from OE *hlinc* hillside + *wudu* WOOD.

Link 1. German and Jewish (Ashkenazic): nickname for a left-handed person, from Ger. *Linke* left hand (MHG *linc* left, OHG *lenka* left hand). In Europe left-handers have long been regarded with suspicion as clumsy, awkward, deviant, and even untrustworthy.

2. English: topographic name, var. of LYNCH 2.

Vars. (of 1): Ger.: **Linke, Linkhand**. Jewish: **Linker**.

Linklater Scots: habitation name from either of the places of this name in the Orkneys, so called from ON *lyng* heather + *klettr* rock.

Var.: **Linkletter**.

Lino Portuguese: from a medieval given name (L *Linus*, from Gk, but of unknown ultimate origin and meaning). According to classical legend this was the name of a celebrated singer and poet, the son of Apollo and the teacher of Orpheus and Hercules. Later it was borne by a 1st-cent. saint, the immediate successor of St Peter as Pope.

Linton English and Scots: habitation name from any of the numerous places so called, found in every part of England and in the Scottish Borders. The second element is in all cases OE *tūn* enclosure, settlement. The first in the case of *Linton* in Northumb. is a Brit. river name, *Lyne* (related to

W *lliant* stream). The other places of this name normally have as their first elements OE *lind* lime tree or *līn* flax, but occasionally perhaps *hlynn* torrent or *hlinc* hillside. On the basis of geographical situation the meaning 'torrent' would be appropriate to *Linton* near Skipton in W Yorks.

Lipin Jewish (E Ashkenazic): patr. from the Yid. male given name *Lipe* (a short form of LIPMAN) + the Slav. suffix *-in*.

Vars.: **Lipovitch, Lipovitz, Lipowicz; Lipso(h)n** (also W Ashkenazic).

Dims.: **Lipkin, Lipkes** (see also LIEBSOHN); **Lipka** (see also LIPPE).

Lipman Jewish (Ashkenazic): from the Yid. male given name *Lipman*, composed of the Yid. words *lib* dear, beloved + *man* man. (In some cases the surname may have been formed directly from these elements.)

Vars.: **Li(e)pmann.**

Patr.: **Lipmanovicz** (E Ashkenazic).

Lipp 1. English: metonymic nickname for someone with large lips or with some deformity of the lips, from ME *lippe* (OE *lippa*).

2. English: perhaps from a ME given name, *Leppe* or **Lippe*, apparently from OE *Lēofa* (see LEAF 1).

3. German: var. of LIPPE 1 and 2.

Patr. (from 2): **Lipson.**

Lippe German: 1. aphetic pet form of PHILIP.

2. from a pet form of any of the various Gmc personal names in which the first element *liut* people, tribe is combined with a second element beginning with *b-*, such as *-berht* famous, *-bald* bold, or *-brand* sword, causing assimilation of the cluster *-tb-* to *-pp-*.

3. habitation name from the duchy of *Lippe*, which became an independent state in the 12th cent. under Bernard, Lord of Lippe. This title was taken from the name of a castle held by the family, which probably has the same origin as in 5 below.

4. topographic name for someone living on the banks of the river *Lippe* in Westphalia, which is of uncertain etymology. It is extremely ancient, being recorded by the Roman historian Tacitus in the form *Lupia*.

5. topographic name (of Slav. origin) for someone who lived among lime trees, from *lipa* lime (cf. LIPSKI).

Cogns. (of 5): Ukr.: **Lipa.** Jewish (E Ashkenazic): **Lipa, Lipnik** (ornamental names).

Dims. (of 1): Ger.: **Lippl.** Low Ger.: **Lipgen.** (Of 5): Ger. (of Slav. origin): **Lip(p)ke, Lipka, Lippek.** Jewish: **Lipka** (see also LIPIN).

Patrs. (from 1): Low Ger.: **Lip(p)s; Lipsius** (Latinized). Flem., Du.: **Lips, Lippen(s).**

Habitation name (from 5): **Liepe** (the name of several places in Brandenburg and Pomerania).

Lippiatt English: habitation name from *Lipiate* in Somerset or *Lypiatt* in Gloucs., both so called from OE *hlīepgeat* 'leap-gate', a gate which was low enough to be jumped by horses and deer but presented an obstacle to sheep and cattle.

Vars.: **Lippiet, Lipyeat.**

Lipschutz Jewish (Ashkenazic): habitation name from *Leobschütz* in Upper Silesia or *Liebeschitz* in Bohemia. The placenames are of Slav. origin, and are probably derived from *lipa* lime (see LIPPE 5).

Vars.: **Lipschütz, Liebschutz, Libschitz, Lipschitz, Lifs(c)hutz, Lifs(c)hitz, Lifshits, Lifchitz, Lifshytz, Lifs(c)hiz, Lifshic, Lifchic, Livschutz, Livs(c)hitz, Livshits, Liwshitz; Lifszec, Lifszic, Lifszyc** (Pol. spellings); **Lüpschütz, Lufschutz** (hypercorrected).

Lipski 1. German and Jewish (E Ashkenazic): habitation name from *Lipsk*, the former name of *Leipzig* in E Germany. The placename derives from the Slav. element *lipa* lime (see LIPPE 5).

2. Polish: habitation name from any of the many places named from Pol. *lipa* lime, for example *Lipno* in N central Poland.

Vars. (of 1): Jewish: **Lipsky, Libsky; Lipsker** ('native or inhabitant of Lipsk'), **Lipskier** (Pol. spelling); **Leipzig(er)** (Ger. forms). (Of 2): **Lipiński, Lipowski.**

Liptrot English: of uncertain origin; according to Harrison it is from a Gmc personal name composed of the elements *liob* dear + *trūt* beloved. The surname is now quite common in Lancs., but seems to be a comparatively recent importation into the county.

Var.: **Liptrott.**

Lis Polish and Jewish (E Ashkenazic): nickname for a cunning person or, in the case of the Jewish name, ornamental name, from Pol. *lis* fox.

Vars.: Pol. **Lisiak; Lisiecki.** Jewish: **Liss, Lys(s), Lis(s)man, Lissak.**

Dims.: Pol.: **Lisek, Lisik.** Ukr.: LYSENKO.

Habitation names: Pol.: **Lisowski, Liszewski.**

Lisboa Portuguese: habitation name from *Lisbon* (Port. *Lisboa*), the principal city of Portugal. The name is first recorded in the L form *Olisipo* and is of uncertain, possibly Carthaginian, origin.

Cogns.: Jewish: **Lisbon(a).**

Lisle English (Norman): 1. topographic name for someone who lived on an island, OF, ME *isle* (L *insula*), with fused def. art. *l'*.

2. habitation name for someone from the Fr. town of *Lille*, which derives its name from OF *isle* (the same word as in 1).

Vars.: **De Lisle, (De) Lyle;** ISLES.

Lison English and French: habitation name from a place in Calvados, Normandy, of obscure etymology.

Vars.: Eng.: **Lysons, Licence.** Fr.: **Liçon.**

List German and Dutch: nickname for a cunning or wily individual, from Ger. *List*, Du. *list* guile, ingenuity, stratagem, device (OHG, MLG *list*).

Var.: Ger.: **Listmann.**

Cogn.: Jewish (Ashkenazic): **Listman.**

Dim.: Ger.: **Listl.**

Lister 1. English: occupational name for a dyer, ME *litster*, an agent deriv. (originally fem.; cf. *Baxter* at BAKER, *Webster* at WEBB) of *lit(t)e(n)* to dye (ON *lita*). The term was used principally in E Anglia and N and E England, and to this day the surname is found principally in these regions, especially in Yorks.

2. Scots: Anglicized form of Gael. **Mac an Fleisdeir** 'son of the arrow-maker'; cf. FLETCHER. The family of this name originated in Drimfearn in the 10th cent.; they served as hereditary arrow-makers to the clan McGregor in Glenorchy. The surname has also been associated with the Gael. vocab. word *leastar* cup, boat, receptacle (used in a figurative sense of people as recipients of divine grace), but this is not the etymology.

3. Jewish (Ashkenazic): of uncertain origin.

Vars.: **Lyster, Lester, Lestor.** (Of 1 only): **Litster, Lidster, Ledster.** (Of 2 only): **McInlester, McLeister, Laister.**

Liston 1. English: habitation name from a place in Essex, so called from the OE personal name **Lissa* (probably a pet form of *Lēofsige*; see LIVESEY 2) + OE *tūn* enclosure, settlement.

2. Scots: habitation name from places in the former counties of W Lothian and Midlothian, which probably have the same origin as in 1.

Liszt Hungarian: 1. metonymic occupational name for baker or miller, from *liszt* flour, perhaps also a nickname for a white-haired person or someone with a very pale complexion.

2. Hungarian spelling of LIST.

Litherland English: habitation name from the district so called near Liverpool, consisting of *Uplitherland* and *Downlitherland*. The placename is derived from ON *hliðar*, gen. of *hlið* slope + *land* land.

Vars.: **Le(a)therland**.

Lithgow Scots: habitation name from *Linlithgow*, between Edinburgh and Falkirk, which was probably named with Brit. words related to W *llyn* lake, pool + *llaith* damp + *cau* hollow. In the 13th and 14th cents. the name appears both with and without the first syllable. It has been assumed that *Lithgow* was the name of the settlement and *Linlithgow* that of the lake. *Lithgow* was associated by folk etymology with Gael. *liath* grey + *cu* dog, and such a figure appears on the medieval borough seal.

Vars.: **Lithgoe**; **Lythgoe** (now commonly found in Lancs.).

Little 1. English: nickname for a small man or distinguishing epithet for the younger of two bearers of the same given name, from ME *littel* (OE *lȳtel*, originally a dim. of *lȳt*; cf. LIGHT 3).

2. Irish: translation of BIGG.

Vars.: **Littell**; **Lyt(t)le** (chiefly N Ireland); **Littler**.

Cogn.: Dan., Norw.: **Litle**.

Littleboy English (E Anglia): occupational nickname from ME *littel* small + *boy* lad, servant; cf. LITTLEPAGE.

Littlefair English: nickname from ME *littel* small + *fere* companion (see FEAR 1).

Littleford English (chiefly W Midlands): habitation name from some minor place named with OE *lȳtel* small + *ford* FORD.

Littlehales English (chiefly W Midlands): habitation name from *Little Hales* near Newport, Shrops., which is named with OE *lȳtel* small + *halh* nook, recess (see HALE 1).

Littlejohn Scots and English: distinguishing epithet for the smallest of two or more bearers of the extremely common given name JOHN; cf. MEIKLEJOHN. In some cases the nickname may alternatively have been bestowed on a large man, irrespective of his actual given name, in allusion to the character in the Robin Hood legend, whose nickname was of ironic application.

Var.: **Litteljohn**.

Patr.: **Littlejohns**.

Littlepage English: occupational nickname from ME *littel* small + PAGE servant, groom.

Littleproud English: unflattering nickname for a person considered to be of slight worth, from ME *littel* small + ME, OF *prod* valiant, gallant (from L *prōdesse* to be of value, use; cf. PROUD).

Before the Industrial Revolution this surname was strongly concentrated in the parish of Attleborough, Norfolk.

Littleton English: habitation name from any of various places, mostly in SW England, but also in Gloucs. and Worcs., so called from OE *lȳtel* small + *tūn* enclosure, settlement.

Var.: **Lyttleton, Lyttelton**.

Lyttleton *has been a Worcs. surname since 1358; it has a long association with Hagley Hall, built by the first Lord Lyttleton.*

Littlewood English (chiefly Yorks.): habitation name from any of several minor places in W Yorks., *Littlewood* in Wooldale being a well-recorded instance. They are named with OE *lȳtel* small + *wudu* WOOD.

Littleworth English: habitation name from any of various places, for example in Berks., Bucks., and Warwicks., so called from OE *lȳtel* small + *worð* enclosure (see WORTH).

Littley English: 1. nickname for someone with disconcertingly small eyes, from ME *littel* small + *ey* eye (OE *ēage*).

2. habitation name from a minor place named with OE *lȳtel* small + *(ge)hæg* enclosure (see HAY 1). There is a lost *Littley* in Kirby Malzeard, W Yorks., which could be the source of the surname.

Litton English: habitation name from any of the places so called, as for example in Derbys., Dorset, Somerset, and W Yorks. In most cases the names are from OE *hlȳde* torrent (from *hlūd* loud, roaring) + *tūn* enclosure, settlement, but some examples may originally have had as their first element *hlid(-geat)* gate (cf. LIDDIATT).

Vars.: **Litten, Lytton**.

Littwak Jewish (E Ashkenazic): regional name from Yid. *Lite* 'Lithuania' (Pol. *Litwa*; see LITWIN 2). In Ashkenazic culture, the region referred to as *Lite* encompassed not only Lithuania but also Latvia, Estonia, Belorussia, parts of the N Ukraine, and parts of NE Poland.

Vars.: **Litwa(c)k, Litva(c)k**, LITWIN; **Lut(t)wak, Lutwick, Lutvak** (hypercorrected forms in S Yid. regions); **Littau, Lit(t)auer, Litewski, Litowski, Litovsky**; **Litai** (Israeli).

Cogns. (meaning 'Lithuanian'): Ukr.: **Litvak**. Russ.: **Litvyakov** (patr.).

Litwin 1. English: probably from an OE personal name, **Lēohtwine*, composed of the elements *lēoht* light, bright + *wine* friend. The name is not attested in pre-Conquest documents, but a certain *Lihtuuinus* is recorded in Domesday Book.

2. Polish: ethnic name for someone from Lithuania, Pol. *Litwa* (of uncertain etymology, perhaps ultimately from a Baltic word meaning 'coast').

3. Jewish (E Ashkenazic): var. of LITTWAK.

Vars. (of 3): **Littwin, Litvin**; **Lutwin** (hypercorrected, from S Yid. regions).

Cogn.: Hung.: **Litván**.

Dims. (of 2): Ukr.: **Litvinenko**. Beloruss.: **Litvinyonok**. (Of 3): Jewish: **Litvintchouk**.

Patrs. (from 2): Pol.: **Litwinowicz**. Russ.: **Litvinov**. (From 3): Jewish: **Litvinov, Litvinoff**.

Lityński Polish: of uncertain origin, perhaps a nickname derived from Pol. *lit* goodwill gift, small bribe.

Livermore English: probably a habitation name from *Livermere* in Suffolk. This is first found in the form *Leuuremer* (*c.*1050), which suggests derivation from OE *lǣfer* rush, reed (see LEVER 2) + *mere* lake. However, later forms consistently show *i* in the first syllable, suggesting OE *lifer* liver, referring either to the shape of the pond or to the coagulation of the water.

Liversidge English (Yorks.): habitation name from *Liversedge* in W Yorks., named in OE as *Lēofheresecg* 'ridge, bank of *Lēofhere*' (see LEVER 3).

Var.: **Liversedge**.

Livesey English (chiefly Lancs.): 1. habitation name from a place in Lancs., so called from ON *hlíf* protection, shelter (or an unrecorded OE cogn.) + OE *ēg* island.

2. possibly in a few cases from an OE personal name composed of the elements *lēof* dear, beloved + *sige* victory.

Vars.: **Livesay, Livsey; Livesley** (influenced by the many placenames and surnames ending in *-ley*).

Livingstone 1. Scots: habitation name from a place in Lothian, originally named in ME as *Levingston*, from an owner called *Levin* (see LEWIN 1), who appears in charters of David I in the early 12th cent.

2. Irish: Anglicized form of Gael. *Ó Duinnshléibhe* and *Mac Duinnshléibhe*; see DUNLEAVY.

3. American: Anglicized form of the Jewish surname *Löwenstein* (see LÖWE 2).

Vars.: **Livingston, Levingston(e)**.

A Scottish family by the name of Livingston *held the titles Earl of Linlithgow and Earl of Callendar. They were descended from Sir William Livingston, who was granted the barony of Callender by David II in 1346. The first Earl was Alexander Livingston (d. 1621), whose younger son James (d. 1674) became 1st Earl of Callendar in 1641. The titles were united in James Livingston (d. 1723) but were forfeited in 1716, when he was attainted for high treason for his part in the Jacobite rebellion of 1715.*

This is also the name of a family who were influential in the post-colonial period in America. The founder was Robert Livingston (1654–1728), who emigrated from Scotland in 1673. His grandsons were Philip (1716–78), who signed the Declaration of Independence, and William (1723–90), 1st Governor of New Jersey, who was a signatory of the Constitution. A great-grandson, Robert R. Livingston (1746–1813), was one of five men who drew up the Declaration of Independence, and he also negotiated the cession of Louisiana by France.

The explorer David Livingstone *(1813–73) belonged to a branch of the McLeays of Appin (see 2 above), a small sept of the Stewarts of Appin.*

Ljung Swedish: ornamental name from Swed. *ljung* heather (ON *lyng*; see LING). This is one of the many Swed. surnames taken in the 19th cent. from vocab. words denoting features of the natural landscape, and used extensively in forming cpd surnames. In the U.S. it has often been Anglicized to YOUNG.

Var.: **Ljungman**.

Cogns.: Dan.: **Lyng(e)**.

Cpds: Swed.: **Ljungberg** ('heather hill'); **Ljungdahl** ('heather valley'); **Ljungren** ('heather branch'); **Ljungholm** ('heather island'); **Ljunglöf** ('heather leaf'); **Ljunqvist** ('heather twig'); **Ljungstedt** ('heather homestead'); **Ljungström** ('heather river').

Lledó Catalan: topographic name for someone who lived near a nettle tree, from Cat. *lledó* nettle fruit (LL *lōto*, gen. *lōtōnis*, for class. L *lōtus*, from Gk). There is a place named with this word in the province of Teruel, which may also be a partial source of the surname.

Var.: **Lladó** (a place in the province of Gerona).

Lloyd Welsh: nickname for a person with grey hair or who habitually dressed in grey, from W *llwyd* grey.

Vars.: **Loyd; Floyd(e), Floyed,** FLOOD.

Cogns.: Corn.: **Loze**. Bret.: **(Le) Louet**.

Patrs.: **Bloyd,** BLOOD, **Blud**.

One of the signatories of the American Declaration of Independence was William Floyd *(1734–1821), a wealthy landowner born on Long Island. His family had first settled there with his great-grandfather Richard Floyd, who emigrated from Wales in the 17th cent. Despite his comfortable circumstances, at the age of 69 Floyd purchased a tract of wilderness in Oneida county and spent the rest of his life as a pioneer.*

Llywelyn Welsh: from an OW personal name, apparently derived from the element *llyw* leader, although the exact formation is unclear.

Vars.: **Llywellin, Llewel(l)yn, Llewel(l)in, Llewhellin, Lewellin, Fluellin;** LEWIS.

Loach English (Midlands): nickname from ME *loch(e)* loach, a type of small fresh-water fish formerly prized as a delicacy (OF *loche*, of uncertain origin).

Loader English: 1. topographic name for someone who lived by a road or a watercourse, OE *lād* (from the verb *lǣdan* to lead, go). In placenames this OE word generally denotes a man-made drainage channel. For the change in the vowel, cf. ROPER.

2. occupational name for a carter, from ME *lode(n)* to carry, transport (deriving phonetically from the word given above, but influenced in its meaning by ME *lade(n)*, from OE *hladan* to load).

Vars.: **Loder, Load(s)man**. (Of 1 only): **Load(e)s** (chiefly E Anglia).

Lobb English: habitation name from a place in Devon, recorded in Domesday Book as *Loba*, apparently a topographical term of uncertain meaning, perhaps 'lump', 'hill'; the village is situated at the bottom of a hill. There is also a place of the same name in Oxon. (recorded in 1208 as *Lobbe*), but the historical and contemporary distribution of the surname makes it unlikely that it ever derives from this place, or from the ME, OE word *lobbe* spider.

Vars.: **Lob(be)**.

The first known bearer of the surname was Goderie Lobb, *recorded in 1136 as the priest of St Anne's Chapel in the parish of Branton Burrows, Devon. In the latter part of the 13th cent. Phillip* de Lobb *was involved in a court case concerning land inheritance. Several later members of the family have been leading figures in the affairs of the region; in 1538 William Lobb signed the deed dissolving Plymouth Carmelite friary, and Richard Lobb served as High Sheriff of Cornwall under Cromwell. The surname is still largely restricted to Devon.*

Lobel 1. French: nickname for a deceitful individual or for a flatterer, from a dim. of OF *lobe* flattery (of Gmc origin; cf. OHG *lob* praise).

2. Jewish (Ashkenazic): pseudo-Germanized form of the Yid. male given name *Leybl*, a dim. of *Leyb* (see LEIB).

Vars. (of 1): **Lobeau**. (Of 2): **Löbel**.

Lochhead Scots: local name for someone who lived at the head of a loch; cf. KINLOCH.

Vars.: **Lochead, Loachead, Lockhead**.

Lock 1. English: metonymic occupational name for a locksmith, from ME, OE *loc* lock, fastening.

2. English: topographic name for someone who lived near an enclosure, a place that could be locked, ME *loke*, OE *loca* (a deriv. of *loc* as in 1). ME *loke* was also used esp. of a barrier on a river, which could be opened and closed at will, and by extension of a bridge. The surname may thus also have been a metonymic occupational name for a lock-keeper.

3. English and German: nickname for a person with fine hair, from OE, OHG *loc* lock (of hair), curl (probably also ultimately identical with *loc* as in 1).

4. N English and Scots: see LUCAS.

Var.: **Locke**. (Of 1 only): Eng.: **Lock(i)er**, **Lockye(a)r** (agent derivs.).

Dim. (of 3): Ger.: **Löckle** (Swabia).

Lockhart Scots: of uncertain origin, probably from a Gmc personal name composed of the elements *loc* lock, bolt (see LOCK 1)+ *hard* hardy, brave, strong.

Var.: **Lockart**.

This surname is found in Scotland from the 13th cent., when Craiglockhart *near Edinburgh is referred to as* Crag (*see* CRAIG) quam Stephanus Locard miles tenuit (*'which Stephen Lockhart, soldier, held'*). Barlockhart *and* Drumlockhart *in the former county of Wigtowns. may also get their final elements from the surname, but it is more likely that in these cases the second element is Gael.* lùchairt *encampment, castle.*

According to family tradition, the surname was acquired when an ancestor conveyed the heart of James Lord Douglas back to Scotland in a locked casket after his death in the Holy Land; their arms accordingly show a heart clasped by a padlock. However, this story is no more than an invention of folk etymology.

Lockley English (W Midlands): habitation name from some minor place, probably *Lockleywood* in Hinstock, Shrops., that gets its name from OE *loca* enclosure (see LOCK 2) + *lēah* wood, clearing.

Lockwood English: habitation name from a place in W Yorks., probably so called from OE *loca* enclosure (see LOCK 2) + *wudu* WOOD. It seems likely that all present-day bearers of the name descend from a single family which originated in this place. There is another place of the same name in Yorks. (Cleveland), first recorded in 1273 as *Locwyt*, from ON *lok* fern + *viðr* wood, brake, but it is not clear whether it has given rise to a surname.

Lodge English: local name for someone who lived in a small cottage or temporary dwelling, ME *logge* (OF *loge*, of Gmc origin). The term was used in particular of a cabin erected by masons working on the site of a particular construction project, such as a church or cathedral, and so it was probably in many cases equivalent to an occupational name for a mason.

Cogns.: Fr.: **Loge**, **Delaloge**, **Logeois**.

Dims.: Fr.: **Logé**, **Logez**.

Aug.: Fr.: **Logeat**.

Löffler German and Jewish (Ashkenazic): occupational name for a maker or seller of spoons, which in the Middle Ages were normally carved from wood, or more rarely from bone or horn. The word is an agent deriv. of Ger. *Löffel* (MHG *leffel*, OHG *leffil*).

Vars.: Ger.: **Leffler**; **Löffel**, **Leffel**. Jewish: **Loeffler**, **Lefler** (occupational); **Leffel** (meaning 'spoon'; reason(s) for adoption uncertain).

Cogns.: Low Ger.: **Löpeler**, **Lep(p)ler**; **Lepel(l)**, **Läpel**.

Loftus 1. English (Yorks.): habitation name from *Loftus* in N Yorks., *Lofthouse* in W Yorks., or *Loftsome* in E Yorks. All get their names from ON *lopt* loft, upper storey + *hús* house, the last deriving from the dat. pl. form. Houses built with an upper story (which was normally used for the storage of produce during the winter) were a considerable rarity among the ordinary people of the Middle Ages.

2. Irish: Anglicized form of *Ó Lachtnáin* (see LACHLAN) or *Ó Lochlainn* (see LOUGHNANE).

Vars. (of 1): **Loft(i)s**, **Lofthouse**.

Logan 1. Scots and N Irish: habitation name from any of the places so called, principally that near Auchinleck. They all get their names from Gael. *lagan*, a dim. of *lag* hollow.

2. Irish: Anglicized form of Gael. **Ó Leocháin** 'descendant of *Leochán*', a personal name of uncertain origin, perhaps a dim. of the OIr. name *Leo*, or akin to *leochail* delicate, fragile.

Vars.: (of 2): **O'Logan**, **O'Loughane**, **O'Lochan**, **O'Lagan(e)**, **Lo(u)ghan**, **Lagan**, **Lohan**.

Logie Scots: habitation name from any of the various places so called, from Gael. *lag* hollow + the local suffix *-ach*.

Var.: **Loggie**.

Lomax English: habitation name from a lost place near Bury in Lancs., recorded in the Middle Ages as *Lumhalghs*, and apparently named with the OE elements *lumm* pool (see LUMB) + *halh* nook, recess (see HALE 1).

Vars.: **Lo(o)mas**, **Loomis**, **Lummis**, **Lummus**.

Lombard English (also Scots and Irish) and French: 1. ethnic name for someone from *Lombardy* in Italy. The region is named from the Gmc tribe which overran the area in the 6th cent. AD; its name is attested only in the Latinized form *Langobardi*, but is clearly composed of Gmc elements meaning 'long-beards' (cf. LONG and BEARD).

2. occupational name for a banker or money-lender. Many of the early It. immigrants to England were involved in such dealings, and the name came to be used from the 14th cent. onward as a generic term for a financier.

Vars.: Eng.: **Lumbard**, **Lumbert**, **Limbert**. Fr.: **Lombart**.

Cogns.: It.: **Lombardi**, **Lombardo** (in Sicily the term is also used of a shopkeeper, and in Genoa of a stupid person); **Langobardi**, **Langobardo** (S Italy). Sp.: **Lombardo**.

Dims.: Fr.: **Lombardet**, **Lombardot**. Prov.: **Lombardy**. It.: **Lombardelli** (Lombardy); **Lombarini**, **Lombarino** (Tuscany).

Bearers of this name are found in Ireland as far back as the 13th cent. In Cork it was the surname of a well-established family of merchants, who provided several mayors of the town from 1380 onward.

Lomonosov Russian: patr. from the nickname *Lomonos* 'Broken Nose' (from *lomit* to break + *nos* nose). The name was presumably originally given to a man whose nose had been broken and had set crooked, but there may possibly be some connection with the plant 'virgin's bower', a kind of clematis, which is called *lomonos* for obscure reasons, probably the result of some lost anecdote.

London 1. English: habitation name for someone who came from *London* or nickname for someone who had made a trip to London or had some other connection with the city. The placename is of Brit. origin and obscure etymology; it is recorded by the Roman historian Tacitus in the Latinized form *Londinium*, and may be connected with the Celt. element *lond* wild, bold, perhaps as a tribal name.

2. Jewish (Ashkenazic): of uncertain origin. It is hardly likely to be of the same origin as 1, since Ashkenazic migration has always been largely from the Continent to Great Britain rather than in the reverse direction. The name may have been chosen to reflect Ashkenazic Hebr. *lamdon*, Yid. *lamdn* Talmudic scholar.

Vars. (of 1): **Lundon**, **Lonnon**, **Lunnon**. (Of 2): **Londin(ski)**, **Londner**.

Long 1. English: nickname for a tall person, from OE *lang*, *long* long, tall (cogn. with L *longus*, from which derive the Romance forms quoted below).

2. Irish: Anglicized form of Gael. *Ó Longáin*; see LANGAN.

Vars. (of 1): **Lang**; **Laing** (Scots); **Longman**, **Langman**.

Cogns. (of 1): Ger.: **Lang(e)**, **Langer**. Flem.: **De Langhe**. Du.: **De Lang(e)**. Dan., Norw.: **Lang(e)**. Swed.: **Lång**. Jewish (Ashkenazic): **Lang(er)(man)**. Fr.: **Long**, **Lelong**. It.: **Longo**, **Longhi**; **Luongo** (Naples); **Lungo**, **Lunghi** (Tuscany); **Slongo** (Feltre). Sp.: **Luengo**. Rum.: **Lungu**. Hung.: **Láng**.

Dims. (of 1): Fr.: **Longeau(x)**, **Longet**, **Longin**, **Lonjon**; **Longuet(eau)**. It.: **Longhin(i)** (Venetia), **Lunghini**, **Longhetti**, **Lunghetti**.

Augs. (of 1): Fr.: **Lonjas**. It.: **Longon(i)** (Lombardy).

Pejs. (of 1): Fr.: **Longeard**, **Longaud**. It.: **Longato** (Venetia).

Patrs. (from 1): Flem.: **Langmans**. It.: **Del Lungo** (Tuscany); **Del Luongo** (Naples).

Cpds (from cogns. of 1, ornamental unless otherwise stated): Jewish (Ashkenazic): **Langbaum** ('tall tree'); **Langbart**, **Langbord**, **Langburt** ('long beard', a nickname); **Langberg** ('long hill'); **Langfuss** ('long foot', a nickname); **Langholz** ('long wood'); **Langleben** ('long life', a 'hopeful' name); **Langent(h)al** ('long valley').

Longbottom English (W Yorks.): topographic name for someone who lived in a long valley, from ME *long* + *bodme* (see BOTTOM). *Longbottom* in Luddenden Foot, W Yorks., may be the origin.

Var.: **Longbotham**.

Longden English: habitation name from any of various places, for example *Longden*, the ME form that underlies *Longdendale* in Ches. and Derbys. This is a cpd of OE *lang*, *long* LONG + *denu* valley (see DEAN 1). A place called *Longden* in Shrops., however, has the same origin as LANGDON, so there has clearly been some confusion between the two forms.

Longfellow English: nickname for a tall person who was a good companion; see LONG 1 and FELLOW.

Longfield English: topographic name for someone who lived by an extensive piece of open country or pastureland; see LONG and FIELD. There is a place so named in Kent, and there are several in W Yorks., where the surname is common. Two places now called *Longville* in Shrops. also have this origin.

Longhurst English: habitation name from any of various places, such as *Longhirst* in Northumb., named with the OE elements *lang*, *long* LONG + *hyrst* wooded hill (see HURST).

Longmire English: habitation name from a minor place in the parish of Windermere, Cumb., so called from ME *long* LONG + *myre*, *myer* marsh, bog (ON *mýrr*).

Var.: **Longmires**.

The first known bearers of the name are William Langmyer, *recorded in Troutbeck in 1545, and another William Langmyer of Longmire Yeat, who died c.1592.*

Longmore English: topographic name for someone who lived in an extensive area of marsh or fen; see LONG and MOORE 1. The surname is now found chiefly in the W Midlands.

Var.: **Longmuir** (Scots).

Longsdon English: habitation name from *Longsdon* in Staffs. or *Longstone* in Derbys. Both seem to derive from the gen. case of a OE hill name *Long* 'Long' + OE *dūn* hill (see DOWN 1).

A family of this name, living at Little Longstone, Derbys., claim descent from Serlo de Longesdon, *who was recorded in the village at the time of the Norman Conquest.*

Longstaff English: apparently an occupational name for a tipstaff or beadle who carried a long staff as a badge of office; perhaps also a nickname for a very tall, thin man, or even an obscene nickname for a man with a long sexual organ. The surname is found chiefly in NE England.

Var.: **Langstaff**.

Longworth English: habitation name from any of various places, for example in Berks. and Lancs., so called from OE *lang*, *long* LONG + *worð* enclosure (see WORTH).

Lönn Swedish: ornamental name from Swed. *lönn* maple tree, one of the many Swed. surnames taken in the 19th cent. from vocab. words denoting features of the natural landscape.

Cpds: **Lönn(e)berg** ('maple hill'); **Lönn(e)gren** ('maple branch'); **Lönnqvist** ('maple twig').

Lonsdale English: habitation name from places in Lancs. and S Cumb., named in OE as *Lunesdæl* 'valley (see DALE) of the river *Lune*'. This ancient Brit. river name is the same as in the first element in LANCASTER, through which city the river runs.

Var.: **Londsdale**.

Loo Low German, Flemish, and Dutch: topographic name for someone who lived in a grove or clearing, MLG, MDu. *lō* (a cogn. of MHG *lōch*, OHG *lōh* (cf. LACHMANN 3 and LEICHER 2) and OE *lēah* (see LEE 1)). The word is a common element in placenames, as for example *Waterloo*, the town in Brabant where Napoleon was finally defeated in 1815.

Vars.: **Lo(e)**, **Loh**, **Zumloh**, **Van (de) Loo**, **Van Loon**, **Looman(n)**.

Loobey Irish: Anglicized form of Gael. **Ó Lúbaigh** 'descendant of *Lúbach*', a byname originally applied to a cunning person.

Looney Irish: Anglicized form of Gael. **Ó Luanaigh** 'descendant of *Luanach*', a personal name derived from *luan* warrior (cf. LANE 3 and LAMB 3).

Vars.: **O'Looney**; **Lowney**; **Loney**, **Luney**, **Lunny** (N Ireland); **Lonie** (Scotland).

Lope Spanish: from a medieval given name. This may be from L *Lupus* 'Wolf', but the manner of derivation is not clear; the Sp. vocab. word has become *lobo* (see LOW 3).

Cogn.: Cat.: **Llop**.

Patrs.: Sp.: **López** (one of the commonest of all Spanish surnames). Cat.: **Llopis**. Port.: **Lopes**.

Lorca Spanish: habitation name from places in the provinces of Murcia and Navarre.

Cogn.: Cat.: **Llorca** (a place in the province of Alicante).

Lord 1. English: nickname for someone who behaved in a lordly manner, or had earned the title in some contest of skill, or had played the part of the 'Lord of Misrule' in the Yuletide festivities. It may also sometimes have been an occupational name for a servant in the household of the lord of the manor, or possibly a status name for a landlord or the lord of the manor himself. The word derives from OE *hlāford*, earlier *hlāf-weard*, lit. 'loaf-keeper', since the lord or chief of a clan was responsible for providing food for his dependants.

2. Irish: translation of Gael. *Ó Tighearnaigh* (see TIERNEY) and *Mac Thighearnáin* (see MCKIERNAN).

An Australian family of this name was founded by Simeon Lord *(1771–1840). He was born in Dobroyd, Yorks., and in 1790 was sentenced to seven years' transportation for stealing tenpence worth of fabric.*

Lordan Irish: Anglicized form of Gael. **Ó Lórdáin** 'descendant of *Lórdán*', a personal name of unknown origin. The surname is particularly common in W Cork.

Lorimer English and Scots: occupational name for a maker and seller of spurs, bits, and other small metal attachments to harness and tackle, from ANF *lorenier*, *loremier* (an agent deriv. of OF *lorain* tackle, harness, LL *lōrānum*, from class. L *lōrum* harness, strap).

Vars.: **Lorrimer**, **Larimer**.

Lorraine French and English: regional name from *Lorraine* in NE France, so called from the Gmc tribal name *Lotharingi* 'people of *Lothar*' (a personal name composed of the elements *hlod* famous, renowned + *hari*, *heri* army); cf. the mod. Ger. name of the region, *Lothringen*.

Vars.: Fr.: **(Le) Lorrain**. Eng.: **Loraine**; **Lor(r)ain**, **Lo(a)ring**. Ger. and Jewish (W Ashkenazic): **Lotring**, **Lot(h)ringer**.

Lorrain is the surname of a French ducal family who held the province of Lorraine continuously from the 11th cent. until 1740.

Lorton English: habitation name from a place in Cumb. The second element of this is clearly OE *tūn* enclosure, settlement; according to Ekwall, the first may be a ON name *Hlóra* 'Roarer' (akin to OE *hlōwan* to low, roar), applied to the beck on which Lorton stands.

Łoś Polish: nickname for a large, ungainly person, from Pol. *łoś* elk.

Var.: **Łosiak**.

Losa Spanish: topographic name for someone who lived by a flat stone slab, perhaps a boundary marker of some kind, Sp. *losa* (of pre-Roman origin, probably Celt.; cf. Gael. *leac*, W *llech*).

Cogn.: Cat.: **Llosa**.

Losada Spanish: topographic name for someone who lived by an area paved with flagstones, Sp. *losada* (from *losar* to pave, a deriv. of LOSA).

Lothian Scots: regional name from the region in SE central Scotland. This is very ancient and is of unknown origin.

Vars.: **Lowthian**, **Louthean**, LOWDEN.

Lott English: from a medieval given name introduced by the Normans, of uncertain origin. It may be the Hebr. personal name *Lot* 'Covering', which was relatively popular in N France, or an aphetic form of various names formed with the dim. suffix *-lot* (originally a combination of *-el* + *-ot*).

Var.: **Lotte**.

Patr.: **Lots**.

Loud English: 1. nickname for a noisy person, from ME *lude* loud (OE *hlūd*), perhaps in part preserving the OE byname *Hlūda* that Ekwall postulates to explain the place-names *Loudham* (Suffolk) and *Lowdham* (Notts.).

2. topographic name for someone who lived by a roaring stream, OE **hlȳde*, or habitation name from any of the places named from this word, e.g. *Lyde* in Hereford and Somerset.

3. habitation name from *Louth* in Lincs., so called from its position on the river *Lud* (OE *Hlūde* 'Loud').

Var.: **Lowde**.

Loughnane Irish: Anglicized form of Gael. **Ó Lachtnáin** 'descendant of *Lachtnán*', a personal name from *lachtna* grey.

Vars.: **O'Lo(u)ghnane**, **O'Loughnan**, **O'Laghnane**, **Lough(nan)**, **Laughnan**.

Loughrey Irish: Anglicized form of Gael. **Ó Luachra** 'descendant of *Luachra*', a personal name derived from *luachair* rushes, sedges.

Vars.: **Loughry**, **Lockery**, **O'Lucry**, **O'Logher**; RUSH.

Dims.: **O'Lucherin**, **O'Loghrane**, **O'Loughran**, **Lough(e)ran**, **Loughren**, **Laugheran**, **Lochrane**, **Loughrane**, **(O')Loran** (Gael. **Ó Luchaireáin**).

Louro Portuguese: nickname for someone with hair of a blonde or light chestnut colour, Port. *louro* (of uncertain etymology; in form it appears to be from L *laurus* laurel (see LAUR 1), but the semantic development is not clear).

Lovatt 1. English (chiefly Staffs.): nickname from ANF *lo(u)vet* wolfcub, young wolf (see LOW 3).

2. Scots: habitation name from *Lovat* near Beauly, in the former county of Inverness, which is from Gael. *lobh* rot, putrefy + *-ait* place.

Vars.: **Lovat**, **Lovett**, **Lovitt**.

Cogns. (of 1): Fr.: **Louvet**. Prov.: **Loubet**. Cat.: **Llobet**. It.: **Lupetti**, **Lobetti**.

Dims. (of 1): Fr..: **Louveton**, **Lovetot**.

Love 1. English: from a ME given name, from the OE female personal name *Lufu* 'Love', or the masc. equivalent *Lufa*. Cf. LEAF 1.

2. English and Scots: nickname from ANF *louve* female wolf (a fem. form of *lou*; cf. LOW 3). This nickname was fairly commonly used for men, in an approving sense. It may have been bestowed on a staunch soldier, with reference to the ferocity with which the she-wolf defends her young. No doubt it was reinforced by crossing with post-Conquest survivals of the masc. version of 1.

3. Irish: erroneous translation of MCKINNON.

Var.: **Luff**.

Cogns. (of 2): Fr.: **Louve**. Prov.: **Lloube**.

Dims. (of 1): Eng.: **Lovekin**, **Lufkin**.

Love is an ancient Kentish surname. A certain Reginald Love owned property around Rochester in the reign of Henry IV.

Loveday English: 1. from the ME female given name *Loveday*, OE *Lēofdæg*, composed of the elements *lēof* dear, beloved + *dæg* day.

2. nickname for someone who had some particular association with a 'loveday'. According to medieval custom this was a day set aside for the reconciliation of enemies and amicable settlement of disputes.

Lovegrove English: apparently a habitation name from an unidentified place named with the OE personal name *Lufa* (see LOVE 1) + OE *grāf* grove, thicket.

Lovelace English: 1. nickname for a philanderer, from ME *lufelesse* loveless, without love (OE *lufu-lēas*), probably in the sense 'fancy free'.

2. some early examples, such as Richard *Lovelas* (Kent 1344), may have as their second element ME *las(se)* girl, maiden (of disputed etymology); cf. TIPLADY.

Vars.: **Loveless**, **Lowles(s)**.

The current spelling is apparently the result of folk etymology, which, perhaps by a process of deliberate bowdlerization, understood the word as a nickname for a dandy fond of lace. *The mod. sense of this word is, however, not attested until the 16th cent. and at the time of surname formation it meant only 'cord', '(shoe)lace' (from OF* las, laz, *LL* lacius, *from class. L* laqueus *noose, snare). It is possible that in some cases the surname derives from ME* lovelas *a cord or belt given as a love token, but there is no evidence to support this suggestion.*

Lovell English: dim. of LOW 3, i.e. a nickname from ANF *lou* wolf (L *lupus*) + the dim. suffix *-el*.

Vars.: **Lovel**, **Lowell**.

Cogns.: Fr.: **Louvel**, **Louveau**. It.: **Lupelli**, **Lovelli**.

The surname Lovell *is found over most of S England, and includes a noble family established in Northants from the 13th to the 16th cent.*

Lowell is the surname of one of America's most distinguished New England families, which has been prominent for over 200 years. Its founder, John Lowell (1743–1802), was a legislator and judge. The town of Lowell, Mass., was named in honour of his son Francis Cabot Lowell (1775–1817).

Lovelock English: nickname for a dandy, from ME *love-lock*, a lock of hair, sometimes an artificial one, curling over the forehead or ears in a variety of fashionable styles.

Var.: **Loveluck**.

Lovely English: nickname for an amiable person, also perhaps sometimes given in an ironical sense, from ME *luvelich* (OE *luf(e)līc*). During the main period of surname formation the word was used in an active sense, 'loving', 'kind', 'affectionate', as well as the passive 'lovable', 'worthy of love'. The meaning 'attractive', 'beautiful' is not clearly attested before the 14th cent., and remained rare throughout the Middle Ages.

Lovick English (Norfolk): from the ME given name *Loveke*, OE *Lufeca*, a deriv. of *Lufa* (see LOVE 1).

Low 1. English: topographic name for someone who lived near a hill, from OE *hlāw* (see LAW 2; for the change of *-ā-* to *-ō-* in the Midland and Southern dialects of ME, cf. ROPER).

2. English: nickname for a short man, from ME *lāh* (ON *lágr*; the word was adopted first into the Northern dialects of ME, where Scand. influence was strong, and then spread south, with regular alteration of the vowel quality).

3. English (Norman): nickname for a crafty or dangerous person, from ANF *lou*, *leu* wolf (L *lupus*). Wolves were relatively common in Britain at the time when most surnames were formed, as there still existed large tracts of uncleared forest.

4. Scots: from a pet form of LAWRENCE; cf. LOWRY 1.

5. Jewish (Ashkenazic): Anglicized form of LÖWE 2.

Var.: **Lowe**.

Cogns. (of 3): Fr.: **Loup**, **Leu**; **Lelou(p)**, **Leleu(x)**. It.: **Lup(p)o**; **Lovo** (N Italy); **Luffi**. Sp., Port.: **Lobo**. Rum.: **Lupu(l)** (in part Jewish, translating WOLF).

Dims. (of 3): Eng.: LOVATT, LEVETT, LOVELL. Fr.: **Loupot**. Prov.: **Louvion**, **Louviot**; **Louvihoux** (Gascony). It.: **Lupi(ci)ni**, **Lup(p)ino**, **Lovini**, **Luvini**; **Lovotti**, **Luvotti**, **Lu(v)otto**; **Lup(p)oli**. Sp., Port.: **Lobato**.

Augs. (of 3): Prov.: **Loubat**. It.: **Lupone**.

Patrs. (from 3) It.: **Lup(p)is**. Rum.: **Lupesco**, **Lupescu** (in part Jewish, translating WOLF). (From 4): Sc.: **Lowson**.

Lowden English (chiefly Northumb.) and Scots: 1. var. of LOTHIAN.

2. habitation name from *Loudoun* near Cunningham in the former county of Ayrs., probably so called from Northern ME *low* flame, beacon (ON *loge*) + *doun* hill (see DOWN 1).

Vars.: **Lowdon**, **Louden**, **Loudon**.

Löwe 1. German: nickname for a brave or regal person, from Ger. *Löwe* lion (MHG *lēwe*, *louwe*, OHG *lēwo*, *louwo*; the word is probably borrowed from L (cf. LYON 1), although the phonetic development is not clear). In some cases the surname may have been originally a house name, from a house distinguished by the sign of a lion.

2. Jewish (Ashkenazic): from Ger. *Löwe* lion, translating the Yid. male given name *Leyb* (see LEIB), or, at least in some cases, chosen because of the association of the animal with the tribe of Judah; in the blessing of Jacob (Gen. 49: 9) Judah is likened to a lion's whelp. There has also been considerable confusion with LEVI, especially among the cpds.

Vars. (of 1): **Löw**; **Leeb** (S Germany); **Löb(e)** (Alsace).

Cogns. (of 1): Low Ger.: **Lau(e)**, **Leu(e)**. Flem., Du.: **(De) Leeuw**, **Louw**. Czech: **Lev**.

Patrs. (of 2): **Lowensohn**, **Lovenzon**.

Cpds (of 2; purely ornamental or, in some cases, ornamental elaborations associated with the given name *Leyb*): **Löwenberg** ('lion hill'; **Leuvenberg** among Dutch Jews); **Lowenhar** ('lion hair', i.e. 'mane'); **Levenherz** ('lion heart'); **Lowenstark** ('strong as a lion'); **Löwenstein**, **Levenstein** ('lion stone', Anglicized LIVINGSTONE); **Löwenthal**, **Leventhal** ('lion valley').

Lown English: 1. from the ME given name *Lovin*, OE *Lēofhūn*, composed of the elements *lēof* dear, beloved + *hūn* bear cub.

2. habitation name from the city of *Louvain* in Belgium (Flem. *Leuven*).

Var.: **Loven**.

Patrs. (from 1): **Lown(e)s**, **Lowndes**; **Loynes** (Norfolk).

Lowry 1. N English and Scots: dim. of LAWRENCE.

2. Irish: Anglicized form of Gael. *Ó Labhradha*; see LAVERY.

Vars.: **Lowery**, **Lowrey**, **Low(e)rie**, **Lor(r)ie**, **Lo(u)ry**, **Lourie**. (Of 2 only): **O'Lowry**, **O'Lawry**.

Patrs. (from 1): **Lowries**, **Lowri(e)son**, **Lorrison**.

'Servant of L. 1': **Lorriman**.

Lowther English: habitation name from a place in Cumb., so called from the river on which it stands. The name is of obscure etymology, perhaps of Brit. origin and equivalent to LAUDER, or from ON *lauðr* froth, foam + *á* river.

This is the surname of the English family who hold the earldom of Lonsdale. They trace their descent from Hugh Lowther *of Westmorland, Attorney General to Edward I in 1292. Hugh Cecil Lowther, 5th Earl of Lonsdale (1857–1944), was a noted sportsman who founded the Lonsdale Belt, a British boxing trophy, in 1909.*

Lowton English: habitation name from a place in Lancs., so called from OE *hlāw* hill + *tūn* settlement, enclosure; cf. LAWTON.

Loyola Spanish form of Basque **Loiola**: habitation name from a place in the province of Guipúzcoa, so called from Basque *loi* mud + the local suffix *-ola*.

Iñigo de Loyola *(1491–1556), founder of the Society of Jesus, was a Spanish nobleman, born on the estate owned by his family at Loyola.*

Lozano Spanish: nickname for an elegant or haughty person, from OSp. *loçano* splendid, later 'good-looking' (LL *lautiānus*, from class. L *lautus*, *lavātus*, originally the past part. of *lavāre* to wash).

Lübbe Low German: short form of the given names LEOPOLD and LUBRECHT.

Var.: **Luppe**.

Dim.: **Lübke**.

Patrs.: **Lübben**, **Lübbing**.

Patrs. (from dims.): **Lübken**, **Lübking**.

Lubbock English: habitation name from the port of *Lübeck* in NW Germany, or nickname for a merchant who had professional connections with the place. Lübeck was a major commercial centre of the Hanseatic League in the Middle Ages. Its name derives from Wendish *Liubice* 'lovely' (cf. LIEB 3).

Lubrecht German: from a Gmc personal name composed of the elements *liut* people, tribe + *berht* bright, famous.

Vars.: **Lubrich(t)**, **Leiprecht**, **Leuprecht**.

Cogn.: Low Ger.: **Lübbert**.

Patrs.: Low Ger.: **Lübbers**, **Lüppertz**, **Lüber(d)ing**.

Lucas English, French, Spanish, Portuguese, and Flemish/Dutch: from the given name *Lucas*, a L form of Gk *Loucas* 'man from *Lucania*'. Lucania was a region of S Italy that was perhaps originally named in an Italic dialect with a word meaning 'bright', 'shining' (cf. Lúcio). The name owed its popularity in the Middle Ages to St Luke the Evangelist.

Vars.: Eng.: **Luke, Luck** (the medieval vernacular forms); **Look,** Lock (N England and Scotland); **Lugg** (Devon). Fr.: **Luc.** Flem., Du.: **Lukas.**

Cogns.: It.: **Luca,** Lucca, **Luc(c)hi, Lucco.** Cat.: **Lluch.** Low Ger.: **Lucks, Lauks, L(a)ux.** Ger. (of Slav. origin): **Luk(e)sch.** Czech: **Lukáš, Lukeš; Káš.** Pol.: **Łukasz, Łukoś; Łuczak.** Ukr.: **Lukash.** Hung.: **Lukács** (partly Jewish, in which case it is an adoption of the Hung. name).

Dims.: Eng.: **Luckett; Locket(t), Lockitt** (N England); **Lockie, Lockey** (Scotland). Fr.: **Lucazeau; Luquet, Lucot.** Prov.: **Lugol.** It.: **Luc(c)helli, Luc(c)hetti, Luc(c)hini, Lucotti.** Low Ger.: **Lauxmann.** Ger. (of Slav. origin): **Lukaschek, Kaschke.** Czech: **Luášek; Kašek, Kašík.** Pol.: **Łukasik, Łulka.** Ukr.: **Lukashenko.** Beloruss.: **Lukashenya.**

Aug.: It.: **Luconi.** Czech: **Kašák.**

Pej.: Fr.: **Lucaud.**

Patrs.: Eng.: **Luckes, Looks, Loukes.** Sc.: **McLucas, McLuga(i)sh, McLugish** (Gael. **Mac Lucais**). Manx: **Clucas.** It.: **De Luca, Di Lucca.** Low Ger.: **Lukasen, Luxen.** Du.: **Lucassen.** Russ.: **Lukin(ov).** Ukr.: **Lukashevich.** Pol.: **Łukaszewicz, Łukasiewicz, Łukowicz.** Croatian: **Luk(ov)ić, Lukač.** Bulg.: **Lukanov.**

Patrs. (from dims.): Sc.: **McLu(c)kie, McLucky.** Russ.: **Lukashev, Lukonin, Lukichyov, Lukinykh.** Pol.: **Łukaszkiewicz, Łuczkiewicz.** Croatian: **Lučić.**

'Servant of L.': Eng.: **Lukeman, Luckman.**

Habitation names: Pol.: **Łukaszewski, Łukowski.**

A family called Lockett *have been established in Ches. for over 600 years. Henry* Loket, *named in a deed dated 1348, held land in Withington, and since the 16th cent. the family has held land at Sweltenham.*

Lucca Italian: 1. cogn. of Lucas.

2. habitation name from the Tuscan city of *Lucca*, or from a smaller place of the same name in Sicily. Both appear to have been originally named with a Celt. element meaning 'marshy'.

Vars. (of 2): **Lucches(in)i** (Tuscany); **Lucchese** (Sicily).

Lucena Spanish: habitation name from any of various places, especially in Andalusia, so called from LL *Lūciēna (villa)* 'estate of *Lūcius*' (see Lúcio).

Lucey 1. English and Irish (Norman), and French: habitation name from any of various places in Normandy and N France originally named with the L personal name *Lūcius* (see Lúcio) + the local suffix *-ācum*.

2. English: from the medieval female given name *Lucie* (L *Lūcia*, a fem. form of *Lūcius*). The name was borne by a young Sicilian maiden and an aged Roman widow, both martyred under Diocletian and venerated as saints.

3. Irish: Anglicized form of Gael. **Ó Luasaigh**, an altered form of *Mac Cluasaigh* 'son of *Cluasach*', a byname originally denoting someone with large ears (from *cluas* ear).

Vars.: **Lucy.** (Of 2 only): Eng.: **Luce** (the normal medieval vernacular form); **Lucia** (Latinized).

Cogns. (of 2): Fr.: **Luce.** It.: **Lucia.**

Dims. (of 2): Fr.: **Lucet(te).**

Metr. (from 2): It.: **De Lucia.**

A powerful Anglo-Norman family called Lucy *took their name from* Lucé *in Orne, Normandy. Richard* de Lucy *(d. 1179) was a baron and chief justiciary of England. He fought in Normandy and commanded the castle of Falaise, returning to England in 1140. His son Godfrey de Lucy (d. 1204) became bishop of Winchester in 1189.*

Lucien French: from a given name (L *Luciānus*, a deriv. of *Lucius*; see Lúcio), borne by a number of minor early Christian martyrs.

Cogns.: Prov.: **Lucian.** It.: **Lucian(i), Luciano.** Sp.: **Luján.** Patrs.: Russ.: **Lukianov.** Ukr.: **Lukianovich.**

Lúcio Portuguese: from a medieval given name (L *Lūcius*, an ancient Roman personal name probably derived from *lux* light, gen. *lūcis*). The name was borne by a large number of early Christian saints, and was accordingly moderately popular in the Middle Ages.

Luckhurst English: of uncertain origin. It is found principally in Kent and may be a habitation name from a place in the parish of Mayfield, Sussex, recorded in 1553 as *Lukkars Croche*. The first part of this seems to be from a family name recorded in 1296 as *Luggere*; the second is ME *croche* cross. The etymology of *Lukkar* or *Luggere* is unknown. If this is really the source of the surname, it has been altered fairly radically by folk etymology, to assimilate to the common placename element Hurst.

Var.: **Lukehurst.**

Lucraft English: habitation name from *Luckcroft* in Ashwater, Devon, named with OE *loca* enclosure (see Lock 2) + *croft* paddock (see Croft).

Var.: **Luckraft.**

The earliest known bearer of the name was Richard de Loccroft *of Ashwater, Devon, recorded in 1332. William and Richard* Lowcrofte *and John* Lowcroffthe *appear in the 1524 Lay Subsidy for Devon, at Harberton and Exeter respectively. The form* Luckraft *first occurs some 30 years later at Stoke Gabriel.*

Ludlow English: habitation name from a place in Shrops., so called from the OE river name *Hlūde* (from *hlūd* loud, roaring) + *hlāw* hill (see Law 2 and Low 1). See also Laidlaw.

Luger 1. German: habitation name from any of the minor places in Germany named from MHG *luoc* hiding place, ambush (from OHG *luogen* to watch, (lie in) wait; cf. OE *lōcian* to look). *Lueg* is a common placename in the Tyrol, and the surname is particularly frequent in Bavaria and Austria.

2. Jewish (Ashkenazic): of uncertain origin, perhaps a derogatory name from mod. Ger. *Lüger* liar, imposed by anti-Semitic government officials in 18th- and 19th-cent. central Europe.

Vars. (of 1): **Lugert; Lueger.**

Lugo Spanish: habitation name from a city in Galicia. This was a Roman settlement under the name of *Lucus Augusti* 'grove, wood of Augustus', but that may have been no more than an adaptation of an earlier name derived from that of the Celt. god *Lugos*.

Luker English: 1. habitation name from *Lucker* in Northumb., so called from ON *ló* sandpiper + *kiarr* marsh, wetland (see Kerr).

2. occupational name for someone who had to watch or look after something, as for example a watchman or a keeper of animals, from ME *luk(en)* to look (OE *lōcian*).

Vars.: **Lo(o)ker.**

Lukov 1. Jewish (Ashkenazic): habitation name from *Lüchow* in Lower Saxony.

2. Russian: patr. from the nickname *Luk* 'Onion' (an early borrowing from a Gmc cogn. of mod. Eng. *leek*), perhaps given originally to a market gardener.

3. Russian: patr. from the nickname *Luk* 'Bow', bestowed on a skilled archer or perhaps on someone with a deformed spine.

Vars. (of 1): **Lukof(f)**, **Luckoff**; **Likoff** (from a S Yid. form of the name); **Lukovsky**, **Lukowsky**.

Cogn. (of 1): Pol. **Lukowski**.

Lumb English: habitation name from places so called in Lancs. and W Yorks., both apparently originally named with OE **lum(m)* pool. The word is not independently attested, but appears also in LOMAX and LUMLEY, and may be reflected in the dial. term *lum* denoting a well for collecting water in a mine. The vars. preserving traces of inflected forms suggest that the surname derives also in part directly from this term used as a vocab. word in the Middle Ages.

Vars.: **Lum**, **Loom**, **Limb**; **Lo(o)mbe**, **Loomes**.

Lumbreras Spanish: metonymic occupational name for a maker of lamps, from the pl. of Sp. *lumbrera* lamp (OSp. *lumnera*, from L *lūmināria*, a deriv. (originally neut. pl. but later taken as fem. sing.) of *lūmen*, gen. *lūminis*, light).

Lumby English (Yorks.): habitation name from a place between Leeds and Selby (now in Humberside), so called from ON *lundr* grove, wood (see LUND) + *býr* farm, settlement.

Lumley N English: habitation name from a place in Co. Durham, so called from OE **lum(m)* pool (see LUMB) + *lēah* wood, clearing.

Var.: **Lumbley**.

This is the surname of a noble English family, who according to tradition are descended from a certain Li(g)ulf, who lost his estates in Northumb. at the time of the Conquest. The surname is first recorded in the 12th cent., when Robert de Lumeleye *witnessed a charter.*

Lumsden Scots: habitation name from a place in the parish of Coldingham, Berwicks. The first element of the placename is of uncertain origin, apparently the gen. case of a personal name; the second is probably OE *denu* valley (see DEAN 1).

Var.: **Lumsdaine**.

Luna Spanish (Aragon) and Jewish (Sefardic): As a Spanish name, a topographic name for someone who lived by an open courtyard, from the Aragonese dial. term *luna* (L *lūmina*, pl. of *lūmen* light); in part it may be a habitation name from a place so called in the province of Saragossa in Aragon. As a Jewish name, its origin is not clear.

Luňák Czech: nickname meaning 'Hawk'.

Lund English, Swedish, and Danish/Norwegian: topographic name for someone who lived in a grove, ON *lundr*; the word was adopted into the Northern dials. of ME and also into ONF. There are a number of places in England named with this word, as for example *Lund* in Lancs. and E and W Yorks., *Lunt* in Lancs., and *Lound* in Lincs., Notts., and Suffolk, and the surname may also derive from any of these. When surnames became obligatory in Sweden in the 19th cent., this was one of the most popular among the many terms denoting features of the natural landscape which were adopted as surnames, usually compounded with some other such term.

Vars.: Eng.: **Lunt** (chiefly Liverpool), **Lunn**. Swed.: **Lundh**, **Lundell**, **Lundén**, **Lundin**, **Lundman**.

Cogns.: Fr.: **Lond(ais)**; **Lalonde** (a frequent placename in Normandy).

Cpds (ornamental): Swed.: **Lundbäck** ('grove stream'); **Lundberg**, **Lundebergh** ('grove hill'); **Lundblad(h)** ('grove leaf'); **Lundbo(h)m** ('grove tree'); **Lundborg** ('grove town'); **Lundahl** ('grove valley'); **Lund(e)gren** ('grove branch'); **Lundholm** ('grove island'); **Lundkvist**, **Lund(e)qvist** ('grove twig'); **Lundmark** ('grove land'); **Lundstedt** ('grove homestead'); **Lundström** ('grove river'); **Lundwall**, **Lundvall** ('grove bank').

Lundy Scots and N Irish: habitation name from any of several places called *Lundie*, for example one near Doune in the former county of Perths. These derive their names from Gael. **lunnd* marsh.

Var.: **Lundie**.

Lupton English: habitation name from a place in the former county of Westmorland, now part of Cumb. The placename is recorded in Domesday Book as *Lupetun*, and probably derives from an OE personal name **Hluppa* (of uncertain origin) + OE *tūn* enclosure, settlement.

The first known bearer of this surname is a certain Adam, son of Guy de Luppton, *who in 1166 was killed in a pole fight, leaving goods worth sixpence. Roger* Lupton *(1456–1540) was the founder of Sedbergh School. The name was brought to America by John Lupton, who sailed from Gravesend on the* Primrose *in 1635, and is recorded in Virginia three years later. On 24 Oct. 1635 Davie Lupton set off on the* Constance *bound for Virginia, but there is no record of his arrival in the New World. One Christopher Lupton was recorded in Suffolk County, Long Island, New York, c.1635, and a large number of Luptons in N Carolina descend from him. An American family of the name settled in the area of Winchester, Virginia, in the mid-18th cent.; they can be traced back to Martin Lupton, who was married in 1630 in the parish of Rothwell, Yorks.*

Luria Jewish (Sefardic and Ashkenazic): of uncertain origin, possibly a habitation name from *Luria* in the province of Treviso, Italy, or *Loria* near Bassano, Italy.

Vars.: **Luriah**, **Lurie**, **Lurya**, **Lurye**, **Loria**, **Lorie**; **Lurja**, **Lurje** (Pol. spellings); **Louria**, **Lourié** (Fr. spellings).

Luscombe English (Devon): habitation name from any of the five villages of this name in Devon, all probably so called from OE *hlōse* pigsty + *cumb* valley (see COOMBE).

Lustgarten Jewish (Ashkenazic): from mod. Ger. *Lustgarten* pleasure garden (a cpd of *Lust* enjoyment, pleasure (cf. LUSTIG) + *Garten* garden), presumably a reference to the Garden of Eden.

Lustig German and Jewish (Ashkenazic): nickname for a person of a cheerful disposition, from Ger. *lustig* merry, carefree (MHG *lustig*, a deriv. of *lust* enjoyment, pleasure).

Vars.: Ger.: **Lust**, **Lüstel**. Jewish: **Lustik**, **Lustig(i)er**, **Lust(ig)man**.

Cogn.: Eng.: **Lusty** (chiefly N Ireland).

Luther 1. German: var. of LEUTHER.

2. English: occupational name for a player on the lute, ME, OF *luthier* (from OF *lut*, via OProv. from Arabic *al ʿūd* 'the wood').

Vars. (of 2): Eng.: **Lut(t)er**.

Cogns. (of 2): Fr.: **Lut(h)ier**, **Luten(i)er**; **Lut(e)rand**. It.: **Lautero**. Ger.: **Laute**; **Lautenschlager**, **Lautenschläger**, **Laudenslayer**.

Luton English: habitation name from the town in Beds. (which derives its name from the river *Lea* + OE *tūn* enclosure, settlement) or, more plausibly in view of the pattern of distribution, from *Luton* in Devon (near Teignmouth), so called from the OE female personal name *Lēofgifu* (composed of the elements *lēof* dear, beloved + *gifu* gift) + *tūn*. A further possible source of the name is *Luton* in Kent, named as the 'settlement (OE *tūn*) associated with *Lēofa*'.

Lutt English: from a medieval given name which probably preserves an OE byname **Lutt*(*a*), derived from *lȳt* small (see LIGHT 3).

Dim.: **Lutkin** (E Anglia).

Lutton English (now found mainly in N Ireland): habitation name from any of the various places so called—in Northants, Devon, Lincs., and elsewhere. The one in Northants is OE *Ludingtūn* 'settlement associated with *Luda*', a personal name of uncertain origin; that in Cornwood, Devon, is OE *Ludantūn* 'Luda's settlement'; that in Lincs is 'pool settlement', from OE *luh* pool (a borrowing from W *llwch*) + *tūn*. *Lutton* in Yorks. is 'settlement on the river *Hlūde*' (see LOUD).

Luttrell English (Norman): nickname from the otter or metonymic occupational name for a hunter of otters (for their pelts), from a dim. form of OF *loutre* otter (L *lutra*).

Cogns.: Fr.: **Loutrel, Leloutrel.**

Geoffrey Luttrell *is named in a deed concerning land at Gamston, Notts., in the 12th cent.; he is also known to have taken part in a rebellion against Richard I. His son Sir Andrew Luttrell was Sheriff of Lincs. in 1251. The manor of East Quantoxhead, NW of Taunton, has been held since 1207 by the Luttrells. Dunster Castle, Somerset, was acquired by Sir Hugh Luttrell in 1404 and remains in the family's possession.*

An Irish family of this name were granted the title Earl of Carhampton in 1785. They had been established in Luttrellstown, Co. Dublin, since the 15th cent. Carhampton is the name of a manor possessed by the Luttrells of Dunster Castle in Somerset. The exact link between the Irish and English families is not clear.

Lutwyche English (W Midlands): habitation name from a place in Shrops., the second element of which is OE *wīc* outlying village (see WICK). According to Ekwall, the first element is from an OE word **lōt*, 'no doubt identical with Du. *loete*, LG *lōte*, a shovel used to remove mud from ditches and canals'.

Luxford English: habitation name from an unidentified place, no doubt named as the FORD belonging to a bearer of the given name or surname *Luke*, *Luck* (see LUCAS).

Luxmoore English (Devon): habitation name from an unidentified place, probably in Devon, recorded in medieval documents as *Lukesmore*, and apparently derived from the gen. case of the given name *Luke*, *Luck* (see LUCAS) + ME *more* marsh, fen (see MOORE 1).

Var.: **Luxmore.**

A family of this name trace their descent from Jordan de Lukesmore, *named in manor rolls in 1296.*

Luxton English: habitation name from a minor place, probably one of two in Devon, so called from the gen. case of the ME given name *Luke*, *Luck* (see LUCAS) + ME *tune*, *tone* settlement (OE *tūn*).

Luz 1. Portuguese: religious byname from a title of the Virgin Mary, *Maria da Luz* 'Mary of Light' (from L *lux*, gen. *lūcis*).

2. Jewish (Israeli): ornamental name from Hebr. *luz* almond, usually if not always a Hebraicization of MANDEL 3.

Luzak Polish: nickname meaning 'Loose Horse', i.e. one not harnessed but led behind the waggon as a spare. It may have been bestowed on someone who was not felt to be doing his fair share of a job of work.

Luzzatto Italian and Jewish (Sefardic): regional name for someone from *Lusatia* (Ger. *Lausitz*), the region between the Elbe in Germany and the Oder in W Poland.

Vars.: **Luzzato, Luzzat(t)i, Lussato.**

Cogns.: Ger.: **(von) Lausitz.**

Lvov Russian: patr. from the name *Lev* (gen. *Lva*) 'Lion' (an early borrowing from Gmc; cf. LÖWE). This word may occasionally have been used as a nickname for a fierce or brave fighter, but normally it was taken as a vernacular equivalent of the given name *Leōn* (see LYON 2).

Dims.: Russ.: **Levkov, Lyov(ysh)kin, Levshukov, Levykin, Levashov, Lyovshin, Levoshin, Levishchev.** Ukr.: **Levchenko** (not patr.). Beloruss.: **Levashenya** (not patr.); **Levanovich** (patr.).

Lwówski Polish and Jewish (E Ashkenazic): habitation name from *Lwów*, the Polish name of the city known in Russ. as *Lvov*, in Ukr. as *Lviv*, and in Ger. as *Lemberg*. It is now in the Ukraine and so part of the Soviet Union, but was for long a major centre of Polish culture.

Vars.: Jewish: **Lwowsky, Lvovski, Lvovsky.**

Lyal Scots: probably from an ON personal name *Liulfr*, composed of an uncertain first element + *úlfr* wolf, although Reaney gives this as a dim. of *Lyon* or *Lionel*.

Vars.: **Lyall, Lyel(l).**

Lynch 1. Irish: Anglicized form of **Ó Loingsigh** 'descendant of *Loingseach*', a personal name (originally a byname) meaning 'Mariner' (from *long* ship; cf. LANGAN).

2. Irish (Anglo-Norman): Anglicized form of Gael. **Linseach**, itself a Gaelicized form of ANF *de Lench*, the version found in old records. This would appear to be a local name, but its origin is unknown. One family of bearers of this name were of Norman origin, but became one of the most important tribes of Galway.

3. English: topographic name for someone who lived on a slope or hillside, OE *hlinc*, or perhaps a habitation name from *Lynch* in Somerset or *Linch* in Sussex, both of which are named with this word.

Vars. (of 1): **(O')Lynchy, O'Lynche, O'Lensie, Linch(e)y,** LINDSAY. (Of 2): **Linch, Lince,** LINK, **Linck.**

Dims. (of 1): **O'Lyneseghane, Lynchaha(u)n, Lynchehan** (Gael. **Ó Loingseacháin**).

The Irish family of Lynch *includes a branch which emigrated to America, one of whom, Thomas (1749–79), was one of the signatories of the Declaration of Independence. The name passed into the English language through General Charles Lynch (1736–96), whose arbitrary and cruel administration of justice in Virginia became known as 'Lynch law'.*

Lyndon English (Midlands): habitation name from a place in Leics. (formerly Rutland), so called from OE *lind* lime tree (cf. LINDE and LINE 1) + *dūn* hill (see DOWN 1).

Lyne 1. English: var. of LINE.

2. Irish: var. of LANE.

3. Scots: habitation name from a place in the former county of Peebles., so called from Gael. *linne* pool, stream.

Var. (of 3): LYNN.

Lyneham 1. English: habitation name from places in Devon, Oxon., and Wilts., all so called from OE *līn* flax + *hām* homestead or *hamm* water meadow.

2. Irish: Anglicized form of Gael. **Ó Laidhghneáin** 'descendant of *Laidhghneán*', a personal name that occurs in OIr. genealogies. It is of uncertain origin, perhaps a dim. of *ladhgh* snow and meaning 'Snowflake'.

Vars.: **Lineham, Lyn(h)am.** (Of 2 only): **Linehan.**

Lynn 1. Scots: var. of LYNE 3.

2. Irish: Anglicized form of Gael. *Mac Fhloinn* and *Ó Fhloinn*; see FLYNN.

3. English: habitation name from any of the various places so called in Norfolk, in particular King's *Lynn*, an important centre of the medieval wool trade. The placename is probably from a Brit. word, an ancestor of W *llyn* lake.

4. Jewish: Anglicization of the Ashkenazic surname **Lin(n)**, which is of unknown origin.

Vars.: **Lynne, Linn, Lenn.**

This surname is common in N Ireland (derivs. 1 and 2) and also in Northumb. (deriv. 1) and Yorks. (deriv. 3, probably brought by workers in the wool trade).

Lyokhin Russian: one of a group of patrs. from dims. of the given name *Aleksei* (see ALEXIS).

Vars.: **Lyoshin; Lyalin, Lyal(ya)kin, Lyalikov, Lyakin, Lya(ki)shev, Lyashutin; Leksin.**

Cogn.: Croatian: **Lek(ov)ić.**

Lyon 1. English and French: nickname for a fierce or brave warrior, from OF, ME *lion* (L *leo*, gen. *leōnis*).

2. English and French: from the name *Leo(n)* (from L *leo* lion, or the cogn. Gk *leōn*), borne by numerous early martyrs and thirteen popes. On the Continent the given name was relatively popular because of the numerous saints who bore it, and also because the lion was the symbol of the evangelist St Mark. In England, however, it was rare throughout the Middle Ages.

3. English and French: habitation name from the town of *Lyon* in central France (sometimes known in mod. Eng. as *Lyons*), or from the smaller *Lyons*(-la-Forêt) in Eure, Normandy. The name of the former place is recorded in the 1st cent. BC as *Lugdunum*, apparently from Gaul. elements meaning 'raven', 'crow' + 'hill', 'fort'.

4. Irish: Anglicized form of Gael. *Ó Laighin*; see LANE 2.

Vars. (of 1–3): Eng.: **Lion, Leon.** Fr.: **Lion, Léon.** (Of 3 only): Eng.: **Lyons.** Fr.: **Lions, Lyonnais.**

Cogns. (of 1 and 2): It.: **Leoni, Leon(e), Lion(e); Liuni, Leo, Lio** (S Italy). Sp.: LEÓN. Cat.: **Lleó.** Port.: **Leão.** (The forms *Lion* and *Leon(i)* are also borne by Jews.)

Dims. (of 1 and 2): Fr.: **Lyonnel, Lion(n)el; Lyonnet, Lion(n)et.** It.: **Leonelli, Leonello, Lionelli, Lionello; Leonetti, Leonetto, Leonotti.**

Patrs. (from 1 and 2): Fr.: **Delion.** It.: **De Leone, Di Lione; De Leonibus** (Latinized); **De Leo, Di Leo; Leoneschi.**

The family name of the Lords of Glamis and Earls of Kinghorne and Strathmore is Lyon. *Sir John Lyon was chamberlain of Scotland 1377–82 and was granted land at Glamis by Robert II. His descendant Patrick Lyon (1575–1615) was created Earl of Kinghorne in 1606, and the designation of the title was changed to Kinghorne and Strathmore by the 3rd Earl in 1677.*

Lysaght Irish: Anglicized form of Gael. **Mac Giolla Iasachta** 'son of the servant of the foreigner', from *iasachta* strange, foreign.

Vars.: **Lysa(ch)t; McLysaght; McGillesachta, McGillisachia, McGillysachtie.**

Lysenko Ukrainian: 1. nickname from a dim. of *lys* fox (cf. LIS).

2. nickname from a dim. of the adj. *lysy* bald (cf. ŁYSIAK).

Łysiak Polish: nickname for a man with a bald pate, from Pol. *łysy* bald + *-iak* noun suffix.

Cogns.: Czech: **Lisý, Lysý; Lis(a).**

Dims.: Pol.: **Łysek.** Beloruss.: **Lysyononok.** Ukr.: LYSENKO.

Lythe English: 1. topographic name for someone who lived on a hillside, from OE *hlið*, ON *hlíð* slope.

2. nickname for a mild or gentle person, from ME *lithe* mild (OE *līðe*).

Lyubimov Russian: patr. from the nickname *Lyubimy* 'Dear', 'Beloved' (from the root *lyub-* love; cf. LIEB 3).

M

Maas Low German and Dutch: 1. aphetic form of THOMAS.

2. topographic name for someone living on the banks of the river *Maas*, which flows through Belgium and Holland. It was originally named as the *Mosa*, a name of apparently Celto-Ligurian origin and uncertain meaning.

Vars. (of 1): MAS, **Ma(a)ss**. (Of 2): **Vermaas**.

Cogns. (of 1): It.: **Masi, Maso**.

Dims. (of 1): Low Ger.: **Massmann, Maascke**. Ger. (of Slav. origin): **Mas(ch)ek, Mas(ch)ke**. Fr.: **Masset, Massin(ot)**, MASSON, **Mass(ic)ot, Massiquot, Massoud**. It.: **Mas(s)ini, Masin(o), Masolini, Maselli, Mas(i)ello, Mas(s)etti, Masetto, Masotti, Masutti, Masutto, Masuzzo, Masucci(o), Masolo, Masullo, Massuli**.

Patrs. (from 1): Low Ger.: **Maasen, Massen(s)**. Flem.: **Maesen**. It.: **Masellis**. Lithuanian: **Masionis**.

Mabb English: from the medieval female given name *Mab(be)*, a short form of ME, OF *Amabel* (from L *amābilis* loveable). This has survived into the 20th cent. in the aphetic form *Mabel*.

Var.: **Mapp**.

Dims.: **Mabbot, Mabbett, Mabbutt**.

Metrs.: **Mabbs, Mabson; Mobbs** (Norfolk).

Mabon 1. Scots: from the medieval given name *Maban*, *Mabon*, which according to Black is cogn. with W *Mabon*, and represents Brit. *Maponos* 'Great Son'. On the other hand the given name could possibly be a dim. of ME *Mab(be)* (see MABB).

2. Jewish: a name borne by French Jews, of unknown origin.

Vars. (of 1): **Maben, Maybin**.

Mac- For Scots and Irish names beginning thus, see Mc-.

Macaire French: from the OF given name *Macaire*, Gk *Makarios* (from *makar* fortunate, blessed) borne by two obscure 4th-cent. Egyptian saints.

Var.: **Maquaire**.

Cogns.: Ger.: **Karius, Karies, Karges** (aphetic forms). Czech: **Maxa**. Ukr.: **Makarenko, Makarushka** (dims.).

Patrs.: Ger.: **Kahrs**. Pol.: **Makarewicz**. Russ.: **Makarov, Makaryev**. Georgian: **Makaradze**. Armenian: **Markarian**.

Patrs. (from dims.): Russ.: **Makarochkin, Makarytsev**. Ukr.: **Makarishin**.

'Son of the wife of M.': Russ.: **Makarikhin**.

Macaluso Italian: status name for a freed serf, from the Sicilian dial. term *macalusciu*, *macaluggiu* freedman (Arabic *maḫlūǧ*, a deriv. of *ḫalaǧa* to free, liberate).

Mace English: from a medieval given name. This was probably originally of Gmc derivation, representing OE *Mæssa* (cf. MASSINGHAM) or the cogn. OHG *Mas(s)o*, but during the Middle Ages it came to be taken as a pet form of MATTHEW.

Var.: **Masse**.

Mach 1. Czech, Polish, and German (of Slav. origin): from the given name *Mach*, a pet form of Czech *Matěj*, Pol. *Maciej*, etc. (see MATTHEW). The Czech name is also a pet form of other names beginning with *Ma-*, e.g. *Marek* (see MARK) and MARTIN.

2. Jewish (Ashkenazic): of unknown origin.

Vars. (of 1): Czech: **Mácha, Máchač, Máchal(a), Macháň, Machoň**. Pol.: **Machała, Machnicki, Machocki**. Ger.: **Mache, Macha**.

Dims.: Czech: **Macháček, Machálek, Machek, Machotka**.

Ernst Mach *(1863–1916), the Austrian physicist who gave his name to the system of speed measurement which uses Mach numbers, was born in Moravia.*

Machado Spanish and Portuguese: metonymic occupational name for a maker, seller, or user of a hatchet, Sp., Port. *machado* (a deriv. of MACHO 2). In part it may also be a habitation name from a place in the province of Lugo, Spain, but alternatively the placename may be derived from the surname rather than the other way about.

Macherzyński Polish: offensive nickname for a man of weak character, from Pol. dial. *macherzyna* bladder, scrotum.

Machiavelli Italian: nickname for a notorious philanderer, from It. *malo* bad (see MALO) + *chiavello* nail, spike (LL *clavellus*, a dim. of class. L *clavus*), also used of the penis. The surname is first recorded in Genoa in 1148 in the Latinized form *Malclavellus* and is found at Savona in the 14th cent. as *Malusclavus*. Today the surname is principally confined to Liguria, Emilia, and Tuscany.

Vars.: **Macchiavelli, Ma(c)chiavello**.

The political philosopher Niccolò Machiavelli *(1469–1527) was from a wealthy and influential family established in Florence since the 13th cent. His father, a lawyer, was from a relatively poor branch of the family. In 1393 his great-great-grandfather had been granted the castle of Montespertoli near Florence, and his father still owned land nearby.*

Machin English: occupational name for a stonemason, ANF *machun* (a Norman var. of OF *masson*; see MASON).

Vars.: **Machon, Machen(t), Meachin, Meachen, Meachem, Meacham, Meecham**.

Macho Spanish: 1. nickname for a virile, bold man, from Sp. *macho* male (L *masculus*; cf. MALE).

2. nickname for a forceful person or metonymic occupational name for a smith, from Sp. *macho* sledgehammer (probably from LL *marculus* hammer (cf. MARTEL), crossed with Sp. MAZA).

Mack 1. Scots (Berwicks.): from the ON personal name *Makkr*, a form of MAGNUS.

2. Chiefly U.S.: simplified form of any of the various Scots and Irish names beginning *Mc-*.

Var. (of 1): **Maccus**.

Mackworth English: habitation name from a place in Derbys., so called from the OE personal name **Macca* (of uncertain origin) + OE *worð* enclosure (see WORTH).

A family of this name can be traced to Mackworth in Derbys., where they also held the manor of Ash (Eisse) *in 1385.*

Maclehose Scots: Anglicized form of Gael. **Mac Gille Thamais** 'son of the servant of (St) THOMAS'.

Mączyński Polish: habitation name from a place named with Pol. *mąka* flour + *-yn* possessive suffix, with the addition of the suffix of local surnames *-ski* (see BARANOWSKI). In effect, it is probably an occupational name for a flour-dealer.

Madariaga Basque: topographic name for someone who lived by a wild pear tree, from Basque *madari* + the local suffix *-aga*.

Madden Irish: Anglicized form of Gael. **Ó Madaidhín** 'descendant of *Madaidhín*', a personal name from a dim. of *madadh* hound, mastiff.

Vars.: **Madine**; **O'Madden, O'Maddane**; **O'Madagane, O'Madigane, Mad(d)igan** (Gael. **Ó Madagáin**).

Madder English: 1. metonymic occupational name for a dyer or seller of dye, from ME *mad(d)er* madder (OE *mædere*), a dark red dye obtained from plant roots.

2. nickname for a person with a ruddy complexion, from the same word used in a transferred sense.

Vars.: **Mader** (also Jewish, of unknown origin); MATHER. (Of 2 only): **Maddern** (an adj. deriv.).

Maddison English: metr. from the medieval female given name *Madde*, a form of *Maud* (see MOULT 1) or of *Magdalen* (see MAUDLING).

Var.: **Madison**.

James Madison *(1751–1836), 4th President of the United States (1809–17), was born in Virginia, the son of a planter. He was descended from John Madison, a ship's carpenter from Gloucester, who had settled in Virginia in about 1653.*

Madeira Portuguese: 1. metonymic occupational name for a carpenter, from Port. *madeira* wood, timber (LL *māteria*, from class. L *māteries* material, substance).

2. nickname for a stupid person, from the same word in a transferred sense, i.e. 'blockhead'.

3. (rarely) local name from the island of *Madeira*, which was named with Port. *madeira* timber because of the timber that grew there. The island was colonized in the 15th cent. under the patronage of Prince Henry the Navigator.

Madeley English: habitation name from any of various places (one in Shrops. and two in Staffs.), so called from the OE byname **Māda* (probably a deriv. of *mād* foolish) + OE *lēah* wood, clearing.

Madoc Welsh: from the OW personal name *Matoc* (possibly a dim. of *mad* fortunate, good), which survives in the mod. W given name *Madog*.

Vars.: **Maddock, Maddick, Mattock, Mattick, Mattuck, Mattack**.

Cogn.: Bret.: **Madec**.

Patrs.: Welsh: **Mad(d)ocks, Maddox, Maddicks, Mattocks, Mattacks**.

Madrid Spanish: habitation name from what is now the principal city of the Spanish peninsula. Throughout the Middle Ages it was of only modest size and importance, and did not become the capital of Spain until 1561. Its name is of uncertain origin, most probably a deriv. of LL *mātrix*, gen. *mātricis*, riverbed, much changed by Arabic mediation; cf. MADRIGAL. There are other, smaller places of the same name in the provinces of Burgos and Santander, and these may also be partial sources of the surname.

Var.: **Lamadrid**.

Madrigal Spanish: habitation name from any of various places, for example in the provinces of Avila, Burgos, Cáceres, and Guadalajara, apparently so called from LL *mātricāle*, a adj. deriv. of *mātrix* womb, riverbed; cf. MADRID.

Madureira Portuguese: habitation name from any of various places so called from LL *mātūrāria* place for ripening fruit and vegetables (a deriv. of *mātūrus* ripe).

Maeterlinck Belgian: occupational name for an official responsible for dispensing corn from a central warehouse, from MDu. *meten* to measure out + the Gmc suffix *-ling* (cf. CHAMBERLAIN).

The Belgian symbolist dramatist Maurice Maeterlinck *(1862–1949) was born in Ghent, the son of a wealthy notary. The family's surname is said to date back to an ancestor who had been in charge of corn distribution during a famine in Renaix in 1395. This ancestor was knighted, and when Maeterlinck was created a count in 1932 he assumed the same arms.*

Magalhaẽs Portuguese: habitation name from any of various minor places. The placename is of uncertain origin; the first element may be akin to Celt. *magal* large.

Ferdinand Magellan, *in Portuguese Fernão* de Magalhaẽs *(?1480–1521), was the navigator who commanded the expedition of which one ship made the first circumnavigation of the world, although Magellan himself was killed by natives in the Philippines. He gave his name to the straits which he discovered between S America and Tierra del Fuego. He was from the lower nobility and spent his boyhood at the court of Queen Leonora of Portugal.*

Magg English (chiefly Somerset and Wilts.): from the medieval female given name *Mag(ge)*, a pet form of *Margaret* (see MARGUERITE).

Vars.: **Mogg**; **Mudge** (Devon).

Metrs.: **Maggs, Magson, Megson**; **Mox(s)on, Mox(s)om, Moxham**.

A family by the name of Mogg *held lands in Somerset from the 13th cent. They included Thomas Mogg, a landowner of Tickenham in 1282. Descendants adopted the surname* Rees-Mogg *when John Rees married Mary Mogg Wooldridge in 1805.*

Magid Jewish (Ashkenazic): occupational name for a preacher, Hebr. *magid*, Yid. *maged*.

Vars.: **Maged** (from Yid. *maged*); **Magit** (reflecting a regional Yid. pronunciation).

Patrs.: **Magidson**; **Magidov(itz)** (E Ashkenazic).

Magnien French: occupational name for an itinerant tinker or locksmith, OF *ma(i)gna(i)n* (lit. 'worker', from a LL deriv. of *machina* work, trade, earlier 'contrivance', 'device').

Vars.: **Meignien, M(e)ignan, Mégni(e)n**; **Lema(i)gnan, Lemaign(i)en**.

Cogns.: Cat.: **Manyà**. It.: **Magnano, Magnan(i), Magnini**.

Dims.: It.: **Magnanelli, Magnanini**.

Magnol French: habitation name from places in Loire, Lot, and Puy-de-Dôme, all so called from a dim. of OProv. *magnan* silkworm (lit. 'worker'; cf. MAGNIEN). The farming of silk worms was an important occupation in S France during the Middle Ages.

The magnolia *tree takes its name from the French botanist Pierre* Magnol *(1638–1715). He was born in Montpellier, the son of an apothecary.*

Magnus 1. English, Swedish, Danish/Norwegian, and German: from the Scandinavian personal name *Magnús*. This was borne by Magnus the Good (d. 1047), king of Norway, who was named after the Emperor Charlemagne, L *Carolus Magnus* 'CHARLES the Great'. The name spread from Norway to the east Scandinavian royal houses, and became popular all over Scandinavia and thence in the English Danelaw.

2. Jewish: of unknown origin. It may be related to the Jewish surname **Magnes**, which is likewise of unknown origin.

Cogns.: Sc.: MACK. Ir.: **Manus**. Fr.: **Ma(i)gne**. It.: **Magni, Magno**; **Manno, Mannu** (Sardinia).

Dims.: Fr.: **Maignet, Maignon**. It.: **Magnetti, Magnozzi**.

Augs.: It.: **Magnoni, Magnone**.

Patrs.: Eng.: **Magnu(s)son**; MANSON. Sc., Ir.: MCMANUS. Swed.: **Magnusson**; **Månsson** (Anglicized in the U.S. as **Monson**). Dan.: **Magnussen**.

Magriñá Catalan: from the medieval given name *Magrinyá* (L *Macrīniānus*, a deriv. of the Roman family name *Macrīnus*, from *macer* lean; cf. MAIGRE).

Magyar Hungarian: name meaning 'Hungarian'. The Magyar people seem to have come originally from the Urals, but between the 5th and 9th cents. they lived in the north Caucasus and were closely associated with the Turkic peoples ther. They were forced to migrate westward as a result of Bulgarian expansionism and settled in their present territory at the end of the 9th cent.

Cogn.: Czech: **Maděra**.

Maher Irish: Anglicized form of Gael. **Ó Meachair** 'descendant of *Meachar*', a byname meaning 'Hospitable'.

Vars.: **O'Meagher, Meacher**.

Mahler 1. German: occupational name for a painter, esp. a painter of stained glass, from an agent deriv. of Ger. *malen* to paint (MHG *mālen*, OHG *mālōn* to mark, from *māl* point, mark).

2. Jewish (Ashkenazic): presumably an adoption of the Ger. surname or an occupational name for an artist or a housepainter. Kaganoff suggests that the name was occasionally used as an equivalent of LEVI, but there seems to be no evidence to support this hypothesis.

Vars.: Ger.: **Mähler**; **Mehler** (Rhineland, Hesse); **Möhler** (Bavaria).

Mahon Irish: 1. Anglicized form of the Gael. personal name or byname *Mathghamhain* 'Bear'.

2. Anglicized form of Gael. *Ó Mocháin*; see MOHAN.

Patr. (from 1): MCMAHON.

'Descendant of M. 1': **(O')Mahon(e)y** (Gael. **Ó Mathghamhna**).

One of those who claimed descent from Brian, King of Munster, was Count Daniel O'Mahony *(d. 1714), a Jacobite who left Ireland in 1692 and entered the service of Spain and France. He was knighted by the pretender James III and ennobled by Louis XIV of France. His son Demetrius (Dermot) was Spanish ambassador to Austria.*

Maia Portuguese: habitation name from any of several places so called. The most important is first recorded in the form *Amaia*, and is probably of pre-Roman origin. Others may get their names from Port. *maia* flowering broom (from *maio* month of MAY).

Maiden English: nickname for a man of effeminate appearance, from ME *maiden*, the usual word for a young girl (OE *mægden*).

Maidment English: occupational name for a servant employed by a (young) woman or at a convent, from ME *maid(en)* + *man*. For the excrescent *-t*, cf. DIAMOND.

Vars.: **Maitment**; **Maidman** (also borne by at least one Ashkenazic Jewish family in the U.S., in which case the origin is unknown).

Maigre French: nickname for a thin person, from OF *maigre* thin, slender (L *macer* delicate).

Var.: **Lemaigre**.

Cogns.: Prov.: **Magre**. Eng.: **Meag(h)er, Megar**. It.: **Magro, Magri**; **Magheri** (Tuscany). Sp., Port.: **Magro**. Ger.: **Mager(mann)**. Jewish (Ashkenazic): **Mager**; **Magier(man)** (Pol. spelling).

Dims.: Fr.: **Maigret, Meigret, Mégret, Maigrot**. Prov.: **Magret, Magrin, Magron, Magrou**. It.: **Magretti, Magrin(i), Magrino, Magherini, Magrotti**. Ger.: **Mägerl(ein), Megerle**.

Augs.: It.: **Magroni, Magrone**.

Patrs.: Eng.: **Meagers**. It.: **Magris** (Venetia); **Del Magro**. Flem., Du.: **Magermans**.

Mailer 1. English: occupational name for an enameller, from an aphetic form of ME *ameillur*, ANF *esmailour* (an agent deriv. of *esmail* enamel, a word of Gmc origin akin to mod. Eng. *(s)melt*).

2. English: occupational name for a maker of chain mail, from ME, OF *maille* mail, mesh (L *macula* mesh, spot, stain).

3. Scots: habitation name from a place in the former county of Perths., perhaps so called from the Gael. elements *maol* bare + *ard* height. It is recorded as *Malere* in 1296 and *Maller* in 1380. The surname is most common around Stirling.

4. Welsh: from the OW personal name *Meilyr*, derived from an original Celt. form **Maglorīx*, composed of the elements *maglos* chief + *rīx* ruler.

5. Welsh: habitation name from *Maelor* in Clwyd, so called from the W personal name *Mael* + W *or* land, territory.

6. Jewish (Ashkenazic): of uncertain origin, possibly an occupational name for a charcoal burner, from mod. Ger. *Meiler* charcoal kiln.

Vars. (of 1–5): **Mailler, Maylor, Meyler**.

Cogn. (of 2): Port.: **Malheiro**.

Maingaut French: from a Gmc personal name, *Magengaut*, composed of the elements *magin* strength (cogn. with Eng. *main*) + the tribal name *Gaut*. For spellings without *-i-*, the first element may be *man* man.

Vars.: **Mangaut, Ma(i)ngaud**.

Mainland Scots: local name found almost exclusively on the Shetland islands, especially in the parish of Dunrossness, and also in parts of the Orkneys. It is a local name from the principal island of the Shetlands, which is so called. The principal island of the Orkneys is also called *Mainland*, but it is probably not the source of the surname.

According to family tradition, the first bearers of the name in Shetland were German immigrants. However, this cannot be checked from parish registers as these began on Shetland only in 1753, by which time the several families bearing this surname had become thoroughly integrated.

Mains Scots and N English: topographic name for a dweller at the chief farm (or home farm) on an estate, Sc. *mains*, or habitation name from any of the various minor places named with this word (originally an aphetic form of *domain*, later associated with the adj. *main* principal).

Mainwaring English (Norman): habitation name from a lost place, of uncertain location, named in ANF as *mesnil Warin* 'domain of *Warin*' (see WARING). The surname has gone through a large number of var. spellings; it is normally pronounced /ˈmænərɪŋ/.

Vars.: **Manwaring, Mannering**. See also MANDRY.

Sir Ralph de Mesnilwarin *was justice of Chester in the 12th cent. and married a daughter of the Earl of Chester. His descendants, bearing this name, can be traced to the present day.*

Mainz Jewish: habitation name from the city of *Mainz* in W Germany, which is so called from the river *Main*, on which it stands. The river name is ancient and has many cogns. throughout Europe, but its meaning is obscure.

Vars.: **Mainzer, Meinzer**; **Magenza** (from a form closer to the L name of the city, *Maguntia*).

Maiorov Russian: 1. patr., of relatively recent origin, from the army rank *maior* major (borrowed in the 16th cent. from Ger.).

2. surname adopted by members of the Orthodox clergy, from the learned nickname *maior* older, senior, with the addition of the normal patr. suffix *-ov*.

Mair 1. Scots: occupational name for an officer of the courts whose functions resembled those of an Eng. beadle and who was known as a *mair* (cf. MAYER 1).

2. Jewish: var. of MAYER 3.

Patr. (from 1): **Mairs** (chiefly N Ireland).

Maites Jewish (Ashkenazic): metr. from the Yid. female given name *Meyte* (from MHG *maget* maiden; cf. MAKIN 2) + the Yid. possessive suffix *-s*.

Vars.: **Mat(t)es, Matus, Matis** (see also MATTHEW); **Meites, Meitus; Maitin, Meitin** (E Ashkenazic).

Metrs. from a dim. (*Meytl*): **Mait(e)les, Ma(j)teles, Mat(a)lis, Meitlis, Maitlis; Majtlis** (Pol. spelling, reflecting the central Yid. pronunciation of the given name); **Matelson; Matlow, Matalovitch, Mat(a)lovsky, Matlovski**.

Maitland Scots and English (Norman): of uncertain origin, possibly a nickname for an ungracious individual, from ANF *maltalent, mautalent* bad temper (LL *malum* bad + *talentum* inclination, disposition). However, there is a place called *Mautalant* in Pontorson, France, so named from its unproductive soil, and this may well be a partial source of the surname. The present spelling is the result of a contracted pronunciation and folk etymological identification with the common topographic element *land*.

The Maitland *family have held the title Earl of Lauderdale since 1624. Their ancestral seat, Thirlstane near Lauder in Cumb., has been in the family for over 700 years. They were an Anglo-Norman family, whose earliest recorded ancestor, Thomas* de Matalan(t), *settled in Berwicks. in the reign of William the Lion between 1165 and 1214. Sir Richard Maitland (1496–1586) was a lawyer and poet. His great-grandson John Maitland (1616–82), 2nd Earl and 1st Duke of Lauderdale, was a statesman who was* de facto *ruler of Scotland. He was a favourite of Charles II, but eventually fell from grace.*

Majewski Polish and Jewish (Ashkenazic): surname adopted with reference to the month of MAY, Pol. *maj*, with the addition of the common surname ending *-ewski*. Surnames derived from months were often taken, for example, by converted Jews to mark the month in which they were converted to Christianity or baptized. In other cases, it simply marks the month in which a surname was registered.

Var.: **Majkowski**.

Major 1. English: from the Norman personal name *Malg(i)er, Maug(i)er*, composed of the Gmc elements *madal* council + *gari, geri* spear.

2. Jewish (E Ashkenazic): var. of MAYER 3.

Vars. (of 1): **Ma(u)ger**.

Makepeace English: nickname for a person known for his skill at patching up quarrels, from ME *mak(en)* to make (OE *macian*) + *pais* peace (see PACE).

Var.: **Makepiece**.

Mäki Finnish: ornamental name from Finn. *mäki* hill, perhaps sometimes chosen as a topographic name by someone who lived on or near a hill.

Vars.: **Mäkelä** (with collective suffix), **Mäkinen** (with gen. suffix).

Cogn.: Estonian: **Mägiste**.

Makin N English (Lancs. and Yorks.): 1. dim. of MAY, which is itself a pet form of MATTHEW.

2. nickname for an effeminate man, from ME *maid(en)* girl, young woman (see MAIDEN) + the dim. suffix *-kin*. It is possible, but unlikely, that it may also have been of more literal application as an occupational name for a female servant.

Vars.: **Maykin; Meakin** (chiefly Notts.), **Meaken; Making**.

Patrs. (from 1): **Makins, Maykin(g)s, Meakin(g)s, Meekin(g)s; Makinson** (Lancs.).

Makowski Polish and Jewish (E Ashkenazic): habitation name from the town of *Maków* (Yid. *Makeve*), so called from Pol. *mak* poppy (a word probably ultimately cogn. with, rather than borrowed from, Gk *mēkon*), + *-ów* possessive suffix used in forming placenames.

Vars.: Pol.: **Makówka**. Jewish: **Ma(c)kover, Makower** (clearly habitation names); **Makov, Makovski, Makowsky, Makovsky** (probably ornamental names from Pol. *mak* poppy).

Cogns.: Czech: **Makovec, Makovička** (from a place called *Makov*).

Malave Jewish (E Ashkenazic): habitation name from *M(e)lave*, Yid. name of the town of *Mława* in Poland.

Vars.: **Mlawer, Melaver; Malavski, Malavsky, Malawsky**.

Malcolm Scots: from the Gael. personal name *Mael-Colum* 'devotee of (St) *Columba*' (see COLOMB).

Var.: **Malcom**.

Patrs.: **Malco(l)mson** (chiefly N Ireland).

Maldonado Spanish: nickname for an ugly or stupid person, from Sp. *mal donado* ill-favoured. The phrase is a cpd of *mal* badly (L *male*, a deriv. of *malus*; see MALO) + *donado* given, endowed (L *donātus*, past part. of *donāre*; cf. DONAT).

Male English: nickname for a particularly virile man, from ME *male* masculine (OF *masle, madle*, L *masculus*).

Vars.: **Mayle, Mayell, Mayall**.

Cogns.: Fr.: **Mâle**. It.: **Maschi(o)** (Venetia); **Mascolo, Mascoli** (S Italy). Sp.: MACHO.

Dims.: Prov.: **Masclet**. It.: **Maschietto, Mascolino**.

Malebranche French: nickname from OF *mal(e)* bad (see MALO) + *branche* branch. The original significance of the name is not easy to determine; there may have been some jocular reference to an illegitimate branch of a noble family.

Malet 1. English: from the medieval female given name *Malet*, a dim. of *Mal(le)*, pet form of *Mary* (see MARIE), and so a var. of MALIN 1 with a different dim. suffix.

2. English: var. of MALLARD 1.

3. English: nickname for an unfortunate person, from OF *maleit* accursed (L *maledictus*, the opposite of *benedictus*; cf. BENNETT).

4. English and French: nickname for a fearsome warrior or metonymic occupational name for a smith, from OF *ma(i)let*, dim. of *ma(i)l* hammer (see MALLE 1).

5. French: from a dim. of the given name *Malo*, which was relatively popular in Brittany in the Middle Ages, having been borne by a 6th-cent. Welsh missionary to the area. His name is also recorded in the Latinized form *Maclovius*, and perhaps has some connection with Celt. *megalos* chief, leader.

Vars.: Eng.: **Mallet(t)**. Fr.: **Mallet, Mallez**.

Cogn. (of 3): Fr.: **Maloit**.

Dim. (of 3): Fr.: **Malouet**.

Malet *was the name of a powerful Anglo-Norman family established in Somerset, where they gave their name to Shepton* Mallet *and Curry* Mallet, *in which places descendants can still be found. William Malet (d.* c.1071*) was from Graville in Normandy. He accompanied William the Conqueror and was responsible for the burial of King Harold at Hastings. His brother Durand also settled* *in England and established a branch of the family in Lincs. William's grandson, also called William, was banished in 1109 and became ancestor of the Malets, Sires de Graville, and of a branch of the family in Jersey.*

Another family called Malet *or* Mallet *were established in England, eventually in Kent, by a Huguenot, Jacques Mallet, in 1797. He was descended from a certain Jean Mallet of Rouen (d.* c.*1593).*

Malherbe French: topographic name for someone who lived on a patch of ground overgrown with weeds, from OF *mal(e)* bad (see MALO) + *herbe* plant (L *herba* grass).

Vars.: **Malherb, Malerbe**; **Malesherbes** (a place in Loiret).

Cogns.: It.: **Malerba, Malerbi.**

Pej.: Fr.: **Malherbaud.**

Malin 1. English: from the medieval female given name *Malin*, a dim. of *Mal(le)*, pet form of *Mary* (see MARIE).

2. Jewish (E Ashkenazic): metr. from the Yid. female given name *Male* (a back-formation from *Malke* (see MALKIN), as if it contained the Slav. dim. suffix *-ke*) + the Slav. metr. suffix *-in*. In a few cases it may originate as in 3 below.

3. Russian: patr. from the nickname *Mala* 'Small One'; see MALÝ.

Vars. (of 1): **Mallin**; **Mallen** (see also MELLON). (Of 2): **Malis.**

Metrs. (from 1): Eng.: **Malli(n)son, Malleson.**

Malinowski Polish and Jewish (E Ashkenazic): habitation name from a place named with Pol. *malina* raspberry, possibly in effect an occupational name for a grower of the fruit. As a Jewish name, it may well be ornamental, one of the many Ashkenazic surnames taken from vocab. words for fruit and plants.

Vars.: Pol.: **Maliński** (also from a nickname). Jewish: **Malina**; **Maliniak**; **Malin(ov)sky, Malinovski, Malinowsky.**

Cogns.: Czech: **Malinovský**; **Malínsky, Malina** (from a nickname).

Patrs. (from a nickname): Russ., Bulg.: **Malinov.** Jewish: **Malinov(itz), Malinowitz.**

Malkin 1. English: from a medieval female given name, a dim. of *Mal(le)* (see MALIN), with the hypocoristic suffix *-kin*.

2. Jewish (E Ashkenazic): metr. from the Yid. female given name *Malke* (from Hebr. *Malka* 'Queen') + the Slav. metr. suffix *-in*.

Vars. (of 1): **Maulkin.** (Of 2): **Malkes**; **Malkind** (influenced by Yid. *kind* child; see SÜSSKIND); **Malkinson** (with a Gmc suffix added to the Slav. one).

Metr. (from 1): Eng.: **Malkinson.**

Mallard English: 1. from the OF personal name *Malhard*, composed of the Gmc elements *madal* council + *hard* hardy, brave, strong. This was introduced to Britain by the Normans.

2. nickname for someone supposedly resembling a drake or male wild duck, ME, OF *malard* (originally a pej. from OF *ma(s)le* MALE).

Vars. (of 1): **Maylard, Maylett,** MALET.

Mallarmé French: nickname for a poorly accoutred warrior, perhaps one who could barely afford the knight's service he had inherited, from OF *mal* badly (L *male*) + *armé* armed (L *armātus*, from *arma* arms).

Vars.: **Malarmé, Mal(l)armey.**

Malle French: 1. metonymic occupational name for a smith, or nickname for a fierce fighter, from OF *ma(i)l* hammer (L *malleus*).

2. metonymic occupational name for a maker of bags or nickname for someone who habitually carried one, from OF *male* bag (of Gmc origin).

Mallory English (Norman): nickname for an unfortunate person, from OF *malheure* unhappy, unlucky. The etymology from *maloret* ill-omened (L *male* badly + *augurātus*) is less likely for the surname that has actually survived, although it does lie behind other medieval Norman surnames, now defunct.

Vars.: **Malory, Mal(l)ary, Mallery, Mallerie, Mallorie.**

The earliest certainly identified bearer of the surname was Richard Mallore, *who is recorded as holding lands in Leics., Northants., and Warwicks. in the mid-12th cent. Geoffrey* Maloret, *recorded in Domesday Book as holding lands in Dorset, is now thought to have belonged to a different family, as is Fulcher* de Maloure, *who held baronies in Rutland and Northants. The* Mallorys *held many manors from 1154 until about 1750, and the surname is now well established in the U.S.A., Canada, and Australia. One of the best known members of the family is Sir Thomas* Malory, *who wrote* Le Morte D'Arthur, *published by Caxton in 1485.*

Mally Irish: Anglicized form of Gael. **Ó Máille** 'descendant of the nobleman', from *mál* prince, champion, poet.

Vars.: **Malley, Meall(e)y, Melly, Melia**; **O'Mall(e)y, O'Mallie, O'Mailie, O'Maely, O'Meal(l)y.**

Malm Swedish: arbitrary or ornamental name, from Swed. *malm* ore (ON *málmr*), adopted in some cases by people having something to do with the copper-mining industry.

Cpds: **Malmberg** ('ore hill'); **Malmborg** ('ore town'); **Malmgren** ('ore branch'); **Malmqvist** ('ore twig'); **Malmsten** ('ore stone'); **Malmström** ('ore river').

Malo Spanish: nickname for an unpleasant individual, from Sp. *malo* bad, evil (L *malus*).

Malone Irish: Anglicized form of Gael. **Ó Maoil Eoin** 'descendant of the devotee of (St) JOHN'.

Var.: **Mallon.**

Malpas English (Norman) and French: habitation name from any of various places named, because of the difficulty of the terrain, from OF *mal pas* bad passage (L *malus passus*). Places in Ches., Cornwall, Gwent, and elsewhere were given this name by Norman settlers. A place in Rousillon which was so called in the 12th cent. was subsequently renamed *Bonpas* for the sake of a better omen.

Vars.: Eng.: **Malpass, Malpuss, Melpuss, Morpuss.** Fr.: **Maupas(sant).**

The family of the French writer Guy de Maupassant *(1850–93) originated in Lorraine. A certain Jean-Baptiste Maupassant was an advisor to King Louis XV and was created a member of the minor nobility in 1752. The aristocratic* de *was dropped at the time of the Revolution, but restored at the insistence of the writer's mother.*

Malpighi Italian: nickname for an idle chatterer or malicious gossip, from It. *mala* (fem.) bad, evil (see MALO) + *piga*, a dial. term for the magpie (L *pica*; cf. PYE 1).

Maltby English: habitation name from *Maltby* in Cleveland, Lincs., and N and W Yorks., or *Mautby* in Norfolk, all so called from the ON byname *Malti* 'Sharp', 'Bitter' + ON *býr* farm, settlement.

Vars.: **Mau(l)tby.**

Malter English: 1. occupational name for a brewer who used malt, from an agent deriv. of ME *malt* malt, germinated barley (OE *mealt*).

2. topographic name for someone who lived on a patch of unprofitable land, from OF *male terre* bad land (L *mala terra*).

Vars. (of 1): **Maltster** (origially a fem. form); **Maltman** (Sc.).

Cogns. (of 1): Ger.: **Mälzer, Melz(l)er, Melzner**; **Mulzer** (Franconia); **Mal(t)z.** Jewish (Ashkenazic): **Mal(t)z, Melz**; **Malc** (Pol. spelling); **Mel(t)zer**; **Melcer** (Pol. spelling); **Maltz-**

man, Meltzman; Malzberg ('malt hill', an ornamental elaboration). Low Ger.: **Molter, Mölter, Multer, Moltmann**. (Of 2): Fr.: **Mal(e)terre**. Prov.: **Malaterre**.

Malthus English: topographic name for someone who lived at a malt-house, ME *malthuse* (from OE *mealt* + *hūs*), and so in effect an occupational name for a brewer. The malt-house was the building in which the cereal was dried in an oven after it had been soaked in water to make it germinate.

Vars.: **Malthouse, Maltus, Maltas**.

Maltravers English (Norman): apparently a local surname from an unidentified place, presumably named from OF *mal travers* bad crossing (LL *malum traversum*), perhaps at the site of a difficult ford. Cf. MALPAS.

Vars.: **Mat(t)ravers, Matraves**.

Malý Czech: from the Czech adj. *malý* small. This was both a nickname for a physically small man and a pet name for a child, which was sometimes retained in adult life. The cogn. noun *malec*, in Pol. as well as Czech, has the additional sense 'young man', which probably also underlies some surnames.

Vars.: **Malec, Maleč, Malecký, Malák, Malát**.

Cogns.: Pol.: **Mały; Malec, Malicki**. Ger. (of Slav. origin): **Mahle, Mahling**. Jewish (E Ashkenazic): **Malenky**.

Dims.: Czech: **Málek, Malík, Maleček**. Pol.: **Malczyk, Małek, Małecki**. Ukr.: **Malko**. Ger. (of Slav. origin): **Ma(h)lke, Malek, Malicke**.

Patrs.: Russ. and Jewish: **Malov**, MALIN. Pol.: **Malisiewicz**.

Patrs. (from dims.): Russ.: **Maltsev, Maltsov, Maleev, Male(n)in, Maleinov, Malnev, Malenkov, Mal(i)kov**, MALIN, **Malyagin, Malyav(k)in, Malyugin, Malyukin, Malyukov, Malyut(k)in, Malyk(h)in, Malygin, Malyshev, Malyshkin, Malushin**. Pol.: **Małkiewicz**. Croatian: **Maletić**.

Habitation names: Pol.: **Malewski, Maliszewski**.

Habitation names (from dims.): Pol.: **Małkowski, Malczewski**.

Mañas Spanish: nickname for a devious character or alternatively for an astute or skilful person, from the pl. form of Sp. *maña* trick, strategem (LL *mania*, a deriv. of *manus* hand).

Mancebo Spanish: occupational or status name for a serf or servant, OSp. *mancebo* (LL *mancipus*, from class. L *mancipium* slave).

Cogns.: Cat.: **Mas(s)ip**.

Manchester English: habitation name from the city in NW England, formerly part of Lancs. This is so called from *Mamucio* (an ancient Brit. name containing the element *mammā* breast, and meaning 'breast-shaped hill') + OE *ceaster* (Roman) fort (L *castra* legionary camp).

Manco Italian: nickname for a left-handed person, from the It. adj. *manco*. The name is found in this form largely in S Italy.

Vars.: **Mango; Manka** (Sardinia); **(Lo) Mancuso, Mancusi, Manguso, Mangusi, Moncuso** (Calabria, Sicily); **Mancosu** (Sardinia).

Dims.: **Mancin(ell)i, Mancinetti** (Tuscany, NW Italy); **Mancin** (Venetia).

Aug.: **Manconi**.

Mandel 1. German and Jewish (Ashkenazic): from Ger. *Mandel* almond or its Yid. cogn. *mandl* (MHG *mandel*, OHG *mandala*, from LL *amandula*, from Gk *amygdale*, probably of Semitic origin). This could have been a topographic name for someone who lived by an almond tree or a metonymic occupational name for a seller of almonds. In the case of the Jewish name, it is one of the many ornamental surnames referring to different types of trees and their fruit.

2. S German and Austrian: dim. of the medieval given name MANN.

Vars. (of 1): Jewish: **Mandell** (U.S.); **Mandelman** (occupational).

Cogn. (of 1): Czech: **Mandlik** (dim.).

Cpds (of 1; ornamental): Jewish: **Mandelbaum, Mandelboim** ('almond tree', Anglicized **Mandlebaum**); **Mandelberg** ('almond hill'); **Mandelblatt** ('almond leaf'); **Mandelblitt** ('almond blossom'); **Mandelmilch** ('almond milk'); **Mandelstam(m)** ('almond trunk'); **Mandeltort** ('almond cake'); **Mandelzweig** ('almond twig').

Mander English: of uncertain origin. It may be a nickname for a beggar, from an agent deriv. of *maund* beg (probably from OF *mendier*, LL *mendicare*); this word is not attested before the 16th cent., but may well have been in use earlier. Alternatively it may be an occupational name for a maker of baskets, from an agent deriv. of ME *maund* basket (OF *mande*, of Gmc origin); or perhaps for someone in some position of authority, from an aphetic form of ME *coma(u)nder* (from *coma(u)nden* to command, ANF *comaunder*, OF *comander*, LL *commandāre*).

Vars.: **Maund(er)**.

Patrs.: **Ma(u)nders, Manderson**.

Mandeville English (Norman): habitation name from any of various places in France called *Mann(e)ville* (from the Gmc personal name *Manno* (see MANN 2) + OF *ville* settlement) or *Magneville* (from OF *magne* great + *ville* settlement).

Vars.: **Manville, Manvell, Manwell**.

Geoffrey de Mandeville (*d. 1144*) *was an English baron, created Earl of Essex in 1141. The exact place from which the family derive their name is not known, but Manneville in Seine Maritime seems the most likely candidate. Geoffrey became very powerful and acquired large estates through reputedly treacherous dealings, first with King Stephen and then with Queen Matilda. After raising a rebellion he became an outlaw in the fens and was killed during a siege. His son, William de Mandeville* (*d. 1189*), *was raised at the court of Philip of Flanders and became Count of Aumale by his marriage in 1179. The earldom of Essex passed to the de Bohun family in the 13th cent.*

Mandry English or Welsh: apparently a var. of MAINWARING. The latter name is pronounced /'mændrɪ/ in the Ammanford district of Wales, but not so spelled there. This spelling is, however, found in Neath. The earliest known record of the name is the marriage of Sarah *Mandrey* in the city of London in 1688.

Mañé Catalan: from a Gmc personal name composed of the elements *magin* strength + *heri*, *hari* army.

Var.: **Mañés**.

Mangan Irish: Anglicized form of Gael. **Ó Mongáin** 'descendant of *Mongán*', originally a byname for someone with a luxurious growth of hair (from *mong* hair, mane).

Mangia Italian: nickname for a glutton, a deriv. of It. *mangiare* to eat (L *manducāre* to chew).

Cogn.: Fr.: **Mangon**.

Dims.: It.: **Mangini** (Tuscany, Liguria); **Mangiullo, Mangiulli**. Fr.: **Mangot, Manguet, Manguin**.

Aug.: It.: **Mangione**.

Mangold 1. English: of uncertain origin. Reaney gives it as a var. of **Mangnall**, which he derives from OF *mangonelle*, a war engine for throwing stones. It may alternatively be identical in origin with the German name in 2 below, but there is no evidence of its introduction to Britain as a given name by the Normans, which is normally the case for English surnames derived from Continental Gmc personal names.

2. German: from a Gmc personal name *Managold*, composed of the elements *manag* much (cogn. with mod. Eng. *many*) + *wald* rule.

Cogn. (of 2): Low Ger.: **Mangel**.

Patrs. (from 2): Low Ger.: **Mangels(en)**, **Mangholz**.

Manjón Spanish: of uncertain origin, perhaps from a LL personal name *Mancio*, gen. *Manciōnis*, a deriv. of *Mancius*.

Manley English: 1. habitation name from places in Devon and Ches., so called from OE *(ge)mǣne* common, shared + *lēah* wood, clearing. The surname is still chiefly found in the regions around these villages.

2. nickname from ME *mannly* manly, virile, brave (OE *mannlīc*, originally 'man-like').

Vars.: **Manly**, **Manleigh**.

Mann 1. English and German: nickname for a fierce or strong man, or for a man contrasted with a boy for some reason, from ME, MHG *man*, mod. Ger. *Mann* (OE *mann*, OHG *man*). In some cases it may have arisen as an occupational name for a servant, from the medieval use of the term to describe a person of inferior social status.

2. English and German: from a Gmc personal name, found in OE as *Manna*. This originated either as a byname or else as a short form of any of the various cpd names containing this element, such as HERMANN.

3. Jewish (Ashkenazic): of uncertain origin. Possibly it is from Hebr. and Yid. *man* manna, and is thus expressive of faith in God. Another possibility is that it comes from the Yid. male given name *Man* (cogn. with the Gmc name mentioned in 2), which is sometimes taken as a short form of the Hebr. given name *Menakhem*. See also MENDEL.

Vars. (of 1): Eng.: **Man**. (Of 3): (E Ashkenazic): **Mannsky**, **Manski**; **Monsky** (reflecting the pronunciation of Yid. *man* found in Podolia, Moldavia, and Bessarabia).

Cogns. (of 1): Flem., Du.: **De Mann**. (Of 2): Fr.: **Man**; **Man(n)on** (from the OF oblique case). It.: **Manni**, **Manno** (see also MAGNUS).

Dims. (of 2): Ger.: MANDEL, **Männel**, **Männle**. Fr.: **Manet(eau)**, **Manin**. It.: **Mannelli**, **Mannello**, **Man(n)ini**, **Man(n)ino**, **Man(n)etti**, **Mannucci**, **Mannuzzi**.

Augs. (of 2): It.: **Mannoni**, **Mannone**.

Patrs. (from 1 and 2): Eng.: **Manning**, MANSON. Ger.: **Mann(e)s**. (From 2): Low Ger.: **Manssen**. It.: **Manneschi**. (From 3): Jewish: **Manzon**, **Manis**, **Manin**.

Manners English (Norman): habitation name from *Mesnières* in Seine-Maritime, recorded in the 13th cent. as *Maneria*, a deriv. of L *manēre* to remain, abide, reside. See also MENZIES.

The Manners *family held the titles Earl and Duke of Rutland and Marquess of Granby. Their ancestry can be traced to Etal or Ethale in Northumb., where documents record a boundary dispute involving the family in 1232.*

Mannheim Jewish (Ashkenazic): habitation name from the city in SW Germany (formerly the residence of the electors Palatine), so called from the Gmc personal name *Manno* (see MANN 2) + OHG *heim* homestead. It seems that all bearers of the surname are Jews who have acquired it relatively recently. Mannheim was not fortified or chartered until the beginning of the 17th cent., until which time it was just a small fishing village.

Vars.: **Manheim**, **Man(n)heimer**.

Mannin Irish: Anglicized form of Gael. **Ó Mainnín** 'descendant of *Mainnín*', probably an assimilated form of *Mainchín*, a dim. of *manch* monk.

Vars.: **Mannion**, **Manning**.

Manrique Spanish: from the medieval given name *Manrique*, composed of the Gmc elements *mann* man + *rīc* power.

Mansell English (chiefly W Midlands): 1. Norman habitation or regional name from OF *mansel* inhabitant of Le *Mans* or the surrounding area of *Maine*. The town was originally named in L *(ad) Ceromannos*, from the name of the Gaul. tribe living there, the *Ceromanni* (of unknown etymology). The name was reduced to *Celmans* and then became *Le Mans* as a result of the mistaken identification of the first syllable with the OF demonstrative adj.

2. status name for a particular type of feudal tenant, ANF *mansel*, who occupied a *manse* (LL *mansa* dwelling), a measure of land sufficient to support one family; cf. HYDE, HUBER.

3. some early examples, such as Thomas *filius Manselli* (Northumb. 1256), point to derivation from a personal name, perhaps the Gmc deriv. of MANN 2 Latinized as *Manzellinus*.

Vars.: **Mansel**, **Mancell**, **Maunsell**.

Cogns. (of 2): Fr.: **Manceau**, **Mançois**, **Mançais**; **Manchel**.

A family of this name trace their descent from Walter Mansel *or* Maunsell *(b. c.1166), who held lands in Little Missenden, Bucks. His son John rose to power as Lord High Justiciar of England and Keeper of the Great Seal in 1246–8.*

Manser English: 1. from the male given name *Manasseh* (Hebr. *Menashe* 'One who causes to forget'), borne occasionally in the Middle Ages by Christians as well as by Jews. Hebr. *Menashe* and its reflexes in other Jewish languages have always been popular among Jews.

2. occupational name for someone who made handles for agricultural and domestic implements, from an agent deriv. of ANF *mance* handle (OF *manche*, LL *manicus*, a deriv. of *manus* hand).

Var.: **Mancer**.

Cogn. (of 1): Jewish (Ashkenazic): **Menashe**.

Dim. (of 1): Jewish (E Ashkenazic): **Menashko** (among Rumanian Jews).

Patrs. (from 1): Jewish: **Menashes**; **Menasherov**; **Manaschewitz**, **Manesewic**.

Mansfield English: habitation name from a place in Notts. The early forms, from Domesday Book to the early 13th cent., show the first element uniformly as *Mam-*, and it is therefore likely that this was a Brit. hill-name meaning 'Breast' (cf. MANCHESTER), with the later addition of OE *feld* pasture, open country (see FIELD) as the second element. The surname is now widespread throughout Midland and S England and is also common in Ireland.

Mansilla Spanish: habitation name from any of various places, for example in the provinces of Burgos, León, Logroño, and Segovia, so called from Sp. *mansilla*, a dim. of LL *mansa* dwelling (class. L *mansio*, a deriv. of *manēre* to remain, abide).

Manso Spanish and Portuguese: nickname for a mild and inoffensive person, from Sp., Port. *manso* tame, docile (LL *mansus*, class. L *mansuētus*, past part. of *mansuescere* to tame, lit. 'accustom to the hand').

Manson 1. Scots: patr. from the given name MAGNUS.

2. English: patr. from the ME nickname or byname MANN.

Mantegna Italian: from an aphetic form of the medieval given name *Diotimantegna* 'God preserve you'.

Mantell 1. English: metonymic occupational name for a maker of overgarments, or nickname for someone who wore a cloak of a particularly conspicuous design, from ANF *mantel* cloak, coat (LL *mantellus*, probably of Celt. origin; cf. W *mantell* cloak).
2. Jewish (Ashkenazic): probably from Ger. *Mantel* or Yid. *mantl* coat, which are related to 1 above.

Vars.: **Mantel**. (Of 1 only): **Mantle**.

Cogns.: Fr.: **Manteau, Mantel**. Ger.: **Mantel**; **Mäntler, Mentler** (agent derivs.). Flem., Du.: **Mantel**.

Dims.: Fr.: **Mantelet, Mantelin**. Jewish: **Mantelik**.

Manthorpe English: habitation name from either of two places in Lincs., so called from the ON personal name *Manni* (a deriv. of *maðr*, gen. *mannes*, man; cf. MANN) + ON *þorp* settlement (see THORPE).

Manton English: habitation name from any of the various places so called, for example in Leics., Lincs., Notts., and Wilts. For the most part the first element is either OE *(ge)mǣne* common, shared (cf. MANLEY), or the OE byname *Mann(a)* (see MANN). However, in the case of *Manton* in Lincs. the early forms show clearly that it was OE *m(e)alm* sand, chalk, with reference to the poor soil of the region. The second element is in each case OE *tūn* enclosure, settlement.

Manzano Spanish: topographic name for someone who lived by an apple tree or orchard, from Sp. *manzano* apple tree (OSp. *maçano*, from *maçana* apple, LL *(māla) Mattiāna* (originally neut. pl., then fem. sing.), a type of apple named in honour of the 1st cent. BC horticultural writer Gaius *Matius*).

Cogn.: Cat.: **Massana**.

Collectives: Sp.: **Manzanares**. Port.: **Macedo**.

Manzo Italian: nickname for someone supposedly resembling an ox, It. *manzo* (from LL *mansus* tame (see MANSO), specialized in the sense of an ox tamed to the plough), or metonymic occupational name for someone who worked with oxen.

Vars.: **Manzi, Mansi**.

Dim.: **Manzitto**.

Aug.: **Manzoni**.

Maple English: topographic name for someone who lived by a maple tree, ME *mapel*, OE *mapul*.

Var.: **Maples**.

Maqueda Spanish: habitation name from a place in the province of Toledo, so called from the Arabic name of a fortress established there, derived from Ar. *makāda* firm, fixed.

Marañón Spanish: habitation name from a place in the province of Navarre, apparently so called from a deriv. of Sp. *maraña* thicket, dense foliage (of uncertain, probably pre-Roman, origin).

Marcelino Portuguese: from a personal name (L *Marcellīnus*, a deriv. of *Marcellus*; see MARCELO) borne by several early saints, including the friend of St Augustine to whom *De Civitate Dei* was dedicated.

Cogn.: Fr.: **Marcel(l)in**.

Marcelo Portuguese: from a personal name (L *Marcellus*, a dim. of *Marcus*; see MARK 1). This was borne by a large number of minor early saints, and consequently became popular as a given name during the Middle Ages.

Vars.: Fr.: **Marcel, Marceau**.

Dims.: Fr.: **Marcel(l)et, Marcel(l)eau, Marcelot, Marcelon**.

March 1. English: topographic name for someone who lived on the border between two territories, esp. in the Marches between England and Wales or England and Scotland, from ANF *marche* boundary (of Gmc origin; cf. MARK 2 and MARQUE 1). In some cases, the surname may be a habitation name from *March* in Cambs., which was probably named from the locative case of OE *mearc* boundary.
2. English: from a nickname or given name for someone who was born or baptized in the month of March (ME, OF *march(e)*, L *Martius (mensis)*, from the name of the god *Mars*) or who had some other special connection with the month, such as owing a feudal obligation then.
3. Catalan: cogn. of MARK 1.

Cogn. (of 2): Sp.: **Marzo**. Pol.: **Marzec**.

Marchant English, French, and Jewish: occupational name for a buyer and seller of goods, from OF, ME *march(e)ant* (LL *mercātans*, pres. part. of *mercātāre*, from *mercātus*, past part. of class. L *mercāri* to trade, from *merx*, gen. *mercis*, commerce, exchange, merchandise). In the Middle Ages the term was used mainly of a wholesale dealer. The surname shows the regular ME, OF change of *-er-* to *-ar-*, although in the Eng. vocab. word the original vowel was later restored under learned (etymological) influence.

Vars.: Eng.: **Marchent, (Le) Marchand, Le Marchant; (Le) Marquand** (from a Norman form); **Merchant**. Fr.: **Marcant, Marc(h)and; Marquant, Marquand**. Jewish: **Marchand**.

Cogns.: It.: **Mercante, Mercanti; Mercatante, Mercatanti** (Tuscany); **Mercadante, Mercadanti** (S Italy). Sp.: **Merchán**. Jewish: **Merkante**.

Dims.: Fr.: **Marchandel, Marcantel, Marchandon, Mercanton**. It.: **Marcantelli, Mercantini**.

Aug.: It.: **Mercantone**.

Patr.: Fr.: **Aumarchand**.

Equivs.: Ger.: HANDLER. Czech: SOUKUP. Pol.: TARGOWNIK. Russ.: KUPTSOV. Rum.: NEGUS.

Marchewa Polish: nickname from Pol. *marchew* carrot (Czech *mrkev*), given no doubt to a person with carrot-coloured hair.

Var.: **Marchwicki**.

Dims.: Pol.: **Marchewka**. Czech: **Mrkvička**.

Patr.: Croatian: **Mrkić**.

Marden English: habitation name from any of various places so called, which have a number of different origins. One in Wilts. is so called from OE *mearc* boundary + *denu* valley; one in Sussex from OE *(ge)mǣre* boundary + *dūn* hill; one in Kent from OE *m(i)ere* mares + *denn* pasture; and one in Herefords. from Brit. *magno-* plain + OE *worðign* enclosure.

Var.: **Mardon**.

Marek Czech: 1. from the personal name *Marek*, the Czech equivalent of MARK. *Marek* is also the usual Pol. form of the given name, but it does not seem to be used as a Pol. surname.
2. from a dim. of MARTIN or *Mauritius* (see MORRIS).

Vars.: **Mareš, Mára**.

Dims.: **Mareček, Maršík, Mařík**.

Marfleet English (Yorks. and Lincs.): habitation name from a village in Humberside, near Hull, which is so called from OE *mere* lake, pond + *flēot* stream.

Var.: **Marflit** (Yorks.).

The earliest known bearer of this surname is Adam de Merflete, *recorded in Holderness 1135–54. William* Merflete *was mayor of nearby Hedon in 1419, and a pedigree of present-day bearers has been traced to John* Marflet *of Fulston, Lincs., who died in 1591.*

Marguerite French: from the LL female personal name *Margarita* 'Pearl' (the vocab. word was borrowed into Greek and Latin from a Semitic source, and is probably of Persian origin). This was borne by several early Christian saints, and became a popular female given name throughout Europe. The usual ME form was *Margerie*.

Vars.: Fr.: **Margueritte, Margeride, Margaride, Margalide, Margerit, Marg(u)erie, Marguery, Margry; Magritte** (Belgium).

Cogns.: Eng.: **Margery, Margary.** Cat.: **Margarit** (from a masc. form). Jewish (ornamental): **Margalit(h); Margoli(e)s, Margolius** (W and NE Ashkenazic); **Marguli(e)s, Margu(i)les, Margulius** (S Ashkenazic); **Margaliyot, Margolioth** (from the Hebr. pl. form).

Dims.: Fr.: **Margeridon; Marg(u)erin, Marg(u)eron; Margot(eau), Margotin, Marguet, Marguin.** Eng.: **Madge,** MAGG; **Madgett, Meggett, Meggitt, Meggat.** Ger.: **Maggi** (Switzerland). Flem., Du.: **Griete.**

Metrs.: Eng.: **Marger(r)ison, Marger(e)son, Margetson, Margesson, Margi(t)son, Marginson; Marget(t)s.**

Marie French: from the extremely popular medieval female given name, L *Maria*. This was the name of the mother of Christ in the New Testament, as well as several other New Testament figures. It derives from Aramaic *Maryam* (Hebr. *Miryam*), but the vernacular forms have been influenced by the Roman family name *Marius* (of uncertain origin). The Hebr. name is likewise of uncertain etymology, but perhaps means 'Wished-for Child', from an Egyptian root *mrj* with the addition of the Hebr. fem. dim. suffix *-am*. St Jerome understood it as a cpd of *mar* drop + *yam* sea, which he rendered as L *stīlla maris*, later altered to *stella maris* star of the sea, whence the liturgical phrase. A Latin masc. adj. form, *Mariānus*, was applied by Christians to devotees of the Virgin Mary, and lies behind several of the surnames listed here.

Cogns.: It.: **Maria.** Sp.: **María.** Port.: **Maria.** Pol.: **Marjański.**

Dims.: Fr.: **Mariel(le), Mariet(te), Mariéton, Marion(eau), Mariot(te), Mariolle.** Eng.: **Mar(r)ion, Maryon, Mar(r)ian, Maryan;** MARRIOTT; **Merrikin.** Pol.: **Marusik.** Czech: **Maroušek, Marušák, Maruška, Maryška.** Ukr.: **Marishenko, Marusyak, Marushak, Marunchak.** Jewish (E Ashkenazic): **Mariamchik** (consists of a central Yid. pronunciation of the Yid. female given name *Miryem* Miriam + the E Yid. dim. ending *-tshik*).

Pejs.: Fr.: **Mariaud, Mariault.**

Metrs.: Eng.: **Marrison** (chiefly Norfolk). Flem.: **Marien.** It.: **De Maria, Di Maria.** Russ.: **Mar(y)in.** Croatian: **Mar(ič)ić, Marjanović.**

Metrs. (from dims.): Eng.: **Marians.** Russ.: **Mariyushkin, Marikhin, Maryakhin, Maryashkin, Maryushkin, Maryasin, Mash(k)in, Mashikhin, Mashenkin, Mashutkin, Man(ikh)in, Manyurin.** Ukr.: **Marusin.** Croatian: **Marušić.**

Habitation name: Pol.: **Maruszewski.**

François Marion *(c.1732–95), partisan leader in the American Revolution, known as 'the Swamp Fox', came of a family of French origin established in S Carolina c.1690 by his grandfather, a Huguenot who was a native of Poitou.*

Marimon Catalan: of uncertain origin. It has been explained as a habitation name from *Miremont* in Garonne, France, so called from OProv. *mirar* to look, watch + *mont* hill (i.e. 'look-out hill'), and as from a medieval given name composed of the Gmc elements *ber(i)* bear + *mund* protection, but neither of these etymologies is very convincing.

Marin 1. French: from a personal name (L *Marīnus*, a Roman family name derived from *Marius*; cf. MARIE). This was borne by several minor early saints.

2. French: occupational name for a sailor, OF *marin* (LL *marīnus*, a deriv. of *mare* sea).

3. Jewish (Ashkenazic): of unknown origin.

Vars. (of 2): **Marinier, Lemari(g)nier.** (Of 3): **Marinberg** (evidently an ornamental elaboration).

Cogns. (of 1): Eng.: **Mar(r)in.** It.: **Marini, Marino; Marin** (Venetia). Sp.: **Marino, Marín.** Cat.: **Marí** (also of 2). Port.: **Marinho.** Rum.: **Marin.** Flem., Du.: **Marinus.** (Of 2): Eng.: **Mar(r)iner, Marner.** It.: **Marinari, Marinaro; Marinai** (Tuscany). Cat.: **Marí** (also of 1); **Mariné.**

Dims. (of 1): It.: **Marin(i)ello, Marinelli, Marinetto, Marinetti, Marinucci, Marinuzzi, Marinolli, Marinotti, Marinotto.** (Of 3): **Marinczik** (E Ashkenazic).

Aug. (of 1): It.: **Marinoni.**

Pejs. (of 1): It.: **Marinacci(o), Marinazzo, Marinato.**

Patrs. (from 1): It.: **De Marini(s).** Rum.: **Marinescu.** Croatian: **Marin(ov)ić.** Bulg.: **Marinov.** Pol.: **Marynowicz.** (Of 3): **Marinoff, Marinow** (E Ashkenazic); **Marinescu** (among Rumanian Jews).

Patr. (from a dim. of 1): Croatian: **Marinković.**

Habitation name: Pol.: **Marynowski.**

Marivaux French: habitation name from places called *Marivaux* in Aisne, Oise, and Seine-et-Oise, or *Marival* in Aisne and Haute-Savoie. The second element is presumably OF *val* valley (see VALE); the first is of uncertain origin.

Var.: **Marival.**

Marjoram English (Norfolk): apparently from the name of the herb, ME *majorane, mageram* (via OF from med. L *majorana*, of obscure derivation).

Marjoribanks Scots: according to Black, this name was adopted by a family previously known as JOHNSTON, when, in the early 16th cent., they acquired the lands of *Ratho-Marjoribankis* in Renfrew. This estate was so called from having been bestowed on Robert the Bruce's daughter *Marjorie* (see MARGUERITE) on her marriage in 1316 to Walter the High Steward. The pronunciation is normally /ˈmɑːtʃbæŋks/.

Var.: **Marchbanks.**

Mark 1. English: from L *Marcus*, the personal name of St Mark the Evangelist, author of the second Gospel. The name was borne also by a number of other early Christian saints. *Marcus* was an old Roman name, of uncertain (possibly non-Italic) etymology; it may have some connection with the name of the war god *Mars* (cf. MARTIN). The given name was not as popular in England in the Middle Ages as it was on the Continent, especially in Italy, where the evangelist became the patron of Venice and the Venetian Republic, and was allegedly buried at Aquileia.

2. English: topographic name for someone who lived on a boundary between two districts (OE *mearc*), or habitation name from any of the various places named with this word, such as *Mark* in Somerset. See also MARCH 1 and MARQUE 1.

3. Jewish (Ashkenazic): in many cases an Anglicization of any of several like-sounding Jewish surnames. However, since *Mark* has also been an Ashkenazic surname in E

Europe, where English influence is out of the question, there must be at least one other explanation too.

Vars. (of 2): **Marke**, MARKS.

Cogns. (of 1): Fr.: **Marc(q)**; **Marcus** (Latinized). It.: **Marco, Marchi**. Sp.: **Marco(s)**. Cat.: MARCH. Port.: **Marcos**. Rum.: **Marcu**. Ger.: **Markus, Marcus**, MARKS. Flem., Du.: **Markus, Marcus, Merck**. Dan., Norw.: **Marcus**. Czech: MAREK. Hung.: **Márk, Markus**. (Of 2): Fr.: **Marck** (a place in Pas-de-Calais), MARQUE. Flem., Du.: **Van der Mark**.

Dims. (of 1): Fr.: **Marquet, Marquot**. It.: **Marchel(li), Marchello, Marchet(ti), Marchetto, Marchitto, Marchitelli, Marchitiello, Marchetiello, Marchin(i), Marcolin(i), Marchiol(i), Marcocci(o), Marcozzi, Marcucci(o), Marcuzzi, Marcuzzo**. Ger.: **Mark(e)l, Merkel, Merkle, Märkli(n)**. Pol.: **Marczyk**. Ukr.: **Marchenko**.

Augs. (of 1): It.: **Marcon(i), Marcone**.

Patrs. (from 1): Eng.: MARKS, **Markson**. Sc.: **McMarquis** (Gael. **Mac Marcuis**). It.: **De Marchi(s)**. Sp.: **Márquez**. Port.: **Marques**. Low Ger.: **Marcussen, Marx(s)en**. Flem., Du.: **Merckx**. Dan., Norw.: **Markussen, Marcussen**. Russ.: **Mark(os)ov**. Ukr.: **Markovich**. Pol.: **Markowicz, Markiewicz**; **Marczak**. Croatian: **Marković**. Bulg.: **Markov**. Jewish: **Markson**; **Marcov, Marcoff, Markovitch, Marcovi(t)ch, Markovic(h), Marcovic, Marcovicz, Marcovitz, Markovitz, Marcovits, Markovits, Marcowi(t)ch, Marcowic(z), Marcowitz, Markowitz, Markewitz, Markovski, Markovsky, Markowsky** (E Ashkenazic); **Marcovici, Markovici** (among Rumanian Jews). Armenian: **Margossian**. Lithuanian: **Morkúnas**.

Patrs. (from 1) (dims.): Russ.: **Markush(k)in, Markushev, Mar(k)tsev, Markisov, Markichev**.

Habitation names: Pol.: **Markowski, Marczewski, Marczyński**.

Marker 1. English: topographic name for someone who lived by a boundary; see MARK 2. It is notable that early examples of the surname tend to occur near borders, for example on the Kent/Sussex boundary. In the U.S.A., the name is also an Anglicization of the Ger. cogns. listed below.

2. English: possibly also an occupational name from an agent deriv. of ME *mark(en)* to put a mark on (OE *mearcian*), although it is not clear what the exact nature of the work of such a 'marker' would be.

3. English: relatively late development of MERCER. There is one family in Clitheroe, Lancs., who spelled their name *Mercer* or *Marcer* (cf. MARCHANT) in the 16th cent., but *Marker* in the 17th.

4. Jewish (Ashkenazic): of unknown origin. Compare MARK 3.

Var. (of 4): **Merker**.

Cogns. (of 1 and 2): Ger.: **Märker, Merker**.

Markey Irish: Anglicized form of Gael. **Ó Marcaigh** 'descendant of *Marcach*', a byname meaning 'Knight', 'Horseman'.

Cogns.: Corn.: **Marrack**. Bret.: **(Le) Mar(r)ec**.

Dims.: Ir.: **O'Markaghaine, O'Marcahan, Marca(ha)n**, MARKHAM (Gael. **Ó Marcacháin**).

Markham 1. English: habitation name from a place in Notts., so called from OE *mearc* boundary (see MARK 2) + *hām* homestead.

2. Irish: Anglicized form of Gael. *Ó Marcacháin*; see MARKEY.

Markland English (Lancs.): habitation name from a place in the parish of Wigan, so called from OE *mearc* boundary (see MARK 2) + *lanu* lane.

Var.: **Martland**. See also MARLAND and MARSLAND.

Marklew English (W Midlands): probably a habitation name from an unidentified place, perhaps named with OE *mearc* boundary (see MARK 2) + *hlǣw* hill (a byform of *hlāw*; cf. LAW 2 and LOW 1). Alternatively, the second element could conceivably be a river name (there is a river *Lliw* in Wales, and a *Lew* in Devon, the names of which are derived from a Celt. element meaning 'bright', 'shining').

Var.: **Martlew**.

Marks 1. English: patr. from MARK 1.

2. English: topographic name, var. of MARK 2.

3. German: contracted form of *Markus*, the Ger. version of MARK 1.

4. Jewish (W Ashkenazic): adoption of the Ger. surname, chosen under the influence of various like-sounding Jewish given names.

Vars. (of 3 and 4): **Marx**.

Markwardt German (common esp. in N Germany): occupational name for a frontier guard, Ger. *Markwart*, from *Mark* frontier, boundary (see MARK 2) + *Wart* guard (MHG, OHG *wart*, cogn. with OE *weard*; see WARD). In MHG folk stories *Markwart* occurs as a nickname for a jay; it is possible that this use influenced the acquisition of the surname to some extent.

Vars.: **Markward, Marquardt**.

Cogn.: Czech: **Markvart** (from the Ger. word).

Patr.: Dan.: **Marquardsen**.

Marland English (S Lancs.): habitation name from a minor place in the parish of Rochdale, so called from OE *mere* lake, pool + *land* land. There may also have been some confusion with MARKLAND.

Marler English: topographic name for someone who lived on a patch of clay soil, ME *marl* (OF *marle*, LL *margīla*, from earlier *marga* (prob. of Gaul. origin), with the ending added under the influence of the synonymous *argilla*).

Var.: **Marlor**.

Marley English: habitation name from any of the various places so called, for example in Devon, Kent, and W Yorks. According to Ekwall, the first element of these placenames is respectively OE *(ge)mǣre* boundary, *myrig* pleasant, and *mearð* (pine) marten. The second element in each case is OE *lēah* wood, clearing.

Vars.: **Marlee**, MARLOW.

This surname was taken to Ireland by a Northumbrian family who settled there in the 17th cent.

Marlow English: 1. habitation name from the town in Bucks., on the Thames, so called from OE *mere* lake, pool + *lāfe* remnants, leavings, i.e. a boggy area remaining after a lake had been drained.

2. var. of MARLEY.

Var.: **Marlowe**.

The Elizabethan dramatist Christopher Marlowe *and his father wrote their name* Marley, *and in some official documents Christopher Marlowe is designated as* Marle *and* Morley.

Marney English (Norman): habitation name from *Marigni* in La Manche, so called from the Gallo-Roman personal name *Marīnius* + the local suffix *-ācum*.

Vars.: **Marnie, De Marney**.

Maroto Spanish: probably a nickname for a lascivious person, from OSp. *marueco* ram (of pre-Roman origin).

Marouzeau Provençal: habitation name from a farm named with the OProv. elements *mas* farm(stead) (see

MAS) + *rouzeau*, a nickname for a red-haired proprietor (cf. RUSSELL).

Vars.: **Marozeau, Marouzé.**

Marple English: habitation name from a place in Ches., so called from OE *(ge)mǣre* boundary + *pōl* pool or *pyll* steam.

Var.: **Marples** (now found chiefly in S Yorks.).

Marque French: 1. topographic name for someone who lived near a boundary, OF *marque* (of Gmc origin; cf. MARK 2 and MARCH 1).

2. metonymic nickname for someone with a noticeable birthmark, or who had suffered the disfigurement of branding (a relatively common medieval punishment; cf. BRENNAN 2), from OF *marque* mark (a transferred sense of 1).

3. metonymic occupational name for a coiner, or nickname with a lost anecdotal origin, from OF *marc*, a coin of high value. The vocab. word is of uncertain etymology, but may be of the same origin as above, from the design marked on it.

Var. (of 1 and 2): **Lamarque.**

Cogn. (of 1): Cat.: **Lamarca.**

Marquis 1. French (Norman) and English: nickname for someone who behaved like a marquess or occupational name for a servant in the household of a marquess, from ONF *marquis*. The title originally referred to the governor of a border territory (cf. MARQUE 1). Marquesses did not form part of the original Fr. feudal structure of nobility; the title was first adopted by the Counts of Toulouse because of their possessions in the border region beyond the Rhône.

2. Scots: var. of *McMarquis* (Gael. *Mac Marcuis*), a patr. from MARK 1.

Vars. (of 1): Fr.: **Lemarquis; Marchis.**

Cogns. (of 1): Prov., Cat.: **Marquès.** Sp.: **Marqués.** It.: **Marquese, Marchese, Marchesi, Marcheso, Marchiso, Marchisi.**

Dims. (of 1): Fr.: **Marquiset.** It.: **Marchisello, Marchiselli, Marchisini** (Emilia); **Marchesin** (Venetia); **Marchesotti.**

Aug. (of 1): It.: **Marchesoni.**

Marr 1. English: habitation name from *Marr* in W Yorks., which is of uncertain etymology. It may have been named with ON *marr*, a rare word used normally of the sea, but perhaps also of a marsh or fen, as reflected in modern dial. forms.

2. Scots: habitation name from *Mar* in the former county of Aberdeens., the etymology of which is equally uncertain, and possibly identical with that of 1.

Vars.: **Marre, Marrs.**

Marriott English: from the medieval female given name *Mariot*, a dim. of *Mary* (see MARIE).

Vars.: MARRYAT, MERRIOT.

Marron Irish: Anglicized form of Gael. **Ó Mearáin** 'descendant of *Mearán*', a personal name from a dim. of *mear* lively.

Marryat English: 1. from a ME given name, *Meryet*, OE *Mǣrgēat*, composed of the element *mǣr* boundary + the tribal name *Gēat* (see JOCELYN).

2. var. of MARRIOTT.

Var.: **Maryatt.** See also MERRIOT.

Marsden English: habitation name from places in Lancs. and W Yorks., so called from OE *mearc* boundary (see MARK 2) + *denu* valley (see DEAN 1), i.e. a valley forming a natural boundary.

Marsh English: topographic name for someone who lived by or in a marsh or fen, OE *mersc* (for the change of *-er-* to *-ar-*, cf. MARCHANT).

Vars.: **Mersh; Mars, Mash; Ma(r)shman.**

Cogns.: Ger.: **Ma(r)sch(mann), Merschmann, Mörsch(ner).** Flem., Du.: **Me(e)rsch, Van der Meersch, Vermeersch.** Fr.: **Marais, Marois; Lemarois; Dumarais, Desmarais.** Prov.: **Marest, Desmarest.**

Dim.: It.: **Marescotti.**

Marshall English and Scots: occupational name from ME, OF *maresc(h)al* marshal. The term is of Gmc origin (cf. OHG *marah* horse, mare + *scalc* servant), and was originally applied to a man who looked after horses. By the heyday of surname formation it referred on the one hand to one of the most important servants in every great household (in the royal household a high official of state), and on the other to a humble shoeing smith or farrier. A similar wide range of meanings is found in other languages: for example, in Polish a *marszałek* can be anything from a field marshal or the chairman of the Polish parliament to the senior servant in a household. The surname is also borne by Jews, presumably as an Anglicization of one or more like-sounding Jewish surnames.

Vars.: **Marschall; Ma(r)skell, Maskall, Mascall, Maskill** (from ANF forms).

Cogns.: Fr.: **Maréchal, Mar(es)chal, Maréchau(x), Marchaux, Marchaud, Ma(r)chaut; Marescal, Marécal, Mari-c(h)al, Marichell, Marescot, Maricot; Menescal, Manescal, Manesc(e)au** (by confusion with SENESCHAL). It.: **Marescalco, Marescalchi, Mariscalco, Maricalchi, Marascalchi** (Venetia); **Manescalchi, Maniscalchi, Maniscalco** (Sicily); **Mascalchi** (Tuscany). Ger.: **Marschal(l), Marschalk, Marschlich.** Flem., Du.: **Maarschalk, De Maerschlack, Maryssal.** Pol.: **Marszał.** Czech: **Maršál.**

Dims.: Fr.: **Marchaudon; Mesclou** (Brittany). Ger. (of Slav. origin): **Marschallek, Marschollek.** Pol.: **Marszałek.** Czech: **Maršálek.**

Marsham English: habitation name from a place in Norfolk, so called from OE *mersc* MARSH + *hām* homestead.

A family of this name were granted the earldom of Romney in 1801. Their descent is traced from John Marsham *(d. 1515) of Stratton Strawless in Norfolk.*

Marsland English (chiefly S Lancs.): habitation name, probably from some place named as being a boggy place, from OE *mersc* MARSH + *land* land. Alternatively, it may be a var. of MARKLAND.

Marston English: habitation name from any of the numerous places so called, of which there are examples in at least sixteen counties. All get their names from OE *mersc* MARSH + *tūn* enclosure, settlement.

Var.: **Marson.**

Martel English and French: 1. from a medieval given name, a dim. of MARTIN or of MARTHE.

2. metonymic occupational name for a smith or nickname for a forceful person, from OF *martel* hammer (LL *martellus*, a var. of *martulus*, *marculus*; cf. MACHO). Charles Martel, the grandfather of Charlemagne, gained his byname from the force with which he struck down his enemies in battle.

Vars.: Eng.: **Martell.** Fr.: **Marteau; Martel(l)ier** (occupational).

Cogns.: It.: **Martelli, Mart(i)ello.**

Dims.: Fr.: **Martelet, Marteret.** It.: **Martellini, Martellino, Martelotti, Martelotto.**

Marthe French and German: from the female name which appears in the Gk New Testament as *Martha* (Aramaic

Marta 'Lady'), borne by the sister of Lazarus and Mary (of Bethany).

Vars.: Ger.: **Morthe, Merta.**

Cogns.: It.: **Marte, Marti.** Port.: **Marta.**

Dims.: Fr.: **Mart(h)on, Martot,** MARTEL, **Marthelot.**

Martial French: from a personal name (L *Martiālis*, originally a family name, apparently derived from that of the war god *Mars*; cf. MARTIN). This was borne by a minor 3rd-cent. saint, the first bishop of Limoges.

Vars.: **Marsal, Marseau, Marsau(l)t, Marsaud.**

Cogns.: Cat.: **Marsal.** Port.: **Marçal.**

Dim.: Fr.: **Marsallon.**

Martin English, Scots, Irish, French, German, Czech, Flemish/Dutch, and Danish/Norwegian: from a personal name (L *Martīnus*, a deriv. of *Mars*, gen. *Martis*, the Roman god of fertility and war, whose name may derive ultimately from a root *mar* gleam). This was borne by a famous 4th-cent. saint, Martin of Tours, and consequently became extremely popular throughout Europe in the Middle Ages. It is one of the few saints' names other than the names of OE saints found in England before the Conquest.

Vars.: Eng.: **Marten, Martyn.** Fr.: **Martine, Lamartine** (fem. forms). Flem., Du.: **Martijn, Martyn, Marten.**

Cogns.: It.: **Martini, Martino; Martina** (fem.). Prov.: **Marti, Marty.** Sp.: **Martín.** Cat.: **Martí.** Port.: **Martinho.** Low Ger.: **Mart(h)en; Mertin, Merten** (hypercorrected forms). Swed.: MORTON. Hung.: **Márton.**

Dims.: Fr.: **Martineau** (also common in Birmingham); **Martinet, Martinon, Martinot; Tinot** (an aphetic form). It.: **Martinello, Martinelli, Martinetto, Martinetti, Martinol(l)i, Martinotti, Martinuzzi.** Ger.: **Märtl, Mertel; Mörtel** (Bavaria); **Marti, Marty** (Switzerland). Low Ger.: **Mertgen; Tienke** (see also AUSTIN). Flem., Du.: **Meert.** Ger. (of Slav. origin): **Martsch(ke), Martschik, Mertsching.** Ukr.: **Martinyuk, Martinets.** Pol.: **Martynka, Marciek.** Czech: **Martínek;** MAREK.

Augs.: Fr.: **Martinat.** It.: **Marti(g)noni, Martignon.** Czech: **Martinec.** Pol.: **Marciniec.**

Patrs.: Eng.: **Martins, Martyns, Martens; Martinson.** Sc.: **McMartin.** It.: **De Martino, Di Martino, De Martini, (De) Martinis.** Sp.: **Martínez.** Port.: **Martins.** Ger.: **Martini** (Latinized). Low Ger.: **Martens(en), Me(h)rtens; Marti(e)n(s)sen** (N Rhineland). Flem., Du.: **Martens, Me(e)rtens.** Dan., Norw.: **Martin(us)sen, Mortensen.** Swed.: **Martinsson, Mårtensson.** Croatian: **Mart(inov)ić.** Pol.: **Marciniak; Marcinowicz, Martynowicz.** Ukr.: **Martinovich.** Russ.: **Martynov.** Lithuanian: **Martinaitis.** Hung.: **Mártonfi, Mártonf(f)y.**

Patrs. (from dims.): Low Ger.: **Mertz; Tienken.** Russ.: **Martyshkin, Mart(y)ushev, Martusov, Martygin, Martyntsev, Martyanychev.** Beloruss.: **Martsinkevich.** Pol.: **Marcinkiewicz.** Lithuanian: **Marcinkus.** Finn.: **Martikainen.**

'Son of the wife of M.': Russ.: **Martynikhin.**

Habitation names: Pol.: **Marcinkowski, Marciszewski.** Czech: **Martinovský.**

The Eng. surname Martin *is first attested in the 12th cent. and is now among the 50 commonest surnames in all areas of the English-speaking world. Within England the name is concentrated most densely in Cornwall and Sussex.*

Harriet Martineau *(1802–76), the English writer, was the daughter of a Norwich manufacturer. She was directly descended from a family of French Huguenots who owned land around Poitou and Touraine in the 15th cent. They included a number of surgeons in the 17th cent. In the 19th cent. a branch of the family was firmly established in Birmingham.*

Martindale English: habitation name from a place in Cumb., first recorded in 1220 in its present form. There is a chapel of St Martin here, and the valley (see DALE) may be named from this. Alternatively, there may have been a landowner here called *Martin*, and the church dedication may be due to popular association of his name with that of the saint.

Martorell Catalan: from a medieval given name of this form and uncertain origin, probably from LL *Martyrellus*, a dim. of *martyr* martyr (originally 'witness (to the faith)', from Gk *martyrein* to bear witness). There are also places in the provinces of Barcelona and Valencia so called from early proprietors, and in some cases the surname may be a habitation name from one of them.

Marvel English: 1. nickname for a person considered prodigious in some way, from ME, OF *merveille* miracle (L *mīrābilia*, originally neut. pl. of the adj. *mīrābilis* admirable, amazing). The nickname was no doubt sometimes given with mocking intent.

2. Norman habitation name, from places called *Merville*. The one in Nord is named from OF *mendre* smaller, lesser (L *minor*) + *ville* settlement; that in Calvados seems to have as its first element a Gmc personal name, probably a short form of a cpd name with the first element *mari*, *meri* famous.

Var.: **Marvell.**

Cogns. (of 1): Fr.: **Merveille.** It.: **Meraviglia.**

The English poet Andrew Marvell *(1621–78) was born near Hull in the village of Winestead, where his father was rector. His ancestry can be traced back to 1279 in the area of Meldreth, Cambs.*

Marwick Scots: habitation name from a place in the Orkneys, so called from ON *marr* sea, lake, marsh (see MARR) + *vík* bay. The surname is also borne in the U.S. by Jews, as an Anglicized form of one or more Ashkenazic surnames.

Marwood English: 1. habitation name from a place so called, probably the one in Co. Durham, which Ekwall derives from OE *māra* greater, larger (cf. mod. Eng. *more*) + *wudu* WOOD.

2. Norman nickname for a person believed to have the power of casting the 'evil eye', from ONF *malreward*, a cpd of *mal* evil, bad + *reward* (OF *regard*) look.

Mas 1. Low German and Dutch: aphetic form of THOMAS.

2. Provençal and Catalan: topographic name for someone who lived in an isolated dwelling in the country, rather than in a village, from OProv., Cat. *mas* farm(stead) (LL *mansum*, *mansus*).

Vars. (of 1): **Masius** (Latinized). (Of 2): Prov.: **Lemas; Duma(i)s, Duma(i)t, Dumès, Dumé(e), Dumeix, Dume(t)z, Dumay, Delmas; Aumas.** Cat.: **Delmàs.**

Cogn. (of 2): It.: **Massa.**

Dims. (of 2): Prov.: **Maset, Masot, Mazet, Dumazet, Mazel, Mazeau, Dumazel, Dumazeau, Mazin, Mazot.** Cat.: **Mas(s)ó** (see also MASON).

Máša Czech: from the given name *Máša*, a pet form of any given name beginning with *Ma-*, in particular *Matěj* (see MATTHEW), MARTIN, and *Mauritius* (see MORRIS). It may also be an aphetic form of *Tomáš* (see THOMAS).

Vars.: **Mašát, Mašata, Mašín.**

Dims.: **Mašek, Maška.**

Masdeu Catalan: habitation name from a farm named with the elements *mas* farm(stead) (see MAS) + *Deu* God (L *deus*); several places were so called in the Middle Ages as a pious invocation of God's blessing on the holding.

Masefield English: apparently a habitation name from an unidentified place, perhaps in the W Midlands, and possibly named with the OE personal name *Mæssa* or the medieval given name MACE + OE *feld*, ME *feild* pasture, open country (see FIELD).

Masheter English: of problematic origin. Reaney's evidence suggests that it derives from the Tudor surname *Masherudder* (York 1517). This would be an occupational nickname for a worker in a brewery, from ME *mash* malt mixed with hot water to form wort (OE *māsc*) + *rudder* (OE *roþer*), i.e. a rudder-shaped implement used to stir the fermenting mass.

Vars.: **Mashiter, Mashe(d)der, Masseter, Messiter.**

Maslin English: 1. from the medieval given name *Masselin*. This originated as an OF dim. of Gmc names with the first element *mathal* speech, counsel. However, it was later used as a dim. of MATTHEW (see MACE). A fem. form, *Mazelina*, was probably originally a dim. of *Matilda*.

2. possibly also a metonymic occupational name. Reaney suggests that this referred to a maker and seller of wooden bowls, from ME, OF *maselin* bowl or goblet of maple wood (a dim. of OF *masere* maple wood, of Gmc origin). It is also possible that in some cases it derives from one of the homonymous dial. terms *maslin*, one of which means 'brass' (OE *mæslen*, *mæstling*; cf. MESSINGER 2), the other 'mixed grain' (OF *mesteillon*, LL *mixtilio*, a deriv. of *mixtus* mixed).

Vars.: **Maslen, Masling.**

Maslov Russian and Jewish (E Ashkenazic): patr. from the Russ. vocab. word *maslo* butter, presumably used as an occupational name for a dairyman, or acquired for some anecdotal reason now lost.

Vars.: Jewish: **Maslow, Maslovitz**; **Maslo** (not a patr.); **Maslovaty** (an adj. deriv.).

Cogn.: Pol.: **Masłowski.**

Mason English and Scots: occupational name for a stonemason, ME, OF *mas(s)on* (apparently of Gmc origin, perhaps akin to OE *macian* to make or *mattuc* mattock). See also MASSON and MACHIN.

Cogns.: Fr.: MASSON, **Maçon**; **Machon** (Normandy); **Lemasson, Lemaçon**. It.: **Massone**. Cat.: **Maçó**; **Mas(s)ó** (see also MAS).

Patr.: Fr.: **Aumasson.**

George Mason *(1725–92), the American Colonial statesman who framed the Virginia Bill of Rights and Constitution, which was used as a model by Jefferson when drafting the Declaration of Independence, was a Virginia planter, fourth in descent from George Mason (?1629–?86), a Cavalier soldier who had received land grants in Virginia. As well as being prominent in the affairs of Virginia, the family also produced the first governor of Michigan.*

Two other men of this name were early English settlers in America. John Mason (1586–1635) was born in King's Lynn, became governor of Newfoundland in 1615, and was one of the founders of New Hampshire. His namesake, John Mason (?1600–72), emigrated before 1633 and was one of the founders of Norwich, Connecticut.

Massey English (Norman) and French: habitation name from any of various places in N France which get their names from the Gallo-Roman personal name *Maccius* + the local suffix *-ācum*.

Vars.: Eng.: **Massy, Mac(e)y.** Fr.: **Macey, Macé, Massé.**

Massingberd English: nickname for someone with a tawny beard, from ME *massing* brass (probably of Scandinavian origin; cf. MESSINGER 2) + BEARD.

Var.: **Massingbird.**

Massingham English: habitation name from a place in Norfolk, so called from OE *Mæssinghām* 'homestead (OE *hām*) associated with **Mæssa*'.

Masson 1. Scots: var. of MASON.

2. French: cogn. of MASON.

3. French: aphetic form of *Thomasson*, dim. of THOMAS (cf. MAAS 1).

Dims. (of 3): Fr.: **Massoneau, Massonet, Massenet.**

Mastalerz Polish: occupational name for a stableman or groom, Pol. *masztalerz*.

Cogn.: Czech: **Maštalíř.**

Master English and Scots: nickname for someone who behaved in a masterful manner, or occupational name for someone who was master of his craft, from ME *maister* (OF *maistre*, L *magister*). In early instances this surname was often borne by people who were franklins or other substantial freeholders, presumably because they had labourers under them to work their lands, and unlike smaller free tenants did not just till their property themselves. In Scotland the eldest sons of barons had this title, and the name may also have been acquired as an occupational nickname by a servant who worked in the household of the eldest son of a baron.

Var.: **Meystre.**

Cogns.: Fr.: **Maistre, Maître**; **Lemaistre, Lemaître**; **Maîtrier.** Prov.: **Mestre, Mistre**; **Mestrier**. It.: **Maestri, Maestro**; **Maistri, Maistro** (Venetia); **Ma(i)sto** (Naples), **Magistri, Magistro** (Lombardy); **Mastro, Marro** (S Italy); **Mascio** (Apulia, Salento); **Lo Mast(r)o** (Sicily). Sp.: **Maestre, Maeso.** Cat.: **Maestre, Mestre(s).** Port.: **Mestre.** Ger.: **Meister.** Low Ger.: **Me(e)ster.** Flem., Du.: **(De) Meester.** Jewish: **Meister, Majster** (Ashkenazic, denoting a rabbi as a leading figure in a Jewish community); **Maestro** (Sefardic, denoting a schoolteacher). Bulg.: **Maistora.** Hung.: **Mester.**

Dims.: Fr.: **Mai(s)tret, Maitrot.** Prov.: **Mestrel, Métreau.** It.: **Maestrello, Maestrelli, Ma(i)strelli, Maistrello, Magistrelli, Magistretti, Maestrini, Mastrillo, Mastrilli, Mastruzzo, Masciullo.**

Aug.: It.: **Maestrone.**

Pej.: It.: **Maestacci.**

Patrs.: Eng.: **Masters**; **Masterson.** Sc.: MCMASTER. Fr.: **Aumaître.** It.: **De Magistri, (De) Magistris.** Low Ger.: **Meistering.** Flem., Du.: **Smeesters, Smeysters.** Russ.: **Mashtakov** (from the vocab. word borrowed via Pol. from Ger.). Croatian: **Majstorović.**

'Servant of the master': Eng.: **Masterman.**

Masterton Scots: habitation name from a place in Fife, so called from the Older Sc. title *maister* (see MASTER) + ME *tune* village, settlement. The lands were once held by a tenant referred to in the Latinized form *Magister Ailricus*, and their name may derive from him.

Mata Spanish, Catalan, and Portuguese: topographic name for someone who lived by a plantation of trees, OSp. *mata* (of uncertain origin).

Vars.: Sp.: **Matas.** Port.: **Matos.** Both these forms are also found as Jewish surnames, but the reasons for their adoption are unclear.

Dim.: Sp.: **Matilla.**

Matchett N Irish: of uncertain origin, possibly a dim. of MATTHEW. The surname **Matches** is found in the Orkney and Shetland islands, and was formerly used as a given name there; it has been supposed to derive from a Scandinavian form of MATTHEW.

Matesanz Spanish: apparently from a combination of the given names *Mate* (see MATTHEW) + *Sanz* (see SANCHO); cf. ROBESPIERRE.

Mather English: 1. occupational name for a mower or reaper of grass or hay, OE *mǣðere* (cf. MEAD 1 and MOWER). Hay was formerly of great importance, not only as feed for animals in winter but also for bedding.

2. in S Lancs., where it has long been a common surname, it is probably a relatively late development of MADDER.

Var.: **Mathur.**

Cogns. (of 1): Ger.: **Ma(h)der, Mä(h)der, Meder.**

Dim. (of 1): Ger.: **Mederle.**

Patr.: Eng.: **Mathers.**

The prominent Mather *family of New England were established in America by Richard Mather (1596–1669) in 1635. He was a Puritan clergyman from a well-established family of Lowton, Lancs. After he emigrated, he was in great demand as a preacher, finally settling in Dorchester, Mass. His son Increase Mather (1639–1723) was a diplomat and president of Harvard. He married his stepsister Maria Cotton, herself the daughter of an eminent Puritan divine, John Cotton. Their son Cotton Mather (1663–1728) bore both family names. The latter was a minister who is remembered for his part in witchcraft trials, but he was also a man of science and a fellow of the Royal Society in London.*

Matthew English and Scots: from the ME given name *Mathew*, of biblical origin, ultimately from the Hebr. male given name *Matityahu* 'Gift of God', recorded in the Gk New Testament in the form *Matth(a)ias*. This was taken into L as both *Matthias* and *Matthaeus*, the former being used for the apostle and the latter for the evangelist. However, the distinction was not consistently made, and in most languages the two forms have completely fallen together again (vernacular forms of the given name, e.g. OF *Matheu*, Sp. *Mateo*, It. *Matteo*, etc., normally being derived from *Matthaeus*).

Vars.: **Mathew; Ma(t)thias** (a learned form, found chiefly in Wales); MAYHEW.

Cogns.: Fr.: **Mat(h)ieu; Mathé(e), Mathey, Mathet; Mathie, Mat(h)y, Matthis, Mat(h)is, Mathys, Matisse; Mat(h)ias, Matyas.** It.: **Mattea, Mattia, Matteo, Mattei; Mattedi, Mattevi; Maffeo, Maffei, Maffi(a), Maffii** (Venetia, Lombardy); **Masseo, Massei, Mazzea, Mazzeo, Mazzei, Mazzi(a)** (S Italy). Sp.: **Mate(o), Mateos; Matías, Macías.** Cat.: **Mateu; Macià.** Port.: **Mateus; Matias.** Rum.: **Matei.** Ger.: **Matthäus, Mattheus, Matthius, Ma(t)the(i)s; Matthesius** (Latinized). Low Ger.: **Matiewe, Matiebe, Tiebe**; see also THIESS. Flem., Du.: **Mattheeuw; Mathys.** Ger. (of Slav. origin): **Mattaus;** MACH. Czech: **Matěj, Matyáš, Matys, Matas, Matouš, Matura, Matula; Macák, Macoun, Macura;** MACH, MÁŠA. Croatian: **Macura.** Pol.: **Matys, Mateja, Matyja; Macieja** (from the usual Pol. form of the given name, *Maciej*); MACH. Ukr.: **Mat(v)iyas.** Beloruss.: **Matei.** Hung.: **Máté; Mátyás** (also Jewish). Jewish: **Mat(t)es, Matis, Matus** (Ashkenazic; see also MAITES); **Matityahu, Mattityah(o)u, Matitiaho(u), Matatyah(o)u** (Israeli).

Dims.: Eng.: **Matt(in), Matten, Mat(t)on, Matkin**; see also MACE and MESLIN. Fr.: **Mathivet, Mathivon, Mathevet, Mathevon; Mathe(lin), Mathely, Mathelon, Math(i)ot, Mathon(net), Matteau; Mat(h)ou** (Brittany). It.: **Mattiello, Mattielli, Matteini, Matt(e)ucci, Matteuzzi, Mattiuzzi, Matt(i)ussi, Matteoli, Mattioli, Matteotti; Maffetti, Maffini, Maf(f)ucci, Maffiol(ett)i, Maffezzoli, Maffiotti, Maffulli; Mazzilli, Mazziotti, Mazzullo.** Ger.: **Matthäi** (Switzerland); **Matz(e)l, Metzel** (Bohemia, Bavaria); see also HIESS and DIESEL. Ger. (of Slav. origin): **Matz(ke), Matschke, Mätschke, Metschke, Metzke, Metzi(n)g, Matschek, Matschuk, Matschoss, Mattschas, Mattke, Mattek.** Czech: **Matěj(í)ček, Matějka, Matiásek, Matoušek, Matuška; Macek, Macourek.** Pol.: **Matuszyk, Matysik, Mateuszczyk, Matyjasik; Macieiczyk, Maciaszek, Maciaszczyk.** Ukr.: **Matveiko, Matyushenko.** Beloruss.: **Matyushonok, Mateiko.** Jewish (E Ashkenazic): **Matuschek.**

Augs.: Fr.: **Mathivat.** It.: **Matteoni, Mattioni; Maffioni, Maff(i)one.**

Pejs.: It.: **Matteacci, Mattiacci, Mattiazzi, Mattiazzo, Mattiassi, Mattiato.**

Patrs.: Eng.: **Ma(t)thew(e)s; Ma(t)thewson.** It.: **De Mattia, De Mattei, Di Mattei, Di Matteo, (De) Matteis.** Rum.: **Mateescu.** Ger.: **Mattäser** (Bavaria). Low Ger.: **Matthiessen, Matthe(e)(s)sen.** Dan., Norw.: **Mathia(s)sen, Mathi(s)sen, Matthie(s)sen.** Swed.: **Matt(h)isson.** Croatian: **Mat(ej)ić, Matij(aš)ević, Matović.** Pol.: **Mackiewicz; Matusiak, Matuszak, Matysiak, Maciejak, Maciak.** Beloruss.: **Mateev.** Russ.: **Matveyev, Matveichev.** Jewish: **Matusson** (Ashkenazic); **Mat(t)usov, Matussov, Matussow, Matusovsky, Matis(s)off, Mattosof, Mattusevich, Matussevich, Matushevitz, Matuszak** (E Ashkenazic). Lithuanian: **Matelyunas, Maciunas, Matelaitis.** Armenian: **Matevosian, Matessian.** Georgian: **Matiashvili.**

Patrs. (from dims.): Eng.: **Mathi(e)s, Ma(t)thys; Matti(n)son, Mattingson, Matterson; Matt(e)s, Ma(t)thes; Matson.** Sc.: **Ma(t)thi(e)son, Matheson.** Low Ger.: **Matzen.** Dan., Norw.: **Madsen.** Swed.: **Mattsson.** Russ.: **Matantsev, Matasov, Matusov, Matyatin, Matyugin, Matyukov, Matyushkin, Matashkin, Matyashev, Matoshin, Matokhin, Matanin, Matonin.** Ukr.: **Matskiv, Matushevich.** Beloruss.: **Matevushev, Matusevich, Matskevich.** Pol.: **Matuszkiewicz; Matczak.** Lithuanian: **Matz(k)aitis, Matz(k)eitis.** Croatian: **Matković; Mašić.**

'Servant of M.': Eng.: **Mat(t)hewman.**

'Relative of M.': Eng.: **Mattimoe** (cf. MAW 2).

Habitation names: Pol.: **Matuszewski, Matuszyński, Maciejewski.** Czech: **Matějovský.**

Mattila Finnish: name borne by a member of a household headed by someone called *Matti* MATTHEW, from the Finn. given name + the local suffix *-la*.

Mattingley English: habitation name from a place in Hants, originally named in OE as *Mattinglēah* 'wood, clearing associated with *Matta*'.

Var.: **Mattingly.**

Maturin French: from a personal name, L *Mātūrīnus* (a deriv. of *Mātūrūs* 'Timely'), borne by a 3rd-cent. saint who was responsible for spreading the gospel in the district of Sens.

Vars.: **Mathurin.**

Dims.: **Mathorel, Mathoré, Mathorez; Matheron.**

Augs.: **Mat(h)erat.**

Maudling English: from the ME vernacular form, *Maudeleyn*, of the Gk female given name *Magdalēnē*. This is a byname, meaning 'woman from *Magdala*' (a village on the Sea of Galilee, deriving its name from Hebr. *migdal* tower, itself from the adj. *gadol* large), which was given in the New Testament to the woman cured of evil spirits by Jesus (Luke 8: 2), who later became a faithful follower. The popularity of the given name increased with the supposed discovery of her relics in the 13th cent.

Cogns.: Fr.: **Ma(g)deleine, Madelin(e), Madolin.** Flem.: **Magdelyn.** Russ.: **Magdalinski** (surname adopted by Orthodox clergy).

Dims.: Fr.: **Ma(g)delon, Madon, Madot, Madoz.**

Metr.: Ger.: **Madlener.**

Metrs. (from dims.): Eng.: MADDISON. Flem.: **Maddens.**

Maufe English: 1. nickname for an untrustworthy person, from the ANF elements *mal*, *mau* bad + *fei*, *foi* faith.

2. variant of MAW 2.

Maughan 1. Scots: habitation name from *Machan* (now also called *Dalserf*) in the former county of Lanarks., named with a dim. form of Gael. *machair* (river) plain.

2. Irish: Anglicized form of Gael. *Ó Mocháin*; see MOHAN.

3. Welsh: habitation name from either of two places in the former county of Monmouths., one of which is called *(St) Maughan* (an Anglicized form of W *Llanfocha*

'Church of St *Mochan*'), and the other *Machen* 'Place of *Cain*'.

Vars.: **Maugham, Ma(u)chan.**

The English novelist Somerset Maugham *(1874–1965) was from a distinguished legal family. His father was a founder of the English Law Society, and his brother Frederick, 1st Viscount Maugham, was Lord Chancellor. Some of his paternal ancestors were more humble: his great-grandfather was a glazier. On his mother's side he claimed to be able to trace descent from King Edward I and Eleanor of Castile.*

Maul German: nickname for someone with a deformed mouth, or for someone who made excessive use of the mouth in eating, drinking, or talking, from Ger. *Maul* mouth, gob (MHG *mūl(e)*, OHG *mūla*). It is also possible that in some cases the surname may derive from MHG *mūl* mule (mod. Ger. *Maultier, Maulesel*) or even MHG *mūl(ber)* mulberry (mod. Ger. *Maulbeere*).

Vars.: **Mäule, Maile.**

Cogns.: Low Ger.: **Muhl(e).**

Dim.: Low Ger.: **Muhlke.**

Mauleverer English (Norman): nickname from OF *mal leverier* bad harrier (L *malus leporārius*). The name is apparently of anecdotal origin, and the reasons for its adoption as a surname are not clear. It is also the name of a place in Seine-Maritime, but this is probably so called from the family name of a Norman family who held it, rather than vice versa.

Maurer 1. German: occupational name for a builder of defensive walls or the walls of substantial buildings from stone or brick, from an agent deriv. of Ger. *Mauer* wall (MHG *mūre*, OHG *mūra*, from L *mūrus*; cf. MURAT). In the Middle Ages the majority of dwellings were built of wood (or lath and plaster); a *Maurer* would have been employed mainly in building defensive walls, castles, churches, and other public buildings.

2. Jewish (Ashkenazic): occupational name for a mason or bricklayer, mod. Ger. *Maurer*.

Vars.: **Meurer, Mauer(mann).**

Cogns.: Low Ger.: **Mührer, Mührmann.** Pol.: **Mularski** (the vocab. word being borrowed from Ger., undergoing dissimilation in the process). Ukr.: **Mulyar.**

Mauriac Provençal: habitation name from any of various places, for example in Cantal and Gironde, so called from the L personal name *Maurus* (see MOORE 3) + the local suffix *-ācum*.

Maus 1. German: nickname for someone supposedly resembling a mouse, in appearance or timidity, or else a metonymic occupational name for a catcher of mice and rats, from Ger. *Maus* mouse (MHG, OHG *mūs*).

2. Jewish (Ashkenazic): from Ger. *Maus* mouse, one of the most common of the unflattering surnames imposed on Jews by non-Jewish government officials in 18th- and 19th-cent. central Europe.

Vars.: Ger.: **Mauser, Meuser; Muser** (Switzerland). Jewish: **Meislish** ('mousy').

Cogns.: Flem., Du.: **(De) Muys, Muis.**

Dims.: Ger.: **Mäusel, Meusel, Meisel, Meissl.** Pol.: **Myszka** (from Pol. *myszka* mouse). Jewish: **Meisel(man), Maizel; Meisel(e)s, Majzels** (patrs. in form; *Majzels* is a Pol. spelling).

Habitation names: Pol.: **Myszk(or)owski.**

Maw English: 1. from the OE personal name *Mawa*, perhaps originally a byname from OE *mǣw* (sea-)mew, or alternatively akin to OE *māwan* to mow.

2. nickname for someone who was related to an important local personality, from ME *maugh, maw* relative, esp. by marriage (from OE *māge* female relative). This element is also found in compound names such as WATMOUGH.

3. topographic name, apparently from OE **māwe* meadow. Some early forms, such as Sibilla *de la Mawe* (Suffolk 1275), clearly indicate a topographic origin, by the preposition and article.

Vars.: **Mawe, Mowe, Mew(e).** (Of 2 only): **Mough,** MAUFE, **Muff.**

Cogns. (of 2): Ger.: **Maag.** Low Ger.: **Moog, Mo(o)gk.** Flem.: **De Maegh.**

Patrs. (from 1): Eng.: **Mawson, Mawsom** (see also MOULT).

Mawdesley English: habitation name from a place in Lancs., recorded in 1219 as *Madesle* and in 1269 as *Moudesley*, i.e. probably 'clearing of *Maud*' (see MOULT 1).

Vars.: **Mawdsley, Maudsley, Maudslay.**

Max German: from a short form of the given name *Maximilian* (L *Maximilliānus*, a deriv. of *Maximillus*, dim. of *Maximus* 'Greatest'), borne by a 3rd-cent. saint venerated particularly in the region of Passau, where he founded a church. This given name was comparatively rare at the most productive period of surname formation; it gained popularity from the Holy Roman Emperor Maximilian I (b. 1459), who was named by his father, Frederick III of Austria, in honour of the Roman heroes Q. Fabius Maximus and Scipio Aemilianus, as if with a combination of their names. The name is also borne by Ashkenazic Jews, presumably as an adoption of the Ger. surname.

Cogns. (patrs., from an aphetic form): Croatian: **Mil(i)jan(ov)ić.**

Maxey English: habitation name from a place in Northants, so called from the gen. case of the N English personal name MACK + OE *ēg* island, low-lying land.

Maxime French: from the personal name (L *Maximus* 'Greatest', superlative of *magnus* great; cf. MAGNUS), borne by a number of minor early Christian saints. The Jewish names mentioned below are adoptions of the non-Jewish surnames.

Vars.: **Maxim** (also Jewish); **Maisme, Mesme** (vernacular forms); **Maismon, Mesmon** (from the oblique case).

Cogn.: It.: **Massimo.**

Dims.: Ukr.: **Maksimonko.** Beloruss.: **Maksimyonok, Maksimuk.**

Patrs.: Russ.: **Maksimov** (also Jewish). Ukr.: **Maksimovich.** Pol.: **Maksymowicz.** Croatian: **Maks(imov)ić.**

Patrs. (from dims.): Russ.: **Maksimychev, Maksakov, Maksyatkin, Maksyutin, Makonin.** Ukr.: **Maksimat.**

The first automatic machine gun took its name from its inventor, Hiram P. Maxim *(1840–1916). He was born in Maine, but emigrated to England in 1881, and was knighted by Queen Victoria in 1901. He could trace his ancestry back four generations to Samuel Maxim of Rochester, New York; family tradition claimed descent from Huguenots who had once lived in Canterbury, England.*

Maxwell 1. Scots: habitation name from a place near Melrose in the former county of Roxburgh. The placename is first recorded in 1144 in the form *Mackeswell* 'spring, stream (see WELL) of MACK'.

2. Jewish: arbitrary adoption of the Scots name, or Anglicization of one or more like-sounding Jewish surnames.

A family of this name, who hold the earldoms of Morton and of Nithsdale, trace their descent from a certain Maccus or Magnus, who in 1107 entered the service of David, Earl of Cumbria, later King of Scotland. The sheriff of Teviotdale in around 1200 was a certain Herbert de Maccuswell, *probably a member of this family. In 1581 John* Maxwell *became Earl of Morton, when his maternal uncle, the 4th Earl, was attainted because of his part in the murder of Lord Darnley. The title was granted to the Douglas family in 1585 but, apparently through an administrative oversight, it had not in fact been removed from the Maxwells. Eventually, to avoid the confusion of two simultaneous holders of the same title, Robert Maxwell (c.1586–1646) exchanged it for the earldom of Nithsdale in 1620.*

An Irish family of this name, descended from Sir Robert Maxwell of Lanarks., were granted the earldom of Farnham in 1763.

May 1. English: pet form of MATTHEW; cf. MAYHEW.

2. English, French, and German: from a nickname or given name from the month of May (ME, OF *mai*, MHG *meie*, from L *Maius* (*mensis*), from *Maia*, a rather obscure goddess of fertility, whose name is derived from the same root as *maius* larger and *maiestas* greatness). This may have been bestowed on someone born or baptized in the month of May, or it may have been used to refer to someone of a particularly sunny disposition, or who had some anecdotal connection with the month of May, such as owing a feudal obligation then.

3. English: nickname from ME *may* young man or woman (of uncertain origin, probably originally meaning kinsman or kinswoman).

4. Jewish (Ashkenazic): ornamental name from Yid. *may* lilac.

Vars.: Eng.: **Maye, Mey(e)**. (Of 2 only): Ger.: **Mai, Mei, Mey**.

Cogns. (of 2): It.: **Maggi(o), Maio**. Sp.: **Mayo**. Port.: **Maio**. Du.: **Van de Mey, Van de Meij**. Pol.: **Maj**, MAJEWSKI.

Dims. (of 1): Eng.: MAKIN; **Maycock, Meacock**. (Of 2): It.: **Maggini, Maggiol(in)i**.

Patrs. (from 1): Eng.: **May(e)s, Mayze, Meyz, Mease**. (From 2): It.: **De Maggio, Di Maggio**. Pol.: **Majewicz**.

Cpds (of 4): **Meibaum** (from Ger. *Maibaum* 'maypole' or Yid. *mayboym* 'lilac tree'); **Mayberg(er), Meiberg** ('(dweller on the) lilac hill'); **Majblat** ('lilac leaf'; Pol. spelling); **Mayblum, Meiblum** ('lilac flower', or based on Ger. *Maiblüme* 'lily of the valley'); **Meit(h)al** ('lilac valley', in Israel often taken as being from Hebr. *mey-tal* dew water).

Maybury English (W Midlands): habitation name, almost certainly not from the place near Woking in Surrey, which is not recorded until 1885 and may well be named from the surname. The origin is probably some unidentified place somewhere farther north.

Mayer 1. English: status name or occupational name for a mayor, ME, OF *mair(e)* (from L *māior* greater, superior; cf. MAYOR). In France the title denoted various minor local officials, and the same is true of Scotland (see MAIR 1). In England, however, the term was normally restricted to the chief officer of a borough, and the surname may have been given not only to a citizen of some standing who had held this office, but also as a nickname to a pompous or officious person.

2. German: occupational name, originally for a village headman or similar official, from MHG *meier* (OHG *meior*, of the same origin as above). The Ger. term also acquired the sense 'steward', 'bailiff', and later came to be used also to denote a (tenant) farmer.

3. Jewish (Ashkenazic): from the Yid. male given name *Meyer* (from Hebr. *Meir* 'Enlightener', a deriv. of Hebr. *or* light).

Vars. (of 1): MAYOR. (Of 2): Ger.: **Maier, Meyer, Meier**. Pol., Czech: **Majer**. (Of 3): Jewish: **Maier, Meyer, Meier, Majer**, MAJOR, **Meyr**; MAIR, **Meir** (not exclusively Ashkenazic); **Meiri, Meiry** (Israeli, with the Hebr. suffix *-i*).

Cogns. (of 1): Fr.: **Maire, Merre; Mayeur, Mayeux; Méar, (Le) Mer** (Brittany). (Of 2): Flem., Du.: **(De) Mayer, (De) Meyer, Mei(j)er**. Hung.: **Major(os)**.

Dims. (of 1): Fr.: **Mairel, Maireau, Mairot, Méret, Mérey, Mérot**. (Of 2): Ger.: **Mayerl, Maierl** (Bavaria, Austria). Pol.: **Majerczyk**. (Of 3): Jewish: **Majerczyk, Majorczyk, Majorchick, Mayorczyk, Mayorchik, Meirtchak** (E Ashkenazic).

Patrs. (from 1): Eng.: **Mayers, M(e)yers, Miers**. (From 2): Ger.: **Mayers**. Low Ger.: **Meggers; Meyering, Meyerinck**. Flem., Du.: **Meyers, Smeyers; Meyerink**. (From 3): Jewish: **Meyers; Mayerso(h)n, Maierson, Meyerso(h)n, Mejerson, Mairson, Meirso(h)n, Me(e)rson; Mayerovitch, Maieroff, Meyerovitch, Meyerovitz, Meyerowitz, Majerowitz, Majerowits, Majerowicz, Mayorovits, Mairoff, Mairov(itch), Mairovitz, Mairowitz, Mairowicz, Meirovic, Meirovi(t)ch, Meirowitch, Meirovitz, Meirowi(t)z, Meirowicz, Meerov, Meerovi(t)ch, Meerovitz, Meerowitz** (E Ashkenazic); **Meirovici** (among Rumanian Jews); **Meirshvili** (among Georgian Jews); **Meirov, Meirow** (not exclusively Ashkenazic).

Mayfield English: habitation name from places in Staffs. and Sussex. The former is so called from OE *mæddre* MADDER + *feld* pasture, open country (see FIELD); the latter has its first element from OE *mægðe* mayweed. The surname itself is common in Notts., and it may be that an additional place of origin is to be sought in this area.

Mayhew English: from the Norman given name *Mahieu*, a var. of *Mathieu*; see MATTHEW.

Vars.: **Mahew, Mehew, Mayo(w)**.

Cogns.: Fr.: **Mahieu(x), Mah(e)u, Maheo, Méhu** (Normandy).

Maynard English (Norman) and French: from the Continental Gmc personal name *Mainard*, composed of the elements *magin* strength + *hard* hardy, brave, strong.

Vars.: Eng.: **Mainerd**. Fr.: **Meynard, Ménard; Mesnard** (hypercorrected).

Cogns.: It.: **Mainardi, Me(i)nardi, Menardo, Minardi, Minardo**. Ger.: **Meinhardt**. Low Ger.: **Meiner(t), Mehnert, Ment(h)(e)**. Fris.: **Minnert, Mint**.

Patrs.: Low Ger.: **Mein(d)ers, Mein(ert)z, Men(t)z, Menzen**. Fris.: **Minners; Meents; Meendsen, Meenzen; Minten**.

An English family called Maynard *trace their descent from Sir Richard* Maynarde *of Kirklevington, Yorks., who fought at Agincourt in 1415.*

Mayne English (Norman): 1. from the Continental Gmc personal name *Maino, Meino*, a short form of the various cpd names with a first element *magin* strength, might (cf., e.g., MAYNARD and MEIFFERT).

2. regional name for someone from the Fr. province of *Maine*; cf. MANSELL 1.

3. nickname for a large man, from ANF *magne, maine* great, tall (L *magnus*).

4. nickname for someone with a deformed or missing hand, from OF *main* hand (L *manus*).

Var.: **Main**.

Cogns. (of 1): Low Ger.: **Mein(e), Meyn(e), Mehn(e), Menne**. Fris.: **Meene, Meye**. It.: **Maino, Maini**.

Dims. (of 1): Ger.: **Meinel, Mein(d)l**. Low Ger.: **Mein(e)(c)ke, Menne(c)ke, Me(h)nke, Menk**. Fris.: **Min(c)k(e), Minkema**. It.: **Mainello, Mainelli, Mainetto, Mainetti, Mainoli**.

Patrs. (from 1): Low Ger.: **Meyns, Me(i)ns; Me(i)nsen; Meynen, Meinen; Menning**. Fris: **Meenen; Minning, Meenenga, Mennenga**. It.: **Mainis**.

Patrs. (from 1) (dims.): Low Ger.: **Mein(e)ken, Mencken; Meineking, Menneking**. Fris.: **Meenken, Meemken**.

The American journalist H. L. Mencken *(1880–1956) was the grandson of a certain Burkhardt Mencken, who had emigrated from Saxony to Baltimore in the early 19th cent.*

Mayol Catalan: topographic name for someone who lived by a plantation of young vines or metonymic occupational name for someone employed to watch over such a plantation, from Cat. *mayol, mallol* young vine, vine shoot (LL *malleolus*).

Mayor 1. English (Lancs.): var. of MAYER 1.

2. Spanish: nickname of the elder of two bearers of the same given name, from Sp. *mayor* elder (L *māior* (*nātū*), lit. 'greater by birth'). The term was also occasionally used as a female given name in Spain in the Middle Ages, and this may be a partial source of the surname.

3. Jewish: of uncertain origin, possibly a var. of MAYER 3.

Mayoral Spanish and Catalan: occupational name for the foreman of a gang of agricultural workers or the leader of a group of herdsmen, Sp., Cat. *mayoral* (LL *māiorālis*, originally an adj. deriv. of *māior*; cf. MAYER and MAYOR).

Var.: Cat.: **Majoral**.

Mayordomo Spanish: occupational name for a steward or butler in a great house, Sp. *mayordomo* (LL *māior domūs* head of the household). Sometimes the same term was used in an extended sense of the headman or mayor of a settlement; cf. MAYER 1.

Maza Spanish: metonymic occupational name for someone who had a mace as a symbol of office or who carried one in ceremonial possessions, from Sp. *maza* mace (LL *mattea*, probably of Gmc origin; cf. OE *mattuc* mattock). In some cases it may have been used as an occupational nickname for a soldier who used a mace in its original function as a weapon.

Mazier Provençal: topographic or status name for the holder of an isolated farmstead, from an agent deriv. of *mas* isolated farm; cf. MAS. The It. cogns. were used as technical terms of feudalism for a tenant farmer; in S Italy the term *Massaro* was also used of a steward managing lands on behalf of an absentee landlord.

Vars.: **Mazié**; **Mazerand, Mazerant**.

Cogns.: It.: **Mas(i)ero, Masieri** (N Italy); **Massoero** (Piedmont); **Massaro, Massari** (S Italy); **Ammassari** (Apulia, Salento); **Massai** (Tuscany).

Dims.: Fr.: **Mazereau, Mazeret, Mazerin**. It.: **Massarelli**; **Massarin(i)** (Venetia); **Massarino** (Liguria); **Massarol(l)i, Massariolo**; **Massarotti, Massarotto**; **Massarut(ti), Massarutto** (Venetia).

Aug.: Fr.: **Mazeyrat**.

Mazo Spanish: nickname for a forceful person or metonymic occupational name for someone who made use of a mallet, Sp. *mazo* (a byform of MAZA; cf. MACHO 2). The surname is also borne by Jews, the reason(s) for its adoption being unclear.

Mazur Polish and Jewish (E Ashkenazic): regional name for someone from one of two provinces of Poland: Masovia (Pol. *Mazowsze*) or Masuria (Pol. *Mazury*) in NE Poland, famous for its lakes. Masuria is so called because it was colonized by settlers from Masovia, replacing the Baltic inhabitants. The primary meaning of *Mazur* in Polish is someone from Masovia.

Vars.: Pol.: **Mazurowski**. Jewish: **Mazer**; **Mazurski, Mazursky**.

Dim.: Pol.: **Mazurek**.

Patr.: Pol.: **Mazurkiewicz**.

Mazza Italian: nickname for a destructive individual, a deriv. of It. *mazzare* to kill, destroy (L *mactāre*).

Dims.: **Mazzetto, Mazzetti, Mazzino, Mazzini, Mazzola, Mazz(u)oli, Mazzoletti, Mazzotta, Mazzotti**.

Augs.: **Mazzone, Mazzoni**.

The numerous cpds, such as **Mazzabue** ('kill bull'), **Mazzacane** ('kill dog'), **Mazzacurati** ('kill curate'), **Mazzagalli** ('kill cock'), **Mazzagreco** ('kill Greek'), **Massalovo** ('kill wolf'), **Mazzanobile** ('kill noble'), **Mazzalorso** ('kill bear'), **Mazzapica** ('kill magpie'), and **Mazzavillani** ('kill churl'), are all elaborations, in some cases no doubt humorous and suggested by some now-forgotten incident.

McAlinden Irish: Anglicized form of Gael. **Mac Giolla Fhiontáin** 'son of the servant of (St) *Fiontán*'. This name, a deriv. of *fionn* white, was borne by various early saints, including 6th-cent. disciples of St Columba and St Comgall.

Vars.: **Linden**; **Lindie, Lundy**.

McAlivery Irish: Anglicized form of Gael. **Mac Giolla Gheimhridh** 'son of the servant of *Geimhreadh*', a byname meaning 'Winter'.

McAra Scots: patr. from the Gael. occupational term *ara* driver, charioteer. The surname is esp. common in the Perth area.

Vars.: **McCar(r)a**, MCAREE.

McArdle Irish: Anglicized form of Gael. **Mac Ardghail**, patr. from the personal name *Ardghal*, composed of the elements *ard* height + *gal* valour.

Vars.: **McArdell, McCardle**.

McAree 1. Irish: Anglicized form of Gael. **Mac Fhearadhaigh**, patr. from the byname *Fhearadhach* 'Manly', 'Brave' (from *fear* man).

2. Scots: var. of MCARA.

Vars. (of 1): **McHarry, Mahorry**; **McKarr(y)e, McKerry, McKeary**; **McCarrie**; **McGarry, Megarry**; **McFaree, McFarry, McFerry**; **McVarry, McVerry**. The name has also been erroneously translated KING, as if from *Mac an Rígh* 'son of the king'.

McAulay Scots: 1. Anglicized form of Gael. **Mac Amhalghaidh**, patr. from the old Gael. personal name *Amhalghadh*.

2. Anglicized form of Gael. **Mac Amhlaoibh** or **Mac Amhlaidh**, patrs. from Gael. forms of the ON personal name *Áleifr*, *Óláfr* Olaf (cf. OLIFF). These names originated in the Hebrides, where Scandinavian influence was particularly strong.

Vars.: **McAull(a)y, McAuley, McAllay, McAlley**; **McCaulay, McCauley, McCally**; **Cawley, Gawley**.

McAuslan Irish and Scots: Anglicized form of Gael. **Mac Ausaláin**, patr. from a Gael. form of the given name ABSOLOM.

Vars.: **McAuslane, McAusland, McAuselan, McA(u)slin, McAslan(d)**; **McCa(u)slan(d), MacCaslane, McCasline**.

The Irish clan of this name was founded in the 11th cent. by Ausalan *Buoy O'Kayn, a chief of a branch of the O'Kanes of Co. Derry.*

McAvinchy Irish: Anglicized form of Gael. **Mac Dhuibhinse**, patr. from the personal name *Duibhinse*, composed of the elements *dubh* black + *inis* island; see also VINCENT.

McBeth Scots: from the Gael. personal name *Mac Beatha* 'Son of Life', i.e. 'man of religion'.

Vars.: **McBeath, McBeith**; **McBay, McBey**; **McVay, McVey, McVeagh, McVeigh, McVie** (Gael. **Mac Bheatha**).

Cogns.: Ir.: **McAbee, McAvey, McAveigh**; **McEvaghe, McEveighe**; **McIv(e)agh** (Gael. **Mac an Bheath(adh)a**).

McCabe Scots and Irish: Anglicized form of Gael. **Mac Cába**, patr. from the byname *Cába* 'Cape' (presumably denoting a wearer of a distinctive cape).

McCafferty Irish: Anglicized form of Gael. **Mac Eachmharcaigh**, patr. from the personal name *Eachmharcach*, composed of the elements *each* horse (see KEOGH) + *marcach* rider, knight (see MARKEY).

Vars.: **McCafferchie, McCafferkie, McCafferky, McCaffarky, McCagherty, McCaugherty, McCaverty, McCaharty, McCaherty, McCaffert; Cafferty, Cafferky.**

McCaffrey Scots and Irish: Anglicized form of Gael. **Mac Gafraidh**, patr. from a Gael. form of an ON personal name composed of the elements *guð* god + *fróðr* wise.

Vars.: **McCaffery, McCaffray, McCaffrae; McGorrie, Gorry, Gorey** (Gael. **Mac Gofraidh**).

McCaig Irish and Scots (Ayr, Galloway): Anglicized form of Gael. **Mac Thaidhg**, patr. from the byname *Tadhg* 'Poet', 'Philosopher'; see also TIGHE and MONTAGU.

Vars.: **McKaig, McKa(i)g(u)e, McKeige, (Mc)Keag(ue), McHaig, McHeigh, Heague, McAig; Keig, Kegg** (Manx).

McCall 1. Irish: Anglicized form of Gael. **Mac Cathmhaoil**, patr. from the personal name *Cathmhaol*, composed of the elements *cath* battle + *maol* chief.

2. Scots: var. of McKAIL.

Vars.: **McCaul(l), McKall,** McGALL, **McAll.**

McCandless Irish: Anglicized form of Gael. **Mac Cuind(i)lis**, patr. from the personal name *Cuindleas*, of uncertain derivation.

Vars.: **McCandlish, C(h)andlish.**

McCann Irish: Anglicized form of Gael. **Mac Cana**, patr. from the byname *Cana* 'Wolf Cub'. There has been considerable confusion with McGANN.

Vars.: **McCanna, (Mc)Canny; McAnn(a).**

McCarney Irish: Anglicized form of Gael. **Mac Cearnaigh**, patr. from the byname *Cearnach* 'Victorious'. See also CARNEY.

McCarrick Irish: Anglicized form of Gael. **Mac Concharraige**, patr. from the personal name *Cúcharraige*, composed of the elements *cú* hound, dog + *carraig* rock.

Vars.: **McCarrach, Carrigy.**

McCarron Irish: Anglicized form of Gael. **Mac Carrghamhna**, patr. from the personal name *Corrghamhain*, composed of the elements *corr* pointed, sharp + *gamhain* calf.

McCarthy Irish: Anglicized form of Gael. **Mac Cárthaigh**, patr. from the byname *Cárthach* 'Loving' (cf. CRADDOCK).

Vars.: **McCarty, McCartie; McCarhie, McCarha; McArthy.**

McCartney Scots and Irish: Anglicized form of Gael. **Mac Artaine** (Sc.), **Mac Artnaigh** (Ir.), patr. from a dim. of the byname *Art* 'Bear', 'Hero' (cf. ARTHUR).

Vars.: **McArtney.** Ir. only: **McCartan, McCarten, McCartin, McArtan, Carton** (Gael. **Mac Artáin**).

McCashin Irish: Anglicized form of Gael. **Mac Caisín**, patr. from the byname *Caisín*, from a dim. of *cas* curly(-headed); cf. CASSIDY.

Vars.: **(Mc)Cassin, Cashi(o)n, Cashe(e)n, McKasshine, Keshin.**

McClatchie Irish and Scots (Ayr, Galloway): Anglicized form of Gael. **Mac Gille Eidich** 'son of the servant of (St) *Eidich*', a personal name of uncertain origin.

Vars.: **McClatch(e)y, McLatchie, McLatchy, McLetchie.**

McClellan Scots and Irish: Anglicized form of Gael. **Mac Gille Fhaolain** (Sc.) and **Mac Giolla Fhaoláin** (Ir.) 'son of the servant of (St) *Faolán*'; see GILFILLAN and WHELAN.

Vars.: **McClelland, McLellan, McLel(l)and, McGillallen;** CLELAND, **Leland.**

McClenaghan Scots: Anglicized form of Gael. **Mac Gille Onchon** 'son of the servant of (St) *Onchú*', an OIr. personal name perhaps meaning 'Mighty Hound'. St Onchú was a 6th-cent. Irish pilgrim and collector of holy relics.

Vars.: **McClanaghan, McClan(n)achan, McLanaghan, McLanachan.**

McClennan Scots: Anglicized form of Gael. **Mac Gille Fhinneain** 'son of the servant of (St) *Fionnán*', a personal name representng a dim. of *fionn* white. There were several early Irish saints of this name, most notably a 7th-cent. bishop who governed the Church established in Northumb. and evangelized parts of S England.

Var.: **McLennan.**

McClintock Scots and Irish: Anglicized form of Gael. **Mac Gille Fhionndaig** (Sc.), **Mac Giolla Fhiontóg** (Ir.) 'son of the servant of (St) *Finndag*', a personal name representing a dim. of *fionn* white.

McClung Scots: Anglicized form of Gael. **Mac Luinge**, patr. from a personal name which is probably derived from *long* ship or the homonymous *long* tall.

Vars.: **McCluny, McLung.**

McClure Scots: 1. Anglicized form of Gael. **Mac Gille Uidhir** 'son of the servant of (St) *Odhar*', whose name means 'Sallow'. Cf. HORAN and McGUIRE.

2. Anglicized form of Gael. **Mac Gille Dheòradha** 'son of the servant of the pilgrim'; cf. DEWAR.

Vars. (of 1): **McCloor, McLure, McLeur, McAlear, McAleer.**

McClurg Scots: Anglicized form of Gael. **Mac Luirg**, patr. from the personal name *Lorg*, of uncertain origin.

Var.: **McLurg.**

McCluskey Irish: Anglicized form of Gael. **Mac Bhloscaidhe**, patr. from the personal name *Bloscadh*, which is probably a deriv. of *blosc* loud noise.

Vars.: **McClusky, McClosk(e)y, McCluskie; McLusky, McLuskie;** GLASGOW.

McCollum Scots: Anglicized form of Gael. **Mac Coluim**, patr. from a Gael. form of the given name *Columba*; see COLOMB.

Vars.: **McCollam, McCallum, McAllum.**

McComb Scots: Anglicized form of Gael. **Mac Thóm**, patr. from a Gael. pet form of the given name THOMAS.

Var.: **McCombe.**

Dims.: **McC(h)ombich, McCom(b)ie, McOmie** (Gael. **Mac Thomaidh**).

McConnell 1. Scots: Anglicized form of Gael. *Mac Dhomhnuill*, patr. from the personal name *Domhnall*; see DONALD and McDONALD.

2. Irish: Anglicized form of Gael. **Mac Conaill**, patr. from the personal name *Conall* (see CONNELL).

Vars.: **McConnel, McConnal** (Of 1 only): **(Mc)Whannell.**

McConville Irish: Anglicized form of Gael. **Mac Conmhaoil**, patr. from the personal name *Conmhaol*, apparently composed of the elements *cú* hound + *maol* bald.

Vars.: **(Mc)Conwell.**

McCord Irish: Anglicized form of Gael. **Mac Cuairt** and **MacCuarta**, patrs. from a personal name of uncertain origin.

Vars.: **McCoard, McCourt.**

McCorry Irish: Anglicized form of Gael. **Mac Gothraidh**, patr. from a Gael. form of the given name GODFREY.

McCosh Scots: Anglicized form of Gael. **Mac Coise**, patr. from the byname *Cos* 'Footsoldier', 'Messenger'.

McCracken N Irish and Scots (Galloway): of uncertain origin, possibly from Gael. **Mac Neachtain** (see McNaughton), with the interchange of *n* and *r* characteristic of Ulster.

Vars.: **McCraken, McCrackan; McGrattan.**

McCrae Scots and Irish: Anglicized form of Gael. **Mag Raith**, patr. from the byname *Rath* 'Grace', 'Prosperity'.

Vars.: **McCray(e), McCrea, McCree, McCrie, McCraw, McCr(e)agh, McCreath, McCraith, McCreith, McCreight; McGra(w), McGragh,** McGrath; **McRay, McRea, McRee, McRie, McRaw, McRaith, McReath; McWray; Magraw, Magragh, Magrath, Megraw, Megrath, Mackereth.** See also Reith.

McCready Irish: Anglicized form of Gael. **Mac Riada**, patr. from the byname *Riada* 'Trained', 'Expert'.

Vars.: **McCre(a)d(d)ie, McReady, McRe(a)die.**

McCreery Scots: Anglicized form of Gael. **Mac Ruidhrí**, patr. from the personal name *Ru(a)idhrí*; see Rory.

Vars.: **McCre(a)ry, McCririe.**

McCrimmon Scots: Anglicized form of Gael. **Mac Ruimein**, patr. from a Gael. form of the ON personal name *Hroðmundr*, composed of the elements *hróð* fame + *mundr* protection.

McCrudden Irish: Anglicized form of Gael. **Mac Rodáin**, patr. from the personal name *Rodán*, a deriv. of *rod* spirited; cf. Roden.

McCrumm Scots: Anglicized form of Gael. **Mac Chruim**, patr. from the byname *Crum* 'Bent', 'Twisted'.

McCulloch Irish and Scots (Glasgow): Anglicized form of a Gael. patr. from a personal name apparently derived from *cullach* wild boar—some families in N Sligo have indeed translated the name as **Boar**. It is, however, possible that it was originally *Cú-Uladh* 'Hound of Ulster' and has undergone alteration as a result of folk etymology.

Vars.: **McCullach, McCullagh, McCullough; McCully, McCullie, McCoulie.**

The first known bearer of the name in Scotland is Thomas Maculagh *of Wigtonshire, who rendered homage in 1296; his seal bore the name in the form* Maccvli.

McCusker Irish: Anglicized form of Gael. **Mac Oscair**, patr. from a Gael. form of the ON personal name *Ásgeirr*, composed of the elements *ans* god + *geirr* spear.

Var.: **McCosker.**

McCutcheon Scots: Anglicized form of Gael. **Mac Uisdein**, patr. from the personal name *Uisdean*, a Gaelicized form of OF *Huchon* (see Hutchin).

Vars.: **McCutchen, McHutche(o)n, McHutchin, McQuistan, McQuisten, McQuistin, McQuiston, McQueston, McQuaston, McWhiston,** Houston.

McDonagh Scots and Irish: Anglicized form of Gael. **Mac Donnchaidh** (Sc.) and **Mac Donnchadha** (Ir.), patrs. from the given name *Donnchadh*; see Donohue.

Vars.: **McDonnagh, McDonaugh, McDon(n)ach, McDono(u)gh, McDona; McDonoghue, McDonnoghie, McDonaghy, McDon(a)chie, McDonachy, McDunphy; McConaghy, McCon(n)achie, McCon(n)echie, McCon(n)ochie, McConoughey, McConachy, McCon(e)chy, McConkey, McKonochie, McOnachie, McOnechy, McOnochie; Dono(u)gh, Don(n)agh.**

McDonald Scots: Anglicized form of Gael. **Mac Dhomhnuill**, patr. from the personal name *Domhnall*; see Donald.

Vars.: **McDon(n)ell, McDona(i)ll, McDaniel;** McConnell.

McDougall Scots: Anglicized form of Gael. **Mac Dhubhghaill**, patr. from the given name *Dubhghall*; see Dougall.

Vars.: **McDougal, McDugal(d), McDoual(l), McDowall, McDo(w)ell, McDuall, McDool; McCool(e), McCole** (see also Cole 3); Coole.

McElhinney Irish: Anglicized form of Gael. **Mac Giolla Choinnigh** 'son of the servant of (St) *Coinneach*' (see Kenny 2).

McEnery Irish: Anglicized form of Gael. **Mac Innéirghe**, patr. from the personal name *Innéirghe*, apparently a deriv. of the verb *éirghe* to arise, ascend.

Vars.: **McEnerie, McEn(i)ry; McIneirie; McKen(n)ery, McKeneyry, McKeniry; McNeiry; Kiniry.**

McEnroe Irish: Anglicized form of Gael. **Mac Conchradha**, patr. from the personal name *Conchradh*, composed of *cú* hound + a second element of uncertain meaning.

Vars.: **McEnchrow,** Crow.

McEntee Irish: Anglicized form of Gael. **Mac an tSaoi** 'son of the scholar, wise man'.

McErlean Scots: Anglicized form of Gael. **Mac an Fhirléighinn** 'son of the lector'; this was the title held by the head of a monastic school.

Vars.: **McErlain, McNerlan, McNerlin.**

McEvoy Irish: Anglicized form of Gael. **Mac Giolla Bhuidhe** 'son of the yellow-haired lad'.

Vars.: **McAvoy, McEabuoy, McElwee,** McKelvey, **Kilboy.**

McFadden Scots and Irish: Anglicized form of Gael. **Mac Phaid(e)in** (Sc.) and **Mac Pháidín** (Ir.), patrs. from Gael. dim. forms of the given name Patrick.

Vars.: **McFadin, McPha(i)den, McFayden, McFeyden, McFadye(a)n, McFadz(e)an, McFadion, McFadyon, McFadzeon, McFadzein, McFadwyn.**

McFall Scots and Irish: Anglicized form of Gael. **Mac Phàil** (Sc.) and **Mac Phóil** (Ir.), patrs. from Gael. forms of the given name Paul.

Vars.: **McFaul, McFail, McVail, McPhail, McPhial, McPhiel, (Mc)Fyall;** Quail.

McFarlane Scots and Irish: Anglicized form of Gael. **Mac Pharthaláin**, patr. from *Parthalán*, a personal name from L *Bartholomaeus* (see Bartholomew).

Vars.: **McFarlan(d), McFarlin, McPharlain, McPharland, McPar(t)lan(d), McParlane, McParlin.**

McFerran Irish: Anglicized form of Gael. **Mac Fearáin**, patr. from the personal name *Fearán*, a dim. of *fear* man.

McFetridge Scots: Anglicized form of Gael. **Mac Pheadruis**, patr. from a Gael. form of the given name Peter.

Vars.: **McPhetrish, McFedri(e)s.**

McGall Scots: 1. var. of McCall.

2. Anglicized form of Gael. **Mac Goill**, patr. from the byname *Gall* 'Stranger'; cf. Gall 1.

McGann Irish: Anglicized form of Gael. **Mag Annaidh**, patr. from the personal name *Annadh*, the meaning of which is unknown. There has been considerable confusion with McCann.

Var.: **Magann** (see also Gahan).

McGarrigle Irish: Anglicized form of Gael. **Mag Fhearhgail**, patr. from the personal name *Fearghal*, composed of the elements *fear* man + *gal* valour.

McGeorge Scots: not a patr. from the given name GEORGE, but an Anglicized form of Gael. **Mac an Deoir** 'son of the pilgrim, relic keeper'; cf. DEWAR.

Vars.: **McJerrow, McJarrow; McIndeor, McIndewer, McKinde(wa)r.**

McGettigan Irish: Anglicized form of Gael. **Mag Eiteagáin**, patr. from the personal name *Eiteagán*, a dim. of *eite* wing (perhaps originally a byname for a swift runner).

Vars.: **Gattin(s), Gaitens.**

McGillicuddy Irish: Anglicized form of Gael. **Mac Giolla Chuda** 'son of the servant of (St) *Chuda*'. This was the name of a 7th-cent. abbot-bishop of Rathin in Westmeath.

Vars.: **McGillacuddy, McElhuddy.**

McGilligan 1. Scots: Anglicized form of Gael. **Mac Gille Fhaolagain** 'son of the servant of (St) *Faolagan*', a personal name representing a double dim. of *faol* wolf (cf. WHELAN and McCLELLAN).

2. Irish: Anglicized form of Gael. **Mac Giollagáin**, patr. from the personal name *Giollagán* (a dim. of *giolla* servant).

Vars.: **McGilligin, McKilligan, McKilligin, McKillican(e).**

McGillivray Scots and Irish: Anglicized form of Gael. **Mac Gille Bhrath** (Sc.) and **Mac Giolla Bhraith** (Ir.), patrs. from a given name meaning 'Servant of Judgment'.

Vars.: **McGillvray, McGilvra(y), McGillavery, McGillivry, McGillivrie, McGil(l)vary, McGilvery.**

The leading negotiator between the Creek tribe and the U.S. government in the years after the American Revolution was a Creek Indian chief who bore the unlikely name Alexander McGillivray *(b. c.1759). He was in fact of mixed descent; his father was Lachlan McGillivray, a Scottish trader, but he owed his position to matrilineal descent through his mother who was half Creek and half French.*

McGinley Irish: Anglicized form of Gael. **Mag Fhionnghaile**, patr. from the personal name *Fionnghal*, composed of the elements *fionn* fair + *gal* valour. According to Black it has no connection with McKINLEY.

McGinn Irish: Anglicized form of Gael. **Mag Fhionn**, patr. from the personal name *Fionn*; see FINN.

Vars.: **McGin(g), McGenn, McKinn, McKing, Maginn, Meggin.**

McGinty Irish: Anglicized form of Gael. **Mag Fhionnachtaigh**, patr. from the personal name *Fionnshneachtaigh*, composed of the elements *fionn* white + *sneachtach* snow.

McGirr Scots and N Irish: Anglicized form of Gael. **Mac an Gheairr** 'son of the short man', sometimes translated into English as SHORT.

The Ulster family of this name are said to have been originally gallowglasses (i.e. mercenary soldiers) from Scotland.

McGlashan Scots: Anglicized form of Gael. **Mac Glasain**, patr. from the personal name *Glasan*, originally a byname from a dim. of *glas* grey, green, blue (see GLASS 2).

Vars.: **McGlashen, McGlasson; Glashen.**

McGoldrick Irish: Anglicized form of Gael. **Mag Ualghairg**, patr. from the personal name *Ualgharg*, apparently composed of old Celt. elements meaning 'proud' + 'fierce'.

Vars.: **McGolrick, Magorlick, McWalrick, Golden.**

McGonigle Irish: Anglicized form of Gael. **Mac Congail**, patr. from the personal name *Congal*, composed of old Celt. elements meaning 'high' and 'valour'.

Var.: **McGonagle.**

McGovern Irish: Anglicized form of Gael. **Mag Shamhr(adh)áin**, patr. from the personal name *Samhradháin*, a dim. of *samhradh* summer.

Vars.: **McGaveran, McGovran, McGivern, McGowran, McGouran, Magover(a)n, Magawran, Magaur(a)n, Magurn, Gooravan, Gorevan, Gorevin.**

McGowan 1. Scots and Irish: Anglicized form of Gael. **Mac Gobhann** (Sc.) and **Mac Gabhann** (Ir.), patrs. from occupational bynames meaning 'Smith'.

2. Scots: Anglicized form of Gael. **Mac Owein**, patr. from the given name *Owen* or EWAN. One family of this name is probably descended from a king of the Strathclyde Britons (killed 1018), recorded by Simeon of Durham in the L form *Eugeni*.

Vars. (of 1): **McGowing, McGow(e)n, McGoun(e), Magowan.** Sc. only: **McAgown, McEgown, McIgo(i)ne** (Gael. **Mac an Ghobhann**); **Gowans.**

McGrath Irish: the normal Ir. form corresponding to Sc. McCRAE.

McGregor Scots: Anglicized form of Gael. **Mac Griogair**, patr. from a Gael. form of the given name GREGORY.

Vars.: **McGr(e)igor.**

The ancestor of the McGregor *clan is supposed to be the 10th-cent. King* Girig. *His name is probably a deriv. of Gael.* cír *comb, crest, but from an early date was associated with* GREGORY *(the king himself associated it rather with* Quiricus*; see* QUILICI*).*

During the Middle Ages the clan had a reputation for lawlessness, and the name was proscribed from 1603 to 1661 and 1693 to 1784, bearers of it being required to take another. Nevertheless, it has survived in large numbers.

McGuigan Irish: Anglicized form of **Mac Guagáin**, an altered version of *Mag Eochagáin*; see GEOGHEGAN.

Vars.: **McG(o)ugan, McGucki(a)n; McWiggan.**

McGuinness Irish: Anglicized form of Gael. **Mag Aonghuis**, patr. from the given name *Aonghus*; see ANGUS.

Vars.: **McGinnis, McEnnesse, McEnnis, McInnes, McInch, McKinch, McHinch; Maguin(n)ess, Maginness, Maginnis, Magennis, Meginniss; Guin(n)ess.**

Cogns.: Manx: **Kennish, Kinnish, Kinch.**

McGuire Irish: Anglicized form of Gael. **Mag Uidhir** 'son of *Odhar*', a byname meaning 'Sallow'. According to legend, St Odhar was St Patrick's charioteer. See also McCLURE and HORAN.

Vars.: **McGwir(e), McGui(v)er, Maguire, Maguier.**

Pierre **Macquer** *(1718–84) was a French chemist who wrote a popular textbook and the first chemical dictionary. He was descended from a Jacobite who had accompanied James II into exile in France. His surname is probably an altered form of* Maguire, *and he may have been related to the Maguires who were Barons of Enniskillen.*

McGurk 1. Scots: Anglicized form of Gael. **Mag Coirc**, patr. from the personal name *Corc* 'Heart'.

2. Irish: Anglicized form of Gael. **Mag Oirc**, patr. from the personal name *Orc*, of uncertain origin, perhaps from *orc* pig.

Vars.: **McGuirk, McCorc.**

McHale Irish: 1. Anglicized form of Gael. **Mac Céile**, patr. from the byname *Céile* 'Companion'.

2. from **Mac Haol**, a Gaelicized form of HOWELL that was adopted by a Welsh family of this name who settled in Co. Mayo.

McHenry Scots and Irish: Anglicized form of Gael. **Mac Eanruig** (Sc.) and **Mac Éinrí, Mac Eanraic** (Ir.), patrs. from Gael. forms of the given name HENRY.

Vars.: **McHendry, McHendrie; McHendrick, McKendrick.**

McIlwaine Scots: Anglicized form of Gael. **Mac Gille Bheathain** 'son of the servant of (St) *Beathan*', a personal name representing a dim. of *beathe* life.

Vars.: **McIlvain(e), McIlvane, McIlvean, McIlveen, McIlvenna, McIlvenny; McElwain; McKilvain; McGilvane.** The name is sometimes further Anglicized as MELVIN.

McIlwraith Scots and Irish: Anglicized form of Gael. **Mac Gille Riabhaich** (Sc.) and **Mac Giolla Riabhaigh** (Ir.) 'son of the brindled lad'; cf. REAVEY.

Vars.: **McIl(w)rath, McIl(a)raith, McIlarith, McIl(le)riach, McIlreach, McIlurick, McIllrick, McGillreich** (Sc.); **McIlravy, McIlrea; McEl(w)reath, McElreavy, McAre(a)vey, McGillereogh, McGilrae, Gallery, McCalreogh, McCalreaghe, McCallerie, Colreavy, Culreavy, Callery, Killery** (Ir.).

McIntosh Scots: Anglicized form of Gael. **Mac an Toisich** 'son of the chief, leader, thane'.

Vars.: **McKintosh, Mackintosh; Tosh, Tos(c)hach, Tosha(c)k.**

McIntyre Scots: Anglicized form of Gael. **Mac an tSaoir** 'son of the carpenter or mason'.

Vars.: **McInteer; McEntire, McEnteer; McAteer; McCateer; McTear, McTier; Matier, Mateer; Tear(e), Tier, Tyr(i)e.**

McKail 1. Scots: Anglicized form of Gael. **Mac Cathail**, patr. from the personal name *Cathal*; see CAHILL.

2. Irish: Anglicized form of Gael. *Mac Céile*; see McHALE.

Vars.: **McKale, McCale, McGale.**

McKane Scots: Anglicized form of Gael. **Mac Iain**, patr. from a Gael. form of the given name JOHN.

Vars.: **McKain, McKean(d), McAne, McEan, McIan.**

McKay Scots and Irish: Anglicized form of Gael. **Mac Aodha**, patr. from the personal name *Aodh* 'Fire', originally the name of a pagan god.

Vars.: **McKoy, McKey, McKee, McKie; McCay, McCoy; McG(h)ee, McGhie; McHugh, McCue; McEa, McAy; Mag(g)ee; Quay(e), Key** (Manx); KEYES; **Hughes, Hueson, Hewson,** (see also HUGH); **Eason** (see also EADE); **Ayson.**

It seems likely that the expression 'the real McCoy' originated with an American boxer, Norman Selby (1873–1940), who adopted the name 'Kid McCoy' as his professional name and wished to distinguish himself from another fighter of the same name.

McKechnie Scots: Anglicized form of Gael. **Mac Eacharna**, patr. from the personal name *Eacharn*, a deriv. of *each* horse.

McKeeman Scots: Anglicized form of Gael. **Mac Eamoinn**, patr. from a Gael. form of the given name EDMOND.

Vars.: **McEdmond, McAimon.**

McKelvey 1. Scots: Anglicized form of Gael. **Mac Shealbhaigh**, patr. from the personal name *Sealbhach*, of uncertain origin.

2. Irish: Anglicized form of Gael. *Mac Giolla Bhuidhe*; see McEVOY.

Vars.: **McKelvy, McKelvie, McKilvie.**

McKenzie Scots: Anglicized form of Gael. **Mac Coinnich**, patr. from the byname *Coinneach* 'Comely' (a deriv. of *cann* fair, bright). The name was formerly pronounced /mə'kenji:/; cf. MENZIES.

Vars.: **McQuenzie; McWhinnie, McW(h)inney, McWeeney, Mawhinney, Mewhinney** (Gael. **Mac Chonnigh**).

McKettrick Scots: Anglicized form of Gael. **Mac Shitrig**, patr. from a Gael. form of the ON personal name *Sigtryggr*, composed of the elements *sigr* victory + *tryggr* true.

Vars.: **McKetterick, McKitt(e)rick, McEtterick.**

McKiernan Irish: Anglicized form of Gael. **Mac Thighearnáin**, patr. from a dim. of the byname *Tighearna* 'Lord', 'Master'; cf. TIERNEY.

Vars.: **K(i)ernan, Kernon, McKernan(e), McCarnon, McHarnon,** LORD.

McKillop Scots: Anglicized form of Gael. **Mac Fhilib**, patr. from a Gael. form of the given name PHILIP.

Vars.: **McGilp, Killip, Keillips.**

McKimm Scots: Anglicized form of Gael. **Mac Shim**, patr. from a Gael. pet form of the given name SIMON.

Var.: **McKim.**

McKinley Scots: Anglicized form of Gael. **Mac Fhionnlaoich**, patr. from the personal name *Fionnlaoch*; see FINLAY.

Vars.: **McKin(d)lay.**

McKinnon Scots and Irish: Anglicized form of Gael. **Mac Fhionghuin**, patr. from an old Gael. personal name meaning 'Fair Born' or 'Beloved Son'. The surname has also been erroneously translated LOVE, as if from Gael. *Mac Ionmhuinn*.

McKinstry N Irish: Anglicized form of Gael. **Mac an Aistrigh**, a simplified version of *Mac an Aistrighthigh* 'son of the traveller'. The name is now largely confined to Ulster, but seems to have originated in Galloway.

McLachlan Scots: Anglicized form of Gael. **Mac Lachlainn**, patr. from the personal name *Lachlann*; see LACHLAN.

Vars.: **McLachlane, McLauchlan(e), McLauchlin, McLaughlan(e); McLaughlin, McLochlin, McLo(u)ghlin, McGloughlin** (Ir.); **Claplin** (Manx).

McLaren Scots: Anglicized form of Gael. **Mac Labhruinn**, patr. from a Gael. form of the given name LAWRENCE.

Vars.: **McLaran, McLauren, McLaurin, McLawring, McClaron.**

McLarnon N Irish: Anglicized form of Gael. **Mac Giolla Earnáin** 'son of the servant of (St) *Ernán*'. The name was borne by several early Irish saints, most notably a nephew of St Columba.

Var.: **McLernon.**

McLay Scots: of uncertain origin, probably an Anglicized and drastically reduced form of Gael. **Mac Dhuinnshléibhe**, patr. from the personal name *Duinnshléibhe*; see DUNLEAVY. On the other hand it is possible that the *McLeay*s of Sutherland are descended from Ferchard *Leche* (see LEACH), recorded in 1386, and in this case the name would be from Gael. *Mac an Léigh* 'son of the physician'.

Vars.: **McLae, McLea(y), McClay.**

McLean Scots and Irish: Anglicized form of Gael. **Mac Gille Eáin** (Sc.) and **Mac Giolla Eóin** (Ir.) 'son of the servant of (St) JOHN'.

Vars.: **McLane, McLain(e), McLune, McLoon(e); McClean(e), McClune, McGlone, McGloin, McAloon.**

McLeod Scots: Anglicized form of Gael. **Mac Leòid**, patr. from a Gael. form of the ON byname *Ljótr* 'Ugly'.

Var.: **McCloud.**

McMahon Irish: Anglicized form of Gael. **Mac Mathghamhna**, patr. from the byname *Mathghamhain*; see MAHON.

Vars.: **McMachon, McMa(c)han, McMaghon(e), McMa(g)hen, McKaghone, McMann; McMahouna, McMaghowney** (Gael. **Mac Mathghamhana**).

McMahon *was the name taken, as a translation of his own, by Reginald FitzUrse when he fled to Ireland after the murder of Thomas à Becket in 1170.*

Patrice, Comte de MacMahon *(1808–93) was Marshal of France and President of the 3rd Republic (1873–93). He was descended from John MacMahon (1715–80), an Irishman who was ennobled as the Marquis d'Equilly for his services to France.*

McManus Irish: Anglicized form of Gael. **Mac Maghnuis**, patr. from a Gael. form of the given name MAGNUS.

Vars.: **McMannas, McMannes, Mayne(s)**.

McMaster Scots: Anglicized form of Gael. **Mac Maighstir**, patr. from the Gael. title *maighstir* MASTER.

Var.: **McMasters**.

McMeekin Irish and Scots (Galloway): Anglicized form of Gael. **Mac Miadhacháin**, patr. from the personal name *Miadhachán*, a dim. of *miadhach* honourable.

Vars.: **McMeeking, McMikin, McMicking, McMeekan, McMei(c)kan, McMi(c)kan, McMeckan, McMeeken, McMi(c)ken, McMeechan, McMeecham, McMichan, McMychen**.

McMenemy Irish: Anglicized form of Gael. **Mac Meanm(n)a**, patr. from a personal name meaning 'Mind', 'Courage', 'Spirit'.

Vars.: **McMenamy, McMenamie**.

Dims.: **McMenamin, McManamon**.

McMichael Scots: Anglicized form of Gael. **Mac Mìcheil**, patr. from a Gael. form of the given name MICHAEL.

Vars.: **McMicheal, McMichail**.

McMillan Scots: Anglicized form of Gael. **Mac Maoláin**, patr. from the byname *Maolán*, a dim. of *maol* bald, tonsured. The name normally referred to a wearer of the tonsure, and, in a transferred sense, to a devotee of a particular saint. See also MULLEN.

Vars.: **McMillen; McMullan, McMullen, McMullin, McMullon; McMowlane, McMoylan**.

McMonagle Irish: Anglicized form of Gael. **Mac Maonghail**, patr. from the personal name *Maonghal*, composed of the elements *maoin* wealth + *gal* valour.

Vars.: **McMunagle, McMenigall**.

McMordie Scots: Anglicized form of Gael. *Mac Muircheartaigh*, patr. from the personal name *Muircheartach*; see MORIARTY.

Vars.: **McMurdo, McMurtough, McMurthoe, McMurty**.

McMorland Scots: Anglicized form of Gael. **Mac Murghalain**, patr. from the personal name *Murghalan*, composed of the elements *muir* sea + *gal* valour + the dim. suffix *-an*.

Var.: **McMoreland**.

McMorrough Irish: Anglicized form of Gael **Mac Murchadha**, patr. from the personal name *Murchadha*, composed of the elements *muir* sea + *cadh* warrior. See also MURPHY.

Vars.: **McMorrow, McMoroghoe, McMurroghowe, (Mc)Murchie, McMurphew; Morrowson, Murchison**.

McMorrough *was the name of the royal house of Leinster. It included Dermot McMorrough (1110–70), whose action in requesting aid from Henry II to regain his kingdom was the immediate cause of the Anglo-Norman invasion of Ireland.*

McMunn Scots: Anglicized form of Gael. **Mac Gille Mhunna** 'son of the servant of (St) *Munnu*'. This name, which is also found in the form *Mundu*, from earlier *Mo-Fhindu*, is a hypocoristic form of *Fionntan* with the affective prefix *mo-* my.

Vars.: **McPhun, McFun(n)**.

McMurray Irish: Anglicized form of Gael. *Mac Muireadhaigh*, patr. from the given name *Muireadhach*; see MURDOCH.

Vars.: **McCurrey, McCurrie**.

McNair 1. Scots: Anglicized form of Gael. **Mac Iain Uidhir** 'son of sallow JOHN'. This form seems to have originated in Ross.

2. Scots: Anglicized form of Gael. **Mac an Oighre** 'son of the heir'. This form seems to have originated in Perthshire.

3. Irish: Anglicized form of Gael. **Mac an Mhaoir** 'son of the steward, keeper'. The principal Irish family of this name held the hereditary post of Keeper of the Book of Armagh at *Ballymoyer* (Gael. *Baile an Mhaoir* 'town of the keeper').

Vars.: **McNeir, McNuir, McNayer, McNuyer, Menair**, WEIR.

McNairn Irish: Anglicized form of Gael. **Mac an Airchinn(igh)** 'son of the *erenagh*', a steward of church lands.

Vars.: **McNern, McNarin, McNaryn, (Mc)Ner(hen)ny, (Mc)Nirney; McInerney; McAnern(y); McEnerny, McEnarhin, McEnerin; McKinnerkin, McKinnertin; Minnerk; Kenerney, Kinerny, Connerny**.

McNally Irish: Anglicized form of Gael. **Mac an Fhailghigh** 'son of the poor man'.

Vars.: **McAn(n)ally, McAnnulla; McInally; McEnally; Manally, Menally; Canally, Kanaly; Nally; McNarry**.

McNamara Irish: Anglicized form of Gael. **Mac Conmara**, patr. from a personal name composed of the elements *cú* hound + *muir* sea.

Vars.: **McNamarra, McNamarrow**.

McNamee Irish: Anglicized form of Gael. **Mac Conmidhe, Mac Conmeadha**, patr. from a personal name meaning 'Hound of Meath'.

Vars.: **McConmea, McConmay, McConvea, (Mc)Convey, (Mc)Convoy; McConomy, McConamy, Conmey, Conmee**, CONWAY; MEE, **Meath** (see also comment at MEAD).

McNaughton Scots: Anglicized form of Gael. **Mac Neachdainn**, patr. from the personal name *Neachdàn*, an old Celt. name of uncertain origin.

Vars.: **McNaughtan, McNaughten, McNauchton, McNauchtan, McNauton, McNachtan, McNaghten; McNaught, McNeight; McKnight, McNutt** (Ulster); **McNitt** (U.S.). See also MCCRACKEN and NAUGHTON.

McNee Scots: Anglicized form of Gael. **Mac Niadh**, patr. from the byname *Nia* 'Champion'.

Vars.: **McNea, McNia, McNey, McNeigh, McNay**.

McNeice Irish: Anglicized form of Gael. **Mac Naois**, a shortened form of *Mac Aonghuis* 'son of ANGUS'.

Vars.: **McNeese, McNess, McNisse, McN(e)ish, Mannish, Mannix, Minnish, Minch; McCreesh** (Ulster); **Neis(s)on, Neeson**.

McNeilly Scots (Galloway) and N Irish: Anglicized form of Gael. **Mac an Fhilidh** 'son of the poet'.

Vars.: **McN(e)illie, McNeely, McNelly, Meneely; Neilly, Neely** (N Ireland).

McNelis Scots: Anglicized form of Gael. **Mac Niallghuis**, patr. from the personal name *Niallghus*, composed of the elements *niall* champion + *gus* choice.

Vars.: **(Mc)Neelis**.

McNidder Scots: Anglicized form of Gael. **Mac an Fhigheadair** 'son of the weaver'.

Var.: **McNider**.

McNucator Scots: Anglicized form of Gael. **Mac an Fhucadair** 'son of the fuller'.

Vars.: **Nucator**, **McKnockatir**.

McNulty Irish: Anglicized form of Gael. **Mac an Ultaigh** 'son of the Ulsterman'.

Vars.: **McAnulty**, **McKnulty**, **Nulty**.

McOmish Scots: Anglicized form of Gael. **Mac Thómais**, patr. from a Gael. form of the given name THOMAS.

Var.: **McComish**.

McPeake Irish: Anglicized form of Gael. **Mac Péice**, patr. from the personal name *Péic*, of uncertain origin.

Var.: **McPake**.

McPherson Scots: Anglicized form of Gael. **Mac an Phearsain** 'son of the parson' (see PARSONS).

Var.: **McPerson**.

McQuaid Irish: Anglicized form of Gael. **Mac Uaid**, patr. from a Gael. form of the given name *Wat* (see WALTER).

Vars.: **McQuade**, **McQuoid**, **Qua(i)d**.

McQuarry Scots: Anglicized form of Gael. **Mac Guaire**, patr. from an old Gael. personal name meaning 'Proud', 'Noble'.

Vars.: **McQuarrey**, **McQuar(r)ie**, **Macquarie**, **McWharrie**. See also QUARRY.

Lachlan Macquarie *(1762–1824), a famous early governor of New South Wales, who encouraged exploration and economic expansion, was born on the Hebridean island of Ulva. His father was a carpenter, a poor tenant of the Duke of Argyll but also a kinsman of the last chief of the clan Macquarie.*

McQueen Scots: Anglicized form of Gael. *Mac Shuibhne*, patr. from the personal name *Suibhne*; see SWEENEY. This name was also used as a Gael. form of the ON byname *Sveinn* (see SWAIN).

McQuillan Irish: Anglicized form of Gael. **Mac Uighilín**, patr. from a Gael. form of OF *Huguelin*, a double dim. of the given name HUGH.

McSharry Irish: Anglicized form of Gael. **Mac Searraigh**, patr. from the byname *Searrach* 'Foal', and sometimes further Anglicized as FOLEY.

Var.: **McSherry**.

McTavish Scots: Anglicized form of Gael. **Mac Támhais**, patr. from a Gael. form of the given name THOMAS.

Vars.: **McCavish**, **McAvish**, **McCaw(i)s**, **McCause** (Gael. **Mac Thámhais**). See also MCOMISH.

McTerrelly Irish: Anglicized form of Gael. **Mac Toirdhealbhaigh**, patr. from the personal name *Toirdhealbhach*, composed of the elements *Tor* Thor + *dealbhach* like, in the shape of.

Vars.: **McTorrilogh**, **McTurlogh**, **McTirlay**, **Torley**, **Turley**; **McTerrens**, **Terrance**, TERRY. See also CURLEY.

McTurk Scots: Anglicized form of Gael. **Mac Tuirc**, patr. from the byname *Torc* 'Boar'.

McVitie Scots (Ayr, Galloway): of uncertain origin, possibly an Anglicized form of Gael. **Mac an Bhiadhtaigh** 'son of the victualler'.

Vars.: **McVittie**, **McVitty**.

McWhirter Scots: Anglicized form of Gael. **Mac Chruiteir**, patr. from the occupational byname *Cruiteir* 'Harpist', 'Fiddler'; cf. CROWTHER.

Var.: **McChruiter**.

McWilliam Scots: Anglicized form of Gael. **Mac Uilleim**, patr. from a Gael. form of the given name WILLIAM.

Vars.: **McWilliams**, **McQuilliam(s)**, **Quilliam**, **McKilliam(s)**, **McIliams**.

Mead English: 1. topographic name for someone who lived near a patch of grassland used as pasture, from ME *mede*, OE *mǣd* meadow.

2. metonymic occupational name for a brewer or seller of mead (OE *meodu*), a type of alcoholic beverage made by fermenting honey.

Vars.: **Meade** (chiefly Ir.; see below). (Of 1 only): **Meads**, **Medd**, **Medding(s)**, MEADOW; **Medland** (W Country).

Cogns. (of 1): Ger.: **Matt(e)**; **Matt(n)er**, **Mattler**; **Mattmann**. (Of 2): Jewish (Ashkenazic): **Meth** (from Ger. *Met* mead); MEDNIK; **Medovoi**, **Medowoy**, **Medovy**.

Dim. (of 1): Ger.: **Mattlin**.

Meade *is the family name of the Earls of Clanwilliam, who were established for centuries in the county and city of Cork. Their name is also found as* Meagh, Miagh, *and* Myagh, *and may in fact be of Irish origin, perhaps a var. of* MCNAMEE. *In 1488 John Miagh established his right through his father and grandfather to a weir in Cork harbour.*

Meadow English: topographic name for someone who lived by a meadow (cf. MEAD 1). The form *meadow* derives from the dative case, *mǣdwe*, of OE *mǣd*.

Vars.: **Meadows**, **Medewe(s)**.

Mealing English: common surname in the Bristol area, of unknown origin. It may be a var. of MELLING.

Meaney Irish: Anglicized form of Gael. **Ó Maonaigh** 'descendant of *Maonach*', a personal name derived from *maoineach* rich.

Vars.: **Meany**, **Meeny**, **O'Mo(o)ney**, **O'Moyney**, **O'Moeney**, **Mooney**, MONEY.

Mear English: 1. topographic name for someone who lived by a pond, OE *mere*; cf. DELAMARE and MEER 1.

2. topographic name for someone who lived near a boundary, OE *(ge)mǣre*.

Vars.: **Mear(e)s**, **Meers**.

Mearns Scots: 1. habitation name from a place in the former county of Renfrews., so called from Gael. *maiorne* office or province of a MAIR.

2. local name for a region more or less coinciding with the former county of Kincardine, called *The Mearns* (apparently of the same origin as in 1).

Meatyard English: of uncertain origin, perhaps from a minor place named with the OE elements *mǣd* meadow (see MEAD 1) + *geard* enclosure. The name is documented in Dorset from the early 13th cent., and seems to have originated around the river Stour, south-west of Shaftesbury.

Vars.: **Met(e)yard**.

Mecklenburg German and Jewish (Ashkenazic): regional name for someone from the province of this name in N Germany, or habitation name from its capital, so called from MLG *mekele* big, great (cf. MEIKLE) + *borch* fortress, city (cf. BURKE). The adj. retains the weak dat. ending used after the lost prepositional phrase *to der* 'at the'.

Vars.: Ger.: **Mäckelburg, Meckelburg, Mechlenburg.**

The former German royal family of this name trace their descent from Niklot, the Slav Prince of the Obotrites (d. 1160), whose grandson Heinrich Borwin I was made a Prince of the Holy Roman Empire in 1170 and became Prince of Mecklenburg in 1179.

Medeiros Portuguese: habitation name from any of various places named with Port. *medeiro* place where shocks of maize are gathered (a deriv. of *meda* shock, stack, L *mēta* (pyramid-shaped) post).

Mediavilla Spanish: topographic name for someone who lived in the centre of a settlement, from Sp. *media* (fem.) middle (L *media*) + *villa* village, settlement (see VILLE).

Medici Italian: occupational name for a physician, It. *medico* (L *medicus*, from *medēre* to cure, heal).

Medina Spanish and Catalan: habitation name from any of the several places, as for example *Medina*-Sidonia in Cádiz and *Medina* del Campo in Valladolid, so called from Arabic *medina* city. The surname is also borne by Sefardic Jews, the reason(s) for its adoption being unclear.

Medler English (Norfolk): habitation name from *Madehurst* in Sussex, which gets its name from OE *mǣd* meadow (see MEAD 1) + *hyrst* wooded hill (see HURST). This placename appears in 12th-cent. records in the Normanized form *Medl(i)ers*. The surname is found in Norfolk as early as the 13th cent. in the form *de Medlers*; the landowning family who bore it were in vassalage to the Earl of Surrey, who had large estates in both Sussex and Norfolk.

Medley English: 1. habitation name, either a var. of MADELEY, or from *Medley* on the Thames in Oxon., so called from OE *middel* middle + *ēg* island.

2. nickname for an aggressive person, from ME, OF *medlee* combat, conflict (LL *misculāta*).

Mednik Jewish (E Ashkenazic): 1. occupational name for a copper-worker, from Pol. *med* copper + *-nik* suffix of occupational names.

2. occupational name for a brewer or seller of mead, a cogn. of Eng. MEAD 2.

Vars.: **Mednikor, Mednicki, Mednitzky, Mednitzki.**

Mędrzak Polish: nickname for a wise man, from Pol. *médrzy* wise, clever, cogn. with Czech *moudrý* wise; cf. Pol. *mędrzec* wise man, philosopher.

Var.: **Mędrzycki** (also Jewish (E Ashkenazic).

Cogns.: Czech: **Moudrý, Mudr(a).**

Medvedev Russian: patr. from the nickname *Medved* 'Bear' (lit. 'Honey-eater'), referring to a large, strong, or clumsy person.

Cogns.: Bulg.: **Mechkov.** Ukr.: **Vedmidski.** Beloruss.: **Myadzvedzki.** Pol.: **Niedźwiedzki, Niedźwiecki.** Czech: **Nedvěd.** Jewish (E Ashkenazic): **Niedzwiedz, Niedzwiecki.**

Dim.: Ukr.: **Medvedko.**

Mee Irish: 1. Anglicized form of Gael. *Mac Conmidhe*; see MCNAMEE.

2. Anglicized form of Gael. **Ó Miadhaigh** 'descendant of *Miadhach*', a byname meaning 'Honourable'.

Dim. (from 2): MEEHAN.

Patr.: **Meeson.**

Meehan Irish: 1. Anglicized form of Gael. **Ó Miadhacháin**, from a dim. of the personal name *Miadhach*; see MEE 2.

2. Anglicized form of Gael. **Ó Maotháin** 'descendant of *Maothán*', a personal name representing a dim. of *maoth* moist, soft, tearful.

Vars.: **O'Meehan, Meegan, Meechan.**

Meek English and Scots: nickname for a self-effacing person or a gentle and compassionate one, from ME *meek* humble, submissive, merciful (ON *mjúkr*).

Var.: **Meeke.**

Patr.: **Meeks.**

Meer 1. Flemish, Dutch: topographic name for someone who lived by a pool or pond, MDu. *mere*; cf. MEAR 1.

2. Jewish: of uncertain origin, possibly a var. of MAYER 3.

Vars. (of 1): **Van der Meer, Vermeer(en), Termeer, Meerman.**

Meersand Jewish (Ashkenazic): ornamental name composed of the Ger. elements *Meer* sea + *Sand* sand, chosen in reference to Gen. 32: 13, where Jacob is promised that his descendants shall be as numerous as the grains of sand on the shore.

Var.: **Mersand** (an Anglicized form).

Megaw Scots and Irish: Anglicized form of Gael. **Mag Ádhaimh**, patr. from a Gael. form of the given name ADAM.

Vars.: **Magaw, McGaw, McCaw.**

Meiffert German: from the Gmc personal name *Mag(in)-frid*, composed of the elements *mag(in)* strength, might + *frid* peace.

Vars.: **Meifert; Meyf(f)arth, Maifahrt.**

Cogns.: Fr.: **Ma(i)nfroi, Ma(i)nfroy.** It.: **Manfredi, Manfredo, Manfre(o), Manfra.**

Dims.: It.: **Manfredini, Manfrin(i), Manfriello, Manfrellotti, Manferlotti, Manfellotti, Manfelloto, Manfrotto.**

Augs.: It.: **Manfr(ed)oni.**

Patrs.: Low Ger.: **Meiferts, Meivers.**

Meikle Scots: nickname for a big man, from Older Sc. *meikle*, *mekill* great, large (ON *mikel*, a cogn. of OE *micel* large).

Vars.: **Mickle; Muckle** (Northumb.).

Meiklejohn Scots: distinguishing name for the largest or eldest (see MEIKLE) of two or more bearers of the given name JOHN.

Vars.: **Micklejohn, Mucklejohn.**

Meireles Portuguese: habitation name from any of several minor places so called. The placename is of unknown origin; an earlier form is *Maioreles*.

Meisner German and Jewish (Ashkenazic): habitation name from the E German town of *Meissen*, earlier *Michsen*, apparently so called from a Slav. element *misna* marsh. The town was famous in the Middle Ages for the fine linen cloth produced there, and the Ger. surname may also be an occupational name for a manufacturer or seller of such wares.

Vars.: Ger.: **Meissner, Me(i)chsner, Me(i)xner.**

Mejía Spanish: religious byname, from a vernacular form of L, Gk *Messias* Messiah.

Vars.: **Mejías, Megía(s).**

Cogn.: Jewish: **Mashia(c)h** (a name taken as an expression of hope for the coming of the Messiah).

Melber German: occupational name for a miller or flour merchant, from an agent deriv. of MHG *mel* (gen. *melwes*) flour (OHG *melo*, gen. *melawes*).

Vars.: **Melbert**; **Möhlber(t)** (Bavaria); **Mehl(mann)**.

Cogns.: Jewish (Ashkenazic): **Me(h)l(man)**, **Mehler**, **Meller**.

Melbourne English: habitation name from any of various places. Melbourne in E Yorks. is recorded in Domesday Book as *Middelburne*, from OE *middel* middle + *burna* stream (see BOURNE); the first element was later replaced by the cogn. ON *meðal*. Melbourne in Derbys. has as its first element OE *mylen* MILL, and *Melbourn* in Cambs. probably OE *melde* milds, a type of plant.

Melchior German and Danish: from the male given name *Melchior* (apparently ultimately derived from Hebr. *melech* king + *or* light, splendour), which was ascribed by popular Christian tradition to one of the Magi. The surname is also borne by Ashkenazic Jews, in which case it represents an adoption of the Ger. surname.

Vars.: Ger.: **Melcher(t)**.

Cogns.: It.: **Melchior(r)i**, **Melchior(r)e**, **Chiorri** (Venetia); **Marchior(r)i**; **Marchionne**, **Marchionni**, **Marchionno** (Lombardy, Tuscany). Sp.: **Melchor**. Ger. (of Slav. origin): **Malcher**. Czech: **Melich(ar)**. Pol.: **Majcher**, **Majchrzycki**.

Dims.: It.: **Chiorrini** (Venetia). Ger. (of Slav. origin): **Malcharek**. Czech: **Melíšek**.

Patrs.: Dan.: **Melchiorsen**. Low Ger., Flem., Du.: **Melchers**. Pol.: **Majchrowicz**, **Majchrzak**.

Habitation name: Pol.: **Majchrowski**.

Meldrum Scots: habitation name from a place in the former county of Aberdeens., first recorded in 1291 as *Melgedrom*, from the OGael. elements *mal(a)g* noble + *druim* ridge.

Melero Spanish: occupational name for a collector or seller of honey, Sp. *melero* (LL *mellārius*, an agent deriv. of *mel*, gen. *mellis*, honey).

Melgar Spanish: topographic name for someone who lived by a field of lucerne, Sp. *melgar* (a collective deriv. of *mielga* lucerne, LL *mēlica*, for class. L *Mēdica* (*herba*) plant from Media). There are several places in Spain named with this word; the surname may be a habitation name from any one of them.

Melhuish English: habitation name from a place in Devon, so called from OE *mǣl(e)* brightly coloured, flowery + *hīwisc* hide of land.

Vars.: **Mell(hu)ish**.

Mellado Spanish: nickname for a gap-toothed person, from the Sp. adj. *mellado* (past. part. of *mellar* to chip, of uncertain, probably pre-Roman, origin).

Mellanby English: habitation name from places in Cumb. and N Yorks. called *Melmerby*. These get their names from the ON personal name *Melmor* (from Ir. *Mael-Muire* 'Devotee of (the Virgin) Mary') + ON *býr* farm, settlement, or, in the case of *Melmerby* near Ripon, from ON *malmr* sandy field + *býr*.

Melling English (Lancs.): habitation name from places near Lancaster and near Liverpool. Both are probably so called from the OE tribal name *Me(a)llingas* 'people of *Mealla*'.

Mellis 1. English: habitation name from a place in Suffolk, so called from OE *mylenas*, plur. of *mylen* MILL.

2. Scots and Irish: from the Gael. personal name *Maol Íosa* 'Devotee of Jesus'.

Vars.: **Melliss**, **Melles**, **Melis**. (Of 2 only): **Malise**; **Mellows** (see also MELLOR).

Mellon Irish: Anglicized form of Gael. **Ó Mealláin** 'descendant of *Meallán*', a personal name representing a dim. of *meall* pleasant.

Vars.: **Mellan**; **Mallen** (see also MALIN).

Mellor English: habitation name from places in Lancs., W Yorks., and Derbys., earlier recorded as *Melver*, and named from ancient Brit. words that are ancestors of W *moel* bare + *bre* hill.

Vars.: **Mellors**; **Mellows** (see also MELLIS).

Melnikov Russian and Jewish (E Ashkenazic): patr. from the occupational term *melnik* miller (from *melit* to grind).

Vars.: Jewish: **Melni(c)k**.

Melrose Scots: habitation name from a place near Galashiels in the Scots Borders, so called from ancient Brit. words that were ancestors of W *moel* bare, barren + *rhos* moor, heath. The Bret. and Ir. cogns. of the second element mean 'hillock', 'promontory', and this may also have been the sense here.

Melton N English: habitation name from any of various places, for example in Leics., Lincs., Norfolk, and E and W Yorks., all of which have the same origin as MIDDLETON, with OE *middel* replaced by ON *meðal* under Scandinavian influence.

Melville 1. Scots (Norman): habitation name from one of the various places in Normandy called *Malleville*, from L *mala* (fem.) bad (see MALO) + *ville* settlement (see VILLE).

2. Irish: Anglicized form of Gael. **Ó Maoil Mhichíl** 'son of the devotee of (St) MICHAEL'.

Vars.: **Melvil**. (Of 1 only): MELVIN. (Of 2 only): **O'Mulmichell**, **O'Mulveill**, **(O')Mulvihil(l)**.

The Norman name was brought to Scotland by a certain Galfridus de Malveill, *whose name appears on several documents at the end of the 12th cent. In 1296 a certain Sir Richard* de Melvill *was forced to swear allegiance to the English king, Edward I. Sir John* Melville *(d. 1548) succeeded his grandfather as laird of Raith in Fife in 1502 and probably accompanied James IV to Flodden. The family were granted the earldom of Melville in 1690, although this later passed to the Leslie family. The American novelist Herman Melville (1819–91) was a direct descendant of the Scottish Melvilles.*

Irish bearers of the name claim descent from Maol Mhichíl, *a chief of Síol Muireadhaigh early in the 9th cent.*

Melvin 1. Scots: var. of MELVILLE 1.

2. Scots: Anglicized form of Gael. *Mac Gille Bheathain*; see MCILWAINE.

3. Irish: Anglicized form of Gael. **Ó Maoil Mhín** 'descendant of the devotee of (St) *Mín*', a personal name derived from *mín* soft, gentle.

Vars. (of 3): **O'Mullwine**, **Mul(l)veen**, **Mulvin**, **Molvin**.

Mena Spanish: habitation name from a place in the province of Burgos, so called from OSp. *mena* battlement (L *minae* (pl.)). The name may also have been used in a transferred sense for anyone who lived on a pinnacle or high spot. It is also borne by Jews, but the reasons for its adoption are not clear.

Menchaca Basque: habitation name from a minor place, so called from a personal name (of uncertain form and meaning) + the local suffix *-aca*.

Mendel Jewish (Ashkenazic): from the Yid. given name *Mendl*, a dim. of *Man* (see MANN 3).

Patrs.: **Mendel(s)so(h)n, Mendelzon; Mendelovi(t)ch, Mendelovic, Mendelovicz, Mendelowicz, Mendelovics, Mendelowisz, Mendelovitz, Mendelowitz, Mendelovits, Mendlovic, Mendelevitch, Mend(e)levitz, Mend(e)lewicz, Mendelevsky, Mendlevich** (E Ashkenazic), **Mendelovici** (among Rumanian Jews).

Mendham English: habitation name from a place in Suffolk, so called from the OE personal name *Mynda* (a byform of *Munda*, a short form of the various cpd names containing the element *mund* protection) + OE *hām* homestead.

Mendieta Basque: habitation name from places in the provinces of Álava and Biscay, so called from *mendi* mountain + the suffix of plurality *-eta*.

Mendizabal Basque: habitation name from a placename composed of the elements *mendi* mountain + *zabal* wide, broad.

Mendoza Spanish (of Basque origin): habitation name from a place in the province of Álava, so called from Basque *mendi* mountain + *otz* cold + the def. art. *-a*.

Cogn.: Port.: **Mendonça**.

The Mendozas *were a powerful Spanish family who provided governors of Granada, as well as many soldiers, explorers, and churchmen, being particularly powerful and influential in Spanish America. The Mendoza Codex took its name from the explorer Pedro de Mendoza (?1487–1537), who founded Buenos Aires in 1536. It is a manuscript history of the Mexican people from 1324–1502, written in Nahuatl with a Spanish translation. Mendoza acquired it for his patron Charles V of Spain, but it was captured as booty by the French and is now in the Bodleian Library, Oxford.*

Menéndez Spanish: patr. from the medieval given name *Menendo*, from the Visigothic personal name *Hermenegild*, composed of the elements *ermen*, *irmen* whole, entire + *gild* tribute. The personal name was borne by a 6th-cent. member of the Visigothic royal house, who was converted from Arianism to the Catholic faith and became an enormously popular saint, as a result of which the given name was very common in Spain in the Middle Ages.

Vars.: **Mélendez, Méndez**.

Cogn.: Port.: **Mendes** (also borne by Sefardic Jews, apparently as an adoption of the non-Jewish surname).

Meneses Spanish and Portuguese: habitation name from any of several places, notably in the province of Palencia, Spain, originally established by settlers from MENA.

Menger German: occupational name for a retail trader in unspecified goods, MHG *mengære*, *mangære* (from LL *mangō* salesman, with the addition of the Gmc agent suffix).

Vars.: **Manger; Menge(l), Meng(e)le(r)**.

Cogns.: Eng.: **Manger, Monger**. Jewish (Ashkenazic): **Manger**.

Patr.: Low Ger.: **Mangers**.

Menshikov Russian: patr. from the disitnguishing nickname *Menshik* (from *menshoi* smaller, younger), often used to distinguish between two bearers of the same given name. Compare BOLSHAKOV.

Vars.: **Mensh(chik)ov**.

Menuhin Jewish (E Ashkenazic): metr. from the Yid. female given name *Menukhe* (from Hebrew *menucha* tranquillity, stillness) + the Slav. suffix *-in*.

Vars.: **M(e)nuchin, M(e)nukhin**.

Dims.: **Mnus(h)kin**.

Menzies Scots (Norman): var. of MANNERS, in which the *z* originally represented ME ȝ, a sound similar to mod. Eng. *y* /j/. The surname is still pronounced /'mɪŋɡɪz/ in Scotland. It has also been Gaelicized **Mèinn**, from which come the Eng. forms **Mein** and **Mien**. The patr. forms **McMenzies, McMon(n)ies, McMin(n)**, and **McMyn** represent adapations of the name to the predominant pattern of Highland surnames.

The first known bearer of the name in Scotland is Robert de Meyners *or* de Meyneiss, *who was created Great Chamberlain of Scotland and witnessed various charters between 1217 and 1248. One of his best-known descendants was Sir Robert* Menzies *(1894–1978), Australian Prime Minister (1939–41; 1949–66), whose grandfather had emigrated to Ballarat from Scotland in the gold rush of the 1850s.*

Mercadier Provençal: occupational name for a tradesman, OProv. *mercadier* (LL *mercātārius*, a agent deriv. of *mercātus* trade; cf. MERCADO 1).

Vars.: **Merchadier, Mercadié**.

Cogns.: Cat.: **Mercader, Mercadé**.

Mercado 1. Spanish: topographic name for someone who lived by a market place, Sp. *mercado* (L *mercātus* trade, commerce, from *mercāri* to trade, deal, aderiv. of *merx* merchandise; cf. MERCADIER and MARCHANT). There are a number of minor places in Spain named with this word, and the surname may also be a habitation name from any of these.

2. Jewish (Sefardic): either of the same origin as 1, or else possibly from the Sefardic male given name *Merkado* 'Bought' (from the past part. of Judezmo *merkar* to buy). This was a name given to or assumed by someone who had escaped some great danger or recovered from a life-threatening illness; he was 'bought' or taken under the protection of a relative or friend, and had his name changed to *Merkado* in order to confuse the Angel of Death, who, it was believed, would make further attempts to take the life of which he had been baulked (cf. *Alt* at OLD).

Var. (of 2): **Merkado**.

Mercer English: occupational name for a trader, from OF *mercier* (LL *mercārius*, an agent deriv. of *merx*, gen. *mercis*, merchandise; cf. MARCHANT, MERCADO). The term was applied in ME particularly to one who dealt in textile fabrics, especially the more costly and luxurious fabrics such as silks, satin, and velvet.

Vars.: **Mercier; Merchier** (from the Norman form); MARKER.

Cogns.: Fr.: **Mercier, Mersier; Lemercier** (with fused def. article *le*). It.: **Merzari, Merzaro** (Emilia); **Merciai** (Tuscany); **Marzari, Marzaro** (Venetia).

Dims.: Fr.: **Merceron, Marceron, Mercereau, Marcereau, Marcireau, Mercerot**.

A family called Mercer *can trace its ancestry to Thomas Mercer, who was empowered by Edward III in 1341 to obtain money from the Constable of Bordeaux to raise troops in Aquitaine.*

Meredith Welsh: from the personal name *Meredydd* or, more commonly, *Maredudd*. The OW form is *Morgetiud*, of which the first element may mean 'pomp, splendour' and the second is *udd* lord. See also BEDDOW.

Vars.: **Merredy, Merriday, Merridew**.

Mérimée French: of uncertain origin. Tradition in the family of the novelist Prosper Mérimée (1803–70) derived the name from an Eng. nickname *Merrymaid*, but this is probably merely fanciful.

Merino Spanish: occupational or status name from Sp. *merino*, the title of a royal or seigneurial functionary who had wide legal and military jurisdiction over a district. The word is from LL *māiorīnus*, a deriv. of *māior* (cf. MAYER and MAYORAL).

Meriton English: habitation name of uncertain origin, probably from places in Shrops. and Co. Durham called *Merrington*. Merrington in Shrops. is from OE *myrge* pleasant (see MERRY) + *dūn* hill (see DOWN 1). *Kirk Merrington* in Co. Durham is from *Mǣringtūn*, 'settlement (OE *tūn*) associated with *Mǣra*', a personal name meaning 'Famous'.

Vars.: **Merrington, Mirrington, Marrington, Morrington; Mannington.**

The earliest known occurrence of this surname is Simon de Mereton *(Patent Rolls, 1242). It is found regularly in both Warwicks. and Yorks. from the 14th cent. onwards.*

Merle French: nickname from OF *merle* blackbird (L *merula*). This bird seems in the Middle Ages to have been regarded at times as a foolish creature like the magpie, and at other times as a cunning rogue like the jackdaw. In Italy today it is generally thought of as shrewd, but in Milan it is a byword for simplicity, and in Sicily it is noted for its timorousness. The surname could have been acquired in any of these senses. It may also in part have been a metonymic occupational name for a catcher of blackbirds for the cooking pot.

Vars.: **Lemerle, Lemesle** (nicknames, with fused def. art. *le*); **Merlier** (occupational).

Cogns.: It.: **Merlo, Merli; M(i)erula** (Trentino, Calabria); **Mirra** (Sicily). Sp.: **Merlo**. Port.: **Melo**.

Dims.: Fr.: **Merlet, Merlot, Merloz, Merleau**. It.: **Merletti, Merletto, Merlini, Merlino, Merlotti**.

Augs.: Fr.: **Merlat**. It.: **Merloni**.

Pejs.: Fr.: **Merlaud, Merlault**.

Patr.: Fr.: **Aumerle** (found chiefly in the *département* of Indre).

Merlin 1. French: from the W personal name *Myrddin*, obtained by back-formation from the placename *Caerfyrddin* (i.e. *Carmarthen*), wrongly analysed as a cpd of W *caer* fort + a personal name *Myrddin*. In fact it represents the Romano-Celtic placename *Moridunum* 'Sea Fort'. *Merlinus* was a Latinized form of *Myrddin* devised by Geoffrey of Monmouth and popularized in the Arthurian romances.

2. Jewish: of unknown origin.

Merrick 1. English: from an OF personal name introduced to Britain by the Normans, composed of the Gmc elements *meri, mari* fame + *rīc* power.

2. Scots: habitation name from a place near Minigaff in Dumfries and Galloway, so called from Gael. *meurach* branch or fork of a road or river.

3. Welsh: from the W given name *Meuric*, a form of *Maurice* (see MORRIS).

Var. (of 3): **Meyrick**.

Merrifield English: habitation name from any of various places, such as *Merryfield* in Devon and Cornwall or *Mirfield* in W Yorks., all named with the OE elements *myrige* pleasant (see MERRY) + *feld* pasture, open country (see FIELD).

Var.: **Mirfield**.

Merrill English: 1. from the female personal name *Muriel*, composed of the Celt. elements *muir* sea + *gael* bright. The given name was particularly common during the Middle Ages in E Anglia, where it was introduced by Bret. settlers accompanying and following William the Conqueror; it was also frequent in N England, where it was brought by Norsemen from Ireland, and in W England, due to Welsh influence.

2. habitation name from any of various minor places named with the OE elements *myrige* pleasant (see MERRY) + *hyll* HILL.

Vars.: **Merril, Merrel, Merrall, Murril, Murrell**.

Metrs. (from 1): **Merrills, Merrells, Merralls, Murrells, Mirralls**.

Merriot English: 1. habitation name from a place in Somerset, so called from OE *(ge)mǣre* boundary or *miere* mare + *geat* gate.

2. var. of MARRIOTT or MARRYAT, as a result of hypercorrection.

Vars.: **Merrett** (W Country); **Merryett, Mer(r)it(t)**.

Merry English: nickname for someone of blithe or cheerful disposition, from ME *merry* lively, happy (OE *myr(i)ge* pleasant, agreeable).

Vars.: **Merriman, Merriment**.

Merryweather English: nickname for someone of a sunny disposition, from ME MERRY + *wether* weather (OE *weder*).

Vars.: **Merrywether, Merriweather, Mereweather**.

Merton English: habitation name from *Merton* in S London, Devon, Norfolk, and Oxon.; *Marton* in Ches., Cleveland, Humberside, Lincs., Shrops., N Yorks., and Warwicks.; or *Martin* in Hants and Lincs. All of them derive their names from OE *mere* lake, pool (see MEAR) + *tūn* enclosure, settlement.

Merwe, van der Dutch: local name from the river *Merwede* in the province of S Holland.

This name was brought from Holland to S Africa, where it is extremely common, by Willem van der Merwe *in 1668.*

Mesa Spanish: topographic name for someone who lived on a plateau, OSp. *mesa* (L *mensa* table), or habitation name from any of the several places named with this term, for example in the provinces of Cadiz, Jaén, and Toledo.

Mesner German: occupational name for a sexton, churchwarden, or verger, S Ger. and Austrian dial. *Mesner* (MHG *mesnære*, OHG *mesināri*, from LL *ma(n)siōnārius*, a deriv. of *mansio*, gen. *mansiōnis*, house (of God), church).

Vars.: **Messner** (a result of association with *Messe* mass; this form is also borne by Ashkenazic Jews, as a translation of Yid. or Hebr. terms for the sexton of a synagogue); **Mes(s)mer** (Swabia, Switzerland; by analogy with surnames in *-mer* from place names in *-heim* homestead); **Mössner, Mössmer** (Bavaria).

Mesquita Portuguese: habitation name from any of various places named during the Moorish occupation with the Port. term *mesquita* mosque (Arabic *másǧid*, from *sáǧad* to prostrate oneself).

Messeguer Catalan: occupational name for a harvester or someone who kept watch over harvested crops, OCat. *messeguer* (LL *messicārius*, agent deriv. of *messis* harvest; cf. MESSER 3).

Messenger English: occupational name, from ME, OF *messag(i)er* carrier of messages (an agent deriv. of *message*, LL *missāticum*, from *missus* sent). For the inserted nasal, cf. PASSENGER.

Vars.: MESSINGER, **Message**.

Cogns.: Fr.: **Message(r)**.

Messer 1. German and Jewish (Ashkenazic): metonymic occupational name for a cutler, from Ger. *Messer* knife or its Yid. cogn. *meser* (MHG *mezzer*, a back-formation from *mezzeres* (taken as a gen. case), OHG *mezzirahs*, *mezzi*-

sahs, a cpd of *maz* food, meat + *sahs* knife, sword, cogn. with OE *meteseax*).

2. German: occupational name for an official in charge of measuring the dues paid in kind by tenants, an agent deriv. of MHG *mezzen* to measure (OHG *mezzan*, from *mez* measure, portion). See also MAETERLINCK.

3. Scots: occupational name for someone who kept watch over harvested crops, Older Sc. *mess(i)er*, from OF *messier* harvest master (LL *messicārius*; cf. MESSEGUER).

Vars. (of 1): Ger.: **Messerer**; **Messerschmidt, Messerschmitt** ('knife smith'; cf. NAYSMITH). Jewish: **Meser, Mes(s)erman**. See also METZ.

Dim. (of 1): Ger.: **Messerle**.

Messina Italian: habitation name from the ancient Sicilian city of this name. It was named *Messana* in the 5th cent. BC when it was captured by Anaxilaos of Rhegium; previously it had been known as *Zancle*.

Vars.: **Messana**; **Messinese**; **Messineo, Messaneo** (S Calabria).

Dims.: **Messinetti, Messanelli**.

Messinger 1. English: var. of MESSENGER.

2. German and Jewish (Ashkenazic): occupational name for a worker in brass, from an agent deriv. of Ger. *Messing* brass (MHG *messinc*, from Gk *Mossynoikos* (*khalkos*) Mossynoecan bronze, named after the people of NE Asia Minor who first produced the alloy).

Var. (of 2): **Messing**.

Métayer French: status name for a tenant farmer who held land on condition of sharing its produce equally with the landlord, OF *meitier* (an agent deriv. of *meitié* half, LL *mediētas*, from *medius* middle).

Vars.: **Métayé, Métoyer, Métadier**; **Mestayé, Mestadier, Mestadié** (hypercorrected forms); **Métais, Lemétais**.

Metcalf English (Yorks.): of uncertain origin, probably from ME *metecalf 'meat calf', i.e. a calf being fattened up to be slaughtered for meat at the end of the summer (from OE *mete* food, meat + *c(e)alf* calf). It is thus either an occupational name for a herdsman or slaughterer, or a nickname for a sleek and plump individual, from the same word in a transferred sense. The variants in *med-* appear early, and suggest that the first element was asssociated by folk etymology with ME *mead* meadow, pasture.

Vars.: **Metcalfe, Medcalf(e), Mitcalfe**.

Methven Scots: habitation name from a place near Perth, recorded in 1150 in the form *Matefen*, at the end of the same cent. as *Mafen*, and at the beginning of the 13th cent. as *Methfen*. The placename is probably derived from Brit. cogns. of W *medd* mead + *maen* (mutated to *faen*) stone, but its significance is not clear.

Var.: **Methuen**.

Métivier French: occupational name for a harvester, or rather a feudal tenant who owed a particular duty of service at the time of the harvest, from an agent deriv. of OF *métive* harvest (L *messis aestiva* summer harvest).

Var.: **Mestivier**.

Metternich German: habitation name from either of two places in the Rhineland. The Austrian statesman and diplomatist Prince Klemens von Metternich (1773–1859) was born in Coblenz into a Rhenish noble family. One ancestor had been elector and archbishop of Trier, and his father was hereditary chamberlain to the archbishop of Mainz and Austrian ambassador to various Rhenish courts.

Metz 1. Jewish (Ashkenazic): habitation name from *Metz* in Lorraine.

2. Low German: occupational name for a cutler, from a regional var. of MESSER 1.

Vars. (of 1): **Metzer**. (Of 2): **Meste**; **Mestemacher**; **Mestwerdt, Mestwarb** (see WRIGHT).

Cogns. (of 2): Flem., Du.: **Mes(man)**.

Metzger German and Jewish (Ashkenazic): occupational name for a butcher, Ger. *Metzger* (MHG *metziger, metzjer*, an agent deriv. of *metzjen* to slaughter, itself a back-formation from the agent noun *metzeller*, from L *macellārius* slaughterer).

Vars.: **Mezger**. Ger. only: **Mezler**.

Meynell English: 1. topographic name for someone who lived not in the main village, but in an isolated dwelling in the country, ME *meinil, mesnil*, OF *mesnil* (LL *mansiōnillum*, a dim. of *mansio* house, dwelling). There are several minor places in France named with this word and the surname may also be a habitation name from any of these. In England the vocab. word was used in particular to denote a fortified manor occupied by a landlord; the surname may also have been an occupational name for someone who was employed at such a manor.

2. from a Norman female personal name composed of the Gmc elements *magin* strength, might + *hild* battle.

Vars.: **Maynell, Maynall, Mennell, Menel**; **Mannell** (Devon).

Cogns. (of 1): Fr.: **Ménil, Mesnil**; **Duménil, Dumesnil**; **Dumany** (Belgium).

Michael 1. English: from the ME given name *Michael* (learned form; cf. MITCHELL). This is ultimately from Hebr. *Micha-el* 'Who is like God?', a name borne by various minor biblical characters as well as by an archangel, the protector of Israel (Dan. 10: 13, 12: 1; Rev. 12: 7). In Christian tradition, Michael was regarded as the warrior archangel, conqueror of Satan, and the given name was correspondingly popular throughout Europe, especially in knightly and military families. See also MYHILL.

2. Jewish: from a Jewish given name such as Hebr. *Michael* or Yid. *Mikhl*. The Hebr. adjectival forms **Michaeli** and **Michaely** are also in use as Jewish surnames.

Cogns.: Fr.: **Michel, Micheau, Mich(e)u**; **Mixhel** (Belgium). It.: **Micheli, Michele**; **Michiel(i)** (Venetia); **Migheli, Mighele, Migali, Migale** (Sardinia); **Mic(i)eli, Micelli, Micello, Micillo**; **Mical(l)i, Micale, Micallo** (S Italy); **Megali, Megale** (Calabria); **Migalli** (Campania). Sp., Port.: **Miguel**. Cat.: **Miquel**. Ger., Flem., Du.: **Michel**. Czech: **Michal**. Pol.: **Michalski**. Jewish (Ashkenazic): **Michel(ski)**. Hung.: **Mihály**.

Dims.: Eng.: MYATT. Sc.: MICHIE. Fr.: **Mich(el)et, Miquelet, Miché, Michey, Michez, Miguet**; **Mich(el)in, Michenet, Michenot**; **Mich(el)ot, Migot**; **Mich(el)on, Chon(n)eau(x), Chonet, Chonez, Chonillon, Mic(h)ou(d), Micoux, Michal(l)on, Miquelon**. It.: **Mich(i)eletti, Mich(i)eletto, Micaletti, Micaletto, Migaleddu**; **Michelini, Michelino, Mich(i)elin, Micalini, Migalini, Megalini**; **Michelutti, Micheluz(zi), Michelucci**; **Michelotti, Michelotto, Michelozzi, Michelozzo**; **Micalizzi, Micalizio, Migalizzi, Megalizzi**; **Michi, Mico, Michetti, Micoli**. Ger. (of Slav. origin): **Mikisch**; **Mich(a)lik, Michling, Michalke, Michelk, Michnik**; **Misch(e), Mischke, Mischok, Mischak, Mischan(ek), Mischnik**. Czech: **Michálek**, MIČKA. Pol.: **Michalczyk, Michalik**. Ukr.: **Mikhalchenko, Mishchenko, Mishurenko**. Beloruss.: **Mikhalenya**. Hung.: **Mikó**.

Augs.: It.: **Micheloni, Michelone, Mic(i)elon, C(h)elon(i)**. Czech: **Michalec**.

Pejs.: Fr.: **Michelaud, Michallaud, Michaut, Michaux**; **Miquelard, Michard**. It.: **Michelacci, Michelazzi, Mich(i)elazzo, Michelassi, Michelato**; **Chelazzi**.

Patrs.: Eng.: **Michaels, Miggles; Michaelson.** Sc.: McMICHAEL. It.: **Michaelis, De Micheli(s).** Port.: **Migueis.** Rum.: **Mihăilescu, Mihaileanu, Mihaileano.** Ger.: **Michel(i)s, Michler.** Low Ger.: **Miche(e)lsen.** Flem., Du.: **Mich(i)els.** Dan., Norw.: **Mich(a)elsen, Mikkelsen.** Swed.: **Mickelsson.** Russ.: **Mikhailov, Mikhailin, Mikhantyev, Mikhailychev, Mikhailichev.** Ukr.: **Mikailiv.** Beloruss.: **Mikalaevich.** Pol.: **Michałowicz, Michalewicz, Mich(n)iewicz; Michalak.** Croatian: **Mihajlović, Mihailović.** Bulg.: **Mikhailov.** Hung.: **Mihályfi.** Jewish: **Michael(i)s, Michaelson; Michaelov(itch); Michaelovici** (Rumanian spelling), **Michaelowici; Michels, Michils, Michlis, Michelson** (Ashkenazic, from Yid. *Mikhl*); **Michlin, Michelevitz** (E Ashkenazic). Gk: **Michaelides.** Armenian: **Mikaelian.** Georgian: **Mikladze.**

Patrs. (from dims.): Russ.: **Mikhalkov,** MISHKIN, **Mishukov, Mishutushkin, Mishechkin, Mishenkin, Mishatkin, Mishenev, Mishunov, Mikhnov, Mikhnev, Mishanin, Mishenin, Mishutin, Mishurov, Mishurin, Mishulin.** Ukr.: **Mitsnovich, Mikhalchat.** Beloruss.: **Mikhnevich.** Croatian: **Mijalković, Mij(at)ović, Mijušković; Mikić, Mihić, Mić(ov)ić, Mićanović.** Pol.: **Michałkiewicz; Miśkiewicz, Miszkiewicz; Miszczak; Misiak.** Ger. (of Slav. origin): **Misch(n)er.** Finn.: **Mikkonen.** Lithuanian: **Mishkunas.** Armenian: **Mikoyan.**

Habitation names: Pol.: **Michalewski, Michałowsky.** Jewish: **Michaelowsky.**

Michie Scots (Aberdeen): from the old Sc. given name *Michie*, a dim. of MICHAEL.

Patrs.: **McMichie, Mich(i)eson, Mitchi(e)son.**

Mička Czech: from a given name, a pet form of *Mikuláš* (see NICHOLAS) or of *Michal* (see MICHAEL).

Vars.: **Micka, Mék, Mičan.**

Micklethwaite English (Yorks.); habitation name from one of several places in W Yorks. named with the ON elements *mekil* great, big (see MEIKLE) + *þveit* meadow (see THWAITE).

Micklewright English (now chiefly W Midlands): distinguishing nickname from Northern ME *mekill* great, big (see MEIKLE) + *wriht* WRIGHT.

Middleditch English: habitation name from a minor place named with the OE elements *midel* middle + *dic* ditch, dyke (see DITCH). This survives as a Cheshire field-name, which may be the source of the surname.

Middlehurst English (Lancs.): probably a habitation name from *Middleforth* in Lancs.; the two placename elements *-hurst* and *-forth* are sometimes confused in surnames in N England.

Middlemass Scots: regional name from a district near Kelso in the Borders region, so called from Northern ME *midelmast* middlemost.

Vars.: **Middlemas, Middlemiss, Middlemist, Middlemost.**

Middler Scots: habitation name from *Midlar* near Aberdeen, which is of unknown derivation. The placename is apparently first recorded in 1513, as *Maidlare*.

Middleton English and Scots: habitation name from any of the places so called. In over thirty instances from many different areas, the name is from OE *midel* middle + *tūn* enclosure, settlement. However, *Middleton* on the Hill near Leominster in Herefords. appears in Domesday Book as *Miceltune*, the first element clearly being OE *micel* large, great (cf. MEIKLE). *Middleton* Baggot and *Middleton* Priors in Shrops. have early spellings that suggest *gemȳðhyll* (from *gemȳð* confluence + *hyll* hill) + *tūn* as its origin.

Var.: **Myddleton.**

A Scottish family of this name derives it from lands at Middleto(u)n *near Kincardine, granted in 1094 by King Duncan II to Malcolm, son of Kenneth, who was the first to be known by the surname.*

Midgley English: habitation name from any of several places in W Yorks., or minor places in Ches., so called from OE *micg(e)* midge + *lēah* wood, clearing.

Midhurst English: habitation name from a place in Sussex, so called from OE *mid* amongst + the pl. of *hyrst* wooded hill (see HURST).

Var.: **Medhurst.**

Mielczarek Polish: 1. occupational name for a maltster, dim. of *mielczarz*, dial. var. of Pol. *mielcarz*.

2. nickname for a dusty person, in particular a miller, from Pol. *miałki* dusty (from *miał* dust, akin to *mielenie* grinding, and ultimately to Eng. MILL).

Vars.: **Milczarek, Mi(e)lczarski.**

Cogns. (of 1): Russ.: **Molodozhnikov** (patr.). Ger.: MOLTKE.

Mierosławski Polish: from a Slav. personal name composed of the elements *mer* great, famous (ultimately cogn. with the Gmc element *meri*, *mari* famous, but early confused with Slav. *mir* peace) + *slav* fame, glory, with the addition of the surname suffix *-ski* (see BARANOWSKI).

Mierzejewski Polish: habitation name from a place called *Mirzejewo* (from Pol. *mierzeja* spit, sandbar + *-ew* possessive suffix) with the addition of *-ski*, suffix of local surnames (see BARANOWSKI).

Mignot French: nickname for an amiable or good-looking person, from OF *mignot* pretty, nice (of uncertain origin).

Vars.: **Me(u)gnot, Migne, Mignon.**

Dims.: **Mignoton, Mignonneau.**

Mikkola Finnish: name borne by a member of a household headed by someone called *Mikko*, Finn. pet form of MICHAEL. The surname is formed from the pet name + the local suffix *-la*.

Míl Czech: 1. affectionate nickname for an attractive person, from Czech *milý* dear, beloved.

2. from a short form of any of the Slav. cpd names containing the element *mil* mercy (cf. MILES 1), as for example *Miloslav* and *Bohumil*.

Var. (of 1): **Milec.**

Cogn. (of 2): Pol.: **Miłosz.**

Dim. (of 1): Czech: **Miláček** (also a vocab. word meaning 'darling', which in some cases may be the source of the surname.

Patrs. (from cogns. of 2): Croatian: **Mil(ošev)ić, Milo(je)vić, Miljević, Milačić, Milćević; Milosavljević, Milisavljević.**

Patrs. (from dims. cogn. with 2): Croatian: **Milekić, Milojković, Miljković.**

Milà Catalan: nickname for a rapacious person, from Cat. *milà* kite (LL *mīlvānus*, a deriv. of class. L *mīlvus*).

Milano Italian (partly Jewish): habitation name for someone who came from Milan, It. *Milano* (from L *Mediolān(i)um*, composed of apparently Celt. elements meaning 'middle' + 'plain').

Vars.: It.: **Milan(i), Milanese, Milanesi.**

Milborne English: habitation name from places in Dorset and Somerset, so called from OE *mylen* MILL + *burna* stream (see BOURNE). See also MELBOURNE, MILBOURNE, and MILBURN.

Milbourne English: habitation name from places in Northumb. and Wilts., so called from OE *mylen* MILL + *burna* stream (see BOURNE). See also MELBOURNE, MILBORNE, and MILBURN.

Milburn English (Northumb. and Cumb.): habitation name from a place in Cumb., so called from OE *mylen* MILL + *burna* stream (see BOURNE). See also MILBO(U)RNE and MELBOURNE.

Mildmay English: nickname for an innocuous individual, from ME *mild(e)* tame, gentle (OE *milde*) + *may* maiden (see MAY 3).

A family of this name claim descent from Hugo de Mildme, *who was stated in a pedigree registered in 1583 to have been living in 1147. Pedigrees of this period, however, are notoriously unreliable.*

Miles 1. English (Norman): via OF from the Gmc personal name *Milo*, of uncertain etymology, but perhaps ultimately akin to the Slav. element *mil-* mercy (cf. MÍL 2). The name was introduced into England by the Normans in the form *Miles* (oblique case *Milon*). In Eng. documents of the Middle Ages the name normally appears in the Latinized form *Milo* (gen. *Milōnis*), but the normal ME form was *Mile*, so the final *-s* must usually represent the possessive ending, i.e. 'son or servant of Mile'.

2. English: patr. from an OF contracted form of MICHAEL (cf. MYHILL).

3. English: occupational name for a servant or retainer, from L *miles* soldier, sometimes used as a technical term in this sense in medieval documents.

4. Jewish: of unknown origin.

Var. (of 1–3): **Myles**.

Cogns. (of 1): Fr.: **Mil(l)e, Mil(l)on**.

Dims. (of 1): Fr.: MILLET, **Mil(l)ot**.

Patrs. (from 1): Eng.: **Mil(e)son, Milsom**.

Milford English: habitation name from any of numerous places, for example in Derbys., Devon, Hants, Norfolk, Staffs., and Surrey, so called from OE *mylen* MILL + *ford* FORD.

Milgrim Jewish (Ashkenazic): ornamental name from Yid. *milgrim, milgroym* pomegranate (ultimately from LL *mille granāta* thousand seeds).

Vars.: **Milgro(u)m, Milgroom, Milgr(a)um, Mil(li)gram**.

Milhaud French (partly Jewish): habitation name from *Millau* in Aveyron, so called from the L personal name *Aemilius* (see ÉMILIEN) + the local suffix *-ācum*.

Vars.: Fr.: **Mil(l)au; Milhavés, Millavois**.

Mill English and Scots: topographic name for someone who lived near a mill, ME *mille, milne*, OE *mylen(e)* (from L *molīna*, a deriv. of *molere* to grind). It was usually in effect an occupational name for a worker at a mill and indeed for the miller himself (cf. MILLER and MILLWARD). The mill, whether powered by water, wind, or (occasionally) animals, was an important centre in every medieval settlement; it was normally operated by an agent of the local landowner, and individual peasants were compelled to come to him to have their corn ground into flour, a proportion of the ground corn being kept by the miller by way of payment.

Vars.: **Mille, Miln(e); Mills** (the commonest form of this name), **Milles, Millis, Miln(e)s, Mil(l)man**; MULLEN.

Cogns.: Fr.: **Mo(u)lin, Moullin, Moulins; Demoulin, Dumo(u)lin, Desmolins**. It.: **Milono, Molin(i), (Da) Mulino, Mulini; Molinese**. Sp.: **Molina, Molino**. Cat.: **Molina, Molins**. Ger.: **Muhl, Mühl(e)**. Low Ger.: **Möhl(e), Mähl(en), Meulen; Termöhlen, Termeulen, T(h)ormühlen, Zurmühlen**. Flem., Du.: **Van der Mo(o)len, Vermolen, Van der Meulen, Vermeulen**. Jewish: **Mu(e)hl, Mühl(e), Mil(l)man(n)** (Ashkenazic); **Molina(s)** (Sefardic).

Dims.: Fr.: **Moulinet, Moulinot, Moulineau**. It.: **Molinelli, Molinetti**. See also MOLYNEUX.

Pej.: It.: **Mullinacci**.

Cpds: Jewish: **Muehlbauer, Milbauer** ('mill builder', occupational name roughly equivalent to Eng. WRIGHT); **Milberg** ('mill hill', probably local); **Milfirer** ('mill director', occupational); **Muehlrad, Mil(e)rad** ('mill wheel', ornamental-occupational); MILLSTEIN.

Miller English: occupational name for a miller. The word represents the Northern ME term, an agent deriv. of *mille, milne* MILL, reinforced by the cogn. ON *mylnari*; in S, W, and Midland England the equivalent MILLWARD was used.

Vars.: **Millar** (Scot.); **Milner** (commonest in Yorks., retaining the *-n-* of the ME and OE word); **Meller**.

Cogns.: Fr.: **Mo(u)lin(i)er; M(e)unier, Meunié, Mugnier, Mounier, Mounié, Maunier; Monnier** (see also MINTER); **Lemeunier, Lemonnier** (with fused def. article *le*); **M(e)usnier** (hypercorrected); **Millour, Mil(l)inaire** (Brittany). It.: **Molinaro, Molinari, Mulinari; Monari, Monaro, Munari** (Venetia); **Mugnaro, Mugnai** (Tuscany, Umbria). Sp.: **Molinero**. Cat.: **Moliner; Munné**. Port.: **Moleiro**. Rum.: **Morariu**. Ger.: **Müll(n)er, Muller, Milner, Molner; Miller** (Bavaria); **Molitor** (Latinized). Low Ger.: **Möller, Moller**. Flem., Du.: **(De) M(e)ulder, De Molder, Moller; Mo(o)lenaar, (De) Mol(d)enaer, De Meulenaer, De Meuleneer**. Dan., Norw.: **Møller**. Swed.: **Möller**. Pol.: **Młynarski, Młyński**. Czech: **Mlynář, Minář**. Hung.: **Molnár** (in part borne by Jews). Jewish (Ashkenazic): **Mu(e)ller, Miler; Miller** (for the most part an Anglicization); **Moller; Milner** (from Yid. *milner* miller); **Mlynarski, Mlinarski** (E Ashkenazic); **Moraru** (among Rumanian Jews).

Dims.: Fr.: **Mugn(er)ot, Mugniot**. It.: **Molinaroli, Molinarolo, Munaretti, Munaretto, Munarin(i), Munerotto, Mugnaini**. Pol.: **Młynarczyk**. Czech: **Mlnařík, Minařík; Mlejnek**.

Aug.: It.: **Muneron** (Venetia).

Patrs.: Eng.: **Mellers** (see also MELLOR). Fr.: **Aumeunier**. Low Ger.: **Möllering**. Flem., Du. : **M(e)ulders, Smulders, Smolders; Molenaers**.

Equivs. (not cogns.): Fr.: CASSEGRAIN, FARINE. Hung.: LISZT.

Millet 1. French and English: metonymic occupational name for a grower or seller of millet or panic grass, from a dim. form of OF *mil* (L *milium*). In some cases it may have been a nickname for someone suffering from a skin disease, with blisters resembling grains of millet (cf. mod. Eng. *miliary* fever).

2. French: dim. of MILES 1.

3. Catalan: topographic name for someone who lived by a field of millet, Cat. *millet* (L *miliētum*, a deriv. of *milium*).

Vars. (of 1): Eng.: **Millett**. Fr.: **Meillet**.

Millichamp English: habitation name from *Millichope* in Shrops., recorded in Domesday Book as *Melicope*, composed of the OE elements *mylen* MILL + *hlinc* hill (see LYNCH 3) + *hop* enclosed valley (see HOPE). It probably referred to location at the foot of a hill with a windmill on it.

Vars.: **Millichap, Millichop(e), Millichip, Millership**.

The first known bearer of the name is Roger Millichap, *whose marriage on 13 June 1555 was recorded in the first year that parish registers were kept for the parish of Munslow, Shrops.*

Millier English (Somerset): of uncertain origin, probably a habitation name from an unidentified place named with the OE elements *mylen* MILL + *gear* weir.

Vars.: **Milliar, Milyear, Melliar, Mel(l)ior**.

It seems likely that all bearers of these names descend from a common ancestor. The first recorded bearer is Thomas Millier, *who was married in 1684 at Yatton, Somerset.*

Milligan Irish: Anglicized form of Gael. **Ó Maolagáin** 'descendant of *Maolagán*', a personal name from a double dim. of *maol* bald, tonsured; cf. MULLEN and MCMILLAN.

Vars.: **Milligen, Millican, Milliken, Millikin, O'Milligane; Mulligan, Mul(la)gan, Mullikin, O'Mullegan, O'Mul(le)g-han; Melican, O'Mellegan; Molohan, O'Mol(l)eghan, O'Mol-legane, O'Moylegane; Malaghan.**

Millington English: habitation name from places in Ches. and E Yorks., so called from OE *mylen* MILL + *tūn* enclosure, settlement. See also MILTON.

Millstein Jewish (Ashkenazic): occupational-ornamental name for a miller, from Yid. *milshteyn* millstone.

Vars.: **Mils(h)tein; Milsztejn** (Pol. spelling).

Millward English (chiefly W Midlands): occupational name for someone in charge of a mill, from OE *mylen* MILL + *weard* guardian. In S(W) England and the W Midlands this was the normal medieval term for a miller.

Vars.: **Milward; Millard** (chiefly Gloucs. and Worcs.); **Mill-wood, Mellard.**

Milton English: habitation name from any of the numerous places so called. The majority, with examples in at least fourteen counties, get the name from OE *middel* middle + *tūn* enclosure, settlement (cf. MIDDLETON); a smaller group, with examples in Cumb., Kent, Northants, Northumb., Notts., and Staffs., have as their first element OE *mylen* mill (cf. MILLINGTON). The surname is most common in Beds.

Milz German: 1. metonymic nickname for a cantankerous, splenetic individual, from Ger. *Milz* spleen (MHG *milz(e)*, OHG *milza*). According to medieval theory of humours, an excess of bile from the spleen was responsible for ill temper.

2. habitation name from a place so called in Thuringia.

Var.: **Miltz.**

Mindel Jewish (Ashkenazic): from the Yid. female given name *Mindl*, a dim. of *Mine* (see MINN).

Metr.: **Mindlin** (E Ashkenazic).

Miner English: occupational name for someone who built mines, either for the excavation of coal and other minerals, or as a technique in the medieval art of siege warfare. The word represents an agent deriv. of ME, OF *mine* mine (apparently of Gaul. origin, cogn. with Gael. *mein* ore, mine).

Var.: **Minor.**

Patrs.: **Miners** (chiefly Cornwall, where there were extensive tin mines), **Minors.**

Equiv. (not cogn.): Czech: HORNÍK.

Mingay English (now chiefly Norfolk): from a Bret. personal name composed of the elements *men* stone + *ki* dog, which was introduced into England by settlers from N France accompanying William the Conqueror and following in his wake.

Var.: **Mingey.**

Cogn.: Fr.: **Menguy.**

Minn English: from the medieval female given name *Minne*. This seems to have been in origin a Gmc personal name from OHG *minna* love, but in the late Middle Ages it was also used as a short form of *Willemina*, a fem. version of WILLIAM.

Var.: **Mynn.**

Dims.: **Minnett, Minnitt.**

Metrs.: **Minns** (chiefly Norfolk). Jewish (Ashkenazic): **Mines(s)** (consisting of the Yid. female given name *Mine* (see MINDEL) + the Yid. possessive suffix *-s*).

Minogue Irish: Anglicized form of Gael. **Ó Muineog** 'descendant of *Muineog*', a personal name representing a dim. of *manach* monk.

Var.: **Minnock.**

Minshull English: habitation name from a pair of villages in Ches., on either side of the river Weaver, recorded in Domesday Book as *Maneshale*, from the gen. case of the OE personal name *Mann* + OE *scylf* shelf, ledge.

Minter English: occupational name for a moneyer, OE *myntere* (cogn. with Ger. *Münzer*, Yid. *mintser*, whence the derivs. listed below), an agent deriv. of *mynet* coin, from LL *monēta* money, originally an epithet meaning 'Counsellor' (from *monēre* to advise) of Juno, at whose temple in Rome the coins were struck. The Eng. term was used at an early date to denote a workman who stamped the coins; later it came to denote the supervisors of the mint, who were wealthy and socially elevated members of the merchant class, and who were made responsible for the quality of the coinage by having their names placed on the coins.

Var.: **Mintor.**

Cogns.: Fr.: **Mon(n)ier, Lemon(n)ier** (see also MILLER). It.: **Moneta.** Sp.: **Monedero.** Ger.: **Münzer.** Jewish (Ashkenazic): **Min(t)zer, Munzer; Min(t)z, Munz, Mun(t)ze** (metonymic), **Minc** (Pol. spelling). Low Ger.: **Münter.** Flem.: **De Mienter, De Munter, De Muntenaer.**

Dims.: Fr.: **Monnereau, Monneret, Monnerot.**

Minto Scots: habitation name from a place near Denholm in the Borders, so called from the Brit. word that became W *mynydd* hill, with the later addition of ME *ho(e)* ridge, hill (OE *hōh*, see HOE) after the original meaning of the first element had been forgotten.

Minton English: habitation name from a place in Shrops., so called from W *mynydd* hill + OE *tūn* enclosure, settlement.

Miralles Catalan: habitation name from any of the various minor places in NE Spain named with Cat. *miralla* watchtower, look-out post (cf. MIRANDA).

Miranda Spanish, Catalan, Portuguese, Jewish (Sefardic), and Italian: habitation name from any of various places so called. The origin of this frequent placename is uncertain. It seems to be from the neut. pl. of L *mīrandus* wondrous, lovely (gerundive of *mīrāri* to wonder at, respect), but it is also possible that it was used in the sense of a watch-tower or look-out post; cf. MIRALLES.

Var.: It.: **Amiranda.**

Mirón Spanish: from a medieval given name of Gmc origin. The name is found in the L form *Miro*, gen. *Mirōnis*, and may represent a short form of the various Gmc cpd names with the first element *meri*, *mari* famous.

Cogns.: Cat.: **Miró, Mir.**

Dim.: Cat.: **Miret.**

Mironov Russian: patr. from the given name *Miron* (Gk *Myron*), borne by a 3rd-cent. saint who was martyred at Cyzicus on the Sea of Marmora, and subsequently venerated in the Orthodox Church.

Cogns.: Rum.: **Mirea; Mironescu** (patr.).

Dims.: Russ.: **Mironichev, Miroshkin** (patrs.).

Mirski Polish and Jewish (E Ashkenazic): nickname for a peaceable individual, from Pol. *mir* peace, respect for others + the general surname suffix *-ski* (see BARA-

NOWSKI). It may also be a habitation name for a native or inhabitant of *Mir*, a town in Belorussia.

Var.: **Mirecki**.

Habitation name: **Mirowski**.

Mishkin 1. Russian: patr. from the given name *Mishka*, a pet form of *Mikhail* MICHAEL.

2. Jewish (E Ashkenazic): patr. from *Mishke*, a pet form of the Yid. given names *Mikhl* MICHAEL and *Moyshe* MOSES.

Var. (of 2): MISKIN.

Cogns. (of 1): Croatian: **Mišković, Mišić**.

Miskin 1. English: nickname for a young man, from ANF, OF *meschin* (via It. *meschino* wretched, small, from Arabic *miskīn* poor). The word seems to have been used to distinguish a younger from an older bearer of the same given name, but it also had a somewhat derogatory connotation.

2. Jewish (E Ashkenazic): var. of MISHKIN.

Mitchell English, Scots, and Irish: from the ME, OF given name *Michel*, the regular vernacular form of MICHAEL.

Vars.: **Mitchel, Michell** (Devon and Cornwall).

Patrs.: Eng.: **Mi(t)chelson**.

Mitchelmore Scots and Irish: distinguishing name for the largest or eldest of several bearers of the given name *Michel* (see MITCHELL), with the addition of the Gael. adj. *mór* big (see MOORE 5).

Var.: **Michelmore**.

Mitford English: habitation name from a place in Northumb., so called from OE *(ge)mȳðe* confluence + *ford* FORD.

A family of this name, holding the title Baron Redesdale, trace their descent from Sir John Mitford (d. 1409) of Mitford, Northumb. He was granted lands by the Earl of Atholl in 1369. His descendants in the 20th cent. included the Mitford sisters, one of whom was the novelist Nancy Mitford. The first Baron Redesdale, John Freeman-Mitford (1748–1830), was Lord Chancellor of Ireland.

Mitrofanov Russian: patr. from the given name *Mitrofan* (Gk *Mētrophanēs*, from *mētēr* mother (sc. of God) + *phainein* to reveal, display). This name was borne by a 4th-cent. bishop of Byzantium, who became a popular saint in the Orthodox Church, although little is known about his life.

Var.: **Mitrofanyev**.

Mittelman Jewish (Ashkenazic): nickname for a wealthy man, from Yid. *mitlman* man of means, from Yid. *mitl* means, resources (Ger. *Mittel*) + *man* man.

Vars.: **Mitelman, Mit(t)elmann; Mittleman** (Anglicized).

Mitter German: topographic name for someone who lived on a farm that was in the middle between two others, esp. if the others were both inhabited by men with the same personal name (e.g. *Mitter Hans*), from the strong form of MHG *mitte* mid, middle (OHG *mitti*).

Var.: **Mitterer**.

Cpds: **Mitterhofer** ('middle farmer'); **Mittermeier** ('middle steward'); **Mittermüller** ('middle miller'); **Mitterreiter, Mitterreuter** ('dweller in the middle clearing').

Mittmann German: (Silesian) status name for a tenant farmer who payed rent, from a dial. pronunciation with short vowel of MHG *miete* rent (OHG *mieta*) + *mann*.

Var.: **Mitter(er)**.

Mitton English: habitation name from places in Lancs., Worcs., and W Yorks., so called from OE *(ge)mȳðe* confluence, place where two streams meet (a deriv. of *mūð* mouth) + *tūn* enclosure, settlement. See also MYTON.

Mizen English: habitation name from *Misson* in Notts., apparently so called from a lost Gmc element denoting a marshy place, akin to MOSS 1 and reflected also in the Belgian placename *Muizen* and the Du. *Mijsen*.

Vars.: **Mizzen, Mizon**.

Mizerski Polish: nickname for a wretchedly poor person, from Pol. *mizerny* poor, wretched, impoverished.

Mizrachi Jewish: from Hebr. *mizrachi* eastern, man from the East.

Vars.: **Mizrahi, Mizrahy, Misra(c)hi**.

Mo Swedish: topographic name for someone who lived on a sand-dune or heathland, Swed. *mo*, or arbitrarily adopted ornamental surname from this word.

Vars.: **Moe, Mo(h)lén, Mo(h)lin**.

Cpds: **Moberg** ('dune hill'); **Mogren** ('dune branch', ornamental).

Moat Scots and N English: habitation name from either of two places in the former county of Dumfries, so called from ME *mote* moat, ditch (originally referring to the whole system of fortifications; see MOTTE). In some cases it may have referred originally to residence in or near some other moated dwelling.

Moberly English: habitation name from *Mobberley* in Ches., so called from OE *(ge)mōt* meeting, assembly + *burh* enclosure, fortification + *lēah* wood, clearing, i.e. a clearing where there was a fortified site at which assemblies were held.

Var.: **Mobley**.

Moczkowski Polish: habitation name from a place named with Pol. *moczary* marsh + *-(e)k* dim. suffix + *-ów* possessive suffix, with the addition of *-ski*, suffix of local surnames (see BARANOWSKI).

Modigliano Italian: probably a habitation name from *Modigliana* in Tuscany. The surname is now most common around Livorno and is to a large extent borne by Jews.

Var.: **Modigliani**.

Modrzejewski Polish: topographic name for someone living in a larch wood, from Pol. *modrzew* larch, or habitation name from a place named with this element.

Var.: **Modrzewski**.

Moët French: nickname of uncertain origin, apparently a dim. of either OF *moe* lip, mouth (of Gmc origin; cf. Du. *mouwe* grimace) or the homonymous OF *moe* seagull (also of Gmc origin; cf. MAW 1).

Vars.: **Mouet, Mouez**.

Cogn.: Eng.: **Mewett**.

The English surname Mewett *is recorded from the late 13th cent. onwards, but it seems that most present-day bearers derive from French families who settled in SE England in the late 16th cent. The name is still most common in the Hastings area.*

Moffatt Scots and N Irish: habitation name from a place in the former county of Dumfries, so called from Gael. *magh* plain, field + *fada* long.

Vars.: **Moffett** (chiefly N Ireland); **Moffitt, Muffatt, Muffett, Meffat, Mefet**.

Mohan Irish: Anglicized form of Gael. **Ó Mocháin** 'descendant of *Mochán*', a personal name from a dim. of *moch* early, timely. It has been occasionally translated into English as EARLY.

Vars.: **O'Mochaine**, **(O')Mo(u)ghan(e)**, **O'Moon**, **Moohan**, **Mo(w)en**, **Moan**, Moon, Maughan, Vaughan.

Moita Portuguese: topographic name for someone who lived at a spot covered with dense undergrowth, Port. *moita* (of uncertain origin, apparently akin to Mata).

Molchanov Russian and Jewish (E Ashkenazic): patr. from the Russ. nickname *Molchan* (from *molchat* to be silent), denoting a taciturn individual. As a Jewish name it may be based on some now irrecoverable minor incident.

Vars.: Jewish: **Molchan(ov)sky**.

Mole English: 1. nickname for someone supposedly resembling the burrowing mammal, ME *mol(le)* (from Du. or Low Ger. *mol*), for example in having poor eyesight.

2. nickname for someone with a prominent mole or blemish on the face, from ME *mōl* (OE *māl*).

Cogn. (of 1): Du.: **Mol**.

Molesworth English: habitation name from a place in Cambs., so called from OE *Mūleswορð* 'enclosure (see Worth) of *Mūl*', a byname meaning 'Mule'. It may also come in part from *Mouldsworth* in Ches., so called from OE *molda* crown of the head, top of a hill + *worð* enclosure.

Mølgård Danish: habitation name from a placename composed of the elements *møl* Mill + *gård* enclosure (see Garth).

Var.: **Mølgaard**.

Moll 1. English (Norfolk): from the medieval female given name *Moll(e)*, a pet form of *Mary* (see Marie).

2. S German: nickname from a Swabian and Alemannic dial. term for a stout person.

3. Catalan: nickname for a weak or ineffective person, from Cat. *moll* soft, weak (L *mollis*).

Molloy Irish: 1. Anglicized form of Gael. **Ó Maolmhuaidh** 'descendant of *Maolmhuadh*', a personal name composed of the elements *maol* chieftain + *muadh* proud.

2. Anglicized form of Gael. **Ó Maol Aodha** 'descendant of the devotee of (St) *Aodh*'; see McKay.

3. Anglicized form of Gael. **Ó Maol Mhaodhóg** 'descendant of the devotee of (St) *Maodhóg*'; see Madoc.

Vars.: **Mulloy**, **Malloy**. (Of 3 only): **Logue** (chiefly N Ireland).

Moloney Irish: 1. Anglicized form of Gael. **Ó Maol Dhomhnaigh** 'descendant of the devotee of the Church'.

2. Anglicized form of Gael. **Mac Giolla Dhomnaigh** 'son of the servant of the Church'. Both names were occasionally used for the illegitimate children of priests.

Vars.: **Molony**, **Maloney**, Downie. (Of 1 only): **Mullo(w)ney**, **Mul(l)downey**. (Of 2 only): **McGildowney**, **McIldowney**, **McEldowney**, **McDowney**.

Molotov Russian: patr. from the nickname *Molot* 'Hammer' (from *molot* to grind), referring to a fierce fighter (cf. Malet 4 and Martel 2) or to someone who used such an implement in his work.

Cogn.: Jewish (E Ashkenazic): **Mlotek** (from Pol. *młotek* hammer).

Dim.: Russ.: **Molotkov**.

Molotov *was the name assumed by Vyacheslav Skryabin, Stalin's foreign minister. He was born in Kukarka in central Russia, where his father, a man of liberal ideas who was related to the composer Aleksandr Skryabin, was a book-keeper in a general store.*

Moltke Low German: metonymic occupational name for a maltster, from a dim. of MLG *molt*, *mout* malt.

Molyneux English and Irish (Norman): habitation name from *Moulineaux* in Seine-Maritime, so called from the pl. form of OF *moulineau*, a dim. of *moulin* Mill.

Vars.: **Molineaux**.

A family of this name have held the earldom of Sefton since 1771. They trace their descent from William de Molines, *a Norman named in the Battle Abbey Roll. They were granted the manor of Sefton in Lancs. by Roger de Poitou* c.*1100. The surname is still particularly common in Lancs. Among other notable members of the family were Adam* de Moleyns *(d. 1450), Keeper of the Privy Seal, and his brother Sir Richard de Moleyns (d. 1439), who distinguished himself at Agincourt.*

This is also the name of an Irish family, descended from Sir Thomas Molyneaux *or* Molinel *(1531–97), who was born in Calais. He settled in Ireland in 1576 and became Chancellor of the Exchequer there.*

Mombrun French and English (Norman): habitation name from places in Aude, Haute-Garonne, Lot, and Lozère called *Montbrun*, from OF *mont* hill (see Mont) + *brun* Brown.

Vars.: Eng.: **Monbrun**, **Monbrum**, **Mombrum**.

The first known bearer of the name in England is Joseph Mombrun, *whose birth is recorded in 1773 in the parish of St Pancras, London. Most present-day bearers seem to be descended from James William Mombrun, whose birth is recorded in the same parish in 1782. There was also a Lewis Mombrun, who was married in Marylebone in 1781. The relationship between these three men has not been established.*

Momigliano Jewish: Italianized form of a habitation name from *Montmélian* in Savoy, so called from OF *mont* hill (see Mont) + the Gaul. name *Mediolanum* (see Milano). This is now no more than a village, but during the Middle Ages it was the capital of a county with a considerable Jewish population. In Italy the name is most common in Piedmont and Lombardy.

Mommsen Low German: patr. from the medieval given name *Mumm(o)*. This is probably a short form of a Gmc personal name composed of *mund* protection + a second element beginning with *m-*, such as *man* man or *muot* courage.

Vars.: **Mummsen**; **Mommen**, **Mummen**.

Monaghan Irish: Anglicized form of Gael. **Ó Manacháin** 'descendant of *Manachán*', a personal name representing a dim. of *manach* Monk.

Vars.: **O'Monaghan**, **(O')Monahan**, **O'Managhane**, **(O')Manahan**, **Minihan(e)**.

Most bearers of these names are descended from Manachán, *a 9th-cent. chief in Connaught.*

Monash Jewish (Ashkenazic): from *Monish*, a pet form of the Yid. male given name *Menakhem*, which is from the Hebr. male given name *Menachem*, lit. 'Consoler'.

Patr.: **Monosson**.

Sir John Monash *(1865–1931), commander of Australian forces in France in the First World War, was born in Melbourne, of Jewish parents who had emigrated from Germany. Monash University in Victoria was named in his honour in 1958.*

Monasterio Spanish: topographic name for someone who lived near a monastery (LL *monastērium*, from Gk *monastērion*, a deriv. of *monos* alone; cf. Monk 1), or occupational name for someone employed in one.

Cogn.: Jewish (E Ashkenazic): **Monastyrski**.

Monclús Catalan: habitation name from any of the places situated on the mountain ridge of *Montclús* in N Spain. The placename is from LL *mons clausus* (en)closed hill, apparently referring to the fact that the high ground is shut in by rivers on either side.

Moncrieff Scots: habitation name from *Moncreiff* near Perth, so called from Gael. *monadh* hill + *craoibhe*, gen. of *craobh* tree.

Vars.: **Moncreiff(e)**.

Sir Matthew de Muncrefe *received lands at Moncreiff from Alexander II in a charter of 1248, and these have been retained in the male line to the present day. It is claimed that Sir Matthew was a member of a cadet branch of a family descended from Maldred, brother of King Duncan and a descendant of Niall of the Nine Hostages, King of Ireland, who lived c.400 in Tara. In the 16th cent. a branch of the family was established in Continental Europe, where it provided archers to the Scots Guard of the Kings of France. French bearers included a Marquis* de Moncrif *who was guillotined in the French Revolution.*

Moncur Scots: evidently a habitation name, possibly of Norman origin. The first known bearer of the name is Michael *de Muncur*, who witnessed a charter in the first half of the 13th cent.

Mondadori Italian: occupational name for a selector of the fleeces to be used in producing wool, from a Venetian dial. form of OIt. *emendatore* corrector (LL *emendātor*, from *emendāre*, a deriv. of *menda* fault).

Monday 1. English: from the ON personal name *Mundi*, a short form of the various cpd names containing the element *mundr* protection.

2. English: nickname for someone who had some particular association with this day of the week (OE *mōnandæg* day of the moon), normally because he owed feudal service then. It was considered lucky to be born on a Monday (and unlucky on a Friday; cf. FREITAG).

3. Irish: Anglicization of *Mac Giolla Eoin* 'son of the servant of Eoin', by confusion of the last part of the name with Irish *Luain* Monday.

Vars.: **Mondy**; **Mund(a)y**.

Cogn. (of 2): Ger. and Jewish (Ashkenazic): **Montag** (as a Jewish name, adopted perhaps with reference to the day of registration of the surname).

Monet French: from an aphetic form of a dim. of either of two given names, *Hamon* (see HAMMOND 1) and *Émon* (see EDMOND).

Var.: **Monnet**.

Money 1. English: nickname for a rich man or metonymic occupational name for a moneyer, from ME *money(e)* money (OF *moneie*, L *monēta*; cf. MINTER).

2. Irish: Anglicized form of Gael. *Ó Maonaigh*; see MEANEY.

Moneypenny English and Scots: probably a nickname for a rich man or a miser, from ME *many* many (OE *manig*, *monig*) + *peny* PENNY (OE *penig*).

Var.: **Monypenny**.

This is the name of a family established since the 13th cent. in Pitmilly, Fife. Ricardus de Moniepennie *was granted these lands, then called Pitmulin, by the Prior of St Andrews in 1211, a grant later confirmed to John* de Monypenny *c.1347.*

Monk 1. English: nickname for someone of monkish habits or appearance, or occupational name for a servant employed at a monastery, from ME *munk*, *monk* monk (OE *munuc*, *munec*, from LL *monachus*, Gk *monakhos* solitary, a deriv. of *monos* alone).

2. Irish: translation of MINOGUE and MONAGHAN.

3. Jewish (Ashkenazic): of unknown origin. The Jewish surnames **Munk(e)** may or may not be related.

Vars.: Eng.: **Monck**, **Mun(c)k**, **Monnick**.

Cogns.: Fr.: **Moine**, **Moyne**, **Lemoine**; **(Le) Manac'h** (Brittany). Prov.: **Monque**, **Monge**. It.: **(Lo) Monaco**, **Monaci**, **Monico**; **Monego** (Venetia). Sp.: **Monge**, **Monje**. Ger.: **Mün(ni)ch**, **Mön(ni)ch**, **Minnich**. Low Ger.: **Mönk(e)**, **Münk**, **Munk**. Flem., Du.: **De Munni(n)k**, **De Mu(y)nck**. Dan., Norw.: **Mun(c)k**, **Munch**. Finn.: **Munkki**.

Dims.: Fr.: **Moinet**, **Moinot**, **Moynet**, **Moynot**, **Moiné**, **Moinel**, **Moineau**. It.: **Monac(h)ello**, **Monacelli**, **Monachino**.

Aug.: Fr.: **Moinat**.

Pejs.: Fr.: **Moinard**, **Moinaud**, **Moynard**, **Moinault**.

Patrs.: Eng.: **Monks**, **Munks**. Fr.: **Aumoine**. It.: **Del Monaco**, **Dal Monaco**.

'Servant of the m.': Eng.: **Monkman**, **Munkman**.

Monkhouse English: topographic name for someone who lived in a house near or owned by a monastery, or occupational name for someone who worked in a house where monks lived, i.e. a monastery.

Monreal Catalan: habitation name from *Montréal* in Aude, France, so called from L *mons rēgālis* royal hill, or from a similarly named place in the province of Tarragona in Spain.

Mont French: topographic name for someone who lived on or near a hill, OF *mont* (L *mons*, gen. *montis*).

Vars.: **Demont**, **Dumont**.

Cogns.: Eng.: **Mount(er)**, **Munt**. It.: **Monte**, **Monti**; **Delmonte** (partly Jewish), **Delmonti**, **Dal Monte**; **Montigiani** (Tuscany); **Montesano** (Campania, Calabria, Apulia). Sp.: **Monte(s)**; **Montesino(s)**. Cat.: **Munt**, **Muns**. Port.: **Montes**. Jewish (Sefardic): **Monte**; **Montesino** (also established in the Netherlands).

Dims.: Fr.: **Montel**, **Monteau(x)**, **Montet**, **Montillon**. It.: **Mont(ic)elli**, **Montello**, **Montin(i)**. Sp.: **Montejo**, **Montilla**.

Aug.: Fr.: **Montat**.

An English family named **Moens**, *said to be derived from the town of* Mons *in Hainault (cf., however, the Flem. name* Moens *at* SIMON), *trace their descent from Godefridus* de Monte. *He is recorded in a charter in 1200 and there is circumstantial evidence that he was related to the Dukes of Brabant. The family were later established in Brussels, where members held high office from 1287, and later still moved to Rotterdam. Jacob Moens (b. 1796) was a W Indies merchant who left Holland to settle in England during the rule of Napoleon I.*

Montagne French: topographic name for someone who lived on or near a hill, from OF *montaine* hill, (small) mountain (LL *montānea*, originally neut. pl. of an adj. deriv. of *mons*; cf. MONT).

Vars.: **Montaigne**; **Monta(g)nier**, **Montagnié**.

Cogns.: Eng.: **Mountain** (chiefly Yorks.). It.: **Monta(g)na**, **Monta(g)ni**, **Montan(o)**. Sp.: **Montaña**; **Montañés**. Rum. (partly Jewish): **Munteanu** (probably regional name denoting a native or inhabitant of *Muntenia*, a district of Rumania).

Dims.: Fr.: **Montagnon**. It.: **Montagnino**, **Montagnini**, **Montanelli**.

Aug.: It.: **Montagnoni**.

Michel Eyquem de Montaigne *(1533–92), the French essayist, was born at the Château de Montaigne de Bordeaux, which had been bought by his grandfather. The family had a number of estates in the area, but they were of very recent nobility, and are said to have been of English origin. The essayist's mother came of a Sefardic Jewish family which had fled the Iberian peninsula.*

Montagu 1. English (Norman) and French: habitation name from a place in La Manche, so called from OF *mont* hill (see MONT) + *agu* pointed (L *acūtus*, from *acus* needle, point).

2. Irish: Anglicized form of Gael. **Mac Taidhg**, patr. from the byname *Tadhg* 'Poet', 'Philosopher'; see TIGHE, and also MCCAIG.

Vars. (of 1): Eng.: **Montague**, **Montacute**. Fr.: **Montaigu**, **Montagut** (also from other places). (Of 2): **McT(e)ague**, **McT(e)igue**.

Cogns. (of 1): Cat.: **Montagut**. Sp.: **Monteagudo**.

Members of the English Montagu *family have held many titles: Dukes of Montagu, Earls of Sandwich, Earls and Dukes of Manchester, Earls of Halifax, and Earls of Beaulieu. They had a common ancestor in Sir Edward Montagu (d. 1557), a distinguished judge, the executor of Henry VIII's will. His grandfather, Richard Montagu, who died before 1485, was also known by the surname* Ladde.

Another family, whose name was originally Montacute, *held the earldom of Salisbury. Their descent can be traced from the Norman baron Drogo* de Montacute, *a companion of William the Conqueror. He received lands in Somerset, and possession of these lands, including Shipton Montacute, was confirmed to his descendant Simon de Montacute (d. 1317) in 1290.*

Montalvo Spanish: habitation name from places in the provinces of Cuenca and Logroño called *Montalbo*, from Sp. *monte* hill (see MONT) + *albo* white (L *albus*).

Montaner Catalan: occupational name for a warden in charge of game forests on a wooded upland, Cat. *muntaner* (LL *montānārius*, a deriv. of *montānea*; cf. MONTAGNE).

Vars.: **Montané, Muntané.**

Montefiore Italian (largely Jewish): either an ornamental name or a habitation name from an unidentified place, from It. *monte* hill (see MONT) + *fiore* flower (L *flōs*, gen. *flōris*).

There is a distinguished English family of Italian Jewish descent who bear this name. Their members include Hugh Montefiore, *formerly Bishop of Birmingham.*

Monteith Scots: habitation name from a place in the former county of Perths., so called from Gael. *mon* hill pasture + *Teith*, a river name of obscure origin.

Vars.: **Menteith, Monteath.**

Montenegro Spanish: habitation name from a place in the province of Soria, so called from Sp. *monte* hill (see MONT) + *negro* black (L *niger*).

Montero Spanish: occupational name for a beater or other assistant at a hunt, from an agent deriv. of Sp. *monte*, which as well as meaning 'hill' (see MONT) was also used in the transferred sense of a game forest on wooded upland (cf. MONTANER). The occupational term was itself also used as a title for various palace functionaries, and some cases of the surname may derive from this.

Cogns.: Cat.: **Monté, Munté.** Port.: **Monteiro.**

Montessori Italian: habitation name from a place in Tuscany, so called from It. *monte* hill (see MONT) + *tessoro* TREASURE.

Monteverde Italian: habitation name from any of various places so called, from It. *monte* hill (see MONT) + *verde* green (L *viridis*).

Var.: **Monteverdi.**

Montfort French and English (Norman): habitation name from any of the numerous places so called, from OF *mont* hill (see MONT) + *fort* strong, impregnable (L *fortis*). A Norman bearer of this name, from *Montfort*-sur-Risle in Eure, near Brionne, accompanied William the Conqueror in his invasion of England.

Vars.: Eng.: **Mountfort, Montford,** MOUNTFORD.

Cogn.: Cat.: **Monfort.**

The English soldier Simon de Montfort, *Earl of Leicester (1208–65), was born in Normandy into the French nobility. He inherited the title through his English grandmother. He led a rebellion of barons against Henry II, and in 1265 summoned a meeting of various barons, knights, and clergy, which may be regarded as the origin of the English Parliament. His father, Simon de Montfort l'Amaury (?1160–1218), fought in the Crusades and also against the Albigensians in Languedoc.*

Montgolfier French: habitation name from a place in Arèche, so called from OF *mont* hill (see MONT) + a Gmc personal name composed of the elements *wulf* wolf + *heri, hari* army.

Jacques (1745–99) and Joseph (1740–1810) Montgolfier, *the pioneer balloonists, were from a wealthy family of paper manufacturers who hailed from Frankenthal in Germany. The family came from Annonay in S France, where they had settled in 1695, but their ancestors came from the Auvergne, where they had had introduced the paper-making process after one of them had learned it in Damascus while a slave there after being captured in the Crusades.*

Montgomery English, Scots, and N Irish (Norman): habitation name from a place in Calvados, so called from OF *mont* hill (see MONT) + a Gmc personal name composed of the elements *guma* man + *rīc* power.

Vars.: **Montgomerie, Montgomry.**

Roger de Montgomery *(d. 1094) was a Norman nobleman who took part in planning the invasion of England in 1066, but remained in Normandy as regent. The following year, however, he was summoned to England by William, being created Earl of Arundel and granted the castle of Arundel with vast estates in Sussex. Later he also received the earldom of Shrewsbury. His father, Roger de Montgomery, was seigneur of St Germain-de-Montgomery in Calvados.*

Montgomerie *is the name of a Scottish family who were granted the earldom of Eglington in 1507. They are descended from a certain Robert* de Montgomerie, *who was granted lands by Walter, High Steward of Scotland, in the latter half of the 12th cent. Through his relationship with the Seton family the 13th Earl, Archibald Montgomerie (b. 1812), also became Earl of Winton in 1859. A branch of the Scottish family was established in Donegal, Ireland, in 1628. A descendant of this branch (born in Australia) was Field Marshal Bernard* Montgomery *(1887–1976), created Viscount Montgomery of Alamein.*

Montilla Spanish: habitation name from a place in the province of Córdoba, so called from L *Montella*, pl. form of *montellum*, a dim. of *mons* hill (see MONT).

Montmorency French: habitation name from a place in Seine-et-Oise, so called from OF *mont* hill (see MONT) + the Gallo-Roman personal name *Maurentius*, apparently a cross between *Maurus* (see MOORE 3) and *Laurentius* (see LAWRENCE).

The name of Montmorency *was borne by one of the most powerful families in France, which provided numerous admirals, cardinals, and constables of France. The first recorded member was Burchard I, Sire de Montmorency in the 10th cent. Baron Matthieu II de Montmorency (d. 1230) was a soldier under Louis VIII, and guardian of the king's heirs.*

Montoliu Catalan: habitation name from either of two places in the province of Lérida, both so called from L *mons olivi* hill of the olive tree (cf. MONT and OLIVA).

Var.: **Montolio.**

Montoro Spanish: habitation name from a place in the province of Córdoba, of uncertain etymology. It was probably originally named with a LL deriv., ***montorium**, of L *mons* hill (see MONT), but the name may possibly be from L *mons aureus* golden hill.

Montserrat Catalan: local name from a hill in the province of Barcelona, so called from Cat. *mont* hill (see MONT) + *serrat* jagged (L *serrātus*, a deriv. of *serra* saw). The frequency of the surname is probably to be explained as a result of its adoption as a religious byname, since the monastery of Montserrat was famous for its shrine of the Black Madonna, regarded as the patroness of Catalonia.

Monzón Spanish: habitation name from a place in the province of Huesca, Aragon, which is of uncertain etymology. Medieval forms include *Mon(t)ssone* and *Montisoni*, and it appears to be a deriv. or cpd of *monte* hill (see MONT).

Moody English: nickname for a courageous, arrogant, or foolhardy person, or one quickly moved to anger, from ME *modie* impetuous, haughty, angry (OE *mōdig* brave, proud, from *mōd* spirit, mind, courage).

Vars.: **Moodey; Moodie** (Scots); **Muddiman, Muddeman.**

Cogns.: Ger.: **Modig.** Swed.: **Modén, Modin; Modig(h).**

Moon 1. English (Norman): habitation name from *Moyon* in La Manche, so called from the Gallo-Roman personal name *Modius* (from L *modus* measure) + the local suffix *-o* (gen. *-ōnis*).

2. English: nickname from ANF *moun* MONK.

3. Cornish: nickname for a slender person, from Corn. *mon* thin.

4. Irish: Anglicized form of Gael. *Ó Mocháin*; see MOHAN.

Vars.: **Moone.** (Of 2 only): **Munn.**

Patrs. (from 2): **Munns, Munson.**

Moorby English: habitation name from a place so called, probably the one in Lincs., which gets its name from ON *mór* marsh, fen (a cogn. of OE *mōr*; see MOORE 1) + *býr* farm, settlement.

Moorcroft English (chiefly Lancs.): habitation name from one of several places in W Yorks., or from a lost place near Ormskirk in Lancs. called *Morcroft*. All derive their names from OE *mōr* marsh, fen (see MOORE 1) + *croft* paddock, smallholding (see CROFT).

Var.: **Moorcraft.**

Moore 1. English: topographic name for someone who lived on a moor or in a fen, both of which were denoted by ME *more* (OE *mōr*), or habitation name from any of the various places named with this word, as for example *Moore* in Ches. or *More* in Shrops.

2. English: nickname for a man of swarthy complexion, from OF *more* Moor, Negro (L *Maurus*, ultimately from Phoenician *mauharim* Eastern).

3. English: from a personal name of the same origin as in 2 above, which was borne by several early saints. The given name was introduced into England by the Normans, but was never as popular in England as on the Continent.

4. Irish: Anglicized form of Gael. **Ó Mórdha** 'descendant of *Mórdha*', a byname meaning 'Great', 'Proud', or 'Stately'.

5. Scots and Welsh: nickname for a large man, from Gael. *mór*, W *mawr* big, great.

Vars.: **Moor.** (Of 1 only): **Mo(o)res, Moors** (rarely perhaps also patrs. from the given name); **Atmore, Amoore; Moorman, Mor(e)man.** See also MUIR. (Of 4 only): **O'Moore, O'Mora, (O')-Morey.** (Of 5 only): Sc.: **Moir** (Aberdeen), **More.**

Cogns. (of 1): Ger.: **Mohr(mann), Moormann; Muhr** (Bavaria). Flem.: **Van der Moeren, Moerman, Moerinck.** (Of 2 and 3): Fr.: **Maur(e), Mor(e),** MORT. It.: **(Lo) Mauro, Maur(i), Moro, Mori.** Sp.: **Moro.** Cat.: **Mauri, Mor.** Port.: **Mouro.** Ger.: **Mohr.** Gk.: **Mavros.** (Of 2 only): Flem., Du.: **(De) Moor(e), Moorman.** (Of 5): Bret.: **(Le) Moer.**

Dims. (of 2 and 3): Eng.: MORRELL; **Mor(r)in, Morren, Mo(o)ring; Moorcock** (perhaps also a nickname from the bird). Fr.: **Maurin, Mo(u)rin, Mor(i)net, Morineau; Mauret, Mouret, Mo(u)ré; Mo(u)rot; Mauron, Moron, Maurou(x).** It.: **Maurino, Maurin(i), Morin(i), Morino; Moret(ti), Moretto, Moriotto, Moriotti, Morozzi, Morucci, Moruzzi, Morucchio.** Ger.: **Mörle.** Low Ger.: **Mö(h)rke, Möri(c)ke.**

Augs. (of 2 and 3): Fr.: **Mauras.** It.: **Moroni.**

Pejs. (of 2 and 3): It.: **Morazzi, Moras(si), Morasso.**

Patrs. (from 2 and 3): It.: **De Mauro, Di Mauro, Del Moro.** Low Ger.: **Mö(h)ring.** Flem.: **Moors.** Russ.: **Mavrov.** Croatian: **Mavrić.**

Patr. (from 2 and 3) (dim.): Russ.: **Mavrishchev.**

The Irish family who came to be granted the titles Earls and Marquesses of Drogheda were established in Ireland in the 16th cent. by four brothers, Owen, George, Thomas, and Edward Moore. *Edward (?1530–1602), grandfather of the first earl, fought in the Irish wars against the Earl of Tyrone. The marquessate was created in 1791.*

Moorfield English (Lancs.): probably an altered version of the Norman baronial name *de Morville*, borne by a family who held land in Yorks. and N Lancs. in the 12th and 13th cents.

Moorhouse English (chiefly Yorks.): habitation name from any of various places, for example in W Yorks., named with the OE elements *mōr* marsh, fen (see MOORE 1) + *hūs* HOUSE.

Vars.: **Morehouse, Morres,** MORRIS.

Mora Spanish and Portuguese: topographic name for someone who lived by a mulberry or blackberry bush, from Sp. *mora* mulberry, blackberry (LL *mōra*, originally the pl. of class. L *mōrum*). There are numerous places named with this word, and the surname may also be a habitation name from any of these. It is also possible that it was used as a nickname, with reference to the dark colour of the berries.

Vars.: Sp.: **Moral(es).** Port.: **Moreira.**

Cogns.: Cat.: **Móra, Morera.** Fr.: **Mourier, Mouriez, Dumouriez.** Prov.: **Maurier, Mauriès, Mouriès; Mourer** (Gascony). It. **Mura** (S Sardinia).

Dims.: Sp.: **Morilla(s).**

Collectives: Sp.: **Moraleda.** Port.: **Morais.**

Moran 1. English: var. of MORANT; the accent is normally on the second syllable.

2. Irish: Anglicized form of Gael. **Ó Móráin** 'descendant of *Mórán*', a personal name meaning 'Great', 'Large' (cf. MOORE 5); the accent is normally on the first syllable.

Vars. (of 2): Ir.: **O'Moraine, O'Moran(e).**

Morant English and French: from an OF personal name of uncertain etymology. It appears to be a byname meaning 'Steadfast', 'Enduring', from the pres. part. of OF *(de)-morer* to remain, stay (cf. DURANT), but this may be no more than the reworking under the influence of folk etymology of some unrecognized Gmc original.

Vars.: Eng.: MORAN. Fr.: **Morand, Mauran(d).**

Cogns.: It.: **Morandi, Morando.** Sp.: **Morante, Morán.** Cat.: **Morà.**

Dims.: Fr.: **Morandeau, Maurandi.** It.: **Morandin(i), Moranduzzo.**

Aug.: Fr.: **Morandat.**

Morata Spanish: habitation name from any of various places so called, for example in the provinces of Jaén, Madrid, Murcia, and Saragossa. The placename is probably from LL *morāta* dwelling, residence (from *morāre* to remain, stay; cf. MORANT).

Dim.: **Moratilla** (the name of two places in the province of Guadalajara).

Moravec Czech: regional name for someone from Moravia (Czech *Morava*, named from the river of the same name), a district of N central Czechoslovakia, which from the 11th cent. onwards was a crownland of the kingdom of

Bohemia. Protestantism has flourished in Moravia since the 16th cent.

Var.: **Morava**.

Dim.: **Moravčík**.

Cogns.: Pol.: **Morawski**, **Morawiec**. Jewish: **Moravia** (borne by descendants of Jews who migrated from Moravia to Italy in the 15th and 16th cents.).

Morcillo Spanish: nickname for someone with dark skin or hair, from Sp. *morcillo* dark, black (LL *mauricellus*, a dim. of class. L *Maurus* Moor; cf. MOORE 2).

Morcombe English: habitation name, probably from *Morecombelake* in Dorset (recorded as *Mortecumbe* in 1240). The second element of this is OE *cumb* short valley (see COOMBE); the first is probably an OE personal name, **Morta* (see MORT). For the third element, see LAKE. The surname is certainly not from *Morecambe* in Lancs., which is named with an 18th-cent. coinage, based on identification of *Morecambe Bay* with Ptolemy's *Morikambē*.

Var.: **Morcom**.

The surname Morcom *has been established in Cornwall since an early date. It was fairly common in Bodmin in the 16th cent. It is not, however, of Cornish origin.*

Mordaunt English (Norman): nickname for a person with a sharp tongue, from ANF *mordaunt* biting, spiteful (pres. part. of OF *mordre* to bite, L *mordere*).

A family called Mordaunt *originated in Beds., where they can be found for example in a catalogue of gentry in the 15th cent. This document records that William Mordaunt was granted permission to enclose a park in 1297. His descendants included John Mordaunt (1598–1643), created Earl of Peterborough in 1628.*

Moreland Scots and N English: habitation name from any of various places, notably in the Borders region and in the former county of Kinross, named with OE *mōr* marsh, fen, moor (see MOORE 1) + *land* land.

Var.: **Morland**.

Moreno 1. Spanish and Portuguese: nickname for someone with dark hair and a swarthy complexion, from Sp., Port. *moreno* dark-haired (of uncertain origin, probably from LL *maurīnus*, a deriv. of class. L *Maurus* Moor; cf. MOORE 2 and MORCILLO).

2. Jewish (Sefardic): probably of the same origin as the Spanish and Portuguese names. It has been suggested that this was a name for a rabbi, from the Hebr. honorific title *morenu* 'our master', but this is unlikely since this Hebr. word would normally give a name ending in *-u*, not *-o*. However, the Hebr. word is probably the source of the Ashkenazic surnames **Moreinu** and **Moreinis** (the latter having Yid. possessive *-s*).

Var. (of 1): Sp.: **Morena** (a fem. form).

Moresby English: habitation name from a place in Cumb., so called from the OF given name *Maurice* (see MORRIS 1) + the Northern ME local element *by* farm, settlement (ON *býr*).

John Moresby *(1830–1922), the English explorer and hydrographer who discovered the natural harbour in New Guinea now called Port Moresby, was born in Allerton, Somerset.*

Morgado Portuguese: distinguishing name for the eldest son of a family, from Port. *morgado* first-born, heir (LL *māioricātus*, a deriv. of *māior*; cf. MAYOR).

Morgan Welsh, Scots, and Irish: from an old Celt. personal name (of which *Morien* is the more usual development in Welsh), apparently composed of elements meaning 'sea' + 'bright' (although 'Great Defender' is also a possible interpretion).

'Descendant of M.': Ir.: **(O')Murchan**, **O'Morghane**, **O'Moraghan**, **Morchan**, **Morkan**, **Morkin**, **Murkin** (Gael. **Ó Murcháin**); FORGAN, HORGAN, ORGAN (Gael. **Ó Mhurcháin**).

Morgan *is one of the oldest and commonest of Welsh names, but there is also a Scots clan Morgan, established from medieval times in Aberdeens., with connections with the Mackays. The Scottish name is thus probably not merely the result of Welsh migration, but was established independently.*

Morgenrot Jewish (Ashkenazic): from mod. Ger. *Morgenrot* dawn, sunrise (lit. 'morning red'), one of a group of Jewish ornamental names taken from words referring to natural phenomena; cf. MORGENSTERN and ABENDROTH.

Var.: **Morgenroth**.

Morgenstern Jewish (Ashkenazic): from mod. Ger. *Morgenstern* morning star, Yid. *morgn-shtern*, one of the class of Jewish ornamental names taken from natural phenomena.

Moriarty Irish: Anglicized form of the Gael. personal name *Muircheartach*, composed of the elements *muir* sea + *ceardach* skilled, i.e. skilled navigator.

Patrs.: **McMoriertagh**, **McMurihertie**, **McMiritee**, **McMreaty**, **McMe(a)rty** (Gael. **Mac Muircheartaigh**). See also MCMORDIE.

'Descendant of M.': **O'Morierty** (Gael. **Ó Muircheartaigh**).

Mörk Swedish: nickname for someone with dark hair or a swarthy complexion, uncharacteristic of Scandinavian people, from Swed. *mörk* dark (ON *myrkr*, whence also ME *murk(y)*).

Cogns.: Dan., Norw.: **Mør(c)k**, **Mørch**.

Morley English: habitation name from any of the various places called *Morley* (e.g. in Ches., Derbys., Co. Durham, Norfolk, and W Yorks.), or *Moreleigh* in Devon, all of which are so called from OE *mōr* marsh, fen (see MOORE 1) + *lēah* wood, clearing.

Vars.: **Moorley**, **Morely**; **Moralee** (Northumb.).

Morling English: of uncertain origin, most likely a double dim. (with the ANF suffixes *-el* and *-in*) of the medieval given name *More*; see MOORE 3 and MORRELL.

Var.: **Morlin**.

The first known bearer of the name is Huga Morlynge, *recorded at Cottenham, Cambs., in 1273. During the Middle Ages the name was mainly confined to Cambs., Suffolk, and Kent, but is now found in every part of Britain, as well as in America, Canada, Australia, and New Zealand.*

Morón Spanish: habitation name from places in the provinces of Seville and Soria. The former, and possibly the latter also, is probably named from Arabic *maurûr* 'hidden', from the past. part. of *wárrà* to hide, bury.

Moroney Irish: Anglicized form of Gael. **Ó Maol Ruanaidh** 'descendant of the devotee of (St) *Ruanaidh*'; see ROONEY.

Vars.: **Morooney**, **Murroney**, **Mulro(o)ney**, **O'Moronie**.

Morpeth English (Northumb.): habitation name from the town of this name, so called from OE *morð* murder + *pæð* path. The reasons for this grisly appellation have long ago been lost.

Var.: **Morpat** (Sc.).

Morpurgo Jewish: habitation name borne by Jews in Italy, either from the city of *Maribor* in Slovenia (known in It. as *Marburgo*, in Ger. as *Markburg*) or from *Marburg* in Germany.

Vars.: **Marpurg**, **Marpurch**.

Morrell English: from the medieval given name *Morel*, a dim. of *More* (see MOORE 3) with the hypocoristic suffix *-el*.

Vars.: **Morel(l)**, **Morrel**, **Mor(r)ill**, **Morrall**, **Murrill**, **Marrel**.

Cogns.: Fr.: **Maurel**, **Morel**, **Moreau**, **Moureau(x)**. It.: **Maur(i)ello**, **Maurel(li)**, **Morelli**, **Morello**. Sp.: **Morillo**. Cat.: **Morell**.

Dims.: Eng.: MORLIN. Fr.: **Morellet**, **Mor(e)let**, **Morel(l)on**, **Mor(e)lot**, **Mourlot**.

The earliest certainly established bearer of the surname Morrell *is Sir Geoffrey Morrell (d. 1321) of Roding in Essex. The name was taken to America by the brothers Abraham and Isaac* Morrill, *who arrived at the Massachusetts Bay Colony in September 1632.*

Morris 1. English, Welsh, Scots, and Irish: from an OF personal name introduced to Britain by the Normans, *Maurice* (L *Mauritius*, a deriv. of *Maurus*; cf. MOORE 3). This was borne by several minor early Christian saints, including a 3rd-cent. Swiss martyr.

2. Jewish: Anglicization of any of various like-sounding Jewish surnames.

Vars. (of 1): **Morriss**, **Morrish**; **Morrice** (Sc., chiefly Aberdeen), **Maurice**; **Morse**, **Morce**, **Morss**. (Of 2): **Morse**.

Cogns. (of 1): Welsh: MEYRICK. Fr.: **Maurice**, **Mauris(se)**, **Maurize**, **Morice**, **Moris(se)**, **Morize**; **Meurice**, **Meuris(se)** (Belgium). It.: **Maurizio**, **Mauriz(z)i**, **Maurici**, **Maurigi**. Port.: **Maurício**. Ger.: **Mori(t)z**. Flem., Du.: **Meuris**; **Risse**. Hung.: **Móricz**.

Dims.: Fr.: **Mauricet**, **Maurisset**, **Moricet**, **Morisset**, **Morizet**, **Maurisseau**, **Maurisson**, **Morisson**, **Maurizot**, **Morizot**. Czech: **Mourek**. Hung.: **Moor**, **Mór(a)**.

Aug.: Fr.: **Maurissat**.

Patrs.: Eng.: **Mor(r)ison** (also Sc.). Sc.: **McMorris** (Gael. **MacMuiris**); **McVarish** (Gael. **Mac Mhuiris**). Ir.: **McMorris**, FITZMAURICE. Ger.: **Moritzer**. Low Ger.: **Moritzen**. Flem., Du.: **Morissen**. Dan., Norw.: **Mouritsen**, **Mouritzen**, **Mauritzen**.

Morris *was the name of an extensive and powerful family in colonial North America, who played a leading part in the emergence of the nation. They were descended from Richard Morris (d. 1672), who had fought in Cromwell's army and then became a merchant in Barbados. His son Lewis (1671–1746) established the 'manor' of Morrisania in New York State. His grandson, Lewis (1726–98), 3rd owner of that manor, was a signatory of the Declaration of Independence. Two other grandsons, Richard and Gouverneur, were also key figures in the Revolution. However, their half-brother Staats Morris (1728–1800) was a general in the British army and governor of Quebec.*

Another signatory of the Declaration, Robert Morris (1734–1806), had emigrated to America from Liverpool at the age of 13. He became known as the 'Financier of the Revolution' and was the founder of the Bank of North America. Despite his reputation, he was personally ruined by unwise (or unfortunate) speculation.

Samuel Morse *(1791–1872), inventor of the electric telegraph and of Morse code, was a direct descendant of Anthony Morse of Wilts., England, who had emigrated to Massachusetts in 1635.*

Morrissey Irish: Anglicized form of **Ó Muirgheas** 'descendant of *Muirgheasa*', a personal name apparently derived from the elements *muir* sea + *geas* taboo, prohibition.

Vars.: **O'Morrissey**, **O'Murrissa**, **O'Morisa**, **Mor(r)issy**, **Morrisey**.

Dims.: **O'Murghesan**, **O'Morrisane** (Gael. **Ó Muirgheasáin**).

Morrow Irish and Scots: Anglicized form of the Gael. personal name *Murchadh*, composed of the elements *muir* sea + *cadh* warrior; cf. MCMORROUGH and MURPHY.

Vars.: **Morrough**, **Murrow**, **Murrough**.

Mort 1. English (Lancs.): of uncertain origin. The most plausible suggestion is that it is a Norman nickname from OF *mort* dead (L *mortuus*), presumably referring to a person of deathly pallor or unnaturally still countenance. However, it could also be the result of survival into the ME period of an OE personal name, **Morta*, postulated by Ekwall to explain various placenames (cf. MORCOMBE and MORTLOCK).

2. French: either a nickname from OF *mort* dead (see above), or alteration, by folk etymology, of the given name *Mor(e)* (see MOORE 3).

Mortiboys English (W Midlands): apparently a Norman habitation name from an unidentified place named with OF *mort* dead (see MORT) + *bois* wood (see BOIS).

Mortimer English (Norman): habitation name from *Mortemer* in Seine-Maritime, so called from OF *mort(e)* dead (see MORT) + *mer* sea (L *mare*). The placename probably referred to a stagnant pond or partly drained swamp; there may also have been an allusion to the biblical Dead Sea seen by crusaders.

Vars.: **Mortimor(e)**, **Murtimer**.

Mortimer *was the name of a powerful Anglo-Norman family who became established in the Welsh marches. The founder was Roger* de Mortimer *(fl. 1054–74), whose name is derived from the castle of Mortemer-en-Brai. His son Ralph Mortimer (d. ?1104) was awarded lands in the marches which had been forfeited by the Earl of Hereford. Another member of this family, Roger de Mortimer, 1st Earl of March (1287–1330), was the lover of Queen Isabella. He invaded England in 1326 and forced her husband, King Edward II, to abdicate in favour of his son, Edward III, but was later executed by the latter.*

Mortlock English: probably a habitation name from *Mortlake* in Surrey, recorded in Domesday Book as *Mortelaga* and *Mortelage*, apparently from the OE byname **Morta* (see MORT 1) + OE *lag* marshy meadow or *lacu* stream (see LAKE).

Morton 1. English and Scots: habitation name from any of the many places called *Mor(e)ton*, from OE *mōr* marsh, fen, moor (see MOORE 1) + *tūn* enclosure, settlement.

2. Swedish: cogn. of MARTIN.

3. Jewish (Ashkenazic): presumably an Anglicization of one or more like-sounding Jewish surnames.

Var. (of 1): Eng.: **Moreton**. See also MURTON.

A family by the name of Moreton *were granted the earldom of Ducie in 1837. They took the name of the peerage from the surname of an ancestor, Sir Robert Ducie (b. 1575), a wealthy banker and Lord Mayor of London, whose granddaughter Elizabeth had married Edward Moreton of Moreton, Staffs.*

The name Morton *was established early in North America. George Morton (1585–1624), one of the Pilgrim Fathers, was probably born in Scrooby, Notts. An early settler of a rather different character was Thomas Morton (d. ?1647), who settled near Plymouth, Massachusetts, in 1625. He was an adventurer, probably trained as a lawyer, who came into conflict with the Puritan settlers over his trade in guns with the Indians and his raising of a maypole. As a result, he was forcibly returned to England in 1628.*

John Morton (c.1724–77), one of the signatories of the Declaration of Independence, was born in Pennsylvania, of Swedish descent. His grandfather, Morten Mortenson, had emigrated from Gothenburg in 1654.

Mosby English (Yorks.): habitation name, probably from *Mosbrough* in S Yorks. (*Moresburh* in Domesday Book), which gets its name from OE *mōres*, gen. sing. of *mōr* marsh, fen, moor (see MOORE 1) + *burh* fortress (see BURY).

Moseley English (chiefly W Midlands): habitation name from one of several places called *Mos(e)ley* in central, W, and NW England. The obvious derivation is from OE *mos* peat bog (see MOSS 1) + *lēah* wood, clearing, but the one in S Birmingham (*Museleie* in Domesday Book) had as its first element OE *mūs* mouse, while one in Staffs. (*Molesleie* in Domesday Book) had the gen. case of the OE byname *Moll*.

Vars.: **Mousley** (Birmingham); **Mosley** (chiefly S Yorks. and Lancs.).

Moses Jewish, English, and French: from the name of the Israelite leader *Moses* in the Book of Exodus, who led the Israelites out of Egypt. The Hebr. form of the name, *Moshe*, is probably of Egyptian origin, a short form of any of the various theophoric personal names, such as *Rameses* and *Tutmosis*, meaning 'conceived by (a certain god)'. However, very early in its history it acquired a folk etymology, being taken as a deriv. of the Hebr. root *mšh* to draw (something from the water), a reference to the story of the infant Moses being discovered among the bullrushes by Pharaoh's daughter. See also Moss 2.

Vars.: Jewish: **Mozes, Moshe**. Eng.: **Moyses**; **Moyse, Moise, Moyce**; **Moyes** (Sc.). Fr.: **Moyse, Moïse**.

Cogns.: It.: **Mo(i)se, Mois(i)o, Moizo, Moze**. Ger.: **Mosse**. Czech: **Mojžíš**.

Dims.: It.: **Moselli, Mosello, Mosetti**. Czech: **Mojžíšek**. Ukr.: **Mosienko**.

Patrs.: Jewish: **Mos(s)esohn, Mosezon, Moshes** (Ashkenazic); **Moise(i)ev, Moisseef, Mosaiov, Mosayov, Moshcyov, Mosheyoff, Moshaiov, Moshaiow, Moshayov, Moshayof, Moshevitch, Moshevitz, Moschowitsch** (E Ashkenazic); **Moisescu** (among Rumanian Jews); **Mosheshvili, Mosheshvily** (among Georgian Jews); **Musayov, Musaiov, Mussaioff, Moussaieff** (via Russ. from the Arabic form). Russ.: **Mo(i)seev, Mos(e)ichev**; **Musin, Musaev, Muzaev** (from the Arabic form *Mūsā* used in the Turkic languages). Croatian: **Mojsilović**. Armenian: **Movesian**.

Patrs. (from dims.): Jewish: **Moskovi(t)ch, Moscovitch, Moskowi(t)ch, Moskovic, Moskowicz, Moscowicz, Moskovicz, Moscovicz, Moskowics, Moskovics, Moskowitz, Moscowitz, Moskovitz, Moscovi(t)z, Moskowits, Moskovits, Moshkovi(t)ch, Moshcovitch, Moshkowich, Moszkowicz** (Pol. spelling), **Moszkovicz, Moshkowitz, Moshkovi(t)z, Moshcovitz** (E Ashkenazic); **Moskovici, Moscovici** (among Rumanian Jews). Russ.: **Mosyagin**. Pol.: **Moszkowicz**.

Moskowski Jewish (E Ashkenazic): ostensibly a habitation name from the city of *Moscow* or regional name from *Muscovy* (both named in Russ. as *Moskva*). However, the reference is probably merely to someone who had been on a trip to Moscow, as there were very few Jews living in Moscow or the surrounding region in the early 19th cent., when most Jews in the Russian Empire adopted family names. Alternatively, the name may in fact be an alteration of *Moskovich* (see patrs. at Moses), under the influence of the placename. The city takes its name from that of the river on which it stands, which seems, like so many old river names, to have originally meant no more than 'damp', 'wet'.

Var.: **Moskowsky**.

Moss 1. English: topographic name for someone who lived by a peat bog (ME, OE *mos*), or habitation name from a place named with this word. It was not until later that the vocab. word came to denote the class of plants characteristic of a peat-bog habitat, under the influence of the ON cogn. *mosi*.

2. English: from the normal medieval vernacular form of the given name Moses.

3. Jewish (Ashkenazic): of uncertain origin. It may be an Anglicization of Moses or some other like-sounding Jewish name.

Vars. (of 1): **Mosse, Mossman**.

Cogns. (of 1): Ger.: **Moos(mann), Mo(o)ser**; **Mies(er)** (Bavaria). Flem., Du.: Most.

Dim. (of 1): Ger.: **Mösl**.

Cpd (of 1; arbitrary or ornamental): Swed.: **Mossberg** ('bog hill').

Most 1. German: metonymic occupational name for a producer or seller of must, i.e. unfermented grape juice, Ger. *Most* (MHG, OHG *most*, from L *mustum* (*vīnum*) young, i.e. fresh, wine). The same term was also used of perry and cider, since these do not keep well and have to be drunk quickly while still fresh.

2. Flemish and Dutch: cogn. of Moss 1.

3. Jewish (E Ashkenazic): from Pol. and Russ. *most* bridge

Vars. (of 1): **Mös(s)t; Mostert, Mustert**. (Of 2): Flem., Du.: **Mostinck, Van der Most**.

Motel 1. Jewish (Ashkenazic): from Yid. *Motl*, a pet form of the Yid. male given name *Mortkhe*, from Hebr. *Mordechay* Mordecai (of Akkadian origin), name of the hero of the Book of Esther in the Bible, who with the help of his cousin Esther saved the Jews of Persia from destruction. Cf. Estersohn.

2. French: dim. of Motte.

Patr. (from 1): **Motelsohn**.

Mothersole English: 1. habitation name from *Moddershall* in Staffs., so called from OE *Mōdrēdeshalh* 'recess (see Hale 1) of *Mōdrēd*', a personal name composed of the elements *mōd* heart, spirit, courage + *rēd* counsel, wisdom.

2. perhaps also a nickname for a person who was in the habit of swearing with the oath 'on my *mother's soul*', but this is probably no more than folk etymology.

Var.: **Mothersill**.

Motion Scots: of unknown origin, perhaps a nickname for a restless person, from ME, OF *motion* movement (LL *mōtio*, gen. *mōtiōnis*, a deriv. of *mōvēre* to move). However, there are difficulties with this suggestion, principally the fact that *motion* was a learned word, and is not attested before the 15th cent.

Motte French and English: topographic name for someone who lived by a fortified stronghold, OF, ME *motte* (of apparently Gaul. origin, referring originally to a hillock or mound; see also Moat). The surname may also be a habitation name from any of the places in France named with this word.

Vars.: Fr.: **Mot(h)e; Lamotte, Lamothe; Delamotte; Mot(t)ier**. Eng.: **Mote, Mott**.

Cogns.: It.: **Mot(t)a; La Motta** (Sicily). Sp.: **Mota** (places in the provinces of Cuenca and Valladolid). Port.: **Mota**.

Dims.: Fr.: Motel, **Mot(t)et, Motton**.

The settlement which became the city of Detroit was founded in 1701 by Antoine de la Mothe, *Sieur de Cadillac (1658–1730), governor of Louisiana. He was born into the minor nobility in Gascony, where his father owned the seigneury of Cadillac.*

Marie Joseph Paul Yves Roch Gilbert du Motier, *Marquis de Lafayette (1757–1834), the French aristocrat who played a leading part in both the French and the American Revolutions, came of a family who had owned the estate of Lafayette in the Auvergne since the 13th cent.*

Mottershead English: habitation name from a lost place in the parish of Mottram, Ches., recorded in the 13th cent. as *Mottresheved*, from the gen. case of the OE byname *Mōtere* 'Speaker' + ME *heved* head(land), hill.

Var.: **Mottishead**.

Mottram English: habitation name from either of two places in Ches. It is possible that the name originally denoted a building where village assemblies were held, from OE *(ge)mōt* meeting + *ærn* house, hall. Other possibilities are that the name derives from OE *(ge)mōt-rūm* 'meeting space', or *(ge)mōt-treum* 'assembly trees'.

Mouche French: nickname from the housefly, OF *mouche* (L *musca*), denoting a small, light person, an insignificant one, or an irritating one.

Vars.: **Mouque**; **Lamouche**, **Lamouque**.

Cogns.: It.: **Mosca**, **Moschi**; **Musca** (Sicily, S Calabria); **Muscas** (S Sardinia). Russ.: MUKHIN (which see for Slav. cogns.).

Dims.: Fr.: **Mouchot(te)**, **Mouchel(et)**, **Mouchet**, **Mouchez**, **Mouquet**. It.: **Moschella**, **Moschelli**, **Moschetta**, **Moschetti**, **Moschetto**, **Moschin(i)**, **Moschino**, **Moschitta**, **Moscolini**, MUSSOLINI.

Augs.: It.: **Moscone**, **Moscon(i)**. Cat.: **Moscardó**.

Pejs.: It.: **Moscardo**, **Moscardi**.

Moult English: 1. from the ME female given name, *Ma(ha)lt*, *Mau(l)d*, a var. of the Norman name *Mathilde*, *Matilda*, composed of the Gmc elements *maht* might, strength + *hild* battle. The learned form *Matilda* was much less common than the vernacular *Mahalt*, *Maud* and the aphetic pet form TILL. The name was borne in England by the daughter of Henry I, who disputed the throne of England with her cousin Stephen for a number of years (1137–48). In Germany the popularity of the name in the Middle Ages was augmented by its being borne by a 10th-cent. saint, wife of Henry the Fowler and mother of Otto the Great.

2. nickname for a bald man, or someone who suffered from some deformity of the skull, from ME *mould* top of the head (OE *molda*).

Vars. (of 1): **Mo(u)ld**, **Moule**, **Moull**, **Ma(u)lt**, **Mald**, **Maud(e)**, MUDD, MOWAT.

Cogns. (of 1): Fr.: **Mathilde**; **Mahau(l)t**, **Mahaux**, **Maho(u)t**, **Mahoux**, **Maheut**, **Méhaut**, **Meheu(st)**. Ger.: **Mechthild**.

Dims. (of 1): Fr.: **Mahoudeau**. Ger.: **Metze**; **Mechel** (Hesse). Low Ger.: **Mett(e)**, **Mettke**.

Metrs. (from 1): Eng.: **Moulds**, **Moulding**; **Maudson**, **Malson**, **Mo(u)lson**; **Mawson**, **Mawsom** (see also MAW).

Metrs. (from 1) (dims.): Ger.: **Metzen**. Low Ger.: **Vermette**.

Moulton English: habitation name from any of the various places with this name, as for example in Ches., Lincs., Norfolk, Northants, Suffolk, and N Yorks. For the most part these are named with the OE byname *Mūla* 'Mule' + OE *tūn* enclosure, settlement, but in some cases they may have been originally farms where mules were reared or kept. for the place in Norfolk the first element was probably a personal name *Mōda*, a short form of the various cpd names with a first element *mōd* spirit, mind, courage (cf. MOODY).

Mounsey English (Norman): habitation name from *Monceaux* in Calvados and Orne, or *Monchaux* in Nord and Seine-Maritime. All get their name from the pl. form of OF *moncel* hillock (LL *monticellum*, a dim. of *mons*; cf. MONT).

Vars.: **Mo(u)ncey**, **Munsey**, **Munchay**; **Mounsie**, **Muncie** (Sc.).

Mountbatten English: translation of the Ger. habitation name **Battenberg**, from a place on the river Eder. The placename consists of the element *bat*, of uncertain meaning, perhaps describing a water-meadow (cf. BATE 3) + OHG *berg* hill.

Admiral of the Fleet Earl Mountbatten *(1900–79), the last viceroy and first governor-general of India, was a great-grandson of Queen Victoria and was related to most of the royal houses of Europe. He was the son of Prince Louis of Battenberg, a title that had been revived in 1851 after it had died out in 1314. The surname was changed in 1917 as a result of anti-German feeling among the populace.*

Mountford English (chiefly W Midlands): 1. Anglicized form of the Norman name MONTFORT.

2. possibly also a habitation name from *Mundford* in Norfolk, so called from the OE personal name *Munda* (from *mund* protection) + *ford* FORD.

Vars.: **Mun(d)ford**, **Mumford**.

Mountney English (Norman): habitation name from any of numerous places called *Montigni*, from the Gallo-Roman personal name *Montinius* + the local suffix *-ācum*.

Moutinho Portuguese: of uncertain origin, possibly a habitation name from a place called *Moitinha*, a dim. of MOITA.

Mowat Scots and N English: 1. from a medieval female given name, *Mohaut*, var. of *Mau(l)d*; see MOULT 1.

2. occupational name for an official in charge of communal pasture land, ME *moward*, *maward*, from OE *māwe* meadow (see MAW 3) + *weard* guardian (see WARD 1).

3. habitation name from any of various places in N France called *Mon(t)haut*, from OF *mont* hill (see MONT) + *haut* high (L *altus*).

Vars.: **Mowatt**, **Mouat(t)**.

Mowbray English (Norman): habitation name from *Montbrai* in La Manche, so called from OF *mont* hill (see MONT) + *brai* mud, slime (of Gaul. origin).

Vars.: **Mowbury**, **Moubray**, **Mumbray**, **Momery**, **Mummery**, **Memory**, **Mulb(e)ry**, **Mulberry**.

Cogn.: Fr.: **Maubray**.

The nephew and heir of Geoffrey de Montbrai, *Bishop of Coutances, Robert* de Mowbray *(d. ?1125), became Earl of Northumberland in c.1080, but was later imprisoned and disinherited for rebellion. His estates passed to a cousin, also bearing the name Mowbray. His descendant Thomas Mowbray (?1366–99) was Marshal of England, created 1st Duke of Norfolk in 1397. The dukedom continued in the family until the death of John Mowbray, 4th Duke, when it passed, via his daughter, to the Howard family.*

Mower English (chiefly Norfolk): occupational name for someone responsible for mowing pasture lands to provide hay, from an agent deriv. of ME *mow(en)* to mow (OE *māwen*; cf. MAW 1 and MATHER 1).

Moyano Spanish: from a medieval given name, LL *Modiānus*, a deriv. of *Modius* (from L *modus* measure).

Cogn.: Cat.: **Moyà** (also from a place originally named as the estate of Modius; cf. MOON 1).

Moyle Cornish: nickname for a bald man, from Corn. *moyl* bald.

Moynihan Irish: Anglicized form of Gael. **Ó Muimhneacháin** 'descendant of *Muimhneachán*', a dim. of the byname *Muimhneach* 'Munsterman'.

Var.: **Moynan**.

Mozart German: of uncertain origin, probably from a Gmc personal name composed of the elements *mōd* spirit, mind, courage + *hard* hardy, brave, strong.

Var.: **Mozet**.

The composer Wolfgang Amadeus Mozart *(1756–91) was born in Salzburg, Austria, but his family had lived in the Augsburg area in Germany for generations. The name was first recorded there with Heinrich* Motzhart *in 1338. His earliest known ancestor was Andris Motzhart, who lived in Augsburg in 1486.*

Mozo Spanish: nickname or occupational name from Sp. *mozo* boy, lad, servant (of uncertain origin, perhaps from L *mustus* young, fresh (cf. MOST 1) or from a pre-Roman element *muts-* pruned, shorn, referring to the custom among youths and lowly individuals of wearing their hair short (cf. PSCHORR and TOUS)).

Mráček Czech: nickname for a person of a gloomy disposition, from Czech *mráček* small dark cloud, dim. of *mrak* cloud, also used in the sense 'gloom'.

Cogn.: Pol.: **Mroczek**.

Habitation name: Pol.: **Mroczkowski**.

Mrówka Polish: nickname from Pol. *mrówka* ant, applied to a person of small stature, or perhaps to a busily active one.

Habitation name: **Mrowiński, Mrówczyński**.

Mróz Polish: 1. from an aphetic form of the Pol. given name *Ambroży* AMBROSE.

2. nickname for a white-haired man or alternatively for one of an icy and unsociable disposition, from Pol. *mróz* hoarfrost.

Cogns. (of 2): Czech: **Mráz**. Russ.: **Morozov** (patr.). Jewish (E Ashkenazic): **Moroz(owski)**, **Maroz** (reason(s) for acquisition not clear).

Dims. (of 1 and 2): Pol.: **Mrozek**. (Of 2 only): Czech: **Mrázek**.

Patr. (from 1): Pol.: **Mrozowicz**.

Habitation names (from 1 or 2): Pol.: **Mrozowski, Mroziński**. (From 1 only): Pol.: **Mrożewski**.

Mucklow English (W Midlands): habitation name from *Mucklows* Hill, to the W of Birmingham, or *Muckley* Corner near Lichfield, Staffs. Both names are from OE *micel* large + *hlāw* hill, here perhaps tumulus.

Mudd English: 1. from a medieval female given name, var. of *Maud*; see MOULT 1.

2. from the OE personal name *Mōd(a)*, a short form of the various cpd names containing the element *mōd* spirit, mind, courage (cf. MOODY).

3. topographic name for someone who lived in a particularly muddy area, from ME *mud* (MLG *mudde*), perhaps also a metonymic occupational name for a dauber (one who constructed buildings of wattle and daub).

Muela Spanish: 1. metonymic occupational name for someone who made or sold mill wheels, from Sp. *muela* mill wheel (L *mola*).

2. topographic name for someone who lived on a hill with a flat top, from the same word used in a topographic sense. There are numerous places called *La Muela*, and the surname may be a habitation name from any of these.

Vars.: **Muelas**. (Of 1 only): **Molero**.

Cogn. (of 2): Cat.: **Mulà**.

Muggeridge English: habitation name from *Mogridge* in Devon. The second element of this placename is clearly OE *hrycg* ridge, spur; the first is probably from an OE personal name *Mogga*.

Vars.: **Mug(g)ridge, Mog(g)ridge, Mockridge**.

Muir Scots and N English: topographic name for someone who lived on a moor, from a Northern dial. var. of ME *more* (see MOORE 1).

Var.: **Mure**.

Muirhead Scots: habitation name from any of the places in S Scotland so called, from Northern ME *muir* moor (see MUIR) + *heid* head, end.

Vars.: **Moorhead** (N Ireland), **Morehead**.

Mukhin Russian: patr. from the nickname *Mukha* 'Fly', denoting a small and irritating person, or someone considered of no importance.

Cogns. (not patrs.): Pol.: **Mucha**. Czech: **M(o)ucha**.

Habitation names: Pol.: **Muszyński**. Jewish (E Ashkenazic): **Muszinsky** (reason(s) for acquisition not clear).

Mulcahy Irish: Anglicized form of Gael. **Ó Maolchathaigh** 'descendant of the devotee of (St) *Cathach*', a byname meaning 'Warlike'.

Vars.: **Cahy**, CAUGHEY.

Mulcreevy Irish: Anglicized form of Gael. **Ó Maolchraoibhe** 'descendant of the devotee of (St) *Craobh*'.

Vars.: **O'Mulcreevy; Mulgrew, Mulgrue, Mulgroo**.

Muldoon Irish: Anglicized form of Gael. **Ó Maoldúin** 'descendant of *Maoldúin*', a personal name composed of the elements *maol* chief + *dún* fortress.

Vars.: **O'Muldoon, Muldon, Meldon**.

Mule English: 1. from a medieval given name, perhaps OE *Mūl* (from OE *mūl* mule, halfbreed). This was the name of a brother of Ceadwalla, King of Wessex (d. 675), and is also found as a placename element. However, it may not have survived to the Conquest, and Domesday Book *Mule*, *Mulo* may instead represent ON *Mūli*, which is probably from ON *mūli* muzzle, snout.

2. nickname for a stubborn person or metonymic occupational name for a driver of pack-animals, from ME *mule* mule (OE *mūl*, from L *mūla*, reinforced by OF *mule*, from the same source).

3. from the medieval female given name *Mulle*, var. of *Molle*, a pet form of *Mary* (see MARIE).

Vars.: **Moule, Mowl(e)**.

Cogns. (of 2): Fr.: **Mule; Mulier, Lemul(l)ier, Mulatier**. Sp.: **Mulero**. Ger.: MAUL.

Dims. (of 2): Eng.: **Mullet(t)**. Fr.: **Mul(l)et, Mulin**.

Pej. (of 2): Fr.: **Mulard**.

Metr. (from 3): Eng.: **Mowles**.

Mulhall Irish: Anglicized form of Gael. **Ó Maolchathail** 'descendant of the devotee of (St) *Cathal*' (see CAHILL).

Mulhern Irish: Anglicized form of Gael. **Ó Maoilchiaráin** 'descendant of the devotee of (St) *Ciarán*' (a byname from a dim. of *ciar* black).

Vars.: **Mulkerrin, Mulkern(s)**.

Mulholland Irish: Anglicized form of Gael. **Ó Maolchalann** 'descendant of the devotee of (St) *Calann*' (see CALLAN).

Mullally Irish: Anglicized form of Gael. **Ó Maolalaidh** 'descendant of *Maolaladh*', a personal name composed of the elements *maol* chieftain + *aladh* speckled, piebald.

Vars.: **O'Mullally, Mullal(e)y, Lally**.

Mullarkey Irish: Anglicized form of Gael. **Ó Maoilearca** 'descendant of the devotee of (St) *Earc*'.

Mullen 1. Irish: Anglicized form of Gael. **Ó Maoláin** 'descendant of *Maolán*', a byname meaning 'Tonsured One', 'Devotee' (from *maol* bald; cf. MILLIGAN and MCMILLAN).

2. English: topographic name for someone who lived by a MILL, or occupational name for a MILLER, from ANF *mo(u)lin*, *mulin* mill.

Vars.: **Mullens, Mullin(s), Mullings, Millen(s)**. (Of 1 only): **Mullan(e), Mulhane, Mullon, Millen, Milling, Mollan, Moylan, Melane, (O')Moylane, O'Mullan(e), O'Mollane, O'Melane**. (Of 2 only): **Molins; Mullin(g)er, Mullin(d)ar** (agent derivs.).

Mullis English (W Midlands): topographic name for someone who lived by a mill(house), from ME *mulle* mill (W dial. form of OE *mylen*) + *hus* house, or occupational name for someone who worked in one.

Mulqueen Irish: Anglicized form of Gael. **Ó Maolchaoine** 'descendant of the devotee of (St) *Caoine*' (see CAIN).

Mulroy Irish: Anglicized form of Gael. **Ó Maolruaidh** 'descendant of *Maolruadh*', a personal name composed of the elements *maol* chief + *ruadh* red.

Mulryan Irish: Anglicized form of Gael. **Ó Maoilríaghain** 'descendant of the devotee of (St) *Ríaghan*' (see RYAN).

Vars.: **Mulryne, Mulrine, Mulran; O'Mulr(o)yan, O'Mulrigan, O'Mulrean.**

Mulvaney Irish: Anglicized form of Gael. **Ó Maoilmheana** 'descendant of the devotee of (St) *Meana*' (a personal name apparently from *mion* mite, small thing).

Vars.: **Mulvenna, Mulvany.**

Mulvey Irish: Anglicized form of Gael. **Ó Maoilmhiadhaigh** 'descendant of the devotee of (St) *Miadhach*' (a byname meaning 'Honourable').

Mumby English: habitation name from a place in Lincs., so called from the ON personal name *Mundi* (see MONDAY 1) + ON *býr* farm, settlement.

Muncaster English: habitation name from a place in Cumb., known in the Middle Ages as *Mulcaster*, from the OE byname *Mūla* 'Mule', or possibly the ON personal name *Múli* (from *múli* muzzle, snout; see MULE 1) + OE *ceaster* (Roman) fort (L *castra* legionary camp).

Var.: **Mulcaster.**

Munden English: habitation name from a place in Herts., so called from the OE personal name *Munda* (a short form of any of the various cpd names containing the element *mund* protection) + OE *denu* valley (see DEAN 1).

Municio Spanish: of uncertain origin, probably from an old given name, which appears in medieval sources in the L forms *Munitius* and *Munnitus* and is probably related to MUÑO.

Munnelly Irish: Anglicized form of Gael. **Ó Maonghaile** 'descendant of *Maonghal*', a personal name composed of the elements *maon* riches + *gal* valour.

Muño Spanish: from an old given name that appears in medieval sources in the L forms *Munnius* and *Monnius*. It is of uncertain origin, perhaps from a Gmc short form of the various cpd personal names with the first element *mund* protection.

Patrs.: **Muñiz, Muñoz.** Port.: **Moniz.**

Munro Scots: local name for someone who had migrated from the mouth of the river *Roe* in Derry, N Ireland; the surname is derived from *mun*, mutated form of Gael. *bun* root, river-mouth + *Rotha*, the Gael. name of the river.

Vars.: **Munroe, Munrow, Monro(e).**

Scottish holders of this name are descended from Donald O'Kane and his sept, who in the 11th cent. migrated from the mouth of the Roe to Ferrindonald in Cromarty, Scotland. There his descendants, as Barons of Foulis and vassals of the Earls of Ross, held lands along the Firth of Cromarty. James Monroe *(1758–1831), 5th President of the United States (1817–25), came from a cadet branch of this family.*

Murat Provençal: habitation name from any of various places so called, from OProv. *murat* fortified (L *mūrātus*, a deriv. of *mūrus* wall; cf. MURO).

Dim.: **Muratet.**

Murcia Spanish: habitation name from the town, or regional name from the province of this name in SE Spain, apparently so called from L (*aqua*) *murcida* stagnant water. Alternatively, it may derive from L *Murcia*, *Murtia*, the name of an obscure Roman or Italic goddess, later used as an epithet of Venus, as if from *myrta*, *murta* myrtle.

Var.: **Murciano** (also borne by Sefardic Jews).

Murdoch Scots: Anglicized form of the Gael. personal name *Muire(adh)ach*, a deriv. of *muir* sea.

Vars.: **Murdock** (N Ireland); **Murdough, Murdow, Murdy, Mortagh, Murt(h)a.** See also MCMURRAY.

Murgatroyd English (W Yorks., chiefly Halifax and Bradford): habitation name from a lost place near Halifax, apparently so called from the medieval female given name *Marg(ar)et* (see MARGUERITE) + Northern ME *royd* clearing (OE *rod*).

Murnane Irish: Anglicized form of Gael. **Ó Murnáin**, a contracted form of *Ó Manannáin* 'descendant of *Manannán*', a name borne in Celt. mythology by a sea-god.

Muro Spanish: topographic name for someone who lived near a fortification (Sp. *muro*, from L *mūrus* wall), or habitation name from any of the numerous places named with this element (cf. MURAT).

Cogn.: Cat.: **Mur.**

Dims.: Sp.: **Muriel, Murillo.**

Murphy Irish: Anglicized form of Gael. **Ó Murchadha** 'descendant of *Murchadh*', a personal name composed of the elements *muir* sea + *cadh* warrior.

Vars.: **O'Murphy, (O')Morphy, O'Morchoe.** See also MORROW and MCMORROUGH.

Murphy *is one of the commonest of all Irish names, widely distributed throughout the English-speaking world, with some 6,000 subscribers in the Ir. telephone directories, around 1,500 in London, some 900 in Chicago, and 680 in Manhattan.*

Murray 1. Scots: regional name from *Moray* in NE Scotland, apparently so called from old Celt. elements meaning 'sea' + 'settlement'.

2. Irish: Anglicized form of Gael. *Mac Muire(adh)aigh*; see MCMURRAY.

3. Irish: Anglicized form of Gael. *Mac Giolla Mhuire*; see GILMORE.

4. English: var. of MERRY; for the varied treatment of OE *-y-*, cf. HILL 1.

Vars.: **Murr(e)y, Murrie.**

The Scottish family of Murray, *the senior branch of which holds the dukedom of Atholl, can be traced to a Flemish settler, Hugh Freskin, who in 1130 obtained extensive grants of land in Morayshire, from which the surname was taken. The earldom of Sutherland was granted to Freskin's grandson, William* Moray, *in 1235. A descendant who acquired lands at Tullibardine, Perths., in 1284 used the name Sir William* de Moravia.

Murton N English: habitation name from any of various places, in Cumb., Co. Durham, N Yorks., and elsewhere, all so called from OE *mōr* marsh, fen, moor (see MOORE 1) + *tūn* enclosure, settlement; cf. MORTON.

Musgrave English: habitation name from a pair of villages in Cumb., so called from OE *mūs* mouse (perhaps a byname) + *grāf* GROVE. The Norman surname *de Muce-*

gros, established in Herefords. and elsewhere in the 12th and 13th cents., is probably unrelated and has died out.

Var.: **Musgrove**.

A family of this name trace their descent from Thomas de Musgrave, *who represented Westmorland in Parliament in 1350.*

Musiał Polish: a fairly common surname, as is its Czech cogn.; both are of uncertain origin. It appears to be a nickname from the masc. sing. past tense of *musieć* must. If this is right, it means something like 'he had to', 'he was forced to', but the circumstances in which this vocab. word gave rise to a surname are not known.

Cogn.: Czech: **Musil**.

Dims.: Pol.: **Musiałek**. Czech: **Musílek**.

Patr.: Pol.: **Musiałowicz**.

Habitation name: Pol.: **Musiałowski**.

Musset French: habitation name from any of various minor places named with a dim. form of OF *musse* hiding-place, ambush (from *musser*, *mucier* to hide, of Gaul. origin).

Vars.: MUSSON, **Mussot**.

Dim.: **Mussillon**.

The French poet and dramatist Alfred de Musset *(1810–57) was from a powerful political family. He could trace his ancestry back to 1140.*

Mussolini Italian: 1. metonymic occupational name for a seller of muslin, It. *mussolina* (Arabic *mauçilīy*, from the name of *Mosul* in Iraq, where it was first manufactured).

2. nickname from a double dim. of *mussa* fly; cf. MOUCHE.

3. from a double dim. of an aphetic form of the given name *Iacomus*; see JAMES.

Musson 1. English (chiefly Notts.): of uncertain origin, ostensibly a patr.

2. French: var. of MUSSET.

Mustard English: metonymic occupational name for a dealer in spices, or nickname for someone with a hot temper or a vicious tongue, from ME, OF *mo(u)starde* mustard (a deriv. of *mo(u)st* unfermented wine (see MOST 1), in which the mustard seeds were originally prepared).

Var.: **Mustart**.

Cogns.: Fr.: **Moutard**; **Mou(s)tardier** (agent derivs.).

Mustoe English: topographic name for someone who lived near a piece of open ground used as a meeting-place, from ME *motestow*, from OE *(ge)mōt* meeting, assembly (a deriv. of *mētan* to meet) + *stōw* place, site (see STOW).

Vars.: **Musto(w)**.

Mustonen Finnish: patr. from the nickname *Musto* 'Black', denoting someone with dark hair or a dark complexion, or who habitually dressed in black.

Mutch Scots: nickname for a large (tall or fat) person, from ME *muche* great, a shortened form (probably a back-formation, as if from a dim. with the ANF suffix *-el*) of *muchel*, OE *mycel* (cf. MEIKLE).

Var.: **Much**.

Mutton English (chiefly Devon): nickname for a gentle but unimaginative person, one thought to resemble a sheep, or metonymic occupational name for a shepherd, from ANF *m(o)uto(u)n* sheep (OF *mouton*, probably of Gaul. origin; cf. Bret. *maout* sheep).

Var.: **Motton**.

Cogns.: Fr.: **Mout(h)on**; **Moutonnier** (an agent deriv.). Prov.: **Moutou**.

Dims.: Fr.: **Moutonneau**, **Moutonnet**, **Mout(h)enet**, **Mouthenot**.

Mužík Czech: affectionate nickname for a man of short stature, from a vocab. word derived from *muž* man.

Myasnikov Russian: patr. from the occupational term *myasnik* butcher (from *myaso* meat).

Cogns.: Bulg.: **Mesarov** (patr.). Czech: **Masák**, **Masaryk**, **Masařík**. Hung.: **Mészáros**. Jewish (E Ashkenazic): **Miasnik**.

Myatt English (chiefly W Midlands): from the ME given name *Myat*, formed from a truncated version of *Mihel* (see MYHILL) + the dim. suffix *-at* (from OF *-et*, crossed with the originally pej. OF *-ard*).

Vars.: **Miatt**, **Myott**, **Miot**.

Myerscough English (Lancs.): habitation name from a place in Lancs., so called from ON *mýrr* marsh, mire + *skógr* copse (cf. SHAW).

Myhill English (Norfolk): from the ME, ANF given name *Mihel*, a vernacular form of MICHAEL.

Vars.: **Mighell**, **Mighill**; **Miell**, **Miall**, **Myall**.

Cogn.: Fr.: **Miel**.

Dim.: Fr.: **Miellet**.

Myslivec Czech: occupational name for a hunter or gamekeeper, from a vocab. word ultimately derived from *mysl* mind.

Dim.: **Myslivеček**.

Myton English: habitation name from *Myton* in Warwicks. or *Mytton* in Shrops., both so called from OE *(ge)mȳðe* confluence, place where two streams meet + *tūn* enclosure, settlement. See also MITTON.

Var.: **Mytton**.

N

Nabais Portuguese: metonymic occupational name for a turnip farmer or topographic name for someone who lived by turnip fields, from the pl. form of Port. *nabal* turnip field (LL *nāpāle*, a deriv. of *nāpus* turnip; cf. NEAPE).

Nabokov Russian: apparently a patr. from a nickname *Nabok*, derived from the phrase *na bok* (with the accent on the preposition) on(to) one's side; the application of the nickname is not clear. Compare BOCZEK.

Nachmann Jewish: from the Hebr. male given name *Nachman*, which is probably a var. of the biblical male given name *Nachum* 'Consoled' (see NAHUM).

Vars.: **Na(c)hman**; **Na(c)hmani**, **Na(c)hmany** (with the Hebr. suffix *-i*).

Patrs.: **Nachmanson** (Ashkenazic); **Nachmanovitz**, **Nachmanowitz**, **Nachminovitch** (E Ashkenazic, the latter reflecting Yid. *Nakhmen*); **Nachmanovici**, **Nachminovici** (Rumanian spellings).

Nadler English, German, and Jewish (Ashkenazic): occupational name for a maker of needles, or in some cases perhaps for a tailor, from an agent deriv. of ME *nadle* needle, Ger. *Nadel* (OE *nǣdle*; MHG *nādel(e)*, OHG *nād(a)la*; cf. NÄHER). Needles in the Middle Ages were comparatively coarse articles made from bone.

Vars.: Eng.: **Needler**; **Ne(e)lder**, **Nayldor**; **Neilder** (mainly Cornwall and Devon); **Needle**. Ger.: **Nold(n)er**, **Nöldner**, **Nöllner**; **Nadel**. Jewish: **Nadel(man)**; **Nodelman** (from Yid. *nodl* needle); **Nudel(man)**, **Nudler** (from a S Yid. pronunciation of *nodl*).

Cogns.: Low Ger.: **Neth(e)ler**.

Cpds: Jewish: **Nadelstecher** ('needle sticker', probably a derogatory nickname for a tailor); **Nadelstern** ('needle star', occupational-ornamental); **Nadelstock** ('needle staff', occupational-ornamental).

The earliest recorded bearer of the surname Neilder *in the South-West of England is Ralf* le Neldere, *whose will was proved at Exeter in 1320. John* Nelder *of Trelowya near St Germans, who lodged a complaint of robbery in 1470, may be an ancestor of present-day bearers in SE Cornwall.*

Nádvorník Czech: occupational name for a chamberlain, head servant, or overseer, from Czech *na* on, over + *dvůr* household, court (see DVOŘÁK) + *-ník* suffix of agent nouns. The vocab. word is more or less equivalent to Ger. HOFMEISTER.

Naftali Jewish: from the Hebr. male given name *Naftali* 'I have struggled', borne by one of the twelve sons of Jacob. On his death bed Jacob blessed him with the words 'Naphtali is a hind let loose: he giveth goodly words' (Gen. 49: 21), and it is possible that in at least some cases surnames meaning 'deer' have been chosen by Jews in allusion to this; see, e.g., CERF 2 and HIRSCH 2.

Vars.: **Naftaly**, **Nafthalie**.

Patrs.: **Naftalis(on)** (Ashkenazic); **Naftalin**, **Naftalovici** (E Ashkenazic; the latter is a Rumanian spelling); **Naftolin** (reflecting the NE Yid. pronunciation of the given name); **Naftulis**, **Naftulin** (reflecting a S Yid. pronunciation of the given name).

Nafz German: nickname for a sleepyhead, from a deriv. of MHG *nafzen* to take a nap (OHG *(h)naffezan*).

Vars.: **Nafz(g)er**, **Nefzger**.

Nagar Jewish (Ashkenazic): occupational name for a carpenter, Hebr. *nagar*.

Vars.: **Naggar**; **Nager** (if this name is indeed related to *Nagar*, it shows alteration of the final vowel under Yid. influence; if not, it is from *Näger* (see NÄHER); **Nagari** (with the Hebr. suffix *-i*).

Patr. (E Ashkenazic): **Nagarin** (with the Slav. suffix *-in*).

Nagy Hungarian and Jewish (Ashkenazic): nickname for a large man, from Hung. *nagy* big. As a Hung. name it is contrasted with KISS and used to describe the older of two bearers of the same given name.

Näher German: occupational name for a tailor, from an agent deriv. of Ger. *nähen* to sew (MHG *najen*, OHG *nājan*; cf. NADLER).

Vars.: **Näger**, **Neher**, **Neger**, **Nei(g)er**; **Nader**, **Näder**; **Nather**, **Nät(h)er**, **Nether**.

Cogns.: Jewish (Ashkenazic): **Neher**, **Neger**, **Nei(g)er**; **Negeris** (presumably a patr.); **Nader**, **Neder**, **Net(t)er**, **Netterman**.

Nahum Jewish: from the Hebr. male given name *Nachum* 'Consoled', borne by a minor prophet, the author of the Book of the Bible that bears his name. The Russ. form of the name, *Naum*, is widespread even among non-Jews, because of folk-etymological association with Russ. *naumnik* genius, from the root *um* mind.

Vars.: **Naum** (from the Russ. given name); **Nahumi** (with the Hebr. ending *-i*).

Dims.: Ukr.: **Naumenko**. Beloruss.: **Navumenko**, **Naumchik**, **Navumchik**.

Patrs.: Jewish: **Nahumson**, **Na(c)himson**, **Nachimzon** (Ashkenazic); **Nakhumovich**, **Na(c)humovsky**, **Nachimovski** (E Ashkenazic); **Nochimowski** (NE Ashkenazic, from Yid. *Nokhem*, a reflex of the Hebr. given name); **Nukhimovich**, **Nuhimovsky** (S Ashkenazic, from a S Yid. pronunciation of the Yid. given name). Russ.: **Naumov**. Beloruss.: **Navumov**. Croatian: **Naumović**.

Patrs. (from dims.): Russ.: **Naumshin**, **Naumychev**.

Nairn Scots: habitation name from the town of this name, east of Inverness, so called from the river at whose mouth it stands. The river name is of ancient and disputed origin.

Var.: **Nairne**.

Nalder English: topographical name for someone who lived by an alder, a var. of ALDER 2 by misdivision from ME *atten al(d)re* at the alder; cf. NASH and NOAKE.

Derivs.: **Naldrett**, **Neldrett** (from *atten al(d)rett* by the alder grove).

Nancarrow Cornish: habitation name from places in the parishes of St Allen and St Michael Penkivel, so called from Corn. *nans* valley + *carow* deer, stag or *garow* rough.

Nangle English and Irish (Norman): var. of ANGLE, from a misdivision of ME *atten angle*.

Vars.: **N(e)agle** (reflecting the OF pronunciation with a nasalized vowel); **de Nógla** (a Gaelicized form).

Gilbert de Angulo *was a Norman baron who settled in Ireland in the 12th cent. Many of his linear male descendants bear the surnames* Nagle *or* Neagle, *and members of the family held estates in Co. Cork and in Connacht.*

Nankervis Cornish: habitation name from a place in St Enoder parish, so called from Corn. *nans* valley + an uncertain second element, possibly **cerwys*, an unattested pl. of *carow* stag. Compare NANCARROW.

Nankivell Cornish: habitation name from a place in the parish of St Mawgan in Pydar, so called from Corn. *nans* valley + a personal name *Cuvel*.

Nanne Low German and Danish: from a Fris. personal name, in origin probably a nursery term, but in the Middle Ages also taken as a short form of various Gmc cpd names containing the element *nand* daring, brave (cf., e.g., FERDINAND).

Dims.: **Nanneke, Nenneke.**

Patrs.: **Nannen, Nansen, Nanning(a).**

Napier Scots, English, and French: occupational name for a seller of table linen or for a 'naperer', the servant in charge of the linen in use in a manor house. The name represents ME, OF *nap(p)ier*, an agent deriv. of OF *nappe* table cloth (L *mappa*, of apparently Punic origin).

Vars.: Eng.: **Nap(p)er.**

An extensive Scottish family called Napier, *who once held the earldom of Lennox, are descended from the hereditary naperers to the Kings of Scotland in the 12th cent.*

Napoleoni Italian: from the Corsican given name *Napoleone*, of uncertain origin. It has been suggested that it is from the Gmc personal name *Nibelung* 'son of Mist, Fog' (see NIEBLICH), but in folk etymology it has been associated with the city of *Naples* (see NAPOLI) + It. *leone* lion.

Vars.: **Napolioni; Nebuloni, Nebulone** (Lombardy); **Nuvoloni, Nuvolone** (Lombardy, Liguria).

Napoli Italian: habitation name from the Campanian city of *Naples* (It. *Napoli*, L *Neapolis*, from Gk *nea* new + *polis* city; it was an ancient Gk colony taken over by the Romans in the 4th cent. BC).

Vars.: **di Napoli; Napoletano, Napolitano.**

Nápravník Czech: status name for a feudal tenant, who held land as of right in return for various duties to his lord, from Czech *na* on, over + *právo* right, entitlement + *-ník* suffix of agent nouns.

Naquet French: occupational name for a young lad or serving man, OF *naquet* (apparently a dim. of *naque* mucus, snot, a word of uncertain origin).

Var.: **Naquin.**

Pej.: **Naquard.**

Naranjo Spanish: metonymic occupational name for a grower of oranges or topographic name for someone who lived by an orange grove, from Sp. *naranjo* orange tree (from *naranja* orange, Arabic *nāránğya*, probably derived via Sanskrit and Persian from a Dravidian language). The word *orange* reached Eng. from Sp. via OF and OProv., in which languages the initial *n-* had already been sporadically lost.

Cogns.: Port.: **Laranjo, Laranjeira.** It.: **Arancio, Arangio; Narangi** (Emilia); **Marangi** (Tarento); **Ranzi.**

Dims.: It.: **Aranzello, Ranzetti.**

Narciso Portuguese: from a medieval given name (L *Narcissus*, from Gk *Narkissos*, the name of a flower). This name was borne, according to classical myth, by a vain youth who was so transfixed by his own beauty that he ignored the blandishments of the nymph Echo and stared at his own reflection in water until he faded away and turned into the pale but lovely flower that bears his name. It was also borne by several early Christian saints, in particular by a bishop who was said to have been put to death, together with his deacon Felix, in Catalonia AD *c.*307. The given name owes its popularity to this saint rather than to the mythological youth.

Cogns.: Jewish: **Narkis(s)** (ornamental names from the word for the flower).

Nardi 1. Italian: from an aphetic form of any of the various medieval It. given names (of Gmc origin) ending in the syllable *-nard(o)*; cf., e.g., BERNARD, LEONARD, and REYNARD.

2. Jewish (Israeli): ornamental name from Hebr. *nerd* nard, an aromatic plant.

Var. (of 1): **Nardo.**

Dims. (of 1): **Nardelli, Nard(i)ello, Nardin(i), Nardulli, Narducci, Narduzzi.** Fr.: **Nardet, Nardeau, Nardin, Nardon(neau), Nardou(x).**

Augs. (of 1): It.: **Nardon(i), Nardone.**

Nascimento Portuguese: religious byname from Port. *nascimento* birth, nativity (LL *nascimentum*, from *nasci* to be born). This was one of the epithets of the Virgin (*Maria do Nascimento*), and was also used as a given name for children born at Christmas.

Nash 1. S English: topographic name for someone who lived by an ash tree, a var. of ASH by misdivision of ME *atten ash* 'at the ash'; cf. NALDER and NOAKE.

2. Jewish: of unknown origin, possibly an Anglicized form of one or more like-sounding Jewish surnames.

Var. (of 1): **Naish** (chiefly Wilts. and Somerset).

The surname Nash *is now also common in Ireland, where it was taken by a family who established themselves in Co. Kerry in the 13th cent., during the second wave of Anglo-Norman settlement.*

Abner Nash (?1740–86), governor of N Carolina, was of Welsh origin, his parents having emigrated to Virginia from Wales in 1730. His brother Francis (?1742–77) was a general in the Continental Army; the town of Nashville, Tennessee, was named in his honour.

Naslednikov Russian: patr. from the nickname *Naslednik* 'Heir' (a deriv. of *(na)sledit* to follow (on)), given perhaps to a man who had inherited a great deal of money, or perhaps merely to someone with great expectations.

Nassau German: habitation name from the small town of *Nassau*, formerly the seat of an independent duchy. The name comes from OHG *nazz* damp, wet + *ouwa* water meadow.

The German royal house of Nassau *traces its descent from Dudo, Count of Lauenberg, who flourished between 1093 and 1117. His family acquired the county of Nassau in the 12th cent.*

Nast German: topographic name for someone who lived in a thickly wooded area, or metonymic occupational name for a woodcutter, from MHG *nast* branch, a regional var. of *ast*, resulting from the misdivision of forms such as *ein ast* 'a branch'.

Var.: **Ast** (also Jewish, of unknown origin, perhaps to be explained in the same way as the Ger. name).

Dim.: **Nestle** (Switzerland), Gallicized as **Nestlé.**

Nathan Jewish and English (Notts.): from the Hebr. male given name *Natan* 'Given' (i.e. by God; cf. *Jonathan* and *Nathaniel*), borne by a minor biblical prophet (2 Sam. 7: 2). The given name was a comparatively rare one among non-Jews in the Middle Ages (although always common among Jews); as a modern surname it is most frequently Jewish.

Vars.: Jewish: **Natan; Nusan, Nusen** (based on S Yid. pronunciations). Eng.: **Natan; Nation** (W Midlands; altered by folk etymology).

Dims.: Jewish: **Nuta** (based on a S Yid. pronunciation).

Patrs.: Jewish: **Nat(h)ans, Nat(h)anso(h)n, Nat(h)anzon, Natenzon, Nathansen, Nusinzon** (Ashkenazic); **Nus(s)inov, Nusynowicz, Nusynowitz, Nusinowitz, Nus(s)inovitz, Nusynowicz** (E Ashkenazic, from S Yid. pronunciations); **Natanov** (not exclusively Ashkenazic).

Patrs. (from dims.): Jewish: **Notes, Notowitz, Nutin; Notkin, Notkovich, Nutkevitch, Nutk(i)ewicz, Nutkewitz, Nutkevitz; Noszkes, Noskes, Noskovitz, Noskowitz.**

Naud 1. French: from an aphetic form of various medieval given names derived from Gmc personal names ending in the element *wald* rule; cf., e.g., ARNOLD and REYNOLD.

2. Provençal: cogn. of the given name NOEL.

3. Provençal: metonymic occupational name for a sailor or boat-builder, from OProv. *nau* boat, ship (L *navis*).

Vars. (of 1): **Naude, Nault.**

Cogns. (of 1): Ger.: **Noldt, Nolde, Nolte, Noll.** It.: **Naldi.**

Dims. (of 1): Fr.: **Naudet, Naudin, Naudot, Naudon.** Low Ger.: **Nöl(de)ke.** It.: **Naldini, Nallini.**

Aug. (of 1): It.: **Naldone.**

Patrs. (from 1): Low Ger.: **Nolten, Nolting, Nölting.**

Patrs. (from 1) (dim.): Low Ger.: **Nölker, Nölken.**

Naughton 1. Irish: Anglicized form of the Gael. personal name *Neachtan*. This was the name of the god of water and the sea in Irish mythology. It has been suggested that the name is derived from L *Neptūnus* Neptune, the Roman sea-god.

2. English: habitation name from a place in Suffolk, so called from OE *nafola* navel, depression + *tūn* enclosure, settlement.

Vars. (of 1): **Naughtan, Na(u)ghten, Nochtin, Nocton, Knockton, Natten, Natton,** NORTON.

'Descendant of N. 1': **O'Naughton, O'Naghtan, O'N(e)aghten** (Gael. **Ó Neachtain**).

Most of the names listed here and at MCNAUGHTON *are today found mainly in Ireland, but it seems that only the* O'Naughtons *are of Irish origin, the* McNaughtons *having originated in Lochow, Scotland, and migrated to Co. Antrim in the 14th cent.*

Naugolnikov Russian: patr. from *Naugolnik*, denoting someone who lived at a corner, from *na* on, at + *ugol* corner + *-nik* suffix of agent nouns.

Nava Spanish: habitation name for someone who lived on a flat, treeless area of upland, Sp. *nava* (a word of pre-Roman origin). There are numerous places named with this element, any of which may also have given rise to the surname. The name is also borne by Sefardic Jews, the reason(s) for its adoption being unknown.

Var. (Sp. only): **Navas.**

Navarrete Spanish: habitation name from places in the provinces of Logroño and Álava, so called from the Basque elements *Nafar* Navarrese (see NAVARRO) + *ate* pass, defile.

Navarro Spanish and Jewish (Sefardic): regional name for someone from Navarre (Sp. *Navarra*), now divided between Spain and France, but in the Middle Ages an independent Basque kingdom. Its name may have some connection with Sp. *nava* treeless plateau (see NAVA).

Vars.: **Nabarro.** Jewish only: **Navaro.**

Cogn.: Fr.: **Navarre.**

Navàs Catalan: habitation name from a place in the province of Barcelona, so called from the pre-Roman element NAVA + the suffix *-às*, which is of Celt. origin and uncertain significance.

Navrátil Czech: nickname from the masc. sing. past tense of the verb *navrátit* to return, perhaps originally used to refer to someone who had returned to his native community after a prolonged absence. The Czech surname does not have the meaning 'Convert' borne by the Pol. cogn. NAWROCKI.

Nawrocki Polish: name adopted by a religious convert, in particular a Jew who had converted to Christianity, from Pol. *nawróc* to turn.

Var.: **Nawrot.**

Naylor English: occupational name for a maker of nails, from an agent deriv. of ME *nayl* nail (OE *nægel*).

Vars.: **Nayler, Naylar.**

Cogns.: Ger.: **Nagler, Nähler; Nagelschmidt** (cf. NAYSMITH); **Nagel, Nägel(e), Negel, Nahl.** Low Ger.: **Nagelmacher, Nagelmaker.** Flem., Du.: **Nagel(smit), Nagelma(e)ker.** Jewish (Ashkenazic): **Nagel, Nagler.**

Patrs.: Flem., Du.: **Nagelma(e)kers.**

Cpds (ornamental elaborations of *Nagel*): Jewish (Ashkenazic): **Nagelberg** ('nail hill'); **Nagelstein** ('nail stone').

Naysmith Scots and English: occupational name for a maker of knives or of nails, from OE *cnīf* knife or *nægel* nail + *smið* SMITH.

Vars.: **Naismith, Na(e)smith, Nasmyth.**

Nazaire French: from the given name *Nazaire*, which was relatively common in the Middle Ages in France as a result of the popularity of a 5th-cent. saint so called, abbot of Lérins. The given name represents a vernacular form of L *Nazareus* or Gk *Nazarios*, a deriv. of *Nazareth* (Hebr. *Natserat*, perhaps from a root meaning 'to guard, protect'), applied to early Christians as followers of Jesus of Nazareth and accepted by them as an honourable personal name.

Cogns.: It.: **Naz(z)ari, Nazzaro.** Pol.: **Nazarski.**

Patrs.: Russ.: **Nazarov, Nazaryev(ykh).** Armenian: **Nazarian.**

Patrs. (from dims.): Ger.: **Zarges, Zerges, Zerr(i)es.** Russ.: **Nazartsev.**

Neal English: var. of NEIL. This is the usual spelling of the surname in S and central England, derived from ME forms of the given name such as *Neel*.

Vars.: **Neale, Neall.**

Patr.: NELSON.

Neame English: 1. var. of ME *eame* uncle (see EAME), arising from misdivision of the common term of address *mine eame* 'my uncle'.

2. nickname for a very short man, from OF *nain* dwarf (L *nānus*). In ME, Fr. nasalized vowels with *n* or *m* were regularly confused.

Cogns. (of 2): Fr.: **Nain, Lenain.**

Dims. (of 2): Fr.: **Nanet, Naneix, Naneau, Nanin, Nanot.**

Pej. (of 2): Fr.: **Nanard.**

Neape English: metonymic occupational name for a grower or seller of turnips and other root vegetables (perhaps also a nickname), from ME *neep* turnip (OE *nǣp*, from L *nāpus*; cf. NABAIS).

Var.: **Neep.**

Cogns.: Fr.: **Nabier, Navier** (occupational).

Collective: Fr.: **Navière.**

Neary Irish: Anglicized form of Gael. **Ó Náraigh** 'descendant of *Nárach*', a byname meaning 'Modest'.

Neat English: metonymic occupational name for a herdsman in charge of cattle or nickname for someone thought to resemble an ox or a cow, from ME *neat* ox, cow (OE *nēat*). The mod. Eng. adj. *neat* (via Fr. from L *nitidus* clean, shining) does not occur before the 16th cent., after the main period of surname formation.

Var.: **Neate**.

Nedergård Danish: habitation name from a placename composed of the elements *neder* lower + *gård* enclosure; cf. OVERGÅRD.

Vars.: **Nedergaard**; **Neegård**, **Neegaard**.

Nee Irish: Anglicized form of Gael. **Ó Niadh** 'descendant of *Nia(dh)*', a byname meaning 'Warrior'.

Vars.: **O'Nee**, **O'Nea**, **O'Ney**, **(O')Knee**. See also NEVILLE.

Need English: probably a nickname for an impoverished person, from ME *nede* poverty, hardship (OE *nēd*).

Needham English: habitation name from places in Derbys., Norfolk, and Suffolk, so called from OE *nēd* need, hardship + *hām* homestead, i.e. a place that provided a poor living.

Var.: **Nedham**.

This is the family name of the Earls of Kilmorey, descendants of Thomas Nedeham *of Needham, Derbys., who was living in 1330. The family included Robert* Needham *of Shrops., who commanded forces in Ireland in the 16th cent.*

Negus 1. English: of uncertain origin. It is conceivably a topographic name for someone who lived in a house that was near but not in a main settlement, from OE *nēah* near + *hūs* house. Other writers claim a Corn. origin for it, but this does not seem plausible.

2. Rumanian: occupational name for a merchant (LL *negōtiātor*, from *negōtiāri* to trade, deal, a deriv. of *negōtium* business, affair).

Var. (of 2): **Negustor**.

Neighbour English: from ME *nechebure* (a cpd of OE *nēah* near + *gebūr* dweller; cf. BAUER). This may have been used as a nickname for someone who was a 'good neighbour', or more probably it derives from the common use of the word as a term of address.

Var.: **Naybour**.

Cogns.: Ger.: **Nachbau(e)r**; **Nachbar** (this is the mod. Ger. form of the vocab. word, and also an Ashkenazic surname, the reasons for its adoption being unknown). Low Ger.: **Nachbur**, **Nabu(h)r**, **Naber**.

Neil Irish, Scots, and English: from a given name of Ir. origin, Gael. *Niall* (gen. *Néill*), thought to mean 'Champion'. This was adopted by Norsemen in the form *Njáll*, and was brought to England both directly from Ireland by Scandinavian settlers and indirectly by the Normans. Among the latter it had taken the form *Ni(h)el*, which was altered by folk etymology to the L form *Nigellus* (see NIGEL).

Vars.: **Neill** (chiefly N Irish; also Scots); **Neild**; NEAL; **Neel(e)**, **Neeld**; NELL; **Niall**, **Niell**, **Niel(d)**, **Nihell**, **Nihill**.

Patrs.: Eng.: **Neels**, **Niles**; **Neilson** (Sc.); **Ni(e)lson**. Sc., Ir.: **McNeil(l)**, **McNeille**, **McNeal(l)**, **McNeale**, **McNeel**, **McNiel**; **McGreal** (Ulster). Manx: **Kneale**. Dan., Norw.: **N(i)elsen**. Swed.: **Ni(e)lsson**.

'Descendant of N.': Ir.: **O'Neil(l)**, **O'Neal** (Gael. **Ó Néill**).

'Descendant of N. (dim.)': Ir.: **(O')Neilane**, **(O')Nillane**, **(O')-Ne(y)lane**, **Ne(i)lan**, **Nilan**, **Nilon**, **Nealon**, **Neylon**, **Neylan(d)**, **N(e)iland**, **Neelan(d)**, **Neelands** (Gael. **Ó Nialláin**).

O'Neill *is the usual Irish form of this very common surname. The O'Neills are a branch of the ancient royal family of Tara. They are said to have the oldest traceable genealogy in Europe, starting from around 360, their surname being the first hereditary surname ever adopted in Ireland; it was assumed by Donell O'Neill, grandson of Niall of the Nine Hostages. The red hand of Ulster is taken from the arms of the O'Neill family. In post-medieval times they held the titles Earl of Tyrone and Earl of Clan Connell. Hugh O'Neill, 2nd Earl of Tyrone* (c.1540–1616) *was the leader of an Irish Catholic revolt against English rule (1593–1603). After the 'flight of the earls' in 1603, some of the family settled in Europe, where descendants included Jorge O'Neill (d. 1901), a peer of Portugal, who was also styled Comte de Tyrone, having been certified by Somerset Herald in 1896 to be a lineal descendant of the royal house of O'Neill.*

Nejedlý Czech: nickname for an unpleasant or unsavoury individual, from the adj. *nejedlý* unappetizing, inedible, from *ne* not + *jedlý* edible.

Nekludov Russian: patr. from the nickname *Neklud* 'Disorder', 'Disarray', referring to an untidy or clumsy person. Uncomplimentary nicknames such as this might also be given by fond parents to their children as familiar names, in the hope that they would discourage evil spirits from paying too much attention (cf. NEKRASOV).

Var.: **Nekhlyudov**.

Nekolný Czech: nickname for a stubborn person, from Czech *ne* not + the rare or obsolete adj. *kolný* unstable (mod. Czech *kolísavý*).

Vars.: **Nekola**, **Nekula**.

Nekrasov Russian: patr. from the nickname *Nekras* 'Ugly' (from the negative particle *ne-* + *kras* beauty, colour, brightness). This seems often to have been given as an apotropaic familiar name, expressing the parents' wish that a child should grow up handsome (cf. NEKLUDOV). The surname is also borne among E Ashkenazic Jews, among whom it presumably represents an adoption of the Russ. surname.

Cogn.: Ukr.: **Nekrashevich** (patr.).

Nell English: from the ME given name *Nel(le)*, a var. of NEIL.

Cogn.: Fr.: **Nel**.

Patr.: Eng.: NELSON.

The S African surname Nel *was first established there in 1690 by a family of Huguenot refugees from Rouen.*

Nelson English: patr. from NELL or NEAL, both of which go back to the same original Ir. personal name, *Niall* (see NEIL).

Nemchinov Russian: patr. from the name *Nemchin* German. In OSlav. this word was evidently used to denote any foreigner, being derived from *nemoi* dumb, referring to an inability to speak intelligibly. The Gk word *barbaros* had a similar meaning (cf. BARBARY).

Var.: **Nemtsev**.

Cogns. (not patrs.): Ukr.: **Nimchuk**. Pol.: **Niemiec**. Czech: **Němec**. Ger. (of Slav. origin): **Niemetz**, **Ni(e)mitz**, **Niem(b)sch**. Jewish (E Ashkenazic): **Niemi(e)c**. Hung.: **Német(h)**.

Cogns. (patrs.): Pol.: **Niemcewicz**. Ger. (of Slavic origin): **Nimzowitz**. Jewish (E Ashkenazic): **Niemocow**.

Dims.: Ukr.: **Nimchenko**. Pol.: **Niemczyk**. Czech: **Němeček**. Ger. (of Slav. origin): **Niemtschke**. Jewish: **Niemczyk**, **Niemtchik**, **Niemchenok**.

Nemes Hungarian: status name or nickname from the adj. *nemes* possessing noble rights and privileges.

Neruda Czech: nickname for a difficult or unsociable individual, from the adj. *neródný* inflexible, surly.

Var.: **Nerud**.

The real name of the Chilean poet Pablo Neruda *(1904–73) was Neftali Ricardo Reyes. He adopted his pen-name in honour of the Czech poet Jan Neruda (1834–91).*

Ness English and Scots: topographic name for someone who lived on a headland or promontory, Northern ME *ness* (ON *nes*), or habitation name from any of the places named with this term, for example *Ness* in Ches. and N Yorks. The name is now most common in Scotland. It coincides in form with the Gael. personal name *Ness*, but there is no evidence to suggest that the two are connected.

Nesterov Russian: patr. from the given name *Nester* (Gk *Nestōr*, the name of an old and wise hero in Homer's *Iliad*). The name is of uncertain etymology, perhaps from Gk *neisthai* to return (safely). It was borne by a 3rd-cent. Pamphilian bishop who became a popular saint in the Orthodox Church.

Var.: **Nesterin.**

Cogn.: Croatian: **Nestorović.**

Dims.: Croatian: **Nešković, Neš(ov)ić.**

Nethercott English: topographic name for someone who lived in a cottage at the lower end of a settlement (from ME *nether(e)* lower (OE *neoðera*) + *cot* cottage (see COATES)), or habitation name from *Nethercote* in Oxon. or *Nethercot* in Northants, both of which are named with these elements.

Netherton English: habitation name from a place named with the OE elements *neoðera* lower + *tūn* enclosure, settlement. This could be the one in Worcs. or the one in Northants, but is more likely to be from one of the eight places so called in Devon, where the surname is most common.

Netherwood English: habitation name from some place named as the 'lower wood', from OE *neoðera* lower + *wudu* WOOD.

Nettlefold English: habitation name from a minor place, probably the lost settlement of *Nettlefold* in Dorking, Surrey. This is named from OE *netele* nettle + *fal(o)d* enclosure (see FOLD) or *feld* pasture, open country (see FIELD).

Var.: **Nettlefield.**

Bearers of the name Nettlefold *can trace their ancestry back to John* de Netoelfeld, *who acquired premises at Dorking, Surrey, in 1310; his descendants can still be found in the area.*

Nettleton English (Yorks.): habitation name from a place so called, probably the one in Lincs., although there is also one in Wilts. The name is derived from OE *netele* nettle + *tūn* enclosure, settlement.

Neubauer 1. German: nickname for an agricultural worker who was new to an area, from MHG *niuwe* new + *gebūre* peasant (see BAUER).

2. Jewish (Ashkenazic): apparently an adoption of the Ger. surname (Jews were not usually agricultural workers at the time when surnames were acquired). Alternatively, the name may have been taken by someone who had just built a new house (from mod. Ger. *neu* new + *bauen* to build), or it may have been intended to express hope for the rebuilding of the Temple in Jerusalem (from mod. Ger. *Neubau* new building, reconstruction).

Vars.: Ger.: **Neuber(t), Neuper(t), Nauber.**

Cogns.: Low Ger.: **Niebu(h)r, Nieber, Nip(p)er.**

Neužil Czech: descriptve nickname for a miser, from Czech *ne* not + *užilý* generous.

Nevado Spanish: nickname for someone with snow-white hair, from Sp. *nevado*, past part. of *nevar* to snow (LL *nivāre*, from *nix* snow, gen. *nivis*; cf. NIEVES).

Nevalainen Finnish: ornamental name from Finn. *neva* marsh + the locative/patr. suffix *-lainen*.

Neve English (Norfolk): from ME *neve* nephew (OE *nefa*), presumably denoting the nephew of some great personage, or perhaps an orphan who was brought up in in the guardianship of his uncle (cf. EAME).

Vars.: **Neave, Neeve.**

Cogns.: Ger.: **Neff(e); Neef(f)** (SW Germany); **Näf** (Switzerland); **Ne(e)be** (Hesse). Low Ger.: **Neeve.** Flem.: **Neve, De Neef(f).**

Dims.: Low Ger.: **Neefken, Nefgen.**

Patrs.: Eng.: **Neaves, Neeves.** Low Ger.: **Neeven.** Flem.: **Neefs, Neven.**

A family by the name Neve *trace their descent from Robert* le Neve, *living in Tivetshall, Norfolk, in the 14th cent.*

Neveu French: from OF *neveu* nephew (L *nepos*, gen. *nepōtis*); for the application(s) as a surname, cf. NEVE.

Vars.: **Neveux, Nepveu; Leneveu.**

Cogns.: Prov.: **Nevoux, Nebout.** Cat.: **Nebot.**

Dim.: Prov.: **Nébodon.**

Neville 1. English and Irish (Norman): habitation name from *Neuville* in Calvados or *Néville* in Seine-Maritime, both so called from OF *neu(f)* new (L *novus*) + *ville* settlement (see VILLE).

2. Irish: a further Anglicization of Gael. *Ó Niadh* (see NEE) and of NEVIN.

Vars.: **Nevile, Nevill; Newell, Newill.**

Cogns. (of 1): Fr.: **Neu(f)ville, Naville** (also from other places in France).

The Anglo-Norman family of Neville *acquired the surname when Robert FitzMaldred, who came of age in 1195, married the heiress to Henry* de Neville, *from Neuville in Calvados; their son was known by his mother's surname. The patrilineal descent can be traced to Dolfin FitzUchtred, who held estates in Northumbria and Scotland in the 11th cent., and was probably related to the Anglo-Saxon earls of Northumbria. The Nevilles became extremely powerful during the Wars of the Roses, supporting each of the factions at various times; Richard Neville, Earl of Warwick (1428–71), was nicknamed 'the Kingmaker'. They have since held the dukedom of Bedford, marquessate of Montagu, and earldoms of Salisbury, Westmorland, Warwick, Kent, and Northumberland. In more recent years they have been Earls and Marquesses of Abergavenny.*

Nevin 1. Scots and Irish: Anglicized form of Gael. **Mac Naoimhín**, patr. from a personal name representing a dim. of *naomh* saint.

2. Irish: Anglicized form of Gael. **Mac Cnáimhín** and **Ó Cnáimhín** 'son' and 'descendant of *Cnámh*', a byname meaning 'Bone', apparently used to refer to a thin man.

Vars.: **Neven, Navin; Niven** (Sc.); NEVILLE. (Of 1 only): **McNevin, McNiven; Nevins, Nevi(n)son** (chiefly Sc.). (Of 2 only): **O'Knavin.**

New English: 1. nickname for a newcomer to an area, from ME *newe* new (OE *nēowe, nīwe*).

2. topographic name for someone who lived by a yew tree, from a misdivision of the ME phrase *atten ew* at the yew (OE *æt ðæm ēowe*).

Cogns. (of 1): Ger.: **Neu, Ney(e), Neyge, Nige.** Jewish (Ashkenazic): **Neu.** Swed.: **Ny(h)lén.**

Patrs. (from 1): Eng.: **Newson** (Norfolk); **Newing.**

Cpds (of 1; mostly ornamental): Swed.: **Nyberg** ('new hill'); **Nyblom** ('new flower'); **Nygren** ('new branch'); **Nyholm** ('new island'); **Nylander** ('dweller on new land'); **Nylund** ('new grove'); **Nyqvist** ('new twig'); **Nystedt** ('new homestead'); **Nyström** ('new river').

Newall English: topographic name for someone who lived at a 'new hall' (cf. NEW 1 and HALL), occupational name for someone who worked in one, or habitation name from a place named with these elements.

Newberry English: habitation name from any of the many places named with the OE elements *nēowe* NEW + *burh* fortress, town (see BERRY 1 and BURY).

Vars.: **Newbery, Newbury, Newb(o)rough, Newburgh.**

Thomas Newberry *emigrated from Devon to Dorchester, Mass., in 1634. Among his descendants were a number of very successful manufacturers and entrepreneurs, including the brothers Oliver (1789–1860) and Walter (1804–68) Newberry, whose prosperity was linked with the growth and development of Chicago.*

Newbold English: nickname for someone who lived in a newly constructed dwelling, from OE *nēowe* NEW + *bold* building (see BOLD 2). There are several places (in Ches., Derbys., Lancs., Leics., Northants, Notts., Warwicks., and Worcs.) named with these elements, and the surname may also be derived from any or all of them.

Vars.: **Newbould, Newbo(u)lt; Newbald** (places in E Yorks.).

Newby English: habitation name from any of the various places in N England named with the ME elements *newe* NEW + *by* farm, settlement (of ON origin); cf. NEWTON.

Newcombe English: nickname for a new arrival in a place, from ME *newe* NEW + *come* comer (OE *cuma*, *cumen*, past part. of *cuman* to come). The intrusive *-b-* is the result of the influence of placenames ending in *-combe* (see COOMBE).

Vars.: **Newcome(n).**

Cogns.: Ger.: **Neukomm, Neukamm, Naukamm.**

Newey English (W Midlands): topographic name for someone who lived at a 'new enclosure', from OE *nēowe* NEW + *haga* enclosure (see HAIG 2), or habitation name from some minor place named with these elements. *Newhay* and *Newhey* occur several times as placenames in Ches.

Var.: **Neway.**

Newham English: habitation name from any of the various places, for example in Northumb. and N Yorks., so called from OE *nēowe* NEW + *hām* homestead.

Vars.: **Newnham, Nuneham** (with the adj. retaining the weak dat. *-an* inflection, originally used after a preposition and article).

Newhouse English: topographic name for someone who lived in a 'new house' (cf. NEW and HOUSE), or habitation name from some minor place named with these elements. See also NEWSOME.

Cogns.: Ger.: **Neuhaus.** Jewish (Ashkenazic): **Neuhaus(er).**

Newland English: topographic name for someone who lived by a patch of land recently brought into cultivation, or recently added to the village, or habitation name from any of a number of settlements called *Newland* for this reason; cf. NEW and LAND 1.

Var.: **Newlands** (as a Scots name this derives from either of two places so called, a barony in Kincardine and a parish in Peebles).

Newman English: nickname for a newcomer to a place, from ME *newe* NEW + *man* man. This form has also been used as an Anglicization of many of the cogns. listed below and of non-cogn. equivalents such as CHODOSH, or more distantly related cogns. such as the group listed at NOVÁK.

Cogns.: Ger.: **Neumann, Naumann; Neander** (a learned calque using Gk *ne-* new + *andr-* man). Low Ger.: **Ni(uw)emann.** Flem., Du.: **Nieman, N(e)ijman, Neyman, Numan.** Dan., Norw., Swed.: **Nyman.** Jewish (Ashkenazic): **Neuman(n), Nauman(n).** Czech (from Ger.): **Najman**; cf. NOVÁK.

Newport English: habitation name from any of several towns so called, from OE *nēowe* NEW + *port* market town (see PORT 2). The name is common in Bristol, where it probably derives from Newport in Gwent, just across the Bristol Channel.

Newsome English (chiefly Yorks.): habitation name from a place named with the OE phrase (*æt ðǣm*) *nēowan hūsum* (at the) new houses. This and some of the vars. listed below are common as placenames in N England.

Vars.: **Newsom, Newsam, Newsum; Newson** (see also NEW); **Newsham** (chiefly Lancs.); **Newsholme** (places in Humberside and Lancs.).

Newstead 1. English: habitation name from any of the various places in Lincs., Notts. (*Newstead* Abbey), and elsewhere, so called from OE *nēowe* NEW + *stede* place (see STEAD 1).

2. Jewish (Ashkenazic): Anglicized form of **Neustadt**, which is equivalent in meaning to NEWTON.

Newton English: habitation name from any of the many places so called, from OE *nēowe* NEW + *tūn* enclosure, settlement. According to Ekwall, this is the commonest Eng. placename. For this reason, the surname has a highly fragmented origin.

Niblett English: of unknown origin, possibly a nickname from a double dim. of ME *nibbe*, dial. form of *neb* beak, referring to someone with a prominent or beaklike nose.

Nice English: nickname from ME, OF *nice* foolish, simple (L *nescius* ignorant). In the 14th cent. the Eng. word also acquired the sense 'wanton' and in the 15th cent. 'coy', 'shy', both of which meanings may be reflected in the surname. The sense 'fastidious', 'precise', 'minute' developed only in the 16th cent., probably too late to have given rise to any surnames, and the present-day sense of general approbation is not clearly attested until the late 19th cent.

Nicholas English and Welsh: from the given name (Gk *Nikolaos*, from *nikān* to conquer + *laos* people). Forms with *-ch-* are the result of hypercorrection (cf. ANTHONY). The name was popular among Christians throughout Europe in the Middle Ages, largely as a result of the fame of a 4th-cent. Lycian bishop, about whom a large number of legends grew up, and who was venerated in the Orthodox Church as well as the Catholic. E European forms of this name are spelled with initial *M-*: Czech *Mikuláš*, Pol. *Mikołaj*. Aphetic short forms (without the first syllable) were also common in most European languages; surnames derived from these are listed at COLL 1 and KLAUS. The normal ME vernacular form was *Nicol*, and this was also sometimes borne by women as well as the feminine forms *Nicole* and *Nicola*.

Vars.: **Nic(o)las** (Wales), **Nickless** (W Midlands); **Nichol(l), Nicoll, Nic(k)ol, Nickal, Nickel(l), Nickle.**

Cogns.: Fr.: **Nic(o)las, Nicolau, Niclaus(se).** Prov.: **Nicol, Nicou(d), Nicoux.** It.: **Nic(c)ola, Nic(c)oli, Nicolli** (Venetia); **Nicolao, Nicolai, Nic(c)olo** (S Italy); **Niccolai** (Tuscany); **Nicora** (Lombardy). Sp.: **Nicolás.** Cat., Port.: **Nicolau.** Rum.: **Nicola(i)e.** Ger.: **Ni(c)k(o)laus, Nicklas, Nücklaus.** Czech: **Mikuláš, Mikula, Mikulanda,** LANDA; **Mikoláš, Mikota.** Pol.: **Mikuła, Mikulski.** Hung.: **Miklós.**

Dims.: Eng.: **Nicklin** (W Midlands, esp. Staffs.). Fr.: **Nicol(l)et, Niclot; Nicollic** (Brittany). Prov.: **Nicolou, Nicloux.** It.: **Nic(c)olini, Nicoletti, Nicorini, Nicorelli, Nic(c)olucci, Nicolussi.** Ger.: **Nick, Nick(e)l, Nigg, Niggl(i); Läule, Laulin** (Switzerland); **Nick(l)isch, Nick(u)sch, Nitsch(k)e, Ni(e)tzsche, Nitzschke, Nitschold, Nietzschold, Niezold, Ni(e)tschmann, Nitzschmann** (of Slav. origin). Czech: **Mikulášek, Mikulík, Mikulka; Míka, Mika, Mikeš, Miksa, Mixa; Mikolášek, Míšek, Miška,** MIČKA. Pol.: **Mikołajczyk.**

Patrs.: Eng.: **Nichol(l)s, Nickol(l)s, Nicolls, Niccols, Nicholes, Nickoles, Nicholds, Nickolds, Nickalls, Nickel(l)s;**

Nic(h)olson, Nickleson. Scot.: **McNicholas; McNic(h)ol(l), McNickle** (Gael. **Mac Neacail**). It.: **De Nicola**. Rum.: **Nicolescu, Niculescu**. Low Ger.: **Nicolassen, Nicklassen, Nickelsen; Nicolaï** (Latinized); **Nicolaisen** (hypercorrected). Dan., Norw.: **Niclasen; Nicolaisen, Nicolajsen, Nikolajsen**. Swed.: **Niklasson**. Russ.: **Nikolaev(ski), Nicolin, Nikulin, Mikulin**. Ukr.: **Mikulich**. Pol.: **Mikołajewicz**. Croatian: **Nikolajević, Nik(ol)ić**. Bulg.: **Nikolaev, Nikolov**. Lithuanian: **Nicoleit, Nickeleit, Mickeleit; Mikolyunas**. Latvian: **Nicolovius**. Gk: **Nicolaou, Nicolaides**. Armenian: **Nicogossian**. Georgian: **Nikolaishvili, Nikoleish(i)vili; Nikolodze**.

Patrs. (from dims.): Eng.: **Nicholetts; Nix** (Notts.), **Nick(e)s**; NIXON; **Nickinson, Nickisson; Nickerson** (Norfolk). Ger.: **Nicks, Nix**. Ger. (of Slav. origin): **Nitsch(k)er**. Russ.: **Nikolyukin, Nikashin**. Croatian: **Nik(š)ić, Nikčević**.

'Servant of N. (dim.)': Eng.: **Nickman**.

Habitation names: Czech: **Mikšovský, Miškovský**. Jewish (E Ashkenazic): **Nikolajewski, Nikolajewsky, Nikolayevski** (either adoptions of non-Jewish surnames, or else from Yid. *Nikelayevsker soldat*, a nickname given to Jews who, during the reign of Tsar Nicholas I, had been required to serve for 25 years in the Russ. army; cf. COHEN, KAPLAN).

Of the most common forms of this name in the British Isles, Nicholas *is found mainly in Wales and the W Country;* Nichol *is characteristic of Northumb.,* Nicholl *of N Ireland, and* Nicol *and* Nicoll *of Scotland.* Nicholson *is esp. common in Northumb. and N England, but is also characteristically Scottish;* Nicholls *is widespread throughout S England and Wales;* Nichols *is even more widespread but slightly less common.*

Nieblich German: from a medieval given name, representing the Gmc clan name *Nibelung* 'son, descendant of Mist (or Fog)' (cf. mod. Ger. *Nebel* mist, fog). In Gmc mythology the Nibelungs were the doomed possessors of an immense hoard of treasure.

Vars.: **Niebli(n)g**.

Cogns.: Low Ger.: **Nebeling, Näbeling, Neveling**.

Nieder German and Jewish (Ashkenazic): topographic name for someone who lived at the lower end of a settlement, from Ger. *nieder* lower (MHG *nider*, OHG *nidar*). In some cases it may have referred to someone who lived on the lower floor of a house of two or more storeys.

Vars.: Ger.: **Niederer** (comp.); **Niederst** (sup.); **Niedermann**. Jewish: **Niederman**.

Cogns.: Low Ger.: **Ternedden** (N Rhineland), **Tornedden** (Westphalia), with fused preposition and article; **Zurnedden** (the Low Ger. prefix being altered to a High Ger. form); **Neddermann, Neerman, Niermann**. Flem., Du.: **(Van) Beneden**.

Niedzielski Polish: nickname from Pol. *niedziela* Sunday, denoting someone baptized or born on a Sunday, or acquired for some anecdotal reason.

Nieminen Finnish: ornamental name from Finn. *niemi* peninsula, headland + the gen. suffix *-nen*. It may in some cases have been chosen as a topographic name, but as this is the second commonest Finnish surname, many adoptions were probably arbitrary.

Vars.: **Niemi(lä)**.

Nierenberg Jewish (Ashkenazic): habitation name from the city of Nuremberg in N Bavaria, Yid. *Nirnberg*, Ger. *Nürnberg*.

Vars.: **Nir(e)nberg; Nur(e)nberg, Nürnberg**.

Nieswand Low German: apparently a habitation name from some minor place, now altered out of all recognition by folk etymological association with *Nies*, a Low Ger. aphetic form of the given name DENNIS + MLG *wand* wall.

Vars.: **Nieswandt, Niesewand(t)**.

Nieto Spanish: nickname for someone descended from a prominent elder in a community, or one whose memory was respected, from Sp. *nieto* grandson (LL *neptus*, for class. L *nepos*, gen. *nep(ō)tis*, grandson, nephew; cf. NEVEU).

Cogn.: Port.: **Neto**.

Nieves Spanish: religious byname, from the title *María de las Nieves* 'Mary of the Snows', given particularly to children born on 5 August, on which date the Virgin allegedly once caused it to snow in Rome. It is possible that the surname also derives from a nickname with the same meaning as NEVADO.

Cogn.: Port.: **Neves**.

Niewiadomski Polish: nickname from Pol. *niewiadomy* unknown, referring to a stranger of unknown origin (i.e. a newcomer to a district), or to a foundling, whose parentage was unknown.

Niewiarowski Polish: nickname for an atheist or unbeliever, from Pol. *nie* not, no + *wiara* faith, religion, with the addition of the surname suffix *-ski* (see BARANOWSKI).

Nigel Scots and English: from the Latinized personal name *Nigellus*, which was popular among the Normans. It is in actual fact a form of NEIL, but was taken by folk etymology to be a dim. of L *niger* black, dark.

Nightingale English: nickname for someone with a good voice, from ME *nichti(n)gale* (OE *nihtegal*, from *niht* night + *galan* to sing; cogn. with Ger. *Nachtigall*).

Var.: **Nightingall**.

Cogns.: Ger.: **Nachtigall**. Flem.: **Nachtergael, Achtergael**. Du.: **Nagtegaal**. Jewish (Ashkenazic): **Nachtigal(l)** (ornamental name, from the mod. Ger. vocab. word).

Florence Nightingale *(1820–1910), the pioneering English nurse who transformed the nursing profession, came from a Derbys. family originally named* Shore. *Her father changed his name to Nightingale on inheriting the fortune of an uncle of that name.*

Nikiforov Russian: patr. from the given name *Nikifor* (Gk *Nikēphoros*, from *nikē* victory + *phorein* to carry, bear). Although of pagan origin, the name was popular among early Christians in allusion to Christ's victory over Death, and was borne in particular by a (possibly fictional) 3rd-cent. martyr of Antioch, as well as various other early saints who helped to make the name a popular one in E Europe.

Nikitin Russian and Ukrainian: patr. from the given name *Nikita* (Gk *Nikētas*, a deriv. of *nikān* to conquer). The name was popular among early Christians for the same reasons as *Nikēphoros* (see NIKIFOROV) and was borne by several saints, including a 4th-cent. converted Ostrogoth and a 5th-cent. missionary to Dacia. Both are more honoured in the Orthodox Church than the Roman Catholic, and the given name is accordingly largely confined to E Europe.

Vars.: Russ.: **Nikitaev, Mikitin**. Ukr.: **Mykyta** (not patr.).

Dims.: Russ.: **Nikitnikov, Nikishov, Mikeshin** (patrs.). Ukr.: **Nikitenko, Nikityuk, Mikitenko, Mikitka**.

Nikodém Czech: from the given name *Nikodém* (Gk *Nikodēmos*, from *nikē* victory + *dēmos* people). The name was adopted in E Europe in honour of the Nicodemus mentioned in the New Testament, a member of the Sanhedrin who helped to bury Christ after he was taken down from the cross.

Vars.: **Nykodým; Kodým, Kodeš, Kodat** (aphetic).

Nimmo Scots: of unknown origin. The earliest forms that belong here are probably *Newmoch* (1459), *Nemoch*

(1490), and *Nemok* (1587). Forms with *-i-* are not found before the 17th cent.

Vars.: **Nemo, Nemmock.**

Niño Spanish: nickname from Sp. *niño* child, boy (of uncertain origin; apparent cogns. are found in various dialects of Catalonia, Provence, and S Italy). This was often given to a first-born son as a familiar name, and in some cases persisted to adulthood.

Cogns.: Jewish (Sefardic): **Nin(i)o, Ninyo** (reason(s) for adoption unknown).

Nisbit Scots and N English: habitation name from any of several places in the Border region called *Nisbit* or *Nesbit(t)*, from Northern ME *nese* nose (from ON) + *bit* mouthful, piece of ground (OE *bita*) or *bit* bend (OE *byht*). The placenames refer either to a piece of raised land sticking up like a nose, or to a bend in a river shaped like a nose.

Vars.: **Nisbet; Nesbit(t)** (esp. N Ireland); **Naisbit(t), Naisbet.**

Nissen 1. Jewish (Ashkenazic): from the Yid. male given name *Nisn*, (from Hebr. *nisan*, the name of a Jewish month), presumably at first given to boys born in that month; cf. ODER 2.

2. German and Danish: patr. from the Scandinavian given name *Niss*, a greatly contracted form of NICHOLAS. This surname is still largely confined to its original home in Schleswig.

Vars. (of 1, not exclusively Ashkenazic): **Nis(s)an; Nissani, Nissany** (with the Hebr. ending *-i*).

Dims. (of 1): **Nis(s)el** (also perhaps from Yid. *nisl*, a dim. of *nus* nut, and so one of the many ornamental surnames derived from plant names).

Patrs. (from 1): **Nissenso(h)n, Nisenzon; Nis(s)anov.**

Patrs. (from 1) (dims.): **Niselovitz, Niselevich; Nusilevitz** (hypercorrected).

Nixon N English, Scots, and N Irish: patr. from the ME given name *Nik(ke)*, a short form of NICHOLAS.

Vars.: **Nickson** (Lancs.), **Nixson.**

Noade English: topographic name resulting from misdivision of ME *atten oade* at the heap (OE *æt ðǣm āde*, from *ād* heap, (funeral) pyre; for the change of *-ā-* to *-ō-*, cf. ROPER). The meaning of OE *ād* is complex: it may refer to an ancient burial mound, a grassed-over refuse heap, a natural mound, or a high spot used as the site for a beacon.

Vars.: **Noad, No(a)des.**

Noake English (chiefly W Midlands): topographic name for someone who lived by an oak tree, from a misdivision of ME *atten oke* at the oak. The form *atten* (from OE *æt ðǣm*) was used more or less indiscriminately in ME as distinctions of grammatical gender ceased to be felt. Strictly, it was used only with masc. nouns, the fem. equivalent being *atter* (OE *æt ðǣre*). Other names resulting from similar misdivision include NALDER and NASH.

Vars.: **Noak, Noke, Nock, Noak(e)s, Nokes.**

Nobb English (Norfolk): from a medieval given name, a pet form of ROBERT.

Patrs.: **Nobbs** (Norfolk), **Nop(p)s, Nobes.**

Patr. (from a dim.): **Nopkins.**

Nobelius Swedish: Latinized form of a habitation name from a place called *Nöbbelöv*. This is one of the rare genuine habitation names in Swedish, as distinct from ornamental coinages, which sometimes look like topographic names.

Var.: **Nobel.**

Noble 1. English, Scots, and French: nickname from ME, OF *noble* high-born, distinguished, illustrious (L *nobilis*), referring to someone of lofty birth or character, or ironically to someone of exceedingly humble birth and station.

2. Jewish (Ashkenazic): in at least one family, an Anglicized form of **Knöbel**, a surname derived from an archaic Ger. word for a servant. This was a famous rabbinical family which came from Wiener Neustadt to Sanok in Galicia in the 17th cent.; several members subsequently emigrated to the U.S.

3. Jewish (Ashkenazic): probably also an Anglicized form of the Ashkenazic surname *Knobel* 'garlic' (see KNOBLOCH).

Var. (of 1): Fr.: **Lenoble.**

Cogns. (of 1): It.: **Nobile, Nobili.** Port.: **Nobre.** Flem., Du.: **De Nobele.**

Patrs. (from 1): Eng.: **Nobles.** Flem., Du.: **Nobels.**

Noblett English (Lancs.): 1. dim. of NOBLE 1.

2. double dim. of NOBB.

Var.: **Noblet.**

Cogns. (of 1): Fr.: **Noblet, Noblot.** It.: **Noblini.**

Noel English and French: nickname for someone who had some particular connection with the Christmas season, such as owing the particular feudal duty of providing a yule-log to the lord of the manor, or having given a memorable performance as the Lord of Misrule; see also YULE. The name is from ME, OF *no(u)el* Christmas (L *natālis (dies)* birthday, from *nasci* to be born). It was also used as a given name for someone born during the Christmas period; cf. NASCIMENTO.

Vars.: Eng.: **Nowell, Nowill.** Fr.: **Nouau, Nou(h)aud.**

Cogns.: Prov.: **Nadal, Nadau(d).** Cat.: **Nadal.** It.: **Natali, Natale, Nadali.**

Dims.: Fr.: **Noellet.** Prov.: **Nadin, Nadot.**

Edward Noel *(?1640-?88) was created Earl of Gainsborough by Charles II in 1682. This was a reward for the family's loyal support during the Civil War. He was descended from Robert, son of Noel, who bought lands in Warwicks. in the 12th cent. The earldom became extinct on the death of the 6th Earl in 1798. His estates passed to the Edwardes family, who adopted the surname Noel by royal licence. The earldom was re-created in 1841 for Charles Noel (d. 1866).*

Nogin Russian: patr. from the nickname *Noga* 'Foot', 'Leg', acquired presumably on account of some lameness or deformity.

Cogns.: Czech: **Noha, Noháč, Nohatý.**

Noir French: nickname for someone with notably dark hair or complexion, from OF *noir* black (L *niger*).

Var.: **Lenoir.**

Cogns.: Prov.: **Nier, Nègre, Lenègre.** It.: **Ne(g)ro, Ne(g)ri, Lo Nero; (Lo) Nigro, Nigri** (S Italy); **Nieddu** (Sardinia). Rum.: **Negrea.** Jewish: **Ne(g)ri, Negro, Negru; Negrin** (Sefardic); **Negrea(nu)** (among Rumanian Jews).

Dims.: Fr.: **Noiret, Noyret, Noirez, Néret, Noiré, Néré, Noireau(x), Noirot, Néreau, Nérot, Noiron, Néron, Noirtin, Nerisson.** Prov.: **Negrel, Negron; Neyret, Neyron, Neyroud.** It.: **Negrelli, Negrello, Ne(g)rini, Negrin(o), Negrotto, Neretti, Nerucci, Nerozzi, Nigrelli, Nigr(i)ello.**

Augs.: Fr.: **Nérat.** Prov.: **Neyrat.** It.: **Ne(g)roni, Ne(g)rone.**

Pejs.: Fr.: **Noiraud, Néraud, Noireau(l)t.** Prov.: **Neyraud.** It.: **Negrato.**

Patrs.: It.: **De Negri(s), Nigris.** Rum.: **Negresco.**

Nolan Irish: Anglicized form of Gael. **Ó Nualláin** 'descendant of *Nuallán*', a personal name representing a dim. of *nuall* famous, noble.

Vars.: **O'No(u)lane, (O')Noland, (O')Nowlan.**

Noon 1. English: nickname for a bright and cheerful person, from ME *none* noon (the time of brightest sunshine). The word is derived from L *nōna* (*hora*), originally denoting the ninth hour, i.e. about three o'clock. The change in meaning of the vocab. word, from mid-afternoon to midday, probably occurred as a result of monastic meal times being brought forward.

2. Irish: var. of NOONE.

Noonan Irish: Anglicized form of Gael. **Ó hIonmhaineáin** 'descendant of *Ionmhaineán*', a personal name derived from *Ionmhain* beloved.

Vars.: **Nunan, Neenan.**

Noone Irish: Anglicized form of Gael. *Ó Nuadháin* 'descendant of *Nuadhán*', a personal name derived from *Nuadha*, the name of several ancient Celt. gods.

Vars.: **O'Now(a)n, O'Nown,** NOON.

Norbury English: habitation name from any of various places, for example in Ches., Derbys., Shrops., Staffs., and Surrey, so called from OE *norð* NORTH + *burh* fortress, town (see BURY).

Norcross English (Lancs.): habitation name from a minor place near Blackpool, so called from OE *norð* NORTH + *cros* CROSS.

Norfolk English: regional name from the county of *Norfolk* in E Anglia, so called from an OE tribal name composed of the elements *norð* NORTH + *folc* people (in contrast to the *sūðfolc* of Suffolk).

Norgård Danish: habitation name from a placename composed of the elements *nord* NORTH + *gård* enclosure.

Vars.: **Norgaard; Norregård, Norregaard.**

Norgrove English (W Country): habitation name from an unidentified place, presumably named with the OE elements *norð* NORTH + *grāf* GROVE.

Noriega Spanish: habitation name for a place in the province of Oviedo, whose name is perhaps akin to Sp. *noria* water-wheel (from Arabic *nā'ûra*, a deriv. of *nā'ar* to creak).

Norman 1. English: name applied either to a Scandinavian settler or to someone from Normandy in N France. The Scandinavian adventurers of the Dark Ages called themselves *norðmenn* (nom. sing. *norðmaðr*) 'men from the North'. When they settled in England and N France the term was adopted by the local population as *Norþmann* and *Norman(t)* respectively. The pre-Conquest Scandinavian settlers in England were fairly readily absorbed, and *Nor(þ)mann* came to be used as a byname and later as a personal name, even among the Saxon inhabitants. It would have been the more easily assimilated because *norð* and *mann* were both Gmc name-forming elements in their own right, so in fact the compound name could have been formed without any specific reference to Scandinavians. The word gained a new use when England was settled by invaders from Normandy, of Scandinavian origin but by now largely integrated with the native population and speaking a Romance language, retaining only their original Gmc name.

2. Jewish (Ashkenazic): of uncertain origin. In at least one case it is an Anglicized form of **Novominsky**, the name of a family from Uman in the Ukraine. On coming to the United States around 1900, a member of this family changed his name to *Norman*, after which some relatives in Russia adopted this name instead of *Novominsky*.

3. Swedish: cogn. of NORTH.

Var. (of 1): **Normand.**

Cogns. (of 1): Fr.: **Normant, Normand, Lenormand.**

Noronha Portuguese: of uncertain origin. In the Middle Ages the name appears as *Loronha*; it is probably related to the Galician placename *Loroño*.

Norrington English: 1. topographic name for someone living to the north of a main settlement, OE *norð in tūne*. According to Reaney, possible sources include *Norrington* near Alvediston, Wilts., *Norrington* End Farm in Redbourn, Herts., and *Northingtown* Farm in Grimley, Worcs., but there were no doubt others, now lost. The form of the name has been influenced by the common placename ending *-ington*.

2. habitation name from the city of *Northampton*, originally named with the elements NORTH + HAMPTON.

Var.: **Nor(th)ington,** NORTON.

There appear to be three distinct groups of Norringtons, *centred in Wilts, Essex, and Kent, from the 15th cent. onwards. The genealogy of one group has been traced to a certain John Norrington, living at Westwell in Kent in 1588–95. A certain innkeeper of Salisbury was married in 1595 as William* Northampton, *received a licence in 1614 as William* Norrington, *and died in 1616 as William* Norington. *At Charminster, Dorset, a certain John* Northampton alias Norenton *was married in 1611 and again in 1614; his successive wives were buried in 1613 and 1619 under the names of* Norinton *and* Norrington.

Norris English and Scots: 1. regional name for someone who had migrated from the North (i.e. further north in England, or from Scotland or Scandinavia), from OF *nor(r)eis* northerner.

2. topographic name for someone who lived in a house on the north side of a settlement or estate, from OE *norð* north + *hūs* house.

3. occupational name for a wet nurse or foster mother, from OF *nurice*, *norrice* (L *nutrix*, gen. *nutricis*).

Vars.: **Noriss, Norrish; Nor(r)ie** (Scots). (Of 1 only): **Norreys.** (Of 3 only): **Nurrish, N(o)urse.**

Some bearers of the surname Norris *trace their ancestry to Richard* de Norrys, *who was cook to Eleanor, wife of Henry III, in the 13th cent. Another ancestor was Henry Norris, who was executed in 1536, convicted of being one of Ann Boleyn's lovers.*

North 1. English: topographic name, from OE *norð* north, for someone who lived in the northern part of a village or to the north of a main settlement (cf. NORRINGTON 1), or regional name for someone who had migrated from the north (cf. NORRIS 1).

2. Irish: regional name for someone from Ulster, the northern area of Ireland, in part as an Anglicized form of Gael. *Mac an Ultaigh* (see MCNULTY).

Vars.: Eng.: **Northe(r)n.**

Cogns.: Ger.: **Nor(d)mann.** Flem., Du.: **Noor(man), Van Noord(en), Van den Noort.** Dan., Norw.: **Nøhr, Nørring.** Swed.: **Nord(h), Nor(d)én, Nor(d)in, Nor(d)ell, Norlin, Nor(d)ling; Norelius;** NORMAN, **Norrman.** Jewish (Ashkenazic): **Nord(man).**

Cpds (mostly arbitrary combinations rather than genuine habitation names): Swed.: **Nor(d)berg** ('north hill'); **Norrby** ('north settlement'); **Nordahl** ('north valley'); **Nor(d)gren** ('north branch'); **Nordlund** ('north grove'); **Nordlöf** ('north leaf'); **Nordmark** ('north land'); **Nordqvist** ('north twig'); **Nor(d)ström** ('north river'); **Nordwall, Nordvall** ('north bank').

Northall English (W Midlands): habitation name from an unidentified place named with the OE elements *norð*

North + *h(e)all* Hall or *h(e)alh* nook, recess (see Hale 1).

Northcott English: habitation name from any of various minor places so called from OE *norð* North + *cot* cottage, shelter (see Coates).

Vars.: **Norcott, Norcutt, Norkutt, Norkett; Northcote; Narracott.**

An old-established Devon family of this name trace their descent from Galfridus Miles, who was living in the county, in the manor of Northcote, in 1103. In 1885 they were granted the earldom of Iddesleigh.

Northey English (Devon): habitation name, probably from *Northay* in Hawkchurch, Devon, named with the OE elements *norð* North + *(ge)hǣg* enclosure (see Hay 1).

Northfield English: habitation name from any of various places, for example in S Birmingham, so called from OE *norð* North + *feld* open country, pasture (see Field).

Northmore English (Devon and Cornwall): topographic name for someone who lived on the northern part of a moor (presumably of Bodmin Moor, Dartmoor, or Exmoor), from ME *north* North + *more* moor (see Moore 1).

Norton English: 1. habitation name from any of the many places so called, from OE *norð* North + *tūn* enclosure, settlement.

2. var. of Norrington.

3. var. of Naughton 1.

Norwood English: habitation name from any of the many places so called, from OE *norð* North + *wudu* Wood.

Var.: **Northwood.**

Nosek Czech: nickname for someone with a noticeable nose, from Czech *nos* nose + the dim. suffix *-ek*. Since the suffix is diminutive, the nose in question could have been either remarkably large or remarkably small.

Var.: **Nosák** ('big nose').

Notley English: habitation name from places, for example in Bucks. and Essex, so called from OE *hnutu* nut + *lēah* wood, clearing.

Notman 1. Scots: probably an occupational name for a dealer in nuts, from ME *not(e)*, *nut* (see Nutt) + *man* (OE *mann*), although Black expresses reservations about this derivation. Maybe it is a var. of Nott.

2. Jewish (Ashkenazic): probably a nickname for a poor man, from mod. Ger. *Not* need, want + *Mann* man.

Vars. (of 2): Jewish: **Nottman, Nothmann.**

Nott English: nickname for a bald man or one who kept his hair extremely close-cropped, from ME *not* bald (OE *hnot*). The word was also used of pollarded cattle and trees, and the surname may perhaps in part be a metonymic occupational name for a herdsman or a topographic name for someone who lived by a stunted tree. See also Knott.

Patrs.: **Notting, Notts.**

Nottage English: nickname from ME *notehache* nuthatch (apparently from OE *hnutu* nut + *haccian* to break, crack).

Var.: **Nottidge.**

Notton English (Wilts.): habitation name from places in Wilts. and Dorset, so called from OE *nēat* cattle (see Neat) + *tūn* enclosure, settlement.

Novais Portuguese: habitation name from any of various minor places so called, from L *Novāles*, pl. of *novālis* clearing, land recently cleared and brought into cultivation (an adj. deriv. of *novus* new; cf. Nuevo).

Novák Czech: nickname from Czech *nový* new, generally referring to a newcomer to a place (cf. Newman). However, the name also denoted a shoemaker who made new shoes (as distinct from a cobbler who repaired old ones). This is the most common Czech surname, and the var. *Novotný* is the third most common. The Pol. cogn. *Nowak* is also extremely common.

Vars.: **Novotný, Nový.**

Cogns.: Pol.: **Nowak, Nowacki, Nowik, Nowicki.** Ger. (of Slav. origin): **Nowa(c)k, Naujock, Nauck(e).** Jewish (E Ashkenazic): **Novak, Nowak, Novik, Novic(k), Nowik, Noveck; Novicki, Novitzki.** Hung.: **Novák.**

Dims.: Czech: **Nováček.** Pol.: **Nowaczyk.** Ukr.: **Novichenko.**

Patrs.: Russ.: **Novikov.** Croatian: **Novaković, Nov(i)čić.** Jewish (E Ashkenazic): **Novikov, Novikoff, Novakovsky.**

Habitation names: Pol.: **Nowakowski, Nowiński.**

Noy 1. English: from ME *Noye*, vernacular form of the Hebr. male given name *Noach* Noah, which is said to mean 'Long-lived'. According to the Book of Genesis, Noah, having been forewarned by God, built an ark into which he took his family and representatives of every species of animal, and so was saved from the flood that God sent to destroy the world because of human wickedness. The given name was not common among non-Jews in the Middle Ages, but the biblical story was an extremely popular subject for miracle plays. In most cases, therefore, the surname probably derives from a nickname referring to someone who had played the part of Noah in a miracle play or pageant, rather than from a given name.

2. Jewish (Israeli): ornamental name from Hebr. *noy* decoration, adornment, in part adopted as a Hebraicized form of various Ashkenazic surnames containing the unrelated Ger. element *neu*, e.g. *Neumann* (see Newman).

Var. (of 1): **Noe.**

Cogns. (of 1): Ger.: **Noah, Noä, Noe.** Flem., Du.: **Noach.** Jewish: **Noa(c)h** (Israeli).

Patrs. (from 1): Eng.: **Noyes, Noyce, Noise, Noice.**

Noyer French: topographic name for someone who lived near a (wal)nut tree, OF *noyer* (LL *nucārius*, from *nux*, gen. *nucis*, nut).

Vars.: **Dunoyer, Desnoyers.**

Cogns.: Prov.: **No(u)guier, Noug(i)er, Nog(u)er, No(u)guès.** Cat.: **Noguer(a), Nogué(s).** Sp.: **Nogue(i)ra, Nogal(es).** Port.: **Nogueira.**

Nudd English: common Norfolk surname, of unknown origin. The suggestion that it is a var. of Hudd with the initial altered under the influence of pairs such as Hobb and Nobb is not very plausible. There are phonological difficulties in accepting it as a var. of Nutt.

Nuevo Spanish: nickname for a newcomer to an area, from Sp. *nuevo* new (L *novus*). The word was also occasionally used in the Middle Ages as a given name, particularly for a child born after the death of a sibling, and this may also be a source of the surname.

Var.: **Novo.**

Cogn.: Port.: **Novo.**

Dims.: Sp.: **Novillo.** Fr.: **Nouvel, Nouveau, Nouvet.** It.: **Nov(i)ello, Novel(li).**

Nugent English and Irish (Norman): habitation name from any of several places in N France, such as *Nogent*-sur-Oise, named with L *Novientum*, apparently an altered form of a Gaul. name meaning 'new settlement'.

The Anglo-Norman family of this name are descended from Fulke de Bellesme, lord of Nogent in Normandy, who was granted large estates around Winchester after the Conquest. His great-grandson was Hugh de Nugent *(d. 1213), who went to Ireland with Hugh de Lacy, and was granted lands in Bracklyn, Westmeath. The family formed themselves into a clan on the Irish model, of which the chief bore the hereditary title of* Uinsheadun, *from their original seat at Winchester. They have been Earls of Westmeath since 1621. The name is now a common one in Ireland, and has been adopted there by some who have no connection with the clan.*

Nunn English: nickname for a pious and demure man, or occupational name for someone who worked at a convent, from ME *nunn* nun (OE *nunne*, from L *nonna*, originally a respectful term of address for an elderly woman. The L word probably originated as a nursery term).

Patr.: **Nunns**.

Nuño Spanish: from a medieval given name, which is first attested in the L forms *Nunnius* and *Nonnius* and is of uncertain origin. There may be some connection with MUÑO.

Cogn.: Port.: **Nuno**.

Patrs.: Sp.: **Núñez**. Port.: **Nunes** (also borne by Sefardic Jews, in which case it is an adoption of the non-Jewish name).

Nuriev Russian: patr. from the Islamic given name *Nuri*, which means 'Light' in Arabic and was originally an epithet of Allah.

Vars.: **Nure(y)ev**.

Nurmi Finnish: ornamental name from Finn. *nurmi* lawn, pasture; one of the many Finn. surnames formed in the 19th cent. from vocab. words denoting natural features.

Var.: **Nurminen**.

Nutt English: from ME *not(e)*, *nut* nut (OE *hnutu*); either a metonymic occupational name for a gatherer and seller of nuts, or nickname for a man supposedly resembling a nut (e.g. in having a rounded head and dark complexion).

Cogn.: Ger.: **Nuss**.

Patr.: Eng.: **Nutting**.

Cpds (meaning 'nut tree'): Ger.: **Nussbaum**, **Nussba(u)mer**. Low Ger.: **Not(te)bohm**, **Näthbom**. Flem., Du.: **Noteboom**. Jewish (Ashkenazic): **Nus(s)(en)baum**, **Nus(s)boim**, **Nis(s)(en)baum**, **Nis(en)boim**, **Nissnbaum**, **Nis(se)lbaum** (all ornamental).

Nuttall English: habitation name from some place named with the OE elements *hnutu* nut (see NUTT) + *h(e)alh* nook, recess (see HALE 1). In some cases this may be *Nuthall* in Notts., but the surname is common mainly in Lancs., and a Lancs. origin is therefore more likely. *Nuttall* in Bury, Lancs., was earlier *Notehogh*, from OE *hnutu* + *hōh* hill-spur (see HOE).

Var.: **Nuthall**.

Nutter English: 1. occupational name for a keeper of oxen, from an agent deriv. of ME *nowt* beast, ox (from ON *naut*, a cogn. of OE *nēat*; cf. NEAT).

2. occupational name for a scribe or clerk, from ME *notere* (OE *nōtere*, from L *notārius*, an agent deriv. of *nota* mark, sign).

Var. (of 1): **Nothard** (see HEARD).

Cogns. (of 2): Fr.: **Not(t)ier**. It.: **Notaro**, **Notari**. Sp.: **Notario**.

Nye English: topographic name arising from a misdivision of ME *atten (e)ye* which means both 'at the river' and 'at the island', from OE *ēa* river and *ēg* island respectively. Both these words were actually fem. in OE, and so should have been preceded only by ME *atter* (see RYE), but distinctions of gender ceased to be carefully maintained in the ME period. Cf. NALDER, NASH, and NOAKE.

Vars.: **Nie**, **Ney**, **Nay**.

Nygård Danish: habitation name from a placename composed of the elements *ny* NEW + *gård* enclosure.

Vars.: **Nygaard**; **Nyegård**, **Nyegaard**.

Nyhan Irish: Anglicized form of Gael. **Ó Niatháin** 'descendant of *Niathán*', a diminutive of *Niath* 'Warrior' (a later spelling of *Nia(dh)*; cf. NEE).

O

Oade English: 1. from a ME given name *Ode*, in which personal names of several different origins have coalesced: principally OE *Od(d)a*, ON *Od(d)a* and Continental Gmc *Odo*, *Otto*. The first two are short forms from names with the first element OE *ord*, ON *odd* point of a weapon. The Continental Gmc names are from a short form of cpd names with the first element *od-* prosperity, riches (cogn. with OE *ēad-*; cf. EADE). The situation is further confused by the fact that all of these names were Latinized as *Odo*. *Odo* was the name of the half-brother of the Conqueror, archbishop of Bayeux, who accompanied the Norman expedition to England and was rewarded with 439 confiscated manors. The German name *Odo* or *Otto* was a hereditary name in the Saxon ruling house, as well as being borne by Otto von Wittelsbach, who founded the Bavarian ruling dynasty in the 11th cent., and the 12th-cent. Otto of Bamburg, apostle of Pomerania.

2. topographic name for someone who lived near a mound or heap; see NOADE.

Vars. (of 1): **Odd(e)**, **Ott**; **Otton**, **Otten**, **Oaten** (from the OF oblique case).

Cogns. (of 1): Fr.: **O(u)don**, **Otton**, **Othon**. It.: **Oddo**, **Od(d)i**; **Od(d)one**, **Od(d)oni**, **Oddono**, **Ottone**, **Ottoni**. Ger.: **Ott(e)**, **Otto**. Low Ger.: **O(h)de**. Fris.: **Ede**. Flem., Du.: **Otte**, **Otto**. Dan., Norw.: **Otto**.

Dims. (of 1): Eng.: **Oddie**, **Odd(e)y**, **Odlin(g)**. Fr.: **Od(el)in**, **Ody**, **Oudin(eau)**, **O(u)dinet**, **O(u)dinot**, **O(u)det**, **Oudot**. It.: **Odello**, **Odetti**, **Oddino**, **Od(d)(ic)ini**, **Odicino**, **Oddenino**, **Ottonello**, **Ottonelli**, **Otanelli**, **Otino**, **Ottin(i)**, **Ottoli**, **Ottolino**, **Ottolin(i)**. Ger.: **Ottel**, **Öttel**, **Öttle**. Low Ger.: **Otke**, **Ötke**, **Odeke**, **Ocke**, **Ödgen**, **Odemann**. Fris.: **Edema**.

Pejs. (of 1): It.: **Odazzi**, **Odazio**, **Odasso**, **Odasi**.

Patrs. (from 1): Eng.: **Oades**, **Oat(e)s**, **Otis**. Low Ger.: **Otten(s)**, **Oden(s)**, **Ottsen**, **O(u)tzen**. Fris.: EDEN, **Edens**, **Edsen**; **Odinga**. Flem., Du.: **Otten(s)**. Dan., Norw.: **Ottesen**, **Ottosen**, **Otzen**. Swed.: **Ottosson**.

Patrs. (from dims. of 1): Ger.: **Ottler**. Low Ger.: **Oetken**, **Oetjen**, **Ötker**, **Öcker**, **Ockens**.

Oak English: topographic name for someone who lived near an oak tree or in an oak wood, from ME *oke* oak (OE *āc*; for the Southern ME change of *-ā- to -ō-*, cf. ROPER), also used in the sing. in a collective sense. In some cases the surname may be a habitation name from minor places named with this word, such as *Oake* in Somerset. It is possible that it was sometimes also used as a nickname for someone 'as strong as oak'.

Vars.: **O(a)ke**, **Oak(e)s**, **Oaker**; **Attoc(k)**, **At(t)ack**; **Aikman** (Scots). See also NOAKE and ROCK 2.

Cogns.: Ger.: **Eich**, **Eich(l)er**, **Aich(l)er**, **Eichner**, **Eichmann**, **Aichmann**, **Eich(l)baum**. Low Ger.: **Eick(er)**, **Eyck**, **Eickmann**. Fris.: **E(y)kstra**. Flem., Du.: **Eike(le)nboom**, **Van Eyk**, **Van Eijk**, **Van der Eycke**, **Vereycke**, **Van Eeke(le)n**, **Eyckman**. Swed.: **Ek**, **Ek(e)man**. Jewish (Ashkenazic, all ornamental): **Eichen**; **Eich(en)baum**, **Eichenboim**, **Aichenbaum**; **Ajchenbaum** (Pol. spelling).

Dims.: Ger.: **Eichele**, **Aichele**. Jewish: **Eichel**, **Aihel(baum)**.

Cpds (ornamental): Swed.: **Ekberg(h)** ('oak hill'); **Ekblad(h)** ('oak leaf'); **Ekblom** ('oak flower'); **Ek(e)dahl** ('oak valley'); **Ek(e)gren**, **Ekengren** ('oak branch'); **Ekholm** ('oak island'); **Eklind** ('oak lime'); **Ek(e)löf**, **Ek(e)löv** ('oak leaf'); **Ek(e)lund(h)** ('oak grove'); **Ekroth** ('oak clearing'); **Ekstedt** ('oak homestead'); **Ekstrand** ('oak shore'); **Ekström** ('oak river'); **Ekwall**, **Ekvall** ('oak bank'). Jewish: **Eichelberg** ('oak hill'); **Eichenblat**, **Aichenblat(t)** ('oak leaf'); **Eichengruen** ('oak green'); **Eich(en)holz**, **Eichengolz**, **Aichenhol(t)z** ('oak wood'; *-golz* under Russ. influence, since Russ. has no /h/ and changes /h/ in borrowed words to /g/); **Eichenstein** ('oak stone'); **Eich(en)wald**, **Aichenwald** ('oak forest').

Aikman *is the name of an old-established Scots family, whose seat is at Aberbrethick, The Ross.*

Oakland English: topographic name for someone who lived on a patch of land marked by its oak tree or trees, from ME *oke* OAK + *land*.

Oakley English: habitation name from any of the numerous places in S and central England named with the OE elements *āc* OAK + *lēah* wood, clearing.

Vars.: **Oakeley**, **Okel(e)y**, OGLEY. See also EAGLE 2.

Oatley English: 1. habitation name from *Oteley* in Ellesmere, Shrops., named with the OE elements *āte* oats + *lēah* wood, clearing.

2. var. of OAKLEY.

Ober German: topographic name for someone who lived at the upper end of a village, from Ger. *ober-* upper (MHG *ober*, *obar* above, OHG *ubar*). In some cases, it may have denoted someone who lived on an upper floor of a building with two or more storeys. Cf. NIEDER.

Vars.: **Oberer** (comparative); **Oberst** (superlative); **Zobrist** (Switzerland); **Obermann** (U.S. **Oberman**).

Cogns.: Low Ger.: **Overmann**, **Avermann**. Flem., Du.: **Van Boven**. Jewish (Ashkenazic): **Oberman** (perhaps an occupational or status name taken by a rabbi; cf. HAUPTMANN).

Oberholz German: topographic name for someone who lived in a place known as the 'upper wood', or on the far side of a wood from the main settlement, from Ger. *ober-* upper or MHG *ober* above, beyond (see OBER) + *Holz* wood (see HOLT).

Var.: **Oberholtz**.

Cogn.: Low Ger.: **Oberholster**.

Oblomov Russian: patr. from the nickname *Oblom* (from *oblomat* to shatter, smash), presumably referring to a strong or clumsy person.

Obolensky Russian: habitation name adopted by a princely family from their estates at *Obolensk*.

Ocaña Spanish: habitation name from places in the provinces of Almería and Toledo. The placename is probably of pre-Roman origin, and may be akin to the North(-Eastern) Italian placenames *Oc(c)a* and *Occagno*, which have been claimed to be of Ligurian derivation.

Ochila Rumanian: nickname for a one-eyed man or for someone with some other defect of the eyes, such as squinting. The name is a deriv. of the word *ochi* eye (L *oc(u)lus*), and is applied also to a one-eyed monster in Rumanian folk-tales.

Cogn.: It.: **Occhi**.

Dims.: Fr.: **Oeuillet**, **Leuillet**, **Leuillot**. It.: **Ochiello**, **Occhillo**, **Occhini**, **Occhino**, **Ochiuzzi**; **Occhiuto**, **Occhiuti** (Calabria).

Aug.: It.: **Occhioni**.

Ochoa Spanish form of Basque **Otxoa**: from a personal name, probably originally a byname from Basque *otso* wolf + the def. art. *-a*.

Ockenden English: habitation name from *Ockendon* in Essex, which appears in Domesday Book as *Wochenduna*, apparently from the gen. case of an OE personal name *Wocca* + OE *dūn* hill (see DOWN 1).

Ocker German: topographic name for someone living on the banks of the river *Ocker* in the Harz mountains, which perhaps derives its name from a Celt. word for the salmon, cogn. with Corn. *ehoc*.

Var.: **Ockermann**.

Odam English: nickname for someone who had done well for himself by marrying the daughter of a prominent figure in the local community, from ME *odam* son-in-law (OE *āðum*).

Vars.: **Odham** (altered by folk etymology as if derived from a placename in *-ham*); **Odom**.

Patrs.: **Od(h)ams**.

Odell English: habitation name from a place in Beds., also called *Woodhill*, from OE *wād* woad (a plant collected for the blue dye that could be obtained from its leaves) + *hyll* HILL.

Vars.: **O'Dell** (altered by folk etymology as if of Ir. origin); WADDELL.

Oder 1. German: topographic name for someone living on the banks of the central European river of this name. It rises in Poland, and its lower course forms the present-day border between Poland and E Germany. Its name is ancient, and is probably from a pre-Slav. element perhaps cogn. with Gk *hydōr* water, Gael. *odhar* dun, sallow, mod. Eng. *otter*.

2. Jewish (Ashkenazic): possibly as in 1, or from a W or NE Yid. pronunciation of Yid. *adar*, the name of a month of the Jewish calendar. This is considered a happy time of year mainly because the festival of Purim is celebrated during this month and because Jewish tradition has it that Moses was born in this month.

Vars. (of 2): **Adar(i)**, **Adary** (with the Hebr. suffix *-i*, from the name of the month); **Oderberg** (presumably an ornamental elaboration).

Offen 1. German: nickname for someone with a straightforward and open nature, from Ger. *offen* open (OHG *offan*).

2. German: metonymic occupational name for a baker, or for someone who had charge of the communal village oven and was empowered to exact payment in kind for its use, from Ger. *Ofen* oven (MHG *oven*, OHG *ovan*).

3. German: habitation name from Buda, part of Budapest in Hungary, which was known in MHG as *Ofen*.

4. Jewish (Ashkenazic): of unclear origin. Any one of the foregoing explanations is possible, but none is certain. In the case of 1, the relevant vocab. words are Ger. *offen* and Yid. *ofn*; in the case of 2, Ger. *Ofen*; and in the case of 3, mod. Ger. *Ofen*.

Vars.: **Ofen**. (Of 2 only): **Of(f)ener**. (Of 4): **Offner**.

Offer 1. English (Norman): occupational name for a goldsmith, from ANF *orfrer*, OF *orfevre* (L *aurifaber*, from *aurum* gold + *faber* maker; cf. FÈVRE).

2. Jewish: of unknown origin; possibly a var. of *Hoffer* (see HOFFMANN 3), reflecting varieties of Yiddish with no /h/. Derivation from the Hebr. male given name *Ofer* is impossible since that is a 20th-cent. coinage.

Var. (of 1): **Orfeur**.

Cogns. (of 1): Fr.: **Orfèvre**, **Orfaure**.

Officer English: 1. occupational name for the holder of any office, from ANF *officer* (an agent deriv. of OF *office* duty, service, L *officium* service, task).

2. occupational name for a sewer of gold embroidery, from ANF *orfroiser* (an agent deriv. of OF *orfrois*, LL *auriphyrigium* Phrygian gold—the Phrygians being famed in antiquity for their gold embroidery).

Var. (of 1): **Office**.

Offord English: habitation name from a place in Cambs., so called from OE *uppe* up(stream) + *ford* FORD.

Ogborne English: habitation name from a pair of villages in Wilts. called *Ogbourne*, from the OE personal name *Oc(c)a* + OE *burna* stream (see BOURNE).

Ogden English: habitation name from some minor place, probably the one in W Yorks., so called from OE *āc* OAK + *denu* valley (see DEAN 1).

Var.: **Oakden**.

Ogg Scots: Anglicized form of a nickname from the Gael. adj. *óg* young, used to distinguish the junior of two bearers of the same given name.

Var.: **Oag**.

Ogilvie Scots: habitation name from a place near Glamis in the former county of Angus, which is first recorded *c.*1205 in the form *Ogilvin*. It probably gets its name from Brit. (pre-Gael.) cogns. of OW *ugl* high + *ma* plain, place (mutated to *fa*) or *ban* hill (mutated to *fan*).

Vars.: **Ogilvy**, **Ogilwy**; **Ogilby** (N Ireland).

Ogilvy *is the name of an ancient Scots family, descended from Gilibride, Earl of Angus (d. c.1187). His sons included Magnus (d. 1239), who became Earl of Caithness, and Gilbert, who was the first to assume the surname, when he was granted the manor of Ogilvy in 1172. The family have held the title Earls of Airlie since 1639, and through the female line they also hold the title Earls of Seafield.*

Ogle Scots and N Irish: habitation name from a place in Northumb., so called from the OE personal name *Ocga* + OE *hyll* HILL.

Var.: **Ogill**.

Oglethorpe English: habitation name from a place in W Yorks., so called from the ON personal name *Oddketill* (composed of the elements *odd* point of a weapon + *ketill* cauldron) + ON *þorp* village, settlement.

The colony of Georgia was founded by an English general, James Oglethorpe *(1696–1785). His stated intention was to establish a place where the poor, with whom he had come into contact in the course of his prison reforms, would be able to begin a new life. He was born in London, the son of Sir Theophilus Oglethorpe, from a long-established Yorks. family.*

Ogley English: 1. var. of OAKLEY.

2. habitation name from a place in Staffs., so called from the OE personal name *Ocga* + OE *lēah* wood, clearing.

Ograbek Polish: nickname, of uncertain application, from Pol. *ograbek*, sing. of *ograbki* remnants, gleanings. This could be a nickname for an insignificant or unwanted person, or perhaps a metonymic occupational name for a gleaner.

Ogrodowski Polish: occupational name (in form a habitation name) for a market gardener or owner of an orchard or smallholding, Pol. *ogród*.

Var.: **Ogrodzki**.

Dim. **Ogrodowczyk**.

Patr.: **Ogrodowicz** (also Jewish (E Ashkenazic).

Ogurtsov Russian: patr. from the nickname *Ogurets* 'Cucumber' (an early borrowing from Gk), given perhaps originally to a grower or seller of these vegetables.

Cogns.: Pol.: **Ogórek**. Jewish (E Ashkenazic): **Ogurek** (from Pol.); **Hurok** (from Beloruss.).

O'Hara Irish: Anglicized form of Gael. **Ó hEaghra** 'descendant of *Eaghra*', a personal name of uncertain derivation; cf. HARE.

Var.: **O'Hora**.

Bearers of this surname claim descent from Eagra, *Lord of Luighne, who died in 926.*

Ohlbaum Jewish (Ashkenazic): ornamental name, from Ger. *Ölbaum* olive tree (lit. 'oil tree').

Vars.: **Elbaum** (mixed Yid.-Ger. form); **Elbum**, **Elbo(i)m**, **Elboym** (from Yid. *eylboym* olive tree).

Ohlenschlager German: occupational name for an extractor of linseed oil. Oil was extracted from linseed by striking the grains with a heavy wooden hammer. The name is thus derived from MHG *oli(e)* oil + *sla(h)en* to strike, smite.

Vars.: **Öhl(en)schlager**, **Öhl(en)schläger**, **Ohligschlager**, **Ohligschläger**, **Öhlschlegel**.

Cogns.: Fris.: **Ölgeschlager**, **Oljeschlager**, **Oldenschläger**. Flem., Du.: **Olieslager**, **Oliesleger**.

Oistrakh Jewish (Ashkenazic): regional name for someone from Austria, from an older pronunciation of Yid. *Estraykh* (Ger. *Österreich*, from OHG *ōstar* eastern + *rīhhi* kingdom).

Vars.: **Ostreich(er)** (syncopated forms); **Estreicher** (Ger.-based romanization of Yid. *estraykher* Austrian); **Österreicher** (from Ger.); **Osterreicher** (from the prec., with omission of umlaut).

Ojala Finnish: topographic name, from Finn. *oja* ditch + the local suffix *-la*.

Ojeda Spanish: topographic name for someone living on the banks of the river *Ojeda* in the province of Soria, which is probably so called from L *folia* leaves (cf. RIOJA) + the collective suffix *-ēta*.

Okeover English: habitation name from a place in Staffs., so called from OE *āc* OAK + *ofer* bank, slope (see OVER).

A family of this name trace their descent from Ormus Helsweyn or Halesoen (presumably someone from Halesowen in Worcs.), living between 1089 and 1138. He held land in Okeover from the abbot of Burton-on-Trent before 1113. He was possibly the son of Eddulf, named as tenant of Okeover in Domesday Book.

Oksanen Finnish: ornamental or arbitarily chosen name, from Finn. *oksa* branch + the gen. suffix *-nen*.

Olalla Spanish: habitation name from a place in the province of Teruel, first recorded in the form *Olalia*, and probably named from the dedication of its church to St *Eulalia* (see HILARY 2).

Old English: from ME *old* (OE *eald*), not necessarily implying old age, but rather used to distinguish an older from a younger bearer of the same given name. See also ELDER.

Vars.: **Ould**; **Auld**, **Ault**, **Aude** (Sc.); **Ol(d)man**.

Cogns.: Ger.: **Alt(er)(man)(n)**. Low Ger.: **Alde(r)**, **Olde(r)**, **Ohle**, **Oldemann**, **Ohlmann**. Flem., Du.: **Oud(e)**, **Ou(d)t**, **Oudeman**. Jewish (Ashkenazic): **Alt**, **Altman(n)**, **Alterman(n)**; **Alter** (in part from the Yid. male given name *Alter* 'Old Man', given to a child born after the death of a sibling or assumed by anyone who was in mortal danger (usually someone ill). The purpose was to confuse the Angel of Death into thinking that the person was old and so not worth claiming as a victim).

Patrs.: Eng.: **O(u)lds**. Low Ger.: **Alden**, **Old(s)en**. Flem., Du.: **Den Olden**, **Den Ouden**. Jewish (from the Yid. male given name *Alter*): **Alters(on)** (Ashkenazic); **Alterovitch**, **Alterowitz**, **Alterovitz** (E Ashkenazic); **Alterovici**, **Alterescu** (among Rumanian Jews).

Metrs.: Jewish: **Altes**, **Altovsky** (from the Yid. female given name *Alte*, fem. equivalent of *Alter*; see above).

Cpds: Jewish: **Altbach** ('old stream'); **Altbauer** (meaning unclear); **Altbaum** ('old tree'); **Altberg** ('old hill'); **Althaus** ('old house'); **Altheim** ('old home'); **Althoff** ('old court'); **Altholz** ('old wood'); **Altsta(e)dter** ('dweller in the old town'); **Altstein** ('old stone'); **Alterthum** ('antiquity').

Oldcastle English: habitation name from a place in Ches., so called from OE *eald* OLD + *castel* fortified settlement (see CASTLE).

A putative ancestor of bearers of this name was the English soldier Sir John Oldcastle (?1378–1417), who has been taken as a possible model for Shakespeare's Falstaff, though the connection is uncertain. He was the son of Sir Richard Oldcastle, whose family owned a manor in Herefords. which included a piece of land called Oldcastle, *probably so named as being the site of a Roman fortification. He inherited the title Baron Cobham in 1408 through his mother. He led the English army against France in 1411, but was hanged and burned as a heretic and Lollard.*

Oldenburg Low German: habitation name from a place so called, from the weak dat. case (originally used after a preposition and article) of MLG *ald*, *old* OLD + MLG *burg* fortress, town (see BURKE).

The royal house of Oldenburg *traces its origin to Egilmar I (fl. 1108), Count of Aldenburg.*

One of only two permanent officers at the inception of the Royal Society was a German, Henry Oldenburg (1618–77), who was its secretary for fifteen years. He was born in Bremen, the son of a teacher, a member of a family who had moved there from Münster in the 16th cent.

Oldfield English: habitation name from any of various minor places so called, from OE *eald* OLD + *feld* pasture, open country (see FIELD). The surname is widespread, but most common in W Yorks.

Vars.: **O(f)field**, **Allfield**.

Cogn.: Jewish: **Altfeld** (reason(s) for acquisition unclear).

Oldham English: habitation name from the place in Lancs., so called from ME *ald*, *old* OLD + *holm* island, dry land in a fen, promontory (see HOLME 2).

Oldroyd English (Yorks.): habitation name from any of various minor places in N England so called from ME *ald*, *old* OLD + *royd* clearing (OE *rod*).

Oliff English: from the ON personal name *Óleifr* Olaf (earlier *Anleifr*), composed of the elements *ans* god + *leifr* relic (from *leifa* to leave). The name was a common Scandinavian one, and became popular also in N Scotland and Ireland, which received Scandinavian colonists at an early date. The name continued to be popular in the Middle Ages, in part as a result of the fame of St Olaf, King of Norway, who brought Christianity to his country *c.*1015.

Vars.: **Ol(l)iffe**, **Olliff**.

Patrs.: Dan., Norw.: **Olufsen**, **Ovesen**, **Olesen**, **Ohlsen**; **Olsen** (also common in Newcastle). Swed.: **Olavsson**, **Olofsson**, **Olausson**, **O(h)lsson**. See also MCAULAY.

Olimpiev Russian: patr. from the given name *Olimpi* (Gk *Olympios*, a deriv. of *Olympos*, the traditional home of the gods), borne by a 4th-cent. saint, bishop of Aenos in Rumelia.

Vars.: **Alimpiev**, **Alimov**.

Oliphant English, Scots, French, and German: from ME, OF, MHG *olifant* elephant (LL *olifantus*, for class. L *elephantus*, Gk *elephas*, gen. *elephantis*; the modern words have been re-formed from the class. L). The circumstances in which this word was applied as a surname are not clear. It may have been a nickname for a large, clumsy individual, or a metonymic occupational name for a worker in ivory, or a house name from a house distinguished with the sign of an elephant.

Vars.: **Olifant**, **Olivant**.

Cogns.: Jewish (Ashkenazic, reasons for acquisition not clear): **Olifant**, **Elefant**, **Elfand**; **Helfant**, **Helfand** (with excrescent *H-*); **Gelfant**, **Gelfand** (under Russ. influence; see GOREN).

Oliphant *is the name of a British family of Norman origin. They originally settled in Northants and Hunts., and later established themselves in Scotland. Their earliest recorded ancestor was Roger* Olifard, *witness to a charter in Northants before 1108. The name is also variously recorded as* Holyfard *and* Olyfard.

Oliva Italian, Spanish, Catalan, and Jewish (Sefardic): topographic name for someone who lived by an olive grove, or metonymic occupational name for a gatherer or seller of olives or an extractor or seller of olive oil, perhaps sometimes also a nickname for someone with a sallow complexion. The vocab. word in all these languages comes from L *olīva* olive; the forms from the LL deriv. *olīvārius* olive tree have been confused with the personal name OLIVER.

Vars.: It.: **Olivi**, **Olivo**; **Uliva** (Venetia); **Ulivi** (Tuscany); **Olivari**. Sp.: **Olivas**; **Olivera**. Cat.: **Olivera**.

Cogns.: Eng.: **Ol(l)ive** (almost always an Anglicized form of one of the Romance names). Fr.: **Olive**. Port.: **Oliveira**. Flem., Du.: **Olijve**, **Olyff**. Jewish (Ashkenazic, ornamental): **Olivenbaum** ('olive tree'); **Olivenstein** ('olive stone'; Anglicized as **Olivestone**).

Dims.: It.: **Olivella**, **Olivelli**, **Olivello**, **Ulivelli**, **Olivetta**, **Olivetti**, **Olivotti**. Prov.: **Olivet**. Cat.: **Olivella**.

Pejs.: It.: **Olivazzi**, **Olivato**.

Collectives: It.: **Oliveto**, **Oliveti**. Sp.: **Olivar(es)**. Cat.: **Olivar**.

Oliver English, Scots, French, Catalan, and German: from the OF given name *Olivier*, which was brought to England by the Normans from France. It was popular throughout Europe in the Middle Ages as having been borne by one of Charlemagne's paladins, the faithful friend of Roland, about whose exploits there were many popular romances. The name ostensibly means 'olive tree' (see OLIVA), but this is almost certainly the result of folk etymology working on a personal name of Gmc origin, perhaps one cogn. with ÁLVARO. The surname is also borne by Jews, apparently as an adoption of the non-Jewish surname.

Vars.: Eng.: **Olver** (Devon). Fr.: **Ol(l)ivier**. Cat.: **Olivé**.

Cogns.: It.: **Oliv(i)eri**, **Oliv(i)ero**, **Oliverio**; **Ulivieri** (Tuscany); **Livieri**, **Liviero** (Emilia, Lombardy); **Vier(i)**, **Viero** (Tuscany, Venetia). Sp.: **Oliveros**. Flem., Du.: **Olivier**.

Dims.: Fr.: **Olivreau**. It.: **Vierin(i)**, **Vierucci**.

Oller Catalan: occupational name for a potter, Cat. *oller* (LL *ollārius*, from *olla* pot; cf. EULER).

Var.: **Ollé**.

Cogns.: Prov.: **Ollier**, **Oulier**.

Ollerenshaw English: habitation name from a place in Derbys., so called from OE *ælren* aldern, of alders (an adj. deriv. of *alor*; see ALDER 2) + *sceaga* wood, copse (see SHAW).

Vars.: **Olerenshaw**, **Olorenshaw**, **Ollarenshaw**; **Ollerearnshaw** (by confusion with EARNSHAW); **Oldershaw**, **Houldershaw**.

Ollerton English (Lancs.): habitation name from places so called in Ches., Notts., and Shrops. The first two are named from OE *alor* ALDER + *tūn* enclosure, settlement. *Ollerton* in Shrops., which is earlier found as *Alvereton*, is from an OE personal name, perhaps *Ælfhere* + OE *tūn* enclosure, settlement.

Olmo Italian and Spanish: topographic name for someone who lived by a conspicuous elm tree (L *ulmus*).

Vars.: It.: **Olmi**. Sp.: **Olmos**.

Collectives: Sp.: **Olmedo**, **Olmeda**.

Olney English: habitation name from places so called in Bucks. and Northants. The former gets its name from OE *Ollanēg* 'island (OE *ēg*) of *Olla*'; the latter from OE *āna* one, single, solitary + *lēah* wood, clearing, with later metathesis of *-nl-* to *-ln-*.

Olszewski 1. Polish: habitation name from one of the places named with Pol. *olcha*, *olsza* alder + *-ew* possessive suffix, with the addition of *-ski*, suffix of local surnames (see BARANOWSKI). It may perhaps also be a topographic name for someone living by an alder.

2. Jewish (E Ashkenazic): ornamental name from Pol. *olcha*, *olsza* alder.

Vars.: Pol.: **Olszak** (topographic only); **Olszacki**, **Olszycki**, **Olszański**, **Olszyński**. Jewish: **Olshevski**, **Olshevsky**, **Olchovski**, **Volchonsky**; **Olcha**, **Olchik**.

Cogns.: Russ.: **Olkhin**, **Volkhin** (patr. in form). Ger.: ELLER.

Öman Swedish: ornamental name from Swed. *ö* island (ON *ey*) + *man* man (ON *maðr*), sometimes adopted as a topographic name by someone who lived on an island.

Var.: **Öhman**.

Cpds (ornamental): **Öberg** ('island hill'); **Ö(h)gren** ('island branch'); **Öqvist** ('island twig'); **Öström** ('island river').

O'Mara Irish: Anglicized form of Gael. **Ó Meadhra** 'descendant of *Meadhra*', a personal name derived from *meadhar* mirth, joy.

Vars.: **(O')Meara**.

Onion 1. Welsh: from the W personal name *Einion*. This is probably from the L personal name *Anniānus*, but no doubt enjoyed its wide popularity as a result of folk etymological associations with W *einion* anvil and *uniawn* upright, just.

2. English: metonymic occupational name for a grower or seller of onions, from ME *oyn(y)on*, *unyon* (OF *oignon*, from L *unio*, gen. *uniōnis*, a deriv. of *unus* one, since the plant produces only a single unit, as contrasted with garlic with its many cloves).

Vars.: **Onyon**. (Of 1 only): **Anyon**, **Anyan**, **Annion**, **Eynon**, **En(n)ion**, **Hennion**.

Patrs. (from 1): **Onions**, **Onians**, **Inions**; **Beynon** (with the Welsh prefix *ap*, *ab*).

Patr. (from 1) (dim.): BAINES.

Onslow English: habitation name from a place in Shrops., which appears in Domesday Book in the form *Andeslave*, and is probably named as the 'hill or burial-mound (OE *hlāw*; see LAW 2 and LOW 1) of *Andhere*', an otherwise unattested personal name composed of the elements *and* spirit, soul + *here* army.

John de Ondeslowe, living in 1203, derived his name from the village of Ondeslowe in Shrops. He was the son of Adam de Andreslawa, *who witnessed a deed in 1174. His descendants received the earldom of Onslow in 1801.*

Openshaw English (Lancs.): habitation name from a place in Greater Manchester, so called from OE *open* open, i.e. not surrounded by a hedge + *sceaga* copse (cf. SHAW).

Opie Cornish: from the medieval given name *Oppy*, *Obby*, a dim. of various names such as OSBORN, *Osbert*, and *Osbald*.

Oppenheim Jewish (W Ashkenazic): habitation name from a place in Hesse, on the Rhine between Mainz and Worms, so called from an obscure first element (Bahlow favours a prehistoric element referring to a marsh or fen) + OHG *heim* homestead.

Vars.: **Oppenhaim**, **Openhaime**, **Openheim**; **Openhajm** (Pol. spelling); **Op(p)enheimer** ('native or inhabitant of Oppenheim').

Sir Ernest Oppenheimer *(1880–1957), the diamond magnate, was born in Friedburg, Germany, the son of a cigar merchant. He became a clerk in a London diamond broker's at the age of 16 and in 1902, at the age of 22, went to S Africa to seek his fortune.*

Oppermann Low German: occupational name for a churchwarden or sexton, with particular reference to his task of taking the collection, from MLG *opper(gilt)* donation (from *oppern* to donate, sacrifice, LL *operāri*) + *mann* man.

Vars.: **Opfermann**; **Offermann** (also Jewish, presumably an occupational name for the sexton of a synagogue).

Cogn.: Flem., Du.: **Offerman**. Jewish: **Offerman**.

Patr.: Low Ger.: **Offermanns**.

O'Prey Irish: Anglicized form of Gael. **Ó Préith**, from a personal name that is probably of Pictish origin.

Vars.: **Prey**, **Pray**.

Orange English: of uncertain origin, discussed by Reaney. A certain William *de Orenge* mentioned in Domesday Book probably derives his name from *Orange* in the *département* of Mayenne. Later medieval examples probably come from a female given name, *Orenge*, of obscure derivation.

Orchard English: topographic name for someone who lived by an orchard, or metonymic occupational name for a fruit grower, from ME *orchard* (OE *ortgeard*, *orceard*, a cpd of *wort*, *wyrt* plant (later associated with L *hortus* garden; see ORT 1) + *geard* yard, enclosure).

Var.: **Norchard** (by misdivision of ME *atten orchard* 'at the orchard').

Ord 1. English (Northumb.): habitation name from a place in Northumb., so called from OE *ord* point; cf. ORT 3.

2. English: from a Gmc personal name; see ORT 2.

3. Scots: habitation name from various minor places named with Gael. *ord* hammer, used as a topographical term for a rounded hill.

Var.: **Orde**.

Ordóñez Spanish: patr. from the medieval given name *Ordoño*, of uncertain origin and meaning.

Orellana Spanish: habitation name from either of two places in the province of Badajoz, probably so called from L *Aurēliāna* (*villa*) 'estate of *Aurēlius*', a Roman family name.

Orff German: 1. habitation name from a place in Hesse, near Kassel, now known as *Urff*, but recorded in 1184 as *Orpha*. Its etymology is obscure.

2. contracted form of a Gmc personal name composed of the elements *ort* point (of a spear, sword) + *wulf* wolf.

3. metonymic occupational name for a fisherman or fishseller, or nickname for a person thought to resemble a fish, from *orf*, a dial. word for a type of fish of the carp family.

Orford English: habitation name from any of various places so called. One in Suffolk gets its name from OE *ōra* shore (see ORR 3) + *ford* FORD, whereas that in Lancs. is from ME *overe* upper (OE *uferra*; cf. OBER) + *ford*. A third example, in Lincs., is recorded as *Erforde* in Domesday Book, but later forms have *I-*, suggesting a derivation from OE *Iraford* 'ford of the Irish'.

Organ 1. English: metonymic occupational name for a player of a musical instrument (not necessarily what is now known as an organ), from ME *organ* (OF *organe*, LL *organum* device, (musical) instrument, Gk *organon* tool, from *ergein* to work, do).

2. English: from a rare medieval given name, attested only in the Latinized forms *Organus* (masc.) and *Organa* (fem.). Its etymology is obscure; it may represent a reworking of a Celt. name.

3. Welsh: see MORGAN.

Var. (of 1): **Organer**.

Oriol Provençal and Catalan: nickname for a man with bright yellow hair, from OProv., Cat. *oriol* oriole, a yellow bird (LL *aureolus*, a dim. of *aureus* golden, from *aurum* gold).

Vars.: Prov.: **Oriou**, **Orieux**, **Oriot**; **Auriol**, **Auriou**; **Loriol**, **Lauriol**, **Lorieu(x)**, **Loriot**.

Orive Spanish form of Basque **Oribe**: topographic name for someone living in the lower part of a village, from *uri*, *iri* settlement (see URIA) + *be(h)e* lower part; cf. URIBE.

Orlov 1. Russian: patr. from the nickname *Oryol* 'Eagle' (cogn. with Pol. *orzeł*, Czech *orel*). This word is a distant cogn. of Gk *ornis* bird, but was specialized in the Slav. languages to denote the king of the birds.

2. Jewish (E Ashkenazic): patr. from the Russ. vocab. word *oryol* eagle, one of the many Ashkenazic ornamental surnames derived from words denoting birds.

Vars.: Russ.: **Orlovski** (surname adopted by Orthodox clergy, in reference to the eagle as a symbol of St John the Evangelist). Jewish: **Orlovitch**, **Orlovitz**, **Orlowitz**; **Orlovsky**, **Orlowsky**, **Orlowski**.

Cogns.: Czech: **Orel**, **Vorel**.

Dims.: Pol.: **Orlik**, **Orlicki**. Czech: **Orlický**, **Vorlický**; **Vorlíček**.

Habitation names: Pol. **Orłowski**, **Orlikowski**, **Orliński**.

The Orlovs *were a powerful Russian family who were close advisers to Catherine the Great and Nicholas I. They gave their name to the Orlov Diamond, a 200-carat stone acquired by Count Gregory Orlov (1734–83) in an attempt to win back Catherine's favour. He and his brother, Aleksei Orlov (1737–1808), had been closely involved in the coup which brought her to power.*

Orme 1. N English: from the ON personal name *Ormr*, originally a byname meaning 'Snake', 'Serpent', 'Dragon' (cogn. with OE *wyrm* worm, which originally had the same range of meanings).

2. French: topographic name for someone who lived near a conspicuous elm tree, from OF *orme* (L *ulmus*; see OLMO).

Vars. (of 1): Eng.: **Oram**, **Or(r)um**. (Of 2): Fr.: **D(h)orme**, **Delorme**.

Cogns. (of 1): Ger.: **Wurm(b)**. Low Ger.: **Worm**.

Dims. (of 1): Ger.: **Würmle**, **Würmlin**. Low Ger.: **Wörm(b)ke**. (Of 2): Fr.: **Ormeau**, **Delormeau**, **Delhommeau(x)**, **Désormeaux**; **Humeau** (E France); **Ormesson**.

Patrs. (from 1): Eng.: **Ormes**. Ger.: **Würmeling**.

Collective (of 2): Fr.: **Dormeuil**.

Ormerod English (Lancs.): habitation name from a place in Lancs., so called from the ON personal name *Ormr* (see

ORME 1) or *Ormarr* (composed of the elements *orm* serpent + *herr* army) + OE *rod* clearing.

Var.: **Ormrod**.

A family of this name trace their descent from Pier de Ormerod, *living in 1495. A branch of the family later settled in Somerset.*

Ormiston Scots: habitation name from places in the former counties of Roxburgh and E Lothian, so called from the gen. case of the ON personal name *Ormr* (see ORME 1) + OE *tūn* enclosure, settlement.

Var.: **Ormston** (Northumb.).

Alan de Ormiston *(d. 1289) was the ancestor of a Scottish family long settled around Roxburgh. He was witness to various charters between 1214 and 1249.*

Ormond Irish (common in the Cork and Waterford areas): Anglicized form of Gael. **Ó Ruaidh** 'descendant of *Ruadh*', a byname meaning 'Red', altered by folk etymology to resemble a regional name from the ancient region of of E Munster known as *Ormond* (Gael. *Ur Mhumhain*).

Vars.: **Ormonde, Orman**.

Ormsby English: habitation name from *Ormsby* in Lincs. and N Yorks., or *Ormesby* in Norfolk, all so called from the gen. case of the ON personal name *Ormr* (see ORME 1) + ON *býr* farm, settlement.

Ormshaw English (Lancs.): habitation name from an unidentified place, apparently named with the personal name ORME and the local element SHAW.

Var.: **Ormesher**.

Orozco Basque: habitation name from a place in the province of Biscay, of unclear etymology; the first element may derive from Basque *oru* plot of land.

Orpin English: metonymic occupational name for a herbalist, from ME, OF *orpin(e)* yellow stonecrop (from LL *auripigmentum* yellow arsenic, lit. 'golden pigment'), a plant widely esteemed for its reputed capacity to heal wounds.

Var.: **Orpen**.

Orr 1. N English, Scots, and N Irish: from the ON byname *Orri* 'Black-cock'.

2. Scots: nickname for someone with a sallow complexion, from Gael. *odhar* pale, dun.

3. English: topographic name for someone who lived on a shore or on the edge of a hill, from OE *ōra* edge, or habitation name from a place named with this word, as for example *Ore* in Sussex or *Oare* in Berks., Kent, and Wilts.

4. Jewish (Israeli): ornamental name from Hebr. *or* light.

Orrick English (Northumb.): from a ME survival of the OE personal name *Ordrīc*, composed of the elements *ord* point (of a sword, spear) + *rīc* power.

Var.: **Orridge** (Notts.).

Orso Italian: nickname for someone thought to resemble a bear (e.g. a large, lumbering person), or local name for someone who lived in a house distinguished with the sign of a bear, from It. *orso* bear (L *ursus*).

Vars.: **Orsi**; **Urso, Ursi** (S Italy).

Cogns.: Fr.: **Ours, Hours, Lours**. Rom.: **Ursul**.

Dims.: It.: **Orselli, Orsello, Orsetti, Ors(ol)ini, Orsolino, Orsolillo, Orsucci, Ursillo, Ursino, Ursini**. Fr.: **Oursel(in), Orsel, Orseau, Hourseau, Orset**.

Augs.: It.: **Orsoni, Orsone**.

Patrs.: It.: **D'Orso, D'Orsi, D'Urso**.

The Orsini *were an ancient and powerful Italian family who included three popes: Celestine III (d. 1198), Nicholas III (d. 1277), and Benedict XIII (d. 1730). Traditionally, they trace their origin to a certain Ursus de Baro, who was living in Rome in 998.*

Ország Hungarian: topographic name from Hung. *ország* land, territory.

Ort 1. Provençal: metonymic occupational name for a gardener or topographic name for someone who lived near an enclosed garden, OProv. *ort* (L *hortus*).

2. German: from a Gmc personal name *Ort*, a short form of the various cpd names with the first element *ord* point (of a sword, spear).

3. German: topographic name for someone who lived at the top of a hill or the end of a settlement, from OHG *ort* (see 2 above), in the transferred sense 'tip', 'extremity'. In mod. Ger. the word has come to mean 'point', 'spot', 'place'.

Vars. (of 1): **Delort, Or(t)s, Des(h)orts**. (Of 3): **Ortner, Ortler**; **Amort, Imort**.

Cogns. (of 1): Cat.: **Orta(s), Horta**. Sp.: **Huerta**. Port.: **Horta**. (Of 3): Low Ger.: **Örder**; **Orth(mann), Ohrt(mann), Ordemann**; **Opdenort(h)**. Flem., Du.: **Van Oort, Van (den) Oord**. Jewish (Ashkenazic): **Ort(s)man, Ortner** (the reasons for the adoption of these names is not known).

Dims. (of 1): Prov.: **Ortet, Orteau(x)**; **Ourtic, Ho(u)rtic**. Cat.: **Ortells, Orteu**. (Of 2): Ger.: **Örtel(t), Ert(e)l, Ertelt, Ordelt, Artelt**.

Ortega Spanish and Catalan: habitation name from any of various places, for example in the provinces of Burgos, La Coruña, and Jaén, of uncertain etymology. It may represent an altered form of Sp. *ortiga* nettle (L *urtīca*), or be from L *hortus* garden, orchard (cf. ORT 1) + the local suffix *-eca*.

Orton English and Scots: habitation name from any of various places so called. All those in England share a second element from OE *tūn* enclosure, settlement, but the first element in each case is more difficult to determine. Examples in Cambs. and Warwicks. are on the banks of rivers, so that there it is probably OE *ōfer* riverbank; in other cases it is impossible to decide between *ofer* ridge and *ufera* upper. Orton in Cumb., exceptionally, probably has as its first element the ON byname *Orri* 'Black-cock' (see ORR 1), and Orton near Fochabers, Scotland, probably gets its name from Gael. *oir*, loc. case of *or* border, edge + *dùin*, gen. case of *dùn* fort.

Ortuño Spanish: from a medieval given name (L *Fortūnius*, a deriv. of *fortūna* chance, (good) fortune).

Orwell 1. English: habitation name from a place in Cambs., so called from the OE topographical term *ord* tip, top, extremity (cf. ORT 3) + *well(a)* spring, stream (see WELL).

2. Scots: habitation name from a place in the former county of Kinross, first recorded in 1330 in the form *Urwell*, probably from Gael. *ùr* new + *baile* (in combination *bhail*) village.

Orzechowski Polish: 1. habitation name from a place named with Pol. *orzech* nut, hazel-nut, + *-ów* possessive suffix, with the addition of the suffix of local surnames *-ski* (see BARANOWSKI). In some cases it may also be a topographic name for someone who lived by a nut-tree.

2. nickname from Pol. *orzechowy* hazel (adj.), applied to the colour of the hair.

Osborn English: from the ON personal name *Ásbjorn*, composed of the elements *ás* god + *björn* bear. This was established in England before the Conquest, in the late OE form *Ōsbern*, and was later reinforced by the Norman *Osbern*.

Vars.: **Osborne, Osbourn(e), Osburn, Osbon, Osband, Usborne, Hosburn.**

Cogns.: Low Ger.: **Ausborn, Asbahr, Osbahr.**

Patr.: Eng.: **Hosbons.**

Oscroft English: apparently a habitation name from an unidentified place, the second element of which appears to be OE *croft* paddock, smallholding (see CROFT). The first element may be a short form of an OE personal name containing the element *ōs* god (e.g. *Oswine*; see OSWIN) or its ON cogn. *ás* (see, e.g., OSBORN).

Osgood English: from the ON personal name *Ásgautr*, composed of the element *ás* god + the tribal name *Gaut* (see JOCELYN). This was established in England before the Conquest, in the late OE forms *Ōsgot* or *Ōsgod*, and was later reinforced by the Norman *Ansgot*.

Vars.: **Angood, Angold; Hosgood, Ho(r)segood.**

Cogns.: Fr.: **Angot, Angaut.**

Osher Jewish (Ashkenazic): from the Yid. male given name *Osher* (Hebr. ASHER 'Blessed').

Vars.: **Osheri** (from Hebr. *osher* happiness + the Hebr. ending *-i*); USHER.

Dim.: **Osherenko** (SE Ashkenazic).

Patrs. (E Ashkenazic): **Osh(e)rov, Osheroff, Oserow, Os(h)erovitch, Os(h)erovitz, Oshrovitz, Osherowitz, Osherowicz, Osherowich, Osherovsky; Oszerowski** (Pol. spelling).

Osiecki Polish: topographic name for someone living by a water meadow, Pol. *osiek*.

Cogn.: Ger. (of Slav. origin): **Ossietzky.**

Osinin Russian: 1. patr. from the given name *Osinya*, a pet form of *Osip*; see JOSEPH.

2. patr. from the nickname *Osina* 'Aspen', used to refer to a very timid person, or to someone who suffered from a nervous tremor.

Cogns. (of 2): Pol.: **Osiński** (habitation name). Jewish (E Ashkenazic): **Osinski** (ornamental name or adoption of the Pol. surname).

Osmond English and French: from the ON personal name *Ásmundr*, composed of the elements *ás* god + *mund* protection. This was established in England before the Conquest, coalescing with the independent OE form *Ōsmund*, and was later reinforced by the Norman *Osmund*.

Vars.: Eng.: **Osmund, Osmon, Osman(t), Osment, Osmint.** Fr.: **O(s)mont.**

Osorio Spanish: from a medieval given name, of uncertain origin. It is probably a metathesized form of L *Orosius* (Gk *Orosios*, a deriv. of *oros* mountain), the name borne by a 4th-cent. Iberian theologian and historian, who was famous in Spain throughout the Middle Ages.

Cogn.: Port.: **Osório.**

Ossowski Polish: common surname of uncertain origin. In form it is a habitation name; it may perhaps be from a place named from a personal nickname derived from Pol. *osowiały* miserable, depressed.

Ostapov Russian: patr. from the given name *Ostap* (Gk *Eustathios*, from *eu* good, well + *stat-* to stand). This rare name was early confused with *Eustakhios* Eustace (see STACE). The forms have been further affected by confusion with *Osip* JOSEPH and other given names.

Vars.: **Astapov, Ostafyev, Astafyev, Evstafyev, Astfimov, Ostanov.**

Dims.: Russ.: **Ostankin, Ostashkin, Ostashkov, Astashkin, Astashov, Astashev, Astachov, Tafintsev** (all patrs.). Ukr.: **Ostashko, Ostapets.** Beloruss.: **Ostepenya, Astapenya, Astapchyonok, Astapchuk.**

'Son of the wife of O.': Ukr.: **Ostapishin.**

Østergård Danish: habitation name from a placename composed of the elements *øster* eastern + *gård* enclosure.

Var.: **Østergaard.**

Ostler English: occupational name for an innkeeper, from ME *(h)osteler* (OF *(h)ostelier*, an agent deriv. of HOSTAL). This term was at first applied to the secular officer in a monastery who was responsible for the lodging of visitors, but it was later extended to keepers of commercial hostelries, and this is probably the usual sense of the surname. The more restricted mod. Eng. sense, 'groom', is also a possible source.

Vars.: **Oastler, Osler; Host(el)ler, Hustler, Horsler.**

Ostrowski Polish: habitation name from any of the many places in different parts of Poland named with Pol. *ostrów*, which denotes both an island in a river and a water meadow bounded by ditches. In some cases it may be a topographical name for someone who lived on a river island or in a water meadow.

Osuna Spanish: habitation name from a place in the province of Seville, so called from Arabic *Oxuna*, perhaps from LL *Ursina* (*villa*) 'estate of *Ursus*', a byname meaning 'Bear'.

Oswald N English and Scots: from an OE personal name composed of the elements *ōs* god (Continental Gmc *ans*) + *weald* power. In the ME period, this fell together with the less common ON cogn. *Ásvaldr*. The name was introduced to Germany from England, as a result of the fame of St Oswald, a 7th-cent. king of Northumb., whose deeds were reported by Celtic missionaries to S Germany. The name was also borne by a 10th-cent. Eng. saint of Dan. parentage, who was important as a monastic reformer.

Cogns.: Ger.: **Oswald, Ostwald, Oschwald.** Fr.: **Ansaud, Ansault.** It.: **Ansaldi, Ansaldo, Anzaldi, Anzaldo.**

Dims.: Ger.: **Ös(ch), Öschlin.**

Oswell English: of uncertain origin, possibly a habitation name, of which the second element appears to be OE *well(a)* spring, stream (see WELL). The first element may be a short form of an OE personal name containing the element *ōs* god (e.g. *Oswine*; see OSWIN) or its ON cogn. *ás* (see, e.g., OSBORN).

A family of this name have been settled in Shrops. since the 15th cent. The earliest known bearer of the name was Roger Wyswall, *who was admitted as a burgess of Shrewsbury in 1450. The name is found in various forms, including* Woosall *and* Wossald.

Oswin English: from a ME survival of the OE personal name *Ōswine*, composed of the elements *ōs* god + *wine* friend.

Otero Spanish: habitation name from any of the numerous places in N and NW Spain so called, from Sp. *otero* height, hill (LL *altārium*, a deriv. of *altus* high).

Otter English: 1. metonymic occupational name for an otter hunter, or nickname for someone supposedly resembling an otter, from ME *oter* (OE *otor*).

2. from the late OE personal name *Ohthere*, a borrowing of ON *Óttar*, composed of the elements *ótti* fear, dread + *herr* army.

Cogn. (of 1): Czech: **Vydra.**

Ottolenghi Italian (Jewish): Italianized form of a habitation name from *Öttlingen* in Bavaria. Jews were repeatedly expelled from this town in the 15th and 16th cents. and many of them settled in N Italy, particularly in Piedmont and Lombardy.

Ottoway English: from either of two Norman personal names: *Otoïs*, composed of the Gmc elements *od* prosperity, riches + *widis* (from *wid* wide or *witu* wood), or *Otewi*, in which the second element is *wīg* war.
Vars.: **Ottaway, Otterway, Ot(t)way.**
Dims.: **Otte(r)well, Ottewill, Ottiwell** (from OF *Otuel*).

Ough English: a fairly common surname in Cornwall, of unknown origin. It is not from the Corn. language.

Ousley S English: apparently a habitation name from an unidentified place, perhaps a cpd of the river name *Ouse* (OE *Usa*, of ancient Brit. origin, from *ud-* water) + OE *lēah* wood, clearing.
Vars.: **Ouseley, Owsley.**
This surname was brought to North America by Major Thomas Owsley *in about 1677; he was born in Stogursey in Somerset.*

Óváry Hungarian: topographic name for someone who lived by an old castle, composed of the elements *ó* old + *vár* castle, or habitation name from a place so named.
Var.: **Óvári.**

Ovejero Spanish: occupational name for a shepherd, Sp. *ovejero* (LL *oviculārius*, agent. deriv. of *ovicula* sheep, a dim. of class. L *ovis*).

Ovenden English: habitation name from a place in W Yorks., so called from the gen. case of the OE personal name *Ofa* + OE *denu* valley (see DEAN 1). In some cases the surname may also derive from *Ovingdean* in Sussex, named as the 'valley of the people of *Ufa*'.

Over English: topographic name for someone who lived on the bank of a river or on a slope (from OE *ōfer* seashore, riverbank, or from the originally distinct word *ofer* slope, bank, ridge). The two terms, being of similar meaning as well as similar form, fell together in the ME period. The surname may also be a habitation name from places named with one or other of these words, which can only be distinguished with reference to their situation. *Over* in Cambs. is on a riverbank, whereas examples in Ches. and Derbys. are not; *Over* in Gloucs. is on the bank of the Severn, but also at the foot of a hill.
Vars.: **Ower(s), Nowers.**
Cogn.: Flem., Du.: **Van den Oever.** See also UFER.

Overall English: topographic name composed of the ME elements *overe*, *uvere* upper (OE *ufera*) + *hall* HALL.
Vars.: **Overal, Overell, Overill.**

Overend English (Yorks.): topographic name for someone who lived at the 'upper end' of a settlement, from ME *overe*, *uvere* upper (OE *ufera*) + *end* end (OE *ende*).

Overgård Danish: habitation name from a placename composed of the elements *over* upper + *gård* enclosure; cf. NEDERGÅRD.
Var.: **Overgaard.**

Overton English: habitation name from any of the numerous places so called. Most get the name from OE *ufere* upper + *tūn* enclosure, settlement; others have the first element from OE *ōfer* riverbank or *ofer* slope (see OVER).

Overy English: habitation name from a place named with the OE phrase *ofer īe* over, across the river, for example *Overy* in Oxon.

Oviedo Spanish: habitation name from the city in N Spain, found in early records in the L form *Ovetum*. It is of unknown origin.

Owczarz Polish: occupational name for a shepherd, Pol. *owczarz*.
Dims.: **Owczarek, Owczarczyk.**

Owen Welsh: from the W personal name *Owain*, in origin probably a borrowing of L *Eugenius* (see EUGÈNE).
Patr.: **Bowen** (*ap Owain*).

Oxenham English (W Country): habitation name from *Oxenham* in S Tawton, Devon, named with OE *oxan*, gen. pl. of *oxa* ox + *hamm* water meadow.

Oxley English: habitation name from any of various places, for example *Oxley* in Staffs. and *Ox Lee* near Hepworth (W Yorks.), so called from OE *oxa* ox + *lēah* wood, clearing.
Var.: **Oxlee.**

Oxnard English: occupational name for a keeper of oxen, from OE *oxan* oxen + *hierde* herdsman (see HEARD).

Oyler English: occupational name for an extractor or seller of oil, from a metathesized form of ANF *olier* (from *oile* oil, L *oleum* (olive) oil; cf. OLIVA). In N England linseed oil obtained from locally grown flax was more common than olive oil.
Var.: **Olier.**
Cogns.: Fr.: **Ol(l)ier.** It.: **Oliari; Dell'Olio, Dall'Oglio.** Ger.: **Ohl(ey)er, Öhler, Ohlmann**; see also OHLENSCHLAGER and ULMAN 2. Flem., Du.: **Olie(mann), Olij.** Czech: **Olejník, Volejník.** Jewish (Ashkenazic): **Ohlmacher** (lit. 'oil maker'); **El(l)man** ('oil man'), **Ejlman** (Pol. spelling).

P

Pacák Czech: 1. nickname for a bungler, from a deriv. of the OCzech verb *pacat* to bungle, botch.

2. habitation name from a place called *Pacov*.

Var. (of 2): **Pacovský**.

Pace English: nickname for a mild-mannered and even-tempered man, from ME *pace*, *pece* peace, concord, amity (ANF *pace*, from L *pax*, gen. *pācis*). There has been considerable confusion with *Pash* (see PASK).

The It. cogn. *Pace* /ˈpɑtʃɛ/ was used as a given name in the Middle Ages, and the many It. derivs. are mostly from this. The Sp. and Port. cogns. were often assumed, as approximate translations of the Hebr. given name *Shelomo* (see SALOMON), by Jews converted to Christianity; in other cases they derive from a title of the Virgin, *María de la Paz* (Sp.), *Maria da Paz* (Port.).

Vars.: **Paice**, PAYS, **Payze**, **Peace**.

Cogns.: Fr.: **Paix**, **Pache**. It.: **Pace**, **Paci**; **Pasi**, **Pase** (N Italy); **Pasio** (Venetia). Sp., Port.: PAZ.

Dims.: Fr.: **Pachot**. Prov.: **Pa(s)choud**. It.: **Pacelli**, **Paciello**, **Pacilli**, **Paselli**, **Pasello**, **Pacetti**, **Pasetti**, **Pasetto**, **Pacitti**, **Pacin(ott)i**, **Pacino**, **Pasin(i)**, **Pasino**, **Pasinetti**, **Pasol(in)i**, **Pasolli**, **Paciotti**, **Pasotti**, **Pasotto**, **Pasutti**, **Pasutto**, **Paciullo**.

Pačes Czech: 1. nickname for someone with an unruly mop of hair, from Czech *pačesy* mop or shock of hair.

2. from an OCzech personal name, *Pačeslav*, composed of the elements *pač* stronger (comparative of *paký* strong) + *slav* glory.

Vars. (of 2): **Pač**, **Páč**.

Pacey English (Norman): habitation name from *Pacy*-sur-Eure, which has the same origin as PASSY.

Var.: **Pacy**.

Pacheco Spanish and Portuguese: of uncertain origin. It is possibly from a dim. of the given name *Francisco* (see FRANCIS); the form *Pachico* is in use in the Basque country, and *Pachón* and *Pachu* are found elsewhere in Spain. Alternatively, it may be related to a root *pag-*, *pak-* found in various Romance languages signifying heaviness or fatness, and so be a nickname for a large, fat man.

Pacholski Polish: occupational name for a manservant, from Pol. *pachoł(ek)* servant + *-ski* suffix of surnames (see BARANOWSKI).

Cogn.: Ger. (of Slav. origin): **Pacholl**.

Dims.: Pol.: **Pacholczyk**. Ger. (of Slav. origin): **Pacholek**, **Pacholke**.

Pacifico 1. Italian: from the medieval given name *Pacifico* 'Peaceful', 'Peace-loving' (L *Pacificus*, from *pax* (gen. *pācis*) peace + *facere* to make, create).

2. Italian (Jewish): surname adopted as an approximate translation of the Hebr. given name *Shelomo* (see SALOMON).

Var.: **Pacifici**.

Pack English (Kentish): from a medieval given name, *Pack*, possibly a survival of the OE personal name **Pacca* (see PACKHAM), although this is found only as a placename element and appears to have died out fairly early on in the OE period. The ME given name is perhaps more likely to be an altered form of PASK.

Vars.: **Packe**, **Paik**; **Patch** (chiefly Bristol).

Packard English: 1. pej. name for a pedlar, from ME *pa(c)k* pack, bundle (see PACKER 2 and PACKMAN 1) + the ANF pej. suffix *-ard*.

2. pej. deriv. of the ME given name PACK.

3. from the Norman personal name *Pachard*, *Baghard*, composed of the Gmc elements *pac*, *bag* fight (see BACON 2) + *hard* hardy, brave, strong.

Cogns. (of 3): Fr.: **Pac(c)ard**.

Packer 1. English: occupational name for a wool-packer, an agent deriv. of ME *pack(en)* to pack (from *pa(c)k* package, from MLG *pak*, of unknown origin).

2. German and Jewish (Ashkenazic): occupational name for a wholesale trader, one who sold goods in large packages rather than broken down into smaller quantities. The term is an agent deriv. of Ger. *Pack* package (of the same MLG origin as the Eng. word).

Packham English: habitation name from *Pagham* in Sussex or *Pakenham* in Suffolk, apparently named as the homesteads (OE *hām*) of bearers of the OE personal names **Pæcga* and **Pac(c)a* respectively. **Pæcga* is an unattested byform of the attested *Pǣga*. **Pac(c)a*, though apparently present in a number of placenames, including PACKWOOD, is unattested in its own right and remains unexplained.

Vars.: **Padgham** (from the place in Sussex); **Pakenham** (from the place in Suffolk).

The surname of the Pakenham *family who hold the title Earl of Longford is derived from the manor in Suffolk, which they held at the end of the 11th cent. The first known bearer of the surname was* Robert de Pakynham, *an illegitimate great-grandson of the founder of the church at Pakenham* (c.1100).

Packman 1. English and Jewish (Ashkenazic): occupational name for a pedlar or hawker, one who carried his pack of goods for sale with him.

2. English: occupational name for the servant of someone called PACK.

Var. (of 1): Jewish: **Pakentreger** (from Yid. *pakn-treger* pack-carrier).

Packwood English: habitation name from a place in Warwicks., so called from the OE personal name **Pac(c)a* (see PACKHAM) + *wudu* WOOD.

Paddock English: 1. topographic name for a dweller in a paddock or enclosed meadow, from ME *parrock* (OE *pearruc*; cf. PARR 1 and PARK 1). The change of *-rr-* to *-dd-* did not occur before the 17th cent., and is not readily explained.

2. nickname for someone considered to resemble a toad or frog, from ME *paddock*, dim. of *pad* (from ON *padda*, apparently from the root *pa(d)* marsh, bog).

Paddon N English: 1. habitation name from some minor place so called, perhaps from OE *pæð* path + *dūn* hill (see DOWN 1).

2. dim. of PATRICK; cf. PATE.

Paderewski E Polish or Ukrainian: habitation name from a place called *Paderew*. The location of this is uncertain, as is the etymology, though this is most likely the same as that of *Padarzewo* in Środa region, i.e. probably from an OPol. personal name *Podarz*.

Var.: W Pol.: **Padarzewski**.

Padfield N English: habitation name from a place in Derbys. (or some other minor place with the same name), so called from the OE personal name *Pad(d)a* (attested, but of disputed origin) + OE *feld* pasture, open country (see FIELD).

Padilla Spanish: habitation name from any of the various minor places, for example in the provinces of Burgos, Guadalajara, and Valladolid, so called from Sp. *padilla* frying-pan, breadpan (L *patella*, a dim. of *patina* shallow dish), a word which was commonly used in the topographical sense of a gentle depression.

Padmore English: 1. habitation name from a place, for example in the parish of Onibury, Shrops., so called from late OE *padde* toad (cf. PADDOCK 2) + OE *mōr* marsh (see MOORE 1).

2. var. of PATMORE.

Padovano Italian (partly Jewish): habitation name from the city of Padua, It. *Padova* (L *Patavium*, of obscure etymology).

Vars.: It.: **Padovan(i)**, **Padoan(i)**, **Paduan(i)**, **Paduano**, **Pavna(i)**. Jewish: **Padova**; **Padover**, **Padawer** (Ashkenazic).

Dims.: It.: **Pavanelli**, **Pavanello**, **Pavanetti**, **Pavanetto**, **Pavanini**.

Pagan N English and Scots: of uncertain origin, probably from a more formal version of the medieval given name *Payne* (see PAIN 1). The name does not occur in this form before the 16th cent., and so probably represents a learned respelling. In America it has often been used as an Anglicization of the Italian surname *Pagano*, itself a cogn. of PAIN 1.

Vars.: **Pagen**, **Pagin**, **Pagon**.

This surname and its vars. are strongly localized in NW England and SW Scotland. However, it is also attested in Devon in the 16th and 17th cents., while the 1634 Heraldic Visitation of London records a certain William Paggin, *whose grandfather came from 'neere Gulick in the Low Countries'.*

Page English and French: occupational name for a young servant, ME, OF *page* (from It. *paggio*, apparently ultimately from Gk *paidion*, dim. of *pais* boy, child). The surname is also common in Ireland, where it has been Gaelicized **Mac Giolla** (see GILL 3).

Vars.: Eng.: **Paige**. Fr.: **Lepage**.

Cogn.: It.: **Paggio**.

Dims.: Eng.: **Paget(t)**, **Padgett**. Fr.: **Pag(en)et**, **Page(n)ot**, **Pajot**, **Pageon**.

Pejs.: Fr.: **Pageard**, **Pageaud**.

Patr.: It.: **Del Paggio**.

A family by the name of Paget, *who hold the marquessate of Anglesey, first became prominent with William Paget (c.1506–63), whose father was said to have been of humble origin from Wednesbury, Staffs. He acquired large estates from Henry VIII on the dissolution of the monasteries. The family also held the title Earl of Uxbridge. This was first granted in 1714, and regranted in 1784 to a relative by marriage, Henry Bayly, who took the name Paget in 1766.*

Pagnol French: ethnic name from an aphetic form of OF *espaignol* Spaniard (L *Hispāniōlus*, from *Hispānia* Spain, a name probably ultimately of Phoenician origin). The It. cogns. were often nicknames referring to people of extreme haughtiness or elegance, which were believed to be characteristics of Spaniards; the painter Giuseppe Maria Crespi (1665–1737) was nicknamed *lo Spagnuolo* because of his foppish dress.

Vars.: **Pagnoul**, **Pagnoux**; **Lespagnol**, **Lespagnoud**, **Lépagnol**, **Lépagneux**.

Cogns.: It.: **Spagn(u)olo**, **Spagnol(i)**, **Spagnul(o)**. Cat.: **Espagnol** (originally applied to Hispano-Goths fleeing northwards from the advancing Moors). Rum.: **Spaniol**. Du.: **Spaans**, **Spanjer**, **Spanjaard**. Pol.: **Hispanski**. Jewish (Ashkenazic): **Spanier(man)** (possibly also in part occupational names from Yid. *shpanyer* brocade).

Dims.: Fr.: **Pagnon**, **Pagnot**. It.: **Spagnoleto**, **Spagnoletti**.

Pej.: Fr.: **Pagnard**.

Paille French: metonymic occupational name for someone who gathered straw or used it to make hats or mattresses, from OF *paille* straw (L *palea*). It may also have been a nickname for someone with straw-coloured hair.

Cogns.: It.: **Pagli(a)**; **Paggia** (Venetia).

Dims.: Eng.: PALLETT. It.: **Pa(gl)ietta**, **Paiola**, **Paiotta**, **Pagliucci**, **Pagliocca**, **Pagliucca**.

Aug.: It.: **Paglione**.

Pejs.: Fr.: **Paillard** (denoting a man who slept on a bed of straw, being too poor to afford anything better; later applied as a general term of abuse for a vagabond or ragamuffin). It.: **Pagliazzi**, **Pagliacci**.

Paillier French: 1. occupational name for someone who gathered or used straw, from an agent deriv. of PAILLE (LL *paleārius*).

2. topographic name for someone who lived near a straw-loft or barn (LL *paleārium*).

Var.: **Pailler**.

Cogns.: Prov.: **Palhier**, **Pa(i)lhié**, **Pailhès**. It.: **Pagliaro**, **Paglia(r)i**, **Paggiaro**, **Paglieri**, **Paiero**. (Of 2 only): Sp.: **Pajares** (also from the numerous places so named). Cat.: **Pallarès** (an adj. deriv. of *Pallars*, a region in the province of Lérida); **Pallàs** (probably from the placename *Pallers*).

Dims.: Fr.: **Pailleret**. It.: **Pagliarolo**, **Pagliaroli**, **Pagliarulo**; **Paggiarin** (Venetia).

Pain 1. English: from a ME given name *Pain(e)*, *Payn(e)* (OF *Paien*, from L *Pāgānus*). The L name is a deriv. of *pāgus* outlying village, and meant at first a rustic, then a civilian as opposed to a soldier, and finally a heathen (one not enrolled in the army of Christ). In spite of its unchristian associations this was a popular name in the early Middle Ages. Some of the Romance cogns. may have originated as topographic names in the original sense 'country-dweller'.

2. French: metonymic occupational name for a baker of bread or for a pantryman (see PANTHER), from OF *pain* bread (L *pānis*).

Vars. (of 1): Eng.: **Pa(i)ne**, **Payn(e)**, **Payen**, **Payan**; PAGAN. (Of 2): Fr.: **Pan(n)ier**, **Pagnier**, **Pagniez**.

Cogns. (of 1): Fr.: **Payen**, **Payan**, **Péan**, **Pacan(t)**. It.: **Pagano**, **Pagan(i)**. Hung.: **Pogány**. (Of 2): Prov.: **Pan**. It.: **Pane**, **Pani**, **Lopane**, **Li Pane**.

Dims. (of 1): Eng.: **Paynell**. Fr.: **Pacandet**. It.: **Paganino**, **Paganin(i)**, **Paganelli**, **Paganetto**, **Paganetti**, **Paganucci**, **Paganuzzi**, **Paganotto**. (Of 2): It.: **Panelli**, **Panello**, **Panetti**, **Pagnotto**, **Panozzo**.

Augs. (of 1): It.: **Paganoni**. (Of 2): It.: **Pagnone**.

Patrs. (from 1): Eng.: **Pa(i)nes**, **Paynes**; **Fitzpayn**.

A certain Thomas Payne, *who was a freeman of the Plymouth Colony in 1639, was the founder of a large American family, which included Robert Treat* Paine *(1731–1814), one of the signatories of the Declaration of Independence.*

Painter English: occupational name for a painter (normally of stained glass), from ME, OF *peinto(u)r*, oblique case of *peintre* (LL *pinctor*, for class. L *pictor*, from *pingere* to paint).
Var.: **Paynter**.
Cogns.: Fr.: **Peintre, Lepeintre, Lepeinteur**. Cat.: **Pintó**.
Dim.: It.: **Pintoricchio**.

Paisley Scots: habitation name from a place in Strathclyde, now a suburb of Glasgow. It is first recorded in 1157 as *Passeleth*, then in 1158 as *Paisleth* and in 1163 as *Passelet*, *Passelay*; it may be derived from LL *basilica* church.

Paiva Portuguese: topographic name for someone living by the river *Paiva* in N Portugal. The river name is recorded in the Middle Ages as *Pavia*, identical in form with the It. town *Pavia* (see PAVEY 2).

Paixão Portuguese: religious byname from Port. *paixão* passion (L *passio*, gen. *passiōnis*, a deriv. of *pati* to suffer), borne in commemoration of Christ's passion, in particular by someone born on Good Friday.

Pajor Polish: nickname for a quarrelsome person, derived from a dial. form of Pol. *pojować* to shout, quarrel.

Pakuła Polish: nickname for someone with tow-coloured hair, or perhaps an occupational name for someone who worked with linen or hemp, from Pol. *pakuły* tow (also called *pacześ*).
Vars.: **Pakulski**; **Pacześ, Paczesny**.

Palacín Spanish: occupational name for someone who was employed at a royal or noble court (cf. COURTIER 1 and HOFFMANN), or nickname for a courteous individual (cf. CURTIS 1 and HÖFLICH). The name is from OSp. *palacin* 'of the palace', the result of a cross between *palatino* and *palaciano* (respectively from L *palātīnus* and LL *palātiānus*, both derivs. of *palātium*; see PALACIO).

Palacio Spanish: topographic name for someone who lived near a royal or noble mansion, or occupational name for someone who was employed in one, from Sp. *palacio* palace, manor, great house (L *palātium*, a vocab. word derived from the *Palātium* or *mons Palātīnus* in Rome (of uncertain etymology), site of the emperor Augustus' golden house).
Vars.: **Palacios**; **Pazos** (Galicia; also from any of the numerous places so called in that region, for example in the provinces of Corunna, Orense, and Pontevedra).
Cogns.: Cat.: **Palau**. Port.: **Passos**. Prov.: **Palais**. It.: **Palazzo, Palazzi**; **Palagi** (Tuscany). Jewish (Sefardic): **Palacci, Pala(t)chi, Palachy, Palache** (possibly not related). Hung.: **Palotai**. Czech: **Palacky**; **Palach**.
Dims.: Cat.: **Palou**. It.: **Palazzetti, Palazzini, Palazzolo, Palazzoli, Palazzotto**.

Pałasz Polish: nickname from Pol. *pałasz* sabre, applied to a fierce or combative individual, or to a soldier.

Palczewski Polish: habitation name from a place called *Palczewo*, named with the element *palec* finger, toe (cf. PALUCH).

Palencia Spanish: habitation name or regional name from the city or region of this name in N Spain, a seat of the Castilian kings during the 12th and 13th cents. It is first recorded in the L forms *Pal(l)antia* and *Pelentia*, and is of uncertain origin.
Cogn.: Jewish (Sefardic): **Palensya**.

Palermi Italian: habitation name from the Sicilian town of *Palermo*, an ancient Phoenician foundation of uncertain etymology.
Var. (also in part Jewish): **Palermo**.

Palethorpe English (Notts.): apparently a habitation name from an unidentified place, the second element of which is ON *þorp* settlement (see THORPE). The first may be the personal name **Pal(l)a*, which Ekwall postulates as an etymon for PALGRAVE in Suffolk.

Paley 1. English: of uncertain origin, probably a habitation name from an unidentified place in Yorks.
2. Jewish (Ashkenazic): of unknown origin.
The English theologian and philosopher William Paley *(1743–1805) was born in Peterborough, but his forebears had been settled for generations on a small estate at Longcliffe in Yorks.*

Palfrey English: metonymic occupational name for a man responsible for the maintenance and provision of saddle-horses, from ME *palfrey* saddle-horse (OF *palefrei*, from LL *paraverēdus*, a cpd of Gk *para* beside + Gaul. *verēd* (light) horse; the L term has also given mod. Ger. *Pferd* horse).
Vars.: **Palfery, Parf(f)rey**; **Palfre(y)man, Palfreeman, Palphreyman, Palframan, Parfrement**.
Cogn.: Fr.: **Palfrène**.

Palgrave English (E Anglia): habitation name from places so called in Norfolk and Suffolk, both of rather doubtful, but clearly distinct, etymology. *Palgrave* in Suffolk appears in Domesday Book as *Palegraua* and is most likely so called from the gen. pl. of OE *pāl* pole + *grāf* grove, though Ekwall also suggests that a personal name, **Pal(l)a*, may underlie the first element. Great and Little *Palgrave* in Norfolk consistently lack the *-l-* in early forms (Domesday Book *Pag(g)raua*), and the first element may be from a personal name of the problematical group discussed at PACKHAM.
Pagrave *occurs in Norfolk as a locative surname in the 12th cent., and is well established as the family name of a powerful and influential Norfolk family, lords of the manor of this place, from the 14th cent. onwards. Bearers of the surname were established at North Barmingham from 1508. The spelling of their surname had changed to* Palgrave *by the end of the 16th cent. Palgrave in Suffolk occurs as a family name from the 14th cent.*

Pałka Polish: from Pol. *pałka* truncheon, club, used as a nickname applied either to a thin, stiff person, or to one renowned for his use of the truncheon.
Habitation name: **Pałczynski**.

Pallejà Catalan: habitation name from a place in the province of Barcelona, so called from LL *Palladiānus (fundus)* estate of *Palladius*, a personal name derived from Gk *Pallas*, gen. *Pallados*, an epithet of the goddess Athene (of unknown origin, probably originally the name of a distinct but obscure goddess).

Pallett English: metonymic occupational name for a maker of straw mattresses or nickname for someone who slept on one (i.e. someone who could not afford a better bed), from ME, OF *pa(i)llet* heap of straw, straw mattress, a dim. of PAILLE straw.

Palliser English: occupational name for a maker of paling and fences, from an agent deriv. of OF *pal(e)is* palisade (from LL *pālicium*, a deriv. of *pālus* stake, pole).
Vars.: **Pal(l)ister, Palser**; **Pallis**.
Cogns.: Fr.: **Paly(s)**.

Pallu French: topographic name for someone who lived near a marsh or fen, OF *palu* (L *palūs*), or habitation name from any of the numerous minor places named with this word.

Vars.: **Palu(t)**, **Palud**; **Lapalu(e)**, **Lapalud**, **Lapalus**.

Dim.: **Paluel**.

Aug.: **Paluat**.

Palmer English: nickname for someone who had been on a pilgrimage to the Holy Land, ME, OF *palmer*, *paumer* (from *palme*, *paume* palm tree, L *palma*). Such pilgrims generally brought back a palm branch as proof that they had actually made the journey, but there was a vigorous trade in false souvenirs, and the term also came to be applied to a cleric who sold indulgences. Some of the European cogns. may also be topographic names referring to dwellers near a palm tree or grove.

Vars.: **Palmar**, **Paumier**; **Palmes**.

Cogns.: Fr.: **Pau(l)mier**. It.: **(De) Palma**; **Palm(i)eri**, **Palmiero**, **Palmerio**, **Parmiero**, **Parmieri**. Sp.: **Palma**; **Palmero**. Cat.: **Palmés**, **Palmer**. Port.: **Palma**; **Palmeiro**. Flem., Du.: **Palm(en)**, **Van der Palme**. Norw., Dan.: **Palm**. Swed.: **Palm(e)**, **Palmér**. Russ.: **Palmov** (surname adopted by Orthodox priests, patr. only in form).

Dims.: It.: **Palmerin(i)**, **Palm(er)ucci**.

Cpds (ornamental): Swed.: **Palmberg** ('palm hill'); **Palmgren** ('palm branch'). Jewish (Ashkenazic): **Palmenbaum** ('palm tree'); **Palmholz** ('palm wood').

A family called Palmer *trace their ancestry to Ralph Palmer (d. 1559), who lived in Marston, Staffs. They have been earls of Selbourne since 1882.*

A family of the name of Palmes *trace their ancestry to Manfred Palmes, who was granted lands in Somerset by Milo, Earl of Hereford, in the 12th cent.*

Palomar Spanish: habitation name from any of the numerous places so called, from Sp. *palomar* pigeon loft, dovecot (LL *palumbāre*, a deriv. of *palumbus* pigeon; see PALOMO).

Var.: **Palomares**.

Palomo Spanish: nickname for a mild and inoffensive individual, or metonymic occupational name for a keeper of pigeons, from Sp. *palomo* pigeon (LL *palumbus*, class. L *palumbēs*). The It. cogn. also has dial. meanings 'butterfly' and 'dogfish', and it is possible that in some cases the nickname has one of these senses.

Var.: **Palomero** (occupational).

Cogns.: It.: **Palombo**, **Palombi**, **Palomba**; **Palumbo** (Naples); **Palumb(i)eri** (occupational). Port.: **Pombo**. Prov.: **Palomer** (occupational). Rum.: **Porumbe**. Jewish (Sefardic): **Palom(b)o**.

Dims.: Sp.: **Palomino**. It.: **Palombella**, **Palombino**, **Palombini**.

Paluch Polish: nickname from Pol. *paluch* thumb (augmentative of *palec* finger). This was used to denote a small person or a dwarf, although it may also have been applied to someone with a deformed or missing thumb.

Cogn.: Czech: **Paleček**.

Patr. (from a dim.): Pol.: **Paluszkiewicz**.

Habitation name: Pol.: **Paluszewski**.

Pamies Catalan: habitation name from *Pamiers* in Ariège, S France, so called from med. L *castrum Appamiae*, a name given to it in the 12th cent. by its lord, Roger II of Foix, in memory of the town of *Apamea* in Syria, where he had fought in the 1st Crusade.

Vars.: **Pàmies**, **Pamias**.

Panadés Catalan: of uncertain origin, probably a habitation name from *Penedès*, a region in the province of Tarragona. The placename probably derives from LL **pinnētense*, a deriv. of **pinnētum*, itself a collective of L *pinna* rock, crag (see PEÑA).

Panek Polish: nickname from a dim. of Pol. *pan* master, used either affectionately, in the sense 'little master', or contemptuously, in the sense 'lordling'.

Var.: **Panas** (not dim.).

Cogns.: Ger. (of Slav. origin): PANK. Czech: **Pánek** (possibly also from the given name *Štěpán*; see STEPHEN).

Patrs.: Pol.: **Pankiewicz**; **Panasewicz** (not dim.). Russ.: **Panov**.

Habitation name: Pol.: **Pankowski**.

Paniagua Spanish: ostensibly a nickname from Sp. *pan y agua* bread and water (L *panis et aqua*), maybe denoting a poor man unable to afford a better diet, or else a miser. It seems more likely, however, that the name is an alteration by folk etymology of the OSp. occupational term *apaniguado* servant, retainer (from the past part. of *apaniguar* to provide bread for, LL *appānificāre*, a deriv. of *pānis* bread; cf. PAIN 2).

Panizo Spanish: metonymic occupational name for a grower or seller of millet, panic grass, or topographic name for someone who lived by a field devoted to the crop, Sp. *panizo* (LL *panīcium*, class. L *panīcum*).

Pank 1. English: from a short form of the medieval given name *Pancras*; see PANKRIDGE.

2. German (of Slav. origin): cogn. of PANEK.

Vars. (of 2): **Pa(h)nke**.

Pankhurst English: the conventional explanation of this name, put forward by Reaney and others, is that it is a var. of PENTECOST, with late assimilation to the local ending *-hurst* (see HURST). However, McKinley has gathered evidence that suggests that it is a habitation name, probably from *Pinkhurst* in Sussex or Surrey. The Sussex place called *Pankhurst* is said to be derived from the surname *Pentecost*, and the hypothesis that it is derived from a surname rather than vice versa is supported by the absence of early forms.

Pankridge English: from the medieval given name *Pancras*, the vernacular form of L *Pancratius* (Gk *Pankratios*, from *pankratēs* all-in wrestler, from *pan* all, every + *kratein* to conquer, subdue, re-analysed by early Christians as meaning 'Almighty' and thus a suitable epithet of Christ). The name was fairly popular in England during the Middle Ages, for in the 7th cent. the relics of an early martyr of this name had been sent to England by the Pope.

Var.: **Panckridge**.

Cogns.: Ger.: **Pankra(t)z**, **Ponkratz**, **Bankratz**, **Bangratz**, **Bongratz**; **Baumkratz** (altered by folk etymological assocation with mod. Ger. *Baum* tree + *kratzen* to scratch). Hung.: **Pongrác(z)**.

Dims.: Eng.: PANK. Ger.: **Kratz** (Latinized as **Kratius**), **Krätzel**. Low Ger.: **Kratzke**, **Kratzmann**.

Patrs.: Ger.: **Pankrazer**. Russ.: **Pankratov**, **Pankratyev**.

Patrs. (from dims.): Ger.: **Kretzing**, **Kratzig**. Russ.: **Pankrushin**, **Pankeev**.

'Son of the wife of P.': Russ.: **Panchishin**.

Pantaleone Italian: from a given name (Gk *Panteleiōn*, from *pas*, gen. *pantos*, all, every + *eleiōn*, pres. part. of *eleein* to forgive, pardon, have mercy). This name was borne by a saint martyred under Diocletian, perhaps at Nicomedia, and regarded as a patron of physicians, having allegedly been one himself. He was honoured in the East as early as the 5th cent., but his cult did not reach the West until the 11th cent., when he was adopted as the patron of

Venice. In the 14th cent. the name was used for a character in the Harlequinade, a foolish old Venetian, and in some later cases the surname may have arisen as a nickname referring to this character. It was from his typical costume that the term *pantaloon(s)* came to be used of a type of loose-fitting breeches, whence the mod. Eng. short form *pants*.

Vars.: **Pantaleo, Pantalone, Pantaloni, Pantele(on)i.**

Cogns.: Ger.: **Pantle(o)n, Bantleon.**

Dims.: Ger.: **Pant(e)l, Pantele, Bantele, Bentele, Bentlin; Bantli** (Switzerland). Low Ger.: **Pantelmann.** Albanian: **Panshi, Pançi.**

Patrs.: Croatian: **Pantelić, Pant(ov)ić.** Bulg.: **Pantleev.**

Patr. (from a dim.): Bulg.: **Pantchev.**

Panther English: 1. occupational name for a servant in charge of the supply of bread and other provisions in a monastery or large household, from ME *panter* (OF *panetier*, from LL *pānitārius*, an expansion of *pānārius*, from *pānis* bread; see PAIN 2).

2. perhaps also a house name from a house bearing the sign of a panther (OF *panthère*, via L from Gk *panthēr*, which was taken in the ancient world to be a cpd of Gk *pan* all, every + *thēr* beast, but more probably represents an independent IE word; cf. Skt *pundarika* tiger).

Cogns.: Fr.: **Pan(n)etier, Pennetier.** It.: **Panattieri.** Sp.: **Panadero.**

Panton English: habitation name from a place in Lincs., for which Ekwall suggests derivation from an unattested OE word **pamp* hill, ridge + OE *tūn* enclosure, settlement.

Panzer 1. German: metonymic occupational name for an armourer, from MHG *panzi(e)r* coat of mail (from OF *pancier* stomach, armour for the stomach, body armour, LL *panticiārium*, from L *pantices* bowels; cf. PAUNCEFOOT).

2. Jewish (Ashkenazic): of unknown origin.

Vars. (of 1): **Panzner; Ban(t)zer** (S Germany).

Papa Italian: nickname from It. *papa* father, priest, pope. In S Italy it is generally a nickname for someone thought to resemble a priest, or in some cases for the illegitimate child of a priest, but in the North it is more often a nickname meaning POPE, denoting a vain or pompous man.

Var.: **Lo Papa.**

Cogn.: Fr., Eng., and Low Ger.: **Pape.**

Dim.: It.: **Papotto.**

Pejs.: S It.: **Papaccio, Papazzo.**

Papillon French and English: nickname for a dainty or inconstant person, from OF *papillon* butterfly (L *papilio*, gen. *papiliōnis*).

Vars.: Fr.: **Parp(a)illon.**

Cogns.: Prov.: **Parpalhol, Perpillou.**

Pejs.: Fr.: **Papillard, Papillaud.**

Papillon *is the name of a Huguenot family descended from Thomas Papillon (d. 1608). He was captain of the guard to Henry IV of France, but because of religious persecution was forced to send his wife and family to England in 1588. They were shipwrecked, and only his two sons survived to become established in England, where descendants live to the present day.*

Papot French: nickname from OF *paper* to munch, eat (LL *pappāre*, in origin a nursery word). The sense of the nickname is not entirely clear, but it may have been given originally to a glutton. The form **Papin** also had the meaning 'pap' or 'pulp', and may have denoted a toothless old man incapable of taking more solid nourishment; **Papon** also meant 'grandfather', 'old man', perhaps for the same reason, or as an independent nursery formation from *papa* father.

Cogns.: It.: **Pappa.** Ger.: **Papp** (Bavaria); **Bapp** (Swabia).

Dims.: Fr.: **Papineau, Papinot, Papponeau, Paponnot.**

Aug.: It.: **Pappone.**

Paprocki Polish: topographic name for someone who lived in a place where ferns grew in abundance, from Pol. *paproć* fern + *-ski* suffix of (originally) local surnames (see BARANOWSKI).

Cogn.: Czech: **Paprotny.**

Papworth English: habitation name from a place in Cambs., so called from an OE personal name *Papa* + OE *worð* enclosure (see WORTH).

Paquet French: 1. dim. of the Fr. given name *Pascal* (see PASCALL).

2. metonymic occupational name for a gatherer or seller of firewood or kindling, from OF *pacquet* bundle (of faggots), dim. of *paque* parcel (from MDu.; cf. PACKER).

Vars.: **Paquette** (fem.); **Pacquet, Paquot, Paquin.**

Dims.: **Paqueteau, Paquetot, Pacteau, Pactot.**

Paquier French: topographic name for someone who lived near a piece of land used for (communal) grazing, OF *pasquier* (LL *pascuārium*, from *pascere* to graze), or habitation name from a place named with this word.

Vars.: **Pasquier, Pasquié; Pasquer** (Brittany); **Dupa(s)quier.**

Dims.: **Paquereau.** Prov.: **Pascarel.**

Paradowski Polish: nickname for a swaggerer, from Pol. *paradować* to swagger (from *parada* parade, display) + *-ski* suffix of surnames (see BARANOWSKI).

Páramo Spanish: topographic name for someone who lived on a patch of waste land or a bare plateau, Sp. *páramo* (found in the LL of the peninsula as *paramus*, but of uncertain origin). The surname may also be a habitation name from one of the places, for example in the provinces of Lugo and Oviedo, named with this element.

Parant 1. French: occupational name for someone involved in the finishing stages of some manufacturing process, from OF *parant*, pres. part. of *parer* to prepare, make ready (L *parāre*; cf. PARMENTER).

2. English and French: var. of PARENT.

Vars. (of 1): **Paran** (also Jewish, of unknown origin; cf. PARENT); **Paraire.**

Dim.: **Paranteau.**

Pardal 1. Portuguese: nickname for someone supposedly resembling a sparrow, presumably a small or chirpy person or one of tawny colouring, from Port. *pardal* sparrow, a deriv. of the adj. *pardo* (see PARDO), referring to the colour of the bird.

2. Jewish: of unknown origin.

Pardo 1. Spanish and Portuguese: nickname for someone with tawny hair, from *pardo* dusky, brown, dark grey (from L *pardus* leopard; in LL this word was joined with the more familiar term *leo* lion to yield the word *leopardus* (see LEPPARD) and the second element, *-pardus*, was taken to be a distinguishing adj. referring to the dark spots and so acquired the status of an independent vocab. element).

2. Jewish: of unknown origin.

Pardoe English: nickname from a favourite oath, OF *par Dieu* by God (LL *de parte Dei* for God's sake), which was adopted into ME in a variety of more or less mangled forms.

Vars.: **Pardew, Pard(e)y, Perdue.** See also PURDY.

Cogns.: Fr.: **Pa(r)dieu, Depardieu, Depardé.**

Paredes Spanish and Portuguese: topographic name for someone who lived in a lean-to built up against the wall of a larger building, from *pared* (house) wall (L *paries*, gen. *parietis*). Servants often lived in buildings of this sort outside manor houses, and masons constructed huts of this kind on the site of their labours, making temporary use of the walls of the new building. There are also a large number of places named with this word, and the surname may also be a habitation name from any of these.

Cogns.: It.: **Pareti, Pareto.**

Parejo Spanish: nickname for a companion or partner in an enterprise, Sp. *parejo* (LL *pāriculus*, a dim. of class. L *pār* equal, like; cf. PEAR 2). The fem. form **Pareja** meant 'wife', and may have denoted a woman who managed the affairs of a household in the absence of her husband.

Parellada Catalan: habitation name from any of various minor places so called, from the name of a measure of land, originally the amount that could be ploughed in a day by a pair of oxen (a deriv. of *parell* pair, from LL *pāriculus*; cf. PAREJO).

Parent English and French: 1. nickname from ME, OF *parent* parent, relative (L *parens*, gen. *parentis*, pres. part. of *parere* to give birth, be a parent), referring to someone who was related to an important member of the community.

2. nickname for someone of striking or imposing appearance, from ME, OF *parent* notable, impressive (L *pārens*, gen. *pārentis*, pres. part. of *pārēre* to appear, seem).

Vars.: Eng.: **Parrent, Parrant,** PARANT.

Cogns. (of 1): It.: **Parenti, Parente** (also Jewish, of unknown origin; cf. PARANT). Sp.: **Pariente** (also Jewish, of unknown origin). Port.: **Parente.**

Dims.: Fr.: **Parentin, Parenteau.**

Pej.: Fr.: **Parentaud.**

Parfitt English: nickname, probably originally denoting an apprentice who had completed his period of training, from ME *parfit* fully trained, well versed (OF *parfit(e)* complete(d), from L *perfectus*, past part. of *perficere* to finish, accomplish). For the change of *-er-* to *-ar-*, cf. MARCHANT. The mod. Eng. vocab. word *perfect* is a learned recoinage from L.

Vars.: **Parf(a)it, Parfect, Perfitt, Perfett, Perfect.**

Pargetter English: occupational name for a (decorative) plasterer, an agent deriv. of OF *pargeter*, *parjeter* to plaster, daub (from *par* (all) over, L *per* + *jeter* to throw, cast, L *iactāre*). Pargetting is a style of house decoration particularly common in E Anglia.

Vars.: **Pargeter, Pargiter.**

Parham English: habitation name from places in Suffolk and Sussex, so called from OE *pere* PEAR + *hām* homestead. For the change of *-er-* to *-ar-*, cf. MARCHANT.

Var.: **Parram.** See also PARNHAM, PERHAM.

Parish English: 1. local name for someone from the French capital, *Paris*, the name of which is derived from that of a Gaul. tribe, recorded in L sources as the *Parisii*; the original meaning of the tribal name cannot even be guessed at.

2. from the rare medieval given name *Paris*, probably in origin an OF form of PATRICK, but associated with the name of the Trojan prince *Paris*, which has been speculatively traced to an original Illyrian form *Voltuparis* or *Assoparis* 'Hawk'.

This, the most common form of the name in Eng., is the result of confusion between *-s* and *-sh* (cf. NORRIS) reinforced by folk etymological association with the mod. Eng. vocab. word *parish* (ME *parosse*, *paroche*, *parissche*, from OF *paroisse*, Gk *paroikia*). In the 17th and 18th cents. the surname was occasionally bestowed on foundlings brought up at the expense of the parish.

Vars.: **Parrish, Par(r)is.**

Cogns. (of 1): Fr.: **Par(r)is,** PARRY; **Parisy, Parizy** (under the influence of the Latin genitive form). It.: **Paris(i), Parissi, Paris(s)e, Paris(i)o, Parigi; Parisiani.** Ger.: **Pari(e)s, Pareis, Bareis; Pariser; Par(r)isius** (Latinized). Flem., Du.: **Van Parijs.** Jewish (Ashkenazic): **Pari(e)ser, Pariz(er).**

Dims. (of 1): Fr.: **Parisel, Parizel, Pariset, Parizet, Parisot, Parizot, Parigot.** It.: **Parisini, Parigini, Parisotti.**

Pejs. (of 1): It.: **Parisato, Parisatti.**

Pařízek Czech: habitation name from a place so called near Sobotka, which derives its name from Czech *pařez* tree stump.

Park English: 1. metonymic occupational name for someone employed in a park (ME, OF *parc*, of Gmc origin; cf. PADDOCK 1), or topographic name for someone who lived in or near a park. In the Middle Ages a park was a large enclosed area where the landowner could hunt game; cf. FORREST.

2. dim. of PETER, a back-formation from PARKIN.

Vars.: **Parke.** (Of 1 only): **Parrock, Parruck, Parrack** (from cogn. vocab. words).

Cogns. (of 1): Fr.: **Duparc(q).**

Dims. (of 1): Fr.: **Parquet, Parquin.**

Patrs. (from 2): Eng.: **Park(e)s, Perks.**

'Servant of P. 2': Eng.: **Parkman.**

Parker 1. English: occupational name for a gamekeeper employed in a medieval park, from a ME agent deriv. of PARK 1.

2. Jewish: presumably an Anglicization of one or more like-sounding Jewish names.

Cogn. (of 1): Fr.: **Parquier.**

A family called Parker *have been established for centuries in Lancs.; Browsholme Hall, near Clitheroe, was first built by Richard* le Parker *in 1380, and is still the family seat. The name is extremely widespread; another well-known family are established in Ches., where their ancestors were keepers of a royal park.*

Parkhill Scots and N Irish: habitation name from a place in the barony of Tarbolton in the former county of Ayrs., presumably a cpd of PARK 1 + HILL.

Parkhouse English: topographic name for someone who lived in a warden's lodge in a park; see PARK 1 and HOUSE.

Parkin English: from the ME given name *Perkin*, *Parkin*, a dim. of PETER with the hypocoristic suffix *-kin*; for the change of *-er-* to *-ar-*, cf. MARCHANT.

Vars.: **Parkyn; Perkin, Perken.**

Patrs.: **Parkins** (also Jewish, presumably an Anglicization of one or more like-sounding Jewish names); **Perkins, Purkins; Parkinson.**

The form Parkin *is commonest in Northumb., Yorks., and the E Midlands;* Parkinson *is widespread, but is very much more frequent in Lancs. than elsewhere.* Perkins *is also widespread, esp. in Kent and the Midlands.*

Parley English and Scots: habitation name from any of various places, for example E and W *Parley* on the Hants-Dorset borders, north of Bournemouth, so called from OE *pere* PEAR + *lēah* wood, clearing.

Vars.: **Parly, Parlie.**

The earliest known bearer of the name is John Parlee *of Lavenham, Suffolk, who died in 1505. The name is largely concentrated in*

Notts. and NE Scotland, from where it was taken to Canada. One family by the name of Parley *are descended from an E Ashkenazic Jew who settled in London in the late 19th cent., but the reason for the selection of the name in this case is not known.*

Parmenter English: occupational name for a maker of facings and trimmings, ME, OF *par(e)mentier* (from *parement* fitting, finishing, LL *parāmentum*, a deriv. of *parāre* to prepare, adorn; cf. PARANT 1).

Vars.: **Parmi(n)ter, Parmeter, Pammenter.**

Cogns.: Fr.: **Parmentier, Parmantier.** It.: **Palminteri.** Jewish (Ashkenazic): **Pas(s)man, Pasmant(ir)er.**

Dims.: Fr.: **Parmentel(ot).** Jewish (E Ashkenazic): **Pas(s)manik.**

Parnell English: from the medieval female given name *Parnell*, a vernacular form of L *Petrōnilla*. This is a dim. of *Petrōnia*, fem. of *Petrōnius*, a Roman family name of uncertain, probably Etruscan, etymology. It was borne by an early Roman martyr about whom very little of historical value is known; a 6th-cent. biography makes her a daughter of St PETER, no doubt as a result of folk etymological association of their names.

Vars.: **Parnall, Parnwell; Purnell** (Gloucs. and Somerset); **Pennell, Pennall.**

Cogns.: Fr.: **Pernelle, Perron(n)elle.** Ger.: **Peternell.**

Dim.: Eng.: PENN.

An Irish family named Parnell *originated in Congleton, Ches.; the title Baron Congleton was selected in 1841 because of this connection. They were established in Ireland after the Restoration, having been prominent supporters of Parliament in the Civil War. Charles Stewart Parnell (1846–91), leader of the Irish Home Rule movement, was a member of this family.*

Parnes Jewish (Ashkenazic): occupational name for the president of a Jewish community, Yid. *parnes* (from Hebr. *parnas*).

Var.: **Parness** (often stressed on the final syllable, under the influence of Eng. words such as *duress* and *caress*); **Parnas(s)** (from the Hebr. form), **Parnasz** (Hung. spelling).

Parnham English: habitation name from a place in Dorset, so called from OE *peren*, adj. from *pere* PEAR + *hām* homestead.

Parr 1. English: habitation name from a place in Lancs., so called from OE **pearr* enclosure (a dim. of which is reflected in PADDOCK 1 and PARK 1).

2. Low German: from MLG *parre* parish, district, perhaps a nickname for a foundling. According to Ekwall, this word is cogn. with the one in 1 above, and has no connection with mod. Eng. *parish* (see PARISH).

Parra Spanish and Catalan: topographic name for someone who lived by an enclosure with some form of trellis or interwoven fencing, OSp., OCat. *parra* (mod. Sp., Cat. *parra* trellis, arbour, vine; the word is of uncertain, possibly Gmc, origin; cf. PARR 1). There are also numerous places named with this word, from which the surname may also derive as a habitation name.

Var.: Sp.: **Parras.**

Cogn.: Port.: **Parreira.**

Dim.: Sp.: **Parrilla** (in part from places so named in the provinces of Cadiz, Córdoba, Málaga, and Valladolid).

Parramon Catalan: from a contracted form of the given names *Pere* (see PETER) + *Ramon* (see RAYMOND).

Parrott English: 1. from a ME given name which took various forms — *Perot, Parot, Paret*, etc., all dims. of PETER. The talking bird seems to get its name from this (cf. the *robin* from a dim. of ROBERT; also the *jackdaw* and *magpie*), but it was not so called until the 16th cent., rather too late to have given rise to a surname. (For names derived from the earlier term for a parrot, see POBGEE.)

2. habitation name from N and S *Perrott* in Somerset, which take their name from the river *Parret* on which they stand. This is of unknown origin.

Vars. (of 1): Eng.: **Parrot, Parret(t), Parratt; Perot(t), Peret(t)** (chiefly Somerset); **Perrat.**

Cogns. (of 1): Fr.: **Pierrot, Perr(i)ot, Peyrot, Pérot; P(i)erret, Pierrez, Pierrey, Péret, Perrès.** It.: **Pe(t)rotto, Pedrotto, Pierotto, Pir(r)otti, Rotti; Pedretti, P(i)eretti, Perretti, Peiretti, Per(r)etto.**

Dims. (of 1): Fr.: **Perrotin, Perroton, Perroteau.** It.: **Pedrotini, Rotellini; Petrettini, Pierettini.**

Parry 1. Welsh: patr., with a reduced form of the W element *ap*, from the given name HARRY.

2. French: cogn. of PARISH 1.

Vars. (of 1): BARRY; **Pend(r)y, Bend(r)y** (from W *ap* HENDRY).

Parslow English (Norman): nickname from an OF phrase composed of the elements *passe(r)* to pass, cross (LL *passāre*, from *passus* step, pace) + *l'ewe* the water (L *(illa) aqua*). The nickname probably at first denoted a merchant who was in the habit of travelling overseas, or else someone who had been on a pilgrimage or crusade; but it may also have been used as a topographic name for someone who lived on the opposite side of a watercourse from the main settlement (cf. PASSMORE).

Vars.: **Parsloe, Paslow, Pa(r)sley,** PASHLEY.

Cogns.: Prov.: **Passeligue, Passelègue, Passelergue.** It.: **Passalacqua.**

The manor of the village of Drayton Parslow in Bucks. is recorded in Domesday Book as being held by Rafe Passacquam, *a L form of the name.*

Parsonage English: topographic name for someone who lived at or by a parson's house, from ME, OF *personage* benefice, living, hence the house and estate held by a parson.

Parsons English: 1. occupational name for the servant of a parish priest or parson, or patr. denoting the child of a parson, from the possessive case of ME *persone, parsoun* (OF *persone*, from L *persōna* person, character). The reasons for the semantic shift from 'person' to 'priest' are not certain; the most plausible explanation is that the local priest was regarded as the representative person of the parish. For the change of *-er-* to *-ar-*, cf. MARCHANT. See also MCPHERSON.

2. Many early examples are found with prepositions (e.g. Ralph *del Persones* 1323); these are habitation names, with the omission of *house*, in effect occupational names for servants employed at the PARSONAGE.

Members of an Irish family called Parsons *were twice created Earl of Rosse; first in 1718, and again in 1806. They settled in Ireland c.1590, when two brothers, William and Laurence Parsons, were granted large estates. Birr Castle, Parsonstown, became the family seat.*

Partanen Finnish: patr. from the nickname *Parta* 'Beard'.

Partington English (Lancs.): habitation name from a place in Greater Manchester, so called from OE *Peartingtūn* 'settlement (OE *tūn*) associated with **Pearta*', a personal name not independently recorded.

Parton English (chiefly W Midlands): habitation name from any of various places so called, which mostly get the name from OE *peretūn* pear orchard (a cpd of *pere* pear + *tūn* enclosure; cf. APPLETON), with later change of *-er-* to

-*ar*- (cf. MARCHANT). There are examples in Gloucs., two in Cumb., and one in Scotland; the last gets its name from Gael. *portan*, a dim. of *port* harbour (see PORT). The distribution of the surname makes it probable that in most cases it is from the place in Gloucs.

Partridge 1. English: from ME *pertriche* partridge (OF *perdriz*, from L *perdix*, gen. *perdicis*), either a metonymic occupational name for a hunter of the bird, or a nickname from some fancied resemblance, or a house name for someone living in a house distinguished by the sign of a partridge. For the change of -*er*- to -*ar*-, cf. MARCHANT.

2. Irish and English: var. of PATRICK.

Vars.: **Partriche, Partrick.**

Cogns. (of 1): Fr.: **Perdrix; Perdriguier** (occupational). Prov.: **Perdiguès** (occupational). Port.: **Perdigão.**

Dims. (of 1): Fr.: **Perdrizet, Perdrizot, Perdrig(e)on, Perdriget.**

Parviainen Finnish: habitation name for someone who lived in an upper storey or in a house with an upper storey, from Finn. *parvi* garret, attic, with the addition of the locative suffix -*ainen*.

Pascall English: from the medieval given name *Pascal* (L *Paschālis*, from *pascha* Easter, via Gk and Aramaic from Hebr. *pesach* Passover; cf. PEISACH). The name was introduced into England from France; it was popular throughout Catholic Europe, mainly in honour of the festival of Christ's crucifixion and resurrection, but also in honour of a 9th-cent. pope and saint who had borne the name.

Vars.: **Paskell, Pasquill.**

Cogns.: Fr.: **Pasc(h)al, Pascau(d), Pascau(l)t, Pasqual, Pascual.** It.: **Pasquali, Pasquale, Pascali, Pascale.** Sp.: **Pascual.** Port.: **Pascoal.** Jewish: **Pascal, Paskal(ski)** (the reason for the adoption of these names is not known; cf. PASK).

Dims.: Eng.: **Pass(e).** Fr.: **Pascalin, Pasquelin, Pascot, Pasquet, Pasquez;** PAQUET. It.: **Pasqualini, Pasqualino, Pascalino, Pasqualetto, Pasqualetti, Pascaletto, Pasqualotto; Quarello.**

Pej.: Fr.: **Pasquard.**

Patrs.: It.: **De Pasquale, (De) Pasqualis, Pascalis.** Rum.: **Pasculesco.**

Blaise Pascal *(1623–62), the French philosopher and mathematician, was born in Clermont-Ferrand, where his father was president of the tax court.*

Pascoe English (Cornwall): from the medieval given name PASK, with -*oe*, -*ow* as a hypocoristic suffix.

Var.: **Pascow.**

Pashley English: 1. habitation name from a place in the parish of Ticehurst, Sussex, so called from an OE personal name **Pæcca* (related to **Pacca*; see PACKHAM) + OE *lēah* wood, clearing. A district of Eastbourne bearing this name derives it from the surname; a family so called had moved there from Ticehurst by the later part of the 13th cent.

2. possibly also a var. of PARSLOW. The surname is now chiefly common in S Yorks, which would anyway raise a question mark over its derivation from a Sussex place-name.

Pask English: nickname for someone who was born at Easter, or had some other particular connection with that time of year, such as owing a feudal obligation then, from ME *paske* Easter (OF *pasque*, L *pascua*, earlier *pascha* (cf. PASCALL); the altered form seems to be the result of association with L *pascuum* pasture (cf. PASTOR)). *Pask*, *Pash*, and *Pack* were sometimes used as vernacular given names in medieval England, equivalent to PASCALL.

Vars.: **Paske, Pasque; Pash(e), Paish** (from the byform *pasche*, L *pascha*).

Cogns.: Fr.: **Pasque(s).** It.: **Pasqua, Pasqui, Pasca, Pasco, Paschi.** Port.: **Páscoa.** Low Ger.: **Paasch(e), Pasche(n), Pas(ch)dag.** Flem., Du.: **Paschen.** Dan.: **Påske, Paaske.** Jewish: **Pasca, Paska** (reason(s) for adoption unknown; it may have to do with the time of year at which the surname was registered).

Dims.: Eng.: **Paskin** (W Midlands); **Patchett, Patchin(g).** It.: **Pasquelli, Pasquetti, Paschetti, Paschetto, Pasquino, Paschini, Pasquin(ell)i, Pascucci, Pascuzzi, Pascuzzo, Pasquinucci, Pasquinuzzi, Pascutti, Pascutto, Pasquotti, Pascotti, Pascullo, Pascol(ett)i, Pascolo, Pascolini, Pascolutti.**

Pejs.: It.: **Pasquazzo, Pasquato, Pasquati.**

Patrs.: Eng.: **Pakes.** It.: **Di Pasqua.**

'Servant of P.': Eng.: PACKMAN, **Paxmann.**

Passenger English: nickname for a traveller (until the 19th cent., the vocab. word *passenger* denoted one who travelled on foot as well as one carried on horseback or in a carriage), from ME, OF *passager* (a deriv. of *passage* journey, LL *passāticum*, from *passāre* to proceed, go, cross; cf. PARSLOW and PASSMORE). For the intrusive -*n*-, cf. MESSENGER. The name was applied to an itinerant merchant or workman who did not stop long in any community, but was always just passing through.

Passmore English (chiefly Devon and Somerset): 1. nickname from ME *pass(en)* to pass, go across (LL *passāre*; cf. PASSENGER) + *more* marsh, fen (see MOORE 1), bestowed no doubt on someone who lived on the far side of a tract of moorland near the main settlement, or on someone who was familiar with the safe routes across a moor.

2. several early forms have -*e*- in place of -*o*- in the second syllable, and may have a different origin. They could represent an ANF nickname *Passemer*, from *passe(r)* to cross (as above) + *mer* sea, ocean (L *mare*), similar in significance to PARSLOW, or the second element could be from OE *mere* lake, marsh.

Var.: **Pasmore.**

Passy French: habitation name from any of the numerous places so called from the Gallo-Roman personal name *Paccius* + the local suffix -*ācum*.

Pasternak Polish, Ukrainian, Russian, and Jewish (E Ashkenazic): from Pol., Ukr., Russ., and E Yid. *pasternak* parsnip (MHG *pastinake*, from L *pastināca*), apparently a nickname or arbitrarily adopted surname taken from the plant. In the case of the Jewish name, this is one of the many ornamental names based on words denoting plants.

Vars.: **Pasternack, Pastinack.**

Paston English: habitation name from any of several places so called. Examples in Norfolk and Northants apparently get the name from OE *pæsc(e)* puddle, pool + *tūn* enclosure, settlement; one in Northumb. is OE *Pallocestūn* 'settlement of **Palloc*', an otherwise unattested personal name.

Pastor 1. English, French, Spanish, and Catalan: occupational name for a shepherd (ANF *pastre* (oblique case *pastour*), Sp., Cat. *pastor*, from L *pastor*, an agent deriv. of *pascere* to graze (trans.)). The religious sense of a spiritual leader was rare in the Middle Ages, and insofar as it occurs at all seems always to be a conscious metaphor; it is unlikely, therefore, that this sense lies behind any examples of the surname.

2. German and Dutch: Latinized form of various vernacular terms meaning 'shepherd' (cf., e.g., SCHÄFER), adopted in the 16th and 17th cents.

3. Jewish: of uncertain origin.

Vars. (of 1): Fr.: **Pastour, Pasteur**; **Pastre**. (Of 3): Jewish: **Paste(u)r**.

Cogns. (of 1): It.: **Pastore, Pastori**. Hung.: **Pásztor**.

Dims. (of 1): Fr.: **Pa(s)tourel, Pa(s)toureau**. It.: **Pastorino, Pastorini, Past(o)rello, Pastorelli**.

Pastukhov Russian: patr. from the occupational term *pastukh* shepherd (from *pasti* to graze (trans.), ultimately a cogn. of L *pascere*; cf. PASTOR).

Cogns.: Ukr.: **Pastushenko** (dim.). Beloruss.: **Pastushik, Pastushonok** (dims.). Pol.: **Pastusiak**; **Pastuszko** (dim.).

Pate English and Scots: 1. from the given name *Pat(t)*, *Pate*, a short form of PATRICK.

2. nickname for a man with a bald head, from ME *pate* head, skull (of unknown origin).

Var. (of 1): **Patt**.

Dims. (of 1): **Patey**; **Pat(t)on**, PADDON, PATTEN.

Patrs. (from 1): **Pates**; **McPhaid, McPhade, McFade, McPhate, McFait, McFeat(e)** (Gael. **Mac Phaid**).

Patrs. (from dims of 1): **Pattinson, Pat(t)ison, Pattyson, Pate(r)son, Paterson**. See also MCFADDEN.

'Servant of P. 1': **Pateman, Pat(t)man**.

The American general George Patton *(1885–1945) was born in San Gabriel, California, into a family with a long military tradition. His earliest American ancestor, Robert Patton, had emigrated from Scotland to Virginia c.1770.*

Pater Dutch: nickname for a solemn or pompous man, from MDu *pater* father superior (in a religious order; from L *pater* father).

Var.: **De Pater**.

Walter Pater *(1839–94), the English writer who advocated the concept of 'art for art's sake', was the son of a physician, born in E London. His family were of Dutch origin, and were said to have come to England with William of Orange. They established themselves in Olney, Bucks.*

Patera Czech: from a blend of the two common given names *Pavel* (see PAUL) and *Petera* (see PETER). The formation was also influenced by the L word *pater* father.

Paternoster English, French, and German: metonymic occupational name for a maker of rosaries, from L *pater noster* Our Father, the opening words of the Lord's Prayer, which is represented by large beads punctuating the rosary. The surname may also have been originally a nickname for an excessively pious individual or for someone who was under a feudal obligation to say paternosters for his master as part of the service by which he held land.

Vars.: Fr.: **Patenôtre, Peternot(te), Paternault**. Ger.: **Ternoster** (an aphetic form).

Cogns.: It.: **Pate(r)nostro**.

Patience 1. English: nickname from ME, OF *patience* (L *patientia*, from *patiens*, gen. *patientis*, patient, pres. part. of *pati* to endure), given perhaps to a notably long-suffering individual or to someone who had represented this abstract virtue in a morality play.

2. Jewish (Ashkenazic): this surname has been used in the U.S. as a translation of GEDULD.

Var.: **Patient**.

Patmore English: habitation name from a place in Herts. which appears in Domesday Book as *Patemere*, from an OE personal name *P(e)atta* (perhaps an assimilated form of *Pearta*; see PARTINGTON) + OE *mere* lake, pool.

Var.: PADMORE.

Patočka Czech: nickname for a beer drinker or metonymic occupational name for a brewer, from a dim. of Czech *patoky* thin beer, porter.

Var.: **Patoka**.

Patora Polish: 1. nickname from Pol. dial. *patorny* bad, evil.

2. nickname from Pol. dial. *patoroczny* clumsy, inept.

Var.: **Patura**.

Patrick English: from a given name (L *Patricius* son of a noble father, member of the patrician class, the Roman hereditary aristocracy). This was the name of a 5th-cent. Romano-Briton who became the apostle of Ireland, and it was largely as a result of his fame that the given name was so popular in the Middle Ages.

Vars.: **Pattrick**, PARTRIDGE.

Cogns.: Fr.: **Patric(e), Patris, Patrix, Patry**. Port.: **Patrício**.

Dims.: Eng., Sc.: PATE; PETRIE; **Padan, Padyn, Pedan, Peden**. Fr.: **Patricot, Patrigeon**.

Patrs.: Sc.: **McPhedric** (Gael. **Mac Phádraig**). Ir.: FITZPATRICK; see also KILPATRICK. Russ.: **Patrikeev**.

Patrs. (from dims.): Sc., Ir.: MCFADDEN. Russ.: **Patrushev, Patrikeivin**.

Patrone Italian: nickname from It. *patrone* master (L *patrōnus*, a deriv. of *pater* father). The term had various senses in the Middle Ages; it was applied, for example, to the master of a ship, and also to the former owner of a freed serf, who still enjoyed certain rights over him.

Vars.: **Patroni, Patrono**; **Paroni, Pa(t)ron** (Venetia); **Patruno** (Apulia).

Cogns.: Fr.: **Patron**. Cat.: **Padró**.

Patte French: nickname, applied presumably to a man with large and clumsy hands or feet, from OF *pat(t)e* paw (of apparently Gaul. origin).

Vars.: **Pat(h)é, Patey, Patez, Patu** ('with paws').

Dims.: **Paton, Patou(x), Patout**.

Augs.: Fr.: **Patat**. Sp.: **Patón**.

Pejs.: Fr.: **Pataud, Patard, Patart**.

Patten English: 1. dim. of PATE 1.

2. metonymic occupational name for a maker or seller of clogs, or nickname for a wearer of them, from ME *paten* clog (OF *patin*, of uncertain origin, but perhaps akin to PATTE).

Var.: **Pattin**.

Cogns. (of 2): Fr.: **Patin(ier)**.

Dims. (of 2): Fr.: **Patinet, Patineau**.

Pattenden English: habitation name from a place in Kent, named in OE as the 'swine pasture (OE *denn*) associated with *Peatta*' (cf. PATMORE).

Patullo Scots: habitation name from either of two places, in the former counties of Fife and Perths., called *Pittilloch*, from the Pictish element *peit* portion (of land) + Gael. *tulach* hill.

Vars.: **Pattullo, Pat(t)illo**.

Pauker German and Jewish (Ashkenazic): occupational name for a drummer, Ger. *Pauker* (MHG *pūkære*, agent deriv. of *pūke* drum (mod. Ger. *Pauke*), of uncertain, possibly imitative, origin).

Vars.: Ger.: **Peuker**; **Peuchert** (Silesia); **Peickert** (Silesia, Saxony); **Baiker(t)**. Jewish (Ashkenazic): **Paucker**.

Paukov Russian: patr. from the nickname *Pauk* 'Spider'.

Cogn.: Pol.: **Pająk**.

Paul English, French, German, and Flemish/Dutch: from the given name (L *Paulus* 'Small'), which has always been popular in Christendom. It was the name adopted by the Pharisee Saul of Tarsus after his conversion to Christianity on the road to Damascus (AD *c.*34). He was a most energetic missionary to the gentiles in the Roman Empire, and perhaps played a more significant role than any other of Christ's followers in establishing Christianity as a major world religion. The name was borne also by numerous other early saints. The surname is also occasionally borne by Jews; the reasons for this are not clear.

Vars.: Eng.: **Paull** (chiefly Devon and Cornwall); **Paule, Pawle,** POOL, POWELL. Fr.: **Pol.** Ger.: **Pahl, Pohl; Paulus** (Latinized). Flem., Du.: **Pau(w)el.**

Cogns.: Prov.: **Pau.** It.: **P(a)oli, P(a)olo, Pauli.** Sp.: **Pablo(s), Polo.** Cat.: POL. Port.: **Paulo; Paula** (fem.). Low Ger.: **Pagel.** Dan., Norw.: **Palle.** Ger. (of Slav. origin): **Pawel, Pabel.** Czech: **Pavel, Pavlata, Pála, Pach, Pachta.** Pol.: **Paweł, Pawelski, Pawlicki, Pawlata.** Hung.: **Pál, Paal.**

Dims.: Eng.: **Paul(l)ey, Pauly,** PAWLEY; **Powley** (E Anglia); **Paulin(g), Paulling, Pawlyn, Pawling, Powling;** PAWLETT. Fr.: **Pauleau, Paulet, Paulin, Pauly, Polin, Paulot, Paulon, Paulou.** It.: **Pa(v)olini, P(a)olino, Polini, Paolinelli, P(a)oletti, Paoletto, Pauletti, Pauletto, Polet(to), P(a)olotti, P(a)olotto, Paolozzi, Paolillo, Paulillo, Pavolillo, P(a)olucci, Paulucci, Pauluzzi, Poluzzi, Paolicchi.** Port.: **Paulino.** Low Ger.: **Paulmann.** Ger. (of Slav. origin): **Paulack, Paulig, Paulich, Pawelke, Pawellek, Pawlick, Pabelik, Paulitschke, Paulisch, Pallas(ch), Pallaske, Palleske, Paulusch, Palluschek, Pavlitschek; Paschek, Paschke, Pache.** Czech: **Pavelka; Pavlí(če)k, Pavlášek; Pávek, Pálek, Pašek.** Pol.: **Pawełek, Pawełczyk, Pawlaczyk, Pawlik, Paszek, Pasek.** Ukr.: **Pavlik, Pavluk, Pavlenko.**

Augs.: Fr.: **Paulat.** It.: **P(a)olon(i), Paolone.** Pol.: **Pawelec.**

Pejs.: Eng.: POLLARD. It.: **P(a)olacci, Paulazzi, P(a)olazzi.**

Patrs.: Eng.: **Paulson, Po(u)lson, Poulsom, Poulsum.** Sc.: McFALL. Manx: QUAIL. Fr.: **Aupol.** It.: **De Paoli(s).** Ger.: **Pauler, Pahler; Pauli, Pauly** (Latinized). Low Ger.: **Pauls(en), Pawels, Pagels(en); Pöhls(en), Pöhling.** Fris.: **Pau(g)els, Paulsen.** Flem., Du.: **Pau(we)ls.** Dan., Norw.: **Paulsen, Pallesen, Poulsen, Povlsen.** Swed.: **Paulsson, På(h)lsson; Pauli** (Latinized). Russ.: **Pavlov, Pavelyev.** Pol.: **Pawłowicz.** Lithuanian: **Paulat(h), Pauleit; Poweleit, Pauluweit** (Ger. spellings). Croatian: **Pavlov(ić), Pav(e)lić, Pavić, Paljić.** Hung.: **Pálf(f)i, Pálf(f)y.** Armenian: **Pogosian, Bogosian.**

Patrs. (from dims.): Eng.: **Pollins.** Russ.: **Pavlen(k)ov, Pavlikov, Pavlishchev, Pavlishintsev, Pavyuchikov, Pavlyuk(h)ov, Pavyushkov, Pavlitsev, Pavlikhin, Pavlukhin, Pavlush(k)in, Pavlygin; Pavshukov, Pavkin, Pavshin; Pashaev, Pashenkov, Pashintsev, Pashinov, Pashkeev, Pashkov, Pashnev, Pashanin, Pashetkin, Pashikhin, Pash(in)(k)in, Pashunin, Pashutin.** Pol.: **Pawełkiewicz, Pawlikiewicz; Paszkiewicz; Pawełczak, Paszak.** Croatian: **Pavličić, Pavičević, Pavković.**

'Son of the wife of P. (dim.)': Russ.: **Pavlikhin, Pashikhin.**

Habitation names: Pol.: **Pawłowski, Pawliński, Pawlikowski; Paszkowski, Pasikowski.** Czech: **Pavlovský.**

Pauncefoot English (Norman): nickname for a man with a large belly, from ANF *paunc(h)e* stomach, gut (OF *paunce*, from L *pantices* bowels, intestines) + *vout*, *vaut* vaulted, arched, rounded (L *volūtus*, past part. of *volvere* to turn).

Vars.: **Pauncefote, Pauncefort; Ponsford** (perhaps also from a place in Devon).

Cogn.: It.: **Panzavuota.**

Paustovski Belorussian: habitation name from any of several minor settlements called *Paustovo*, from the dedication of the local church to St *Faustus* (see FAUST 2).

Pavey English: 1. from the medieval female given name *Pavia*, which is of uncertain origin.

2. habitation name from the It. town of *Pavia* in Lombardy, N Italy.

Vars.: **Pavy, Pavie.**

Cogns. (of 2): Fr.: **Pavie, Pavy.** It.: **Pavese.**

Dims. (of 1): Eng.: **Pavett, Pavitt.**

Pavier English: occupational name for a layer of paving, from ME, OF *pavier* (an agent deriv. of OF *paver* to pave, L *pavīre* to beat, ram down; the difference in declension suggests that the OF verb may be a back-formation from *pavement* laid floor, L *pavīmentum*).

Vars.: **Pav(y)er, Pavio(u)r.**

Paw English: 1. nickname from ME *pawe*, OE *pāwa* PEACOCK.

2. var. of PAUL.

Var.: **Pawe.**

Patr. (from 2): **Pawson** (Yorks).

Pawlett English: 1. dim. of PAUL.

2. habitation name from a place in Somerset, apparently so called from OE *pāl* pole + *flēot* stream, i.e. a stretch of water with mooring posts or with piles to support the banks.

Vars.: **Paulet.**

Most present-day bearers of this surname are descended from Sir John Paulet *(d. 1356). Various branches of the family were ennobled and their titles include Marquess of Winchester and Earl* Poulett.

Pawley English: 1. Norman habitation name from *Pavilly* in Seine-Maritime, which is so called from the Gallo-Roman personal name *Pavilius* + the local suffix *-ācum*.

2. dim. of PAUL.

Vars. (of 1): **Pav(e)l(e)y.**

Paxton English and Scots: habitation name from places in Cambs. and the former county of Berwicks., so called from OE *Pæccestūn* 'settlement of *Pæcc*', a personal name related to the **Pacca* discussed at PACKWOOD.

Pay S English: 1. var. of *Pea*, *Pee* (see PEACOCK).

2. from an early medieval given name, apparently masc. but of uncertain origin, perhaps derived from 1 (cf. PAW).

Var.: **Pey.**

'Servant of P.': **Payman, Peyman.**

Payeur French: occupational name for an official responsible for settling accounts, from OF *payeur* (LL *pācātor*, from *pācāre* to appease, requite, a deriv. of *pax*, gen. *pācis*, peace, concord).

Var.: **Payer.**

Dims.: **Payet, Payot, Payon.**

Payler English: occupational name for a maker of pots and pans, from an agent deriv. of ME *pail(e)* (OF *paelle* frying pan, cooking pan; cf. PADILLA).

Vars.: **Paler, Paylor.**

Pays 1. French: occupational name for a peasant farmer or agricultural labourer, OF *pays* peasant (LL *pāgēnsis*, a deriv. of *pāgus* village, country district; cf. PAIN 1).

2. English: var. of PACE.

Vars. (of 1): **Paysan(t), Paisant.**

Cogn. (of 1): Cat.: **Pagès.**

Payton English: habitation name from *Peyton* in Sussex (so called from the OE personal name *Pǣga* + OE *tūn* enclosure, settlement) or from some other place similarly named. The surname is common in the W Midlands. *Peyton* in Essex has probably not contributed; it is recorded in

Domesday Book as *Pachenhou* 'ridge, spur (see HOE) of *Pac(c)a*', and even in the 16th cent. it was still *Pakenho* or *Patenhall*.

Paz 1. Spanish and Portuguese: cogn. of PACE.
2. Jewish (Israeli): ornamental name from Hebr. *paz* pure gold.
Cpd (of 2): **Har-Paz** (translation of GOLDBERG, with Hebr. *har* mountain).

Pazdera Czech: 1. occupational name for a flax-dresser, from Czech *pazdero* flax.
2. nickname for an untidy person or a person of ill repute, from metaphorical uses of the preceding word.
Var.: **Pazdernik**.

Peabody English: probably a nickname for a showy dresser, from ME *pē* PEACOCK + *body* BODY, person.

Peachey English: nickname for a reprobate, probably given more often in jest than as a mark of censure, from OF *pech(i)e* sin (L *peccātum*, past part. of *peccāre* to sin, err).
Vars.: **Pe(t)chey**; **Peach(e)**, **Peech**, **Petch(e)**.

Peacock English: nickname for a vain, strutting person or for a dandy, from ME *pē*, *pā*, *pō* peacock (OE *pēa*, *pāwa*, ON *pá*; cogn. with or taken from L *pāvo*, gen. *pāvōnis*), with the later disambiguating addition of *cok* male bird (see COCK). In some cases it may be a house name from a house distinguished by the sign of a peacock.
Vars.: **Peacocke**, **Peecock**, **Pacock**, **Pocock(e)**; PAW, PAY, POWE; **Poe** (from ON *pá*); **Pea**, **Pee**.
Cogns. (of 1): Fr.: **Pabon**. Sp.: **Pavón**. It.: **Pa(v)one**, **Pavoni**. Rum.: **Paun**. Ger.: **Pfau**, **Pfoh**; **Pfab** (Bavaria). Low Ger.: **Pauw**; **Pagelon**, **Pagelun**. Flem.: **De Pa(e)uw**. Du.: **De Pa(a)uw**. Russ.: **Pavsky** (surname adopted by Orthodox clergy).

Peak English: topographic name for someone living by a pointed hill, or regional name from the *Peak* District (OE *Pēaclond*) in Derbys., from OE *pēac* peak, pointed hill (found only in placenames). This word is not directly related to OE *pīc* point(ed hill), which yielded PIKE; there is, however, evidence of confusion between the two surnames.
Vars.: **Peake(r)**, **Peakman**; **Peek** (Norfolk); PECK.
Major concentrations of the surname Peak *are found in Staffs. and in the West Country. Among the earliest known bearers are Richard* del Pech *or* del Pek *(d. 1196), son of Rannulf, Sheriff of Nottingham, and Willielmus* Piec *(Winchester 1194). A century later,* c.*1284, a certain Richard* del Peke *settled in the former county of Denbighs. (now part of Clwyd), receiving lands from Henry de Lacey, Earl of Lincoln, in return for helping to control the region. His descendants, who bear the name* Peak(e), *can be traced to the present day, and are found in New Zealand and Canada as well as in Britain.*
Peake *is also the name of a family descended from John* Pyke, *who paid rent to the Abbot of Leicester in 1477. The name took various forms, such as* Peke *and* Pick, *settling as* Peak *in the 17th cent.*

Pear English: 1. metonymic occupational name for a grower or seller of pears, or topographic name for someone who lived by a pear tree or pear orchard, from ME *pe(e)re* pear (OE *pere*, *peru*, from L *pirum*).
2. nickname from ME *pere* peer, companion (OF *pe(e)r*, from L *pār* equal).
Vars. (mostly of 1): **Pee(a)r**, **Pere**; **Pearman**, **Pearmund**; **Peartree**. See also PERRY.
Cogns. (of 1): Fr.: **Poir(r)ier**, **Poirriez**, **Dupoirier**. Prov.: **(Le) Périer**, **Pér(i)é**, **Pérès**. It.: **Pera**, **La Pira**, **Delpero**; **Piras** (Sardinia); **Piraro**. Sp.: **Perera**; **Pereira** (W Spain); **Peral(es)**. Cat.: **Perera**, **Parera**, **Parés**. Port.: **Pereira** (also Jewish, a common N Sefardic surname). Ger.: **Pirner** (Bavaria); see also BIRNBAUM. (Of 2): Prov.: **Par(i)er**; **Parès** (Gascony); **Parésy** (Latinized).
Dims. (of 1): Fr.: **Poirot**. It.: **Peretto** (see also PARROTT), **Piretto**; **Predda**, **Prodda**, **Piroddi** (Sardinia). Sp.: **Perella**. Cat.: **Perellas**. (Of 2): Prov.: **Pari(o)n**, **Pariot**.
Collectives (of 1): Prov.: **Lapérière**. Sp.: **Pereda**.

Pearce English: from the ME given name *Piers*, the regular vernacular form of PETER. Since the given name ends in *-s*, surnames that originated as patrs. in *-s* are indistinguishable from those derived directly from the base form.
Vars.: **Pears(e)** (chiefly Cornwall); **Pierce**, **Piers(e)** (chiefly Ireland); **Peers**, **Perce**, **Pers(s)e**, **Perris**.
Patrs.: **Pearson**, **Pierson**.
A family called Piers *became established in Ireland when William* Piers *(d. 1603) was granted estates there by Elizabeth I in 1566, including the abbey of Tristernagh, Westmeath.*

Pearl 1. English: metonymic occupational name for a trader in pearls, which in the Middle Ages were fashionable among the rich for the ornamentation of clothes, from ME, OF *perle* (LL *perla*, perhaps from *perna* mussel (originally 'ham'; the sense transfer was no doubt due to a supposed similarity in shape)).
2. Jewish (Ashkenazic): ornamental name, or Anglicized form of the Yid. female given name *Perl* 'Pearl', a translation of Hebr. *Margalit* (see MARGUERITE).
Vars.: Jewish: **Per(e)l**, **Perle**; **Per(e)lman(n)** (Anglicized **Pearlman**); **Perelsman**, **Perlesman** ('husband of *Perl*').
Cogns.: It.: **Perla**, **Perli**; **(La) Perna** (S Italy). Ger.: **Perl(er)**, **Parler**. Pol.: **Perliński**.
Metrs. (from the given name): Jewish: **Perles**, **Perlis**, **Perlus**, **Perelson**; **Perlov**, **Perlow(ski)**, **Perlin(ski)** (Anglicized **Pearlin**).
Cpds (ornamental): Jewish: **Perlberg(er)** ('pearl hill'); **Perlgut** ('pearl good(s)'); **Per(e)lmut(t)er**, **Mutterperl** ('mother of pearl'); **Perlrot(h)** ('pearl red'); **Perlschein** ('pearl shine'); **Per(e)lstein** ('pearl stone', partly Anglicized as **Pearlstine**); **Perlszweig** ('pearl twig').

Peart N English and Scots: of uncertain origin, perhaps a habitation name from *Pert* on the North Esk near Montrose, so called from a Pictish or Celtic term for a wood or copse.

Pease English: metonymic occupational name for a grower or seller of peas, or nickname for a small and insignificant man, from ME *pese*, originally a collective singular (OE *peose*, *pise*, from L *pisa*), from which the mod. E vocab. word *pea* is derived by folk etymology, the singular having been taken as a plural.

Péchels Provençal: habitation name from an unidentified place named with the pl. form of a dim. of OProv. *pech* hill, plateau (see PUY).
Pechell *is the name of a Huguenot family established in Ireland, but originally from Montauban, Languedoc. Samuel* de Péchels *(1645–1732) was imprisoned and transported to the French W Indies, but escaped and reached England in 1688. He accompanied William III's forces to Ireland and was given estates in Kildare.*

Pecher 1. German and Jewish (Ashkenazic): occupational name for a boiler of pitch, from an agent deriv. of Ger. *Pech*, Yid. *pekh* pitch (MHG *pech*, OHG *peh*, from L *pix* pitch; cf. PÈGUE).
2. German: metonymic occupational name for a turner of wooden vessels, from MHG *becher* beaker, goblet, pitcher, jug (cf. BECHER 1). For the alternation of /p/ and /b/, cf. BIRNBAUM and its vars.

3. German: nickname for an unlucky fellow, from Ger. *Pech* bad luck (a transferred sense of the same word as in 1) + *-er* suffix of agent nouns.

Vars. (of 1): Jewish: **Pechner**; **Pechwasser** ('pitch water').

Cogns.: Czech: **Pechar**. (Of 1 only): Prov.: **Peg(h)aire**.

Pêcheur French: occupational name for a fisherman, from an agent deriv. of OF *pesche* fish (see PESCE).

Vars.: **Pêcheux**, **Pescheur**, **Pescheux**; **Pe(c)queur**, **Pe(c)queux** (Normandy, Picardy); **Pesque(u)r**, **Pesqueux**, **Lepesqueur** (Brittany).

Cogns.: Prov.: **Pesquier**, **Pescaire**, **Pescadou**. It.: **Pescatore**, **Pescatori**. Sp.: **Pescador**. Port.: **Peixero**.

Peck English: 1. metonymic occupational name for someone who dealt in weights and measures, for example a corn factor, from ME *pekke* peck (an old measure of dry goods equivalent to eight quarts or a quarter of a bushel).

2. topographic name, a var. of PEAK.

Peckham English: habitation name from one of the places so called, in Kent and S London, possibly from OE *pēac* hill (see PEAK) + *hām* homestead.

Pecora Italian: metonymic occupational name for a keeper of flocks of sheep and goats, from It. *pecora* flock (from L *pecus*, gen. *pecoris*).

Vars.: **Pecori**, **Peguri**; **Pecoraro**, **Pecora(r)i**, **Pegoraro**, **Pegorari**, **Pegorer**.

Dims.: **Pecorella**, **Pecorelli**, **Pegoretti**, **Pecorini**, **Pegorin(i)**.

Pedler English: 1. occupational name for a pedlar, from ME *pedler*, *pedlar*, apparently a dissimilated var. of *pedder*, *peddar*, from *pedde* pannier, basket (of uncertain origin), in which goods were carried from place to place.

2. nickname for a fleet runner, from OF *pie de lievre* hare's foot (LL *pēs de lepore*); cf. PEDLEY.

Vars.: **Pedlar**, **Pegler**, **Pidler**. (Of 1 only): **Pedder**, **Peddar**.

Cogn. (of 2): It.: **Pedilepore**.

Equivs. (not cogn.): Fr.: TROSSIER. Ger.: TRAGER, KORB. Du.: DEVENTER. Jewish: GEIER. Pol.: BEDWINEK. Czech: KABELÁČ. Russ.: PESHKOV.

Pedley English (Norman): nickname for a stealthy person, from OF *pie de leu* wolf's foot (LL *pēs de lupo*); cf. PEDLER 2.

Var.: **Pedlow**, **Pellew**, PELLOW.

Pedró Catalan: habitation name from any of several minor places so called from Cat. *pedró* large stone, pedestal (LL *petro*, gen. *petrōnis*, a deriv. of *petra* stone; cf. PIERRE 2).

Pedrosa Spanish, Catalan, and Portuguese: habitation name from any of various places, for example in the provinces of Burgos, Lugo, and Orense, so called from LL *Petrōsa* 'Place of Stones' (neut. pl. or fem. sing. of *petrōsus*, an adj. deriv. of *petra* stone; cf. PIERRE 2).

Vars.: Cat.: **Padrós**. Port.: **Pedroso**.

Pędziwiatr Polish: nickname for a restless person given to impractical and fanciful schemes, from Pol. *pędzić* to chase + *wiatr* the wind.

Peebles Scots: habitation name from the town on the river Tweed in SE Scotland, or from a smaller place of the same name in the parish of St Vigeans, Angus. Both places probably get the name from a Brit. element that became W *pebyll* tent, pavilion, to which the Eng. pl. *-s* has been added.

Peel English: nickname for a tall thin man, from ANF *pel* stake, pole (OF *piel*, from L *pālus*). It may also have been a topographic name for someone who lived by a stake fence or in a property defended by one, or a metonymic occupational name for a builder of such fences (cf. PALLISER).

Vars: **Peele**, **Peale**, **Piele**, **Peile**.

Cogns.: Fr.: **Pieu**. Ger.: **Pfahl(er)**, **Pfähler**. Low Ger.: **Pahl(mann)**.

Dims.: Fr.: **Pieuchot**. Prov.: **Pallet**, **Pallez**. Low Ger.: **Pahlke**.

Pegg English: metonymic occupational name for a maker or seller of wooden pegs, from ME *pegge* (from MDu., of uncertain origin), perhaps also a nickname for a person with a wooden leg.

Pègue Provençal: metonymic occupational name for a boiler of pitch (cf. PECHER 1) or nickname for someone with very dark, 'pitch-black' hair, from OProv. *pegue* pitch (L *pix*, gen. *picis*).

Dims.: **Pegeon**, **Pe(u)geot**, **Peguet**.

Pej.: **Pegeaud**.

Peinado Spanish: nickname for a well-groomed person or for someone with naturally smooth rather than curly hair, from Sp. *peinado*, past. part. of *peinar* to comb (LL *pectināre*, a deriv. of *pecten* comb, gen. *pectinis*, itself a deriv. of class. L *pectere* to comb).

Peisach Jewish (Ashkenazic): from the Yid. male given name *Peysekh* (from Hebr. *pesach* Passover).

Vars.: **Pes(s)a(c)h**.

Patrs.: **Pesahson**; **Peisachovitz**, **Peisachowitch**, **Pesachov**, **Pesakhowich**, **Pessahov(itz)**, **Pesa(c)hovitz** (E Ashkenazic).

Peiser 1. English: var. of PEYZER.

2. Jewish (Ashkenazic): of unknown origin.

Pękala Polish: nickname from the Pol. dial. term *pękal* short, fat man.

Var.: **Pękalski**.

Pěkný Czech: nickname for a man who was either fair-haired or handsome, Czech *pěkný*.

Pelayo Spanish: from a medieval given name, from Gk *Pelagios* (a deriv. of *pelagos* (open) sea). The name was borne by a 10th-cent. Christian martyr, a young boy tortured and killed by the Moors of Córdoba for refusing to renounce his faith. His fame led to the given name being very popular in Spain in the Middle Ages; it was borne also by the semi-legendary first king of the Reconquest. The name was also borne by various other early martyrs, but in other European countries it has not been popular because of its association with the British heretic *Pelagius*.

Cogns.: Ger.: **Bolay**, **Boley** (S Germany).

Patrs.: Sp.: **Peláez**, **Páez**, **Báez**. Port.: **Pais**.

Pełczyński Polish: habitation name, probably from *Pełczyn*, a placename derived from PEŁKA army, or *Pełczyce* in NW Poland, the Ger. name of which is BERNSTEIN.

Pelham English: habitation name from a place in Herts., so called from the OE personal name *Pēotla* (a deriv. of *Pēot*, perhaps a short form of the various cpd personal names with the first element *Peoht* Pict) + OE *hām* homestead.

The manor of Pelham in Herts was held by Walter de Pelham *in the reign of Edward I (1272–1307). His descendants became constables of Pevensey Castle, Sussex, and were so influential that their badge, the buckle, is seen in at least eleven of the county's churches, and as a decoration on iron chimney-backs in Sussex farmhouses. Various branches of the family were ennobled and their titles include Earl of Chichester and Earl of Yarborough. The family also once held the dukedom of Newcastle and the marquessate of Clare.*

Pelikán Czech: house name from a house marked with the sign of a pelican (Czech *pelikán*). The pelican was regarded as a symbol of Christian piety: the female pelican was supposed, in medieval religious folklore, to feed her young with her own blood by plucking the feathers from her breast.

Pelisse French: metonymic occupational name for a maker of fur garments or nickname for a wearer, from OF *pellice* fur cloak (LL *pellīcia* from *pellis* skin, fur; cf. PELLETIER).
Vars.: **Pel(l)isier, Pélissier, Pélissié, Pelicier, Pélicier; Plissonier.**
Cogns.: Cat.: **Pellicer, Pelliser, Pellisé.** It.: **Pellicci(a), Pel(l)izza, Pel(l)izzi, Pellicchio; Pellicceri, Pel(l)izzeri, Pel(l)issero, Pelisseri, Pellic(ci)ari, Pellicciaro, Pellicaio, Pel(l)izzari, Pel(l)izzaro.** Eng.: PILCHER.
Dims.: Fr.: **Pellisson, P(é)lisson, Plissoneau, Plichon, Plichet.** It.: **Pellicciotta.**
Augs.: It.: **Pelliccioni, Pel(l)izzon(i), Pellissoni, Pellissone.**

Pełka Polish: apparently from a short form of a given name containing the element *pełka* army. This is found in several Slav. compound names such as *Świętopełk* ('holy' + 'army'). Alternatively, this name may simply be a dial. var. of PAŁKA.

Pell English: 1. from the ME given name *Pell*, a pet form of PETER.
2. metonymic occupational name for a dealer in furs, from ME, OF *pel* skin (cf. PELLETIER and PILCHER).
3. topographic name, a var. of PILL 1.
Dim. (of 1): **Pelly.**

Pellé French: nickname for a bald man, from OF *pelé* (past part. of *peler* to peel, strip (esp. of hair), L *(de)pilāre*, from *pilus* hair; the spelling has been influenced by L *pellis* skin, hide).
Var.: **Pelé.**
Cogns.: Prov.: **Pel(l)at.**
Pej.: Fr.: **Pelard.**

Pelletier French: occupational name for a furrier, from OF *pelletier* (a deriv. of *pellet*, dim. of *pel* skin, hide, from L *pellis*).
Var.: **Peltier.**
Cogns.: Eng.: **Pelter, Pilter** (rare). Du.: **(Van) Pelt.** It.: **Pellitteri, Pillitteri; Impellitteri, Impelizzeri** (S Italy).

Pelling English: 1. habitation name from *Peelings*, a minor place in Sussex, recorded in Domesday Book as *Pellinges*, apparently from the OE tribal name *Pydelingas* 'people of *Pydel*', a personal name which may be derived from the root *pud-* to swell, be fat.
2. See HAYLING.
The first known bearer of the name is Hammyng de Pellyng, *recorded at Lewes, Sussex, in 1265/6.*

Pellow 1. Cornish: deriv. of PELL 1; for the ending, cf. PASCOE.
2. English: var. of PEDLEY.

Peltonen Finnish: ornamental or topographic name from *pelto* field + the gen. suffix *-nen*.
Var.: **Peltola** (with a local suffix).

Pemberton English: habitation name from a place in Greater Manchester, so called from the Brit. element *penn* hill, head + OE *bere* barley + *tūn* enclosure, settlement (see BARTON).
There seem to have been several families called de Pemberton *in the Wigan area as early as the beginning of the 13th cent., notably that of Adam de Pemberton, a substantial landowner.*

Peña Spanish: topographic name for someone who lived near a large jutting rock or crag, Sp. *peña* (probably from L *penna*, *pinna* pinnacle, battlement, originally 'feather', or else of Celt. origin (cf. PENDLEBURY)). The surname is no doubt also a habitation name from any of the numerous minor places named with this term.
Vars.: **Peñas; Pina** (a place in the province of Saragossa).
Cogns.: Cat., Port.: **Pena, Pina** (of Aragonese origin). Prov.: **Sapena.** It.: PENNA, **Penni, Lapenna.**
Dims.: Sp.: **Pinilla** (see also PINE). It.: **Pennella, Pennelli, Penniello, Pennetta, Pennetti, Pennino, Pennini.**
Augs.: It.: **Pennone, Pennoni.**
Pejs.: It.: **Pennacci, Pennazzi.**

Pendlebury English (Lancs.): habitation name from a place in Greater Manchester so called from the hill name *Pendle* (composed of the Brit. element *penn* hill, head + a tautologous OE *hyll*) + OE *burh* fort, town (see BURY).

Pendleton English: habitation name from a place near PENDLEBURY, or another in Lancs., both of which are so called from the hill name *Pendle* + OE *tūn* enclosure, settlement.
Var.: **Pendelton.**

Pendreigh Scots: habitation name from any of various places apparently named with the Brit. phrase *pet an drych* croft of the view.
Vars.: **Pendrigh, Pendrich; Pittendr(e)igh, Pettendrich.**

Penfold English (mainly Kentish): metonymic occupational name for someone in charge of a pound where stray animals were kept, from ME *punfold*, OE *pundfald* (cf. POUND and FOLD), or topographic name for someone who lived by such a pound.
Var.: **Pinfold.**

Pengelly Cornish: habitation name from any of the places (in thirteen parishes) so called from Corn. *pen* head, top, end + *kelly* (mutated *gelly*) copse, grove.
Vars.: **Pengelley, Pengill(e)y.**

Penhaligon Cornish: habitation name from a place in the parish of Bodmin, so called from Corn. *pen* head, top, end + *helygen* willow treee.

Penman Scots: habitation name from a lost place in the Border region, apparently derived from the Brit. elements *penn* hill, head + *maen* stone.

Penn English: 1. metonymic occupational name for a shepherd or an impounder, from ME, OE *penn* (sheep) pen.
2. habitation name from various places, e.g. *Penn* in Bucks. and Staffs., named with the Brit. element *pen* hill, which was apparently adopted into OE.
3. pet form of PARNELL.
Var.: (of 1): **Penner.** See also PINDER.
Patrs. (from 3): **Pen(n)son.**
The state of Pennsylvania was founded in 1681 by an English Quaker, William Penn (1644–1718), who was born in London into a family of Gloucs. origin. His grandfather was a merchant and sea-captain, and his father was an admiral on the Parliamentary side during the Civil War, who later served King Charles II after the Restoration.

Penna 1. Cornish: of uncertain origin. The form *Pennow* is recorded in 1524, and this name is probably derived from it. This seems to be Corn. *pennow* heads, pl. of *penn* head, but it may be Corn. *penn* + the ME dim. suffix *-oe* (see PASCOE).
2. Italian: topographic name from a cogn. of Sp. PEÑA.

Pennington English: habitation name from places in Lancs., Cumb., and Hants. The latter two are so called from OE *pening* PENNY (used as a byname or from a tribute due on the land) + *tūn* enclosure, settlement. The place of this name in the parish of Leigh in Lancs. is recorded in the 13th cent. as *Pinington* and *Pynington*, and may be from OE *Pinningtūn* 'settlement associated with *Pinna*'; the var. **Pinnington** derives specifically from this place.

Penny English: nickname from the coin (OE *peni(n)g*, cogn. with OHG *pfenning*, ON *penningr*). This was the common Gmc unit of value when money was still an unusual phenomenon, and by no means denoted a coin of little value, as it does today. It was the only unit of coinage in England until the early 14th cent., when the groat and the gold noble were introduced. It was a silver coin of considerable value, and the nickname may therefore have denoted a person of some substance. There is some evidence that the word for the coin was used in OE times as a byname (cf. PENNINGTON).

Vars.: **Penney**, **Pennie**, **Penning**.

Cogns.: Ger.: **Pfenni(n)g**, **Fenning**. Low Ger., Du.: **Penning**. Flem., Du.: **Penninck**. Jewish (Ashkenazic): **Fenig** (from Yid. *fenig* pfennig; reason for adoption unknown; cf. GREITZER and *Rubel* at RUBLYOV).

Patrs.: Eng.: **Pennings**. Jewish: **Fenigson**.

'Servant of P.': **Pennyman**, **Penniman**, **Pannaman**.

Pennycuick Scots: habitation name from *Penycuik* near Edinburgh, recorded in 1250 as *Penicok* and in 1296 as *Penycoke*, apparently from Brit. cogns. of W *pen* hill and *cog* cuckoo.

Vars.: **Penneycuik**, **Pennecuik**, **Pennycook**, **Pennycock**.

Penrose Cornish and Welsh: habitation name from any of the places so called, in ten parishes of Cornwall, several times in Wales, and in Herefords. near the Welsh border. All are so called from the Celt. elements *pen* head, top, end + *ros* heath, moor.

Penswick English: habitation name from *Painswick* in Gloucs., so called from the possessive case of the ME given name PAIN + ME *wick* outlying settlement (see WICK). The place is recorded in Domesday Book simply as *Wiche*, but was later held by Pain FitzJohn (d. 1137), from whose name the first element of the placename is derived. The surname is now most common in Lancs., where it was introduced apparently as late as the 19th cent. and ramified exceptionally rapidly.

Pentecost English: nickname for someone who was born at Whitsuntide or had some particular connection with that time of year, such as owing a feudal obligation then. The name is from ME, OF *pentecost* (Gk *pentēcostē (hēmera)* fiftieth (day) (after Easter)).

Vars.: **Pentercost**, **Penticost**, **Pentycross**, **Perrycost**. See also PANKHURST.

Cogns.: Fr.: **Pantecôte**. Ger.: **Pfingst(en)**, **Pfingstner**, **Pfingstmann**.

Pentland Scots: habitation name from a place in the former county of Midlothian, of uncertain etymology, perhaps from ME *pent* (i.e. enclosed) *land*.

Pentreath Cornish: habitation name from a place in the parish of Breage, so called from Corn. *pen* head, top, end + *treth* beach, shore.

Penty W English: of uncertain origin, perhaps a back-formation from ME *pentis*, *pent(h)us* penthouse, and so a topographic name for someone who lived in one. This form of the vocab. word is found in W *penty* penthouse.

Vars.: **Pentey**, **Painty**.

The earliest known bearer of the name is Willemus de la Penty, *recorded in Dorset in 1231.*

A similar surname (Pentyth, *with modern forms* **Penteth** *and* **Paintiff**) *is also found in Yorks. in the 16th cent.; the alternation seems similar to that in* DAINTITH, *but no suitable ANF abstract noun has been identified.*

Penwarne Cornish: habitation name from places in the parishes of Mawnan, Cuby, and Mevagissey, all so called from Corn. *pen* head, top, end + *gwern*, which means both 'marsh' and 'alder trees'.

Var.: **Penwarden** (a place in the parish of South Hill).

Peplow English: habitation name from a place in Shrops., recorded in Domesday Book as *Papelau*. This may be from OE *pyppel* pebble + *hlāw* hill (see LAW 2 and LOW 1).

Var.: **Peploe** (chiefly Scots.).

A direct male line of this family has been traced back to William Peplowe *(d. 1552), yeoman and tenant of Sir Andrew Corbett in Shawbury, Shrops. He is also the ancestor of Scottish bearers of the name* Peploe.

Pepper 1. English: metonymic occupational name for a spicer, from ME *peper*, *piper* pepper (OE *piper*, *pipor*, from L *piper*). The surname may also be a nickname for a small man or one with a fiery temper, or anecdotal for someone who paid a peppercorn rent.

2. Jewish (Ashkenazic): Anglicized form of **Pfef(f)er**, derived from Ger. *Pfeffer* pepper, or **Fef(f)er**, from Yid. *fefer*. These are ornamental names, belonging to the large class of Ashkenazic names taken from words denoting plants. It is also possible that it may represent a punning translation of Hebr. *pilpul*, lit. 'pepper', fig. 'Talmudic debate', with reference to someone who was a sharp reasoner.

Vars.: Eng.: **Peppar**; **Peever**, **Peffer(s)** (from ANF *pivre*). Jewish: **Peper**; **Peperman**, **Fef(f)erman**; **Peperni(c)k** (E Ashkenazic, an agent deriv.).

Cogns.: Prov.: **Poivre**. Cat.: **Pebre**. Ger.: **Pfeffer(mann)**; **Pföffer** (Bavaria); **Feffer** (Silesia, Bohemia). Low Ger.: **Pepper**.

Dims.: Eng.: **Peperel**, **Pepp(e)rell**, **Pepperall**, **Peperwell**; **Pevere(l)(l)**, **Peverill**, **Peverall**. Fr.: **Peuvret**, **Prevel**. Ger.: **Pfefferle(in)**.

Cpds (not clear whether merely ornamental, or ornamental extensions of 'pepper' with reference to a sharp reasoner): Jewish: **Pfefferbaum** ('pepper tree'); **Feferberg** ('pepper hill'); **Pfefferbluth** ('pepper blossom'); **Feferkichen** ('pepper cake'); **Pfefferkranz** ('pepper wreath').

Pepys English: from the OF personal name *Pepis*, oblique case *Pepin*, introduced to Britain by the Normans. It is of uncertain origin, perhaps originally a byname meaning 'Terrible', 'Awe-inspiring', from a root *bib-* to tremble. It was borne by several Frankish kings, most notably Pepin le Bref, father of Charlemagne, and remained popular throughout the early Middle Ages. The pronunciation is normally /pi:ps/.

Vars.: **Pep(p)in**, **Pippin**, **Pipon**.

Cogns.: Fr.: **Pépi(n)**, **Pepy**. It.: **Pepino**.

Dims.: Eng.: **Pepall**, **Peaple**, **People**, **Peopall**; **Peppett**, **Peppiatt**, **Peppiett**. Fr.: **Pépineau(x)**, **Pépinot**.

Patr. (from a dim.): Eng.: **Peoples**.

Pepys *is the family name of the Earls of Cottenham, which title was granted in 1850. Records of the manor of Cottenham, Cambs., show bearers of the name living there as early as 1290. The diarist Samuel Pepys was a member of this family.*

Peralta Spanish, Catalan, and Portuguese: habitation name from any of various places, for example in the provinces of Huesca and Navarre, so called from L *petra alta* high rock.

Percival English: from the personal name *Perceval*, first found as the name of the hero of an epic poem by the 12th-cent. Fr. poet Crestien de Troyes, describing the quest for the holy grail. The origin of the name is uncertain; it may be associated with the Gaul. personal name *Pritorīx* or it may be an alteration of the Celt. name *Peredur* (perhaps from OW *peri* spears + *dur* hard, steel). It seems to have been altered as the result of folk etymological association with OF *perce(r)* to pierce, breach (LL *pertūsiāre*, reformed from *pertūsus*, past part. of class. L *pertundere*) + *val* valley (see VALE); cf. PERCY 2. The same hero was celebrated by the German epic poet Wolfram von Eschenbach under the name *Parzifal*, and with the spread of Arthurian romance the name became popular throughout W Europe.

Vars.: **Perceval, Percifull, Passifull, Purcifer.**

Cogns.: Fr.: **Perceval, Percevau(x), Percevaut, Perseval.** It.: **Percival(l)e, Percivalli, Perciavalle, Perciavalli, Perciballi, Percipalli, Princivalle, Princivalli, Prinzivalle, Prinzivalli, Principalli, Princigalli.** Ger.: **Parseval, Partzefall.**

The English Prime Minister Spencer Perceval *(1762–1812), who was assassinated in the House of Commons, was born into a powerful landowning family in Cork, Ireland, the grandson of the 1st Earl of Egmont.*

Percy English (Norman): habitation name from any of various places in N France, so called from the Gallo-Roman personal name *Persius* + the local suffix *-ācum*. The suggestion has also been made that it is a nickname from OF *perce(r)* to pierce, breach (cf. PERCIVAL) + *haie* hedge, enclosure (cf. HAY 1), referring either to a soldier remembered for his breach of a fortification, or in jest to a poacher who was in the habit of breaking into a private park.

Vars.: **Percey, Persay, Pearc(e)y, Pears(e)y, Pierc(e)y, Peircey; Pursey** (Somerset).

Percy *is the name of a leading Northumbrian family who were instrumental in holding the English border against the Scots, from their stronghold at Alnwick. Their founder was a Norman, William* de Percy *(?1030–96), 1st Baron Percy, who accompanied William the Conqueror. Sir Henry Percy (1342–1408), 1st Earl of Northumberland, and his son Sir Henry Percy (1364–1403), known as Harry Hotspur, helped place Henry IV on the throne. Hotspur later revolted and was killed at the battle of Shrewsbury. The earldom, created in 1377, has continued, on two occasions through female members, in the same family to the present day.*

A family spelling their name Piercy *have been established at Malton, N Yorks., since at least the 16th cent.*

Perek Polish: of uncertain origin, probably a nickname or metonymic occupational name from a dim. of the Poznań dial. word *perka, pyrka* potato.

Var.: **Perka.**

Habitation name: **Perkowski.**

Perelló Catalan: topographic name for someone who lived by a wild pear tree, from Cat. *perelló* wild pear (a double dim. of *pera* PEAR). There are places named with this word in the provinces of Tarragona and Valencia, and the surname may in part derive from them.

Perepyolkin Russian: patr. from a dim. of the nickname *Perepel* 'Quail', denoting presumably either a hunter of quails or an individual thought to be as timid as a quail.

Cogns.: Ukr.: **Perepelitsa.** Jewish (E Ashkenazic): **Perepelizky** (one of the many ornamental names taken from vocab. words denoting birds and animals).

Perevodchikov Russian: patr. from the occupational term *perevodchik* interpreter, translator (from *perevodit* to translate, from *pere-* across + *vodit* to lead, a calque of Fr. *traduire*, from L *tra(ns)ducere*).

Perham English: habitation name from any of various places (for example those in Suffolk and Sussex now called PARHAM as the result of a regular ME development) originally named with the OE elements *peru* PEAR + *hām* homestead.

Vars.: **Perram.**

Permenter German: occupational name for a preparer or seller of parchment, an agent deriv. of Ger. *Pergament* parchment (so called from the ancient city of *Pergamon* in Asia Minor, where the technique of producing the material originated). Parchment was in general use well into the 15th cent.

Vars.: **Pergament; Berm(it)ter.**

Cogn.: Jewish (Ashkenazic): **Parmet** (from Yid. *parmet* parchment); **Pergament(er).**

Perov Russian: patr. from the nickname *Pero* 'Feather', 'Pen', denoting either a small, light person, or a clerk, on account of his use of a quill pen.

Cogns.: Czech: **Peroutka, Peřina** (also in the sense 'bundle of feathers, feather bed').

Perrier French: occupational name for a quarryman, OF *perrier*, an agent deriv. of *pierre* stone, rock (see PIERRE 2).

Vars.: **Pierrier; Peirier.**

Perrin English and French: from the ME, OF given name *Perrin*, a dim. of PETER.

Vars.: Eng.: **Perring** (chiefly Devon), **Perryn, Perren, Parren.** Fr.: **Perrain, Perrein, Prin.**

Cogns.: It.: **Pie(t)rini, Petrin(i), Pe(d)rin(i), Per(r)ino, Rini.**

Dims.: Fr.: **Perrinet, P(é)rinet; Perrineau, Périnel; Perren(n)et, Pernet, Pernin, Pernot, Pernod, Pernollet.** It.: **Pe(d)rinelli, Perinello, Rinelli, P(e)rinetti, Rinetti, Rinucc(in)i.**

Patr.: Eng.: **Perrins** (chiefly W Midlands).

Perrowne English: Huguenot name, from the F given name *Perron*, a S French dim. of PIERRE.

Vars.: **Perron, Perowne.**

Perry 1. English: topographic name for someone who lived near a pear tree, ME *per(r)ie* (OE *pyrige*, a deriv. of *pere* pear).

2. Welsh: patr., with the W prefix *ap-*, from the medieval given name *Herry*, an assimilated form of HENRY.

3. Jewish (Israeli): ornamental name from Hebr. *peri* fruit, reward.

Vars. (of 1): **Pery, Perrie; Pir(r)ie** (Scots); **Pur(r)y; Per(r)yman, Per(r)iman, Perriment.** (Of 3): **Pery, Per(r)i.**

Pery *is the family name of the Earls of Limerick. They are said to have originated in Brittany, and first became prominent in the reign of Henry VII. The present title was first granted to Edmond Pery (1758–1844).*

Pertek Polish: nickname from the Pol. dial. term *pertek*, referring to a small, sprightly man.

Patr.: **Pertkiewicz.**

Pertwee English (Norman): habitation name from any of the various places in N France called *Pert(h)uis, Pertuy*, or *Pertus*, from OF *pertuis* ravine, gorge, cave (LL *pertūsium*, from *pertūsus*, past part. of *pertundere* to pierce, breach; cf. PERCIVAL and PERCY 2). The Fr. cogns. can also be topographic names for someone living by a ravine.

Var.: **Pertuce.**

Cogns.: Fr.: **Pert(h)uis, Perthuy, Pertus.**

Dims.: Fr.: **Pertuiset, Pertuisot.**

Pesce Italian: metonymic occupational name for a fisherman or fishmonger (cf. PÊCHEUR) or nickname for someone supposedly resembling a fish, It. *pesce* (L *piscis*).

Vars.: **Peschi(o)**.

Cogns.: Prov.: **Peix**. Sp.: **Peces**.

Dims.: It.: **Pescetto, Pesc(iol)ini**. Fr.: **Poisson(net), Poissenot, Poyssenot**. Prov.: **Peisson, Peysson(eau)**. Port.: **Peixoto, Peixinho**. Jewish (Sefardic): **Peixotto** (reason for adoption unknown).

Aug.: It.: **Peschione**.

Peshin Jewish (E Ashkenazic): metr. from the Yid. female given name *Peshe*, *Pesye*, which is of uncertain origin; it may be an altered form of *Bashe*, *Basye*, from Hebr. *Batya* 'daughter of God'; cf. BASKIN.

Var.: **Peshes**.

Dims.: **Pessel; Pesselov, Pes(h)kin** (metrs.).

Peshkov Russian: patr. from the nickname *Peshki* 'Pedestrian', 'Foot-traveller', denoting someone who travelled about but was too poor to be able to afford the humblest form of transport, for example a pedlar.

Cogn.: Pol.: PIECHOTA.

Peso Spanish: nickname for a heavy person or metonymic occupational name for someone responsible for testing weights and measures, from Sp. *peso* weight (LL *pensum*, from the past part. of *pendere* to weigh; cf. PEYZER).

Pessoa Portuguese: nickname from Port. *pessoa* person, human being (L *persōna*; cf. PARSONS). The original application of the nickname is not clear; it may have had contemptuous overtones, or it may have denoted an important personage.

Pestalozzi Italian: nickname for a butcher, from It. *pesta(re)* to pound, crush (LL *pistāre*, a reformation from *pistus*, past part. of class. L *pinsere*) + the dial. term *lozzo* bone.

The name is relatively common in Zurich today; the family of Johann Heinrich Pestalozzi *(1746–1827), the educational reformer, moved there in the 16th cent.*

Pestana Portuguese: nickname for someone who had long eyelashes or bushy eyebrows, from Port. *pestana* eyelash, also used in the Middle Ages of the eyebrow; the word is of unknown origin, probably from a pre-Roman term.

Peter English, German, and Flemish/Dutch: from the given name (Gk *Petros*, from *petros* rock, stone, a byform of *petra*; cf. PERRIER and PIERRE 2). The name was extremely popular throughout Christian Europe in the Middle Ages, as it had been bestowed by Christ as a byname on the apostle Simon bar Jonah, the brother of Andrew. The name, chosen by Christ for its symbolic significance, is a translation of Aramaic *kefa* rock (John 1: 42, Matt. 16: 18); St Peter is regarded as the founding father of the Christian Church in view of Christ's comment, 'Thou art Peter and upon this rock I will build my Church'. In Christian Germany in the early Middle Ages this was the most frequent given name of non-Gmc origin, being overtaken in the 14th cent. by JOHN and NICHOLAS. In England the vernacular form *Piers* (from OF *Piers*, oblique case *Pierre*) was usual at the time when surnames were being assumed; see PEARCE. The usual form of the given name in mod. Fr. is *Pierre*; in It. *Pietro*; in Sp. and Port. *Pedro*; in Russ. *Pyotr*; in Pol. *Piotr*; and in Czech *Petr*. The surname is also occasionally borne by Jews, in which case it represents an adoption of a non-Jewish surname.

Vars.: Eng.: **Petre**; **Pether** (Cornwall). Flem., Du.: **Peeter, Pieter, Peer**.

Cogns.: Fr.: PIERRE. Sp., Port.: **Pedro**. Cat.: **Pei(d)ró, Pere**. It.: **P(i)e(t)ri, Preto, Pretti, Pedri, P(i)erri, Pierro, Pero, Pei(re), P(e)iro, Pirri, Peyro**. Rum.: **Petru**. Low Ger.: PETTER, **Peer**. Swed.: **Petré(n)**. Ger. (of Slav. origin): **Petran**. Czech: **Petr, Petera, Pet(r)ák, Petrás, Petráň, Petrů; Pešák, Peš**. Pol.: **Piotr, Pietras**. Hung.: **Péter(i)**.

Dims.: Eng.: **Peet, Peat**; PELL; **Peattie, Pe(a)ddie** (N England and Scotland); **Perell, Parell**; PERROWNE; PERRIN; PARROTT; PARKIN; PETHICK (Cornwall); PETRIE (Scotland). It.: **Pe(t)relli, Pitrelli, Perrelli, Pe(t)r(i)ello, Pe(t)rilli, Pe(t)rillo, Pitrillo, Pirello, Pirelli, Perrillo, Pedr(i)elli, Perillio, Petrelluzzi; Petrozz(in)i, Pedrozzi, P(i)erozzi, Pirozzi, Pirozzolo, P(e)rozzo, Prozillo, Perocci; Petrucco, P(i)etrucci, Pedrucci, P(i)erucci, Prucci, Pieruccio, Perrucci(o), Petruccelli, Petrucc(h)ini, Petruzzi, P(i)eruzzi, Pe(t)ruzzo, Petruzzio, Petuzzo, Petruzzelli, Petruzziello, Perut(ti), Perutto, Petruzziello, Petrussi, Prusso; Petrizz(ell)i, Periz(zi), Pedrizzoli; Petroccello, Petroselli, Petriccelli, Petroccini, Petriccini, Petricciolo, Petrocchi, Pedrocco, Pedrocchi, Pirocchi; Petrol(in)i, Petrol(in)o, Pedrol(in)i, Pe(t)rolo, Pedrioli, Pe(i)roli, Pirioli, Pirolini, Pittoli, Petrolli, Pedrollo, Pe(t)rullo, Perrulo, Perulli, Perruli**; see also PARROTT and PERRIN. Ger.: **Pischel** (Silesia); **Pöschel** (Bavaria). Low Ger.: **Pe(e)termann**. Fris.: **Pie(te)rsma**. Flem., Du.: **Pie(t), Pee**. Ger. (of Slav. origin): **Pet(e)rick, Petrusch, Pietruschka, Pet(r)asch, P(i)etsch, Pietz(ke), Petz(old), Petzolt, Pötzold, Patzelt, Pes(s)olt, Pessold, Piesold, Pessel, Posselt, Poss(e), Possa, Possek, Pe(t)schel(t), Peschke, Peschka, Peschmann; Pech(e), Pecht, Pächt, Pechan, Pech(h)old; Piche, Pioch, Piech(a), Piechnik, Pichan, Pichmann; Perschke, Pers(i)cke, Persich, Persian**. Czech: **Petráček, Petrášek, Petrásek, Petránek; Petřík, Petříček, Petřína; Pešek, Pešík; Pech(a); Pecháček**. Pol.: **Pietrzyk, Pietrzycki, Pietrasik, Pietraszek, Pietruszka, Pietranek**. Ukr.: **Petrus, Petrik, Petrenko, Petrushanko, Petlyura**. Beloruss.: **Petruk**. Jewish (E Ashkenazic, adoptions of non-Jewish surnames): **P(i)etruszka, Petrus(h)ka**. Hung.: **Pet(t)kó, Petö, Petri**.

Augs.: It.: **P(i)etroni, Troni, Pedron(i), Spedroni, P(i)eroni, Peron(e), Perroni, Perrone, Pirrone, Peirone, Pitone**.

Pejs.: It.: **Petrazzi, Trazzi, Pedrazzi, P(i)erazzi, Pirazzi, Perazzo, Petracc(h)i, Spedracci, Pieracci, Raccio, Pe(t)racco, Pe(t)rasso, Pitrasso, Perassi**.

Patrs.: Eng.: **Peters(on); Pethers, Pithers** (Cornwall). Sc.: MCFETRIDGE. It.: **De Pietri, De Pietro, Di Pietro, Di Pierro, De Pero, (De) Petris, Perris**. Sp.: **Pérez**. Cat.: **Peris, Piris**. Port.: **Peres, Pires**. Rum.: **Petrescu**. Ger.: **Petri, Petry** (Latinized). Low Ger.: **Pet(t)ers, Pieters, Peers**. Fris.: **Pietringa**. Flem., Du.: **Pe(e)ters, Pieters; P(i)eterse(n); Petri**. Norw., Dan.: **Petersen, Pedersen**. Swed.: **Pet(t)ersson, Pe(h)rsson**. Pol.: **Pietrowicz, Piotrowicz; Pietrzak, Pietrasiak, Pietrusiak**. Russ.: **Petrov(ykh)**. Croatian: **Petr(ov)ić; Per(ov)ić, Pešić**. Bulg.: **Petrov**. Jewish (E Ashkenazic, adoptions of non-Jewish surnames): **Petrov, Petroff**. Lithuanian: **Petráitis, Petrulis, Petronis, Petráuskas**. Gk: **Petrou(lis)**. Armenian: **Petrosian, Bedrosian**. Hung.: **Péterf(f)y, Petöfi**.

Patrs. (from dims.): Flem., Du.: **Pien(s), Pergens**. Ger. (of Slav. origin): **Pietzker, Pietzner, Pessler, Pässler, Passler**. Russ.: **Petra(ch)kov, Petrash(k)ov, Petrishchev, Petryashov, Petrun(k)in, Pet(r)aev, Pet(ru)ichev, Petin(ov), Petugin, Petyakov, Petyan(k)in**. Pol.: **Pietruszewicz, Pietrusikiewicz, Pietrkiewicz**. Ukr.: **Petrus(k)evich, Petrichat**. Beloruss.: **Petrush(k)evich, Petrashkevich**. Croatian: **Petković; Perišić**. Bulg.: **Petkov**.

Habitation names: Pol.: **Piotrowski, Pietrowski, Pietruszewski; Pietrzykowski; Petrykowski**. Jewish (E Ashkenazic): **Piotrkowski, Piotrkowsky, Piotrkovski, Piotrkovsky**.

Pethick Cornish: from the Corn. given name *Petroc* or *Pedrek*, a dim. of PETER. St Petroc is a local saint, of whom very little of historical value is known, but who is commemorated in several placenames, including *Padstow* (earlier *Sancte Petroces stow*).

Vars.: **Petherick, Pedrick**.

Pethybridge English (Cornwall and Devon): habitation name from a place near Lustleigh in S Devon, so called from the OE personal name *Pyd(d)a* or *Pidda* (cf. PIDDINGTON) + ME *brigge* BRIDGE.

Petipa French: 1. nickname for a man with a mincing gait, from OF *petit* small (see PETTIT) + *pas* step, stride (L *passus*).
2. habitation name from any of the various minor places named with the OF elements *petit* small, narrow + *pas* passage (L *passus*, originally the same word as in 1 above).

Petrie Scots: 1. dim. of PETER.
2. dim. of PATRICK.

Petter 1. English (Norman): nickname for a flatulent person, from an agent deriv. of OF *peter* to fart (from *pet* a fart, L *peditum*, past part. of *pedere* to fart).
2. Low German: var. of PETER.
Vars. (of 1): **Pet(t)our**.
Dims. (of 1): Fr.: **Pét(a)in, Péton, Pétot**.
Aug. (of 1): Fr.: **Pétat**.
Pejs. (of 1): Fr.: **Pétard, Pethard, Pétaud**.

Pettifer English (Norman): nickname from OF *pie de fer* iron foot (LL *pēs de ferro*), given perhaps to someone with an artificial foot or leg, or to a tireless walker.
Vars.: **Pettyfer, Pettipher, Pettefer, Pettiver, Pettyfor, Pettafor, Pettiford, Pettifar, Pettefar, Puddifer; Pot(t)iphar** (altered by folk etymology to conform to the name of Pharaoh's captain of the guard in Gen. 39).
Cogn.: It.: **Pedeferro**.

Pettigrew Scots (Norman): apparently a nickname for a small man, from OF *petit* little, small (see PETTIT) + *cru* growth (past part. of *creistre* to grow, increase, L *crescere*). Another explanation is that it is a nickname for a man with long thin legs, from OF *pie de grue* crane's foot (LL *pēs de gruā*).
Vars.: **Petticrew, Petticrow, Pettigree, Pet(t)egree**.
The first known bearer of the name is Thomas Petykreu *of Lanarks., recorded in 1296.*

Pettingell English: ethnic name for someone from Portugal. The name derives from LL *Portucale*, originally referring only to the area around the trading base of Oporto (*Portus Cales*, from L *portus* port, harbour (see PORT 2) + *Cales*, the ancient name of the town). In some cases the surname may be no more than a nickname for someone who had business connections with Portugal.
Vars.: **Pettingall, Pettingale, Pettingill, Pettengell, Pettengill, Puttergill, Portingale, Portugal**.
Cogns.: Port.: **Portugal**. It.: **Portogallo, Portoghese, Portoghesi**. Flem., Du.: **Portugaels**. Jewish: **Portugal; Portugues(e), Portuguez, Portugheis, Portugais; Portugali, Portugaly** (with the Hebr. ending *-i*).

Pettit English: nickname for a small person, or for the younger of two bearers of the same given name, from ANF *petit* small (a word of obscure and isolated origin, probably a nursery word).
Vars.: **Petit, Petyt, Pettitt, Pettet, Pittet, Petty, Pettie**.
Cogns.: Fr.: **Petit, Lepetit**. Cat.: **Petit**.
Dims.: Fr.: **Petiteau, Peti(t)et, Peti(t)on, Peti(t)ot, Petetot, Petetin, Pit(t)iot; Péchin, Péchon, Pechon, Péchou(x), Péchot, Pechot**.
Patr.: Fr.: **Aupetit**.

Petukhov Russian: patr. from the nickname *Petukh* 'Cock' (from *pet* to sing), denoting a lusty or self-important person.
Cogns.: Beloruss.: **Pyatuch**. Pol.: **Pietucha**. Jewish (E Ashkenazic): **P(i)etuchowski** (reason for adoption unknown).

Peutherer Scots and English: occupational name for a pewterer, someone who made articles of pewter (an alloy of tin and lead), from ME *peutrer* (OF *peautrier*, an agent deriv. of *peau(l)tre* pewter, the further etymology of which is unknown).
Vars.: **Pewterer, Powter, Pouter**.

Pevzner Jewish (Ashkenazic): of uncertain origin, possibly from Yid. *Poyzner*, a habitation name from the city of *Poznań* (Ger. *Posen*, Yid. *Poyzn*) in Poland. See POZNAŃSKI.
Var.: **Pevsner**.

Pewsey English: habitation name from a place so called in Wilts., recorded in Domesday Book as *Pevesie*, apparently from the gen. case of an OE personal name ***Pefe*, not independently attested + OE *ēg* island.
Var.: PUSEY.

Peyzer English: occupational name for an official in charge of weights and measures, especially one whose duty it was to weigh rent or tribute received, from ANF *peiser*, *poiser* weigher (LL *pensārius*, a deriv. of *pensāre* to weigh, for class. L *pendere*, past. part. *pensus*).
Vars.: **P(e)iser, Peizer, Pyser, Pyzer, Po(y)ser, Poyzer; Penzer** (with *-n-* reflecting a trace of the L word).

Pfeidler S German and Austrian: occupational name for a maker of goatskin garments, S Ger. dial. *Pfeidler* (mod. sense 'shirtmaker'), an agent deriv. of a dim. of MHG *pfeit* goatskin cloak (OHG *pfeit*, from Gk *baitē*).
Vars.: **Pfeitler, Pfaitler, Feidler**.

Pfeil German: metonymic occupational name for an arrowsmith, or perhaps a nickname for a tall thin man, from Ger. *Pfeil* arrow (MHG, OHG *pfīl*, from L *pīlum* spike, javelin; cf. PILE 1).
Vars.: **Pfeiler; Pfeilschmidt** (see SMITH).
Cogns.: Low Ger.: **Piel(mann), Pyl**. Flem., Du.: **Van den Pijl(l), Pijlman**. Dan., Norw., Swed.: **Pi(e)hl**.
Dims.: Low Ger.: **Pielk(e)**.

Pfirsich German: metonymic occupational name for a grower or seller of peaches, from Ger. *Pfirsich* peach (MHG *pfersich*, from LL *persica*, for class. L *persicum* (*malum*) Persian apple).
Vars.: **Pfersich, Pfirsching, Pfersching, Pförsching; Pershing** (U.S.).
General John Pershing *(1860–1948), the commander of American forces in the First World War, was descended from Alsatian Huguenots whose name was originally* Pfoersching.

Pfister S German: occupational name for a baker, southern MHG *pfister* (from L *pistor* baker, miller, from *pinsere*, past part. *pistus*, to grind, mill).
Var.: **Pfisterer** (with the addition of the Ger. agent suffix).
Cogns.: Low Ger.: **Pister**. Flem.: **De Pester, Pisterman**. Fr.: **Pisteur** (Switzerland). It.: **Pistor(i), Pistore, Pistorio**.
Dims.: It.: **Pistorello, Pistorino, Pistorini**.

Pfützer German: topographic name for someone who lived by a well or a pond, MHG *pfütze* (mod. Ger. *Pfütze* puddle; from L *puteus* well; cf. PUITS).
Vars.: **Pfützner; Pfitz(n)er** (Austria); **Fitzner** (Silesia); **Pfützmann, Pfitzmann**.
Cogns.: Flem., Du.: **(Van den) Put, Van (den) Putten, Putter**.

Philbert French: from *Filibert*, a Gmc personal name composed of the elements *filu* very + *berht* bright, famous, which was borne by a 7th-cent. saint, abbot of Jumièges. The spelling has been influenced by the various given names of Gk origin containing the element *phil-* love; cf. e.g. PHILIP.

Var.: **Philibert**.

Philip English, French, Dutch/Flemish, and Danish/Norwegian: from the Gk name *Philippos* (from *philein* to love + *hippos* horse), borne by one of the apostles, as well as by various other early saints. Unusually for a common Christian name, it seems to owe its popularity more to the medieval romances about Alexander the Great, whose father was Philip of Macedon, than to any saint. The surname is also occasionally borne by Jews, in which case it represents an adoption of a non-Jewish surname or an Anglicization of some like-sounding Jewish surname.

Vars.: Eng.: **Philipp, Phillip, Phil(l)p, Phelp, Phalp**. Fr.: **Philippe, Phélip, Félip, Phélit, Phelip, Phalip**. Flem., Du.: **Filip**. Jewish: **Philipp, Phillip, Filip**.

Cogns.: It.: **Filippo, Filippi; Filpo, Filpi** (S Italy); **Firpo, Firpi** (Liguria); **Lippi, Lippo** (Tuscany). Sp., Port.: **Felipe**. Cat.: **Felip**. Ger.: **Philipp**; LIPPE. Pol., Czech: **Filip**. Hung.: **Fülep, Fülöp**.

Dims.: Eng.: PHILPOTT, **Philott; Phippin, Phippen; Philcock, Philcott**. Fr.: **Philip(p)eau(x), Phélipeau, Philip(p)et, Philip(p)on, Phlipon**. It.: **Filippini, Lippini, Filippelli, Filippello, Lippiello, Filippetti, Filippucci, Filipputti, Filippozzi**. Czech: **Filípek**. Pol.: **Filipek**. Ukr.: **Pilipyak, Pilipets, Pikhno**.

Augs.: It.: **Filippone, Filipponi**.

Pejs.: Fr.: **Philip(p)ault, Philip(p)art, Philip(p)ard**. It.: **Filippazzo**.

Patrs.: Eng.: **Phil(l)ip(p)s, Phillis; Phil(l)ps; Phel(i)ps** (S and SW England); **Phip(p)s; Philip(p)son, Phillipson; Phipson**. Sc.: **McPhilip, McPhillips**, MCKILLOP. It.: **De Filippo, De Filippi(s), Di Filippo**. Ger.: **Philippi** (Latinized). Low Ger.: **Philipps(en), Ph(i)lips, Flips(en)**. Flem., Du.: **Philips, Flippen**. Dan., Norw.: **Philipsen**. Swed.: **Philipsson**. Jewish (Ashkenazic): **Phil(l)ips, Philip(p)sohn, Filipson**. Russ.: **Filippov, Filip(p)yev**. Pol.: **Filipowicz; Filipczak, Filipiak**. Croatian: **Filip(ov)ić, Pilipović**. Bulg.: **Filipov**. Gk.: **Philippou**.

Patrs. (from dims.): Eng.: **Fills, Philson, Filson; Phillins**, FILKINS, **Phil(l)cox**. Low Ger.: **Lipgens**. Russ.: **Filipchikov, Filipychev, Fil(k)ov, Fil(ya)ev, Fil(k)in, Filyakov, Filyukov, Filchakov, Filinkov, Filyushkin, Filyashin, Filchagin, Filisov, Filasov, Filochov, Filintsev, Filshin, Khilkov**. Croatian: **Piletić**.

Habitation name: Pol.: **Filipczyński**.

The Phipps *family, who are Marquesses of Normanby and Earls of Mulgrave, are descended from Constantine Phipps (1656–1723), who was Lord Chancellor of Ireland. A more humble cousin, Sir William Phip(p)s (1651–95), was born in Maine, America, where his parents had emigrated. He was originally a ship's carpenter, but was knighted by Charles II, and rose to become governor of Massachusetts.*

The form Phipson *is rare, being found almost exclusively in the Stourbridge area of Worcs. in the late 18th and early 19th cents. It seems likely that all present-day bearers are descended from a certain Richard Phipson, living at Bewdley at the end of the 17th cent. The first known bearer of the name is Edward Phipson, who was married in 1564 at Ludlow, Shrops., and may have been an earlier ancestor.*

The form Filson *is recorded in Dartmouth, Devon, in 1600, when Thomas Filson married Joane Reade.* Philson *is the name of a large Protestant family of Magheraboy, Co. Donegal, whose earliest known member is Robert Philson, b. c.1700; his descendants are now found in the U.S.A. and New Zealand, as well as Ireland.*

Phillimore English: from a Norman personal name, *Filimor*, composed of the Gmc elements *filu* very + *meri, mari* famous. The spelling has been altered under the influence of PHILIP.

Vars.: **Fil(l)more**.

Philosoph Jewish (Ashkenazic): Germanized form of a Yid. nickname from *filesof, pilesof* philosopher, also used ironically to mean 'ignoramus'.

Vars.: **Philossoph, Philozof, Filosof(f), Filozof, Pilos(s)of**.

Philpott English (mainly Kentish): from the ME given name *Phil(i)pot*, a dim. of PHILIP with the hypocoristic suffix *-ot*.

Vars.: **Phillpott, Phil(l)pot, Phillippot**, POTT.

Cogns.: Fr.: **Philip(p)ot, Phélipot, Flipot**.

Patrs.: Eng.: **Phil(l)pots, Philpotts**.

Piaget French: metonymic occupational name for the keeper of a toll booth. The surname is found principally around Lyon, and represents a local pronunciation of OF *péaget*, a dim. of *péage* toll (booth) (from LL *pediaticum* right to cross, set foot on, from *pēs*, gen. *pedis*, foot).

Piasecki Polish: topographic name for someone who lived in a sandy place, from Pol. *pias(ek)* sand, or habitation name from a place named with this element.

Vars.: **Piaskowski; Piasny; Piaseczny** (probably a habitation name from *Piaseczno*, just S of Warsaw); **Piaskowiak** (also an occupational name for a dealer in sand).

Piątkowski Polish: from the Pol. given name *Pątek* 'Friday', with the addition of the common surname ending *-owski*. Illegitimate children were often given the name of the day of the week on which they were baptized; even more frequently, converted Jews took as a surname the name of the day on which they were baptized.

Var.: **Piątek**.

Cogn.: Czech: **Pátek**.

Patr.: Pol.: **Piątkiewicz**.

Picazo Spanish: nickname from Sp. *picazo* magpie, given perhaps to a talkative or thievish person, or to someone who had a streak of white among black hair. The word seems to derive from L *pīca* (see PYE 1), but the suffix is obscure.

Cogn.: Cat.: **Picassó**.

Piccini Italian: nickname for a small person, from It. *piccino* small (of uncertain etymology, perhaps related to the group of words discussed at PIKE).

Vars.: **Piccin, Pizzin(i)** (Venetia); **Piccinni, Piccinno** (Tuscany); **Picc(i)oli, Picc(i)olo, Pizz(i)oli, Pizz(i)olo, Picci(o)tto, Picciocchi, Picciulli, Picciullo, Picciuzzo**.

Cogn.: Sp.: **Pequeño**.

Dims.: It.: **Piccinelli, Pizzinelli, Piccinin(i), Piccinino, Pizzinini; Piccolin(i), Piccolino, Picolotto**.

Patr.: It.: **Del Piccolo**.

Piccolomo Italian: nickname for a small man, from It. *piccolo* small (see PICCINI) + *uomo* man (L *homo*, gen. *hominis*).

Var.: **Piccolomini**.

Pick 1. English: metonymic occupational name for someone who made or used a pick or pickaxe as an agricultural or excavating tool, from ME *pi(c)k*. This is probably from OE *pīc* (see PIKE 3), although the shortening of the vowel is something of a mystery. See also PEAK.

2. Jewish (E Ashkenazic): of unknown origin.

Dims. (of 1): **Pickin, Picken**.

Pickard English: 1. regional name for someone from Picardy (Fr. *Picardie*) in N France, a region adjoining

Normandy, from which many of William the Conqueror's companions and followers came.

2. some early examples, such as Paganus *filius Pichardi* (Hants 1160), seem to point to derivation from a Gmc personal name, probably composed of the elements *bic* sharp point, pointed weapon + *hard* hardy, brave, strong.

Var. (of 2): PITCHER.

Cogns.: Fr.: **Picard** (partly Jewish), **Piccard, Piquard, Picart, Piquart, Lepicard**. It.: **Pic(c)ardi, Pic(c)ardo**. Ger.: **Pikhar(d)t**.

Dims.: It.: **Pic(c)ardino**.

Pickerden English: of uncertain origin. From its form it would appear to be a habitation name, but no suitable placename is known. The first known bearer is a certain William Pickerden of Hastings, Sussex, recorded in 1591, and if the William *Picardin* whose will was proved at Hastings in 1593 is the same person, it may be a dim. of PICKARD. The surname has been strongly concentrated in E Sussex from its first occurrence to the present day, and it seems likely that all bearers belong to a single family.

Pickerell English: nickname for a sharp and aggressive person, from ME *pykerell* young pike (from ME *pyke* pike (the fish) + *-ell* dim. suffix).

Vars.: **Pick(e)rill, Pickrell**.

Pickering English: habitation name from a town in N Yorks., so called from an OE tribal name *Piceringas*. Ekwall suggests that this is earlier *Pīcōringas* 'people on the ridge (see ORR 3) of the pointed hill (see PIKE 1)'.

Var.: **Pickerin**.

Pickersgill English (Yorks.): habitation name from a place in W Yorks., apparently originally named as 'Robber's Ravine', from ME *pyker* thief + *gill* gully (see GILL 2).

Var.: **Pickersgil**.

Pickford English: habitation name, perhaps from *Pickforde* 'pig ford' in Ticehurst, Sussex. The surname is now most common in the Manchester region, but it does not seem to have reached there before the 17th cent.

Pickholz Jewish (Ashkenazic): ornamental name from Yid. *pikholts* woodpecker (from Ger. *picken* to peck + *Holz* wood), one of the large group of Ashkenazic surnames taken from words denoting birds and animals.

Var.: **Pikholz**.

Pickles English (Yorks.): topographic name for someone who lived by a small field or paddock, ME *pigh(t)el* (of obscure origin).

Vars.: **Pickless, Pighills**.

Pickup English: habitation name from a place in Lancs., so called from OE *pīc* point (see PIKE 1) + *copp* top, i.e. a hill with a sharp peak.

Picton English: habitation name from any of various places, for example in Ches. and N Yorks., so called from OE *pīc* point, peak (or the derived byname *Pīca*; see PIKE 1 and 6) + *tūn* enclosure, settlement.

Var.: **Pickton**.

Pidal Spanish: topographic name for someone who lived by a plant nursery or metonymic occupational name for a nurseryman, from OSp. *pibdal* nursery (LL *pīpītāle*, a deriv. of *pīpīta* seed, class. L *pītuīta* gum exuded from trees).

Piddington English: habitation name from places so called in Northants and Oxon., both from OE *Pydingtūn* 'settlement (OE *tūn*) associated with *Pyda*'.

Pidgeon English: 1. metonymic occupational name for a hunter of wood pigeons, or nickname for a foolish or gullible person, since the birds were easily taken. ME *pigeon* (from OF *pijon* young bird, LL *pipio*, gen. *pipiōnis*, an imitative formation) was also used to denote a young DOVE.

2. from *Pet(y)jon*, a nickname from ME *pety* small (see PETTIT) + the given name JOHN. Cf. LITTLEJOHN.

Vars. (of 1): **Pid(e)on, Pidgen, Piggin**.

Cogns. (of 1): Fr.: **Pigeon, Pichon, Pichou(nier)**. It.: **Piccioni, Piccione, Piggini**.

Piechota Polish: 1. nickname for someone who travelled about on foot, from Pol. *na piechotę* on foot (the vocab. word is not found in the nominative). Cf. Russ. PESHKOV.

2. from a pet form of *Piotr* PETER.

Var.: **Piechocki**.

Patr. (from 2): **Piechowiak**.

Piedade Portuguese: religious byname from Port. *piedade* compassion, pity (L *pietas*, gen. *pietātis*), an attribute of the Virgin Mary, *Maria da Piedade*.

Piekarski Polish: occupational name for a baker, from Pol. *piekarz* baker + *-ski* suffix of surnames (see BARANOWSKI).

Var.: **Piekarz**.

Cogns.: Czech: **Pekař**. Croatian: **Pek(ov)ić** (patrs.).

Dim.: Czech: **Pekárek**.

Pieńkowski Polish: topographic name for someone who lived where hemp was grown, from Pol. *pieńka* hemp + *-ów* possessive suffix, + *-ski* suffix of local surnames (see BARANOWSKI).

Piera Catalan: habitation name from a place in the province of Barcelona, so called from an aphetic form of OCat. *apiera* beehive (L *apiāria*, a deriv. of *apis* bee). In some cases it may also derive from the vocab. word and be a metonymic occupational name for a beekeeper.

Var.: **Pié**.

Pierre French: 1. from the Fr. given name *Pierre*, a cogn. of PETER.

2. topographic name for someone who lived on a patch of stony soil or by a large outcrop of rock, from OF *pierre* stone, rock (L *petra*, from Gk). It may also be a metonymic occupational name for a quarryman or stone-carver; cf. PERRIER.

Vars. (of 2): **Lapierre, Delapierre**.

Cogns. (of 1) Prov.: **P(i)eyre, Peire**. (Of 2): Prov.: **Peyre, Lapière, Lapeyre; Sapeyre** (Rousillon). It.: **Dellapietra**. Sp.: **Piedra**.

Dims. (of 1): Fr.: **Pérel, Péreau, Perreau; P(i)erron, Perronet, P(ey)ron(et), Péronel, Perronel, Péroneau, Perron(n)eau, Peyroneau, Perron(n)in, Peyronin, Pe(y)rony, Perronot; Perruc, Peyruc** (Brittany). Prov.: **Pe(d)ron, Pezron, Pierrou, Perroux**. See also PARROTT and PERRIN.

Augs. (of 1): Fr.: **P(i)errat, Piérat**.

Pejs. (of 1): Fr.: **P(i)errard, P(i)érard; Perrau(l)t, Perriault, Pérau(l)t, Peyraud**.

Collectives (of 2): Sp.: **Pedraza** (places in the provinces of Lugo and Segovia), **Pedrera** (a place in the province of Sevilla), **Pedreira** (Galicia). Port.: **Pedreira**.

Pierrepont French and English (Norman): habitation name from any of various places, for example in Aisne and Calvados, so called from OF PIERRE stone + PONT bridge.

Vars.: Eng.: **Pierrepoint, Pierpon(t), Pearpoint, Pairpoint**.

Pierzchała Polish: nickname for a harum-scarum or hothead, from a deriv. of the verb *pierzchać*, which in OPol.

meant 'to be angry' (it has since acquired the meaning 'to run away').

Var.: **Pierzchalski**.

Pigg English (Northumb.): metonymic occupational name for a swineherd or nickname for someone supposedly resembling a pig or young hog, ME *pigge* (of uncertain origin; although an OE form is not attested, there is oblique evidence for it in the word *picbrēd* pigfood, i.e. acorns).

Piggott English: from the ME, OF given name *Picot*, *Pigot*, a dim. of *Pic* (see PIKE 6). In ME, the form *Piket* (OF *Picquet*) was also common.

Vars.: **Pigott**, **Pig(g)ot**, **Pygott**, **Picot**; **Pi(c)kett**, **Pykett** (Notts.).

Cogns.: Fr.: **Pigot**, **Pic(qu)ot**, **Pichot**; **Pi(c)quet**, **Piet**. It.: **Pi(c)chetti**; **Pigotti**, **Pigozzi**, **Pigozzo**.

Dim.: Fr.: **Piqueton**.

A family by the name of Pigott *trace their descent from Richard* Pigot, *who was justiciar of Chester in 1431. They were established for eight generations in Butley, Ches., from 1189.*

Pike English: 1. topographic name for someone who lived near a hill with a sharp point, from OE *pīc*, which was a relatively common placename element (cf. PICKERING and PICKUP).

2. metonymic occupational name for a pike fisherman or nickname for a predatory individual, from ME *pike* (OE **pīc*, the fish being named from its pointed jaw).

3. metonymic occupational name for a user of a pointed tool for breaking up the earth, ME *pike* (cf. PICK).

4. metonymic occupational name for a medieval foot-soldier who used a pike, a weapon consisting of a sharp pointed metal end on a long pole, ME *pic* (OF *pique*, of Gmc origin).

5. nickname for a tall, thin person, from a transferred sense of one of the above.

6. from a Gmc personal name (derived from the root 'sharp', 'pointed' underlying all of the above), found in ME and OF as *Pic*.

7. nickname from OF *pic* woodpecker (from L *pīcus*, perhaps named from its pointed beak and so ultimately cogn. with the other words of this group; see also PYE, SPEIGHT, and PICKHOLZ).

Var.: **Pyke**. See also PICK and PEAK.

Cogns.: Fr.: **Pic(q)**, **Pique**, **Pigue**; **Lepic**. Ger.: **Picher(t)**. Low Ger.: **Pee(c)k**. Fris.: **Pieksma**. (Of 1 only): Fr.: **Dupic**. (Of 2, 3, and 4 only): Prov.: **Piquer**. Cat.: **Piquer**, **Piqué**. (Of 6 only): It.: **Picchi(o)**, **Pighi**.

Dims.: Fr.: **Picon**, **Pichon**, **Pichonneau**. (Of 2 only): Eng.: PICKERELL. (Of 6 only): Eng.: PIGGOTT.

Augs. (of 6): It.: **Picchioni**, **Pigoni**.

Pejs.: Fr.: **Pic(h)ard** (see also PICKARD); **Pic(h)aud**, **Pic(h)ault**, **Pigault**.

Pilcher English (Kentish): occupational name for a maker or seller of *pilches*, or nickname for a habitual wearer of one of these. A *pilch* was a kind of coarse leather garment with the hair or fur still on it (OE *pylece*, from LL *pellīcia*, a deriv. of *pellis* skin, hide, from which Ger. *Pelz* hide (OHG *pelliz*) is also derived). Cf. FELL. In early 17th-cent. English, *pilcher* was a popular term of abuse, being confused or punningly associated with the unrelated verb *pilch* to steal and with the unrelated noun *pilchard* a kind of fish.

Vars.: **Pilger**; **Pilch**.

Cogns. (occupational names for a tanner of hides): Ger.: **Pel(t)zer**, **Bel(t)zner**; **Pel(t)z**, **Bel(t)z**. Du.: **Pelser**. Jewish (Ashkenazic): **Pel(t)z**, **Pelzner**, **Pelzman(n)**. Fr.: PELISSE.

Pile 1. English: topographic name for someone who lived near a stake or post serving as a landmark, ME *pile* (OE *pīl*, from L *pīlum* spike, javelin; cf. PFEIL).

2. French: topographic name for someone who lived in a depression or hollow, from OF *pile* trough, mortar (L *pīla* mortar; both *pīlum* and *pīla* are derivs. of *pinsere* to grind, crush (cf. PFISTER and PISTOL)). The surname may perhaps also have been a metonymic occupational name for someone who made or used such vessels.

Var. (of 1): **Pyle**.

Dims. (of 2): **Pil(l)et**, **Pil(l)ot**, **Pil(l)on**.

Pilgrim English: nickname for a person who had been on a pilgrimage to the Holy Land (cf. PALMER) or to some seat of devotion in Europe such as Santiago de Compostella or Rome (cf., e.g., KUMSTELLER and ROMAN), or to one nearer home, for example the tomb of St Thomas à Becket at Canterbury. Such pilgrimages were often imposed as penances, graver sins requiring more arduous journeys. The word *pilgrim* is from ME *pilegrim*, *pelgrim*, OF *pelegrin* (L *peregrīnus* traveller, a deriv. of *peregre* abroad, from L *per agros* lit. 'through the fields', from *ager* field). Pilgrim was also occasionally used as a given name, and the surname may in some cases be derived from this use.

Vars.: **Pilgram**, **Peagrim**, **Piggrem**, **Pigram**, **P(e)agram**, **Peg(g)ram**, **Pegrum**, **Pi(e)grome**; **Pelerin**; **Peregrine**, **Paragreen**.

Cogns.: Fr.: **Pellegrin**, **Pélégrin**, **Pelgrin**. Prov.: **Péle(g)rin**, **Péligry**, **Pelegry**, **Pelegri**. It.: **Pelle(g)rini**, **Pelle(g)rino**. Sp.: **Pelegrín**, **Peregrín**. Cat.: **Pelegrí**. Port.: **Peregrino**. Ger.: **Pilgrim**, **Pilgram**. Low Ger.: **Pehlgrimm**, **Pälegrimm**. Flem., Du.: **Pelgrim**, **Pelgram**.

Dims.: It.: **Pellegrinelli**, **Pellegrinetti**, **Pellegrinotti**.

Pilkington English: habitation name from a place in the parish of Prestwich, Lancs., so called from OE *Pīlecingtūn* 'settlement (OE *tūn*) associated with *Pīleca*'.

This is the name of a landowning family traceable in the region around Salford to the 14th cent.

Pill English (Devon and Cornwall): 1. topographic name for someone who lived by a stream or creek, OE *pyll*.

2. nickname for a small, round person, from ME, OF *pil(l)e* ball (LL *pilula*, a dim. of class. L *pila*).

Vars. (of 1): PELL; **Piller**, **Peller**, **Puller**; **Pillman**, **Pel(l)man**, **Pul(l)man**; **Pilling**.

Pillay English: habitation name from either of two places now called *Pilley*. One in S Yorks. is recorded as *Pillei* in Domesday Book and as *Pillay* in the late 12th cent. It is probably from OE *pīl* pile, post (see PILE 1) + *lēah* wood, clearing, i.e. a wood where timber for piles could be obtained. One in Hants appears in Domesday Book as *Piste(s)lei*, but has later spellings resembling those for *Pilley* in Yorks., and may have the same etymology.

Var.: **Pilley**.

Pilshchikov Russian: patr. from the occupational term *pilshchik* sawyer (from *pilit* to saw).

Cogns. (not patrs.): Beloruss. and Jewish (E Ashkenazic): **Pilnik**. Pol.: **Pilarski**; **Piłat**. Czech: **Pilař**, **Pilát**. Ger. (of Slav. origin): **Pilar(tz)**.

Dims.: Pol.: **Pilarczyk**, **Pilarek**.

Pilz German and Jewish (Ashkenazic): metonymic occupational name for a gatherer or grower of mushrooms, from Ger. *Pilz* mushroom (MHG *bül(e)z*, OHG *buliz*, from L *bōlētus*).

Vars.: **Piltz**. Ger. only: **Bilz**. Jewish only: **Pilzer**.

Cogns.: Low Ger.: **Pils**. Pol.: **Pilc**.

Pimenta Portuguese: metonymic occupational name for a grower of peppers, from Port. *pimenta* red pepper (LL *pigmenta*, from class. L *pigmentum* paint, pigment, a deriv. of *pingere* to paint; cf. PAINTER and PINTO). The fruit was so called because of its bright colour. The surname may also have arisen as a nickname for someone with a red face or a quick temper or wit.

Dim.: **Pimentel** (also Jewish (N Sefardic), reason for adoption unknown). The Jewish name has also been altered to **Pimenthal** by association with the many ornamental Ashkenazic names ending in *-t(h)al* valley.

Pimm English: from the medieval female given name *Pymme*, *Pimme*, vernacular short forms of *Euphemia*, a Gk name composed of the elements *eu* well + *phēnai* to speak, i.e. to avoid words of ill omen. The name was adopted by early Christians in the sense 'praise of God' or 'good repute', and was borne by a 4th-cent. virgin martyr burnt at the stake in Chalcedon. It was popular in England in the Middle Ages, official documents usually recording only the learned form.

Vars.: **Pim**, **Pym(m)**.

Dims.: **Pim(b)let(t)** (chiefly Lancs.); **Pim(b)lott**.

Pinard French: nickname from OF *pinard*, a small medieval coin, so called because it bore the device of a pine cone (see PINE). The name may have denoted someone who paid a rent of this amount; the term seems also to have been used as a derogatory term for a rich man or miser.

Var.: **Pinart**.

Dims.: **Pinardel**, **Pinardeau**, **Pinardon**.

Pinch English: nickname for a chirpy person, from ME *pinch*, *pink* (chaf)finch (OE *pinc(a)*; cf. FINCH and FINK).

Var.: **Pin(c)k**.

Cogn.: Czech: **Pěnkava**.

Dim.: Eng.: **Pinkett**.

Patr.: Eng.: **Pinks**.

Pinchas Jewish: from the Hebr. male given name *Pinechas* (of Egyptian origin).

Vars.: **Pinhas**; **Pinches** (from the Yid. form *Pinkhes*); **Pinchasi**, **Pinhas(s)i**, **Pinhasy** (with the Hebr. ending *-i*). See also FINCH.

Dim.: **Pinko** (from Yid. *Pinke*).

Patrs.: **Pin(c)hasov**, **Pinchasow**, **Pinhassof**, **Pinhasovi(t)ch**, **Pinhassovitch**, **Pinhassovitz** (E Ashkenazic).

Patrs. (from dims.): (Ashkenazic): **Pin(n)es**, **Pinus**, **Pinas**, PINSON (from Yid. *Pinye*); **Pineles** (from Yid. *Pinyele*). (E Ashkenazic, from E Yid. *Pinke*): **Pinkus**, **Pincus**, **Pinkas**, **Pincas**, **Pinkason**; **Pincov**, **Pincovich**, **Pinkowitz**, **Pincowitz**, **Pink(as)ovitz**, **Pincowski**; **Pincovici** (among Rumanian Jews); **Pinkoffs**, **Pincoffs** (with double suffix: Slav. *-ov* + Yid. *-s*).

Pinchbeck English: habitation name from a place in Lincs., apparently so called from OE *pinc(a)* (chaf)finch (see PINCH) + *bæc* back, ridge.

Var.: **Pinchback**.

Pincher English: nickname from ME *pinch(en)* to pinch, grip (from a Norman version of OF *pincier*, from LL *punctiāre* to prick, pierce, punch (freq. of *pungere*, past part. *punctus*), with the vowel altered by crossing with words of the PIKE group). The verb also had the transferred senses 'carp', 'cavil', and 'dispense meanly', and this may well be the origin of the surname.

Pejs.: Fr.: **Pinsard**; **Pinchard**, **Pinchart**, **Pinchaut** (Normandy).

Pinder English: occupational name for an official who was responsible for rounding up stray animals and placing them in a pound, from an agent deriv. of ME *pind(en)* to shut up, enclose (OE *pyndan*).

Vars.: **Pindar**, **Pindor**, **Pender**.

Pine English: topographic name for someone who lived by a conspicuous pine tree or in a pine forest, from ME *pine* (OE *pīn*, from L *pīnus*, reinforced by OF *pin* from the same source). It may also be a habitation name from various places named with this word, such as *Le Pin* in Calvados; in other cases it may originally have been a nickname for a tall, thin man, supposedly resembling a pine tree.

Var.: **Pyne**.

Cogns.: Fr.: **Pin**, **Dupin**; **Pinier**, **Pinié**. Prov.: **Py**, **Delpy**, **Alpy**, **Aupy**. It.: **Pin(i)**, **Pino**. Sp.: **Pino**, **Piñe(i)ro**; **Piña** ('pine cone'). Cat.: **Pi**. Port.: **Pinho**; **Pinheiro** (also Jewish (Sefardic); Anglicized as **Pinero**).

Dims.: Eng.: **Pinnell**, **Pinel**. Fr.: **Pineau(x)**, **Pinet**, **Pinot(eau)**, **Pinon**. Prov.: **Pinets**. It.: **Pinelli**, **Pinello**, **Pinetti**, **Pinotti** (all in part also from aphetic dim. forms of given names such as JACOB, JOSEPH, and PHILIP). Sp.: **Pinilla** (see also PEÑA). Cat.: **Piñol**.

Aug.: Fr.: **Pinat**.

Collectives: Fr.: **Pinoy**. Prov.: **Pinède**. Sp.: **Pinedo**, **Pineda**, **Pinar**. Cat.: **Pineda**. Port.: **Pinhal**.

The English dramatist Sir Arthur Wing Pinero *(1855–1934) was born in London of Sefardic descent; his family's name was originally* Pinheiro.

Pinkerton Scots and N Irish: habitation name from a place near Dunbar in the former county of E Lothian. The placename is probably of Eng. origin, with a final element from OE *tūn* enclosure, settlement, but the first part is obscure.

Pinkney English (Norman): habitation name from *Picquigny* in Somme, so called from a Gmc personal name *Pincino* (of obscure derivation) + the local suffix *-(i)ācum*.

Var.: **Pinckney**.

Pinner English: 1. occupational name for a maker of pins or pegs, from an agent deriv. of ME *pin* (OE *pinn*, apparently from L *pinna*; cf. PEÑA).

2. occupational name for a maker or user of combs, ANF *peigner* (from *peigne* comb, L *pecten*; cf. PEINADO).

3. habitation name from *Pinner*, now part of NW London, which derives its name from OE *pinn* pin, peg + *ōra* slope, ridge. The first element probably denoted a topographical projection, although it is also possible that it represents a byname.

Pinson 1. English and French: nickname from OF *pinson* finch (LL *pincio*, gen. *pinciōnis*, apparently of Gmc origin; cf. PINCH), perhaps applied to a bright and cheerful person.

2. English and French: metonymic occupational name for someone who made use of pincers or forceps in his work, from OF *pinson* pincers (a deriv. of *pincier* to pinch; cf. PINCHER).

3. Jewish (Ashkenazic): patr. from *Pine*, a pet form of the Yid male given name *Pinkhes* (see PINCHAS).

Vars. (of 1 and 2): Eng.: **Pinshon**, **Pinch(e)on**, **Pinchin(g)**, **Pinchen** (Norman forms); **Pinsent**. Fr.: **Pinçon**; **Pinchon** (Normandy, Picardy).

Pinto Spanish, Portuguese, Italian, and Jewish (Sefardic): nickname for a person with a blotchy complexion or pepper-and-salt hair, from *pinto* mottled (LL *pinctus*, for class. L *pictus*, past part. of *pingere* to paint).

Vars.: Sp.: **Pintado**. Port.: **Pinta** (partly Jewish, Anglicized **Pinter**). It.: **Pintus**, **Lo Pinto**, **La Pinta** (Sicily).

The English playwright Harold Pinter *(b. 1930) was born in E London, the son of a Sefardic Jewish tailor, whose family had migrated to London from Portugal, where they had borne the surname* Pinta.

Piper English: occupational name for a player on the pipes, ME *pipere*, OE *pīpere* (an agent deriv. of *pīpe* pipe (cogn.

with Ger. *Pfeife* whistle, pipe, OHG *pfīfa*), from LL *pīpa*, from *pīpāre* to pipe, squeak, of imitative origin; cf. PIDGEON).

Vars.: **Pyper**; **Pipe(s)**.

Cogns.: Ger.: **Pfeif(f)er**; **Pfiffer** (Switzerland); **Pfeuffer** (E Franconia); **Feiffer** (U.S.). Low Ger.: **Pi(e)per**; **Peiper** (N Rhineland); **Peifer** (Rhineland, Nassau). Flem., Du.: **De Pypere**, **Pieper**. Jewish (Ashkenazic): **Pfeiffer**, **Pfeuffer**; **Feifer** (from Yid. *fayfer* piper).

Patrs.: Low Ger.: **Pi(e)pers**, **Peipers**.

Pisani Italian: habitation name from the city of *Pisa* in Tuscany. This was probably founded by Greek colonists, but before coming under Roman control it was in the hands of the Etruscans, who seem to have given it its name. At any rate, the placename is of obscure meaning.

Vars.: **Pisano**; **Pisanu** (Sardinia); **Pisa**.

Dims.: **Pisanelli**, **Pisan(i)ello**.

Pisarski Polish: occupational name for a clerk or scribe, Pol. *pisarz* (from *pisać* to write), with the addition of the surname suffix *-ski* (see BARANOWSKI). Cf. SCHREIBER and SOFER for names with similar meanings.

Vars.: **Pisarz**, **Pisera**.

Cogns.: Czech: **Písař**. Ukr.: **Pisarevski**.

Dims.: Pol.: **Pisarek**, **Pisarczyk**. Czech: **Písařík**. Ukr.: **Pis(s)arenko**.

Patrs.: Russ.: **Pisarev**. Jewish (E Ashkenazic): **Pisareff**.

Patr. (from a dim.): Pol.: **Pisarkiewicz**.

Piskač Czech: metonymic occupational name or nickname for someone who played a fife or penny whistle, from Czech *piskač* (also *pištec*) whistle.

Var.: **Píštěk**.

Dim.: **Piskáček**.

Pistol English: metonymic occupational name for an apothecary or grocer, from ME, OF *pistel*, *pestel* pestle (L *pistillum*, later *pestillum*, from *pinsere*, past part. *pistus*, to crush, grind).

Var.: **Pestell**.

Cogns.: Fr.: **Peste(i)l**, **Peytel**, **Pétel**; **Pe(s)tre**, **Lepêtre**; **Pesteur**, **Lepesteur**, **Pestour**, **Peytou(r)**.

Dims.: Fr.: **Pétrel**, **Pétron**; **Pestureau**.

Augs.: Fr.: **Pétel(l)at**, **Pételaz**, **Pettelat**.

Pej.: Fr.: **Pestelard**.

Pitarch Catalan: of uncertain origin, apparently from the Fr. surname *Pitard*; see PYTHON.

Pitcher English (chiefly E Anglia): 1. occupational name for a caulker, one who sealed the seams of a ship with pitch, from an agent deriv. of ME *pich* (OE *pic*; cf. PECHER 1 and PÈGUE).

2. var. of PICKARD 2.

Patr.: **Pitchers**.

Pitchford English: habitation name from a place near Shrewsbury, where there was a bituminous well; the name is derived from OE *pic* pitch (see PITCHER) + *ford* FORD.

Var.: **Pitchforth**.

Pite English: of uncertain origin, probably a var. of PITT.

The earliest known bearer is William Pite, who was married in 1549 in the parish of Ilketshall St Margaret, Suffolk. It seems likely that all present-day bearers of this rare surname are descended from this man.

Pitkänen Finnish: patr. from the nickname *Pitkä* 'Tall'.

Pitt English: topographic name for someone who lived by a pit or hollow, OE *pytt*, or habitation name from a place named with this word, e.g. *Pitt* in Hants or *Pett* in E Sussex. For the variation in the vowel, cf. HILL 1.

Vars.: **Pitts**, **Pett(s)**; **Putt(s)** (Devon and Cornwall); **Pit(t)man**, **Pettman**, **Putman**; **Pitter**, **Putter**.

Pittaway English (W Midlands): of uncertain origin, probably a habitation name from an unidentified place named with the OE elements *pytt* pit, hollow (see PITT) + *weg* path (see WAY).

Piwoński Polish: ostensibly an ornamental nickname from *piwonia* peony, this is probably a 'polite' alteration of **Piwocha** 'beer drinker'.

Cogns.: Czech: **Pivoňka** ('peony'); **Pivec**, **Pivko**, **Pivník** ('beer drinker').

Piwowarski Polish: occupational name for a brewer, Pol. *piwowar* (from *piwo* beer + *warić* to brew), with the addition of the surname suffix *-ski* (cf. BARANOWSKI).

Cogn.: Czech: **Pivovař**.

Pizarro Spanish: topographic name for someone who lived near a slate quarry or occupational name for someone who worked in one; perhaps also a topographic name for someone who lived in a house with a roof of slate, or a nickname from the colour. The name is from Sp. *pizarra* slate, of uncertain etymology. It seems to be taken from Basque, and may have been originally *lapitz-arri*, a cpd of the borrowed L *lapideus* (an adj. deriv. of *lapis* stone) + the native *arri* stone, with the initial syllable being lost by folk etymology, it being taken as the fem. form of the Sp. definite article.

Cogns.: Port.: **Piçarra**, **Pissarra**.

Place English and French: 1. topographic name for someone who lived in the main market square of a town or village, ME, OF *place* (LL *platea* (*via*) broad street, from Gk *platys*, fem. *plateia*, broad, wide).

2. metonymic occupational name for a fishmonger, or perhaps a nickname for a thin person, from ME, OF *plaise* plaice, flat fish (LL *platessa*, apparently akin to 1).

3. topographic name for someone who lived near a quickset fence, ME, OF *pleis* (L *plexum*, past part. of *plectere* to plait, weave, intertwine).

Vars.: Eng.: **Plaice**. (Of 1 only): Fr.: **Plasse**, **Laplace**, **Delaplace**. (Of 3 only): Eng.: **Pl(e)ass**, **Pleace**, **Pleece**.

Cogns. (of 1): It.: **Piazza**, **Piaz(zi)**, **Del Piaz(zo)**; **Piazzese**, **Piazzesi**. Sp.: **Plaza**. Ger.: **Platz(er)**, **Platzmann**. Flem., Du.: **Van der Plaetse(n)**, **Verplaetse(n)**, **Van de Plaats**. Jewish (Ashkenazic, exact meaning unclear): **Plaz(man)**, **Platzner**. (Of 3): Fr.: **Plaix**, **Play**, **Pleix**, **Plez**, **Plesse**, **Ploix**; **Leplay**; **Deplaix**, **Duplaix**, **Duplay**, **Duple(i)x**; **Plessis**, **Plessix**, **Plessy**, **Duplessis**, **Duplessix**, **Duplessy**; **Plessier**, **Duplessier**. Flem.: **Van der Placke**.

Dims. (of 1): It.: **Piazzini**, **Piazzol(l)a**, **Piazzoli**.

Armand-Jean du Plessis, *Cardinal de Richelieu (1585–1642), was chief minister to Louis XIII and virtual ruler of France. The du Plessis family had risen by intermarriage to a position where they could purchase the seigneury of Richelieu in Poitou. The surname is also well established in S Africa.*

Plaček Czech: nickname for a discontented, miserable person, from Czech *plaček* moaner, weeper, from *pláč* to cry, bewail one's lot.

Plachý Czech: nickname for a shy, timid person, from Czech *plachý* shy.

Var.: **Plachký**.

Plackett English (Notts.): probably a nickname from early mod. Eng. *placket* (from OF, a deriv. of *plaquier* to lay flat). The word denoted an extra piece of material in a garment or a slit in the top of a skirt, also the female sex organs, and hence a woman considered as an object of sexual desire. The word is not attested in OED until Shakespeare, for whom it clearly had bawdy connotations, but it was probably in colloquial use earlier. The surname is presumably of obscene origin, perhaps a nickname for a person noted for sexual activity.

Plain French: topographic name for someone who lived on a plain or plateau, OF *plan* (L *plānum*, from the adj. *plānus* flat, level).

Vars.: **Plan, Plaine; Duplain, Duplan(t).**

Cogns.: Eng.: **Plane** (Norfolk). Prov.: **Plana(s), Planaz.** It.: **(La) Piana, (Lo) Piano, Pian(i), Del Piano, Delle Piane; Pianese** (Campania); **Piangiani** (Tuscany). Sp.: **Llano(s).** Cat.: **Plana(s), Pla.**

Dims.: Fr.: **Planet, Planeix, Planel(le), Planeau.** It.: **Pianella, Pianelli, Pianetti.** Cat.: **Planella, Planells.**

Augs.: It.: **Pianon(e).**

Planche French: from OF *planche* plank (LL *planca*, akin to L *plancus* flat-footed, which was a Roman family name, and Gk *plax*, gen. *plankos*, flat surface, *platys* broad, flat; cf. PLACE 1). It is not clear how this word was applied as a surname: it may be a topographic name for someone who lived near a plank-bridge over a stream, a metonymic occupational name for a carpenter, or a nickname for a thin person, i.e. one seen as being as flat as a board.

Vars.: **Planque; Laplanche, Laplanque; De(la)planche, Desplanches, De(la)planque.**

Cogns.: Eng.: **Plank.** Ger.: **Plan(c)k, Plänker, Plankmann.** Flem., Du.: **Plancke.**

Dims.: Fr.: **Planchet(te), Planquette, Planchon, Plançon, Plancon.** Ger.: **Plankl.**

Pej.: Fr.: **Planchard.**

Plant English: 1. metonymic occupational name for a gardener, from ME *plant* young tree, herb (OE *plante*, from L *planta* cutting, shoot, reinforced by OF *plante* from the same source).

2. perhaps also a nickname for a tender or delicate individual, from the same word in a transferred sense.

Var.: **Plante.**

An early bearer of the name Plant *in Wales was Ricardo Plant, recorded in 1301 at Ewelowe in the former county of Flints. (now part of Clwyd). He was perhaps connected with the Plant family of Macclesfield, Ches., whose earliest known ancestor is Ranulf* Plont, *recorded in 1383.*

Plas, van den Dutch: topographic name for someone who lived by a dip in a road, which filled up with water in the winter months, from MDu. *plas* puddle, pool, plash.

Plaster English: 1. metonymic occupational name for a plasterer, from ME *plaster* (OF *plastre*, from L *(em)plastrum*, Gk *emplastron*, a deriv. of *emplassein* to shape, form).

2. habitation name from any of various places called *Plaistow* (in E London, Derbys., Sussex, and elsewhere), from OE *plegestōw* playground (cf. PLAYER and STOW).

Vars. (of 2): **Pla(i)stow.**

Platonov Russian: patr. from the given name *Platon*. The Gk byname *Platōn* 'Flat(-footed)' (from *platys* broad, flat; cf. PLACE 1 and PLATT) was borne not only by the ancient philosopher known in Eng. as *Plato*, but also by a 4th-cent. Christian martyr venerated in the Orthodox Church, and for this reason the given name became fairly common in Russia.

Dims: **Platon(n)ikov, Platoshkin, Platygin** (all patrs.).

'Son of the wife of P.': **Platonikhin.**

Platt 1. English: nickname for a thin man, from OF *plat* flat (LL *plat(t)us*, from Gk *platys* broad, flat; cf. PLACE 1). It may also be a topographic name for someone who lived on a piece of flat land or by a plank-bridge; *Platt* Bridge in Lancs. is named from this dial. sense of the ME word, and may well be the main source of the surname, which is still found principally in the surrounding area.

2. Jewish (Ashkenazic): of unknown origin.

Var. (of 1): **Platts.**

Cogns. (of 1): Fr.: **Plat(te), Laplatte, Duplat, De(la)platte** (topographic names). Ger.: **Plath** (a placename in Mecklenburg).

Dims. (of 1): Eng.: **Platten** (Norfolk). Fr.: **Platel, Plateau.**

Pejs. (of 1): Fr.: **Plat(t)ard.**

Many present-day English bearers of the name Platt *are descended from a family called* de Platt, *who held lands at Platt in the parish of Rusholme, Manchester, from* c.*1260.*

Player English: occupational name for an actor or musician or nickname for a successful competitor in contests of athletic or sporting prowess, from an agent deriv. of ME *pleyen* to play (OE *plægian, plegan*).

Playfair Scots: 1. var. of PLAYFORD.

2. nickname for an enthusiastic participant in athletic activities, from ME *pley* sport, play (cf. PLAYER) + *fere* companion (see FEAR 1).

Var.: **Playfer.**

The earliest known bearer of the name is William Playefayre, *a servant of the Earl of Orkney at the end of the 13th cent.*

Playford English: habitation name from a place in Suffolk, so called from OE *plæga, plega* sport, play + *ford* FORD. The reason for the name is not clear; the place may have been the site of sporting contests, or it may have been so named from animals playing there.

Var.: PLAYFAIR.

Pleasance English: 1. from the medieval female given name *Plaisance* 'Pleasantness', regarded as a specifically fem. form of the much rarer *Plaisant* (pres. part. of OF *plaire*, from L *placere* to please), of common gender (cf. CONSTANT and CONSTANCE).

2. habitation name from the N Italian city of *Piacenza*, so called from L *Placentia* (neut. pl. of the pres. part. of *placere*).

Var.: **Pleasaunce.**

Cogns.: Fr.: **Plaisance.** It.: **Piacenza; Piacentini, Piacentino, Piasentin(i)** (habitation names only).

Plechatý Czech: nickname for a bald-headed man, from Czech *plechatý, plešatý* bald.

Var.: **Plecháč.**

Plecitý Czech: nickname for someone with broad shoulders, from Czech *plecitý* broad-shouldered.

Plemyannikov Russian: patr. from the nickname *Plemyannik* 'Nephew', 'Kinsman', denoting someone who was related to some prominent member of the community or who had inherited wealth from a relative.

Plenderleith Scots: habitation name from a place in the former county of Roxburgh, the name of which is of uncertain derivation. It may be from Brit. *pren* timber + *dre* farm, plus an uncertain final element, possibly a river name meaning 'Broad' (see LEITH).

Var.: **Plenderleath.**

Plenty English: nickname from ME *plente(th)* plenty, abundance (OF *plentet*, from LL *plēnitas*, gen. *plēnitātis*, a deriv. of *plēnus* full), given perhaps to a wealthy man or else to a heavy drinker or eater. The word was also used as an adj. in the Middle Ages; cf. DAINTITH.

Płoński Polish: habitation name from the town of *Płońsk*, NW of Warsaw.

Płoszaj Polish: occupational name for someone whose job was to frighten birds away from crops, from a deriv. of Pol. *płoszyć* to frighten.

Vars.: **Płoszajski**; **Płoszyński** (formally a habitation name).

Plotka Jewish (E Ashkenazic): from Pol. *płotka*, dim. of *płoć* roach, one of the many ornamental names based on fish names.

Vars.: **Plotke**; **Plotkin** (formally a patr.).

Plotnik Jewish (E Ashkenazic): occupational name from Russ. *plotnik* carpenter (originally a maker of wattles and wooden fences, from *plot* plaited, woven object).

Vars.: **Plotnick**; **Plotnicki**, **Plotni(t)zki**, **Plotni(t)zky**; **Plot(t)**.

Patrs.: **Plotnikov**, **Plotnicov**.

Plouvier French: 1. topographic name for someone who lived near a gutter or drainage channel, OF *plo(u)vier* (LL *pluviārium*, from *pluvia* rain).

2. nickname from the plover or rainbird, OF *plo(u)vier* (LL *pluviarius*).

Var.: **Plovier**.

Plowden English: habitation name from a place in Shrops., so called from OE *plæga*, *plega* play, sport + *denu* valley (see DEAN 1); cf. PLAYFORD. The vowel of the first syllable is not easy to explain, but it occurs as early as 1286, a single generation after the unambiguous *Plaueden*, *Pleweden* of 1252.

A family of this name trace their descent from Roger de Plowden, *who is said to have been present at the siege of Acre in 1191. His son, Philip de Plowden, lived in the village of that name in Shrops. He witnessed a charter in c.1220. The family seat is Plowden Hall, which was built as a hunting lodge in the 11th or 12th cent.*

Plowman English: occupational name, from OE *plōh* plough + *mann* man; it was probably given more often to a PLOWRIGHT than to a ploughman in the modern sense, since ploughing was shared at the appropriate season by virtually all male members of the agricultural community.

Vars.: **Pleuman**; **Plows**, **Plews**.

Cogns.: Ger.: **Pflug**; **Pflüger**, **Pflugner**, **Pfliegner**. Low Ger.: **Plo(o)g**; **Plöger**; **Pleuger** (N Rhineland). Flem., Du.: **Ploeg(er)**. Dan.: **Ploug**. Czech: **Pluhař**.

Plowright English: occupational name for a maker of ploughs, from OE *plōh* plough + *wyrhta* WRIGHT.

Var.: **Plewright**.

Equivs.: Low Ger.: **Plomaker**, **Plögemaker**; **Pluymaker**, **Plümaker** (Rhineland).

Płuciennik Polish: occupational name for a linen-draper, Pol. *płóciennik*, from *płótno* linen + *-nik* suffix of agent nouns.

Var.: **Płóciennik**.

Plum English: topographic name for someone who lived by a plum tree, from OE *plūme* plum (L *prūna*, originally a neut. pl., but later taken as fem. sing.).

Vars.: **Plumb**, **Plum(b)e**; **Plum(p)tre(e)**.

Cogns.: Ger.: **Pflaum**; **Pfläumer**, **Pfräumer**; **Pflaumbaum**, **Pfraumbaum**, **Prum(en)baum**. Low Ger.: **Plum(e)**; **Plümer**; **Plumbohm**. Flem., Du.: **Pruim(boom)**, **Proemen**. Jewish (Ashkenazic, ornamental): **Pflaum**; **Flaum(enboim)**, **Flom(enbaum)** (of mixed Ger. and Yid. origin); **Floumanboum**; **Flamenb(a)um** (a hypercorrected form). Fr.: **Prune**, **Lapru(g)ne**; **Prunier**.

Dims.: Ger.: **Pflimlin** (Switzerland). Low Ger.: **Plum(e)ke**, **Plümecke**. Fr.: **Prunel**, **Pruneau**, **Prunet**.

William de Plumptre, *mentioned in documents of 1330 and 1345, is an ancestor of a family associated for centuries with Notts. Their name is derived from the village of* Plumptre *in the county, now spelled* Plumtree.

Plumley English: habitation name from any of various places so called, the chief of which is in Ches. near Knutsford. The name is derived from OE *plūme* PLUM + *lēah* wood, clearing.

Vars.: **Plomley**, **Plumbley**.

Plummer English: 1. topographic name for someone who lived near a plum tree; see PLUM.

2. occupational name for a dealer in feathers, from an agent deriv. of ME, OE *plume* feather (L *plūma*).

3. occupational name for a worker in lead, especially a maker of lead pipes and conduits, a plumber (ANF *plom(m)er*, *plum(m)er*, from *plom(b)*, *plum(b)* lead, L *plumbum*).

Vars.: **Plumer**; **Plomer** (pronounced /ˈpluːmə(r)/); **Plimmer** (W Midlands).

Cogns. (of 2): Du.: **Van der Pluijm**, **Van der Pluym**.

Plumstead English: habitation name from any of various places, for example in Norfolk, so called from OE *plūme* PLUM + *stede* site (see STEAD).

Plunkett English and Irish (Norman): 1. habitation name from a metathesized form of *Plouquenet* in Ille-et-Villaine, Brittany, so called from Bret. *plou* parish (from L *plebs* people) + *Guenec*, the personal name (a dim. of *guen* white) of a somewhat obscure saint.

2. An alternative explanation is that this is a metonymic occupational name for a maker or seller of blankets, from ME *blaunket* (ANF *blancquet*, a dim. of *blanc* white), but replacement of /b/ by /p/ is not usual in English.

Vars.: **Plunket**, **Plumkett**, **Plucknett**; **Pluincéid** (a Gaelicized form).

Plunkett *is the name of a family who settled in Beaulieu or Bewley in Co. Meath, Ireland, in the early 13th cent. They have held the barony of Dunsany since around 1462, and received the earldom of Fingall in 1628.*

Pluta Polish: nickname from the Pol. dial. term *pluta* bad weather, rain, sleet, or puddle, perhaps denoting someone of a gloomy temperament.

Habitation name: **Pluciński**.

Plzák Czech: habitation name for someone from the city of Pilsen in Czechoslovakia, Czech *Plzeň*.

Pobgee English: nickname from ME *popinjay*, *papejai* parrot (OF *papageai*, from Arab. *bab(b)aghā*, perhaps of imitative origin; the ending was altered by folk etymological association with JAY). The nickname was probably acquired by a talkative person or by someone who habitually dressed in bright colours, but occasionally it may have denoted one who was connected with or who excelled at the medieval sport of tilting or shooting at a wooden parrot on a pole.

Vars.: **Pebjoy**, **Pobjoy**, **Pop(e)joy**, **Papigay**.

Cogns.: It.: **Pappagallo**. Czech: **Papoušek**. Pol.: **Papuziński** (in form a habitation name, from Pol. *papuga* parrot). Jewish (E Ashkenazic): **Papigai** (ornamental name or nickname).

Patr.: Russ.: **Popugaev**.

Poch Catalan: nickname for a small man, from Cat. *poch* little, small (L *paucus*).

Pockney English (Sussex): habitation name, probably from *Puckney* Gill in the parish of Charlwood, Surrey, which is so called from the gen. pl. of OE *pūca* goblin + OE *ēg* island. The surname is first found in Sussex in 1332 as *atte Pukenegh*, and occurs also in Surrey at about the same date. From the 14th to the 17th cent. it was largely confined to a small area of central Sussex around W Grinstead.

Vars.: **Pokney**, **Pocknee**.

Podczaski Polish: occupational name from Pol. *podczaszy* butler, wine steward, one who served drinks and organized weddings.

Podgórski Polish: topographic name for someone who lived at the foot of a hill, from the elements *pod* under + *góra* hill, mountain + *-ski*, suffix of local surnames (see BARANOWSKI).

Cogns.: Czech: **Podhorský**. Ger. (of Slav. origin): **Podgora**, **Podgorny**. Jewish (E Ashkenazic): **Podgor**, **Podgur**.

Podkidyshev Russian: patr. from the nickname *Podkidysh* 'Foundling' (from *podkidyvat* to abandon a baby, a cpd of *pod* under, secretly + *kidat* to throw).

Podlesiak Polish: topographic name for someone who lived near a wood, from Pol. *pod* near + *les* wood + *-(i)ak* suffix denoting human nouns. The two vars. listed below are probably regional names from the district of *Podlasie* in Poland, which gets its name from these elements.

Vars.: **Podlasiak**, **Podlaski** (regional names).

Cogns.: Czech: **Podlešák**. Jewish: (E Ashkenazic): **Podlashuk**.

Podmore English: habitation name from *Podmore* in Staffs. or *Podimore* in Somerset, both of which are of uncertain origin, possibly from a rare ME word *pod*, *pad* frog (cf. PADDOCK 2) + *more* fen, marsh (see MOORE 1).

Podolski Polish and Jewish (E Ashkenazic): regional name for someone from Podolia in the Ukraine (Pol. *Podole*, Yid. *podolye*), a region which had a large Jewish population from the Middle Ages up to the Second World War. It is also possible that in some cases the Jewish names listed here derive from *Podol*, the only district of Kiev in which Jews were permitted to live in the 1880s. However, since all Ashkenazic Jews in the Russian Empire had surnames by that decade, it would have to be shown that Jews were living in Podol earlier (at least by 1844) if this explanation is to be established as correct.

Vars.: Jewish: **Podolsky**; **Podoly**, **Podell**, **Podol(i)er** (from Yid. *podolyer* native or inhabitant of Podolia); **Podolov**, **Podoloff**.

Podroužek Czech: from a dim. form of Czech *podruh*, a status term denoting a tenant on an estate who held his land in return for labour rather than for a cash rent.

Poggs English: metr. from the ME female given name *Pogg(e)*, var. of *Mogg(e)*, a dim. of *Margaret* (cf. mod. Eng. *Peggy*).

Vars.: **Pogson**, **Poxon**.

Pogoński Polish: nickname for a Lithuanian, from Pol. *pogoń* the Lithuanian coat of arms.

Patr.: **Pogonowicz**.

Pogorzelski Polish: nickname for someone who had lost his home and his property in a fire, from a deriv. of *pogorzeć* to burn down. It may also be a habitation name from the town of *Pogorzela* in W Poland, which gets its name from this word.

Cogn.: Czech: **Pohořelý**.

Poincaré French: nickname for a fierce fighter, from OF *poing carré* square fist (L *pugnus quadrātus*). The surname is found mainly in the Meuse and Champagne regions.

Poinçon French: metonymic occupational name for a maker or user of any pointed instrument, OF *poinson* (LL *punctio*, gen. *punctiōnis*, from *pungere* to pierce, punch; cf. PINSON 2).

Vars.: **Poinson**, **Poinçot**, **Poinsot**; **Poinset** (Anglicized **Poinsett**, see below).

Cogn.: Eng.: **Punshon**.

Dims.: Fr.: **Poincelin**, **Poincelot**, **Poincelet**; **Poinsignon**, **Poincignon**.

The poinsettia *takes its name from an American diplomat, Joel* Poinsett *(1779–1851), who was a keen amateur botanist and who brought the flower back from Mexico, where he was ambassador. He was born in Charleston, S Carolina, and was descended from a Huguenot, Peter* Poinset, *who was born near La Rochelle and settled in Charleston c.1700.*

Pointer English (E Anglia): occupational name from ME *pointer* point maker, an agent deriv. of *point*, a kind of lace used to fasten together the doublet and hose (OF *pointe* point, sharp end, LL *puncta*, from *pungere* to pierce).

Var.: **Poynter**.

Pointon English: habitation name from a place in Lincs., so called from OE *Pohhingtūn* 'settlement (OE *tūn*) associated with *Pohha*', a byname apparently meaning 'Bag' (cf. POKE).

Var.: **Poynton**.

Points English (Norman): 1. from the medieval given name *Ponc(h)e*, *Pons*, ultimately from *Pontius*, a Roman family name of uncertain origin, perhaps an ethnic name for someone from *Pontus* (named from Gk *pontos* ocean) in Asia Minor, or an Italic cogn. of L *Quintus* 'Fifth(-born)'. The name was borne by two 3rd-cent. saints, a Carthaginian deacon and a martyr of Nice, but was not widely popular in the Middle Ages because of the inhibiting influence of the even more famous Pontius Pilate. In some cases, though, the surname may have been originally used for someone who had played the part of this character in a religious play.

2. habitation name from *Ponts* in La Manche and Seine-Maritime, Normandy; see PONT.

Vars.: **Poyntz**. (Of 1 only): **Punch**.

Cogns. (of 1): Fr.: **Pons**, **Ponce**, **Point**. It.: **Ponzi**, **Ponz(i)o**, **Punzi**, **Punz(i)o**. Sp.: **Ponce**. Cat.: **Pons**. Flem., Du.: **Pons**, **Poms**.

Dims. (of 1): Eng.: **Pointel**. Fr.: **Ponci(n)**, **Poncy**, **Poncet**, **Punchet**, **Punchon**. It.: **Ponzetti**, **Punzetti**, **Punzetto**.

Augs. (of 1): It.: **Ponzoni**, **Ponzone**, **Punzone**.

Pejs. (of 1): Eng.: **Ponsard**. Fr.: **Punchard**.

Patr. (from 1): Eng.: **Ponson**.

The surname Poyntz *is borne by descendants of a certain* Pons *or* Poinz, *living before 1086, who gave lands to the abbey at Westminster. His son, Drogo* FitzPons, *held lands in Devon from the bishop of Coutances. The surname is first recorded in its present form with Hugh Poyntz, who served in Ireland in 1210.*

Poireau French: metonymic occupational name for a grower or seller of leeks, from OF *poireau* leek (LL *porrellum*, a dim. of class. L *porrum*; the first syllable seems to have been altered by the influence of *poire* PEAR).

Vars.: **Poirel**, **Poiraux**, **Po(u)reau**, **Pouriau**, **Pouriel**, **Pourrel**.

Cogns.: Ger.: **Pforr**. Low Ger.: **Porr(mann)**.

Poke English: metonymic occupational name for a maker of bags and purses, or nickname for someone who was in the habit of carrying a distinctive bag or purse, from ME *poke*

purse, bag (ANF *poque*, of Gmc origin, cogn. with OE *pohha*).
Vars.: **Pouch(er)**, **Pougher**.
Cogns.: Fr.: **Po(c)que**, **Poche**.
Dims.: Eng.: **Pocket(t)**. Fr.: **Pocquet**, **Po(u)chet**, **Po(u)chon**, **Pochot**.

Pokorný Czech: nickname for a humble or self-effacing person, from Czech *pokorný* lowly, humble, meek.
Cogns.: Jewish (Ashkenazic): **Pokorny**. Pol.: **Pokora**, **Pokorski**. Ger. (of Slav. origin): **Bockhorny**.

Pokrovski Russian: surname adopted by members of the Orthodox clergy, formed from *pokrov* feast of the Intercession of the Holy Virgin (lit. 'covering', 'protection', from *pokryt* to cover over). This feast, celebrated on 1 October, commemorates the salvation of Constantinople from the Saracens in the mid-10th cent., allegedly as the result of an apparition of the Holy Virgin.

Pol 1. Dutch: topographic name for someone who lived by a grassy mound, from MDu. *pol* tussock.
2. Catalan: cogn. of Paul.
Vars. (of 1): **Poll**, **Pols**, **Van den Pol(l)**; **Polman** (also Jewish).

Polak Polish and Jewish (Ashkenazic): ethnic name for a Pole or regional name for someone from Poland. In the case of the Ashkenazic name and its vars., the reference is to a Jew from Poland or other Slav.-speaking region. The name of the country (Pol. *Polska*) derives from a Slav. element *pole* field, open country, cleared land (cf. Polański); to this has been added *-ak*, suffix denoting a human subject.
Vars.: Pol.: **Pol**, **Polka**; **Pol(a)kowski**. Jewish: **Polack**, **Pollack**, **Polliak**, Pollock; **Bollack**, **Bol(l)ag** (W Ashkenazic); **Polski**, **Polsky**; **Pol(a)kowski**; Pool.
Cogns.: Czech: **Polák**. Ger. (of Slav. origin): **Polla(c)k**, Pollock, Polk, **Pollag**. Swiss Ger.: **Bol(l)ag**. Flem.: **Polenaer**. Du.: **Polak**, Pool.
Dims.: Pol.: **Polaczek**. Czech: **Poláček**, **Polášek**. Jewish: **Pola(t)chek**, **Polatshek**, **Pol(l)atsek**, **Polacek**.
Patrs.: Jewish: **Polyakov**, **Poliakov(e)**, **Poliakow**; **Polakevitch**, **Polakiewicz**. Russ.: **Polyakov**.

Polański Polish: 1. ethnic name (with the surname suffix *-ski*: see Baranowski) for a Pole, or more specifically for a descendant of the *Polanie*, one of the original Polish tribes.
2. topographic name for someone who lived in a clearing, from *polana* glade, clearing (a deriv. of *pole* field).
Vars.: **Polanowski**, **Poliński**; **Polczynski**; **Polawski**.
Cogns.: Russ.: **Polyanski**. Czech: **Polanský**, **Polanecký**. Jewish (Ashkenazic): **Polanski**, **Polansky**. Bulg.: **Polyanov**.
Cpd (of 2): Jewish: **Dolgopolski** ('long field').

Polglase Cornish: habitation name from any of several places whose name is composed of the Corn. elements *pol* pool, pond + *glās* blue, green, grey.

Polívka Czech: apparently a nickname from Czech *polevka* soup, broth, stock, perhaps denoting a cook or seller of broth.

Polk 1. German (of Slav. origin): from a dim. of a short form of a Slav. personal name composed of the elements *bole* great, large + *slav* glory. This name was a favourite during the Middle Ages among the Silesian ruling class and was widely imitated by their subjects.
2. German: ethnic name for a Pole; see Polak.
3. U.S.: contracted form of Pollock.
Vars. (of 1): **Polke**, **Polka**, **Pulke**.
The American president James Polk *(1795–1849) was of Scots descent. His family reached America from Ireland, where their name had been contracted from* Pollok *to* Polk. *The first American bearer, Robert Bruce Polk, emigrated from Ireland to Maryland in the late 17th cent.*

Polkinghorne Cornish: habitation name from a place in the parish of Gwinear, recorded in 1316 as *Polkenhoern*, from Corn. *pol* pool, pond + the OCorn. personal name *Kenhoern* (literally 'Hound-Iron').

Pollard English: 1. nickname for a person with a large or unusually shaped head, from ME *poll* head (MLG *polle* (top of the) head) + the pej. suffix *-ard*. The term *pollard* denoting an animal that has had its horns lopped is not recorded before the 16th cent., and of a tree similarly truncated not until the 17th cent., so both these senses are almost certainly too late to have contributed to the surname.
2. pej. of Paul.

Pollock 1. Scots: habitation name from a place in Strathclyde, apparently so called from a dim. of a Brit. cogn. of Gael. *poll* pool, pit.
2. Jewish (Ashkenazic) and German: ethnic name for someone from Poland. In the case of the Ashkenazic name, the reference is to a Jew from Poland or from some other Slav.-speaking region; cf. Polak.
Var.: **Pollok**.

Polly English (Norman): nickname for a courteous or amiable person (perhaps also sometimes given ironically to a boor), from OF *poli* agreeable, polite (lit. 'polished', past part. of OF *polir*, L *polīre*).
Var.: **Polley**.
Cogns.: Fr.: **Pol(l)i**, **Pol(l)y**. It.: **Puliti** (Tuscany). Sp.: **Pulido** ('smart', 'neat', 'handsome').
Dims.: Fr.: **Pol(l)iet**, **Pol(l)iot**.
Pej.: Fr.: **Poliard**.

Polster German: metonymic occupational name for a maker or seller of cushions, or nickname for a plump man, from Ger. *Polster*, *Bolster* cushion, pillow, bolster (OHG *polstar*).
Var.: **Bolster**.
Dim.: **Pölsterl**.

Polyblank English (Norman): apparently a nickname for someone with fair hair, from OF *poil* hair (L *pilus*) + Blanc white. However, the name consistently shows an extra syllable in the middle (represented normally as *y*, sometimes as *i* or *e*, in isolated cases as *o*, *a*, *ay*, *ey* and *er*), which is not easy to explain.
Vars.: **Pulleyblank**, **Pulliblank**.
The name is almost exclusively confined to S Devon, where the earliest known bearers are Walter Polyblaunk *(Ermington 1332) and William* Poleblank *(Chillaton 1386).*

Pomerantz 1. German: metonymic occupational name for an importer or seller of bitter (Seville) oranges, Ger. *Pomeranze* (MHG *pomeranz*, med. L *pōmarancia*, composed of **arancia*, the name imported with the fruit (cf. Naranjo), with the explanatory L *pōmum* apple, fruit (cf. Pomeroy)).
2. Jewish (Ashkenazic): from Yid. *pomerants* orange, one of the many ornamental names taken from plants.
Vars.: **Pomeranz**. (Of 2 only): **Pomerants**, **Pomeranc(e)**, **Pomrince**, **Pomrinse**; **Marantz**, **Maranc**, **Marans** (from the aphetic Yid. form *marants*).
Cogn.: Pol.: **Pomarański**.
Dims.: Jewish: **Pomeranzik**, **Pomaranzik**, **Pomeranchik**.
Cpds (ornamental): Jewish: **Maranțenboim** ('orange tree'; the spelling is Rumanian); **Pomeranzblum**, **Pomerancblum** ('orange flower').

Pomeroy English (Norman; found mainly in Devon): habitation name from any of the various places in NE France named with OF *pommeroie*, *pommeraie* apple orchard (collective of *pomme* apple, L *pōmum*).

Vars.: **Pomery**, **Pomroy**, **Pummery**.

Cogns.: Fr.: **Pommeray(e)**, **Pommerais**, **Pommery**. Prov.: **Pomarède**.

The Pomeroy *family of Devon trace their descent from Ralph* de la Pomerai, *a close associate of William the Conqueror. His descendants lived for over 500 years after the Conquest in the castle of Berry Pomeroy, near Totnes, Devon. A branch of the family was established in Ireland when Arthur Pomeroy accompanied the Earl of Essex there in 1573.*

Pomfret English: habitation name from *Pontefract* in W Yorks., so called from OF *pont freit* broken bridge (from L *pons* (gen. *pontis*) bridge + *fractus*, past part. of *frangere* to break). The name is recorded in the medieval period in L (*Pontefracto* 1090) and in Fr. (*Puntfreit* 1226). The modern placename spelling derives from the L form, while the local pronunciation is from the Fr.

Vars.: **Pomfrett**, **Pumfrett**, **Pomphrett**, **Pontefract**.

Pomorski Polish: regional name from *Pomerania* in NW Poland (Pol. *Pomorze*, Ger. *Pommern*, from Pol. *po-* up to, beside + *morze* the sea).

Cogns.: Ger.: **Pommerehne**, **Pommerening**; **Pommerschein** (from Pol. *Pomerzyn*, altered by folk etymology as if from Ger. *Schein* brightness).

Dim.: Ger.: **Pommerenke**.

Pomphrey Welsh: patr., with a reduced form of the W element *ap*, from the given name HUMPHREY.

Vars.: **Pomfrey**, **Pomphray**, **Pumphrey(s)**, **Pumphery**, **Pumfray**.

The name was early taken to Scotland, David Pumfray *being admitted as a burgess of Lanark in 1488.*

Pond English: topographic name for someone who lived beside a pond or lake, from ME *pond* enclosed expanse of water, especially a man-made one (an altered form of POUND).

Var.: **Ponder**.

Ponomaryov Russian: patr. from the occupational term *ponomar* sexton, churchwarden (from Late Gk *paramonarios*, a deriv. of *paramonē* service, support, from *paramenein* to remain beside, support; the Gk prefix has been replaced by a Slav. one of similar meaning, and the nasals have undergone metathesis).

Dim.: Ukr.: **Ponomarenko** (not patr.).

Ponsonby English: habitation name from a place in Cumb., so called from the ME nickname, *Puncun*, of a 12th-cent. owner (see POINÇON) + northern ME *by* settlement (ON *býr*).

This is the name of a family, originally from Cumberland, who were established in Ireland with Sir John Ponsonby *(1608–78). He was colonel of a cavalry regiment which accompanied Cromwell in 1649. A descendant, Brabazon Ponsonby (1679–1758), was created Earl of Bessborough in 1739.*

Pont English, French, and Catalan: topographic name for someone who lived near a bridge, ANF, OF, Cat. *pont* (L *pons*, gen. *pontis*).

Vars.: Fr.: **Depont**, **Dupont**.

Cogns.: It.: **Ponti**, **Dalponte**, **Delponte**. Sp.: **Puente(s)**. Port.: **Ponte(s)**.

Dims.: Eng.: **Pontin(g)**. Fr.: **Pontet**, **Pontel**, **Pontin**, **Pont(ill)on**. It.: **Pontello**, **Pontel(li)**, **Pontillo**, **Pontini**; **Ponticiello**, **Ponticeli** (Naples).

Augs.: It.: **Ponton(i)**.

Pook English: nickname from ME *pook*, *puck* goblin, evil spirit (OE *pūca*; cf. POCKNEY).

Vars.: **Pouck**, **Pooke**.

Pool 1. English: topographic name for someone who lived near a pool or pond, OE *pōl*.

2. English: var. of PAUL.

3. Dutch (largely Jewish): ethnic name for someone from Poland. In the case of the Jewish name, the reference is to a Jew from Poland or from some other Slav.-speaking region; cf. POLAK.

Vars. (of 1): Eng.: **Poole**, **Po(o)lman**.

Cogns. (of 1): Ger.: **Pfuhl(mann)**, **Pfuhler**. Low Ger.: **Pohl(mann)**, **Puhl(mann)**, **Pöhler**. Fris.: **Po(e)lstra**. Flem., Du.: **Van de(r) Poel**, **Poelman**.

Pooley English: 1. habitation name from a place so called in Warwicks. No forms of the name are recorded before the 13th cent., when *Povele*, *Poueleye*, *Powelee*, *Pouelee*, and *Poleye* are all found. The second element is OE *lēah* wood, clearing; the first is a word *pofel*, found occasionally in placenames, the meaning of which has not been established.

2. habitation name from *Pooley* Bridge in Cumb., so called from OE *pōl* POOL + ON *haugr* hill, mound.

Pope English: nickname from the ecclesiastical title for the head of the Roman Catholic Church, ME *pope* (OE *pāpa*, from LL *pāpa* bishop, pope, from Gk *pappas* father, in origin a nursery word; for the change of *-ā-* to *-ō-* cf. ROPER). In the early Christian Church, the L term was at first used as a title of respect for male clergy of every rank, but in the Western Church it gradually came to be restricted to bishops, and then only to the bishop of Rome; in the Eastern Church it continued to be used of all priests (see POPOV). The nickname would have been used for a vain or pompous man, or for someone who had played the part of the pope in a pageant or play.

Cogns.: Fr.: PAPE, **Lepape**. Ger.: **Pabst**, **Babst**; **Pfaffe**. Low Ger.: **Paff(e)** (Rhineland). Czech: **Papež**. Pol.: **Papież**; **Papierz** (a deliberate mis-spelling, assimilated to the form of agent nouns, to avoid *lèse-majesté*); **Papis**. Flem., Du.: **De Paepe**. Finn.: **Pappi**. Hung.: **Pap(p)**.

Dims.: Ger.: **Pfäffle**, **Pfeffel(in)**. Low Ger.: **Pa(a)pke**, **Päpke**.

Patrs.: Ger.: **Papen**, **Paffen**. Croatian: **Papić**.

Habitation name: Pol.: **Papiewski**.

Popham English: habitation name from a place in Hants, so called from an unexplained first element *pop* + OE *hām* homestead.

Popkiss English: of uncertain origin, ostensibly an assimilated form of *Popkins*, from W *ap Hopkin* 'son of *Hopkin*' (see HOBB). It is a rare surname, which has not been traced before the 18th cent. and has always been strongly localized in the Dover area. It is probable that all bearers descend from a certain Peter *Popkes*, who was married at Dover in 1748; it has not been possible to discover anything of his origins.

Var.: **Popkess**.

Popławski Polish: topographic name for someone who lived by a water-meadow, from Pol. *popław* water-meadow + *-ski* suffix of local surnames (see BARANOWSKI).

Popov 1. Russian, Bulgarian, and Croatian: patr. from the occupational term *pop* priest (from Gk *pappas*; see POPE). The name may occasionally derive from a nickname, but celibacy was not enjoined on priests of the Orthodox Church and so the name normally means literally 'son of the priest'.

2. Jewish: of unknown origin, probably an adoption of the Russ. surname.

Vars.: Bulg.: **Papatov**. Croatian: **Pop(ov)ić**.

Cogns.: Rum.: **Pop(a)**; **Popescu(l)**.

Dim.: Ukr.: **Popenko**.

Popp 1. German: from a Gmc personal name *Poppo*, *Boppo*, of uncertain origin and meaning, perhaps originally a nursery word. It was a hereditary given name among the counts of Henneberg and Babenberg in E Frisia between the 9th and 14th cents.

2. Jewish (Ashkenazic): habitation name from either of the cities called *Frankfurt*, on the Main and on the Oder. These are both named from OHG *Frankena furt* 'FORD of the FRANKS'. In Jewish writings the placename was commonly abbreviated to *Ff* and read as /pop/, since in unpointed Hebr. and Yid. the same letter can be read as /f/ or as /p/.

Vars. (of 1): **Poppe**, **Bopp**, **Bopf**. (Of 2): **Popper**.

Dims. (of 1): Ger.: **Pöpp(e)l**, **Böppel**, **Böpple**. Fris.: **Popkema**. Czech: **Popel(ka)** (the Czech word *Popelka* is the equivalent of Cinderella, being associated with the vocab. word *popel* ashes).

Patrs. (from 1): Ger.: **Popper**. Low Ger.: **Poppen**. Fris.: **Poppinga**.

Patrs. (from 1) (dim.): Low Ger.: **Popken**.

Poppleton English (W Yorks.): habitation name from a place in W Yorks., so called from OE *popel* pebble + *tūn* enclosure, settlement.

Popplewell English (W Yorks.): habitation name from any of several places in W Yorks., for example in the parish of Cleckheaton. The second element is OE *well(a)* spring, stream (see WELL); the first may be *popel* pebble, or a word meaning 'bubbling spring'.

Porcher English and French: occupational name for a swineherd, ME, OF *porch(i)er* (LL *porcārius*, an agent deriv. of *porcus* pig; cf. PURCELL).

Vars.: Fr.: **Pourcher**, **Po(u)rquier**, **Porché**, **Pourquié**, **Porchez**.

Cogns.: It.: **Porcari**, **Porcaro**; **Purcaro** (Naples).

Dims.: Fr.: **Porcheron**. Prov.: **Pourcheiroux**.

Porras Spanish and Catalan: nickname for a thickset or belligerent person, from the pl. form of Sp., Cat. *porra* cudgel, club (probably from L *porrum* leek (see POIREAU), because of similarity in shape).

Port 1. English: topographic name for someone who lived near the gates of a town (and in many cases was in charge of them; thus in part a metonymic occupational name equivalent to PORTER 1), from ME *port* gateway, entrance (OF *porte*, from L *porta* door, entrance).

2. English: topographic name for someone who lived near a harbour or in a market town, from the homonymous ME *port* (OE *port* harbour, market town, from L *portus* harbour, haven, reinforced in ME by OF *port*, from the same source).

3. Jewish: of unknown origin.

Vars. (of 1 and 2): **Porte**; **Portman**.

Cogns. (of 1): Fr.: **Porte**, **Laporte**, **Delaporte**, **Desportes**. Prov.: **Porta**, **Saporta** (Rousillon). Sp.: **Puerta(s)**. Cat.: **Porta**, **Laporta**, **Saporta**. Jewish (Sefardic): **Saporta**, **Sa(s)portas**. It.: **(La) Porta**, **Della Porta**, **Dallaporta**. Low Ger.: **Portmann**. Du.: **Poort**, **Van Poorten**. (Of 2): Sp.: **Puerto**. Port.: **Porto** (also used of a mountain pass). It.: **Porto**, **Porti**; **Puorto**, **Da(l)porto** (Naples).

Dims. (of 1): Sp.: **Portela**, **Portilla**. Cat.: **Portella**. Port.: **Portela**. (Of 2): Sp.: **Portillo**. Cat.: **Portell**. It.: **Portelli**.

A Somerset family by the name of Portman *still bear the arms first granted to Thomas Portman by Edward I in the 13th cent. His descendants include Sir William Portman (d. 1555), who rose to be Lord Chief Justice of England.*

Portail French: topographic name for someone who lived near the gates of a town, or metonymic occupational name for a gatekeeper, from OF *portal* gateway (LL *portāle*, a deriv. of *porta* door, entrance); cf. PORT 1 and PORTER 1.

Var.: **Duportail** (with fused preposition and def. art.).

Cogns.: Prov.: **Portal(ier)**, **Duportal**, **Dupo(u)rtau**.

Portal *is the name of a Huguenot family who settled in England when Jean François Portal (1642–1705) took refuge in London. His sons included Henri Portal (b. 1690), born in Poitiers, who was granted the right to make paper for Bank of England notes, a privilege held by a number of subsequent generations.*

Portch English: topographic name for someone who lived in a building with a covered entrance, or nickname for a beggar who was in the habit of stationing himself in the porch of a church, from ME *porch* (OF *porche*, LL *porticus*, a deriv. of *porta* door, entrance; cf. PORT 1 and PORTER 1).

Porteous Scots: of uncertain origin, perhaps a topographic name for someone who lived in the lodge at the entrance to a manor house, from ME *port* gateway, entrance (see PORT 1) + *hous* HOUSE.

Porter English: 1. occupational name for the gatekeeper of a town or the door-keeper of a large house, ME *porter* (OF *portier*, LL *portārius*, an agent deriv. of *porta* door, entrance; cf. PORT 1).

2. occupational name for a man who carried loads for a living, esp. one who used his own muscle power rather than a beast of burden or a wheeled vehicle (see CARTER). This sense is from OF *porteo(u)r* (LL *portātor*, from *portāre* to carry, convey).

Cogns. (of 1): Fr.: **Po(u)rtier**. Port.: **Porteiro**. Ger.: **Pförtner**, **Pfertner**. Low Ger.: **Portner**, **Pörtner**. Flem., Du.: **Portenaer**. (Of 2): Fr.: **Porteu(r)**; **Porzier**, **(Le) Porz**, **Le Porn** (Brittany).

Dims. (of 1): Fr.: **Portereau**, **Port(e)ret**, **Porterot**, **Port(e)ron**.

Aug. (of 1): Fr.: **Porterat**.

Equivs. (of 1): Prov.: BADIER. Ger.: DÜRER, GITTER.

Portnov Russian and Jewish (Ashkenazic): patr. from the occupational term *portnoi* tailor (an adj. deriv. of *port* uncut cloth).

Vars.: Russ.: **Portnyakov**, **Portnyagin**. Jewish: **Portnoi**, **Portnoy**, **Portnoj** (not patrs.)

Poruchikov Russian: patr. from the occupational term *poruchik* lieutenant, deputy, steward (from *poruchit* to hand over, entrust, from *ruka* hand).

Posada Spanish: metonymic occupational name for an innkeeper or for someone who worked at an inn, from Sp. *posada* inn (a deriv. of *posar* to rest, stay, LL *pausāre*, from Gk).

Cogns.: It.: **Positero**, **Pusateri** (Sicily).

Pospíšil Czech: nickname for a busy or active individual, from Czech *pospíšit* to be in a hurry.

Cogns.: Pol.: **Pośpiech**, **Pośpieszyński**.

Post 1. Low German: topographic name for someone who lived near a post or pole (MLG *post*, from L *postis*), presumably one of some significance, e.g. serving as a landmark or boundary.

2. Jewish: of unknown origin.

Cogns (of 1): Ger.: **Pfost**. Fris.: **Post(e)ma**. Du.: **(Van der) Post**. Fr.: POSTE.

Dim. (of 1): Ger.: **Pföstl**.

Poste French: apparently a topographic name from OF *poste* post, pole (L *postis*; see Post). However, the word in Fr. was used also of the pillory, and so the surname may in part be a metonymic occupational name for the official in charge of overseeing the punishment, or a nickname for someone who had frequently suffered it.

Dims.: **Po(s)tel, Po(s)teau, Pouteau.**

Postgate English (Yorks.): habitation name from a place in N Yorks., so called from northern ME *post(e)* post, pole (from OF; see Poste) + *gate* road (ON *gata*), i.e. a road marked by posts.

Vars.: **Posgate, Poskett, Poskitt.**

Postigo Spanish: topographic name for someone who lived by a minor opening in the walls of a city, as opposed to the main gateway, from Sp. *postigo* postern gate (LL *postīcum*, a deriv. of *post* behind).

Postle English: nickname from an aphetic form of ME *apostel* apostle (OE *apostol*, via L from Gk *apostolos* messenger, delegate, from *apostellein* to dispatch). The nickname may have been used for someone who had played the part of one of the twelve apostles in a play or pageant, or for a particularly zealous Christian. The word seems also to have been occasionally used as a personal name; cf. Postlethwaite.

Vars.: **Post(h)ill, Possell.**

Cogns.: Fr.: **Apostol, Lapostol(l)e, Lapostoile.** Ger.: **Apostel, Aposter.**

Postlethwaite English: habitation name from a minor place in the parish of Millom, Cumb. The name is not recorded until the 13th cent. The first element is probably from ME *apostel* apostle, used as a nickname or personal name (see Postle). Alternatively, it may represent a survival of an OE personal name, *Possel*. The second element is northern ME *thwaite* clearing (ON *þveit*; see Thwaite).

Vars.: **Posselwhite, Posnett(e).**

Potocki Polish and Jewish (E Ashkenazic): topographic name for someone who lived by a brook or stream, from Pol., Czech *potok* stream.

Var.: Jewish: **Potok.**

Cogns.: Czech: **Potocký, Potočník; Potůček.** Hung.: **Pataki, Pataky** (from the numerous placenames containing this element).

Pott English: 1. from a medieval given name, an aphetic form of Philpott.

2. topographic name for someone who lived by a depression in the ground, from ME *pot* (cf. Potter) used in this transferred sense, or habitation name from one of the minor places deriving their name from this element.

Dims. (of 1): **Potkin; Pottle, Potell.**

Patr. (from 1): **Potts.**

Patr. (from 1) (dim.): **Potkins.**

'Servant of P. 1': **Pot(is)man.**

Potter English: occupational name for a maker of drinking and storage vessels, from an agent deriv. of ME *pot* (OE *pott*, from LL *pottus* (perhaps an altered form of *pōtus* drink, draught), reinforced by OF *pot* from the same source). In the Middle Ages the term covered workers in metal as well as earthenware and clay.

Cogns.: Fr.: **Po(u)t(h)ier, Pottier, Potiez; Pode(u)r** (Britanny). Low Ger.: **Pötter; Pottbecker** ('pot baker'); **Pottgieter, Pottgiesser** ('pot founder'). Flem., Du.: **De Potter; Pottebakker; Potgieter.**

Dim.: Fr.: **Poterot.**

Equivs. (not cogns.): Sp.: Cantarero. It.: Vasari. Ger. and Jewish (Ashkenazic): Hafner, Kachler, Töpfer, Euler. Russ.: Goncharov. Pol.: Zduniak.

Pottinger English: occupational name for a maker or seller of potage, a thick soup or stew. The name represents ME, OF *potagier* (an agent n. from *potage*, a deriv. of *pot*; see Potter). For the intrusive *-n-*, cf. Messenger and Passenger.

Var.: **Pottage.**

Potton English: habitation name from a place in Beds., so called from OE *pott* pot + *tūn* enclosure, settlement. The significance of the first element is not clear; this may have been a place where pots were made, or the word may have been used in a topographical sense of a hollow depression.

Potvin English: regional name from OF *Poitevin*, denoting someone from *Poitou* in W France, so called from L *Pictāvum*, the region of the *Pictāvi* or *Pictōnes*. The name of this Gaul. tribe was probably cogn. with, if not identical to, that of the Brit. *Picts*, but the meaning is unknown.

Vars.: **(Le) Poidevin, Le Poideven, Pod(e)vin, Patvine, Potwin, Portwin(e), Putwaine, Puddifin, Puddifant, Puttifent.**

Cogns.: Fr.: **Poit(t)evin, Poitvin, Pitavin, Pétavin, Pétavy, Peytavi(n).**

Potyomkin Russian: patr. from the nickname *Potyomki* 'Darkness', 'Nightfall' (from *tyomni* dark), which was probably originally given for some anecdotal reason.

Pou 1. French: nickname from OF *poiul* louse, flea (LL *pediculus*, *peduculus*, a dim. of class. L *pedis*), denoting a small or despised person, or someone who was infested with lice or fleas.

2. Catalan: cogn. of Puits.

Vars. (of 1): **P(ed)oux, Pezout; Pouilleux.** (Of 2): **Pous.**

Dims. (of 1): **Pouillet, Pouillot, Poillon.**

Pejs. (of 1): **Pouillard, Pouillaud.**

Poule French: metonymic occupational name for a breeder of chickens or nickname for a timorous person, from OF *poule* chicken (LL *pulla (avis)* young bird; cf. Pullen).

Vars.: **Poul(le).**

Cogns.: It.: **Pollo; Pudda, Puddu** (Sardinia). Eng.: **Poulter** (occupational).

Dims.: Fr.: **Poulin, Poul(l)et, Poul(l)ot, Poul(e)teau.** It.: **Pollini; Puddinu** (Sardinia).

Augs.: Fr.: **Poulat, Poulas.** It.: **Polloni.**

Pejs.: Fr.: **Poulard, Poulastre.**

Poulton English: habitation name from any of the various places, for example in Ches., Gloucs., Kent, and Lancs., so called from OE *pōl* Pool + *tūn* enclosure, settlement.

Var.: **Poolton.**

Pound English: topographic name for someone who lived near an enclosure in which animals were kept, ME *p(o)und* (of uncertain, presumably native, origin; cf. Penfold), or metonymic occupational name for an official responsible for rounding up stray animals and placing them in a pound.

Vars.: **Pounds, Pund; Pounder, Poynder.**

Pountney English: habitation name from a place in Leics. now known as *Poultney*, but recorded in Domesday Book as *Pontenei*. The Domesday form shows the common Norman French substitution of *-n-* for OE *-l-*. The placename derives from the gen. case of the OE personal name *Pulta* + OE *ēg* island.

Vars.: **Poul(t)ney, Pulteney.**

Poussin French: nickname from OF *poussin* chick (LL *pullicīnus*, a deriv. of *pullus*; cf. Poule and Pullen), apparently denoting a small man.

Var.: **Pouchin**.

Dims.: **Pous(s)ineau, Pouzinot, Poussinet**.

Povarov Russian: patr. from the occupational term *povar* cook (from *povarit* to cook, boil).

Cogn.: Jewish (E Ashkenazic): **Povarsky**.

Poveda Spanish: topographic name for someone who lived near a grove of poplars, OSp. *poveda*, a collective of *povo*, *pobo* (white) poplar (LL *pōpus*, a back-formation from class. L *populus*, taken as a dim.). There are also several places named with this word, and they may have contributed to the surname.

Povey English: of uncertain origin; according to Smith it is a nickname deriving from a dial. term for the owl. The name is most common in London and Birmingham, with a smaller concentration in Bristol.

Powe English: 1. nickname from ME *pō* Peacock.

2. Welsh: patr., with a reduced form of the W element *ap*, from the given name Howe, a var. of Hugh.

Var.: **Pow** (chiefly Scots.).

Powell 1. Welsh: patr., with a reduced form of the W element *ap*, from the given name *Hywel* (see Howell).

2. English: var. of Paul.

Vars. (of 1): **Powles**; Bowell.

A Welsh family bearing the name Powell *claim descent from the Welsh chieftain known as Coel Hen Gotebauc 'the Old Protector', who probably ruled an area of Britain under the Romans around the year 400. The first recorded occurrence of the surname in its modern form is Roger* ap Howell, alias Powell, *named in a lawsuit in 1563. He was the grandson of Howell ap John (d. 1535). Later members of the family include the novelist Anthony Powell (b. 1905).*

Power 1. English and Irish (Norman): habitation name from OF *Pohier* native of *Pois*, a town in Picardy, apparently so called from OF *pois* fish (cf. Pesce) because of its well-stocked rivers.

2. English: nickname for a poor man, or ironically for a miser, from ME, OF *povre*, *poure* poor (L *pauper*).

Vars.: **Powers**; **Poor(e)**.

Cogns. (of 2): It.: **(Il) Povero**.

Dims. (of 2): Fr.: **Pouv(e)reau**. It.: **Poverelli**.

The surname Power *is very common in Munster, where it goes back to a bearer of the name* le Poer *who came to Ireland with Strongbow. It is sometimes Gaelicized to* **de Paor**.

Pownall English: habitation name from a place in Ches., first recorded in the 12th cent. as *Pohenhale*, from the gen. case of the OE personal name *Pohha* + OE *halh* nook, recess (see Hale 1).

Var.: **Powney**.

Poyner 1. English (Norman): nickname for someone who was handy with his fists, from OF *poigneor* fighter (L *pugnātor*, from *pugnāre* to fight, a deriv. of *pugnus* fist).

2. Welsh: Anglicized form of the patr. phrase *ab Ynyr* son (W *ab*, *ap*) of *Ynyr* (a personal name, apparently from L *Honorius*; cf. Honoré).

Vars. (of 1): **Poynor, Punyer**. (Of 2): **Bonner, Bunner**.

Poznański Polish and Jewish (Ashkenazic): habitation name from the city of *Poznań* (Ger. *Posen*) in W central Poland, + *-ski* suffix of local surnames (see Baranowski). The name of the city is said to be derived from the verb *poznać sié* to get to know someone, and is associated with the story of the meeting of the Polish king Bolesław Chrobry and the German emperor Otto III at the funeral of St Wojciech in the 11th cent.

Vars.: Jewish: **Posner**; Pevzner.

Praetorius German: Latinized form of various surnames meaning 'leader' or 'headman', e.g. Mayer and Schultz; it is a deriv. of L *praetor*, the title of various officials in republican and imperial Rome (probably a contracted form of *praeitor*, from *praeire* to go before).

Var.: **Pretorius**.

Cogns.: Eng.: **Pr(e)ater, Pretor**.

Prager Jewish (Ashkenazic) and German: habitation name from the city of Prague (Ger. *Prag*, Czech *Praha*), the capital of Czechoslovakia. The name may also have been applied to or taken by someone who came from elsewhere in Bohemia, the name of the nearest large town being preferred to a more precise local designation. It is possible that in some cases the name may derive from *Praga* on the Vistula opposite Warsaw, known in Yid. as *Prage*.

Vars.: Jewish: **Pragerman**; **Proger** (from the Yid. name of the Bohemian city, *Prog*); **Van Praag(h)** (among Jews in Holland).

Cogns.: Czech: **Pražák, Praž(an)ský**.

Prášek Czech: occupational nickname for a miller's apprentice, from Czech *prášek* dust, flour (a dim. of *prach* powder, cogn. with Pol. *proch*; cf. Prochownik).

Prata 1. Italian: cogn. of Pré.

2. Portuguese: metonymic occupational name for a worker in silver, Port. *prata* (LL *plata* sheet metal, apparently from *plat(t)us* flat, from Gk; cf. Platt).

Var. (of 2): **Pratas**.

Pratt English: nickname for a clever trickster, from OE *prætt* trick, which is found in use as a byname in the 11th cent. ME *pratt(e)* is not recorded as a vocab. word until the 15th cent.

Dims.: **Pratten, Pratlett**.

Pratt *is the family name of the Marquesses and Earls Camden. They are descended from John Pratt (d. 1573) of Devonshire. The first Earl, Sir Charles Pratt (1714–94), was a childhood friend of the elder Pitt. His son was created Marquess in 1786.*

Prazeres Portuguese: religious byname, from Port. *prazeres* joys (from L *placēre* to please, delight); the reference is to the Seven Joys of the Blessed Virgin (cf. Dores for the complement).

Prchal Czech: nickname for a fugitive or deserter, Czech *prchal*, from *prchat* to run away.

Dim.: **Prchlík**.

Pré French: topographic name for someone who lived near a meadow, OF *pred* (L *prātum*; the fem. forms are from LL *prāta*, originally the pl. of this word), or habitation name from any of the numerous minor places named with this word.

Vars.: **Prée, Prey, Prez**; **Laprée, Lapraye**; **Dupré, Després, Desprez**.

Cogns.: Prov.: **Pra(t)(z), Pra(t)x, Prats, Prade**; **Lapraz, Laprade**; **Duprat, De(l)prat, Delaprade**. It.: **Prati, (Dal) Prato, Del Prato**, Prata; **Prado, Prada** (N Italy); **(Dal) Pra** (Venetia). Sp.: **Prado(s), Prada**. Cat.: **Prat(s), Prada(s), Prades**.

Dims.: Fr.: **Préau(x), Pr(é)el**. Prov.: **Pradeau(x), Pradel(le), (De) Lapradelle, Pradine, Prad(ill)on, Pradoux**. It.: **Pratelli, Pratella, Pradel(la), Pradetto, Pratolini, Pradolin**. Sp.: **Pradillo**.

Prebble English (chiefly Kent): of uncertain origin. It may be a habitation name from a Norman place named with the

elements PRÉ + VILLE, but this theory has not been supported by evidence in the shape of early forms.
Vars.: **Preble**, **Pribul**.

Precious English (mainly Yorks. and Norfolk): nickname for a valued member of the community (perhaps sometimes used ironically), from ME, OF *precios* (LL *pretiōsus*, a deriv. of *pretium* price, prize). It may also derive from a medieval female given name, originally an affectionate nickname.
Var.: **Pretious**.
Cogns.: Jewish (Sefardic): **Preciado** (ornamental); **Pers(s)iado** (hypercorrected forms).

Preedy Welsh: 1. occupational name for a bard, W *prydudd*.
2. from the personal name *Predyr*, *Peredur*, which was borne, in Arthurian legend, by one of the knights of the Round Table; see also PERCIVAL.
Var.: **Pridd(e)y**, **Preddy**.

Prendergast English: of uncertain origin; said by its bearers to be the name of Flemish settlers in Normandy, who took their name from a lost place, *Brontegeest* (*Prentagast*) in Flanders near Ghent.
Vars.: **Pendergast**, **P(r)endegast**, **P(r)end(er)grast**, **Prendergrass**, **Prendeguest**, **Prendergat**.
The name is said to have been brought to England by one Prenliregast, *a follower of William the Conqueror. His son Philip was given lands in Pembrokeshire, renamed as* Prendergast Castle. *Prenegast in Berwicks. also apparently takes its name from this family. A member of the Welsh branch, Maurice* de Prendergast, *played a prominent part with Strongbow, Earl of Pembroke, in the invasion of Ireland in May 1169, and it is possible that many, if not all, present-day Prendergasts are descended from him and his wife, who was a Fitzgerald. His younger son William acquired New Castle near Clonmel in Co. Tipperary, which was the family seat for several centuries.*

Prentice 1. English and (esp.) Scots: nickname from an aphetic form of ME, OF *aprentis* apprentice (from OF *aprendre* to learn, understand, L *appre(he)ndere* to understand, grasp).
2. Irish: Anglicized form of *Ó Pronntaigh*; see PRUNTY.
Vars. (of 1): **Prentis(s)**.

Prescott English: habitation name from any of the places so called, in SW Lancs. (now Merseyside), Gloucs., Oxon., and Shrops. (two), all of which are named from OE *prēost* PRIEST + *cot* cottage, dwelling (see COATES). The surname is most common in N England, and so it seems likely that the first of these places is the most frequent source.
Vars.: **Prescot**, **Priscott**, **Preskett**, **Prescod**.

Presland English: topographic name for someone who farmed land held by the Church, from OE *prēost* PRIEST + *land* land.
Vars.: **Pressland**, **Priestland**.

Preston N English: habitation name from any of the extremely numerous places (most notably one in Lancs.) so called from OE *prēost* PRIEST + *tūn* enclosure, settlement; the meaning may have been either 'village with a priest' or 'village held by the Church'.

Prestwich English: habitation name from places in Lancs. (now Greater Manchester) and Northumb., so called from OE *prēost* PRIEST + *wīc* outlying settlement (see WICK). Cf. PRESTON.
Var.: **Prestige**.
A family by the name of Prestige *trace their descent from Robert* de Prestwych, *who died before 1206. He held the manor of Prestwich in Lancs. from 1193. The name is first recorded in its present form with John Prestige (b. ?1615).*

Pretty English (chiefly E Anglia): nickname for a fine or handsome fellow, from ME *prety*, *prity* fine, pleasing, excellent (OE *prættig* clever, artful, wily, from *prætt* trick; see PRATT).
Vars.: **Pritty**; **Pret(t)yman** (E Anglia).
A family by the name of Pretyman *have been established in Suffolk since at least the 14th cent. William* Praytman *of Bacton was named in a charter in 1393.*

Preuss German and Jewish (Ashkenazic): regional name for someone from Prussia (Ger. *Preussen*), a former state of N Germany, so called from the tribal name of the *Prūsen*, a Baltic tribe displaced by the Germans during the 13th cent. Their name is of unknown origin, although it has been suggested that it may be connected with that of the Frisians (see FRIES).
Vars.: Ger.: **Preussner**, **Preussler**; **Preiss(ner)**, **Preissler** (S Germany); **Prutz** (E Germany). Jewish: **Preis(s)**, **Prais(s)**, **Preiser**, **Preissler**, **Preissman** (from Yid. *Prays* Prussia, or from a S Ger. pronunciation of *Preuss*); PRICE (Anglicized).
Cogns.: Low Ger.: **Prüss(e)**, **Prüssmann**, **Prüssing**. Flem., Du.: **(De) Pruis**, **Pruijs**, **Pruys**. Pol.: **Prus(ki)**. Hung.: **Porosz**.
Patr.: Jewish: **Preiserowicz** (E Ashkenazic).
Habitation names: Pol.: **Prusz(cz)yński**.

Preux French: nickname for a much admired man, perhaps also sometimes given in a spirit of irony, from OF *proz* good, excellent (LL *prodis*, a back-formation from the impersonal verb *prodesse* to be (to the) good; the verb is in fact a cpd of *pro-* for, advantageous + *esse* to be, with epenthetic *-d-*, but was reinterpreted as a contraction of *prode esse*, from which the masc. form of the adj. was derived).
Vars.: **Lepreux**, **Prou(x)**, **Leproux**.
Cogn.: Eng.: PROWSE.

Prevost French: occupational name for any of various officials in a position of responsibility, from OF *prevost* (L *praepositus*, past part. of *praeponere* to place in charge).
Vars.: **Prévost**, **Prévôt**, **Le Prevost**.
Dims.: **Prévostel**, **Prévo(s)teau**, **Prévotet**.
A family by the name of Prevost, *said to be from Poitou, settled in England from Geneva with General Augustine Prevost (1723–86). His family is recorded in Switzerland back to 1572. The general served in the British army in N America and fought under Wolfe at Quebec.*

Price 1. Welsh: one of the commonest of W surnames, a patr., with a reduced form of the W element *ap*, from the given name RHYS.
2. English: the name is also found very early in parts of England far removed from Welsh influence (e.g. Richard *Prys*, Essex 1320), and in such cases presumably derives from ME, OF *pris* price, prize (L *pretium*; cf. PRECIOUS).
3. Jewish (Ashkenazic): Anglicized form of any of the Jewish surnames listed at PREUSS.
Vars.: **Pryce**. (Of 1 only): **Preece**.

Prideaux Cornish: habitation name from a place in the parish of Luxulyan, which is first recorded in the 12th and 13th cents. in the form *Pridias*, perhaps from Corn. *prȳ* clay + an unknown word. Later forms of the placename, and hence the surname, show the results of folk etymological assimilation to Fr. *près d'eaux* 'near waters' or *pré d'eaux* 'meadow of waters'.
Var.: **Priday**.

Pridham English (Norman): nickname from OF *prud'homme* wise, sensible man, a cliché term of approbation from the chivalric romances. It is a cpd of OF *proz*, *prod* good (cf. PREUX), with the vowel influenced by crossing with *prudent* wise (L *prūdens*, gen. *prūdentis*, from *providēre* to foresee) + *homme* man (L *homo*, gen. *hominis*).

Vars.: **Prodham**, **Prudham**, **Prudhomme**; **Purdham**, **Purdom**, **Purdon** (metathesized forms).

Cogns.: Fr. (all also with apostrophes between the two elements): **Pr(e)udhomme**, **Prodhomme**, **Pro(u)dhon**, **Prud(h)on**.

Dim.: Fr.: **Prudhommeau**.

Priest English: nickname from ME *pr(i)est* minister of the Church (OE *prēost*, from L *presbyter*, Gk *presbyteros* elder, counsellor, cpd of *presbys* old man). It may also have been an occupational name for someone in the service of a priest, and occasionally it may have been used to denote someone suspected of being the son of a priest.

Vars.: **Preist**, **Prest(t)**, **Press**, **Prust**; **Prester**, **Presser** (from OF forms).

Cogns.: Fr.: **Prestre**, **Prêtre**, **Prettre**; **Leprestre**, **Leprêtre**. Prov.: **Prouvaire**, **Prouvère**, **Prouhère**, **Prouvéze**. It.: **(Lo) Prete**, **Preti**; **Preite** (Apulia); **Previ**, **Preve** (N Italy); **Previti**, **Previte**, **Previto**, **Prevete**, **Previtero**, **Proviteri**; **(Lo) Presto**, **(Lo) Presti** (S Italy); **Prest(i)eri**. Ger.: **Priester**. Low Ger.: **Pre(i)ster**. Jewish (Ashkenazic): **Priester** (perhaps a name given in jest to a rabbi by anti-Semitic government officials).

Dims.: It.: **Privitelli**; **Prevedel(lo)** (Venetia); **Prestino**.

Patrs.: It.: **Del Prete**, **De Pretis**.

'Servant of the p.': Eng.: **Priestman**; **Pres(s)man** (also Jewish, of unknown origin).

Priestley English: habitation name from any of the various minor places so called, especially the one in N Yorks. These are named from OE *prēost* PRIEST + *lēah* wood, clearing, i.e. a wood or clearing belonging to the Church.

Vars.: **Priestly**, **Pressl(e)y**, **Presley**, **Presslee**, **Presslie**, **Prisley**.

Prieto Spanish: nickname for a dark-haired or dark-skinned man, from OSp. *prieto* dark, black (from the verb *apretar* to squeeze, compress, a metathesized form of *apetrar*, LL *appectorāre* to hold close to the chest (from *pectus*, gen. *pectoris*, chest)). The use as a colour term seems to have derived originally from its application to rainclouds and fog.

Cogn.: Port.: **Preto**.

Primak Jewish (E Ashkenazic): from Slavic *primak* adopted member of a family. The exact application of the name is unclear. It could have been taken by or given to an adopted child or by a married student of Jewish law, supported, following Jewish tradition, by his father-in-law so that he would be free to devote all his time to his studies.

Vars.: **Primack**, **Prema(c)k**.

Prime English: from a ME personal name or nickname. The personal name existed in OE, and is probably derived from OE *prim* early morning (from L *prīmus* first, used as the name of one of the canonical hours). A possible source of the word as an ME nickname is ME, OF *prim(e)* fine, excellent (L *prīmus* first, best).

Vars.: **Prin(n)**, **Pring**, **Prinne**, **Prynn(e)**.

Cogn.: Fr.: **Prin** (see also PERRIN).

Primrose Scots: habitation name from a place in the parish of Dunfermline, so called from Brit. equivalents of W *pren* tree + *rhos* moor, later altered by folk etymological association with the name of the flower (LL *prima rosa* first(-flowering) rose).

Var.: **Primerose**.

A family of this name has been established in Perths. since before the Reformation. An ancestor, Henry Primrose, *was named in a charter in 1543; the family later received the earldom of Rosebery.*

Prince 1. English and French: nickname from ME, OF *prince* (L *princeps*, gen. *principis*, from *prīmus* first + *capere* to take), presumably denoting someone who behaved in a regal manner or who had won the title in some contest of skill.

2. Jewish (Ashkenazic): Anglicized form of the ornamental name *Prinz* (see below; compare GRAF, BARON, HERZOG, KAISER, etc.).

Vars.: Eng.: **Prins**. Fr.: **Leprince**.

Cogns.: It.: **Principe**, **Principi**, **Prencipe**. Sp.: **Principe**. Ger. (also Ashkenazic ornamental names): **Prin(t)z**. Flem., Du.: **(De)-Prins**.

Patr.: It.: **Del Principe**. Flem., Du.: **Prinsen**, **Prinzen**.

Pringle Scots and English (Northumb.): habitation name from a place near Stow in the former county of Roxburghs., formerly called *Hop(p)ringle*, from ME *hop* enclosed valley (see HOPE) + a name of ON origin composed of the byname *Prjónn* 'Pin', 'Peg' + *gil* narrow valley, ravine (see GILL 2).

A family of this name trace their descent from Robert Pringle, *squire to the Earl of Douglas, who fought at the battles of Otterburn (1388) and of Verneuil in Normandy (1424).*

Prior English: nickname or occupational name from ME *prior* prior, a monastic official immediately subordinate to an abbot (OE *prior*, from L *prior* superior, reinforced by OF *pri(o)ur* from the same source). The surname probably most often originated as an occupational name for a servant of a prior.

Vars.: **Prier**, **Pryer**, **Pryor**.

Cogns.: Fr.: **Prieur**, **Leprieur**, **Prieu(x)**. Prov.: **Prior**, **Priou(x)**, **Prio(u)l**. It.: **(Lo) Priore**, **Prior(i)**; **Priuli** (Venetia); **Priolo** (S Calabaria, Sicily).

Pritchard Welsh: patr., with a reduced form of the W element *ap*, from the given name RICHARD.

Var.: **Prichard**.

Privat French: from the given name (L *Prīvātus* 'Secluded', 'Withdrawn', from the past part. of *prīvāre* to deprive) borne by a 3rd-cent. saint and martyr, bishop of Mende, as well as various other early saints.

Vars.: **Privé**, **Privey**, **Privez**.

Privett English: habitation name from a place in Hants, which seems to get its name from an OE word **pryfet* privet copse. This element is thought to occur in other place-names, including *Privett* Farm in Standlynch, Wilts., which may also be a partial source of the surname, but the vocab. word for the shrub is not recorded before the 16th cent.

Probert Welsh: patr., with a reduced form of the W element *ap*, from the given name ROBERT.

This is the name of a Welsh family said to be directly descended from Ynyr, King of Gwent. Jenkin ap Howell was a courtier of Richard, Duke of York in 1436, his son was Robert ap Jenkin (d. 1509), and his grandson was Thomas Probert *(d. 1536).*

Procházka Czech: occupational name for an itinerant tradesman, especially a travelling butcher, literally a 'walker', from a deriv. of Czech *procházet* to walk, stroll, saunter. It could also be a nickname for an idle person, from the same word in the sense of one who sauntered idly from place to place. This is one of the most common Czech surnames.

Prochownik Polish and Jewish (E Ashkenazic): occupational name for a manufacturer of or trader in any type of powder, especially gunpowder, from an agent deriv. of *proch* powder.

Var.: Pol.: **Prochowski**.

Cogn.: Czech: **Prachař**.

Proctor English (most common in the north): occupational name for a steward, ME *prok(e)tour* (contracted from OF *procurateour*, L *prōcūrātor* agent, from *prōcūrāre* to manage, a cpd of *prō* for, on behalf of + *cūrāre* to deal with). The term was used most commonly of an attorney in a spiritual court, but also of other officials such as collectors of taxes and agents licensed to collect alms on behalf of lepers and enclosed orders of monks.

Vars.: **Procktor**, **Proc(k)ter**.

Profumo Italian (Liguria): metonymic occupational name for a maker or seller of scents and aromatic oils, from It. *profumo* perfume (from *perfumare* to perfume, L *perfūmāre* to smoke through, with change of prefix). The name may also have been a nickname for someone who made liberal use of perfume, or ironically for someone who was exceptionally evil-smelling even by medieval standards. It was also used as an affectionate familiar name, since perfume was very precious in the Middle Ages.

Proietto Italian: nickname given to a foundling, from It. *proietto* rejected, abandoned (L *prōiectus*, past part. of *prōicere* to cast forth). The surname is found mainly in Rome, and is still relatively frequent, in spite of its transparently unfavourable meaning. Cf. Esposito.

Var.: **Proietti**.

Prokhorov Russian: patr. from the given name *Prokhor* (Gk *Prokhoros*, from *pro* before, in front + *khorein* to dance, sing). This is the name supposedly borne by a 1st-cent. saint ordained by the apostles, who is said to have subsequently become bishop of Nicomedia and been martyred at Antioch.

Dims.: Russ.: See at Prokop. Beloruss.: **Prokhorchik** (not patr.).

'Son of the wife of P.': Russ.: **Prokhorikhin**.

Prokop Czech, Polish, Ukrainian, and Belorussian: from the given name *Prokop* (Gk *Prokopios*, from *pro* before, in front + *kopē* cut; i.e. 'Pioneer'). This was the name of the first victim of Diocletian's persecutions in Palestine in AD 303. He was greatly venerated in the Orthodox Church, whence the popularity of the Russ. given name *Prokofi* (a hypercorrected version of the Gk name, since Russian *p* was often used for Gk *ph*; cf. Stephen). The popularity of the name in central Europe is largely due to a later St *Prokop*, the patron saint of Bohemia, who founded the Sazaba abbey in Prague in the 11th cent.

Cogns.: Ger. (of Slav. origin): **Prokop(f)**, **Brokof**, **Brokuff**, **Brokob**.

Dims.: Czech: **Prokůpek**; **Průcha**, **Průša**; **Prokoš**, **Prokeš**, **Prošek**. Pol.: **Prokopczyk**. Beloruss.: **Prokopchik**, **Prakepyonok**. Ger. (of Slav. origin): **Prok(i)sch**, **Prox**; **Broksch**, **Bruck(i)sch**, **Brox**.

Aug.: Czech: **Prokopec**.

Patrs.: Ukr., Beloruss.: **Prokopovich**. Russ.: **Prokofyev**. Bulg.: **Prokofiev**.

Patrs. (from dims.): Russ.: **Prokoshkin**, **Prokoshev**, **Prokonov**, **Prokunin**, **Prokhnov**; **Pron(yak)ov**, **Pron(k)in**, **Pronichkin**, **Pronyaev**, **Pronchishchev**, **Pronichev**, **Proshchin** (shared with Prokhorov). Croatian: **Prokić**, **Kopčić**.

Pronk Dutch: nickname for an ostentatious dresser, from MDu. *prunk*, *pronk* finery, show, display.

Proom English: of uncertain origin, perhaps an importation, via the Low Countries, of a habitation name derived from *Prüm* near Trier in Germany.

Var.: **Proome** (a 20th-cent. alteration).

The first known bearer of the name in England is John Prom, *who died in 1454 at Brockford, Suffolk. All present-day bearers of the name seem to be descended from him. They are found during the 15th and 16th cents. in the area around Stowmarket, Suffolk, and in the 17th, 18th, and 19th cents. around Harwich, Essex.*

Prosser Welsh: patr., with a reduced form of the W element *ap*, from the given name *Rhosier*, the W form of Roger.

Protais French: from the OF given name *Protais* (from Gk *Protāsios*, a deriv. of *Protās*, a short form of various cpd personal names with the first element *prōtos* first). This was the name of a 1st-cent. saint martyred together with his brother Gervasius (see Jarvis 1), as well as of a 4th-cent. bishop of Milan and a 6th-cent. bishop of Avence.

Vars.: **Prothais**, **Protas**, **Protat**.

Dims.: **Proteau(x)**, **Protet**, **Prothin**, **Prothon**.

Protheroe Welsh: patr., with a reduced form of the W element *ap*, from the given name *Rhydderch* (see Roderick 2).

Vars.: **Prothero**, **Protherough**, **Pretheroe**; **Prydderch**, **Prytherch**, **Prytherick**; **Plutheroe**.

Protopopov Russian: patr. from the occupational term *protopop* arch-priest (Late Gk *prōtopappas*, from *prōtos* first + *pappas* priest; cf. Pope and Popov).

Proud English (chiefly Northumb.): nickname for a vain or haughty man, from ME *prod*, *prud* proud (late OE *prūd*, from the oblique form of OF *proz*; see Preux and Pridham).

Vars.: **Proude**; **Prout** (Cornwall).

Proudfoot Scots and English: nickname for someone with a haughty gait, from ME *prod*, *prud* Proud + *fote* Foot.

Provan Scots: habitation name from a place near Glasgow, so called from ME *provend*, *prebend* land providing revenue for a holder of religious office (OF *probende*, *prebende*, LL *praebenda* supplies, things to be supplied, from the neut. pl. form of the gerundive of *praebēre* to provide, furnish; for the alteration in the prefix, cf. Provost). The place was formerly held by the prebendary of Barlanark, one of the canons of Glasgow cathedral.

Vars.: **Provand**, **Proven**.

Provazník Czech: occupational name for a rope-maker, from Czech *provaz* rope + *-ník* suffix of agent nouns.

Province English: regional name for someone from *Provence* in S France, which is so called from L *prōvincia* province, sphere of office, because it was the first Roman province to be established outside Italy.

Var.: **Provins**.

Cogns.: Fr.: **Provençal**, **Provensal**, **Provensau(x)**. It.: **Provenza**; **Provenzale**, **Provenzal(i)**, **Provinciali**; **Provenzano**, **Provenzani**. Port.: **Proença** (also from two towns in Portugal, apparently so called because they were originally established by settlers from Provence).

Provost English: occupational name for the head of a religious chapter or educational establishment, or, since such officials were usually clergy and celibate, a nickname for a self-important person who behaved like a headmaster. The ME word *provost* (OE *profost*, reinforced by OF *provost*) is from L *prōpositus*, a byform of *praepositus* (see Prevost).

Vars.: **Provest**, **Provis**, **Proust**.

Cogns.: Fr.: **Pro(u)vo(s)t, Pruvo(s)t, Leprovo(s)t, Proust, Leproust, Pro(o)st, Prot**. Ger.: **Probst** (also borne by Ashkenazic Jews, the reason for this being unclear). Low Ger.: **Praast, Prakst, Pragst**. Flem.: **De Proot, De Prof**. Du.: **Pro(o)st**.

Prowse English: nickname for a redoubtable warrior, from ME *prou(s)* brave, valiant (OE *proux, preux*; see PREUX).

Vars.: **Prouse, Prewse, Pruce; Prow, Prew, Prue**.

Dims.: **Prewett, Pruett, Pruitt**.

Prudhoe English: habitation name from a place in Northumb., so called from the late OE byname *Prūda* (from *prūd* PROUD) + OE *hōh* ridge (see HOE).

Pruen English: of uncertain origin, probably Dutch or Flemish.

Vars.: **Pruin, Pruyn**.

The first known bearer of the name in England is William Pruyne *(d. 1493), buried in St Mary-at-Hill, in the city of London. Since the 17th cent. the family have been established in Gloucs.*

Prunty Irish: Anglicized form of Gael. **Ó Proinntigh** 'descendant of *Proinnteach*', a personal name meaning 'Bestower' (originally a byname denoting a generous person).

Vars.: **Pronty, Brunty, Brontë**, PRENTICE.

Pryde English and Scots: nickname from ME *pryde, pride* (late OE *prȳde*, a deriv. of *prūd* PROUD), denoting an arrogant man, or referring to someone who had played the part of this personified vice in a pageant of the Seven Deadly Sins.

2. Welsh: nickname from *prid* precious, dear.

Pryke English: metonymic occupational name for a maker or user of any of various pointed instruments, or nickname for a tall, thin man, from ME *prik(e), prich* point, prick (OE *pric(a)*).

Dims.: **Prickett, Pritchet(t), Pritchatt**.

Przybysz Polish: nickname for someone who had recently arrived in a district, from Pol. *przybysz* newcomer. Cf. NEWMAN, NOVÁK.

Vars.: **Przbył(a), Przybyłak; Przybyłski** (a common Pol. name, said by Bystroń to have been frequently given to foundlings).

Cogns.: Czech: **Přibyl; Přibáň, Přibík**.

Dim.: Pol.: **Przybyłek**.

Habitation names: Pol.: **Przybyłowski, Przybyszewski**.

Przygoda Polish: apparently a nickname from Pol. *przygoda* adventure, although the application is not clear. It probably refers to some now forgotten incident, but may have been used for an adventurous individual.

Vars.: **Przygodzki, Przygocki**.

Cogn.: Czech: **Příhoda**.

Pschorr S German: nickname for a person with close-cropped hair, from MHG *beschorner* shorn, strong form of the past part. of *(be)schern* to shear. In the Middle Ages this would have indicated lowly status, for only free men had the right to wear their hair long; cf. TOUS.

Vars.: **Pschorn, Beschor(e)n, Beschorner**.

Ptáčník Czech: occupational name for a fowler, from Czech *pták* bird + *-ník* suffix of agent nouns.

Pták Czech: nickname for a small, light person, from Czech *pták* bird.

Dim.: Czech: **Ptáček**.

Ptaszyński Polish: habitation name from a place named *Ptaszyn*, from Pol. *ptak* bird, or alternatively from a place where someone nicknamed *Ptaszek* 'Little Bird' lived. The nickname has the additional sense 'Cunning Rogue'.

Var.: **Ptasiński**.

Puccini Italian: aphetic form of a double dim. of any of various given names with the final consonant *p*, as for example *Filippo* (see PHILIP), *Giuseppe* (see JOSEPH), and *Iacopo* (see JACOB).

Puddephat English: nickname for someone compared in shape to a round barrel, from ME PUDDY round-bellied + *fat* vat.

Vars.: **Pudephat, Puddefoot, Pud(d)ifoot, Puttifoot**.

Puddy English: nickname for a rotund person, from ME *puddy* round-bellied (of uncertain immediate origin, but evidently akin to the Gmc element *pud-* to swell, bulge).

Puebla Spanish: habitation name from any of the many places in Spain so called, from OSp. *puebla* village, settlement (a deriv. of *poblar* to settle, populate, LL *populāre*, from *populus* people). The term was applied to a variety of deliberate settlements and resettlements, including those established in border areas or set up by foreigners or Jews.

Puey Catalan: nickname for a young person, or the younger of two bearers of the same given name, from Cat. *puey* boy (LL *puellus*, a dim. of class. L *puer*).

Pugachyov Russian: patr. from the nickname *Pugach* 'Owl' (of imitative origin, or from *pugat* to frighten, alarm).

Cogns.: Ukr.: **Pugach**. Jewish (E Ashkenazic): **Puga(t)ch, Pugatz(ky), Pugatchov** (all ornamental).

Pugh Welsh: patr., with a reduced form of the W element *ap*, from the given name HUGH.

Vars.: **Pughe, Pudge, Pew**, POWE, PYE.

Pugmire English: habitation name from a lost place in Yardley, E Birmingham, recorded in 1645 as *Puggmyre* Farm. This derives from the name of its 13th-cent. landlord, Robert *Pugg*, whose surname is of unknown etymology + ME *myre* mire, bog.

Puits French: topographic name for someone who lived by a well, OF *puts* (L *puteus* well, pit).

Vars.: **Puis, Dupui(t)s**.

Cogns.: Prov.: **Pou(t)s, Poux, Dupoux**. It.: **(Del) Pozzo, Dal Pozzo, Pozzi; (Della) Pozza** (Venetia); **Puzzu** (Sardinia). Sp.: **Pozo, Poza(s)**. Cat.: POU. Port.: **Poça**.

Dims.: Prov.: **Pouzet, Pouzin, Pouzol**. It.: **Pozetti, Pozetto** (also nicknames for a pock-marked man); **Pozzoli, Pozzolo** (see also PUY); **Puzzolo, Puzzulu** (Sardinia). Sp.: **Pozuelo**.

Pujadas Catalan: topographic name for someone who lived on a piece of rising ground, Cat. *pujada* (a deriv. of *puig*; see PUY).

Cogns.: Prov.: **P(o)ujade**.

Pulford English: habitation name from a place in Ches., so called from OE *pōl* POOL + *ford* FORD.

Pulham English: habitation name from places in Dorset and Norfolk, so called from OE *pōl* POOL + *hām* homestead.

Pullen English: metonymic occupational name for a horse-breeder or nickname for a frisky person, from OF *poulain* colt (LL *pullāmen*, a deriv. of *pullus* young animal; cf. POULE).

Vars.: **Pullein(e), Pulleyn, Pullin, Pullan**.

Cogns.: Fr.: **Poul(l)ain, Poulan, Poulenc**.

Pulver German and Jewish (Ashkenazic): metonymic occupational name for an apothecary who dispensed various types of medicinal powder, from Ger. *Pulver* powder (LL *pulver*, for class. L *pulvis*, gen. *pulveris*). From the

15th cent. it may also have been used of a manufacturer of gunpowder.

Var.: **Pulvermacher.**

Pulvertaft Irish: of uncertain origin, possibly a var. of the extinct Lincs. surname *Pulvertoft*, which may have been a habitation name from some lost place. *Pulver* is probably an old stream name, preserved also in *Pulverbatch*, Shrops., derived from ON *puldra* to gush; *-toft* is a common N English placename element, from ON *topt* homestead, although in the earliest known instance of the surname the second element seems to be CROFT.

The first known bearers of the name are Robert and John Pulvertaft, *who married in Cork in 1753 and 1765 respectively. All modern bearers of the name, which is found in the U.S., Australia, S Africa, and Denmark, as well as Ireland and England, seem to be descended from Thomas Pulvertaft, who was married* c.*1840*.

Pummell English: of uncertain origin. It appears to derive from ME, OF *pomel* bump, hillock (LL *pōmellum*, dim. of *pōmum* apple, fruit), perhaps as a topographic name.

Punainen Finnish: patr. from the nickname *Puna* 'Red', denoting a man with red hair.

Var.: **Punanen.**

Punton Scots and N English: of uncertain origin, probably a habitation name from *Ponton* or PANTON in Lincs., both of which have the same etymology.

Purcell English: metonymic occupational name for a swineherd or nickname, perhaps affectionate in tone, from OF *pourcel* piglet (L *porcellus*, a dim. of *porcus*; cf. PORCHER).

Cogns.: Fr.: **Pourcel, Pourceau.** It.: **Porc(i)ello, Porcelli, Purcelli.** Rum.: **Purčel.**

Dims.: It.: **Porcellino, Porcellini, Porcellotto, Porcelletti.**

Pej.: It.: **Porcellazzi.**

Purchase English: metonymic occupational name for an official responsible for obtaining the supplies required by a monastery or manor house, from ANF *purchacer* to acquire, buy (OF *pourchacier*, from *chacier* to chase, catch (L *captāre*; cf. CATCHPOLE) with the addition of the intensive prefix *p(o)ur*, L *prō*).

Vars.: **Purchas, Purches(e); Purkis(s), Purkess, Pirkis(s), Porkiss.**

Purdy English: nickname for someone who made frequent use of the ANF oath *pur die*, from OF *p(o)ur Dieu* by God (L *prō Deo*).

Vars.: **Purdey, Purdye, Purday, Purdu(e); Purdie** (Scots).

Cogn.: Fr.: **Pourdieu.**

Purser 1. English: occupational name for someone who made or sold purses and bags, or for an official in charge of expenditure, from an agent deriv. of ME *purse* (OE *purse*, from LL *bursa*).

2. Scots: translation of Gael. *Mac Sparáin*; see SPORRAN.

Var.: **Purse.**

Cogn.: Fr.: BOURSIER.

Purton English: habitation name from any of the places so called, in Gloucs., Staffs., and Wilts., from OE *pirige* pear tree (see PERRY 1) + *tūn* enclosure, settlement; cf. PARTON.

Purves Scots and N English: probably a metonymic occupational name for an official responsible for obtaining the supplies required by a monastery or manor house, from ME *purveys* provisions, supplies (from *purvey(en)*, OF *porveoir* to provide, supply, L *prōvidēre* to foresee, anticipate). According to Black it is a topographic name from ME, OF *parvis* church portico (from an altered form of L *paradīsus* Paradise), but the consistent *u* or *o* of the first syllable in early forms is hard to reconcile with this explanation.

Vars.: **Purvis** (Northumb.); **Purvess; Purvey.**

Pusey 1. English: habitation name from *Pusey* in Berks., so called from OE *peose*, *piosu* pea(s) (see PEASE) + *ēg* island, low-lying land.

2. French: habitation name from *Pusey* in Haute-Saône, so called from a Gallo-Roman personal name *Pusius* + the local suffix *-ācum*.

Vars. (of 1): **Peasey, Pezey, Piz(z)ey, Pizzie**; PEWSEY. (Of 2): **Puss(e)y.**

Edward Pusey *(1800–82), one of the leaders of the Oxford Movement, was originally named* Bouverie, *but inherited the estates on which he was born, at Pusey, Berks., from an aunt on condition that he assumed the surname Pusey.*

Pushkar Jewish (E Ashkenazic): occupational name for a gunsmith or cannon maker; cf. PUSHKIN.

Cogn.: Hung.: **Puskás.**

Dims.: Ukr.: **Pushkarenko.** Beloruss.: **Pushkarchuk.**

Patrs.: Russ.: **Pushkarev.** Beloruss.: **Pushkarevich.**

Pushkin Russian: patr. from the nickname *Pushka* 'Cannon' (originally 'container', 'magazine', from OHG *buhsa* box, L *buxis*; see BOX), denoting a bombastic person or used as an occupational name for a gunner or gunsmith.

The Russian poet and novelist Aleksandr Pushkin *(1799–1837) was born into a prosperous family in Moscow. His maternal great-grandfather was Abram Hannibal, an Abyssinian slave, said to be a prince, brought from Constantinople to Russia, where he became a great favourite of Peter the Great.*

Pustelnik Polish: nickname for a solitary individual, from Pol. *pustelnik* hermit.

Putnam English: habitation name from either of the places, in Herts. and Surrey, called *Puttenham*, from the gen. case of the OE byname *Putta* 'Kite' + OE *hām* homestead.

Var.: **Puttenham.**

Putterill English: metonymic occupational name for someone responsible for keeping horses, or nickname for a frisky and high-spirited person, from OF *poutrel* colt (LL *pultrellus*, from *pullus* young animal; cf. PULLEN).

Vars.: **Puttrell, Poutrel, Potterall, Pott(e)rill, Powdrell, Powd(e)rill; Purtill.**

A family called Poutrel *or* Powdrill *held the manor of Thrumpton, Notts., from the time of Domesday Book until 1604, when it was confiscated in view of the family's well-known Catholic sympathies. Members of the family then moved to W Hallam, Derbys., but the direct line died out in 1666. The name had also spread into Leics. and Lincs. by the early 14th cent., and is still found mainly in this region.*

Puttfarken Low German: nickname for a dirty or slovenly person, from MLG *put(t)* puddle (see PFÜTZER) + *farken* piglet (dim. of a cogn. of OE *fearh*).

Var.: **Putfarken.**

Puttock English: nickname for a rapacious or greedy person, from ME *puttock* kite (a dim. of OE *putta*; cf. PUTNAM).

Vars.: **Puttick, Puttack, Puttuck, Pottock.**

Puy Provençal and Catalan: topographic name for someone who lived at a high place, or habitation name from any of the numerous places in S France and NE Spain named with OProv., Cat. *puy* hill(ock) (L *podium* platform, from Gk *podion*, a dim. of *pous*, gen. *podis*, foot).

Vars.: Prov.: **Peu(x)**, **Pey**, **Pou(e)y**, **Poy**, **Pu(e)ch**, **Pe(u)ch**, **Pioch**, **Poueigh**, **Poeuf**; **Lepeu(t)**; **Dupeux**, **Dupouy**, **Delpu(e)ch**, **Delpech**. Cat.: **Puig**.

Cogns.: Sp.: **Pueyo** (Aragonese). It.: **Poggi(o)**.

Dims.: Prov.: **Puechon**, **Puget**, **Pugin**; see also PÉCHELS. Cat.: **Puyol**, **Pujol**. It.: **Poggetti**, **Poggini**, **Poggiol(in)i**; **Pozzol(in)i**, **Pozzolo** (from places in Tuscany and Liguria; see also PUITS).

Pye 1. English (especially common in Lancs. and E Anglia): nickname (for a talkative or thievish person) from the magpie, ME, OF *pie*, *pye* (L *pīca*). The mod. Eng. name of the bird, not found before the 17th cent., is from the earlier dial. term *maggot-pie*, formed by the addition of a dim. of the female given name *Margaret*.

2. English: metonymic occupational name for a baker or seller of pies, from ME *pie* (of unknown origin, possibly from the bird).

3. Welsh: patr., with a reduced form of the W element *ap*, from the given name HUGH.

Cogn. (of 1): It.: **Pica**.

Pytel Polish: metonymic occupational name for a bolter of flour, from Pol. *pytel* bolting cloth, sieve.

Python French: nickname for an unfortunate individual, from a dim. of OF *pite* pitable, from *pité* pity, mercy, LL *pietās*.

Vars.: **Pit(h)on**, **Pitou**; **Pitet**, **Pitel**.

Pejs.: **Pitard**, **Pitault**.

Q

Quail 1. English: nickname from the bird, ME, OF *quaille* (LL *quacula*, probably of imitative origin), no doubt denoting a timorous, lecherous, or fat person, all of which qualities were ascribed to the bird.

2. Irish: var. of QUILL 1.

3. Irish and Manx: Anglicized form of Gael. *Mac Phóil*; see MCFALL.

4. Jewish: in one family this is an Anglicized form of the Ashkenazic ornamental surname **Kvalvaser** (Yid.: 'spring water').

Vars.: **Quaile, Qua(y)le.**

Cogns. (of 1): Fr.: CAIL. It.: **Quaglia**; **Quaglieri** (occupational name for a hunter of quail). Flem., Du.: **Quackel.**

Dims. (of 1): It.: **Quaglino, Quagliotto, Quaglietta.**

Qualtrough Manx: from an aphetic form of Gael. **Mac Ualtair**, patr. from the given name WALTER, with the addition of the adj. suffix *-agh*, in a collective or patronymic sense.

Vars.: **Qualterough**; **Qualter(s).**

The surname is first recorded in the form Mac Qualtroughe *in 1430. The Manx placename* Kentraugh *is derived from the surname, which is now found also in America, Canada, Australia, and New Zealand, as well as elsewhere in the British Isles.*

Quant English: nickname for a person admired for his good sense or skill, or regarded as cunning or crafty, or noted for elegance and fine dress, from ME, OF *cointe*, *quointe* (L *cognitus* known (past part. of *cognōscere* to discover), later used also in the active sense 'knowing', 'clever', 'cunning'). The OF word developed the sense 'skilfully made', 'attractive', and this meaning was also taken into ME, eventually developing into 'unusual' (mod. Eng. *quaint*).

Cogns.: Fr.: **Coint(r)e, Lecoint(r)e, Coind(r)e, Lecoindre, Quinde.**

Dim.: Eng.: QUANTRILL.

Augs.: Fr.: **Cointat, Coindat.**

Quantrill English (E Anglia): nickname for a dandy or an elegant person, from ME, OF *cointerel*, a deriv. of *coint* skilled, attractive (see QUANT).

Vars.: **Quantrell, Quintrell.**

Cogns.: Fr.: **Coint(e)rel, Coint(e)reau, Cointeau, Coind(r)eau, Cointet.**

Quaresma Portuguese: religious byname for someone born during Lent, Port. *quaresma* (LL *quadrāgēsima*, from *quadrāgēsimus*, a deriv. of *quadrāginta* forty, referring to the forty days of Lent, commemorating Christ's forty days in the wilderness).

Quark 1. German: metonymic occupational name for a maker and seller of curd cheese, Ger. *Quark* (MHG *quark*, from Slav. *tvarog*, borrowed first into E Ger. dialects and then spreading throughout the German-speaking lands during the Middle Ages).

2. Manx: aphetic form of Gael. **Mac Mhairc**, patr. from the given name MARK.

Vars. (of 1): **Quarch, Quarg.**

Quarles English: habitation name from a place in Norfolk, recorded in Domesday Book as *Hueruelès*, from OE *hwerflas*, pl. of *hwerfel* circle. The name perhaps originally referred to a prehistoric stone circle, although no trace of any such feature remains today.

Quarrell English: 1. metonymic occupational name for a maker of crossbow bolts or nickname for a short, stout man, from ME, OF *quar(r)el* bolt for a crossbow (LL *quadrellum*, a dim. of *quadrum* square). Cf. BOLT 2.

2. nickname for a troublemaker, from ME, OF *querel* complaint, accusation (LL *querella*, for class. L *querūla*, a deriv. of *queri* to complain). For the change of *-er-* to *-ar-*, cf. MARCHANT.

Cogns. (of 1): Fr.: **Car(r)el, Car(r)eau.**

Dim. (of 1): Fr.: **Carrelet.**

Quarry 1. English (Norman): nickname for a thickset or portly man, from ONF *quaré* square-shaped (L *quadrātus*, from *quadrum* square); cf. CARRÉ.

2. English: topographic name for someone who lived near a stone quarry, or metonymic occupational name for someone who worked in one, from ME *quarey*, *quarer(e)* (ONF *quarrere*, a deriv. of *quaré* in the specialized sense 'dressed stone').

3. Manx: aphetic form of Gael. *Mac Guaire*; see MCQUARRY.

Var.: **Quarrie.**

Quartermain English (Norman): nickname meaning 'four hands', perhaps denoting a person who was in the habit of wearing heavy gloves, esp. of mail, or one who worked so fast or was so dextrous that he seemed to have four hands, from OF *quatre* four (L *quattuor*) + *main* hand (L *manus*).

Vars.: **Quartermaine, Quarterman, Quatermain(e).**

Queille French: habitation name from any of the places called *La Queille*, of which there is one in Calvados and another in Corrèze, or one called *Laqueille* in Puy-de-Dôme. All were originally named *l'accueil*, from OF *accueil* welcome (from *accueillir* to welcome, LL *accolligere* to gather (together) to oneself) with fused def. art. and consequent misdivision.

Var.: **Queuille.**

Quêne French: 1. nickname from Norman forms of OF *chiene* bitch (fem. of *chien* dog, L *canis*).

2. topographic name for someone who lived by an oak tree, from a Norman or Picard form of CHÊNE.

3. aphetic var. of the given name *Jacqème*; see JAMES.

Vars. (of 2): **Quesne, Duquesne.**

Dims. (of 2): **Quesnet, Quénet, Quesnel, Quénel, Quesneau, Quéneau, Quesnot.**

Collectives (of 2): **Quesnay, Quesney, Quesnoy; Duquesnay, Duquesnoy.**

Quennell English: from the ME female given name *Quenilla*, *Quenilde*, from OE *Cwēnhild*, composed of the elements *cwēn* woman + *hild* battle.

Vars.: **Quenell, Quinell.**

Quer Catalan: habitation name from any of various places named with the OCat. element *quer* rock (of pre-Roman origin and apparently akin to Basque *arri*).

Dims.: **Querol, Queró.**

Queralt Catalan: habitation name from any of various places so called from OCat. *quer* rock (see QUER) + *alt* high (L *altus*).

Quesada Spanish: habitation name from a place in the province of Jaén, of uncertain etymology. There may be some connection with OSp. *requexada* corner, tight spot, apparently a deriv. of *quexar* to afflict, oppress (L *quassāre* to shake, break, frequentative of *quatere* to shake).

Quested English: of uncertain origin, probably a habitation name from the lost village of *Questers* (earlier *Quernstede*) in the parish of Sampford, Essex, so called from OE *cweorn* quern, hand-mill + *stede* site (see STEAD).

Quick 1. English: nickname for a lively or agile person, from ME *quik*, OE *cwic* alive, lively.

2. English: topographic name for someone who lived by one of the various types of vegetation named from this word: couch grass, which grows rapidly and is difficult to eradicate (OE *cwice*); the aspen, whose leaves tremble as if they are alive (OE *cwictrēow*); or the poplar, which is widely used to make quickset fences (OE *cwicbēam*).

3. English: topographic name for someone who lived at an outlying dairy farm, from OE *cū* cow + *wīc* outlying settlement (see WICK).

4. Cornish: topographic name for someone who lived in a wood, Corn. *gwyk*, or habitation name from a minor place named with this word, as for example *Gweek* in the parish of Constantine.

Vars.: Eng.: **Quicke**. (Of 1 only): QUICKLEY.

Quickley 1. English: var. of QUICK 1, from ME *quiklich*, OE *cwiclīc* lively.

2. Irish: Anglicized form of Gael. **Ó Coigligh** 'descendant of *Coigleach*', a byname apparently representing a simplified form of *coigeallach* untidy person.

Vars. (of 2): **(O')Quigl(e)y**, **O'Cwigley**, **(O')Cogley**, **O'Coigley**, **(O')Kegley**.

Quijada Spanish: nickname for a person with a prominent jaw, Sp. *quijada* (a deriv. of OSp. *quexa*, from LL *capsea*, itself a deriv. of *capsa* box (cf. CASE 1)).

Quilici Italian: from the given name *Quilico*, an altered form of *Quirico*, borne by a (probably fictitious) 4th-cent. infant saint, said to have been martyred at Tarsus with his mother Julitta, who was honoured in the Middle Ages as a patron of children. The name is of uncertain origin. It seems to result from the crossing of two other names, both borne by several early saints: L *Quirīnus*, originally a title borne by Romulus, founding father of Rome, which is derived from the Sabine city of *Cures*, and Gk *Kyriakos*, a deriv. of *kyrios* lord, master.

Vars.: **Quilico**, **Quirico**.

Dim.: **Quilichini**.

Aug.: **Quiriconi**.

Patrs.: Sp.: **Quílez**. Cat.: **Quiles**, **Quilis**.

Quill 1. Irish: Anglicized form of Gael. **Ó Cuill** 'descendant of *Coll*', a personal name from *coll* hazel tree.

2. Scots: Anglicized form of Gael. **Mac Cuill** 'son of *Coll*', the same name as in 1.

Vars. (of 1): QUAIL, **O'Quill**, **O'Cuill**. (Of 2): **McColl**.

Dims. (of 1): **Quill(ig)an**, **Col(l)gan**.

Quilly Irish: 1. Anglicized form of Gael. **Mac Conchoille** 'son of *Cú Choille*', a personal name from *cú* dog + *coille*, gen. of *coill* wood, forest.

2. Anglicized form of Gael. **Mac an Choiligh** 'son of the cock', from *coileach* cock.

Vars.: **McQuilly**. (Of 2 only): **McAnchelly**, **McInchelly**, **McEnkelly**, **McAckolly**.

Quilter English: occupational name for a maker of quilts and mattresses, and also of the quilted garments worn in battle by those who could not afford armour made of metal, from an agent deriv. of ME, OF *cuilte*, *coilte* quilt, mattress (L *culcita* mattress).

Quincey English (Norman): habitation name from any of several places in France deriving their names from the Gallo-Roman personal name *Quintus* 'Fifth(-born)' + the local suffix *-ācum*. The earliest bearers of the name in England were from *Cuinchy* in Pas-de-Calais, but other stocks may be from *Quincy*-sous-Sénard in Seine-et-Oise or *Quincy*-Voisins in Seine-et-Marne.

Vars.: **De Quincey**, **Quincy**, **Quinsey**, **Quinsee**.

The English writer Thomas De Quincey *(1785–1859) was born in Manchester, the son of a businessman, into a family of Norman origin. In the 13th cent. his ancestors had held the earldom of Winchester, but they later sank into obscurity. The prefix* De *was adopted by the author.*

The American Quincy *family were established in Massachusetts by Edmund Quincy in 1633. Fifth in descent was Josiah Quincy (1744–75), a leading patriot, who was sent to England to argue the colonists' case in 1774. His son Josiah (1772–1864) was a powerful opponent of slavery, president of Harvard, and mayor of Boston, a post also held by several of his descendants. This family traditionally pronounces the name* /ˈkwɪnzɪ/.

Quinlan Irish: 1. Anglicized form of Gael. **Ó Caoindealbháin** 'descendant of *Caoindealbhán*' a personal name composed of the elements *caoin* comely, fair + *dealbh* form + the dim. suffix *-án*.

2. Anglicized form of **Ó Conailláin** 'descendant of *Conaillán*' a personal name representing a dim. of *Conall*; see CONNELL.

Vars.: **O'Connellaine**, **Connellan**, **(O')Conlan**, **Conlon**, **Conlin**. (Of 1 only): **O'Quinelane**, **O'Guindelane**, **O'Kenolan**, **(O')Kennellan**, **Quinlivan**, **Quinlevan**, **Kin(del)lan**, **Kenlan**.

Quinn Irish: Anglicized form of Gael. **Ó Cuinn** 'descendant of *Conn*', a byname meaning 'Leader', 'Chief'.

Vars.: **(O')Quin(e)**, **O'Quyn**.

Quin *is the name of an ancient Irish family, whose forebears were once chiefs of the clan Heffernan. One of their earliest recorded ancestors is Donogh Quin, living in 1551. They are unusual in being one of the few Celtic families in the peerage, holding the titles Earl of Dunraven and Mountearl.*

Quiñones Spanish: topographic name for someone who lived on a piece of land that was shared out among a group of co-tenants for sowing, Sp. *quiñón* (L *quīnio*, gen. *quīniōnis*, group of five, a deriv. of *quinque* five).

Quintana Spanish and Catalan: topographic name for someone who lived on a piece of land subject to rent of one-fifth of its produce, from Sp., Cat. *quintana* a fifth (LL *quintāna*, a deriv. of *quintus* fifth). There are numerous places named with this word, and the surname may also be a habitation name from any of these.

Cogn.: Port.: **Quintas**.

Dim.: Sp.: **Quintanilla**.

Quinton English: 1. habitation name from any of the places, for example in Gloucs., Northants, and Birmingham, so called from OE *cwēn* queen + *tūn* enclosure, settlement (cf. KINGSTON).

2. from the OF given name *Quentin*, *Quintin* (L *Quintīnus*, a deriv. of *Quintus* 'Fifth(-born)'; cf. QUINCEY), which was introduced into England by the Normans, but never became widely popular.

3. Norman habitation name from any of the places in N France named from St Quentin of Amiens, a 3rd-cent. Roman missionary to Gaul, as for example *Saint-Quentin* in La Manche or *Saint-Quentin*-en-Tourmont in Somme, the site of his martyrdom.

Cogns. (of 2): Fr.: **Quintin**, **Quentin**, **Quantin**. It.: **Quintino**, **Quintini**.

Quirke Manx and Irish: Anglicized form of Gael. **Ó Cuirc** 'descendant of *Corc*', a personal name from *corc* heart, or *curc* tuft of hair. It is sometimes translated **Oates**, as if from *coirce* oats.

Vars.: **Quirk**; **O'Quirk(e)**, **O'Cuirk**.

The family of Sir Randolph Quirk (*b. 1920*), *formerly Professor of English Language at the University of London, have farmed the same piece of land, Lambfell, on the Isle of Man since 1654.*

Quiroga Spanish: habitation name from places (of unknown etymology) in the provinces of Lugo and Orense.

Quirós Spanish: habitation name from any of various places in W Spain, most notably one in the province of Oviedo. The placename is of unknown origin; there may be some connection with the Galician dial. term *queiroa*, which denotes a kind of heather.

Cogn.: Port.: **Queirós**.

Qvist Swedish: ornamental surname, from Swed. *quist* twig (ON *kvistr*). When surnames were adopted on a large scale in the 19th cent. in Sweden, *qvist* was one of the elements that were widely used in combination with other words denoting natural features to form surnames such as *Lindqvist* and *Blomqvist*.

Vars.: **Quist**, **Kvist**.

R

Rabadán Spanish: occupational name for a shepherd boy, Sp. *rabadán* (Arabic *rabb ad-da'n* 'the one with the sheep').

Rabaud French: from the OF personal name *Radbaud*, *Rabbaud*, composed of the Gmc elements *rād* counsel, advice + *bald* bold, brave.

Var.: **Rabault**.

Cogns.: Ger.: **Rappold**, **Rapholdt**, **Rappelt**. Low Ger.: **Rabbold**.

Dims.: Low Ger.: **Rabbe(ke)** (see also RABBITT).

Patr.: Ger.: **Rappolder** (Austria).

Rabbitt 1. English: dim. of *Rabb*, a pet form of ROBERT.

2. English: from the Norman personal name *Radbode*, *Rabbode*, composed of the Gmc elements *rād* counsel, advice + *bodo* message, tidings, introduced by the Normans.

3. Irish: erroneous translation of Gael. *Ó Coinín*; see KINNEEN.

Vars. (of 1): **Rabet**. (Of 3): **Rabbitte**.

Cogn. (of 2): Ger.: **Rappot**.

Dims. (of 2): Low Ger.: **Rabbe(ke)** (see also RABAUD).

Patrs. (from 1 and 2): Eng.: **Rabbit(t)s**, **Rabet(t)s**, **Rabbatts**.

Rabin Jewish (E Ashkenazic): status name from Pol. *rabin* rabbi (ultimately from Hebr. *rav*).

Vars.: **Rabinski**, **Rabinsky**; **Ravin(sky)**, **Ravinzki** (from Russ. *ravin*); **Rabiner** (from Ger. *Rabbiner*; also W Ashkenazic); **Raff** (W Ashkenazic; from Low Ger.); **Rab(b)ino** (among It. Jews, from the It. word for 'rabbi'); **Rabenu** (a Hebr. phrase meaning 'our rabbi'); ROBIN.

Patrs.: **Rabin(er)son**, **Rabinsohn**, **Robinso(h)n**, **Robinzon** (Ashkenazic); **Rabinow**, **Rabinov**, **Robinov**, **Robinow**, **Rabinowicz**, **Ravinovicz**, **Rabinowit(s)ch**, **Rabinovi(t)ch**, **Rabinovitsh**, **Rabinowitz**, **Rabinovitz**, **Rabinovits**, **Rabinovics**, **Robinovich**, **Robinovitz** (E Ashkenazic), **Rabinovici** (among Rumanian Jews).

Rachet French: nickname for a bald man, from a dim. of North-Eastern OF *rache* bald (of uncertain origin, perhaps from L *rāsus* clean-shaven, past part. of *rādere* to scrape; cf. RAYER 2). The surname is found largely in the Burgundy and Champagne regions.

Var.: **Rachez**.

Racine French: metonymic occupational name for a grower or seller of root vegetables, or nickname for a tenacious and stubborn person, from OF *racine* root (LL *rādīcīna*, a deriv. of class. L *rādix*, gen. *rādīcis*).

Vars.: **Rachine** (Normandy); **Rassinier**, **Racineux**, **Rassineux** (agent derivs.).

Dims.: **Racinet**; **Rachinel** (Normandy).

Rackham English: habitation name from a place in Sussex, so called from OE *hrēac* mound, (hay)rick (probably the name of a nearby hill) + *hām* homestead.

Rackley English: apparently a habitation name from an unidentified place, which would derive its name from OE *hrēac* mound (cf. RACKHAM) or *hraca* throat, gulley + *lēah* wood, clearing.

Rácz Hungarian: from Hung. *rác* Serbian, derived from the Serbian placename *Ras*, the capital of medieval Serbia.

Raczyński Polish: habitation name from a village called *Raczyn* or *Raczyno*.

Radecki Polish: from a dim., *Radek*, of any of various Slav. personal names containing a first element *rad* glad. In Pol., the most common such names are *Radosław* (Czech *Radoslav*), in which the second element means 'glory' and *Radomierz* (Czech *Radomír*), in which the second element means 'great, famous'.

Vars.: **Radek**, **Radke**.

Cogns.: Czech: **Rada**. Rum.: **Radu**. Hung.: **Radó**.

Patrs.: Pol.: **Radkiewicz**. Croatian: **Radić**, **Radović**, **Radojević**, **Radoj(i)čić**; **Radojković**; **Radošević**, **Radišić**; **Radunović**, **Radjenović**, **Radonjić**, **Radenković**, **Radaković**; **Radulović**; **Radovanović**; **Rad(o)manović**. Bulg.: **Raikov**. Rum.: **Rădulescu**, **Rad(u)lesco**. Hung.: **Radics**.

Radecký Czech: habitation name from any of several places in Bohemia, for example *Hradec* (*Králové*) (Ger. *Königgrätz*) or *Radeč*.

Vars.: **Hradecký**, **Hradec**.

Cogn.: Ger.: **Radetzky**.

The Austrian military leader Count Josef Radetzky von Radetz *(1766–1858) was born in Trebnice, Bohemia.*

Rademaker Low German and Dutch: occupational name for a wheelwright, from MLG, MDu. *rat* wheel + *makære* maker. The term was also used by extension for a builder of carts, and so is an equivalent of N Ger. STELLMACHER and S Ger. WAGNER.

Vars.: Low Ger.: **Rademacher**, **Ra(h)maker**, **Ramacker**, **Ramecker**; **Re(de)ker**.

Cogns.: Flem.: **Rae(de)maeker**.

Patrs.: Low Ger.: **Ra(h)makers**, **Ramachers**, **Rameckers**, **Rademächers**. Flem.: **Raemakers**.

Radford English: habitation name from any of the various places so called, for example in Devon, Notts., Oxon., Warwicks., and Worcs. Most are named from OE *rēad* red (see READ 1) + *ford* FORD, but it is possible that in some cases the first element may be a deriv. of OE *rīdan* to ride, with the meaning 'ford that can be crossed on horseback'.

Vars.: **Radforth**, **Radfirth**, **Ratford**; **Red(di)ford**, **Retford**.

Radigue Provençal: of uncertain origin. It is largely confined to Gascony and is perhaps a deriv. of OProv. *razigar* to tear out, uproot (L *ērādīcāre*, from *rādix*, gen. *rādīcis*, root; cf. RACINE); if so, it is presumably a topographic name for someone who lived on a patch of cleared land.

Dims.: **Radiguet**, **Radigon**.

Radley English: habitation name from a place so called from OE *rēad* red (see READ 1) + *lēah* wood, clearing; cf. REDSHAW and REDWOOD. There are places of this name in Berks. and Devon.

Var.: **Radleigh**. See also RALEIGH.

Radmore English (Devon): habitation name from an unidentified place, apparently originally named with the OE elements *rēad* red (see READ 1) + *mōr* moor (see MOORE 1).

Radnedge English: habitation name, probably from *Radnage* in Bucks., which gets its name from OE (*æt þǣm*) *rēadan ǣc* '(at the) red oak'.

Radomski Polish: habitation name from the city of *Radom* in central Poland, S of Warsaw. The placename is derived from the OSlav. personal name *Radomir*.

Radziejewski Polish: habitation name from the town of *Radziejów* in N central Poland, so called from an OPol. personal name *Radziej* (derived from the suffix *rad(z)-* together) + *-ów*, *-ew* possessive suffix, with the addition of the surname suffix *-ski* (see BARANOWSKI).

Vars.: **Radzikowski, Radziński.**

Dims. (of the personal name): **Radzik, Radzicki.**

Radziwiłł Polish: from Lithuanian *radvila* foundling. In spite of its humble origin, this surname has enjoyed considerable prestige as the name of one of the leading noble families of Poland.

Vars.: **Radziwilski, Radziwił(ł)owski** (from placenames derived from this surname); **Radziwill** (U.S.).

Raeburn Scots: habitation name from a place in the Scottish Borders, so called from Northern ME *ray* roebuck (see RAY 2) + *burn* stream (see BOURNE).

Rafferty Irish (esp. Ulster): Anglicized form of Gael. **Ó Rabhartaigh** or **Ó Robhartaigh** 'descendant of *Robhartach*', a personal name apparently meaning 'Wielder of Prosperity'.

Ragazzo Italian: occupational name for a servant, from It. *ragazzo* boy, lad, servant.

Vars.: **Ragazzi, Regazzi, Regazzo.**

Dims.: **Ragazzini, Regazzini.**

Augs.: **Ragazzoni, Ragazzone, Regazzoni.**

Raggett English: nickname for a person of unkempt appearance, from ME *ragged* shaggy, rough (from ON *roggvaðr* tufted); the noun *rag* is a back-formation from this. The surname is localized in the Odiham area of Hants. in the 17th cent.

Rahn German: 1. nickname for a person with dark hair or a swarthy complexion, from MHG, OHG *rān*, *rām* soot, dirt.

2. nicknickname for a thin person, from MHG *rān* slender (of uncertain origin).

3. from a short form of any of various Slav. personal names, such as *Ranoslav* and *Ranomir*, with the first element *rano* early.

Dims. (of 3): **Rahncke, Ran(t)ke, Ranek, Rahnsch, Ranisch, Ranusch, Ränisch.**

Raikes English: topographic name for someone who lived by a narrow pass or cleft in a hillside, from OE *hraca* throat, also commonly used with this transferred sense.

Vars.: **Rake(s).**

Rainbird English: from an OF personal name, *Rainbert*, composed of the Gmc elements *ragin* counsel + *berht* bright, famous. This was introduced to Britain by the Normans. The form of the name has been affected by folk etymological association with *rainbird*, a vernacular name of the plover (cf. PLOUVIER 2).

Vars.: **Raynbird, Rambert, Ram(b)art.**

Cogns.: Fr.: **Ra(i)mbert, R(e)imbert, Rembert.** Ger.: **Regenprecht, Reiprecht, Reiprich.** Low Ger.: **Re(i)mbert, Rei(m)pert, Reimert, Remmert.** Fris.: **Reemt.**

Rainbow 1. English: from an OF personal name, *Rainbaut*, composed of the Gmc elements *ragin* counsel + *bald* bold, brave. This was introduced to Britain by the Normans. The form of the name has been affected by folk etymological association with the natural phenomenon.

2. Jewish (Ashkenazic): Anglicized form of **Regenbogen** (mod. Ger. 'rainbow'), one of the group of ornamental names based on natural phenomena.

Vars. (of 1): **Rambaut, Rimbault, Renbold, Ramble, Rammell, Raybould.**

Cogns. (of 1): Fr.: **Ra(i)mbaud, Ra(i)mbault, R(e)imbaud, Rembaud, Reimbold, Reinbold.** Ger.: **Re(i)mbold; Römbold** (Swabia). Low Ger.: **Reimelt.** It.: **Rambaldi, Rambaudi.**

Raine 1. English and French: from a short form of any of the various Gmc personal names with the first element *ragin* counsel (see, e.g., RAYMOND, REYNOLD).

2. English: from the medieval female given name *Reine* (from OF *reine* queen, L *rēgīna*).

3. Jewish (Ashkenazic): from the Yid. female given name *Rayne*, cognate with 2 and used as a translation of Hebr. *Malka* 'Queen'.

4. English and French: nickname from OF *raine* frog (L *rāna*).

5. Scots: habitation name from *Raine* in the former county of Aberdeens., so called from Gael. *rath chàin* ford of the tax or tribute.

Vars.: Eng.: **Rayne, Rain.** (Of 1 only): Fr.: **Renne; Rainon, Renon** (from the oblique case).

Cogns. (of 1): Ger.: **Rein.** Low Ger.: **Rehn, Renn(e).** (Of 2): Fr.: **Reine, Reyne.** It.: **Regina; Reina** (Sicily). Sp., Cat.: **Reina.**

Dims. (of 1): Eng.: **Raincock.** Fr.: **Raineau, Ragoneau(x), Rag(on)ot, Ragueneau, Ragu(en)et, Raguin.** Ger.: **Reinel, Reinle, Rein(d)l; Rein(t)sch, Re(i)nisch, Rentsch(ke); Rön(t)sch, Rönisch.** Low Ger.: **Reinmann, Rai(n)mann; Reine(c)ke, Reinick(e), Reinege, Reinke, Renneke.** It.: **Ranucci, Ranuzzi.**

Patrs. (from 1): Eng.: **Raines.** Low Ger.: **Reins, Reinen, Rehnen, Reenen, Rennen.**

Metrs. (from 3): Jewish: **Rainin** (E Ashkenazic); **Raines, Ra(i)nis, Reines, Reinis, Reinuss, Renus.**

Patrs. (from 1) (dims.): Low Ger.: **Reine(c)ken, Reinicken, Reinken(s), Rennsen, Reining, Rennings, Rein(e)king.** Fris.: **Reininga, Reinkena.**

Rainey Scots and Irish: from a dim. of a short form of any of the various Gmc personal names with a first element *rand* (shield) rim (cf. RAND 1) or *ragin* counsel. The given name was most frequently used as a form of RANDOLF and REYNOLD.

Vars.: **Rainy, Rain(n)ie, Raney, Rannie, Rean(n)(e)y, Ren-n(e)y, Rennie.**

Patrs: **Renison; Creaney** (Gael. **Mac Raighne**); **McCrank, McGrane, McGrain** (Gael. **Mac Raing**).

'Descendant of R.': **O'Reaney** (Gael. **Ó Ráighne, Ó Raighne**).

Rainford English: habitation name from a place in Lancs., so called from **Regna*, a short form, not independently attested, of OE cpd personal names with the first element *regen* counsel + OE *ford* FORD.

Var.: **Rainsford.**

Raison English and French: nickname for an intelligent person, from ME, OF *raison* reasoning, intellectual faculty (L *ratio*, gen. *ratiōnis*, a deriv. of *rēri* to think).

Vars.: Eng.: **Reason.** Fr.: **Raisonnier.**

Raistrick English: habitation name from *Rastrick* in W Yorks., the origin of which is obscure; it may mean 'resting-place ridge'.

Var.: **Rastrick.**

Rajala Finnish: topographic name for someone living near a border, from Finn. *raja* boundary, border + the local suffix *-la*.

Rajski Polish and Jewish (Ashkenazic): 1. topographic name for someone living in a marshy or muddy spot, from OPol. *raj(a)* marsh, mud + *-ski* suffix of surnames (see BARANOWSKI).

2. nickname for someone who lived in a pleasant spot or in happy circumstances, from Pol. *raj* paradise + *-ski*. As a Jewish name, this may well be ornamental in origin.

Var.: **Raj**.

Habitation names: **Rajewski**. Pol. only: **Rajkowski** (from a dim.).

Rak Polish, Czech, and Jewish (E Ashkenazic): apparently from the Slav. vocab. word *rak* crab, crayfish. The reasons for its acquisition as a surname are not clear. It may be a nickname, and in areas where crabs were familiar may have been applied to someone who did not walk straight or to one who was not entirely 'straight' in his dealings. In some cases it represents a translation of Ger. *Krebs* (see CRABBE), and as an Ashkenazic name may have been one of the unflattering surnames bestowed on Jews by non-Jewish government officials in 18th- and 19th-cent. Eastern Europe.

Dim.: Pol.: **Raczek**.

Habitation names: Pol. and Jewish: **Rakowski** (from any of several places called *Raków*, including one S of Warsaw and another in Belorussia, which was a frontier town between Poland and the Soviet Union 1921–39). Pol. only: **Rakowiecki** (from *Rakowiec*, S of Warsaw).

Habitation name (from the dim. *raczek*): Pol. and Jewish: **Raczkowski**.

Rakhmaninov Russian: patr. from the ORuss. ethnic name *rakhmanin* Indian (ultimately from Skt *brāhmana* Brahmin), used as a nickname for someone of swarthy appearance.

Rákos Czech: 1. topographic name for someone who lived by a reedbed or patch of bulrushes, Czech *rákos*.

2. metonymic occupational name for a basketmaker, from the same word in the sense of cane or wickerwork.

Vars.: **Rokos**. (Of 2 only): **Rákosník**.

Rakušan Czech: ethnic name for an Austrian, from a deriv. of Czech *Rakousko* Austria.

Raleigh English: habitation name from *Raleigh* in Devon, recorded in Domesday Book as *Radeleia*, from OE *rēad* red (see READ 1) + *lēah* wood, clearing; cf. RADLEY. The placename is pronounced /ˈrɔːlɪ/, and this is also the traditional pronunciation of the surname (James I punned the name of Sir Walter with *rarely*); nowadays the pronunciations /ˈrɑːlɪ/ and /ˈrælɪ/ are also found.

Vars.: **Ralegh**, RAYLEIGH; **Ra(w)ley**, **Rall(e)y**.

The English explorer Sir Walter Raleigh *(?1552–1618) was born in Hayes Barton, Devon, into a family of Devon gentry. He was related to most of the W Country's important families, including that of Sir Francis Drake. His half-brother was the explorer Sir Humphrey Gilbert.*

Ralph English: from an ON personal name composed of the Gmc elements *rad* counsel, advice + *wolf* wolf. This was first introduced into England by Scandinavian settlers in the ON form *Ráðúlfr*, and was reinforced after the Conquest by the Norman form *Ra(d)ulf*.

Vars.: **Ralf(e)**; **Rafe**, **Raff**; RAW, **Rawle**, **Rawll**.

Cogns.: Fr.: **Raoul(t)**, **Ra(o)ux**, **Rault**. Prov.: **Radou**; **Razou(l)(s)**, **Razoux**, **Razout**. Ger.: **Radolf**. Low Ger.: **Radloff**, **Rahl(of)f**.

Dims.: Eng.: RAWLING. Fr.: **Raulet**; **Raulic** (Brittany).

Patrs.: Eng.: **Ralphs**, **Ralfs**; **Raves**; **Ra(w)les**, **Ralls**; **Ralphson**. Low Ger.: **Ralf(e)s**, **Ralwes**.

Ram 1. English: nickname for a forceful or lusty individual, from ME, OE *ram(m)* male sheep (in part perhaps representing a continued use of an OE byname). It may also occasionally have been a metonymic occupational name for a shepherd, or a house name for someone who lived 'at the sign of the ram'.

2. French: topographic name for someone who lived in a thickly wooded area, from OF *ra(i)m* branch (L *rāmus*). It seems likely that it was also used as a nickname for someone who had some particular connection with Palm Sunday, for which the Fr. term is *(dimanche des) rameaux*, and there may in some cases have been some reference to the 'branches' of a family tree.

3. Swedish: topographic name for someone who lived near a border or boundary, Swed. *ram*.

4. Jewish (Israeli): ornamental name from Hebr. *ram* lofty.

Vars. (of 1 and 4): **Ramm**. (Of 2): **Rame(s)**.

Cogns. (of 1): Ger.: **Ramm(e)**. (Of 2): Prov.: **Ramas**. It.: **Rama**. Sp., Port.: **Ramos**.

Dims. (of 1): Eng.: **Ramplin(g)**. (Of 2): Fr.: **Ramel(et)**, **Rameau(x)**, **Ram(e)lot**, **Ramet**, **Ramey**. Port.: **Ramalhete**.

Pej. (of 2): Fr.: **Ramard** (the sense is probably as in RAMAGE).

Collective (of 2): Port.: **Ramalho**.

Cpds (of 3, topographic or ornamental): Swed.: **Ramberg** ('border hill'); **Ramstedt** ('border homestead'); **Ramström** ('border river').

Ramage Scots: nickname for a savage or unpredictable individual, from ME, OF *ramage* wild (of a bird of prey) (LL *rāmaticus*, from *rāmus* branch; cf. SAVAGE).

Ramsbottom N English: habitation name from a place in Lancs., so called from OE *hramsa* wild garlic + *boðm* valley (see BOTTOM).

Var.: **Ramsbotham**.

Ramsdale N English: habitation name from a place in N Yorks., so called from OE *hramsa* wild garlic (or possibly the gen. case of the byname *Ram(m)* 'RAM') + *dæl* valley (see DALE).

Ramsden N English: habitation name from any of various places so called from OE *hramsa* wild garlic (or possibly the gen. case of the OE byname *Ram(m)* 'RAM') + *denu* valley (see DEAN 1). There are villages so named in Essex, Kent, Oxon., and Warwicks., but the surname is most common in Yorks., where there are several minor places so called, *Ramsden* in the parish of Kirkburton being a well-recorded instance.

Ramsey Scots: 1. habitation name from places in Hunts. (now part of Cambs.) and Essex, so called from OE *hramsa* wild garlic + *ēg* island, low-lying land.

2. habitation name from a place in the parish of Whithorn, in the former county of Wigtown, so called from the gen. case of the OE byname *Ram(m)* 'RAM' + *ēg*.

Var.: **Ramsay**.

The first bearer of the name recorded in Scotland was Simundus de Ramsay, *a Norman baron from Hunts., England, who was a retainer of David, Earl of Huntingdon, brother of King Alexander I of Scotland (cf.* LINDSAY*). Simundus was granted lands in Midlothian by the earl, and he is recorded as a witness to a charter in 1140. Among his descendants are the earls of Dalhousie.*

Another family of the same name have possessed lands in NE Scotland in the direct male line since the 13th cent. These lands, near Banff, were granted in 1232 to Neis de Ramsey, *who was physician to King Alexander II of Scotland.*

Ramshaw English: habitation name from a place in Co. Durham, probably so called from OE *hramsa* wild garlic + *sceaga* wood, copse (cf. SHAW).

Ramskill English (Yorks.): habitation name from *Ramsgill* in W Yorks., so called from OE *hramsa* wild garlic (or possibly the gen. case of the OE byname *Ram(m)* 'RAM' or the ON byname *Hrafn* 'RAVEN') + ON *gil* ravine (see GILL 2).

Rand English: 1. from the ME given name *Rand(e)*, a short form of any of the various Gmc cpd personal names with the first element *rand* (shield) rim, as for example RANDOLPH.

2. topographic name for someone who lived on the margin of a settlement or on the bank of a river (from OE *rand* rim, used in a topographical sense), or habitation name from a place named with this word, as for example *Rand* in Lincs. and *Rand* Grange in N Yorks.

Vars.: **Rant**. (Of 1): **Randon** (from the OF oblique case).

Cogn. (of 2): Ger.: **Randt** (also a metonymic occupational name for a maker of shields).

Dims. (of 1): Eng.: RANDALL, RANKIN; **Randy**, RAINEY.

Patrs. (from 1): Eng.: **Rands**, **Rance**; **Ranson**, **Ransom(e)** (chiefly E Anglia).

The surname Randon *is found as a name of yeoman farmers and framework knitters in Leics. back to the 17th cent.*

Randall English: from the ME given name *Randel*, a dim. of RAND with the ANF hypocoristic suffix *-el*.

Vars.: **Randell**, **Randle**; **Rendall**, **Rendell**, **Rendle**.

Patrs.: **Randles**; **Randlesome**, **Randerson**.

Randolph English: from a Gmc personal name composed of the elements *rand* rim (of a shield), shield + *wolf* wolf. This was first introduced into England by Scandinavian settlers in the ON form *Rannúlfr*, and was reinforced after the Conquest by the Norman form *Randolf*.

Cogn.: Ger.: **Ranolff**.

Patr.: Eng.: **Fitzrandolph**.

An American family bearing the surname Randolph *is descended from William Randolph (?1651–1711), a planter and merchant from a Sussex family, who emigrated from Warwicks. to Virginia c.1673. He was a forebear of Thomas Jefferson and Robert E. Lee. Randolph had seven sons, each of whom inherited an estate, the name of which was sometimes added to their own, such as Sir John Randolph of Tazewell. His great-grandsons included Edmund Randolph (1753–1813), first attorney general of the United States and one of the framers of the American constitution, and the diplomat and statesman John Randolph of Roanoke (1773–1833), who served as U.S. minister to Russia.*

Ranger English: occupational name for a gamekeeper or warden, ME *ranger*, an agent deriv. of *range(n)* to arrange, dispose (OF *ranger*, from *rang* rank, of Gmc origin).

Var.: **Rainger**.

Rank English: 1. nickname for a powerfully built man or someone of violent emotions, from the ME adj. *rank* (OE *ranc* proud, rebellious).

2. from a medieval given name, a back-formation from the dim. RANKIN.

Rankin Scots and N English: from the medieval given name *Rankin*, a dim. of RAND 1, with the hypocoristic suffix *-kin* (of Low Ger. or Du. origin).

Vars.: **Rankine**, **Ranking**, **Ranken**.

Ranta Finnish: ornamental name, perhaps chosen for topographic reasons by someone who lived near the coast, from Finn. *ranta* shore.

Vars.: **Rantala**, **Rantanen**.

Rapa Italian: 1. metonymic occupational name for a grower or seller of turnips, from It. *rapa* turnip (LL *rāpa* (fem.), originally the pl. form of class. L *rāpum* (neut.)).

2. derogatory nickname for a stupid person, from the same word in a transferred sense.

Vars.: **Rapi**; **Rava**, **Ravi** (N Italy).

Cogns.: Fr.: **Rabier**, **Ravier** (agent derivs.). Du.: **Raap**.

Dims.: It.: **Rapetti**, **Rapetto**, **Rapini**, **Rapino**, **Rapucci**, **Rappuzzi**; **Ravetta**, **Ravetti**, **Ravina**, **Ravella**, **Ravelli**.

Raphael Jewish, English, and French: from the Hebr. male given name *Refael*, composed of the elements *rafa* to heal + *el* God. This name was borne by one of the archangels, but for some reason it was less popular among Christians in the Middle Ages than the other names of archangels, MICHAEL and GABRIEL, except perhaps in Italy. Such currency as it did enjoy was largely the result of the part played by the angel in the Apocryphal tale of Tobias.

Vars.: Jewish: **Rafael**, **Rephael**, **Refael**; **Raphaeli**, **Rephaeli**, **Rafaeli**, **Refaeli**, **Raphael(l)y**, **Rafaely**, **Refaely** (Israeli, with the Hebr. ending *-i*). Fr.: **Raphel**. Eng.: **Raffel**, **Raffle**, **Raffield**.

Cogns.: It.: **Raffaello** (N Italy); **Raffaele**, **Raffaeli** (S Italy); **Raffelli**, **Rafeli**. Port.: **Rafael**. Pol.: **Rachwał**, **Rafalski**, **Rafacz**.

Patrs.: Jewish (E Ashkenazic): **Raphaelov**, **Raphaelof(f)**, **Rafaelof(f)**, **Rafaelovich**, **Rafaelovitz**, **Refaelov(e)**, **Refalovicz**, **Refalovitch**; **Rafaelovici** (a Rumanian spelling). Croatian: **Rafajlović**. Eng.: **Raffles**.

Raposo Portuguese: nickname for a cunning person, or else for someone with reddish brown hair, from Port. *raposo* fox, a deriv. of *rabo* tail, with reference to the spectacular brush of the animal. The origin of *rabo* is not clear, but it has been suggested that it is from L *rāpum* turnip (cf. RAPA), because of the resemblance between the shaggy tap root of the turnip and the tail of an animal.

Rapp 1. Swedish: 'soldier's name', one of the monosyllabic names adopted by soldiers in the 17th cent., before surnames became general in Sweden, from Swed. *rapp* quick, prompt.

2. German and Jewish (Ashkenazic): cogn. of RAVEN.

Rappaport Jewish (Ashkenazic): of uncertain origin. Most people bearing this name are descended from Avrom-Menakhem Ben-Yankev Hakoyen Rapa, who lived in Porto, Italy, at the beginning of the 16th cent. In his case *Rapa* was an ornamental name, from Ger. *Rappe* RAVEN. According to one explanation his descendants added the name of their city, Porto, in order to distinguish themselves from unrelated Jews surnamed *Rapa*; according to another, there was a marriage between the *Rapa* and *Porto* families, and the issue of this union took the cpd name. In any case, because this was a distinguished family, some unrelated Jews adopted may have the surname for the sake of its prestige.

Vars.: **Rapaport**, **Rap(p)oport**.

Rasch 1. German: nickname for a nimble person, from Ger. *rasch* quick (OHG *rasc*; cf. ON *róskr* bold).

2. German (of Slav. origin): dim. from a short form of any of various Slav. personal names with the first element *rad* glad (see RADECKI) or *rano* early (see RAHN 3).

Cogns. (of 1): Du.: **Ras**. Swed.: **Rask** (a 'soldier's name'). (Of 2): Czech: **Raš**.

Dims. (of 2): Ger.: **Raschke**, **Raschka**, **Ratzke**, **Ratzka**, **Raschek**, **Ratzek**, **Rassek**. Czech: **Rašek**, **Raška**.

Rash 1. English: var. of Ash; the name has arisen as the result of the misdivision of ME *atter ashe* 'at the ash tree' (OE *æt þǣre æsce*).

2. Jewish: of unknown origin.

Rasp German: probably a nickname for a miser, from MHG *raspen* to scrape together (OHG *raspōn*).

Rasputin Russian: patr. from a nickname composed of the elements *raz* apart, away + *put* journey, which is capable of various interpretations. On the one hand *rasputye* is a road-fork or parting of the ways, and it seems likely that the most famous bearer of the name, the monk Grigori Yefimovich Rasputin (1872–1916), himself derived the name from this, since his birthplace is said to have been situated on a road fork. His enemies, however, took it to be from *rasputny* deviant, debauched, and it is likely that he himself enjoyed the ambiguity, since he was a member of the Khlysty sect, who believed that sinning was a prerequisite of salvation.

Rat 1. French: nickname for a sly and agile individual, from OF *rat* rat (apparently of Gmc origin).

2. German and Jewish (Ashkenazic): nickname for a wise person, from Ger. *Rat* counsel, advice (MHG, OHG *rāt*).

3. German: from a short form of any of the various Gmc cpd personal names with the first element *rāt* counsel, advice.

Vars. (of 1): **Lerat**. (Of 2): Jewish: **Rath**. (Of 2 and 3): Ger.: **Rath(e)**.

Cogns. (of 1): It.: **Ratti, Ratto**. Port.: **Rato** ('mouse', perhaps denoting someone with mouse-coloured hair). (Of 3): Fr.: **Radon** (oblique case).

Dims. (of 1): Fr.: **Ratet**, Rateau, **Rat(ill)on, Ratin(eau), Raty**. (Of 3): Ger.: **Rack(e)l**. Low Ger.: **Rademann, Rade(c)ke, Redeke, Rathke, Rathgen, Rathje(n)**. Fr.: **Radet, Radot**.

Cpds (of 2): Jewish: **Rathaus(e)** (topographic name for someone who lived by a town hall; Anglicized as **Rathouse**).

Ratajski Polish: occupational name for a ploughman, from Pol. *rataj* ploughman + *-ski* suffix of surnames (see Baranowski).

Cogn.: Czech: **Rataj**.

Dim.: Pol.: **Ratajczyk**.

Ratcliffe English (chiefly Lancs.): habitation name from any of the places, in various parts of England, called *Ratcliff(e)*, *Radcliffe*, *Redcliff*, or *Radclive*, all of which derive their names from OE *rēad* red (see Read 1) + *clif* cliff, slope, riverbank (see Clive).

Vars.: **Rat(t)cliff, Radcliff(e), Radclyffe, Ratliff(e), Rack(c)liff(e); Red(i)cliffe, Redclift, Reddecliff**.

A family called Radcliffe *trace their descent from Sir Nicholas* de Radclyffe, *a knight in the service of Baron de Marsey in the 11th cent. He was earlier known as Nicholas de Tailbois, but after he had been granted the manor of Radcliffe in Lancs. (now part of Greater Manchester), he acquired the surname Radclyffe.*

Rateau French: 1. metonymic occupational name for someone who made or used rakes, or nickname for a tall, thin man, from OF *rastel* rake (LL *rastellum*, a dim. of class. L *rastrum*).

2. dim. of Rat 1.

Vars.: **Ra(s)tel, Ratheau, Rateaux, Rateaud**.

Cogns. (of 1): It.: **Rast(r)elli, Rast(i)ello**.

Rathbone English: apparently a habitation name from *Radbourn* in Warwicks. or *Radbourne* in Derbys., both of which seem to get their names from OE *hrēod* reeds (a collective sing.) + *burna* stream (see Bourne).

Vars.: **Ra(d)bone; Rathbourn, Rathborne**.

Ratner Jewish (Ashkenazic): habitation name from *Ratno* in the Ukraine or *Rathenau* near Brandenburg.

Vars.: **Rattner; Rathenau** (from the Ger. placename).

Rattigan Irish: Anglicized form of **Ó Reachtagáin** 'descendant of *Reachtagán*', a personal name from a dim. of *reachtaire* steward, administrator.

Vars.: **O'Raghtagan, Roghtigan, Ra(c)tigan, Ratican, Rhatigan, Rhategan**.

Rattray Scots: habitation name from a feudal barony in the former county of Perths., apparently so called from Brit. cogns. of Gael. *rath* fortress + W *tref* settlement.

A family of this name still hold the ruined Rattray Castle. Family tradition has it that the lands were first granted by Malcolm III, who reigned 1057–93. However, the first laird in existing records is Alan de Ratheriff, *who witnessed charters in the late 12th cent.*

Räuber German: derogatory nickname (hardly an actual occupational name) from Ger. *Räuber* robber, bandit, highwayman (MHG *roubære*, OHG *roubari*, from *roub*, *roup* booty, spoils; cf. Ropero).

Vars.: **Rauber; Raiber** (Austria; also born by Ashkenazic Jews).

Cogns.: Low Ger.: **Röver, Röwer**. Flem., Du.: **Roof**.

Dim.: Ger.: **Raible** (Swabia).

Rauch German and Jewish (Ashkenazic): nickname for a shaggy or unkempt person, from Ger. *rauch* rough, hairy (MHG, OHG *rū(h)*).

Vars.: Ger.: **Rau(h)**. Jewish: **Rau**.

Cogns.: Low Ger.: **Ruhe, Ruge**. Eng.: **Rough** (mainly Scotland).

Rautainen Finnish: patr. from the Finn. adj. *rautainen* 'made of iron', used as an ornamental name, as a nickname referring to the strength or colour of the metal, or as an occupational name for a blacksmith.

Rautenbach German: habitation name from a place in Saxony, so called from MLG *rūte* rue (L *rūta*) + *bach* stream (see Bach).

Ravaillac French: habitation name from a lost place in SW France, so called from the Gallo-Roman personal name *Ravilius* + the local suffix *-ācum*.

Ravano Italian: metonymic occupational name for a grower or seller of horse-radish, It. *ravano* (L *raphanus*, from a Gk word akin to the roots of Rapa and Repin).

Vars.: **Rava(g)ni**.

Dims.: **Ravanelli, Ravanello**. Fr.: **Ravenel, Raveneau, Raffenel, Raffeneau, Rappeneau, Raphanel, Rafanel**.

Ravel 1. French: metonymic occupational name or nickname from OF *ravel*, a dim. of *rabe*, *rave* turnip (see Rapa). In part it may also be a habitation name from a place named with this word, as for example *Ravel* in Puy-de-Dôme.

2. Provençal: habitation name from a place in Drôme, so called from OProv. *revel* rebel (L *rebellis*, from *re-* again, back + *bellum* war).

Vars. (of 1): **Raveau; Rabel, Rabeau**. (Of 2): **Revel**.

Raven English: nickname for a thievish or dark-haired person, from ME *raven* (OE *hræfn*). In some cases it may be from a personal name derived from this element, a survival into ME of the ON byname *Hrafn* or of an unattested OE cogn. name (**Hræfn*), which is probably present in placenames such as Ravenscroft and Rawnsley. In central European languages, the cogns. are also found in use as nicknames. In England, a few early forms such as William *atte Raven* (London 1344) suggest that it may also in part be derived from a house sign.

Var.: **Revan**.

Cogns.: Ger. and Jewish (Ashkenazic): **Rabe**, **Rapp(e)** (reasons for adoption unclear, perhaps ornamental names from the word for the bird). Low Ger.: **Rave**, **Raaf**. Flem., Du.: **De Raeve**. Dan.: **Rafn**, **Ravn**. Czech: **Havrán**, **Harván**.

Dims.: Ger.: **Rabl**, **Rappl**, **Räppli**. Czech: **Havránek**, **Harvánek**.

Patrs.: Eng.: **Ravening**; **Ravens**, **Revans**, **Revens**.

Ravenscroft English: habitation name from a place in Ches., so called from the gen. case of the OE byname *Hræfn* 'RAVEN' + OE *croft* paddock, smallholding (see CROFT).

Raventós Catalan: of uncertain origin, perhaps an altered form of the rarer surname **Revoltós**, a nickname from Cat. *revoltós* rebellious, difficult (a deriv. of *revolt* revolt, rebellion; cf. REVUELTA). The alteration of the surname may have come about partly to avoid the unfavourable connotations, partly as a result of connection with VENTÓSA.

Raw English: 1. from a medieval given name, a var. of RALPH.

2. topographic name, a northern var. of ROWE 1.

Var.: **Rawe**.

Patrs. (from 1): **Raw(e)s**, **Rawse**; **Rawson** (chiefly S Yorks.).

The form Rawes *is most common in the Lake District, where the earliest known occurrences are in the 16th cent. (e.g. Windermere 1560, Patterdale 1568). There is a small, apparently unconnected group of bearers of the name* Rawes *in Dorset.*

Rawcliffe English: habitation name from places in Lancs. and N and W Yorks., so called from ON *rauðr* red (probably replacing the cogn. OE *rēad*; cf. RATCLIFFE) + OE *clif* cliff, slope, riverbank (see CLIVE).

Vars.: **Rawcliff**, **Rawlcliffe**.

Rawling English: from the ME given name *Rawlin*, OF *Raulin*, a double dim. of RAW 1, with the ANF suffixes *-el* and *-in*.

Vars.: **Rawlin**, **Raulin**, **Rallin(g)**.

Cogns.: Fr.: **Ra(o)ulin**.

Patrs.: Eng.: **Rawlin(g)s**, **Rawlyns**, **Rawlence**, **Raulins**, **Rallin(g)s**; **Rawlin(g)son**, **Rawlison**, **Rallison**.

Rawnsley English: habitation name from a place in W Yorks., apparently so called from the gen. case of the OE byname **Hræfn* 'RAVEN' + OE *hlāw* hill (see LAW 2).

Var.: **Ransley**.

Rawsthorne English: habitation name from *Rostherne* in Ches., so called from the gen. case of the ON byname *Rauðr* 'Red' + ON or OE *þorn* thorn bush.

Vars.: **Rawsthorn**, **Rawstorn(e)**, **Rawstron**, **Rosthorne**, **Rostron**, **Rostern(e)**.

Ray 1. English (Norman): nickname from OF *rey*, *roy* king (from L *rex*, gen. *rēgis*), denoting someone who behaved in a regal fashion or who had earned the title in some contest of skill or by presiding over festivities.

2. English: nickname for a timid person, from ME *ray* female roe deer (OE *rǣge*) or northern ME *ray* roebuck (OE *rā*; for the vowel development, cf. ROPER).

3. English: topographic name, a var. of RYE (1 and 2).

4. English: habitation name, a var. of WRAY.

5. Jewish (Ashkenazic): of unknown origin.

Vars. (of 1–4): **Raye**, **Rey**. (Of 1 only): ROY. (Of 2 only): **Roe(buck)**.

Cogns. (of 1): Fr.: **Rey**, **Reix**, ROY, **Leroy**; **Roué** (Brittany). It.: **(Lo) Ré**, **Rege**. Sp.: **Rey(es)**. Cat.: **Rey**, **Reig**. Port.: **Rei(s)**. (Of 2): Flem., Du.: **De Ree**.

Patrs. (from 1): Eng.: FITZROY. It.: **Del Ré**, **De Rege**, **(De) Regis**, **(De) Regibus**.

Rayer 1. English: from the Norman personal name *Raher*, composed of the Gmc elements *rad* counsel, advice + *heri*, *hari* army.

2. French: occupational name for a barber, OF *raier* (from *rère* to shave, L *rādere*).

Vars. (of 2): **Rayeur**, **Rahier**.

Cogns. (of 1): Fr.: **Rat(h)ier**, **Rathié**.

Rayleigh English: 1. habitation name from a place in SE Essex, so called from OE *rǣge* female roe deer (see RAY 2) + *lēah* wood, clearing.

2. var. of RALEIGH.

Raymond English and French: from the Norman personal name *Raimund*, composed of the Gmc elements *ragin* counsel + *mund* protection.

Vars.: Eng.: **Raymont**, **Rayment**, **Raiment**. Fr.: **Raimond**, **Reymond**, **Rémon(d)**, **Rémont**, **Ramon(d)**.

Cogns.: It.: **Ra(i)mondi**, **Ra(i)mondo**; **Ramundi** (S Italy); **Rimondi** (Emilia). Sp.: **Ramón**. Cat.: **Ramon**. Port.: **Raimundo**. Ger.: **Rei(n)mund**; **Raimund**, **Raymund** (Austria).

Dims.: Fr.: **Remondeau**, **Remondon**. Prov.: **Ramondou**, **Ramon(d)enc**, **Raymonenc(q)**, **Ramonic**. It.: **Raimo**; **Ramondelli**, **Ramondini**, **Ramondino**, **Rimondini**. Ger.: **Reim**.

Patrs.: Ir.: **Redmond(s)** (Gael. **Mac Réamoinn**).

Rayner 1. English: from the Norman personal name *Rainer*, composed of the Gmc elements *ragin* counsel + *hari*, *heri* army.

2. Jewish (Ashkenazic): apparently an ornamental name from mod. Ger. *rein* or Yid. *reyn* pure.

Vars. (of 1): **Raynor**, **Rainer**, **Reyner**, **Reiner**, **Ranner**, RENNER. (Of 2): **Reiner**, **Rainer**; **Rajnerman** (Pol. spelling).

Cogns. (of 1): Fr.: **Rainer**, **Reyn(i)er**, **Reiner**, **Rei(g)nier**, **Régnier**, **Re(i)nié**, **Renier**. It.: **Ra(i)nieri**, **Ra(i)niero**; **Raineri**, **Rainero** (NW Italy); **Raneri** (Sicily); **Renieri** (S Italy, Tuscany, Emilia); **Raner**, **Renier** (Venetia); **Rinero** (Piedmont). Ger.: **Reiner**, **Rainer**, RENNER. Flem., Du.: **Reiner**.

Patrs. (from 1): Ger., Flem., Du.: **Reiners**. Swed.: **Ragnarsson**.

Razgovorov Russian: patr. from the nickname *Razgovor* 'Conversation', denoting a gossip or chatterbox.

Read English: 1. nickname for a person with red hair or a ruddy complexion, from ME *re(a)d*, OE *rēad* red (the shortening of the vowel in the mod. Eng. vocab. word is not well explained, though it is parallelled in *bread*, *dead*, and *lead*, where the spelling is more conservative).

2. topographic name for someone who lived in a clearing in woodland, OE *rīed*, *rȳd*; cf. RHODES and REUTER 1.

3. habitation name from various places: *Read* in Lancs., the name of which is a contracted form of OE *rǣghēafod*, from *rǣge* female roe deer + *hēafod* head(land); *Rede* in Suffolk, so called from OE *hrēod* reeds; or *Reed* in Herts., so called from OE *rȳht* brushwood.

Vars. (of 1): **Reade**, **Reed**, **Red(d)**; **Reid** (Scots); **Re(a)dman** (see also READER). (Of 2): **Ride**, **Ryde**; RIDER; **Attride**, **Attryde**.

Cogn. (of 1 and 2): Ger.: ROTH.

A family called Read *were established in America in the early 18th cent. by John Read, who was born in Dublin, sixth in descent from Sir Thomas Read of Berks., England. His son, George Read (1733–98), was one of the signatories of the Declaration of Independence, and as a lawyer helped frame the Constitution.*

Reader English: occupational name for someone who thatched cottages with reeds, from an agent deriv. of ME *rēd(en)* to cover with reeds (from OE *hrēod* reed).

Vars.: **Re(e)der**; **Reedman**, **Readman** (see also READ).

Patrs.: **Readers**, **Reeders**.

Reading English: 1. habitation name from the county town of Berks., which gets its name from OE *Rēadingas* 'people of *Rēad(a)*', a byname meaning 'Red' (see READ 1).

2. topographic name for someone who lived in a clearing, from OE *ryding*, a deriv. of *rīed*, *rȳd* (see READ 2).

Vars.: **Red(d)ing**. (Of 2 only): **Rid(d)ing**, **Ryding(s)** (Lancs.).

Ready 1. English: nickname for a provident man, from ME *readi* prepared, prompt (OE *(ge)rǣde*, of uncertain origin, perhaps a deriv. of *rǣd* counsel, advice).

2. Scots: habitation name from *Reedie* in the former county of Angus, whose name is of uncertain origin.

3. Irish: Anglicized form of Gael. **Ó Rodaigh** 'descendant of *Rodach*', a personal name probably derived from *rod* spirited, furious (cf. RODEN 1).

Vars.: **Readey**, **Re(a)ddie**, **Re(a)ddy**, **Raddie**. (Of 2 only): **Reedie**, **Reiddie**, **Reidy**. (Of 3 only): **(O')Roddy**, **(O')Ruddy**, **O'Reddie**.

Dims. (of 3): **O'Rodeghan**, **Rodaughan**, **Rudihan**, **Rudican**, **Redehan**, **Redahan** (Gael. **Ó Rodacháin**).

Real Spanish: 1. habitation name from any of the numerous places so called, from Sp. *real* encampment, rural property (Arabic *rah(á)l* farmhouse, cabin).

2. nickname for someone who behaved in a regal manner or occupational name for someone in the service of the king, from Sp. *real* royal (L *rēgālis*, from *rex*, gen. *rēgis*, king; cf. RAY 1).

Cogns. (of 1): Cat.: **Ràfols**. (Of 2): Fr.: **Réal**, **Réau(lt)**, **Reaux**, **Réjau(d)**. It.: **Reale**, **Reali**.

Réaumur French: habitation name from a place in Vendée, so called from OF *réal* royal (see REAL 2) + *mur* fortress, redoubt (L *mūrus* wall, fortification).

Reavey Irish: Anglicized form of Gael. *Riabhach*, a byname meaning 'Brindled', 'Grizzled'.

Patrs.: **McReavy**, **McCreavy**, **McCreevy**, **McCreve(y)**, **McKrevie**, **McGreavy**, **McGreevy**, **McGrievy**, **McGrevye**, **McGreave**, **Magreavy**, **Magreevy** (Gael. **Mac Riabhaich**).

'Descendant of R.': **O'Revoay**, **O'Reogh**, **O'Ria**, **O'Ree** (Gael. **Ó Riabhaigh**).

Rebelo Portuguese: habitation name from the medieval town of *Rabelo*, perhaps so called from a deriv. of Port. *rabo* tail (cf. RAPOSO), i.e. a projecting strip of land.

Rebhun 1. German: metonymic occupational name for a hunter of partridges or nickname for someone supposedly resembling a partridge in some way, from Ger. *Rebhuhn* male partridge (MHG *rephuon*, OHG *reb(a)huon*).

2. Jewish (Ashkenazic): ornamental name from the word denoting the bird, Ger. *Rebhuhn*, one of the many Ashkenazic surnames derived from words for birds and animals.

Var.: **Rebhahn** (from Ger. *Rebhahn* female partridge).

Rebmann German: occupational name for a vine-dresser, from Ger. *Rebe* vine, young shoot (MHG *rebe* planting, esp. of a vine, OHG *reba*) + *Mann* man.

Rebollo Spanish: habitation name from any of various places, for example in the provinces of Segovia and Soria, so called from Sp. *rebollo* shoot (LL **repullus*, from class. L *pullus* young animal; cf. POULE and PULLEN). It is possible that in some cases it may have been a nickname in the sense 'offspring', 'son'.

Rebours French: nickname for someone with bushy and unkempt hair, from OF *rebours* shaggy (LL *reburrus*, probably from *burrus* coarse cloth (see BOURE); later *rebursus*, by hypercorrection and crossing with *reversus*, past part. of *revertere* to turn back).

Vars.: **Rebour**, **Rebous**, **Rebout**.

Dims.: **Rebourseau(x)**, **Rebourset**, **Reboussin**.

Récamier French: occupational name for an embroiderer, from an agent deriv. of OF *recamer* to embroider.

Var.: **Racamier**.

Recasens Catalan: from a Visigothic personal name composed of the elements *rīc* power + *sinðs* way, path. In view of its frequency it is probably in part also a habitation name from either of the two places in the province of Gerona called *Requesens*, from an early proprietor.

Recio Spanish: nickname for a strong or tough man, from the Sp. adj. *recio* (apparently related to L *rigidus* stiff, hard, but the phonetic development is not clear).

Reddick Scots and N Irish: habitation name from *Rerrick* or *Rerwick* in the former county of Kirkcudbright, probably so called from OE *reafere* robber, reiver + *wīc* outlying settlement (see WICK). It is also possible that the first element was ON *rauðr* red, partially replaced by the native equivalent, which would better explain the pronunciation preserved in the surname.

Var.: **Riddick**.

Nicholas de Reraik *held land in Kircudbright* c.1280, *but the first known bearer of the name in its current form seems to be William* Redik *of Dalbatye, recorded in 1577*.

Reddington English: probably a var. of READING 1, from the placename + the ME suffix *-tune* (OE *tūn* settlement). However, the surname is quite common in Lancs. and Yorks., and so perhaps a northern place named as the 'settlement associated with *Rēad(a)*' is to be sought.

Reddish English: habitation name from *Reddish* in Lancs. or *Redditch* in Worcs., which are respectively 'reed ditch' (OE *hrēod* + *dīc*) and 'red ditch' (cf. READ 1). The surname is now common in Notts.

Redfern English: habitation name from *Redfern* near Rochdale, Greater Manchester, so called from OE *rēad* red + *fearn* fern, bracken.

Var.: **Redfearn**.

Redgate English (Notts.): habitation name from an unidentified place probably deriving its name from OE *rēad* red + ON *gata* road; cf. REDPATH. There is a *Redgate* Wood in Kirklington, Notts., but this placename may be of comaparatively recent origin.

Redgrave English (E Anglia): habitation name from a place in Suffolk, so called from OE *hrēod* reed + *græf* excavation, ditch or OE *rēad* red + *grāfa* grove.

Redhead English and Scots: nickname for someone with red hair, from ME *re(a)d* red (see READ 1) + *heved* head (OE *hēafod*). In some cases it is possibly also a topographic name with the sense 'red headland'.

Var.: **Readhead**.

Redmayne English: habitation name from *Redmain* in Cumb., near Cockermouth, the derivation of which is uncertain. Ekwall suggests that it may be from ME *re(a)d* red + the N Eng. dial. term *man* cairn (of Celt. origin). Another suggestion is W *rhyd* ford + *main* stone.

Redouté French: nickname for a formidable individual, from the past part. of OF *redouter* to fear (LL *redubitāre*, from the intensive prefix *re-* + *dubitāre* to hesitate, waver).

Redpath Scots: habitation name from a place in the former county of Berwicks., probably so called from OE *rēad* red + *pæð* path; cf. REDGATE.

Var.: **Ridpath**.

Redshaw N English: habitation name, perhaps from *Radshaw* Gill in Fewston, W Yorks., named with the OE elements *rēad* red + *sceaga* copse; cf. RADLEY and REDWOOD.

Redwin English: from an OE personal name composed of the elements *rǣd* counsel, advice + *wine* friend.

Var.: **Readwin**.

Cogns.: Fr.: **Radouin, Radouan, Redouin**.

Redwood S English: apparently a habitation name from some minor place so called, probably from OE *rēad* red + *wudu* WOOD; cf. RADLEY and REDSHAW. The reference is probably to birch trees as they appear in the spring.

Reekie Scots: of uncertain origin, possibly a habitation name from *Reikie* in the former county of Aberdeens., or an altered spelling of *Rikie*, a dim. of RICHARD. It is also possible that it originated as a nickname meaning 'Smoky', from the Sc. dial. term *reek* smoke.

Reeve English (most common in E Anglia): occupational name for a steward or bailiff, the precise character of whose duties varied from place to place and at different periods. The vocab. word is from ME *reeve* (OE *(ge)rēfa*, the etymology of which is disputed; there is apparently no connection with Ger. GRAF). See also GRIEVE, GRAVE 1, and SHERIFF.

Reeves English: 1. patr. from REEVE.

2. topographic name for someone who lived on the margin of a wood, from a misdivision of the ME phrase *atter eaves* at the edge (OE *æt þære efese*).

Vars.: **Reaves, Revis**.

Refoy English: of uncertain origin; the first known bearer in England is Francis Refoy, who was living at Slindon, Sussex, in 1740. The family are Catholics, and may well have immigrated from Continental Europe.

Regan Irish: Anglicized form of Gael. **Ó Ríagáin** 'descendant of *Riagán*', a personal name of uncertain origin, perhaps akin to *ríodhgach* impulsive, furious. Bearers of the surname sometimes claim descent from a nephew of Brian Boru called Riagán. See also RYAN.

Vars.: **(O')Reagan, O'Regan(e), O'Riegaine**.

The American President Ronald Reagan *(b. 1911) was born in Tampico, Illinois, of Irish Catholic descent; his great-grandfather, Michael Reagan (b. 1829), was born in Ballyporeen, Co. Tipperary.*

Reger 1. German: nickname from MHG *re(i)ger* heron (OHG *(h)reigaro*), no doubt bestowed on a tall, thin person with long spindly legs.

2. German: nickname for a passionate person, from an agent deriv. of MHG *regen* to be excited, moved.

3. Jewish (Ashkenazic): nickname from mod. Ger. *rege* industrious, quick, nimble.

Var. (of 3): **Regerman**.

Cogn. (of 1): Flem.: **Reyger**.

Regidor Spanish: occupational name for an alderman or similar official, Sp. *regidor* (from *regir* to rule, govern; cf. RÉGIS 1).

Régis French: 1. occupational name for a local dignitary, a deriv. of OF *régir* to rule, manage (L *regere*; cf. REGIDOR).

2. from L *rēgis*, gen. case of *rex* king (see RAY 1); perhaps an occupational name for someone employed in the royal household, or a patr. from a nickname.

Vars. (of 1): **Régissier, Regisser**.

Cogn. (of 2): Eng.: **Regis**.

Rego Portuguese: topographic name for someone who lived by a ditch or channel used for irrigation or drainage, Port. *rego* (of pre-Roman origin).

Řehák Czech: ostensibly a nickname meaning 'Redstart', a kind of field warbler. However, in many cases this may well be a pet form of the given name *Řehoř*, the Czech form of GREGORY.

Dim.: **Řeháček**.

Reichenbach German and Jewish (Ashkenazic): habitation name from any of various minor places, particularly in Baden-Württemberg, so called from OHG *rīhhi* rich, powerful (i.e. strongly-flowing; cf. RICH 1) + *bah* stream (see BACH); the adj. retains the weak dat. ending originally used after a preposition and def. art.

Reilly Irish: Anglicized form of the Gael. personal name *Raghailleach*, OIr. *Roghallach*, of unknown origin.

Vars.: **Reily, Rielly, Real(l)y, Reely**; RILEY.

Patrs.: **McReilly, Crilly** (Gael. **Mac Raghailligh**).

'Descendant of R.': **O'Reil(l)y, O'Rielly, O'Riellie, O'Rahilly, O'Real(l)y, O'Reallye, O'Reely, O'Reyley** (Gael. **Ó Raghailligh**).

Reinmar German: from a Gmc personal name composed of the elements *ragin* counsel + *meri*, *mari* fame.

Cogns: Low Ger.: **Re(i)mer** (see also RIEMER). Sp.: **Ramiro**.

Patrs.: Low Ger.: **Re(i)mers**. Flem., Du.: **Reijmers, Reymers, Remmers**. Sp.: **Ramírez**.

Reis 1. German: topographic name for someone who lived in an overgrown area, from MHG, OHG *rīs* undergrowth, brushwood (mod. Ger. *Reis*).

2. Jewish (Ashkenazic): of unclear origin: possibly an ornamental name from Ger. *Reis* twig, branch (the same word as in 1 in a transferred sense). Cf. ZWEIG. It may also be a metonymic occupational name for a dealer in rice, from mod. Ger. *Reis* rice.

3. Portuguese: nickname meaning 'King'; see RAY.

Vars. (of 2): **Reiss, Reisman(n)**.

Reisen Jewish (Ashkenazic): 1. possibly an ornamental name from NE Yid. *reyzn* roses (Standard Yid. *royzn*); see ROSE 3.

2. possibly also a habitation name from *Reisen*, which is the Ger. name of *Rydzyna* in the province of Poznań, Poland.

Var. (of 2): **Reisner**.

Reith 1. Scots: of uncertain origin, possibly a var. of *McCreath* (see MCCRAE), with the loss of the patr. prefix.

2. German: var. of REUTER 1.

Relph English: from the OF personal name *Riulf*, composed of the Gmc elements *rīc* power + *wulf* wolf. This was introduced to Britain by the Normans.

Vars.: **Relf(e), Realff**.

Remy French: from a medieval given name, which represents a falling together of two distinct L names: 1. *Rēmigius* (a deriv. of *rēmex*, gen. *rēmigis*, rower, oarsman, from *rēmus* oar + *agere* to wield); this was borne by a 6th-cent. bishop of Rheims who brought Christianity to the W Franks and who baptized Clovis.

2. *Remedius* (from *remedium* cure, remedy, a deriv. of (*re*)*medēri* to treat, heal), which was borne by various minor saints of the 8th to 10th cents.

Var.: **Remi** (also Jewish, of unknown origin).

Cogns.: Ger.: **Rehm, Rem(m)y, Remeis, Romeis**. (Of 2 only): It.: **Remedi(o), Rimedi(o)**.

Dims: Fr.: **Remi(ll)on, Remiot**. (Of 1 only): Fr.: **Remigeau, Remigeon**. (Of 2 only): It.: **Rimediotti**.

Patr.: Flem.: **Remiens**.

Render N English: of uncertain origin, perhaps an occupational name for a woodcutter or a butcher, from an agent deriv. of ME *rend(en)* to divide, split (OE *rendan*).

René French: from a given name (L *Renātus* 'Reborn') borne by a 4th-cent. saint, and popular in France throughout the Middle Ages because of its transparent reference to Christian spiritual rebirth.

Var.: **Resnais** (a hypercorrected form).

Cogn.: Prov.: **Renat**.

Renner English and German: 1. occupational name for a messenger, normally a mounted and armed military servant, from an agent deriv. of ME, MHG *rennen* to run.

2. var. of RAYNER 1.

Renouard French: from *Reginward*, a Gmc personal name composed of the elements *ragin* counsel + *ward* guard.

Vars.: **Reynouard, Raynouard**.

Cogns.: Ger.: **Reinwarth, Reinwerth**. Low Ger.: **Reineward, Renward**.

Rensburg, van Dutch: habitation name from *Rendsburg* in the province of Holstein.

Cogn.: Jewish (Ashkenazic): **Rendsburg**.

A family of this name have long been established in S Africa, the founding father being Nicolaas Janse van Rensburg, *who emigrated from the province of Holland in the 17th cent.*

Renshaw English: habitation name from *Renishaw* in Derbys., so called from the ME given name REYNOLD + *shawe* copse (see SHAW). The name is still chiefly common in Derbys., S Yorks., and Lancs.

Vars.: **Ra(ve)nshaw, Ravenshear; Renshall, Renshell**.

Renton Scots: habitation name from a place in the former county of Berwicks., 'settlement (OE *tūn*) associated with *Regna*' (a short form of the various cpd personal names with the first element *regen* govern).

Renwick English and Scots (pronounced /'rɛnɪk/): habitation name from a place in Cumb., so called from the OE byname *Hræfn* 'RAVEN' + *wīc* outlying settlement (see WICK).

Repin Russian: patr. from the nickname *Repa* 'Turnip' (cogn. with Pol. *rzepa* and Czech *řepa*, and ultimately with It. RAPA), denoting a grower or seller of the vegetable or an impassive or slow-witted individual. The Pol. cogn. is also a nickname for a sturdy, vigorous person (cf. the expression *zdrowy jak rzepka* 'healthy as a turnip').

Cogns. (not patrs.): Pol.: **Rzepa, Rzepecki**. Czech: **Řepa, Řípa**.

Dims.: Pol.: **Rzepka**. Czech: **Řepka**.

Habitation names: Pol.: **Rzepkowski, Rzepczyński**.

Repton English: habitation name from a place in Derbys., so called from OE *Hrypa*, gen. pl. of the tribal name *Hreope* (cf. RIPPON) + *dūn* hill (see DOWN 1).

Requena Spanish: habitation name from places in the provinces of Palencia and Valencia, apparently so called from a short form of any of the various Visigothic cpd personal names with the first element *rīc* power, with the addition of the local suffix *-ena*.

Resende Portuguese: habitation name from any of various places, for example in the province of Beira, so called from the gen. case of a Visigothic personal name composed of the elements *rēðs* counsel, advice + *sinðs* way, path.

Restorick Cornish: habitation name from a farm called *Restowrack* in the parish of St Dennis, named from Corn. *ros* hill-spur + *dowrek* watery.

Retallack Cornish: habitation name from any of four places in Cornwall. Two of them are from Corn. *res* ford + *helyk* willow trees; the other two are either from *res* + *halek* muddy, marshy, or from *res* + *talek* steep-browed (which also occurs as a personal name).

Var.: **Retallick**.

Rétif French: nickname for an obstinate or awkward individual, from OF *restif* unmoving, stubborn (LL *restīvus*, from *restāre* to remain still).

Vars.: **Restif, Réty; Retief** (S Africa).

Cogns.: It.: **Restivo, Restifo** (Sicily).

Retter 1. English: occupational name for someone who prepared flax to be made into linen, from an agent deriv. of ME *rett(en)* to soak flax stems in water (in order to rot the soft parts and release the linen fibres).

2. English: occupational name for a maker of fishing nets, OF *retier* (L *rētiārius* (earlier, a gladiator who fought with a net), a deriv. of *rēta* net).

3. Jewish (Ashkenazic): probably from Ger. *Retter* rescuer, saviour (an agent deriv. of *retten* to save). The reasons for its adoption as a surname are unknown: it is probably anecdotal, based on some now irrecoverable incident.

Cogn. (of 2): Fr.: **Rettier**.

Rettig 1. German: metonymic occupational name for a grower or seller of radishes, from Ger. *Rettich* radish (MHG *rætich*, OHG *rātih*, from L *rādix*, gen. *rādīcis*, root; cf. RACINE).

2. Jewish (Ashkenazic): occupational or ornamental name from the Ger. word for the plant.

Vars. (of 1): **Rettich**. (Of 2): **Retig**.

Cogns.: Low Ger.: **Reddig, Reddich**.

Reuben Jewish: from the Hebr. given name *Reuven* (interpreted in Gen. 29: 32 as *reu* behold + *ben* son). This biblical name may well have influenced the selection of Ashkenazic surnames that are ostensibly derived from mod. Ger. *Rubin* ruby, Yid., Pol., Russ., Ukr. *rubin* (from LL *rubīnus* (*lapis*), a deriv. of *rubeus* red; cf. RUDGE 3); see the cpds listed below.

Vars.: **Ruben, Rubin(sky), Reuven**.

Cogns.: Czech: **Ruben, Rubeš**.

Dims.: Jewish: **Rubel, Ruvel** (from a NE Yid. form); **Rivel, Rival** (from a S Yid. form); **Rubenchik, Rubenczyk, Rubenczik, Rubinchik, Rubi(ne)k, Rubanenko** (E Ashkenazic).

Patrs.: Jewish: **R(e)ub(b)ens** (see also ROBERT), **Rubinsohn** (Ashkenazic); **Rivenzon** (S Ashkenazic); **Rub(e)nov, Rubinov, Rubinow, Rubenovic, Rubinowicz, Rubinowitz, Rubinowi(t)ch, Rubinowitsch, Rubinovi(t)sch, Rubinivitz** (E Ashkenazic); **Rubinovici** (among Rumanian Jews).

Patrs. (from dims.): Jewish: **Riveles, Rivilis, Rivlin** (S Ashkenazic; see also RIFKIN).

Cpds (ornamental): Jewish: **Rubinfeld, Rubenfeld** ('ruby field'); **Rubinfajn** ('ruby fine'); **Rubinlicht** ('ruby light'); **Rubinsaft** ('ruby juice'); **Rubins(h)tein, Rubinsztein** ('ruby stone').

Reuss German: ethnic name for someone from Russia, from Ger. *Reusse*, MHG *riusse* Russian (cf. RUSAKOV 1). In some cases, as shown by the example below, it was merely a nickname for someone who had some connection with an E Slav. region.

A German noble family called Reuss *trace their descent from Erkenbert, Lord of Weida, who was living in 1122. His descendants were appointed imperial stewards at Weida, Gera, and Plauen by the Emperor Heinrich VI, in whose honour every male child in the family was named Heinrich. Heinrich the Young, Vogt of Plauen (1276–92), was bynamed* der Reusser *'the Russian' because he was the son-in-law of Sophie, daughter of Daniel, King of Galicia.*

Reuter 1. German: topographic name for someone who lived in a clearing or occupational name for a clearer of woodland, from an agent deriv. of MHG *(ge)riute* clearing (OHG *riuti*; cf. READ 2 and RHODES).

2. German: derogatory nickname (hardly an actual occupational name) from MHG *riutære* footpad, highwayman (MDu. *ruiter*, *rütær*, from LL *ruptuārius*, a deriv. of *rupta* (*via*) road, lit. 'broken way').

3. Jewish (Ashkenazic): of uncertain origin, possibly as in 1 or 2, possibly an adoption of the German surname.

Vars. (of 1): **Reuther**; **Reit(h)er**, REITH, **Reithmann**, **Reiten**; **Rauter**, **Rauth(mann)**; **Greut(er)**, **Greither**, **Kreith(er)**, **Kreuter**. (Of 3): **Reiten**, **Rauth(mann)**, **Rautman**, **Kreuter**.

Cogns. (of 2): Du.: **De Ruijter**, **De Ruyter**.

Patrs. (from 2): Low Ger.: **Reuters**, **Rüters**.

Baron Paul Julius von Reuter *(1816–99), founder of the news agency which still bears his name, was born Jisroel-Ber Josafat. He changed his name on being baptized as a Christian in 1844, but it is not known why he adopted the surname* Reuter.

Revell English: nickname for a boisterous person, from ME, OF *revel* festivity, tumult, riot (from OF *reveler* to revel, LL *rēbellāre* to rebel, riot; cf. RAVEL 2).

Vars.: **Revel(s)**, **Revill(e)**, **Reavell**.

Revilla Spanish: habitation name from any of the numerous places so called, from OSp. *revilla* dependent settlement (a deriv. of *villa*; see VILLE).

Revuelta Spanish: nickname for a quarrelsome or argumentative person, from Sp. *revuelta* squabble (LL *revolta* revolt, rebellion, from the past part. of *revolvere* to turn round; cf. RAVENTÓS).

Reynard English and French: from a Gmc personal name composed of the elements *ragin* counsel + *hard* hardy, brave, strong, which was introduced into England by the Normans in the form *Re(i)nard*. This was the name borne by the cunning fox in the popular medieval cycle of beast-tales, with the result that from the 13th cent. it began to replace the previous OF word for the animal (see GOUPIL). Some Fr. examples may be nicknames for crafty individuals, referring to the fox's reputation for cunning.

Vars.: Eng.: **Renhard**, **Rennard**, **Renyard**. Fr.: **Reinard**, **Raynard**, **Rainard**, **Rena(r)d**, **Re(i)gnard**.

Cogns.: Ger.: **Regenhardt**, **Reinhart**; **Reinhard(t)** (also Jewish). Low Ger.: **Reinert**, **Rehnert**, **Rennert**; **Reint**, **Renet**, **Rente**. Flem., Du.: **Reinaert**, **Reynaert**.

Dims.: Fr.: **Renardet**, **Renardin**, **Renardeau**, **Renardot**. Ger.: **Reindel**. Fris.: **Reintsema**.

Patrs.: Ger.: **Reinartz**. Low Ger.: **Reinerts**; **Reinerding**, **Renting**. Fris.: **Reints**, **Reents**.

Patr. (from a dim.): Low Ger.: **Reintjes**.

Reynold English: from a Gmc personal name composed of the elements *ragin* counsel + *wald* rule, which was first introduced to England by Scandinavian settlers in the ON form *Rögnvaldr* (see RONALD), and greatly reinforced after the Conquest by the Norman forms *Reinald*, *Reynaud*. The surname is occasionally also borne by Jews, in which case it presumably represents an Anglicization of one or more like-sounding Jewish surnames.

Vars.: **Reynell**, **Rennell**, **Rennoll**, **Rennold**; **Renaud**, **Renaut**.

Cogns.: Fr.: **Reynaud**, **Raynaud**, **Rainaud**, **Reynal**; **Re(i)(g)naud**, **Re(g)nault**, **Reneaud**, **Reneault**, **Renaut**, **Rign(e)ault**, **Renaux**. It.: **R(a)inaldo**, **R(a)inaldi**, **Rinallo**, **Rinaudi**, **Renaldi**, **Ranaldi**, **Ranalli**, **Ranaldo**, **Ranaudo**, **Ranauro**, **Ranaulo**, **Ranavolo**, **Reynaudi**; **Rainoldi**, **Renoldi** (N Italy). Ger.: **Rein(h)old** (also Jewish, presumably adoptions of the Ger. surname); **Regenold**, **Rien(h)olt**, **Reinholdt**, **Re(i)nelt**. Low Ger.: **Reinwald(t)**, **Reinwold**.

Dims.: Fr.: **Renaudel**, **Renaudeau**, **Renaudet**, **Renaudin**, **Renaudot**, **Renaudon**; **Renauleau**, **Renolleau**. It.: **Rinaldelli**, **Rinaldin(i)**, **Renaldini**, **R(a)inalducci**, **Rinalduzzi**.

Patrs.: Eng.: **Reynolds**, **Reynalds**, **Rennolds**, **Renals**, **Rennels**; **Reynoldson**. It.: **R(a)inaldis**; **Rinaldeschi** (Tuscany). Ger.: **Ra(i)nalder**, **Rainalter**; **Reinhol(t)z**; **Rainals** (Austria). Low Ger.: **Rei(n)elts**. Fris.: **Reendels**.

Řezáč Czech: occupational name for a woodcutter, an agent noun from the verb *řezat* to cut, trim, lop, and so a byform of *Řezník* butcher (see RZEŹNIK).

Rhein German: topographic name for someone who lived by the river *Rhine*, which is first recorded in the Roman period in the form *Rhenus*; it may be derived from a Celt. element meaning 'to flow'.

Cogns.: Low Ger.: **Riemann**. Du.: **Van R(h)yn**, **Van Rijn**.

Rhodes English (chiefly Yorks.): topographic name for someone who lived in a clearing in woodland, OE *rod*. This most common form of the name has been influenced in spelling by the Gk island of *Rhodes* (Gk *Rhodos*, perhaps ultimately akin to ROSE 1). There does not seem to be any connection with mod. Eng. *road* (OE *rād* 'riding'), which was not used of a thoroughfare on land until the 16th cent.

Vars.: **Rhoades**, **Road(s)**; **Royds**; **Rodd**.

Cogns.: Low Ger.: RODE. Flem., Du.: **Van Rode**, **Van Ro(o)ij**, **Van Ro(o)y**; **Van Ro(o)ijen** (common in S Africa); **Van Rooyen**.

Rhys Welsh: from one of the most common of OW personal names, *Rīs* 'Fiery Warrior'. This was the name of the last ruler of an independent kingdom of Wales, Rhys ap Tewder, who died in 1093 unsuccessfully opposing the Norman advance.

Vars.: **Rees(e)**, **Reece**, **Rease**, **Rice**.

Patr.: PRICE.

Ribalta Catalan: topographic name for someone who lived by a high riverbank, from Cat. *riba* bank (see RIVE) + *alta* (fem.) high (L *alta*). There are various minor places in E Spain named with these elements, and the surname may also derive from any of them.

Ribaud French: nickname for a notorious reprobate, from a pej. deriv. of OF *riber* to live licentiously (of Gmc origin). The term was also used to denote a member of the lowest class of servants, who had to carry out the most unpleasant and dangerous tasks, so that it may in part also have been originally an occupational name.

Vars.: **Ribau(l)t**, **Riboud**, **Ribout**; **Ribard**.

Cogns.: Cat.: **Ribot**, RIBÓ. It.: **Ribaud(o)**, **Rebaudo**, **Rebaudi**, **Robaudo**, **Robaldo**.

Dims.: Fr.: **Ribot(on)**, **Ribon**, **Ribet**.

Ribbentrop German: habitation name from a place in Lippe, recorded in 1564 in the form *Ribbrachtingdorp*, i.e. 'village (see THORPE) of the people of *Ribbracht*', a Gmc personal name composed of the elements *rīc* power + *berht* bright, famous; cf. RIPPERT.

Ribó Catalan: 1. nickname, a var. of *Ribot*; see RIBAUD.
2. topographic name, a dim. of *Riba*; see RIVE.

Ricci Italian: nickname for a person with curly hair, from It. *ricco* curly.

Vars.: **(Lo) Riccio, Rizzi, (Lo) Rizzo**; **Risso** (Liguria).

Dims.: **Riccelli, Rizzelli, Rizz(i)ello, Rizzillo, Riccetti, Rizzetti, Rizzetto**; **Riccini** (partly Jewish), **Rizzini, Riciol(in)i, Ricciolino, Rizz(i)oli, Rizzolo, Rissolo, Ricciulli, Ricciotti, Rizzotti, Rizzotto**.

Augs.: **Riccioni, Rizzon(i), Rizzone, Rissone**.

Rich English: 1. nickname for a wealthy man (or perhaps in some case an ironic nickname for a pauper), from ME, OF *riche* rich, wealthy (of Gmc origin, akin to Gmc *rīc* power).
2. from a medieval given name, a short form of RICHARD, or less commonly of some other cpd name with this first element (cf., e.g., RICHER).
3. habitation name from the lost village of *Riche* in Leics., apparently so called from an OE element **rīc* stream or, here, drainage channel. Some early forms of the surname, such as Ricardus *de la riche* (Hants 1200) and Alexander *atte Riche* (Sussex 1296) probably derive from minor places named with this element in southern counties, as for example Glynde *Reach* in Sussex.

Vars.: **Riche, Ritch**; **Richman** (see also RICHMOND). (Of 2 only): **Rick**.

Cogns. (of 1): Fr.: **Riche, Leriche**. Prov.: **Ric(q), Ricque**. It.: **Ricco, Richi**. Sp.: **Rico**; **Rica** (fem.). Ger.: **Reich(e), Reicher** (see also RICHER); **Reichmann**. Low Ger.: **Rieke, Rieckmann**. Flem.: **De Righe, De Ryche**. Du.: **De Rijk(e)**. Jewish (Ashkenazic, nickname): **Reich(er), Reichman(n)**; **Rajcher, Rajchman** (Pol. spellings); **Richman** (Anglicization). (Of 1 and 2): Pol.: **Rajch**. Czech: **Reich, Raich**. (Of 2): Ger.: **Ritz(e)**. Low Ger.: **R(e)ick(e)**. Flem., Du.: **Rikke**.

Dims. (of 1): Fr.: **Richet(on), Richez, Richon, Richou**. It.: **Ricchini, Ricchino**. Ger.: **Reichel, Reichlin**. (Of 2): Eng.: **Ritchie** (chiefly Scots); **Ricket(t), Reckitt**. Ger.: **Reichel(t), Reickl, Rietsche(l)**. Fris.: **Ritzke**.

Augs. (of 1): It.: **Riccone**. Sp.: **Ricote**.

Patrs. (from 2): Eng.: **Riches**; **Ricks(on)**, RIX, **Rixon**. Ger.: **Ritzer, Ritzen, Ritscher, Ritschen**. Low Ger.: **Ricks, Rix(en), Ricken(s)**. Fris.: **Rickena, Rykena**.

Patrs. (from 2) (dims.): Eng.: **Richies**; **Ricketts** (chiefly W Midlands). Sc.: **McRitchie**. Ger.: **Reichler**.

Cpds (from cogns. of 1; ornamental unless otherwise stated): Jewish (Ashkenazic): **Reichbach** ('rich stream', may also be topographic; see also REICHENBACH); **Reichbart, Reichbard, Rajchbart** ('rich beard', nickname; *Rajchbart* is a Pol. spelling); **Reichenbaum** ('rich tree'); **Reich(en)berg** ('rich hill'); **Reichfeld** ('rich field'); **Reichgold** ('rich gold'); **Reichgott** ('rich God'); **Reichkind** ('rich child'); **Reichnadel, Reichnudel** ('rich needle', perhaps ornamenal-occupational for a tailor); **Reich(en)stein** ('rich stone'); **Reichent(h)al** ('rich valley'); **Reichtaler** ('rich dollar' or 'dweller in a rich valley').

Several different lines of bearers of the surname Ricketts *have been traced, in particular one to Robert Ricketts of North Nibley, Gloucs., who died before 1567. The surname* Rickett *is already found widely distributed throughout England in the 16th cent.*

Richard English, French, German, and Flemish/Dutch: from a Gmc personal name composed of the elements *rīc* power + *hard* hardy, brave, strong. This is found in OE, but was popularized in England by the Normans. See also DICK and HICK. There was considerable confusion with the rarer RICHER (for a similar situation, cf. SIMON).

Vars.: Eng.: **Ritchard, Ricard(e), Riccard**; **Rickard** (Devon and Cornwall); **Rickerd, Rickert**. Fr.: **Ricard, Rig(u)ard**. Ger.: **Reich(h)ardt, Reichert, Richardt**. Flem.: **Rickaert, Rykert**.

Cogns.: It.: **Ricc(i)ardi, Ricc(i)ardo**; **Rizzardi, Rizzardo** (S Italy); **Licc(i)ardi, Licc(i)ardo** (Naples, Sicily); CIARDO. Port., Sp., Jewish (Sefardic): **Ricardo**. Cat.: **Ricart**. Low Ger.: **Ricker(t), Riggert**. Fris.: **Richt**. Pol.: **Rajchert**. Czech: **Reichert**.

Dims.: Fr.: **Richardeau, Rigardeau, Ric(h)ardet, Ric(h)ardin, Ric(h)ardon, Ric(h)ardot, Ricardou**. It.: **Ricc(i)ardelli, Ricciardello, Riccardini**; **Ricciardiello** (Naples); **Rizzardini**; **Licciard(i)ello**.

Patrs.: Eng.: **Richard(e)s, Ric(k)ards, Rickardes**; **Richardson**; **Ritson** (Northumb. and Yorks). Welsh: PRITCHARD. Ger.: **R(e)ichar(t)z, Reicherz**. Low Ger.: **Rickertsen**. Fris.: **Richten, Rigts**. Swed.: **Rickardsson, Richardsson**.

A family by the name of Ricardo *were prominent in the Sefardic Jewish community of medieval Andalusia. They were driven from Spain by the Inquisition, when Daniel Ricardo fled to Italy, later settling in Amsterdam, where a branch of the family had been established since the early 16th cent. Another branch was established in England by Abraham Ricardo (b. 1733), whose son David (1773–1832) was one of the founders of modern economic theory. He broke with his father after adopting the Christian faith.*

Richer English (chiefly Essex): from a Gmc personal name composed of the elements *rīc* power + *heri*, *hari* army, introduced into England by the Normans in the form *Richier*, but largely absorbed by the much more common RICHARD.

Vars.: **Reacher, Ricker**.

Cogns.: Fr.: **Rich(i)er**. Prov.: **Riquier, Riquiez**. Ger.: **Reicher**.

Patr.: Eng.: **Rickers**.

Richmond English: habitation name from any of the numerous places so called, in N France as well as in England. These are named with the OF elements *riche* rich, splendid (see RICH 1) + *mont* hill (see MONT). Richmond in N Yorks. was named after a *Richmont* in France immediately after the Norman Conquest, and in many if not most cases the Eng. surname can be derived from this place. Richmond in SW London received this name only in the reign of Henry VII, in honour of the king, who had been Earl of Richmond until he came to the throne. Previously the place was known as *Sheen*; it is unlikely to be the source of the surname of anyone called *Richmond*.

Vars.: **Richmont**; **Richman** (see also RICH).

Cogns.: Fr.: **Richemont, Richemond**.

Richter 1. German: occupational or status name for an arbiter or judge, Ger. *Richter* (MHG *rihtære*, from *rihten* to make right). The term was mostly used in the Middle Ages to denote a part-time settler of disputes rather than a full-time legal official. Such communal conciliators held a position of considerable esteem in rural communities; in E Germany the term came to denote a village headman, which was often a hereditary office. It is in this region that the surname is most frequent.
2. Jewish (Ashkenazic): translation of DAYAN.

Cogns. (of 1): Flem.: **De Rechter**. Du.: **Rigter**. Pol.: **Rychter** (when Jewish, a Pol. spelling of 2). Czech: **Rychtář, Rychtera**.

Dim. (of 1): Czech: **Rychtářík**.

Patrs. (from 1): Low Ger.: **Richters** (N Rhineland); **Richtering** (Westphalia).

Rickwood English: 1. from *Richold*, a Norman personal name composed of the Gmc elements *rīc* power + *wald* rule. Reaney also cites *Ricolda* as a fem. name, from Gmc *rīc* power + *hild* battle.
2. from *Richward*, a Norman personal name composed of the Gmc elements *rīc* power + *ward* guard. Both names

were introduced into England by the Normans, but neither became particularly popular, and they were confused early.

Vars. (of 1): **Richold**. (Of 2): **Rickward, Rickword, Record**.

Cogns. (of 1): Fr.: **Ric(h)aud, Ricaut, Rigau(l)t, Ricaux, Rigaux**. Prov.: **Rigal**. Ger.: **Reichwald, Reich(h)old**. Low Ger.: **Rickelt**.

Dims. (of 1): Fr.: **Rigaudet, Rigaudin**.

Patrs. (from 1): Ger.: **Reicholz**. Low Ger.: **Rickolts, Rickelts**. (From 2): Eng.: **Records**.

Riddell Scots and N English: 1. regional name from *Ryedale* in N Yorks., the valley (see DALE) of the river *Rye* (which bears a Brit. name).

2. from a Norman personal name, *Ridel*. Reaney explains this as a nickname from OF *ridel* small hill (a dim. of *ride* fold, of Gmc origin), but a more probable source is a Gmc personal name derived from the element *rīd* ride.

Vars.: **Riddel, Riddle, Riddall, Rid(e)al**.

A family called Riddell *have been established at Whitton in the former county of Roxburghs. since the mid-12th cent., when Walter* de Riddel *(of Ryedale in Yorks.) accompanied King David I (1124–53) from England and was appointed sheriff of the county.*

The Riddels *of Cranstoun Riddel near Edinburgh are quite separate, and are descended from a certain Gervase* Ridel, *also a retainer of King David I. He (or his father) is said to have come originally from Gascony.*

Another family of this name have been established in Northumb. since at least the 14th cent. An ancestor, Sir William de Riddell, *was sheriff of the county, and was appointed constable of Norham castle in 1314.*

Rider English: 1. occupational name for a mounted warrior or messenger, late OE *rīdere* (from *rīdan* to ride), a term quickly displaced after the Conquest by the new sense of KNIGHT. As an Ir. surname it is a translation of a Gael. name; see MARKEY.

2. topographic name for someone who lived in an clearing in woodland; cf. READ 2.

Var.: **Ryder**.

Cogns. (of 1): Ger.: **Ritter**. Low Ger.: **Ridder**. Flem., Du.: **De Rid(d)er(e)**. Dan.: **Rytter**. Czech: **Rytíř**. Jewish (Ashkenazic): **Ritter(man)** (the reason for the adoption of these names is not clear).

Patrs. (from 1): Low Ger.: **Ridders, Ritters, Riddering**.

Ridge 1. English: topographic name for someone who lived on or by a ridge, ME *rigge*, OE *hrycg*.

2. Irish: translated form of Gael. **Mac Con Iomaire** 'son of *Cú Iomaire*', a byname meaning 'Hound (i.e. watchdog) of the Ridge (i.e. border)'. This surname is common in Galway.

Vars. (of 1): **Rigg(e), Riggs** (northern, from an ON cogn.; cf. RIGBY); RUDGE, **Ruggs, Rugman**; **Atteridge**.

Ridgewell English: habitation name from *Ridgewell* in Essex, so called from OE *hrēod* reed + *well(a)* spring, stream (see WELL).

Vars.: **Ridgwell, Redg(e)well**.

Ridgway English (chiefly Lancs.): topographic name for someone who lived on an ancient way along a ridge, from OE *hrycg* RIDGE + *weg* path, road (see WAY), or habitation name from some minor place of this name.

Var.: **Ridgeway**.

Ridler English: occupational name for a sifter of flour and meal, from an agent deriv. of ME *rid(e)len* to sift (from OE *hriddel* sieve).

Ridley English: habitation name from any of various places in England so called, esp. the one in Northumb., which, like that in Ches., is clearly derived from OE *geryd* channel + *lēah* wood, clearing. Those in Essex and Kent appear in Domesday Book as *Retleia* and *Redlege* respectively, and get their names from OE *hrēod* reed + *lēah*.

The Ridleys *of Unthank Hall, Northumb., are an old-established border family, whose members include Bishop Nicholas Ridley (?1500–55), who was burned at the stake in the reign of Mary I because he refused to recant his Protestant beliefs.*

Ridout English: of uncertain origin. It might seem to be an occupational nickname for a rider, from ME *rid(en)* to ride + *out* out, forth, but this is probably no more than folk etymology.

Vars.: **Rideout, Ridoutt**.

Ridsdale English (Yorks.): habitation name from *Ridsdale* or *Redesdale* in Northumb., so called from its position in the valley (see DALE) of the river *Rede*, whose name is derived from OE *rēad* red.

Riefenstahl Low German: occupational nickname for a polisher of weapons and armour, from the MLG phrase *wrīve den stāl* polish the steel, from *wrīven* to rub, polish + *den* (acc.) def. art. + *stāl* STEEL.

Var.: **Riefstahl**.

Riemer German and Jewish (Ashkenazic): occupational name for a maker of leather reins and similar articles, Ger. *Riemer* and Yid. *rimer* belt-maker (MHG *riemære*, an agent deriv. of *rieme(n)* strap, belt, thong, OHG *riomo*).

Vars.: Ger.: **Rieme, Rie(h)m** (metonymic); **Riem(en)schneider** (see SCHNEIDER). Jewish: RIMER; **Rymer** (E Ashkenazic, a Pol. spelling); **Rimerman**.

Cogns.: Low Ger.: **Re(h)mer** (see also REINMAR); **Rehm(e)**; **Remensnider**. Fris.: **Riemersma**. Flem., Du.: **Riemsnijder**.

Riera Catalan: topographic name for someone who lived by a flood-stream, Cat. *riera* (LL *rīvāria*, a deriv. of *rīvus* stream; cf. RIEU). There are various places in N Spain named with this word, for example in the province of Tarragona, and the surname may also be a habitation name from any of these.

Riesco Spanish: topographic name for someone who lived near an outcrop of rock or nickname for a hard-hearted individual, from OSp. *riesco* steep crag (of uncertain origin, perhaps akin to L *resecāre* to cut; cf. RIESGO).

Var.: **Risco**.

Riese Jewish (Ashkenazic): nickname for an exceptionally tall or bulky person, from mod. Ger. *Riese* giant. In some cases the name may have been used to refer ironically to a particularly short man.

Vars.: **Ries, Riz** (from Yid. *riz* giant). The name has sometimes been Anglicized as REESE (see also RHYS).

Riesgo Spanish: nickname for an awkward or quarrelsome person, from OSp. *riesgo* discord (perhaps akin to L *resecāre* to cut, divide; cf. RIESCO).

Rietveld Dutch: topographic name for someone living by a reedbed, from Du. *riet* reed (OSax. *hriod*) + *veld* uncultivated land (see FIELD).

Rieu Provençal: topographic name for someone who lived near a stream, OProv. *rieu* (L *rīvus*), or habitation name from any of the numerous places named with this word.

Vars.: **Rieux, Rieuf; Rio(u); Larieu, Sarieu; Delrieu, Durrieu; Duriz, Duruz, Dury** (Switzerland).

Cogns.: Sp.: **Río(s)** ('river'). Cat.: **Riu(s)**. Port.: **Rios**. It.: **De Rivo; Del Rio, De Riu** (S Sardinia).

Dims.: Prov.: **Riol(s), Rivol(l)et**. It.: **Rivolo, Da Riolo; Rivelli; Riet(t)i, Riozzi**.

Rifkin Jewish (E Ashkenazic): metr. from the Yid. female given name *Rifke* (from the Hebr. name *Rivka* Rebecca, meaning 'Heifer'), with the addition of the Slav. metr. suffix *-in*.

Vars.: **Rifkind, Rivkin(d), Ryvkin(d)** (for the excrescent *-d*, see SÜSSKIND); **Rivkovich, Rivkes; Rives** (from the female given name *Rive*, a back-formation from *Rivke*, taken as a supposed dim.); **Riveles, Rivelis, Rivlin** (from *Rivele*, a pet from of *Rive*; see also REUBEN).

Rigby English (chiefly Lancs.): habitation name from *Rigby* in Lancs, named with ON *hryggr* ridge + *býr* farm, settlement.

Rikin Jewish (E Ashkenazic): metr. from the Yid. female given name *Rike* (of uncertain origin) + the Slav. metr. suffix *-in*.

Vars.: **Rykowicz; Riklin, Riklis** (from the dim. *Rikl*).

Riley 1. Irish: var. of REILLY.

2. English: habitation name from *Ryley* in Lancs., so called from OE *ryge* RYE + *lēah* wood, clearing. There is a *Riley* with the same meaning in Devon, but it does not seem to have contributed to the surname, which is more common in N England.

Var. (of 2): **Ryley**.

Rimer 1. English (Lancs.): occupational name for a poet, minstrel, or balladeer, from an agent deriv. of ME *rime(n)* to compose or recite verses (OF *rimer*, from *rime* metre, L *rhythmus*).

2. Jewish (Ashkenazic): var. of RIEMER.

Var. (of 1): Eng.: **Rimmer**.

Rimmington English: habitation name from *Rimington* in Yorks., so called from the old name of the stream on which it stands (OE *Riming* 'Boundary Stream') + OE *tūn* enclosure, settlement.

Var.: **Remington**.

The American painter Frederic Remington *(1861–1909) was descended from a certain John Remington, living in Massachusetts in 1639.*

Rimon Jewish (Israeli): ornamental name from Hebr. *rimon* pomegranate, in part a Hebraicization of MILGRIM and *Granat* (see GARNETT 1).

Var.: **Rimmon**.

Rincón Spanish: topographic name for someone who lived by a corner, Sp. *rincón* (OSp. *re(n)cón*, from Arabic *ruk(ú)n*).

Rind 1. Scots: habitation name from a small place in the former county of Perths. called *Rhynd*, from Gael. *roinn* point of land.

2. Jewish (Ashkenazic): of uncertain origin, possibly from Ger. *Rind*, Yid. *rind* head of cattle, or a shortening of the ornamental Ashkenazic surname **Baumrind** (from Ger. *Baumrinde* tree-bark).

Vars. (of 1): **Rhind, Rhynd**.

Ring English, German, Danish/Norwegian, and Swedish: metonymic occupational name for a maker of rings (from OE, OHG *hring*, ON *hringr*), either to be worn as jewellery or as component parts of chain-mail, harnesses, and other objects. In part it may also have arisen as a nickname for a wearer of a ring. Latterly, in Scandinavia it was adopted as an ornamental name.

Vars.: Eng.: **Rings**. Ger.: **Rin(c)k(e)**.

Dims.: Ger.: **Ringel, Ringle**.

Ringer English: 1. from the OF personal name *Reinger, Rainger*, composed of the Gmc elements *ragin* counsel + *geri, gari* spear. This was introduced to Britain by the Normans.

2. occupational name for a maker of rings (see RING) or for a bell-ringer (from ME *ring(en)* (trans.), OE *hringan* (intrans.)).

Var. (of 1): **Rainger**.

Cogns. (of 2): Ger.: **Rinker; Ringger** (Switzerland).

Ringrose English: of uncertain origin. It is first attested in Norwich in 1259 as *Ringerose*, and later forms show no significant variation. Unless it had already been drastically altered by folk etymology at that early date, it is probably from ME RING + ROSE, but if so the original meaning is far from clear.

Rintoul Scots: habitation name from a minor place now lost, which was in Fife near Kinross. The etymology of the placename is obscure.

Var.: **Rentoul**.

Rioja Spanish: regional name for someone from the region of *Rioja* in N Castile, which is centered on Logroño. The region is named from the river *Oja*, which flows through it; the Sp. word *río* river has become fused with the river name. This is first recorded in the form *Ol(i)a*, and may possibly be derived from L *folia* leaves (cf. OJEDA).

Riordan Irish: Anglicized form of Gael. **Ó Ríoghbhárdáin** 'descendant of *Ríoghbhárdán*', a byname composed of *ríogh-* royal + a dim. of *bárd* bard, poet.

Vars.: **O'Riordan, O'Riourdane, O'Riverdan, O'Reedan, Reardon, Rearden**.

Most bearers of this surname claim descent from an eponymous ancestor killed at Aherlow in 1058, who was a son of Cucoirne, lord of Ely O'Carroll.

Ripley English: habitation name from any of various places, esp. one in W Yorks., so called from OE *ripel* strip of land + *lēah* wood, clearing.

Ripoll Catalan: habitation name from a place in N Spain, the site of a famous medieval monastery, originally named with the L elements *rivus* stream (see RIEU) + *pullus* dark grey.

Var.: **Ripollès**.

Rippe 1. French: nickname for a sufferer from scabies, OF *ripe* (from *riper* to itch, scratch, tear, of Gmc origin).

2. Low Ger.: dim. of the given name RIPPERT.

Dims. (of 1): Fr.: **Ripot(eau), Ripon, Ripoche**.

Ripper English: occupational name for someone who made or sold baskets, or else carried wares about in a basket, from an agent deriv. of ME *(h)rip* basket (ON *hrip*).

Rippert French and Low German: from a Gmc personal name composed of the elements *rīc* power + *berht* bright, famous.

Vars.: Fr.: **Ripert, Ribert**. Low Ger.: **Ribbert**.

Dims.: Low Ger.: RIPPE, **Ribbe, Rip(p)ke**. Fris.: **Riepe**.

Patrs. (from dims.): Low Ger.: **Rippen(s), Ripping**. Fris.: **Riepen(a)**.

Rippon English: habitation name from *Ripon* in N Yorks., so called from OE *Hrypum*, dat. pl. (originally used after a preposition) of a tribal name of obscure etymology; cf. REPTON.

Risby English: habitation name from any of various places, for example in Lincs., Suffolk, and E Yorks., so called from ON *hrís* brushwood (cf. REIS 1 and RISLEY) + *býr* farm, settlement.

Riseborough English (Norfolk): habitation name, of uncertain origin. It could be from Princes *Risborough* in Bucks. (from OE *hrīsen*, an adj. deriv. of *hrīs* brushwood + *beorgas* hills).

Var.: **Risebrow**.

Risley English: habitation name from *Risley* in Derbys. and Lancs., or *Riseley* in Beds. and Berks., all so called from OE *hrīs* brushwood + *lēah* wood, clearing.

Rita Portuguese: from a female given name, an aphetic form of *Margharita* Margaret (see MARGUERITE), chosen in particular in honour of a 15th-cent. It. saint who bore the name in this form.

Rive French: topographic name for someone who lived on the bank of a river or the shore of a lake, OF *rive* (L *rīpa*).

Vars.: **Rives**; **Larive**, **Delarive**.

Cogns.: Prov.: **Ribe(s)**. It.: **Riva**; **Rivani**, **Rivano**. Sp.: **Riva(s)**. Cat.: **Riba(s)**, **Ribes**.

Dims.: Fr.: **Rivet**, **Riveau**, **Rivelon**. It.: **Rivetti**. Cat.: RIBÓ.

Rivero Spanish: topographic name for someone who lived on a patch of raised land beside a river, Sp. *ribero* (LL *rīpārium*, a deriv. of *rīpa*; see RIVE).

Cogns.: Cat.: **Ribé**. Port.: **Ribeiro** ('creek', 'brook'). Fr.: **Rivier**, **Derivier**.

Rivers English (Norman): habitation name from any of various places in N France called *Rivières*, from the pl. form of OF *rivière* river (originally meaning 'riverbank', from L *rīpāria*, a deriv. of *rīpa* bank; cf. RIVE and RIVERO). The absence of Eng. forms without the final *-s* makes it unlikely that it is ever from the borrowed ME vocab. word *river*, but the French and other Romance cogns. do normally have this sense.

Cogns.: Fr.: **Rivière**, **Larivière**, **De(la)rivière**, **Rivierre**. Prov.: **Rivoire**; **Ribière**, **Ribeyre**. It.: **Riviera** ('bank'). Sp.: **Rivera** ('bank'). Cat.: **Ribera** ('bank').

Dims.: Prov.: **Ribereau**, **Riberole**, **Ribe(y)rolles**.

Aug.: Prov.: **Ribeyras**.

A Huguenot family named Rivière *settled in England around 1689. They were originally merchants from Nérac, Gascony.* **Revere**, *originally* De Revoire *or* Rivoire, *is the name of another Huguenot family, descended from Apollos De Revoire, who settled in America in the early 18th cent. He was a silversmith, as was his son, the American patriot Paul Revere (1735–1818).*

Rivett English (E Anglia): metonymic occupational name for a metalworker, from ME, OF *rivet* small nail or bolt (from OF *river* to fix, secure, of unknown origin).

Var.: **Revett**.

Rix English (E Anglia): 1. patr. from the given name *Rick*, a var. of RICH 2.

2. topographic name for someone who lived on a piece of land thickly grown with rushes, from OE (W Saxon) *rixe* rush (coll. sing.), a metathesized form of *rysc*; cf. RUSH 1.

Roach English: topographic name for someone who lived by a rocky crag or outcrop, from ME, OF *roche* (later replaced in England by *rock*, from the Norman byform *rocque*; cogns. are found in other Romance languages, but the origin is unknown). Some early examples of the surname derive from various places in Normandy, as for example *Les Roches* in Seine-Maritime, named with this word.

Var.: **Roche** (Irish).

Cogns.: Fr.: **Roche**, **Roc**; **Laroche**, **De(la)roche**, **Desroches**. Prov.: **Roca**, **Ro(c)que(s)**, **Laro(c)que**, **Larroque**, **De(la)roque**, **Desroques**. Sp.: **Roca**; **Rocha** (Galicia). Cat.: **Roca**. Port.: **Rocha**. It.: **(La) Rocca**, **Della Rocca**.

Dims.: Eng.: **Rochelle**, **Rotchell**, **Rockell**, **Rockall**. Fr.: **Rochel(le)**, **Larochelle**, **Rochet(te)**, **Larochette**, **Rochon**; **Rohel**, **(Le) Roël** (Brittany). Prov.: **Ro(c)quet(te)**; **Rouchet**, **Rouché**, **Rouchès**, **Rouchon**, **Rouchoux**, **Rouchousse**.

Roadknight English: occupational name for a mounted retainer, ME *rōdknicht* (OE *rādcniht*, from *rād*, an abstract deriv. of *rīdan* to ride + *cniht* servant (see KNIGHT)).

Var.: **Rodknight**.

Robalo Portuguese: metonymic occupational name for a fisherman, or nickname, from Port. *robalo* snook (*Centropomus undecimalis*, a marine fish). The word is of uncertain origin, perhaps a metathesized form of **lobarro*, a deriv. of *lobo* wolf (cf. LOW 3).

Robert English, French, Catalan, Low German, and Dutch: from a Gmc personal name composed of the elements *hrōd* renown + *berht* bright, famous. This is found occasionally in England before the Conquest, but in the main it was introduced into England by the Normans and quickly became popular among all classes of society. See also DOBB, HOBB, and NOBB. The surname is also occasionally borne by Jews, as an Anglicization of one or more like-sounding Jewish surnames.

Vars.: Eng.: **Robart**. Fr.: **Robart**, **Robard**, **Rebert**; ROPER, **Ro(s)pars**, **Ropartz** (Brittany); **Flobert**, **Flaubert** (from a byform with the first element *hlōd*; cf. LEWIS). Low Ger.: **Robbert**, **Rub(b)ert**, **Ropert**, **Rup(p)ert**.

Cogns.: Prov.: **Roubert**, **Roubeix**. It.: **Roberti**, **Roberto**; **Ruberti**, **Ruberto**, **Ruperto** (S Italy); **Luberti**, **Luberto**, **Luparti**, **Luparto**. Port.: **Roberto**. Ger.: **Rup(p)recht**, **Rüpprecht**, **R(a)uprich**. Flem.: **Robberecht**. Hung.: **Róbert**.

Dims.: Eng.: **Robb**, **Rabb**; ROBIN; ROBY (Scotland); RABBITT, **Roblett**, **Roblin**, **Rablin**, **Rablan**. Fr.: **Robertet**, **Robardet**, **Robardey**, **Robertot**; **Robet**, **Robé**, **Robey**, **Robez**, **Robel(in)**, **Roblin**, **Rob(e)let**, **Rob(e)lot**, **Rob(i)ot**, **Robion**, **Robiou**, **Robeçon**, **Robichon**, **Rebichon**, **Robuchon**; **Robic** (Brittany). It.: **Robertelli**, **Rubertelli**, **Rubartelli**, **Robertucci**. Ger.: **Ropp**, **Robbel**, **Rupp(el)**, **Rüpel**, **Rüppele** (Swabia); **Rüppeli(n)** (Switzerland); **Riep(e)l** (Bavaria); **Reubel**, **Reuble** (see also REUBEN). Low Ger.: **Robbe**, **Röpe**, **Röb(be)ke**, **Röp(c)ke**, **Rübke**, **Rüpke**.

Pejs.: It.: **Robertacci**, **Robertazzi**.

Patrs.: Eng.: **Roberts** (also Jewish), **Robers**, **Robarts**, **Robberds**; **Rober(t)son** (especially common in Scotland). Sc.: **McRobert(s)**. Welsh: PROBERT. Fr.: **Derobert**. It.: **De Roberto**, **Di Roberto**, **(De) Robertis**, **Rubertis**. Ger.: **Ruprechter**; **Ruperti** (Latinized). Low Ger.: **Roberts(en)**, **Robberts**, **Rubberts**; **Robertz**, **Ruppertz** (N Rhineland). Swed.: **Robertsson**.

Patrs. (from dims.): Eng.: **Robbs**; **Rob(e)son** (Northumb.); **Rabson**; **Rapson** (Cornwall); **Ropkins**, **Rapkins**. Sc.: **McRobb**. Low Ger.: **Robben**, **Röbken**, **Röbker**, **Röpkes**, **Röpking**. Flem., Du.: **Rops**, **Rub(b)ens**.

A Scottish family by the name of Robertson *trace their descent from Crinan, Lord of Atholl (d. c.975). A family tradition has it that they acquired the family name Robertson as a result of their crucial support of Robert the Bruce at Bannockburn in 1306, after which he is reputed to have said that thereafter they should be regarded as his children.*

Robertshaw English (W Yorks.): habitation name from a lost place in Heptonstall, W Yorks., taking its name from an owner ROBERT + ME *shawe* copse (OE *sceaga*).

Var.: **Robshaw**.

Robespierre French: from a combination of the given names ROBERT and PIERRE. The spelling with *-s-* is the result of hypercorrection of the form *Robépierre*, from earlier *Rober(t)pierre*.

Robin 1. English and French: from the medieval given name *Robin*, a dim. of ROBERT, from the short form *Rob* + the hypocoristic suffix *-in*.

2. Jewish (Ashkenazic): possibly a var. of RABIN.

Vars. (of 1): Eng.: **Robbin, Robyn.**

Cogns. (of 1): Prov.: **Roubin, Rouby.**

Dims. (of 1): Fr.: **Robinet, Robinot, Robineau.** Prov.: **Roubineau, Roubinet.**

Patrs. (from 1): Eng.: **Rob(b)ins, Rob(b)ens, Robyns; Robi(n)son.** Sc.: **McRobin.** Welsh: **Probin, Brobin, Broben.**

Robusti Italian: nickname for a strong and hardy person, from the It. adj. *robusto* (L *rōbustus*, from *rōbur* (heart of) oak; cf. ROUVRE).

Roby English and Scots: 1. dim. of ROBERT.

2. habitation name from *Roby* in Lancs. (now Merseyside), so called from ON *rá* pole, boundary mark + *býr* farm, settlement.

Vars. (of 1): **Rob(b)ie.** (Of 2): **Rab(e)y, Rabie** (also from *Raby* in Ches. and Co. Durham, with the same etymology).

Patr. (from 1): Sc.: **McRobbie.**

Roch 1. French: from a Gmc personal name of uncertain origin. It may have been originally a byname meaning 'Crow' (cf. OHG *hruoh*, OE *hrōc*, an imitative formation), but Dauzat derives it from a root *hroc* rest. The name was reasonably common in the Middle Ages and was often given in honour of a 14th-cent. saint of Montpellier remembered for his miraculous healings during an outbreak of the plague.

2. Jewish: of unknown origin.

Var. (of 1): **Roz** (see also ROSE).

Cogns. (of 1): It.: **Ruocco, Rocc(h)i.** Port.: **Roque.** Low Ger.: **Roch(us).**

Dims. (of 1): It.: **Rocchelli, Rocchetti, Rocchini, Rocuzzo.**

Augs. (of 1): It.: **Roccon(i).**

Patrs. (from 1): Low Ger.: **Rochs, Rochussen.**

Rochester English: habitation name from the town in Kent, recorded by Bede (*c*.730) under the names of both *Dorubrevi* and *Hrofæcæstre*. The former represents the original Brit. name, composed of the elements *duro-* fortress and *brīvā* bridge. The second represents a contracted form of this (possibly affected by folk etymological connection with OE *hrōf* roof) combined with an explanatory OE *cæster* Roman fort (from L *castra* military camp). There is a much smaller place in Northumb. also called *Rochester*, which seems to have been named in imitation of the more important one, but which is a more than occasional source of the surname. In a few cases there may also have been confusion with *Wroxeter* in Shrops., recorded in Domesday Book as *Rochecestre*.

Vars.: **Rogister, Rossiter.**

Rochford English: habitation name from either of two places so called, in Essex and Worcs. In both cases the name probably derives from the gen. case of OE *ræcc* hunting dog (perhaps a byname) + OE *ford* FORD, but its development has been influenced by the common Fr. placename composed of the elements *roche* rock (see ROACH) + *fort* strong (L *fortis*).

Vars.: **Ratchford, Retchford.**

Rochlin Jewish (NE Ashkenazic): metr. from the Yid. female given name *Rokhl* (from the Hebr. female name *Rachel* 'Ewe') + the Slav. metr. suffix *-in*.

Var.: **Rachlin** (a Hebraicized form found in Israel).

Rock English: 1. topographic name for someone who lived near a notable crag or outcrop, from ME *rocc* rock (see ROACH), or habitation name from a place named with this word, as for example *Rock* in Northumb.

2. topographic name for someone who lived near a large oak tree (see OAK), from a misdivision of ME *atter oke* at the oak. *Rock* in Worcs. gets its name in this way, and the surname may in some cases be a habitation name from this source.

3. metonymic occupational name for a spinner of wool or a maker of distaffs, from ME *rok* distaff (from ON *rokkr* or MDu. *rocke* or an unattested OE cogn.).

Vars.: **Rocke; Rocks.** (Of 2 only): **Ro(a)ke.** (Of 3 only): **Rocker, Rooker, Rucker.**

Rockefeller German: habitation name from the village of *Rockenfeld* near Neuwied in the Rhineland (so called from MHG *rocke* RYE (OHG *rocko*) + *feld* open country; see FIELD) + *-er* suffix denoting a native or inhabitant.

The first immigrants to bring this name to America arrived in America in 1734. One of their descendants, the American millionaire industrialist John D. Rockefeller *(1839–1937), founder of Standard Oil, was born in Richmond, New York, of New England descent; his father was a commodities dealer and farm-owner. He also had some German blood, and his mother was Scottish.*

Rockley English (Notts.): habitation name from a place near Retford, so called from OE *hrōc* rook (perhaps a byname) + *lēah* wood, clearing. There is also a place so called in Wilts., which is a possible alternative source of the surname.

Rockwell English: habitation name from places in Bucks. and Somerset. The former was earlier *Rockholt*, and is so called from OE *hrōc* rook (perhaps a byname) + *holt* wood. The second element of the Somerset place is probably (and more predictably) OE *well(a)* spring, stream (see WELL).

Roddam English: habitation name from *Roddam* Hall near Alnwick in Northumb., which is named from the dat. pl., *rodum* (originally used after a preposition) of OE *rod* clearing (see RHODES).

Var.: RODEN.

A family of this name have been established for centuries at Roddam Hall. William of Roddam was recorded in 1296, and the descent to present-day bearers can be traced from Sir John Roddam, *who died in battle in 1461.*

Rode 1. French: from a short form of any of the various Gmc personal names with the first element *hrod* reknown (cf. ROTH 3).

2. French: topographic name for someone who lived in a clearing in woodland, OF *rode* (of Gmc origin; cf. RHODES).

3. Low German: cogn. of RHODES.

4. Danish and Norwegian: cogn. of ROTH 1 and 2.

5. Provençal: metonymic occupational name for a wheelwright or topographic name for someone who lived by a water-wheel, from OProv. *rode* wheel (L *rota*).

Vars. (of 1): **Rodon** (from the oblique case). (Of 3 and 4): **Rohde.** (Of 5): **Ro(u)dier, Ro(u)dié.**

Cogns. (of 5): Fr.: **Ro(u)yer, Leroyer.** Sp.: **Rueda; Roa** (León). Cat.: **Roda.** Rum.: **Roata.**

Dims. (of 1): Fr.: **Rodin, Rodot, Rodilon.** Ger.: **Rüdel, Riedel.** (Of 5): Prov.: **Rodel, Ro(u)det, Roudeix.**

Patrs. (from 1): Low Ger.: **Röd(d)ing.** Flem., Du.: **Rutten.**

Roden 1. Irish: Anglicized form of Gael. **Ó Rodáin** 'descendant of *Rodán*', a personal name derived from *rod* hearty, lively, furious, spirited; cf. READY 3.

2. English: var. of RODDAM.

Vars.: **Rodden, Rod(d)an.** (Of 1 only): **O'Rodane, O'Ruddane, (O')Rudden, Ruddon, Reddan, Reddin.**

Ródenas Spanish: habitation name from a place in the province of Teruel, so called from a fem. pl. form of the adj. *rodeno*, a Mozarabic dial. form of OSp. *roano* reddish (see RUANO); the noun *tierras* land is probably to be understood.

Rodera Spanish: topographic name for someone who lived by a cart track, Sp. *rodera* (LL *rotāria*, a deriv. of *rota* wheeel; cf. RODE 5).

Var.: **Roderas** (more frequent).

Roderick 1. English: from the Gmc personal name *Hrōdrīc*, composed of the elements *hrōd* renown + *rīc* power, introduced into England by the Normans in the form *Rodric*, but not frequent during the Middle Ages.

2. Welsh: Anglicized form of the personal name *Rhydderch*, originally a byname meaning either 'Reddish-brown' or else 'Very Famous'.

Cogns. (of 1): Sp.: **Rodrigo**. It.: **Rod(e)rigo**, **Roderighi**; **Rodolico** (Sicily). Jewish (Sefardic): **Rodrig(ue)** (shortened forms of the Sp. and It. names).

Patrs. (from 1): Sp.: **Rodríguez**, **Ruiz**. Port.: **Rodrigues**. Jewish (Sefardic): **Rodriques**, **Rodriguez** (adoptions of the Sp. and Port. names). (From 2): Welsh: PROTHEROE.

Rodés Catalan: habitation name from a place in the province of Lérida. This probably has the same origin as *Rodez* in the *département* of Aveyron, France, which is first recorded in the 6th cent. in the L form *Rutensis*, apparently from the Gaul. tribal name *Ruteni*, of unknown origin.

Rodney English: habitation name from a minor place in Somerset, an area of land in the marshes near Markham. This is first recorded in the form *Rodenye*; it derives from the gen. case of the OE personal name *Hroda* (a short form of the various cpd names with the first element *hrōð* renown; cf. RODE 1) + OE *ēg* island, dry land in a fen.

The Rodney *family of Stoke Rodney, Somerset, can be traced back to Richard* de Rodney (*b.* c.*1270*). *Among his descendants was the naval commander Admiral George Rodney* (*1718–92*).

Rodway English: habitation name from a place in Somerset, so called from OE *rād* riding (a deriv. of *rīdan* to ride) + *weg* way, path, i.e. a path suitable for passage on horseback as well as on foot.

Var.: **Rodaway**.

Rodwell English (chiefly E Anglia): apparently a habitation name from an unidentified place (probably not the district of Weymouth in Dorset), perhaps so called from the OE personal name *Hroda* (see RODNEY) + OE *well(a)* spring, stream.

Rofé Jewish: occupational name from Heb. *rofe* physician (a deriv. of *rafa* to heal; cf. RAPHAEL).

Vars.: **Rofe(h)**, **Rophe**, **Roff(e)** (see also ROLF); **Harofé**, **Harofe** (with the Hebr. def. article).

Roffey English: habitation name from a place in Sussex, near Horsham, so called from OE *rūh* rough (cf. RAUCH) + *(ge)hæg* enclosure (see HAY 1).

Rogacki Polish: topographic name for someone who lived on a 'horn' of land, i.e. an outlying, projecting edge of a settlement or administrative division, from Pol. *róg* horn, projection, with the surname suffix *-ski* (see BARANOWSKI).

Vars. (also Jewish (E Ashkenazic)): **Rogowski**, **Rogaczewski**.

Rogalski 1. Polish: from the Pol. dial. term *rogala* ox (a deriv. of *róg* horn), with the surname suffix *-ski* (see BARANOWSKI). This was perhaps applied as a nickname for a large, strong man, or taken from a house sign showing an ox or a pair of horns.

2. Jewish (Ashkenazic): the reasons for its adoption as a Jewish surname are unclear; it may be an ornamental name.

Vars.: **Rogulski**, **Rogala**; **Rogaliński** (possibly also a habitation name from the town of *Rogalin* in Great Poland).

Cogn.: Czech: **Rohlík** ('crescent', probably from a house sign).

Patr.: Pol.: **Rogalewicz**.

Rogala *is a very old Polish family name, recorded since the 13th cent. in Silesia and Little Poland. Bystroń mentions a historical record saying that the Rogala family in Kujawy changed their name to* Rogaliński.

Roger 1. English, French, Catalan, and Low German: from a Gmc personal name composed of the elements *hrōd* renown + *geri*, *gari* spear, which was introduced into England by the Normans in the form *Rog(i)er*. The cogn. ON *Hróðgeirr* was a reinforcing influence in Normandy. See also DODGE and HODGE.

2. Irish: Anglicized form of *Mac Ruaidhrí*; see RORY.

Vars. (of 1): Eng.: **Rodgier**, **Rogger**; **Rodger** (Scotland); **Rosser** (Wales). Fr.: **Rogier**, **Rogez**. Low Ger.: **Rogger**, **Röttger**, **Röttcher**, **Rödi(n)ger**.

Cogns. (of 1): Prov.: **Roug(i)er**, **Rougé**, **Rotgé**. It.: **Rugg(i)eri**, **Rugg(i)ero**, **Ruggier** (Venetia); **Rugieri**, **Rugiero** (Naples); **Rogg(i)eri**, **Rogg(i)ero** (NW Italy); **Roglieri**, **Rogliero** (Apulia). Ger.: **Rüdi(n)ger**, **Rüger**, **Rückert**, **Rie(di)ger**; **Rückhard** (with change of suffix, from the 16th cent.).

Dims. (of 1): Eng.: **Rodge(tt)**, RUDGE. Fr.: **Rogeron**, **Rogerot**, **Roget**, **Rogeon**. Flem., Du.: **Rogge**.

Aug. (of 1): It.: **Roggerone**.

Patrs. (from 1): Eng.: **Rogers(on)**; **Rodgers(on)** (Scotland, N Ireland). Welsh: PROSSER. It.: **De Rugg(i)ero**, **Di Rugg(i)ero**. Low Ger.: **Ruttgers**, **Röttgers**. Flem., Du.: **Rutgers**, **Roggers**.

'Servant of R. 1 (dim.)': Eng.: **Rodgeman**, **Roggeman**.

Rogov Jewish (E Ashkenazic): habitation name from *Raguva* near Kaunas in Lithuania, formerly known by the Russ. name *Rogovo*.

Vars.: **Rogoff**, **Rogow**; **Rogowski**, **Rogowsky**, **Rogovsky**; **Rogover** (from Yid *Rogever* native or inhabitant of *Rogeve*, the Yid. name of the town).

Rogoziński Polish and Jewish (E Ashkenazic): habitation name from some place named with Pol. *rogoża* bulrush, for example *Rogoźnica*, *Rogoźnik*, *Rogoźno*, or *Rogożno*.

Rohan 1. French: habitation name from a place in Morbihan, in Brittany. There is also another place of the same name in Deux-Sèvres, which may have contributed to the surname.

2. Irish: var. of RUANE.

A French family of this name, which originated in Morbihan, claim kinship with the early kings of Brittany. Members of the family have included the Duc de Montbazon (1568–1654), who was governor of Paris; Henri, duc de Rohan (*1579–1638*), *a Huguenot leader; and Louis, cardinal de Rohan (1734–1803).*

Rohr 1. German: topographic name for someone who lived in an area thickly grown with reeds, from Ger. *Rohr* reed, MHG *rōr* (a collective sing.), or habitation name from one of the several places named with this word.

2. Jewish: of uncertain origin, possibly as in 1.

Vars. (of 1): **Röhr**, **Rohrer**, **Rohrmann**.

Cogn. (of 1): Low Ger.: **Röring**.

Dims. (of 1): Ger.: **Röhrle**. Low Ger.: **Röhreke**.

Collectives (of 1): Ger.: **Röhrich(t)**, **Rörig**.

Rojas Spanish: from the fem. pl. form of *rojo* red (see ROUSE). It is probably a topographic name, with some noun to be understood such as *tierras* land (cf. Ródenas) or *aguas* water.

Rojek Polish and Jewish (E Ashkenazic): apparently a nickname from Pol. dial. *rojek*, a kind of small ox from the mountain regions of S Poland (a deriv. of *róg* horn; see Rogalski). As a Jewish name, it is probably purely ornamental.

Habitation name: **Rojewski**.

Rolf English: from the ME given name *Rolf*, composed of the Gmc elements *hrōd* renown + *wulf* wolf. This name was especially popular among Nordic peoples in the contracted form *Hrólfr*, and seems to have reached England by two separate channels; partly through its use among pre-Conquest Scandinavian settlers, partly through its popularity among the Normans, who, however, generally used the form *Rou(l)* (see Rollo).

Vars.: **Ro(a)lfe**, **Rolph**, **Rulf**; **Roff(e)**, **Ruff**, **Roaf**, **Rofe**, **Roof(e)**, **Rouf(f)**, **Rove**.

Cogns.: Fr.: **Rodolphe**. It.: **R(e)olfi**, **R(e)olfo**, **Riolfi**, **Riolfo** (N Italy); **Rodolfi** (Emilia); **Redolfi** (Venetia); **Ridolfi**, **Ridolfo** (Tuscany); **Ridulfo** (Sicily). Ger.: **Rudolf**, **Rudloff**, **Rodolf**, **Ro(h)loff**, **Rotlauf**; **Ruf(f)**, **Ruoff**, **Rief** (Switzerland). Low Ger.: **Rohlf**.

Dims.: Eng.: **Ruffell**, **Ruffle** (Essex). It.: **Rolfini**. Ger.: **Rüffli**, **Rieflin** (Switzerland).

Patrs.: It.: **Firidolfi**. Ger.: **Rudolfer**. Low Ger.: **Ro(h)lfs**, **Rohfsen**, **Rohlfing**. Flem., Du.: **Roelofs(en)**, **Roelvink**.

Patr. (from a dim.): Eng.: **Ruffles**.

Rollo English: from a Latinized form, common in early medieval documents, of *Rou(l)*, the usual Norman form of Rolf.

Vars.: **Roll(e)**, Rule, Rowe.

Cogns.: Fr.: **Ro(u)l**, **Rol(l)e**; **Rol(l)on**. It.: **Rao(li)**, **Rau** (S Italy); **Raho** (Salento). Low Ger.: **Röhl**, **Rölle**; **Rühl(e)**; **Rahl**. Flem., Du.: **Roele**.

Dims.: Eng.: **Rollet(t)**, **Rollit(t)**, **Rowlett**, **Rowlatt**; **Rol(l)in(g)**, **Rowling**. Fr.: **Ro(u)l(l)et**, **Rol(l)in**, **Relin**, **Roul(l)y**, **Rollot**, **Roulot**. It.: **Raucci(o)**. Low Ger.: **Rollman**, **Rullmann**, **Rühlemann**, **Rahlmann**; **Rö(h)lke**, **Rühlicke**, **Rülke**, **Rahlke**.

Patrs.: Eng.: **Rolls**, **Rol(l)es**, **Rowles**; **Rowlson**, **Roulson**. It.: **Firrao**, **De Rao**. Low Ger.: **Rohls(en)**, **Rahls**; **Röhli(n)g**, **Rohling**.

Patrs. (from dims.): Eng.: **Rollin(g)s(on)**, **Rollison**, **Roli(n)son**, **Rollerson**, **Rollason**, **Rowlings(on)**, **Rowli(n)son**, **Rowlerson**.

A family called Rollo *have been established in Perths., Scotland, for centuries. In 1380/1 John* Rollo(k) *was granted land there by the Earl of Strathearn, to whom he was secretary. The surname was later spelled* Rollock, *but when the family were granted a barony in the mid-17th cent., they re-adopted the older form* Rollo.

Rolo Portuguese: 1. nickname for a person with curly hair, from Port. *rolo* roll, coil, curl (LL *rotulus*, a dim. of *rota* wheel; cf. Rode 3).

2. nickname for a troublesome or obstreperous person, from the same word used in the sense 'rumpus', 'uproar'.

Cogn. (of 1): Cat.: **Rull**.

Rolston English: habitation name from any of various places, such as *Rowlston* on the coast in Humberside, *Rolleston* in Leics., Notts., and Staffs., or *Rowlstone* in Herefords., near the Welsh border. Most of these are so called from the gen. case of the ON personal name *Hrólfr* (see Rolf) or of the OE cogn. name *Hrōðwulf* + OE *tūn* enclosure, settlement. In the case of the Notts. place, however, the first element is from the gen. case of the ON personal name *Hróald* (see Rowett).

Vars.: **Rolleston**, **Rolstone**, **Roulston**, **Row(le)ston(e)**.

Romagosa Catalan: habitation name from any of several places in N Spain, so called from *romagosa*, fem. of Cat. *romagós*, *romegós* thistly, prickly (LL *rumicōsus*, from *rumex*, gen. *rumicis*, sorrel); a noun such as 'land' is presumably to be understood.

Roman 1. English, French, Catalan, Rumanian, Polish, Ukrainian, and Belorussian: from the L personal name *Rōmānus* (originally an ethnic byname from *Rōma* Rome, of obscure, probably pre-Italic, origin), borne by several early saints, including a 7th-cent. bishop of Rouen. It was also the baptismal name of St Boris (see Borisov). The name was popular in N France in the early Middle Ages and was introduced into England by the Normans, but did not become common.

2. English, French, and Catalan: regional or ethnic name for someone from Rome or from Italy in general, or nickname for someone who had some connection with Rome, as for example having been there on a pilgrimage (cf. Romero).

Vars. (of 1 and 2): Eng.: **Romain(e)**, **Romayn(e)**. Fr.: **Romain**, **Romand**. Cat.: **Romà**. (Of 1 only): Pol.: **Romański**. (Of 2 only): Eng.: **Rome**, **Room(e)**. Fr.: **Rom(m)e**.

Cogns. (of 1 and 2): Sp.: **Román**. Port.: **Romão**. It.: **Romano**, **Romani**. Flem., Du.: **Rom(e)ijn**, **Romeyn**. (Of 1 only): Ger.: **Romahn**, **Ruhmann**. Hung.: **Román**. (Of 2 only): Prov.: **Roume**. It.: **Roma**. Pol.: **Rzymski**. Jewish: **Romi**, **Romano**.

Dims. (of 1 and 2): Fr.: **Romanet**. It.: **Romanelli**, **Roman(i)ello**, **Romanetti**, **Romanino**, **Romanin(i)**, **Romanucci**. (Of 1 only): Ukr.: **Romaniuk**, **Romanchuk**, **Romanets**. Beloruss.: **Romanenya**.

Pej. (of 1 and 2): It.: **Romanazzi**.

Patrs. (from 1 and 2): Eng.: **Romans**. (From 1 only): Russ.: **Romanov**, **Rominov**; **Romanoff** (U.S.). Ukr., Beloruss.: **Romanovich**. Pol.: **Romanowicz**.

Patrs. (from 1) (dims.): Russ.: **Romanychev**, **Romin**, **Romashov**. Ukr.: **Romanitsa**, **Romanchat**.

'Son of the wife of R. 1': Russ.: **Romanikhin**.

Habitation name: Pol.: **Romanowski**.

The Romanov *dynasty began its rule of Russia in 1613 with Michael Romanov (d. 1645), and ended with the execution of Nicholas II and his family at Yekaterinburg in July 1918. The family was descended from a Muscovite boyar, Andrei Kobyla, who had emigrated in the 14th cent. from Prussia. They took the name from Roman Yurievich (d. 1543), whose daughter Anastasia Romanovna was the first wife of Ivan the Terrible. Her brother Nikita was regent after Ivan's death, and after years of disorder Nikita's grandson Michael Romanov was elected tsar in 1613.*

Romero Italian and Spanish: 1. regional or ethnic name for a Roman or more generally for an Italian (cf. Roman 2), from L *Rōmaeus*, Gk *Rōmaios*, with the ending influenced by the common L agent suffix *-ārius*.

2. nickname for a pilgrim. The vocab. word came to have this sense because it was originally applied to travellers from the Western (Roman) Empire who had to pass through the Eastern (Byzantine) Empire on their way to the Holy Land. Later it was also used of pilgrims to Rome and to Santiago de Compostella.

Vars.: It.: **Romerio**, **Romeo**, **Romei**.

Cogns.: Fr.: **Ro(u)mier**, **Roumieu(x)**. Prov.: **Romeu(f)**. Cat.: **Romeu**. Eng.: **Ro(o)mer**, **Rummer**. Ger.: **Rö(h)mer**, **Ro(h)mer**. Flem., Du.: **Romer**. Dan.: **Rømer**.

Romilly 1. English (Norman) and French: habitation name from any of various places in N France, as for example *Romilly* in Eure or *Remilly* in La Manche, so called from the Gallo-Roman personal name *Rōmilius* (a deriv. of *Rōmulus*, the founding father of Rome) + the local suffix *-ācum*.

2. habitation name from *Romiley* in Greater Manchester, so called from OE *rūm(ig)* spacious, roomy + *lēah* wood, clearing.

This is the name of a Huguenot family, originally from Montpelier. They were established in England by Stephen Romilly *(1678–1733), who settled in Hoxton, Middlesex, c.1701. A number of his descendants became prominent in the English legal profession.*

Rommel Low German, Flemish, and Dutch: nickname for an obstreperous person, from MLG, MDu. *rummeln*, *rumpeln* to make a noise, create a disturbance (of imitative origin).

Vars.: **Römmele, Römmler; Rummel, Rümmele, Rümmler.**

Romney English: habitation name from a place in Kent, so called from an obscure first element *Rumen* + OE *ēa* river (see RYE).

Var.: **Rumney.**

Romo Spanish: nickname for someone with a snub nose, from Sp. *romo* blunt, foreshortened (of uncertain etymology, perhaps from L *rhombus*, itself a borrowing from Gk, with reference to the two obtuse angles of this figure).

Ronald Scots: Anglicized form of the Gael. personal name *Raonull*, which is a borrowing from ON *Rögnvaldr* (see REYNOLD).

Var.: **Ranald.**

Patrs.: **Ronaldson, Ranaldson; McRanald, McRannal, Magrannell, Grannell, (Mc)Crandle, (Mc)Crindle, McCrindell, McGrandell, (Mc)Crangle, (Mc)Cringle, Crennall** (Gael. **Mac Raonuill**).

Ronan Irish: Anglicized form of Gael. **Ó Rónáin** 'descendant of *Rónán*', a personal name apparently representing a dim. of *rón* seal.

Vars.: **(O')Rona(y)ne.**

Cogns.: Fr.: **Renan(d)** (Brittany; *Loc Ronan* in Brittany takes its name from a solitary Ir. saint of uncertain date).

Roncero Spanish: nickname for a deceitful person or a flatterer, from the OSp. adj. *roncero* (a deriv. of *ronce* deception, flattery, from Arabic *ramz*, *rumz* allusion, figurative expression (as opposed to plain speech)).

Roncin French: metonymic occupational name for someone in charge of horses used as pack-animals or for pulling carts rather than for riding, from OF *roncin* workhorse (of obscure etymology). The word also developed the meaning 'drudge', and so may also have been a nickname for a hard-pressed servant.

Var.: **Ronsin.**

Cogns.: Eng.: **Runcie; Runci(e)man, Runchman.**

Pej.: Fr.: **Ronsard.**

Rongier French: nickname from an agent deriv. of OF *ronger* to gnaw (from L *rumigāre* to ruminate, with the vowel influenced by crossing with *rōdere* to gnaw). The significance of the name is not entirely clear. It may have been bestowed on a usurer or a grumbler or for some more anecdotal reason.

Dims.: **Rongeron, Ronget.**

Rønne Danish: topographic name for someone who lived in a very humble dwelling, from Dan. *rønne* hovel.

Var.: **Rønn.**

Rook English: 1. nickname from the bird (OE *hrōc*), given to a person with very dark hair, or for some other reason.

2. some early examples, such as Robert *of ye Rook* (London 1318) and Henry *del Rook* (Staffs. 1332), point clearly to a local name of some kind. The first of these could be from a house sign, the second may well be a var. of ROCK 1.

Vars.: **Rooke, Ruck.**

Patrs. (from 1): **Rook(e)s.**

Rooney Irish: Anglicized form of Gael. **Ó Ruanaidh** 'descendant of *Ruanaidh*', a byname meaning 'Champion'.

Vars.: **O'Rownoe, (O')Roney,** ROWNEY.

Roosevelt Dutch: topographic name for someone living by an area of uncultivated land overgrown with roses, from Du. *roose* ROSE + *velt* open country (cf. FIELD).

The two American Presidents Theodore Roosevelt *(1858–1919) and Franklin Delano Roosevelt (1882–1945) and the latter's wife Eleanor Roosevelt (1884–1962) were all descended from a common ancestor, Claes Martenzen* van Rosenvelt *or* Roosevelt, *who had settled in New Amsterdam (now New York) from Holland in 1644. He was the son of Maertin Cornelisse Geldersman, who had bought the farm of* Rosevelt *in Tholen, Zeeland, from Pieter Jorisse* op het Rosevelt *and his son Joris Pieterse. The family became prosperous with the growth of Manhattan. Theodore Roosevelt was born in New York City; his mother was of Irish and Huguenot descent. Franklin Delano Roosevelt was his 5th cousin. His mother's family, the Delanos, were descended from Philippe de la Noye of Luxembourg, who arrived at Plymouth in 1621 with the Pilgrim Fathers. He married his distant cousin, Eleanor, whose maiden name was also Roosevelt. She was a niece of Theodore Roosevelt, who gave her away at the wedding.*

Root 1. English: nickname for a cheerful person, from ME *rote* glad (OE *rōt*).

2. English: metonymic occupational name for a player on the rote, an early medieval stringed instrument (ME, OF *rote*, of uncertain origin but apparently ultimately akin to W *crwth*; cf. CROWTHER).

3. Dutch: topographic name for someone who lived by a retting place (Du. *root*, a deriv. of *ro(o)ten* to ret, akin to mod. Eng. *rot*), where flax was soaked in tubs of water until the stems rotted to release the linen fibres.

Vars. (of 1 and 2): Eng.: **Roote, Rutt.** (Of 2 only): Eng.: RUTTER. (Of 3 only): Du.: **Rooth.**

Patrs. (from 1): **Root(e)s.**

Rootham English: habitation name from *Wrotham* in Kent, so called from the OE byname **Wrōta* (from *wrōt* snout) + OE *hām* homestead. The spelling of the surname reflects the present pronunciation of the placename.

The main family bearing this name are firmly established in N Beds., where the name occurs as early as 1206, when a certain William de Wrotham *is mentioned in connection with Harrold Priory. The first recorded bearer is Geoffrey de Wrotham, who came from Baddenville near Wrotham, and was employed as a domestic servant by several successive Archbishops of Canterbury in the 12th cent. One of them, Hubert Walter, granted him lands near Wrotham. His son William de Wrotham (d. ?1208) rose to become Sheriff of Devon (1198–9), and his grandson, another William de Wrotham, was Archdeacon of Taunton and one of the organizers of King John's navy.*

Roper 1. English: occupational name for a maker or seller of rope. The word is an agent deriv. of OE *rāp*; in the SE Midland dialect of Eng., which became standard, OE *-ā-* /ɑː/ became ME *-ō-* /ɔː/ and eventually mod. Eng. /əʊ/, whereas in the N Eng. dialects it was preserved, becoming mod. Eng. /eɪ/, so that the var. **Raper** is still common in Yorks., in spite of its obvious undesirable modern connotations.

2. French (Brittany): var. of ROBERT.

Vars. (of 1): **Rooper; Rope(s), Roop(e).**

Cogns. (of 1): Low Ger.: **R(i)eper; Rep(p), Reef.** Flem., Du.: **Reep(er); Reepmaeker.**

Equivs. (not cogn.): Ger.: SEILER. Czech: PROVAZNÍK.

A family by the name of Rooper *trace their descent in the male line from Robert de Fourneaux, who was living in the reign of Henry I (1100–35). Their surname became* Ro(o)per *on the marriage in 1428 of Richard Furneaux of Deighton, Yorks., to the heiress of a certain John Rooper of Derbys.*

Ropero Spanish: occupational name for a seller of clothes or for someone who was in charge of the working clothing held in common by a group of workers, from an agent deriv. of Sp. *ropa* clothes (of Gmc origin; the meaning was originally 'spoils', 'plunder'; cf. RÄUBER).

Rory Scots and Irish: Anglicized form of the Gael. personal name *Ruaidhrí*, originally composed of Celt. elements meaing 'red' (also 'powerful', 'mighty') and 'rule'.

Vars.: **Rorie**; ROGER.

Patrs.: **Rorison**; **McRo(o)ry**, **McRury**, **McCrory**, **McGrory**, MCCREERY (Gael. **Mac Ruaidhrí**).

Rosa 1. Italian and Catalan: cogn. of ROSE 1.

2. Polish and Czech: apparently from Pol., Czech *rosa* dew, perhaps applied as a nickname. However, in the Mazovian dial. of Polish *rosa* also means a cornflower, and the Pol. name may therefore be of topographic origin, while the Czech word also has other meanings, including waste from a mill or the outflow of a millstream. Moldanová suggests also that it may also be a short form of the given name *Rostislav*.

Vars.: Pol.: **Rosiak**, **Roszak**, **Rosicki**. Czech: **Rosák**.

Dims.: Pol.: **Roszczyk**. Czech: **Rosík**.

Habitation names: Pol.: **Roszkowski**; **Rosiński**.

Rosado Spanish and Portuguese: nickname for someone with a notably 'pink and white' complexion, from Sp., Port. *rosado* pink (LL *rosātus*, a deriv. of *rosa* ROSE).

Cogns.: Fr. **Rosé**, **Ro(u)zé**.

Rosal Spanish: topographic name for someone who lived by a rose bush, Sp. *rosal* (LL *rosāle*, a deriv. of *rosa* ROSE). There are numerous places named with this word, for example in the provinces of Granada, Huelva, Orense, and Pontevedra, and the surname may also derive from any of these.

Var.: **Rosales**.

Rosário Portuguese: religious byname from *rosário* rosary, given in particular to someone who was born on the festival of Our Lady of the Rosary, celebrated on the 1st Sunday in October. The word derives from LL *rosārium* rose garden (a deriv. of *rosa* ROSE), and was transferred to a set of devotions dedicated to the Virgin Mary as the result of the medieval symbolism which constantly compared her to a rose.

Roscoe English: habitation name from a place in Lancs., so called from ON *rá* roebuck (see RAY 2) + *scógr* copse (see SHAW).

Rose 1. English, French, and German: from the name of the flower, ME, OF *rose*, Ger. *Rose*, MHG *rose* (L *rosa*), in various applications. In part it is a topographic name for someone who lived at a place where wild roses grew. In a town, it can also be a house name from a house bearing the sign of the rose. It is also found, especially in Europe, as a nickname for a man with 'rosy' complexion. Latterly, in Scandinavia the cogns. were adopted as ornamental names.

2. English: from the medieval female given name *Rose*, *Royse*, popularly associated with the flower, but in fact originally from a Gmc personal name. This is recorded in Domesday Book in the form *Rothais*, and is apparently composed of the elements *hrōd* renown + *haid(is)* kind, sort.

3. Jewish (Ashkenazic): ornamental surname from the word for the flower (Ger. *Rose*, Yid. *royz*), or metronymic from the Yid. female given name *Royze*, derived from the word for the flower.

Vars. (of 1): Fr.: **Roze**, **Larose**, **Laroze**; **Roz** (Brittany; see also ROCH). (Of 2): Eng.: **Royse**, **Royce**. (Of 3): Jewish: **Rois(en)**, **Roiz**, **Roiz(i)n**, REISEN; ROSEMAN.

Cogns. (of 1): It.: **Rosa(s)**, **La Rosa**, **Rosi**. Sp., Port.: **Rosas**. Cat.: **Rosa**, **Larrosa**. Low Ger.: **Roos**. Flem., Du.: **(De) Roos**, **Roose**, **Rooze**. Swed.: **Ro(o)s**, **Rosell**, **Rosén**; **Ros(s)ander**. Pol. and Jewish (E Ashkenazic): **Różański**, **Różalski**; **Różycki** (also a habitation name from the town of *Rozhishche* (Pol. *Rożyszcze*) in the Ukraine; as a Jewish name, may be ornamental). Czech: **Růžička** (one of the commonest Czech surnames). Croatian: **Ružić** (patr.). Finn.: **Ruusa**. Hung.: **Rózsa**.

Dims. (of 1): Fr.: **Roset**, **Ro(u)zet**, **Rosin**; **Rozec** (Brittany). It.: **Rosell(in)i**, **Rosiello**, **Rosett(in)i**, **Rosina**, **Rosin(i)**, **Rosita**. Ger.: **Rösel**, **Rösle(n)**. Low Ger.: **Rösgen**. Czech: **Růžek**.

Augs. (of 1): It.: **Rosone**, **Roson(i)**.

Cpds (ornamental): Swed.: **Ros(en)berg** ('rose hill'); **Rosenblad(h)** ('rose leaf'); **Rosencran(t)z** ('rose wreath, rosary'); **Rosendahl** ('rose valley'); **Rosengren** ('rose branch'); **Ros(en)qvist** ('rose twig'). Jewish: **Rosenbaum**, **Rosenboim**, **Rosenbojm**, **Roizenbaum** ('rose tree'); **Rosenberg(er)**, **Rosenbarg**, **Reisenberg** ('(inhabitant of) rose hill'); **Rosenblatt**, **Rosenblat(h)** ('rose leaf'); **Rosenblum** (U.S. **Rosenbloom**; 'rose flower'); **Rosenbus(c)h** ('rose bush'); **Rosendorf** ('rose village'); **Rosenfarb** ('rose colour'); **Rosenfeld(er)** ('(inhabitant of) rose field', partly or completely Anglicized as **Rose(n)field**); **Rosenfrucht** ('rose fruit'); **Rosengart(en)** ('rose garden'); **Rosenhaupt** ('rose head'); **Rosenhaus** ('rose house'); **Rosenkran(t)z**, **Rosenkranc(e)** ('rose wreath'); **Rosensaft** ('rose juice'); **Rosenschein** (U.S. **Rosenshine**; 'rose shine'); **Rosens(h)tein**, **Reisenstein** ('rose stone'); **Rosenstengel** ('rose stem'); **Rosenstiel** ('rose stalk'); **Rosens(h)to(c)k** ('rose bush'); **Rosenshtrom** ('rose river'); **Rosent(h)al**, **Rosent(h)ol(er)** ('(inhabitant of) rose valley'); **Rosenwald** ('rose wood'); **Rosenwasser**, **Rosenvasser** ('rose water'); **Rosenzweig**, **Rosenzveig**, **Rosencwaig** ('rose twig').

Roselló Catalan: habitation name from a place in the province of Lérida or a region in S France (*Rousillon*). Both places first appear in the L form *Ruscino*, gen. *Ruscinōnis*. They are of pre-Roman origin and obscure meaning.

Var.: **Rosselló**.

Roseman 1. English: from the medieval female given name *Rosemunde*, apparently originally a Gmc cpd of the elements *hros* horse + *mund* protection, but early associated in the popular mind with the L phrase *rosa munda* pure rose, an epithet of the Virgin Mary.

2. Jewish (Ashkenazic): ornamental name or name adopted by the husband of a woman bearing the Yid. given name *Royze* (see ROSE 3).

Vars. (of 1): **Rosoman**; **Rosamond** (also Fr., and in London and elsewhere partly of Huguenot origin). (Of 2): **Rosemann**, **Roisman**, **Roizman**, **Royzman**; **Rosenman(n)** (the latter is probably only ornamental).

The earliest known bearer of this group of English surnames is Godfrey Rosamound, *whose will was proved in London in 1287. Family tradition has it that the surname is from a manor in Fulham that had belonged to Rosamond Clifford, but firm evidence is lacking.*

Roses Catalan: habitation name from a place in the province of Gerona, of uncertain etymology (it has been guessed to have some connection with the name of the Gk island of *Rhodes*, which is perhaps distantly related to ROSE 1).

Var.: **Rosas**.

Roseveare Cornish: habitation name from either of two places so called. The one in St Austell is so called from

Corn. *ros* moor + *mur* great, large; the other, in St Mawgan in Meneage, is from *res* ford + *mur*. In both cases, the initial *m*- of the adj. is mutated to *v*-.

Vars.: **Rosevear, Roseveer, Roseveor.**

Rosewall Cornish: habitation name from a place in the parish of Towednack, recorded in 1327 in the form *Ryswal*, from Corn. *res* ford + possibly *(g)wall* rampart.

Var.: **Rosewell.**

Roskilly Cornish: habitation name from a place in the parish of St Keverne, so called from Corn. *ros* moor + *kelly* grove.

Var.: **Roskelly.**

Ross 1. English and Scots (Norman): habitation name from *Rots* near Caen in Normandy, probably named with the Gmc element *rod* clearing; cf. RHODES. This was the original home of a family *de Ros*, who were established in Kent in 1130.

2. English and Scots: habitation name from any of various places called *Ross* or *Roos(e)*, deriving the name from W *rhós* upland or moorland, or from a Brit. ancestor of this word, which also had the sense 'promontory'. This is the sense of the cogn. Gael. word *ros*. Known sources of the surname include *Roos* in E Yorks (now Humberside) and the region of N Scotland known as *Ross*, part of the former county of Ross and Cromarty. Other possible sources are *Ross*-on-Wye in Herefords., *Ross* in Northumb. (which is on a promontory), and *Roose* in Lancs.

3. English and German: from the Gmc personal name *Rozzo*, a short form of the various cpd names with the first element *hrōd* renown, introduced into England by the Normans in the form *Roce*.

4. German: metonymic occupational name for a breeder or keeper of horses, from S Ger. *Ross* horse (MHG *ros*, OHG *hros*), perhaps also a nickname for someone thought to resemble a horse or a house name for someone who lived at a house distinguished by the sign of a horse.

5. Jewish (Ashkenazic): in some cases, of the same origin as in 4, in others an Anglicization of any of the Jewish surnames listed at ROSE.

Vars. (of 2): **Roos(e).**

Cogns. (of 4): Jewish (Ashkenazic): **Ros(s)man, Rossler, Ros(s)ner** (occupational names); **Rosswald** ('horse wood', an ornamental cpd).

The name Ross *was taken to Scotland from Yorks. in the 12th cent., when large territories in Ayrs. were held by a family* de Ros, *who were apparently so called from the place in Yorks. They are distinct from the family descended from the lairds of Balnagown, who adopted the surname* Ross *after the earldom of Ross (to which they considered themselves rightful heirs) had passed into other hands through the female line.*

Rossall English: habitation name from *Rossall* in Lancs. and Shrops, so called from OE *hros*, *hors* horse + *halh* nook, recess (see HALE 1).

Rossignol French: nickname for a person with a good singing voice, or ironically for a raucous person, from OF *rossignol* nightingale (OProv. *rossinhol*, from LL *lusciniōlus*, class. L *lusciniōla*, dim. of *luscinia*).

Vars.: **Roussignol, Rossignon, Rossigneux.**

Cogns.: Cat.: **Russinyol, Rusiñol.** It.: **Rosignuoli, Usignuolo, Lisignoli.**

Rossington English: habitation name from a place in W Yorks., apparently named in OE as *Rosingtūn* 'enclosure, settlement associated with a moor' (the first element being akin to W *rhôs* moor, heath).

Rostaing French: from a Gmc personal name composed of the elements *hrōd* renown + *stān* stone.

Vars.: **Roustaing, Ro(u)stang, Rostand, Roustan.**

Rostropovich Belorussian: patr. from the nickname *Rastrop* 'Shock-headed person'; the vowel of the first syllable has been hypercorrected under Russ. influence, since in that language unaccented *o* is pronounced as *a*.

Rotgerber German and Jewish (Ashkenazic): occupational name for someone who dressed leather with tannin (cf. BARKER 1 and TANNER 1), as opposed to using alum salts (cf. WEISSGERBER and WHITTIER). The word is a cpd of Ger. *rot* red (see ROTH 1) + GERBER.

Roth 1. German and Jewish (Ashkenazic): nickname for a person with red hair, from Ger. *rot* red (MHG, OHG *rōt*; a cogn. of READ 1). As a Jewish surname it is also at least partly ornamental: its frequency as a Jewish surname is disproportionate to the number of Jews who one may reasonably assume were red-headed during the period of surname adoption.

2. German and English: topographic name for someone who lived in a clearing; see RHODES.

3. German: from a short form of any of the various Gmc personal names with the first element *hrōd* reknown; cf. RODE 1 and ROSS 3.

Vars. (of 1): Ger.: **Rothe, Rother(t).** Jewish: **Rot(er); Roit(er), Royter** (from Yid. *royt*), **Rojter** (Pol. spelling); **Rot(h)man(n), Rottmann, Rot(t)erman, Roitman; Reitman** (from the NE Yid. pronunciation of Yid. *royt* red); **Redman** (Anglicized); **Rothmensch, Rotmensh, Rotmench; Rotmensz** (Pol. spelling). See also ROTHMANN.

Cogns. (of 1 and 2): Dan., Norw.: RODE. (Of 1 only): Du.: **Rood(e), De Roo.**

Dims. (of 1): Ger.: **Röthel, Rethel, Röthlein.** Low Ger.: **Rötchen.**

Cpds (of cogns. of 1, ornamental except where otherwise stated): Jewish: **Rotapel** ('red apple'); **Rot(er)band** ('red ribbon'); **Rotbart(h), Rotbard, Reitbard, Reitbord** ('red beard', nickname); **Rotbaum** ('red tree'); **Rotblat, Reitblatt** ('red leaf'); **Ro(i)tblit** ('red blossom'); **Rotblum** ('red flower'); **Rotfarb** ('red colour'); **Rot(h)feld, Rottfeld** ('red field'); **Rotgold** ('red gold'); **Rotholz, Rotgolz** ('red wood'); **Rotkirch** ('red church', probably topographic); **Rot(h)kopf, Roitkof** ('red head', nickname); **Rotleder** ('red leather', perhaps ornamental-occupational); **Rotermund** ('red mouth', perhaps nickname or anecdotal); **Rotrubin** ('red ruby'); **Rot(h)stein, Rotshtein, Rotsztein, Rotsztejn** ('red stone'); **Rotwald** ('red forest').

Rothenberg Jewish (Ashkenazic): habitation name from a place so called in W Bavaria, or possibly from some other place similarly named, e.g. one in Upper Lusatia in East Germany. The placename is from OHG *rōt* red (with the weak dat. ending *-en*, originally used after a preposition and def. art.) + *Berg* hill.

Vars. (also merely ornamental, composed of the elements *rot* red + *berg* hill): **Rot(t)enberg, Rut(t)enberg; Routenberg** (Fr. spelling); **Rothenberger; Rothberg, Rutberg; Reitberg(er)** (from the NE Yid. pronunciation of Yid. *royt* red).

Rotherham English: habitation name from the town in S Yorks., so called from the ancient Brit. river name *Rother* (of obscure meaning) + OE *hām* homestead.

Var.: **Rotheram.**

Rothmann German: 1. var. of ROTH, in any of its senses.

2. (in Saxony and Silesia) occupational name for a counsellor or nickname for a man respected for his opinions and advice, from a dial. var. of Ger. *Rat* counsel (MHG *rāt*) + *Mann* man.

Cogns. (of 1): Low Ger.: **Roodman**, **Rudmann** ('red man'). (Of 2): Ger.: **Rathmann**.

Rothschild Jewish (Ashkenazic): house name from a house distinguished with a red sign (see ROTH 1 and SCHILD 2). The famous banking family of this name took it from a house so marked in the Jewish quarter of Frankfurt-am-Main, but the name has also been adopted by many Ashkenazic Jews unrelated to the family. In Britain the surname is normally given the spelling pronunciation /ˈrɒθstʃaɪld/; the original pronunciation is /ˈroːtʃɪlt/.

Vars.: **Rotschild**; **Rothchild** (U.S.).

The Rothschild *dynasty of bankers was founded by Meyer Amschel Rothschild (1744–1812). He abandoned his original intention to become a rabbi after his father's early death, and became a factor to the Landgrave of Hesse-Kassel. His five sons established branches of the banking business, and of the family, in several European countries. They were made barons of the Austrian Empire; successive generations in Britain produced the first practising Jew to sit in Parliament and the first to be raised to the peerage.*

Rothwell English: habitation name from any of the places, in Lincs., Northants, N Yorks., and elsewhere, so called from OE **roð(u)* clearing (a byform of *rod*; cf. RHODES) + *well(a)* spring, stream (see WELL).

Var.: ROWELL (representing the local pronunciation of the place in Northants).

Roubíček Czech and Jewish (Ashkenazic): nickname for a cringing person, from a dim. of the vocab. word *roub* graft, binding (cf. the expression *svázat do roubu* to bind someone's arms and legs), akin to the verb *roubat* to cut.

Rouček Czech (Moravian): nickname for someone with a deformed or missing hand, from the vocab. word *roučka* handle.

Round English (chiefly W Midlands): nickname for a plump person, from ME, OF *rond*, *rund* fat, round (L *rotundus*, a deriv. of *rotāre* turn, from *rota* wheel; cf. RODE 3).

Cogns.: Fr.: **Rond**, **Lerond**. Prov.: **Redon**. Sp.: **Redondo**. Cat.: **Rodon**. Du.: **De Rond**, **(De) Ronde**.

Dims.: Eng.: **Roundell**, RUNDLE. Fr.: **Rondel**, **Lerondel**, **Rondeau**, **Lerondeau**, **Rond(el)et**, **Rondot**, **Rondou**. Prov.: **Redondet**, **Redon(n)et**, **Redondin**.

Patrs.: Eng.: **Rounds**, **Rounce**.

The first known bearer of the surname Rounce *is recorded in 1319 at Haveringsand, Norfolk. It is still most common in Norfolk and Suffolk.*

Rourke Irish: Anglicized form of the Gael. personal name *Ruarc*, perhaps from *ruarc* heavy shower of rain.

Var.: **Rorke**.

Patrs.: **Groarke** (Gael. **Mac Ruiarc**).

'Descendant of R.': **O'Ro(u)rke**, **O'Ro(w)warke** (Gael. **Ó Ruairc**).

Rouse English: nickname for a person with red hair, from ME, OF *rous* red(-haired) (L *russ(e)us*). For Slav. cogns., see RUDAKOV.

Vars.: **Rous**, **Rowse**, **Russ**.

Cogns.: Fr.: **Rous**, **Roux**, **Leroux**; **(Le) Rouz** (Brittany); **Larousse** (fem.). It.: **Rossi**, **Rosso**; **Russi**, **(Lo) Russo** (S Italy); **Ru(gg)iu**, **Ruju** (Sardinia). Sp.: **Rojo**. Cat.: **Ros** (but with the sense 'blond', 'fair'). Rum.: **Rusu**. Flem., Du.: **De Rosse**. Jewish (Sefardic): **Russo**.

Dims.: Eng.: RUSSELL (which also see for further Eng., Fr., and It. dims.). Fr.: **Ro(u)sset**, **Rossey**, **Roussin(eau)**, **Roussy**, **Rosson**, **Roussot**; **(Le) Rouzic**, **Rousic** (Brittany). It.: **Rossett(in)i**, **Rossett(o)**, **Rossitti**, **Rossitto**, **Russetti**, **Rossin(i)**, **Rossino**, **Russino**, **Rossotti**, **Rossotto**, **Russotti**, **Russotto**.

Augs.: It.: **Rosson(i)**, **Rossone**.

Patrs.: Fr.: **Auroux**. It.: **De Rossi** (partly Jewish; reasons for adoption unclear); **Del Rosso**, **De Russi**.

Gabriele Rossetti *(1783–1854) was an Italian refugee in England who had a number of remarkable children; Dante Gabriel (1828–82), the poet and painter, Michael (1829–1919), a founder of the Pre-Raphaelite Brotherhood, and Christina (1830–94), also a poet. Their father, born in Vasto, was an opera librettist who was sentenced to death for his revolutionary activities and became a professor of English at King's College, London.*

Rout English (now chiefly E Anglia): probably a topographic name for someone who lived by a patch of rough ground, from a hypothetical OE word **rū(we)t* or *rūhet*, derivs. of *rūh* rough, overgrown; cf. RAUCH. There are places called *Ruffet(t)* in Surrey and Sussex which are thought to have this origin.

Routledge English and Scots: of uncertain origin. If it is a habitation name, the location and etymology of the place from which it derives are obscure. The name is found mainly on the English/Scottish borders. The place in Cumb. now called *Routledge* Burn seems to have received its name in the 16th cent. from a member of the family rather than vice versa.

Vars.: **Rutledge**, **Rudledge**, **Rookledge**, **Rucklidge**.

Rouvre Provençal: topographic name for someone who lived by a notable oak tree or in an oak forest, from OProv. *rouvre* oak (L *robur*; cf. ROBUSTI).

Vars.: **Roure**, **Durou(v)re**, **Delroure**.

Cogns.: It.: **(Della) Rovere**, **Roveri**, **Rever**, **Rua**. Sp.: **Robles**. Cat.: **Roura**, **Roure**.

Dims.: Fr.: **Rouvreau**, **Rouvet**, **Rouveix**.

Collectives: Fr.: **Rouvroy**, **Rouvray**, **Rouvrais**, **Rouvière**, **Rouveyre**. Sp.: **Robledo**, **Robredo**. Cat.: **Rovira**.

Rover English: 1. occupational name for someone who constructed or repaired roofs, from an agent deriv. of ME *roof* (OE *hrōf*). In the Middle Ages roofs might be thatched with reeds or straw, or covered with tiles, slates, or wooden shingles.

2. nickname for an unscrupulous individual, from ME *rover* pirate, robber (from MLG *rōver*; cf. RÄUBER). The verb *rove* to wander is probably a back-formation from this, and is not attested before the 16th cent., so it is unlikely to lie behind any examples of the surname.

Var. (of 1): **Ruffer**.

Rowbottom English: topographic name for someone living in an overgrown valley, from OE *rūh* rough, overgrown (cf. RAUCH) + *boðm* valley (see BOTTOM). The surname is now most common in Lancs., but does not seem to be found there before 1500. The surname may be a habitation name from an unidentified place so called.

Vars.: **Robottom**, **R(o)ubottom**, **Rowbottam**, **Roobottam**, **Rowbotham**, **Roebotham**, **Robatham**, **Robathan**.

Rowden English: habitation name from a place near Hereford, so called from OE *rūh* rough, overgrown (cf. RAUCH) + *dūn* hill (see DOWN 1).

Rowe English: 1. topographic name for someone who lived by a hedgerow or in a row of houses built next to one another, from ME *row* (Northern ME *raw*, from OE *rāw*).

2. from the medieval given name *Row*, a var. of *Rou(l)* (see ROLLO) or a short form of ROWLAND.

Vars.: **Row**. (Of 1 only): RAW; **Rew**, RUE (from the OE byform *rǣw*).

Dims. (of 2): ROWELL, ROWETT.

Patrs. (from 2): **Rowes**, **Rowson**.

Rowell English: 1. habitation name, a var. of ROTHWELL.
2. habitation name from a place in Devon, so called from OE *rūh* rough, overgrown (cf. RAUCH) + *hyll* HILL.
3. from a medieval given name, a dim. of ROWE 2.

Rowett English: from a medieval given name composed of the Gmc elements *hrōd* renown + *wald* rule, which was introduced into England by Scandinavian settlers in the form *Hróaldr*, and again later by the Normans in the form *Ro(h)ald*. This name has absorbed a much rarer one with the second element *hard* hardy, brave, strong, which was introduced into England by the Normans in the form *Ro(h)ard*. It has also sometimes been used a dim. of ROWE 2, itself both a var. of ROLLO and a short form of ROWLAND.

Vars.: **Rowet, Rowat(t)**.

Rowland English: 1. from *Rol(l)ant*, a Norman personal name composed of the Gmc elements *hrōd* renown + *land* land, territory. This was popular throughout Europe in the Middle Ages as a result of the fame of Charlemagne's warrior of this name, who was killed at Roncesvalles in AD 778.
2. habitation name from places in Derbys. and Sussex, so called from ON *rá* roebuck (see RAY 2) + *lundr* wood, grove (see LUND).

Vars.: **Rol(l)and**.

Cogns. (of 1): Fr.: **Ro(u)l(l)and, Rollant, Rollang**. It.: **Rolandi, Rolendi; Orlando, Orlandi**. Sp.: **Roldán**. Ger.: **Roland, Ru(h)land**. Hung.: **Loránd, Lóránt**.

Dims. (of 1): Fr.: **Rolandeau, Relandeau**. It.: **Rolandino; Orlandini, Orlandelli, Orlanducci**.

Aug.: It.: **Orlandoni**.

Patrs.: Eng.: **Rowlands, Rolance, Rollons; Rowlandson, Ro(w)nson**. Flem., Du.: **Roeland(t)s**.

Rowley English: habitation name from any of the various places, in Devon, Co. Durham, Staffs., and Yorks., so called from OE *rūh* rough, overgrown (cf. RAUCH)+ *lēah* wood, clearing.

Var.: **Roughley** (Lancs.).

A family of this name trace their descent from William de Roulowe, *whose name is found in the rolls of the guild of Shrops. merchants in 1252.*

Rowney 1. English: habitation name from a place in Herts. so called from OE *rūh* rough, overgrown (with the remains of the weak dat. ending *-en*, originally used after a preposition and def. art.) + *(ge)hæg* enclosure (see HAY 1), or from various other minor places of the same origin.
2. Irish: Anglicized form of Gael. *Ó Ruanaidh*; see ROONEY.

Rowntree English: topographic name for someone who lived by a rowan or mountain ash, from ME *rown* (ON *rogn*) + *tree* (OE *trēow*).

Vars.: **Roun(d)tree; Rowen**.

Cogn.: Swed.: **Rönn** (probably ornamental rather than topographic).

Cpds (ornamental): Swed.: **Rönnberg(h)** ('rowan hill'); **Rönnqvist** ('rowan twig').

A Quaker family of this name have long been prominent in the affairs of the city of York. Joseph Rowntree *(1801–59), who with his son Joseph (1836–1925) built up a prosperous grocery business, founded two well-known schools there. The family became involved in the cocoa trade in 1862 and set up a sweet factory, earning a reputation as enlightened employers.*

Roxburgh Scots: habitation name from a place near Kelso, so called from the gen. case of the OE byname *Hrōc* 'ROOK' + OE *burh* fort, manor (see BURY).

Roy 1. Scots: nickname for a person with red hair, from Gael. *ruadh* red (ultimately cogn. with READ 1, ROTH 1, RUDAKOV, and RUDD).
2. English (Norman): var. of RAY 1.
3. French: cogn. of RAY 1.

Royle English (chiefly Lancs.): habitation name from a place in Lancs., so called from OE *rā* roe deer (see RAY 2) + *hyll* HILL.

Vars.: **Royal(l); Ryal(l), Ryle, Ryhill** (also in part from places such as *Ryal* and *Ryle* in Northumb. and *Ryhill* in Humberside and W Yorks., so called from OE *ryge* RYE + *hyll*).

Royston English: 1. habitation name from a place in Herts., recorded in 1262 as *Croyroys*, from OF *croiz* cross (L *crux*, gen. *crucis*) + the female given name *Royse* (see ROSE 2). Ekwall mentions forms from only twenty years later in which the placename first more or less assumes its modern form. It is not clear, however, whether this is to be interpreted as 'Royse's stone' (with the second element ME *stōn*, from OE *stān*) or 'settlement at (Croiz) Royse' (with the second element ME *toun*, from OE *tūn*).
2. habitation name from a place in W Yorks., so called from the gen. case of the OE byname *Hrōr* 'Vigorous' (or its ON cogn. *Róarr*) + OE *tūn* enclosure, settlement.
3. Jewish (Ashkenazic): presumably an Anglicization of one or more like-sounding Jewish surnames.

Rozas Spanish: habitation name from any of various places so called, from the pl. form of Sp. *roza* cleared land ready for ploughing (from *rozar* to clear, plough, LL *ruptiāre*, from the past part. *ruptus* of class. L *rumpere* to break).

Rozdestvenski Russian: surname adopted by members of the Orthodox clergy in honour of the feast of Christmas, Russ. *rozdestvo* (from *roditsya* to be born).

Var.: **Rozestvenski**.

Rozwadowski Polish: habitation name from the town of *Rozwadów* in SE Poland.

Ruane Irish: Anglicized form of Gael. **Ó Ruadháin** 'descendant of *Ruadhán*', a personal name from a dim. of *ruadh* red (cf. ROY 1).

Vars.: **O'Ruane, O'Rowane, (O')Roan, Ro(u)ane, Rowan**, ROHAN, **Rewan, Royan, Raun, Roon**.

Ruano Spanish: 1. occupational name for a common soldier, OSp. *ruano* (apparently a deriv. of *ru(g)a* street (see RUE 1), perhaps because such soldiers were recruited in the street).
2. nickname for someone with reddish hair, from Sp. *roano*, *ruano* reddish, roan (apparently from a Goth. cogn. of READ 1 and ROTH 1).

Rubbra English: habitation name from any of various places, such as *Roborough* in Devon, *Rowberrow* and *Ruborough* Hill in Somerset, *Rubery* near Birmingham, and *Rowborough* in the Isle of Wight, named from OE *rūh* rough, overgrown + *beorg* hill.

Vars.: **Ribra, Ruber(r)y, Rowb(er)ry, Rowbury**.

Rübel German: metonymic occupational name for a cultivator of rape, grown for use as a fodder crop and for the oil obtained from its seeds. The name represents a dim. form of MHG *ruobe* (L *rāpum*; cf. RAPA and RAVEL). It is possible that the surname may in some cases derive from a nickname given with reference to the bright yellow flowers or unpleasant smell of the plant.

Rublyov Russian: patr. from the nickname *Rubl* 'Rouble', a unit of currency, denoting someone who payed a rent or tax of this amount, or acquired for some more anecdotal reason. The etymology of the word is uncertain: it may be a deriv. of *rubit* to chop, hack, and so may mean 'portion', 'fraction', but others have connected it with the Indian *rupee*, from Skt *rūpya* wrought silver.

Cogn.: Jewish (Ashkenazic): **Rubel** (reason for adoption unknown; cf. GREITZER and *Fenig* at PENNY).

Rudakov Russian: patr. from the nickname *Rudak* 'Red-haired man' (from *rudy* red(-haired), akin to *ruda* ore; cf. READ 1, ROTH 1, and RUDD 1).

Cogns.: Ukr.: **Rudy**. Pol.: **Ruda**, **Rudniak**, **Rudzki**.

Dims.: Ukr.: **Rudeiko**, **Rudenko**. Beloruss.: **Rudzko**, **Rudyonok**; **Rudzevich** (patr.).

Habitation names: Pol.: **Rudnicki**; **Rudziński** (from the town of *Rudnik* in SE Poland, or from some other place similarly named with the Slav. word *rudy* red).

Rudd 1. English: nickname for a person with red hair or a ruddy complexion, from ME *rudde*, OE *rud(ig)* red, ruddy.

2. Jewish (Ashkenazic): Anglicized, shortened form of various surnames beginning with the syllable *Rud-*.

Vars. (of 1): **Ruddy**, **Rudman**.

Dims. (of 1): **Rudkin**, **Rudling**.

Ruddock English: nickname from the robin, ME *ruddock* (OE *ruddoc*, *rudduc*, a dim. of *rud(ig)* red; cf. RUDD 1).

Var.: **Ruddick** (Northumb.).

Rudge English (W Midlands): 1. topographic name from West Midland ME *rugge*, a var. of *rigge* RIDGE, or habitation name from the village of *Rudge* in Shrops., which is named with this element.

2. from a medieval given name, a dim. of ROGER.

3. nickname for a person with red hair or a ruddy complexion, from OF *r(o)uge* red (L *rubeus*).

Var. (of 3): **Lerouge**.

Cogns. (of 3): Fr.: **Rouge**. Prov.: **Rouy**. Sp.: **Rubio**, **Rubia** ('blond'); **Royo**. Cat.: **Roig**. Port.: **Ruivo**.

Dims. (of 3): Fr.: **Rouget(et)**, **Rougeau(x)**, **Rougeot**, **Roujon**, **Roujou**.

Patr. (from 2) (dim.): Eng.: **Ruggles**.

Rue 1. French: topographic name for someone who lived on a track or pathway, OF *rue* (L *rūga* crease, fold).

2. English: var. of *Rew*; see ROWE 1.

Vars. (of 1): Fr.: **Larue**, **De(la)rue**, **Delrue**, **Desrues**.

Ruffin French: from a personal name (L *Rūfinus*, a deriv. of *Rūfus*; see RUFFO 1), borne and popularized by various minor early saints, including a 3rd-cent. martyr of Soissons and a 4th-cent. Church Father.

Var.: **Rufin**.

Cogns.: It.: **Ruf(f)ini**, **Ruf(f)ino**.

Dim.: It.: **Ruffinelli**.

Aug.: It.: **Ruffinoni**.

Ruffo S Italian: 1. from a personal name (L *Rūfus*, originally a nickname for someone with red hair, from a byform of *rubeus* (see RUDGE 3), taken from another Italic dialect). This name was borne by various minor early saints, and occasionally used as a given name in the Middle Ages.

2. from a personal name of Gmc origin but uncertain form and meaning. The Calabrian noble family of this name are said to have come to S Italy with the Normans.

Var.: **Ruffi**.

Cogn. (of 1): Sp.: **Rufo** (also a nickname).

Dims.: It.: **Ruf(f)olo**, **Ruffoli**.

Rule 1. English: from a medieval given name, a var. of *Rou(l)*; see ROLLO.

2. Scots: habitation name from a place in the former county of Roxburghs., so called from the stream on which it stands. This name is of uncertain origin, possibly cogn. with W *rhull* hasty, rash.

Rumbelow English: habitation name from any of two or three minor localities originally named with OE *þrēom* (dat. of *þrēo* three) + *hlǣwum* (dat. pl. of *hlǣw* hill, tumulus (see LAW 2)), i.e. 'at the three tumuli'. The word *rumbelow* is attested from the 14th cent. as a meaningless combination of syllables sung by sailors to keep time while rowing, and the surname used to be thought to be a generic name for a sailor, but Reaney has produced convincing evidence in favour of the local-name hypothesis; a certain Richard *Thrimelowe* (1334) lived in Aston (Birmingham), where there is a locality called *the Rumbelow*.

Vars.: **Rumbellow**, **Rombulow**.

Rumbold English: from the Norman personal name *Rumbald*, composed of the Gmc elements *rūm* wide, spacious (or, more plausibly, a byform of *hrūm* renown) + *bold* bold, brave.

Vars.: **Rumbolt**, **Rumbol(l)**, **Rumball**, **Rumbell**, **Rumble**, **Rumpole**.

Cogns.: Fr.: **Romboud**, **Rombaut**, **Rombeau**. Ger.: **Rumpold**, **Rumpel(t)**.

Patrs.: Eng.: **Rumbles**. Ger.: **Rumpler**, **Rümpler**, **Rimpler**. Flem.: **Rombouts**; **Boudts**.

Rump English: nickname for a person with a large behind, from OE *rumpe* buttocks. Despite the faintly obscene or derogatory connotations of the vocab. word, the surname survives in Norfolk.

Rumsey English: habitation name from *Romsey* in Hants, so called from the gen. case of the OE personal name *Rūm* (a short form of cpd names with the first element *rūm*) + OE *ēg* island, dry land in a fen.

Vars.: **Romsey**, **Romsay**, **Rumsay**.

Runacres English: topographic name for someone who lived by a field where rye was grown, from OE *rygen*, an adj. deriv. of *ryge* RYE + *æcer* cultivated land (see ACKER). *Renacres* near Liverpool (*Runacres* in 1284) is a possible source.

Vars.: **Runnacles**, **Runicles**, **Runagle**, **Runnagall**.

Rundle English (Devon and Cornwall): 1. nickname, a dim. of ROUND.

2. habitation name from *Rundale* in the parish of Shoreham, Kent, so called from OE *rūm(ig)* roomy, spacious + *dæl* valley.

Vars.: **Rundell**, **Rundall**.

Runge German: from MHG *runge* staff, stick (OHG *runga*). The precise sense of the surname is not clear, but the vocab. word was used in particular of the handle by which a horse-drawn waggon was led by someone walking beside it; thus it is possibly a metonymic occupational name for a carter.

Ruotsalainen Finnish: name for a Swedish-speaker or someone from Sweden, from Finn. *ruotsalainen* Swede, from *Ruotsala* Sweden + *-ainen* locative suffix.

Rusakov Russian: 1. patr. from the name *Rusak* (Great) Russian. The name derives ultimately from a Scandinavian term meaning 'rower', 'oarsman', the Russian state having been first established in the 9th cent. by Varangian (i.e. Norse) settlers who rowed up the rivers from the Baltic.

2. patr. from the nickname *Rusak*, a deriv. of *rusi* light brown (akin to the vocab. words that lie behind RUDAKOV and RYZHAKOV).

Var. (of 1): **Rusinov**.

Cogns. (of 1): Pol.: **Ruszczak**; **Rusiecki**. Czech: **Rus**. Croatian: **Rosić** (patr.). Jewish (E Ashkenazic): **Rus(s)ak**. Rum.: **Russesco** (patr.). Ger.: REUSS. Flem., Du.: **Rus(man)**. Hung.: **Orosz** (via Turkic *urus*).

Dims. (of 1): Pol.: **Rusek, Ruszczyk, Rusin**. Czech: **Rusek**.

Patrs. (from dims. of 1): Pol.: **Ruszkiewicz, Rusinkiewicz**.

Habitation names (from dims. of 1): Pol.: **Ruszkowski, Ruszczyński**.

Rush 1. English: topographic name for someone who lived near a clump of rushes, from ME *rush* (a collective sing., OE *rysc*).

2. Irish: Anglicized form of Gael. **Ó Ruis** 'descendant of *Ros*', a personal name perhaps from *ros* wood. In S and SW Ulster it has also been used as a translation of *Ó Fuada* (see FOODY), and in Connaught for *Ó Luachra* (see LOUGHREY).

Vars. (of 1): **Rusher, Rischer**.

Cogns. (of 1): Ger.: **Risch(e)**. Low Ger.: **Röschen, Röschmann**. Flem., Du.: **Ruys**.

Rushforth English (W Yorks.): habitation name from an unidentified place, possibly *Rushford* in Devon, Norfolk, or Warwicks. However, in view of the distribution of the surname, a more likely source is *Ryshworth* in Bingley, W Yorks., which was earlier called *Rushford* (from OE *rysc* rushes + *ford* FORD).

Var.: **Rushfirth**.

Rushmer English (E Anglia): habitation name from *Rushmere* in Suffolk, near Lowestoft, so called from OE *rysc* rushes + *mere* pond, lake.

Var.: **Rushmere**.

Rushton English: habitation name from any of the various places, for example in Ches., Northants, and Staffs., so called from OE *rysc* rushes + *tūn* enclosure, settlement.

Rushworth English (W Yorks.): habitation name from *Rishworth* in W Yorks., so called from OE *rysc* rushes + *worð* enclosure (see WORTH).

Rusk Scots: of uncertain origin, probably a topographic name from the Gael. element *riasg* marsh, bog.

Var.: **Risk**.

Ruskin 1. English: probably a dim. of the medieval given name ROSE 2.

2. Scots: occupational name for a tanner, from Gael. *rusg(aire)an*, dim. form of *rusgaire* peeler (of bark).

Russell English, Scots, and Irish: from *Rousel*, a common ANF nickname for someone with red hair, representing a dim. of ROUSE with the hypocoristic suffix *-el*.

Vars.: **Russel, Rous(s)el(l), Rowsell, Russill**.

Cogns.: Fr.: **Roussel, Rouxel, Leroussel, Rousseau(x), Lerousseau**. It.: **Rosselli, Rossi(e)llo, Russello**. Cat.: **Ros(s)ell**.

Dims.: Fr.: **Rouselet, Rousselin, Rousselot**. It.: **Rossellini**.

Patrs.: Fr.: **Aurousseau**. Flem.: **Rosseels**.

Russell *is the name of a prominent English family, originally established in Dorset. Their earliest recorded ancestor was Stephen Russell, bailiff of Weymouth in 1388, who is also known to have owned property in Dorchester. Henry Russell was a merchant in the Bordeaux wine trade in the 15th cent. The family rose to prominence with his great-grandson, John Russell* (c.*1486–1555*), *who attracted the notice of Henry VIII when he accompanied the shipwrecked King of Castile to court. He was eventually created Earl of Bedford by Edward VI. Other titles acquired by his descendants include Duke of Bedford, Marquess of Tavistock, and Earl Russell. The 3rd Earl Russell is better known as the philosopher Bertrand Russell (1872–1970).*

Another Dorset family called Russell held Kingston Russel in 1212, and later (1551) acquired lands in Devon. The Jack Russell terrier is named after a member of this family, a famous hunting parson, who bred the dog. He was born in Dartmouth in 1795, and was still hunting until a few years before his death in 1883.

Rust English (chiefly E Anglia) and Scots: nickname for someone with red hair or a ruddy complexion, from OE *rūst* rust (from a Gmc root meaning 'red'; cf. READ 1 and ROTH 1).

Ruston English: habitation name from any of the various places so called, for example in Norfolk, N Yorks., and Humberside. The two villages of this name in Norfolk are recorded in Domesday Book as *Ristuna*, and are from OE *hrīs* brushwood + *tūn* enclosure, settlement; *Ruston* Parva in Humberside appears in Domesday Book as *Roreston*, from the gen. case of the ON byname *Hrór* 'Vigorous' + OE *tūn*; *Ruston* in N Yorks. is *Rostune* in Domesday Book, apparently from OE *hrōst* roost, roof + *tūn*, referring to a building with an unusual roof.

Rutecki Polish: topographic name for someone who lived by a patch of rue, Pol. *ruta* (L *rūta*).

Vars.: **Ruta**.

Habitation name: **Ruciński**.

Ruth English: nickname for a charitable person, or for a wretched one, from ME *reuthe* pity (a deriv. of *rewen* to pity, OE *hrēowan*). The given name *Ruth* was little used in the Middle Ages among non-Jews, and is unlikely to have had any influence on the surname.

Cogn.: Du.: **Rouw**.

Rutherford Scots: habitation name from a place in the Scottish Borders near Roxburgh, so called from OE *hryðer* cattle + *ford* FORD. There is another place of the same name and etymology in N Yorks., but this does not seem to have contributed to the surname, which is principally found in the Borders and Lowlands of Scotland.

Vars.: **Rutherfoord, Rutherfurd, Rutterford, Rotherforth, Ruddiforth, Rudeforth**.

Ruthven Scots: habitation name, traditionally pronounced /'ri:vən/, from various places in Scotland, esp. one near Coldstream in the Borders region, and one near Perth. There are two possible etymologies: from ON *rauðr* red + *fen* fen, marsh, or from Gael. *ruadh* red + *abhuinn* river.

Ruthven *is the name of a Scottish family who trace their ancestry to Thor, the Scandinavian overlord of an area of Clydesdale, whose name is recorded in charters dating from between 1127 and 1150. The surname in this case is derived from a barony near Perth, granted by William I of Scotland (1165–1214); it was assumed around 1234 by Sir Walter of Ruthven. The family was granted the earldom of Gowrie, but because of what became known as 'the Gowrie Conspiracy' the title was forfeited and from 1600 to 1641 the surname itself was proscribed. The title was later restored to the family, and the present Earl of Gowrie bears the surname* Ruthven.

Rutkowski Polish: habitation name from a village called *Rutki*, which according to Rospond is derived from the personal name *Rudek*. This is either a byname meaning 'Red-haired' (see RUDAKOV), or a short form of a cpd personal name with *rudy* red as its first element.

Patr. (from *Rudek*): **Rutkiewicz**.

Rutland English: regional name from the former English county of this name, so called from the OE byname *Rōta* (from *rōt* cheerful, glad; see ROOT 1) + *land* land, territory.

Rutter English: 1. occupational name for a player on the rote; see ROOT 2.

2. nickname for an unscrupulous person, from OF *ro(u)-tier* robber, highwayman, footpad (see REUTER 2).

Cogns. (of 1): Fr.: **Rot(t)ier**. Ger.: **Rotter**.

Ruysdael Dutch: habitation name from a minor place, so called from MDu. *ruis* rush + *dal* valley.

Var.: **Ruisdael**.

Ryan Irish (one of the commonest surnames in Ireland): 1. simplified form of MULRYAN. The surname from this source is particularly common in Tipperary.

2. Anglicized form of Gael. **Ó Riain** 'descendant of *Rian* or *Riaghan*', a personal name of uncertain origin. There has been considerable confusion with REGAN.

Vars.: **O'Ryan**, **Rian**.

Ryba Polish, Czech, and Jewish (E Ashkenazic): metonymic occupational name, nickname, or ornamental name from the Slav. term *ryba* fish. As an occupational name it may have denoted a fisherman (cf. RYBAK) or a seller of fish. As a nickname it may have been bestowed on account of some fancied physical resemblance to a fish.

Vars.: Pol.: **Rybicki**. Czech: **Rybín**, **Rybka**. Jewish: **Riba**, **Ryb(icki)**.

Cogns.: Ger. (of Slav. origin): **Riebe**, **Reibe**.

Dims.: Ger. (of Slav. origin): **Reibke**, **Riebisch**, **Reibisch**.

Patrs.: Pol.: **Rybowicz**. Russ.: **Rybin**.

Patr. (from a dim.): Russ.: **Ryb(ush)kin**.

Habitation names: Pol.: **Rybiński**, **Rybczyński**.

Rybak Polish, Ukrainian, and Jewish (E Ashkenazic): occupational name for a fisherman, an agent deriv. of RYBA fish.

Vars.: Pol.: **Rybarz**. Jewish: **Riba(c)k**.

Cogns.: Czech: **Rybář**, **Rybák**. Croatian: **Ribar**. Ger. (of Slav. origin): **Ribback**, **Ribbeck**, **Ribach**; **Rieban(d)**, **Reiban(d)**.

Dims.: Pol.: **Rybarczyk**, **Rybiałek**. Ukr.: **Rybal(chen)ko**.

Patrs.: Pol.: **Ryba(r)kiewicz**. Ukr.: **Rybalka**. Jewish: **Rybalow**. Russ.: **Rybakov**, **Ryba(l)kin**.

Rybniček Czech: topographic name for someone who lived by a fishpond, from a dim. of Czech *rybnik* fishpond.

Rycroft English: topographic name for someone who lived by a smallholding (see CROFT) where RYE was grown.

Vars.: **Rycraft**; **Roycroft**, **Roycraft** (chiefly Irish).

Rye English: 1. topographic name for someone who lived on an island or patch of firm ground surrounded by fens, from a misdivision of the ME phrase *atter ye* at the island (OE *æt þǣre īge*, from *ēg* island).

2. topographic name for someone who lived near a river or stream, from a misdivision of the ME phrase *atter eye* at the river (OE *æt þǣre eǣ* at the river, from *ēa* river).

3. topographic name for someone living at a place where rye (OE *ryge*) was grown, or perhaps a metonymic occupational name for someone who grew it.

Vars. (of 1 and 2): RAY, **Rea(y)**; **R(a)yman**, RAIMAN, **Reaman**, **Reeman**. See also NYE.

Cogns. (of 3): Pol.: **Rżanek** (from OPol. *rżany* of rye (adj.)). Czech: **Rež**, **Režný**.

Ryland English: topographic name for someone who lived near a piece of land where rye was grown, from OE *ryge* RYE + *land* land.

Vars.: **Rylands**, **Rylance**.

Rysev Russian: patr. from the nickname *Rys* 'Lynx', given perhaps to a sly person. The lynx was native to the forests of E Europe until the 19th cent., and in Russ. was originally named from its colour; cf. RYZHAKOV.

Var.: **Rysin**.

Cogn.: Czech: **Rys**.

Ryzhakov Russian: patr. from the nickname *Ryzhak* 'Red-haired man' (from *ryzhi* red, lit. rust-coloured; the name is akin to the roots mentioned at RUSAKOV 2 and RUDAKOV, and is ultimately cogn. with L *russ(e)us* (see ROUSE)).

Vars.: **Ryzh(i)kov**, **Ryzhochin**, **Ryzhov**, **Ryzhago**.

Cogns.: Pol.: **Reszka**. Czech: **Ryšavý** (adj.); **Rezek**. Jewish (E Ashkenazic): **Rezik**.

Dim.: Czech: **Ryšánek**.

Rzetelski Polish: nickname for a man noted for his honesty and fair dealing, from Pol. *rzetelny* honest, fair + the surname suffix *-ski* (see BARANOWSKI), or else from the same word in the sense 'likeable' or 'handsome'.

Rzeźnik Polish: occupational name for a butcher, Pol. *rzeźnik*, from a deriv. of Pol. *rzeźać* to slaughter (cf. Czech *řezat* to cut and the surname ŘEZÁČ).

Var.: **Rzeźnicki**.

Cogns.: Czech: **Řezník**; **Řezníček** (dim.). Jewish (E Ashkenazic): **Reznik**, **Resnick**; **Reznikov**, **Reznikoff**.

S

Saarinen Finnish: ornamental name from Finn. *saari* island + the gen. suffix *-nen*, chosen in some cases as a topographic name by someone who lived on or by an island.

Var.: **Saari**.

Saavedra Spanish (Galicia): habitation name composed of the dial. words *saa* hall (see SALE 1) + *vedra* (fem.) old (L *vetus*, gen. *veteris*).

Sabbato Italian: from a nickname or given name bestowed on someone born on a Saturday, which was considered a good omen, from It. *sabbato* Saturday (LL *sabbatum*, Gk *sabbaton*, from Hebr. *shabaton* Sabbath, a deriv. of *shabat* rest).

Var.: **Sabato**.

Cogns.: Cat.: **Sàbat**. Jewish: **S(h)abat(h)**, **Shabatt**, **Shabato(n)**, **Shabatov**, **Shabathoff**, **Sabatov(ski)**, **Sabatowski** (E Ashkenazic); **Shabes** (from Yid. *shabes*).

Dims.: It.: **Sab(b)atini**, **Sab(b)atino**, **Sab(b)atelli**, **Sabatello**, **Sab(b)atiello**, **Sab(b)atucci**; **Zabatino** (Sicily); **Sab(b)adin(i)** (N Italy).

Sabberton English (E Anglia): probably a habitation name from any of the various places, in Derbys., Gloucs., Lincs., and Sussex, called *Sapperton*, from OE *Sāperatūn* 'settlement (OE *tūn*) of the soap-makers' (cf. SOPER). The place in Sussex is frequently found in forms such as *Saberton* and *Sabirton* as late as the 16th cent. The place in Lincs. is the most likely source of the E Anglian surname, as there was a good deal of migration from that region in connection with the medieval wool-trade.

Sabin 1. English and French: from the OF masc. given name *Sabin* or the fem. *Sabine* (L *Sabīnus*, *Sabīna*, member of the Sabine tribe, an ancient Italic people of central Italy whose name is of uncertain origin). The masc. name was borne by at least ten early saints, but the fem. form was more common in England in the Middle Ages.

2. Jewish (Ashkenazic): of unknown origin.

Vars. (of 1): Eng.: **Sab(b)en**, **Saban**; **Sabine**. Fr.: **Savin**, **Sevi(n)**; **Sabine**, **Savine**, **Sevène** (fem. forms); **Sabina** (fem., Brittany). (Of 2): **Sabine** (an Anglicized form).

Cogns.: Prov.: **Sabi**, **Sab(b)y**. It.: **Savini**, **Savin(i)o**; **Sabini**, **Sabino** (S Italy); **Savina** (fem.). Port.: **Sabino**. Flem., Du.: **Seven**.

Dims.: Eng.: **Sablin(e)**. Fr.: **Savineau**, **Savignon**, **Sevenet**.

Patrs.: Flem., Du.: **Sevens**. Russ.: **Savinov**, **Savinykh**. Bulg.: **Savov**.

Sabrier Provençal: occupational name for a preparer or seller of spiced foods, from an agent deriv. of OProv. *sabre* flavour (L *sapor*; cf. SAVOUREUX). The denotation of this word was extended to sauces, bacon, and other highly flavoured foodstuffs, which were extremely common in the Middle Ages, since the spices functioned as preservatives as well as flavourings.

Var.: **Sabrié**.

Saburov Russian: patr. from the Turkic given name *Sabur*, from Arabic *Sābūr* 'the Patient one', an epithet of Allah.

Sacerdote Italian (Jewish): name assumed by a member of the priestly caste (see COHEN), from It. *sacerdote* priest (L *sacerdōs*, gen. *sacerdōtis*).

Sacher Jewish (Ashkenazic): of uncertain origin, possibly from: 1. the Yid. male given name *Skharye*, from the Hebr. name *Zecharya*; see ZACHARY.

2. the Yid. male given name *Sokher*, from the Hebr. name *Yissachar* (Eng. *Issachar*) 'Hired'.

3. the Yid. occupational term *soykher* merchant (from Hebr. *socher*). However, none of these three explanations is really convincing, for phonological reasons.

Var.: **Sachar**.

Patrs.: **Sachers**; **Sacharov**, **Sacharow** (E Ashkenazic).

Sachs 1. German: regional name from Saxony, Ger. *Sachsen*. The region is called after the Gmc tribe which settled there in Roman times; they in turn seem to have been named from a kind of knife or dagger that they used (see MESSER 1).

2. Jewish (Ashkenazic): of uncertain origin, possibly as in 1 above, or else adopted in memory of persecuted forebears, an acronym of the Hebr. phrase *Zera Kodesh SHemo* 'his name is of the seed of holiness'.

Vars. (of 1): **Sachse**. (Of 2): **Zaks**, **Sa(c)ks**, **Sax**.

Cogns. (of 1): Low Ger.: **Sass(e)**. Welsh: **Sayce**, **Seys** (applied to English settlers, from OW *sais* Saxon, i.e. English). Fr.: **Sa(i)sson**; **(Le) Saux**, **Le Sauz** (most common in Brittany). It.: **Sassone**, **Sasson(i)**; **Sasso**. Pol.: **Sas(s)**, **Sasiak**, **Sasin**. Czech: **Sasák**, **Saska**. Hung.: **Szász(y)** (partly Jewish; often Anglicized as **Sas(s)**). Finn.: **Saksi**.

Dims. (of 1): Fr.: **Sachsé**, **Saisset**. It.: **Sassoli**.

Sack 1. English: metonymic occupational name for a maker of sacks or bags, from OE *sacc* (LL *saccus*, Gk *sakkos*, probably ultimately of Semitic origin).

2. Jewish (Ashkenazic): of uncertain origin, possibly an acronym of the Hebr. phrase *Zera Keshodim* 'Seed of the Holy'.

Vars. (of 1): **Sa(t)ch**; **Sa(c)ker**, **Sackur**, SECKER. (Of 2): **Sackheim**, **Zakheim**, **Zakheym** (ornamental extensions).

Cogns. (of 1): It.: **(Lo) Sacco**, **Sacchi**; **Sacch(i)eri**.

Dims. (of 1): Eng.: **Sackett**; **Satchel(l)**. Fr.: **Sachet**, **Sachot**. Prov.: **Saquet(oux)**. It.: **Sacchet(ti)**, **Sacchetto**, **Sacchini**, **Saccucci**.

Augs. (of 1): It.: **Saccon(i)**, **Saccone**.

Sackville English (Norman): habitation name from *Saqueneville* in Eure, so called from the Gmc personal name *Sachano* (apparently a deriv. of the element *sakō* quarrel, dispute) + OF *ville* settlement (see VILLE).

Var.: **Sackwild**.

Cogn.: Fr.: **Saqueville**.

Bearers of this surname are members of a single family, deriving the name from a manor near Dieppe. Herbrand de Sauqueville *was recorded in Domesday Book as the holder of lands in Bucks. He is said to have received them in* c.1070 *from the lord of Longueville, in whose household he was a steward. The family held the earldom and dukedom of Dorset, rising to prominence when John* Sackville *(d. 1557) married into the powerful Boleyn family. The 1st Earl, Thomas Sackville (1536–1608), was second cousin to Queen Elizabeth I. She granted him an estate at Knole in Kent in 1566, and through the female line this is the family seat of the barons Sack-*

ville. The dukedom and earldom became extinct in 1843. The name continued in the female line and was adopted by the 5th Earl de la Warr after he married the daughter of the 3rd Duke of Dorset in 1813.

Sacramento Portuguese: religious byname from Port. *sacramento* sacrament (L *sacrāmentum* oath, a transparent deriv. of *sacer* sacred, re-analysed in Christian terminology).

Sadd English (E Anglia): nickname for a serious or solemn person, from ME *sad* serious, grave (OE *sæd* weary, tired). The mod. Eng. sense 'unhappy' did not develop until the 15th cent.

Saddington English: habitation name from a place in Leics., recorded in Domesday Book in the forms *Sadintone* and *Setintone*. The first element may be a reduced form of an OE personal name; Ekwall suggests *Sǣgēat* (from *sǣ* sea + the tribal name *Gēat*), in which case the etymology is 'settlement (OE *tūn*) associated with *Sǣgēat*'.

Sade French: 1. habitation name from the village of *Saddes* in Avène.

2. nickname for a pleasant or amiable person, from OF *sade* agreeable (originally of taste, from L *sapidus*; cf. SAVOUREUX).

Sadler English and Low German: occupational name for a maker of saddles, from an agent deriv. of ME, MLG *sadel* (OE *sadol*, OSax. *zadel*).

Vars.: Eng.: **Saddler**; **Sadlier** (chiefly common in Ireland). Low Ger.: **Sedler**; **Sadelmacher**.

Cogns.: Ger.: **Sattler, Sättler**; **Sattel**. Flem.: **De Sadelaer**; **Saelman, Saelemaeker**. Du.: **Zadelaar**. Jewish (Ashkenazic): **Satler, Satelman, Zatelman**; **Zutler** (S Ashkenazic, from a S Yid. pronunciation of Yid. *zotler* saddlemaker).

Sadowski Polish, German (of Slav. origin), and Jewish (E Ashkenazic): habitation name from any of several places named with Pol. *sad* orchard + the possessive suffix *-ów*, such as *Sadowa* in NE Poland, with the addition of the suffix of local surnames *-ski* (see BARANOWSKI).

Vars.: Jewish: **Sadowsky, Sadovski, Sadovsky**; **Sadovnik, Sadownik** (occupational names).

Cogns. (patrs.): Russ.: **Sadovnikov, Sadovshchikov**.

Saffer English (Norman): nickname for a greedy person, from OF *saffre* glutton (of unknown etymology).

Cogns.: Fr.: **Saf(f)re, Lesaffre**.

Safran 1. German: metonymic occupational name for a spicer or nickname for someone with blond hair, from Ger. *Safran* saffron, a spice which is bright yellow or orange in colour (MHG *saffrān*, from OF *safran*, Arabic *zaʿfarān*).

2. Jewish (Ashkenazic): occupational name as in 1, or ornamental name (one of the many taken from words denoting plants).

Vars.: **Saffran**. Jewish only: **Shafran(ski), S(h)afranovitch, Zaf(f)ren**.

Cogns.: Pol.: **Szafran, Szafrański**. Hung.: **Sáfrán(y)**.

Dim.: Czech: **Šafrănek**.

Sagan Polish: metonymic occupational name for a maker of pots and pans, from Pol. *sagan* kettle, or nickname from the same word in a less clear application.

Var.: **Sagański** (with *-ski* suffix of surnames; see BARANOWSKI).

Habitation name: **Saganowski**.

Sage English and French: nickname for a wise man, from ME, OF *sage* learned, sensible (LL *sapius*, from *sapere* to taste, discern, discriminate).

Var.: Fr. **Lesage**.

Cogns.: Prov.: **Sa(i)ve**. It.: **Saggio**; **Savi(o), Lo Savio**; **Sapio** (S Italy).

Dims.: Fr.: **Sagel, Saget, Sageon, Sageot**. Prov.: **Saivet**. It.: **Saviotti, Savioli, Saviozzi**.

Patrs.: It.: **Del Savio**; **Dal Savio** (Venetia, where *savio* was a title of office for the city councillors during the Middle Ages).

Sagne Provençal: topographic name for someone who lived by a patch of marshy land, from OProv. *sagne* fen, bog (from *sagnier* to bleed, L *sanguināre*, a deriv. of *sanguis*, gen. *sanguinis*, blood).

Vars.: **Saigne, Sagnes, Desagnes**; **Sa(n)gnier, Saignier, Sannier, Sannié**.

Sainsbury English: habitation name from *Saintbury* in Gloucs., recorded in the 12th cent. as *Seynesbury*. The placename is probably from the gen. case of the OE male personal name *Sǣwine* (composed of the elements *sǣ* sea + *wine* friend) + OE *burh* fort, town (see BURY).

Vars.: **Saintsbury, Sainsberry, Sinisbury**.

Saint English and French: nickname for a notably pious individual, from ME, OF *saint*, *seint* (L *sanctus* blameless, holy). The vocab. word was occasionally used in the Middle Ages as a given name, esp. on the Continent, and this may have given rise to some instances of the surname.

Vars.: Eng.: **Sa(u)nt**. Fr.: **Sant, Sa(i)ns**.

Cogns.: It.: **Sant(i), Santo**. Sp.: **Santos** (from a byname or nickname for someone born on All Saints' Day; cf. SANTORO and TOUSSAINT). Port.: **Santo** (in most cases in combination with **Espírito**, and so a religious byname referring to the Holy Spirit); **Santos** (very common). Flem., Du.: **Sint**. Hung.: **Szente** ('pious').

Dims.: Fr.: **Sainteau, Saintin, Saint(ign)on, Santot**; **Sansuc** (Brittany). It.: **Santel(li), Santello, Santilli, Santillo, Santulli, Santullo, Santin(i), Santino, Santucci, Santuzzo**.

Augs.: It.: **Santon(i)**.

Patrs.: It.: **De Santi** (Venetia); **De San(c)tis** (S Italy). Swed.: **Santesson**.

Sainte-Beuve French: habitation name from a place in Seine-Maritime, Normandy, so called from the dedication of its church to a 7th-cent. saint, abbess of Rheims, who bore the Gmc personal name *Bova*, which is of uncertain etymology.

Saint-Exupéry French: habitation name from either of the places, in Corrèze and Gironde, so called from the dedication of their churches to a 5th-cent. archbishop of Toulouse, St *Exsuperius* (a deriv. of LL *exsuper* (far) above).

Var.: **Saint-Supéry**.

Saint-Georges French: habitation name from any of the numerous places so called from the dedication of their churches to St GEORGE.

Cogn.: Eng. (Norman): **St George**. Hung.: **Szentgyörgyi**.

A family by the name of St George, *established in Cambs. as early as the reign of Henry II (1154–89), derive their surname from the barony of Saint-Georges near Limoges, France. They are said to have settled in England with Baldwin St George at the time of the Norman Conquest.*

Sainthill English: habitation name from a hamlet in Devon, recorded in the 13th cent. as *Sengethill*, from OE *senget* place cleared by burning (from *sencgan* to burn) + *hyll* HILL. Later forms of the name include *Se(i)nthill*, *Sainthyll*, and *St Hill*.

John Seynthill *represented Honiton in Parliament in 1300–11.*

Saint-Jean French: habitation name from any of the extremely numerous places so called from the dedication of their churches to a St JOHN.

Cogns.: Eng. (Norman): **St John**. Sp.: **San Juan**. Cat.: **Sanjuan**.

St John *is the family name of Viscount Bolingbroke. They trace their descent in the male line from Hugh de Port (d. 1096), who was at the court of Normandy in 1085. His descendant, Adam de Port (d. before 1213) was a powerful baron, governor of Southampton Castle. He married the heiress of the St John family, at the same time adopting her surname. This family had settled in England at the Conquest; its name was taken from the manor of* Saint-Jean-*le-Thomas near Arranches, Normandy*.

Saint-Just French: habitation name from any of the numerous places so called from the dedication of their churches to a 4th-cent. bishop of Lyons, St *Justus* (see JUST).

Saint-Laurent French: habitation name from any of the numerous places so called from the dedication of their churches to St LAWRENCE.

Saint-Saëns French: habitation name from a place near Rouen in Seine-Maritime, Normandy, so called from the abbey founded there under a 7th-cent. Irishman, St *Sidōnius*, whose name is of obscure origin. It is probably in origin a L ethnic name from the Phoenician city of *Sidon*, but was widely associated with Gk *sindon* winding sheet, shroud (cf. SENDALL).

Saladin French: nickname for a blustering or tyrannical individual, from the Arabic title, *Salāh-ad-Dīn* 'Justice of the Faith', of the great Moslem leader Yusuf ibn-Ayyub, who opposed, for the most part successfully, the Crusades undertaken by Richard I of England and Philip II of France, and became in popular French imagination a monster as great as Herod.

Cogns.: It.: **Salad(d)ino, Sala(n)dini, Salardino, Salatino, Salatino.**

Salamanca Spanish: habitation name from the city of *Salamanca* in W Spain, which is of pre-Roman foundation and obscure etymology. During the Middle Ages it was one of the leading cultural centres of Europe, and the surname may in some cases have been been a respectful nickname for someone who had visited the city.

Salazar Spanish and Portuguese: habitation name, ultimately of Basque origin, from Romance *sala* hall (see SALE 1) + Basque *zahar* old; cf. SAAVEDRA. In some cases the surname may derive from a place so called in the province of Burgos.

Sale English: 1. occupational name for someone employed at a manor house, ME *sale* (from OE *sæl* hall, reinforced by OF *salle*, also of Gmc origin).

2. topographic name for someone who lived by a sallow tree, ME *sale* (OE *salh*; cf. SAUCE), or habitation name from a place named with this word, for example *Sale* in Greater Manchester.

Vars.: SALES, SEAL, **Sall(es)**.

Cogns. (of 1): Fr.: **Salle**, LASALLE, **Delasalle**. It.: **Sala**. Sp.: **Sala(s)**. Cat.: **Sala(s)**, SALES. Port.: **Sá**. Rum.: **Sala**. Flem., Du.: **Zaal**. Swed.: **Sahlin, Sa(h)lén**. Pol.: **Salski**. (Of 2): Ger.: **Salch; Salch(n)er**.

Dims. (of 1): Fr.: **Sal(l)et, Sallez**. Prov.: **Salon, Salou, Salot**.

Cpds (of 1, ornamental): Swed.: **Sahlberg** ('hall hill'); **Sahlström** ('hall river').

Salé French: 1. nickname for an amusing or witty person, from the OF adj. *salé*, lit. salted, salty (LL *salātus*, from *sal* salt).

2. topographic name for someone who lived in a salt marsh, from the same word used in a literal sense.

Var.: **Sallé**.

Cogns.: Prov., Cat.: **Salat**. Sp.: **Salado** (habitation name, from a place in the province of Murcia); **Salgado** (nickname, from LL *salicātus*, past part. of *salicāre* to give salt to). Port.: **Salgado**.

Sales 1. English and Catalan: topographic name; see SALE 2.

2. Portuguese: habitation name from a place that is probably so called from a Gmc personal name of uncertain form and derivation.

3. Portuguese: religious byname adopted since the 17th cent. in honour of St Francis of *Sales* (1567–1622), who was born at the Château de *Sales* in Savoy.

Salguero Spanish: 1. topographic name for someone who lived by a weeping willow, Sp. *salguero* (LL *salicārius*, a deriv. of class. L *salix*, gen. *salicis*, willow; see SAUCE).

2. it is also possible that the name is sometimes derived from a homonymous archaic term denoting a spot where salt was given to cattle (LL *salicārium*, a deriv. of *salicāre* to give salt to, from *sal* salt; cf. SALÉ).

Cogn.: Port.: **Salgueiro**.

Salido Spanish: nickname for an exile, OSp. *salido*, past part. of *salir* to go out (L *salīre* to leap; cf. SAUTOUR and SAYLOR). The name may also have been acquired by someone who had spent a period abroad.

Salinas Spanish: topographic name for someone who lived near a salt works, Sp. *salinas* (L *salīnae*, a deriv. of *sal* salt; cf. SALÉ), or occupational name for someone who worked at one.

Var.: **Salinero** (an agent deriv.).

Salinger 1. English (Norman): habitation name from *Saint-Léger* in La Manche or *Saint-Léger*-aux-Bois in Seine-Maritime, both so called from the dedication of their churches to St Leger (see LEDGER), the martyred 7th-cent. bishop of Autun.

2. Jewish (Ashkenazic): of uncertain origin, possibly an altered form of a habitation name from *Solingen* in N Germany. The expected deriv. of *Solingen* is *Solinger*, but this apparently does not occur as a surname.

Vars. (of 1): **Salingar, Sallagar, Seli(n)ger, Sellinger**. (Of 2): **Salingar, Selinger**.

Cogns. (of 1): Fr.: **Saint-Léger, Saint-Lagar**.

Salisbury English: 1. habitation name from the city in Wilts., the Roman name of which was *Sorviodūnum* (of Brit. origin). In the OE period the second element (from Celt. *dūn* fortress) was dropped and *Sorvio-* (of unsolved meaning) became *Searo-* in OE as the result of folk etymological association with OE *searu* armour; to this an explanatory *burh* fortress, manor, town (see BURY) was added. The town is recorded in Domesday Book as *Sarisberie*; the change of *-r-* to *-l-* is a later result of dissimilation.

2. habitation name from *Salesbury* in Lancs., so called from OE *salh* willow (see SALE 2) + *burh* fortress, manor.

Vars.: **Salisberry, Salesbury, Sal(u)sbury**.

Salked N English: habitation name from *Salkeld* in Cumb., so called from OE *salh* willow (see SALE 2) + *hylte* wood.

Salminen Finnish: ornamental name from Finn. *salmi* strait + the gen. suffix *-nen*, perhaps chosen in some cases as a topographic name by someone who lived by a strait.

Var.: **Salmi**.

Salmon 1. English and French: from the ME, OF given name *Salmon*, *Saumon*, a contracted form of SALOMON.

2. Jewish (Ashkenazic): from the Yid. male given name *Zalmen*, derived via a German form from Hebr. *Shelomo*; see SALOMON.

3. Irish: translated form of Gael. *Ó Bradáin*; see BRADEN.

Vars. (of 1): Eng.: **Salmond, Salman, Salmen.** Fr.: **Salman, Solmon.** (Of 2): Jewish: **Salman, Zalmon, Zalman, Zalmen.**

Cogns. (of 1): It.: **Salmone, Salmon(i).** Ger.: **Sal(l)man, Sahlmann.**

Patrs. (from 1): Eng.: **Salmons, Sammon(d)s.** Swed.: **Salmonsson.** (From 2): Jewish: **Salmanso(h)n, Salmenson, Zalmanson; Salmonov, Salmanov, Zalmonovich, Zalmanov, Zalmanoff, Zalmanovi(t)ch, Zalmanovicz, Zalmanovics, Zalmanowitz, Zalmanovitz, Zalmenov(itz)** (E Ashkenazic); **Zalmanovici** (a Rumanian spelling).

Salomon Jewish, English, French, Venetian, German, Danish/Norwegian, Polish, and Hungarian: ultimately from the Hebr. male given name *Shelomo* (a deriv. of *shalom* peace; cf. SHOLEM), which was fairly widespread in the Middle Ages among Christians and has for generations been a popular Jewish name. Among Christians it was also used as a nickname for a man who was considered wise, and for someone who had played the part of King Solomon in a miracle play.

Vars.: Jewish: **Salamon, Salaman,** SALMON; **Suliman** (from the Arabic form of the given name). Eng.: **Salamon, Salaman,** SALMON. Fr.: **Salamon, Solomon,** SALMON; **Salaün** (Brittany). It.: **Salomone, Salomon(i), Salamone, Salamon(i); Salamo** (Calabria). Ger.: **Saleman.** Pol.: **Salamon.** Czech: **Šalamoun.** Hung.: **Salamon.**

Dims.: Jewish: **Salomonczyk; Slomka** (from Yid. *s(h)loyme*). Czech: **Šach, Šalda, Šálek.**

Patrs.: Jewish: **Salomonson; Salomonof, Salomonivitch, Salom(on)owicz, Salomonovitz, Salomonowitz, Salam(on)ovitz, Salamonovits; Sulimanof(f); Sulimani** (with the Arabic suffix *-i*); **Sulimanian** (among Iranian Jews); **Shlomov, Shlomof; Shlomowitz, S(h)lomovitz, Szlomowicz, Schlomovitz, S(h)lomovits, Shlomovics, Schlomovich, Shlomovi(t)ch, Schlomowich; S(h)lomovici** (a Rumanian spelling); **Shlemovich, Sleymovich** (from NE Yid. forms). Eng.: **Salomons, Salamans.** Flem., Du.: **Salomons.** Norw., Dan.: **Salomonsen.** Swed.: **Salomonsson.**

Patrs. (from dims.): Jewish (E Ashkenazic): **Shlomkowitz, Shlomkovitz, Schlomkowich.**

Salonen Finnish: ornamental name from Finn. *salo* forested wilderness + the gen. suffix *-nen*, perhaps chosen in some cases as a topographic name by someone who lived by such a place.

Var.: **Salo.**

Salt English: metonymic occupational name, a var. of SALTER 1, or habitation name from a place in Staffs., so called from a salt pit there.

Vars.: SAULT, **Saltman.**

Cogns. (occupational): Ger.: **Sal(t)z(mann).** Low Ger.: **Soltmann, Soldmann.** Jewish (Ashkenazic): **Sal(t)z(man), Salzmann, Salts(man), Zal(t)z(man), Zals(man); Zalc(man)** (a Polish spelling); **Salc** (a mixed German and Polish spelling).

Cpds (ornamental elaborations): Jewish (Ashkenazic): **Salzberg, Zalt(z)berg, Zalcberg, Zalsberg** ('salt hill'); **Salzstein, Zalcstein** ('salt stone'); **Zalcwasser** ('salt water').

Salter English: 1. occupational name for an extractor and seller of salt (OE *s(e)alt*), a precious commodity in medieval times.

2. metonymic occupational name for a player on the psaltery, ME, OF *saltere* (L *psaltērium*, Gk *psaltērion*, from *psallein* to sound), a kind of stringed instrument.

Var.: SAUTER.

Cogns. (of 1): Fr.: **Sau(l)nier, Salinier, Lesau(l)nier.** It.: **Salieri.** Ger.: **Salzer, Sel(t)zer.** Low Ger.: **Solter, Sölter.** Pol.: **Solarz, Solarski.** Jewish (Ashkenazic): **Salzer; Solarz, Solarski** (E Ashkenazic); **Salzhandler** ('salt dealer'); **Salzhauer** ('salt cutter').

Dim.: Pol.: **Solarek** (also means 'salt-barrel').

Habitation names: Pol.: **Solecki** (from any of a number of places called *Solec*); **Soliński.**

Salter *is the name of a family of Shrops. origin, where John* de le Sel *was recorded at Shrewsbury Abbey in 1211. The family's wealth was derived from the manufacture of salt, as was its surname. They owned salt-springs in Shrops. and Ches., but around 1475 these were sold, the proceeds were divided, and the family dispersed.*

Salthouse English (Lancs.): occupational name for a worker at a salt-works, topographic name for someone who lived by a salt-works, or habitation name from one of the minor places named from a salt-works. There are examples in Lytham St Annes and in Furness, among other places.

Var.: **Salters** (chiefly N Ireland).

Saltykov Russian: patr. from the Turkic byname *Satyq, Satuq* 'Sold', presumably borne originally by a serf or someone who had been sold into slavery.

Salvador Spanish, Catalan, and Portuguese: from a popular medieval and modern given name (L *Salvātor* 'Saviour', a deriv. of *salvāre* to save; cf. SAUVÉ), borne in honour of Christ. The given name is also popular in Italy, esp. in the south, partly as a result of Sp. influence.

Cogns.: It.: **Salvadori, Salvadore; Salvator(i), Salvatore.**

Dims.: It.: **Salvatorello, Salvatorelli.**

Salvi French and Italian: from a personal name (L *Salvius*, a deriv. of *salvus* safe; cf. SAUVÉ) borne by various early saints, among them a 6th-cent. bishop of Albi and a 7th-cent. bishop of Amiens.

Vars.: Fr.: **Salvy, Sauvy.** It.: **Salv(i)o.**

Dims.: It.: **Salvetti, Salvin(ell)i, Salvinello, Salvioli, Salvucci.**

Augs.: It.: **Salvioni, Salvione.**

Patr: It.: **Di Salvo.**

Šámal Czech: nickname for someone with some peculiarity of the gait, from a deriv. of Czech *šámat* to shuffle or limp.

Sambrook English: habitation name from a place in Shrops., so called from OE *sand* SAND + *brōc* stream (see BROOK).

Samet 1. German and Jewish (Ashkenazic): metonymic occupational name for a maker or seller of velvet, Ger. *Samt*, Yid. *samet* (MHG *samet*, ultimately from Gk *hexamiton*, a cpd of *hex* six + *mitos* thread).

2. Jewish: acronymic name from the Hebr. letters SMT, representing the phrase *SiMan Tov* 'lucky sign', 'good omen' or *Sor Mera vaase Tov* 'turn from evil and do good', which was inscribed on the lecterns of the reader's desk in Ashkenazic synagogues in E Europe.

Vars. (of 1): Ger.: **Sameth, Samm(e)t, Sambeth.** Jewish (E Ashkenazic): **Sametnik** (an agent deriv.).

Sampaio Portuguese: habitation name from a place named from the dedication of its church to St *Pelagius*; see PELAYO.

Samper English (Norman): habitation name from any of the various places in N France called *Saint-Pierre*, from the dedication of their churches to St PETER.

Vars.: **Samber, Semper, Sember, Simper, Symber.**

Cogns.: Fr.: **Saint-Pierre, Saint-Père, Saint-Pé.** It.: **Sampier(i), Sampie(t)ro.** Sp.: **San Pedro, Sampedro.**

Samson English, French, German, Jewish, and Flemish/Dutch: from the biblical name *Samson* (Hebr. *Shimshon*, a dim. of *shemesh* sun). Among Christians it may sometimes have been chosen as a given name or nickname in direct reference to the great strength of the biblical character, but a more common association was with the 6th-cent. Welsh bishop *Samson*, who travelled to Brittany, where he died and was greatly venerated. His name, which may be an altered form of a Celt. original, was popularized in England by Bret. followers of William the Conqueror, and to some extent independently from Wales.

Vars.: Eng.: **Sampson, Samsin; Sansom(e), Sansum, Sansam** (chiefly Somerset). Fr.: **Sa(i)nson**. Ger.: SIMSON. Jewish: **Shimshon; Shimsoni, Shimsony** (with the Hebr. suffix *-i*).

Cogns.: It.: **Sansone, Sanson(i), Sanzone; Sanzonio, Sanzogno** (Venetia). Cat.: **Samsó**.

Dims.: Eng.: **Sam(me), Sanne, Sankin**. Fr.: **Sansot, Sansonnet**. It.: **Sansonetti**.

Patrs.: Jewish (E Ashkenazic): **Samsonov(ich), Samsonovitz; Szimszewicz, Shimshovits** (from Yid. *Shimshn*).

Samuel English, French, German, and Jewish: from the biblical male given name *Samuel* (Hebr. *Shemuel* 'Name of God').

Vars.: Eng.: **Samwell**. Ger.: **Samel**. Jewish: **Schmuel, Szmu(e)l; Shmil** (a S Yid. form); **S(c)hmueli, S(c)hmuely** (with the Hebr. suffix *-i*); **Shmouel, Schmoueli** (semi-Gallicized spellings).

Cogns.: It.: **Samuel(l)i**. Pol.: **Samul(ski), Smulski**. Hung.: **Sámuel**.

Dims.: Pol.: **Samulczyk, Smulczyk**. Czech: **Samek**. Ukr.: **Samus**. Beloruss.: **Samuilyonok**. Hung.: **Samu**.

Patrs.: Eng.: **Samuels(on)**. Dan., Norw.: **Samuelsen**. Swed.: **Samuelsson**. Jewish: **Sam(u)elsohn; S(h)mulevich, Szmulewicz, Szmulewitz, Shmuilov(ich)** (NE Ashkenazic); **Shmilovitch, Shmilovitz** (S Ashkenazic). Russ.: **Samylov, Samoilov, Samylin**. Pol.: **Smuliewicz; Samulak**. Lithuanian: **Samelionis**. Armenian: **Smulian**.

Patrs. (from dims.): Eng.: **Sam(m)s**. Jewish: **Schmelkes, Schmelkin** (E Ashkenazic). Russ.: **Samoshkin, Samyshkin, Samokhin, Samukhin, Samonin, Samunin, Samus(y)ev, Samugin, Simulev**. Beloruss.: **Samusev**.

Samways English: nickname for a stupid person, from ME *samwis* dull, foolish (OE *sāmwīs*, from *sām* half + *wīs* wise).

Sanahuja Catalan: habitation name from *Sanaüja* in the province of Lérida. The placename is certainly not of Romance origin and more than one Basque etymology has been proposed.

Sancho Spanish and Portuguese: from an extremely common medieval given name (L *Sanc(t)ius*, seemingly a deriv. of *sanctus* (see SAINT), but in fact probably an approximation to an earlier pre-Roman personal name (cf. DIEGO)). The given name was borne by a 9th-cent. martyr of Cordova.

Var.: **Sanz**.

Cogns.: Cat.: **Sanz, Sans**. It.: **Sanzio**.

Patrs.: Sp.: **Sánchez, Sáe(n)z, Sái(n)z; Sánchiz** (Aragon). Cat.: **Sanchís, Sanchis, Sanchiz**. Port.: **Sanches**.

Sand 1. English, Scots, German, Danish/Norwegian, and Swedish: topographic name for someone who lived on patch of sandy soil, from ME, Ger., Dan., Swed. *sand* (OE *sand*, OHG *sant*, ON *sandr*).

2. English, Scots, and Danish/Norwegian: short form of ALEXANDER (cf. SANDER).

3. Jewish (Ashkenazic): ornamental name, perhaps adopted in reference to God's promise to the Jewish people that they would be as many as the grains of sand upon the shore of the sea; cf. MEERSAND.

Vars. (of 1): Eng.: **Sand(e)s, Sandys** (also patrs. from 2). Ger.: **Sande, Sandt; Sand(e)mann, San(n)mann, Samman; Sandner**. Swed.: **Sandh, Sandin, Sandén, Sandman**, SANDELL. (Of 3): Jewish: **Zand**.

Cogns. (of 1): Du.: **Van den Sande, Van den Zande, Van (den) Zanden**.

Cpds (of 1, ornamental elaborations): Swed.: **Sandberg** ('sand hill'); **Sandgren** ('sand branch'); **Sandlund** ('sand grove'); **Sandmark** ('sand territory'); **Sandquist** ('sand twig'); **Sandström** ('sand river'). (Of 3): Jewish: **Sandberg, Zandberg** ('sand hill'); **Sandgarten** ('sand garden'); **Sandhaus** ('sand house'; Anglicized **Sandhouse**); **Sandstein, Zandsztajn** ('sand stone'; the latter is a Pol. spelling).

Sir Edwin Sandys *(1561–1629) was a founder of Virginia, the brother of the poet George Sandys (1578–1664), who was treasurer of the colony in 1621. They were born into a Lancs. family, the sons of an archbishop of York. Sir Edwin was knighted in 1603 by James I, but became one of the king's leading opponents. He joined the Virginia Company in 1607, and supported the request of the Leiden group to be allowed to settle there.*

Sandak Jewish: from Hebr. *sandak* godfather (Gk *syndikos* defendant's advocate, from *syn* with + *dikē* judgement), a role normally undertaken by some particularly respected member of the family or of the Jewish community.

Vars.: **Sandek, Sandik** (from Yid. *sandek*).

Sandbach English: habitation name from a place in Ches., so called from OE *sand* SAND + *bæce* stream (see BACH).

Sandell 1. English: topographic name for someone who lived by a sand-hill or sandy slope, from OE *sand* SAND + *hyll* HILL or *hylde* slope.

2. Swedish: ornamental name, from Swed. *sand* SAND + the element *-el(l)* abstracted arbitrarily from other surnames such as *Nobel*.

Vars. (of 2): **Sandel(in), Sandelius**.

Sander English, Scots, and German: from the medieval given name *Sander*, an aphetic form of ALEXANDER.

Var.: Sc.: **Saunder**.

Cogns.: Fr.: **Sandre**. It.: **Sandre, Sandri**. Hung.: **Sándor**. Jewish (Ashkenazic): **Sender** (from the E Yid. form of the name).

Dims.: Eng.: **Sandercock** (Devon); **Sandow** (Cornwall). Fr.: **Sandrin**. Prov.: **Sandeyron**. It.: **Sandrelli, Sandrin(i), Sandrolini, Sandrucci**.

Augs.: It.: **Sandron(i)**.

Patrs.: Eng., Sc.: **Sa(u)nders, Sandars; Sa(u)nderson, Sandeson, Sandi(e)son**. Low Ger.: **Sanders(en), Sandering**. Jewish: **Senders, Senderov(ski), Senderowsky, Senderoff, Senderovitch, Send(e)rovitz, Send(e)rowitz, Send(e)rowicz, Senderovicz, Senderovits** (E Ashkenazic). Croatian: **Sand(ov)ić**.

'Servant of S.': Eng.: **Sande(r)man**.

Hereditary surnames, as opposed to identifying patronymics, did not become established in the Shetland Islands until the 18th cent. One family of Shetland Sandisons *are descended from* Alexander *Harrison, b. c.1700 at Delting, and another from Christopher* Alexanderson, *b. 1681 at Northmarine, himself presumably the son of an Alexander.*

Sandford English: habitation name from any of the various places, for example in Berks., Devon, Dorset, Oxon., and Shrops., so called from OE *sand* SAND + *ford* FORD.

Vars.: **Sanford; Sampford** (places in Devon, Essex, and Somerset); **Sandiford** (a lost place, probably in Yorks.), **Sandeford, Sandifer, Sandever, Sandyfirth**.

A Shrops. family called Sandford *trace their descent from a Norman, Thomas* de Saundford, *who was granted lands at Sandford, Shrops., shortly after the Conquest.*

Sandham N English: apparently a habitation name, perhaps from an unidentified place named with the OE elements *sand* SAND + *hām* homestead. Alternatively, it may be from any of the several places in Yorks. called *Sandholme*, named from ON *sandr* sand + *holmr* island.

Sandilands Scots: habitation name from a district in Clydesdale, so called from the sandy soil.

The Sandilands *family, who hold the title Baron Torphichen, were confirmed in their ownership of the lands from which they derive their name by the Lord of Douglas in 1348.*

Sandler 1. English (Norman): habitation name from *Saint-Hilaire*-du-Harcouët in La Manche, which gets its name from the dedication of its church to St HILARY, or alternatively from either of the places, in La Manche and Somme, called *Saint-Lô*. Both of the latter are named from a 6th-cent. St *Lauto*, bishop of Coutances; his name is of variable form in the sources and uncertain etymology.

2. Jewish (Ashkenazic): occupational name for a shoemaker or cobbler, Yid. *sandler* (from Hebr. *sandelar*, from LL *sandalārius*, an agent deriv. of *sandalium* shoe, a word that is apparently ultimately of Persian origin).

Vars. (of 1): **Santler**, **Sendler**. (Of 2): **Sandlerman**; **Sandlar** (from the Hebr. word).

Cogns. (of 1): Fr.: **Saint-Hil(l)aire**; **Saint-Lo**, **Saint-Laux**.

Sandoval Spanish: habitation name from a place in the province of Burgos, earlier called *Sannoval*, from L *saltus* grove, wood (see SAULT) + *novālis* newly cleared land (see NOVAIS).

Sandy English: 1. habitation name from a place in Beds., so called from OE *sand* SAND + *ēg* island, dry land in a fen.

2. from the ON personal name *Sand(i)*, a short form of the various cpd names with a first element that is either *sand* truth or *sandr* sand.

Sanger 1. English: occupational name for a singer or chorister, or nickname for a person who was always singing, from OE *sangere*, *songere* singer (a deriv. of *singan* to sing); the var. **Singer** represents a ME recoinage from the verb *sing(en)*.

2. Jewish (Ashkenazic): occupational name for a cantor, from Ger. *Sänger* singer. See also KAZAN.

Vars.: Eng.: **Songer**; **Sangster** (Scots; in form, early ME *-ster* is a fem. agent suffix, contrasted with the masc. *-er*, but by the period of surname formation, the distinction was pretty well lost). Jewish: **Zing(h)er** (from Yid. *zinger*); **Singman**.

Cogns.: Ger.: **Sänger**, **Senger**, **Singer**. Flem., Du.: **Sanger**, **Senger**, **Zanger**.

Dim.: Jewish (E Ashkenazic): **Zingerenko** (with the Ukr. dim. suffix *-enko*).

Patrs.: Eng.: **Singers**. Flem., Du.: **Sangers**, **Sengers**, **Zangers**. Jewish (E Ashkenazic): **Zingerevich**, **Zingerevitz**.

San José Spanish: habitation name from any of various places, for example in the provinces of Almería, Cadiz, and Seville, so called from the dedication of their churches to St JOSEPH.

Sankey 1. English: habitation name from a place in Lancs., apparently so called from a Brit. river name, perhaps meaning 'Sacred', 'Holy'.

2. Irish: Anglicized form of Gael. **Mac Seanchaidhe** 'son of the chronicler'. The name is nevertheless not common in Ireland.

Var.: **Sanky**.

San Martín Spanish: habitation name from any of the numerous places so called from the dedication of their churches to St MARTIN.

Cogns.: Cat.: **Sanmartí**. Fr.: **Saint-Martin** (the most frequent of the names of this type).

San Miguel Spanish: habitation name from any of the numerous places so called from the dedication of their churches to St MICHAEL.

Cogns.: Fr.: **Saint-Mihiel**, **Saint-Mieux**.

San Román Spanish: habitation name from any of the numerous places so called from the dedication of their churches to St ROMAN.

Cogn.: Fr.: **Saint-Romans**.

San Segundo Spanish: habitation name from some minor place so called from the dedication of its church to St *Secundus* (see SEGOND).

Santa María Spanish: habitation name from any of the extremely numerous places so called from the dedication of their churches to the Blessed Virgin Mary, or to some other St Mary (cf. MARIE).

Cogns.: Cat.: **Santamaria**. Fr.: **Sainte-Marie**.

Santana Spanish, Catalan, and Portuguese: habitation name from any of the numerous places so called from the dedication of their churches to St *Anne* (see HANNA).

Santiago Spanish and Portuguese: habitation name from any of the numerous places so called from the dedication of their churches to St JAMES. The apostle St James the Greater is the patron of Spain, following a 9th-cent. legend that he visited and evangelized the country after the death of Christ, rather than meeting a speedy end under Herod Agrippa. The scene of his alleged burial at Compostela was a place of pilgrimage from all over Europe throughout the Middle Ages.

Var.: Port.: **Tiago** (an aphetic form, the result of misdivision).

Santoro Italian: from a nickname or given name for someone who was born on All Saints' Day, It. *santoro* (LL *sanctorum (omnium dies festus)*).

Vars.: **Santori(o)** (Naples); **Santorum** (Trentino).

Dims.: **Santorelli**, **Santoriello**, **Santorini**.

Sanvoisin French: nickname for someone who lived in a remote situation, from OF *sans* without (L *sine*, apparently crossed with *absens*, pres. part. of *abesse* to be absent, lacking) + *visin* neighbour (see VOISIN).

Sapin French: topographic name for someone who lived near a fir tree, or in a coniferous forest, from OF *sapin* fir (LL *sapīnus*). The OF byform *sap* may be a back-formation from a supposed dim., but it may also represent the survival of an earlier form of the word, of Gaul. origin, to which was added the L adj. ending *-īnus*, perhaps as a result of association with *pīnus* PINE.

Vars.: **Sapy**; **Dusapin**; **Dusap(t)**.

Sapiński Polish: nickname for someone who wheezed a lot, from OPol. *sapać* to wheeze, hiss, or habitation name from a place named with this element in the sense 'quagmire'.

Var.: **Sapieha** (traditionally derived from Gk *sophia* wisdom, but this is no more than folk etymology).

Sapir Jewish (Ashkenazic): 1. ornamental name from Hebr. *sapir* sapphire.

2. said to be a habitation name from the Ger. town of *Speyer* (Eng. *Spires*), which had a large Jewish population in the Middle Ages; cf. SHAPIRO, SPIER, and SPIRE. However, there are phonological problems with this explanation.

Vars. (of 1): **Saphir(e)**; **Saphyr** (influenced by the spelling of Eng. *zephyr*); **Saperstein**.

Sapozhnikov Russian and Jewish (E Ashkenazic): patr. from Russ. *sapozhnik*, occupational name for a cobbler, an agent noun from *sapog* boot.

Vars.: Jewish: **Saposhnikov**, **Sapochnikov**, **Sapoznikov**, **Sapoznikow**, **Sapojnikov**, **Sapojnikoff** (patrs.); **Saposhnik**, **Sapoznik**.

Sapsford English: habitation name from *Sawbridgeworth* in Herts., which is recorded in 1568 as *Sapsforde*. The first element represents the gen. case of the OE personal name *Sǣbeorht*, composed of the elements *sǣ* sea + *beorht* bright, famous; the second is from OE *worð* enclosure (see WORTH), but has been confused with *ford* FORD.

Saraiva Portuguese: of uncertain origin, possibly a habitation name from *Sarabia* in Galicia.

Sardinha Portuguese: metonymic occupational name for a fisher of sardines (or perhaps a nickname), from Port. *sardinha* sardine (L *sardīna*, from Gk; the further etymology of the vocab. word is unclear, but it may be connected with the name of the island of *Sardinia*; cf. SARDOU).

Sardou Provençal: ethnic name for someone from Sardinia, a dim. of OProv. *sarde* Sardinian. The name of the island is of uncertain origin; cf. SARDINHA.

Vars.: **Sardet**, **Sardin**.

Cogns.: It.: **Sardi**, **Sardo**.

Sarfatti Jewish: ethnic name adopted in Italy by migrants from France and Spain, from Hebr. *Tsarefati*, a deriv. of *Tsarefat*, originally designating a Phoenician city on the eastern shore of the Mediterranean mentioned in the Book of Obadiah (rendered in the Vulgate as *Sarepta*). Under the influence of Gk *Hesperides* 'Western Islands', Jews associated the name *Tsarefat* first with France, then with France and the Iberian Peninsula (beginning in the 10th cent.), and finally with the whole of Western Europe (from about the 14th cent.). In today's Hebr. the meaning of the word is 'France'.

Vars.: **Sarfati**, **Sarfat(t)y**, **Zarfat(t)i**, **Zarfaty**, **Serfati**, **Serfaty**.

Sarmiento Spanish: apparently a nickname for a tall, thin person, from Sp. *sarmiento* vine shoot (L *sarmentum* shoot, from *sarpere* to trim, prune).

Cogn.: Port.: **Sarmento**.

Sarrail Provençal: metonymic occupational name for a locksmith, from OProv. *sarrail* lock (LL *serrālium*, a deriv. of *serra* bolt, bar). For the change of *-er-* to *-ar-*, cf. MARCHANT.

Vars.: **Sarraille**, **Sarralh**; **Sarraillier**, **Sarraillié**, **Sarralhier**, **Sarralhié**.

Sarson English: 1. nickname for someone of swarthy appearance, or for an unruly person, or perhaps for someone who had taken part in a Crusade, from ME, OF *sarrazin* Saracen (via L and Gk from a Semitic term, perhaps akin to Arab. *sharq* sunrise, east, from *shāraqa* to rise).

2. patr. from the medieval male given name *Sa(h)er*; see SAYER.

3. metr. from the Hebr. female given name *Sara* 'Princess', borne by the wife of Abraham. This given name was not common in the Middle Ages except among Jews; cf. SORIN.

Cogns. (of 1): Fr.: **Sar(r)asin**, **Sar(r)azin**. It.: **Saracino**, **Saracini**, **Saraceno**, **Saraceni** (S Italy); **Sarracino** (Naples); **Sara(s)in**, **Sarazin**, **Serasin(i)**, **Serraino**, **Sarci(no)** (Venetia); **Sar(r)aino** (Sicily); **Ser(r)acino**, **Seracini** (Naples). Ger.: **Sar(r)azin**, **Sarassin**.

Dim. (of 1): It.: **Sarcinelli**.

Patr. (from 1): Eng.: **Sarsons**.

Sartre French: occupational name for a tailor, OF *sartre* (oblique case *sartor*, from L *sartor*, a deriv. of *sarcīre* (past part. *sartus*) to mend, patch).

Vars.: **Sa(s)tre**, **Sarthre**; **Sartor**.

Cogns.: It.: **Sarto(re)**, **Sart(or)i**, **Sartorio**, **Sertorio**; **Sartorius** (Latinized). Sp.: **Sastre**.

Dims.: Fr.: **Sart(h)on**, **Sart(h)ou**. It.: **Sartorelli**, **Sartoret(to)**, **Sartini**, **Sartucci**.

Aug.: It.: **Sartoni**.

Šašek Czech: nickname meaning 'fool' or 'buffoon'.

Sashin Russian: patr. from the given name *Sasha*, one of a group of aphetic pet forms and dims. of ALEXANDER.

Vars.: **San(yut)in**, **Sa(kh)nov**.

Dims.: **Sashkin**, **Sash(en)kov**, **San(ich)kin**, **Sankov**.

Sason Jewish (non-Ashkenazic): from the Hebr. male given name *Sason* 'Joy', or ornamental name from the vocabulary word.

Vars.: **Sasson**; **Sassoon** (an Anglicized spelling); **Sassoun** (a Gallicized spelling); **Sassoni** (with the Hebr. adj. suffix *-i*).

Patrs.: **Ben-Sasson**; **Sassonov**.

A family called Sassoon *were prominent in the Jewish community in Baghdad, where they were chief banker to the government. However, they were forced to flee persecution in the 18th cent., settling first in Persia, then Bombay. A branch was established in Britain, where Albert Sassoon (1818–96) was created a baronet. This family includes the writer Siegfried Sassoon (1886–1967) and the hairstylist Vidal Sassoon.*

Satterthwaite English: habitation name from a place in the Lake District, so called from OE *sætr* shieling + ON *þveit* pasture (see THWAITE).

Vars.: **Satterfitt**, **Setterfield**.

Saturnin French: from a given name (L *Saturnīnus*, a Roman family name, from *Saturnus*, the god of agriculture and vegetation, whose name is a deriv. of the root *sat-* plant, sow). This was borne by a large number of early saints, including the 3rd-cent. first bishop of Toulouse.

Vars.: **Sernin**, **Sornin**, **Cernin**, **Cerny**.

Cogns.: Prov.: **Sadournin**, **Sadourny**.

Satz Jewish (Ashkenazic): acronym from the Hebr. phrase *Zera TSadikim* 'seed of the righteous', assumed in a spirit of pious respect for one's ancestors. See also SCHATZ.

Vars.: **Zatz**; **Zac** (a Polish spelling).

Sauber German and Jewish (Ashkenazic): nickname for a tidy or well-groomed person, from Ger. *sauber* clean (MHG *sūber* smart, neat).

Vars.: Ger.: **Saubert**; **Säuberlich**, **Seuberlich**, **Seiberlich**. Jewish: **Sauberman**; **Soiberman**, **Zoiberman** (from Yid. *zoyber*).

Sauce French: topographic name for someone who lived by a willow tree, OF *saus* (L *salix*, gen. *salicis*; cf. SALE).

Vars.: **Sausse**, **Sauze**.

Cogns.: It.: **Sal(i)ce**, **Sal(i)ci**. Sp.: **Saz**.

Dims.: Fr.: **Saucet**, **Saucey**, **Sausset**, **Sauzet**. It.: **Sal(ic)etti**, **Sal(ic)ini**, **Salizzoli**.

Collectives: Fr.: **Saussure**; **Saulxures** (Lorraine). It.: **Saliceti**. Sp.: **Salcedo** (places in the provinces of Álava, Lugo, and Oviedo).

Sauer German and Jewish (Ashkenazic): nickname for a cross or cantankerous person, from Ger. *sauer* sour (MHG *sūr*, cogn. with Eng. *sour*, OE *sūr*).

Vars.: Ger.: **Sauermann**. Jewish: **Sauerman(n)**; **Zoyer** (from Yid. *zoyer*).

Cogns.: Low Ger.: **Suhr(mann)**. Dan., Norw.: **Suhr**.

Dims.: Ger.: **Säuerle**, **Seyerlin**.

Cpds: Jewish (reason for adoption unknown, perhaps bestowed by non-Jewish government officials): **Sauerbrunn** ('sour well'); **Sauerquell** ('sour spring'); **Sauerstrom** ('sour river'); **Sauerteig** ('sour dough').

Saul English, French, German, and Italian: from the given name *Saul* (Hebr. *Shaul* 'Asked-for (child)'), the name of the king of Israel whose story is recounted in the first book of Samuel. In spite of his success in uniting Israel and his military prowess, Saul had a troubled reign, not least because of his long conflict with the young David, who eventually succeeded him. Perhaps for this reason, the given name was not particularly common in medieval times; hence the surname too is comparatively rare. A further disincentive to its popularity as a Christian name was the fact that it was the original name of St Paul, borne by him while he was persecuting Christians, and rejected by him after his conversion to Christianity. It may in part have arisen as a nickname for someone who had played the part of the biblical king in a religious play.

Vars.: Eng.: **Saull, Sawle.** It.: **Saul(l)e, Saul(l)i, Saullo.**

Cogns.: Jewish: **Shaul; Shauli, Shauly** (with the Hebr. suffix *-i*); **Shaulsky** (E Ashkenazic).

Dims.: It.: **Saulino.** Jewish: **Shaulick** (E Ashkenazic).

Patrs.: Jewish: **Shaulson** (Ashkenazic); **Shaulov, Shauloff** (E Ashkenazic).

Sault 1. English: var. of SALT.

2. French: topographic name for someone who lived near a grove or small wood, OF *saut* (L *saltus*).

Vars. (of 2): Fr.: **Dussau(l)t, Dussaud; Duss(e)aux, Duseau(x).**

Cogns. (of 2): Sp.: **Soto.** Port.: **Souto.**

Dims. (of 2): It.: **Saltilo.** Sp.: **Sotelo, Sotillo(s).**

Sauter 1. German: occupational name for a shoemaker or cobbler (rarely a tailor), from MHG sūter, *siuter*, *sūtære* (from L *sūtor*, an agent deriv. of *suere* to sew). See also SCHUSTER.

2. English: var. of SALTER.

Vars. (of 1): **Seut(t)er; Seiter** (Swabia); **Sutter(er)** (Switzerland); **Saut(t).** (Of 2): **Saulter, Sautter.**

Cogns. (of 1): Eng.: **Sutor, Sut(t)er, Seuter, Sewter; Sout(t)er, Sout(t)ar, Sowter** (Scots). Fr.: **Suire; Sueur, Lesueur.** Prov.: **Sudre; Sudour.**

Dims. (of 1): Ger.: **Seuterle, Seuterlin, Seit(t)erle, Sütterle, Sütterlin.**

Sautour French: occupational name for a tumbler or acrobat, OF *sauteour* (L *saltor*, an agent deriv. of *salīre*, past part. *saltus*, to spring, leap; cf. SAYLOR).

Dims.: **Saut(e)reau, Sauterel, Sauteron.**

Sauvé French: nickname for someone who had had a narrow escape, or from a given name with a religious significance referring to Christian salvation, from OF *sauvé* saved (past part. of *sauver* to save, L *salvāre*).

Cogns.: Prov.: **Sauvat, Salvat.** Cat.: **Salvat.** Sp., Port.: **Salvado.**

Savage English: nickname for a wild or uncouth person, from ME, OF *salvage*, *sauvage* untamed (LL *salvaticus*, a deriv. of L *silva* wood, influenced by L *salvus* whole, i.e. natural).

Vars.: **Sauvage, Salvage, Sa(l)vidge, Savege.** The surname is also relatively common in Ireland, where it has been Gaelicized **Sabhaois** and **Sabháiste.**

Cogns.: Fr.: **Salvage, Sauvage, Lesauvage.** It.: **Salvaggi, Selvaggi(o), Selvatici.**

Dims.: Fr.: **Sauvageon, Sauvageau, Sauvageot.** It.: **Selvaggini.**

Savatier French: occupational name for a shoemaker or cobbler, OF *savatier* (an agent deriv. of *savate* slipper, shoe, a borrowing from Arabic or some oriental language). The term also acquired the pej. sense 'botcher' and in some cases the surname may perhaps have arisen as an abusive nickname with this meaning.

Var.: **Savetier.**

Cogns.: Prov.: **Sab(b)atier, Sabattier, Sabathier, Sabater, Sabatié, Sabat(h)é.** It.: **Zavattaro, Zavattari, Zavattiero, Zavat(i)eri, Zavitteri, Ciabatteri.** Sp.: **Zapatero.** Cat.: **Sabater, Sabaté(s), Zapater.** Rumanian (Jewish): **Ci(o)botaru, Ciobotaro, Ciobutaru, Ciobutaro, Ciubutaro.**

Savelyev Russian: patr. from the given name *Saveli* (L *Sabellius*). Sabellius (*fl.* 215) was an early Christian theologian who was excommunicated by Pope Calixtus I, but whose ideas enjoyed a considerable cult in the East. The name *Sabellius* is an ethnic term, of uncertain origin, denoting a member of a minor Italic tribe that was subdued by the Romans in ancient times; cf. SABIN.

Var.: **Savyolov.**

Cogns.: It.: **Savelli, Sabelli.**

Dims.: Russ.: **Savlichev** (patr.). It.: **Savellini.**

Savignac French: habitation name from any of the various places, mostly in SW France, so called from the Gallo-Roman personal name *Sabinius* (a deriv. of *Sabinus*; see SABIN) + the local suffix *-ācum*.

Vars.: **Savignat, Savigny.**

Friedrich von Savigny *(1779–1861), the leading figure in the formulation of modern civil law in Germany, was born in Frankfurt into a landed noble family. His ancestors had emigrated to Germany from Lorraine.*

Saville English (Norman): habitation name from a place in N France, of which the identity is not clear. It is probably *Sainville* in Eure-et-Loire, so called from OF *saisne* Saxon (see SACHS 1) + *ville* settlement (see VILLE).

Vars.: **Savil(l), Savile, Save(a)ll, Seville.**

Savoie French: regional name from Savoy, Fr. *Savoie*, which was consolidated in the 11th cent. by Count Humbert the White-handed, feudal lord of the kingdom of Arles. His descendants formed the great European noble house of Savoy, with large holdings in France, Switzerland, and Italy. Piedmont was closely connected with Savoy as early as the 11th cent., since Humbert acquired a number of possessions there through marriage.

Vars.: **Savoye, Savois; Savoyer, Savoyen, Savoyant.**

Cogns.: It.: **Savoia; Savoiardi.**

Savory English: from a Gmc personal name composed of the elements *saba*, of uncertain meaning + *rīc* power, which was introduced into England by the Normans in the form *Savaric*.

Vars.: **Savoury, Savary, Savery, Severy.**

Cogns.: Fr.: **Savaric, Savarit, Savary; Saf(f)ré, Saffroy.**

One of the earliest Australian novels, Quintus Servington *(1831), was written by an English-born convict, Henry* Savery *(1791–1842). He had been convicted of forgery and when his death-sentence was commuted he was transported to Australia in 1825. Savery was borne in Butcombe, Somerset, the son of a banker, and had been a businessman and sugar refiner. In Australia he fell into debt and was again imprisoned, during which time he wrote his sketches of colonial life.*

Savoureux French: nickname for a pleasant or amiable person, from OF *savoureux* tasty, agreeable (LL *saporōsus*, from *sapor* flavour, taste).

Vars.: **Savreux; Savouré.**

Cogns.: Prov.: **Saboureux; Sabourand.**

Dims.: Fr.: **Savouret, Savourez**. Prov.: **Sabouret, Saboureau, Sabourin**.

Aug.: Fr.: **Savourat**.

The name Sabourin *was introduced into England through Huguenot immigration. One present-day family trace their descent from a certain Pierre Sabourin, who arrived in England c.1750 from Saint-Maixent and became a silk-weaver in Bethnal Green, London. An earlier immigrant was Aaron Sabourin, recorded in 1682 in the archives of the French Protestant Church, London.*

Sawicki Polish: from the given name *Sawa* (from Gk *Sabbas*, the name of a saint who died in 532), with the addition of *-ski*, suffix of surnames (see BARANOWSKI).

Dim.: Pol.: **Sawczyk**.

Patrs.: Pol.: **Sawicz**. Croatian: **Savić, Savićević**.

Patr. (from a dim.): Croatian: **Savković**.

Sawyer English: occupational name for someone who earned his living from sawing wood, ME *saghier*, an agent deriv. of *sagh(en)* to saw (from OE *sagu* a saw); for the inserted glide, cf. BOWYER. The ME word absorbed the ANF term for a sawyer, *syour* (see SEWER 3).

Var.: **Sawer**; see also SAYER.

Cogns.: Ger.: **Säger**. Low Ger.: **Sager**. Flem., Du.: **Saeger, Saegaert**. Jewish (Ashkenazic): **Seger, Sager**; **Zegman** (from Yid. *zeg* saw).

Patr.: Eng.: **Sawyers**.

Equivs. (not cogn.): Fr.: GACHE. Pol.: TRACZ. Russ.: PILSHCHIKOV.

Saxby English: 1. habitation name from places in Leics. and Lincs., so called from the ON byname *Saksi* 'Saxon' (or the gen. of the OE folk-name *Seaxe*, ON *Saksar*; cf. SACHS 1) + ON *býr* farm, settlement.

2. from ME *sakespey*, OF *sacquespee*, a nickname for someone quick to take offence and draw his sword, from OF *sacque(r)* to draw, extract (from *sac* SACK) + *espee* sword (L *spatha*; cf. ESPADA).

Cogn. (of 2): Fr.: **Sacquépée**.

Saxon English (Lancs.): 1. var. of SAXTON.

2. from the medieval given name *Saxon*, originally an ethnic byname for someone from Saxony; cf. SACHS 1.

Saxton English: 1. habitation name from places in Cambs. and W Yorks., both so called from OE *Seaxe* Saxons (cf. SACHS 1) + *tūn* enclosure, settlement.

2. occupational name, a var. of SEXTON 1.

Say English: 1. Norman habitation name from *Sai* in Orne or *Say* in Indre, perhaps so called from a Gaul. personal name *Saius* + the local suffix *-ācum*.

2. metonymic occupational name for a maker or seller of *say*, a kind of finely textured cloth (from OF *saie*, L *saga*, pl. of *sagum* military cloak). The surname may also have denoted a habitual wearer of clothes made of this material.

Var.: **Saye**.

Sayer 1. English: from the ME personal name *Saher* or *Seir*. This is probably a Norman introduction of the Continental Gmc personal name *Sigiheri*, composed of the elements *sigi* victory + *heri* army. However, it could also represent a ME survival of an unrecorded OE name, **Sǣhere*, composed of the elements *sǣ* sea + *here* army.

2. English: occupational name for a woodcutter, from ME *saghier* (see SAWYER) or OF *seieor* (see SEWER 3).

3. English: occupational name for a professional reciter, from an agent deriv. of ME *say(en)*, *sey(en)* to say (OE *secgan*).

4. English: occupational name for an assayer of metals or a taster of food, from an aphetic form of ME *assayer* (an agent deriv. of *assay* trial, test, OF *essay*, from LL *exagium*, a deriv. of *exagmināre* to weigh).

5. English: occupational name for a maker or seller of the type of cloth known in ME as *say*; cf. SAY 2.

6. Welsh: occupational name from W *saer* wright, artificer, carpenter (cf. MCINTYRE).

Vars.: **Sa(y)re, Saer, Se(e)ar**.

Cogns. (of 1): Fr.: **Sig(u)ier, Ség(ui)er, Sohier, Soyer, Soyez**. Ger.: **Sieger(t), Se(e)ger(t), Segger**.

Patrs.: Eng.: **Sayers, Seyers**; **Sear(e)s, Seers**; **Searson**, SARSON. (From 1 only): Low Ger.: **Siegers, Se(e)gers**. Dan., Norw.: **Sejersen**.

Saylor English: occupational name for a dancer or acrobat, OF *sailleor* (L *salītor*, from *salīre* to jump, leap; cf. SAUTOUR).

Vars.: **Sailer**, SEILER.

Cogns.: Fr.: **Saillier; Saillant**.

Scaife N English: nickname for an awkward or difficult man, a tyke, or else one who was physically misshapen, from Northern ME *skafe* misshapen, crooked; awkward, difficult (ON *skeifr*).

Vars.: **Skaife, Scafe**.

Scammell English: of uncertain origin, perhaps from a ME given name **Skammel*, dim. of an ON byname from *skammr* short.

Scannell Irish: Anglicized form of Gael. **Ó Scannail** 'descendant of *Scannal*', a byname meaning 'Contention'.

Vars.: **O'Scandall, O'Scannill, O'Scannell**.

Dims.: **O'Scanlaine, (O')Scanlan, (O')Scan(d)lon** (Gael. **Ó Scannláin**).

Scantlebury English (W Country): of unknown origin, perhaps a habitation name from *Kentisbury* or *Kentisbeare* in Devon, with excrescent initial *S-*. Both these places derive their first element from the OE personal name *Cǣntel*; the second is in the one case *burh* fort (see BURY) and in the other *bearu* grove (see BEER).

Scarborough English: habitation name from the town on the coast of N Yorks., so called from the ON byname *Skarði* (see SCARTH 2) + ON *borg* fortress, town.

Scarfe English: nickname for someone bearing some supposed resemblance to a cormorant, Northern ME *scarfe* (ON *skarfr*), or else a survival into ME of the ON byname *Scarfi*, from the same source.

Vars.: **Scarf(f), Scarffe**.

Scargill English: habitation name from a place in N Yorks., so called from the ON bird name *skraki*, a diving duck + ON *gil* valley, ravine (see GILL 2).

Scarisbrick English: habitation name from a place near Liverpool, so called from the gen. case of the ON personal name *Skar* + ON *brekka* slope, hill.

Vars.: **Sizebrick, Siosbrick**.

It is probable that all present-day bearers of these names are descended from Gilbert de Scaresbrec, *who held the manor of Scarisbrick in the 13th cent.*

Scarlett English: metonymic occupational name for a dyer or for a seller of rich, bright fabrics, from OF *escarlate* scarlet cloth (LL *scarlāta*, *scarlētum*, of uncertain, probably Semitic, origin).

Var.: **Scarlet**.

Cogns.: It.: **Scarlata, Scarlato, Scarlat(t)i**. Ger.: **Scharlach**.

Scarso Italian: nickname for a poor man or for a miser, from It. *scarso* scarse, scant (LL *excarpsus*, for class. L *excarptus*, past part. of *excarpere* to excerpt, pick out).
Var.: **Scarsi**.
Dims.: **Scarsello**, **Scarselli**, **Scarsini**.

Scarth N English and Scots (esp. Orkneys): 1. habitation name from any of the various places named with the ON topographical term *skarð* gap, notch.
2. from the ON byname *Skarði* 'Hare-lipped', a deriv. of the element given above.
This is the name of a family who settled in Orkney from Norway in the 15th cent. They took their name from lands at Scarth *or* Settiscarth *in the Orkneys. An early ancestor, Alvar Haraldsson (1340–1412), was secretary to King Håkon of Norway.*

Scatchard English: of uncertain origin, perhaps a derisory nickname for a long-legged man, from ANF *(e)scache* stilt + the pej. suffix *-ard*.

Scattergood English: nickname for a man who was careless and free with money, perhaps a philanthropist who gave his goods to the poor, from ME *skater(en)* to squander, dissipate (apparently a byform, under Scandinavian influence, of *shatter*) + *gode* property, goods, wealth.

Schadow German: habitation name from a place in the Spreewald, whose name is of Slav. origin.
A German family of this name produced a number of artists in the late 18th and 19th cents. Johann Schadow *(1764–1850) was born in Berlin and became Prussian court sculptor; his work included the crowning piece on the Brandenburg Gate. His son Rudolf Schadow (1786–1822) was born in Rome and was also a sculptor; another son, Wilhelm von Schadow (1788–1862), made a prosperous living as a painter of historical and religious subjects.*

Schäfer 1. German: occupational name for a shepherd, Ger. *Schäfer*, an agent deriv. of *Schaf* sheep (MHG *schāf*, OHG *scāf*).
2. Jewish (Ashkenazic): because of the small number of Jewish shepherds at the time when most Ashkenazic Jews adopted surnames (in the late 18th and early 19th cents.), it is unlikely that this common Jewish surname can be given a literal interpretation. Perhaps it was adopted as a reference to God ('The Lord is my Shepherd'; Ps. 23: 1), or perhaps in allusion to King David, who was a shepherd in his boyhood.
Vars.: Jewish: **Schaf(f)er**, **S(c)hef(f)er**; **Szefer** (a Pol. spelling); Sheferman.
Cogns.: Low Ger.: **Schaper**, **Schäper**, **Scheper**. Flem., Du.: **Schaper**, **(De) Scheper**. See also SHIPMAN.
Patrs.: Low Ger.: **Schäpers**, **Sche(e)pers**, **Schiepers**. Flem., Du.: **Schepers**.

Schaffer 1. German: occupational name for a steward or baliff, from an agent deriv. of Ger. *schaffen* to manage, run (OHG *scaffan*, *scaffōn*).
2. Jewish (Ashkenazic): var. of SCHÄFER.
Vars. (of 1): **Schaffner**, **Scheffner**, **Schäffer**, **Schöfer**.
Cogn. (of 1): Czech: **Šafář**.
Dims. (of 1): Ger.: **Schafferlin**. Czech: **Šafařík**.
Patr. (from 1): Low Ger.: **Scheffers**.

Schäffler German (Bavaria): occupational name for a cooper, an agent deriv. of *Schäffl*, dim. of the S Ger. dial. term *Schaff* tub, butt.
Vars.: **Scheffler**, **Schöffler**; **Scheff(e)l**, **Schöffel**.
Cogns.: Jewish (Ashkenazic): **Schaffler**, **S(c)hefler**. Czech: **Šefl**.

Schalk German: occupational name for a servant or, more specifically, a jester, MHG *schalk* (OHG *scalc*); cf. also GOTTSCHALK, MARSHALL, SENESHAL. Later the word came to be used as a term of reproach, 'knave', and some cases of the surname may reflect this use.
Var.: **Schalch**.
Dims.: **Schalkl**, **Schälkle**.

Scharnhorst German: habitation name from any of various places, for example near Dortmund in Westphalia and also near Verden and to the north of Celle, apparently so called from the Gmc elements *skarn* damp, dirty + *horst* wood(ed hill) (cf. HURST).

Scharrer German: 1. occupational name for a carder of wool, from an agent deriv. of Ger. *scharren* to scrape, scratch (akin to OHG *scerran*).
2. habitation name from any of the various places, such as *Scharr* in Switzerland and the Upper Palatinate or *Scharre* in Saxony, named from OHG *scara* wooded area, with the suffix *-er* denoting an inhabitant of a place.

Schatz 1. German: metonymic occupational name for a treasurer, from Ger. *Schatz* treasure (MHG *scha(t)z*, OHG *skaz*). It may also have been a nickname for a rich man (or ironically for a miser), or else for a well-liked person or a ladies' favourite, from the use of the vocab. word as a term of endearment.
2. Jewish (Ashkenazic): acronymic name from the Hebr. phrase *SHeliach-TSibur* 'emissary of the congregation', an epithet of the cantor.
Vars. (of 1): **Schatz(l)er**, **Schätz(l)er**; **Schatzmann**. (Of 2): **Shatz**, **Szatz**; **Shatski**, **Shatsky** (E Ashkenazic adjectival forms); **Shatzov**, **Shatzkin** (patrs., the latter based on a dim. form).
Cogns. (of 1): Low Ger.: **Schatt**. Jewish (Ashkenazic): **S(c)hatzman** (probably ornamental; alternatively an elaboration of 2).
Dims. (of 1): Ger.: **Schatzl**, **Schätzl**.
Cpd (of 1, ornamental): Jewish (Ashkenazic): **S(c)hatzberg** ('treasure hill').

Schauer 1. German: occupational name for an official inspector, for example the official overseer of a market, MHG *schouwer*, agent deriv. of *schouwen* to look, inspect (OHG *scouwōn*).
2. Jewish (W Ashkenazic): ornamental name from a W Yid. pronunciation of Hebr. *shor* ox, perhaps taken by bearers of the given name JOSEPH because the biblical character of this name is compared to an ox in Deut. 33: 17: 'His glory is like the firstling of his bullock'. See also BICK 2.
Vars. (of 1): **Schauert**, **Schauber**. (Of 2): **S(c)hor(r)**, **Schorman(n)**; **Szor** (a Pol. spelling); **S(c)hory**, **Shori** (with the Hebr. suffix *-i*); SHORE.

Schechter Jewish (Ashkenazic): occupational name for a ritual slaughterer, Ger. *Schächter* (agent deriv. of *schächten*, from the Yid. verb *shekhtn*, whose stem is from Hebr. *shachat* to slaughter). See also SHOIKHET.
Vars.: **Schächter**, **Scha(e)chter**, **Schacter**, **Shechter**, **Schecter**, **Szechter**, **Schechner**, **S(c)hecht(er)man**.

Schecker German: occupational name for an armourer, an agent. deriv. of MHG *schecke* quilted jacket, coat of mail.
Vars.: **Scheck(e)**, **Schegg**, **Schöck**; **Scheckenmacher**, **Scheggenmacher**.

Scheidt German: topographic name for someone who lived near a boundary or watershed, MHG *scheide* (OHG *sceida*, from *sceidan* to part, divide), or habitation name from any of the numerous places named with this word.
Vars.: **Scheit**, **Schaid(t)**; **Scheid(l)er**.

Scheinis Jewish (Ashkenazic): metr. from the Yid. female given name *Sheyne* (from Yid. *sheyn* beautiful, which is from MHG *schoene*; cf. SCHÖN) + the Yid. possessive suffix -*s*.

Vars.: **Sheinis**, **S(c)heines**; **Sheinenson**, **Scheineson**; **Szenes**, **S(c)heinin** (E Ashkenazic).

Dims.: **Sche(i)ndel** (from Yid. *Sheyndel*); **Scheinkin** (metr., from Yid. *Sheynke*).

Schell German: nickname for a wild or obstreperous person, from MHG *schel* noisy, loud.

Vars.: **Schelle(r)**, **Schöll(er)**; **Schellig**, **Schölig**.

Cogn.: Jewish (Ashkenazic): **Scheller**.

Schemmel German: metonymic nickname for a cripple, from MHG *schemel* crutch (also meaning 'bench' or 'stool', OHG *scamil*, from L *scamillus* raised platform).

Var.: **Schemel**.

Schenke German: occupational name for a cup-bearer or server of wine, MHG *schenke* (OHG *scenko*, from *scenken* to pour out, serve). The vocab. word was also used as an occupational name for a tavern keeper (hence the sense of the mod. Ger. word, 'inn, tavern'). In another development, the word came to be used as an honorary title for a high court official (cf. BUTLER); the surname may additionally derive from either of these senses.

Vars.: **Schenk**, **Schenck(e)**; **Schenker** ('tavern keeper').

Cogns.: Jewish (Ashkenazic, all meaning 'tavern keeper'; a very common group of names because at one time only Jews were allowed to sell alcohol in the Russian Empire): **Shenker**, **Sche(i)nker**, **Sheinker**, **She(i)nkar**; **Szenkier** (Pol. spelling); **Sche(i)nkman**, **Szeinkman**, **Shenk(man)**, **She(i)nkerman**. Ukr.: **Shinkar**.

Scherzer 1. German: occupational name for a jester or nickname for a facetious person, an agent deriv. of Ger. *Scherz* joke (MHG *scherz* amusement, game).

2. Jewish (E Ashkenazic): possibly a habitation name from *Scierza* in Galicia, Poland, or an occupational name akin to 1, referring to an entertainer at Jewish weddings.

Vars.: **Schertzer**; **Scher(t)z** (metonymic).

Scheuer 1. German: topographic name for someone who lived near a tithe-barn, or metonymic occupational name for an official responsible for receiving the tithes of agricultural produce rendered, from MHG *schiur(e)*, *schiuwer* barn, granary (OHG *scūra*, *sciura*).

2. Jewish (Ashkenazic): of uncertain origin, perhaps taken by someone who lived near or owned a barn.

Vars. (of 1): **Scheurer**, **Scheuermann**. (Of 2): **Scheuerman(n)**; **Scheier**, **Schaier** (presumably from Yid. *shayer* barn).

Vars.: Low Ger.: **Verschuer**, **Terschüren**; **Scheu(ne)mann**, **Schü(ne)mann**. Flem.: **Van der Schueren**; **Schuerman**. Du.: **Verschoor**, **Verschuren**, **Schuurman**.

Schiaparelli Italian: occupational name for a woodcutter, from a dim. of the Ligurian dial. term *sciaparo* (an agent deriv. of *sciapà* to split, cleave).

Schick 1. German: nickname for a pleasant and well-behaved person, from Ger. *schick* polished, courteous, proper, fitting (from Ger., MHG *schicken* to be fitting or appropriate; the Fr. adj. *chic* is from the Ger.).

2. Jewish (Ashkenazic): of uncertain origin, either of similar derivation to 1 above, or perhaps an acronym of the Hebr. phrase *SHem yisrael Kodesh* 'the name of Israel is holy'.

Vars. (of 1): **Schicke**, **Schicker(t)**. (Of 2): **Shi(c)k**.

Dims. (of 1): **Schick(e)l**, **Schickele**.

Schief German: nickname for someone suffering from some deformity, from Ger., MLG *schief* crooked.

Vars.: **Scheef(e)**, **Scheff**, **Scheve**, **Scheewe**.

Schild 1. German: metonymic occupational name for a maker or painter of shields, from Ger. *Schild* shield (MHG *schilt*, OHG *scilt*).

2. Jewish (Ashkenazic): of uncertain origin, probably a house name for someone who lived in a house marked with a sign, from Ger. *Schild*, Yid. *shild* sign; cf. ROTHSCHILD and SCHWARZSCHILD.

Vars.: **Schildt**, **Schilder**, **Schilter**. (Of 2 only): **Schildhaus**.

Cogns.: Eng.: SHIELD. Swed.: **Sk(j)öld**, **Skiöld**.

Dim.: Low Ger.: **Schilgen**.

Schiller 1. German: nickname for a person with a squint, from an agent deriv. of MHG *schilhen* to squint (from *schelh* squinting, OHG *scelah*).

2. Jewish (S Ashkenazic): see SCHULER 2.

Vars. (of 1): **Schilcher**. (Of 2): **Shil(l)er**.

Cogns. (of 1): Low Ger.: **Scheel(e)**, **Schiel(e)**, **Schelch(er)**, **Schölch**, **Schelb(er)**, **Schelbert**.

Schilling German: nickname from the coin, Ger. *Schilling* (MHG *schilling*, OHG *scilling*, a deriv. of *scilt* shield). The surname may have referred originally to a rent or fee owed, or have some other anecdotal origin, now irrecoverable.

Vars.: **Schelling**. (Under Slav. influence): **Schilla(c)k**, **Schellack**, **Schellach**, **Schillok**, **Schilloga**.

Cogns.: Jewish (Ashkenazic): **Shiling**. Eng.: **Shilling**. Flem., Du.: **Schellinck**.

Patr.: Flem.: **Schellinckx**.

Schimmel 1. German and Dutch: nickname for a man with grey or white hair, from MHG, MDu. *schimel*, a term used to denote both mildew and a white horse. OHG forms are not found, and the semantic development is not entirely clear.

2. Jewish (Ashkenazic): of uncertain origin, probably an unflattering nickname, meaning 'mildew', imposed by a non-Jewish government official.

Schimpf 1. German: nickname for a humorous or playful person, from MHG *schimpf* sport, play, amusement (OHG *scimpf*).

2. Jewish (Ashkenazic): of uncertain origin, probably an unflattering nickname from mod. Ger. *Schimpf* insult, complaint, imposed by a non-Jewish government official.

Vars: Ger.: **Schimpp**, **Schempf**, **Schempp**; **Schimpfer**.

Dim.: Ger.: **Schimpfle**.

Schlecht German: 1. nickname for a straightforward person, from MHG, OHG *sleht* direct, natural (which later came to mean 'defective', 'bad'; a cogn. of SLIGHT 1).

2. habitation name from any of various minor places, named from OHG *sleht* in the sense 'flat'. There are places so named for example in Mecklenburg and the Upper Palatinate.

Vars.: **Schlicht(e)**, **Schlichter**, **Schlichtmann**.

Cogn.: Flem., Du.: **Slegt**.

Patrs. (from 1): Low Ger.: **Schlichting**. Flem., Du.: **Slechten**.

Schlegel German: metonymic occupational name for a smith, or nickname for a forceful person, from MHG *slegel* sledgehammer (OHG *slegil*, a deriv. of *slahan* to strike).

Vars.: **Schlegl**, **Schlögl**.

Schleicher German and Jewish (Ashkenazic): nickname for a furtive or stealthy person, from an agent deriv. of Ger. *schleichen* to creep silently (MHG *slīchen*, OHG *slīhhan*).

Vars.: Ger.: **Schleich**. Jewish: **Shleicher**.

Cogn.: Low Ger.: **Schlieker**.

Schleier German: metonymic occupational name for a maker or seller of veils, from Ger. *Schleier* veil or headscarf (MHG *sleier*, *sloier*, of uncertain origin).

Vars.: **Schleyer**, **Schlayer**; **Schleirmacher**.

Schleifer 1. German: occupational name for a polisher of swords and armour (cf. FROBISHER), or a grinder of knives or diamonds, from an agent deriv. of Ger. *schleifen* to grind, polish (MHG *slîfen*, OHG *slīfan*).

2. German and Jewish (Ashkenazic): habitation name for someone who came from *Schleife* in Silesia.

Vars. (of 1): Ger.: **Schleif**. Jewish: **Schleifman**.

Cogns. (of 1): Low Ger.: **Schliep(er)**. Eng.: **Slipper**.

Schlein Jewish (Ashkenazic): ornamental or occupational-ornamental name from Yid. *shlayn* tench (Ger. *Schlei(e)*, MHG *slī(g)e*, *slīhe*, OHG *slīo*). This is one of the many Ashkenazic ornamental names taken from words denoting fishes.

Cogn.: Low Ger.: SCHLIEMANN.

Schlessinger German: regional name for someone from Silesia (Ger. *Schlesien*, *Schlesing*, Pol. *Śląsk*), so called from the *Silingae*, a Gmc tribe which occupied the region before being expelled by Slavs in the 4th cent. AD. The region is now part of Poland, but was formerly under German administration. Other places named with the same element include *Schleusingen* in Saxony, *Schlenzig* in Pomerania, and *Schlenz* in Silesia itself, and it is possible that in some instances the surname derives from one of these.

Vars.: **Sles(s)inger**, **Slazenger** (Anglicized forms); **Schlensok**, **Schlensog** (of Slav. origin).

Cogns.: Pol.: **Śląski**, **Ślązak**, **Ślęzak**. Czech: **Slezák**. Jewish (Ashkenazic): **S(c)hlesinger**; **Szlezyng(i)er** (Pol. spellings); **Slezak**; **Shla(n)sky**, **Shlanski**, **Shlonsky**.

Schlick 1. German: nickname for a glutton, a deriv. of MHG *slicken* to gulp, swallow (OHG **sluckōn*).

2. Low German: topographic name for someone who lived in a marshy area, from MLG *slik* slime, bog.

3. Jewish (Ashkenazic): of uncertain origin, probably an unflattering name from mod. Ger. *Schlick* slime, mud, imposed by a non-Jewish government official.

Vars. (of 1): **Schluck(er)**. (Of 2): **Schlicke**, **Schlickmann**, **Schlich**.

Schliemann 1. Low German: occupational name for a seller of freshwater fish, from MLG *slîe* tench + *mann* man.

2. German: topographic name for someone who lived near a sloe tree, or occupational name for someone who sold sloes, from MHG *slēhe* sloe (OHG *slēha*, *slēwa*) + *mann* man.

Vars. (of 1): **Schlie**. (Of 2): **Schlee(mann)**.

Cogns. (of 1): Ger.: **Schlei**, **Schley**. Jewish (Ashkenazic): SCHLEIN.

Schliesser 1. German: occupational name for a jailer, Ger. *Schliesser*, or for a chatelain or steward in charge of the keys to the pantry and storerooms, MHG *sliezer*, agent deriv. of *sliezen* to shut, lock (OHG *sliozan*).

2. Jewish (Ashkenazic): of uncertain origin, perhaps an adoption of the relatively common German surname.

Var.: Ger.: **Schleusser**.

Cogns.: Low Ger.: **Schleuter**, **Schlüter**.

Schloss 1. German: metonymic occupational name for a locksmith, from Ger. *Schloss* lock (MHG, OHG *sloz*, a deriv. of *sliozen* to shut, lock; cf. SCHLIESSER).

2. German: topographic name for someone who lived in or near a castle, or who or was employed at a castle, Ger. *Schloss* castle (originally the same word as in 1).

3. Jewish (Ashkenazic): of uncertain origin, either an occupational cogn. of 1 or an ornamental name related to 2.

Vars. (of 1 and 2): **Schlösser**, **Schlossmann**. (Of 1 only): **Schlossmacher**, **Schlosshauer**.

Cogns. (of 1 and 2): Flem., Du.: **Slot**. Dan., Norw.: **Sloth**. (Of 1 only): Flem., Du.: **Slotma(e)ker**. See also ŚLUSARSKI.

Schlossberg Jewish (Ashkenazic): habitation name from any of various places in Germany so called, because they were the sites of castles (see SCHLOSS 2) on hills (see BERG).

Var.: **Szlosberg** (a Pol. spelling).

Schlunk German: topographic name for someone who lived in a narrow valley or ravine, MHG dial. *slunk* (cogn. with mod. Ger. *Schlund* throat, chasm), or perhaps a nickname from this word.

Schmalz 1. German: metonymic occupational name for a chandler, from Ger. *Schmalz* tallow, grease, fat (MHG, OHG *smalz*), or perhaps a nickname for a fat or unctuous man.

2. Jewish (Ashkenazic): of uncertain origin, perhaps a nickname from Ger. *Schmalz* or Yid. *shmalts* animal fat.

Vars.: Ger.: **Schmaltz**; **Schmolz** (Bavaria). Jewish: **Schmalzer** (apparently an occupational name for someone who dealt in animal fat).

Cogns.: Low Ger.: **Schmalt**, **Schmol(d)t**.

Dims.: Ger.: **Schmalzl**, **Schmälzle**; **Schmolzl** (Bavaria).

Schmuck German: metonymic nickname for someone who wore a prominent jewel or ornament, from Ger. *Schmuck* jewel, ornament (MHG *smuc* jewel, finery).

Cogn.: Low Ger.: **Schmugge**.

Schnabel German and Jewish (Ashkenazic): nickname for a gossip or a glutton, or for someone with a long nose, from Ger. *Schnabel* beak, mouth (MHG *snabel*, OHG *snabul*).

Cogns.: Czech: **Šnobl**, **Šnábl**.

Schneck German and Jewish (Ashkenazic): nickname for a slow or indolent worker, from Ger. *Schneck(e)*, Yid. *shnek* snail (MHG *snecke*, OHG *snecko*). The same Ger. vocab. word was also used to denote slugs and leeches, and the surname may in some cases refer to one of these creatures, e.g. as a nickname for a 'slimy' or clinging person, or in the case of the Jewish name, simply an unflattering name imposed by a non-Jewish government official.

Vars.: Ger.: **Schnicke**; **Schnegg(e)**, **Schnigge**, **Schnegel** (chiefly S German and Austrian).

Schneider German and Jewish (Ashkenazic): occupational name for a tailor, Ger. *Schneider*, Yid. *shnayder* (MHG *snīdære*, an agent deriv. of *snīden* to cut, OHG *snīdan*). The vocab. word is probably a loan translation of OF *tailleur* (see TAYLOR), replacing the earlier *nātære*, from *nāten* to sew.

Vars.: Ger.: **Schneidermann**. Jewish: **Snider**, **Snyder** (Anglicized forms); **Schneid(er)man**; **Sznajderman** (a Pol. spelling).

Cogns.: Eng.: **Snider(man)**, **Snyder**. Low Ger.: **Schnie(de)r**. Flem.: **Sn(e)yder**, **Snieder**. Du.: **Sneider**, **Sniyder**. Czech: **Šnajdr**. Pol.: **Sznajder** (from the Ger. vocab. word).

Patrs.: Jewish: **Shneiderov** (E Ashkenazic). Low Ger.: **Schneiders**, **Schnie(de)rs**. Flem.: **Sn(e)yders**, **Snieders**. Du.: **Snijders**. Eng.: **Sniders**, **Snyders**.

Schneir Jewish (Ashkenazic): from the Yid. male given name *Shneyer* (ultimately from L SENIOR 'Elder').

Vars.: **Schneu(e)r**, **Shneur**, **Shneor**; **Sznejor** (a Pol. spelling).

Patrs.: **Schneerso(h)n, Schneurso(h)n, Shneerson; Schneirovitz** (E Ashkenazic).

Schnitzer German and Jewish (Ashkenazic): occupational name for a woodworker, from an agent deriv. of Ger. *schnitzen* to cut, carve (MHG *snitzen*).

Vars.: Ger.: **Schnitz(ler); Schnetz, Schnetz(l)er.** Jewish: **Schnitzler.**

Schnur German and Jewish (Ashkenazic): metonymic occupational name for a maker of cords and rope, from Ger. *Schnur*, Yid. *shnur* cord, rope (MHG *snuor*).

Vars.: Ger.: **Schnürer; Schnierer** (Bavaria). Jewish: **Shnur, Schnurman, Schnurmacher; Schnirr, Schnirman, Schnirer** (from a S Yid. pronunciation).

Cogn.: Low Ger.: **Schnoor.**

Dims.: Ger.: **Schnürle; Schnierl** (Bavaria). Low Ger.: **Schnürchen.**

Schnurrer German: of uncertain origin, possibly: 1. occupational name for a jester or nickname for a merry prankster, from MHG *snurrære* jester.

2. occupational name for a busker, one who begged by playing the *Schnurrpfeife*, an instrument similar to a penny whistle.

3. nickname for someone with something odd about his mouth, from Ger. *Schnurre* mouth (MLG *snurre*).

4. occupational name for a night-watchman, an agent deriv. of Ger. *Schnurre* rattle; night-watchmen carried rattles.

Vars.: **Schnurr(e); Schnorr(er).**

Schofield English (mainly Northern): habitation name from any of various minor places, in Lancs. and elsewhere, named from ME *sc(h)ole* hut (see SCHOLES) + *feld* pasture, open country (see FIELD).

Vars.: **Sc(h)ol(e)field, Scoefield, Sco(f)field.**

Scholar English: Reaney makes this a local name from ON *skáli* hut (see SCHOLES) + *erg* shieling. However, it seems equally probable that it is a nickname for a person who could read and write, in the days when education was the exception rather than the rule; cf. SCHULER, SCULLY.

Vars.: Eng.: **Scholer, Scollard; Scoular** (Scots).

Cogns. (referring to minor clerics): Sp.: **Escolar.** Cat.: **Escolà.**

Scholes N English: topographic name for someone who lived in a rough hut or shed, Northern ME *scale*, later also *sc(h)ole* (from ON *skáli*), or habitation name from one of the various places named with this word, as for example *Scholes* in W Yorks. or *Scales* in Lancs. and Cumb.

Vars.: **Schoales, Scoles, Scale(s); Scoyles** (Norfolk).

Scholey N English: topographic name for someone who lived in a wood or clearing with a hut in it, from ON *skáli* hut (see SCHOLES) + OE *lēah* wood, clearing. This cpd occurs several times as a minor placename in W Yorks.

Scholl 1. German: nickname for a lumpish person, from Ger. *Scholle* clod of earth (OHG *scolla, scollo*).

2. Jewish (Ashkenazic): cogn. of 1, or acronymic surname from the Hebr. phrase *SHevach Leel* 'praise to God'.

Var. (of 2): **Shol.**

Schön German: nickname for a handsome or pleasant man, from Ger. *schön* fine, beautiful; bright; refined, friendly, nice (MHG *schœne*, OHG *skōni*).

2. Jewish (Ashkenazic): ornamental name from the same vocab. word as in 1, in any of its senses.

Vars.: Ger.: **Schöne, Schöner(t), Schonert, Schön(e)mann; Schönherr.** Jewish: **S(c)ho(e)n; S(c)hein(er), Scheyn, Shain, Szejn, Szajn(er)**; (from Yid. *sheyn*; *Szajn* is a Pol. spelling); **Scheinman(n), S(c)heinerman, Sheinman, Schainman; Schen(man).**

Cogns.: Low Ger.: **Schoon, Schömann.** Flem., Du.: **De Schoone.**

Dims.: Ger.: **Schönle(in), Schinle.** Low Ger.: **Schöneke.**

Patr.: Low Ger.: **Schöning.**

Cpds (ornamental): Jewish: **Scho(e)nbach, S(c)heinbach, Shainbach** ('lovely stream'); **Scho(e)nbaum, S(c)heinbaum, Sheynbaum, Shainbaum, Szejnbojm** ('lovely tree'); **Sheinbein, Schenbein** ('lovely bone'); **Schönberg, S(c)ho(e)nberg(er), S(c)heinberg(er), Shainberg, Sheinerberg, Szejnberg, Schenberg** ('lovely hill'); **Scheinblatt** ('lovely leaf'); **Schonblum** ('lovely flower'); **Sho(e)nbrot, Szenbrot** ('lovely bread'); **Scheinbrun** ('lovely well'); **S(c)hondorf** ('lovely village'); **S(c)heinfein** ('lovely and fine'); **Scho(e)nfeld, Shoenfeld, Sche(i)nfeld, Sheinfeld, Shainfeld, Sze(i)nfeld, Szainfeld** ('lovely field'); **Scheinfuchs** ('lovely fox'); **S(c)heingarten** ('lovely garden'); **Scho(e)ngut, Shongut, Scheingut** ('lovely and good'); **Sheinhaus** ('lovely house'); **Schoenherz, Scheinherz** ('lovely heart'); **Scho(e)nholz, S(c)heinholz** ('lovely wood'); **Schoenhorn, S(c)heinhorn** ('lovely horn'); **Shainkind, Sheinkinder** ('lovely child(ren)'); **Schonkopf** ('lovely head'); **Schoenlicht** ('lovely light'); **Schoenrock, Scheinrok, Szeinrok** ('lovely coat'); **S(c)honshein** ('lovely shine'); **Schonstadt** ('lovely city'); **Shonstein** ('lovely stone'); **Schonthal, Sheintal, Schenthal** ('lovely valley'); **S(c)heintuch** ('lovely cloth'); **Schoenwald, Scheinwald** ('lovely forest').

Schöngauer German: regional name from *Schöngau* in Upper Bavaria, so called from OHG *skōni* lovely (see SCHÖN) + *gewi* region, area.

Schramm German and Jewish (Ashkenazic): metonymic nickname for a person with a prominent scar, from Ger. *Schramme*, Yid. *shram* scar (MHG *schram(me)*).

Vars.: Ger.: **Schramme; Schrimp(f), Schrempf, Schrempp.**

Cogn.: Pol.: **Szram** (from the Ger. word).

Dims.: Ger.: **Schrammel, Schremmel.** Low Ger.: **Schramke.** Czech: **Šrámek.**

Schreiber 1. German: occupational name for a clerk, from an agent deriv. of Ger. *schreiben* to write (MHG *schrīben*, OHG *scrīban*, from L *scribere*; see also SCRIBE and SCRIVEN).

2. Jewish (Ashkenazic): from Ger. *Schreiber*, Yid. *shrayber* writer, adopted as a translation of Hebr. SOFER scribe (cf. *Pisareff* at PISARSKI).

Vars.: Ger.: **Schreber** (Saxony). Jewish: **Szreiber, Schreibman(n).**

Cogns.: Low Ger.: **Schrieber, Schriever, Schriefer, Schriewer.** Du.: **Schrijver.** Dan., Norw.: **Skriver.**

Patr.: Low Ger.: **Schrievers.**

A family by the name of Schreiber *were established in England c.1721 by Carl Schreiber (1680–1760), a native of Durlach in Swabia.*

Schreier 1. German: occupational name for a town crier, or nickname for a noisy individual, from an agent deriv. of Ger. *schreien* to shout, cry (MHG *schrī(e)n*, OHG *scrīan*).

2. Jewish (Ashkenazic): from Ger. *Schreier*, Yid. *shrayer* shouter, either a nickname for a noisy person, or, possibly, an occupational name for a person whose duty it was to summon Jews to public worship.

Vars.: Ger.: **Schreiert, Schrei.** Jewish: **Shreier, Szrayer.**

Schreiner German: occupational name for a joiner, Ger. *Schreiner* (MHG *schrīnære*, an agent deriv. of *schrīn* chest, box, OHG *skrīni*, from L *scrinium* bookcase). The vocab. word and the surname are found mainly in W parts

of Germany; the term in N, E, and S German-speaking regions was TISCHLER.
Var.: **Schreinert**.
Cogns.: Low Ger.: **Schreinemaker**. Flem.: **Schrijnma(e)ker**, **De Schrijnwerker**. Pol.: **Skrzynecki**; **Szrajner**, **Szrejner**.

Schröder N German: occupational name for a tailor, from an agent deriv. of MLG *schrōten*, *schrāten* to cut. The same term was also occasionally used to denote a shoemaker, whose work included cutting leather, and, for reasons that are not clear, also a drayman, one who delivered beer and wine in bulk to customers. The surname may have been acquired in any of these senses.
Vars.: **Schröter**, **Schrader**.
Cogns.: Low Ger., Flem., Du.: **Schreu(de)r**, **Schroier**. Jewish (Ashkenazic): **Schrötter**.
Patrs.: Low Ger., Flem., Du.: **Schreu(de)rs**, **Schrörs**.

Schübel German: apparently from MHG *schubel*, *schübel* bunch, clump, tuft; of uncertain application. It may have been a topographic name for someone who lived near a hillock or a clump of trees. In Bavaria it seems also to have been a nickname for a plump little fellow, from the same vocab. word used in a transferred sense.
Var.: **Schübler**.

Schubert German and Jewish (Ashkenazic): occupational name for a shoemaker or cobbler, from MHG *schuoch* shoe (see SCHUH) + *würhte* maker (see WRIGHT). The sound /b/ was often substituted for /v/ in southern and south-eastern dialects of German.
Vars.: **Schubart**, **Schubort**, **Schuwart**, **Schuchert**, **Schuckert**, **Schuh(h)ardt**.
Cogns.: Pol.: **Szubert**. Czech: **Šubrt**.

Schuh German: metonymic occupational name for a maker or repairer of shoes, from Ger. *Schuh* shoe (MHG *schuoch*, OHG *scuoh*); see also SCHUBERT and SCHUSTER.
Vars.: **Schuch**, **Schuck**, **Schug**; **Schu(h)mann**, **Schuckmann**; **Schu(h)macher** (Anglicized **S(c)hoemaker**).
Cogns.: Low Ger.: **Schau(mann)**, **Schaumaker** (Westphalia); **Scho(e)mann**, **Schomaker**. Flem., Du.: **Schoen(mann)**, **Schoe(n)maker**. Jewish (Ashkenazic): **Shuchman**; **Schichman(n)**, **Szichman** (representing a S Yid. pronunciation of Yid. *shukh*); **Schumacher**, **Shuchmacher**.
Dims.: Ger.: **Schü(h)le**, **Schühlein**, **Schü(c)hel**, **Schügl**, **Schiegel**, **Schigl**; **Schiele** (Swabia); **Schieli** (Switzerland).

Schuler 1. German: occupational name for a scholar or a student training to be a priest, from an agent deriv. of Ger. *Schule* school (MHG *schuol(e)*, OHG *scuola*, from L *schola* sect, Gk *skholē* leisure, pastime).
2. Jewish (Ashkenazic): occupational name for a Talmudic scholar or the sexton of a synagogue, from an agent deriv. of Yid. *shul* synagogue (likewise ultimately from L *schola*).
Vars. (of 1): **Schuller** (Latinized **Schullerus**), **Schül(l)er**. (Of 2): **Schuller**, SCHILLER, **Schulman**, **Szulman**, **Shi(e)lman**; **S(z)koler**, **Szkolerman**; **S(c)hkolnik**, **Szkolnik**, **Skolni(c)k**, **Scolnik**, **Scolnic**, **Skulnik**, **Skoolnik**, **Schoolnik** (E Ashkenazic); **Schulsinger**, **Szulsinger** (names adopted by cantors; cf. *Singer* at SANGER).
Cogns. (of 1): Low Ger.: **Schöler(mann)**. Du.: **Schuyler**.
Patrs. (from 2): Jewish: **Skolnikov**.
Schuyler *is the name of one of the oldest and wealthiest Dutch families of New York, established there by Philip Pieterse Schuyler from Amsterdam; his marriage was recorded in America in 1650. He was a merchant and colonial administrator. Four generations later one of his best-known descendants was Philip Schuyler (1733–1804), a congressman and senator, and a leading figure in the American Revolution.*

Schulmeister Jewish (Ashkenazic): occupational name for a teacher in a Jewish school, from mod. Ger. *Schulmeister* schoolmaster.

Schultz 1. German: status name for a village headman, from a contracted form of MHG *schultheize* (OHG *sculdheizo*). The term originally denoted a man responsible for collecting dues and paying them to the lord of the manor; it is a cpd of *sculd(a)* debt, due + a deriv. of *heiz(z)an* to command.
2. Jewish (Ashkenazic): reason for adoption uncertain, perhaps taken by or given to a rabbi, seen as the head of a Jewish community (cf. HAUPTMANN and *Oberman* at OBER).
Vars. (of 1): **Schulz**, **Schul(t)ze**, **Schulthe(i)ss**; **Scholz**, **Scholtis** (Saxony, Silesia). (Of 2): **Schulz**.
Cogns. (of 1): Low Ger.: **Schulte**, **Schout**. Flem.: **Scholte**, **Schout(hede)**. Du.: **Schulte**, **Scholte**, **Schoute**; **Scholtz**, **Scolts**. Pol.: **Szulc**; **Sołtys**, **Sołtysiak**. Czech: **Šulc**, **Šolc**; **Šolta**, **Šoltys**.
Dims. (of 1): Ger.: **Schölzel**, **Schelzel**. Pol.: **Sołtysik**.
Patrs. (from 1): Low Ger.: **Schulten**, **Schülting**. Flem.: **Schouteden**, **Scholts**. Du.: **Scholten(s)**, **Schouten**.
Habitation name: Pol.: **Szulczewski**.

Schüssel 1. German: metonymic occupational name for a turner, from MHG *schüssel(e)* small wooden bowl (OHG *skussila*).
2. Jewish (Ashkenazic): from mod. Ger. *Schüssel* dish. The reason for its assumption is not known, but the fact that it is not a common surname suggests that it may be an anecdotal name derived from some now irrecoverable minor incident.
Var.: Ger.: **Schüssler**.
Cogns.: Low Ger.: **Schötte**; **Schöttler**; **Schöteldreyer** (see DREIER 2).

Schuster German and Jewish (Ashkenazic): occupational name for a maker or repairer of shoes, from Ger. *Schuster*, Yid. *shuster* (MHG *schuochsūtære*, a cpd of *schuoch* shoe (see SCHUH) + *sūtære* sewer (see SAUTER)).
Vars.: Jewish: **Shuster**, **S(c)husterman**.
Cogns.: Flem., Du.: **De Zuzter**. Pol.: **Szuster**. Czech: **Šusta**. See also SZEWC.
Dims.: Ger.: **Schüst(er)l**, **Schiesterl**, **Schiest(e)l**.

Schutz 1. German: occupational name for a watchman or guard, from a deriv. of MHG *schützen* to guard, protect; the word originally denoted either the warden of a park or piece of common land or a night-watchman in a town.
2. Jewish (Ashkenazic): of uncertain origin, possibly an adoption of the relatively common Ger. surname.
Vars.: Jewish: **Schutzer**, **Schutzman**.
Cogn.: Du.: **Schut**.

Schützbier German: nickname for a belligerent person, from MHG *schüt(t)en* to brandish, flourish, shake (OHG *skutten*) + *sper* SPEAR (cf. SHAKESPEARE). A knight named Diderich *Schuzcesper* is recorded in 1316 in Hessen, and a Low Ger. Reimbert *Scudesper* in 1174. In more recent times the surname has been altered by folk etymological association with mod. Ger. *schützen* to protect (see SCHUTZ) and *Bier* beer.

Schütze German: occupational name for a bowman, Ger. *Schütze* (MHG *schütze*, OHG *scuzz(i)o*, from *skiozan* to shoot).
Var.: **Schütz**.
Cogns.: Low Ger.: **Schütt(e)**. Eng.: SHUTT.
The German composer Heinrich Schütz *(1585–1672) was born in Köstritz into a family originally from Franconia, but who settled in*

Saxony after the mid-15th cent. His grandfather owned the inn in the town of Gera, which his father later took over.

Schwab German and Jewish (Ashkenazic): regional name for someone from Swabia, Ger. *Schwaben*, so called from a Gmc tribe recorded from the 1st cent. BC in the L form *Suebi* or *Suevi*, of uncertain origin. This region in S Germany was an independent duchy from the 10th cent. until 1313, when the territory was broken up.

Vars.: Ger.: **Schwob**. Jewish: **Schwabe**.

Cogns.: Low Ger.: **Schwaf**. Flem., Du.: **Swaab**. It.: **Soave, Soavi**. Czech: **Šváb**. Hung.: **Sváb**.

Dims.: Ger.: **Schwäble; Schwabel** (also Jewish, of uncertain origin).

Schwand German: topographic name for someone who lived in a glade or clearing, MHG *swand* (from *swinden* to thin out, disappear, OHG *swintan*).

Vars.: **Schwandt, Schwende(mann); Schwand(n)er, Gschwandtner, Schwend(n)er, Schwendler**.

Schwarz German and Jewish (Ashkenazic): nickname for someone with black hair or a dark complexion, from Ger. *schwarz*, Yid. *shvarts* dark, black (MHG, OHG *swarz*, a cogn. of OE *swart* dark, swarthy).

Vars.: **Schwartz, Schwar(t)ze(r), Schwar(t)zmann**.

Cogns.: Low Ger.: **Schwart(e), Schward(e)**. Flem., Du.: **(De) Swart(e), (De) Zwart**. Pol.: **Szwarc**. Czech: **Švarc**.

Dim.: Ger.: **Schwärzel**.

Patrs.: Low Ger.: **Schwarten, Schwarting**. Flem.: **Swerts**. Du.: **Zwarts**.

Patr. (from a dim.): Du.: **Zwartjes**.

Schwarzkopf German and Jewish (Ashkenazic): nickname for someone with dark hair, from Ger. *schwarz* black, dark (see SCHWARZ) + *kopf* head (see KOPF).

Var.: **Schwartzkopf**.

Cogn.: Low Ger.: **Schwartekopp**.

Schwarzschild Jewish (Ashkenazic): from Ger. SCHWARZ black + SCHILD sign; in at least some cases this was a house name for someone who lived in a house marked by a black sign. Cf. ROTHSCHILD.

A German family of Jewish origin trace their descent from Liebmann zum swarzen shilte *of Frankfurt, who died in 1594. His descendants included the astronomers Karl* Schwarzschild *(1873–1916) and his son Martin (b. 1912).*

Schwebel 1. German: apparently a dim. of SCHWAB.

2. Jewish (Ashkenazic): of uncertain origin, possibly from Yid. *shvebl* sulphur, in which case the reason for its assumption is unknown.

Schweder German: ethnic name for a Swede (cf. SVEDIN).

Var.: **Schwed**.

Cogns.: Pol.: **Szwed**. Czech: **Švejda**.

Habitation name: Pol.: **Szwedziński**.

Schweiger German and Jewish (Ashkenazic): nickname for a somewhat taciturn or 'deep' person, from an agent deriv. of Ger. *schweigen*, Yid. *shvaygn* to be silent.

Schweitzer German and Jewish (Ashkenazic): ethnic name for a Swiss, Ger. *Schweizer*, from Ger. *Schweiz* + the suffix *-er* denoting a native or inhabitant of a place. As a Jewish name, it denotes a Jew from Switzerland. The Polish cogn. vocab. word acquired the additional senses of a commissionaire and a verger in a church.

Vars.: **Schweizer**. Jewish only: **Szweitzer**.

Cogns.: Flem., Du.: **Switser, De Zwitser**. Pol.: **Szwajcer**. Czech: **Švejcar**.

Schwemmer German: 1. occupational name for someone who floated logs downstream from the forests where they were felled, from an agent deriv. of MHG *swemmen*, causative of *swimmen* to float, swim.

2. topographic name for someone who lived by a deep ford where horses could be made to swim across, MHG *swem(me)*, from the same word as in 1.

Cogn.: Low Ger.: **Swemmer**.

Schwepe Low German: metonymic occupational name for a roof-builder, from MLG *swepe* rafter.

Vars.: **Schweppe** (also Jewish); **Schwepenhauer**.

Schwimmer German and Jewish (Ashkenazic): nickname for a good swimmer, from an agent deriv. of Ger. *schwimmen*, Yid. *shvimen* to swim.

Var.: Jewish: **Schwimer**.

Schwippe German: metonymic occupational name for a driver or nickname for a brutal man, from early mod. Ger. *schwuppe* whip (of Gmc origin, probably akin to mod. Eng. *sweep* and *swoop*), now replaced as a vocab. word by the Slav. borrowing *Peitsche*.

Vars.: **Schwibbe, Schwöpe**.

Dims.: **Schwippl**. Low Ger.: **Schwippke**.

Scobie Scots: habitation name from a lost place in the former county of Perths., so called from Gael. *sgolbach* thorny place.

Scopes English: of uncertain origin, perhaps a topographic name from ME *scōpe* scoop, ladle, shovel (of Low Ger. origin), used in the transferred sense of a hollow in the ground. However, this does not occur as a placename element. According to Barber it is a patr. from OE *scōp* poet, minstrel, a word last attested at the beginning of the 13th cent. before its revival as a conscious archaism in the 19th cent.

Scorer N English: 1. occupational name for someone who kept accounts, from an agent deriv. of ME *score(n)* to record (ON *skora*).

2. occupational name for a scout or a spy, ME *scorer* (OF *escoreor*, an agent deriv. of *escorir* to reconnoitre, L *excurrere* to run out, make a sally).

Vars.: **Scorrer, Scorah**.

Scorza Italian: occupational name for a tanner or nickname for a vicious man, from a deriv. of It. *scorzare* to skin, flay (L *excoriāre*, from *corium* skin, hide).

Var.: **Scorcia**.

Dims.: **Scorzelli, Scorziello, Scorzetti**.

Augs.: **Scorzon(e), Scorsone**.

Scothern English: habitation name from a place in Lincs., recorded in Domesday Book as *Scotstorne*, from the gen. case of the OE byname *Scott* 'Irishman' (see SCOTT) + OE *þorn* thornbush (see THORN 1).

Scotland 1. English: ethnic name for someone from Scotland (cf. SCOTT).

2. English: from the rare Norman personal name *Escotland*, composed of the ethnic name *Scot* + *land* territory.

3. Scots: habitation name from *Scotland(well)* near Loch Leven in Kinross.

Cogns. (of 1): Jewish (Ashkenazic; reason for adoption unclear, perhaps indicative of trade relations with Scotland): **Schottlander, Shottlender; Szotland** (a Pol. spelling).

Scott English and Scots: ethnic name for someone from Scotland or, more commonly, for a Gaelic-speaker within Scotland. The Gaelic-speaking peoples in Scotland came originally from Ireland, and it is possible that their name is connected with OW *ysgthru* to cut, carve, referring to their habit of tatooing themselves with iron points.

Cogns.: Fr.: **Escot**, **Lescot**, **Lécot**, **Lescaut**, **Lescaux**. It.: **Scoto**, **Scoti**; **Scuotto** (Campania). Ger.: **Schott(e)**. Flem., Du.: **Schot**. Norw., Dan.: **Skotte**.

Dim.: Ger.: **Schöttle**.

Patrs.: Eng.: **Scotts**, **Scotson**.

The Scott *family who hold the dukedoms of Buccleuch and Queensberry trace their descent from Sir Richard* le Scot(t) *(1249–85). They also hold the earldom of Doncaster. The writer Sir Walter Scott (1771–1832) came from a cadet branch of this family.*

There is a manuscript of 1587 which says that a family spelling their name Schot *were descended from Heinrich of Eysenrodt, Nassau, who owned iron mines in the 12th cent. Heinrich is said to have been a descendant of one of a group of Scotsmen, attendant on two noble ladies, who settled in a village in Franconia. The effigies of some of them can still be seen in the church in the village, which is called* Schotten *after them.*

There is also a pedigree of 1570 in Lorraine which traces a family called Schott *to Mathieu or Matthias Schott, living early in the 15th cent. There does not seem to be any connection between this man and Heinrich of Eysenrodt, however.*

Scougall Scots: habitation name from *Scoughall* on the coast near North Berwick, so called from ON *skógr* wood (cf. SHAW) + OE *halh* nook, recess (see HALE 1).

Scrase English: of unknown origin. It is an established surname in E Sussex as early as the 13th cent., and is still relatively common in the W Country, but none of the early forms give any clue as to its meaning.

Screech English (Devon and Cornwall): of uncertain origin, perhaps a nickname for a person with a strident voice, from early mod. Eng. *screche* screech, or just possibly a habitation name from *Screek* Wood in the parish of St Martin by Looe. This place was earlier known as *Loscruk*, from Corn. *lost* tail + *cruc* barrow (the first element referring to the long, thin shape of the feature).

The surname is first recorded in Devon in the form Skreche *in 1524 and* Scryche *in 1525. It occurs as* Screche *in 1569 in Calstock.*

Scribe French: occupational name for a clerk or copyist, OF *scribe* (L *scrība*, a deriv. of *scrībere* to write; cf. SCHREIBER and SCRIVEN).

Var.: **Scrive**.

Cogns.: Ger.: SCHREIBER. Eng.: SCRIVEN.

Dim.: Fr.: **Scribot**.

Equivs. (not cogn.): Jewish (Ashkenazic): PISARSKI, SOFER. Russ. PEROV.

Scrimgeour Scots and English: occupational name for a fencer or fencing-master, from OF *eskermisseo(u)r* fencer (from *eskermir* to fence, skirmish, fight hand-to-hand, of Gmc origin; cf. OHG *skirmen* to defend). Fencing-masters always found plentiful employment in medieval England, although they were officially banned from the City of London because of their dangerous influence.

Vars.: **Scrimgeoure**, **Scrymgeo(u)r**, **Scrimger**, **Scrimi(n)ger**, **Skrimshire**, **Scrimshaw**; **Skirmer**, **Skermer**, **Scurmer** (the last three being derivs. of ME *skirme(n)* to fight).

Cogns.: Ger.: **Schirm(er)**, **Schürmer**; **Schörmer** (Bavaria). Low Ger., Du.: **Schermer**.

A family by the name of Scrimgeour *or* Scrymgeour *held the position of hereditary standard-bearers of Scotland. For his services in this office, Sir Alexander Scrymgeour was granted lands in Forfar in 1298, and became Constable of Dundee. Through marriage the family inherited the estates of the Wedderburn family in 1788, and it is under the surname Scrymgeour-Wedderburn that they hold the title Earls of Dundee.*

Scriven English: occupational name for a clerk or copyist, from OF *escrivein*, *escrivain* writer, scribe (LL *scrībānus*, for class. L *scrība*; cf. SCRIBE).

Vars.: **Scrivener**, **Scrivenor** (with the addition of the ME agent suffix); **Scribner**.

Cogns.: Prov.: **Escriva(n)**. Sp.: **Escribano**. Cat.: **Escribà**, **Escrivà**.

Patrs.: Eng.: **Scrivens**, **Scrivin(g)s**.

The Scribner *family who founded the American publishing house were established in America by one Benjamin Scrivener, who settled in Norwalk, Conn., in 1680. The present form of the name was adopted after 1742. The firm was established in 1846 by Charles Scribner (1821–71), who was born in New York, where his father was established as a prosperous merchant.*

Scrope English: of uncertain origin, said to be from an ON byname meaning 'Crab'.

A branch of this family has adopted a crab as its heraldic crest. They held lands at Barton-on-Humber, Lincs., where Robert Scrope *was living in 1166. Another Robert Scrope was a Crusader who died at Acre in 1190. The family held a number of baronies between 1350 and 1630, and for a time in the 14th cent. they were sovereign in the Isle of Man.*

Scruton English: habitation name from a place in N Yorks., so called from the ON byname *Skurfa* 'Scurf' + OE *tūn* enclosure, settlement.

Var.: **Scrutton**.

Scudamore English (West Country): of uncertain origin, perhaps a habitation name from an unidentified place so called from OE *scīte* shit, dung + *mōr* moor, fen.

Vars.: **Skidmore**, **Skitmore**.

A family of this name trace their descent from Ralph, who in 1086 held Opetone, Wilts., later known as Upton Scudamore. *His son, who died before 1148, was known as Reginald* Escudemor.

Scull English: nickname for a bald-headed man or someone of cadaverous appearance, from ME *sc(h)olle*, *sc(h)ulle* skull (probably of Scandinavian origin).

Scully Irish: Anglicized form of Gael. **Ó Scolaidhe** 'descendant of the scholar', from *scolaidhe* scholar.

Vars.: **O'Scully**, **O'Scollee**, **Skelly**, **Skally**, **Scally**.

Dims.: **Scull(i)on**, **Scallan**, **Scalon** (Gael. **Ó Scoláin**).

Scutt English: 1. occupational name for a scout or spy, ME *scut* (OF *escoute*, from *escouter* to listen, L *auscultāre*).

2. nickname for a swift runner, from ME *scut* hare (of uncertain origin).

Vars. (of 1): **Scudder** (with the addition of the ME agent suffix). (Of 2): **Skitt**.

Seabra Portuguese: apparently a habitation name from *Senabria* in Spain, which was perhaps originally named with the Celt. elements *sena* old + *briga* height, hill.

Seabrook English: habitation name from a place in Bucks., so called from the OE river name *Sǣge*, apparently meaning 'Trickling', 'Slow-moving' + OE *brōc* stream (see BROOK).

Seacombe English: habitation name from a place in Ches., named with the OE elements *sǣ* sea + *cumb* valley (see COOMBE).

Seagar English: from the ME given name *Segar*, OE *Sǣgar*, composed of the elements *sǣ* sea + *gār* spear.

Vars.: **Seager**, **Seegar**, **Se(e)ger**; **Sagar**, **Sa(i)ger**; **Segger**.

Patrs.: **Seagars**, **Seagers**, **Saggers**.

Seagrave English: habitation name from a place in Leics., recorded in Domesday Book as *Satgrave* and *Setgraue*, probably from OE *(ge)set* fold, pen or *sēað* pit, pool + *grāf* grove or *græf* ditch.

Vars.: **Segrave, Seagrove, Seagrief.**

A family by the name of Segrave *trace their descent from Thomas* de Segrave, *recorded in Domesday Book as jointly holding the manor of Seagrave, Leics. Among his descendants was Sir Stephen de Segrave, who was chief justiciar of England in the 13th cent.*

Seal English: 1. topographic name; var. of SALE.

2. metonymic occupational name for a maker of seals or signet rings, from ME, OF *seel* seal (L *sigillum*, a dim. of *signum* sign).

3. metonymic occupational name for a maker of saddles, from OF *seele* saddle (see SELLER 2).

4. nickname for a plump or ungainly person, from the aquatic mammal, ME *sele* (OE *seolh*).

Vars.: **Seale, Seel, Zeal(e).** (Of 2 and 3): **Sealer.**

Cogns. (of 2): Ger.: SIEGEL, **Siegler.** Low Ger.: **Segler.** It.: **Sigliente.**

Patrs. (from 4): Eng.: **Seal(e)s, Seels.**

'Servant of S. 4': Eng.: SELMAN.

Sealey English: nickname for a person with a cheerful disposition, from ME *seely* happy, fortunate (OE *sǣlig*, from *sǣl* happiness, good fortune), which was also occasionally used as a female given name during the Middle Ages. The sense 'pitiable', which developed into mod. Eng. *silly*, is not attested before the 15th cent.

Vars.: SELLEY; **Seal(l)y, Seel(e)y, Seelly, Sill(e)y, Sellick; Ceel(e)y, Ceiley, Cely; Zeal(l)ey, Zelley;** SELMAN.

Cogns.: Ger.: SELIG. Low Ger.: **Salge, Selge.** Swed.: **Säll.**

Cpd (ornamental): Swed.: **Sälström** ('lovely river').

Seaman English (Norfolk): 1. from *Sǣmann*, an OE personal name composed of the elements *sǣ* sea + *mann* man.

2. occupational name for a sailor.

Vars.: **Se(e)man, Seyman, Sayman, Seamenn.**

Patrs.: **Se(m)mens** (Devon and Cornwall), **Semmence; Seamons.**

Searle English: from the Norman personal name *Serlo*, Gmc *Sarilo, Serilo*. This was probably originally a byname cogn. with ON *Sorli*, and akin to OE *searu* armour, meaning perhaps 'Defender', 'Protector'.

Vars.: **Searl, Serle, Serrell.**

Patrs.: **Searl(e)s.**

Seaton English and Scots: habitation name from any of the various places so called. The majority, for example those in Cumb., Devon, Co. Durham, Northumb., and E and N Yorks., are named with OE *sǣ* sea, lake + *tūn* enclosure, settlement. One in Leics. (formerly Rutland), however, seems to have as its first element a stream name *Sǣge* (see SEABROOK) or a personal name *Sǣga*, a short form of a cpd name such as SEAGAR. One in Kent is named with OE *seten* plantation, cultivated land (from *settan* to set, plant). The Scottish place of this name, near Longniddry, is so named because it was held from the 12th cent. by a Norman family *de Sey*, from *Say* in Indre (see SAY 1).

Var.: **Seton.**

Seton *was the name of a powerful Scots family, who held the earldoms of Eglinton and Winton. There are differing theories concerning the origin of the surname. It is first recorded in Scotland with Alexander* Setone or de Seaton, *who was witness to a charter granted to King David I* c.*1150. Some sources say the name is derived from the 'sea town' of Tranent, E Lothian, where the family originated, but this is extremely implausible. Derivation from one of the places mentioned above is more likely to be correct. Through marriage the earldom is now held by the Montgomerie family.*

Sebastian German: from the given name *Sebastian* (L *Sebastiānus*, originally an ethnic name meaning 'man from *Sebastia*', a city in Pontus named from Gk *sebastos* revered). The name was borne by a 3rd-cent. martyr who became the patron saint of Nuremberg, hence (in part) its popularity in Germany. The surname is also sometimes born by Jews, presumably as an adoption of the Ger. surname.

Vars.: **Sebass; Ba(u)stian, Paustian.**

Cogns.: Flem.: **Bastiaen.** Du.: **Bastiaan.** Eng.: **Basti(a)n, Bast(i)en, Bastion.** Fr.: **Sébastien; Bastien.** Prov.: **Sébastian; Bastian.** Sp.: **Sebastián.** Cat.: **Sebastià.** Port.: **Sebastião.** It.: **Sebastiani, Sebastiano; Bastiani, Bastiano.** Pol.: BACH. Czech: **Šebesta, Bašta;** BACH. Croatian: **Basta.** Hung.: **Sebestyén.**

Dims.: Ger.: **Bast, Bästl(e),** BEST, **Pest(lin).** Low Ger.: **Bastke, Bes(t)gen.** It.: **Sebastianelli, Sebastianini, Sebastianutto, Sebastianutti; Bastianel(li), Bastiaelli, Bastia(n)ello, Bastianetto, Bastianini, Bastianutti, Bastianutto.** Czech: **Šebek.** Hung.: **Sebök.**

Augs.: Fr.: **Bastiat.** It.: **Bastianon.**

Patrs.: Flem.: **Basteyns.** Du.: **Bastiaanse(n).** It.: **De Bastiani.** Russ.: **Savasteev.**

Patrs. (from dims.): Low Ger.: **Basten, Basting, Bestges.** Russ.: **Savoskin, Savonichev.**

Seccombe English (Devon): habitation name from either of two places in Devon, both so called from the OE personal name *Secca* + OE *cumb* valley (see COOMBE).

Var.: **Secombe.**

Secker 1. English: var. of *Sacker*; see SACK.

2. Low German: topographic name for someone who lived in an area of wetland, MLG *seck*.

3. Jewish (Ashkenazic): of unknown origin, possibly as in 1.

Seco Spanish: nickname for a thin and apparently bloodless person, from Sp. *seco* dry (L *siccus*).

Dims.: Fr.: **Sechet, Séchet.**

Seddon English: of uncertain origin, perhaps a habitation name from an unidentified place, the last element of which could well be OE *dūn* hill. Without early forms, it is impossible even to speculate what the first element might be. The surname is extremely common in Lancs., esp. in the Manchester area, where it was first recorded in the 14th cent.

Richard Seddon *(1845–1906), Prime Minister of New Zealand, known as 'King Dick', was born in St Helens, Lancs., and served an engineering apprenticeship. He went to the Australian goldfields in 1863, and then on to New Zealand. His father was a schoolteacher who became a greengrocer.*

Sedge English: topographic name for someone who lived in a place overgrown with sedge and reeds, or metonymic occupational name for someone who made use of these materials in thatching, from OE *secg* sedge.

Vars.: **Sedger, Sedgeman.**

Sedgley English (W Midlands): habitation name from a place near Dudley, so called from the OE byname *Secg* 'Warrior' + OE *lēah* wood, clearing.

Sedgwick English: habitation name from *Sedgwick* in Cumb., so called from the ME personal name *Sigg(e)* (from ON *Siggi* or OE *Sicg*, short forms of the various cpd names with the first element 'victory') + OE *wīc* outlying settlement, dairy farm (see WICK); or from *Sedgewick* in Sussex, so called from OE *secg* SEDGE + *wīc*.

Vars.: **Sedgewick(e), Sedwick, Sidg(e)wick.**

Sedlák Czech: occupational or status name for a peasant or farmer, Czech *sedlák*, the equivalent of Ger. BAUER. A

sedlák was a comparatively rich farmer, with more land than a *zahradník* (smallholder) or a *chaloupník* (cotter).
Dim.: Czech: **Sedláček**.

Sedov Russian: patr. from the nickname *Sedoi* 'Grey (-haired)'.
Cogns.: Jewish (E Ashkenazic): **Sedoff, Sedow**. Czech: **Šedivý; Šeda**.

Sędzicki Polish: 1. occupational name from Pol. *sędzia* judge, or nickname for a wise person.
2. nickname from *sędziwy* grey-haired. There is no direct cogn. relationship between this Pol. word and Russ. *sedoi* (see SEDOV), although they both mean 'grey-haired'. The connection between *sędziwy* and *sędzia* is also unclear, although presumably it has something to do with the association between judges and grey hair. The Pol. cogn. of *sedoi* is *szady*, which also means 'grey-haired'.
Vars.: **Sędicki, Sędziński**.
Patr.: **Sędkiewicz**.
Habitation name: **Sędkowski**.

See English: topographic name for someone who lived by the sea-shore or beside a lake, from ME *see* sea, lake (OE *sǣ*).
Cogns.: Du.: **Van (der) Zee, Zeeman**. Norw., Dan.: **Søe**. Swed.: **Sjölin, Sjödin, Sjödén; Sjöman**. Jewish (Ashkenazic): **Seeman(n)**.
Cpds (mostly ornamental): Swed.: **Sjöberg** ('sea hill'); **Sjöborg** ('sea town'); **Sjöblom** ('sea flower'); **Sjögren** ('sea branch'); **Sjöholm** ('sea island'); **Sjölund** ('sea grove'); **Sjöqvist** ('sea twig'); **Sjöstedt** ('sea homestead'); **Sjöstrand** ('sea shore'); **Sjöström** ('sea river').

Seed English (chiefly Lancs.): metonymic occupational name for a gardener or husbandman, or nickname for a small person, from ME *sede* seed (OE *sǣd*).
Vars.: **Se(e)dman, Seeds**.

Seerey Irish: Anglicized form of Gael. **Ó Saoraidhe** 'descendant of *Saoraidhe*', a personal name derived from *saordha* noble.
Vars.: **Seery; O'Seyry, O'Serie; O'Shirie, O'Shyry, O'Shrue; Earner** (a translated form, the result of erroneous association with *saothraidhe* worker, earner).

Sefton English: habitation name from a place in Lancs., so called from ON *sef* rush + OE *tūn* enclosure, settlement.
Var.: **Sephton**.

Segal 1. Jewish (Ashkenazic): acronym of the Hebr. phrase *SeGan Levia* 'second-rank Levite'.
2. French: metonymic occupational name for a grower or seller of rye, OF *segal* (L *secale*).
Vars. (of 1): **Sagal, Se(i)gel**, SIEGEL, **Chagal(l); Segelstein** (an ornamental elaboration). (Of 2): **Ségal, Segall, Sigal**.
Dim. (of 1): **Segalczyk**.
Patrs. (from 1): **Segals(on); Segalescu** (Rumanian); **Segalov, Segalovi(t)ch, Segalowitz, Segalovitz, Segalowitsch, Sagalov(ich), Shagalov** (E Ashkenazic).

Segarra Catalan: habitation name from a place of uncertain etymology (possibly derived from Basque *sagar* apple tree + the def. art. *-a*, although the alteration of the first vowel cannot be readily explained).
Var.: **Sagarra**.

Segond French: from the medieval given name *Segond* (L *Secundus* 'Second(-born)' or 'Favourable', a deriv. of *sequi* to follow), borne in honour of various minor early saints.
Var.: **Second**.
Dims.: **Segondin, Segondy**.
Aug.: **Secondat**.

Segovia Spanish: habitation name from the town in central Spain of this name, which is of uncertain origin (possibly containing the Celt. element *sego* victory).
Var.: **Segoviano**.

Seguí Catalan: from a Gmc personal name composed of the elements *sigi* victory + *wine* friend.
Cogns.: Prov.: **Séguin, Ségui(s), Séguy**. Ger.: **Siegwein**.
Dims.: Prov.: **Séguineau, Séguinot, Séguiniol**.

Ségur Provençal: habitation name from any of various minor places so called from OProv. *ségur* safe, well-defended (L *sēcūrus* carefree, from *sē-* without + *cūra* care, anxiety).
Var.: **Ségura**.
Cogn.: Cat.: **Segura**.
Dims.: Prov.: **Séguret, Siguret**.

Seide German: metonymic occupational name for a manufacturer or seller of silk, Ger. *Seide* (MHG *sīde*, from LL *sēta*, originally denoting animal hair).
Vars.: **Seidemann, Seidler**.
Cogns.: Jewish (Ashkenazic): **Seid(en)(man), Seideman, Seidmann, Zaidman** (partly ornamental); **Seidler, Seidner; Seidweber** ('silk weaver'). Pol.: **Zajdler**.
Cpds (ornamental): Jewish (Ashkenazic): **Seidenband** ('silk ribbon'); **Seidenbaum** ('silk tree'); **Seidenberg** ('silk hill'); **Seidenfeld** ('silk field'); **Seidenschnir, Zajdensznir** ('silk rope', the latter a Pol. spelling); **Seidenwurm, Zajdenvorm** ('silk worm', the latter a partly Pol. spelling).

Seigneur French: derisive nickname for a peasant who gave himself airs and graces, or occupational name for someone in the service of a great lord, from OF *segneur* lord (L *senior* elder). The It. cogns. came to be used also as titles of respect for professional men such as notaries.
Vars.: **Sieur, Lesieur, Lesieux; Sire, Lesire**.
Cogns.: Eng.: SENIOR. It.: **Signori, Signore; Sire, Seri**.
Dims.: Fr.: **Seigneuret, Seigno(u)ret; Siret, Siron, Sirot(eau)**. It.: **Signorini, Signorino, Signorelli, Signor(i)ello, Signoretti**.
Aug.: It.: **Signoroni**.
Pej.: It.: **Signoraccio**.
Patr.: Fr: **Duseigneur**.

Seiler 1. German: occupational name for a rope-maker, from an agent deriv. of Ger. *Seil* rope (MHG, OHG *seil*).
2. Jewish (Ashkenazic): of unknown origin, possibly an occupational name as in 1 above, or possibly a surname adopted as an (imperfect) anagram of the Hebr. given name *Yisrael* (see ISRAEL). The latter explanation is the less convincing one.
3. English: var of SAYLOR.
Vars. (of 3): **Seyler, Seiller**.
Cogns. (of 1): Low Ger.: **Seel(er)**.

Seixas Portuguese and Jewish (Sefardic): topographic name for someone who lived on a patch of stony ground, from Port. *seixas* rocks, pl. of *seixa* (L *saxa*, originally itself the pl. of the neut. noun *saxum*, but later taken as a fem. sing.).

Séjournant French: nickname for a newcomer or temporary visitor to a community, from the pres. part. of OF *séjourner* to sojourn, stay (LL *subdiurnāre* to spend the day, from *diēs* day).
Vars.: **Séjourné, Séjournet**.

Selby English: habitation name from a place in W Yorks., so called from ON *selja* willow (cf. SALE 2) + *býr* farm, settlement. The surname is now very common in Notts.
Vars.: **Selbey, Selbie**.

Seld S German: topographic name for an inhabitant of a croft (a hut with a small kitchen-garden, but no agricultural land attached), MHG *selde*.

Vars.: **Seldt(e)**: **Seldner**, **Sellner**, **Söldner**, **Söllner**; **Seldmann**, **Seltmann**.

Selden English: habitation name from *Selden* Farm in the parish of Patching, Sussex, probably so called from OE *s(e)alh* willow (see SALE 2) + *denu* valley (see DEAN 1).

Vars.: **Seldon**, **Seldom**.

Self English (E Anglia): from the ME given name *Saulf*, OE *Sǣwulf*, composed of the elements *sǣ* sea + *wulf* wolf.

Var.: **Selfe**.

Selfridge English: of uncertain origin, perhaps a habitation name from an unidentified minor place, which might be so called from OE *scelf* shelf + *hrycg* ridge.

Selig 1. German: cogn. of SEALEY.

2. Jewish (Ashkenazic): from the Yid. male given name *Zelik* 'Fortunate', 'Blessed' or from the mod. Ger. vocabulary word *selig* of the same meaning (cf. SEALEY).

Vars. (of 1): **Seelig**, **Se(e)liger**, **Seligmann**. (Of 2): **Sellig**, **Zelig**, **Seligman(n)**, **Zeligman(n)**, **Zelik**.

Patrs. (from the given name): Jewish: **Seligso(h)n**, **Zeligson**, **Selikson**; **Zelikov**, **Zelikovi(t)ch**, **Zelikowicz**, **Zelikovitz**; **Zelicovici** (a Rumanian spelling); **Zeligowski**, **Zelikowsky**, **Zelicovski**, **Zelichovsky**, **Zelichowski**, **Zelikin**, **Zelicki**, **Zelitzki** (E Ashkenazic).

Selkirk Scots: habitation name from the town of *Selkirk* in the Borders region of Scotland, so called from ME *sale*, *sele* hall, manor (see SALE 1) + *kirk* church (see KIRK).

Var.: **Selcraig** (an altered form of the placename current in the 16th–18th cents.).

Alexander Selkirk *(1676–1721), the Scottish sailor who was the model for the fictional Robinson Crusoe, was also known as* Selcraig. *He was born in Largo, Fife, the son of a shoemaker.*

Sell 1. English: topographic name for someone who lived in a rough hut of the type normally occupied by animals, ME *selle*, OE *(ge)sell*. In many cases the name may have been in effect an occupational name for a herdsman.

2. U.S.: Anglicized form of SZÉLL.

Vars. (of 1): **Selle**, **Sells**, **Zell(e)**; SELLER.

Seller English and Scots: 1. topographic name, a var. of SELL 1.

2. occupational name for a saddler, ANF *seller* (OF *sellier*, L *sellārius*, a deriv. of *sella* seat, saddle, from *sedēre* to sit).

3. metonymic occupational name for someone employed in the cellars of a great house or monastery, from ANF *celler* cellar (OF *cellier*, LL *cellārium*, a deriv. of *cella* small room, store-room, from *celāre* to hide), or a reduction of the ME agent deriv. *cellerer*.

4. occupational name for a tradesman or merchant, from an agent deriv. of ME *sell(en)* to sell (OE *sellan* to hand over, deliver).

Vars.: **Sellar**, **Sellier**, **Cellier**.

Cogns. (of 2): Fr.: **Sellier**, **Lesellier**. Cat.: **Sellés**. It.: **Sellaro**, **Sellaio**. (Of 3): Fr.: **Cellier**, **Ducellier**; **Cellerier**, **Célerier**, **Célarier**, **Célarié**. Ger.: KELLNER. Flem., Du.: **Kelder**.

Dims. (of 2): Fr.: **Selleret**. It.: **Sellaroli**.

Patrs.: Eng.: **Sellers**, **Sellars**, **Sellors**. (From 2 only): It.: **Del Sellaio**.

Selley English: 1. (chiefly Devon) var. of SEALEY.

2. habitation name from *Selly* Oak in Birmingham, which is a var. of SHELLEY by origin.

Var.: **Selly**.

Selman English: 1. nickname for a happy or fortunate man; see SEALEY.

2. occupational name for a servant employed by a bearer of the name SEALEY or SEAL 4.

Vars.: **Sellman**, **Sil(l)man**.

Cogns. (of 1): Jewish (Ashkenazic): **Sel(l)man**, **Zelman** (from mod. Ger. *Seele* happiness, good fortune).

Selous English: of uncertain origin, perhaps a habitation name from an unidentified place named with the OE elements *s(e)alh* willow (see SALE 2) + *hūs* house.

Selway English: from a ME given name, *Salewi*, probably from an unattested OE personal name, **Sǣlwīg*, composed of the elements *sǣl* good fortune (cf. SEALEY) + *wīg* war.

Vars.: **Sal(la)way**, **Salloway**, **Salwey**.

Selwood English: habitation name from a place in Somerset, so called from OE *s(e)alh* willow (see SALE 2) + *wudu* WOOD.

Var.: **Sellwood**.

Selwyn English: 1. from the ME, OF given name *Seluein* (L *Silvānus*, a deriv. of *silva* wood; cf. SILVA), bestowed in honour of various minor early Christian saints.

2. from a ME given name, *Selewyne*, from the OE personal name *Selewine*, composed of the elements *sele* hall + *wine* friend.

Vars.: **Selwyne**, **Selwin(e)**. (Of 1 only): **Sa(l)vin**, **Sauva(i)n**, **Sauven**, **Sylvaine**.

Cogns. (of 1): Fr.: **Seuvan**, **Sauva(i)n**, **Sauvent**, **Silva(i)n**, **Silvant**, **Sylvain**. It.: **Silva(g)ni**, **Silva(g)no**, **Salva(g)ni**, **Salva(g)no**. Sp.: **Silván**. Cat.: **Salvà**.

Dims. (of 1): Eng.: SILL. Fr.: **Sauvignon**, **Sauvanet**, **Sauvanon**. It.: **Salva(g)nini**. Beloruss.: **Selivonok**, **Salivonok**.

Aug. (of 1): It.: **Salvagnoni**.

Patrs. (from 1): It.: **Salvagneschi**. Russ.: **Selivanov**, **Selifanov**, **Selifonov**.

Semmel German and Jewish (Ashkenazic): metonymic occupational name for a baker of white rolls (Ger. *Semmel*, Yid. *zeml*), from fine wheat-flour, MHG *semel(e)*, *simel* (OHG *semala*, *simila*, from L; ultimately, via Gk, from Arabic). Such rolls were in contrast to the coarse rye-bread that was and is the norm in many households. The Ger. surname may also be an occupational name for a dealer in fine wheat-flour.

Vars.: Ger.: **Semel**, **Simmel**; **Sem(m)ler**, **Simmler**, **Semmelmann**; **Semmelweis** (with MHG *weize* wheat). Jewish: **Semel**, **Simel**, **Zemel**; **Semler**, **Simler**, **Zemler**, **Zimler**; **Zemelman**.

Cogns.: It.: **Sem(m)ola**, **Simula**, **Simbola**, **Simbula**.

Dims.: It.: **Semolini**. Fr.: **Sim(o)ulin**.

Semple 1. Scots, N Irish, and English (Norman): habitation name from any of various places in Normandy called *Saint-Paul* or *Saint-Pol*, from the dedication of their churches to St PAUL.

2. nickname from ME, OF *simple* simple, straightforward, humble (L *simplus*).

Vars. (of 1): **Sempill**, **Sample**, **Sambell**, **Simble**, **Simpole**.

Cogns. (of 1): Fr.: **Saint-Paul**, **Saint-Pol**. It.: **Sampaoli**, **Sampaolo**, **Sampaolesi**, **Sampo**. (Of 2): Fr.: **Simple**. It.: **Semplici**, **Semplice**.

Dims. (of 2): Fr.: **Simplot**. It.: **Semplicini**.

A Scottish family of this name held the hereditary post of Sheriff of Renfrewshire from the 13th cent. The 1st Lord Sempill *(d. 1513) was raised to the nobility by James IV around 1489, and died at Flodden.*

Semrád Czech: from a Czech personal name, *Sěmirad*, composed of the elements *sěmi* person + *rad* nimble, swift.

Vars.: **Semerád, Semirád.**

Cogn. (patr.): Croatian: **Samardžić.**

Sena Portuguese: apparently a religious byname adopted in honour of St Catherine of *Siena* (Port. *Sena*). This saint was born in 1347 at Siena in Tuscany, the daughter of a wool-dyer with the surname Benincasa, and combined her work among the poor of the town with an influential role in ecclesiastical politics.

Sénac French: habitation name from a place in Hautes-Pyrénées, so called from the Gaul. personal name *Senos* (from the root *sen-* old) + the local suffix *-ācum*.

Sendall English: probably a metonymic occupational name for a merchant dealing in fine silk, ME, OF *sendal* (apparently ultimately from Gk *sindōn* fine linen cloth, winding sheet, shroud). The meaning 'winding sheet, shroud' also attached to the ME word, and so it is possible that in some cases the surname originated as an occupational name for an undertaker.

Sendra Catalan: 1. from a Gmc (Visigothic) personal name composed of the elements *sinðs* path + *rēðs* counsel, attested in placenames such as *Vilasendra*.

2. nickname for someone with grey hair or an unhealthy complexion, from Cat. *cenda* cinders, ash (L *cinis*, gen. *cineris*).

Seneschal English: nickname for an officious man or occupational name for a seneschal, an official in a large household who was responsible for overseeing day-to-day domestic arrangements, ME, OF *seneschal* (of Gmc origin, composed of the elements *sini* old (ultimately cogn. with the root of SEIGNEUR) + *scalc* servant (see SCHALK)). The seneschal of a royal or ducal household in the Middle Ages was a very powerful man indeed, often having control over the administration of justice, among other things.

Vars.: **Seneschall, Senchell, Sene(s)cal, Senskell, Sensicall, Sensicle.**

Cogns.: Fr.: **Sénéc(h)al, Senescal, Sénéchau(l)t, Sénécaut, Sénécaux.** It.: **Siniscalco, Siniscalchi.**

Senf German: 1. metonymic occupational name for a dealer in mustard or nickname for someone with a fiery temper, from Ger. *Senf(t)* mustard (MHG *sen(e)f*, OHG *senef*, from L *sinapi*, a borrowing from Gk and probably ultimately from an oriental language).

2. nickname for a helpful or friendly person, from MHG *senfte* soft, accommodating (OHG *semfti*), mod. Ger. *sanft*.

Vars.: **Sempf, Senff, Senft.** (Of 2): **Senftleber** ('easy liver'); **Senftleben, Sanftleben** ('easy life').

Cogns. (of 1): Jewish (Ashkenazic): **Senft; Zenftman** (from Yid. *zeneft* mustard).

Senior 1. English: nickname for a peasant who gave himself airs and graces, from ANF *segneur* lord (see SEIGNEUR).

2. English: distinguishing nickname for the elder of two bearers of the same given name (e.g. father and son or two brothers), from L *senior* elder.

3. Jewish (Ashkenazic): reason for adoption unknown.

Vars.: Eng. (mainly of 1): **Seignior, Senier, Senyard, Sinyard, Sinyer, Seyner, Seynor, Sainer, Seanor, Seener, Seeney.**

The English surname Senior *is now most common in Yorkshire.*

Sentís Catalan: habitation name from a place whose name is of uncertain origin. It may derive from the dedication of the local church to St *Thyrsus*, a 3rd-cent. martyr of Apollonia in Phrygia, who was honoured with a full office in the Mozarabic liturgy. Alternatively, it may be from L *senticētum* thorn brake (a collective of *sentis* thorn bush, briar).

Sentry English: topographic name for someone who lived near a shrine, ME, OF *seintuarie* (LL *sanctuārium*, a deriv. of *sanctus* holy; cf. SAINT), or a nickname for someone who had had occasion to take sanctuary in a church or monastery, where he would have been afforded immunity from arrest or injury. The mod. Eng. occupational term *sentry* 'guardsman' is not attested before the 17th cent., and so is unlikely to be the source of the surname.

Vars.: **Santry, Sanctuary.**

Seppälä Finnish: topographic name for someone who lived in the house of a smith, from *seppä* (black)smith + the local suffix *-la*.

Seppänen Finnish: patr. from the occupational term *seppä* (black)smith.

Seppings English (E Anglia): nickname meaning 'sevenpence' (recorded in the form *Sevenpen(n)ys* in 1524), bestowed on someone who paid a rent of this amount or for some now irrecoverable anecdotal reason.

Var.: **Sippings.**

Sepúlveda Spanish: habitation name from any of various places so called, for example in the provinces of Salamanca and Segovia. The name is probably a deriv. of Sp. *sepultar* to bury (LL *sepultāre*, for class. L *sepelīre*, past part. *sepultus*), but the ending has not been satisfactorily explained.

Sequeira Portuguese: topographic name for someone who lived by a patch of dry, infertile land or a piece of land used for drying crops or bleaching clothes in the sun. The term derives from LL *siccāria*, a deriv. of *siccus* dry (see SECO), and has named various places, which may also be sources of the surname.

Serafim Portuguese: from a medieval given name, L *Seraphīnus*, from Hebr. *serafim*. This term was applied to the six-winged creatures described in Isaiah 6, and regarded in the Middle Ages as a class of angels; it is the pl. form of Hebr. *saraf*, probably a deriv. of *saraf* to burn. In part the Port. surname may represent a religious byname adopted in honour of the Capuchin monk St Seraphinus (1540–1604, formally canonized in 1767).

Cogns.: Pol.: **Serafin, Serafiński; Serafiniuk.**

Patr.: Pol.: **Serafinowicz.**

Serbinov Russian: patr. from the name *serbin* Serb. The Serbs originally came from what is now Galicia in Poland, and migrated to the Balkan peninsula in the 6th and 7th cents. AD.

Cogns.: Czech: **Srb(a).** Hung.: **Szerb.** Rum.: **Sarbesco** (patr.).

Dims.: Czech: **Srbek, Srbík.**

Sergeant English and French: occupational name for a servant, ME, OF *sergent* (L *serviens*, gen. *servientis*, pres. part. of *servīre* to serve). The surname probably originated for the most part in this general sense, but the word also developed various specialized meanings (being used for example as a technical term for a tenant by military service below the rank of a knight, and as the name for any of certain administrative and legal officials in different localities). For the change of *-er-* to *-ar-*, see MARCHANT.

Vars.: Eng.: **Sergeaunt**, **Sergean**, **Sergant**, **Sergent**, **Serje(a)nt**, **Seargeant**, **Searjeant**, **Sarg(e)ant**, **Sarge(au)nt**, **Sargint**, **Sarjant**, **Sarjent**. Fr.: **Sergent**, **Sargent**.

Cogns.: Cat.: **Sirvent**, **Servent**.

Patrs.: Eng.: **Serjeantson**, **Sarge(a)ntson**, **Sarjantson**, **Sergenson**, **Serginson**, **Sarginson**, **Sargeson**, **Sargi(s)son**, **Surgison**.

A family by the name of Sargeant *trace their descent from John* le Sergeant, *who held the office of sergeant of the forest of Dean from about 1357. However, the exact line of descent is uncertain; the earliest ancestor who can be verifed with any certainty is John* Sargeaunt *(d. 1541) of Mitcheldean, Gloucs.*

Sergio Italian: from the L family name *Sergius* (of uncertain, possibly Etruscan, origin), borne by a 4th-cent. Christian saint martyred in Cappadocia under Diocletian. The given name was hereditary in the ducal houses of Amalfi and Naples between the 11th and 13th cents. In the form *Sergei* it is also extremely popular in Russia.

Var.: **Sergi**.

Cogns.: Port.: **Sérgio**. Ger.: **Sergius**, **Serries**, **Sörries**.

Patrs.: Russ.: **Sergeev**; **Sergievski** (a clerical name). Beloruss.: **Syarkeev**. Gk: **Sergiou**. Armenian: **Sarkis(s)ian**.

Patrs. (from dims.): Russ.: **Sergevin**, **Serganov**, **Sergachyov**, **Sergun(k)ov**, **Sergunchikov**, **Seryozhechkin**, **Seryozhichev**.

Sermon English: metonymic occupational name for a preacher, or perhaps a nickname for a long-winded and pompous person, from ME *serm(o)un* sermon (OF *sermon*, from L *sermo*, gen. *sermōnis*, speech, discourse). The agent derivs. attested in the Middle Ages do not seem to have survived as modern surnames.

Vars.: **Surmon**, **Surman**, **Sirmon**, **Sirman**, **Sermin**, **Serman**.

A modern family of this name trace their line back to a certain Edmund Sermon, *recorded in 1644 in the parish register at Naunton Beauchamp, Worcs. A later William Sermon of Worcs. served as physician to Charles II. Before the Industrial Revolution the name was rare outside the Cotswolds. Richard* le Sermoner *is recorded at Sibford Gower, Oxon., in 1212.*

Serna Spanish: feudal status name for someone who worked on a plot of land owned by the lord of the manor and cultivated for him as part of the prescribed feudal service, Sp. *serna* (OSp. *senera*, apparently of Celt. origin, composed of the separative prefix *sen-* + *ar* to plough, cultivate). There are several places in Spain named with this word, and the surname could also be a habitation name from any of these.

Serpe French: metonymic occupational name for a maker or seller of scythes and other agricultural implements, from OF *sarpe* (hypercorrected to *serpe*) scythe, sickle (LL *sarpa*, from *sarpere* to trim, cut).

Dims.: **Sarpot**, **Serpot**, **Serpeau**, **Serpin(et)**, **Serpy**, **Serpette**. Eng.: **Serpell**.

Serrat Catalan: topographic name for someone who lived on a wooded upland, Cat. *serrat* (a deriv. of *serra* chain, range of hills; see SERRE).

Cogn.: Prov.: **Sarrat**.

Serre Provençal: topographic name for someone who lived on or near a ridge or chain of hills, OProv. *serre* (L *serra* saw).

Vars.: **Serres**, **Sarre**; **Sarran**.

Cogns.: Sp.: **Sierra**; **Serrano**. Cat.: **Serra**; **Serrà**, **Sarrà**. Port.: **Serra(s)**; **Serrano**, **Serrão**. It.: **(De) Serra**, **Serri**; **Serrano**, **Serresi**.

Dims.: Prov.: **Serreau**, **Sarreau**, **Serret**, **Sarret**, **Sarrey**, **Sarron**, **Sarrot**, **Sarrin**, **Sarry**. It.: **Serretta**, **Serrini**, **Serrotti**.

Aug.: It.: **Serrone**.

Servadio Italian (Jewish): from a given name composed of the It. elements *servare* to serve + *Dio* God, representing a calque of the Hebr. male given name *Ovadya* (Eng. *Obadiah*).

Servis English: metonymic occupational name for a brewer or a tavern-keeper, from ANF *cerveise* ale (OF *cervoise*, of apparently Gaul. origin).

Vars.: **Service**, **Servais**, **Sarvis**.

Cogn.: Fr: **Servoise**.

Sessions English: habitation name from *Soissons* in N France, so called from the Gaul. tribe who once inhabited the area, and whose name is recorded in L documents in the form *Suessiones*, of uncertain derivation.

Cogn.: Fr.: **Soissons**.

Šesták Czech: from *šesták*, name of an old coin (literally 'sixer'; it was at one time worth six kreuzers). The surname would have been acquired by someone who had to pay rent of this amount or for some other anecdotal reason. Cf. SHOSTAKOVICH.

Settle English: habitation name from a place in W Yorks., so called from OE *setl* seat, dwelling.

Seuss German: habitation name representing a S Ger. pronunciation of *Seis*, a place in the Tyrol.

Vars.: **Seis(er)**.

Séverin French: from a given name (L *Severīnus*, from the same root as *Severus*; see SEVEROV). This was borne by several early Christian saints, including bishops of Trèves (2nd cent.), Cologne (4th cent.), Bordeaux (5th cent.), and Santempeda (6th cent.), and hermits of Paris (6th cent.) and Tivoli (8th cent.), as well as a 5th-cent. apostle of Austria.

Vars.: **Sévrin**, **Sevrain**, **S(e)urin**.

Cogns.: It.: **Severin(i)**, **Severino**. Port.: **Severino**. Eng.: SEVERN. Ger.: **Severin(g)**, **Seffrin(g)**, **Siffrin(g)**. Flem., Du.: **Severyn**. Dan., Norw.: **Sö(h)ren**. Swed.: **Severin**, **Sewerin**. Pol.: **Seweryn**, **Seweryński**.

Dims.: Fr.: **Seuret**, **Seurot**.

Aug.: Fr.: **Seurat**.

Patrs.: Low Ger.: **Vrings**, **Frin(g)s**, **Freins**. Flem., Du.: **Severyns**. Dan., Norw.: **Severinsen**, **Sørens(en)**. Swed.: **Sörensson**. Pol.: **Seweryniak**.

An English family by the name of **Sorensen** *originated in Denmark. They trace their descent from Søren of Silkeborg (c.1815–75), whose son Jens (James) Sørensen (1840–1919) moved to England, where he became a blacksmith in Islington, London.*

Severn English: 1. cogn. of Fr. SÉVERIN.

2. topographic name for someone living on the banks of the river *Severn*, which flows from Wales through much of W England to the Bristol Channel. The river name is recorded as early as the 2nd cent. AD in the form *Sabrina*. This is one of Britain's most ancient river names; the original meaning is uncertain, but it may have been 'Slow-moving'.

Var.: **Severne**.

Severov Russian: surname adopted by Orthodox priests, from the L personal name *Severus* (in L meaning 'Harsh, Austere'). This was the name of several Roman Emperors, including Alexander Severus (d. 235), born in Syria, who was noted for his virtuous and studious character and his tolerance towards Christians. The given name enjoyed some popularity among early Christians. Its adoption as a Russian priestly surname was reinforced by the Russ. vocab. word *sever* North.

Cogns.: Czech: **Severa**. Pol.: **Siewiera**, **Siewierski** (reinforced not only by the vocab. words *siewierz* north and *siewier* north wind, but also by *siewiarz* sower).

Sévigné French: habitation name from a place in Ille-et-Vilaine, so called from the Gallo-Roman personal name *Sabinius* (a deriv. of L *Sabinus*; see SABIN) + the local suffix *-ācum*.

Sevilla Spanish: habitation name from the city of this name in SW Spain, the capital of Andalusia. The city is extremely ancient, having reputedly been founded by the Phoenicians. The origin of the name is obscure, presumably Phoenician. It is first recorded in the L form *Hispalis*, which was adopted into Arabic as *Isbilia*, and thence into Sp. as *Sibilia*, now *Sevilla*.

Var.: **Sevillano**.

Cogns.: Jewish (Sefardic): **Sevil(l)ia, Sevilya**. It.: **Sivi(g)lia, Sivilla, Sivilli, S(c)ibilia, Sibiglia, Sibilio, S(c)ibilla, Sibillo** (see also SIBLEY); **Sibil(l)ano**.

Seward 1. English: from a ME given name representing two originally distinct personal names, *Siward* and *Seward*, OE *Sigeweard* and *Sǣweard*, composed of the elements *sige* victory and *sǣ* sea + *weard* guard, protect. They became confused in the late OE period.

2. English: occupational name for a swineherd, from OE *sū* pig + *hierde* herdsman (see HEARD).

3. Irish: Anglicized form of Gael. **Ó Suaird, Ó Suairt** 'descendant of *Suart*', a personal name derived from an ON cogn. of OE *Sigeweard*; cf. 1 above.

Vars. (of 3): **O'Swerte, O'Sworde**, SWORD.

Sewell English: 1. from the ME given names *Siwal(d)* and *Sewal(d)*, OE *Sigeweald* and *Sǣweald*, composed of the elements *sige* victory and *sǣ* sea + *weald* rule.

2. habitation name from *Sewell* in Beds., *Showell* in Oxon., or *Seawell* or *Sywell* in Northants, all of which are so called from OE *seofon* seven + *wella* spring (cf. CIFUENTES).

Vars.: **Sewall, Sewill, Sa(y)well**.

Henry Sewell *(1807–79), the first Prime Minister of New Zealand, was born in Newport, Isle of Wight, the son of a solicitor. He became secretary of the Association for the Colonization of New Zealand, and went there in 1852, returning to England in 1876.*

Sewer English: 1. occupational name for a shoemaker or cobbler, an agent deriv. of ME *sew(en)* to sew (OE *si(o)wan*), reinforced by ANF *suo(u)r* (L *sūtor*; cf. SAUTER). The OE term was also used to denote a tailor; cf. SOUSTER.

2. occupational name for an official in charge of banqueting arrangements, from ANF *seour*, an aphetic form of OF *asseour* (from *asseoir* to seat, L *adsīdere* to sit down (to)).

3. occupational name for a sawyer, from ANF *syour* (OF *seior*, L *secātor*, from *secāre* to cut). Compare SAWYER.

Cogn. (of 1): Ger.: SAUTER.

Equivs. (of 1, not cogn.): Ger. and Jewish: SCHUSTER. Pol.: SZEWC.

Sexton 1. English: occupational name for a sexton or churchwarden, ME *sexteyn* (OF *secrestein*, from L *sacristānus*).

2. Irish: Anglicized form of Gael. **Ó Seastnáin** 'descendant of *Seastnán*', a personal name of uncertain origin; it may have been originally a byname meaning 'Bodyguard', from *seasuighim* to resist, defend.

Vars. (of 1): **Sexten, Sex(st)on, Seckerson, Secretan**, SAXTON, SAXON. (Of 2): **O'Sesnane, O'Shesnan, Shasnan**.

Cogns. (of 1): Fr.: **Sagrestain, Segrestan, Segréta(i)n, Segrétin, Secréta(i)n**. Prov.: **Sacriste, Sacreste**. Sp.: **Sacristán**. Cat.: **Sagristà**. Ger.: **Si(e)grist, Siegeris(t)**.

Equivs. (of 1, not cogn.): Ger.: GLOCKNER, KIRCHNER, KÜSTER, MESNER. Russ.: PONOMARYOV.

Seymour English: 1. Norman habitation name from *Saint-Maur*-des-Fossées in Seine, N France, so called from the dedication of the church there to St *Maur* (see MOORE 3).

2. habitation name from either of two places in N Yorks. called *Seamer*, from OE *sǣ* sea, lake + *mere* lake, pond. Ekwall postulates that the original name in OE was simply *Sǣ* 'the Lake', the second element being added when the denotation of the first came to be restricted to a body of salt water. There are also places called *Semer* in Norfolk, Suffolk, and N Yorks., which have the same origin and may lie behind some instances of the surname.

Vars.: **Seymo(u)re, Seymer**.

Cogn. (of 1): Fr.: **Saint-Maur**.

A family of the name Seymour, *who hold the title Dukes of Somerset, originated in* Saint-Maur. *Some sources say this was the place in Seine mentioned above, others identify it as Saint-Maur-sur-Loire in Touraine. The family is said to have come to England with the Conqueror, and in 1240 William* de Saint Maur *held lands in Monmouth. They also held the earldom and dukedom of Hertford, and rose to prominence under the Tudors. Edward Seymour (?1506–52) held high office under Henry VIII, who was married to Seymour's sister, Jane (?1509–37). He was Lord Protector in the reign of Edward VI, but was beheaded for treason on charges laid by his rival, the Earl of Warwick.*

Shackell English: 1. metonymic occupational name for a maker of fetters, from ME *schackel* chain, bond (OE *sceacol*).

2. from the medieval given name *Schackel*, an Anglicized form of the ON byname *Skokull* 'Wagon-pole' (a cogn. of 1), given perhaps to a tall, thin man.

Vars.: **Shackel, Shackle, Skakle**.

Patr. (from 2): **Shackles**.

Shacklady English (Lancs.): of uncertain origin, probably a bawdy nickname for a man who was suspected of having made love to a lady higher than him in social rank, from ME *schak(k)en*, *schag(g)en* to shake, toss (cf. SHAKESPEARE) + *ladie* lady (OE *hlǣfdige*, literally 'loaf kneader').

Var.: **Shakelady**.

Shackleton English: habitation name from a place in the parish of Halifax, W Yorks., so called from OE **scacol* tongue of land (a cogn. of ON *skekill*) + *tūn* enclosure, settlement.

The British Antarctic explorer Sir Ernest Shackleton *(1874–1922) was born in Kilkee, Ireland; his father's Quaker family came from Yorkshire.*

Shacklock English (Derbys.): metonymic occupational name for a jailer, from ME *shaklock* fetter (apparently a cpd of *schackel* (see SHACKELL 1) + LOCK). According to the OED the vocab. word is first found in an isolated instance from the 16th cent.

Shade Scots and English: 1. local name for someone who lived near a boundary, OE *scēad* (from *scēadan* to divide; cf. SCHEIDT).

2. nickname for a very thin man, from ME *schade* shadow, wraith (OE *sceadu*, gen. *scead(u)we*).

Var.: **Schade**.

Shadwell English: habitation name from any of the places so called, in London, Norfolk, and W Yorks. The first is named from OE *sceald* shallow + *well(a)* spring, stream (see WELL), the latter two from *scēad* boundary (see SHADE 1) + *well(a)*.

The English dramatist Thomas Shadwell *(?1642–92) was appointed Poet Laureate in 1688. He was born in Norfolk, the son of a landowner and attorney-general of Connacht. His family lost a great deal of property because of their support for the King in the Civil War. They are said to have originated in Staffs.*

Shaftoe English: habitation name from a place in Northumb., probably so called from OE *sceaft* shaft (presumably a post marking a boundary) + *hōh* ridge (see HOE).

Shakespeare English: nickname for a belligerent person or perhaps a bawdy name for an exhibitionist, from ME *schak(k)en* to brandish (OE *sc(e)acan*) + *speer* spear (OE *spere*).

Vars.: **Schakespear, Shakspeare.**

The most famous of all English dramatists, William Shakespeare *(1564–1616), was born in Stratford-on-Avon, Warwicks. The surname is still found in Warwicks. and the W Midlands.*

Shale English (W Midlands): apparently a nickname from ME *shale* shell (OE *scealu*), perhaps denoting someone considered of little value, as in the ME phrase *vayled not of a schale* 'not worth a shell'.

Shallcross English: habitation name from a place named after an ancient stone cross in the High Peak forest of Derbys., in the parish of Chapel en le Frith, known as the *Shackelcross*. The first element in this name appears to be from OE *sceacol* (see SHACKELL 1), perhaps denoting a cross to which penitents could be fettered.

Vars.: **Shalcross, Shallcrass, Shellcross; Shawcross.**

Shand Scots: of uncertain origin, perhaps from a short form of ALEXANDER (see SAND 2), or a Norman habitation name from *Chandai* in Orne, recorded in the early 12th cent. as *Canziacum*, from the Gallo-Roman personal name *Candius* + the local suffix *-ācum*.

Shane Irish: 1. Anglicized form of Gael. **Mac Seáin** 'son of *Seán*', a form of JOHN.

2. Anglicized form of Gael. **Ó Seanaigh** 'descendant of *Seanach*', a byname meaning 'Old', 'Wise'.

Vars. (of 1): **McShane.** (Of 2): **O'Shanna, O'Shann(e)y, O'Sheny; Shannagh, Shann(e)y, Sheeny.**

Dims. (of 2): **O'Sheanaghaine, O'Shanahan, Shana(g)han, Shanghan, Shan(ih)an** (Gael. **Ó Seanacháin**); **O'Shenane, O'Shennan, (O')Shannon, (O')Shanan** (Gael. **Ó Seanáin**).

Shanks N English and Scots: nickname for someone with long legs or some peculiarity of gait, from OE *sceanca* shin-bone, leg. This vocab. word was preserved in Scotland, whereas in England it was replaced by ON *leggr* (see LEGG). See also CRUIKSHANK and SHEEPSHANKS.

Var.: **Shank.**

Shanley Irish: Anglicized form of the Gael. personal name *Seanlaoch*, composed of the elements *sean* old + *laoch* hero.

Var.: **Shanly.**

Patrs.: **McShanl(e)y.**

'Descendant of S.': **O'Shanley.**

Shapcott English (Somerset): topographic name for someone who lived by a sheepcote (from OE *scēap, scīp* sheep + *cot* shelter), no doubt equivalent to an occupational name for a shepherd.

Shaper English: occupational name for a tailor, from an agent deriv. of ME *schap(en)* to form, mould (a back-formation from *schap*, OE *(ge)sceap*, from **sciepan* to create).

Vars.: **Shapster, Shipster** (fem. forms).

Shapiro Jewish (Ashkenazic): 1. possibly an ornamental name, from Hebr. *shapir* fair, lovely.

2. habitation name from the German town of *Speyer*, which had a large Jewish population in the Middle Ages; cf. SAPIR, SPIER, and SPIRE.

Vars.: **Schapiro, Shapero, Shapira; Chapiro** (a Fr. spelling); **Szapiro, Szapira** (Pol. spellings); **Shapir.**

Shapochnikov Russian: patr. from *shapochnik*, occupational name for a hatter, an agent noun from *shapka* hat (from OF *chape, chapel* hat, via MHG *schäpel* and Pol. *czapka*).

Var.: **Shaposhnikov.**

Cogns.: Jewish (E Ashkenazic): **Shaposhnik, Schaposchnik** (not patrs.); **Szaposznik** (a Pol. spelling).

Shardlow English: habitation name from a place in Derbys., so called from OE *sceard* notched + *hlāw* hill, tumulus (see LAW 2 and LOW 1), i.e. a hill or tumulus with an indentation in its outline.

Sharkey Irish: Anglicized form of Gael. **Ó Searcaigh** 'descendant of *Searcach*', a byname meaning 'Beloved'.

Sharp English: nickname from ME *scharp* keen, active, quick (OE *scearp*).

Vars.: **Sharpe; Shairp** (Scots).

Cogns.: Ger.: **Scharf(f), Scharfe, Sharpf.** Low Ger.: **Scharp.** Flem., Du.: : **Scherp.** Jewish (Ashkenazic): **Scharf(man); Szarf** (Pol. spelling).

Patrs.: Eng.: **Sharps.** Low Ger.: **Scharping, Schärping, Scherping.**

Cpds (arbitrary elaborations): Jewish: **Scharfherz, Szarfherc, Szarfharc** ('sharp heart'); **Scharfstein, Szarfstein** ('sharp stone').

Sharples English (very common in Lancs.): habitation name from *Sharples* Hall near Bolton, probably so called from OE *scearp* sharp, i.e. steep + *lǣs* pasture.

Var.: **Sharpless.**

Shaughnessy Irish: Anglicized form of Gael. **Ó Seachnasaigh** 'descendant of *Seachnasach*', a personal name of uncertain origin, perhaps derived from *seachnach* elusive.

Vars.: **O'Shaughnessy, O'Shoughnessy, (O')Shannessy, O'Shanesy.**

The main branch of the once-powerful O'Shaughnessy *clan died out in the 18th cent. The early 16th-cent. head of the clan, Dermot O'Shaughnessy, had been knighted by Henry VIII in 1533 and confirmed in possession of his lands, but just over a century later these were confiscated by Cromwell. The clan had these lands returned to them in 1660, on the restoration of the Stuart monarchy, but finally lost them in 1697 for supporting the Stuart cause. The last chief, Colonel William O'Shaughnessy, died in France in 1744.*

Shaw 1. English: topographic name for someone who lived by a copse or thicket, OE *sceaga*, or habitation name from one of the numerous minor places named with this word.

2. Scots and Irish: Anglicized form of any of various surnames derived from the Gael. personal name *Sithech* 'Wolf'.

Vars. (of 1): **Shawe, Shay, Shay(e)s, Shave(s), Shafe.**

Cogns. (of 1): Dan., Norw.: **Skov, Skou, Schou.** Swed.: **Sko(o)g(h).**

The Irish writer George Bernard Shaw *(1856–1950) was born in Dublin into a Protestant family established in Ireland by William Shaw, a captain in William III's army, who went there c.1689.*

Shcherbakov Russian: patr. from the nickname *Shcherbak* (from *shcherba* hole, tear, scar), denoting a man disfigured by pockmarks or scars.

Var.: **Shcherbatov.**

Cogns.: Ukr.: **Shcherbak, Shcherban.** Beloruss.: **Shcharbakov** (patr.).

Shchukin Russian: patr. from the nickname *Shchuka* 'Pike', denoting a sharp or malicious person.

Cogns.: Ukr., Beloruss.: **Shchupak**. Pol.: **Szczupak**. Jewish (E Ashkenazic): **Szczupak**, **Shupa(c)k** (ornamental); **Szczupakiewicz** (formally a patr.).

Shea Irish: Anglicized form of Gael. **Ó Séaghdha** 'descendant of *Séaghdha*', a byname meaning 'Fine', 'Fortunate'.

Vars.: **Shee**; **O'Shea** (the most common form), **O'Shee**.

Shear English: nickname for a beautiful or radiant person, or one with fair hair, from ME *scher*, *schir*, OE *scīr* bright, fair.

Vars.: **Sheer**, **She(e)re**, **Sher(r)**.

Patrs.: **Shear(e)s**, **Sheer(e)s**; **Shires** (Yorks.); **Shearing** (E Anglia).

Sheard English (W Yorks.): topographic name for someone who lived by a gap between hills, OE *sceard* (a deriv. of *sceran* to cut, shear).

Vars.: **Shard**, **Sheards**.

Shearer Scots and N English: occupational name for a sheep-shearer or someone who used scissors to trim the surface of finished cloth and remove excessive nap, from an agent deriv. of ME *schere(n)* to shear (OE *sceran*). ME *schere* denoted shears and scissors of all sizes.

Vars.: **Sherer**, **Sharer**, **Shirer**, **She(a)ra**.

Cogns.: Ger.: **Sche(e)rer**, **Scherrer**. Jewish (Ashkenazic): **Sherer**; **Szerer** (a Pol. spelling).

Equivs. (not cogn.): Ger.: FUGGER. Fr.: TONDEUR.

Sheddon Scots: of uncertain origin, perhaps a habitation name from *Sheddens* in the former county of Renfrews. This placename contains a first element of uncertain derivation + ME *den* hollow, valley (OE *denu*; see DEAN 1).

Vars.: **Shedden**, **Sheddan**.

Sheedy Irish: Anglicized form of Gael. **Ó Síoda** 'descendant of *Síoda*', a byname meaning 'Silk'.

Vars.: **O'Shydie**, **Shead**; SILK.

Sheehan Irish: Anglicized form of Gael. **Ó Síodhacháin** 'descendant of *Síodhachán*', a personal name representing a dim. of *síodhach* peaceful.

Vars.: **O'Shiegane**, **O'Shehane**, **O'Sheehan**, **(O')Sheahan**, **She(e)an**, **Sheane**, **Sheen**, **Shine**.

Sheehy Scots and Irish: Anglicized form of the Gael. personal name *Sítheach*, probably originally a byname from the adj. *sítheach* relating to fairies, eerie, mysterious.

Vars.: **Sheekey**, **Sheach**, **Shiach**, **Se(a)th**.

Patrs.: **McShee(hy)**, **McShiehie**, **McShihy** (Gael. **Mac Síthigh**); **McKeith**.

The name was first established in Ireland by a branch of the Scottish McDonnells, descended from Sithich, *great-grandson of Domhnaill, who came to Ireland early in the 14th cent.*

Most bearers of the name in the Highlands of Scotland claim descent from Sithich, *son of Gilchrist, son of John, son of Angus, the 6th chief of the McIntoshes.*

Sheepshanks N English and Scots: nickname for someone with an odd, shambling gait, from Northern ME *schep* sheep + SHANKS.

Sheffield English: habitation name from the city in S Yorks., so called from the river name *Sheaf* (from OE **scēað* boundary, a byform of *scēad*; see SHADE 1) + OE *feld* pasture, open country (see FIELD). There are also minor places of the same name in Sussex (from OE *scēap*, *scīp* sheep + *feld*) and Berks. (from OE *scēo* shelter, shed + *feld*), which may have contributed to the surname.

Shelby English: of uncertain origin, either a var. of SELBY, or a habitation name from an unidentified place named with the Northern ME elements *schēle* hut (see SHIELD 2) + *by* settlement, farm (ON *býr*). The surname is now more common in the U.S. than in England.

Sheldon English: habitation name from any of the various places so called. The main source is probably the one in Derbys., recorded in Domesday Book as *Scelhadun*, formed by the addition of the OE distinguishing term *scylf* shelf to the placename *Haddon* (from OE *hǣð* heath(er) + *dūn* hill). There are also places called *Sheldon* in Devon (from OE *scylf* shelf + *denu* valley) and Birmingham (from OE *scylf* + *dūn* hill).

Sheldrake English (chiefly E Anglia): nickname for a vain or showy person, from a type of brightly coloured duck, ME *scheldrake* (from the E Anglian dial. term *scheld* variegated (MLG *schelede*, past part. of *schelen* to differ) + *drake* male duck (apparently also of Low Ger. origin)).

Vars.: **Shildrake**, **Sheldrick**, **Shildrick**.

Shelley English: habitation name from any of various places, for example in Sussex, Suffolk, Essex, and W Yorks., all so called from OE *scylf* shelf + *lēah* wood, clearing. The surname is now as common in the W Midlands as it is in E Anglia and London.

Var.: **Shelly**.

The family of Percy Bysshe Shelley *(1792–1822) had been established in Sussex for centuries. They took their name from a minor place near Crawley, and the poet was born at nearby Horsham.*

Shelton English (most common in Notts.): habitation name from any of various places, for example in Notts., Beds., Norfolk, Shrops., and Staffs., all apparently so called from OE *scylf* shelf + *tūn* enclosure, settlement. See also SHILTON and SKELTON.

Shenton English: habitation name from a place in Leics., originally named as the settlement (OE *tūn*) on the river *Sence*. This river name is a Normanized form of OE *Scenc* 'Drinking Cup', referring to its abundance of potable water.

Sheppard English: occupational name for a shepherd, ME *schepherde*, from OE *scēap*, *scīp* sheep + *hierde* herdsman (see HEARD) or *weard* guardian (see WARD 1).

Vars.: **Shephe(a)rd**, **Shep(h)ard**, **Shepe(a)rd**, **Shepperd**, **Shippard**.

Cogn.: Flem.: **Schaapherder**.

Patrs.: Eng.: **Sheppardson**, **Shepper(d)son**, **Shep(h)erdson**.

Sheraton English: habitation name from a place in Co. Durham, found in 11th-cent. records as *Scurufatun*, and hence probably of the same origin as SCRUTON.

Sherborne English: habitation name from any of various places, for example in Dorset, Gloucs., Hants, and Warwicks., all so called from OE *scīr* bright (see SHEAR) + *burna* stream (see BOURNE).

Vars.: **Sherbourne**, **Sherborn**; **Sherburn** (Yorks.).

A family by the name of Sherborn *has been established in the area of Ashford, Middlesex, for centuries, originally in the parish of Bedfont. The name is first recorded there in the Middlesex Muster Rolls of 1338, when John Sherborn was required to do service as an archer.*

Sheremetyev Russian: patr. from a Turkic given name, from Arab. *Ahmad* (see AKHMATOV), with the addition of the title *Shir* 'Lion' (of Persian origin).

Var.: **Sheremetev**.

Sheridan Irish: Anglicized form of Gael. **Ó Sirideáin** 'descendant of *Sirideán*', a personal name of uncertain origin, possibly akin to *sirim* to seek.

Vars.: **Sherridan, O'Sheridane, O'Shiridane.**

Sheriff English: occupational name for a sheriff, a word derived from OE *scīr* shire, administrative district (the original sense being '(sphere of) office, duty') + *(ge)rēfa* REEVE. In some cases it may also have arisen as a nickname. In England before the Norman Conquest the sheriff was the king's representative in a county, responsible for every aspect of local administration. Gradually the duties of the office became restricted, until by the 19th cent. they were more or less confined to the administration of county courts and prisons, this being something of a sinecure. In some counties the office was hereditary, a practice which continued in Westmorland until 1850. Similar officials were found in Scotland in the Middle Ages, and from the 16th cent. in Ireland.

Vars.: **Sherriff, Shir(r)eff, Shiriff, Shirra, Shre(e)ve, Sch(r)ieve, Schrive.**

Patrs.: **Sher(r)iffs, Shirref(f)s, Shreeves, Schrieves, Shrives.**

Sherington English: habitation name from a place in Bucks., so called from OE *Scīringtūn* 'settlement associated with *Scīra*', a byname meaning 'Bright', 'Fair' (see SHEAR).

Vars.: **Sherrington** (now found chiefly in Lancs.), **Shrimpton.**

Sherlock English: nickname for someone with fair hair or a lock of fair hair, ME *schirloc*, from OE *scīr* bright, fair (see SHEAR) + *loc* lock (of hair).

Var.: **Shurlock.**

Sherman 1. English: occupational name for a sheep-shearer or someone who used shears to trim the surface of finished cloth and remove excess nap, ME *shereman*; cf. SHEARER.

2. Jewish (Ashkenazic): occupational name for a tailor, from Yid. *sher* scissors + *man* man.

Vars. (of 1): **Sh(e)arman, Sheerman, Shurman.** (Of 2): **Shermann, Szerman, Shermeister.**

Roger Sherman *(1722–93), the only man to sign all four documents at the foundation of the American republic (the Declaration of Independence, the Articles of Association and Confederation, and the Constitution itself), was born in Newton, Mass., a descendant of Captain John Sherman, who had emigrated in about 1636 to Massachusetts from Dedham, Essex, where his father was a farmer, following his brother Edmund, who had emigrated two years previously.*

A descendant of Edmund Sherman was the American general William Tecumseh Sherman (1820–91), who led the Union March through Georgia. He was born in Lancaster, Ohio, the son of a judge; his middle name was bestowed in honour of a Shawnee chieftain.

Sherratt English: of uncertain origin, apparently a deriv. of ME *shere* bright, fair (see SHEAR) with the addition of the ANF pej. suffix *-ard*.

Vars.: **Sharratt; Sherrett, Sherott, Sherrad, Sherred, Sherr(e)ard, Sherard.**

Sherwin English: nickname for a swift runner, from ME *schere(n)* to shear + *wind*; the Ger. surname **Schneidewin(d)** 'cut wind' provides a semantic parallel. The Eng. surname is sometimes translated in medieval sources into the ANF form *Tranchevent*.

Var.: **Sherwen.**

Sherwood English: habitation name from a place in Notts., around which once stood the famous Sherwood Forest. The place is so called from OE *scīr* shire (see SHERIFF) or *scīr* bright (see SHEAR) + *wudu* WOOD.

Var.: **Shearwood.**

Shield 1. English: metonymic occupational name for an armourer; cf. SCHILD 1.

2. English: habitation name from places in Northumb. and Co. Durham (now both in Tyne and Wear) called respectively N and S *Shields*, from ME *schēle* shed, hut, shelter (OE *scēol*). Some examples of the surname may be topographic names, derived directly from the vocab. word.

3. English: topographic name for someone who lived near the shallow part of a river, from OE *scieldu* shallows, a deriv. of *sceald* shallow.

4. Irish: Anglicized form of Gael. **Ó Siaghail, Ó Siadhail** 'descendant of *Siadhal*', a well-attested personal name of unknown derivation.

Vars. (mainly of 2): **Shiel(ds); Shiel(l)s** (chiefly Sc.); **Sheil(ds), Sheal(s).** (Of 4): **O'Siegall, O'Shiel(l), O'Sheal, O'Shill, Sheil(d)s.**

Shillingford English: habitation name from places so called, in Devon and Oxon., which are of uncertain etymology. The second element is clearly OE *ford* FORD; Ekwall proposes that the first is probably a tribal name, *Scillingas* 'people of **Sciell(a)*', a byname from OE *sciell* resounding.

Shillito English: of uncertain meaning. This surname seems to have a single origin in the parish of Featherstone, W Yorks.

Vars.: **Sillito(e).**

Shilton English: habitation name from any of various places (in Berks., Leics., Oxon., and Warwicks.) which have the same origin as SHELTON.

Shingler English: occupational name for someone who laid wooden tiles (shingles) on roofs, an agent deriv. of ME *schingle* shingle (OE *scingel*, from L *scindula, scandula*).

Var.: **Shingles.**

Cogns.: Ger.: **Schindler, Schind(e)l.** Jewish (Ashkenazic): **Schindler, Schindel(man).** Czech: **Šindelář.**

Equiv.: Pol.: SZKUDLAREK.

Shipley English: habitation name from any of the various places, for example in Derbys., Co. Durham, Northumb., Shrops., Sussex, and W Yorks., so called from OE *scēap, scīp* sheep + *lēah* wood, clearing.

Vars.: **Shiplee, Shapley.**

Shipman English: 1. occupational name for a shepherd, ME *schepman*, from OE *scēap, scīp* sheep + *mann* man. See also SHEPPARD.

2. occupational name for a mariner, or occasionally perhaps for a boat-builder, ME *schipman*, from OE *scip* ship + *mann*.

Vars. (of 1): **Sheep.** (Of 2): **Ship(p).**

Cogns. (of 1): Ger.: **Scha(a)f.** Low Ger.: **Schaap.** Flem.: **Schaepman.** See also SCHÄFER. (Of 2): Ger.: **Schiff(er), Schiffmann.** Flem., Du.: **Schip(per).** Jewish (Ashkenazic): **Schiffman(n).**

Shippam English: habitation name from *Shipham* in Somerset, so called from OE *scēap, scīp* sheep + *hām* homestead.

Shippen English: habitation name from any of various places named from OE *scypen* cattleshed, such as *Shippen* in W Yorks. and *Shippon* in Berks., or topographical name derived directly from the vocab. word. In some cases it may originally have been acquired as an occupational name for a cowman, who in medieval times would often have shared the quarters of his charges.

Shipside English: of uncertain origin. It may be a habitation name from some unidentified place, perhaps so called from OE *scēap*, *scīp* sheep + *sīde* slope. The earliest known bearers of the name are found as far apart as Worcs. and Co. Durham. Another possibility is that it may derive from *Shepshed* in Leics., recorded in Domesday Book as *Scepe(s)hefde*, and derived from OE *scēap* sheep + *hēafod* head, hill.

Var.: **Shipsides**.

The earliest known bearer of the name was George Shipside, *whose marriage is recorded in 1538. A present-day family by the name of* Shipsides *trace their descent to William Shipsides (b. 1661), the son of John Shipside (b. 1621); both men were born in Gotham, Notts., not far from Shepshed. John Shipside was the son of another John, who spelled his surname indiscriminately with and without the final* -s *and does not seem to have been born in Gotham.*

Shipstone English: habitation name, probably from *Shipston* on Stour in Warwicks., which is recorded in Domesday Book as *Shepwestun*, from OE *scēapwæsc* place for washing sheep + *tūn* enclosure, settlement.

Shipton English: habitation name from any of the various places, for example in Dorset, Gloucs., Hants, Oxon., and Shrops., so called from OE *scēap*, *scīp* sheep + *tūn* enclosure, settlement.

Shipway English (Gloucs.): probably a topographic name for someone who lived by a road along which sheep were regularly driven, from ME *schip* sheep + *way* path, road (see WAY).

Shirley English: habitation name from any of various places, for example in Derbys., Hants, Surrey, and the W Midlands, all so called from OE *scīr* bright + *lēah* wood, clearing; cf. SHERWOOD.

The Shirley *family of Earl Ferrers are said to be descended from a certain Sewallis (d. 1129), holder of the manor of Shirley, Derbys. His grandfather, Sewallis (d. c.1085), had held lands in Northants, Lincs., and Derbys.*

Shoesmith English: occupational name for a blacksmith who specialized in the shoeing of horses, ME *schosmith*, from OE *scōh* shoe (cf. SCHUH) + *smið* SMITH.

Var.: **Shoosmith**.

Shoikhet Jewish (Southern Ashkenazic): occupational name for a ritual slaughterer, Yid. *shoykhet*.

Vars.: **Shoichet**; **S(c)hochet**, **Shohet** (E Ashkenazic); **Szochet** (a Pol. spelling); **Schauchet** (reflecting a W Yid. pronunciation); **Shohetman**.

Patr.: **Szochatowicz**.

Sholem Jewish (Ashkenazic): from the Yid. male given name *Sholem* (from Hebr. *shalom* peace).

Vars.: **Shulem** (reflecting a S Yid. pronunciation); **Shalom** (Israeli).

Patrs.: **Shulimson** (reflecting a S Yid. pronunciation); **Sholemoff** (NE Ashkenazic); **Shalomoff** (a partly Hebraicized form).

Sholl 1. Cornish: of uncertain origin. It may perhaps be from Corn. *is* under + *hall* moor.

2. Anglicized form of Ger. or Jewish SCHOLL.

The earliest known bearer of the name is John Shole, *who was baptized in the parish of St Minver, near Padstow, Cornwall, in 1500. The name is now well established in Australia.*

Sholokhov Russian: patr. from the nickname *Sholokh* 'Stir', 'Bustle' (of imitative origin), denoting an officious or self-important person.

Var.: **Sholokov**.

Shooter English (now chiefly E Midlands): occupational name for a marksman, from an agent deriv. of ME *schoot(en)* to shoot (OE *scēotan*).

Vars.: **Shotter**, **Shut(t)er**; see also SHUTT.

Shore 1. English: topographic name for someone who lived by the sea-shore, ME *schore* (of uncertain origin, from Low Ger. or the native *scora* below).

2. English: topographic name for someone who lived by a bank or steep slope, from OE *scora*. There are minor places named with this word in Lancs. and W Yorks., and the surname may also be a habitation name from one of these.

3. Jewish (Ashkenazic): Anglicized spelling of *S(c)hor(r)* and *Szor*; see SCHAUER 2.

Var. (of 1 and 2): **Shores**.

Shorrock English (Lancs.): habitation name from *Shorrock* Green in Lancs., probably so called from OE *scora* bank + *āc* oak.

Vars.: **Shorrocks**, **Sharrock(s)**, **Shurrock**.

Short 1. English: nickname for a person of low stature, from ME *schort*, OE *sceort* short.

2. Irish: translation of Gael. *Mac an Ghirr*; see MCGIRR.

Vars. (of 1): **Shortman** (Somerset). (Of 2): **Shortt**.

Comparative (of 1): **Shorter**.

Shortall Irish: re-Anglicized form of Gael. *Soirtéil*, itself a Gaelicized form of an Eng. surname, *Shorthals*. This name, which was brought to Ireland in the reign of Edward I, was originally a nickname from ME *schort* SHORT + *halse* neck (see HALS). It survives in England only in the form SHORTHOUSE.

Vars.: **Scorthals**, **Shorthall**, **Shortle**, **Sertell**, **Sertill**, **Surtill**; **Shorten** (Gael. **Seartáin**; an altered form common in Co. Cork).

Shorthouse English (now chiefly W Midlands): 1. nickname from a peculiarity of dress, from ME *schort* SHORT + *hose* (OE *hosa*; cf. HOSIER). Hose were the regular medieval leg covering, varying in kind from a garment rather like a pair of tights to *half hose*, which reached only to the knee. Compare CURTIS 2.

2. nickname for someone with a short neck, a var. of SHORTALL.

Vars. (chiefly of 1): **Shorthose**, **Shorters**, **Shortis**.

Shoshin Jewish (E Ashkenazic): metr. from the Yid. female given name *Shoshe* (from the Hebr. name *Shoshana*, from *shoshan* lily) + the Slav. metr. suffix *-in*.

Vars.: **Sosin**; **Sosis** (Ashkenazic); **Shoshkin**, **Soskin**, **Shoshkes** (E Ashkenazic, from a dim. form, *Shoshke*, of the given name).

Shostakovich Belorussian: patr. from the nickname *Shastak*, a deriv. of *shast* six. The application of the nickname is uncertain; it may have denoted a person with six fingers on one hand, or it may have had some anecdotal reference to the coin (worth three copeks) so called. The surname has been given a Great Russ. form by the substitution of (unstressed) *o* for *a* in the first syllable.

Cogns. (not patrs.).: E Ger.: **Shostag**. Pol.: **Szostak**, **Szostek**. Jewish (E Ashkenazic): **Shosta(c)k**, **Shustak**, **Shustek**; **Szostak**. See also ŠESTÁK.

Shotton English (chiefly Northumb.): habitation name from any of various places in Co. Durham and Northumb., so called from OE *Scotta-tūn* 'settlement of the Scots' (from *Scotta* Scots), or *Scēot-tūn* 'settlement at a steep place' (from *scēot* quick, steep, a deriv. of *scēotan* to shoot), or *Scēat-tūn* 'settlement in a projection of a parish or other administrative division' (from *scēat* projection, corner, promontory). *Shotton* in the parish of Glendale, Northumb., is 'hill of the Scots', with the second element OE *dūn* hill (see Down 1). There are also two minor places in the W Midlands — *Shotten* on the Welsh border and *Shotton* in Hadnall, Shrops — that may lie behind some instances of the surname in this area. There is also a *Shotton* in Clwyd.

Shovell English: metonymic occupational name for a maker or seller of shovels, or for someone who regularly used a shovel in his work, from ME *schovel* (OE *scofl*, a deriv. of *scūfan* to push, shove).

Vars.: **Shovel, Showell, Showl; Shoveller, Showler, Shouler.**

Shroff English: although this is for the most part an Asian name (from a Hindi word for a money-changer or money-lender), it was already well established in England in the 19th cent. (see below), and may also be of Eng. origin. The etymology is unknown; it may be connected with *shroffe (metal)* old copper or brass (a term first recorded in the 16th cent., perhaps derived from Ger. *Schroff* fragment).

The earliest known English bearer is a certain William Shroff, *b. c.1855 in Saxmundham or Snape, Suffolk. A contemporary of his, William Homey Shroff, was born in 1866 in Sunderland.*

Shtul Jewish (Ashkenazic): 1. apparently a metonymic occupational name for a maker of chairs, from Ger. *Stuhl*, Yid. *shtul* chair.

2. possibly also from a S Yid. pronunciation of Yid. *shtol* Steel.

Vars.: **Shtull, Shtulman.**

Shufflebottom English: habitation name from *Shipperbottom* in Lancs., which derives its name from OE *scēpwœlla* spring where sheep are washed + *boðm* valley (see Bottom).

Vars.: **Shufflebot(h)am, Shovelbottom, Shipperbottom, Shoebottom, Shoebotham, Shubotham.**

Shugg Cornish: of unknown origin.

This name is first recorded in the form Shuge *at North Tamerton in Cornwall in 1569, and appears in its present-day form at Gwinear in 1641.*

Shute English: habitation name from *Shute* in Devon, so called from OE **sciete*, a var. form of *scēat* projection. There are minor places in Wilts. and Berks. named with this word; their modern forms are *Shute* and *Shoot* respectively.

Shutt English: occupational name for an archer, ME *schut(te)*, *schit(te)*, OE *scytta*, a primary deriv. of *scēotan* to shoot.

Vars.: **Shut(te)**. See also Shooter.

Cogn.: Ger.: Schütze.

Patr.: Eng.: **Shutts.**

Shuttleworth English: habitation name from any of several places so called (in Lancs., Derbys., and W Yorks.), which derive their name from OE *scyttel(s)* bar, bolt + *worð* enclosure (see Worth).

Var.: **Shettlesworth.**

A family of this name trace their descent from Henry de Shuttleworth, *recorded in 1300. His son, Ughtred, lived at Gawthorpe, near Burnley, Lancs., where one branch of the family can still be found. Ughtred has survived as a standard given name in this family into modern times.*

Sibbald Scots and N English: from the ME given name *Sybald*, OE *Sigebeald*, composed of the elements *sige* victory + *beald* bold, brave, reinforced in the early Middle Ages by the Norman introduction of a Continental cogn.

Cogns.: Fr.: **Sibaud, Sébaud, Sibault, Sibaux.** Fris.: **Sibbelt, Siebel.**

Patr.: Fris.: **Siebels.**

Sibbett Scots and English: from the early mod. Eng. given name *Sebode*, probably from an unattested OE personal name **Sigeboda*, composed of the elements *sige* victory + *boda* messenger. However, there has been some confusion with Sibbald.

Vars.: **Sibbit(t).**

Sibley English: from the popular medieval female given name *Sibley*, a vernacular form of L *Sibilla*, from Gk *Sibylla*, a title (of obscure origin) borne by various oracular priestesses in Classical times. In Christian mythology the sibyls came to be classed as pagan prophets, and hence the name was a respectable one to be bestowed on a child.

Vars.: **Sibly, Sebley; Sibble.**

Cogns.: Fr.: **Sibille, Sébille, Sébire.** Pol.: **Sibilski, Sibiński.**

Dims.: Fr.: **Sibilleau, Sibillot, Sébilleau, Sébillot, Sébillon, Sébline, Subileau.**

Aug.: Fr.: **Sibillat.**

Metrs.: Eng.: **Sibbles; Sibson** (from a pet form).

Sicilia Italian and Spanish: name for someone from the island of Sicily, which formed part of the kingdom of Aragon from 1282 to 1713.

Vars.: It.: **Siciliano, Siciliani.**

Siddall N English: habitation name from places in Lancs. (in the parish of Middleton) and W Yorks. (part of Halifax) called *Siddal*, from OE *sīd* wide + *halh* nook, recess (see Hale 1).

Vars.: **Siddle, Sidell.**

Sidebottom N English: habitation name from a place in Ches., so called from OE *sīd* wide + *boðm* valley (see Bottom).

Var.: **Sidebotham.**

Sidney English: 1. habitation name from *Sidney* in Surrey and Lincs., so called from OE *sīd* wide + *ēg* island, dry land in a fen, with the adj. retaining traces of the weak dat. ending, originally used after a preposition and def. art. Two places in Ches. called *Sydney* are from OE *sīd* + *halh* nook, recess (see Hale 1) and may also be partial sources of the surname.

2. possibly also a habitation name from a place in Normandy called *Saint-Denis*, from the dedication of its church to St *Dionysius* (see Dennis). There is, however, no evidence to support this derivation beyond occasional early mod. Eng. forms such as *Seyndenys*, which may equally well be the result of folk etymology.

Var.: **Sydney.**

A family of this name, who hold the title Viscount de l'Isle, trace their descent from John de Sydenie, *who held lands c.1280 at Alford, Surrey, where* Sidney *Farm and* Sidney *Wood are situated. His descendants include Sir William Sidney (?1482–1554), a commander at Flodden, who was granted Penshurst Place, Kent, by Edward VI. The poet Sir Philip Sidney (1554–86) was a descendant, born at Penshurst.*

Siebert German: from a Gmc personal name composed of the elements *sigi* victory + *berht* bright, famous. There has been some confusion between forms of this name and those of the more common Siegfried.

Vars.: **Siegbert; Segebrecht, Sägebrecht, Siebrecht, Zieprecht, Zyprecht.**

Cogns.: Low Ger.: **Seiber(t), Sibbert, Seg(e)barth, Sägerbarth, Seebarth.** Flem., Du.: **Sebrecht.**

Dims.: Low Ger.: **Sieb(e), Sibbe, Sipp, Siebeck(e), Sieb(e)ke, Seibicke.** Fris.: **Segelke.**

Patrs.: Low Ger.: **Segbers, Siebers, Siebertz, Seibers, Seibertz, Zeiberts, Sibbers(en)**. Flem., Du.: **Sebrechts, Sibers**.

Patrs. (from dims.): Low Ger.: **Siebs, Sieben(s), Siebken**.

Sieczkowski Polish: habitation name from a place called *Sieczków* (named from Pol. *sieczka* chaff + the possessive suffix *ów*), with the addition of the suffix of local surnames *-ski* (see BARANOWSKI).

Siedlecki Polish and Jewish (Ashkenazic): habitation name from the town of *Siedlce* in E Poland, which gets its name from OPol. **siedlo* abode, dwelling place.

Sieff Jewish (W Ashkenazic): said to be from the Yid. male given name *Zev* (from Hebr. *Zeev*, literally 'Wolf', the symbolic animal associated with the tribe of BENJAMIN), but this explanation is problematic because the Yid. given name has /ɛ/, whereas *Sieff* and *Seef* have /i/ and *Ziff* has /ɪ/. Only *Zevin* is clearly from the given name.

Vars.: **Seef, Ziff**.

Patr. (E Ashkenazic): **Zevin**.

Siegel 1. German: metonymic occupational name, a cogn. of SEAL 2.

2. German: from a medieval given name, a dim. of a short form of the various Gmc cpd personal names with the first element *sigi* victory; cf., e.g., SIEBERT, SIEGFRIED, SIEGHARD, SIEGMUND, and SIEMER.

3. Jewish (Ashkenazic): var. of SEGAL 1.

Vars. (of 2): **Siegl, Sigle, Sick(el); Siedl, Seidl**. (Of 3): **Siegelman**.

Cogns. (of 2): Low Ger.: **Siegmann, Seeck**. Fris.: **Zeeck, Sickama, Sieh, Sy(e)**. Czech: **Seidl**. Pol.: **Zajdel**. It.: **Sic(c)a, Sicco**.

Patrs. (from 2): Ger.: **Sicks, Seggeling**. Fris.: **Segelken**.

Siegfried German: from a Gmc personal name composed of the elements *sigi* victory + *fridu* peace. The Ger. surname has also occasionally been adopted by Ashkenazic Jews.

Vars.: **Seefried, Seifer(t), S(e)iffert, Sey(f)fahrt, Seifart(h), Seuffert**.

Cogns.: Low Ger.: **S(i)evert, Siewert**. Fris.: **Suffert**. It.: **Sif(f)redi, Segafredo, Seganfreddo**. Pol.: **Zajfert**.

Dims.: Ger.: **Seiferlin**. Low Ger.: **S(i)efke, S(i)eveke**. Fris.: **Süfke**.

Patrs.: Low Ger.: **Siever(t)s, Siefers, Siewers, Seevers, Seffers; Siever(t)sen, Siewertsen; Siever(d)ing**. Dan., Norw.: **Sivertsen**.

Patrs. (from dims.): Low Ger.: **Siefken; Söf(f)ker; Sieveking, Söffing**.

Sieghard German: from a Gmc personal name composed of the elements *sigi* victory + *hard* hardy, brave, strong.

Vars.: **Sichardt, Si(e)ghart, Siehard**.

Cogns.: Low Ger.: **Sigert, Sickert, Sichert**. Fr.: **Sic(h)ard, Segard, S(é)card**. It.: **Sic(c)ardi, Siccardo**.

Siegmund German: from a Gmc personal name composed of the elements *sigi* victory + *mund* protection. There has also been some confusion in the vars. and cogns. with SIMON.

Vars.: **S(i)egemund; Sigismund; Siemund, Seemund, Simond**.

Cogns.: Eng.: **Sim(m)ond**, SIMON. Fr.: **Simond, Sémond**. It.: **Si(gi)smondi, Si(gi)smondo, Simondi**. Czech: **Zikmund**. Pol.: **Zygmunt, Zygmański**. Hung.: **Zsigmond**.

Dims.: It.: **Simondini**. Czech: **Zich, Zika, Zíka, Zýka, Zikán, Zykán; Žižka**. Pol.: **Zygmuńczyk; Zych, Zychoń**.

Patr.: Pol.: **Zygmuntowicz**.

Patr. (from a dim.): Pol.: **Zychowicz**.

Habitation name (from a dim.): Pol.: **Zychowski**.

Siekiera Polish: metonymic occupational name for a wood-cutter or axeman, one who wielded an axe, from Pol. *siekiera* axe, hatchet. It may also in part represent a nickname.

Vars.: **Sierkierski; Skierski**.

Sielski Polish: regional name for someone from *Sioło* eastern Poland, or nickname for a rural or rustic person, from Pol. *sielski* rural, pastoral.

Siemer German: from the Gmc personal name *Siegmar*, composed of the elements *sigi* victory + *mari*, *meri* famous.

Cogns.: Fris.: **Ziemer**. Fr.: **Simar(d), Sémard, Seymard**.

Dims.: Low Ger.: **Siem(ann)**.

Patr.: Low Ger: **Siemers**.

Patrs. (from dims.): Low Ger.: **Siems, Siem(s)sen, Siemen(s), Siemensen**.

Siemiński Polish: from a short form of any of various OPol. personal names such as *Siemisław*, *Siemomyśl*, *Siemirad* (see SEMRÁD), having OSlav. *sěmb* person as a first element.

Var.: **Simiński**.

Patr. (from a dim.): **Sienkiewicz**.

Sieradzki Polish: habitation name from the town of *Sieradz* in W central Poland, which gets its name from a OPol. personal name, *Sie(mi)rad* (see SEMRÁD).

Sierota Polish and Jewish (E Ashkenazic): nickname for an orphan, Pol. *sierota*.

Vars.: Pol.: **Sierocki, Sieroń, Sierant**. Jewish: **Sirota; Sieroszewski, Szereszewski, Sher(e)shevski, Shershevsky, Scherschewski**.

Dims.: Czech: **Sirotek**. Ukr.: **Sirotyuk, Sirotenko**.

Patrs.: Russ.: **Sirot(in)in**.

Patr. (from a dim.): Russ.: **Sirotkin**.

Habitation names: Pol.: **Sieroszewski, Sieroczewski, Sierociński**.

Sigsworth English (Yorks.): habitation name from *Sigsworth* Moor, near Pately Bridge, so called from the gen. case of the ON personal name *Síkr* + OE *ford* FORD.

Sikora Polish and Jewish (Ashkenazic): nickname for a small, dark person, from Pol. *sikora* titmouse, coalmouse, or, in the case of the Jewish name, an ornamental name.

Var.: **Sikorski**.

Cogn.: Czech: **Sýkora**.

Šilhavý Czech: nickname for a boss-eyed person, Czech *šilhavý* (adj.).

Var..: **Šilhan**.

Dim.: **Šilhánek**.

Silk 1. English: metonymic occupational name for a merchant dealing in silk, OE *seolc* (L *sēricum*).

2. English: from a medieval given name, a back-formation from *Silkin*; see SILL.

3. Irish: translation of Gael. *Ó Síoda*; see SHEEDY.

Var.: **Silke**.

Silkstone English: habitation name from a place in S Yorks., so called from the gen. case of the OE personal name *Sigelāc* (composed of the elements *sigi* victory + *lāc* play, sport) + OE *tūn* enclosure, settlement.

Sill English: from a medieval given name, a short form of SILVESTER or *Silvanus* (see SELWYN 1).

Dims.: **Sillett** (E Anglia), **Silkin, Silcock**.

Patr.: **Sills**.

Patrs. (from dims.): **Silcocks, Silcox**.

Silva Spanish and Portuguese: topographic name for someone who lived in a wood, OSp., OPort. *silva* (L *silva*). During the Middle Ages the Sp. term was replaced by *bosque* (see Bois), but in the west of the Peninsula it survived with the altered sense 'bramble bush', 'thicket', and in some cases this may have been the meaning of the surname.

Cogns.: Cat.: **Selva**. Prov.: **Selve, La(s)selve**. It.: **Selva, Selvi; Silva** (Latinized).

Collective: Port.: **Silveira**.

Silver 1. English: nickname for a rich man or for someone with silvery grey hair, from ME *silver*, OE *seolfor* silver. Sometimes, too, it may have originated as a metonymic occupational name for a silversmith.

2. English: topographic name from any of the various streams in different parts of England named with this word, from the silvery appearance of the water.

3. Jewish (Ashkenazic): Anglicized form of **Silber** (from Ger. *Silber*, Yid. *zilber* silver), an ornamental name.

Cogns.: Ger.: **Silber(t), Silbermann**. Pol.: **Sylburski**. Jewish: **Zylber** (a Polish spelling); **Silberman(n), Zylberman** (Anglicized **Silverman**); **Silberschmidt** ('silversmith', an occupational name; partly Anglicized **Silvershmid**); **Silberdi(c)k, Zylberdik** (from Yid. *zilberdik* silvery).

Patr.: Eng.: **Silvers**.

Cpds (ornamental): Jewish: **Silberbach** ('silver stream'); **Silberbaum, Zylberbaum** ('silver tree'); **Silberberg, Zylberberg** ('silver hill'; partly Anglicized **Silverberg**); **Silberblatt** ('silver leaf'); **Silberbusch** ('silver bush'); **Silberfaden** ('silver thread'); **Silberfarb, Zylberfarb** ('silver colour'); **Silberfeld** ('silver field'); **Silberfreund** ('silver friend'); **Silberher(t)z** ('silver heart'); **Silberlicht** ('silver light'); **Silbermin(t)z, Zilbermin(t)z** ('silver coin'); **Silbernadel** ('silver needle'); **Silberpfennig, Silberfenig, Silberphenig** ('silver penny'); **Zylbering** ('silver ring'); **Silbers(c)hatz** ('silver treasure'); **Silbershein** ('silver shine'); **Silberschlag** ('silver stroke'); **Silberso(h)n** ('son of silver'); **Silberspitz, Zylberspic** ('silver point'); **Silberstein, Zylbers(z)tein, Zylbersztejn, Zylbersztajn** ('silver stone'; partly Anglicized **Silverstein**; see also Silverstone); **Zylberstrom** ('silver stream'); **Silberwasser** ('silver water'); **Silberzahn** ('silver tooth'); **Silberzweig** ('silver twig').

Silvério Portuguese: from a medieval given name (L *Silverius*, a deriv. of *silva* wood; cf. Selwyn 1 and Silvester), borne in honour of a 6th-cent. pope, who met a premature end as the result of the enmity of the Empress Theodora, but was subsequently revered as a saint.

Silverstone 1. English: habitation name from a place in Northants, recorded in Domesday Book as *Silvetone* and *Selvestone*, from the gen. case of an OE personal name, either *Sǣwulf* (see Self) or *Sigewulf* ('victory wolf') + OE *tūn* enclosure, settlement.

2. Jewish (Ashkenazic): Anglicized form of *Silberstein*; see Silver.

Vars. (of 1): **Silverston, Silveston**.

Silverthorne English (Bristol): apparently a habitation name from some unidentified minor place deriving its name from OE *seolfor* Silver + *þorn* thorn bush (see Thorn).

Silverton English: of uncertain origin, apparently a habitation name. The surname is first recorded in Kent and Suffolk in the 17th cent., which lends no support to the theory that it is a var. of Silverstone.

The earliest known bearers of the name Silverton *are the brothers Thomas and William Silverton, baptized on 9 Sept., 1612, in St Clement's, Hastings.*

Silverwood English (Yorks.): apparently a habitation name, perhaps from *Silver Wood* in Ravenfield, W Yorks. (although that is not recorded until 1764). The placename may be referring to a wood of silver birches.

Silvester English and German: from a given name (L *Silvester*, a deriv. of *silva* wood; cf. Selwyn 1 and Silvério). This was borne by three popes, including a contemporary of Constantine the Great.

Vars.: Eng.: **Selvester, Sylvester; Siviter** (W Midlands), **Seveter**. Ger.: **Ve(h)ster, Fe(h)ster** (aphetic forms).

Cogns.: Fr.: **Silvestre, Sylvestre, Sivestre, Sevestre**. It.: **Sivestri, Sivestre, Silvestro, Vestri**. Sp., Cat., Port.: **Silvestre**. Dan., Norw.: **Sylvest**. Pol.: **Sylwester**.

Dims.: It.: **Silvestrelli, Silvestrini, Vestrini, Vestrucci**. Pol.: **Symbestyrek**.

Aug.: It.: **Silvestroni**.

Patrs.: Low Ger.: **Festersen**. It.: **De Silvestri, (De) Silvestris, Vestris**. Russ.: **Silvestrov, Silverstov, Seliverstov**. Beloruss.: **Silvestrovich**. Pol.: **Sylwestrowicz, Sylwestrzak**.

Habitation name: Pol.: **Sylwestrowski**.

Sim Scots and N English: from the ME given name *Sim(me)*, a short form of Simon.

Vars.: **Simm** (Lancs. and Northumb.); **Sime, Syme**.

Dims.: **Simmie** (chiefly Scots); Simkin; **Simcock, Sincock, Sincoe** (chiefly W Midlands).

Patrs.: Simson, McKimm.

Patrs. (from dims.): **Simcocks, Simcox, Symcox**.

Simkin 1. English (W Midlands): from the ME given name of this form, a dim. of Sim.

2. Jewish (E Ashkenazic): metr. from *Simke*, a pet form of the Yid. female given name *Sime*, from Hebr. *Simcha* 'Joy', with the Slav. metr. suffix *-in*.

Vars. (of 1): **Simpkin, Sinkin, Semkin**. (Of 2): **Simkovic(h), Simkovitz, Simkievitz, Simkovits**.

Patrs. (from 1): **Sim(p)kins, Sim(p)kiss, Sinkin(g)s, Sempkins, Simpkinson, Sinkinson**.

Simon English, French, German, Flemish/Dutch, Czech, Hungarian, and Jewish (Ashkenazic): from the Hebr. personal name *Shim'on*, which is probably derived from the verb *sham'a* to hearken. In the Vulgate and in many vernacular versions of the Old Testament, this is usually rendered as *Simeon*. In the New Testament, however, the name is normally rendered *Simōn*, partly as a result of association with the pre-existing Gk byname *Sīmōn* (from *sīmos* snub-nosed). Both *Simon* and *Simeon* were in use as given names in W Europe from the Middle Ages onwards. However, the former was far more popular, no doubt because of its associations with the apostle Simon Peter, the brother of Andrew. In Britain there was also confusion from an early date with Anglo-Scandinavian forms of *Sigmund* (see Siegmund), a name whose popularity was reinforced at the Conquest by the Norman form *Simund*. This confusion is also found in other languages, e.g. Italian.

Vars.: Eng.: **Simeon, Simion; Symon** (Scots); **Simmen**. Fr.: **Simeon**. Ger.: **Simmon, Siemon**. Jewish: **S(c)himon, Szymon, Szimon; S(h)imoni, S(h)imony, Schimoni, Szimoni, Szymoni** (with the Hebr. suffix *-i*).

Cogns.: It.: **Sim(e)oni, Sim(e)one; Simion(i), Simione, Mion(i)** (Venetia); **Scimo(ne), Scimoni** (Sicily). Sp.: **Simón**. Cat.: **Simó**. Port.: **Simão**. Ger. (of Slav. origin): **Schimon, Schimann**. Czech: **Šimon, Šíma, Šimák, Šiman**. Pol.: **Szymański**. Hung.: **Simonyi**.

Dims.: Eng.: Sim, **Sim(o)nett, Sim(m)onite, Simnel(1)**. Fr.: **Simonel, Sim(e)nel, Simoneau, Simon(n)et, Simounet, Simenet, Simon(et)on, Simonou, Simenon, Simon(n)ot, Simenot, Simon(n)in, Simony, Sémonin**. It.: **Simonetti,**

Simonetto, Simonitto, Simonutti, Simon(c)elli, Simoncello, Scimonelli, Simon(c)ini, Simeoli, Simioli; Monetti, Monelli, Monini. Ger.: **Siemandl, Siemantel** (Bavaria). Low Ger.: **Simmgen.** Fris.: **Zie(h)m, Ziemke.** Ger. (of Slav. origin): **Schimonek, Schimank, Schimmang, Simmank, Schimek, Simmig, Schim(p)ke, Schimaschke; Zima, Zimek; Manske, Manntschke.** Czech: **Šimek, Šimeček, Šimáček, Šimánek, Šimůnek; Ších(a).** Pol.: **Szymczyk; Szymanek, Szymanczyk.** Ukr.: **Simchenko, Senchenko, Semechik.** Beloruss.: **Shimuk.** Jewish: **Simanenko, Simko.** Hung.: **Simó, Simka, Simkó.**

Pejs.: Fr.: **Simonard.** It.: **Simonazzi, Simonassi, Sim(i)onato.**

Patrs.: Eng.: **Sim(m)on(d)s, Simeons; Sym(m)ons** (Devon); **Symonds** (chiefly E Anglia); **Simmens, Simmins, Sim(m)ans, Simmance; Simonson, Symondson, Simison, Simyson; Fitzsimmons.** It.: **De Simone, De Simoni, Simoneschi.** Port.: **Simões.** Rum.: **Simionescu.** Low Ger.: **Simons(en).** Flem.: **Simo(e)ns, Moens.** Du.: **Si(e)mons, Sijmons.** Norw., Dan.: **Simonsen.** Swed.: **Simonsson.** Ger. (of Slav. origin): **Schiemen(t)z.** Pol.: **Szymanowicz, Szymonowicz, Szymaniak.** Ukr.: **Simonich, Semenovich.** Beloruss.: **Simonich, Shimonov, Semyanovich.** Russ.: **Sim(e)onov, Semyonov, Semanov.** Lithuanian: **Simonaitis, Semenas.** Hung.: **Simonf(f)y.** Croatian: **Sim(on)ović, Simić, Šimić.** Armenian: **Simonian.** Jewish: **Simons, Simonso(h)n** (Ashkenazic); **Simonov, Simonof, Simonow, Simonovitch, Simonowicz, Simonowitz, Simon(ov)itz, Shimonoff, Shimonov(ich), Shimonovitz, S(c)himonowitz, Szymonowicz** (E Ashkenazic); **Simonovici** (a Rum. spelling).

Patrs. (from dims.): Eng.: **Syson** (Notts.). Sc.: **McKimmie** (Gael. **Mac Shimidh**). Fris.: **Zie(h)ms, Ziemens, Ziemsen.** Russ.: **Simonin, Sim(ak)ov, Simukov, Simushin, Simulin, Sim(y)agin, Simarov, Semyonychev, Semichev, Semakin, Semyashkin, Semchishchev, Sem(en)ischev, Semen(n)ikov, Semenyutin, Sementsov, Semendyaev, Senyagin, Senyavin, Sentyurin, Syomin.** Pol.: **Szymankiewicz, Szymczykiewicz; Szymczak.** Lithuanian: **Schimkat, Schimkus.** Jewish (E Ashkenazic): **Simkovic(h), Simkovitz, Szymkiewicz, Shimkevicz, Shimkevich, Shimkewitz, Shimkevitz** (based on the E Yid. pet form *Shimke*).

'Son of the wife of S.': Russ.: **Semyonikhin.**

'Son of the wife of S. (dim.)': Russ.: **Semchikhin, Sentyurikhin.** Ukr.: **Semchishin.**

Habitation names: Pol.: **Szymanowski, Szymczewski, Szymczyński.** Czech: **Šimononský.**

Simson 1. English: patr. from the medieval given name SIM.

2. German and Jewish (Ashkenazic): var. of SAMSON.

Vars. (of 1): **Simpson; Sim(m)s, Sym(m)s; Simes, Symes.**

Sinatra Italian: from a given name borne by both men and women in Sicily and S Calabria. The name was apparently in origin a nickname from L *senātor* member of the Roman senate (L *senātus*, a deriv. of *senex* old), which later came to be used as a title of magistrates in various It. states.

Var.: **Sinatora.**

Sinclair 1. Scots and English (Norman): habitation name from *Saint-Clair*-sur-Elle in La Manche or *Saint-Clair*-l'Évêque in Calvados, so called from the dedication of their chuches to St *Clarus* (see CLARE 1).

2. French: habitation name from the same places as in 1 above or from others of the same name in other parts in France.

Vars.: Eng.: **Sinclaire, Saint-Clair, Saint-Clare.** Fr.: **Sainclair, Saint-Clair.**

The Scottish Sinclair *family, which includes the Earls of Caithness, originally held the Norman barony of Saint-Clair. Sir William Saint-Clair (?1240–?1303) was a leader of a rebellion against Edward I of England. By marriage the family also obtained the earldom of Orkney; and in 1379 Sir Henry Sinclair (d. ?1400) was created Prince of Orkney by King Haakon of Norway. His grandson ceded his rights over the Orkneys to James III of Scotland.*

Singleton English: habitation name from places in Lancs. and Sussex. The former seems from the present-day distribution of the surname to be the major source, and is named from OE *scingel* shingle(s) + *tūn* enclosure, settlement; the latter gets its name from OE *sengel* burnt clearing + *tūn*.

Lancs. bearers of this surname are descended from Ughtred de Sinleton, *who held land in Amounderness* c.*1160–90*.

Sinnott English and Irish: from the ME given name *Sinod*, OE *Sigenōð*, composed of the elements *sige* victory + *nōð* brave.

Vars.: **Synot, Synnot(t), Sinnett, Sinnatt, Senet, Sennett, Sennitt.**

Although this name is of Eng. origin, it is now far more common in Ireland than in England, and has been Gaelicized as **Sionóid.**

Sinton Scots: habitation name from a place near Selkirk, also spelled *Synton*. In the 12th and 13th cents. it is recorded several times as *Sintun*. The origin of the first element is uncertain; the second is clearly OE *tūn* enclosure, settlement.

Šíp Czech: from Czech *šíp* arrow, perhaps applied as a nickname for a thin man or a swift runner, or as a metonymic occupational name for an archer.

Dim.: **Šípek** (as a vocab. word, this also means 'dogrose' or 'briar', the thorns being likened to little arrows; the surname may therefore also be topographic for someone who lived by a briar patch).

Sisley English: from the medieval female given name *Sisley*, *Cecilie* (L *Caecilia*, fem. form of the Roman family name *Caecilius*, originally a deriv. of *caecus* blind). This was the name of a Roman virgin martyr of the 2nd or 3rd cent., who came to be regarded as the patron saint of music.

Var.: **Sicely.**

Cogns.: Fr.: **Cécil(l)e, Cicil(l)e.** Ger.: **Cäcilie.**

Dim.: Eng.: **Sisson.**

Metrs. (from dims.): Eng.: **Sissons, Sissens; Sisterson** (Northumb.; from earlier *Sissotson*, altered by folk etymology).

Sitarz Polish: occupational name for a maker or seller of sieves, Pol. *sitarz* (from *sito* sieve).

Var.: **Sitarski.**

Dim.: **Sitarek.**

Sittart, van Dutch: habitation name from a place in the province of Limburg.

The English **Vansittart** *family are descended from a Dutch merchant adventurer who settled in London* c.*1670. Their members included Henry Vansittart (1732–70), governer of Bengal, and his son Nicholas (1766–1851), who rose to be chancellor of the exchequer and was created Baron Boxley in 1823.*

Sittich German: 1. nickname for a courteous person, from Ger. *sittig* demure, well-behaved (MHG *sitec*, a deriv. of *site* custom, use, OHG *situ*).

2. nickname for someone supposedly resembling a parrot, from Ger. *Sittich* parakeet (MHG, OHG *sitich*, L *psittacus*, from Gk).

Sitwell English: of uncertain origin. It would appear to be a habitation name from an unidentified place with a second element from OE *well(a)* spring, stream, but on the other hand early forms are found without prepositions, so it may be a phrasal nickname.

Var.: **Sidwell.**

An early ancestor of the Sitwell *family of Yorks. was Roger* Cytewelle, *recorded in 1310. Through a marriage into the Reresby family in 1693, they are also descended from an 11th-cent. baron, Hugh FitzOsbern. The direct line died out with William Sitwell in 1776, when his nephew and heir Francis Hurt assumed the arms and surname of Sitwell. The family have in their time been connected with many noble families, and have held an estate at Renishaw since the 14th cent.*

Siwiec Polish: nickname for a grey-haired man, Pol. *siwiec*, from *siwy* grey.
Dim.: **Siwek**.
Cogns. (patrs.): Russ.: **Sivtsov**, **Sivachyov**, **Sivyakov**, **Sivochin**; **Sivolobov** ('grey brow').
Habitation name: Pol.: **Siwiński**.

Six 1. French and German: from a given name (L *Sixtus*, a var. of *Sextus* 'Sixth(-born)'), borne by various saints and popes in the early cents. of the Christian era, and subsequently adopted in their honour.
2. French: nickname from OF *six* six (L *sex*), given for some anecdotal reason now lost (cf. SHOSTAKOVICH); the surnames **Deux** ('Two'), **Huit** ('Eight'), and **Dix** ('Ten') also exist, but all are rare. In English, the surname **Eighteen** is attested, of similarly obscure anecdotal origin.
Vars. (of 1): Ger.: **Sixt(us)**.
Cogns. (of 1): It.: **Sisto**, **Sist(i)**, **Sesti**, **Sesto**. Czech: **Sixta**.
Dims. (of 1): Ger.: **Sixl** (Bavaria). It.: **Sestini**.

Sixsmith English (Lancs.): apparently an occupational name for a SMITH, but with a first element of obscure origin. It may conceivably be from ME *sikel* sickle (OE *sicel*, *sicol*), in which case it denotes a maker of sickles. The surname is first attested in 1590.

Skalski Polish: topographic name for someone who lived by a rock or crag, Pol. *skała*.
Var.: **Skałecki**.
Cogns.: Czech: **Skála**; **Skalicky** (from a placename, *Skalice* or *Skalička*); **Skalník**.

Škarda Czech: nickname for a sullen individual, from Czech *škaredý* sullen, sour-faced.

Skeat N English: from the ON byname *Skjótr* 'Swift'.
Vars.: **Skeate**, **Skeet(e)**, **Skate**; **Skett** (W Midlands).
Patrs.: **Skeat(e)s**, **Skates**.

Skeffington English: habitation name from a place in Leics., so called from OE *Scēaftingtūn* 'settlement (OE *tūn*) associated with *Scēaft*', a byname meaning 'Shaft', 'Spear'. The initial consonant cluster has been modified from /ʃ/ to /sk/ as a result of Scandinavian influence.
Vars.: **Skiffington**, **Skevington**, **Skivington**.
A family by the name of Skeffington *are Viscounts Massereene. They acquired the title in 1654 through marriage; the daughter of Sir John Clotworthy, the 1st Viscount, married a Skeffington. Clotworthy has since been used as a given name in this family.*

Skegg N English: from the ON byname *Skegg* 'Beard'.
Patr.: **Skeggs**.

Skelding English: habitation name from a place in W Yorks., near Ripon, also known as *Skelden*. It is so called from the river name *Skell* (ON *Skjallr* 'Resounding'; cf. SHILLINGFORD) + OE *denu* valley (see DEAN 1).

Skeldon Scots and N English: habitation name from a place in Ayrs., probably so called from OE *scylf* shelf, ledge + *dūn* hill, with later change of /ʃ-/ to /sk-/ under Scandinavian influence; cf. SHELDON.

Skelton N English: habitation name from places in Cumb. and Yorks., originally named with the same elements as SHELTON, but with later change of /ʃ-/ to /sk-/ under Scandinavian influence.
Var.: **Skilton** (N England and Yorks., also N Ireland).

Skene Scots: habitation name from a place in the former county of Aberdeens., so called from Gael. *sceathin* bush.
Vars.: **Skeen(e)**.

Skiba Polish: topographic name from Pol. *skiba* ridge.
Var.: **Skibicki**.
Habitation name: **Skibiński**.

Skinner English: occupational name for someone who stripped the hide from animals, to be used in the production of fur garments or to be tanned for leather, from an agent deriv. of ME *skin* hide, pelt (ON *skinn*). The much rarer var. **Shinner** is from the OE cogn. *scinn*, displaced in the ME period by the Scandinavian form.
Vars.: **Skyn(n)er**, **Skin**; **Shinn**, **Shynn**.

Skipper English (chiefly Norfolk): 1. occupational name for the master of a ship, ME *skipper* (from MLG, MDu. *schipper*; cf. SHIPMAN 2).
2. occupational name for an acrobat or professional tumbler, or nickname for a high-spirited person, from an agent deriv. of ME *skip(en)* to jump, spring (apparently of Scandinavian origin).
3. occupational name for a basket-maker, from an agent deriv. of ME *skipp(e)*, *skepp(e)* basket, hamper (ON *skeppa*; cf. SCHÄFFLER).
Vars. (of 3): **Skepper**; **Skipp**.

Skipsey English (Northumb.): habitation name from *Skipsea* in N Yorks., so called from Northern ME *skip* ship (ON *skip*) + *see* lake, pond (OE *sǣ*).

Skipwith English (Yorks.): habitation name from a place in Yorks., recorded in Domesday Book as *Schipwic*, from OE *scēap*, *scīp* sheep + *wīc* outlying settlement (see WICK). Under later Scandinavian influence the initial /ʃ-/ became /sk-/ and the second element was changed to *-with* (ON *viðr* wood).
Var.: **Skipworth** (Lincs.).
The main Skipwith *family held the manor of Skipwith in the early Middle Ages, and direct descendants can be traced to the present day. In the 13th cent. they moved from Yorks. to Lincs., where their principal seat was at S Ormsby. In the early 17th cent. there was further migration, to Leics., Warwicks., and across the Atlantic to Virginia. Other bearers of the name seem to have been tenants of Lincs. manors held by the* Skipworth *family, and to have taken the surname of their overlords.*

Skoczylas Polish: topographic name for someone who lived by a dam on a stream or river in a forest, from an OPol. word composed of the elements *skok-* dam (akin to *skoczy-* to leap) + *las* forest.

Škoda Czech: from the vocab. word *skoda* damage, loss; apparently a nickname denoting someone whose property had been damaged or who had a financial claim on someone else.

Skóra Polish: metonymic occupational name for a leather-worker or tanner, from Pol. *skóra* leather.
Vars.: **Skórski**, **Skórnik**.
Dims.: **Skórka**, **Skórek**, SKOREK.
Habitation name: **Skórzewski**.

Skorek Polish: 1. var. of *Skórek*, dim. of SKÓRA.
2. nickname from Pol. *skory* eager.
3. offensive nickname meaning 'Earwig'.
Cogn. (of 3): Czech: **Škvor**.

Skorokhodov Russian: patr. from the nickname *Skorokhod*, denoting a runner or messenger, from *skoro* swiftly + *khodit* to go, walk.

Cogns.: Jewish (E Ashkenazic): **Skoro(c)hod** (reason for adoption unknown).

Skorupa Polish: nickname for someone with a rough skin or a skin disease, or for a 'crusty' individual, from Pol. *skorupa* crust, shell.

Var.: **Skorupski**.

Cogn.: Czech: **Skořepa**.

Skovgård Danish: habitation name from a place so called from the elements *scov* copse (cf. SHAW) + *gård* enclosure, farm (cf. GARTH).

Skowron Polish: nickname for a happy, cheerful person, from Pol. *skowronek* skylark.

Var.: **Skowroński**.

Cogn.: Czech: **Skřivan**.

Dim.: Czech: **Skřivánek**.

Skrzydlewski Polish: habitation name from some place named with Pol. *skrzydło* wing, probably in the sense of a 'wing-shaped' piece of land + *-ew* possessive suffix, with the addition of *-ski*, suffix of local surnames (see BARANOWSKI).

Skrzypek Polish: occupational name for a violinist or fiddler, Pol. *skrzypek* (from *skrzypieć* to creak, groan, ultimately cogn. with Eng. *scrape*).

Var.: **Skrzypczak**.

Cogns. (patrs.): Russ.: **Skripkin**, **Skrypkin**.

Habitation names: **Skrzypiński**, **Skrzypczyński**.

Skupień Polish: apparently from Pol. *skupić* to buy up (perhaps a nickname for a shrewd businessman), or from another word of the same form, meaning 'to mass or concentrate in one place'.

Var.: **Skupiński**.

Skuse Cornish: habitation name from any of various minor places named with Corn. *skaw* elder bush + the suffix of location *-es*.

Vars.: **Scuce**, **Skew(e)s**, **Skewis**.

Skvortsov Russian: patr. from the nickname *Skvorets* 'Starling' (of apparently imitative origin).

Skwara Polish: apparently a nickname from OPol. *skwara* scorching heat, *skwarny* scorching, although the application is not clear. It may have been applied to a 'hot-tempered' person.

Vars.: **Skwarski**, **Skwarnecki**.

Dim.: **Skwarnek**.

Słaby Polish: nickname for a weak and feeble individual, from Pol. *słaby* weak.

Vars.: **Słabicki**, **Słabiak**.

Cogn.: Czech: **Slabý**.

Slack English (chiefly N Midlands): 1. topographic name for someone who lived in a shallow valley, Northern ME *slack* (ON *slakki*) or habitation name from one of the places named with this term, for example near Stainland and near Hebden Bridge in W Yorks.

2. nickname for an idle or indolent person, from ME *slack* lazy, careless (OE *slæc*).

Var.: **Slacke**.

Slade S English: topographic name for someone who lived in a small valley, OE *slæd*, or habitation name from any of the minor places named with this word, for example in Devon and Somerset, or *Slad* in Gloucs.

Var.: **Slader**.

Sládek Czech: occupational name for a maltster, from Czech *slad* malt.

Vars.: **Sladovník**, **Sladovský**.

Sladen English: probably a habitation name from an unidentified place. The original form is *Sloden*, perhaps from OE elements *slōh* slough (see SLOW 1) + *denu* valley (see DEAN 1).

Var.: **Sladden**.

A family called Sladen *trace their descent from Henry* Sloden (*b.* c.*1390*), *who served as a juror at Lyminge, Kent, in 1449. The spelling* Sladen *began to appear in the 16th cent.*

Slater English: occupational name for someone who covered roofs with slate, from an agent deriv. of ME *s(c)late* slate (OF *esclate*, a var. of *esclat* splinter, slat, of Gmc origin, akin to OHG *sleizen* to tear).

Vars.: **Slator**, **Sclater**, **Slatter**, **Slate**.

Slattery Irish: Anglicized form of Gael. **Ó Slat(ar)ra** 'descendant of *Slatra*', a byname meaning 'Robust', 'Strong', 'Bold'.

Vars.: **O'Slattery**, **O'Slattra**.

Slaughter English: 1. occupational name for a slaughterer of animals, ME *slahter* (a agent deriv. of *slaht* killing, OE *slēaht*).

2. topographic name for someone who lived by a muddy spot, ME *sloghtre* (OE **slōhtre*, a deriv. of *slōh*; see SLOW 1), or habitation name from a place named with this term, for example Upper and Lower *Slaughter* in Gloucs.

3. topographic name for someone who lived by a sloe tree, OE *slāhtrēow* (cf. SLOW 3).

Vars.: **Slagter**, **Slafter**. (Of 1 only): **Slayter**, **Slaytor**, **Sleator**.

Cogns. (of 1): Ger.: **Schlachter**, **Schlächter**. Flem., Du.: **Slachter**, **Slagter**. Jewish (Ashkenazic): **S(c)lachter**, **S(c)hlechter**; **Szlachter** (a Pol. spelling).

Slavin Jewish (E Ashkenazic): metr. from the Yid. female given name *Slave* (from the Slav. word *slava* glory, fame, praise) + the Slav. metr. suffix *-in*.

Vars.: **Slawin**; **Slovin**, **Slowes** (from the variant given name *Slove*).

Sławiński Polish: from any of the numerous Pol. given names containing the element *sław* glory, fame, praise. The surname has the form of a habitation name.

Cogn. (patr. from a dim.): Croatian: **Slavković**.

Slay English: 1. metonymic occupational name for someone who made slays, instruments used in weaving to push the weft thread that had just been laid tightly against the thread of the preceding pass of the shuttle. The name is from ME *slaye* (OE *slege*, from *slēan* to strike).

2. topographic name for someone who lived by a grassy slope, ME *slay* (OE **slēa*).

Var. (of 1): **Slaymaker**.

Slevin Irish: Anglicized form of Gael. **Ó Sléibhín** 'descendant of *Sléibhín*', a personal name representing a dim. of *sliabh* mountain (perhaps originally a short form of *Dunnshléibhe*; see DUNLEAVY).

Slight Scots: 1. nickname from Northern ME *sleght*, *slyght* smooth, sleek, slender, slim (apparently of ON origin).

2. nickname from ME *sleghth* craft, cunning, dexterity, adroitness (ON *slǿgð*, a deriv. of *slǿgr* SLY).

Slim English: topographic name for someone who lived in a muddy area, from OE *slīm* slime, mud. The mod. Eng.

adj. *slim* slender (from Low Ger. or Du.) is not found before the 17th cent.

Slinger N English: occupational name for a soldier or hunter armed with a sling, or nickname for someone who was a particularly good shot with this weapon, from an agent deriv. of ME *sling* strap for hurling stones (of Low Ger. origin).

Slingsby English: habitation name from a place in N Yorks., so called from the gen. case of the ON byname *Slengr* 'Idle' + ON *býr* farm, settlement.

Śliwa Polish: metonymic occupational name for a grower or seller of plums, from Pol. *śliwa* plum, or possibly a nickname from the same word.

Cogn.: Jewish (E Ashkenazic): **Sliva** (probably an ornamental name, one of the many taken from plant names).

Habitation name: Pol.: **Śliwiński**.

Sloan Scots and N Irish: Anglicized form of the Gael. personal name *Sluaghadhán*, a dim. of *Sluaghadh* (see SLOWEY).

Vars.: **Sloane, Slo(y)ne, Slowan, Sloyan**.

A family by the name of Sloane *emigrated from Scotland to Ireland in the reign of James I. An earlier spelling was* Slowan *or* SLOWMAN. *A member of this family was Sir Hans* Sloan *(1660–1753), whose collection of manuscripts, curios, and books formed the nucleus of what became the British Museum.*

Slocombe English (W Country): habitation name from a place, as for example *Slocum* on the Isle of Wight and in Devon, named with the OE elements *slāh* sloe (see SLOW 3) + *cumb* valley (see COOMBE).

Vars.: **Slocom, Slocum**.

Słodski Polish: nickname meaning 'Sweet, Lovely', with the addition of the surname suffix *-ski* (see BARANOWSKI).

Var.: **Słodak**.

Cogn.: Czech: **Sladký**.

Patr. (from a dim.): Pol.: **Słodkiewicz**.

Słomkowski Polish: habitation name from a place named with Pol. *słomka* woodcock + *-ów* possessive suffix, with the addition of *-ski*, suffix of local surnames (see BARANOWSKI).

Słomski Polish: from Pol. *słoma* straw + *-ski* suffix of surnames (see BARANOWSKI). The application as a surname is not clear; it may be an occupational name for a dealer in straw or a nickname for someone with straw-coloured hair (cf. STRAW).

Habitation names: **Słomiński**; **Słomczewski, Słomczyński** (the latter two could also be vars. of SŁOMKOWSKI).

Cogn.: Czech: **Sláma**.

Sloper English: occupational name for a maker of loose overgarments, from an agent deriv. of ME *slop(e)* overall (apparently of OE origin, akin to *slūpan* to slip, reinforced by a MLG cogn.).

Slovák Czech: ethnic name for someone from Slovakia (Czech *Slovensko*); the name is possibly derived from the Slav. element *slov-* speak, talk.

Dim.: **Slováček**.

Slow English: 1. topographic name for someone who lived near a swamp or bog, from OE *slōh* slough, or habitation name from one of the various places, for example *Slough* in Berks., named with this word.

2. nickname for a sluggish or stupid person, from ME *slōw* (OE *slāw*; for the change of vowel, cf. ROPER).

3. topographic name for someone who lived by a sloe tree, ME *slōh* (OE *slāh*).

Vars.: **Slowe**, SLOWMAN. (Of 1 only): **Slough**.

Slowey Irish: Anglicized form of Gael. **Ó Sluaghadhaigh** 'descendant of *Sluaghadhach*', a personal name derived from *sluaghadh* expedition, raid.

Vars.: **O'Slowey, Slo(e)y**.

Słowik Polish: nickname for a good singer, or else a night-time reveller, from Pol. *słowik* nightingale.

Cogn.: Czech: **Slavík** (also borne by Ashkenazic Jews, in which case it is possibly a name taken by a cantor).

Dim.: Czech: **Slavíček**.

Habitation names: Pol.: **Słowikowski; Słowiński** (there are cases on record of the Ger. surname *Nachtigall* (see NIGHTINGALE) being altered to *Słowiński*).

Slowman 1. English: var. of SLOW.

2. Scots: var. of SLOAN.

Vars. (of 1): Eng.: **Sloman, Sluman**.

Sluis Dutch: topographic name for someone who lived by a lock or weir, MDu. *sluis* (OF *escluse*, from LL *exclūsa (aqua)*, past part. of *exclūdere* to dam, keep out). Some examples of the name may derive from a town in the province of Zeeland, founded in the 13th cent. and named with this word.

Vars.: **Van der Sluis, Van (der) Sluijs, Van (der) Sluys, Versluі(j)s, Versluys**.

Ślusarski Polish: occupational name for an ironworker or locksmith, Pol. *ślusarz*, with the addition of *-ski*, suffix of surnames (see BARANOWSKI).

Cogn.: Beloruss.: **Slyusar**.

Dims.: Pol.: **Ślusarczyk, Ślusarek**.

Slutsky Jewish (NE Ashkenazic): habitation name from *Slutsk*, a city in the province of Minsk, Belorussia.

Vars.: **Slutski, Slutzk(y), Slucky, Slucki; Slutzker**.

Sly English (chiefly W Midlands): nickname for a cunning or crafty individual, from Midland and Southern ME *sligh* sly (earlier *slegh*, from ON *slǿgr*).

Vars.: **Sligh, Slyman, Sliman, Slimmon, Slimming; Slee(man), Slemming** (N England); **Sleith, Sleath** (Yorks.).

Patrs.: **Slemmings, Slemmonds**.

Small English: nickname for a person of slender build or diminutive stature, from ME *smal* thin, narrow, small (OE *smæl*).

Vars.: **Smale** (Cornwall), **Smaile** (Scotland); **Smeal(l)**.

Cogns.: Ger.: **Schmal(l), Schmahl**. Low Ger.: **Smal**. Flem., Du.: **Smal(le), (De) Smaele**.

Patrs.: Eng.: **Small(e)s, Smales; Smailes** (Northumb.), **Smiles** (Scotland). Low Ger.: **Schmeling**.

Smalley English: habitation name from places in Derbys. and Lancs, so called from OE *smæl* narrow (see SMALL) + *lēah* wood, clearing.

Var.: **Smally**; SMILEY.

Smallman English: ostensibly a nickname for a small man, but the vocab. word was also used as a technical term of feudalism to denote an inferior tenant, and so the surname may in fact be a status name with this origin.

Var.: **Smalman**.

Smallshaw English (Lancs.): habitation name from a place in W Yorks., so called from OE *smæl* narrow (see SMALL) + *sceaga* copse (see SHAW).

Smallwood English (chiefly W Midlands): habitation name from a place in Ches., so called from OE *smæl* narrow (see SMALL) + *wudu* WOOD.

Smart English: nickname for a brisk or active person, from ME *smart* quick, prompt (OE *smeart* stinging, painful, from *smeortan* to sting, hurt).
Var.: **Smartman**.
A N English family called Smart *claim to be descended from Sir John Smart, who was a Garter Knight in the reign of Edward IV (1461–83). The religious poet Christopher Smart (1722–71) was a member of this family.*

Smeaton English and Scots: habitation name from any of various places, notably *Smeaton* near Edinburgh and in N and W Yorks., or *Smeeton* in Leics., all so called from OE *Smiðatūn* 'settlement (OE *tūn*) of the smiths'.
Vars.: **Smeeton**, **Smieton**.

Smedley English (Notts): apparently a habitation name from an unidentified place, perhaps so called from OE *smēðe* smooth (see SMEETH) + *lēah* wood, clearing.

Smeeth English: ostensibly a topographic name for someone who lived on a piece of smooth, level ground, from ME *smethe* smooth (OE *smēðe*), or a nickname from the same word used in a transferred sense for someone of an amiable disposition. However, it is more probably simply a spelling var. of SMITH.
Vars.: **Smee(d)**, **Smead**, **Smeath(man)**.

Šmejkal Czech: apparently a deriv. of Czech *smýkat* to drag, perhaps a nickname for someone with a bad limp.

Smerdon English (Devon): habitation name from *Smeardon* Down in the parish of Petertavy, so called from OE *smeoru* butter + *dūn* hill.

Smetana Czech and Jewish (E Ashkenazic): nickname from Czech *smetana* soured cream, given perhaps to someone who was particularly fond of this food. It may also have been a metonymic occupational name for a trader in dairy products.
Var.: Jewish: **Smetanka**.
Cogns.: Pol.: **Śmietan(k)a**. Ger.: **Schmetten**.

Smethurst English (Lancs.): habitation name from a minor place near Manchester, so called from OE *smēðe* smooth (see SMEETH) + *hyrst* (wooded) hill (see HURST).

Śmiałkowski Polish: habitation name from a place named with Pol. *śmiałek* brave man, hero (from *śmiały* brave) + *-ów* possessive suffix, with the addition of *-ski*, suffix of local surnames (see BARANOWSKI).
Cogn.: Czech: **Smělý** (a nickname).

Śmiech Polish: nickname for a cheerful person who was always laughing, from Pol. *śmiech* laughter.
Cogn.: Czech: **Smíšek**.
Patr.: Pol.: **Śmiechowicz**.
Habitation name: Pol.: **Śmiechowski**.

Smiley Scots: of uncertain origin, probably a var. of SMILLIE, but perhaps a habitation name representing a var. of SMALLEY, or a nickname from ME *smile* smile, grin (probably of Scand. origin).
Var.: **Smylie**.

Smillie Scots: nickname for someone notorious for giving off a smell that was obnoxious even by medieval standards, or for someone who made great use of perfumes and pomanders to counteract this tendency in an age when such measures were not generally considered necessary. The word is a deriv. of ME *smil*, *smel* odour.
Var.: **Smellie**.

Smirnyagin Russian: patr. from the nickname *Smirnyaga*, denoting a quiet, humble person (from the adj. *smirnoi*, a deriv. of the Slav. element *mera* measure, restraint, but early associated by folk etymology with *mir* peace, quiet).
Var.: **Smirnov**.

Smith English: occupational name for a worker in metal, ME *smith*, OE *smið* (probably a deriv. of *smītan* to strike, hammer). Metal-working was one of the earliest occupations for which specialist skills were required, and its importance ensured that this term and its cogns. and equivalents were perhaps the most widespread of all occupational surnames in Europe. Medieval smiths were important not only in making horseshoes, ploughshares, and other domestic articles, but above all for their skill in forging swords, other weapons, and armour. Brett has calculated that there are about 187,000 subscribers named *Smith* in British telephone directories; his regional study shows that the name is most common in the Aberdeen area, with a distribution of 184 per 10,000, and that it is also common throughout the Midlands and again in E Anglia. It is least common in Wales and the W Country.
Vars.: **Smyth**, SMYTHE; **Smither** (with the ME agent suffix *-er*).
Cogns.: Ger.: **Schmid(t)**, **Schmitt**. Flem.: **(De) Smid**, **(De) Smet**, **Desmeth**. Du.: **Smit**, **Smid(t)**, **Smed**, **Smut**. Dan., Norw.: **Smidth**, **Smed**. Pol.: **Szmi(d)t**, **Szmyt**. Czech: **Šmíd**. Jewish (Ashkenazic): **S(c)hmidt**, **Szmidt**; **Shmidman**, **Szmidman**; **Schmieder**, **Shmider** (from Yid. *shmider*).
Dims.: Ger.: **Schmiedel**, **Schmiedle**. Low Ger.: **Schmedeke**, **Schmädicke**, **Schmedtje**. Czech: **Šmídek**.
Patrs.: Eng.: **Smithson**, **Smythson**, **Smisson**; **Smithers**. Ger.: **Schmitz**. Low Ger.: **Smets**, **Smuts**; **S(ch)meder**; **Schmedding**. Flem., Du.: **Smits**, **Smets**.
Patrs. (from a dim.): Flem.: **Smeken(s)**.
'Servant of the smith': Eng.: **Smidman**, **Smitherman**.
Cpds: Eng.: **Blacksmith**, SHOESMITH (working in iron, usually for domestic purposes); **Brownsmith**, COPPERSMITH; **Greensmith** (working in lead); **Redsmith**, GOLDSMITH; SIXSMITH; **Whitesmith** (working in tin).
Equivs. (of 1, not cogn.): Celtic: GOUGH. Fr.: FÈVRE. Pol.: KOWALSKI. Russ.: KUZNETSOV. Finn.: SEPPÄNEN. Lithuanian: KÁLVAITIS.
In addition to its frequency as a native English surname, Smith *is also one of the commonest surnames adopted by Gypsies in Britain, in part translating Romany* **Petulengro**, *which means 'smith'.*
The Smithsonian Institution in Washington was founded with a bequest from the English chemist and mineralogist James Smithson *(1765–1829). He was born James Lewes Macie, the illegitimate son of Hugh Smithson Percy, Duke of Northumberland. His mother, Elizabeth Macie, a widow, was a direct descendant of Henry VIII; through her family James Smithson inherited a fortune.*

Smolarek Polish: occupational name for a distiller of pitch, from a dim. of Pol. *smolarz* pitch-burner, from *smoła* pitch.
Cogn.: Czech and Jewish (Ashkenazic): **Smola**.
Dim.: Czech: **Smolík**.

Smoleński Polish: habitation name from the city of *Smolensk* in Russia, which was a great trade centre in medieval times. The placename probably derives from Slav. *smola* pitch, because of tar pits in the region.

Smollett English and Scots: nickname for a person with delicate features or of meagre intelligence, from ME *smal* SMALL + *heved* head (OE *hēafod*).

Smrček Czech: topographic name for someone who lived by a clump of spruce trees, Czech *smrček* (a deriv. of *smrk* spruce), or habitation name from a place named with this word.
Var.: **Smrčka**.

Smutný Czech: nickname for a person with a gloomy disposition, from Czech *smutný* sad.

Smythe English: 1. topographic name for someone who lived by a forge, ME *smithe* (OE *smiðđe*), or occupational name for someone employed at a forge.

2. spelling var. of SMITH.

Vars.: **Smithe**. (Of 1 only): **Smithies**, **Smithyes**, **Smythyes**; **Athersmith**.

Cogns. (of 1): Ger.: **Schmied(er)**. Low Ger.: **Tersmeden**.

Snaith English: habitation name from a place in Humberside near Goole (formerly in W Yorks.), so called from ON *sneið* piece of land, or from the same word used independently in other minor place names. The surname is commonest in the Newcastle and Sunderland areas.

Vars.: **Sneath**; **Snee(d)**, **Snead**, **Sneyd** (apparently from a cogn. OE **snǣd*); **Snoad**, **Snode** (from OE **snād*).

Snape 1. N English and Scots: habitation name from any of various places in N England and S Scotland, for example in N Yorks. near Bedale and in the Lowlands near Biggar, so called from ON *snap* poor grazing, winter pasture.

2. habitation name from any of various minor places in S England named with the cogn. OE word *snæp*. In Sussex the dial. term *snape* is still used of boggy uncultivable land.

Snell English: nickname for a brisk or active person, from ME *snell* quick, lively, in part representing a survival of the OE personal name *Snell* or the cogn. ON *Snjallr*.

Vars.: **Snel(l)man** (also 'servant of S.').

Cogns.: Ger.: **Schnell(mann)**; **Schnöll** (Bavaria). Low Ger., Du.: **Snel**. Jewish (Ashkenazic): **Schneller**.

Patrs.: Eng.: **Snelling**; **Snelson**.

Snellgrove English: apparently a habitation name from an unidentified place, perhaps so called from OE *snæg(e)l* snail (cf. SCHNECK) + *grāf* grove.

Vars.: **Snelgrove**, **Snellgrave**.

Śniady Polish: nickname for a person with dark hair or a dark complexion, from Pol. *śniady* tawny, swarthy.

Snoddy Scots and N Irish: nickname from Northern ME *snod* neat, trim, smart (probably of Scand. origin; cf. SNODGRASS) + a dim. suffix.

Var.: **Snoddie**.

Snodgrass Scots: habitation name from a minor place near Irvine in the former county of Ayrs., so called from Northern ME *snod* smooth, sleek, even (probably of Scand. origin; cf. ON *snoðinn* bald) + *grass* grass.

Var.: **Snodgers**.

Snook English: topographic name for someone who lived on a projecting piece of land, ME *snoke* (OE **snōc*). It is possible that this term was also used as a nickname for someone with a long nose.

Cogn.: Du.: **Snoek** ('pike', so called from its pointed snout).

Patr.: Eng.: **Snooks**.

Snow 1. English: nickname denoting someone with very white hair or an exceptionally pale complexion, from OE *snāw* snow.

2. Jewish (Ashkenazic): Anglicized and shortened form of any of the ornamental cpds listed below.

Cogns.: Ger.: **Schnee(weiss)**.

Dims.: Eng.: **Snowling**. Ger.: **Schneele**, **Schnelli** (Swiss).

Cpds (ornamental): Jewish: **Shneebaum**, **Schneibaum**, **Schneubaum** ('snow tree'); **Schneeberg**, **Sznejberg** ('snow hill', the latter a Pol. spelling); **Schneeweiss** ('snow white').

Snowball English (Northumb.): apparently a nickname from ME *snawball* snowball, given either for some anecdotal reason now irrecoverable, or (as Reaney suggests) with reference to a white streak or bald spot in dark hair.

Snowden English: habitation name from a place in W Yorks., so called from OE *snāw* SNOW + *dūn* hill (see DOWN 1), i.e. a hill where snow lies long.

Vars.: **Snawdon**; **Snowdon** (a place in Devon, and the name of the highest mountain in Wales, as well as the former name of *Snow End* in Herts. and *Snow Hill* in Windsor, Berks.); **Snoddon**, **Sneddon**, **Snedden**, **Snadden** (Scots, from a place near Dumfries).

Soame English: habitation name from places in Cambs. and Suffolk called *Soham*, from OE *sā* sea, lake (a byform of *sǣ*) + *hām* homestead.

Vars.: **So(a)mes**.

Soane English: distinguishing epithet for a son (ME *sone*, OE *sunu*) who shared the same given name as his father.

Vars.: **Son(n)**, **Sone**, **Soan**.

Cogn.: Ger.: **Sohn**.

Dims.: Ger.: **Söhnlein**, **Söhndl**. Low Ger.: **Söhnchen**, **Söhngen**, **Söhnke**.

Patrs.: Eng.: **Soan(e)s** (Norfolk), **Sones**. Low Ger.: **Sohns**, **Söhns**.

Patrs. (from dims.): Low Ger.: **Sohnker**, **Sönnecken**, **Sönnischen**, **Sönksen**.

Soar English (chiefly Notts.): 1. topographic name for someone who lived by the river *Soar*, which is of Brit. origin, probably from a root **sar-* to flow.

2. nickname for a person with reddish hair, from ANF *sor* chestnut (of Gmc origin, apparently referring originally to the colour of dry leaves).

Cogns. (of 2): Fr.: **Sor**, **Saur**. Cat.: **Saura**.

Dims. (of 2): Eng.: **Sorrel(l)**, **Sorrill**. Fr.: **Sorel**, **Soreau**, **Saurel**, **Soret**, **Sauret**, SORIN, **Saurin**, **Saury**.

Aug. (of 2): Fr.: **Saurat**.

Patrs. (from 2): Eng.: **Soar(e)s**.

Sobel Jewish (E Ashkenazic): nickname from Pol. *sobol*, a type of marten with handsome fur. The Eng. word *sable* derives from this source, via OHG *zobel* and OF *soble*, *sable*. In some cases the surname may have arisen as a metonymic occupational name for a trader in furs, but the name is too frequent and the number of Ashkenazic furriers too low at the time when surnames were taken for this explanation to be plausible in most cases. It is, rather, for the most part ornamental.

Vars.: **Sobol**, **Zobel**; **Sobelman**; **Soibelman** (from Yid. *soybl*).

Cogn. (habitation name): Pol.: **Sobolewski**.

Patrs.: Jewish: **Soboliev**, **Sobolewitz**.

Sobieraj Polish: anecdotal nickname for someone who coped well in difficult circumstances, from Pol. *sobie radzić* to manage, make shift.

Var.: **Sobierajski**.

Sobota 1. Polish and Czech: from Pol., Czech *Sobota* Saturday, a name bestowed on or taken by someone who was born, baptized, or registered on a Saturday, esp. a new convert to Christianity.

2. Czech: deriv. of the personal name *Soběslav*, composed of elements meaning 'take for oneself', 'appropriate', 'usurp' + 'glory'.

Cogns. (of 2): Pol.: **Sobiech**, **Sobieski**, **Sobański**, **Sobiński**, **Sobalski**.

Dims.: Czech: **Sobotka**. (Of 2 only): Pol.: **Sobek**, **Sobczyk**, **Sobieszek**.

Patrs. (from 2): Pol.: **Sobusiak**; **Sob(iesz)czak**, **Sobkiewicz** (from dims.).

Habitation name (from 2): Pol.: **Sobczyński**.

Jan Sobieski *(1629–96), king of Poland from 1674 and one of the most brilliant military leaders of his time, was born at Olesko, near Lwów, the son of the castellan of the Wawel Castle in Cracow.*

Sobral Portuguese: topographic name for someone who lived by a grove of cork oaks, Port. *sobral*, a collective of *sobro* cork oak (L *sūber*).

Sobrino Spanish: nickname from Sp. *sobrino*, a term of relationship applied to nephews and, in the Middle Ages, also to second and third cousins (L *sobrīnus* second cousin; cf. *consobrīnus* first COUSIN). The name was probably originally applied to someone who was related in this way to an important member of the community.

Socha 1. Polish and Czech: metonymic occupational name for a ploughman, from Pol., Czech *socha* a kind of simple plough.

2. Czech: nickname for a strong man, from *socha* bar, column (var. of SOCHOR).

Vars. (of 1): Pol.: **Sochacki**, **Sochala**.

Sochor Czech: nickname for a man of exceptional strength, from a metaphorical use of the vocabulary word *sochor* strong pole, crowbar.

Dim.: **Sochůrek**.

Sofer Jewish: occupational name for a scribe, Hebr. *sofer*.

Vars.: **Soffer**; **Soferman** (Ashkenazic); **Soifer** (S Ashkenazic).

Søgård Danish: habitation name from a placename composed of the elements *sø* sea + *gård* enclosure, farm.

Vars.: **Søegård**, **Sø(e)gaard**.

Soikin Russian: patr. from the nickname *Soika*, a dim. of *soya* jay, presumably denoting a garrulous or garishly dressed person.

Cogn.: Jewish (E Ashkenazic): **Sojka** (one of the many Ashkenazic ornamental surnames taken from animal names).

Sokol 1. Czech: nickname from *sokol* falcon, or metonymic occupational name for a falconer.

2. Jewish (E Ashkenazic): from Slav. *sokol* falcon, one of the many Ashkenazic ornamental surnames taken from animal names.

Vars.: Jewish: **Sokoll**, **Sokole**, **Socol**; **Sokolski**, **Sokolsky**.

Cogns.: Pol.: **Sokół(ski)**, **Sokal(ski)**.

Dim.: Jewish: **Sokolik**.

Patrs.: Russ.: **Sokolov**. Pol.: **Sokołowicz**. Jewish: **Sokolov**, **Socolov**, **Sokolow**, **Socolow**, **Sokolof(f)**, **Socolof(f)**. Croatian: **Sokolović**, **Sokić**.

Habitation name: Pol.: **Sokołowski**.

Sol 1. Provençal: topographic name for someone who lived by a communal threshing-floor, OProv. *sol* (from L *solum* bottom, floor, ground).

2. Spanish and Catalan: nickname for someone with a sunny personality, from *sol* sun (L *sōl*). This was also sometimes used as a female given name in medieval Spain, and some examples of the surname may derive from this use.

3. Catalan: nickname from OCat. *sàul* saved (L *salvus*; cf. SAUVÉ).

4. Jewish: of unknown origin.

Var. (of 1): **Delsol**.

Solano Spanish: habitation name from any of various places, for example in the provinces of Burgos and Malaga, so called from OSp. *solano* place exposed to the sun (LL *sōlānum*, a deriv. of *sōl* sun; cf. SOL 2).

Var.: **Solana**.

Cogns.: Cat.: **Solà**, **Solana(s)**, **Solan(e)s**. Prov.: **Soula(n)**.

Dim.: Prov.: **Soulanet**.

Soldevila Catalan: topographic name for someone who lived in the lower part of a settlement, from Cat. *sòl* bottom (L *solum*) + *de* of (L *de* from) + *vila* village, settlement (L *villa* country house, estate).

Var.: **Soldevilla**.

Sole English: 1. topographic name from OE *sol* muddy place, or habitation name from one of the places named with this word, as for example *Soles* in Kent.

2. nickname for an unmarried man, from ME, OF *soul* single, unmarried (L *sōlus* alone).

Vars.: **Soal(l)**. (Of 1 only): **Soles**.

Soler Provençal and Catalan: habitation name from any of numerous minor places so called, from *soler* site, plot (LL *solārium*, a deriv. of *solum* bottom, ground).

Vars.: Prov.: **Sol(l)ier**. Cat.: **Solé**.

Cogns.: It.: **Solaro**, **Solari(o)**, **Solero**, **Sol(i)eri**.

Dims.: It.: **Solarino**, **Solaroli**.

Solignac French: habitation name from any of the various places, for example in Haute-Vienne and Haute-Loire, so called from the Gallo-Roman personal name *Sollemnius* (a deriv. of L *sollemnis* solemn, sacred) + the local suffix *-ācum*.

Var.: **Solinhac** (Prov. spelling).

Solis 1. English: from a medieval given name bestowed on a child born after the death of a sibling, from ME *solace* comfort, consolation (OF *solas*, from L *sōlācium*). The word also came to have the sense 'delight', 'amusement', and so the surname may in some cases have been originally given as a nickname to a playful or entertaining person.

2. Jewish (Sefardic): of unknown origin.

Vars.: **Soliss**, **Solass**.

Cogn.: Fr.: **Soulas**.

Solovey Jewish (E Ashkenazic): ornamental name from Yid. *solevey* nightingale (of Slav. origin, probably referring originally to the colour of the bird, 'yellowish brown'). This is one of the large class of Ashkenazic surnames taken from the names of birds; in some cases it may have been chosen as a nickname by a cantor.

Vars.: **Solovei**, **Solovej**; **Soloway** (an Anglicized form); **Solvay**.

Dims.: **Solov(ei)chik**, **Soloveitshik**, **Soloweiczyk**, **Solowieczyk**, **Solovieczyk**, **Solovitzik**.

Solsona Catalan: habitation name from a place in the province of Lérida. The placename is of pre-Roman origin and unknown meaning.

Solzhenitsyn Russian: of uncertain origin. Unbegaun suggests that it may be connected with *solod* malt. The Soviet writer of this name is of Cossack descent.

Somerscales N English: topographic name for someone who lived in a shelter (on upland pastures) inhabited only in the summer, from ON *sumar* SUMMER + *skáli* hut, shelter (see SCHOLES).

Vars.: **Somerscale**, **Summerscale(s)**, **Summerskill**, **Summersgill**.

The name seems to have originated in W Yorks., and is still most common in that county. It is possible that it has a single origin in the hamlet of Somerscales *near Hazlewood, by Bolton Abbey; the first known bearer of the name is Robert* de Somerscales, *recorded in 1298 in the parish of Hazlewood.*

Somerset English: regional name from the county of this name, so called from OE *Sumor(tūn)sǣte* 'dwellers at the summer settlement'.

Vars.: **Som(m)ersett, Summersett.**

The Somerset *family who are Dukes of Beaufort are descended from the Plantagenets. The surname was assumed by Charles Somerset (1460–1520), illegitimate son of Henry Beaufort, Duke of Somerset. The latter was himself descended illegitimately from Edward III through John of Gaunt. A later member of the family was Fitzroy Somerset (1788–1855), who, as Lord Raglan, was the commander of British forces in the Crimea, one of the men responsible for the charge of the Light Brigade.*

Somerville 1. Scots (Norman): habitation name, probably from (Graveron) *Sémerville* in Nord, so called from the Gmc personal name *Sigimar* (see SIEMER) + OF *ville* settlement (see VILLE).

2. Irish: Anglicized form of Gael. *Ó Somacháin*; see SUMMERLY.

Vars. (of 1): **Sommerville, Summerville, Somervail(le), Somervell; Summerfield** (see also SUMMER).

The surname was brought to Scotland in the 12th cent. by William de Somerville, *a retainer of David, Earl of Huntingdon, brother of King Alexander I of Scotland (cf.* LINDSAY*).*

Somoza Spanish: habitation name from any of various places so called, in the provinces of La Coruña, Orense, and Pontevedra.

Søndergård Danish: habitation name from a place named with the elements *sønder* southern + *gård* enclosure, farm.

Var.: **Søndergaard.**

Sønderup Danish: habitation name from a place named with the elements *sønder* southern + *rup* settlement.

Sonnenschein 1. German: nickname for a person of a friendly or cheerful temperament, from Ger. *Sonnenschein*, composed of the MHG elements *sunne* sun (OHG *sunna*) + *schīn* shine (OHG *skīn*). It may also in part be a topographic name for someone who lived at a place which caught the sun, or a house name from a house marked with the sign of the sun.

2. Jewish (Ashkenazic): ornamental name from the Ger. word meaning 'sunshine'; cf. the less frequent **Sonnenstein** ('sun stone') and **Mondschein** ('moonshine'). According to Kaganoff, it was selected because of a supposed phonetic association with SAMSON, or a semantic one with the various Hebr. given names referring to light, such as *Uri* and *Meir*. There is no evidence to support either of these speculations.

Vars. (of 2): **Sonschein, Sunshine, Zonens(c)hein, Zonenshine.**

Sonnier French: occupational name for a bell-ringer, OF *sonnier* (LL *sonārius*, an agent deriv. of *sonāre* to sound, ring).

Vars.: **Son(n)eur.**

Sonntag German and Jewish (Ashkenazic): nickname for someone who had some particular connection with Sunday, Ger. *Sonntag* (MHG *sun(nen)tac*, OHG *sunnūn tag* day of the sun). The Ger. word was sometimes used as a given name for a child born on a Sunday, for this was considered as lucky as Friday (see FREITAG) was unlucky. Among Jews, it seems to have been one of the group of names referring to days of the week that were distributed at random by government officials.

Var.: **Sontag.**

Cogns.: Low Ger.: **Zondagh.** Flem., Du.: **Zondag.**

Sopeña Spanish: topographic name for someone who lived at the foot of a cliff, from OSp. *so* below, under, hard by (L *sub*) + *peña* cliff, rock (L *pinna* pinnacle, battlements).

Cogn.: Cat.: **Sopena.**

Soper English (chiefly Cornwall): occupational name for someone who manufactured soap, by boiling oil or fat together with potash or soda. The name is from an agent deriv. of ME *sōpe* (OE *sāpe*, apparently of Celt. origin).

Vars.: **Soaper, Sopper.**

Cogns.: Fr.: **Savon.** It.: **Saponaro, Saponari, Saponieri; Saoner** (Venetia). Sp.: **Jabonero.** Ger.: **Seif(f).** Jewish: **Seif(er), Seifman, Zeif(er), Zeifman, Zaif(man),** (Ashkenazic); **Zajf** (Central Ashkenazic, with a Pol. spelling reflecting the Central Yid. pronunciation of Yid *zeyf* soap); **Saponaru, Soponaru** (among Rumanian Jews). Hung.: **Szappanos.**

Sorbier French: topographic name for someone who lived near a sorb or service tree, OF *sorbier* (L *sorbārium*, a deriv. of *sorbus* service berry), or habitation name from a place named with this word.

Cogn.: It.: **Sorba.**

Dims.: Fr.: **Sorbet, Sorbon.**

Robert de Sorbon *(1201–74), who founded the Sorbonne in Paris in 1253 as a theological seminary, was born in the village of Sorbon near Rethel, from which he took his surname, and became confessor to Louis IX.*

Sorge German: nickname for a careworn individual, from Ger. *Sorge* care, concern, worry, anxiety (MHG *sorge*, OHG *sor(a)ga*).

Var.: **Sorg.**

Cogns.: Flem., Du.: **Sorg(h)e.** Jewish (Ashkenazic): **Sorger** ('Worrier').

Dim.: Ger.: **Sörgel.**

Soria Spanish and Jewish (Sefardic): habitation name from a city of this name in Castile, of uncertain etymology.

Vars.: **Soriano, Soreano; Soriyano** (Jewish only).

Sorin 1. Jewish (NE Ashkenazic): metr. from the Yid. female given name *Sore* Sarah (from the Hebr. female given name *Sara* 'Princess'), with the Slav. metr. suffix *-in*.

2. French: dim. of *sor*; see SOAR.

Vars. (of 1): **Sorenson** (with a double suffix, Slav. *-in* + mod. Ger. *-sohn*); **Surin, Suris, Surizon** (S Ashkenazic).

Dims. (of 1): **Sorkin, Surkin, Sirkin, Zirkin, Sarkin; Zirlin, Serlin, Cerlin; S(o)urkes, Surkis, Sorkis, Sirkes, Zerkus.**

Sorley Scots: Anglicized form of the Gael. personal name *Somhairle*, itself a Gael. form of the ON name discussed at SUMMERLAD.

Vars.: **Sorlie, Sorrie.**

Patr.: **McSorley.**

Soroff Jewish (NE Ashkenazic): apparently a metr. from the Yid. female given name *Sore*; see SORIN. It may also be an ornamental name deriving from the NE Ashkenazic pronunciation of Hebrew *saraf* seraph (cf. SERAFIM).

Sorokin Russian and Jewish (E Ashkenazic): patr. from the nickname *Soroka* 'Magpie', denoting a garrulous or thievish person, or someone with a streak of white among black hair. In the case of the Jewish surname it is normally an ornamental name, one of the many taken from bird names.

Vars. (not patrs.): Jewish: **Soroka, Soroko; Soroker** (elaborated with an agentive suffix).

Cogn.: Ukr.: **Soroka.**

Sorribas Catalan: topographic name for someone who lived on the bank of a river, from Cat. *so* below, hard by (L *sub*) + *ribas* banks (L *ripae*).

Var.: **Sorribes** (the name of two places in the province of Lérida).

Sosnin Russian: patr. from the nickname *Sosna* 'Pine', given perhaps to a tall, thin person.

Cogns.: Pol.: **Sosnowski** (habitation name). Jewish (E Ashkenazic): **Sosna, Sosner, Sosn(i)ak, Sosnick(i)** (ornamental names); **Sosnowiec, Sosnovitz, Sosnevits, Sosnovsky, Sosnowski** (habitation names from *Sosnowiec* near Katowice in Poland, whose Yid. name is *Sosnevits*).

Sotheby N English: topographic name for someone who lived in the southern part of a settlement, from ON *suðr í bý* south in the village.

Vars.: **Sutherby, Suddaby**.

Soubeyre Provençal: topographic name for someone who lived in an elevated position, from OProv. *soubeyre* (L *superior*, comp. of *super* above).

Vars.: **Soubrier**; **Soub(e)iran, Soub(ey)ran**; **Soubeyrol, Soubayrol, Soubirou(s)**.

Cogns.: Cat.: **Subirà, Subirats**; **Subirana** (fem.). It.: **Sobrero, Subrero**.

Soukup Czech (a common Czech surname): occupational name for a merchant or dealer, Czech *soukup*, from Slav. *sou-* with + *kup-* buy (from Gmc *kaupjan* (mod. Ger. *kaufen*), which is from L *caupō* shopkeeper). The Czech word also acquired the sense 'one who aids or abets a thief', but this probably did not affect the development of the surname.

Soul French: 1. nickname for a habitual drunkard, from OF *soul* drunk, satiated (LL *salullus*, a dim. form of *salur* full, class. L *satur*).

2. habitation name from places in Cantal and Lorrèze, so called because they catch the sun (OF, L *sol*; cf. SOL 2 and SOLANO).

Var. (of 1): **Saoul**.

Pej. (of 1): **Soulard**.

Soulier French: 1. topographic name for someone who lived in a house with more than one storey, something of a rarity in the Middle Ages, from a deriv. of OF *soule* platform, storey (L *solium* throne, dais).

2. metonymic occupational name for a shoemaker, from OF *soulier* shoe, sandal (LL *sublelārius* open sandal, from *sublel* arch of the foot).

Vars.: **Soullier, Soul(i)é**.

Soulsby English (Northumb.): of uncertain origin, perhaps a habitation name from either of two places called *Soulby*, one near Penrith and the other near Kirkby Stephen. These are probably named from ON *súl* post + *býr* farm, settlement. There is, however, no reason why either of the placenames should have developed an *s* in it.

Soult French: probably a nickname for a man who had separated from his wife, from OF *soult* free, detached (L *solūtus*, past part. of *solvere* to loose, untie).

Souness Scots: habitation name from a locality near Blainslie in the former county of Roxburghs.

Vars.: **Sounness, Soonhouse**.

Sourd French: nickname for a deaf man, from OF *sourd* deaf (L *surdus* muffled).

Var.: **Lesourd**.

Cogns.: It.: **Sordi, Sordo, Surdi, (Lo) Surdo**.

Dims.: Fr.: **Sourdeau, So(u)rdet, Sourdin, Sourdou, Sourdillon**. It.: **Sordini**.

Augs.: Fr.: **Sourdat**. It.: **Sordon(i)**.

Sousa Portuguese: habitation name from any of various minor places so called. The placename is of uncertain origin; it was probably applied originally to a salt-marsh, a var. of *sausa* (fem.) salty (L *salsa*), with the word *agua* water (L *aqua*) understood.

Vars.: **Souza** (also a Sefardic name); **De Souza, D'Souza**.

John Philip Sousa *(1854–1932), the American composer, was born in Washington DC, the son of a U.S. Marines bandmaster. His father was born in Spain, the son of a Portuguese refugee, and had emigrated to America in the 1840s.*

Souster English: occupational name for a tailor, from ME *soustere* sewer, from OE *si(o)wan* to sew (see SEWER) + *-ster* agent suffix. The *-ster* ending was originally feminine, but by the Middle English period it was applied equally to both sexes. See also SEWER.

South English: topographic name for someone who lived to the south of a settlement, or regional name for someone who had migrated from the south, from ME *s(o)uth* (OE *sūð*).

Vars.: **Sowman**; **Southern, S(o)uther(i)n, Suthren, Sother(a)n, Sotheron, Southorn**; **Southan, Southon**; **Sudran, Sudron**.

Cogns.: Ger.: **Sudermann, Sondermann**. Fris.: **Zuidema**. Swed.: **Söder(ling), Södermann**. Norw., Dan.: **Sønder**.

Cpds (mostly arbitrary elaborations rather than genuine habitation names): Swed.: **Söderbäck** ('south stream'); **Söderberg** ('south hill'); **Söderblom** ('south flower'); **Södergren** ('south branch'); **Söderholm** ('south island'); **Söderlind(h)** ('south lime'); **Söderlund** ('south grove'); **Söderqvist** ('south twig'); **Söderstöm** ('south river').

Southall English (chiefly W Midlands): habitation name from any of the various places so called, from OE *sūð* SOUTH + *halh* nook, recess (see HALE 1). This might be the town that is now a district of W London, but the distribution of the surname makes a Warwicks. origin more likely. Places called *Southall* in Doverdale, Worcs., and Billingsley, Shrops., are also possible sources.

Southam English: habitation name from places in Gloucs. and Warwicks., so called from OE *sūð* SOUTH + *hām* homestead.

Var.: **Sotham**.

Southcott English (W Country): habitation name from any of various places, for example *Southcot* in Devon or *Southcott* in Devon (of which spelling there are three occurrences) and Cornwall, named with the OE elements *sūð* SOUTH + *cot* cottage, shelter (see COATES).

Southey English: habitation name from any of various places, for example *Southey* in the parish of Culmstock, Devon, in Ecclesford, W Yorks., *Southey* Green in Essex, or *Southey* Wood in Ufford, Northants. All of these get their names from OE *sūð* SOUTH + *(ge)hæg* enclosure (see HAY 1).

Var.: **Southee** (mainly Kent, centred on Canterbury).

The English poet Robert Southey *(1774–1843) was born in Bristol, the son of a linen-draper. His family can be traced back as drapers and clothiers to the early 17th cent. in Somerset.*

The name Southee *is relatively common in Kent from the late 17th cent. onwards, probably as the result of migration. Many bearers of the name in this spelling, including several in New Zealand, are descended from John Southee, who became a master baker in Canterbury in 1836.*

Southgate English: 1. habitation name from a place in Norfolk, so called from OE *sūð* SOUTH + *geat* gate; the village was situated near the southern entrance to a large medieval enclosed forest.

2. topographic name for someone who lived near the south gate of a medieval walled town or other enclosed place.

Vars. (of 2): **Suggate**; **Suggett**, **Suggitt** (chiefly Yorks.).

Southwell English: habitation name from a place in Notts., so called from OE *sūð* SOUTH + *well(a)* spring, stream (see WELL), or topographic name from the same vocab. elements used independently.

Southwood English: habitation name from a place in Norfolk, so called from OE *sūð* SOUTH + *wudu* WOOD, or topographic name from the same vocab. elements used independently.

Southworth English (Lancs.): habitation name from a place in Ches. (formerly S Lancs.), so called from OE *sūð* SOUTH + *worð* enclosure (see WORTH).

Var.: **Southward**.

Sowa Polish: nickname meaning 'Owl', perhaps denoting a bookish or knowledgeable person, or arising out of some fancied physical resemblance.

Vars.: **Sowała**, **Sowiak**.

Cogn.: Czech: **Sova**.

Habitation name: Pol.: **Sowiński**.

Sowden English: nickname from ME, OF *soudan* sultan (Arabic *sultān* ruler), either for someone who behaved in an outlandish and autocratic manner, or for someone who had played the part of a sultan in a pageant.

Vars.: **Soden**, **Soldan**, **Sultan**.

Cogns.: Fr.: **Soudan(t)**. It.: **Soldano**, **Soldan(i)**. Hung.: **Zoltán**.

Sowerby English: habitation name from any of various places in N England named with the ON elements *saurr* sour ground + *býr* farm, settlement.

Vars.: **Sowersby**, **Sor(s)bie**, **Sor(s)by**, **Surby**.

Spaak Dutch: metonymic occupational name for someone who made spokes for wheels, from MDu. *spaak* spoke (OSax. *spece*; cf. OE *spāca*).

Var.: **Spock** (Anglicized).

The American paediatrician Dr Benjamin Spock *(b. 1903) was of Dutch descent; his ancestors, whose name was* Spaak, *were early settlers in the Hudson River Valley.*

Špaček Czech: nickname from a vocab. word meaning 'starling'.

Spain English and Irish (Norman): 1. habitation name from *Épaignes* in Eure, recorded in the L form *Hispānia* in the 12th cent. It seems to have been so called because it was established by colonists from Spain during the Roman Empire.

2. habitation name from *Espinay* in Ille-et-Vilaine, Brittany, so called from a collective of OF *espine* thorn bush.

3. (rarely) ethnic name for a Spaniard; see PAGNOL.

Spalding English: habitation name from a place in Lincs., so called from the OE tribal name *Spaldingas* 'people of the district called *Spald*'. The district name probably means 'Ditches', referring to drainage channels in the fenland.

Vars.: **Spaulding**, SPAUGHTON.

The surname Spalding *was brought to Scotland in the 13th cent. by* Radulphus de Spalding. *His descendants prospered, and the name is still common in Scotland.*

Spanton English (Norfolk): habitation name from *Spaunton* in E Yorks., so called from ON *spánn* shingle, wooden tile (cf. SPOONER) + OE *tūn* settlement, i.e. 'settlement with shingled roofs'.

Spargo Cornish: habitation name from Higher or Lower *Spargo*, in the parish of Mabe, so called from Corn. *spern* thorn bushes + **cor* enclosure.

Spark 1. English: from the ON byname *Sparkr* 'Sprightly', 'Vivacious'.

2. Low German: cogn. of SPARROW.

Vars. (of 1): **Sparke**; **Sprake**, **Sprague**, **Spragg(e)** (metathesized forms). (Of 2): **Spahr**, **Spaar**.

Patrs. (from 1): Eng.: **Spark(e)s**.

Sparrow English: nickname, perhaps for a small, chirpy person, or else for someone bearing some fancied physical resemblance to a sparrow, ME *sparewe*, OE *spearwa*.

Var.: **Sparrowe**.

Cogns.: Ger.: SPEER, **Spervogel**, **Sper(c)k**. Low Ger.: SPARK. Flem., Du.: **Spreeuw**.

Dims.: Eng.: **Sparling**, **Sperling**, **Spurling**. Ger.: **Sperl(ing)**, **Spierling**, **Sperlich**; **Spörl** (Bavaria). Jewish (Ashkenazic): **Sperling** (an ornamental name).

Patr.: Flem., Du.: **Verspreeuwen**.

Sperling *is a well-established surname on the S Baltic coast. Bearers of it settled in Sweden, where they were raised to the nobility as barons in 1653, and as counts in 1687. A member of this family, Henry Sperling (1657–1737), settled in England, where his descendants can still be found.*

Spasski Russian: 1. habitation name from any of the numerous places called *Spasskoe*, from the dedication of their churches to the Saviour, ORuss. *Spas(itel)* (from *spasti* to save, a calque of Gk *sōtēr*, from *sōzein* to save).

2. surname adopted by Orthodox priests, affirming their dedication to Jesus Christ as Saviour.

Cogns. (patrs.): Croatian: **Spasić**, **Spasojević**.

Spath German: nickname for a tardy person, from Ger. *spät* late (MHG *spæte*, OHG *spāti*).

Vars.: **Späth(e)**, **Späthmann**, **Speth(mann)**.

Spaughton English: of uncertain origin, from its form apparently a habitation name. The suggestion has been put forward that it is a var. of SPALDING, assimilated by folk etymology to the common placename ending *-ton*. The name *de Spotton* is well established in the Malden-Tolworth-Chessington area of Surrey from the 13th cent. onwards, so perhaps a local Surrey origin should be sought. However, no suitable placename in this area is known.

Vars.: **Spawton**, **Sporton**, **Spotton**, **Spolton**, **Spalton**.

All present-day bearers of the surname Spaughton *are apparently descended from a London family living in the parish of St Mary, Newington, in the mid-18th cent.*

Speak English: nickname from the woodpecker, ME *spek(e)* (an aphetic form of OF *espeche(e)*, of Gmc origin; cf. SPEIGHT).

Vars.: **Spe(a)ke**, **Speek**; SPECK, **Spick**.

Patrs.: **Speaks**, **Speeks**.

Espec *or* Espek *is recorded as a nickname or byname in Normandy from 1036. By 1086 ancestors of the Speke family were in possession of lands in Yorks., where Walter Espec founded Kirkham and Rivaulx abbeys in the 12th cent. The present family trace their descent from Richard Espec, steward of the Fitzregis family* c.*1160. A later member of the family was the explorer John Hanning Speke (1827–64), who identified the source of the Nile. He was born in Bideford, into a branch of the Yorks. family which had migrated to the W Country in the 15th cent.*

Speakman English (chiefly Lancs.): nickname or occupational name for someone who acted as a spokesman, from

ME *spekeman* advocate, spokesman (from OE *specan* to speak + *mann* man).

Var.: **Spackman**.

Spear English: nickname for a tall, thin person, or else for a skilled user of the hunting spear, from ME, OE *spere* spear. In part it may also have been a metonymic occupational name for a maker of spears.

Vars.: **Speare**; **Speir**, SPIER (Scotland); **Speer** (N Ireland).

Cogn.: Ger.: SPEER.

Patrs.: Eng.: **Spearing**, **Spear(e)s**; **Speirs**, **Spiers** (Scotland); **Speers** (N Ireland).

Spearman English: 1. occupational name for a soldier armed with a spear, from ME *spere* SPEAR + *man*.

2. from a ME, OE personal name *Spereman*, of the same origin as the occupational name above.

Speck 1. German: metonymic occupational name for a seller of bacon or a pork butcher, from Ger. *Speck* bacon (MHG *spec* bacon, OHG *spek*), or nickname for someone who was particularly fond of this food.

2. English: var. of SPEAK.

Var. (of 1): **Speckesser** ('bacon eater').

Cogns. (of 1): Low Ger.: **Speckäter**, **Speck(e)ter**. Du.: **Van der Spek**. Jewish (Ashkenazic): **Spekman** (possibly an offensive name assigned by a non-Jewish government official, since pork is forbidden to Jews).

Dim. (of 1): Ger.: **Speckle**.

Spector Jewish (E Ashkenazic): of uncertain origin. It is possibly an occupational name for someone who inspected meat to ensure that it conformed with Jewish dietary laws; the Yid. name for this officer was *mazhgiekh* (Hebr. *mashgiach*). According to Kaganoff the name was taken by a tutor in the household of a rich Jew who had special permission to reside in the large cities of Russia where other Jews could not live, but this is unlikely since 'inspector' and 'tutor' are semantically distinct.

Vars.: **Spektor**, **Inspektor**, **Spectorman**.

Spedding N English and Scots: of uncertain origin, possibly a patr. from the OE byname *Spēd* 'Success', 'Prosperity' (cf. SPEED). However, Black is not able to quote forms earlier than 1502, which makes this hypothesis very doubtful.

Speed 1. English: nickname for a fortunate person, from ME *sped* (OE *spēd*) success, good fortune, smooth progress (hence the mod. meaning 'swiftness').

2. English: nickname for a swift runner, from the derived sense of ME *sped* mentioned above.

3. Irish: translation of Gael. *Ó Fuada*; see FOODY.

Dim. (of 2): **Speedie** (Scotland).

Speer 1. N Irish: var. of SPEAR.

2. German: cogn. of SPEAR, from Ger. *Speer* spear (MHG *sper*, *spar(e)*, OHG *sper*).

3. German: cogn. of SPARROW, from MHG *spar(e)* (OHG *sparo*).

4. Jewish (Ashkenazic): of unknown origin, probably an adoption of the German name.

Speight English (now chiefly Yorks.): nickname from ME *speght* woodpecker (presumably from an unrecorded OE **speoht*, apparently akin to OE *specan* to speak, talk, chatter).

Vars.: **Sp(e)aight**, **Spieght**.

Cogn.: Ger.: **Specht**.

Speiser 1. German: occupational name for a steward in charge of the supply and distribution of provisions in a great house or monastery, from an agent deriv. of Ger. *Speise* food, supplies (MHG *spīse*, OHG *spīsa*, from an aphetic form of LL *expe(n)sa* (*pecunia*) (money) expended). Cf. SPENCE and SPENDER.

2. Jewish (Ashkenazic): occupational name for a grocer, from a later semantic development of the same word as in 1.

Vars. (of 2): **Spieser**, **Speis(man)**, **Speizman**; **Szpajzer** (a Pol. spelling).

Cogn. (of 1): Low Ger.: **Spieser**.

Speller English: occupational name for a reciter, from an agent deriv. of ME *spell(en)* to tell, relate (OE *spellian*). There has probably been some confusion with SPILLER.

Vars.: **Spelar**, **Spel(l)man**.

Spence English: metonymic occupational name for a servant employed in the pantry of a great house or monastery, from ME *spense* larder, storeroom (an aphetic form of OF *despense*, from a LL deriv. of *dispendere*, past part. *dispensus*, to weigh out, dispense). Cf. SPEISER and SPENDER.

Vars.: **Spens** (Scots); **Spencer**, **Spenser**; **Despenser**.

Spens *is the name of a family of Scottish origin, with exceptionally widespread branches in Europe, especially France and Sweden. They are said to be descended from the ancient Earls of Fife. One line, originally recorded in Boddam, Aberdeens., in the 15th cent., settled in Silesia in the 17th cent. They became known as* von Boden, *and were granted the title Reichsfreiherr of the Kingdom of Bohemia in 1781. A branch of the family from Strathallan, Scotland, is represented by the Barons* de Spens *d'Estignols. They are descended from Henry de Spens (d. c.1300), who was compelled to submit to Edward I of England in 1296. The family was established in France when Patrick de Spens went there in 1450 as an officer in Charles VII's bodyguard of Scots Guards. He settled in Gascony and married the heiress of Estignols. The château Estignols is still the family seat. Another branch of the family was established in Sweden by Sir James Spens, sent there originally as an ambassador of James I of England. He was created Baron of Orreholmen in 1635. His descendant, Baron Jacob Spens, was general of the Swedish forces and was created a count in 1719. Members of the family are still living in Sweden.*

There is some dispute about the origins of the Spencer *family whose most famous present-day member is the Princess of Wales, formerly Lady Diana Spencer (b. 1961). Some sources say that they are descended from William the Conqueror's steward, Robert* Despencer. *What is clear is that by the 15th cent. they had become prosperous from sheep-farming in Northants. Robert Spencer (d. 1627) was said to be the wealthiest man in England. Their titles have included Earls of Sunderland and Earls Spencer; and through the female line the 5th Earl of Sunderland also became Duke of Marlborough in 1733. This connection was the result of the marriage, in 1700, of the 3rd Duke of Sunderland to the daughter of John Churchill, 1st Duke of Marlborough. The youngest son of this union, John Spencer (1708–46), was the father of the 1st Earl Spencer (1734–83), the title now held by the Princess of Wales' family.*

Spender English: occupational name for a steward in charge of the supply of necessities in a great house or monastery, from an aphetic form of ME, OF *despendeour* dispenser (L *dispenditor*, from *dispendere* to weigh out, dispense). Cf. SPEISER and SPENCE.

Spendlove English: nickname for someone who was free with his affections, from ME *spend(en)* to spend, squander (OE *spendan*) + *love* love (OE *lufu*).

Vars.: **Spen(d)low**.

Spengler German: occupational name for a metal-worker, from an agent deriv. of a dim. form of MHG *spange* clasp, buckle, ornamental fastening. In S Germany, Austria, and Switzerland the mod. Ger. vocab. word *Spengler* means 'plumber', but in earlier times it had a wider range of meanings.

Var.: **Spengel**.

Sperber 1. German: nickname for a small but pugnacious person, from Ger. *Sperber* sparrowhawk (MHG *sperwære*, OHG *sparwāri*, a cpd of *sparw* SPARROW + *āri* 'eagle'; cf. ADLER and EARNSHAW).

2. Jewish (Ashkenazic): ornamental name from the mod. Ger. bird name.

Var. (of 2): **Sperberg** (influenced by the many Ashkenazic surnames ending in the element *-berg* hill).

Sperrin English: metonymic occupational name for a maker of spurs, from ME *sperun* spur (OF *(e)speron*, of Gmc origin; cf. SPOHRER and SPURR).

Vars.: **Sperryn**, **Spurren**, **Spearon**, **Sperring**, **Spurring**.

Spicer English: occupational name for a seller of spices, ME *spic(i)er* (an aphetic form of OF *espicier*, LL *speciārius*, an agent deriv. of *speciēs* spice, groceries, merchandise).

Var.: **Spice**.

Cogns.: Fr.: **Lépicier**, **Lépissier**; **Lépice**. It.: **Speziale**, **Speziali**, **Speciale**, **Speciali**.

Equivs. (not cogn.): Prov.: SABRIER. Jewish (Ashkenazic): GEWIRTZ.

Spiegler German and Jewish (Ashkenazic): occupational name for a maker or seller of mirrors, from an agent deriv. of Ger. *Spiegel*, Yid. *shpigl* (OHG *spiagal*, from L *speculum*, a deriv. of *specere* to look, see).

Vars.: Ger.: **Spieg(e)l**, **Spiegelmann**. Jewish: **Spigler**, **Spi(e)gel(man)**.

Cogns.: Low Ger.: **Spegel**. Flem., Du.: **Spiegheleer**. Sp.: **Espejo**.

Spielberg German and Jewish (Ashkenazic): habitation name from any of the various places so called, from a contracted form of MHG *spiegel* look-out point (L *speculum*; cf. SPIEGLER) + *berg* hill.

Vars.: Jewish: **Spielberger**; **Szpilberg** (a Pol. spelling).

Spier 1. English: occupational name for a lookout or watchman, or nickname for a nosy person, from an agent deriv. of ME *(e)spi(en)* to watch, observe (OF *espier*, of Gmc origin).

2. Scots: var. of SPEAR.

3. Jewish (Ashkenazic): of uncertain origin, possibly a habitation name from the Ger. city of *Speyer*; cf. SPIRE 2.

Var. (of 3): **Spierer**.

Spillane Irish: Anglicized form of Gael. **Ó Spealáin** 'descendant of *Spealán*', a personal name representing a dim. of *speal* scythe.

Vars.: **O'Spillane**, **O'Spallane**, **(O')Spollane**, **Spellane**, **Spalane**, **Spollan**, **Spollen**; **Spla(i)ne**; **Smallen**, **Smollan**, **Smullen**.

Spiller English: 1. occupational name for a tumbler or jester, from an agent deriv. of ME *spill(en)* to play, jest, sport (OE *spilian*).

2. nickname for a destructive or wasteful person, from an agent deriv. of the homonymous ME *spill(en)* to spoil, waste, squander (OE *spillan*).

Cogns. (of 1): Ger.: **Spieler**, **Spielmann**, **Spillmann**. Low Ger.: **Spelmann**. Jewish (Ashkenazic): **Spielman(n)**, **S(z)pilman** (occupational names for a musician).

Spilling English (Norfolk): of uncertain origin, apparently from a medieval given name, perhaps from an OE patr., **Spilling*, of a personal name **Spill(a)*. Evidence for an ON byname **Spilli*, from *spillir* squanderer, profligate (cf. SPILLER 2), may be found in the placename *Spilsby* (Lincs.).

Patr.: **Spillings**.

The earliest known bearer of the surname is Edmund Spyllyng, *recorded in 1522 at Brooke and Bedingham, Norfolk. Later in the 16th cent. the manor of Bedingham was held by a bearer of the name in the current form* Spilling.

Spillman English: from a ME given name Spileman, which was originally an OE byname meaning 'Juggler', 'Tumbler', 'Actor' (cf. SPILLER).

Spilsbury English: habitation name from *Spelsbury* in Oxon., apparently so called from the gen. case of an OE byname **Spēol* 'Watchful' + OE *burh* town, fortress.

Spindler English, German, and Jewish (Ashkenazic): occupational name for a maker or user of spindles, from an agent deriv. of ME *spindle*, Ger. *Spindel*, Yid. *shpindl* (OE *spinel*, MHG *spinnele*, OHG *spin(n)ila*, all derived from a Gmc verb meaning 'to spin').

Var.: Jewish: **Spindel**.

Spink English: nickname from ME *spink* chaffinch (of uncertain, probably imitative, origin), bestowed on account of some fancied resemblance to the bird.

Var.: **Spinke**.

Patr.: **Spinks**.

Spire 1. English: nickname for a tall, thin man, from ME *spir* stalk, stem (OE *spīr*). This was apparently used as a personal name or byname, in view of the fact that there are patr. derivs. In some ME dialects this word also denoted reeds, and the surname may in part have been originally a topographic name for someone who lived in a marshy area. The application to a church steeple is not attested before the 16th cent., and is not a likely source of the surname.

2. Jewish (Ashkenazic): Anglicized form of **Speyer**, a habitation name from the German town so called, which had a large Jewish population in the Middle Ages; cf. SAPIR, SHAPIRO, and SPIER 3.

Vars. (of 2): **Spiro**, **Spira**, **Spirer**.

Dims. (of 1): Eng.: **Spirett**, **Spirit**.

Patrs. (from 1): Eng.: **Spiring**; **Spires**.

Spittle English: occupational name for someone who was employed at a lodging house, ME *spital* (an aphetic form of OF *hospital*, LL *hospitāle*, from *hostis*, gen. *hospitis*, guest).

Vars.: **Spittel**, **Spital(l)**, **Spittles**; **Spitt(e)ler**.

Cogns.: It.: **Spit(al)eri**. Ger.: **Spittel**; **Spitt(e)ler**. Jewish (E Ashkenazic): **Spitalnik**.

Spitz 1. German: topographic name for someone who lived by a pointed hill or by a field with an acute angle, from Ger. *spitz* pointed (OHG *spizzi*). There are numerous minor places throughout Germany named with this word, and the surname may also be a habitation name from any of these.

2. Jewish (Ashkenazic): of uncertain origin, perhaps of similar derivation to the German name, or from Yid. *shpitsn* lace.

Vars.: Ger.: **Spitz(l)er**. Jewish: **S(c)hpitz**, **S(h)pitzer**, **Spitzman**.

Spitzweg German: metonymic occupational name for a baker who specialized in a particular type of pastry baked in a pointed shape, MHG *spitzweck* (from SPITZ + *wecke* wedge).

Spivak Jewish (E Ashkenazic): occupational name from Ukr. *spivák* singer, used as a translation of KAZAN.

Vars.: **Spivack**; **Spi(e)wak**, **Spievak** (from the cogn. Pol. *śpiewak*; **Spivakovsky**.
Cogn.: Pol.: **Śpiewak**.

Spjut Swedish: nickname from Swed. *spjut* spear, lance, pike, javelin; this is one of the 'soldiers' names' assumed during military service in the 17th and 18th cents. before surnames came into regular use in Sweden.
Var.: **Spjuth**.

Spode English: habitation name from *Spoad* in Shrops., the name of which is of obscure origin.

Spofforth English: habitation name from a place in N Yorks., recorded in Domesday Book as *Spoford* and perhaps so called from OE *splott* spot, plot of land + *ford* FORD.
Vars.: **Spofford, Spoffard, Spawforth**.

Spohrer German: occupational name for a maker of spurs, from an agent deriv. of MHG *spor* spur (OHG *sporo*; mod. Ger. *Sporn*).
Vars.: **Spör(n)er**, **Spehrer**, **Sperner**; **Spohr**, **Spehr** (metonymic); **Spo(h)rmann**.
Cogns.: Low Ger.: **Sparmann**. Flem.: **Spoormaeker**. Du.: **Spoor**. Eng.: SPURR.

Spooner English: occupational name for someone who covered roofs with wooden shingles, from an agent deriv. of ME *spoon* chip, splinter (OE *spōn*). However, from the 14th cent., under Scandinavian influence, the word had also begun to acquire its modern sense denoting the eating utensil, and the surname may therefore in some cases have been acquired by someone who made these articles from wood or horn.
Cogns.: Ger.: **Spener**; **Spahn, Spohn**.

Sporran Irish: Anglicized form of Gael. **Mac Sparáin** 'son of *Sparán*', a byname meaning 'Purse' (ultimately from L *bursa*; cf. PURSER). The main family of this name held the hereditary post of purse-bearers to the McDonnells of the Isles.
Vars.: **McSporran**; **McSparran** (Ulster).

Spottiswoode Scots: habitation name from a place in the parish of Gordon, Berwicks., first recorded in 1249 as *Spottiswode*. The second element is ME *wode* WOOD; the first appears to derive from a personal name.
Vars.: **Spottiswood, Spotswood**.
All bearers of this surname are probably descended from Robert de Spotswood (fl. c.*1300*). *Alexander* Spotswood *was governor of Virginia in 1710*.

Spratt English: nickname for a small and insignificant person, from ME *sprat* sprat (of uncertain origin, possibly a deriv. of OE *spryt*, *sprot* sprout, young shoot; see SPROTT).

Spray English (Notts. and Derbys.): nickname for a thin person, from ME *spray* slender branch (of uncertain origin).
Patr.: **Sprason**.

Sprigg English: nickname for a tall, thin, bony person, from ME *sprigge* twig, branch (apparently of ON or Low Ger. origin, first recorded as a vocab. word in Eng. in the 15th cent.).
Patr.: **Spriggs**.

Spring English: of uncertain origin. Early examples, as for example William *Spring* (Yorks. 1280), all point to a personal name or nickname, perhaps going back to an OE byname derived from the verb *springan* to jump, leap (see SPRINGER 1). Reaney derives the surname from the season, but there is a difficulty in that the word is not attested in this sense until the 16th cent., the usual ME word being *lenten* (cf. LENZ).
Dims.: **Springett, Springate**.

Springall English: 1. nickname from ME *springal(d)* youth, stripling (of uncertain origin, perhaps from SPRING with the addition of the OF suffix *-ald*).

2. nickname for a violent and destructive individual or metonymic occupational name for an operator of the medieval siege-engine known in ME as a *springalde* (OF *espringalle*, apparently from a Gmc root cogn. with OE *springan* to jump, leap). The engine worked like a giant catapult, hurling missiles against fortifications.
Vars.: **Springhall, Springell, Springle**.

Springer 1. English, German, Dutch, and Jewish (Ashkenazic): nickname for a lively person, from an agent deriv. of ME, Ger. *springen*, MDu. *springhen*, Yid. *shpringen* to jump, leap (OE, OHG, OSax. *springan*).

2. English: topographic name for someone who lived by a fountain or the source of a stream, from ME *spring* (OE *spring*, *spryng*, a deriv. of the verb given above). The word *spring* was also used of a plantation of young trees, and this may in some cases be the source of the surname.
Vars. (of 1): Ger.: **Spranger**. Jewish: **Shpringer**.
Cogn. (of 1): Low Ger.: **Sprenger**.

Springfield English: habitation name from a place in Essex, recorded in Domesday Book as *Springinghefelda* as well as *Springafelda*, apparently from OE *Springingafeld* 'pasture (see FIELD) of the people who live by a spring'.

Sprott Scottish and N English: from the ME, OE personal name *Sprot*, of uncertain origin. It may be derived from OE *sprot* sprout, young shoot.
Var.: **Sproat**.

Spruce English: ethnic name for someone from Prussia, the ME name for which was *Spruce* or *Sprewse*; cf. PREUSS. The adj. *spruce* neat, dapper, which probably derives from an attrib. use of the name of the country, is not recorded until the late 16th cent., too late for it to be a likely source of the surname. The tree (earlier *Spruce fir*) has likewise only come to be known by this name in the last couple of cents.

Spry English: apparently a nickname for an active, brisk, or smart person. Although *spry* is not recorded in OED until the 18th cent., it was probably in colloquial use in the W Country dialect and in Scots much earlier. The word is of obscure origin. The surname is found mainly in Devon, but there is also a modest concentration of bearers in NE England.

Spurr English (now chiefly Yorks.): metonymic occupational name for a maker of spurs, from ME *spore*, *spure* spur (OE *spora*, *spura*). Cf. SPERRING.
Vars.: **Spurrs**; **Spore**, **Spoor(s)** (Northumb.); **Spurrier** (from a ME agent deriv.).

Spurway English: habitation name from a place in Devon, apparently so called from OE *sprǣg* brushwood + *weg* path, way.
This is the name of an ancient Devon family, one of whose ancestors, Robert Grede, alias Spurway, *is known to have owned lands at E Spurway in 1242*.

Spychalski Polish: nickname for an idle worker, a 'buck passer', Pol. dial. *spychacz*, from *spychać* to push down.

2. topographic name for someone living by a precipice, Pol. dial. *spych*, also from *spychać*.

Var.: **Spychała**.

Squibb English: perhaps a nickname for a sarcastic, witty, or spiteful person, from early mod. Eng. *squibbe* lampoon, satirical attack. The word, which is probably of imitative origin, is not recorded until the 16th cent.; the original sense was 'firework'.

Squire English: status name for a man belonging to the social rank immediately below that of knight, from ME *squyer*, an aphetic form of OF *esquier* shield-bearer (L *scūtārius*, a deriv. of *scūtum* shield). At first it denoted a young man of good birth attendant on a knight, or by extension any attendant or servant, but by the 14th cent. the meaning had been generalized, and referred to social status rather than age. By the 17th cent., the term denoted any member of the landed gentry, but this is unlikely to have influenced the development of the surname.

Vars.: **Squier, Swire, Swyer**.

Cogns.: Fr.: **Écuyer, Lécuyer, Escuyer, Lescuyer**. Prov.: **Escudier, Escudié**. It.: **Scud(i)eri, Scudiero, Scut(i)eri, Scutiro**. Sp.: **Escudero**. Cat.: **Escuder, Escudé**.

Patrs.: Eng.: **Squires, Squiers, Squeers, Swires, Swiers**.

Squirrel English: nickname from ME *squirel* squirrel, an aphetic form of OF *esquirel* (LL *scūriōlus*, a dim. from Gk *skiouros*, from *skia* shadow + *oura* tail). This was presumably bestowed on someone bearing some resemblance to a squirrel, such as puffy cheeks and big eyes.

Vars.: **Squir(rel)l, Scurrell**.

Cogns.: Fr.: **Ecureuil, Lécureuil, Lécureux**. Prov.: **Esquirol, Esquirou**. Cat.: **Esquirol**.

Sroka Polish: nickname for a thievish or insolent person, from Pol. *sroka* magpie.

Cogn.: Czech: **Straka**.

Habitation name: Pol.: **Sroczyński**.

Stabe German: nickname for a tall, thin person, or metonymic occupational name for anyone who carried a staff of office, a reminder of his right to inflict physical discipline, from Ger. *Stab* rod, staff (MHG *stap*, OHG *stab*).

Vars.: **Staab, Staap**.

Cogn.: Eng.: **Staff** (mainly Norfolk).

Dim.: Ger.: **Stäble**.

Stables English: topographic name for someone who lived by a stable, or occupational name for someone employed in one, from ME *stable* (an aphetic form of OF *estable*, from L *stabulum*, a deriv. of *stāre* to stand). In ME the term was used of the quarters occupied by cattle as well as those reserved for horses.

Vars.: **Stable, Stab(e)ler**.

Stace English: from the medieval male given name *Stace*, an aphetic vernacular form of *Eustace* (L *Eustacius*, from Gk *Eustakhios* 'Fruitful', crossed with the originally distinct *Eustathios* 'Orderly'). The name was born by various genuine minor saints, but nothing of historical value is known of the most famous St Eustace, said to have been converted by the vision of a crucifix between the antlers of a hunted stag.

Var.: **Eustace**.

Cogns.: Fr.: **Eustac(h)e, Eustaze, Hustache**. Ger.: **Stach**. Low Ger.: **Staas, Staat**. Flem., Du.: **Staes, Taes**. Pol.: **Ostaszewski** (in form, a habitation name).

Dims.: Eng.: **Stacey, Eustie**. Ger.: **Stachl, Stächelin**.

Patrs.: Low Ger.: **Staasen, Staats**. Flem., Du.: **Staesen**.

Stach Polish and Czech: from the given name *Stach*, a pet form of Pol. *Stanisław*, Czech *Stanislav* (see STANISŁAWSKI).

Vars.: Pol.: **Stachura, Stachurski**.

Patrs.: Pol.: **Stachowicz; Stachowiak**.

Habitation names: Pol.: **Stachowski, Stachlewski**.

Stack English: nickname for a large, well-built man, from ME *stack* haystack (ON *stakkr*).

Vars.: **Stak(e)** (Ireland).

This surname is now less common in England than in Ireland (esp. Co. Kerry), where it was first taken in the 13th cent.; it has been Gaelicized **Stac**.

Stackpoole Irish: habitation name from a place called *Stackpole* 'Pool by the Rock' in the former county of Pembrokes., Wales, from which settlers of Norman descent made their way into Ireland. The name is recorded in Dublin as early as 1200, and has been Gaelicized as **de Stacapúl**; bearers were also known as **Galldubh** ('Black Stranger'; see also STAPLETON).

Vars.: **Stackpole, Stacpoole**.

Staddon English (W Country): habitation name from any of half a dozen places in Devon, all earlier found as *Stoddon*, from OE *stod* stud or *stott* bullock + *dūn* hill.

Var.: **Stadden**.

Stadler German: topographic name for someone who lived near a barn or granary, or occupational name for an official who was responsible for receiving tithes into the manorial storehouse, from a deriv. of MHG *stadel* barn, granary (OHG *stadal*). Cf. SCHAUER. The surname is also occasionally borne by Ashkenazic Jews, apparently as an adoption of the Ger. surname.

Vars.: Ger. only: **Stadel(mann), Stadtler, Städtler**.

Cogns.: Flem., Du.: **Stad(t)mann**.

Stafford English: habitation name from any of the various places so called, which do not all share the same etymology. The county town of Staffs. (which is probably the main source of the surname) gets its name from OE *stæð* landing place + *ford* FORD. Examples in Devon seem to have as their first element OE *stān* STONE, and one in Sussex is probably named with OE *stēor* STEER.

Var.: **Staffurth**.

Stagg English: nickname from OE *stagga* male deer, stag. In N dials. of ME the term was also used of a young horse, perhaps under Scandinavian influence, and in some cases this meaning may lie behind the original application of the name.

Stainburn N English: habitation name from a place in Cumb., so called from ON *steinn* or OE *stān* STONE + OE *burna* stream (see BOURNE).

Stainer English: occupational name for a dyer, particularly of glass rather than fabrics, from an agent deriv. of ME *steyn(en)*, an aphetic form of *disteyn(en)* (OF *disteindre*, L *distingere*, from *tingere* to dye; cf. TEINTURIER).

Vars.: **Steiner, Steinor**.

Staines English: habitation name from a place on the Thames west of London, apparently so called from OE *stān* stone. The reference may be to a milestone on the Roman road that ran through the town, while the vocalic development seems to be the result of Norman influence.

Stainsby English: habitation name from either of two places, one in Derbys. (*Steinesbi* in Domesday Book) and one in Lincs. (*Stafnebi* in 12th-cent. records). The former

is so called from the ON personal name *Steinn* 'Stone' + ON *býr* farm, settlement, the latter from the ON personal name *Stafn* 'Stem' + *býr*.
Var.: **Stansbie**.

Stainthorpe English: habitation name from *Staindrop* in Co. Durham, which Ekwall derives from OE *stǣner* stony ground + *hop* enclosed valley (see HOPE). If this is correct, the second syllable has been assimilated by folk etymology to the common habitation element THORPE.

Stait English (W Midlands): topographic name for someone who lived by a landing stage, ME *sta(i)the* (OE *stæð*; cf. STATHAM).

Stakes English: apparently a topographic name for someone who lived by a prominent post or stake, ME *stake* (OE *staca*). The stake in question may well have been a boundary marker.

Stakhanov Russian: patr. from the given name *Stakhan* (from Gk *Stakhys* 'Bunch of Grapes', with the addition of the suffix from *Stepan* STEPHEN). *Stakhys* was the name of a 1st-cent. Christian, traditionally regarded as the first bishop of Byzantium, and so an important figure in the Orthodox Church.
Vars.: **Stakheev**, **Stasov**; **Stashinin** (from a dim.).
Cogns.: Beloruss.: **Stakhevich**, **Stakhovich**.

Stalder German: topographic name for someone who lived on a steep slope, MHG *stalde*, or habitation name for someone from a place named with this word, as for example *Stalden* in Switzerland.

Stalker Scots and N English: occupational name for a trapper or nickname for a stealthy person, from an agent deriv. of ME *stalk(en)* to stalk, approach stealthily (OE **stealcian*, a deriv. of *stelan* to steel).

Stallard English: nickname for a valiant or resolute person, from ME *stalward*, *stalworth* (OE *stǣlwierðe*, a cpd of *stǣl* place + *wierðe* worthy).
Vars.: **Stollard**, **Stallwood**; **Stal(l)worthy**, **Stolworthy**; **Stal(l)ey**.

Stamm Jewish (Ashkenazic): 1. ornamental name from Ger. *Stamm* stem, stock (MHG, OHG *stam*), or perhaps in some cases a short form of names such as *Aronstam* 'stock of AARON' (the first high priest), **Kohenstam** 'stock of the kohenim' (see COHEN), and **Löwenstam** 'stock of the Levites' (see LEVI and LÖWE 2).

2. acronym of the Hebr. phrase *(sofer) Sifre-tora, Tefilim uMezuzot*, an occupational title for a scribe (see SOFER) who wrote scrolls of the law, phylacteries, and mezuzas.
Var.: **Stam**.

Stammer 1. English: from the OE personal name *Stānmǣr*, composed of the elements *stān* stone + *mǣr* famous.

2. English: habitation name from *Stanmer* in Sussex, so called from OE *stān* STONE + *mere* lake.

3. Jewish (Ashkenazic): of unknown origin.
Var. (of 2): **Stanmore** (a place in the former county of Middlesex).
Patr. (from 1): **Stammers**.

Stamp English (Norman): habitation name from *Étampes* in Seine-et-Oise, a placename apparently of Celt. origin; the meaning is uncertain.
Var.: **Stamps**.

Stanbridge English: habitation name from any of various places, for example in Beds. and Hants, so called from OE *stān* STONE + *brycg* BRIDGE, i.e. a bridge built of stone rather than wood.

Stanbury English (Devon): habitation name from *Stanborough* in Devon, so called from OE *stān* STONE + *beorg* hill, tumulus. There is a place called *Stanbury* in W Yorks. near Haworth, but it does not seem to have given rise to the surname.
Vars.: **Stanborough**, **Stanberry**, **Stanbra**.

Stancliffe English (W Yorks.): habitation name, probably from a minor place such as *Stonecliff* or *Stancliffe* in Agbrigg, W Yorks., so called from OE *stān* STONE + *clif* slope (see CLIVE).

Standen English: habitation name from any of various places, for example in Berks., Lancs., and Wilts., so called from OE *stān* STONE + *denu* valley (see DEAN 1), or from another on the Isle of Wight, the second element of which is OE *dūn* hill (see DOWN 1).
Var.: **Standing** (chiefly Sussex; also Lancs., where it is a place name).

Standeven English: one of the several ME nicknames for an independent and resolute person, derived from the verb *stand(en)* to stand (OE *standan*) + *even* firm, balanced (OE *efen*). Others include **Standfast** and **Standwell**.

Standish English: habitation name from a place in Lancs. (now part of Greater Manchester), so called from OE *stān* STONE + *edisc* pasture. There is another place so named in Gloucs., but it does not seem to be the source of the surname.
Vars.: **Standage**, **Standidge**.
Miles Standish *(?1584–1656) was a soldier of fortune, from 1620 military leader of the Pilgrim Fathers. Little is known of his origins and early life, but in his will he claimed to be descended from a leading Catholic family, the Standishes of Standish, Lancs. He also claimed to have been deprived of his inheritance, a claim which has not been confirmed.*

Stanford English: habitation name from any of the various places, for example in Beds., Berks., Essex, Herts., Kent, Norfolk, Northants, Notts., and Worcs., so called from OE *stān* STONE + *ford* FORD.
Vars.: **Stamford**, **Standford**, **Staniford**, **Staniforth**, **Stanyforth**.

Stanger 1. English (Newcastle and Durham): of uncertain origin, probably a deriv. of Northern ME *stang* pole (ON *stongr*). Possible meanings include a topographic name for someone who lived by a pole or stake (cf. STAKES) or an occupational name for someone armed with one. It may alternatively be a nickname for someone who had 'ridden the stang', i.e. been carried on a pole through the streets as an object of derision, in punishment for some misdemeanour. However, this custom is of uncertain antiquity.

2. Jewish (Ashkenazic): of unknown origin.

Stanhope English: habitation name from a place in Co. Durham, so called from OE *stān* STONE + *hop* enclosed valley (see HOPE).
This is the family name of the Earl of Harrington, and was also the name of the Earls of Chesterfield. The first Earl of Chesterfield was a Royalist soldier in the English Civil War. His half-brother was the great-grandfather of the 1st Earl of Harrington.

Stanier English (chiefly Staffs.): occupational name for a stonecutter, one who cut and dressed stone, ME *stanyer* (from *stan* stone (OE *stān*) + a reduced form of *hewer*, agent deriv. of *hew(en)* to cut, chop (OE *hēawan*), assimilated to the agent suffix *-(i)er*).
Vars.: **Stanyer**, **Stonier**.

The surname Stanier *has been found in various forms, but the main family now bearing it can be traced back to John* Stonhewer, *living in Staffs. in 1560. The name has also occurred in the spellings* Stonhewing *and* Stonyer. *Francis Stonyer (1737–1805) changed the spelling of his name to* Stanier.

Stanisławski Polish: from the given name *Stanisław* (composed of the Slav. elements *stan* become + *slav* glory, fame, praise) + the surname suffix *-ski* (see BARANOWSKI).

Cogns.: Czech: **Stanislav**. Russ.: **Stanislavsky**. Jewish (E Ashkenazic): **Stanislavsky** (either an adoption of the Pol. surname or, probably more commonly, a habitation name indicating some connection with the town of *Stanisławów* in the Carpathian foothills.

Dims.: Pol.: **Stanek**, **Stan(i)ecki**, **Stańczyk**, **Staniaszek**, **Staniaszczyk**, **Stanisz**; STACH, **Staszczyk**. Czech: **Staněk**, STACH. Jewish (E Ashkenazic): **Stashevsky**, **Stashevski**, **Stas(h)ewsky**, **Stas(h)ewski** (probably adoptions of the Pol. surnames, but also possibly habitation names from *Staszów* in Poland, whose Yid. name is *Stashev*).

Patrs.: Pol.: **Staniak**; **Stasiak**, **Staszak**; **Stanilewicz**. Croatian: **Stanisavljević**, **Stanić**.

Patrs. (from dims.): Pol.: **Stankiewicz** (also adopted as an E Ashkenazic surname); **Staszkiewicz**, **Staśkiewicz**; **Stańczak**. Croatian: **Stanković**, **Stanišić**.

Habitation names: Pol.: **Staniszewski**, **Staszewski**, **Stasiński**, **Stan(i)kowski**, **Stańczykowski**.

Stanley English: habitation name from any of the various places, for example in Derbys., Co. Durham, Gloucs., Staffs., Wilts., and W Yorks., so called from OE *stān* STONE + *lēah* wood, clearing.

Vars.: **Stanly**, **Standley**, **Stanleigh**.

The Stanley *family who hold the earldom of Derby trace their descent from a companion of William the Conqueror, Adam de Aldithley. Some of his descendants became known by the surname Audley, but another branch took the name Stanley when Adam de Aldithley's grandson married the heiress to the manor of Stanley in Staffs. The founder of the family's fortune was Sir John Stanley (?1350–1414), who married an heiress of W Derby, Lancs. He became Lord Lieutenant of Ireland, and was granted sovereignty over the Isle of Man by Henry IV. His great-grandson, Thomas Stanley (?1435–1504), was created Earl of Derby in 1485 by Henry VII, his wife's son by an earlier marriage.*

Stannard English (E Anglia): from the ME given name *Stanhard*, OE *Stānheard*, composed of the elements *stān* stone + *heard* hardy, brave, strong.

Vars.: **Ston(h)ard**, **Stannett**.

Stansfield English: habitation name from a place in W Yorks., so called either from the gen. case of the OE personal name *Stān* (a byname or short form of the various cpd names with this first element; cf., e.g., STAMMER I and STANNARD) + OE *feld* pasture, open country (see FIELD), or else from a cpd meaning 'open land of the stone', with reference to a monolith. There are other places so called, e.g. in Suffolk, but the distribution suggests that the Yorks. one is the source of the surname.

Var.: **Stansfeld**.

A family of this name trace their descent from Roger de Stansfeld *of Stansfield, Yorks, whose grandson, John de Stansfeld, was living in 1276.*

Stanton English: habitation name from any of the extremely numerous places throughout England so called from OE *stān* STONE + *tūn* enclosure, settlement. Most of them get the name from their situation on stony ground, but in the case of *Stanton* Harcourt in Oxon. and *Stanton* Drew in Avon the reference is to the proximity of prehistoric stone monuments. The name has also sometimes been chosen by Ashkenazic Jews as an Anglicization of various like-sounding Jewish surnames.

Vars.: **Staunton** (places in Gloucs., Herefords., Leics., Notts., Somerset and Worcs.); **Stainton** (from various places in N England, where the first element has been influenced by the cogn. ON *steinn* stone); **Stenton** (see also STENSON).

A family by the name of Staunton *have been established for centuries at Staunton, Notts. This manor is recorded in Domesday Book as belonging to a certain Mauger, and the family claim descent from him. However, the evidence for this claim depends on a 14th-cent. copy of a 12th-cent. charter, and is not reliable.*

Staunton *is also a particularly common surname in Ireland, where it was taken by early settlers who obtained large estates in Co. Mayo. They quickly became assimilated to the Gaelic way of life and formed a clan, one branch of which took the surname* **Mac an Mhílidh** *'son of the warrior', because of its similarity in sound to the name of their ancester* Milo de Stanton. *The surname has also been Gaelicized* **Stundún**, *and it is still very common in Mayo and Galway.*

Staple English: topographic name for someone who lived near a boundary post, ME *staple* (OE *stapol*), or habitation name from some place named with this word, as for example *Staple* in Kent or *Staple* Fitzpaine in Somerset.

Var.: **Staples**.

Stapleton English and Irish: habitation name from any of the various places, as for example in Cumb., Gloucs., Herefords., Leics., Shrops., Somerset, and N and W Yorks., so called from OE *stapol* post (see STAPLE) + *tūn* enclosure, settlement.

Var.: **Stapylton**.

The surname Stapleton *is now particularly common in Ireland. Some members of the family adopted the Gael. surnames* **Galldubh** *'Black Stranger' and* **Mac an Ghaill** *'Son of the Stranger', which have in turn been re-Anglicized as* GALL.

Stapley English: habitation name from *Stapeley* in Ches. or *Stapely* in Hants, so called from OE *stapol* post (see STAPLE) + *lēah* wood, clearing. The reference may have been to a place where timber was got for posts.

Starikov Russian: patr. from the nickname *Starik* 'Old Man' (from *stary* old).

Cogns. (not patrs.): Pol.: **Starski**, **Starzycki**, **Staroń**. Czech: **Starý**. Jewish (Ashkenazic): **Starik**, **Starski**.

Cogns. (patrs.): Bulg.: **Starov**. Jewish (Ashkenazic): **Starikov**, **Staricoff**.

Dims.: Pol.: **Starek**, **Starzyk**, **Starczyk**. Czech: **Stárek**. Ukr.: **Starshenko**. Croatian: **Starčević** (patr.). Ger. (of Slav. origin): **Staroske**.

Habitation names: Pol.: **Starzyński**, **Starczewski**.

Stark N English and Scots: nickname for a stern, determined, or physically strong person, from ME *stark* firm, unyielding (OE *stearc*, ON *sterkr*). The Continental cogns. have the sense 'strong', 'brave'.

Cogns.: Ger.: **Star(c)k(e)**, **Stärck**, **Starker**, **Starkmann**. Flem.: **(De) Star(c)ke**. Du.: **Sterk**. Jewish (Ashkenazic): **S(h)tark(er)**, **S(h)tarkman(n)**.

Dims.: Eng.: **Starkie**, **Starkey**. Ger.: **Stärkel**, **Stärkle**.

Patrs.: Eng.: **Starcks**; **Starkings**. Flem.: **Stercken(s)**, **Sterckx**, **Ster(c)kmans**.

Starling English: nickname from some fancied resemblance to the bird, ME *starling* (OE *stær(ling)*; for the suffix, cf. CHAMBERLAIN).

Cogn.: Norw., Dan.: **Stæhr**.

Starosta Polish and Czech: status name for the headman of a village or district, a deriv. of *stary* old (cf. STARIKOV).

Var.: Pol.: **Starostecki**.

Starr English: nickname from ME *sterre*, *starre* star (OE *steorra*). The word was also used in a transferred sense of a patch of white hair on the forehead of a horse, and so perhaps the name denoted someone with a streak of white hair. It is possibly also a house name, for someone who lived at a house distinguished by the sign of a star.

Var.: **Starman** (also 'servant of S.').

Cogns.: Ger.: STERN. Du.: **Van de Star**, **Van der Ster**, **Verster**. Jewish (Ashkenazic): STERN, **Shtern** (ornamental); **Sztern** (a Pol. spelling).

Cpds (ornamental, except where indicated): Swed.: **Stjernqvist** ('star twig'); **Stjernström** ('star river'). Jewish: **Sternbach**, **Sternbuch** ('star stream'); **Sternbaum**, **Szterenbojm** ('star tree'); **S(h)ternberg**, **Sterenberg**, **Sternberger** ('(dweller on a) star hill'); **Sternblitz** ('star lightning'); **Sternfeld** ('star field'); **S(z)ternfinkel**, **Sternfinkiel** ('star sparkle'); **Sternglanz** ('star radiance'); **Sternglass**, **Shterenglass** ('star glass'); **Sternheim** ('star homestead'); **Sternhell** ('star bright'); **Sternhertz**, **Shterngartz** ('star heart', the latter from Slav. regions lacking /h/); **Sternklar** ('star clear'); **Sternkuker** ('star gazer', apparently a nickname based on some now irrecoverable minor incident); **Sternli(e)b** ('star love'); **Sternlicht** ('star light'); **Sternschein** ('star shine'); **Sternschuss**, **Shternshuss**, **Sternshos** ('star shot'); **Sternt(h)al**, **Sterental** ('star valley'); **Ster(e)nzis**, **Szternzys** ('star sweet').

Start English: habitation name from any of the various minor places, for example in Devon, so called from OE *steort* tail, apparently in the transferred sense of a promontory or a spur of a hill.

Vars.: **Starte**, **Stert**, **Sturt**; **Starrett**, **Sterritt** (N Ireland).

Cogns.: Ger.: **Stertz**. Low Ger.: **Ster(d)t**, **Steert**.

Dim.: Ger.: **Stertzel**.

Startin Scots (Aberdeen): habitation name from *Stirton* near Cupar in the former county of Fife. The placename is of unknown origin.

Var.: **Stirton**.

Šťastný Czech: from a given name representing a Czech vocab. word meaning 'happy', 'fortunate', or 'lucky', used as a translation of L FELIX.

Cogn.: Pol.: **Szczęsny**.

Patrs.: Pol.: **Szczęśnowicz**; **Szczęśniak**, **Szcześniak** (also nicknames meaning 'lucky fellow').

Patr. (from a dim.): Pol.: **Szczęścikowicz**.

Statham English: habitation name from a place in Ches., so called from the dat. pl. *stæðum* of OE *stæð* landing stage (see STAIT), i.e. 'at the landing stages'.

Stauche German: nickname for someone who was distinguished by some peculiarity of dress, from MHG *stūche*, a term used to denote both a type of wide sleeve and a headcovering (OHG *stūhha*, denoting any wide, flat object).

Vars.: **Stauch**, **Steichen**.

Staude German: topographic name for someone who lived by a patch of uncleared dense undergrowth, from MHG *stūde* thicket, wilderness (OHG *stūda*).

Vars.: **Staudt**, **Stäuder**, **Stüde(r)**.

Cogns.: Low Ger.: **Stüdemann**, **Stühmann**.

Dims.: Ger.: **Stäudle**, **Stüdle**, **Steidle**, **Steudle**.

Stauffer German: 1. occupational name for a maker or seller of beakers or mugs, from an agent deriv. of Ger. *Stauf* beaker, stoop (MHG, OHG *stouf*).

2. habitation name from any of the various minor places named with this word; the reference is to hills thought to resemble a beaker in shape.

Vars.: **Staufer(t)**.

Stawski Polish: topographic name for someone who lived by a pond, from Pol. *staw* pond + *-ski* suffix of local surnames (see BARANOWSKI).

Vars.: **Stawicki**, **Stawiak**.

Habitation names: **Stawiński**, **Stawowski**, **Stawiszyński**.

Stead English (chiefly W Yorks.): 1. habitation name from *Stead* in W Yorks., or from some other place taking its name from OE *stede* estate, farm, place.

2. from ME *steed* stud horse, stallion (OE *stēda*), applied as a nickname to a lusty person or as an occupational name to someone responsible for looking after stallions.

Vars.: **Steed(e)**, **Stede**, **Steeds**. (Of 2 only): **Ste(a)dman**; **Steedman** (chiefly Scotland); **Stedmont**.

Cogns. (of 1): Du.: **Stad**; **Steeman**.

Stebbing English (E Anglia): topographic name for someone who lived in a clearing in woodland, from ME *stebbing*, *stubbing* clearing (OE *stybbing*, a deriv. of *stubb* tree stump; see STUBBE), or habitation name from some minor place deriving its name from this element.

Vars.: **Stebbings**, **Stubbin(g)s**.

Steckler Jewish (Ashkenazic): occupational name for a glass worker or glazier, from Russ. *steklo* glass (cf. SZKLAR) + the Ger., Yid. agent suffix *-er*.

Vars.: **Stekler**, **Steckl**, **Steckelman**, **Steckelmacher**.

Steel English and Scots: nickname for someone considered as hard and durable as steel, or metonymic occupational name for a foundry worker, from ME *stele* steel (OE *stȳle*). The name has also been used as an Anglicization of the Jewish forms listed below.

Var.: **Steele**.

Cogns.: Ger.: **Stahl(er)**, **Stähler**. Du., Flem.: **Staal**. Dan., Norw.: **Stål**, **Staal**. Swed.: **Ståhl(e)**.

Dims.: Ger.: **Stählin**, **Stäheli(n)**.

Patr.: Eng.: **Steels**.

Cpd (ornamental): Swed.: **Stå(h)lberg** ('steel hill').

Steeples English (E Midlands): topographic name for someone who lived by a tall tower, ME *stepel* (OE *stēpel*). The term was first used of a church spire in the 15th cent.; this sense is unlikely to lie behind many examples of the surname.

Steer English: nickname for a truculent person or metonymic occupational name for someone who was responsible for tending bullocks, from ME *steer* bullock (OE *stēor*).

Vars.: **Steere**, **Stear**; **Ste(a)rman** (occupational only).

Cogns.: Ger.: **Stier**. Low Ger.: **Stiehr**, **Steer**. Flem., Du.: **Stier**. Jewish (Ashkenazic): **Stier(man)** (reason for adoption uncertain).

Dim.: Ger.: **Stierle**.

Patrs.: Eng.: **Steers**, **Stears**.

Steiger German: 1. topographic name for someone who lived by a path running up a hillside, from an agent deriv. of Ger. *Steig* steep path or track (MHG, OHG *stīc*, from OHG *stīgan* to climb).

2. topographic name for someone who lived by a plank bridge, from a deriv. of MHG *stec* (OHG *steg*, from the same verb as in 1).

Vars.: **Staiger**, **Steg(n)er**; **Steg(e)mann**.

Cogns.: Low Ger.: **Steeg**, **Stieger**; **Testeegen**, **Zumsteeg**. Fris.: **Stegena**. Flem., Du.: **Van der Steeg(en)**, **Versteeg**, **Stegeman**. Jewish (Ashkenazic): **Ste(i)g(man)**.

Stein 1. German and Jewish (Ashkenazic): cogn. of STONE.

2. Scots: from a contracted form of the given name STEPHEN.

Vars. (of 2): Sc.: **Steen, Stain.**

Patr. (from 2): Sc.: **Steenson.** See also STENSON.

Cpds (of 1): See STONE.

Steinmetz German and Jewish (Ashkenazic): occupational name for a mason or worker in stone, Ger. *Steinmetz* stonemason (MHG *steinmetze*, OHG *steinmezzo*, a cpd of *stein* STONE and *mezzo* MASON).

Vars.: Ger.: **Stainmetz, Stamitz.** Jewish: **Stienmetz, Stienmets.**

Dims.: Ger.: **Steinmetzel, Steinmeissel, Steinmassel.**

A family of musicians by the name of Stamitz, *established in Mannheim, originated in Maribor, Slovenia, and moved to Mannheim via Bohemia. Martin Stamitz settled in Pardubice in Bohemia in 1665. The best-known member of the family was his son Karl Philipp Stamitz (1745–1801).*

Steinweg German: habitation name from an unidentified place named with the OHG elements *stein* STONE + *weg* path (see WAY).

Var.: **Steinway** (Anglicized).

The well-known firm of piano-makers called Steinway *was founded by Heinrich* Steinweg *(1797–1871) in Brunswick in 1835. He was born in Wolfshagen, Germany, and in 1849 moved with his three sons to New York, changing his name to* Steinway. *The firm expanded with new designs by Theodore Steinway (1825–89) and remained in family ownership until 1972.*

Stejskal Czech: nickname for a miserable, unhappy, or complaining person, a deriv. of the verb *stejskat, stýskat* to be unhappy, lonely, or grumpy.

Stella Italian: from It. *stella* star (L *stella*). In most cases it probably derives from a medieval given name or nickname, but it may also have been a house name for someone who lived at a house distinguished by this sign, or a topographic name for someone who lived at a place from which roads radiated out in various different directions.

Vars.: It.: **Stelli; La Stella** (Apulia).

Cogns.: Fr.: **Estoile, Étoile; Détoile, Delétoile.** Sp.: **Estrella.** Port.: **Estrela.**

Dims.: It.: **Stellin(i), Stellino.**

Augs.: It.: **Stellon(i).**

Pej.: It.: **Stellacci.**

Stellmacher German: occupational name for a cartwright, Ger. *Stellmacher*, from MHG *stelle* carriage (originally 'frame', 'chassis') + *macher* maker. The term originated in Silesia and spread across northern Germany during the Middle Ages, though it never displaced WAGNER in the south.

Vars.: **Stellmach, Stallmach.**

Cogns.: Pol.: **Stelmach, Stelmasiak.** Ukr.: **Stelmach.** Jewish (Ashkenazic): **Stel(l)mach.**

Dims.: Pol.: **Stelmaszczyk.** Ukr.: **Stelmashenko.** Beloruss.: **Stelmashonok.**

Stendal Jewish (Ashkenazic): probably a habitation name from a place near Magdeburg so called from MLG *steen* STONE + *dal* valley (see DALE).

Vars.: **Stendahl, Stendhal, Stendel.**

Stenhouse Scots: habitation name from a former barony near Falkirk, whose name has the same origin as STONEHOUSE.

Stenning English: habitation name from *Steyning* in Sussex, so called from OE *Stǣningas* 'people of *Stān*', a byname or short form of the various cpd personal names with the first element *stān* stone.

Stenson English: 1. patr. from a contracted form of the given name STEPHEN (cf. STEIN 2).

2. habitation name from a place in Derbys., recorded in Domesday Book as *Steintune*, later as *Steineston*, from the ON personal name *Steinn* 'Stone' + OE *tūn* enclosure, settlement.

Vars. (of 1): **Stinson, Stim(p)son.** (Of 2): **Stenton** (see also STANTON).

Stephen English: from the ME given name *Stephen, Steven* (Gk *Stephanos* 'Crown'). This was a popular name throughout Christendom in the Middle Ages, having been borne by the first Christian martyr, stoned to death at Jerusalem three years after the death of Christ.

Vars.: **Steven, Stiven, Steffen, Steffan.** See also STEIN 2.

Cogns.: Fr.: **Stephan, Stéphane; Estienne, Étienne.** Prov.: **Estiévan(t), Etiévant, Tiévant, Thevan(d); Estéban, Eséva, Estèbe, Estève, Et(h)ève, Etiève, Etiemble, Thièble.** It.: **Stefano, Stifano, Stephano, St(i)evano; Stef(f)ani, Stifani, Stephani, Stevani, Stivani, Schivani, Stefi, Steno.** Sp.: **Esteban.** Cat.: **Esteva, Esteve.** Port.: **Estêvão.** Rum.: **Stefan.** Ger.: **Stephan; Stöffen** (Bavaria). Low Ger.: **Steven, Steffen.** Flem.: **Stevaen.** Ger. (of Slav. origin): **Steppan, Steppuhn, Schep(p)an(g), Schippan(g), Zschepang, Schoppan.** Czech: **Štefan; Štěpán.** Pol.: **Stefanski; Szczepański.**

Dims.: Fr.: **Stevenet, Thévenet, Theuvenet, Thouv(en)et, Thevet, Thivet, Touvet, Étiennet, Thenet; Theuveney, Étienney; Thévenot, Thouvenot, Thevot, Thieblot, Étiennot, T(h)ienot, Thénot, Tenot; Thevenon, Thouvignon, T(h)enon; Stevenin, Thévenin, Thouvenin, Thiévin, Thevin, Thieblin; The(u)veny, Théveny; Stevenel, Théveneau, Thouvenel.** It.: **Stefanelli, Stifanelli, Stephanelli, Stevanelli, Stivanelli, Stephanello, Stef(f)anini, Stevanini, Stivanini, Stef(an)utti, Stefanutto.** Ger.: **Steff(l),** STIEFEL. Flem., Du.: **Sties.** Ger. (of Slav. origin): **Stepke, Steffke, Steffek, Staffke, Stief(ke), Schep(p)e, Scheppe, Tschepe, Tschäpe, Schäp(k)e, Zschäpe, Schepke, Schip(p)ke, Schipek, Schippig, Schoppe, Schoppa, Schöpe, Tschöp(p)e.** Czech: **Štěpánek; Štefek; Štěpnicka, Štěch; Štícha.** Pol.: **Stefanek, Stefanczyk; Szczepanik, Szczepanek.** Ukr.: **Stepanenko, Steshenko, Stepyuk, Stetsyuk, Stepura, Stetsyura.** Beloruss.: **Stepanets, Stachvanyonok.**

Aug.: It.: **Stefanoni.**

Pejs.: Fr.: **Estévenard, Stiévenard, Stiévenart, Thév(en)ard, Thénard, Thénau(l)t.**

Patrs.: Eng.: **Stephens, Stevens, Steffens; Stephenson, Stephinson, Stevenson, Stevinson, Steverson;** STENSON. It.: **De Stefani(s).** Sp.: **Estébanez.** Cat.: **Estévez.** Port.: **Esteves.** Rum.: **Stefanescu.** Low Ger.: **Stevens, Steffens(en).** Fris.: **Stevinga.** Flem., Du.: **Stevens.** Dan., Norw.: **Steffensen, Stefansen, Stephensen, Stephansen.** Russ.: **Stepanov.** Bulg.: **Stefanov.** Pol.: **Stefanowicz; Stefaniak; Szczepanowicz; Szczepaniak.** Lithuanian: **Stepanaitis.** Armenian: **Stapanian.** Croatian: **Stepanović, Stefanović, Stevanović; Šćepanović.**

Patrs. (from dims.): Russ.: **Stepanchikov, Stepanychev, Step(an)ichev, Step(an)ishchev, Stepunin, Stepynin, Stepurin, Stepykin, Stepyryov, Stepulev, Styopushkin, Styokhin.** Ukr.: **Stepovich, Stetskiv.** Pol.: **Stefankiewicz; Szczepankiewicz.** Bulg.: **Penev.** Croatian: **Stev(ov)ić.**

Habitation names: Pol.: **Stefanowski; Szczepanowski.**

The var. Stiven *arose in Scotland at the beginning of the 19th cent. A certain John Stephen of Charleston, near Glamis Castle, began to keep a journal in 1780 under the spelling* Stephen, *but by the time he came to write his last entry in 1830 he was signing himself John Stiven.*

Stępień Polish: of uncertain origin, possibly an occupational name for a herbalist or other user of a pestle and mortar, from Pol. *stępor* mortar.

Vars.: **Stępiński, Stępni(a)k.**

Habitation names: **Stępniewski, Stępczyński, Stęp(k)owski, Stęplewski.**

Štěrba Czech: probably a nickname for someone with a front tooth missing, from Czech *štěrba* gap.

Cogns.: Pol.: **Szczerba, Szczerbiak**.

Stern 1. German and Jewish (Ashkenazic): cogn. of STARR.

2. English: nickname for a severe person, from ME *stern(e)* strict, austere (OE *styrne*).

Vars. (of 2): Eng.: **Sterne, Stearn(e)**.

Patrs. (from 2): Eng.: **Ste(a)rns**.

The novelist Laurence Sterne *(1713–68), author of* Tristram Shandy *(1759), was born into a poor family in Clonmel, Co. Tipperary. His father was a low-ranking English army officer who had married a poor Irishwoman in Flanders. His grandfather, however, was Archbishop of York, and it was around this city that Sterne's career in the church was centred.*

Štětina Czech: 1. nickname for a shoemaker, from the vocab. word *štětina* bristle, thread (i.e. the thread used to sew shoes with, which was made from bristles).

2. nickname for a person with thick, spiky hair (from the same word as in 1).

Steventon English: habitation name from *Steventon* in Berks., Hants, and Shrops., or *Stevington* in Beds. and Essex, probably all originally meaning 'settlement associated with *Stīf(a)*'. The surname is most common in Birmingham, where it probably derives from the Shrops. placename.

Stewart Scots: occupational name for an administrative official, from ME *stiward*, OE *stigweard*, *stīweard*, a cpd of *stig* house(hold) + *weard* guardian (see WARD). In OE times this title was used of an officer controlling the domestic affairs of a household, esp. of the royal household; after the Conquest it was also used more widely as the native equivalent of SENESCHAL for the steward of a manor or manager of an estate.

Vars.: **St(e)uart; Steward** (England).

Patrs.: **Stewartson, Stewardson**.

Stuart *or* Stewart *is the surname of one of the great families of Scotland, the royal family of Scotland from the 14th cent., and of England from 1603, when James VI of Scotland acceded to the English throne as James I. They remained the royal family through many vicissitudes to the death of Queen Anne in 1714, and thereafter were Pretenders to the throne, instigating rebellions against the Hanoverians in 1715 and 1745. The surname is derived from the hereditary office of steward, which family members first held under the lords of Dol in Brittany in the 11th cent., although they did not acquire the surname until the 13th cent. in Scotland. Their Breton ancestor Alan was living c.1045; fourth in descent from him was Walter FitzAlan (d. 1177), who was created Great Steward of Scotland by King David I of Scotland. The Stuarts became the ruling family of Scotland through the marriage of the sixth Great Steward, Walter (1293–1326), to the daughter of Robert Bruce in 1315. Their son Robert (1316–90) became King Robert II of Scotland in 1371. Their claim to the English throne arose through the marriage of James IV of Scotland to a daughter of Henry VII. There were many minor branches of the family left in Britain after the flight of James II in 1688, but not every bearer of the surname can claim relationship with the royal house, even in Scotland. Every great house in medieval England and Scotland had its steward, and in many cases the office gave rise to a hereditary surname. The fall of the house of Stuart in Britain, conversely, led to the establishment of several highly placed branches bearing this surname in Continental Europe, which are in most cases related to the old Scottish royal family.*

Stibor Czech: from an OCzech given name composed of the elements *cti*, gen. of *čest* honour + *bor* warrior.

Var.: **Ctibor**.

Stiddolph English (Northumb.): from the OE personal name *Stīðwulf*, composed of the elements *stīð* stiff, hard + *wulf* wolf.

Var.: **Stidolph**.

Stiefel 1. German and Jewish (Ashkenazic): metonymic occupational name for a maker of boots or nickname for someone who wore boots, from Ger. *Stiefel*, Yid. *shtivl* boot (MHG *stivel*, OHG *stival*, from LL *aestivale* light shoe, a deriv. of *aestas* summer).

2. German: from a given name, a dim. of STEPHEN.

Vars. (of 1): Jewish: **Shtivel; Stiefler, Stiffelman, Stivelman** (occupational).

Stiff English: nickname for someone who had difficulty in bending, from ME *stif* rigid, inflexible (OE *stīf*). The term was also used in a transferred sense of character (generally in the approving sense 'resolute', 'steadfast') from the 12th cent., and this use may lie behind many examples of the surname.

Stigand English: from an ON personal name composed of the element *stígr* path, way + the suffix *-and* (cf. WIGGIN).

Vars.: **Stigant; Styan**.

Patrs.: **Stiggants, Stiggins; Styants, Styance**.

Still 1. English and German: nickname for a placid person, from ME, MHG *still* calm, quiet (OE *stille*, OHG *stilli*).

2. English: topographic name for someone who lived by a fish trap in a river, ME *still*, *stell* (OE *stiell*).

Vars. (of 1 and 2): Eng.: **Stille, Stillman**. (Of 1 only): Ger.: **Stille, Stiller(t)**. (Of 2 only): Eng.: **Stiller, Stell**.

Cogns. (of 1): Jewish (Ashkenazic): **Shtil(l)(er), Stil(l)man, Shtilerman**.

Stillingfleet English: habitation name from a place in E Yorks., recorded in Domesday Book as *Steflingefled* 'stream (OE *flēot*; see FLEET) of the people of **Stȳfel*', a dim. of the attested byname *Stūf* (of uncertain origin).

This was the name of a family who came originally from Stillingfleet, Yorks. Members included an author and botanist, Benjamin Stillingfleet *(1702–71). It was to him, and not to a woman, that the term 'blue-stocking' was first applied.*

Stinchcombe English: habitation name from a village in Gloucs., recorded in the 12th cent. as *Stintescombe*, from the dial. term *stint* sandpiper + *cumb* narrow valley (see COOMBE).

Stirk English: nickname for someone resembling a bullock or metonymic occupational name for someone who had charge of bullocks, from ME *stirk* bullock (OE *styr(i)c*, *steorc*).

Stirling Scots: habitation name from the city in central Scotland, recorded in the 12th cent. as *Strevelin*. The name is of problematic etymology, perhaps from a river name.

Var.: **Sterling**.

Stirrup English (Lancs.): 1. possibly a metonymic occupational name for a maker of stirrup irons or stirrup leathers (or both), from OE *stīgrāp* stirrup (a cpd of *stīgan* to rise + *rāp* rope). However, there is no evidence that stirrup-making had any special status as an occupation in the Middle Ages.

2. habitation name from *Styrrup* in Northants, which is probably so called from OE *stīgrāp* stirrup because of a stirrup-shaped ridge near which it stands.

Stirzaker English (Lancs.): habitation name from *Stirzacre* in the parish of Garstang, N Lancs., so called from the gen. case of the ON personal name *Styrr* + OE *æcer* cultivated land (see ACKER) or the ON cogn. *akr*.

Vars.: **Stirsacre**, **Sturzaker**, **Stursaker**, **Stersaker**, **Sturraker**, **Staziker**.

Stobbart English (Northumb.): from a medieval given name. This is first recorded in Domesday Book as *Stubart*. It is probably a late OE formation from *stubb* stump, which seems to have been in use as a byname (see STUBBE), + *-heard* hardy, brave, strong.

Vars.: **Stobart**, **Stubbert**.

Stobie Scots: habitation name from *Stobo* near Peebles in S Scotland, so called from OE *stubb* tree stump + *holh* hollow (see HOLE) or *halh* nook, recess (see HALE 1).

Var.: **Stobo**.

Stock English: probably for the most part a topographic name for someone who lived near the uprooted trunk or stump of a large tree, OE *stocc*. In some cases the reference may be to a primitive foot-bridge over a stream consisting of a felled tree trunk. Some early examples without prepositions may point to a nickname for a stout, 'stocky' man or a metonymic occupational name for a keeper of punishment stocks.

Vars.: **Stocke**, **Stocks**; **Stocker**; **Stockman**.

Cogns.: Ger.: **Stock(en)**, **Stöcken**; **Stocker**, **Stöcker**; **Stockmann**, **Stöckmann**. Flem., Du.: **Stok**, STOKER, **Stockman**.

Dims.: Ger.: **Stökel**, **Stöckle**.

Stockdale English: habitation name from a valley in Cumb. and N Yorks., so called from OE *stocc* tree trunk (see STOCK) + *dæl* valley (see DALE).

Vars.: **Stogdale**, **Stockdill**.

Stockley English: habitation name from any of various places, for example in Devon, Co. Durham, and Staffs., called *Stockleigh* or *Stockley*, from OE *stocc* tree trunk (see STOCK) + *lēah* wood, clearing.

Vars.: **Stockleigh**, **Stokel(e)y**.

Stockton English: habitation name from any of the places, for example in Ches., Co. Durham, Herts., Norfolk, Shrops., Warwicks., Wilts., Worcs., and N and W Yorks., so called from OE *stocc* tree trunk (see STOCK) or *stoc* dependent settlement (see STOKE) + *tūn* enclosure, settlement. It is not possible to distinguish between the two first elements on the basis of early forms.

A family of this name was established in America by an English Quaker, Richard Stockton, *in 1656. He bought large tracts of land around Princeton, New Jersey, and founded an estate on which his great-grandson, Richard Stockton (1730–81), a leading colonial lawyer and one of the signers of the Declaration of Independence, was born.*

Stockwell English: habitation name from a place now in S London, so called from OE *stocc* tree trunk, plank bridge (see STOCK) + *well(a)* spring, stream (see WELL).

Stoddart English (Northumb.): occupational name for a breeder or keeper of horses, from OE *stōd* stud (see STUDD) or *stott* inferior kind of horse (see STOTT) + *hierde* herdsman, keeper (see HEARD). There is a difficulty in deriving this name from OE *stōd* in that *stud* is not recorded in the sense 'collection of horses bred by one person' until the 17th cent.; before that it denoted a place where horses were kept for breeding, but that sense does not combine naturally with 'herdsman'.

Vars.: **Stod(h)art**, **Stoddard**, **Studart**, **Studd(e)ard**, **Studdert**, **Stiddard**, **Stothard**, **Stothart**, **Stothert**, **Stuttard**.

Stoke English: habitation name from any of the numerous places throughout England named from ME *stoke* (OE *stoc*). The exact sense in individual cases is not clear; it seems to have meant originally merely 'place', and to have been used mainly for an outlying hamlet or dependent settlement.

Vars.: **Stokes**, **Stoak(s)**, **Stook(es)**, STOKER.

Stoker 1. English: habitation name, a var. of STOKE.

2. Flemish and Dutch: cogn. of STOCK.

3. Scots: occupational name for a trumpeter, from Gael. *stocaire*, an agent deriv. of *stoc* Gaelic trumpet. The name is borne by a sept of the McFarlanes.

Patrs. (from 3): **McInstocker**, **McStoker** (Gael. **Mac an Stocaire**).

Stokoe English: habitation name from *Stockhow* in Cumb. The placename is first attested in 1581 as *Stackay*; in the absence of earlier forms it is not possible to suggest an etymology with any confidence.

Stokowski Polish: habitation name from a place named with Pol. *stok* hillside, slope + *-ów* possessive suffix, with the addition of *-ski* suffix of local surnames (see BARANOWSKI). It may also be a topographic name for someone who lived on a hillside.

Stolarski Polish and Jewish (E Ashkenazic): occupational name for a joiner, Pol. *stolarz* (a calque of Ger. TISCHLER, from Pol. *stół* table), with the addition of the surname suffix *-ski* (see BARANOWSKI).

Vars.: Pol.: **Stolarz**. Jewish: **Stol(i)ar**; **Stol(l)er**, **Stolersky** (from E Yid. *stolyer*).

Cogn.: Russ.: **Stolyarov** (patr.).

Dims.: Pol.: **Stolarek**, **Stolarczyk**.

Stolz German and Jewish (Ashkenazic): nickname for a proud or haughty person, from Ger. *stolz*, Yid. *shtolts* proud.

Vars.: Ger.: **Stoltz(e)**, **Stolze**. Jewish: **Shtolzer**; **Sztolc** (a Pol. spelling).

Cogns.: Low Ger.: **Stolt(e)**, **Stoldt**, **Stolter**. Swed.: **Stolt**.

Dims.: Ger.: **Stöl(t)zel**.

Patrs.: Low Ger.: **Stolten**, **Stolting**, **Stölting**.

Stone English: from OE *stān* stone, in any of several uses. It is most commonly a topographic name, for someone who lived either on stony ground or by a notable outcrop of rock or a stone boundary-marker or monument, but it is also found as a metonymic occupational name for someone who worked in stone, a mason or stonecutter. There are various places in S and W England named with this word, for example in Bucks., Gloucs., Hants, Kent, Somerset, Staffs., and Worcs., and the surname may also be a habitation name from any of these. The form *Stone* is also found as an Anglicization of the various Jewish surnames listed below, including compounds.

Vars.: **Stones**; **Stoner**, **Stenner**; **Stoneman** (Devon); ASTON.

Cogns.: Ger.: STEIN, **Steiner(t)**, **Stein(e)mann**, **Steimann**. Low Ger.: **Steen(mann)**, **Stehn(mann)**, **Stehmann**. Fris.: **Steenstra**. Flem., Du.: **Van (den) Steen**, **Steenman**. Swed.: **Ste(e)n**, **Stehn**, **Stenman**; **Stenius** (Latinized). Jewish (Ashkenazic): STEIN, **Sztajn** (a Pol. spelling), **Sztein**; **Steiner**, **Steinman**, **Sztejnman** (apparently occupational); **Steinig(er)** ('stony').

Dims.: Ger.: **Steinl(e)**, **Steindl**. Low Ger.: **Steinchen**, **Steinke**, **Steine(c)ke**, **Steinicke**, **Steenke(n)**, **Stehnke**.

Cpds (ornamental): Swed.: **Stenbäck** ('stone stream'); **Stenberg** ('stone hill'); **Stenholm** ('stone island'); **Stenmark** ('stone territory'); **Stenqvist** ('stone twig'); **Stenström** ('stone river'). Jewish: **Steinbach** ('stone stream'); **Steinbaum**, **Sztajnbaum**, **Sztejnbaum** ('stone tree'); **S(z)teinberg**, **Sztajnberg**, **Sztejnberg**, **Steinberger** ('(dweller on a) stone hill'); **Steinfeld**, **Stienfeld** ('stone field'); **Steingart(en)** ('stone garden'); **Steingold** ('stone gold'; cf. GOLDSTEIN); **Steinhard(t)** ('stone hard'); **Steinher(t)z** ('stone heart'); **Steinhorn** ('stone horn'); **Steinreich** ('stone rich'); **Steinwurzel, Steinwercel** ('stone root').

Thomas Stone *(1743–87), one of the signatories of the Declaration of Independence, was born into a prosperous family at Poynton Manor, Maryland. He was a descendant of William Stone (b. c.1603), who had emigrated to Virginia from Northants in England around 1628 and later became governor of Maryland.*

Stoneham English: habitation name from a pair of villages in Hants, so called from OE *stān* STONE + *hām* homestead.

Var.: **Stonham** (a place in Suffolk).

Stonehouse 1. English: topographic name (from OE *stān* STONE + *hūs* HOUSE for someone who lived in a house built of stone, something of a rarity in the Middle Ages, or habitation name from a place so named, for example in Devon and Gloucs. See also STENHOUSE.

2. Jewish (Ashkenazic): Anglicized form of **Steinhaus** 'stone house', a topographic name for someone who lived in a house made of this material; see STONE.

Var. (of 2): **Steinhouse**.

Stonor English: habitation name from a place in Oxon., so called from OE *stān* STONE + *ōra* slope (see ORR 3).

The Stonors *are an ancient family who lived at Stonor Park, Oxon., for over 800 years. They hold the title Baron Camoys, which was in abeyance for some 400 years, from 1426 until it was regranted in 1839. Their earliest ancestors include Richard* de Stonore, *mentioned in records 1177–85, and Ralph de Camoys (d. 1259).*

Stopford English: habitation name from *Stockport* in Greater Manchester, which used to be locally pronounced /'stɒpfɔ:d/. The placename is recorded in the 12th cent. as *Stokeport*, probably from OE *stoc* hamlet, dependent settlement (see STOKE) + *port* market place (see PORT). The confusion of the second element with *ford* appears in 1288, and the form *Stopford* is recorded in 1347.

Vars.: **Stopforth, Stop(p)ard, Stopper**.

Storer English: occupational name for an official in charge of dispensing provisions in a great house or monastery, or who collected rents paid in kind, from an agent deriv. of ME *stor* provisions, supplies (an aphetic form of OF *estor*, from the verb *estorer* to lay in, store, L *instaurāre* renew, replace). The word *stor* was also used in the Middle Ages for livestock, and the surname may sometimes have denoted a keeper of animals.

Vars.: **Storrar, Storah, Storror, Storrow; Stores**.

Storey N English: from the ON byname *Stóri* (from *storr* big, large), also used as a given name in N England in the early Middle Ages.

Vars.: **Story; Stor(r)ie** (Scotland); **Storr** (from *storr* 'big' used as a nickname).

Stork English: nickname for a thin man with long legs, from the bird (OE *storc*), or perhaps occasionally a house name from a house distinguished by the sign of a stork.

Cogns.: Ger., Jewish (Ashkenazic): **Storch** (one of the many ornamental surnames taken from bird names). Low Ger.: **Storck**.

Dims.: Ger.: **Störchel, Störkel**.

Storm English, Low German, Flemish/Dutch, and Danish/Norwegian: nickname for a man of blustery temperament, from OE, OSax. *storm*, ON *stormr* storm.

Vars.: Eng.: **Storme**. Flem., Du.: **Van den Storm**.

Cogns.: Ger.: **Sturm**. Jewish (Ashkenazic): **S(h)turm** (reason for adoption unknown).

Dims.: Ger.: **Stürmle; Sturm(l)i** (Switzerland).

Patrs.: Eng.: **Stormes**. Flem., Du.: **Storms**.

Stott English: nickname from ME *stott* steer, bullock (OE *stott* inferior kind of horse), or metonymic occupational name for a keeper of the animals. The term was also occasionally used in ME of a horse or of a heifer (and so as a term of abuse for a woman), and these senses may also lie behind some examples of the surname.

The earliest known bearer of the name is Gamell Stot, *who in 1165 failed an ordeal by water in Yorks. For at least the last 400 years the surname has been largely confined to a relatively small area around Rochdale, Lancs., where one resident in 50 bears this name at the present day. A much smaller group is found in Somerset, probably of independent origin.*

Stourton English: habitation name from any of various places, in Staffs., Warwicks., and Wilts., so called from their situation on different rivers *Stour* + OE *tūn* enclosure, settlement. The river name is of Gmc origin, and seems to have originally meant 'Strong', 'Powerful'.

This is the name of a family whose earliest known ancestor is William de Stourton, *living in 1325. Their name is derived from the manor of Stourton in Wilts. They hold the baronies of Mowbray, Segrave, and Stourton.*

Stout English: 1. nickname for a brave or powerfully built man, from ME *stout* steadfast (an aphetic form of OF *estout*, from a Gmc cogn. of STOLZ).

2. from the ON byname *Stútr* 'Gnat', denoting a small and insignificant person.

3. possibly also a habitation name from a minor place named with the OE element **stūt* stumpy hillock, which is found as a component in various Devon placenames.

Vars.: **Stoute, St(o)utt**.

Stow 1. English: habitation name from any of the numerous places, for example in Cambs., Essex, Gloucs., Lincs., Norfolk, Shrops., and Suffolk, so called from OE *stōw*, a word akin to *stoc* (see STOKE), with the specialized meaning 'meeting place', frequently referring to a holy place or church. Places in Bucks., Cambs., Lincs., Northants, and Staffs. having this origin use the spelling *Stowe*, but the spelling difference cannot be relied on as an indication of locality of origin. The final *-e* in part represents a trace of the OE dat. inflection.

2. Jewish (Ashkenazic): Anglicized form of various like-sounding Jewish surnames.

Var.: **Stowe**.

Strachan Scots: habitation name from a place in the parish of Banchory, near Kincardine, which is first recorded in 1153 in the form *Strateyhan*, and perhaps gets its name from Gael. *srath* valley + *eachain*, gen. case of *eachan* foal (dim. of *each* horse; cf. KEOGH). The pronunciation is traditionally /strɔ:n/.

Vars.: **Strahan; Straughan** (Northumb.); **Strain** (N Ireland).

Stradivari Italian: topographic name for someone who lived in a street with many bends, from It. *strada* STREET + *vara* (fem.) bent, crooked (L *vāra*). Both parts of the name have been assimilated to the most common surname ending *-i*.

Strahl Jewish (Ashkenazic): ornamental name from Yid. *shtral* or Ger. *Strahl* ray of light, sunbeam (MHG *strāle* flash of lightning, arrow, OHG *strāla*). It is possible that the name was adopted as a translation of any of the various

Hebr. given names referring to light, such as *Uri* and *Meir*, but there is no evidence for this.
Var.: **Strahler**.

Strand Danish, Norwegian, and Swedish: topographic name for someone who lived by the sea-shore, or arbitrarily chosen ornamental surname, from Dan., Swed. *strand* shore (ON *strond*).
Var.: Swed.: **Strandh**.
Cpds: Swed.: **Strandberg, Strindberg** ('shore hill').

Strange English: nickname for a newcomer to the area, from ME *strange* foreign (an aphetic form of OF *estrange*, L *extrāneus*, from *extra* outside).
Vars.: **Strainge, Lestrange, Stranger**.
Cogns.: Fr.: **Lestrange, Létrange**. It.: **Stran(e)o, Strani(o), Stragio; Straniero, Stranieri**.

Strangeways English: habitation name from a place near Manchester, so called from OE *strang* STRONG + *(ge)wæsc* wash, current.
Vars.: **Strangways, Strangeway, Strangewick**.
The name Strang(e)ways *is borne by a Lancs. landowning family traceable back to the 14th cent.*

Stránský Czech: topographic name for someone living on a hillside, Czech *stráň*, or habitation name from a place named with this element, for example *Strán*, *Strana*, or *Stránka*.

Stratfield English: habitation name from places in Berks. and Hants, so called from OE *strǣt* (Roman) road (see STREET) + *feld* pasture, open country (see FIELD).
Vars.: **Stre(a)tfield**.

Stratford English: habitation name from any of various places, for example in Greater London, Beds., Bucks., Northants, Suffolk, Wilts., and Warwicks., so called from OE *strǣt* (Roman) road (see STREET) + *ford* FORD.
Var.: **Strafford**.

Stratton English: habitation name from any of various places, for example in Beds., Dorset, Hants, Norfolk, Oxon., Somerset, Suffolk, Surrey, and Wilts., so called from OE *strǣt* (Roman) road (see STREET) + *tūn* enclosure, settlement. A place of the same name in Cornwall, which may also be a partial source of the surname, probably has as its first element Corn. *stras* valley.
Var.: **Stretton** (the name of places in Ches., Derbys., Herefords., Leics., Shrops., Staffs., and Warwicks.).

Straub German: nickname for a shock-headed man, from MHG *strūp* rough, unkempt (OHG *strūb*).
Cogns.: Low Ger.: **Strube, Struwe, Strufe**. Jewish (Ashkenazic): **Strauber**.
Dims.: Ger.: **Sträuble, Strubel, Strobel**.
Patrs.: Low Ger.: **Strübing, Strüwing, Strüfing**.

Strauss 1. German: nickname for an awkward or belligerent person, from Ger. *Strauss* quarrel, complaint (MHG *strūz*; cf. STRUTT).

2. German: house name from a house distinguished by the sign of an ostrich, Ger. *Strauss* (MHG *strūze*, OHG *strūz*, from L *strūthio*, Gk *strouthion*), or nickname for someone who wore a hat decorated with an ostrich feather.

3. Jewish (Ashkenazic): ornamental name from Ger. *Strauss* ostrich, one of the many Ashkenazic surnames taken from bird names.
Var.: **Straus**. (Of 3 only): **Shtrauss; Strausz** (a Hung. spelling); **Straussman(n), Strusman**.
Cogns.: Low Ger.: **Struss**. Flem., Du.: **(Van der) Struys, (Van der) Struijs**. Swed.: **Strutz** (a 'soldier's name').
Dims.: Ger.: **Sträussle, Streissle**. Low Ger.: **Strussgen**.

Straw English (chiefly Notts.): metonymic occupational name for a dealer in straw (OE *strēaw*), or nickname for an exceptionally thin man or someone with straw-coloured hair.
Cogns.: Ger.: **Stroh(mann)**. Jewish (Ashkenazic): **Shtroy, Shtroi** (from the S Yid. pronunciation of Yid. *shtroy* straw); **Strohman**.
Dim.: Ger.: **Ströhlein**.

Streatley English: habitation name from any of various places, for example in Beds. and Berks., so called from OE *strǣt* (Roman) road (see STREET) + *lēah* wood, clearing.
Vars.: **Streetley** (a place in Essex); **Streetly** (places in Cambs. and Warwicks.); **Strelley** (a place in Notts.).

Streek English: nickname for a stern or obstinate person, from ME *streke* severe, unyielding (OE *stræc*, *strec*).
Var.: **Streake**.

Streep Dutch: nickname for someone marked in some way with a stripe or streak, MDu. *strīpe*.

Street English: habitation name from any of the various places, for example in Herts., Kent, and Somerset, so called from OE *strǣt* Roman road (L *strāta* (*via*), from the past part. of *sternere* to strew, cover, surface). In the Middle Ages the word also came to denote the main street in a village, and so the surname may also have been a topographic name for someone who lived on the main street.
Vars.: **Streat** (a place in Sussex); **Strete** (places in Devon); **Streete, Streets; Streeter, Streater**.
Cogns. (topographic): Fr.: **Estrée, Lestrée, Destrée, Delestrée; Listrée, Listray** (Belgium). Prov.: **Estrade, Étraz, Lestrade, Létraz, Détraz, Delétraz, Deletrez; Estradier, Estradère**. It.: **(Della) Strada, Stradi**. Sp.: **Estrada**. Cat.: **Estrada; Estrader, Estradé**. Ger.: **Strass(n)er, Strässner, Strässler, Strassmann**. Low Ger.: **Straeter, Strat(h)mann, Stradtmann, Straatman**. Flem.: **Van der Straeten, Verstraete**. Du.: **Van Stra(a)ten, Straatman; Strating**. Jewish (Ashkenazic): **Strass(l)er, Strassmann, Strasman**.
Dims. (topographic): It.: **Stradella**. Flem.: **Straetje(s)**.

Streltsov Russian: patr. from the occupational term *strelets* marksman, musketeer (a deriv. of *strelyat* to shoot, originally with arrows, from *strela* arrow, an ultimate cogn. of STRAHL).
Cogns. (not patrs.): Beloruss.: **Strelchuk, Strelchenko** (dims.). Pol.: **Strzelczyk** (dim.). Czech: **Střelka** (lit., 'arrow'). Ger. (of Slav. origin): **Streletz**.
Habitation names: Pol.: **Strzelecki** (from either of two towns called *Strzelce*). Jewish (E Ashkenazic): **Strelec**.

Strettell English: probably a habitation name from an unidentified place named with the OE elements *strǣt* (Roman) road (see STREET) + *hyll* HILL.
Robert de Mara or de la Mere was a landowner who, around 1210, gave lands at somewhere called Strettle *or* Strethull, *probably in Ches., to his two sons, Philip and Gilbert. The name later occurs as* de Stretle, Stretley, *and* Stratley, *and there has probably been some confusion with* STREATLEY. *There is a family living today who claim descent from these two early bearers, but so far the line can only be traced with any certainty back to Edward Strettell (d. 1626) of Mobberley, Ches.*

Strickland English: habitation name from a place in Cumb., so called from OE *styr(i)c*, *steorc* bullock (see STIRK) + *land* land, pasture.
Var.: **Stirland** (common in Notts.; perhaps from a different (unidentified) place of the same etymology).
A family of this name trace their descent from Sir Walter de Stirkeland, *holder of the manor of Stirkland, Cumb., who was licensed to maintain a domestic chapel in 1230. The name has also been common in Lancs. from as early as the 14th cent.*

Stride English: apparently a nickname for someone with long legs or whose gait had a purposeful air, from ME *stride* (long) pace (from *stride(n)* to walk with long steps, OE *strīdan* to straddle.

Striker English: occupational name for someone whose job was to fill level measures of corn by passing a flat stick over the brim of the measure, thus removing any heaped excess, from an agent deriv. of ME *strike(n)* to stroke, smooth (OE *strīccan*).

Vars.: **Strike** (a metonymic name from the stick used); **Straker** (from the OE byform *strācian*).

Cogns.: Ger.: **Streicher, Kornstreicher**. Flem.: **De Strycker**.

Stringer English: occupational name for a maker of string, from an agent deriv. of ME *string* string (OE *streng*).

Var.: **String** (metonymic).

Stringfellow English (Lancs.): nickname for a powerful man, from ME *streng* mighty, STRONG + *felaw* FELLOW.

Strnad Czech: nickname for someone bearing some fancied resemblance to a bunting, Czech *strnad*.

Stroev Russian: patr. from the ORuss. term of relationship *stroi* uncle. The word was also used as an affectionate nickname and even as a given name in some parts of Russia, whereas in others it was used to describe a cripple or beggar, and the surname may also derive from either of these senses.

Stroganov Russian: patr. from the nickname *Strogan*, which may derive either from the adj. *strogi* stern, severe, or from the past part. *stroganni* of the verb *strogat* to shave.

Vars.: **Strogonov**; **Stroganoff** (a Fr. spelling).

The Stroganovs *were a Russian merchant family whose personal ambitions also assisted the country's territorial expansion and economic growth. The name is first found on commercial documents, connected with trade in Novgorod, in the 15th cent. They gained extensive grants of land from Ivan the Terrible, and played a leading role in the accession of Michael Romanov. Gregory Stroganov (1650–1715) was an adviser of Peter the Great.*

Strohane Irish: Anglicized form of Gael. **Ó Sruthάin** 'descendant of *Sruthán*', a personal name from a dim. of *sruth* sage, elder (or, less likely, of the homonymous *sruth* stream).

Ström Swedish: topographic name for someone who lived by a river, or arbitrarily adopted ornamental name, from *ström* river (ON *straumr*, a cogn. of OE *strēam*, mod. Eng. *stream*).

Cogn.: Jewish (Ashkenazic): **S(h)trom**; **Sztrom** (a Pol. spelling); **Stromwasser, Wasserstrom**.

Cpds (ornamental): **Strömbäck** ('river stream'); **Strömberg** ('river hill'); **Strömblad** ('river leaf'); **Strömblom** ('river flower'); **Strömbom** ('river tree'); **Strömgren** ('river branch'); **Strömqvist** ('river twig'); **Strömwall, Strömvall** ('river bank').

Stronach Scots: nickname for an interfering person, from Gael. *sronach* nosey.

Strong English: nickname for a strong man, or perhaps sometimes ironically for a weakling, from ME, OE *strong*, *strang* strong.

Vars.: **Stronge**; **Strang** (Scots; according to Black a var. of STRANGE); **Strangman**.

Cogns.: Flem., Du.: **Strang**. Jewish (Ashkenazic): **Streng** ('strict').

Stroud English: habitation name from places in Gloucs. and Middx, so called from an OE element *strōd*, used to describe marshy ground overgrown with brushwood. *Strood* in Kent is named with the same word, and some examples of the surname are no doubt derived from this term in independent use.

Vars.: **Strood, Strode**.

Stróżyński Polish: habitation name referring to a place where a gate-keeper lived, from Pol. *stróż* gatekeeper + *-yn* possessive suffix + *-ski* suffix of local surnames (see BARANOWSKI). In effect, it is normally an occupational name for a gate-keeper or watchman.

Strudwick English: habitation name from an unidentified minor place, so called from OE *strōd* damp land (see STROUD) + *wīc* dairy farm (see WICK). *Strudgewick* in the parish of Kirdford, Sussex, was earlier *Strodwike*, and may be a partial source of the surname.

Strumiłło Polish: topographic name for someone who lived by a stream, from Pol. *strum-* (cf. mod. Pol. *strumień*), with the Lithuanian ending *-i(e)łło* (cf. RADZIWIŁŁ).

Var.: **Strumiński**.

Struthers Scots: topographic name from Northern ME *strother* damp land (from OE *strōd*, the same word as in STROUD), or habitation name from any of the various places named with this element, as for example *Struther* near Stonehouse, Lanarks., *Sruthers* in Fife, or *Srother* in Northumb.

Strutt English: of uncertain origin, probably from the ON byname *Strútr* (from a vocab. word referring to a cone-like ornament on a headdress or cap). Alternatively it may be a nickname for an argumentative person, from ME *strut(t)* quarrel (cf. STRAUSS 1).

Strzałkowski Polish: habitation name referring to a place where an archer or musketeer lived, from a dim. of Pol. *strzał* shot, archery (cf. STRELTSOV) + *-ów* possessive suffix + *-ski* suffix of local surnames (see BARANOWSKI). In effect, it is probably an occupational name for an archer or musketeer.

Stubbe English: topographic name for someone who lived near the stump of a large felled tree, or nickname for a short, stout man, from OE *stub(b)* tree stump.

Vars.: **Stubber** (local); **Stobbe**.

Cogns.: Low Ger.: **Stübe, Stüve, Stüwe**.

Patrs. (from the nickname): Eng.: **Stubbs, Stobbs** (also vars. of the topographic name). Low Ger.: **Steuben, Stüven**.

Stubley English: habitation name from any of several places so called, from OE *stub(b)* tree stump (see STUBBE) + *lēah* wood, clearing, i.e. a patch where the trees had been felled, leaving only stumps; cf. STUKELEY. The surname is commonest in Yorks., and the source is probably most often *Stubley* in Heckmondwike.

Studd English: topographic name for someone who lived on a stud farm, or occupational name for someone who was employed on one, from ME *stode*, *stud(d)e* stud (OE *stōd*; cf. STODDART).

Vars.: **Stitt** (Scotland and N Ireland); **Studman**.

Studley English: habitation name from any of various places, in Oxon., Warwicks., Wilts., and W Yorks., so called from OE *stōd* stud farm + *lēah* wood, clearing, pasture.

Studziński Polish: topographic name for someone who lived beside a well, from Pol. *studzień* well + *-ski* suffix of local surnames (see BARANOWSKI).

Vars.: **Studzieński**; **Studnicki**.

Dim.: **Studniarek** (occupational name for a well-sinker).

Stukeley English: habitation name from a place in the former county of Hunts., now part of Cambs., so called from OE *styfic* stump + *lēah* wood, clearing; cf. STUBLEY. *Stewkley* in Bucks. has the same origin and may also be a partial source of the surname.

Vars.: **Stukely, Stucley.**

A family by the name of Stucley *can be traced to Richard Stucley (d. 1441), who is also found in records as Richard* Styuecle. *He lived in Hunts., and is probably the son of John Styuecle of Great Stukeley in the same county.*

Stümbke N German: habitation name from the village of *Steimbke*, near Sachsenhagen, Hesse.

Vars.: **Stümbcke, Stümpke, Stüm(c)ke.**

The first known instance of the name Stümbke *is found in a document in the records of the Bishop of Minden in 1400. In 1795 a family bearing this name migrated from Hesse to England, where the name is still found in the forms* **Stumbke** *and* **Stumcke**. *The latter form is also found in Boston, Mass., while* **Stumke** *is a fairly frequent surname in S Africa.*

Stump English: of similar meaning to STUBBE, from ME *stump* tree stump (a borrowing from MLG *stump(e)*, obscurely related to OE *stub(b)*).

Sturdy English: nickname for an impetuous or hot-headed man, from ME *st(o)urdi* reckless, rash (an aphetic form of OF *est(o)urdi*, past part. of *estourdir* to daze, stupify, LL *exturdīre*, a deriv. of *turdus* thrush, which was thought to be a stupid bird, dazed and drunken from its diet of grapes).

Vars.: **Sturdee, Stordy.**

Sturgeon English: metonymic occupational name for a fishmonger, or possibly a nickname, from ME *sturgeon* (an aphetic form of OF *estourgeon*, of Gmc origin, which replaced the native cogn. *styrga*).

Cogn.: Du.: **Steur.**

Sturgess English: apparently from the ON personal name *Þorgils*, composed of the divine name *Þorr* + *gils* hostage, pledge. However, the inorganic initial *S-* is not easily explained; it may be the result of OF influence.

Vars.: **Sturges, Sturgis, Sturge; Turgoose.**

Cogns.: Fr.: **T(o)urgis.**

Sturman 1. English: occupational name for a navigator, from ON *stýrimaðr* steersman (a cpd of *stýra* to steer + *maðr*, gen. *manns*, man).

2. English: from a OF dim. form **Esturmin* of a Gmc byname meaning 'STORM'.

3. Jewish (Ashkenazic): of unknown origin.

Sturrock Scots (Dundee): Black comments that this name is an occupational name for a sheep-farmer or store-master, but he gives no further explanation. The connection, if any, with ME *stor*, OF *estor* (see STORER) is by no means clear.

Patr.: **Sturrocks.**

Sturtivant English: apparently a nickname for a hasty individual, from ME *stert(en)* to start, leap (OE *styrtan*) + ANF *avaunt* forward (LL *abante*, a cpd of class. L *ab* away + *ante* in front).

Vars.: **Sturtevant, Sturdevant, Startifant.**

Stuyvesant Dutch: probably a nickname for a blustering person or for a keen horseman, from MDu. *stūven* to stir up (cf. MHG *stieben*, OHG *stioban*) + *sant* sand.

Cogns.: Low Ger.: **Steubesand, Stöbesand, Stövesand, Stöwesand.**

Styczyński Polish: from Pol. *styczeń* January, a name taken by or bestowed on someone who was born or baptized in January, esp. a convert to Christianity.

Styles English: 1. topographic name for someone who lived near a steep ascent, OE *stigol* (a deriv. of *stīgan* to climb; cf. STEIGER).

2. topographic name for someone who lived near a stile, OE *stigel* (from the same verb).

Vars.: **Style, Stile(s), Stileman; Stiggles, Stygal(l), Stickel, Stickel(l)s, Stickles, Stegel(l), Steggle(s), Steggall(s), Steggals, Ste(c)kel, Stekles.**

Cogns.: Ger.: **Sti(e)gler.**

Suc Provençal: topographic name for someone who lived on a hillock or mound, OProv. *suc*.

Var.: **Delsuc.**

Dims.: **Suquet, Suchet.**

Aug.: **Suchat.**

Such English: from ME, OF *s(o)uche* tree stump (probably of Gaul. origin, apparently ultimately related to Eng. STOCK). The original application of this word as a surname is not clear; it may be a topographic name for someone who lived by a tree stump, or else a nickname for a man of stumpy build.

Vars.: **Souch, Sutch, Zouch; Chuck(s)** (from the Norman form *chouque*).

Cogns.: Fr.: **Souche, Lasouche, De(la)souche;** CHOQUE, **Chouque** (Normandy). Prov.: **Souque.** It.: **Zocca, Zocco, Zocchi.**

Dims.: Fr.: **Souchet, Dusouchet, Souchon.** Prov.: **So(u)quet, Socquet, Socquin.** It.: **Zoccoli.**

Augs.: It.: **Zocconi, Zoccone.**

Suchý Czech: nickname for a thin man, from Czech *suchý*, the original meaning of which is 'dry'.

Var.: **Suchan.**

Cogns.: Pol.: **Suchecki, Suchocki** (habitation names from a place named as 'dry').

Dim.: Czech: **Suchánek.**

Suckling English: nickname for a person who was childish in appearance or behaviour, from ME *suckling* infant at the breast (from OE *sūcan* to suck + the Gmc suffix *-ling* (cf. CHAMBERLAIN), probably under the influence of MDu. *sūgeling*). The surname is attested from the 13th cent., although the vocab. word does not appear until the 15th cent.

Sudell N English: probably a habitation name from an unidentified place, possibly *Sud Hill* in Hunmanby, E Yorks. (*Suddale* in the 12th cent.), which is named with OE *sūð* or ON *suðr* SOUTH + OE *dæl* or ON *dalr* valley (see DALE).

Sudworth English (Lancs.): habitation name from the depopulated village of *Southworth* near Winwick in Ches., so called from OE *sūð* SOUTH + *worð* enclosure (see WORTH).

Suero Spanish: from a medieval given name of Gmc origin, attested in the Latinized form *Suerius*. The first element is of obscure origin, the second is *heri*, *hari* army.

Cogn.: Port.: **Soeiro.**

Patrs.: Sp.: **Suárez.** Port.: **Soares.**

Sugden English: habitation name from a place in W Yorks., so called from OE *sucga* sparrow (or other small bird) + *denu* valley (see DEAN 1).

Var.: **Sugdon.**

Sugrue Irish: Anglicized form of Gael. **Ó Siochfhradha** 'descendant of *Siochfhradh*', a personal name representing a Gaelicized form of an ON cogn. of SIEGFRIED. The surname is largely confined to Co. Kerry.

Var.: **Shugrue**.

Suk Czech: from the vocab. word *suk* knot, knar, applied either as a topographic name for someone who lived by a tree with a knotty trunk, or as a nickname for a powerful, unyielding man or a stubborn, awkward one, from the same word in a transferred sense.

Cogn.: Pol.: **Sęk**.

Dim.: Czech: **Souček**.

Habitation names: Pol.: **Sękowski**; **Sęczkowski** (from a dim., *sęczek*).

Sulley English (Notts.): habitation name from an unidentified place named with the OE elements *sūð* SOUTH + *lēah* wood, clearing.

Sullivan Irish: Anglicized form of Gael. **Ó Súileabháin** 'descendant of *Súileabhán*', a personal name composed of the elements *súil* eye + *dubh* black, dark + the dim. suffix *-án*.

Vars.: **O'Sullivan, Sullevan, Soolivan**.

Sully 1. French: habitation name from any of various places, for example in Calvados, Loiret, and Oise. The first of these is recorded in 1180 as *Silleium*, from the Gallo-Roman personal name *Silius* or *Cilius* + the local suffix *-ācum*. The others are from a personal name *Sol(l)ius* + *-ācum*.

2. S English: of uncertain origin; possibly a habitation name imported from France and so identical with 1, or alternatively a var. of SULLEY. It may also be from the parish of *Sully* in the former county of Glamorgan, Wales, so called either from ON *sul* cleft + *ey* island or from the Norman family name *de Sulley* (as in 1), which is found in Glamorgan in the 12th cent.

Summer 1. English: nickname for someone of a warm or sunny disposition, or for someone associated with the season of summer in some other way, from ME *sum(m)er* summer (OE *somer*); cf. WINTER.

2. English: assimilated var. of SUMNER.

3. English: assimilated var. of SUMPTER.

4. Irish: translation of Gael. **Ó Samhraidh** 'descendant of *Samhradh*', a byname meaning 'Summer'.

Vars.: **Som(m)er**; **Simmer** (Scots). (Of 4 only): **O'Sawrie, O'-Sawra**.

Cogns. (of 1): Ger.: **Sommer**. Flem., Du.: **De Somer**. Dan., Norw.: **Sommer**. Jewish (Ashkenazic, either ornamental or belonging in the group of names referring to the seasons that were bestowed on Jews more or less at random by government officials in 18th- and 19th cent. central Europe; cf. WINTER, HERBST, and FRULING): **Som(m)er(man)**, **Zom(m)er**, **Zomerman** (from Ger. *Sommer*); **Zum(m)er** (from Yid. *zumer*).

Patrs. (from 1): Eng.: **Summers, Som(m)ers, Simmers, Sym(m)ers; Summerson**.

Cpds (of 1): Jewish: **Somerfreund** ('summer friend'); **Sommerfeld(t)** ('summer field'; Anglicized **Summerfield**, see also SOMERVILLE); **Somerschein** ('summer sunshine'); **Som(m)erstein** ('summer stone)'.

Summerhayes S English: probably a topographic name referring to an enclosure (on upland pasture), where animals were kept in summer; for the second element (from OE *(ge)hæg* enclosure) see HAY 1.

Summerhill S English: probably a habitation name from an unidentified minor place named with the OE elements *somer* SUMMER + *hyll* HILL, i.e. hill used for summer grazing.

Summerlad English: from an ON personal name composed of the elements *sumar* summer + *líðr* warrior; the second element has been variously altered by folk etymology.

Vars.: **Summerland, Sommerlat, Som(m)erlad**.

Summerly Irish: Anglicized form of Gael. **Ó Somacháin** 'descendant of *Somachán*', a byname originally denoting a soft, fat person.

Var.: SOMERVILLE.

Sumner English (now common mainly in Lancs.): occupational name for an official who was responsible for ensuring the appearance of witnesses in court, ME *sumner*, *sumnor* summoner (OF *sumoneor*, L *submonitor*, from *submonēre* to remind discreetly).

Vars.: **Sumpner, Somner, Simner, Simnor**, SUMMER.

Sumpter English: occupational name for a carrier, from ME *sum(p)ter* (driver of a) pack animal (OF *som(m)etier*, from LL *sagmatārius*, a deriv. of *sagma*, gen. *sagmatis*, pack saddle, from Gk).

Vars.: **Sunter**, SUMMER.

Sund Swedish: arbitrarily adopted or ornamental surname from the Swed. vocab. word *sund* sound, strait (ON *sund*), perhaps in some cases adopted as a topographic name by someone who lived by a strait.

Vars.: **Sundh, Sundén, Sundin, Sundell, Sundelius, Sundelin, Sundman**.

Cpds (ornamental): **Sundberg** ('strait hill'); **Sundblad** ('strait leaf'); **Sundgren** ('strait branch'); **Sundqvist** ('strait twig'); **Sundstedt** ('strait homestead'); **Sundström** ('strait river'); **Sundwall, Sundvall** ('strait slope').

Sunderland English: habitation name from any of various places so called, especially the city at the mouth of the river Wear. This, like other places so called in Cumb., Lancs., and S Scotland, derives its name from OE *sundor* separate + *land* land; a further example in Northumb. has the same origin as SUTHERLAND.

Sunyer Catalan: from a Gmc personal name composed of the elements *sunj* truth + *heri*, *hari* army.

Vars.: **Suñer, Sunyé, Suñé**.

Suominen Finnish: ostensibly a patr. from the word meaning 'Finn', this surname was apparently adopted in a spirit of patriotism. *Suomi* Finland is a deriv. of *suomaa* marshland.

Sureau French: topographic name for someone who lived by an elder tree, from a dim. of OF *seür* elder (originally *seü*, *saü*, from L *sa(m)būcus*, but apparently altered by association with the adj. *sur* sour, of Gmc origin).

Vars.: **Surel; Saüc, Sahuc, Sahut; Sahu(c)quet**.

Surgeon English: occupational name for a person who performed operations, mostly amputations, ME, OF *sur(ri)gien* (LL *chirurgiānus*, from *chirurgia* handiwork, Gk *kheirourgia*, a cpd of *kheir* hand + *ourgia* work, from *ergein* to perform, do). Before the advent of anaesthetics, only crude surgery was possible, and the calling was often combined with that of the BARBER or bath-house attendant (cf. BADER).

Vars.: **Surgey; Surge(o)ner, Surgenor** (with ME agent suffixes).

Cogn.: Jewish (Ashkenazic): **Chirurg** (it is unclear whether this is an occupational name).

Surowiec Polish: nickname for a serious, grim, or unrefined person, from a deriv. of Pol. *surowy* raw, serious. The word *surowiec* also means 'raw material'.

Var.: **Surowiecki.**

Cogn.: Czech: **Syrový** (adj.).

Surridge English: 1. from a ME given name, *Seric*, which represents a coalescence of two OE personal names, *Sǣrīc* (composed of the elements *sǣ* sea + *rīc* power) and *Sigerīc* (composed of the elements *sige* victory + *rīc* power). This would normally have given mod. Eng. *Serrich*, but the form has been altered under the influence of OF *surreis* southerner (see 2 below).

2. regional name for someone who had migrated from the South, from OF *surreis* southerner; cf. NORRIS.

3. habitation name from a place in the parish of Morebath, Devon, so called from OE *sūð* SOUTH + *hrycg* RIDGE.

Vars. (of 1): **Surrage, S(e)arch, Sarge, Ser(ri)ck, Sark, Sea(w)right.**

Surtees English (Northumb.): topographic name from ANF *sur* on, by (L *super* on, over) + *Tees* (a river in N England, so called from a Brit. term cogn. with Gael. *teas* heat, and so probably meaning 'boiling', 'surging'). Some early forms, as for example Randulf *de Super Teise* (Northants 1174), seem to point to a lost placename composed of these elements.

Süsskind Jewish (Ashkenazic): 1. ornamental name from Ger. *süss* SWEET + *kind* child.

2. metr. from the Yid. dim. female given name *Ziske* (see ZISIN), altered by folk etymology to conform to 1. Many Jewish surnames ending in *-kin* (actually from the dim. given name ending *-k(e)* + the Slav. possessive ending *-in*) acquired an excrescent *-d* as a result of folk-etymological association with Yid. *kind* child.

Vars.: **Susskind; Siskind; Zusskind, Zyskind, Zis(s)kind.**

Sutcliffe English: habitation name from any of the three places in W Yorks. so called from OE *sūð* SOUTH + *clif* riverbank, slope, cliff (see CLIVE).

Var.: **Sutcliff.**

Sutherland Scots: regional name from the former county of this name, so called from ON *suðroen* southern + *land* land; the territory was so named because it lay south of Scandinavia and the earlier Norse colonies in the Orkney and Shetland Islands.

Vars.: **Southerland, Sutherlan.**

Sutton English: habitation name from any of the extremely numerous places so called, from OE *sūð* SOUTH + *tūn* enclosure, settlement.

Through a pedigree first recorded in 1569, a family called Sutton *claim descent from Seward, lord of the manor of Sutton in Holderness, Yorks., at the time of the Conquest. Unfortunately, Tudor pedigrees are notoriously unreliable, and this genealogy has not been confirmed independently.*

Suwalski Polish: habitation name from the town of *Suwałki* in NE Poland.

Svatoš Czech: from any of the Czech personal names with a first element *svat-* holy (cf. ŚWIĄTEK), for example *Svatomír* ('holy' + 'great'), *Svatoslav* ('holy' + 'glory'), and *Svatobor* ('holy' + 'warrior').

Vars.: **Svatoň, Svačina; Švanda** (altered by folk etymology to conform with the vocab. word *švanda* joke, fun).

Dims.: **Svátek, Svášek, Sváček; Svach.**

Svedin Swedish: ornamental name, ostensibly from Swed. *sved* (burnt) clearing (past. part. of *svedja* to singe, scorch). This was perhaps sometimes chosen as a topographic name by someone who lived in or near such a clearing, but far more often no doubt it was adopted, on the basis of folk etymology, for patriotic reasons, because of the similarity of this vocab. word to L *Suedia* Sweden. The Swed. name of Sweden is *Sverige*, from *Sve(ar)* Swede(s) + *rige* kingdom. In LL the name of the country occurs variously as *Suedia*, *Sueonia*, and *Suecia*.

Cpds: **Svedberg, Swedberg** ('clearing hill'); **Swedenborg** ('clearing town'); **Swedlund** ('clearing grove').

Svehla Czech: nickname for a twittering person, from a deriv. of OCzech *švehlat* to twitter.

Var.: **Švehlák.**

Dims.: **Švehlík, Švehelka.**

Svoboda Czech: the third most common Czech surname, from a noun literally meaning 'freedom'. This was a technical term in the feudal system for a freeman, i.e. a peasant who was not a serf.

Swaby English: habitation name from a place in Lincs., so called from the ON ethnic byname *Sváfi* 'Swabian' + ON *býr* farm, settlement.

Swain English: 1. occupational name for a servant or attendant, ME *swein* (ON *sveinn*, a cogn. of OE *swān*; cf. SWAN 2). Not until the 16th cent. did the word *swain* develop the senses 'young rustic' and hence 'rustic lover', 'wooer'.

2. from the ON personal name *Sveinn*, originally a byname meaning 'Boy', 'Servant' (cf. 1 above).

Vars.: **Swaine, Swayn(e).**

Cogns.: Low Ger.: **Schwen(n).**

Patrs.: Eng.: **Swe(y)nson, Swainson.** Low Ger.: **Schwennen, Schwenn(e)sen.** Dan., Norw.: **Svendsen, Svenningsen.** Swed.: **Svensson.**

Swallow English: 1. nickname for someone thought to resemble a swallow, perhaps in swiftness and grace, from ME *swal(e)we*, *swalu* (OE *swealwe*).

2. habitation name from a place in Lincs., so called from the river *Swallow* on which it stands, whose name is apparently ultimately akin to that of the bird, presumably with some transferred meaning such as 'swirling' or 'rushing'.

Cogns. (of 1): Ger.: **Schwalb(e).** Low Ger.: **Swalke.** Flem.: **Swaelu, Swaluwe.** Jewish (Ashkenazic; ornamental names): **Schwalbe** (from Ger. *Schwalbe*), **S(c)hwalb, Szwalb** (from Yid. *shvalb*, the latter a Pol. spelling).

Dim. (of 1): Ger.: **Schwälble.**

Patr. (from 1): Flem.: **Swaelus.**

Swan English: 1. nickname for a person noted for purity or excellence (which were taken to be attributes of the swan), or resembling a swan in some other way, from OE *swan*, *swon* swan. In some cases it may be a house name for someone who lived at a house with the sign of a swan.

2. occupational name for a servant or retainer; cf. SWAIN 1. In part it may be from an OE byname, preserved into the Middle Ages as a given name.

Var.: **Swann.**

Cogns. (of 1): Ger.: **Schwa(h)n.** Flem.: **De Swaen.** Du.: **De Swaan, (De) Zwaan, Van den Swaan, Van den Zwaan.** Dan., Norw.: **Svane.** Swed.: **Svahn, Swahn.**

Dims. (of 1): Low Ger.: **Schwan(e)ke, Schwank, Schwen(e)ke.** (Of 2): Sc.: **Swanie, Swanney.**

Patr. (from 2): Eng.: **Swanson.**

Cpds (of cogns. of 1, ornamental): Swed.: **Svanberg** ('swan hill'); **Svanström** ('swan river'). Jewish (Ashkenazic): **Schwanenfeld, Shvanenfeld** ('swan field').

An English family by the name of **Swahn**, *living in Deptford, London, are apparently descended from John August* Svahn, *a Scandinavian immigrant who was married in Rotherhithe in 1860. He was the son of Carl Svahn, a ship's chandler. See also* ŚWIĄTEK.

Swannell English: from an ON female personal name, *Svanhildr*, composed of the elements *svanr* swan + *hild* battle.

Var.: **Swonnell**.

Swansborough English: probably a habitation name from an unidentified place, named from the gen. case of the OE byname *Swān* (see SWAN 2) + OE *burh* fortress, town.

Var.: **Swansbury**.

Swanston 1. Scots: habitation name from a place near Edinburgh, probably so called from the gen. case of the OE byname *Swān* (see SWAN 2) + OE *tūn* enclosure, settlement.

2. English: var. of SWANTON.

Swanton English: habitation name from one of the places, in Kent and Norfolk, so called from OE *Swānatūn* 'settlement (OE *tūn*) of the retainers (see SWAN 2)'; cf. CHARLTON and KNIGHTON.

Var.: SWANSTON.

Swanwick English: habitation name from a place in Derbys., so called from OE *Swānawīc* 'outlying settlement (see WICK) of the retainers (see SWAN 2)'.

Swarbrick English (Lancs.): habitation name from a place in the parish of Kirkham, Lancs., so called from the ON byname *Svartr* 'Black' + ON *brekka* slope.

Sweeney Irish: Anglicized form of Gael. **Mac Suibhne** 'son of *Suibhne*', a byname meaning 'Pleasant'.

Vars.: **McSeveny**, **McSween(ey)**, **(Mc)Swiney**, **McSwine**; **McQueenie**, MCQUEEN, **McQueyn**, **McQuine**, **Magueen**, **(Mc)Whin**, **McWhan** (Gael. **Mac Shuibhne**).

Sweet English (most common in the W Country): nickname for a popular person, from ME *swete* sweet, pleasant, agreeable (OE *swēte*, cogn. with MHG *süeze*, Ger. *süss*); cf. SWEETING. The OE bynames *Swēt(a)* (masc.) and *Swēte* (fem.) derived from this word survived into the early ME period, and may also be sources of the surname.

Vars.: **Swett**; **Swe(e)tman**, **Sweatman**; **Swatman** (Norfolk).

Cogns.: Ger.: **Süss(e)**, **Süssmann**; **Siess** (Bavaria). Low Ger.: **Söth**, **Söte**, **Seute(mann)**. Flem.: **De Soete**, **De Zoete**. Du.: **De Soet**, **Zoet**. Jewish (Ashkenazic): **Suss(er)**, **Zis**, **Zis(s)er**, **Zisserman** (ornamental, from Ger. *süss* sweet or its Yid. cogn. *zis*; see also SÜSSKIND); **Sussman(n)**, **Zus(s)man**, **Sissman**, **Zisman** (possibly ornamental, but more probably derived from the Yid. male given name *Zusman*, lit. 'Sweet Man').

Patrs.: Jewish (from the Yid. male given name *Zusman*): **Zusmans**; **Zusmanovitch**, **Zusmanovitz**, **Zusmanovics**, **Sussmanowitz** (E Ashkenazic).

Cpds (ornamental): Jewish (Ashkenazic): **Sussapfel**, **Zisapel** ('sweet apple'); **Zisberg** ('sweet hill'); **Zuserblum** ('sweet flower'); **Sussholz**, **Zishol(t)z** ('sweet wood'); **Sissmilch** ('sweet milk').

Sweeting English: 1. from a medieval given name, originally an OE patr. from *Swēt(a)*; see SWEET.

2. nickname for a popular and attractive person, or for somebody who habitually addressed people with the ME term *sweting* darling, sweetheart.

Sweetsir English: nickname from ME *swete* pleasant, agreeable (see SWEET) + *sire* lord, master (see SEIGNEUR). The name was probably ironical in tone and given either to someone of condescending manner or to someone who habitually used this form of address.

Vars.: **Sweetsur**, **Sweetzer**, **Switsur**, **Switzer**.

Świątek Polish: name taken by someone, esp. a convert to Christianity, who was baptized on a holy day or feast day, Pol. *świątek* (from *święty* saint (n.), holy (adj.)).

Var.: **Świątczak**.

Habitation names: **Świątkowski**; **Święcicki** (from *Święcice* in Mazovia, named as a 'holy' place).

One British family by the name of SWAN *is of Polish origin, and originally bore the surname* Święcicki; *their name was changed by deed poll in 1919. Ancestors of this family were widely dispersed in E Europe; some are recorded as hving migrated to Lithuania with Martin Święcicki (d. 1569), and some later settled in Canada.*

Świderski Polish: nickname for a boss-eyed person, from Pol. *świder* drill, gimlet + the surname suffix *-ski* (see BARANOWSKI).

Dim.: **Świderek**.

Świercz Polish: nickname for a diminutive, chirpy person, from Pol. *śwircz* cricket (the insect).

Habitation name: **Świerczyński**.

Swift 1. English: nickname for a rapid runner, from ME, OE *swift* fleet.

2. Irish: translation of Gael. *Ó Fuada*; see FOODY.

Swinburn English: habitation name from a place in Northumb., so called from OE *swīn* pig, wild boar + *burna* stream (see BOURNE).

Vars.: **Swinburne**, **Swinbourn(e)**.

Swindells English (Lancs.): of uncertain origin, in spite of being a very common name in Lancs. It is possibly a habitation name from *Swindale* in Skelton, N Yorks., so called from OE *swīn* pig, wild boar + *dæl* valley (see DALE).

Var.: **Swindell**.

Swindlehurst English (Lancs.): probably a habitation name from *Swinglehurst* in Bowland Forest, W Yorks., so called from OE *swīn* pig, wild boar + *hyll* hill + *hyrst* wooded ridge.

Var.: **Swinglehurst**.

Swingler English (W Midlands): occupational name for someone who made or used a certain type of wooden instrument used for beating hemp, ME *swingle* (MDu. *swinghel*, from the verb 'to swing').

Swinley English: habitation name from a place in Lancs., near Manchester, so called from OE *swīn* pig, wild boar + *lēah* wood, clearing.

In 1410 William de Swyndeley *of Liverpool owned property at Swinley in Lancs., from which the family derives its name. However, a direct line of descent for the present family can only be traced back to the 18th cent.*

Swinnerton English: habitation name from *Swynnerton* in Staffs., so called from OE *swīn* pig, wild boar + *ford* FORD + *tūn* enclosure, settlement.

Vars.: **Swinerton**, **Swyn(n)erton**, **Swinarton**, **Swenerton**, **Swinnington**.

The earliest known bearer of the name is Robert de Swynnerton, *who held the manor of this place from 1190 to 1203.*

Swinscoe English: habitation name from a place in Staffs., so called from ON *svín* pig, wild boar + *skógr* copse (cf. SHAW).

Swinton English and Scots: habitation name from any of various places, for example in Lancs. and N and S Yorks., so called from OE *swīn* pig, wild boar + *tūn* enclosure, settlement.

A family who derive their name from lands at Swinton *in the former county of Berwicks., now part of Borders region, were first granted them* c.*1098 by King Edgar of Scotland. Members of the family were lords of Bamburgh and held sway over the area between the Tyne and Forth known as Bernicia. The first lord was Eadwulf (d. 912).*

Swithenbank English (Yorks.): habitation name from an unidentified place, so called from ME *swithen* land cleared by burning (from ON *sviðinn* burnt) + *bank* slope (see BANKS).

Sword 1. English and Scots: metonymic occupational name for an armourer, from ME *swerd*, *sword*, OE *sweord* sword.

2. Irish: Anglicized form of Gael. *Ó Suaird*; see SEWARD 3.

Vars. (of 1): **Soord**; **Sworder** (largely concentrated in E Herts. and W Essex). (Of 2): **Sworde**.

Cogns.: Ger.: **Schwert**. Swed.: **Svärd(h)** (a 'soldier's name').

Dim.: Ger.: **Schwertl**.

Sydenham English: habitation name from any of various places, for example in Devon, Oxon., and Somerset, so called from OE *sīd* wide + *hamm* water meadow, with the adj. retaining traces of the weak dat. ending originally used after a preposition and def. art. A further example in S London is a late alteration of *Chippenham* 'homestead of *Cippa*', and is not likely to have contributed to the surname.

Vars.: **Syddenham**, **Sid(d)enham**.

A family of this name, originally from Sydenham in Somerset, settled at Wynford Eagle, Dorset. This estate had been bought in the time of Henry VIII. Descendants included Thomas Sydenham *(1624–89), who is regarded as the founder of clinical medicine.*

Sykes N English: topographic name for someone who lived by a marshy stream or damp gully, ME *syke* (from OE *sīc* or the cogn. ON *sík*).

Vars.: **Sikes**; **Si(t)ch**, **Seach** (S Eng. forms, with palatalization of the OE final consonant).

Symington Scots: habitation name from either of two places, one near Glasgow and the other near Ayr, so called from the given name SIMON + ME *toun* settlement (OE *tūn*). Both places were held in the late 12th cent. by a certain Simon Loccard or Lockhart, from whom they presumably derive their name.

Sypniewski Polish: habitation name from a place named *Sypniewo*, from Pol. *sypn-* heap up, build (an embankment or dike) + the possessive suffix *-ew*, with the addition of *-ski*, suffix of local surnames (see BARANOWSKI).

Syrett English: 1. from the ME male given name *Syred*, OE *Sigerǣd*, composed of the elements *sige* victory + *rǣd* counsel.

2. from the ME female personal name *Sigerith*, ON *Sigríðr*, a contraction of *Sigfríðr*, composed of the elements *sige* victory + *fríðr* lovely.

Vars.: **Sirett(e)**, **Sired**, **Syred**, **Syrad**, **Syratt**.

Szablewski Polish: habitation name from a place named with Pol. *szabla* sabre + the possessive suffix *-ew*, with the addition of *-ski*, suffix of local surnames (see BARANOWSKI). The name would have been applied either to a sabre-shaped piece of land or to a place where a noted swordsman lived.

Vars.: **Szabłowski**, **Szabliński**.

Szabó Hungarian (partly Ashkenazic Jewish): occupational name for a tailor, Hung. *szabó*.

Szadkowski Polish: habitation name from a place called *Szadków* or *Szadkowo*, from *szady* grey.

Szántó Hungarian (partly Ashkenazic Jewish): occupational name for a ploughman or farmer, Hung. *szántó* (from *szánt* to plough).

Szczeciński Polish (partly Ashkenazic Jewish): 1. habitation name from the great seaport of *Szczecin* in NW Poland (Ger. *Stettin*), which probably gets its name either from Pol. *szczeć*, a species of sharp spiky grass, or from *szczecina* pine needles or bristles.

2. habitation name derived directly from either of the two vocab. words mentioned above.

A Jewish family bearing this name went from Poland to Wupperthal, Germany, and later to Israel, where one member Hebraicized his name to the like-sounding but otherwise unrelated name **Shani** *('red thread').*

Szczygiel Polish: nickname for a person with bright yellow hair, from Pol. *szczygiel* goldfinch.

Var.: **Szczygielski**.

Cogns.: Czech: **Stehlík**. Ger. (of Slav. origin): **Stieglitz**. Jewish (Ashkenazic): **Stieglitz**, **S(h)tiglitz** (ornamental names).

Széll Hungarian (partly Ashkenazic Jewish): topographic name for someone who lived in a spot exposed to the wind, from Hung. *szél* wind.

Var.: **Szeles**.

Szewc Polish: occupational name for a shoemaker, from a deriv. of Pol. *szewać* to sew (*szew* seam). The word is ultimately cogn. with MHG *sūtære* sewer (see SAUTER, SCHUSTER).

Cogns.: Czech: **Švec**, **Ševc**. Ukr.: **Shvets**.

Dims.: Pol.: **Szewczyk**. Czech: **Ševčík**. Ukr.: **Shevchenko**, **Shevchuk**. Beloruss.: **Shevchik**.

Patrs.: Russ.: **Shvetsov**, **Shevtsov**.

Szigeti Hungarian: topographic name for someone who lived on or near an island, Hung. *sziget*, or habitation name from a place named with this word.

Szklar Polish (partly E Ashkenazic Jewish): occupational name for a glazier, Pol. *szklarz*, an agent deriv. of *szkło* glass.

Var.: **Szklarski**.

Cogns.: Czech: **Sklář**, **Sklenář**. See also STECKLER.

Dim.: Pol.: **Szklarek**.

Szkudlarek Polish: occupational name for a maker of shingles (wooden roof tiles), from a dim. of Pol. *szkudlarz* SHINGLER, a deriv. of *szkudła* shingle.

Szmigiel Polish: 1. nickname for a fast and furious driver of a horse-drawn vehicle, from Pol. *śmigać* to crack the whip.

2. nickname for a tall, thin man, from Pol. dial. *śmigły* tall and thin, gangly.

Vars.: **Szmigielski**, **Śmigielski**.

Szuba Polish: from Pol. *szuba* fur-lined coat, a nickname for someone who habitually wore one or a metonymic occupational name for a dealer in fur-lined coats.

Var.: **Szubski**.

Szurgot Polish: nickname for a dirty, untidy person, or one who talked nonsense, from Pol. *szurgot* ragamuffin, buffoon.

Szürke Hungarian: nickname for a grey-haired man or for someone who habitually dressed in grey, from Hung. *szürke* grey.

Szydłowski Polish: in form, a habitation name referring to a place where a worker in leather lived, especially a shoemaker, from Pol. *szydło* awl + *-ów* possessive suffix + *-ski* suffix of local surnames (see BARANOWSKI). In practice this would often have amounted to an occupational name for a shoemaker.

Var.: **Szydłowiecki**.

Cogn.: Czech: **Šidlo** (occupational name for a shoemaker).

T

Tabak German and Jewish (Ashkenazic): metonymic occupational name for a seller of tobacco, from Ger. *Tabak*, Yid. *tabik* (both ultimately from Sp. *tabaco*, of Caribbean origin). As a Ger. surname, this is of relatively late formation, since tobacco was not introduced into Europe until the 16th cent.

Vars.: Jewish: **Tabakman, Tabekman**; **Tabatchnik, Tabacznik, Tabatznik** (E Ashkenazic); **Tabakero** (Sefardic).

Patrs.: Jewish: **Tabatchnikov, Tabashnikov** (E Ashkenazic).

Tabard English and French: nickname for a habitual wearer of a *tabard*, a long sleeveless coat of heavy material, or occupational name for a maker or seller of such garments. Originally the normal outdoor wear of peasants and soldiers, the tabard was later adopted by knights as an outer garment emblazoned with armorial bearings, and hence by the 16th cent. had become specialized as the official coat of a herald.

Vars.: Eng.: **Tabbitt**. Fr.: **Tabart**.

Cogn.: Ger.: **Tappert**.

Dims.: Fr.: **Tabarel, Tabareau, Tabarin, Tabary**.

Taboada Spanish (Galicia): habitation name from any of various places, for example in the province of Lugo, so called from the dial. term *taboada* plot of land marked out with drainage channels (Sp. *tablada*, L (*terra*) *tabulāta*, a deriv. of *tabula* board, writing tablet, record; the reference is to the division of the land into strips like the columns of accounts or lists).

Tabor 1. English: metonymic occupational name for a drummer, from ME, OF *tabo(u)r* drum (of uncertain origin, perhaps ultimately from Pers. *tabīr*).

2. Jewish (Israeli): ornamental name taken from Mount *Tabor* (Hebr. *Tavor*), in Israel.

Vars. (of 1): **Taber, Tabah**; **Tab(b)erer, Tabborah, Tabrar** (with the addition of ME agent suffixes); **Tab(b)erner, Tab(i)ner** (from the ME verb *tabourn(en)* to drum, OF *tabourner*). (Of 2): **Tavor**; **Tabori, Tabory, Tavori, Tavory** (all with the Hebr. adj. ending *-i*, but among Hung. Jews adopted under the influence of the Hung. surname *Tábori*; see TABORSKI).

Cogns. (of 1): Fr.: **Tab(o)ur, Tambur**; **Tambourier**; **Tabournier**. It.: **Tambur(r)i, Tamburo**. Jewish (Rumanian): **Tamb(o)ur**.

Dims. (of 1): Fr.: **Tabourel, Taboureaux, Ta(m)bourin, Tab(o)uret, Tabourot**. It.: **Tamburelli, Tamburello, Tammurello, Tambur(l)ini, Tamburino, Tamborino**.

Taborski Polish: topographic name for someone who lived at a minor settlement, from Pol. *tabor* camp, encampment + *-ski* suffix of local surnames (see BARANOWSKI).

Cogns.: Czech: **Táborský**. Hung.: **Tábori**.

Tache French: nickname for someone with a birthmark or scar, from OF *tache*, *teche* spot, stain (probably of Gmc origin). The word also had different technical meanings in various medieval crafts and trades, and in some cases the surname may have originated as an occupational name connected with one of these.

Vars.: **Taché**; **Taque** (Normandy).

Dims.: **Tachet, Tacheau, Tachon, Tachot**; **Taquet** (Normandy).

Tadié French: from a vernacular form of the given name *Thaddeus*. This is the name given in St Mark's Gospel to one of Christ's disciples, referred to elsewhere as Judas son of James. It represents an Aramaic form *Thaddai*, of uncertain origin; it may be of Hebr. origin and mean 'Beloved', 'Desired', but it is also possible that it is an adaptation of the Gk name *Theodōros* (see THÉODORE).

Var.: **Thaddée**.

Cogns.: Eng.: **Thaddey, Taddye**. It.: **Tad(d)ei, Tad(d)eo, Taddio, Taddia**. Pol.: **Tadeusz**.

Dims.: It.: **Taddeini, Tad(ol)ini, Taddeucci**. Pol.: **Tadeusik**.

Patrs.: Pol.: **Tadeusiewicz**; **Tadeusiak**. Russ.: **Fad(n)eev, Fadeichev, Khadeev**.

Patrs. (from dims.): Russ.: **Fadyshin**. Croatian: **Tadić**.

Taggart Scots and N Irish: Anglicized form of Gael. **Mac an t-Sagairt** 'son of the priest', from *sagart* priest. Marriage by members of the clergy was illegal and invalid after the 12th cent., but was frequently practised nevertheless.

Vars.: **McEntaggart, McIntaggart, McTaggart, (Mc)Taggert, Taggairt, Tagart, Taggard, Target**.

Tagliavini Italian: apparently a nickname for an alleged adulterator of wine, from It. *taglia(re)* to cut (see TAILLANT) + *vino* wine (L *vīnum*).

Taillant French: occupational name for a tailor or nickname for a good swordsman, from *taillant* cutting, pres. part. of OF *tailler* to cut (LL *taliāre*, from *talea* (plant) cutting; cf. TALLIS and TAYLOR).

Cogn.: Eng. (Norman): **Tallant**.

Pejs.: Fr.: **Ta(i)llard**.

Tait Scots and N English: nickname for a cheerful person, from ON *teitr* cheerful, gay. This surname is quite distinct in origin from TATE.

Var.: **Teyte**.

Talavera Spanish: habitation name from any of several places, in the provinces of Badajóz, Cáceres, Lérida, and Toledo, all of which seem to be so called from the (attested) pre-Roman personal name *Talavus*, *Talevus* + the L local suffix *-āria*; cf. TÀVARES.

Talbot English (Norman): of much disputed origin, but probably from a Gmc personal name composed of the elements *tal* destroy (cf. TALLEYRAND) + *bod* message, tidings (cf. BOTHA), i.e. 'messenger of destruction'.

Vars.: **Talbott, Talbut(t), Taulbut**.

Cogns.: Fr.: **Tal(a)bot** (apparently reintroduced by Eng. immigrants to France in the 14th and 15th cents.).

Talbot *is the name of an ancient Irish family of Norman origin, who have held the earldoms of Shrewsbury and Waterford since the 15th cent. They were granted the baronial estate of Malahide, near Dublin, by Henry II (1154–89), an estate which they held for over 850 years. They trace their descent from Richard* de Talbott, *mentioned in Domesday Book. His son, Hugh* de Talbot *or* Talebot'h, *became governor of Plessis Castle, Normandy, in 1118.*

Talboys English: 1. occupational name for a woodcutter, from OF *taille(r)* to cut (see TAILLANT) + *bosc*, *bois* wood (see BOIS).

2. habitation name from *Taillebois* in Orne, Normandy, so called from OF *taille* clearing (see TALLIS) + *bosc*, *bois* wood.

Vars.: **Tallboy(s)**.

Cogn.: Fr.: **Taillbois**.

Tall English: nickname for a respectable or decent person, or else a good-looking one, both these senses belonging to ME *tall* (OE *getæl* swift, prompt). The mod. sense 'of high stature' did not develop until the end of the 16th cent.; the usual ME equivalents were LONG and HIGH.

Talleyrand French: of uncertain origin, perhaps from a Gmc personal name composed of the elements *tal* destroy (cf. TALBOT) + *rand* (shield) rim, shield.

Tallis 1. English (Norman): habitation name from some minor locality named with ANF *taillis* clearing in an area of woodland (a deriv. of *tailler* to cut; cf. TAILLANT).

2. Jewish (Ashkenazic): from Yid. *tales* prayer shawl (from Hebr. *talit*).

Vars. (of 2): **Talis(man)**; **Talisnik** (E Ashkenazic); **Talit(man)** (Israeli).

Cogns. (of 1): Fr.: **Tailly, Taillé, Taille**. Prov.: **Taillade, Talhade**.

Tallon English and Irish (Norman), and French: 1. from a Gmc personal name derived from the element *tal* destroy, either as a short form of a cpd name with this first element (cf. TALBOT and TALLEYRAND) or as an independent byname.

2. metonymic nickname for a swift runner or for someone with a deformed heel, from OF *talon* heel (a dim. of *tal*, L *tālus*).

Vars.: Ir.: **Talún** (a Gaelicized form). Fr.: **Talon**.

Talma French: habitation name from *Talmas* in Somme, Picardy, so called from L *templum Martis* temple of *Mars*, the Roman god of war.

Tamblyn English (chiefly Devon and Cornwall): from the ME given name *Tamlin*, a double dim., with the ANF suffixes *-el* and *-in*, of *Tam*, *Tom*, itself a short form of THOMAS.

Vars.: **Tamblin(g), Tamplin**; **Tamlin, Tamlyn**.

Tame English: 1. nickname for a quiet and gentle person, from ME *tame* tame, domesticated (OE *tam*).

2. habitation name from *Thame* in Oxon., so called from a Brit. river name, meaning possibly 'dark'.

Tamminen Finnish: ornamental name from Finn. *tammi* oak + the genitive suffix *-nen*, perhaps sometimes chosen as a topographic name by someone who lived by an oak tree.

Tancred English: from an OF personal name, *Tancred*, composed of the Gmc elements *þank* thought + *rēd* counsel. This was introduced to Britain by the Normans. There has been some confusion with TANKARD.

Cogns.: Fr.: **Tancrède**. It.: **Tancredi**; **Tangredi** (Naples).

A family by the name of Tancred *trace their descent from William* Tanckard, *steward of Knaresborough Forest in the reign of Henry III (1216–72). He held lands in Yorks., where his family had already been established for several generations; his great-grandfather, Richard* Tankard, *lived at Boroughbridge*.

Taney English (Norman): habitation name from Saint-Aubin-du-Thennay or Saint-Jean-du-Thennay in Eure, Normandy, both so called from an uncertain first element (possibly a Gallo-Roman personal name or the Gaul. element *tann* oak, holly; cf. TANNER 1) + the local suffix *-ācum*.

Var.: **Tawney**.

Tanguy Breton, English (Norman), and French: from a Bret. personal name composed of the elements *tān* fire + *ci* dog, borne by a 6th-cent. Christian saint associated with Paul Aurelian. The name was introduced into England at the time of the Norman Conquest, and was reintroduced into Cornwall independently at a later date.

Vars.: Eng.: **Tangye, Tingay, Tingey, Tengue**; **Tangney** (Ireland). Fr.: **Tanneguy, Tinguy**.

Tankard English: 1. from a Norman personal name, *Tancard*, composed of the Gmc elements *þank* thought + *hard* hardy, brave, strong. See also TANCRED.

2. metonymic occupational name for a maker of barrels and drinking vessels, or nickname for a hardened drinker, from ME *tankard* tub, cup (apparently a borrowing from MDu.).

Tann 1. German: topographic name for someone who lived in a forest, Ger. *Tann* (MHG *tan*). This was originally a distinct word from TANNE pine tree, and denoted a forest of any kind. Inevitably, however, the two became confused, with the result that *Tann* now denotes only coniferous forests; it is a rather rare and literary word.

2. English (E Anglia): occupational name, a var. of TANNER.

Tanne German: topographic name for someone who lived near a conspicuous pine tree or among pine trees, Ger. *Tanne* pine (MHG *tanne*, OHG *tanna*).

Cogn.: Low Ger.: **Dannemann**.

Cpds (ornamental): Jewish (Ashkenazic): **Tan(n)enbaum, Tanenboim** ('pine tree'); **Tanenholz** ('pine timber'); **Tannenwald** ('pine forest'); **Tanenwurzel** ('pine root').

Tanner 1. English: occupational name for a tanner of skins, ME *tanner* (OE *tannere*, from LL *tannārius*, reinforced by OF *taneor*, from LL *tannātor*; both LL forms derive from a verb *tannāre*, possibly from a Celt. word for the oak, whose bark was used in the process).

2. German: topographic name, a var. of TANN and TANNE.

3. Finnish: ornamental name from Finn. *tanner* open field, or topographic name chosen by someone who lived by an open field, Finn. *tanner*.

4. Jewish (Ashkenazic): of unknown origin.

Vars. (of 2): **Thanner, T(h)enner**.

Cogns. (of 1): Fr.: **Tanneur, Letanneur**. (Of 2): Low Ger.: **Danner, Denner(t)**.

Dims. (of 1): Fr.: **Tan(ne)ret, Tanron**.

Equivs. (of 1, not cogns.): Prov.: ESCOFFIER. It.: SCORZA. Ger.: GERBER, LAUER. Hung.: TIMÁR.

Tansey Irish and Scots: Anglicized form of Gael. **Mac an Tánaiste** 'son of the *tanist*' (*tanist* denoted the heir presumptive to a throne).

Tansley English: habitation name from a place in Derbys., so called from OE *tān* branch(ing valley) + *lēah* wood, clearing.

Tanzer 1. German: nickname for a skilled or enthusiastic dancer, or occupational name for a professional acrobat, from Ger. *Tanzer* dancer, an agent deriv. of MHG *tanzen* to dance (from OF *danser*, of disputed origin; the initial *t-* is the result of hypercorrection of a presumed Low Ger. form).

2. Jewish (Ashkenazic): apparently of similar origin to the German name. There were, however, no Jewish acrobats, and Jews generally danced only at weddings. The name may have been taken by Chasidim, since members of

this branch of Jewry (which arose in the 18th cent.) do place great emphasis on dancing.

Vars. (of 1): **Tänz(l)er, Tenzer; Dantzer, Dentz(ler)**. (Of 2): **Tantzer, Ten(t)zer, Tantzman; Tanc(man)** (Polish spelling).

Cogns.: Eng.: **Dance(r)**. Fr.: **Danse**.

Dims.: Ger.: **Denzel, Denzle**. Fr.: **Danset(te), Dancet(te), Dansin**.

Tapia Spanish: topographic name for someone who lived by a mud wall, Sp. *tapia* (of uncertain origin), or, more commonly, a habitation name from one of the places named with this word, in the provinces of Burgos, León, and Oviedo.

Var.: **Tapias**.

Cogns.: Cat.: **Tàpia(s), Tàpies**. Prov.: **Tapie, Latapie; Tapié**.

Tapp English: from an OE personal name *Tæppa*, of uncertain origin and meaning.

Var.: **Tappe**.

Dims.: **Tap(l)in**.

Patrs.: **Tapping** (Bucks.); **Tapps(on)**.

Tappenden English: habitation name from an unidentified place, probably so called from the gen. case of the OE personal name *Tæppa* (see TAPP) + OE *denu* valley (see DEAN 1).

Tapster English: 1. occupational name for a wine merchant, tavern keeper, or hostess in a tavern, ME *tapster* (an agent deriv. (formally fem.) of *tappen* to draw off, from *tap* tap).

2. occupational name for a weaver or seller of carpets or figured cloths, from ANF *tap(is)ser* (LL *tapētiārius*, an agent deriv. of *tapētium* carpet, Gk *tapētion*, dim. of *tapēs*, gen. *tapētis*).

Var. (of 1): **Tapper**.

Tarasov Russian: patr. from the given name *Taras* (Gk *Tarasios* 'Native of *Taras*', a place in S Italy now known as *Taranto*), which was borne by an 8th-cent. patriarch of Constantinople much venerated in the Eastern Church.

Vars.: **Tarasyev, Taranov**.

Cogn.: Beloruss.: **Taras** (not patr.).

Dims.: Russ.: **Tarasikov** (patr.). Ukr.: **Tarasyuk**. Beloruss.: **Tarasenya, Tarasyonok; Tarashkevich** (patr.).

Tarbock English: habitation name from a place in Lancs., so called from OE *þorn* thorn bush (see THORN 1) + *brōc* BROOK; in Domesday Book it is already *Torboc*, but the form *Thornebrooke* occurs as late as the mid-13th cent., when Sir Henry *de Torbok*, bailiff of the territory between the Ribble and Mersey, is recorded also as Henry *de Thornebrooke*.

Vars.: **Tarbuck, Tarbox, Terbocke**.

Tarczyński Polish: habitation name from a place called *Tarczyn* (there is one SW of Warsaw, and another is now in the Soviet Union), named from Pol. *tarcz* shield + *-yn* possessive suffix, with the addition of *-ski* suffix of local surnames (see BARANOWSKI).

Tarde French: habitation name from *Tardes* in Creuse, probably so called from LL *Tarda* (*villa*) 'settlement (see VILLE) of *Tardus*', a byname meaning 'Slow' (cf. TARDIF).

Tardif English and French: nickname for a sluggish person, from ME, OF *tardif* slow (LL *tardīvus*, for class. L *tardus*).

Vars.: Eng.: **Tardew**. Fr.: **Tardy, Tardieu**.

Dims.: Fr.: **Tardiveau, Tardivel, Tard(iv)on**.

Targownik Polish: occupational name for a merchant or trader, Pol. *targownik* (from *targ* market, trade).

Var.: **Targowski**.

Tarkowski Polish: habitation name, probably from a place named with OPol. *tarkać* to rattle, chatter, whirr + *-ów* possessive suffix, with the addition of *-ski* suffix of local surnames (see BARANOWSKI).

Tarleton English: 1. habitation name from *Tarleton* in Lancs., near Croston, so called from the ON personal name *Þórvaldr* (see THOROLD) + OE *tūn* enclosure, settlement.

2. habitation name from *Tarlton* in Gloucs., recorded in Domesday Book as *Tornentone* and *Torentune*, and of the same origin as THORNTON 1.

Var.: **Tarlton**.

Tarling English: habitation name from *Terling* in Essex, apparently so called from the OE tribal name *Tyrhtelingas* 'people of *Tyrhtel*'.

Tarn N English: topographic name for someone who lived by a tarn, a small lake or pool, Northern ME *tarne* (ON *tarnu*).

Tarnowski Polish and Jewish (E Ashkenazic): habitation name from one of the places called *Tarnów*, named with Pol. *tarn* blackthorn + *-ów* possessive suffix, with the addition of *-ski* suffix of local surnames. There are at least two places so named; in the case of the Jewish surname, the source is usually, if not exclusively, the city in Galicia.

Vars.: Jewish: **Tarnovski, Tarnovsky**; TURNER.

Tarpey Irish: Anglicized form of Gael. **Ó Tarpaigh** 'descendant of *Tarpach*', a byname originally denoting a sturdy person.

Var.: **Torpy**.

Tarr English (Bristol): apparently from the vocab. word *tar* (OE *te(o)ru*), and applied perhaps to someone who worked with tar or bitumen in waterproofing ships.

Tarragó Catalan: habitation name from the city of *Tarragona* in NE Spain. The placename is first recorded in L as *Tarraco* (gen. *Tarracōnis*), but the meaning is unknown. It is an extremely ancient city, captured by the Romans from the Carthaginians in the Second Punic War (218 BC).

Cogns.: Jewish (Sefardic): **Taragan(o)**.

Tarrant 1. English: topographic name for someone living on the banks of the river *Tarrant* in Dorset, which is of the same origin as TRENT. As well as giving rise to a surname, it has been added as a distinguishing epithet to several Dorset placenames.

2. Irish: Anglicized form of Gael. **Ó Toráin** 'descendant of *Torán*', a personal name from a dim. of *tor* hero, champion.

Tarrés Catalan: habitation name from a place in the province of Lérida, of uncertain origin. It is probably from the pl. form of a var. of Cat. *terrer* plot of land (LL *terrārium*, a deriv. of *terra* land).

Tartaglia Italian: nickname for a stammerer, from It. *tartagliare* to stammer, stutter.

Tartakowski Polish: habitation name from a place named with Pol. *tartak* sawmill + *-ów* possessive suffix, with the addition of *-ski* suffix of local surnames (see BARANOWSKI).

Tartier French: occupational name for a baker or seller of filled pastries, from an agent deriv. of OF *tarte* pastry, pie (of unknown origin).

Var.: **Tartière** (a fem. form).

Augs.: **Tart(e)rat**.

Tash English: topographic name for someone who lived by an ash tree, from the ME phrase *at(te) asche* at (the) Ash.

Vars.: **Tasche, Tesh(e)**.

Tasker English: occupational name for someone who did piece-work, from an agent deriv. of ANF *tasque* task (OF *tasche*, LL *taxa*, of uncertain origin), applied particularly to someone who threshed corn with a flail.

Cogn.: Fr.: **Tascher**.

Dim.: Fr.: **Taschereau**.

Tasse French: metonymic occupational name for a maker or seller of purses and bags, or nickname for a rich man or a miser, from OF *tasse* purse (apparently of Arabic origin).

Vars.: **Tassier, Tassié** (agent derivs.).

Cogn.: Du.: **Tasman**.

Dims.: Fr.: **Tasset, Tassin, Tasson, Tassot**.

Pejs.: Fr.: **Tassard, Tassaud**.

Tasso Italian: 1. topographic name for someone who lived near a prominent yew tree, It. *tasso* (L *taxus*, gen. *taxi*).

2. nickname for a person thought to resemble a badger in some way, for example in his nocturnal habits, from It. *tasso* badger (LL *taxo*, gen. *taxōnis*, of Gmc origin; cf. Dachs).

3. from a Gmc personal name derived from the obscure element *tāt* (possibly akin to OHG *tāt* deed; see also Tate).

Var.: **Tassi**.

Cogns. (of 2): Fr.: **Taisson, Tesson**.

Dims.: It.: **Tasselli, Tassetto, Tassino, Tassotto**; **Tasin(i)** (Venetia). (Of 2 only): Fr.: **Tessel**.

Collectives (of 1): Sp.: **Tejeda** (the name of places in the provinces of Cáceres and Salamanca). Port.: **Teixeira**.

Tatarinov Russian: patr. from the name *tatarin* Tatar (apparently ultimately from a Turkic word meaning 'Stammerer'). The word came to be used in languages outside Russia (e.g. Czech and Italian) as a nickname for a wild or uncontrolled person. However, in English, this use did not develop until the late 16th or early 17th cent., and there are no surnames derived from it.

Var.: **Tatarintsev**.

Cogns. (not patrs.): Pol.: **Tatarski**. Czech: **Tatar**.

Cogns. (nicknames): It.: **Tartari, Tartaro**.

Cogns. (patrs.): Pol.: **Tatarowicz, Tatar(ki)ewicz**.

Dims.: Czech: **Tatárek**. It.: **Tartarini, Tartarino, Tarterini, Tartarelli**.

Aug.: It.: **Tartaroni**.

Tate English: from the OE personal name *Tāta*, possibly a short form of various cpd names with the obscure first element *tāt*, or else a nursery formation.

This surname is widespread and common; the chief areas of concentration are Yorks. and Northumb.

Tatham English: habitation name from a place in N Lancs., so called from the OE personal name *Tāta* (see Tate) + OE *hām* homestead.

Vars.: **Tatam, Tatem, Tatum**.

Tatishchev Russian: patr. from the ORuss. nickname *Tatishche*, a dim. of *tat* thief. Family tradition, however, prefers to derive the name from the phrase *tat ishchi* 'seek out the thief', allegedly a nickname denoting a minor official who pursued a vigorous policy of law and order.

The French actor Jacques **Tati** *(1908–82) was of Russian origin; his grandfather was Count Dmitri* **Tatischeff**, *an attaché at the Russian embassy in Paris, who married a Frenchwoman.*

Tatler English: of uncertain origin. It would seem to be a nickname for someone who was unsteady in either his gait or his speech, from ME *tatelen* to falter, stammer (from MDu., of imitative origin). The sense 'gossip' did not develop until the 16th cent.

Vars.: **Tattler, Tatlar, Tatlor**.

The first known bearer of the name is Christopher Tatler, *recorded in 1491 at Mabelthorpe, Lincs. The surname is most common in E Staffs. and S Derbys., and is now found also in the U.S.A., Canada, Australia, and New Zealand.*

Tattersall English: habitation name from *Tattershall* in Lincs., so called from the gen. of the OE personal name *Tāthere* (composed of an obscure element *tāt* + *here* army) + OE *halh* nook, recess (see Hale 1). The surname has been common in Lancs. from an early period.

Vars.: **Tattershall, Tattershaw, Tattersill, Tettersell, Tetsall**.

Tattersfield English: probably a habitation name from *Tatsfield* in Surrey, so called from the gen. case of an OE personal name *Tātel* + OE *feld* pasture, open country (see Field).

Tatton English: habitation name from places in Ches. and Dorset, so called from the OE personal name *Tāta* (see Tate) + OE *tūn* enclosure, settlement.

Taube 1. German and Jewish (Ashkenazic): 1. from Ger. *Taube* pigeon, dove (MHG *tūbe*, OHG *tūba*; cogn. of Eng. Dove). This is either a metonymic occupational name for a keeper of doves or pigeons, a nickname for a mild and gentle person, or, in the case of the Jewish surname, an ornamental adoption of the vocab. word or its Yid. cogn. *toyb*.

2. Jewish (Ashkenazic): from the Yid. female given name *Toybe* (from Yid. *toyb* dove).

Vars. (of 1): Ger.: Tauber, **Taubner, Taubert, Täuber(t), Teuber(t), Taubner, Teubner**; **Daube, Dauber(t), Däubler, Deubler, Deibler, Deubner, Deibner**. Jewish: **Taubman** (see also Tauber 2). (Of 2): **Daube**.

Metrs. (from 2): **Toibin** (E Ashkenazic, with the Slavic suffix *-in*), **Tojbin** (Pol. spelling); **Tobis** (S Ashkenazic, from a regional pronunciation of *Toybe*, with Yid. possessive *-s*); **Taubes, Taubin** (Germanized forms).

Metr. (from a dim. of 2): **Taubkin** (from the Yid. dim. female given name *Toybke*).

Cpds (ornamental): Jewish: **Tauberg** ('dove hill'); **Taubenblat(t)** ('dove leaf'); **Taubenfeld** ('dove field'); **Taubenhaus** ('dove house', partly Anglicized as **Taubenhouse**); **Taubenschlag** ('dovecot').

Tauber 1. German and Jewish (Ashkenazic): var. of Taube 1, from an agent noun deriv. ending in *-er*.

2. German and Jewish (Ashkenazic): nickname for a deaf person, from Ger. *taub* deaf (MHG *toup*), with the strong inflectional ending *-er*, originally used before a male given name. The adj. also had the sense 'stupid', and this may lie behind some examples of the Ger. name.

3. German: occupational name for a player of the horn or a similar musical instrument, MHG *toubære*.

Vars. (of 1 and 2): Ger.: **Taub(mann), Daub(mann)**. Jewish: **Taub(man)** (see also Taube).

Cogns. (of 2 only): Low Ger.: Dove, **Dowe, Duwe, Do(o)be**. Flem., Du.: **De Duve, De Doove**.

Patr. (from 2): Flem., Du.: **Den Dooven**.

Taufer German: name for a member of the Anabaptist sect, who believed in adult rebaptism, from an agent deriv. of Ger. *taufen* to baptize (MHG *toufen*, a cogn. of mod. Eng. *dip* and a calque of LL *baptizāre*, from Gk *baptein* to dip).
Vars.: **Tauffer, Täufer**.

Taupin French: nickname for a short-sighted or stupid person, or for someone who habitually dressed in a brownish grey colour, from a dim. of OF *taupe* mole (L *talpa*).
Var.: **Taupeau**.
Dims.: **Taupenot, Taupeneau**.
Pej.: **Taupinard**.

Tavares Portuguese: habitation name from any of at least seven minor places so called, first recorded in the forms *Taavares* and *Thalavares*. It is probably a deriv. of the personal name *Talavus* (see TALAVERA).

Taverner English: occupational name for an innkeeper, ANF *taverner* (OF *tavernier*, LL *tabernārius* from *taberna* shop, inn). OIt. *taverna* was also used of a stable, and in Tuscany of a slaughterhouse, and the It. cogns. may have referred to someone employed at one of these places.
Vars.: **Tavernor, Taven(n)er, Tavenor, Tav(i)ner, Tavender**.
Cogns.: Fr.: **Taver(g)nier, Letavernier; Taverne**. It.: **Taverna(r)i, Tavernieri; Taverna, Taverni**. Sp.: **Tabernero**. Cat.: **Taberner**. Ger.: **Taferner**.

Tawyer English: occupational name for a dresser of white leather, cured with alum rather than tanned with bark, from an agent deriv. of ME *taw(en)* (OE *tawian* to prepare, make ready). See also WHITTIER.
Var.: TOWER.

Taylor English: occupational name for a tailor, from OF *tailleur* (LL *tāliātor*, from *tāliāre* to cut; cf. TAILLANT). The surname is extremely common and widespread, and its numbers have been swelled by its adoption as an Anglicized form of various equivalent names such as SCHNEIDER, SZABÓ, and PORTNOV.
Vars.: **Tayler, Tailour, Taylour**.
Cogns.: Fr.: **Tailleur, Letailleur; Taillandier, Tallendier** (all these terms have a wider meaning than the Eng. one, and may originally have referred to a woodcutter rather than a cloth-cutter).
Patrs.: Eng.: **Taylorson, Taylerson**.
Equivs. (not cogn.): Fr.: SARTRE, COUTURIER. Ger. and Jewish: SCHNEIDER. Ger.: SCHRÖDER. Pol. and Jewish: KRAWIEC. Hung. and Jewish: SZABÓ. Russ. and Jewish: PORTNOV. Jewish: CHAIT.

Tchernovitz Jewish (E Ashkenazic): habitation name from *Czernowitz*, the Ger. name of the city of *Chernovtsy* in the Ukraine, which is named from Slav. *cherny* black (see CHERNYAKOV).

Teacher English: occupational name for an instructor in any branch of learning, or nickname for a wise or a pompous man, from an agent deriv. of ME *teche(n)* to teach (OE *tǣcan*).

Teague 1. Cornish: nickname for a handsome person, from Corn. *tek* fair, beautiful (cf. TEGG 1).
2. Irish: var. of TIGHE.

Teale English: nickname for a person considered to resemble the water-bird in some way, from ME *tele* teal (of uncertain origin).
Vars.: **Teal(l)**.

Tearle English: of uncertain origin, probably a var. of TYRRELL.
The earliest known bearer of the name is Richard Terle, *who was a tenant at Alciston in Sussex in 1335. A certain John Terle is recorded in 1475 at Stanbridge, Beds., and the surname seems to have been concentrated largely in that county.*

Teasdale English: regional name from *Teesdale* in Co. Durham and N Yorks., so called from the river name *Tees* (see SURTEES) + OE *dæl* valley (see DALE).

Tedd English: of uncertain origin, perhaps from a medieval given name, but not the short form of EDWARD represented in mod. Eng. *Ted*. It may have been a short form of an OE or Norman name beginning with the Gmc element **þeudō-* people. An OE name *Teoda* is on record, but there is some controversy whether any of the pre-Conquest *Theod-* names are really OE or whether they are Continental importations. More probably, given the early distribution, it is a habitation name from *Tydd* in Lincs., south of the Wash, which is named from OE *titt* teat, with reference to a small hill.
Patr.: **Teds**.
The earliest known bearers of the name are Robert Tedde *(Fillongley, Warwicks. 1327) and Witto* Ted *(Hundleby, Lincs. 1395).*

Tedesco Italian and Jewish: name for someone of Ger. origin or who spoke German, from It. *tedesco* German (OHG *diutisc*; see DEUTSCH). As a Jewish name, it was given to or taken by Ashkenazic Jews in Italy, or is based on a nickname given to a Jew who had been to Italy.
In Lucca the vars. **Todesco** and **To(d)eschi** were also nicknames for a stammerer; in Naples the var. **Todisco** was a nickname for a tippling simpleton.
Vars. (in addition to those mentioned above): Italian and Jewish: **Tedeschi**. Italian only: **Tudisco** (Sicily, Calabria).
Dims.: Italian and Jewish: **Todeschini**. Italian only: **Tedeschini**.
The Austrian-Jewish industrialist and philanthropist Hermann Todesco *(1792–1844) took this surname after he had acquired the nickname* Todesco *as a result of numerous trips to Italy.*

Tedstone English: habitation name from a pair of places (*Tedstone* Delamere and *Tedstone* Wafre) in NE Herefords. The placename is recorded in Domesday Book as *Tedesthorne*, from the gen. case of an OE personal name of uncertain form (see TEDD) + *þorn* thorn bush (see THORN 1).

Tegg 1. Welsh: nickname for a handsome person, from W *teg* fair, beautiful (cf. TEAGE 1).
2. English: occupational name for a shepherd, from ME *tegge* sheep in its second year (OE *tegga*).
Var. (of 2): **Tigg**.

Teggart English: occupational name for a shepherd, from ME *tegge* young sheep (see TEGG 2) + HEARD herdsman.
Var.: **Tegart**.

Teich German and Jewish (Ashkenazic): topographic name for someone who lived by a pond or lake, Ger. *Teich* (MHG *tīch*, a cogn. of DITCH). See also WEIHER, the equivalent term used in S and W Germany during the Middle Ages. The Jewish name also denoted someone who lived near a river: in Yid. *taykh* means 'river'.
Vars.: Ger.: **Teicher(t), Teichner, Teichler, Teichmann**. Jewish: **Teich(n)er, Teichman(n); Tajchman** (Pol. spelling).

Teig Jewish (Ashkenazic): metonymic occupational name for a baker, from mod. Ger. *Teig* dough, Yid. *teyg*.
Vars.: **Teigman, Taigman; Teigfeld** ('dough field', an ornamental elaboration).

Teil French: topographic name for someone who lived near a lime tree, OF *teil* (L *tilia*).

Vars.: **Theil, Thil(l), Til; Dut(h)(e)il, Dut(h)euil, Duteille; Tilleul** (from the LL dim. *tiliōlus*); **Dut(h)illeul, Dutilleux; T(h)illier**.

Cogns.: Prov.: **Delt(h)eil, Delthil**.

Dims.: Fr.: **Teillet, T(h)illet, T(e)illon, Tillou, Til(le)quin; Dut(h)(e)illet**.

Pejs.: Fr.: **Te(i)lhard, Teillard, T(h)illard, Teillaud**.

Collectives: Fr.: **Thillaye, Theilley, Tilloy; Dutillay, Dutilloy**. Sp.: **Tejada** (the name of places in the provinces of Burgos and Salamanca).

Teinturier French: occupational name for a dyer, from OF *teint(e)ur* (L *tinctor*, from *tingere*, past part. *tinctus*, to dye, stain), with the later addition of the OF agent suffix *-ier* (L *-ārius*).

Vars.: **Tainturier; Leteinturier, Letainturier**.

Cogns.: It.: **Tintore**. Jewish (Ashkenazic): **Tint(n)er** (of uncertain meaning, possibly an occupational name for an ink-maker).

Dims.: It.: **Tintorello, Tintoretto**.

Teitelbaum Jewish (Ashkenazic): ornamental name from Yid. *teytlboym* date palm (from MHG *tahtel* date (OHG *dahtil*, from Gk *daktylos* finger) + *boum* tree). The name may sometimes have been chosen in reference to Psalm 92: 12 'the righteous shall flourish like the palm tree'.

Vars.: **Teitelbo(i)m, Tejtelbaum, Taitelbaum, Taytelboim, Ta(j)telbaum; Teitel(man), Taitel(man), Deitel, Tatelman; T(a)ytel**.

Telegin Russian: patr. from the nickname *Telega* 'Cart', 'Waggon', given presumably as an occupational name to a carter.

Cogn.: Ukr.: **Teliga** (not patr.).

Dim.: Russ.: **Telezhkin** (patr.).

Telfer English (chiefly Northumb.) and Scots: nickname for a strong man or ferocious warrior, from OF *taille(r)* to cut (see TAILLANT) + *fer* iron (L *ferrum*).

Vars.: **Taillefer, Telfair, Tulliver, Tolver**; TELFORD.

Cogns.: Fr.: **Taillefer, Talifert**. It.: **Tagliaferro**.

Telford Scots and English (Northumb.): not, as its form would imply, a habitation name, even though there is a town in Shrops. so called, but a var. of TELFER, assimilated to the pattern of habitation names in *-ford*. The Shrops. place is a 'new town', named after the celebrated Scottish civil engineer Thomas Telford (1757–1834).

Vars.: **Tilfo(u)rd, Talfourd**.

Tell 1. Low German: dim. of *Dietrich*; see DERRICK and TERRY 1.

2. Low German: habitation name from any of the various minor places so called from MLG *telg(e)* branch, twig.

3. Jewish: of unknown origin.

Vars. (of 2): **Telle, Telge**; TELLER; **Tellmann, Telgmann**.

Cogn. (of 2): Eng.: **Tellow**.

Teller 1. Low German: habitation name, a var. of TELL 2.

2. Jewish (Ashkenazic): of uncertain origin, possibly an occupational name for a barber-surgeon, derived from the sign of the platter (Ger. *Teller*, Yid. *teler*), with which barber-surgeons' shops were distinguished in central Europe.

Var. (of 2): **Teler**.

Tello Spanish: from a medieval given name, which is probably of Gmc origin, and may be akin to the Gmc personal name represented by OE *Tila* (cf. TILBROOK, TILBURY, and TILDEN).

Patrs.: Sp.: **Téllez**. Port.: **Teles**.

Tempest English: nickname for someone of blustery temperament, from ME, OF *tempest(e)* storm (L *tempestas* weather, season, a deriv. of *tempus* time).

Cogns.: It.: **Tempesta, Tempesti**.

Dim.: It.: **Tempestini**.

The Tempest *family have been established at Skipton in Craven, Yorks., since at least the 12th cent. An ancestor, Roger Tempest, who held lands there, was witness to a document in 1120.*

Temple 1. English and French: occupational name or habitation name for someone who was employed at or lived near one of the houses ('temples') maintained by the Knights Templar, a crusading order so named because they claimed to occupy in Jerusalem the site of the old temple (ME, OF *temple*, L *templum*, a deriv. of *temere* to cut, referring originally to a sacred enclosure). The order was founded in 1118 and flourished for 200 years, but was suppressed as heretical in 1312.

2. English: name given to foundlings baptized at the Temple Church, London, so called because it was originally built on land belonging to the Templars.

3. Scots: habitation name from the parish of *Temple* in Edinburgh, likewise so called because it was the site of the local headquarters of the Knights Templar.

Vars.: Eng.: **Templar, Templer** (Somerset); **Templeman**. Fr.: **Templier**.

Cogns.: Flem., Du.: **Tempelaar**. Jewish (Ashkenazic): **Tempelman** (reason for adoption as a Jewish surname unknown).

Templeton Scots: habitation name from a place near Dundonald, in the former county of Ayrs. (now part of Strathclyde region), so called from ME *temple* house of the Knights Templar + *toun* settlement (OE *tūn*). There are also places in Wales, Berks. and Devon so called, but these do not seem to be the source of any surnames.

Tena 1. Spanish: topographic name from the dial. term *tena* rough farm building (e.g. a cattle-shed or barn). The word is probably from L *tigna*, pl. of *tignum* beam, plank. There is a place so named in the province of Huesca, and the surname may in part be a habitation name from this.

2. Catalan: metonymic occupational name for a shopkeeper, from OCat. *tena* shop (LL *tenda*).

3. Jewish: of unknown origin.

Tendler German and Jewish (Ashkenazic): occupational name for a dealer in second-hand goods, Ger. *Tändler*, MHG *tendelære*, an agent deriv. of MHG *tändeln* to deal, trade, ultimately from LL *tantum* price (originally meaning 'so much', correlative to *quantum* 'how much'; cf. GANTER). The Ger. vocab. word and the surname are restricted largely to Bavaria, Austria, and the Sudeten Germans.

Vars.: **Tandler, Dandler**.

Tennant English: status name for a farmer who held his land from an overlord by obligations of rent or service, from OF, ME *tenant* (pres. part. of OF *tenir* to hold, L *tenere*). This was the normal situation for landholders in the Middle Ages, since under the feudal system all land belonged ultimately to the king and use of it was granted in return for financial or military support.

Vars.: **Tennent; Tenner** (from an agent noun).

Cogns.: Fr.: **Tenant; Teneur**. Sp.: **Teniente**.

Patr.: Eng.: **Tennents**.

Tenney English (Yorks.): from a medieval given name, a dim. of DENNIS 1. The variation in initial seems to have been occasioned by the model of Gmc personal names with initial *Þ-*, which were often introduced to England in doublet forms with initial *D-* and *T-*; cf., e.g., DERRICK and TERRY 1.

Patrs.: **Tennyson, Tennison, Tenneson.**

This name was taken to America in 1638 by Thomas Tenney, *a member of a party led by the Rev. Ezekiel Rogers from Rowley, Yorks., to found Rowley, Mass. Most (probably all) modern American families with this name are descended from him.*

Tenniel English: of uncertain origin; it may be a var. of DANIEL (cf. the form *Denial* quoted there, and, for the altered initial, TENNEY).

Teplý Czech: nickname for an eager or enthusiastic person, from the Czech adj. *teplý* warm.

Tereshkov Russian: patr. from the given name *Tereshko*, a dim. form of *Terenti* (L *Terentius*, an old Roman family name). This name was borne by numerous early Christian saints.

Terrón Spanish: topographic name for someone who lived by a plot of agricultural land, Sp. *terrón* (a deriv. of L *terra* land; cf. TARRÉS).

Terry 1. English: from the common Norman personal name, *T(h)erry* (OF *Thierri*), composed of the Gmc elements **þeudō-* people, race + *rīc* power. Theodoric was the name of the Ostrogothic leader (*c*.454–526) who invaded Italy in 488 and established his capital at Ravenna in 493. His name was often taken as a deriv. of Gk *Theodōros* (see THÉODORE).

2. Irish: Anglicized form of Gael. *Mac Toirdhealbhaigh*; see MCTERRELLY and CURLEY.

3. Provençal: occupational name for a potter, from OProv. *terrin* earthenware vase (a dim. of *terre* earth, L *terra*).

Vars. (of 1): **Terrey, Tarry, Torr(e)y, Torrie, Todrick.** See also DERRICK.

Cogns. (of 1): Fr.: **Thierry, Thi(é)ry, T(h)éry.** Fris.: **Tiark, Tjark, Jar(c)k.**

Dims. (of 1): Fr.: **Thiriet, Thiriez, Theuriet, Thiriot, Thériot, Thirion, Thir(i)eau.** Ger.: **Tietze(l), Thielsch, Tilke, Tillich.** Low Ger.: **T(h)iede, Tiedmann, Thie(de)mann, Theimann, The(d)e; Thieke, Tieck(e), Theeck; Tietz(e), Tietzmann, Titze, Tetze; Thiel(e), Tiel, Thielmann, Theil(e), Theilemann, Theel(e), Thele(mann), Telemann, Thälmann,** TELL, TILL; **Thieleke, Thieleck, Tilke.** Fris.: **T(h)ode, Thöl(e), T(h)ölke; Thede; Thade.**

Pejs. (of 1): Fr.: **Thierrard, Thiérard, Thierrart, Thiérart.**

Patrs. (from 1): Eng.: **Torris.** Fris.: **Tiarks, Tjarcks, Jarcks.**

Patrs. (from dims. of 1): Ger.: **Thielscher.** Low Ger.: **The(e)den(s), Th(i)elen(s), Tillmanns; The(e)ding, Thielking; Theeder, Tielker.** Fris.: **Thoden, Tholen, Thölen, T(h)ölken; Todsen; Thedinga.** Flem.: **Tits.**

Teruel Spanish: habitation name from the city of this name in E Spain, so called from L *Turiolum*, a dim. formation from the pre-Roman element *tur* hill (found also in Fr. placenames, and akin to OE *torr*, of Brit. origin). See also THÉRON.

Tess German (of Slav. origin): short form of the various Slav. personal names with a first element *tech* comfort, consolation, e.g. *Techomir* (with a second element meaning 'great', 'famous'), which has itself given the Ger. surname **Tes(s)mer.**

Vars.: **Tessmann, Tetzmann, Tech, Teck.**

Dims.: **Teske, Tetzke, Tetzel, Techel, Teckel.**

Patrs.: **Tessen, Techen.**

Teste French: nickname for someone with a large or ugly head, from OF *teste* head (LL *testa*, originally used to describe an earthenware pot).

Vars.: **Tête; Testu, Tétu.**

Cogns.: It.: **Testa, Testi.**

Dims.: Fr.: **Testot, Tétot, Teston.** It.: **Testini, Testino.**

Augs.: It.: **Testoni, Testone.**

Pejs.: Fr.: **Testard, Tétard, Testart, Tétart, Testaud, Têtaud.** Eng.: **Tester, Testar.**

Tetley English (Yorks.): apparently a habitation name from an unidentified place, perhaps named from the OE byname *Tǣta* or its ON cogn. *Teitr* (cf. TAIT) + OE *lēah* wood, clearing.

Tew 1. English: habitation name from a place in Oxon., named from an OE element *tīewe* row, ridge.

2. Welsh: nickname for a fat man, from W *tew* plump.

Thacker English (W Midlands): occupational name for a THATCHER, from an agent deriv. of Northern ME *thack* thatch (ON *þak*).

Vars.: **Thak(k)er, Thakkar, Thackore; Thaxter** (formally fem., largely confined to Norfolk).

Thackeray English: habitation name from *Thackray* in the parish of Great Timble, W Yorks., now submerged in Fewston reservoir. It was named with the ON elements *þak* thatching, reeds + *(v)rá* nook, corner. The surname is found principally in Yorks. and Cumb.

Vars.: **Thacker(e)y, Thack(w)ray, Thack(a)ra, Thackrah.**

This is an ancient Yorks. name, recorded in the area of Knaresborough Forest in the 14th cent. Its forms included Thakras *and* Thakwras. *Probably the most famous bearer of the name was the novelist William Makepeace* Thackeray *(1811–63), author of* Vanity Fair *(1848). His given names commemorated an ancestor, William Makepeace, a Protestant martyr in the reign of Mary Tudor.*

Thain Scots and English: occupational name for a noble retainer or attendant, ME *thayn* (OE *þeg(e)n*). In Scotland the term was used in the later Middle Ages to denote someone who held land directly from the king.

Vars.: **Thaine, Thayne.**

Thake English: occupational name for a THATCHER, or habitation name for someone who lived in a house with a thatched roof when this was something of a rarity in the neighbourhood. The name is from ME *thake* thatch (OE *ðæc*).

Thatcher English: occupational name for a thatcher, someone who covered roofs in straw, from an agent deriv. of ME *thach(en)* to thatch (OE *þæccan* to cover, roof). See also THACKER and THEAKER, and DECKER 1 for cogns.

Theaker English (Yorks.): occupational name for a THATCHER, from an agent deriv. of Northern ME *theke(n)* to thatch (ON *þekja* to cover, roof).

Thelwall English: habitation name from a place in Ches., so called from OE *þel* plank (bridge) + *wǣl* pool, deep part of a river.

Var.: **Thelwell.**

Theobald English: learned form, re-created from Fr. *Théobald*, of the common medieval given name *Tebald*, *Tibalt* (OF *Teobaud*, *Tibaut*), from a Gmc personal name composed of the elements **þeudō-* people, race + *bald* bold, brave.

Vars.: **Theobold, Tudbald, Tudball, Tidbold, Ti(d)bald, Ti(d)ball, Tibble, Tippell, Tipple, Tebbell, Tebble, Dybald, Dyball, Diboll, Dybell, Dib(b)le, Dyble, Dipple; Tibbett,**

Tibbitt, Tibbott, Tebbet(t), Tebbit(t), Tebbut(t), Debutt, Teboth; Tippett (Cornwall).

Cogns.: Fr.: **Thibaud, Thibout, T(h)ibault, Th(i)ébaud, Thébault; Thépaud** (Brittany); **Thibou** (Belgium). It.: **Te(o)baldi, Tibaldi, Tiboldi, Tipaldi, Tolaldi, Tolaldo**. Ger.: **Theo(d)bald, D(i)ebald, Dewald, Theobold, Diebold, Theopold, Diepold, Tippold, Dippolt, Debelt, Diepelt, Dippelt**. Low Ger.: **Tiepel, Diepel, Dipp(e)l, Teupel; Dibelius** (Latinized). Fris.: **Tiedebohl, Tietböhl**. Flem.: **Debbaut, Dibbaut**. Hung.: **Tibold, Divold**.

Dims.: Eng.: **Tebb, Tibb, Tipp**. Fr.: **Thibaudeau, Thibaudet, Thibaudin**. It.: **Tebaldini**.

Aug.: Fr.: **Thibaudat**.

Patrs.: Eng.: **Theobalds, Tibballs, Tibbles, Tipples; Tibbat(t)s, Tibbet(t)s, Tippetts, Tibbit(t)s, Tibbotts**. It.: **Fittipaldi, Fittipoldi; Tebaldeschi**. Low Ger.: **Diepolder, Diebels**. Flem.: **Dibbauts**.

Patrs. (from dims.): Eng.: **Tebbs, Tibb(in)s, Tippins, Tipson**.

Théodore French: from the given name *Théodore* (Gk *Theodōros*, a cpd of *theos* God + *dōron* gift), relatively popular in the Middle Ages because of its auspicious meaning; cf. DIEUDONNÉ. There has been considerable confusion with the Gmc personal name *Theodoric*; see TERRY. Gk *Th*- regularly gives Russ. *F*-, hence the common Russ. given name *Fyodor*.

Cogns.: Welsh: **Tudor**. It.: **Teodori, Teodoro; Toderi, Todeo, Todari, Todaro** (NE Italy); **Totaro** (S Italy). Port.: **Teodoro**. Rum.: **Tudor**. Ger.: **Joder** (chiefly Swiss). Pol.: **Teodorski; Fedorski, Fedyński**. Hung.: **Tódor**.

Dims.: Fr.: **Doret, Dorot, Dorin**. It.: **Toderini, Todarini, Todarello**. Ger.: **Jöderli** (Swiss). Ukr.: **Tedorenko, Fedoronko, Fedorchenko, Fedorchik, Fesenko, Fedko, Khvedko**. Beloruss.: **Fedorinchik, Fedchonok**. Pol.: **Teodorczyk, Fedorczyk, Fedorko, Fedyszyn; Chwedko, Chodźko**.

Patrs.: Russ.: **Fyodorov(ykh)**. Ukr.: **Khodorovich**. Beloruss.: **Teodorovich**. Pol.: **Teodorowicz; F(i)edorowicz**. Croatian: **T(e)odorović**. Bulg.: **Todorov**. Georgian: **Tedoradze**. Armenian: **Torosian**. Rum.: **Teodorescu, Theodoresco**. Greek: **Theodoridis, Theodorakis**.

Patrs. (from dims.): Russ.: **Fedorushov, Fedorishchev, Fedorintsev, Fed(k)in, Fed(i)kov, Fedyakin, Fedyakov, Fedyanin, Fedyash(k)in, Fedya(sh)ev, Fedyukin, Fedyukov, Fedyun(k)in, Fedunov, Fedyunyaev, Fedyush(k)in, Fedichkin, Fedinin, Fedyshin, Fed(e)nev, Fedchin, Fedishchev**. Beloruss.: **Fedorkevich, Khodasevich, Khadkevich**. Pol.: **Chodkiewicz**.

Habitation name: Pol.: **Fedorowski**.

Habitation name (from a dim.): Pol.: **Chwedkowski**.

Théron French: habitation name from a place in the Massif Central, apparently named with a Gaul. element *turon* height, hill (see TERUEL). There seems to have been some confusion with **Thirion**, which is derived from a medieval given name of uncertain origin. Both surnames were borne by Huguenot refugees to England in the 17th–18th cents.

Var.: **Thérond**.

Thewlis English (chiefly Yorks.): nickname for an ill-mannered person, from the northern ME adj. *thewless* badly behaved, immoral (OE *þēawlēas*, a cpd of *þēaw* custom, correct behaviour + *-lēas* lacking, without).

Vars.: **Thewles(s); Thowless** (Scotland).

Thiess Low German: from an aphetic short form of the given name *Mathiess*; see MATTHEW.

Vars.: **Thies(e), Dies(s); Theuss, Deuss; T(h)ew(e)s, Thevs; Theis(s)**.

Cogns.: Fris.: **Thees**. Flem., Du.: **Th(ew)ys**.

Dims.: Low Ger.: **Theismann, Deissmann**.

Patrs.: Low Ger.: **Thies(s)en, Tiessen, Th(i)esing, Diesing; The(u)ssen, Deussen, Deesen, Deus(s)ing; The(u)vissen, Thewissen, Thywissen, Thevessen, Devissen; Theissen, T(h)yssen, Thaysen**. Fris.: **Theesinga**. Flem., Du.: **T(h)ijssen, Diessens, Teewen**. Dan., Norw.: **Thiesen, Theisen, Thuesen, Thygesen**.

Thin English: nickname for a slender man, from ME *thinne* thin (OE *þynne*).

Vars.: **Thynn(e)**.

Cogns.: Ger.: **Dünne**. Flem., Du.: **(De) Dun(ne)**. Jewish (Ashkenazic): **Dinner, Dinman** (from Yid. *din*).

The Thynne *family who are Marquesses of Bath are a branch of the Norman* Botfield *or* Boteville *family of Church Stretton, Shrops. According to family tradition, the name derives from a contraction of ME* (at) the inn, *since an ancestor is supposed to have resided at one of the Inns of Court. However, this is more probably a folk-etymological legend than the true origin of the surname.*

Thirkill English: from the ON personal name *Þorkell*, a contracted form of a name composed of the divine name *Þórr* (see THOR 2) + *ketill* cauldron. The given name *Thurkill* or *Thirkill* was in use throughout England in the Middle Ages; in N England it had been introduced directly by Scandinavian settlers, whereas in the South it was the result of Norman influence. Surnames of this group are especially common in E Anglia, where Norman-French settlement was heavy.

Vars.: **Thurkettle, Thurkittle, Thirkettle; Thurtell, Turtill, Thurtle, Thirtle**, TURTLE, **Tuttle; Thurkell, Thirkell, Turkel, T(h)urgell, Turkill, Thirkhill, Turgill, Thorkell, Toghill**.

Cogns.: Fr.: **Turquetil, Turquety**.

Patrs.: Sc.: **McCorquodale, McCorkindale; McCorkell, McCork(h)ill, McCorkle**. Dan.: **T(h)erkelsen, T(h)erkildsen**.

Thirwell English (Northumb.): probably a habitation name from *Thirlwall* in Northumb., so called from OE *þerel* hollow, perforated + *weall* WALL. The placename apparently referred to a gap in the Roman wall, which passes through the settlement.

Thistlewaite English (Lancs.): habitation name from a minor place in the parish of Lancaster called *Thistlethwaite*, from ME *thistle* (OE *þistel*) + *thwaite* meadow (see THWAITE), i.e. a meadow overgrown with thistles.

Thistlewood English: habitation name from *Thistleworth* farm in the parish of W Grinstead, Sussex, so called from OE *þistel* thistle (cf. DISTEL) + *worð* enclosure (see WORTH).

Thomas English (and Welsh and Cornish), French, German, Dutch/Flemish, and Danish/Norwegian: from the popular medieval given name, of biblical origin. The *-h-* is organic, the initial letter of the name in the Gk New Testament being a theta. The universal Eng. pronunciation as /t/ rather than /θ/ is the result of Fr. influence from an early date. The biblical name was originally an Aramaic byname meaning 'Twin', borne by one of the disciples of Christ, best known for his scepticism about Christ's resurrection (John 20: 24–9). This disciple is stated by Eusebius, on no scriptural authority, to have borne the given name *Judah*. Aphetic forms are common in most European languages; see MAAS.

Vars.: Eng.: **Tomas**. Fr.: **Thoumas**. It.: **Tom(m)asi, Tommaseo, Tom(m)ei, Tom(m)eo, Toma, Tome**. Ger.: **Thoma, Thome**.

Cogns.: Sp.: **Tomás**. Port.: **Tomé**. Cat.: **Tomàs**. Rum.: **Toma**. Czech: **Tůma; Toman, Tomáš, Tomeš, Toms(a)**. Pol.: **Tomas(z), Tomala, Tom(a)**. Hung.: **Tamás(i)**.

Dims.: Eng.: **Thomazin; T(h)om(p)sett; Thom** (Scotland); **Tom(a)lin, Tomblin(g)**, TAMBLYN; **Tom(p)kin, Tonkin** (W Country). Fr.: **Thomasset, Thom(az)et, Thomé; Thomassin,**

Thomelin; Tho(u)masson, Thomazon, Thom(es)son; Thomasseau, Thomazeau. It.: **Tomas(s)ini, Tommasini, Tom(m)asino, Tom(ad)ini, Tomaini, Tomaino, Tumini; Tom(m)aselli, Tom(m)asello, Tomaelli, Tomaello, Tuminelli; Tomas(s)etti, Tommasetti, Tumiotto, Tomasutti, Tom(m)asuzzi, Tomasicchio.** Ger.: **Thömel, Dömel; Theml** (Bavaria); **Teml** (Austria); **Dehmel, Demel(t), Thämel(t), Dähmel, Thümnel.** Low Ger.: **Thomann, Do(h)mann, Themann, Demann, Thumann; Thomke, Domke, Demke, Demchen, Dumke.** Ger. (under Slav. influence): **Tom(as)ek, Domaschek, Tomaschke, Domaschke, Damaschke, Demschke, Tomisch.** Pol.: **Tomaszczyk, Tomaszek, Tomasik, Tomalczyk, Tomanek, Tomczyk, Tomik.** Ukr.: **Khomik.** Czech: **Tomášek, Tománek, Tomeček; Tomek.**

Augs.: It.: **Tomas(s)oni, Tommasoni, Tomadoni.**

Patrs.: Eng.: **Thomas(s)on, Thomerson.** Sc.: McTavish, McOmish. Dan., Norw.: **Thoma(s)sen.** Swed.: **Thomasson.** Beloruss.: **Tomashov, Tomashevich.** Pol.: **Tomaszewicz, Tomasiewicz; Tomowicz.** Lithuanian: **Tomaskunas, Tomaskaitis.** Czech: **Tomšů.** Croatian: **Tomašević, Tom(ov)ić.** Armenian: **Tomasian, Tumasian.**

Patrs. (from dims.): Eng.: **Toms** (chiefly W Country); **Thoms** (chiefly Scots); **Tombs, Toomb(e)s, Tomes, Tommis; Tomlins, Tomblings; Tom(p)kins, Tom(p)kiss, Tomkies, Tomkys; Tonks** (Midlands); **T(h)om(p)son, Tomsen, Thombleson, T(h)omlinson, Tom(p)kinson, Townson.** Sc.: McComb. Low Ger.: **Thoms(en), Thömen, Dohms, Dohmer.** Fris.: **Thöminga.** Flem.: **Tommen.** Dan., Norw.: **Thomsen.** Swed.: **Thomsson.** Russ.: **Fominov, Fom(ush)kin, Fomichkin, Fomichyov.** Beloruss.: **Tomich, Khomich, Khomin, Tomashkov.** Pol.: **Tomaszkiewicz, Tomkowicz, Tomczykiewicz, Tomankiewicz; Chomicz; Tomczak.** Armenian: **Tumayan.**

'Son of the wife of T.': Ukr.: **Khomishin.**

Habitation names: Pol.: **Tomaszewski, Tomaszyński, Tomicki, Chomicki, Chomiński, Chomiszewski.**

Habitation names (from dims.): Pol.: **Tomczyński, Tomczykowski; Tomankowski.**

The most common names in this group in Britain are Thomas *itself and* Thompson. *Both are widely distributed throughout the country,* Thomas *being especially common in Wales and Cornwall, while* Thompson *is rather more common in N England. The form* Thomson *is especially common in Scotland (although not exclusively Scottish).*

Thon 1. German: from an aphetic form of the given name *Ant(h)on*; see Anthony and Toney.

2. Jewish (E Ashkenazic): of unknown origin.

Vars. (of 1): Toni, **Thön; Theng, Deng** (Switzerland, Swabia).

Cogn. (of 1): Low Ger.: **Theun.**

Dim. (of 1): Low Ger.: **Dohnke.**

Patrs. (from 1): Low Ger.: **Thönes, Tön(is)sen. Tönsing.** Du.: **Teunisse(n), Theunissen.**

Patrs. (from dims. of 1): Low Ger.: **T(h)onjes, Thönges, Dönges.**

Thor 1. German: habitation name for someone who lived near the gates of a town or metonymic occupational name for someone responsible for guarding them, from MHG *thor*, OHG *tor* gate (mod. Ger. *Tor*).

2. Swedish: from a given name, a short form of any of the various Scand. personal names containing as their first element *Thor* (ON *Þórr*), the name of the god of thunder in Scandinavian mythology (cf. names such as Thorburn and Thorogood).

Vars. (of 1): **Thormann; Thorwart(h)** (for the second element cf. Ward 1).

Cogns. (of 1): Low Ger.: **Dohr, Do(h)rmann, Dorwart; Amdohr, Amthor.** Flem.: **De Deurwaerder.**

Dims. (of 1): **Thörl; Dörl** (Franconia, Thuringia).

Patrs. (from 2): Swed.: **T(h)or(e)sson, T(h)uresson.** Dan., Norw.: **Thorsen.**

Thorburn Scots and N English: from a Northern ME given name (ON *Þórbjörn*, composed of the divine name *Þórr* (see Thor 2) + *björn* bear, warrior).

Vars.: **Thoburn, Thurburn, Thurbon, Thurban, Thubron, Turbin, Tarbun, Tarbin.**

Thorel French: 1. nickname for a strong or violent individual, from OF *t(h)or(el)* bull; see Toro.

2. from a dim. of an aphetic short form of the given name Maturin.

Vars.: **Thoreau, Thoret, Thoré, Thorez.**

Thorley N English: habitation name. There are places called *Thorley* in Herts. (near Bishop's Stortford) and in the Isle of Wight. However, the surname almost certainly derives from *Thornley* in Lancs. The origin of all of these is OE *þorn* thorn bush (see Thorn 1) + *lēah* wood, clearing.

Var.: **Thornley.**

Thorn 1. English and Danish: topographic name for someone who lived by a thorn bush or hedge (OE, ON *þorn*), or habitation name from a place named with this word, for example *Thorne* in Somerset or *Thorns* in Suffolk.

2. Low German and Danish: topographic name for someone who lived near a tower, from MLG *torn* tower (see Thurn).

3. German: habitation name from the city of *Thorn*, now *Toruń* in Poland, the name of which is from MHG *torn* tower (see Thurn).

Vars. (of 1): Eng.: **Thorne, Thorn(e)s.** (Of 3): **Thörner.**

Cogns. (of 1): Ger.: **Dorn.** Flem., Du.: **Van Doorn, Van den Doorne, Doorneman.** Jewish (Ashkenazic; perhaps assigned as offensive names by anti-Semitic officials): **Dorn(er), Derner, Dornbus(c)h.**

Thornber English: habitation name from *Thornborough* in N Yorks. (*Thornebergh* in 12th-cent. records) or *Thornbrough* in Northumb. and N Yorks. (*T(h)orneburg* in 13th-cent. records). The former is probably so called from OE *þorn* thorn bush + *berg* hill; the latter from *þorn* + *burh* fort. There are other places in England bearing these names, but they are less likely to be the source of the surname.

Vars.: **Thornberry, Thornbury, Thornburgh, Thornborough, Thornborrow.**

Thorndike English: habitation name from some minor place so called from OE *þorn* thorn bush + *dīc* ditch, dyke, or topographic name for someone who lived by a defencework consisting of a thorn hedge and a ditch.

Vars.: **Thorndyke, Thorndick.**

Thornhill English: habitation name from any of various places, for example in Dorset, Wilts., Derbys., and W Yorks., so called from OE *þorn* thorn bush + *hyll* Hill.

Var.: **Thornell** (Wilts.).

A family of the name Thornhill *trace their ancestry to Thomas* de Thornhill (fl. *1338*), *who held the manor of Thornhill in W Yorks.*

Thornton 1. English and Scots: habitation name from any of the numerous places throughout England and Scotland so called, from OE *þorn* thorn bush + *tūn* enclosure, settlement.

2. Irish: translation of Gael. **Mac Sceacháin** 'son of *Sceachán*', a personal name from a dim. of *sceach* thornbush.

3. Irish: Anglicized form of Gael. *Ó Draighneáin*; see Drennan.

Thorogood English: from the Northern ME given name *Thurgod* (ON *Þorgautr*, composed of the divine name *Þórr* (see THOR 2) + the ethnic name *Gautr*; see JOCELYN). The derivation from ME *thur(og)h* completely (OE *þur(u)h*) + *gode* good (OE *gōd*), supported by Ekwall among others, is less plausible.

Vars.: **Thorou(gh)good**, **Thor(r)owgood**; **Thorgood**, **Thurgood**, **Thurgate**.

Cogn.: Fr.: **Turgot**.

Thorold English: from the ME given name *Turold* (ON *Þorvaldr*, composed of the divine name *Þórr* (see THOR 2) + *valdr* rule).

Vars.: **Thorrold**, **Thourault**, **Torode**.

Cogns.: Fr.: **T(h)ouroude**, **Théroude**, **Troude**.

Dims.: Fr.: **Trudon**, **Trudeau**.

Patr.: Dan.: **Thorvaldsen**.

A family by the name of Thorold *trace their descent from Sir Richard* de Thorold, *who lived in Selby, Yorks., in the reign of Edward III.*

Thorpe English: habitation name from any of the numerous places in England named with the ON element *þorp* hamlet, village, or the rarer OE cogn. *þrop*.

Vars.: **Thorp**, **Tharp**, **Turp**; **Thro(u)p**, **T(h)rupp**, **Thripp**. See also TROUP.

Cogns.: Dan., Norw.: **Torp**. Ger.: **Dorfer**, **Dörfer(t)**, **Derfert**. Low Ger.: **Dorp**. Fris.: **Dorpma**. Flem., Du.: **Van Dorp**, **Van den Dorpe**, **Van't Deurp**. Jewish (Ashkenazic): **Dorf**, **Dorf(s)man(n)**.

Dims.: Ger.: **Dörfle(in)**. Jewish: **Derfler** (from Yid. *derfl*, dim. of *dorf* village).

A family named Thorpe *are descended from Sir Robert Thorpe of Thorpe Waterville in Northants, who became a knight before 1315. One of his sons became Lord Chancellor, the other Lord Chief Justice. They were of English rather than Norman descent; one of their forebears, Thurstan, was a bondman who won his freedom in around 1200.*

Thrane Danish: nickname for someone who was thought to resemble a crane (Dan. *trane*, ON *trani*) in some way, most probably in having long spindly legs.

Threadgold English: occupational nickname for someone who embroidered fine clothes with gold thread, from ME *thred(en)* to thread (from OE *þrǣd* thread) + *gold* GOLD.

Vars.: **Threadgould**, **Threadgill**, **Threadgall**, **Threadkell**, **Thridgould**, **Tre(a)dgold**.

Threapleton English (Yorks.): apparently a habitation name from an unidentified place, the etymology of which is unclear. The last element is OE *tūn* enclosure, settlement; the first may represent a personal name *Þrȳðbeald* (composed of the elements *þrȳð* might + *beald* bold, brave), or it may be akin to OE *þrēapland* land over which there was some dispute (from *þrēapian* to quarrel).

Var.: **Thrippleton**.

Threlfall English (Lancs.): habitation name from a place near Kirkham, so called from ME *thrall* serf (ON *þráll*) + *fall* clearing, place where the trees had been felled.

Var.: **Trelfall**.

Thrower S English: occupational name for someone who made silk thread from raw silk, from an agent deriv. of ME *thrōw(en)* (OE *þrāwan* to twist). From the 13th cent. the verb began to be used in its mod. sense, including throwing clay in pottery, and so the surname may also have originated as an occupational name for a potter.

Var.: **Trower**.

Thrussell English: nickname from ME *throstle* thrush (OE *þrostle*), given probably to a cheerful person, the bird being noted for its cheerful song.

Vars.: **Thrustle**, **Throssell**; **Thrush** (OE *þrysce*).

Cogn.: Jewish (Ashkenazic): **Dres(s)ler** (ornamental; from Yid. *dresler* thrush; see also DRECHSLER).

Thumb 1. English: nickname for someone with a missing or deformed thumb, or for someone of very small size, from ME *thum* thumb (OE *þūma*; cf. DAUM).

2. German: nickname for a foolish person, from MHG *tump* ignorant, stupid (OHG *tumb* dumb).

Vars. (of 1): **Thum**. (Of 2): **Thumm**, **Dummer**, **Dummann**.

Thurlow English: habitation name from a place in Suffolk, recorded in Domesday Book as *Tritlawa* and *Tridlauua*, and apparently named from the OE elements *þrȳð* troop, assembly + *hlāw* hill.

Var.: **Thurloe**.

Thurman English: from the ME given name *Thurmond*, ON *Þormundr*, composed of the divine name *Þórr* (see THOR 2) + *mundr* protection.

Vars.: **Thurmand**, **Thorman**.

Thurn German: topographic name for someone who lived near a watch tower or metonymic occupational name for someone responsible for manning it, from MHG *turn*, *torn* tower (from OF *torn*, a byform of *torz*; see TOWER). Some examples may derive from the town of *Thurn* in Austria, named with this word. See also THORN 3.

Vars.: **Thurm**; **Thurner**, **Thurmer**, **Thörmer**.

The German noble family von Thurn und Taxis *came from Milan, and originally bore the name* Della Torre. *They acquired the office of Hereditary Grand Postmasters General of the Holy Roman Empire in 1595, and the rank of Princes of the Empire a century later.*

Thursfield English (W Midlands): habitation name from *Thursfield* (now New Chapel) near Newcastle in Staffs., so called from the ON personal name *Þorvaldr* (see THOROLD) + OE *feld* pasture, open country (see FIELD).

Thurston English: 1. from a medieval given name (ON *Þorsteinn*, composed of the divine name *Þórr* (see THOR 2) + *steinn* stone).

2. habitation name from a place in Suffolk, so called from the gen. case of the ON personal name *Þori* (see THOR 2) + OE *tūn* enclosure, settlement.

Vars. (of 1): **Thurstan**, **Thursting**; **Tustain**, **Tustian**, **Tustin(g)**, **Dusting**; **Tutin(g)**, **Tut(t)on**.

Cogns. (of 1): Fr.: **To(u)(s)tain**, **Toutin**.

Patrs. (from 1): Eng.: **Thurstans**. Swed.: **T(h)orstensson**. Dan., Norw.: **Torstensen**.

Thwaite N English: topographic name for someone who lived by a clearing or patch of pasture land, ME *thwaite* (ON *þveit*), or habitation name from any of the various places named with this word, in N England and in Norfolk and Suffolk.

Vars.: **Thwaites**, **Thwaytes**, **Thoytes**; **Twaite**, **Twatt**, **Twait(e)s**, **Tweats**, **Twite**.

Tichborne English: habitation name from a place in Hants, so called from OE *ticce(n)* goat, kid + *burna* stream (see BOURNE).

Vars.: **Tichbourne**, **Tichbon**, **Tichband**.

Tickle English: habitation name from *Tickhill* in S Yorks., so called from the OE personal name or byname *Tica* (of uncertain origin) or *ticce(n)* kid + *hyll* HILL.

Vars.: **Tickel(l)**.

Tidman English: 1. status name for the head of a tithing, OE *tēoðingmann* (from *tēoðing* tithing, group of households, originally ten households, + *mann* man). According to the medieval system of frankpledge, every member of a tithing was responsible for every other, so that for example if one of them committed a crime the others had to help pay for it.

2. from the ME, OE given name *Tideman*, composed of the OE elements *tīd* time, season + *mann* man.

Vars.: **Tiddeman, Tydeman, Tit(t)man.**

Tidmarsh English: habitation name from a place in Berks., whose name means 'marsh of the people', from OE *þēod* nation + *mersc* MARSH.

Tidy English: nickname for a handsome or admirable person, from ME *tīdi* fine, excellent (a deriv. of OE *tīd* (due) season).

Tierney Irish (esp. common in Galway): Anglicized form of Gael. **Ó Tíghearnaigh** 'descendant of *Tighearnach*', a byname meaning 'Lord', 'Master'.

Vars.: **Tierny, O'Tiern(e)y, (O')Te(a)rney**; LORD.

Dims.: **(O')Tiernan, O'Ternane, Ternan** (Gael. **Ó Tíghearnáin**).

Tiers French: 1. name for a third-born son, from OF *tiers* third (L *tertius*).

2. habitation name from any of various places named from OF *tierce* third part (L *tertia (pars)*), either because they formed part of estates divided into three, or because they were subject to a rent of one-third of the produce raised.

Var.: **Thiers.**

Tiffin English: from the medieval female given name *Tiffania* (OF *Tiphaine*, from Gk *Theophania*, a cpd of *theos* God + *phainein* to appear). This name was often given to girls born around the feast of Epiphany.

Vars.: **Tiffen, Tiffany, Tiffney.**

Cogns.: Fr.: **Tiphai(g)ne, Tiphine, Thiéfaine.**

Dims.: Fr.: **Tif(f)en(n)eau, Tipheneau, Tifon, Tiphon.**

Tighe Irish: Anglicized form of Gael. **Ó Taidhg** 'descendant of *Tadhg*', a byname meaning 'Bard', 'Poet', 'Philosopher'. See also MCCAIG.

Vars.: TEAGUE, **Tague, T(e)igue, Teige, Teage, Teek.**

Dims.: **Teahan, Teehan** (Gael. **Ó Tadhgán**).

Tighe is the name of an Irish family said to be descended from Tadhg, brother of Connor O'Connor (d. 973), King of Connacht. Other sources trace their ancestry to a son of Cathair Mor, King of Ireland in AD 119. The name also took the form O'Teig, *and a branch established in England was known as* de Teye *and* Tiyge. *It is possible that some of them were brought to England as hostages after the treaty of Windsor in 1175.*

Tikhonov Russian: patr. from a given name, *Tikhon* (Gk *Tykhōn*, a deriv. of *tynkhanein* to hit, succeed). This was borne by a 5th-cent. bishop of Cyprus, who finally suppressed the cult of Aphrodite. The popularity of the given name in Russia may have been enhanced by folk-etymological associations with *tikh* quiet, calm, a common element in Slav. cpd personal names.

Var.: **Tikhanov.**

Cogn.: Pol.: CICHY.

Dims.: Russ.: **Tishutkin, Tisheev** (patrs.). Ukr.: **Tishchenko.**

Tilbrook English: habitation name from a place in the former county of Hunts. (now part of Cambs.), so called from the OE byname *Tila* (from *til* capable) + OE *brōc* BROOK.

Tilbury English: habitation name from the port on the Thames in Essex, so called from the OE byname *Tila* (cf. TILBROOK) + OE *burh* fortress (see BURY).

Tilden English: probably a habitation name from an unidentified place, apparently so called from the OE byname *Tila* (cf. TILBROOK) + OE *denu* valley (see DEAN 1).

Tiler English: occupational name for a maker or layer of tiles, from an agent deriv. of ME *tile* tile (OE *tigele*, from L *tēgula*, a deriv. of *tegere* cover). In the Middle Ages tiles were widely used in floors and pavements, and to a lesser extent in roofing, where they did not really come into their own until the 16th cent.

Vars.: **Tyler, Tylor.** See also TILLER.

Cogns.: Fr.: **T(h)uil(l)ier, Tivol(l)ier, Thiolier, Thioller, Théolier, Teulier, Teulié, Tullier, Tulliez.** Sp.: **Tejero.** Ger. and Jewish (Ashkenazic): ZIEGLER. Low Ger.: **Teg(e)ler, Tiegeler.** Du.: **Tichelaar.**

Wat Tyler *(d. 1381), the leader of the English Peasants' Revolt, is referred to in Thomas Walsingham's* Chronicon Angliae *as Walterus* Helier *(see* HELLIER*), which suggests that the name by which he is now generally known was not a hereditary surname but simply a reference to his occupation.*

Till 1. English: from a common medieval female given name, a short form of *Matilda* (see MOULT 1).

2. Low German: dim. of *Dietrich*; see DERRICK and TERRY 1.

Var.: **Tille.** (Of 2 only): **Tillmann.**

Dims. (of 1): TILLEY, **Tillet(t), Tillot(t), Til(l)cock.**

Metrs. (from 1): TILSON.

Tiller English: occupational name for a husbandman, from ME *til(l)er*, a secondary deriv. of OE *tilian* to till, cultivate (cf. TILLEY 3). There has been some confusion with TILER.

Vars.: **Tillier, Til(l)yer, Tillyard; Tillman.**

Tilley English: 1. Norman habitation name from any of various places in N France called *Tilly* (*Tiliācum* in medieval records). Examples in Eure and Calvados are so called from a Gallo-Roman personal name *Tilius* (perhaps from L *tilia* lime tree; cf. TEIL) + the local suffix *-ācum*; one in Seine-et-Oise gets its name from the personal name *Attilius* (a deriv. of *Attalus*, a hereditary name of uncertain origin used by the kings of Pergamum and adopted occasionally in the Roman Empire) + *-ācum*.

2. habitation name from *Tilley* in Shrops., so called from OE *telg(e)* branch, bough (cf. TELL 2) + *lēah* wood, clearing.

3. occupational name for a husbandman, ME *tilie* (OE *tilia*, a primary deriv. of *tilian* to till, cultivate; cf. TILLER).

4. from a medieval female given name, a dim. of TILL.

Vars.: **Tilly** (see also TULLY), **Tillie, Til(e)y, Tyley.**

Cogn. (of 1): Fr.: **Tilly.**

Tilling English: from a medieval given name, possibly a dim. (originally in *-in*) of TILL, but more probably a patr. deriv. of the OE byname *Tila* (see TILBROOK).

Tilson 1. English: metr. from the medieval female given name TILL.

2. Jewish (Ashkenazic): metr. from the Yid. female given name *Tile* (from the Hebr. name *Tehila* 'Splendour').

Vars. (of 1): **Tills(on).** (Of 2): **Til(l)es, Tillis, Tilas, Till(e)son.**

From dims. (of 1): **Tillotson.** (Of 2): **Tilkin.**

Timár Hungarian: occupational name for a tanner, Hung. *timár* (a deriv. of *tim(só)* alum).

Timberlake English: habitation name from a lost place in the parish of Bayton, Worcs., so called from OE *timber* timber, wood + *lacu* stream (see LAKE).

Var.: **Timblick**.

Timbrell English: from ME *tumbrel* cart typically used for carting away and tipping out dung (OF *tomberel*, from *tomber* to fall, let fall), and so a metonymic occupational name for a maker of tip-up carts or for someone who had the job of collecting and transporting dung.

Timm 1. English: probably from an otherwise unrecorded OE personal name, cogn. with the attested Continental Gmc form *Timmo*. This is of uncertain origin, perhaps a short form of DIETMAR. The given name *Timothy* (see TIMOFEEV) was not in use in England until Tudor times, and is therefore not a likely source of this group of surnames.

2. Low German: from a short form of the medieval given name DIETMAR.

Vars. (of 1): **Timme, Tym(m)**. (Of 2): **Thimm, Timme**.

Dims. (of 1): **Timblin, Timkin**. (Of 2): **Thimmann, Thiemeke**.

Patrs. (from 1): **Tim(m)s, Timmes, Tymms; Tim(p)son**.

Patrs. (from 1) (dims.): TIMMONS; **Timmins, Timmi(e)s** (chiefly W Midlands); **Timkiss**.

Timmons 1. English: patr. from a dim. of the given name TIMM.

2. Irish: Anglicized form of Gael. **Mac Toimín** 'son of *Toimín*', a dim. form of *Tomás* THOMAS.

3. Irish: Anglicized form of Gael. **Ó Tiomáin** 'descendant of *Tiomán*', a personal name from a dim. of *tiom* pliant, soft.

4. Irish: Anglicized form of Gael. *Ó Tiománaidhe*; see TIMONY.

Timofeev Russian: patr. from the given name *Timofei* Timothy (Gk *Timotheos*, from *timān* to honour + *theos* God), which was bestowed in honour of various early saints, notably the companion of St Paul and first bishop of Ephesus.

Cogns. (patrs.): Beloruss.: **Tsimafeev**. Croatian: **Timotijević**.

Cogns. (not patrs.): Pol.: **Tyma, Tymański, Tymowski** (all from the Pol. given name *Tymoteusz*). Cat.: **Timoteu**.

Dims.: Ukr.: **Timoshchuk, Timoshenko, Timchenko**. Hung.: **Timkó**.

Patrs. (from dims.): Russ.: **Timoshkov, Timosh(k)in, Timochin, Timonin, Tim(k)in, Timshin, Timakov, Timachyov, Tim(y)ashaev, Timu(sh)ev, Timeshov**. Pol.: **Tymkiewicz**.

'Son of the wife of T. (dim.)': Ukr.: **Timchishin**.

Timony Irish: Anglicized form of Gael. **Ó Tiománaidhe** 'descendant of *Tiománaidhe*', a byname meaning 'Driver'.

Vars.: **Tymmany, (Mc)Timney**, TIMMONS.

Timpany English: metonymic occupational name for a player on the tympany (ME *timpan(e)*, OE *timpana*, from L *tumpanon*, from Gk), a kind of drum or tambourine.

Vars.: **Tympany, Tumpany, Tempany, Tempeny, Tenpen(n)y**.

Cogns.: It.: **Timpano; Timpanaro**.

Dim.: It.: **Timpanelli**.

Timperley English: habitation name from *Timperley* in N Ches., which is so called from OE *timber* timber, wood + *lēah* wood, clearing, i.e. a clearing where timber for building was obtained.

Tindale English: regional name for someone who lived in *Tynedale*, the valley of the river Tyne, or habitation name from a place so called in Cumb., situated on a tributary of the S *Tyne*. The name derives from a Brit. river name *Tina* (apparently from a Celt. root meaning 'to flow') + OE *dæl* valley (see DALE).

Vars.: **Tyndale, Tindal(l), Tyndall, Tindell, Tindle, Tindill**.

Tingle English: metonymic occupational name for a maker of nails or pins, or nickname for a small, thin man, from ME *tingle*, a kind of very small nail (of Low Ger. origin).

Var.: **Tingler** (an agent deriv.).

Tinker English: occupational name for a mender of pots and pans, ME *tink(l)er* (of uncertain origin).

Var.: **Tinkler**.

Tinney Irish: Anglicized form of Gael. **Mac an tSionnaigh** 'son of the fox', from *sionnach* fox.

Vars.: **McAsinagh; Shin(n)agh, Shinnock, Shinnick, Shinwick, Shonnagh, Shunnagh, Shunny**.

Tinsley English: habitation name from a place in S Yorks. near Rotherham, so called from the gen. case of the unattested OE personal name **Tynni* (a byform of the attested *Tunne*, of uncertain origin) + OE *hlāw* hill, mound, barrow (see LAW 2 and LOW 1).

Tioli Italian (Venetia): from an aphetic dim. of the given name *Matio*; see MATTHEW.

Vars.: **Tiozzi, Tiosso, Tiussi**.

Tiplady English: nickname for a lecherous man or one who was reputed to have achieved sexual success with a woman of higher rank, from ME *tȳpe(n)* to knock over (of obscure origin) + *lady*; cf. SHACKLADY.

Vars.: **Toplady, Topley**.

Tipper English: probably an occupational name for a maker of arrowheads, from an agent deriv. of ME *tippe* tip, head. On the other hand it may possibly be a bawdy nickname comparable to TIPLADY.

Tipping English: from a medieval given name, originally an OE patr. from a personal name or byname *Tippa*, for which there is evidence in placenames such as *Tiptree*, but which is of uncertain origin.

Patrs.: **Tippings**.

Tipton English: habitation name from a place in the W Midlands, recorded in Domesday Book as *Tibintone*, from the gen. case of an unrecorded OE personal name **Tibba* (of obscure origin, possibly akin to *Tippa*; see TIPPING) + *tūn* enclosure, settlement.

Tirado Spanish: probably a nickname for someone with long limbs, from Sp. *tirado* stretched (past part. of *tirar* to pull; cf. TYRRELL). The nickname may also have had the sense of Sp. *estirado* lofty, haughty, difficult.

Tirpitz German: habitation name from *Tirpitz* near Küstrin, Brandenburg, or from *Türpitz* in Silesia, recorded in the 13th cent. as *Tirpiz*. Both placenames are of Slav. origin.

Var.: **Türpitz**.

Tischbein German: metonymic occupational name for a furniture maker, from Ger. *Tischbein* table leg, a cpd formed from MHG *tisch* table (see TISCHLER) + *bein* leg.

Tischler German and Jewish (Ashkenazic): occupational name for a joiner, from an agent deriv. of Ger. *Tisch* table (MHG *tisch*, OHG *tisc*). This was the normal term for the craftsman in N and E Germany and in Austria and Switzerland during the Middle Ages; in the W, from Bavaria to the Dutch border, the equivalent was SCHREINER.

Vars.: **Tischmann**. Ger.: **Tisch(n)er**. Jewish: **Tishler**, **Tishman(n)**, **Tischman**, **Teszler**, **Tes(s)ler**.

Cogn.: Low Ger.: **Discher**.

Tisdall English: apparently a habitation name from an unidentified place, perhaps named with the OE personal name *Tissi* (contracted form of *Tīdsige*, composed of the elements *tīd* season + *sige* victory) + OE *dæl* valley (see DALE).

Tissier French: occupational name for a weaver, OF *tissier* (LL *texārius*, a deriv. of *texere* to weave).

Vars.: **Te(i)ssier**, **Teyssier**, **Tixier**, **Te(i)xier**, **Letessier**; **Tisserand**, **Tesserand**.

Cogns.: Prov.: **Teissaire**, **Teyssaire**, **Teisseire**, **Teysseyre**; **Teissèdre**, **Teyssèdre**, **Tixidre**; **Tissandier**, **Teysandier**, **Texandier**. Eng.: **Tisser**. It.: **Tessier(i)**; **Tes(si)tore**, **Tes(si)tori**, **Tess(i)ore**; **Tessa(d)ro**. Sp.: **Tejedor**. Cat.: **Teixidor**, **Teixidó**. Rum.: **Tesator**.

Dims.: Fr.: **Tessereau**, **Texereau**; **Tissot**. Prov.: **Teysédou**. It.: **Tesserin(i)**, **Tessarin(i)**, **Tessarotto**, **Tessarolo**, **Tessaroli**.

Patrs.: Fr.: **Autissier**, **Autixier**, **Autessier**.

Titchener English: topographic name for someone who lived at a crossroads or a fork in the road, OE *twicen(e)* (a deriv. of *twā* two).

Vars.: **Tutchener**, **Tichner**, **Tickner**; **Twitchen**, **Twitching(s)**, **Tutchings**.

Titford English: habitation name from an unidentifed place. This may well be *Tetford* in Lincs., so called from OE *þēod* people + *ford* FORD, i.e. the public ford that everybody used. However, the surname is associated chiefly with Wilts., and a connection with early Lincs. bearers has not been established.

Var.: **Tatford** (an altered form first occurring in Hants in the late 18th cent.).

The first known bearer of the name is Alured de Titford, *whose son William held land in Lincs. in 1195. Almost all modern bearers of the name seem to be descendants of one of four brothers by the name of* Titford *or* Tutford *living at Bratton in Wilts. in the mid-16th cent.*

Titley English: habitation name from a place in Herefords., so called from the OE personal name *Titta* (apparently a short form of the various cpd names with the first element *tīd* season) + OE *lēah* wood, clearing.

Titmus English: nickname for a small person, from ME *titmōse* titmouse (composed of the prefix *tit-*, probably of ON origin, indicating small size, + OE *māse*, the original name of the bird).

Vars.: **Titmuss**, **Titmas**.

Tito 1. Italian: from a medieval given name (L *Titus*, probably Etruscan in origin). The name was popular in the Middle Ages since it had been borne by a disciple of St Paul who became bishop of Crete.

2. Jewish: of unknown origin, possibly an adoption of the Italian name.

Var.: **Titi**.

Dim.: It.: **Titolo**.

Aug.: It.: **Titone**.

Patrs.: Russ.: **Titov**, **Titaev**, **Titanov**; **Kitov**, **Kitaev**, **Kit(m)anov** (forms found from the late 15th cent.; the reason for the substitution of initial *K-* for *T-* is unknown; there may have been some association with Russ. *kit* whale, from Gk *kētos*). Beloruss.: **Tsitov(ich)**.

Patrs. (from dims.): Russ.: **Titkov**, **Titkin**, **Titushin**.

Titterington English: habitation name from *Tytherington* in Ches., so called from OE *Tydringtūn* 'settlement (OE *tūn*) associated with *Tȳdre*', a personal name of uncertain meaning.

Tiziano Italian: from a medieval given name (LL *Titiānus*, a deriv. of *Titus*; cf. TITO). The name was popular in the Middle Ages as it had been borne by a 6th-cent. bishop of Brescia and a 7th-cent. bishop of Oderzo. The surname is particularly common in Naples.

Vars.: **Tizziano**, **Tiz(z)iani**.

Dim.: **Tizzanini**.

Tkach Ukrainian and Jewish (E Ashkenazic): occupational name for a weaver, Ukr. *tkach*, a deriv. of *tkaty* to weave (cogn. with Pol. *tkać*, Czech *tkát*, etc.).

Vars.: Jewish: **Tkatsh**, **Tekach**, **Tkacz**.

Cogns.: Pol.: **Tkacz**. Czech: **Kadlec**. Hung.: **Takács**.

Dims.: Ukr.: **Tkachuk**. Pol.: **Tkaczyk**. Czech: **Kadleček**.

Tobel German and Jewish (Ashkenazic): topographic name for someone who lived near a ravine or gorge, from MHG southern dial. *tobel* gorge.

Vars.: Ger.: **Tobler** (esp. Swiss); **Zumtobel**; DOBEL.

Tobias English, French, German, and Jewish: from a Gk form of the Hebr. male given name *Tovya* 'Jehovah is good', which, together with various deriv. forms, have been popular among Jews for generations. Other derivs. were occasionally used by Christians in the Middle Ages.

Vars.: Eng.: **Tob(e)y**, **Tooby**. Fr.: **Tobie**. Ger.: **Tobis**; **Töbi** (Switzerland). Jewish: **Tovia(s)**; **Tuvia**, **Tuvya(hu)**.

Cogns.: Sp.: **Tobías**. Pol.: **Tobiasz**; **Tobiański**, **Tobola**. Czech: **Dobiáš**, **Dobeš**. Hung.: **Tóbiás**.

Dims.: Eng.: TOBIN. Ger.: **Döbl** (Bavaria). Ger. (of Slav. origin): **Tob(i)sch**, **Tobusch**, **Topsch**, **Dobisch**, **Dopsch**.

Patrs.: Pol.: **Tobiasewicz**, **Tobolewicz**.

Tobin 1. English: dim. of the given name TOBIAS.

2. Irish: Anglicized form of Gael. *Tóibín*, which is itself an aphetic Gaelicized version of a Norman habitation name from *Saint-Aubin* in Brittany (so called from the dedication of its church to St ALBIN).

Tocqueville French: habitation name from any of the places, in Eure, Manche, and Seine-Maritime, so called from the ON personal name *Tóki* (see TOOKE) + OF *ville* settlement (see VILLE).

The French political writer Alexis **de Tocqueville** *(1805–59) was born in Verneuil into an ancient Norman family, who claimed descent from one of the companions of William the Conqueror in the conquest of England.*

Todd English: nickname for someone thought to resemble a fox in some way, for example in cunning or slyness, or perhaps more obviously in having red hair, from Northern ME *tod(de)* fox (of unknown origin).

Var.: **Tod** (Scots).

Todhunter English (Cumb.): nickname for a keen hunter of foxes, from Northern ME *tod(de)* fox (see TODD) + HUNTER.

Toft English: habitation name from any of the various places, for example in Cambs., Lincs., Norfolk, and Warwicks., so called from ME *toft* homestead (ON *topt*, *tomt*).

Vars.: **Tofts**; **Taft**.

Cogns.: Dan.: **Toft(e)**.

Toivonen Finnish: patr. from the OFinn. personal name *Toivo* 'Hope'.

Tokarz Polish: occupational name for a turner, Pol. *tokarz*.

Var.: **Tokarski**.

Cogns.: Jewish (E Ashkenazic): **To(c)ker** (from Yid. *toker*); TUCKER (Anglicized).

Dims.: Pol.: **Tokarczyk, Tokarek**.

Patrs.: Pol.: **Tokarzewicz**. Beloruss.: **Tokarevich**.

Tolbert French and English (Norman): from a Continental Gmc personal name composed of a first element of uncertain meaning + *berht* bright, famous.

Toledo Spanish and Jewish (Sefardic): habitation name from the city in central Spain, which was the capital of the Visigothic state and afterwards of the kingdom of Castile between the 11th and 16th cents. It was a major cultural and political centre throughout the Middle Ages, and was also the home of an important Jewish community. The placename, first recorded in L as *Tolētum*, is of obscure etymology, possibly connected with *Toleto* in Piedmont; Jewish tradition connects it with Hebr. *toledot* generations, but this is no more than folk etymology.

Var.: **Toledano**.

Tollemache English: apparently a metonymic occupational name for an itinerant merchant, from OF *talemasche* knapsack (of uncertain origin).

Vars.: **Tallemach, Tallamach, Talma(d)ge, Tammage**. (The form *Talmadge* has also been used as an Anglicized form of one or more like-sounding Jewish surnames.)

Tollemache *is the name of an E Anglian family, established in Bentley, Suffolk, from the early 13th cent. An early spelling of their name was* Talemasche.

Toller 1. English: occupational name for a toll taker or tax gatherer, from an agent deriv. of ME *toll* tax, payment (OE *toln*, from LL *tolōneum*, *telōneum*, a deriv. of Gk *telos* tax).

2. habitation name from *Toller* in Dorset, so called from a Brit. river name, apparently composed of elements akin to W *toll* hollow, pierced + *dw(f)r* stream.

Vars. (of 1): **Towler, Towner; Towlard**.

Cogns. (of 1, meaning 'toll taker'): Ger.: **Zoll(n)er, Zöll(n)er, Zollmann**. Low Ger.: **Töllner**. Fris.: **Tolsma**. Du.: **Van (den) Tol**. Jewish (Ashkenazic): **Zoller, Zollman(n), Zolman; Colman** (Pol. spelling).

The surname Towlard *was for centuries associated with Arkendale, near Knaresborough in W Yorks. John* Toller *is recorded there in 1379; by 1588 the surname is recorded as* Tollert *and in 1602 as* Towlerde. *From the 1640s it was* Towlard. *It has now died out in Yorks. and is not common elsewhere.*

Tolmachev Russian: patr. from the occupational term *tolmach* interpreter, a word of Turkic origin.

Var.: **Talmachev**.

Cogns. (occupational): Ger. (of Slav. origin): **Dolmetsch**. Jewish: **Tolmatcz** (E Ashkenazic); **Talmaciu, Talmacio** (among Rumanian Jews); **To(u)rgeman, Torjman, Tourjeman, Turg(e)man** (Arabic).

Tolstoy Russian and Jewish (E Ashkenazic): nickname for a plump man, from Russ. *tolstoi*, a dial. var. of *tolsty* fat.

Cogns.: Pol.: **Tłusty, Tłustowski**. Czech: **Tlustý**.

Patrs.: Russ.: **Tolst(yak)ov, Tolstenev, Tolstykh**.

Tomelty Irish: Anglicized form of Gael. **Mac Tomhaltaigh** and **Ó Tomhaltaigh** 'son' and 'descendant of *Tomaltach*', a byname apparently meaning 'Glutton'.

Vars.: **Tumelty, Timothy**.

Tondeur French: occupational name for a sheep-shearer, OF *tondeur* (L *tonditor*, from *tondere* to shear; cf. TIJERINA).

Cogns.: Eng.: **Thunder**. Sp.: **Tundidor**.

Toner 1. English: topographic name for someone who lived in a village, as opposed to an outlying farm or hamlet, from ME *tune*, *tone* (OE *tūn*, which originally meant 'fence' and then 'enclosure', although the sense 'settlement, village' was already firmly established in the OE period). The Ger. cogns. (see ZAUNER) retain the sense 'fence', whereas the Du. ones (see below) have the meaning 'garden'.

2. Irish: Anglicized form of Gael. **Ó Tomhrair** 'descendant of *Tomhrar*', a personal name from *tomhra(r)* protection.

Vars. (of 1): Eng.: **Town(e), Toon(e), Tune, Town(e)s; Towning**.

Cogns. (of 1): Du.: **(Van den) Tuin, Tui(j)nman, Tuynman**.

Toney English: from the medieval given name *Ton(e)y*, an aphetic form of ANTHONY.

Cogns.: Fr.: **T(h)oin(e)**. Prov., Cat.: **Toni**. It.: **To(g)ni; Ton** (Venetia). Ger.: THON.

Dims.: Fr.: **T(h)oinet, Tonet, T(h)oinot, Tonin, Tony**. It.: **Tone(ll)i, Tognello, Ton(i)celli; Ton(i)etti, Tognetti, Tugnetti, Tonitto; To(g)nini; Tonicchi; Ton(i)olo, Tognoli, Tunioli, Tugnoli, Ton(i)olli; Tonizzo, Tonizzi, Tonissi, Tonussi, Ton(i)utti, Ton(ell)otto**.

Pejs.: It.: **Toniacci, Tognacci, Toniazzi, Tognazzi, Tonassi**.

Patrs.: It.: **De Toni**. Russ.: **Toneev, Taneev**.

Tong English: 1. metonymic occupational name for a maker or user of tongs (OE *tang(e)*).

2. habitation name from any of the various places, for example in Lancs., Shrops., and W Yorks., called *Tong* from their situation by a fork in a road or river.

3. nickname for a chatterbox or a scold or for someone with some deformity of the tongue, ME, OE *tunge*.

4. topographic name for someone who lived on a tongue of land, or habitation name from a place named with this word, for example *Tonge* in Leics.

Vars.: **Tong(u)e, Tongs**.

Cogns. (of 1): Flem., Du.: **Tang**. Dan., Norw.: **Tange**. (Of 3): Jewish (Ashkenazic): **Tzung, Cung** (from Yid. *tsung* tongue); **Tzinger** (from the Yid. pl. *tsinger*); **Zingel** (from the Yid. dim. *tsingl*, but see also ZINGLER).

Tonnellier French: occupational name for a cooper, OF *tonnellier* (LL *tunnellārius*, from *tunnella*, dim. of *tunna* cask, vat, of Celt. origin).

Var.: **Tonelier**.

Toogood English: apparently a nickname from ME *to* exceedingly + *gode* GOOD, perhaps ironic in application.

Vars.: **Towgood, Tugwood**.

Tooke English (Norfolk): from the ON personal name or byname *Tóki*, of uncertain origin, perhaps a short form of THIRKILL.

Vars.: **Took, Tuck, Toke, Tuke; Tookey, Tuckey**.

Toole 1. Irish: Anglicized form of Gael. **Ó Tuathail** 'descendant of *Tuathal*', an old Celt. personal name composed of elements meaning 'people', 'tribe' + 'rule'.

2. English: var. of TOWLE.

Vars. (of 1): **O'Toole, O'Tuale, (O')Tou(g)hill, (O')Twohill, To(o)hill, Tohall, Toal(e)**.

Toop English: from the ON personal name *Tópi*, *Túpi*, probably a short form of a personal name with a first element consisting of the divine name *Þórr* (see THOR 2) + a second element with initial *b*-, for example *björn* bear, warrior (see THORBURN).

Var.: **Toope**.

Tootell English (Lancs.): topographic name for someone who lived by a hill used as a look-out station, from OE **tōt-*

look-out (apparently akin to *tōtian* to protrude, peep, or peer) + *hyll* HILL, or habitation name from some place named with these elements, e.g. *Tootle* Heights in Lancs.
Vars.: **Tootill, Tootal, Tootle, Tottle; Tothill.**

Tooth 1. English (W Midlands): nickname for someone with a prominent tooth or teeth, from ME *tōth* (OE *tōð*).
2. Irish: Anglicization of Gael. *Mac Confhiaclaigh*; see TUITE.

Töpfer German: occupational name for a maker of metal or earthenware pots, from Ger. *Töpfer* potter, an agent deriv. of *Topf* pot, vessel (MHG *topf(e)*, first attested in the 12th cent., and at first confined to the E Ger. dialects). See also EULER, HAFNER, KACHLER, and POTTER.
Vars.: **Töpper, Tepfer, Döpfner, Döp(p)ner, Döpfler.**
Cogns.: Jewish (Ashkenazic): **Toper; Tep(p)er, Teperman, Teppermann** (from Yid. *teper* potter); **Tepperberg** ('potter hill', an ornamental elaboration).
Patr.: Jewish: **Teperson.**

Topham English: habitation name from a place in Yorks., near Snaith. The final element is probably OE *hām* homestead, and the first may be the personal name *Toppa* (see TOPP).

Topol 1. Czech: topographic name for someone who lived by a poplar tree, Czech *topol* (Pol. *topola*).
2. Jewish (E Ashkenazic): ornamental name from the tree.
Vars. (of 2): **Topiol; Topol(i)ansky, Topolski, Topolsky.**
Cogn. (of 1): Pol.: **Topolski.**

Topp English: from the OE byname *Topp* 'Tuft', 'Crest', or the cogn. ON *Toppr*.
Patr.: **Topping** (common in Lancs. and N Ireland).

Toribio Spanish: from a medieval given name, *Toribio* (L *Turibius*, of apparently Gmc (Visigothic) origin, but uncertain derivation), bestowed in honour of two Spanish saints. St Turibius of Astorga was a 5th-cent. bishop who championed Catholic doctrine against the Priscillianist heresy. St Turibius of Palencia was the 6th-cent. founder of the famous abbey of Liébana in Asturias.

Tormo Catalan: topographic name for someone who lived by a crag or boulder, OCat. *tormo* (of uncertain, probably pre-Roman, origin). There are various places named with forms of this word, for example *Tormos* in Alicante, *El Tormo* in Castellón, and *Torms* in Lérida, and the surname may also be a habitation name from any of these.

Toro 1. Italian and Spanish: nickname for a lusty person or metonymic occupational name for a tender of bulls, from It., Sp. *toro* bull (L *taurus*).
2. Italian: from a medieval given name, an aphetic short form of various names such as VICTOR and SALVADOR.
Var.: It.: **Tori.**
Dims.: It.: **Toretto, Toritto; Torelli, Torello** (Tuscany); **Toriello, Turiello.** (Of 1 only): Fr.: **Taurel, Taureau,** THOREL.

Torquemada Spanish: habitation name from a place in the province of Logroño, so called from Sp. *torre* TOWER + *quemada* (fem.) burnt (from the past part. of *quemar* to burn, L *cremāre*).

Torr English: 1. topographic name for someone who lived by a tor or rocky hilltop (OE *torr*, of Celt. origin; cf. TERUEL and THÉRON).
2. nickname for someone thought to resemble a bull, ANF *tor* (see TORO).

Torrado Spanish and Portuguese: nickname for an exceptionally dark-skinned person, from Sp., Port. *torrado* toasted, roasted (past part. of *torrar*, LL *torrāre*, for class. L *torrēre* to burn, parch; cf. TORRENTE).

Torralba Spanish and Catalan: habitation name from any of the numerous places so called from Sp., Cat. *torre* TOWER + OSp., OCat. *alba* (fem.) white.

Torrance Scots and N Irish: habitation name from either of two places (one near E Kilbride, the other north of Glasgow under the Campsie Fells), so called from Gael. *torran* hillock, mound, with the later addition of the Eng. pl. /s/.
Vars.: **Torrence, Torrens.**
A family called Torrens, *important in Australian history, owned land in Ireland in the 18th cent., having been established in Londonderry by a Swedish cavalry officer, Count Torrens, who fought with William III in 1690. He was probably of Scot. ancestry. His descendants included Robert Torrens (1780–1864), a noted advocate of Australian colonization, after whom a lake and a river were named, and the latter's son Sir Robert Torrens (1814–84), born in Cork, who put his father's principles into practice and emigrated to Australia in 1840.*

Torrente Spanish: topographic name for someone who lived by a flood stream, Sp. *torrente* (L *torrens*, gen. *torrentis*, from the pres. part. of *torrēre* to rush, seethe (originally 'to burn, parch'; cf. TORRADO)).
Cogns.: Fr.: **Torrent.** Prov.: **Torrens.** Cat.: **Torrent, Torren(t)s.**

Tort French, Provençal, and Catalan: nickname for a crippled or deformed man, from OF, Prov., Cat. *tort* twisted, crooked (L *tortus*, past part. of *torquēre* to turn, twist). The Cat. word also has the sense 'one-eyed'.
Var.: Fr.: **Letort.**
Cogns.: It.: **Torti, Storti, Storto.**
Dim.: Fr.: **Torteau.**
Augs.: Fr.: **Tortat.** It.: **Stortone.**

Tortosa Catalan: habitation name from a place in the province of Tarragona, recorded in L as *Dertosa*, but of pre-Roman origin and unknown meaning.

Toscano Italian: regional name for someone from Tuscany, It. *Toscana*.
Vars.: **Toscan(i), Tuscano; Toscanese, Toscanesi; Tosco, Toschi.**
Dims.: **Toscanello, Toscanelli, Toscanino, Toscanini.**

Toth German: 1. nickname from MHG *tōt* DEATH.
2. nickname from MHG *tote* godfather (OHG *toto*, in origin apparently a nursery word).
Vars.: **Todt, Tott.**
Dim.: **Töttel.**

Tóth Hungarian: name for a Slavonian, Slovak, or Slovene, from Hung. *tót* Slav, ultimately related to DEUTSCH German.
Var.: **Tót.**

Touche French: topographic name for someone who lived by a grove or thicket, OF *touche* (of unknown origin).
Vars.: **Latouche, Letouche, Delatouche, Destouches.**
Dims.: **Touchet, Touchon.**
Collectives: **Tou(c)quoy, To(c)quoy** (Picardy).

Tough 1. Scots: topographic name for someone who lived on a hillside, from Gael. *tulach* hill, mound, or habitation name from a minor place named with this word. The Scots surname is pronounced /tu:x/.
2. English: nickname for a valiant or stubborn person, from ME *togh* steadfast (OE *tōh*).
Vars. (of 2): **Tow(e).**
Patr. (from 2): **Towes.**

Toulouse French: habitation name from the city in Haute-Garonne, whose name is of uncertain, apparently Celt., etymology.

Vars.: **de Toulouse**, **Toul(ou)ze**; **Toulousa(i)n**, **Toulousy**, **Toulza(n)**.

Cogn.: It.: **Tolosa**.

The French painter and lithographer Henri de Toulouse Lautrec (1864–1901) was born into a wealthy aristocratic family, descended from the Counts of Toulouse. They claim to be able to trace their ancestry back to the time of Charlemagne.

Tourte French: metonymic occupational name for a baker, or nickname for a short, dumpy man, from OF *tourte* round loaf (of uncertain origin).

Vars.: **Tourtier**; **Tourtel(l)ier**, **Tortellier**.

Dims.: **To(u)rtel**, **Tourteau**.

Tous French: nickname from OF *tous* clean-shaven, close-cropped (L *tonsus*, past part. of *tondere* to cut, shear; cf. TONDEUR). In the later Middle Ages it was for some time the fashion for young men to cut their hair close, while their elders preferred a longer style.

Cogns.: It.: **Tosi**, **To(n)so**.

Dims.: Fr.: **Touzel**, **Touzeau**, **Letouzel**, **Touzet**, **Touzé**, **Letouzé**, **Letouzey**, **Touz(el)in**. It.: **Toselli**, **Tosetti**, **Tosetto**, **Tos(ol)ini**, **Tositti**.

Aug.: It.: **Tosoni**.

Pejs.: Fr.: **Touzard**. It.: **Tosat(t)o**, **Tosatti**.

Toussaint French: from a nickname or given name composed of the elements *tous* (pl.) all + *saints* saints. The name was given to someone who was born on All Saints' Day (1 November), or chosen as an invocation of the protection of all the saints of the calendar. Cf. SANTORO.

Tovar Spanish: topographic name for someone who lived by a quarry of pumice stone, OSp. *tovar* (LL *tōfāre*, a deriv. of *tōfus* tufa, porous stone).

Tovell English (E Anglia): from a Scandinavian female personal name of an unusual type, *Tōfa-Hildr* '*Hildr* the daughter of *Tōfi*' (see TOVEY).

Tovey English: from the ON personal name *Tófi*, a short form of any of various cpd names whose first element is the divine name *Þórr* (see THOR 2), while the second begins with *f* or *v*, for example *valdr* rule (see THOROLD).

Vars.: **Toovey**, **Tuvey**, **Tovee**.

Toward N English (Northumb.) and Scots: nickname for a meek, obedient person, from ME *toward* docile, biddable.

Tower English: 1. topographic name for someone who lived near a tower, usually a defensive fortification or watchtower, from ME, OF *tūr* (L *turris*).

2. occupational name for a maker of white leather, a var. of TAWYER.

Cogns. (of 1): Fr.: **Tour**, **Latour**, **Delatour**. Prov.: **Torrès**. It.: **(La) Torre**, **Torri**, **Turri**, **Della Torre**; **Torrese**, **Torresi**, **Torrisi**, **Turrisi**. Sp.: **Torre(s)**. Cat.: **Torre(s)**, **Torra(s)**. Port.: **Torres**. Jewish (Sefardic): **Torres** (reasons for adoption unknown). See also THURN.

Dims. (of 1): Fr.: **Touret(te)**, **Tourot**, **Tourry**. It.: **Toretta**, **Toretti**, **Torritti**, **Torrini**, **Turrini**, **Torricina**, **Torricella**. Sp.: **Torrecilla(s)**, **Torrijos**, **Torrejón**.

Towers English: 1. var. of TOWER, with later *-s*.

2. habitation name from *Tours* in Eure-et-Loire, N France, so called from the Gaul. tribal name *Turones*, of uncertain etymology.

Cogn. (of 2): Fr.: **Tournois**.

Towle English (Notts.): from the ME given name *Toll*, OE *Toll*, or ON *Tóli*, the latter being derived from a short form of some cpd name such as *Þórleifr* (composed of the divine name *Þórr* (see THOR 2) + *leifr* relic) or *Þōrleikr* (composed of the elements *Þórr* + *leikr* sport, play).

Vars.: **Tow(e)ll**, TOOLE, **Tole**, **Toll**.

Dims.: **Tol(l)ey** (chiefly W Midlands), **Tooley**.

Patrs.: **Towlson** (Notts.), **Tolson** (Yorks.), **Toulson**.

Townley English: habitation name from *Towneley* near Burnley in Lancs., which is named with the OE elements *tūn* enclosure, settlement + *lēah* wood, clearing.

Vars.: **Towneley**, **Townsley**.

Towneley *is the name of a family who for many years provided lay deans for Whalley Abbey, Lancs. Around the year 1200 they received lands at Towneley from the Earl of Lincoln.*

Townsend English: topographic name for someone who lived at the extremity of a village, from ME *tone*, *tune* village, settlement (see TONER) + *end* end (OE *ende*).

Vars.: **Townshend** (Norfolk), **Townend** (Yorks.), **Townen**.

Toy English: nickname for a light-hearted or frivolous person, from ME *toy* play, sport (of uncertain origin).

Var.: **Toye**.

Tozer English: occupational name for a comber or carder of wool, from an agent deriv. of ME *tōse(n)* to tease (OE *tāsian*, a byform of *tǣsan*). For the change of *-ā-* to *-ō-*, cf. ROPER.

Tracey 1. English (Norman): habitation name from *Tracy*-Bocage or *Tracy*-sur-Mer in Calvados, both so called from the Gallo-Roman personal name *Thracius* (a deriv. of L *Thrax*, gen. *Thracis*, 'Thracian') + the local suffix *-eium*.

2. Irish: var. of TREACY.

Var.: **Tracy**.

Trachtenberg Jewish (Ashkenazic): of unknown origin. The less common **Trachtenbroit** and **Trachtengot**, **Trachtingot** would seem to be related. *-berg* hill is a very common ornamental ending of Yiddish surnames; *-broit* clearly reflects the S Yiddish pronunciation of Yid. *broyt* bread; and *-got* is presumably Yid. *got* or Ger. *Gott* God. Trachten-, however, is unclear. The following vocab. words have been considered, but none of them seems appropriate: Yid. *trakhtn* to think, Ger. *trachten* to endeavour, Ger. *Trachten* endeavours, Ger. *Trachten* loads.

Tracz Polish: occupational name for a sawyer, Pol. *tracz*.

Dim.: **Traczyk** (also Jewish (E Ashkenazic)).

Tradescant English: of unknown origin. The names *Tradesskin* and *Tredeskin*, found as early as the 11th cent. in the parishes of Walberswick and Harleston, Suffolk, are apparently early forms of this name.

This was the name of a family of noted naturalists and gardeners, including John Tradescant (1608–62), who was gardener to Charles I. He was born in Meopham, Kent, and his father was known as 'the Dutch gardener', although the reasons for this are unclear.

Trafford English: habitation name from any of various places so called. One in Northants is named with the OE elements *træppe* (fish-)trap + *ford* FORD. The places called *Trafford* in Ches. have as their first element OE *trog* trough, valley (see TROW 3); while *Trafford* in Lancs. was originally called STRATFORD. Nevertheless, most cases of the surname probably derive from the last of these places; a landowning family can be traced there to the 13th cent.

Trager German and Jewish (Ashkenazic): occupational name for someone who carried a load, a pedlar or porter, from Ger. *Träger*, Yid. *treger*, agent derivs. of Ger. *tragen* to carry (OHG *tragan*).

Vars.: Ger.: **Trage, Träger**. Jewish: **Treger(man)**.

Cogns.: Low Ger.: **Dräger**. Flem.: **Dra(e)ger**.

Trainor 1. N English, Scots, and N Irish: occupational name for a trapper, from an agent deriv. of ME *train(e)* trap, snare (from OF *trainer* to draw, allure, LL *tragināre*, a deriv. of class. L *trahere*).

2. Irish: Anglicized form of Gael. **Mac Thréinfhir** 'son of *Thréinfhear*', a byname meaning 'Champion' (from *tréan* strong + *fear* man).

Vars.: **Trainer**. (Of 2 only): **Traynor, Treanor, McCranor**.

Tranchant French: occupational name for a butcher, or nickname for a violent person, from the pres. part. of OF *trenchier* to cut, hack, slice (L *truncāre*, a deriv. of *truncus* lopped, short).

Vars.: **Tranchand, Trenchant; Tranchaire**.

Dims.: **Tranch(ill)on**.

Pejs.: **Tranchard, Trenchard; Tranquard, Trincard** (Normandy).

Tranter English: occupational name for a pedlar or hawker, esp. one equipped with a horse and cart, ME *traunter, traventer* (LL *trāvetārius*, of uncertain origin, possibly derived from L *transvehere* to convey).

Var.: **Trenter**.

Trappe 1. English: metonymic occupational name for a trapper, from a deriv. of ME *trapp* trap (OE *træppe*, reinforced by MDu. *trappe*).

2. German: nickname for a stupid person, from MHG *trappe* bustard (of Slav. origin).

Var.: **Trapp**.

Traub 1. German: metonymic occupational name for a wine-grower, from Ger. *Traube* grape (MHG *trūbe* bunch of grapes, OHG *t(h)rūba*). In some cases it may originally have been a house name, for someone who lived at a house marked with the sign of a bunch of grapes.

2. Jewish (Ashkenazic): ornamental name or, occasionally perhaps, metonymic occupational name for a wine-grower, from Ger. *Traube*.

Vars.: Ger.: **Traube; Trübner** (Switzerland). Jewish: **Traube, Traubner, Traubnik, Traubmann**.

Dims.: Ger.: **Traubel, Treibel, Träuble**.

Travers 1. English and French: topographic name for someone who lived by a bridge or ford, or occupational name for a gatherer of tolls exacted for the right of passage, from ME, OF *travers* passage, crossing (from OF *traverser* to cross, LL *transversāre*).

2. Irish: Anglicized form of Gael. *Ó Treabhair*; see TREVOR 2.

Vars. (of 1): Eng.: **Traves, Travis(s), Trevis**. Fr.: **Traverse, Traver(t)**.

Cogns. (of 1): It.: **Traversa, Traverso, Traversi**. Sp.: **Travieso**.

Dim. (of 1): It.: **Traversini**.

Many modern bearers of the name Travers *are descended from a certain Robert Travers who held lands at Whiston in the parish of Prescot, Lancs., in the 12th cent.*

Trawiński Polish: habitation name from some place named for its fine grass, from Pol. *trawa* grass, lawn + *-in* possessive suffix + *-ski* suffix of local surnames (see BARANOWSKI).

Var.: **Trawczyński**.

Cogn.: Czech: **Trávníček**.

Treacher English: nickname for a devious or unreliable person, from OF *tricheor* trickster, cheat (from *trichier* to cheat, trick, of uncertain origin). See also TRICK.

Treacy Irish: Anglicized form of Gael. **Ó Treasaigh** 'descendant of *Treasach*', a personal name meaning 'Warlike', 'Fierce'.

Vars.: TRACEY, **Treasey, O'Trasey, (O')Trassy, (O')Tressy**.

Treadwell English (chiefly W Midlands): occupational nickname for a fuller, from ME *tred(en)* to tread (OE *tredan*) + *well* well (OE *wel(l)*).

Vars.: **Tredwell, Tretwell, Trad(e)well**.

Treasure English: 1. metonymic occupational name for a treasurer or person in charge of financial administration, from ME *tresor* treasure, wealth, riches (OF *trésor*, from L *thēsaurus* hoard).

2. affectionate nickname for a loved or valued person, from ME *tresor* used as a term of endearment.

Cogns. (of 1): Fr.: **Tensorier, Tansorier** (Brittany). It.: **Tesauro**.

Trebilcock Cornish: habitation name from a place in the parish of Roche, apparently so called from Corn. *tre* homestead, settlement + a mutated form of the ME term of endearment *pilicock* darling.

Tredinnick Cornish: habitation name from any of various places, for example near Bodmin, Liskeard, and St Issey. Some of these get the name from Corn. *tre* homestead, settlement + **dynek* fortified (a deriv. of *dyn* fort; cf. DOWN 1); in other cases the second element is **eythynek* overgrown with gorse or **redenek* overgrown with bracken.

Treen Cornish: habitation name from places in the parishes of Zennor and St Levan, both of which appear earlier in the form *Trethyn*, from Corn. *tre* homestead, settlement + *dyn* fort (cf. DOWN 1).

Trefusis Cornish: habitation name from a place in the parish of Mylor, recorded in 1346 as *Trevusus*, from Corn. *tre* homestead, settlement + a second element of unknown form and meaning.

Tregear Cornish: habitation name from any of various places so called, from Corn. *tre* homestead, settlement + a mutated form of **ker* farmstead encircled by a hedge.

Vars.: **Tregeare, Tregears, Tregair, Tregare**.

Tregenza Cornish: habitation name from a place in the parish of Creed, so called from Corn. *tre* homestead, settlement + a second element **kensyth* of unknown meaning (possibly a personal name).

Tregoning Cornish: habitation name from any of various places so called, from Corn. *tre* homestead, settlement + a mutated form of the personal name CONAN.

Vars.: **Tregonning, Tregon(n)an**.

Tregunna Cornish: habitation name, probably from a place in the parish of St Breock, so called from Corn. *tre* homestead, settlement + a second element of unknown form and meaning (possibly *gonyow*, pl. of *goon* down). This name, or its vars., may also be from various places called *Tregon(n)a* or *Tregenna*, which are likewise from *tre* + an unknown second element.

Vars.: **Tregunno** (a place in the parish of Breage), **Tregonnowe**, **Tregon(n)a**.

Trehearne Welsh: from the personal name *Trahaearn*, composed of the elements *tra* most, very + *haearn* iron. This personal name has also given rise to a placename, spelled *Trehaearn* as if containing the element *tre(f)* homestead, settlement, and so in some cases the surname may be a habitation name with this origin.

Var.: **Traherne**.

Treille French: topographic name for someone who lived near a vineyard or in a house with an ornamental vine, from OF *treille* lattice used to support vines (LL *trichila* arbour, bower).

Vars.: **Treilles**, **Trille**, **Latr(e)ille**.

Cogn.: Cat.: **Trias**.

Dims.: Fr.: **Tr(e)illet**.

Aug.: Fr.: **Trillat**.

Trelawney Cornish: habitation name from *Trelawny* in the parish of Altarnun, so called from Corn. *tre* homestead, settlement + a second element of unknown form and meaning.

Var.: **Trelawny**.

Treleaven Cornish: habitation name from a place in the parish of Mevagissey, so called from Corn. *tre* homestead, settlement + a second element of unknown form and meaning (possibly *leven* level, flat).

Var.: **Treleven**.

Tremaine Cornish: habitation name from any of various places so called, from Corn. *tre* homestead, settlement + *men* stone.

Vars.: **Tremayne**; **Tremain** (also Welsh, from a place in the former county of Cardigan named with W *tre* homestead, settlement + *main* stones).

Trembath Cornish: habitation name from a place in the parish of Madron, so called from Corn. *tre an bagh* 'homestead of the corner'.

Trembeth Cornish: habitation name from *Trembleath* in the parish of St Mawgan in Pydar, recorded in 1327 as *Trenbeth*, from Corn. *tre an beth* 'homestead of the grave'.

Tremble 1. French: topographic name for someone who lived near an aspen, OF *tremble* (from *trembler* to quiver, LL *tremulāre*, a deriv. of *tremulus*, from class. L *tremere*).

2. English: var. of TRUMBULL.

Vars. (of 1): **Trémo(u)ille**, **Trimouille**.

Dims. (of 1): **Tremblet**, **Tremblot**.

Collective (of 1): Fr.: **Tremblay**.

Tremenheere Cornish: habitation name from any of various places named with the Corn. elements *tre* homestead, settlement + **menhyr* menhir, standing stone (a cpd of *men* stone + *hyr* long).

Vars.: **Tremenhere**, **Tremenheer**.

Tremlett English (Norman): habitation name from Les *Trois Minettes* in Calvados, apparently so called from three mines of some sort.

Vars.: **Trimlett**, **Tremblet**.

Tremlett *is the name of an old-established Devon family, who have held lands in the county since the early 12th cent. Olivarus* de Tremblet, *probably an early ancestor, was witness to a charter for Earl Roger de Poitou in 1094. Another early bearer is William* Tremenet, *recorded in documents dating from 1165.*

Trench English (of French origin): habitation name from La *Tranche* in Poitou, so called from the OF topographical term *trenche*, a deriv. of the verb *trenchier* to cut (LL *truncāre*; cf. TRANCHANT). The noun denoted both a ditch and a track cut through a forest.

The Trench *family who hold the earldom of Clancarty trace their descent from Frederic* de la Tranche, *who settled in Northumb. from France c.1575. They were established in Ireland in the 17th cent., when Frederick Trench went there and purchased an estate in Galway in 1631.*

Trenerry Cornish: habitation name from a place in the parish of St Allen, so called from Corn. *tre* homestead, settlement + a second element of uncertain form and meaning.

Trent English: topographic name for someone living on the banks of any of the several rivers so called. The river name is of Brit. origin; it may be composed of the elements **tri* through, across + **sant-* travel, journey (cogn. with W *hynt* road); alternatively it may mean 'traveller' or 'trespasser', a reference to frequent flooding. There is also a village in Dorset of this name, on the river *Trent* or Piddle, and the surname may therefore also be a habitation name derived from this.

Trepat Catalan: presumably a nickname for someone who was scarred with pock-marks or else one who dressed in rags, from Cat. *trepat* full of holes (past part. of *trepar* to pierce, LL *trepāre*). It may also be a topographic name for someone who lived in a house with some form of openwork decoration.

Trerise 1. Cornish: habitation name from any of various places so called. Most get the name from Corn. *tre* homestead, settlement + *rid*, **rys* ford; in some cases the second element may be the personal name **Rys*, equivalent to W RHYS.

2. Welsh: habitation name from W *tre(f)* homestead, settlement + the personal name RHYS.

Var.: **Trerice**.

Tresidder Cornish: habitation name from places in the parishes of St Buryan and Constantine, so called from Corn. *tre* homestead, settlement + a second element of uncertain form and meaning.

Třešňák Czech: habitation name from *Třešně*, near Písek in S Bohemia. The placename means 'cherries' or 'cherry trees'; it is a Slav. borrowing from Old Bavarian **chersia*, which is from LL *ceresia*.

Trethewey Cornish: habitation name from any of various places so called, from Corn. *tre* homestead, settlement + a mutated form of the personal name *Dewi* DAVID.

Vars.: **Trethewy**; **Trethevy**.

Trethowan Cornish: habitation name from a place in the parish of Constantine, recorded in 1195 in the form *Treðewen* and in 1327 as *Trethouen*, from Corn. *tre* homestead, settlement + what is perhaps a mutated form of a personal name **Dewin*, equivalent to W *Dewin* 'Magician', 'Wizard'.

Tretyakov Russian: patr. from *Tretyak*, presumably originally a byname for a third child or third son, from Russ. *treti* third.

Vars.: **Tretnikov**, **Tretilov**, **Tretyukhin**; **Tryoshnikov**.

Cogns.: Ukr.: **Tretyak**. Beloruss.: **Tratsyakov** (patr.). Pol.: **Trzeciak**. Croatian: **Tr(e)čić** (patr.).

Trevail Cornish: habitation name from places in the parishes of Cubert, Ladock, and Zennor called *Treveal(e)*, from Corn. *tre* homestead, settlement + a mutated form of a personal name equivalent to Bret. *Mael* 'Chief', 'Leader'.

Trevaldwyn Welsh: habitation name from the town and former county of Montgomery, known in Welsh as *Trefaldwyn*, from *tre(f)* homestead, settlement + *Faldwyn*, a mutated form of the personal name BALDWIN. Montgomery was granted to Baldwin de Bollers in 1102 and the castle of Montgomery became known as *Castell Baldwin* in Welsh. The town was called *Trefaldwyn* by the 16th cent.

Trevarthen 1. Cornish: habitation name from places in the parishes of St Hilary and Newlyn East, so called from Corn. *tre(v)* homestead, settlement + a personal name equivalent to W *Arthen*.

2. Welsh: habitation name from W *tre(f)* homestead, settlement + the personal name *Arthen*.

Trevaskis Cornish: habitation name from *Trevaskis* in the parish of Gwinear or *Trevascus* in the parish of Goran, both so called from Corn. *tre* homestead, settlement + a mutated form of a personal name equivalent to Bret. *Maelscuet*.

Vars.: **Tregaskis(s)**.

Trevelyan Cornish: habitation name from a place in the parish of St Veep, apparently so called from Corn. *tre* homestead, settlement + a mutated form of *melin* mill.

Vars.: **Trevell(y)an**; **Trevellion** (a place near Bodmin, in the parish of Luxulian).

The Trevelyan *family have held the manor from which they derive their name for centuries. Ancestors include Sir John Trevelyan, who was High Sheriff of Cornwall in the reign of Henry VI (1422–71).*

Trevena Cornish: habitation name from any of various places so called, from Corn. *tre* homestead, settlement + a mutated form of *meneth* mountain, hill.

Vars.: **Trevenna**, **Treven(n)er**.

Treverrow Cornish: habitation name from *Trevarra* in the parish of St Minver, recorded in 1233 in the form *Treveru*, from Corn. *tre(v)* homestead, settlement + *erw* acre, ploughed land.

Trevethan Cornish: habitation name from places in the parishes of Budock, St Eval, and Gwennap, all so called from Corn. *tre* homestead, settlement + a second element of uncertain form and meaning (possibly a mutated form of *budin*, **buthyn* meadow).

Trevithick Cornish: habitation name from any of various places, in the parishes of St Columb Major, St Columb Minor, Perranzabuloe, and St Ewe, so called from Corn. *tre* homestead, settlement + various personal names; in the case of the last-mentioned place, the second element may be from a mutated form of *methek* doctor.

Var.: **Trevethick**.

Trevor 1. Welsh: habitation name from any of the numerous places, for example in the former counties of Denbigh and Cardigan, so called from W *tre(f)* homestead, settlement + a mutated form of *mawr* large.

2. Irish: Anglicized form of Gael. **Ó Treabhair** 'descendant of *Treabhar*', a byname meaning 'Industrious', 'Prudent'.

Vars. (of 2): **O'Trevir**, **O'Trover**, **Treyor**, **Trower**, **Trevors**, **Travor(s)**, TRAVERS.

Trevorrow Cornish: habitation name from a place in the parish of Ludgvan, so called from Corn. *tre* homestead, settlement + a second element of uncertain form and meaning.

Trewhella Cornish: habitation name from *Trewhella* in the parish of St Hilary or *Trewhela* in the parish of St Enoder, both apparently so called from Corn. *tre* homestead, settlement + a deriv. of *hwilen* beetle.

Var.: **Trewheela**.

Trewin Cornish: habitation name from any of the various places called *Trewen*; most get their names from Corn. *tre* homestead, settlement + various second elements, for example the vocabulary word *gwynn* white, fair and the personal name *Gwen*.

Trezise Cornish: habitation name from *Trezise* in the parish of St Martin in Meneage or *Tresayes* in the parish of Roche, both so called from Corn. *tre* homestead, settlement + **Seys* Englishman.

Vars.: **Trezize**, **Tresize**, **Tresise**.

Trick English: metonymic nickname for a cunning or crafty person, from ME *trick* strategem, device (from a Norman form of OF *triche*; cf. TREACHER).

Var.: **Tricker** (an agent deriv.).

Dim.: **Trickett**.

Trigg English: from the ON byname *Triggr* 'Trustworthy', 'Faithful', a cogn. of TROW 1.

Var.: **Trigge**.

Cogn.: Swed.: **Trygg** (in part a 'soldier's name', one of the group of monosyllabic names adopted by peasants on military service in the 17th and 18th cents., and subsequently retained by their families).

Patr.: Eng.: **Triggs**.

Trigo Spanish and Portuguese: occupational name for a grower or seller of wheat, Sp., Port. *trigo* (L *trīticum*, from *terere* to grind, past part. *trītus*).

Var.: Sp.: **Triguero** (an agent deriv.).

Trillo Spanish: 1. metonymic occupational name for a thresher, from Sp. *trillo* threshing-sledge (L *trībulum*).

2. habitation name from a place in the province of Guadalajara, presumably so called from some similarity of shape.

Cogns. (of 1): Fr.: **Triboul**, **Tribo(u)t** (also used in a fig. sense, meaning 'torment' or 'affliction', and so perhaps a nickname for a tormented, emotionally troubled person or a tormentor of others).

Dims. (of 1): Fr.: **Triboulet**, **Triboulot**.

Pej. (of 1): Fr.: **Tribouillard**.

Trim English: apparently a nickname for a well-turned-out person, from the adj. *trim* well-equipped, neatly made. The word is first attested in the early 16th cent. (cf. TRIMMER), but may well have been in colloquial use much earlier.

Trimmer English: occupational name, probably for a trimmer of cloth. The verb *trim* is not attested in its mod. sense before the early 16th cent., but the surname form William *le Trymmere* is found in the 14th cent., and this seems to be continuous with OE *trymian*, *trymman* to strengthen, confirm (from *trum* strong, firm).

Trindade Portuguese: religious byname adopted in honour of the Holy Trinity, and given in particular to children born on Trinity Sunday. The name is from Port. *trindade* trinity (LL *trīnitās*, gen. *trīnitātis*, a deriv. of *trēs* three).

Trinder English: occupational name for a braider or a spinner, from an agent deriv. of ME *trend(en)* to twist, plait (OE *trendan* to turn round, roll).

Tripconey Cornish: habitation name from a place in the parish of St Columb Major, now known as *Trekenning*. The placename is recorded in 1294 in the form

Trehepkenyn, probably from Corn. *tre* homestead, settlement + a personal name **Hepkenyn*. The form of the surname has been affected by folk etymology: the family arms registered in 1573 by John *Tripconie* of Gulval, fifth in descent from Ralph *Tripcony* who lived in the reign of Edward III (1327–77), feature three black conies (rabbits).

The surname is now most common in the St Keverne district.

Tripp English: 1. metonymic occupational name for a dancer, or nickname for someone with an odd gait, from ME *trip(p)(en)* to step lightly, skip, hop (OF *triper*, of Gmc origin; cf. OE *treppan* to tread).

2. metonymic occupational name for a butcher or tripe-dresser, from ME, OF *trip(p)e* tripe (of unknown origin).

Vars: **Tripper**. (Of 2 only): **Tripe**.

Cogns. (of 2): Fr.: **Tripier, Tripié**.

Dims. (of 2): Fr.: **Tripet(te), Tripon, Tripeau**.

Pejs. (of 1): Fr.: **Trépard, Trépaud**.

Tříska Czech: nickname for a thin man, one who was 'as thin as a splinter', from Czech *tříska* splinter.

Var.: **Tříška**.

Trnka Czech: 1. topographic name for someone living by a sloe or blackthorn, Czech *trnka*.

2. nickname for someone with eyes as dark as sloes, from the same word in a trasferred sense.

Trock Jewish (E Ashkenazic): habitation name from *Trok*, the Yid. name of a town in Lithuania (Lithuanian *Trakai*, Russ. *Troki*), which had a large Jewish population.

Vars.: **Trocker** (from Yid. *troker* inhabitant of *Trok*); **Trocki, Trotski, Trotsky** (from Russ. *trotskii*, adj., relating to *Troki*).

Trofimov Russian: patr. from the given name *Trofim* (Gk *Trophimos* 'Nursling', from *trophein* to raise, rear). The personal name was borne by various early Christian saints martyred at Rome and in the East under the emperors Probus and Diocletian.

Cogns. (patrs.): Beloruss.: **Trakhimovich**. Pol.: **Trochimowicz**.

Dims.: Russ.: **Tronyaev, Trishkin** (patrs.). Ukr.: **Troshchenko**. Beloruss.: **Trokhinchik; Atrakhovich, Atrashkevich** (patrs.).

Troitski Russian: surname originally adopted by Orthodox priests in honour of the Holy Trinity, from ORuss. *troitsa* group of three (a calque of Gk *trias*; cf. TRINDADE) + the (originally local) suffix *-ski*. In recent years it has also been adopted in the Soviet Union by bearers of the name *Trotski* (see TROCK), which was felt to be politically undesirable.

Trojan Czech: from an OSlav. personal name, *Trojan*, apparently a form of L *Traiānus*, the name of a Roman emperor (53–117), who extended the Roman Empire east into Dacia (mod. Rumania). In early Slav. records the name is also found denoting a mythical creature or deity.

Dims.: **Trojánek, Trojášek, Trojančík, Trojek**.

Cogns.: Pol.: **Trojanowski** (habitation name from a place called *Trojanówka*). Croatian: **Trajković** (patr. from a dim.).

Trollope English: habitation name from the former name of Troughburn in Northumb., from ON *troll* imp, supernatural being (cf. TROUILLET) + OE *hop* enclosed valley (see HOPE).

Var.: **Trollop**.

A family of this name trace their descent from John Tro(w)lope, *who lived at Thornlaw, Co. Durham, and before 1390 had acquired the manor of Morden in the same county. The novelist Anthony* Trollope *(1815–82) was one of his descendants.*

Trossier French: occupational name for a pedlar, from an agent deriv. of OF *tro(u)sse* pack, bundle (of uncertain origin).

Var.: **Troussié**.

Cogns.: Eng.: **Truss(man)**.

Trost 1. German: from a medieval given name or byname often bestowed on a child born after the death of a sibling, from Ger. *Trost* comfort, consolation (MHG *trōst*, OHG *trōst* confidence, trust); cf. SOLIS.

2. Jewish (Ashkenazic): ornamental name from mod. Ger. *Trost* comfort, consolation.

Vars.: Ger.: **Tröster**. Jewish: **Treister, Traister, Trejster** (from Yid. *treyster* comforter, consoler); **Trostman, Treistman, Traistman, Trajstman** (coined from Yid. *treyst* comfort, consolation + *-man* man).

Cogns.: Flem., Du.: **(Van) Troost**. Dan., Norw.: **Trøst**.

Troth English (Worcs., centred on Bromsgrove): nickname from ME *trowthe*, *trouthe* good faith, loyalty (OE *trēowð* truth, a deriv. of *trēow* true; cf. TROW 1). *By my troth* was a common phrase emphasizing the veracity of an assertion, and the nickname may have been bestowed on someone who used it habitually or to excess.

Trotter 1. English and Scots: occupational name for a messenger, from an agent deriv. of ME *trot(en)* to walk fast (OF *troter*, of Gmc origin, akin to 2 below).

2. German: occupational name for a grape-treader, from an agent deriv. of MHG *trot(t)e* winepress (OHG *trot(t)a*, from *trottōn* to tread, trample). The vocab. word and the surname are confined largely to Alsace, Lorraine, Switzerland, and Swabia.

Vars. (of 1): **Trott, Trotman**. (Of 2): **Trott, Trot(t)mann**.

Cogns. (of 1): Fr.: **Trot(t)ier**.

Dims. (of 1): Fr.: **Trottereau, Trotteleau; Trotot, Trotin, Trotignon**.

Trotter *is a name well established in Edinburgh, Northumb., and the Scottish Borders. The vars.* Trott *and* Trotman *occur mainly in S England.*

Troughton English: habitation name from *Troughton* Hall in the parish of Kirkby Ireleth, Lancs., so called from OE *trog* trough, hollow (see TROW 3) + *tūn* enclosure, settlement.

Var.: **Trouton**.

Trouillet French: metonymic nickname for a devious character, from a dim. of OF *trouille* trickery, sorcery (of Gmc origin, apparently akin to ON *troll* imp, supernatural being).

Vars.: **Trouillot, Trouillon**.

Cogns.: Ger.: **Trull, Trüll(er); Trültsch, Tröltsch, Triltsche** (Swabia).

Pej.: Fr.: **Trouillard**.

Troup Scots: habitation name from a place in the parish of Gamrie, near Banff. The place is situated on a headland affording some sheltered anchorage, and may get its name from ME *true hope*; however, when first recorded in 1296 it already appears as *Trup*, and so is more likely to be of the same origin as THORPE.

Vars.: **Troupe, Troop**.

Trout English: metonymic occupational name for a fisherman, or nickname for someone supposedly resembling this freshwater fish, ME *trowte* (OE *trūht*).

Trouvé French: nickname for a foundling, from the past part. of OF *trouver* to find (of uncertain origin, probably from L *turbāre* to disturb, the semantic development being a result of the practice of disturbing water to catch fish).

Cogns.: Prov.: **Trouvat, Troubat.** It.: **Trovato, Trovati.**

Dims.: Fr.: **Trouvin.** It.: **Trovatello, Trovatelli.**

Trow English (chiefly W Midlands): 1. nickname for a trustworthy person, from ME *trow(e)*, *trew(e)* faithful, steadfast (OE *trēowe*).

2. topographic name for someone who lived near a conspicuous tree, ME *trow*, *trew* (OE *trēow*).

3. topographic name for someone who lived near a depression in the ground, from ME *trow* trough, hollow (OE *trog*).

Vars. (mostly of 1): **Trew, True.** See also TRUEMAN. (Of 2 only): **Tree(s), Treece.**

Cogns. (of 1): Ger.: **Treu(e).** Jewish (Ashkenazic): **Treu(mann), Treiman; Getreuer; Getroir, Getrouer** (from Yid. *getray*, influenced by Ger. *treu*); **Treuherz** ('true heart').

Trowbridge English: habitation name from a place in Wilts., so called from OE *trēow* tree (see TROW 2) + *brycg* BRIDGE; the name probably referred to a felled trunk serving as a rough-and-ready bridge.

Vars.: **Tro(u)bridge, Trubridge.**

Troy 1. Irish: Anglicized form of Gael. **Ó Troighthigh** 'descendant of *Troightheach*', a byname meaning 'Foot Soldier'.

2. Jewish (E Ashkenazic): presumably an Anglicized form of some like-sounding Jewish surname or an Anglicized spelling of *Treu* (see TROW).

Var. (of 1): **O'Trehy.**

Truc Provençal: topographic name for someone who lived near or on a hill or elevation, OProv. *t(r)uc* (a word of Gaul. origin commonly found in placenames).

Vars.: **Tuc; Dut(r)u(c), Dutrut, Duthu; Tusse** (SE France).

Dims.: **T(r)uquet, Truchet(et), Truchon, Truchot, Truchy; Tusseau, Tussaud.**

Trudgeon English (Cornwall): habitation name from *Tregian* in the parish of St Ewe, earlier *Trudgeon*. The placename is recorded in 1331 in the form *Trehydian*, from Corn. *tre* homestead, settlement + a personal name similar in form to the attested *Hedyn*.

Var.: **Trudgian.**

Trudgill English (Norfolk): of uncertain origin. According to Barber it is from an OE personal name composed of the elements *þrȳð* might + *hild* battle.

Trueman English (common esp. in the Midlands): nickname for a trustworthy man, from ME *trew(e)*, *trow(e)* faithful (see TROW 1) + *man* man. This was apparently also used as a given name during the Middle Ages, and some instances of the surname may derive from this use. The name is also found among Ashkenazic Jews as an Anglicization of any of the various Jewish surnames listed at TROW.

Vars.: **Truman, Trewman; Tro(w)man** (W Midlands, esp. Staffs.).

Cogn.: Ger.: **Treumann.**

Patrs.: Eng.: **Tro(w)mans** (Staffs.).

Truffault French: nickname for a joker or a trickster, from a pej. deriv. of OF *trufe* deceit, abuse, teasing (of uncertain origin).

Vars.: **Truffaut, Truffot, Triffault; Truffaudier** (with an agent suffix).

Truhlář Czech: occupational name for a joiner, Czech *truhlář*, agent noun from *truhla* chest, coffer, a borrowing from Ger. *Truhe* chest.

Trujillo Spanish: habitation name from places in the provinces of Cáceres and Seville, first recorded in L as *Turgalium* and of unknown, presumably pre-Roman, origin.

Trumbull English and Scots: from an OE personal name, **Trumbeald*, composed of the elements *trum* strong, firm + *beald* bold, brave. See also TURNBULL, which is thought by some to be a var. of this.

Vars.: **Trumble,** TREMBLE; **Trimble** (N Ireland).

Trunchion English: nickname for a short, fat man, from ME, OF *tronchon* piece broken off (LL *trunciō*, gen. *truncīōnis*, from *truncus* lopped, cut short). It is just possible that the nickname also denoted someone who carried a staff or cudgel as a symbol of office, but this sense of the word is not attested in Eng. before the 16th cent.

Vars.: **Tro(u)nson.**

Cogns.: Fr.: **Tronchon, Tronson, Troncin.**

Truscott Cornish: habitation name from a place in the parish of St Stephens by Launceston, so called from Corn. *dres* beyond + *cuit* wood.

Trussell English (E Midlands): of uncertain origin, perhaps a metonymic occupational name for a pedlar, from a dim. of ME *truss* bundle, package (cf. TROSSIER), or else a nickname representing a var. of THRUSSELL.

Vars.: **Trussel, Truswell.**

Tryon English, of Dutch origin and uncertain derivation.

A Northants family of this name trace their descent from Peter Trieon *(d. 1611), who came to England from the Netherlands* c.*1562. His son, Moses Tryon, was High Sheriff of Northants in 1624.*

Trzciński Polish: habitation name from a place called *Trzcian(a)* or another called *Trzcin*, both of which are named from Pol. *trzcina* reed.

Var.: **Trzcieński.**

Trzepałkowski Polish: habitation name from a place named from the nickname *Trzepałek*, meaning either 'Thrasher' or 'Chatterer', from Pol. *trzepać* to beat, thrash, or chatter.

Var.: **Trzepiński.**

Tsadok Jewish: from the Hebr. male given name *Tsadok* (from Hebr. *tsadik* pious, saintly man, whence Yid. *tsadik*; see ZADIK). The Eng. word *Sadducee* is related.

Vars.: **Tzadok, Zadok; Tsodek** (NE Ashkenazic; from the Yid. form, *Tsodek*, of the given name); **Tzudick** (S Ashkenazic). name).

Patr.: **Zudkevitz** (S Ashkenazic).

Tsyganov Russian: patr. from the name *tsygan* Gipsy. The vocab. word is of uncertain origin; it may have come from India at the same time as the Gipsies themselves. In any event, it reached Russ. by way of Byzantine Gk, where it had been associated by folk etymology with *athinganos* untouchable.

Cogns.: Pol.: **Cygan.** Ger.: **Zigeuner.** Hung.: **Czigány.**

Tubb English: from the ME given name *Tubbe*, apparently derived from either ON *Tubbi* or OE **Tubba* (evidence for which is found in the placename *Tubney*, Berks.). There is no evidence to support the suggestion that it might be a metonymic occupational name or nickname from ME *tub* barrel (of Low Ger. origin).

Var.: **Tubby** (Norfolk, of ON origin).

Patr.: **Tubbs.**

Tuček Czech: nickname for a plump person, from a dim. form of Czech *tučný* fat.

Tuchmann German and Jewish (Ashkenazic): occupational name for a maker or seller of cloths, from Ger. *Tuch* cloth (MHG *tuoch*) + *mann* man.

Vars.: Ger.: **Tucher(t)**. Jewish: **Tuchman, Tuchler; Tuchmacher** ('cloth maker'); **Tuchschneider, Tuchsznajder** ('cloth cutter'; the second form is a Pol. spelling (E Ashkenazic)).

Tucker 1. English (chiefly W Country): occupational name for a fuller, from an agent deriv. of ME *tuck(en)* to full cloth (OE *tūcian* to torment). This was the term used for the process in the Middle Ages in SW England, and the present-day distribution of the surname still reflects this (see also FULLER and WALKER).

2. English: occasionally perhaps a nickname for a brave or generous man, from OF *tout* all (L *tōtus*) + *coeur* heart (L *cor*).

3. Jewish (Ashkenazic): Anglicized form of *To(c)ker*; see TOKARZ.

Tuckwell English: apparently an occupational nickname for a TUCKER; cf. TREADWELL.

Var.: **Tugwell**.

Tuddenham English (E Anglia): habitation name from a group of places in Norfolk and Suffolk, so called from the gen. case of the OE personal name *Tudda* + OE *hām* homestead.

Var.: **Tudman**.

Tudela Spanish and Catalan: habitation name from any of various places, for example in the provinces of Lérida, Navarre, Oviedo, and Valladolid. The placename is of pre-Roman origin and unknown meaning.

Tuháček Czech: nickname for a stiff or unbending person, from Czech *tuhý* stiff, rigid.

Tuite Irish: in origin apparently a Norman habitation name, from an unknown place (see below), but from an early date it was taken as an Anglicization of Gael. **Mac Confhiaclaigh** 'son of *Cú Fhiaclach*', a personal name meaning 'Large-toothed Hound', the essential element of which was translated into Eng. as TOOTH, of which *Tuite* came to be taken as a variant.

This is the name of an Irish family established in Ireland by Sir Richard de Tuite *(d. 1211), a member of the force which accompanied Strongbow's invasion of Ireland in 1172.*

Tull English: of uncertain origin, possibly from an unrecorded late survival of the OE personal name *Tula*.

Tulloch Scots: habitation name from a place near Dingwall on the Firth of Cromarty, so called from Gael. *tulach* hillock, or from any of various other minor places named with this element.

Vars.: **Tullock, Tulloh**. See also TOUGH 1.

Tully Irish: 1. Anglicized form of Gael. **Ó Taithlagh** 'descendant of *Taithleach*', a byname meaning 'Quiet', 'Peaceable'.

2. Anglicized form of Gael. **Ó Maol Tuile** 'descendant of the devotee of (St) *Tuile*', a personal name derived from *toil* will (of God).

Vars.: **Tilly** (see also TILLEY). (Of 1 only): **Tally**. (Of 2 only): **O'Multully, O'Multilly**; FLOOD (the result of erroneous association with the vocab. word *tuile* flood).

Tumanov Russian: patr. from the nickname *Tuman* 'Mist', 'Fog' (a Turkic borrowing), perhaps denoting a dim-witted person.

Tungate English (Norfolk): habitation name from a minor place near N Walsham, so called from ME *tune*, *tone* village, settlement (OE *tūn*) + *gate* GATE.

Tunik Jewish (E Ashkenazic): habitation name from a town so called near Minsk in Belorussia.

Var.: **Tunick**.

Tunney Irish: Anglicized form of Gael. **Ó Tonnaigh** 'descendant of *Tonnach*', a personal name meaning either 'Billowy' (from *tonn* wave) or 'Shining' or 'Swamp'.

Tunnicliffe English: habitation name from *Tonacliffe* in Lancs., recorded in 1246 as *Tunwal(e)clif*, from OE *tūn* enclosure, settlement + *wœll(a)* spring, stream + *clif* bank, slope.

Vars.: **Tunnicliff, Dunnicliff(e)**.

Tunstall English: habitation name from any of the numerous places, for example in Lancs., N Yorks., Co. Durham, Humberside, Kent, Norfolk, Shrops., Staffs., and Suffolk, so called from OE *tūn* enclosure, settlement + *st(e)all* site. The surname is found chiefly in Lancs. and Yorks.

Vars.: **Tunstell, Tunstill**. See also DUNSTALL.

Tuohy Irish: Anglicized form of Gael. **Ó Tuathaigh** 'descendant of *Tuathach*', a byname meaning 'Chief', 'Lord' (i.e. ruler over a *tuath* tribe, territory).

Vars.: **O'Towie, (O')Twohy, T(w)oohy, Tuhy, Tooey, Towey**.

Tuominen Finnish: ornamental name from Finn. *tuomi* bird cherry (*Prunus padus*) + the gen. suffix *-nen*. Cf. Swed. HÄGG.

Tupper 1. English: occupational name for a herdsman who had charge of rams, from an agent deriv. of ME *to(u)pe* ram (of uncertain origin).

2. German: of uncertain origin, possibly a cogn. of 1.

This is the name of a family descended from two brothers, originally from Kassel in Upper Saxony. They fled religious persecution in the 16th cent., settling in the Netherlands, where a descendant became burgomaster of Rotterdam in 1813. A branch of the family settled in England at Sandwich, Kent, whence another descendant, Thomas Tupper, *went to America in 1635, and helped to found the town of Sandwich, Mass., in 1637.*

Turgenev Russian: patr. from the Mongol nickname *Türgen* 'Swift'.

The Russian novelist and dramatist Ivan Turgenev *(1818–83) came of a family of the middle nobility. The name is recorded in the 15th cent. as that of a Tatar Khan who served Duke Vassily the Blind.*

Turk 1. English: nickname for a rowdy or unruly person, from ME, OF *turc* Turk (of unknown ultimate origin). The non-Jewish Continental cogns. listed below are also house names, derived from the use of a picture of a Turk as a house sign, and nicknames for someone who had taken part in the wars against the Turks. The Jewish names mean 'Jew from Turkey'.

2. English: from a medieval given name, apparently a back-formation from THIRKILL, misanalysed as containing the OF dim. suffix *-el*.

3. Scots: Anglicized form of Gael. *Mac Torc*; see MCTURK.

Cogns. (of 1): Fr.: **Turc(q), Leturc, Leturque**. It.: **Turco, Turc(h)i; Turchio** (Sicily, Calabria). Rum.: **Turcu(l)**. Ger.: **Turck, Türk, Thürch**. Flem., Du.: **De Turk**. Jewish: **Turk(isher)** (Ashkenazic); **Turkow, Turkov** (E Ashkenazic); **Turcu, Turco** (in Rumania). Pol., Czech: **Turek**. Hung.: **Török**.

Dims. (of 1): Fr.: **Turquet, Turquin**. It.: **Turchelli, Turchetti, Turchetto, Turchini**. Ger. and Jewish (Ashkenazic): **Terkel**. Czech: **Tureček**.

Patrs. (from 1): It.: **Del Turco, Turcheschi**. Pol.: **Turkiewicz**; **Turczak**.

Habitation name: Pol.: **Turkowski**.

Turkington N Irish: of uncertain origin, apparently a habitation name from *Torkington* in Ches., but now much more common in N Ireland than anywhere else. It may have been used as an Anglicized form of Sc. McTurk.

Turnbull N English (chiefly Northumb.) and Scots: apparently a nickname for a man thought to be strong and brave enough to turn back a charging bull, from ME *turn(en)* to turn (OE *turnian*, reinforced by OF *torner*, both from L *tornāre*, a deriv. of *tornus* lathe; cf. Turner) + *bul(l)e* Bull.

Var.: **Turnbill**.

Turner 1. English and Scots (extremely common and widespread): occupational name for a maker of small objects of wood, metal, or bone by turning on a lathe, from ANF *torner* (OF *tornier*, L *tornārius*, a deriv. of *tornus* lathe). The surname may also derive from various other senses of ME *turn* and have originally described a turnspit, translator or interpreter, or tumbler.

2. English and Scots (rarely): nickname for a fast runner, from ME *turnen* to turn + Hare; cf. Turnbull.

3. English and Scots: occupational name for an official in charge of a tournament, OF *tornei* (in origin akin to 1).

4. Jewish (Ashkenazic): habitation name from a S Yid. pronunciation of Yid. *Torner*, denoting a native or inhabitant of the city of *Tarnów* (Yid. *Torne*), in Galicia (see Tarnowski).

5. Jewish (Ashkenazic): translation or Anglicized form of any of various other Jewish surnames.

Vars. (of 1): **Turno(u)r**.

Cogns. (of 1): Fr.: **To(u)rnier**; **Tourneur, Tourneux, Letourneur, Letourneux**. Prov.: **Tornadou(r), Tournadre**.

Equivs. (not cogn.): Ger. and Jewish: Drechsler. N Ger.: Dreier. Pol.: Tokarz.

Turney English (Norman): habitation name from any of various places in N France called *Tournai* (Orne), *Tournay* (Calvados), or *Tourny* (Eure), all from the pre-Roman personal name *Turnus* (probably meaning 'Height', 'Eminence'; cf. Teruel and Théron) + the local suffix *-ācum*.

Var.: **Tournay**.

Turnham English: habitation name from *Turnham* in E Yorks or *Turnham* Green in W London, both of which are so called from OE *trun* circular + *hamm* water meadow or *hām* homestead.

Turov Russian: patr. from the nickname *Tur* 'Aurochs' (ultimately cogn. with L *taurus* bull; see Toro).

Cogns.: Beloruss.: **Tur**. Pol.: **Tur(al)ski, Turała** (not patrs.). Jewish (E Ashkenazic; all ornamental): **Turuk, Turo(c)k** (augs.); **Turowicz, Turovetz** (patrs. in form); **Turowski**.

Dim.: Pol.: **Turajczyk**.

Turpin English and French: from a Norman French form of the ON personal name *Þorfinnr*, composed of the divine name *Þórr* (see Thor 2) + the ethnic name *Finnr*. This may have absorbed another name, *Turpius*, *Turpinus* (from L *turpis* ugly, base), one of the self-abasing names adopted as a mark of humility by the early Christians. It was borne by the archbishop of Rheims in the Charlemagne legend.

Vars.: Fr.: **Tourpin, Trupin**.

Dim.: Scots: **Turpie**.

Turtle English: 1. var. of Thirkill.

2. nickname for a mild and gentle or affectionate person, from ME *turtel* turtle dove (OE *turtla*, *turtle*, from L *turtur*, apparently of imitative origin).

3. nickname for a crippled or deformed person, from OF *tourtel*, a dim. of *tourt* crooked (L *tortus*, past part. of *torquere* to twist).

Cogns. (of 2): It.: **Tortora, Turtura, Turturo**.

Dims. (of 2): It.: **Tortorella, Tortorello, Tortorelli; Torturiello, Turturiello** (Naples).

Turton English: habitation name from a place in Lancs., so called from the ON personal name *Þóri* (see Thor 2) + OE *tūn* enclosure, settlement. The surname is now as common in the Midlands as it is in Lancs. and Yorks.

Turvey English: habitation name from a place in Beds., so called from OE *turf* turf, grass + *ēg* island, low-lying land.

Tuson English (Lancs.): apparently a patr. from the given name *Tuwe* or *Tywe*, which occurs in Lancs. in the 14th cent., but is of unknown origin.

Var.: **Tewson**.

Tutt English: from an OE personal name or byname *Tutta*, preserved in placenames such as *Tutnall* (Worcs.) and *Tuttington* (Norfolk), and apparently persisting into the Middle Ages. Its origin and meaning are unclear.

Tutty Irish: Anglicized form of Gael. **Ó Tuataigh** 'descendant of *Tuatach*', a byname meaning 'Rustic', 'Boorish'.

Tvrdík Czech: nickname for an obstinate or severe person, from a deriv. of Czech *tvrdý* hard.

Cogns.: Pol.: **Twardy**. Jewish (E Ashkenazic): **Tward**.

Patrs.: Russ.: **Tvyordyshev, Tverdashov, Tverdyukov**.

Habitation name: Pol.: **Twardowski**.

Cpd: Jewish (E Ashkenazic): **Twardogora** ('hard hill'; reason for adoption unknown).

Tweddle N English and Scots: regional name for someone who lived in the valley (see Dale) of the river Tweed.

Vars.: **Tweddell, Tweed(a)le, Twaddle, Twaddell**.

Tweed N English and Scots: topographic name for someone living on the banks of the river *Tweed*, which flows between NE England and SE Scotland, and bears a Brit. name of uncertain meaning. It may be akin to W *twyad* hemming in (from *twy* check, bound), with reference to the deep and narrow valley at points along its course, or it may derive from a lost Brit. word cogn. with an Indo-European root meaning 'to swell, be powerful'.

Tweedie Scots: habitation name from a place in the parish of Stonehouse, south of Glasgow, the name of which is of uncertain origin.

Var.: **Tweedy**.

For centuries the Tweedie *family had their home in the valley of the river Tweed, and assumed that their surname was derived from the river. However, Black has shown that this is not the case, and the origin is as above.*

Twigg English: nickname for a thin person, from ME, OE *twigge* twig, shoot. Since the word occurs only late in the OE period and was initially confined to Northern dialects, it may be a borrowing from ON. The surname is found mainly in the Midlands.

Var.: **Twigge**.

Cogns.: Ger.: **Zweig**. Jewish (Ashkenazic): **Zweig**; **Cwaig** (forms with *Cw-* are E Ashkenazic, being Pol. in spelling); **Zweig(en)haft, Cwajg(en)haft, Cwaigenhaft** ('twig-like'). Low Ger.: **Tweig**.

Dims.: Ger.: **Zweigle**. Jewish: **Zweig(e)l**.

Cpds (ornamental): Jewish: **Zweigenbaum** ('twig tree'); **Zweigenberg, Cwajgenberg** ('twig hill').

Twin English: name for one of a pair of twins, from ME *twinn* (OE *(ge)twinn* twofold, double, a deriv. of *twā* two).

Var.: **Twinn**.

Twist English (chiefly Lancs. and W Midlands): of uncertain origin, possibly a metonymic occupational name for someone in the cotton-spinning industry, whose responsibility was to combine threads into a strong cord, a sense of *twist* recorded from the 16th cent.

Var.: **Twiss**.

Twomey Irish: Anglicized form of Gael. **Ó Tuama** 'descendant of *Tuama*', a personal name probably derived from *tuaim* hill, small mountain.

Vars.: **Twoomy, Tuomy, Towmey, O'Twomey, (O')Toomey**.

Twyford English: habitation name from any of the numerous places, for example in Berks., Bucks., Derbys., Hants, Leics., Lincs., Middx, and Norfolk, so called from OE *twī-* double (cf. TWIN) + *ford* FORD.

Tyas English: ethnic name of early date (12th cent. onwards) for someone from Germany or the Low Countries, from ANF *tieis*, *tiois* German (OHG *tiutisc*; cf. DEUTSCH and TEDESCO).

Var.: **Tyers**.

Tye English: 1. topographic name for someone who lived by a common pasture, ME *tye* (OE *tēag*).

2. topographic name for someone who lived by a river or on an island, from a misdivision of ME *at(te) ye*, *at(te) ey*; cf. NYE and RYE.

Vars.: **Tey, Tee**.

Tyldesley English: habitation name from a place in Lancs., near Leigh, so called from the gen. case of the OE personal name *Tilweald* (composed of the elements *til* good + *weald* rule) + OE *lēah* wood, clearing. The surname has been common in the surrounding area since the 14th cent.

Vars.: **Tyldeslegh, Tydsley, Tild(e)sley, Til(l)sley, Tilzey**.

Tynan Irish: Anglicized form of Gael. **Ó Teimhneáin** 'descendant of *Teimhneán*', a dim. form of the OIr. personal name *Teimhean* 'Dark'.

Tyrer English (Lancs.): of unknown origin. It is possible that it arose as an occupational name for an official in charge of the wardrobe of a great personage, from an agent deriv. of ME *tire(n)* to equip, dress (an aphetic form of OF *atir(i)er*, from the phrase *a tire* in order, which is itself of uncertain origin). However, there is no early evidence for this.

Tyringham English: habitation name from a place in Bucks., probably so called from OE *Tīdheringahām* 'homestead (OE *hām*) of the people of *Tīdhere*', a personal name composed of the elements *tīd* time + *here* army. Alternatively, the proprietor may have borne the shorter name of *Tīr(a)*, a short form of the rare cpd names with the first element *tīr* glory.

A family of this name held lands at Tyringham in the late 12th cent. They trace their line from Giffard de Tyringham, *who donated the living from the church at Tyringham to a nearby priory in* c.*1187*.

Tyrrell English and Irish: of uncertain origin, probably a Norman nickname for a stubborn person, from OF *tirel*, used of an animal which pulls on the reins, a deriv. of *tirer* to pull (cf. TIRADO).

Vars.: **Tyrell, Tirrell, Terrill, Terrell, Terrall, Turrell, Tearall; Tirial** (a Gaelicized form).

Cogns.: Fr.: **Tirand, Tirant** (pres. parts.); **Tirard** (pej.).

Tyrwhitt English: habitation name from *Trewhitt* in Northumb., so called from ON *tyri* dry resinous wood + *þvít* meadow, piece of land (see THWAITE).

Var.: **Truett**.

Tyson English: 1. var. of *Dyson*; see DYE.

2. nickname for someone of a fiery temperament, from OF *tison* firebrand (L *titio*, gen. *titiōnis*).

Cogn. (of 2): Fr.: **Tison**.

Tyzack English (of French origin): habitation name from *Tizac* in Gironde, Aquitaine, so called from the L personal name *Titius* (a deriv. of *Titus*; see TITO) + the local suffix *-ācum*.

U

Uccello Italian: metonymic occupational name for a bird-catcher or a nickname for a small birdlike person, from It. *uccello* bird (LL *avicellus*, a dim. of class. L *avis*).

Vars.: **Uccelli, Ulcelli, Uzielli; Auc(i)ello, Aucelli, Augello, Ausielli; Oselli.**

Cogns.: Fr.: **Oiseau, Loiseau, Loisel(le), Loizeau, Loyseau, Loysel; Loisellier, Loisselier, Loiseleur** (agent derivs.). Prov.: **Lausel, Laugel; Laudet** (Gascony). Eng. (Norman): **Ussell, Uzzell.**

Dims.: It.: **Uccelletti; Augelluzzi; Oseletti.** Fr.: **Loiselet, Loisillon, Loizillon.**

The painter Paolo Uccello *(1397–1475) was born in Pratovecchio near Florence, the son of a barber-surgeon. His original identifying name was* di Dono; *the reason why he acquired the name Uccello is not known.*

Uceda Spanish: habitation name from a place in the province of Guadalajara, so called from a collective deriv. of the Sp. dial. term *uz*, denoting a kind of heather (L *ulex*, gen. *ulicis*).

Uciński Polish: habitation name from a place probably named from Pol. *ucinać* to cut off, dock, with the addition of *-ski*, suffix of local surnames (see BARANOWSKI).

Udall English: habitation name from *Yewdale* in Lancs., so called from OE *īw* yew tree + *dæl* valley (see DALE).

Vars.: **Udell, Uvedale.**

Uddin English: of uncertain origin, probably a dim. of the given name HUDD. The name is relatively common in the London area, but rare elsewhere.

Ufer German: topographic name for someone who lived on a riverbank, Ger. *Ufer*, MHG *uover* (not attested in OHG, but cf. OVER), or habitation name from one of the various places named with this word, of which there are two in Austria and one near Cologne.

Vars.: **Ufert, Ufermann.**

Ufford English: habitation name from places in Northants and Suffolk, so called from the OE personal name *Uffa* (of uncertain origin) + OE *worð* enclosure (see WORTH).

Ugalde Basque: topographic name for someone who lived near water, from Basque *ur* water + *alde* place, direction, side. In the dialect of Navarre the combination has the sense 'river', and this may sometimes lie behind the surname.

Ugarte Basque: topographic name for someone who lived on an island or piece of land between two rivers, Basque *ugarte* (from *ur* water + *arte* intervening space). There are places so named in the provinces of Álava and Biscay, and the surname may also be a habitation name from one of these.

Uhlíř Czech: occupational name for a coal merchant or, at an earlier date, a charcoal burner, an agent deriv. of Czech *uhlí* coal, charcoal.

Dim.: **Uhlík.**

Ukraintsev Russian: patr. from the name *ukrainets* Ukrainian. The Ukraine (Russ. *Ukraina*) gets its name from the Slav. elements *u* at + *kraina* boundary, edge, i.e. 'border territory'.

Cogns. (not patrs.): Jewish (E Ashkenazic): **Ukrainetz, Okrainetz; Krainer, Kreiner** (aphetic forms).

Cogn. (patr.): Jewish: **Krainovitz** (aphetic).

Dim.: Ukr.: **Ukraïnko.**

Ulanov Russian: 1. patr. from the occupational term *ulan* lancer, uhlan (from a Turkic word meaning 'youth').

2. Russianized form of the Mongol (Kalmuck) byname *Ulan*, meaning 'Red'.

Cogns. (of 1): Pol.: **Ulański, Ułański** (not patrs.).

Habitation name: Pol.: **Ulanowski.**

Ulatowski Polish: apparently a habitation name, of uncertain origin, perhaps from a place deriving its name from OPol. *ulatać* to yield, defer (meaning 'to fly away' in mod. Pol.).

Ulman Jewish (Ashkenazic): habitation name from the city of *Ulm* in Baden-Württemberg, with the suffix *-man* man, which is occasionally found as a surname-forming element with placenames, denoting a native or inhabitant of a place.

Var.: **Ullman.**

Ulrich German: from the given name *Ulrich*, OHG *Odalrīc*, composed of the elements *odal* prosperity, fortune + *rīc* power. The name was borne by a 10th-cent. saint, bishop of Augsburg, whose fame contributed greatly to the popularity of the given name in German- and Slavic-speaking areas in the Middle Ages.

Vars.: **Ull(e)rich; Uhlich, Uhlig, Urich, Urech, U(h)rig** (under Slav. influence).

Cogns.: Low Ger.: **Ohlerich, Öll(e)rich.** Czech: **Oldřich, Voldřich.** Pol.: **Ulik, Ulejski.**

Dims.: Ger.: **U(h)de, Uhl(e), Uli, Ühl(e)in; Utz, Ützle; Ullmann.** Ger. (under Slav. influence): **Ulisch, Ul(t)sch, Ulusch; Jedele.** Low Ger.: **Ullmann, Uhl(e)mann, Utzmann; Ulke, Jehle.** Czech: **Volek.**

Patrs.: Ger.: **Ulrici** (Latinized). Low Ger.: **Öhlrichs.**

Patrs. (from dims.): Low Ger.: **Öhlerking, Öllerking; Ulkes, U(l)ken.** Fris.: **Ukena.**

Umfreville English and Scots (Norman): habitation name from a place in La Manche, so called from the OF personal name *Umfroi* (see HUMPHREY) + OF *ville* settlement (see VILLE).

Vars.: **Umfraville, Umphraville.**

Robert de Umfreville *was granted the manor of Redesdale in Northumb. by William the Conqueror to hold by service of defending the region 'from wolves and the king's enemies'. The direct line seems to have become extinct in 1820 with the death of his last descendant, a ship's master, the son of a Newcastle ship's chandler.*

Umpleby English (Yorks.): habitation name from *Anlaby* in E Yorks., recorded 1234 as *Anlaweby* but in Domesday Book as *Umloueby*. The place is named from the ON personal name *Anláfr, Óláfr* (see OLIFF) + ON *býr* farm, settlement.

Unbehauen German: nickname for an ill-mannered or boorish individual, from the MHG adj. *unbehouwen*, lit. 'not hewn into shape', i.e. rough, crude.

Vars.: **Unbehaun; Unbegaun** (in regions such as Russia, where the local Slav. language substitutes /g/ for /h/).

Uncle English: 1. nickname for an avuncular man, from the term of relationship, ME *uncle* (OF *oncle*, L *avunculus*), which eventually displaced the native EAME.

2. from the ON personal name *Úlfketil*, composed of the elements *úlfr* wolf + *ketill* cauldron. This was reasonably common as a given name in N England in the early Middle Ages, especially in the contracted form *Úlfkell*.

Cogn. (of 1): Flem.: **Nonckel**.

Dim. (of 1): Flem.: **Onckelet**.

Patrs. (from 1): Eng.: **Uncles, Ungles(s)**. Rom.: **Onciulesco**.

Underhill English (most common in the W Midlands, but also found in the W Country and elsewhere): topographic name for someone who lived at the foot of a hill, from ME *under* + HILL, or habitation name from a place named with these elements, for example in Devon.

Var.: **Undrell**.

Underwood English and Scots: topographic name for someone who lived at the edge of a wood, from ME *under* + WOOD, or habitation name from a place named with these elements, for example in Derbys., Notts., and the former county of Ayrs.

Unger German, Czech, and Jewish (Ashkenazic): name for a Magyar or someone from Hungary (Ger. *Ungarn*, Yid. *Ungern*), perhaps also in some cases a nickname for someone who had some trading or other connection with Hungary.

Vars.: Ger. and Jewish: **Ungar, Hunger, Hungar; Ungerer, Ungermann**. Jewish only: **Ungerland** (from Yid.), **Ungerman**; INGER; **Hungerer, Hungerland** (the initial *H-* generally added under Eng. influence).

Cogns.: Hung.: **Ungár**. Czech: **Uher**. Pol.: **Węgier(ski), Węgrzyn**. Russ.: **Veng(e)rov**. Jewish (E Ashkenazic): **Weng(i)er, Wengerik**. It.: **Ungaro, Ungari; Ongaro, Ongari** (Venetia); **Ungherese**.

Dims.: Ger.: **Hüngerle**. It.: **Ongarelli, Ungarelli, Ungherelli, Ungaretti**.

Patrs.: Jewish: **Ungerson; Ingerov** (S Ashkenazic). It.: **Dell'Ongaro**.

Unruh German: nickname for a restless or quarrelsome person, from Ger. *Unruhe* disturbance, unrest (MHG *unrou(we)*, *unrāwa*, OHG *unrāwa*, from the negative prefix *un-* + *ruowa* rest, calm).

Cogn.: Low Ger.: **Unrau**.

Unsworth English (Lancs.): habitation name from a place in Greater Manchester, so called from the gen. case of the OE byname *Hund* 'Dog' + OE *worð* enclosure (see WORTH).

Unwin English: from the OE personal name *Hūnwine*, composed of the elements *hūn* bearcub + *wine* friend. Later in the OE or early ME period, this name came to be confused with the word *unwine* enemy (from the negative prefix *un-* + *wine* friend), and this is no doubt the source of the surname in some cases.

Var.: **Hunwin**.

Upjohn Welsh: patr. from JOHN, with the prefix *ap* son of.

This is the name of an Exeter family who were watch- and clock-makers for over 300 years, from the late 17th cent. There is now a branch in Australia, still involved in clock-making.

Upton English: habitation name from any of the numerous places so called. The majority of them get the name from OE *up-* upper + *tūn* enclosure, settlement. One in Essex, however, was originally named with the phrase *upp in tūne* up in the settlement, i.e. the higher part of the settlement; and one in Worcs. is probably so called from the OE personal name *Ubba* (of uncertain origin) + *tūn*.

An Irish family of this name trace their ancestry to Henry Upton, *who served in Ireland under the Earl of Essex in 1598 and settled in Co. Antrim. In this particular case, the surname is derived from Upton in S Devon.*

Urban English, French, Czech, Polish, Belorussian, and Jewish (E Ashkenazic): from a medieval given name (L *Urbānus* 'City-dweller', a deriv. of *urbs* town, city). The name was borne by a 4th-cent. saint, the patron of vines, and by seven early popes. The Jewish names are adoptions of the Polish or Belorussian surname.

Vars.: Eng.: **Urben**. Fr.: **Urb(a)in**. Pol.: **Urbański; Urbaniec**.

Cogns.: It.: **Urbani, Urbano**. Sp., Port.: **Urbano**. Ger.: **Turban, Durban, Thurbahn, Thorbahn** (by misdivision from *Sankt Urban* St Urban). Ger. (under Slav. influence): **Hurban, Horban, Orbahn, Wurban, Jurband, Jorband, Jorbahn**. Hung.: **Urbán**.

Dims.: It.: **Urbaniello**. Ger. (under Slav. influence): **Urbanek, Urbanke, Hurbank, Wurbank; Urbasch, Urbisch, Horbasch**. Czech: **Urbánek**. Pol.: **Urbańczyk, Urbanek**.

Aug.: Czech: **Urbanec**.

Patrs.: Pol.: **Urbanowicz; Urbaniak**. Beloruss.: **Urbanovich**. Russ.: **Urbanov**. Jewish: **Urbanovsky**.

Patrs. (from dims.): Russ.: **Urbantsov, Urbantsev, Urmantsov, Urmantsev**.

Habitation name: Pol.: **Urbanowski**.

Ure Scots: from the Older Scots given name *Ure*, a var. of IVOR.

Patr.: **McUre**.

Uren Cornish: from the Brittonic personal name recorded as *Urbgen* in OW and as *Urbien* and *Urien* in OBret. The first element is unexplained; the second represents the root *gen* birth, born. In Cornwall the name may be a survival from the Celtic period or, more probably, an import from Brittany.

Vars.: **Urien, Urren, Urene, Urion, Ur(r)on, Urian, Ur(r)an, Urane, Urrin, Urin(e), Uring, Uryn, Urne, Youren, Youron, Yourn(e), Euren, Eweren**.

Patrs.: **Yourenson, Youronson**.

The earliest known record of the surname is in the forms Uryn *and* Urine *in 1524 in the borough of Helston and the parish of Sancreed.*

Ureña Spanish: habitation name from any of various places, for example in the provinces of Salamanca and Segovia, called *Urueña*. These are first recorded in the L form *Oronia*, and are of uncertain, presumably pre-Roman, origin.

Uría Spanish form of Basque **Uria**: topographic name for someone who lived in a village rather than the open countryside, from Basque *uri* settlement (a western dial. var. of *iri*; cf. IRIGOYEN) + the def. art. *-a*.

Uriarte Basque: topographic name for someone who lived between two settlements, from *uri* settlement (see URIA) + *arte* intervening space.

Var.: **Iriarte**.

Uribarri Basque: habitation name from any of various places, for example in the provinces of Álava, Biscay, and Guipúzcoa, so called from *uri* settlement (see URIA) + *barri* new.

Uribe Basque: topographic name for someone who lived in the lower part of a village, from *uri* settlement (see URIA) + *be(h)e* lower part.

Urquhart Scots: habitation name from a place in the former county of Inverness, on Loch Ness, apparently named with cogns. of W *ar* on, upon + *cardden* thicket.

Bearers of this common Scottish surname trace their descent from William de Urchard, *the earliest known bearer, who fought for Robert the Bruce between 1297 and 1328.*

Urquijo Spanish form of Basque **Urkiza, Urkizu**: topographic name for someone who lived by a group of birch trees, from Basque *urki* birch tree + the suffix of abundance *-zo*, *-zu*.

Urrutia Basque: topographic name for someone who lived at some distance from the main settlement, from *urruti* distant + the def. art. *-a*.

Urzędowski Polish: habitation name from the town of *Urzędów* SW of Lublin (so called from Pol. *urząd* office + *-ów* possessive suffix), with the addition of *-ski*, suffix of local surnames (see BARANOWSKI).

Var.: **Urzędowicz** (patr. in form, probably meaning 'son of the official').

Ushakov Russian: patr. from the nickname *Ushak*, a deriv. of *ukh* ear, pl. *ushi*. The nickname may have been used for a man with large or conspicuous ears, or perhaps for someone who had good hearing or who was given to eavesdropping.

Usher 1. English, Scots, and Irish: occupational name for a janitor or gate-keeper, ME *usher* (ANF *usser*, OF *ussier*, *huissier*, from LL *ustiārius*, a deriv. of class. L *ostium* door, gate). The term was also used in the Middle Ages of a court official charged with accompanying a person of rank on ceremonial occasions, and this may be a partial souce of the surname.

2. Jewish (S Ashkenazic): from a S Yid. pronunciation of the Yid. male given name OSHER (Hebr. ASHER).

Vars. (of 1): **Ussher, Husher**; **Lusher** (with the OF def. art.).

Patrs. (from 2): **Usherov(itz)**, **Usherowicz**; **Uszerowicz** (Pol. spelling).

There is a tradition among Irish bearers of the name Ussher *that they are descended from the Neville family, one of whose members served King John when he went to Ireland in 1210. The name is first recorded in Ireland with John* le Ussher, *who was constable of Dublin Castle in 1302.*

Utley N English: habitation name from a place in Yorks., near Keighley, so called from the OE personal name *Utta* (see UTTING) + OE *lēah* wood, clearing.

Var.: **Uttley**.

Utting English (Norfolk): from the OE personal name **Utting*, in origin a patr. from the attested *Utta*, which is of uncertain origin. The name is also discussed by Black as Scots, though it does not now seem to be common north of the border.

Var.: **Uttin**.

Uttridge English: from the OE personal name *Ūhtrīc*, composed of the elements *ūht* dawn + *rīc* power.

Vars.: **Ut(te)ridge**; **Out(te)ridge, Ou(gh)tright**.

Uys Flemish and Dutch: nickname for a belligerent individual or occupational name for a professional champion, from MDu. *huys* fighter.

Var.: **Uijs**.

V

Vaandrager Dutch: occupational name for a standard bearer, from MDu. *vann* flag (cf. GONFALONIERI) + *draghen* to carry (OSax. *dragan*).

Patr.: **Vendricks**.

Vacca Italian: nickname from It. *vacca* cow (L *vacca*), denoting a cowherd (see VACCARO) or a gentle person.

Var.: **Vacchi**.

Cogns.: Sc. (Norman): **Ve(i)tch**. Sp.: **Vaca(s), Baca**.

Dims.: It.: **Vacchelli**. Fr.: **Vachet(te)**; **Vachey** (Burgundy); **Vachez** (N France); **Vachon, Vachot, Vachoux** (E France); **Vacquez, Vacquin** (Normandy).

Vaccaro Italian: occupational name for a cowherd, It. *vaccaro* (LL *vaccārius*, a deriv. of *vacca* cow; see VACCA).

Vars.: **Vaccari**; **Vaccai** (Tuscany); **Vaccher, Vaguer** (Venetia).

Cogns.: Fr.: **Vach(i)er, Vaché**; **Va(c)quier** (Normandy). Prov.: **Vaquié**; **Baquer, Baqué** (Gascony). Eng. (Norman): **Va(t)cher, Vacha**. Sp.: **Vaquer(iz)o, Baquero**. Cat.: **Vaquer, Vaqué, Baqué**. Port.: **Vaqueiro**. Rum.: **Vacar**.

Dims.: It.: **Vaccarino, Vaccarini, Vaccar(i)ello, Vaccarelli**. Fr.: **Vacheret, Vache(y)ron, Vacherot**; **Vacquerel**.

Augs.: Fr.: **Vacherat**. It.: **Vaccaroni**.

Václav Czech: from the Czech given name *Václav*, OCzech *Vęceslav* (cogn. with Pol. *Więcław, Wacław*; Anglicized as *Wenceslas*). It is composed of the elements *vęce* greater + *slav* glory. It was borne by a 10th-cent. duke of Bohemia who fought against a revival of paganism in his territory, and after his death became patron saint of Bohemia.

Vars.: **Vacula**; **Vácha(l), Vach(e)l, Vása, Vašák**; **Vaňa, Vaňáč, Vančata, Vančura**; **Vaniš, Vaňous**.

Cogns.: Pol.: **Wacławski, Więcławski**.

Dims.: Czech: **Vacek, Vacík**; **Václavek, Václavík**; **Vacuík**; **Vachek**; **Vašek, Vašíček, Vaško**; **Vaňek, Vaníček, Vaněček, Vaňásek**.

Patrs.: Czech: **Václavů**. Pol.: **Więclawicz**.

Habitation name: Czech: **Václavovský**.

Vadimov Russian: patr. from the given name *Vadim*, a shortened form of the Slav. personal name *Vadimir*, composed of the elements *vad-* to tame + *mir* peace or *mer* great. This name was not accepted by the Orthodox Church as a baptismal name, but it was commonly used in the Middle Ages as a familiar name borne in addition to an official given name.

Vainio Finnish: ornamental name from Finn. *vainio* field, in some cases perhaps chosen as a topographic name by someone who lived by a field.

Vair French: nickname for someone with a blotchy complexion, or who made a habit of dressing in clothes of different colours, from OF *vair* variegated (L *varius*). The same word was also used in the Middle Ages of a type of variegated fur, probably that of the Russian squirrel (cf. the Czech word VEVERKA 'Squirrel'), and the surname may also have denoted someone who traded in furs. According to an early version of the fairy tale, Cinderella's slippers were made of this fur, but when the word fell out of use and was no longer understood, it was changed to the less plausible *verre* glass (cf. VERRIER).

Var.: VER.

Dims.: **Vairel, Vérel, Vairet, Vér(el)et, Verlet, Vairon, Veyron**.

Vaisey English: nickname for a cheerful person, from an aphetic form of ANF *enveisié* playful, merry (OF *envoisié*, past part. of *envoisier* to sport, enjoy oneself, from LL *invitiāre*, a deriv. of *vitium* pleasure (originally 'vice', 'fault')).

Vars.: **Vaizey, Vasey, Veas(e)y, Veazey, Ve(y)sey, Vezey, Voisey, Voizey, Voysey, Voyzey**; **F(e)asey, F(e)acey, Feazy, Feesey, Foizey**; **Pha(i)sey, Phazey, Pheasey, Pheazey, Pheysey**; **Lenfestey**.

Vajda 1. Hungarian: status name from Hung. *vajda* leader, governor, a word of Slav. origin (cf. VEJVODA).

2. Jewish (Ashkenazic): adoption of the Hung. name, presumably taken by a rabbi; cf. HAUPTMANN.

Var. (of 2): **Vaida**.

Valbuena Spanish: habitation name from any of various places, for example in the provinces of Palencia, Salamanca, and Valladolid, so called from OSp. *val* valley (see VALE) + *buena* (fem.) good, pleasant, attractive (see BON).

Vars.: **Balbuena**; **Balboa** (Galicia).

Valcárcel Spanish: habitation name from a place in the province of León now called *Valcarce*, from OSp. *val* valley (see VALE) + *cárcel* prison (L *carcer*), the second element being used in the transferred sense of a confined space, i.e. a narrow gorge.

Var.: **Valcarce**.

Valderrama Spanish: habitation name from a place in the province of Burgos, first recorded as *Val de Rama* 'valley (see VALE) of *Rama*'; it is not clear whether the final element represents Sp. *rama* branch (see RAM 2) or a personal name.

Vale English (chiefly S England and Midlands): topographic name for someone who lived in a valley, ME *vale* (OF *val*, from L *vallis*). The surname is now also common in Ireland, where it has been Gaelicized as **de Bhál** (see also WALL 3). The Fr. cogn. was originally fem., as in L, but later became masc., perhaps under the influence of MONT.

Cogns.: Fr.: **Val, Vaux**; **Laval(le), Lav(e)au, Lavaux, Lavaud, Lavault**; **Leval, Lev(e)au** (see also VEAL); **De(la)val, Delav(e)au, Delavault, Duval, Duv(e)au, De(s)vaux, Deveaux**; VALOIS. It.: **Valle, Valli, Valla**; **La Valle**; **Da Valle** (and by misdivision **D'Avalle**), **Della Valle**; **Valles(i), Vallese** (Venetia); **Vallar(i)o** (Campania). Sp.: **Val, Valle(s)**. Cat.: VALL; VALLÈS. Port.: **Vale**. Rum.: **Valeano**.

Dims.: Fr.: VALLET, **Val(l)ette, Lavallette, Duvallet, Delavalette, Vallon**. It.: **Valetta, Valletti**; **Val(l)otto** (Venetia); **Vallillo** (Campania); **Vallarino, Vallarini**. Sp.: **Vallejo**.

Augs.: It.: **Vallone, Valloni**.

Valencia Spanish: habitation name from any of various places so called, principally the major city in E Spain, which was formerly the capital of an independent Moorish kingdom of the same name. The city was named by the Romans as *Valentia*, a deriv. of the personal name *Valens* (see VALENTE).

Var.: **Valenciano**.

Cogns.: Cat.: **València**. It.: **Valenza**, **Valenzi**; **Valenz(i)ano**, **Valenzani**.

Dim.: Sp.: **Valenzuela** (places in the provinces of Ciudad Real and Córdoba).

Valente Italian and Portuguese: from the medieval given name *Valente* (L *Valens*, gen. *Valentis*, pres. part. of *valēre* to be strong, healthy). The name was especially popular in medieval Italy, in honour of a 6th-cent. bishop of Verona.

Cogns.: Sp.: **Valiente**. Jewish: **Valenti** (Sefardic, reasons for adoption unknonwn).

Valentine English and Scots: from a medieval given name (L *Valentīnus*, a deriv. of *Valens*; see VALENTE), which was never common in England, but is occasionally found from the end of the 12th cent., probably as the result of Fr. influence. The name was borne by a 3rd-cent. saint and martyr, whose chief claim to fame is that his feast falls on 14 February, the date of a traditional celebration of spring going back to the Roman fertility festival of Juno Februata. A 5th-cent. missionary bishop of Rhaetia of this name was venerated esp. in S Germany, being invoked as a patron against gout and epilepsy.

Vars.: **Valentin**, **Vallentin(e)**, **Val(l)intine**, **Vallantine**.

Cogns.: Fr.: **Val(l)entin**, **Val(l)antin**. It.: **Valentino**, **Valentin(i)**. Sp.: **Valentín**. Cat.: **Valentí**. Port.: **Valentim**. Jewish: **Valentini**. Ger.: **Val(en)tin**, **Faltin**, **Foltin**. Swed.: **Vallentin**, **Wallentin**. Dan., Norw.: **Valentin**. Czech: **Valenta**, **Vála**, **Valeš**, **Valíš**. Pol.: **Walent(a)**; **Walas**, **Walak**, **Walicki** (shortened forms). Hung.: **Bálint**.

Dims.: It.: **Valentinelli**, **Valentinetti**, **Valentinuzzi**. Ger.: **Valtl**, **Veltl**. Low Ger.: **Velte**. Czech: **Válek**; **Valášek**. Pol.: **Walaszczyk**, **Walasik**, **Waliszek**.

Patrs.: Pol.: **Walentynowicz**, **Walewicz**.

Patrs. (from dims.): Low Ger.: **Velten**, **Felten**. Fris.: **Veltjes**. Pol.: **Walentkiewicz**, **Walkiewicz**; **Walczak**, **Walisiak**.

Habitation names: Pol.: **Walewski**, **Walczyński**, **Waliszewski**, **Walkowski**.

Valera Spanish: habitation name from any of various places so called from LL *Valēria (villa)* 'homestead of *Valērius*' (cf. VALERIO), for example in the province of Cuenca.

Valeriano Italian: from a medieval given name (L *Valēriānus*, a deriv. of *Valērius*; see VALERIO). The name was borne by various minor Christian saints, most notably 4th-cent. bishops of Aquileia and Auxerre.

Var.: **Valeriani**.

Cogn.: Fr.: **Valérian**.

Patr.: Russ.: **Valerianov**.

Valerio Italian: from a medieval given name (L *Valērius*, a Roman family name probably connected with L *valēre* to flourish, be strong, healthy; cf. VALENTE). The name was borne by several minor Christian saints, among them 4th-cent. bishops of Trier and Saragossa and 5th-cent. bishops of Sorrento and of Antibes in S France.

Vars.: **Valeri**; **Valleri** (Tuscany); **Val(i)er** (Venetia).

Cogns.: Fr.: **Valère**; **Valéri**, **Valéry** (Latinized). Prov.: **Val(l)ier**. Sp., Cat.: **Valero** (also Jewish (Sefardic); reasons for adoption unknown). Port.: **Valério**. Ger.: **Valerius**.

Dim.: It.: **Valerini**. Hung.: **Valkó**.

Valiant English: nickname for a stalwart or courageous person, from ME *vailaunt*, *valiaunt* sturdy, brave (OF *vail(l)ant*, pres. part. of *vail(l)ir* to be strong, healthy, L *valēre*; cf. VALENTE).

Cogns.: Fr.: **Vaillant**, **Levaillant**.

Vall Catalan: 1. topographic name for someone who lived in a valley (a cogn. of VALE).

2. topographic name for someone who lived by a ditch (in form a cogn. of WALL 1, but for the meaning cf. VALLAT).

Var.: **Valls**.

Vallance English and Scots (Norman): habitation name from *Valence* in Drôme, which probably has the same origin as VALENCIA.

Vars.: **Valance**, **Vallans**.

Vallat Provençal: topographic name for someone who lived by a ditch, OProv. *vallat* (LL *vallātum*, a deriv. of *vallum* palisade, fortification composed of both a mound and a ditch).

Vars.: **Valat**, **Val(l)adier**, **Val(l)ayer**; **Balat**, **Albalat**, **Delbalat** (Gascony).

Dim.: **Valadon**.

Vallender German: habitation name from *Valandar* near Koblenz, which according to Bahlow is so called from a prehistoric river name *Val-andra* 'stagnant water'.

Vallès Catalan: regional name for someone from a region of Catalonia centred on Granollers in the province of Barcelona, called *El Vallès*. In a few cases the surname may be a habitation name from a village of the same name in the province of Valencia. In both cases the placename is from L *vallēnsis*, an adj. deriv. of *vallis* valley; cf. VALE and VALOIS.

Vallet 1. French and English: occupational name for a manservant, ME, OF *vaslet*, *val(l)et* (a dim. of *vassal* serf; see VASS, VASSALL and VAVASOUR).

2. French: dim. of *val* valley (see VALE).

Vars. (of 1): Eng.: **Valet(t)**. Fr.: **Va(y)let**, **Leval(l)et**, **Val(l)ot**, **Vaslet**, **Vaslot**, **Varlet**, **Levarlet**, **Varlot**.

Dims.: Fr.: **Val(le)teau**, **Val(e)ton**, **Valtot**, **Valtin**.

Vallverdú Catalan: local name composed of the elements VALL valley + the placename *Verdú* (see VARDON).

Valois French: topographic name for someone who lived in a valley, or habitaion name from any of the various places called *Val(l)ois*, or regional name from the district in N France so called, which was once an independent duchy. In all cases the source is an adj. deriv. of OF *val* valley (see VALE).

Var.: **Levallois**.

Cogn.: Eng. (Norman): **Vallis**.

Valverde Spanish: habitation name from any of the numerous places so called from OSp. *val* valley (see VALE) + *verde* green (see VERDE). The reference is to particularly lush pastures in a well-watered valley.

Vannier French: occupational name for a winnower, or more often, since this was a highly seasonal activity, for a maker and seller of winnowing fans, from an agent deriv. of OF *vanne* winnowing fan (L *vannus*) or the verb *van(n)ier* to winnow. Cf. FANNER.

Vars.: **Vanier**, **Levannier**; **Vanneur**, **Levanneur**.

Dim.: **Vannereau**.

Vara Spanish: nickname from Sp. *vara* rod, stick (LL *vāra* forked stick, probably a deriv. of *vārus* bent, twisted). The nickname may have been given to a keeper of animals, who used a stick to urge his charges on, or to an official who carried a rod as a symbol of his office, but it is also possible that it had a sexual connotation (cf., e.g., HARDSTAFF and WAGSTAFF).

Var.: **Varas**.

Dim.: **Varela** (also Port.).

Vardon English (Norman): habitation name from any of various places in France called *Verdun*. The placename is probably of Gaul. origin, and probably derives from the elements *ver(n)* alder (see VER 1) + *dūn* hill, fortress. Some early bearers of the name certainly came from a place of this name in La Manche, others possibly from one in Eure. For the ME change of *-er-* to *-ar-*, cf. MARCHANT.

Vars.: **Varden**; **Verdon**, **Verden**, **Verd(u)in**, **Verduyn**.

Cogns.: Fr.: **Verdu(n)**. Cat.: **Verdú** (a place in the province of Lérida).

Varga Hungarian: occupational name from Hung. *varga* cobbler, shoemaker.

Vargas Spanish and Portuguese: topographic name from Sp., Port. *varga*, a dial. term used in the northern part of the Peninsula in various senses: hut, slope, fenced pasture-land which becomes waterlogged in winter. These different senses were apparently originally represented by two or three distinct pre-Roman words, but they fell together too early for their history to be reconstructed. Cf. BÁRCENA.

Varley English: of uncertain origin, probably a habitation name from *Verly* in Aisne, Picardy, so called from the Gallo-Roman personal name *Virilius* (a deriv. of *virilis* male, from *vir* man) + the local suffix *-ācum*. For the ME change of *-er-* to *-ar-*, cf. MARCHANT. The surname is now most common in W Yorks.

Vars.: **Verley**, **Virley**.

Varney English (Norman): habitation name from Saint-Paul-du-Vernay in Calvados or any of various other places in N France of the same name. All are apparently so called from the Gaul. element *ver(n)* alder (see VER 1) + the local suffix *-ācum*. For the ME change of *-er-* to *-ar-*, cf. MARCHANT.

Vars.: **Vernay**, **Vern(e)y**.

Cogns.: Fr.: **Vernay**, **Verney**.

Vasari Italian: occupational name for a potter, It. *vasaro* (LL *vāsārius*, a deriv. of *vās* vessel, jar, pot).

Vásári Hungarian: topographic name for someone who lived by a market-place or in a market town, or occupational name for a trader, from Hung. *vásár* market.

Var.: **Vásáry**.

Vasco 1. Italian: ethnic name for someone from the Basque region in S France and N Spain. The inhabitants of this region are first recorded in L sources as the *Vascōnes*, a word of unknown origin (see also GASCOIGNE). The Basques' own name for themselves is *Euskaldun*.

2. Jewish: of unknown origin.

Var.: **Lo Vasco** (Sicily).

Cogns.: Fr.: **Basque**. Prov.: **Basq**.

Dims.: It.: **Vaschetti**, **Vaschini**. Fr.: **Basquet**, **Basquin**. Prov.: **Bascou(l)**.

Vasconcelos Portuguese: habitation name from a place near Braga, so called because it was originally settled by Basques. The placename is from the pl. of a dim. form of the adj. *vasconço* Basque (see VASCO).

Vass 1. English: status name for a serf, ME, OF *vass(e)* (LL *vassus*, of Celt. origin; cf. W *gwas* boy, Gael. *foss* servant).

2. English: var. of VAUSE.

3. Swedish: var. of WASS (2 and 3).

Var. (of 1): **Vasse**.

Cogn. (of 1): Fr.: **Vasse**.

Dims. (of 1): Fr.: **Vacelet**, **Vasselin**, **Vasselot**.

Pej. (of 1): Fr.: **Vassard**.

Vassall English: status name for a servant or retainer, ME, OF *vassal* (LL *vassallus*, a deriv. of *vassus*; see VASS).

Cogns.: Fr.: **Vassal**. It.: **Vassallo**, **Vassalli**.

Vattiato Italian (Sicily): nickname for a devout Christian, from the Sicilian dial. form, *vattiatu*, of It. *battezzato* baptized (L *baptizātus*, past part. of *baptizāre* to baptize, from Gk *baptizein*, a deriv. of *baptein* to dip).

Vars.: **Battiato**, **Battiati**.

Vaughan 1. Welsh: dim. of BAUGH, with mutation of the initial consonant to *f*.

2. Irish: Anglicized form of various Gael. surnames, such as *Ó Mocháin* (see MOHAN), **Ó Macháin**, and **Ó Beacháin**.

Vars.: **Vaughn**, **Vaugham**.

Vaughan *is the name of a Welsh family who have held the same estate, Trawscoed, for almost 800 years. They are said to have originated with Adda* Vychan, *who married the daughter of Ievan Gôch in 1200.*

Vauquelin French: of uncertain origin. Dauzat derives it from a Gmc personal name *Walklino*, a dim. formation from the element *walk* to full (cf. WALKER). The surname is most common in Normandy, especially in the *département* of Calvados.

Var.: **Gauquelin** (Picardy).

Vaur French: habitation name from any of various minor places that derive their names from the Gaul. element *vober*, *vaber* stream, watercourse, ravine.

Vars.: **Vaure**, **Vaurs**, **Vabre**, **Vaivre**, **Voivre**; **Duvaur**, **Delavaivre**, **Desvoivres**.

Vause English and Scots (Norman): habitation name from any of various places in N France called *Vaux*, from the OF pl. of *val* valley (see VALE). Reaney explains a few early English examples with arts. rather than preps. as being from a southern form of ME *faus* false, untrustworthy (late OE *fals*, from L *falsus*, reinforced by OF *fals*, *faus* from the same source).

Vars.: **Vaus(s)**, **Vaux**; VASS; **Waus(s)**.

Vavasour English: from ME, OF *vavasour*, a technical term of the feudal system for a tenant ranking immediately below a baron. Such a tenant would have been a prosperous man, and the surname may have been used for someone in his service more often than for the man himself. The term is probably derived from med. L *vassus vassorum* 'vassal of vassals', i.e. vassal-in-chief; cf. VASS and VASSALL.

Var.: **Vavasseur**.

Cogns.: Fr.: **Vavasseur**; **Vasseur**, **Levasseur**, **Vassor**, **Levassor(t)**. It.: **Valvassori**.

Dim.: Fr.: **Vasserot**.

Vaysse French: habitation name from any of the various minor places, mainly in the Massif Central, that get their names from the Gaul. element *vas* hazel.

Vars.: **Vaisse**; **Vayssier**, **Vaissier**, **Veyssier**, **Vayssié**, **Vaissié**, **Veyssié**.

Dims.: **Vayset(te)**, **Vaisset(te)**, **Veyset(te)**, **Voisset**.

Aug.: **Vaissat**.

Collectives: **Vayssière**, **Vaissière**, **Veyssière**. Prov.: **Vayssade**, **Vaissade**, **Veyssade**.

Veal English (Norman): 1. nickname for an old man, or for the elder of two bearers of the same given name, from ANF *viel* old (OF *vieil*, from LL *vetulus*, a dim. of class. L *vetus*).

2. metonymic occupational name for a calf-herd or nickname for a docile, calf-like person, from ANF *ve(e)l* calf (OF *veel*, from LL *vitellus*, a dim. of class. L *vitulus*).

Vars.: **Veall, Veel.**

Cogns. (of 1): Fr.: **Vieil, Vieux.** It.: **Vecchi(o); Veggi** (Genoa); **Becciu, Betzu** (Sardinia); **Lo Vecchio, Li Vecchi** (S Italy). Sp.: **Viejo.** (Of 2): Fr.: **Veau(x), Leveau** (see also VALE). Prov.: **Vedel.** It.: **Vit(t)ello, Vit(t)elli** (in part borne by Jews, among whom it may sometimes have been chosen as a partial anagram of *Levito*; see LEVI). Rum.: **Vitel.**

Dims. (of 1): Fr.: **Vieillot.** It.: **Vecchini, Vecchiett(in)i, Vecchiotto, Vecchiotti, Vecchiuzzo.** (Of 2): Fr.: **Vellet, Vélo(t).**

Augs. (of 1): It.: **Vecchioni, Vecchione.**

Patrs. (from 1): It.: **De Vecchi; Del Vecchio** (in part borne by Jews; according to tradition this name was taken by various Jewish families long established in Italy (allegedly since the capture of Jerusalem by the Romans in AD 70) to distinguish themselves from later arrivals who migrated there on being expelled from the Iberian Peninsula after 1492).

Veerman Dutch: 1. occupational name for a trader in feathers, from MDu. *veder(e)* FEATHER + *man* man. The omission of dentals between vowels is a common development in Low Ger. and Du.

2. occupational name for a ferryman, from MDu. *vēre* ferry + *man* man.

Var.: **Van de Veer.**

Vega Spanish: topographic name for someone who lived by a meadow, Sp. *vega* (of pre-Roman origin, apparently originally denoting irrigated land, and perhaps akin to the Basque elements *ibai* river + the gen. suffix *-ko, -ka*).

Vars.: **Vegas, Veiga.**

Cogn.: Port.: **Veiga.**

Végh Hungarian: topographic name for someone who lived at the end of a village, from Hung. *vég* end.

Veil 1. English: occupational name for a watchman, from ANF *veil(le)* watch, guard (L *vigilia* watch, wakefulness).

2. Jewish (W Ashkenazic): of uncertain origin, according to Kaganoff perhaps chosen as an anagram of LEVI. See also WEIL 2.

Vars. (of 1): **V(e)ail.**

Cogns. (of 1): Fr.: **Veillier.** Sp.: VELA.

Dims. (of 1): Fr.: **Veillet(et), Veillon, Veillot.**

Vejvoda Czech: status name for the administrative head of a district, Czech *Vojevoda*, originally the commander of an army, from Czech *voj* army + *vodič* leader (see VODIČKA).

Cogns.: Pol.: **Wojewoda, Wojewódzki.** Croatian: **Vojvodić** (patr.).

Vela Spanish: 1. from a medieval given name, of Gmc (Visigothic) origin. The name represents a reduced from of *Vigila*, from a short form of the various cpd names with a first element *wīg* war.

2. occupational name for a watchman, a cogn. of VEIL 1.

Patrs. (from 1): Sp.: **Vélez.** Port.: **Velez.**

Velasco Spanish: from a very common medieval given name of Basque origin, from *bela* crow + the dim. suffix *-sko*.

Cogn.: Jewish (Sefardic): **Belasco** (an adoption of the Sp. surname).

Patrs.: Sp.: **V(el)ázquez.** Port.: **Vasques, Vaz.**

Velík Czech: from a dim. given name, derived from a short form of any of the OCzech personal names containing the first element *veli-* great (see VELIKOV), for example *Velislav* 'great glory' or *Velimir* 'great fame' (or 'great peace').

Vars.: **Velek, Velíšek.**

Cogns. (patrs.): Croatian: **Velj(ov)ić; Veljković, Veličković; Velimirović** (from the given name *Velimir*).

Velikov 1. Russian and Bulgarian: patr. from the nickname *Veliki* 'Great', denoting a large man.

2. Jewish (E Ashkenazic): adoption of the Slav. name. Kaganoff suggests that was it was used as a translation of the Hebr. male given name *Gedalya* 'God is great', but offers no evidence in support of this hypothesis.

Vars. (Jewish): **Velikovski, Velkovics, Welkovitz, Welkovitch.**

Vellacott English: habitation name from a place in Devon, so called from the OE personal name *Willa* (a short form of the various cpd names containing the first element *will* will, desire) + OE *cot* cottage, dwelling (see COATES).

Veloso Portuguese: nickname for a hirsute individual, from Port. *veloso* hairy (L *villōsus*, a deriv. of *villus* (shaggy) hair).

Venables English (Norman): habitation name from a place in Eure, probably so called from LL *vēnābulum* hunting ground (a deriv. of *vēnāri* to hunt; cf. VENÂNCIO and VENNER 2).

Venâncio Portuguese: from a medieval given name (L *Vēnantius*, a deriv. of *vēnans*, gen. *vēnantis*, pres. part. of *vēnari* to hunt, chase), borne in honour of various early saints of the 3rd–6th cents.

Vendrell Catalan: habitation name from a place in the province of Tarragona, which derives its name from the OCat. personal name *Venrello* (LL *Venerellus*, a dim. of *Venereus* 'of Venus'). The personal name seems usually to have denoted someone born or baptized on a Friday (LL *Veneris dies* 'Venus' day').

Vendryes French: habitation name from a place in Quercy, apparently so called from LL *Veneriānus (fundus)* '(estate) of *Venerius*', a personal name derived from that of the goddess *Venus* (cf. VENDRELL).

Venezia Italian (partly Jewish): habitation name or regional name from the city of Venice or the region of Venetia, both called *Venezia* in It., from L *Venetia*. The name derives from the tribal name, of obscure origin, of the *Veneti*, a probably Celt. tribe who inhabited this area before the Roman expansion.

Vars.: It.: **Veneziano, Venezian(i).**

Venner English: 1. topographic name for someone who lived in a fen or marsh; see FENN.

2. occupational name for a huntsman, from OF *veneo(u)r* (L *venātor*, a deriv. of *venāri* to hunt).

Var. (of 2): **Venour.**

Ventosa Spanish and Catalan: habitation name from any of various places, for example in the provinces of Burgos, Cuenca, and Salamanca, so called from their exposed and windy situation; the placename is from LL *ventōsa*, a deriv. of *ventus* wind.

Ventre French: nickname for a man with a large paunch, from OF *ventre* belly (L *venter*).

Dim.: **Ventrillon.**

Ventris English: probably a nickname for a daring person, from an aphetic form of ME *aventurous* bold, venturesome (a deriv. of ME, OF *aventure*; see VENTURE). The vocab.

word *aventurous* is attested from the 14th cent. onwards, the aphetic form *venturous* from the 16th.
Vars.: **Ventress**; **Venters** (Scots: Fife).

Ventura 1. Italian (partly Jewish): cogn. of VENTURE.
2. Italian, Spanish, Catalan, and Portuguese: from a medieval given name, a short form of *Bonaventura* 'Good Fortune'. The name was borne in honour of a saint (1221–74) who was given this nickname by St Francis of Assisi when he cured him miraculously as a child.
Vars.: It.: **Venturi**; **Tura**.
Dims.: It.: **Venturella**, **Venturelli**, **Venturino**, **Venturin(i)**, **Venturoli**, **Venturucci**; **Turella**, **Turello**, **Turelli**.

Venture English: nickname for a bold or venturesome person, from an aphetic form of ME, OF *aventure* chance, hazard, exploit (LL *adventūra* chance happening, a deriv. of *advenīre* to happen, come about, lit. arrive, come on the scene). The normal vocab. word in ME was *aventure*, found from the 13th cent.; the aphetic form *venture* occurs from the 15th, shortly before the reintroduction of the L root as mod. Eng. *adventure*.
Var.: **Ventur**.
Cogns.: Ger.: **Abenteuer**, **Ebenteuer**; **Hebentheier** (Austria). It.: VENTURA.

Venus English (Norman): habitation name from *Venoix* in Calvados, the name of which is of uncertain origin. The surname in this spelling is now found principally in NE England.
Vars.: **Venes(s)**, **Venis(e)**.

Ver French: 1. habitation name from any of the numerous places named with the Gaul. element *ver(n)* alder; cf. VARDON, VARNEY, and VERNON.
2. from the medieval given name *Ver* (L *Vērus* 'True'), which enjoyed some slight currency in honour of a 4th-cent. bishop of Vienne.
3. var. of VAIR.
4. var. of *Vert*; see VERDE.
Vars. (of 1): **Verne(s)**, **Vergne**, **Vernhe**; **Lavergne**; **Duverne**; VERNIER.
Cogns. (of 1): Eng.: **Ve(a)re** (see also WEIR 4). Prov.: **Vergna(s)**; **Lavergna**, **Lasvergnas**.
Dims. (of 1): Fr.: **Vernet**, **Vergnol(le)**.
Collective (of 1): Fr.: **Vernière**.

Vera Spanish: topographic name for someone who lived on a river bank, Sp. *vera* (of pre-Roman origin), or habitation name from one of the several places named with this word.
Var.: **Veras**.

Verdaguer Catalan: topographic name for someone who lived by a meadow or grassy spot, OCat. *verdeguer* (LL *viridicārium*, a deriv. of *viridis* green; cf. VERDIER).
Var.: **Verdeguer**.

Verde Italian: from It. *verde* green (L *viridis*, akin to *virēre* to bloom, flourish), presumably a nickname for someone who habitually dressed in this colour.
Vars.: **Verdi**; **Virde**, **Virdi** (Sicily); **Lo Verde** (S Italy).
Cogns.: Fr.: **Vert**, **Verd**, VER, **Levert**.
Dims.: It.: **Verdelli**, **Verdini**, **Verdicchio**. Fr.: **Verdel**, **Verd(el)et**, **Verdin**, **Verdon(net)**.
Aug.: It.: **Verdone**.
Pej.: It.: **Verdacci**.
Patr.: It.: **Virdis** (Sicily).

Verdier 1. English (Norman) and French: occupational name for a forester, OF *verdier* (LL *viridārius*, a deriv. of *viridis* green; see VERDE). The officials were so called from their green costumes, which may be regarded as an early example of camouflage.
2. Provençal: topographic name for someone who lived near an orchard or garden, or occupational name for someone who was employed in one, from OProv. *verdier* orchard (LL *virid(i)ārium*).
Vars. (of 1): Eng.: **Varder**. (Of 2): **Verdié**; **Vergès**, **Bergès** (Gascony).
Cogns. (of 2): Cat.: **Vergés**. Fr.: **Verg(i)er**, **Duverg(i)er**, **Duverg(i)é**, **Duvergey**.

Verdugo Spanish: occupational name for an officer of justice or public executioner, Sp. *verdugo*. The name has been transferred to denote an individual from the rod or staff of office he held, OSp. *verdugo* (LL *vir(i)dūcum* switch, shoot, a deriv. of *viridis* green; cf. VERDE).

Vergara Spanish form of Basque **Bergara**: habitation name from places so called (earlier *Virgara*) in the provinces of Guipúzcoa and Navarre, which are of uncertain derivation. The second element is *gara* hill, height, eminence, but the first has not been satisfactorily identified.

Veríssimo Portuguese: from a medieval given name (L *Vērissimus*, superlative of *vērus* true; cf. VER 2), borne in honour of a saint who was martyred at Lisbon at the beginning of the 4th cent. AD in the persecution instigated by the emperor Diocletian.

Verity English (Yorks.): nickname for a truthful person, or perhaps rather for someone who was in the habit of insisting repeatedly on the truth of the stories he told, from ME *verite* truth(fulness) (OF *verité*, from L *vēritās*, a deriv. of *vērus* true; cf. VER 2). The surname may also sometimes have been acquired by someone who had acted the part of the personified quality of Truth in a mystery play or pageant.
Var.: **Varty**.

Verlaine Belgian: of uncertain origin, perhaps a Gallicized form of Flem. *Verlaen*; see LANE 1.

Verner Scots: of uncertain origin, probably a var. of WARNER (cf. VERNIER 2). Another possibility is that it may be a habitation name from *Vernours* in the former county of Midlothian, but it seems more likely that this placename is derived from the family name.
A branch of this family was established in Ireland in the 17th cent.

Vernier French: 1. topographic name for someone who lived near an alder tree; see VER 1.
2. hypercorrected form of *Varnier*, the version of WARNER found in E France.

Vernon 1. English (Norman): habitation name from *Vernon* in Eure, so called from the Gaul. element *ver(n)* alder (see VER 1) + the Gallo-Roman local suffix *-o* (gen. *ōnis*).
2. French: habitation name from the same place as in 1 or from one of the numerous other places in France with the same name and etymology.
Vars.: Eng.: **Vernum**, **Varnon**. Fr.: **Vernou**.

Verona Italian: habitation name or regional name from the city and province in NE Italy, L *Vērōna*. The town was an important settlement long before its capture by the Romans in 89 BC; its name is of uncertain origin.
Vars.: **Veronese**, **Veronesi**.

Verran Cornish: of uncertain origin, possibly a habitation name from *Treverran* in the parish of Tywardreath, so called from Corn. *tre* homestead, settlement + a second element of unknown original form and meaning. Alternatively it may derive from *Veryan* near Tregony. This latter placename is a shortened version of *St Veryan*, itself the result of a misinterpretation of the form *Symphorianus* recorded from 1278 onwards. The church there was dedicated to a certain St Symphorianus, probably the 2nd-cent. martyr of Autun revered in France.

Verrier English (Norman) and French: occupational name for a maker of glass objects, OF *verrie(o)r* (from *verre*, *voir(r)e* glass, L *vitrum*).

Vars.: Eng.: **Verriour**. Fr.: **Veyrier, Leverrier**.

Cogns.: Prov.: **Veyradier**. It.: **Vetraio**.

Vershinin Russian: patr. from the nickname *Vershina* 'Mountain Peak', given presumably to a particularly tall person or to someone who lived at the top of a hill.

Very English: habitation name from an unidentified place in N France named with the Gaul. element *ver(n)* alder (see VER 1, and cf. VARNEY) or the Gallo-Roman personal name *Vērus* (see VER 2) + the local suffix *-ācum*.

Veselov Russian: patr. from the nickname *Vesyoly* 'Cheerful'.

Var.: **Veselago** (for the ending, cf. ZHIVAGO).

Cogns. (patrs.): Croatian: **Veselinović; Ves(ov)ić**.

Cogns. (not patrs.): Czech: **Veselý** (a very common Czech surname). Jewish (E Ashkenazic, ornamental or nicknames): **Ves(s)ely, Wesseley**.

Dim.: Pol.: **Wesołek**.

Habitation name: Pol.: **Wesołowski**.

Vespucci Italian: nickname for a waspish individual, from a dim. form of It. *vespa* wasp (L *vespa*).

The name of the continent of America *is traditionally believed to be derived from the given name of the Florentine navigator Amerigo* Vespucci *(?1454–1512), who sailed with Columbus on at least one of his voyages. In his account of his travels, published in 1507, he asserted that he had independently discovered the American mainland in 1497. However, doubt has been cast on this claim. He was born in Florence, the son of a notary; in 1491 he was sent to Spain by the Medicis, and in 1505 he became a Spanish citizen.*

Vessey English (Norman): habitation name from a place in La Manche, so called from the Gallo-Roman personal name *Vessius* or *Vettius* (of uncertain origin) + the local suffix *-ācum*.

Var.: **Vessie** (Scotland).

Vetrov Russian: patr. from the nickname *Veter* 'Wind' (earlier also 'Storm'), perhaps denoting someone with a blustery or an inconstant temperament (cf. the Czech vocab. word *větroplach* madcap, devil-may-care).

Cogns.: Czech: **Větrovec, Větrovský** (not patrs.). Croatian: **Vetranović** (patr.).

Vetter German: nickname from MHG *veter(e)* uncle, nephew (i.e. father's brother or brother's son). The word is from OHG *fetiro* (a deriv. of *fater* father), which was used more generally of various male relatives; the meaning of the mod. Ger. word *Vetter* is 'cousin'. In N Germany the vocab. word was sometimes used as a given name, and this may lie behind some cases of the surname.

Var.: **Vötter** (Bavaria).

Dims.: **Vetterle; Vötterl** (Bavaria).

Veverka Czech: nickname meaning 'squirrel', applied either to someone who bore a fancied resemblance to a squirrel, or perhaps to someone who habitually dressed in squirrel fur (cf. Fr. VAIR).

Viana Portuguese: habitation name from *Viana* do Castelo, a city in the province of Minho, or *Viana* do Alentejo, a town in the province of Alto Alentejo.

Vicario Italian: occupational name for a parish priest (see VICKAR), or for any ecclesiastical or civil official who carried out duties on behalf of an absentee office-holder or who deputized for a magistrate.

Vars.: **Vicaro, Vicari**.

Cogns.: Fr.: **Vicaire; Voye(u)r, Voyeu(x), Levoyer**. Prov.: **Vig(u)ier, Vig(u)ié**. Port.: **Vigário**. Hung.: **Vikár**.

Vickar 1. English: occupational name for a parish priest, ME *vica(i)re*, *vikere* (OF *vicaire*, from L *vicārius* substitute, deputy, a deriv. of *vices* place, turn). The word was originally used to denote someone who carried out pastoral duties on behalf of the absentee holder of a benefice. It became a regular word for a parish priest because in practice most benefice-holders were absentees. See also VICARIO.

2. Irish: surname used as an approximate translation of Gael. *Mac an Abadh* 'son of the abbot'; see ABBÉ.

Vars. (of 1): **Vicker, Vicar; Vicar(e)y, Viccary, Vickary, Vickery** (S and W English, from a ME var. *vicarie*, derived directly from L *vicārius*).

Patrs. (from 1): Eng.: VICKERS. Sc.: **McVicar, McVicker** (Gael. **Mac Bhiocair**).

Vickers English: patr. for the son of a vicar or, perhaps in most cases, occupational name for the servant of a vicar, from ME *vicare* (see VICKAR) + the possessive ending *-s*. In many cases it may also represent an elliptical form of a topographic name; cf. PARSONS.

Vars.: **Vic(c)ars, Vickars; Vickarman** (occupational name only).

Vico Italian: 1. topographic name for someone who lived in a village as opposed to an outlying farmstead, from OIt. *vico* settlement, village (L *vīcus*).

2. aphetic short form of the medieval given name *Lodovico*; see LEWIS 1.

Vars.: **Vigo, Vig(g)hi** (N Italy). (Of 1 only): **Da Vico; Vig(i)ano, Vigiani, Vigato**.

Dims.: **Vigetti, Vigotti, Vigutto, Viguzzi, Vigolo**.

Augs.: **Vigone, Vigoni**.

Patr. (from 2 only): **De Vico**.

Victor French: from a medieval given name (L *Victor* 'Conqueror', an agent deriv. of *vincere* to win, defeat). Early Christians often bore this name in reference to Christ's victory over sin and death, and there are a large number of saints so called. Some of the principal ones, who contributed to the popularity of the given name in the Middle Ages, are a 2nd-cent. pope, a 3rd-cent. Mauritanian martyr, and a 5th-cent. bishop of Cologne. See also AVIGDOR.

Cogns.: It.: **Vittore, Vittor(i), Vettor(i)**. Port.: **Vítor**. Czech: **Viktora**. Pol.: **Wiktor(ski)**.

Dims.: Prov.: **Victouron**. It.: **Vittorelli, Vettorello, Vettorel(li), Vettoretti, Vettoretto**. Port.: **Vitorino**. Czech: **Vích**. Pol.: **Wiktorczyk**.

Patrs.: It.: **De Vettori**. Swed.: **Victorsson**. Pol.: **Wiktorowicz**. Beloruss.: **Viktorevich**. Croatian: **Vitorović**.

Habitation name: Pol.: **Wiktorowski**.

Videira Portuguese: topographic name for someone who lived by a vineyard or in a house distinguished by an ornamental vine, from Port. *videira* vine (LL *vītāria*, a deriv. of class. L *vītis*).

Vidler English: 1. var. of *Fidler* (see FIEDLER), with the voiced initial consonant characteristic of S dialects of ME.

2. nickname from the ANF phrase *vis de leu* 'Wolf-face' (from *vis* face, L *vīsus* appearance + *de* of, L *de* from + *leu* wolf, L *lupus*).

Viegas Portuguese: of uncertain derivation, probably a macaronic name, the first letter representing a reduced form of the Arabic prefix *ibn* son of, the remainder being the medieval given name *Egas*, patr. from the personal name *Egga*. The source of this is not clear; it may be of Gmc origin (cf. Eck 2).

Cogns.: Sp.: **Venegas, Benegas.**

Vieira Portuguese: 1. religious byname from Port. *veiria* scallop (LL *veneria*, a deriv. of the name of *Venus* (cf. Vendrell and Vendryes); the goddess was often depicted riding on a scallop). The scallop was a symbol of the pilgrim who had been to the shrine of Santiago de Compostela.

2. habitation name from any of various minor places so called because they were situated in scallop-shaped depressions.

Viggars English: nickname for a sturdy person, from ME *vigrus* strong, lusty (OF *vigoro(u)s*, a deriv. of *vigour* strength, vitality, L *vigor*, from *vigēre* to flourish). There may have been some confusion with Vickers.

Vars.: **Vigars, Vig(g)ers, Vigo(u)rs, Vigu(r)s, Vigrass.**

Cogns.: Fr.: **Vig(ou)reux, Vig(ou)roux.**

Vilagrassa Catalan: habitation name from a place in the province of Lérida, so called from Cat. *vila* settlement (see Ville) + *grassa* (fem.) lush, fertile (L *grassa*).

Var.: **Villagrasa.**

Vilalta Catalan: habitation name from any of various places, for example in the province of Lérida, so called from Cat. *vila* settlement (see Ville) + *alta* (fem.) high (L *alta*).

Vilaplana Catalan: habitation name from a place in the province of Tarragona, so called from Cat. *vila* settlement (see Ville) + *plana* (fem.) flat (L *plāna*).

Vilaseca Catalan: habitation name from places in the provinces of Barcelona and Tarragona, so called from Cat. *vila* settlement (see Ville) + *seca* (fem.) dry (L *sicca*).

Villain English and French: from ME, OF *vilein*, *vilain* feudal serf, peasant owing personal service to his lord (LL *villānus*, a deriv. of *villa* estate; see Ville). The low status of such serfs led to the semantic decline of the vocab. word to mod. Eng. *villain* rogue, evildoer, mod. Fr. *vilain* ugly, naughty, but these sense developments occurred late and are unlikely to lie behind any cases of the surname.

Vars.: Eng.: **Vilain, Villin.** Fr.: **Vilain, Vil(l)an, Levillain.**

Cogns.: It.: **Villano, Villan(i).**

Dims.: Fr.: **Villaneau.** It.: **Villanelli, Villanello, Villanetti.**

Villalba Spanish: habitation name from any of the numerous places so called from Sp. *villa* settlement (see Ville) + *alba* (fem.) white (L *alba*).

Cogn.: Cat.: **Vilalba.**

Villalobos Spanish: habitation name from a place in the province of Zamora, so called from LL *villa* settlement (see Ville) + the personal name *Lupus* 'Wolf'.

Villanueva Spanish: habitation name from any of the numerous places so called, which get their name from Sp. *villa* settlement (see Ville) + *nueva* (fem.) new (L *nova*).

Cogns.: Cat.: **Vilanova.** It.: **Villanova.** Fr.: **Villeneuve.** Prov.: **Villenave.**

Villarreal Spanish: habitation name from any of various places, for example in the province of Badajoz, so called from Sp. *villa* settlement (see Ville) + *real* royal (L *rēgālis*). The places were so named from having some particular connection with the Crown.

Villarrubia Spanish: habitation name from places in the provinces of Ciudad Real, Cuenca, and Toledo, so called from Sp. *villa* settlement (see Ville) + *rubia* (fem.) red(dish) (L *rubea*).

Villate Basque: habitation name composed of the elements *villa* settlement (a Romance borrowing; see Ville) + *ate* door; the name seems to have referred to a settlement situated by a pass between hills.

Villaverde Spanish: habitation name from any of the numerous places so called, from Sp. *villa* settlement (see Ville) + *verde* green (see Verde).

Ville French: topographic name for someone who lived in a village as opposed to an isolated farmhouse, or in the town as opposed to the countryside, from OF *ville* settlement (L *villa* country house, estate, later used of a group of houses forming a settlement).

Vars.: **Laville, De(la)ville, Desvilles.**

Cogns.: Prov.: **Vialle, Viala, Lavialle.** It.: **Villa.** Sp.: **Villa(s).** Cat.: **Vila(s); Vilà.**

Dims.: Fr.: **Vil(l)ette, Devillette, Desvillettes; Villon, Villot.** It.: **Villetti, Villino, Villotta, Villotti.** Cat.: **Vilella.** Port.: **Vilela.**

Villefranche French: habitation name from any of various places, in more than a dozen *départements*, so called from OF *ville* settlement (see Ville) + *franche* (fem.) free (see Frank 2). The settlements were so named because they were exempt from certain feudal taxes or obligations, normally as a reward for some special service.

Cogn.: Prov.: **Villefranque.**

Villegas Spanish: habitation name from places in the provinces of Albacete and Burgos, so called from Sp. *villa* settlement (see Ville) + the personal name *Egas* (see Viegas).

Villena Spanish: habitation name from a place in the province of Alicante, so called from LL *Belliēna*, a deriv. of the personal name *Bellius*, of uncertain origin.

Cogn.: Port.: **Vilhena.**

Villiers English (Norman) and French: habitation name from any of the numerous places in France called *Vil-l(i)er(s)*, from LL *villāre* outlying farm, dependent settlement, a deriv. of *villa* village, settlement (see Ville, and cf. Casa and Casale).

Vars.: Eng.: **Villers, Villar(s), Villis.** Fr.: **Villers; Devilliers, Deviller, Divill(i)er.**

Cogns.: Prov.: **Villar(d), Villars; Duvil(l)ard.** Sp.: **Villar, Vilà.** Cat.: **Vilar(es).** Port.: **Vilar.** Ger.: **Weiler(t).**

Dims.: Prov.: **Vil(l)aret, Villarel, Villaron.** Cat.: **Vilardell, Vilaró.**

The English family of Villiers *once held great power and influence, being Dukes of Buckingham under the Stuarts. They are possibly related to the Norman family which held the title Seigneurs de l'Isle Adam.*

Vinagre Portuguese: nickname for a man of sour temperament, from Port. *vinagre* vinegar (L *vīnum acre* sour wine).

Vincent 1. English and French: from a medieval given name (L *Vincentius*, a deriv. of *vincens*, gen. *vincentis*, pres. part. of *vincere* to conquer; cf. Victor). The name was borne by a 3rd-cent. Sp. martyr widely venerated in the Middle Ages and by a 5th-cent. monk and writer of Lérins, as well as various other early saints. In E Europe the name was popular in honour of Wincenty Kadłubek (d. 1223), a bishop of Cracow and an early chronicler; he was venerated especially in Silesia and his head was believed to rest in Wrocław.

2. Irish: Anglicized form of Gael. *Mac Dhuibhinse*; see McAvinchy.

Vars. (of 1): Eng.: **Vincett**; **Vinsen, Vinson, Vinsun**. Fr.: **Vincens**; **Vinson, Vinçon**.

Cogns. (of 1): It.: **Vincenti, Vincenzi**; **Vicenzo, Vicenzi** (Naples); **Cenzi**. Sp., Port.: **Vicente**. Cat.: **Vicens, Vicent**. Ger.: **Vinzenz**. Ger. (under Slav. influence): **Viezenz**.

Dims. (of 1): Eng.: **Vince** (E Anglia). Fr.: **Vincendeau, Vincendet, Vincendon, Vincenot, Vinçonneau, Vinsonneau, Vincot**. It.: **Vinci, Venzi**; **Vincenzot(to)**. Ger.: **Vinz(el), Finzel**; **Zen(t)z**. Ger. (under Slav. influence): **Vietze, Fietz(e)**; **Wien(t)zek, Fietzek, Fietzke**. Pol.: **Więcek**; **Winceniuk**. Hung.: **Vinc(z)e**.

Aug. (of 1): It.: **Cenzon**.

Patrs. (from 1): It.: **De Vincenzo** (S Italy). Pol.: **Wincentowicz**. Croatian: **Vićentijević**.

Patrs. (from dims. of 1): It.: **Da Vinci**. Low Ger.: **Zensen**. Pol.: **Wi(ę)czkiewicz, Węcewicz, Węczkowicz**.

Habitation names: Pol.: **W(i)ęckowski**.

Vine English: topographic name for someone who lived near a vineyard, or metonymic occupational name for a vine dresser, from ME *vine* vine(yard) (OF *vi(g)ne*, from L *vīnea*, a deriv. of *vīnum* wine). Vine growing was formerly more common in England than it is now, and there are several minor places in S England named from their vineyard, any of which may be partial sources of the surname. See also Winyard.

Vars.: **Vines, Vigne(s)**; **Viner, Vyner** (agent derivs.).

Cogns.: Fr.: **Vigne(s)**; **Lavigne**; **Delavigne, Desvignes**; **Vignier, Vign(i)é**. It.: **Vigna**; **Vigneri**. Sp.: **Viña(s)**. Cat.: **Vinya(s)**. Czech: **Vinař**.

Dims.: Fr.: **Vigneau, Vignon, Vignol(le)**. It.: **Vignini, Vignola, Vignol(in)i, Vignolo, Vignot(t)o, Vignozzi**.

Augs.: It.: **Vignone, Vignoni**.

Habitation names: Czech: **Vinecký, Vinický** (from places named *Vinec* and *Vinice* respectively, both from the vocab. word *vinice* vineyard).

Viney English: apparently a habitation name from some place in N France named from LL *vīnētum* vineyard, a deriv. of *vīnea* vine (see Vine).

Vinogradov Russian and Jewish (E Ashkenazic): patr. from Russ. *vinograd* grape(s), raisin(s) (a collective singular, ultimately a borrowing from a Gmc cogn. of Winyard; an earlier meaning was 'vine' and before that 'vineyard'). The name may occasionally have been taken as an occupational name, but for the most part it is ornamental (cf. Wein).

Vars.: Jewish: **Winogradow**; **Winograd, Vinogradski**; **Weingrod** (influenced by Ger. *Wein* or Yid. *vayn* wine); **Wajngrod** (Pol. spelling).

Vinokur Jewish (E Ashkenazic): occupational name for a distiller, Russ. *vinokur* (from *vino* wine, earlier used also of spirits (L *vīnum*, borrowed by way of a Gmc intermediary; cf. Vinogradov) + *kurit* to distil (in mod. Russ. 'to smoke')).

Vars.: **Winokur, Winocur**; **Winocour** (a Fr. spelling).

Vinuesa Spanish: habitation name from a place in the province of Soria. The name is probably of Italic origin, identical with that of *Venosa* in Italy (L *Venusia*), a town on the borders of Apulia and Lucania, birthplace of the poet Horace.

Vinyals Catalan: habitation name from any of various minor places so called from a pl. form of Cat. *vinyal* land planted with vines (LL *vineāle*, a deriv. of *vinea* vineyard; cf. Vine).

Var.: **Viñals** (Spanish spelling).

Viola Italian and Spanish: 1. from a medieval female given name, originally an affectionate nickname, from It., Sp. *viola* violet (L *viola*).

2. metonymic occupational name for a player of the musical instrument of this name (from LL *vītula*; see Fiedler).

Vars.: It.: **Violi**; **La Viola** (Apulia).

Cogns.: Fr.: **Viol(l)e**.

Dims.: It.: **Violetta, Violetti, Violino, Violin(i)**. Fr.: **Violleau, Viol(l)et, Viol(l)ot**.

Virgili Catalan: from a medieval given name (L *Virgilius, Vergilius*, a Roman family name of unknown derivation; perhaps from *virga* stick or *virgo* virgin, or of Etruscan origin). This was the name of the most famous of all Roman poets, who in the Middle Ages was considered to have been a fount of all kinds of wisdom and virtue, and thus almost an honorary Christian. However, the given name may also have been bestowed in honour of a 7th-cent. Christian saint, Virgilius of Arles.

Virgo English: of uncertain origin. The surname coincides in form with L *virgo*, gen. *virginis*, maiden, from which is derived (via OF) mod. Eng. *virgin*. It is possible that the surname was originally a nickname for someone who had played the part of the Blessed Virgin Mary in a mystery play. This, and the vernacular vars. listed below, may also have been nicknames for shy young men, or possibly ironically for notorious lechers.

Vars.: **Virgoe, Vergo**; **Virgin, Vergin(e)**.

Cogn.: Cat.: **Verge**.

Virtanen Finnish: ornamental name from Finn. *virta* stream + the gen. suffix *nen*, perhaps in some cases chosen as a topographic name by someone who lived by a stream. This is the most common Finnish surname.

Virtue English and Scots: nickname from ME, OF *vertu* moral worth or goodness (L *virtūs* manliness, valour, worth, a deriv. of *vir* man). This may have been bestowed on a good or pious person, it may alternatively have been a sarcastic nickname for a prig, or it may have been borne by someone who had played the part of Virtue in a medieval mystery play.

Var.: **Verty** (Scots).

Visconte Italian: from It. *visconte*, a title of rank (med. L *vicecomes* deputy of a Count). Unusually (since most noble families took their surnames from their estates), the surname was sometimes of literal application, but it is also no doubt in part a nickname for someone who gave himself airs and graces, and in part an occupational name for someone employed by a viscount.

Vars.: **Visconti**; **Bisconti** (S Italy); **Viceconte, Viceconti** (learned alterations).

The Viscontis *were rulers of Milan for almost 200 years, from 1277 to 1447, and took their name from their hereditary office. They traced their descent from Desiderius, whose daughter married Charlemagne. They were related to the royal houses of Valois, Tudor, and Habsburg as a result of marriages arranged by Duke Gian Visconti (1351–1402). His son was the last of the direct line, and in 1447 the Duchy passed to the Sforza family.*

Visdomini Italian: occupational name for the steward of an estate or the headman of a village, from med. L *vicedominus* deputy, local representative of the lord.

Vars.: **Bisdomini**; **Vicedomino**, **Vicedomini**, **Vicidomini** (learned alterations).

Cogns.: Ger.: **Vitzethum**, **Fitzthum**. Jewish (Ashkenazic): **Witzt(h)um**.

Vita 1. Italian: from a medieval female given name, originally an affectionate nickname, from It. *vita* life (L *vita*).

2. Jewish (Ashkenazic): from the Yid. female given name *Vite* (of Romance origin, adopted as a translation of the Hebr. name *Chaya* 'Life'; cf. VITALE 2).

Var. (of 1): It.: **Vida** (N Italy).

Metrs. (from 1): **De Vita**. (From 2): **Vitas**, **Vites**, **Wit(t)es**; **Vitin** (E Ashkenazic).

Metrs. (from dims. of 2): **Wittels**, **Vitelson**, **Witelson**, **Witelzon**, **Vitalzon**, **Vit(t)lin**, **Vitlov** (from the Yid. dim. given name *Vitl*; the last two are E Ashkenazic); **Vitkes** (from the E Yid. dim. given name *Vitke*), **Vitkin(d)**, **Witkin(d)** (showing influence of Yid. *kind* child; see SÜSSKIND). See also VITO.

Vitale 1. Italian: from a medieval given name (L *Vitālis*, a deriv. of *vita* life; cf. VITA). The name was popular with Christians as a symbol of their belief in eternal life, and was borne by a dozen early saints.

2. Jewish: borrowing of the It. name, adopted as a translation of the Hebr. male given name *Chayim* 'Life'; cf. HYAM.

Vars.: It.: **Vitali**; **Vidale**, **Vidali** (N Italy); **Vidal**, **Viale**, **Vial(i)** (Venetia); **Biale** (Liguria). Jewish: **Vitalis**.

Cogns.: Fr.: **Vital(is)**, **Vitau**; **Vidal**, **Vid(e)au**; **Vial**, **Viau(d)**, **Viaux**, **Viault**, **Viel**, **Vié**. Eng.: **Vitall**, **Vidal(l)**, **Vial(l)**, **Viel**. Sp., Cat.: **Vidal**. Port.: **Vidal**, **Vital**.

Dims.: It.: **Vitaletti**, **Vitalitti**, **Vitalini**; **Vialetto**. Fr.: **Vidalin**, **Vi(d)alet**, **Vid(al)on**, **Vialon**, **Vid(al)ot**, **Vialot**.

Augs.: It.: **Vitalone**, **Vitaloni**.

Patr.: Eng.: **Vials**.

Vito Italian: from a medieval given name (L *Vitus*, from *vita* life; cf. VITA). The name was popular in the Middle Ages as the result of the cult of an early Christian martyr in S Italy, about whom very little of historical value is known. He was regarded as a patron against epilepsy and the nervous tremor named after him, 'St Vitus' dance'. His cult spread into Germany and thence through E Europe, where the name was reinforced by native Slav. names such as *Vitoslav* and *Vitomír*, with a first element derived from OSlav. *vitati* inhabit or welcome.

Vars.: It.: **Vit(t)i**; **Vidi**, **Vi(d)o** (N Italy; see also GUY); **Bitto**, **Bit(t)i** (S Italy).

Cogns.: Ger.: **Veit(h)**, **Veidt**, **Fei(d)t**; **Vaith** (Bavaria). Low Ger.: **Viet(h)**, **Viett**. Czech: **Vít**, **Vitouš**.

Dims.: It.: **Vitelli**, **Vitello** (see also VEAL); **Vitillo**, **Vitullo**, **Vitulli**, **Vitolo**, **Vitucci**, **Vitussi**, **Vittozzi**, **Vitt(u)ozzo**; **Vidollo**, **Vidos(si)**, **Vidusso**, **Vi(d)us(si)**, **Vidotti**, **Vidotto** (N Italy); **Viel(li)** (Venetia); **Vietti**, **Vietto**, **Viotti**, **Viotto** (NW Italy); **Bitelli**, **Bitetti**, **Bitetto**, **Bittini**, **Bittolo** (S Italy). Ger.: **Veitle**; **Vaitl** (Bavaria). Czech: **Vítek**, **Vitáček**, **Vitášek**, **Vitoušek**; **Víšek**. Pol.: **Witek**, **Witaszek**.

Augs.: It.: **Vitone**, **Vitoni**, **Vidoni**.

Patrs.: It.: **De Vito**, **De Viti**; **De Vit**, **De Vio** (Venetia). Ger.: **Vix**, **F(e)ix**. Low Ger.: **Vieten**, **Viets(en)**. Pol.: **Witasiak**, **Witczak**. Czech: **Vítů**. Croatian: **Vit(ov)ić**, **Vid(ov)ić**.

Patrs. (from dims.): It.: **Vitelleschi**. Low Ger.: **Vietken**, **Vietjen**. Pol.: **Witkiewicz**. Croatian: **Vidaković**. Jewish (E Ashkenazic): **Witkovitz**, **Witkowitz**, **Vitkovski**, **Vitkovsky**, **Wit(t)kowski**, **Wit(t)kowsky**, **Witkovsky** (in part adoptions of the non-Jewish surname, but more often derivs. of VITA 2).

Habitation names: Pol.: **Witkowski**. Czech: **Vítovec**, **Vítovský**.

Vitry French: habitation name from any of various places, for example in Aube, Loiret, Marne, and Seine, so called from the Gallo-Roman personal name *Victorius* (a deriv. of VICTOR) + the local suffix *-ācum*.

Var.: **Vitrey** (places in Haute-Saône and Meurthe-et-Moselle).

Cogns.: Prov.: **Vitrac**, **Vitrat**.

Vivaldi Italian: from a Gmc personal name composed of the elements *wīg* war + *wald* rule.

Vivas Catalan: from a medieval given name or byname bestowed on children for the sake of a good omen, from the expression *vivas* 'may you live', found in Catalan, Spanish, and in Latin.

Var.: **Vives**.

Cogn.: Jewish (Sefardic): **Bivas** (from Judezmo *bivas* 'may you live').

Vivian English and French: from a medieval given name (L *Viviānus*, a deriv. of *vivus* living, alive; cf. VITO and VITALE). The name was borne by a 5th-cent. bishop of Saintes, and was popular among the Normans, by whom it was introduced to England.

Vars.: Eng.: **Vivien**, **Vyvyan**; **Videan**, **Vidge(o)n**, **Vigeon**; **Fiddian**, **Fidge(o)n**; **Phyt(h)ian**, **Phethean**. Fr.: **Vivien**, **Viviand**, **Vivant**, **Vivie**.

Cogns.: It.: **Vi(vi)an(i)**, **Vi(vi)ano**, **Vivan**.

Dims.: Eng.: **Fidkin**, **Fitkin**. Fr.: **Viennet**, **Viénet**, **Vianey**, **Viennot**, **Viénot**. It.: **Vianello**, **Vianelli**, **Vianini**.

Patr.: Eng.: **Vivians**.

Vizcaíno Spanish: habitation name or regional name for someone from the town or province of Biscay (Sp. *Vizcaya*) in N Spain. The placename derives from Basque *bizkai* ridge + the def. art. *-a*.

Vlach Czech: from *vlach* Italian. This vocab. word originally meant 'foreigner'; it is cogn. with Ger. *welsch* Latin, Romance-speaking, and ultimately with OE *wælisc* foreign and mod. Eng. *Welsh*; see WALSH. At the time when surnames were formed, the Czech word was applied chiefly to Italians, but also to the Rumanians (Walachians).

Cogns.: Pol.: **Włoch**, **Włoski**; **Wołosz(yn)** ('Walachian'). Ger.: **Walch**, **Wel(t)scher**; **Wloch**, **Floch**, **Bloch**, **Ploch**. Jewish (Ashkenazic): **Wallakh**, **Wal(l)ach**, **Walloch**, **Wol(l)ach**, **Wolloch**, **Volach**, **Volloch**; **Bloch** (often Anglicized as BLOCK); **Wolichman**, **Volichman**; **Walsch**, **Wellisch**, **Weltsch**, **Wel(t)scher** (the last four are from the Ger. word and applied to Jews from Italy and France). Hung.: **Olasz**, **Oláh**.

Dims.: Czech: **Vlášek**, **Vlašánek**, **Vlašín**. Pol.: **Włoszek**.

Patrs.: Croatian: **Vlahović**, **Vlašić**, **Vlajić**. Pol.: **Włochowicz**. Russ.: **Volokhov**, **Volosh(en)inov**.

Patr. (from a dim.): Croatian: **Vlajković**.

Habitation name: Czech: **Vlachovský**.

Vladimirov Russian and Bulgarian: patr. from the given name *Vladimir*, which is composed of the Slav. elements *vlad-* wealth, rule + *mer* famous, glorious. This was one of the very few Slav. names acceptable for baptism in the Orthodox Church, due to the acceptability to the Church of the immensely popular St Vladimir (d. 1015), the first Christian Grand Duke of Kiev (who, as a matter of fact, himself bore the baptismal name *Vasili*).

Var.: Russ.: **Volodimerov**.

Cogns. (not patrs.): Pol.: **Włodzimi(e)rski**. Jewish (E Ashkenazic, adoptions of the non-Jewish surname): **Vladimirski**, **Vladimirsky**.

Cogns. (patrs.): Rum.: **Vladimiresco**, **Vladimirescu**.

Dims. (not patrs.): Ukr.: **Volodko**. Beloruss.: **Volodzhko**. Pol.: **Włodek**, **Wołodko**. Ger. (of Slav. origin): **Wlodasch**, **Wlotzka**, **Wlotzke**.

Dims. (patrs.): Russ.: **Volodin, Volodichev**. Ukr.: **Volodich**. Pol.: **Wołodkiewicz, Włodkowicz**. Rumanian (of Slav. origin): **Vladescu**.

Vladyka Czech: occupational name approximately equivalent to Eng. *steward* (see STEWART). The Czech vocab. word *vladyka* also came to denote a minor rank of aristocracy, while in the larger cities it was a term for an alderman, and the surname in many cases is probably a status name from one of these.

Vlasák Czech: nickname for a man with thick or long hair, from Czech *vlas* hair + *-ák* suffix denoting human nouns, or occupational name for a buyer of hair, where the suffix is agentive.

Var.: **Vlas**.

Dim.: **Vlásek**.

Vobora Czech: 1. topographic name for someone who lived by an enclosure, Czech (*v*)*obora*. The vocab. word came to denote specifically an enclosed forest in which red deer were kept for hunting, and the surname may also be a metonymic occupational name for a gamekeeper.

2. habitation name from a place called *Obora*, named with Czech (*v*)*obora* enclosure.

Vars. (of 1): **Voborník**. (Of 2): **Voborský**.

Vobořil Czech: nickname for an irritable person, from Czech (*v*)*obořit se* to speak angrily or gruffly.

Vodička Czech: topographic name for someone living by a body of water, or a nickname for a teetotaller, from a dim. of Czech *voda* water. The name was also used as a humorous nickname for an innkeeper.

Vodopyanov Russian: patr. from the nickname *Vodopyan* 'Water-drinker' (from *voda* water + *pit* to drink), presumably denoting a teetotaller. Cf. BOILEAU and DRINKWATER.

Vogel 1. German and Dutch/Flemish: metonymic occupational name for a bird-catcher or nickname for a timid person, from Ger. *Vogel* bird (MHG, MLG *vogel*, OHG *fogul*; cf. FOWLE).

2. Jewish (Ashkenazic): ornamental name from mod. Ger. *Vogel* bird.

Vars.: Du., Flem.: **De Vogel, (De) Voogel**. Flem. only: **(De) Voghel**. Jewish: **Fogiel** (a Pol. spelling); **Vogelman, Fogel(man)**; **Feigelman** (from Yid. *feygl* birds, which in NE Yid. also had a sing. meaning); **Fogelmanas** (with Lithuanian nom. sing. ending *-as*).

Cogns.: Low Ger.: **Vagel**. Dan., Norw.: **Fugl**.

Dims.: Ger.: **Vögele(in)**; **Vögeli** (Switzerland).

Patrs.: Du.: **Vogels**. Flem.: **Voghels, Veughelen**.

Cpds (ornamental): Swed.: **Fogelberg** ('bird hill'); **Fogelström** ('bird river'). Jewish: **Fogelbaum** ('bird tree'); **Vogelblat** ('bird leaf'); **Vogelfang** ('bird claw'); **Fogelfuss, Feigelfuss** ('bird foot'); **Fogelhut** ('bird hat'); **Fogelnest** ('bird nest'); **Vogelsang, Fogelsang** ('bird song'); **Fogelstein, Feigelstein** ('bird stone'); **Feigelstock** ('bird stick').

Vogt German: occupational name for a bailiff or farm manager, MHG *voget* (LL *advocātus*, past part. of *advocāre* to call up (to help); cf. AVOGADRO). The term originally described someone who appeared before a court on behalf of some party not permitted to make direct representations, often an ecclesiastical body which was not supposed to have any dealings with temporal authorities.

Vars.: **Vögt, Voi(g)t, Voigh(t)**; **Vauth, Faut(h), Fath(mann)** (Franconia, Hesse).

Cogns.: Low Ger.: **Voogd, Vagd**. Flem., Du.: **(De) Voogd, (De) Voogt, De Vocht, Vagt**. Dan., Norw.: **Foged**.

Dims.: Ger.: **Vögtle; Voitl** (Bavaria).

Patrs.: Low Ger.: **Vogts, Vögting**. Flem., Du.: **Vagts, Vagedes**.

Voisin English (Norman) and French: from OF *voisin* (ANF *veisin*) neighbour (L *vicinus*, a deriv. of *vicus* village, district; cf. VICO). The application is uncertain; it may be a nickname for a 'good neighbour', or for someone who used this word as a frequent term of address.

Var.: Eng.: **Vezin**.

Cogns.: Prov.: **Bezi(n)**. It.: **Vicini, Vicino; Visin(i)** (Venetia).

Dim.: It.: **Vicinelli**.

Patr.: Fr.: **Duvoisin** (with fused prep. and article *du* 'of the').

Vojtěch Czech: from a Czech personal name, *Vojtěch*, composed of the elements *voi* soldier + *tech* comfort, consolation. This, along with its Pol. cogn. *Wojciech* and the Ger. form *Wozzek*, was a popular given name among Christians in E Europe, mainly because of the cult of St Vojtěch (*c*.955–97). The latter was bishop of Prague from 982 onwards. In 995 he was expelled from Bohemia and in 996 he went to Poland on a mission to the Prussians (members of a heathen Baltic-speaking people, not the German-speakers who later took their name). He was killed by the Prussians in 997, and was canonized in 999. He is regarded as the first Polish saint; in Polish he is known as St Wojciech, in German as St Adalbert (or Albert) of Prague.

Vars.: **Vojtek, Vojtěk, Vojtík, Vojta(s), Vojtaš; Vojka**.

Cogns.: Pol. **Wojciech, Wojtych, Wojtak, Wojtas, Wojtecki; Wojtan, Wojtera, Wojtala, Wojtyła, Wojtyło**. Beloruss.: **Voitekh**. Rum.: **Voicu**. Ger. (of Slav. origin): **Woitschek, Woitzik, Wutschik; Wo(i)tek, Wozzek, Woyzek; Wehtag** (the last has been altered by folk etymology as if derived from vocab. words meaning 'day of woe').

Dims.: Czech: **Vojtíšek, Vojtášek, Vojtárek**. Pol.: **Wojcieszek; Wojtczyk, Wojtasik, Wojtylak; Woś, Wosik, Woszczyk**. Ger. (of Slav. origin): **Wuttschke, Wutzke, Woitke**.

Patrs.: Pol.: **Wojciechowicz, Wojtowicz, Wojtanowicz, Wojtczak, Wojtysiak**. Beloruss.: **Voit(s)ekhov**.

Patrs. (from dims.): Pol.: **Wojtkiewicz; Wojtkowiak; Woszczak**.

Habitation names: Pol.: **Wojciechowski, Wojtaszewski, Wojtanowski, Wojtkowski**. Czech: **Vojtěchovský**.

Vokoun Czech: 1. nickname for someone supposedly bearing some resemblance to a perch (the fish), from Czech (*v*)*okoun* perch.

2. nickname for someone with prominent eyes, from a deriv. of Czech *oko* eye.

Volák Czech: occupational name for a keeper of or dealer in oxen, from Czech *vůl* ox (cogn. with Pol. *wół*).

Cogn.: Pol.: **Wołowiec** (oxherd).

Habitation name: Pol.: **Wołowski**.

Völgyi Hungarian: topographic name for someone who lived in a valley, Hung. *völgy*.

Volk 1. German: from a medieval given name, a short form of various Gmc personal names with the first element *folk* people (cf. FOULKES).

2. Jewish (Ashkenazic): apparently from the mod. Ger. vocab. word *Volk* people or an adoption of the Ger. surname, but perhaps also influenced by Pol. *wilk* wolf, Czech *vlk* (see WILK).

Vars. (of 1): **Folk, Volke, Voll(e), Völke**. (Of 2): **Volkman(n), Folk(man)**.

Dims. (of 1): Ger.: **Völkel, Velkel, Fölkel, Felkel; Vol(t)z, Völ(t)z, Völzle** (Swabia). Low Ger.: **Volkmann**. Fris.: **Fokema**. Ger. (of Slav. origin): **Völsch, Vözke, Fölsch, Fölske**.

Patrs. (from 1): Low Ger.: **Focken(s), Focks**, Fox. Fris.: **Focken, Focken(g)a**.

Patrs. (from 1) (dims.): Ger.: **Völser, Fölser**.

Volmer German: from the Gmc personal name *Folkmar*, composed of the elements *folk* people, race + *meri*, *mari* famous.

Vars.: **Vollmer, Vol(l)mert, Völlmer, Volk(a)mer, Völkmer, Vollmar, Völlmar, Volkmar; Volkmeier.**

Dims.: **Völm(le)**; **Völmy, Felmy** (Switzerland). Low Ger.: **Völlmeke.**

Volpe 1. Italian: nickname for a crafty person, from It. *volpe* fox (L *vulpes*, an ultimate cogn. of WOLF; see also GOUPIL).

2. Jewish (E Ashkenazic): habitation name from a town in Belorussia, SE of Grodno, the Yid. name of which is *Volp(e)* (Beloruss., Russ. *Volpa*, Pol. *Wołpa*).

Vars. (of 1): **Volpi, Vulpi, La Volpe.** (Of 2): **Volper, Wolpe(r).**

Dims. (of 1): **Volpino, Volpin(i), Volp(ic)ella, Volp(ic)elli.**

Augs. (of 1): **Volpone, Volponi.**

Patrs. (from 1): **Volpis, Vulpis; Della Volpe, Dalla Volpe.**

Volpert 1. Low German: from the Gmc personal name *Folkberht*, composed of the elements *folk* people, race + *berht* bright, famous.

2. Jewish (Ashkenazic): adoption of the name in 1 above, or possibly a var., with excrescent *-t*, of *Volper* (see VOLPE 2).

Vars. (of 1): **Volber(t).** (Of 2): **Wolpert.**

Cogns.: Fris.: **Volpt.** Ger.: **Volprecht, Vol(l)brecht, Fulbrecht, Fulpracht, Vol(l)bracht, Vol(l)barth, Vol(l)borth, Volbrod; Fulbright** (Anglicized).

Dims.: Ger.: **Völpel, Vopel, Vaupel, Vaubel.**

Patrs.: Low Ger.: **Volper(t)s, Volbers; Volberding, Volb(e)ring.** Fris.: **Völpts.**

Volta Italian: habitation name from any of the numerous minor places so called from their situation on a bend in a road or a river. The name is from It. *volta* curve, bend (LL *volūta*, a deriv. of *volvere* to turn).

Vars.: **Della Volta, Dalla Volta.**

Voorzanger Dutch (Jewish): name taken by a cantor. See KAZAN and SANGER 2.

Vorobyov Russian: patr. from the nickname *Vorobei* 'Sparrow', denoting a small, chirpy individual.

Cogns.: Ukr.: **Vorobets, Gorobets.** Beloruss.: **Vorobei, Verabei.** Pol.: **Wróbel** (also Jewish (E Ashkenazic), in which case it is an ornamental name). Czech: **Brabec, Vrabec.** Ger. (of Slav. origin): **Wrob(b)el.**

Habitation name: Pol. **Wróblewski** (also a Jewish ornamental name).

Voronin Russian: patr. from the nickname *Vorona* 'Crow', denoting a raucous person or someone with very dark hair. The stress is on the second syllable.

Cogns.: Pol.: **Wrona, Wroński.** Czech: **Vrána.** Jewish (E Ashkenazic): **Vorona, Worona, Vronsky, Wronski, Wronsky; Vronovitz** (patr.). Croatian: **Vraneš; Vranić** (patr.).

Dims.: Ger. (of Slav. origin): **Wronka, Wronek.**

Habitation name: Pol.: **Wronowski.**

Voronov Russian: patr. from the nickname *Voron* 'Raven', denoting someone with very dark hair. The stress is on the first syllable.

Cogns.: Ukr.: **Voronich, Voronevski.** Beloruss.: **Voronich.**

Vörös Hungarian: nickname for a man with red hair, from Hung. *vörös* red.

Vars.: **Veres(s), Weöres.**

Vorotnikov Russian: patr. from the occupational term *vorotnik* gatekeeper (a deriv. of *vorota* gates, ultimately a cogn. of OE *worð* fence, enclosure; see WORTH).

Cogn.: Czech: **Vrátný.**

Vosátka Czech: status name for the leader of a new settlement, from a dim. of Czech *osada* settlement (originally meaning 'people').

Vostrý Czech: nickname for a quick-minded person, from Czech *(v)ostrý* sharp, keen, acute.

Vars.: **Ostrý; Vostřák** (also means 'hobby', a kind of falcon).

Dim.: **Vostárek.**

Votava Czech: 1. topographic name for someone living by the river *Otava*.

2. from the Czech vocab. word *(v)otava*, lit. 'aftermath', i.e. a second crop of grass from the same field, after a first crop has been mown in early summer. As a surname, this may be a topographic name or an anecdotal nickname. The vocab. word also means 'convalescence', and this meaning may alternatively lie behind the surname.

Var.: **Otava.**

Votruba Czech: nickname for a stupid person, from Czech *(v)otruby* bran, husks of corn, which has the figurative sense 'blockhead'.

Vrba Czech: 1. topographic name for someone who lived by a conspicuous willow tree or among willow trees, from Czech *vrba* willow.

2. nickname for a timid person, with reference to the trembling leves of the willow tree.

Cogns. (of 1): Jewish (Ashkenazic): **Verba, Werba** (ornamental).

Dims. (of 2): Czech: **Vrbík, Vrbka.**

Habitation names: Czech: **Vrb(en)ský.** Pol.: WIERZBICKI. Ger.: FRÖBE.

Vršecký Czech: habitation name from any of several places named with Czech *vršek*, dim. of *vrch* hill.

Vuorinen Finnish: ornamental name from Finn. *vuori* mound, hill + the gen. suffix *-nen*, perhaps sometimes chosen as a topographic name by someone who lived on a hillock.

Výborný Czech: nickname for a good person, from Czech *výborný* good, excellent, or more probably for a habitual user of the exclamation *výborně* 'Excellent!', 'Well done!'

Vyskočil Czech: from the past tense of the verb *vyskočit* to jump up. The application of this word as a surname is uncertain; it may be a nickname for one who had risen in social status.

W

Wace 1. Scots and English: from the Norman personal name *Wazo*, apparently derived from a compound Gmc name with a first element *wad* to go (cf. WADE 1).

2. Welsh: status name for a servant, W *(g)was* (cf. VASS).

Vars.: WASE, WASS. (Of 1 only): **Waison, Wayson, Was(s)on** (from the OF oblique case); **Gaze** (E Anglia), GASS, **Ga(i)sh, Gas(s)on, Gashion** (from central Fr. forms).

Dims. (of 1): **Was(se)lin, Wastling.**

Wachsmann German: occupational name for a gatherer or seller of beeswax, from Ger. *Wachs* wax (MHG, OHG *wahs*) + *Mann* man. Wax was important in former times, being used for example to make candles and for sealing letters.

Vars.: **Wachs, Was(s)mann.**

Cogns.: Eng.: **Wax(man).** Du.: **Wassenaar.** Jewish (Ashkenazic): **Wachs(man), Waks(man), Wax(man), Vacks, Vaks(man), Vax(man)** (from mod. Ger. *Wachs*, Yid. *vaks*).

Wachtel 1. German: nickname for a timorous or stupid person, from Ger. *Wachtel* quail (MHG *wachtele*, OHG *wahtala*, of imitative origin; cf. QUAIL).

2. Jewish (Ashkenazic): ornamental name taken from Ger. *Wachtel* or Yid. *vakhtl* quail. According to Kaganoff the name was adopted in reference to the quails miraculously provided for the Israelites in the wilderness (Exod. 16: 13), but the name is more likely to be simply one of the large number of Jewish ornamental names derived from words for animals and birds, or, in view of the connotations of the Ger. word, it may have been one of the derogatory surnames imposed on Jews by non-Jewish government officials in central Europe.

Wachter 1. German: occupational name for a watchman, Ger. *Wachter*, an agent deriv. of MHG *wachte* watch, guard (OHG *wahta*; cf. WAITE).

2. Jewish (Ashkenazic): from Ger. *Wachter* watchman, possibly adopted as an occupational name by a synagogue beadle (Yid. *shames*).

Vars.: Ger.: **Wächter, Wachtmann.** Jewish: **Wachtman(n).**

Waddell Scots: habitation name from *Wedale* (now Stow) near Edinburgh. The origins of this placename are uncertain. The second element is evidently OE *dæl* or ON *dalr* valley (see DALE). The first element might conceivably be OE *wedd* pledge, security or its ON cogn. *veð* (although this is not found elsewhere as a placename element). In Scotland the stress normally falls on the first syllable of the surname, but elsewhere the name is often accented on the second syllable to avoid association with the vocabulary word *waddle*.

Vars.: **Waddel, Waddle, Weddel(l), Woddell; Weddle** (Northumb.).

Waddingham English: habitation name from a place in Lincs., recorded in Domesday Book as *Wadingeham*, i.e. 'homestead (OE *hām*) of the people of *Wada*' (see WADE 1).

Waddington N English: habitation name from any of various places. One near Clitheroe in Lancs. and another in Lincs. (*Wadintune* in Domesday Book) were originally named in OE as the 'settlement (OE *tūn*) associated with *Wada*' (see WADE 1); cf. WADDINGHAM.

Var.: **Wadington.**

Wade English: 1. from the ME given name *Wade*, OE *Wada*, from the verb *wadan* to go. (*Wada* was the name of a legendary sea-giant.)

2. topographic name for someone who lived near a ford, OE *(ge)wæd* (of cogn. origin to 1), or habitation name from a place named with this word, as for example *Wade* in Suffolk.

Var.: **Waide.**

Cogns. (of 2): Ger.: **Wademann.** Flem., Du.: **Vad.** Fr.: **Gué, Legué, Dugué.** Sp.: **Vado.**

Dims. (of 1): Fr.: **Vadet, Vadé, Vadez, Vadon, Vadel; Vatel(ot), Vat(t)in, Vaton; Wat(t)el, Watteau, Watelet, Watelot, Wat(t)in.** (Of 2): Sp.: **Vadillo.**

Patrs. (from 1): Eng.: **Wadeson, Waidson.**

Wader English: occupational name for a gatherer or seller of woad, from an agent deriv. of ME *wade* woad (OE *wād*, reinforced by OF *waisde*, likewise of Gmc origin). This plant produces a powerful blue dye, which was widely used in the Middle Ages.

Var.: **Waider; Wad(e)man, Wodeman.**

Cogns.: Ger.: WEITER.

Wadham English: apparently a habitation name from an unidentified place, perhaps so called from the OE personal name *Wada* (see WADE 1) + OE *hām* homestead. It may be a contracted form of WADDINGHAM.

Wadley English: habitation name from a place in Berks., so called from OE *wād* woad (see WADER) or the personal name *Wada* (see WADE 1) + *lēah* wood, clearing.

Wäger German: occupational name for an official responsible for weighing produce, esp. that offered as rent in kind, or else for one who was in charge of checking weights and measures used by merchants. The vocab. word is an agent deriv. of MHG *wegen* to weigh (OHG *wegan*).

Vars.: **Waage** (from MHG *wāge* scales); **Wag(e)mann.**

Cogns.: Jewish (Ashkenazic): **Weger; Wagman, Vagman; Wegman** (it is not clear whether this name belongs here, or at WAY; cf. mod. Ger. *Weg*, Yid. *veg* way, path)

Waghorn English and Scots: according to Reaney, this is an occupational nickname for a hornblower or trumpeter, from ME *wag(gen)* to brandish, shake (OE *wagian*) + *horn* HORN. It is also quite possible that it was originally an obscene nickname with *horn* in the sense 'penis'; cf. WAGSTAFF. Black states that the name, recorded in Scotland in the 14th cent., is of local origin, with *horn* in a topographical sense.

Var.: **Waghorne.**

Wagner German and Jewish (Ashkenazic): occupational name for a carter or cartwright, from an agent deriv. of Ger. *Wagen* cart, waggon (MHG *wagen*, OHG *wagan*).

Vars.: Ger.: **Wagener, Wahner, Wähner(t), Wehner(t), Wainer, Woiner; Wag(g)oner** (a recently Anglicized form; mod. Eng. *waggon* was borrowed in the 16th cent. from Du.).

Cogns.: Low Ger.: **Weg(e)ner**, **Weg(e)ler**. Flem.: **Wagenaer**. Du.: **Wagenaar**. Eng.: **Wainer**; see also WAIN. Czech: **Vágner**, **Vognar**, **Vojnar**. Pol.: **Wojnar**. Hung.: **Bognár**.

Habitation name: Pol.: **Wojnarowski**.

Wągrowski Polish: habitation name from *Wągrowiec*, a town SW of Poznań (which probably derives its name from Pol. *wągroda* enclosed pasture), with the addition of *-ski*, suffix of local surnames (see BARANOWSKI).

Wagstaff English (chiefly Midlands and Yorks.): 1. occupational nickname for some official who carried a staff of office, from ME *wag(gen)* to brandish, shake (OE *wagian*) + *staff* staff, rod (OE *stæf*).

2. obscene nickname for a medieval 'flasher', one who brandished his 'staff' publicly; cf. WAGHORN.

Var.: **Wagstaffe**.

Wahl 1. Jewish (Ashkenazic): according to Jewish tradition, this name is taken from Ger. *Wahl* election (MHG *wal(e)*, OHG *wala* choice), and was adopted by people who claimed descent from Saul Katzenellenbogen (1541-*c*.1617), who according to a Jewish legend was elected king of Poland for a single day at the time when Poland was an elective monarchy (hence *Wahl* election).

2. Swedish: var. of WALL 4.

Wain English: metonymic occupational name for a carter or cartwright, from ME *wain* cart, waggon (OE *wægen*). Occasionally it may have been a house name for someone who lived at a house distinguished with this sign, probably from the constellation of the Plough, known in the Middle Ages as *Charles's Wain*, the reference being to Charlemagne.

Vars.: **Waine(s)**, **Wayne**; **Wane** (Lancs.); **Wainman**, **W(h)enman**.

Cogns.: Ger.: **Wagenmann**; see also WAGNER.

Wainwright English (chiefly Lancs. and Yorks.): occupational name for a maker of carts or waggons; see WAIN + WRIGHT.

Vars.: **Wainewright**, **Wainrig(h)t**.

Waite English: occupational name for a watchman, ANF *waite* (of Gmc origin; cf. WACHTER), or from the same word in its original abstract/collective sense, 'the watch'. There may also have been some late confusion with WHITE.

Vars.: **Wait**, **Wayt(e)**, **Waight(e)**.

Cogns.: Fr.: **Guet**, **Guez**, **Guey**; **Guettier**, **Guestier**; **Guettand**, **Guétan**; **Leguet**; **Duguet**, **Duguez**, **Duguey**.

Patrs.: Eng.: **Wait(e)s**, **Wa(y)tes**, **Whait(e)s**; **Gaites**.

Wake N English: apparently from the ON byname *Vakr* 'Wakeful', 'Vigilant' (from *vaka* to remain awake), or perhaps from a cogn. OE *Waca* (apparently attested in placenames such as WAKEFORD, WAKEHAM, and WAKELEY). In the case of the noble family of this name, however, it is apparently of Continental origin; see below.

Wake *is the name of an English family who held a very early Norman barony. They trace their descent from Geoffrey* Wac *or Wake, who was living in 1099 and is believed to have been of Flemish origin.*

Wakefield English: habitation name from the city in W Yorks., and perhaps also from a place of the same name in Northants. Both are so called from OE *wacu* vigil, festival (a deriv. of *wac(i)an* to watch, wake; cf. WAKEMAN) + *feld* pasture, open country, i.e. a patch of open land where a fair was held.

One of the founders of New Zealand was Edward Gibbon Wakefield *(1796–1862), an enthusiastic advocate of Antipodean colonization. He was born in London, the son of a farmer and land agent, and was transported in 1827 after being found guilty of abduction. His first writing on colonial expansion,* A Letter from Sydney, *was written in 1829. In 1837 he formed the New Zealand Association, and was one of the founders of Canterbury, New Zealand.*

Wakeford English: habitation name from an unidentified place, presumably so called from the OE byname *Waca* 'Watchful' (see WAKE) + OE *ford* FORD. There was one place of this name (now lost) near WAKEHAM in Sussex.

Wakeham English: habitation name from places in Devon and Sussex, both so called from the OE byname *Waca* 'Watchful' (see WAKE) + OE *hām* homestead.

Var.: **Wakem**.

Wakeley English: habitation name from a place in Herts., so called from the OE byname *Waca* 'Watchful' (see WAKE) + OE *lēah* wood, clearing.

Vars.: **Wakely**, **Wa(c)kley**.

Wakeling English: from the medieval given name *Walquelin*, an ANF dim. of the Gmc byname *Walho* 'Foreigner' (cf. WALLACE).

Vars.: **Wakelin**, **Wa(l)kling**, **Walklin**, **Walklyn**, **Wakelam**.

Wakeman English: occupational name for a watchman, from ME *wake* watch, vigil (OE *wacu*; see WAKEFIELD) + *man* man (OE *mann*). This was the title of the mayor of Ripon until the 16th cent.

Cogns.: Ger.: **Wachmann**. Jewish (Ashkenazic): **Wachman(n)** (occupational name for a synagogue beadle; cf. WACHTER).

Walburg German: from a Gmc female personal name composed of the elements *wald* rule + *burg* fortress. St Walburga (d. 779) was an Eng. missionary who accompanied St Boniface on his mission to Germany, and became abbess of Heidenheim. Her cult became very popular in N Germany in the early Middle Ages, with consequent effects on the frequency of the given name. Her bodily remains were later transferred to Eichstätt, according to legend on 1 May, which thus came to be known as *Walpurgisnacht*. This is also the date of an extremely ancient pagan fertility festival, welcoming the return of summer, and associated with witchcraft and revelry.

Vars.: **Wallburg**, **Wolburg**.

Cogn.: It.: **Valperga** (NE Italy).

Dims.: Ger.: **Walpl**, **Wabbel**. Low Ger.: **Wobbe**, **Wöbb**, **Wöb(c)ke**.

Metrs. (from dims.): Low Ger.: **Wobben**, **Wöbken**, **Wöbbeking**.

Walcot English: habitation name from any of various places, for example in Berks., Lincs., Northants, Oxon., Shrops., Warwicks., and Wilts., all so called from OE *wealh* foreigner, Briton, serf (see WALLACE) + *cot* cottage, shelter (see COATES).

Vars.: **Walcott** (places in Norfolk and Worcs.); **Walcote** (a place in Leics.).

Wald 1. English and German: topographic name for someone who lived in or near a forest (OE *w(e)ald*, OHG *wald*). After the extensive clearances of forests in England before the Norman Conquest, the OE term *w(e)ald* also came to be used in ME to denote open uplands (*wolds*) and waste land not brought into cultivation.

2. Jewish (Ashkenazic): in most cases, an ornamental name from the Ger. vocab. word *Wald* forest. Very few Jews would have been living in or near forests at the time when they acquired surnames. However, the forms ending in *-man(n)* or *-ner* are more probaby explained as in 1 or as

metonymic occupational names for someone whose job was connected with wood, such as a woodcutter or lumber merchant.

Vars.: Eng.: **Walde, Waud; Wo(u)ld(e), Wo(u)lds; We(a)ld, Weild; Waldman, Walder, Walding**. Ger.: **Walde, Waldmann, Wald(n)er, Wallner**. Jewish: **Waldman(n), Waldner, Vald(man)**.

Cogns.: Low Ger.: **Wohld, Verwohl, Wohltmann**. Fris.: **Woldstra, Woud(str)a**. Flem., Du.: **Van de Woude, Verwoude, Van't Woud, Woudman**.

Cpds (ornamental): Jewish: **Valdberg** ('forest hill'); **Valdboim** ('forest tree'); **Waldfogel** ('forest bird'); **Waldhorn** ('forest horn'); **Waldstein** ('forest stone').

A family by the name of Weld *trace their descent from William* de Welde *who was sheriff of London in 1352.*

Waldeck German and Jewish (Ashkenazic): habitation name from a place in Hesse, on the river Eder, apparently so called from OHG *wald* wood + *ecka, egga* corner, recess. However, Bahlow interprets the earliest recorded forms of the name, *Waldegg* and *Waldei*, as pointing to an ancient term for a stretch of water.

The noble family of this name trace their descent from Widukind III, Count of Schwalenberg (fl. *1116–37*). *His descendants acquired the Castle of Waldeck* c.*1150 and took their name from it.*

Waldegrave English: habitation name from *Walgrave* in Northants, recorded in Domesday Book as *Waldgrave* 'grove (OE *grāf*) belonging to *Old*'. *Old* is a nearby place, so called from OE *w(e)ald* forest (see WALD 1). The surname is often pronounced /'wɔlgreɪv/, as though it had the same spelling as the modern form of the place name.

This is the name of a family who trace their descent from Sir Richard Waldegrave *of Smallbridge, Suffolk, speaker of the House of Commons in the 14th cent. They now hold the title Earl Waldegrave.*

Walden English: habitation name from any of the places, in Essex, Herts., and N Yorks., so called from OE *wealh* foreigner, Briton, serf (see WALLACE) + *denu* valley (see DEAN 1).

Waldorf German: habitation name from any of at least three places, all apparently so called from OHG *wald* forest + *dorf* village, settlement (see THORPE).

Waldron English: 1. from a Gmc personal name composed of the elements *walh* foreigner + *hrafn* raven.

2. habitation name from a place in Sussex, so called from OE *w(e)ald* forest + *ærn* house, dwelling. The surname is now also common in Ireland, esp. in Connacht.

Vars. (of 1): **Waldren, Waldram, Waldrum, Walrand, Walrond, Wallraven**.

Cogns. (of 1): Ger.: **Wallrabe, Wollrabe, Wohlrab**. Low Ger.: **Walrafen, Wallraff, Waldraff**. Flem., Du.: **Walraven**.

Wale English: 1. from a Gmc personal name *Walo*, either a byname meaning 'Foreigner' (see WALLACE), or else a short form of the various cpd names with this first element (cf., e.g., WALDRON 1). See also WAKELING and GALE 2.

2. nickname for a well-liked person, from ME *wale* good, excellent (originally 'choice'; cf. WAHL 1).

3. topographic name for someone who lived near an embankment, ME *wale* (OE *walu*).

Patrs. (from 1): **Wa(i)les**.

Walford English: habitation name from any of various places so called. Examples in Herefords. and Shrops. are so called from OE (W Midlands) *wæll(a)* spring, stream (see WALL 2) + *ford* FORD. A second place in Herefords. of the same name originally had as its first element OE *w(e)alh* foreigner, Briton, serf (see WALLACE), and one in Dorset had OE *wealt* unsteady, difficult.

This is the name of an English family who held the manor of Walford, Herts. One of the earliest holders was Sir Hugo de Walford, *recorded in 1109.*

Walkden English (Lancs.): habitation name from a place near Rochdale, probably so called from an OE streamname *Wealce* (from *wealcan* to roll along) + *denu* valley (see DEAN 1).

Walker English and Scots: 1. occupational name for a fuller, ME *walkere*, OE *wealcere*, an agent deriv. of *wealcan* to walk, tread. This was the regular term for the occupation during the Middle Ages in W and N England (cf. FULLER and TUCKER), but now the surname is fairly widespread. The highest concentrations are in a patch of NW England centred on Leeds, and in the Grampian region of Scotland. As a Scots surname it has also been used as a translation of Gael. *Mac an Fhucadair*; see MCNUCATOR.

2. habitation name from a place in Northumb., so called from ME *wall* (Roman) wall (see WALL 1) + *kerr* marsh (see KERR).

Cogns. (of 1): Ger.: **Wal(c)ker**. Low Ger.: **Welcker**.

Walkingshaw Scots: habitation name from *Walkinshaw* in the former county of Renfrews., which is probably named from OE *wealcere* fuller (see WALKER) + *sceaga* copse (see SHAW).

Vars.: **Walkinshaw; Wakenshaw** (Northumb.).

Wall 1. English: topographic name for someone who lived by a stone-built wall, e.g. one used to fortify a town or to keep back the encroachment of the sea (OE *w(e)all*, from L *vallum* rampart, palisade).

2. N English: topographic name for someone who lived by a spring or stream, Northern ME *wall(e)* (OE (W Midlands) *wæll(a)*; cf. WELL).

3. Irish: var. of VALE, a re-Anglicized form of Gael. *de Bhál*.

4. Swedish: ornamental name from Swed. *wall, vall* grassy bank, pasture, or grazing ground, perhaps adopted in some cases as a topographic name by someone who lived by a grassy bank.

Vars. (of 1 and 2): Eng.: **Walle, Walls**, WALLER, **Wallman**. (Of 4): Swed.: WAHL; **Wallén, Wallin, Wallenius; Wallner, Wallman, Wallander**.

Cogns. (of 1): Low Ger.: **Wall(mann)**. Flem., Du.: **Van den Wall**.

Cpds (of 4, mainly ornamental): Swed.: **Wall(en)berg, Wahlberg** ('pasture hill'); **Wallgren, Wahlgren** ('pasture branch'); **Wahlquist** ('pasture twig'); **Wahlsted** ('pasture homestead'); **Wallström, Wahlström** ('pasture river').

Wallace Scots, Irish, and English: name for a Celt, from ANF *waleis* (from a Gmc cogn. of OE *wealh* foreign). In different parts of Britain this term was used to denote variously Scotsmen, Welshmen, and Bretons, as well as the small pocket of Strathclyde Britons who persisted into the Middle Ages. English placenames containing *wealh* (as for example WALCOT, WALDEN, WALFORD, and WALLINGTON) are believed to refer to enclaves of Welsh-speaking people noted by the Anglo-Saxons. The surname has also been adopted in the 19th and 20th cents. as an Anglicized form of various Ashkenazic Jewish surnames.

Vars.: **Wallice, Wallis, Walles, Wallas**. See also WALSH and WAUGH.

Cogns.: Fr.: **Gal(l)ais, Gal(l)ois**. Flem., Du.: **De Wall** ('Walloon'). See also VLACH and GALL 1.

The surname Wallace *is particularly common in the Lowlands of Scotland, where it apparently referred to people from south of the Border as well as to Highlanders. The earliest known bearer is Richard* Walas *(Paisley 1160), who had migrated from Shropshire to Riccarton in Ayrs., and whose surname may indicate Welsh origin.*

Sir William Wallace (?1272–1305), who defeated Edward I in 1297, was born in Paisley, probably a descendant of the Richard Wallace referred to above. His surname also appeared in the forms Wallays *and* Wallensis.

Wallbank N English: apparently a topographic name for someone who lived by a bank with a wall on it, from ME *wall* (see WALL 1) + *bank* (see BANKS). Alternatively, the first element may be Northern ME *wall(e)* spring, stream (see WALL 2), in which case the surname would denote someone who lived on the banks of a stream.

Vars.: **Wallbanks**, **Walbank**, **Walbanck(e)**.

Waller English: 1. topographic name, a var. of WALL 1, or occupational name for a mason.

2. topographic name, a var. of WALL 2; see also WELL.

3. occupational name for someone who boiled sea water to extract the salt, from an agent deriv. of ME *well(en)* to boil (OE *weallan*).

4. nickname for a good-humoured person, ANF *wall(i)er* (an agent deriv. of OF *galer* to make merry, of Gmc origin; cf. GALE 1 and GAILLARD).

Vars. (of 4): **Gall(i)er**, **Gallear** (from central Fr. forms).

A genealogy for an English family by the name of Waller *claims that it is descended from one Alured* de Waller *(d. 1183) of Newark, Notts.; another early member is said to be David* de Waller, *Master of the Rolls in 1327. However, more recent research has not been able to confirm the existence of either of these individuals. The name was taken to Ireland by Robert Waller, recorded in 1291.*

Wallington English: habitation name from any of various places so called, with perhaps as many as four different origins. Those in Berks., Hants, and Surrey are probably all so called from the gen. pl. of OE *wealh* foreigner, Briton (see WALLACE) + OE *tūn* enclosure, settlement. One in Northumb. was originally OE *Wealingtūn* 'settlement associated with *Wealh*', a personal name or byname (cf. WALE 1). One in Herts. was named as the 'settlement of the people of *Wændel*', while one in Norfolk was probably the 'settlement of the dwellers by the wall'; see WALL 1.

Wallop English: 1. habitation name from a place in Hants, so called from OE (W Midlands) *wæll(a)* spring, stream (see WALL 2) + *hop* enclosed valley (see HOPE). There are also minor places of the same name and etymology in Gloucs. and Shrops., and these may be partial sources of the surname.

2. var. of GALLOP.

This is the name of a Hants family who are said to have lived in the place from which their name is derived since before the Norman Conquest. One of their earliest recorded members is Matthew de Wallop, *living in the 13th cent. They were granted the earldom of Portsmouth in 1743.*

Wallwork English (Lancs.): habitation name of uncertain origin. Thomas *de Wallerwork* was living in Lancs. *c.*1324, and throughout the Middle Ages forms in *-work* alternate with ones in *-worth*. No similarly named place in Lancs. has been identified, and it is possible that the surname derives from places in Co. Durham or Greater London called *Walworth*, from OE *w(e)alh* foreigner, Briton (see WALLACE) + *worð* enclosure (see WORTH).

Walmsley English: habitation name from *Walmersley* near Bury in Lancs., which according to Ekwall is so called from OE *wald* wood + *mere* lake or *(ge)mǣre* boundary + *lēah* wood, clearing. However, it is perhaps more plausibly from the gen. case of an OE personal name *Wealhmǣr* 'Foreign-famous' or *Wealdmǣr* 'Rule-famous' + OE *lēah*.

Vars.: **Walmesley**, **Walmisley**, **Wa(r)msley**, **Waumsley**.

Walpole English: habitation name from either of two places, in Norfolk and Suffolk. The first element of the former is OE *w(e)all* wall (see WALL 1), while the first element of the latter is *wealh* foreigner, Briton (see WALLACE); they share the second element OE *pōl* pool.

Vars.: **Wolpole**, **Waple(s)**.

The English statesman Sir Robert Walpole, *1st Earl of Orford (1676–1745), was born into a prosperous family at Houghton Hall, Norfolk. The family fortunes had been established by Ralph* de Walpole *(d. 1302), who became bishop of Ely.*

Walsh 1. English: name for a Celt, from ME *walsche* Celtic, foreign (OE *wælisc*, a deriv. of *wealh* foreign; cf. WALLACE and WAUGH). This word is cogn. with Ger. *welsch* foreign, southern European, Romance-speaking, so ultimately with Czech *Vlach*.

2. Irish: translation of the Gael. name *Breathnach* 'British', 'Welsh'; cf. BRANNICK.

Vars. (mostly of 1): **Walshe**, **Welsh**, **Walch**, **Welch**, **Wals(h)man**.

Cogns.: See VLACH.

Walshaw English (Yorks.): habitation name from a place in W Yorks., near Hebden Bridge, so called from OE *w(e)alh* foreigner, Briton (see WALLACE) + *sceaga* copse (see SHAW).

Walsingham English: habitation name from a place in Norfolk, so called from OE *Wælsingahām* 'homestead (OE *hām*) of the people of *Wæls*', a personal name of uncertain origin, which occurs in *Beowulf*.

Walter English: from a Gmc personal name composed of the elements *wald* rule + *heri*, *hari* army, introduced into England by the Normans in the form *Walt(i)er*, *Waut(i)er*. The normal vernacular pronunciation of the Middle Ages reflected the latter of these forms.

Vars.: WATER; **Gualter** (from the central Fr. form).

Cogns.: Fr.: **Ga(u)ltier**, **Galtié**, **Gaut(h)ier**, **Gauthiez**, **Gaudier**, **Vaut(h)ier**. It.: **G(u)altieri**, **Gualtiero**; **Gualdieri**, **Gualdiero** (Campania, Calabria); **Valtieri**, **Valter** (Venetia); **T(i)eri**, **Tiero**. Ger.: **Walt(h)er**, **Waldherr**. Low Ger.: **Welter**, **Wolter**, **Wolder**, **Wöhlder(t)**, **Wohler(t)**. Flem., Du.: **Wauter**, **Wouter**.

Dims.: Fr.: **Gaut(h)ereau**, **Gautreau**, **Gaudr(i)eau**, **Gautr(el)et**, **Gaut(h)eron**, **Gautron**, **Gaud(e)ron**, **Gaut(h)erot**, **Gautrot**, **Vautrot**, **Gaut(h)erin**, **Vaut(h)rin**, **Vautrin(ot)**. It.: **Galtierotti**. Ger.: **Wal(t)z**, **Wäl(t)z**, **Walzel**, **Welz(el)**; **Wälti**, **Welti** (Switzerland). Low Ger.: **Wolterke**, **Wöldeke**, **Wöhlk(e)**, **Wölke**, **Wöhl(e)**.

Patrs.: Eng.: **Walters**, **Walterson**; **Fitzwa(l)ter**. Sc.: **McWalter**, **McWatters** (Gael. **Mac Uaitéir**). Low Ger.: **Welters**, **Wo(h)lters**, **Wolders**, **Wohlers**; **Woltering**, **Woldering**, **Wollring**. Flem., Du.: **Wauters**, **Wouters(en)**.

Patrs. (from dims.): Low Ger.: **Wolterkes**, **Wölterges**; **Wöhlken(s)**, **Wölken**, **Wöhl(k)ing**. Fris.: **Wöltjes**, **Wöljen**. Flem., Du.: **Wouts**.

Fitzwalter *is the name of an English family of Norman origin, descendants of Godfrey, Count of Brionne. His grandson Richard Fitz-Gilbert (?1035–?90) accompanied William the Conqueror and was made Lord of Clare, because of which he was also known as Richard* de Clare. *His great-grandson Robert FitzWalter was one of the barons who guaranteed the Magna Carta (1215); the latter's grandson Robert Fitzwalter (b. 1247) was the first holder of the barony of Fitzwalter.*

Walthew English: from a widespread Anglo-Scandinavian personal name *Wælþeof* (ON *Valþiófr*), composed of the elements *val* battle + *þiofr* thief, i.e. one who snatched victory out of battle.

Vars.: **Waltho, Waldy, Waldo; Waddy.**

Walton English: habitation name from any of the numerous places so called. The first element in these names was variously OE *wealh* foreigner, Briton (see WALLACE), *w(e)ald* wood (see WALD), *w(e)all* wall (see WALL 1), or *wæll(a)* spring, stream (see WALL 2).

Vars.: **Walten, Wauton.**

George Walton *(1741–1804) was one of those who signed the American Declaration of Independence. He was born in Prince Edward County, Virginia, whither his grandfather had emigrated from England in 1682.*

Wander 1. German: occupational name for a builder, one who built walls, from an agent deriv. of Ger. *Wand* wall (MHG, OHG *want* wall, from OHG *wenten* to wind, weave; the earliest domestic walls were of wattle and daub construction, made from woven hurdles packed with clay).

2. German: occupational name for a maker or seller of cloth, from an agent deriv. of an aphetic form of Ger. *Gewand* cloth, garment (MHG *gewant*, OHG *giwant*, likewise a deriv. of *wenten* to weave).

3. Jewish (Ashkenazic): of uncertain origin, possibly a cogn. of 1 or 2.

Vars. (of 1): **Wand(t).** (Of 2): **Wand.**

Wang 1. German: topographic name for someone who lived near a meadow, from the Low Ger. and Austrian/Bavarian dial. term *wang*.

2. Jewish (Ashkenazic): either a cogn. of 1, or else a habitation name for a Jew from Hungary (cf. Russ. *Vengria* Hungary).

Vars. (of 1): **Wang(n)er, Wäng(l)er.**

Cogns. (of 1): Dan., Norw.: **Wang, Vang.**

Wanner German: occupational name for a maker or seller of winnowing fans, from an agent deriv. of MHG *wanne* (OHG *wanna*, from L *vannus*; cf. FANNER).

Cogns.: Low Ger.: **Wannamaker, Wennmaker.**

Waplington English: habitation name from a place in E Yorks. (now Humberside), so called from OE *Wapolingtun* 'settlement (OE *tūn*) associated with a pond or march', from OE *wapol* pond, marsh.

Warboys English: 1. occupational name for a forester, from ANF *warde(r)* to guard (see WARDEN) + *bois* wood (see BOIS).

2. habitation name from a place in the former county of Hunts. (now part of Cambs.), so called from ON *varði* beacon + *buski* brushwood, bushes. Both elements are cogn. with those in 1.

Vars.: **Warboy, Worboys.**

Warburton English: habitation name from a place in Ches., so called from the OE female personal name *Wǣrburh* (composed of the elements *wǣr* pledge + *burh* fortress) + OE *tūn* enclosure, settlement.

Var.: **Warbutton** (Bristol).

Ward 1. English: occupational name for a watchman or guard, from OE *weard* guard (used as both an agent noun and an abstract noun).

2. Irish: Anglicized form of Gael. *Mac an Bhaird*; see BARD.

3. Jewish (Ashkenazic): Anglicization of *Warszawczyk* (see WARSZAWSKI).

Vars. (of 1): Eng.: **Warde, Wardman, Wordman.**

Patr. (from 1): Eng.: **Wards.**

Nathaniel Ward *(1578–1652), one of the authors of the first legal code to be enacted in New England, was born in Haverhill in Suffolk, England.*

Warden English: 1. occupational name for a watchman or guard, from ANF *wardein* (a deriv. of *warder* to guard, of Gmc origin; cf. WARD 1 and GUARD).

2. habitation name from any of various places, for example in Beds., Co. Durham, Kent, Northumb., and Northants, so called from OE *weard* watch + *dūn* hill; cf. WARDHAUGH, WARDLAW, and WARDLE 1.

Cogns. (of 1): Fr.: **Gardien, Gardenc.**

Dim. (of 1): Fr.: **Gardiennet.**

Wardhaugh English (Northumb.) and Scots: habitation name from some minor place so called, presumably from ON *varða* beacon + *haugr* hill; cf. WARDEN 2, WARDLAW, and WARDLE 1.

Wardlaw Scots: habitation name from any of several minor places so called, from OE *weard* watch + *hlāw* hill; cf. WARDEN 2, WARDHAUGH, and WARDLE 1.

Wardle English: 1. habitation name from places in Ches. and Lancs., so called from OE *weard* watch + *hyll* hill; cf. WARDEN 2, WARDHAUGH, and WARDLAW.

2. regional name from *Weardale* in Co. Durham, so called from the river *Wear* (named with a Brit. word apparently meaning 'liquid', 'water') + OE *dæl* valley (see DALE).

Vars.: **Wardel(l), Wardill, Wardall, Wardale.**

Wardley English: habitation name from a place in the former county of Rutland (now part of Leics.), apparently so called from OE *wær* weir (see WARE 1) + *lēah* wood, clearing; the *-d-* does not appear before the late 13th cent., and is apparently excrescent.

Wardrop English and Scots: metonymic occupational name for someone who was in charge of the garments worn by a feudal lord and his household, from ANF *warde(r)* to keep, guard (cf. WARDEN and GUARD) + *robe* garment (cf. ROPERO).

Vars.: **Wardrope, Wardrupp, Whatrup, Wardrobe; Wardrop(p)er, Waredraper.**

Ware English: 1. topographic name for someone who lived by a dam or weir on a river (OE *wær*, *wer*), or habitation name from a place named with this word, such as *Ware* in Herts.

2. nickname for a cautious person, from ME *war(e)* wary, prudent (OE *(ge)wær*).

Vars. (of 1): **Wares,** WEAR, WEIR, **W(h)ere.**

Wareham English: habitation name from a place in Dorset, so called from OE *wær* weir (see WARE 1) + *hām* homestead.

Var.: **Warham** (places in Herefords. and Norfolk).

Warfield English: habitation name from a place in Berks., recorded in Domesday Book as *Warwelt*, from OE *wær* weir (see WARE 1) + *feld* pasture, open land (see FIELD).

Waring English: from the Norman personal name *Warin*, derived from the Gmc element *war(in)* guard, and used as a short form of various cpd names with this first element (cf., e.g., WARNER 2). The name was popular in France and among the Normans, partly as a result of the fame of the Carolingian lay *Guérin de Montglave*.

Vars.: **Wareing, Warring, Wearing, Werring, W(h)arin, Werren; Guerin** (Ireland, from a central Fr. form; sometimes Gaelicized **Geran**).

Cogns.: Fr.: **Guérin, Guerne, Garin, Garne**. It.: **Guarino, Guarini, Guerino, Guerini** (S Italy); **Garin** (NW Italy); **Varin(i)** (Venetia).

Dims.: Fr.: **Guérineau, Guérinet, Guérinon, Guérinot**. It.: **Guariniello** (Naples).

Aug.: It.: **Guarinoni** (Venetia).

Patrs.: Eng.: **Fitzwarin**. It.: **Gaureschi**.

Wark English (Northumb.) and Scots: habitation name from *Wark* on the river Tweed, which gets its name from OE *(ge)weorc* (earth)works, fortification.

Var.: **Warke**.

Warman English: 1. occupational name for a merchant or trader, from ME *ware* wares, articles of trade (OE *waru*, a collective noun, apparently from the root *war-* guard; cf. WARD 1 and WARING) + *man* man.

2. from the OE personal name *Wǣrmund*, composed of the elements *wǣr* pledge + *mund* protection.

3. Jewish (Ashkenazic): probably an ornamental name from Ger. *wahr* true + *Mann* man.

Warmington English: habitation name from either of two places so called. The one in Warwicks. was originally named in OE as *Wǣrmundingtūn* 'settlement (OE *tūn*) associated with *Wǣrmund*' (see WARMAN 2). That in Northants was *Wyrmingtūn* 'settlement associated with *Wyrm*', a byname meaning 'Serpent', 'Dragon'.

Warne English: habitation name from a place in Devon, first recorded in 1194 as *Wagefen*, apparently from an OE deriv. of *wagian* to shake, quiver (cf. WAGHORN and WAGSTAFF) + *fen* bog, marsh (see FENN).

Vars.: **Warn, Wearne**.

Warner English (Norman): 1. from a Gmc personal name composed of the Gmc elements *war(in)* guard + *heri*, *hari* army, introduced into England by the Normans in the form *Warnier*. See also GARNER.

2. contracted form of *Warrener*; see WARREN 2.

Cogns. (of 1): Fr.: **Garnier, Gasnier, Guernier**; see also VERNIER. It.: **Guarnier(i), Guarniero, Guarneri(o)**; **Varnier(i)** (Venetia). Ger.: **Wern(h)er**; **Wörner, Wörnhör** (Bavaria). Low Ger.: **Warner, Warnherr**.

Dims. (of 1): Fr.: GARNON, **Garnot(el), Garnotin**. It.: **Varnerin(i)** (Venetia). Ger.: **Wer(n)lein, Wernle, We(h)rle, Werndl, We(r)n(t)z, Wertz**; **Wöhrle(in), Wörlin, Wörn(d)le, Wörn(z)** (Bavaria); **Wehrli** (Switzerland). Low Ger.: **Warn(e)(c)ke, Werne(c)ke, Warremann**. Fris.: **Warntje, Wessel(mann)**.

Patrs. (from 1): Low Ger.: **Warn(d)ers**.

Patrs. (from 1) (dims.): Low Ger.: **Warn(ke)s**; **Warnken**; **War-n(ek)ing, Warninck, Wern(ek)ing, Warnkönig**. Fris.: **Warrentjes, Werntjes, Wessels**; **Warntjen, Werntjen**; **Wesseling**.

Warnes English (E Anglia): of uncertain origin. In one modern family of this name there is a tradition that it is of Low Ger. origin, and it is possibly in origin a patr. from a short form of WARNER 1. There was fairly extensive migration from the Low Counties to E Anglia during the Middle Ages in connection with the wool trade.

Warnock Scots: Anglicized form of Gael. **Mac Gille Mheàrnaig** 'son of the servant of (St) *Meàrnag*', a personal name possibly representing a dim. form of *mear* wild, solitary.

Vars.: **Warnoch**; **McGilvernock, McIlvernock, McVarnock**.

Warr English: nickname for a belligerent person or for a valiant soldier, from ANF *werr(e)* war (OF *guerre*, of Gmc origin); for the change of *-er-* to *-ar-*, cf. MARCHANT.

Vars.: **Warre**; **W(h)arrier, Warrior**.

Cogns.: Fr.: **Gu(i)erre, Laguerre**; **Guerrier**. Sp.: **Guerra**; **Guerrero**. Port.: **Guerra**; **Guerreiro**. It.: **Guerra, Guerri**; **Guerrieri, Guerriero**; **Guerreru** (Sicily).

Dims.: Fr.: **Guerreau, Guerrin, Guerry**.

Pej.: It.: **Guerrazzi**.

The American state of Delaware *is named after Thomas West, Baron* de la Warr *(1577–1618), who was governor of Virginia at the time when the region was first explored.*

Warren English: 1. Norman habitation name from *La Varrenne* in Seine-Maritime, so called from a Gaul. element probably descriptive of alluvial land or sandy soil.

2. topographic name for someone who lived by a game-park, or occupational name for someone employed in one, from ANF *warrene* warren, piece of land for breeding game (of uncertain origin, perhaps akin to 1, or to the Gmc element *war(in)-* guard, preserve).

Vars.: Eng.: **Warran(d), Warrant, Warrenne**. (Of 2 only): **Warren(d)er, Warriner**, WARNER.

Cogns. (of 1): Fr.: **Varenne**. (Of 2): Fr.: **Garenne, Lagarenne**; **Gar(e)nier**.

Warrington English: habitation name from the town in Lancs., probably named in OE as *Wæringtun* 'settlement by the weir', from OE *wæring*, a deriv. of *wær* (see WARE 1) + *tūn* settlement.

Warsop English: habitation name from the town of Market *Warsop* in Notts., recorded in Domesday Book as *Wareshope*, from the gen. case of the OE name *Wær* or *Wǣr* + OE *hop* enclosed valley (see HOPE).

Warszawski Polish and Jewish (E Ashkenazic): habitation name from the city of Warsaw (Pol. *Warszawa*), which became the capital of Poland at the end of the 16th cent., after the destruction of Cracow by fire.

Vars.: Pol.: **Warszakowski**. Jewish: **Warszavski, Wars(c)haw(ski), Wars(c)hawsky, Wars(c)havski, Wars(c)havsky**; **Warszawiak, Warshawiak, Warshaviak**; **Warschauer** (a Ger. form); **Warscher** (from W Yid. *varsher* 'native or inhabitant of Warsaw'); **Warschawer, Warszawer** (from E Yid. *varshever* 'native or inhabitant of Warsaw', the *a* in the second syllable being the result of the influence of the Pol. form).

Dim.: Jewish: **Warszawczyk**.

Warth 1. English: habitation name from any of various minor places named with the ON term *varða* beacon (a deriv. of *varða* to guard; cf. WARD 1).

2. German: habitation name from any of various minor places named with an OHG cogn. of this element.

Vars. (of 2): Ger.: **Warthe(r)**.

Many English bearers of the name Warth *are descended from a certain Robert Warth who was buried at Chatteris, Cambs., on 2 January 1616. Others are descended from a certain Bartholomaus Warth (1630–1707), who was mayor of Untertürkheim in Württemberg, some of whose descendants settled in England.*

Warwick English: 1. habitation name from the county town of Warwicks., or regional name from the county itself. The town was originally named as the 'outlying settlement (see WICK) by the weir'; cf. WARRINGTON.

2. habitation name from a much smaller place of the same name in Cumb., so called from OE *waroð* slope, bank + *wīc*.

Vars.: **W(h)arrick**.

Wase 1. Scots and English: var. of WACE.

2. German: topographic name for someone who lived on a patch of reclaimed marshland (which generally provided rich pasture land), MHG *wase* (from OHG *waso* marsh; cf. OE *wāse* mud).

Vars. (of 2): Ger.: **Was(n)er, Wasmer**.

Cogns. (of 2): Swed.: WASS. Jewish (Ashkenazic): **Wasner**.

Washbourne English: 1. habitation name from *Washbourne* in Devon, so called from OE *wæsce* washing (an abstract noun from *wæscan* to wash; cf. WASHER) + *burna* stream (see BOURNE), i.e. stream where washing was done.
2. habitation name from *Washbourne* in Gloucs., so called from OE *wæsse* alluvial land (cf. WASE 2) + *burna*. See also WASHBURN.
Var.: **Washbourn.**

Washbrook English: habitation name from any of various places, for example in Lancs., Somerset, and Suffolk, so called from OE *wæsce* washing + *brōc* BROOK; cf. WASHBOURNE 1.

Washburn N English: topographic name for someone living on the banks of the river *Washburn* in W Yorks., so called from the OE personal name *Walc* + OE *burna* stream (see BOURNE). The river name is first recorded as *Walke(s)burna* in the early 12th cent. There is no evidence of any confusion with the S English name WASHBOURNE, although this is of course possible.
Var.: **Washburne.**

Washer English: occupational name for a laundryman, or for someone who washed raw wool before spinning, from an agent deriv of ME *wasch(en)* to wash (OE *wæscan*). In some cases it may have denoted a man who washed or dipped sheep; some tenants on the manor of Burpham, near Worthing, in Sussex (where the surname is found from an early date), had as part of their feudal service to wash the flocks of their master.
Cogns.: Ger.: **Wascher, Wescher.**

Washington English: habitation name from either of the places so called, in Tyne and Wear and in W Sussex. The latter is from OE *Wassingatūn* 'settlement (OE *tūn*) of the people of *Wassa*', a personal name apparently representing a short form of some cpd name such as *Wāðsige*, composed of the elements *wāð* hunt + *sige* victory. Washington in Tyne and Wear is from OE *Wassingtūn* 'settlement associated with *Wassa*'.
George Washington *(1732–99), first President of the United States (1789–97), was born at Bridges Creek, Virginia. His great-grandfather had settled in the colony after emigrating from Dillicar in Westmorland in 1658, after the family's fortunes had suffered in the English Civil War because of its Royalist sympathies. His earliest recorded ancestor was William de Hertburn, who served the bishop of Durham and who in 1185 was granted the manor of Washington in return for the service of attending the episcopal hunt with four greyhounds. The family lived on the estate for 400 years, but in 1613 it was sold back to the Church.*

Wąsik Polish: nickname for a man with a particularly fine or noticeable moustache, from Pol. *wąs* moustache + *-ik* dim. suffix.
Cogns.: Jewish (E Ashkenazic): **Wons, Vons.**
Patrs.: Pol.: **Wąs(ik)iewicz, Wąsowicz.** Russ.: **Usatchov, Usatych.**
Habitation name: Pol.: **Wąs(ik)owski.**

Wass 1. Scots and English: var. of WACE.
2. Swedish: from Swed. *vass* sharp, keen. This is a 'soldier's name', one of the identifying names adopted by Swed. soldiers in the 17th and 18th cents., before the use of surnames became general in Scandinavia.
3. Swedish: ornamental name from Swed. *vass* reed, marsh (cf. WASE 2), one of the many Swed. surnames derived from vocab. words denoting features of the natural landscape.
Var. (of 2 and 3): VASS.
Cpds (of 3, ornamental): **Wassberg, Vassberg** ('marsh hill').

Wastell English: 1. metonymic occupational name for a baker of fancy breads, from ANF *wastel* cake (mod. Fr. *gâteau*, apparently of Gmc origin).
2. habitation name from *Wasthills* in Worcs., so called from OE *weardsetl* guardhouse.
Vars.: **Wastall, Waistell, Washtell, Wassell, Wassall.** (Of 1 only): **Gastall** (from the central Fr. form).

Water 1. English: var. of WALTER, representing the normal medieval pronunciation of the name.
2. English: topographic name for someone who lived by a stretch of water (OE *wæter*).
3. Irish: Anglicized form of Gael. *Ó Fuarisc(e)*; see FOURISH.
Var.: **Waters** (commonly a patr. from 1 as well as a var. of 2 and 3).
Cogns. (of 2): Ger., Jewish (Ashkenazic): **Wasser.** Flem., Du.: **Van den Water.**
Patrs. (from 1): Eng.: **Wat(t)ers, Warters, Worters; Wat(t)erson; Fitzwater.**

Waterfield English (Norman): habitation name from *Vatierville* in Seine-Maritime, so called from the personal name WALTER + OF *ville* settlement (see VILLE).

Waterhouse English (chiefly Yorks., Lancs., and Midlands): topographic name for someone who lived in a house by a stretch of water.

Waterman 1. English: occupational name for the servant of a bearer of the given name *Wa(l)ter*; see WATER 1.
2. English and Flemish/Dutch: occupational name for a boatman or a water-carrier, or topographic name for someone who lived by a stretch of water; see WATER 2.
3. Jewish (Ashkenazic): Anglicized form of **Wasserman**, occupational surname given to a water-carrier; cf. 2 above.
Cogns. (of 2): Ger. **Wassermann.** Low Ger.: **Watermann.**

Waterton English: habitation name from *Waterston* in Dorset, recorded in the early 13th cent. as *Walterton*, named from the ME personal name *Wa(l)ter* + ME *tone, tune* settlement.
A number of bearers of this name trace their descent from Sir Robert Waterton, who fought in the Crusades in 1191.

Waterworth English (chiefly Lancs.): ostensibly a habitation name from a place deriving its name from OE *wæter* water + *worð* enclosure, but in fact, as McKinley has shown, an occupational name for a water bailiff, earlier **Waterward**, from ME *water* + WARD 1. All the early examples occur on the banks of Martin Mere, a large freshwater lake (now drained) in W Lancs.

Watford English: habitation name from the town in Herts. or from the much smaller one in Northants. Both derive their name from OE *wāð* hunt + *ford* FORD.

Watman 1. English: occupational name for the servant of someone called *Wat(t)*; see WATT.
2. English: from a ME given name, *W(h)atman, Wheteman*, a survival of OE *Hwætmann*, composed of the elements *hwæt* bold, brave + *mann* man.
3. Jewish (Ashkenazic): of unknown origin.
Vars. (of 2): **Wh(e)atman, W(h)eetman.**

Watmough English (chiefly Yorks.): name for someone who was related to a bearer of the given name *Wat(t)*; see WATT. The ME term *maugh, mough* was used of various relatives, normally those connected by marriage rather than by blood.
Vars.: **Whatmough, W(h)atmaugh, W(h)atmuff, Wha(r)tmouth;** WHATMORE.

Watt English and Scots: from an extremely common ME given name, *Wat(t)*, a short form of WALTER.
Dims.: **Watkin(g)**; **Watlin(g)**, **Whatling**.
Patrs.: **Watt(i)s**, **Watson**.
Patrs. (from dims.): **W(h)atkins**, **Watkiss**, **Watkeys**; **Gwatkins** (Wales); **Swatkins** (Gloucs.); **Watkinson** (widespread, but commonest in Lancs. and S Yorks.).

Waugh Scots and N English: of disputed origin. It is most likely from OE (Anglian) *walh* foreign (see WALLACE), perhaps applied originally to the Strathclyde Britons who survived as a separate group in Scotland well into the Middle Ages.

Wavell English (Norman): habitation name from *Vauville* in Calvados and La Manche, both so called from the Gmc personal name *Walo* (see WALE 1) + OF *ville* settlement (see VILLE).
Vars.: **Wevell**, **We(a)vill**.

Way English (chiefly Southern): topographic name for someone who lived near a road or path, OE *weg* (cogn. with ON *vegr*, OHG *weg*), or habitation name from some minor place named with this word.
Vars.: **Waye**, **Whay**, **Wey**, **Waigh**, **Weigh**; **Attaway**, **Byway**, BYTHEWAY, **Bythway**, **Bidaway**.
Cogns.: Ger.: **Wegmann**. Fris.: **Wegstra**. Flem., Du.: **Van de Weg**, **Van der Weghe**, **Van der Wegen**, **Wegman**. Jewish (Ashkenazic): **Wegsman** (perhaps from Yid. *vegsman* traveller); **Wegman** (see also WÄGER).

Weake English: 1. topographic or habitation name, a var. of WICK.
2. nickname for a poor physical specimen, from ME *wayke* weak, feeble (ON *veikr*).
Vars.: **Week**. (Of 1 only): **Week(e)s**, **Wheeker**.

Wear English (Northumb.): 1. topographic name for someone who lived by the N English river of this name. The river name occurs in the form *Vedra* in Ptolemy's *Geographia*. It is probably a Celt. word meaning simply 'water'.
2. topographic name for someone who lived near a dam or weir, a var. of WARE 1.
Vars.: **Weare**, **Wears**.

Wearden English (Lancs.): habitation name from *Worden* in Lancs, so called from OE *wær*, *wer* weir (see WARE 1) + *denu* valley (see DEAN 1).

Wearne English: habitation name from a place so called in Somerset, which gets its name from the river that runs through it. The river name is of Brit. origin, from the element *ver(n)* alder; cf. VER 1.

Weather English: nickname from ME *wether* wether, (castrated) ram (OE *weðer*), denoting a man supposedly resembling a wether in some way, esp. in lacking sexual prowess. In some cases, however, it may be no more than a metonymic occupational name for a shepherd.
Patr.: **Weathers**.

Weatherall English: habitation name from *Wetheral* in Cumb., so called from OE *weðer* wether, ram (see WEATHER) + *halh* nook, recess (see HALE 1).
Vars.: **Wetherall**, **Wetherald**, **We(a)therell**, **Wetheril(l)**, **Weather(h)ill**, **We(a)therilt**, **Weatheritt**, **Weathrall**, **Wealthall**, **Wederell**.

Weatherhead English and Scots: according to Reaney this is an occupational name for a shepherd, from ME *wether* wether, ram (see WEATHER) + *herd* herdsman (see HEARD). His only evidence for this interpretation of the final syllable is alternation in the late 15th cent. between *Weydurherd* and *Wedirhed*. Black quotes numerous later forms that undoubtedly belong to this name; they divide fairly evenly between endings in *-heid* (representing the normal Scots pronunciation of mod. Eng. *head*) and *-at*. He supposes that the name derives from an unidentified minor hill in the former county of Berwicks.
Vars.: **Wetherhead**, **Wethered**.

Weatherley Scots and English: habitation name, probably from *Wedderlie* in the former county of Berwicks., so called from OE *weðer* wether, ram (see WEATHER) + *lēah* wood, clearing.
Var.: **Weatherly**.

Weathersby English: habitation name from *Wetherby* in W Yorks., so called from ON *veðr* wether, ram (cf. WEATHER) + *býr* farm, settlement.
Vars.: **We(a)therby**, **Witherby**, **Wetherbee**.

Weaver English: 1. occupational name, from an agent deriv. of ME *weven* to weave (OE *wefan*); cf. WEBB.
2. habitation name from a place on the river *Weaver* in Ches., now called *Weaver* Hall (recorded simply as *Weuere* in the 13th and 14th cents.). The river name is from OE *wēfer(e)* winding stream.
Var.: **Weafer**.
Cogns. (of 1): Ger.: **We(h)ber**; **Wöber**, **Wober** (Bavaria); **Waber** (Silesia). Low Ger.: **Wever**, **Wefer**. Flem., Du.: **(De) Weber**, **(De) Wever**. Jewish (Ashkenazic): **Web(b)er(man)**, **Webman**, WEBB.
Patrs. (from 1): Eng.: **Weavers**. Low Ger.: **Wewers**, **Wevers**, **We(i)fers**, **Weverinck**. Flem., Du.: **Web(b)ers**, **Wevers**.
Equivs.: Scot.: MCNIDDER. Fr.: TISSIER. Ukr. and Jewish: TKACH.

Webb 1. English: occupational name for a weaver, early ME *webbe*, from OE *webba* (a primary deriv. of *wefan* to weave; cf. WEAVER 1). This word survived into ME long enough to give rise to the surname, but was already obsolescent as an agent noun; hence the secondary forms with the (redundant) agent suffixes -*(st)er*.
2. Jewish (Ashkenazic): Anglicizations of the various Jewish names given at WEAVER.
Vars. (of 1): **Webbe**; **Webber** (chiefly W Country); **Webster** (chiefly Yorks., Lancs., and Midlands). (Of 2): **Web**.
Noah Webster *(1758–1843), the American lexicographer, was born in Hertford, Connecticut, the son of a prosperous landowner descended from one of the founders of the city and the state, John Webster (d. 1661). The latter had emigrated from England to Massachusetts c.1631, and had become governor of Connecticut in 1656.*
Daniel Webster (1782–1852), the American politician and orator, was born in Salisbury, New Hampshire, a descendant of Thomas Webster, a prominent 17th-cent. citizen of Ipswich, Mass., whose family had settled there around 1635, while he was still a child.

Webley English (Gloucs.): of uncertain origin, perhaps a habitation name from *Weobley* in Herefords. (*Webbeley* 1242, *Wibelai* in Domesday Book), in which the first element is probably from a byform, **Weobba* or **Wiobba*, of the attested personal name *Wibba* (of uncertain origin).

Websdale English: of uncertain origin, apparently a habitation name from a place whose name contains as its second element ME DALE. The first element, however, has not been identified.

Wechsler German and Jewish (Ashkenazic): occupational name for a money-changer, Ger. *Wechsler*, an agent deriv.

of Ger. *wechseln* to exchange (MHG *wehseln*, OHG *wehsalōn*).

Vars.: Jewish: **Weksler** (Pol. spelling); **Wexler** (Anglicized spelling); **Vexler**; **Wechselman(n)**, **Wekselman**, **Vexelman**.

Cogns.: Low Ger.: **Wesseler**, **Wissler**.

Cpds (ornamental): Jewish: **Wexelbaum**, **Vexelbaum** ('exchange tree'); **Wechselberg** ('exchange hill'); **Wechselfis(c)h** ('exchange fish').

Wedderburn Scots: habitation name from a place in the former county of Berwicks., so called from OE *weðer* wether, ram (see WEATHER) + *burna* stream (see BOURNE), i.e. probably a place where sheep were washed.

Var.: **Weatherburn**.

The earliest known bearer of this name is Walter de Wederburne, *who is recorded as having sworn an oath of loyalty to Edward I in 1296.*

Wedekind Low German: from a Gmc personal name composed of the elements *widu* wood + *kind* child. The name became famous as that of a Duke of Lower Saxony who was an opponent of Charlemagne, and was consequently popular in N Germany as a given name throughout the Middle Ages.

Vars.: **Widdekind**, **Witekind**, **Wehkind**.

Dims.: **Weck(e)**, **Weckl(e)in**.

Patrs. (from dims.): **Weckes**, **Wecken**, **Wecking**, **Wekking**.

Wedge English: of uncertain origin, possibly from ME *wegge* wedge (OE *wecg*) used as a topographic name for someone who lived on a wedge-shaped (i.e. triangular) piece of land. However, this suggestion must be regarded as extremely doubtful since *wecg* is not recorded as an element in English placenames.

Var.: **Wegg** (Norfolk).

Wedgewood English: apparently a habitation name from an unidentified place, perhaps named with the OE elements *wice* wych elm (see WICH 2) + *wudu* WOOD.

Var.: **Wedgwood**.

The family of pottery makers of this name can trace its descent from Stephen de Wedgewood, *who was living in Brerehurst, Staffs., in 1358. They settled in Burslem, the centre of its industry, in 1612, and the factory at Etruria (so named by Josiah* Wedgwood *in admiration of Etruscan pottery) was established in 1771.*

Weedon English: habitation name from places in Bucks. and Northants, so called from OE *wēoh* pagan temple + *dūn* hill (see DOWN 1).

Var.: **Weeden**.

Weekley English: habitation name from a place in Northants, so called from OE *wīc* settlement (perhaps in this case a Roman *vīcus*; see WICKHAM) + *lēah* wood, clearing.

Var.: **Weekly**.

Weide 1. German: topographic name for someone who lived by a conspicuous willow or by a group of willow trees, from Ger. *Weide* willow (MHG *wīde*, OHG *wīda*; cf. WITHEY, WYTHE).

2. German: topographic name for someone who lived by a patch of pasture land or by a hunting ground, Ger. *Weide* (MHG *weide*, OHG *weida* feeding, grazing, hunting; cf. OE *wāð*).

3. Jewish (Ashkenazic): ornamental name from Ger. *Weide* willow tree.

Vars.: Jewish: **Weid(en)**, **Waide**, **Weid(l)er**, **Weidman(n)**. (Of 2 only): Ger.: **Weidner**, **Weid(t)ler**, **W(e)idmann** (also occupational names for a huntsman).

Cogns. (of 1): Swed.: **Widell**, **Videll**, **Widén**, **Widman**. Low Ger.: **Wiede**, **Wied(e)mann**, **Wiemann**; **Beiderwieden**. Flem.: **Van der Weyden**, **Verweyden**. Du.: **Wei(j)de**, **Van der Weide**, **Verweij**, **Verwey**, **Terweij**, **Terwey**, **Van den Weijden**, **Van den Weyden**.

Dims.: Ger.: **Weidel**, **Weidle**.

Cpds (ornamental): Swed.: **Wid(e)gren** ('willow branch'); **Widerberg** ('willow hill'); **Widholm** ('willow island'); **Widlund** ('willow grove'); **Widmark** ('willow land'); **Widerström** ('willow river'). Jewish: **Weidenbaum**, **Wajdenbaum** ('willow tree'; the second form is a Pol. spelling); **Weidberg** ('willow hill'); **Weidenfeld**, **Waidenfeld** ('willow field'); **Weidhorn** ('willow horn'); **Weidenkopf** ('willow head'); **Weidwasser** ('willow water').

Weiher German: topographic name for someone who lived by a fish pond, Ger. *Weiher* (MHG *wīher*, *wī(w)er*, OHG *wī(w)āri*, from L *vīvārium*, a deriv. of *vivus* alive).

Cogns.: Low Ger.: **Weier**, **Weyer**. Du.: **(De) Weijer**, **(De) Weyer**, **Weijers**, **Van den Weijer**. Fr.: **Vivier**, **Duvivier**. Prov.: **Vivès**. Sp.: **Vivar** (a place in the province of Burgos). Cat.: **Viver(s)**. Port.: **Viveiro**.

Weil 1. German: habitation name from any of various places, in Baden, Württemberg, and Bavaria, so called from L *villa* (see VILLE).

2. Jewish (Ashkenazic): according to Kaganoff, this name was sometimes selected as an anagram of *Lewi*, but there does not seem to be any evidence supporting this conjecture, and it is far more likely that it is a habitation name as in 1, esp. in view of the fact that the vars. ending in *-er* (see below) are clearly habitational.

Vars.: Ger.: **Weill**, **Weile**. Jewish: **Weill**, **Weil(l)er**.

Wein 1. German: metonymic occupational name for a producer or seller of wine, from Ger. *Wein* wine, vine (MHG *wīn*; cf. VINE).

2. Jewish (Ashkenazic): largely an ornamental name, reflecting the prominence of wine in the Jewish Scriptures and its use in several Jewish ceremonies. It has been suggested that the surname has been adopted because of the symbolic association of the vine with the Hebr. personal name ISRAEL ('they shall thoroughly glean the remnant of Israel as a vine', Jer. 6: 9), but since wine is mentioned over nine hundred times in the Jewish Scriptures it is unwise to try to find one passage to explain all the ornamental occurrences of this name.

Vars: Ger.: **Weiner**, **Wei(n)mann**. Jewish: **Weiner(man)**, **Wainer(man)**, **Veiner**, **Vainer(man)**, **Weinman(n)**, **Veinman**, **Wainman**, **Wajner(man)** (occupational, the last being a Pol. spelling); **Weinbren(n)** (occupational name for a distiller; cf. BRENNER 1); **Weinschenk(er)**, **Wainshenker** (occupational names for an innkeeper; cf. SCHENKE); **Weinis(c)h** (an adj. deriv.).

Cogns.: Du.: **De Wijn**, **De Wyn**, **Wijnen**. Pol.: **Winiarski**, **Winiecki**.

Cpds (mostly ornamental): Jewish: **Weinapel**, **Wainapel** ('wine apple'); **Weinbach** ('wine stream'); **Weinbaum**, **Veinbaum**, **Wainbaum**, **Wajnbaum** ('wine tree'); WEINBERG; **Weinblatt**, **Weinblot** ('wine leaf'); **Weinblum** ('wine flower'); **Weinblut** ('wine blood', or perhaps 'wine blossom', from Ger. *Blute*); **Weindorf** ('wine village'); **Weinfeld**, **Wainfeld** ('wine field'); **Waingart(en)**, **Waingarten** ('wine garden' or 'vineyard'); **Weingold** ('wine gold'); **Weingrub** ('wine dig'); **Weinhaus** ('wine house'); **Weinhol(t)z** ('wine wood'); **Weinkeller** ('wine cellar'); **Winekran(t)z** ('wine garland'); **Weinlager** ('wine store'); **Weinpres** ('wine press'); **Weinreb(e)**, **Weinrib**, **Wainryb**, **Wajnryb**, **Weinraub**, **Weinrieber**, **Weinrober**, **Wainrober** ('wine branch'); **Weinrot** ('wine red'); **Weinsaft**, **Wainsaft** ('wine juice'); **Weinshnabel** ('wine snout'); **Weinstein(er)**, **Veinstein**, **Vainstein**, **Wainshtein**, **Wajnsztajn** ('wine stone'); **Weinsto(c)k**, **Weinshtock**, **Wainshtok**, **Wajnsztok** ('grape vine'); **Weint(h)al**, **Waintal**, **Vaintal** ('wine valley'); **Vaynzof** ('wine guzzle', presumably a nickname for a heavy drinker of wine); **Weinzweig** ('wine twig'). Swed.: **Winblad(h)**, **Vinblad(h)** ('vine leaf'); **Winquist** ('vine twig').

Weinberg 1. German: topographic name for someone who lived near a vineyard on a hillside, or occupational name for someone who worked in one, from Ger. *Weinberg* vineyard (MHG *wīnberc*, a cpd of *wīn* vine + *berc* hill; vineyards were normally built on hillsides).

2. Jewish (Ashkenazic): ornamental combination of the elements WEIN + BERG, or topographic or ornamental name as in 1.

Vars.: Jewish: **Weinberger**, **Veinberg**, **Wainberg(er)**, **Vainberg(er)**, **Wajnberg**; **Wijnbergen** (Dutch).

Cogns. (of 1): Du.: **Wijnberg**. Dan., Norw., Swed.: **Win(n)-berg**.

Weinreich Jewish (Ashkenazic): ornamental name, either a combination of the Ger. elements WEIN wine + *Reich* kingdom, or from mod. Ger. *weinreich* abounding in wine, vines, or a modification of Yid. *vayrekh* incense (Ger. *Weihrauch*).

Vars.: **Weinrich**, **Weinrauch**, **Wainrauch**.

Weinschel Jewish (Ashkenazic): ornamental name, from Yid. *vaynshl* sour cherry (a deriv. of *vayn* wine; cf. WEIN).

Vars.: **Weinshel**, **Weinschal(l)**; **Weins(c)helbaum**, **Wajnszelbaum** ('sour cherry tree', the latter form being a Pol. spelling).

Weintraub Jewish (Ashkenazic): ornamental name, representing a Germanized form of Yid. *vayntroyb* grape (Ger. *Weintraub*).

Vars.: **Weintrob**, **Waintraub**, **Waintrob**; **Wajntraub**, **Wajntrob** (Pol. spellings).

Weir 1. English: topographic name for someone who lived by a dam or weir on a river, a var. of WARE 1.

2. Irish: Anglicized form of Gael. *Mac an Mhaoir* 'son of the steward'; see McNAIR.

3. Irish: Anglicized form, based on an erroneous translation (as if from Gael. *core* weir, stepping stones), of various Gael. names such as *Ó Corra* and *Ó Comhraidhe* (see CORR and CORY 2).

4. Scots: according to Black this name is of Norman origin, from various places in Calvados, Manche, Eure-et-Loire, and Orne called *Vere*, from ON *ver* dam, which makes it ultimately cogn. with 1 above. However, cf. VER 1.

Weisselfisch Jewish (E Ashkenazic): either an ornamental name or an anecdotal nickname based on some now irrecoverable event, composed of the Yid. elements *Vaysl* Vistula (the river that flows through Poland) + *fish* fish.

Var.: **Vajselfisz** (Pol. spelling).

Weissgerber German and Jewish (Ashkenazic): occupational name for a dresser of white leather, one whose job was to cure the fine leather from the hide of goats and kids with alum salts; cf. ROTGERBER. The word is a cpd of Ger. *weiss* white + *Gerber* leather-dresser (see GERBER); cf. WHITTIER.

Weiter 1. German: occupational name for a gatherer or seller of woad, from an agent deriv. of MHG, OHG *weit* woad; cf. WADER.

2. Jewish (Ashkenazic): apparently an anecdotal nickname, commemorating some now forgotten incident, from mod. Ger. *weiter* farther, or its Yid. cogn. *vayter*.

Weland Scots: of uncertain origin, apparently from a personal name. According to Black it is a form of VALENTINE, but it seems more likely that it is a var. of Wieland.

Var.: **Welland**.

Welbourne English: habitation name from *Welbourn* in Lincs., *Welborne* in Norfolk, or *Welburn* in N Yorks., all so called from OE *well(a)* spring (see WELL) + *burna* stream (see BOURNE).

Var.: **Welburn**.

Welcome English: 1. habitation name from places in Devon and Warwicks. called *Welcombe*, from OE *well(a)* spring, stream (see WELL) + *cumb* broad, straight valley (see COOMBE).

2. nickname for a well-liked person or one noted for his hospitality, from ME *welcume*, a calque of OF *bienvenu* or ON *velkominn*.

Vars.: **Welcomme**, **Wellcome**.

Weldon English: habitation name from a place in Northants, so called from OE *well(a)* spring, stream (see WELL) + *dūn* hill (see DOWN 1).

Vars.: **Welldon**, **Wel(l)den**.

This name is now also relatively common in Ireland, where it has sometimes been Gaelicized as **de Bhéalatún** *and re-Anglicized as* **Veldon** *and* BELTON.

Welford English: habitation name from any of the places so called, of which there are instances in Berks., Gloucs., Northants, and elsewhere. The first is so called from OE *welig* willow + *ford* FORD; the latter two seem to have the first element *well(a)* spring, stream (see WELL). The surname is now found chiefly on Tyneside.

Welham English: habitation name from any of the places so called, of which there are instances in Leics., Notts., and E Yorks. The first gets its name from OE *well(a)* spring, stream (see WELL) + *hām* homestead; the latter two from the dat. pl. *wellum*, originally used after a preposition.

Vars.: **Wellam**, **Wellum**.

Well English: topographic name for someone who lived near a spring or stream, ME *well(e)* (OE *well(a)*).

Vars.: **Wells**, **Weller**, **Welling(s)**, **Wel(l)man**; WALL, WILL, WOOL.

Cogns.: Low Ger.: **Welle(r)**, **Wellmann**. Du.: **Van (der) Wel(s)**, **Welman**.

Wellesley English: apparently a habitation name from an unidentified place, so called from the gen. case of the OE byname *Wealh* 'Foreigner' (cf. WALE 1) + OE *lēah* wood, clearing.

Wellington English: habitation name from any of the three places so called, in Herts., Shrops., and Somerset. All are considered by Ekwall to have been originally named in OE as *Wēolingatūn* 'settlement (OE *tūn*) of the *Wēolingas*', a tribal name apparently apparently derived from OE *wēoh* (pagan) temple + *lēah* wood, clearing. This origin is disputed, however, and the meaning is actually quite uncertain.

Welton English: habitation name from any of various places, for example in Cumb., Lincs., Northants, and E Yorks., so called from OE *well(a)* spring, stream (see WELL) + *tūn* enclosure, settlement.

Wemyss Scots: habitation name from places in the former counties of Fife and Argylls., so called from OGael. *uaim* cave, with the addition of the ME pl. suffix *-s*. The pronunciation is /wi:mz/.

Vars.: **Weems**, **Wemes**.

Wendt German: name for a Wend, MHG *wind(e)* (OHG *winida*, of unknown origin). The Wends once occupied a large area of NE Germany, and many Ger. placenames and surnames are of Wendish origin. Their Slav. language is still spoken in the SE part of E Germany, around Bautzen and Cottbus.

Vars.: **Wend(e)**, WIND; **Wendisch**; **Windisch** (the name of an Austrian noble family, also sometimes adopted by Ashkenazic Jews); **Winsch**, **Wündisch**, **Wünsch(e)**; **Wentscher**, **Wintscher**, **Wünscher**; **Win(di)schmann**, **Wünschmann**; **Wendland(t)**, **Wendländer**.

Cogns.: Czech: **Vindiš, Vinš**.

Wenham English: habitation name from places so called in Suffolk and Sussex, both of which seem to have as their first element OE *wenn* tumour, used of a tumulus or hill. The former is probably 'homestead (OE *hām*) by a hill', the latter 'watermeadow (OE *hamm*) with tumuli'.

Wenig German and Jewish (Ashkenazic): nickname for a small or insignificant man, from Ger. *wenig* little or, in the case of the Ger. name, from MHG *wēnec*, *weinec* puny, pitiable (OHG *wēnag*, *weinag*, from *weinōn* to weep).

Var.: **Weniger** (an inflected form).

Went English: topographic name for someone who lived by a road or path, ME *went* (a deriv. of OE *wendan* to turn).

Var.: **Whent**.

Wentworth English: habitation name from places in Cambs. and S Yorks., probably so called from the OE byname *Wintra* 'WINTER' + OE *worð* enclosure (see WORTH). It is, however, also possible that the name referred to a settlement inhabited only in winter; cf. WINTERBOTTOM and SOMERSCALES.

William Wentworth *(1793–1872), known as 'the Australian patriot' because of his advocacy of Australian self-government, was a lawyer and proprietor of the newspaper* The Australian. *His mother had been transported in 1788 (for stealing clothes) and had travelled on the same ship as his father, D'Arcy Wentworth (?1762–1827). The latter was a physician who had been tried but acquitted on charges of highway robbery. He nevertheless took passage to Botany Bay, where he played a leading role in the development of New South Wales. He was born near Portadown in Ireland; the Irish Wentworths had been established in the reign of Charles II by the Irish agent to Wentworth Dillon, 4th Earl of Roscommon; they had owned land at Fyanstown Castle, Co. Meath, but had declined in prosperity by the 18th cent. Their further ancestry has been traced to Robert Wentworth of Woodhouse in Yorks., living in the 13th cent.*

Wenzel German (of Slav. origin): from the given name *Wenzel*, a dim. (with the Ger. dim. suffix *-el*) of the MHG given name *Wenze*, a borrowing from Slavic representing a short form of the OCzech personal name *Vęceslav* (see VÁCLAV); the borrowing took place before Czech lost its nasal vowels.

Vars.: **Wentzel**, **Wanzel**, **Fenzl(ein)**; **Wetzel**, **Wötzel**, **Wätzold**; **Wen(t)zke**, **Wen(t)zig**, **Wetz(ig)**.

Cogn.: Czech: **Vencl** (Czech spelling of the Ger. name, which is in turn derived from Czech).

Dims.: Ger.: **Wenz**, **Wach(e)**, **Fach(e)**, **Fech(e)**. Czech: **Venclík**; **Venc**.

Patrs.: Ger.: **Wen(t)zler**; **Fech(t)ner**, **Fechler**.

Wepner German: occupational name for a maker or seller of offensive and defensive weaponry, or for an armed official or a shield-bearer, from an agent deriv. of MHG *wāpen* weapon, shield (a borrowing from Low Ger., used alongside the original High Ger. byform *wāfen*).

Vars.: **Weppner**, **Weppler**.

Werf, Van der Dutch: topographic name for someone who lived by a wharf, MDu. *werf* (cf. OE *hwearf*; in mod. Du. the word means 'shipyard').

Var.: **Van der Werff**.

Werth 1. German: topographic name for someone who lived on an island in a river, or on a riverbank, or on a patch of dry land in a fen, all of which were senses of the MHG term *wert*, *werder* (OHG *werid* island, a cogn. of OE *waroð* shore, bank, apparently from the Gmc root *war-* guard).

2. English: var. of WORTH.

Vars. (of 1): **Werder**.

Wertheim Jewish (W Ashkenazic): habitation name from a place on the Main, so called from OHG *werid* island (see WERTH) + *heim* homestead.

Vars.: **Werthajm** (Pol. spelling); **Wertheimer**, **Werthaimer**, **Werthammer**.

Wesker 1. Scots: var. of WISHART.

2. English: topographic name for someone who lived on a patch of damp land to the west of a settlement, from ME *west* WEST + *kerr* marshland (see KERR). The name has also been adopted as a Jewish surname.

Wesley English: habitation name from any of various places named with the OE elements *west* WEST + *lēah* wood, clearing, as for example *Westley* in Cambs. and Suffolk, and *Westleigh* in Devon and Greater Manchester.

Vars.: **Westl(e)y**.

West English and German: topographic name for someone who lived to the west of a settlement, or regional name for one who had migrated from further west, from ME, MHG *west* west.

Vars.: Eng.: **Western**, **Westren**, **Westron** (from the OE adj. *westerne*); **Westman**, **Wester**; **Westerman** (chiefly Yorks.). Ger.: **Weste(r)**, **Westermann**, **West(erl)ing**.

Cogns.: Low Ger.: **Thorwest(en)**, **Zurwesten** (with fused preposition and article, 'to the west'). Fris.: **Westra**. Flem., Du.: **Van West(en)**, **Wester(man)**, **Westerink**. Dan., Norw.: **West(h)**, **Vest(er)**. Swed.: **Wester**, **Westin**, **West(er)man**, **Westling**. Jewish (Ashkenazic): **Westman**.

Cpds (mostly ornamental elaborations rather than habitation names): Swed.: **West(er)berg** ('western hill'); **Westerdahl** ('western valley'); **Westergren** ('western branch'); **West(er)holm** ('western island'); **Westerlind** ('western lime'); **West(er)lund** ('western grove'); **Westermark** ('western land').

Westbrook English: habitation name from any of various places, for example in Berks., Kent, and the Isle of Wight, so called from OE *west* WEST + *brōc* BROOK.

Vars.: **Westbrooke**, **Westbrock**.

Westbury English: habitation name from any of various places, for example in Bucks., Gloucs., Hants, Shrops., Somerset, and Wilts., so called from OE *west* WEST + *burh* fortress, town (see BURY).

Westby English: habitation name from any of various places, for example in Lancs., Lincs., and W Yorks., so called from ON *vestr* WEST + *býr* settlement.

Westcott English: habitation name from any of various minor places, for example *Westcott* in Surrey and Berks., named with the OE elements *west* WEST + *cot* cottage, shelter (see COATES).

Vars.: **Westcot** (another place in Berks.), **Westacott**, **Westicott**, **Wescot(t)**, **Weskett**, **Waistcoat**; **Westcote** (places in Gloucs., Hants, and Warwicks.), **Westcoate**.

Westgate English: 1. topographic name for someone who lived by the west gate of a city, from ME *west* WEST + *gate*

Gate. From the present-day distribution of the surname, the city in question in many if not all cases was probably Norwich.

2. habitation name from any of various places, for example in Co. Durham, Kent, and Northumb., named with these elements.

Westhead English (Lancs.): habitation name from a minor place near Ormskirk, Lancs., presumably so called from ME *west* West + *heved* headland (see Head 2).

Westhuizen, van der Dutch: habitation name from places in the provinces of Gelderland and Overijssel, so called from the MDu. elements *west* West + *huis* House.

Westlake English: topographic name for someone who lived to the west of a streamlet, from ME *by weste lake* (see Lake). The place of this name in Devon derives from the surname, rather than the other way about.

Var.: **Weslake**.

Westmorland N English: regional name for someone from the former county of this name, originally named in OE as *Westmōringaland* 'territory of the people living west of the moors' (i.e. the Pennines).

Var.: **Westmoreland**.

Weston English and Scots: habitation name from any of the very many places so called, from OE *west* West + *tūn* enclosure, settlement. In some cases (see below), it may be from the Leics. or Middlesex villages called *Whetstone* or the Derbys. village of *Wheston*, all of which are so called from OE *hwetstān* whetstone. This supposition is supported by forms of the Leics. placename recorded in the 13th and 14th cents., although in Domesday Book it is called *Westham*.

Var.: **Wesson** (Midlands).

Most bearers of the name Wesson *seem to come originally from Leics. The first occurrence of this assimilated form is in 1626, when the parish register for Burton Overy records the baptism of Theophilus, son of Nathaniel Wesson, but this spelling did not become firmly established until the late 18th cent. The Burton Overy family can probably trace its descent to Peter* de Weston, *who was living in the neighbouring village of Carlton Curlieu in 1278 and probably came originally from* Whetstone, *Leics. (see above).*

Westray 1. English: regional name for someone who migrated from the west, from the ANF adj. *westreis*.

2. Scots: local name from one of the islands in the Orkneys, so called from ON *vestr* west + *ey* island.

Westrop English: probably a habitation name from *Westrip* in Gloucs. or *Westrop* in Wilts., both originally named with ME *west* West + *thorp*, *throp* village (see Thorpe). However, see also below.

This is the name of a family established in Ireland by Montifort Westrop *in 1657. One of its earliest recorded ancestors is Nicholas* de Westhorp, *who was living in Lincs. in the 13th cent. This suggests origin from* Westhorpe *in nearby Notts., which has ON* þorp *as its final element.*

Westwood English and Scots: habitation name from any of various places so called, from OE *west* West + *wudu* Wood.

Wettin German: the noble family of this name (see Windsor) trace their descent from Burkhard, Count in the Grabfeld (d. 908). The castle of *Wettin*, on the river Saale near Halle, was acquired by his descendants in the 11th cent., but sold to the Archbishop of Magdeburg in 1288.

Wetton English: habitation name from a place in Staffs., so called from OE *wēt* wet + *dūn* hill (see Down 1).

Wężyk Polish: unflattering nickname from a dim. of Pol. *wąż* snake, applied presumably to an astute, cunning, or untrustworthy person.

Var.: **Wąż**.

Whale English: nickname for a large, ungainly person, from ME *hwal* whale (OE *hwæl*).

Var.: **Whall**.

Patr.: **Whales**.

Whalley English: habitation name from *Whalley* in Lancs. or *Whaley* in Derbys., both so called from OE *hwealf* vault, arch, hill + *lēah* wood, clearing. In some cases it may also be from *Waley* in Ches., which has as its first element OE *weg* path, road (see Way).

Vars.: **Whaley**, **Wal(l)ey**.

Wharmby English (E Midlands): habitation name from *Quarmby* in W Yorks., recorded in Domesday Book as *Cornebi*, apparently from ON *kvern* handmill + *býr* farm, settlement.

Var.: **Quarmby**.

Wharton English: habitation name from any of various places so called. Examples in Ches. and Herefords. are from an OE river name *Wæfer* (derived from *wæfre* wandering, winding) + OE *tūn* settlement; another in Lincs. has as its first element OE *wearde* beacon or *waroð* shore, bank; one in the former county of Westmorland (now in Cumb.) is from OE *hwearf* wharf, embankment + *tūn*.

Whatmore English: 1. var. of Watmough.

2. habitation name from *Whatmoor* in Shrops., apparently so called from OE *wēt* wet + *mōr* marsh.

Vars.: **Watmore**, **W(h)atmoor**.

Wheat English (chiefly Notts.): metonymic occupational name for a grower or seller of wheat, from OE *hwǣte* wheat (a deriv. of *hwīt* white, because of its use in making white flour).

Vars.: **W(h)eate**, **Whate**, **Weet**.

Cogns.: Ger.: **Weitz(mann)**, **Weitzner**. Jewish (Ashkenazic): **Weitz(ner)**, **Wei(t)zman(n)**, **Weitzhändler**, **Weitzhendler** (all occupational).

Cpds: Jewish (ornamental, possibly adopted by or assigned to millers or bakers): **Weitzberg** ('wheat hill'); **Weitzfeld** ('wheat field').

Wheatcroft English: habitation name from some place so called from OE *hwǣte* Wheat + *croft* paddock, smallholding (see Croft). There is one such place in Derbys.; the surname is most common in Notts.

Var.: **Whitcroft**.

Wheatley English: habitation name from any of various places, for example in Essex, Lancs., Notts., Oxon., and W Yorks., so called from OE *hwǣte* Wheat + *lēah* wood, clearing.

Vars.: **Wheatly**, **Wheatleigh**; **Whately** (a place in Warwicks.), **Whateley**; **Whatley** (a place in Somerset), **Whatly**, **Watley**.

Wheaton English: of uncertain origin, apparently a habitation name, perhaps from an unidentified place named with the OE elements *hwǣte* Wheat + *tūn* enclosure, settlement.

Wheel English: from ME *whele* wheel (OE *hwēol*, *hweowol*), generally no doubt a metonymic occupational name for a maker of wheels (cf. Wheeler), but perhaps occasionally a topographic name for someone who lived near a water-wheel.

Vars.: **Wheele**, **Wheels**, **Wheal(e)**, **Wheals**, **While**, **Whewell**.

Cogn.: Flem., Du.: **Wieleman**.

Wheeldon English: habitation name from *Wheeldon* in Derbys. or *Whielden* in Bucks. The former is so called from OE *hwēol* WHEEL (referring perhaps to a rounded shape) + *dūn* hill (see DOWN 1), the latter from *hwēol* + *denu* valley (see DEAN 1).

Vars.: **Wh(i)eldon, W(he)ildon, Wheelden.**

Wheeler English: occupational name for a maker of wheels (for vehicles or for use in spinning or various other manufacturing processes), from an agent deriv. of ME *whele* WHEEL.

Vars.: **Wheeller, Whe(al)ler, Whaler, Wailer, Wayler, W(h)iler, Wyler; Wheelwright** (see WRIGHT); **W(h)ilesmith** (see SMITH).

Equivs.: Low Ger. and Du.: RADEMAKER. Pol.: KOŁODZIEJ.

The name Wheeler *is particularly common on the Isle of Wight; on the mainland it is concentrated in the neighbouring region of central S England. It is fairly evenly distributed over the rest of S England, but much less common in the North.*

Wheelhouse English (Yorks. and E Midlands): habitation name, composed of the ME elements *whele* WHEEL + *hous* HOUSE. According to Reaney, the reference is often to a house near a dammed-up stream where a cutler ground his knives on a small water-wheel. The cpd is not attested as a vocab. word in this or any other sense before the 19th cent, although the surname William *de Whelehous* is found in 1379.

Whelan Irish: Anglicized form of Gael. **Ó Faoláin** 'descendant of *Faolán*', a personal name representing a dim. of *faol* wolf.

Vars.: **Wheelan, Whelehan, O'Whealane, (O')Whalen; O'-F(e)olane, (O')Fylan; O'Phelane, Phelan, Philan; Heelan;** WOLF.

Whipp English: of uncertain origin, perhaps a metonymic occupational name for someone who carried out judicial floggings, from ME *whip* (probably of Low Ger. origin, from a Gmc root indicating quick movement).

Whipple English: of uncertain origin, perhaps a topographic name for someone who lived by a whipple tree. Chaucer lists the *whippletree* together with the maple, thorn, beech, hazel, and yew; the word apparently denotes the cornel tree, and is a cogn. of MLG *wipelbōm*.

William Whipple *(1730–85) was one of those who signed the American Declaration of Independence. He was born in Kittery, Maine, descended from an Englishman, Matthew Whipple, who had settled in America before 1638.*

Whistler English: occupational name for a player on a pipe or flute, from an agent deriv. of ME *whistle* (OE *hwistle*, of imitative origin). Alternatively, it may be a nickname for someone noted for his habit of whistling cheerfully.

Var.: **Wissler.**

Whiston English: habitation name from any of various places so called. Examples in Lancs. and W Yorks. are named from OE *hwīt* white + *stān* stone, while one in Staffs. is from the gen. case of the OE byname *Hwīt* 'White' + OE *tūn* enclosure, settlement. Another place of the same name, in Northants, was probably named as the settlement associated with *Hwicce*, an OE personal name from the tribal name *Hwicce*.

Whitbread English: metonymic occupational name for a baker of the finer sorts of bread, from ME *whit* WHITE or *whete* WHEAT + *bred* bread (OE *brēad*). For the confusion between the two first elements, cf. WHITTAKER.

A number of bearers of this name trace their descent from Roger Wytbred, *recorded in Gravenhurst, Beds., in 1254. His name is also found in the ANF form* Blaunpayne *(cf.* BLANC *and* PAIN 2*).*

Whitby English: habitation name from the port in N Yorks., so called from ON *hvítr* white + *býr* farm, settlement, or from a place of the same name in Ches., originally named with OE *hwīt* white (i.e. stone-built) + *burh* manor-house, fortified place.

Whitchurch English: habitation name from any of several places so named from having a 'white' church, i.e. one built of stone.

Whitcombe English: habitation name from any of various places so called, for example in Dorset and the Isle of Wight. The former means 'wide valley' (see WITCOMB), the latter 'white valley', from OE *hwīt* + *cumb*.

Vars.: **Whitcomb** (used in S Fermanagh as an Anglicized form of Gael. *Mac Thighearnáin* (see TIERNEY), perhaps because the contracted form *Kiernáin* was associated with *cíor* comb); **Witcomb(e).**

White English, Scots, and Irish: nickname for someone with white hair or an unnaturally pale complexion, from ME *whit* white (OE *hwīt*). In some cases it may represent the ME use as a given name of an OE byname, *Hwīt(a)*, of this origin. As a Sc. and Ir. surname it has been widely used as a translation of various Gael. names derived from the elements *bán* white (see BAIN 1) or *fionn* fair (see FINN 1). There has also been some confusion with WIGHT. It has also been adopted by Ashkenazic Jews as an Anglicization of any of the various Jewish surnames listed below.

Vars.: **Whyte** (esp. Sc. and Ir.); **Whitt(e)** (Notts.), **Witt(e).**

Cogns.: Ger.: **Weiss(e), Weisser(t); Wyss** (Switzerland); **Weissmann.** Low Ger.: **Witt(e).** Flem., Du.: **(De) Witt(e), De Wit.** Dan., Norw.: **Hvid(t).** Pol.: **Wajs, Wajsowski.** Jewish (Ashkenazic): **Weiss(e), Waiss, Weisz; Veisser, Vajser; Weis(man), Veis(man), Vais(man), Wajs(man), Weissman(n), Wais(s)man.**

Dims.: Low Ger.: **Wittke, Wittje, Wittgen.** Pol.: **Wajsczyk.**

Patrs.: Eng.: **Whit(e)ing, W(h)itting; Whites, Witts; Whit(e)son, Whitsun** (chiefly Sc.). Low Ger.: **Witten, Witting.**

Patr. (from a dim.): Low Ger.: **Wittgens.**

Cpds (mostly ornamental elaborations): Jewish: **Weissadler** ('whie eagle'); **Weissbaum, Weisbom, Waissbaum, Wajsbaum** ('white tree'); **Weissbecher** ('white goblet'); **Weis(s)becker, Wajsbecker** (occupational name from Ger. *Weissbäcker* fancy baker); **Weis(s)bein, Veisbein** ('white bone'); **Weis(s)berg(er), Wajsberg, Waysberg, Weiszberger** ('white hill'); **Weissblat(t), Weisblat, Waisblat** ('white leaf'); **Weissblech** ('white tin'); **Weis(s)blum, Weissbloom** (white flower'); **Weissbluth** ('white blossom'); **Weis(s)brem** ('white eyebrow); **Weissbrod, Weisbrod(t), Waisbrot, Waysbrot** ('white bread', occupational name for a baker); **Weissbrun** ('white brown'); **Weis(s)buch, Veisbuch** ('white book', or perhaps from mod. Ger. *Weissbuche* hornbeam); **Weissburg** ('white town'); **Weis(s)feld, Vaisfeld, Wajsfeld** ('white field', partly Anglicized as **Weisfield**); **Weis(s)fisch** ('white fish'); **Wajsfogiel** ('white bird'); **Weisgarten** ('white garden'); **Weis(s)glas, Weisglass, Wajsglus** ('white glass'); **Wajsgras** ('white grass'); **Weishaus** ('white house'); **Weisshaut** ('white skin'); **Weisshof, Wajshof** ('white court'); **Weisskirch** ('white church'); **Weis(s)kopf, Weiszkopf** ('white head'); **Weissmel, Wajsmehl** ('white flour'); **Weisrosen** ('white roses'); **Weissalz** ('white salt'); **Waissztein** ('white stone'); **Weistuch, Waistuch** ('white cloth'); **Weiswasser** ('white water'); **Waiswohl** ('white wool', or perhaps from Yid. *veys voyl* knows well).

Peregrine White *(1620–1704) was born in Cape Cod Harbour on board the* Mayflower, *thus becoming the first child of English descent to be born in New England.*

John White who settled in Cambridge, Mass., in 1632 and who was later one of the founders of Hartford, Conn., is the ancestor of a noted American family, including the architect Stanford White (1853–1906).

Whitecross Scots: habitation name from any of various minor places that get their names from a cross of white stone, perhaps principally *Whitecross* in the parish of Chapel in the former county of Aberdeens.

Whiteford Scots: habitation name from a place named with the elements WHITE + FORD, in most cases apparently from *Whitefoord* near Paisley, outside Glasgow.

Whitehead 1. English and Scots: nickname for someone with fair or prematurely white hair, from ME *whit* WHITE + *heved* HEAD.
2. Irish (Connacht): erroneous translation of CANAVAN, as if it were from Gael. *ceann* head + *bán* white.
Var.: **Whytehead**.

Whitehorn Scots: habitation name from *Whithorn* near Wigtown, so called from OE *hwīt* WHITE + *ærn* house. The settlement is said to have been established in the 5th cent. by St Ninian, and named from the white stone church built by him.
Vars.: **Whitehorne, Whithorn**.

Whitehouse English (widespread, but especially common in the W Midlands): topographic name for someone who lived in a white house, from ME *whit* WHITE + *hous* HOUSE, or habitation name from a place named with these elements, as for example *Whittus* in Cumb.
Vars.: **Whithous, Whitters**.

Whitelaw Scots and N English: habitation name from any of various places in the Borders so called, from OE *hwīt* WHITE + *hlāw* hill (see LAW 2).
Vars.: **Whitlaw, Whyt(e)law**.

Whiteley English (chiefly Yorks.): habitation name from any of various places, mostly now spelled *Whitley*, named with the OE elements *hwīt* WHITE + *lēah* wood, clearing.
Vars.: **Whitely, Whit(t)ley, Whit(t)la, Witley**.

Whiter English: occupational name for a bleacher or a whitewasher, from an agent deriv. of ME *whit* WHITE.
Vars.: **Whitter** (Lancs.), **Whitta**.

Whiteside English (Lancs.) and Scots (also N Ireland): probably a habitation name from any of various minor places so called, from OE *hwīt* WHITE + *sīde* slope of a hill. Reaney, however, quotes early forms without prepositions and derives the surname from a nickname.
Var.: **Whitesides**.

Whitfield English: habitation name from any of various places, for example in Derbys., Kent, Northants, and Northumb., so called from OE *hwīt* WHITE + *feld* pasture, open country (see FIELD), because of their chalky soil.
Var.: **Whitefield** (places in Lancs. and the Isle of Wight).

Whitford English: habitation name from a place in Devon, so called from OE *hwīt* WHITE + *ford* FORD, or possibly also from some other place similarly named.

Whitgift English: habitation name from a place in Humberside, so called from the ON byname *Hvíti* 'White' + ON *gipt* gift, dowry.

Whitlam English: nickname for an inoffensive individual, from ME *whit* WHITE + *lam* LAMB. Some examples may be house names from houses marked with such a sign, in origin a reference to the paschal lamb.
Vars.: **Whitelam, Whit(e)lum**.

Whitlock English: 1. nickname for someone with white or fair hair, from ME *whit* WHITE + *lock* tress, curl; cf. SHERLOCK.
2. from an OE personal name composed of the elements *wiht* creature, demon + *lāc* play, sport.
Vars. (of 1): **Whitelock(e)**.

Whitman English: from ME *whit* white + *man* man, either a nickname with the same sense as WHITE, or else an occupational name for a servant of a bearer of the nickname WHITE.
Vars.: **Whiteman, Wittman**.
The American poet Walt Whitman *(1819–92) was descended from Joseph Whitman, who had settled in Stratford, Conn., from England around 1660.*

Whitmarsh English: habitation name from a place in the parish of Sedgehill, Wilts., so called from OE *hwīt* WHITE (i.e. phosphorescent) + *mersc* MARSH; cf. WHITMORE.

Whitmore English: 1. habitation name from any of various places, for example in Staffs., so called from OE *hwīt* WHITE + *mōr* moor (see MOORE 1).
2. in some cases, bearers of the name are apparently descended from John of *Whytenmere*, Shrops., who lived in the 13th cent. This form may represent a poor spelling for *Whittimere* on the Staffs.-Shrops. border, the name of which perhaps means 'pool associated with someone called *Hwīta*'.
Vars. (of 1): **Whitemore; Whittemore, Whit(t)amore, Whittimore, Wittamore** (Devon forms, probably from *Whitmoor* in that county). (Of 2): **Whitmer**.

Whitney English: habitation name from a place in Herefords., the etymology of which is uncertain. The second element is OE *ēg* island, low-lying land; the first appears to be *hwītan*, which is either the gen. sing. of an OE byname *Hwīta* 'White', or the weak dat. case (originally used after a preposition and article) of the adj. *hwīt* white.
A prominent American family of this name are descended from John Whitney, *who emigrated from England to Watertown, Mass., in 1635.*

Whittaker English: habitation name from any of various places named from OE *hwīt* WHITE or *hwǣte* WHEAT + *æcer* cultivated land (see ACKER), as for example *Whitaker* in Lancs. and *Whitacre* in Warwicks. (both 'white field') or *Whiteacre* in Kent and *Wheatacre* in Norfolk (both 'wheat field').
Vars.: **Whit(e)aker; Whitticase**.

Whittier English: occupational name for a white-leather dresser, from ME *whit* WHITE + *taw(i)er* TAWYER (cf. WEISSGERBER).
Vars.: **Whit(t)ear, Whit(c)hair, Whithear**.

Whittingham English and Scots: habitation name from places in Lancs., Northumb., and the former county of E Lothian, originally named in OE as *Hwītingahām* 'homestead (OE *hām*) of the people of *Hwīta*', a byname meaning 'WHITE'.

Whittington English: habitation name from any of a large number of places so called, for example in Gloucs., Worcs., Warwicks., Shrops., Staffs., Derbys., Lancs., and Northumb. The placename could mean '*Hwīta*'s settlement' (OE *Hwītantūn*), 'settlement associated with *Hwīta*' (OE *Hwītingtūn*), or '(at the) white settlement' (OE (*æt ðǣm*) *hwītan tūne*).
Var.: **Whitington**.
Dick Whittington *is still the subject of English pantomime, but he was in fact a historical figure. He was an English merchant who was three times Lord Mayor of London. His wealth and position were partly the result of favourable loans to Henry IV and Henry V.*

He was the son of a knight from Gloucester, where the family held land into the 20th cent.

Whittle English (chiefly Lancs.): 1. habitation name from any of various places, especially one in Lancs., so called from OE *hwīt* WHITE + *hyll* HILL.
2. var. of WHITWELL.

Whitton Scots and English: habitation name from any of various places, for example in the former county of Roxburghs., Co. Durham, Northumb., Shrops., Suffolk, and SW London, so called from the OE byname *Hwīta* 'WHITE' (or the adj. *hwīt* white) + OE *tūn* enclosure, settlement.

Whitty English: of uncertain origin, possibly: 1. habitation name from an unidentified place named with the OE elements *hwīt* WHITE + *(ge)hæg* enclosure (see HAY 1).
2. nickname for someone with unusually pale eyes, from ME *whit* WHITE + *eye* eye (OE *ēaga*).
Vars.: **Whit(t)ey, Whitie.**

Whitwell English: habitation name from any of various places, for example in Dorset, Herts., Leics. (formerly Rutland), Norfolk, and N Yorks., so called from OE *hwīt* WHITE + *well(a)* spring, stream (see WELL).
Vars.: **Whit(t)ell,** WHITTLE.

Whitworth English: habitation name from any of several places so called, from the OE byname *Hwīta* 'WHITE' (or the adj. *hwīt* white) + OE *worð* enclosure (see WORTH). The chief places of this name are in Co. Durham and Lancs., but the surname is fairly evenly distributed throughout N England and the Midlands.

Whybrow English: from the ME female given name *Wyburgh*, OE *Wīgburh*, composed of the elements *wīg* war + *burh* fortress.
Vars.: **Whybro, Wybrow, Wibrow, Wibroe.**

Wich 1. English: topographic or habitation name, from a palatalized form of OE *wīc*; see WICK.
2. English: topographic name for someone who lived by a wych elm tree, OE *wice*.
3. Polish: from the given name *Wich*, shortened form of the given names *Wincenty* (see VINCENT) and *Węcesław* (see VÁCLAV).
Vars. (of 1 and 2): **Wych, Wee(t)ch.** (Of 3): **Wichan; Wiech.**

Wick English: topographic name for someone who lived in an outlying settlement dependent on a larger village, OE *wīc* (L *vīcus*; cf. VICO 1), or habitation name from a place named with this word, of which there are examples in Berks., Gloucs., Somerset, and Worcs. The term seems to have been used especially of an outlying dairy farm or a salt works.
Vars.: **Whick, Wi(c)ke, Wyke,** WEAKE; **Wick(e)s, Wix, Wykes; Wicken(s), Wickins** (from the OE dat. pl. *wīcum*, with the addition of the ME pl. suffix *-s*); **W(h)icker, W(h)ickman; Att(w)ick.**
Cogns.: Ger.: **Wieck.** Flem.: **(Van) Wyck, Wyckman.** Du.: **(Van) Wijk.**

Wickham English: habitation name from any of various places so called, for example in Cambs., Suffolk, Essex, Herts., Kent, Hants, Berks., and Oxon. It has been established that *wīchām* was an OE term for a settlement (OE *hām*) associated with a Romano-British town, *wīc* in this case being an adaptation of L *vīcus*. Childs *Wickham* in Gloucs. bears a British name with a different etymology.
Vars.: **Wykeham; Wigham** (Northumb. and Scotland).

The surname is now also common in Ireland (esp. Co. Wexford), where it was taken by followers of Cromwell; it also occurs there in the form **Wycomb.**

Widdow English: nickname for a widow or widower, both described in ME by the term *widow(e)* (OE *widewe* fem., *widewa* masc.).
Cogns.: Ger.: **Wittwer, Witt(i)ber** (masc.). Low Ger.: **Wedewer, Wettwer** (masc.). Flem., Du.: **De Weduwe, De Vieuw** (masc.). It.: **Vedo(v)a** (fem.); **Vedovato, Vedovati.** Pol.: **Wdowiak** (masc.).
Dims.: It.: **Vedovelli, Vedovetto, Vedovotto.** Pol.: **Wdowczak.** Ukr.: **Udov(ich)enko, Vdovenko.** Beloruss.: **Udovchik.**
Metrs. (or patrs.): Eng.: **Widdow(e)s, Widders, Widdess, Widdas; Wid(d)owson, Widde(r)son, Widdison.** It. (metr. only): **Della Vedova.** Russ. (metr. only): **Vdovin.**

Widdrington English (Northumb.): habitation name from a place in Northumb., so called from OE *Wuduheringatūn* 'settlement (OE *tūn*) of the people of *Wuduhere*', a personal name composed of the elements *wudu* wood + *here* army.

Wieczorek Polish: nickname for someone supposedly resembling a bat, from Pol. dial. *wieczorek* bat, dim. of *wieczor* evening (cogn. with Czech (Moravian) *večeřek*, dim. of *večer* evening).
Cogns.: Czech: **Večeřek, Večerka.**
Patr.: Pol.: **Wieczorkiewicz.**
Habitation name: Pol.: **Wieczorkowski.**

Wieland 1. German: from a Gmc personal name composed of the elements *wīg* war + *land* land, territory. This name was borne by the supernaturally skilled smith of Gmc folk legend, and for this reason it may in part have been given as a nickname to smiths.
2. Jewish (Ashkenazic): presumably an adoption of the Ger. surname.
Var.: **Weiland.**

Wien German and Jewish (Ashkenazic): habitation name from the city of Vienna (Ger. *Wien*, Yid. *Vin*). The placename is first recorded in the L form *Vindobona*, and is of Celt. origin. Before the Holocaust there was a large Jewish population in Vienna; from the 17th cent. onwards the Leopoldstadt district was officially designated as a Jewish quarter, and many families bearing this surname no doubt originated there.
Var.: **Wiener.**

Wierzbicki Polish: habitation name from *Wierzbica*, a town in Poland S of Radom (the name of which is derived from Pol. *wierzba* willow; cf. Czech VRBA), or topographic name for someone who lived among willow trees.
Var.: **Wierzbowski.**

Wiese German: topographic name for someone who lived by a patch of meadowland, Ger. *Wiese* (MHG *wise*, OHG *wisa*).
Vars.: **Wieser, Wies(e)ner, Wiesemann.**
Cogns.: Low Ger.: **Interwies.** Jewish (Ashkenazic): **Wiesner; Wiesen** (possibly ornamental; cf. the cpds below).
Cpds (ornamental): Jewish: **Wiesenberg** ('meadow hill'); **Wiesenfeld** ('meadow field'); **Wiesengrund** ('meadow ground'); **Wiesenthal** ('meadow valley'); **Wiesenstern** ('meadow star').

Wiffen English: of uncertain origin, possibly a habitation name from an unidentified place named with the OE elements *hwīt* white, i.e. phosphorescent + *fen* marsh; cf. WHITMARSH and WHITMORE 1.
Vars.: **Whiffen, Whiffin.**

Wigg English (E Anglia): 1. nickname from ME *wigge* beetle, bug (OE *wicga*; cf. mod. Eng. *earwig*).

2. metonymic occupational name for a maker of fancy breads baked in rounds and then divided up into wedge-shaped slices, ME *wigge* (from MDu. *wigge* wedge(-shaped cake); cf. SPITZWEG).

Var. (of 2): **Wigger**.

Patr. (from 1): **Wiggs**.

Wiggin English: 1. from the Bret. personal name *Wiucon*, composed of elements meaning 'worthy' + 'high', 'noble', which was introduced into England by followers of William the Conqueror.

2. from the Gmc personal name *Wīgant*, originally a byname meaning 'Warrior', from the pres. part. of *wīgan* to fight, likewise introduced to England in the wake of the Conquest.

Vars.: **Wigin**, **Wigan(d)**.

Cogns. (of 1): Ger.: **Weigand**, **Weigang**; **Weigt** (Silesia); **Weicht** (Saxony). Low Ger.: **Wi(e)gand(t)**, **Wiegank**.

Dims. (of 2): Ger.: **Weigel(t)**, **Weigl**; **Witzel**.

Patrs.: Eng.: **Wiggins**, **Wiggans**, **Wigens**.

Wigglesworth English (W Yorks.): habitation name from a place in Ribblesdale, recorded in Domesday Book as *Winchelesuuorde*, from the gen. case of the OE byname *Wincel* 'Child' + OE *worð* enclosure (see WORTH).

Wight Scots and N English: 1. nickname for a strong-willed or brave man, from ME *wigt* valiant, stalwart (ON *vígt*).

2. topographic name for someone who lived by a bend or curve in a river or road, OE *wiht* (a deriv. of *wican* to bend). There does not seem to be any connection between modern bearers of this surname and the Isle of *Wight* (the name of which is apparently of Brit. origin, perhaps meaning 'watershed').

Vars. (of 1): **W(e)ightman**.

Wigley English: habitation name from places in Derbys. and Hants, so called from the OE byname *Wicga* 'Beetle', 'Bug' (cf. WIGG 1) + *lēah* wood, clearing.

Wigmore English: habitation name from a place in Herefords., so called from OE *wicga* (see WIGG 1) in the sense 'something moving' + *mōr* marsh (see MOORE 1).

Wignal English (Lancs.): habitation name from a minor place near Holmes in the parish of Croston, so called from the gen. case of the OE byname *Wicga* 'Beetle', 'Insect' (cf. WIGG 1) + OE *h(e)alh* nook, corner, recess (see HALE 1). The surname occurs in the surrounding area from the 14th cent., and had already become frequent there by the 16th.

Wik Swedish: ornamental name from Swed. *vik* bay (ON *vík*), perhaps sometimes chosen as a topographic name by someone who lived by a bay.

Vars.: **Wi(c)kmann**, **Vi(c)kmann** (of which **Wikander** is a Graecized form); **Wikner**.

Cpds: **Wi(c)kberg** ('bay hill'); **Wi(c)klund** ('bay grove'); **Wi(c)kström**, **Vi(c)kström** ('bay river').

Wilberfoss English: habitation name from a place in Humberside, so called from the OE female personal name *Wilburh* (composed of the elements *wil* will, desire + *burh* fortress) + OE *foss* ditch (see FOSS).

Var.: **Wilberforce**.

Wilbert English: from a Gmc personal name composed of the elements *wil* will, desire + *berht* bright, famous. The native form, *Wilbeorht*, is attested before the Conquest, but was greatly reinforced in the early Middle Ages by the introduction of the Continental cogn. by the Normans.

Cogns.: Ger.: **Wilbrecht**. Low Ger.: **Wilbert**, **Wilbarth**. Fr.: **Guilbert**, **Guilbard**.

Dims.: Fr.: **Guilbon**, **Guilbot**.

Patrs.: Low Ger.: **Wilbertz**, **Wilbers**; **Wilberding**.

Wilby English: habitation name from any of various places so called. One in Norfolk probably represents a contracted form of WILLOUGHBY; one in Suffolk is from OE *wilig* willow + *bēag* ring, circle; and one in Northants is from the ON personal name *Vili* (a short form of various cpd names with the first element *vil* will, desire) + ON *býr* settlement. The surname is found in E Anglia, but is most common in W Yorks.

Wilcock English (chiefly Lancs. and Yorks.): from a medieval given name, a dim. of WILL 1 with the addition of the hypocoristic suffix *-cock* (see COCK 1).

Vars.: **Willcock** (Devon), **Wilcocke**.

Patrs.: **Wil(l)cocks**, **Wil(l)cox** (widespread throughout England); **Wil(l)cockson**, **Wil(l)cox(s)on**.

Wild English: 1. nickname for a man of violent and undisciplined character, from ME *wild* wild, uncontrolled (OE *wilde*).

2. topographic name for someone who lived on a patch of uncultivated land left in a state of nature.

Vars.: **Wilde**, **Whild(e)**, **Wyld(e)**; **Wilder**, **Wildman**.

Cogns. (of 1): Ger.: **Wild(t)**, **Wilde(r)**, **Wildemann**. Flem., Du.: **De Wildt**, **(De) Wilde**, **Wildeman**. Jewish (Ashkenazic): **Wild(mann)**, **Wilder(man)**.

Patrs. (from 1): Eng.: **Wyld(e)s**.

The writer Oscar Wilde *(1854–1900) was born in Dublin, descended from Ralph Wilde, a builder from Walsingham near Durham, who had moved to Ireland in the 17th cent.*

Wildig English: of uncertain origin, possibly a var. of WILDING. The name has not been found in records before the late 16th cent.; John *Wildigge* was married at Wybunbury, Ches., in 1581, and the name is still concentrated in that area.

Vars.: **Wildigg**, **Willdig(g)**.

Several modern bearers of the surname Willdig *are descended from Thomas* Willidge *who was married in 1837 at Walsall; he signed himself thus in the marriage register, but his children were all baptized as Willdig. The surname is now found in Argentina as well as the U.S., Canada, Australia, New Zealand, and elsewhere.*

Wilding English (now chiefly Lancs.): from the OE personal name **Wilding*, a deriv. of OE *wilde* wild, savage (see WILD 1). It is also possible that it may be from a topographical term derived from the same vocab. word (cf. WILD 2), but early forms with prepositions are not found.

Var.: **Wilden**.

Wildish English: topographic name for someone who lived in an area of wooded land, from OE *wealdisc*, an adj. deriv. of *weald* wood (see WALD).

Var.: **Wildash**.

Wildy English: of uncertain origin. Reaney claims that it is a var. of WALTHEW, but this is by no means certain.

Var.: **Willday**.

The earliest known occurrence of this surname is the baptism of Thomas Wildy, *son of John Wildy, at Tamworth, Staffs., in 1572. Willielmus Wildy was married at Alrewas in Staffs. in 1577. The var.* Willday *arose at Mancetter, Warwicks., in the mid-18th cent.*

Wileman English: occupational name for a trapper or hunter, or nickname for a devious person, from ME *wile* trap, snare (late OE *wīl* contrivance, trick, possibly of Scandinavian origin) + *man* man (OE *mann*).

Vars.: **Wiles**, **Wyles**.

Wilk 1. English: from a medieval given name, a back-formation from WILKIN, as if that contained the ANF dim. suffix *-in*.

2. Polish: from Pol. *wilk* WOLF, probably from an OSlav. personal name containing this element, but perhaps also applied as a nickname for someone thought to resemble a wolf or connected with wolves in some other way.

Vars. (of 1): **Wilck, Wilke.**

Cogns. (of 2): Ukr.: **Vovk.** Czech: **Vlk.** Ger. (of Slav. origin): **Wolk.**

Dims. (of 1): Eng.: **Wilkie** (Scotland). (Of 2): Pol.: **Wilczek.** Ukr.: **Vovchenko.** Beloruss.: **Volchik.** Czech: **Vlček.**

Patrs. (from 1): Eng.: **Wilk(e)s.** (From 2): Pol.: **Wilkowicz; Wilczak.** Ukr.: **Vovkovich.** Russ.: **Volkov.** Bulg.: **Vulkov, Vluchkov.** Croatian: **Vuk(ov)ić, Vukotić.**

Patrs. (from dims. of 1): Eng.: **Wilkieson** (Scotland). (From dims. of 2): Croatian: **Vuk(i)č(ev)ić, Vukelić; Vučić, Vučković, Vučinić, Vučenović, Vučetić, Vučićević.**

Habitation name (from 2): Pol.: **Wilczyński.**

Wilkin English: from a medieval given name, a short form of WILL with the addition of the hypocoristic suffix *-kin* (of Low Ger. origin).

Var.: **Wilken.**

Patrs.: **Wilkins, Wilkens; Wilkinson, Wilkenson, Wilkerson.**

Will 1. Scots and N English: from the medieval given name *Will*, a dim. of WILLIAM. In a few cases it may be from one of the other medieval given names with this first element; cf., e.g., WILBERT and WILLARD.

2. S and SW English: topographic name for someone who lived by a spring or stream, ME *will* (from the W Saxon form, *wiell(a)*, of OE *well(a)*; see WELL).

Cogns. (of 1): Fr.: **Guille.** Low Ger.: **Will(e).** Flem., Du.: **Wil.**

Dims. (of 1): Eng.: WILCOCK, WILKIN; **Willet(t), Willitt, Willott;** GILLET. Fr.: **Guillet(on), Willet; Guillot(eau), Guillotin, Guilloton, Will(i)ot, Vuillot, Vuillod; Guillon(eau), Guillou(x), Guilloud; Guill(a)in, Guilly, Vuillin.** Low Ger.: **Wil(l)mann, Wilke.** Flem., Du.: **Wilman, Willeke.** Pol.: **Wilmański, Wilmanowski.**

Patrs. (from 1): Eng.: **Will(e)s, Willis, Wyllis; Wilson, Will(e)son, Willison.** Low Ger.: **Willing(s).** Flem., Du.: **Wils(ens).** Swed.: **Wil(l)sson, Vil(l)sson.**

Patrs. (from 1) (dims.): Eng.: **Willetts** (esp. W Midlands), **Wilets, Willats.** Low Ger.: **Willmanns, Wilken(s).** Flem., Du.: **Willekens.**

Although the surname Will *is comparatively infrequent and more or less confined to Scotland, with a smaller concentration in the W Country, the associated derivative* Wilson *is one of the most common of all Britain's surnames, being especially common in N England, Scotland, and N Ireland.*

Willard English: from a Gmc personal name composed of the elements *wil* wil, desire + *hard* brave, hardy, strong.

Var.: **Wyllarde.**

Cogns.: Fr.: **Guil(l)ard.** Low Ger.: **Willer(t).**

Patrs.: Low Ger.: **Willers, Willerding.**

Willerton English: habitation name from *Willoughton* in Lincs., so called from OE *wilig* willow + *tūn* enclosure, settlement; cf. WILTON.

This surname has always been closely associated with Lincs., with some spreading into E Yorks. A branch of the Alford family of this name was established in London from the early 18th cent.

Willey English: habitation name from any of various places so called. Those in Ches., Herefords., Shrops., and Warwicks. are named from OE *wilig* willow + *lēah* wood, clearing; one in Devon probably has as its first element OE *wīðig* willow, while one in Surrey has OE *wēoh* pagan temple.

Willgress English (E Anglia): apparently a nickname from ME *wild* WILD + *grise* pig (see GRICE 2).

Vars.: **Wilgress, Wilgrass, Willgross.**

William English: from the Norman form of an OF personal name composed of the Gmc elements *wil* will, desire + *helm* helmet, protection. This was introduced into England at the time of the Conquest, and within a very short period it became the most popular given name in England, mainly no doubt in honour of the Conqueror himself. The given name has also enjoyed considerable popularity in Germany (as *Wilhelm*), France (as *Guillaume*), Spain (as *Guillermo*), and Italy (as *Guglielmo*, with numerous dims.).

Vars.: **Welliam; Gill(i)am, Gil(l)ham, Gillum** (from central Fr. forms).

Cogns.: Welsh: **Gwill(i)am, Gwiliam, Gwilym.** Fr.: **Guillaume; Willaume, Willème** (NE France); **Wil(l)ame** (Belgium); **Guillelme, Guillerme** (Brittany); **V(u)illaume, V(u)illerme** (E France); **Vuilleaume** (Switzerland). Prov.: **Guillem, Guilhem, Guilen, Guilhen.** Sp.: **Guillermo, Guillén.** Cat.: **Guillem, Guillén.** Port.: **Guilherme.** It.: **Guglielmo, Guglielmi; G(hi)elmo, G(hi)elmi, Vielmi** (Venetia, Lombardy); **Guiglia, Ghiglia** (Liguria); **Viglia** (Piedmont, Emilia, Campania); **Biglia, Biglio** (Lombardy, Emilia, Campania); **Lelmi, Lemmi, Lembi, Lemmo, Lembo** (Tuscany); **Mem(m)i, Mem(m)o.** Ger.: **Wilhelm, Wilhalm, Wilharm.** Low Ger.: **Wil(l)m.** Flem., Du.: **Wilhelm, Willem.** Czech: **Vilím.**

Dims.: Eng.: **Willmett, Wil(l)mot(t), Willimott, Willmutt, Wil(l)min, Will(i)ment, Willament, Willimont** (from OF forms; see WILL for native derivs., and also WYATT). Fr.: **Guillaumet, Guil(le)met, Willemet, Vuillaumet, Vuille(r)met; Guillaumot, Guil(le)mot, Willemot, Vuille(r)mot; Guillaumin, Guil(le)min(ot), Willemin, Vuillaumin, Vuillem(a)in, Vuilleminet, Vuilleminot, Vuillemenot; Guillaumeau; Guillermou, Guillermic** (Brittany). It.: **Guglielmin(ett)i, Guglielmino, Gelmini, Vielmini, Ghiglino, Viglini; G(ugli)elmetti, Vielmetti, Viglietto, Viglietti, Biglietto, Biglietti; Guglielmotti, Ghilgliotti, Vigliotto, Vigliotti; Guglielmelli; Guglielmucci; Memoli** (Campania). Cat.: **Guillemet.** Port.: **Guilhermino.** Czech: **Vilímek.**

Augs.: Fr.: **Guillaumat.** It.: **Guglielmoni, Guglielmone, Ghiglione, Viglione; Memon** (Venetia).

Patrs.: Eng.: **Williams** (also very common in Wales); **Willems; Wiliems** (Wales); **Williamson; Fitzwilliam(s).** Sc.: McWILLIAM. Fr.: **Aguillaume.** It.: **De Guglielmo.** Ger.: **Wilhelmer; Wilhelmi** (Latinized). Low Ger.: **Wil(he)lms(en).** Flem., Du.: **Willems, Wil(l)ms, Willemse(n).** Dan., Norw.: **Wilhelmsen, Vilhelmsen, Willumsen, Villumsen.** Swed.: **Wilhelmsson, Vilhelmsson.**

Patrs. (from dims.): Eng.: **Willmetts, Willmotts.**

Habitation names: Pol.: **Wilimowski, Wiliński.** Czech: **Vilímovský.**

Willmore English: habitation name from *Wildmore* in Lincs. or the *Weald Moors* in Shrops., both named with the OE elements *wild* wild, uncultivated (see WILD 2) + *mōr* moor, marsh (see MOORE 1).

Var.: **Wilmore.**

Willner 1. German: habitation name from any of various places, for example in Saxony, Upper Franconia, the Upper Palatinate, and Upper Austria, called *Wildenau*, from OHG *wildi* wild, uncultivated (with the adj. retaining the weak dat. ending originally used after a preposition and article) + *ouwa* wet land, marsh.

2. Jewish (E Ashkenazic): habitation name from Yid. *vilner* native or inhabitant of the Lithuanian city of Vilnius (Yid. *Vilne*).

Vars. (of 1): **Wil(d)ner.** (Of 2): **Wilner, Vilner; Vilnai** (Israeli, a Hebr. form).

Willock Scots and English: from the ME and OE personal name *Willoc*, dim. from a short form of the various cpd names with the first element *willa* will, desire. In the Middle Ages it was used as a dim. of the given name WILLIAM.

Patrs.: **Willocks, Willox.**

Willoughby English: habitation name from any of the various places, for example in Leics., Lincs., Notts., and Warwicks., so called. This is from OE *wilig* willow + ON *býr* farm, settlement, or perhaps in some cases from *wilig* + OE *bēag* ring (cf. WILBY).

This is the name of an ancient family who originated in Lincs. One branch trace their descent from William de Willoughby, *whose name is recorded in law suits in 1200 and 1202. They hold the titles Earls Ancaster and Barons Middleton.*

Wilton English: habitation name from any of various places so called. Most, including those in Cumb., Herefords., Norfolk, and E and N Yorks., are named from OE *wilig* willow + *tūn* enclosure, settlement. One in Somerset and another in Wilts. have as their first element OE *wiell(a)* spring, stream (see WILL 2), and the one that has given its name to WILTSHIRE derives its name from that of the river *Wylye*, on which it stands (an ancient Brit. river name, perhaps meaning 'Capricious').

Wiltshire English: regional name from the county of Wiltshire in SW central England, which gets its name from WILTON, once its principal town, + OE *scīr* district, administrative division.

Vars.: **Wiltsh(i)er, Wiltshear, Will(i)shire, Wilshire, Wil(l)sher(e), Willshear, Wilcher, Wiltshaw, Wil(l)shaw.**

Wimpenny English: nickname for an acquisitive person, from ME *winn(en)* to gain (OE *winnan* to conquer, defeat) + *penny* PENNY.

Var.: **Winpenny.**

This surname is first recorded in Ripon in 1379. A family by the name of Wimpenny *moved to Huddersfield in the late 16th cent., probably as a result of the decline in the wool trade in Ripon, and the name is now mainly confined to Huddersfield.*

Wimpey English: of uncertain origin. Sir Elijah IMPEY, a well-known 18th-cent. judge, had an illegitimate son who used this name, but it may simply have been selected as an existing surname approximating to his father's.

Winch English: 1. in examples such as William *de la Winche* (Worcs. 1275) evidently a topographic name, perhaps for someone who lived at a spot where boats were hauled up onto the land by means of pulleys, from ME *winche* reel, roller (OE *wince*).

2. in examples such as William *le Wynch* (Sussex 1327) it appears to be a nickname, perhaps from the lapwing, OE *(hlēap)wince*.

Vars.: **Wynch; Wink.**

Winchester English: habitation name from the city in Hants, so called from the addition of OE *ceaster* Roman town (L *castra* legionary camp) to the Romano-British name *Venta*, of disputed etymology.

Oliver Winchester *(1810–80), owner of the arms company which produced the Winchester rifle, was born in Boston, a fifth-generation descendant of John Winchester, who had settled in America by 1637.*

Winckel German: metonymic occupational name for someone who kept a corner shop, especially one that dealt in second-hand items, or topographic name for someone who lived on a corner of land in the countryside or on a street corner in a town, from Ger. *Winkel* corner (MHG *winkel*, OHG *winkil*).

Vars.: **Winkel, Win(c)kler, Win(c)kelmann, Zumwinkel.**

Cogns.: Flem.: **Van (de) Winckel, Van Wynkel.** Du.: **(Van der) Winkel, Winkelaar, Winkler, Winkelman.** Czech: **Vinklář.** Jewish (Ashkenazic): **Winckler, Vinckler; Winkelsberg, Winkelstein** (ornamental elaborations).

Wind 1. English: topographic name for someone who lived near a pathway, alleyway, or road, OE *(ge)wind* (from *windan* to go, proceed).

2. English: nickname for a swift runner, from ME, OE *wind* wind (cf. SHERWIN).

3. German: var. of WENDT.

Vars. (of 3): **Winde, Windt.**

Winder English: 1. occupational name for a winder of wool, from an agent deriv. of ME *wind(en)* to wind (OE *windan* to go, proceed; cf. WIND 1). The verb was also used in the Middle Ages of various weaving and plaiting processes, so that in some cases the name may have referred to a maker of baskets or hurdles.

2. habitation name from any of the various minor places in N England so called, from OE *vindr* wind + *erg* hut, shelter, i.e. a shelter against the wind.

Windle English (Lancs. and Yorks.): habitation name from *Windhill* in W Yorks. or *Windle* in Lancs., both so called from OE *wind* wind + *hyll* HILL, i.e. a mound exposed to fierce gusts.

Var.: **Wintle** (Gloucs.).

Windsor English: habitation name from places in Berks. and Dorset, named from OE **windels* windlass + *ōra* bank.

Vars.: **Winsor** (places in Devon and Hants); **Winser, Winzor, Winzer, Winzar.**

Windsor *is the surname of the present British royal family, adopted in place of* Wettin *in 1917 as a response to anti-German feeling during the First World War. The surname of Edward VII (and hence of George V up to 1917) was Wettin, his father, Prince Albert, being Prince Wettin of Saxe-Coburg-Gotha. The name Windsor was taken from the town in Berks., where Windsor Castle is a royal residence. It had been an ordinary English habitation surname for centuries before these events.*

Winfield English: habitation name from any of various places now called *Wingfield*. N and S Wingfield in Derbys. seem to be named from OE **wynn* meadow, pasture + *feld* pasture, open country (see FIELD); an example in Beds. may have as it first element a topographical term or bird name *wince* (see WINCH); and one in Suffolk was probably either the 'field of the people of *Wīga*', a short form of the various cpd names with a first element *wīg* war, or else derives its first element from OE *wēoh* pagan temple.

Var.: **Wingfield.**

Wing English: habitation name from places in Bucks. and Leics. (formerly Rutland). The former is probably a drastically contracted form of OE *Wihthūningas* 'people of *Wihthūn*', a personal name composed of the elements *wiht* creature + *hūn* bearcub; the latter is from ON *vengi*, a deriv. of *vangr* field (cf. WANG).

Wingate Scots and N English: habitation name from places so called, for example in Northumb. and Co. Durham, from OE *wind* wind + *geat* gate, i.e. a place where the wind howls through a narrow pass.

Vars.: **Wingett, Wynniatt, Wynyates.**

The British general Orde Wingate *(1903–44) was from an old Stirlings. family.*

Wingrove English: habitation name from *Wingrave* in Bucks., so called from the nearby village of WING + OE *grāf* GROVE.

Winn English: from the OE personal name and byname *Wine* 'Friend', in part a short form of various cpd names with this first element.

Vars.: **Wynn(e)**.

Patrs.: Eng.: **Wyn(n)es, Wyness**.

Winnick Jewish (E Ashkenazic): occupational name for a distiller of brandy, Yid. *vinik*, Ukr. *vinnik*, from the Slav. element *vino* wine (cf. WEIN) + the agent suffix *-nik*.

Vars.: **Winnik, Wini(c)k(man), Vinnik; Winitzky, Winicki, Vinitzky, Venezkey**.

Patrs.: **Winikov, Winnikow, Winikoff**.

Winrow English (Lancs.): of uncertain origin, perhaps a habitation name from an unidentified minor place named with the ON elements *hvin* whin, gorse + *vrá* nook, corner.

Vars.: **Whinrow, Whin(w)ray, Whiner(a)y, Whinnerah**.

Winslow English: habitation name from a place in Bucks., so called from the gen. case of the OE personal name or byname *Wine* (see WINN) + OE *hlāw* hill, mound, barrow (see LAW 2 and LOW 1).

Edward Winslow *(1595–1655), one of the founders of the Plymouth colony who sailed from Leiden on the* Mayflower *in 1617, was born in Droitwich, Worcs. He was a governor of the colony and also served as agent of the Massachusetts Bay Company in France. In 1621 he married the widow of Sir Sanna White, the first marriage in New England. Their son Josiah* (c.*1629–80) was the first native-born governor in America.*

Winstanley English (Lancs.): habitation name from a place near Manchester, so called from the OE personal name *Wynnstān* (see WINSTON 1) + OE *lēah* wood, clearing.

Winston 1. English: from an OE personal name composed of the elements *wynn* joy + *stān* stone.

2. English: habitation name from any of various places called *Winston* or *Winstone*, from various OE personal names + OE *tūn* enclosure, settlement, or, in the case of *Winstone* in Gloucs., OE *stān* stone.

3. Jewish (Ashkenazic): Anglicized form of *Weinstein*; see WEIN.

Var. (of 1 and 2): **Winstone**.

Sir Henry Winston *of Standish in Gloucs. was the father of Sarah Winston, who was the mother of Sir Winston Churchill (b. 1620), himself the father of the 1st Duke of Marlborough.*

Winter 1. English, German, and Danish/Norwegian: nickname or byname for someone of a frosty or gloomy temperament, variously from ME, MHG, or Dan./Norw. *winter* (OE *winter*, OHG *wintar*, ON *vetr*).

2. Jewish (Ashkenazic): from Ger. *Winter* winter, either an ornamental name or one of the group of names denoting the seasons, which were distributed at random by government officials; cf. SUMMER, FRULING, and HERBST.

3. Irish: translation of Gael. *Mac Giolla-Gheimhridh*; see MCALIVERY.

Vars.: Eng.: **Wynter, Wintour**. Dan., Norw.: **Vinter**.

Cogn.: Flem., Du.: **De Winter**.

Dims.: Ger.: **Winterl(e), Winterlein**.

Patrs.: Eng.: **Winters, Wynters; Winterson**. Flem., Du.: **Winters**.

Cpds (ornamental elaborations): Jewish: **Winterberg, Winterstein**.

Winterbottom English: topographic name, esp. in the hilly regions of Lancs. and Yorks., for someone whose principal dwelling was in a valley inhabited only in winter (the summer being spent in temporary shelters on the upland pasture), from ME *winter* WINTER + *bottom* valley (see BOTTOM). In many cases, the surname is a habitation name from the place of this name in Ches.

Var.: **Winterbotham**.

Winterbourne English: habitation name from any of the various places, for example in Berks., Dorset, Sussex, and Wilts., so called from OE *winter* WINTER + *burna* stream (see BOURNE), i.e. a watercourse which dried up in summer.

Vars.: **Winterborne** (places in Dorset); **Winterburn** (a place in W Yorks.); **Winterbo(u)rn**.

Winterton English: habitation name from places in S Humberside and Norfolk, so called from OE *winter* winter + *tūn* enclosure, settlement, referring perhaps to a place inhabited only in winter (cf. WINTERBOTTOM), or named from a proprietor who bore this byname (see WINTER 1).

Winthrop English: habitation name from places in Lincs. and Notts. called *Winthorpe*. The former is so called from the OE personal name or byname *Wina* (see WINN) + OE *þorp* settlement (see THORPE). In the latter the first element represents a contracted form of the OE personal name *Wīgmund*, composed of the elements *wīg* war + *mund* protection.

John Winthrop *(1588–1649) was the first governor of the Massachusetts Bay Colony. He kept a detailed journal, an invaluable source for historians. He was born into a family of Suffolk gentry whose fortunes were founded by his grandfather Adam Winthrop (d. 1562) of Lavenham. In 1544 the latter acquired a 500-acre estate which had been part of the monastery of Bury St Edmunds. John Winthrop emigrated to America in 1629 because of Charles I's anti-Puritan policies. By the time of his death he had had four wives and 16 children, the most notable of whom was his son John (1606–76), a scientist and governor of Connecticut. His descendants were prominent in politics and science, including John Winthrop (1714–79), an astronomer, and Robert Winthrop (1809–94), a senator and Speaker of the House of Representatives.*

Winton English and Scots: habitation name from any of various places so called. Those in N Yorks. and near Edinburgh are so called from the OE byname or personal name *Wine* (see WINN) + OE *tūn* enclosure, settlement; one in Westmorland (now Cumb.) probably has as its first element OE **wynn* pasture; and one in Lancs. has OE *wiðigen* 'growing with willows'. In S England it is the name of a place just outside Bournemouth.

Winyard English: topographic name for someone who lived by a vineyard, or occupational name for someone who worked in one, from ME *winyard* (a cpd of OE *wīn* wine, vine + *geard* yard, enclosure). Wine growing was formerly more common in England than it is now.

Vars.: **Wynyard, Wingard; Winnard** (Lancs.).

Cogns.: Ger.: **Weingardt, Weingartz, Wingert; Weingart(n)er, Weingärtner**. Flem.: **Wijnyaerd, Van de Wijngaerden**. Du.: **Wijngaard, Van Wijngaarden**. Jewish (Ashkenazic): **Weingart(en)** (partly ornamental). Dan., Norw.: **Wiingård, Wiingaard**.

Wirth 1. German and Jewish (Ashkenazic): occupational name for an innkeeper, from Ger. *Wirt* host (MHG *wirt*).

2. German: status name for a man who was the head of a family and the master of his own household, from the same word in the sense 'provider'.

Var.: Ger.: **Würth**.

Dims.: Ger.: **Würthle**. Low Ger.: **Wirthgen**.

Patrs.: Low Ger.: **Wirtz, Wirths**.

Wise 1. English: nickname for a wise or learned person, or in some cases a nickname for someone suspected of being acquainted with the occult arts, from ME *wise* wise (OE *wīs*).

2. U.S.: Anglicized form of Ger. and Jewish (Ashkenazic) *Weiss*; see WHITE.

Vars. (of 1): **Wyse**; **Wiseman**; **Wisdom**.

Cogns.: Ger.: **Weis(e)**, **Weiser**, **Weismann**. Flem.: **De Wyse**. Du.: **De Wijs**, **De Wijze**, **Wijsman**.

Wishart Scots: from the Norman form, *Wischard*, of the OF personal name *Guiscard*. This was formed in Normandy from the ON elements *viskr* wise + *hard* hardy, brave, bold (or possibly the OF suffix *-ard*).

Vars.: **Whiscard**, **Wysard**, **Vizard**; **Wiskar**, **W(h)isker**, WESKER.

Cogn.: Fr.: **Guiscard**.

Wiśniak Polish: topographic name for someone who lived by a cherry tree, from Pol. *wiśnia* cherry tree (see WIŚNIEWSKI) + *-ak* suffix of agent nouns. The Pol. vocab. word *wiśniak* also means 'cherry brandy', and in some cases the surname may be an occupational name for a seller of this or a nickname for a habitual drinker of it.

Wiśniewski 1. Polish: habitation name from a place called *Wiśniewo* (named with Pol. *wiśnia* cherry tree), with the addition of *-ski*, suffix of local surnames (see BARANOWSKI).

2. Jewish (E Ashkenazic): ornamental name from Pol. *wiśnia* cherry tree, or habitation name as in 1.

Vars.: **Wiszniewski**, **Wiśniowski**, **Wiśniowiecki**.

Witham English: habitation name from any of various places so called. N and S *Witham* in Lincs. derive the name from the river on which they stand, which is of ancient Brit. origin and uncertain meaning. *Witham* on the Hill in Lincs., along with other examples in Essex and Somerset, was probably originally named with an OE byname *Wit(t)a* (presumably from *wit(t)* wits, mind) + OE *hām* homestead. However, the first element may instead have been OE *wiht* bend (see WIGHT 2).

Vars.: **Withams**, **Wittams**.

Wither English: 1. from the ON personal name *Víðarr*, composed of the elements *víð* wide + *árr* messenger.

2. topographic name for someone who lived near a willow tree, a deriv. of ME *wyth(e)*; see WYTHE.

Patr. (from 1): **Withers**.

Witherspoon Scots: of uncertain origin, perhaps a habitation name from an unidentified place named with ME *wether* sheep, ram (see WEATHER) + *spong*, *spang*, a dial. term for a narrow strip of land.

Vars.: **We(a)therspoon**, **Wedderspoon**, **Wotherspoon**.

The first known bearer of the name is Roger Wythirspon, *mentioned in a document of the late 13th cent.*

Withey English: topographic name for someone who lived by a willow tree, ME *withy* (OE *wīðig*; cf. WEIDE 1 and WYTHE).

Var.: **Withy**.

Withington English: habitation name from any of several places so called. The majority, including those in Ches., Herefords., Lancs., and Shrops., get the name from derivs. of OE *wīðig* willow (see WITHEY) + *tūn* enclosure, settlement; *Withington* in Gloucs. appears in Domesday Book as *Widindune*, from the gen. case of an OE personal name *Widia* + OE *dūn* hill (see DOWN 1).

Withnell English (Lancs.): habitation name from a place near Blackburn, so called from OE *wīðegn* willow wood + *hyll* HILL.

Withycombe English: habitation name from any of various places, for example in Devon and Somerset, so called from OE *wīðig* willow (see WITHEY) + *cumb* valley (see COOMBE).

Vars.: **Withecombe**, **Withacombe**, **Widdicombe**, **Widdecombe**.

Witney English: habitation name from a place in Oxon., so called from the gen. case, *Wit(t)an*, of the OE personal name *Wit(t)a* (cf. WITHAM) + OE *ēg* island, raised land in a marsh.

Wittelsbach German: habitation name from the village and former castle of *Wittelsbach* in Upper Bavaria.

The house of Wittelsbach *was for centuries one of the great noble families of German-speaking Europe, including counts, dukes, and kings of Bavaria. It is probably descended from a certain Margrave Luitpold (d. 907), a relative of the Carolingian Emperor Arnulf. Luitpold's son, another Arnulf, was Duke of Bavaria 907–37, but his successors lost the duchy and became Counts of Scheyern. In 1180 the Emperor Friedrich I bestowed a greatly reduced duchy of Bavaria on Count Otto of Wittelsbach, who was probably a descendant of Luitpold. Otto's descendants ruled Bavaria continuously until 1918.*

Witty English: nickname for a bright or inventive person, from ME *witty* clever, ingenious (OE *(ge)wittig* learned, from *wit(t)* wits, mind). It is possible that some early examples may represent a survival into ME of OE *wītega* soothsayer, and there may also have been some confusion with WHITTY.

Var.: **Wittey**.

Włodarski Polish: occupational name for a steward, from Pol. *włodarz* (a deriv. of *włodać* to govern, rule, order), with the addition of the (originally local) suffix of surnames *-ski* (see BARANOWSKI).

Dims.: **Włodarczyk**, **Włodarek**.

Wnuk Polish: from Pol. *wnuk* grandson, presumably a name either for the grandson of an important personage or for someone who was brought up by his grandparents after being left an orphan.

Cogn.: Czech: **Vnouček**.

Wodzyński Polish: habitation name from Pol. *wódz* military commander + *-yn* possessive suffix, with the addition of *-ski*, suffix of local surnames (see BARANOWSKI).

Wogan Welsh: from the OW personal name (still used as a given name during the Middle Ages) *Gwgan*, *Gwgon*, originally a byname (probably a dim. of *gwg* scowl, i.e. 'Little Scowler'). The name was taken early on from Wales to Ireland, where it is common.

Wohl Jewish (Ashkenazic): ornamental name adopted in a spirit of optimism, from mod. Ger. *Wohl* wellbeing.

Vars.: **Wohlman(n)**.

Cpds (mostly ornamental, although some may be based on now irrecoverable minor events and anecdotes): **Wohlberg** ('good hill'); **Wohlfarth** ('good journey'); **Wohlfeld** ('good field'); **Wohlfinger** ('good finger'); **Wohlgemueth** ('good mood'); **Wohlspiegel** ('good mirror'); **Wohlsta(e)dter** ('good city'); **Wohlstein** ('good stone').

Wójcik Polish: status name from a dim. of Pol. *wójt* village headman, a borrowing of Ger. VOGT. There has probably

been some confusion with derivs. of the given name *Wojciech* (see VOJTĚCH).
Vars.: **Wójcicki, Wójt.**
Patrs.: **Wójcikiewicz; Wójtowicz.**
Habitation names: **Wójcikowski, Wójciński.**

Wolf 1. English and German: from a short form of the various Gmc cpd names with a first element *wolf* wolf, or a byname or nickname with this meaning. The wolf was native throughout the forests of Europe, including Britain, until comparatively recently, and played an important role in Gmc mythology, being regarded as one of the sacred beasts of Woden.

2. Jewish (Ashkenazic): from the Yid. male given name *Volf* 'Wolf', which is associated with the Hebr. given name *Binyamin* (see BENJAMIN). This association stems from Jacob's dying words 'Benjamin shall ravin as a wolf: in the morning he shall devour the prey, and at night he shall divide the spoil' (Gen. 49: 27).

3. Irish: translation of Gael. *Ó Faoláin*; see WHELAN.
Vars. (of 1): Eng.: **Wo(u)lfe** (also an Ir. var. of 3); **Woolf(e), Woof(f); Ulph** (Norfolk, from the ON byname *Ulfr*). Ger.: **Wolff.** (Of 2): Jewish: **Wolff, Wulf(f), Volf; Wolfman(n), Volfman.**
Cogns.: Low Ger.: **Wulf(f).** Flem., Du.: **(De) Wulf(e), De Wolf(f).** Dan., Norw.: **Wulff, Wolff.** Czech: **Volf.** Pol.: WILK.
Dims.: Ger.: **Wölfel, Wölfle, Wölf(f)lin.** Low Ger.: **Wülfke, Wolfgen.**
Patrs.: Eng.: **Wolfes, Wolfson.** Low Ger.: **Wulfen, Wolfen, Wolfsen, Wulfing.** Dan., Norw. **Volfing.** Jewish: **Wolf(f)sohn, Wolfenso(h)n, Wolfson, Wulfsohn; Wolfin, Wolfovitch, Wolfowi(t)ch, Wolfowicz, Wulfowicz, Wolfowitz, Wolfovitz, Wolfovits, Volfovich, Wolfovsky, Volfovski, Volfovsky, Vulfov(ich)** (E Ashkenazic); **Volfovici** (Rumanian spelling).
Patr. (from a dim.): Low Ger.: **Wülfken.**
Cpds (ornamental elaborations): Jewish: **Wolfberg** ('wolf hill'); **Wolfheim** ('wolf home'); **Wolfstein** ('wolf stone').

Wolfenden English: habitation name from a place in the parish of Newchurch-in-Rossendale, Lancs., apparently so called from the OE personal name *Wulfhelm* (composed of the elements *wulf* wolf + *helm* helmet, protection) + OE *denu* valley (see DEAN 1).
Vars.: **Woolfenden, Woffenden, Woffendon, Woffindon, Woffindin, Woofinden.**

Wolfit English: from the ME given name *Wolfet, Wolfat*, OE *Wulfgēat*, composed of the element *wulf* wolf + the ethnic name *Gēat* (see JOCELYN).
Vars.: **Woolfit(t), Woffit, Wool(v)ett, Wo(o)llett, Woolatt; Ul(l)yett, Ulyet, Ullett, Ul(l)yatt, Ullyat(e), Ulyate, Ullyott, Ulyot, Uliot** (found in Notts. and Lincs., and to a lesser extent in Yorks. and Derbys., where there was Scandinavian influence; cf. *Ulph* at WOLF).

Wolfram English and German: from the Gmc personal name *Wolfram*, composed of the elements *wolf* wolf + *hrafn* raven. Both these creatures played an important role in Gmc mythology. They are usually represented in battle poetry as scavengers of the slain, while Woden (Odin) is generally accompanied by the wolves Geri and Freki and the ravens Hugin and Munin.
Vars.: Ger.: **Wolfrum, Wolfrom, Wohlfromm, Wolfgram, Wulfgram.**

Wollaston English: habitation name from any of various places so called. Those in Northants (Domesday Book *Wilavestone*) and Shrops. (Domesday Book *Willavestune*) get the name from the gen. case of the OE personal name *Wīglāf* (composed of the elements *wīg* war + *lāf* relic) + OE *tūn* enclosure, settlement. The one in Worcs. (first recorded in 1275 as *Wollaueston*) has as its first element the gen. case of the OE personal name *Wulflāf* (composed of the elements *wulf* wolf + *lāf* relic).
Var.: **Woollaston.**

Wolniak Polish: status name for a freedman, one who had been released from the feudal obligations of serfdom, from Pol. *wolny* free + *-ak* suffix of animate nouns. The vocab. word *wolniak* also denoted an unmarried man, but this is less likely to lie behind the surname.
Var.: **Wolnicki.**
Cogn.: Czech: **Volný.**
Patr.: Pol.: **Wolniewicz.**

Wolsey English: from the ME given name *Wulsi*, OE *Wulfsige*, composed of the elements *wulf* wolf + *sige* victory.
Vars.: **Woo(l)sey.**

Wolstenholme English: habitation name from a place in Lancs., so called from the OE personal name *Wulfstān* (see WOOLSTON 1) + ON *holmr* island, dry land in a fen (see HOLME 2).
Vars.: **Wolstonholm(e), Wolstanholme, Wo(o)lstenhulme, Worstenholme, Wostenholm, Wusteman, Woosnam, Woosman, Worsman.**

Wolstonecraft English: habitation name from *Woolstencroft* in Ches., so called from the OE personal name *Wulfstān* (see WOOLSTON 1) + OE *croft* paddock, smallholding (see CROFT).
Vars.: **Wollstonecraft, Wolstoncraft, Wo(o)lstencroft, Wors(t)encroft, Wosencroft, Wozencroft.**

Wombwell English: habitation name from a place in S Yorks., so called from the OE byname *Wamba* 'Belly' (or this vocab. word used in a transferred topographical sense) + OE *well(a)* spring, stream (see WELL).
Vars.: **Womwell, Wo(o)mbell, Woombill, Woomble.**

Womersley English (Yorks.): habitation name from a place near Pontefract, recorded in Domesday Book as *Wilmereslege*, probably from the gen. case of the OE personal name *Wilmǣr* (composed of the elements *willa* will, desire + *mǣr* famous) + OE *lēah* wood, clearing. However, since this personal name is not definitely instanced in England before the Conquest, Ekwall suggests that the first part may alternatively be composed of the elements *wil(i)g* willow + *mere* pond, lake.

Wood English and Scots: 1. in the overwhelming majority of cases a topographic name for someone who lived in or by a wood or a metonymic occupational name for a woodcutter or forester, from ME *wode* wood (OE *wudu*).

2. nickname for a mad, eccentric, or violent person, from ME *wōd* mad, frenzied (OE *wād*), as in Adam *le Wode* 'Adam the Mad', Worcs. 1221.
Vars. (of 1): **Woode, Woods; Wooder,** WOODMAN; **Wooding(s), Wood(d)in;** ATTWOOD, **Bywood.**
Cogns. (of 1): Low Ger.: **Widde, We(h)de, Weh(e), Wedemann, Wehmann.** Swed.: **Wedin, Vedin.**
Cpd (of a cogn. of 1): Swed.: **Wedberg** ('wood hill').

Woodard English: 1. from the ME given name *Wodard, Udard, Hudard*, OE **Wuduheard*, composed of the elements *wudu* wood + *heard* hardy, brave, strong.

2. occupational name for someone who tended pigs feeding on mast in a wood, from OE *wudu* WOOD + *hierde* herdsman (see HEARD).

3. var. of WOODWARD.
Var.: **Huddart.**

Woodbridge English: habitation name from a place in Suffolk, so called from OE *wudu* WOOD + *brycg* BRIDGE, i.e. a bridge made of timber or one near a wood.

Woodburn Scots and N English: habitation name from places in the former counties of Ayrs., Kincardines., and Midlothian, and in Northumb., so called from OE *wudu* WOOD + *burna* stream (see BOURNE), i.e. a stream flowing through a wood.

Var.: **Woodburne**.

Woodcock English: 1. nickname for a guileless or stupid person, from ME *woodcock* (a cpd of OE *wudu* wood + *cocc* cock, bird), a bird easily caught.

2. habitation name from any of various places named with the OE elements *wudu* WOOD + *cot* cottage, shelter (see COATES), as for example *Woodcott* in Ches. and Hants or *Woodcote* in Hants, Surrey, Oxon., Warwicks., and Shrops.

Var. (of 2): **Woodcott**.

Patr. (from 1): **Woodcocks**.

Woodfield 1. English: topographic name that originated in the parish of Napton-on-the-Hill, Warwicks. In the earliest parish registers it is found as *Woodhull* (with minor variations), from OE *wudu* WOOD + *hyll* HILL. By 1620, however, the change to *Woodfield* was established. The surname has always been largely confined to Warwicks., but is now found also in Australia and New Zealand.

2. Scots: Black derives this name from a place near Annan in the former county of Dumfries, citing a certain Roger *Wodyfelde* who held land in Dumfries in 1365.

Woodford English and Scots: habitation name from any of various places, as far apart as Essex, Wilts., Cornwall, Northants, Ches., and Roxburghs., so called from OE *wudu* WOOD + *ford* FORD.

Vars.: **Woodforde**, **Woodfords**.

Woodgate English: topographic name for someone who lived by a gate leading into an enclosed wood, from ME *wode* WOOD + *gate* GATE.

Vars.: **Woodgates**, **Woodget(t)**, **Woodjetts**, **Woodyatt**.

Woodhall English and Scots: habitation name from any of various places, for example in Herts., Lincs., N Yorks., Dumfries, and E Lothian, so called from OE *wudu* WOOD + *hall* HALL.

Var.: **Woodall** (chiefly Staffs.).

Woodham English: habitation name from any of various places so called. Most, as for example those in Essex and Surrey, are named from OE *wudu* WOOD + *hām* homestead; one in Bucks., however, probably has as its second element OE *hamm* water meadow, and one in Co. Durham is from *wudum*, the dat. pl. of *wudu*, originally used after a preposition.

Vars.: **Wo(o)dhams**.

Woodhatch English: topographic name for someone who lived by a gate into an enclosed forest (cf. WOODGATE), from OE *wudu* WOOD + *hæcc* gate (see HATCH), or habitation name from any of the places, for example in Essex and Surrey, named with these elements.

Woodhead English and Scots: habitation name from any of various minor places, for example in W Yorks. and Strathmore, so called from OE *wudu* WOOD + *hēafod* head(land), top, extremity.

Woodhouse English and Scots: habitation name from any of numerous places, for example in Leics., Peebles., and W Yorks., so called from OE *wudu* WOOD + *hūs* HOUSE.

Vars.: **Wodehouse**, **Wooders**, **Woodus**.

The writer P.G. Wodehouse *(1881–1975) was born into a Norfolk family first recorded in the county in 1402. Their earliest known ancestor was John* de Woodhouse *living in Rastrick, Yorks., at the end of the 13th cent.*

Woodland English: topographic name for someone living in an area of woodland, from OE *wudu* WOOD + *land* land, or habitation name from any of the numerous places, for example in Devon, named with these elements.

Var.: **Woodlands** (the name of places in Kent, Dorset, and Somerset).

Woodley English: habitation name from *Woodleigh* in Devon, *Woodley* in Berks., or some other place named with the OE elements *wudu* WOOD + *lēah* clearing, pasture.

Var.: **Woodleigh**.

Woodlock Irish and English: from an OE personal name, *Wudlāc*, composed of the elements *wudu* wood + *lāc* play, sport.

Vars.: **Woodlake**, **Wedlock**.

The name Woodlock *or* Wodelock *was taken to Ireland as early as 1172 by the brothers Torsten and Reginaldus* Utlag, *the sons of a Wilts. landowner named* Wudulach. *Their descendants held large estates in Tipperary and Co. Dublin during the Middle Ages. In the 18th cent. they suffered greatly from the restrictions placed on Catholics, and several bearers of the name emigrated to France and Spain, and in the 19th cent. to Canada, the U.S., Australia, and New Zealand.*

Woodman English and Scots: topographic name, a var. of WOOD 1, or specifically occupational name for a woodcutter or a forester (cf. WOODWARD). In a few cases, it is possible that it derives from the OE personal name *Wudumann*.

Woodrow English: habitation name for someone who lived in a row of cottages near a wood, from OE *wudu* WOOD + *rāw* row, line. There are places bearing this name in Dorset, Wilts., Bucks., and Worcs., but the surname is found mainly in Norfolk.

Woodruff English: topographic name for someone who lived on a patch of land thickly grown with woodruff, OE *wudurofe* (apparently a cpd of *wudu* wood with a second element of unknown origin). The leaves of the plant have a sweet smell and the surname may also have been a nickname for one who used it as a perfume, or perhaps an ironical nickname for a malodorous person.

Vars.: **Woodruffe**, **Woodrup**, **Woodroff(e)**, **Woodroof(e)**, **Woodrooffe**, **Woodrough**.

Woodside Scots and N Irish: habitation name for any of various minor places, for example in the former county of Ayrs., so called from OE *wudu* WOOD + *sīde* slope of a hill.

Woodward English: 1. occupational name for a forester employed to look after the trees and game, ME *woodward* (a cpd of OE *wudu* WOOD + *weard* guardian, protector; see WARD 1).

2. occasionally perhaps from an OE personal name *Wuduweard*, composed of the vocab. elements mentioned in 1.

Var.: WOODARD.

Wookey English (Somerset): habitation name from a place in the Mendip Hills, apparently named with the rare OE word *wōcig* snare, trap.

Wool English: 1. metonymic occupational name for a worker in wool, ME *woll* (OE *wull*).

2. in SW England, a topographic name for someone who lived by a spring or stream, from ME *woll*, *wull* spring, stream, a western dial. development of OE (W Saxon) *wiell(a)* (see WILL 2).

Vars.: **Wo(o)ll, Wool(l)er, Woller, Woolman, Wol(l)man.**

Cogns. (of 1): Ger.: **Wolle, Woll(n)er, Wollmann.** Low Ger.: **Wulle.** Jewish (Ashkenazic): **Wol(ner)(man); Wolmansky** (E Ashkenazic).

Woolcott English: habitation name from *Woolcot* in Somerset, which is named from ME *woll* spring, stream (see WOOL 2) + *cot* cottage, shelter (see COATES).

Vars.: **Woolcot, Wolcott, Woollcott, Woolcock.**

Oliver Wolcott *(1726–97), one of the signatories of the American Declaration of Independence, was a descendant of Henry Wolcott, a clothier who had settled in Windsor, Conn., in 1636.*

Wooldridge English: from the ME given name *Wol(f)rich*, OE *Wulfrīc*, composed of the elements *wulf* wolf + *rīc* power.

Vars.: **Wo(o)lveridge, Woolridge, Wo(o)lrich, Woolright; Ur(r)y, Urey, Urie, Ourry, Orr(e)y, Hurr(e)y, Hurrie, Horr(e)y** (from Norman forms).

Woolford English: 1. from the ME given name *Wol(f)ward*, OE *Wulfweard*, composed of the elements *wulf* wolf + *weard* guardian, protector.

2. habitation name from *Wolford* in Warwicks., apparently named with the same two elements as in 1, perhaps in the sense of an enclosure to protect livestock from marauding wolves.

Vars.: **Wolford, Woolforde, Woolforth, Woolfarth, Woolfoot, Woolward, Wool(l)ard, Wollard.**

Woolgar English: from the ME given name *Wol(f)gar*, OE *Wulfgār*, composed of the elements *wulf* wolf + *gār* spear.

Vars.: **Woolgard, Woolger.**

Woolley English: habitation name from any of various places so called. Most, including those in Berks., Cambs. (formerly Hunts.), and W Yorks., get the name from OE *wulf* wolf (or perhaps the personal name or byname *Wulf*; see WOLF) + *lēah* wood, clearing; one example in Somerset, however, has as its first element ME *woll*, *wull* spring, stream (see WOOL 2).

Vars.: **Wooley, Wolley.**

Woollin English (W Yorks.): of uncertain origin. Reaney derives a large number of similar names (**Woollan, Woollon(s), Wool(l)en**) from minor places named with the OE elements *wōh* curved, crooked + *land* land. The surname is found mainly in Wakefield.

Woolnough English (chiefly E Anglia): from the ME given name *Wo(o)lnoth*, *Wulnaugh*, *Wulnod*, OE *Wulfnōð*, composed of the elements *wulf* wolf + *nōð* daring.

Vars.: **Woolnoth, Woolner, Wolfner.**

Woolston English (chiefly E Anglia): 1. from the ME given name *Wol(f)stan*, OE *Wulfstān*, composed of the elements *wulf* wolf + *stān* stone.

2. habitation name from any of a large number of places called *Woolston(e)* or *Wollston*, all of which are named from OE personal names containing the first element *Wulf* (*Wulfhēah*, *Wulfhelm*, *Wulfrīc*, *Wulfsige*, and *Wulfweard*) + OE *tūn* enclosure, settlement.

Vars.: **Woolstone, Woollston, Wolston.**

Wooster English: habitation name from the city of *Worcester*, so called from the addition of OE *ceaster* Roman fort (L *castra* legionary camp) to a Brit. tribal name of uncertain origin.

Vars.: **Wostear, Wor(ce)ster.**

Wootton English: habitation name from any of the extremely numerous places so called from OE *wudu* WOOD + *tūn* enclosure, settlement.

Vars.: **Wooton, Woot(t)en, Wotton.**

Worden English (Lancs.): habitation name from a place near Chorley. Early forms consistently show the first syllable as *Wer-*, and the name is probably derived from OE *wer* weir (see WARE 1) + *denu* valley (see DEAN 1).

Wordsworth English: habitation name from *Wadsworth* near Halifax, W Yorks., so called from the OE personal name *Wæddi* (related to *Wada*; see WADE 1) + *worð* enclosure (see WORTH).

Var.: **Wadsworth.**

Worgan Welsh: from the personal name *Gorgan*, *Gwrgan*, of uncertain origin.

Workman English: ostensibly an occupational name for a labourer, from ME *work* (OE *weorc*) + *man* (OE *mann*). According to a gloss cited by Reaney the term was used in the Middle Ages to denote an ambidextrous person, and the surname may also be a nickname in this sense.

Worley English: apparently a habitation name, from a place that has not been identified with certainty. It is perhaps a var. of WORTLEY, or is from places in Essex and Somerset called *Warley*, from OE *wær*, *wer* weir (see WARE 1) + *lēah* wood, clearing, or from *Warley* in the West Midlands, which is from OE *weorf* yoke oxen + *lēah*.

Wormald English (Yorks.): habitation name from places so called in the parishes of Barkisland and Rishworth, both so called from the OE female personal name *Wulfrūn* (composed of the elements *wulf* wolf + *rūn* secret) + northern OE *wæll(a)* spring, stream (see WALL 2); the excrescent *-d* is not found before the middle of the 17th cent. Some of the vars. may also derive from *Wormill* in Derbys., so called from OE *wyrm* serpent, reptile (perhaps a byname) + *hyll* HILL.

Vars.: **Wormal, Wormhall, Wormell, Wormull, Warmoll.**

Worrall English: habitation name from a place in S Yorks., so called from OE *wīr* bog myrtle + *halh* nook, recess (see HALE). The *Wirrall* peninsula in Ches. has the same origin and may well be the source of the surname in some cases. The surname is now especially common in Lancs. and the W Midlands as well as in S Yorks.

Vars.: **Worral, Whorall, Worrell, Worril.**

Worsfold English: of uncertain origin, probably a habitation name from an unidentified place.

Var.: **Worsfield.**

The first known bearer of the name is Robert Wersfelde *(d. 1522), of Abynworth in the parish of Abinger, Surrey. It is still mainly confined to Surrey, Sussex, and Kent.*

Worsley English: habitation name from places in Lancs. and Worcs. The former, which appears to be the main source of the surname, is probably named from the gen. case of an OE personal name of uncertain form (probably with a first element *weorc* work, fortification) + OE *lēah* wood, clearing. The latter apparently gets its first element from the gen. case of OE *weorf* draught cattle (a collective noun).

Worsthorne English: habitation name from a place in Lancs., so called from the gen. case of the OE byname *Wurð* 'Worthy' + OE *þorn* thorn bush (see THORN).

Worswick English (Lancs.): habitation name from *Urswick* in Lancs., so called from OE *ūr* wild ox, bison, aurochs + *sǣ* lake + *wīc* (dependent) settlement.

Var.: **Worsick**.

Wort English: metonymic occupational name for a grower or seller of vegetables or of medicinal herbs and spices, from ME *wurt*, *wort* plant (OE *wyrt*; cf. OHG *wurz*).

Vars.: **Wortt**, **Worts**; WORTMAN.

Cogns.: Ger.: **Wurz(er)** (seller of vegetables and herbs); **Wür(t)z**, **Würz(n)er** (seller of spices). Jewish (Ashkenazic, metonymic occupational names for a seller of spices, herbs, or vegetables; the precise nature of the products sold is unclear): **Wurzer**, **Wurzman**, **Wurzel(man)**; **Wurcel** (Pol. spelling).

Worth English: habitation name from any of the various places, for example in Ches., Dorset, Sussex, and Kent, so called from OE *worð* enclosure, settlement. The vocab. word probably survived into the Middle English period in the sense of a subsidiary settlement dependent on a main village, and in some cases the surname may be a topographic name derived from this use.

Var.: WERTH.

Cogn.: Du.: **Verwoerd**.

Worthington English: habitation name from places in Lancs. and Leics.; both may have originally been named in OE as *Wurðingtūn* 'settlement (OE *tūn*) associated with *Wurð*' (cf. WORSTHORNE), but it is also possible that the first element was OE *worðign*, a deriv. of *worð* enclosure (see WORTH and WORTHY 1).

Worthy English: 1. habitation name from any of various minor places so called from OE *worðig*, a deriv. of *worð* enclosure (see WORTH).

2. nickname for a respected member of the community, from ME *worthy* valuable (a deriv. of *worth* value, merit, OE *weorð*).

Wortley English: habitation name from either of two places so called in W Yorks. The one near Barnsley gets its name from OE *wyrt* plant, vegetable (see WORT) + *lēah* wood, clearing; the one near Leeds probably has as its first element an OE personal name **Wyrca*, perhaps a short form of a cpd name with a first element *weorc* work, fortification (cf. WORSLEY).

Wortman 1. English: var. of WORT.

2. Jewish (Ashkenazic): nickname for a reliable person who could be trusted to keep his word, from Yid. *vort*, mod. Ger. *Wort* word + *man*, *Mann* man.

Vars. (of 2): **Vortman**; **Vortsman**, **Vortzman** ('man of his word'); **Worthalter** (based on Yid. *haltn vort* to keep one's word).

Worton English: habitation name from any of various places so called. Most get the name from OE *wyrt* plant, vegetable (see WORT) + *tūn* enclosure, i.e. a kitchen garden, but in some cases the first element may be OE *worð* enclosure (see WORTH), and in the case of Nether and Over *Worton* in Oxon (*Hortone* in Domesday Book, *Orton* in other early sources), it is OE *ōra* bank, slope.

Woźniak Polish: 1. occupational name for a coachman, driver, or carter, Pol. *woźinica* (from *wozić* to convey, carry).

2. occupational name for a bailiff, Pol. *woźny* (likewise from *wozić*, in the transferred sense 'carry out (a magistrate's decisions)'.

Vars.: **Woźni(a)cki**, **Wońicko**. (Of 2 only): **Woźny**.

Cogn. (of 1): Czech: **Vozka**.

Patr.: Pol.: **Woźniakiewicz**.

Habitation name: Pol.: **Woźniakowski**.

Wraith N English: nickname for someone with a violent temper, from Northern ME *wrath* angry (OE *wrāð*). Reaney cites John *Wrayth*, recorded in 1587 as the son of Thomas *Wrath*. The S English forms **Wro(a)th** are far less common (for the vowel, cf. ROPER).

Cogns.: Low Ger.: **Wreth**, **Wre(d)e**.

Wray N English: habitation name from any of various minor places in N England, so called from ON *vrá* nook, corner, recess.

Vars.: **Wra**, **Wrey**, **Wroe**, RAY.

Wren 1. English: nickname from the bird (ME *wrenne*, OE *wrenna*, *wrænna*), probably in reference to its small size.

2. Irish: Anglicized form of Gael. **Ó Rinn** 'descendant of *Rinn*', a personal name from *rinn* star, constellation.

Vars.: **Wrenn**. (Of 2 only): **(O')Rinne**, **Rynn(e)**, **Wrynn**.

Wrigglesworth English: habitation name from a place in W Yorks., now called *Woodlesford* but recorded in the 12th cent. as *Wridelesford*, apparently from OE **wrīdels*, a deriv. of *wrīd* bush, thicket + *ford* FORD. The change of the final element in the surname is a relatively late development.

Vars.: **Wriglesworth**, **Rigglesford**, **Riggulsford**.

Wright English and Scots: common occupational name for a maker of machinery or objects, mostly in wood, of any of a wide range of kinds, from OE *wyrhta*, *wryhta* craftsman (a deriv. of *wyrcan* to work, make). The term is found in several combinations (cf., e.g., CARTWRIGHT and WAINWRIGHT), but when used in isolation it generally referred to a builder of windmills or watermills.

Vars.: **Wrighte**, **Wraight(e)**, **Wreight**, **Wrate**.

Patrs.: **Wrightson**, **Wrixon**.

Wrigley English (Lancs.): habitation name from *Wrigley* Head near Salford, the second element of which is presumably OE *lēah* wood, clearing; the first may be a personal name or topographical term from OE *wrigian* to strive, bend, turn.

Var.: **Rigley** (Notts.).

Wring English (Bristol): topographic name for someone living on the river in Somerset formerly known as the *Wring* (now called the Yeo). The river name is of uncertain derivation, perhaps from a Brit. word meaning 'twisted', 'crooked'.

Wrocławski Polish: habitation name from the city of *Wrocław* in W Poland (Ger. BRESLAU), with the addition of the surname suffix *-ski* (see BARANOWSKI). The placename is attested in the 11th cent. as *Wortizlaua*, i.e. castle of *Wortislav*, a Slav. personal name. Later this became *Wrocisław*, and eventually contracted to *Wrocław*.

Wrottesley English: habitation name from a place in Staffs., apparently so called from the gen. case of an OE personal name **Wrott* + OE *lēah* wood, clearing.

Vars.: **Wriottesley**, **Wrothesley**.

Many bearers of this name are of Norman ancestry and can be traced to Simon, son of William de Coctune, who held the manor of Wrottesley c.1165. It was his son, known initially as William de Verdon, who is first recorded with the surname de Wrottesle.

Wrzesiński Polish: from Pol. *wrzesień* September + *-ski* suffix of surnames (see BARANOWSKI). The name was generally acquired by someone born or baptized in September, in particular a convert who adopted Christianity in that month.

Vars.: **Wrzesieński**.

Habitation name: **Wrześniewski**.

Wunderlich 1. German: nickname for an eccentric or moody person, from Ger., MHG *wunderlich* odd, capricious, unpredictable (a deriv. of *wunder*, OHG *wundar* puzzle, marvel).

2. Jewish (Ashkenazic): probably an anecdotal nickname from Yid. *vunderlekh* wonderful, marvellous, based on some now irrecoverable event, but possibly also a descriptive nickname from Ger. *wunderlich* odd, strange.

Vars. (of 1): **Wünderlich, Winderlich**.

Wundt German: nickname for a maimed or crippled person, from MHG, OHG *wunt* wounded, disabled.

Würfel German: nickname for an enthusiastic gambler, from Ger. *Würfel* die, dice (MHG *würfel*, OHG *wurfil*, a deriv. of *werfan* to throw). In some cases it may have originated as a metonymic occupational name for a maker of dice.

Var.: **Werfel** (Bohemia; also Jewish).

Cogn.: Low Ger.: **Wörpel**.

Wurst German: from Ger. *Wurst* sausage (MHG, OHG *wurst*, a collective noun), either a metonymic occupational name for a butcher who specialized in the production of spiced sausages, or a nickname for a plump person or someone who was particularly fond of such sausages.

Vars.: **Wurst(n)er, Wurstler** (agent derivs.).

Cogns.: Low Ger., Du.: **Worst**.

Dim.: Ger.: **Würstl(e)**.

Württemberg German: habitation name from a castle and town in S Germany, which gave its name to the state of which Stuttgart was the capital. The surname may also be a regional name from this state. The castle is first recorded as *Wirteneberg*; the final element is clearly OHG *berg* hill, and Bahlow suggests that the first may represent an ancient element meaning 'reeds', 'rushes'.

The German noble house of Württemberg *trace their descent from Konrad* von Wirtemberg, *who was living at the end of the 11th cent.*

Wüst German: topographic name for someone who lived on a piece of waste land, from Ger. *Wüste* empty, uncultivated land (MHG *wüeste*, OHG *wuosti*).

Vars.: **Wüst(n)er, Wiestner; Wüstemann, Wustmann**.

Cogns.: Low Ger.: **Wöst(e), Weuste, Wöstmann**. Flem.: **Verwaest**.

Wyatt English: from the medieval given name *Wiot*, *Wyot*, *Gyot*, which derives from the OE personal name *Wīgheard*, composed of the elements *wīg* war + *heard* hardy, brave, strong. Under Norman influence it was also adopted as a dim. of both Guy 1 and William.

Vars.: **Whyatt, W(h)yard; Guyat(t), Gyatt**.

Cogns.: Fr.: **Guyard, Gui(h)ard, Guyart**.

Dim.: Fr.: **Guyardeau**.

An English family called Wyatt *were closely linked with the Boleyn family and through them with Henry VIII. Sir Henry Wyatt was joint Constable of Norwich Castle with Thomas Boleyn, whose daughter Anne was raised with Sir Henry's son, Sir Thomas Wyatt (?1503–42). The latter's great-grandson, Sir Francis Wyatt (?1588–1644) became governor of Virginia. His wife's family had great influence with the London Virginia Company, and Wyatt was named the Company's governor in 1621 and became the first Royal Governor in 1624.*

Wycliffe English: habitation name from a place in N Yorks., situated on a bend in the Tees, and probably named from OE *wiht* bend (see Wight 2) + *clif* slope, bank (see Clive).

Wye English: 1. habitation name from a place in Kent, so called from the dat. case (originally used after a preposition) of OE *wēoh* pagan temple.

2. var. of Guy.

Wygodarz Polish: occupational name for an innkeeper, Pol. *wygodarz* (an agent deriv. of *wygoda* comfort, convenience, inn).

Cogns.: Jewish (E Ashkenazic): **Wigod(n)er, Vigodner, Wigodman**.

Wyman English: from the ME given name *Wymund*, OE *Wīgmund* (composed of the elements *wīg* war + *mund* protection), reinforced by the cogn. ON form *Vígmundr*, introduced by Scandinavian settlers in N England.

Vars.: **Wymann, Whyman(t), W(h)ayman, Whaymand, Whaymond, W(h)aymont, Whamond, Weyman, Weymont**.

Patr.: **Wymans**.

Wymer English: 1. from the ME given name *Wymer*, OE *Wīgmǣr* (composed of the elements *wīg* war + *mǣr* famous), reinforced by the cogn. Continental Gmc form *Wigmar*, introduced into England by the Normans.

2. from the OBret. personal name *Wiumarch*, composed of the elements *uuiu* worthy + *march* horse. The name was borne by both men and women and became relatively popular in E Anglia during the early Middle Ages as a result of the influence of Bretons who settled there in the wake of the Conquest.

Vars. (of 1): Guymer. (Of 2): **W(a)ymark**.

Cogns.: Fr.: **Guimar(d)**.

Patr. (from 1): Du.: **Wimmers**.

Wyndham 1. English: habitation name from a place in W Sussex, near W Grinstead, apparently so called from an OE personal name *Winda* + OE *hamm* water meadow; or from *Wymondham* in Leics. and Norfolk, so called from the OE personal name *Wīgmund* (see Wyman) + OE *hām* homestead. The name *de Wyndem* is found in Westmorland as early as 1284, and the surname may additionally derive from some unidentified place in N England.

2. Irish: Anglicized form of various Gael. names derived from *gaoith* wind; cf. e.g. Gahan 2.

Var.: **Windham**.

Wypych Polish: occupational name for a judicial investigator or a spy, from OPol. *wypych*, a deriv. of *wypytać* to find out (from *wy-* out + *pytać* to ask).

Wyrębski Polish: topographic name for someone who lived in a clearing in a wood, from Pol. *wyrąb* clearing (a deriv. of *wyrąbeć* to fell, cut down) + *-ski* suffix of surnames (see Baranowski).

Wyrzkowski Polish: habitation name from a place called *Wyrzeka*, from Pol. *wyrzek* source (of a river), with the addition of *-ski*, suffix of local surnames (see Baranowski).

Wysocki Polish and Jewish (E Ashkenazic): habitation name from a placename such as *Wysocko* or *Wysoko* (named from Pol. *wysoki* high), with the addition of *-ski*, suffix of local surnames (see BARANOWSKI).

Var.: Pol.: **Wysokiński**.

Wyszyński Polish: occupational name for an innkeeper or seller of alcoholic drinks, from Pol. *wyszynk* sale of alcoholic drinks + *-ski* suffix of surnames (see BARANOWSKI).

Wythe English: topographic name for someone who lived by a willow tree, ME *wythe* (OE *wiððe*, a byform of *wīðig*; cf. WITHEY).

Vars.: **Wyth, With(e)**.

American bearers of the surname Wythe *trace their ancestry to Thomas Wythe, who emigrated from England to Virginia in 1680. One of his descendants was the judge George Wythe (1726–1806), mentor of Jefferson and one of the signatories of the Declaration of Independence.*

Xenakis Greek: patr. from the nickname *Xenos* 'Stranger', denoting a newcomer to a locality.

Y

Yagodin Russian: patr. from the nickname *Yagoda* 'Berry', given perhaps to a small, wizened man, or to someone who gathered and sold berries, or to someone who lived by a tree that produced them.

Cogns.: Beloruss.: **Yahadzinski**. Pol.: **Jagodziński**, **Jagodzki**; **Jagoda**. Czech: **Jahoda** ('strawberry'). Croatian: **Jagodič** (patr.). Jewish (Ashkenazic): **Yagoda**; **Yagodnick** (occupational for a seller of berries); **Yagodjinski**, **Jagodzinski**.

Dim.: Russ.: **Yagodkin** (patr.).

Yagüe Spanish: apparently a religious byname for someone who was born on St James' Day, from OSp. *Santi Yague*, a frequent medieval form of SANTIAGO.

Yale Welsh: habitation name for someone who lived in the commote of *Iâl* (near Wrexham in NE Wales), so called from W *iâl* fertile or arable upland.

Yale *University in America takes its name from an early benefactor, Elihu Yale (1649–1721), an American merchant of Welsh ancestry. He was born in Boston into a family who originated in Wrexham, Wales; his father, David Yale, had settled in New Hampshire in 1637. The Yale lock was invented by Linus Yale (1821–68), ultimately a member of the same family. He was born in Salisbury, New York, descended from Thomas Yale, who settled in New Hampshire in 1637, probably a brother of David.*

Yallop English (Norfolk): of unknown origin. According to Barber it derives from the ON personal name or byname *Hjálpr* 'Help', whereas Harrison believes that it is a topographic name composed of the ME elements *yelow*, *yalow* yellow + *hop(e)* enclosed valley (see HOPE).

Yapp English (chiefly W Midlands): nickname for a clever or cunning person, from the ME adj. *yap* devious (OE *gēap*). The OE word, which seems to have meant originally 'open', 'wide', also had the sense 'curved', 'bent', but this does not appear to have survived into the period of surname formation.

Var.: **Yap**.

Yarbrough English: habitation name from places in Lincs. called *Yarborough* and *Yarburgh*, from OE *eorðburg* earthworks, fortifications (a cpd of *eorð* earth, soil + *burh* fortress, stronghold).

Var.: **Yarborough**.

Yard English: 1. topographic name for someone who lived by an enclosure of some kind, ME *yard(e)* (OE *geard*; cf. GARTH).

2. nickname from ME *yard* rod, stick (OE (Anglian) *gerd*), probably with reference to a rod or staff carried as a symbol of authority.

3. from the same word as in 2, used to denote a measure of land. The surname probably denoted someone who held this quantity of land, and as it was quite a large amount (varying at different periods and in different places, but generally approximately 30 acres, a quarter of a hide), such a person would have been a reasonably prosperous farmer.

Var.: **Yarde**.

Yardley English (W Midlands): habitation name from any of various places, for example *Yardley* in the W Midlands, Essex, Northants, etc., or *Yarley* in Somerset, so called from OE *gerd* pole, stick (see YARD 2) + *lēah* wood, clearing. The cpd apparently referred to a forest where timber could be gathered.

Vars.: **Year(d)ley**.

Yarham English (Norfolk): apparently a habitation name from some unidentified minor place, perhaps on the river *Yare*. If so, it would be named from the river (a Brit. river name of uncertain meaning; possibly, according to Ekwall, 'Babbling') + OE *hām* homestead or *hamm* water meadow.

Yarrow English: 1. topographic name for someone who lived by a river of this name in Lancs. or by one in the Border region of Scotland, both apparently so called from a Brit. cogn. of W *garw*, Gael. *garbh* rough. The one in Scotland has also given its name to a town that stands by it.

2. topographic name for someone who lived in a place overgrown with the plant yarrow, OE *gearwe*.

Yarwood English (Lancs.): habitation name, probably from *Yarwood* in Ches. Despite its modern frequency and concentration, the surname does not seem to be recorded in Lancs. before the 17th cent., when it is found as *Ye(a)rwood*.

Var.: **Yearwood**.

Yastrebov Russian: patr. from the nickname *Yastreb* 'Hawk', given perhaps to a cruel or rapacious man. The vocab. word derives from an element meaning originally 'swift'.

Var.: **Yastrebtsov**.

Cogns.: Pol.: **Jastrzębski**. Jewish (E Ashkenazic): **Jastrzebski**, **Jastrzabski** (ornamental names).

Yate N English: topographic name for someone who lived near a gate or metonymic occupational name for a gatekeeper, from OE *geat* gate; cf. GATES.

Vars.: **Yates**, **Yeat(e)s**, **Yetts**; **Y(e)atman**, **Yetman**.

Yaxley English (E Anglia): habitation name from a place so called, of which there is one in Suffolk and another in Cambs. (formerly Hunts.). The name is derived from the gen. case of OE *gēac* cuckoo (perhaps a byname) + *lēah* wood, clearing.

Yeadon English (Yorks.): habitation name from a place in W Yorks. Ekwall suggests that the placename may come from OE *hēah* high + *dūn* hill.

Yefimov Russian: patr. from the given name *Yefim*, a Russ. form of Gk *Euthumios* 'Cheerful' or 'Bold' (composed of the elements *eu* good, well + *thumos* heart, mind, spirit). This name was borne by various early saints, among them Euthumios the Great (378–473), an Armenian monk highly revered in the Orthodox Church.

Vars.: **Yevfimov**, **Yefimyev**, **Yefimanov**, **Nefimanov**, **Nefimonov**.

Dims.: **Yefimychev**, **Yefimochkin**, **Yefimtsev**, **Yefintsov**, **Fimichev**, **Khimichev** (all patrs.).

Yefremov Russian: patr. from the given name *Yefrem*, a Russ. form of Hebr. *Efrayim* Efraim (lit., 'Meadows'). In the Bible this name is borne by the younger son of Joseph. In W Europe the given name is found mainly among Jews. In the Orthodox Church, however, it is much more widespread, as a result of having been borne by a 4th-cent. Syrian saint famous for his biblical commentaries and mariological hymns.

Var.: **Afremov**.

Cogn. (not patr. in form): Jewish (Ashkenazic): **Froim** (from *Froyim*, an aphetic Yid. form of the given name).

Cogns. (patrs.): Jewish (Ashkenazic): **Efroimson**, **Yefroimovich**, **Froimovitch**, **Frojmowicz**, **Froimowitz**, **Froimovitz**, **Froimovits**; **Froimovici** (Rumanian spelling). Croatian: **Jevremović**.

Dims. (patrs.): Russ.: **Yefremushkin**. Jewish (E Ashkenazic): **Fromc(h)enko**; **Froikin** (from the Yid. dim. given name *Froyke*).

Yelland English (Devon): habitation name from any of several places called *Yelland* (from OE *ēald* old + *land* land), or conceivably from *Yealand* in Lancs. (so called from OE *hēah* high + *land* land).

Var.: **Yealland**.

Yeo English (chiefly Devon and Somerset): topographic name for someone who lived near a stream, from OE *ēa* stream, river (cf. NYE, RYE 1, and TYE 1), which became *ya* or *yo* in the ME dials. of Somerset and Devon, and gave rise to several river names and minor placenames in this region.

Vars.: **Yeoh**, **Yea**; **Attyea**; YEOMAN.

Yeoman English: 1. status name, from ME *yoman*, *yeman*, used of an attendant of relatively high status in a noble household, ranking beween a SERGEANT and a GROOM, or between a SQUIRE and a PAGE. The word appears to derive from a cpd of OE *geong* YOUNG + *mann* man. Later in the ME period it came to be used of a modest independent freeholder, and this latter sense may well lie behind some examples of the surname.

2. topographic name, a var. of YEO.

Vars. (of 1): **Youngman**, **Younkman** (Norfolk; also simply a nickname). (Of 2): **Ye(a)man**.

Patr. (from 1): **Yeomans** (chiefly Midlands).

Yepifanov Russian: patr. from the given name *Yepifan*, a Russ. form of Gk *Epiphanios* (from *epiphanē* epiphany, manifestation, from *epiphainein* to show, display). This name was borne by a 4th-cent. bishop of Salamis, venerated in the Orthodox Church.

Var.: **Yepifanyev**.

Dims.: **Yepish(ch)ev**, **Yepishin**, **Yepikhin** (all patrs.).

Yerburgh English: habitation name from a place in Lincs., probably so called from OE *g(i)erd*, a land measure (see YARD 3) + *burh* fortress, town.

A family of this name trace their descent back to a certain Germund, who held lands at Grainthorpe, Lincs., between 1040 and 1089.

Yerushalmi Jewish: from the Hebr. habitational name *Yerushalmi* Jerusalemite, from Hebr. *Yerushalayim* Jerusalem. The name may have been adopted by Jews in exile as a symbol of the longed-for homeland, or have referred to someone who had made a pilgrimage to the Holy Land, or have been adopted by someone who was born there and later migrated elsewhere.

Vars.: **Yero(u)shalmi**, **Yerushalmy**, **Jerushalmi**, **Jerushalmy**, **Ieroushalmi**, **Urshalimi**; **Yerushamsky**; **Jerozolimski** (from the Pol. adj. derived from the placename).

Leon **Uris** *(b. 1924), the American novelist, was born in Baltimore, Maryland. His parents were E Ashkenazic Jews; his mother was a first-generation American, and his father, a shopkeeper whose name was originally* Yerushalmi, *settled in America after emigrating from Poland after the First World War.*

Yevdokimov Russian: patr. from the given name *Yevdokim*, a Russ. form of Gk *Eudokimos* 'Respected' (from *eu* good, well + *dokein* to seem). The name was borne by a 9th-cent. saint, governor of Cappodocia, much revered in the Orthodox Church.

Var.: **Ovdkimov**.

Dims.: **Evdakov**, **Evdonin**, **Evdoshin**, **Avdakov**, **Aldakov**, **Avdon(k)in**, **Aldonin**, **Aldoshin** (all patrs.). Beloruss.: **Evdokinchik**.

Yevtikhiev Russian: patr. from the given name *Yevtikhi*, a Russ. form of Gk. *Eutykhios* 'Fortunate' (from *eu* good, well + *tykhē* chance, fortune). This name was borne by various early Christian saints, notably a 6th-cent. bishop of Constantinople much revered in the Orthodox Church.

Vars.: **Yevtikhov**, **Yev(s)tikheev**, **Yev(s)tifeev**, **Yestifeev**, **Yevtyukhov**, **Ovtukhov**, **Oltukhov**, **Avtukhov**, **Altukhov**, **Altufyev**, **Antifeev**.

Cogns.: Croatian: **Jevt(ov)ić**, **Jeftić**.

Dims.: Russ.: **Yevteev**, **Yevtyugin** (patrs.). Ukr.: **Yevtushenko**.

Yezhov Russian: patr. from the nickname *Yozh* 'Hedgehog', presumably denoting a man of prickly, shy, or unapproachable temperament.

Cogns.: Pol.: **Jeż**, **Jeżak**.

Dims.: Czech: **Ježek**.

Habitation names: Pol.: **Jeżewski**, **Jeżowski** (either 'place of the hedgehog' or 'place where a man nicknamed Hedgehog lived').

Yoel Jewish: from the Hebr. male given name *Yoel* (Eng. *Joel*), borne by a biblical prophet.

Vars.: **Joel** (see also JEKYLL); **Yoeli**, **Joeli**, **Joely** (with the Hebr. suffix *-i*).

Dim.: **Yolleck** (E Ashkenazic).

Patrs.: **Joels(on)**, **Yoelson**, **Yolles**, **Jol(l)es** (Ashkenazic).

Al **Jolson** *(1886–1950), the singer and actor, was originally called Asa* Yoelson. *He was born in Russia, the son of a rabbi who emigrated to America in 1894.*

Yolkin Russian: 1. patr. from the given name *Yolka*, dim. of any of the various Russ. names beginning with the syllable *Yel-*. None of these names is individually very frequent; they include *Yelevferi* (Gk *Eleutherios* 'Free') and *Yelizar* (Hebr. *Eliezer*; see LAZAR).

2. patr. from the nickname *Yolka* 'Fir' (a dim. of the common noun *yel*, cogn. with Pol. *jodła* fir, spruce), given perhaps to a tall, thin man, or to someone who lived by a fir tree.

Cogns. (of 1): Croatian: **Jel(ič)ić**. (Of 2): Czech: **Jedlička**, **Jehlička**. Jewish (E Ashkenazic): **Jodla**, **Yodla** (both ornamental).

Habitation name (cogn. with 2): Pol.: **Jodłowski**.

York English: habitation name from the city of York in N England, or perhaps in some cases regional name from the county of Yorkshire. The surname is now widespread throughout England. Originally, the town bore the Brit. name *Eburăcum*, which probably meant 'yew-tree place'. This was altered by folk etymology into OE *Eoforwīc* (from the elements *eofor* wild boar + *wīc* outlying settlement (see WICK)). This name was taken over by Scandinavian settlers in the area, who altered it back to opacity in the form *Iorvík* and eventually *Iork*, in which form it was finally settled by the 13th cent. The surname has also been adopted by Jews as an Anglicization of various like-sounding Jewish surnames.

Var.: Eng.: **Yorke**.

Yorkston Scots (Edinburgh): habitation name from a place near the village of Corstorphine, recorded in 1354 as

Yokistoun, in 1374 as *Yorkeston*, apparently from the gen. case of the ON personal name *Jórek* + ME *toun* settlement.

Vars.: **Yo(u)rston, Yorstoun, Yorkson.**

Young English: distinguishing name, from ME *yunge*, *yonge* young (OE *geong*), for the younger of two bearers of the same given name, usually a son who bore the same name as his father. In ME this name is often found with the ANF def. art., e.g. Robert *le Yunge*.

Vars.: **Younge, Yong(e).**

Cogns.: Ger.: **Jung(e), Junk.** Flem., Du.: **(De) Jong(h)(e), Jonk.** Jewish (Ashkenazic): **Jung(er), Jungerman(n)** (given to or assumed by people who were young at the time of surname assumption).

Patrs.: Eng.: **Youngs** (common in Norfolk). Flem., Du.: **Jongen.**

Younger English: 1. distinguishing name, a var. of Young, from the comparative of OE *geong* young.

2. Anglicized form of MDu. *jonghheer* young nobleman (a cpd of *jong(h)* young + *herr* master, lord; cf. Ger. *Junker*). The term was used of a member of the European nobility who had not yet assumed knighthood.

Cogns. (of 2): Ger.: **Jun(c)ker.** Flem., Du.: **(De) Jonckheere, Jonker.**

Patrs. (from 2): Ger.: **Junkers.** Flem., Du.: **Jonkers.**

Yubero Spanish: occupational name for an oxherd or muleteer, from Sp. *yubero*, a dial. var. of *yuguero* (LL *iugārius*, an agent deriv. of *iugum* yoke).

Yule Scots and English: nickname for someone who was born on Christmas Day or had some other connection with this time of year, from ME *yule* Christmastide (OE *gēol*, reinforced by the cogn. ON *jól*). This was originally the name of a pagan midwinter festival, which was later appropriated by the Christian Church for celebration of the birth of Christ. Its further etymology is unknown.

Vars.: **Youle, Youel, You(hi)ll, Yoell, Yeowell, Y(e)uell, Yuile, Yuill(e).**

Cogns.: Dan., Norw.: **Juul, Juhl, Juel.** Swed.: **Ju(h)lin.**

Patrs.: Eng.: **Youles, Youels.**

Z

Zabala Spanish: habitation name from a place in the province of Biscay, so called from Basque *zabal* small square + the def. art. *-a*. In some cases the surname may derive directly from the vocab. word.

Var.: **Zaballa** (places in the provinces of Burgos and Logroño).

Zaborowski Polish: habitation name from a place near Leszno called *Zaborowo* (probably named with the Pol. elements *za* beyond + *bór* forest + *-owo* suffix of place-names, but alternatively perhaps from *zabór* sequestration). It could alternatively be a topographic name for someone who lived 'on the other side of the forest'.

Var.: **Zaborski**.

Cogn.: Jewish (E Ashkenazic): **Zaborovsky**.

Zábranský Czech: topographic name for someone who lived 'behind the gate' (*za branou*) of a town, or at a place named *Zábraní*, from these elements.

Var.: **Zábrana**.

Zachary Jewish, Polish, and English: from the Hebr. male given name *Zecharya*, composed of the elements *zachar* to remember + *ya* God. This name was borne by a biblical prophet and by the father of John the Baptist, and for that reason it achieved a modest popularity among Gentiles during the Middle Ages. The given name has always been popular among Jews.

Vars.: Jewish: **Za(c)haria**, **Zachari(a)s** (Ashkenazic); **Zachariasz**, **Zachari(a)sh**, **Sachariasch** (E Ashkenazic). Pol.: **Zachara**, **Zachariasz**; **Zacharski**.

Cogns.: Ger.: **Zacher(t)**, SACHER; **Zacharias**, **Zachri(e)s**, **Zachreis**. Czech: **Zachariáš**. Rum.: **Zaharia**. Hung.: **Zakariás**. Gk: **Zacharia(s)**. It.: **Zaccaria**.

Dims.: Ger.: **Zacherl**, **Sacherl**, **Zecherle**, **Zechel**. Czech: **Zach**. It.: **Zaccariello**, **Zaccarielli**, **Zaccarino**, **Zaccarini**, **Zaccherini**, **Zacchiroli**.

Aug.: It.: **Zaccheroni**.

Patrs.: Eng.: **Ackery**, **Ackary** (apparently the result of misdivision of the extinct *FitzZackery*). Dan., Norw.: **Zachariessen**. Swed.: **Za(c)krisson**, **Zachrisson**. Jewish: **Zacharin**, **Zacharovitch**, **Zaharovich**, **Zacharowicz**, **Zacharowitz**, **Zacharovitz**, **Zacharovits** (E Ashkenazic); **Zahareanu**, **Zaharianu** (among Rumanian Jews). Russ.: **Zakharov**, **Sakharov**, **Zakharyev**, **Zakharyin**. Bulg.: **Zakhariev**. Gk: **Zachariou**, **Zachariades**.

Zadik Jewish: from Yid. *tsadik* pious, saintly man (cf. TSADOK).

Vars.: **Tzadik**, **Tsaddik**, **Zadek**; **Zadiki** (with the Hebr. suffix *-i*).

Patrs.: **Zadikov**, **Zadikoff**, **Zadickoviz**; **Tzadikian** (among Iranian Jews).

Zafra Spanish: habitation name from any of various places so called, notably one in the province of Extremadura. The placename is from OSp. *zafra*, *çafra* rock, crag (of Arabic origin). In some cases the surname may be a topographic name derived directly from the vocab. word.

Zagórski Polish and Jewish (E Ashkenazic): topographic name composed of the Pol. elements *za* beyond, on the other side of + *góra* hill (see GÓRSKI) + the local surname suffix *-ski* (see BARANOWSKI), or habitation name from a place named with the elements *za* + *góra*.

Vars.: Pol.: **Zagórny**, **Zagórowski**. Jewish: **Zagorsky**, **Zagursky**.

Cogns.: Czech: **Záhora**; **Záhorský** (habitation name). Croatian: **Zagorac**.

Zahn German and Jewish (Ashkenazic): nickname for someone with a large or peculiar tooth or a remarkable or defective set of teeth, from Ger. *Zahn* tooth (MHG *zan(t)*).

Var.: Ger.: **Zandt**.

Dims.: Ger.: **Zähnle**, **Zehnle**.

Zahradník Czech: occupational name for a person who farmed on a small scale, from *zahrada* smallholding, orchard, or garden. A *zahradník* held lands larger than those of a cotter (*chalupník*) but smaller than those of a farmer (*sedlák*).

Dim.: **Zahradníček**.

Habitation name: **Zahrádka** (from a place named with this word in its earlier sense 'enclosure').

Zähringen German: habitation name from a place so called near Freiburg in Breisgau.

The title Duke of Zahringen *was first assumed in 1100 by Berchtold, a descendant of Berchtold I, Count in Breisgau 962–8. From them descends the former Grand Ducal house of Baden.*

Zaitsev Russian: patr. from the nickname *Zayats* (gen. *Zaitsa*) 'Hare', denoting a swift runner. (The Slav. term meant originally 'jumper', 'leaper'.)

Cogns. (not patrs.): Pol.: **Zając**. Czech: **Zajíc**. Croatian: **Zec**. Jewish (E Ashkenazic): **Zaitz**, **Zajac** (ornamental names). Ger. (of Slav. origin): **Zajac**, **Zajec**.

Cogns. (patrs.): Croatian: **Zečević**. Jewish (E Ashkenazic): **Zai(t)zov**, **Zaitsov**.

Dims.: Pol.: **Zajączek**. Czech: **Zajíček**. Jewish: **Zaicik**, **Zajczyk**. Ger. (of Slav. origin): **Zajacek**, **Zajecek**.

Habitation name (from a dim.): Pol.: **Zajączkowski** (also borne by Karaites in Poland, presumably an adoption of the Pol. surname).

Żak Polish: nickname for a youthful or studious person, from Pol. *żak* student, schoolboy. The original meaning of this word was 'novice, candidate for the priesthood', and so in some cases it is perhaps a nickname for one who had been destined for holy orders.

Cogn.: Czech: **Žák**.

Dim.: Czech: **Žáček**.

Aug.: Czech: **Žákovec**.

Patr.: Pol.: **Żakiewicz**.

Habitation names: Pol.: **Żakowski**. Czech: **Žákovský**.

Zákostelecký Czech: topographic name for someone who lived 'behind the church', from Czech *za* behind + *kostel* church + *-ec* suffix of animate nouns + *-ský* adjectival suffix applied used in forming local names.

Zakrzewski Polish: habitation name from a place called *Zakrzewie* (from Pol. *za* beyond + *krzewie* thicket, collective noun from *kierz* bush), with the addition of *-ski*, suffix of local surnames (see BARANOWSKI).

Var.: **Zakrzeski**.

Załęcki Polish: topographic name for someone who lived 'on the other side of the meadow', from Pol. *za* beyond + *łąka* meadow + *-ski* suffix of local surnames (see BARANOWSKI).

Var.: **Załęski**.

Zaleski Polish: 1. topographic name for someone who lived 'on the other side of the wood', from Pol. *za* beyond + *les*, *las* wood, with the addition of *-ski*, suffix of local surnames (see BARANOWSKI), or habitation name from a place, *Zalesie*, named with the elements *za* + *les*.
2. var. of ZALEWSKI.
Vars. (of 1): **Zalasa, Zalasik.**
Cogns. (of 1): Czech: **Záleský.** Jewish (E Ashkenazic): **Zalesky.**

Zalewski Polish: topographic name for someone who lived by a flood plain or bay, Pol. *zalew*, or habitation name from a place named with this element, with the addition of *-ski*, suffix of local surnames (see BARANOWSKI). There has been considerable confusion with ZALESKI.
Cogn.: Jewish (E Ashkenazic): **Zalewsky.**

Zaliznyak Ukrainian: occupational name for an ironmonger or, less commonly, a blacksmith. The vocab. word is an agentive deriv. from Ukr. *zalizo* iron.
Var.: **Zheleznyak.**
Cogns.: Beloruss.: **Zhaleznyakov** (patr., Russianized as **Zheleznyakov**). Pol.: **Żelaski, Żelazny.** Czech: **Železný.** Jewish (E Ashkenazic): **Zelazo; Zalaznik, Zelezniak.**
Habitation name: Pol.: **Żelazowski.**

Zámečník Czech: occupational name for a locksmith, Czech *zámečník*, agent noun derived from *zámek* lock (which also means 'castle').
Var.: **Zámek** (also a topographic name for someone who lived in or by a castle).

Zammit Jewish (E Ashkenazic): regional name from *Zamet*, the Yid. name of Samogitia, an area of Lithuania.

Zamora Spanish: habitation name from a city in NW Spain, the name of which is of Arabic origin, apparently from *azemur* wild olive.
Var.: **Zamorano.**

Zangwill Jewish (Ashkenazic): ornamental name from Hebr. *zangvil* ginger.
Var.: **Zangvil.**

Zappa Italian: metonymic occupational name for an agricultural worker, from It. *zappa* mattock.
Var.: **Zappi.**
Dims.: **Zappell(in)i, Zappetta, Zappett(in)i, Zappini, Zappino; Zapp(ar)oli** (Emilia); **Zapulla, Zappulli** (Sicily).

Zaragoza Spanish: habitation name from *Zaragoza*, Sp. name of the city of Saragossa in NE Spain, the ancient capital of the kingdom of Aragon. The name derives, via Arabic, from L *Caesarea Augusta*, the name bestowed in the 1st cent. AD by the Emperor Augustus, from two of the names belonging to the imperial house (cf. CESARE and AGOSTI).
Cogns.: Jewish (Sefardic): **Saragos(s)i, Sargossi, Saragosti, Saragusti.**

Zárate Spanish form of Basque **Zarate**: habitation name from a place in the province of Álava, so called from the elements *zara* (oak) wood + *ate* pass, defile.

Zaremba Polish: occupational name for a woodcutter, a deriv. of Pol. *zarębać* to hack, chop.
Vars.: **Zaręba; Zarębski, Zarembski.**
Cogn.: Czech: **Záruba** (also a topographic name for someone living by an enclosure).

Zarraga Basque: topographic name for someone who lived by a slag heap, from *zarra* slag + the local suffix *-aga*.

Zarza Spanish: topographic name for someone who lived on a patch of land overgrown with brambles, from Sp. *zarza* bramble (of pre-Roman origin).

Zarzecki Polish and Jewish (E Ashkenazic): topographic name for someone who lived 'on the other side of the river', from Pol. *za* beyond + *rzek(a)* river, with the addition of *-ski*, suffix of local surnames (see BARANOWSKI). The Jewish surname may possibly also be a habitation name from the city of *Shklov Zaretski* in the Ukraine, which bore the distinguishing epithet to differentiate it from *Shklov Dneprovski*, a town of the same name situated on the banks of the Dnieper. However, this is only conjecture: when Ashkenazic surnames are based on compound placenames, it is as a rule only the first element of the placename that forms the basis for the surname.
Vars.: Pol.: **Zarzycki.** Jewish: **Zarecki, Zarecky, Zaretski, Zare(t)zki.**

Zasada Polish: status name for a person who organized a new settlement, OPol. *zasadźca*. The name has been altered by folk etymology to conform to the mod. Pol. word *zasada* principle, basis (which formerly meant 'trap' or 'ambush').
Habitation name: **Zasadziński.**

Zatorski Polish: habitation name from the town of *Zator* near Oświęcim in S Poland.
Cogn.: Jewish (E Ashkenazic): **Zatorsky.**

Zauner German: occupational name for a fence-builder, from an agent deriv. of Ger. *Zaun* fence, hedge, enclosure (MHG, OHG *zūn*, a cogn. of OE *tūn* enclosure, settlement). The vocab. word denoted in particular the enclosure built surrounding a village as a defence against marauding animals and strangers. In some cases the surname may also be a topographic name for someone who lived by such a fence.
Vars.: **Zäuner, Zeuner.**
Cogns.: Flem., Du.: **Tuyn(s).**

Zavetaev Russian: patr. from the nickname *Zavetai* 'Heir' (a deriv. of *zavet* will, testament), denoting someone who had inherited or was due to inherit a substantial estate or fortune.
Cogn.: Czech: **Zavěta.**

Zawadzki Polish and Jewish (E Ashkenazic): nickname for a troublesome or troubled person, from Pol. *zawada* difficulty, obstacle, with the addition of the surname suffix *-ski* (see BARANOWSKI). In some cases it may be a topographic name for someone who lived by a physical obstruction.
Vars.: **Zawada, Zawadski.** Jewish only: **Zavadzki, Zavatzky, Zawacki; Zawader.**
Cogns.: Czech: **Závada, Zavadil.**
Habitation name: Pol.: **Zawadowski.**

Zawierucha Polish and Jewish (E Ashkenazic): nickname or, as a Jewish name, ornamental name from Pol. *zawierucha* snowstorm, blizzard.

Zawiślak Polish: 1. topographic name for someone who lived on the 'far side' of the River Vistula, from Pol. *za* beyond + *wiśl-* (from *Wisła* Vistula) + *-ak* suffix denoting animate nouns.
2. nickname for a hanger-on, from Pol. *zawisły* dependent.

Zayas Jewish (Ashkenazic): ornamental name, derived from the Ashkenazic pronunciation, *zayis*, of Hebr. *zayit* olive.

Zazo Spanish: nickname for someone with a lisp. The adj. is of imitative origin, representing the pronunciation of /s/ as /θ/ (written in Sp. as *z*).

Zdeněk Czech: from the OSlav. personal name *Zdeněk*, pet form of *Zdeslav*, composed of the elements *zde* here + *slav* glory, i.e. bringer of glory.
Vars.: **Zděnek**; **Zděnovec**.
Cogn.: Pol.: **Zdan**.
Patr.: Pol.: **Zdanowicz**.
Habitation name: Pol.: **Zdanowski**.

Zdrojewski Polish: habitation name from a place naemd with Pol. *zdrój* spring, source+ *-ew* possessive suffix, with the addition of *-ski* suffix of local surnames (see BARANOWSKI). It may also be a habitation name from a place named with this word.

Zduniak Polish: 1. habitation name from the town of *Zduny*, SW of Kalisz.
2. occupational name for a potter or maker of stoves, from Pol. *zdun* potter + the redundant agent suffix *-iak*.
Dims.: **Zduńczyk**, **Zdunek**.
Patr. (from a dim.): **Zdunkiewicz**.

Żebrowski Polish: 1. habitation name from some place named with Pol. *żebry* penury, poverty, perhaps because of its poor soil.
2. nickname for a beggar, Pol. *żebrak* (from the same root as in 1).
Cogn. (of 2): Jewish (E Ashkenazic): **Zebrak**.

Zedník Czech: occupational name for a mason, Czech *zedník*.
Cogn.: Rum.: **Zidar**.
Dim.: Czech: **Zedníček**.
Patr.: Bulg.: **Zidarov**.

Zehender German: occupational name for an official responsible for collecting, on behalf of the lord of the manor, tithes of agricultural produce owed as rent. The more prosperous tenants had to contribute wine and corn, those with smaller holdings fruit, vegetables, milk, cheese, beer, and poultry. The MHG term for this official was *zehendære*, a deriv. of *zehende* tenth part, tithe (OHG *zehanto*, from *zehan* ten). The surname is most common in Bavaria, Austria, Switzerland, and Württemberg.
Vars.: **Zehe(n)tner**, **Zehner**, **Zent(n)er**, **Center**.
Cogns.: Low Ger.: **Tegeder**, **Tägeder**; **Tegtmann**. Ger. (of Slav. origin): **Zentnerowski**. Jewish (Ashkenazic): **Zentner** (it is not clear whether this is an occupational name or an adoption of the Ger. surname).

Zehrer German: unflattering nickname for a sponger, spendthrift, or prodigal, from an agent deriv. of Ger. *zehren* to live off, feed on, sap (MHG *(ver)zern* to consume, use up, OHG *zeren*).

Zeiss German: nickname for a gentle person, from MHG *zeiss* tender, kind.
Vars.: **Zeisse**, **Zaiss**.
Dim.: **Zaissle**.

Zeitlin Jewish (E Ashkenazic): metr. from the Yid. female given name *Tseytl*, which is of uncertain origin, with the addition of the Slav. metr. suffix *-in*.
Vars.: **Tzeitlin**; **Ceitlin** (a Pol. spelling).

Zeldes Jewish (Ashkenazic): metr. from the Yid. female given name *Zelde* (from MHG *sælde* fortunate, blessed) + the Yid. possessive suffix *-s*.
Vars.: **Zeldis**, **Seldes**, **Seldis**; **Zeldin**, **Seldin**, **Zeld(ov)ich** (E Ashkenazic).

Zeller German and Jewish (Ashkenazic): topographic name for someone who lived by a shrine or at the site of a hermit's cell, Ger. *Zelle* (MHG *zelle*, from L *cella* small room), or habitation name from any of the various places named with this word, most notably the town of *Celle* near Hanover. In some cases it may also have been an occupational name for someone who owned or was employed at a small workshop, and this is the most likely source of the Jewish surname.
Vars.: **Zellmann**. Jewish only: **Zelman**.

Zeman Czech: status name for a yeoman farmer or small landowner, Czech *zeman* (a deriv. of *zem* land). This is one of the most common Czech surnames.
Dims.: **Zemánek**, **Zemek**.

Zenger German: nickname for a lively or active person, from MHG *zenger*, *zanger* sharp, biting.
Vars.: **Zenker** (also Jewish), **Zanger**, **Zänger**.
Dims.: **Zengerle**, **Zangerl**, **Zängerle**; **Zingerle** (Tyrol).

Zeppelin German: habitation name from the town of *Zepelin* in Mecklenburg, so called from a Slav. word cogn. with Pol. *Czaplin* 'place of herons' (cf. CHAPLIN 2).
Var.: **Zeplin**.

Zeuthen Danish: habitation name from the town of *Søften* in Jutland.
The surname Søften *was first adopted in the 16th cent. by Laurids Sørenson (d. 1578), who was the parish priest in the village of this name. His son, Jens Lauridsen, Latinized the name, according to the prevailing fashion, as* Zeuthen(nius). *A later member of this family, Christian Frederick Zeuthen, was created Baron in 1843.*
Jens Rasmus Theodor Zeuthen (1823–77) was born at Kastrup, near Copenhagen, the son of Peter Laurantius Zeuthen (1783–1839), a Royal Ranger, and was apprenticed at Copenhagen on a schooner registered at Whitby, England. On completion of his apprenticeship he settled in England, adopting Whitby as his supposed place of birth and Anglicizing his name to James **Zenthon**. *He died in Greenwich, and his English descendants may be traced to the present day.*

Žežulka Czech: nickname from the vocab. word *žežulka* cuckoo.
Vars.: **Zezulka**, **Zezulák**, **Zezula**.

Zhavoronkov Russian: patr. from the nickname *Zhavoronok* 'Lark' (probably from a dim. of the same stem as in *voron* raven (see VORONOV) and *vorona* crow (see VORONIN), with the addition of an obscure prefix). The nickname probably denoted an early riser or else someone with a fine singing voice.
Cogn.: Beloruss.: **Zhavruk**.

Zhidovinov Russian: patr. from the ORuss. name *zhidovin* Jew.
Var.: **Zhidovtsev**.
Cogns.: Beloruss.: **Zhydovich** (patr.). Pol.: **Żydowicz** (patr.); **Żydak**. Czech: **Žid**.
Dim.: Czech: **Žídek**.

Zhivago Russian: nickname from Russ. *zhivoi* lively, brisk, quick. The ending is unusual; it perhaps represents an OSlav. gen. case of this word, or it may be an alteration of a deriv. in *-aga*, under the influence of Beloruss. and Ukr. dims. in *-o*.
Vars.: **Zhivagin** (patr.); **Zhivchikov** (patr., from a dim.).
Cogns.: Croatian: **Živanović**, **Živojnović**, **Živić** (patrs.); **Živković** (patr. from a dim.).

Zhukov Russian: patr. from the nickname *Zhuk* 'Beetle', presumably denoting someone bearing some supposed resemblance to a beetle.
Cogns. (not patrs.): Ukr.: **Zhuk**. Pol.: **Żuk**.

Cogns. (patrs.): Beloruss.: **Zhukovich, Zhukevich**. Croatian: **Žikić**.

Dims.: Ukr.: **Zhuchenko**.

Patr. from a dim.: Beloruss.: **Zhuchkevich**.

Habitation names: Pol.: **Żukowski**. Ukr., Beloruss.: **Zhukovski**.

Zieger German: metonymic occupational name for a preparer or seller of goat's curd cheese, MHG *ziger(kæse)*. The word is of problematic etymology, apparently being of neither Gmc nor Romance origin; it may derive from one of the Celt. elements preserved in the Alpine region.

Vars.: **Ziegert, Ziegerer**.

Ziegler German and Jewish (Ashkenazic): occupational name for a tiler, from an agent deriv. of Ger. *Ziegel* roof tile (MHG *ziegel*, OHG *ziagal*, from L *tēgula*). In the Middle Ages the term came to denote bricks as well as tiles, and so in some cases the term may have denoted a brickmaker or bricklayer rather than a tiler. Cf. CEGIELSKI.

Vars.: Jewish: **Tsigler, Cigler, Cygler, Cygel, Ziegel(man), Cygielman** (from Yid. *tsigl* brick or mod. Ger. *Ziegel* tile).

Cogn.: Czech: **Cihelka**.

Zielak Polish: 1. var. of ZIELIŃSKI.

2. occupational name for a herbalist, from a deriv. of Pol. *ziele* herb (related to *zielony* green; see ZIELIŃSKI).

Var.: **Ziołek** (from the var. vocab. word *ziółko*).

Patr.: **Ziółkiewicz**.

Habitation names: **Ziółkowski, Zielewski**.

Zieliński Polish and Jewish (E Ashkenazic): from the vocab. word *zielony* green, in various applications. As a Pol. name it seems primarily to have been a nickname for a person with a sickly 'greenish' complexion. It may also have been a nickname for someone who habitually dressed in green, or who was 'green' in the sense of being immature or inexperienced. Additionally, it may be a habitation name from a place named with this word. As a Jewish name it is mainly an ornamental name.

Vars.: **Zielonka**; **Zieleniewski**; ZIELAK.

Cogns.: Czech: **Zelenka, Zelinka**; **Zelený**. Russ.: **Zelyony**. Jewish (E Ashkenazic, ornamental): **Zielony**.

Patrs.: Pol.: **Zielen(k)iewicz**.

Zima Czech: 1. from the vocab. word *zima* winter, cold, probably a nickname from someone with a gloomy or unapproachable personality, but possibly also a topographic name for someone living in a particularly cold spot.

2. from a short form of the given name *Erazim* ERASMUS.

Cogns.: Pol.: **Zimny** ('cold, bleak'); **Zimniak, Zimnicki**.

Zimbalist German and Jewish (Ashkenazic): occupational name for a player on the cymbals, from an agent deriv. of Ger. *Zimbal* cymbal (MHG *zymbel(e)*, OHG *zymbala*, from Gk *kymbala* (pl.)). As a Jewish surname it refers specifically to a cymbalist in a band that provided music at a wedding feast (cf. KLEZMER).

Vars.: Jewish (E Ashkenazic): **Cymbalist(a), Cimbalist(a)**, (Pol. spellings); **Zimbalista, Zymbalist(a)**; **Cimbal, Zimbal(er)**.

Zimmermann German and Jewish (Ashkenazic): occupational name for a carpenter, Ger. *Zimmermann* (MHG *zimbermann*, a cpd of *zimber*, *zimmer* timber, wood + *mann* man).

Vars.: Ger.: **Zimmer(er)**. Jewish: **Zim(m)erman**; **Cimerman, Cymerman** (Pol. spellings); **Cymmermann, Cimmermann, Timmerman(n)**.

Cogns.: Low Ger.: **Timmer(mann)**. Flem., Du.: **(De) Timmerman, Temmerman**.

Patr.: Flem., Du.: **Timmermans**.

The American singer and song-writer Bob Dylan (b. 1941) is of Jewish descent; he was born Robert Zimmerman, *in Duluth, Minnesota, where his father was a businessman. He adopted the surname Dylan in 1962 in honour of the Welsh poet Dylan Thomas.*

Zingler German and Jewish (Ashkenazic): topographic name for someone who lived by the outermost defensive wall of a town or city, from MHG *zingel* (from L *cingula* belt, from *cingere* to surround, encompass) + *-er* suffix denoting human nouns.

Vars.: Ger.: **Zingel(mann)**. Jewish: **Zingel** (but this may also be a deriv. of Yid. *tsingl* 'little tongue'; see TONG).

Zink German: from Ger. *Zinke* tip, point, prong (MHG *zinke*, OHG *zinko*), acquired either as a topographic name by someone who lived on a pointed piece of land or as a nickname for a man with a singularly pointed nose (cf. mod. Ger. slang *Zinken* 'hooter'). The same word was used to denote the cornet, although the semantic development is not clear, and the surname may sometimes have been metonymic for a player of this instrument. It was not until the 16th cent. that the metal *zinc* was discovered and named (apparently from its jagged appearance in the furnace), so this is unlikely to lie behind the surname.

Vars.: **Zinke, Zingg**.

Zinn German and Jewish (Ashkenazic): metonymic occupational name for a worker in tin, Ger. *Zinn*, Yid. *tsin* (MHG, OHG *zin*). In medieval times the metal was used to make cups and vessels for use in the more prosperous households, while the majority of the population had to make do with wooden utensils.

Vars.: Ger.: **Zinner(t)**. Jewish: **Zin, Tzin, Tsin, Zin(n)er**.

Zinovyev Russian: patr. from the given name *Zinovi*, a Russ. form of Gk *Zēnobios*, composed of the elements *Zeus*, gen. *Zēnos*, the name of the principal god in the ancient Gk pantheon + *bios* life. In spite of its pagan overtones, the name was borne by several early Christian saints, including a 4th-cent. bishop of Florence. Its popularity in E Europe is largely due to the veneration in the Orthodox Church of an early Christian martyr, a priest and physician who was killed in Asia Minor at the end of the 3rd cent.

Var.: **Zinovichev**.

Cogns.: It.: **Zenob(b)i**; **Zanob(b)i** (Tuscany); **Zob(b)i** (NE Italy).

Dims.: Russ.: **Zinkov, Zinichev, Zinyukhin** (all patrs.). Ukr.: **Zin(chen)ko, Zinchuk**. It.: **Zanobelli, Zanobetti**; **Zobin(i), Zob(b)oli, Zob(b)olo, Zobele**.

Zirkler German: occupational name for a town watchman, from an agent deriv. of MHG *zirk(e)len* to do the rounds (OHG *zirkilan*, from L *circulāre*, a deriv. of *cīrculus* circle, dim. of *circus* ring).

Vars.: **Zirkel**; **Zürcklert** (Saxony).

Zisin Jewish (E Ashkenazic): metr. from the Yid. female given name *Zise* (from Yid. *zis* sweet) + the Slav. metr. suffix *-in*.

Vars.: **Zissin, Susin, Zisovich, Ziszovics**.

Dims. (metrs.): **Ziske, Ziskis, Ziskin, Zyskin, Siskin, Suskin, Süsskin, Ziskovi(t)ch, Ziskovitz, Zuscovitch, Susskovitch, Suskovitz** (all from the Yid. dim. female given name *Ziske*; see also the derivs. listed at SÜSSKIND); **Zislis, Zislin, Sislin, Zisslowicz** (from the Yid. dim. female given name *Zisl*). Forms with *ü* show the influence of mod. Ger. *süss* sweet; forms with *u* are derivs. of *süss* or are S Yid. hypercorrections.

Zistler German: occupational name for a basket-maker, from an agent deriv. of MHG *zistel* small basket (from L *cistella*, a dim. of *cistis* bag, box, basket, from Gk *kystis* pouch, bladder).

Zito S Italian: from the medieval given name *Zito*, originally a nickname from the S It. dial. term *zito*, *zite*, *zitu* young bachelor.

Vars.: **Lozito, Losito, Loseto** (nicknames, with fused def. art.).

Dims.: **Zitello, Zitelli**.

Zlatanović Croatian: patr. from a Croat. given name, *Zlatan* 'Golden', from Croat. *zlato* gold, cogn. with Russ. *zoloto*; cf. ZOLOTARYOV.

Var.: **Zlatić**.

Patr. from a dim.: **Zlatković**.

Zlatin Jewish (E Ashkenazic): metr. from the Yid. female given name *Zlate* (from the Czech word meaning 'gold'; cf. ZOLOTARYOV) + the Slav. metr. suffix *-in*.

Vars.: **Slatin(e)**.

Metrs. (from dims.): **Zlatkin, Slatkin(e), Zlatkes, Zlatkis**.

Zola 1. Italian: habitation name from any of various minor places called *Zol(l)a*, named with a dial. term for a mound or bank of earth.

2. Jewish: of unknown origin.

Vars. (of 1): **Zolla, Zol(l)i; Zolese, Zolesi**.

The French novelist Émile Zola *(1840–1902) was born in Paris, the son of an Italian immigrant, and did not become a French citizen until 1862. His father, a civil engineer, had left Italy because of his opposition to Austrian rule, and in 1842 moved to Aix-en-Provence, where he worked on building a canal; his death in 1847 left the family destitute.*

Zolotaryov Russian: patr. from the occupational term *zolotar* goldsmith (a deriv. of *zoloto* gold).

Cogns. (not patrs.): Pol.: **Złotnik**. Czech: **Zlatník**. Jewish (E Ashkenazic): **Zolotar, Zoloter, Zlattner; Zlotnik, Slotni(c)k**.

Cogns. (patrs.): Croatian: **Zlatarić**. Jewish: **Zolotariov, Zolotaref, Zlatarov, Zlatnikov**.

Dims.: Ukr.: **Zolotarenko**. Beloruss.: **Zolotarenko, Zolotaryonok**. Czech: **Zlatníček**.

Zoppo Italian: nickname for a lame man, from It. *zoppo* lame.

Var.: **Zoppi**.

Dims.: **Zopetti, Zoppetto, Zoppini, Zoppino**.

Zoref Jewish: occupational name for a goldsmith, Hebr. *tsoref*.

Vars.: **Zoreff, Soref(f)**.

Zorn German and Jewish (Ashkenazic): nickname for a short-tempered man, from Ger. *Zorn* anger (MHG *zorn*).

Var.: Ger.: **Zorndt**.

Dims.: Ger.: **Zörnle, Zerndl**. Low Ger.: **Zörnchen**.

Zorrilla Spanish: nickname for a crafty or devious person, from a dim. of Sp. *zorra* vixen. The Sp. name of the fox means literally 'the lazy one', from OSp. *zorro* lazy (from *zorrar* to drag, apparently of imitative origin), and it is likely that the nickname was sometimes given in this original sense.

Zuazo Basque: topographic name for someone who lived by a group of trees, from *zuaitz* tree + the suffix of abundance *-zo*, *-zu*. There are several places in the Basque country so called, and the surname may also derive from any of them.

Zubakov Russian: patr. from the nickname *Zubak* 'Toothy' (a deriv. of *zub* tooth), denoting someone with something odd or noticeable about his teeth.

Vars.: **Zubin; Zubarev, Zubavin**.

Cogns.: Ukr.: **Zuban**. Beloruss.: **Zub**. Czech: **Zub**.

Dims.: Russ.: **Zubkin**. Ukr.: **Zubko**. Czech: **Z(o)ubek**. Beloruss.: **Zubashkevich**.

Zubiaur Basque: habitation name from either of two places in the province of Biscay, so called from the elements *zubi* bridge + *aurre* front part, i.e. a settlement in front of a bridge.

Zuccheri Italian: metonymic occupational name for a dealer in sugar or for a confectioner or seller of sweatmeets, from It. *zucchero* sugar (of Arabic and probably ultimately of Skt origin).

Vars.: **Zuccari, Zuccaro** (S Italy); **Zucaro** (Naples).

Cogns.: Ger., Jewish: ZUCKER. Russ.: **Sakharov** (patr. in form); see also ZACHARY.

Dims.: It.: **Zuccherini, Zuccherino, Zuccarini, Zuccarino, Zuccarelli, Zuccarello**.

Zucchi Italian: in part a metonymic occupational name for a grower and seller of gourds (squashes or marrows), from It. *zucca* gourd (LL *cucutia*, for class. L *cucurbita*). More often, however, it is a nickname from the same word used in its colloquial transferred sense 'head'.

Vars.: **Zucca, Zucco**.

Dims.: **Zucchelli, Zucchello, Zucchetti, Zucchetto, Zucchetta, Zucchini, Zucchino, Zuccol(in)i, Zuccolo, Zuccotti, Zuccotto**.

Aug.: **Zucconi**.

Zucker 1. German: metonymic occupational name for a dealer in sugar or a confectioner, from MHG *zucker* sugar (cf. ZUCCHERI).

2. Jewish (Ashkenazic): generally an ornamental surname from mod. Ger. *Zucker*, Yid. *zuker* sugar, but possibly also an occupational name as in 1.

3. German: offensive nickname for somene thought to be a thief, from MHG *zuckære* thief, an agent deriv. of *zucken* to snatch, grab (OHG *zucchen*, an intensive formation from *ziohan* to pull, draw).

Vars.: Jewish (those ending in *-man* and *-nik* are occupational; the rest may be ornamental): **Zuker, Tzuker; Zuckerman(n), Zuk(i)erman, Czukerman** (Anglicized **Sugarman**); **Cuk(i)er(man)** (Pol. spellings); **Zukernik, Cukiernik** (E Ashkenazic); **Zukerovitz** (patr. in form).

Cogns. (of 1): Flem.: **Suiker(man)**.

Dim. (of 2): Jewish: **Cukerl**.

Patr. (from 1): Flem.: **Suikermans**.

Cpds (of 2, ornamental): Jewish: **Zuckerbaum** ('sugar tree'); **Zuckerberg(er), Zukerberg** ('sugar hill'); **Zuckerblum** ('sugar flower'); **Zuckerbrot** ('sugar bread'; also a metonymic occupational name for a fancy baker); **Zukerfein** ('sugar fine'); **Zu(c)kerkandel** ('sugar candy'); **Zuckerstein, Cukierstein** ('sugar stone'); **Zukerwasser** ('sugar water').

Zulueta Basque: habitation name from a place in the province of Navarre, so called from *zulo* hole + the suffix of abundance *-eta*, i.e. presumably an area where the ground was full of pits and indentations.

Zunder German and Jewish (Ashkenazic): metonymic occupational name for a seller of kindling wood, from Ger. *Zunder* tinder (MHG *zunder*, OHG *zuntara*, a cogn. of OE *tynder*).

Dims.: Ger.: **Zundel, Zündel; Zundler, Zündler**.

Zunz Jewish: probably a habitation name from *Zons*, a town situated on the Rhine not far from Cologne and Düsseldorf, although the reason for the change in the vowel is not clear. The placename is of uncertain origin, traced by Bahlow to an ancient element *san*, *sen*, *sin*, *son*, *sun*, meaning '(stagnant) water'.

Vars.: **Zuntz; Zunser** (with the habitational ending *-er*).

Żuraw Polish: nickname for a tall, gangling person, from Pol. *żuraw* crane (cogn. with Czech *jeřáb*). The term was also used as a nickname for a chimney-sweep, referring to the crane's habit of nesting on chimneys.

Var.: **Żurawski**.

Cogn. (dim.): Czech: **Jeřábek**.

Zurdo Spanish: nickname for a left-handed person, Sp. *zurdo* (of pre-Roman origin, apparently related to Basque *zurrun* heavy, sluggish, clumsy).

Zurita Spanish: habitation name from any of several places so called. The placename is of uncertain origin; it may have some connection with Basque *zuri* white, or with Sp. *zurita* dove (allegedly of imitative origin).

Zvezdochyotov Russian: patr. from the ORuss. occupational term *zvezdochyot* astrologer (from *zvezda* star + *chet* to read).

Zwiebel 1. German: metonymic occupational name for a grower or seller of onions, Ger. *Zwiebel* onion (MHG *z(w)ibolle*, *zwifel* from LL *cēpulla*, dim. of class. L *cēpa*). In the Pomeranian dialect the word and the surname were accented on the second syllable.

2. Jewish (Ashkenazic): metonymic occupational name for a grower or seller of onions, or unflattering surname bestowed at random by non-Jewish government officials, or just one of the large number of Jewish ornamental names referring to plants.

Vars.: Ger.: **Zwibel, Swibel; Zieboll, Zibell, Zibill; Zwiebler, Zwiebelmann; Zwiefel, Zwiefler** (Bavaria). Jewish: **Zwibel; Cibula, Cybula; Zibulsky, Cibulski** (E Ashkenazic).

Cogns. (of 1): Czech: **Cibulka**. Pol.: **Cybulski**. Ukr.: **Tsibulya**. Sp.: CEBOLLA.

Dim.: Russ.: **Tsybulkin** (patr.). Jewish (E Ashkenazic): **Zibulkin** (patr. in form).

Zwierzchowski Polish: habitation name from a place named with Pol. *zwierzchni* upper + *-ów* possessive suffix, with the addition of *-ski* suffix of local surnames (see BARANOWSKI), or else a topographic name for someone who lived on an upper storey.

Zwierzyński Polish: habitation name from *Zwierzyna*, a district of Cracow, named with Pol. *zwierzę* animal, or from some other place named with this element.

Zwilling German and Jewish (Ashkenazic): nickname for a twin, Ger. *Zwilling*, Yid. *tsviling* (MHG *zwillinc*, OHG *zwiniling*, a deriv. of *zwinal* double, from *zwēne* two).

Cogn.: Low Ger.: **Dwilling**.

Dim.: Ger.: **Zwingli** (Switzerland).

Patr.: Ger.: **Zwillinger**.

Zwolski Polish: probably a habitation name from any of the various places in Poland called *Wola*, with fused preposition *z*; *z Woli* means 'from Wola'.

Vars.: **Wolski; Zwoliński**.

Zyablikov Russian: patr. from the nickname *Zyablik* 'Finch', given perhaps to a cheerful or birdlike man. The word itself is said to derive from an element meaning 'to freeze', because the finch appears as soon as the winter snows begin to melt, and disappears again when ice and frost return.

Cogns.: Pol.: **Zięba, Ziemba** (nicknames).

Zyl, van Dutch: topographic name for someone who lived by a patch of stagnant water, i.e. a lake or canal.

Vars.: **Van der Zyl, Van Zijl, Zylman**.

Cogn.: Fris.: **Zylstra**.

INDEX

To facilitate use of the dictionary, this Index lists all names appearing in the text, both headwords and those listed as variant forms within other entries.

A

Adamović, *Adam*
Adamovich, *Adam*
Adamovicz, *Adam*
Adamovitch, *Adam*
Adamovitz, *Adam*
Adamovský, *Adam*
Adamowicz, *Adam*
Adamowitz, *Adam*
Adams, *Adam*
Adamsen, *Adam*
Adamski, *Adam*
Adamsky, *Adam*
Adamson, *Adam*
Adamsson, *Adam*
Adán, *Adam*
Adanet, *Adam*
Adanez, *Adam*
Adão, *Adam*
Adar, *Oder*
Adari, *Oder*
Adary, *Oder*
Adburgham
Adcock, *Adam*
Adcocks, *Adam*
Addams, *Adam*
Adde, *Adel*
Addekin, *Adam*
Adderley
Addess, *Adam*
Addey, *Adam*
Addie, *Adam*
Addington
Addionisio, *Dennis*
Addionizio, *Dennis*
Addis, *Adam*
Addison, *Adam*
Addy, *Adam*
Addyman, *Adam*
Ade, *Adam, Adel*
A'Deane, *Dean*
Adeane, *Dean*
Adeau, *Allis*
Adel
Adelaar, *Adler*
Adelbaum, *Adel*
Adèle, *Allis*
Adelheid, *Allis*
Adeline, *Allis*
Adell
Adelman, *Adel*
Adelmann, *Adel*
Adelsberg, *Adel*
Adelsburg, *Adel*
Adelstein, *Adel*
Adelung, *Adel*
Adema, *Adel*
Ademar, *Aylmer*
Aden, *Adel*
Adena, *Adel*
Adenauer
Adenet, *Adam*
Adenot, *Adam*
Ades, *Adam*
Adeson, *Adam*
Adey, *Adam*
Adger, *Edgar*
Adhams, *Adam*
Adhémar, *Aylmer*
Adie, *Adam*
Adima, *Aylmer*
Adinolfi, *Adolf*
Adkin, *Adam*
Adkins, *Adam*
Adlam, *Alleaume*
Adlard, *Allard*
Adler
Adlerberg, *Adler*
Adlerman, *Adler*
Adlerstein, *Adler*
Adlington
Admar, *Aylmer*
Adné, *Adam*
Adnet, *Adam*
Adnett, *Adam*
Adnitt, *Adam*
Adnot, *Adam*
Ado, *Adel*
Adolf
Adolfi, *Adolf*
Adolfino, *Adolf*
Adolfsen, *Adolf*
Adolfsson, *Adolf*
Adon, *Adel*
Adorján, *Adrian*
Adornetti, *Adorno*
Adorno
Adrados
Adrià, *Adrian*
Adriaan, *Adrian*
Adriaans, *Adrian*
Adriaanse, *Adrian*
Adriaansen, *Adrian*
Adriaansz, *Adrian*
Adriaen, *Adrian*
Adriaens, *Adrian*
Adrián, *Adrian*
Adrian
Adriani, *Adrian*
Adriano, *Adrian*
Adrianov, *Adrian*
Adrião, *Adrian*
Adrien, *Adrian*
Adriyashev, *Adrian*
Adshead
Advokat, *Avogadro*
Ady, *Adam*
Adye, *Adam*
Aebracht, *Albert*
Aebrechts, *Albert*
Aegten, *Aggis*
Aeles, *Allis*
Aelion
Afanasov, *Afanasyev*
Afanasyev
Afferrante, *Farrant*
Affery, *Aubrey*
Affleck, *Auchinleck*
Affuso, *Alfonso*
Afonchikov, *Afanasyev*
Afonchin, *Afanasyev*
Afonichev, *Afanasyev*
Afonso, *Alfonso*
Afonyushkin, *Afanasyev*
Afremov, *Yefremov*
Agace
Agache, *Agace*
Agaciak, *Aggis*
Agapeev, *Agapov*
Agapov
Agapyev, *Agapov*
Agar, *Edgar*
Ågård
Agard, *Haggard*
Agars, *Edgar*
Agas, *Aggis*
Agass, *Aggis*
Agasse, *Agace*
Agassis, *Agace*
Agassiz, *Agace*
Agate
Agatestein
Agathe, *Aggis*
Agati, *Aggis*
Agatiello, *Aggis*
Agatini, *Aggis*
Agatoni, *Aggis*
Agatz, *Achatz*
Agazzi, *Agace*
Agazzini, *Agace*
Ageasse, *Agace*
Ager, *Edgar*
Agethe, *Aggis*
Agethen, *Aggis*
Aggas, *Aggis*
Aggass, *Aggis*
Agger, *Acker*
Agget, *Aggis*
Aggett, *Aggis*
Aggis
Aghini, *Eck*
Aghinolfi, *Egiloff*
Ägidi, *Giles*
Agiss, *Aggis*
Aglieri, *Aillier*
Agneau, *Agnew*
Agneesen, *Annis*
Agneesens, *Annis*
Agnel, *Agnew*
Agnelli, *Agnew*
Agnellini, *Agnew*
Agnellotti, *Agnew*
Agnelutti, *Agnew*
Agnes, *Annis*
Agnesen, *Annis*
Agnesetti, *Annis*
Agnesi, *Annis*
Agnesini, *Annis*
Agness, *Annis*
Agnete, *Annis*
Agneter, *Annis*
Agnew
Agnoletti, *Angel*
Agnolo, *Angel*
Agnoloni, *Angel*
Agnolozzi, *Angel*
Agosti
Agostinetti, *Austin*
Agostinho, *Austin*
Agostini, *Austin*
Agostinone, *Austin*
Ágoston, *Austin*
Agostoni, *Agosti*
Agotz, *Achatz*
Agricola
Agrifoul, *Griffoul*
Agrillo, *Grill*
Agron, *Aaron, Heron*
Agronski, *Aaron*
Aguado
Agudo
Águeda, *Aggis*
Agüero
Aguiar, *Aguilar*
Aguilar
Aguilera, *Aguilar*
Aguillaume, *William*
Aguiló
Aguinaga
Aguirre
Agulló
Agustí, *Austin*
Agustín, *Austin*
Agusto, *Agosti*
Agustoni, *Agosti*
Agut, *Agudo*
Agutter
Aharoni, *Aaron*
Ahearne, *Ahern*
Ahern
Aherne, *Ahern*
Ahl
Ahlberg, *Ahl*
Ahlbom, *Ahl*
Ahlborg, *Ahl*
Ahlenius, *Ahl*
Ahlers, *Allard*
Ahlert, *Allard*
Ahlf, *Adolf*
Ahlfors, *Ahl*
Ahlfs, *Adolf*
Ahlgren, *Ahl*
Ahlhelm, *Alleaume*
Ahlman, *Ahl*
Ahlmark, *Ahl*
Ahlqvist, *Ahl*
Ahlsén, *Ahl*
Ahlstedt, *Ahl*
Ahlström, *Ahl*
Ahlwardt, *Aylward*
Ahmel, *Amery*
Ahmelmann, *Amery*
Ahmels, *Amery*
Ahmling, *Amery*
Ahonen
Ahrén
Ahrend, *Arnold*
Ahrendsen, *Arnold*
Ahrens, *Arnold*
Åhs
Åhsberg, *Åhs*
Aicard, *Achard*
Aichele, *Oak*
Aichenbaum, *Oak*
Aichenblat, *Oak*
Aichenblatt, *Oak*
Aichenholtz, *Oak*
Aichenholz, *Oak*
Aichenwald, *Oak*
Aicher, *Oak*
Aichison, *Adam*
Aichler, *Oak*
Aichmann, *Oak*
Aicken, *Adam*
Aides, *Edel*
Aidess, *Edel*
Aidler, *Edel*
Aiello
Aigle, *Eagle*
Aigner, *Eigner*
Aigrefeuille, *Griffoul*
Aigron, *Heron*
Aihel, *Oak*
Aihelbaum, *Oak*
Aiken, *Adam*
Aikin, *Adam*
Aikman, *Oak*
Aillier
Ailmer, *Aylmer*
Ailward, *Aylward*
Ailwyn, *Alwyn*
Aimar, *Aylmer*
Aimé, *Amey*
Aimer, *Aylmer*
Aimeric, *Henry*
Aimers, *Aylmer*
Aimetti, *Hammond*

Aimino, *Hammond*
Aimo, *Hammond*
Aimon, *Hammond*
Aimond, *Hammond*
Aimoni, *Hammond*
Aimonino, *Hammond*
Aindrias, *Andrew*
Aindriú, *Andrew*
Ainger
Ainhorn, *Einhorn*
Ainscough
Ainscow, *Ainscough*
Ainslee, *Ainslie*
Ainsley, *Ainslie*
Ainslie
Ainstein, *Einstein*
Ainsworth
Aiolfi, *Egiloff*
Air, *Ayer*
Airaldi, *Harrod*
Airaudo, *Harrod*
Aires, *Arias*
Airey
Airoldi, *Harrod*
Airy, *Airey*
Aisenberg, *Eisen*
Aish, *Ash*
Aiskew, *Askew*
Aiskowitz, *Isaac*
Aïstov
Aitchison, *Adam*
Aitken, *Adam*
Aitkin, *Adam*
Aizen, *Eisen*
Aizenbaum, *Eisen*
Aizenberg, *Eisen*
Aizenfeld, *Eisen*
Aizengart, *Eisen*
Aizenman, *Eisen*
Aizenshtain, *Eisen*
Aizenshtat, *Eisenstadt*
Aizenstark, *Eisen*
Aizenstat, *Eisenstadt*
Aizenstein, *Eisen*
Aizental, *Eisen*
Aizic, *Isaac*
Aizicovitch, *Isaac*
Aizik, *Isaac*
Aizikov, *Isaac*
Aizikovich, *Isaac*
Aizikovitch, *Isaac*
Aizikovitz, *Isaac*
Aizikowicz, *Isaac*
Aizin, *Eisen*
Aizlewood, *Hazelwood*
Aizner, *Eisen*
Ajam, *John*
Ajasse, *Agace*
Ajchenbaum, *Oak*
Ajean, *John*
Ajello, *Aiello*
Ajolfi, *Egiloff*
Ajsenberg, *Eisen*
Ajsenman, *Eisen*
Ajsik, *Isaac*
Ajzen, *Eisen*
Ajzenbaum, *Eisen*
Ajzenberg, *Eisen*
Ajzenfisz, *Eisen*
Ajzenkranz, *Eisen*
Ajzenman, *Eisen*
Ajzenstadt, *Eisenstadt*
Ajzenstat, *Eisenstadt*
Ajzensztad, *Eisenstadt*
Ajzensztein, *Eisen*
Ajzental, *Eisen*
Ajzinberg, *Eisen*
Ajzner, *Eisen*
Aker, *Acker*
Åkerberg, *Acker*
Åkerblom, *Acker*
Åkerlind, *Acker*
Åkerlund, *Acker*
Akerman, *Ackerman*
Åkerman, *Ackerman*
Akeroyd, *Ackroyd*
Akers, *Acker*
Åkerstedt, *Acker*
Åkerström, *Acker*
Akess, *Acker*
Akhmatov
Akimakin, *Joachim*
Akimchev, *Joachim*
Akimchin, *Joachim*
Akimikhin, *Joachim*
Akimkin, *Joachim*
Akimochkin, *Joachim*
Akimov, *Joachim*
Akimushkin, *Joachim*
Akimychev, *Joachim*
Akker, *Acker*
Akkeringa, *Acker*
Akkerman, *Ackerman*
Akkers, *Acker*
Akred, *Ackroyd*
Akroyd, *Ackroyd*
Aksanov, *Aksyonov*
Aksentijević, *Aksyonov*
Aksentsev, *Aksyonov*
Aksentsov, *Aksyonov*
Aksentyev, *Aksyonov*
Aksyanov, *Aksyonov*
Aksyonov
Aksyutin, *Aksyonov*
Alabarbe, *Barbe*
Alabaster
Aladerne
Alain, *Allen*
Alaire, *Hilary*
Alais, *Allis*
Alaman, *Alman*
Alamanno, *Alman*
Alameda, *Álamo*
Álamo
Alan, *Allen*
Alarcó, *Alarcón*
Alarcón
Alard, *Allard*
Alari, *Alaric*
Alaric
Alastar, *Alexander*
Alauze
Alaway, *Alloway*
Alayrac
Albà, *Alban*
Alba
Albain, *Alban*
Albalat, *Vallat*
Alban
Albanell, *Alban*
Albanelli, *Alban*
Albani, *Alban*
Albano, *Alban*
Albareda, *Albaret*
Albarède, *Albaret*
Albaret
Albaric, *Aubrey*
Albarracín
Albarrán
Albee
Albeisser, *Altbüsser*
Alberdi
Alberding, *Albert*
Albéric, *Aubrey*
Alberic, *Aubrey*
Alberich, *Aubrey*
Alberici, *Aubrey*
Alberighi, *Aubrey*
Alberigi, *Aubrey*
Albers, *Albert*
Albert
Albertazzi, *Albert*
Albertelli, *Albert*
Alberti, *Albert*
Albertinelli, *Albert*
Albertini, *Albert*
Alberto, *Albert*
Albertocci, *Albert*
Albertoli, *Albert*
Albertolli, *Albert*
Albertoni, *Albert*
Albertos, *Albert*
Albertotti, *Albert*
Alberts, *Albert*
Albertsen, *Albert*
Albertuzzi, *Albert*
Alberty, *Albert*
Albien, *Albin*
Albiez, *Altbüsser*
Albin
Albinelli, *Albin*
Albinet, *Albin*
Albinetti, *Albin*
Albini, *Albin*
Albino, *Albin*
Albinoni, *Albin*
Albinotti, *Albin*
Albinowski, *Albin*
Albiński, *Albin*
Albinson, *Albin*
Albinuzzi, *Albin*
Albiol
Albioni, *Albin*
Albisser, *Alabaster*
Albohn, *Alban*
Albon, *Alban*
Alboreto, *Albaret*
Alborn, *Alban*
Albrecht, *Albert*
Albrechtsen, *Albert*
Albrich, *Aubrey*
Albrici, *Aubrey*
Albright, *Albert*
Albrigi, *Aubrey*
Albrigio, *Aubrey*
Albrink, *Albert*
Albrisi, *Aubrey*
Albrisio, *Aubrey*
Albrizi, *Aubrey*
Albrizzi, *Aubrey*
Albrook, *Holbrook*
Albrooks, *Holbrook*
Albuquerque
Albutt
Alby, *Albee, Albin*
Alcaide
Alcalá
Alcalde
Alcàntara, *Alcántara*
Alcántara
Alcaraz
Alcázar
Alcocer
Alcock
Alcoe, *Alcock*
Alcolea
Alcott
Alcox, *Alcock*
Alda, *Aldous*
Aldakov, *Yevdokimov*
Aldar, *Adler*
Alday
Alde, *Old*
Aldea
Aldecoa
Alden
Alden, *Old*
Alder
Alder, *Old*
Alderdice, *Allardyce*
Alderman
Alders, *Alder*
Alderson, *Alder*
Alderton
Aldhouse, *Aldous*
Aldi, *Aldous*
Aldin, *Alden*
Aldine, *Alden*
Aldini, *Aldous*
Aldis, *Aldous*
Aldiss, *Aldous*
Aldobrandi
Aldobrandini, *Aldobrandi*
Aldonin, *Yevdokimov*
Aldoshin, *Yevdokimov*
Aldous
Aldovrandi, *Aldobrandi*
Aldred, *Aldritt*
Aldritt
Aldrovandi, *Aldobrandi*
Aldus, *Aldous*
Alecci, *Alexis*
Alecock, *Alcock*
Alegre, *Allegri*
Alegret, *Allegri*
Alegría, *Allegri*
Alegria, *Allegri*
Aleixo, *Alexis*
Alejandre, *Alexander*
Alejandro, *Alexander*
Alejo, *Alexis*
Alekhov, *Alexis*
Aleksakhin, *Alexander*
Aleksandrev, *Alexander*
Aleksandrikhin, *Alexander*
Aleksandrov, *Alexander*
Aleksandrovich, *Alexander*
Aleksandrowicz, *Alexander*
Aleksankin, *Alexander*
Aleksankov, *Alexander*
Aleksanov, *Alexander*
Aleksashin, *Alexander*
Alekseev, *Alexis*
Alekseichik, *Alexis*
Aleksić, *Alexander*
Aleksich, *Alexis*
Aleksidze, *Alexis*
Alemán, *Alman*
Alemanno, *Alman*
Alemañy, *Alman*
Alemany, *Alman*
Alemão, *Alman*
Alen, *Allis*
Alenchikov, *Alexander*
Alenichev, *Alexander*
Alenikov, *Alexander*

Alenin, *Alexander*
Alenius, *Ahl*
Alennikov, *Alexander*
Alenov, *Alexander*
Alenshev, *Alexander*
Alentyev, *Alexander*
Alesci, *Alexis*
Alescio, *Alexis*
Aleshintsev, *Alexis*
Aleshkov, *Alexis*
Alesi, *Alexis*
Alesin, *Alexis*
Alesio, *Alexis*
Alessandrelli, *Alexander*
Alessandretti, *Alexander*
Alessandri, *Alexander*
Alessandrini, *Alexander*
Alessandrone, *Alexander*
Alessandrucci, *Alexander*
Alessi, *Alexis*
Alessio, *Alexis*
Aleth, *Allis*
Alévêque, *Bishop*
Alexander
Alexandersen, *Alexander*
Alexandersson, *Alexander*
Alexandre, *Alexander*
Alexandrescu, *Alexander*
Alexandrou, *Alexander*
Alexandrowicz, *Alexander*
Alexis
Alf, *Adolf*
Alfaric, *Aubrey*
Alfaro
Alfonsetti, *Alfonso*
Alfonsini, *Alfonso*
Alfonso
Alfonsoni, *Alfonso*
Alfonzo, *Alfonso*
Alford
Alfors, *Ahl*
Alfred
Alfredo, *Alfred*
Alfreds, *Alfred*
Alfredson, *Alfred*
Alfredsson, *Alfred*
Alfrey, *Aubrey*
Alfry, *Aubrey*
Alfs, *Adolf*
Alfuso, *Alfonso*
Algar, *Alger*
Alger
Algren, *Ahl*
Alguacil
Alhard, *Allard*
Alheit, *Allis*
Aliaga
Aliberti, *Albert*
Aliberto, *Albert*
Alice, *Allis*
Aliman, *Alman*
Alimanesco, *Alman*
Alimov, *Olimpiev*
Alimpiev, *Olimpiev*
Aline, *Allis*
Aliot, *Ellis*
Aliperti, *Albert*
Alis, *Allis*
Alischer, *Allis*
Alise, *Allis*
Alisen, *Allis*
Alison
Alix, *Allis*
Allain, *Allen*
Allaire, *Hilary*
Allais, *Allis*
Allaman, *Alman*
Allamand, *Alman*
Allamanno, *Alman*
Allan, *Allen*
Allanson, *Allen*
Allard
Allardes, *Allardyce*
Allardice, *Allardyce*
Allardyce
Allart, *Allard*
Allatt, *Allis*
Allaway, *Alloway*
Allbon, *Alban*
Allbond, *Alban*
Allbone, *Alban*
Allborn, *Alban*
Allbright, *Albert*
Allbutt, *Albutt*
Allcoat, *Alcott*
Allcock, *Alcock*
Allcott, *Alcott*
Allcox, *Alcock*
Alldis, *Aldous*
Alldiss, *Aldous*
Alle, *Hall*
Alleaume
Allebrach, *Albert*
Allègre, *Allegri*
Allégret, *Allegri*
Allegretti, *Allegri*
Allegrezza, *Allegri*
Allegri
Allegria, *Allegri*
Allegrini, *Allegri*
Allegroni, *Allegri*
Allegrucci, *Allegri*
Allem, *Alleaume*
Alleman, *Alman*
Allemand, *Alman*
Allemandet, *Alman*
Allemandou, *Alman*
Allemano, *Alman*
Allen
Allenby
Allende
Allenson, *Allen*
Allerding, *Albert*
Allers, *Allard*
Allert, *Allard*
Allerton
Allerts, *Allard*
Allet, *Allis*
Allex, *Allis*
Alleyne, *Allen*
Allez, *Allis*
Allfield, *Oldfield*
Allford, *Alford*
Alliaume, *Alleaume*
Allilaire, *Hilary*
Allimant, *Alman*
Allin, *Allen*
Alline, *Allen*
Alline, *Allis*
Allinson, *Allen*
Alliot, *Ellis*
Allis
Allison, *Alison, Allen*
Alliss, *Allis*
Allix, *Allis*
Alliz, *Allis*
Allman, *Alman*
Allmand, *Alman*
Allmann, *Alman*
Allmen, *Alman*
Allment, *Alman*
Allmers, *Aylmer*
Alloard, *Aylward*
Allodi, *Alauze*
Alloisi, *Lewis*
Alloisio, *Lewis*
Alloiso, *Lewis*
Allot, *Allis*
Allott, *Allis*
Allouard, *Aylward*
Alloway
Allred, *Aldritt*
Allsep, *Allsop*
Allsepp, *Allsop*
Allsop
Allsopp, *Allsop*
Allston, *Alston*
Allstone, *Alston*
Alluard, *Aylward*
Allué, *Alloway*
Allured, *Alfred*
Allvey, *Alvey*
Allward, *Aylward*
Allway, *Alloway*
Allwood, *Ellwood*
Allwyn, *Alwyn*
Alm, *Alleaume*
Almagro
Alman
Almand, *Alman*
Almann, *Alman*
Almanno, *Alman*
Almazán
Almazov
Almberg, *Elm*
Almeida
Almén, *Elm*
Almendro
Almendros, *Almendro*
Alment, *Alman*
Almer, *Aylmer*
Almers, *Aylmer*
Almgren, *Elm*
Almirall
Almon, *Alman*
Almond
Almqvist, *Elm*
Almroth, *Elm*
Almstedt, *Elm*
Almström, *Elm*
Aloigi, *Lewis*
Alois, *Lewis*
Aloisi, *Lewis*
Aloisio, *Lewis*
Aloiso, *Lewis*
Alonso, *Alfonso*
Alonzo, *Alfonso*
Alòs, *Alós*
Alós
Aloshechkin, *Alexis*
Aloshikin, *Alexis*
Aloshkin, *Alexis*
Alov
Alovisi, *Lewis*
Aloway, *Alloway*
Alper, *Alpert, Heilbronn*
Alperin, *Heilbronn*
Alpern, *Heilbronn*
Alperovich, *Heilbronn*
Alperovitch, *Heilbronn*
Alperovitsh, *Heilbronn*
Alperovitz, *Heilbronn*
Alperowich, *Heilbronn*
Alperowicz, *Heilbronn*
Alpers, *Albert*
Alperson, *Heilbronn*
Alperstein, *Heilbronn*
Alpert
Alphege, *Elphick*
Alpin
Alpine, *Alpin*
Alpron, *Heilbronn*
Alpy, *Pine*
Alred, *Aldritt*
Alric, *Alaric*
Alscher, *Allis*
Alschner, *Allis*
Alsén, *Ahl*
Alshioner, *Alexander*
Alsina, *Encina*
Alsop, *Allsop*
Alsopp, *Allsop*
Alstead, *Halstead*
Alston
Alstone, *Alston*
Alt, *Old*
Altbach, *Old*
Altbauer, *Old*
Altbaum, *Old*
Altberg, *Old*
Altbüsser
Alter, *Old*
Alterescu, *Old*
Alterman, *Old*
Altermann, *Old*
Altern, *Old*
Alterovici, *Old*
Alterovitch, *Old*
Alterovitz, *Old*
Alterowitz, *Old*
Alters, *Old*
Alterson, *Old*
Alterthum, *Old*
Altés
Altes, *Old*
Altfeld, *Oldfield*
Althaus, *Old*
Altheim, *Old*
Althoff, *Old*
Altholz, *Old*
Altimari, *Aylmer*
Altman, *Old*
Altmann, *Old*
Altn, *Old*
Altomari, *Aylmer*
Alton
Altovsky, *Old*
Altscher, *Allis*
Altschul
Altschuler, *Altschul*
Altschuller, *Altschul*
Altshuler, *Altschul*
Altstadter, *Old*
Altstaedter, *Old*
Altstein, *Old*
Altufyev, *Yevtikhiev*
Altukhov, *Yevtikhiev*
Alty, *Auty*
Aluard, *Aylward*
Aluigi, *Lewis*
Aluisio, *Lewis*
Aluiso, *Lewis*
Alured, *Alfred*
Alvar, *Álvaro*
Álvares, *Álvaro*
Álvarez, *Álvaro*

Álvaro
Alven, *Alwyn*
Alverichs, *Aubrey*
Alves, *Álvaro*
Alvey
Alvigi, *Lewis*
Alvin, *Alwyn*
Alvisi, *Lewis*
Alvisio, *Lewis*
Alvy, *Alvey*
Alway, *Alloway*
Alwen, *Alwyn*
Alwin, *Alwyn*
Alwyn
Alyokhin, *Alexis*
Alyonov, *Alexander*
Alyoshin, *Alexis*
Alyukin, *Alexis*
Alyushin, *Alexis*
Alyutin, *Alexis*
Amaddei, *Amadei*
Amaddio, *Amadei*
Amadé, *Amadei*
Amade, *Amadei*
Amadei
Amadi, *Amadei*
Amadieu, *Amadei*
Amadini, *Amadei*
Amadio, *Amadei*
Amado, *Amey*
Amador, *Amatore*
Amadore, *Amatore*
Amadorucci, *Amatore*
Amadoruzzi, *Amatore*
Amalfi
Amalfitano, *Amalfi*
Amalric, *Amery*
Aman, *Amand*
Amand
Amann, *Amand, Ammann*
Amant
Amante, *Amant*
Amanti, *Amant*
Amantino, *Amant*
Amar, *Aylmer*
Amaral
Amaro, *Amery*
Amat, *Amey*
Amati, *Amey*
Amato, *Amey*
Amatore
Amatori, *Amatore*
Amatucci, *Amey*
Amatulli, *Amey*
Amaurich, *Amery*
Amaury, *Amery*
Ambihl, *Bühler*
Ambler
Ambresin, *Ambrose*
Ambridge
Ambrodi, *Ambrose*
Ambroes, *Ambrose*
Ambrogelli, *Ambrose*
Ambrogetti, *Ambrose*
Ambrogi, *Ambrose*
Ambrogini, *Ambrose*
Ambrogio, *Ambrose*
Ambrogioli, *Ambrose*
Ambrogioni, *Ambrose*
Ambrogiotti, *Ambrose*
Ambrois, *Ambrose*
Ambroise, *Ambrose*
Ambroisin, *Ambrose*
Ambroix, *Ambrose*
Ambros, *Ambrose*
Ambrosch, *Ambrose*
Ambrose
Ambrosetti, *Ambrose*
Ambrosi, *Ambrose*
Ambrosini, *Ambrose*
Ambrosio, *Ambrose*
Ambrosoli, *Ambrose*
Ambrosoni, *Ambrose*
Ambrož, *Ambrose*
Ambrożewicz, *Ambrose*
Ambroziak, *Ambrose*
Ambrozik, *Ambrose*
Ambrus, *Ambrose*
Ambühl, *Bühler*
Amdohr, *Thor*
Amé, *Amey*
Amédée, *Amadei*
Amedei, *Amadei*
Ameling, *Amery*
Amelrich, *Amery*
Amelung, *Amery*
Amend, *Ende*
Amende, *Ende*
Ament, *Amant*
Ameri, *Aylmer*
Americi, *Henry*
Amerighi, *Henry*
Amerio, *Aylmer*
Amery
Ames, *Amis*
Amey
Amez, *Amey*
Amezaga
Amherst
Ami, *Amis*
Amiard, *Amis*
Amicelli, *Amis*
Amicino, *Amis*
Amico, *Amis*
Amiconi, *Amis*
Amie, *Amey*
Amiel, *Amis*
Amies, *Amis*
Amiet, *Amis*
Amietti, *Amis*
Amighetti, *Amis*
Amighini, *Amis*
Amigó, *Amis*
Amigoni, *Amis*
Amigotti, *Amis*
Amiguet, *Amis*
Amioni, *Amis*
Amiot, *Amis*
Amiranda, *Miranda*
Amis
Amison, *Amis*
Amiss, *Amis*
Amman, *Amand*
Ammann
Ammassari, *Mazier*
Ammon, *Amond*
Ammonds, *Amond*
Amo
Amoddeo, *Amadei*
Amoddio, *Amadei*
Amodeo, *Amadei*
Amodio, *Amadei*
Amon, *Amond*
Amond
Amoore, *Moore*
Amor
Amore, *Amor*
Amorelli, *Amor*
Amores, *Amor*
Amorese, *Amoureux*
Amoretti, *Amor*
Amorielli, *Amor*
Amorim
Amorini, *Amor*
Amorós, *Amoureux*
Amoroselli, *Amoureux*
Amorosini, *Amoureux*
Amoroso, *Amoureux*
Amort, *Ort*
Amoruso, *Amoureux*
Amory, *Amery*
Amos
Amour, *Amor*
Amoureux
Amouroux, *Amoureux*
Amphlet, *Fleet*
Amphlett, *Fleet*
Amschel
Amschler, *Amsler*
Amsel
Amsler
Amson, *Amis*
Amsterdam, *Amsterdam, van*
Amsterdamer, *Amsterdam, van*
Amsterdamski, *Amsterdam, van*
Amsterdam, van
Amszel, *Amschel*
Amthor, *Thor*
Amundsen, *Amond, Hammond*
Amy, *Amey, Amis*
Amyot, *Amis*
Anacleto
Anastácio, *Anstice*
Anastaise, *Anstice*
Anastase, *Anstice*
Anastasi, *Anstice*
Anastasijević, *Anstice*
Anastasio, *Anstice*
Anastasiou, *Anstice*
Anastay, *Anstice*
Anaya
Anceau, *Ancel*
Anceaux, *Ancel*
Ancel
Ancelet, *Ancel*
Ancelevitch, *Ancel*
Ancelin, *Ancel*
Ancelle, *Ancel*
Ancellet, *Ancel*
Ancellin, *Ancel*
Ancelot, *Ancel*
Anchel, *Amschel*
Anděl, *Angel*
Andelman, *Handler*
Andelsman, *Handler*
Anderbrügge, *Bridge*
Anderer, *Andrew*
Anderfur, *Ford*
Anderl, *Andrew*
Anders, *Andrew*
Andersch, *Andrew*
Andersen, *Andrew*
Anderson, *Andrew*
Andersson, *Andrew*
Anderton
Andino, *Andrew*
Andjelić, *Angel*
Andjelković, *Angel*
Andor, *Andrew*
Andrade
Andrag, *Andrew*
András, *Andrew*
Andrasch, *Andrew*
Andrássy, *Andrew*
Andrat, *Andrew*
Andraud, *Andrew*
Andrault, *Andrew*
André, *Andrew*
Andre, *Andrew*
Andrea, *Andrew*
Andreacci, *Andrew*
Andreaccio, *Andrew*
Andreas, *Andrew*
Andreasen, *Andrew*
Andreassen, *Andrew*
Andreasson, *Andrew*
Andreazzi, *Andrew*
Andree, *Andrew*
Andreelli, *Andrew*
Andreetti, *Andrew*
Andreev, *Andrew*
Andrei, *Andrew*
Andreichik, *Andrew*
Andreini, *Andrew*
Andreix, *Andrew*
Andrejević, *Andrew*
Andrejs, *Andrew*
Andrelli, *Andrew*
Andrén, *Andrew*
Andreoletti, *Andrew*
Andreoli, *Andrew*
Andreolli, *Andrew*
Andreone, *Andrew*
Andreotti, *Andrew*
Andreou, *Andrew*
Andrés, *Andrew*
Andres, *Andrew*
Andresen, *Andrew*
Andress, *Andrew*
Andresser, *Andrew*
Andretti, *Andrew*
Andreu, *Andrew*
Andreucci, *Andrew*
Andreutti, *Andrew*
Andreuzzi, *Andrew*
Andrew
Andrewartha
Andrewes, *Andrew*
Andrews, *Andrew*
Andrey, *Andrew*
Andrez, *Andrew*
Andri, *Andrew*
Andria, *Andrew*
Andrić, *Andrew*
Andrich, *Andrew*
Andrichak, *Andrew*
Andrichuk, *Andrew*
Andrick, *Andrew*
Andries, *Andrew*
Andriesse, *Andrew*
Andriessen, *Andrew*
Andrieu, *Andrew*
Andrieux, *Andrew*
Andrík, *Andrew*
Andrin, *Andrew*
Andrini, *Andrew*
Andrioletti, *Andrew*
Andrioli, *Andrew*
Andriolli, *Andrew*
Andrioni, *Andrew*
Andriss, *Andrew*
Andriulis, *Andrew*
Andriuzzi, *Andrew*
Andriveaux, *Andrew*

Andrivel, *Andrew*
Andrivot, *Andrew*
Androck, *Andrew*
Androletti, *Andrew*
Androli, *Andrew*
Androlli, *Andrew*
Androsik, *Andrew*
Andrusov, *Andrew*
Andrusyak, *Andrew*
Andrys, *Andrew*
Andrýsek, *Andrew*
Andrysiak, *Andrew*
Andryszczak, *Andrew*
Andryunin, *Andrew*
Andryushchenko, *Andrew*
Andryushin, *Andrew*
Andrzej, *Andrew*
Andrzejak, *Andrew*
Andrzejczak, *Andrew*
Andrzejewski, *Andrew*
Andrzejowski, *Andrew*
Anese, *Annis*
Anfossi, *Alfonso*
Anfuso, *Alfonso*
Anfusso, *Alfonso*
Angaut, *Osgood*
Ange, *Angel*
Angear, *Ainger*
Angeau, *Angel*
Ángel, *Angel*
Angel
Angelet, *Angel*
Angeletti, *Angel*
Angelillo, *Angel*
Angelin, *Angel*
Angelini, *Angel*
Angell, *Angel*
Angelo, *Angel*
Ângelo, *Angel*
Angelopoulos, *Angel*
Angelot, *Angel*
Angelotti, *Angel*
Angelov, *Angel*
Angelozzi, *Angel*
Anger, *Ainger*
Anghel, *Angel*
Angheloni, *Angel*
Angier, *Ainger*
Angilbert, *Engelbert*
Angioletti, *Angel*
Angioli, *Angel*
Angiolillo, *Angel*
Angiolini, *Angel*
Angiolotti, *Angel*
Angioni, *Angel*
Angiuli, *Angel*
Anglada, *Anglade*
Anglade
Anglais, *English*
Angle
Anglebert, *Engelbert*
Anglès, *English*
Angless, *English*
Anglichaud, *English*
Anglish, *English*
Angliss, *English*
Angloes, *English*
Angold, *Osgood*
Angood, *Osgood*
Angot, *Osgood*
Angove, *Gough*
Angrick, *Andrew*
Angrock, *Andrew*
Ångström, *Eng*
Anguera
Ángulo, *Angle*
Angus
Angwin
Angyal, *Angel*
Aniceto
Anjos, *Angel*
Anketell, *Ashkettle*
Ankettle, *Ashkettle*
Ankill, *Ashkettle*
Ankin, *Ashkettle*
Annas, *Annis*
Annatt, *Annis*
Anne
Anness, *Annis*
Annets, *Annis*
Annett, *Annis*
Annion, *Onion*
Annis
Annison, *Annis*
Annott, *Annis*
Anouilh
Anquetil, *Ashkettle*
Anquetin, *Ashkettle*
Anquier, *Ainger*
Ansaldi, *Oswald*
Ansaldo, *Oswald*
Ansalm, *Ansell*
Ansaud, *Oswald*
Ansault, *Oswald*
Anseau, *Ancel*
Anseaume, *Ansell*
Anseaux, *Ancel*
Anselet, *Ancel*
Anselin, *Ancel*
Ansell
Anselm, *Ansell*
Anselmann, *Ansell*
Anselme, *Ansell*
Anselmi, *Ansell*
Anselmini, *Ansell*
Anselmo, *Ansell*
Anselot, *Ancel*
Anserme, *Ansell*
Ansermet, *Ansell*
Anshell, *Ansell*
Ansiau, *Ancel*
Ansiaume, *Ansell*
Ansill, *Ansell*
Ansle, *Ansell*
Ansli, *Ansell*
Anslow
Anslyn, *Ansell*
Ansquer, *Ainger*
Anstett, *Anstice*
Anstey
Ansteys, *Anstice*
Anstice
Anstie, *Anstey*
Anstis, *Anstice*
Anstiss, *Anstice*
Anstruther
Ansty, *Anstey*
Antal, *Anthony*
Antalffy, *Anthony*
Antão, *Anthony*
Antczak, *Anthony*
Antecki, *Anthony*
Antell, *Ashkettle*
Anthes, *Anthony*
Anthoin, *Anthony*
Anthoine, *Anthony*
Anthon, *Anthony*
Anthoney, *Anthony*
Anthonies, *Anthony*
Anthonsen, *Anthony*
Anthony
Antić, *Anthony*
Antifeev, *Yevtikhiev*
Antill, *Ashkettle*
Antin, *Ashkettle*
Antipin, *Antipov*
Antipov
Antipyev, *Antipov*
Antognazzi, *Anthony*
Antognelli, *Anthony*
Antognetti, *Anthony*
Antognini, *Antonini*
Antognoli, *Anthony*
Antognoni, *Anthony*
Antognozzi, *Anthony*
Antoin, *Anthony*
Antoinat, *Anthony*
Antoine, *Anthony*
Antoinet, *Anthony*
Antolí, *Antonini*
Antolín, *Antonini*
Antón, *Anthony*
Antoň, *Anthony*
Anton, *Anthony*
Antona, *Anthony*
Antonacci, *Anthony*
Antonas, *Anthony*
Antonat, *Anthony*
Antonazzi, *Anthony*
Antonchik, *Anthony*
Antonczyk, *Anthony*
Antonelli, *Anthony*
Antonellini, *Anthony*
Antonescu, *Anthony*
Antonetti, *Anthony*
Antoney, *Anthony*
Antongini, *Antonini*
Antoni, *Anthony, Antonini*
Antoniades, *Anthony*
Antoniak, *Anthony*
Antoniazzi, *Anthony*
Antonich, *Anthony*
Antonietti, *Anthony*
Antoniewicz, *Anthony*
Antoniewski, *Anthony*
Antonijević, *Anthony*
Antonik, *Anthony*
Antonikov, *Anthony*
Antonín, *Anthony*
Antonin, *Antonini*
Antonini
António, *Anthony*
Antonio, *Anthony*
Antonioli, *Anthony*
Antonioni, *Anthony*
Antoniotti, *Anthony*
Antoniou, *Anthony*
Antoniutti, *Anthony*
Antonnikov, *Anthony*
Antonopoulos, *Anthony*
Antonov, *Anthony*
Antonović, *Anthony*
Antonowicz, *Anthony*
Antonsen, *Anthony*
Antonsson, *Anthony*
Antonucci, *Anthony*
Antonutti, *Anthony*
Antony, *Anthony, Antonini*
Antonyev, *Anthony*
Antoons, *Anthony*
Antoš, *Anthony*
Antosch, *Anthony*
Antoshin, *Anthony*
Antosik, *Anthony*
Antoszczyk, *Anthony*
Antoszewski, *Anthony*
Antowski, *Anthony*
Antrack, *Andrew*
Antrag, *Andrew*
Antrobus
Anttila
Antuk, *Anthony*
Antuñano
Antunes, *Anthony*
Antúnez, *Anthony*
Antuoni, *Anthony*
Antusch, *Anthony*
Antushev, *Anthony*
Antyshev, *Anthony*
Antyukhin, *Anthony*
Antzilewitz, *Amschel*
Anyan, *Onion*
Anyon, *Onion*
Anzaldi, *Oswald*
Anzaldo, *Oswald*
Anzelmi, *Ansell*
Aoustin, *Austin*
Aparici, *Aparicio*
Aparício, *Aparicio*
Aparicio
Apel, *Albert*
Apelbaum, *Apple*
Apelbe, *Appleby*
Apelblat, *Apple*
Apelboim, *Apple*
Apelbom, *Apple*
Apeloig, *Apple*
Apfel, *Apple*
Apfelbaum, *Apple*
Apfelberg, *Apple*
Apfelmann, *Apple*
Apfelschnitt, *Apple*
Apfler, *Apple*
Apostel, *Postle*
Aposter, *Postle*
Apostol, *Postle*
Appel, *Albert*
Appel, *Apple*
Appelbaum, *Apple*
Appelberg, *Apple*
Appelblat, *Apple*
Appelbohm, *Apple*
Appelboim, *Apple*
Appelbom, *Apple*
Appelboom, *Apple*
Appelgren, *Apple*
Appelkvist, *Apple*
Appelman, *Apple*
Appelmann, *Apple*
Apple
Applebaum, *Apple*
Applebe, *Appleby*
Applebee, *Appleby*
Applebey, *Appleby*
Appleby
Applegarth
Applegate, *Applegarth*
Applegath, *Applegarth*
Appleman, *Apple*
Applethwaite
Appleton
Applewhaite, *Applethwaite*
Applewhite, *Applethwaite*
Appleyard
Apps
Aprahamian, *Abraham*

April
Aps, *Apps*
Apsel, *Absalom*
Apsey, *Apps*
Apt
Apter, *Apt*
Apterman, *Apt*
Aquila, *Eagle*
Aquili, *Eagle*
Aquilini, *Eagle*
Aquilone, *Eagle*
Aquiloni, *Eagle*
Aquilotti, *Eagle*
Aragão, *Aragón*
Aragon, *Aragón*
Aragón
Aragona, *Aragón*
Aragone, *Aragón*
Aragonés, *Aragón*
Aragonès, *Aragón*
Aragonese, *Aragón*
Aragoneses, *Aragón*
Aragou, *Aragón*
Araldi, *Harrod*
Aramburu
Arampuru, *Aramburu*
Aran, *Arana*
Arana
Arancio, *Naranjo*
Aranda
Arangio, *Naranjo*
Aranguren
Aranzello, *Naranjo*
Arasimovich, *Gerasimov*
Araújo
Arbatov
Arbaud, *Herbaud*
Arber, *Harber*
Arblaster, *Alabaster*
Arbós
Arbuckle
Arbus
Arbusman, *Arbus*
Arbuss, *Arbus*
Arbuthnot
Arbuthnott, *Arbuthnot*
Arbuz, *Arbus*
Arbuzov
Arca, *Arcas*
Arcari, *Arcas*
Arcaro, *Arcas*
Arcas
Arce
Arceri, *Archer*
Archa, *Arcas*
Archambault, *Archibald*
Archbald, *Archibald*
Archbell, *Archibald*
Archbold, *Archibald*
Archbould, *Archibald*
Archbutt, *Archibald*
Archdale
Archer
Archetti, *Arco*
Archetto, *Arco*
Archi, *Arco*
Archibald
Archibould, *Archibald*
Archier, *Archer*
Archimbaud, *Archibald*
Archimbeaud, *Archibald*
Archini, *Arco*
Arcieri, *Archer*
Arco
Arcone, *Arco*
Arconi, *Arco*
Arcos, *Arco*
Arct, *Arzt*
Arcucci, *Arco*
Arcy, *Darcy*
Arden
Ardenghi, *Harding*
Ardes, *Allardyce*
Ardin, *Harding*
Arding, *Harding*
Ardinghi, *Harding*
Ardini, *Ardouin*
Ardleigh, *Ardley*
Ardley
Ardoini, *Ardouin*
Ardouin
Ardouini, *Ardouin*
Ardovini, *Ardouin*
Ardura
Areles, *Aaron*
Arellano
Arena, *Arenas*
Arenas
Arend, *Arnold*
Arends, *Arnold*
Arendse, *Arnold*
Arendsen, *Arnold*
Arendt, *Arnold*
Arenella, *Arenas*
Arenello, *Arenas*
Areni, *Arenas*
Areniello, *Arenas*
Arenillas, *Arenas*
Arens, *Arnold*
Arent, *Arnold*
Arents, *Arnold*
Ares
Aresti
Arévalo
Argemí
Argent
Argenti, *Argent*
Argüello
Argyle
Arheur, *Arcas*
Ariaan, *Adrian*
Ariaen, *Adrian*
Arianello, *Adrian*
Arianetto, *Adrian*
Ariani, *Adrian*
Arias
Ariaudo, *Harrod*
Arillo, *Grill*
Arillotta, *Grill*
Ariñó
Ariza
Arkell, *Arkle*
Arkenbout, *Archibald*
Arkhipov
Arkhipyev, *Arkhipov*
Arkill, *Arkle*
Arkin, *Aaron*
Arkle
Arkley, *Arkle*
Arkow, *Aaron*
Arkwright
Arlet, *Arnold*
Arling, *Harling*
Arlot, *Arlott*
Arlott
Arlt, *Arnold*
Arman, *Hermann*
Armand, *Hermann*
Armandin, *Hermann*
Armanetti, *Hermann*
Armani, *Hermann*
Armanini, *Hermann*
Armanino, *Hermann*
Armanni, *Hermann*
Armanno, *Hermann*
Armano, *Hermann*
Armant, *Hermann*
Armborster, *Alabaster*
Armbriester, *Alabaster*
Armbrüster, *Alabaster*
Armbruster, *Alabaster*
Armbster, *Alabaster*
Armburster, *Alabaster*
Armengaud, *Armengol*
Armengault, *Armengol*
Armengol
Armengou, *Armengol*
Armer
Armero, *Armer*
Armes, *Armin*
Armetrading, *Armetriding*
Armetriding
Armett, *Hermite*
Armgardt, *Ermgard*
Armin
Arminot, *Armin*
Arminson, *Armin*
Armison, *Armin*
Armistead
Armit, *Hermite*
Armitage
Armitt, *Hermite*
Armor, *Armour*
Armour
Armson, *Armin*
Armstead, *Armistead*
Armster, *Alabaster*
Armstrong
Armytage, *Armitage*
Arnáez, *Arnold*
Arnáiz, *Arnold*
Arnal, *Arnold*
Arnald, *Arnold*
Arnaldi, *Arnold*
Arnaldo, *Arnold*
Arnaldy, *Arnold*
Arnall, *Arnold*
Arnao, *Arnold*
Arnason, *Arnold*
Arnatt, *Arnold*
Arnau, *Arnold*
Arnaud, *Arnold*
Arnaudet, *Arnold*
Arnaudi, *Arnold*
Arnaudin, *Arnold*
Arnaudon, *Arnold*
Arnaudot, *Arnold*
Arnauduc, *Arnold*
Arnaudy, *Arnold*
Arnault, *Arnold*
Arnaut, *Arnold*
Arnbuckle, *Arbuckle*
Arndell, *Arundel*
Arndt, *Arnold*
Arndtsen, *Arnold*
Arnecke, *Arnold*
Arnell, *Arnold*
Arnhold, *Arnold*
Arnholdt, *Arnold*
Arnholtz, *Arnold*
Arnholz, *Arnold*
Arni, *Arnold*
Arnison, *Arnold*
Arnke, *Arnold*
Ärnli, *Arnold*
Arno, *Arnold*
Arnold
Arnoldi, *Arnold*
Arnoll, *Arnold*
Arnot, *Arnott*
Arnott
Arnou
Arnoud, *Arnold*
Arnoul, *Arnou*
Arnould, *Arnold*
Arnoulf, *Arnou*
Arnoult, *Arnold*
Arnout, *Arnold*
Arnoux, *Arnou*
Arnow, *Aaron*
Arnowicz, *Aaron*
Arnowitz, *Aaron*
Arnson, *Arnold*
Arntz, *Arnold*
Arntzen, *Arnold*
Arnull, *Arnold*
Arold, *Arnold*
Aroldi, *Harrod*
Aroldt, *Arnold*
Aron, *Aaron*
Aronde, *Hiron*
Arondeau, *Arundel*
Arondel, *Arundel*
Arondello, *Arundel*
Aronin, *Aaron*
Aronoff, *Aaron*
Aronov, *Aaron*
Aronovich, *Aaron*
Aronovitz, *Aaron*
Aronow, *Aaron*
Aronowicz, *Aaron*
Aronowitz, *Aaron*
Arons, *Aaron*
Aronsohn, *Aaron*
Aronson, *Aaron*
Aronstam, *Aaron*
Aronstein, *Aaron*
Aróstegui
Arpin, *Harper*
Arpino, *Harper*
Arqué, *Archer*
Arquer, *Archer*
Arquero, *Archer*
Arqués, *Archer*
Arquet, *Arco*
Arquier, *Archer*
Arquin, *Arco*
Arragon, *Aragón*
Arrandale, *Arundel*
Arranz
Arrault, *Arnold*
Arregui
Arrhenius, *Ahrén*
Arrheur, *Arcas*
Arriba
Arribas, *Arriba*
Arrichiello, *Henry*
Arriero
Arrieta
Arrighetti, *Henry*
Arrighi, *Henry*
Arrighini, *Henry*
Arrigo, *Henry*
Arrigucci, *Henry*
Arrington
Arriola, *Arrieta*

Attwooll, *Attwell*
Atty, *Athey*
Attyea, *Yeo*
Atwell, *Attwell*
Atwill, *Attwell*
Atwood, *Attwood*
Atwool, *Attwell*
Atz, *Ace*
Atze, *Ace*
Atzen, *Ace*
Aubain, *Alban*
Auban, *Alban*
Aubanel, *Alban*
Aubé, *Albert*
Aubel, *Beau*
Aubelet, *Albert*
Aubelin, *Albert*
Auber, *Albert*
Aubert, *Albert*
Aubertin, *Albert*
Auberton, *Albert*
Auberty, *Albert*
Aubery, *Aubrey*
Aubey, *Albert*
Aubin, *Albin*
Aubineau, *Albin*
Aubinet, *Albin*
Aublet, *Albert*
Aublin, *Albert*
Aubray, *Aubrey*
Aubreton, *Brett*
Aubrey
Aubriet, *Aubrey*
Aubriot, *Aubrey*
Aubrun, *Brown*
Aubry, *Aubrey*
Aubryet, *Aubrey*
Aubury, *Aubrey*
Auby, *Albin*
Aucelli, *Uccello*
Aucello, *Uccello*
Auchamp, *Champ*
Auchinleck
Auciello, *Uccello*
Auclerc, *Clark*
Aucoc, *Cock*
Aucock, *Alcock*
Aucott, *Alcott*
Aucourt, *Court*
Aucutt, *Alcott*
Auda, *Aldous*
Aude, *Old*
Auden, *Alden*
Audenis, *Dennis*
Audi, *Aldous*
Audier, *Edgar*
Audini, *Aldous*
Audinucci, *Aldous*
Audis, *Aldous*
Audley
Audo, *Aldous*
Audrey, *Awdrey*
Audritt, *Aldritt*
Audsley
Auduc, *Duke*
Auerbach
Auerbacher, *Auerbach*
Aufaure, *Fèvre*
Aufauvre, *Fèvre*
Auffray, *Aubrey*
Aufray, *Aubrey*
Aufrède, *Alfred*
Aufroix, *Aubrey*
Aufroy, *Aubrey*
Augagneux, *Gagneux*
Augé, *Alger*
Augello, *Uccello*
Augelluzzi, *Uccello*
Auger, *Alger*
Augereau, *Alger*
Augeri, *Edgar*
Augero, *Edgar*
Augeron, *Alger*
Auggieri, *Edgar*
Auggiero, *Edgar*
Augié, *Alger*
Augier, *Alger, Edgar*
Augieri, *Edgar*
Augiero, *Edgar*
Augras, *Grass*
Augros, *Gross*
Augst, *Agosti*
Augstein, *Austin*
August, *Agosti*
Auguste, *Agosti*
Augustin, *Austin*
Augustine, *Austin*
Augustinello, *Austin*
Augusto, *Agosti*
Augustowicz, *Austin*
Augustowski, *Austin*
Augustsson, *Agosti*
Augustyn, *Austin*
Augustyniak, *Austin*
Augustynowicz, *Austin*
Augustyński, *Austin*
Aujean, *John*
Aujouanet, *John*
Auld, *Old*
Auler, *Euler*
Aulner, *Euler*
Ault, *Old*
Aumaître, *Master*
Aumarchand, *Marchant*
Aumari, *Aylmer*
Aumas, *Mas*
Aumasson, *Mason*
Aumerle, *Merle*
Aumeunier, *Miller*
Aumoine, *Monk*
Aumonier
Aunay, *Delaney*
Auneau, *Delaney*
Aunger, *Ainger*
Aupetit, *Pettit*
Aupol, *Paul*
Aupy, *Pine*
Auric, *Alaric*
Auriol, *Oriol*
Auriou, *Oriol*
Aurousseau, *Russell*
Auroux, *Rouse*
Aurrecoechea
Aury, *Alaric*
Ausborn, *Osborn*
Ausielli, *Uccello*
Austen, *Austin*
Auster, *Easter*
Austerling, *Easter*
Austerlitz
Austermann, *Easter*
Austin
Austins, *Austin*
Auston, *Austin*
Autessier, *Tissier*
Authier, *Edgar*
Autier, *Edgar*
Autin, *Austin*
Autissier, *Tissier*
Autixier, *Tissier*
Auty
Auvray, *Albaret, Aubrey*
Auxten, *Austin*
Avann, *Fenn*
Avans, *Evan*
Avdakov, *Yevdokimov*
Avdonin, *Yevdokimov*
Avdonkin, *Yevdokimov*
Aveline, *Evelyn*
Aveling, *Evelyn*
Avenel, *Avoine*
Avenet, *Avoine*
Avenier, *Avoine*
Avenne, *Avoine*
Avenol, *Avoine*
Averbach, *Auerbach*
Averback, *Auerbach*
Averbouch, *Auerbach*
Averbuch, *Auerbach*
Averbuj, *Auerbach*
Averies, *Aubrey*
Averill, *April*
Avermann, *Ober*
Avery, *Aubrey*
Avesalomov, *Absalom*
Avesque, *Bishop*
Aveyard
Avigdor
Avila
Avilés, *Avila*
Avilin, *Babel*
Avilov, *Babel*
Avis
Avison, *Avis*
Avksentyev, *Aksyonov*
Avner, *Avoine*
Avnet
Avogadro
Avogaro, *Avogadro*
Avoine
Avory, *Aubrey*
Avraam, *Abraham*
Avraham, *Abraham*
Avrahami, *Abraham*
Avrahamian, *Abraham*
Avrahamof, *Abraham*
Avrahamoff, *Abraham*
Avrahamov, *Abraham*
Avrahamy, *Abraham*
Avrahm, *Abraham*
Avram, *Abraham*
Avramchik, *Abraham*
Avramian, *Abraham*
Avramov, *Abraham*
Avramović, *Abraham*
Avramovich, *Abraham*
Avramovitz, *Abraham*
Avramovsky, *Abraham*
Avramow, *Abraham*
Avramy, *Abraham*
Avrashin, *Abraham*
Avrashkov, *Abraham*
Avrasin, *Abraham*
Avrial, *April*
Avril, *April*
Avrillon, *April*
Avschalom, *Absalom*
Avseev, *Eusébio*
Avshalom, *Absalom*
Avtukhov, *Yevtikhiev*
Avvocato, *Avogadro*
Awcock, *Alcock*
Awdrey
Awdry, *Awdrey*
Awerbach, *Auerbach*
Awerbuch, *Auerbach*
Axell, *Ashkettle*
Axelsen, *Ashkettle*
Axelsson, *Ashkettle*
Axtell, *Ashkettle*
Ayasse, *Agace*
Ayckbourn
Ayer
Ayers, *Ayer*
Aykroyd, *Ackroyd*
Aylard, *Allard*
Aylen, *Ayling*
Ayler, *Aillier*
Ayliff
Ayliffe, *Ayliff*
Aylin, *Ayling*
Ayling
Aylmer
Aylmore, *Aylmer*
Aylward
Aylwen, *Alwyn*
Aylwin, *Alwyn*
Aymar, *Aylmer*
Aymer, *Aylmer*
Aymeric, *Henry*
Aymerich, *Henry*
Aymery, *Amery*
Aymon, *Hammond*
Aymonic, *Hammond*
Aynauld, *Einold*
Aynsley, *Ainslie*
Ayo
Ayr, *Ayer*
Ayre, *Ayer*
Ayres, *Ayer*
Ayris, *Ayer*
Ayscough, *Askew*
Aysh, *Ash*
Aysik, *Isaac*
Ayson, *McKay*
Ayuso
Azam, *Adam*
Azarian, *Lazar*
Azcárate
Azcona
Azcorra
Azcue
Aze, *Ace*
Azéma, *Aylmer*
Azémar, *Aylmer*
Azevedo, *Acevedo*
Aznar
Azyornikov, *Jeziorski*
Azzi, *Ace*
Azzini, *Ace*
Azzoli, *Ace*
Azzolini, *Ace*
Azzoni, *Ace*

B

Baack, *Baud*
Baade, *Bothu*
Baaij, *Bay*
Baake, *Baud*
Baal, *Baud*
Baamonde
Baanders, *Bannerman*
Baaren, *Barr*
Baark, *Birch*

Baarmann, *Bermann*
Baars, *Barr*
Baars, *Bass*
Baart, *Beard*
Baartman, *Beard*
Baas
Baasch, *Baas*
Baba, *Babin*
Babák, *Babin*
Babb
Babbitt, *Babb*
Babbs, *Babb*
Babcock, *Babb*
Babeau, *Babel*
Babel
Babelet, *Babel*
Babelin, *Babel*
Babelon, *Babel*
Babenko, *Babin*
Baber
Babet, *Babb*
Babeuf
Babić, *Babin*
Babič, *Babin*
Babich, *Babin*
Babický, *Babin*
Babics, *Babin*
Babicz, *Babin*
Babin
Babington
Babiński, *Babin*
Babitch, *Babin*
Babits, *Babin*
Babitt, *Babb*
Babka, *Babin*
Babkin, *Babin*
Bablet, *Babel*
Babli, *Babel*
Bablin, *Babel*
Bablon, *Babel*
Bably, *Babel*
Babot, *Babb*
Babović, *Babin*
Babski, *Babin*
Babst, *Pope*
Babukhin, *Babin*
Babushkin, *Babin*
Baca, *Vacca*
Baccelieri, *Bachelor*
Baccellieri, *Bachelor*
Bacchus
Bacciglieri, *Bachelor*
Baccilieri, *Bachelor*
Baccus, *Bacchus*
Bach
Bacha, *Bartholomew*
Bachański, *Bach*
Bacharach
Bache, *Bach*
Bachelard, *Bachelor*
Bacheler, *Bachelor*
Bachelet, *Bachelor*
Bachelier, *Bachelor*
Bachelin, *Bachelor*
Bacheller, *Bachelor*
Bachelor
Bachelot, *Bachelor*
Bacher, *Bach, Baker*
Bacherach, *Bacharach*
Bacherich, *Bacharach*
Bacherig, *Bacharach*
Bachiller, *Bachelor*
Bachman, *Bach*
Bachmann, *Bach*
Bachnik, *Bartholomew*
Bachofen
Bachrach, *Bacharach*
Bachrameev, *Bartholomew*
Bachrich, *Bacharach*
Bachs, *Bach*
Bächtold, *Berthold*
Bachura, *Bartholomew*
Baciglieri, *Bachelor*
Bacilieri, *Bachelor*
Bäck, *Beck*
Back
Backe, *Baud*
Backen, *Baud*
Bäcker, *Baker*
Backer, *Back*
Backes, *Backhouse*
Backhaus, *Backhouse*
Backhouse
Backhus, *Backhouse*
Backler, *Bachelor*
Bäcklund, *Beck*
Backlund, *Banks*
Bäckman, *Beck*
Backman, *Back*
Backner, *Bacon*
Backof, *Bachofen*
Backofen, *Bachofen*
Backouse, *Backhouse*
Backs, *Back, Backhouse*
Bäckström, *Beck*
Backström, *Banks*
Backus, *Backhouse*
Bacon
Baconnier, *Bacon*
Bączyk, *Bąk*
Badaire, *Badier*
Badanes
Badaud
Badault, *Badaud*
Badcock, *Bade*
Badcoe, *Bade*
Baddams, *Adam*
Baddeley
Badé, *Badier*
Bade
Bade, *Botha*
Bädeke, *Böttcher*
Badeke, *Botha*
Bädeker, *Böttcher*
Baden, *Botha*
Badenius, *Botha*
Bäder, *Bader*
Bader
Badger
Badgers, *Badger*
Badham
Badia, *Abbey*
Badier
Bading, *Botha*
Badini, *Abbé*
Badiou, *Badaud*
Badman
Badner
Badoc, *Badaud*
Badoche, *Badaud*
Badolle, *Badaud*
Badou, *Badaud*
Badrick, *Betteridge*
Badrock, *Betteridge*
Baeck, *Beck*
Bael, *Baud*
Baelde, *Baud*
Baena
Baer, *Bear*
Baert, *Bartholomew*
Baerts, *Bartholomew*
Baeta
Baeten, *Béatrice*
Báez, *Pelayo*
Baeza
Baffin, *Baughan*
Bage, *Bagge*
Bagehot, *Bacon*
Bagenal, *Bagnall*
Bager, *Badger*
Bagg, *Bagge*
Baggaley, *Bagley*
Baggallay, *Bagley*
Baggally, *Bagley*
Baggarley, *Bagley*
Baggat, *Bathgate*
Bagge, *Bacon*
Bagge
Bagger, *Badger*
Bagges, *Bacon*
Baggesen, *Bacon*
Baggett, *Bacon*
Baggot, *Bacon*
Baggott, *Bacon*
Bagguley, *Bagley*
Bagieński, *Bagiński*
Bagiński
Bagley
Bagliardi, *Bailey*
Baglietti, *Bailey*
Baglini, *Bailey*
Baglio, *Bailey*
Baglione, *Bailey*
Baglivo, *Bailey*
Bagnacci, *Bain*
Bagnall
Bagnell, *Bagnall*
Bagnesi, *Bain*
Bagni, *Bain*
Bagnold, *Bagnall*
Bagnoli, *Bain*
Bagnone, *Bain*
Bagnulo, *Bain*
Bagnuolo, *Bain*
Bagot, *Bacon*
Bagott, *Bacon*
Bagradian, *Bagratian*
Bagratian
Bagration, *Bagratian*
Bagshaw
Bagshawe, *Bagshaw*
Baguley, *Bagley*
Bahamonde, *Baamonde*
Bahdanovich, *Bogdanov*
Bahde, *Botha*
Bahl, *Baud*
Bahlke, *Baud*
Bahlmann, *Baud*
Bahls, *Baud*
Bähr, *Bear*
Bahring, *Bear*
Bahrmann, *Bermann*
Bai, *Bay*
Baião
Baiard, *Bayard*
Baibakov
Baier, *Bayer*
Baijer, *Bayer*
Baijerman, *Bayer*
Baiker, *Baker, Pauker*
Baikert, *Pauker*
Bail, *Bailey*
Baile, *Bailey*
Bailes, *Bailey*
Bailess, *Bailey*
Bailet, *Bailey*
Bailey
Bailie, *Bailey*
Bailif, *Bailey*
Bailiff, *Bailey*
Bailin, *Beilin*
Baill, *Bailey*
Baillaud, *Bailey*
Baille, *Bailey*
Baillet, *Bailey*
Bailli, *Bailey*
Baillie, *Bailey*
Baillif, *Bailey*
Bailliff, *Bailey*
Baillivet, *Bailey*
Baillot, *Bailey*
Bailloud, *Bailey*
Bailloux, *Bailey*
Bailly, *Bailey*
Bailo, *Bailey*
Bailone, *Bailey*
Bails, *Bailey*
Baily, *Bailey*
Bain
Bainbridge
Baine, *Bain*
Baines
Bains, *Baines*
Baird, *Bard*
Bairnsfather
Bairstow
Baise, *Bass*
Baish, *Bach*
Baistow, *Bairstow*
Baitson, *Bate*
Baivier, *Bayer*
Baivy, *Bayer*
Baiwir, *Bayer*
Bajard, *Bayard*
Bajo, *Bass*
Bajol, *Bay*
Bajolet, *Bay*
Bak, *Back*
Bąk
Bakalář, *Bachelor*
Bakehouse, *Backhouse*
Bäker, *Böttcher*
Baker
Bakewell
Bakhrushin, *Bartholomew*
Bakhrushkin, *Bartholomew*
Bakhuijsen, *Backhouse*
Bakhuizen, *Backhouse*
Bakhuysen, *Backhouse*
Bakić, *Bąk*
Bakker, *Baker*
Baklanov
Bakmann, *Baker*
Bąkowski, *Bąk*
Bakulin, *Bakunin*
Bakunin
Bal
Balaam
Baláč, *Balthasar*
Baladier, *Bal*
Balagué, *Balaguer*
Balaguer
Balák, *Balthasar*
Balakirev
Balaňá
Baland, *Bal*

Balandier, *Bal*
Balanesco, *Blanc*
Baláš, *Balthasar*
Balassa, *Blaise*
Balassi, *Blaise*
Balat, *Vallat*
Baláž, *Balthasar*
Balázs, *Blaise*
Balb, *Baube*
Balbaud, *Baube*
Balbet, *Baube*
Balboa, *Valbuena*
Balbuena, *Valbuena*
Balcar, *Balthasar*
Balcárek, *Balthasar*
Balcells
Balcer, *Balthasar*
Balcerek, *Balthasar*
Balcerski, *Balthasar*
Balcewicz, *Balthasar*
Balch
Balcher, *Balch*
Balchin, *Balch*
Balcombe
Bald, *Ball, Baud*
Baldacchi, *Baud*
Baldacco, *Baud*
Baldassari, *Balthasar*
Baldasserini, *Balthasar*
Baldasseroni, *Balthasar*
Baldassi, *Baud*
Baldazzi, *Baud*
Balde, *Baud*
Baldelli, *Baud*
Balder, *Baudier*
Balderston
Balderstone, *Balderston*
Baldes, *Balthasar*
Baldessari, *Balthasar*
Baldetti, *Baud*
Baldewein, *Baldwin*
Baldi, *Baud*
Baldick, *Baldock*
Balding, *Baud*
Baldini, *Baud*
Baldinotti, *Baud*
Baldissari, *Balthasar*
Baldisseri, *Balthasar*
Baldisserotto, *Balthasar*
Baldocci, *Baud*
Baldock
Baldoin, *Baldwin*
Baldoni, *Baud*
Baldovino, *Baldwin*
Baldrey, *Baldry*
Baldrich, *Baldry*
Baldrick, *Baldry*
Baldry
Balducci, *Baud*
Balduini, *Baldwin*
Baldung, *Baud*
Baldus, *Balthasar*
Baldwin
Bale, *Bailey*
Balek, *Balthasar*
Bales, *Bailey*
Balestier, *Ballaster*
Balestra, *Ballaster*
Balestracci, *Ballaster*
Balestrassi, *Ballaster*
Balestrazzi, *Ballaster*
Balestrelli, *Ballaster*
Balestreri, *Ballaster*
Balestrieri, *Ballaster*
Balestrini, *Ballaster*
Balet, *Bal*
Balfe
Balfour
Balík, *Balthasar*
Bálint, *Valentine*
Baliol, *Balliol*
Balistreri, *Ballaster*
Balivan, *Balfe*
Balke, *Baud*
Balkwill
Ball
Ballaam, *Balaam*
Balladier, *Bal*
Ballaire, *Bal*
Balland, *Bal*
Ballandier, *Bal*
Ballantine, *Ballantyne*
Ballantyne
Ballard, *Ball*
Ballaster
Balle, *Ball*
Ballendine, *Ballantyne*
Ballentine, *Ballantyne*
Baller, *Ball*
Ballesta, *Ballaster*
Ballesté, *Ballaster*
Ballester, *Ballaster*
Ballestero, *Ballaster*
Ballesteros, *Ballaster*
Ballestreri, *Ballaster*
Ballestrieri, *Ballaster*
Ballet, *Bal*
Ballin, *Hayling*
Balling, *Ball*
Ballinger, *Beringer*
Ballintine, *Ballantyne*
Ballintyne, *Ballantyne*
Balliol
Ballista, *Ballaster*
Ballister, *Ballaster*
Ballon, *Bal*
Ballot, *Bal*
Ballou, *Bal*
Balls, *Ball*
Ballwein, *Baldwin*
Ballwen, *Baldwin*
Bally, *Bailey*
Balma, *Balme*
Balmadier, *Balme*
Balme
Balmer
Balmette, *Balme*
Balmforth, *Bamford*
Balog, *Balogh*
Balogh
Balon, *Bal*
Balot, *Bal*
Balou, *Bal*
Balp, *Baube*
Bals, *Balthasar*
Balsam, *Balmer*
Balsari, *Balthasar*
Balsells, *Balcells*
Balser
Balster, *Ballaster*
Baltasar, *Balthasar*
Baltazar, *Balthasar*
Baltes, *Balthasar*
Balthas, *Balthasar*
Balthasar
Balthasard, *Balthasar*
Balthazar, *Balthasar*
Balthazard, *Balthasar*
Baltrushaitis, *Bartholomew*
Baltus, *Balthasar*
Baltz, *Balthasar*
Baltzer, *Balthasar*
Baltzersen, *Balthasar*
Baluet, *Blewett*
Baluhet, *Blewett*
Balz, *Balthasar*
Balzac
Balzari, *Balthasar*
Balzarini, *Balthasar*
Balzarotti, *Balthasar*
Balzel, *Balthasar*
Balzer, *Balthasar*
Balzl, *Balthasar*
Bälzle, *Balthasar*
Balzli, *Balthasar*
Bamber
Bamberger
Bambrough
Bamford
Bamforth, *Bamford*
Bampford, *Bamford*
Bampforth, *Bamford*
Bampfylde
Bampton
Banach, *Bennett*
Bañales, *Bain*
Banan, *Bannan*
Banane, *Bannan*
Bañares, *Bain*
Banaś, *Bennett*
Banasevich, *Bennett*
Banasiak, *Bennett*
Banasik, *Bennett*
Banaszczyk, *Bennett*
Banaszewski, *Bennett*
Banaszkiewicz, *Bennett*
Banbury
Bancroft
Band
Bande, *Band*
Bandeira, *Bannerman*
Bandeiras, *Bannerman*
Bandel, *Band*
Bandelman, *Band*
Bandle, *Band*
Bandler, *Band*
Bandman, *Band*
Bandmann, *Band*
Bandner, *Band*
Bandt, *Band*
Banes, *Baines*
Banfather, *Bairnsfather*
Banfield
Bang
Bangratz, *Pankridge*
Bangs, *Banks*
Banham
Banim, *Bannan*
Banin, *Bannan*
Banisch, *Bennett*
Banish, *Bennett*
Banishevitz, *Bennett*
Banister, *Bannister*
Bank, *Banks*
Banke, *Banks*
Banker, *Banks*
Bankes, *Banks*
Bankhead
Banković, *Bańkowski*
Bańkowski
Bankratz, *Pankridge*
Banks
Bannan
Banner, *Bannerman*
Bannerman
Bannester, *Bannister*
Bannion, *Bannan*
Bannister
Bannon, *Bannan*
Bañón, *Bain*
Baños, *Bain*
Bansfather, *Bairnsfather*
Bantele, *Pantaleone*
Bantleon, *Pantaleone*
Bantli, *Pantaleone*
Bantzer, *Panzer*
Banuelos, *Bain*
Banwell
Banyard
Banzer, *Panzer*
Bapp, *Papot*
Baptie, *Baptiste*
Baptist, *Baptiste*
Baptista, *Baptiste*
Baptiste
Baque, *Bacon*
Baqué, *Vaccaro*
Baquelin, *Bacon*
Baquer, *Vaccaro*
Baquero, *Vaccaro*
Baqulin, *Bacon*
Bär, *Bear*
Bar, *Bard*
Bara, *Barrett*
Barabino
Barada, *Barr*
Baradas, *Barr*
Baradat, *Barr*
Baradeau, *Barr*
Baradel, *Barr*
Baradulin, *Borodin*
Baradzeya, *Borodin*
Baragwanath
Baragwaneth, *Baragwanath*
Barahona
Barajas
Baran, *Baranov*
Baranchik, *Baranov*
Baranchuk, *Baranov*
Baranda
Baraniek, *Baranov*
Baranov
Baranovich, *Baranov*
Baranovitz, *Baranov*
Baranovski, *Baranowski*
Baranovsky, *Baranowski*
Baranowicz, *Baranov*
Baranowitz, *Baranov*
Baranowski
Baranski, *Baranov*
Bárány, *Baranov*
Barasch, *Barish*
Barash, *Barish*
Barat, *Barrett*
Barata, *Barrett*
Barateau, *Barrett*
Barateri, *Barrett*
Baratier, *Barrett*
Baratieri, *Barrett*
Baratin, *Barrett*
Baraton, *Barrett*
Baratoux, *Barrett*
Baratta, *Barrett*
Baratte, *Barrett*
Barattini, *Barrett*
Barattoni, *Barrett*

Barattucci, *Barrett*
Baraux, *Baril*
Barba, *Barbe*
Barbacci, *Barbe*
Barbadillo, *Barbe*
Barbado, *Barbe*
Barbanchon, *Brabazon*
Bárbara, *Barbary*
Barbarà, *Barberà*
Barbara, *Barbary*
Barbaracci, *Barbary*
Barbaraci, *Barbary*
Barbarelli, *Barbary*
Barbarin, *Barbary*
Barbarino, *Barbary*
Barbarolli, *Barber*
Barbarotto, *Barbary*
Barbarou, *Barbary*
Barbaroux, *Barbary*
Barbarulo, *Barbary*
Barbary
Barbas, *Barbe*
Barbat, *Barbe*
Barbato, *Barbe*
Barbé, *Barbe*
Barbe
Barbeiro, *Barber*
Barbella, *Barbe*
Barber
Barberà
Barberàn, *Barberà*
Barbereau, *Barber*
Barberet, *Barber*
Barberi, *Barber*
Barberini, *Barber*
Barbero, *Barber*
Barberon, *Barber*
Barberot, *Barber*
Barbery, *Barbary*
Barbet, *Barbe*
Barbetti, *Barbe*
Barbié, *Barber*
Barbier, *Barber*
Barbieri, *Barber*
Barbiers, *Barber*
Barbieux, *Barber*
Barbin, *Barbe*
Barbini, *Barbe*
Barbolini, *Barbe*
Barbon, *Barbe*
Barbone, *Barbe*
Barbosa
Barboso, *Barbe*
Barbot, *Barbe*
Barbour, *Barber*
Barbu, *Barbe*
Barbuat, *Barbe*
Barbucci, *Barbe*
Barbudo, *Barbe*
Barbulesco, *Barbe*
Barbut, *Barbe*
Barbuto, *Barbe*
Barbuzzi, *Barbe*
Barby, *Barbe*
Barcan, *Cohen*
Barceló
Bárcena
Bárcenas, *Bárcena*
Barcenilla, *Bárcena*
Barcina, *Bárcena*
Barclay
Barco
Bar-Cohen, *Cohen*
Barcroft
Barczewski, *Bartholomew*
Barczyński, *Bartholomew*
Bard
Bardacci, *Bard*
Bar-Dayan, *Dayan*
Bardazzi, *Bard*
Barde
Bardell, *Bardwell*
Bardelli, *Bard*
Bardellini, *Bard*
Barden
Bardet, *Bard*
Bardetti, *Bard*
Bardi, *Bard*
Bardineau, *Bard*
Bardinet, *Bard*
Bardinon, *Bard*
Bardinot, *Bard*
Bardioni, *Bard*
Bardolph, *Bertolf*
Bardon, *Bard*
Bardoni, *Bard*
Bardonneau, *Bard*
Bardonnet, *Bard*
Bardot, *Bard*
Bardotti, *Bard*
Bardsley
Barducci, *Bard*
Bardwell
Bardy, *Bard*
Bareau, *Barr*
Bareel, *Baril*
Barefoot, *Barfoot*
Bareham, *Barham*
Bareis, *Parish*
Barella, *Barr*
Barelli, *Bear*
Barellini, *Bear*
Barenbaum, *Birnbaum*
Barenboim, *Birnbaum*
Barends, *Bernard*
Barendts, *Bernard*
Barendtsen, *Bernard*
Barenholtz, *Birnbaum*
Barenholz, *Birnbaum*
Bärenreiter
Barens, *Bernard*
Barense, *Bernard*
Barensen, *Bernard*
Barents, *Bernard*
Barentsen, *Bernard*
Barettino, *Bear*
Baretto, *Bear*
Barfaut, *Barfoot*
Barff, *Barrow*
Barfield
Barfod, *Barfoot*
Barfoed, *Barfoot*
Barfoot
Barfoth, *Barfoot*
Barfuss, *Barfoot*
Barg, *Berg*
Bargalló
Barge
Bargeman, *Barge*
Bargeton, *Barge*
Bargh, *Barrow*
Bargmann, *Berg*
Barham
Barhams, *Barham*
Barhem, *Barham*
Barhems, *Barham*
Barhims, *Barham*
Barial, *Baril*
Bariglietti, *Baril*
Bariglione, *Baril*
Baril
Barilaro, *Baril*
Barile, *Baril*
Bariletti, *Baril*
Barilini, *Baril*
Barillaro, *Baril*
Bariller, *Baril*
Barillet, *Baril*
Barilli, *Baril*
Barillier, *Baril*
Barillon, *Baril*
Barillot, *Baril*
Barilone, *Baril*
Barilotti, *Baril*
Barilucci, *Baril*
Baring, *Bear*
Barini, *Bear*
Barish
Barizeret, *Basil*
Barjon, *Barge*
Barjot, *Barge*
Barjou, *Barge*
Bark, *Birch*
Barkan, *Cohen*
Barker
Barkley, *Barclay*
Barlee, *Barley*
Barlet, *Baril*
Barletta, *Baril*
Barletti, *Baril*
Barley
Barleyman, *Barley*
Barling, *Burling*
Barlon, *Baril*
Barlot, *Baril*
Barlow
Barme, *Balme*
Barna, *Barnaby*
Barnaba, *Barnaby*
Barnabé, *Barnaby*
Barnabe, *Barnaby*
Barnabee, *Barnaby*
Barnabei, *Barnaby*
Barnabucci, *Barnaby*
Barnaby
Barnacle, *Coyne*
Barnaclough, *Barraclough*
Barnard, *Bernard*
Barnaud, *Beraud*
Barne, *Barnes*
Barneby, *Barnaby*
Barnes
Barness, *Barnes*
Barnet
Barnett, *Barnet*
Barnewall, *Barnwell*
Barnfather, *Bairnsfather*
Barnfield
Barnham, *Barnum*
Barnhart, *Bernard*
Barnholz, *Birnbaum*
Barni, *Barnaby*
Barnini, *Barnaby*
Barnobi, *Barnaby*
Barns, *Barnes*
Barnsfather, *Bairnsfather*
Barnsley
Barnum
Barnwell
Baró, *Baron*
Barocci, *Bear*
Baroen, *Baron*
Bärold, *Beraud*
Barón, *Baron*
Baron
Baroncelli, *Baron*
Baroncini, *Baron*
Barone, *Baron*
Baronio, *Baron*
Baronnet, *Baron*
Barontini, *Baron*
Barotti, *Bear*
Barou, *Baron*
Baroux, *Baron*
Barque, *Barge*
Barquero, *Barco*
Barr
Barraclough
Barradas, *Bard*
Barragán
Barrailler, *Baril*
Barral, *Baril*
Barralier, *Baril*
Barranco
Barrass, *Barrow*
Barrat, *Barrett*
Barratt, *Barrett*
Barrau, *Baril*
Barraud, *Baril*
Barrault, *Baril*
Barraut, *Baril*
Barraux, *Baril*
Barre, *Barr*
Barré
Barreau, *Barr*
Barrée, *Barr*
Barreira, *Barrera*
Barreiros, *Bard*
Barrel, *Barr*
Barrelet, *Barr*
Barrell, *Baril*
Barrella, *Barr*
Barrelle, *Barr*
Barrena
Barrenechea
Barrera
Barret, *Barr, Barrett*
Barreto, *Bard*
Barrett
Barri, *Barry*
Barrick, *Barwick*
Barrie, *Barry*
Barriga
Barril, *Baril*
Barrile, *Baril*
Barrilero, *Baril*
Barrillon, *Baril*
Barrington
Barrio
Barriol, *Barry*
Barrion, *Barry*
Barrios, *Barrio*
Barritt, *Barrett*
Barron, *Baron*
Barros, *Bard*
Barros
Barroso, *Bard*
Barrot, *Barr*
Barrow
Barrowcliff, *Barraclough*
Barrowcliffe, *Barraclough*
Barrowclough, *Barraclough*
Barrowman, *Burkman*
Barrows, *Barrow*
Barry
Barryman, *Burkman*

Barsham, *Basham*
Barski
Barson, *Bartholomew*
Barstow, *Bairstow*
Barsuk, *Barsukov*
Barsukov
Barszczewski, *Bartholomew*
Bart, *Bard, Bartholomew, Beard*
Bárta, *Bartholomew*
Bàrta, *Bartholomew*
Barták, *Bartholomew*
Bàrtal, *Bartholomew*
Bartaletti, *Bartholomew*
Bartali, *Bartholomew*
Bartalini, *Bartholomew*
Bartaloni, *Bartholomew*
Bartalucci, *Bartholomew*
Bartas, *Barthe*
Bartczak, *Bartholomew*
Barte, *Barthe*
Bartek, *Bartholomew*
Bartel, *Bartholomew*
Bartélemy, *Bartholomew*
Bartelet, *Bartholomew*
Bartelli, *Bartholomew*
Bartélmy, *Bartholomew*
Bartels, *Bartholomew, Berthold*
Barten, *Barton*
Bartens, *Bartholomew*
Bartet, *Barthe*
Barth, *Bartholomew, Beard*
Barthas, *Barthe*
Barthe
Barthel, *Bartholomew*
Barthélemy, *Bartholomew*
Barthelet, *Bartholomew*
Barthelme, *Bartholomew*
Barthelmes, *Bartholomew*
Barthélmy, *Bartholomew*
Barthels, *Bartholomew, Berthold*
Barthès, *Barthe*
Barthet, *Barthe*
Barthod, *Bartholomew*
Barthol, *Bartholomew*
Bartholat, *Bartholomew*
Barthold, *Berthold*
Bartholdy, *Berthold*
Bartholin, *Bartholomew*
Bartholomä, *Bartholomew*
Bartholomäus, *Bartholomew*
Bartholomew
Bartholomieu, *Bartholomew*
Barthot, *Bartholomew*
Bartie, *Bartholomew*
Bartke, *Bartholomew*
Bartkiewicz, *Bartholomew*
Bartkowiak, *Bartholomew*
Bartl, *Bartholomew*
Bartlam, *Bartholomew*
Bartle, *Bartholomew*
Bartleet, *Bartholomew*
Bartlet, *Bartholomew*
Bartlett, *Bartholomew*
Bartley
Bartłomieczak, *Bartholomew*
Bartłomiej, *Bartholomew*
Bartłomiejczyk, *Bartholomew*
Bartocci, *Bartholomew*
Bartod, *Bartholomew*
Bartók, *Bartholomew*
Bartol, *Bartholomew*
Bartolacci, *Bartholomew*
Bartolat, *Bartholomew*
Bartold, *Berthold*
Bartoletti, *Bartholomew*
Bartoleyn, *Bartholomew*
Bartoli, *Bartholomew*
Bartolić, *Bartholomew*
Bartolijn, *Bartholomew*
Bartolin, *Bartholomew*
Bartolini, *Bartholomew*
Bartolomä, *Bartholomew*
Bartolomäus, *Bartholomew*
Bartolomé, *Bartholomew*
Bartolomeazzi, *Bartholomew*
Bartolomeo, *Bartholomew*
Bartolomeoni, *Bartholomew*
Bartolomeotti, *Bartholomew*
Bartolomeu, *Bartholomew*
Bartolomieu, *Bartholomew*
Bartolomivis, *Bartholomew*
Bartolommeo, *Bartholomew*
Bartolomucci, *Bartholomew*
Bartolozzi, *Bartholomew*
Bartomeu, *Bartholomew*
Bartomieu, *Bartholomew*
Bartoň, *Bartholomew*
Barton
Bartoš, *Bartholomew*
Bartosch, *Bartholomew*
Bartošek, *Bartholomew*
Bartoshevich, *Bartholomew*
Bartosiak, *Bartholomew*
Bartosik, *Bartholomew*
Bartosiński, *Bartholomew*
Bartosz, *Bartholomew*
Bartoszek, *Bartholomew*
Bartoszewicz, *Bartholomew*
Bartoszewski, *Bartholomew*
Bartosziński, *Bartholomew*
Bartot, *Bartholomew*
Bartozzi, *Bartholomew*
Bartram, *Bertram*
Bartrum, *Bertram*
Barts, *Bartholomew*
Barttrum, *Bertram*
Bartul, *Bartholomew*
Bartůnek, *Bartholomew*
Bartušek, *Bartholomew*
Barty, *Bartholomew*
Bartz, *Bartholomew*
Bartzen, *Bartholomew*
Barucci, *Bear*
Baruch
Baruchsohn, *Baruch*
Baruchson, *Baruch*
Barugh, *Barrow*
Barukh, *Baruch*
Barusso, *Bear*
Barutti, *Bear*
Baruzzi, *Bear*
Barwell
Barwick
Baryła
Barylski, *Baryła*
Barysevich, *Borisov*
Baryshnikov
Barz, *Bartholomew*
Barzen, *Bartholomew*
Bas, *Bass, Bard*
Basch
Bascio, *Bass*
Bascou, *Vasco*
Bascoul, *Vasco*
Base, *Bass*
Baseggio, *Basil*
Basei, *Basil*
Bašek, *Bach*
Bäseke, *Basil*
Baseley, *Basil*
Baseli, *Basil*
Baselio, *Basil*
Baselli, *Basil*
Basely, *Basil*
Basezzi, *Basil*
Basford, *Bashford*
Bash, *Bach*
Basham
Bashford
Basil
Basile, *Basil*
Basilevich, *Basil*
Basili, *Basil*
Basílio, *Basil*
Basilio, *Basil*
Basillon, *Basil*
Basilone, *Basil*
Basilotta, *Basil*
Basin, *Basil*
Basire, *Basil*
Baskerfield, *Baskerville*
Baskerful, *Baskerville*
Baskerville
Basketfield, *Baskerville*
Baskin
Baskind, *Baskin*
Baskwell, *Baskerville*
Bason, *Bate*
Basq, *Vasco*
Basque, *Vasco*
Basquet, *Vasco*
Basquin, *Vasco*
Bass
Basse, *Bass*
Basset, *Bass*
Bassett, *Bass*
Bassetti, *Bass*
Bassford, *Bashford*
Bassham, *Basham*
Bassi, *Bass*
Bassil, *Basil*
Bassilashvili, *Basil*
Bassill, *Basil*
Bassini, *Bass*
Bassis, *Bass*
Basso, *Bass*
Bassoli, *Bass*
Bassolino, *Bass*
Bassone, *Bass*
Bassot, *Bass*
Bassotti, *Bass*
Bast, *Sebastian*
Bašta, *Sebastian*
Basta, *Sebastian*
Bastable
Bastaerd, *Bastard*
Bastard
Bastardeau, *Bastard*
Bastardo, *Bastard*
Bastardon, *Bastard*
Basten, *Sebastian*
Basterfield, *Baskerville*
Basterra
Basterrechea
Basteyns, *Sebastian*
Basthart, *Bastard*
Bastiaan, *Sebastian*
Bastiaanse, *Sebastian*
Bastiaansen, *Sebastian*
Bastiaelli, *Sebastian*
Bastiaello, *Sebastian*
Bastiaen, *Sebastian*
Bastian, *Sebastian*
Bastianel, *Sebastian*
Bastianelli, *Sebastian*
Bastianello, *Sebastian*
Bastianetto, *Sebastian*
Bastiani, *Sebastian*
Bastianini, *Sebastian*
Bastiano, *Sebastian*
Bastianon, *Sebastian*
Bastianutti, *Sebastian*
Bastianutto, *Sebastian*
Bastiat, *Sebastian*
Bastida, *Bastide*
Bastide
Bastidon, *Bastide*
Bastie, *Bastide*
Bastien, *Sebastian*
Bastin, *Sebastian*
Basting, *Sebastian*
Bastion, *Sebastian*
Bastke, *Sebastian*
Bästl, *Sebastian*
Bästle, *Sebastian*
Bastow, *Bairstow*
Baszek, *Bach*
Baszkiewicz, *Bach*
Baszniak, *Bach*
Bataillard, *Bataille*
Bataille
Batailler, *Bataille*
Bataillier, *Bataille*
Bataillon, *Bataille*
Batalha, *Bataille*
Bâtard, *Bastard*
Bâtardeau, *Bastard*
Batch, *Bach*
Batchelder, *Bachelor*
Batcheldor, *Bachelor*
Batcheler, *Bachelor*
Batcheller, *Bachelor*
Batchellor, *Bachelor*
Batchelor, *Bachelor*
Batcock, *Batt*
Bate
Bateman, *Bate*
Bates, *Bate*
Bateson, *Bate*
Batey, *Bate*
Bath
Bathas, *Balthasar*
Bathgate
Bathurst
Bâtie, *Bastide*
Batie, *Bate*
Batisse, *Baptiste*
Batista, *Baptiste*
Batistelli, *Baptiste*
Batistetti, *Baptiste*
Batistini, *Baptiste*
Batistio, *Baptiste*
Batistoni, *Baptiste*
Batistotti, *Baptiste*
Batistucci, *Baptiste*
Batistuzzi, *Baptiste*
Bätjer, *Böttcher*
Batley
Batllé, *Bailey*
Batman, *Batt*
Baton, *Batt*
Batram, *Bertram*
Batrick, *Betteridge*
Batsford
Batson, *Batt*

Batt
Battaglia, *Bataille*
Battaglieri, *Bataille*
Battaglini, *Bataille*
Battaia, *Bataille*
Battaiglioli, *Bataille*
Battaiglioni, *Bataille*
Battaiioli, *Bataille*
Battaiioni, *Bataille*
Battaillard, *Bataille*
Battaille, *Bataille*
Battailler, *Bataille*
Battaillier, *Bataille*
Battaillon, *Bataille*
Battaini, *Bataille*
Battala, *Bataille*
Battaler, *Bataille*
Battell, *Battle*
Batten, *Batt*
Batterham, *Bertram*
Battersby
Batteson, *Batt*
Battiati, *Vattiato*
Battiato, *Vattiato*
Battie, *Batt*
Battigne, *Beaton*
Battin, *Batt*
Battine, *Beaton*
Batting, *Batt*
Battisford
Battista, *Baptiste*
Battistelli, *Baptiste*
Battistetti, *Baptiste*
Battistini, *Baptiste*
Battistio, *Baptiste*
Battistoni, *Baptiste*
Battistotti, *Baptiste*
Battistucci, *Baptiste*
Battistuzzi, *Baptiste*
Battle
Battmann, *Batt*
Batton, *Batt*
Battram, *Bertram*
Battrick, *Betteridge*
Batts, *Batt*
Battson, *Batt*
Battu
Battut, *Battu*
Batty, *Batt*
Battye, *Batt*
Batu, *Battu*
Batut, *Battu*
Baty, *Batt*
Baubard, *Baube*
Baubault, *Baube*
Baube
Bauberon, *Baube*
Baubet, *Baube*
Baubier, *Baube*
Baubot, *Baube*
Bauch
Bauche
Bauchet, *Bauche*
Bäuchle, *Bauch*
Baucutt, *Baud*
Baud
Baudacci, *Baud*
Baudassi, *Baud*
Baudasso, *Baud*
Baude, *Baud*
Baudeau, *Baudel*
Baudel
Baudelaire
Baudelier, *Baudel*
Baudeloche, *Baudel*
Baudeloque, *Baudel*
Baudelot, *Baudel*
Baudereau, *Baudier*
Bauderon, *Baudier*
Baudesson, *Baud*
Baudet, *Baud*
Baudewijn, *Baldwin*
Baudewijns, *Baldwin*
Baudi, *Baud*
Baudic, *Baud*
Baudichon, *Baud*
Baudié, *Baudier*
Baudier
Baudin, *Baud*
Baudinelli, *Baud*
Baudinet, *Baud*
Baudino, *Baud*
Baudinot, *Baud*
Baudon, *Baud*
Baudone, *Baud*
Baudou, *Baud*
Baudouin, *Baldwin*
Baudoux, *Baud*
Baudrey, *Baldry*
Baudri, *Baldry*
Baudric, *Baldry*
Baudrick, *Baldry*
Baudrin, *Baudier*
Baudron, *Baudier*
Baudry, *Baldry*
Baudts, *Baud*
Bauduccio, *Baud*
Bauducco, *Baud*
Bauduin, *Baldwin*
Baudy, *Baud*
Bauer
Bäuerle, *Bauer*
Baugh
Baugham, *Baughan*
Baughan
Baughen, *Baughan*
Baughn, *Baughan*
Baulch, *Balch*
Baulcher, *Balch*
Bauld, *Baud*
Bault, *Baud*
Baum
Baumadier, *Balme*
Bauman, *Bauer*
Baumann, *Bauer*
Baumat, *Balme*
Baume, *Balme*
Bäumer, *Baum*
Baumer, *Baum*
Baumert, *Baum*
Baumgard, *Baumgarten*
Baumgart, *Baumgarten*
Baumgarte, *Baumgarten*
Baumgarten
Baumgartner, *Baumgarten*
Baumier, *Balme*
Baumkratz, *Pankridge*
Bäumler, *Baum*
Baun, *Bain*
Baussaro, *Balthasar*
Baustian, *Sebastian*
Bautesar, *Balthasar*
Bautista, *Baptiste*
Bautiste, *Baptiste*
Bauwen, *Baldwin*
Bauwens, *Baldwin*
Bauzaro, *Balthasar*
Bavel, *Babel*
Baverel, *Bayer*
Baverey, *Bayer*
Baverez, *Bayer*
Baverstock
Bavier, *Bayer*
Bavli, *Babel*
Bavly, *Babel*
Bavridge, *Beveridge*
Bawcock, *Baud*
Bawcutt, *Baud*
Bawdon, *Bowden*
Bawli, *Babel*
Bawly, *Babel*
Bawn, *Bain*
Bax, *Back, Backhouse*
Baxendale
Baxter, *Baker*
Bay
Bayard
Bayart, *Bayard*
Baybutt
Bayer
Bayerle, *Bayer*
Bayerlein, *Bayer*
Bayes, *Bay*
Bayet, *Bay*
Bayeux, *Bewes*
Bayfield
Bayford
Bayl, *Bailey*
Baylay, *Bailey*
Bayle, *Bailey*
Bayles, *Bailey*
Bayless, *Bailey*
Baylet, *Bailey*
Bayley, *Bailey*
Bayliff, *Bailey*
Bayliffe, *Bailey*
Baylis, *Bailey*
Bayliss, *Bailey*
Baylot, *Bailey*
Bayls, *Bailey*
Bayly, *Bailey*
Baynard, *Banyard*
Bayne, *Bain*
Baynes, *Baines*
Bayo, *Bay*
Bayol, *Bay*
Bayoux, *Bay*
Bays, *Bay*
Bazelaire, *Baudelaire*
Bazeley, *Basil*
Bazell, *Basil*
Bazelle, *Basil*
Bazenet, *Bazin*
Bazile, *Basil*
Bazilev, *Basil*
Bazille, *Basil*
Bazin
Bazinet, *Bazin*
Bazini, *Bazin*
Bazley, *Basil*
Bazy, *Bazin*
Bazylets, *Basil*
Bazylewski, *Basil*
Beach, *Beech*
Beacham, *Beauchamp*
Beachamp, *Beauchamp*
Beacom, *Beauchamp*
Beadel, *Beadle*
Beadell, *Beadle*
Beadle
Beadles, *Beadle*
Beake
Béal
Beal
Beale, *Beal*
Beales, *Beal*
Bealeson, *Beal*
Bealle, *Beal*
Bealles, *Beal*
Bealls, *Beal*
Beals, *Beal*
Bealson, *Beal*
Beaman, *Beeman*
Beamand, *Beaumont*
Beamant, *Beaumont*
Beament, *Beaumont*
Beames, *Beamish*
Beamish
Beamiss, *Beamish*
Beamond, *Beaumont*
Beamont, *Beaumont*
Beams, *Beamish*
Bean
Beanland
Bear
Beard
Beardmore
Beards, *Beard*
Beardsley
Beardsworth
Beardwell, *Bardwell*
Beardwood, *Beardsworth*
Beare, *Beer*
Bearman
Bearsmore, *Beardmore*
Beasley
Beaston, *Beeston*
Beaten, *Beaton*
Beatey, *Beatty*
Beaton
Béatrice
Beatrijs, *Béatrice*
Béatrix, *Béatrice*
Beatson, *Bate*
Beattey, *Beatty*
Beattie, *Beatty*
Beatty
Beaty, *Beatty*
Beau
Beauchamp
Beauchet, *Bauche*
Beauclerk
Beaufils, *Beavis*
Beaufort
Beaulieu
Beaulieux, *Beaulieu*
Beauman, *Beaumont, Bowman*
Beaumant, *Beaumont*
Beaumarchais
Beaumarchaix, *Beaumarchais*
Beaumarcheix, *Beaumarchais*
Beaument, *Beaumont*
Beaumont
Beauregard
Beaurepaire
Beaushaw, *Belcher*
Beausire, *Bowser*
Beauvoir, *Beaver*
Beauvois, *Beaver*
Beaver
Beaves, *Beavis*
Beavin, *Bevin*
Beavis
Beazleigh, *Beasley*
Beazley, *Beasley*
Bebbington

Beber, *Beaver*
Bebert, *Beaver*
Bec, *Beck*
Bécard, *Beck*
Beccai, *Butcher*
Beccaio, *Butcher*
Beccari, *Butcher*
Beccaro, *Butcher*
Beccheri, *Butcher*
Becciu, *Veal*
Becerra
Becerril, *Becerra*
Becerro, *Becerra*
Bech, *Becher*
Béchard, *Beck*
Béché, *Beck*
Bécher, *Beck*
Becher
Béchereau, *Beck*
Bécherel, *Beck*
Bécherelle, *Beck*
Becherini, *Butcher*
Becheroni, *Butcher*
Béchet, *Beck*
Béchillon, *Beck*
Bechor
Bechstein
Bechtloff, *Bertolf*
Bechtold, *Berthold*
Bechtolf, *Bertolf*
Béchu, *Beck*
Beck, *Becher*
Beck
Becke, *Beck*
Becken, *Bach*
Becker, *Bach, Baker, Becher*
Beckerman, *Baker*
Beckermann, *Baker*
Beckers, *Baker*
Becket, *Beckett*
Beckett
Beckford
Beckham
Beckhard, *Bègue*
Beckhardt, *Bègue*
Beckles
Beckley
Beckman, *Beck*
Beckmann, *Bach, Beck*
Beckwith
Beckx, *Bach*
Becq, *Beck*
Becque, *Beck*
Becquelin, *Beck*
Becquereau, *Beck*
Becquerel, *Beck*
Becquet, *Beck*
Bécu, *Beck*
Bečvář, *Bednarz*
Bedal, *Béal*
Bedau, *Béal*
Beddall, *Beadle*
Beddard, *Edward*
Beddell, *Beadle*
Beddis, *Beddow*
Beddoe, *Beddow*
Beddoes, *Beddow*
Beddow
Beddowes, *Beddow*
Beddows, *Beddow*
Bedé, *Beadle*
Bede, *Bennett*
Bedeau, *Beadle*
Bedel, *Beadle*
Bedell, *Beadle*
Beder, *Bader*
Bedford
Bedingfeld
Bedle, *Beadle*
Bedmond, *Edmond*
Bednář, *Bednarz*
Bednarczyk, *Bednarz*
Bednarek, *Bednarz*
Bednařík, *Bednarz*
Bednarowicz, *Bednarz*
Bednarsh, *Bednarz*
Bednarski, *Bednarz*
Bednarsky, *Bednarz*
Bednarz
Bednyakov
Bedo, *Beddow*
Bedrosian, *Peter*
Bedward, *Edward*
Bedwell
Bedwinek
Bedworth
Bee
Beeby
Beech
Beecham, *Beauchamp*
Beechaman, *Beech*
Beecher, *Beech*
Beechey
Beechman, *Beech*
Beeck, *Bach*
Beecke, *Bach*
Beecker, *Bach*
Beecroft
Beedle, *Beadle*
Beek, *Bach*
Beeke, *Bach*
Beeker, *Bach*
Beekman, *Bach*
Beel, *Beal*
Beels, *Beal*
Beem, *Böhm*
Beeman
Beemer, *Böhm*
Been, *Bain*
Beenen, *Bain*
Beentjes, *Bennett*
Beer
Beerbohm, *Birnbaum*
Beere, *Beer*
Beerhold, *Beraud*
Beerli, *Bear*
Beernaert, *Bernard*
Beernt, *Bernard*
Beerold, *Beraud*
Beers, *Bear*
Beert, *Bernard*
Beesley, *Beasley*
Beeston
Beetham
Beethoven
Beeton, *Beaton*
Beever, *Beaver*
Beevers, *Beaver*
Beevis, *Beavis*
Beeviss, *Beavis*
Beevor, *Beaver*
Bégard, *Bègue*
Begbeder, *Beaver*
Begg
Beggan, *Begg*
Beggi, *Basil*
Beggin, *Begg*
Beggini, *Basil*
Beggio, *Basil*
Beggs, *Begg*
Béghard, *Bègue*
Beghe, *Butcher*
Bégin, *Bègue*
Begley
Begliuomini, *Belham*
Begnudelli, *Benvenuti*
Bégon, *Bègue*
Bégot, *Bègue*
Bégouin, *Bègue*
Bègue
Béguen, *Bègue*
Béguet, *Bègue*
Béguin, *Bègue*
Behaim, *Böhm*
Beham, *Böhm*
Behan, *Bean*
Behan
Behenna
Behets, *Béatrice*
Behm, *Böhm*
Behn, *Bennett*
Behncke, *Bennett*
Behncken, *Bennett*
Behne, *Bennett*
Behnecke, *Bennett*
Behnecken, *Bennett*
Behneke, *Bennett*
Behneken, *Bennett*
Behninck, *Bennett*
Behning, *Bennett*
Behnke, *Bennett*
Behnken, *Bennett*
Behrbohm, *Birnbaum*
Behrend, *Bernard*
Behrends, *Bernard*
Behrendsen, *Bernard*
Behrens, *Bernard*
Behrensen, *Bernard*
Behring, *Bear*
Behringer, *Beringer*
Behrman, *Bermann*
Behrmann, *Bermann*
Beiderwieden, *Weide*
Beier, *Bayer*
Beierle, *Bayer*
Beierlein, *Bayer*
Beil, *Bill*
Beiles, *Beilin*
Beilin
Beilis, *Beilin*
Beiliss, *Beilin*
Beillard, *Bélier*
Beilschmidt, *Bill*
Beimbrinke, *Brink*
Beimfohr, *Ford*
Bein, *Bain, Bennett*
Beincke, *Bennett*
Beincken, *Bennett*
Beine, *Bennett*
Beininck, *Bennett*
Beining, *Bennett*
Beinisch, *Bennett*
Beinke, *Bennett*
Beinken, *Bennett*
Beinosovitch, *Bennett*
Beirne, *Byrne*
Beisley, *Beasley*
Bejarano
Bejerano, *Bejarano*
Bek
Beker, *Baker*
Bekerman, *Baker*
Bekker, *Becher*
Bekman, *Beck*
Bel, *Beau*
Belaigue, *Bellew*
Belami, *Bellamy*
Belasco, *Velasco*
Belaygue, *Bellew*
Belch, *Balch*
Belcham, *Belchem*
Belchamp, *Beauchamp*
Belchem
Belcher
Belchère, *Belcher*
Belenger, *Beringer*
Belet, *Beau*
Belfort, *Beaufort*
Belgrave
Belham
Belhomme, *Belham*
Béliard, *Bélier*
Belić, *Białas*
Bélier
Bělík, *Białas*
Belin, *Bélier, Beilin*
Belingeri, *Beringer*
Belingheri, *Beringer*
Belinghieri, *Beringer*
Belingieri, *Beringer*
Belinson, *Beilin*
Béliot, *Bélier*
Belison, *Beilin*
Belisson, *Bélier*
Belk, *Balch*
Belkin
Belkind, *Belkin*
Belkis, *Belkin*
Bell
Bella, *Beau*
Bellacci, *Beau*
Bellam, *Belham*
Bellamy
Bellanger, *Beringer*
Bellas, *Bellhouse*
Bellat, *Beau*
Bellay
Bellazzi, *Beau*
Belle, *Beau*
Belleau, *Bellew*
Belleken, *Beau*
Belleli, *Beau*
Bellelli, *Beau*
Bellenger, *Beringer*
Beller, *Bell*
Belleschi, *Beau*
Bellet, *Beau*
Belletti, *Beau*
Bellettini, *Beau*
Bellew
Bellham, *Belham*
Bellhanger, *Beringer*
Bellhouse
Belli, *Beau*
Bellido
Bellinger, *Beringer*
Bellingeri, *Beringer*
Bellingham
Bellingheri, *Beringer*
Bellinghieri, *Beringer*
Bellingieri, *Beringer*
Bellini, *Beau*
Bellino, *Beau*
Bellis, *Ellis*
Belliss, *Ellis*
Bellman, *Bell*

Belló, *Beau*
Bello, *Beau*
Belloc, *Beaulieu*
Bellocci, *Beau*
Belloch, *Beaulieu*
Belloli, *Beau*
Bellomo, *Belham*
Bellon, *Beau*
Belloni, *Beau*
Bellot, *Beau*
Bellotti, *Beau*
Belloy, *Bellay*
Bellozzi, *Beau*
Bellsham, *Belchem*
Bellsyer, *Bowser*
Bellucci, *Beau*
Belluccio, *Beau*
Belluomo, *Belham*
Belluschi, *Beau*
Bellutti, *Beau*
Belluzzi, *Beau*
Bellver, *Beaver*
Bellwood
Belman, *Bell*
Belmont, *Beaumont*
Belmonte, *Beaumont*
Belmunt, *Beaumont*
Belo, *Beau*
Beloff, *Białas*
Bělohlávek, *Białas*
Belon, *Beau*
Belot, *Beau*
Belov, *Białas*
Belsham, *Belchem*
Belshaw, *Belcher*
Belshire, *Bowser*
Belsire, *Bowser*
Belton
Beltram, *Bertram*
Beltramelli, *Bertram*
Beltrametti, *Bertram*
Beltrami, *Bertram*
Beltramini, *Bertram*
Beltrán, *Bertram*
Beltran, *Bertram*
Beltrand, *Bertram*
Beltrandi, *Bertram*
Beltrani, *Bertram*
Beltrijs, *Béatrice*
Beltrine, *Béatrice*
Beltz, *Pilcher*
Beltzner, *Pilcher*
Beluchot, *Beau*
Belvedere, *Beaver*
Belvezer, *Beaver*
Belvoir, *Beaver*
Belyaev, *Białas*
Belyak, *Białas*
Belyanchikov, *Białas*
Belz, *Pilcher*
Belzner, *Pilcher*
Beman, *Beeman*
Bemand, *Beaumont*
Bemmand, *Beaumont*
Ben-Aharon, *Aaron*
Ben-Amos, *Amos*
Bénard, *Bernard*
Benard, *Bernard*
Bénardeau, *Bernard*
Benavent, *Benavente*
Benavente
Benavides
Bénazet, *Bennett*
Benbow
Bench
Benck, *Bennett*
Bencroft, *Bancroft*
Benda, *Bennett*
Bendall, *Benthall*
Ben-Dayan, *Dayan*
Bendell, *Benthall*
Bendetti, *Bennett*
Bendick, *Bennett*
Bendig, *Bennett*
Bendík, *Bennett*
Benditt, *Bennett*
Benditti, *Bennett*
Bendix, *Bennett*
Bendixen, *Bennett*
Bendle, *Benthall*
Bendry, *Parry*
Bendsen, *Bennett*
Bendtsen, *Bennett*
Benduhn, *Bennett*
Bendy, *Parry*
Bené, *Bennett*
Benech, *Bennett*
Benedek, *Bennett*
Beneden, *Nieder*
Benedetti, *Bennett*
Benedettini, *Bennett*
Bénédict, *Bennett*
Benedict, *Bennett*
Bénédicte, *Bennett*
Benedicto, *Bennett*
Benedikt, *Bennett*
Benediktovich, *Bennett*
Benediktsson, *Bennett*
Bénédit, *Bennett*
Bénédite, *Bennett*
Benedito, *Bennett*
Benedyktowicz, *Bennett*
Benegas, *Viegas*
Beneix, *Bennett*
Beneš, *Bennett*
Benes, *Bennett*
Beneshevich, *Bennett*
Bénet, *Bennett*
Benet, *Bennett*
Beneteau, *Bennett*
Benetelli, *Bennett*
Benetollo, *Bennett*
Benettelli, *Bennett*
Benettini, *Bennett*
Benettollo, *Bennett*
Beneyto, *Bennett*
Benez, *Bennett*
Bénézeit, *Bennett*
Bénézet, *Bennett*
Bénézit, *Bennett*
Benfield, *Banfield*
Benger, *Beringer*
Bengoa
Bengoechea
Bengtsen, *Bennett*
Bengtson, *Bennett*
Bengtsson, *Bennett*
Benham
Beniamini, *Benjamin*
Bénier, *Berner*
Beniesh, *Bennett*
Benini, *Bennett*
Benítez, *Bennett*
Benito, *Bennett*
Benjamens, *Benjamin*
Benjámin, *Benjamin*
Benjamin
Benjamini, *Benjamin*
Benjaminov, *Benjamin*
Benjaminowitsch, *Benjamin*
Benjamins, *Benjamin*
Benjaminy, *Benjamin*
Benkö, *Bennett*
Benn, *Bennett*
Benn
Benne, *Bennett*
Bennedick, *Bennett*
Bennedsen, *Bennett*
Bennen, *Bennett*
Bennet, *Bennett*
Bennets, *Bennett*
Bennett
Bennetto, *Bennett*
Bennetts, *Bennett*
Benney, *Benn*
Bennie, *Benn*
Bennike, *Bennett*
Benninck, *Bennett*
Benning, *Bennett*
Benninger, *Beringer*
Bennink, *Bennett*
Bennis, *Benn*
Bennison, *Benson*
Benns, *Benn*
Bennson, *Benson*
Benoîton, *Bennett*
Ben-Sasson, *Sason*
Benson
Benstead
Bensted, *Benstead*
Bent
Bentall, *Benthall*
Bente, *Bennett*
Bentele, *Pantaleone*
Benthall
Bentham
Bentinck
Benting, *Bentinck*
Bentje, *Bennett*
Bentjens, *Bennett*
Bentjes, *Bennett*
Bentke, *Bennett*
Bentley
Bentlin, *Pantaleone*
Bento, *Bennett*
Benton
Bentsen, *Bennett*
Bentson, *Bennett*
Bentz, *Bennett, Berthold*
Bentzen, *Bennett*
Benvegnu, *Benvenuti*
Benveneste, *Benveniste*
Benvenishte, *Benveniste*
Benveniste
Benvenisti, *Benveniste*
Benvenisty, *Benveniste*
Benvenuti
Benyamin, *Benjamin*
Benyamini, *Benjamin*
Benyaminov, *Benjamin*
Benz, *Bennett, Berthold*
Benzies, *Benn*
Béquet, *Beck*
Ber, *Bernard*
Béral, *Beraud*
Beraldi, *Beraud*
Beraldini, *Beraud*
Berán, *Bernard*
Beránek, *Baranov*
Beránek, *Bernard*
Béranger, *Beringer*
Berard, *Bernard*
Berardt, *Bernard*
Bérau, *Beraud*
Béraud, *Beraud*
Beraud
Beraudi, *Beraud*
Bérault, *Beraud*
Berault, *Beraud*
Beraut, *Beraud*
Berchthold, *Berthold*
Berckman, *Birch*
Berdiev, *Berdyaev*
Berdyaev
Berdyev, *Berdyaev*
Bere, *Beer*
Berebaum, *Birnbaum*
Berecloth, *Barraclough*
Berenblum, *Birnbaum*
Berends, *Bernard*
Berendsen, *Bernard*
Berenfeld, *Birnbaum*
Berengari, *Beringer*
Berengario, *Beringer*
Bérenger, *Beringer*
Bérengier, *Beringer*
Bérenguié, *Beringer*
Bérenguier, *Beringer*
Berenholc, *Birnbaum*
Berenholltz, *Birnbaum*
Berenhollz, *Birnbaum*
Berenholtz, *Birnbaum*
Berenholz, *Birnbaum*
Berenicky, *Bereznikov*
Berens, *Bernard*
Berenshtein, *Bernstein*
Berenstein, *Bernstein*
Berensztejn, *Bernstein*
Beresford
Berez, *Bereznikov*
Bereza, *Bereznikov*
Berezin, *Bereznikov*
Berezinski, *Bereznikov*
Berezko, *Bereznikov*
Berezniak, *Bereznikov*
Bereznik, *Bereznikov*
Bereznikov
Berezov, *Bereznikov*
Berezovitz, *Bereznikov*
Berezovski, *Bereznikov*
Berezovsky, *Bereznikov*
Berezowicz, *Bereznikov*
Berezowski, *Bereznikov*
Berezowsky, *Bereznikov*
Berg
Bergdahl, *Berg*
Bergdolt, *Berthold*
Berge
Bergeau, *Berge*
Bergeest, *Geest*
Bergen, *Berg*
Bergén, *Berg*
Bergendahl, *Berg*
Bergeon, *Berge*
Berger, *Barker, Berg*
Bergereau, *Barker*
Bergeret, *Barker*
Bergerioux, *Barker*
Bergeron, *Barker*
Bergeronneau, *Barker*
Bergerot, *Barker*
Bergès, *Verdier*
Berget, *Barker*
Bergey, *Barker*
Berggren, *Berg*
Bergholm, *Berg*

Bergier, *Barker*
Bergin, *Berg*
Bergin
Berglin, *Berg*
Berglind, *Berg*
Berglöf, *Berg*
Berglund, *Berg*
Bergman, *Berg*
Bergmann, *Berg*
Bergogne, *Bourgoin*
Bergognon, *Bourgoin*
Bergoin, *Bourgoin*
Bergougnan, *Bourgoin*
Bergougnon, *Bourgoin*
Bergougnou, *Bourgoin*
Bergougnoux, *Bourgoin*
Bergqvist, *Berg*
Bergsma, *Berg*
Bergstedt, *Berg*
Bergsten, *Berg*
Bergstrand, *Berg*
Bergström, *Berg*
Berguier, *Barker*
Bergvall, *Berg*
Berhold, *Beraud*
Bering, *Bear*
Beringeli, *Beringer*
Beringer
Beringheli, *Beringer*
Beringheri, *Beringer*
Beringhieri, *Beringer*
Berisford, *Beresford*
Berk, *Birch*
Berka, *Bernard*
Berke, *Birch*
Berkeley, *Barclay*
Berkemann, *Birch*
Berkenblit, *Birch*
Berkenfeld, *Birch*
Berkhout
Berkley, *Barclay*
Berkman, *Birch*
Berkmann, *Birch*
Berkner, *Birch*
Berkovich, *Bear*
Berkovitz, *Bear*
Berkowicz, *Bear*
Berkutov
Berlanczyk, *Brillant*
Berland, *Brillant*
Berle
Berlet, *Berle*
Berlier, *Berle*
Berliet, *Berle*
Berlin
Berliner, *Berlin*
Berlinger, *Beringer*
Berlingheri, *Beringer*
Berlinghieri, *Beringer*
Berlinguer, *Beringer*
Berlinski, *Berlin*
Berlinsky, *Berlin*
Berlioz, *Berle*
Berlitz, *Bert*
Berlot, *Berle*
Berman
Bermann
Bermejo
Bermingham, *Birmingham*
Bermitter, *Permenter*
Bermon, *Berman*
Bermond, *Berman*
Bermter, *Permenter*
Bermúdez, *Berman*
Bermudo, *Berman*
Bern, *Bernard*
Bernaba, *Barnaby*
Bernabé, *Barnaby*
Bernabe, *Barnaby*
Bernabeo, *Barnaby*
Bernabeu, *Barnaby*
Bernabo, *Barnaby*
Bernaciak, *Bernard*
Bernadé, *Bernard*
Bernadet, *Bernard*
Bernadette, *Bernard*
Bernadon, *Bernard*
Bernadot, *Bernard*
Bernadotte, *Bernard*
Bernadou, *Bernard*
Bernadoux, *Bernard*
Bernadzki, *Bernard*
Bernaert, *Bernard*
Bernakiewicz, *Bernard*
Bernal, *Beraud*
Bernáldez, *Bernard*
Bernaldo, *Bernard*
Bernard
Bernardeau, *Bernard*
Bernardelli, *Bernard*
Bernardes, *Bernard*
Bernardeschi, *Bernard*
Bernardet, *Bernard*
Bernardette, *Bernard*
Bernárdez, *Bernard*
Bernardi, *Bernard*
Bernardin, *Bernard*
Bernardinelli, *Bernard*
Bernardini, *Bernard*
Bernardino, *Bernard*
Bernardo, *Bernard*
Bernardon, *Bernard*
Bernardoni, *Bernard*
Bernardos, *Bernard*
Bernardot, *Bernard*
Bernardotte, *Bernard*
Bernardotti, *Bernard*
Bernardou, *Bernard*
Bernardoux, *Bernard*
Bernardy, *Bernard*
Bernášek, *Bernard*
Bernát, *Bernard*
Bernat, *Bernard*
Bernáth, *Bernard*
Bernaud, *Beraud*
Bernberg, *Birnbaum*
Bernblum, *Birnbaum*
Berndsen, *Bernard*
Berndt, *Bernard*
Berndtssen, *Bernard*
Berndtsson, *Bernard*
Berne, *Byrne*
Bernelin, *Berner*
Berner
Berneret, *Berner*
Bernerette, *Berner*
Bernerin, *Berner*
Berneron, *Berner*
Berners, *Berner*
Bernet, *Bernard*
Bernette, *Bernard*
Bernetti, *Bernard*
Berney, *Bernard, Burney*
Bernfeld, *Birnbaum*
Bernhard, *Bernard*
Bernhardi, *Bernard*
Bernhardsson, *Bernard*
Bernhardt, *Bernard*
Bernhart, *Bernard*
Berni, *Bernard*
Bernier, *Berner*
Bernini, *Bernard*
Bernli, *Bernard*
Bernlin, *Bernard*
Bernocchi, *Bernard*
Bernolet, *Bernard*
Bernollet, *Bernard*
Bernon, *Bernard*
Bernot, *Bernard*
Bernotti, *Bernard*
Bernreith, *Bärenreiter*
Bernreut, *Bärenreiter*
Bernreuth, *Bärenreiter*
Berns, *Bernard*
Bernshtein, *Bernstein*
Bernstein
Bernstejn, *Bernstein*
Bernt, *Bernard*
Bernth, *Bernard*
Berntssen, *Bernard*
Berntsson, *Bernard*
Bernucci, *Bernard*
Bernuzzi, *Bernard*
Berold, *Beraud*
Béron, *Bear*
Béronneau, *Bear*
Berresford, *Beresford*
Berrick, *Barwick*
Berridge, *Beveridge*
Berrier, *Berry*
Berrigan, *Bergin*
Berriman, *Bury*
Berringer, *Beringer*
Berrisford, *Beresford*
Berrocal
Berrow, *Barrow*
Berrueix, *Berry*
Berruer, *Berry*
Berruex, *Berry*
Berry
Berrycloth, *Barraclough*
Berryer, *Berry*
Berryman, *Bury*
Bersohn, *Bear*
Berson, *Bear*
Bert
Bertacchi, *Bert*
Bertacco, *Bert*
Bertalan, *Bertram*
Bertalti, *Berthold*
Bertamini, *Bertram*
Bertaneu, *Bertram*
Bertarini, *Berthier*
Bertaud, *Berthold*
Bertaudet, *Berthold*
Bertault, *Berthold*
Bertaux, *Berthold*
Bertel, *Bartholomew, Bert*
Bertelémot, *Bartholomew*
Bertélemy, *Bartholomew*
Bertelet, *Bartholomew*
Bertelin, *Bert*
Bertelli, *Bert*
Bertélmy, *Bartholomew*
Bertelot, *Bert*
Bertels, *Bert*
Bertenghi, *Bert*
Berterman, *Bertram*
Bertero, *Berthier*
Berteron, *Berthier*
Berterou, *Berthier*
Berteroux, *Berthier*
Bertet, *Bert*
Berthaud, *Berthold*
Berthaudet, *Berthold*
Berthault, *Berthold*
Berthaux, *Berthold*
Berthel, *Bartholomew, Bert*
Berthelémot, *Bartholomew*
Berthélemy, *Bartholomew*
Berthelet, *Bartholomew*
Berthelin, *Bert*
Berthélmy, *Bartholomew*
Berthelot, *Bert*
Berthels, *Bert*
Bertheron, *Berthier*
Bertherou, *Berthier*
Bertheroux, *Berthier*
Berthier
Berthilet, *Bert*
Bertholat, *Bertolf*
Berthold
Berthold, *Bennett*
Bertholet, *Bertolf*
Bertholin, *Bartholomew*
Berthollet, *Bertolf*
Berthomé, *Bartholomew*
Berthomier, *Bartholomew*
Berthomieu, *Bartholomew*
Berthoneau, *Bert*
Berthot, *Bartholomew*
Berthou, *Bertolf*
Berthoulet, *Bertolf*
Berthouloume, *Bartholomew*
Berthoux, *Bertolf*
Berti, *Bert*
Bertie, *Bert*
Bertier, *Berthier*
Bertiero, *Berthier*
Bertilet, *Bert*
Bertillon, *Bert*
Bertilon, *Bert*
Bertilsson, *Berthold*
Bertinetti, *Bert*
Bertinghi, *Bert*
Bertini, *Bert*
Bertinotti, *Bert*
Bertl, *Bert*
Bertleff, *Bertolf*
Bertocchi, *Bert*
Bertocchini, *Bert*
Bertocci, *Bert*
Bertoccini, *Bert*
Bertogli, *Berthold*
Bertoglio, *Berthold*
Bertók, *Bartholomew*
Bertolat, *Bertolf*
Bertoldi, *Berthold*
Bertolet, *Bertolf*
Bertoletti, *Berthold*
Bertolf
Bertoli, *Berthold*
Bertolin, *Bartholomew, Bert*
Bertolini, *Berthold*
Bertollet, *Bertolf*
Bertollio, *Berthold*
Bertollo, *Berthold*
Bertolucci, *Berthold*
Bertoluzzi, *Berthold*
Bertomé, *Bartholomew*
Bertomeu, *Bartholomew*
Bertomier, *Bartholomew*
Bertomieu, *Bartholomew*
Berton, *Bert*
Bertoneau, *Bert*
Bertoni, *Bert*

Bertorelli, *Bert*
Bertot, *Bartholomew*
Bertou, *Bertolf*
Bertoud, *Berthold*
Bertoul, *Bertolf*
Bertoulet, *Bertolf*
Bertouloume, *Bartholomew*
Bertozzi, *Bert*
Bertram
Bertrami, *Bertram*
Bertran, *Bertram*
Bertrand, *Bertram*
Bertrandeau, *Bertram*
Bertrandet, *Bertram*
Bertrandi, *Bertram*
Bertrandon, *Bertram*
Bertrandot, *Bertram*
Bertranet, *Bertram*
Bertron, *Berthier*
Bertrou, *Berthier*
Bertuccelli, *Bert*
Bertucci, *Bert*
Bertuccini, *Bert*
Bertuccioli, *Bert*
Bertuzzi, *Bert*
Bertwistle, *Birtwistle*
Berwald, *Beraud*
Berwick, *Barwick*
Beryozkin, *Bereznikov*
Berzal
Berzon, *Bear*
Bès
Besançon
Besant
Beschoren, *Pschorr*
Beschorn, *Pschorr*
Beschorner, *Pschorr*
Beseke, *Basil*
Besemer, *Bessemer*
Besgen, *Sebastian*
Besnard, *Bernard*
Besnardeau, *Bernard*
Besnier, *Berner*
Besque, *Bishop*
Bessant, *Besant*
Besse, *Bès*
Besseau, *Bès*
Bessède, *Bès*
Besseire, *Bès*
Bessell
Bessemer
Bessent, *Besant*
Besser
Besserer, *Besser*
Besset, *Bès*
Bessey, *Bès*
Besseyre, *Bès*
Bessière, *Bès*
Bessières, *Bès*
Besson
Bessonat, *Besson*
Bessonaud, *Besson*
Bessoneau, *Besson*
Bessonet, *Besson*
Bessoni, *Besson*
Bessou, *Besson*
Best
Bestar, *Best*
Bestau, *Best*
Bestaux, *Best*
Beste, *Best*
Besteau, *Best*
Besteaux, *Best*
Besteiro, *Ballaster*
Bestel, *Best*
Bestelle, *Best*
Bester, *Best*
Bestgen, *Sebastian*
Bestges, *Sebastian*
Bestiman, *Best*
Bestman, *Best*
Bestwick, *Beswick*
Beswick
Betancourt, *Bettencourt*
Betau, *Béal*
Betaudé, *Berthold*
Betbeder, *Beaver*
Betham, *Beetham*
Bethaudé, *Berthold*
Bethe, *Bert*
Bethell
Bethke, *Bert*
Bethmann, *Bert*
Béthune, *Beaton*
Bétiau, *Best*
Betje, *Bennett*
Betjeman, *Bennett*
Betjens, *Bennett*
Betjes, *Bennett*
Betke, *Bennett*
Bétran, *Bertram*
Bett
Bettencourt
Bettenson, *Bett*
Betteridge
Betteriss, *Betteridge*
Bettis, *Bett*
Bettison, *Bett*
Betton, *Beaton*
Bettridge, *Betteridge*
Betts, *Bett*
Bettson, *Bett*
Betz, *Bernard, Berthold*
Betzu, *Veal*
Beuchel, *Bauch*
Beuerle, *Bauer*
Beukema, *Buch*
Beuker, *Buch*
Beurs, *Boursier*
Beuscher, *Belcher*
Beushaw, *Belcher*
Beushire, *Belcher*
Beuvin, *Bevin*
Beuvo, *Beaver*
Bevacqua, *Boileau*
Bevan
Bevans, *Bevan*
Bevar, *Beaver*
Bever, *Beaver*
Beveridge
Beverley
Beverly, *Beverley*
Beves, *Beavis*
Beviacqua, *Boileau*
Bevilacqua, *Boileau*
Bevin
Bevington
Bevir, *Beaver*
Bevis, *Beavis*
Beviss, *Beavis*
Bevivino, *Bevin*
Bevor, *Beaver*
Bew, *Bewes*
Bewer, *Beaver*
Bewes
Bewick
Bewicke, *Bewick*
Bewley, *Beaulieu*
Bewshaw, *Belcher*
Bewshea, *Belcher*
Bewson, *Beau*
Bex, *Bès*
Bexon, *Beck*
Beyer, *Bayer*
Beyle, *Bailey*
Beylet, *Bailey*
Beylot, *Bailey*
Beyn, *Bain, Bennett*
Beyne, *Bennett*
Beynke, *Bennett*
Beynken, *Bennett*
Beynon, *Onion*
Bez, *Bès*
Bezal, *Béal*
Bezançon, *Besançon*
Bezant, *Besant*
Bezarra, *Becerra*
Bezault, *Béal*
Bezděk
Bezi, *Voisin*
Bezin, *Voisin*
Bezobrazov
Bezou, *Bès*
Bezout, *Bès*
Bezuidenhout
Bezzant, *Besant*
Biagelli, *Blaise*
Biagetti, *Blaise*
Biaggelli, *Blaise*
Biaggetti, *Blaise*
Biaggi, *Blaise*
Biaggioli, *Blaise*
Biaggioni, *Blaise*
Biaggiotti, *Blaise*
Biagi, *Blaise*
Biagini, *Blaise*
Biagioli, *Blaise*
Biagioni, *Blaise*
Biagiotti, *Blaise*
Białas
Białasiewicz, *Białas*
Białasik, *Białas*
Białasiński, *Białas*
Białczyk, *Białas*
Biale
Biale, *Vitale*
Białecki, *Bielski*
Bialecky, *Bielski*
Białek, *Białas*
Bialer, *Biale*
Biali, *Biale*
Bialik, *Białas*
Bialinski, *Bielski*
Bialistock
Bialistocki, *Bialistock*
Bialistotzki, *Bialistock*
Bialistotzky, *Bialistock*
Bialkovits, *Białas*
Bialkovitz, *Białas*
Białkowski, *Białas*
Bialo, *Biale*
Białobrzeski
Białoskórski
Bialostatzki, *Bialistock*
Bialostocki, *Bialistock*
Bialostocky, *Bialistock*
Bialostotsky, *Bialistock*
Bialostotzky, *Bialistock*
Bialostozki, *Bialistock*
Bialovchik, *Białas*
Bialovitch, *Białas*
Bialovitz, *Białas*
Białowąs
Bialowice, *Białas*
Bialowitz, *Białas*
Bialski, *Bielski*
Bialy, *Biale*
Bialystocky, *Bialistock*
Biamini, *Benjamin*
Biancardi, *Blanchard*
Bianchetti, *Blanc*
Bianchi, *Blanc*
Bianchini, *Blanc*
Bianchinotti, *Blanc*
Bianciardi, *Blanchard*
Bianco, *Blanc*
Biancoli, *Blanc*
Biancolini, *Blanc*
Bianconi, *Blanc*
Biancotti, *Blanc*
Biancucci, *Blanc*
Biard
Biardeau, *Biard*
Biardot, *Biard*
Biasetti, *Blaise*
Biasi, *Blaise*
Biasini, *Blaise*
Biasio, *Blaise*
Biasioli, *Blaise*
Biasioni, *Blaise*
Biasotti, *Blaise*
Biavo, *Beaver*
Bibb, *Bibby*
Bibby
Biber, *Beaver*
Biberfeld, *Beaver*
Biberman, *Beaver*
Biberstein, *Beaver*
Bicard, *Biard*
Bicha, *Best*
Bichet
Bichl, *Bühler*
Bichler, *Bühler*
Bick
Bickel, *Bick*
Bicker
Bickerdike
Bickers, *Bicker*
Bickerstaff
Bickerstaffe, *Bickerstaff*
Bickersteth, *Bickerstaff*
Bickerton
Bickford
Bickhardt, *Biard*
Bickle, *Bickley*
Bickley
Bicknell
Bicksteth, *Bickerstaff*
Bidaway, *Way*
Biddell, *Beadle*
Biddle, *Beadle*
Biddlecombe
Biddles, *Beadle*
Biddulph
Biddwell, *Bedwell*
Bider, *Biedermann*
Biderman, *Biedermann*
Bidewell, *Bedwell*
Bidjerano, *Bejarano*
Bidwell, *Bedwell*
Bié, *Béal*
Bie, *Bee*
Bieber, *Beaver*
Bieberfeld, *Beaver*
Bieder, *Biedermann*
Biederman, *Biedermann*

Biedermann
Bief, *Béal*
Biegel, *Bühler*
Biegler, *Bühler*
Biehler, *Bühler*
Biehlmann, *Bühler*
Biela, *Białas*
Bielak, *Białas*
Bielawski, *Bielski*
Bielecki, *Bielski*
Bielensky, *Bielski*
Bieler, *Biale*
Bielicki, *Bielski*
Bieliński, *Bielski*
Bielinski, *Bielski*
Bielinsky, *Bielski*
Bielostocki, *Bialistock*
Bielski
Biemann, *Beeman*
Bien, *Bee*
Bien
Bienemann, *Beeman*
Bienenstock, *Bienstock*
Biener, *Bien*
Bienstein, *Bien*
Bienstock
Bier
Bierbaum, *Birnbaum*
Bierhold, *Beraud*
Bierman, *Bier*
Biermann, *Bier*
Biernacki, *Bernard*
Biernat, *Bernard*
Biernatowicz, *Bernard*
Biers, *Byers*
Biétrix, *Béatrice*
Biétron, *Béatrice*
Bieuvo, *Beaver*
Biever, *Beaver*
Biez, *Béal*
Bigard, *Biard*
Bigaud
Bigault, *Bigaud*
Bigaut, *Bigaud*
Bigg
Biggerstaff, *Bickerstaff*
Biggin
Biggings, *Biggin*
Biggins, *Biggin*
Biggio, *Biss*
Biggs, *Begg*
Bigio, *Biss*
Biglia, *William*
Biglietti, *William*
Biglietto, *William*
Biglio, *William*
Bignall, *Bicknell*
Bignami, *Benjamin*
Bignamini, *Benjamin*
Bignat, *Bignon*
Bignaud, *Bignon*
Bignauld, *Bignon*
Bignell, *Bicknell*
Bignold, *Bicknell*
Bignon
Bigot
Bigotteau, *Bigot*
Bigrave, *Bygrave*
Bigraves, *Bygrave*
Bigwood, *Bigaud*
Bihard, *Biard*
Bijelić, *Białas*
Bijl, *Bill*
Bijlsma, *Bill*
Bikker, *Bicker*
Bikovski, *Bick*
Bikovsky, *Bick*
Bíl, *Białas*
Bilan, *Białas*
Bilard, *Billard*
Bilbao
Bilczak, *Białas*
Bílek, *Białas*
Biles
Biletzki, *Bielski*
Bilewicz, *Białas*
Bilharz, *Billard*
Bilinski, *Bielski*
Bilinsky, *Bielski*
Bilko, *Białas*
Bilkowitz, *Białas*
Bill
Billard
Billardon, *Billard*
Billaud
Billaudel, *Billaud*
Billaudet, *Billaud*
Billault, *Billaud*
Billaut, *Billaud*
Bille, *Bill*
Biller, *Bill*
Billes, *Bill*
Billet
Billett, *Billet*
Billing, *Bill*
Billingham
Billings, *Bill*
Billingsley
Billington
Billion, *Billon*
Billo, *Jacob*
Billon
Bills, *Bill*
Billsborough
Billson, *Bill*
Billung, *Bill*
Bilsborrow, *Billsborough*
Bilski, *Bielski*
Bilt
Bilton
Bílý, *Białas*
Bily, *Białas*
Bilz, *Pilz*
Bimpson, *Binn*
Bimson, *Binn*
Bin, *Bien*
Binch, *Binks*
Binchy
Binder
Binderman, *Binder*
Bindig, *Bennett*
Binenbaum, *Bien*
Binenfeld, *Bien*
Binenkopf, *Bien*
Binenshtok, *Bienstock*
Binenstock, *Bienstock*
Binenstok, *Bienstock*
Bines
Bing
Bingham
Biniamini, *Benjamin*
Biniaminovitz, *Benjamin*
Binkin, *Bines*
Binks
Binman, *Bien*
Binn
Binney
Binnie, *Binney*
Binning, *Bing*
Binns, *Binn*
Binovitch, *Bines*
Binshtock, *Bienstock*
Binshtok, *Bienstock*
Binstein, *Bien*
Binstock, *Bienstock*
Binstok, *Bienstock*
Binyamin, *Benjamin*
Binyamini, *Benjamin*
Binyaminov, *Benjamin*
Binyaminovich, *Benjamin*
Biondelli, *Blunt*
Biondellini, *Blunt*
Biondetti, *Blunt*
Biondi, *Blunt*
Biou, *Boeuf*
Biram, *Byron*
Birbaum, *Birnbaum*
Birbeck, *Birkbeck*
Birch
Birchall
Bircham
Birchental, *Birch*
Bircher, *Birch*
Birchett, *Birkett*
Birchner, *Birch*
Birck, *Birch*
Birckmann, *Birch*
Bird
Birdsall
Birdwhistell, *Birtwistle*
Birenbach, *Birnbaum*
Birenbaum, *Birnbaum*
Birenberg, *Birnbaum*
Birenblat, *Birnbaum*
Birenboim, *Birnbaum*
Birencvaig, *Birnbaum*
Birencwaig, *Birnbaum*
Birencwajg, *Birnbaum*
Birencweig, *Birnbaum*
Birendorf, *Birnbaum*
Birenholc, *Birnbaum*
Birenzwaig, *Birnbaum*
Birenzweig, *Birnbaum*
Birk, *Birch*
Birkbeck
Birkby
Birkdale
Birkenfeld, *Birch*
Birkenshaw, *Burkinshaw*
Birkental, *Birch*
Birkett
Birkin, *Burkin*
Birkle, *Birch, Burkett*
Birkner, *Birch*
Birks, *Birch*
Birling, *Burling*
Birmingham
Birn, *Birnbaum*
Birnbach, *Birnbaum*
Birnbaum
Birnberg, *Birnbaum*
Birnboim, *Birnbaum*
Birnboum, *Birnbaum*
Birnboym, *Birnbaum*
Birndorf, *Birnbaum*
Birney, *Birnie*
Birnfeld, *Birnbaum*
Birnholz, *Birnbaum*
Birnie
Birnstein, *Birnbaum*
Birnstock, *Birnbaum*
Birnzweig, *Birnbaum*
Bíró, *Biró*
Biró
Biron, *Byron*
Biron
Birrell, *Bourrel*
Birt, *Burt*
Birtenshaw, *Burkinshaw*
Birtwhistle, *Birtwistle*
Birtwistle
Bisard, *Biss*
Bischof, *Bishop*
Bischoff, *Bishop*
Bischop, *Bishop*
Biscio, *Biss*
Bisco, *Bishop*
Bisconti, *Visconte*
Bisdomini, *Visdomini*
Biselli, *Biss*
Biset, *Biss*
Bisetti, *Biss*
Bish, *Bush*
Bishell, *Bissell*
Bishop
Bishton
Bisi, *Biss*
Bisini, *Biss*
Bisio, *Biss*
Biskup, *Bishop*
Biskupek, *Bishop*
Biskupiak, *Bishop*
Biskupski, *Bishop*
Bismarck
Bisot, *Biss*
Bisp, *Bishop*
Bispham
Bispo, *Bishop*
Biss
Bisschop, *Bishop*
Bissell
Bisset, *Biss*
Bissett, *Biss*
Bissex, *Isaac*
Bissill, *Bissell*
Bisson, *Buisson*
Bitelli, *Vito*
Bitetti, *Vito*
Bitetto, *Vito*
Bithell, *Bethell*
Biti, *Vito*
Bitner, *Büttner*
Bittcher, *Böttcher*
Bittel, *Beadle*
Bitti, *Vito*
Bittini, *Vito*
Bittner, *Büttner*
Bitto, *Vito*
Bittolo, *Vito*
Biundo, *Blunt*
Biunno, *Blunt*
Bivan, *Bevin*
Bivas, *Vivas*
Bivin, *Bevin*
Bizard, *Biss*
Bizet, *Biss*
Bizot, *Biss*
Bjelić, *Białas*
Bjerg, *Berg*
Björk, *Birch*
Björke, *Birch*
Björkén, *Birch*
Björklund, *Birch*
Björkman, *Birch*
Björkqvist, *Birch*
Björling, *Birch*

Bloxsome, *Bloxham*
Bloyd, *Lloyd*
Blücher
Bluck
Blud, *Lloyd*
Blue, *Blau*
Bluehstein, *Blaustein*
Bluestein, *Blaustein*
Bluestone, *Blaustein*
Bluet, *Blewett*
Bluhm, *Blum*
Blühmke, *Blum*
Blum
Blumberg, *Blum*
Blumberger, *Blum*
Blume, *Blum*
Blumenberg, *Blum*
Blumenfarb, *Blum*
Blumenfeld, *Blum*
Blumenfeldt, *Blum*
Blumenfield, *Blum*
Blumenfrucht, *Blum*
Blumenkopf, *Blum*
Blumenkranc, *Blum*
Blumenkrantz, *Blum*
Blumenkranz, *Blum*
Blumenkrohn, *Blum*
Blumensohn
Blumenstein, *Blum*
Blumensztajn, *Blum*
Blumental, *Blum*
Blumenthal, *Blum*
Blumenzweig, *Blum*
Blumer, *Bloom*
Blumfeld, *Blum*
Blumfeldt, *Blum*
Blümke, *Blum*
Blumkin, *Blumensohn*
Blumkind, *Blumensohn*
Blumkine, *Blumensohn*
Blumovitz, *Blumensohn*
Blumrosen, *Blum*
Blumstein, *Blum*
Blund, *Blunt*
Blundell, *Blunt*
Blunden
Blundo, *Blunt*
Blunno, *Blunt*
Blunt
Bluntschli
Bluschke, *Blaise*
Blushtein, *Blaustein*
Blustein, *Blaustein*
Blusztain, *Blaustein*
Blusztein, *Blaustein*
Blusztejn, *Blaustein*
Blut, *Blüthner*
Bluth, *Blüthner*
Blüthner
Bluthstein, *Blüthner*
Blutman, *Blüthner*
Blutner, *Blüthner*
Blutreich, *Blüthner*
Blutstein, *Blüthner*
Bluvstein, *Blaustein*
Bly, *Bligh*
Blyde, *Blythe*
Blye, *Bligh*
Blyth, *Blythe*
Blythe
Bo, *Boeuf*
Boada
Boakes, *Balch*
Boal, *Bowler*
Boaler, *Bowler*
Board, *Boarder*
Boarder
Boardman, *Boarder*
Boarer, *Bower*
Boas
Boase, *Boas*
Boasson, *Boas*
Boast
Boater, *Bate, Bowater*
Boatman, *Bate*
Boatte, *Bate*
Boavida, *Bonnevie*
Boays, *Boas*
Boaz, *Boas*
Boazi, *Boas*
Bobé, *Bouvier*
Bober, *Bobrov, Bouvier*
Boberg, *Boman*
Boberman, *Bobrov*
Bobo
Bobroff, *Bobrov*
Bobrov
Bobrovitz, *Bobrov*
Bobrovitzki, *Bobrov*
Bobrovsky, *Bobrov*
Bobrow, *Bobrov*
Bobrowski, *Bobrov*
Bobrowsky, *Bobrov*
Bocanegra, *Boccanegra*
Bocca
Boccacci, *Bocca*
Boccaccia, *Bocca*
Boccaccio, *Bocca*
Boccanegra
Boccardi, *Burkett*
Bocchetta, *Bocca*
Bocchi, *Bocca*
Bocchiardi, *Burkett*
Bocchini, *Bocca*
Bocciardi, *Burkett*
Boccieri, *Butcher*
Boccone, *Bocca*
Boccotti, *Bocca*
Boccucci, *Bocca*
Boccuzzi, *Bocca*
Boček
Bocheński
Bochner, *Buch*
Bocian
Bocianowski, *Bocian*
Böck, *Beck*
Bock, *Buck*
Böcker, *Böttcher*
Bockett, *Burkett*
Bockhorny, *Pokorný*
Böcking, *Buch*
Böckler
Böcklin, *Buck*
Böckmann, *Buch*
Bočko, *Boček*
Bocock, *Baud*
Bocquel, *Buck*
Bocquet, *Buck*
Boczek
Boczkowski, *Boczek*
Bodanis, *Badanes*
Bodankin, *Badanes*
Bodanoff, *Badanes*
Bodas
Boddie, *Body*
Boddington
Boddy, *Body*
Bode, *Botha*
Bodechon, *Baud*
Bodega, *Böttcher*
Bodeke, *Botha*
Bödeker, *Böttcher*
Bodén, *Booth*
Boden, *Botha*
Bodesson, *Baud*
Bodey, *Body*
Bodfish
Bodie, *Body*
Bodin, *Booth*
Bodle, *Boodle*
Bodleigh, *Bodley*
Bodley
Bodmer, *Bodner*
Bodner
Bodros
Bodson, *Baud*
Body
Boe, *Boeuf*
Boehm, *Böhm*
Boehme, *Böhm*
Boeing, *Boye*
Boelli, *Boeuf*
Boer, *Bauer*
Boere, *Bauer*
Boering, *Bauer*
Boerma, *Bauer*
Boerman, *Bauer*
Boermans, *Bauer*
Boers, *Bauer*
Boersma, *Bauer*
Boesen, *Boye*
Boesma, *Bauer*
Boeter, *Bowater*
Boetto, *Boeuf*
Boeuf
Boey, *Boeuf*
Boez, *Boeuf*
Boff, *Boeuf*
Boffin, *Baughan*
Bofill
Bogaard, *Baumgarten*
Bogaarde, *Baumgarten*
Bogaart, *Baumgarten*
Bogacki, *Bogatov*
Bogaert, *Baumgarten*
Bogaerts, *Baumgarten*
Bogarde, *Baumgarten*
Bogardt, *Baumgarten*
Bogart, *Baumgarten*
Bogartz, *Baumgarten*
Bogat, *Bogatov*
Bogatas, *Bogatov*
Bogatch, *Bogatov*
Bogatov
Bogdahn, *Bogdanov*
Bogdán, *Bogdanov*
Bogdan, *Bogdanov*
Bogdanov
Bogdanović, *Bogdanov*
Bogdanowicz, *Bogdanov*
Bogdanowitch, *Bogdanov*
Bogdański, *Bogdanov*
Bogdanski, *Bogdanov*
Bogdassarian, *Balthasar*
Bogdassian, *Balthasar*
Bogdikian, *Balthasar*
Böger, *Bow*
Bogert, *Baumgarten*
Boggers, *Boggis*
Boggis
Boggs, *Boggis*
Bøgh, *Buch*
Boghan, *Bowen*
Bogie
Bögl, *Bow*
Bögle, *Bow*
Bogle
Bögler, *Bow*
Bognár, *Wagner*
Bögner, *Bow*
Bogner, *Bow*
Bogosavljević, *Bogusławski*
Bogosian, *Paul*
Bogoslavitz, *Bogusławski*
Bogoslavski, *Bogusławski*
Bogoslawicz, *Bogusławski*
Bogoslawski, *Bogusławski*
Bogouslavsky, *Bogusławski*
Bogren, *Boman*
Bogucki, *Bogusławski*
Bogus, *Bogusławski*
Bogusławski
Bogusz, *Bogusławski*
Boháč, *Bogatov*
Boháček, *Bogatov*
Bohane, *Bowen*
Bohata, *Bogatov*
Bohdal, *Bocian*
Bohdanchik, *Bogdanov*
Bohdanets, *Bogdanov*
Bohdanovich, *Bogdanov*
Bohden, *Botha*
Böhe, *Boye*
Bohl, *Baud*
Bohlens, *Baud*
Bohlin, *Boman*
Böhling, *Baud*
Bohlje, *Baud*
Böhlke, *Baud*
Bohlmann, *Baud*
Bohls, *Baud*
Bohlsen, *Baud*
Bohm, *Böhm*
Böhm
Bohman, *Boman*
Böhme, *Böhm*
Böhmer, *Böhm*
Bohmer, *Böhm*
Bohmgahren, *Baumgarten*
Böhmig, *Böhm*
Böhmisch, *Böhm*
Bohnhoff, *Bonhoff*
Bohr, *Bauer*
Böhrnsen, *Bear*
Bohun, *Boon*
Bohuslav, *Bogusławski*
Boi, *Boeuf*
Boice, *Boyce*
Boie, *Boye*
Boieiro, *Bouvier*
Boieldieu
Boileau
Boilève, *Boileau*
Boilevin, *Bevin*
Boilleau, *Boileau*
Boin, *Boudin*
Boineau, *Boudin*
Bois
Boisard, *Bissell*
Boise, *Boyce*
Boisen, *Boye*
Boisin, *Bois*
Boislève, *Boileau*
Boislevin, *Bevin*
Boisot, *Bois*
Boissard, *Bissell*

Boisseau, *Bissell*
Boissel, *Bissell*
Boisselat, *Bissell*
Boisselet, *Bissell*
Boisselier, *Bissell*
Boissereau, *Boissier*
Boissier
Boisson, *Buisson*
Boissonet, *Buisson*
Boissy
Boisvin, *Bevin*
Boiteau, *Boiteux*
Boitel, *Boiteux*
Boiteux
Boivin, *Bevin*
Boivinet, *Bevin*
Boix, *Box*
Bøje, *Boye*
Boje, *Boye*
Bojens, *Boye*
Bojesen, *Boye*
Bojsen, *Boye*
Bok, *Buck*
Bokma, *Buck*
Boksbaum, *Buchs*
Boksenbaum, *Buchs*
Boksenboum, *Buchs*
Bolag, *Polak*
Bolam
Bolan, *Hayling*
Boland
Bolaños
Bolay, *Pelayo*
Bold
Böldeke, *Baud*
Boldero, *Baldry*
Bolderoe, *Baldry*
Bolderstone, *Balderston*
Bolding, *Baud*
Boldizsár, *Balthasar*
Boldra, *Baldry*
Boldry, *Baldry*
Boldt, *Baud*
Bole, *Boyle*
Boleček, *Bolesławski*
Bolek, *Bolesławski*
Bolens, *Baud*
Boler, *Bowler*
Boleslavski, *Bolesławski*
Boleslavsky, *Bolesławski*
Boleslawski, *Bolesławski*
Bolesławski
Bolesma, *Baud*
Boley, *Pelayo*
Boleyn, *Bullen*
Bolgar, *Bolger*
Bolger
Bolin, *Boman*
Bolinder, *Boman*
Bolingbroke
Bolino, *Jacob*
Bolitho
Bolívar
Bölke, *Baud*
Bollack, *Polak*
Bollag, *Polak*
Bolland, *Boland*
Bollands, *Boland*
Bolle, *Baud*
Bollen, *Bullen*
Bolletti, *Jacob*
Bollini, *Jacob*
Bollwagen, *Baldwin*
Bollwahn, *Baldwin*
Bolmann, *Baud*
Bologna, *Bolognese*
Bolognese
Bols, *Baud*
Bolsen, *Baud*
Bolshakov
Bolshov
Bolster, *Polster*
Bolt
Bölte, *Baud*
Bolte, *Baud*
Bolter, *Bolt*
Boltflower
Bölting, *Baud*
Bolton
Boltwood
Bolwahn, *Baldwin*
Bolwell
Bolzen, *Baud*
Bolzmann, *Baud*
Bömak, *Böhm*
Boman
Boman, *Bowman*
Bommicino, *Bonvoisin*
Bompard
Bompas, *Bumpas*
Bomphrey, *Humphrey*
Bomptaň, *Bontemps*
Bon
Bonacci, *Bon*
Bonaccio, *Bon*
Bonaccorsi, *Bonaccorso*
Bonaccorso
Bonaccurso, *Bonaccorso*
Bonacorsi, *Bonaccorso*
Bonacorso, *Bonaccorso*
Bonacurso, *Bonaccorso*
Bonafede, *Bonnefoi*
Bonagente
Bonaiuto
Bonallo, *Bonally*
Bonally
Bonaparte
Bonar
Bonard, *Bon*
Bonarelli, *Bonar*
Bonaro, *Bonar*
Bonassi, *Bon*
Bonavita, *Bonnevie*
Bonay, *Bonnet*
Bonazzi, *Bon*
Bonchrestien, *Bonchrétien*
Bonchrétien
Boncoeur, *Bunker*
Boncore, *Bunker*
Bond
Bondar
Bondarovich, *Bondar*
Bonde, *Bond*
Bonder, *Bondar*
Bonderefsky, *Bondar*
Bonderman, *Bondar*
Bonderoff, *Bondar*
Bonderow, *Bondar*
Bondesen, *Bond*
Bondfield, *Bonfield*
Bondia, *Bonjour*
Bondiou
Bondivenne, *Bondiou*
Bonds, *Bond*
Bone
Bonefaas, *Boniface*
Bonehill
Bonella, *Bonally*
Bonelli, *Bon*
Bonello, *Bonally*
Bonenfant
Boner, *Bonar*
Bones, *Bunin*
Bonet, *Bonnet*
Bonett, *Bonnet*
Bonetti, *Bonnet*
Bonex, *Bonnet*
Boney, *Bonnet*
Bonez, *Bonnet*
Bonfà, *Boniface*
Bonfante, *Bonenfant*
Bonfatti, *Boniface*
Bonfield
Bongaerts, *Baumgarten*
Bongard, *Bongars*
Bongardt, *Baumgarten*
Bongars
Bongart, *Baumgarten*
Bongartz, *Baumgarten*
Bongarzoni, *Bongars*
Bongers, *Baumgarten*
Bongi, *Budgen*
Bongianni, *Budgen*
Bongini, *Budgen*
Bongino, *Budgen*
Bongioanni, *Budgen*
Bongiorno, *Bonjour*
Bongiovanni, *Budgen*
Bongratz, *Pankridge*
Bonham
Bonheur
Bonheure, *Bonheur*
Bonhoff
Bonhöffer, *Bonhoff*
Bonhomme, *Bonham*
Bonhommet, *Bonham*
Boniello, *Bon*
Bonifacci, *Boniface*
Boniface
Bonifaci, *Boniface*
Bonifacino, *Boniface*
Bonifácio, *Boniface*
Bonifacio, *Boniface*
Bonifas, *Boniface*
Bonifati, *Boniface*
Bonifazio, *Boniface*
Bonilla
Bonin, *Bon*
Bonini, *Bon*
Bonioli, *Bon*
Boniotti, *Bon*
Bónis, *Boniface*
Bonis, *Bunin*
Bonito, *Bon*
Bonjean, *Budgen*
Bonjour
Bonjovi, *Budgen*
Bonn, *Bone*
Bonnaire, *Bonar*
Bonnar, *Bonar*
Bonnard, *Bon*
Bonnat, *Bon*
Bonnaud, *Bon*
Bonnay, *Bonnet*
Bonne, *Bon, Bond*
Bonnefoi
Bonnella, *Bonally*
Bonner, *Bonar, Poyner*
Bonnesen, *Bond*
Bonnet
Bonnetain, *Bonnet*
Bonnetaud, *Bonnet*
Bonneteau, *Bonnet*
Bonnetin, *Bonnet*
Bonneton, *Bonnet*
Bonnetot, *Bonnet*
Bonnett, *Bonnet*
Bonnevie
Bonnex, *Bonnet*
Bonney, *Bonnet*
Bonney
Bonnez, *Bonnet*
Bonniface, *Boniface*
Bonnin, *Bon*
Bonnineau, *Bon*
Bonnington
Bonnot, *Bon*
Bono, *Bon*
Bonomelli, *Bonomo*
Bonometti, *Bonomo*
Bonomini, *Bonomo*
Bonomo
Bonomolo, *Bonomo*
Bonomone, *Bonomo*
Bononi, *Bon*
Bonot, *Bon*
Bonotti, *Bon*
Bonpas, *Bumpas*
Bonser
Bontant, *Bontemps*
Bontein, *Bunting*
Bontempelli, *Bontemps*
Bontempo, *Bontemps*
Bontemps
Bonthuys
Bontine, *Bunting*
Bonuccello, *Bon*
Bonucci, *Bon*
Bonutti, *Bon*
Bonvicino, *Bonvoisin*
Bonville, *Bonfield*
Bonvoisin
Bonzoumet, *Bonham*
Boocock, *Baud*
Boodle
Boogaart, *Baumgarten*
Boogard, *Baumgarten*
Boogert, *Baumgarten*
Boogman, *Bowman*
Boohan, *Bowen*
Bookbinder, *Binder*
Booker
Bookman, *Buch*
Bookspan, *Buchs*
Bool, *Bull*
Boole, *Bull*
Boolsen, *Baud*
Boom, *Baum*
Boomgard, *Baumgarten*
Boon
Boone, *Boon*
Boonstra, *Bean*
Boontje, *Bean*
Boord, *Boarder*
Boorer, *Bower*
Boorman, *Bower*
Boorne, *Bourne*
Boosey
Boosie, *Boosey*
Boost, *Boast*
Boot
Boote, *Boot*
Booth
Boothby
Boothe, *Booth*
Boothman, *Booth*

Boothroyd
Bootle
Bootsma, *Bate*
Bootsman, *Bate*
Bopf, *Popp*
Bopp, *Popp*
Böppel, *Popp*
Böpple, *Popp*
Boquel, *Buck*
Boquer, *Butcher*
Boquet, *Buck*
Boqvist, *Boman*
Boras, *Boure*
Borbély, *Barber*
Borbón, *Bourbon*
Borch, *Birch*
Borchard, *Burkett*
Borchardt, *Burkett*
Borcherding, *Burkett*
Borchers, *Burkett*
Borchert, *Burkett*
Bord, *Borodin*
Borda, *Boarder, Borodin*
Bordas, *Boarder*
Bordasse, *Boarder*
Borde, *Boarder*
Bordeaux
Bordel, *Boarder*
Bordelier, *Boarder*
Bordelle, *Boarder*
Borden
Border, *Boarder*
Bordey, *Boarder*
Bordier, *Boarder*
Bordillon, *Boarder*
Bordillot, *Boarder*
Bordils, *Boarder*
Bordiu, *Boarder*
Borecki, *Borowski*
Boreham
Borek, *Borkowski*
Borel, *Bourrel*
Boreland, *Borland*
Boreley, *Borley*
Borelli, *Bourrel*
Borenshtain, *Bernstein*
Borenshtein, *Bernstein*
Borenstain, *Bernstein*
Borenstein, *Bernstein*
Borensztein, *Bernstein*
Borer, *Bower*
Boret, *Burrett*
Borg, *Burke*
Borgazzo, *Burke*
Borgeest, *Geest*
Borgen, *Burke*
Börger, *Burger*
Borger, *Burger*
Borgers, *Burger*
Borgert, *Burkett*
Borges
Borgesio, *Burgess*
Borgh, *Burke*
Borghard, *Burkett*
Borghardt, *Burkett*
Borghese, *Burgess*
Borghesetti, *Burgess*
Borghesini, *Burgess*
Borghetti, *Burke*
Borghi, *Burke*
Borghini, *Burke*
Borgmann, *Burkman*
Borgne
Borgnet, *Borgne*
Borgniol, *Borgne*
Borgnol, *Borgne*
Borgnot, *Borgne*
Borgo, *Burke*
Borgogni, *Bourgoin*
Borgoni, *Burke*
Borgotti, *Burke*
Borgström, *Burke*
Borić, *Borowski*
Borichev, *Borisov*
Borin, *Borisov*
Borisavljević, *Borisov*
Borishchenko, *Borisov*
Borishchev, *Borisov*
Borisov
Borisovich, *Borisov*
Borisyak, *Borisov*
Borja
Bork, *Birch*
Borkett, *Burkett*
Borkowski
Borland
Borley
Borman, *Bower*
Bormann, *Bourne*
Born, *Bourne*
Bornard, *Borgne*
Börne, *Bourne*
Borne, *Borgne, Bourne*
Bornemann, *Bourne*
Börner, *Bourne*
Borner, *Bourne*
Bornet, *Borgne*
Bornman, *Bourne*
Bornot, *Borgne*
Börnsen, *Bear*
Bornshtain, *Bernstein*
Bornshtein, *Bernstein*
Bornstein, *Bernstein*
Bornsztein, *Bernstein*
Borochov, *Baruch*
Borochovich, *Baruch*
Borochovitch, *Baruch*
Borochovitz, *Baruch*
Borochovski, *Baruch*
Borochowski, *Baruch*
Boroda, *Borodin*
Borodin
Borodulin, *Borodin*
Borohov, *Baruch*
Borohovich, *Baruch*
Borokhov, *Baruch*
Börold, *Beraud*
Boronat
Borovski, *Borowski*
Borovsky, *Borowski*
Borowicki, *Borowski*
Borowicz, *Borowski*
Borowiec, *Borowski*
Borowiński, *Borowski*
Borowski
Borowsky, *Borowski*
Borrêgo, *Borrego*
Borrego
Borreguero, *Borrego*
Borrel, *Bourrel*
Borrell, *Bourrel*
Borrelli, *Bourrel*
Borrett, *Burrett*
Borritt, *Burrett*
Borroman, *Burkman*
Borromei, *Borromeo*
Borromeo
Borrow, *Burrows*
Borrowman, *Burkman*
Borrows, *Burrows*
Borsche, *Borisov*
Borschke, *Borisov*
Borsig, *Borisov*
Borský, *Borowski*
Borthram, *Bertram*
Borthwick
Bortol, *Bartholomew*
Bortolazzi, *Bartholomew*
Bortoletti, *Bartholomew*
Bortoli, *Bartholomew*
Bortolini, *Bartholomew*
Bortolomei, *Bartholomew*
Bortoloni, *Bartholomew*
Bortolotti, *Bartholomew*
Bortolozzi, *Bartholomew*
Bortolussi, *Bartholomew*
Bortolutti, *Bartholomew*
Bortoluzzi, *Bartholomew*
Borton, *Burton*
Boruchov, *Baruch*
Boruchson, *Baruch*
Borucki, *Borowski*
Boruhov, *Baruch*
Borwick, *Barwick*
Borysewicz, *Borisov*
Borysiewicz, *Borisov*
Borzig, *Borisov*
Borzik, *Borisov*
Bos
Bosanquet
Bosc, *Bois*
Boscâ, *Bois*
Boscaino, *Boissier*
Boscarello, *Boissier*
Boscari, *Boissier*
Boscarino, *Boissier*
Boscariolo, *Boissier*
Boscaro, *Boissier*
Boscaroli, *Boissier*
Boscawen
Bösch, *Bush*
Bosch, *Bois, Bush*
Bosche, *Bush*
Boschello, *Bois*
Boscher, *Boissier*
Boscherini, *Boissier*
Boschero, *Boissier*
Boschet, *Bois*
Boschetti, *Bois*
Boschetto, *Bois*
Böschgen, *Bush*
Boschi, *Bois*
Boschier, *Boissier*
Boschieri, *Boissier*
Boschiero, *Boissier*
Boschini, *Bois*
Boschmann, *Bush*
Boschot, *Bois*
Bosco, *Bois*
Boscolo, *Bois*
Boscos, *Bois*
Boscq, *Bois*
Bose, *Bos*
Boselli, *Bos*
Bosetti, *Bos*
Boshell, *Bissell*
Bosher, *Boissier*
Boshere, *Boissier*
Boshier, *Boissier*
Bosi, *Bos*
Bosinelli, *Bos*
Bosini, *Bos*
Bosio, *Bos*
Bosk, *Bush*
Bosker, *Bush*
Bosma, *Bush*
Bosman, *Bush*
Boson, *Bos*
Bosone, *Bos*
Bosonnet, *Bos*
Bosotti, *Bos*
Bosq, *Bois*
Bosqué, *Bois*
Bosque, *Bois*
Bosquer, *Boissier*
Bosquero, *Boissier*
Bosquet, *Bois*
Bosquier, *Boissier*
Boss, *Bossut*
Bossaert, *Bossard*
Bossard
Bosse, *Bossut, Burkett, Bush*
Bossé, *Bossut*
Bossel, *Bissell*
Bosseux, *Bossut*
Bosshardt, *Bossard*
Bossuat, *Bossut*
Bossut
Bossuyt, *Bossut*
Bost, *Bois*
Bostock
Boston
Boström, *Boman*
Bosuet, *Bossut*
Bosutti, *Bos*
Boswall, *Boswell*
Boswell
Bosworth
Botas
Bote
Botelho
Botella, *Butler*
Boter, *Bowater*
Botfish, *Bodfish*
Botflower, *Boltflower*
Both, *Botha*
Botha
Botham, *Bottom*
Bothe, *Botha*
Bothner, *Bodner*
Bothwell
Botija, *Botas*
Botje, *Botha*
Bötjer, *Böttcher*
Botler, *Butler*
Botlero, *Butler*
Botma, *Botha*
Boto, *Botas*
Bott
Botta, *Boot*
Bottams, *Bottom*
Böttcher
Botte, *Boot*
Bottell, *Butler*
Botten, *Bouton*
Botterell, *Bottrell*
Botterill, *Bottrell*
Böttger, *Böttcher*
Botticelli, *Jacob*
Bötticher, *Böttcher*
Bottinelli, *Jacob*
Botting, *Bott*
Bottini, *Jacob*
Bottle, *Butler*
Bottman, *Bate*
Bottom

Bottomley
Bottoms, *Bottom*
Bottrell
Bottrill, *Bottrell*
Bou, *Boeuf*
Bouc, *Buck*
Bouch, *Budge*
Bouchard, *Burkett*
Bouché, *Butcher*
Boucher, *Butcher*
Bouchereau, *Butcher*
Boucheron, *Butcher*
Boucherot, *Butcher*
Bouchey, *Butcher*
Bouchez, *Butcher*
Bouchier, *Butcher*
Boucker, *Butcher*
Boud, *Bold*
Bouda, *Buzek*
Boudeau, *Boudon*
Boudericks, *Baldry*
Boudet
Boudewijn, *Baldwin*
Boudewijns, *Baldwin*
Boudin
Boudineau, *Boudin*
Boudinier, *Boudin*
Boudinot, *Boudin*
Boudon
Boudot, *Boudon*
Boudts, *Rumbold*
Boudy, *Boudin*
Boué, *Bouvier*
Bouet, *Boeuf*
Boufard, *Bouffard*
Bouffard
Bouffaud, *Bouffard*
Bougan, *Bowen*
Bough
Boughan, *Bowen*
Boughflower, *Boltflower*
Boughtflower, *Boltflower*
Boughton
Bouillard, *Bouille*
Bouillat, *Bouille*
Bouillé, *Bouille*
Bouille
Bouillet, *Bouille*
Bouillette, *Bouille*
Bouillon, *Bouille*
Bouillot, *Bouille*
Bouin, *Boudin*
Bouis, *Box*
Bouisson, *Buisson*
Bouissou, *Buisson*
Bouix, *Box*
Boul
Boulais, *Boul*
Boulanger
Boulay, *Boul*
Bould, *Bold*
Boulderstone, *Balderston*
Boulding, *Baud*
Boule, *Boul, Bowler*
Bouleau, *Boul*
Boules, *Bowler*
Boulet, *Boul*
Bouley, *Boul*
Boulez, *Boul*
Boulger, *Bolger*
Boulle, *Boul*
Boullen, *Bullen*
Boullet, *Boul*
Boullin, *Bullen*
Boullot, *Boul*
Boulois, *Boul*
Boulot, *Boul*
Bouloy, *Boul*
Boulsher, *Bolger*
Boult, *Bolt*
Boultby
Boulter, *Bolt*
Boultflower, *Boltflower*
Boulting, *Baud*
Boulton, *Bolton*
Bouma, *Bauer*
Bouman, *Bauer*
Boumans, *Bauer*
Boumphrey, *Humphrey*
Bounaud, *Bon*
Bound, *Bond*
Boundey, *Bond*
Bounds, *Bond*
Boundy, *Bond*
Bounin, *Bon*
Bouniol, *Bon*
Bouquet, *Buck*
Bouquier, *Butcher*
Bour, *Bower*
Bourbon
Bourbonnais, *Bourbon*
Bourbonneux, *Bourbon*
Bourcard, *Burkett*
Bourcart, *Burkett*
Bourchaert, *Burkett*
Bourchard, *Burkett*
Bourcier, *Boursier*
Bourda, *Boarder*
Bourdas, *Boarder*
Bourdasse, *Boarder*
Bourdel, *Boarder*
Bourdelier, *Boarder*
Bourdelin, *Boarder*
Bourdelle, *Boarder*
Bourdet, *Boarder*
Bourdier, *Boarder*
Bourdillon, *Boarder*
Bourdillot, *Boarder*
Boure
Bourg, *Burke*
Bourgat, *Burke*
Bourgeas, *Burke*
Bourgeat, *Burke*
Bourgeix, *Burgess*
Bourgel, *Burke*
Bourgeois, *Burgess*
Bourgès, *Burgess*
Bourget, *Burke*
Bourgey, *Burgess, Burke*
Bourgogne, *Bourgoin*
Bourgoin
Bourgouin, *Bourgoin*
Bourguignon, *Bourgoin*
Bourjois, *Burgess*
Bourke, *Burke*
Bourn, *Bourne*
Bourne
Bourner, *Bourne*
Bourquet, *Burke*
Bourreau, *Bourrel*
Bourrel
Bourse, *Boursier*
Boursereau, *Boursier*
Bourseret, *Boursier*
Bourseron, *Boursier*
Bourserot, *Boursier*
Bourset, *Boursier*
Boursier
Boursillon, *Boursier*
Boursin, *Boursier*
Bourson, *Boursier*
Bourstin, *Burstin*
Bourthouloume, *Bartholomew*
Bourthoumieux, *Bartholomew*
Bourton, *Burton*
Bourtouloume, *Bartholomew*
Bourtoumieux, *Bartholomew*
Bourzec, *Boursier*
Bourzeix, *Burgess*
Bouscarel, *Boissier*
Bouscatier, *Boissier*
Bouscayre, *Boissier*
Bouscayrol, *Boissier*
Boušek, *Bogusławski*
Bousfield
Bousie, *Boosey*
Bouška, *Bogusławski*
Bousquet, *Bois*
Bousquier, *Boissier*
Boussard, *Bossard*
Boussardon, *Bossard*
Boutcher, *Butcher*
Bouteiller, *Butler*
Bouteillier, *Butler*
Boutflower, *Boltflower*
Boutillier, *Butler*
Bouton
Boutonier, *Bouton*
Boutonneau, *Bouton*
Boutonnet, *Bouton*
Boutonnier, *Bouton*
Bouts, *Baud*
Bouvel, *Boeuf*
Bouvelet, *Boeuf*
Bouvelot, *Boeuf*
Bouveret, *Bouvier*
Bouverie
Bouveron, *Bouvier*
Bouvery, *Bouverie*
Bouvet, *Boeuf*
Bouvier
Bouvon, *Boeuf*
Bouvot, *Boeuf*
Bouvret, *Bouvier*
Bouvron, *Bouvier*
Bouvry, *Bouverie*
Bouwen, *Baldwin*
Bouwer, *Bauer*
Bouwijn, *Baldwin*
Bouwman, *Bauer*
Bouwmeester, *Bauer*
Bouyer, *Bouvier*
Bouzek, *Buzek*
Bouzic, *Box*
Bouzit, *Box*
Bouzon, *Bos*
Bovary, *Bouverie*
Bové, *Bouvier*
Bove, *Boeuf*
Bovell, *Bovill*
Bovelli, *Boeuf*
Bover, *Bouvier*
Boverie, *Bouverie*
Bovetto, *Boeuf*
Bovi, *Boye*
Bovier, *Bouvier*
Bovill
Boville, *Bovill*
Bovingdon
Bovington
Bovino, *Boeuf*
Bovio, *Boye*
Bovis, *Beavis*
Bovo, *Boye*
Bovoli, *Boeuf*
Bow
Bowater
Bowcock, *Baud*
Bowcott
Bowcutt, *Baud*
Bowden
Bowdery, *Baldry*
Bowdidge, *Bowditch*
Bowditch
Bowdon, *Bowden*
Bowe, *Bow*
Bowell
Bowells, *Bowell*
Bowen
Bowen, *Owen*
Bower
Bowerer, *Bower*
Bowering, *Bower*
Bowerman, *Bower*
Bowers, *Bower*
Bowes
Bowick, *Bewick*
Bowie
Bowker
Bowland, *Boland*
Bowlands, *Boland*
Bowle, *Bowell, Bowler*
Bowler
Bowles, *Bowell*
Bowles, *Bowler*
Bowley
Bowller, *Bowler*
Bowman
Bown, *Boon*
Bowne, *Boon*
Bowra, *Bower*
Bowrah, *Bower*
Bowrer, *Bower*
Bowring, *Bower*
Bowser
Bowsher, *Belcher*
Bowton, *Bovingdon*
Bowyer
Box
Boxall
Boxboim, *Buchs*
Boxell, *Boxall*
Boxenbaum, *Buchs*
Boxer, *Box*
Boxhall, *Boxall*
Boyce
Boycott
Boyd
Boyda, *Boyd*
Boyde, *Boyd*
Boydell, *Boodle*
Boyé, *Bouvier*
Boye
Boyens, *Boye*
Boyer, *Bouvier*
Boyero, *Bouvier*
Boyes, *Boyce*
Boyk, *Boye*
Boyke, *Boye*
Boykin, *Boye*
Boyle
Boyles, *Boyle*
Boys, *Boyce*
Boyse, *Boyce*
Boysen, *Boye*
Boyson, *Boyce*

Boyton
Bozon, *Bos*
Bozounet, *Bos*
Braak, *Brach*
Braakman, *Brach*
Braaksma, *Brach*
Braam, *Brahm*
Braams, *Abraham*
Braban, *Brabham*
Brabanchon, *Brabazon*
Brabançon, *Brabazon*
Braband, *Brabham*
Brabander, *Brabham*
Brabandt, *Brabham*
Brabandter, *Brabham*
Brabant, *Brabham*
Brabanter, *Brabham*
Brabazon
Brabban, *Brabham*
Brabbant, *Brabham*
Brabben, *Brabham*
Brabbin, *Brabham*
Brabbon, *Brabham*
Brabbyn, *Brabham*
Brabec, *Vorobyov*
Braben, *Brabham*
Brabham
Brabin, *Brabham*
Brabiner, *Brabham*
Brabner, *Brabham*
Brabon, *Brabham*
Brabyn, *Brabham*
Brac, *Brack*
Braccaro, *Brack*
Bracchi, *Brack*
Bracco, *Brack*
Brace
Bracegirdle
Bracer, *Brasher*
Bracewell
Brach
Bracher, *Brach*
Brachet, *Brack*
Brachmann, *Brach*
Brachner, *Brach*
Brack
Brackan, *Bracken*
Bracken
Brackenridge
Bracket, *Brack*
Brackley
Brackner, *Brack*
Brackpool
Braconnet, *Brack*
Braconnier, *Brack*
Braconnot, *Brack*
Bracq, *Brack*
Brada, *Borodin*
Bradáč, *Borodin*
Bradane, *Braden*
Bradatý, *Borodin*
Bradberry, *Bradbury*
Bradbery, *Bradbury*
Bradbrook
Bradbury
Bradden, *Braden*
Braddigan, *Brady*
Braddock
Braddon
Brade, *Broad*
Bradekin, *Brady*
Braden
Bradey, *Brady*
Bradfield
Bradford
Bradforth, *Bradford*
Bradić, *Brother*
Bradič, *Borodin*
Bradican, *Brady*
Bradie, *Brady*
Bradlaugh, *Bradley*
Bradley
Bradly, *Bradley*
Bradman
Bradshaw
Bradstreet
Bradwell
Brady
Braga
Bragg
Braham, *Brahm, Bream*
Brahame, *Bream*
Brahams, *Abraham*
Brahm
Brahms, *Abraham, Brahm*
Braibant, *Brabham*
Braid, *Broad*
Braiden, *Braden*
Braidford, *Bradford*
Braidman, *Bradman*
Braille
Brailsford
Braime, *Bream*
Brain
Braine, *Brain*
Braines
Brainin, *Braines*
Braisher, *Brasher*
Braitbart, *Breit*
Braithwait, *Braithwaite*
Braithwaite
Braitman, *Breit*
Braizier, *Brasher*
Brajtbard, *Breit*
Brajtman, *Breit*
Brake
Brakspear, *Breakspear*
Bramah, *Bramall*
Bramall
Bramble, *Bramall*
Brame, *Bream*
Bramhall, *Bramall*
Bramham, *Bream*
Bramley
Brammall, *Bramall*
Brammer, *Bramall*
Bramo, *Abraham*
Brampton
Bramsen, *Abraham*
Bramson, *Abraham, Brand*
Bramwell
Branagan, *Brannigan*
Branagh, *Brannick*
Branca, *Branch*
Brancas, *Branch*
Branch
Branche, *Branch*
Branchet, *Branch*
Branchflower, *Blanchflower*
Branco, *Blanc*
Brancusi, *Branch*
Brand
Brandacci, *Brand*
Brandassi, *Brand*
Brandeis, *Brandejs*
Brandejs
Brändel, *Brand*
Brandel, *Brand*
Brandes, *Brand, Brandejs*
Brandi, *Brand*
Brandin, *Brand*
Brandini, *Brand*
Brandino, *Brand*
Brändle, *Brand*
Brändli, *Brand*
Brando, *Brand*
Brandolini, *Brand*
Brandon
Brandone, *Brand*
Brandoni, *Brand*
Brands, *Brand*
Brandsen, *Brand*
Brandsma, *Brand*
Brandt, *Brand*
Brandts, *Brand*
Brandwain, *Bronfman*
Brandwainman, *Bronfman*
Brandwein, *Bronfman*
Brandweinhendler, *Bronfman*
Brandweinman, *Bronfman*
Brandwin, *Bronfman*
Brangwin, *Brangwyn*
Brangwyn
Braniff
Branigan, *Brannigan*
Brankin, *Brannigan*
Brannagh, *Brannick*
Brannan, *Brennan*
Branni, *Brand*
Brannick
Brannigan
Branno, *Brand*
Branque, *Branch*
Branquet, *Branch*
Bransom, *Brand*
Branson, *Brand*
Branston
Brant, *Brand*
Brantham, *Bream*
Brantl, *Brand*
Braque, *Brack*
Braquennier, *Brack*
Braquet, *Brack*
Brás, *Blaise*
Brasch, *Barish*
Brash
Brashaw, *Bradshaw*
Brasher
Brasier, *Brasher*
Brass, *Brace*
Brasseur, *Brasher*
Brassill, *Brazil*
Brassington
Bratcher, *Brach*
Bratley, *Bradley*
Bratly, *Bradley*
Bratt
Braud, *Beraud*
Braude, *Brodski*
Braudel, *Beraud*
Braudey, *Beraud*
Bräuer, *Brewer*
Brauer, *Brewer*
Brauermann, *Brewer*
Brauers, *Brewer*
Brault, *Beraud*
Braumann, *Brewer*
Braun, *Brown*
Braund, *Brand*
Braunds, *Brand*
Brauner, *Brown*
Braunfeld, *Brown*
Brauning, *Browning*
Bräunle, *Brown*
Bräunlein, *Brown*
Braunroth, *Brown*
Brauns, *Brown*
Braunschweig
Braunstein, *Brown*
Braunstein
Braunthal, *Brown*
Bravard, *Bravo*
Bravetti, *Bravo*
Bravo
Brawley, *Brolly*
Brawnick, *Brannick*
Braxton
Bray
Braybrook, *Bradbrook*
Braybrooke, *Bradbrook*
Brayham, *Bream*
Brayne, *Brain*
Brayshaw, *Bradshaw*
Brayshay, *Bradshaw*
Brazier, *Brasher*
Brazil
Brazovsky, *Bereznikov*
Breach, *Brach*
Breacher, *Brach*
Bready, *Brady*
Breakell, *Breakwell*
Breakspear
Breakwell
Bream
Brear
Brearley, *Brierley*
Breassell, *Brazil*
Breathnach, *Brett*
Brébant, *Brabham*
Brebner, *Brabham*
Brech, *Brach*
Brecher, *Brach*
Brecht, *Albert*
Breckan, *Bracken*
Breckenridge, *Brackenridge*
Breddy
Brede, *Breed*
Bredon, *Breedon*
Breed
Breede, *Breed*
Breeder, *Breed*
Breedon
Breeds, *Breed*
Breem, *Bream*
Breen
Breese, *Breeze*
Breeze
Breger, *Brewer*
Bregman
Brei, *Brewer*
Breier, *Brewer*
Breil, *Brühl, Breuil*
Breilmann, *Brühl*
Breines, *Braines*
Breinl, *Brown*
Breinlein, *Brown*
Breit
Breitbard, *Breit*
Breitbart, *Breit*
Breitholz, *Breit*
Breitman, *Breit*
Breitmann, *Breit*
Breitstein, *Breit*
Brejcha
Brekonridge, *Brackenridge*
Brel, *Breuil*

Brelford, *Brailsford*
Brellisford, *Brailsford*
Bremner
Brémond, *Berman*
Brémont, *Berman*
Brenane, *Brennan*
Brenchley
Brend, *Brent*
Brendeke, *Brand*
Brendel, *Brand*
Brener, *Brenner*
Brenguié, *Beringer*
Brenguier, *Beringer*
Brenman, *Brenner*
Brennach, *Brannick*
Brennan
Brennand
Brenneke, *Brand*
Brenner
Brent
Brentnall
Brenton
Brereton
Brés, *Brice*
Breslane, *Brazil*
Breslau
Breslauer, *Breslau*
Breslav, *Breslau*
Breslavski, *Breslau*
Breslaw, *Breslau*
Breslawski, *Breslau*
Bresler, *Breslau*
Breslin, *Brazil*
Breslow, *Breslau*
Bresset, *Brice*
Bressington
Bresslauer, *Breslau*
Bressler, *Breslau*
Bresson, *Brice*
Bressot, *Brice*
Bret, *Brett*
Bretagne, *Brett*
Bretange, *Brett*
Bretanha, *Brett*
Bretaud, *Brett*
Breteau, *Brett*
Bretécher
Bretegnier, *Brett*
Bretel, *Brett*
Bretherick
Bretherton
Brethiot, *Brett*
Brétillon, *Brett*
Breton, *Brett*
Bretonel, *Brett*
Bretoni, *Brett*
Bretonneau, *Brett*
Bretonnel, *Brett*
Bretonnier, *Brett*
Brett
Brettell, *Brett*
Brettle, *Brett*
Bretton
Breu, *Brewer*
Breuel, *Brühl*
Breuer, *Brewer*
Breuers, *Brewer*
Breughel, *Brühl*
Breuil
Breuilh, *Breuil*
Breuillard, *Breuil*
Breuillat, *Breuil*
Breuillaud, *Breuil*
Breuillet, *Breuil*
Breuillon, *Breuil*
Breuillot, *Breuil*
Breul, *Brühl*
Breulet, *Breuil*
Breuls, *Brühl*
Breuning, *Browning*
Brew
Brewer
Brewin, *Breen*
Brewis
Brewster, *Brewer*
Breyer, *Brewer*
Breymann, *Brewer*
Březa, *Bereznikov*
Brezack, *Bereznikov*
Brezak, *Bereznikov*
Brezenoff, *Bereznikov*
Brezhnev
Březina, *Bereznikov*
Brezinski, *Bereznikov*
Brezner, *Bereznikov*
Brezniak, *Bereznikov*
Breznik, *Bereznikov*
Breznitz, *Bereznikov*
Brezny, *Bereznikov*
Bri, *Bric*
Briamo, *Abraham*
Brian, *Bryan*
Briand, *Bryan*
Briandet, *Bryan*
Briant, *Bryan*
Briar, *Brear*
Briard
Briarley, *Brierley*
Briarly, *Brierley*
Briars, *Brear*
Briaud, *Briard*
Briault, *Briard*
Bric
Bricard, *Bric*
Bricaud, *Bric*
Bricault, *Bric*
Brice
Brickdale, *Birkdale*
Brickett, *Birkett*
Brickman, *Bridge*
Brickmann, *Bridge*
Brickner, *Bridge*
Bricks, *Brice*
Bricon, *Bric*
Bricq, *Bric*
Bride, *Bird*
Bridel, *Bridle*
Bridell, *Bridle*
Bridewell, *Bridle*
Bridge
Bridgeman, *Bridge*
Bridgens, *Bridge*
Bridger, *Bridge*
Bridges, *Bridge*
Bridgewater
Bridgman, *Bridge*
Bridgwater, *Bridgewater*
Bridle
Bridson, *Kilbride*
Brie, *Briard*
Briel, *Brühl*
Brien, *Bryan*
Briend, *Bryan*
Brier, *Brear*
Brière, *Bruyère*
Brierley
Brierly, *Brierley*
Brierre, *Bruyère*
Briers, *Brear*
Brigden
Brigetson, *Kilbride*
Brigg, *Bridge*
Brigginshaw, *Burkinshaw*
Briggs, *Bridge*
Bright
Brighten, *Brighton*
Brightman, *Bright*
Brighton
Brightwell
Brigman, *Bridge*
Brik, *Bridge*
Bril, *Brill*
Brilant, *Brillant*
Briliant, *Brillant*
Brill
Brillant
Brilleman, *Brill*
Brilliant, *Brillant*
Brim
Brimm, *Brim*
Brimner, *Bremner*
Brinan, *Brennan*
Brinane, *Brennan*
Brinch, *Brink*
Brinck, *Brink*
Brinckman, *Brink*
Brinckmann, *Brink*
Brind, *Brent*
Brindle
Brindley
Brington
Bringuier, *Beringer*
Brink
Brinkema, *Brink*
Brinken, *Brink*
Brinkley
Brinkman, *Brink*
Brinkmann, *Brink*
Brinksma, *Brink*
Brinkstra, *Brink*
Brinton
Brion
Bris, *Brice*
Brisard
Brisbane
Brisch, *Barish*
Brisco, *Briscoe*
Briscoe
Brisk
Brisker, *Briscoe*
Brisker, *Brisk*
Briskey, *Briscoe*
Briskin, *Brisk*
Briskman, *Brisk*
Brissard, *Brice*
Brissaud, *Brice*
Brisse, *Brice*
Brisset, *Brice*
Brisson, *Brice*
Brissonneau, *Brice*
Brissot, *Brice*
Brister, *Bristow*
Bristo, *Bristow*
Bristoe, *Bristow*
Bristow
Bristowe, *Bristow*
Britch, *Brach*
Britcher, *Brach*
Britnor, *Brittain*
Brito
Britt, *Brett, Brice*
Brittain
Brittan, *Brittain*
Britten, *Brittain*
Brittin, *Brittain*
Brittle, *Brett*
Brittner, *Brittain*
Britton, *Brittain*
Brix, *Brice*
Brixle, *Brice*
Bříza, *Bereznikov*
Broad
Broadbent
Broadely, *Bradley*
Broadfield, *Bradfield*
Broadhead
Broadhurst
Broadie, *Brady*
Broadly, *Bradley*
Broady, *Brady*
Broben, *Robin*
Broberg, *Brolin*
Brobin, *Robin*
Brobson, *Brabazon*
Broc
Broca, *Broc*
Brocard, *Broc*
Brocart, *Broc*
Brocas, *Broc*
Broccardi, *Burkett*
Brochard, *Broc*
Brochart, *Broc*
Broche, *Broc*
Brocher, *Broc*
Brochet, *Broc*
Brochier, *Broc*
Brochon, *Broc*
Brochot, *Broc*
Brock
Brockenshaw, *Burkinshaw*
Bröcker, *Brock*
Brockhole
Brockie, *Brock*
Brocklebank
Brocklehurst
Brocklesby
Brockman, *Brock*
Brockmann, *Brock*
Brockmon, *Brock*
Brockwell
Brocque, *Broc*
Brocquet, *Broc*
Brod, *Brodski*
Broda, *Borodin, Brodski*
Brode, *Brodski*
Brodecki, *Borodin*
Broder, *Brodski, Brother*
Broders, *Brother*
Brodersen, *Brother*
Broderson, *Brodski*
Broderzon, *Brodski*
Brodewicz, *Borodin*
Brodi, *Brodski*
Brodie
Brodigan, *Brady*
Brodman, *Brodski*
Brodniewicz, *Borodin*
Brodowski, *Brodski*
Brodski
Brodsky, *Brodski*
Brodt, *Brodski*
Brody, *Brodski*
Brodziński, *Brodski*
Broeders, *Brother*
Broek, *Brook*
Broekema, *Brook*

Broekman, *Brook*
Broekstra, *Brook*
Broere, *Brother*
Broeren, *Brother*
Bröers, *Brother*
Broerse, *Brother*
Broersen, *Brother*
Broersma, *Brother*
Broertjes, *Brother*
Brogan
Brogden
Brögel, *Brühl*
Brogelli, *Ambrose*
Brögelmann, *Brühl*
Brogetti, *Ambrose*
Broggi, *Ambrose*
Broggini, *Ambrose*
Broggio, *Ambrose*
Broghel, *Brühl*
Brogi, *Ambrose*
Brogini, *Ambrose*
Brogio, *Ambrose*
Brogioni, *Ambrose*
Brogiotti, *Ambrose*
Brohlin, *Brolin*
Brohoon, *Brain*
Broida, *Brodski*
Broide, *Brodski*
Broido, *Brodski*
Broinlich, *Brown*
Brok, *Brock*
Broke, *Brook*
Brokenshaw, *Burkinshaw*
Brokob, *Prokop*
Brokof, *Prokop*
Broksch, *Prokop*
Brokuff, *Prokop*
Brolin
Brollaghan, *Brolly*
Brolly
Bromage
Broman, *Brolin*
Bromberg
Bromberger, *Bromberg*
Brome, *Broom*
Bromfield, *Broomfield*
Bromidge, *Bromage*
Bromiley, *Bromley*
Bromilow, *Bromley*
Bromley
Brommage, *Bromage*
Broms
Bromwich, *Bromage*
Bron, *Bear*
Bronfin, *Bronfman*
Bronfman
Bronfmann, *Bronfman*
Broniewski
Bronisz, *Broniewski*
Broniszewski, *Broniewski*
Bronowski
Bronshtein, *Braunstein*
Bronson
Bronstein, *Braunstein*
Bronstejn, *Braunstein*
Bronstien, *Braunstein*
Bronsztejn, *Braunstein*
Brontë, *Prunty*
Brook
Brooke, *Brook*
Brooker, *Brook*
Brookes, *Brook*
Brookfield
Brooking, *Brook*
Brookman, *Brook*
Brookmann, *Brook*
Brooks, *Brook*
Brooksbank
Brooksby
Brookstra, *Brook*
Broom
Broome, *Broom*
Broomfield
Broomhall
Broomhead
Broose, *Ambrose*
Brophy
Broque, *Broc*
Broquet, *Broc*
Broquier, *Broc*
Bros, *Ambrose*
Brosch, *Ambrose, Barish*
Broschek, *Ambrose*
Broschke, *Ambrose*
Bröse, *Ambrose*
Brose, *Ambrose*
Bröseke, *Ambrose*
Broseke, *Ambrose*
Brösel, *Ambrose*
Broseman, *Ambrose*
Brosenius, *Ambrose*
Brosetti, *Ambrose*
Brosi, *Ambrose*
Brosini, *Ambrose*
Brosio, *Ambrose*
Brosius, *Ambrose*
Broske, *Ambrose*
Brosnahan
Brosnan, *Brosnahan*
Brosoli, *Ambrose*
Brossard, *Brosse*
Brosse
Brosses, *Brosse*
Brosset, *Ambrose, Brosse*
Brossier, *Brosse*
Brossolette, *Brosse*
Brossollet, *Brosse*
Broster, *Bruster*
Broström, *Brolin*
Broszkiewicz, *Ambrose*
Brother
Brotherston, *Brotherstone*
Brotherstone
Brouard
Brouardel, *Brouard*
Brough
Brougham
Broughton
Broun, *Brown*
Broune, *Brown*
Brouss, *Brosse*
Broussard, *Brosse*
Brousseau, *Brosse*
Brousseloux, *Brosse*
Brousset, *Brosse*
Broussot, *Brosse*
Broussoux, *Brosse*
Brouwer, *Brewer*
Brouwers, *Brewer*
Brower, *Brewer*
Brown
Browne, *Brown*
Brownell, *Brownhill*
Brownett, *Brown*
Brownfield, *Brown*
Brownhall, *Brownhill*
Brownhill
Brownill, *Brownhill*
Browning
Brownings, *Browning*
Brownridge
Brownsmith, *Smith*
Brownson, *Bronson*
Brownstein, *Braunstein, Brown*
Brownstone, *Braunstein*
Brox, *Prokop*
Broxholme
Broy, *Brophy*
Broyers, *Brewer*
Brož, *Ambrose*
Brożek, *Ambrose*
Brožek, *Ambrose*
Bru, *Brown*
Bruce
Bruch, *Brook*
Brücher, *Brook*
Bruchmann, *Brook*
Brück, *Bridge*
Bruck, *Bridge, Brook*
Bruckental, *Bridge*
Bruckenthal, *Bridge*
Brucker, *Bridge, Brook*
Bruckisch, *Prokop*
Bruckman, *Bridge*
Brückmann, *Bridge*
Bruckmann, *Bridge*
Brückner, *Bridge*
Bruckner, *Bridge*
Brucksch, *Prokop*
Bruckstein, *Bridge*
Brudenell
Bruder, *Brother*
Bruderman, *Brother*
Brudersohn, *Brother*
Bruderson, *Brother*
Bruel, *Breuil*
Bruère, *Bruyère*
Brueton, *Bruton*
Bruff, *Brough*
Brüg, *Bridge*
Bruger, *Bruyère*
Brugère, *Bruyère*
Brugerolle, *Bruyère*
Brugerolles, *Bruyère*
Brugeron, *Bruyère*
Brügge, *Bridge*
Bruggeman, *Bridge*
Brüggemann, *Bridge*
Brügger, *Bridge*
Brugh, *Brough*
Brugier, *Bruyère*
Brugière, *Bruyère*
Brugman, *Bridge*
Brügmann, *Bridge*
Brugnot, *Brown*
Brugsma, *Bridge*
Bruguera, *Bruyère*
Brühl
Brühler, *Brühl*
Bruhn, *Brown*
Brühnicke, *Brown*
Bruhnke, *Brown*
Bruhns, *Brown*
Bruhnsen, *Brown*
Bruin, *Brown*
Bruine, *Brown*
Bruineman, *Brown*
Bruinen, *Brown*
Bruins, *Brown*
Bruinsma, *Brown*
Brulard, *Brûlé*
Brûlé
Bruley, *Brûlé*
Brulin, *Brûlé*
Brullon, *Brûlé*
Brulon, *Brûlé*
Brulot, *Brûlé*
Brummell, *Bramall*
Brun, *Brown*
Bruna, *Brown*
Brundu, *Blunt*
Bruneau, *Brown*
Brunel, *Brown*
Brunelleschi, *Brown*
Brunelli, *Brown*
Brunesco, *Brown*
Brunet, *Brown*
Bruneton, *Brown*
Brunetti, *Brown*
Bruni, *Brown*
Brünicke, *Brown*
Brüning, *Browning*
Bruning, *Browning*
Bruninga, *Browning*
Brünings, *Browning*
Brunini, *Brown*
Brunke, *Brown*
Brunn, *Bourne, Brown*
Brunnberg, *Bourne*
Brunnemann, *Bourne*
Brünner, *Bourne*
Brunner, *Bourne*
Brunning, *Browning*
Bruno, *Brown*
Brunon, *Brown*
Brunone, *Brown*
Brunot, *Brown*
Brunotti, *Brown*
Bruns, *Brown*
Brunschvieg, *Braunschweig*
Brunsen, *Brown*
Brunson, *Bronson*
Brunswick, *Braunschweig*
Brunt, *Brent*
Brüntje, *Brown*
Brüntjen, *Brown*
Brunton
Brunty, *Prunty*
Brusch, *Brush*
Brush
Brusin, *Ambrose*
Bruslé, *Brûlé*
Bruster
Bruton
Bruttner, *Brittain*
Bruun, *Brown*
Bruwer, *Brewer*
Bruxby, *Brooksby*
Bruyer, *Brewer*
Bruyère
Bruyn, *Brown*
Bruyne, *Brown*
Bruyninckx, *Browning*
Bruyns, *Brown*
Bruyntjes, *Brown*
Bry, *Bric*
Bryan
Bryans, *Bryan*
Bryant, *Bryan*
Bryce, *Brice*
Bryceson, *Brice*
Brydson, *Kilbride*
Bryer, *Brear*
Bryers, *Brear*
Bryl, *Brühl*
Bryla, *Brühl*

Brymner, *Bremner*
Bryn, *Brown*
Bryning
Bryns, *Brown*
Bryson
Brzeski
Brzezicki, *Bereznikov*
Brzeziński, *Bereznikov*
Brzezinski, *Bereznikov*
Brzoza, *Bereznikov*
Brzózka, *Bereznikov*
Brzozowski, *Bereznikov*
Bua, *Boeuf*
Bubb
Bube
Bübelin, *Bube*
Buberl, *Bube*
Bucca, *Bocca*
Buccello, *Bocca*
Bucchi, *Bocca*
Buccieri, *Butcher*
Bucco, *Bocca*
Buccolini, *Bocca*
Buch
Buchan
Buchanan
Buchbinder, *Binder*
Buche, *Budge*
Büchelmann, *Bühler*
Bücher, *Buch*
Bucher, *Buch, Butcher*
Buchert, *Buch*
Buchholtz, *Buch*
Buchholz, *Buch*
Büchler, *Bühler*
Büchmann, *Buch*
Buchmann, *Buch*
Büchner, *Buch*
Buchner, *Buch*
Buchs
Buchsbaum, *Buchs*
Buchsenbaum, *Buchs*
Buchsenboim, *Buchs*
Buchwald, *Buch*
Buck
Buck, *Bauch*
Buckell, *Buckle*
Buckett, *Burkett*
Buckingham
Buckland
Buckle
Buckleigh, *Buckley*
Buckler, *Böckler, Buckle*
Buckles, *Buckle*
Buckley
Buckman
Buckmaster
Buckminster, *Buckmaster*
Bucknall, *Bucknell*
Bucknell
Bucksboim, *Buchs*
Buckspan, *Buchs*
Buckston, *Buxton*
Buckstone, *Buxton*
Buczak, *Bukowski*
Buczek, *Bukowski*
Buczko, *Bukowski*
Buczkowski, *Bukowski*
Buczyński, *Bukowski*
Buda, *Buzek*
Budcock, *Budd*
Budd
Budde, *Büttner*
Buddell, *Beadle*
Büddenbinder, *Binder*
Buddenbrock
Buddenbrook, *Buddenbrock*
Buddenbrooks, *Buddenbrock*
Budding, *Budd*
Buddle, *Beadle, Boodle*
Buddles, *Beadle*
Budds, *Budd*
Budek, *Buzek*
Budge
Budgen
Budgeon, *Budgen*
Budgett, *Burkett*
Budík, *Buzek*
Budil, *Buzek*
Budleigh, *Bodley*
Bue, *Boeuf*
Bueb, *Bube*
Buendía, *Bonjour*
Bueno, *Bon*
Buero, *Bouvier*
Buey, *Boeuf*
Bueyero, *Bouvier*
Bufton, *Bovingdon*
Bugdahn, *Bogdanov*
Bugdan, *Bogdanov*
Bugg
Bugh, *Bewes*
Bühel, *Bühler*
Buhilly, *Buckley*
Bühl, *Bühler*
Buhl
Buhle, *Buhl*
Bühler
Bühlmann, *Bühler*
Buhmann, *Bauer*
Bührmann, *Bauer*
Bührs, *Bauer*
Buhrs, *Bauer*
Buick, *Bewick*
Buijs, *Buss*
Buijsman, *Buss*
Buijzer, *Buss*
Buini, *Boeuf*
Buis, *Box, Buss*
Buisman, *Buss*
Buisse, *Box*
Buisson
Buissonnet, *Buisson*
Buissonnière, *Buisson*
Buitrago
Bujnowicz, *Bunin*
Buk, *Bauch*
Bukov, *Bukowski*
Bukovitz, *Bukowski*
Bukovski, *Bukowski*
Bukovský, *Bukowski*
Bukowiecki, *Bukowski*
Bukowitz, *Bukowski*
Bukowski
Bukowsky, *Bukowski*
Buksbaum, *Buchs*
Buksboim, *Buchs*
Buksenbaum, *Buchs*
Bukspan, *Buchs*
Bukszpan, *Buchs*
Bul, *Bull*
Bulgakov
Bulganin, *Bulgakov*
Bulger, *Bolger*
Bull
Bullan, *Bullen*
Bullant, *Bullen*
Bullar, *Buller*
Bullcock, *Bull*
Bulle, *Bull*
Bullen
Bullent, *Bullen*
Buller
Bullers, *Buller*
Bulley
Bulleyn, *Bullen*
Bullick
Bullier, *Buller*
Bullin, *Bullen*
Bullman, *Bulman*
Bullock
Bullon, *Bullen*
Bully, *Bulley*
Bulman
Bulmer
Bulstrode
Bumann, *Bauer*
Bumpas
Bumphries, *Humphrey*
Bunbury
Bunch
Bunche, *Bunch*
Buncombe
Bunde, *Bond*
Bundey, *Bond*
Bundy, *Bond*
Bunim, *Bonham*
Bunimovitz, *Bonham*
Bunin
Bunis, *Bunin*
Bunker
Bunkin, *Bunin*
Bunkum, *Buncombe*
Bunn, *Bone*
Bunner, *Poyner*
Bunnett
Bunney
Bunnion, *Bunyan*
Bunnyt, *Bunnett*
Bunomovitz, *Bonham*
Buntain, *Bunting*
Bunten, *Bunting*
Bunter
Buntin, *Bunting*
Buntine, *Bunting*
Bunting
Bunton, *Bunting*
Bunyan
Bunyard, *Banyard*
Bunyon, *Bunyan*
Bunz
Bunzel, *Bunz*
Bünzli, *Bunz*
Buo, *Boeuf*
Buonaparte, *Bonaparte*
Buonarroti
Buoncristiano, *Bonchrétien*
Buongiorno, *Bonjour*
Buongiovanni, *Budgen*
Buono, *Bon*
Buonsangue
Buontempo, *Bontemps*
Buosi, *Bos*
Buosio, *Bos*
Buou, *Boeuf*
Bur, *Bauer*
Burbage
Burbidge, *Burbage*
Burch, *Birch*
Burchall, *Birchall*
Burchard, *Burkett*
Burchardt, *Burkett*
Burchatt, *Burkett*
Burchert, *Burkett*
Burchett, *Birkett, Burkett*
Burchfield
Burckhard, *Burkett*
Burckhardt, *Burkett*
Bürcklin, *Birch*
Burd, *Bird*
Burda
Burdák, *Burda*
Burdekin, *Bird*
Burden, *Burdon*
Burdon
Bure, *Boure*
Bureš, *Burian*
Burford
Burg, *Burger*
Burge
Burgemeester, *Burgemeister*
Burgemeister
Bürger, *Burger*
Burger
Bürgers, *Burger*
Burgers, *Burger*
Burges, *Burgess*
Burgess
Burgh, *Burke*
Burghard, *Burkett*
Burghardt, *Burkett*
Burgher, *Burger*
Burgin, *Bourgoin*
Burgis, *Burgess*
Burgisi, *Burgess*
Burgiss, *Burgess*
Burgmann, *Burger, Burkman*
Burgo, *Burke*
Burgoin, *Bourgoin*
Burgoine, *Bourgoin*
Burgon, *Bourgoin*
Burgos, *Burke*
Burgoyne, *Bourgoin*
Burian
Buriánek, *Burian*
Bürk, *Burkett*
Burk, *Birch*
Burkart, *Burkett*
Burke
Bürkel, *Burkett*
Burker, *Burger*
Burkert, *Burkett*
Burkett
Burkhard, *Burkett*
Burkhardt, *Burkett*
Burkin
Burkinshaw
Burkitt, *Burkett*
Bürkli, *Burkett*
Burkman
Burleigh, *Burley*
Burley
Burling
Burman, *Burkman*
Bürmann, *Bauer*
Burmann, *Bauer*
Burn, *Bourne*
Burnand, *Brennand*
Burne, *Bourne*
Burnell, *Brown*
Burner, *Bourne*
Burness, *Burns*
Burnet, *Brown*
Burnett, *Brown*
Burney
Burnham

Burnhouse, *Burns*
Burnie, *Burney*
Burnley
Burns
Burnside
Burquès, *Burgess*
Burr
Burrage, *Burridge*
Burrel, *Bourrel*
Burrell, *Bourrel*
Burrett
Burridge
Burris, *Burrows*
Burrough, *Burrows*
Burroughes, *Burrows*
Burroughs, *Burrows*
Burrow, *Burrows*
Burrowes, *Burrows*
Burrows
Burs, *Bauer*
Burshtain, *Burstin*
Burshtein, *Burstin*
Burshtin, *Burstin*
Burshtyn, *Burstin*
Bursian, *Borisov*
Burski, *Borowski*
Burstain, *Burstin*
Burstein, *Burstin*
Bursten, *Burstin*
Burstin
Burstyn, *Burstin*
Bursztein, *Burstin*
Bursztejn, *Burstin*
Bursztin, *Burstin*
Bursztyn, *Burstin*
Burt
Burtenshaw, *Burkinshaw*
Burton
Burtwistle, *Birtwistle*
Bury
Burýšek, *Burian*
Burzyński
Busboom, *Buchs*
Busby
Buscaino, *Boissier*
Buscarino, *Boissier*
Busch, *Bush*
Büscher, *Bush*
Büschgen, *Bush*
Busck, *Bush*
Busco, *Bois*
Bušek, *Buzek*
Bush
Bushby
Bushbye, *Bushby*
Bushell, *Bissell*
Busher, *Boissier*
Bushill, *Bissell*
Busk, *Bush*
Busquet, *Bois*
Busquets, *Bois*
Buss
Busse, *Burkett, Buss*
Bussel, *Bissell*
Bussey
Bussière, *Box*
Bussy, *Boissy*
Bustamante
Bustillos, *Busto*
Busto
Bustos, *Busto*
Butchard, *Burkett*
Butcher
Butler
Butlin
Butner, *Bouton*
Butor, *Butter*
Butrimovich, *Bartholomew*
Butson, *Butt*
Butt
Büttel, *Beadle*
Butter
Butterfield
Butteriss, *Bottrell*
Butteriss
Butterman, *Butter*
Butters
Butterworth
Butting, *Butt*
Buttle, *Boodle, Butler*
Büttner
Button, *Bouton*
Buttress, *Butteriss*
Buttrey, *Butteriss*
Buttrice, *Butteriss*
Buttriss, *Butteriss*
Buttrum, *Bertram*
Butts, *Butt*
Buuck, *Bauch*
Buuk, *Bauch*
Buur, *Bauer*
Buurman, *Bauer*
Bux, *Buchs*
Buxbaum, *Buchs*
Buxó, *Box*
Buxtehude
Buxton
Buy, *Bye*
Buye, *Bye*
Buysman, *Buss*
Buyzer, *Buss*
Buzek
By, *Bye*
Byatt
Býček, *Bick*
Bye
Byers
Byfield
Byford
Bygrave
Bygraves, *Bygrave*
Býk, *Bick*
Byk, *Bick*
Bykoff, *Bick*
Bykovski, *Bick*
Bykowski, *Bick*
Byles, *Biles*
Byng, *Bing*
Bynnan, *Bannan*
Byram, *Byron*
Byran, *Byron*
Byrch, *Birch*
Byrd, *Bird*
Byres, *Byers*
Byrne
Byrnes, *Byrne*
Byrom, *Byron*
Byron
Bysh, *Bush*
Bysshe, *Bush*
Bythell, *Bethell*
Bytheway
Bythway, *Way*
Bywater
Bywaters, *Bywater*
Byway, *Way*
Bywood, *Wood*

C

Ca, *Casa*
Cabaço
Caballé, *Chevalier*
Caballer, *Chevalier*
Caballero, *Chevalier*
Caballo, *Cavallo*
Caban, *Cabane*
Cabaña, *Cabane*
Cabana, *Cabane*
Cabanais, *Cabane*
Cabañas, *Cabane*
Cabanas, *Cabane*
Cabane
Cabanel, *Cabane*
Cabanès, *Cabane*
Cabanes, *Cabane*
Cabanié, *Cabane*
Cabanillas, *Cabane*
Cabanne, *Cabane*
Cabanon, *Cabane*
Cabanot, *Cabane*
Cabeça, *Cabeza*
Cabel, *Cable*
Cabello
Cabellos, *Cabello*
Cabestany
Cabeza
Cabezas, *Cabeza*
Cabezón, *Cabeza*
Cabezudo, *Cabeza*
Cabezuelo, *Cabeza*
Cabiron, *Cheever*
Cabiten, *Capitaine*
Cable
Cabo, *Cap*
Caboi, *Capon*
Caboni, *Capon*
Cabot
Cabotin, *Cabot*
Caboto, *Cabot*
Cabotto, *Jacob*
Cabras, *Cheever*
Cabré, *Cheever*
Cabre, *Cheever*
Cabreiro, *Cheever*
Cabrer, *Cheever*
Cabrera
Cabrerizo, *Cheever*
Cabrero, *Cheever*
Cabrié, *Cheever*
Cabrier, *Cheever*
Cabriol, *Chevreuil*
Cabriolé, *Chevreuil*
Cabrioler, *Chevreuil*
Cabrit, *Cheever*
Cabrita, *Cheever*
Cabrol, *Chevreuil*
Caçador, *Chase*
Cacci, *Jack*
Cáceres
Căcilie, *Sisley*
Cadbury
Cadd, *Cade*
Caddel, *Cadell*
Caddell, *Cadell*
Caddick, *Caddock*
Caddock
Cade
Cadel
Cadell
Cadena
Cadéo, *Cadiou*
Cadge, *Cage*
Cadieu, *Cadiou*
Cadilhac, *Cadillac*
Cadilhon, *Cadillac*
Cadilhou, *Cadillac*
Cadillac
Cadio, *Cadiou*
Cadiot, *Cadiou*
Cadiou
Cadioux, *Cadiou*
Cadle, *Cadell*
Cadman, *Cade*
Cadogan, *Caddock*
Cadwallader
Cadwell, *Caldwell*
Cadwgan, *Caddock*
Caeiro, *Calero*
Caen, *Cain*
Caesman, *Cheeseman*
Caesmans, *Cheeseman*
Caetano, *Gaetano*
Caff, *Chaff*
Cafferky, *McCafferty*
Cafferty, *McCafferty*
Caffin, *Coffin*
Caffyn, *Kyffin*
Cagan, *Cohen*
Caganovitz, *Cohen*
Cage
Cager, *Cage*
Cagliari, *Callegaro*
Cagliarotti, *Callegaro*
Caglieri, *Callegaro*
Caglieris, *Callegaro*
Cagliero, *Callegaro*
Caglierotti, *Callegaro*
Cagney
Cahalan, *Callan*
Cahalane, *Callan*
Cahan, *Cohen*
Cahana, *Cohen*
Cahane, *Keane*
Cahani, *Cohen*
Cahanoff, *Cohen*
Cahanov, *Cohen*
Cahanovitch, *Cohen*
Cahanovitz, *Cohen*
Cahansky, *Cohen*
Cahany, *Cohen*
Cahen, *Cohen*
Caherny, *Carney*
Cahill
Cahn, *Cohen*
Cahouet, *Chouan*
Cahu, *Chouan*
Cahuet, *Chouan*
Cahy, *Mulcahy*
Caiger, *Cage*
Cail
Caill, *Cail*
Caillard, *Cail*
Caillat, *Cail*
Caillaux, *Cail*
Cailleaux, *Cail*
Cailleteau, *Cail*
Cailleton, *Cail*
Caillette, *Cail*
Cailliat, *Cail*
Caillier, *Cail*
Cailliot, *Cail*
Caillot, *Cail*
Caillotin, *Cail*
Caillouet, *Cail*
Cailloux, *Cail*

Cailly, *Cayley*
Cain
Caine, *Cain*
Caines, *Keynes*
Cains, *Keynes*
Caird
Cairnduff
Cairns
Caistel, *Ashkettle*
Cajel, *Cage*
Cajelot, *Cage*
Cajet, *Cage*
Cajot, *Cage*
Cakebread
Calabrese, *Calabria*
Calabresi, *Calabria*
Calabri, *Calabria*
Calabria
Calabro, *Calabria*
Calado
Calamel, *Challamel*
Calamelle, *Challamel*
Calandraud, *Calendri*
Calandre, *Calendri*
Calandreau, *Calendri*
Calandrini, *Calendri*
Calandrino, *Calendri*
Calatayud
Calçada, *Chaussée*
Calcott, *Caldicott*
Calcut, *Caldicott*
Calcutt, *Caldicott*
Caldairou, *Calderon*
Caldairoux, *Calderon*
Caldaro, *Calderon*
Caldas
Caldayrou, *Calderon*
Caldayroux, *Calderon*
Caldbeck, *Colbeck*
Caldecot, *Caldicott*
Caldecott, *Caldicott*
Caldecourt, *Caldicott*
Caldeira, *Calderon*
Calder
Caldera, *Calderon*
Caldero, *Calderon*
Calderón, *Calderon*
Calderon
Calderone, *Calderon*
Calderonello, *Calderon*
Calderwood
Caldeyroux, *Calderon*
Caldicot, *Caldicott*
Caldicott
Caldor, *Calder*
Caldroni, *Calderon*
Caldwell
Calegari, *Callegaro*
Calendar, *Callander*
Calendra, *Calendri*
Calendreau, *Calendri*
Calendri
Caleri, *Callegaro*
Calero
Calet, *Callot*
Caley, *Cayley*
Calf
Calgari, *Callegaro*
Calgaris, *Callegaro*
Calgaro, *Callegaro*
Calhau, *Cail*
Calhoun, *Colquhoun*
Caliari, *Callegaro*
Calieri, *Callegaro*
Caliero, *Callegaro*
Caligari, *Callegaro*
Caligaris, *Callegaro*
Calladine
Callaghan
Callahan, *Callaghan*
Callan
Callanan, *Calnan*
Callander
Callaway, *Calloway*
Callcott, *Caldicott*
Calle
Callegari, *Callegaro*
Callegarin, *Callegaro*
Callegarini, *Callegaro*
Callegaris, *Callegaro*
Callegaro
Callegher, *Callegaro*
Calleja, *Calle*
Callejas, *Calle*
Callejo, *Calle*
Callen, *Callan*
Callendar, *Callander*
Callender, *Callander*
Calleri, *Callegaro*
Callero, *Callegaro*
Callery, *McIlwraith*
Calles, *Calle*
Callet, *Callot*
Calley, *Cayley*
Callf, *Calf*
Calliari, *Callegaro*
Callicot, *Caldicott*
Callie, *Cayley*
Callieri, *Callegaro*
Callierotti, *Callegaro*
Calligan, *Callaghan*
Calligari, *Callegaro*
Calligaro, *Callegaro*
Calligher, *Callegaro*
Callin, *Callan*
Callinan, *Calnan*
Callister, *Alexander*
Callot
Callow
Calloway
Callowe, *Callow*
Callum, *Coleman*
Calme, *Chaume*
Calmel, *Chaume*
Calmels, *Chaume*
Calmette, *Chaume*
Calnan
Caloe, *Callow*
Calon, *Callot*
Calonge, *Cannon*
Calot, *Callot*
Calow, *Callow*
Calowe, *Callow*
Calterone, *Calderon*
Caluwaert, *Kahl*
Caluwe, *Kahl*
Calvão, *Chaff*
Calvard, *Calvert*
Calve, *Chaff*
Calvelli, *Chaff*
Calvello, *Chaff*
Calver
Calverd, *Calvert*
Calverley
Calvert
Calvet, *Chaff*
Calvetti, *Chaff*
Calvi, *Chaff*
Calvietti, *Chaff*
Calvillo, *Chaff*
Calvini, *Chaff*
Calvino, *Chaff*
Calvó, *Chaff*
Calvo, *Chaff*
Calway, *Calloway*
Calwell, *Caldwell*
Calza, *Chausse*
Calzada, *Chaussée*
Calzetta, *Chausse*
Calzette, *Chausse*
Calzetti, *Chausse*
Calzo, *Chausse*
Calzolai, *Chausse*
Calzolari, *Chausse*
Cam, *Chaume*
Camacho
Cámara, *Chambers*
Câmara, *Chambers*
Câmarão, *Chambers*
Camard, *Camoys*
Camarero, *Chambers*
Camarillo, *Chambers*
Camarinho, *Chambers*
Camarino, *Chambers*
Camb, *Camber*
Cambden, *Camden*
Cambell, *Campbell*
Camber
Camberlin, *Chamberlain*
Cambet, *Gambe*
Cambin, *Gambe*
Camble, *Campbell*
Cambra, *Chambers*
Cambran, *Chambers*
Cambrand, *Chambers*
Cambre, *Chambers*
Cambreleng, *Chamberlain*
Cambret, *Chambers*
Cambrette, *Chambers*
Cambrillon, *Chambers*
Cambrin, *Chambers*
Cambron, *Chambers*
Camden
Camel
Camelin, *Campling*
Camell, *Camel*
Camellini, *Campling*
Camelo, *Camel*
Camera, *Chambers*
Camerino, *Chambers*
Camerlenghi, *Chamberlain*
Camerlengo, *Chamberlain*
Camerlinghi, *Chamberlain*
Camerlingo, *Chamberlain*
Camerlynk, *Chamberlain*
Camerman, *Chambers*
Cameron
Camí, *Chemin*
Cami, *Chemin*
Camidge, *Gamage*
Camilo
Camin, *Chemin*
Caminel, *Chemin*
Caminero, *Chemin*
Camino, *Chemin*
Camis, *Camoys*
Cammell, *Camel*
Cammer, *Camber*
Cammidge, *Gamage*
Cammis, *Camoys*
Cammish, *Camoys*
Camoens, *Camões*
Camões
Camoletto, *James*
Camolli, *James*
Camosso, *James*
Camous, *Camoys*
Camoys
Camozzi, *Camoys*
Camozzini, *Camoys*
Camp, *Champ*
Campacci, *Champ*
Campaccio, *Champ*
Campagne, *Champney*
Campai, *Champ*
Campari, *Champ*
Campassi, *Champ*
Campasso, *Champ*
Campazzi, *Champ*
Campazzo, *Champ*
Campbell
Campeggi, *Champ*
Camper, *Champ*
Campese, *Champ*
Campesi, *Champ*
Campetti, *Champ*
Campi, *Champ*
Campieri, *Champ*
Campillo, *Champ*
Campino, *Champ*
Campion
Campione, *Campion*
Campise, *Champ*
Campisi, *Champ*
Camplin, *Campling*
Campling
Campo, *Champ*
Campoli, *Champ*
Campolo, *Champ*
Campone, *Champ*
Camponi, *Champ*
Campos, *Champ*
Camps, *Champ*
Campus, *Champ*
Camus, *Camoys*
Camusat, *Camoys*
Camuscio, *Camoys*
Camuseau, *Camoys*
Camuset, *Camoys*
Camuso, *Camoys*
Camussat, *Camoys*
Camuzat, *Camoys*
Camuzeau, *Camoys*
Camuzet, *Camoys*
Camy, *Chemin*
Can, *Chaume*
Caña, *Cain*
Canaan, *Cannon*
Cañada, *Cain*
Cañadas, *Cain*
Canal, *Chenal*
Canales, *Chenal*
Canaletto, *Chenal*
Canalini, *Chenal*
Canally, *McNally*
Canals, *Chenal*
Cañamero, *Chenevier*
Canapai, *Chenevier*
Canapari, *Chenevier*
Canaparo, *Chenevier*
Cañas, *Cain*
Canas, *Cain*
Canau, *Chenal*
Canaud, *Chenal*
Canault, *Chenal*
Canavan

Cancelier, *Chancellor*
Cancellario, *Chancellor*
Cancellieri, *Chancellor*
Cancellor, *Chancellor*
Candeias, *Chandler*
Candela, *Chandler*
Candelari, *Chandler*
Candelario
Candelaro, *Chandler*
Candelas, *Chandler*
Candelier, *Chandler*
Candelieri, *Chandler*
Candeliez, *Chandler*
Candeloro, *Candelario*
Cândido
Candiloro, *Candelario*
Candish, *Cavendish*
Candlish, *McCandless*
Cane, *Chêne, Cain*
Canela, *Chandler*
Canelas, *Cain*
Canele, *Chenal*
Caneli, *Chenal*
Cañellas, *Cain*
Canepari, *Chenevier*
Caneparo, *Chenevier*
Cañero, *Cain*
Canet
Cañete, *Cain*
Canevari, *Chenevier*
Canevaro, *Chenevier*
Canham
Cani, *Chenu*
Cañizares, *Cain*
Cann
Cannan, *Cannon*
Cannavan, *Canavan*
Canner, *Cann*
Canning
Cannon
Cannons, *Cannon*
Canny, *McCann*
Cano, *Chenu*
Caño
Canon, *Cannon*
Canonaco, *Cannon*
Canone, *Cannon*
Canonge, *Cannon*
Canonici, *Cannon*
Canonico, *Cannon*
Canonne, *Cannon*
Canourge, *Cannon*
Canova, *Casanova*
Cànovas, *Casanova*
Cant
Cantalejo
Cantalupo, *Cantellow*
Cantarero
Cantello, *Cantellow*
Cantellow
Cantelo, *Cantellow*
Canteloube, *Cantellow*
Canteloup, *Cantellow*
Cantelue, *Cantellow*
Canter, *Cant, Kantor*
Cantera, *Canto*
Cantero, *Canto*
Cantie, *Cant*
Cantle, *Cantwell*
Cantlow, *Cantellow*
Cantó
Canto
Cantor, *Cant, Kantor*
Cantos, *Canto*
Cantrowitz, *Kantor*
Cantwell
Canty, *Cant*
Canu, *Chenu*
Canudet, *Chenu*
Canudi, *Chenu*
Canudo, *Chenu*
Canuel, *Chenu*
Canuet, *Chenu*
Canut, *Chenu*
Canuti, *Chenu*
Canuto, *Chenu*
Cáp, *Chaplin*
Cap
Capaccio, *Cap*
Capain, *Chaplin*
Capard, *Cap*
Caparròs
Capart, *Cap*
Capasso, *Cap*
Capdevielle
Capdevila, *Capdevielle*
Capdeville, *Capdevielle*
Cape, *Capper, Chape*
Čapek, *Chaplin*
Capel, *Chape, Chappell*
Capela, *Chappell*
Capelaan, *Kaplan*
Capelain, *Chaplin*
Capelan, *Chaplin*
Capelen, *Chaplin*
Capelin, *Chaplin*
Capeling, *Chaplin*
Capell, *Chape, Chappell*
Capellà, *Chaplin*
Capella, *Chappell*
Capellán, *Chaplin*
Capellaro, *Chape*
Capellé, *Chape*
Capelle, *Chappell*
Capeller, *Chape*
Capellero, *Chape*
Capelletti, *Chape*
Capelli, *Chape*
Capello, *Chape*
Capellozzi, *Chape*
Capelon, *Chape*
Caper, *Chape*
Capéran, *Chaplin*
Caperon, *Capron*
Capers, *Chape*
Capes, *Capper*
Capewell, *Chappell*
Capez, *Chape*
Capilla, *Chappell*
Capinetti, *Jacob*
Capini, *Jacob*
Capitain, *Capitaine*
Capitaine
Capitán, *Capitaine*
Capitan, *Capitaine*
Capitand, *Capitaine*
Capitanelli, *Capitaine*
Capitaneo, *Capitaine*
Capitani, *Capitaine*
Capitanin, *Capitaine*
Capitanio, *Capitaine*
Capitanucci, *Capitaine*
Capiten, *Capitaine*
Caplan, *Kaplan*
Caplen, *Chaplin*
Caplin, *Chaplin*
Caplot, *Chape*
Capo, *Cap*
Capoen, *Capon*
Capoens, *Capon*
Capon
Capone, *Cap, Capon*
Caponi, *Cap, Capon*
Capot, *Chape*
Capote, *Chape*
Capou, *Capon*
Capozzi, *Jacob*
Capp, *Capper*
Cappa, *Chape*
Capparo, *Chape*
Cappe, *Chape*
Cappel, *Chappell*
Cappell, *Chappell*
Cappella, *Chappell*
Cappellari, *Chape*
Cappellaro, *Chape*
Cappelle, *Chappell*
Cappelleri, *Chape*
Cappelletti, *Chape*
Cappelli, *Chape*
Cappellieri, *Chape*
Cappellini, *Chape*
Cappello, *Chape*
Cappellozzi, *Chape*
Cappelluti, *Chape*
Cappellutti, *Chape*
Capper
Cappiello, *Chape*
Cappilli, *Chape*
Cappini, *Chape*
Cappoen, *Capon*
Cappoens, *Capon*
Cappon, *Capon*
Cappone, *Capon*
Capponi, *Capon*
Capppellari, *Chape*
Capps, *Capper*
Cappucci, *Chape*
Cappuccini, *Chape*
Cappuza, *Chape*
Capra, *Cheever*
Caprari, *Cheever*
Capraro, *Cheever*
Capretti, *Cheever*
Caprin, *Cheever*
Caprini, *Cheever*
Caprino, *Cheever*
Caprioli, *Chevreuil*
Capriolo, *Chevreuil*
Capriotti, *Cheever*
Capro, *Cheever*
Capron
Caproni, *Cheever*
Capronnier, *Capron*
Caprotti, *Cheever*
Capruzzi, *Cheever*
Capstack, *Capstick*
Capstake, *Capstick*
Capstick
Captal, *Cheptel*
Capucci, *Chape*
Capucciaro, *Chape*
Capuccini, *Chape*
Capus, *Chapuis*
Caputi, *Cap*
Caputo, *Cap*
Capuyn, *Capon*
Capuyns, *Capon*
Carabajal, *Carballo*
Caraballo, *Carballo*
Caradeau, *Craddock*
Caradec, *Craddock*
Carado, *Craddock*
Caradot, *Craddock*
Carass, *Carus*
Caravajal, *Carballo*
Caravajales, *Carballo*
Carazo, *Caro*
Carbajal, *Carballo*
Carbajo, *Carballo*
Carballeda, *Carballo*
Carballedo, *Carballo*
Carballo
Carberry
Carbery, *Carberry*
Carbó, *Carbonell*
Carbone, *Carbonell*
Carboneau, *Carbonell*
Carbonel, *Carbonell*
Carbonell
Carbonelli, *Carbonell*
Carbonetti, *Carbonell*
Carbonin, *Carbonell*
Carbonini, *Carbonell*
Carbonkel, *Gorfinkel*
Carbonnel, *Carbonell*
Carbry, *Carberry*
Carceller
Carcopino
Card
Cardante, *Carding*
Carde, *Card*
Cardeal, *Cardinal*
Carden, *Carding, Carwardine*
Cardenal, *Cardinal*
Cárdenas
Carder, *Card*
Cardet, *Ciardo*
Cardew
Cardin, *Ciardo*
Cardinaels, *Cardinal*
Cardinal
Cardinale, *Cardinal*
Cardinaletti, *Cardinal*
Cardinali, *Cardinal*
Cardinall, *Cardinal*
Cardinau, *Cardinal*
Cardinaux, *Cardinal*
Cardineau, *Ciardo*
Cardinet, *Ciardo*
Carding
Cardis, *Carruthers*
Cardnell, *Cardinal*
Cardo, *Carding*
Cardoeiro, *Carding*
Cardon, *Carding, Ciardo*
Cardona
Cardone, *Carding*
Cardoni, *Carding*
Cardoso, *Carding*
Cardot, *Ciardo*
Cardou, *Carding*
Cardoux, *Carding*
Cardus, *Carruthers*
Cardwell, *Caldwell*
Cardy, *Cardew*
Careaga
Careau, *Quarrell*
Carel, *Quarrell*
Careless, *Carless*
Carelli, *Caro*
Carello, *Caro*
Caress, *Carus*
Carette, *Charrette*
Caretti, *Caro*
Caretto, *Charrette*

Carew
Carey
Cargill
Cari, *Caro*
Carillo, *Caro*
Carini, *Caro*
Carino, *Caro*
Cariss, *Carus*
Caritat
Caritato, *Caritat*
Carl, *Charles*
Carlavara, *Carnevali*
Carle, *Charles*
Carlens, *Charles*
Carles, *Charles*
Carlesi, *Charles*
Carless
Carlesso, *Charles*
Carlet, *Charles*
Carleton, *Carlton*
Carletti, *Charles*
Carletto, *Charles*
Carlevari, *Carnevali*
Carlevarini, *Carnevali*
Carlevarino, *Carnevali*
Carleveri, *Carnevali*
Carlier, *Charlier*
Carlile, *Carlisle*
Carlill, *Carlisle*
Carlin, *Charles*
Carlin, *Charles*
Carlin
Carliner, *Karlin*
Carlini, *Charles*
Carlino, *Charles*
Carlisi, *Charles*
Carlisle
Carlo, *Charles*
Carlon, *Charles*
Carlone, *Charles*
Carloni, *Charles*
Carlos, *Charles*
Carlotti, *Charles*
Carlotto, *Charles*
Carlozzi, *Charles*
Carlsen, *Charles*
Carlsson, *Charles*
Carlton
Carlucci, *Charles*
Carluccio, *Charles*
Carluzzi, *Charles*
Carlvaro, *Carnevali*
Carlyle, *Carlisle*
Carlyon
Carman
Carmans, *Carman*
Carme, *Carne*
Carmichael
Carmo
Carmody
Carmona
Carmoy, *Charme*
Carnall, *Carnell*
Carnavale, *Carnevali*
Carnduff, *Cairnduff*
Carné
Carne
Carnegie
Carnegy, *Carnegie*
Carneiro, *Carnero*
Carnell
Carnero
Carnes, *Cairns*
Carnevale, *Carnevali*
Carnevali
Carnevalini, *Carnevali*
Carney
Carniceiro, *Carnicero*
Carnicer, *Carnicero*
Carnicero
Carnier, *Carnero*
Carnovale, *Carnevali*
Carnovali, *Carnevali*
Carnoy, *Charme*
Carns, *Cairns*
Carnu, *Carné*
Carnus, *Carné*
Caro
Carolan, *Carlin*
Caroli, *Charles*
Carollo, *Caro*
Caron
Carone, *Caro*
Caronet, *Caron*
Caroni, *Caro*
Caroselli, *Caruso*
Carosello, *Caruso*
Carosi, *Caruso*
Carosiello, *Caruso*
Carosio, *Caruso*
Carosoni, *Caruso*
Carothers, *Carruthers*
Carotti, *Caro*
Carp, *Karpov*
Carpanelli, *Charme*
Carpaneto, *Charme*
Carpanini, *Charme*
Carpano, *Charme*
Carpanoni, *Charme*
Carpe, *Charme*
Carpene, *Charme*
Carpeneti, *Charme*
Carpeneto, *Charme*
Carpenetti, *Charme*
Carpenter
Carpentié, *Carpenter*
Carpentier, *Carpenter*
Carpentiere, *Carpenter*
Carpentieri, *Carpenter*
Carpentiero, *Carpenter*
Carpes, *Karpov*
Carpi, *Charme*
Carpine, *Charme*
Carpinelli, *Charme*
Carpineti, *Charme*
Carpineto, *Charme*
Carpini, *Charme*
Carpino, *Charme*
Carpinteiro, *Carpenter*
Carpinteri, *Carpenter*
Carpintero, *Carpenter*
Carpintieri, *Carpenter*
Carpintiero, *Carpenter*
Carpio
Carr
Carracedo, *Carrizo*
Carradice, *Carruthers*
Carrai, *Carrier*
Carraretto, *Carrier*
Carrari, *Carrier*
Carrarini, *Carrier*
Carraro, *Carrier*
Carraroli, *Carrier*
Carras, *Carus*
Carrascal, *Carrasco*
Carrascó, *Carrasco*
Carrasco
Carrasquilla, *Carrasco*
Carrasquillo, *Carrasco*
Carratié, *Carter*
Carratier, *Carter*
Carré
Carreau, *Quarrell*
Carrec, *Carrier*
Carreira, *Carrière*
Carreiras, *Carrière*
Carreiro, *Carrier*
Carrel, *Quarrell*
Carrelet, *Quarrell*
Carreman, *Carman*
Carrer, *Carrier*
Carrera, *Carrière*
Carreras, *Carrière*
Carrère, *Carrière*
Carreri, *Carrier*
Carrero, *Carrier*
Carreter, *Carter*
Carretero, *Carter*
Carretier, *Carter*
Carrey, *Carré*
Carrez, *Carré*
Carriage, *Kendrick*
Carricchio, *Caro*
Carrick, *Craig*
Carriço, *Carrizo*
Carrié, *Carrier*
Carrier
Carriere, *Carrier*
Carrière
Carrieri, *Carrier*
Carriero, *Carrier*
Carriez, *Carrier*
Carrigy, *McCarrick*
Carrilho, *Carrillo*
Carrillo
Carrington
Carrió, *Carrión*
Carrión
Carriss, *Carus*
Carrizo
Carro, *Carman*
Carrocci, *Caro*
Carrodus, *Carruthers*
Carrol, *Carroll*
Carroll
Carron, *Charron*
Carrothers, *Carruthers*
Carruthers
Carryer, *Carrier*
Carslake
Carson
Carstairs
Carsten, *Christian*
Carstens, *Christian*
Carstensen, *Christian*
Carswell, *Creswell*
Carter
Carteret, *Carter*
Carteron, *Carter*
Carthew, *Cardew*
Cartier, *Carter*
Cartledge
Cartlidge, *Cartledge*
Cartmell
Cartmill, *Cartmell*
Carton, *McCartney*
Cartret, *Carter*
Cartron, *Carter*
Cartwright
Carucci, *Caro*
Caruccio, *Caro*
Carulli, *Caro*
Carullo, *Caro*
Carus
Caruselli, *Caruso*
Carusello, *Caruso*
Carusi, *Caruso*
Carusio, *Caruso*
Caruso
Carusone, *Caruso*
Caruth, *Carruthers*
Carvajal, *Carballo*
Carvajales, *Carballo*
Carvalhal, *Carballo*
Carvalheira, *Carballo*
Carvalho, *Carballo*
Carvell, *Carvill*
Carver
Carvill
Carville, *Carvill*
Carwardine
Cary, *Carey*
Carye, *Carey*
Casa
Casacchia, *Casa*
Casacci, *Casa*
Casaccia, *Casa*
Casaccio, *Casa*
Casado
Casagli, *Casale*
Casaglia, *Casale*
Casal, *Casale*
Casalari, *Casale*
Casalaro, *Casale*
Casale
Casaletti, *Casale*
Casaletto, *Casale*
Casali, *Casale*
Casalin, *Casale*
Casalini, *Casale*
Casalino, *Casale*
Casalone, *Casale*
Casaloni, *Casale*
Casals, *Casale*
Casanova
Casanovas, *Casanova*
Casanueva, *Casanova*
Casar, *Casale*
Casares, *Casale*
Casari, *Cheeseman*
Casaril, *Cheeseman*
Casarile, *Cheeseman*
Casarin, *Cheeseman*
Casarini, *Cheeseman*
Casarino, *Cheeseman*
Casaro, *Cheeseman*
Casaroli, *Cheeseman*
Casas, *Casa*
Casassa, *Casa*
Casaubon
Casazza, *Casa*
Case
Casel, *Casa*
Casella, *Casa*
Casellas, *Casa*
Caselli, *Casa*
Casello, *Casa*
Casement
Caseneuve, *Casanova*
Caser, *Cheeseman*
Caseri, *Cheeseman*
Casero, *Casa*
Cases, *Casa*
Caset, *Casa*
Casetta, *Casa*
Casetti, *Casa*

Casewell, *Creswell*
Casey
Cash, *Case*
Casheen, *McCashin*
Cashen, *McCashin*
Cashin, *McCashin*
Cashion, *McCashin*
Cashman
Cashmore
Casiello, *Casa*
Casier, *Cheeseman*
Casieri, *Cheeseman*
Casiero, *Cheeseman*
Casillas, *Casa*
Casillo, *Casa*
Casimir, *Kaźmierczak*
Casimiro, *Kaźmierczak*
Casin, *Casa*
Casina, *Casa*
Casine, *Casa*
Casini, *Casa*
Casino, *Casa*
Casiroli, *Cheeseman*
Caslake, *Carslake*
Caso, *Casa*
Casola, *Casa*
Casolla, *Casa*
Cason, *Casa*
Casone, *Casa*
Casoni, *Casa*
Casotti, *Casa*
Caspary, *Kaspar*
Casper, *Kaspar*
Casperri, *Kaspar*
Caspers, *Kaspar*
Cass
Cassagnade, *Cassagne*
Cassagnau, *Cassagne*
Cassagne
Cassagnol, *Cassagne*
Cassagnou, *Cassagne*
Cassaigne, *Cassagne*
Cassan, *Cassagne*
Cassard
Cassart, *Cassard*
Cassé, *Casse*
Casse
Cassedy, *Cassidy*
Cassegrain
Cassel, *Castle*
Cassell, *Castle*
Cassells, *Castle*
Cassels, *Castle*
Cassen, *Christian*
Cassens, *Christian*
Casserley, *Cassidy*
Casserly, *Cassidy*
Casses, *Casse*
Casset, *Casse*
Cassidy
Cassie, *Cass*
Cassignol, *Cassagne*
Cassin, *Casse, McCashin*
Cassini, *Casse*
Cassirer, *Case*
Casson, *Cass*
Casswell, *Creswell*
Castagna, *Castan*
Castagnaro, *Castan*
Castagnasso, *Castan*
Castagné, *Castan*
Castagneri, *Castan*
Castagnet, *Castan*
Castagneto, *Castan*
Castagnetta, *Castan*
Castagnetto, *Castan*
Castagnier, *Castan*
Castagno, *Castan*
Castagnoli, *Castan*
Castagnone, *Castan*
Castagnotto, *Castan*
Castaignet, *Castan*
Castaing, *Castan*
Castan
Castana, *Castan*
Castañé, *Castan*
Castañeda, *Castan*
Castañer, *Castan*
Castanet, *Castan*
Castangia, *Castan*
Castanho, *Castan*
Castanié, *Castan*
Castaño, *Castan*
Castañón, *Castan*
Castaños, *Castan*
Castanyer, *Castan*
Castejón
Castel, *Castle*
Castela, *Castille*
Castelain, *Castellan*
Castelan, *Castellan*
Castelão, *Castellan*
Castelari, *Châtelier*
Castelarin, *Châtelier*
Castelarini, *Châtelier*
Castelaro, *Châtelier*
Castel-Branco
Castelein, *Castellan*
Casteleyn, *Castellan*
Castelhano, *Castellan*
Castelijn, *Castellan*
Castelin, *Castellan*
Castell, *Ashkettle*
Castell, *Castle*
Castellà, *Castellan*
Castellacci, *Castle*
Castellaccio, *Castle*
Castellain, *Castellan*
Castellan
Castellani, *Castellan*
Castellano, *Castellan*
Castellanos, *Castellan*
Castellari, *Châtelier*
Castellarin, *Châtelier*
Castellarini, *Châtelier*
Castellaro, *Châtelier*
Castellazzi, *Castle*
Castellazzo, *Castle*
Castellet, *Castle*
Castelletti, *Castle*
Castelletto, *Castle*
Castelli, *Castle*
Castellini, *Castle*
Castellino, *Castle*
Castello, *Castle*
Castellone, *Castle*
Castellotti, *Castle*
Castellotto, *Castle*
Castells, *Castle*
Castellucci, *Castle*
Castelluccio, *Castle*
Castelluzzi, *Castle*
Castelluzzo, *Castle*
Castellví, *Castelvieil*
Castelnau
Castelnovi, *Castelnau*
Castelnovo, *Castelnau*
Castelnuovo, *Castelnau*
Castelo, *Castle*
Castelo-Branco, *Castel-Branco*
Castelot, *Castle*
Castels, *Castle*
Castelvecchi, *Castelvieil*
Castelvecchio, *Castelvieil*
Castelvetri, *Castelvieil*
Castelvetro, *Castelvieil*
Castelvieil
Casterot, *Castle*
Casterou, *Castle*
Castiello, *Castle*
Castiglio, *Castille*
Castiglione, *Castille*
Castiglioni, *Castille*
Castilho, *Castle*
Castilla, *Castille*
Castille
Castillejo, *Castle*
Castillo, *Castle*
Castillón, *Castle*
Castillon, *Castle*
Castillos, *Castle*
Castillou, *Castle*
Castle
Castleman, *Castle*
Castles, *Castle*
Castling, *Castellan*
Castri, *Castro*
Castrillo, *Castro*
Castro
Caswall, *Creswell*
Caswell, *Creswell*
Caswill, *Creswell*
Cata, *Catlin*
Catagnetti, *Castan*
Català, *Catalán*
Catala, *Catalán*
Catalan, *Catalán*
Catalán
Catalani, *Catalán*
Catalano, *Catalán*
Catalanotti, *Catalán*
Catalão, *Catalán*
Catalina, *Catlin*
Catalogne, *Catalán*
Catan, *Katan*
Catanheira, *Castan*
Catarinea, *Catlin*
Catarino, *Catlin*
Cataruzza, *Catlin*
Cataruzzi, *Catlin*
Catchpol, *Catchpole*
Catchpole
Catchpool, *Catchpole*
Catchpoole, *Catchpole*
Catchpoule, *Catchpole*
Cate, *Catlin*
Cateau, *Catlin*
Catelain, *Castellan*
Catelani, *Catalán*
Catelet, *Catlin*
Catelin, *Catlin*
Cateline, *Catlin*
Catelon, *Catlin*
Catelot, *Catlin*
Catenat, *Catlin*
Catenot, *Caton*
Cater
Catera, *Catlin*
Caterin, *Catlin*
Caterina, *Catlin*
Caterine, *Catlin*
Caterini, *Catlin*
Caterino, *Catlin*
Cates
Catesby
Catet, *Catlin*
Cathala, *Catalán*
Cathalan, *Catalán*
Cathcart
Catheau, *Catlin*
Cathelat, *Catlin*
Cathelet, *Catlin*
Cathelin, *Catlin*
Catheline, *Catlin*
Cathelineau, *Catlin*
Cathelon, *Catlin*
Cathelot, *Catlin*
Cathelyn, *Catlin*
Cathenod, *Caton*
Catherall, *Catterall*
Catheraud, *Catlin*
Catherin, *Catlin*
Catherine, *Catlin*
Catherinet, *Catlin*
Catheron, *Catlin*
Catherou, *Catlin*
Catheroux, *Catlin*
Cathet, *Catlin*
Cathrall, *Catterall*
Catillon, *Catlin*
Catin, *Catlin*
Catinat, *Catlin*
Catinaud, *Catlin*
Catineau, *Catlin*
Catlin
Catling, *Catlin*
Caton
Catonné, *Caton*
Catonnet, *Caton*
Cator, *Cater*
Catriene, *Catlin*
Catron, *Catlin*
Catrou, *Catlin*
Catroux, *Catlin*
Cats, *Catt*
Catt
Catta, *Catlin*
Cattagni, *Capitaine*
Cattan, *Katan*
Cattanei, *Capitaine*
Cattaneo, *Capitaine*
Cattani, *Capitaine*
Cattano, *Capitaine*
Cattarin, *Catlin*
Cattarini, *Catlin*
Cattarossi, *Catlin*
Cattaruccia, *Catlin*
Cattarulla, *Catlin*
Catte, *Catlin*
Cattell, *Cadell, Catlin*
Catten, *Catlin*
Cattera, *Catlin*
Catterall
Catterell, *Catterall*
Catterill, *Catterall*
Cattermole
Cattermoul, *Cattermole*
Catteroll, *Catterall*
Cattin, *Catlin*
Cattini, *Catlin*
Cattlin, *Catlin*
Catton
Cattonnet, *Caton*
Cattozzo, *Catlin*
Cattrall, *Catterall*
Cattrell, *Catterall*

Cattroll, *Catterall*
Cattuzza, *Catlin*
Caublance, *Koblenz*
Cauce, *Chausse*
Cauchie, *Chaussée*
Cauchy, *Chaussée*
Caudell, *Caldwell*
Caudle, *Caldwell*
Caudor, *Calder*
Caudwell, *Caldwell*
Cauffin, *Coffin*
Caughey
Caujol, *Cage*
Caujolle, *Cage*
Caulcutt, *Caldicott*
Caulder, *Calder*
Cauldfield, *Caulfield*
Cauldor, *Calder*
Cauldron, *Calderon*
Cauldwell, *Caldwell*
Caulfield
Caulkett, *Caldicott*
Caumont
Caunce, *Chance*
Caunt, *Cant*
Causer, *Chaucer*
Causey
Caussade, *Chaussée*
Causton, *Cawston*
Cava, *Cave*
Caval, *Cavallo*
Cavalacci, *Cavallo*
Cavalcanti
Cavaleiro, *Chevalier*
Cavaletti, *Cavallo*
Cavaletto, *Cavallo*
Cavalheiro, *Chevalier*
Cavalié, *Chevalier*
Cavalier, *Chevalier*
Cavaliere, *Chevalier*
Cavalieri, *Chevalier*
Cavaliero, *Chevalier*
Cavallacci, *Cavallo*
Cavallar, *Chevalier*
Cavallaro, *Chevalier*
Cavalleri, *Chevalier*
Cavallero, *Chevalier*
Cavalli, *Cavallo*
Cavallié, *Chevalier*
Cavallier, *Chevalier*
Cavalliere, *Chevalier*
Cavallieri, *Chevalier*
Cavalliero, *Chevalier*
Cavallin, *Cavallo*
Cavallini, *Cavallo*
Cavallino, *Cavallo*
Cavallio, *Cavallo*
Cavallo
Cavallone, *Cavallo*
Cavallucci, *Cavallo*
Cavalluccio, *Cavallo*
Cavalotti, *Cavallo*
Cavalotto, *Cavallo*
Cavaluzzi, *Cavallo*
Cavan, *Keefe*
Cavana, *Cabane*
Cavanagh, *Kavanagh*
Cavanaugh, *Kavanagh*
Cavani, *Cabane*
Cavanillas, *Cabane*
Cavanna, *Cabane*
Cavanni, *Cabane*
Cavaretta, *Cheever*
Cavari, *Cave*
Cave
Caveau, *Cave*
Cavel, *Cave*
Cavell, *Chaff*
Cavendish
Cavenett
Cavero
Cavestany, *Cabestany*
Cavier, *Cave*
Cavill
Cavin, *Cave*
Cavolini, *Jacob*
Cavoto, *Jacob*
Cavozzi, *Jacob*
Cavra, *Cheever*
Cavrini, *Cheever*
Cavrotti, *Cheever*
Cavrulli, *Cheever*
Cavy, *Cave*
Cawcutt, *Caldicott*
Cawdell, *Caldwell*
Cawker, *Chalk*
Cawley, *McAulay*
Cawood
Cawsey, *Causey*
Cawston
Cawthorn
Cawthorne, *Cawthorn*
Caxton
Cayla, *Châtelier*
Cayley
Cayzer, *Kaiser*
Cazal, *Casale*
Cazalet, *Casale*
Cazalin, *Casale*
Cazaubon, *Casaubon*
Cazaux, *Casale*
Caze, *Casa*
Cazeaux, *Casale*
Cazelle, *Casa*
Cazelles, *Casa*
Cazenave, *Casanova*
Cazenove, *Casanova*
Cazet, *Casa*
Cazette, *Casa*
Cazin, *Casa*
Cazot, *Casa*
Cazotte, *Casa*
Cea
Cebolla
Cebollas, *Cebolla*
Cebollero, *Cebolla*
Cebrià, *Cebrián*
Cebrián
Cecchetelli, *Francis*
Cecchi, *Francis*
Ceccoli, *Francis*
Ceccucci, *Francis*
Ceccuzzi, *Francis*
Čech
Cecil
Cécile, *Sisley*
Cécille, *Sisley*
Cecucci, *Francis*
Ceder
Cederbaum, *Ceder*
Cederberg, *Ceder*
Cederblad, *Ceder*
Cederboim, *Ceder*
Cedergren, *Ceder*
Cederholm, *Ceder*
Cederlöf, *Ceder*
Cederlöv, *Ceder*
Cederlund, *Ceder*
Cederquist, *Ceder*
Cederstrand, *Ceder*
Cederström, *Ceder*
Cederwall, *Ceder*
Cedgren, *Ceder*
Cedlöf, *Ceder*
Cedlöv, *Ceder*
Cedwall, *Ceder*
Ceeley, *Sealey*
Ceely, *Sealey*
Cefariello, *Cifaro*
Cefaro, *Cifaro*
Cegiełkowski, *Cegielski*
Cegielski
Ceiley, *Sealey*
Ceitlin, *Zeitlin*
Ceja
Čejka, *Czajkowski*
Cela, *Celle*
Celada
Célarié, *Seller*
Célarier, *Seller*
Celaya
Célerier, *Seller*
Cella, *Celle*
Cellai, *Celle*
Cellani, *Celle*
Cellari, *Celle*
Celle
Cellerier, *Seller*
Celles, *Celle*
Cellesi, *Celle*
Celletti, *Celle*
Celli, *Celle*
Cellier, *Seller*
Cellin, *Celle*
Cellini, *Celle*
Cellon, *Celle*
Celloni, *Celle*
Cellotto, *Celle*
Cellucci, *Celle*
Celon, *Michael*
Celoni, *Michael*
Cely, *Sealey*
Centeno
Center, *Zehender*
Cenzi, *Vincent*
Cenzon, *Vincent*
Cepeda
Cerasa, *Cerisier*
Cerasi, *Cerisier*
Ceraso, *Cerisier*
Cerasola, *Cerisier*
Cerasoli, *Cerisier*
Cerasuola, *Cerisier*
Cercott, *Circuit*
Cerda
Cereceda, *Cerisier*
Cerera, *Cerisier*
Ceresa, *Cerisier*
Ceresero, *Cerisier*
Cereseto, *Cerisier*
Ceresi, *Cerisier*
Cereso, *Cerisier*
Ceresoli, *Cerisier*
Ceresolo, *Cerisier*
Cereti, *Carrasco*
Cereto, *Carrasco*
Cerezo, *Cerisier*
Cerf
Cerfon, *Cerf*
Cérié, *Cerisier*
Cerisier
Cerisola, *Cerisier*
Cerlin, *Sorin*
Čermák
Černický, *Chernyakov*
Černík, *Chernyakov*
Cernin, *Saturnin*
Černohlávek, *Chernyakov*
Černý, *Chernyakov*
Cerny, *Saturnin*
Cerqueira
Cerrillo, *Cerro*
Cerro
Cersini, *Cerisier*
Cervantes
Červenka, *Czerwiński*
Červeny, *Czerwiński*
Cervera
Cerveró, *Cervera*
Cervi, *Cerf*
Cervini, *Cerf*
Červinka, *Czerwiński*
Cervo, *Cerf*
Cervoni, *Cerf*
César, *Cesare*
Cesar, *Cesare*
Césard, *Cesare*
Cesare
Cesarelli, *Cesare*
Cesari, *Cesare*
Cesarić, *Kaiser*
Cesarin, *Cesare*
Cesarini, *Cesare*
Cesaro, *Cesare*
Cesarone, *Cesare*
Cesaroni, *Cesare*
Cesarotti, *Cesare*
Ceschelli, *Francis*
Ceschi, *Francis*
Ceschini, *Francis*
Cesco, *Francis*
Cescon, *Francis*
Cesconi, *Francis*
Cescot, *Francis*
Cescotti, *Francis*
Céspedes
Ceyssen, *Francis*
Cézanne
Cézar, *Cesare*
Cézard, *Cesare*
Chabanas, *Cabane*
Chabanat, *Cabane*
Chabane, *Cabane*
Chabaneix, *Cabane*
Chabanes, *Cabane*
Chabanet, *Cabane*
Chabanier, *Cabane*
Chabanne, *Cabane*
Chabannes, *Cabane*
Chabanon, *Cabane*
Chabre, *Cheever*
Chabres, *Cheever*
Chabri, *Cheever*
Chabrié, *Cheever*
Chabrier, *Cheever*
Chabrol, *Chevreuil*
Chabrolle, *Chevreuil*
Chabroullet, *Chevreuil*
Chabroux, *Chevreuil*
Chace, *Chase*
Chacón
Chadash, *Chodosh*
Chaddock, *Chadwick*
Chaderton, *Chatterton*
Chadwell, *Caldwell*
Chadwick

Chadwyck, *Chadwick*
Chafen, *Chaff*
Chaff
Chaffe, *Chaff*
Chaffin, *Chaff*
Chagal, *Segal*
Chagall, *Segal*
Chagas
Chagne, *Chêne*
Chagneaux, *Chêne*
Chagnol, *Chêne*
Chagnon, *Chêne*
Chagnot, *Chêne*
Chagnoux, *Chêne*
Chaifetz, *Heifetz*
Chaigne, *Chêne*
Chaikovski, *Czajkowski*
Chaillet, *Cail*
Chaillot, *Cail*
Chaillou, *Cail*
Chaillouet, *Cail*
Chailloux, *Cail*
Chaim, *Hyam*
Chaimsohn, *Hyam*
Chaimson, *Hyam*
Chainey, *Chêne*
Chaise, *Casa*
Chait
Chaitchik, *Chait*
Chaitin, *Chait*
Chaitow, *Chait*
Chaitowitz, *Chait*
Chaize, *Casa*
Chajat, *Chait*
Chajczuk, *Chait*
Chajczyk, *Chait*
Chalamel, *Challamel*
Chalamelle, *Challamel*
Chalamet, *Challamel*
Chalcot, *Caldicott*
Chaldcott, *Caldicott*
Chalice, *Challis*
Chalk
Chalke, *Chalk*
Chalker, *Chalk*
Chalkley
Challace, *Challis*
Challamel
Challen, *Challenor*
Challender, *Challenor*
Challener, *Challenor*
Challenor
Challens, *Challenor*
Challes, *Challis*
Challice, *Challis*
Challin, *Challenor*
Challinor, *Challenor*
Challis
Challiss, *Challis*
Challoner, *Challenor*
Chalmers
Chaloner, *Challenor*
Chalonin, *Bartholomew*
Chaloupek
Chaloupka, *Chaloupek*
Chaloupník, *Chaloupek*
Chalumeau, *Challamel*
Chalupa, *Chaloupek*
Chalupník, *Chaloupek*
Chalve, *Chaff*
Chalveron, *Chaff*
Chalvet, *Chaff*
Chalvin, *Chaff*
Chalvon, *Chaff*
Chalvron, *Chaff*
Chambellan, *Chamberlain*
Chambelland, *Chamberlain*
Chamberlain
Chamberlaine, *Chamberlain*
Chamberland, *Chamberlain*
Chamberlayne, *Chamberlain*
Chamberlen, *Chamberlain*
Chamberlin, *Chamberlain*
Chambers
Chambet, *Gambe*
Chambin, *Gambe*
Chambly, *Cholmondeley*
Chambonneau, *Gambe*
Chambonnet, *Gambe*
Chambras, *Chambers*
Chambre, *Chambers*
Chambrier, *Chambers*
Chamin, *Chemin*
Chamizo
Chamorro
Champ
Champagne, *Champney*
Champaigne, *Champney*
Champain, *Champney*
Champeau, *Champ*
Champeaux, *Champ*
Champeix, *Champ*
Champel, *Champ*
Champenois, *Champney*
Champerlen, *Chamberlain*
Champet, *Champ*
Champion, *Campion*
Championnet, *Campion*
Champness, *Champney*
Champney
Champneys, *Champney*
Champniss, *Champney*
Champollion, *Champouillon*
Champon, *Champ*
Champonnet, *Champ*
Champonnois, *Champney*
Champot, *Champ*
Champouillon
Champs, *Champ*
Chanal, *Chenal*
Chanau, *Chenal*
Chanault, *Chenal*
Chance
Chancelier, *Chancellor*
Chancellor
Chandelier, *Chandler*
Chandler
Chandlish, *McCandless*
Chaneles, *Hanna*
Chaney, *Chêne*
Chanin, *Hanna*
Chankin, *Hanna*
Chanlewicz, *Hanna*
Channer, *Challenor*
Channon
Chanoine, *Cannon*
Chanson
Chant, *Cant*
Chantalou, *Cantellow*
Chantaloup, *Cantellow*
Chantelouve, *Cantellow*
Chanter, *Cant*
Chanteraine
Chanterenne, *Chanteraine*
Chantler, *Chandler*
Chantraine, *Chanteraine*
Chantreine, *Chanteraine*
Chanu, *Chenu*
Chanudet, *Chenu*
Chanut, *Chenu*
Chapaev
Chapé, *Chape*
Chape
Chapeau, *Chape*
Chapel, *Chape*
Chapelain, *Chaplin*
Chapelet, *Chape*
Chapelier, *Chape*
Chapelin, *Chaplin*
Chapell, *Chappell*
Chapelle, *Chappell*
Chapellier, *Chape*
Chaperlin, *Chaplin*
Chaperling, *Chaplin*
Chaperon, *Capron*
Chapet, *Chape*
Chapey, *Chape*
Chapez, *Chape*
Chapier, *Chape*
Chapiro, *Shapiro*
Chapla, *Chaplin*
Chaplain, *Chaplin*
Chapleteau, *Chape*
Chaplin
Chapling, *Chaplin*
Chaplot, *Chape*
Chapman
Chapon, *Capon*
Chaponeau, *Capon*
Chaponet, *Capon*
Chappe, *Chape*
Chappel, *Chappell*
Chappell
Chappelle, *Chappell*
Chapper, *Chapman*
Chapple, *Chappell*
Chappon, *Capon*
Chapponeau, *Capon*
Chapponet, *Capon*
Chapron, *Capron*
Chaptal, *Cheptel*
Chapu, *Chape*
Chapuis
Chapuisat, *Chapuis*
Chapuiseau, *Chapuis*
Chapuiset, *Chapuis*
Chapuisot, *Chapuis*
Chapus, *Chapuis*
Chapuset, *Chapuis*
Chapusot, *Chapuis*
Chaput, *Chape*
Chapuzet, *Chapuis*
Chapuzot, *Chapuis*
Charameau, *Challamel*
Charamon, *Challamel*
Charater, *Carter*
Charbonel, *Carbonell*
Charbonell, *Carbonell*
Charbonneau, *Carbonell*
Charbonneaux, *Carbonell*
Charbonnet, *Carbonell*
Chard, *Chart*
Chardel, *Ciardo*
Chardenot, *Carding*
Chardet, *Ciardo*
Chardin, *Ciardo*
Chardineau, *Ciardo*
Chardon, *Carding, Ciardo*
Chardoneau, *Carding*
Chardonel, *Carding*
Chardonet, *Carding*
Chardonnay, *Carding*
Chardonneau, *Carding*
Chardonnel, *Carding*
Chardonnet, *Carding*
Chardonnière, *Carding*
Chardonnot, *Carding*
Chardot, *Ciardo*
Chardron, *Carding*
Chardy, *Ciardo*
Chareour, *Carrier*
Chareter, *Carter*
Charette, *Charrette*
Charle, *Charles*
Charles
Charleston, *Charles*
Charlesworth
Charlet, *Charles*
Charleton, *Charlton*
Charley, *Charles*
Charlier
Charlin, *Charles*
Charlo, *Charles*
Charlon, *Charles*
Charlot, *Charles*
Charlton
Charmay, *Charme*
Charme
Charmes, *Charme*
Charmet, *Charme*
Charmey, *Charme*
Charmoy, *Charme*
Charne, *Charme*
Charnes, *Chernyakov*
Charney, *Chernyakov*
Charni, *Chernyakov*
Charniak, *Chernyakov*
Charnietzky, *Chernyakov*
Charnley
Charnobroda, *Chernyakov*
Charnock
Charnu, *Carné*
Charnut, *Carné*
Charny, *Chernyakov*
Charnyak, *Chernyakov*
Charnylas, *Chernyakov*
Charpantier, *Carpenter*
Charpenay, *Charme*
Charpentereau, *Carpenter*
Charpentier, *Carpenter*
Charpentreau, *Carpenter*
Charraire, *Carrière*
Charrandier, *Charron*
Charrayre, *Carrière*
Charretier, *Carter*
Charrette
Charreyre, *Carrière*
Charreyron, *Carrière*
Charrier, *Carrier*
Charrière, *Carrière*
Charrington, *Cherrington*
Charron
Charrondier, *Charron*
Chart
Charter, *Carter*
Charteris
Charters, *Charteris*
Chartier, *Carter*
Chartres, *Charteris*
Charvát, *Horváth*
Charve, *Chaff*
Charvet, *Chaff*
Charvin, *Chaff*
Chasan, *Chazan*
Chasanoff, *Chazan*
Chase, *Casa*

Chase
Chasen, *Chazan*
Chasier, *Cheeseman*
Chasin, *Chazan*
Chasinoff, *Chazan*
Chasins, *Chazan*
Chaskelovic, *Ezekiel*
Chasle, *Charles*
Chasles, *Charles*
Chasnoff, *Chazan*
Chason, *Chazan*
Chassagne, *Cassagne*
Chassagnol, *Cassagne*
Chassaigne, *Cassagne*
Chassaing, *Cassagne*
Chassan, *Cassagne*
Chassang, *Cassagne*
Chassant, *Cassagne*
Chasseigne, *Cassagne*
Chasseur, *Chase*
Chassin, *Cassagne*
Chassinat, *Cassagne*
Chastagnier, *Castan*
Chastaing, *Castan*
Chastan, *Castan*
Chastand, *Castan*
Chastanet, *Castan*
Chastang, *Castan*
Chasteau, *Castle*
Chastel, *Castle*
Chastelain, *Castellan*
Chastellain, *Castellan*
Chastenet, *Castan*
Chaster, *Chester*
Chaston, *Castan*
Chataigneaux, *Castan*
Châtaignier, *Castan*
Chataignon, *Castan*
Châtaignoux, *Castan*
Chatain, *Castan*
Châtainier, *Castan*
Chatal, *Cheptel*
Château, *Castle*
Chateau, *Cheptel*
Chateaubriand
Châteauneuf, *Castelnau*
Châteauvieux, *Castelvieil*
Châtel, *Castle*
Châtelain, *Castellan*
Chatelain, *Castellan*
Châtelet, *Castle*
Châtelier
Chatellier, *Châtelier*
Châtelot, *Castle*
Châtenay, *Castan*
Châtenet, *Castan*
Chatenier, *Castan*
Chater, *Cater*
Chatfield
Chatham
Chatin, *Castan*
Chatres, *Charteris*
Chatt, *Catt*
Chattaway
Chatteris, *Charteris*
Chatterley
Chatters, *Charteris*
Chatterton
Chatto
Chattock, *Chadwick*
Chatwin, *Chetwynd*
Chaucer
Chaudrelle, *Calderon*
Chaudret, *Calderon*
Chaudron, *Calderon*
Chaulk, *Chalk*
Chaulme, *Chaume*
Chaulmes, *Chaume*
Chaumat, *Chaume*
Chaume
Chaumeil, *Chaume*
Chaumeix, *Chaume*
Chaumel, *Chaume*
Chaumet, *Chaume*
Chaumeton, *Chaume*
Chaumette, *Chaume*
Chaumié, *Chaume*
Chaumier, *Chaume*
Chaumillon, *Chaume*
Chaumont, *Caumont*
Chaumot, *Chaume*
Chaunce, *Chance*
Chausard, *Chausse*
Chauser, *Chaucer*
Chaussaire, *Chausse*
Chaussat, *Chausse*
Chaussé, *Chausse*
Chausse
Chaussec, *Chausse*
Chaussée
Chaussier, *Chausse*
Chausson, *Chausse*
Chaustov, *Faust*
Chauvard, *Chaff*
Chauvat, *Chaff*
Chauve, *Chaff*
Chauveau, *Chaff*
Chauvel, *Chaff*
Chauvelet, *Chaff*
Chauvelin, *Chaff*
Chauvelon, *Chaff*
Chauvelot, *Chaff*
Chauvenet, *Chaff*
Chauveron, *Chaff*
Chauvet, *Chaff*
Chauvillon, *Chaff*
Chauvin, *Chaff*
Chauvineau, *Chaff*
Chauvon, *Chaff*
Chauvron, *Chaff*
Chavalier, *Chevalier*
Chavallier, *Chevalier*
Chavane, *Cabane*
Chavaneau, *Cabane*
Chavanel, *Cabane*
Chavanes, *Cabane*
Chavanne, *Cabane*
Chavannes, *Cabane*
Chávarri, *Echeverría*
Chavarría, *Echeverría*
Chavau, *Cavallo*
Chavaux, *Cavallo*
Chave, *Chaff*
Chavenon, *Cabane*
Chaves
Chavialle, *Capdevielle*
Chavkin, *Khavke*
Chawner, *Challenor*
Chayat, *Chait*
Chaytor, *Cater*
Chazal, *Casale*
Chazan
Chazanoff, *Chazan*
Chazanow, *Chazan*
Chazaux, *Casale*
Chazelle, *Casa*
Chazelles, *Casa*
Chazen, *Chazan*
Chazerand, *Cheeseman*
Chazereau, *Cheeseman*
Chazet, *Casa*
Chazette, *Casa*
Chazier, *Cheeseman*
Chazot, *Casa*
Chazotte, *Casa*
Ché, *Cap*
Cheadle
Cheak, *Cheek*
Cheake, *Cheek*
Cheasman, *Cheeseman*
Cheater
Cheatham, *Cheetham*
Chebanier, *Cabane*
Checchetelli, *Francis*
Checchi, *Francis*
Checcucci, *Francis*
Checkley
Checo, *Francis*
Checucci, *Francis*
Chédeville, *Capdevielle*
Cheek
Cheeke, *Cheek*
Cheeld, *Child*
Cheenay, *Chêne*
Cheeper, *Chapman*
Cheesbrough
Cheese, *Cheeseman*
Cheeseman
Cheeseright, *Cheeseman*
Cheesewright, *Cheeseman*
Cheesman, *Cheeseman*
Cheeswright, *Cheeseman*
Cheetham
Cheever
Cheevers, *Cheever*
Chef, *Cap*
Chefdeville, *Capdevielle*
Chefetz, *Heifetz*
Cheftel, *Cheptel*
Chegwin
Chegwyn, *Chegwin*
Cheifetz, *Heifetz*
Cheke, *Cheek*
Chekhov, *Čech*
Chelazzi, *Michael*
Chelon, *Michael*
Cheloni, *Michael*
Cheltzov, *Cherntsov*
Chemin
Chemineau, *Chemin*
Cheminel, *Chemin*
Chênai, *Chêne*
Chênais, *Chêne*
Chenal
Chenau, *Chenal*
Chenaud, *Chenal*
Chenault, *Chenal*
Chenaux, *Chenal*
Chenay, *Chêne*
Chêne
Chéneau, *Chêne*
Chénel, *Chêne*
Chênelot, *Chêne*
Chenery, *Chêne*
Chénet, *Chêne*
Chenevier
Cheney, *Chêne*
Chénier, *Chêne*
Chénière, *Chêne*
Chénières, *Chêne*
Chennevier, *Chenevier*
Chênois, *Chêne*
Chénot, *Chêne*
Chenoweth
Chênoy, *Chêne*
Chentsov, *Cherntsov*
Chenu
Chenudeau, *Chenu*
Chenueau, *Chenu*
Chenuet, *Chenu*
Chenuil, *Chenu*
Chenut, *Chenu*
Cheptel
Cherbonneau, *Carbonell*
Cherici, *Clark*
Cheriton, *Cherrington*
Chernakov, *Chernyakov*
Chernavin, *Chernyakov*
Chernenko, *Chernyakov*
Chernev, *Chernyakov*
Cherniak, *Chernyakov*
Chernichowsky, *Chernyakov*
Chernigin, *Chernyakov*
Chernik, *Chernyakov*
Chernishev, *Chernyakov*
Chernobelski, *Chernyakov*
Chernomorski, *Chernyakov*
Chernomorsky, *Chernyakov*
Chernov, *Chernyakov*
Chernovsky, *Chernyakov*
Cherntsov
Chernukhin, *Chernyakov*
Cherny, *Chernyakov*
Chernyaev, *Chernyakov*
Chernyagin, *Chernyakov*
Chernyak, *Chernyakov*
Chernyakin, *Chernyakov*
Chernyakov
Chernyatin, *Chernyakov*
Chernyonok, *Chernyakov*
Chernyshevski, *Chernyakov*
Chernyshyov, *Chernyakov*
Chéron, *Caron*
Cheroneau, *Caron*
Cheronnet, *Caron*
Cherrett, *Cheeseman*
Cherrie, *Cherry*
Cherriman, *Cherry*
Cherrington
Cherritt, *Cheeseman*
Cherry
Cherryman, *Cherry*
Cheseldine
Cheseman, *Cheeseman*
Chesher, *Cheshire*
Cheshir, *Cheshire*
Cheshire
Chesier, *Cheeseman*
Chesman, *Cheeseman*
Chesnais, *Chêne*
Chesnay, *Chêne*
Chesné, *Chêne*
Chesne, *Chêne*
Chesneau, *Chêne*
Chesnel, *Chêne*
Chesnet, *Chêne*
Chesnier, *Chêne*
Chesnière, *Chêne*
Chesnot, *Chêne*
Chesnoy, *Chêne*
Chesser, *Cheshire*
Chesshire, *Cheshire*
Chesshyre, *Cheshire*
Chessman, *Cheeseman*
Chessor, *Cheshire*
Chesswright, *Cheeseman*

Chester
Chesters, *Chester*
Chesterton
Chestworth
Cheswright, *Cheeseman*
Cheteau, *Cheptel*
Chétel, *Cheptel*
Chetter, *Cheater*
Chettle, *Cheadle*
Chetwode
Chetwood, *Chetwode*
Chetwynd
Cheuret, *Cheever*
Cheval, *Cavallo*
Chevalard, *Cavallo*
Chevaleau, *Cavallo*
Chevalet, *Cavallo*
Chevalier
Chevalin, *Cavallo*
Chevallard, *Cavallo*
Chevallereau, *Chevalier*
Chevalleret, *Chevalier*
Chevallet, *Cavallo*
Chevalley, *Cavallo*
Chevalon, *Cavallo*
Chevau, *Cavallo*
Chevaux, *Cavallo*
Cheverall, *Cheever*
Cheverell, *Cheever*
Cheverill, *Cheever*
Chevers, *Cheever*
Chevin, *Chaff*
Chèvre, *Cheever*
Chevreau, *Cheever*
Chevrel, *Cheever*
Chevret, *Cheever*
Chevretot, *Cheever*
Chevreuil
Chevreul, *Chevreuil*
Chevreux, *Cheever*
Chevrey, *Cheever*
Chevrier, *Cheever*
Chevrill, *Cheever*
Chevrillon, *Cheever*
Chevrolet, *Chevreuil*
Chevrolier, *Chevreuil*
Chevrollat, *Chevreuil*
Chevrollier, *Chevreuil*
Chevrot, *Cheever*
Chew
Cheyne, *Chêne*
Cheyney, *Chêne*
Chèze, *Casa*
Chezel, *Casale*
Chézelle, *Casa*
Chézelles, *Casa*
Chezier, *Cheeseman*
Chiabra, *Cheever*
Chiabrero, *Cheever*
Chiara, *Clare*
Chiarella, *Clare*
Chiarelli, *Clare*
Chiari, *Clare*
Chiariello, *Clare*
Chiarini, *Clare*
Chiarizia, *Claridge*
Chiaro, *Clare*
Chiaroni, *Clare*
Chiarotti, *Clare*
Chiarulli, *Clare*
Chiarutti, *Clare*
Chicchelli, *Francis*
Chicco, *Francis*
Chicharro
Chichester
Chick
Chicken, *Chick*
Chico
Chicote, *Chico*
Chicotti, *Francis*
Chidgley
Chiechio, *Francis*
Chieco, *Francis*
Chierego, *Clark*
Chiericetti, *Clark*
Chierici, *Clark*
Chiese, *Cheeseman*
Chiesman, *Cheeseman*
Chièze, *Casa*
Chilcott
Child
Childe, *Child*
Childerhouse, *Childers*
Childers
Childress, *Childers*
Childs, *Child*
Chiles, *Child*
Chill, *Child*
Chilles, *Child*
Chilton
Chilver
Chilvers, *Chilver*
Chimenti, *Clement*
Chimienti, *Clement*
Chinery, *Chêne*
Chinn
Chinnery, *Chêne*
Chiommienti, *Clement*
Chiorri, *Melchior*
Chiorrini, *Melchior*
Chipman, *Chapman*
Chippendale
Chipper, *Chapman*
Chipperfield
Chippindale, *Chippendale*
Chippindall, *Chippendale*
Chirac
Chirurg, *Surgeon*
Chisholm
Chisholme, *Chisholm*
Chisman, *Cheeseman*
Chismon, *Cheeseman*
Chisnall
Chisolm, *Chisholm*
Chiswell
Chittenden
Chittey, *Chitty*
Chitteye, *Chitty*
Chittie, *Chitty*
Chittock, *Chitty*
Chitty
Chiumenti, *Clement*
Chiva
Chiverall, *Cheever*
Chiverell, *Cheever*
Chivers, *Cheever*
Chivrall, *Cheever*
Chlebowski, *Khlebnikov*
Chmel, *Chmielewski*
Chmela, *Chmielewski*
Chmelař, *Chmielewski*
Chmelenský, *Chmielewski*
Chmelíček, *Chmielewski*
Chmelík, *Chmielewski*
Chmiel, *Chmielewski*
Chmiela, *Chmielewski*
Chmielecki, *Chmielewski*
Chmielewski
Chmieliński, *Chmielewski*
Chmielnicki, *Chmielewski*
Chmielowiec, *Chmielewski*
Choc, *Choque*
Chocq, *Choque*
Chocque, *Choque*
Chodakowski
Chodkiewicz, *Théodore*
Chodosh
Chodźko, *Théodore*
Choice
Choise, *Choice*
Choiseul
Chojnacki
Chojnowski, *Chojnacki*
Chol, *Kohl*
Cholain, *Kohl*
Cholé, *Kohl*
Choleau, *Kohl*
Cholet, *Kohl*
Cholewicki, *Cholewiński*
Cholewiński
Cholier, *Kohl*
Cholin, *Kohl*
Chollet, *Kohl*
Cholley, *Kohl*
Chollez, *Kohl*
Chollier, *Kohl*
Cholmeley, *Cholmondeley*
Cholmondeley
Cholomin, *Bartholomew*
Cholot, *Kohl*
Choloux, *Kohl*
Cholton, *Chorlton*
Cholwell, *Caldwell*
Chomel, *Chaume*
Chomet, *Chaume*
Chomette, *Chaume*
Chomicki, *Thomas*
Chomicz, *Thomas*
Chomiński, *Thomas*
Chomiszewski, *Thomas*
Chomont, *Caumont*
Chomski, *Chomsky*
Chomsky
Choneau, *Michael*
Choneaux, *Michael*
Chonet, *Michael*
Chonez, *Michael*
Chonillon, *Michael*
Chonneau, *Michael*
Chonneaux, *Michael*
Chopin
Chopinel, *Chopin*
Chopinet, *Chopin*
Choppen, *Chopin*
Choppin, *Chopin*
Chopping, *Chopin*
Chopy, *Chopin*
Choquard, *Choque*
Choque
Choqueneau, *Choque*
Choquenet, *Choque*
Choquet, *Choque*
Chorley
Chorlton
Chorni, *Chernyakov*
Chorny, *Chernyakov*
Chossaire, *Chausse*
Chossec, *Chausse*
Chou, *Kohl*
Chouan
Chouanard, *Chouan*
Chouard, *Chouan*
Chouet, *Chouan*
Chouette, *Chouan*
Choulet, *Kohl*
Choupin, *Chopin*
Chouque, *Such*
Chouvet, *Chaff*
Chouvin, *Chaff*
Choux, *Kohl*
Choveau, *Chaff*
Chovel, *Chaff*
Chovet, *Chaff*
Chovin, *Chaff*
Choyce, *Choice*
Choyse, *Choice*
Chrestian, *Christian*
Chrestin, *Christian*
Chrétien, *Christian*
Chrétinat, *Christian*
Chrichton, *Creighton*
Chrismas, *Christmas*
Chrisp, *Crisp*
Chrispin, *Crispin*
Christaen, *Christian*
Christaller, *Christian*
Christauffour, *Christopher*
Christensen, *Christian*
Christensson, *Christian*
Christey, *Christian*
Christiaens, *Christian*
Christian
Christiane, *Christian*
Christiansen, *Christian*
Christiansson, *Christian*
Christie, *Christian*
Christin, *Christian*
Christiné, *Christian*
Christine, *Christian*
Christinet, *Christian*
Christison, *Christian*
Christler, *Christian*
Christmas
Christofe, *Christopher*
Christoffe, *Christopher*
Christoffels, *Christopher*
Christoffer, *Christopher*
Christofides, *Christopher*
Christofle, *Christopher*
Christofol, *Christopher*
Christofor, *Christopher*
Christoforou, *Christopher*
Christol, *Christopher*
Christon, *Christopher*
Christophe, *Christopher*
Christopher
Christophers, *Christopher*
Christophersen, *Christopher*
Christopherson, *Christopher*
Christophle, *Christopher*
Christou, *Christian, Christopher*
Christy, *Christian*
Chroust, *Khrushchev*
Chruściel
Chruścielewski, *Chruściel*
Chrystal, *Cristal*
Chrystall, *Cristal*
Chrzanowski
Chrząszcz, *Khrushchev*
Chrząszczyński, *Khrushchev*
Chuanard, *Chouan*
Chuant, *Chouan*
Chuard, *Chouan*
Chuat, *Chouan*
Chubb
Chuck, *Such*

Chucks, *Such*
Chudzik
Chue, *Chew*
Chuet, *Chouan*
Chuette, *Chouan*
Chumbly, *Cholmondeley*
Chumley, *Cholmondeley*
Chupin, *Chopin*
Church
Churchard, *Churchyard*
Churcher, *Church*
Churchill
Churchman, *Church*
Churchyard
Churm
Chwedko, *Théodore*
Chwedkowski, *Théodore*
Chynoweth, *Chenoweth*
Ciabatteri, *Savatier*
Ciambellani, *Chamberlain*
Ciamberlini, *Chamberlain*
Cianelli, *John*
Ciani, *John*
Cianni, *John*
Ciardelli, *Ciardo*
Ciardello, *Ciardo*
Ciardetti, *Ciardo*
Ciardi, *Ciardo*
Ciardiello, *Ciardo*
Ciardin, *Ciardo*
Ciardini, *Ciardo*
Ciardo
Ciardon, *Ciardo*
Ciardone, *Ciardo*
Ciardulli, *Ciardo*
Ciardullo, *Ciardo*
Cibotaru, *Savatier*
Cibrario, *Cheever*
Cibula, *Zwiebel*
Cibulka, *Zwiebel*
Cibulski, *Zwiebel*
Ciccetti, *Francis*
Cicchetto, *Francis*
Cicchillo, *Francis*
Cicchinelli, *Francis*
Cicchini, *Francis*
Cicchitello, *Francis*
Cicci, *Francis*
Cicciotti, *Francis*
Ciccitti, *Francis*
Cicco, *Francis*
Ciccolini, *Francis*
Ciccolo, *Francis*
Cicconetti, *Francis*
Ciccotti, *Francis*
Ciccottini, *Francis*
Cicculi, *Francis*
Cicetti, *Francis*
Cichecki, *Cichy*
Cichle, *Keighley*
Cichocki, *Cichy*
Cichoń, *Cichy*
Cichończyk, *Cichy*
Cichosz, *Cichy*
Cichowicz, *Cichy*
Cichy
Cicile, *Sisley*
Cicille, *Sisley*
Cicolini, *Francis*
Cicotti, *Francis*
Cicottini, *Francis*
Cicullo, *Francis*
Cicutto, *Francis*
Cid
Ciervo, *Cerf*
Ciesielski, *Cieślak*
Cieśla, *Cieślak*
Cieślak
Cieslar, *Cieślak*
Cieślewicz, *Cieślak*
Cieślik, *Cieślak*
Cifarelli, *Cifaro*
Cifariello, *Cifaro*
Cifaro
Cifero, *Cifaro*
Cifuentes
Cigler, *Ziegler*
Čihák
Cihelka, *Ziegler*
Cihlář, *Cegielski*
Cimbal, *Zimbalist*
Cimbalist, *Zimbalist*
Cimbalista, *Zimbalist*
Cimerman, *Zimmermann*
Cimmermann, *Zimmermann*
Cinefra, *Juniper*
Cinelli, *Francis*
Cino, *Francis*
Cioban, *Ciobanu*
Ciobanu
Ciobotaro, *Savatier*
Ciobotaru, *Savatier*
Ciobutaro, *Savatier*
Ciobutaru, *Savatier*
Ciotto, *Francis*
Cipolla, *Cebolla*
Cipran, *Cebrián*
Ciprano, *Cebrián*
Cipriano, *Cebrián*
Ciraldo, *Garrett*
Cirasa, *Cerisier*
Ciraso, *Cerisier*
Circuit
Císař, *Kaiser*
Císarovský, *Kaiser*
Cisco, *Francis*
Cisneros
Cissen, *Francis*
Ciszewski
Citrin, *Citroen*
Citrinbaum, *Citroen*
Citroen
Citron, *Citroen*
Citronowicz, *Citroen*
City
Ciubutaro, *Savatier*
Ciurana
Čížek, *Czyż*
Claasen, *Klaus*
Claasens, *Klaus*
Clachar
Clacher, *Clachar*
Clack
Claesen, *Klaus*
Claesens, *Klaus*
Claeskens, *Klaus*
Claessens, *Klaus*
Claesson, *Klaus*
Claffey
Claffy, *Claffey*
Clague, *Clegg*
Clair, *Clare*
Claire, *Clare*
Clairet, *Clare*
Clairin, *Clare*
Clairot, *Clare*
Clake, *Cleak*
Clamp
Clancy
Clap, *Clapp*
Clapham
Claplin, *McLachlan*
Clapp
Clappe, *Clapp*
Clappison, *Clapp*
Clapson, *Clapp*
Clar, *Clare*
Clara, *Clare*
Clarage, *Claridge*
Claramunt, *Clermont*
Clare
Claret, *Clare*
Claretti, *Clare*
Clarey, *Clare*
Clarges
Clargis, *Clarges*
Clari, *Clare*
Clarice, *Claridge*
Claridge
Clarin, *Clare*
Clarini, *Clare*
Claris, *Claridge*
Clariss, *Claridge*
Clarisse, *Claridge*
Clarisseau, *Claridge*
Clarizia, *Claridge*
Clark
Clarke, *Clark*
Clarkins, *Cleary*
Clarkson, *Clark*
Clarkstone, *Clark*
Claro, *Clare*
Claron, *Clare*
Clarot, *Clare*
Clarotti, *Clare*
Clarson, *Clark*
Clasbery, *Clasby*
Clasbey, *Clasby*
Clasbie, *Clasby*
Clasbury, *Clasby*
Clasby
Clasbye, *Clasby*
Clasen, *Klaus*
Classen, *Klaus*
Classon, *Klaus*
Clatworthy
Claud, *Claude*
Claude
Claudel, *Claude*
Claudet, *Claude*
Claudin, *Claude*
Claudino, *Claude*
Cláudio, *Claude*
Claudon, *Claude*
Claudot, *Claude*
Claughton
Claus, *Close, Klaus*
Clausen, *Klaus*
Clausewitz, *Klaus*
Clausius, *Klaus*
Claussen, *Klaus*
Claux, *Claude, Close*
Clauzel, *Close*
Clauzet, *Close*
Clauzié, *Close*
Clauzier, *Close*
Clauzin, *Close*
Clavareau, *Clavero*
Claveau, *Cravo*
Clavel, *Cravo*
Claver, *Clavero*
Clavereau, *Clavero*
Clavero
Clavié, *Clavero*
Clavier, *Clavero*
Claxton
Clay
Clayden, *Claydon*
Claydon
Claye, *Clay*
Clayman, *Clay*
Clayton
Cleak
Cleake, *Cleak*
Clear, *Clare*
Cleare, *Clare*
Cleary
Cleatherow, *Clitheroe*
Cleave, *Clive*
Cleaver
Cleaves, *Clive*
Clee
Cleeick, *Cleak*
Cleek, *Cleak*
Cleeke, *Cleak*
Cleene, *Klein*
Cleeve
Cleever, *Cleaver*
Cleeves, *Cleeve*
Cleft, *Clift*
Clegg
Cleghorn
Cleik, *Cleak*
Cleike, *Cleak*
Cleke, *Cleak*
Cleland
Clelland, *Cleland*
Clem, *Clement*
Clemanceau, *Clement*
Clemançon, *Clement*
Clemans, *Clement*
Clemas, *Clement*
Clemen, *Clement*
Clémence, *Clement*
Clemence, *Clement*
Clemenceau, *Clement*
Clemencet, *Clement*
Clemençon, *Clement*
Clemendet, *Clement*
Clemendot, *Clement*
Clemens, *Clement*
Clemensen, *Clement*
Clemenson, *Clement*
Clément, *Clement*
Clement
Clemente, *Clement*
Clémentel, *Clement*
Clémentet, *Clement*
Clementi, *Clement*
Clementini, *Clement*
Clements, *Clement*
Clementson, *Clement*
Clementucci, *Clement*
Clemenza, *Clement*
Clemenzi, *Clement*
Clemenzo, *Clement*
Clemerson, *Clement*
Clemetson, *Clement*
Clemett, *Clement*
Clemetts, *Clement*
Cleminson, *Clement*
Clemitt, *Clement*
Clemm, *Clement*
Clemmans, *Clement*
Clemmen, *Clement*
Clemmens, *Clement*

Clemmensen, *Clement*
Clemmey, *Clement*
Clemmo, *Clement*
Clemmow, *Clement*
Clemo, *Clement*
Clemons, *Clement*
Clemonts, *Clement*
Clémot, *Clement*
Clemow, *Clement*
Clempson, *Clement*
Clemson, *Clement*
Clench, *Clinch*
Clendennen, *Glendinning*
Clendenning, *Glendinning*
Cler, *Clare*
Clerc, *Clark*
Clerckx, *Clark*
Clercq, *Clark*
Clercx, *Clark*
Clercy, *Clarges*
Clère, *Clare*
Clere, *Clare*
Cléret, *Clare*
Clergé, *Clarges*
Clergeau, *Clark*
Clergeon, *Clark*
Clergeot, *Clark*
Clerget, *Clark*
Clergier, *Clarges*
Clergue, *Clark*
Clericetti, *Clark*
Clerici, *Clark*
Clerihan, *Cleary*
Clerihew
Clérin, *Clare*
Clériot, *Clare*
Clérisse, *Claridge*
Clerjot, *Clark*
Clerk, *Clark*
Clerkan, *Cleary*
Clerke, *Clark*
Clerkin, *Cleary*
Clerkx, *Clark*
Clermont
Clérot, *Clare*
Clerx, *Clark*
Clery, *Cleary*
Cléry
Cleugh, *Clough*
Cleve, *Cleeve*
Cleveland
Cleveley, *Cleverley*
Cleverley
Cleverly, *Cleverley*
Clew, *Clough*
Clewer
Clewes, *Clough*
Clews, *Clough*
Cleynaert, *Klein*
Cleyne, *Klein*
Cleynman, *Klein*
Click, *Cleak*
Cliff, *Clive*
Cliffe, *Clive*
Clifford
Clifforth, *Clifford*
Clift
Clifton
Climance, *Clement*
Climas, *Clement*
Climenson, *Clement*
Climent, *Clement*
Climie, *Clement*
Climo, *Clement*
Climpson, *Clement*
Clinch
Clindening, *Glendinning*
Cline, *Klein*
Clingerman, *Klinger*
Clink, *Clinch*
Clinker, *Clinch*
Clinton
Cliquet
Cliquot, *Cliquet*
Clitheroe
Clitherow, *Clitheroe*
Clive
Clives, *Clive*
Cloarec, *Clark*
Cloche, *Glock*
Clocke, *Glock*
Clodic, *Claude*
Clodius, *Claude*
Cloerec, *Clark*
Clohessy
Cloke, *Clough*
Cloot, *Claude*
Cloots, *Claude*
Cloquet, *Cliquet*
Cloquette, *Cliquet*
Clos, *Close*
Closa, *Close*
Closas, *Close*
Close
Closeau, *Close*
Closel, *Close*
Closier, *Close*
Closon, *Cloud*
Closs, *Close*
Closset, *Close*
Closson, *Close*
Clot
Clotet, *Clot*
Clother, *Clothier*
Clothier
Clotten, *Claude*
Clottens, *Claude*
Clotworthy, *Clatworthy*
Clou, *Cloud*
Cloud
Cloude, *Cloud*
Clouet, *Cloud*
Clough
Clouseau, *Close*
Clousel, *Close*
Clousier, *Close*
Clout
Clouter, *Clout*
Cloutier, *Cravo*
Cloutman, *Clout*
Cloutot, *Cravo*
Cloutrier, *Cravo*
Cloutt, *Clout*
Cloux, *Close, Cloud*
Clouzeau, *Close*
Clouzel, *Close*
Clouzier, *Close*
Clover, *Cleaver*
Clow, *Clough*
Clowes
Clowser, *Close*
Cloy, *Lewis*
Clozeau, *Close*
Clozel, *Close*
Clozier, *Close*
Clucas, *Lucas*
Cluderay, *Clitheroe*
Clue, *Clough*
Cluff, *Clough*
Clune
Cluse, *Close*
Clusel, *Close*
Clutterbuck
Cluzeau, *Close*
Cluzeaux, *Close*
Cluzel, *Close*
Clyde
Clyma, *Clement*
Clymer, *Clement*
Clymo, *Clement*
Clyne
Clynes
Clynman, *Klein*
Clynmans, *Klein*
Clyve, *Clive*
Coad
Coady, *Cody*
Coakley
Coales, *Cole*
Coard, *Corde*
Coate, *Coates*
Coates
Coatman, *Coates*
Coats, *Coates*
Coatts, *Coates*
Cob, *Cobb*
Coba, *Cave*
Cobas, *Cave*
Cobb
Cobbald, *Cobbold*
Cobbe, *Cobb*
Cobbett, *Cobbold*
Cobbold
Cobden
Cobelli, *Jacob*
Cobello, *Jacob*
Cobham
Coblance, *Koblenz*
Cobleigh, *Cobley*
Coblence, *Koblenz*
Coblentz, *Koblenz*
Coblenz, *Koblenz*
Cobley
Cobo
Cobos, *Cobo*
Coburn, *Cockburn*
Cocci, *Dominique*
Coccimano, *Kuzmin*
Cochet, *Cock*
Cocheteau, *Cock*
Cochey, *Cock*
Cochez, *Cock*
Cochin, *Cock*
Cochineau, *Cock*
Cochran, *Cochrane*
Cochrane
Cochren, *Cochrane*
Cochy, *Cock*
Coci, *Cook*
Cock, *Cook*
Cock
Cockarill, *Cock*
Cockayne
Cockburn
Cockcroft
Cockell
Cocker
Cockerell, *Cock*
Cockerham
Cockerill, *Cock*
Cockill, *Cockell*
Cocking, *Cock*
Cockle, *Cockell*
Cocklin, *Cock*
Cockling, *Cock*
Cockman, *Cook*
Cockrell, *Cock*
Cockrill, *Cock*
Cockroft, *Cockcroft*
Cocks, *Cock*
Coclet, *Cock*
Coclin, *Cock*
Coco, *Cook*
Cocquet, *Cock*
Cocqueteau, *Cock*
Cocteau, *Cock*
Cocuccio, *Cook*
Codd
Code, *Coad*
Codgbrook
Codina
Codlin
Codling, *Codlin*
Codman, *Codd*
Codrington
Codron, *Calderon*
Cody
Coe
Coeheert, *Coward*
Coelho, *Coney*
Coelli, *Jacob*
Coello, *Coney*
Coen, *Cohen*
Coenraets, *Konrad*
Coeur
Coeuret, *Coeur*
Coey, *Cowie*
Coffee, *Coffey*
Coffey
Coffin
Coffineau, *Coffin*
Coffinel, *Coffin*
Coffinet, *Coffin*
Coffinier, *Coffin*
Cofin, *Coffin*
Cogan
Coggan, *Cogan*
Coggeshall, *Coxall*
Coggin, *Cogan*
Coggins, *Cogan*
Coghill
Coghlan, *Coughlan*
Cogley, *Quickley*
Coglin, *Coughlan*
Cogo, *Cook*
Cogolo, *Cook*
Cogoni, *Cook*
Cogswell, *Coxall*
Cogut, *Kochetov*
Cohan, *Cohen*
Cohane, *Cohen*
Cohani, *Cohen*
Cohansky, *Cohen*
Cohen
Cohener, *Cohen*
Cohn, *Cohen*
Cohr, *Konrad*
Cohrs, *Konrad*
Coillard, *Couillet*
Coillau, *Couillet*
Coillaud, *Couillet*
Coimbra
Coindat, *Quant*
Coinde, *Quant*
Coindeau, *Quantrill*
Coindre, *Quant*

Coindreau, *Quantrill*
Cointat, *Quant*
Cointe, *Quant*
Cointeau, *Quantrill*
Cointereau, *Quantrill*
Cointerel, *Quantrill*
Cointet, *Quantrill*
Cointre, *Quant*
Cointreau, *Quantrill*
Cointrel, *Quantrill*
Cok, *Cook*
Coke, *Cook*
Coker
Col, *Coll*
Cola, *Coll*
Colaço
Colade, *Collado*
Coladon, *Collado*
Colange, *Coulange*
Colao, *Coll*
Colard, *Coll*
Colaucci, *Coll*
Colaussi, *Coll*
Colauzzi, *Coll*
Colbeck
Colborn, *Colbourne*
Colborne, *Colbourne*
Colbourn, *Colbourne*
Colbourne
Colburn, *Colbourne*
Colburne, *Colbourne*
Colby
Colclough
Colcock, *Coll*
Colcot, *Caldicott*
Colcott, *Caldicott*
Colcut, *Caldicott*
Colcutt, *Caldicott*
Coldham
Coldicott, *Caldicott*
Coldron, *Calderon*
Cole
Colebeck, *Colbeck*
Coleclough, *Colclough*
Coleçon, *Coll*
Colelli, *Coll*
Coleman
Colen, *Coll*
Colenso
Coleridge
Coles, *Cole*
Coleson, *Cole*
Colet, *Coll, Kohl*
Coletti, *Jack*
Coley
Colgan, *Quill*
Colhoun, *Colquhoun*
Coli, *Coll*
Colichio, *Coll*
Colicot, *Caldicott*
Colignon, *Coll*
Colijn, *Coll*
Colin, *Coll*
Colinet, *Coll*
Coling, *Colling*
Colini, *Coll*
Colino, *Coll*
Colinon, *Coll*
Colinot, *Coll*
Colkett, *Caldicott*
Colkin, *Coll*
Coll
Colla, *Coll*
Collacot, *Caldicott*
Collacott, *Caldicott*
Collado
Collan, *Cullen*
Collange, *Coulange*
Collard, *Coll*
Collazzo, *Coll*
Colle, *Coll*
Collec, *Coll*
Collechon, *Coll*
Collecott, *Caldicott*
Colleer, *Collier*
Collell, *Coll*
Colleman, *Coleman*
Collen, *Coll*
Collenot, *Coll*
Colleran
Colleson, *Coll*
Collet, *Coll*
Collett, *Coll*
Colleu, *Coll*
Colleuc, *Coll*
Colley, *Coley*
Collgan, *Quill*
Colliar, *Collier*
Colliard, *Collier*
Collicutt, *Caldicott*
Collie, *Coley*
Collier
Collin, *Coll*
Collinet, *Coll*
Colling
Collinge, *Colling*
Collings, *Colling*
Collingwood
Collingworth, *Collingwood*
Collinot, *Coll*
Collins
Collinson, *Collins*
Collinwood, *Collingwood*
Collis, *Collins*
Collison, *Collins*
Collman, *Coleman*
Collom, *Colomb*
Collomb, *Colomb*
Collomp, *Colomb*
Collon, *Colomb*
Collonge, *Coulange*
Collongues, *Coulange*
Collot, *Coll*
Colls, *Coll*
Collucello, *Coll*
Colluciello, *Coll*
Collyear, *Collier*
Collyer, *Collier*
Collyns, *Collins*
Colman, *Coleman, Toller*
Colmenar
Colmenarejo, *Colmenar*
Colmenares, *Colmenar*
Colmenero, *Colmenar*
Colocott, *Caldicott*
Colom, *Colomb*
Coloma, *Colomb*
Colomb
Colomba, *Colomb*
Colombain, *Coleman*
Colomban, *Coleman*
Colombari, *Colomb*
Colombat, *Colomb*
Colombazzi, *Colomb*
Colombeau, *Colomb*
Colombel, *Colomb*
Colombet, *Colomb*
Colombetta, *Colomb*
Colombetti, *Colomb*
Colombier, *Colomb*
Colombin, *Colomb*
Colombini, *Colomb*
Colombo, *Colomb*
Colombot, *Colomb*
Colomé, *Colomb*
Colomer, *Colomb*
Colomès, *Colomb*
Colomi, *Colomb*
Colomic, *Colomb*
Colomiès, *Colomb*
Colomines, *Coromina*
Colomo, *Colomb*
Colón, *Colomb*
Colon, *Colomb*
Colonge, *Coulange*
Colotti, *Coll*
Colozzi, *Coll*
Colqueran, *Cochrane*
Colquhoun
Colreavy, *McIlwraith*
Cols, *Coll*
Colson, *Coll*
Colston
Colt
Coltart, *Coulthard*
Colter, *Colt*
Colthard, *Coulthard*
Colthart, *Coulthard*
Coltherd, *Coulthard*
Colthert, *Coulthard*
Coltman, *Colt*
Colton
Colucci, *Coll*
Coluccio, *Coll*
Columban, *Coleman*
Columbani, *Coleman*
Columberi, *Colomb*
Columbo, *Colomb*
Colussi, *Coll*
Colusso, *Coll*
Colvill, *Colville*
Colville
Colwell
Colwill, *Colwell*
Colyer, *Collier*
Coma, *Coombe*
Comas, *Coombe*
Comazzo, *James*
Combas, *Coombe*
Combe, *Coombe*
Combeau, *Coombe*
Combelle, *Coombe*
Combelles, *Coombe*
Comber, *Camber*
Comber, *Coombe*
Combes, *Coombe*
Combet, *Coombe*
Combette, *Coombe*
Combier, *Coombe*
Combin, *Coombe*
Combot, *Coombe*
Comboul, *Coombe*
Combs, *Coombe*
Come, *Coombe*
Côme, *Kuzmin*
Comeau, *Coombe*
Comelini, *James*
Comella, *Coombe*
Comellas, *Coombe*
Comelli, *James*
Comellini, *James*
Comello, *James*
Comer, *Camber*
Comerford
Comet, *Coombe*
Cometti, *James*
Cometto, *James*
Comfort
Comi, *James*
Cominello, *James*
Cominetti, *James*
Comings, *Cumming*
Comini, *James*
Comino, *James*
Cominoli, *James*
Cominotti, *James*
Comins, *Cumming*
Comisk, *Comerford*
Comisky, *Comerford*
Comizzoli, *James*
Comley
Commane, *Cumming*
Commin, *Cumming*
Commings, *Cumming*
Commins, *Cumming*
Commiskey, *Comerford*
Commons, *Cumming*
Como, *James*
Comoletti, *James*
Comolli, *James*
Compagni, *Compagnon*
Compagnini, *Compagnon*
Compagnino, *Compagnon*
Compagno, *Compagnon*
Compagnon
Compagnone, *Compagnon*
Compagnoni, *Compagnon*
Compagnucci, *Compagnon*
Compain, *Compagnon*
Compaing, *Compagnon*
Companys
Compin, *Compagnon*
Comport, *Comfort*
Compte, *Count*
Compton
Comrie
Comte, *Count*
Comtet, *Count*
Comti, *Count*
Comucci, *James*
Comusso, *James*
Comuzzo, *James*
Comyn, *Cumming*
Conagan, *Cunningham*
Conaghan, *Cunningham*
Conally, *Connolly*
Conan
Conant, *Conan*
Conaty
Conaughton, *Conaty*
Conca, *Conche*
Concannon
Conceição
Concepción, *Conceição*
Concha, *Conche*
Conche
Conches, *Conche*
Conchon, *Conche*
Conciglieri, *Counsel*
Concilieri, *Counsel*
Condamin, *Condamine*
Condamine
Conde, *Count*
Condell
Condemine, *Condamine*
Condes, *Count*

Corlett
Corley, *Curley*
Corley
Cormack
Cormican, *Cormack*
Cormick, *Cormack*
Cormieau, *Cormier*
Cormieaud, *Cormier*
Cormier
Cormillot, *Cormier*
Cormode, *Dermott*
Cormoul, *Cormier*
Cornaert, *Corne*
Cornah, *Cornier*
Cornall
Cornard, *Corne*
Cornat, *Corne*
Cornaud, *Corne*
Corné, *Corne*
Corne
Cornec, *Corne*
Cornehl, *Corneille*
Corneil, *Corneille*
Corneille
Cornejo, *Corneille, Cornier*
Cornel, *Corneille*
Cornelis, *Corneille*
Cornelisse, *Corneille*
Cornelissen, *Corneille*
Cornelius, *Corneille*
Corneliussen, *Corneille*
Corneljes, *Corneille*
Cornell
Cornelleau, *Corneille*
Cornels, *Corneille*
Cornély, *Corneille*
Corner, *Cornier*
Cornes, *Cornish*
Cornet, *Corne*
Cornett, *Corne*
Cornette, *Corne*
Corney, *Corne*
Corney
Cornez, *Corne*
Cornfeld, *Korn*
Cornfield, *Korn*
Cornfoot, *Cornforth*
Cornford
Cornforth
Cornhill
Cornic, *Corne*
Cornier
Cornil, *Corneille*
Cornill, *Corneille*
Cornille, *Corneille*
Cornilleau, *Corneille*
Cornillot, *Corneille*
Cornils, *Corneille*
Cornish
Cornoueil, *Cornier*
Corns, *Cornish*
Cornu, *Corne*
Cornuau, *Corne*
Cornuchet, *Corne*
Cornudet, *Corne*
Cornuel, *Corne*
Cornuet, *Corne*
Cornut, *Corne*
Cornwall, *Cornwell*
Cornwell
Corobi, *Cuervo*
Coromina
Corominas, *Coromina*
Coromines, *Coromina*
Corona
Coronado, *Corona*
Coronas, *Corona*
Coropi, *Cuervo*
Corot
Corr
Corradengo, *Konrad*
Corradeschi, *Konrad*
Corradetti, *Konrad*
Corradi, *Konrad*
Corradini, *Konrad*
Corradino, *Konrad*
Corrado, *Konrad*
Corragan, *Corr*
Corral
Corrales, *Corral*
Corran, *Curran*
Corrao, *Konrad*
Corré, *Konrad*
Correa
Correas, *Correa*
Corredor
Correia, *Correa*
Corrie
Corrigan, *Corr*
Corrin, *Curran*
Corro, *Konrad*
Corry, *Corrie*
Corsan, *Carson*
Corselli, *Bonaccorso*
Corsellini, *Bonaccorso*
Corsello, *Bonaccorso*
Corsetti, *Bonaccorso*
Corsi, *Bonaccorso*
Corsini, *Bonaccorso*
Corso, *Bonaccorso*
Corson, *Carson, Curzon*
Corssen, *Konrad*
Corstgens, *Christian*
Cort, *Court*
Cortada
Cortadellas, *Cortada*
Cortázar
Corte, *Court*
Cortella, *Court*
Cortelletti, *Court*
Cortelli, *Court*
Cortellini, *Court*
Cortellino, *Court*
Cortello, *Court*
Corten, *Court*
Corteney, *Courtenay*
Cortens, *Court*
Côrte-Real
Cortés, *Curtis*
Cortès, *Curtis*
Cortese, *Curtis*
Cortesi, *Curtis*
Cortesini, *Curtis*
Corti, *Court*
Corticelli, *Court*
Cortijo, *Court*
Cortina, *Court*
Cortinas, *Court*
Cortini, *Court*
Cortnay, *Courtenay*
Cortney, *Courtenay*
Corts, *Court*
Corver, *Korb*
Corvetto, *Corbett*
Corvi, *Cuervo*
Corvietto, *Corbett*
Corvini, *Cuervo*
Corvino, *Cuervo*
Corvisier, *Courvoisier*
Corvisy, *Courvoisier*
Corvo, *Cuervo*
Cory
Coryton
Cosby
Coscor, *Cusker*
Cosens, *Cousin*
Cosgrave, *Cosgrove*
Cosgreave, *Cosgrove*
Cosgriff, *Cosgrove*
Cosgrive, *Cosgrove*
Cosgrove
Cosgry, *Cosgrove*
Cosimelli, *Kuzmin*
Cosimi, *Kuzmin*
Cosimini, *Kuzmin*
Cosimo, *Kuzmin*
Cosin, *Cousin*
Cosker, *Cusker*
Coskeran, *Cosgrove*
Coskerry, *Cosgrove*
Coskery, *Cosgrove*
Cosma, *Kuzmin*
Cosmani, *Kuzmin*
Cosmano, *Kuzmin*
Cosmao, *Kuzmin*
Cosme, *Kuzmin*
Cosmelli, *Kuzmin*
Cosmi, *Kuzmin*
Cosmin, *Kuzmin*
Cosmini, *Kuzmin*
Cosmo, *Kuzmin*
Cossentine, *Constantine*
Cossins, *Cousin*
Cossons, *Cousin*
Costa, *Coste*
Costache, *Constantine*
Costain
Costanti, *Constant, Constantine*
Costantino, *Constantine*
Costanza, *Constance*
Costanzi, *Constant*
Costanzo, *Constant*
Costard, *Constantine*
Costas, *Coste*
Costatin, *Constantine*
Coste
Costean, *Costain*
Costel, *Coste*
Costelle, *Coste*
Costello
Costelloe, *Costello*
Costellow, *Costello*
Costen, *Costain*
Coster
Costes, *Coste*
Costi, *Coste*
Costil, *Coste*
Costilhe, *Coste*
Costilla, *Coste*
Costily, *Costello*
Costin, *Costain*
Costings, *Constantine*
Costins, *Constantine*
Costiou, *Coste*
Costley, *Costello*
Coston, *Coste*
Costons, *Constantine*
Costy, *Coste*
Cosyns, *Cousin*
Cot
Cotard, *Cot*
Côte, *Coste*
Cote, *Coates*
Coteau, *Coste*
Cotel, *Coste*
Cotentin, *Constantine*
Cotes, *Coates*
Cotet, *Cot*
Cotherill, *Cotter*
Cotin, *Cot*
Cotineau, *Cot*
Cotler, *Kessel*
Cotman, *Coates, Cotter*
Coton, *Cot, Cotton*
Cotot, *Cot*
Cots, *Cot*
Cotsbrooke, *Codgbrook*
Cottam, *Cotton*
Cottard, *Cotte*
Cottarel, *Cotter*
Cotté, *Cotte*
Cotte
Cotteaux, *Coste*
Cottel, *Coste*
Cottel, *Cottle*
Cottell, *Cottle*
Cottem, *Cotton*
Cottenet, *Cotte*
Cottenot, *Cotte*
Cotter
Cottereau, *Cotter*
Cotterel, *Cotter*
Cotterell, *Cotter*
Cotterill, *Cotter*
Cottet, *Cotte*
Cottey, *Cotte*
Cottez, *Cotte*
Cottier, *Cotter*
Cottin, *Cotte*
Cottineau, *Cotte*
Cottis, *Coates*
Cottle
Cottom, *Cotton*
Cotton
Cottot, *Cotte*
Cottreau, *Cotter*
Cottrel, *Cotter*
Cottrell, *Cotter*
Cottrill, *Cotter*
Cottu, *Cotte*
Cotty, *Coste*
Coty, *Coste*
Couaillet, *Cail*
Couaillier, *Cail*
Couch
Coucha, *Couch*
Couche, *Couch*
Coucher, *Couch*
Couchman, *Couch*
Couder, *Coudert*
Couderc, *Coudert*
Coudert
Coudrais, *Cowdrey*
Coudray, *Cowdrey*
Coudroy, *Cowdrey*
Coudure, *Couturier*
Coudurier, *Couturier*
Coudwell, *Caldwell*
Coufal
Couffin, *Coffin*
Couffinel, *Coffin*
Couffinet, *Coffin*
Coufin, *Coffin*
Cough, *Couch*
Coughan, *Coughlan*
Coughlan

Coughlin, *Coughlan*
Couillard, *Couillet*
Couillau, *Couillet*
Couillaud, *Couillet*
Couilleau, *Couillet*
Couillet
Couillette, *Couillet*
Couillon, *Couillet*
Couillot, *Couillet*
Coulange
Coulangeon, *Coulange*
Coulanges, *Coulange*
Coulbeck, *Colbeck*
Couldwell, *Caldwell*
Coules, *Cole*
Coulet
Coull, *Cole*
Coullomp, *Colomb*
Coullon, *Colomb*
Coulman, *Coleman*
Coulomb, *Colomb*
Coulombat, *Colomb*
Coulombe, *Colomb*
Coulombeau, *Colomb*
Coulombel, *Colomb*
Coulombet, *Colomb*
Coulombot, *Colomb*
Coulomp, *Colomb*
Coulon, *Colomb*
Coulonge, *Coulange*
Coulonges, *Coulange*
Couloumbe, *Colomb*
Coulson, *Cole, Coole*
Coulston, *Colston*
Coult, *Colt*
Coultar, *Coulter*
Coultas
Coulter
Coulthard
Coulthart, *Coulthard*
Coulthurst
Coulton
Coumas, *Coombe*
Coumat, *Coombe*
Coumbe, *Coombe*
Coume, *Coombe*
Coumes, *Coombe*
Coumet, *Coombe*
Coumoul, *Coombe*
Councel, *Counsel*
Councell, *Counsel*
Council, *Counsel*
Counihan, *Cooney*
Counsel
Counsell, *Counsel*
Count
Coupar
Coupe, *Cooper*
Couper, *Coupar*
Coupland, *Copeland*
Coupman, *Copeman*
Cour, *Court*
Courage
Courage, *Kendrick*
Courageot, *Courage*
Courajot, *Courage*
Courbat, *Courbe*
Courbaud, *Courbe*
Courbe
Courbet, *Courbe*
Courbin, *Courbe*
Courbon, *Courbe*
Courbot, *Courbe*
Courcelle, *Courcelles*
Courcelles
Courdurié, *Couturier*
Courdurier, *Couturier*
Courné, *Corne*
Cournet, *Corne*
Cournu, *Corne*
Couronnaud, *Corona*
Couronne, *Corona*
Courseaux, *Courcelles*
Coursel, *Courcelles*
Courselle, *Courcelles*
Coursey, *Decourcey*
Court
Courtade, *Cortada*
Courtadon, *Cortada*
Courtauld, *Court*
Courtenay
Courtès, *Curtis*
Courthès, *Curtis*
Courtier
Courtil
Courtilier, *Courtil*
Courtille, *Courtil*
Courtillet, *Courtil*
Courtillier, *Courtil*
Courtilloles, *Courtil*
Courtillols, *Courtil*
Courtillon, *Courtil*
Courtman, *Court*
Courtney, *Courtenay*
Courtois, *Curtis*
Courts, *Court*
Courvoisier
Cousen, *Cousin*
Cousens, *Cousin*
Cousi, *Cousin*
Cousin
Cousinet, *Cousin*
Cousiney, *Cousin*
Cousinot, *Cousin*
Cousinou, *Cousin*
Cousins, *Cousin*
Cousou, *Cousin*
Cousteau, *Coste*
Coustet, *Coste*
Coustille, *Coste*
Couston, *Coste*
Cousture, *Couturier*
Cousturier, *Couturier*
Cousyn, *Cousin*
Coutance, *Constance*
Coutanceau, *Constant*
Coutans, *Constant*
Coutanson, *Constant*
Coutant, *Constant*
Coutas, *Coste*
Coutet, *Cot*
Couthon, *Cot*
Coutinet, *Cot*
Coutinho, *Couto*
Coutisson, *Cot*
Couto
Couton, *Cot*
Coutou, *Cot*
Coutout, *Cot*
Coutts
Couture, *Couturier*
Couturié, *Couturier*
Couturier
Couturieux, *Couturier*
Couvert
Couvrant, *Couvreur*
Couvreur
Couvreux, *Couvreur*
Couzens, *Cousin*
Couzi, *Cousin*
Couzineau, *Cousin*
Couzinet, *Cousin*
Couzy, *Cousin*
Couzyn, *Cousin*
Cove
Covelli, *Jacob*
Covello, *Jacob*
Coveney
Coventry
Cover, *Couvreur, Cuvier*
Coverdale
Coviello, *Jacob*
Covillo, *Cobo*
Covington
Covino, *Jacob*
Covo, *Cobo*
Covolini, *Jacob*
Covotti, *Jacob*
Cowan
Coward
Cowburn
Cowcha, *Couch*
Cowdell, *Caldwell*
Cowden
Cowderoy, *Cowdrey*
Cowdery, *Cowdrey*
Cowdray, *Cowdrey*
Cowdrey
Cowdron, *Calderon*
Cowdroy, *Cowdrey*
Cowdry, *Cowdrey*
Cowell
Cowen, *Cowan*
Cowey, *Coffey*
Cowherd, *Coward*
Cowhey, *Coffey*
Cowhiy, *Coffey*
Cowie
Cowles, *Cole*
Cowley
Cowling, *Colling*
Cowlishaw, *Culshaw*
Cowlson, *Cole*
Cowman, *Cumming*
Cowney, *Cooney*
Cowper, *Coupar*
Cowpland, *Copeland*
Cox
Coxall
Coxen, *Cock*
Coxon, *Cock*
Coxwell, *Coxall*
Coy
Coyle, *Cole*
Coyle
Coyne
Cozens, *Cousin*
Cozins, *Cousin*
Cozzi, *Dominique, Jack*
Cozzini, *Jack*
Cozzolini, *Jack*
Crab, *Crabbe*
Crabb, *Crabbe*
Crabbe
Crabe, *Cheever*
Crabet, *Cheever*
Crabette, *Cheever*
Crabot, *Cheever*
Crabtree, *Crabbe*
Crackel, *Cracknell*
Cracknall, *Cracknell*
Cracknell
Craddock
Cradduck, *Craddock*
Cradick, *Craddock*
Cradock, *Craddock*
Craey, *Crow*
Craft, *Croft*
Crafts, *Croft*
Cragg, *Craig*
Craggs, *Craig*
Craig
Craigie, *Craig*
Craik, *Craig*
Craker, *Croaker*
Crambe, *Chambers*
Crambes, *Chambers*
Cramer, *Creamer, Krämer*
Cramp, *Crome*
Crampton, *Crompton*
Crandle, *Ronald*
Crane
Cranfield
Crangle, *Ronald*
Crank
Crankshaw
Cranmer
Cranshaw, *Crankshaw*
Cranston
Cranstone, *Cranston*
Cranstoun, *Cranston*
Crapa, *Cheever*
Crapper, *Cropper*
Crapulli, *Cheever*
Crashaw, *Crawshaw*
Crasswell, *Creswell*
Crassweller, *Creswell*
Craswall, *Creswell*
Craswell, *Creswell*
Crathorne
Crauford, *Crawford*
Craufurd, *Crawford*
Crava, *Cheever*
Cravari, *Cheever*
Crave, *Cheever*
Craveiro, *Cravo*
Craven
Craveri, *Cheever*
Cravero, *Cheever*
Cravetta, *Cheever*
Cravetti, *Cheever*
Cravin, *Cheever*
Cravini, *Cheever*
Cravino, *Cheever*
Craviotto, *Cheever*
Cravo
Cravoisier, *Courvoisier*
Cravotta, *Cheever*
Craw, *Crow*
Crawcour, *Croaker*
Crawetz, *Krawiec*
Crawford
Crawforth, *Crawford*
Crawfurd, *Crawford*
Crawley, *Crowley*
Crawshaw
Crawshay, *Crawshaw*
Cray
Craythorne, *Crathorne*
Creagh, *Cray*
Creamer
Creamer, *Krämer*
Crean, *Creggan*
Creane, *Creggan*
Creaney, *Rainey*
Crease

Creasey, *Crease*
Creavagh, *Cray*
Creaven, *Cray*
Creavin, *Cray*
Crebbin, *Cribbin*
Creddon, *Creggan*
Cree, *Creggan*
Creedon
Creeghan, *Creggan*
Creegor, *Croaker*
Creemer, *Krämer*
Creemers, *Krämer*
Crees, *Crease*
Creese, *Crease*
Creevey, *Cray*
Creevy, *Cray*
Cregan, *Creggan*
Creggan
Cregor, *Croaker*
Crehan, *Creggan*
Creigan, *Creggan*
Creighton
Cremer, *Krämer*
Cremers, *Krämer*
Cremin
Crenel, *Carnell*
Crenell, *Carnell*
Crennall, *Ronald*
Crenshaw, *Crankshaw*
Crépet, *Crisp*
Crépey, *Crisp*
Crépin, *Crispin*
Crepin, *Crispin*
Crépon, *Crisp*
Crépy
Crès
Crescent
Cresp, *Crisp*
Crespel, *Crisp*
Crespet, *Crisp*
Crespí, *Crispin*
Crespi, *Crisp*
Crespi, *Crispin*
Crespin, *Crispin*
Crespini, *Crispin*
Crespino, *Crispin*
Crespo, *Crisp*
Crespon, *Crisp*
Crespoul, *Crisp*
Crespy, *Crispin*
Cressall, *Creswell*
Cressan, *Crescent*
Cressant, *Crescent*
Cresseau, *Crès*
Cresseaux, *Crès*
Cressel, *Creswell*
Cressent, *Crescent*
Cresset, *Crès*
Cressin, *Crès*
Cresson, *Crès*
Cressot, *Crès*
Cresswell, *Creswell*
Cressy, *Crès*
Cresta, *Creste*
Cresté, *Creste*
Creste
Crestian, *Christian*
Crestien, *Christian*
Crestin, *Christian*
Creswell
Crétat, *Creste*
Crété, *Creste*
Crète, *Creste*
Créteau, *Creste*
Créteaux, *Creste*
Cretet, *Creste*
Crétin, *Christian*
Crétinon, *Christian*
Crétinot, *Christian*
Cretté, *Creste*
Creus, *Cross*
Creuse, *Creux*
Creuset, *Creux*
Creusot, *Creux*
Creux
Creuze, *Creux*
Creuzet, *Creux*
Creuzot, *Creux*
Creveau, *Crible*
Crèvecoeur, *Croaker*
Crevel, *Crible*
Crevelier, *Crible*
Crew
Crewe, *Crew*
Crewes, *Cruise*
Crews, *Cruise*
Crewther, *Crowther*
Criado
Cribbin
Cribbins, *Cribbin*
Cribellier, *Crible*
Cribier, *Crible*
Crible
Criblier, *Crible*
Crich
Crichten, *Creighton*
Crichton, *Creighton*
Crick, *Crich*
Crighton, *Creighton*
Crilly, *Reilly*
Crimond
Crimp
Crindle, *Ronald*
Cringle, *Ronald*
Cripin, *Crispin*
Crippen, *Crispin*
Crippes, *Crisp*
Crippin, *Crispin*
Cripps, *Crisp*
Crips, *Crisp*
Cripwell
Crisp
Crispe, *Crisp*
Crispi, *Crisp*
Crispim, *Crispin*
Crispin
Crispo, *Crisp*
Crispoul, *Crisp*
Crissel, *Creswell*
Crist, *Christian*
Cristal
Cristea, *Christopher*
Cristescu, *Christopher*
Cristiana, *Christian*
Cristiani, *Christian*
Cristiano, *Christian*
Cristina, *Christian*
Cristini, *Christian*
Cristino, *Christian*
Cristóbal, *Christopher*
Cristofalo, *Christopher*
Cristofanini, *Christopher*
Cristofano, *Christopher*
Cristofari, *Christopher*
Cristofaro, *Christopher*
Cristoferi, *Christopher*
Cristoffersen, *Christopher*
Cristòfol, *Christopher*
Cristofolini, *Christopher*
Cristofolo, *Christopher*
Cristòfor, *Christopher*
Cristofor, *Christopher*
Cristoforetti, *Christopher*
Cristofori, *Christopher*
Cristoforo, *Christopher*
Cristol, *Christopher*
Cristou, *Christopher*
Cristóvão, *Christopher*
Criswell, *Creswell*
Critchley, *Crutchley*
Crivelier, *Crible*
Crivelli, *Crible*
Crivosei, *Krivov*
Crnčić, *Chernyakov*
Crnić, *Chernyakov*
Crnko, *Chernyakov*
Crnković, *Chernyakov*
Croaker
Croasdale
Croattini, *Horváth*
Croatto, *Horváth*
Crobath, *Horváth*
Crobu, *Cuervo*
Croc, *Crook*
Croce, *Cross*
Crocetti, *Cross*
Crochard, *Crook*
Croche, *Crook*
Crochet, *Crook*
Crochon, *Crook*
Crochot, *Crook*
Croci, *Cross*
Crockatt, *Crockett*
Crocker
Crockett
Crockford
Croes, *Kraus*
Croese, *Kraus*
Croft
Crofter, *Croft*
Crofton
Crofts, *Croft*
Croisier, *Crozier*
Croitoru, *Krawiec*
Croix, *Cross*
Croizier, *Crozier*
Croke, *Crook*
Croket, *Crockett*
Croll, *Kroll*
Crolla, *Crowley*
Crolly, *Crowley*
Croly, *Crowley*
Cromack, *Crummock*
Cromb, *Crome*
Crombie
Crome
Cromeeke, *Crummock*
Cromie, *Crombie*
Crommelinck, *Crome*
Crommen, *Crome*
Crompton
Cromwell
Crone, *Corona, Cronin*
Cronholm, *Corona*
Cronin
Cronk, *Crank*
Cronkite, *Kranke*
Cronkshaw, *Crankshaw*
Cronquist, *Corona*
Cronshaw, *Crankshaw*
Cronstedt, *Corona*
Cronström, *Corona*
Cronvall, *Corona*
Cronwall, *Corona*
Crook
Crooke, *Crook*
Crooker, *Crook*
Crookes, *Crook*
Crooks, *Crook*
Crookshank, *Cruikshank*
Crookshanks, *Cruikshank*
Crookson, *Crook*
Croom, *Crome*
Croome, *Crome*
Cropper
Croque, *Crook*
Cros, *Creux*
Crosbie, *Crosby*
Crosby
Crosdale, *Croasdale*
Crose, *Creux, Cross*
Croser, *Crozier*
Croset, *Creux*
Crosetti, *Cross*
Crosetto, *Cross*
Crosfield, *Crossfield*
Croshaw, *Crawshaw*
Crosier, *Crozier*
Crosio, *Cross*
Crosland, *Crossland*
Cross
Crossan, *Cross*
Crossby, *Crosby*
Crossdale, *Croasdale*
Crosse, *Cross*
Crosseland, *Crossland*
Crossey, *Cross*
Crossfield
Crossin, *Cross*
Crossland
Crossley
Crossman, *Cross*
Crossthwaite
Crosston
Crosswaite, *Crossthwaite*
Crosthwaite, *Crossthwaite*
Crotch, *Crouch*
Crother, *Crowther*
Crothers, *Carruthers, Crowther*
Crotty
Crouch
Croucher, *Crouch*
Crouchman, *Crouch*
Crouse, *Cruise*
Crousié, *Crozier*
Crousier, *Crozier*
Crouvezier, *Courvoisier*
Crouvisier, *Courvoisier*
Crouvoisier, *Courvoisier*
Croux, *Cross*
Crouzet, *Creux*
Crouzier, *Crozier*
Crovato, *Horváth*
Crovatto, *Horváth*
Crovelli, *Cuervo*
Crovetti, *Corbett*
Crovetto, *Corbett*
Crovi, *Cuervo*
Crovo, *Cuervo*
Crow
Crowdace, *Carruthers*
Crowder, *Crowther*
Crowe, *Crow*
Crowell
Crowest, *Crowhurst*
Crowfoot

Crowhurst
Crowle
Crowley
Crowsher, *Crawshaw*
Crowther
Croxford
Croz, *Creux*
Crozat, *Creux*
Croze, *Creux*
Crozel, *Creux*
Crozes, *Creux*
Crozet, *Creux*
Crozier
Cruce, *Cross*
Cruces, *Cross*
Crucetti, *Cross*
Crucitti, *Cross*
Cruddace, *Carruthers*
Cruddas, *Carruthers*
Crudgington
Cruft, *Croft*
Crufts, *Croft*
Cruickshank, *Cruikshank*
Cruickshanks, *Cruikshank*
Cruikshank
Cruikshanks, *Cruikshank*
Cruise
Crumb, *Crome*
Crumbie, *Crombie*
Crummack, *Crummock*
Crummay, *Crombie*
Crummey, *Crombie*
Crummie, *Crombie*
Crummock
Crummy, *Crombie*
Crump, *Crome*
Crumpton, *Crompton*
Cruse, *Creux, Cruise*
Cruset, *Creux*
Crutch, *Crouch*
Crutchley
Crutzen, *Cross*
Cruveilher, *Crible*
Cruveilhier, *Crible*
Cruvel, *Crible*
Cruvelhier, *Crible*
Cruvelier, *Crible*
Cruwys, *Cruise*
Cruz, *Cross*
Cryer
Crystal, *Cristal*
Crystall, *Cristal*
Crystol, *Cristal*
Császár, *Kaiser*
Cseh, *Čech*
Ctibor, *Stibor*
Cuadrado, *Carré*
Cubas, *Cuvier*
Cubbino, *Jacob*
Cubells, *Cuvier*
Cubero, *Cuvier*
Cubillo, *Cuvier*
Cubinelli, *Jacob*
Cubo, *Cuvier*
Cubucci, *Jacob*
Cucci, *Jack*
Cuckson, *Cook*
Cudbird, *Cuthbert*
Cudby, *Cuthbert*
Cudd, *Cuthbert*
Cuddehy, *Cody*
Cuddihy, *Cody*
Cuddy, *Cuthbert*
Cudihy, *Cody*
Cudmore
Cuenca, *Conche*
Cuerda, *Corde*
Cuerden
Cuervo
Cuesta, *Coste*
Cueto
Cueva, *Cave*
Cuevas, *Cave*
Cuff
Cuffe, *Cuff*
Cugat
Cugini, *Cousin*
Cuijpers, *Cooper*
Cuisin, *Cuisine*
Cuisinaire, *Cuisine*
Cuisine
Cuisinier, *Cuisine*
Cuker, *Zucker*
Cukerl, *Zucker*
Cukerman, *Zucker*
Cukier, *Zucker*
Cukierman, *Zucker*
Cukiernik, *Zucker*
Cukierstein, *Zucker*
Culebras
Culhane, *Cullen*
Cull, *Culling*
Cullane, *Cullen*
Culle, *Coll*
Cullen
Cullicchi, *Coll*
Cullin, *Cullen*
Cullinan, *Cullen*
Cullinane, *Cullen*
Culling
Cullingworth
Cullo, *Coll*
Cullon, *Cullen*
Cullpeper, *Culpepper*
Cullum, *Coleman*
Cully
Culpeper, *Culpepper*
Culpepper
Culreavy, *McIlwraith*
Culshaw
Culter, *Coulter*
Culver
Culverhouse, *Culver*
Culwen, *Curwen*
Cumberbatch
Cumberpatch, *Cumberbatch*
Cumeskey, *Comerford*
Cumesky, *Comerford*
Cumine, *Cumming*
Cuming, *Cumming*
Cumings, *Cumming*
Cumins, *Cumming*
Cumish, *Comerford*
Cumiskey, *Comerford*
Cumisky, *Comerford*
Cummane, *Cumming*
Cummerford, *Comerford*
Cummin, *Cumming*
Cummine, *Cumming*
Cumming
Cummings, *Cumming*
Cummins, *Cumming*
Cumo, *James*
Cumpton, *Compton*
Cunard
Cundy, *Condy*
Cung, *Tong*
Cunha
Cuní, *Coney*
Cunihan, *Cunningham*
Cunill, *Coney*
Cunillé, *Coney*
Cuningham, *Cunningham*
Cuninghame, *Cunningham*
Cunliffe
Cunnahan, *Cunningham*
Cunnea, *Cooney*
Cunnell, *Gunnell*
Cunnigan, *Cunningham*
Cunningham
Cunninghame, *Cunningham*
Cunnington
Cunnliffe, *Cunliffe*
Cunradi, *Konrad*
Cunrado, *Konrad*
Cunti, *Count*
Cunto, *Count*
Cuoco, *Cook*
Cuocolo, *Cook*
Cuoghi, *Cook*
Cuogo, *Cook*
Cuorvo, *Cuervo*
Cupper, *Cooper*
Curd
Curl, *Kroll*
Curland, *Kurland*
Curle, *Kroll*
Curless, *Carless*
Curley
Curm, *Curme*
Curme
Curnow, *Cornwell*
Curran
Currao, *Konrad*
Curreen, *Curran*
Currey, *Curry*
Currie, *Curry*
Currigan, *Corr*
Currm, *Curme*
Curro, *Konrad*
Currom, *Curme*
Currum, *Curme*
Curry
Curson, *Curzon*
Curt, *Court*
Curtain, *Curtin*
Curtayne, *Curtin*
Curter, *Courtier*
Curti, *Court*
Curtin
Curtis
Curtiss, *Curtis*
Curtius, *Court*
Curtó, *Court*
Curto, *Court*
Curwen
Curwin, *Curwen*
Curzon
Cusack
Cushen, *Cousin*
Cusheon, *Cousin*
Cushing, *Cousin*
Cushion, *Cousin*
Cushworth, *Cusworth*
Cusimano, *Kuzmin*
Cusin, *Cuisine*
Cusinier, *Cuisine*
Cusins, *Cousin*
Cusker
Cuskern, *Cosgrove*
Cuskery, *Cosgrove*
Cusmano, *Kuzmin*
Cuss, *Constance, Kiss*
Cusse, *Constance, Kiss*
Cussen, *Constance, Cousin, Cuthbert*
Cussens, *Constance, Cousin, Cuthbert*
Cussins, *Cousin*
Cusson, *Constance, Cousin, Cuthbert*
Cussons, *Constance, Cousin, Cuthbert*
Cust, *Constance*
Custance, *Constance*
Custer, *Küster*
Custers, *Küster*
Custerson, *Constance*
Custódio
Cusumano, *Kuzmin*
Cusworth
Cutbirth, *Cuthbert*
Cuthbe, *Cuthbert*
Cuthbert
Cuthbertson, *Cuthbert*
Cutlack, *Gullick*
Cutler
Cutlock, *Gullick*
Cutmore, *Cudmore*
Cutress, *Gutteridge*
Cutt, *Cuthbert*
Cuttelar, *Cutler*
Cuttell, *Cottle*
Cutteridge, *Gutteridge*
Cuttill, *Cottle*
Cutting, *Cuthbert*
Cuttles, *Cottle*
Cuttridge, *Gutteridge*
Cuttriss, *Gutteridge*
Cutts, *Cuthbert*
Cuvier
Cuxon, *Cook*
Cuxson, *Cook*
Cuyp, *Cooper*
Cuyper, *Cooper*
Cuypere, *Cooper*
Cuypers, *Cooper*
Cuyvers, *Cuvier*
Cuzen, *Cousin*
Cuzons, *Cousin*
Cuzzi, *Jack*
Cwaig, *Twigg*
Cwaigenhaft, *Twigg*
Cwajgenberg, *Twigg*
Cwajgenhaft, *Twigg*
Cwajghaft, *Twigg*
Cybula, *Zwiebel*
Cybulski, *Zwiebel*
Cygan, *Tsyganov*
Cygel, *Ziegler*
Cygielman, *Ziegler*
Cygler, *Ziegler*
Cymbalist, *Zimbalist*
Cymbalista, *Zimbalist*
Cymerman, *Zimmermann*
Cymmermann, *Zimmermann*
Cytrinik, *Citroen*
Cytron, *Citroen*
Cytryn, *Citroen*
Cytrynbaum, *Citroen*
Cytrynowicz, *Citroen*
Cytrynowitz, *Citroen*
Czajka, *Czajkowski*
Czajkowski
Czapla, *Chaplin*
Czaplicki, *Chaplin*

Czapliński, *Chaplin*
Czapnik, *Chaplin*
Czapski, *Chaplin*
Czarnecki, *Chernyakov*
Czarniecki, *Chernyakov*
Czarninski, *Chernyakov*
Czarnobroda, *Chernyakov*
Czarnoczapka, *Chernyakov*
Czarnolewski, *Chernyakov*
Czarny, *Chernyakov*
Czarnyląs, *Chernyakov*
Czech, *Čech*
Czechowicz, *Čech*
Czechowski, *Čech*
Czernas, *Chernyakov*
Czernek, *Chernyakov*
Czerniak, *Chernyakov*
Czerniawski, *Chernyakov*
Czernichowski, *Chernyakov*
Czernicki, *Chernyakov*
Czernik, *Chernyakov*
Czernilov, *Chernyakov*
Czernin, *Chernyakov*
Czerninski, *Chernyakov*
Czerno, *Chernyakov*
Czernobilski, *Chernyakov*
Czernocki, *Chernyakov*
Czernov, *Chernyakov*
Czerny, *Chernyakov*
Czerwieński, *Czerwiński*
Czerwiński
Czigány, *Tsyganov*
Czukerman, *Zucker*
Czupryniak
Czupryński, *Czupryniak*
Czyż
Czyżewski, *Czyż*
Czyżo, *Czyż*
Czyżykowski, *Czyż*

D

Daalman, *Dale*
D'Abadie, *Abbey*
D'Abbadie, *Abbey*
Dabbs, *Dobb*
Dąbek, *Dubnikov*
Däbel, *Doppler*
Däbeler, *Doppler*
Dabelsteen, *Doppler*
Dabelstein, *Doppler*
Dabinett, *Dobb*
Dąbkowski, *Dubnikov*
Dabney, *Daubeney*
D'Aboville, *Abonville*
D'Abramo, *Abraham*
Dąbrowski
Dabs, *Dobb*
Dabson, *Dobb*
Da Ca, *Casa*
Da Canal, *Chenal*
Da Canale, *Chenal*
Dacca, *Casa*
D'Accardo, *Achard*
D'Accorso, *Bonaccorso*
D'Accursio, *Bonaccorso*
D'Accurso, *Bonaccorso*
Dach
Da Cha, *Casa*
Dacher, *Dach*
Dacheux
Dachmann, *Dach*
Dachner, *Dach*
Dachs
Dack
Da Costa, *Coste*
Dacre
D'Adamo, *Adam*
Dadd, *Dodd*
D'Adda, *Adam*
Daddow, *Dando*
Dadds, *Dodd*
Dade, *David*
Dadswell
Dael, *Dale*
Daelman, *Dale*
Daen, *Daniel*
Daenen, *Daniel*
Daens, *Daniel*
D'Aeth, *Death*
Daffey, *David*
Daft
Dafydd, *David*
D'Agata, *Aggis*
Dagg
Daggett, *Dagg*
Dagless, *Dalgleish*
Daglish, *Dalgleish*
D'Agnello, *Agnew*
D'Agnese, *Annis*
D'Agniello, *Agnew*
D'Agnolo, *Angel*
Dagon, *Dagg*
Dagonet, *Dagg*
Dagonneau, *Dagg*
Dagot, *Dagg*
Dagueneau, *Dagg*
Daguenet, *Dagg*
Daguet, *Dagg*
Daguin, *Dagg*
Daguinot, *Dagg*
Dahl, *Dale*
Dahlbäck, *Dale*
Dahlberg, *Dale*
Dahlbom, *Dale*
Dahlborg, *Dale*
Dahlén, *Dale*
Dahler, *Dale*
Dahlgren, *Dale*
Dahlin, *Dale*
Dahlman, *Dale*
Dahlquist, *Dale*
Dahlstedt, *Dale*
Dahlstrand, *Dale*
Dahlström, *Dale*
Dähmel, *Thomas*
Dahmke, *Adam*
Dähn, *Dench*
Dähne, *Dench*
Dahnert, *Deinhard*
Dähnhard, *Deinhard*
Dähnhardt, *Deinhard*
Dähnick, *Daňek*
Dähnicke, *Daňek*
Dahnke, *Daňek*
Daid, *David*
D'Aiello, *Aiello*
Daile, *Dale*
Dailey, *Daly*
Daily, *Daly*
Daimler
Dain
Daine, *Dain*
Daines, *Dain*
Dainese, *Dench*
Dainesi, *Dench*
Dainteth, *Daintith*
Daintith
Daintree, *Daintry*
Daintrey, *Daintry*
Daintry
Dainty, *Daintith*
Dairson, *Dear*
D'Ajello, *Aiello*
Dakhno, *Daniel*
Dakhov, *Daniel*
Dakin, *Day*
Daladerne, *Aladerne*
Daladier, *Aladerne*
D'Alayrac, *Alayrac*
D'Albert, *Albert*
D'Alberti, *Albert*
Dal Bo, *Boeuf*
Dal Borgo, *Burke*
Dalby
Dal Degan, *Dean*
Dale
Daleman, *Dale*
Dales, *Dale*
D'Alesco, *Alexis*
D'Alesio, *Alexis*
D'Alessandro, *Alexander*
D'Alessio, *Alexis*
Daley, *Daly*
Dal Fabbro, *Fèvre*
Dalfin, *Dauphin*
Dalfinelli, *Dauphin*
Dalfini, *Dauphin*
Dalfino, *Dauphin*
Dal Fiore, *Flower*
Dalgetty
Dalgety, *Dalgetty*
Dalgleas, *Dalgleish*
Dalgleish
Dalgliesh, *Dalgleish*
Dalglish, *Dalgleish*
Dalhousie
Dalí, *Adell*
D'Alisi, *Lewis*
Dalkeith
Dall, *Dale, Dallas*
Dalla Ca, *Casa*
Dalla Casa, *Casa*
Dalla Cha, *Casa*
Dalla Corte, *Court*
Dalla Costa, *Coste*
Dalla Fior, *Flower*
Dallamore, *Delamare*
Dallaporta, *Port*
Dallas
Dalla Volpe, *Volpe*
Dalla Volta, *Volta*
Dallaway
Dalle Donne, *Dame*
Dalley, *Daly*
Dallicoat, *Coates*
Dallicote, *Coates*
Dallimore, *Delamare*
Dallmann, *Dale*
Dall'Oglio, *Oyler*
Dallow, *Dallaway*
Dally, *Daly*
Dalmace, *Dalmas*
Dalmais, *Dalmas*
Dalmann, *Dale*
Dalmas
Dalmases, *Dalmas*
Dalmasso, *Dalmas*
Dalmau, *Dalmas*
Dalmay, *Dalmas*
Dal Monaco, *Monk*
Dal Monte, *Mont*
D'Aloisio, *Lewis*
Dalphy, *Dauphin*
Dalponte, *Pont*
Dalporto, *Port*
Dal Pozzo, *Puits*
Dal Pra, *Pré*
Dal Prato, *Pré*
Dalrymple
Dal Savio, *Sage*
D'Alton, *Dalton*
Dalton
Daltrey, *Daltry*
Daltry
D'Aluisio, *Lewis*
Daly
Dalyell, *Dalziel*
Dalyiel, *Dalziel*
Dalzell, *Dalziel*
Dalziel
Dam
Damace, *Dalmas*
D'Amante, *Amant*
Damanti, *Amant*
Damas, *Dalmas*
Damas, *Dame*
Damaschke, *Thomas*
D'Amato, *Amey*
D'Ambrogi, *Ambrose*
D'Ambrogio, *Ambrose*
D'Ambrosi, *Ambrose*
D'Ambrosio, *Ambrose*
Dame
Damen, *Dam*
D'Ameri, *Aylmer*
D'Amerio, *Aylmer*
Damero, *Aylmer*
Dametti, *Adam*
Dami, *Adam*
Damiaens, *Damyon*
Damian, *Damyon*
Damiani, *Damyon*
Damiano, *Damyon*
D'Amici, *Amis*
D'Amico, *Amis*
Damien, *Damyon*
Damjanović, *Damyon*
Damm, *Dam*
Damman, *Dam*
Dammen, *Dam*
Dammer, *Dam*
Dammers, *Dankmar*
Dammert, *Dankmar*
Damon, *Damyon*
D'Amore, *Amor*
Damper, *Dampier*
Dampier
Dampierre, *Dampier*
Dams, *Damyon*
Damson, *Dame*
Damstra, *Dam*
Da Mulino, *Mill*
Damyanov, *Damyon*
Damyon
Danais, *Dench*
Danard, *Dench*
D'Anastasio, *Anstice*
Danay, *Dench*
Danays, *Dench*
Danby
Dance, *Tanzer*
Dancer, *Tanzer*
Dancet, *Tanzer*
Dancette, *Tanzer*

Dancey, *Dansie*
Danchenko, *Daniel*
Danciger, *Danzig*
Dancigerkron, *Danzig*
Dancigier, *Danzig*
Dancy, *Dansie*
Dancyg, *Danzig*
Dancyger, *Danzig*
Dancygier, *Danzig*
Dand, *Andrew*
Dandie, *Andrew*
Dandison, *Andrew*
Dandler, *Tendler*
Dando
D'Andrea, *Andrew*
Dandy, *Andrew*
Dané, *Dench*
Dane, *Dean, Dench*
Dänecke, *Daňek*
Dänecke, *Deinhard*
Danehl, *Daniel*
Daňek
Danelet, *Daniel*
Danell, *Daniel*
Danello, *Daniel*
Danels, *Daniel*
Danelut, *Daniel*
Danelutti, *Daniel*
Danès, *Dench*
Danes, *Dean*
Danese, *Dench*
Danesi, *Dench*
Danet, *Jordan*
Danev, *Daniel*
Daney, *Dench*
Dangel, *Daniel*
D'Angelo, *Angel*
Dangerfield
Dangl, *Daniel*
Daňhel, *Daniel*
Dani, *Daniel*
Daniau, *Daniel*
Daničić, *Daňek*
Danick, *Daniel*
Dániel, *Daniel*
Daniel
Danielczyk, *Daniel*
Daniele, *Daniel*
Danieli, *Daniel*
Danielian, *Daniel*
Danielis, *Daniel*
Danielkiewicz, *Daniel*
Daniell, *Daniel*
Danielli, *Daniel*
Daniello, *Daniel*
Daniellot, *Daniel*
Daniells, *Daniel*
Daniélou, *Daniel*
Danielovitch, *Daniel*
Daniels, *Daniel*
Danielsen, *Daniel*
Danielski, *Daniel*
Danielsky, *Daniel*
Danielsohn, *Daniel*
Danielson, *Daniel*
Danielsson, *Daniel*
Danielut, *Daniel*
Daniely, *Daniel*
Danigel, *Daniel*
Danihel, *Daniel*
Danihelka, *Daniel*
Däniken, *Daňek*
Danilchenko, *Daniel*
Danilchev, *Daniel*
Danilchik, *Daniel*
Danilenko, *Daniel*
Danilevich, *Daniel*
Danilewicz, *Daniel*
Danilin, *Daniel*
Danilishin, *Daniel*
Danilov, *Daniel*
Danilović, *Daniel*
Danilovich, *Daniel*
Danilovitch, *Daniel*
Daniłowicz, *Daniel*
Danilyak, *Daniel*
Danilyuk, *Daniel*
Danis, *Daniel*
Danise, *Dench*
Danisi, *Dench*
Dankmar
Dankó, *Daniel*
Dankov, *Daniel*
Danks, *Daniel*
Danne, *Dame*
Dannehl, *Daniel*
Danneil, *Daniel*
Dannel, *Daniel*
Dannemann, *Tanne*
Danner, *Tanner*
Dannet, *Jordan*
Danniel, *Daniel*
Danniell, *Daniel*
Dannöhl, *Daniel*
Dannot, *Jordan*
Danois, *Dench*
Danon, *Jordan*
Danot, *Jordan*
Danovich, *Daniel*
Danse, *Tanzer*
Danset, *Tanzer*
Dansette, *Tanzer*
Dansey, *Dansie*
Danshin, *Daniel*
Dansie
Dansin, *Tanzer*
Danson, *Andrew, Daniel*
Dantas
Dante, *Durant*
Dantec, *Dent*
Danti, *Durant*
Dantini, *Durant*
Danton
D'Antoni, *Anthony*
D'Antonio, *Anthony*
D'Antuoni, *Anthony*
Dantzer, *Tanzer*
Dantzig, *Danzig*
Danvers
Dany, *Daniel*
Danz, *Danzig*
Danzger, *Danzig*
Danzig
Danziger, *Danzig*
Danzik, *Danzig*
Daoust, *Davout*
Daout, *Davout*
Daporto, *Port*
D'Aquila, *Eagle*
Daragon, *Aragón*
Daragona, *Aragón*
Daras, *Darras*
Darbey, *Darby*
Darbishire, *Darbyshire*
Darby
Darbyshire
Darcet, *Darcy*
Darcey, *Darcy*
Darche, *Arco*
D'Arco, *Arco*
D'Arcy, *Darcy*
Darcy
Dard
Darde
Dardel, *Darde*
Dardelet, *Darde*
Dardelin, *Darde*
Dardet, *Darde*
Dardol, *Darde*
Dare, *Dear*
Dareau, *Darell*
Darel, *Darell*
Darell
Dargan
Da Riolo, *Rieu*
Dark
Darke, *Dark*
Darkes, *Dark*
Darky, *Darcy*
Darley
Darling
Darlington
Darlot, *Arlott*
Darmody, *Dermott*
Da Rold, *Harrod*
Da Rolt, *Harrod*
Darrach, *Darroch*
Darragh, *Darroch*
Darragon, *Aragón*
Darras
D'Arrigo, *Henry*
Darroch
Darrow, *Darroch*
Dart
Darvell, *Darvill*
Darvill
Darwen, *Darwin*
Darwin
Das, *Dachs*
Dash
Dashkov, *Daniel*
Dashkovich, *Daniel*
Dashwood
Daszkiewicz, *Daniel*
D'Aton, *Dalton*
Daton, *Dalton*
Daub, *Tauber*
Daube, *Taube*
Daubeney
Daubeny, *Daubeney*
Dauber, *Taube*
Daubert, *Taube*
Däubler, *Taube*
Daubmann, *Tauber*
D'Aubney, *Daubeney*
Daubney, *Daubeney*
Dauchez
Daud, *David*
Daudé, *Daudet*
Daudet
Daudov, *David*
Dauffard, *Dauphin*
Daugherty, *Doherty*
Daughtery, *Daltry*
Daughton, *Dalton*
Daughtrey, *Daltry*
Daughtry, *Daltry*
Daukes, *Daw*
Daulton, *Dalton*
Daultrey, *Daltry*
Daum
Daumann, *Daum*
Daumard, *Daumier*
Daumet, *Daumier*
Daumier
Däumler, *Daimler*
Daunay, *Delaney*
Dauncey, *Dansie*
Daunderer, *Donner*
Dauney, *Delaney*
Dauphin
Daurat, *Doré*
Dautun, *Dalton*
Davage, *David*
Daval
Davall, *Deville*
D'Avalle, *Vale*
Da Valle, *Vale*
Davau, *Daval*
Davault, *Daval*
Davaux, *Daval*
Daveau, *Daval*
Daveine, *Avoine*
Daveisne, *Avoine*
Davell, *Deville*
Davenne, *Avoine*
Davenport
Daventry, *Daintry*
Davet, *David*
Da Vico, *Vico*
Dávid, *David*
David
Davidai, *David*
Davidde, *David*
Daviddi, *David*
Davide, *David*
Davídek, *David*
Davidesco, *David*
Davidescu, *David*
Davidge, *David*
Davidi, *David*
Davidian, *David*
Davidman, *David*
Davidof, *David*
Davidoff, *David*
Davidofski, *David*
Davidou, *David*
Davidov, *David*
Davidove, *David*
Davidović, *David*
Davidovic, *David*
Davidovich, *David*
Davidovici, *David*
Davidovics, *David*
Davidovicz, *David*
Davidovitch, *David*
Davidovits, *David*
Davidovitz, *David*
Davidovsky, *David*
Davidow, *David*
Davidowich, *David*
Davidowitz, *David*
Davidowsky, *David*
Davids, *David*
Davidsen, *David*
Davidsohn, *David*
Davidson, *David*
Davidsson, *David*
Davidy, *David*
Davidzon, *David*
Davie
Davies, *David*
D'Avigdor, *Avigdor*
Dávila, *Avila*
Davin, *David, Devane*
Da Vinci, *Vincent*

Davine, *Devane*
Davinet, *David*
Daviö, *David*
Davion, *David*
Daviot, *David*
Davioud, *David*
Davis, *David*
Davison, *David*
Davisson, *David*
Davitashvili, *David*
Davitt, *David*
Davitti, *David*
Davoll, *Deville*
Davoud, *Davout*
Davous, *Davout*
Davoust, *Davout*
Davout
Davson, *David*
Davy, *David*
Davydenko, *David*
Davydkov, *David*
Davydochkin, *David*
Davydov, *David*
Davydychev, *David*
Davydzenko, *David*
Davys, *David*
Daw
Dawber
Dawe, *Daw*
Dawes, *Daw*
Dawid, *David*
Dawidman, *David*
Dawidowich, *David*
Dawidowicz, *David*
Dawidowitsch, *David*
Dawidowitz, *David*
Dawidowsky, *David*
Dawidsohn, *David*
Dawkes, *Daw*
Dawkin, *Daw*
Dawkins, *Daw*
Dawnay, *Delaney*
Dawney, *Delaney*
Daws, *Daw*
Dawson, *Daw*
Dawton, *Dalton*
Dawtrey, *Daltry*
Dawtry, *Daltry*
Dax, *Dack*
Day
Dayan
Dayczman, *Deutsch*
Daye, *Day*
Daykin, *Day*
Dayman, *Day*
Dayment, *Diamond*
Daymond, *Diamond*
Dayne, *Dain*
Daynes, *Dain*
Dayson, *Day*
D'Azeglio, *Aiello*
D'Azzi, *Ace*
Dea, *Daw*
Deacon, *Deakin*
Deacy, *Deasy*
Deadman, *Debenham*
De Agostini, *Austin*
Deák, *Deakin*
Deakan, *Deakin*
Deakes, *Ditch*
Deakin
Deakins, *Deakin*
Deal, *Dale*
De Albertis, *Albert*
Dealtry, *Daltry*
Deam, *Dempster*
De Ambrosi, *Ambrose*
De Ambrosis, *Ambrose*
Deamer, *Dempster*
De Amicis, *Amis*
Dean
De Andreis, *Andrew*
Deane, *Dean*
Deaner, *Dean*
De Angelis, *Angel*
Deans, *Dean*
De Antoni, *Anthony*
Dear
Dearden
Deare, *Dear*
Deares, *Dear*
Dearing, *Dear*
Dearling, *Darling*
Dearman, *Dear*
Dearson, *Dear*
Dearth, *Death*
Deason, *Day*
Deasy
Dêat, *Dieudonné*
D'Eath, *Death*
De Ath, *Death*
Death
Deathridge
Deavall, *Deville*
Deaville, *Deville*
Deavin, *Devin*
De Baat, *Batt*
De Backer, *Baker*
De Baecker, *Baker*
Debald, *Theobald*
Debanc, *Debank*
Debank
Debanks, *Debank*
De Barberi, *Barber*
De Barberis, *Barber*
De Barbieri, *Barber*
De Bas, *Bass*
De Bassis, *Bass*
De Bastiani, *Sebastian*
Debbage
Debbaut, *Theobald*
Debec, *Beck*
De Becker, *Baker*
Dębecki, *Dubnikov*
De Beer, *Bear*
De Bei, *Beau*
De Bel, *Beau*
De Belli, *Beau*
De Bellis, *Beau*
Debelt, *Theobald*
De Benedetti, *Bennett*
De Benedictis, *Bennett*
De Beneditti, *Bennett*
Debenham
De Berk, *Birch*
De Bernardi, *Bernard*
De Bernardis, *Bernard*
De Bever, *Beaver*
De Biaggi, *Blaise*
De Biagi, *Blaise*
De Bianchi, *Blanc*
De Biasi, *Blaise*
De Biasio, *Blaise*
Dębicki, *Dubnikov*
De Bij, *Bee*
De Bischop, *Bishop*
De Bisschop, *Bishop*
De Blanke, *Blanc*
De Blase, *Blaise*
De Blasi, *Blaise*
De Blasiis, *Blaise*
De Blasio, *Blaise*
De Blauw, *Blau*
De Bleeker, *Blacker*
De Blond, *Blunt*
Debnam, *Debenham*
De Bock, *Buck*
De Boeck, *Buck*
De Boer, *Bauer*
De Boni, *Bon*
De Bonis, *Bon*
De Bono, *Bon*
Debov, *Dubnikov*
Dębowski, *Dubnikov*
De Brabandere, *Brabham*
De Brave, *Bravo*
Debray, *Debrie*
Debrie, *Briard*
Debrie
Debrosse, *Brosse*
Debrousse, *Brosse*
De Brouwer, *Brewer*
De Bruijn, *Brown*
De Bruijne, *Brown*
De Bruin, *Brown*
De Bruine, *Brown*
De Bruyn, *Brown*
De Bruyne, *Brown*
De Bul, *Bull*
De Burger, *Burger*
De Burgh, *Burke*
De Burgher, *Burger*
Debussy
Debutt, *Theobald*
De Cae, *Kay*
De Caluwe, *Kahl*
Decamp, *Champ*
Decamps, *Champ*
De Carli, *Charles*
De Carlo, *Charles*
De Caro, *Caro*
De Caroli, *Charles*
De Carolis, *Charles*
De Castri, *Castro*
De Castris, *Castro*
De Cat, *Catt*
De Cauw, *Kay*
Decaux
Decaze, *Casa*
De Cesare, *Cesare*
De Cesaris, *Cesare*
Dechambre, *Chambers*
Dechamp, *Champ*
Dechandt, *Dean*
Dechant, *Dean*
Decharme, *Charme*
Déchaux
Déchelette, *Eschelle*
Déchelle, *Eschelle*
Dechêne, *Chêne*
Dechesne, *Chêne*
De Chiara, *Clare*
Decker
Deckers, *Decker*
Deckert, *Decker*
Deckwarth, *Decker*
Deckwer, *Decker*
Deckwerth, *Decker*
De Cleene, *Klein*
De Clemente, *Clement*
De Clerck, *Clark*
De Clercq, *Clark*
De Clerk, *Clark*
De Clerq, *Clark*
De Cleyne, *Klein*
De Cock, *Cook*
De Cola, *Coll*
De Conynck, *König*
De Copman, *Chapman*
De Costanzo, *Constant*
Decour, *Court*
Decourcey
De Courcy, *Decourcey*
De Coursey, *Decourcey*
Decourt, *Court*
De Craen, *Crane*
De Creemer, *Krämer*
De Cremer, *Krämer*
De Cristofalo, *Christopher*
De Cristoforo, *Christopher*
De Croes, *Kraus*
Decroix, *Cross*
De Crom, *Crome*
De Curti, *Court*
De Curtis, *Court*
De Cuyper, *Cooper*
De Cuypere, *Cooper*
Dede, *Derrick*
De Decker, *Decker*
Dedek, *Dudek*
Dedeke, *Derrick*
De Deken, *Dean*
Dedekind, *Derrick*
Dedeking, *Derrick*
Dederich, *Derrick*
De Deurwaerder, *Thor*
De Dick, *Dick*
De Diere, *Dear*
Dedman, *Debenham*
De Domenicis, *Dominique*
De Domenico, *Dominique*
De Dominici, *Dominique*
De Dominicis, *Dominique*
De Dona, *Donat*
De Donato, *Donat*
De Doove, *Tauber*
De Dresseler, *Drechsler*
De Dun, *Thin*
De Dunne, *Thin*
De Duve, *Tauber*
Dee
Deegan
Deegin, *Deegan*
Deehan, *Deegan*
Deeken, *Derrick*
Deeker, *Ditch*
Deekes, *Ditch*
Deeks, *Ditch*
Deeley
Deem, *Dempster*
Deemer, *Dempster*
Deeming, *Dempster*
Deen, *Dean, Dench*
Deeney, *Denny*
Deeny, *Denny*
Deer, *Dear*
Deere, *Dear*
Deere, *Dwyer*
Deering, *Dear*
Deery
Deesen, *Thiess*
Deetch, *Ditch*
Deetcher, *Ditch*
Deeth, *Death*
Deevey, *Devoy*
Deevy, *Devoy*

Deex, *Ditch*
De Facci, *Boniface*
De Falco, *Faulkes*
De Fant, *Infante*
Defau, *Fage*
Defaux, *Fage*
De Fazio, *Boniface*
De Felice, *Felix*
De Felici, *Felix*
De Ferrari, *Farrar*
De Ferraris, *Farrar*
Deffou, *Fage*
Deffoux, *Fage*
De Filippi, *Philip*
De Filippis, *Philip*
De Filippo, *Philip*
De Florian, *Floriano*
De Florio, *Fleury*
Defond, *Font*
Defont, *Font*
Defontaine, *Fontaine*
Deforest, *Forrest*
Deforge, *Forge*
De Fraine, *Frain*
De Franceschi, *Francis*
De Francesco, *Francis*
De Franchi, *Frank*
De Franchis, *Frank*
De Francisci, *Francis*
De Franciscis, *Francis*
De Franco, *Frank*
de Freitas, *Freitas*
Defrêne, *Frain*
Defresne, *Frain*
De Freyne, *Frain*
De Fries, *Fries*
Dega, *Dean*
De Gan, *Dean*
Degan, *Dean*
Degand, *Gaunt*
Degani, *Dean*
Degano, *Dean*
De Gans, *Goose*
Degant, *Gaunt*
Deganu, *Dean*
Deganut, *Dean*
Deganutti, *Dean*
Degas, *Dean*
De Gaspari, *Kaspar*
De Gasperi, *Kaspar*
De Gast, *Guest*
De Geest, *Geist*
Degenhard, *Deinhard*
Degenschein
Degenszajn, *Degenschein*
Degenszejn, *Degenschein*
De Gentenaer, *Gaunt*
De Germano, *German*
Deghel, *Igel*
De Gier, *Geier*
De Giglio, *Lilly*
De Gioia, *Joy*
De Giorgi, *George*
De Giorgio, *George*
De Giorgis, *George*
De Giovanni, *John*
De Giuli, *Júlio*
Degli Abati, *Abbé*
Degli Abbati, *Abbé*
Degli Antoni, *Anthony*
De Gobbi, *Gobbi*
De Gobbis, *Gobbi*
De Gobi, *Gobbi*
De Gobis, *Gobbi*
De Goede, *Good*
Degoes, *Goose*
De Graeve, *Graf*
De Graf, *Graf*
De Graff, *Graf*
De Grandi, *Grant*
De Grandis, *Grant*
De Grassi, *Grass*
De Greef, *Graf*
De Gregoli, *Gregory*
De Gregorio, *Gregory*
De Griek, *Greco*
De Grijse, *Grice*
De Groot, *Gross*
De Groote, *Gross*
De Gruyter, *Grüter*
De Gryse, *Grice*
De Guglielmo, *William*
De Haan, *Hahn*
De Haas, *Hare*
De Haese, *Hare*
De Hals, *Hals*
De Harde, *Hard*
Dehaye, *Hay*
De Heer, *Herr*
De Herdt, *Hart*
De Hertog, *Herzog*
De Hertoghe, *Herzog*
Dehl, *Derrick*
Dehling, *Derrick*
Dehls, *Derrick*
Dehlsen, *Derrick*
Dehm, *Adam*
Dehmel, *Thomas*
Dehn, *Deinhard, Dench*
Dehncke, *Deinhard*
Dehne, *Dench*
Dehnecke, *Deinhard*
Dehnert, *Deinhard*
Dehnhardt, *Deinhard*
Dehning, *Deinhard*
Dehns, *Deinhard*
Dehondt, *Hund*
De Hoog, *Hoch*
De Hooghe, *Hoch*
Deibel, *Deville*
Deibler, *Taube*
Deibner, *Taube*
Deichman, *Deutsch*
Deickstra, *Ditch*
Deifel, *Deville*
Deighan, *Deegan*
Deighton
Deimler, *Daimler*
Dein, *Deinhard*
Deindl, *Deinhard*
Deinert, *Deinhard*
Deinhard
Deinhardt, *Deinhard*
Deinlein, *Deinhard*
Deissmann, *Thiess*
Deitch, *Deutsch*
Deitchman, *Deutsch*
Deitel, *Derrick, Teitelbaum*
Deitsch, *Deutsch*
Deitschman, *Deutsch*
De Jager, *Jäger*
De Jode, *Jude*
De Jonckheere, *Younger*
De Jong, *Young*
De Jonge, *Young*
De Jongh, *Young*
De Jonghe, *Young*
De Kale, *Kahl*
De Kat, *Catt*
Deken, *Derrick*
Dekena, *Derrick*
Dekens, *Dean*
De Kesel, *Kiesel*
De Keyser, *Kaiser*
Dekker, *Decker*
Dekkers, *Decker*
De Klerk, *Clark*
De Knaap, *Knapp*
De Kneght, *Knight*
De Kock, *Cook*
De Kok, *Cook*
De Koker, *Cook*
De Koning, *König*
De Kort, *Court*
Dekownik, *Decker*
De Kriger, *Krieger*
De Krijger, *Krieger*
De Kuyper, *Cooper*
Delabarre, *Barr*
Delabaye, *Abbey*
Delabbaye, *Abbey*
De Laborde, *Boarder*
Delabrierre, *Bruyère*
Delabrosse, *Brosse*
Delabrousse, *Brosse*
Delabruyère, *Bruyère*
De Lacey, *Lacey*
Delachambre, *Chambers*
Delachaume, *Chaume*
Delachaussée, *Chaussée*
Delachenal, *Chenal*
Delacombe, *Coombe*
Delacoste, *Coste*
Delacôte, *Coste*
Delacour, *Court*
Delacourt, *Court*
Delacroix, *Cross*
Delacroux, *Cross*
De Lacy, *Lacey*
Delafenestre, *Fenster*
Delafield, *Field*
Delafon, *Font*
Delafont, *Font*
Delafontaine, *Fontaine*
Delaforce, *Force*
Delaforest, *Forrest*
Delaforêt, *Forrest*
Delaforge, *Forge*
Delafosse, *Fosse*
Delafoy, *Foy*
Delagneau, *Agnew*
Delahalle, *Hall*
Delahaye, *Hay*
Delahunt, *Delahunty*
Delahunty
Delaistre, *Delâtre*
Delaite, *Delaitre*
Delaitre
Delaloge, *Lodge*
Delamar, *Delamare*
Delamare
Delamarre, *Delamare*
Delamere, *Delamare*
Delamore, *Delamare*
Delamotte, *Motte*
Delaney
De Lang, *Long*
De Lange, *Long*
De Langhe, *Long*
Delany, *Delaney*
Delapierre, *Pierre*
Delaplace, *Place*
Delaplanche, *Planche*
Delaplanque, *Planche*
Delaplatte, *Platt*
Delaporte, *Port*
Delaprade, *Pré*
De Lapradelle, *Pré*
Delarive, *Rive*
Delarivière, *Rivers*
Delaroche, *Roach*
Delaroque, *Roach*
Delarue, *Rue*
Delasalle, *Sale*
Delasouche, *Such*
Delastre, *Delâtre*
Delatouche, *Touche*
Delatour, *Tower*
Delâtre
Delatte, *Delaitre*
Delattre, *Delâtre, Delaitre*
Delaunay, *Delaney*
Delauney, *Delaney*
Delaunois, *Delaney*
Delaunoy, *Delaney*
Delauny, *Delaney*
De Laurentis, *Lawrence*
De Laurenzis, *Lawrence*
Delavaivre, *Vaur*
Delaval, *Vale*
Delavalette, *Vale*
Delavau, *Vale*
Delavault, *Vale*
Delaveau, *Vale*
Delavenne, *Avoine*
Delavigne, *Vine*
Delaville, *Ville*
Delay, *Dunleavy*
Delbalat, *Vallat*
Delbec, *Beck*
Del Beccaro, *Butcher*
Delbecq, *Beck*
Del Bello, *Beau*
Delbergue, *Berge*
Del Bianco, *Blanc*
Del Bono, *Bon*
Del Borgo, *Burke*
Delbos, *Bois*
Del Bosco, *Bois*
Delboscq, *Bois*
Delbouille, *Bouille*
Delbourg, *Burke*
Del Bue, *Boeuf*
Del Buono, *Bon*
Delcambre, *Chambers*
Delcamino, *Chemin*
Delcamp, *Champ*
Delcassé, *Casse*
Delcasse, *Casse*
Delcastel, *Castle*
Del Castello, *Castle*
Del Castiglio, *Castille*
Delcauchie, *Chaussée*
Del Checolo, *Francis*
Del Coco, *Cook*
Del Conte, *Count*
Del Corso, *Bonaccorso*
Delcros, *Creux*
Del Duca, *Duke*
Delea, *Dunleavy*
Deleaney, *Delaney*
Delee, *Dunleavy*
De Leeman, *Lehmann*
De Leener, *Lehmann*
De Leenman, *Lehmann*
De Leeuw, *Löwe*

De Lellis, *Lelli*
De Lello, *Lelli*
De Leo, *Lyon*
De Leonardi, *Leonard*
De Leonardis, *Leonard*
De Leone, *Lyon*
De Leonibus, *Lyon*
Delépine, *Épine*
Delestre, *Delâtre*
Delestrée, *Street*
Delétang, *Etang*
Delétoile, *Stella*
Delétraz, *Street*
Deletrez, *Street*
Del Fabbro, *Fèvre*
Del Fante, *Infante*
Del Felice, *Felix*
Delfini, *Dauphin*
Delfino, *Dauphin*
Delforce, *Force*
Delgadillo, *Delgado*
Delgado
Del Giudice, *Judge*
Del Grande, *Grant*
Del Greco, *Greco*
Del Grosso, *Gross*
Delhommeau, *Orme*
Delhommeaux, *Orme*
Delhostal, *Hostal*
Delhoustal, *Hostal*
Delhoustau, *Hostal*
D'Elia, *Ellis*
D'Elias, *Ellis*
De Liberto, *Albert*
Delicate, *Coates*
De Lichte, *Light*
Delion, *Lyon*
De Lisle, *Lisle*
Delius, *Derrick*
Dell
Dell'Abate, *Abbé*
Dell'Abbate, *Abbé*
Della Bella, *Beau*
Dellac, *Lake*
Della Casa, *Casa*
Della Corte, *Court*
Della Costa, *Coste*
Della Croce, *Cross*
Dell'Agata, *Aggis*
Dell'Agnol, *Angel*
Dell'Agostino, *Austin*
Dell'Amore, *Amor*
Dellapietra, *Pierre*
Della Porta, *Port*
Della Pozza, *Puits*
Dell'Aquila, *Eagle*
Dellar, *Dell*
Dell'Arco, *Arco*
Della Rocca, *Roach*
Della Rovere, *Rouvre*
Della Scala, *Eschelle*
Della Strada, *Street*
Della Torre, *Tower*
Della Valle, *Vale*
Della Vedova, *Widdow*
Della Volpe, *Volpe*
Della Volta, *Volta*
Delle Donne, *Dame*
Delle Grazie, *Grace*
Delleman, *Delman*
Delle Piane, *Plain*
Deller, *Dell*
Dello Iacono, *Deakin*
Dello Jacono, *Deakin*
Dell'Olio, *Oyler*
Dell'Ongaro, *Unger*
Del Lungo, *Long*
Del Luongo, *Long*
Del Magro, *Maigre*
Delman
Delmàs, *Mas*
Delmas, *Mas*
Del Monaco, *Monk*
Delmonte, *Mont*
Delmonti, *Mont*
Del Moro, *Moore*
De Lorenzis, *Lawrence*
De Lorenzo, *Lawrence*
Delorme, *Orme*
Delormeau, *Orme*
Delort, *Ort*
Del Paggio, *Page*
Delpech, *Puy*
Delpero, *Pear*
Delphin, *Dauphin*
Delphy, *Dauphin*
Del Piano, *Plain*
Del Piaz, *Place*
Del Piazzo, *Place*
Del Piccolo, *Piccini*
Delponte, *Pont*
Del Pozzo, *Puits*
Delprat, *Pré*
Del Prato, *Pré*
Del Prete, *Priest*
Del Principe, *Prince*
Delpuch, *Puy*
Delpuech, *Puy*
Delpy, *Pine*
Del Ré, *Ray*
Delrieu, *Rieu*
Del Rio, *Rieu*
Del Rosso, *Rouse*
Delroure, *Rouvre*
Delrue, *Rue*
Del Savio, *Sage*
Del Sellaio, *Seller*
Delsen, *Derrick*
Delsol, *Sol*
Delsuc, *Suc*
Delteil, *Teil*
Deltheil, *Teil*
Delthil, *Teil*
Del Turco, *Turk*
De Luca, *Lucas*
De Lucia, *Lucey*
De Luisi, *Lewis*
Del Vecchio, *Veal*
De Lyle, *Lisle*
De Maegh, *Maw*
De Maerschlack, *Marshall*
Demageard, *Dominique*
De Maggio, *May*
De Magistri, *Master*
De Magistris, *Master*
Demakov, *Damyon*
Demanche, *Dominique*
Demange, *Dominique*
Demangeat, *Dominique*
Demangel, *Dominique*
Demangeon, *Dominique*
Demangeot, *Dominique*
Demangin, *Dominique*
De Mann, *Mann*
Demann, *Thomas*
Demant, *Diamond*
D'Emanuele, *Emmanuel*
De Marchi, *Mark*
De Marchis, *Mark*
Démare, *Delamare*
Demare, *Delamare*
De Maria, *Marie*
De Marini, *Marin*
De Marinis, *Marin*
De Marney, *Marney*
De Martini, *Martin*
De Martinis, *Martin*
De Martino, *Martin*
De Mattei, *Matthew*
De Matteis, *Matthew*
De Mattia, *Matthew*
De Mauro, *Moore*
De Mayer, *Mayer*
Demb, *Dubnikov*
Demba, *Dubnikov*
Dembak, *Dubnikov*
Dembe, *Dubnikov*
Dembiak, *Dubnikov*
Dembin, *Dubnikov*
Dembinsk, *Dubnikov*
Dembiński, *Dubnikov*
Dembinsky, *Dubnikov*
Dembitzer
Dembo, *Dubnikov*
Dembovich, *Dubnikov*
Dembovitz, *Dubnikov*
Dembowitz, *Dubnikov*
Dembowski, *Dubnikov*
Dembowsky, *Dubnikov*
Dembrover, *Dąbrowski*
Dembski, *Dubnikov*
Demby, *Dubnikov*
Demčák, *Dmitriev*
Demchen, *Thomas*
Demchenko, *Damyon*
Demchinyat, *Damyon*
Demčík, *Dmitriev*
Deme, *Dmitriev*
De Meester, *Master*
De Meis, *Bartholomew*
Demel, *Thomas*
Demelt, *Thomas*
Demény, *Damyon*
Demer, *Dempster*
Demers, *Dempster*
Demeshko, *Damyon*
Demeter, *Dmitriev*
Demetr, *Dmitriev*
Demetriades, *Dmitriev*
Demetriou, *Dmitriev*
De Meulder, *Miller*
De Meulenaer, *Miller*
Dc Meuleneer, *Miller*
De Meyer, *Mayer*
De Micheli, *Michael*
De Michelis, *Michael*
Demidas, *Demidov*
Demidov
Demidyonok, *Demidov*
De Mienter, *Minter*
Deming, *Dempster*
De Minico, *Dominique*
De Mitri, *Dmitriev*
De Mitris, *Dmitriev*
Demitrowski, *Dmitriev*
Demjén, *Damyon*
Demke, *Thomas*
Demko, *Dmitriev*
Demkov, *Damyon*
Demkowicz, *Dmitriev*
Demkowski, *Dmitriev*
Demoge, *Dominique*
Demogeot, *Dominique*
De Moldenaer, *Miller*
De Molder, *Miller*
De Molenaer, *Miller*
Demonge, *Dominique*
Demongeot, *Dominique*
Demont, *Mont*
De Moor, *Moore*
De Moore, *Moore*
Demougeot, *Dominique*
Demougin, *Dominique*
Demoulin, *Mill*
Dempsey
Dempster
Dempsy, *Dempsey*
Demschke, *Thomas*
De Mulder, *Miller*
De Munck, *Monk*
De Munnik, *Monk*
De Munnink, *Monk*
De Muntenaer, *Minter*
De Munter, *Minter*
De Muynck, *Monk*
De Muys, *Maus*
Demyanchuk, *Damyon*
Demyanets, *Damyon*
Demyanok, *Damyon*
Demyanov, *Damyon*
Demykin, *Damyon*
Denaghy, *Donohue*
Denbeigh, *Denby*
Denbigh, *Denby*
Den Broeder, *Brother*
Denby
Dence, *Dench*
Dench
Den Dooven, *Tauber*
Denecke, *Deinhard*
De Neef, *Neve*
De Neeff, *Neve*
De Negri, *Noir*
De Negris, *Noir*
Dénes, *Dennis*
Deng, *Thon*
Dengler
Denham
den Hoed, *Huth*
Denholm
Denholme, *Denholm*
Denial, *Daniel*
Deniau, *Daniel*
Deniaud, *Daniel*
Denicke, *Deinhard*
De Nicola, *Nicholas*
Deniel, *Daniel*
Denis, *Dennis*
Denisard, *Dennis*
Deniseau, *Dennis*
Denisenya, *Dennis*
Deniset, *Dennis*
Denisevich, *Dennis*
Denisi, *Dennis*
Deniskevich, *Dennis*
Denison, *Dennis*
Denisot, *Dennis*
Denisov, *Dennis*
Denisovich, *Dennis*
Deniss, *Dennis*
Denisyev, *Dennis*
Denisyuk, *Dennis*
Denizet, *Dennis*
Denizot, *Dennis*
Denley
Denly, *Denley*

Denman
Denn, *Dennis*
Denne, *Dennis*
Dennehy, *Donohue*
Dennell, *Daniel*
Denner, *Dean, Tanner*
Dennerlein, *Deinhard*
Dennert, *Deinhard*
Dennert, *Tanner*
Dennery
Dennes, *Dennis*
Denness, *Dennis*
Dennet, *Dennis*
Dennett, *Dennis*
Denney, *Denny*
Denning, *Dineen*
Dennington
Dennis
Dennish, *Dench*
Dennison, *Dennis*
Denniss, *Dennis*
Denniston
Dennitts, *Dennis*
Denns, *Dench*
Denny
Dennys, *Dench*
De Nobele, *Noble*
de Nógla, *Nangle*
Den Olden, *Old*
Den Ouden, *Old*
D'Enrico, *Henry*
Densey, *Dansie*
Densie, *Dansie*
Denson, *Dean*
Densum, *Dean*
Dent
Dentch, *Dench*
Dentith, *Daintith*
Denton
Dentu, *Dent*
Denty, *Daintith*
Dentz, *Tanzer*
Dentzler, *Tanzer*
Deny, *Dennis*
Denyagin, *Dennis*
Denyakin, *Dennis*
Denyer
Denys, *Dennis*
Denyukhin, *Dennis*
Denzel, *Tanzer*
Denzey, *Dansie*
Denzle, *Tanzer*
Déodat, *Dieudonné*
Deodati, *Dieudonné*
Deodato, *Dieudonné*
De Paauw, *Peacock*
De Paepe, *Pope*
De Paeuw, *Peacock*
De Palma, *Palmer*
De Paoli, *Paul*
De Paolis, *Paul*
Depardé, *Pardoe*
Depardieu, *Pardoe*
De Pasquale, *Pascall*
De Pasqualis, *Pascall*
De Pater, *Pater*
De Pauw, *Peacock*
De Pero, *Peter*
De Pester, *Pfister*
De Petris, *Peter*
De Pietri, *Peter*
De Pietro, *Peter*
Deplaix, *Place*
Deplanche, *Planche*
Deplanque, *Planche*
Deplatte, *Platt*
Depont, *Pont*
De Potter, *Potter*
Deprat, *Pré*
De Pretis, *Priest*
DePrins, *Prince*
De Prof, *Provost*
De Proot, *Provost*
De Pruis, *Preuss*
De Pypere, *Piper*
De Quincey, *Quincey*
De Raeve, *Raven*
De Rao, *Rollo*
Derby, *Darby*
Derbyshire, *Darbyshire*
De Rechter, *Richter*
De Ree, *Ray*
De Rege, *Ray*
De Regibus, *Ray*
De Regis, *Ray*
De Renzis, *Lawrence*
Derering, *Derrick*
Derfert, *Thorpe*
Derfler, *Thorpe*
Dericks, *Derrick*
De Ridder, *Rider*
De Riddere, *Rider*
De Rider, *Rider*
De Ridere, *Rider*
De Righe, *Rich*
De Rijk, *Rich*
De Rijke, *Rich*
Dering, *Dear*
De Riu, *Rieu*
Derivier, *Rivero*
Derivière, *Rivers*
De Rivo, *Rieu*
Derk, *Derrick*
Derks, *Derrick*
Derksen, *Derrick*
Dermody, *Dermott*
Dermott
Derner, *Thorn*
Derobert, *Robert*
De Robertis, *Robert*
De Roberto, *Robert*
Deroche, *Roach*
De Rond, *Round*
De Ronde, *Round*
De Roo, *Roth*
De Roos, *Rose*
Deroque, *Roach*
De Rosse, *Rouse*
De Rossi, *Rouse*
Derouet, *Drew*
Derouin, *Drew*
Derrick
D'Errico, *Henry*
Derue, *Rue*
De Ruggero, *Roger*
De Ruggiero, *Roger*
De Ruijter, *Reuter*
De Russi, *Rouse*
De Ruyter, *Reuter*
De Ryche, *Rich*
De Sadelaer, *Sadler*
Desagnes, *Sagne*
De Sanctis, *Saint*
De Santi, *Saint*
De Santis, *Saint*
Desarches, *Arco*
Desargues, *Arco*
Desbarres, *Barr*
Desbois, *Bois*
Desborough
Descamps, *Champ*
Descartes
Descazes, *Casa*
Deschamps, *Champ*
Deschelle, *Eschelle*
De Scheper, *Schäfer*
De Schoone, *Schön*
De Schrijnwerker, *Schreiner*
Desclouzeaux, *Close*
Desclozeaux, *Close*
Descombes, *Coombe*
Descroix, *Cross*
Desdoights, *Douet*
Desdouets, *Douet*
Desdouits, *Douet*
De Serra, *Serre*
Désesquelle, *Eschelle*
Desessard, *Essart*
Desessarts, *Essart*
Desfaux, *Fage*
Desfontaines, *Fontaine*
Desforges, *Forge*
Desfossés, *Fosse*
Desfoux, *Fage*
Deshayes, *Hay*
Deshorts, *Ort*
Desideri, *Didier*
Desiderio, *Didier*
De Silvestri, *Silvester*
De Silvestris, *Silvester*
De Simone, *Simon*
De Simoni, *Simon*
Desjardins, *Gardener*
De Smaele, *Small*
Desmarais, *Marsh*
Desmarest, *Marsh*
De Smet, *Smith*
Desmeth, *Smith*
De Smid, *Smith*
Desmolins, *Mill*
Desmond
Desnoyers, *Noyer*
De Soet, *Sweet*
De Soete, *Sweet*
De Somer, *Summer*
Désormeaux, *Orme*
Desorts, *Ort*
Desouche, *Such*
De Souza, *Sousa*
Despenser, *Spence*
Desplanches, *Planche*
Desportes, *Port*
Després, *Pré*
Desprez, *Pré*
Desroches, *Roach*
Desroques, *Roach*
Desrues, *Rue*
Dessewffy, *Didier*
Destaing, *Etang*
Destan, *Etang*
De Starcke, *Stark*
De Starke, *Stark*
D'Este, *Este*
De Stefani, *Stephen*
De Stefanis, *Stephen*
Destombe, *Destombes*
Destombes
Destouches, *Touche*
Destrée, *Street*
De Strycker, *Striker*
Desvaux, *Vale*
Desvignes, *Vine*
Desvilles, *Ville*
Desvillettes, *Ville*
Desvoivres, *Vaur*
De Swaan, *Swan*
De Swaen, *Swan*
De Swart, *Schwarz*
De Swarte, *Schwarz*
Détang, *Etang*
Detels, *Derrick*
Detheridge, *Deathridge*
De Timmerman, *Zimmermann*
Détoile, *Stella*
Detombes, *Destombes*
De Toni, *Toney*
de Toulouse, *Toulouse*
Détraz, *Street*
Dettmer, *Dietmar*
Dettmers, *Dietmar*
De Turk, *Turk*
Deubel, *Deville*
Deubler, *Taube*
Deubner, *Taube*
Deubov, *Dubnikov*
Deudat, *Dieudonné*
Deufel, *Deville*
Deus, *Dios*
Deusch, *Deutsch*
Deusing, *Thiess*
Deuss, *Thiess*
Deussen, *Thiess*
Deussing, *Thiess*
Deutsch
Deutscher, *Deutsch*
Deutschländer, *Deutsch*
Deutschman, *Deutsch*
Deutschmann, *Deutsch*
Deval, *Vale*
De Valkener, *Faulkner*
Devall, *Deville*
Devane
Devaney
Devany, *Devaney*
Devaux, *Vale*
Deveaux, *Vale*
De Vecchi, *Veal*
De Veer, *Feather*
Devenish, *Devonshire*
Devenny, *Devaney*
Deventer
Dever, *Dwyer*
Deveraux, *Devereux*
Devereaux, *Devereux*
Devereu, *Devereux*
Devereux
Deverose, *Devereux*
Deveroux, *Devereux*
De Verver, *Färber*
De Vettori, *Victor*
De Veuster, *Forrest*
Devey, *Devoy*
Devèze
De Vico, *Vico*
De Vieuw, *Widdow*
Devill, *Deville*
De Ville, *Deville*
Deville
Deville, *Ville*
Deviller, *Villiers*
Devillette, *Ville*
Devilliers, *Villiers*
Devin
De Vincenzo, *Vincent*
De Vinck, *Fink*
Devine, *Devin*

De Vink, *Fink*
Devinn, *Devin*
De Vio, *Vito*
De Vis, *Fish*
De Visch, *Fish*
De Visscher, *Fisher*
Devissen, *Thiess*
De Visser, *Fisher*
De Vit, *Vito*
De Vita, *Vita*
De Viti, *Vito*
De Vito, *Vito*
Devitt, *David*
Devkin, *Devin*
De Vlaminck, *Fleming*
De Vleesauwer, *Flesher*
De Vleeschauwer, *Flesher*
De Vleeschouwer, *Flesher*
De Vleesouwer, *Flesher*
De Vlesave, *Flesher*
Devlin
Devochkin, *Devin*
De Vocht, *Vogt*
De Vogel, *Vogel*
De Voghel, *Vogel*
De Voller, *Fuller*
Devon, *Devonshire*
Devonish, *Devonshire*
Devonshire
De Voogd, *Vogt*
De Voogel, *Vogel*
De Voogt, *Vogt*
De Vos, *Fox*
Devoskin, *Dvorin*
Devoy
De Vré, *Fried*
De Vree, *Fried*
De Vrees, *Fries*
De Vreese, *Fries*
De Vrient, *Friend*
De Vries, *Fries*
De Vroom, *Fromm*
De Vroome, *Fromm*
De Vuono, *Bon*
Devushkin, *Devin*
De Vuyst, *Faust*
Dew, *Duff*
Dewald, *Theobald*
De Wall, *Wallace*
Dewan, *Devane*
Dewar
De Weber, *Weaver*
De Weduwe, *Widdow*
De Weijer, *Weiher*
De Wever, *Weaver*
Dewey
De Weyer, *Weiher*
Dewhirst, *Dewhurst*
Dewhurst
Dewi, *David*
De Wijn, *Wein*
De Wijs, *Wise*
De Wijze, *Wise*
De Wilde, *Wild*
De Wildt, *Wild*
De Winter, *Winter*
De Wit, *White*
De Witt, *White*
De Witte, *White*
De Wolf, *Wolf*
De Wolff, *Wolf*
De Wulf, *Wolf*
De Wulfe, *Wolf*
De Wyn, *Wein*
De Wyse, *Wise*
Dexter, *Dyer*
Dey, *Day*
D'Eye, *Day*
Deyes, *Day*
Deyns, *Dain*
Deyville, *Deville*
De Zoete, *Sweet*
Dezsö, *Didier*
Dezsöffi, *Didier*
De Zuani, *John*
De Zuzter, *Schuster*
De Zwaan, *Swan*
De Zwart, *Schwarz*
De Zwitser, *Schweitzer*
Dhorme, *Orme*
Dhôtel, *Hostal*
D'Hozier, *Dozier*
Diaconescu, *Deakin*
Diacono, *Deakin*
Diaghilev, *Dzięgielewski*
Diago, *Diego*
Diagonetti, *Deakin*
Diamand, *Diamond*
Diamandstein, *Diamond*
Diamant, *Diamond*
Diamantstein, *Diamond*
Diament, *Diamond*
Diamond
Diamont, *Diamond*
Diamontstein, *Diamond*
Di Antonio, *Anthony*
Dias, *Diego*
Diat, *Dieudonné*
Díaz, *Diego*
Di Bartoli, *Bartholomew*
Di Bartolomeo, *Bartholomew*
Di Bartolommeo, *Bartholomew*
Di Batista, *Baptiste*
Di Battista, *Baptiste*
Di Baudi, *Baud*
Dibb
Dibbaut, *Theobald*
Dibbauts, *Theobald*
Dibble, *Theobald*
Dibbs, *Dibb*
Dibden
Dibelius, *Theobald*
Di Bello, *Beau*
Di Bernardo, *Bernard*
Di Biagio, *Blaise*
Di Biasi, *Blaise*
Di Biasio, *Blaise*
Dible, *Theobald*
Diboll, *Theobald*
Di Bono, *Bon*
Di Buono, *Bon*
Di Carlo, *Charles*
Di Caro, *Caro*
Di Cesare, *Cesare*
Di Chiara, *Clare*
Dichter
Dick
Dickason, *Dick*
Dicke, *Dick*
Dickels, *Dick*
Dicken, *Dick*
Dickens, *Dick*
Dickenson, *Dick*
Dickenstein, *Dick*
Dicker
Dickerman, *Dick*
Dickerson, *Dick*
Dickert, *Dicker*
Dickeson, *Dick*
Dicketts, *Dick*
Dickey, *Dick*
Dickhoff, *Dick*
Dickie, *Dick*
Dickin, *Dick*
Dickings, *Dick*
Dickins, *Dick*
Dickinson, *Dick*
Dickison, *Dick*
Dickman, *Dick*
Dickman, *Ditch*
Dickmann, *Dick*
Dickons, *Dick*
Dicks, *Dick*
Dicksee, *Dixie*
Dickson, *Dick*
Dickstein, *Dick*
Di Clemente, *Clement*
Di Cola, *Coll*
Di Contino, *Count*
Di Costanzo, *Constant*
Di Curti, *Court*
Didden, *Derrick*
Diddens, *Derrick*
Didelet, *Didier*
Didelot, *Didier*
Dideriks, *Derrick*
Dideron, *Didier*
Diderot, *Didier*
Didier
Didion, *Didier*
Didiot, *Didier*
Di Domenico, *Dominique*
Di Donato, *Donat*
Didot, *Didier*
Didriksen, *Derrick*
Didrot, *Didier*
Diebald, *Theobald*
Diebels, *Theobald*
Diebold, *Theobald*
Dieck, *Ditch*
Dieckmann, *Ditch*
Diede, *Derrick*
Diederich, *Derrick*
Diedericks, *Derrick*
Diedericksen, *Derrick*
Dief, *Dieudonné*
Diegnan, *Deegan*
Diego
Diéguez, *Diego*
Diehl, *Derrick*
Diehlmann, *Derrick*
Diehls, *Derrick*
Diehm, *Derrick*
Diel, *Derrick*
Diem, *Dietmar*
Diemant, *Diamond*
Diemar, *Dietmar*
Diemer, *Dietmar*
Dienes, *Dennis*
Dienl, *Deinhard*
Diepel, *Theobald*
Diepelt, *Theobald*
Diepold, *Theobald*
Diepolder, *Theobald*
Dier, *Dear*
Dierck, *Derrick*
Diercks, *Derrick*
Dierckx, *Derrick*
Dierich, *Düring*
Diericks, *Derrick*
Dierickx, *Derrick*
Dierix, *Derrick*
Dierking, *Derrick*
Dierks, *Derrick*
Dierksen, *Derrick*
Dies, *Thiess*
Diesch, *Derrick*
Diesel
Diesing, *Thiess*
Diess, *Thiess*
Diessens, *Thiess*
Diestel, *Distel*
Diestelmann, *Distel*
Diet, *Derrick, Dieudonné*
Dieterich, *Derrick*
Dieterle, *Derrick*
Dieth, *Derrick*
Dietjen, *Derrick*
Dietle, *Derrick*
Dietlein, *Derrick*
Dietler, *Derrick*
Dietmann, *Derrick*
Dietmar
Dietreich, *Derrick*
Dietrich, *Derrick*
Diets, *Derrick*
Dietsch, *Derrick*
Dietschi, *Derrick*
Dietz, *Derrick*
Dietze, *Derrick*
Dieudonné
Dieulafé, *Dieulafoy*
Dieulafoy
Díez, *Diego*
Diez, *Dieudonné*
Di Falco, *Faulkes*
Di Fazio, *Boniface*
Di Felice, *Felix*
Di Filippo, *Philip*
Di Fiore, *Flower*
Di Folca, *Foulkes*
Di Francesco, *Francis*
Di Franco, *Frank*
Di Frisco, *Francis*
Di Gaetano, *Gaetano*
Digan, *Deegan*
Digan, *Dick*
Digance, *Dick*
Digby
Di Gennaro, *January*
Digg
Diggan, *Dick*
Diggen, *Dick*
Diggens, *Dick*
Digges, *Digg*
Diggin, *Deegan*
Diggings, *Dick*
Diggins, *Dick*
Diggle, *Digg*
Diggles, *Digg*
Diggon, *Dick*
Dightham, *Deighton*
Dighton, *Deighton*
Di Giacomettino, *James*
Di Giacomo, *James*
Digin, *Deegan*
Di Gioia, *Joy*
Di Giorgio, *George*
Di Giulio, *Júlio*
Digman, *Dick, Ditch*
Dignam, *Deegan*
Dignan, *Deegan*
Dignen, *Deegan*
Di Gratia, *Grace*
Di Gregorio, *Gregory*
Dihl, *Derrick*

Di Iorio, *George*
Dijkema, *Ditch*
Dijkman, *Ditch*
Dijkstra, *Ditch*
Dik, *Dick*
Dike, *Ditch*
Dikerman, *Dick*
Dikes, *Ditch*
Dikfeld, *Dick*
Dikken, *Dick*
Dikkes, *Dick*
Dikman, *Dick*
Dikshtein, *Dick*
Dikstein, *Dick*
Diksztejn, *Dick*
Di Lauro, *Laur*
Di Lazzari, *Lazar*
Di Leo, *Lyon*
Di Leonardi, *Leonard*
Di Lione, *Lyon*
Dilks, *Dillon*
Dillamore, *Delamare*
Dillane, *Dillon*
Dilling, *Dowling*
Dillon
Dilmann, *Derrick*
Di Lorenzo, *Lawrence*
Di Lucca, *Lucas*
Di Luisi, *Lewis*
Dilworth
Di Maggio, *May*
Dimanche, *Dominique*
Dimant, *Diamond*
Dimantstein, *Diamond*
Di Maria, *Marie*
Di Martino, *Martin*
Di Mattei, *Matthew*
Di Matteo, *Matthew*
Di Mauro, *Moore*
Dimblebee, *Dimbleby*
Dimbleby
Dimbledee, *Dimbleby*
Diment, *Diamond*
Dimentstein, *Diamond*
Di Meo, *Bartholomew*
Dimet, *Diamond*
Dimetbarg, *Diamond*
Dimetman, *Diamond*
Dimetstein, *Diamond*
Dimić, *Dmitriev*
Dimitresco, *Dmitriev*
Dimitrie, *Dmitriev*
Dimitriev, *Dmitriev*
Dimitrijević, *Dmitriev*
Dimitrov, *Dmitriev*
Dimmack, *Dymock*
Dimmick, *Dymock*
Dimmock, *Dymock*
Dimock, *Dymock*
Dimond, *Diamond*
Dimont, *Diamond*
Din, *Dennis*
Dinan, *Dineen*
di Napoli, *Napoli*
Dineen
Dines, *Dain*
Dines
Dinesen, *Dennis*
Dinesohn, *Dines*
Dineson, *Dines*
Diness, *Dines*
Dingle
Dingott
Dinin, *Dines*
Dinis, *Dennis*
Dinjes, *Dennis*
Dinman, *Thin*
Dinn, *Dennis*
Dinneen, *Dineen*
Dinner, *Thin*
Dinnies, *Dennis*
Dinniges, *Dennis*
Dinnis, *Dennis, Dines*
Dinovitz, *Dines*
Dinowitz, *Dines*
Dins, *Dennis*
Dinsdale
Dinse, *Dennis*
Dinswoodie, *Dunwoodie*
Dinu, *Constantine*
Dinwiddie, *Dunwoodie*
Dinwoodie, *Dunwoodie*
Dinzey, *Dansie*
Dinzon, *Dines*
Diodati, *Dieudonné*
Diodato, *Dieudonné*
Diogo, *Diego*
Dion
Dionet, *Dion*
Dionis, *Dennis*
Dionisetti, *Dennis*
Dionisetto, *Dennis*
Dionisi, *Dennis*
Dionísio, *Dennis*
Dionisio, *Dennis*
Dioniso, *Dennis*
Dionne, *Dion*
Dionnet, *Dion*
Dios
Dioudonnat, *Dieudonné*
Di Pasqua, *Pask*
Di Pierro, *Peter*
Di Pietro, *Peter*
Dippel, *Theobald*
Dippelt, *Theobald*
Dippl, *Theobald*
Dipple, *Theobald*
Dippolt, *Theobald*
Dirand, *Durant*
Dirks, *Derrick*
Dirksen, *Derrick*
Di Roberto, *Robert*
Di Ruggero, *Roger*
Di Ruggiero, *Roger*
Di Salvo, *Salvi*
Discher, *Tischler*
Disley
Disney
Disraeli, *Israel*
Diss
Distel
Distelfeld, *Distel*
Distelman, *Distel*
Distelmann, *Distel*
Distler, *Distel*
Ditch
Ditchburn
Ditcher, *Ditch*
Ditchfield
Dittmaier, *Dietmar*
Dittmair, *Dietmar*
Dittman, *Derrick*
Dittmann, *Dietmar*
Dittmar, *Dietmar*
Dittmer, *Dietmar*
Dittmers, *Dietmar*
Dittmeyr, *Dietmar*
Ditton
Dittrich, *Derrick*
Divall, *Deville*
Dive, *Dives*
Divell, *Deville*
Diver
Divers, *Diver*
Dives
Diviller, *Villiers*
Divillier, *Villiers*
Divín, *Dennis*
Divína, *Dennis*
Divine, *Devin*
Divíš, *Dennis*
Divíšek, *Dennis*
Divold, *Theobald*
Dix, *Dick*
Dixcee, *Dixie*
Dixcey, *Dixie*
Dixey, *Dixie*
Dixi, *Dixie*
Dixie
Dixon, *Dick*
Dixson, *Dick*
Dizier, *Didier*
Djaković, *Jacob*
Djekić, *Jacob*
Djeković, *Jacob*
Djokić, *Jacob*
Djoković, *Jacob*
Djordjević, *George*
Djorić, *George*
Djurdjević, *George*
Djurdjić, *George*
Djurić, *George*
Djuričić, *George*
Djurišić, *George*
Djurković, *George*
Djurović, *George*
Dkány, *Dean*
Dlouhý, *Dolgov*
Dlug, *Dolgov*
Dlugacz, *Dolgov*
Dlugatch, *Dolgov*
Dlugatz, *Dolgov*
Dlugin, *Dolgov*
Długosz, *Dolgov*
Długoszewski, *Dolgov*
Dlugovitzky, *Dolgov*
Dmíšek, *Dmitriev*
Dmiterko, *Dmitriev*
Dmitrichenko, *Dmitriev*
Dmitrienko, *Dmitriev*
Dmitriev
Dmitrievski, *Dmitriev*
Dmitrović, *Dmitriev*
Dmitruk, *Dmitriev*
Dmych, *Dmitriev*
Dmytryk, *Dmitriev*
Do, *Dodd*
Doag, *Doig*
Doak, *Doig*
Doane, *Devane*
Dobb
Dobbe, *Dobb*
Dobbelstein, *Doppler*
Dobbie, *Dobb*
Dobbin, *Dobb*
Dobbing, *Dobb*
Dobbings, *Dobb*
Dobbins, *Dobb*
Dobbinson, *Dobb*
Dobbison, *Dobb*
Dobbs, *Dobb*
Dobby, *Dobb*
Dobbyn, *Dobb*
Dobe, *Tauber*
Dobel
Dobell, *Dobel*
Dobelmann, *Dobel*
Dobeš, *Tobias*
Dobey, *Dobb*
Dobiáš, *Tobias*
Dobie, *Dobb*
Dobieson, *Dobb*
Dobing, *Dobb*
Dobinson, *Dobb*
Dobisch, *Tobias*
Dobkin
Döbl, *Tobias*
Doble, *Dobel*
Dobler, *Dobel*
Dobney, *Daubeney*
Dobre, *Dobrý*
Dobrescu, *Dobrý*
Dobrić, *Dobrý*
Dobrin
Dobroń, *Dobrý*
Dobroniak, *Dobrý*
Dobronravov
Dobrovev, *Dobrynin*
Dobrovich, *Dobrynin*
Dobrovichev, *Dobrynin*
Dobrovolný, *Dobrovolski*
Dobrovolski
Dobrovský
Dobrowolski, *Dobrovolski*
Dobrý
Dobrynin
Dobryshin, *Dobrynin*
Dobrzyński
Dobson, *Dobb*
Doby, *Dobb*
Dočekal
Docharty, *Doherty*
Docherty, *Doherty*
Dočkal, *Dočekal*
Döcker, *Decker*
Docker
Dockeray, *Dockray*
Dockerty, *Doherty*
Dockery, *Dockray*
Dockett, *Doggett*
Dockray
Dockry, *Dockray*
Docq, *Joyce*
Docwra, *Dockray*
Docwray, *Dockray*
Dod, *Dodd*
Dodd
Dodding, *Dodd*
Doddington
Dodds, *Dodd*
Dode, *Dodd, Dude*
Dodell, *Dodd*
Doden, *Dude*
Dodet, *Dodd*
Dodge
Dodgeon, *Dodge*
Dodgeoon, *Dodge*
Dodgin, *Dodge*
Dodgshon, *Dodge*
Dodgshun, *Dodge*
Dodgson, *Dodge*
Dodin, *Dodd*
Dodinet, *Dodd*
Dodman, *Dodd*
Dodon, *Dodd*
Dods, *Dodd*

Dodson, *Dodd*
Dodsworth
Doe
Doeg, *Doig*
Doey, *Duffy*
Dogerty, *Doherty*
Doggart, *Doherty*
Doggett
Doghartie, *Doherty*
Dogherty, *Doherty*
Doherty
Dohmann, *Thomas*
Dohmer, *Thomas*
Dohmjan, *Damyon*
Dohms, *Thomas*
Dohnal
Dohnke, *Thon*
Dohr, *Thor*
Döhring, *Düring*
Dohrmann, *Thor*
Doidge, *Dodge*
Doig
Doige, *Dodge*
Doin, *Dodd*
Doke, *Digg*
Dolamore, *Delamare*
Dolan
Dolat, *Dolé*
Dolce, *Duce*
Dolcetta, *Duce*
Dolcetti, *Duce*
Dolci, *Duce*
Dolcini, *Duce*
Dolcino, *Duce*
Dolciotti, *Duce*
Dolcis, *Duce*
Dolé
Dolejš
Dolejšek, *Dolejš*
Dolejší, *Dolejš*
Doley, *Doyley*
Doležal
Doležel, *Doležal*
Dolfini, *Dauphin*
Dolfino, *Dauphin*
Dolgin, *Dolgov*
Dolgopolov
Dolgopolski, *Polański*
Dolgov
Doliński
Dolittle
Dolk
Dölker
Doll
Dollamore, *Delamare*
Dollat, *Dolé*
Dollé, *Dolé*
Dollemore, *Delamare*
Dolley, *Doyley*
Dolleymore, *Delamare*
Dollimore, *Delamare*
Dolling, *Dowling*
Dollman, *Doll*
Dollymore, *Delamare*
Dolman, *Doll*
Dolmetsch, *Tolmachev*
Dolohunty, *Delahunty*
Dolomieu
Dolphin, *Duffin*
Domagała
Domagalski, *Domagała*
Dománek, *Dominique*
Domange, *Dominique*
Domann, *Thomas*
Domański, *Dominique*
Domański
Domaschek, *Thomas*
Domaschke, *Thomas*
Domb, *Dubnikov*
Dombe, *Dubnikov*
Dombek, *Dubnikov*
Dombovsky, *Dubnikov*
Dombrovski, *Dąbrowski*
Dombrovsky, *Dąbrowski*
Dombrowski, *Dąbrowski*
Dombrowsky, *Dąbrowski*
Döme, *Dmitriev*
Dome, *Dempster*
Domec, *Domecq*
Domecq
Domek, *Dominique*
Dömel, *Thomas*
Domenc, *Dominique*
Domènech, *Dominique*
Domeneghetti, *Dominique*
Domeneghini, *Dominique*
Domenge, *Dominique*
Domenget, *Dominique*
Domengue, *Dominique*
Domenichelli, *Dominique*
Domenichetti, *Dominique*
Domenichini, *Dominique*
Domenici, *Dominique*
Domenico, *Dominique*
Domenicone, *Dominique*
Domenicucci, *Dominique*
Domerc, *Dominique*
Domerq, *Dominique*
Domerque, *Dominique*
Domian, *Damyon*
Domichelli, *Dominique*
Domico, *Dominique*
Domiczek, *Dominique*
Dominec, *Dominique*
Dominelli, *Dominique*
Dominetti, *Dominique*
Domingo, *Dominique*
Domingos, *Dominique*
Domingues, *Dominique*
Domínguez, *Dominique*
Domini, *Dominique*
Dominiak, *Dominique*
Dominicacci, *Dominique*
Dominichelli, *Dominique*
Dominichetti, *Dominique*
Dominichini, *Dominique*
Dominici, *Dominique*
Dominico, *Dominique*
Dominigazzo, *Dominique*
Dominighi, *Dominique*
Dominik, *Dominique*
Dominique
Dominka, *Dominique*
Domján, *Damyon*
Domke, *Thomas*
Dommerque, *Dominique*
Domnick, *Dominique*
Domokos, *Dominique*
Domonkos, *Dominique*
Dömötör, *Dmitriev*
Domvile, *Dumville*
Domville, *Dumville*
Don, *Dodd, Dunn*
Dona, *Donat*
Donachie, *Donohue*
Donadini, *Donat*
Donadon, *Donat*
Donadoni, *Donat*
Donagh, *McDonagh*
Donaghey, *Donohue*
Donaghie, *Donohue*
Donaghoe, *Donohue*
Donaghue, *Donohue*
Donaghy, *Donohue*
Donahue, *Donohue*
Donald
Donaldson, *Donald*
Donát, *Donat*
Donat
Donatelli, *Donat*
Donáth, *Donat*
Donath, *Donat*
Donati, *Donat*
Donatiello, *Donat*
Donatini, *Donat*
Donato, *Donat*
Donatoni, *Donat*
Donaty, *Donat*
Donavan, *Donovan*
Donavin, *Donovan*
Donder, *Donner*
Donderer, *Donner*
Donegan
Donelan, *Donald*
Donellan, *Donald*
Donet, *Donat*
Doney, *Donat*
Dönges, *Thon*
Dönhardt, *Deinhard*
D'Onise, *Dennis*
Donisetti, *Dennis*
Donisetto, *Dennis*
D'Onisi, *Dennis*
Donisi, *Dennis*
Doniso, *Dennis*
Donizeau, *Dennis*
Donk, *Dung*
Donker
Donkers, *Donker*
Donlan, *Donald*
Donleavy, *Dunleavy*
Donlon, *Donald*
Donn, *Dunn*
Donna, *Dame*
Donnagh, *McDonagh*
Donnan, *Dunn*
Donnat, *Donat*
Donnay, *Donat*
Donné, *Donat*
Donne, *Dunn*
Donneely, *Donnelly*
Donnell, *Donald*
Donnellan, *Donald*
Donnelly
Donner
Donnerer, *Donner*
Donnet, *Donat*
Donnett, *Donat*
Donney, *Donat*
Donogh, *McDonagh*
Donoghue, *Donohue*
Donohoe, *Donohue*
Donohue
Donoso
Donough, *McDonagh*
Donov, *Dorofeev*
Donovan
Dons, *Donat*
Doobe, *Tauber*
Doody, *Duddy*
Doohan, *Duggan*
Dooks, *Digg*
Doolan
Doole, *Donald*
Doolen, *Doolan*
Dooley
Doolin, *Doolan*
Doolittle, *Dolittle*
Dooly, *Dooley*
Doone, *Devane*
Doonican, *Donegan*
Doorneman, *Thorn*
Döpfler, *Töpfer*
Döpfner, *Töpfer*
Dopkin, *Dobrin*
Döpner, *Töpfer*
Doppelstein, *Doppler*
Doppler
Döppner, *Töpfer*
Dopsch, *Tobias*
Dopson, *Dobb*
Dorado, *Doré*
Doran
Dorant, *Durant*
Dorat, *Doré*
Dorcey, *Darcy*
Doré
Dore
Doree, *Doré*
Dores
Doret, *Théodore*
Dorey, *Doré*
Dorf, *Thorpe*
Dörfer, *Thorpe*
Dorfer, *Thorpe*
Dörfert, *Thorpe*
Dörfle, *Thorpe*
Dörflein, *Thorpe*
Dorfman, *Thorpe*
Dorfmann, *Thorpe*
Dorfsman, *Thorpe*
Dorfsmann, *Thorpe*
Dorgan
Dörges, *Isidore*
Dörich, *Düring*
Dorin, *Dorofeev, Théodore*
Döring, *Düring*
Doring, *Dear*
Dorival
Dörk, *Derrick*
Dörken, *Derrick*
Dorkin, *Dorofeev*
Dörks, *Derrick*
Dörksen, *Derrick*
Dörl, *Thor*
Dorling, *Darling*
Dorman, *Dear*
Dormann, *Thor*
Dorme, *Orme*
Dormer
Dormeuil, *Orme*
Dorn, *Thorn*
Dornan
Dornbusch, *Thorn*
Dornbush, *Thorn*
Dorner, *Thorn*
Dorofankin, *Dorofeev*
Dorofanov, *Dorofeev*
Dorofeev
Doroshaev, *Dorofeev*
Doroshenko, *Dorofeev*
Doroshev, *Dorofeev*
Doroshevich, *Dorofeev*
Doroshkevich, *Dorofeev*
Doroshko, *Dorofeev*
Doroszewski, *Dorofeev*

Dorot, *Théodore*
Dorp, *Thorpe*
Dorpma, *Thorpe*
Dorran, *Doran*
Dorrance, *Durant*
Dorrell, *Darell*
Dorrian, *Doran*
Dörries, *Isidore*
Dorrington
Dorrins, *Durant*
Dörscher, *Drescher*
Dorset, *Dorsett*
Dorsett
Dorsey
D'Orsi, *Orso*
Dorsman, *Drescher*
D'Orso, *Orso*
Dorval, *Dorival*
Dorwart, *Thor*
Döscher, *Drescher*
Dossett, *Dorsett*
Dostál
Dostanić, *Dostál*
Dostoevski
Dotson, *Dodd*
Doubble, *Dobel*
Doubec, *Dubnikov*
Doubek, *Dubnikov*
Doubell, *Dobel*
Double, *Dobel*
Doubrava, *Dąbrowski*
Douce, *Duce*
Doucet, *Duce*
Douch, *Duce*
Douche, *Duce*
Douchet, *Duce*
Douchez, *Duce*
Douchin, *Duce*
Doucin, *Duce*
Doucinel, *Duce*
Doud, *David*
Douet
Douetteau, *Douet*
Dougal, *Dougall*
Dougall
Dougan, *Duggan*
Dougharty, *Doherty*
Dougherty, *Doherty*
Doughtery, *Daltry*
Doughty
Dougill, *Dougall*
Douglas
Douglass, *Douglas*
Douillard, *Douillet*
Douillet
Douillot, *Douillet*
Douin, *Dodd*
Douis, *Douet*
Douit, *Douet*
Doull, *Donald*
Doumenc, *Dominique*
Doumer, *Dominique*
Doumerc, *Dominique*
Doumerque, *Dominique*
Doumic, *Dominique*
Dourado, *Doré*
Doussain, *Duce*
Doussaint, *Duce*
Doussard, *Duce*
Doussaud, *Duce*
Dousset, *Duce*
Doussin, *Duce*
Doussinaud, *Duce*
Doussinel, *Duce*
Doussinelle, *Duce*
Doussinet, *Duce*
Doussot, *Duce*
Douty, *Doughty*
Douy, *Douet*
Dove
Dover
Dovermann, *Dover*
Dovey, *Duffy*
Dovidaitis, *David*
Dovydénas, *David*
Dow
Dowall, *Dougall*
Dowcett, *Duce*
Dowd, *Duddy*
Dowden, *Dowding*
Dowdeswell, *Dadswell*
Dowding
Dowe, *Dow, Tauber*
Dowell, *Dougall*
Dowey, *Duffy*
Dowie, *Duffy*
Dowlan, *Dolan*
Dowler
Dowley, *Dooley*
Dowlin, *Dolan*
Dowling
Dowman, *Dow*
Down
Downe, *Down*
Downer, *Down*
Downes, *Dunn*
Downey, *Downie*
Downie
Downing, *Dunn*
Downman, *Down*
Downs, *Dunn*
Downton, *Dunton*
Dowse, *Duce*
Dowsett, *Duce*
Dowson, *Dow, Duce*
Dowtry, *Daltry*
Dowty, *Doughty*
Doyen, *Dean*
Doyle, *Dougall*
Doyley
Dozier
Draack, *Drake*
Draaijer, *Dreier*
Draaisma, *Dreier*
Draak, *Drake*
Draayer, *Dreier*
Dráb
Drabble
Drábeček, *Dráb*
Drábek, *Dráb*
Dracke, *Drake*
Draco, *Dragon*
Draconet, *Dragon*
Draeger, *Trager*
Drage
Dräger, *Trager*
Drager, *Trager*
Draghetti, *Dragon*
Draghetto, *Dragon*
Draghi, *Dragon*
Drago, *Dragon*
Dragon
Dragoner, *Dragon*
Dragotti, *Dragon*
Dragotto, *Dragon*
Drahonnet, *Dragon*
Draijer, *Dreier*
Drain, *Drane*
Drake
Drakes, *Drake*
Draksler, *Drechsler*
Drane
Dransfield
Drape, *Draper*
Drapeau, *Draper*
Draper
Draperon, *Draper*
Drapier, *Draper*
Drapper, *Draper*
Drappier, *Draper*
Drapy, *Draper*
Draschner, *Drescher*
Draxler, *Drechsler*
Draycott
Drayer, *Dreier*
Drayton
Dreassi, *Andrew*
Drechsler
Dredge, *Drage*
Drees, *Andrew*
Dreesen, *Andrew*
Dreessen, *Andrew*
Drefus, *Dreyfuss*
Dreger, *Dreier*
Dreher, *Dreier*
Drei, *Andrew*
Dreier
Dreifus, *Dreyfuss*
Dreifuss, *Dreyfuss*
Dreigher, *Dreier*
Dreinan, *Drennan*
Dreini, *Andrew*
Drejer, *Dreier*
Dreng, *Dring*
Drennan
Dreoni, *Andrew*
Dreossi, *Andrew*
Drescher
Dreschner, *Drescher*
Dresher, *Drescher*
Dresler, *Drechsler, Thrussell*
Dressler, *Drechsler, Thrussell*
Dreus, *Andrew*
Dreux, *Drew*
Drew
Drewe, *Drew*
Drewell, *Drew*
Drewery, *Drury*
Drewes, *Drew*
Drewett, *Drew*
Drewing, *Andrew*
Drewitt, *Drew*
Drewry, *Drury*
Drexler, *Drechsler*
Dreyer, *Dreier*
Dreyfus, *Dreyfuss*
Dreyfuss
Dri, *Andrew*
Driburg
Dries, *Andrew*
Driesch
Drieschmann, *Driesch*
Driesen, *Andrew*
Driessen, *Andrew*
Drieu, *Andrew*
Driewer, *Driver*
Driffel, *Driffield*
Driffield
Driker, *Drucker*
Drinan, *Drennan*
Dring
Drinkwater
Drinnan, *Drennan*
Drioli, *Andrew*
Driscoll
Driussi, *Andrew*
Driutti, *Andrew*
Driuzzi, *Andrew*
Driver
Drobek, *Drobný*
Drobník, *Drobný*
Drobnik, *Drobný*
Drobnjak, *Drobný*
Drobný
Drohan
Drohane, *Drohan*
Drohun, *Drohan*
Droin, *Drew*
Dromey, *Drummy*
Drompt, *Drew*
Dron, *Drew*
Droniou, *Drew*
Droohan, *Drohan*
Droop
Dröscher, *Drescher*
Drossaerd, *Droste*
Drossart, *Droste*
Drossate, *Droste*
Drössler, *Drechsler*
Drost, *Droste*
Droste
Drouet, *Drew*
Drouhet, *Drew*
Drouhin, *Drew*
Drouilly
Drouin, *Drew*
Drouineau, *Drew*
Drouon, *Drew*
Drovandi, *Aldobrandi*
Droz, *Drew*
Drozd, *Drożdż*
Drozda, *Drożdż*
Drozdowski, *Drożdż*
Drożdż
Dru, *Drew*
Druce, *Drew*
Druck, *Drucker*
Drucker
Druckier, *Drucker*
Druckmann, *Drucker*
Druery, *Drury*
Druett, *Drew*
Druitt, *Drew*
Druker, *Drucker*
Drukman, *Drucker*
Drukmann, *Drucker*
Drumm, *Drummy*
Drummond
Drummy
Druon, *Drew*
Druot, *Drew*
Drury
Drut, *Drew*
Dryden
Drynan, *Drennan*
Drysdale
Drzewiecki
D'Souza, *Sousa*
Duan, *Devane*
Duane, *Devane*
Duart, *Edward*
Duarte, *Edward*
Dub, *Dubnikov*
Dubarry, *Barry*
Dubček, *Dubnikov*
Dubec, *Beck*

Dubec, *Dubnikov*
Du Bellay, *Bellay*
Du Bief, *Béal*
Dubík, *Dubnikov*
Dubin, *Dubnikov*
Dubnikov
Dubois, *Bois*
Dubonnet, *Bonnet*
Dubos, *Bois*
Duboscq, *Bois*
Dubost, *Bois*
Dubouis, *Box*
Du Boulay, *Boul*
Du Bouloy, *Boul*
Dubourg, *Burke*
Dubourquet, *Burke*
Dubov, *Dubnikov*
Dubovoi, *Dubnikov*
Dubreuil, *Breuil*
Dubrovin, *Dubnikov*
Dubrovsky, *Dąbrowski*
Dubrule, *Breuil*
Dubský, *Dubnikov*
Dubuis, *Box*
Dubuisson, *Buisson*
Duc, *Duke*
Duca, *Duke*
Ducaen, *Cain*
Ducami, *Chemin*
Ducamin, *Chemin*
Ducamp, *Champ*
Ducamy, *Chemin*
Du Cane, *Chêne*
Ducarme, *Carne*
Ducarne, *Carne*
Ducarpe, *Charme*
Ducasse, *Casse*
Ducastel, *Castle*
Ducayla, *Châtelier*
Ducazeau, *Casale*
Ducazeaux, *Casale*
Duce
Ducellier, *Seller*
Duch, *Dušek, Duke*
Ducháček, *Dušek*
Duchamp, *Champ*
Duchaň, *Dušek*
Ducharme, *Charme*
Ducharne, *Charme*
Duchasteau, *Castle*
Duchâteau, *Castle*
Duchâtel, *Castle*
Duchâtelier, *Châtelier*
Duchatellier, *Châtelier*
Duché, *Duchier*
Duchefdelaville, *Capdevielle*
Duchek, *Dušek*
Duchemin, *Chemin*
Duchêne, *Chêne*
Duchenois, *Chêne*
Duchenoy, *Chêne*
Ducher, *Duchier*
Ducheron, *Duchier*
Duchesne, *Chêne*
Duchet, *Duke*
Duchey, *Duke*
Duchez, *Duke*
Duchi, *Duke*
Duchier
Duchini, *Duke*
Duchoň, *Dušek*
Duchon, *Duke*
Duck, *Digg*
Duckenfield
Ducker
Duckes, *Digg*
Ducket, *Duckett*
Duckett
Duckit, *Duckett*
Duckitt, *Duckett*
Duckworth
Duclaux, *Close*
Duclerc, *Clark*
Duclert, *Clark*
Duclos, *Close*
Duclot, *Close*
Ducloux, *Close*
Duclouzeau, *Close*
Ducluzeau, *Close*
Ducos, *Ducost*
Ducost
Ducoudray, *Cowdrey*
Ducoudré, *Cowdrey*
Ducquet, *Duke*
Ducrès, *Crès*
Ducreux, *Creux*
Ducroc, *Crook*
Ducrocq, *Crook*
Ducros, *Creux*
Ducrot
Duda
Dudaczyk, *Duda*
Dudák, *Duda*
Dudar, *Duda*
Dudarov, *Duda*
Dudás, *Duda*
Duddell, *Dodd*
Dudden, *Dude*
Duddle, *Dodd*
Duddy
Düde, *Dude*
Dude
Dudek
Dudel, *Duda*
Dudelsak, *Duda*
Dudelzak, *Duda*
Duden, *Dude*
Duder
Dudgeon
Dudić, *Duda*
Dudin, *Duda*
Dudka, *Dudek*
Dudke, *Dudek*
Dudkevich, *Dudek*
Dudkevitz, *Dudek*
Dudkeviz, *Dudek*
Dudkewich, *Dudek*
Dudkewitz, *Dudek*
Dudkewiz, *Dudek*
Dudkiewicz, *Dudek*
Dudkin, *Duda*
Dudko, *Dudek*
Dudley
Dudman, *Dodd, Duda*
Dudnik, *Duda*
Dudoit, *Douet*
Dudorov, *Duda*
Dudouet, *Douet*
Dudouit, *Douet*
Dudouyt, *Douet*
Dudovitz, *Duda*
Dudoy, *Douet*
Dudson, *Dodd*
Dudyshkin, *Duda*
Düe, *Dude*
Dueñas
Duenias, *Dueñas*
Duerden, *Dearden*
Dufau, *Fage*
Dufaure, *Fèvre*
Dufay, *Fage*
Dufayard, *Fage*
Dufayel, *Fage*
Dufayet, *Fage*
Dufays, *Fage*
Dufer, *Ferro*
Duff
Duffeau, *Fage*
Duffeaux, *Fage*
Duffell, *Duffield*
Duffey, *Duffy*
Duffie, *Duffy*
Duffield
Duffill, *Duffield*
Duffin
Duffy
Duflo, *Duflocq*
Duflocq
Duflos, *Duflocq*
Duflot, *Duflocq*
Dufossés, *Fosse*
Dufosset, *Fosse*
Dufragne, *Frain*
Dufraisne, *Frain*
Dufraisse, *Frain*
Dufrègne, *Frain*
Dufrêne, *Frain*
Dufrenne, *Frain*
Dufresne, *Frain*
Dufresnoy, *Frain*
Dufty, *Doughty*
Dugage, *Gage*
Dugald, *Dougall*
Dugall, *Dougall*
Dugan, *Duggan*
Dugard, *Gardener*
Dugardin, *Gardener*
Dugas, *Gast*
Dugast, *Gast*
Dugdale
Dugenest, *Genest*
Dugenet, *Genest*
Duggan
Duggen, *Duggan*
Duggins, *Duggan*
Duggon, *Duggan*
Dugmore
D'Ugo, *Hugh*
Dugué, *Wade*
Duguet, *Waite*
Duguey, *Waite*
Duguez, *Waite*
Duguid
Duhm, *Daum*
Duhme, *Daum*
Duhoux, *Hilse*
Dührig, *Düring*
Dühring, *Düring*
Duigan, *Deegan*
Duignam, *Deegan*
Duignan, *Deegan*
Duigo, *Duff*
Duim, *Daum*
Duin
Dujardin, *Gardener*
Dukas, *Duke*
Duke
Dukes, *Duke*
Dulac, *Lake*
Dulanty, *Delahunty*
Duley, *Doyley*
Dulinty, *Delahunty*
Dullea, *Dunleavy*
Dullforce, *Force*
Duly, *Doyley*
Dumais, *Mas*
Dumait, *Mas*
Dumany, *Meynell*
Dumarais, *Marsh*
Dumas, *Mas*
Dumat, *Mas*
Dumay, *Mas*
Dumazeau, *Mas*
Dumazel, *Mas*
Dumazet, *Mas*
Dumé, *Mas*
Dumée, *Mas*
Dumeix, *Mas*
Duménil, *Meynell*
Dumès, *Mas*
Dumesnil, *Meynell*
Dumetz, *Mas*
Dumez, *Mas*
Dumini, *Dominique*
Dumitrescu, *Dmitriev*
Dumitru, *Dmitriev*
Dumke, *Thomas*
Dummann, *Thumb*
Dummer, *Thumb*
Dumolin, *Mill*
Dumont, *Mont*
Dumoulin, *Mill*
Dumouriez, *Mora*
Dumville
Dun, *Dunn, Thin*
Dunan, *Dunant*
Dunant
Dunbar
Duncan
Duncanson, *Duncan*
Dunckel, *Donker*
Dunckelmann, *Donker*
Duncker, *Donker*
Duncombe
Dundas
Dunderdale
Dundrer, *Donner*
Dune, *Devane*
Dunegain, *Donegan*
Dunegaine, *Donegan*
Dunfield, *Dumville*
Dunford
Dung
Düngen, *Dung*
Dungs, *Dung*
Dunham
Dunić, *Dunin*
Dunin
Dunk, *Dung*
Dunker, *Donker*
Dunkin, *Dunin*
Dunkinson, *Duncan*
Dunkley
Dunkmann, *Dung*
Dunlap, *Dunlop*
Dunlavy, *Dunleavy*
Dunlea, *Dunleavy*
Dunleavy
Dunleevy, *Dunleavy*
Dunlevy, *Dunleavy*
Dunlop
Dunman, *Down*
Dunn
Dunne, *Dunn, Thin*
Dünne, *Thin*
Dunnet, *Dunn*

Dunnett, *Dunn*
Dunnicliff, *Tunnicliffe*
Dunnicliffe, *Tunnicliffe*
Dunnigan, *Donegan*
Dunning
Dunnion, *Dineen*
Dunoyer, *Noyer*
Dunsford
Dunstable
Dunstall
Dunstan
Dunster
Dunton
Dunville, *Dumville*
Dunwoodie
Duny, *Downie*
Dupaquier, *Paquier*
Duparc, *Park*
Duparcq, *Park*
Dupasquier, *Paquier*
Dupeux, *Puy*
Dupic, *Pike*
Dupin, *Pine*
Duplain, *Plain*
Duplaix, *Place*
Duplan, *Plain*
Duplant, *Plain*
Duplat, *Platt*
Duplay, *Place*
Dupleix, *Place*
Duplessier, *Place*
Duplessis, *Place*
Duplessix, *Place*
Duplessy, *Place*
Duplex, *Place*
Dupoirier, *Pear*
Dupont, *Pont*
Duportail, *Portail*
Duportal, *Portail*
Duportau, *Portail*
Dupourtau, *Portail*
Dupoux, *Puits*
Dupouy, *Puy*
Duprat, *Pré*
Dupré, *Pré*
Dupuis, *Puits*
Dupuits, *Puits*
Duque, *Duke*
Duquemin, *Chemin*
Duquesnay, *Quêne*
Duquesne, *Quêne*
Duquesnoy, *Quêne*
Duquet, *Duke*
Dur, *Duro*
Duráes, *Durant*
Durán, *Durant*
Duran, *Durant*
Durand, *Durant*
Durandeau, *Durant*
Durandet, *Durant*
Durandin, *Durant*
Durando, *Durant*
Duranseau, *Durant*
Durant
Durante, *Durant*
Duranteau, *Durant*
Durantel, *Durant*
Durantet, *Durant*
Duranthon, *Durant*
Duranti, *Durant*
Durantini, *Durant*
Duranton, *Durant*
Durany, *Durant*
Durão, *Durant*
Durban, *Urban*
Durcan
Durden, *Dearden*
Dureau
Durel, *Dureau*
Dürer
Duret, *Dureau*
Durham
Duri, *Duro*
Dürich, *Düring*
Durie
Durin, *Duro*
During, *Düring*
Düring
Durini, *Duro*
Duriz, *Rieu*
Durk, *Dark*
Durkan, *Durcan*
Durkheim
Durkheimer, *Durkheim*
Durkin, *Durcan*
Durman, *Dear*
Durnin, *Dornan*
Duro
Duroure, *Rouvre*
Durouvre, *Rouvre*
Durram, *Durham*
Durran, *Durant*
Durrance, *Durant*
Durrand, *Durant*
Durrans, *Durant*
Durrant, *Durant*
Durrel, *Dureau*
Durrell, *Dureau*
Dürrenmatt
Durrieu, *Rieu*
Dursley
D'Urso, *Orso*
Durtnell
Duruflé
Duruz, *Rieu*
Dury, *Rieu*
Dušák, *Dušek*
Dusap, *Sapin*
Dusapin, *Sapin*
Dusapt, *Sapin*
Duseau, *Sault*
Duseaux, *Sault*
Duseigneur, *Seigneur*
Dušek
Dusouchet, *Such*
Dussaud, *Sault*
Dussault, *Sault*
Dussaut, *Sault*
Dussaux, *Sault*
Dusseaux, *Sault*
Dusting, *Thurston*
Dutartre, *Dutetre*
Duteil, *Teil*
Duteille, *Teil*
Duteillet, *Teil*
Dutetre
Duteuil, *Teil*
Duteutre, *Dutetre*
Dutheil, *Teil*
Dutheillet, *Teil*
Dutheuil, *Teil*
Duthie, *Duffy*
Duthil, *Teil*
Duthillet, *Teil*
Duthilleul, *Teil*
Duthu, *Truc*
Duthy, *Duffy*
Dutil, *Teil*
Dutillay, *Teil*
Dutillet, *Teil*
Dutilleul, *Teil*
Dutilleux, *Teil*
Dutilloy, *Teil*
Dutkiewicz, *Dudek*
Dutkowski, *Dudek*
Dutru, *Truc*
Dutruc, *Truc*
Dutrut, *Truc*
Dutsch, *Deutsch*
Dutschke, *Deutsch*
Dutton
Dutu, *Truc*
Dutuc, *Truc*
Dutz, *Deutsch*
Dutzke, *Deutsch*
Duursma, *Dear*
Duval, *Vale*
Duvallet, *Vale*
Duvau, *Vale*
Duvaur, *Vaur*
Duveau, *Vale*
Düvel, *Deville*
Duvergé, *Verdier*
Duverger, *Verdier*
Duvergey, *Verdier*
Duvergié, *Verdier*
Duvergier, *Verdier*
Duverne, *Ver*
Duvilard, *Villiers*
Duvillard, *Villiers*
Duvivier, *Weiher*
Duvoisin, *Voisin*
Duwe, *Tauber*
Düwel, *Deville*
Duxberry, *Duxbury*
Duxbury
Duym, *Daum*
Dvoirin, *Dvorin*
Dvojres, *Dvorin*
Dvoraček, *Dvořák*
Dvořák
Dvorin
Dvorkin, *Dvorin*
Dvorský, *Dvořák*
Dvoskin, *Dvorin*
Dvossis, *Dvorin*
Dwilling, *Zwilling*
Dwire, *Dwyer*
Dworak, *Dvořák*
Dworakowski, *Dvořák*
Dworczak, *Dvořák*
Dworczyk, *Dvořák*
Dworkin, *Dvorin*
Dworkis, *Dvorin*
Dwornik, *Dvořák*
Dworzyński, *Dvořák*
Dwoskin, *Dvorin*
Dwyer
Dwynn, *Dunn*
Dwyr, *Dwyer*
Dyachenko, *Deakin*
Dyagilev, *Dzięgielewski*
Dyakonov, *Deakin*
Dyason, *Dye*
Dyatlov, *Dzięciełowski*
Dybald, *Theobald*
Dyball, *Theobald*
Dybell, *Theobald*
Dyble, *Theobald*
Dychterman, *Dichter*
Dydek, *Dudek*
Dye
Dyer
Dyers, *Dyer*
Dyerson, *Dye*
Dyerson, *Dyer*
Dyet, *Dye*
Dyett, *Dye*
Dyhr, *Dear*
Dyhring, *Dear*
Dyke, *Ditch*
Dykema, *Ditch*
Dykes, *Ditch*
Dykierman, *Dick*
Dykman, *Ditch*
Dykstra, *Ditch*
Dymant, *Diamond*
Dymantsztain, *Diamond*
Dymecki, *Dymowski*
Dymek, *Dymowski*
Dyment, *Diamond*
Dymentsztain, *Diamond*
Dymetman, *Diamond*
Dymetsztain, *Diamond*
Dymick, *Dymock*
Dymidowicz, *Dmitriev*
Dymkowski, *Dymowski*
Dymock
Dymocke, *Dymock*
Dymoke, *Dymock*
Dymond, *Diamond*
Dymont, *Diamond*
Dymowski
Dyne, *Dain*
Dyomichev, *Damyon*
Dyomin, *Damyon*
Dyominov, *Damyon*
Dyomkin, *Damyon*
Dyomshin, *Damyon*
Dyomyshev, *Damyon*
Dyoshin, *Damyon*
Dyott, *Dye*
Dyrling, *Darling*
Dysart
Dyson, *Dye*
Dyster, *Dyer*
Dzenisenya, *Dennis*
Dzeniskevich, *Dennis*
Dzięciełowski
Dziedzic
Dziedziczak, *Dziedzic*
Dzięgielewski
Dzierżawa, *Dzierżyński*
Dzierżawski, *Dzierżyński*
Dzierżyński
Dzikowski
Dziwisz, *Dennis*
Dzugashvili
Dzyak, *Deakin*

E

Eacock, *Eade*
Ead, *Eade*
Eade
Eaden, *Eden*
Eades, *Eade*
Eadie, *Eade*
Eadmeades, *Edmead*
Eadmeads, *Edmead*
Eadon, *Eden*
Eads, *Eade*
Eady, *Eade*
Eagan, *Higgins*
Eagar, *Edgar*

Eager, *Edgar*
Eagers, *Edgar*
Eagger, *Edgar*
Eagle
Eaglen, *Eagle*
Eagles
Eagling, *Eagle*
Eakin, *Eade, Higgins*
Eakins, *Eade*
Ealey, *Ely*
Ealy, *Ely*
Eame
Eames, *Eame*
Eardley, *Ardley*
Earl
Earle, *Earl*
Earles, *Earl*
Earley, *Early*
Early
Earner, *Seerey*
Earnshaw
Earwaker
Earwicker, *Earwaker*
Easey, *Easy*
Easman, *Hayes*
Eason, *Eade, McKay*
Easson, *Eade*
East
Eastabrook, *Easterbrook*
Eastbrook, *Easterbrook*
Easter
Easterbrook
Easterling, *Easter*
Eastes, *East*
Eastham
Eastman
Eastment, *Eastman*
Easton
Eastwood
Easy
Eaton
Eatwell
Eaves, *Eve*
Eayres, *Ayer*
Eayrs, *Ayer*
Ebbe, *Eggebrecht*
Ebbeke, *Eggebrecht*
Ebben, *Eggebrecht*
Ebbena, *Eggebrecht*
Ebbers, *Eggebrecht*
Ebbert, *Eggebrecht*
Ebbesen, *Eggebrecht*
Ebbets, *Hibbs*
Ebbetts, *Hibbs*
Ebbing, *Eggebrecht*
Ebbinga, *Eggebrecht*
Ebblewhite, *Hebblethwaite*
Ebbrecht, *Eggebrecht*
Ebden, *Ebdon*
Ebdon
Ebe, *Everard*
Ebeling, *Eggebrecht*
Ebenteuer, *Venture*
Eberhard, *Everard*
Eberhardt, *Everard*
Eberhart, *Everard*
Eberl, *Everard*
Eberle, *Everard*
Eberlein, *Everard*
Ebermann, *Everard*
Ebers, *Everard*
Ebert, *Eggebrecht, Everard*
Ebertz, *Everard*
Eberwein, *Irvine*
Eberz, *Everard*
Ebhard, *Everard*
Ebi, *Everard*
Ebke, *Eggebrecht*
Ebkema, *Eggebrecht*
Eble, *Everard*
Eblein, *Everard*
Ebler, *Everard*
Ebner
Ebrard, *Everard*
Ebrech, *Eggebrecht*
Ebrecht, *Eggebrecht*
Ebsen, *Eggebrecht*
Ebstein, *Epstein*
Eby, *Everard*
Eccles
Eccleston
Echabe, *Echave*
Echalié, *Eschelle*
Echalier, *Eschelle*
Echallié, *Eschelle*
Echallier, *Eschelle*
Echarri, *Echeverría*
Echávarri, *Echeverría*
Echave
Echeandía
Echébarri, *Echeverría*
Echebarría, *Echeverría*
Echéberri, *Echeverría*
Echeberría, *Echeverría*
Échelle, *Eschelle*
Echévarri, *Echeverría*
Echevarría, *Echeverría*
Echeverría
Echt, *Čech*
Echterling, *Achtermann*
Echtermann, *Achtermann*
Eck
Eckart, *Eckhardt*
Eckbrett, *Eggebrecht*
Ecke, *Eck*
Eckebrecht, *Eggebrecht*
Eckehard, *Eckhardt*
Eckenbrecher, *Eggebrecht*
Ecker, *Eck*
Eckerling, *Eck*
Eckerman, *Eck*
Eckersley
Eckert, *Eckhardt*
Eckes, *Eck*
Eckhard, *Eckhardt*
Eckhardt
Eckhaus, *Eck*
Eckheizer, *Eck*
Eckloff, *Egiloff*
Eckmann, *Eck*
Ecks, *Eck*
Eckstein
Ecles, *Eccles*
Ecroyd, *Ackroyd*
Ecureuil, *Squirrel*
Écuyer, *Squire*
Edard, *Edward*
Eddie, *Eddy*
Eddington
Eddison, *Eade*
Eddow, *Beddow*
Eddowes, *Beddow*
Eddy
Ede, *Eade*
Ede, *Oade*
Edel
Edeler, *Edel*
Edelheid, *Edel*
Edelheit, *Edel*
Edelman, *Edel*
Edelmann, *Edel*
Edelsohn, *Edel*
Edelson, *Edel*
Edelstein, *Adel*
Edema, *Oade*
Eden
Edens, *Eden, Oade*
Eder
Ederer, *Eder*
Edert, *Edward*
Edes, *Eade*
Edeson, *Eade*
Edess, *Beddow*
Edgar
Edgard, *Edgar*
Edgars, *Edgar*
Edge
Edgeley
Edger, *Edgar*
Edgerton, *Egerton*
Edgeworth
Edgington
Edgley, *Edgeley*
Edgworth, *Edgeworth*
Edington
Edison, *Eade*
Edkins, *Eade*
Edler, *Edel*
Edlestone
Edmead
Edmeades, *Edmead*
Edmeads, *Edmead*
Edmed, *Edmead*
Edmenson, *Edmond*
Edmett, *Edmead*
Edminson, *Edmond*
Edmond
Edmonds, *Edmond*
Edmondson, *Edmond*
Edmons, *Edmond*
Edmonson, *Edmond*
Edmont, *Edmond*
Edmott, *Edmead*
Edmund, *Edmond*
Edmunds, *Edmond*
Edmundson, *Edmond*
Edon, *Eden*
Edouard, *Edward*
Edrich
Edridge, *Edrich*
Edsel, *Albert*
Edsen, *Oade*
Edson, *Eade*
Eduardo, *Edward*
Edvardsen, *Edward*
Edvardsson, *Edward*
Edvinsson, *Edwin*
Edward
Edwarde, *Edward*
Edwardes, *Edward*
Edwards, *Edward*
Edwardson, *Edward*
Edwin
Edwing, *Edwin*
Edwyn, *Edwin*
Edzard, *Eckhardt*
Edzart, *Eckhardt*
Eely, *Ely*
Eerikäinen, *Herrick*
Effertz, *Everard*
Efroimson, *Yefremov*
Efron
Efroni, *Efron*
Efronny, *Efron*
Efrony, *Efron*
Egan, *Higgins*
Egar, *Edgar*
Egarr, *Edgar*
Egbert, *Eggebrecht*
Egberts, *Eggebrecht*
Ege, *Eck*
Egelolf, *Egiloff*
Egenlauf, *Egiloff*
Egenolf, *Egiloff*
Egenolff, *Egiloff*
Eger, *Edgar*
Egerton
Egg, *Eck*
Eggar, *Edgar*
Eggars, *Edgar*
Egge, *Eck*
Eggebrecht
Eggehart, *Eckhardt*
Eggen, *Eck*
Eggena, *Eck*
Eggens, *Eck*
Egger, *Eck*
Egger, *Eckhardt*
Egger, *Edgar*
Eggerding, *Eckhardt*
Eggers, *Eckhardt*
Eggert, *Eckhardt*
Eggert, *Eggebrecht*
Eggerton, *Egerton*
Egges, *Eck*
Egging, *Eck*
Eggink, *Eck*
Eggle, *Eck*
Eggleston
Egglestone, *Eggleston*
Eggleton
Eggli, *Eck*
Egi, *Eck*
Egido
Egidy, *Giles*
Egiloff
Eginolf, *Egiloff*
Egle, *Eagle*
Eglehaaf, *Egiloff*
Eglehaf, *Egiloff*
Eglese, *Eagles*
Egleston, *Eggleston*
Egli, *Eck*
Egloff, *Egiloff*
Eguía
Egúsquiza
Egyde, *Giles*
Egyed, *Giles*
Eha, *Eame*
Eham, *Eame*
Ehebrecht, *Eggebrecht*
Eheim, *Eame*
Ehem, *Eame*
Ehemann, *Ehmann*
Ehlebracht, *Eggebrecht*
Ehlend, *Elend*
Ehler, *Ehlert*
Ehlerding, *Ehlert*
Ehlermann, *Ehlert*
Ehlers, *Ehlert*
Ehlert
Ehmann
Ehmcke, *Amery*
Ehmecke, *Amery*
Ehn
Ehnert, *Eckhardt*

Ehnlund, *Ehn*
Ehnlundh, *Ehn*
Ehnqvist, *Ehn*
Ehnström, *Ehn*
Ehre, *Ehrmann*
Ehrenberg, *Ehrmann*
Ehrenfeld, *Ehrmann*
Ehrenfreund, *Ehrmann*
Ehrenfried, *Ehrmann*
Ehrenhalt, *Ehrmann*
Ehrenhaus, *Ehrmann*
Ehrenkranz, *Ehrmann*
Ehrenmann, *Ehrmann*
Ehrenpreis, *Ehrmann*
Ehrenreich, *Ehrmann*
Ehrenstein, *Ehrmann*
Ehrental, *Ehrmann*
Ehrenthal, *Ehrmann*
Ehrenwort, *Ehrmann*
Ehrenzweig, *Ehrmann*
Ehrlich
Ehrmann
Ehwalt, *Ewald*
Eich, *Oak*
Eichbaum, *Oak*
Eichel, *Oak*
Eichelberg, *Oak*
Eichele, *Oak*
Eichen, *Oak*
Eichenbaum, *Oak*
Eichenblat, *Oak*
Eichenboim, *Oak*
Eichengolz, *Oak*
Eichengruen, *Oak*
Eichenholz, *Oak*
Eichenstein, *Oak*
Eichenwald, *Oak*
Eicher, *Oak*
Eichholz, *Oak*
Eichhorn
Eichlbaum, *Oak*
Eichler, *Oak*
Eichmann, *Oak*
Eichner, *Oak*
Eichwald, *Oak*
Eick, *Oak*
Eicker, *Oak*
Eickmann, *Oak*
Eida, *Edel*
Eidelheit, *Edel*
Eidelman, *Edel*
Eidels, *Edel*
Eidelson, *Edel*
Eidler, *Edel*
Eidtner, *Aggis*
Eierding, *Eckhardt*
Eiffel
Eiffler, *Eiffel*
Eifler, *Eiffel*
Eigner
Eikelenboom, *Oak*
Eikenboom, *Oak*
Eilbert, *Eggebrecht*
Eilbracht, *Eggebrecht*
Eildermann, *Ehlert*
Eilderts, *Ehlert*
Eilebrecht, *Eggebrecht*
Eiler, *Ehlert*
Eilerding, *Ehlert*
Eilers, *Ehlert*
Eilersen, *Ehlert*
Eilert, *Ehlert*
Eilertsen, *Ehlert*
Eilts, *Ehlert*
Einbinder, *Binder*
Einert, *Eckhardt*
Einhart, *Eckhardt*
Einhorn
Einold
Einolf, *Egiloff*
Einsiedel
Einstein
Eiselt, *Izard*
Eisen
Eisenbach, *Eisen*
Eisenbart, *Isambert*
Eisenbaum, *Eisen*
Eisenbein
Eisenberg, *Eisen*
Eisenberger, *Eisen*
Eisenboum, *Eisen*
Eisenfarb, *Eisen*
Eisenfeld, *Eisen*
Eisenfish, *Eisen*
Eisengrein
Eisenhandler
Eisenhardt, *Eisen, Isnard*
Eisenhart, *Isnard*
Eisenhauer
Eisenhendler, *Eisenhandler*
Eisenhouwer, *Eisenhauer*
Eisenhower, *Eisenhauer*
Eisenkeit, *Eisen*
Eisenkraft, *Eisen*
Eisenman, *Eisen*
Eisenmann, *Eisen*
Eisenmenger, *Ironmonger*
Eisenpresser, *Eisen*
Eisenreich, *Eisen*
Eisenscher, *Eisen*
Eisenschmidt, *Eisen*
Eisenschreiber, *Eisen*
Eisensher, *Eisen*
Eisenstadt
Eisenstein, *Eisen*
Eisental, *Eisen*
Eisenthal, *Eisen*
Eisenzweig, *Eisen*
Eiser, *Eisen*
Eisermann, *Eisen*
Eisig, *Isaac*
Eisik, *Isaac*
Eisikowitch, *Isaac*
Eisikowitz, *Isaac*
Eiskovitsh, *Isaac*
Eisler, *Eisen*
Eismann, *Eisen*
Eisner, *Eisen*
Eisold, *Izard*
Eisolde, *Izard*
Eitel
Eithner, *Aggis*
Eitner, *Aggis*
Ejido, *Egido*
Ejlman, *Oyler*
Ek, *Oak*
Ekberg, *Oak*
Ekbergh, *Oak*
Ekblad, *Oak*
Ekbladh, *Oak*
Ekblom, *Oak*
Ekdahl, *Oak*
Eke
Ekedahl, *Oak*
Ekegren, *Oak*
Ekelöf, *Oak*
Ekelöv, *Oak*
Ekelund, *Oak*
Ekelundh, *Oak*
Ekeman, *Oak*
Ekengren, *Oak*
Eker, *Eck*
Ekerling, *Eck*
Ekerman, *Eck*
Ekgren, *Oak*
Ekhaizer, *Eck*
Ekhajzer, *Eck*
Ekhaus, *Eck*
Ekhause, *Eck*
Ekholm, *Oak*
Ekins, *Eade*
Ekler, *Eck*
Eklind, *Oak*
Eklöf, *Oak*
Eklöv, *Oak*
Eklund, *Oak*
Eklundh, *Oak*
Ekman, *Oak*
Ekroth, *Oak*
Ekstedt, *Oak*
Eksteen, *Eckstein*
Ekstein, *Eckstein*
Ekstien, *Eckstein*
Ekstra, *Oak*
Ekstrand, *Oak*
Ekström, *Oak*
Eksztajn, *Eckstein*
Ekvall, *Oak*
Ekwall, *Oak*
Elbaum, *Ohlbaum*
Elbel, *Albert*
Elberding, *Eggebrecht*
Elbers, *Eggebrecht*
Elbert, *Eggebrecht*
Elbertz, *Eggebrecht*
Elboim, *Ohlbaum*
Elbom, *Ohlbaum*
Elborough
Elboym, *Ohlbaum*
Elbra, *Elborough*
Elbracht, *Eggebrecht*
Elbrecht, *Eggebrecht*
Elbro, *Elborough*
Elbrow, *Elborough*
Elbum, *Ohlbaum*
Elcock, *Ellis*
Elcy, *Elsey*
Elder
Eldred, *Aldritt*
Eldrett, *Aldritt*
Eldritt, *Aldritt*
Elebrecht, *Eggebrecht*
Elefant, *Oliphant*
Elejalde, *Elizalde*
Elen, *Ellen*
Elend
Elent, *Elend*
Eles, *Ellis*
Elesander, *Alexander*
Eley, *Eloy*
Eley, *Ely*
Elfand, *Oliphant*
Elfick, *Elphick*
Elfin, *Alpin*
Elford
Elgar, *Alger*
Elger, *Alger*
Elia, *Ellis*
Eliahu, *Ellis*
Elías, *Ellis*
Eliáš, *Ellis*
Elias, *Ellis*
Élias, *Ellis*
Eliasen, *Ellis*
Eliassen, *Ellis*
Eliasson, *Ellis*
Eliasz, *Ellis*
Élie, *Ellis*
Elies, *Ellis*
Eliesco, *Ellis*
Éliet, *Ellis*
Éliez, *Ellis*
Elijah, *Ellis*
Elijahu, *Ellis*
Elin, *Ellen*
Elington, *Ellington*
Élion, *Ellis*
Eliot, *Elliott*
Eliott, *Elliott*
Elis, *Ellis*
Eliyahu, *Ellis*
Elizalde
Elizondo
Elkin
Elkington
Elkins, *Elkin*
Ellard, *Allard*
Ellen
Ellend, *Elend*
Ellens, *Ellen*
Eller
Elleray, *Hilary*
Elleri, *Hilary*
Ellerman, *Elman*
Ellermann, *Eller*
Ellero, *Hilary*
Ellert, *Allard*
Ellery, *Hilary*
Elley, *Eloy*
Elleyne, *Ellen*
Ellice, *Ellis*
Ellif, *Ayliff*
Elliff, *Ayliff*
Elliman, *Elman*
Ellin, *Ellen*
Ellingham
Ellings, *Ellen*
Ellington
Ellins, *Ellen*
Elliot, *Elliott*
Elliott
Ellis
Ellison, *Ellis*
Elliss, *Ellis*
Ellissen, *Ellis*
Ellisson, *Ellis*
Elliston, *Ellis*
Ellman, *Oyler*
Elloway, *Alloway*
Elloy, *Eloy*
Ellson, *Elson*
Ellsworth, *Elsworth*
Ellwood
Elm
Elman
Elman, *Oyler*
Elmar, *Aylmer*
Elmer, *Aylmer*
Elmers, *Aylmer*
Elmes, *Elm*
Elmhirst
Elmhurst, *Elmhirst*
Elmore
Elms, *Elm*
Elmsley, *Emslie*
Elmslie, *Emslie*

Elmsly, *Emslie*
Elofsson, *Egiloff*
Eloi, *Eloy*
Elorduy
Elorriaga
Elorza, *Elorduy*
Eloy
Elperin, *Heilbronn*
Elpern, *Heilbronn*
Elphey, *Alvey*
Elphick
Elphicke, *Elphick*
Elphinston
Elphinstone, *Elphinston*
Elray, *Hilary*
Elsässer
Elsey
Elshenar, *Alexander*
Elsie, *Elsey*
Elsip, *Allsop*
Elson
Elsop, *Allsop*
Elston
Elsworth
Elsy, *Elsey*
Elter, *Elder*
Eltermann, *Elder*
Elton
Eltringham
Elvey, *Alvey*
Elvidge, *Elphick*
Elvin, *Alwyn*
Elvira
Elvy, *Alvey*
Elwell
Elwes
Elwess, *Elwes*
Elwin, *Alwyn*
Elwood, *Ellwood*
Elwyn, *Alwyn*
Ely
Elyahu, *Ellis*
Elys, *Ellis*
Elzas, *Elsässer*
Elzesser, *Elsässer*
Emanuel, *Emmanuel*
Emanuele, *Emmanuel*
Emanueli, *Emmanuel*
Emanuelli, *Emmanuel*
Emanuelov, *Emmanuel*
Emanulsson, *Emmanuel*
Emary, *Amery*
Emberry, *Amery*
Embery, *Amery*
Emblem, *Emmett*
Embleton
Emblin, *Emmett*
Embling, *Emmett*
Embrey, *Amery*
Embrich, *Amery*
Embry, *Amery*
Emburey, *Amery*
Embury, *Amery*
Emeline, *Emmett*
Emelrich, *Amery*
Emeric, *Amery*
Emerick, *Amery*
Emerson, *Amery*
Emery, *Amery*
Emet, *Emmett*
Émilian, *Émilien*
Emiliani, *Émilien*
Emiliano, *Émilien*
Émilien
Émilion, *Émilien*
Emlyn, *Emmett*
Emmanuel
Emmanuele, *Emmanuel*
Emmanueli, *Emmanuel*
Emmatt, *Emmett*
Emmel, *Amery*
Emmelot, *Emmett*
Emmerich, *Amery*
Emmet, *Emmett*
Emmett
Emmison, *Emmett*
Emmitt, *Emmett*
Emmlein, *Amery*
Emmott, *Emmett*
Emms, *Emmett*
Émon, *Edmond*
Émond, *Edmond*
Émonet, *Edmond*
Émonot, *Edmond*
Émont, *Edmond*
Emory, *Amery*
Empereur
Empson, *Emmett*
Emslie
Emson, *Emmett*
Enault, *Einold*
Enaux, *Einold*
Encabo
Encarnação, *Encarnación*
Encarnación
Encina
Encinar, *Encina*
Encinas, *Encina*
Endacott, *Endecott*
Ende
Endecott
Endemann, *Ende*
Enderby
Enderl, *Andrew*
Enderle, *Andrew*
Enderlein, *Andrew*
Enders, *Andrew*
Endersby, *Enderby*
Enderson, *Andrew*
Endicott, *Endecott*
Endler, *Andrew*
Endlich
Endres, *Andrew*
Endresser, *Andrew*
Endricci, *Henry*
Endrici, *Henry*
Endrighi, *Henry*
Endrizzi, *Henry*
Enevoldsen, *Einold*
Enfant, *Infante*
Enfantin, *Infante*
Eng
Engberg, *Eng*
Engblom, *Eng*
Engborg, *Eng*
Engdahl, *Eng*
Engel
Engelander, *English*
Engelberg, *Engel*
Engelbert
Engelbertz, *Engelbert*
Engelbracht, *Engelbert*
Engelbrecher, *Engelbert*
Engelbrecht, *Engelbert*
Engelbrett, *Engelbert*
Engelchin, *Engel*
Engelen, *Engel*
Engelhard
Engelhardt, *Engelhard*
Engelhart, *Engelhard*
Engelken, *Engel*
Engelking, *Engel*
Engelman, *Engel*
Engelmann, *Engel*
Engelmayer, *Engel*
Engelowitch, *Engel*
Engelrad, *Engel*
Engels, *Engel*
Engelsberg, *Engel*
Engelsman, *Engel*
Engelsmann, *Engel*
Engelsrath, *Engel*
Engelstein, *Engel*
Engesma, *Engel*
Engh, *Eng*
Engholm, *Eng*
Englaender, *English*
England, *English*
Englander, *English*
Englebert, *Engelbert*
Englefield
Engleke, *Engel*
Englender, *English*
Engler, *Engel*
Englerding, *Engelhard*
Englert, *Engelhard*
Englibert, *Engelbert*
Engling, *Engel*
English
Englisher, *English*
Englmann, *Engel*
Englund, *Eng*
Engman, *Eng*
Engqvist, *Eng*
Engstrand, *Eng*
Engström, *Eng*
Engvall, *Eng*
Engwall, *Eng*
Engwers, *Inger*
Enion, *Onion*
Enjalbert, *Engelbert*
Enjeubert, *Engelbert*
Enlund, *Ehn*
Enlundh, *Ehn*
Ennion, *Onion*
Ennis, *Innes*
Enoch, *Enock*
Enochsson, *Enock*
Enock
Enocksson, *Enock*
Enoksson, *Enock*
Enqvist, *Ehn*
Enrdigo, *Henry*
Enric, *Henry*
Enrich, *Henry*
Enrico, *Henry*
Enrietto, *Henry*
Enright
Enrigo, *Henry*
Enrique, *Henry*
Enriques, *Henry*
Enríquez, *Henry*
Ensle, *Ansell*
Ensli, *Ansell*
Enslin, *Ansell*
Ensor
Enström, *Ehn*
Ent, *Ende*
Enterl, *Andrew*
Enterle, *Andrew*
Enterlein, *Andrew*
Entissle, *Entwistle*
Entreis, *Andrew*
Entres, *Andrew*
Entwhistle, *Entwistle*
Entwisle, *Entwistle*
Entwistle
Enys, *Innes*
Eötvös
Epel, *Apple*
Epelbaum, *Apple*
Epelman, *Apple*
Ephron, *Efron*
Ephrony, *Efron*
Épinay, *Épine*
Épine
Épinoy, *Épine*
Episcopio, *Bishop*
Episcopo, *Bishop*
Epp, *Eggebrecht*
Eppel, *Apple*
Eppen, *Eggebrecht*
Eppens, *Eggebrecht*
Eppers, *Eggebrecht*
Eppert, *Eggebrecht*
Epping, *Eggebrecht*
Eppink, *Eggebrecht*
Epple, *Everard*
Eppmann, *Eggebrecht*
Epps, *Apps*
Eppstein, *Epstein*
Epstein
Epsztajn, *Epstein*
Epsztejn, *Epstein*
Erard, *Erhard*
Eras, *Erasmus*
Erasmi, *Erasmus*
Erasmus
Erbe, *Ive*
Erbst, *Herbst*
Erdelt, *Artaud*
Erdtelt, *Artaud*
Erenberg, *Ehrmann*
Erenfried, *Ehrmann*
Erenreich, *Ehrmann*
Erental, *Ehrmann*
Ergang, *Irrgang*
Erhard
Erhardt, *Erhard*
Erhart, *Erhard*
Erich, *Herrick*
Erichs, *Herrick*
Erichsen, *Herrick*
Ericsson, *Herrick*
Eriksen, *Herrick*
Eriksson, *Herrick*
Erlanger
Erlbaum, *Eller*
Erle, *Alder*
Erleigh, *Early*
Erler, *Alder*
Erley, *Early*
Erlich, *Ehrlich*
Erlichgerecht, *Ehrlich*
Erlichman, *Ehrlich*
Erlichson, *Ehrlich*
Erly, *Early*
Erman, *Hermann*
Ermani, *Hermann*
Ermanni, *Hermann*
Ermanno, *Hermann*
Ermano, *Hermann*
Ermengard, *Ermgard*
Ermengarde, *Ermgard*
Ermenjard, *Ermgard*
Ermenjon, *Ermgard*

Ermgard
Ermin, *Armin*
Ernau, *Ernaud*
Ernaud
Ernaul, *Ernaud*
Ernest, *Ernst*
Erni, *Arnold*
Ernke, *Arnold*
Ernlib, *Ehrmann*
Ernmonger, *Ironmonger*
Ernout, *Ernaud*
Ernst
Ernstein, *Ehrmann*
Ernster, *Ernst*
Ernstig, *Ernst*
Ernsting, *Ernst*
Ernwert, *Ehrmann*
Erpel
Errichelli, *Henry*
Errichi, *Henry*
Errichiello, *Henry*
Erricker, *Earwaker*
Errico, *Henry*
Errigo, *Henry*
Errington
Erskine
Erszman, *Hirsch*
Ertel, *Ort*
Ertelt, *Ort*
Ertl, *Ort*
Ervin, *Irvine*
Ervine, *Irvine*
Erving, *Irvine*
Erwin, *Irvine*
Esburnham, *Ashburnham*
Escala, *Eschelle*
Escalada
Escalante, *Eschelle*
Escale, *Eschelle*
Escalera, *Eschelle*
Escalero, *Eschelle*
Eschalette, *Eschelle*
Eschalotte, *Eschelle*
Eschelle
Eschels, *Ashkettle*
Eschelsen, *Ashkettle*
Escher, *Ash*
Escobar
Escobedo, *Escobar*
Escoda
Escoffier
Escofié, *Escoffier*
Escofier, *Escoffier*
Escolà, *Scholar*
Escolar, *Scholar*
Escorial
Escot, *Scott*
Escribà, *Scriven*
Escribano, *Scriven*
Escrivà, *Scriven*
Escriva, *Scriven*
Escrivan, *Scriven*
Escudé, *Squire*
Escuder, *Squire*
Escudero, *Squire*
Escudié, *Squire*
Escudier, *Squire*
Escuyer, *Squire*
Eséva, *Stephen*
Esh, *Ash*
Esherwood, *Isherwood*
Eskenazi, *Ashkenazi*
Esmond, *Eastman*
Esmonde, *Eastman*
Espada
Espadas, *Espada*
Espadaté, *Espada*
Espadater, *Espada*
Espadero, *Espada*
Espagnol, *Pagnol*
Espasa, *Espada*
Espejo, *Spiegler*
Espí, *Épine*
Espín, *Épine*
Espin, *Épine*
Espina, *Épine*
Espinal, *Épine*
Espinar, *Épine*
Espinas, *Épine*
Espinay, *Épine*
Espinazo, *Épine*
Espine, *Épine*
Espinel, *Épine*
Espinet, *Épine*
Espinha, *Épine*
Espinheira, *Épine*
Espinho, *Épine*
Espino, *Épine*
Espínola, *Épine*
Espinós, *Épine*
Espinos, *Épine*
Espinosa, *Épine*
Espírito, *Saint*
Esposi, *Esposito*
Esposito
Esposti, *Esposito*
Esposto, *Esposito*
Esposuto, *Esposito*
Esquerrà, *Ezquerra*
Esquirol, *Squirrel*
Esquirou, *Squirrel*
Esquivel
Essart
Essartier, *Essart*
Essert, *Essart*
Essertel, *Essart*
Essertier, *Essart*
Essex
Esslin, *Ansell*
Esson, *Eade*
Estagnol, *Etang*
Estaing, *Etang*
Estang, *Etang*
Este
Estéban, *Stephen*
Esteban, *Stephen*
Estébanez, *Stephen*
Estèbe, *Stephen*
Esterbrook, *Easterbrook*
Esterházy
Esterin, *Estersohn*
Esterkin, *Estersohn*
Estersohn
Esterson, *Estersohn*
Esteva, *Stephen*
Estêvão, *Stephen*
Estève, *Stephen*
Esteve, *Stephen*
Estévenard, *Stephen*
Esteves, *Stephen*
Estévez, *Stephen*
Estienne, *Stephen*
Estiévan, *Stephen*
Estiévant, *Stephen*
Estival
Estivalet, *Estival*
Estivau, *Estival*
Estivaux, *Estival*
Estoile, *Stella*
Estourneau, *Étourneau*
Estournel, *Étourneau*
Estrada, *Street*
Estradé, *Street*
Estrade, *Street*
Estrader, *Street*
Estradère, *Street*
Estradier, *Street*
Estrée, *Street*
Estreicher, *Oistrakh*
Estrela, *Stella*
Estrella, *Stella*
Estrin, *Estersohn*
Etang
Etchells
Etève, *Stephen*
Etheridge, *Edrich*
Etherington, *Hetherington*
Ethève, *Stephen*
Etiemble, *Stephen*
Étienne, *Stephen*
Étiennet, *Stephen*
Étienney, *Stephen*
Étiennot, *Stephen*
Etiévant, *Stephen*
Etiève, *Stephen*
Étoile, *Stella*
Étournaud, *Étourneau*
Étourneau
Étraz, *Street*
Ettwein, *Edwin*
Etzel, *Albert*
Eugène
Euler
Eulner, *Euler*
Eunson, *Ewan*
Euren, *Uren*
Eusébio
Eustace, *Stace*
Eustache, *Stace*
Eustaze, *Stace*
Eustie, *Stace*
Euvrard, *Everard*
Eva, *Eve*
Evan
Evance, *Evan*
Evans, *Evan*
Evason, *Eve*
Evatt, *Eve*
Evdakov, *Yevdokimov*
Evdokinchik, *Yevdokimov*
Evdonin, *Yevdokimov*
Evdoshin, *Yevdokimov*
Eve
Eveking, *Everard*
Eveleens, *Evelyn*
Evelegh
Evelyn
Even, *Evan*
Evens, *Evan*
Évêque, *Bishop*
Evéquot, *Bishop*
Ever, *Everard*
Everaert, *Everard*
Everaerts, *Everard*
Everard
Everatt, *Everard*
Everdey, *Everard*
Everding, *Everard*
Evered, *Everard*
Everest
Everett, *Everard*
Everid, *Everard*
Everill
Everiss, *Everest*
Everist, *Everest*
Everitt, *Everard*
Everix, *Everest*
Everling, *Everard*
Evermann, *Everard*
Evers, *Everard*
Everson, *Eve*
Evert, *Everard*
Everts, *Everard*
Evertz, *Everard*
Everwin, *Irvine*
Eves, *Eve*
Eveson, *Eve*
Evesque, *Bishop*
Evett, *Eve*
Evetts, *Eve*
Evison, *Eve*
Evitt, *Eve*
Evitts, *Eve*
Evrard, *Everard*
Evras, *Everard*
Evrat, *Everard*
Evreux, *Everest*
Evron, *Efron*
Evroni, *Efron*
Evstafyev, *Ostapov*
Ewald
Ewan
Ewart
Ewen
Ewens, *Ewan*
Ewer
Eweren, *Uren*
Ewermann, *Everard*
Ewers, *Everard, Ewer*
Ewert, *Everard*
Ewin, *Ewan*
Ewing, *Ewan*
Ewings, *Ewan*
Ewins, *Ewan*
Ewold, *Ewald*
Ewols, *Ewald*
Ewolsen, *Ewald*
Exley
Expósito, *Esposito*
Eyck, *Oak*
Eyckman, *Oak*
Eydel, *Eitel*
Eyer, *Ayer*
Eyers, *Ayer*
Eykstra, *Oak*
Eyles, *Isles*
Eynaud, *Einold*
Eynault, *Einold*
Eynon, *Onion*
Eyre, *Ayer*
Eyres, *Ayer*
Eyrs, *Ayer*
Eytel, *Eitel*
Eyth, *Aggis*
Eythner, *Aggis*
Eyton, *Eaton*
Ezekiel
Ezquerra
Ezquerro, *Ezquerra*
Eztelt, *Artaud*

F

Faas, *Boniface, Jarvis*
Faasen, *Boniface*
Fabbiani, *Fabian*
Fabbiano, *Fabian*
Fabbretti, *Fèvre*
Fabbri, *Fèvre*
Fabbrin, *Fèvre*
Fabbrini, *Fèvre*
Fabbrizzi, *Fabrizio*
Fabbroni, *Fèvre*
Fabbrucci, *Fèvre*
Fabel, *Fabian*
Faber, *Fèvre*
Fabert, *Fèvre*
Fabetto, *Fèvre*
Fabián, *Fabian*
Fabian
Fabiańczyk, *Fabian*
Fabianek, *Fabian*
Fabiani, *Fabian*
Fabianke, *Fabian*
Fabianowicz, *Fabian*
Fabiański, *Fabian*
Fabicki, *Fabian*
Fabien, *Fabian*
Fabig, *Fabian*
Fabigan, *Fabian*
Fabijan, *Fabian*
Fabijańczyk, *Fabian*
Fabijanowicz, *Fabian*
Fabijański, *Fabian*
Fábiń, *Fabian*
Fabion, *Fabian*
Fabisch, *Fabian*
Fabiszewski, *Fabian*
Fabjan, *Fabian*
Fabra, *Fèvre*
Fabre, *Fèvre*
Fàbrega, *Forge*
Fàbregas, *Forge*
Fabretti, *Fèvre*
Fabretto, *Fèvre*
Fabri, *Fèvre*
Fabricant, *Fabrikant*
Fabrici, *Fabrizio*
Fabricius, *Fabrizio*
Fabriczy, *Fabrizio*
Fabrikant
Fabrini, *Fèvre*
Fabritius, *Fabrizio*
Fabritzius, *Fabrizio*
Fabrizi, *Fabrizio*
Fabrizio
Fabrizzi, *Fabrizio*
Fabron, *Fèvre*
Fabrucci, *Fèvre*
Fabry, *Fèvre*
Fabrykant, *Fabrikant*
Facci, *Boniface*
Faccini, *Boniface*
Faccio, *Boniface*
Faccioli, *Boniface*
Faccione, *Boniface*
Facciotti, *Boniface*
Faceto, *Fage*
Facey, *Vaisey*
Fach, *Wenzel*
Fache, *Wenzel*
Facini, *Boniface*
Facon, *Falcon*
Fadeev, *Tadié*
Fadeichev, *Tadié*
Fadneev, *Tadié*
Fadyshin, *Tadié*
Fae, *Fage*
Faedi, *Fage*
Faedo, *Fage*
Faers, *Fair*
Faes, *Boniface*
Faeta, *Fage*
Faeti, *Fage*
Faeto, *Fage*
Faetto, *Fage*
Faga, *Fage*
Fagan
Fage
Fageau, *Fage*
Fagerberg, *Fair*
Fagerlund, *Fair*
Fagerström, *Fair*
Fages, *Fage*
Faget, *Fage*
Fagette, *Fage*
Fagg
Fagge, *Fagg*
Faggi, *Fage*
Faggin, *Fage*
Faggini, *Fage*
Faggio, *Fage*
Faggiola, *Fage*
Faggioli, *Fage*
Faggion, *Fage*
Faggioni, *Fage*
Faggiotto, *Fage*
Fagin, *Feige*
Fagione, *Fage*
Fago, *Fage*
Fagon, *Fagot*
Fagone, *Fage*
Fagot
Fagotti, *Fage*
Fagotto, *Fage*
Faguet, *Fagot*
Faherty
Fahey, *Fahy*
Fahy
Faia, *Fage*
Faibis, *Faivish*
Faibish, *Faivish*
Faier, *Fayerman*
Faierman, *Fayerman*
Faiers, *Fair*
Faierstein, *Feuerstein*
Faiertag
Faig, *Feige*
Faigenbaum, *Feige*
Faigenberg, *Feige*
Faigenblat, *Feige*
Faigenboum, *Feige*
Faigin, *Feige*
Failes
Faille
Faillon, *Faille*
Faillot, *Faille*
Fails, *Failes*
Fainan, *Finn*
Fainer, *Fenier*
Fainnan, *Finn*
Fair
Fairbairn
Fairbairns, *Fairbairn*
Fairbank
Fairbanks, *Fairbank*
Fairbarns, *Fairbairn*
Fairbourn, *Fairburn*
Fairbourne, *Fairburn*
Fairbrother
Fairburn
Fairburne, *Fairburn*
Fairchild
Faircliff, *Fairclough*
Faircliffe, *Fairclough*
Faircloth, *Fairclough*
Fairclough
Faire, *Fair*
Faires, *Fair*
Fairest, *Fairhurst*
Fairfax
Fairgrieve
Fairhead
Fairhurst
Fairlamb
Fairlem, *Fairlamb*
Fairless, *Fairlie*
Fairley, *Fairlie, Farley*
Fairlie
Fairman
Fairn, *Fern*
Fairnie, *Fernie*
Fairs, *Fair*
Fairtlough, *Fairclough*
Fairweather
Fairy, *Feary*
Faist
Faistl, *Faist*
Faistle, *Faist*
Faith
Faithful, *Faith*
Faithfull, *Faith*
Faito, *Fage*
Faivelson, *Faivish*
Faivisevitz, *Faivish*
Faivish
Faivre, *Fèvre*
Faivret, *Fèvre*
Faivuschevitch, *Faivish*
Faivuszevicz, *Faivish*
Fajard, *Fage*
Fajardo, *Fage*
Fajer, *Fayerman*
Fajeraizen
Fajerman, *Fayerman*
Fajgenbaum, *Feige*
Fajgenblat, *Feige*
Fajn, *Fein*
Fajner, *Fein*
Fajngold, *Fein*
Fajnholtz, *Fein*
Fajnholz, *Fein*
Fajntuch, *Fein*
Fajnzylber, *Fein*
Fajon, *Fage*
Fajwlewich, *Faivish*
Fajwlewicz, *Faivish*
Fajwshewitz, *Faivish*
Fake, *Faulkes*
Fakes, *Faulkes*
Falameev, *Bartholomew*
Falcão, *Falcon*
Falchetti, *Faulkes*
Falchi, *Faulkes*
Falchini, *Faulkes*
Falc'hun, *Falcon*
Falciatori, *Faucheur*
Falck, *Falcon*
Falckner, *Faulkner*
Falcó, *Falcon*
Falco, *Faulkes*
Falcón, *Falcon*
Falcon
Falconar, *Faulkner*
Falconat, *Falcon*
Falcone, *Falcon*
Falconer, *Faulkner*
Falconet, *Falcon*
Falconetto, *Falcon*
Falconi, *Falcon*
Falconieri, *Faulkner*
Falconio, *Falcon*
Falconnat, *Falcon*
Falconnet, *Falcon*
Falconnier, *Faulkner*
Falcou, *Falcon*
Falcucci, *Faulkes*
Falcus, *Faulkes*
Fales, *Failes*
Falge, *Fallow*
Falguera, *Fougère*
Falgueras, *Fougère*
Falk, *Falcon*
Falke, *Falcon*
Falkenberg, *Falcon*
Falkenflik, *Falcon*
Falkenstein, *Falcon*
Falkhus, *Faulkes*
Falkievich, *Falcon*
Falkiner, *Faulkner*
Falkingham
Falkman, *Falcon*
Falkner, *Faulkner*
Falkoff, *Falcon*
Falkous, *Faulkes*
Falkov, *Falcon*
Falkovitch, *Falcon*
Falkovitz, *Falcon*
Falkovski, *Falcon*
Falkovsky, *Falcon*
Falkowicz, *Falcon*
Falkowitz, *Falcon*
Falkowsky, *Falcon*
Falkus, *Faulkes*
Fall
Fallas
Falle, *Fall*
Fallis, *Fallas*
Fallon
Falloon, *Fallon*
Fallow
Fallowes, *Fallow*
Fallows, *Fallow*
Falls, *Fallas*
Fälman, *Fell*
Faloon, *Fallon*
Falquière, *Fougère*
Faltin, *Valentine*
Falvey, *Feely*
Fanagan, *Finn*
Fancello, *Infante*
Fanciulli, *Infante*
Fanciullo, *Infante*
Fandrey, *Andrew*
Fandrich, *Andrew*
Fane
Fanier, *Fenier*
Fann, *Fenn*
Fanner
Fannin, *Finn*
Fanning, *Fenn*
Fannon, *Finn*
Fanon
Fanshaw, *Featherstonehaugh*
Fanshawe, *Featherstonehaugh*
Fant, *Infante*
Fantacci, *Infante*

Fantazzi, *Infante*
Fante, *Infante*
Fantes, *Infante*
Fanti, *Infante*
Fantin, *Infante*
Fantinelli, *Infante*
Fantini, *Infante*
Fantino, *Infante*
Fantocci, *Infante*
Fanton, *Infante*
Fantone, *Infante*
Fantoni, *Infante*
Fantou, *Infante*
Fantozzi, *Infante*
Fantucci, *Infante*
Fantuzzi, *Infante*
Fanty, *Infante*
Faraday, *Fereday*
Faragher, *Farquhar*
Faraker, *Farquhar*
Faraquhart, *Farquhar*
Farb, *Färber*
Farber, *Färber*
Färber
Farbersohn, *Färber*
Farberson, *Färber*
Farbiarz, *Färber*
Farbiasz, *Färber*
Farbman, *Färber*
Farbrother, *Fairbrother*
Farbstein, *Färber*
Farbsztein, *Färber*
Fare, *Farrar*
Farebrother, *Fairbrother*
Fareweather, *Fairweather*
Farey, *Feary*
Fargas, *Forge*
Farge, *Forge*
Fargeon, *Forge*
Farges, *Forge*
Fargette, *Forge*
Fargher, *Farquhar*
Fargier, *Forge*
Fargo
Fargue, *Forge*
Fargues, *Forge*
Faria
Farias, *Faria*
Farina, *Farine*
Farinacci, *Farine*
Farinari, *Farine*
Farinaro, *Farine*
Farinasso, *Farine*
Farinaux, *Farine*
Farinazzo, *Farine*
Farine
Farineau, *Farine*
Farinel, *Farine*
Farinela, *Farine*
Farinella, *Farine*
Farinelli, *Farine*
Farinet, *Farine*
Farinetti, *Farine*
Farinez, *Farine*
Farinha, *Farine*
Farini, *Farine*
Farinier, *Farine*
Farinola, *Farine*
Farinon, *Farine*
Farinone, *Farine*
Farinotti, *Farine*
Farjat, *Forge*
Farjon, *Forge*
Farkache, *Farkas*
Farkas
Farkash, *Farkas*
Farlam, *Fairlamb*
Farleigh, *Farley*
Farley
Farman
Farmar, *Farmer*
Farmer
Farmery
Farn, *Fern*
Farnall, *Farnell*
Farnaux, *Farine*
Farndon
Farneau, *Farine*
Farnel, *Farine*
Farnell
Farnes, *Farnese*
Farnes, *Fern*
Farnese
Farnham
Farnhill, *Farnell*
Farnier, *Farine*
Farnill, *Farnell*
Farnorth, *Farnworth*
Farnsworth, *Farnworth*
Farnworth
Faro
Farquar, *Farquhar*
Farquarson, *Farquhar*
Farquhar
Farquharson, *Farquhar*
Farr
Farra, *Farrar*
Farragher, *Farquhar*
Farragut, *Ferragut*
Farrah, *Farrar*
Farran, *Farrant*
Farrance, *Farrant*
Farrand, *Farrant*
Farrant
Farrants, *Farrant*
Farrar
Farràs
Farré, *Farrar*
Farrel, *Farrell*
Farrell
Farrelly, *Farrell*
Farren
Farreny, *Farràs*
Farrer, *Farrar*
Farrera, *Ferrers*
Farreras, *Ferrers*
Farreres, *Ferrers*
Farrés, *Farrar*
Farrey, *Farrar*
Farrier, *Farrar*
Farrimond
Farrin, *Farren*
Farrington
Farris, *Fergus*
Farrissy, *Fergus*
Farrow, *Farrar*
Farthing
Fasey, *Vaisey*
Fäsi, *Jarvis*
Fäsin, *Jarvis*
Fass
Fassbender, *Fassbinder*
Fassbinder
Fassbinder, *Binder*
Fässer, *Fass*
Fasset, *Fawcett*
Fassi, *Boniface*
Fassini, *Boniface*
Fassio, *Boniface*
Fassioli, *Boniface*
Fässler, *Fass*
Fassnidge
Fassone, *Boniface*
Fastnedge, *Fassnidge*
Fastolf
Fath, *Vogt*
Fathmann, *Vogt*
Fau, *Fage*
Faucett, *Fawcett*
Faucheur
Faucheux, *Faucheur*
Faucon, *Falcon*
Fauconneau, *Falcon*
Fauconnet, *Falcon*
Fauconnier, *Faulkner*
Faugère, *Fougère*
Faughnan
Faughy, *Fahy*
Faugière, *Fougère*
Faul, *Fall*
Faulconnier, *Faulkner*
Faulder, *Fold*
Faulds, *Fold*
Faulkener, *Faulkner*
Faulkes
Faulkner
Faulknor, *Faulkner*
Faull, *Fall*
Faultley, *Fautley*
Faunt, *Infante*
Fauquer, *Faucheur*
Fauquex, *Faucheur*
Faur, *Fèvre*
Faura, *Fèvre*
Fauré, *Fèvre*
Faure, *Fèvre*
Faurel, *Fèvre*
Fauron, *Fèvre*
Faurou, *Fèvre*
Faury, *Fèvre*
Fausset, *Fawcett*
Faussett, *Fawcett*
Faust
Fäustel, *Faust*
Faustino
Fäustlein, *Faust*
Faustov, *Faust*
Faustsev, *Faust*
Faut, *Vogt*
Fauth, *Vogt*
Fautley
Fautly, *Fautley*
Fauveau, *Fauvel*
Fauvel
Faux, *Faulkes*
Favard
Favardel, *Favard*
Favardin, *Favard*
Favardon, *Favard*
Favaretti, *Fèvre*
Favari, *Favier*
Favarin, *Fèvre*
Favaro, *Favier*
Favaroli, *Fèvre*
Favaron, *Fèvre*
Favarone, *Fèvre*
Favart, *Favard*
Favel, *Fauvel*
Favell, *Fauvel*
Favereau, *Favier*
Faveri, *Fèvre*
Favier
Favill, *Fauvel*
Favre, *Fèvre*
Favreau, *Fèvre, Favier*
Favrel, *Fèvre*
Favret, *Fèvre*
Favretin, *Fèvre*
Favretti, *Fèvre*
Favri, *Fèvre*
Favrichon, *Fèvre*
Favrin, *Fèvre*
Favron, *Fèvre*
Favruzzi, *Fèvre*
Favshevitz, *Faivish*
Favstov, *Faust*
Fawcett
Fawcitt, *Fawcett*
Fawke, *Faulkes*
Fawkes, *Faulkes*
Fawle, *Fall*
Fawlks, *Faulkes*
Fawsett, *Fawcett*
Fawssett, *Fawcett*
Fay, *Fage*
Fay
Fayard, *Fage*
Faybish, *Faivish*
Faydel, *Feydit*
Faydit, *Feydit*
Faye, *Fage, Fay*
Fayel, *Fage*
Fayer, *Fair, Fayerman*
Fayerbrother, *Fairbrother*
Fayerman, *Fairman*
Fayerman
Fayers, *Fair*
Fayerstein, *Feuerstein*
Fayet, *Fage*
Fayette, *Fage*
Fayne, *Fane*
Faynes, *Fane*
Fayol, *Fage*
Fayolle, *Fage*
Fayon, *Fage*
Fayot, *Fage*
Fayre, *Fair*
Fazackerly, *Fazakerley*
Fazakerley
Fazi, *Boniface, Fage*
Fazio, *Boniface*
Fazzi, *Boniface*
Fazzini, *Boniface*
Fazzio, *Boniface*
Fazzioli, *Boniface*
Fazzuoli, *Boniface*
Feacey, *Vaisey*
Feakes, *Fitch*
Feaks, *Fitch*
Fealey, *Feely*
Fealy, *Feely*
Feamaster, *Femister*
Feamster, *Femister*
Feane, *Fee*
Fear
Feare, *Fear*
Fearey, *Feary*
Fearn, *Fern*
Fearnall, *Farnell*
Fearne, *Fern*
Fearnley, *Farley*
Fearnside
Fearon
Fears, *Fear*
Feary
Feasey, *Vaisey*

Feather
Featherston, *Featherstone*
Featherstone
Featherstonehaugh
Featherstonhaugh, *Featherstonehaugh*
Featley, *Fairclough*
Feavearyear, *Feverel*
Feaver, *Fèvre*
Feavers, *Fèvre*
Feaveryear, *Feverel*
Feaviour, *Fèvre*
Feazy, *Vaisey*
Fèbre, *Fèvre*
Febreau, *Fèvre*
Febry, *Feverel*
Febvre, *Fèvre*
Fech, *Wenzel*
Feche, *Wenzel*
Fechler, *Wenzel*
Fechner, *Wenzel*
Fechtner, *Wenzel*
Feck, *Frederick*
Fecke, *Frederick*
Fecken, *Frederick*
Fedchin, *Théodore*
Fedchonok, *Théodore*
Fedde, *Frederick*
Feddeke, *Frederick*
Feddema, *Frederick*
Fedder, *Feather*
Feddercke, *Frederick*
Feddersen, *Frederick*
Feddinga, *Frederick*
Fedenev, *Théodore*
Feder, *Feather*
Federbusch, *Feather*
Federbush, *Feather*
Federer, *Feather*
Federgreen, *Feather*
Federgrin, *Feather*
Federgrün, *Feather*
Federici, *Frederick*
Federico, *Frederick*
Federighi, *Frederick*
Federigi, *Frederick*
Federigo, *Frederick*
Federle, *Feather*
Federman, *Feather*
Federmann, *Feather*
Federschneider, *Feather*
Federzoni, *Frederick*
Fedichkin, *Théodore*
Fedikov, *Théodore*
Fedin, *Théodore*
Fedinin, *Théodore*
Fedishchev, *Théodore*
Fedkin, *Théodore*
Fedko, *Théodore*
Fedkov, *Théodore*
Fednev, *Théodore*
Fedorchenko, *Théodore*
Fedorchik, *Théodore*
Fedorczyk, *Théodore*
Fedorinchik, *Théodore*
Fedorintsev, *Théodore*
Fedorishchev, *Théodore*
Fedorkevich, *Théodore*
Fedorko, *Théodore*
Fedoronko, *Théodore*
Fedorowicz, *Théodore*
Fedorowski, *Théodore*
Fedorski, *Théodore*
Fedorushov, *Théodore*
Fedotikhin, *Fedotov*
Fedotov
Fedotyev, *Fedotov*
Fedrici, *Frederick*
Fedrigo, *Frederick*
Fedrigon, *Frederick*
Fedrigoni, *Frederick*
Fedrix, *Frederick*
Fedrizzi, *Frederick*
Fedunov, *Théodore*
Fedyaev, *Théodore*
Fedyakin, *Théodore*
Fedyakov, *Théodore*
Fedyanin, *Théodore*
Fedyashev, *Théodore*
Fedyashin, *Théodore*
Fedyashkin, *Théodore*
Fedyński, *Théodore*
Fedyshin, *Théodore*
Fedyszyn, *Théodore*
Fedyukin, *Théodore*
Fedyukov, *Théodore*
Fedyunin, *Théodore*
Fedyunkin, *Théodore*
Fedyunyaev, *Théodore*
Fedyushin, *Théodore*
Fedyushkin, *Théodore*
Fee
Feehally, *Fitzhenry*
Feehan, *Fee*
Feeharry, *Fitzhenry*
Feehely, *Feely*
Feehily, *Feely*
Feek, *Fitch*
Feeks, *Fitch*
Feeley, *Feely*
Feely
Feemster, *Femister*
Feeney
Feenstra, *Fenn*
Feesey, *Vaisey*
Feest, *Faist*
Feferberg, *Pepper*
Feferkichen, *Pepper*
Feferman, *Pepper*
Feffer, *Pepper*
Fefferman, *Pepper*
Fegan, *Fee*
Feghan, *Fee*
Fehan, *Fee*
Fehane, *Fee*
Fehely, *Feely*
Fehér
Fehst, *Faist*
Fehster, *Silvester*
Fei, *Feo*
Feibel, *Faivish*
Feibelovitz, *Faivish*
Feibischoff, *Faivish*
Feibish, *Faivish*
Feibusch, *Faivish*
Feibush, *Faivish*
Feibushewitz, *Faivish*
Feicht
Feichter, *Feicht*
Feichtner, *Feicht*
Feidler, *Pfeidler*
Feidt, *Vito*
Feierle, *Feuer*
Feifer, *Piper*
Feiffer, *Piper*
Feig, *Feige*
Feige
Feigel
Feigelewitz, *Feigel*
Feigelfuss, *Vogel*
Feigelman, *Vogel*
Feigelsohn, *Feigel*
Feigelson, *Feigel*
Feigelstein, *Vogel*
Feigelstock, *Vogel*
Feigenbaum, *Feige*
Feigenberg, *Feige*
Feigenblat, *Feige*
Feigenblatt, *Feige*
Feigenboim, *Feige*
Feigenson, *Feige*
Feiges, *Feige*
Feighery
Feigin, *Feige*
Feiglewitz, *Feigel*
Feiglin, *Feigel*
Feigman, *Feige*
Feijoo
Feild, *Field*
Feilden, *Field*
Feilding, *Field*
Feiler, *Filer*
Feimster, *Femister*
Fein
Feinberg, *Fein*
Feinblatt, *Fein*
Feinbrun, *Fein*
Feinburg, *Fein*
Feinbusch, *Fein*
Feinbush, *Fein*
Feindeitsch, *Fein*
Feine, *Fein*
Feiner, *Fein, Fenier*
Feinert, *Fein*
Feingang, *Fein*
Feingold, *Fein*
Feinholz, *Fein*
Feinkind, *Fein*
Feinkoch, *Fein*
Feinle, *Fein*
Feinman, *Fein*
Feinmann, *Fein*
Feinmesser, *Fein*
Feinschreiber
Feinsilber, *Fein*
Feinstein, *Fein*
Feintuch, *Fein*
Feinwachs, *Fein*
Feinzak, *Fein*
Feio
Feirer, *Feuer*
Feirn, *Fern*
Feist, *Faist*
Feistel, *Faust*
Feistle, *Faust*
Feit, *Vito*
Feito
Feivel, *Faivish*
Feivelson, *Faivish*
Feivlovitz, *Faivish*
Feiwel, *Faivish*
Feiwlewicz, *Faivish*
Feiwlowicz, *Faivish*
Feix, *Vito*
Fejér, *Fehér*
Fejgin, *Feige*
Fekete
Feking, *Frederick*
Fekkena, *Frederick*
Felber
Felberbaum, *Felber*
Felbert, *Felber*
Felczyk, *Felix*
Felczykowski, *Felix*
Feld, *Field*
Feldbau, *Field*
Feldbaum, *Field*
Feldberg, *Field*
Feldberger, *Field*
Feldblum, *Field*
Feldbrin, *Field*
Felder, *Field*
Felderer, *Field*
Feldfisher, *Field*
Feldhammer, *Field*
Feldharker, *Field*
Feldheim, *Field*
Feldhorn, *Field*
Feldhuhn, *Field*
Feldklein, *Field*
Feldman, *Field*
Feldmann, *Field*
Feldmark, *Field*
Feldmeser, *Field*
Feldmesser, *Field*
Feldmus, *Field*
Feldner
Feldscher
Feldstein, *Field*
Feldstern, *Field*
Felhandler, *Fell*
Féli, *Felix*
Felice, *Felix*
Felices, *Felix*
Felicetti, *Felix*
Felici, *Felix*
Feliciano
Felicini, *Felix*
Felicioli, *Felix*
Felicioni, *Felix*
Feliciotti, *Felix*
Felicjan, *Feliciano*
Felicjaniak, *Feliciano*
Felickson, *Felix*
Feliks, *Felix*
Feliksiak, *Felix*
Felińczak, *Feliński*
Feliński
Félip, *Philip*
Felip, *Philip*
Felipe, *Philip*
Felis, *Felix*
Felise, *Felix*
Felisiak, *Felix*
Félissot, *Felix*
Feliu, *Felix*
Félix, *Felix*
Fèlix, *Felix*
Felix
Feliz, *Felix*
Félizet, *Felix*
Félizon, *Felix*
Félizot, *Felix*
Felkel, *Volk*
Felkner, *Faulkner*
Fell
Fella, *Fell*
Feller, *Fell*
Fellerer, *Fell*
Fellermann, *Fell*
Fellman, *Fell*
Fellmann, *Fell*
Fellner, *Feldner*
Fellner, *Fell*
Fellow
Fellowes, *Fellow*

Fellows, *Fellow*
Fells, *Fell*
Felman, *Fell*
Felmy, *Volmer*
Felner, *Fell*
Fels, *Fell*
Felser, *Fell*
Felsmann, *Fell*
Felstead, *Felsted*
Felsted
Felt, *Filzer*
Felten, *Valentine*
Felter, *Filzer*
Feltham
Felton
Feltz, *Fell*
Feltzmann, *Fell*
Felzer, *Fell*
Felzner, *Fell*
Femister
Fenaghty
Fenayre, *Fenier*
Fenayrol, *Fenier*
Fenayroux, *Fenier*
Fenchel, *Fennell*
Fenck
Fend, *Infante*
Fendel, *Infante*
Fenderico, *Frederick*
Fendt, *Infante*
Fenech, *Fenck*
Fenegan, *Finn*
Fenellosa, *Fennell*
Fénelon, *Fenlon*
Fenelon, *Fenlon*
Fenemore, *Finnemore*
Feneron, *Fenier*
Fenêtre, *Fenster*
Fenié, *Fenier*
Fenier
Fenig, *Penny*
Fenigson, *Penny*
Fenimore, *Finnemore*
Fenix, *Fenwick*
Fenkohl, *Fennell*
Fenlon
Fenn
Fennekohl, *Fennell*
Fennel, *Fennell*
Fennell
Fennelly, *Fennell*
Fennemore, *Finnemore*
Fenner, *Fenn*
Fennessy
Fennick, *Fenwick*
Fenning, *Fenn, Penny*
Fenocchio, *Fennell*
Fenoglietto, *Fennell*
Fenoglio, *Fennell*
Fenoll, *Fennell*
Fenoller, *Fennell*
Fenster
Fensterer, *Fenster*
Fenstermacher, *Fenster*
Fenstermann, *Fenster*
Fenteman, *Fentiman*
Fentiman
Fenton
Fenwich, *Fenwick*
Fenwick
Fenyves, *Fenyvesi*
Fenyvesi
Fenyvessy, *Fenyvesi*
Fenzl, *Wenzel*
Fenzlein, *Wenzel*
Feo
Feofilaktov, *Filatov*
Feoli, *Feo*
Fer, *Ferro*
Féral
Ferber, *Färber*
Ferberov, *Färber*
Ferdico, *Frederick*
Ferdinand
Fere, *Farrar*
Fereday
Ferenc, *Francis*
Ference, *Farrant*
Ferenci, *Francis*
Ferencowicz, *Francis*
Ferencz, *Francis*
Ferenczi, *Francis*
Ferenczy, *Francis*
Ferens, *Farrant, Francis*
Ferentz, *Francis*
Ferfers, *Färber*
Fergie, *Fergus*
Fergus
Ferguson, *Fergus*
Fergusson, *Fergus*
Fergyson, *Fergus*
Férié, *Farrar*
Férier, *Farrar*
Fériot, *Frederick*
Fermer, *Farmer*
Fermier, *Farmer*
Fermín, *Firmin*
Fermin, *Firmin*
Fermor, *Farmer*
Fern
Fernán, *Ferdinand*
Fernandes, *Ferdinand*
Fernández, *Ferdinand*
Fernandez, *Ferdinand*
Fernando, *Ferdinand*
Fernant, *Ferdinand*
Fernão, *Ferdinand*
Ferne, *Fern*
Fernel, *Fearon*
Fernet, *Fearon*
Fernez, *Fearon*
Fernie
Fernier, *Fearon*
Ferns, *Fern*
Ferragu, *Ferragut*
Ferragus, *Ferragut*
Ferragut
Ferrai, *Farrar*
Ferrán, *Farrant*
Ferran, *Farrant*
Ferrand, *Farrant*
Ferrández, *Ferdinand*
Ferrandi, *Farrant*
Ferrándiz, *Ferdinand*
Ferrando, *Farrant*
Ferrans, *Farrant*
Ferrant, *Farrant*
Ferrante, *Farrant*
Ferrantelli, *Farrant*
Ferrantello, *Farrant*
Ferranti, *Farrant*
Ferrantin, *Farrant*
Ferrantini, *Farrant*
Ferrantino, *Farrant*
Ferrão, *Farrant, Ferdinand*
Ferrar, *Farrar*
Ferrara, *Ferrers*
Ferraraccio, *Farrar*
Ferrarello, *Farrar*
Ferrarese, *Ferrers*
Ferraresi, *Ferrers*
Ferraretto, *Farrar*
Ferrari, *Farrar*
Ferrarin, *Farrar*
Ferrarini, *Farrar*
Ferrario, *Farrar*
Ferraro, *Farrar*
Ferraron, *Farrar*
Ferrarone, *Farrar*
Ferrarotti, *Farrar*
Ferras, *Ferro*
Ferraz, *Farrant*
Ferré, *Farrar*
Ferre, *Farrar*
Ferrea, *Ferrers*
Ferreira, *Ferrers*
Ferreiró, *Farrar*
Ferreiro, *Farrar*
Ferreli, *Farrar*
Ferrell, *Farrell*
Ferrer, *Farrar*
Ferrera, *Ferrers*
Ferreras, *Ferrers*
Ferreres, *Ferrers*
Ferreri, *Farrar*
Ferrerio, *Farrar*
Ferreró, *Farrar*
Ferrero, *Farrar*
Ferrers
Ferrés, *Farrar*
Ferretti, *Ferro*
Ferrettini, *Ferro*
Ferrettino, *Ferro*
Ferretto, *Ferro*
Ferrey, *Ferry*
Ferri, *Ferro*
Ferriaud, *Frederick*
Ferrie, *Ferry*
Ferrier, *Farrar*
Ferrier
Ferrière, *Ferrers*
Ferrières, *Ferrers*
Ferrieri, *Farrar*
Ferriero, *Farrar*
Ferrighi, *Frederick*
Ferrillo, *Ferro*
Ferriman, *Ferry*
Ferrin, *Ferro*
Ferrini, *Ferro*
Ferrino, *Ferro*
Ferriot, *Frederick*
Ferris, *Fergus*
Ferro
Ferroli, *Ferro*
Ferron, *Fearon, Ferro*
Ferrone, *Ferro*
Ferronel, *Fearon*
Ferronet, *Fearon*
Ferroni, *Ferro*
Ferronier, *Fearon*
Ferrotti, *Ferro*
Ferrucci, *Ferro*
Ferrulli, *Ferro*
Ferruzzi, *Ferro*
Ferry
Ferryman, *Ferry*
Ferstel, *Fürst*
Ferster, *Forster*
Fertig
Ferver, *Färber*
Fervers, *Färber*
Fery, *Feary*
Fesenko, *Théodore*
Fessler, *Fass*
Fester, *Silvester*
Festersen, *Silvester*
Fetherston, *Featherstone*
Fetherstonhaugh, *Featherstonehaugh*
Fett
Fetter, *Fett*
Fettermann, *Fett*
Fetting, *Fett*
Fettman, *Fett*
Feubre, *Fèvre*
Feuchère, *Fougère*
Feucht, *Feicht*
Feuchtner, *Feicht*
Feuchtwanger
Feuer
Feuerbach
Feuerlein, *Feuer*
Feuerman, *Feuer*
Feuermann, *Feuer*
Feuerstein
Feugère, *Fougère*
Feugière, *Fougère*
Feuquières, *Fougère*
Feure, *Fèvre*
Feurer, *Feuer*
Fever, *Fèvre*
Feverel
Fevers, *Fèvre*
Feveyear, *Feverel*
Fèvre
Févret, *Fèvre*
Fevret, *Fèvre*
Févrichaud, *Fèvre*
Février, *Feverel*
Fevyer, *Feverel*
Fewkes, *Foulkes*
Fewster, *Forster*
Fewtrell
Fey, *Fage, Fay*
Feydeau, *Feydit*
Feydel, *Feydit*
Feydit
Feyel, *Fage*
Feyer, *Fair*
Feyeux, *Fage*
Fiala
Fialek, *Fiala*
Fialho
Fialka, *Fiala*
Fiammenghi, *Fleming*
Fibonacci
Fiche
Fichet, *Fiche*
Fichot, *Fiche*
Ficht, *Feicht*
Fichte, *Feicht*
Fichter, *Feicht*
Fichtner, *Feicht*
Fick, *Fitch, Frederick*
Ficken, *Fitch*
Fickett, *Fitch*
Fickin, *Fitch*
Fickins, *Fitch*
Fidalgo, *Hidalgo*
Fiddes
Fiddian, *Vivian*
Fiddler, *Fiedler*
Fiddy
Fidge, *Fitch*
Fidgen, *Vivian*
Fidgeon, *Vivian*

Fidget, *Fitch*
Fidkin, *Vivian*
Fidler, *Fiedler*
Fido, *Fiddy*
Fidoe, *Fiddy*
Fieback
Fiebeck, *Fieback*
Fiebich, *Fieback*
Fiebig, *Fieback*
Fiebiger, *Fieback*
Fiederer, *Feather*
Fiedler
Fiedorowicz, *Théodore*
Fieger, *Füger*
Fiegert, *Füger*
Fiegner, *Füger*
Fiehn, *Fein*
Field
Fielden, *Field*
Fielder, *Field*
Fieldhouse
Fielding, *Field*
Fields, *Field*
Fien, *Fein*
Fienes, *Fiennes*
Fiennes
Fierman, *Fairman*
Fierro, *Ferro*
Fietz, *Vincent*
Fietze, *Vincent*
Fietzek, *Vincent*
Fietzke, *Vincent*
Fiévet
Fievez, *Fiévet*
Fife, *Fyfe*
Figadère, *Feige*
Figairol, *Feige*
Figarol, *Feige*
Figdor, *Avigdor*
Figg, *Feige*
Figge, *Feige*
Figgess, *Figgis*
Figgis
Figiovanni, *John*
Figliovanni, *John*
Figueira, *Feige*
Figueiras, *Feige*
Figueiredo, *Feige*
Figuera, *Feige*
Figueras, *Feige*
Figuère, *Feige*
Figueredo, *Feige*
Figuères, *Feige*
Figueroa, *Feige*
Figuerola, *Feige*
Figuier, *Feige*
Figuière, *Feige*
Fihelly, *Feely*
Fijałkowski
Fiks, *Fox*
Fiksel, *Fox*
Fiksman, *Fox*
Filakhtov, *Filatov*
Filasov, *Philip*
Filatov
Filatyev, *Filatov*
Filbee, *Filby*
Filbey, *Filby*
Filby
Filc, *Filzer*
Filchagin, *Philip*
Filchakov, *Philip*
Filcman, *Filzer*
Fild, *Filzer*
Fildes
Fildrey, *Fillery*
Filer
Filev, *Philip*
Filhon, *Fillon*
Filice, *Felix*
Filin, *Philip*
Filinkov, *Philip*
Filintsev, *Philip*
Filip, *Philip*
Filipchikov, *Philip*
Filipczak, *Philip*
Filipczyński, *Philip*
Filípek, *Philip*
Filipek, *Philip*
Filipiak, *Philip*
Filipić, *Philip*
Filipov, *Philip*
Filipović, *Philip*
Filipowicz, *Philip*
Filippazzo, *Philip*
Filippelli, *Philip*
Filippello, *Philip*
Filippetti, *Philip*
Filippi, *Philip*
Filippini, *Philip*
Filippo, *Philip*
Filippone, *Philip*
Filipponi, *Philip*
Filippov, *Philip*
Filippozzi, *Philip*
Filippucci, *Philip*
Filipputti, *Philip*
Filippyev, *Philip*
Filipson, *Philip*
Filipychev, *Philip*
Filipyev, *Philip*
Filisov, *Philip*
Filkin, *Philip*
Filkins
Filkov, *Philip*
Fillary, *Fillery*
Fillery
Fillingham
Fillion, *Fillon*
Fillis, *Felix*
Fillmore, *Phillimore*
Fillon
Fills, *Philip*
Filmore, *Phillimore*
Filochov, *Philip*
Filosof, *Philosoph*
Filosoff, *Philosoph*
Filov, *Philip*
Filozof, *Philosoph*
Filpi, *Philip*
Filpo, *Philip*
Filshin, *Philip*
Filson, *Philip*
Filt, *Filzer*
Filter, *Filzer*
Filtser, *Filzer*
Filyaev, *Philip*
Filyakov, *Philip*
Filyashin, *Philip*
Filyukov, *Philip*
Filyushkin, *Philip*
Filz, *Filzer*
Filzer
Fimichev, *Yefimov*
Fimister, *Femister*
Fin
Finan, *Finn*
Finar, *Finer*
Finch
Fincham
Findl, *Findling*
Findlater
Findlay, *Finlay*
Findley, *Finlay*
Findling
Findlow, *Finlay*
Fine, *Fin*
Finegan, *Finn*
Finel, *Fin*
Finer
Finet, *Fin*
Finger
Fingerhut
Fingerman, *Finger*
Fingerreich, *Finger*
Fingeryk, *Finger*
Fingherman, *Finger*
Finigan, *Finn*
Fink
Finkel, *Fink, Funke*
Finkelberg, *Funke*
Finkelbrand, *Funke*
Finkelkraut, *Funke*
Finkelman, *Funke*
Finkels, *Funke*
Finkelstein, *Funke*
Finkelstejn, *Funke*
Finkelsztain, *Funke*
Finker, *Fink*
Finkiel, *Funke*
Finkielstejn, *Funke*
Finkle, *Fink*
Finkler, *Fink*
Finkman, *Fink*
Finlaison, *Finlay*
Finlason, *Finlay*
Finlater, *Findlater*
Finlator, *Findlater*
Finlay
Finlayson, *Finlay*
Finley, *Finlay*
Finlow, *Finlay*
Finn
Finnan, *Finn*
Finne, *Finn*
Finnegan, *Finn*
Finnemore
Finnerty, *Fenaghty*
Finney
Finnick, *Fenwick*
Finnie, *Finney*
Finnigan, *Finn*
Finocchi, *Fennell*
Finocchiaro, *Fennell*
Finocchio, *Fennell*
Finoccietti, *Fennell*
Finot, *Fin*
Finsen, *Finn*
Finster
Finsterbush, *Finster*
Finsterer, *Finster*
Finsterle, *Finster*
Finsterlin, *Finster*
Finucane, *Finn*
Finzel, *Vincent*
Fior, *Flower*
Fiora, *Flower*
Fiore, *Flower*
Fiorella, *Flower*
Fiorelli, *Flower*
Fiorellini, *Flower*
Fiorellino, *Flower*
Fiorello, *Flower*
Fiorentin, *Florence*
Fiorentini, *Florence*
Fiorentino, *Florence*
Fioretti, *Flower*
Fioretto, *Flower*
Fiori, *Flower*
Fioriglio, *Flower*
Fiorillo, *Flower*
Fiorini, *Flower*
Fiorito, *Flower*
Fioritto, *Flower*
Fiorone, *Flower*
Fioroni, *Flower*
Fiorotto, *Flower*
Fiorucci, *Flower*
Fioruzzi, *Flower*
Fiquenet, *Fiche*
Fiquet, *Fiche*
Firbank
Fireman, *Fairman*
Fireman
Firenze, *Florence*
Firestein, *Feuerstein*
Firestone, *Feuerstein*
Firidolfi, *Rolf*
Firk, *Firth*
Firkin
Firkins, *Firkin*
Firks, *Firth*
Firman, *Firmin*
Firmin
Firmino, *Firmin*
Firpi, *Philip*
Firpo, *Philip*
Firrao, *Rollo*
Firsht, *Fürst*
First, *Fürst*
Firstenberg, *Fürstenberg*
Firstenfeld, *Fürst*
Firszt, *Fürst*
Firth
Fisch, *Fish*
Fischauf, *Fish*
Fischbach, *Fish*
Fischbein
Fischel, *Fish*
Fischelewitz, *Fish*
Fischelovitch, *Fish*
Fischelovitz, *Fish*
Fischelson, *Fish*
Fischer, *Fisher*
Fischers, *Fisher*
Fischfanger, *Fisher*
Fischgrund, *Fish*
Fischhof, *Fish*
Fischhofer, *Fish*
Fischl, *Fish*
Fischleiber, *Fish*
Fischlein, *Fish*
Fischler, *Fisher*
Fischlin, *Fish*
Fischman, *Fish*
Fischmann, *Fish*
Fischov, *Fish*
Fischsohn, *Fish*
Fischzang, *Fish*
Fišer, *Fisher*
Fišera, *Fisher*
Fish
Fishbach, *Fish*
Fishbain, *Fischbein*
Fishbaum, *Fish*
Fishbein, *Fischbein*

Fishberg, *Fish*
Fishbin, *Fischbein*
Fishburger, *Fish*
Fishe, *Fish*
Fishel, *Fish*
Fishelberg, *Fish*
Fishelevitz, *Fish*
Fishelov, *Fish*
Fishelson, *Fish*
Fishelzon, *Fish*
Fisher
Fisherhofer, *Fish*
Fisherman, *Fisher*
Fisherovich, *Fisher*
Fishfanger, *Fisher*
Fishfeder, *Fish*
Fishgrund, *Fish*
Fishkin, *Fish*
Fishkind, *Fish*
Fishkinhorn, *Fish*
Fishkov, *Fish*
Fishl, *Fish*
Fishlein, *Fish*
Fishler, *Fisher*
Fishlevitz, *Fish*
Fishlovitz, *Fish*
Fishlsin, *Fish*
Fishman, *Fisher*
Fishner, *Fisher*
Fishof, *Fish*
Fishov, *Fish*
Fishson, *Fish*
Fishstein, *Fish*
Fishtal, *Fish*
Fishthal, *Fish*
Fishwick
Fisk
Fiske, *Fisk*
Fisker, *Fisher*
Fisser, *Fisher*
Fist, *Faust*
Fisz, *Fish*
Fiszel, *Fish*
Fiszelewicz, *Fish*
Fiszer, *Fisher*
Fiszhof, *Fish*
Fiszow, *Fish*
Fitch
Fitchell, *Fitch*
Fitchen, *Fitch*
Fitcher, *Fitch*
Fitchet, *Fitch*
Fitchett, *Fitch*
Fitchew, *Fitzhugh*
Fitchie, *Fitzhugh*
Fiter, *Fitter*
Fiterman, *Fitter*
Fithie, *Fitzhugh*
Fithye, *Fitzhugh*
Fitkin, *Vivian*
Fitschen, *Frederick*
Fitt
Fitter
Fittipaldi, *Theobald*
Fittipoldi, *Theobald*
Fitton
FitzAlan, *Allen*
Fitzclarence
Fitzgerald
Fitzgibbon
Fitzharry, *Fitzhenry*
Fitzhenry
FitzHerbert, *Herbert*
Fitzhugh
Fitzhugues, *Fitzhugh*
Fitzmaurice
Fitzner, *Pfützer*
Fitzpatrick
Fitzpayn, *Pain*
Fitzrandolph, *Randolph*
Fitzroy
Fitzsimmons
Fitzsimmons, *Simon*
Fitzsimon, *Fitzsimmons*
Fitzsimons, *Fitzsimmons*
Fitzsymon, *Fitzsimmons*
Fitzsymonds, *Fitzsimmons*
Fitzsymons, *Fitzsimmons*
Fitzthum, *Visdomini*
Fitzwalter, *Walter*
Fitzwarin, *Waring*
Fitzwater, *Walter, Water*
Fitzwilliam, *William*
Fitzwilliams, *William*
Fix, *Vito*
Fjällström, *Fell*
Fjell, *Fell*
Fjellander, *Fell*
Fjellman, *Fell*
Fjellstedt, *Fell*
Fjellström, *Fell*
Flachard, *Flash*
Flachat, *Flash*
Flache, *Flash*
Flachet, *Flash*
Flachot, *Flash*
Flachs, *Flax*
Flachser, *Flax*
Flachsmann, *Flax*
Flächsner, *Flax*
Flack
Flacke, *Flack*
Flackmann, *Flack*
Flacks, *Flax*
Flagg
Flagherty, *Flaherty*
Flaherty
Flähming, *Fleming*
Flaisher, *Flesher*
Flajszer, *Flesher*
Flaks, *Flax*
Flakser, *Flax*
Flaksman, *Flax*
Flaman, *Fleming*
Flamand, *Fleming*
Flamank, *Fleming*
Flamant, *Fleming*
Flamard, *Fleming*
Flamen, *Fleming*
Flamenbaum, *Plum*
Flamenbum, *Plum*
Flamenc, *Fleming*
Flamenck, *Fleming*
Flament, *Fleming*
Flaming, *Fleming*
Flammang, *Fleming*
Flammant, *Fleming*
Flamstead
Flamstede, *Flamstead*
Flamsteed, *Flamstead*
Flanagan
Flanaghan, *Flanagan*
Flander, *Fleming*
Flanders, *Fleming*
Flandre, *Fleming*
Flandrois, *Fleming*
Flannagan, *Flanagan*
Flannally, *Flannery*
Flannery
Flannigan, *Flanagan*
Flarity, *Flaherty*
Flasch, *Flaschner*
Flasche, *Flaschner*
Flaschner
Flash
Flasher, *Flash*
Flashman, *Flash*
Flashner, *Flaschner*
Flass, *Flax*
Flassmann, *Flax*
Flatman, *Flatt*
Flatt
Flaubert, *Robert*
Flaum, *Plum*
Flaumenboim, *Plum*
Flavell
Flaverty, *Flaherty*
Flavian, *Flavien*
Flaviano, *Flavien*
Flavien
Flavin
Flax
Flaxer, *Flax*
Flaxman, *Flax*
Flèche, *Fletcher*
Flécher, *Fletcher*
Fléchier, *Fletcher*
Fleck
Flecker, *Fleck*
Fleckman, *Fleck*
Fleckner, *Fleck*
Fleeman, *Fleming*
Fleeming, *Fleming*
Fleet
Fleetjer, *Fleet*
Fleetwood
Flehmig, *Fleming*
Flehmke, *Fleming*
Fleisch, *Flesher*
Fleischer, *Flesher*
Fleischhack, *Flesher*
Fleischhacker, *Flesher*
Fleischhauer, *Flesher*
Fleischman, *Flesher*
Fleischmann, *Flesher*
Fleischner, *Flesher*
Fleisher, *Flesher*
Fleishhacker, *Flesher*
Fleishner, *Flesher*
Fleissner, *Flesher*
Flek, *Fleck*
Fleksman, *Flax*
Flement, *Fleming*
Fleming
Fleminger, *Fleming*
Fleminks, *Fleming*
Flemisch, *Fleming*
Flemmig, *Fleming*
Flemming, *Fleming*
Flemons, *Fleming*
Flemyng, *Fleming*
Flescher, *Flesher*
Fleschler, *Flaschner*
Fleschmann, *Flesher*
Fleschner, *Flaschner*
Flesher
Fleshner, *Flaschner, Flesher*
Fletcher
Flett
Fleur, *Flower*
Fleurance, *Florence*
Fleurant, *Florent*
Fleureau, *Flower*
Fleurel, *Flower*
Fleurelle, *Flower*
Fleurent, *Florent*
Fleuret, *Flower*
Fleurette, *Flower*
Fleurinck, *Flower*
Fleuriot, *Fleury*
Fleuron, *Flower*
Fleurot, *Flower*
Fleury
Flewett, *Flewitt*
Flewitt
Flexer, *Flax*
Flexman, *Flax*
Flexner, *Flax*
Flinck, *Flink*
Flinders, *Fleming*
Flindt, *Flint*
Flink
Flinker, *Flink*
Flinn, *Flynn*
Flins, *Flint*
Flinsch, *Flint*
Flint
Flipot, *Philpott*
Flippen, *Philip*
Flips, *Philip*
Flipsen, *Philip*
Flizet, *Felix*
Flizot, *Felix*
Flobert, *Robert*
Floch, *Vlach*
Flockhart
Flockton
Flodén, *Flood*
Flodin, *Flood*
Flodquist, *Flood*
Flodström, *Flood*
Floire, *Flower*
Flom, *Plum*
Flomenbaum, *Plum*
Flood
Flook
Flor, *Flower*
Florance, *Florence*
Florant, *Florent*
Florczak, *Floriano*
Florczyk, *Floriano*
Flore, *Flower*
Florea, *Fleury*
Florean, *Floriano*
Floreani, *Floriano*
Floreano, *Floriano*
Florek, *Floriano*
Florel, *Flower*
Florelle, *Flower*
Florén, *Flower*
Florence
Florêncio, *Florence*
Florensa, *Florence*
Florent
Florentin
Florenty, *Florentin*
Florenz, *Florence*
Flores, *Flórez, Flower*
Florescu, *Fleury*
Florey, *Fleury*
Flórez
Flori, *Flower*
Flórián, *Floriano*
Florián, *Floriano*
Florian, *Floriano*
Floriani, *Floriano*

Floriano
Florianowicz, *Floriano*
Floricke, *Flower*
Florin, *Flower*
Flöring, *Flower*
Florino, *Fleury*
Florio, *Fleury*
Flóris, *Floriano*
Floris, *Flower*
Florjan, *Floriano*
Florjanić, *Floriano*
Florke, *Flower*
Florkowski, *Floriano*
Flörl, *Flower*
Floro, *Flower*
Florov, *Flower*
Flory, *Fleury*
Florysiak, *Floriano*
Floto, *Flotow*
Flotow
Floud, *Flood*
Floumanboum, *Plum*
Flourens, *Florent*
Flouret, *Flower*
Flourette, *Flower*
Flouriot, *Fleury*
Floury, *Fleury*
Floutard, *Flewitt*
Flower
Flowers, *Flower*
Flowitt, *Flewitt*
Floyd, *Lloyd*
Floyde, *Lloyd*
Floyed, *Lloyd*
Fluck, *Flook*
Flucker, *Flockhart*
Fludd, *Flood*
Flude, *Flood*
Fluellin, *Llywelyn*
Flury, *Fleury*
Flux, *Flook*
Flynn
Fo, *Fage*
Foakes, *Foulkes*
Foard, *Ford*
Fobian, *Fabian*
Fobianke, *Fabian*
Foch
Fochs, *Fox*
Focken, *Volk*
Fockena, *Volk*
Fockenga, *Volk*
Fockens, *Volk*
Focks, *Volk*
Foddy, *Foody*
Fodor
Foet, *Fage*
Foffano, *Christopher*
Fog, *Fogg*
Fogarty
Fogaty, *Fogarty*
Foged, *Vogt*
Fogel, *Vogel*
Fogelbaum, *Vogel*
Fogelberg, *Vogel*
Fogelfuss, *Vogel*
Fogelhut, *Vogel*
Fogelman, *Vogel*
Fogelmanas, *Vogel*
Fogelnest, *Vogel*
Fogelsang, *Vogel*
Fogelson, *Feigel*
Fogelstein, *Vogel*
Fogelström, *Vogel*
Fogerty, *Fogarty*
Fogg
Foggarty, *Fogarty*
Foggin
Foggon, *Foggin*
Fogh, *Fogg*
Fogiel, *Vogel*
Fogler, *Fowler*
Fohr, *Ford*
Fohrmann, *Ford*
Foin, *Fouine*
Foinard, *Fouine*
Foine, *Fouine*
Foineau, *Fouine*
Foing, *Fouine*
Foisneau, *Fouine*
Foister, *Forster*
Foix, *Foch*
Foizey, *Vaisey*
Fokanov, *Fokin*
Fokema, *Volk*
Fokes, *Foulkes*
Fokin
Fokinov, *Fokin*
Folan, *Foley*
Folc, *Foulkes*
Folceri, *Fulcher*
Folch, *Foulkes*
Folchetti, *Foulkes*
Folchi, *Foulkes*
Folchieri, *Fulcher*
Folchini, *Foulkes*
Folcieri, *Fulcher*
Folcini, *Foulkes*
Folcio, *Foulkes*
Folco, *Foulkes*
Fold
Folder, *Fold*
Foldes, *Fold*
Földes
Földesi, *Földes*
Folds, *Fold*
Foletti, *Christopher*
Foley
Folgado, *Holgado*
Folger, *Fulcher*
Folgieri, *Fulcher*
Foli, *Christopher*
Folini, *Christopher*
Foljambe
Folk, *Foulkes, Volk*
Folkard
Folkart, *Folkard*
Folke, *Foulkes*
Fölkel, *Volk*
Folker, *Fulcher*
Folkerts, *Folkard*
Folkes, *Foulkes*
Folkierski, *Folkard*
Folkman, *Volk*
Folks, *Foulkes*
Folkson, *Foulkes*
Foll
Folladore, *Fuller*
Follert, *Folkard*
Follet, *Foll*
Follett, *Foll*
Folletti, *Christopher*
Folli, *Christopher*
Follis, *Follows*
Follit, *Foll*
Follitt, *Foll*
Follows
Folomeev, *Bartholomew*
Folomin, *Bartholomew*
Folomkin, *Bartholomew*
Folonin, *Bartholomew*
Fölsch, *Volk*
Fölser, *Volk*
Fölske, *Volk*
Foltin, *Valentine*
Fomichkin, *Thomas*
Fomichyov, *Thomas*
Fominov, *Thomas*
Fomkin, *Thomas*
Fomushkin, *Thomas*
Fonaryov
Fonck, *Funke*
Fönekold, *Fennell*
Fonin, *Afanasyev*
Fonk, *Funke*
Fonkin, *Afanasyev*
Fonnell, *Fennell*
Fons, *Font*
Fonseca
Fonsèque, *Fonseca*
Fonso, *Alfonso*
Font
Fontaine
Fontana, *Fontaine*
Fontanals, *Fontaine*
Fontanari, *Fontaine*
Fontanazzi, *Fontaine*
Fontane, *Fontaine*
Fontanel, *Fontaine*
Fontanella, *Fontaine*
Fontanellas, *Fontaine*
Fontanelli, *Fontaine*
Fontanes, *Fontaine*
Fontanesi, *Fontaine*
Fontanet, *Fontaine*
Fontani, *Fontaine*
Fontanier, *Fontaine*
Fontanillas, *Fontaine*
Fontanin, *Fontaine*
Fontanini, *Fontaine*
Fontanino, *Fontaine*
Fontanot, *Fontaine*
Fontanotti, *Fontaine*
Fonte, *Font*
Fontein, *Fontaine*
Fontel, *Font*
Fontelle, *Font*
Fontelles, *Font*
Fontenay, *Fontaine*
Fonteneau, *Fontaine*
Fontenel, *Fontaine*
Fontenelle, *Fontaine*
Fontenet, *Fontaine*
Fontenier, *Fontaine*
Fontenieu, *Fontaine*
Fontenille, *Fontaine*
Fontenoy, *Fontaine*
Fontes, *Font*
Fonteyne, *Fontaine*
Fontijn, *Fontaine*
Fontin, *Font*
Fonts, *Font*
Fontyn, *Fontaine*
Fonzo, *Alfonso*
Fonzone, *Alfonso*
Foody
Fookes, *Foulkes*
Fooks, *Foulkes*
Foord, *Ford*
Foorish, *Fourish*
Foot
Foote, *Foot*
Footitt, *Foot*
Foran
Forasté, *Forrest*
Forastié, *Forrest*
Forastier, *Forrest*
Forber, *Frobisher*
Forbes
Forca, *Fourche*
Forcada, *Fourche*
Forcadell, *Fourche*
Force
Forcella, *Fourche*
Forcelli, *Fourche*
Forcellini, *Fourche*
Forcher
Forchert, *Forcher*
Forchheimer
Forchner, *Forcher*
Forcone, *Fourche*
Ford
Forde, *Ford*
Forder, *Ford*
Fordham
Fordyce
Forel, *Forell*
Forell
Foreman, *Forman*
Forés, *Forrest*
Forest, *Forrest*
Forester, *Forrest*
Forestier, *Forrest*
Forêt, *Forrest*
Forgan
Forge
Forgette, *Forge*
Forgrave, *Fairgrieve*
Forgrieve, *Fairgrieve*
Forgue, *Forge*
Forichon, *Forrest*
Fóris, *Floriano*
Forjonnel, *Forge*
Forker, *Farquhar*
Forlong, *Furlong*
Forman
Formánek, *Forman*
Formanek, *Forman*
Formanski, *Forman*
Formansky, *Forman*
Formby
Formenti, *Froment*
Formentin, *Froment*
Formentini, *Froment*
Formento, *Froment*
Formenton, *Froment*
Formentone, *Froment*
Forn, *Fournier*
Fornai, *Fournier*
Fornari, *Fournier*
Fornarini, *Fournier*
Fornarino, *Fournier*
Fornario, *Fournier*
Fornaris, *Fournier*
Fornaro, *Fournier*
Fornarotti, *Fournier*
Forné, *Fournier*
Forner, *Fournier*
Forneris, *Fournier*
Fornero, *Fournier*
Fornés, *Fournier*
Forns, *Fournier*
Forrest
Forrester, *Forrest*
Forrestier, *Forrest*
Forrestor, *Forrest*

Fors
Forsberg, *Fors*
Forsdick, *Fosdyke*
Forsdike, *Fosdyke*
Forsdyke, *Fosdyke*
Forse, *Fors*
Forselius, *Fors*
Forsell, *Fors*
Forsgren, *Fors*
Forshaw
Forslin, *Fors*
Forsling, *Fors*
Forslund, *Fors*
Forsman, *Fors*
Forss, *Fors*
Forssell, *Fors*
Forssén, *Fors*
Forsström, *Fors*
Foršt, *Forrest*
Forst, *Forrest*
Förstel, *Fürst*
Förster, *Forster*
Forster
Forstner, *Forster*
Forsyth
Forsythe, *Forsyth*
Fořt, *Forrest*
Fort
Forte, *Fort*
Forteau, *Fort*
Fortes, *Fort*
Fortescue
Fortesquieu, *Fortescue*
Fortet, *Fort*
Fortgang
Forth, *Ford*
Förther, *Ford*
Forthmann, *Ford*
Forti, *Fort*
Fortier
Förtig, *Fertig*
Fortin, *Fort*
Fortini, *Fort*
Fortino, *Fort*
Fortis, *Fort*
Fortnam, *Fortnum*
Fortner, *Ford*
Fortnum
Fortoly, *Fort*
Forton, *Fort*
Fortoul, *Fort*
Fortugno, *Fortune*
Fortuna, *Fortune*
Fortunat, *Fortunato*
Fortunati, *Fortunato*
Fortunato
Fortuné, *Fortunato*
Fortune
Fortuni, *Fortune*
Fortunio, *Fortune*
Fortuny, *Fortune*
Fortuzzi, *Fort*
Fortwängler, *Furtwanger*
Forward
Forwood, *Forward*
Foschi, *Fusco*
Foschini, *Fusco*
Fosco, *Fusco*
Foscoli, *Fusco*
Foscolo, *Fusco*
Fosdyke
Foskett
Foskew, *Fortescue*
Foss, *Fors, Fosse*
Fossa, *Fosse*
Fossat, *Fosse*
Fossé, *Fosse*
Fosse
Fosset, *Fawcett, Fosse*
Fossey, *Fosse*
Fossez, *Fosse*
Fossi, *Fosse*
Fossit, *Fawcett*
Fossitt, *Fawcett*
Fosso, *Fosse*
Foster
Foth, *Foot*
Fothergill
Fotheringham
Fothringham, *Fotheringham*
Fou, *Fage*
Foucard, *Folkard*
Foucart, *Folkard*
Foucaud, *Foucault*
Foucauld, *Foucault*
Foucault
Foucaut, *Foucault*
Fouchard, *Folkard*
Fouchareau, *Fulcher*
Fouché, *Fulcher*
Foucher, *Fulcher*
Fouchère, *Fougère*
Fouchereau, *Fulcher*
Fouchet, *Foulkes*
Fouchier, *Fulcher*
Foucque, *Foulkes*
Foucques, *Foulkes*
Foucrat, *Fulcher*
Foucreau, *Fulcher*
Foucret, *Fulcher*
Foudy, *Foody*
Fouet, *Fage*
Fougerat, *Fougère*
Fougère
Fougeron, *Fougère*
Fouin, *Fouine*
Fouinat, *Fouine*
Fouine
Fouineau, *Fouine*
Foukx, *Foulkes*
Foulcque, *Foulkes*
Foulcques, *Foulkes*
Fould, *Fold*
Fouldes, *Fold*
Foulds, *Fold*
Foulerton, *Fullerton*
Foulger, *Fulcher*
Foulkes
Foullon, *Fuller*
Foulon, *Fuller*
Foulonneau, *Fuller*
Foulser, *Fulcher*
Fountain, *Fontaine*
Fountaine, *Fontaine*
Fouqué, *Foulkes*
Fouque, *Foulkes*
Fouqueau, *Foulkes*
Fouquerat, *Fulcher*
Fouquereau, *Fulcher*
Fouqueret, *Fulcher*
Fouques, *Foulkes*
Fouquet
Fouquíe, *Fulcher*
Fouquière, *Fougère*
Fourcade, *Fourche*
Fourche
Fourest, *Forrest*
Fourestier, *Forrest*
Fourié, *Fourrier*
Fourier, *Fourrier*
Fourish
Fournel, *Furneaux*
Fourneret, *Fournier*
Fourneyron, *Fournier*
Fournié, *Fournier*
Fournier
Fournival, *Furnival*
Fourquet, *Fourche*
Fourquier, *Fourche*
Fourrier
Fourteau, *Fort*
Fourtier, *Fortier*
Fourtoul, *Fort*
Foussat, *Fosse*
Foussé, *Fosse*
Fousse, *Fosse*
Foux, *Foulkes*
Fowell, *Fowle*
Fowells, *Fowle*
Fowkes, *Foulkes*
Fowlds, *Fold*
Fowle
Fowler
Fowles, *Fowle*
Fowls, *Fowle*
Fox
Foxall
Foxe, *Fox*
Foxen, *Foulkes*
Foxley
Foxman, *Fox*
Foxon, *Foulkes*
Foxton
Foxwell
Foy
Foyle
Foyster, *Forster*
Fozard, *Fozzard*
Fozzard
Frabbetti, *Fèvre*
Frabboni, *Fèvre*
Frabet, *Fèvre*
Fraboni, *Fèvre*
Frąckiewicz, *Francis*
Frączak, *Francis*
Frączek, *Francis*
Frączkiewicz, *Francis*
Fradin, *Freidis*
Fradis, *Freidis*
Fradkin, *Freidis*
Fradlin, *Freidis*
Fraga, *Fragoso*
Fragapane, *Frangipane*
Fragino, *Francis*
Fragneau, *Frain*
Fragonard
Fragoso
Fragua, *Forge*
Fraguas, *Forge*
Frahm, *Fromm*
Frähmke, *Fromm*
Fraigne, *Frain*
Fraigneau, *Frain*
Fraile, *Freer*
Frain
Fraine, *Frain*
Fraisne, *Frain*
Fraisse, *Frain*
Frame
Främke, *Fromm*
Frampton
Franc, *Francis, Frank*
França, *Francis*
Français, *Francis*
Francello, *Francis*
Francés, *Francis*
Francès, *Francis*
Frances, *Francis*
Francesc, *Francis*
Francesch, *Francis*
Franceschelli, *Francis*
Franceschetti, *Francis*
Franceschi, *Francis*
Franceschielli, *Francis*
Franceschini, *Francis*
Franceschino, *Francis*
Francesco, *Francis*
Francescoccio, *Francis*
Francesconi, *Francis*
Francescotti, *Francis*
Francescozzi, *Francis*
Francescuccio, *Francis*
Francescuzzi, *Francis*
Francey, *Francis*
Franch, *Frank*
Franchelli, *Frank*
Franchet, *Frank*
Franchetti, *Frank*
Franchi, *Frank*
Franchineau, *Frank*
Franchini, *Frank*
Franchioni, *Francis*
Franchitti, *Frank*
Francholini, *Frank*
Franchyonok, *Francis*
Francie, *Francis*
Francies, *Francis*
Francillo, *Francis*
Francillon, *Frank*
Francin, *Frank*
Francine, *Frank*
Francino, *Francis*
Francioli, *Francis*
Francione, *Francis*
Franciotti, *Francis*
Franciotto, *Francis*
Francis
Francisco, *Francis*
Franciskiewicz, *Francis*
Franck, *Frank*
Francke, *Frank*
Francken, *Frank*
Francklin, *Franklin*
Francklyn, *Franklin*
Franco, *Frank*
François, *Francis*
Francom, *Francombe*
Francombe
Françon, *Frank*
Francon, *Frank*
Francone, *Frank*
Franconi, *Frank*
Francos, *Frank*
Francou, *Frank*
Francoul, *Frank*
Francucci, *Frank*
Frandsen, *Francis*
Frane, *Frain*
Franěk, *Francis*
Franey, *Frain*
Frangello, *Francis*
Frangione, *Francis*
Frangipane
Franiak, *Francis*
Frank
Frankcom, *Francombe*

Frankcombe, *Francombe*
Franke, *Frank*
Fränkel, *Frank*
Frankel, *Frank*
Frankema, *Francis*
Franken, *Frank*
Frankenheim, *Frank*
Frankenschein, *Frank*
Frankenstein, *Frank*
Frankental, *Frank*
Frankenthal, *Frank*
Frankham, *Francombe*
Frankiewicz, *Francis*
Fränkl, *Frank*
Frankl, *Frank*
Frankland
Fränkle, *Frank*
Franklen, *Franklin*
Franklin
Frankling, *Franklin*
Franklyn, *Franklin*
Franko, *Frank*
Frankom, *Francombe*
Frankovits, *Frank*
Frankowski, *Francis*
Franks, *Frank*
Franquesa, *Frank*
Franquet, *Frank*
Franscini, *Francis*
Franscioni, *Francis*
Franseco, *Francis*
Fransecone, *Francis*
Fransema, *Francis*
Fransen, *Francis*
Franses, *Francis*
Fransevich, *Francis*
Fransinelli, *Francis*
Fransman, *Francis*
Fransoni, *Francis*
Franssen, *Francis*
Fransson, *Francis*
Frantsev, *Francis*
Frantz, *Francis*
Frantzen, *Francis*
Franz, *Francis*
Fränzel, *Francis*
Franzelini, *Francis*
Franzen, *Francis*
Franzetto, *Francis*
Franzewitch, *Francis*
Franzini, *Francis*
Franzitti, *Francis*
Franzke, *Francis*
Franzoli, *Francis*
Franzolini, *Francis*
Franzonello, *Francis*
Franzonetti, *Francis*
Franzotto, *Francis*
Frary, *Frederick*
Fraschetti, *Francis*
Frascini, *Francis*
Frascone, *Francis*
Fraser
Frasse, *Frain*
Frątczak, *Francis*
Fratkin, *Freidis*
Frau
Frauenhof, *Fraunhofer*
Fraunhof, *Fraunhofer*
Fraunhofer
Frawley, *Farrell*
Frayne, *Frain*
Fraysse, *Frain*
Frazer, *Fraser*
Frazier, *Fraser*
Freak, *Firth*
Freake, *Firth*
Freaker, *Firth*
Frean, *Frain*
Frear, *Freer*
Frears, *Freer*
Frearson, *Freer*
Freathy
Frebel
Frech
Freche, *Frech*
Freck, *Frech*
Frecke, *Frech*
Freckmann, *Frech*
Fredberg, *Fried*
Fredderich, *Frederick*
Frede, *Frederick*
Fredeke, *Frederick*
Fredeking, *Frederick*
Frédéric, *Frederick*
Frederich, *Frederick*
Frederichs, *Frederick*
Frederichsen, *Frederick*
Frederick
Fredericks, *Frederick*
Frederickx, *Frederick*
Frederico, *Frederick*
Frederiks, *Frederick*
Frederiksen, *Frederick*
Frederiksson, *Frederick*
Frederix, *Frederick*
Frederking, *Frederick*
Fredholm, *Fried*
Fredlund, *Fried*
Fredric, *Frederick*
Fredrich, *Frederick*
Fredrichs, *Frederick*
Fredrick, *Frederick*
Fredriksson, *Frederick*
Free
Freear, *Freer*
Freebern, *Freeborn*
Freeberne, *Freeborn*
Freebody, *Free*
Freeborn
Freeborne, *Freeborn*
Freeburn, *Freeborn*
Freed, *Firth, Fried*
Freeder, *Firth*
Freedman
Freegard
Freeguard, *Freegard*
Freeland
Freeman, *Free*
Freemantle, *Fremantle*
Freen, *Frain*
Freeney, *Frain*
Freer
Freercks, *Frederick*
Freericks, *Frederick*
Freericksson, *Frederick*
Freeriksson, *Frederick*
Freerks, *Frederick*
Freerksen, *Frederick*
Freese, *Fries*
Freestone
Freeth, *Firth*
Freethy, *Freathy*
Freeville, *Freville*
Fregapane, *Frangipane*
Frehse, *Fries*
Frei, *Free*
Freidin, *Freidis*
Freidis
Freidkin, *Freidis*
Freidlin, *Freidis*
Freier, *Free*
Freilach, *Fröhlich*
Freilich, *Fröhlich*
Freilichman, *Fröhlich*
Freiling
Freiman, *Free*
Freimann, *Free*
Freins, *Séverin*
Freire, *Freer*
Freitag
Freitas
Freixa, *Frain*
Freixas, *Frain*
Freixes, *Frain*
Freixo, *Frain*
Freke, *Firth*
Freke, *Frederick*
Fremantle
Frémeau, *Frémond*
Frémin, *Firmin*
Frémon, *Frémond*
Frémond
Frémont, *Frémond*
Frênais, *Frain*
Frênay, *Frain*
French
Frend, *Friend*
Frêne, *Frain*
Fréneau, *Frain*
Frénel, *Frain*
Freney, *Frain*
Frenkel, *Frank*
Frenkental, *Frank*
Frenkiel, *Frank*
Frenking, *Frank*
Frênoy, *Frain*
Frensch, *Francis*
Frensche, *Francis*
Frentz, *Lawrence*
Frenzel, *Francis*
Frenzl, *Francis*
Frercks, *Frederick*
Frere, *Freer*
Frericks, *Frederick*
Freriks, *Frederick*
Frerk, *Frederick*
Frerking, *Frederick*
Frerks, *Frederick*
Frerksen, *Frederick*
Fréry, *Frederick*
Freschi, *Francis*
Freschini, *Francis*
Fresco, *Frisch*
Frescobaldi
Frese, *Fries*
Freseman, *Fries*
Freshwater
Fresko, *Frisch*
Fresnay, *Frain*
Fresne, *Frain*
Fresneau, *Frain*
Fresneda, *Frain*
Fresneix, *Frain*
Fresnel, *Frain*
Fresnet, *Frain*
Fresnillo, *Frain*
Fresno, *Frain*
Fresnoy, *Frain*
Fresse, *Frain*
Frethey, *Freathy*
Fretwell
Freud
Freude, *Freud*
Freudemann, *Freud*
Freudenberger, *Freud*
Freudenfels, *Freud*
Freudenstein, *Freud*
Freudental, *Freud*
Freudenthal, *Freud*
Freudiger, *Freud*
Freudman, *Freud*
Freund, *Friend*
Freundl, *Friend*
Freundlich, *Friend*
Freundschaft, *Friend*
Frevel, *Frebel*
Freville
Frew
Frewen, *Frewin*
Frewin
Frewing, *Frewin*
Frey, *Free*
Freye, *Free*
Freyer, *Free*
Freyman, *Free*
Freymann, *Free*
Freyne, *Frain*
Freyse, *Fries*
Freysse, *Frain*
Freysz, *Frederick*
Freytag, *Freitag*
Friar, *Freer*
Frias, *Frías*
Frías
Frick, *Frederick*
Fricke, *Frederick*
Frickel, *Frederick*
Fricker
Frickle, *Frederick*
Frickmann, *Frederick*
Frid, *Firth, Fried*
Friday, *Freitag*
Fridaye, *Freitag*
Fridberg, *Fried*
Fridd, *Firth*
Fridell, *Fried*
Fridén, *Fried*
Fridenberg, *Fried*
Fridh, *Fried*
Fridlander, *Friedland*
Fridlender, *Friedland*
Fridman, *Fried*
Fridmann, *Fried*
Fridnik, *Fried*
Fridrich, *Frederick*
Fridwald, *Fried*
Frie, *Free*
Friebe, *Fröbe*
Friebel, *Fröbe*
Frieben, *Fröbe*
Frieber, *Fröbe*
Friebner, *Fröbe*
Fried
Friedag, *Freitag*
Frieday, *Freitag*
Friedberg, *Fried*
Friede, *Frederick*
Friedel, *Frederick*
Friedeman, *Fried*
Friedemann, *Fried*
Friedenberg, *Fried*
Friedenreich, *Fried*
Friedenstein, *Fried*
Friedental, *Fried*
Friedenthal, *Fried*

Friederich, *Frederick*
Friederichs, *Frederick*
Friederichsen, *Frederick*
Friedfertig, *Fried*
Friedgut, *Fried*
Friedhaber, *Fried*
Friedheim, *Fried*
Friedhof, *Fried*
Friediger, *Fried*
Friedl, *Frederick*
Friedland
Friedländer, *Friedland*
Friedlander, *Friedland*
Friedlein, *Frederick*
Friedler, *Fried*
Friedlich, *Fried*
Friedman, *Fried*
Friedmann, *Fried*
Friedreicher, *Frederick*
Friedrich, *Frederick*
Friedrichs, *Frederick*
Friedsch, *Frederick*
Friedsche, *Frederick*
Friedstein, *Fried*
Friedwald, *Fried*
Friehe, *Free*
Friel
Frieling, *Fruling*
Friemann, *Free*
Friend
Frier, *Freer*
Frierson, *Freer*
Fries
Friese, *Fries*
Frieseke, *Fries*
Friesel, *Fries*
Frieslander, *Fries*
Friesz, *Frederick*
Frift, *Firth*
Frige, *Free*
Frigge, *Free*
Frighi, *Frederick*
Fright, *Firth*
Frigo, *Frederick*
Friis, *Fries*
Friling, *Fruling*
Friman, *Free*
Frind, *Friend*
Frings, *Séverin*
Frins, *Séverin*
Fris, *Fries*
Frisby
Frisch
Frischberg, *Frisch*
Frische, *Frisch*
Frischer, *Frisch*
Frischler, *Frisch*
Frischling, *Frisch*
Frischman, *Frisch*
Frischmann, *Frisch*
Frischwasser, *Frisch*
Frisell, *Fries*
Friser, *Fries*
Frish, *Frisch*
Frishberg, *Frisch*
Frisher, *Frisch*
Frishler, *Frisch*
Frishling, *Frisch*
Frishman, *Frisch*
Frishmann, *Frisch*
Frishtag, *Frisch*
Friss, *Fries*
Frith, *Firth*
Fritsch, *Frederick*
Fritsche, *Frederick*
Fritschler, *Frederick*
Fritz, *Frederick*
Fritze, *Frederick*
Fritzel, *Frederick*
Fritzl, *Frederick*
Fritzle, *Frederick*
Fritzler, *Frederick*
Fritzmann, *Frederick*
Fritzsch, *Frederick*
Fritzsche, *Frederick*
Frizner, *Fries*
Frizzell
Frizzi, *Frederick*
Frizzone, *Frederick*
Frizzotti, *Frederick*
Fröba, *Fröbe*
Fröbe
Fröbel, *Fröbe*
Fröber, *Fröbe*
Frober, *Fröbe*
Frobisher
Fröbner, *Fröbe*
Frödden, *Froud*
Fröde, *Freud, Froud*
Frodon, *Froud*
Frodsham
Frodson, *Frodsham*
Froehlich, *Fröhlich*
Froelich, *Fröhlich*
Froggatt
Frogget, *Froggatt*
Fröhlck, *Fröhlich*
Frohlich, *Fröhlich*
Fröhlich
Fröhlking, *Fröhlich*
Frohm, *Fromm*
Frohme, *Fromm*
Fröhmke, *Fromm*
Froikin, *Yefremov*
Froim, *Yefremov*
Froimovici, *Yefremov*
Froimovitch, *Yefremov*
Froimovits, *Yefremov*
Froimovitz, *Yefremov*
Froimowitz, *Yefremov*
Froissant
Froissard, *Froissant*
Froissart, *Froissant*
Fröjd, *Freud*
Frojmowicz, *Yefremov*
Frol, *Flower*
Fröleke, *Fröhlich*
Frölich, *Fröhlich*
Frolkin, *Flower*
Frolkov, *Flower*
Frolochkin, *Flower*
Frolov, *Flower*
Frolovski, *Flower*
From, *Fromm*
Fromcenko, *Yefremov*
Fromchenko, *Yefremov*
Frome, *Froome*
Fromel, *Fromm*
Froment
Fromentas, *Froment*
Fromenteau, *Froment*
Fromentin, *Froment*
Fromer, *Fromm*
Fromerman, *Fromm*
Frömke, *Fromm*
Fromkin, *Frumin*
Fromm
Frommann, *Fromm*
Fromme, *Fromm*
Frommel, *Fromm*
Frömmer, *Fromm*
Frommer, *Fromm*
Frommerman, *Fromm*
Frömming, *Fromm*
Frommke, *Fromm*
Fron, *Froud*
Fronczak, *Francis*
Fröndt, *Friend*
Froněk, *Francis*
Frontczak, *Francis*
Fronzek, *Francis*
Frood, *Froud*
Froom, *Froome*
Froome
Frosdick, *Fosdyke*
Frossard, *Froissant*
Frost
Frot, *Froud*
Froud
Froude, *Froud*
Frouin, *Froud*
Froumentin, *Froment*
Froumenty, *Froment*
Froumin, *Frumin*
Frowd, *Froud*
Frowde, *Froud*
Frowen, *Frewin*
Frowing, *Frewin*
Fruchard, *Frutos*
Fruchon, *Frutos*
Fruchou, *Frutos*
Frucht, *Frutos*
Fruchtbaum, *Frutos*
Fruchtenbaum, *Frutos*
Fruchtenboim, *Frutos*
Fruchter, *Frutos*
Fruchtgarten, *Frutos*
Fruchtlander, *Frutos*
Fruchtman, *Frutos*
Fruchtmann, *Frutos*
Fruchtnis, *Frutos*
Fruchtzweig, *Frutos*
Früdden, *Froud*
Frude, *Froud*
Fruen, *Frewin*
Frugier, *Frutos*
Fruhling, *Fruling*
Fruin, *Frewin*
Fruit, *Frutos*
Fruitier, *Frutos*
Fruling
Frum, *Fromm*
Frumak, *Fromm*
Frumento, *Froment*
Frumer, *Fromm*
Frumerman, *Fromm*
Frumin
Frumkes, *Frumin*
Frumkin, *Frumin*
Frumkis, *Frumin*
Frumson, *Frumin*
Fründ, *Friend*
Fründt, *Friend*
Früngen, *Friend*
Frutos
Fry
Fryazinov
Fryd, *Firth*
Frydrich, *Frederick*
Frydrych, *Frederick*
Frydrychowicz, *Frederick*
Frydrychowski, *Frederick*
Frye, *Fry*
Fryer, *Freer*
Frymer, *Fromm*
Fryś, *Frederick*
Fryszczyk, *Frederick*
Fryszer, *Frisch*
Fryszkiewicz, *Frederick*
Fuche, *Fulcher*
Fucher, *Fulcher*
Fuchs, *Fox*
Füchsel, *Fox*
Fuchsman, *Fox*
Füchter, *Feicht*
Fuckart, *Fugger*
Fucker, *Fugger*
Fuckert, *Fugger*
Fucks, *Fox*
Fudge, *Fulcher*
Fudger, *Fulcher*
Fuente, *Font*
Fuentes, *Font*
Fuerte, *Fort*
Fuertes, *Fort*
Fuge, *Fulcher*
Fugener, *Füger*
Fuger, *Fulcher*
Füger
Fugger
Fuggle, *Fowle*
Fuggles, *Fowle*
Fugl, *Vogel*
Fugler, *Fowler*
Fugner, *Füger*
Führ, *Führer*
Fuhr, *Ford*
Führer
Fuhrman, *Forman*
Fuhrmann, *Führer*
Fuhrmann, *Forman*
Fuke, *Foulkes*
Fuks, *Fox*
Fuksman, *Fox*
Fulbrecht, *Volpert*
Fulbright, *Volpert*
Fulcher
Fulcieri, *Fulcher*
Fulco, *Foulkes*
Fulcoli, *Foulkes*
Fulconi, *Foulkes*
Fülep, *Philip*
Fulford
Fulger, *Fulcher*
Fulgeri, *Fulcher*
Fulgieri, *Fulcher*
Fulk, *Foulkes*
Fulke, *Foulkes*
Fulker, *Fulcher*
Fulkes, *Foulkes*
Fulks, *Foulkes*
Fullagar, *Fulcher*
Fullarton, *Fullerton*
Fullbrook
Fulleger, *Fulcher*
Fuller
Fullerton
Fulljames, *Foljambe*
Fulloon, *Fuller*
Fullwood
Fülöp, *Philip*
Fulpracht, *Volpert*
Fulsher, *Fulcher*
Fulton
Fulwood, *Fullwood*
Funck, *Funke*

Funcke, *Funke*
Funikov, *Afanasyev*
Funk, *Funke*
Funke
Funkenstein, *Funke*
Funnell, *Fennell*
Furbank, *Firbank*
Furber, *Frobisher*
Fureau, *Furet*
Fürer, *Führer*
Furet
Furey
Furgeri, *Fulcher*
Furgieri, *Fulcher*
Furish, *Fourish*
Furlong
Furlonge, *Furlong*
Furlonger, *Furlong*
Furman, *Firmin, Forman*
Furmańczyk, *Forman*
Furmanek, *Forman*
Furmaniak, *Forman*
Furmann, *Forman*
Furmanov, *Forman*
Furmański, *Forman*
Furmanski, *Forman*
Furmansky, *Forman*
Furnari, *Fournier*
Furnass, *Furness*
Furneaux
Furnell, *Furneaux*
Furner, *Fournier*
Furneri, *Fournier*
Furness
Furnifall, *Furnival*
Furniss, *Furness*
Furnival
Furnivall, *Furnival*
Furon, *Furet*
Fursdon
Fursdonne, *Fursdon*
Furse
Furseman, *Furse*
Furst, *Fürst*
Fürst
Fürstenberg
Furt, *Ford*
Furtado, *Hurtado*
Furter, *Ford*
Fürterer, *Ford*
Furterer, *Ford*
Fürther, *Ford*
Furtner, *Ford*
Furtwanger
Furtwängler, *Furtwanger*
Fury, *Furey*
Furze, *Furse*
Furzeman, *Furse*
Furzer, *Furse*
Fuschi, *Fusco*
Fuschillo, *Fusco*
Fuschini, *Fusco*
Fusco
Fuscoli, *Fusco*
Fuscolo, *Fusco*
Fuscone, *Fusco*
Fusconi, *Fusco*
Fuss, *Foot*
Füssel, *Foot*
Fussell
Füssle, *Foot*
Füssli, *Foot*
Fust, *Faust*
Fusté, *Forster*
Fuster, *Forster*
Futcher, *Fulcher*
Fux, *Fox*
Fuxsman, *Fox*
Fyall, *McFall*
Fyers, *Fair*
Fyfe
Fyffe, *Fyfe*
Fylan, *Whelan*
Fyldes, *Fildes*
Fynes, *Fiennes*
Fynn, *Finn*
Fyodorov, *Théodore*
Fyodorovykh, *Théodore*
Fysh, *Fish*

G

Gabai, *Gabbai*
Gabain, *Gavin*
Gabaldà, *Gavaldà*
Gabaldón
Gabara, *Gabriel*
Gabarkiewicz, *Gabriel*
Gabarró
Gabay, *Gabbai*
Gabbai
Gabbay, *Gabbai*
Gabbin, *Gabin*
Gabbrielli, *Gabriel*
Gabbriello, *Gabriel*
Gabel, *Gabler*
Gaber, *Gabriel*
Gaber, *Haber*
Gaberl, *Gabriel*
Gaberle, *Gabriel*
Gäberlein, *Gabriel*
Gaberman, *Haber*
Gabert, *Gebhardt*
Gabet, *Gabin*
Gabin
Gabion, *Gabriel*
Gabison, *Gabin*
Gabizon, *Gabin*
Gable
Gäbler, *Gabler*
Gabler
Gablonz, *Jabłoński*
Gábor, *Gabriel*
Gabot, *Gabin*
Gabotti, *Jacob*
Gabovitch, *Gabin*
Gabowicz, *Gabin*
Gabreli, *Gabriel*
Gabriałowicz, *Gabriel*
Gabrich, *Gabriel*
Gabrié, *Gabriel*
Gabriel
Gabriele, *Gabriel*
Gabrieli, *Gabriel*
Gabrielian, *Gabriel*
Gabrielini, *Gabriel*
Gabrielli, *Gabriel*
Gabriellini, *Gabriel*
Gabriello, *Gabriel*
Gabrieloff, *Gabriel*
Gabrielov, *Gabriel*
Gabrielow, *Gabriel*
Gabrielsen, *Gabriel*
Gabrielski, *Gabriel*
Gabrielsson, *Gabriel*
Gabriely, *Gabriel*
Gabrilewicz, *Gabriel*
Gabrilovitz, *Gabriel*
Gabriš, *Gabriel*
Gabris, *Gabriel*
Gabrisch, *Gabriel*
Gabrusyonok, *Gabriel*
Gabry, *Gabriel*
Gabryel, *Gabriel*
Gabryjańczyk, *Gabriel*
Gabryłowicz, *Gabriel*
Gabryś, *Gabriel*
Gabrys, *Gabriel*
Gabrysiak, *Gabriel*
Gabrysiewicz, *Gabriel*
Gabrysz, *Gabriel*
Gaby, *Gabriel*
Gache
Gachenot, *Gache*
Gachet, *Gache*
Gachlin, *Gache*
Gachon, *Gache*
Gack, *Geach*
Gackl, *Geach*
Gäckle, *Geach*
Gädcke, *Gott*
Gadd
Gadde, *Gott*
Gaddesden
Gäde, *Gott*
Gade, *Gate, Gott*
Gadea, *Aggis*
Gädecke, *Gott*
Gädeke, *Gott*
Gaden, *Gott*
Gäderts, *Goddard*
Gadesden, *Gaddesden*
Gadsby
Gadsden, *Gaddesden*
Gadsdon, *Gaddesden*
Gädt, *Gott*
Gädtke, *Gott*
Gaetani, *Gaetano*
Gaetano
Gaffey, *Caughey*
Gaffican, *Gavigan*
Gaffikin, *Gavigan*
Gaffney
Gagan, *Gahan*
Gagarin
Gage
Gagelin, *Gage*
Gageot, *Gage*
Gager, *Gage*
Gagern
Gaget, *Gage*
Gagey, *Gage*
Gagg, *Geach*
Gagliardi, *Gaillard*
Gagliardini, *Gaillard*
Gagliardone, *Gaillard*
Gagliarducci, *Gaillard*
Gagnaire, *Gagneux*
Gagneau, *Gagneux*
Gagneron, *Gagneux*
Gagnerot, *Gagneux*
Gagnet, *Gagneux*
Gagneux
Gagnier, *Gagneux*
Gagnieur, *Gagneux*
Gagnot, *Gagneux*
Gago
Gahagan, *Gavigan*
Gahan
Gahr, *Geary*
Gahrmann, *Geary*
Gai, *Gay*
Gaiger, *Gage*
Gaigneux, *Gagneux*
Gaignoux, *Gagneux*
Gail, *Gale*
Gailer, *Gale*
Gailhard, *Gaillard*
Gaillard
Gaillardet, *Gaillard*
Gaillardon, *Gaillard*
Gaillé, *Gale*
Gaillet, *Gale*
Gaillochet, *Gale*
Gaillot, *Gale*
Gaillourdet, *Gaillard*
Gain
Gaine, *Gain*
Gaines, *Gain*
Gainsborough
Gairdner, *Gardener*
Gaish, *Wace*
Gaiss, *Geist*
Gaisser, *Geist*
Gait, *Gate*
Gaitán, *Gaetano*
Gaite, *Gate*
Gaitens, *McGettigan*
Gaiter, *Gate*
Gaites, *Waite*
Gaitskell, *Gaskell*
Gaitskill, *Gaskell*
Gaitt, *Gate*
Gajda
Gajek, *Hájek*
Gajer, *Geier*
Gajewicz, *Gajownik*
Gajewski, *Gajownik*
Gajić, *Gajownik*
Gajowiak, *Gajownik*
Gajownik
Gál, *Gall*
Gal, *Gall*
Gala, *Gale, Gall*
Galais, *Wallace*
Galamb, *Golubev*
Galán, *Galland*
Galan, *Galland*
Galanciak, *Galland*
Galand, *Galland*
Galandin, *Galland*
Galant, *Galland*
Galante, *Galland*
Galasby, *Gillespie*
Gałązka
Galbán, *Galván*
Galbraith
Galbreath, *Galbraith*
Galcerà, *Galceran*
Galceran
Gałczyński, *Gall*
Galdós
Gale
Gałecki, *Gall*
Galego, *Gallego*
Galer, *Gale*
Galera
Galet, *Gale*
Galewicz, *Gall*
Galewski, *Gall*
Galey, *Galley*
Gálffy, *Gall*
Gálfi, *Gall*
Galhard, *Gaillard*
Galià, *Galiano*

Galiana
Galiano
Galić, *Gall*
Galichet, *Gale*
Galichon, *Gale*
Galicki, *Gall*
Galilee, *Galley*
Galimard, *Gallimard*
Galíndez, *Galindo*
Galindo
Galiński, *Gall*
Gałka
Gałkiewicz, *Gałka*
Galkin
Gałkowski, *Gałka*
Gáll, *Gall*
Gall
Gallaccio, *Gallo*
Gallacher, *Gallagher*
Gallagher
Gallaher, *Gallagher*
Gallais, *Wallace*
Gallally, *Galley*
Galland
Gallandon, *Galland*
Gallant, *Galland*
Gallard, *Gaillard*
Gallardo, *Gaillard*
Gallart, *Gaillard*
Gallasch, *Gall*
Gallatly, *Golightly*
Galle, *Gall*
Gallé, *Gale*
Gallear, *Waller*
Gallego
Gallegos, *Gallego*
Gallelli, *Gallo*
Gallen
Galler, *Gall, Waller*
Gallery, *McIlwraith*
Gallet, *Gale*
Galletley, *Golightly*
Galletly, *Golightly*
Galletti, *Gallo*
Galley
Galliard, *Gaillard*
Gallic, *Gall*
Gallico, *Gallego*
Gallie, *Galley*
Gallier, *Waller*
Galliford, *Gulliver*
Galligai, *Callegaro*
Galligan
Galligari, *Callegaro*
Galliker, *Gallagher*
Gallimard
Gallini, *Gallo*
Gallinotti, *Gallo*
Galliou, *Gall*
Galliver, *Gulliver*
Gallmann, *Gall*
Gallo
Gallo, *Gall*
Gallogher, *Gallagher*
Gallois, *Wallace*
Gallon, *Gale*
Gallone, *Gallo*
Galloni, *Gallo*
Gallop
Gallot, *Gale*
Gallotti, *Gallo*
Galloway
Gallozzi, *Gallo*
Gallucci, *Gallo*
Galluccio, *Gallo*
Gallup, *Gallop*
Gallussi, *Gallo*
Galluzzi, *Gallo*
Gally, *Galley*
Galofre
Galois, *Wallace*
Gálos, *Gall*
Galper, *Heilbronn*
Galperin, *Heilbronn*
Galpern, *Heilbronn*
Galsery, *Galsworthy*
Galsworthy
Galt
Galtié, *Walter*
Galtier, *Walter*
Galtieri, *Walter*
Galtierotti, *Walter*
Galton
Galuschke, *Gall*
Galván
Galvani, *Gavin*
Galvano, *Gavin*
Galvão, *Galván*
Galve
Gálvez, *Galve*
Galvin
Gama
Gamache, *Gamage*
Gamage
Gaman, *Game*
Gamba, *Gambe*
Gambaccini, *Gambe*
Gambassi, *Gambe*
Gambe
Gambell, *Gamble*
Gambella, *Gambe*
Gambet, *Gambe*
Gambetta, *Gambe*
Gambi, *Gambe*
Gambier
Gambin, *Gambe*
Gambino, *Gambe*
Gambitta, *Gambe*
Gamble
Gambles, *Gamble*
Gamblin, *Gamble*
Gambling, *Gamble*
Gambon, *Gambe*
Gambone, *Gambe*
Gambourg, *Hamburg*
Gambozza, *Gambe*
Gamburg, *Hamburg*
Gambuzza, *Gambe*
Game
Gameiro, *Gamero*
Gamero
Gámez, *Gamo*
Gamlane, *Gamble*
Gamlen, *Gamble*
Gamlin, *Gamble*
Gamling, *Gamble*
Gammage, *Gamage*
Gamman, *Game*
Gammell, *Gamble*
Gammidge, *Gamage*
Gammil, *Gamble*
Gammon
Gammond, *Gammon*
Gamo
Gamon, *Gammon*
Ganc, *Goose*
Gance
Gancel, *Gance*
Gand, *Gaunt*
Gandee, *Gandy*
Gandelis, *Handler*
Gandelman, *Handler*
Gander
Gandey, *Gandy*
Gandler, *Handler*
Gandois, *Gaunt*
Gandrich, *Andrew*
Gandy
Gandz, *Goose*
Gane, *Gain*
Ganelin, *Gabriel*
Gange
Ganichev, *Gabriel*
Ganin, *Gabriel*
Gannon
Gans, *Goose*
Gansel, *Goose*
Ganser, *Goose*
Gansl, *Goose*
Gänsler, *Goose*
Gansler, *Goose*
Gänsli, *Goose*
Gansmann, *Goose*
Gansner, *Goose*
Ganson, *Gance*
Ganson, *Gavin*
Gant, *Gaunt*
Ganter
Gantier, *Gaunt*
Gantois, *Gaunt*
Gantz, *Goose*
Ganyushkin, *Gabriel*
Ganz, *Goose*
Ganzel, *Goose*
Gapeev, *Agapov*
Gapper
Gara, *Geary*
Garabedian
Garabetian, *Garabedian*
Garand
Garandel, *Garand*
Garanin, *Gerasimov*
Garant, *Garand*
Garanton, *Garand*
Garard, *Garrett*
Garaseev, *Gerasimov*
Garasimchuk, *Gerasimov*
Garasimov, *Gerasimov*
Gárate
Garavin, *Garvin*
Garay
Garbade, *Garbutt*
Garbar, *Gerber*
Garbe, *Garber*
Garber
Garberding, *Garbett*
Garbers, *Garbett*
Garbett
Garbo
Garbrecht, *Garbett*
Garbutt
Garcés, *García*
Garci, *García*
Garcia, *García*
García
Garcin, *Gars*
Garcioux, *Gars*
Garçon, *Gars*
Garçonnet, *Gars*
Garçonnot, *Gars*
Gard, *Gardener, Guard*
Garde, *Guard*
Garden, *Gardener*
Gardenc, *Warden*
Gardener
Gardes, *Guard*
Gardet, *Guard*
Gardey, *Guard*
Gardien, *Warden*
Gardiennet, *Warden*
Gardin, *Gardener*
Gardiner, *Gardener*
Gardinier, *Gardener*
Gardinor, *Gardener*
Gardner, *Gardener*
Gardot, *Guard*
Gardyne, *Gardener*
Gareau, *Garet*
Gareis, *Gregory*
Garel, *Garet*
Garelick, *Gorelik*
Garelik, *Gorelik*
Garenier, *Warren*
Garenne, *Warren*
Garet
Garey, *Geary*
Garfield
Garfinkel, *Gorfinkel*
Garforth
Garfunkel, *Gorfinkel*
Gargan
Garibaldi, *Garbutt*
Gariboldi, *Garbutt*
Garimoldi, *Garbutt*
Garin, *Gerasimov, Waring*
Garinov, *Gerasimov*
Gariot, *Garet*
Gariou, *Garet*
Garit, *Garet*
Garke, *Geary*
Garken, *Geary*
Garlach, *Garlick*
Garland
Garlant, *Garland*
Garlic, *Garlick*
Garlich, *Garlick*
Garlick
Garlicke, *Garlick*
Garman, *Gorman*
Garmendia
Garment, *Gorman*
Garnar, *Garner*
Garne, *Waring*
Garner
Garnet, *Garnett*
Garnett
Garnham
Garnier, *Garner, Warner, Warren*
Garnon
Garnons, *Garnon*
Garnot, *Warner*
Garnotel, *Warner*
Garnotin, *Warner*
Garrad, *Garrett*
Garrals, *Garrett*
Garralts, *Garrett*
Garrard, *Garrett*
Garratt, *Garrett*
Garred, *Garrett*
Garrels, *Garrett*
Garrelts, *Garrett*
Garretson, *Garrett*
Garrett
Garretts, *Garrett*
Garrettson, *Garrett*

Garric, *Jarry*
Garrido
Garriga, *Jarry*
Garrigou, *Jarry*
Garrigue, *Jarry*
Garrioux, *Jarry*
Garrique, *Jarry*
Garrish, *Geary*
Garrison, *Garrett*
Garrit, *Garrett, Jarry*
Garrod, *Garrett*
Garrold, *Garrett*
Garrote
Garrould, *Garrett*
Garry, *Geary*
Gars
Garshin, *Gerasimov*
Garside
Garson, *Gars*
Garsonnin, *Gars*
Garstang
Garston
Gartenmann, *Gardener*
Garth
Gartmann, *Gardener*
Gärtner, *Gardener*
Gartner, *Gardener*
Garton
Gartside, *Garside*
Gartzman, *Herz*
Garvan, *Garvin*
Garvey
Garvie, *Garvey*
Garvin
Garwin, *Garvin*
Garwood
Gary, *Geary*
Garza, *García*
Garzón, *Gars*
Garzonetti, *Gars*
Garzoni, *Gars*
Gas, *Gass*
Gasbarri, *Kaspar*
Gasbarrini, *Kaspar*
Gascard, *Gascoigne*
Gasch, *Gascoigne*
Gascó, *Gascoigne*
Gascogne, *Gascoigne*
Gascoigne
Gascoin, *Gascoigne*
Gascón, *Gascoigne*
Gascon, *Gascoigne*
Gascone, *Gascoigne*
Gascoyne, *Gascoigne*
Gascuel, *Gascoigne*
Gash, *Wace*
Gashion, *Wace*
Gashkov, *Gabriel*
Gąsior
Gąsiorek, *Gąsior*
Gąsiorkiewicz, *Gąsior*
Gąsiorowicz, *Gąsior*
Gąsiorowski, *Gąsior*
Gąsiorski, *Gąsior*
Gaskell
Gasken, *Gascoigne*
Gaskens, *Gascoigne*
Gaskill, *Gaskell*
Gaskin, *Gascoigne*
Gasking, *Gascoigne*
Gasnier, *Warner*
Gason, *Wace*
Gáspár, *Kaspar*
Gaspar, *Kaspar*
Gaspard, *Kaspar*
Gaspardi, *Kaspar*
Gaspardini, *Kaspar*
Gaspardis, *Kaspar*
Gaspardo, *Kaspar*
Gasparelli, *Kaspar*
Gasparetti, *Kaspar*
Gaspari, *Kaspar*
Gasparin, *Kaspar*
Gasparinetti, *Kaspar*
Gasparini, *Kaspar*
Gasparo, *Kaspar*
Gasparoli, *Kaspar*
Gasparoni, *Kaspar*
Gasparotti, *Kaspar*
Gasparoux, *Kaspar*
Gasparri, *Kaspar*
Gasparrini, *Kaspar*
Gasparro, *Kaspar*
Gasperetti, *Kaspar*
Gasperi, *Kaspar*
Gasperin, *Kaspar*
Gasperini, *Kaspar*
Gaspero, *Kaspar*
Gasperoni, *Kaspar*
Gasperotti, *Kaspar*
Gasq, *Gascoigne*
Gasquet, *Gascoigne*
Gasquié, *Gascoigne*
Gasquiel, *Gascoigne*
Gass
Gässer, *Gass*
Gasser, *Gass*
Gassmann, *Gass*
Gässner, *Gass*
Gassner, *Gass*
Gasson, *Wace*
Gast
Gastall, *Wastell*
Gastfreund, *Gast*
Gastl, *Guest*
Gästle, *Guest*
Gaston
Gastou, *Gaston*
Gate
Gateacre
Gatehouse
Gately
Gatenby
Gater, *Gate*
Gates
Gath, *Garth*
Gäthgens, *Gott*
Gato, *Catt*
Gatsby, *Gadsby*
Gatter, *Gatterer*
Gatterer
Gattermann, *Gatterer*
Gatti, *Catt*
Gattin, *McGettigan*
Gattinelli, *Catt*
Gattini, *Catt*
Gattins, *McGettigan*
Gatto, *Catt*
Gattone, *Catt*
Gattullo, *Catt*
Gatward
Gaubert, *Jaubert*
Gauceran, *Galceran*
Gauceron, *Galceran*
Gaudefroy, *Galofre*
Gauderon, *Walter*
Gaudier, *Walter*
Gaudreau, *Walter*
Gaudrieau, *Walter*
Gaudron, *Walter*
Gaufré, *Galofre*
Gaufré, *Jeffrey*
Gaufre, *Galofre, Jeffrey*
Gaufreteau, *Galofre*
Gaufridy, *Galofre*
Gaufroy, *Galofre*
Gaugain, *Gaugin*
Gauge, *Gage*
Gauge, *Gaugin*
Gauggele, *Jougleux*
Gaughan, *Gahan*
Gaughran
Gaught, *Galt*
Gaugier, *Gaugin*
Gaugin
Gaugler, *Jougleux*
Gaukele, *Jougleux*
Gaukeler, *Jougleux*
Gaul, *Gall*
Gauld, *Galt*
Gaule, *Gall*
Gaulle, de
Gault, *Galt*
Gaultier, *Walter*
Gaumond, *Gaumont*
Gaumont
Gaunson, *Gavin*
Gaunt
Gaunter, *Gaunt*
Gauquelin, *Vauquelin*
Gaureschi, *Waring*
Gaus, *Goose*
Gauser, *Goose*
Gäusgen, *Goose*
Gaut, *Galt*
Gaute, *Galt*
Gautereau, *Walter*
Gauterin, *Walter*
Gauteron, *Walter*
Gauterot, *Walter*
Gauthereau, *Walter*
Gautherin, *Walter*
Gautheron, *Walter*
Gautherot, *Walter*
Gauthier, *Walter*
Gauthiez, *Walter*
Gautier, *Walter*
Gautreau, *Walter*
Gautrelet, *Walter*
Gautret, *Walter*
Gautron, *Walter*
Gautrot, *Walter*
Gauvain, *Gavin*
Gauvin, *Gavin*
Gauvreau, *Gavin*
Gauvrit, *Gavin*
Gauvry, *Gavin*
Gauwain, *Gavin*
Gauzeran, *Galceran*
Gavaghan, *Gavigan*
Gavaldà
Gavaldó, *Gavaldà*
Gavarró, *Gabarró*
Gavecan, *Gavigan*
Gaven, *Gavin*
Gävert, *Gebhardt*
Gaveshin, *Gabriel*
Gavigan
Gavilà, *Gavilán*
Gavilán
Gavin
Gavini, *Jacob*
Gavino, *Gavin*
Gavozzi, *Jacob*
Gavrić, *Gabriel*
Gavriel, *Gabriel*
Gavrieli, *Gabriel*
Gavrielli, *Gabriel*
Gavrielly, *Gabriel*
Gavriely, *Gabriel*
Gavrikov, *Gabriel*
Gavrilchik, *Gabriel*
Gavrilechko, *Gabriel*
Gavrilenko, *Gabriel*
Gavrilichev, *Gabriel*
Gavrilik, *Gabriel*
Gavrilin, *Gabriel*
Gavrilov, *Gabriel*
Gavrilović, *Gabriel*
Gavrilyuk, *Gabriel*
Gavrishchev, *Gabriel*
Gavrishev, *Gabriel*
Gavrys, *Gabriel*
Gavryutin, *Gabriel*
Gavshikov, *Gabriel*
Gavurin, *Gabriel*
Gaw, *Gall*
Gaweł, *Gall*
Gawen, *Gavin*
Gawenson, *Gavin*
Gäwert, *Gebhardt*
Gawley, *McAulay*
Gawlik, *Gall*
Gawlikowski, *Gall*
Gawliński, *Gall*
Gawłowski, *Gall*
Gawn, *Gavin*
Gawne, *Gavin*
Gawroński
Gawryelov, *Gabriel*
Gawrysiak, *Gabriel*
Gawryszczak, *Gabriel*
Gawthorpe
Gawthrop, *Gawthorpe*
Gay
Gayard, *Gay*
Gayaud, *Gay*
Gaye, *Gay*
Gayer, *Geier*
Gayet, *Gay*
Gaylard, *Gaillard*
Gayle, *Gale*
Gayler, *Gale*
Gaylor, *Gale*
Gaylord, *Gaillard*
Gaynor
Gayo, *Guy*
Gayon, *Gay*
Gayot, *Gay*
Gayter, *Gate*
Gaytor, *Gate*
Gaze, *Wace*
Gazeley
Gazza, *Agace*
Gazzini, *Agace*
Gazzola, *Agace*
Gdanski, *Danzig*
Gdansky, *Danzig*
Gé, *Geary*
Geach
Geai, *Jay*
Geaix, *Jay*
Geake, *Geach*
Geaney
Gear, *Geary*
Geare, *Geary*

Gearing, *Geary*
Gearty, *Geraghty*
Geary
Geaves, *Jeeves*
Geay, *Jay*
Gebb, *Gebhardt, Jeffrey*
Gebbe, *Gebhardt*
Gebbers, *Gebhardt*
Gebbert, *Gebhardt*
Gebecke, *Gebhardt*
Geber, *Gebhardt*
Geberding, *Gebhardt*
Geberl, *Gebhardt*
Gebers, *Gebhardt*
Gébert, *Garbett*
Gebert, *Gebhardt*
Gebhard, *Gebhardt*
Gebhardt
Gębicki, *Gębski*
Gebken, *Gebhardt*
Gebrt, *Gebhardt*
Gębski
Gebühr, *Bauer*
Gecht, *Hecht*
Geck, *Geach*
Gedanski, *Danzig*
Gedansky, *Danzig*
Geddes
Geddie
Geddis, *Geddes*
Gedge
Gee
Geer, *Geary*
Geeraert, *Garrett*
Geerdts, *Garrett*
Geere, *Geary*
Geeren, *Geary*
Geerhaert, *Garrett*
Geering, *Geary*
Geerits, *Garrett*
Geerling, *Garrett*
Geeroom, *Jerome*
Geerooms, *Jerome*
Geers, *Geary*
Geertje, *Garrett*
Geerts, *Garrett*
Geertsen, *Garrett*
Geertz, *Garrett*
Geest
Geestman, *Geest*
Geestra, *Geest*
Geeve, *Gebhardt*
Geeves, *Jeeves*
Gefen
Geffe, *Gebhardt*
Geffers, *Gebhardt*
Geffert, *Gebhardt*
Geffroy, *Jeffrey*
Gefken, *Gebhardt*
Gegg, *Geach*
Geghan, *Gahan*
Gegner
Gehler, *Geller*
Gehlert, *Geller*
Gehr, *Geary*
Gehrbracht, *Garbett*
Gehrbrecht, *Garbett*
Gehre, *Geary*
Gehrels, *Garrett*
Gehrich, *Geary*
Gehricke, *Geary*
Gehrigh, *Geary*
Gehring, *Geary*
Gehrke, *Geary*
Gehrlein, *Geary*
Gehrmann, *Geary*
Gehrs, *Geary*
Gehrt, *Garrett*
Gehrts, *Garrett*
Gehrtz, *Garrett*
Geier
Geierman, *Geier*
Geiger
Geil, *Gale*
Geiler, *Gale*
Geilert, *Gale*
Geindre, *Gendre*
Geipel, *Gilbert*
Geipelt, *Gilbert*
Geippel, *Gilbert*
Geisel, *Gilbert*
Geiselbrecht, *Gilbert*
Geiss, *Geist*
Geissel, *Gilbert*
Geisselbrecht, *Gilbert*
Geisser, *Geist*
Geist
Geister, *Geist*
Geistert, *Geist*
Gel, *Geller*
Gelabert, *Gilbert*
Gelardi, *Garrett*
Gelatly, *Golightly*
Gelb, *Geller*
Gelband, *Geller*
Gelbard, *Geller*
Gelbart, *Geller*
Gelbaum, *Geller*
Gelbein, *Geller*
Gelber, *Geller*
Gelberg, *Geller*
Gelberman, *Geller*
Gelbermann, *Geller*
Gelberson, *Geller*
Gelbert, *Geller, Gilbert*
Gelbfisch, *Geller*
Gelbgieser, *Geller*
Gelbgiesser, *Geller*
Gelbgiser, *Geller*
Gelbhar, *Geller*
Gelbman, *Geller*
Gelbmann, *Geller*
Gelbord, *Geller*
Gelbort, *Geller*
Gelbrecht, *Gilbert*
Gelbrun, *Geller*
Gelbstein, *Geller*
Gelbwachs, *Geller*
Geldard, *Geldart*
Geldart
Gelder, *Geldart, Geller*
Gelderland, *Geller*
Gelderman, *Geller*
Geldermann, *Geller*
Geldner, *Gold*
Geldstein, *Held*
Geler, *Geller*
Gelerman, *Geller*
Gelerstein, *Geller*
Geles
Gelfand, *Oliphant*
Gelfant, *Oliphant*
Gelfarb, *Geller*
Gelin, *Geles*
Gélis, *Giles*
Gelis, *Geles*
Gelkop, *Geller*
Gelkopf, *Geller*
Gell, *Geller, Julian*
Gellan, *Gilfillan*
Gelland, *Gilfillan*
Gelle, *Julian*
Geller
Gellerman, *Geller*
Gellermann, *Geller*
Gellerstein, *Geller*
Gellért, *Garrett*
Gellert, *Geller*
Gelles, *Geles*
Gelless, *Geles*
Gelletly, *Golightly*
Gelli, *Aiello*
Gellibrand, *Gillibrand*
Gelling, *Lewin*
Gellion, *Julian*
Gellis, *Geles*
Gellman, *Geller*
Gellmann, *Geller*
Gellner, *Gold*
Gelly, *Giles*
Gelman, *Geller*
Gelmann, *Geller*
Gelmetti, *William*
Gelmi, *William*
Gelmini, *William*
Gelmo, *William*
Gelmond, *Geller*
Gelmont, *Geller*
Gelperin, *Heilbronn*
Gelstein, *Geller*
Geltzer, *Geldart*
Geluk, *Glück*
Gély, *Giles*
Gelzer, *Geldart*
Gembicki, *Gębski*
Gemeau, *Jumeau*
Gemeaux, *Jumeau*
Gemelli, *Jumeau*
Gemignani, *Jumeau*
Gemini, *Jumeau*
Geminiani, *Jumeau*
Gemmell, *Gamble*
Gemmill, *Gamble*
Gemson, *James*
Gencke, *John*
Gend, *Gaunt*
Gendebein, *Jennewein*
Gendelman, *Handler*
Gendelsman, *Handler*
Gendler, *Handler*
Gendlerman, *Handler*
Gendre
Gendreau, *Gendre*
Gendrich, *Henry*
Gendricke, *Henry*
Gendrin, *Gendre*
Gendron, *Gendre*
Gendrot, *Gendre*
Gendry, *Gendre*
Gendt, *Gaunt*
Genébrier, *Juniper*
Genès
Genest
Genestà, *Genest*
Genestat, *Genest*
Genestay, *Genest*
Geneste, *Genest*
Geneston, *Genest*
Genestou, *Genest*
Genestoux, *Genest*
Genestre, *Genest*
Genet
Genetay, *Genest*
Geneton, *Genest*
Genevai, *Genevois*
Genevard, *Genevois*
Genevay, *Genevois*
Genève, *Genevois*
Genevois
Genevoix, *Genevois*
Genévrier, *Juniper*
Genewein, *Jennewein*
Genicke, *John*
Geniès, *Genès*
Genike, *John*
Genís, *Genès*
Genke, *John*
Genn, *Jane, Juniper*
Gennai, *January*
Gennarelli, *January*
Gennarino, *January*
Gennaro, *January*
Genner, *Jenner*
Gennerich, *Henry*
Gennewein, *Jennewein*
Gennrich, *Henry*
Genoese, *January*
Genova, *January*
Genovese, *January*
Genower, *Jenner*
Genre, *Gendre*
Gens, *Goose*
Genslein, *Goose*
Gensler, *Goose*
Gent, *Gaunt, Gentle*
Gente, *Gentle*
Gentet, *Gentle*
Genthon, *Gentle*
Gential, *Gentle*
Gentil, *Gentle*
Gentile, *Gentle*
Gentili, *Gentle*
Gentilini, *Gentle*
Gentilleau, *Gentle*
Gentillotti, *Gentle*
Gentillucci, *Gentle*
Gentizon, *Gentle*
Gentle
Genton, *Gentle*
Gentot, *Gentle*
Gentry, *Gentle*
Gentsch, *John*
Genty, *Gentle*
Gentzsch, *John*
Genua, *January*
Genzel, *Goose*
Genzman, *Goose*
Geoffré, *Jeffrey*
Geoffre, *Jeffrey*
Geoffrey, *Jeffrey*
Geoffreys, *Jeffrey*
Geoffrion, *Jeffrey*
Geoffroy, *Jeffrey*
Geofroy, *Jeffrey*
Geoghegan
Géolier, *Gale*
Geolier, *Gale*
Georg, *George*
Georgé, *George*
George
Georgeau, *George*
Georgel, *George*
Georgelin, *George*
Georgeon, *George*
Georgeot, *George*
Georgeou, *George*

Georger, *George*
Georges, *George*
Georgescu, *George*
Georgeson, *George*
Georget, *George*
Georghescu, *George*
Georghiou, *George*
Georgi, *George*
Georgiades, *George*
Georgiev, *George*
Georgievski, *George*
Georgiou, *George*
Georgius, *George*
Gepfert, *Godfrey*
Gepp, *Jeffrey*
Geppert, *Godfrey*
Gepson, *Jeffrey*
Géquel, *Jekyll*
Gera, *German*
Geraghty
Gerakhov, *Gerasimov*
Gérald, *Garrett*
Gerald, *Garrett*
Geraldes, *Garrett*
Geraldi, *Garrett*
Geraldini, *Garrett*
Geran, *Waring*
Geranichev, *Gerasimov*
Geranin, *Gerasimov*
Gerankin, *Gerasimov*
Gérard, *Garrett*
Gerard, *Garrett*
Gérardeaux, *Garrett*
Gérardet, *Garrett*
Gerardi, *Garrett*
Gérardin, *Garrett*
Gérardot, *Garrett*
Gerasch, *George*
Gerasimchuk, *Gerasimov*
Gerasimenko, *Gerasimov*
Gerasimenya, *Gerasimov*
Gerasimov
Gerasov, *Gerasimov*
Gerasyutin, *Gerasimov*
Geratt, *Garrett*
Geraty, *Geraghty*
Géraud, *Garrett*
Géraudel, *Garrett*
Géraudy, *Garrett*
Gérault, *Garrett*
Gerb, *Gerber*
Gerbaud, *Garbutt*
Gerbault, *Garbutt*
Gerbaux, *Garbutt*
Gerbe, *Garber*
Gerbeau, *Garber*
Gerbeaux, *Garber*
Gerber
Gerberding, *Garbett*
Gerberich, *Garbett*
Gerberon, *Garber*
Gerbert, *Garbett*
Gerbet, *Garber*
Gerbier, *Garber*
Gerbl, *Gerber*
Gerbod, *Garbutt*
Gerbold, *Garbutt*
Gerboth, *Garbutt*
Gerboud, *Garbutt*
Gercken, *Geary*
Gerckens, *Geary*
Gerdes, *Garrett*
Gerding, *Garrett*
Gerdts, *Garrett*
Gerecke, *Geary*
Gereev, *Gerasimov*
Gereke, *Geary*
Gerencsér, *Goncharov*
Gerety, *Geraghty*
Gerg, *George*
Gerge, *George*
Gergely, *Gregory*
Gerger, *George*
Gergler, *George*
Gergolet, *Gregory*
Gergus, *George*
Gerhard, *Garrett*
Gerhardt, *Garrett*
Gerhartz, *Garrett*
Gerhold, *Garrett*
Gerholz, *Garrett*
Géricault, *Geary*
Géricot, *Geary*
Gerigh, *Geary*
Gérin, *Geary*
Gerin, *Geary*
Gering, *Geary*
Gerish, *Geary*
Gerity, *Geraghty*
Gerken, *Geary*
Gerkens, *Geary*
Gerking, *Geary*
Gerlach, *Garlick*
Gerlacher, *Garlick*
Gerle, *Geary*
Gerlein, *Geary*
Gerler, *Geary*
Gerli, *Geary*
Gerlich, *Garlick*
Gerlicher, *Garlick*
Gerling, *Geary*
Gerlts, *Garrett*
Germain, *German*
Germaine, *German*
Germán, *German*
German
Germaneau, *German*
Germani, *German*
Germanini, *German*
Germanino, *German*
Germann, *Geary, German*
Germano, *German*
Germanoff, *Hermann*
Germanov, *Hermann*
Germanovitz, *Hermann*
Germineau, *German*
Germinet, *German*
Germing, *German*
Germiny, *German*
Germly, *Gormley*
Gerner, *Garner*
Gernet, *Geary*
Gernon, *Garnon*
Gerö, *Gregory*
Gerok, *George*
Gerold, *Garrett*
Geroldi, *Garrett*
Geroldini, *Garrett*
Géròme, *Jerome*
Geron, *Geary, Girona*
Gérondeau, *Geary*
Geronimi, *Jerome*
Geronnet, *Geary*
Gerpott, *Garbutt*
Gerrad, *Garrett*
Gerram, *Jerome*
Gerrard, *Garrett*
Gerratsch, *George*
Gerred, *Garrett*
Gerrels, *Garrett*
Gerrelt, *Garrett*
Gerrelts, *Garrett*
Gerren, *Geary*
Gerrens, *Geary*
Gerressen, *Garrett*
Gerrets, *Garrett*
Gerretsen, *Garrett*
Gerrett, *Garrett*
Gerretz, *Garrett*
Gerrey, *Geary*
Gerrie, *Geary*
Gerriet, *Garrett*
Gerriets, *Garrett*
Gerrish, *Geary*
Gerrit, *Garrett*
Gerritse, *Garrett*
Gerritsen, *Garrett*
Gerritsma, *Garrett*
Gerritzen, *Garrett*
Gerry, *Geary*
Gers, *Geary*
Gersch, *Hirsch*
Gerschenfus, *Hirsch*
Gerschfeld, *Hirsch*
Gerschonowitz, *Gershon*
Gersh, *Hirsch*
Gershanovits, *Gershon*
Gershenowitz, *Gershon*
Gershensohn, *Gershon*
Gershevich, *Hirsch*
Gershkevich, *Hirsch*
Gershman, *Hirsch*
Gershom, *Gershon*
Gershon
Gershoni, *Gershon*
Gershonov, *Gershon*
Gershonowitz, *Gershon*
Gershony, *Gershon*
Gershov, *Hirsch*
Gershun, *Gershon*
Gershuny, *Gershon*
Gerson, *Gershon*
Gerszonowicz, *Gershon*
Gert, *Garrett*
Gertsen, *Garrett*
Gerty, *Geraghty*
Gertz, *Garrett, Herz*
Gertzberg, *Herz*
Gertzog, *Herzog*
Gerung, *Geary*
Gervais, *Jarvis*
Gervaise, *Jarvis*
Gervaiseau, *Jarvis*
Gervas, *Jarvis*
Gervase, *Jarvis*
Gervasing, *Jarvis*
Gervasinho, *Jarvis*
Gervasini, *Jarvis*
Gervasoni, *Jarvis*
Gervasutti, *Jarvis*
Gerver, *Gerber*
Gervex, *Jarvis*
Gervis, *Jarvis*
Gervois, *Jarvis*
Gervot, *Jarvis*
Gesche, *Gilbert*
Geschen, *Gilbert*
Gese, *Gilbert*
Gesecke, *Gilbert*
Gesell
Gesellewitz, *Gesell*
Gesen, *Gilbert*
Gesenius, *Gilbert*
Gessner, *Gass*
Gething, *Gitting*
Gethings, *Gitting*
Getreuer, *Trow*
Getroir, *Trow*
Getrouer, *Trow*
Gettens, *Gitting*
Gettings, *Gitting*
Gettins, *Gitting*
Getty
Geve, *Gebhardt*
Geverc, *Gewirtz*
Gevercman, *Gewirtz*
Gevers, *Gebhardt*
Gevert, *Gebhardt*
Gevertz, *Gewirtz*
Gevertzman, *Gewirtz*
Gevirtz, *Gewirtz*
Gevirtzer, *Gewirtz*
Gevirtzman, *Gewirtz*
Gewers, *Gebhardt*
Gewert, *Gebhardt*
Gewirc, *Gewirtz*
Gewirtz
Gewirtzman, *Gewirtz*
Gewirtzmann, *Gewirtz*
Gewirzer, *Gewirtz*
Gewirzman, *Gewirtz*
Gewirzmann, *Gewirtz*
Gewuerz, *Gewirtz*
Gewurtz, *Gewirtz*
Gewurtzman, *Gewirtz*
Gewurz, *Gewirtz*
Geyer, *Geier*
Gheeraert, *Garrett*
Gheerhaert, *Garrett*
Ghelardi, *Garrett*
Ghelardoni, *Garrett*
Ghelarducci, *Garrett*
Ghelerdini, *Garrett*
Gheorgescu, *George*
Gheorghe, *George*
Gheorghescu, *George*
Gheorghie, *George*
Gheraldi, *Garrett*
Gherardelli, *Garrett*
Gherardesci, *Garrett*
Gherardi, *Garrett*
Gherardini, *Garrett*
Gherarducci, *Garrett*
Gherman, *German*
Ghershensohn, *Gershon*
Ghetti, *Jack*
Ghidelli, *Guy*
Ghidetti, *Guy*
Ghidini, *Guy*
Ghidoli, *Guy*
Ghidoni, *Guy*
Ghidotti, *Guy*
Ghielmi, *William*
Ghielmo, *William*
Ghiglia, *William*
Ghiglino, *William*
Ghiglione, *William*
Ghilardi, *Garrett*
Ghilardini, *Garrett*
Ghilgliotti, *William*
Ghillebaert, *Gilbert*
Ghinazzi, *Ghini*
Ghinelli, *Ghini*
Ghinello, *Ghini*
Ghinetti, *Ghini*
Ghini

Ghinsberg, *Ginsberg*
Ghinzberg, *Ginsberg*
Ghinzburg, *Ginsberg*
Ghio, *Guy*
Ghion, *Guy*
Ghione, *Guy*
Ghioni, *Guy*
Ghiotti, *Guy*
Ghiotto, *Guy*
Ghiraldi, *Garrett*
Ghirardi, *Garrett*
Ghiriardelli, *Garrett*
Ghirigori, *Gregory*
Ghiroldi, *Garrett*
Ghys, *Gilbert*
Ghyselen, *Gilbert*
Ghysen, *Gilbert*
Giacchello, *Jack*
Giacchi, *Jack*
Giacchini, *Jack*
Giaccone, *Jack*
Giacconi, *Jack*
Giachetti, *Jack*
Giachi, *Jack*
Giachini, *Jack*
Giachinotti, *Jack*
Giacobazzi, *Jacob*
Giacobbini, *Jacob*
Giacobbo, *Jacob*
Giacobelli, *Jacob*
Giacobillo, *Jacob*
Giacobini, *Jacob*
Giacobo, *Jacob*
Giacoboni, *Jacob*
Giacobucci, *Jacob*
Giacobuzzi, *Jacob*
Giacoletti, *Jack*
Giacomasso, *James*
Giacomazzo, *James*
Giacomelli, *James*
Giacomello, *James*
Giacometti, *James*
Giacomi, *James*
Giacomini, *James*
Giacomo, *James*
Giacomoni, *James*
Giacomozzo, *James*
Giacomucci, *James*
Giacomuzzi, *James*
Giacomuzzo, *James*
Giacone, *Jack*
Giaconi, *Jack*
Giacopazzi, *Jacob*
Giacopello, *Jacob*
Giacopetti, *Jacob*
Giacopini, *Jacob*
Giacoponi, *Jacob*
Giacoppello, *Jacob*
Giacoppo, *Jacob*
Giacoppoli, *Jacob*
Giacovazzo, *Jacob*
Giacovelli, *Jacob*
Giacovetti, *Jacob*
Giacozzi, *Jack*
Giacubbo, *Jacob*
Giametti, *James*
Giamitti, *James*
Giammelli, *James*
Giamo, *James*
Giamusso, *James*
Giamuzzi, *James*
Gianasi, *John*
Gianassi, *John*
Gianazzo, *John*
Gianelli, *John*
Gianello, *John*
Gianeti, *John*
Gianetti, *John*
Gianettini, *John*
Giani, *John*
Gianiello, *John*
Gianilli, *John*
Gianini, *John*
Gianinotti, *John*
Giannassi, *John*
Giannazzi, *John*
Giannelli, *John*
Gianneschi, *John*
Giannetti, *John*
Gianni, *John*
Giannini, *John*
Giannoni, *John*
Giannotti, *John*
Giannucci, *John*
Gianolini, *John*
Gianolo, *John*
Gianotti, *John*
Gianucci, *John*
Gianulli, *John*
Gianullo, *John*
Gianuzzi, *John*
Giardinaro, *Gardener*
Giardini, *Gardener*
Giardinieri, *Gardener*
Giardino, *Gardener*
Giardinu, *Gardener*
Gibard, *Gebhardt*
Gibb
Gibbard, *Gebhardt*
Gibbe, *Gilbert*
Gibbels, *Gilbert*
Gibben, *Gibbon*
Gibbens, *Gibbon*
Gibbens, *Gilbert*
Gibbes, *Gibb*
Gibbeson, *Gibb*
Gibbin, *Gibbon*
Gibbings, *Gibbon*
Gibbins, *Gibbon*
Gibbon
Gibbons, *Gibbon*
Gibbs, *Gibb*
Gibert, *Gilbert*
Gibertin, *Gilbert*
Giberton, *Gilbert*
Gibke, *Gebhardt*
Gibki
Giblett, *Gibb*
Giblin, *Gibb*
Gibling, *Gibb*
Gibney
Gibson, *Gibb*
Giddings
Gide
Gidel, *Gide*
Gidi, *Giles*
Gidon, *Gide*
Gidy, *Giles*
Gié, *Geary*
Giebecke, *Gebhardt*
Giel, *Giles*
Giele, *Giles*
Gielen, *Giles*
Gieles, *Giles*
Gieling, *Giles*
Gier, *Geary*
Gieraths, *Garrett*
Gierck, *Garrett*
Giercke, *Garrett*
Gierek, *Garrett*
Gierhard, *Garrett*
Gierke, *Garrett*
Giermann, *Geary*
Gierok, *Garrett*
Gierth, *Garrett*
Gies, *Gilbert*
Giese, *Gilbert*
Giesebrecht, *Gilbert*
Giesecke, *Gilbert*
Giesel, *Gilbert*
Gieselmann, *Gilbert*
Giesges, *Gilbert*
Gietz, *Garrett*
Giffard
Giffaut, *Giffard*
Gifford
Giggle, *Jekyll*
Gigli, *Lilly*
Giglietti, *Lilly*
Giglietto, *Lilly*
Giglio, *Lilly*
Giglioli, *Lilly*
Giglioni, *Lilly*
Gigliotti, *Lilly*
Gigliucci, *Lilly*
Gigon, *Gigot*
Gigot
Giguet, *Gigot*
Gijsbers, *Gilbert*
Gijsen, *Gilbert*
Gijzen, *Gilbert*
Gil, *Giles*
Gilabert, *Gilbert*
Gilardengo, *Garrett*
Gilardi, *Garrett*
Gilardini, *Garrett*
Gilardoni, *Garrett*
Gilbain, *Gilbert*
Gilbard, *Gilbert*
Gilbart, *Gilbert*
Gilbeart, *Gilbert*
Gilberd, *Gilbert*
Gilbers, *Gilbert*
Gilbert
Gilbertin, *Gilbert*
Gilberton, *Gilbert*
Gilberts, *Gilbert*
Gilbertson, *Gilbert*
Gilbertz, *Gilbert*
Gilbey, *Gilby*
Gilbird, *Gilbert*
Gilblum, *Geller*
Gilbon, *Gilbert*
Gilbracht, *Gilbert*
Gilbrecht, *Gilbert*
Gilbride, *Kilbride*
Gilburd, *Gilbert*
Gilburt, *Gilbert*
Gilby
Gilcher, *Giles*
Gilchrist
Gilcriest, *Gilchrist*
Gildea, *Kildea*
Gilder, *Gold*
Gildernew
Gildersleeve
Gildersleve, *Gildersleeve*
Gilduff
Gile, *Giles*
Giles
Gilet, *Giles*
Giletto, *Giles*
Gilfedder, *Kilfeather*
Gilfillan
Gilfilland, *Gilfillan*
Gilfoil
Gilfoyle, *Gilfoil*
Gilg, *Giles*
Gilger, *Giles*
Gilgmann, *Giles*
Gilgryst, *Gilchrist*
Gilham, *William*
Gilhespy, *Gillespie*
Gilhool, *Cole*
Gilhool
Gilhooley, *Gilhool*
Gilhooly, *Gilhool*
Gili, *Giles*
Giliat, *Gillett*
Gilibert, *Gilbert*
Giliberti, *Gilbert*
Gilio, *Giles*
Gilioli, *Giles*
Giliot, *Gillett*
Gilis, *Giles*
Gilkes, *Gilchrist*
Gilkison, *Gilchrist*
Gilks, *Gilchrist*
Gill
Gillam, *William*
Gillanders, *Andrew*
Gillard, *Giles*
Gillaspy, *Gillespie*
Gillatt, *Gillett*
Gillbard, *Gilbert*
Gillbride, *Kilbride*
Gillcrist, *Gilchrist*
Gille, *Giles*
Gillebrand, *Gillibrand*
Gillen, *Giles*
Gillequin, *Giles*
Gilles, *Giles*
Gilleson, *Giles*
Gillespey, *Gillespie*
Gillespie
Gillespy, *Gillespie*
Gillet, *Giles, Gillett*
Gillett
Gillette, *Gillett*
Gillham, *William*
Gilli, *Giles*
Gilliam, *William*
Gillian, *Julian*
Gilliatt, *Gillett*
Gillibrand
Gillick, *Gullick*
Gillier, *Giles*
Gilliéron, *Giles*
Gillies
Gillig, *Giles*
Gilliger, *Gallagher*
Gillilan, *Gilfillan*
Gilliland, *Gilfillan*
Gilling
Gillingham
Gillings, *Julian*
Gillio, *Giles*
Gillion, *Giles, Julian*
Gillions, *Julian*
Gilliot, *Gillett*
Gillis, *Giles, Gillies*
Gillison, *Gillies*
Gillmor, *Gilmore*
Gillmore, *Gilmore*
Gillo, *Giles*
Gillon, *Giles*

Gillot, *Giles, Gillett*
Gillott, *Gillett*
Gillotte, *Giles*
Gillou, *Giles*
Gillouin, *Giles*
Gillow
Gillson, *Giles*
Gillum, *William*
Gilly, *Giles*
Gillyatt, *Gillett*
Gillyns, *Giles*
Gilmartin
Gilmer, *Gilmore*
Gilmore
Gilmour, *Gilmore*
Giloteau, *Giles*
Gilotin, *Giles*
Gilotot, *Giles*
Gilpin
Gilquin, *Giles*
Gilroy
Gilson, *Giles*
Gilveil, *Bell*
Gilyot, *Gillett*
Gilyott, *Gillett*
Gimbel, *Gimpel*
Gimel, *Jumeau*
Gimelstein, *Himmel*
Giménez, *Jimeno*
Gimeno, *Jimeno*
Gimignani, *Jumeau*
Gimpel
Gimpelevitch, *Gimpel*
Gimpl, *Gimpel*
Gimplevitch, *Gimpel*
Gimson, *James*
Gincbarg, *Ginsberg*
Gincberg, *Ginsberg*
Gindre, *Gendre*
Giné, *January*
Giner, *January*
Ginés, *Genès*
Ginest, *Genest*
Ginestà, *Genest*
Ginestat, *Genest*
Gineste, *Genest*
Ginestou, *Genest*
Ginestoux, *Genest*
Ginet, *Genest*
Ginevri, *Juniper*
Gingell
Gingle, *Gingell*
Gingold, *Gingell*
Ginn
Ginner, *Jenner*
Ginsberg
Ginsberger, *Ginsberg*
Ginsborg, *Ginsberg*
Ginsborski, *Ginsberg*
Ginsbourg, *Ginsberg*
Ginsburg, *Ginsberg*
Ginsburski, *Ginsberg*
Ginzberg, *Ginsberg*
Ginzbourg, *Ginsberg*
Ginzburg, *Ginsberg*
Ginzburski, *Ginsberg*
Ginzbursky, *Ginsberg*
Gioacchini, *Joachim*
Gioachini, *Joachim*
Gioan, *John*
Gioanetti, *John*
Gioani, *John*
Gioannini, *John*
Gioffre, *Godfrey*
Gioffredo, *Godfrey*
Giofre, *Godfrey*
Gioia, *Joy*
Gioiella, *Joy*
Gioiello, *Joy*
Giorda, *Jordan*
Giordan, *Jordan*
Giordano, *Jordan*
Giorgeschi, *George*
Giorgetti, *George*
Giorgi, *George*
Giorgini, *George*
Giorgio, *George*
Giorgione, *George*
Giorgioni, *George*
Giorgiutti, *George*
Giorielli, *George*
Gioriettto, *George*
Giorio, *George*
Giottini, *Francis*
Giotto, *Francis*
Giovacchini, *Joachim*
Giovachini, *Joachim*
Giovanardi, *John*
Giovanazzi, *John*
Giovanelli, *John*
Giovanetti, *John*
Giovani, *John*
Giovanitti, *John*
Giovanizio, *John*
Giovannacci, *John*
Giovannardi, *John*
Giovannazzi, *John*
Giovannelli, *John*
Giovannetti, *John*
Giovanni, *John*
Giovannilli, *John*
Giovannini, *John*
Giovannoni, *John*
Giovinazzo, *Jeune*
Giovine, *Jeune*
Giovinetti, *Jeune*
Gipa, *Job*
Gipp, *Gibb*
Gipps, *Gibb*
Gipson, *Gibb*
Giquel, *Jekyll*
Giquelle, *Jekyll*
Giral, *Garrett*
Giráldez, *Garrett*
Giraldo, *Garrett*
Giraldon, *Garrett*
Giralt, *Garrett*
Girard, *Garrett*
Girardeau, *Garrett*
Girardengo, *Garrett*
Girardet, *Garrett*
Girardetti, *Garrett*
Girardey, *Garrett*
Girardez, *Garrett*
Girardi, *Garrett*
Girardin, *Garrett*
Girardini, *Garrett*
Girardoni, *Garrett*
Girardot, *Garrett*
Girardy, *Garrett*
Giraths, *Garrett*
Giraud, *Garrett*
Giraudat, *Garrett*
Giraudeau, *Garrett*
Giraudel, *Garrett*
Giraudo, *Garrett*
Giraudot, *Garrett*
Giraudou, *Garrett*
Giraudoux, *Garrett*
Giraudy, *Garrett*
Girauld, *Garrett*
Girault, *Garrett*
Giraume, *Jerome*
Giraut, *Garrett*
Giraux, *Garrett*
Girbal, *Garbutt*
Girbe, *Garber*
Girbeau, *Garber*
Girbet, *Garber*
Girdwood
Gire, *Giles*
Girhard, *Garrett*
Giri, *Giles*
Giriardelli, *Garrett*
Giriat, *Giles*
Giribaldi, *Garbutt*
Girke, *Garrett*
Girlach, *Garlick*
Girling, *Codlin*
Giró, *Girona*
Girod, *Garrett*
Girodias, *Garrett*
Girodier, *Garrett*
Girodin, *Garrett*
Girodon, *Garrett*
Girolami, *Jerome*
Giroldi, *Garrett*
Girome, *Jerome*
Girón, *Girona*
Giron, *Geary*
Girona
Girond, *Geary*
Gironès, *Girona*
Girsch, *Hirsch*
Girsh, *Hirsch*
Girshevich, *Hirsch*
Girshfeld, *Hirsch*
Girshkevich, *Hirsch*
Girshkovich, *Hirsch*
Girshov, *Hirsch*
Girshovich, *Hirsch*
Girshtein, *Hirsch*
Girstejn, *Hirsch*
Girth, *Garrett*
Girtin, *Gurton*
Girton, *Gurton*
Girvan, *Garvin*
Girvin, *Garvin*
Girwin, *Garvin*
Giry, *Giles*
Gisbert, *Gilbert*
Gisbertz, *Gilbert*
Gispert, *Gilbert*
Gissel, *Gilbert*
Gissing
Gite, *Gute*
Giter, *Good*
Giterman, *Goodman*
Gitlin, *Gute*
Gittel, *Gute*
Gittelson, *Gute*
Gittens, *Gitting*
Gitter, *Good*
Gitter
Gitterman, *Gitter*
Gitterman, *Goodman*
Gitting
Gittings, *Gitting*
Gittins, *Gitting*
Gittoes, *Griffith*
Gittus, *Griffith*
Giubba, *Job*
Giubbini, *Job*
Giudice, *Judge*
Giuffre, *Godfrey*
Giuffri, *Godfrey*
Giuli, *Júlio*
Giulianelli, *Julian*
Giulianini, *Julian*
Giuliano, *Julian*
Giulietti, *Júlio*
Giulio, *Júlio*
Giulioni, *Júlio*
Giuliotti, *Júlio*
Giuliuzzi, *Júlio*
Giurin, *George*
Giurini, *George*
Giurio, *George*
Giustini, *Justin*
Giusto, *Just*
Givenchy
Głąb, *Głąbski*
Głąbicki, *Głąbski*
Głąbowski, *Głąbski*
Głąbski
Glace, *Glass*
Glad
Gladden, *Glad*
Gladding, *Glad*
Gladh, *Glad*
Gladhill, *Gledhill*
Glading, *Glad*
Gladman, *Glad*
Gladstone
Gladwin
Gladwyn, *Gladwin*
Glaisher, *Glass*
Glaister
Glancy, *Clancy*
Glandfield, *Glanville*
Glanfield, *Glanville*
Glantz
Glantzmann, *Glantz*
Glanvill, *Glanville*
Glanville
Glanz, *Glantz*
Glanzberg, *Glantz*
Glanzer, *Glantz*
Glanzman, *Glantz*
Gläre, *Hilary*
Gläri, *Hilary*
Glari, *Hilary*
Glaris, *Hilary*
Glas, *Glass*
Glasberg, *Glass*
Glasby, *Gillespie*
Glascott
Gläsener, *Glass*
Gläser, *Glass*
Glaser, *Glass*
Glaserman, *Glass*
Glasgow
Glashen, *McGlashan*
Glasius, *Glass*
Glasman, *Glass*
Glasner, *Glass*
Glass
Glassberg, *Glass*
Glassbrook, *Glazebrook*
Glasscock, *Glascott*
Glasscoe, *Glasgow*
Glasscote, *Glascott*
Glasser, *Glass*
Glassgold, *Glass*
Glassheib, *Glass*
Glassman, *Glass*

Glasson, *Glass*
Glastra, *Glass*
Glatz
Glätzel, *Glatz*
Glatzer, *Glatz*
Glauber, *Klug*
Glauer, *Klug*
Glauert, *Klug*
Glave, *Gleave*
Glaves, *Gleave*
Glaysher, *Glass*
Glazachov, *Glazurin*
Glazatov, *Glazurin*
Glaze, *Glass*
Glazebrook
Glazeev, *Glazurin*
Glazer, *Glass*
Glazier, *Glass*
Glazov, *Glazurin*
Glazovoi, *Glazurin*
Glazunov, *Glazurin*
Glazurin
Glazyer, *Glass*
Glazyrin, *Glazurin*
Glazzon, *Glass*
Gleadell, *Gledhill*
Gleadle, *Gledhill*
Gleasan, *Gleesan*
Gleason, *Gleesan*
Gleave
Gleaves, *Gleave*
Głębocki, *Głąbski*
Glebov
Głębowski, *Głąbski*
Głębski, *Głąbski*
Gledall, *Gledhill*
Glede, *Gleed*
Gledhill
Gledstane, *Gladstone*
Gleed
Gleesan
Gleeson, *Gleesan*
Glejzer, *Glass*
Glekfeld, *Glück*
Glen
Glendening, *Glendinning*
Glendenning, *Glendinning*
Glendinning
Glenn, *Glen*
Glew
Gley, *Eloy*
Glezer, *Glass*
Glick, *Glück*
Glickin
Glicklich, *Glück*
Glickman, *Glück*
Glicksberg, *Glück*
Glicksman, *Glück*
Glickson, *Glickin*
Glickstein, *Glück*
Gliddon
Glide, *Gleed*
Gligoraci, *Gregory*
Gligori, *Gregory*
Gligorić, *Gregory*
Gligorijević, *Gregory*
Glik, *Glück*
Gliker, *Glück*
Glikin, *Glickin*
Glikman, *Glück*
Glikner, *Glück*
Glikovsky, *Glickin*
Gliksam, *Glück*
Gliksberg, *Glück*
Gliksman, *Glück*
Glikson, *Glickin*
Glikstein, *Glück*
Glock
Glocke, *Glock*
Glöckel, *Glock*
Glocker, *Glock*
Glöckl, *Glock*
Glöckle, *Glock*
Glockle, *Glock*
Glöckler, *Glock*
Glöckner, *Glock*
Glockner, *Glock*
Glodeau, *Claude*
Glogau, *Głogowski*
Gloger, *Głogowski*
Glogger, *Glock*
Glöggl, *Glock*
Głogowski
Glohr, *Hilary*
Glomski, *Głąbski*
Glöre, *Hilary*
Glori, *Hilary*
Glorius, *Hilary*
Glossop
Gloster
Glover
Głowacki
Głowacz, *Głowacki*
Głowiński, *Głowacki*
Gloy, *Eloy*
Glozman, *Glass*
Gluck, *Glück*
Glück
Glucker, *Glück*
Gluckman, *Glück*
Gluckmann, *Glück*
Glucksam, *Glück*
Gluckshtin, *Glück*
Glucksman, *Glück*
Gluckstein, *Glück*
Glue, *Glew*
Glueck, *Glück*
Gluecklich, *Glück*
Glueckman, *Glück*
Glueckselig, *Glück*
Gluecksmann, *Glück*
Glueckstadt, *Glück*
Glueckstern, *Glück*
Gluekson, *Glickin*
Glusman, *Glass*
Gluz, *Glass*
Gluzband, *Glass*
Gluzberg, *Glass*
Gluzer, *Glass*
Gluzman, *Glass*
Gluzmann, *Glass*
Gluzschneider, *Glass*
Glyde, *Gleed*
Glyn, *Glynn*
Glyne, *Glynn*
Glynn
Glynne, *Glynn*
Gnatowski, *Ignace*
Gnudi, *Benvenuti*
Gnuti, *Benvenuti*
Goate, *Gate*
Goater, *Gate*
Goatman, *Gate*
Gobart, *Godbert*
Göbbel, *Godbert*
Gobbel, *Godbert*
Göbbels, *Godbert*
Göbbert, *Godbert*
Gobbert, *Godbert*
Gobbetti, *Gobbi*
Gobbetto, *Gobbi*
Gobbi
Gobbini, *Gobbi*
Gobbo, *Gobbi*
Gobeau, *Gobel*
Gobeaux, *Gobel*
Göbel, *Godbert*
Gobel
Gobelet, *Gobel*
Gobelin, *Gobel*
Gobelot, *Gobel*
Goberman, *Haber*
Gobert, *Godbert*
Gobet
Gobetti, *Gobbi*
Göbhardt, *Gebhardt*
Gobin, *Godbert*
Gobinot, *Godbert*
Goble, *Godbold*
Göbler, *Godbert*
Gobrecht, *Godbert*
Goch, *Gogh*
Göcken, *Gott*
Göcker, *Gott*
Göcking, *Gott*
Göcks, *Gott*
Godar, *Goddard*
Godard, *Goddard*
Godart, *Goddard*
Godball, *Godbold*
Godber, *Godbert*
Godbert
Godbold
Godbolt, *Godbold*
Goddard
Godde, *Gott*
Gödden, *Goddard*
Godden, *Godin*
Göddert, *Goddard*
Goddert, *Goddard*
Göddertz, *Goddard*
Goddman, *Goodman*
Göde, *Gott*
Gode, *Good, Gott*
Godebert, *Godbert*
Godebrecht, *Godbert*
Godeferding, *Godfrey*
Godefrey, *Godfrey*
Godefroi, *Godfrey*
Godefroy, *Godfrey*
Godehard, *Goddard*
Gödeke, *Gott*
Gödel, *Gott*
Godemann, *Goodman*
Godemar, *Gomer*
Godemer, *Gomer*
Gödens, *Gott*
Göder, *Gott*
Goder, *Gott*
Göders, *Gott*
Godet, *Gott*
Godevaard, *Godfrey*
Godey, *Gott*
Godfer, *Godfrey*
Godfrain, *Godfrey*
Godfray, *Godfrey*
Godfree, *Godfrey*
Godfrey
Godfried, *Godfrey*
Godfrin, *Godfrey*
Godfroid, *Godfrey*
Godfroy, *Godfrey*
Godin
Godineau, *Godin*
Godinet, *Godin*
Godínez, *Godin*
Godinho, *Godin*
Godino, *Godin*
Godinou, *Godin*
Godinoux, *Godin*
Godley
Godly, *Godley*
Godman, *Goodman*
Godmard, *Gomer*
Godmer, *Gomer*
Godolphin
Godon, *Gott*
Godot, *Gott*
Godoy
Godrich, *Gutteridge*
Godridge, *Gutteridge*
Godschalk, *Gottschalk*
Godson
Godt, *Gott*
Godtfring, *Godfrey*
Gödtke, *Gott*
Godunov
Godwin, *Goodwin*
Godwyn, *Goodwin*
Gody, *Godin*
Goed, *Good*
Goedhard, *Goddard*
Goedhart, *Goddard*
Goedkoop, *Goodchap*
Goefrain, *Godfrey*
Goefraint, *Godfrey*
Goemans, *Goodman*
Goens, *Gott*
Goerty, *Fogarty*
Gofer, *Hoffmann*
Goff, *Gough*
Goffarth, *Godfrey*
Goffe, *Gough*
Goffer, *Godfrey, Hoffmann*
Goffic, *Gough*
Goffin, *Gough*
Goffman, *Hoffmann*
Goffredo, *Godfrey*
Gofman, *Hoffmann*
Gofton
Gogan, *Cogan*
Gogarty, *Fogarty*
Gogerty, *Fogarty*
Goggin, *Cogan*
Gogh
Gogol
Gogolewski, *Gogol*
Goguel, *Goguin*
Goguelat, *Goguin*
Goguillon, *Goguin*
Goguin
Goguineau, *Goguin*
Goguy, *Goguin*
Gohde, *Gott*
Gohdens, *Gott*
Gohdes, *Gott*
Gohert, *Goddard*
Gohier, *Gower*
Gohin, *Godin*
Göhring, *Geary*
Gohrt, *Goddard*
Goïc, *Gough*
Goichman, *Hoch*
Goicoechea
Goin, *Godin*
Goiri

Goitia
Gołąb, *Golubev*
Gołąbek, *Golubev*
Gołąbik, *Golubev*
Golagley, *Golightly*
Goland, *Holland*
Golański, *Golec*
Golby
Gold
Golda, *Golde*
Goldbach, *Gold*
Goldband, *Gold*
Goldbaum, *Gold*
Goldberg, *Gold*
Goldberger, *Gold*
Goldblat, *Gold*
Goldbloom, *Gold*
Goldblum, *Gold*
Goldboim, *Gold*
Goldbrener, *Gold*
Goldbrenner, *Gold*
Goldbruch, *Gold*
Golde
Golden, *Gold*
Golden, *McGoldrick*
Goldenberg, *Gold*
Goldenfarb, *Gold*
Goldenfeld, *Gold*
Goldenholtz, *Gold*
Goldenholz, *Gold*
Goldenhorn, *Gold*
Goldenrot, *Gold*
Goldenstein, *Gold*
Goldenthal, *Gold*
Golder
Goldernberg, *Gold*
Goldes, *Golde*
Goldfaber, *Gold*
Goldfaden, *Gold*
Goldfajn, *Gold*
Goldfarb, *Gold*
Goldfeder, *Gold*
Goldfein, *Gold*
Goldfeld, *Gold*
Goldfinch
Goldfine, *Gold*
Goldfinger, *Gold*
Goldfisch, *Gold*
Goldfischer, *Gold*
Goldfish, *Gold*
Goldfisher, *Gold*
Goldflam, *Gold*
Goldfleiss, *Gold*
Goldfoot, *Gold*
Goldfracht, *Gold*
Goldfrid, *Gold*
Goldfried, *Gold*
Goldfus, *Gold*
Goldgart, *Gold*
Goldgewicht, *Gold*
Goldglass, *Gold*
Goldgraber, *Gold*
Goldgrub, *Gold*
Goldhaber, *Gold*
Goldhamer, *Gold*
Goldhammer, *Gold*
Goldhand, *Gold*
Goldhar, *Gold*
Goldhecht, *Gold*
Goldhirsch, *Gold*
Goldhirsh, *Gold*
Goldie
Goldin, *Golde*
Golding
Goldingay
Goldis, *Golde*
Goldkind, *Gold*
Goldklang, *Gold*
Goldkorn, *Gold*
Goldkranc, *Gold*
Goldkrantz, *Gold*
Goldlust, *Gold*
Goldmacher, *Gold*
Goldman, *Gold*
Goldmann, *Gold*
Goldminc, *Gold*
Goldmintz, *Gold*
Goldminz, *Gold*
Goldmund, *Gold*
Goldnadel, *Gold*
Göldner, *Gold*
Goldner, *Gold*
Goldney, *Goldie*
Goldrat, *Gold*
Goldrath, *Gold*
Goldreich, *Gold*
Goldring
Goldrosen, *Gold*
Golds, *Gold*
Goldsand, *Gold*
Goldsby
Goldschein, *Gold*
Goldschlaeger, *Gold*
Goldschlager, *Gold*
Goldsmith
Goldsobel, *Gold*
Goldspink
Goldstein, *Gold*
Goldstern, *Gold*
Goldstoff, *Gold*
Goldston, *Goldstone*
Goldstone
Goldstrom, *Gold*
Goldstuck, *Gold*
Goldthorpe
Goldvasser, *Gold*
Goldwasser, *Gold*
Goldwater, *Gold*
Goldwein, *Gold*
Goldweitz, *Gold*
Goldweiz, *Gold*
Goldwerger, *Gold*
Goldwin
Goldwirth, *Gold*
Goldworm, *Gold*
Goldwyn, *Goldwin*
Goldzimmer, *Gold*
Goldzweig, *Gold*
Gołębiewski, *Golubev*
Gołębiowski, *Golubev*
Golec
Golembiewski, *Golubev*
Golembo, *Golubev*
Golender, *Holland*
Goligher, *Golightly*
Golightly
Goligly, *Golightly*
Goliński, *Golec*
Golis, *Golec*
Gollan, *Jekyll*
Golland, *Jekyll*
Golley, *Gully*
Gollin, *Jekyll*
Gollins, *Jekyll*
Göllner, *Gold*
Gollub, *Golubev*
Golob, *Golubev*
Golobič, *Golubev*
Golobiwsky, *Golubev*
Golobov, *Golubev*
Golobovich, *Golubev*
Golobow, *Golubev*
Golomb, *Golubev*
Golombek, *Golubev*
Golombik, *Golubev*
Golombovitz, *Golubev*
Golomburskу, *Golubev*
Goloubow, *Golubev*
Goloubowitz, *Golubev*
Golson, *Goldstone*
Golston, *Goldstone*
Golsworthy, *Galsworthy*
Golty, *Goulty*
Goltz, *Holt*
Goltzer, *Holt*
Goltzman, *Holt*
Golubev
Golubić, *Golubev*
Golubinski, *Golubev*
Golubović, *Golubev*
Golz, *Holt*
Gölzer, *Geldart*
Golzer, *Holt*
Golzman, *Holt*
Gomà, *Gomer*
Gomar, *Gomer*
Gombart, *Gombert*
Gombert
Gombrich, *Gombert*
Gomer
Gomersall
Gomes, *Gomme*
Gómez, *Gomme*
Gomis, *Gomme*
Gomm, *Gomme*
Gomme
Gommert, *Gombert*
Gompers, *Gombert*
Gompert, *Gombert*
Gompertz, *Gombert*
Gomperz, *Gombert*
Gomułka, *Homolka*
Gon, *Hugh*
Gonard, *Hugh*
Gonçaves, *Gonzalo*
Goncharov
Goneau, *Hugh*
Gonel, *Hugh*
Gonet, *Hugh*
Gonfalonieri
Gonin, *Hugh*
Gonnard, *Hugh*
Gonneau, *Hugh*
Gonnel, *Hugh*
Gonnet, *Hugh*
Gonnin, *Hugh*
Gonser, *Goose*
Gontier, *Gunter*
González, *Gonzalo*
Gonzalo
Gonzálvez, *Gonzalo*
Gonzalvo, *Gonzalo*
Gooch, *Gough*
Good
Gooda, *Gooder*
Goodale, *Goodall*
Goodall
Goodanew, *Goodenough*
Gooday
Goodayle, *Goodall*
Goodbaudy, *Goodbody*
Goodboddy, *Goodbody*
Goodbody
Goodby
Goodchap
Goodcheap, *Goodchap*
Goodchild
Gooddy, *Goodey*
Goode, *Good*
Goodee, *Goodey*
Gooden
Goodenough
Gooder
Goodere, *Gooder*
Gooderham, *Goodrum*
Gooderick, *Gutteridge*
Gooderidge, *Gutteridge*
Gooders, *Gooder*
Goodeve, *Goodey*
Goodey
Goodfellow
Goodfriend
Goodge, *Gough*
Goodger, *Goodyear*
Goodhall, *Goodall*
Goodhew
Goodhue, *Goodhew*
Goodhugh, *Goodhew*
Goodier, *Goodyear*
Goodiff, *Goodey*
Gooding, *Good*
Goodinge, *Good*
Goodings, *Good*
Goodison, *Goodey*
Goodlad
Goodlake, *Gullick*
Goodlatt, *Goodlad*
Goodleigh, *Godley*
Goodlet, *Goodlad*
Goodlett, *Goodlad*
Goodley, *Godley*
Goodluck, *Gullick*
Goodly, *Godley*
Goodman
Goodner, *Goodenough*
Goodnow, *Goodenough*
Goodram, *Goodrum*
Goodrich, *Gutteridge*
Goodrick, *Gutteridge*
Goodridge, *Gutteridge*
Goodrum
Goodsir
Goodson
Goodswen
Goodwill
Goodwin
Goodwright, *Gutteridge*
Goody, *Goodey*
Goodyear
Goodyer, *Goodyear*
Goold, *Gold*
Goolden, *Gold*
Goom, *Gomme*
Goonan, *Gaffney*
Goonane, *Gaffney*
Goor, *Gregory*
Gooravan, *McGovern*
Goos, *Goose*
Goose
Gooseman, *Goose*
Goosen, *Gosse*
Goosens, *Gosse*
Goosey
Goosmann, *Goose*
Goossen, *Gosse*
Goossens, *Gosse*

Goozee, *Goosey*
Göpfert, *Godfrey*
Goppel, *Godbert*
Goppelt, *Godbert*
Göppert, *Godfrey*
Gora, *Górski*
Goracci, *Gregory*
Górak, *Górski*
Góral, *Górski*
Góralczyk, *Górski*
Goralnick, *Gorelik*
Goralnik, *Gorelik*
Góralski, *Górski*
Goranov, *Górski, Gregory*
Goraud, *Gore*
Gorb, *Cuervo*
Gorce, *Gorse*
Gorch, *Gorge*
Görcke, *George*
Górczak, *Górski*
Górczyk, *Górski*
Gord, *Goddard*
Gordeev
Gordet, *Gordon*
Gordge, *Gorge*
Gordienko, *Gordeev*
Gordillo, *Gordo*
Gordin, *Gordon*
Gordo
Gordón, *Gordo*
Gordon
Gordonoff, *Gordon*
Gordonowitz, *Gordon*
Gore
Gorcau, *Gorc*
Górecki, *Górski*
Goreham
Göreis, *Gregory*
Gorel, *Gore*
Gorelick, *Gorelik*
Gorelik
Gorelli, *Gregory*
Goren
Gorenn, *Goren*
Gorenstein, *Goren*
Gorer, *Gore*
Göres, *Gregory*
Goret, *Gore*
Goretti, *Gregory*
Goretzki, *Górski*
Gorevan, *McGovern*
Gorevin, *McGovern*
Gorey, *McCaffrey*
Gorfinkel
Gorfunkel, *Gorfinkel*
Gorge
Gorgeau, *Gorge*
Görgel, *George*
Görgen, *George*
Gorgeon, *Gorge*
Gorgeot, *Gorge*
Görger, *George*
Görges, *George*
Gorges, *Gorge*
Gorghetto, *Gregory*
Görgl, *George*
Görgler, *George*
Gorham, *Goreham*
Görhardt, *Garrett*
Gori, *Gregory*
Gorichon, *Gore*
Gorick, *George*
Göricke, *George*
Gorillot, *Gore*
Gorin, *Gore, Goring*
Göring, *Geary*
Goring
Goringe, *Goring*
Gorini, *Gregory*
Gorioli, *Gregory*
Goriot, *Gore*
Gork, *George*
Görke, *George*
Gorke, *George*
Görl, *Geary*
Görlach, *Garlick*
Görlacher, *Garlick*
Görler, *Geary*
Görlich, *Garlick*
Görling, *Geary*
Gorlnik, *Gorelik*
Gorman
Gormilly, *Gormley*
Gormley
Gornall
Górniak, *Górski*
Górnicki, *Górski*
Górniok, *Górski*
Górny, *Górski*
Gornykh, *Górski*
Gorobets, *Vorobyov*
Gorochov, *Gorokhov*
Gorochovski, *Gorokhov*
Gorohovski, *Gorokhov*
Gorokhov
Goron, *Gore*
Goroni, *Gregory*
Gorostiaga
Gorostiza
Górowski, *Górski*
Görres, *Gregory*
Görries, *Gregory*
Gorriessen, *Gregory*
Gorringe, *Goring*
Görrissen, *Gregory*
Gorron, *Gore*
Gorry, *McCaffrey*
Görs, *Gregory*
Gorse
Górski
Gorsky, *Górski*
Gorsse, *Gorse*
Gorst, *Gorse*
Gorstidge, *Gossage*
Gorsuch, *Gossage*
Gorton
Gorusso, *Gregory*
Gorwitz, *Horowitz*
Gory, *Gore*
Gorzki, *Horký*
Gorzkiewicz, *Horký*
Gorzkowski, *Horký*
Gosálvez, *Gonzalo*
Gösch, *Gottschalk*
Gosch, *Gottschalk*
Gösche, *Gottschalk*
Göschel, *Gottschalk*
Göschen, *Gottschalk*
Goseling, *Gosling*
Gösgen, *Goose*
Gosland, *Gosling*
Goslich, *Gottschalk*
Goslin, *Gosling*
Gosling
Gosmin, *Kuzmin*
Gosney
Goss, *Gosse*
Gossage
Gossart
Gösse, *Gosse*
Gosse
Gosselin, *Gosling*
Gosselk, *Gottschalk*
Gosset, *Gosse*
Gossett, *Gosse*
Gossin, *Gosse*
Gossling, *Gosling*
Gostage, *Gossage*
Gostellow
Gostling, *Gosling*
Got, *Hugh*
Got
Gotajner, *Got*
Gotesdiner, *Got*
Gotesman, *Got*
Gotfert, *Godfrey*
Gotfredsen, *Godfrey*
Gotfreund, *Got*
Gotfrey, *Godfrey*
Gotfrid, *Got*
Gotfried, *Godfrey*
Gotfried, *Got*
Gotfryd, *Got*
Göth, *Gott*
Gothárd, *Goddard*
Gothard
Göthe, *Gott*
Gothelf, *Got*
Gothilf, *Got*
Gothmann, *Goodman*
Götke, *Gott*
Gotkind, *Got*
Gotlib, *Gottlieb*
Gotlibovski, *Gottlieb*
Gotlibowicz, *Gottlieb*
Gotlieb, *Gottlieb*
Gotsforcht, *Got*
Gotshal, *Got*
Gott
Gottdenker, *Got*
Gottdiener, *Got*
Gotte, *Gott*
Gottehrer, *Got*
Gottel, *Gott*
Göttert, *Goddard*
Gottesdiener, *Got*
Gottesdiner, *Got*
Gottesdonner, *Got*
Gottesfeld, *Got*
Gottesgnade, *Got*
Gottesman, *Got*
Gottesmann, *Got*
Gottessegen, *Got*
Gottfried, *Godfrey, Got*
Göttgens, *Gott*
Gotthárd, *Goddard*
Gotthard, *Goddard*
Gotthardt, *Goddard*
Gottheil, *Got*
Gotthelf, *Got*
Gotthilf, *Got*
Göttjens, *Gott*
Gottl, *Gott*
Göttler, *Gott*
Gottlib, *Gottlieb*
Gottlieb
Gottreich, *Got*
Gotts, *Gott*
Gottschald, *Gottschalk*
Gottschalk
Gottschall, *Gottschalk*
Gottschlich, *Gottschalk*
Gottschling, *Gottschalk*
Gottsegen, *Got*
Gottselig, *Got*
Götz, *Gott*
Götze, *Gott*
Gouasquet, *Gascoigne*
Goubeau, *Gobel*
Goubel, *Gobel*
Goubert, *Jaubert*
Goubet, *Gobet*
Goublier, *Gobel*
Gouda, *Gooder*
Goudard, *Goddard*
Goude, *Good*
Goudge, *Gough*
Goudie, *Goldie*
Goudier, *Goodyear*
Goudman, *Goodman*
Goudon, *Gott*
Goudsmet, *Goldsmith*
Goudsmid, *Goldsmith*
Goudsmit, *Goldsmith*
Goudy, *Goldie*
Gouge, *Gough*
Gougeon, *Goujon*
Gough
Gouïc, *Gough*
Gouin, *Godin, Gwyn*
Gouineau, *Godin*
Goujon
Goujou, *Goujon*
Gould, *Gold*
Goulden, *Gold*
Gouldie, *Goldie*
Gouldstone, *Goldstone*
Gouldy, *Goldie*
Goulet
Gouley, *Goulet*
Goulston, *Goldstone*
Goulstone, *Goldstone*
Goulty
Gounard, *Hugh*
Goundry, *Grundy*
Gounel, *Hugh*
Gounet, *Hugh*
Gounin, *Hugh*
Gounod, *Hugh*
Gounot, *Hugh*
Gouny, *Hugh*
Goupil
Goupillet, *Goupil*
Goupillon, *Goupil*
Goupy, *Goupil*
Gourdon, *Gordon*
Goureau, *Gore*
Gouret, *Gore*
Gourlay
Gourley, *Gourlay*
Gourlie, *Gourlay*
Goury, *Gore*
Gous
Goussard, *Gous*
Goussaud, *Gous*
Gousset, *Gous*
Goussin, *Gous*
Gousson, *Gous*
Gouveia
Gouvernaire, *Gouverneur*
Gouverneur
Govaard, *Godfrey*
Govan
Govenlock, *Gowanlock*
Gover
Govers, *Godfrey*

Govert, *Godfrey*
Goverts, *Godfrey*
Govic, *Gough*
Govini, *Jacob*
Govinlock, *Gowanlock*
Gow, *Gough*
Gowanlock
Gowans, *McGowan*
Gowar, *Gower*
Goward, *Gough*
Gowen, *Gough*
Gowenlock, *Gowanlock*
Gower
Gowers, *Gower*
Goya
Gozalo, *Gonzalo*
Gozzard, *Gossart*
Gozzett, *Gossart*
Gozzi, *Dominique*
Gozzini, *Dominique*
Gozzoli, *Dominique*
Graap, *Grape*
Grab, *Grabowski*
Grabarczyk, *Graber*
Grabarz, *Graber*
Grabau, *Grabowski*
Gräber, *Graber*
Graber
Graberman, *Graber*
Grabert, *Graber*
Grabner, *Graber*
Grabovski, *Grabowski*
Grabowicz, *Grabowski*
Grabowski
Grabski, *Grabowski*
Graby, *Gabriel*
Graça, *Grace*
Grace
Gracey, *Grass*
Gràcia, *Grace*
Gracià, *Gratien*
Gracia, *Grace*
Gracie, *Grass*
Graczyk
Gradillas
Grady
Graell, *Gradillas*
Graells, *Gradillas*
Graeme, *Graham*
Graf
Grafchikov, *Graf*
Gräfe, *Graf*
Grafe, *Graf*
Graff
Grafman, *Graf*
Grafton
Grage, *Gray*
Graham
Grahame, *Graham*
Grahe, *Gray*
Grahmann, *Gray*
Grahn, *Gran*
Grail
Graille, *Grail*
Graillet, *Grail*
Graillon, *Grail*
Graillot, *Grail*
Grailot, *Grail*
Grainge, *Grange*
Grainger, *Granger*
Graley, *Grealey*
Gralhon, *Grail*
Gralnick, *Gorelik*
Gralnik, *Gorelik*

Gram
Gramann, *Gray*
Grame
Gramme, *Grame*
Gran
Granado
Granat, *Garnett*
Granath, *Garnett*
Granatov, *Garnett*
Granatstein, *Garnett*
Granberg, *Gran*
Granche, *Grange*
Grancher, *Granger*
Grand, *Grant*
Granda
Grande, *Grant*
Grandeau, *Grant*
Grandel, *Grant*
Grandet, *Grant*
Grandi, *Grant*
Grandinetti, *Grant*
Grandini, *Grant*
Grandis, *Grant*
Grandison
Grando, *Grant*
Grandon, *Grant*
Grandone, *Grant*
Grandoni, *Grant*
Grandot, *Grant*
Grandotto, *Grant*
Granel, *Granet*
Granet
Grangé, *Granger*
Grange
Granger
Grangié, *Granger*
Grangier, *Granger*
Granholm, *Gran*
Granillo, *Granet*
Granja, *Grange*
Granlöf, *Gran*
Granlund, *Gran*
Grann, *Gran*
Grannell, *Ronald*
Granquist, *Gran*
Granström, *Gran*
Grant
Grantham
Granville, *Greenfield*
Grap, *Grape*
Grape
Gräper, *Grape*
Grapes
Gras, *Grass*
Gräser, *Grass*
Graser, *Grass*
Grasigli, *Grass*
Grass
Grasselli, *Grass*
Grassellini, *Grass*
Grasset, *Grass*
Grassetti, *Grass*
Grassi, *Grass*
Grassick, *Grass*
Grassie, *Grass*
Grassilli, *Grass*
Grassin, *Grass*
Grassini, *Grass*
Grassmann, *Grass*
Grasso, *Grass*
Grasson, *Grass*
Grassot, *Grass*
Grassotti, *Grass*
Gratien

Grattan, *Gratton*
Gratten, *Gratton*
Gratton
Grau, *Gray*
Grau
Graubard, *Gray*
Graubart, *Gray*
Grauberg, *Gray*
Grauer, *Gray*
Grauert, *Gray*
Grauf, *Graf*
Graumann, *Gray*
Grauweis, *Gray*
Graux, *Grau*
Grauzalc, *Gray*
Grave
Gravel, *Grave*
Graveleau, *Grave*
Gravelin, *Grave*
Graveline, *Grave*
Graveling, *Grave*
Gravelle, *Grave*
Graver, *Graber*
Gravereau, *Graverend*
Gravereaux, *Graverend*
Graverend
Graveron, *Graverend*
Graves, *Grave*
Gravesen, *Graf*
Graveson, *Grave*
Graveston, *Grave*
Gravier, *Grave*
Gravot, *Grave*
Graw, *Gray*
Grawe, *Gray*
Gray
Grayham, *Graham*
Grayley, *Grealey*
Grayshon, *Grave*
Grayson, *Grave*
Grayston, *Grave*
Grazi, *Grace*
Grazia, *Grace*
Graziani, *Gratien*
Graziano, *Gratien*
Grazioli, *Grace*
Graziotti, *Grace*
Grazzi, *Grace*
Grazziani, *Gratien*
Grazziano, *Gratien*
Grazzini, *Grace*
Grbić, *Hrb*
Grčić, *Gregory*
Grealey
Grealish, *Grealey*
Grealy, *Grealey*
Greasley, *Gresley*
Greathead
Greatorex, *Greatrex*
Greatrex
Greave
Greaves, *Greave*
Greavison, *Grieve*
Grebe, *Graf*
Greber, *Graber*
Grebert, *Graber*
Grec, *Greco*
Grechi, *Greco*
Greci, *Greco*
Greco
Gredley, *Grealey*
Greef, *Grieve*
Greehy, *Griffin*
Greeley, *Grealey*

Greelish, *Grealey*
Greely, *Grealey*
Green
Greenacre
Greenalf, *Greenhalgh*
Greenaway
Greenbaum, *Green*
Greenberg, *Green*
Greenberger, *Green*
Greenblat, *Green*
Greenblatt, *Green*
Greenbom, *Green*
Greene, *Green*
Greener
Greenfeld, *Green*
Greenfield
Greenglass, *Green*
Greengrass
Greenhalgh
Greenhall, *Greenhalgh*
Greenham
Greenhill
Greenhoiz, *Green*
Greenholtz, *Green*
Greenhorn
Greenhorne, *Greenhorn*
Greenhough
Greenhouse
Greening, *Green*
Greenland
Greenlee, *Grindley*
Greenley, *Grindley*
Greenly, *Grindley*
Greenman, *Green*
Greenmon, *Green*
Greenough, *Greenhough*
Greenslade
Greensmith
Greensmith, *Smith*
Greenspan, *Grünspan*
Greenspon, *Grünspan*
Greenstein, *Green*
Greenstien, *Green*
Greenwald, *Green*
Greenway, *Greenaway*
Greenwell
Greenwood
Greenzweig, *Green*
Greep
Greer, *Grier*
Greerson, *Grier*
Greeson, *Grieve*
Greet
Greeves, *Greave*
Greffuelhe, *Griffoul*
Greffulhe, *Griffoul*
Greg, *Gregory*
Greger, *Gregory*
Gregersen, *Gregory*
Gregg, *Gregory*
Greggersen, *Gregory*
Greggor, *Gregory*
Greggs, *Gregory*
Gregh, *Gregory*
Greghi, *Greco*
Gregi, *Greco*
Grego, *Greco*
Grégoire, *Gregory*
Gregol, *Gregory*
Gregoletti, *Gregory*
Gregoli, *Gregory*
Gregolin, *Gregory*
Gregor, *Gregory*
Gregorace, *Gregory*

Gregoraci, *Gregory*
Gregorczyk, *Gregory*
Gregorek, *Gregory*
Gregoretti, *Gregory*
Gregori, *Gregory*
Gregorin, *Gregory*
Gregorini, *Gregory*
Gregório, *Gregory*
Gregorio, *Gregory*
Gregoriou, *Gregory*
Gregorowicz, *Gregory*
Gregorutti, *Gregory*
Gregory
Grégr, *Gregory*
Gregs, *Gregory*
Gregson, *Gregory*
Greguol, *Gregory*
Greibel, *Gribov*
Greibke, *Gribov*
Greif
Greiff, *Greif*
Greifman, *Greif*
Greifner, *Greif*
Greig, *Gregory*
Greim, *Graham, Grime*
Greimbl, *Grime*
Greimel, *Grime*
Greis, *Grice*
Greise, *Grice*
Greither, *Reuter*
Greitzer
Grelak, *Gregory*
Grêlé, *Grealey*
Grelik, *Gregory*
Grelka, *Gregory*
Grelley, *Grealey*
Grellon, *Grealey*
Grelon, *Grealey*
Grelot, *Grealey*
Grémaud, *Grimaud*
Gren
Grene, *Green*
Grenet, *Granet*
Grenetton, *Granet*
Grenfell, *Greenfield*
Grenkov, *Gregory*
Grennan, *Garnon*
Grenon, *Garnon*
Grenot, *Granet*
Grenow, *Greenaway*
Grenville, *Greenfield*
Gresch, *Gregory*
Greschik, *Gregory*
Greschke, *Gregory*
Gresham
Greslé, *Grealey*
Greslet, *Grealey*
Gresley
Greslon, *Grealey*
Greson, *Grieve*
Gretton
Greut, *Reuter*
Greuter, *Reuter*
Greuzard, *Greuze*
Greuze
Greve, *Graf, Greave*
Greveke, *Graf*
Greves, *Greave*
Gréville, *Greville*
Greville
Greving, *Graf*
Grew
Grewcock, *Grew*
Grewe, *Graf, Grew*
Grewing, *Graf*
Grey, *Gray*
Greyes, *Gregory*
Grgić, *Gregory*
Gribaldi, *Garbutt*
Gribaud, *Grimble*
Gribaudo, *Garbutt*
Gribaut, *Grimble*
Gribbell, *Grimble*
Gribben, *Cribbin*
Gribbin, *Cribbin*
Gribble, *Grimble*
Gribbon, *Cribbin*
Gribov
Griboyedov
Grice
Grichukhin, *Gregory*
Gricks, *Gregory*
Gridin
Gridley, *Grealey*
Gridnev, *Gridin*
Gridnin, *Gridin*
Gridunov, *Gridin*
Griebke, *Gribov*
Griebler, *Gruber*
Griebner, *Gribov*
Griebsch, *Gribov*
Grieco, *Greco*
Grief, *Grieve*
Grieff, *Grieve*
Grieg, *Gregory*
Grieger, *Gregory*
Griem, *Grime*
Griep, *Greif*
Grier
Grierson, *Grier*
Griese, *Grice*
Griete, *Marguerite*
Grieu, *Greco*
Grieux, *Greco*
Grieve
Grieves, *Grieve*
Grieveson, *Grieve*
Griffard, *Griffe*
Griffaud, *Griffe*
Griffaut, *Griffe*
Griffe
Griffey, *Griffin*
Griffin
Griffis, *Griffith*
Griffith
Griffiths, *Griffith*
Griffoen, *Griffin*
Griffon, *Griffe*
Griffoul
Griffy, *Griffin*
Grifoul, *Griffoul*
Grifuel, *Griffoul*
Grigaut, *Gregory*
Grigg, *Gregory*
Griggi, *Grice*
Griggs, *Gregory*
Grignard, *Grignon*
Grignon
Grigoire, *Gregory*
Grigolashvili, *Gregory*
Grigoletti, *Gregory*
Grigoli, *Gregory*
Grigolli, *Gregory*
Grigolon, *Gregory*
Grigor, *Gregory*
Grigore, *Gregory*
Grigorescu, *Gregory*
Grigorey, *Gregory*
Grigori, *Gregory*
Grigorian, *Gregory*
Grigoriev, *Gregory*
Grigoriis, *Gregory*
Grigorio, *Gregory*
Grigorkin, *Gregory*
Grigorov, *Gregory*
Grigorushkin, *Gregory*
Grigoryev, *Gregory*
Grigson, *Gregory*
Grikhanov, *Gregory*
Gril, *Grill*
Grilhot, *Grill*
Grill
Grillard, *Grill*
Grille, *Grill*
Grillet, *Grill*
Grilletti, *Grill*
Grilletto, *Grill*
Grilli, *Grill*
Grillini, *Grill*
Grillo, *Grill*
Grillon, *Grill*
Grillone, *Grill*
Grilloni, *Grill*
Grillot, *Grill*
Grills, *Grill*
Grilo, *Grill*
Grim, *Grimm*
Grimal, *Grimaud*
Grimaldi, *Grimaud*
Grimaldo, *Grimaud*
Grimason, *Grime*
Grimaud
Grimaudi, *Grimaud*
Grimaudo, *Grimaud*
Grimault, *Grimaud*
Grimaux, *Grimaud*
Grimble
Grime
Grimes, *Grime*
Grimley
Grimm
Grimme, *Grimm*
Grimmer
Grimmert, *Grimmer*
Grimod, *Grimaud*
Grimoldi, *Grimaud*
Grimshaw
Grimson, *Grime*
Grimston
Grimstone, *Grimston*
Grimwade, *Grimward*
Grimward
Grimwood, *Grimward*
Grinaugh, *Greenhalgh*
Grinbaum, *Green*
Grinberg, *Green*
Grinblat, *Green*
Grinblatt, *Green*
Grinboim, *Green*
Grinbom, *Green*
Grinder
Grindley
Griner, *Green*
Grinfas, *Green*
Grinfass, *Green*
Grinfeld, *Green*
Grinfield, *Green*
Gringart, *Green*
Gringarten, *Green*
Gringlas, *Green*
Gringlass, *Green*
Gringras, *Green*
Gringrass, *Green*
Grinhaus, *Green*
Grinheim, *Green*
Grinholc, *Green*
Grinhut, *Green*
Grinikhin, *Gregory*
Grinin, *Gregory*
Grinishin, *Gregory*
Grinkraut, *Green*
Grinlay, *Grindley*
Grinley, *Grindley*
Grinman, *Green*
Grinnell, *Greenhill*
Grinnikov, *Gregory*
Grinov, *Gregory*
Grinshpan, *Grünspan*
Grinshpon, *Grünspan*
Grinspan, *Grünspan*
Grinspanholz, *Grünspan*
Grinspon, *Grünspan*
Grinspoon, *Grünspan*
Grinstein, *Green*
Grinszpan, *Grünspan*
Grint, *Grinter*
Grinter
Grintuch, *Green*
Grinvald, *Green*
Grinwald, *Green*
Grinwurcel, *Green*
Grinyakin, *Gregory*
Grinyov, *Gregory*
Grioli, *Gregory*
Gripon, *Griffin*
Grippaldi, *Garbutt*
Grippaudo, *Garbutt*
Grippon, *Griffin*
Gris, *Grice*
Grisard, *Grice*
Grise, *Grice*
Griseau, *Grice*
Grisel, *Grice*
Griselain, *Grice*
Griselin, *Grice*
Griset, *Grice*
Grisez, *Grice*
Grishaev, *Gregory*
Grishagin, *Gregory*
Grishakin, *Gregory*
Grishakov, *Gregory*
Grishanin, *Gregory*
Grishankov, *Gregory*
Grishanov, *Gregory*
Grishechkin, *Gregory*
Grishelyov, *Gregory*
Grishenkov, *Gregory*
Grishin, *Gregory*
Grishinov, *Gregory*
Grishka, *Grushin*
Grishkov, *Gregory*
Grishmanov, *Gregory*
Grishukhin, *Gregory*
Grishukov, *Gregory*
Grishunin, *Gregory*
Grisi, *Grice*
Grisini, *Grice*
Grislain, *Grice*
Grison, *Grice*
Grisoni, *Grice*
Grisonnet, *Grice*
Grisot, *Grice*
Griss, *Grice*
Grissin, *Grice*
Grissom, *Grice*
Grisson, *Grice*

Grist
Gritsaev, *Gregory*
Gritskov, *Gregory*
Gritsunov, *Gregory*
Gritten, *Gretton*
Gritton, *Gretton*
Grivé, *Grivel*
Griveau, *Grivel*
Grivel
Grivelet, *Grivel*
Grivet, *Grivel*
Grivori, *Gregory*
Grivot, *Grivel*
Grix, *Gregory*
Grizard, *Grice*
Grizeau, *Grice*
Grizon, *Grice*
Groarke, *Rourke*
Grob
Grobard, *Gray*
Grobbelaar, *Grobelaer*
Grobe, *Grob*
Grobelaar, *Grobelaer*
Grobelaer
Grober, *Grob*
Groberman, *Grob*
Grobler, *Grobelaer*
Grobman, *Grob*
Grobmann, *Grob*
Groce, *Gross*
Grochocki, *Gorokhov*
Grochowski, *Gorokhov*
Grochulski, *Gorokhov*
Grocock, *Grew*
Grocott, *Grew*
Grodzicki, *Grodzki*
Grodziński, *Grodzki*
Grodzki
Groen, *Green*
Groeneveld, *Greenfield*
Groenveld, *Greenfield*
Groffmann, *Grob*
Grogan
Gröger, *Gregory*
Groggan, *Grogan*
Grohmann, *Gray*
Gröhn, *Green*
Gröhne, *Green*
Groleau, *Grail*
Grolleau, *Grail*
Grollet, *Grail*
Grolms, *Jerome*
Gromann, *Gray*
Gromek, *Gromyko*
Gromeko, *Gromyko*
Grommes, *Jerome*
Groms, *Jerome*
Gromykin, *Gromyko*
Gromyko
Grøn, *Green*
Grönberg, *Green*
Grönblad, *Green*
Grönbladh, *Green*
Gröndahl, *Green*
Grönkvist, *Green*
Grönlund, *Green*
Grono, *Greenaway*
Gronow, *Greenaway*
Grönskog, *Green*
Grönstedt, *Green*
Grönvall, *Green*
Grönwall, *Green*
Groocock, *Grew*
Groogan, *Grogan*
Groom
Groombridge
Groome, *Groom*
Groos, *Gross*
Groot, *Gross*
Grootaers, *Gross*
Groote, *Gross*
Grootmans, *Gross*
Grope, *Grape*
Gröper, *Grape*
Gropius, *Grape*
Gröpper, *Grape*
Gros, *Gross*
Grosbaum, *Gross*
Grosberg, *Gross*
Grosboim, *Gross*
Grose, *Cross*
Grosetti, *Gross*
Grosfeld, *Gross*
Grosgluck, *Gross*
Grosgold, *Gross*
Groshev, *Grosz*
Groskopf, *Gross*
Grosman, *Gross*
Gross
Grossard, *Gross*
Grossbaum, *Gross*
Grossberg, *Gross*
Grosse, *Gross*
Grosser, *Gross*
Grossert, *Gross*
Grosset, *Gross*
Grossfeld, *Gross*
Grossglick, *Gross*
Grossgold, *Gross*
Grosshaus, *Gross*
Grossi, *Gross*
Grossin, *Gross*
Grosskopf, *Gross*
Grossman, *Gross*
Grossmann, *Gross*
Grosso, *Gross*
Grosson, *Gross*
Grossu, *Gross*
Grossvogel, *Gross*
Grosswasser, *Gross*
Grosvenor
Grósz, *Gross*
Grosz
Grote, *Gross*
Groth, *Gross*
Grothe, *Gross*
Grotius, *Gross*
Groucutt, *Grew*
Groussaud, *Gross*
Grousset, *Gross*
Groussin, *Gross*
Grousson, *Gross*
Groussot, *Gross*
Grout
Grove
Grovemann, *Grob*
Grover, *Grove*
Groves, *Grove*
Grow, *Grob*
Growcock, *Grew*
Growcott, *Grew*
Growe, *Grob*
Groy, *Gray*
Grüb, *Gruber*
Grub, *Gruber*
Grubard, *Gray*
Grubb
Grubbe, *Grubb*
Grube, *Gruber*
Grüber, *Gruber*
Gruber
Grubišić, *Grob*
Grübler, *Gruber*
Grübner, *Gruber*
Grubner, *Gruber*
Grudziński
Grudzinsky, *Grudziński*
Gruen, *Green*
Gruenbaum, *Green*
Gruenberg, *Green*
Gruenberger, *Green*
Gruenblat, *Green*
Gruenebaum, *Green*
Gruener, *Green*
Gruenewald, *Green*
Gruenfeld, *Green*
Gruengras, *Green*
Gruenhut, *Green*
Gruenkraut, *Green*
Gruenspan, *Grünspan*
Gruenstein, *Green*
Gruenwald, *Green*
Gruenwurzel, *Green*
Gruet, *Grew*
Grüger, *Gregory*
Gruhn, *Green*
Gruiters, *Grüter*
Grulms, *Jerome*
Grumble, *Grimble*
Grumell, *Grimble*
Grumley, *Gormley*
Grummes, *Jerome*
Grün, *Green*
Grun, *Green*
Grünbaum, *Green*
Grunbaum, *Green*
Grünberg, *Green*
Grunberg, *Green*
Grunberger, *Green*
Grunblat, *Green*
Grünblatt, *Green*
Grunblatt, *Green*
Grundy
Grüne, *Green*
Grunebaum, *Green*
Gruner, *Green*
Grünewald, *Green*
Grunfarb, *Green*
Grünfeld, *Green*
Grunfeld, *Green*
Grunglas, *Green*
Grunhaus, *Green*
Grünheim, *Green*
Grünholtz, *Green*
Grünholz, *Green*
Grunhut, *Green*
Grunkraut, *Green*
Grunseid, *Green*
Grunspan, *Grünspan*
Grünspan
Grünstein, *Green*
Grunstein, *Green*
Grünwald, *Green*
Grunwall, *Green*
Grunwurzel, *Green*
Grunzweig, *Green*
Gruot, *Grew*
Grusche, *Grushin*
Gruschka, *Grushin*
Gruschkewitz, *Grushin*
Grushevski, *Grushin*
Grushevsky, *Grushin*
Grushin
Grushka, *Grushin*
Grushkewitch, *Grushin*
Grushkewitz, *Grushin*
Grushko, *Grushin*
Gruson, *Greuze*
Gruszczak, *Grushin*
Gruszczyński, *Grushin*
Gruszecki, *Grushin*
Gruszka, *Grushin*
Gruszko, *Grushin*
Grut, *Grout*
Grute, *Grout*
Grüter
Grüters, *Grüter*
Grutter, *Grüter*
Gruzinov
Gruzintsev, *Gruzinov*
Gryglewski, *Gregory*
Grygorcewicz, *Gregory*
Grygorwicz, *Gregory*
Grylls, *Grill*
Grynszpan, *Grünspan*
Grzegorczyk, *Gregory*
Grzegorek, *Gregory*
Grzegorzecki, *Gregory*
Grzegorzewicz, *Gregory*
Grzegorzewski, *Gregory*
Grzelak, *Gregory*
Grzelczak, *Gregory*
Grzelczyk, *Gregory*
Grzelewski, *Gregory*
Grześ, *Gregory*
Grzesiak, *Gregory*
Grzesiewicz, *Gregory*
Grześkowski, *Gregory*
Grzeszczak, *Gregory*
Grzeszczyk, *Gregory*
Grzyb, *Gribov*
Grzybek, *Gribov*
Grzybowski, *Gribov*
Grzywacz
Grzywaczewski, *Grzywacz*
Gsänger
Gschaider, *Gscheid*
Gscheid
Gscheider, *Gscheid*
Gschwandtner, *Schwand*
Gsell, *Gesell*
Gsöll, *Gesell*
Guadalupe
Guagliardo, *Gaillard*
Gual
Gualdieri, *Walter*
Gualdiero, *Walter*
Gualter, *Walter*
Gualtieri, *Walter*
Gualtiero, *Walter*
Guanter, *Gaunt*
Guard
Guardi, *Guard*
Guàrdia, *Guard*
Guardia, *Guard*
Guardiola, *Guard*
Guarducci, *Guard*
Guarini, *Waring*
Guariniello, *Waring*
Guarino, *Waring*
Guarinoni, *Waring*
Guarneri, *Warner*
Guarnerio, *Warner*
Guarnier, *Warner*
Guarnieri, *Warner*
Guarniero, *Warner*

Guasch, *Gascoigne*
Gubbin, *Gibbon*
Gubbins, *Gibbon*
Guber, *Huber*
Guberblit, *Huber*
Guberman, *Huber*
Gucci
Guccini, *Gucci*
Guckenheim, *Guggenheim*
Gudd, *Good*
Gudden, *Goddard*
Gude, *Good*
Gudemann, *Goodman*
Gudge, *Gough*
Gudgeon, *Goujon*
Gudger, *Goodyear*
Gudgin, *Goujon*
Gudmundsson, *Goodman*
Gué, *Wade*
Guedes
Güell
Guen, *Gwyn*
Guenec, *Gwyn*
Guennec, *Gwyn*
Guérin, *Waring*
Guerin, *Waring*
Guérineau, *Waring*
Guérinet, *Waring*
Guerini, *Waring*
Guerino, *Waring*
Guérinon, *Waring*
Guérinot, *Waring*
Guerne, *Waring*
Guernier, *Warner*
Guerpillon, *Goupil*
Guerra, *Warr*
Guerrazzi, *Warr*
Guerre, *Warr*
Guerreau, *Warr*
Guerreiro, *Warr*
Guerrero, *Warr*
Guerreru, *Warr*
Guerri, *Warr*
Guerrier, *Warr*
Guerrieri, *Warr*
Guerriero, *Warr*
Guerrin, *Warr*
Guerry, *Warr*
Guest
Guestier, *Waite*
Guet, *Waite*
Guétan, *Waite*
Guettand, *Waite*
Guettier, *Waite*
Guevara
Guey, *Waite*
Guez, *Waite*
Gugenheim, *Guggenheim*
Guggenheim
Guggenheimer, *Guggenheim*
Guglielmelli, *William*
Guglielmetti, *William*
Guglielmi, *William*
Guglielminetti, *William*
Guglielmini, *William*
Guglielmino, *William*
Guglielmo, *William*
Guglielmone, *William*
Guglielmoni, *William*
Guglielmotti, *William*
Guglielmucci, *William*
Guiard, *Wyatt*
Guichard
Guichardet, *Guichard*
Guichardin, *Guichard*
Guichardon, *Guichard*
Guichardot, *Guichard*
Guichet, *Guichard*
Guicheteau, *Guichard*
Guichon, *Guichard*
Guichot, *Guichard*
Guidelli, *Guy*
Guidetti, *Guy*
Guidi, *Guy*
Guidini, *Guy*
Guido, *Guy*
Guidone, *Guy*
Guidoni, *Guy*
Guidotti, *Guy*
Guiducci, *Guy*
Guiduzzi, *Guy*
Guierre, *Warr*
Guiet, *Guy*
Guiglia, *William*
Guignard
Guignardeau, *Guignard*
Guignet, *Guignard*
Guigneux, *Guignard*
Guignier, *Guignard*
Guignon, *Guignard*
Guignot, *Guignard*
Guihan, *Gahan*
Guihard, *Wyatt*
Guijarro
Guilard, *Willard*
Guilbard, *Wilbert*
Guilbert, *Wilbert*
Guilbon, *Wilbert*
Guilbot, *Wilbert*
Guilen, *William*
Guilfoyle, *Gilfoil*
Guilhem, *William*
Guilhen, *William*
Guilherme, *William*
Guilhermino, *William*
Guillain, *Will*
Guillamon
Guillard, *Willard*
Guillaumat, *William*
Guillaume, *William*
Guillaumeau, *William*
Guillaumet, *William*
Guillaumin, *William*
Guillaumot, *William*
Guille, *Will*
Guillelme, *William*
Guillem, *William*
Guillemet, *William*
Guillemin, *William*
Guilleminot, *William*
Guillemot, *William*
Guillén, *William*
Guillerme, *William*
Guillermic, *William*
Guillermo, *William*
Guillermou, *William*
Guillet, *Will*
Guilleton, *Will*
Guillin, *Will*
Guillon, *Will*
Guilloneau, *Will*
Guillot, *Will*
Guilloteau, *Will*
Guillotin, *Will*
Guilloton, *Will*
Guillou, *Will*
Guilloud, *Will*
Guilloux, *Will*
Guilly, *Will*
Guilmet, *William*
Guilmin, *William*
Guilminot, *William*
Guilmot, *William*
Guimar, *Wymer*
Guimarães
Guimard, *Wymer*
Guinan
Guinane, *Guinan*
Guinard, *Guignard*
Guiness, *McGuinness*
Guinnard, *Guignard*
Guinness, *McGuinness*
Guion, *Guy*
Guiot, *Guy*
Guirado, *Garrett*
Guirao, *Garrett*
Guirard, *Garrett*
Guirardin, *Garrett*
Guirau, *Garrett*
Guiraud, *Garrett*
Guiry, *Geary*
Guisado
Guiscard, *Wishart*
Guise
Guitard, *Guitart*
Guitart
Guitel, *Guy*
Guitet, *Guy*
Guiton, *Guy*
Guitonneau, *Guy*
Guittard, *Guitart*
Guitte, *Guy*
Guittet, *Guy*
Guitton, *Guy*
Guiu, *Guy*
Guiver
Gulick, *Gullick*
Gullberg, *Gold*
Gullick
Gullickson, *Gullick*
Gulliford, *Gulliver*
Gulliver
Gullström, *Gold*
Gully
Gullyes, *Gully*
Gulson, *Goldstone*
Gulston, *Goldstone*
Gulyaev
Gumb, *Gomme*
Gumbel
Gumberich, *Gombert*
Gumbert, *Gombert*
Gumbley, *Gumbel*
Gumbrecht, *Gombert*
Gumbrich, *Gombert*
Gumm, *Gomme*
Gumme, *Gomme*
Gummer, *Gomer*
Gummerson, *Gomer*
Gummert, *Gombert*
Gumpert, *Gombert*
Gumpertz, *Gombert*
Gumperz, *Gombert*
Gumprecht, *Gombert*
Gumprich, *Gombert*
Gun, *Gunn*
Gunda, *Konrad*
Gundelach, *Gullick*
Gundersen, *Gunter*
Gundlach, *Gullick*
Gundlack, *Gullick*
Gundloch, *Gullick*
Gundrey, *Grundy*
Gundry, *Grundy*
Gunkel
Gunn
Gunnar, *Gunter*
Gunnarsson, *Gunter*
Gunnell
Gunner
Gunnet, *Gunn*
Gunnett, *Gunn*
Gunning, *Connell*
Gunns, *Gunn*
Gunsberg, *Ginsberg*
Gunsberger, *Ginsberg*
Gunson, *Gunn*
Gunter
Gunther, *Gunter*
Gunton
Güntzel, *Gunter*
Gunz, *Gunter*
Gunzberg, *Ginsberg*
Günzel, *Gunter*
Günzelmann, *Gunter*
Günzl, *Gunter*
Günzlein, *Gunter*
Günzler, *Gunter*
Guppey, *Guppy*
Guppie, *Guppy*
Guppy
Gura, *Górski*
Guralnick, *Gorelik*
Guralnik, *Gorelik*
Gurdon, *Gordon*
Guretzky, *Górski*
Gurevich, *Horowitz*
Gurfinkiel, *Gorfinkel*
Gurg, *George*
Gurgian, *Gruzinov*
Gurko, *George*
Gurling, *Codlin*
Gurnay
Gurney, *Gurnay*
Gurovich, *Horowitz*
Gurrado, *Konrad*
Gurski, *Górski*
Gursky, *Górski*
Gurton
Gurvich, *Horowitz*
Gurvitz, *Horowitz*
Gurys, *George*
Gusakov, *Gusev*
Gusev
Gusman, *Gusev*
Gusmani, *Kuzmin*
Gusmão, *Guzmán*
Gusmin, *Kuzmin*
Gustafsen, *Gustavsson*
Gustafsson, *Gustavsson*
Gustavsson
Gustin, *Austin*
Gustowski, *Austin*
Gut, *Good*
Gutch, *Gough*
Gute
Gutenberg, *Guttenberg*
Gutenberger, *Guttenberg*
Guter, *Good*
Guterman, *Goodman*
Gutermann, *Goodman*
Guterson, *Goodson*
Gutfreund, *Goodfriend*
Guth, *Good*
Guthe, *Good*
Guthrie

Guthrum, *Goodrum*
Gutiérrez
Gutjahr, *Goodyear*
Gutkind, *Goodchild*
Gutman, *Goodman*
Gutmann, *Goodman*
Gutridge, *Gutteridge*
Gutsch, *Gottschalk*
Gutschalk, *Gottschalk*
Gutsche, *Gottschalk*
Gutscher, *Gottschalk*
Gutschke, *Gottschalk*
Gutschler, *Gottschalk*
Gutschmann, *Gottschalk*
Gutschner, *Gottschalk*
Guttenberg
Guttentag, *Gooday*
Gutter, *Good*
Gutteridge
Gutterman, *Goodman*
Guttfreund, *Goodfriend*
Guttman, *Goodman*
Guttmann, *Goodman*
Guttridge, *Gutteridge*
Guwer, *Gower*
Guy
Guyard, *Wyatt*
Guyardeau, *Wyatt*
Guyart, *Wyatt*
Guyat, *Wyatt*
Guyatt, *Wyatt*
Guye, *Guy*
Guyet, *Guy*
Guyler
Guymer
Guyon, *Guy*
Guyonneau, *Guy*
Guyonnet, *Guy*
Guyot, *Guy*
Guys, *Guy*
Guyson, *Guy*
Guyton
Guyver, *Guiver*
Guz, *Guzek*
Guzek
Guzewicz, *Guzek*
Guziak, *Guzek*
Guzicki, *Guzik*
Guzik
Guzman, *Guzmán*
Guzmán
Guzowski, *Guzek*
Guzzetti, *Gucci*
Guzzi, *Gucci*
Guzzini, *Gucci*
Guzzo, *Gucci*
Guzzolini, *Gucci*
Gwatkins, *Watt*
Gwiazda
Gwiazdowski, *Gwiazda*
Gwiliam, *William*
Gwillam, *William*
Gwilliam, *William*
Gwilym, *William*
Gwinn, *Gwyn*
Gwinnett
Gwioneth, *Gwinnett*
Gwizdała, *Gwizdka*
Gwizdka
Gwyn
Gwyneth, *Gwinnett*
Gwynn, *Gwyn*
Gwynne, *Gwyn*
Gwyre, *Geary*
Gyatt, *Wyatt*
Gye, *Guy*
Gyenes, *Dennis*
Gyles, *Giles*
Gyllenhammar, *Gold*
Gyllensten, *Gold*
Gynn, *Ginn, Juniper*
Györffy, *George*
György, *George*
Gypps, *Gibb*
Gypson, *Gibb*
Gyselbrecht, *Gilbert*
Gyselbrechts, *Gilbert*
Gyurkó, *George*
Gyurkovics, *George*
Gzik

H

Haack, *Hake*
Haacker, *Hake*
Haag, *Haig*
Haagen, *Haig*
Haagensen, *Hain*
Haagsma, *Haig*
Haahr, *Haar*
Haak, *Hake*
Haar
Haaren, *Haar*
Haarla
Haart, *Hardt*
Haas, *Hare*
Haase, *Hare*
Habbe, *Habbert*
Habbema, *Habbert*
Habben, *Habbert*
Habberjam, *Habersham*
Habbert
Habbes, *Habbert*
Habbeshaw, *Habersham*
Habbing, *Habbert*
Habbishaw, *Habersham*
Habbrecht, *Habbert*
Habeck, *Hawk*
Habecker, *Hawker*
Habel, *Gall*
Habenicht
Haber
Haberberg, *Haber*
Habercorn, *Haber*
Häberer, *Haber*
Haberer, *Haber*
Haberfeld, *Haber*
Haberfield, *Haber*
Haberkorn, *Haber*
Haberl, *Haber*
Häberle, *Haber*
Häberlein, *Haber*
Haberman, *Haber*
Habermann, *Haber*
Habersham
Habershon, *Habersham*
Habershtoub, *Haber*
Haberstaub, *Haber*
Habert, *Habbert*
Habeshaw, *Habersham*
Häbich, *Hawk*
Habich, *Hawk*
Häbicher, *Hawker*
Habicht, *Hawk*
Habig, *Hawk*
Habishaw, *Habersham*
Hablet, *Habbert*
Hablot, *Abel, Habbert*
Habnit, *Habenicht*
Habs, *Habbert*
Habsburg
Hach, *Hache*
Hache
Hachet, *Hache*
Hachette, *Hache*
Hachin, *Hache*
Hachnek, *Hache*
Hachner, *Hans*
Hachnik, *Hache*
Hachon, *Hache*
Hack
Häcker, *Hacker*
Hacker
Hackett
Hacking
Hackman, *Hackmann*
Hackmann
Hackwood
Hacon
Hadaway, *Hathaway*
Hadcock, *Adam*
Hadden, *Howden*
Haddleton
Haddock
Haddon
Haddow
Haddrell, *Hatherell*
Haddrill, *Hatherell*
Haddy, *Adam*
Hadeke, *Habbert*
Haden
Hader
Haderer, *Hader*
Häderle, *Hader*
Haderlin, *Hader*
Hadermann, *Hader*
Hadewig, *Hathaway*
Hadfield, *Hatfield*
Hadgkiss, *Hodge*
Hädicke, *Heydrich*
Hadkins, *Adam*
Hadlee, *Hadley*
Hadleigh, *Hadley*
Hadley
Hadlow
Hädrich, *Heydrich*
Hadrill, *Hatherell*
Hädscher, *Hathaway*
Haensch, *Hans*
Haerinck, *Herring*
Haesen, *Hans*
Hafer, *Haber*
Haffner, *Hafner*
Häfke, *Hawk*
Häfner, *Hafner*
Hafner
Haft
Haftel, *Haft*
Haftenmacher, *Haft*
Hafter, *Haft*
Haftmann, *Haft*
Hag, *Haig*
Hagan
Hagard, *Haggard*
Hagberg, *Haig*
Häge, *Haig*
Hage, *Haig*
Hagedoorn, *Hawthorn*
Hagedorn, *Hawthorn*
Hageman, *Haig*
Hagemann, *Haig*
Hagen, *Haig, Hain*
Hagenaar, *Haig*
Hågensen, *Hain*
Häger, *Haig*
Hager, *Haig*
Hagerty, *Hegarty*
Hägg
Haggan, *Hagan*
Haggar, *Haggard*
Haggard
Haggart, *Haggard*
Haggarty, *Hegarty*
Haggas, *Haggis*
Häggberg, *Hägg*
Häggblad, *Hägg*
Häggblom, *Hägg*
Hagger, *Haggard*
Haggerty, *Hegarty*
Haggett, *Hackett*
Haggis
Haggish, *Haggis*
Haggitt, *Hackett*
Hägglund, *Hägg*
Häggmark, *Hägg*
Häggqvist, *Hägg*
Häggström, *Hägg*
Hägle, *Haig*
Haglund, *Haig*
Hagman, *Haig*
Hagstedt, *Haig*
Hagstrand, *Haig*
Hagström, *Haig*
Hague
Hahn
Hahncke, *Hans*
Hahnecke, *Hans*
Hahneke, *Hans*
Hahnel, *Hans*
Hahnelt, *Hans*
Hahnemann, *Hans*
Hahner, *Hahn*
Hahnert, *Hahn*
Hahnke, *Hans*
Haid, *Heath*
Haider, *Heath*
Haidler, *Heath*
Haidmann, *Heath*
Haidner, *Heath*
Haiduk, *Hajdú*
Haiem, *Hyam*
Haifetz, *Heifetz*
Haig
Haigh, *Haig*
Haighwood, *Hogwood*
Haigwood, *Hogwood*
Haile, *Hale*
Hailes
Hailey, *Haley*
Haill, *Hale*
Hails, *Hailes*
Hailwood
Haily, *Haley*
Haim, *Hyam*
Haime, *Hammond*
Haimes, *Hammond*
Haimon, *Hammond*
Haimovich, *Hyam*
Hain
Haine, *Hain*
Haines
Haining, *Henning*
Hainning, *Henning*
Hainon, *Hain*
Hainsworth

Haipt, *Head*
Hair, *Hare*
Haire, *Hare*
Hairon, *Heron*
Haiselden, *Hazelden*
Haisell, *Hazel*
Haiss, *Hiess*
Haitlie, *Heatley*
Haizelden, *Hazelden*
Hajdú
Hajduk, *Hajdú*
Hajdukiewicz, *Hajdú*
Hajduković, *Hajdú*
Hájek
Hajný, *Hájek*
Hak, *Hake*
Hakala
Hake, *Hook*
Hake
Haker, *Hacker, Hake*
Hakes, *Hake*
Hakkarainen
Häkkinen
Håkonsen, *Hacon*
Håkonsson, *Hacon*
Hal, *Hall*
Hála, *Gall*
Halary, *Alaric*
Hałas
Halász
Hałaszczyk, *Hałas*
Halbrook, *Holbrook*
Halbrooks, *Holbrook*
Halcón, *Falcon*
Häld, *Halder*
Hald, *Halder*
Haldane
Hälde, *Halder*
Halden, *Haldane*
Halder
Haldermann, *Halder*
Haldin, *Haldane*
Haldner, *Halder*
Hale
Hálek, *Gall*
Haler, *Hayler*
Hales, *Hailes*
Halévi, *Levi*
Halevy, *Levi*
Haley
Halford
Halfpenny
Halicki, *Halicz*
Halicz
Haliday, *Halliday*
Halík, *Gall*
Halket, *Hackett*
Halkett, *Hackett*
Häll
Hall
Halladey, *Halliday*
Hallady, *Halliday*
Hallaghan, *Hallahan*
Hallahan
Hallam
Hallard, *Allard*
Hallary, *Alaric*
Hallas, *Hailes*
Hallaway, *Alloway*
Hallawell, *Halliwell*
Hallberg, *Hall*
Hallding, *Haldane*
Hallé, *Hall*
Halle, *Hall*
Halleday, *Halliday*
Hallén, *Hall*
Haller, *Hall*
Hallet, *Allard, Hall*
Hallett, *Allard*
Hallewell, *Halliwell*
Halley
Hallez, *Hall*
Hällgren, *Häll*
Hallgren, *Hall*
Halliday
Halligan, *Hallahan*
Hallihane, *Hallahan*
Hallin, *Allen*
Hallin, *Hall*
Hallinan
Hallis, *Allis*
Hallison, *Allen*
Hallissey
Halliwell
Hallman, *Hall*
Hallmann, *Hall*
Hallon, *Fallon*
Halloran
Halloway, *Alloway*
Hallowell, *Halliwell*
Hallowes, *Hailes*
Hallows, *Hailes*
Hallqvist, *Hall*
Halls, *Hall*
Hällström, *Häll*
Hallström, *Hall*
Hallsworth, *Hallworth*
Hallu
Hallum, *Hallam*
Hallworth
Hally, *Halley*
Halmann, *Hall*
Halmshaw, *Hampshire*
Halonen
Halpen, *Alpin*
Halpenny, *Alpin*
Halpeny, *Alpin*
Halper, *Alpert, Heilbronn*
Halperin, *Heilbronn*
Halpern, *Heilbronn*
Halpert, *Heilbronn*
Halpin, *Alpin*
Halprin, *Heilbronn*
Hals
Halsall
Halsband, *Hals*
Halse, *Hals*
Halsema, *Hals*
Halsey
Halstead
Halsted, *Halstead*
Halstuch, *Hals*
Halt, *Halder*
Halter, *Halder*
Halton
Haly, *Haley*
Ham
Hamblen, *Hambly*
Hamblet, *Hamlett*
Hamblett, *Hamlett*
Hambley, *Hambly*
Hamblin, *Hambly*
Hambling, *Hambly*
Hambly
Hamblyn, *Hambly*
Hamborch, *Hamburg*
Hamborg, *Hamburg*
Hambro
Hambrook
Hamburg
Hamburger, *Hamburg*
Hamburgh, *Hanbury*
Hambury, *Hanbury*
Hame, *Hammond*
Hamel
Hamelet, *Hamel*
Hamelin, *Hamel*
Hamelly, *Hambly*
Hamelmann, *Hamel*
Hamelot, *Hamel*
Hamer
Hamerschmidt, *Hammer*
Hamersma, *Hammer*
Hames, *Hammond*
Hamill
Hamilton
Hamlet, *Hamlett*
Hamlett
Hamley, *Hambly*
Hamlin, *Hambly*
Hamling, *Hambly*
Hamly, *Hambly*
Hamlyn, *Hambly*
Hamm, *Hammer*
Hammann, *Hoffmann*
Hammar, *Hammer*
Hammarbäck, *Hammer*
Hammarberg, *Hammer*
Hammargren, *Hammer*
Hammarlund, *Hammer*
Hammarskjöld, *Hammer*
Hammarstedt, *Hammer*
Hammarstrand, *Hammer*
Hammarström, *Hammer*
Hamme, *Hammer*
Hammel
Hammer
Hammerich, *Henry*
Hammerl, *Hammer*
Hämmerle, *Hammer*
Hammerman, *Hammer*
Hammermann, *Hammer*
Hammerschlag, *Hammer*
Hammerschmidt, *Hammer*
Hammerstein
Hammerstone, *Hammerstein*
Hammerton
Hammill, *Hamill*
Hammon, *Hammond*
Hammond
Hamnet, *Hammond*
Hamnett, *Hammond*
Hamon, *Hammond*
Hamoneau, *Hammond*
Hamonet, *Hammond*
Hamonic, *Hammond*
Hampden
Hampe
Hampel, *Hampe*
Hampl, *Hampe*
Hamprecht, *Hampe*
Hampshaw, *Hampshire*
Hampshire
Hampson, *Hammond*
Hampton
Hamrén, *Hammer*
Hamrin, *Hammer*
Hamshar, *Hampshire*
Hamshaw, *Hampshire*
Hamsher, *Hampshire*
Hamshere, *Hampshire*
Hamson, *Hammond*
Hán, *Hans*
Hanák, *Hans*
Hanau, *Hanauer*
Hanauer
Hanbury
Hance
Hancell, *Ansell*
Hancock
Hancocks, *Hancock*
Hancox, *Hancock*
Hańczak, *Hans*
Hand
Handasyde, *Handyside*
Handbury, *Hanbury*
Handcock, *Hancock*
Handcocks, *Hancock*
Händel, *Hans*
Handel, *Hans*
Handeles, *Handler*
Handelman, *Handler*
Handelsman, *Handler*
Handford
Handforth, *Handford*
Handl, *Hans*
Handler
Handley
Handlon, *Hanlon*
Handrek, *Andrew*
Handrick, *Andrew*
Handrik, *Andrew*
Handrock, *Andrew*
Handrok, *Andrew*
Hands, *Hand*
Handschiegl, *Handschuh*
Handschu, *Handschuh*
Handschuh
Handsford, *Hansford*
Handy
Handyside
Hánek, *Hans*
Hanel, *Hans*
Hanelt, *Hans*
Hanes, *Haines*
Haneson, *Hanna*
Hanfirth, *Handford*
Hanford, *Handford*
Hanforth, *Handford*
Hänggi, *Hans*
Hanham
Hanich, *Hans*
Hanik, *Hans*
Hanin, *Hanna*
Haning, *Henning*
Haninkes, *Hanna*
Hanis, *Hanna*
Hänisch, *Hans*
Hanke, *Hans*
Hankes, *Hanna*
Hankiewicz, *Hans*
Hankin
Hanking, *Hankin*
Hankins, *Hankin*
Hankinson, *Hankin*
Hanks
Hanlan, *Hanlon*
Hanley, *Handley*
Hanlon
Hanly, *Handley*
Hanmann, *Hans*
Hanmer
Hann
Hanna
Hannaford, *Handford*
Hannah, *Hanna*

Hannan, *Hanna*
Hannay, *Hanna*
Hanne, *Hans*
Hanneen, *Hanna*
Hanneke, *Hans*
Hanneken, *Hans*
Hannema, *Hans*
Hannemann, *Hans*
Hannessen, *Hans*
Hannigan, *Hanna*
Hänniger, *Henry*
Hänninen
Hanning, *Henning*
Hannington
Hannon, *Hanna*
Hannover
Hannusch, *Hans*
Hannuschik, *Hans*
Hanoch, *Enock*
Hanochi, *Enock*
Hanochov, *Enock*
Hanochow, *Enock*
Hanokhov, *Enock*
Hanousek, *Hans*
Hanover, *Hannover*
Hanower, *Hannover*
Hanrahan
Hanratty
Hanry, *Henry*
Hans
Hansard
Hansch, *Hans*
Hanschke, *Hans*
Hanschuch, *Handschuh*
Hanse, *Hans*
Hansel, *Ansell, Hans*
Hänsel
Hänselin, *Hans*
Hansell, *Ansell*
Hansemann, *Hans*
Hansen, *Hans*
Hansford
Hansi, *Hans*
Hansill, *Ansell*
Hansing, *Hans*
Hansl, *Hans*
Hanslick, *Hans*
Hanslik, *Hans*
Hansmann, *Hans*
Hansom, *Hann*
Hanson, *Hann, Hanna*
Hanssen, *Hans*
Hansson, *Hans*
Hantsch, *Hans*
Hantschke, *Hans*
Hantusch, *Andrew*
Hanuš, *Hans*
Hanus, *Hans*
Hanusch, *Hans*
Hanuschik, *Hans*
Hanusz, *Hans*
Hanuszkiewicz, *Hans*
Hanvey
Hanzal, *Hans*
Hanzálek, *Hans*
Hanzel, *Hans*
Hanzl, *Hans*
Hanzlík, *Hans*
Hapke, *Habbert*
Happel, *Habbert*
Happert, *Habbert*
Happs, *Apps*
Haps, *Habbert*
Hapsburg, *Habsburg*
Haquin, *Isaac*
Harald, *Harrod*
Haraldsson, *Harrod*
Haran, *Hanrahan, Herring*
Harand, *Herring*
Harant, *Herring*
Harbage, *Harber*
Harbard, *Herbert*
Harbaud, *Herbaud*
Harbaut, *Herbaud*
Harbaux, *Herbaud*
Harbelot, *Herbert*
Harber
Harberd, *Herbert*
Harberding, *Herbert*
Harberer, *Harber*
Harbers, *Herbert*
Harbert, *Herbert*
Harbertson, *Herbert*
Harbidge, *Harber*
Harbinson, *Herbert*
Harbird, *Herbert*
Harbisher, *Harber*
Harbison, *Herbert*
Harbor, *Harber*
Harbord, *Herbert*
Harborne
Harbot, *Herbaud*
Harbott, *Herbaud*
Harbottle
Harbour, *Harber*
Harbring, *Herbert*
Harbron, *Harborne*
Harbs, *Herbert*
Harbud, *Herbaud*
Harbulot, *Herbert*
Harburtson, *Herbert*
Harbut, *Herbaud*
Harbutt, *Herbaud*
Harck, *Herbert*
Harcourt
Harcus, *Herkes*
Hård, *Hard*
Hard
Hardacre, *Hardaker*
Hardaker
Hardcastle
Hardeman, *Hardiman*
Harden
Hardenberg
Harder, *Hard*
Hardes, *Hards*
Hardess, *Hards*
Hardesty, *Hardisty*
Hardeweg, *Hartwig*
Hardewig, *Hartwig*
Hardey, *Hardy*
Hardi, *Hardy*
Hardie, *Hardy*
Hardiman
Hardin
Harding
Hardion, *Hardy*
Hardisty
Hardman
Hardoin, *Ardouin*
Hardouin, *Ardouin*
Hardres, *Hards*
Hardress, *Hards*
Hards
Hardstaff
Hardt
Härdtle, *Hard*
Hardwick
Hardwicke, *Hardwick*
Hardwig, *Hartwig*
Hardy
Hare
Har-El, *Harel*
Harel
Hareli, *Harel*
Harell, *Harel*
Harely, *Harel*
Harenc, *Herring*
Hareng, *Herring*
Harenger, *Herring*
Harewood, *Harwood*
Harford
Harfst, *Herbst*
Hargent, *Argent*
Hargrave, *Hargreaves*
Hargraves, *Hargreaves*
Hargreave, *Hargreaves*
Hargreaves
Hargreves, *Hargreaves*
Hargrove, *Hargreaves*
Hargroves, *Hargreaves*
Harich, *Herbert*
Harina, *Farine*
Haring, *Herring*
Harington, *Harrington*
Hariot, *Henry*
Harju
Harker
Harkes, *Herkes*
Harkess, *Hard, Herkes*
Harkin, *Hard*
Harkins, *Hard*
Harkiss, *Hard*
Harkness
Harlan, *Harland*
Harland
Härle, *Haar*
Harle
Harley
Harlin, *Harling*
Harling
Harlock, *Horlock*
Harlot, *Arlott*
Harlow
Harm, *Hermann*
Harman, *Hermann*
Harmand, *Hermann*
Harmaning, *Hermann*
Harmant, *Hermann*
Harmar, *Harmer*
Harmel, *Hermelin*
Harmelin, *Hermelin*
Harmen, *Hermann*
Harmer
Harmgardt, *Ermgard*
Harmolin, *Hermelin*
Harmon, *Hermann*
Harms, *Hermann*
Harmsen, *Hermann*
Harmsworth
Harn, *Hearn*
Harnett, *Arnold*
Harney
Harniman, *Hearn*
Harnott, *Arnold*
Haro
Harofé, *Rofé*
Harofe, *Rofé*
Harold, *Harrod*
Harong, *Herring*
Haroughton, *Harrington*
Harp, *Harper*
Har-Paz, *Paz*
Harper
Harpham
Harpin, *Harper*
Harpour, *Harper*
Harpur, *Harper*
Harr, *Herbert*
Harraden, *Harradine*
Harradine
Harral, *Harrod*
Harrald, *Harrod*
Harralt, *Harrod*
Harran, *Heron*
Harrap, *Harrop*
Harraughton, *Harrington*
Harre, *Herbert*
Harrel, *Harrod*
Harrell, *Harrod*
Harrema, *Henry*
Harridine, *Harradine*
Harries, *Harris*
Harriman
Harrington
Harriot, *Herriot*
Harris
Harrismith, *Arrowsmith*
Harrison, *Harris*
Harrod
Harrold, *Harrod*
Harroll, *Harrod*
Harron, *Heron*
Harrop
Harrow
Harrowar, *Harrower*
Harroway, *Harrower*
Harrower
Harrowsmith, *Arrowsmith*
Harrup, *Harrop*
Harry
Harsch
Harschbarger, *Hirschberg*
Harschberger, *Hirschberg*
Harscher, *Harsch*
Harshbarger, *Hirschberg*
Harshberger, *Hirschberg*
Harshkowitch, *Hirsch*
Härst, *Hurst*
Harst, *Harsch*
Harster, *Harsch*
Hart
Hartaud, *Artaud*
Harte, *Hart*
Härtel, *Hard*
Hartell, *Hartill*
Härtelt, *Artaud*
Hartelt, *Artaud*
Hartig, *Hartwig*
Hartigan, *Hart*
Hartill
Hartisch, *Hard*
Hartland
Härtle, *Hard*
Hartle, *Hartill*
Hartley
Hartly, *Hartley*
Hartmann, *Hart*
Hartnell
Hartnett
Hartoch, *Herzog*
Hartog, *Herzog*
Hartogs, *Herzog*
Hartogsohn, *Herzog*
Hartogson, *Herzog*
Hartrick, *Arkwright*

Hartshorn
Hartshorne, *Hartshorn*
Hartung, *Harding*
Hartvig, *Hartwig*
Hartvigsen, *Hartwig*
Hartwell
Härtwig, *Hartwig*
Hartwig
Hartwiger, *Hartwig*
Hartwigsen, *Hartwig*
Hartwright, *Arkwright*
Harty
Hartz, *Hardt*
Hartzer, *Hardt*
Hartzog, *Herzog*
Harván, *Raven*
Harvánek, *Raven*
Harvard
Harvey
Harvie, *Harvey*
Harward, *Harvard*
Harwood
Harz, *Hardt*
Harzbach, *Herz*
Harzer, *Hardt*
Harzfeld, *Herz*
Harzmann, *Hardt*
Harzstark, *Herz*
Haš, *Hašek*
Háša, *Hašek*
Hasard
Hasch, *Hans*
Hasche, *Hans*
Haschke, *Hans*
Hase, *Hare*
Hašek
Hasel, *Hazel*
Haselar, *Hazel*
Haselden, *Hazelden*
Haseldene, *Hazelden*
Haseldine, *Hazelden*
Haseler, *Hazel*
Hasell, *Hazel*
Haseltine, *Hazelden*
Haselton, *Hazelton*
Haselup, *Heslop*
Haselwood, *Hazelwood*
Haskel, *Ashkettle, Ezekiel*
Haskelevic, *Ezekiel*
Haskell, *Ashkettle, Ezekiel*
Haskew, *Askew*
Haskey, *Askew*
Haskilewitz, *Ezekiel*
Haskin, *Ashkettle*
Hasking, *Ashkettle*
Haskings, *Ashkettle*
Haskins, *Ashkettle*
Haslam
Hasleden, *Hazelden*
Haslem, *Haslam*
Haslen, *Haslam*
Hasler, *Hazel*
Haslett, *Hazlett*
Haslewood, *Hazelwood*
Haslin, *Hasling*
Hasling
Haslip, *Heslop*
Haslitt, *Hazlett*
Haslop, *Heslop*
Haslum, *Haslam*
Haslup, *Heslop*
Hason, *Hasson*
Haspineall, *Aspinall*
Hass
Hassall
Hassard, *Hasard*
Hasse, *Hass*
Hassel, *Hazel*
Hasselberg, *Hazel*
Hasselblad, *Hazel*
Hasselgren, *Hazel*
Hassell, *Hassall*
Hasselqvist, *Hazel*
Hassett, *Hasard*
Hasson
Hastain, *Hastings*
Hastie, *Hasty*
Hastin, *Ashkettle*
Hasting, *Hastings*
Hastings
Hastins, *Ashkettle*
Hastleton, *Hazelton*
Hasty
Haswell
Hatch
Hatchard, *Achard*
Hatcher, *Hatch*
Hateley, *Hatley*
Hatfeild, *Hatfield*
Hatfield
Hatful, *Hatfield*
Hatfull, *Hatfield*
Hathaway
Hatherall, *Hatherell*
Hatherell
Hatherill, *Hatherell*
Hatherley
Hathorne, *Hawthorn*
Hathway, *Hathaway*
Hatin, *Hatton*
Hatje, *Habbert*
Hatley
Haton, *Hatton*
Hatot, *Hatton*
Hatry, *Daltry*
Hatt
Hatté, *Hatton*
Hatter, *Hatt*
Hattersley
Hatton
Hattrick, *Arkwright*
Hattwich, *Hartwig*
Hattwig, *Hartwig*
Hatzkel, *Ezekiel*
Hau, *Fage*
Haubt, *Head*
Hauch, *Hugh*
Hauck, *Hugh*
Haucke, *Hugh*
Haueis, *Eisenhauer*
Haueisen, *Eisenhauer*
Hauenschild, *Hauschild*
Hauer
Hauff, *Hale*
Haufschild, *Hauschild*
Haug, *Hugh*
Hauger, *Hugh*
Haugg, *Hugh*
Haugh, *Hale*
Haughey
Haughton
Haulbrook, *Holbrook*
Häupl, *Head*
Haupt, *Head*
Häuptel, *Head*
Hauptman, *Hauptmann*
Hauptmann
Haur, *Fèvre*
Haure, *Fèvre*
Haurillon, *Fèvre*
Haurwitz, *Horowitz*
Hauschild
Hause, *House*
Hauser, *House*
Häusler, *House*
Hausman, *House*
Hausmann, *House*
Hausner, *House*
Hausser, *House*
Haussner, *House*
Haüy
Hauzer, *House*
Hauzman, *House*
Hävecke, *Hawk*
Havekoss, *Havekost*
Havekost
Havel, *Gall*
Havelock
Havemann, *Hoffmann*
Havemeister, *Hofmeister*
Havemester, *Hofmeister*
Havenith, *Habenicht*
Haver, *Haber*
Haversham, *Habersham*
Havet
Havighorst, *Havekost*
Havinga, *Hofer*
Havisham, *Habersham*
Havken, *Khavke*
Havkin, *Khavke*
Havlíček, *Gall*
Havlík, *Gall*
Havlin, *Khavke*
Havon, *Havet*
Havot, *Havet*
Havrán, *Raven*
Havránek, *Gawroński*
Havránek, *Raven*
Haw
Haward, *Hayward, Howard*
Hawdon
Hawe, *Haw*
Häwecker, *Hawker*
Hawes
Häwicke, *Hawk*
Hawk
Hawke, *Hawk*
Hawken, *Hawkin*
Hawker
Hawkes, *Hawk*
Hawkesford
Hawkeswood
Hawkett, *Hawk*
Hawkin
Hawking
Hawkinge
Hawkings, *Hawkin*
Hawkins, *Hawkin*
Hawkitt, *Hawk*
Hawkley
Hawkshaw
Hawksworth
Hawkyns, *Hawkin*
Hawley
Haworth
Hawrane, *Hanrahan*
Hawson, *Haw*
Hawtayne, *Hawtin*
Hawthorn
Hawthorne, *Hawthorn*
Hawtin
Hawtry, *Daltry*
Hawyes, *Hawes*
Hay
Hayat, *Chait*
Haycock
Hayday
Hayden
Haydin, *Hayden*
Haydn, *Heiden*
Haydon, *Hayden*
Haydorn, *Hawthorn*
Haydu, *Hajdú*
Hayduk, *Hajdú*
Haye, *Hay*
Hayem, *Hyam*
Hayer, *Ayer*
Hayes
Hayesman, *Hayes*
Hayet, *Hay*
Hayfield
Hayhoe
Hayhow, *Hayhoe*
Hayhurst
Hayim, *Hyam*
Hayler
Hayles, *Hailes*
Haylet, *Hay*
Haylett, *Hay*
Hayley, *Haley*
Hayling
Hayller, *Hayler*
Haylock, *Hale*
Haylor, *Hayler*
Haym, *Hammond, Hyam*
Hayman
Haymes, *Hammond*
Hayn, *Hain*
Hayne, *Hain*
Haynes, *Haines*
Hayns, *Haines*
Hayon, *Hay*
Hayot, *Hay*
Hays, *Hayes*
Hayselden, *Hazelden*
Hayter, *Height*
Hayton
Haytor, *Height*
Hayward
Haywood
Hayzelden, *Hazelden*
Hayzeldene, *Hazelden*
Hazan, *Chazan*
Hazard, *Hasard*
Hazart, *Hasard*
Hazel
Hazeldeane, *Hazelden*
Hazelden
Hazeldene, *Hazelden*
Hazeldine, *Hazelden*
Hazeldon, *Hazelden*
Hazelgrave
Hazell, *Hazel*
Hazeltine, *Hazelden*
Hazelton
Hazelwood
Hazkel, *Ezekiel*
Hazkelevitch, *Ezekiel*
Hazkelevitz, *Ezekiel*
Hazledine, *Hazelden*
Hazlett
Hazlewood, *Hazelwood*
Hazlitt, *Hazlett*
Hazzan, *Chazan*
Hazzard, *Hasard*
Hazzeldine, *Hazelden*

Hazzledine, *Hazelden*
Hazzlewood, *Hazelwood*
Heacock, *Haycock*
Head
Headford
Headley
Heads, *Head*
Heafield, *Highfield*
Heague, *McCaig*
Heal, *Hale*
Heald
Heale, *Hale*
Heales, *Hailes*
Healey
Heals, *Hailes*
Healy, *Healey*
Heam, *Eame*
Heams, *Eame*
Heaney
Heany, *Heaney*
Heap
Heape, *Heap*
Heaps, *Heap*
Heard
Hearder, *Heard*
Heardman, *Heard*
Hearl, *Earl*
Hearle, *Earl*
Hearmon, *Hermann*
Hearn
Hearne, *Hearn*
Hearst, *Hurst*
Heart, *Hart*
Hearty, *Harty*
Heaseman, *Hayes*
Heasey, *Easy*
Heasler, *Hazel*
Heaslett, *Hazlett*
Heaslewood, *Hazelwood*
Heaslip, *Heslop*
Heasman, *Hayes*
Heasy, *Easy*
Heath
Heathcoat, *Heathcote*
Heathcote
Heathcott, *Heathcote*
Heather, *Heath*
Heatherington, *Hetherington*
Heathfield
Heathman, *Heath*
Heatley
Heatlie, *Heatley*
Heaton
Heavan, *Evan*
Heavans, *Evan*
Heaven, *Evan*
Heavens, *Evan*
Heazel, *Hazel*
Heazell, *Hazel*
Hebard, *Herbert*
Hebb, *Herbert*
Hebbard, *Herbert*
Hebbert, *Herbert*
Hebblethwaite
Hebblewaite, *Hebblethwaite*
Hebblewhite, *Hebblethwaite*
Hebborn, *Hepburn*
Hebbourne, *Hepburn*
Hebburn, *Hepburn*
Hebden
Hebdon, *Hebden*
Hebecker, *Hawker*
Hebentheier, *Venture*
Heberl, *Haber*
Heberle, *Haber*
Heberlein, *Haber*
Hébert, *Herbert*
Hébertet, *Herbert*
Hébertot, *Herbert*
Hebich, *Hawk*
Hebson, *Herbert*
Hec, *Hedge*
Hecht
Hechtkopf, *Hecht*
Hechtl, *Hecht*
Heck, *Hedge*
Hecker, *Hacker, Hedge*
Heckerle, *Hacker*
Heckerlein, *Hacker*
Heckingbottom, *Higginbottom*
Heckmann, *Hedge*
Heckner, *Hake*
Hecq, *Hedge*
Hector
Hed, *Heath*
Hedberg, *Heath*
Hedderich, *Hetterich*
Hede, *Heath*
Hedecke, *Heydrich*
Hedegaard, *Hedegård*
Hedegård
Hedemann, *Heath*
Hedén, *Heath*
Hedenberg, *Heath*
Hedenström, *Heath*
Hederich, *Hetterich*
Hedewig, *Hathaway*
Hedge
Hedgecock, *Hick*
Hedgecote, *Hick*
Hedgeman, *Hedge*
Hedger, *Hedge*
Hedges, *Hedge*
Hedh, *Heath*
Hedian, *Hayden*
Hedin, *Heath*
Hedley, *Headley*
Hedlund, *Heath*
Hedman, *Heath*
Hedqvist, *Heath*
Hedström, *Heath*
Hedwig, *Hathaway*
Hee, *Heath*
Heed, *Head, Heath*
Heede, *Heath*
Heeder, *Heath*
Heegaard, *Hedegård*
Heegan, *Higgins*
Heegård, *Hedegård*
Heekt, *Hecht*
Heelan, *Whelan*
Heeley, *Healey*
Heelis, *Ellis*
Heely, *Healey*
Heeney, *Heaney*
Heer, *Herr*
Heere, *Herr*
Heeren, *Herr*
Heeschen, *Hathaway*
Heese, *Hayes*
Heesemann, *Hayes*
Heester, *Heister*
Hefets, *Heifetz*
Hefetz, *Heifetz*
Heffer
Hefferan, *Heffernan*
Hefferman, *Heffer*
Heffernan
Heffernon, *Heffernan*
Heffner, *Hafner*
Hefner, *Hafner*
Hegan, *Higgins*
Hegarty
Hegedüs
Hegel, *Haig, Hugh*
Hegele, *Haig*
Hegemann, *Haig*
Hegerty, *Hegarty*
Heggemann, *Haig*
Heginbotham, *Higginbottom*
Heginbottom, *Higginbottom*
Hegner, *Hedge*
Hehir, *Hare*
Hehl
Hehle, *Hehl*
Hehler, *Hehl*
Hehlke, *Hehl*
Hehnke, *Henry*
Heichman, *Hoch*
Heid, *Heath*
Heide, *Heath*
Heidecke, *Heydrich*
Heidecker, *Heidegger*
Heidegger
Heidel, *Heydrich*
Heidema, *Heath*
Heidemann, *Heath*
Heiden
Heidenreich, *Heydrich*
Heidenrich, *Heydrich*
Heider, *Heath*
Heidorn, *Hawthorn*
Heidreich, *Heydrich*
Heidrich, *Heydrich*
Heidt, *Heath*
Heifetz
Heigho, *Hayhoe*
Height
Heigl, *Hugh*
Heij, *Heath*
Heijden, *Heiden*
Heijer, *Heath*
Heijman, *Heath*
Heijne, *Henry*
Heijnen, *Henry*
Heikkilä
Heikkinen, *Henry*
Heilborn, *Heilbronn*
Heilbron, *Heilbronn*
Heilbronn
Heilbronner, *Heilbronn*
Heilbrun, *Heilbronn*
Heilbruner, *Heilbronn*
Heilbrunn, *Heilbronn*
Heilpern, *Heilbronn*
Heilprun, *Heilbronn*
Heilsen, *Hehl*
Heim, *Hammond, Hyam*
Heimann, *Henry*
Heimberger, *Heimbürge*
Heimbürge
Heimbürger, *Heimbürge*
Heimburger, *Heimbürge*
Hein, *Henry*
Heindl, *Henry*
Heindle, *Henry*
Heindrich, *Henry*
Heindrick, *Henry*
Heine, *Henry*
Heinecke, *Henry*
Heineke, *Henry*
Heineken, *Henry*
Heineking, *Henry*
Heinel, *Henry*
Heineman, *Henry*
Heinemann, *Henry*
Heinen, *Henry*
Heiner, *Henry*
Heinert, *Henry*
Heinicke, *Henry*
Heinig, *Henry*
Heining, *Henry*
Heinisch, *Henry*
Heinke, *Henry*
Heinl, *Henry*
Heinle, *Henry*
Heinlein, *Henry*
Heino, *Henry*
Heinonen, *Henry*
Heinreich, *Henry*
Heinrich, *Henry*
Heinrici, *Henry*
Heinritz, *Henry*
Heinritze, *Henry*
Heins, *Henry*
Heinsch, *Henry*
Heinschke, *Henry*
Heinsen, *Henry*
Heinsius, *Henry*
Heinssen, *Henry*
Heintsch, *Henry*
Heintze, *Henry*
Heintzsch, *Henry*
Heinz, *Henry*
Heinze, *Henry*
Heinzel, *Henry*
Heinzler, *Henry*
Heiptmann, *Hauptmann*
Heireth, *Harrod*
Heirold, *Harrod*
Heisel, *Hiess*
Heiser, *House*
Heisler, *House*
Heiss, *Hiess*
Heisser, *House*
Heissner, *House*
Heister
Heitz, *Henry*
Hejda, *Hajdú*
Hejduk, *Hajdú*
Hejfec, *Heifetz*
Hejna, *Hájek*
Hejný, *Hájek*
Hejtmánek, *Hetman*
Heker, *Hacker*
Hekman, *Hedge*
Held
Heldenberg, *Held*
Heldman, *Held*
Heldmann, *Held*
Heldstein, *Held*
Heldt, *Held*
Hele, *Hale*
Helen, *Ellen*
Heler, *Heller*
Helerman, *Heller*
Helfand, *Oliphant*
Helfant, *Oliphant*
Helian, *Ellis*
Hélie, *Ellis*
Hélier, *Hilary*
Héliet, *Ellis*
Hélin, *Ellis*
Héliot, *Ellis*
Helis, *Ellis*
Hell, *Hill*

Hellcat, *Ellis*
Helle, *Heller*
Hellen, *Ellen*
Hellens, *Ellen*
Heller
Hellerman, *Heller*
Hellerstein, *Heller*
Helliar, *Hellier*
Hellier
Hellin, *Ellen*
Hellings
Hellis, *Ellis*
Helliwell, *Halliwell*
Hellman, *Heller*
Hellmund, *Helmund*
Hellmundt, *Helmund*
Hellyer, *Hellier*
Helm
Helman, *Heller*
Helmchen, *Helm*
Helmcke, *Helm*
Helme, *Helm*
Helmecke, *Helm*
Helmel, *Helm*
Helmholt, *Helmold*
Helmholtz, *Helmold*
Helmholz, *Helmold*
Helmker, *Helm*
Helmle, *Helm*
Helmold
Helmolt, *Helmold*
Helmont, *Helmund*
Helms, *Helm*
Helmsen, *Helm*
Helmsley, *Hemsley*
Helmund
Helper, *Heilbronn*
Helpern, *Heilbronn*
Helprin, *Heilbronn*
Helps
Helsby
Helyer, *Hellier*
Helyn, *Hayling*
Hembrey, *Amery*
Hembry, *Amery*
Heme, *Eame*
Hemelaar, *Himmel*
Hémeret, *Henry*
Hemerijk, *Henry*
Hemery, *Amery*
Hemes, *Eame*
Hemesley, *Hemsley*
Hemingway
Hemmann, *Hans*
Hemmett, *Emmett*
Hemming
Hemminga, *Hemming*
Hemmings, *Hemming*
Hemmingsen, *Hemming*
Hemmingsson, *Hemming*
Hemmingway, *Hemingway*
Hémon, *Hammond*
Hémond, *Hammond*
Hémonnot, *Hammond*
Hémonot, *Hammond*
Hempe, *Hampe*
Hempel, *Hampe*
Hemphill
Hempill, *Hemphill*
Hempl, *Hampe*
Hemprecht, *Hampe*
Hemprich, *Hampe*
Hems
Hemsley
Hemson, *Emmett*
Hemstock
Hemsworth
Hemus
Henchcliff, *Hinchcliffe*
Henchcliffe, *Hinchcliffe*
Henchey, *Hennessy*
Henchy, *Hennessy*
Hencke, *Henry*
Henday, *Hendy*
Hendel, *Handler*
Hendel, *Hans*
Hendelman, *Handler*
Henderson
Hendeschuh, *Handschuh*
Hendey, *Hendy*
Hendisson, *Hendy*
Hendl, *Hans*
Hendlerski, *Handler*
Hendlersky, *Handler*
Hendra
Hendrey, *Henry*
Hendrich, *Henry*
Hendrichs, *Henry*
Hendrick, *Henry*
Hendricks, *Henry*
Hendrickx, *Henry*
Hendrie, *Henry*
Hendrik, *Henry*
Hendriks, *Henry*
Hendrikse, *Henry*
Hendriksen, *Henry*
Hendrix, *Henry*
Hendry, *Henry*
Hendy
Henegan, *Heneghan*
Heneghan
Heneries, *Henry*
Henesey, *Hennessy*
Henessey, *Hennessy*
Henessy, *Hennessy*
Henesy, *Hennessy*
Heney, *Heaney*
Henggi, *Hans*
Hengst
Hengstmann, *Hengst*
Hénin
Henke, *Henry*
Henken, *Henry*
Henkens, *Henry*
Henker, *Henry*
Henkin, *Henn*
Henkmann, *Henry*
Henle, *Hans*
Henley
Henly, *Henley*
Henn
Henne, *Hans*
Hennecke, *Hans*
Henneke, *Hans*
Hennemann, *Henry*
Henner, *Henry*
Hennesey, *Hennessy*
Hennessen, *Hans*
Hennessey, *Hennessy*
Hennessy
Hennesy, *Hennessy*
Henniger, *Henry*
Hennin, *Hénin*
Henning
Hennion, *Onion*
Hénon, *Hain*
Henrey, *Henry*
Henri, *Henry*
Henric, *Henry*
Henrichs, *Henry*
Henrichsen, *Henry*
Henricsson, *Henry*
Henries, *Henry*
Henriet, *Henry*
Henriksen, *Henry*
Henriksson, *Henry*
Henrion, *Henry*
Henriot, *Henry*
Henrique, *Henry*
Henriques, *Henry*
Henriquet, *Henry*
Henrot, *Henry*
Henry
Henrych, *Henry*
Henryson, *Henry*
Hens, *Henry*
Henschler, *Hans*
Hensel, *Hans*
Hensemann, *Hans*
Hensen, *Hans*
Hensgen, *Hans*
Henshall, *Henshaw*
Henshaw
Henshell, *Henshaw*
Hensher, *Henshaw*
Hensing, *Hans*
Hensman, *Hengst*
Hensmann, *Hans*
Hensmans, *Henry*
Hensolt, *Hans*
Henson, *Henn*
Henssen, *Hans*
Henton
Henty
Hentze, *Henry*
Hentzeler, *Henry*
Hentzer, *Henry*
Hentzler, *Henry*
Henwood
Henze, *Henry*
Henzer, *Henry*
Hepburn
Hepden, *Hebden*
Hepner, *Höpfner*
Heppell, *Hepple*
Heppenstall, *Heptinstall*
Heppl, *Head*
Hepple
Hepplewhite, *Hebblethwaite*
Heppner, *Höpfner*
Heptinstall
Heptner, *Höpfner*
Hepton, *Hebden*
Heptonstall, *Heptinstall*
Hepworth
Hequet, *Hedge*
Heraghty
Heral, *Harrod*
Herald, *Harrod*
Heran, *Heron*
Heras
Héraud, *Harrod*
Héraudet, *Harrod*
Herauld, *Harrod*
Hérault, *Harrod*
Herbage, *Harber*
Herbaud
Herbault, *Herbaud*
Herbaut, *Herbaud*
Herbaux, *Herbaud*
Herbelet, *Herbert*
Herbelin, *Herbert*
Herbelot, *Herbert*
Herberg, *Harber*
Herberger, *Harber*
Herbert
Herbertson, *Herbert*
Herbertz, *Herbert*
Herbet, *Herbert*
Herbin, *Herbert*
Herbinson, *Herbert*
Herbison, *Herbert*
Herbit, *Herbert*
Herbold, *Herbaud*
Herbot, *Herbert*
Herbrecht, *Herbert*
Herbreteau, *Herbert*
Herbrich, *Harber*
Herbricht, *Herbert*
Herbrig, *Harber*
Herbst
Herbstman, *Herbst*
Herc, *Herz*
Herceg, *Herzog*
Hercegh, *Herzog*
Hercenberg, *Herz*
Herche, *George*
Herck, *Herbert*
Hercock, *Herbert*
Hercog, *Herzog*
Hercus, *Herkes*
Hercwolf, *Herz*
Herczeg, *Herzog*
Herczegh, *Herzog*
Herd, *Heard*
Herder, *Heard*
Herdman, *Heard*
Herdwick, *Hardwick*
Heredero
Heredia
Herenzon, *Herr*
Heretage, *Heritage*
Hereward, *Harvard*
Herfahrt
Herfart, *Herfahrt*
Herfert, *Herfahrt*
Herforth, *Herfahrt*
Herfst, *Herbst*
Herfurth, *Herfahrt*
Herget, *Herrgott*
Hergot, *Herrgott*
Hergt, *Herrgott*
Herholdt, *Harrod*
Herholz, *Harrod*
Heribertz, *Herbert*
Hérichon, *Hérisson*
Hering, *Herring*
Heriot, *Herriot*
Hérisson
Heritage
Herkes
Herkheimer, *Herkommer*
Herkimer, *Herkommer*
Herkommer
Herl, *Hermann*
Herle, *Hermann*
Herlein, *Hermann*
Herlet, *Harrod*
Herley, *Herlihy*
Herlihy
Herling, *Hermann*
Herlt, *Harrod*
Herm, *Hermann*
Heřman, *Hermann*
Herman, *Hermann*
Heřmánek, *Hermann*

Hermann
Hermanoff, *Hermann*
Hermanowicz, *Hermann*
Hermanowski, *Hermann*
Hermans, *Hermann*
Hermansen, *Hermann*
Hermansson, *Hermann*
Hermansz, *Hermann*
Hermanszoon, *Hermann*
Hermecke, *Hermann*
Hermel, *Hermann, Hermelin*
Hermele, *Hermelin*
Hermelin
Hermer, *Harmer*
Hermes, *Hermann*
Hermès
Hermichen, *Hermann*
Hermida
Hermier, *Hermès*
Hermitage, *Armitage*
Hermite
Hermitte, *Hermite*
Hermke, *Hermann*
Hermle, *Hermann*
Hermon, *Hermann*
Hermoso
Herms, *Hermann*
Hermsen, *Hermann*
Hern, *Hearn*
Hernáez, *Ferdinand*
Hernáiz, *Ferdinand*
Hernaman, *Hearn*
Hernán, *Ferdinand*
Hernández, *Ferdinand*
Hernando, *Ferdinand*
Hernanz, *Ferdinand*
Herne, *Hearn*
Herniman, *Hearn*
Herod, *Herrod*
Herold, *Harrod*
Héron, *Heron*
Heron
Herpeux, *Harper*
Herpin, *Harper*
Herpoldt, *Herbaud*
Herr
Herráez, *Farrant*
Herráiz, *Farrant*
Herrald, *Harrod*
Herrán, *Farrant*
Herran, *Heron*
Herranz, *Farrant*
Herre, *Herr*
Herrema, *Henry*
Herrenson, *Herr*
Herrenzon, *Herr*
Herrera, *Ferrers*
Herrero, *Farrar*
Herreros, *Farrar*
Herrfart, *Herfahrt*
Herrfert, *Herfahrt*
Herrforth, *Herfahrt*
Herrfurth, *Herfahrt*
Herrgen, *Herr*
Herrgott
Herrick
Herring
Herrington
Herriot
Herrl, *Hermann*
Herrle, *Hermann*
Herrlein, *Herr*
Herrlen, *Herr*
Herrler, *Hermann*
Herrling, *Hermann*
Herrmann, *Hermann*
Herrod
Herrold, *Harrod*
Herron, *Heron*
Herroun, *Heron*
Hersch, *Hermann, Hirsch*
Herschbaum, *Hirsch*
Herschbein, *Hirsch*
Herschberg, *Hirschberg*
Herschel, *Hermann*
Herschel, *Hirsch*
Herschfeld, *Hirsch*
Herschko, *Hirsch*
Herschkorn, *Hirsch*
Herschkovic, *Hirsch*
Herschkovici, *Hirsch*
Herschkowitz, *Hirsch*
Herschman, *Hirsch*
Herschmann, *Hermann, Hirsch*
Herschowitz, *Hirsch*
Herscovici, *Hirsch*
Herscovics, *Hirsch*
Herscovitch, *Hirsch*
Herscovitz, *Hirsch*
Herscowicz, *Hirsch*
Herscowitz, *Hirsch*
Herse, *Hirsemann*
Hersenson, *Hirsch*
Hersh, *Hirsch*
Hershbein, *Hirsch*
Hershberg, *Hirschberg*
Hershcopf, *Hirsch*
Hershcovitz, *Hirsch*
Hershel, *Hirsch*
Hershenbaum, *Hirsch*
Hershenhaus, *Hirsch*
Hershenhorn, *Hirsch*
Hershenov, *Hirsch*
Hershenson, *Hirsch*
Hershenstrauss, *Hirsch*
Hershfang, *Hirsch*
Hershfeld, *Hirsch*
Hershfinger, *Hirsch*
Hershfinkel, *Hirsch*
Hershinson, *Hirsch*
Hershko, *Hirsch*
Hershkoff, *Hirsch*
Hershkopf, *Hirsch*
Hershkovich, *Hirsch*
Hershkovits, *Hirsch*
Hershkovitz, *Hirsch*
Hershkowitz, *Hirsch*
Hershman, *Hirsch*
Hershorn, *Hirsch*
Herskovits, *Hirsch*
Hersovich, *Hirsch*
Herst, *Hurst*
Herszenbaum, *Hirsch*
Herszenhaut, *Hirsch*
Hertel, *Hard*
Herter, *Heard*
Hertlein, *Hard*
Hertog, *Herzog*
Hertoghe, *Herzog*
Hertogs, *Herzog*
Hertwig, *Hartwig*
Hertz, *Herz*
Hertzberg, *Herz*
Hertzburg, *Herz*
Hertzel, *Herz*
Hertzenberg, *Herz*
Hertzhaft, *Herzhaft*
Hertzheim, *Herz*
Hertzig, *Herzig*
Hertziger, *Herzig*
Hertzlich, *Herzlich*
Hertzmann, *Herz*
Hertzog, *Herzog*
Hervás, *Jarvis*
Hervé, *Harvey*
Herve, *Harvey*
Hervet, *Harvey*
Hervey, *Harvey*
Hervié, *Harvey*
Hervieux, *Harvey*
Hervo, *Harvey*
Hervochon, *Harvey*
Hervouet, *Harvey*
Herz
Herzbaum, *Herz*
Herzberg, *Herz*
Herzberger, *Herz*
Herzel, *Herz*
Herzen, *Herz*
Herzenberg, *Herz*
Herzenstein, *Herz*
Herzer, *Herz*
Herzfeld, *Herz*
Herzhaft
Herzig, *Herzog*
Herzig
Herziger, *Herzig*
Herzl, *Herz*
Herzlich
Herzman, *Herz*
Herzmann, *Herz*
Herzog
Herzstein, *Herz*
Herzweig, *Herz*
Heschold, *Hermann*
Heselden, *Hazelden*
Heseldin, *Hazelden*
Heseltine, *Hazelden*
Heselton, *Hazelton*
Heselwood, *Hazelwood*
Heskel, *Ezekiel*
Hesketh
Heskett, *Hesketh*
Heskitt, *Hesketh*
Heslam, *Haslam*
Hesleden, *Hazelden*
Hesleham, *Haslam*
Heslep, *Heslop*
Heslewood, *Hazelwood*
Heslin, *Hasling*
Hesling, *Hasling*
Heslip, *Heslop*
Heslop
Hesp, *Apps*
Hespe, *Apps*
Hess
Hesse, *Hess*
Hessel, *Hazel, Hermann*
Hesselberg, *Hazel*
Hesselblad, *Hazel*
Hesselden, *Hazelden*
Hesselgren, *Hazel*
Hessels, *Hazel*
Hesseltine, *Hazelden*
Hesselwood, *Hazelwood*
Hession
Hessling, *Hasling*
Hester, *Heister*
Hesterman, *Heister*
Hetherington
Hetman
Hêtre, *Heister*
Hêtreau, *Heister*
Hétroy, *Heister*
Hetschold, *Hermann*
Hetterich
Hettmann, *Hauptmann*
Hetzel, *Hermann*
Hetzold, *Hermann*
Heubt, *Head*
Heucheux, *Huchet*
Heuer, *Hauer*
Heugel, *Hugh*
Heugh
Heugle, *Hugh*
Heupl, *Head*
Heuptmann, *Hauptmann*
Heurtebise
Heuse
Heuser, *House*
Heuvel, *Hill*
Heuvelman, *Hill*
Heuzé, *Heuse*
Heuze, *Heuse*
Heuzey, *Heuse*
Hevesi, *Hevesy*
Hevesy
Hew, *Hugh*
Hewar, *Hauer*
Heward, *Howard*
Hewart, *Howard*
Hewartson, *Howard*
Hewat, *Hewitt*
Hewe, *Hugh*
Hewer, *Hauer*
Hewertson, *Howard*
Hewes, *Hugh*
Hewet, *Hewitt*
Hewetson, *Hewitt*
Hewett, *Hewitt*
Hewin, *Ewan*
Hewins, *Ewan*
Hewison, *Hewitt*
Hewit, *Hewitt*
Hewitson, *Hewitt*
Hewitt
Hewkin, *Hugh*
Hewlett
Hewlings, *Hugh*
Hewlins, *Hugh*
Hewlitt, *Hewlett*
Hews, *Hugh*
Hewson, *Hugh, McKay*
Hey, *Hay, Heath*
Heycock, *Haycock*
Heyd, *Heath*
Heyde, *Heath*
Heydemann, *Heath*
Heyden, *Heiden*
Heydenrych, *Heydrich*
Heydicke, *Heydrich*
Heydon, *Hayden*
Heydorn, *Hawthorn*
Heydrich
Heye, *Hay*
Heyem, *Hyam*
Heyer, *Ayer, Heath*
Heyes, *Hayes*
Heyhoe, *Hayhoe*
Heyim, *Hyam*
Heym, *Hammond, Hyam*
Heyman, *Hayman, Heath*
Heymann, *Henry*
Heyn, *Henry*
Heyne, *Henry*
Heynel, *Henry*

Heynen, *Henry*
Heynes, *Haines, Hynes*
Heynl, *Henry*
Heyns, *Henry*
Heyo, *Hayhoe*
Heys, *Hayes*
Heyseler, *House*
Heyward, *Hayward*
Heywood
Heyworth
Hezlet, *Hazlett*
Hezlett, *Hazlett*
Hibbard, *Hibbert*
Hibbe, *Hibbert*
Hibben, *Hibbert*
Hibberd, *Hibbert*
Hibbert
Hibbing, *Hibbert*
Hibbs
Hibler, *Hill*
Hibsh, *Hübsch*
Hibsher, *Hübsch*
Hibshman, *Hübsch*
Hibshmann, *Hübsch*
Hichens, *Hick*
Hichisson, *Hick*
Hick
Hicken, *Hick*
Hickenbotham, *Higginbottom*
Hickes, *Hick*
Hickeson, *Hick*
Hickey
Hickie, *Hickey*
Hickin, *Hick*
Hickinbottom, *Higginbottom*
Hicking, *Hick*
Hicklin, *Hick*
Hickling
Hickman, *Hick*
Hickmott
Hickock, *Hick*
Hickox, *Haycock*
Hicks, *Hick*
Hickson, *Hick*
Hicky, *Hickey*
Hidalgo
Hidde, *Hibbert*
Hiddleston, *Huddleston*
Hiddlestone, *Huddleston*
Hide, *Hyde*
Hidler, *Hüttler, Hiedler*
Hie, *High*
Hiebel, *Hill*
Hiebl, *Hill*
Hiebler, *Hill*
Hiedl, *Hiedler*
Hiedle, *Heydrich*
Hiedler
Hiegel, *Hill*
Hield, *Heald*
Hields, *Heald*
Hiemer, *Huber*
Hien, *Hühne*
Hierl, *Hermann*
Hiermann, *Hermann*
Hieronimus, *Jerome*
Hieronymus, *Jerome*
Hierro, *Ferro*
Hiersemann, *Hirsemann*
Hies, *Hiess*
Hiesel, *Hiess*
Hiesler, *Hiess*
Hiess
Hifferan, *Heffernan*
Hiffernan, *Heffernan*
Higenbotham, *Higginbottom*
Higenbottam, *Higginbottom*
Higerty, *Hegarty*
Higgenbottom, *Higginbottom*
Higgens, *Higgins*
Higgett, *Hick*
Higginbotham, *Higginbottom*
Higginbottam, *Higginbottom*
Higginbottom
Higgins
Higginson, *Higgins*
Higgitt, *Hick*
Higgon, *Hick*
Higgs, *Hick*
High
Higham
Highe, *High*
Highet
Highfield
Highland, *Hyland*
Highman, *High*
Higho, *Hayhoe*
Hight, *Height*
Highton
Higinbothom, *Higginbottom*
Higman, *Hick*
Hignett
Higonnet, *Hugh*
Higounet, *Hugh*
Higson, *Hick*
Higuera, *Feige*
Higueras, *Feige*
Hihn, *Hühne*
Hilaire, *Hilary*
Hilari, *Hilary*
Hilário, *Hilary*
Hilary
Hilber, *Hibbert*
Hilbering, *Hibbert*
Hilbers, *Hibbert*
Hilbert, *Hibbert*
Hilbertz, *Hibbert*
Hilbrand, *Hildebrand*
Hilbrands, *Hildebrand*
Hilbrich, *Hibbert*
Hilbricht, *Hibbert*
Hilbrig, *Hibbert*
Hilbring, *Hibbert*
Hilbrink, *Hibbert*
Hild, *Hildebrand*
Hildebrand
Hildebrands, *Hildebrand*
Hildebrecht, *Hibbert*
Hildenbrand, *Hildebrand*
Hilderbrand, *Hildebrand*
Hildesheim
Hildesheimer, *Hildesheim*
Hildt, *Hildebrand*
Hildyard, *Hilliard*
Hill
Hillaire, *Hilary*
Hillaireau, *Hilary*
Hillairet, *Hilary*
Hillairin, *Hilary*
Hillam, *Hill*
Hillard, *Hilary*
Hillary, *Hilary*
Hillcoat, *Ellis*
Hille, *Hill*
Hilleard, *Hilliard*
Hillebrand, *Hildebrand*
Hillebrenner, *Hildebrand*
Hillel, *Hilary*
Hillemann, *Hill*
Hillemans, *Hill*
Hillen, *Hill*
Hiller, *Hill*
Hillerbrand, *Hildebrand*
Hilleret, *Hilary*
Hillerin, *Hilary*
Hillery, *Hilary*
Hillesheim, *Hildesheim*
Hilliar, *Hellier*
Hilliard
Hillier
Hillion, *Hilary*
Hillis, *Hills*
Hillman, *Hill*
Hillmann, *Hill*
Hills
Hillyar, *Hellier*
Hillyard, *Hilliard*
Hillyer, *Hellier*
Hilmann, *Hill*
Hilpert, *Hibbert*
Hilpl, *Hibbert*
Hilprecht, *Hibbert*
Hilse
Hilson, *Hills*
Hilster, *Hilse*
Hilt, *Hildebrand*
Hiltebrandt, *Hildebrand*
Hiltl, *Hildebrand*
Hiltle, *Hildebrand*
Hilton
Hiltunen
Hilty, *Hildebrand*
Hilyer, *Hellier*
Himel, *Himmel*
Himelberg, *Himmel*
Himelbrand, *Himmel*
Himelfarb, *Himmel*
Himelman, *Himmel*
Himelschein, *Himmel*
Himelshine, *Himmel*
Himelstein, *Himmel*
Himelsztajn, *Himmel*
Himlich, *Himmel*
Himmel
Himmelbaum, *Himmel*
Himmelblau, *Himmel*
Himmelbrand, *Himmel*
Himmelburg, *Himmel*
Himmeler, *Himmel*
Himmelfarb, *Himmel*
Himmelmann, *Himmel*
Himmelreich, *Himmel*
Himmelschein, *Himmel*
Himmelstein, *Himmel*
Himml, *Himmel*
Himmler, *Himmel*
Hinchcliff, *Hinchcliffe*
Hinchcliffe
Hinchliff, *Hinchcliffe*
Hinchliffe, *Hinchcliffe*
Hinchsliff, *Hinchcliffe*
Hinchy, *Hennessy*
Hinckesman, *Hengst*
Hinckley
Hind
Hinde, *Hind*
Hindeley, *Hindley*
Hindels, *Hindes*
Hinden, *Hindes*
Hindenburg
Hinder
Hinderer, *Hinder*
Hindermann, *Hinder*
Hindes
Hindin, *Hindes*
Hindle
Hindley
Hindmarch, *Hindmarsh*
Hindmarsh
Hindrich, *Henry*
Hindrick, *Henry*
Hinds, *Hind*
Hindson, *Hind*
Hine
Hiner, *Hyner*
Hines, *Hynes*
Hingle, *Ingle*
Hingley, *Hinckley*
Hingst, *Hengst*
Hingstmann, *Hengst*
Hingston
Hinken, *Henry*
Hinkens, *Henry*
Hinkley, *Hinckley*
Hinks
Hinksen, *Henry*
Hinksey
Hinkson, *Hinks*
Hinner, *Hinder*
Hinnerk, *Henry*
Hinners, *Henry*
Hinojo, *Fennell*
Hinojosa
Hinrich, *Henry*
Hinrichs, *Henry*
Hinrichsen, *Henry*
Hinsch, *Henry*
Hinsche, *Henry*
Hinsey, *Hennessy*
Hinsley, *Hinckley*
Hinson, *Hinks*
Hintner, *Hinder*
Hinton
Hintz, *Henry*
Hintze, *Henry*
Hintzer, *Henry*
Hinz, *Henry*
Hinze, *Henry*
Hinzer, *Henry*
Hiort, *Hart*
Hiorth, *Hart*
Hipkin, *Herbert*
Hipkins, *Herbert*
Hipkiss, *Herbert*
Hipólito
Hippolyte, *Hipólito*
Hipsch, *Hübsch*
Hipsh, *Hübsch*
Hipsher, *Hübsch*
Hipshman, *Hübsch*
Hipworth, *Hepworth*
Hirche, *George*
Hircock, *Herbert*
Hird, *Heard*
Hireth, *Harrod*
Hirnyak, *Górski*
Hirois, *Ireland*
Hiron
Hirons, *Hiron*
Hirsch
Hirschbein, *Hirsch*
Hirschberg
Hirschberger, *Hirschberg*
Hirschel, *Hirsch*
Hirschenbach, *Hirsch*
Hirschenboim, *Hirsch*

Hirschenson, *Hirsch*
Hirschenstein, *Hirsch*
Hirscher, *Hirsemann*
Hirschfeld, *Hirsch*
Hirschfield, *Hirsch*
Hirschhorn, *Hirsch*
Hirschkop, *Hirsch*
Hirschkorn, *Hirsch*
Hirschle, *Hirsch*
Hirschman, *Hirsch*
Hirschmann, *Hirsch*
Hirschorn, *Hirsch*
Hirschstein, *Hirsch*
Hirschtal, *Hirsch*
Hirschthal, *Hirsch*
Hirsemann
Hirser, *Hirsemann*
Hirsfeld, *Hirsch*
Hirsh, *Hirsch*
Hirshberg, *Hirschberg*
Hirshfeld, *Hirsch*
Hirshin, *Hirsch*
Hirshman, *Hirsch*
Hirshprung, *Hirsch*
Hirst, *Hurst*
Hirt, *Heard*
Hirtel, *Heard*
Hirter, *Heard*
Hirth, *Heard*
Hirtle, *Heard*
Hirtz, *Hirsch*
Hirtzel, *Hirsch*
Hirvonen
Hirz, *Hirsch*
Hischenboim, *Hirsch*
Hischke, *Henry*
Hiscock, *Hick*
Hiscocks, *Hick*
Hiscoke, *Hick*
Hiscott, *Hick*
Hiscox, *Hick*
Hiscutt, *Hick*
Hisel, *Hiess*
Hiskett, *Hick*
Hislop, *Heslop*
Hispanski, *Pagnol*
Hita, *Laffitte*
Hitch, *Hick*
Hitchcock, *Hick*
Hitchcoe, *Hick*
Hitchcott, *Hick*
Hitchcox, *Hick*
Hitchen, *Hick*
Hitchens, *Hick*
Hitcheon, *Hick*
Hitches, *Hick*
Hitchin, *Hick*
Hitching, *Hick*
Hitchings, *Hick*
Hitchins, *Hick*
Hitchisson, *Hick*
Hitchman, *Hick*
Hitchmough, *Hickmott*
Hitchmouth, *Hickmott*
Hitchon, *Hick*
Hite, *Height*
Hiter, *Hüter*
Hitler, *Hüttler*
Hitscher, *Henry*
Hitschke, *Henry*
Hitter, *Hüter*
Hittler, *Hüttler*
Hitzke, *Henry*
Hitzschke, *Henry*
Hixon, *Hick*
Hjort, *Hart*
Hjorth, *Hart*
Hladík
Hladký, *Hladík*
Hlava
Hlaváč, *Głowacki*
Hlaváček, *Głowacki*
Hlavatý, *Hlava*
Hlouch, *Hloušek*
Hloucha, *Hloušek*
Hloušek
Hloužek, *Hloušek*
Hnát, *Ignace*
Hnátek, *Ignace*
Hnatik, *Ignace*
Hnatovich, *Ignace*
Hnatyuk, *Ignace*
Hoad
Hoadley
Hoar, *Hoare*
Hoare
Hoath, *Hoad*
Hoather, *Hoad*
Hob, *Hobb*
Hoban
Hobart, *Hubert*
Hobb
Hobbart, *Habbert*
Hobbe, *Habbert*
Hobbema, *Habbert*
Hobben, *Habbert*
Hobbert, *Habbert*
Hobbes, *Hobb*
Hobbin, *Hobb*
Hobbing, *Habbert*
Hobbins, *Hobb*
Hobbis, *Hobb*
Hobbiss, *Hobb*
Hobbs, *Hobb*
Hobday
Hobdey, *Hobday*
Höbel, *Hill*
Hobemann, *Hoffmann*
Hober, *Haber*
Hoberman, *Haber*
Hobkin, *Hopkin*
Hobkins, *Hopkin*
Hobkinson, *Hopkin*
Hobkirk, *Hopkirk*
Hoblin, *Hobb*
Hobling, *Hobb*
Hoblyn, *Hobb*
Hobson, *Hobb*
Hocek, *Hodek*
Hoch, *Hodek*
Hoch
Hochard, *Hoche*
Hochbaum, *Hoch*
Hochberg, *Hoch*
Hochberger, *Hoch*
Hochboim, *Hoch*
Hochbojm, *Hoch*
Hochdorf, *Hoch*
Hoche
Hochedé, *Hoche*
Hochedel, *Hoche*
Hocherman, *Hoch*
Hochet, *Hoche*
Hochfeld, *Hoch*
Hochfelder, *Hoch*
Hochgeborn, *Hoch*
Hochgelernter, *Hoch*
Hochgraf, *Hoch*
Hochhauser, *Hoch*
Hochman, *Hoch*
Hochmann, *Hoch*
Hochmanovich, *Hoch*
Hochner, *Hoch*
Hochon, *Hoche*
Hochrad, *Hoch*
Hochschild, *Hoch*
Hochsinger, *Hoch*
Hochstadt, *Hoch*
Hochstadter, *Hoch*
Hochstein, *Hoch*
Hochstim, *Hoch*
Hochstrasser, *Hoogstraeten*
Höcht, *Hecht*
Hochteil, *Hoch*
Höchtl, *Hecht*
Hochwald, *Hoch*
Hochzeit
Höck, *Hedge*
Hocke, *Hake*
Höcker, *Hake*
Hockey
Hockley
Höckner, *Hake*
Hodač, *Hodek*
Hodáček, *Hodek*
Hodas, *Hodes*
Hodd, *Hood*
Hodde, *Hood*
Hodder
Hoddes, *Hood*
Hoddesdon, *Hodsdon*
Hoddinott
Hodds, *Hood*
Hodeček, *Hodek*
Hodek
Hodemacher, *Huth*
Hodermann, *Hader*
Hodes
Hodess, *Hodes*
Hodesson, *Hodes*
Hodgdon, *Hodsdon*
Hodge
Hodgekinson, *Hodge*
Hodgen, *Hodge*
Hodgens, *Hodge*
Hodgeon, *Hodge*
Hodges, *Hodge*
Hodgeskinson, *Hodge*
Hodgett, *Hodge*
Hodgetts, *Hodge*
Hodgin, *Hodge*
Hodgins, *Hodge*
Hodgkiess, *Hodge*
Hodgkin, *Hodge*
Hodgkins, *Hodge*
Hodgkinson, *Hodge*
Hodgkison, *Hodge*
Hodgkiss, *Hodge*
Hodgkisson, *Hodge*
Hodgshon, *Hodge*
Hodgskins, *Hodge*
Hodgson, *Hodge*
Hodinott, *Hoddinott*
Hodis, *Hodes*
Hodison, *Hodes*
Hodkin, *Hodge*
Hodkinson, *Hodge*
Hodnett, *Hoddinott*
Hodouš, *Hodek*
Hodoušek, *Hodek*
Hodsden, *Hodsdon*
Hodsdon
Hodskin, *Hodge*
Hodson, *Hodge*
Hodt, *Huth*
Hodus, *Hodes*
Hodys, *Hodes*
Hoe
Hoedt, *Huth*
Hoef, *Head*
Hoeft, *Head*
Høeg, *Hawk*
Høegh, *Hawk*
Hoeksema, *Hook*
Hoekstra, *Hook*
Hoes, *Huff*
Hoet, *Huth*
Hoetje, *Huth*
Hoetmech, *Huth*
Hoey, *Howey*
Höf, *Head*
Hofen, *Hoffnung*
Hofenberg, *Hoffnung*
Höfer, *Hofer*
Hofer, *Hoffmann*
Hofer
Hofert, *Hofer*
Hoff, *Hofer*
Hoffenberg, *Hoffnung*
Hoffer, *Hofer, Hoffmann*
Hoffert, *Hofer*
Hoffman, *Hoffmann*
Hoffmann
Hoffmitz, *Hoffnung*
Hoffner, *Höpfner, Hoffmann*
Hoffnung
Hoffrichter, *Hofrichter*
Hoffschläger
Höfler, *Hofer*
Höflich
Hofman, *Hoffmann*
Hofmann, *Hoffmann*
Hofmeister
Höfner, *Hofer*
Hofner, *Hofer, Hoffmann*
Hofnung, *Hoffnung*
Hofrichter
Hofstra, *Hofer*
Höft, *Head*
Høg, *Hawk*
Hög, *Hoch*
Hogan
Hogart, *Fogarty*
Hogarth
Hogarty, *Fogarty*
Hogben
Högberg, *Hoch*
Hogbin, *Hogben*
Höge, *Hoch*
Hoge, *Hoch*
Hogemann, *Hoch*
Högen, *Hoch*
Hogens, *Hoch*
Hogerty, *Fogarty*
Högg, *Hedge*
Hogg
Hoggar, *Hogg*
Hoggard
Hoggart, *Hoggard*
Hoggarth, *Hogarth*
Hogge, *Hogg*
Hogger, *Hogg*
Høgh, *Hawk*
Hoghton, *Hutton*
Höglund, *Hoch*
Högman, *Hoch*

Högström, *Hoch*
Hogwood
Hohenzollern
Hoher, *Hoch*
Hohl, *Hole*
Hohlbein, *Holbein*
Hohler, *Hole*
Höhmann, *Hoch*
Hohmann, *Hoch*
Höhrold, *Harrod*
Høier, *Hoch*
Hoile, *Hoyle*
Hoiles, *Hoyle*
Høj, *Hoch*
Højer, *Hoch*
Hojman, *Hoch*
Hök, *Hawk*
Hol, *Hole*
Holá, *Golec*
Holah, *Hole*
Holan, *Golec*
Holand, *Holland*
Holander, *Holland*
Holas, *Golec*
Holbeche
Holbein
Holberd, *Hulbert*
Holbert, *Hulbert*
Holbird, *Hulbert*
Holbrock, *Holbrook*
Holbrook
Holbrooke, *Holbrook*
Holc, *Holt*
Holcberg, *Holt*
Holcblat, *Holt*
Holcer, *Holt*
Holcman, *Holt*
Holcom, *Holcombe*
Holcomb, *Holcombe*
Holcombe
Holcroft, *Holdcroft*
Holcstein, *Holt*
Holdane, *Haldane*
Holdaway, *Holloway*
Holdbrook, *Holbrook*
Holdcroft
Holden
Holder
Holderbaum, *Holder*
Holderer, *Holder*
Hölderle, *Holder*
Hölderlein, *Holder*
Hölderlin, *Holder*
Holdermann, *Holder*
Holderness
Holdford, *Holford*
Holdforth, *Holford*
Holdin, *Holden*
Holding, *Holden*
Holdmann, *Holt*
Holdroyd, *Holroyd*
Holdrup
Holdsworth, *Hallworth*
Holdt, *Holt*
Holdup, *Holdrup*
Hole
Holebrook, *Holbrook*
Holec, *Golec*
Holeček, *Golec*
Holeman, *Holman*
Holer, *Hole*
Holesworth, *Hallworth*
Holford
Holgado
Holgate
Holíček, *Golec*
Holiday, *Halliday*
Holík, *Golec*
Holla, *Hole*
Holladay, *Halliday*
Hollaender, *Holland*
Holland
Hollande, *Holland*
Hollander, *Holland*
Hollands, *Holland*
Hollard, *Hollier*
Hollaway, *Holloway*
Holleman, *Holman*
Hollen, *Hollis*
Hollens, *Hollis*
Hollenzer, *Holland*
Holles, *Hollis*
Holley, *Hollis*
Holliday, *Halliday*
Hollier
Hollies, *Hollis*
Holling, *Hollis*
Hollings, *Hollis*
Hollingshead, *Hollinshead*
Hollingshed, *Hollinshead*
Hollingsworth
Hollington
Hollingworth, *Hollingsworth*
Hollins, *Hollis*
Hollinshead
Hollinshed, *Hollinshead*
Hollis
Holliss, *Hollis*
Hollister, *Hollier*
Holliwell, *Halliwell*
Hollman, *Holman*
Holloran, *Halloran*
Hollow, *Hole*
Holloway
Hollowell, *Halliwell*
Hollway, *Holloway*
Holly, *Hollis*
Hollyer, *Hollier*
Hollyhock, *Holyoak*
Hollyoak, *Holyoak*
Hollyoake, *Holyoak*
Hollywood
Holm, *Holme*
Holman
Holmberg, *Holme*
Holme
Holmén, *Holme*
Holmen, *Holme*
Holmer, *Holme*
Holmes, *Holme*
Holmgren, *Holme*
Holmin, *Holme*
Holmlund, *Holme*
Holmqvist, *Holme*
Holmstedt, *Holme*
Holmsten, *Holme*
Holmstrand, *Holme*
Holmström, *Holme*
Holness, *Holderness*
Holopainen
Holoubek, *Golubev*
Holoway, *Holloway*
Holroyd
Holroyde, *Holroyd*
Holst
Holste, *Holst*
Holsworth, *Hallworth*
Holt
Holtappel, *Holzapfel*
Holten, *Holt*
Holter, *Holt*
Höltgen, *Holt*
Holtham
Hölting, *Holt*
Höltje, *Holt*
Holtmann, *Holt*
Holton
Holtsman, *Holt*
Holttum, *Holtum*
Holtum
Holtz, *Holt*
Holtzberg, *Holt*
Holtzer, *Holt*
Holtzman, *Holt*
Holtzmann, *Holt*
Holub, *Golubev*
Holubec, *Golubev*
Holubovich, *Golubev*
Holý, *Golec*
Holyday, *Halliday*
Holyoak
Holyoake, *Holyoak*
Holz, *Holt*
Holzapfel
Holzberg, *Holt*
Holzblat, *Holt*
Holzdorf, *Holt*
Hölzer, *Holt*
Holzer, *Holt*
Holzhendler, *Holt*
Hölzl, *Holt*
Hölzle, *Holt*
Hölzler, *Holt*
Holzman, *Holt*
Holzmann, *Holt*
Hölzner, *Holt*
Holzner, *Holt*
Holzstein, *Holt*
Homan, *Holman*
Homann, *Hoch*
Homburg
Homburger, *Homburg*
Home, *Holme*
Homer
Homewood
Homfray, *Humphrey*
Homm, *Humm*
Hommeister, *Hofmeister*
Hommel, *Hummel*
Hommen, *Humm*
Hommer, *Humbert*
Hommers, *Humbert*
Hommes, *Humm*
Hommester, *Hofmeister*
Homola
Homolka
Homs, *Elm*
Hönack, *Henry*
Hönatsch, *Henry*
Honchar, *Goncharov*
Hondt, *Hund*
Höne
Hone
Hönecke, *Höne*
Honecker, *Honegger*
Honeen, *Hooney*
Honegger
Hönemann, *Höne*
Honer, *Hone*
Hones, *Hone*
Honey
Honeyball
Honeycombe
Honeyfield
Honeyman, *Honey*
Hönig, *Henry*
Honig, *Honey*
Honigbaum, *Honey*
Honigberg, *Honey*
Honigman, *Honey*
Honigmann, *Honey*
Honigsberg, *Honey*
Honigsfeld, *Honey*
Honigstein, *Honey*
Honigwachs, *Honey*
Honikman, *Honey*
Honing, *Honey*
Honingh, *Honey*
Hönisch, *Henry*
Hönk, *Höne*
Honkanen
Hönks, *Höne*
Honneybell, *Honeyball*
Honneyman, *Honey*
Honniball, *Honeyball*
Honnorat, *Honoré*
Honorat, *Honoré*
Honoré
Hönsch, *Henry*
Honse, *Hans*
Hont, *Font*
Hoo
Hood
Hoods, *Hood*
Hooe, *Hoo*
Hoof, *Huff*
Hooff, *Huff*
Hooft, *Head*
Höög, *Hoch*
Hoogland
Hoogma, *Hoch*
Hoogman, *Hoch*
Hoogstraeten
Höök, *Hawk*
Hook
Hooke, *Hook*
Hooker, *Hook*
Hookes, *Hook*
Hookins, *Hugh*
Hooks, *Hook*
Hookway
Hoole, *Hooley*
Hooley
Hooney
Hooper
Hoose, *House*
Hooson, *Hugh*
Hoover, *Huber*
Hopcroft
Hope
Hopes, *Hope*
Hopf, *Höpfner*
Höpfer, *Höpfner*
Hopfer, *Höpfner*
Höpfli, *Höpfner*
Hopfner, *Höpfner*
Höpfner
Hopkin
Hopkins, *Hopkin*
Hopkinson, *Hopkin*
Hopkirk
Hopman, *Höpfner*
Hopp, *Hobb*
Hoppe, *Höpfner*
Hopper, *Hüpfer*
Hopping, *Hope*

Höppner, *Höpfner*
Hopson, *Hobb*
Höptner, *Höpfner*
Hopton
Hopwood
Hora, *Górski*
Horáček, *Górski*
Horák, *Górski*
Horálek, *Górski*
Horan
Hörauf
Horban, *Urban*
Horbasch, *Urban*
Horcajada
Horcajo
Horche, *George*
Horčička, *Horký*
Horčík, *Horký*
Hordienko, *Gordeev*
Hore, *Hoare*
Hořejš
Hořejší, *Hořejš*
Horen, *Horn*
Horenstein, *Horn*
Höreth, *Harrod*
Horetski, *Górski*
Horgan
Hörholz, *Harrod*
Horick, *George*
Höring, *Herring*
Horisky, *Fourish*
Horkan, *Hanrahan*
Horkheimer, *Herkommer*
Horký
Hörl, *Hermann*
Horlacher
Horley
Horlick, *Horlock*
Horlock
Hormaeche
Hormaechea, *Hormaeche*
Hörmann, *Hermann*
Hormann, *Horn*
Horn
Hornby
Horncastle
Horne, *Horn*
Hornemann, *Horn*
Hörner, *Horn*
Horner, *Horn*
Hornet, *Arnold*
Hornett, *Arnold*
Hornfeld, *Horn*
Hörnfeldt, *Horn*
Horníček, *Horník*
Hornik, *Horn*
Horník
Horniker, *Horn*
Horniman, *Hearn*
Hörnle, *Horn*
Hornlein, *Horn*
Hornmann, *Horn*
Hornor, *Horn*
Hörnqvist, *Horn*
Hornreich, *Horn*
Hornsby
Hornstein, *Horn*
Hornsztajn, *Horn*
Horovitz, *Horowitz*
Horowitz
Horrey, *Wooldridge*
Horridge
Horrigan, *Hanrahan*
Hörring, *Hermann*
Horrocks
Horry, *Wooldridge*
Horsburgh
Horseford
Horseforth, *Horseford*
Horsegood, *Osgood*
Horseman, *Horsman*
Horsey
Horsfall
Horsfield
Horshalyov, *Goncharov*
Horský, *Górski*
Horsler, *Ostler*
Horsley
Horsman, *Hurst*
Horsman
Horst, *Hurst*
Horsten, *Hurst*
Horstman, *Hurst*
Horstmann, *Hurst*
Hort, *Hardt, Hart*
Horta, *Ort*
Hörter, *Heard*
Horter, *Hardt*
Hortic, *Ort*
Hörtle, *Hard*
Horton
Horvát, *Horváth*
Horvat, *Horváth*
Horváth
Horwell
Horwich, *Horridge*
Horwitz, *Horowitz*
Horwood
Hosbons, *Husband, Osborn*
Hosburn, *Osborn*
Hose, *Huff*
Hoseason
Hosegood, *Osgood*
Hošek, *Hodek*
Hosey, *Hussey*
Hosford, *Horseford*
Hosgood, *Osgood*
Hosie, *Hussey*
Hosier
Hosken, *Hoskin*
Hoskin
Hosking, *Hoskin*
Hoskings, *Hoskin*
Hoskins, *Hoskin*
Hoskison, *Hoskin*
Hoskisson, *Hoskin*
Hoskyn, *Hoskin*
Hoskyns, *Hoskin*
Hoskys, *Hoskin*
Høst, *Herbst*
Hostal
Hostaux, *Hostal*
Hosteaux, *Hostal*
Hosteller, *Ostler*
Hostler, *Ostler*
Hotchen, *Hutchin*
Hotchkin, *Hodge*
Hotchkins, *Hodge*
Hotchkis, *Hodge*
Hotchkiss, *Hodge*
Hôtel, *Hostal*
Hoth, *Huth*
Hother, *Hoad*
Hothersall
Houard
Houchen, *Hutchin*
Houdard
Houdart, *Houdard*
Houdek, *Hudec*
Houdin, *Houdard*
Houdinet, *Houdard*
Houdon, *Houdard*
Houdot, *Houdard*
Houdsworth, *Hallworth*
Houf, *Huff*
Houfe, *Huff*
Hougaard, *Hougård*
Hougård
Hough
Houghney, *Hooney*
Houghton
Houghy, *Howey*
Houie, *Gilduff*
Houlbrook, *Holbrook*
Houlbrooke, *Holbrook*
Houlcroft, *Holdcroft*
Houldcroft, *Holdcroft*
Houlden, *Holden*
Houlder, *Holder*
Houldershaw, *Ollerenshaw*
Houldin, *Holden*
Houldsworth, *Hallworth*
Houle, *Hole*
Houlford, *Holford*
Houlihan
Houliston
Hoult, *Holt*
Houneen, *Hooney*
Hourcade, *Fourche*
Hourigan, *Hanrahan*
Hourihan, *Hanrahan*
Hourihane, *Hanrahan*
Hours, *Orso*
Hourseau, *Orso*
Hourtic, *Ort*
Housa, *Goose*
House
Housego, *House*
Household, *House*
Householder, *House*
Houseman, *House*
Houser, *House*
Houska, *Goose*
Housley
Housman, *House*
Houssais, *Hilse*
Houssay, *Hilse*
Houssaye, *Hilse*
Houssel, *Hilse*
Housset, *Hilse*
Houssière, *Hilse*
Houssin, *Hilse*
Houston
Houstoun, *Houston*
Hout, *Holt*
Houtman, *Holt*
Houton, *Hutton*
Houtsma, *Holt*
Houzard, *Heuse*
Houzé, *Heuse*
Houzeaux, *Heuse*
Houzel, *Heuse*
Houzet, *Heuse*
Hövel, *Hill*
Hovemeister, *Hofmeister*
Hovemester, *Hofmeister*
Hövet, *Head*
Hovgaard, *Hougård*
Hovgård, *Hougård*
Hovorka
How, *Howe*
Howard
Howarth
Howat, *Hewitt*
Howatson, *Hewitt*
Howatt, *Hewitt*
Howchin, *Hutchin*
Howcroft
Howden
Howe
Howel, *Howell*
Howell
Howells, *Howell*
Howels, *Howell*
Howes
Howet, *Hewitt*
Howetson, *Hewitt*
Howett, *Hewitt*
Howey
Howgate
Howick
Howie, *Howey*
Howieson, *Howey*
Howison, *Howey*
Howitt, *Hewitt*
Howkins, *Hugh*
Howl, *Howell*
Howland, *Holland*
Howlden, *Holden*
Howlett, *Hewlett*
Howlin, *Hugh*
Howling, *Hugh*
Howlings, *Hugh*
Howorth, *Howarth*
Howourth, *Howarth*
Howroyd, *Holroyd*
Howse, *Howes*
Howson, *Hugh*
Høy, *Hoch*
Hoy, *Howey*
Høyer, *Hoch*
Hoyland, *Holland*
Hoyle
Hoyles, *Hoyle*
Hoyo
Hoyos, *Hoyo*
Hoz
Hrabáč, *Hrabák*
Hrabáček, *Hrabák*
Hrabák
Hrabánek, *Hrabák*
Hrabě, *Graf*
Hrabek, *Graf*
Hrach, *Gorokhov*
Hrachovec, *Gorokhov*
Hradec, *Radecký*
Hradecký, *Radecký*
Hrádek, *Grodzki*
Hradil, *Grodzki*
Hradský, *Grodzki*
Hráský, *Gorokhov*
Hrb
Hrba, *Hrb*
Hrbáč, *Hrb*
Hrbáček, *Hrb*
Hrbatý, *Hrb*
Hrbek, *Hrb*
Hrdina, *Hrdý*
Hrdlička
Hrdý
Hriban, *Gribov*
Hribko, *Gribov*
Hrihorovich, *Gregory*
Hrinchenko, *Gregory*
Hrinchishin, *Gregory*
Hrinishin, *Gregory*

Hrishanok, *Gregory*
Hrishchenko, *Gregory*
Hristić, *Christian*
Hritzko, *Gregory*
Hritzkov, *Gregory*
Hrnčír, *Goncharov*
Hrobat, *Horváth*
Hroch, *Hron*
Hromačík, *Gromyko*
Hromas, *Gromyko*
Hromek, *Gromyko*
Hromíř, *Gromyko*
Hron
Hroněk, *Hron*
Hroník, *Hron*
Hroz, *Hron*
Hrubant, *Grob*
Hrubec, *Grob*
Hrubeš, *Grob*
Hrubý, *Grob*
Hruš, *Grushin*
Hrušík, *Grushin*
Hruška, *Grushin*
Hrvat, *Horváth*
Hrycek, *Gregory*
Hryckiewicz, *Gregory*
Hryńcewicz, *Gregory*
Hryńczyk, *Gregory*
Hryniewicki, *Gregory*
Hryniewicz, *Gregory*
Huard
Huart, *Howard*
Huartson, *Howard*
Huba, *Gębski*
Hubáček, *Gębski*
Hubach, *Jacob*
Hubál, *Gębski*
Hubálek, *Gębski*
Hubatsch, *Jacob*
Hubaud, *Hubble*
Hubault, *Hubble*
Hubaut, *Hubble*
Hubball, *Hubble*
Hubbard, *Hubert*
Hubbart, *Hubert*
Hübbe, *Hubert*
Hubbe, *Hubert*
Hübben, *Hubert*
Hübbers, *Hubert*
Hubbert, *Hubert*
Hubbertz, *Hubert*
Hubble
Hubbold, *Hubble*
Hubeau, *Hubert*
Hübel, *Hill*
Hubel, *Hubert*
Hubelet, *Hubert*
Hubelin, *Hubert*
Hubelot, *Hubert*
Hubený
Hüber, *Huber*
Huber
Huberdeau, *Hubert*
Huberman, *Huber*
Hübers, *Hubert*
Hubers, *Huber*
Hübert, *Hubert*
Hubert
Hübgen, *Hubert*
Hübgens, *Hubert*
Hubin, *Hubert*
Hubinet, *Hubert*
Hübler, *Hill*
Hublin, *Hubert*
Hublot, *Hubert*
Hübner, *Huber*
Hubner, *Huber*
Hubrecht, *Hubert*
Hubsch, *Hübsch*
Hübsch
Hübscher, *Hübsch*
Hubscher, *Hübsch*
Hübschle, *Hübsch*
Hubschman, *Hübsch*
Hübschmann, *Hübsch*
Hubsher, *Hübsch*
Huby, *Hubert*
Huc, *Hugh*
Huchard, *Huchet*
Huchet
Hucheux, *Huchet*
Huchez, *Huchet*
Huchier, *Huchet*
Huchon, *Hugh*
Huchot, *Huchet*
Huck
Hucke, *Huck*
Huckel, *Huck*
Huckell, *Huck*
Hucker
Huckes, *Huck*
Huckfield
Huckin, *Hugh*
Huckle, *Huck*
Hucknall
Hucks, *Huck*
Hudd
Huddart, *Woodard*
Huddle, *Hudd*
Huddleston
Huddlestone, *Huddleston*
Huddy, *Hudd*
Hudec
Hudeček, *Hudec*
Hudek, *Hudec*
Hudson, *Hudd*
Hudus, *Hodes*
Hue, *Hugh*
Huebmer, *Huber*
Huelin, *Hugh*
Huemer, *Huber*
Huerta, *Ort*
Huertson, *Howard*
Hueson, *McKay*
Huet, *Hewitt, Hugh*
Huete
Huetson, *Hewitt*
Huett, *Hewitt*
Huey, *Howey*
Huff
Hüffner, *Huber*
Huffton
Hüfner, *Huber*
Hug, *Huck, Hugh*
Hüge, *Hugh*
Hügel, *Hill*
Hügelmann, *Hill*
Huget, *Hugh*
Hugett, *Hugh*
Huggard, *Hugh*
Hüggel, *Hill*
Hüggelmann, *Hill*
Huggens, *Hugh*
Huggin, *Hugh*
Huggins, *Hugh*
Huggon, *Hugh*
Huggons, *Hugh*
Hugh
Hughes, *Hugh, McKay*
Hughf, *Huff*
Hughff, *Huff*
Hughlin, *Hugh*
Hughs, *Hugh*
Hughson, *Hugh*
Hugk, *Hugh*
Hügle, *Hugh*
Hügler, *Hill*
Hügli, *Hugh*
Hüglin, *Hugh*
Huglin, *Hugh*
Hugman, *Huck*
Hugo, *Hugh*
Hugon, *Hugh*
Hugonet, *Hugh*
Hugonin, *Hugh*
Hugonneau, *Hugh*
Hugonnet, *Hugh*
Hugonot, *Hugh*
Hugot, *Hugh*
Huguenet, *Hugh*
Huguenin, *Hugh*
Hugues, *Hugh*
Huguet, *Hugh*
Huguin, *Hugh*
Hühn, *Hühne*
Hühne
Huie, *Gilduff*
Huijsman, *House*
Huijsmans, *House*
Huis, *House*
Huise, *House*
Huisinga, *House*
Huisman, *House*
Huismans, *House*
Huison, *Hewitt*
Huitson, *Hewitt*
Huitt, *Hewitt*
Huizinga, *House*
Hukin, *Hugh*
Hukins, *Hugh*
Hulance, *Hugh*
Hulbert
Hulburd, *Hulbert*
Hulett, *Hewlett*
Hulin, *Hugh*
Hull
Hullah, *Hull*
Hüllebrand, *Hildebrand*
Huller, *Hull*
Hüllerbrand, *Hildebrand*
Hulles, *Hull*
Hullin, *Hugh*
Hullins, *Hugh*
Hullot, *Hewlett*
Hulls, *Hull*
Hullyer, *Hollier*
Hulme, *Holme*
Hulmes, *Holme*
Hüls, *Hilse*
Hülse, *Hilse*
Hulse
Hülsemann, *Hilse*
Hulsenboom, *Hilse*
Hulsman, *Hilse*
Hulson, *Hull*
Hülss, *Hilse*
Hülst, *Hilse*
Hülster, *Hilse*
Hult, *Holt*
Hulton
Hum, *Humm*
Humbelot, *Humbert*
Humber
Humberdot, *Humbert*
Humberston, *Humberstone*
Humberstone
Humbert
Humble
Humblestone, *Humberstone*
Humblot, *Humbert*
Humboldt
Humbolt, *Humboldt*
Humbrecht, *Humbert*
Hume, *Holme*
Humeau, *Orme*
Humerstone, *Humberstone*
Humfress, *Humphrey*
Humfrey, *Humphrey*
Humfrid, *Humphrey*
Huml, *Hummel*
Humm
Hummel
Hummen, *Humm*
Hummer, *Humbert*
Hummers, *Humbert*
Hummerston, *Humberstone*
Hummerstone, *Humberstone*
Humperdinck, *Humbert*
Humperding, *Humbert*
Humpert, *Humbert*
Humpertz, *Humbert*
Humpherson, *Humphrey*
Humpherston, *Humphrey*
Humphery, *Humphrey*
Humphrey
Humphreys, *Humphrey*
Humphries, *Humphrey*
Humphris, *Humphrey*
Humphriss, *Humphrey*
Humphry, *Humphrey*
Humphrys, *Humphrey*
Humprecht, *Humbert*
Hund
Hundt, *Hund*
Hüne, *Hühne*
Huneen, *Hooney*
Hungar, *Unger*
Hüngen, *Hund*
Hüngens, *Hund*
Hunger, *Unger*
Hungerer, *Unger*
Hungerland, *Unger*
Hüngerle, *Unger*
Hunnable, *Honeyball*
Hunneyball, *Honeyball*
Hunneybell, *Honeyball*
Hunnibal, *Honeyball*
Hunnibell, *Honeyball*
Hunt
Hunte, *Hunt*
Hunter, *Hunt*
Huntingdon, *Huntington*
Huntington
Huntinton, *Huntington*
Huntley
Huntly, *Huntley*
Hunwin, *Unwin*
Huon, *Hugh*
Huonic, *Hugh*
Huot, *Hugh*
Hupe, *Hubert*
Hupen, *Hubert*
Hüper, *Hüpfer*
Hupf, *Hüpfer*
Hupfauf, *Hüpfer*
Hupfer, *Hüpfer*

Hüpfer
Hüpgen, *Hubert*
Hüpgens, *Hubert*
Hupje, *Hubert*
Hupka, *Jacob*
Hupp, *Hüpfer*
Hüpper, *Hüpfer*
Huppers, *Hubert*
Huppert, *Hubert*
Huppertz, *Hubert*
Hupprecht, *Hubert*
Huprecht, *Hubert*
Huquet, *Huchet*
Huqueux, *Huchet*
Hurard, *Huré*
Hurban, *Urban*
Hurbank, *Urban*
Hürch, *George*
Hurch, *George*
Hürche, *George*
Hurd, *Heard*
Hurdman, *Heard*
Huré
Hureau, *Huré*
Hurel, *Huré*
Hurford
Hurich, *George*
Hurle, *Earl*
Hurlen, *Harling*
Hurles, *Earl*
Hurley
Hurlin, *Harling*
Hurling, *Harling*
Hurll, *Earl*
Hurly, *Hurley*
Hurman, *Hearn*
Hurn, *Hearn*
Hurne, *Hearn*
Hurok, *Ogurtsov*
Huron, *Huré*
Hurot, *Huré*
Hurran, *Huré*
Hurrell, *Huré*
Hurren, *Huré*
Hurrey, *Wooldridge*
Hurrie, *Wooldridge*
Hurry, *Wooldridge*
Hurst
Hurt, *Hart*
Hurtado
Hurwitz, *Horowitz*
Hus, *Gusev*
Husák, *Gusev*
Husband
Husbands, *Husband*
Huse, *House*
Húsek, *Gusev*
Hüseler, *House*
Hüsemann, *House*
Husemann, *House*
Husey, *Hussey*
Hüsgen, *House*
Husher, *Usher*
Huskinson, *Hoskin*
Huskisson, *Hoskin*
Hüsmann, *House*
Husmann, *House*
Huss, *Gusev*
Husset, *Hugh*
Hussey
Hussmann, *House*
Husson, *Hugh*
Hussy, *Hussey*
Hustache, *Stace*
Hustin
Hustler, *Ostler*
Huston, *Houston*
Hut, *Huth*
Hutcheon, *Hutchin*
Hutcherson, *Hutchin*
Hutcheson, *Hutchin*
Hutchin
Hutchings, *Hutchin*
Hutchingson, *Hutchin*
Hutchins, *Hutchin*
Hutchinson, *Hutchin*
Hutchison, *Hutchin*
Hütel, *Huth*
Hüter, *Huth*
Huter, *Huth*
Hüter
Huth
Huther, *Huth*
Huthmann, *Huth*
Hutin
Hutineau, *Hutin*
Hutinel, *Hutin*
Hutiner, *Hutin*
Hutinet, *Hutin*
Hutman, *Huth*
Hutner, *Huth*
Hutnet, *Hutin*
Hutnik, *Huth*
Hutson, *Hudd*
Hutt, *Hudd, Huth*
Hütter, *Hüttler*
Hutter, *Huth*
Hutterer, *Huth*
Hüttler
Huttman, *Huth*
Hutton
Huws, *Hugh*
Huxley
Huyben, *Hubert*
Huybens, *Hubert*
Huybrecht, *Hubert*
Huybrechts, *Hubert*
Huyge, *Hugh*
Huygen, *Hugh*
Huygens, *Hugh*
Huyghe, *Hugh*
Huysman, *House*
Huysmans, *House*
Huyton
Huzard, *Heuse*
Huzette, *Heuse*
Hvid, *White*
Hvidt, *White*
Hyam
Hyams, *Hyam*
Hyat, *Chait*
Hyatt, *Chait, Highet*
Hyde
Hyett, *Highet*
Hyland
Hylands, *Hyland*
Hylton, *Hilton*
Hyman, *Hyam*
Hynd, *Hind*
Hyndman, *Hind*
Hynds, *Hind*
Hyne, *Hine*
Hyner
Hynes
Hyrois, *Ireland*
Hyslop, *Heslop*

I

Iacabucci, *Jacob*
Iacavone, *Jacob*
Iaccacci, *Jack*
Iaccello, *Jack*
Iacchi, *Jack*
Iacchini, *Jack*
Iacchino, *Jack*
Iachelli, *Jack*
Iachetti, *Jack*
Iachi, *Jack*
Iacielli, *Jacob*
Iacini, *Jack*
Iacivelli, *Jacob*
Iacobacci, *Jacob*
Iacobassi, *Jacob*
Iacobelli, *Jacob*
Iacobetto, *Jacob*
Iacobini, *Jacob*
Iacobo, *Jacob*
Iacoboni, *Jacob*
Iacobucci, *Jacob*
Iacofo, *Jacob*
Iacoletti, *Jack*
Iacollo, *Jack*
Iacolo, *Jack*
Iacolucci, *Jack*
Iacomelli, *James*
Iacometti, *James*
Iacomi, *James*
Iacomini, *James*
Iacomo, *James*
Iacone, *Jack*
Iacono, *Deakin*
Iacopetti, *Jacob*
Iacopini, *Jacob*
Iacopo, *Jacob*
Iacopucci, *Jacob*
Iacotti, *Jack*
Iacovacci, *Jacob*
Iacovaccio, *Jacob*
Iacovazzi, *Jacob*
Iacovelli, *Jacob*
Iacovides, *Jacob*
Iacoviello, *Jacob*
Iacovini, *Jacob*
Iacovino, *Jacob*
Iacovo, *Jacob*
Iacovolo, *Jacob*
Iacovone, *Jacob*
Iacovozzo, *Jacob*
Iacovucci, *Jacob*
Iacovuzzi, *Jacob*
Iacozzo, *Jack*
Iacucci, *Jack*
Iacuzzi, *Jack*
Iacuzzio, *Jack*
Iago, *Jack*
Iain, *John*
Iamitti, *James*
Ian, *John*
Ianelli, *John*
Ianetti, *John*
Ianiello, *John*
Ianittello, *John*
Ianitti, *John*
Ianizzi, *John*
Iannazzi, *John*
Ianne, *John*
Iannelli, *John*
Iannello, *John*
Iannetti, *John*
Ianni, *John*
Ianniello, *John*
Iannilli, *John*
Iannini, *John*
Ianniti, *John*
Ianno, *John*
Iannone, *John*
Iannoni, *John*
Iannuzzelli, *John*
Iannuzzi, *John*
Ianoni, *John*
Ianson, *John*
Ianuccelli, *John*
Ianussi, *John*
Iapico, *Jacob*
Iardino, *Gardener*
Iashvili, *Ellis*
Ibán, *John*
Ibáñez, *John*
Ibarra
Ibarruri
Ibbers, *Hibbert*
Ibberson, *Hibbs*
Ibbeson, *Hibbs*
Ibbetson, *Hibbs*
Ibbison, *Hibbs*
Ibbots, *Hibbs*
Ibbotson, *Hibbs*
Ibbotts, *Hibbs*
Ibbs, *Hibbs*
Iben, *Ive*
Ibens, *Ive*
Ibing, *Hibbert*
Ibraimov, *Abraham*
Ibsen, *Hibbert*
Ibson, *Hibbs*
Icemonger, *Ironmonger*
Icigson, *Isaac*
Ick, *Hick*
Icke, *Hick*
Ickes, *Hick*
Ickov, *Isaac*
Ickovic, *Isaac*
Ickovici, *Isaac*
Ickovicz, *Isaac*
Ickovits, *Isaac*
Ickovitz, *Isaac*
Ickowics, *Isaac*
Ickowicz, *Isaac*
Iczkovits, *Isaac*
Iczkovitz, *Isaac*
Iddins, *Iddon*
Iddison, *Iddon*
Iddon
Ide
Idel, *Idle, Jude*
Idelchek, *Jude*
Idell, *Idle*
Idelman, *Jude*
Idelovici, *Jude*
Idelovitch, *Jude*
Idelovitz, *Jude*
Idels, *Jude*
Idelsohn, *Jude*
Idelson, *Jude*
Iden, *Ide*
Ideson, *Ide*
Iding, *Ide*
Idle
Idtensohn, *Ide*
Iemolo, *Jumeau*
Ientile, *Gentle*
Ierardi, *Garrett*
Ieroushalmi, *Yerushalmi*
Ifans, *Evan*

Igel
Igelberg, *Igel*
Igelfeld, *Igel*
Igielski, *Igolkin*
Ignác, *Ignace*
Ignace
Ignácz, *Ignace*
Ignaczak, *Ignace*
Ignaev, *Ignace*
Ignashev, *Ignace*
Ignatides, *Ignace*
Ignatov, *Ignace*
Ignatowicz, *Ignace*
Ignatowski, *Ignace*
Ignatyev, *Ignace*
Ignatz, *Ignace*
Ignaz, *Ignace*
Ignjatović, *Ignace*
Ignoti, *Ignoto*
Ignoto
Igolkin
Igonet, *Hugh*
Igonin, *Ignace*
Igoshin, *Ignace*
Igounet, *Hugh*
Ihde, *Ide*
Ihden, *Ide*
Ihnatchik, *Ignace*
Ihnazcnya, *Ignace*
IJzer, *Eisen*
Ikin, *Ide*
Ikonnikov
Ilari, *Hilary*
Ilario, *Hilary*
Ilbert, *Hibbert*
Ilchenko, *Ellis*
Ilchmann, *Giles*
Ilchuk, *Ellis*
Iles, *Isles*
Ilewicz, *Ellis*
Ilg, *Giles*
Ilgen, *Giles*
Illán, *Julian*
Illés, *Ellis*
Illes, *Giles, Isles*
Illichmann, *Giles*
Illies, *Giles*
Illig, *Giles*
Illige, *Giles*
Illingworth
Illmann, *Giles*
Illyés, *Ellis*
Ilmanov, *Ellis*
Il Povero, *Power*
Ilroy, *Gilroy*
Ilsley
Ilyasov, *Ellis*
Ilyenko, *Ellis*
Ilyin, *Ellis*
Ilyinichnin, *Ellis*
Ilyinski, *Ellis*
Ilyinykh, *Ellis*
Ilyuchyov, *Ellis*
Ilyukhov, *Ellis*
Ilyunin, *Ellis*
Ilyushkin, *Ellis*
Imber
Imberman, *Ingber*
Imbery, *Amery*
Imbrey, *Amery*
Imbrie, *Amery*
Imbrogno
Imery, *Amery*
Imhof, *Hofer*
Imhoff, *Hofer*
Imm
Immer
Immermann, *Immer*
Imms, *Imm*
Imort, *Ort*
Impelizzeri, *Pelletier*
Impellitteri, *Pelletier*
Imperadore, *Empereur*
Imperatore, *Empereur*
Imperatrice, *Empereur*
Impey
Impy, *Impey*
Imray, *Amery*
Imre, *Amery*
Imrie, *Amery*
Ims, *Imm*
Inácio, *Ignace*
Inber, *Ingber*
Ince, *Innocenti*
Ince
Inch, *Innes*
Incháustegui, *Inchausti*
Inchausti
Inchbald
Incze, *Innocenti*
Indruch, *Andrew*
Inés, *Annis*
Inês, *Annis*
Ineson, *Iddon*
Infante
Infantes, *Infante*
Infantino, *Infante*
Infantolino, *Infante*
Ing
Ingall, *Ingle*
Ingbar, *Ingber*
Ingber
Ingberg, *Ingber*
Ingberman, *Ingber*
Inge, *Ing*
Ingegneri, *Jenner*
Ingelbrecht, *Engelbert*
Ingels, *Engel*
Ingenkamp, *Champ*
Inger
Ingerman, *Inger*
Ingerov, *Unger*
Ingersoll, *Inkersall*
Ingham
Ingigneri, *Jenner*
Ingle
Ingleby
Inglés, *English*
Ingles, *Ingle*
Inglese, *English*
Ingleson, *Ingle*
Inglis, *English*
Inglish, *English*
Ingold, *Ingle*
Ingoldsby
Ingram
Ingrams, *Ingram*
Ingres
Ingrosso, *Gross*
Ings, *Ing*
Ingsole, *Inkersall*
Ingward, *Inger*
Ingwer, *Inger*
Ingwers, *Inger*
Ingwersen, *Inger*
Ingwertsen, *Inger*
Iniesta, *Genest*
Iñigo, *Ignace*
Iñíguez, *Ignace*
Inions, *Onion*
Inizan, *Innes*
Inker, *Inger*
Inkersall
Inkersole, *Inkersall*
Inkerson, *Inger*
Inman
Innes
Inness, *Innes*
Innett, *Iddon*
Innis, *Innes*
Inniss, *Innes*
Innocenti
Innocentini, *Innocenti*
Inns, *Innes*
Inskeep, *Inskip*
Inskip
Inskipp, *Inskip*
Insley
Inspektor, *Spector*
Instone
Interwies, *Wiese*
Intveen, *Fenn*
Inverarity
Ioan, *John*
Ioannidis, *John*
Ioannou, *John*
Iodice, *Judge*
Iohananof, *John*
Ioia, *Joy*
Iomelli, *Jumeau*
Ion, *John*
Ionesco, *John*
Ionescu, *John*
Ionnidis, *John*
Ionnisian, *John*
Ions, *John*
Iordanesco, *Jordan*
Iordanski, *Jordan*
Iori, *George*
Iorillo, *George*
Iorio, *George*
Iorizzo, *George*
Iorrizzi, *George*
Ioselev, *Joseph*
Ioselevich, *Joseph*
Iovane, *Jeune*
Iovene, *Jeune*
Iovine, *Jeune*
Iovinelli, *Jeune*
Iozefovich, *Joseph*
Ippoliti, *Hipólito*
Ippolito, *Hipólito*
Ippolitov, *Hipólito*
Ipsen, *Hibbert*
Irby
Ireby, *Irby*
Iredale
Iredell, *Iredale*
Ireland
Iremonger, *Ironmonger*
Ireton
Irgang, *Irrgang*
Iriarte, *Uriarte*
Irigoyen
Irish, *Ireland*
Irisov
Irmgard, *Ermgard*
Irmingard, *Ermgard*
Irois, *Ireland*
Ironbuckle, *Arbuckle*
Ironde, *Hiron*
Irondelle, *Arundel*
Ironmonger
Irons
Ironside
Irrgang
Irton, *Ireton*
Irvin, *Irvine*
Irvine
Irving, *Irvine*
Irwin, *Irvine*
Irwine, *Irvine*
Irwing, *Irvine*
Isaac
Isaacs, *Isaac*
Isaacson, *Isaac*
Isaak, *Isaac*
Isaaksohn, *Isaac*
Isac, *Isaac*
Isachkov, *Isaac*
Isacoff, *Isaac*
Isacov, *Isaac*
Isacq, *Isaac*
Isacson, *Isaac*
Isacson, *Isaac*
Isacsson, *Isaac*
Isak, *Isaac*
Isaki, *Isaac*
Isakof, *Isaac*
Isakoff, *Isaac*
Isakov, *Isaac*
Isaković, *Isaac*
Isakovitch, *Isaac*
Isakower, *Isaac*
Isakowitz, *Isaac*
Isaksen, *Isaac*
Isakson, *Isaac*
Isaksson, *Isaac*
Isambard, *Isambert*
Isambert
Isard, *Izard*
Isarn, *Isern*
Isasi
Isbert, *Isambert*
Isbrecht, *Isambert*
Iscowitz, *Isaac*
Isembert, *Isambert*
Isemonger, *Ironmonger*
Iser, *Israel*
Iserles, *Israel*
Iserlis, *Israel*
Isern
Iserovich, *Israel*
Iserson, *Israel*
Ishak, *Isaac*
Ishaki, *Isaac*
Ishchenko, *Joseph*
Isherwood
Isidor, *Isidore*
Isidore
Isidoro, *Isidore*
Isidro, *Isidore*
Iskov, *Joseph*
Iskow, *Isaac*
Iskowitz, *Isaac*
Isles
Islip
Isnard
Isoldi, *Izard*
Ison, *Ide*
Isotti, *Izard*
Israel
Israelashvili, *Israel*
Israeler
Israelevitch, *Israel*
Israelevitz, *Israel*

Israelewicz, *Israel*
Israelewitz, *Israel*
Israeli, *Israeler*
Israelit, *Israeler*
Israelith, *Israeler*
Israeloff, *Israel*
Israelov, *Israel*
Israelovich, *Israel*
Israelovici, *Israel*
Israelovitch, *Israel*
Israelovitz, *Israel*
Israelow, *Israel*
Israelowicz, *Israel*
Israelowitz, *Israel*
Israels, *Israel*
Israelski, *Israel*
Israelson, *Israel*
Israely, *Israeler*
Isreeli, *Israeler*
Isrelof, *Israel*
Isreloff, *Israel*
Issac, *Isaac*
Issacof, *Isaac*
Issacov, *Isaac*
Issacson, *Isaac*
Issak, *Isaac*
Issakov, *Isaac*
Issard, *Izard*
Issart, *Essart*
Issarte, *Essart*
Issarteaux, *Essart*
Issartel, *Essart*
Isser, *Israel*
Isserl, *Israel*
Isserles, *Israel*
Isserlin, *Israel*
Isseroff, *Israel*
Issersohn, *Israel*
Isserson, *Israel*
Issert, *Essart*
Issett, *Izard*
Issit, *Izard*
Issitt, *Izard*
Issolt, *Izard*
Issot, *Izard*
Iszczak, *Isaac*
Itelson, *Ittelson*
Itensohn, *Ide*
Ithel, *Jekyll*
Ithell, *Idle*
Itkin, *Ittelson*
Itschakov, *Isaac*
Itscovitz, *Isaac*
Itshak, *Isaac*
Itskovitz, *Isaac*
Itt, *Ide*
Ittelson
Ittensohn, *Ide*
Iturbe
Itzakovitz, *Isaac*
Itzakson, *Isaac*
Itzchak, *Isaac*
Itzchaki, *Isaac*
Itzchaky, *Isaac*
Itzcovich, *Isaac*
Itzhaiek, *Isaac*
Itzhaik, *Isaac*
Itzhak, *Isaac*
Itzhaki, *Isaac*
Itzhaky, *Isaac*
Itzhayek, *Isaac*
Itzig, *Isaac*
Itzigsohn, *Isaac*
Itzik, *Isaac*
Itzikson, *Isaac*
Itzkin, *Isaac*
Itzkov, *Isaac*
Itzkovich, *Isaac*
Itzkovici, *Isaac*
Itzkovitch, *Isaac*
Itzkovsky, *Isaac*
Itzkowicz, *Isaac*
Itzkowitch, *Isaac*
Itzkowitz, *Isaac*
Iuli, *Júlio*
Iuliano, *Julian*
Iuorio, *George*
Ivachyov, *John*
Ivain, *Ive*
Ivakhin, *John*
Ivakhno, *John*
Ivakhnov, *John*
Ivakin, *John*
Ivan, *Ive*
Ivanaev, *John*
Ivančević, *John*
Ivanchenkov, *John*
Ivanchev, *John*
Ivanchikov, *John*
Ivanchin, *John*
Ivanchov, *John*
Ivanenko, *John*
Ivanenkov, *John*
Ivanets, *John*
Ivanichev, *John*
Ivanikhin, *John*
Ivanikov, *John*
Ivanilov, *John*
Ivanin, *John*
Ivanishchev, *John*
Ivanishev, *John*
Ivanishin, *John*
Ivanisov, *John*
Ivanitsa, *John*
Ivankin, *John*
Ivanko, *John*
Ivankov, *John*
Ivanković, *John*
Ivannikov, *John*
Ivanonko, *John*
Ivanov, *John*
Ivanović, *John*
Ivanshin, *John*
Ivanshintsev, *John*
Ivantsov, *John*
Ivantyev, *John*
Ivanushka, *John*
Ivanusyev, *John*
Ivanyukov, *John*
Ivanyushin, *John*
Ivanyushkin, *John*
Ivanyutin, *John*
Ivarsson, *Ivor*
Ivasechko, *John*
Ivashchenko, *John*
Ivashechkin, *John*
Ivashev, *John*
Ivashin, *John*
Ivashinnikov, *John*
Ivashintsov, *John*
Ivashkin, *John*
Ivashkov, *John*
Ivashnikov, *John*
Ivashnyov, *John*
Ivashov, *John*
Ivasyushkin, *John*
Ivatt, *Ive*
Ivchenko, *John*
Ive
Ivelain, *Ive*
Iven, *Ive*
Ivens, *Ive*
Ivers, *Ivor*
Iversen, *Ivor*
Iverson, *Ivor*
Ivery, *Ivory*
Ives, *Ive*
Iveson, *Ive*
Ivey
Ivi, *Ive*
Ivić, *John*
Ivie, *Ivey*
Ivings, *Evan*
Ivins, *Evan*
Ivison, *Ive*
Ivković, *John*
Ivolgin
Ivone, *Ive*
Ivonnet, *Ive*
Ivor
Ivory
Ivoshin, *John*
Ivshin, *John*
Ivushkin
Ivy, *Ivey*
Iwańczyk, *John*
Iwanicki, *John*
Iwanowicz, *John*
Iwanowski, *John*
Iwański, *John*
Iwarsson, *Ivor*
Iwaszkiewicz, *John*
Iwe, *Ive*
Iwen, *Ive*
Iwers, *Ivor*
Iwiński, *John*
Izaac, *Isaac*
Izac, *Isaac*
Izachenko, *Isaac*
Izachik, *Isaac*
Izacov, *Isaac*
Izaguirre
Izak, *Isaac*
Izakov, *Isaac*
Izakovitz, *Isaac*
Izakowicz, *Isaac*
Izaks, *Isaac*
Izakson, *Isaac*
Izard
Izarn, *Isern*
Izat, *Izard*
Izatt, *Izard*
Izchaki, *Isaac*
Izdebski
Izhak, *Isaac*
Izhaki, *Isaac*
Izhakov, *Isaac*
Izhaky, *Isaac*
Izhayek, *Isaac*
Izikov, *Isaac*
Izikovitz, *Isaac*
Izkoveski, *Isaac*
Izkovici, *Isaac*
Izkovicz, *Isaac*
Izkovitch, *Isaac*
Izkovitz, *Isaac*
Izon, *Ide*
Izquierdo
Izrael, *Israel*
Izraeler, *Israeler*
Izraeli, *Israeler*
Izraely, *Israeler*
Izreeli, *Israeler*
Izsák, *Isaac*
Izsak, *Isaac*
Izydorczyk, *Isidore*
Izygson, *Isaac*
Izzard, *Izard*
Izzett, *Izard*

J

Jaan, *John*
Jablin, *Jabłoński*
Jabłkiewicz, *Jabłoński*
Jabłkowski, *Jabłoński*
Jablon, *Jabłoński*
Jablonec, *Jabłoński*
Jabloner, *Jabłoński*
Jabłonka, *Jabłoński*
Jabłonowicz, *Jabłoński*
Jabłonowski, *Jabłoński*
Jablons, *Jabłoński*
Jablonski, *Jabłoński*
Jabłoński
Jablonsky, *Jabłoński*
Jablow, *Jabłoński*
Jabonero, *Soper*
Jabouille
Jač, *Jach*
Jaccoud, *Jack*
Jaccoux, *Jack*
Jaček, *Jach*
Jacek
Jäch, *Jach*
Jach
Jacháček, *Jach*
Jachek, *Jach*
Jächel, *Jach*
Jachel, *Jach*
Jachimczak, *Joachim*
Jachimowicz, *Joachim*
Jachisch, *Jach*
Jächle, *Jach*
Jachler, *Jach*
Jachmann, *Jach*
Jachner, *Jach*
Jachowicz, *Jach*
Jachsch, *Jach*
Jachymski, *Joachim*
Jacinto, *Jacek*
Jack
Jačka, *Jach*
Jacka, *Jack*
Jackaman, *Jackman*
Jackett, *Jack*
Jacketts, *Jack*
Jackiewicz, *Jacek*
Jackl, *Jach*
Jäcklein, *Jach*
Jäcklin, *Jach*
Jacklin, *Jack*
Jackling, *Jack*
Jackman
Jackner, *Jach*
Jackowiak, *Jacek*
Jackowicz, *Jacek*
Jackowski, *Jacek*
Jacks, *Jack*
Jackson, *Jack*
Jacmar, *James*
Jacmard, *James*
Jacob
Jacobb, *Jacob*
Jacobbe, *Jacob*

Jacobi, *Jacob*
Jacobovitch, *Jacob*
Jacobovits, *Jacob*
Jacobovitz, *Jacob*
Jacobowits, *Jacob*
Jacobowitz, *Jacob*
Jacobs, *Jacob*
Jacobsen, *Jacob*
Jacobskind, *Jacob*
Jacobsohn, *Jacob*
Jacobson, *Jacob*
Jacobsson, *Jacob*
Jacobsz, *Jacob*
Jacoby, *Jacob*
Jacocks, *Jack*
Jacono, *Deakin*
Jacot, *Jack*
Jacotet, *Jack*
Jacotin, *Jack*
Jacoton, *Jack*
Jacotot, *Jack*
Jacoutot, *Jack*
Jacox, *Jack*
Jacq, *Jack*
Jacquard, *Jack*
Jacque, *Jack*
Jacqueau, *Jack*
Jacquel, *Jack*
Jacquelain, *Jack*
Jacquelet, *Jack*
Jacquelin, *Jack*
Jacquelot, *Jack*
Jacquemar, *James*
Jacquemard, *James*
Jacquème, *James*
Jacquemet, *James*
Jacqueminet, *James*
Jacqueminot, *James*
Jacquemot, *James*
Jacquemy, *James*
Jacquenet, *Jack*
Jacquenod, *Jack*
Jacquenot, *Jack*
Jacques, *Jack*
Jacqui, *Jack*
Jacquin, *Jack*
Jacquinel, *Jack*
Jacquinet, *Jack*
Jacquinot, *Jack*
Jacquot, *Jack*
Jacquotet, *Jack*
Jacquotin, *Jack*
Jacquoton, *Jack*
Jacquotot, *Jack*
Jacquoutot, *Jack*
Jaczewski, *Jacek*
Jadczak, *Anthony*
Jadczyk, *Anthony*
Jäde, *Gott*
Jädecke, *Gott*
Jaén
Jaffray, *Jeffrey*
Jaffré, *Jeffrey*
Jaffre, *Jeffrey*
Jaffrennou, *Jeffrey*
Jaffrès, *Jeffrey*
Jaffrey, *Jeffrey*
Jaffrezic, *Jeffrey*
Jaffrézo, *Jeffrey*
Jæger, *Jäger*
Jager, *Jäger*
Jäger
Jagerman, *Jäger*
Jagg, *Jack*
Jagger
Jaggers, *Jagger*
Jaggi, *John*
Jäggli, *John*
Jaggs, *Jack*
Jagieła, *Jagiełło*
Jagiełło
Jagielski, *Jagiełło*
Jaglom
Jago, *Jack*
Jagoda, *Yagodin*
Jagodič, *Yagodin*
Jagodziński, *Yagodin*
Jagodzinski, *Yagodin*
Jagodzki, *Yagodin*
Jagoe, *Jack*
Jagson, *Jack*
Jahan, *John*
Jaher, *John*
Jahier, *Jayet*
Jahn, *John*
Jähncke, *John*
Jähndel, *John*
Jahndel, *John*
Jähne, *John*
Jähnel, *John*
Jahnel, *John*
Jähner, *John*
Jähnig, *John*
Jähnisch, *John*
Jahnisch, *John*
Jähnke, *John*
Jahns, *John*
Jähnsch, *John*
Jahnsch, *John*
Jahnsen, *John*
Jahoda, *Yagodin*
Jahrmann, *Geary*
Jaillard, *Jaillet*
Jailler, *Gale*
Jaillet
Jaillon, *Jaillet*
Jaime, *James*
Jaimez, *James*
Jain, *Jane*
Jaine, *Jane*
Jakab, *Jacob*
Jake, *Jack*
Jakeman, *Jackman*
Jakes, *Jack*
Jakimovski, *Joachim*
Jakimovsky, *Joachim*
Jakimowski, *Joachim*
Jakings, *Jack*
Jakins, *Jack*
Jákó, *Jacob*
Jakob, *Jacob*
Jakobs, *Jacob*
Jakobsen, *Jacob*
Jakobsson, *Jacob*
Jakoub, *Jacob*
Jakoubeč, *Jacob*
Jakoubek, *Jacob*
Jakov, *Jacob*
Jakovlevitch, *Jacob*
Jakovljević, *Jacob*
Jakovljevic, *Jacob*
Jakowczyk, *Jach*
Jakšić, *Jacob*
Jakubczak, *Jacob*
Jakubczyk, *Jacob*
Jakubiak, *Jacob*
Jakubovics, *Jacob*
Jakubovicz, *Jacob*
Jakubovitch, *Jacob*
Jakubovits, *Jacob*
Jakubovitz, *Jacob*
Jakubovski, *Jacob*
Jakubowicz, *Jacob*
Jakubowitz, *Jacob*
Jakubowski, *Jacob*
Jakubowsky, *Jacob*
Jakubski, *Jacob*
Jakucewicz, *Jacob*
Jakuszewski, *Jacob*
Jambrozek, *Ambrose*
James
Jameson, *James*
Jamet, *James*
Jamieson, *James*
Jamin, *Benjamin*
Jaminet, *Benjamin*
Jaminot, *Benjamin*
Jamison, *James*
Jamme, *James*
Jammes, *James*
Jammet, *James*
Jamot, *James*
Jamrowicz, *Ambrose*
Ján, *John*
Jan, *John*
Janáček, *John*
Janák, *John*
Janas, *John*
Janasik, *John*
Janaszewski, *John*
Janaszkiewicz, *John*
Janata, *John*
Janatka, *John*
Janaud, *John*
Janaways, *January*
Janč, *John*
Janča, *John*
Jančar, *John*
Jančić, *John*
Jančík, *John*
Jäncke, *John*
Jancsó, *John*
Janczak, *John*
Janczewski, *John*
Janczyk, *John*
Janda, *John*
Jandač, *John*
Jandák, *John*
Jändel, *John*
Jandera, *John*
Jandl, *John*
Jand'ourek, *John*
Jäne, *John*
Jané, *January*
Jane
Janeček, *John*
Janecki, *John*
Janeczek, *John*
Janeiro, *January*
Janek, *John*
Jänel, *John*
Janel, *John*
Jäner, *John*
Janer, *January*
Janes, *Jane*
Janet, *Jane*
Janiak, *John*
Janić, *John*
Janíček, *John*
Janićijević, *John*
Janicki, *John*
Jänig, *John*
Janík, *John*
Janik, *John*
Janikowski, *John*
Janin, *John*
Jänisch, *John*
Janisch, *John*
Janisson, *John*
Janiszewski, *John*
Janjić, *John*
Janjušević, *John*
Jänke, *John*
Jankel, *Jacob*, *Jankoff*
Jankelevitz, *Jankoff*
Jankelewicz, *Jankoff*
Jankelewitz, *Jankoff*
Jankell, *Jankoff*
Jankeloff, *Jankoff*
Jankelovicz, *Jankoff*
Jankelovits, *Jankoff*
Jankelowitz, *Jankoff*
Jankielewicz, *Jankoff*
Jankielowicz, *Jankoff*
Jankiewicz, *John*
Jankilevitz, *Jankoff*
Jankilewicz, *Jankoff*
Jankin, *Jane*
Janklewitz, *Jankoff*
Janklowicz, *Jankoff*
Jankó, *John*
Jankoff
Jankolovits, *Jankoff*
Jankolowitz, *Jankoff*
Janković, *John*
Jankovich, *Jankoff*
Jankovitch, *Jankoff*
Jankovitz, *Jankoff*
Jankovský, *John*
Jankowicz, *Jankoff*
Jankowitz, *Jankoff*
Jankowski, *John*
Janks, *Jenks*
Janků, *John*
Jankulovits, *Jankoff*
Janman, *John*
Jann, *John*
Jannach, *John*
Jannasch, *John*
Jannel, *John*
Jannequin, *John*
Jannin, *John*
Janning, *John*
Jannings, *Jennings*
Jannis, *Jane*
Jannuschek, *John*
Janny, *John*
Janoch, *John*
Janodet, *John*
Janoš, *John*
Janoschek, *John*
Janošević, *John*
Janota, *John*
Janouch, *John*
Janouš, *John*
Janoušek, *John*
Janout, *John*
Janovský, *John*
Janowicz, *John*
Janowski, *John*
Jans, *Jane*, *John*
Jansa, *John*
Jänsch, *John*
Jansch, *John*
Janse, *John*
Jansema, *John*

Jansen, *John*
Jansens, *John*
Janský, *John*
Janson, *Jane*
Janssen, *John*
Janssens, *John*
Jansson, *John*
Jantel, *John*
Jantet, *John*
Janton, *John*
Jantot, *John*
Jantz, *John*
Jantzen, *John*
Janů, *John*
Januário, *January*
January
Janus, *John*
Januschek, *John*
Janusik, *John*
Janusz, *John*
Januszewicz, *John*
Januszewski, *John*
Januszkiewicz, *John*
Janvier, *January*
Jany, *John*
Janz, *John*
Janzen, *John*
Jaouen, *John*
Jaquard, *Jack*
Jaqueau, *Jack*
Jaquel, *Jack*
Jaquelain, *Jack*
Jaquelet, *Jack*
Jaquelin, *Jack*
Jaquelot, *Jack*
Jaquemar, *James*
Jaquemard, *James*
Jaqueminet, *James*
Jaqueminot, *James*
Jaquemy, *James*
Jaquenet, *Jack*
Jaquenod, *Jack*
Jaquenot, *Jack*
Jaques, *Jack*
Jaquin, *Jack*
Jaquinel, *Jack*
Jaquinet, *Jack*
Jaquinot, *Jack*
Jaquith, *Jack*
Jaquot, *Jack*
Jara
Jarad, *Garrett*
Jaram, *Jerome*
Jaraszek, *Jarosz*
Jarck, *Terry*
Jarcks, *Terry*
Jard, *Gardener*
Jarden, *Jordan*
Jardeni, *Jordan*
Jardeny, *Jordan*
Jardier, *Gardener*
Jardim, *Gardener*
Jardin, *Gardener*
Jardine, *Gardener*
Jardinier, *Gardener*
Jarecki, *Jarosz*
Jared, *Garrett*
Jareš, *Jarosz*
Jarewicz, *Jarosz*
Jarić, *Jarosz*
Jark, *Terry*
Jarl, *Earl*
Jarmain, *German*
Jarmains, *German*
Jarman, *German*
Jarmay, *Jeremy*
Jarmey, *Jeremy*
Jarmy, *Jeremy*
Jarolím, *Jerome*
Jarolímek, *Jerome*
Jaroś, *Jarosz*
Jaros, *Jarosz*
Jarosik, *Jarosz*
Jarosz
Jaroszczak, *Jarosz*
Jaroszek, *Jarosz*
Jaroszewski, *Jarosz*
Jaroszyński, *Jarosz*
Jarrard, *Garrett*
Jarratt, *Garrett*
Jarre
Jarred, *Garrett*
Jarrelt, *Garrett*
Jarren, *Geary*
Jarres, *Geary*
Jarret, *Jarre*
Jarrett, *Garrett*
Jarrier, *Jarre*
Jarrige, *Jarry*
Jarrijon, *Jarry*
Jarritt, *Garrett*
Jarrod, *Garrett*
Jarrold, *Garrett*
Jarron, *Jarre*
Jarrott, *Garrett*
Jarrs, *Geary*
Jarry
Jarsen, *Geary*
Jarušek, *Jarosz*
Jaruszewicz, *Jarosz*
Jarvie, *Jarvis*
Järvinen
Jarvis
Jarý, *Jarosz*
Jary, *Jarry*
Jarząbek, *Jarzębowski*
Jarzębowski
Jarzębski, *Jarzębowski*
Jaš, *Jach*
Jäsche, *Jach*
Jasche, *Jach*
Jaschek, *Jach*
Jaschke, *Jach*
Jašek, *Jach*
Jashinovsky, *Jasiński*
Jashunsky, *Jasiński*
Jasiak, *John*
Jasieński, *Jasiński*
Jašík, *Jach*
Jasik, *John*
Jasiński
Jaška, *Jach*
Jaśkiewicz, *John*
Jason, *Jasiński*
Jaspar, *Kaspar*
Jaspars, *Kaspar*
Jasparsen, *Kaspar*
Jasper, *Kaspar*
Jaspers, *Kaspar*
Jaspersen, *Kaspar*
Jassen, *Jasiński*
Jassin, *Jasiński*
Jassinowsky, *Jasiński*
Jastrov, *Jastrow*
Jastrow
Jastrzabski, *Yastrebov*
Jastrzębski, *Yastrebov*
Jastrzebski, *Yastrebov*
Jasyn, *Jasiński*
Jaszczak, *John*
Jatczak, *John*
Jatta, *Catt*
Jaubert
Jauer, *Jaworski*
Jauernick, *Jaworski*
Jauernig, *Jaworski*
Jauernik, *Jaworski*
Jauert, *Jaworski*
Jauffred, *Jeffrey*
Jauffret, *Jeffrey*
Jaufred, *Jeffrey*
Jauković, *Jacob*
Jaulme, *James*
Jaulmes, *James*
Jaume, *James*
Jaumes, *James*
Jaumet, *James*
Jaunard, *Jaune*
Jaunasse, *Jaune*
Jaune
Jauneau, *Jaune*
Jaunet, *Jaune*
Jáuregui
Jaus, *Joyce*
Javier
Jávor, *Jaworski*
Javor, *Jaworski*
Jávorka, *Jaworski*
Javorský, *Jaworski*
Javůrek, *Jaworski*
Jawerbaum, *Jaworski*
Jaworowski, *Jaworski*
Jaworski
Jay
Jayes, *Jay*
Jayet
Jayez, *Jayet*
Jayne, *Jane*
Jaynes, *Jane*
Jayot, *Jayet*
Jays, *Jay*
Jayume, *James*
Jeacock, *Jack*
Jeacop, *Jacob*
Jeakings, *Jack*
Jeakins, *Jack*
Jean, *Jane*
Jean, *John*
Jeandeau, *John*
Jeandel, *John*
Jeandet, *John*
Jeandillou, *John*
Jeandin, *John*
Jeandon, *John*
Jeandot, *John*
Jeaneau, *John*
Jeanel, *John*
Jeanenet, *John*
Jeanequin, *John*
Jeanes, *Jane*
Jeanesson, *John*
Jeanet, *John*
Jeanin, *John*
Jeannard, *John*
Jeannaud, *John*
Jeanneau, *John*
Jeannel, *John*
Jeannenet, *John*
Jeannequin, *John*
Jeannesson, *John*
Jeannet, *John*
Jeannin, *John*
Jeannon, *John*
Jeannot, *John*
Jeanon, *John*
Jeanot, *John*
Jeans, *Jane*
Jearey, *Jarry*
Jeary, *Jarry*
Jeavon
Jeavons, *Jeavon*
Jebb, *Jeffrey*
Jebbs, *Jeffrey*
Jebson, *Jeffrey*
Jech, *Jach*
Jeche, *Jach*
Jecheskel, *Ezekiel*
Jechezkieli, *Ezekiel*
Jechimczyk, *Joachim*
Jecht, *Jach*
Jeckell, *Jekyll*
Jeckells, *Jekyll*
Jecks, *Geach*
Jecock, *Jack*
Jecop, *Jacob*
Jedele, *Ulrich*
Jedlička, *Yolkin*
Jędrachowicz, *Andrew*
Jędras, *Andrew*
Jędrasik, *Andrew*
Jędraszczyk, *Andrew*
Jędraszek, *Andrew*
Jędruch, *Andrew*
Jędrych, *Andrew*
Jędrychowski, *Andrew*
Jędryka, *Andrew*
Jędrys, *Andrew*
Jędrysik, *Andrew*
Jędrzaszkiewicz, *Andrew*
Jędrzej, *Andrew*
Jędrzejczak, *Andrew*
Jędrzejczyk, *Andrew*
Jędrzejewicz, *Andrew*
Jędrzéjewski, *Andrew*
Jędrzejkiewicz, *Andrew*
Jeeks, *Geach*
Jeens, *Jane*
Jeeves
Jefcoat, *Jeffrey*
Jefcock, *Jeffrey*
Jefcote, *Jeffrey*
Jefcott, *Jeffrey*
Jeff, *Jeffrey*
Jeffcoat, *Jeffrey*
Jeffcock, *Jeffrey*
Jeffcote, *Jeffrey*
Jeffcott, *Jeffrey*
Jeffe, *Jeffrey*
Jefferd, *Giffard*
Jefferies, *Jeffrey*
Jefferis, *Jeffrey*
Jeffers, *Jeffrey*
Jefferson, *Jeffrey*
Jeffery, *Jeffrey*
Jefferyes, *Jeffrey*
Jefferys, *Jeffrey*
Jeffes, *Jeffrey*
Jefford, *Giffard*
Jeffray, *Jeffrey*
Jeffree, *Jeffrey*
Jeffress, *Jeffrey*
Jeffrey
Jeffries, *Jeffrey*
Jeffroy, *Jeffrey*
Jeffry, *Jeffrey*
Jeffryes, *Jeffrey*

Jeffrys, *Jeffrey*
Jeffs, *Jeffrey*
Jeftić, *Yevtikhiev*
Jeger, *Jäger*
Jeggo, *Jack*
Jeggons, *Jekyll*
Jehaes, *John*
Jehan, *John*
Jehle, *Ulrich*
Jehlička, *Yolkin*
Jekel, *Jacob*
Jekyll
Jelbart, *Gilbert*
Jelbert, *Gilbert*
Jelen
Jelenić, *Jelen*
Jelić, *Yolkin*
Jeličić, *Yolkin*
Jelin, *Jelen*
Jelinak, *Jelen*
Jelínek, *Jelen*
Jelinek, *Jelen*
Jelinowicz, *Jelen*
Jeliński, *Jelen*
Jelinsky, *Jelen*
Jell, *Julian*
Jellard, *Giles*
Jellett, *Gillett*
Jelley, *Julian*
Jellicoe, *Julian*
Jellin, *Jelen*
Jellinek, *Jelen*
Jellings, *Julian*
Jellis, *Giles*
Jellison, *Julian*
Jelliss, *Giles*
Jelonek, *Jelen*
Jelonka, *Jelen*
Jemison, *James*
Jencke, *John*
Jenckes, *Jenks*
Jencks, *Jenks*
Jendrach, *Henry*
Jendrássik, *Henry*
Jendrich, *Henry*
Jendricke, *Henry*
Jendrusch, *Andrew*
Jendrusch, *Henry*
Jendrys, *Andrew*
Jeneson, *Jane*
Jeníček, *John*
Jenicke, *John*
Jeník, *John*
Jenike, *John*
Jenison, *Jane*
Jenke, *John*
Jenken, *Jenkin*
Jenkerson, *Jenkin*
Jenkes, *Jenks*
Jenkin
Jenkins, *Jenkin*
Jenkinson, *Jenkin*
Jenkison, *Jenkin*
Jenks
Jenman, *John*
Jenn, *Jane*
Jenne, *Jane, John*
Jennemann, *John*
Jennens, *Jennings*
Jenner
Jenness, *Jane*
Jennett, *Jane*
Jennewein
Jennings
Jennins, *Jennings*
Jennison, *Jane*
Jennrich, *Henry*
Jenns, *Jane*
Jenoure, *Jenner*
Jensen, *John*
Jent, *Gentle*
Jenteau, *John*
Jentel
Jentet, *John*
Jentgens, *John*
Jentges, *John*
Jentin, *John*
Jentle, *Gentle*
Jenton, *John*
Jentsch, *John*
Jentzsch, *John*
Jephcote, *Jeffrey*
Jephcott, *Jeffrey*
Jephson, *Jeffrey*
Jepp, *Jeffrey*
Jeppe, *Jeffrey*
Jeppesen, *Jacob*
Jeppeson, *Jeffrey*
Jepps, *Jeffrey*
Jepsen, *Jacob*
Jepson, *Jeffrey*
Jepsson, *Jacob*
Jeřábek, *Zuraw*
Jerche, *George*
Jerdan, *Gardener*
Jerdein, *Gardener*
Jerden, *Gardener*
Jerdon, *Gardener*
Jereatt, *Garrett*
Jeremiahu, *Jeremy*
Jeremias, *Jeremy*
Jeremić, *Jeremy*
Jeremies, *Jeremy*
Jeremović, *Jeremy*
Jeremy
Jerety, *Geraghty*
Jerez
Jerg, *George*
Jerger, *George*
Jerich, *George*
Jerisch, *George*
Jerke, *George*
Jerman, *German*
Jermas, *Jeremy*
Jermatz, *Jeremy*
Jermey, *Jeremy*
Jermine, *German*
Jermis, *Jeremy*
Jermulowicz, *Jeremy*
Jermy, *Jeremy*
Jermyn, *German*
Jermynn, *German*
Jeroch, *George*
Jerok, *George*
Jérôme, *Jerome*
Jerome
Jeromes, *Jerome*
Jeroms, *Jerome*
Jerónimo, *Jerome*
Jerosch, *George*
Jerozolimski, *Yerushalmi*
Jerram, *Jerome*
Jerrams, *Jerome*
Jerran, *Jerome*
Jerrans, *Jerome*
Jerrard, *Garrett*
Jerratsch, *George*
Jerratt, *Garrett*
Jerred, *Garrett*
Jerrold, *Garrett*
Jerrolt, *Garrett*
Jerrom, *Jerome*
Jerrome, *Jerome*
Jerromes, *Jerome*
Jerroms, *Jerome*
Jersch, *George*
Jerschke, *George*
Jertz, *Garrett*
Jerushalmi, *Yerushalmi*
Jerushalmy, *Yerushalmi*
Jervis, *Jarvis*
Jerzak, *George*
Jerzyk, *George*
Jerzykiewicz, *George*
Jerzykowski, *George*
Ješ, *Jach*
Jesche, *Jach*
Jeschek, *Jach*
Jeschke, *Jach*
Jeschner, *John*
Ješek, *Jach*
Jesionek, *Jesionowski*
Jesionowski
Jesper, *Kaspar*
Jespers, *Kaspar*
Jespersen, *Kaspar*
Jess, *Joseph*
Jesse, *Joseph*
Jessel, *Joseph*
Jessen, *Jacob*
Jessep, *Joseph*
Jessett, *Joseph*
Jesson, *Joseph*
Jessop, *Joseph*
Jessup, *Joseph*
Jestice, *Justice*
Jesus
Jetson, *Jordan*
Jeude, *Jude*
Jeuffroy, *Jeffrey*
Jeulin, *Julian*
Jeullin, *Julian*
Jeune
Jeuneau, *Jeune*
Jeunet, *Jeune*
Jevain, *Jouvin*
Jeves, *Jeeves*
Jevin, *Jouvin*
Jevon, *Jeavon*
Jevons, *Jeavon*
Jevremović, *Yefremov*
Jevtić, *Yevtikhiev*
Jevtović, *Yevtikhiev*
Jew, *Jude, Julian*
Jewell, *Jekyll*
Jewels, *Jekyll*
Jewesson, *Julian*
Jewett, *Jowett*
Jewhurst, *Dewhurst*
Jewison, *Julian*
Jewitt, *Jowett*
Jewkes, *Jekyll*
Jewry, *Jury*
Jewson, *Julian*
Jex, *Geach*
Jeynes, *Jane*
Jeż, *Yezhov*
Jeżak, *Yezhov*
Ježek, *Yezhov*
Jézéquel, *Jekyll*
Jezerski, *Jeziorski*
Jezersky, *Jeziorski*
Jeżewski, *Yezhov*
Jezierski, *Jeziorski*
Jeziorny, *Jeziorski*
Jeziorski
Jeżowski, *Yezhov*
Jhering, *Geary*
Jibson, *Jeffrey*
Jícha, *Jach*
Jickells, *Jekyll*
Jickles, *Jekyll*
Jickling, *Jekyll*
Jiggen, *Jekyll*
Jiggins, *Jekyll*
Jiggle, *Jekyll*
Jiguet, *Gigot*
Jílek, *Giles*
Jiles, *Giles*
Jillard, *Giles*
Jillett, *Gillett*
Jillings, *Julian*
Jillions, *Julian*
Jillitt, *Gillett*
Jilson, *Julian*
Jilý, *Giles*
Jiménez, *Jimeno*
Jimeno
Jimpson, *James*
Jimson, *James*
Jína, *Henry*
Jinda, *Henry*
Jindáček, *Henry*
Jindra, *Henry*
Jindráček, *Henry*
Jindrák, *Henry*
Jindřich, *Henry*
Jindrich, *Henry*
Jinkin, *Jenkin*
Jinkins, *Jenkin*
Jinks, *Jenks*
Jíra, *George*
Jira, *George*
Jiráček, *George*
Jirák, *George*
Jirak, *George*
Jiráň, *George*
Jiránek, *George*
Jiras, *George*
Jirásek, *George*
Jirek, *George*
Jiří, *George*
Jiříček, *George*
Jiřička, *George*
Jiřík, *George*
Jirka, *George*
Jirkovský, *George*
Jirků, *George*
Jirmyahu, *Jeremy*
Jiroudek, *George*
Jiroušek, *George*
Jirousek, *George*
Jiroutek, *George*
Jiroutka, *George*
Jirsa, *George*
Jírů, *George*
Jiruch, *George*
Jiruš, *George*
Jirušek, *George*
Jirzik, *George*
Jizhaki, *Isaac*
Joachim
Joachimi, *Joachim*
Joachimiak, *Joachim*
Joachimowicz, *Joachim*
Joachimsen, *Joachim*

Joachinsohn, *Joachim*
Joan, *John*
Joanaud, *John*
Joaneton, *John*
Joanic, *John*
Joanin, *John*
Joanisson, *John*
Joannet, *John*
Joanneton, *John*
Joannic, *John*
Joannin, *John*
Joannisson, *John*
Joannot, *John*
Joanny, *John*
Joanot, *John*
Joans, *Jones*
Joany, *John*
João, *John*
Joaquim, *Joachim*
Joaquin, *Joachim*
Joas, *Joyce*
Joass, *Joyce*
Jób, *Job*
Job
Jobar, *Job*
Jobber, *Job*
Jobbins, *Job*
Jobe, *Job*
Jobelin, *Job*
Jobert, *Jaubert*
Jobes, *Job*
Jobet, *Job*
Jobey, *Job*
Jöbgen, *Job*
Jöbges, *Job*
Jobin, *Job*
Jobineau, *Job*
Jobke, *Jacob*
Jöbken, *Job*
Joblin, *Job*
Jobling, *Job*
Jobot, *Job*
Jobson, *Job*
Joce, *Joyce*
Jocelyn
Jochanany, *John*
Jocheim, *Joachim*
Jöchel, *Jach*
Jochel, *Jach*
Jochem, *Joachim*
Jochen, *Joachim*
Jochens, *Joachim*
Jochimowich, *Joachim*
Jochimowicz, *Joachim*
Jochims, *Joachim*
Jochimsen, *Joachim*
Jochmann, *Jach*
Jochum, *Joachim*
Jocić, *John*
Jockelson, *Jekyll*
Jockle, *Jekyll*
Jockumsen, *Joachim*
Jodar
Joder, *Théodore*
Jöderli, *Théodore*
Jodla, *Yolkin*
Jodłowski, *Yolkin*
Jodrellec, *Calderon*
Joe, *Joseph*
Joel, *Jekyll, Yoel*
Joeli, *Yoel*
Joell, *Jekyll*
Joels, *Jekyll, Yoel*
Joelson, *Jekyll, Yoel*
Joely, *Yoel*
Joensen, *John*
Joffre, *Jeffrey*
Joffrey, *Jeffrey*
Joffrin, *Jeffrey*
Jofré, *Jeffrey*
Jofre, *Jeffrey*
Jogla, *Jougleux*
Joglar, *Jougleux*
Johan, *John*
Johanan, *John*
Johananoff, *John*
Johananov, *John*
Johanchon, *John*
Johann, *John*
Johannes, *John*
Johannesen, *John*
Johannesson, *John*
Johanning, *John*
Johannsen, *John*
Johansen, *John*
Johanssen, *John*
Johansson, *John*
Johäntges, *John*
John
Johncock
Johncook, *Johncock*
Johnigan, *John*
Johnikin, *John*
Johnke, *John*
Johns, *John*
Johnsen, *John*
Johnson, *John*
Johnsson, *John*
Johnston
Johnstone, *Johnston*
Johst, *Joyce*
Joice, *Joyce*
Joie, *Joy*
Join, *Jouvin*
Joindeau, *Jouvin*
Joineau, *Jouvin*
Joiner
Joiners, *Joiner*
Joinet, *Jouvin*
Joinson, *John*
Joire, *George*
Joiris, *George*
Joisce, *Joyce*
Joisse, *Joyce*
Joisson, *Joyce*
Jojić, *John*
Jokel, *Jacob*
Jokinen
Jokisch, *Jach*
Jokl, *Jacob*
Joksch, *Jach*
Jokusch, *Jach*
Joles, *Yoel*
Jolet, *Jolly*
Joli, *Jolly*
Joliet, *Jolly*
Jolif, *Jolly*
Jolin, *Jekyll, Jolly*
Jolion, *Jolly*
Joliveau, *Jolly*
Jolivel, *Jolly*
Jolivet, *Jolly*
Jolivot, *Jolly*
Joll, *Julian*
Jolland, *Jekyll*
Jollands, *Jekyll*
Jolle, *Julian*
Jolles, *Julian, Yoel*
Jollet, *Jolly*
Jolley, *Jolly*
Jollie, *Jolly*
Jolliff, *Jolly*
Jolliffe, *Jolly*
Jollin, *Jekyll, Jolly*
Jolliot, *Jolly*
Jolly
Jollye, *Jolly*
Jolson, *Jekyll*
Joly, *Jolly*
Jon, *John*
Jona, *Jonas*
Jonah, *Jonas*
Jonák, *Jonas*
Jónás, *Jonas*
Jonáš, *Jonas*
Jonas
Jonasen, *Jonas*
Jonasson, *Jonas*
Jonchay
Jonchère, *Jonchay*
Joncherie, *Jonchay*
Jončić, *John*
Joncière, *Jonchay*
Jonckheere, *Younger*
Joncock, *Johncock*
Joncook, *Johncock*
Jończyk, *John*
Jone, *John*
Jones
Jonet, *Jeune*
Jong, *Young*
Jonge, *Young*
Jongen, *Young*
Jongh, *Young*
Jonghe, *Young*
Jonigan, *John*
Jonikin, *John*
Jönk, *John*
Jonk, *Young*
Jönke, *John*
Jonker, *Younger*
Jonkers, *Younger*
Jonnart, *Jeune*
Jonneau, *Jeune*
Jonnet, *Jeune*
Jonquères, *Jonchay*
Jonquières, *Jonchay*
Jonsen, *John*
Jonson, *John*
Jönsson, *John*
Jonsson, *John*
Jonuzi, *John*
Joontjes, *John*
Joos, *Joyce*
Jooss, *Joyce*
Jooste, *Joyce*
Joosten, *Joyce*
Jope, *Job*
Jopke, *Jacob*
Joplin, *Job*
Jopling, *Job*
Jopp, *Job*
Joppich, *Jacob*
Jopson, *Job*
Jorat, *George*
Jorba
Jorbahn, *Urban*
Jorband, *Urban*
Jörck, *George*
Jorczyk, *George*
Jordà, *Jordan*
Jordain, *Jordan*
Jordán, *Jordan*
Jordan
Jordana, *Jordan*
Jordanet, *Jordan*
Jordaney, *Jordan*
Jordanov, *Jordan*
Jordans, *Jordan*
Jordański, *Jordan*
Jordão, *Jordan*
Jördens, *Jordan*
Jordens, *Jordan*
Jordi, *George*
Jordi, *Jordan*
Jordin, *Jordan*
Jordon, *Jordan*
Jordt, *Goddard*
Jore, *George*
Joreau, *George*
Joret, *George*
Jorey, *George*
Jorez, *George*
Jörg, *George*
Jorg, *George*
Jorge, *George*
Jörgensen, *George*
Jörger, *George*
Jørgesen, *George*
Jori, *George*
Jorin, *George*
Jorio, *George*
Joriot, *George*
Jorioz, *George*
Joris, *George*
Jorissen, *George*
Jörn, *George*
Joron, *George*
Jorry, *George*
Jory, *George*
Joscelyn, *Jocelyn*
Joscelyne, *Jocelyn*
José, *Joseph*
Jose, *Joyce*
Josef, *Joseph*
Josefer, *Joseph*
Joseff, *Joseph*
Josefovic, *Joseph*
Josefowicz, *Joseph*
Josefs, *Joseph*
Josefsen, *Joseph*
Josefsohn, *Joseph*
Josefson, *Joseph*
Josefsson, *Joseph*
Joseland, *Jocelyn*
Joselevitch, *Joseph*
Joselevitz, *Joseph*
Joselin, *Jocelyn*
Joselovitch, *Joseph*
Joselson, *Joseph*
Joseph
Josephi, *Joseph*
Josephoff, *Joseph*
Josephov, *Joseph*
Josephs, *Joseph*
Josephsen, *Joseph*
Josephson, *Joseph*
Josephy, *Joseph*
Josey, *Joseph*
Josifović, *Joseph*
Josifovitz, *Joseph*
Josilevich, *Joseph*
Josilowski, *Joseph*
Josipović, *Joseph*
Josipovitz, *Joseph*
Joska, *Joseph*

Joskovitch, *Joseph*
Joskowicz, *Joseph*
Joskowitz, *Joseph*
Josland, *Jocelyn*
Joslen, *Jocelyn*
Joslin, *Jocelyn, Joseph*
Josling, *Jocelyn*
Joslow, *Joseph*
Josofovitz, *Joseph*
Josovich, *Joseph*
Josovitz, *Joseph*
Josowitz, *Joseph*
Josquin, *Joyce*
Joss, *Joyce*
Josse, *Joyce*
Jossel, *Joseph*
Josselin, *Jocelyn*
Josseline, *Jocelyn*
Josselsohn, *Joseph*
Josselson, *Joseph*
Josselyn, *Jocelyn*
Jossequin, *Joyce*
Josset, *Joyce*
Jossic, *Joyce*
Jossin, *Joyce*
Josskovitz, *Joseph*
Josskoviz, *Joseph*
Josson, *Joyce*
Jossot, *Joyce*
Jost, *Joyce*
Jöstel, *Joyce*
Jostel, *Joyce*
Josten, *Joyce*
Jostes, *Joyce*
Jösting, *Joyce*
Josupeit, *Joseph*
Josuweit, *Joseph*
Jou, *Jover*
Jouan, *John*
Jouandeau, *John*
Jouandet, *John*
Jouaneau, *John*
Jouanet, *John*
Jouaneton, *John*
Jouanin, *John*
Jouanisson, *John*
Jouanneton, *John*
Jouannin, *John*
Jouannisson, *John*
Jouannot, *John*
Jouanny, *John*
Jouanot, *John*
Jouany, *John*
Joubert, *Jaubert*
Joubertin, *Jaubert*
Jouberton, *Jaubert*
Joucla, *Jougleux*
Joudren, *Jordan*
Jouen, *John*
Jouet, *Jouvin*
Joufrion, *Jeffrey*
Jougla, *Jougleux*
Jouglar, *Jougleux*
Jouglas, *Jougleux*
Jougleux
Jouhan, *John*
Jouhandeau, *John*
Jouhaneau, *John*
Jouin, *Jouvin*
Jouisse, *Joyce*
Joulain, *Julian*
Joule, *Jekyll*
Joules, *Jekyll*
Joulin, *Julian*
Joullain, *Julian*
Joullin, *Julian*
Jouon, *Jouvin*
Jouot, *Jouvin*
Jourdain, *Jordan*
Jourdan, *Jordan*
Jourdanet, *Jordan*
Jourdaney, *Jordan*
Jourde, *Jordan*
Jourdin, *Jordan*
Jourdineau, *Jordan*
Jourdon, *Jordan*
Jousse, *Joyce*
Jousselin, *Jocelyn*
Jousseline, *Jocelyn*
Jousserand, *Galceran*
Jousset, *Joyce*
Joussin, *Joyce*
Jousson, *Joyce*
Joussot, *Joyce*
Joutaitis, *Joseph*
Joutapaitis, *Joseph*
Joutapavicius, *Joseph*
Jouve, *Jeune*
Jouveau, *Jeune*
Jouvel, *Jeune*
Jouven, *Jeune*
Jouvenel, *Jeune*
Jouvenet, *Jeune*
Jouvenot, *Jeune*
Jouvet, *Jeune*
Jouvin
Jouxson, *Jekyll*
Jovanović, *John*
Jovašević, *John*
Jové, *Jover*
Jove, *Jeune*
Jovelet, *Jouvin*
Jovelin, *Jouvin*
Jover
Jovers, *Godfrey*
Jović, *John*
Jovićević, *John*
Jovičić, *John*
Jovignet, *Jouvin*
Jovin, *Jouvin*
Jovinet, *Jouvin*
Jovović, *John*
Jowett
Jowitt, *Jowett*
Jowle, *Jekyll*
Jowling, *Jekyll*
Joy
Joyce
Joye, *Joy*
Joyes, *Joy*
Joyet, *Joy*
Joyner, *Joiner*
Joynes, *Jones*
Joynson, *John*
Jozaitis, *Joseph*
Józef, *Joseph*
Józefczak, *Joseph*
Józefiak, *Joseph*
Józefowicz, *Joseph*
Józsa, *Joseph*
József, *Joseph*
Józsika, *Joseph*
Jóźwiak, *Joseph*
Jóźwicki, *Joseph*
Jóźwik, *Joseph*
Juan, *John*
Juanes, *John*
Juanico, *John*
Jubb, *Job*
Jubber, *Job*
Jubert, *Jaubert*
Juby, *Job*
Jud, *Jude*
Judas, *Jude*
Judd, *Jordan*
Jude
Judeikin, *Jude*
Judelevich, *Jude*
Judelevitch, *Jude*
Judelevitz, *Jude*
Judelewitz, *Jude*
Judelman, *Jude*
Juden, *Jordan*
Juderías, *Jury*
Judet, *Jude*
Judevitch, *Jude*
Judge
Judges, *Judge*
Judin, *Jude*
Judkes, *Jude*
Judkevitz, *Jude*
Judkewich, *Jude*
Judkiewicz, *Jude*
Judkovicz, *Jude*
Judkowski, *Jude*
Jüdl, *Jude*
Judlin, *Jude*
Judon, *Jude*
Judovitch, *Jude*
Judovits, *Jude*
Judovitz, *Jude*
Judson, *Jordan*
Judt, *Jude*
Juel, *Yule*
Juell, *Jekyll*
Juett, *Jowett*
Juez, *Judge*
Juge, *Judge*
Jugeau, *Judge*
Jugelet, *Judge*
Juget, *Judge*
Jugg, *Jekyll*
Juggins, *Jekyll*
Juggler, *Jougleux*
Juhász
Juhel, *Jekyll*
Juhl, *Yule*
Juhlin, *Yule*
Juhre, *George*
Juhrich, *George*
Juhrke, *George*
Juillard, *Julian*
Juillet, *Julian*
Juillot, *Julian*
Jukes, *Jekyll*
Jule, *Júlio*
Jules, *Júlio, Julian*
Julhe, *Júlio*
Julhes, *Júlio*
Julià, *Julian*
Julián, *Julian*
Julian
Julians, *Julian*
Juliard, *Julian*
Julien, *Julian*
Juliffe, *Jolly*
Julin, *Yule*
Júlio
Juliot, *Julian*
Juliussen, *Júlio*
Jull, *Julian*
Jullens, *Julian*
Jullian, *Julian*
Jullien, *Julian*
Jullings, *Julian*
Julyan, *Julian*
Jumeau
Jumel, *Jumeau*
Jumelet, *Jumeau*
Jůn, *Jun*
Jun
Jůna, *Jun*
Juna, *Jun*
Juncà, *Jonchay*
Juncker, *Younger*
Juncosa, *Jonchay*
Junek, *Jun*
Jung, *Young*
Junge, *Young*
Junger, *Young*
Jungerman, *Young*
Jungermann, *Young*
Junifer, *Juniper*
Juniper
Junk, *Young*
Junker, *Younger*
Junkers, *Younger*
Junkin, *Jenkin*
Junkinson, *Jenkin*
Junkison, *Jenkin*
Junquera, *Jonchay*
Juorio, *George*
Jupe, *Job*
Jupp, *Job*
Jura, *George*
Jurado
Juraitis, *George*
Juránek, *George*
Jurásek, *George*
Jurasz, *George*
Jurband, *Urban*
Jurča, *George*
Jurczak, *George*
Jurczik, *George*
Jurczyk, *George*
Jurd, *Jordan*
Jurek, *George*
Jurewicz, *George*
Jurgaitis, *George*
Jürgen, *George*
Jurgen, *George*
Jürgens, *George*
Jurgens, *George*
Jürgensen, *George*
Jurgensen, *George*
Jurgenson, *George*
Jürges, *George*
Jurich, *George*
Jurick, *George*
Jurik, *George*
Juris, *George*
Jurisch, *George*
Jurišić, *George*
Jurkiewicz, *George*
Jurkowski, *George*
Jürn, *George*
Jurn, *George*
Jürres, *George*
Jürries, *George*
Jürs, *George*
Jursch, *George*
Jury
Jurzyk, *George*
Juschka, *George*
Juschke, *George*
Juson, *Julian*

K

Kanner, *Kannengiesser*
Kanngiesser, *Kannengiesser*
Kantarovitch, *Kantor*
Kantarovitz, *Kantor*
Kantarowicz, *Kantor*
Kantarowitch, *Kantor*
Kanter, *Kantor*
Kanterman, *Kantor*
Kanterovich, *Kantor*
Kanters, *Kantor*
Kántor, *Kantor*
Kantor
Kantorovich, *Kantor*
Kantorovitch, *Kantor*
Kantorovitz, *Kantor*
Kantorovsky, *Kantor*
Kantorowicz, *Kantor*
Kantorowitch, *Kantor*
Kantorowitsh, *Kantor*
Kantorowitz, *Kantor*
Kantrow, *Kantor*
Kantrowicz, *Kantor*
Kantrowitz, *Kantor*
Kánya, *Kania*
Kanzler, *Chancellor*
Kapaun, *Capon*
Kapelushnik, *Chape*
Kapelusz, *Chape*
Kapetanović, *Kapitonov*
Kapf
Kapfer, *Kapf*
Kapferer, *Kapf*
Kaphahn, *Capon*
Kapitán, *Capitaine*
Kapitány, *Capitaine*
Kapitonov
Kaplan
Kaplanowicz, *Kaplan*
Kaplanski, *Kaplan*
Kaplin, *Kaplan*
Kaplinski, *Kaplan*
Kaplinsky, *Kaplan*
Kappe, *Chape*
Käppel, *Chape*
Käppele, *Chape*
Käppner, *Chape*
Kappuhn, *Capon*
Kapr, *Karpov*
Kapras, *Karpov*
Kaprilian, *Gabriel*
Kapteijn, *Capitaine*
Kaptein, *Capitaine*
Kapteyn, *Capitaine*
Kapuściak, *Kapusta*
Kapuściński
Kapusta
Karapetian, *Garabedian*
Karas, *Karaś*
Karaś
Karásek, *Karaś*
Karasek, *Karaś*
Karasiewicz, *Karaś*
Karasiński, *Karaś*
Karaszewicz, *Karaś*
Karatygin, *Korotygin*
Karaus, *Karaś*
Karban
Karbowiak
Karbownik, *Karbowiak*
Karbowski, *Karbowiak*
Karch
Kärcher, *Karch*
Karcher, *Karch*
Karchmer, *Kretschmar*
Karczewski
Karczmar, *Kretschmar*
Karczmarczyk, *Kretschmar*
Karczmarek, *Kretschmar*
Karczmarski, *Kretschmar*
Karczmer, *Kretschmar*
Kardinael, *Cardinal*
Kardinal, *Cardinal*
Kardos
Karel, *Charles*
Karer, *Karmann*
Kareš, *Charles*
Karfunkel, *Gorfinkel*
Karfunkiel, *Gorfinkel*
Karg
Kärgel, *Karg*
Karger, *Karg*
Karges, *Macaire*
Kargman, *Karg*
Karies, *Macaire*
Karius, *Macaire*
Karjalainen
Kärkkäinen
Karl, *Charles*
Karle, *Charles*
Karlíček, *Charles*
Karlík, *Charles*
Karlin
Karliner, *Karlin*
Karlinski, *Karlin*
Karlinsky, *Karlin*
Karlovský, *Charles*
Karłowicz, *Charles*
Karłowski, *Charles*
Karlsen, *Charles*
Karlsson, *Charles*
Karmann
Karmeli, *Carmo*
Karolak, *Charles*
Karolczak, *Charles*
Karolczyk, *Charles*
Karolewski, *Charles*
Károly, *Charles*
Karolyi, *Charles*
Karp, *Karpov*
Karpe, *Karpov*
Karpeev, *Karpov*
Karpel, *Karpov*
Karpeles, *Karpov*
Karpenko, *Karpov*
Karpenya, *Karpov*
Karpets, *Karpov*
Karpf, *Karpov*
Karpfen, *Karpov*
Karpik, *Karpov*
Karpinen, *Karpov*
Karpiński, *Karpov*
Karpio, *Karpov*
Karpísek, *Karpov*
Karpman, *Karpov*
Karpoff, *Karpov*
Karpov
Karppi, *Karpov*
Karpukhin, *Karpov*
Karpunichev, *Karpov*
Karpushkin, *Karpov*
Karputkin, *Karpov*
Karpychev, *Karpov*
Karpyshev, *Karpov*
Kärrström, *Kerr*
Karsch, *Kirsch*
Karschenstein, *Kirsch*
Karsh, *Kirsch*
Karshen, *Kirsch*
Karshon, *Kirsch*
Karski
Karslake, *Carslake*
Karśnicki, *Karski*
Karssen, *Christian*
Karst, *Christian*
Karsten, *Christian*
Karstens, *Christian*
Karstensen, *Christian*
Kartschmer, *Kretschmar*
Kartsev, *Karpov*
Karwacki
Karwański, *Karwacki*
Karwat, *Karwacki*
Karwatek, *Karwacki*
Karwowski, *Karwacki*
Käs, *Cheeseman*
Kas, *Case*
Káš, *Lucas*
Kašák, *Lucas*
Kaschke, *Lucas*
Käse, *Cheeseman*
Kašek, *Lucas*
Käser, *Cheeseman*
Kashman, *Cashman*
Kašík, *Lucas*
Käsmann, *Cheeseman*
Kašpar, *Kaspar*
Kaspar
Kašpárek, *Kaspar*
Kasparek, *Kaspar*
Kasparkiewicz, *Kaspar*
Kasparov, *Kaspar*
Kasparski, *Kaspar*
Kasper, *Kaspar*
Kasperek, *Kaspar*
Kasperov, *Kaspar*
Kasperovich, *Kaspar*
Kasperski, *Kaspar*
Kasprowiak, *Kaspar*
Kasprowicki, *Kaspar*
Kasprowicz, *Kaspar*
Kasprzak, *Kaspar*
Kasprzycki, *Kaspar*
Kasprzyk, *Kaspar*
Kasprzykiewicz, *Kaspar*
Kassel, *Castle*
Kassidy, *Cassidy*
Kassierer, *Case*
Kassirer, *Case*
Kast, *Christian*
Kaštánek, *Castan*
Kastel, *Castle*
Kasten, *Christian*
Kastens, *Christian*
Kastensen, *Christian*
Kasting, *Christian*
Kästner, *Kastner*
Kastner
Kašuba, *Kaszuba*
Kaszczyk, *Kaspar*
Kaszper, *Kaspar*
Kaszuba
Kaszubski, *Kaszuba*
Kat, *Catt*
Kataev
Katalan, *Catalán*
Kataloni, *Catalán*
Katan
Kate, *Catlin*
Kater, *Catt*
Katerinich, *Catlin*
Katerinin, *Catlin*
Katerinov, *Catlin*
Katerinyuk, *Catlin*
Kates, *Cates*
Käther, *Cotter*
Kather, *Cotter*
Kathman, *Coates*
Kathrein, *Catlin*
Kathreiner, *Catlin*
Katona
Katrevich, *Catlin*
Katrich, *Catlin*
Katrin, *Catlin*
Kats, *Catt*
Katsevman, *Katzev*
Kattan, *Katan*
Katte, *Catt*
Katusov, *Constantine*
Katynin, *Catlin*
Katyushin, *Catlin*
Katyushkin, *Catlin*
Katz
Katzeff, *Katzev*
Katzenellenbogen
Katzenelson, *Katzenellenbogen*
Katzenstein, *Katz*
Katzev
Katziff, *Katzev*
Katzman, *Katz*
Katzmann, *Katz*
Katznelson, *Katzenellenbogen*
Katzoff, *Katzev*
Katzowitch, *Katzev*
Katzowitz, *Katzev*
Kaubisch, *Jacob*
Kaucký, *Koutský*
Kauf, *Chapman*
Käufel, *Chapman*
Käufer, *Chapman*
Kaufer, *Chapman*
Kauffman, *Chapman*
Kauffmann, *Chapman*
Käufler, *Chapman*
Kaufman, *Chapman*
Kaufmann, *Chapman*
Kaufner, *Kiefer*
Kauppinen, *Chapman*
Kautský, *Koutský*
Kavanagh
Kave, *Cave*
Kavka, *Kafka*
Kawa, *Kafka*
Kawczyński, *Kafka*
Kawecki, *Kafka*
Kawiński, *Kafka*
Kawka, *Kafka*
Kay
Kaye, *Kay*
Kayes, *Keyes*
Kayley, *Cayley*
Kayne, *Cain*
Kays, *Keyes*
Kayser, *Kaiser*
Kayzer, *Kaiser*
Kazan, *Chazan*
Kazanov, *Chazan*
Kazanovich, *Chazan*
Kazanovski, *Chazan*
Kazanowitz, *Chazan*
Kazimierczak, *Kaźmierczak*
Kazimierowicz, *Kaźmierczak*
Kazimierski
Kazimiersky, *Kazimierski*
Kazimierz, *Kazimierski*
Kazimirov, *Kaźmierczak*
Kazimirski, *Kazimierski*

Kazimirsky, *Kazimierski*
Kazkiewicz, *Kaźmierczak*
Kázmér, *Kaźmierczak*
Kaźmierczak
Kaźmierski, *Kazimierski*
Keable, *Keble*
Keach, *Keech*
Keag, *McCaig*
Keague, *McCaig*
Kealahan, *Callaghan*
Kealey, *Keeley*
Kealy, *Keeley*
Kean, *Keane*
Keane
Kearney
Kearns
Kearsley
Keary, *Carey*
Keast
Keat, *Kite*
Keatch, *Keech*
Keate, *Kite*
Keates, *Kite*
Keating
Keatley, *Keighley*
Keats, *Kite*
Keaty
Keavane, *Keefe*
Keay, *Kay*
Keays, *Keyes*
Kebbell, *Keble*
Kebble, *Keble*
Kebell, *Keble*
Kebert, *Gebhardt*
Keble
Keddie, *Adam*
Keddy, *Adam*
Kedge
Kedie, *Adam*
Kędziak, *Kudravtsev*
Kędzierski, *Kudravtsev*
Kędzior, *Kudravtsev*
Kędziora, *Kudravtsev*
Keeble, *Keble*
Keech
Keefe
Keeffe, *Keefe*
Keegan
Keel, *Keeler*
Keeler
Keeley
Keeling
Keely, *Keeley*
Keemish, *Camoys*
Keen
Keene, *Keen*
Keenlyside
Keep
Keerl, *Charles*
Keery, *Carey*
Keese, *Cheeseman*
Keeser, *Keser*
Keesman, *Cheeseman*
Keet, *Kite*
Keetch, *Keech*
Keetley, *Keighley*
Keevane, *Keefe*
Keevil
Keeys, *Keyes*
Kegan, *Keegan*
Kegg, *McCaig*
Keggin, *Keegan*
Keggins, *Keegan*
Kegley, *Quickley*
Kehl
Kehoe, *Keogh*
Kehoe, *Kew*
Kehrl, *Charles*
Keig, *McCaig*
Keighley
Keighly, *Keighley*
Keight, *Kite*
Keightley, *Keighley*
Keijser, *Kaiser*
Keijzer, *Kaiser*
Keil
Keillips, *McKillop*
Keinrat, *Konrad*
Keir, *Kerr*
Keiser, *Kaiser*
Keiserman, *Kaiser*
Keitch, *Keech*
Keith
Keitley, *Keighley*
Keizer, *Kaiser*
Keizman, *Cheeseman*
Kelaghan, *Callaghan*
Kelberer, *Calf*
Kelberman, *Calf*
Kelble, *Calf*
Kelder, *Seller*
Kelemen, *Clement*
Keler, *Kellner*
Kelerman, *Kellner*
Kelermann, *Kellner*
Kell, *Kettle*
Kellar, *Kellner*
Kellart, *Kellner*
Kellaway, *Calloway*
Kelleher
Keller, *Kellner*
Kellerman, *Kellner*
Kellermann, *Kellner*
Kellert, *Kellner*
Kellet, *Kellett*
Kellett
Kelleway, *Calloway*
Kelley, *Kelly*
Kelliher, *Kelleher*
Kellitt, *Kellett*
Kellman, *Kalman*
Kellner
Kello
Kelloch, *Kelly*
Kellock, *Kelly*
Kellog, *Kellogg*
Kellogg
Kellow
Kells, *Kettle*
Kelly
Kelman, *Kalman*
Kelner, *Kellner*
Kelsall
Kelsey
Kelso
Kelway, *Calloway*
Kember, *Camber*
Kemble
Kemelman, *Camber*
Kemelman, *Kemmelman*
Kemény
Kemmelman
Kemmer, *Camber*
Kemmis, *Camoys*
Kemmler, *Camber*
Kemp
Kempa
Kempe, *Kemp, Kempa*
Kemper, *Champ, Kemp*
Kempers, *Kemp*
Kempf, *Kemp*
Kempfle, *Kemp*
Kempiński, *Kempa*
Kempinski, *Kempa*
Kempner, *Kemp*
Kemppainen, *Kemp*
Kempski, *Kempa*
Kempson, *Kemp*
Kempster, *Camber*
Kempton
Kendal, *Kendall*
Kendall
Kendell, *Kendall*
Kendle, *Kendall*
Kendler, *Kändler*
Kendrew, *Andrew*
Kendrick
Kendzersky, *Kudravtsev*
Kenerney, *McNairn*
Kenlan, *Quinlan*
Kenna, *Kenny*
Kennan, *Kenny*
Kennard
Kennaway
Kenneally
Kennealy, *Kenneally*
Kennedy
Kennellan, *Quinlan*
Kennelly, *Kenneally*
Kennely, *Kenneally*
Kennett
Kenney, *Kenny*
Kenngott
Kennigan, *Cunningham*
Kenning, *Keen*
Kennish, *McGuinness*
Kenny
Kenrick, *Kendrick*
Kent
Kentish, *Kent*
Kenton
Kenward, *Kennard*
Kenway, *Kennaway*
Kenwood, *Kennard*
Kenworthy
Kenwrick, *Kendrick*
Kenyeres
Kenyon
Keogan, *Keogh*
Keogh
Keoghan, *Keogh*
Keoghoe, *Keogh*
Keohane, *Keogh*
Keough, *Keogh*
Keown, *Ewan*
Kępa, *Kempa*
Kępczyński, *Kempa*
Kępiński, *Kempa*
Kępka, *Kempa*
Kepler, *Chape*
Keppel, *Chape*
Keppie
Keppler, *Chape*
Keppner, *Chape*
Kępski, *Kempa*
Ker, *Kerr*
Kerber, *Corbeil, Korb*
Kerbey, *Kirby*
Kerbler, *Korb*
Kerby, *Kirby*
Kercher, *Karch*
Kerfed, *Kerfoot*
Kerfod, *Kerfoot*
Kerfoot
Kergan, *Kerrigan*
Kerigan, *Kerrigan*
Kerk, *Kirk*
Kerl, *Charles*
Kerley, *Curley*
Kermeen, *Curwen*
Kermode, *Dermott*
Kern
Kernaghan
Kernan, *McKiernan*
Kerner
Kernerman, *Kerner*
Kernohan, *Kernaghan*
Kernon, *McKiernan*
Kerr
Kerrage, *Kendrick*
Kerrich, *Kendrick*
Kerrick, *Kendrick*
Kerridge, *Kendrick*
Kerrigan
Kerrison, *Kendrick*
Kerry, *Kendrick*
Kersaw, *Kershaw*
Kersch, *Kirsch*
Kerschenbaum, *Kirsch*
Kerschman, *Kirsch*
Kerschner, *Kürschner*
Kersey
Kersh, *Kirsch*
Kershaw
Kershenblat, *Kirsch*
Kershman, *Kirsch*
Kershner, *Kürschner*
Kerslake, *Carslake*
Kersner, *Kürschner*
Kerst, *Christian*
Kerstein, *Kirsch*
Kersten, *Christian*
Kerstens, *Christian*
Kerstgens, *Christian*
Kersting, *Christian*
Kerswell, *Creswell*
Kerswill, *Creswell*
Kertész
Keser, *Kaiser*
Keser
Keserling, *Kiessling*
Keshin, *McCashin*
Keslake, *Carslake*
Kesler, *Kessel*
Kesper, *Kaspar*
Kespers, *Kaspar*
Kessel
Kesseler, *Kessel*
Kesselman, *Kessel*
Kessler, *Kessel*
Kest, *Christian*
Kestell, *Castle*
Kesten, *Christian*
Kestenbaum, *Castan*
Kesterton, *Chesterton*
Kesting, *Christian*
Kestle, *Castle*
Kestner, *Kastner*
Ketch, *Kedge*
Ketchen, *Kitchen*
Ketchin, *Kitchen*
Ketel, *Kessel*
Ketels, *Kettle*
Ketelsen, *Kettle*
Ketill, *Kettle*
Ketley

Kett
Kettel, *Kessel, Kettle*
Kettell, *Kettle*
Kettelson, *Kettle*
Kettle
Kettler, *Kessel*
Kettles, *Kettle*
Kettless, *Kettle*
Kettlewell
Ketts, *Kite*
Kettunen
Keune, *Konrad*
Keuneke, *Konrad*
Keunemann, *Konrad*
Keuning, *Konrad*
Keuntje, *Konrad*
Kevane, *Keefe*
Kevans, *Keefe*
Kevern
Kew
Kewley, *Cowley*
Key, *Kay, McKay*
Keye, *Kay*
Keyes
Keyfetz, *Heifetz*
Keyho, *Kew*
Keyhoe, *Kew*
Keynes
Keys, *Keyes*
Keyser, *Kaiser*
Keysers, *Kaiser*
Keysor, *Kaiser*
Keyte, *Kite*
Keyworth
Keyzer, *Kaiser*
Keyzman, *Cheeseman*
Keyzor, *Kaiser*
Khachaturian
Khadeev, *Tadié*
Khadkevich, *Théodore*
Khaet, *Chait*
Khaimovich, *Hyam*
Khait, *Chait*
Khaitovich, *Chait*
Khanele, *Hanna*
Khaninke, *Hanna*
Khanke, *Hanna*
Khavke
Khavkin, *Khavke*
Khazan, *Chazan*
Khazanov, *Chazan*
Khazanovich, *Chazan*
Khazanovski, *Chazan*
Khilkov, *Philip*
Khimichev, *Yefimov*
Khlebnikov
Khmelnytsky, *Chmielewski*
Khodasevich, *Théodore*
Khodorovich, *Théodore*
Khomich, *Thomas*
Khomik, *Thomas*
Khomin, *Thomas*
Khomishin, *Thomas*
Khrenov, *Chrzanowski*
Khrishtafovich, *Christopher*
Khrishtanovich, *Christian*
Khristich, *Christian*
Khristin, *Christian*
Khristinin, *Christian*
Khristoforov, *Christopher*
Khristyukhin, *Christopher*
Khrushchev
Khvedko, *Théodore*
Kiær, *Kerr*
Kibbel, *Keble*
Kibble, *Keble*
Kibel, *Keble*
Kid, *Kidd*
Kidd
Kidde, *Kidd*
Kiddell, *Kiddle*
Kiddie, *Adam*
Kiddle
Kiddy, *Adam*
Kidman, *Kidd*
Kidney, *Devane*
Kidson, *Kidd*
Kief, *Kiefer*
Kiefer
Kiefner, *Kiefer*
Kiehne, *Konrad*
Kiehnelt, *Konrad*
Kiełbasa
Kiełbasiak, *Kiełbasa*
Kiełbasiński, *Kiełbasa*
Kiely
Kiendl, *Konrad*
Kienl, *Konrad*
Kienle, *Konrad*
Kienlein, *Konrad*
Kienzle, *Konrad*
Kieran
Kierans, *Kieran*
Kierevan, *Kirwan*
Kierkegaard, *Churchyard*
Kiernan, *McKiernan*
Kierschner, *Kürschner*
Kiervan, *Kirwan*
Kiesel
Kieselstein, *Kiesel*
Kieser
Kieserling, *Kiessling*
Kiesewetter
Kieslich, *Kiessling*
Kiesling, *Kiessling*
Kiesslich, *Kiessling*
Kiessling
Kiezler, *Konrad*
Kigel, *Kugel*
Kighel, *Kugel*
Kightley, *Keighley*
Kihlberg, *Keil*
Kihlén, *Keil*
Kihlgren, *Keil*
Kihlin, *Keil*
Kihlström, *Keil*
Kilbane
Kilberg, *Keil*
Kilbey, *Kilby*
Kilboy, *McEvoy*
Kilbride
Kilburn
Kilbuy, *Kilby*
Kilby
Kilcoyne
Kildaire, *Kildare*
Kildare
Kildea
Kilduff, *Gilduff*
Kilén, *Keil*
Kilfeather
Kilfedder, *Kilfeather*
Kilfillan, *Gilfillan*
Kilfoyle, *Gilfoil*
Kilgore, *Kilgour*
Kilgour
Kilgren, *Keil*
Kilgus, *Killeen*
Kilián, *Killeen*
Kilian, *Killeen*
Kilin, *Keil*
Kilius, *Killeen*
Kiljan, *Killeen*
Kiljański, *Killeen*
Kill, *Killeen*
Killby, *Kilby*
Killduff, *Gilduff*
Killeavy, *Dunleavy*
Killeen
Killen, *Killeen*
Killery, *McIlwraith*
Killian, *Killeen*
Killick
Killigrew
Killik, *Killick*
Killingback, *Killingbeck*
Killingbeck
Killington
Killip, *McKillop*
Kilmartin, *Gilmartin*
Kilminster
Kilmore, *Gilmore*
Kilner
Kilpatrick
Kilroy, *Gilroy*
Kilshaw, *Kelsall*
Kilsson, *Kettle*
Kilström, *Keil*
Kilvert
Kilvington
Kimber
Kimberley
Kimberly, *Kimberley*
Kimbrough, *Kimber*
Kimel, *Kümmel*
Kimelfeld, *Kümmel*
Kimelheim, *Kümmel*
Kimelman, *Kümmel*
Kimelmann, *Kümmel*
Kimmel, *Kümmel*
Kimmelfield, *Kümmel*
Kimmelman, *Kümmel*
Kimpton
Kinaghan, *Cunningham*
Kinahan, *Cunningham*
Kinavan, *Canavan*
Kincade, *Kincaid*
Kincaid
Kincaidie, *Kincaid*
Kincey, *Kinsey*
Kinch, *McGuinness*
Kind
Kindall, *Kendall*
Kindel, *Kind*
Kindell, *Kendall*
Kindellan, *Quinlan*
Kinder
Kinderlehrer
Kinderlerer, *Kinderlehrer*
Kindl, *Kind*
Kindle, *Kendall*
Kindon, *Kingdon*
Kindrick, *Kendrick*
Kindt, *Kind*
Kine, *Coyne*
Kineally, *Kenneally*
Kinerny, *McNairn*
King
Kingdon
Kinge, *King*
Kingeter, *Kenngott*
Kingett, *King*
Kinggett, *King*
Kingham
Kinghan, *Cunningham*
Kinghorn
Kinghorne, *Kinghorn*
Kingman, *King*
Kings, *King*
Kingsberg, *Königsberg*
Kingsbury
Kingscote
Kingscott, *Kingscote*
Kingsley
Kingson, *King*
Kingston
Kingstone, *Kingston*
Kington
Kingwell
Kinig, *König*
Kinigel, *König*
Kinigsberg, *Königsberg*
Kinigson, *König*
Kinigstein, *König*
Kiniry, *McEnery*
Kinkade, *Kincaid*
Kinkaid, *Kincaid*
Kinkead, *Kincaid*
Kinkel, *Gunkel*
Kinlan, *Quinlan*
Kinloch
Kinlock, *Kinloch*
Kinnaird
Kinnan, *Finn*
Kinne, *Kenngott*
Kinneally, *Kenneally*
Kinnear
Kinneavy
Kinneen
Kinnegan, *Cunningham*
Kinneir, *Kinnear*
Kinney, *Kenny*
Kinnie, *Kenny*
Kinnighan, *Cunningham*
Kinnish, *McGuinness*
Kinny, *Kenny*
Kinscher, *Kenngott*
Kinsella
Kinsey
Kinshela, *Kinsella*
Kinsley, *Kinsella*
Kinsman
Kintish, *Kent*
Kintscher, *Kenngott*
Kintzel, *Konrad*
Kinzel, *Konrad*
Kinzie, *Kinsey*
Kiper, *Copper*
Kiperbaum, *Copper*
Kiperman, *Copper*
Kipling
Kipper, *Copper*
Kippie, *Keppie*
Király, *Król*
Királyfi, *Król*
Kirby
Kirch, *Kirk*
Kirchner
Kirchstein, *Christian*
Kirckman, *Kirk*
Kireenko, *Kirilov*
Kireev, *Kirilov*
Kireiko, *Kirilov*
Kirichev, *Kirilov*
Kirichkov, *Kirilov*
Kirilenko, *Kirilov*

Kirilichev, *Kirilov*
Kirilin, *Kirilov*
Kirillin, *Kirilov*
Kirillitsev, *Kirilov*
Kirillov, *Kirilov*
Kirilochkin, *Kirilov*
Kirilov
Kiriltsev, *Kirilov*
Kirilyuk, *Kirilov*
Kirin, *Kirilov*
Kirisov, *Kirilov*
Kirivan, *Kirwan*
Kirk
Kirkbride
Kirkbright, *Kirkbride*
Kirkby, *Kirby*
Kirke, *Kirk*
Kirkeby, *Kirby*
Kirkebye, *Kirby*
Kirkegaard, *Churchyard*
Kirkegård, *Churchyard*
Kirkham
Kirkin, *Kirilov*
Kirkland
Kirkley
Kirkman, *Kirk*
Kirkpatrick
Kirkup
Kirkwood
Kirley, *Curley*
Kirner, *Kürner*
Kirrage, *Kendrick*
Kirsanin, *Kirilov*
Kirsanov, *Kirilov*
Kirsblum, *Kirsch*
Kirsch
Kirschbaum, *Kirsch*
Kirschblum, *Kirsch*
Kirsche, *Kirsch*
Kirschenbaum, *Kirsch*
Kirschenberg, *Kirsch*
Kirschenblatt, *Kirsch*
Kirschenblut, *Kirsch*
Kirschenhaut, *Kirsch*
Kirschensaft, *Kirsch*
Kirschholz, *Kirsch*
Kirschman, *Kirsch*
Kirschner, *Kürschner*
Kirschstein, *Christian*
Kirschstein, *Kirsch*
Kirsenovitz, *Kirsch*
Kirsh, *Kirsch*
Kirshaw, *Kershaw*
Kirshbaum, *Kirsch*
Kirshberg, *Kirsch*
Kirshblum, *Kirsch*
Kirshbom, *Kirsch*
Kirshenbaum, *Kirsch*
Kirshenberg, *Kirsch*
Kirshenblat, *Kirsch*
Kirshenblatt, *Kirsch*
Kirshenblut, *Kirsch*
Kirshenboim, *Kirsch*
Kirshenbom, *Kirsch*
Kirshenfeld, *Kirsch*
Kirshenzweig, *Kirsch*
Kirshin, *Kirilov*
Kirshman, *Kirsch*
Kirshner, *Kürschner*
Kirsholz, *Kirsch*
Kirshonovitz, *Kirsch*
Kirshov, *Kirilov*
Kirshtein, *Kirsch*
Kirsner, *Kürschner*
Kirst, *Christian*
Kirstain, *Kirsch*
Kirstan, *Christian*
Kirstegen, *Christian*
Kirstein, *Christian*
Kirstein, *Kirsch*
Kirsten, *Christian*
Kirstens, *Christian*
Kirstgen, *Christian*
Kirsz, *Kirsch*
Kirszberg, *Kirsch*
Kirszenbaum, *Kirsch*
Kirszenzweig, *Kirsch*
Kirszholc, *Kirsch*
Kirton
Kirtsov, *Kirilov*
Kirvan, *Kirwan*
Kirwan
Kirwen, *Kirwan*
Kirwin, *Kirwan*
Kiryaev, *Kirilov*
Kiryakin, *Kirilov*
Kiryanov, *Kirilov*
Kiryukhin, *Kirilov*
Kiryunchev, *Kirilov*
Kiryupin, *Kirilov*
Kiryushin, *Kirilov*
Kiryushkin, *Kirilov*
Kiryutin, *Kirilov*
Kis, *Kiss*
Kisch, *Kiss*
Kisel, *Kiselyov*
Kiselstein, *Kiesel*
Kiselyov
Kish, *Kiss*
Kisiel, *Kiselyov*
Kisielewski, *Kiselyov*
Kiślański, *Kiselyov*
Kiss
Kissa, *Kiss*
Kissack, *Isaac*
Kissane
Kisser, *Kiss*
Kissinger
Kissock, *Isaac*
Kisswetter, *Kiesewetter*
Kist, *Christian*
Kisten, *Christian*
Kisting, *Christian*
Kit, *Christopher*
Kitaev, *Tito*
Kitanov, *Tito*
Kitcheman, *Kitchen*
Kitchen
Kitchener, *Kitchen*
Kitchin, *Kitchen*
Kitching, *Kitchen*
Kitchingman, *Kitchen*
Kitchinman, *Kitchen*
Kitchman, *Kitchen*
Kite
Kiteley
Kitell, *Kettle*
Kites, *Kite*
Kitlee, *Keighley*
Kitley, *Keighley*
Kitmanov, *Tito*
Kitov, *Tito*
Kitschelt, *Christian*
Kitscher, *Christian*
Kitschold, *Christian*
Kitson, *Christopher*
Kitt, *Christopher*
Kittan, *Christian*
Kittle, *Kettle*
Kitto, *Christopher*
Kittow, *Christopher*
Kitts, *Christopher*
Kitzer, *Christian*
Kjäll, *Käll*
Kjällberg, *Käll*
Kjällén, *Käll*
Kjällgren, *Käll*
Kjällman, *Käll*
Kjällqvist, *Käll*
Kjällström, *Käll*
Kjær, *Kerr*
Kjeldsen, *Kettle*
Kjell, *Käll*
Kjellander, *Käll*
Kjellberg, *Käll*
Kjellén, *Käll*
Kjellgren, *Käll*
Kjellin, *Käll*
Kjellman, *Käll*
Kjellqvist, *Käll*
Kjellström, *Käll*
Klaas, *Klaus*
Klaasen, *Klaus*
Klaassen, *Klaus*
Klaes, *Klaus*
Klaesen, *Klaus*
Klaesson, *Klaus*
Klaffs, *Klaus*
Klage, *Klaus*
Klageman, *Klaus*
Klages, *Klaus*
Klagge, *Klaus*
Klagges, *Klaus*
Klahr, *Klar*
Klaiman, *Klayman*
Klain, *Klein*
Klainer, *Klein*
Klainman, *Klein*
Klais, *Klaus*
Klaiser, *Klaus*
Klajman, *Klayman*
Klämbt, *Clement*
Klambt, *Clement*
Klamman, *Klaus*
Klammt, *Clement*
Klampfer, *Klempner*
Klampferer, *Klempner*
Klampke, *Clement*
Klampt, *Clement*
Klamt, *Clement*
Klapper
Klapperman, *Klapper*
Klappert, *Klapper*
Klar
Klarfeld, *Klar*
Klarman, *Klar*
Klarmann, *Klar*
Klarreich, *Klar*
Klarsfeld, *Klar*
Klas, *Klaus*
Klasen, *Klaus*
Klasing, *Klaus*
Klass, *Klaus*
Klassmann, *Klaus*
Klasson, *Klaus*
Klaudius, *Claude*
Klaus
Klausen, *Klaus*
Klausewitz, *Klaus*
Klausner, *Klaus*
Klaussen, *Klaus*
Klaver, *Klee*
Klaves, *Klaus*
Kläwi, *Klaus*
Klayman
Klazenenga, *Klaus*
Klebes, *Klaus*
Klečák
Klečka, *Klečák*
Klee
Kleeman, *Clement*
Kleeman, *Klee*
Kleemann, *Klee*
Kleen, *Klein*
Klehn, *Klein*
Kleij, *Clay*
Kleijn, *Klein*
Kleiman, *Klayman*
Kleimann, *Klein*
Klein
Kleinbaum, *Klein*
Kleinberg, *Klein*
Kleinberger, *Klein*
Kleine, *Klein*
Kleiner, *Klein*
Kleinerman, *Klein*
Kleinert, *Klein*
Kleinfeld, *Klein*
Kleingrub, *Klein*
Kleinhändler
Kleinhaus, *Klein*
Kleinhaut, *Klein*
Kleinhendler, *Kleinhändler*
Kleinholz, *Klein*
Kleinlerer
Kleinman, *Klein*
Kleinmann, *Klein*
Kleinmintz, *Klein*
Kleinmuntz, *Klein*
Kleinpeltz, *Klein*
Kleinplac, *Klein*
Kleinplatz, *Klein*
Kleinschmidt
Kleinsinger, *Klein*
Kleinstein, *Klein*
Kleinstern, *Klein*
Kleinstub, *Klein*
Kleint, *Klein*
Kleinzweig, *Klein*
Kleis, *Klaus*
Kleisel, *Klaus*
Kleiser, *Klaus*
Kleisle, *Klaus*
Kleist
Klejna, *Klein*
Kleman, *Klee*
Klemenčić, *Clement*
Klemensiewicz, *Clement*
Klement, *Clement*
Klementz, *Clement*
Klemenz, *Clement*
Klemke, *Clement*
Klemmt, *Clement*
Klemper, *Klempner*
Klemperer, *Klempner*
Klempert, *Klempner*
Klempke, *Clement*
Klempner
Klemps, *Clement*
Klemptner, *Klempner*
Klems, *Clement*
Klemt, *Clement*
Klemz, *Clement*
Klene, *Klein*
Klepáč, *Klapper*
Kleper, *Klepper*

Klepper
Klerk, *Clark*
Kles, *Klaus*
Klesel, *Klaus*
Klesl, *Klaus*
Kless, *Klaus*
Klesse, *Klaus*
Klessel, *Klaus*
Klessmann, *Klaus*
Klewi, *Klaus*
Kley, *Clay*
Kleyn, *Klein*
Kleynen, *Klein*
Kleynermans, *Klein*
Klich, *Clement*
Kliche, *Clement*
Klicher, *Clement*
Klička, *Klika*
Kliegel, *Klug*
Klieger, *Klug*
Kliegerman, *Klug*
Kliegman, *Klug*
Kliemann, *Clement*
Kliemchen, *Clement*
Kliemke, *Clement*
Kliemt, *Clement*
Kliger, *Klug*
Kligerman, *Klug*
Kligman, *Klug*
Klijn, *Klein*
Klik, *Klika*
Klika
Klíma, *Clement*
Klima, *Clement*
Klimas, *Clement*
Klimashevich, *Clement*
Klimaszewski, *Clement*
Klimchuk, *Clement*
Klimczak, *Clement*
Klimecki, *Clement*
Klimek, *Clement*
Kliment, *Clement*
Klimentov, *Clement*
Klimentyev, *Clement*
Klimentyonok, *Clement*
Klimeš, *Clement*
Klimke, *Clement*
Klimkiewicz, *Clement*
Klimkin, *Clement*
Klimko, *Clement*
Klimkov, *Clement*
Klimkovich, *Clement*
Klimkowski, *Clement*
Klimmek, *Clement*
Klimochkin, *Clement*
Klimontovich, *Clement*
Klimov, *Clement*
Klimovich, *Clement*
Klimowicz, *Clement*
Klimowski, *Clement*
Klimpke, *Clement*
Klimpt, *Clement*
Klimsch, *Clement*
Klimschak, *Clement*
Klimt, *Clement*
Klimuk, *Clement*
Klimus, *Clement*
Klimushev, *Clement*
Klincksieck
Kline, *Klein*
Kliner, *Klein*
Kling, *Klinge, Klinger*
Klinge
Klingel, *Klinger*
Klingemann, *Klinge*
Klingenstein, *Klinger*
Klinger
Klingerman, *Klinger*
Klinghofer, *Klinger*
Klinghoffer, *Klinger*
Klingman, *Klinger*
Klingsberg, *Klinger*
Klingstein, *Klinger*
Klingweil, *Klinger*
Klisch, *Clement*
Klishin, *Clement*
Klöber, *Klöver*
Klöcking, *Klug*
Klöckner, *Glock*
Kloek, *Klug*
Klohr, *Hilary*
Kloisner, *Klaus*
Klok, *Glock*
Klokke, *Glock*
Klokman, *Glock*
Klonowicz, *Klonowski*
Klonowski
Klonymus, *Kalman*
Klook, *Klug*
Kloosterman, *Klostermann*
Kloot, *Klotz*
Klooth, *Klotz*
Klopstock
Klör, *Hilary*
Klor, *Klar*
Klorfeld, *Klar*
Klos, *Klaus*
Kłos
Klosa, *Klaus*
Klöser, *Klaus*
Kloser, *Klaus*
Klösges, *Klaus*
Kłosiński, *Kłos*
Kloska, *Klaus*
Kłosowski, *Kłos*
Klöss, *Klaus*
Klossek, *Klaus*
Klössel, *Klaus*
Klösser, *Klaus*
Klossmann, *Klaus*
Klostermann
Kloth, *Klotz*
Klots, *Klotz*
Klotz
Klötzel, *Klotz*
Klotzman, *Klotz*
Klotzmann, *Klotz*
Klouček
Kloud, *Claude*
Klouda, *Claude*
Klousner, *Klaus*
Klouz, *Klaus*
Klöver
Klöwer, *Klöver*
Klucznik
Kluczyński, *Klucznik*
Klug
Kluge, *Klug*
Klügel, *Klug*
Kluger, *Klug*
Klugman, *Klug*
Klurglus, *Klar*
Klurman, *Klar*
Klus, *Klaus*
Kluss, *Klaus*
Klut, *Klotz*
Kluth, *Klotz*
Klüver, *Klöver*
Klüwer, *Klöver*
Klyn, *Klein*
Klyne, *Klein*
Kment, *Clement*
Kmetz, *Kmieć*
Kmieć
Kmieciak, *Kmieć*
Kmiecik, *Kmieć*
Kmoch
Knabbe, *Knapp*
Knabben, *Knapp*
Knabe, *Knapp*
Knäble, *Knapp*
Knable, *Knapp*
Knacht, *Knight*
Knaepen, *Knapp*
Knaggs
Knap, *Knapp*
Knapen, *Knapp*
Knapik, *Knapp*
Knäple, *Knapp*
Knapman, *Knapp*
Knapp
Knappe, *Knapp*
Knapper, *Knapp*
Knappman, *Knapp*
Knapton
Knatchbull
Knauer, *Knorr*
Knauert, *Knorr*
Knaus
Knäusle, *Knaus*
Knaut, *Knott*
Knauth, *Knott*
Kneale, *Neil*
Knecht, *Knight*
Knee, *Nee*
Kneebone
Knef
Kneib, *Knef*
Kneif, *Knef*
Kneip, *Knef*
Kneipp, *Knef*
Kneisel, *Knaus*
Kneissel, *Knaus*
Kneissl, *Knaus*
Kneler, *Kneller*
Knell, *Knill*
Kneller
Knepel, *Knopf*
Knepler, *Knopf*
Kneppel, *Knopf*
Kneussel, *Knaus*
Knevet, *Knight*
Knevett, *Knight*
Knežević, *Kníže*
Knief, *Knef*
Kníěk, *Kníže*
Kniep, *Knef*
Kniepe, *Knef*
Knieper, *Knef*
Knife, *Knef*
Knight
Knighten, *Knighton*
Knightley
Knightly, *Knightley*
Knighton
Knights, *Knight*
Knill
Knipe
Knivett, *Knight*
Knivit, *Knight*
Kníže
Knobel, *Knobloch*
Knobeloch, *Knobloch*
Knoblauch, *Knobloch*
Knobler, *Knobloch*
Knoblich, *Knobloch*
Knobloch
Knochenhauer
Knock, *Knox*
Knocker, *Knox*
Knockton, *Naughton*
Knode, *Knott*
Knödel, *Knott*
Knödgen, *Knott*
Knöfel, *Knopf*
Knöffel, *Knopf*
Knoflach, *Knobloch*
Knöfler, *Knopf*
Knoll
Knollys, *Knowles*
Knoop, *Knopf*
Knop, *Knopf*
Knopf
Knöpfel, *Knopf*
Knopfelmacher, *Knopf*
Knöpfle, *Knopf*
Knöpfler, *Knopf*
Knopfler, *Knopf*
Knöpfli, *Knopf*
Knopfloch, *Knobloch*
Knopfmacher, *Knopf*
Knöpken, *Knopf*
Knopl, *Knopf*
Knopmacher, *Knopf*
Knopp, *Knopf*
Knöre, *Knorr*
Knorn, *Knorr*
Knörndl, *Knorr*
Knorr
Knörre, *Knorr*
Knot, *Knott*
Knote, *Knott*
Knotek
Knötel, *Knott*
Knoth, *Knott*
Knothe, *Knott*
Knott
Knotts, *Knott*
Knottson, *Knott*
Knowlder, *Knoll*
Knowler, *Knoll*
Knowles
Knowling, *Knowles*
Knowlman, *Knoll*
Knowlson, *Knowles*
Knox
Knuckey
Knudsen, *Knott*
Knull, *Knill*
Knür, *Knorr*
Knürle, *Knorr*
Knut, *Knott*
Knuth, *Knott*
Knutsson, *Knott*
Knyll, *Knill*
Knyvett, *Knight*
Kob, *Jacob*
Koba, *Jacob*
Kobel, *Köbler*
Kobelmann, *Köbler*
Kobera, *Jacob*
Kobes, *Jacob*
Köbi, *Jacob*
Kobiera, *Jacob*
Kobierecki, *Jacob*
Kobierski, *Jacob*

Kobierzycki, *Jacob*
Kobisch, *Jacob*
Köbke, *Jacob*
Koblenc, *Koblenz*
Koblence, *Koblenz*
Koblentz, *Koblenz*
Koblenz
Koblenzer, *Koblenz*
Kobler, *Köbler*
Köbler
Kobs, *Jacob*
Kobsch, *Jacob*
Kobus, *Jacob*
Kobylak, *Kobyłecki*
Kobyłański, *Kobyłecki*
Kobyłecki
Kobyliński, *Kobyłecki*
Kočar, *Kocsis*
Kočarek, *Kocsis*
Koch, *Cook*
Koch
Kochanek
Kochaniak, *Kochanek*
Kochanowicz, *Kochanek*
Kochanowski, *Kochanek*
Kochański, *Kochanek*
Köchel
Kocher, *Koch*
Kochetov
Köchl, *Köchel*
Köchle, *Koch*
Köchler, *Köchel*
Kochman, *Cook*
Kochmann, *Cook, Koch*
Kočí, *Kocsis*
Kociński, *Catt*
Kociszewski, *Catt*
Kock, *Cook*
Kocks, *Cook*
Kocour, *Catt*
Kocourek, *Catt*
Kocsis
Kodat, *Nikodém*
Kodeš, *Nikodém*
Kodým, *Nikodém*
Koefoed, *Kofoed*
Koekemoer
Koene, *Konrad*
Koenen, *Konrad*
Koenraad, *Konrad*
Koeppe, *Jacob*
Koeppke, *Jacob*
Kofahl, *Kowalski*
Kofax, *Kowalski*
Kofod, *Kofoed*
Kofoed
Kofoth, *Kofoed*
Kofránek, *Kofroň*
Kofrň, *Kofroň*
Kofroň
Kogan, *Cohen*
Kogel
Kogen, *Cohen*
Kögler, *Kogel*
Kogler, *Kogel*
Kogut, *Kochetov*
Kogutov, *Kochetov*
Kogutovski, *Kochetov*
Kohaner, *Cohen*
Kohanoff, *Cohen*
Kohardt, *Coward*
Kohen, *Cohen*
Kohener, *Cohen*
Koherde, *Coward*
Kohhardt, *Coward*
Kohl
Kohl, *Collier*
Köhl, *Kohl*
Kohlberg, *Collier*
Kohlenberg, *Collier*
Kohlenbrenner, *Collier*
Köhler, *Collier*
Kohler, *Collier*
Kohlmann, *Coleman, Collier*
Kohn, *Cohen*
Köhn, *Konrad*
Köhne, *Konrad*
Köhneke, *Konrad*
Köhnemann, *Konrad*
Köhnen, *Konrad*
Kohnen, *Konrad*
Kohnert, *Konrad*
Köhnke, *Konrad*
Köhnmann, *Konrad*
Kohout, *Kochetov*
Kohoutek, *Kochetov*
Kohrding, *Konrad*
Köhring, *Konrad*
Kohrs, *Konrad*
Kohrsen, *Konrad*
Kohrt, *Konrad*
Kohrts, *Court*
Kohut, *Kochetov*
Koifman, *Chapman*
Koilman, *Collier*
Koivisto
Kojfman, *Chapman*
Kok, *Cook*
Kokeš, *Kochetov*
Kokkonen
Kokoscha, *Kochetov*
Kokoschka, *Kochetov*
Kokoška, *Kochetov*
Kokoszka, *Kochetov*
Kokoszko, *Kochetov*
Kokotek, *Kochetov*
Kokott, *Kochetov*
Kokutak, *Kochetov*
Kołacki, *Kołacz*
Kołacz
Kołak, *Klaus*
Kolaković, *Klaus*
Kołakowski, *Klaus*
Kolař, *Kołodziej*
Kolařík, *Kołodziej*
Kolařský, *Kołodziej*
Kolasa
Kolasiński, *Kolasa*
Kolatsch, *Kołacz*
Kolczyński, *Klaus*
Koleš, *Klaus*
Kolijn, *Coll*
Kolín, *Klaus*
Kolin, *Klaus*
Kolinský, *Klaus*
Koliš, *Klaus*
Köll, *Cullen*
Kollach, *Klaus*
Kollas, *Klaus*
Kollasch, *Klaus*
Kollaschek, *Klaus*
Kollatsch, *Klaus*
Köllen, *Cullen*
Köller, *Collier*
Koller, *Collier*
Kölling, *Cullen*
Kollman, *Kalman*
Köllmann, *Cullen*
Köllner, *Cullen*
Kolman, *Coleman, Kalman*
Kołodziej
Kołodziejczak, *Kołodziej*
Kołodziejczyk, *Kołodziej*
Kołodziejski, *Kołodziej*
Kölsch, *Cullen*
Kolushev, *Klaus*
Kolyagin, *Klaus*
Komar, *Komarov*
Komárek, *Komarov*
Komaroff, *Komarov*
Komarov
Komarow, *Komarov*
Komer, *Komarov*
Komorowski
Kömpf, *Kemp*
Kön, *Konrad*
Konárek, *Konarski*
Koňarík, *Konarski*
Konarowski, *Konarski*
Konarski
Konarzewski, *Konarski*
Kondić, *Constantine*
Kondrachenko, *Konrad*
Kondrakov, *Kondratyev*
Kondrashikhin, *Kondratyev*
Kondrashov, *Kondratyev*
Kondrat, *Konrad*
Kondratenko, *Konrad*
Kondratenya, *Konrad*
Kondratov, *Kondratyev*
Kondratovich, *Konrad*
Kondratowicz, *Konrad*
Kondratyev
Kondratyuk, *Konrad*
Kondrichev, *Kondratyev*
Kondrushkin, *Kondratyev*
Kondryukhov, *Kondratyev*
Kondzyereyonok, *Kudravtsev*
Köne, *Konrad*
Konečný, *Konieczny*
Köneke, *Konrad*
Könemann, *Konrad*
Konerding, *Konrad*
Konert, *Konrad*
Konertz, *Konrad*
Köngeter, *Kenngott*
Konieczny
König
Königsberg
Konigsberger, *Königsberg*
Konijn, *Coney*
Konings, *König*
Konίř, *Konarski*
Konjević, *Constantine*
Konjović, *Constantine*
Könke, *Konrad*
Könmann, *Konrad*
Könneke, *Konrad*
Könngott, *Kenngott*
Konopka
Konovalchik, *Konovalov*
Konovalets, *Konovalov*
Konovalik, *Konovalov*
Konovalov
Konovalyuk, *Konovalov*
Konrád, *Konrad*
Konrad
Konstancin, *Constantine*
Konstantinov, *Constantine*
Konstantinović, *Constantine*
Konstantynowicz, *Constantine*
Konzel, *Konrad*
Konzelmann, *Konrad*
Koock, *Cook*
Kooi, *Kooy*
Kooij, *Kooy*
Kooijman, *Kooy*
Kooiman, *Kooy*
Kooistra, *Kooy*
Kook, *Cook*
Kool, *Kohl*
Koole, *Kohl*
Koomans, *Chapman*
Koop, *Jacob*
Kooper, *Cooper*
Koopman, *Chapman*
Koopmans, *Chapman*
Kooy
Kooyman, *Kooy*
Kop, *Copp, Jacob*
Kopa, *Jacob*
Kopáč, *Jacob*
Kopaček, *Jacob*
Kopacki, *Kopczyński*
Kopal, *Jacob*
Kopčić, *Prokop*
Kopczyński
Kopeć
Kopečka, *Kopczyński*
Kopecký, *Kopczyński*
Kopečný, *Kopczyński*
Köper, *Chapman*
Koper, *Copper*
Koper
Kopernik, *Koper*
Koperski, *Koper*
Kopf
Köpfel, *Kopf*
Köpfle, *Kopf*
Kopfstein, *Kopf*
Kopiec, *Copp*
Kopisch, *Jacob*
Kopka, *Copp, Kopczyński*
Köpke, *Jacob*
Kopman, *Kopf*
Kopmann, *Chapman*
Kopp, *Copp, Jacob*
Koppe, *Jacob*
Köppel, *Kopf*
Köppen, *Jacob*
Koppen, *Jacob*
Koppens, *Jacob*
Kopper, *Copper*
Koppermann, *Copper*
Koppmann, *Chapman*
Kopps, *Jacob*
Kopřiva
Koprowski, *Koper*
Kops, *Jacob*
Kopstein, *Kopf*
Kopta, *Kopeć*
Koptík, *Kopeć*
Koralyov, *Król*
Kořán
Kořánek, *Kořán*
Korb
Korbel, *Korb*
Körbel, *Korb*
Korbelář, *Korb*
Körber, *Corbeil, Korb*
Korber, *Korb*
Körbler, *Korb*
Korda
Kordač, *Korda*
Kordes, *Konrad*
Kordewan, *Cordonnier*

Kordík, *Korda*
Kording, *Konrad*
Kordova, *Córdoba*
Kordovani, *Córdoba*
Kordt, *Konrad*
Koreček, *Korecky*
Korecky
Korejs, *Corneille*
Koreš, *Corneille*
Korf, *Corbeil, Korb*
Körfer, *Korb*
Körfers, *Korb*
Korff, *Corbeil*
Korff, *Korb*
Korfgen, *Korb*
Korfmaker, *Korb*
Korfmakers, *Korb*
Korfman, *Korb*
Korfmann, *Korb*
Korhonen
Kořínek
Korland, *Kurland*
Korlander, *Kurland*
Korlansky, *Kurland*
Korlát, *Konrad*
Kormann, *Korn*
Korn
Kornacki, *Corneille*
Kornalík, *Corneille*
Kornberg, *Korn*
Kornblatt, *Korn*
Kornblau, *Korn*
Kornblitt, *Korn*
Kornblum, *Korn*
Kornblume, *Korn*
Körndle, *Korn*
Korneev, *Corneille*
Korneichik, *Corneille*
Korneichuk, *Corneille*
Kornel, *Corneille*
Korneluk, *Corneille*
Kornemann, *Korn*
Körner, *Korn*
Kornfein, *Korn*
Kornfeld, *Korn*
Kornfield, *Korn*
Korngold, *Korn*
Korngruen, *Korn*
Kornhaber, *Korn*
Kornhauser, *Korn*
Kornhendler, *Korn*
Kornilov, *Corneille*
Kornilyev, *Corneille*
Körnle, *Korn*
Kornmehl, *Korn*
Kornoušek, *Corneille*
Kornreich, *Korn*
Kornstein, *Korn*
Kornstreicher, *Striker*
Kornwasser, *Korn*
Kornweiss, *Korn*
Kornweitz, *Korn*
Kornyakov, *Corneille*
Kornyshev, *Corneille*
Kornzweig, *Korn*
Korolenko, *Król*
Korolyonok, *Król*
Korolyov, *Król*
Korostelyov
Korostylyov, *Korostelyov*
Korot, *Korotygin*
Korotchenko, *Korotygin*
Korotich, *Korotygin*
Korotkikh, *Korotygin*
Korotkin, *Korotygin*
Korotky, *Korotygin*
Korotygin
Korous, *Corneille*
Korovnikov
Korsakov
Körschkes, *Christian*
Körschner, *Kürschner*
Korst, *Christian*
Korsten, *Christian*
Korstiaan, *Christian*
Korstinens, *Christian*
Kort, *Court, Konrad*
Korte, *Court*
Korthase, *Curtis*
Körting, *Konrad*
Korts, *Court*
Kortwright, *Cartwright*
Körver, *Korb*
Korver, *Korb*
Korzeniowski, *Kořán*
Kos
Kosa, *Kos*
Košar, *Košnář*
Kosch, *Jacob*
Koschek, *Jacob*
Koscher, *Klaus*
Köschges, *Christian*
Koschke, *Jacob*
Kościelski
Kościuk, *Constantine*
Kościuszko, *Constantine*
Kosík, *Kos*
Kosiński, *Kos*
Koskela, *Koskinen*
Koski, *Koskinen*
Koskinen
Koslofsky, *Kozlov*
Koslovitz, *Kozlov*
Koslovsky, *Kozlov*
Koslow, *Kozlov*
Kosmala
Kosmalski, *Kosmala*
Kosmin, *Kuzmin*
Kosminski, *Kuzmin*
Košnar, *Košnář*
Košnář
Kosorotov
Kössler, *Kessel*
Kost, *Constantine*
Košt'ák, *Košt'ál*
Košt'ál
Košt'álek, *Košt'ál*
Kostański, *Constantine*
Kostashchuk, *Constantine*
Kostecki, *Constantine*
Kostenko, *Constantine*
Köster, *Küster*
Koster, *Küster*
Köstering, *Küster*
Kostermann, *Küster*
Kösters, *Küster*
Kosters, *Küster*
Kostić, *Constantine*
Kostikov, *Constantine*
Kostin, *Constantine*
Kostiuk, *Constantine*
Kostka, *Constantine*
Kostkiewicz, *Constantine*
Kostko, *Constantine*
Köstner, *Kastner*
Kostrzewa
Kostrzewski, *Kostrzewa*
Kostyunin, *Constantine*
Kostyura, *Constantine*
Kostyushin, *Constantine*
Kosygin
Koszta, *Constantine*
Kosztka, *Constantine*
Kot, *Catt*
Kotal, *Catt*
Kotas, *Catt*
Kot'átko, *Catt*
Kotecki, *Catt*
Kotek, *Catt*
Kotev, *Catt*
Koth, *Coates*
Kothe, *Coates*
Köther, *Cotter*
Kother, *Cotter*
Kotík, *Catt*
Kotkiewicz, *Catt*
Kotkowski, *Catt*
Kotlar, *Kessel*
Kotlarski, *Kessel*
Kotlarsky, *Kessel*
Kotler, *Kessel*
Kotliar, *Kessel*
Kotlicki, *Kotliński*
Kotliński
Kotlyar, *Kessel*
Kotlyarchuk, *Kessel*
Kotlyarevski, *Kessel*
Kotlyarov, *Kessel*
Kotowicz, *Catt*
Kotowski, *Catt*
Kotrba
Kotrbatý, *Kotrba*
Kotrc, *Kotrč*
Kotrč
Kott, *Catt*
Kötter, *Cotter*
Kotter, *Cotter*
Kouba, *Jacob*
Koubek, *Jacob*
Koucký, *Koutský*
Koudela
Kough, *Keogh*
Koukenheim, *Guggenheim*
Kout, *Koutský*
Koutecký, *Koutský*
Koutek, *Koutský*
Koutník, *Koutský*
Koutný, *Koutský*
Koutský
Kováč, *Kowalski*
Kovač, *Kowalski*
Kovac, *Kowalski*
Kovačević, *Kowalski*
Kovách, *Kowalski*
Kovačić, *Kowalski*
Kovács, *Kowalski*
Kovacs, *Kowalski*
Koval, *Kowalski*
Kovalchuk, *Kowalski*
Kovalenya, *Kowalski*
Kovalevich, *Kowalski*
Kovalevski, *Kowalski*
Kovalski, *Kowalski*
Kovalsky, *Kowalski*
Kovalyonok, *Kowalski*
Kovalyov, *Kowalski*
Kovanda
Kovanko, *Kowalski*
Kovář, *Kowalski*
Kovaříček, *Kowalski*
Kovařík, *Kowalski*
Kováts, *Kowalski*
Kovel, *Kowalski*
Kovelman, *Kowalski*
Köver, *Cuvier*
Ković, *Kowalski*
Kowahl, *Kowalski*
Kowal, *Kowalski*
Kowalczyk, *Kowalski*
Kowalczyński, *Kowalski*
Kowalewicz, *Kowalski*
Kowalewski, *Kowalski*
Kowalik, *Kowalski*
Kowaliński, *Kowalski*
Kowalke, *Kowalski*
Kowaloff, *Kowalski*
Kowalski
Kowalsky, *Kowalski*
Kowlowitz, *Kowalski*
Kox, *Cook*
Koyfman, *Chapman*
Koza, *Kozák*
Kozák
Kozak
Kozakiewicz, *Kozak*
Kozel, *Kozlov*
Kozelka, *Kozlov*
Koziara, *Kozlov*
Koziarski, *Kozlov*
Koziarz, *Kozlov*
Kozieł, *Kozlov*
Kozin, *Kozlov*
Koziol, *Kozlov*
Kozlík, *Kozlov*
Kozloff, *Kozlov*
Kozlov
Kozlović, *Kozlov*
Kozlovitz, *Kozlov*
Kozlovski, *Kozlov*
Kozlow, *Kozlov*
Kozłowski, *Kozlov*
Kozlowski, *Kozlov*
Kozma, *Kuzmin*
Kozmin, *Kuzmin*
Kra, *Crow*
Kraaij, *Crow*
Kraan, *Crane*
Kraay, *Crow*
Krabat, *Horváth*
Krabbe, *Crabbe*
Krach, *Crow*
Kracht, *Kraft*
Kračmar, *Kretschmar*
Kračmarík, *Kretschmar*
Kráčmer, *Kretschmar*
Kraemer, *Krämer*
Kraemers, *Krämer*
Krafchik, *Krawiec*
Krafchinsky, *Krawiec*
Krafft, *Kraft*
Kräft, *Crabbe*
Kraft
Krag, *Crow*
Kragelić, *Król*
Kragh, *Crow*
Kräh, *Crow*
Krah, *Crow*
Krähe, *Crow*
Krahe, *Crow*
Krahl, *Król*
Krahn, *Crane*
Kraindels
Krainer, *Ukraintsev*
Krainin, *Kraindels*
Krainis, *Kraindels*
Krainovitz, *Kraindels*

Krainovitz, *Ukraintsev*
Kraitor, *Krawiec*
Krajča, *Krawiec*
Krajčí, *Krawiec*
Krajčír, *Krawiec*
Krajewski
Krajíček, *Krawiec*
Krajina, *Krajewski*
Krajník, *Krajewski*
Krajnik, *Krajewski*
Krajnis, *Kraindels*
Krajný, *Krajewski*
Krakauer, *Krakowiak*
Krakowiak
Krakowski, *Krakowiak*
Král, *Król*
Kral, *Król*
Kraliček, *Królik*
Králík, *Królik*
Kralik, *Król*
Kraljević, *Król*
Kramář, *Krämer*
Kramar, *Krämer*
Kramarchuk, *Krämer*
Kramarenko, *Krämer*
Kramarov, *Krämer*
Kramer, *Krämer*
Krämer
Kramerman, *Krämer*
Kramers, *Krämer*
Krammer, *Krämer*
Kranc, *Kranz*
Krancberg, *Kranz*
Krancenblum, *Kranz*
Kranch, *Crane*
Kranewitter, *Kronewitter*
Kranich, *Crane*
Kranke
Kränkel, *Crane*
Krankheid, *Kranke*
Krankheit, *Kranke*
Krantz, *Kranz*
Krantzberg, *Kranz*
Krantzcke, *Kranz*
Krantzke, *Kranz*
Krantzler, *Kranz*
Kranz
Kranzbaum, *Kranz*
Kranzberg, *Kranz*
Kranzdorf, *Kranz*
Kränzel, *Kranz*
Kränzl, *Kranz*
Kranzlbinder, *Kranz*
Kränzle, *Kranz*
Kränzler, *Kranz*
Kranzler, *Kranz*
Krapf
Krapfl, *Krapf*
Krapotkin, *Kropotkin*
Krapp, *Krapf*
Krappel, *Krapf*
Krarup
Krása, *Krasnikov*
Krasavchikov, *Krasnikov*
Krasilnikov
Krasilshchikov, *Krasilnikov*
Krasne, *Krasnikov*
Krasner, *Krasnikov*
Krasnianski, *Krasnikov*
Krasniansky, *Krasnikov*
Krasnick, *Krasnikov*
Krasnicki, *Krasnikov*
Krasnikov
Krasnitzki, *Krasnikov*
Krasno, *Krasnikov*
Krasnoff, *Krasnikov*
Krasnov, *Krasnikov*
Krasnove, *Krasnikov*
Krasnovsky, *Krasnikov*
Krasnow, *Krasnikov*
Krasnowski, *Krasnikov*
Krásný, *Krasnikov*
Krasny, *Krasnikov*
Krasnykh, *Krasnikov*
Krasoń, *Krasnikov*
Krassner, *Krasnikov*
Krasukhin, *Krasnikov*
Kraszewski
Kratěna, *Korotygin*
Kratius, *Pankridge*
Krátký, *Korotygin*
Kratochvíl
Kratschmer, *Kretschmar*
Kratz, *Pankridge*
Krätzel, *Pankridge*
Kratzig, *Pankridge*
Kratzke, *Pankridge*
Kratzmann, *Pankridge*
Kraus
Krause, *Kraus*
Krauser, *Kraus*
Kraushaar, *Kraus*
Kraushar, *Kraus*
Krauskopf, *Kraus*
Krausman, *Kraus*
Krauspe, *Crisp*
Krauss, *Kraus*
Krausz, *Kraus*
Krauszman, *Kraus*
Kraut
Krautberg, *Kraut*
Krautblatt, *Kraut*
Krautenberg, *Kraut*
Krauter, *Kraut*
Krauth, *Kraut*
Krauthamer, *Kraut*
Krautheim, *Kraut*
Krautheimer, *Kraut*
Kräutl, *Kraut*
Krautman, *Kraut*
Krauz, *Kraus*
Krauze, *Kraus*
Krauzer, *Kraus*
Krauzhar, *Kraus*
Krauzman, *Kraus*
Kravchenko, *Krawiec*
Kravchick, *Krawiec*
Kravchook, *Krawiec*
Kravchuk, *Krawiec*
Kravcich, *Krawiec*
Kravczich, *Krawiec*
Kravet, *Krawiec*
Kravetsky, *Krawiec*
Kravett, *Krawiec*
Kravette, *Krawiec*
Kravetz, *Krawiec*
Kravetzky, *Krawiec*
Kravietz, *Krawiec*
Kravit, *Krawiec*
Kravits, *Krawiec*
Kravitsky, *Krawiec*
Kravitt, *Krawiec*
Kravitz, *Krawiec*
Kravtchik, *Krawiec*
Kravtchinsky, *Krawiec*
Kravtshuk, *Krawiec*
Kravtsov, *Krawiec*
Kravzik, *Krawiec*
Krawath, *Horváth*
Krawatsky, *Krawiec*
Krawchick, *Krawiec*
Krawchuk, *Krawiec*
Krawczuk, *Krawiec*
Krawczyk, *Krawiec*
Krawczyński, *Krawiec*
Krawet, *Krawiec*
Krawetz, *Krawiec*
Krawicki, *Krawiec*
Krawiec
Krawiecki, *Krawiec*
Krawiecky, *Krawiec*
Krawietz, *Krawiec*
Krawitt, *Krawiec*
Krawitz, *Krawiec*
Kräwt, *Crabbe*
Krawzow, *Krawiec*
Kray, *Crow*
Krč
Krčál, *Krč*
Krček, *Krč*
Krčma, *Kretschmar*
Krčmář, *Kretschmar*
Krčmarík, *Kretschmar*
Kreber, *Korb*
Krebs, *Crabbe*
Krechmer, *Kretschmar*
Krečmar, *Kretschmar*
Krečmer, *Kretschmar*
Kreft, *Crabbe*
Krehe, *Crow*
Krei, *Crow*
Kreiner, *Ukraintsev*
Kreinin, *Kraindels*
Kreisel
Kreisler, *Kreisel*
Kreitchman, *Kretschmar*
Kreitenberger, *Kraut*
Kreiter, *Kraut*
Kreith, *Reuter*
Kreither, *Reuter*
Kreitler, *Kraut*
Kreitman, *Kraut*
Kreitner, *Kraut*
Krejčí, *Krawiec*
Krejčík, *Krawiec*
Krejčíř, *Krawiec*
Krejnis, *Kraindels*
Křemen, *Krzemiński*
Kremer, *Krämer*
Kremerman, *Krämer*
Kremerov, *Krämer*
Kremers, *Krämer*
Křen, *Chrzanowski*
Křenek, *Chrzanowski*
Krenkel, *Crane*
Krenzle, *Kranz*
Krepel, *Krapf*
Kreppel, *Krapf*
Krestyaninov, *Christian*
Krestyanov, *Christian*
Kret, *Krtil*
Kretchmer, *Kretschmar*
Kretschmann, *Kretschmar*
Kretschmar
Kretschmer, *Kretschmar*
Kretschmeyer, *Kretschmar*
Kretshmer, *Kretschmar*
Kretzing, *Pankridge*
Kretzschmer, *Kretschmar*
Kreuter, *Reuter*
Kreutz, *Cross*
Kreutzer, *Cross*
Kreuz, *Cross*
Kreuzer, *Cross*
Kreuziger, *Cross*
Krey, *Crow*
Krieger
Kriegman, *Krieger*
Kriegsman, *Krieger*
Kriesten, *Christian*
Kriger, *Krieger*
Krigier, *Krieger*
Krigman, *Krieger*
Krigsman, *Krieger*
Krijger, *Krieger*
Krijgsman, *Krieger*
Krikorian, *Gregory*
Krimmel, *Crome*
Krimpke, *Crome*
Krisch, *Christian*
Krischan, *Christian*
Krische, *Christian*
Krischke, *Christian*
Krischpin, *Crispin*
Krishtopaitis, *Christopher*
Krisp, *Crisp*
Krispien, *Crispin*
Křist'ál, *Christian*
Kristall, *Cristal*
Kristeller, *Christian*
Kristen, *Christian*
Kristensen, *Christian*
Kristensson, *Christian*
Kristersson, *Christian*
Kristiansen, *Christian*
Kristiansson, *Christian*
Krištof, *Christopher*
Kristóf, *Christopher*
Kristoffersen, *Christopher*
Kristoffersson, *Christopher*
Krištůfek, *Christopher*
Křiva, *Krivov*
Křivak, *Krivov*
Křivan, *Krivov*
Křivánek, *Krivov*
Krivchenko, *Krivov*
Krivenko, *Krivov*
Křivka, *Krivov*
Krivoshei, *Krivov*
Krivov
Krivtzov, *Krivov*
Kříž, *Christian*
Křížek, *Christian*
Krob, *Grob*
Krochmann, *Krüger*
Kroes, *Kraus*
Kroese, *Kraus*
Kroeze, *Kraus*
Krog, *Krüger*
Kroge, *Krüger*
Kröger, *Krüger*
Kroger, *Krüger*
Krogh, *Krüger*
Krogmann, *Krüger*
Kroh, *Crow*
Krohe, *Crow*
Krohn, *Crane*
Krohnson, *Kraindels*
Kroin, *Corona*
Kroinik, *Corona*
Kroitoru, *Krawiec*
Krojn, *Corona*
Krojtor, *Krawiec*
Krol, *Król, Kroll*
Król
Królak, *Król*

Królewicz, *Król*
Krolick, *Królik*
Krolik, *Królik*
Królik
Krolikov, *Królik*
Królikowski, *Królik*
Krolitzki, *Królik*
Krolizki, *Królik*
Krolizky, *Królik*
Krøll, *Kroll*
Kroll
Krom, *Crome*
Krömer, *Krämer*
Kromer, *Krämer*
Kron, *Corona*
Kronberg, *Corona*
Krone, *Corona*
Kronebitter, *Kronewitter*
Kronenberg, *Corona*
Kronenberger, *Corona*
Kronenbitte, *Kronewitter*
Kronenblat, *Corona*
Kronenfeld, *Corona*
Kronental, *Corona*
Kronenthal, *Corona*
Kronenwetter, *Kronewitter*
Kronewitter
Kronfeld, *Corona*
Krongold, *Corona*
Krongrad, *Corona*
Kronkop, *Corona*
Kronkopf, *Corona*
Kronkopp, *Corona*
Kronnberg, *Corona*
Kronnenfeld, *Corona*
Kronquist, *Corona*
Kronson, *Kraindels*
Kronstein, *Corona*
Kronymus, *Jerome*
Kronzon, *Kraindels*
Krook, *Crook*
Kroon, *Corona*
Kropaček
Kropotkin
Krotil, *Kraus*
Kroupa, *Krupa*
Krousa, *Kraus*
Kroutil, *Kraus*
Kroužek, *Kraus*
Kroužil, *Kraus*
Krs, *Karski*
Kršák, *Karski*
Kršek, *Karski*
Krsek, *Karski*
Krška, *Karski*
Kršňák, *Karski*
Krt, *Krtil*
Krtek, *Krtil*
Krtil
Kruczkowski, *Kruk*
Krug, *Krüger*
Krügel, *Krüger*
Kruger, *Krüger*
Krüger
Krügle, *Krüger*
Krugliakov, *Kruglov*
Kruglin, *Kruglov*
Kruglov
Krugman, *Krüger*
Krugmann, *Krüger*
Kruijs, *Cross*
Kruis, *Cross*
Kruk
Krukowski, *Kruk*
Krul, *Kroll*
Krula, *Kroll*
Krulick, *Królik*
Krulik, *Królik*
Kruliš, *Kroll*
Krulitzky, *Królik*
Krull, *Kroll*
Krümel, *Crome*
Krümmel, *Crome*
Krump, *Crome*
Krumpp, *Crome*
Krupa
Krupička, *Krupa*
Krupiński, *Krupa*
Krupka, *Krupa*
Krupke, *Krupa*
Krupp, *Cripwell*
Kruppa, *Krupa*
Krüppel, *Cripwell*
Krupski, *Krupa*
Krusch, *Grushin*
Krusche, *Grushin*
Kruschel, *Grushin*
Kruschka, *Grushin*
Kruschke, *Grushin*
Kruse, *Kraus*
Krushchyov, *Khrushchev*
Kruskopf, *Kraus*
Kruspe, *Crisp*
Kruszyewski, *Kruszyński*
Kruszyński
Krůta
Kruták, *Krůta*
Krutský, *Krůta*
Kruuse, *Kraus*
Kryger, *Krieger*
Krygier, *Krüger*
Krylov
Krylovich, *Krylov*
Krysiak, *Christopher*
Kryska, *Christopher*
Krýsl, *Christian*
Krystek, *Christopher*
Kryštof, *Christopher*
Kryszka, *Christopher*
Kryszkiewicz, *Christopher*
Krysztof, *Christopher*
Krysztofiak, *Christopher*
Krysztofowicz, *Christopher*
Krysztowczyk, *Christopher*
Krywoshej, *Krivov*
Kryzhov, *Cross*
Krzemień, *Krzemiński*
Krzemieniewski, *Krzemiński*
Krzemieński, *Krzemiński*
Krzemiński
Krzemionka, *Krzemiński*
Krzeszewski
Krzysztof, *Christopher*
Krzysztofiak, *Christopher*
Krzywański, *Krivov*
Krzywicki, *Krivov*
Krzywiec, *Krivov*
Krzyżaniak, *Cross*
Krzyżanowski, *Cross*
Krzyżowski, *Cross*
Ksandr, *Alexander*
Książek
Kuba, *Jacob*
Kubáček, *Jacob*
Kubach, *Jacob*
Kubacki, *Jacob*
Kubal, *Jacob*
Kubala, *Jacob*
Kubalek, *Jacob*
Kuban, *Jacob*
Kubánek, *Jacob*
Kubas, *Jacob*
Kubásek, *Jacob*
Kubasiewicz, *Jacob*
Kubát, *Jacob*
Kubatsch, *Jacob*
Kubczak, *Jacob*
Kubec, *Jacob*
Kubečka, *Jacob*
Kubek, *Jacob*
Kubelka, *Jacob*
Kubera, *Jacob*
Kubeš, *Jacob*
Kubetz, *Kuptsov*
Kubiak, *Jacob*
Kubica, *Jacob*
Kubíček, *Jacob*
Kubička, *Jacob*
Kubicki, *Jacob*
Kubiczek, *Jacob*
Kubík, *Jacob*
Kubik, *Jacob*
Kubín, *Jacob*
Kubin, *Jacob*
Kubiš, *Jacob*
Kubis, *Jacob*
Kubisch, *Jacob*
Kubišta, *Jacob*
Kubisz, *Jacob*
Kubů, *Jacob*
Kubyszek, *Jacob*
Kučera
Kuchař, *Cook*
Kucharczyk, *Cook*
Kucharek, *Cook*
Kucharski, *Cook*
Kuchciak, *Cook*
Küchenmeister, *Kitchen*
Küchmeister, *Kitchen*
Kuchta, *Cook*
Kuchynka, *Kitchen*
Kuciński
Kuczyński, *Kitchen*
Kudelski, *Kudravtsev*
Kudła, *Kudravtsev*
Kudlik, *Kudravtsev*
Kudliński, *Kudravtsev*
Kudravtsev
Kudrna, *Kudravtsev*
Kudrnáč, *Kudravtsev*
Kudroff, *Kudravtsev*
Kudrowitz, *Kudravtsev*
Küfer, *Kiefer*
Küffner, *Kiefer*
Küfler, *Kiefer*
Küfner, *Kiefer*
Kugel
Kugelman, *Kugel*
Kugelmann, *Kugel*
Kugler, *Kugel*
Kuglovitz, *Kugel*
Kuhardt, *Coward*
Kuhert, *Coward*
Kühfuss, *Kofoed*
Kuhfuss, *Kofoed*
Kühl, *Kuhl*
Kuhl
Kühle, *Kuhl*
Kuhlemann, *Kuhl*
Kühlen, *Kuhl*
Kuhlmann, *Kuhl*
Kühn, *Konrad*
Kuhn, *Konrad*
Kühndel, *Konrad*
Kühne, *Konrad*
Kühnel, *Konrad*
Kuhnert, *Konrad*
Kuhnhardt, *Konrad*
Kuhnke, *Konrad*
Kuhnt, *Konrad*
Kuijper, *Cooper*
Kuijpers, *Cooper*
Kuiper, *Cooper*
Kuipers, *Cooper*
Kujawa
Kujawiak, *Kujawa*
Kujawski, *Kujawa*
Kukhar, *Cook*
Kukharenko, *Cook*
Kukharov, *Cook*
Kukla
Kuklík, *Kukla*
Kukuła
Kukulski, *Kukuła*
Kulaszyński, *Kulesza*
Kulawczyk, *Klečák*
Kulawiak, *Klečák*
Kulawik, *Klečák*
Kulawiński, *Klečák*
Kulemann, *Kuhl*
Kulesza
Kulič, *Klaus*
Kulíček, *Klaus*
Kulig
Kuligowicz, *Kulig*
Kuligowski, *Kulig*
Kulík, *Klaus*
Kulik
Kulikiewicz, *Kulik*
Kulikov, *Kulik*
Kulikowski, *Kulik*
Kuliš, *Klaus*
Kulišek, *Klaus*
Kulka, *Kulik*
Kull, *Konrad*
Kullmann, *Konrad*
Kulon, *Kulik*
Kummel, *Kümmel*
Kümmel
Kümmelmann, *Kümmel*
Kumsteller
Kún, *Cohen*
Kuna, *Konrad*
Kunat, *Konrad*
Kunath, *Konrad*
Kunc, *Konrad*
Kundert, *Konrad*
Kundt, *Konrad*
Kunert, *Konrad*
Kuneš, *Konrad*
Kunigunde, *Kenngott*
Kunisch, *Konrad*
Künkel, *Gunkel*
Kunkel, *Gunkel*
Künkler, *Gunkel*
Künne, *Kenngott*
Künneke, *Konrad*
Kunrád, *Konrad*
Kunrad, *Konrad*
Küntscher, *Kenngott*
Kunz, *Konrad*
Kunze, *Konrad*
Künzel, *Konrad*
Künzelmann, *Konrad*
Künzler, *Konrad*
Kupča, *Kuptsov*

Kupčak, *Kuptsov*
Kupczyk, *Jacob*
Kupec, *Jacob*
Kupec, *Kuptsov*
Küper, *Cooper*
Kuper, *Copper*
Kuperbaum, *Copper*
Kuperberg, *Copper*
Kuperboim, *Copper*
Kuperfish, *Copper*
Kuperman, *Copper*
Kupermintz, *Copper*
Küpers, *Cooper*
Kuperschlak, *Copper*
Kuperschmidt, *Coppersmith*
Kupershmid, *Coppersmith*
Kupershmidt, *Coppersmith*
Kupershmit, *Coppersmith*
Kupershtein, *Copper*
Kuperstein, *Copper*
Kuperstock, *Copper*
Kuperwasser, *Copper*
Kupets, *Kuptsov*
Kupetz, *Kuptsov*
Kupfer, *Copper*
Kupferberg, *Copper*
Kupferman, *Copper*
Kupfermann, *Copper*
Kupferminc, *Copper*
Kupferschmidt, *Coppersmith*
Kupferschmiedt, *Coppersmith*
Kupfershmid, *Coppersmith*
Kupfershmidt, *Coppersmith*
Kupferstein, *Copper*
Kupferstock, *Copper*
Kupferstok, *Copper*
Kupferwasser, *Copper*
Kupiec, *Kuptsov*
Kupiecki, *Kuptsov*
Kupietz, *Kuptsov*
Kupis, *Jacob*
Kupisz, *Jacob*
Kupitz, *Kuptsov*
Kupka, *Jacob*
Kupke, *Jacob*
Kupker, *Cooper*
Küpper, *Cooper*
Kupper, *Copper*
Kupperberg, *Copper*
Kupperman, *Copper*
Kuppermintz, *Copper*
Küppers, *Cooper*
Kupperschmidt, *Coppersmith*
Kupperstein, *Copper*
Kuptsov
Kurasov, *Kirilov*
Kurczewski, *Kurek*
Kurdvani, *Córdoba*
Kurek
Kureš, *Corneille*
Kurikhin, *Kirilov*
Kurikov, *Kirilov*
Kurilas, *Kirilov*
Kurilchikov, *Kirilov*
Kurilin, *Kirilov*
Kurilkin, *Kirilov*
Kurilov, *Kirilov*
Kuriltsev, *Kirilov*
Kurilyov, *Kirilov*
Kurin, *Kirilov*
Kurinov, *Kirilov*
Kurisov, *Kirilov*
Kuritsin, *Kurek*
Kuritsky, *Kurek*
Kuritzky, *Kurek*
Kurka, *Kurek*
Kurkiewicz, *Kurek*
Kurkowski, *Kurek*
Kurland
Kurlander, *Kurland*
Kurlandski, *Kurland*
Kurlansky, *Kurland*
Kurlender, *Kurland*
Kurliandcik, *Kurland*
Kurliandschick, *Kurland*
Kurlov, *Kirilov*
Kürner
Kurowski, *Kurek*
Kursanov, *Kirilov*
Kürschner
Kurshin, *Kirilov*
Kurshner, *Kürschner*
Kürssner, *Kürschner*
Kürsten, *Christian*
Kürstgens, *Christian*
Kurt, *Konrad*
Kürten, *Konrad*
Kurth, *Konrad*
Kurtz, *Court*
Kurtze, *Court*
Kuryanov, *Kirilov*
Kurylkin, *Kirilov*
Kurylyov, *Kirilov*
Kurysev, *Kirilov*
Kuryshev, *Kirilov*
Kurz, *Court*
Kurze, *Court*
Kůs, *Kos*
Kus, *Kos*
Kusch, *Jacob*
Kuscha, *Jacob*
Kuschack, *Jacob*
Kuschak, *Jacob*
Kusche, *Jacob*
Kuschel, *Jacob*
Kuschke, *Jacob*
Kuschner, *Kürschner*
Kushner, *Kürschner*
Kushnir, *Kürschner*
Kusiak, *Kos*
Kuśnierz, *Kürschner*
Küssewetter, *Kiesewetter*
Kuster, *Küster*
Küster
Küstermann, *Küster*
Kustermann, *Küster*
Küsters, *Küster*
Kutuzov
Kuusi
Kuusinen, *Kuusi*
Küver, *Cuvier*
Kuyper, *Cooper*
Kuypers, *Cooper*
Kužel
Kužela, *Kužel*
Kuzemchikov, *Kuzmin*
Kuzichkin, *Kuzmin*
Kuzik, *Kuzmin*
Kužilek, *Kužel*
Kuzin, *Kuzmin*
Kuzishchin, *Kuzmin*
Kuzkin, *Kuzmin*
Kuzmanović, *Kuzmin*
Kuzmich, *Kuzmin*
Kuzmichyov, *Kuzmin*
Kuzmin
Kuzminov, *Kuzmin*
Kuźmiński, *Kuzmin*
Kuzminsky, *Kuzmin*
Kuzmishchev, *Kuzmin*
Kuzmishin, *Kuzmin*
Kuzmyanko, *Kuzmin*
Kuznetsov
Kuznetzky, *Kuznetsov*
Kuzniak, *Kuznetsov*
Kuznicki, *Kuznetsov*
Kuźnik, *Kuznetsov*
Kuznits, *Kuznetsov*
Kuznitsky, *Kuznetsov*
Kuznitz, *Kuznetsov*
Kuznitzki, *Kuznetsov*
Kuzyakin, *Kuzmin*
Kuzyutin, *Kuzmin*
Kvapil, *Kwapisz*
Květ, *Kwiatek*
Kveťon, *Kwiatek*
Kviat, *Kwiatek*
Kviatek, *Kwiatek*
Kviatkovsky, *Kwiatkowski*
Kvieťon, *Kwiatek*
Kvist, *Qvist*
Kwapiński, *Kwapisz*
Kwapisiewicz, *Kwapisz*
Kwapisz
Kwaśniak
Kwaśniewski, *Kwaśniak*
Kwiat, *Kwiatek*
Kwiatek
Kwiatkowski
Kwiatosiński, *Kwiatkowski*
Kwiecień
Kwieciński, *Kwiecień*
Kwietniewski, *Kwiatkowski*
Kyd, *Kidd*
Kydd, *Kidd*
Kydds, *Kidd*
Kyffin
Kyle
Kyncl, *Konrad*
Kyne, *Coyne*
Kynsey, *Kinsey*
Kyrke, *Kirk*
Kyryshkin, *Kirilov*
Kyte, *Kite*

L

Laack, *Lake*
Laackmann, *Lake*
Laakso
Laaksonen, *Laakso*
Laan, *Lane*
Laba, *Abbé*
Labadini, *Abbé*
Labarile, *Baril*
Labarre, *Barr*
Labarrée, *Barr*
Labarree, *Barr*
Labarte, *Barthe*
Labarthe, *Barthe*
Labastida, *Bastide*
La Bastie, *Bastide*
Labate, *Abbé*
La Bâtie, *Bastide*
Labaye, *Abbey*
Labba, *Abbé*
Labbate, *Abbé*
Labbaye, *Abbey*
Labbé, *Abbé*
Labbey, *Abbé*
Labbez, *Abbé*
Łabęcki, *Lebedev*
Łabędzki, *Lebedev*
La Bella, *Beau*
Labelle, *Beau*
Labère, *Beau*
Laberenz, *Lawrence*
Labern, *Leyburn*
Labitte
Labonne, *Bon*
Laborda, *Boarder*
Laborde, *Boarder*
Laborier
Laborieux, *Laborier*
Labrador, *Laborier*
Labrencis, *Lawrence*
Labrenz, *Lawrence*
Labretesche, *Bretécher*
Labrosse, *Brosse*
Labrousse, *Brosse*
Labruyère, *Bruyère*
La Bua, *Boeuf*
Lac, *Lake*
Lacaille, *Cail*
Lacam, *Chaume*
Lacambra, *Chambers*
Lacambre, *Chambers*
Lacan, *Chaume*
Lacanal, *Chenal*
Lacanau, *Chenal*
La Capruccia, *Cheever*
Lacasa, *Casa*
Lacase, *Casa*
Lacassagne, *Cassagne*
Lacaussade, *Chaussée*
Lacave, *Cave*
Lacaze, *Casa*
Lace, *Glass*
Laček, *Lach*
Lacerda, *Cerda*
Lacey
Lach
Lacha, *Lach*
Lachaize, *Casa*
Lachambre, *Chambers*
Lachassagne, *Cassagne*
Lachaume, *Chaume*
Lachaussée, *Chaussée*
Lachenal, *Chenal*
Lachenaud, *Chenal*
Lacher, *Lake, Leicher*
Lachèvre, *Cheever*
Lachèze, *Casa*
Lachlan
Lachman, *Lachmann*
Lachmann
Lachmanovici, *Lachmann*
Lachner, *Lake, Leach, Leicher*
Lachout, *Lach*
Lachowicz, *Lach*
Lachowski, *Lach*
Lachs, *Lax*
Lachser, *Lax*
Lachsman, *Lax*
Lacina
Lack, *Lake*
Lackemann, *Lake*
Lackenby
Lacklinson, *Lachlan*
Lacklison, *Lachlan*
Lackmann, *Lake*
Lacks, *Lax*
Lacombe, *Coombe*
Lacome, *Coombe*
Lacomme, *Coombe*

Lacorne, *Corne*
La Corte, *Court*
Lacorte, *Court*
Lacoste, *Coste*
Lacotte, *Cotte*
Lacour, *Court*
Lacourt, *Court*
Lacourte, *Court*
Lacquet, *Lake*
Lacrambe, *Chambers*
La Croce, *Cross*
Lacroix, *Cross*
Lacrouts, *Cross*
Lacroutz, *Cross*
Lacroux, *Cross*
Lacy, *Lacey*
Ladbrooke
Ladd
Ladds, *Ladd*
Lade, *Lewis*
Ladefoged
Ladel, *Ladler*
Ladell, *Ladler*
Lademann, *Lewis*
Ladevèze, *Devèze*
Ladewig, *Lewis*
Ladler
Ladson, *Ladd*
Ladwig, *Lewis*
Lafage, *Fage*
Lafagette, *Fage*
Lafargue, *Forge*
Lafay, *Fage*
Lafaye, *Fage*
Lafayette, *Fage*
Laffage, *Fage*
Laffan, *Lavin*
Laffargue, *Forge*
Laffay, *Fage*
Lafferty, *Laverty*
Laffin, *Lavin*
Laffite, *Laffitte*
Laffitte
Lafflin, *Lachlan*
Laffling, *Lachlan*
La Fiore, *Flower*
Lafon, *Font*
Lafond, *Font*
Lafont, *Font*
Lafontaine, *Fontaine*
La Fontant, *Fontaine*
Laforest, *Forrest*
Laforêt, *Forrest*
Laforge, *Forge*
Laforgue, *Forge*
Lafosse, *Fosse*
Lafourcade, *Fourche*
Lafoy, *Foy*
Lafrentz, *Lawrence*
Lafrenz, *Lawrence*
Lafuente, *Font*
Lagache, *Agace*
Lagan, *Logan*
Lagarde, *Guard*
Lagarenne, *Warren*
Lagasse, *Agace*
Lage
Lager
Lagerbäch, *Lager*
Lagerberg, *Lager*
Lagerborg, *Lager*
Lagercrantz, *Lager*
Lagerdahl, *Lager*
Lagerfeldt, *Lager*
Lagerfelt, *Lager*
Lagerfors, *Lager*
Lagergreehn, *Lager*
Lagergreen, *Lager*
Lagergrehn, *Lager*
Lagergren, *Lager*
Lagerholm, *Lager*
Lagerkrantz, *Lager*
Lagerkranz, *Lager*
Lagerlöf, *Lager*
Lagerlund, *Lager*
Lagerman, *Lager*
Lagerquist, *Lager*
Lagerstedt, *Lager*
Lagerstrandt, *Lager*
Lagerström, *Lager*
Lagervall, *Lager*
Lagerwall, *Lager*
Lages, *Lage*
Laghlan, *Lachlan*
Lagioia, *Joy*
Lagneau, *Agnew*
Lagnel, *Agnew*
Lagnese, *Annis*
Lago, *Lake*
Lagorce, *Gorse*
Lagore, *Gore*
Lagrange, *Grange*
Laguardia, *Guard*
Laguerre, *Warr*
Laguna
Lagunas, *Laguna*
Lahache, *Hache*
Lahalle, *Hall*
Lahaye, *Hay*
Lahger, *Lager*
Lahitte, *Laffitte*
Lähr, *Hilary*
Lahr, *Hilary*
Lahrs, *Lawrence*
Lahti, *Lahtinen*
Lahtinen
Laicher, *Leicher*
Laichner, *Leicher*
Laidlaw
Laidler, *Ladler, Laidlaw*
Laidley, *Laidlaw*
Laigle, *Eagle*
Laigneau, *Agnew*
Laignel, *Agnew*
Laikin, *Lakin*
Lain, *Lane*
Laine
Lainer, *Lanier*
Laing, *Long*
Laiper, *Leapman*
Laird
Laister, *Lister*
Laithwaite
Laitinen
Laitner, *Leitner*
Laity, *Lawty*
Lajarrige, *Jarry*
Lajos, *Lewis*
Lake
Lakeman, *Lake*
Laker
Lakes, *Lake*
Lakin
Lakins, *Lakin*
Lakser, *Lax*
Laksman, *Lax*
Lally, *Mullally*
Lalonde, *Lund*
Lalor, *Lawlor*
Lalour, *Lawlor*
Lam
Lama
Lamadrid, *Madrid*
La Magna, *Alman*
La Manna, *Alman*
Lamarca, *Marque*
Lamard, *Delamare*
Lamare, *Delamare*
Lamarque, *Marque*
Lamarre, *Delamare*
Lamartine, *Martin*
Lamas, *Lama*
Lamb
Lamba, *Lambert*
Lambard, *Lambert*
Lambart, *Lambert*
Lambarth, *Lambert*
Lambe, *Lamb*
Lambert
Lambertazzi, *Lambert*
Lambertenghi, *Lambert*
Lamberteschi, *Lambert*
Lamberti, *Lambert*
Lambertini, *Lambert*
Lamberto, *Lambert*
Lambertoni, *Lambert*
Lamberts, *Lambert*
Lambertsen, *Lambert*
Lambertson, *Lambert*
Lambertz, *Lambert*
Lambie, *Lamb*
Lambin, *Lambert*
Lambinet, *Lambert*
Lambkin, *Lamb*
Lamblin, *Lambert*
Lamblot, *Lambert*
Lamborn, *Lambourne*
Lamborne, *Lambourne*
Lambot, *Lambert*
Lambotin, *Lambert*
Lambourn, *Lambourne*
Lambourne
Lambrecht, *Lambert*
Lambrechts, *Lambert*
Lambregts, *Lambert*
Lambrich, *Lambert*
Lambricht, *Lambert*
Lambrick, *Lambert*
Lambson, *Lamb*
Lambton
Lamburn, *Lambourne*
Lamburne, *Lambourne*
Lamby, *Lamb*
Lamcke, *Lambert*
Lamcken, *Lambert*
Lameiras, *Lama*
Lamers, *Lambert*
Lamerton
Laming, *Lemon*
Lamke, *Lambert*
Lamkin, *Lamb*
Lamm, *Lamb*
Lammekins, *Lamb*
Lämmel, *Lamb*
Lammel, *Lamb*
Lammeling, *Lamb*
Lammenga, *Lambert*
Lammens, *Lamb*
Lammerding, *Lambert*
Lammerich, *Lambert*
Lammering, *Lambert*
Lammers, *Lambert*
Lammert, *Lambert*
Lammerts, *Lambert*
Lammertse, *Lambert*
Lammertz, *Lambert*
Lammey, *Lamb*
Lammie, *Lamb*
Lammin, *Lamb*
Lamming, *Lamb*
Lämmle, *Lamb*
Lammond, *Lamont*
Lamond, *Lamont*
Lamont
Lamothe, *Motte*
La Motta, *Motte*
Lamotte, *Motte*
Lamouche, *Mouche*
Lamouque, *Mouche*
Lamoureux, *Amoureux*
Lamouroux, *Amoureux*
Lamp, *Lambert*
Lampaert, *Lambert*
Lampard, *Lambert*
Lampart, *Lambert*
Lampe, *Lambert*
Lampel, *Lambert*
Lampen, *Lamb*
Lampens, *Lambert*
Lamperd, *Lambert*
Lampert, *Lambert*
Lamperti, *Lambert*
Lampet
Lampin, *Lamb*
Lamping, *Lambert*
Lampitt, *Lampet*
Lampke, *Lambert*
Lampkin, *Lamb*
Lämpl, *Lambert*
Lampl, *Lambert*
Lamprecht, *Lambert*
Lamps, *Lambert*
Lampson, *Lamb*
Lamputt, *Lampet*
Lamson, *Lamb*
Lamy, *Amis*
Lança, *Lancia*
Lancaster
Lancastle, *Lancaster*
Lance
Lancel, *Ancel*
Lancia
Lancini, *Lancia*
Lancioni, *Lancia*
Lanciotti, *Lancia*
Lanctin, *Ashkettle*
Land
Landa
Landau, *Lander*
Landauer, *Lander*
Landberg, *Land*
Lande, *Lander*
Landegren, *Land*
Landelius, *Land*
Landell, *Land*
Landén, *Land*
Lander
Landesman, *Landmann*
Landesmann, *Landmann*
Landeta, *Landa*
Landgren, *Land*
Landh, *Land*
Landi, *Lance*
Landin, *Land*
Landini, *Lance*
Landino, *Lance*

Landman, *Landmann*
Landmann
Lando, *Lance*
Landoj, *Lander*
Landone, *Lance*
Landoni, *Lance*
Landow, *Lander*
Landowski, *Lander*
Landquist, *Land*
Landrieu, *Andrew*
Landseer
Landsman, *Landmann*
Landsmann, *Landmann*
Landström, *Land*
Landt, *Land*
Landucci, *Lance*
Landuzzi, *Lance*
Lane
Lanes, *Lane*
Láng, *Long*
Lång, *Long*
Lang, *Long*
Langan
Langbart, *Long*
Langbaum, *Long*
Langberg, *Long*
Langbord, *Long*
Langburt, *Long*
Langcaster, *Lancaster*
Langcastle, *Lancaster*
Langdon
Lange, *Long*
Langenscheid, *Langenscheidt*
Langenscheidt
Langental, *Long*
Langenthal, *Long*
Langer, *Long*
Langerman, *Long*
Langford
Langfuss, *Long*
Langham
Langholz, *Long*
Langin, *Langan*
Langlais, *English*
Langlands
Langleben, *Long*
Langlebert, *Engelbert*
Langley
Langlois, *English*
Langloy, *English*
Langman, *Long*
Langmans, *Long*
Langnese
Langobardi, *Lombard*
Langobardo, *Lombard*
Langridge
Langsford, *Langford*
Langstaff, *Longstaff*
Langston
Langton
Langtree
Lanham, *Langham*
Lanier
Lanigan, *Lennon*
Lankester, *Lancaster*
Lannan, *Lennon*
Lannen, *Lennon*
Lanni, *Lance*
Lannigan, *Lennon*
Lannin, *Lennon*
Lannino, *Lance*
Lanno, *Lance*
Lannon, *Lennon*
Lanon, *Lennon*
Lanquetin, *Ashkettle*
Lansdown
Lansky, *Lánský*
Lánský
Lansman, *Landmann*
Lant
Lantz, *Lance*
Lanyon
Lanz, *Lance*
Lanza, *Lancia*
Lanzetta, *Lancia*
Lanzi, *Lance*
Lanzini, *Lance*
Lanzl, *Lance*
Lanzo, *Lance*
Lanzola, *Lancia*
Lanzone, *Lance*
Lanzoni, *Lance*
Laoust, *Davout*
Lapage, *Lawrence*
Lapalu, *Pallu*
Lapalud, *Pallu*
Lapalue, *Pallu*
Lapalus, *Pallu*
Läpel, *Löffler*
Lapenna, *Peña*
Lapérière, *Pear*
La Perna, *Pearl*
Lapeyre, *Pierre*
La Piana, *Plain*
Lapid
Lapides, *Lapidus*
Lapidos, *Lapidus*
Lapidot, *Lapidus*
Lapidoth, *Lapidus*
Lapidus
Lapiduss, *Lapidus*
Lapière, *Pierre*
Lapierre, *Pierre*
Lapin, *Łapiński*
Lapiner, *Łapiński*
Lapinski, *Łapiński*
Łapiński
Lapinsky, *Łapiński*
La Pinta, *Pinto*
La Pira, *Pear*
Lapkin, *Łapiński*
Laplace, *Place*
Laplanche, *Planche*
Laplanque, *Planche*
Laplatte, *Platt*
La Porta, *Port*
Laporta, *Port*
Laporte, *Port*
Lapostoile, *Postle*
Lapostole, *Postle*
Lapostolle, *Postle*
Lappage, *Lawrence*
Lappalainen
Läpple, *Lepper*
Laprade, *Pré*
Lapradelle, *Pré*
Lapraye, *Pré*
Lapraz, *Pré*
Laprée, *Pré*
Laprugne, *Plum*
Laprune, *Plum*
Lapworth
Laquièvre, *Cheever*
Lara
Laranjeira, *Naranjo*
Laranjeira
Laranjo, *Naranjo*
Larcher
Larder
Lardge, *Large*
Lardiner, *Larder*
Lardner, *Larder*
Lareur, *Arcas*
Large
Largeau, *Large*
Largeault, *Large*
Largent, *Argent*
Largeot, *Large*
Larget, *Large*
Largeteau, *Large*
Largey, *Large*
Largman, *Large*
Larher, *Arcas*
Larieu, *Rieu*
Larimer, *Lorimer*
Larius, *Hilary*
Larive, *Rive*
Larivière, *Rivers*
Lark
Larke, *Lark*
Larkin
Larking, *Larkin*
Larkman, *Lark*
Larmer, *Armer*
Larmor, *Armour*
Larmour, *Armour*
Larnach
Larnack, *Larnach*
Larner
La Rocca, *Roach*
Laroche, *Roach*
Larochelle, *Roach*
Larochette, *Roach*
Larocque, *Roach*
Laronde, *Hiron*
Laroque, *Roach*
La Rosa, *Rose*
Larose, *Rose*
Larour, *Arcas*
Larousse, *Rouse*
Laroze, *Rose*
Larpin, *Harper*
Larquier, *Archer*
Larrazabal
Larrea
Larrett, *Lawrence*
Larreur, *Arcas*
Larrie, *Lawrence*
Larrinaga, *Larrea*
Larroque, *Roach*
Larrosa, *Rose*
Larrour, *Arcas*
Larrouy, *Arroyo*
Lars, *Lawrence*
Larsen, *Lawrence*
Larson, *Lawrence*
Larsson, *Lawrence*
Lartigue, *Artiga*
Larue, *Rue*
Laš, *Lach*
Las, *Lawrence*
Lasa
Lasalle, *Lassalle*
Lasar, *Lazar*
Lasbordas, *Boarder*
Lascelles
Lascombes, *Coombe*
Łasek, *Łaski*
Laselve, *Silva*
Lasenby, *Lazenby*
Laser, *Lazar*
Lashford, *Latchford*
Laska, *Laskowski*
Laskar, *Laskowski*
Laskau, *Laskowski*
Laske, *Łaski*
Lasker, *Laskowski*
Łaski
Laskier, *Laskowski*
Laśkiewicz, *Lasoń*
Laśkiewicz, *Lazar*
Laskov, *Laskowski*
Laskovski, *Laskowski*
Laskow, *Laskowski*
Laskowski
Lasky, *Łaski*
Lasnier, *Lanier*
Laso
Lasocki, *Lasoń*
Lasoń
Lasota, *Lasoń*
Lasouche, *Such*
La Spina, *Épine*
Lass, *Lax*
Lassalle
Lassandri, *Alexander*
Lasselve, *Silva*
Lassen, *Lawrence*
Lasseter, *Leicester*
Lassey, *Lacey*
Lassiter, *Leicester*
Last
La Stella, *Stella*
Laster, *Last*
Lastra
Lastras, *Lastra*
Lasvergnas, *Ver*
Łaszczewski
Łaszkiewicz, *Lazar*
Latapie, *Tapia*
Latch, *Leek*
Latches, *Leach*
Latches, *Leek*
Latchford
Lateiner
Latek
Latham
Lathem, *Latham*
Lathom, *Latham*
Latimer
Latimier, *Latimer*
Latimore, *Latimer*
Latinier, *Latimer*
Latkowski, *Latek*
Latner, *Latimer*
La Torre, *Tower*
Latouche, *Touche*
Latour, *Tower*
Latreille, *Treille*
Latrille, *Treille*
Latta, *Latto*
Latter
Latterman, *Latter*
Lattey, *Latto*
Lattimer, *Latimer*
Lattner, *Latimer, Latter*
Latto
Laturner, *Latimer*
Latzarus, *Lazar*
Lau, *Löwe*
Laubreton, *Brett*
Lauckhardt, *Legard*
Laudenslayer, *Luther*
Lauder
Laudet, *Uccello*
Laue, *Löwe*

Lauer
Lauersen, *Lawrence*
Lauesen, *Lawrence*
Laufer, *Läufer*
Läufer
Laugé, *Ledger*
Laugel, *Uccello*
Lauger, *Ledger*
Laugesen, *Lawrence*
Laugheran, *Loughrey*
Laughlan, *Lachlan*
Laughland, *Lachlan*
Laughlin, *Lachlan*
Laughnan, *Loughnane*
Laughton
Laugier, *Ledger*
Laukkanen
Lauks, *Lucas*
Läule, *Nicholas*
Laulin, *Nicholas*
Laumonier, *Aumonier*
Launay, *Delaney*
Launder, *Lavender*
Launois, *Delaney*
Launoy, *Delaney*
Laur
Laurain, *Laur*
Lauraire, *Laborier*
Laurance, *Lawrence*
Laurand, *Lawrence*
Laurant, *Lawrence*
Lauras, *Laur*
Laure, *Laur*
Laureau, *Laur*
Laurel, *Laur*
Lauren, *Lawrence*
Laurence, *Lawrence*
Laurenceau, *Lawrence*
Laurencet, *Lawrence*
Laurencin, *Lawrence*
Laurençon, *Lawrence*
Laurençot, *Lawrence*
Laurendeau, *Lawrence*
Laurendin, *Lawrence*
Laurens, *Lawrence*
Laurenson, *Lawrence*
Laurent, *Lawrence*
Laurenti, *Lawrence*
Laurentin, *Lawrence*
Laurentino, *Lawrence*
Laurentis, *Lawrence*
Laurenty, *Lawrence*
Laurenz, *Lawrence*
Laurenzi, *Lawrence*
Lauri, *Laur*
Laurich, *Lawrence*
Lauridsen, *Lawrence*
Laurie, *Lawrence*
Lauriello, *Laur*
Laurier, *Laur*
Laurin, *Laur*
Laurinaitis, *Lawrence*
Laurini, *Laur*
Laurino, *Laur*
Lauriol, *Oriol*
Laurisch, *Lawrence*
Laurito, *Lawrence*
Lauritsen, *Lawrence*
Lauritzen, *Lawrence*
Lauro, *Laur*
Laurot, *Laur*
Laursen, *Lawrence*
Lausel, *Uccello*
Lausen, *Lawrence*
Lausitz, *Luzzatto*
Laute, *Luther*
Lautenschläger, *Luther*
Lautenschlager, *Luther*
Lautero, *Luther*
Lautrec
Laux, *Lucas*
Lauxmann, *Lucas*
Laval, *Vale*
La Valle, *Vale*
Lavalle, *Vale*
Lavallette, *Vale*
Lavandier, *Lavender*
Lavator, *Lavender*
Lavau, *Vale*
Lavaud, *Vale*
Lavault, *Vale*
Lavaux, *Vale*
Laveau, *Vale*
Lavell, *Lavelle*
Lavelle
Lavender
Lavenier, *Avoine*
Lavenne, *Avoine*
Laver
Laverack, *Lark*
Laverentz, *Lawrence*
Laverenz, *Lawrence*
Lavergna, *Ver*
Lavergne, *Ver*
Laverick, *Lark*
Lavers, *Laver*
Laverty
Lavery
Lavialle, *Ville*
Lavigne, *Vine*
Laville, *Ville*
Lavin
La Viola, *Viola*
Lavis, *Laver*
Laviss, *Laver*
Lavoine, *Avoine*
Lavoinne, *Avoine*
Lavoisier
La Volpe, *Volpe*
Lavoratore, *Laborier*
Lavrador, *Laborier*
Lavrenčić, *Lawrence*
Lavrenov, *Lawrence*
Lavrin, *Lawrence*
Lavrinov, *Lawrence*
Lavrishchev, *Lawrence*
Lavrov, *Laur*
Lavrukhin, *Lawrence*
Lavrushin, *Lawrence*
Law
Lawder, *Lauder*
Lawer, *Flower*
Lawes, *Law*
Lawford
Lawler, *Lawlor*
Lawless
Lawley
Lawlor
Lawman, *Lamont*
Lawn, *Land*
Ławnicki
Ławniczak, *Ławnicki*
Lawrance, *Lawrence*
Lawrence
Lawrenson, *Lawrence*
Lawrenz, *Lawrence*
Lawrey, *Lawrence*
Lawrie, *Lawrence*
Lawry, *Lawrence*
Laws, *Law*
Lawson, *Law*
Lawter, *Lauder*
Lawther, *Lauder*
Lawtie, *Latto*
Lawton
Lawty
Lax
Laxer, *Lax*
Laxman, *Lax*
Lay, *Lee*
Layborn, *Leyburn*
Laybourn, *Leyburn*
Laycock
Laye, *Lee*
Layland, *Leyland*
Layman, *Lee*
Layne, *Lane*
Laytham, *Latham*
Layton
Lázár, *Lazar*
Lazăr, *Lazar*
Lazar
Lazarchuk, *Lazar*
Łazarczyk, *Lazar*
Lazard, *Lazar*
Lazare, *Lazar*
Łazarek, *Lazar*
Lazarev, *Lazar*
Lazarević, *Lazar*
Lazarin, *Lazar*
Lázaro, *Lazar*
Lazaroff, *Lazar*
Lazarofsky, *Lazar*
Lazarov, *Lazar*
Lazarovici, *Lazar*
Lazarovitch, *Lazar*
Lazarovitz, *Lazar*
Lazarow, *Lazar*
Lazarowics, *Lazar*
Łazarowicz, *Lazar*
Lazarowicz, *Lazar*
Lazarowitz, *Lazar*
Łazarski, *Lazar*
Lazarson, *Lazar*
Lazart, *Lazar*
Lazaruk, *Lazar*
Lazarus, *Lazar*
Lazenby
Lazer, *Lazar*
Lazere, *Lazar*
Lazerowitz, *Lazar*
Lazerson, *Lazar*
Lazerus, *Lazar*
Lazić, *Lazar*
Lazović, *Lazar*
Lazrus, *Lazar*
Lazzarelli, *Lazar*
Lazzaretti, *Lazar*
Lazzari, *Lazar*
Lazzarin, *Lazar*
Lazzarini, *Lazar*
Lazzarino, *Lazar*
Lazzaro, *Lazar*
Lazzarone, *Lazar*
Lazzaroni, *Lazar*
Lazzarotti, *Lazar*
Lazzarotto, *Lazar*
Lazzarutti, *Lazar*
Lazzeretti, *Lazar*
Lazzeri, *Lazar*
Lazzerini, *Lazar*
Lazzero, *Lazar*
Lazzeroni, *Lazar*
Lea, *Lee*
Leach
Leacock, *Laycock*
Leacy, *Lacey*
Leadbeater, *Leadbetter*
Leadbeatter, *Leadbetter*
Leadbetter
Leadbitter, *Leadbetter*
Leader
Leaf
Leafe, *Leaf*
Leahy
Leak, *Leek*
Leake, *Leek*
Leaker, *Leek*
Leal
Leale, *Leal*
Lealman, *Leal*
Leaman, *Lemon*
Leaming, *Lemon*
Leamon, *Lemon*
Lean
Leane, *Lean*
Leão, *Lyon*
Leaper, *Leapman*
Leapman
Lear
Learmond, *Learmonth*
Learmont, *Learmonth*
Learmonth
Learnard, *Leonard*
Learned, *Leonard*
Learoyd
Leary
Leask
Leason, *Lees*
Leatham, *Latham*
Leathead, *Leithead*
Leathem, *Latham*
Leather
Leatherbarrow
Leatherland, *Litherland*
Leatherman, *Leather*
Leathers, *Leather*
Leathley
Léautard, *Leuthard*
Léauthier, *Leuther*
Leaver, *Lever*
Leaves, *Leaf*
Leavesley
Leavett, *Levett*
Leavey, *Levy*
Leavis, *Leaf*
Leavitt, *Levett*
Leavy, *Dunleavy, Levy*
Lebail, *Bailey*
Lebaillif, *Bailey*
Lebailly, *Bailey*
Lebart, *Leppard*
Lebas, *Bass*
Le Bâtard, *Bastard*
Lebbel, *Beau*
Lebbell, *Beau*
Lebeau, *Beau*
Lebec, *Beck*
Lebecq, *Beck*
Lebed, *Lebedev*
Lebeda, *Lebedev*
Lebedev
Lebedevich, *Lebedev*
Lebedinski, *Lebedev*
Lebedinsky, *Lebedev*
Lebedkin, *Lebedev*

Lebedoff, *Lebedev*
Lebègue, *Bègue*
Le Bel, *Beau*
Lebert, *Leppard*
Leblanc, *Blanc*
Lebleu, *Blau*
Le Blond, *Blunt*
Le Blonde, *Blunt*
Leboeuf, *Boeuf*
Leboff, *Boeuf*
Lebon, *Bon*
Lebordais, *Boarder*
Leborgne, *Borgne*
Leborne, *Borgne*
Lebouc, *Buck*
Leboucq, *Buck*
Lebourdais, *Boarder*
Lebourg, *Burke*
Le Brasseur, *Brasher*
Lebret, *Brett*
Lebreton, *Brett*
Lebrun, *Brown*
Lebyadzevich, *Lebedev*
Lecalm, *Chaume*
Lecalme, *Chaume*
Lecamus, *Camoys*
Lecanu, *Chenu*
Le Canuel, *Chenu*
Lecanut, *Chenu*
Lecapelain, *Chaplin*
Lecaplain, *Chaplin*
Lecarpentier, *Carpenter*
Le Carré, *Carré*
Lecat, *Catt*
Lecerf, *Cerf*
Lech
Lechapelain, *Chaplin*
Lechardon, *Carding*
Lecharpentier, *Carpenter*
Lechat, *Catt*
Leche, *Leach*
Léchelle, *Eschelle*
Lechêne, *Chêne*
Lechesne, *Chêne*
Lechevalier, *Chevalier*
Lechevallier, *Chevalier*
Lechner, *Lehmann*
Leck, *Leek*
Leckey, *Leckie*
Łęcki
Leckie
Lecky, *Leckie*
Leclair, *Clark*
Lecler, *Clark*
Leclerc, *Clark*
Leclercq, *Clark*
Leclert, *Clark*
Lecoc, *Cock*
Lecocq, *Cock*
Lecoindre, *Quant*
Lecointe, *Quant*
Lecointre, *Quant*
Lecombe, *Coombe*
Lecomber, *Camber*
Lecomte, *Count*
Leconde, *Count*
Le Corbeiller, *Corbeil*
Lecorbusier, *Courvoisier*
Lecordier, *Corde*
Lecornu, *Corne*
Lécot, *Scott*
Lecount, *Count*
Lecour, *Coeur*
Lecourt, *Court*
Lecreux, *Creux*
Lecroc, *Crook*
Lecrocq, *Crook*
Lecue
Lécureuil, *Squirrel*
Lécureux, *Squirrel*
Lécuyer, *Squire*
Le Dantec, *Dent*
Ledbetter, *Leadbetter*
Ledder, *Leader*
Leddy
Ledentu, *Dent*
Leder, *Leather*
Lederaich, *Leather*
Lederberg, *Leather*
Ledereich, *Leather*
Lederer, *Leather*
Lederfajn, *Leather*
Lederhandler, *Leather*
Lederkramer, *Leather*
Lederle, *Leather*
Lederman, *Leather*
Ledermann, *Leather*
Lederstein, *Leather*
Ledesma
Ledger
Ledoux, *Duce*
Ledoyen, *Dean*
Ledru, *Drew*
Ledster, *Lister*
Leduc, *Duke*
Le Duigo, *Duff*
Ledur, *Duro*
Lee
Leeb, *Löwe*
Leeburn, *Leyburn*
Leece, *Lees*
Leech, *Leach*
Leedam, *Latham*
Leeder, *Leader*
Leedham, *Latham*
Leedom, *Latham*
Leeds
Leefe, *Leaf*
Leehan, *Lehane*
Leehane, *Lehane*
Leek
Leeke, *Leek*
Leeks, *Leek*
Leeman, *Lehmann, Lemon*
Leeming
Leenders, *Leonard*
Leendert, *Leonard*
Leenderts, *Leonard*
Leenerts, *Leonard*
Leeper, *Leapman*
Lees
Leese, *Lees*
Leeson, *Lees*
Leestman, *Last*
Leetch, *Leach*
Leeuw, *Löwe*
Le Faou, *Fage*
Lefaucheur, *Faucheur*
Lefaucheux, *Faucheur*
Lefauquer, *Faucheur*
Lefauquex, *Faucheur*
Lefeaver, *Fèvre*
Lefébure, *Fèvre*
Lefebvre, *Fèvre*
Lefeubre, *Fèvre*
Lefeure, *Fèvre*
Lefeuvre, *Fèvre*
Lefever, *Fèvre*
Lefevre, *Fèvre*
Leffeck, *Levick*
Leffel, *Löffler*
Leffler, *Löffler*
Lefkovich, *Lewkowicz*
Lefkovits, *Lewkowicz*
Lefkovitz, *Lewkowicz*
Lefkowicz, *Lewkowicz*
Lefkowits, *Lewkowicz*
Le Fleming, *Fleming*
Lefler, *Löffler*
Lefort, *Fort*
Lefoulon, *Fuller*
Lefournié, *Fournier*
Lefournier, *Fournier*
Lefranc, *Frank*
Lefridge, *Leveridge*
Legagneur, *Gagneux*
Legagneux, *Gagneux*
Le Gall, *Gall*
Le Galle, *Gall*
Le Gallic, *Gall*
Le Gallo, *Gall*
Legard
Legat, *Leggatt*
Legate, *Leggatt*
Legatt, *Leggatt*
Legay, *Gay*
Legeay, *Jay*
Legendre, *Gendre*
Legentil, *Gentle*
Léger, *Ledger*
Leger, *Ledger*
Légeret, *Ledger*
Légeron, *Ledger*
Légerot, *Ledger*
Legg
Leggate, *Leggatt*
Leggatt
Legge, *Legg*
Legget, *Leggatt*
Leggett, *Leggatt*
Leggitt, *Leggatt*
Leggott, *Leggatt*
Legh, *Leigh*
Légier, *Ledger*
Le Goff, *Gough*
Legood, *Good*
Legori, *Lever*
Le Grand, *Grant*
Legrand, *Grant*
Legras, *Grass*
Legrey, *Gray*
Le Grice, *Grice*
Legris, *Grice*
Legrix, *Grice*
Legros, *Gross*
Le Grys, *Grice*
Leguay, *Gay*
Legué, *Wade*
Le Guen, *Gwyn*
Le Guenec, *Gwyn*
Le Guennec, *Gwyn*
Leguet, *Waite*
Leguey, *Gay*
Legwood, *Leggatt*
Lehane
Leherne, *Heron*
Lehéron, *Heron*
Lehêtre, *Heister*
Lehigh, *Leahy*
Lehman, *Lehmann*
Lehmann
Lehner, *Lehmann*
Lehnert, *Leonard*
Lehnertz, *Leonard*
Lehnhard, *Leonard*
Lehoux, *Hilse*
Lehr, *Lehrer*
Lehrer
Lehrmann, *Lehrer*
Lehtinen
Lehto, *Lehtonen*
Lehtonen
Leib
Leibel, *Leib*
Leibin, *Leib*
Leibl, *Leib*
Leiblowicz, *Leib*
Leibnitz
Leibniz, *Leibnitz*
Leibold, *Leopold*
Leibov, *Leib*
Leibovic, *Leib*
Leibovich, *Leib*
Leibovici, *Leib*
Leibovicz, *Leib*
Leibovitch, *Leib*
Leibovitz, *Leib*
Leibow, *Leib*
Leibowics, *Leib*
Leibowicz, *Leib*
Leibowitch, *Leib*
Leibowitsch, *Leib*
Leibowitz, *Leib*
Leibsohn, *Leib*
Leibson, *Leib*
Leibush, *Leib*
Leicester
Leichart, *Legard*
Leicher
Leichert, *Legard*
Leichner, *Leicher*
Leicht, *Light*
Leichtl, *Light*
Leichtle, *Light*
Leickard, *Legard*
Leif, *Leaf*
Leigh
Leighton
Leikart, *Legard*
Leikert, *Legard*
Leikin, *Lakin*
Leinardi, *Leonard*
Leinardo, *Leonard*
Leiner
Leino, *Leinonen*
Leinonen
Leipelt, *Leopold*
Leiper, *Leapman*
Leipold, *Leopold*
Leipoldt, *Leopold*
Leiprecht, *Lubrecht*
Leipzig, *Lipski*
Leipziger, *Lipski*
Leirer
Leirmonth, *Learmonth*
Leish, *Lees*
Leishman, *Lees*
Leisk, *Leask*
Leist, *Last*
Leistenmacher, *Last*
Leistenschneider, *Last*
Leitão
Leitch, *Leach*
Leite
Leiter, *Leader*
Leiter, *Leitner*

Leitert, *Leuthard*
Leith
Leithead
Leither, *Leuther*
Leithhead, *Leithead*
Leitner
Leiva
Leivers, *Lever*
Leivick, *Levi*
Leivik, *Levick*
Lejay, *Jay*
Lejderman, *Leather*
Lejeune, *Jeune*
Le Keux, *Kew*
Lekić, *Lyokhin*
Leković, *Lyokhin*
Leksin, *Lyokhin*
Leland, *McClellan*
Lelarge, *Large*
Leleu, *Low*
Leleux, *Low*
Lelièvre, *Lever*
Lelikov, *Lenin*
Lelkin, *Lenin*
Lelli
Lelmi, *William*
Lelong, *Long*
Le Lorrain, *Lorraine*
Lelou, *Low*
Le Louet, *Lloyd*
Leloup, *Low*
Leloutrel, *Luttrell*
Lely, *Lilly*
Lelyakin, *Lenin*
Lelyakov, *Lenin*
Lelyanov, *Lenin*
Lelyashin, *Lenin*
Lelyukhin, *Lenin*
Lemaçon, *Mason*
Lemagnan, *Magnien*
Lemaignan, *Magnien*
Lemaignen, *Magnien*
Lemaignien, *Magnien*
Lemaigre, *Maigre*
Lemaistre, *Master*
Lemaître, *Master*
Leman, *Lehmann, Lemon*
Le Manac'h, *Monk*
Le Marchand, *Marchant*
Le Marchant, *Marchant*
Le Marec, *Markey*
Lemarignier, *Marin*
Lemarinier, *Marin*
Lemarois, *Marsh*
Le Marquand, *Marchant*
Lemarquis, *Marquis*
Le Marrec, *Markey*
Lemas, *Mas*
Lemasson, *Mason*
Lembcke, *Lambert*
Lembi, *William*
Lembke, *Lambert*
Lembo, *William*
Lemcke, *Lambert*
Lemel, *Lamb*
Lemelson, *Lamb*
Le Mer, *Mayer*
Lemercier, *Mercer*
Lemerle, *Merle*
Lemesle, *Merle*
Lemétais, *Métayer*
Lemeunier, *Miller*
Lemm, *Lambert*
Lemme, *Lambert*
Lemmel, *Lamb*
Lemmen, *Lambert*
Lemmens, *Lambert*
Lemmers, *Lambert*
Lemmertz, *Lambert*
Lemmi, *William*
Lemmo, *William*
Lemmon, *Lemon*
Le Moer, *Moore*
Lemoine, *Monk*
Lemon
Lemonier, *Minter*
Lemonnier, *Miller*
Lemonnier, *Minter*
Lemos
Lempel, *Lambert*
Lempereur, *Empereur*
Lempert, *Lambert*
Lempertz, *Lambert*
Lempke, *Lambert*
Lempl, *Lambert*
Lemppl, *Lambert*
Lemprière, *Empereur*
Lemulier, *Mule*
Lemullier, *Mule*
Lenaghan, *Lenihan*
Lenahan, *Lenihan*
Lenain, *Neame*
Lenan, *Lennon*
Lenane, *Lennon*
Lenarczyk, *Leonard*
Lénard, *Leonard*
Lenard, *Leonard*
Lenardi, *Leonard*
Lenardon, *Leonard*
Lenardoni, *Leonard*
Lenarduzzi, *Leonard*
Lénars, *Leonard*
Lénárt, *Leonard*
Lenart, *Leonard*
Lenartovich, *Leonard*
Lenartowicz, *Leonard*
Lenchenko, *Alexander*
Lendeke, *Lance*
Lendl, *Lance*
Lenègre, *Noir*
Lenehan, *Lenihan*
Leneveu, *Neveu*
Lenfant, *Infante*
Lenfestey, *Vaisey*
Lenglard, *English*
Lenglé, *English*
Lenglet, *English*
Lenglin, *English*
Lengliney, *English*
Lengyel
Lenhard, *Leonard*
Lenhardt, *Leonard*
Lenhart, *Leonard*
Lenihan
Lenin
Lenk, *Lance*
Lenke, *Lance*
Lenkin, *Lenin*
Lenkov, *Lenin*
Lenn, *Lynn*
Lennahan, *Lenihan*
Lennan, *Lennon*
Lennane, *Lennon*
Lennard, *Leonard*
Lennartsson, *Leonard*
Lennartz, *Leonard*
Lennerts, *Leonard*
Lennie
Lennihan, *Lenihan*
Lennikov, *Lenin*
Lennon
Lennox
Lenny, *Lennie*
Lenoble, *Noble*
Lenoir, *Noir*
Lenormand, *Norman*
Lenov, *Lenin*
Lenox, *Lennox*
Lensch, *Lawrence*
Lenshin, *Lenin*
Lente, *Lenz*
Lenthéric
Lenton
Lentsch, *Lawrence*
Lentsov, *Lenin*
Leny, *Lennie*
Lenz
Leo, *Lyon*
Léon, *Lyon*
Leon, *Lyon*
León
Léonard, *Leonard*
Leonard
Leonardelli, *Leonard*
Leonardi, *Leonard*
Leonardini, *Leonard*
Leonardo, *Leonard*
Leonarduzzi, *Leonard*
Leone, *Lyon*
Leonelli, *Lyon*
Leonello, *Lyon*
Leoneschi, *Lyon*
Leonetti, *Lyon*
Leonetto, *Lyon*
Leonhard, *Leonard*
Leonhardt, *Leonard*
Leonhart, *Leonard*
Leoni, *Lyon*
Leonidov
Leonotti, *Lyon*
Leontyev
Leopard, *Leppard*
Leopardi, *Leppard*
Leopardo, *Leppard*
Leopold
Leotard, *Leuthard*
Lepage, *Page*
Lépagneux, *Pagnol*
Lépagnol, *Pagnol*
Lepape, *Pope*
Lepeinteur, *Painter*
Lepeintre, *Painter*
Lepel, *Löffler*
Lepell, *Löffler*
Le Périer, *Pear*
Lepesqueur, *Pêcheur*
Lepesteur, *Pistol*
Lepetit, *Pettit*
Lepêtre, *Pistol*
Lepeu, *Puy*
Lepeut, *Puy*
Lephay, *Fage*
Lepic, *Pike*
Lepicard, *Pickard*
Lépice, *Spicer*
Lépicier, *Spicer*
Lépinay, *Épine*
Lépine, *Épine*
L'Episcopio, *Bishop*
L'Episcopo, *Bishop*
Lépissier, *Spicer*
Leplay, *Place*
Lepler, *Löffler*
Le Poideven, *Potvin*
Le Poidevin, *Potvin*
Lepore, *Lever*
Lepori, *Lever*
Leporini, *Lever*
Leporino, *Lever*
Le Porn, *Porter*
Le Porz, *Porter*
Leppänen
Leppard
Lepper
Lepperd, *Leppard*
Leppers, *Lepper*
Lepple, *Lepper*
Leppler, *Löffler*
Lepre, *Lever*
Leprestre, *Priest*
Leprêtre, *Priest*
Lepreux, *Preux*
Le Prevost, *Prevost*
Lepri, *Lever*
Leprieur, *Prior*
Leprince, *Prince*
Leproni, *Lever*
Leprotti, *Lever*
Leproust, *Provost*
Leproux, *Preux*
Leprovost, *Provost*
Leprovot, *Provost*
Lequeux, *Kew*
Lerat, *Rat*
Lerch, *Lark*
Lerche, *Lark*
Lercher, *Larcher*
Leriche, *Rich*
Lerner
Le Roël, *Roach*
Lerond, *Round*
Lerondeau, *Round*
Lerondel, *Round*
Lerouge, *Rudge*
Lerousseau, *Russell*
Leroussel, *Russell*
Leroux, *Rouse*
Le Rouz, *Rouse*
Le Rouzic, *Rouse*
Leroy, *Ray*
Leroyer, *Rode*
Lesaffre, *Saffer*
Lesage, *Sage*
Lesaulnier, *Salter*
Lesaunier, *Salter*
Lesauvage, *Savage*
Le Saux, *Sachs*
Le Sauz, *Sachs*
Lescaut, *Scott*
Lescaux, *Scott*
Leschelle, *Eschelle*
Lescop, *Bishop*
Lescot, *Scott*
Lescuyer, *Squire*
Lešek, *Alexander*
Lesellier, *Seller*
Leser, *Lazar*
Lesiak, *Leśniak*
Lesieur, *Seigneur*
Lesieux, *Seigneur*
Lesire, *Seigneur*
Leskinen
Lesley, *Leslie*
Leslie
Leśniak
Leśnicki, *Leśniak*

Leśniczak, *Leśniak*
Leśniewicz, *Leśniak*
Leśniewski, *Leśniak*
Leśnik, *Leśniak*
Leśnikowski, *Leśniak*
Lesourd, *Sourd*
Lespagnol, *Pagnol*
Lespagnoud, *Pagnol*
Less, *Leśniak*
Lessard, *Essart*
Lessart, *Essart*
Lessells, *Lascelles*
Lesseps
Lessing, *Leśniak*
Lessiter, *Leicester*
Lesslie, *Leslie*
Lessnick, *Leśniak*
Lesson, *Lees*
Lester, *Lister*
Lestor, *Lister*
Lestrade, *Street*
Lestrange, *Strange*
Lestrée, *Street*
Lesueur, *Sauter*
Leszczyński
Letailleur, *Taylor*
Letainturier, *Teinturier*
Letanneur, *Tanner*
Letavernier, *Taverner*
Letch, *Leek*
Letcher, *Leach, Leek*
Letchford, *Latchford*
Leteinturier, *Teinturier*
Letessier, *Tissier*
Leth, *Light*
Lethaby
Letham, *Latham*
Letherland, *Litherland*
Letort, *Tort*
Letouche, *Touche*
Létourneau, *Étourneau*
Letourneur, *Turner*
Letourneux, *Turner*
Letouzé, *Tous*
Letouzel, *Tous*
Letouzey, *Tous*
Létrange, *Strange*
Létraz, *Street*
Letsom, *Lett*
Letson, *Lett*
Lett
Lettey, *Lett*
Letts, *Lett*
Letty, *Lett*
Leturc, *Turk*
Leturque, *Turk*
Leu, *Löwe, Low*
Leue, *Löwe*
Leuillet, *Ochila*
Leuillot, *Ochila*
Leukart, *Legard*
Leupold, *Leopold*
Leupoldt, *Leopold*
Leuprecht, *Lubrecht*
Leutert, *Leuthard*
Leuthard
Leuther
Leuthner, *Leitner*
Leuty, *Lawty*
Leuvenberg, *Löwe*
Lev, *Löwe*
Levaillant, *Valiant*
Levák, *Lewy*
Levak, *Levick*
Levakov, *Levick*
Leval, *Vale*
Levalet, *Vallet*
Levallet, *Vallet*
Levallois, *Valois*
Levanidov, *Leonidov*
Levanneur, *Vannier*
Levannier, *Vannier*
Levanovich, *Lvov*
Levarlet, *Vallet*
Levashenya, *Lvov*
Levashov, *Lvov*
Levasseur, *Vavasour*
Levassor, *Vavasour*
Levassort, *Vavasour*
Levau, *Vale*
Levchenko, *Lvov*
Leve, *Levi*
Leveau, *Vale*
Leveau, *Veal*
Levecque, *Bishop*
Leven, *Levi, Lewin*
Lévenard, *Leonard*
Levene, *Levi*
Levenherz, *Löwe*
Levens, *Lewin*
Levenson, *Levi*
Levenstein, *Löwe*
Leventhal, *Löwe*
Levenzon, *Levi*
Lévêque, *Bishop*
Lever
Levere, *Lever*
Leverentz, *Lawrence*
Leverenz, *Lawrence*
Leverett
Leveri, *Lever*
Leverich, *Leveridge*
Leverick, *Leveridge*
Leveridge
Leveritt, *Leverett*
Levermann, *Lieb*
Leverrier, *Verrier*
Levert, *Verde*
Leverton
Levesque, *Bishop*
Levet, *Levett*
Levett
Levey, *Levy*
Levéziel, *Lavoisier*
Lévi, *Levi*
Levi
Levick
Levie, *Levi*
Levict, *Levi*
Leviev, *Levi*
Le Vigne, *Levi*
Levikson, *Levick*
Levillain, *Villain*
Levin, *Levi*
Levinberg, *Levi*
Le Vine, *Levi*
Levine, *Levi*
Levingston, *Livingstone*
Levingstone, *Livingstone*
Levinov, *Levi*
Levinsen, *Levi*
Levinski, *Levi*
Levinsky, *Levi*
Levinsohn, *Levi*
Levinson, *Levi*
Levinstein, *Levi*
Levinthal, *Levi*
Lévis, *Levy*
Levis, *Levi*
Levishchev, *Lvov*
Levison, *Levi*
Levit, *Levi*
Lévitan, *Levi*
Levitan, *Levi*
Levitansky, *Levi*
Levitas, *Levi*
Lévite, *Levi*
Levite, *Levi*
Levites, *Levi*
Levitin, *Levi*
Leviton, *Levi*
Levitov, *Levi*
Levitsky, *Levi*
Levitt, *Levett*
Levitt, *Levi*
Levittan, *Levi*
Lévitte, *Levi*
Levkov, *Lvov*
Levkovits, *Lewkowicz*
Levkovitz, *Lewkowicz*
Levkowitz, *Lewkowicz*
Levontyev, *Leontyev*
Levorin, *Lever*
Levorini, *Lever*
Levoshin, *Lvov*
Levoyer, *Vicario*
Levrard, *Everard*
Levrini, *Lever*
Levrotto, *Lever*
Levshukov, *Lvov*
Lévy, *Levi*
Levý, *Lewy*
Levy
Levykin, *Lvov*
Lewandowski
Lewark, *Lark*
Lewellin, *Llywelyn*
Lewen, *Lewin*
Lewens, *Lewin*
Lewer, *Ewer*
Lewerenz, *Lawrence*
Lewi, *Lewy*
Lewiak, *Lewy*
Lewicki, *Lewkowicz*
Lewin
Lewins, *Lewin*
Lewiński, *Lewkowicz*
Lewis
Lewit, *Levi*
Lewitt, *Levi*
Lewkovitz, *Lewkowicz*
Lewkowicz
Lewkowitz, *Lewkowicz*
Lewtey, *Lawty*
Lewty, *Lawty*
Lewy
Lexa, *Alexander*
Ley, *Eloy*
Ley
Leybish, *Leib*
Leyborne, *Leyburn*
Leyburn
Leycester, *Leicester*
Leyden
Leydon, *Leyden*
Leyeles, *Lakin*
Leyes, *Ellis*
Leyh, *Eloy*
Leyhane, *Lehane*
Leyland
Leyman, *Lee*
Leynaert, *Leonard*
Leyne, *Lane*
Leyrer, *Leirer*
Leyten, *Allis*
Leyton
Lhéraud, *Harrod*
Lhérault, *Harrod*
Lhermite, *Hermite*
Lhermitte, *Hermite*
Lhirondel, *Arundel*
Lhirondelle, *Arundel*
Lhostal, *Hostal*
Lhota, *Lhoták*
Lhoták
Lhotský, *Lhoták*
Lhozier, *Dozier*
Liautard, *Leuthard*
Liautier, *Leuther*
Li Bassi, *Bass*
Libby
Liber, *Lieb*
Liberfreund, *Lieb*
Liberman, *Lieb*
Libermann, *Lieb*
Libermensch, *Lieb*
Libermensh, *Lieb*
Libersohn, *Lieb*
Liberson, *Lieb*
Libertal, *Lieb*
Liberti, *Albert*
Libertini, *Albert*
Libertucci, *Albert*
Libes
Libest, *Lieb*
Libig, *Lieb*
Libin, *Libes*
Libing, *Lieb*
Libis, *Libes*
Libkowicz, *Libes*
Liblein, *Lieb*
Liblich, *Lieb*
Libling, *Lieb*
Libman, *Lieb*
Libov, *Libes*
Libovici, *Libes*
Libovits, *Libes*
Libovitz, *Libes*
Libowicz, *Libes*
Libschitz, *Lipschutz*
Libsky, *Lipski*
Libsohn, *Lieb*
Libson, *Lieb*
Libst, *Lieb*
Li Cari, *Caro*
Licastri, *Castro*
Liccardi, *Richard*
Liccardo, *Richard*
Licciardello, *Richard*
Licciardi, *Richard*
Licciardiello, *Richard*
Licciardo, *Richard*
Licence, *Lison*
Lichfield
Licht
Lichtbach, *Licht*
Lichtblau, *Licht*
Lichtbrun, *Licht*
Lichtenbaum, *Licht*
Lichtenberg, *Licht*
Lichtenfeld, *Licht*
Lichtenholz, *Licht*
Lichtenstein, *Licht*
Lichtensztein, *Licht*
Lichtenthal, *Licht*
Lichter, *Licht*

Lichterman, *Licht*
Lichtermann, *Licht*
Lichtfoth, *Lightfoot*
Lichtig, *Licht*
Lichtiger, *Licht*
Lichtman, *Licht*
Lichtmann, *Licht*
Lichtner, *Licht*
Lichtschein, *Licht*
Lichtstein, *Licht*
Lichtszain, *Licht*
Lichtszajn, *Licht*
Lichtzer
Lichtzieher, *Lichtzer*
Liçon, *Lison*
Li Conti, *Count*
Lidbetter, *Leadbetter*
Liddall, *Liddell*
Liddel, *Liddell*
Liddell
Liddiard
Liddiatt
Liddicoat
Liddle, *Liddell*
Liddy, *Leddy*
Lidell, *Liddell*
Lidgate, *Liddiatt*
Lidgett, *Liddiatt*
Lidster, *Lister*
Lidstone
Lieb
Liebe, *Lieb*
Lieber, *Lieb*
Lieberman, *Lieb*
Liebermann, *Lieb*
Liebermensch, *Lieb*
Liebermensh, *Lieb*
Liebermensz, *Lieb*
Liebersohn, *Lieb*
Lieberson, *Lieb*
Liebfreund, *Lieb*
Liebig, *Lieb*
Liebing, *Lieb*
Liebis, *Libes*
Liebisch, *Lieb*
Lieblein, *Lieb*
Lieblich, *Lieb*
Liebling, *Lieb*
Liebman, *Lieb*
Liebmann, *Lieb*
Liebsch, *Lieb*
Liebschutz, *Lipschutz*
Liebsohn, *Lieb*
Liebson, *Lieb*
Liechtenstein
Lief, *Leaf*
Liénard, *Leonard*
Lienhard, *Leonard*
Lienhardt, *Leonard*
Liepe, *Lippe*
Liepmann, *Lipman*
Liermann, *Leirer*
Liétard, *Leuthard*
Lievers, *Lever*
Lièvre, *Lever*
Lifchic, *Lipschutz*
Lifchitz, *Lipschutz*
Life, *Leaf*
Liff, *Leaf*
Lifschitz, *Lipschutz*
Lifschiz, *Lipschutz*
Lifschutz, *Lipschutz*
Lifshic, *Lipschutz*
Lifshits, *Lipschutz*
Lifshitz, *Lipschutz*
Lifshiz, *Lipschutz*
Lifshutz, *Lipschutz*
Lifshytz, *Lipschutz*
Lifszec, *Lipschutz*
Lifszic, *Lipschutz*
Lifszyc, *Lipschutz*
Liger, *Ledger*
Ligereau, *Ledger*
Ligeron, *Ledger*
Ligerot, *Ledger*
Liget, *Ledger*
Ligez, *Ledger*
Liggat, *Liddiatt*
Liggatt, *Liddiatt*
Liggett, *Liddiatt*
Light
Lightbody
Lightfoot
Lightman, *Light*
Lightoller, *Lightowler*
Lightollers, *Lightowler*
Lightowler
Lightowlers, *Lightowler*
Ligier, *Ledger*
Ligtvoet, *Lightfoot*
Lihane, *Lehane*
Likht, *Licht*
Likhtiger, *Licht*
Likhtikman, *Licht*
Likoff, *Lukov*
Lilburn
Liley, *Lilly*
Lilian, *Lilly*
Lilie, *Lilly*
Lilien, *Lilly*
Lilienberg, *Lilly*
Lilienblum, *Lilly*
Lilienfeld, *Lilly*
Lilienstein, *Lilly*
Liliental, *Lilly*
Lilienthal, *Lilly*
Lilja, *Lilly*
Lilje, *Lilly*
Liljeberg, *Lilly*
Liljeblad, *Lilly*
Liljebladh, *Lilly*
Liljedahl, *Lilly*
Liljegren, *Lilly*
Liljenberg, *Lilly*
Liljendahl, *Lilly*
Liljenström, *Lilly*
Liljeqvist, *Lilly*
Liljeroos, *Lilly*
Liljeros, *Lilly*
Liljestrand, *Lilly*
Liljeström, *Lilly*
Lille, *Lilly*
Lilley, *Lilly*
Lilleyman, *Lilly*
Lillicrap, *Lillicrop*
Lillicrop
Lillie, *Lilly*
Lilliman, *Lilly*
Lillis, *Lilly*
Lillo
Lilly
Lillyman, *Lilly*
Lillywhite
Lilywhite, *Lillywhite*
Lima
Liman, *Lemon*
Limb, *Lumb*
Limbert, *Lombard*
Limon, *Lemon*
Limpert, *Lambert*
Limpertz, *Lambert*
Limprecht, *Lambert*
Limprich, *Lambert*
Limpricht, *Lambert*
Linacre
Linaker, *Linacre*
Linardi, *Leonard*
Linardo, *Leonard*
Linardon, *Leonard*
Linares
Linbohm, *Linde*
Linbom, *Linde*
Lince, *Lynch*
Lincey, *Lindsay*
Linch, *Lynch*
Linchey, *Lynch*
Linchy, *Lynch*
Linck, *Lynch*
Lincoln
Lind, *Linde*
Lind, *Line*
Lindahl, *Linde*
Lindal, *Linde*
Lindbäck, *Linde*
Lindberg, *Linde*
Lindbergh, *Linde*
Lindblad, *Linde*
Lindbladh, *Linde*
Lindblom, *Linde*
Lindborg, *Linde*
Linde
Lindeberg, *Linde*
Lindeboom, *Linde*
Lindeborg, *Linde*
Lindegaard, *Lindegård*
Lindegård
Lindegren, *Linde*
Lindell, *Linde*
Lindelöf, *Linde*
Lindeman, *Linde*
Lindemann, *Linde*
Lindén, *Linde*
Linden, *Linde*
Linden, *McAlinden*
Lindenbaum, *Linde*
Lindenberg, *Linde*
Lindenblat, *Linde*
Lindenblatt, *Linde*
Lindenbluth, *Linde*
Lindenboim, *Linde*
Lindenfeld, *Linde*
Lindenman, *Linde*
Lindenstrauss, *Linde*
Linder, *Linde, Line*
Lindermann, *Linde*
Linderot, *Linde*
Linderoth, *Linde*
Linders, *Leonard*
Lindevall, *Linde*
Lindewall, *Linde*
Lindfors, *Linde*
Lindgren, *Linde*
Lindh, *Linde*
Lindhardt
Lindhe, *Linde*
Lindholm, *Linde*
Lindie, *McAlinden*
Lindl, *Linde*
Lindley
Lindman, *Linde*
Lindmark, *Linde*
Lindner, *Linde*
Lindop
Lindqvist, *Linde*
Lindroos, *Linde*
Lindros, *Linde*
Lindrot, *Linde*
Lindroth, *Linde*
Lindsay
Lindsell
Lindsjö, *Linde*
Lindskog, *Linde*
Lindstedt, *Linde*
Lindstrand, *Linde*
Lindström, *Linde*
Lindvall, *Linde*
Lindwall, *Linde*
Lindwasser, *Linde*
Line
Linegar, *Linacre*
Lineham, *Lyneham*
Linehan, *Lyneham*
Linek, *Leonard*
Lineker, *Linacre*
Lines, *Line*
Linfoot, *Linforth*
Linford, *Linforth*
Linforth
Ling
Lingen
Linglay, *English*
Linglet, *English*
Lingley, *Lindley*
Lingner, *Linde*
Lingwood
Linhart, *Leonard*
Liniker, *Linacre*
Linikov, *Kalinin*
Link
Linka, *Leonard*
Linke, *Link*
Linker, *Link*
Linkhand, *Link*
Linkin, *Lincoln*
Linklater
Linkletter, *Linklater*
Linkov, *Kalinin*
Linley, *Lindley*
Linn, *Lynn*
Linnane, *Lennon*
Linnartz, *Leonard*
Linné, *Linde*
Linne, *Linde*
Linnecar, *Linacre*
Linnegar, *Linacre*
Linneman, *Linde*
Linnemann, *Linde*
Linnér, *Linde*
Linnert, *Leonard*
Linnikov, *Kalinin*
Lino
Linsey, *Lindsay*
Linton
Lio, *Lyon*
Lion, *Lyon*
Lione, *Lyon*
Lionel, *Lyon*
Lionelli, *Lyon*
Lionello, *Lyon*
Lionet, *Lyon*
Lionnel, *Lyon*
Lionnet, *Lyon*
Lions, *Lyon*
Liotard, *Leuthard*
Liotier, *Leuther*
Lipa, *Lippe*

Li Pane, *Pain*
Lipgen, *Lippe*
Lipgens, *Philip*
Lipin
Lipiński, *Lipski*
Lipka, *Lipin, Lippe*
Lipke, *Lippe*
Lipkes, *Lipin*
Lipkin, *Lipin*
Lipman
Lipmann, *Lipman*
Lipmanovicz, *Lipman*
Lipnik, *Lippe*
Lipovitch, *Lipin*
Lipovitz, *Lipin*
Lipowicz, *Lipin*
Lipowski, *Lipski*
Lipp
Lippard, *Leppard*
Lippe
Lippek, *Lippe*
Lippen, *Lippe*
Lippens, *Lippe*
Lippi, *Philip*
Lippiatt
Lippiello, *Philip*
Lippiet, *Lippiatt*
Lippini, *Philip*
Lippke, *Lippe*
Lippl, *Lippe*
Lippo, *Philip*
Lipps, *Lippe*
Lips, *Lippe*
Lipschitz, *Lipschutz*
Lipschütz, *Lipschutz*
Lipschutz
Lipsius, *Lippe*
Lipsker, *Lipski*
Lipski
Lipskier, *Lipski*
Lipsky, *Lipski*
Lipsohn, *Lipin*
Lipson, *Lipin*
Lipson, *Lipp*
Liptrot
Liptrott, *Liptrot*
Lipyeat, *Lippiatt*
Liron, *Hiron*
Lironde, *Hiron*
Lirondelle, *Arundel*
Lis, *Łysiak*
Lis
Lisa, *Łysiak*
Lisboa
Lisbon, *Lisboa*
Lisbona, *Lisboa*
Lisciandro, *Alexander*
Lisciardelli, *Alexander*
Lisek, *Lis*
Lisiak, *Lis*
Lisiecki, *Lis*
Lisignoli, *Rossignol*
Lisik, *Lis*
Liška, *Leszczyński*
Lisle
Lisman, *Lis*
Lison
Lisowski, *Lis*
Liss, *Lis*
Lissak, *Lis*
Lissandre, *Alexander*
Lissandri, *Alexander*
Lissandrini, *Alexander*
Lissiter, *Leicester*
Lissman, *Lis*
Lisson, *Lees*
List
Lister
Listl, *List*
Listman, *List*
Listmann, *List*
Liston
Listray, *Street*
Listrée, *Street*
Lisý, *Łysiak*
Liszewski, *Lis*
Liszt
Litai, *Littwak*
Litauer, *Littwak*
Litchfield, *Lichfield*
Litewski, *Littwak*
Litherland
Lithgoe, *Lithgow*
Lithgow
Litle, *Little*
Litman, *Light*
Litovsky, *Littwak*
Litowski, *Littwak*
Litster, *Lister*
Littau, *Littwak*
Littauer, *Littwak*
Litteljohn, *Littlejohn*
Littell, *Little*
Litten, *Litton*
Little
Littleboy
Littlefair
Littleford
Littlehales
Littlejohn
Littlejohns, *Littlejohn*
Littlepage
Littleproud
Littler, *Little*
Littleton
Littlewood
Littleworth
Littley
Littman, *Light*
Litton
Littwak
Littwin, *Litwin*
Litvack, *Littwak*
Litvak, *Littwak*
Litván, *Litwin*
Litvin, *Litwin*
Litvinenko, *Litwin*
Litvinoff, *Litwin*
Litvinov, *Litwin*
Litvintchouk, *Litwin*
Litvinyonok, *Litwin*
Litvyakov, *Littwak*
Litwack, *Littwak*
Litwak, *Littwak*
Litwin
Litwinowicz, *Litwin*
Lityński
Litzmann, *Lewis*
Liuni, *Lyon*
Li Vecchi, *Veal*
Livens, *Lewin*
Livermore
Liversedge, *Liversidge*
Liversidge
Livery, *Leveridge*
Livesay, *Livesey*
Livesey
Livesley, *Livesey*
Livett, *Levett*
Livick, *Levick*
Livieri, *Oliver*
Liviero, *Oliver*
Livingston, *Livingstone*
Livingstone
Livitt, *Levett*
Livock, *Levick*
Livschitz, *Lipschutz*
Livschutz, *Lipschutz*
Livsey, *Livesey*
Livshits, *Lipschutz*
Livshitz, *Lipschutz*
Liwshitz, *Lipschutz*
Ljung
Ljungberg, *Ljung*
Ljungdahl, *Ljung*
Ljungholm, *Ljung*
Ljunglöf, *Ljung*
Ljungman, *Ljung*
Ljungren, *Ljung*
Ljungstedt, *Ljung*
Ljungström, *Ljung*
Ljunqvist, *Ljung*
Lladó, *Lledó*
Llama, *Lama*
Llamas, *Lama*
Llano, *Plain*
Llanos, *Plain*
Llauradó, *Laborier*
Llavero, *Clavero*
Lledó
Lleó, *Lyon*
Lleonart, *Leonard*
Llewelin, *Llywelyn*
Llewellin, *Llywelyn*
Llewellyn, *Llywelyn*
Llewelyn, *Llywelyn*
Llewhellin, *Llywelyn*
Llinares, *Linares*
Llobet, *Lovatt*
Llop, *Lope*
Llopart, *Leppard*
Llopis, *Lope*
Llorca, *Lorca*
Llorens, *Lawrence*
Llorente, *Lawrence*
Lloret, *Laur*
Llosa, *Losa*
Lloube, *Love*
Lloyd
Lluch, *Lucas*
Lluís, *Lewis*
Llywellin, *Llywelyn*
Llywelyn
Lo, *Loo*
Loach
Loachead, *Lochhead*
Loader
Loades, *Loader*
Loadman, *Loader*
Loads, *Loader*
Loadsman, *Loader*
Loan, *Lane*
Loaring, *Lorraine*
Löb, *Löwe*
Lob, *Lobb*
Lo Bascio, *Bass*
Lo Basso, *Bass*
Lobato, *Low*
Lobb
Lobbe, *Lobb*
Löbe, *Löwe*
Lobeau, *Lobel*
Löbel, *Lobel*
Lobel
Lobello, *Beau*
Lobetti, *Lovatt*
Lo Bianco, *Blanc*
Lobo, *Low*
Lo Bono, *Bon*
Lo Bue, *Boeuf*
Lo Buono, *Bon*
Lo Casto, *Castro*
Lo Castro, *Castro*
Lochead, *Lochhead*
Lochhead
Lochrane, *Loughrey*
Lock
Lockart, *Lockhart*
Locke, *Lock*
Locker, *Lock*
Lockery, *Loughrey*
Locket, *Lucas*
Lockett, *Lucas*
Lockey, *Lucas*
Lockhart
Lockhead, *Lochhead*
Lockie, *Lucas*
Lockier, *Lock*
Lockitt, *Lucas*
Löckle, *Lock*
Lockley
Lockwood
Lockyear, *Lock*
Lockyer, *Lock*
Lo Conte, *Count*
Lo Cuoco, *Cook*
LoCurto, *Court*
Lode, *Lewis*
Lödeke, *Lewis*
Lodemann, *Lewis*
Loder, *Loader*
Lodewig, *Lewis*
Lodewijk, *Lewis*
Lodewijks, *Lewis*
Lodge
Löding, *Lewis*
Lo Dolce, *Duce*
Lodovichetti, *Lewis*
Lodovichi, *Lewis*
Lodovici, *Lewis*
Lodovico, *Lewis*
Lodovisi, *Lewis*
Lo Duca, *Duke*
Lodwig, *Lewis*
Loe, *Loo*
Loeffler, *Löffler*
Löf, *Leaf*
Löfberg, *Leaf*
Löfdahl, *Leaf*
Löffel, *Löffler*
Löffler
Loffreda, *Godfrey*
Loffredo, *Godfrey*
Löfgren, *Leaf*
Lo Forto, *Fort*
Löfquist, *Leaf*
Löfstedt, *Leaf*
Löfstrand, *Leaf*
Löfström, *Leaf*
Lofthouse, *Loftus*
Loftis, *Loftus*
Lofts, *Loftus*
Loftus
Logan
Lo Gatto, *Catt*
Logé, *Lodge*

Loge, *Lodge*
Logeat, *Lodge*
Logeois, *Lodge*
Logez, *Lodge*
Loggie, *Logie*
Loghan, *Logan*
Loghlan, *Lachlan*
Loghlen, *Lachlan*
Loghlin, *Lachlan*
Logie
Logiudice, *Judge*
Lo Grande, *Grant*
Lo Grasso, *Grass*
Lo Greco, *Greco*
Logue, *Molloy*
Loh, *Loo*
Lohan, *Logan*
Löhde, *Lewis*
Lohde, *Lewis*
Löhner, *Lehmann*
Lohner, *Lehmann*
Löhnert, *Lehmann*
Lohrensen, *Lawrence*
Löhrke, *Lawrence*
Lo Iacono, *Deakin*
Loiodice, *Judge*
Loiseau, *Uccello*
Loisel, *Uccello*
Loiselet, *Uccello*
Loiseleur, *Uccello*
Loiselle, *Uccello*
Loisellier, *Uccello*
Loisi, *Lewis*
Loisillon, *Uccello*
Loisselier, *Uccello*
Loiudice, *Judge*
Loix, *Lewis*
Loizeau, *Uccello*
Loizillon, *Uccello*
Lo Jacono, *Deakin*
Loker, *Luker*
Lo Mancuso, *Manco*
Lomas, *Lomax*
Lo Masto, *Master*
Lo Mastro, *Master*
Lo Mauro, *Moore*
Lomax
Lombard
Lombardelli, *Lombard*
Lombardet, *Lombard*
Lombardi, *Lombard*
Lombardo, *Lombard*
Lombardot, *Lombard*
Lombardy, *Lombard*
Lombarini, *Lombard*
Lombarino, *Lombard*
Lombart, *Lombard*
Lombe, *Lumb*
Lo Monaco, *Monk*
Lomonosov
Lonardi, *Leonard*
Lonardo, *Leonard*
Loncaster, *Lancaster*
Lond, *Lund*
Londais, *Lund*
Londin, *London*
Londinski, *London*
Londner, *London*
London
Londsdale, *Lonsdale*
Lo Nero, *Noir*
Lones, *Lane*
Loney, *Looney*
Long
Longan, *Langan*
Longato, *Long*
Longaud, *Long*
Longbotham, *Longbottom*
Longbottom
Longcaster, *Lancaster*
Longden
Longdon, *Langdon*
Longeard, *Long*
Longeau, *Long*
Longeaux, *Long*
Longet, *Long*
Longfellow
Longfield
Longford, *Langford*
Longham, *Langham*
Longhetti, *Long*
Longhi, *Long*
Longhin, *Long*
Longhini, *Long*
Longhurst
Longin, *Long*
Longley, *Langley*
Longman, *Long*
Longmire
Longmires, *Longmire*
Longmore
Longmuir, *Longmore*
Longo, *Long*
Longon, *Long*
Longoni, *Long*
Longridge, *Langridge*
Longsdon
Longstaff
Longton, *Langton*
Longtown, *Langton*
Longuet, *Long*
Longueteau, *Long*
Longworth
Lonie, *Looney*
Lo Nigro, *Noir*
Lonjas, *Long*
Lonjon, *Long*
Lönn
Lönnberg, *Lönn*
Lönneberg, *Lönn*
Lönnegren, *Lönn*
Lönngren, *Lönn*
Lonnon, *London*
Lönnqvist, *Lönn*
Lonsdale
Loo
Loobey
Lööf, *Leaf*
Look, *Lucas*
Looker, *Luker*
Looks, *Lucas*
Loom, *Lumb*
Looman, *Loo*
Loomann, *Loo*
Loomas, *Lomax*
Loombe, *Lumb*
Loomes, *Lumb*
Loomis, *Lomax*
Looney
Loos, *Lewis*
Lopane, *Pain*
Lo Papa, *Papa*
Lope
Löpeler, *Löffler*
Löper, *Läufer*
Lopes, *Lope*
López, *Lope*
Lo Piano, *Plain*
Lo Pinto, *Pinto*
Lo Presti, *Priest*
Lo Presto, *Priest*
Lo Prete, *Priest*
Lo Priore, *Prior*
Lorain, *Lorraine*
Loraine, *Lorraine*
Loran, *Loughrey*
Lorand, *Lawrence*
Loránd, *Rowland*
Lorans, *Lawrence*
Lorant, *Lawrence*
Lóránt, *Rowland*
Lorat, *Lawrence*
Lorca
Lorck, *Lawrence*
Lord
Lordan
Lo Ré, *Ray*
Loreit, *Lawrence*
Lorek, *Lawrence*
Lorenc, *Lawrence*
Lorence, *Lawrence*
Lorenceau, *Lawrence*
Lorens, *Lawrence*
Lorensot, *Lawrence*
Lorent, *Lawrence*
Lorente, *Lawrence*
Lorentowicz, *Lawrence*
Lorentsen, *Lawrence*
Lorentz, *Lawrence*
Lorentzen, *Lawrence*
Lorentzson, *Lawrence*
Lorenz, *Lawrence*
Lorenzen, *Lawrence*
Lorenzetti, *Lawrence*
Lorenzetto, *Lawrence*
Lorenzi, *Lawrence*
Lorenzin, *Lawrence*
Lorenzini, *Lawrence*
Lorenzo, *Lawrence*
Lorenzon, *Lawrence*
Lorenzoni, *Lawrence*
Lorenzut, *Lawrence*
Lorenzutti, *Lawrence*
Loria, *Luria*
Lo Riccio, *Ricci*
Loricke, *Lawrence*
Lorie, *Lowry*
Lorie, *Luria*
Lorieu, *Oriol*
Lorieux, *Oriol*
Lorimer
Lorin, *Laur*
Lörinc, *Lawrence*
Lörincz, *Lawrence*
Lörincze, *Lawrence*
Lorinez, *Lawrence*
Loring, *Lorraine*
Loriol, *Oriol*
Loriot, *Oriol*
Lo Rizzo, *Ricci*
Lorkin, *Larkin*
Lorking, *Larkin*
Lornsen, *Lawrence*
Lorrain, *Lorraine*
Lorraine
Lorrie, *Lowry*
Lorriman, *Lowry*
Lorrimer, *Lorimer*
Lorrison, *Lowry*
Lorton
Lörtz, *Lawrence*
Lortz, *Lawrence*
Lörtzing, *Lawrence*
Lortzing, *Lawrence*
Lo Russo, *Rouse*
Lory, *Lowry*
Los, *Lewis*
Łoś
Losa
Lo Sacco, *Sack*
Losada
Lo Savio, *Sage*
Lose, *Lewis*
Loseke, *Lewis*
Lösel, *Lewis*
Losemann, *Lewis*
Löser, *Lazar*
Loseto, *Zito*
Łosiak, *Łoś*
Losier, *Dozier*
Losito, *Zito*
Lossman, *Lewis*
Lo Surdo, *Sourd*
Lothian
Lothringer, *Lorraine*
Lotring, *Lorraine*
Lotringer, *Lorraine*
Lots, *Lott*
Lott
Lotte, *Lott*
Lotze, *Lewis*
Loubat, *Low*
Loubet, *Lovatt*
Louckx, *Lewis*
Loud
Louden, *Lowden*
Loudon, *Lowden*
Louet, *Lloyd*
Lough, *Loughnane*
Loughan, *Logan*
Lougheran, *Loughrey*
Loughlan, *Lachlan*
Loughlen, *Lachlan*
Loughlin, *Lachlan*
Loughnan, *Loughnane*
Loughnane
Loughran, *Loughrey*
Loughrane, *Loughrey*
Loughren, *Loughrey*
Loughrey
Loughry, *Loughrey*
Louichon, *Lewis*
Louis, *Lewis*
Louiset, *Lewis*
Louisot, *Lewis*
Loukes, *Lucas*
Loup, *Low*
Loupot, *Low*
Loureiro, *Laur*
Lourenço, *Lawrence*
Lourens, *Lawrence*
Louria, *Luria*
Lourié, *Luria*
Lourie, *Lowry*
Louro
Lours, *Orso*
Loury, *Lowry*
Loustal, *Hostal*
Loustalet, *Hostal*
Loustalot, *Hostal*
Loustau, *Hostal*
Louthean, *Lothian*
Loutrel, *Luttrell*
Louve, *Love*
Louveau, *Lovell*
Louvel, *Lovell*

Louvet, *Lovatt*
Louveton, *Lovatt*
Louvihoux, *Low*
Louvion, *Low*
Louviot, *Low*
Louw, *Löwe*
Louy, *Lewis*
Louys, *Lewis*
Löv, *Leaf*
Lovascio, *Bass*
Lo Vasco, *Vasco*
Lovat, *Lovatt*
Lovatt
Lövberg, *Leaf*
Lövdahl, *Leaf*
Love
Lo Vecchio, *Veal*
Loveday
Lovegrove
Lovekin, *Love*
Lovel, *Lovell*
Lovelace
Loveless, *Lovelace*
Lovell
Lovelli, *Lovell*
Lovelock
Loveluck, *Lovelock*
Lovely
Loveman, *Lemon*
Loven, *Lown*
Lovenzon, *Löwe*
Lo Verde, *Verde*
Loveredge, *Leveridge*
Loveridge, *Leveridge*
Lovetot, *Lovatt*
Lovett, *Lovatt*
Lövgren, *Leaf*
Lovick
Lovini, *Low*
Lovitt, *Lovatt*
Lovo, *Low*
Lo Voi, *Boeuf*
Lovotti, *Low*
Lövquist, *Leaf*
Lövstedt, *Leaf*
Löw, *Löwe*
Low
Lowde, *Loud*
Lowden
Lowdon, *Lowden*
Lowe, *Low*
Löwe
Lowell, *Lovell*
Lowen, *Lewin*
Löwenberg, *Löwe*
Lowenhar, *Löwe*
Lowensohn, *Löwe*
Lowenstark, *Löwe*
Löwenstein, *Löwe*
Löwenthal, *Löwe*
Lower, *Flower*
Lowerie, *Lowry*
Lowery, *Lowry*
Lowin, *Lewin*
Lowis, *Lewis*
Lowles, *Lovelace*
Lowless, *Lovelace*
Lowman, *Lemon*
Lown
Lowndes, *Lown*
Lownes, *Lown*
Lowney, *Looney*
Lowns, *Lown*
Lowrance, *Lawrence*
Lowrey, *Lowry*
Lowrie, *Lowry*
Lowries, *Lowry*
Lowrieson, *Lowry*
Lowrison, *Lowry*
Lowry
Lowson, *Low*
Lowther
Lowthian, *Lothian*
Lowton
Loy, *Eloy*
Loyd, *Lloyd*
Loynes, *Lown*
Loyola
Loyseau, *Uccello*
Loysel, *Uccello*
Lozano
Loze, *Lloyd*
Lozerus, *Lazar*
Lozito, *Zito*
Luášek, *Lucas*
Lübbe
Lübben, *Lübbe*
Lübbers, *Lubrecht*
Lübbert, *Lubrecht*
Lübbing, *Lübbe*
Lubbock
Lubelli, *Beau*
Lubello, *Beau*
Lüberding, *Lubrecht*
Lübering, *Lubrecht*
Luberti, *Robert*
Luberto, *Robert*
Lübke, *Lübbe*
Lübken, *Lübbe*
Lübking, *Lübbe*
Lubrecht
Lubrich, *Lubrecht*
Lubricht, *Lubrecht*
Luc, *Lucas*
Luca, *Lucas*
Lucas
Lucassen, *Lucas*
Lucaud, *Lucas*
Lucazeau, *Lucas*
Lucca
Lucchelli, *Lucas*
Lucchese, *Lucca*
Lucchesi, *Lucca*
Lucchesini, *Lucca*
Lucchetti, *Lucas*
Lucchi, *Lucas*
Lucchini, *Lucas*
Lucco, *Lucas*
Luce, *Lucey*
Lucena
Lucet, *Lucey*
Lucette, *Lucey*
Lucey
Luchelli, *Lucas*
Luchetti, *Lucas*
Luchi, *Lucas*
Luchini, *Lucas*
Lucia, *Lucey*
Lucian, *Lucien*
Luciani, *Lucien*
Luciano, *Lucien*
Lučić, *Lucas*
Lucien
Lúcio
Luck, *Lucas*
Luckard, *Legard*
Luckes, *Lucas*
Luckett, *Lucas*
Luckhurst
Lucking, *Levick*
Luckman, *Lucas*
Luckoff, *Lukov*
Luckraft, *Lucraft*
Lucks, *Lucas*
Luconi, *Lucas*
Lucot, *Lucas*
Lucotti, *Lucas*
Lucraft
Lucy, *Lucey*
Łuczak, *Lucas*
Łuczkiewicz, *Lucas*
Lüdders, *Leuther*
Lude, *Lewis*
Lüder, *Leuther*
Lüders, *Leuther*
Ludewig, *Lewis*
Lüdgering, *Ledger*
Ludkiewicz, *Lewis*
Ludl, *Lewis*
Ludlow
Ludovici, *Lewis*
Ludovico, *Lewis*
Ludovisi, *Lewis*
Ludvigsen, *Lewis*
Ludvík, *Lewis*
Ludwicki, *Lewis*
Ludwiczak, *Lewis*
Ludwig, *Lewis*
Ludwikiewicz, *Lewis*
Ludwisiak, *Lewis*
Lueger, *Luger*
Luengo, *Long*
Lüer, *Leuther*
Lüers, *Leuther*
Lüersen, *Leuther*
Luff, *Love*
Luffery, *Leveridge*
Luffi, *Low*
Luffman, *Lemon*
Lufkin, *Love*
Lufschutz, *Lipschutz*
Luger
Lugert, *Luger*
Lugg, *Lucas*
Lugo
Lugol, *Lucas*
Lühr, *Leuther*
Lührig, *Leuther*
Lühring, *Leuther*
Lührs, *Leuther*
Lührsen, *Leuther*
Luickinga, *Lewis*
Luigi, *Lewis*
Luís, *Lewis*
Luis, *Lewis*
Luiselli, *Lewis*
Luisetti, *Lewis*
Luisi, *Lewis*
Luiso, *Lewis*
Luithardt, *Leuthard*
Luitpold, *Leopold*
Luizard, *Lewis*
Luizet, *Lewis*
Luján, *Lucien*
Lukač, *Lucas*
Lukács, *Lucas*
Lukanov, *Lucas*
Lukáš, *Lucas*
Lukas, *Lucas*
Lukaschek, *Lucas*
Lukasen, *Lucas*
Lukash, *Lucas*
Lukashenko, *Lucas*
Lukashenya, *Lucas*
Lukashev, *Lucas*
Lukashevich, *Lucas*
Łukasiewicz, *Lucas*
Łukasik, *Lucas*
Łukasz, *Lucas*
Łukaszewicz, *Lucas*
Łukaszewski, *Lucas*
Łukaszkiewicz, *Lucas*
Luke, *Lucas*
Lukehurst, *Luckhurst*
Lukeman, *Lucas*
Luker
Lukeš, *Lucas*
Lukesch, *Lucas*
Lukianov, *Lucien*
Lukianovich, *Lucien*
Lukić, *Lucas*
Lukichyov, *Lucas*
Lukin, *Lucas*
Lukinov, *Lucas*
Lukinykh, *Lucas*
Lukof, *Lukov*
Lukoff, *Lukov*
Lukonin, *Lucas*
Łukoś, *Lucas*
Lukov
Luković, *Lucas*
Lukovsky, *Lukov*
Łukowicz, *Lucas*
Łukowski, *Lucas*
Lukowski, *Lukov*
Lukowsky, *Lukov*
Luksch, *Lucas*
Łulka, *Lucas*
Lum, *Lumb*
Lumb
Lumbard, *Lombard*
Lumbert, *Lombard*
Lumbley, *Lumley*
Lumbreras
Lumby
Lumley
Lummis, *Lomax*
Lummus, *Lomax*
Lumsdaine, *Lumsden*
Lumsden
Luna
Luňák
Lunardelli, *Leonard*
Lunardi, *Leonard*
Lunardo, *Leonard*
Lunardon, *Leonard*
Lunardoni, *Leonard*
Lund
Lundahl, *Lund*
Lundbäck, *Lund*
Lundberg, *Lund*
Lundblad, *Lund*
Lundbladh, *Lund*
Lundbohm, *Lund*
Lundbom, *Lund*
Lundborg, *Lund*
Lundebergh, *Lund*
Lundegren, *Lund*
Lundell, *Lund*
Lundén, *Lund*
Lundeqvist, *Lund*
Lundgren, *Lund*
Lundh, *Lund*
Lundholm, *Lund*
Lundie, *Lundy*
Lundin, *Lund*

Lundkvist, *Lund*
Lundman, *Lund*
Lundmark, *Lund*
Lundon, *London*
Lundqvist, *Lund*
Lundstedt, *Lund*
Lundström, *Lund*
Lundvall, *Lund*
Lundwall, *Lund*
Lundy, *McAlinden*
Lundy
Luney, *Looney*
Lunghetti, *Long*
Lunghi, *Long*
Lunghini, *Long*
Lungo, *Long*
Lungu, *Long*
Lunn, *Lund*
Lunnon, *London*
Lunny, *Looney*
Lunt, *Lund*
Luongo, *Long*
Luotto, *Low*
Luparti, *Robert*
Luparto, *Robert*
Lupelli, *Lovell*
Lupesco, *Low*
Lupescu, *Low*
Lupetti, *Lovatt*
Lupicini, *Low*
Lupini, *Low*
Lupino, *Low*
Lupis, *Low*
Lupo, *Low*
Lupoli, *Low*
Lupone, *Low*
Luppe, *Lübbe*
Lüppertz, *Lubrecht*
Luppino, *Low*
Luppis, *Low*
Luppo, *Low*
Luppoli, *Low*
Lüpschütz, *Lipschutz*
Lupton
Lupu, *Low*
Lupul, *Low*
Luquet, *Lucas*
Luria
Luriah, *Luria*
Lurie, *Luria*
Lurja, *Luria*
Lurje, *Luria*
Lürsen, *Leuther*
Lurya, *Luria*
Lurye, *Luria*
Luscombe
Lusher, *Usher*
Lussato, *Luzzatto*
Lust, *Lustig*
Lüstel, *Lustig*
Lustgarten
Lustig
Lustiger, *Lustig*
Lustigier, *Lustig*
Lustigman, *Lustig*
Lustik, *Lustig*
Lustman, *Lustig*
Lusty, *Lustig*
Lutener, *Luther*
Lutenier, *Luther*
Luter, *Luther*
Luterand, *Luther*
Lütge, *Leuther*
Lütgen, *Leuther*
Lütger, *Ledger*
Lütgert, *Ledger*
Luthard, *Leuthard*
Luthardt, *Leuthard*
Luther
Lüthge, *Leuther*
Lüthgens, *Leuther*
Luthier, *Luther*
Lüthke, *Leuther*
Lutier, *Luther*
Lütje, *Leuther*
Lütjen, *Leuther*
Lütjens, *Leuther*
Lütkens, *Leuther*
Lutkin, *Lutt*
Lutman, *Light*
Luton
Lutrand, *Luther*
Lutsch, *Lewis*
Lütt, *Light*
Lutt
Lutter, *Luther*
Lüttgen, *Leuther*
Lüttgens, *Leuther*
Lüttger, *Ledger*
Lüttgert, *Ledger*
Luttman, *Light*
Lutton
Luttrell
Luttwak, *Littwak*
Lutvak, *Littwak*
Lutwak, *Littwak*
Lutwick, *Littwak*
Lutwin, *Litwin*
Lutwyche
Luty, *Lawty*
Lutz, *Lewis*
Lutzmann, *Lewis*
Luvini, *Low*
Luvotti, *Low*
Luvotto, *Low*
Lux, *Lucas*
Luxen, *Lucas*
Luxford
Luxmoore
Luxmore, *Luxmoore*
Luxton
Luyck, *Lewis*
Luyckx, *Lewis*
Luytgaeren, *Ledger*
Luytgaerens, *Ledger*
Luz
Luzak
Luzzati, *Luzzatto*
Luzzato, *Luzzatto*
Luzzatti, *Luzzatto*
Luzzatto
Lvov
Lvovski, *Lwówski*
Lvovsky, *Lwówski*
Lwowicz, *Lewkowicz*
Lwówski
Lwowsky, *Lwówski*
Lyakin, *Lyokhin*
Lyakishev, *Lyokhin*
Lyal
Lyalikov, *Lyokhin*
Lyalin, *Lyokhin*
Lyalkin, *Lyokhin*
Lyall, *Lyal*
Lyalyakin, *Lyokhin*
Lyashev, *Lyokhin*
Lyashutin, *Lyokhin*
Lyburn, *Leyburn*
Lydall, *Liddell*
Lydiate, *Liddiatt*
Lydon, *Leyden*
Lye, *Lee*
Lyel, *Lyal*
Lyell, *Lyal*
Lyhan, *Lehane*
Lyhane, *Lehane*
Lykke, *Glück*
Lyle, *Lisle*
Lyman, *Lee*
Lynam, *Lyneham*
Lynch
Lynchahan, *Lynch*
Lynchahaun, *Lynch*
Lynchehan, *Lynch*
Lynchy, *Lynch*
Lynde, *Line*
Lyndon
Lynds, *Line*
Lyne
Lyneham
Lynes, *Line*
Lyng, *Ljung*
Lynge, *Ljung*
Lynham, *Lyneham*
Lynn
Lynne, *Lynn*
Lyokhin
Lyon
Lyonnais, *Lyon*
Lyonnel, *Lyon*
Lyonnet, *Lyon*
Lyons, *Lyon*
Lyoshin, *Lyokhin*
Lyosik, *Alexis*
Lyovkin, *Lvov*
Lyovshin, *Lvov*
Lyovyshkin, *Lvov*
Lys, *Lis*
Lysacht, *Lysaght*
Lysaght
Lysat, *Lysaght*
Łysek, *Łysiak*
Lysenko
Łysiak
Lysons, *Lison*
Lyss, *Lis*
Lyster, *Lister*
Lysý, *Łysiak*
Lysyononok, *Łysiak*
Lyte, *Light*
Lyteman, *Light*
Lythe
Lythgoe, *Lithgow*
Lytle, *Little*
Lyttelton, *Littleton*
Lyttle, *Little*
Lyttleton, *Littleton*
Lytton, *Litton*
Lyubimov

M

Maag, *Maw*
Maarschalk, *Marshall*
Maas
Maascke, *Maas*
Maasen, *Maas*
Maass, *Maas*
Mabb
Mabbett, *Mabb*
Mabbot, *Mabb*
Mabbs, *Mabb*
Mabbutt, *Mabb*
Maben, *Mabon*
Mabon
Mabson, *Mabb*
Mac-
Mac Adaidh, *Adam*
Mac Adaim, *Adam*
MacAfee, *Duffy*
Mac Aileáin, *Allen*
Mac Ailín, *Allen*
Mac Ailpín, *Alpin*
Mac Aindrín, *Andrew*
Macaire
Macák, *Matthew*
Mac Alastair, *Alexander*
Mac Alastraim, *Alexander*
Macalpin, *Alpin*
Macalpine, *Alpin*
Macaluso
Mac Ambróis, *Ambrose*
Mac an Aba, *Abbott*
Mac an Abadh, *Abbott*
Mac an Baird, *Bard*
Mac an Bhaird, *Bard*
Mac an Bheatha, *McBeth*
Mac an Bheathadha, *McBeth*
Mac an Bhreatnaich, *Brett*
Mac an Easpuig, *Bishop*
Mac an Ghobhann, *McGowan*
Mac an Ghoill, *Gall*
Mac an Stocaire, *Stoker*
Mac Artáin, *McCartney*
Mac Artair, *Arthur*
Mac Ascaidh, *Ashkettle*
Mac Asgaill, *Ashkettle*
Mac Beathain, *Bean*
Mac Bheatha, *McBeth*
Mac Bheathain, *Bean*
Mac Bhiocair, *Vickar*
Mac Biorna, *Burney*
Mac Briain, *Bryan*
Maccaffie, *Duffy*
Mac Calmáin, *Coleman*
Mac Carlais, *Charles*
MacCaslane, *McAuslan*
Mac Cearbhaill, *Carroll*
Macchiavelli, *Machiavelli*
Macchiavello, *Machiavelli*
Mac Chonnigh, *McKenzie*
Mac Cionaodha, *Kenny*
Mac Cionaodháin, *Kenny*
Mac Cléirich, *Cleary*
Mac Coimín, *Cumming*
Mac Colmáin, *Coleman*
Mac Cormaic, *Cormack*
Maccus, *Mack*
Mac Cúthbhréith, *Cuthbert*
Mac Daibhéid, *David*
Mac Diarmid, *Dermott*
Macé, *Massey*
Mace
Mac Ealair, *Hilary*
Macedo, *Manzano*
Macek, *Matthew*
Mac Eocháin, *Keogh*
Mac Eòghainn, *Ewan*
Macey, *Massey*
Mac Fearchair, *Farquhar*
Mac Fhionnáin, *Finn*
Mac Fhógartaigh, *Fogarty*
Mac Gairbheith, *Garvey*
Mac Gairbhith, *Garvey*
MacGarvey, *Garvey*

Mac Gille Andrais, *Andrew*
Mac Gille Iosa, *Gillies*
Mac Giobúin, *Gibbon*
Mac Giolla Aindréis, *Andrew*
Mac Giolla Dhuinn, *Dunn*
Mac Giolla Dubhthaigh, *Duffy*
Mac Giolla Fhionnain, *Finn*
Mac Giolla Íosa, *Gillies*
Mac Gobha, *Gough*
Mac Gofraidh, *McCaffrey*
MacGorman, *Gorman*
Mach
Mácha, *Mach*
Macha, *Mach*
Máchač, *Mach*
Macháček, *Mach*
Machado
Machaffie, *Duffy*
Máchal, *Mach*
Máchala, *Mach*
Machała, *Mach*
Machálek, *Mach*
Macháň, *Mach*
Machan, *Maughan*
Machaut, *Marshall*
Mache, *Mach*
Machek, *Mach*
Machen, *Machin*
Machent, *Machin*
Macherzyński
Machiavelli
Machiavello, *Machiavelli*
Machin
Machnicki, *Mach*
Macho
Machocki, *Mach*
Machoň, *Mach*
Machon, *Machin*
Machon, *Mason*
Machotka, *Mach*
Macià, *Matthew*
Maciak, *Matthew*
Macías, *Matthew*
Maciaszczyk, *Matthew*
Maciaszek, *Matthew*
Macieiczyk, *Matthew*
Macieja, *Matthew*
Maciejak, *Matthew*
Maciejewski, *Matthew*
MacIlvreed, *Kilbride*
MacIlvride, *Kilbride*
Maciunas, *Matthew*
MacIvor, *Ivor*
Mack
Mackelbreed, *Kilbride*
Mäckelburg, *Mecklenburg*
MacKeller, *Hilary*
Mackereth, *McCrae*
Mackiewicz, *Matthew*
Mackintosh, *McIntosh*
Mackover, *Makowski*
Mackworth
Mac Laomuinn, *Lamont*
Maclehose
Mac Lucais, *Lucas*
Mac Marcuis, *Mark*
Mac Mathghamhana, *McMahon*
Mac Mhuiris, *Morris*
Mac Muircheartaigh, *Moriarty*
MacMuiris, *Morris*
Mac na Ceardadh, *Caird*
Mac Neacail, *Nicholas*
Maçó, *Mason*
Maçon, *Mason*
Macoun, *Matthew*
Macourek, *Matthew*
Mac Phádraig, *Patrick*
Mac Phaid, *Pate*
Macquarie, *McQuarry*
Mac Raghailligh, *Reilly*
Mac Raighne, *Rainey*
Mac Raing, *Rainey*
Mac Raonuill, *Ronald*
Mac Réamoinn, *Raymond*
Mac Riabhaich, *Reavey*
Mac Ruaidhrí, *Rory*
Mac Ruiarc, *Rourke*
Mac Sheumais, *James*
Mac Shimidh, *Simon*
Mac Shuibhne, *Sweeney*
Mac Síthigh, *Sheehy*
Mac Thámhais, *McTavish*
Mac Thomaidh, *McComb*
Mac Uaitéir, *Walter*
Macura, *Matthew*
Macy, *Massey*
Mączyński
Madariaga
Maddei, *Amadei*
Madden
Maddens, *Maudling*
Madder
Maddern, *Madder*
Maddick, *Madoc*
Maddicks, *Madoc*
Maddigan, *Madden*
Maddison
Maddock, *Madoc*
Maddocks, *Madoc*
Maddox, *Madoc*
Madec, *Madoc*
Madei, *Amadei*
Madeira
Madeleine, *Maudling*
Madeley
Madelin, *Maudling*
Madeline, *Maudling*
Madelon, *Maudling*
Mäder, *Mather*
Mader, *Madder*
Mader, *Mather*
Maděra, *Magyar*
Madge, *Marguerite*
Madgett, *Marguerite*
Madigan, *Madden*
Madine, *Madden*
Madison, *Maddison*
Madlener, *Maudling*
Madoc
Madocks, *Madoc*
Madolin, *Maudling*
Madon, *Maudling*
Madot, *Maudling*
Madoz, *Maudling*
Madrid
Madrigal
Madsen, *Matthew*
Madureira
Maesen, *Maas*
Maeso, *Master*
Maestacci, *Master*
Maestre, *Master*
Maestrelli, *Master*
Maestrello, *Master*
Maestri, *Master*
Maestrini, *Master*
Maestro, *Master*
Maestrone, *Master*
Maeterlinck
Maffei, *Matthew*
Maffeo, *Matthew*
Maffetti, *Matthew*
Maffezzoli, *Matthew*
Maffi, *Matthew*
Maffia, *Matthew*
Maffii, *Matthew*
Maffini, *Matthew*
Maffioletti, *Matthew*
Maffioli, *Matthew*
Maffione, *Matthew*
Maffioni, *Matthew*
Maffiotti, *Matthew*
Maffone, *Matthew*
Maffucci, *Matthew*
Maffulli, *Matthew*
Mafucci, *Matthew*
Magahan, *Gahan*
Magaheran, *Gaughran*
Magahern, *Gaughran*
Magalhaẽs
Magann, *Gahan, McGann*
Magauran, *McGovern*
Magaurn, *McGovern*
Magaw, *Megaw*
Magawran, *McGovern*
Magdalinski, *Maudling*
Magdeleine, *Maudling*
Magdelon, *Maudling*
Magdelyn, *Maudling*
Mageachrane, *Gaughran*
Maged, *Magid*
Magee, *McKay*
Magennis, *McGuinness*
Magennure, *Gaynor*
Magenor, *Gaynor*
Magenza, *Mainz*
Mager, *Maigre, Major*
Mageraghty, *Geraghty*
Mägerl, *Maigre*
Mägerlein, *Maigre*
Magermann, *Maigre*
Magermans, *Maigre*
Magg
Maggee, *McKay*
Maggi, *Marguerite, May*
Maggini, *May*
Maggio, *May*
Maggioli, *May*
Maggiolini, *May*
Maggs, *Magg*
Magheri, *Maigre*
Magherini, *Maigre*
Magid
Magidov, *Magid*
Magidovitz, *Magid*
Magidson, *Magid*
Magier, *Maigre*
Magierman, *Maigre*
Magill, *Gall*
Maginn, *McGinn*
Maginness, *McGuinness*
Maginnis, *McGuinness*
Maginnoire, *Gaynor*
Maginot, *Dominique*
Mägiste, *Mäki*
Magistrelli, *Master*
Magistretti, *Master*
Magistri, *Master*
Magistris, *Master*
Magistro, *Master*
Magit, *Magid*
Magnan, *Magnien*
Magnanelli, *Magnien*
Magnani, *Magnien*
Magnanini, *Magnien*
Magnano, *Magnien*
Magne, *Magnus*
Magnetti, *Magnus*
Magni, *Magnus*
Magnien
Magnini, *Magnien*
Magno, *Magnus*
Magnol
Magnone, *Magnus*
Magnoni, *Magnus*
Magnozzi, *Magnus*
Magnus
Magnuson, *Magnus*
Magnussen, *Magnus*
Magnusson, *Magnus*
Magorlick, *McGoldrick*
Magoveran, *McGovern*
Magovern, *McGovern*
Magowan, *McGowan*
Magragh, *McCrae*
Magrannell, *Ronald*
Magrath, *McCrae*
Magraw, *McCrae*
Magre, *Maigre*
Magreavy, *Reavey*
Magreevy, *Reavey*
Magret, *Maigre*
Magretti, *Maigre*
Magri, *Maigre*
Magrin, *Maigre*
Magriñá
Magrini, *Maigre*
Magrino, *Maigre*
Magris, *Maigre*
Magritte, *Marguerite*
Magro, *Maigre*
Magron, *Maigre*
Magrone, *Maigre*
Magroni, *Maigre*
Magrotti, *Maigre*
Magrou, *Maigre*
Magson, *Magg*
Magueen, *Sweeney*
Maguier, *McGuire*
Maguiness, *McGuinness*
Maguinness, *McGuinness*
Maguire, *McGuire*
Magurn, *McGovern*
Magyar
Mahault, *Moult*
Mahaut, *Moult*
Mahaux, *Moult*
Mähder, *Mather*
Mahder, *Mather*
Maheo, *Mayhew*
Maher
Maheu, *Mayhew*
Maheut, *Moult*
Mahew, *Mayhew*
Mahieu, *Mayhew*
Mahieux, *Mayhew*
Mähl, *Mill*
Mahle, *Malý*
Mählen, *Mill*
Mähler, *Mahler*
Mahler
Mahling, *Malý*
Mahlke, *Malý*
Mahon

Mahoney, *Mahon*
Mahony, *Mahon*
Mahood, *Hood*
Mahorry, *McAree*
Mahot, *Moult*
Mahoudeau, *Moult*
Mahout, *Moult*
Mahoux, *Moult*
Mahu, *Mayhew*
Mai, *May*
Maia
Maiden
Maidman, *Maidment*
Maidment
Maier, *Mayer*
Maierl, *Mayer*
Maieroff, *Mayer*
Maierson, *Mayer*
Maifahrt, *Meiffert*
Maigne, *Magnus*
Maignet, *Magnus*
Maignon, *Magnus*
Maigre
Maigret, *Maigre*
Maigrot, *Maigre*
Maile, *Maul*
Mailer
Mailler, *Mailer*
Main, *Mayne*
Mainardi, *Maynard*
Mainelli, *Mayne*
Mainello, *Mayne*
Mainerd, *Maynard*
Mainetti, *Mayne*
Mainetto, *Mayne*
Mainfroi, *Meiffert*
Mainfroy, *Meiffert*
Maingaud, *Maingaut*
Maingaut
Maini, *Mayne*
Mainis, *Mayne*
Mainland
Maino, *Mayne*
Mainoli, *Mayne*
Mains
Mainwaring
Mainz
Mainzer, *Mainz*
Maio, *May*
Maiorov
Mair
Maire, *Mayer*
Maireau, *Mayer*
Mairel, *Mayer*
Mairoff, *Mayer*
Mairot, *Mayer*
Mairov, *Mayer*
Mairovitch, *Mayer*
Mairovitz, *Mayer*
Mairowicz, *Mayer*
Mairowitz, *Mayer*
Mairs, *Mair*
Mairson, *Mayer*
Maisme, *Maxime*
Maismon, *Maxime*
Maisto, *Master*
Maistora, *Master*
Maistre, *Master*
Maistrelli, *Master*
Maistrello, *Master*
Maistret, *Master*
Maistri, *Master*
Maistro, *Master*
Maiteles, *Maites*
Maites
Maitin, *Maites*
Maitland
Maitles, *Maites*
Maitlis, *Maites*
Maitment, *Maidment*
Maître, *Master*
Maitret, *Master*
Maîtrier, *Master*
Maitrot, *Master*
Maizel, *Maus*
Maj, *May*
Majblat, *May*
Majcher, *Melchior*
Majchrowicz, *Melchior*
Majchrowski, *Melchior*
Majchrzak, *Melchior*
Majchrzycki, *Melchior*
Majer, *Mayer*
Majerczyk, *Mayer*
Majerowicz, *Mayer*
Majerowits, *Mayer*
Majerowitz, *Mayer*
Majewicz, *May*
Majewski
Majkowski, *Majewski*
Major, *Mayer*
Major
Majoral, *Mayoral*
Majorchick, *Mayer*
Majorczyk, *Mayer*
Majoros, *Mayer*
Majster, *Master*
Majstorović, *Master*
Majteles, *Maites*
Majtlis, *Maites*
Majzels, *Maus*
Makaradze, *Macaire*
Makarenko, *Macaire*
Makarewicz, *Macaire*
Makarikhin, *Macaire*
Makarishin, *Macaire*
Makarochkin, *Macaire*
Makarov, *Macaire*
Makarushka, *Macaire*
Makaryev, *Macaire*
Makarytsev, *Macaire*
Mäkelä, *Mäki*
Makepeace
Makepiece, *Makepeace*
Mäki
Makin
Mäkinen, *Mäki*
Making, *Makin*
Makins, *Makin*
Makinson, *Makin*
Makonin, *Maxime*
Makov, *Makowski*
Makovec, *Makowski*
Makover, *Makowski*
Makovička, *Makowski*
Makovski, *Makowski*
Makovsky, *Makowski*
Makower, *Makowski*
Makówka, *Makowski*
Makowski
Makowsky, *Makowski*
Maksakov, *Maxime*
Maksić, *Maxime*
Maksimat, *Maxime*
Maksimonko, *Maxime*
Maksimov, *Maxime*
Maksimović, *Maxime*
Maksimovich, *Maxime*
Maksimuk, *Maxime*
Maksimychev, *Maxime*
Maksimyonok, *Maxime*
Maksyatkin, *Maxime*
Maksymowicz, *Maxime*
Maksyutin, *Maxime*
Malaghan, *Milligan*
Malák, *Malý*
Malarmé, *Mallarmé*
Malarmey, *Mallarmé*
Malary, *Mallory*
Malát, *Malý*
Malaterre, *Malter*
Malave
Malavski, *Malave*
Malavsky, *Malave*
Malawsky, *Malave*
Malc, *Malter*
Malcharek, *Melchior*
Malcher, *Melchior*
Malcolm
Malcolmson, *Malcolm*
Malcom, *Malcolm*
Malcomson, *Malcolm*
Malczewski, *Malý*
Malczyk, *Malý*
Mald, *Moult*
Maldonado
Mâle, *Male*
Male
Malebranche
Maleč, *Malý*
Malec, *Malý*
Maleček, *Malý*
Małecki, *Malý*
Malecký, *Malý*
Maleev, *Malý*
Malein, *Malý*
Maleinov, *Malý*
Málek, *Malý*
Małek, *Malý*
Malek, *Malý*
Malenin, *Malý*
Malenkov, *Malý*
Malenky, *Malý*
Malerba, *Malherbe*
Malerbe, *Malherbe*
Malerbi, *Malherbe*
Malesherbes, *Malherbe*
Malet
Maleterre, *Malter*
Maletić, *Malý*
Malewski, *Malý*
Malfi, *Amalfi*
Malfitano, *Amalfi*
Malheiro, *Mailer*
Malherb, *Malherbe*
Malherbaud, *Malherbe*
Malherbe
Malicke, *Malý*
Malicki, *Malý*
Malík, *Malý*
Malikov, *Malý*
Malin
Malina, *Malinowski*
Maliniak, *Malinowski*
Malinov, *Malinowski*
Malinovitz, *Malinowski*
Malinovski, *Malinowski*
Malinovský, *Malinowski*
Malinovsky, *Malinowski*
Malinowitz, *Malinowski*
Malinowski
Malinowsky, *Malinowski*
Maliński, *Malinowski*
Malínsky, *Malinowski*
Malinsky, *Malinowski*
Malis, *Malin*
Malise, *Mellis*
Malisiewicz, *Malý*
Maliszewski, *Malý*
Malke, *Malý*
Malkes, *Malkin*
Małkiewicz, *Malý*
Malkin
Malkind, *Malkin*
Malkinson, *Malkin*
Malko, *Malý*
Malkov, *Malý*
Małkowski, *Malý*
Mallard
Mallarmé
Mallarmey, *Mallarmé*
Mallary, *Mallory*
Malle
Mallen, *Malin, Mellon*
Mallerie, *Mallory*
Mallery, *Mallory*
Malleson, *Malin*
Mallet, *Malet*
Mallett, *Malet*
Malley, *Mally*
Mallez, *Malet*
Mallin, *Malin*
Mallinson, *Malin*
Mallison, *Malin*
Mallon, *Malone*
Mallorie, *Mallory*
Mallory
Malloy, *Molloy*
Mally
Malm
Malmberg, *Malm*
Malmborg, *Malm*
Malmgren, *Malm*
Malmqvist, *Malm*
Malmsten, *Malm*
Malmström, *Malm*
Malnev, *Malý*
Malo
Maloit, *Malet*
Malone
Maloney, *Moloney*
Malory, *Mallory*
Malouet, *Malet*
Malov, *Malý*
Malpas
Malpass, *Malpas*
Malpighi
Malpuss, *Malpas*
Malson, *Moult*
Malt, *Moult*
Maltas, *Malthus*
Maltby
Malter
Malterre, *Malter*
Malthouse, *Malthus*
Malthus
Maltman, *Malter*
Maltravers
Maltsev, *Malý*
Maltsov, *Malý*
Maltster, *Malter*
Maltus, *Malthus*
Maltz, *Malter*
Maltzman, *Malter*
Malushin, *Malý*
Mały, *Malý*

Marchitelli, *Mark*
Marchitiello, *Mark*
Marchitto, *Mark*
Marchwicki, *Marchewa*
Marciek, *Martin*
Marciniak, *Martin*
Marciniec, *Martin*
Marcinkiewicz, *Martin*
Marcinkowski, *Martin*
Marcinkus, *Martin*
Marcinowicz, *Martin*
Marcireau, *Mercer*
Marciszewski, *Martin*
Marck, *Mark*
Marco, *Mark*
Marcocci, *Mark*
Marcoccio, *Mark*
Marcoff, *Mark*
Marcolin, *Mark*
Marcolini, *Mark*
Marcon, *Mark*
Marcone, *Mark*
Marconi, *Mark*
Marcos, *Mark*
Marcov, *Mark*
Marcovic, *Mark*
Marcovich, *Mark*
Marcovici, *Mark*
Marcovicz, *Mark*
Marcovitch, *Mark*
Marcovits, *Mark*
Marcovitz, *Mark*
Marcowic, *Mark*
Marcowich, *Mark*
Marcowicz, *Mark*
Marcowitch, *Mark*
Marcowitz, *Mark*
Marcozzi, *Mark*
Marcq, *Mark*
Marcu, *Mark*
Marcucci, *Mark*
Marcuccio, *Mark*
Marcus, *Mark*
Marcussen, *Mark*
Marcuzzi, *Mark*
Marcuzzo, *Mark*
Marczak, *Mark*
Marczewski, *Mark*
Marczyk, *Mark*
Marczyński, *Mark*
Marden
Mardon, *Marden*
Mare, *Delamare*
Marec, *Markey*
Marécal, *Marshall*
Mareček, *Marek*
Maréchal, *Marshall*
Maréchau, *Marshall*
Maréchaux, *Marshall*
Marek
Mareš, *Marek*
Marescal, *Marshall*
Marescalchi, *Marshall*
Marescalco, *Marshall*
Mareschal, *Marshall*
Marescot, *Marshall*
Marescotti, *Marsh*
Marest, *Marsh*
Marfleet
Marflit, *Marfleet*
Margalide, *Marguerite*
Margalit, *Marguerite*
Margalith, *Marguerite*
Margaliyot, *Marguerite*
Margaride, *Marguerite*
Margarit, *Marguerite*
Margary, *Marguerite*
Margereson, *Marguerite*
Margeride, *Marguerite*
Margeridon, *Marguerite*
Margerie, *Marguerite*
Margerin, *Marguerite*
Margerison, *Marguerite*
Margerit, *Marguerite*
Margeron, *Marguerite*
Margerrison, *Marguerite*
Margerson, *Marguerite*
Margery, *Marguerite*
Margesson, *Marguerite*
Margets, *Marguerite*
Margetson, *Marguerite*
Margetts, *Marguerite*
Marginson, *Marguerite*
Margison, *Marguerite*
Margitson, *Marguerite*
Margolies, *Marguerite*
Margolioth, *Marguerite*
Margolis, *Marguerite*
Margolius, *Marguerite*
Margossian, *Mark*
Margot, *Marguerite*
Margoteau, *Marguerite*
Margotin, *Marguerite*
Margry, *Marguerite*
Marguerie, *Marguerite*
Marguerin, *Marguerite*
Marguerite
Margueritte, *Marguerite*
Margueron, *Marguerite*
Marguery, *Marguerite*
Marguet, *Marguerite*
Marguiles, *Marguerite*
Marguin, *Marguerite*
Margules, *Marguerite*
Margulies, *Marguerite*
Margulis, *Marguerite*
Margulius, *Marguerite*
Mari, *Aylmer*
Marí, *Marin*
María, *Marie*
Maria, *Marie*
Mariamchik, *Marie*
Marian, *Marie*
Marians, *Marie*
Mariaud, *Marie*
Mariault, *Marie*
Marić, *Marie*
Marical, *Marshall*
Maricalchi, *Marshall*
Marichal, *Marshall*
Marichell, *Marshall*
Maričić, *Marie*
Maricot, *Marshall*
Marie
Mariel, *Marie*
Marielle, *Marie*
Marien, *Marie*
Mariet, *Marie*
Mariéton, *Marie*
Mariette, *Marie*
Mařík, *Marek*
Marikhin, *Marie*
Marimon
Marín, *Marin*
Marin
Marin, *Marie*
Marinacci, *Marin*
Marinaccio, *Marin*
Marinai, *Marin*
Marinari, *Marin*
Marinaro, *Marin*
Marinato, *Marin*
Marinazzo, *Marin*
Marinberg, *Marin*
Marinczik, *Marin*
Mariné, *Marin*
Marinelli, *Marin*
Marinello, *Marin*
Mariner, *Marin*
Marinescu, *Marin*
Marinetti, *Marin*
Marinetto, *Marin*
Marinho, *Marin*
Marini, *Marin*
Marinić, *Marin*
Mariniello, *Marin*
Marinier, *Marin*
Marinković, *Marin*
Marino, *Marin*
Marinoff, *Marin*
Marinolli, *Marin*
Marinoni, *Marin*
Marinotti, *Marin*
Marinotto, *Marin*
Marinov, *Marin*
Marinović, *Marin*
Marinow, *Marin*
Marinucci, *Marin*
Marinus, *Marin*
Marinuzzi, *Marin*
Mariolle, *Marie*
Marion, *Marie*
Marioneau, *Marie*
Mariot, *Marie*
Mariotte, *Marie*
Mariscalco, *Marshall*
Marishenko, *Marie*
Marival, *Marivaux*
Marivaux
Mariyushkin, *Marie*
Marjanović, *Marie*
Marjański, *Marie*
Marjoram
Marjoribanks
Márk, *Mark*
Mark
Markarian, *Macaire*
Marke, *Mark*
Markel, *Mark*
Märker, *Marker*
Marker
Markewitz, *Mark*
Markey
Markham
Markichev, *Mark*
Markiewicz, *Mark*
Markisov, *Mark*
Markl, *Mark*
Markland
Marklew
Märkli, *Mark*
Märklin, *Mark*
Markosov, *Mark*
Markov, *Mark*
Marković, *Mark*
Markovic, *Mark*
Markovich, *Mark*
Markovici, *Mark*
Markovitch, *Mark*
Markovits, *Mark*
Markovitz, *Mark*
Markovski, *Mark*
Markovsky, *Mark*
Markowicz, *Mark*
Markowitz, *Mark*
Markowski, *Mark*
Markowsky, *Mark*
Marks
Markson, *Mark*
Marktsev, *Mark*
Markus, *Mark*
Markushev, *Mark*
Markushin, *Mark*
Markushkin, *Mark*
Markussen, *Mark*
Markvart, *Markwardt*
Markward, *Markwardt*
Markwardt
Marland
Marlee, *Marley*
Marler
Marley
Marlor, *Marler*
Marlow
Marlowe, *Marlow*
Marner, *Marin*
Marney
Marnie, *Marney*
Marois, *Marsh*
Maroto
Maroušek, *Marie*
Marouzé, *Marouzeau*
Marouzeau
Maroz, *Mróz*
Marozeau, *Marouzeau*
Marple
Marples, *Marple*
Marpurch, *Morpurgo*
Marpurg, *Morpurgo*
Marquand, *Marchant*
Marquant, *Marchant*
Marquardsen, *Markwardt*
Marquardt, *Markwardt*
Marque
Marqués, *Marquis*
Marquès, *Marquis*
Marques, *Mark*
Marquese, *Marquis*
Marquet, *Mark*
Márquez, *Mark*
Marquis
Marquiset, *Marquis*
Marquot, *Mark*
Marr
Marrack, *Markey*
Marre, *Marr*
Marrec, *Markey*
Marrel, *Morrell*
Marrian, *Marie*
Marrin, *Marin*
Marriner, *Marin*
Marrington, *Meriton*
Marrion, *Marie*
Marriott
Marrison, *Marie*
Marro, *Master*
Marron
Marrs, *Marr*
Marryat
Mars, *Marsh*
Maršál, *Marshall*
Marsal, *Martial*
Maršálek, *Marshall*
Marsallon, *Martial*
Marsaud, *Martial*
Marsault, *Martial*

Marsaut, *Martial*
Marsch, *Marsh*
Marschal, *Marshall*
Marschalk, *Marshall*
Marschall, *Marshall*
Marschallek, *Marshall*
Marschlich, *Marshall*
Marschmann, *Marsh*
Marschollek, *Marshall*
Marsden
Marseau, *Martial*
Marsh
Marshall
Marsham
Marshman, *Marsh*
Maršík, *Marek*
Marskell, *Marshall*
Marsland
Marson, *Marston*
Marston
Marszał, *Marshall*
Marszałek, *Marshall*
Marta, *Marthe*
Marte, *Marthe*
Marteau, *Martel*
Martel
Martelet, *Martel*
Martelier, *Martel*
Martell, *Martel*
Martelli, *Martel*
Martellier, *Martel*
Martellini, *Martel*
Martellino, *Martel*
Martello, *Martel*
Martelotti, *Martel*
Martelotto, *Martel*
Marten, *Martin*
Martens, *Martin*
Martensen, *Martin*
Mårtensson, *Martin*
Marteret, *Martel*
Marthe
Marthelot, *Marthe*
Marthen, *Martin*
Marthon, *Marthe*
Martí, *Martin*
Marti, *Marthe, Martin*
Martial
Martić, *Martin*
Martiello, *Martel*
Martiensen, *Martin*
Martienssen, *Martin*
Martignon, *Martin*
Martignoni, *Martin*
Martijn, *Martin*
Martikainen, *Martin*
Martín, *Martin*
Martin
Martina, *Martin*
Martinaitis, *Martin*
Martinat, *Martin*
Martindale
Martine, *Martin*
Martineau, *Martin*
Martinec, *Martin*
Martínek, *Martin*
Martinelli, *Martin*
Martinello, *Martin*
Martinet, *Martin*
Martinets, *Martin*
Martinetti, *Martin*
Martinetto, *Martin*
Martínez, *Martin*
Martinho, *Martin*
Martini, *Martin*
Martinis, *Martin*
Martino, *Martin*
Martinoli, *Martin*
Martinolli, *Martin*
Martinon, *Martin*
Martinoni, *Martin*
Martinot, *Martin*
Martinotti, *Martin*
Martinović, *Martin*
Martinovich, *Martin*
Martinovský, *Martin*
Martins, *Martin*
Martinsen, *Martin*
Martinson, *Martin*
Martinssen, *Martin*
Martinsson, *Martin*
Martinussen, *Martin*
Martinuzzi, *Martin*
Martinyuk, *Martin*
Märtl, *Martin*
Martland, *Markland*
Martlew, *Marklew*
Márton, *Martin*
Marton, *Marthe*
Mártonffy, *Martin*
Mártonfi, *Martin*
Mártonfy, *Martin*
Martorell
Martot, *Marthe*
Martsch, *Martin*
Martschik, *Martin*
Martschke, *Martin*
Martsev, *Mark*
Martsinkevich, *Martin*
Martushev, *Martin*
Martusov, *Martin*
Marty, *Martin*
Martyanychev, *Martin*
Martygin, *Martin*
Martyn, *Martin*
Martynikhin, *Martin*
Martynka, *Martin*
Martynov, *Martin*
Martynowicz, *Martin*
Martyns, *Martin*
Martyntsev, *Martin*
Martyshkin, *Martin*
Martyushev, *Martin*
Marunchak, *Marie*
Marušák, *Marie*
Marushak, *Marie*
Marušić, *Marie*
Marusik, *Marie*
Marusin, *Marie*
Maruška, *Marie*
Marusyak, *Marie*
Maruszewski, *Marie*
Marvel
Marvell, *Marvel*
Marwick
Marwood
Marx, *Marks*
Marxen, *Mark*
Marxsen, *Mark*
Maryakhin, *Marie*
Maryan, *Marie*
Maryashkin, *Marie*
Maryasin, *Marie*
Maryatt, *Marryat*
Maryin, *Marie*
Marynowicz, *Marin*
Marynowski, *Marin*
Maryon, *Marie*
Maryška, *Marie*
Maryssal, *Marshall*
Maryushkin, *Marie*
Marzari, *Mercer*
Marzaro, *Mercer*
Marzec, *March*
Marzo, *March*
Mas
Máša
Masák, *Myasnikov*
Masařík, *Myasnikov*
Masaryk, *Myasnikov*
Mašát, *Máša*
Mašata, *Máša*
Mascalchi, *Marshall*
Mascall, *Marshall*
Masch, *Marsh*
Maschek, *Maas*
Maschi, *Male*
Maschietto, *Male*
Maschio, *Male*
Maschke, *Maas*
Maschmann, *Marsh*
Mascio, *Master*
Masciullo, *Master*
Masclet, *Male*
Mascoli, *Male*
Mascolino, *Male*
Mascolo, *Male*
Masdeu
Masefield
Mašek, *Máša*
Masek, *Maas*
Maselli, *Maas*
Masellis, *Maas*
Masello, *Maas*
Masero, *Mazier*
Maset, *Mas*
Masetti, *Maas*
Masetto, *Maas*
Mash, *Marsh*
Mashedder, *Masheter*
Masheder, *Masheter*
Mashenkin, *Marie*
Masheter
Mashiach, *Mejía*
Mashiah, *Mejía*
Mashikhin, *Marie*
Mashin, *Marie*
Mashiter, *Masheter*
Mashkin, *Marie*
Mashman, *Marsh*
Mashtakov, *Master*
Mashutkin, *Marie*
Masi, *Maas*
Mašić, *Matthew*
Masiello, *Maas*
Masieri, *Mazier*
Masiero, *Mazier*
Mašín, *Máša*
Masin, *Maas*
Masini, *Maas*
Masino, *Maas*
Masionis, *Maas*
Masip, *Mancebo*
Masius, *Mas*
Maška, *Máša*
Maskall, *Marshall*
Maske, *Maas*
Maskell, *Marshall*
Maskill, *Marshall*
Maslen, *Maslin*
Maslin
Masling, *Maslin*
Maslo, *Maslov*
Maslov
Maslovaty, *Maslov*
Maslovitz, *Maslov*
Maslow, *Maslov*
Masłowski, *Maslov*
Masó, *Mas, Mason*
Maso, *Maas*
Masolini, *Maas*
Masolo, *Maas*
Mason
Masot, *Mas*
Masotti, *Maas*
Mass, *Maas*
Massa, *Mas*
Massai, *Mazier*
Massalovo, *Mazza*
Massana, *Manzano*
Massarelli, *Mazier*
Massari, *Mazier*
Massarin, *Mazier*
Massarini, *Mazier*
Massarino, *Mazier*
Massariolo, *Mazier*
Massaro, *Mazier*
Massaroli, *Mazier*
Massarolli, *Mazier*
Massarotti, *Mazier*
Massarotto, *Mazier*
Massarut, *Mazier*
Massarutti, *Mazier*
Massarutto, *Mazier*
Massé, *Massey*
Masse, *Mace*
Massei, *Matthew*
Massen, *Maas*
Massenet, *Masson*
Massens, *Maas*
Masseo, *Matthew*
Masset, *Maas*
Masseter, *Masheter*
Massetti, *Maas*
Massey
Massicot, *Maas*
Massimo, *Maxime*
Massin, *Maas*
Massingberd
Massingbird, *Massingberd*
Massingham
Massini, *Maas*
Massinot, *Maas*
Massip, *Mancebo*
Massiquot, *Maas*
Massmann, *Maas*
Massó, *Mas, Mason*
Massoero, *Mazier*
Masson
Massone, *Mason*
Massoneau, *Masson*
Massonet, *Masson*
Massot, *Maas*
Massoud, *Maas*
Massuli, *Maas*
Massy, *Massey*
Mastalerz
Maštalíř, *Mastalerz*
Master
Masterman, *Master*
Masters, *Master*
Masterson, *Master*
Masterton
Masto, *Master*
Mastrelli, *Master*
Mastrilli, *Master*

Mastrillo, *Master*
Mastro, *Master*
Mastruzzo, *Master*
Masucci, *Maas*
Masuccio, *Maas*
Masullo, *Maas*
Masutti, *Maas*
Masutto, *Maas*
Masuzzo, *Maas*
Mata
Matalis, *Maites*
Matalovitch, *Maites*
Matalovsky, *Maites*
Matanin, *Matthew*
Matantsev, *Matthew*
Matas, *Mata, Matthew*
Matashkin, *Matthew*
Matasov, *Matthew*
Matatyahou, *Matthew*
Matatyahu, *Matthew*
Matchett
Matczak, *Matthew*
Máté, *Matthew*
Mate, *Matthew*
Mateer, *McIntyre*
Mateescu, *Matthew*
Mateev, *Matthew*
Matei, *Matthew*
Mateiko, *Matthew*
Matěj, *Matthew*
Mateja, *Matthew*
Matějček, *Matthew*
Matejić, *Matthew*
Matějíček, *Matthew*
Matějka, *Matthew*
Matějovský, *Matthew*
Matelaitis, *Matthew*
Mateles, *Maites*
Matelson, *Maites*
Matelyunas, *Matthew*
Mateo, *Matthew*
Mateos, *Matthew*
Materat, *Maturin*
Mates, *Maites, Matthew*
Matesanz
Matessian, *Matthew*
Mateu, *Matthew*
Mateus, *Matthew*
Mateuszczyk, *Matthew*
Matevosian, *Matthew*
Matevushev, *Matthew*
Mathé, *Matthew*
Mathe, *Matthew*
Mathée, *Matthew*
Matheis, *Matthew*
Mathelin, *Matthew*
Mathelon, *Matthew*
Mathely, *Matthew*
Mather
Matherat, *Maturin*
Matheron, *Maturin*
Mathers, *Mather*
Mathes, *Matthew*
Matheson, *Matthew*
Mathet, *Matthew*
Mathevet, *Matthew*
Mathevon, *Matthew*
Mathew, *Matthew*
Mathewes, *Matthew*
Mathewman, *Matthew*
Mathews, *Matthew*
Mathewson, *Matthew*
Mathey, *Matthew*
Mathias, *Matthew*
Mathiasen, *Matthew*
Mathiassen, *Matthew*
Mathie, *Matthew*
Mathies, *Matthew*
Mathieson, *Matthew*
Mathieu, *Matthew*
Mathilde, *Moult*
Mathiot, *Matthew*
Mathis, *Matthew*
Mathisen, *Matthew*
Mathison, *Matthew*
Mathissen, *Matthew*
Mathivat, *Matthew*
Mathivet, *Matthew*
Mathivon, *Matthew*
Mathon, *Matthew*
Mathonnet, *Matthew*
Mathoré, *Maturin*
Mathorel, *Maturin*
Mathorez, *Maturin*
Mathot, *Matthew*
Mathou, *Matthew*
Mathur, *Mather*
Mathurin, *Maturin*
Mathy, *Matthew*
Mathys, *Matthew*
Matías, *Matthew*
Matias, *Matthew*
Matiásek, *Matthew*
Matiashvili, *Matthew*
Matić, *Matthew*
Matiebe, *Matthew*
Matier, *McIntyre*
Matieu, *Matthew*
Matiewe, *Matthew*
Matijašević, *Matthew*
Matijević, *Matthew*
Matilla, *Mata*
Matis, *Maites, Matthew*
Matisoff, *Matthew*
Matisse, *Matthew*
Matissoff, *Matthew*
Matitiaho, *Matthew*
Matitiahou, *Matthew*
Matityahu, *Matthew*
Matiyas, *Matthew*
Matkin, *Matthew*
Matković, *Matthew*
Matlis, *Maites*
Matlovski, *Maites*
Matlovsky, *Maites*
Matlow, *Maites*
Matokhin, *Matthew*
Maton, *Matthew*
Matonin, *Matthew*
Matos, *Mata*
Matoshin, *Matthew*
Matou, *Matthew*
Matouš, *Matthew*
Matoušek, *Matthew*
Matović, *Matthew*
Matravers, *Maltravers*
Matraves, *Maltravers*
Matschek, *Matthew*
Mätschke, *Matthew*
Matschke, *Matthew*
Matschoss, *Matthew*
Matschuk, *Matthew*
Matskevich, *Matthew*
Matskiv, *Matthew*
Matson, *Matthew*
Matt, *Matthew, Mead*
Mattack, *Madoc*
Mattacks, *Madoc*
Mattäser, *Matthew*
Mattaus, *Matthew*
Matte, *Mead*
Mattea, *Matthew*
Matteacci, *Matthew*
Matteau, *Matthew*
Mattedi, *Matthew*
Mattei, *Matthew*
Matteini, *Matthew*
Matteis, *Matthew*
Mattek, *Matthew*
Matten, *Matthew*
Matteo, *Matthew*
Matteoli, *Matthew*
Matteoni, *Matthew*
Matteotti, *Matthew*
Matter, *Mead*
Matterson, *Matthew*
Mattes, *Maites, Matthew*
Matteucci, *Matthew*
Matteuzzi, *Matthew*
Mattevi, *Matthew*
Matthäi, *Matthew*
Matthäus, *Matthew*
Mattheesen, *Matthew*
Mattheessen, *Matthew*
Mattheeuw, *Matthew*
Mattheis, *Matthew*
Matthes, *Matthew*
Matthesen, *Matthew*
Matthesius, *Matthew*
Matthessen, *Matthew*
Mattheus, *Matthew*
Matthew
Matthewes, *Matthew*
Matthewman, *Matthew*
Matthews, *Matthew*
Matthewson, *Matthew*
Matthias, *Matthew*
Matthiesen, *Matthew*
Matthieson, *Matthew*
Matthiessen, *Matthew*
Matthis, *Matthew*
Matthison, *Matthew*
Matthisson, *Matthew*
Matthius, *Matthew*
Matthys, *Matthew*
Mattia, *Matthew*
Mattiacci, *Matthew*
Mattiassi, *Matthew*
Mattiato, *Matthew*
Mattiazzi, *Matthew*
Mattiazzo, *Matthew*
Mattick, *Madoc*
Mattielli, *Matthew*
Mattiello, *Matthew*
Mattila
Mattimoe, *Matthew*
Mattin, *Matthew*
Mattingley
Mattingly, *Mattingley*
Mattingson, *Matthew*
Mattinson, *Matthew*
Mattioli, *Matthew*
Mattioni, *Matthew*
Mattison, *Matthew*
Mattisson, *Matthew*
Mattityahou, *Matthew*
Mattityahu, *Matthew*
Mattiussi, *Matthew*
Mattiuzzi, *Matthew*
Mattke, *Matthew*
Mattler, *Mead*
Mattlin, *Mead*
Mattmann, *Mead*
Mattner, *Mead*
Mattock, *Madoc*
Mattocks, *Madoc*
Matton, *Matthew*
Mattosof, *Matthew*
Mattravers, *Maltravers*
Matts, *Matthew*
Mattschas, *Matthew*
Mattsson, *Matthew*
Mattucci, *Matthew*
Mattuck, *Madoc*
Mattusevich, *Matthew*
Mattusov, *Matthew*
Mattussi, *Matthew*
Matula, *Matthew*
Matura, *Matthew*
Maturin
Matus, *Maites, Matthew*
Matuschek, *Matthew*
Matusevich, *Matthew*
Matushevich, *Matthew*
Matushevitz, *Matthew*
Matusiak, *Matthew*
Matuška, *Matthew*
Matusov, *Matthew*
Matusovsky, *Matthew*
Matussevich, *Matthew*
Matusson, *Matthew*
Matussov, *Matthew*
Matussow, *Matthew*
Matuszak, *Matthew*
Matuszewski, *Matthew*
Matuszkiewicz, *Matthew*
Matuszyk, *Matthew*
Matuszyński, *Matthew*
Matveichev, *Matthew*
Matveiko, *Matthew*
Matveyev, *Matthew*
Matviyas, *Matthew*
Maty, *Matthew*
Mátyás, *Matthew*
Matyáš, *Matthew*
Matyas, *Matthew*
Matyashev, *Matthew*
Matyatin, *Matthew*
Matyja, *Matthew*
Matyjasik, *Matthew*
Matys, *Matthew*
Matysiak, *Matthew*
Matysik, *Matthew*
Matyugin, *Matthew*
Matyukov, *Matthew*
Matyushenko, *Matthew*
Matyushkin, *Matthew*
Matyushonok, *Matthew*
Matz, *Matthew*
Matzaitis, *Matthew*
Matzeitis, *Matthew*
Matzel, *Matthew*
Matzen, *Matthew*
Matzkaitis, *Matthew*
Matzke, *Matthew*
Matzkeitis, *Matthew*
Matzl, *Matthew*
Maubray, *Mowbray*
Mauchan, *Maughan*
Maud, *Moult*
Maude, *Moult*
Maudling
Maudslay, *Mawdesley*
Maudsley, *Mawdesley*
Maudson, *Moult*
Mauer, *Maurer*

Mauermann, *Maurer*
Maufe
Mauger, *Major*
Maugham, *Maughan*
Maughan
Maul
Mäule, *Maul*
Mauleverer
Maulkin, *Malkin*
Mault, *Moult*
Maultby, *Maltby*
Maund, *Mander*
Maunder, *Mander*
Maunders, *Mander*
Maunier, *Miller*
Maunsell, *Mansell*
Maupas, *Malpas*
Maupassant, *Malpas*
Maur, *Moore*
Mauran, *Morant*
Maurand, *Morant*
Maurandi, *Morant*
Mauras, *Moore*
Maure, *Moore*
Maurel, *Morrell*
Maurelli, *Morrell*
Maurello, *Morrell*
Maurer
Mauret, *Moore*
Mauri, *Moore*
Mauriac
Maurice, *Morris*
Mauricet, *Morris*
Maurici, *Morris*
Maurício, *Morris*
Mauriello, *Morrell*
Maurier, *Mora*
Mauriès, *Mora*
Maurigi, *Morris*
Maurin, *Moore*
Maurini, *Moore*
Maurino, *Moore*
Mauris, *Morris*
Maurissat, *Morris*
Maurisse, *Morris*
Maurisseau, *Morris*
Maurisset, *Morris*
Maurisson, *Morris*
Mauritzen, *Morris*
Maurize, *Morris*
Maurizi, *Morris*
Maurizio, *Morris*
Maurizot, *Morris*
Maurizzi, *Morris*
Mauro, *Moore*
Mauron, *Moore*
Maurou, *Moore*
Mauroux, *Moore*
Maury, *Amery*
Maus
Mäusel, *Maus*
Mauser, *Maus*
Mautby, *Maltby*
Mavrić, *Moore*
Mavrishchev, *Moore*
Mavros, *Moore*
Mavrov, *Moore*
Maw
Mawdesley
Mawdsley, *Mawdesley*
Mawe, *Maw*
Mawhinney, *McKenzie*
Mawsom, *Maw, Moult*
Mawson, *Maw*
Mawson, *Moult*
Max
Maxa, *Macaire*
Maxey
Maxim, *Maxime*
Maxime
Maxwell
May
Mayall, *Male*
Mayberg, *May*
Mayberger, *May*
Maybin, *Mabon*
Mayblum, *May*
Maybury
Maycock, *May*
Maye, *May*
Mayell, *Male*
Mayer, *Mayer*
Mayer
Mayerl, *Mayer*
Mayerovitch, *Mayer*
Mayers, *Mayer*
Mayersohn, *Mayer*
Mayerson, *Mayer*
Mayes, *May*
Mayeur, *Mayer*
Mayeux, *Mayer*
Mayfield
Mayhew
Maykin, *Makin*
Maykings, *Makin*
Maykins, *Makin*
Maylard, *Mallard*
Mayle, *Male*
Maylett, *Mallard*
Maylor, *Mailer*
Maynall, *Meynell*
Maynard
Mayne, *McManus*
Mayne
Maynell, *Meynell*
Maynes, *McManus*
Mayo, *May, Mayhew*
Mayol
Mayor
Mayoral
Mayorchik, *Mayer*
Mayorczyk, *Mayer*
Mayordomo
Mayorovits, *Mayer*
Mayow, *Mayhew*
Mays, *May*
Mayze, *May*
Maza
Mazeau, *Mas*
Mazel, *Mas*
Mazer, *Mazur*
Mazerand, *Mazier*
Mazerant, *Mazier*
Mazereau, *Mazier*
Mazeret, *Mazier*
Mazerin, *Mazier*
Mazet, *Mas*
Mazeyrat, *Mazier*
Mazié, *Mazier*
Mazier
Mazin, *Mas*
Mazo
Mazot, *Mas*
Mazur
Mazurek, *Mazur*
Mazurkiewicz, *Mazur*
Mazurowski, *Mazur*
Mazurski, *Mazur*
Mazursky, *Mazur*
Mazza
Mazzabue, *Mazza*
Mazzacane, *Mazza*
Mazzacurati, *Mazza*
Mazzagalli, *Mazza*
Mazzagreco, *Mazza*
Mazzalorso, *Mazza*
Mazzanobile, *Mazza*
Mazzapica, *Mazza*
Mazzavillani, *Mazza*
Mazzea, *Matthew*
Mazzei, *Matthew*
Mazzeo, *Matthew*
Mazzetti, *Mazza*
Mazzetto, *Mazza*
Mazzi, *Matthew*
Mazzia, *Matthew*
Mazzilli, *Matthew*
Mazzini, *Mazza*
Mazzino, *Mazza*
Mazziotti, *Matthew*
Mazzo, *James*
Mazzola, *Mazza*
Mazzoletti, *Mazza*
Mazzoli, *Mazza*
Mazzone, *Mazza*
Mazzoni, *Mazza*
Mazzotta, *Mazza*
Mazzotti, *Mazza*
Mazzullo, *Matthew*
Mazzuoli, *Mazza*
McAbee, *McBeth*
McAbrahams, *Brain*
McAbreham, *Brain*
McAckolly, *Quilly*
McAdam, *Adam*
McAddie, *Adam*
McAdie, *Adam*
McAffer, *Duffy*
McAgill, *Gall*
McAgown, *McGowan*
McAhuie, *Gilduff*
McAig, *McCaig*
McAimon, *McKeeman*
McAirter, *Arthur*
McAlary, *Cleary*
McAlaster, *Alexander*
McAlea, *Dunleavy*
McAlear, *McClure*
McAleary, *Cleary*
McAleavy, *Dunleavy*
McAleece, *Gillies*
McAleenan, *Finn*
McAleer, *McClure*
McAleese, *Gillies*
McAlery, *Cleary*
McAlester, *Alexander*
McAlinden
McAline, *Allen*
McAlish, *Gillies*
McAlister, *Alexander*
McAlivery
McAll, *McCall*
McAllan, *Allen*
McAllaster, *Alexander*
McAllay, *McAulay*
McAlley, *McAulay*
McAllister, *Alexander*
McAllum, *McCollum*
McAloon, *McLean*
McAlroy, *Gilroy*
McAnally, *McNally*
McAnaspie, *Bishop*
McAnchelly, *Quilly*
McAncrossane, *Cross*
McAndrew, *Andrew*
McAne, *McKane*
McAneave, *Gildernew*
McAnern, *McNairn*
McAnerny, *McNairn*
McAnleavy, *Dunleavy*
McAnlevy, *Dunleavy*
McAnn, *McCann*
McAnna, *McCann*
McAnnally, *McNally*
McAnnulla, *McNally*
McAnulty, *McNulty*
McAra
McArdell, *McArdle*
McArdle
McAreavey, *McIlwraith*
McAree
McArevey, *McIlwraith*
McArtair, *Arthur*
McArtan, *McCartney*
McArthur, *Arthur*
McArthy, *McCarthy*
McArtney, *McCartney*
McAsgill, *Ashkettle*
McAsinagh, *Tinney*
McAskie, *Ashkettle*
McAskill, *Ashkettle*
McAslan, *McAuslan*
McAsland, *McAuslan*
McAslin, *McAuslan*
McAteer, *McIntyre*
McAulay
McAuley, *McAulay*
McAullay, *McAulay*
McAully, *McAulay*
McAuselan, *McAuslan*
McAuslan
McAusland, *McAuslan*
McAuslane, *McAuslan*
McAuslin, *McAuslan*
McAveigh, *McBeth*
McAvey, *McBeth*
McAvinchy
McAvish, *McTavish*
McAvoy, *McEvoy*
McAward, *Bard*
McAy, *McKay*
McBain, *Bean*
McBay, *McBeth*
McBayne, *Bean*
McBean, *Bean*
McBeath, *McBeth*
McBeith, *McBeth*
McBeth
McBey, *McBeth*
McBirney, *Burney*
McBlain, *Blain*
McBratney, *Brett*
McBratnie, *Brett*
McBrayne, *Brain*
McBrehon, *Brain*
McBreive, *Brew*
McBride, *Kilbride*
McBrien, *Bryan*
McBrohoon, *Brain*
McBryde, *Kilbride*
McBurney, *Burney*
McCabe
McCaddie, *Adam*
McCadie, *Adam*
McCaet, *David*
McCaffarky, *McCafferty*

McCaffer, *Duffy*
McCafferchie, *McCafferty*
McCafferkie, *McCafferty*
McCafferky, *McCafferty*
McCaffert, *McCafferty*
McCafferty
McCaffery, *McCaffrey*
McCaffrae, *McCaffrey*
McCaffray, *McCaffrey*
McCaffrey
McCagherty, *McCafferty*
McCaharty, *McCafferty*
McCaherty, *McCafferty*
McCahey, *Caughey*
McCahy, *Caughey*
McCaig
McCairtair, *Arthur*
McCale, *McKail*
McCall
McCallan, *Callan*
McCallerie, *McIlwraith*
McCallister, *Alexander*
McCallum, *McCollum*
McCally, *McAulay*
McCalman, *Coleman*
McCalmon, *Coleman*
McCalmont, *Coleman*
McCalreaghe, *McIlwraith*
McCalreogh, *McIlwraith*
McCambridge, *Ambrose*
McCandless
McCandlish, *McCandless*
McCann
McCanna, *McCann*
McCanny, *McCann*
McCanon, *Cannon*
McCara, *McAra*
McCaragher, *Farquhar*
McCardle, *McArdle*
McCarha, *McCarthy*
McCarhie, *McCarthy*
McCarlish, *Charles*
McCarney
McCarnon, *McKiernan*
McCarra, *McAra*
McCarrach, *McCarrick*
McCarrick
McCarrie, *McAree*
McCarroll, *Carroll*
McCarron
McCartair, *Arthur*
McCartan, *McCartney*
McCarten, *McCartney*
McCarter, *Arthur*
McCarthy
McCartie, *McCarthy*
McCartin, *McCartney*
McCartney
McCarty, *McCarthy*
McCarvill, *Carroll*
McCashin
McCaskell, *Ashkettle*
McCaskie, *Ashkettle*
McCaskil, *Ashkettle*
McCaskill, *Ashkettle*
McCaslan, *McAuslan*
McCasland, *McAuslan*
McCasline, *McAuslan*
McCassin, *McCashin*
McCateer, *McIntyre*
McCaubrey, *Cuthbert*
McCaugherty, *McCafferty*
McCaughey, *Caughey*
McCaul, *McCall*
McCaulay, *McAulay*
McCauley, *McAulay*
McCaull, *McCall*
McCause, *McTavish*
McCauslan, *McAuslan*
McCausland, *McAuslan*
McCaverty, *McCafferty*
McCavish, *McTavish*
McCavitt, *David*
McCaw, *Megaw*
McCawis, *McTavish*
McCaws, *McTavish*
McCay, *McKay*
McChlery, *Cleary*
McChombich, *McComb*
McChruiter, *McWhirter*
McClacher, *Clachar*
McClanachan, *McClenaghan*
McClanaghan, *McClenaghan*
McClannachan, *McClenaghan*
McClaron, *McLaren*
McClatchey, *McClatchie*
McClatchie
McClatchy, *McClatchie*
McClave, *Claffey*
McClay, *McLay*
McClean, *McLean*
McCleane, *McLean*
McCleary, *Cleary*
McCleery, *Cleary*
McClellan
McClelland, *McClellan*
McClements, *Lamont*
McClemment, *Lamont*
McClenaghan
McClennan
McClery, *Cleary*
McClew, *Dunleavy*
McClintock
McClone, *Clune*
McCloone, *Clune*
McCloor, *McClure*
McCloskey, *McCluskey*
McClosky, *McCluskey*
McCloud, *McLeod*
McCloy, *Lewis*
McClune, *McLean*
McClung
McCluny, *McClung*
McClure
McClurg
McCluskey
McCluskie, *McCluskey*
McClusky, *McCluskey*
McClymond, *Lamont*
McClymont, *Lamont*
McCoard, *McCord*
McCole, *Cole, McDougall*
McColl, *Quill*
McCollam, *McCollum*
McColley, *Dunleavy*
McCollum
McComb
McCombe, *McComb*
McCombich, *McComb*
McCombie, *McComb*
McComie, *McComb*
McComish, *McOmish*
McComisky, *Comerford*
McConachie, *McDonagh*
McConachy, *McDonagh*
McConaghy, *McDonagh*
McConamy, *McNamee*
McConchy, *McDonagh*
McCone, *Ewan*
McConechie, *McDonagh*
McConechy, *McDonagh*
McConkey, *McDonagh*
McConloy, *Dunleavy*
McConmay, *McNamee*
McConmea, *McNamee*
McConnachie, *McDonagh*
McConnal, *McConnell*
McConnechie, *McDonagh*
McConnel, *McConnell*
McConnell
McConnochie, *McDonagh*
McConochie, *McDonagh*
McConomy, *McNamee*
McConoughey, *McDonagh*
McConvea, *McNamee*
McConvey, *McNamee*
McConville
McConvoy, *McNamee*
McConwell, *McConville*
McCool, *Cole, McDougall*
McCoole, *Cole*
McCoole, *McDougall*
McCorc, *McGurk*
McCord
McCorkell, *Thirkill*
McCorkhill, *Thirkill*
McCorkill, *Thirkill*
McCorkindale, *Thirkill*
McCorkle, *Thirkill*
McCorley, *Curley*
McCormack, *Cormack*
McCormick, *Cormack*
McCorquodale, *Thirkill*
McCorry
McCosdalowe, *Costello*
McCosh
McCosker, *McCusker*
McCostalaighe, *Costello*
McCostelloe, *Costello*
McCoubrey, *Cuthbert*
McCoubrie, *Cuthbert*
McCoubry, *Cuthbert*
McCoulie, *McCulloch*
McCourt, *McCord*
McCovie, *Duffy*
McCovvie, *Duffy*
McCown, *Ewan*
McCoy, *McKay*
McCrackan, *McCracken*
McCracken
McCrae
McCragh, *McCrae*
McCraith, *McCrae*
McCraken, *McCracken*
McCrandle, *Ronald*
McCrangle, *Ronald*
McCrank, *Rainey*
McCranor, *Trainor*
McCraw, *McCrae*
McCray, *McCrae*
McCraye, *McCrae*
McCrea, *McCrae*
McCreaddie, *McCready*
McCreadie, *McCready*
McCready
McCreagh, *McCrae*
McCreary, *McCreery*
McCreath, *McCrae*
McCreavy, *Reavey*
McCreddie, *McCready*
McCredie, *McCready*
McCree, *McCrae*
McCreery
McCreesh, *McNeice*
McCreevy, *Reavey*
McCreight, *McCrae*
McCreith, *McCrae*
McCrery, *McCreery*
McCreve, *Reavey*
McCrevey, *Reavey*
McCrie, *McCrae*
McCrimmon
McCrindell, *Ronald*
McCrindle, *Ronald*
McCringle, *Ronald*
McCririe, *McCreery*
McCrory, *Rory*
McCrossan, *Cross*
McCrudden
McCrumm
McCruttan, *Curtin*
McCrutten, *Curtin*
McCrystal, *Cristal*
McCubbin, *Gibbon*
McCubbine, *Gibbon*
McCubbing, *Gibbon*
McCue, *McKay*
McCullach, *McCulloch*
McCullagh, *McCulloch*
McCullie, *McCulloch*
McCulloch
McCullough, *McCulloch*
McCully, *McCulloch*
McCumesky, *Comerford*
McCumisky, *Comerford*
McCune, *Ewan*
McCure, *Ivor*
McCurlye, *Curley*
McCurrey, *McMurray*
McCurrie, *McMurray*
McCurtain, *Curtin*
McCusker
McCutchen, *McCutcheon*
McCutcheon
McDade, *David*
McDaid, *David*
McDairmid, *Dermott*
McDairmond, *Dermott*
McDaniel, *McDonald*
McDarmid, *Dermott*
McDavid, *David*
McDavitt, *David*
McDearmid, *Dermott*
McDearmont, *Dermott*
McDermaid, *Dermott*
McDermand, *Dermott*
McDerment, *Dermott*
McDermid, *Dermott*
McDermit, *Dermott*
McDermont, *Dermott*
McDermot, *Dermott*
McDermott, *Dermott*
McDevitt, *David*
McDiarmond, *Dermott*
McDoell, *McDougall*
McDona, *McDonagh*
McDonach, *McDonagh*
McDonachie, *McDonagh*
McDonachy, *McDonagh*
McDonagh
McDonaghy, *McDonagh*
McDonaill, *McDonald*
McDonald
McDonall, *McDonald*
McDonaugh, *McDonagh*
McDonchie, *McDonagh*

McDonell, *McDonald*
McDonnach, *McDonagh*
McDonnagh, *McDonagh*
McDonnell, *McDonald*
McDonnoghie, *McDonagh*
McDonogh, *McDonagh*
McDonoghue, *McDonagh*
McDonough, *McDonagh*
McDool, *McDougall*
McDoual, *McDougall*
McDouall, *McDougall*
McDougal, *McDougall*
McDougall
McDowall, *McDougall*
McDowell, *McDougall*
McDowney, *Moloney*
McDuall, *McDougall*
McDuff, *Duff*
McDuffie, *Duffy*
McDugal, *McDougall*
McDugald, *McDougall*
McDunphy, *McDonagh*
McEa, *McKay*
McEabuoy, *McEvoy*
McEan, *McKane*
McEbrehowne, *Brain*
McEcrossan, *Cross*
McEdmond, *McKeeman*
McEever, *Ivor*
McEevor, *Ivor*
McEgaine, *Keegan*
McEgan, *Keegan*
McEgill, *Gall*
McEgown, *McGowan*
McElane, *Allen*
McElderry, *Kildare*
McEldoon, *Dunn*
McEldowney, *Moloney*
McElduff, *Gilduff*
McElharan, *Heron*
McElhinney
McElhuddy, *McGillicuddy*
McElistrim, *Alexander*
McElistrum, *Alexander*
McEllar, *Hilary*
McEllen, *Allen*
McEller, *Hilary*
McElmurray, *Gilmore*
McElreath, *McIlwraith*
McElreavy, *McIlwraith*
McElroy, *Gilroy*
McElvride, *Kilbride*
McElwain, *McIlwaine*
McElwee, *McEvoy*
McElwreath, *McIlwraith*
McEnally, *McNally*
McEnarhin, *McNairn*
McEnchrow, *McEnroe*
McEnerie, *McEnery*
McEnerin, *McNairn*
McEnerny, *McNairn*
McEnery
McEniry, *McEnery*
McEnkelly, *Quilly*
McEnleavy, *Dunleavy*
McEnleive, *Dunleavy*
McEnleve, *Dunleavy*
McEnlevie, *Dunleavy*
McEnnesse, *McGuinness*
McEnnis, *McGuinness*
McEnroe
McEnry, *McEnery*
McEntaggart, *Taggart*
McEntee
McEnteer, *McIntyre*
McEntire, *McIntyre*
McEoghoe, *Keogh*
McErchar, *Farquhar*
McErlain, *McErlean*
McErlean
McEtterick, *McKettrick*
McEvaghe, *McBeth*
McEveighe, *McBeth*
McEvoy
McEvrehune, *Brain*
McEwan, *Ewan*
McEwen, *Ewan*
McEwing, *Ewan*
McFadden
McFade, *Pate*
McFadin, *McFadden*
McFadion, *McFadden*
McFadwyn, *McFadden*
McFadyean, *McFadden*
McFadyen, *McFadden*
McFadyon, *McFadden*
McFadzan, *McFadden*
McFadzean, *McFadden*
McFadzein, *McFadden*
McFadzeon, *McFadden*
McFail, *McFall*
McFait, *Pate*
McFall
McFaree, *McAree*
McFarlan, *McFarlane*
McFarland, *McFarlane*
McFarlane
McFarlin, *McFarlane*
McFarquar, *Farquhar*
McFarquhar, *Farquhar*
McFarry, *McAree*
McFaul, *McFall*
McFayden, *McFadden*
McFeat, *Pate*
McFeate, *Pate*
McFedries, *McFetridge*
McFedris, *McFetridge*
McFee, *Duffy*
McFerran
McFerry, *McAree*
McFetridge
McFeyden, *McFadden*
McFie, *Duffy*
McFun, *McMunn*
McFunn, *McMunn*
McFyall, *McFall*
McGaffey, *Caughey*
McGaffigan, *Gavigan*
McGahan, *Gahan*
McGahey, *Caughey*
McGahran, *Gaughran*
McGahy, *Caughey*
McGale, *McKail*
McGall
McGann
McGarran, *Gaughran*
McGarrigle
McGarrity, *Geraghty*
McGarry, *McAree*
McGaughey, *Caughey*
McGaughie, *Caughey*
McGaughran, *Gaughran*
McGauhy, *Caughey*
McGaveran, *McGovern*
McGaw, *Megaw*
McGawran, *Gaughran*
McGee, *McKay*
McGenn, *McGinn*
McGeogh, *Keogh*
McGeorge
McGeown, *Ewan*
McGeraghty, *Geraghty*
McGerety, *Geraghty*
McGerity, *Geraghty*
McGerraghty, *Geraghty*
McGerrity, *Geraghty*
McGettigan
McGhee, *McKay*
McGhie, *McKay*
McGibbon, *Gibbon*
McGilbride, *Kilbride*
McGilchrist, *Gilchrist*
McGildowie, *Duffy*
McGildowney, *Moloney*
McGilduff, *Gilduff*
McGill, *Gall*
McGillacoell, *Gilhool*
McGillacuddy, *McGillicuddy*
McGillallen, *McClellan*
McGillaroe, *Gilroy*
McGillarowe, *Gilroy*
McGillaroy, *Gilroy*
McGillaspick, *Gillespie*
McGillavery, *McGillivray*
McGillbride, *Kilbride*
McGillecole, *Gilhool*
McGilleduff, *Gilduff*
McGilleghole, *Gilhool*
McGilleguff, *Gilduff*
McGillereogh, *McIlwraith*
McGillesachta, *Lysaght*
McGillicuddy
McGilligan
McGilligin, *McGilligan*
McGillisachia, *Lysaght*
McGillivray
McGillivrie, *McGillivray*
McGillivry, *McGillivray*
McGillreich, *McIlwraith*
McGillvary, *McGillivray*
McGillvray, *McGillivray*
McGillvrid, *Kilbride*
McGillvride, *Kilbride*
McGillworry, *Gilmore*
McGillysachtie, *Lysaght*
McGilmore, *Gilmore*
McGilmour, *Gilmore*
McGilmurry, *Gilmore*
McGilp, *McKillop*
McGilrae, *McIlwraith*
McGilroy, *Gilroy*
McGilvane, *McIlwaine*
McGilvary, *McGillivray*
McGilveil, *Bell*
McGilvernock, *Warnock*
McGilvery, *McGillivray*
McGilvra, *McGillivray*
McGilvray, *McGillivray*
McGimpsey, *Dempsey*
McGin, *McGinn*
McGing, *McGinn*
McGinley
McGinn
McGinnis, *McGuinness*
McGinty
McGirr
McGivern, *McGovern*
McGlashan
McGlashen, *McGlashan*
McGlasson, *McGlashan*
McGloin, *McLean*
McGlone, *McLean*
McGloughlin, *McLachlan*
McGoldrick
McGolrick, *McGoldrick*
McGonagle, *McGonigle*
McGonigle
McGorley, *Curley*
McGorrie, *McCaffrey*
McGougan, *McGuigan*
McGoun, *McGowan*
McGounasan, *Gordon*
McGoune, *McGowan*
McGouran, *McGovern*
McGournaghan, *Gordon*
McGovern
McGovran, *McGovern*
McGow, *Gough*
McGowan
McGowe, *Gough*
McGowen, *McGowan*
McGowing, *McGowan*
McGown, *McGowan*
McGowran, *McGovern*
McGra, *McCrae*
McGragh, *McCrae*
McGrain, *Rainey*
McGrandell, *Ronald*
McGrane, *Rainey*
McGrath
McGrattan, *McCracken*
McGraw, *McCrae*
McGreal, *Neil*
McGreave, *Reavey*
McGreavy, *Reavey*
McGreevy, *Reavey*
McGregor
McGreigor, *McGregor*
McGrevye, *Reavey*
McGrievy, *Reavey*
McGrigor, *McGregor*
McGrory, *Rory*
McGuckian, *McGuigan*
McGuckin, *McGuigan*
McGuffie, *Duffy*
McGugan, *McGuigan*
McGuggy, *Caughey*
McGuier, *McGuire*
McGuigan
McGuinness
McGuire
McGuirk, *McGurk*
McGuiver, *McGuire*
McGuone, *Ewan*
McGurk
McGwir, *McGuire*
McGwire, *McGuire*
McGynnowar, *Gaynor*
McHaffie, *Duffy*
McHaffy, *Duffy*
McHaig, *McCaig*
McHale
McHarnon, *McKiernan*
McHarry, *McAree*
McHeagan, *Keegan*
McHeever, *Ivor*
McHeigh, *McCaig*
McHendrick, *McHenry*
McHendrie, *McHenry*
McHendry, *McHenry*
McHenry
McHinch, *McGuinness*
McHugh, *McKay*
McHutchen, *McCutcheon*
McHutcheon, *McCutcheon*
McHutchin, *McCutcheon*

McIan, *McKane*
McIgoine, *McGowan*
McIgone, *McGowan*
McIlaraith, *McIlwraith*
McIlarith, *McIlwraith*
McIlderry, *Kildare*
McIldoon, *Dunn*
McIldowie, *Duffy*
McIldowney, *Moloney*
McIlduff, *Gilduff*
McIlghuie, *Gilduff*
McIlheron, *Heron*
McIliams, *McWilliam*
McIlleriach, *McIlwraith*
McIllrick, *McIlwraith*
McIlmurray, *Gilmore*
McIlraith, *McIlwraith*
McIlrath, *McIlwraith*
McIlravy, *McIlwraith*
McIlrea, *McIlwraith*
McIlreach, *McIlwraith*
McIlriach, *McIlwraith*
McIlroy, *Gilroy*
McIlurick, *McIlwraith*
McIlvain, *McIlwaine*
McIlvaine, *McIlwaine*
McIlvane, *McIlwaine*
McIlvean, *McIlwaine*
McIlveen, *McIlwaine*
McIlvenna, *McIlwaine*
McIlvenny, *McIlwaine*
McIlvernock, *Warnock*
McIlwaine
McIlwraith
McIlwrath, *McIlwraith*
McInally, *McNally*
McInch, *McGuinness*
McInchelly, *Quilly*
McIndeor, *McGeorge*
McIndewer, *McGeorge*
McIneirie, *McEnery*
McInerney, *McNairn*
McIngill, *Gall*
McInlester, *Lister*
McInnes, *McGuinness*
McInstocker, *Stoker*
McIntaggart, *Taggart*
McInteer, *McIntyre*
McIntosh
McIntyre
McIsaac, *Isaac*
McIvagh, *McBeth*
McIveagh, *McBeth*
McIver, *Ivor*
McJames, *James*
McJarrow, *McGeorge*
McJerrow, *McGeorge*
McKage, *McCaig*
McKaghone, *McMahon*
McKaguc, *McCaig*
McKaig, *McCaig*
McKaige, *McCaig*
McKaigue, *McCaig*
McKail
McKain, *McKane*
McKale, *McKail*
McKall, *McCall*
McKane
McKarre, *McAree*
McKarrill, *Carroll*
McKarrye, *McAree*
McKaskil, *Ashkettle*
McKaskill, *Ashkettle*
McKasshine, *McCashin*
McKay
McKeag, *McCaig*
McKeagan, *Keegan*
McKeague, *McCaig*
McKeamish, *James*
McKean, *McKane*
McKeand, *McKane*
McKeaney, *Kenny*
McKeary, *McAree*
McKechnie
McKee, *McKay*
McKeegan, *Keegan*
McKeeman
McKeggan, *Keegan*
McKehoe, *Keogh*
McKeige, *McCaig*
McKeith, *Sheehy*
McKellan, *Allen*
McKellar, *Hilary*
McKellen, *Allen*
McKelvey
McKelvie, *McKelvey*
McKelvy, *McKelvey*
McKendrick, *McHenry*
McKenery, *McEnery*
McKeney, *Kenny*
McKeneyry, *McEnery*
McKeniry, *McEnery*
McKenna, *Kenny*
McKennan, *Kenny*
McKennery, *McEnery*
McKenny, *Kenny*
McKenzie
McKeo, *Keogh*
McKeogh, *Keogh*
McKeoghoe, *Keogh*
McKeon, *Ewan*
McKeough, *Keogh*
McKeown, *Ewan*
McKeracher, *Farquhar*
McKerchar, *Farquhar*
McKercher, *Farquhar*
McKerichar, *Farquhar*
McKericher, *Farquhar*
McKerley, *Curley*
McKerlie, *Curley*
McKernan, *McKiernan*
McKernane, *McKiernan*
McKerracher, *Farquhar*
McKerricher, *Farquhar*
McKerry, *McAree*
McKetterick, *McKettrick*
McKettrick
McKevitt, *David*
McKey, *McKay*
McKibben, *Gibbon*
McKibbin, *Gibbon*
McKibbon, *Gibbon*
McKie, *McKay*
McKiegan, *Keegan*
McKiegane, *Keegan*
McKiernan
McKilduff, *Gilduff*
McKillbride, *Kilbride*
McKilliam, *McWilliam*
McKilliams, *McWilliam*
McKillican, *McGilligan*
McKillicane, *McGilligan*
McKilligan, *McGilligan*
McKilligin, *McGilligan*
McKillop
McKillroe, *Gilroy*
McKilroy, *Gilroy*
McKilvain, *McIlwaine*
McKilvie, *McKelvey*
McKim, *McKimm*
McKimm
McKimmie, *Simon*
McKinch, *McGuinness*
McKinder, *McGeorge*
McKindewar, *McGeorge*
McKindlay, *McKinley*
McKing, *McGinn*
McKinlay, *McKinley*
McKinley
McKinn, *McGinn*
McKinna, *Kenny*
McKinnawe, *Kinneavy*
McKinnerkin, *McNairn*
McKinnertin, *McNairn*
McKinney, *Kenny*
McKinnie, *Kenny*
McKinnon
McKinny, *Kenny*
McKinstry
McKintosh, *McIntosh*
McKisack, *Isaac*
McKissack, *Isaac*
McKitterick, *McKettrick*
McKittrick, *McKettrick*
McKnight, *McNaughton*
McKnockatir, *McNucator*
McKnulty, *McNulty*
McKonochie, *McDonagh*
McKough, *Keogh*
McKoy, *McKay*
McKrevie, *Reavey*
McKynnan, *Finn*
McKyrrelly, *Curley*
McLachlan
McLachlane, *McLachlan*
McLae, *McLay*
McLain, *McLean*
McLaine, *McLean*
McLamon, *Lamont*
McLamont, *Lamont*
McLanachan, *McClenaghan*
McLanaghan, *McClenaghan*
McLane, *McLean*
McLaran, *McLaren*
McLaren
McLarnon
McLatchie, *McClatchie*
McLatchy, *McClatchie*
McLauchlan, *McLachlan*
McLauchlane, *McLachlan*
McLauchlin, *McLachlan*
McLaughlan, *McLachlan*
McLaughlane, *McLachlan*
McLaughlin, *McLachlan*
McLauren, *McLaren*
McLaurin, *McLaren*
McLaverty, *Laverty*
McLawring, *McLaren*
McLay
McLea, *McLay*
McLean
McLeary, *Cleary*
McLeavy, *Dunleavy*
McLeay, *McLay*
McLeery, *Cleary*
McLees, *Gillies*
McLeish, *Gillies*
McLeister, *Lister*
McLeland, *McClellan*
McLellan, *McClellan*
McLelland, *McClellan*
McLennan, *McClennan*
McLeod
McLernon, *McLarnon*
McLeroy, *Gilroy*
McLese, *Gillies*
McLetchie, *McClatchie*
McLeur, *McClure*
McLise, *Gillies*
McLish, *Gillies*
McLochlin, *McLachlan*
McLoghlin, *McLachlan*
McLoon, *McLean*
McLoone, *McLean*
McLoughlin, *McLachlan*
McLucas, *Lucas*
McLuckie, *Lucas*
McLucky, *Lucas*
McLugaish, *Lucas*
McLugash, *Lucas*
McLugish, *Lucas*
McLukie, *Lucas*
McLune, *McLean*
McLung, *McClung*
McLure, *McClure*
McLurg, *McClurg*
McLuskie, *McCluskey*
McLusky, *McCluskey*
McLysaght, *Lysaght*
McMachan, *McMahon*
McMachon, *McMahon*
McMaghen, *McMahon*
McMaghon, *McMahon*
McMaghone, *McMahon*
McMaghowney, *McMahon*
McMahan, *McMahon*
McMahen, *McMahon*
McMahon
McMahouna, *McMahon*
McManamon, *McMenemy*
McMann, *McMahon*
McMannas, *McManus*
McMannes, *McManus*
McManus
McMarquis, *Mark*
McMartin, *Martin*
McMaster
McMasters, *McMaster*
McMearty, *Moriarty*
McMeckan, *McMeekin*
McMeecham, *McMeekin*
McMeechan, *McMeekin*
McMeekan, *McMeekin*
McMeeken, *McMeekin*
McMeekin
McMeeking, *McMeekin*
McMeickan, *McMeekin*
McMeikan, *McMeekin*
McMenamie, *McMenemy*
McMenamin, *McMenemy*
McMenamy, *McMenemy*
McMenemy
McMenigall, *McMonagle*
McMerty, *Moriarty*
McMichael
McMichail, *McMichael*
McMichan, *McMeekin*
McMicheal, *McMichael*
McMichie, *Michie*
McMickan, *McMeekin*
McMicken, *McMeekin*
McMicking, *McMeekin*
McMikan, *McMeekin*
McMiken, *McMeekin*
McMikin, *McMeekin*
McMillan

McMillen, *McMillan*
McMiritee, *Moriarty*
McMonagle
McMordie
McMoreland, *McMorland*
McMoriertagh, *Moriarty*
McMorland
McMoroghoe, *McMorrough*
McMorris, *Morris*
McMorrough
McMorrow, *McMorrough*
McMowlane, *McMillan*
McMoylan, *McMillan*
McMreaty, *Moriarty*
McMullan, *McMillan*
McMullen, *McMillan*
McMullin, *McMillan*
McMullon, *McMillan*
McMunagle, *McMonagle*
McMunn
McMurchie, *McMorrough*
McMurdo, *McMordie*
McMurihertie, *Moriarty*
McMurphew, *McMorrough*
McMurray
McMurroghowe, *McMorrough*
McMurthoe, *McMordie*
McMurtough, *McMordie*
McMurty, *McMordie*
McMychen, *McMeekin*
McNab, *Abbott*
McNabb, *Abbott*
McNabo, *Abbott*
McNachtan, *McNaughton*
McNaghten, *McNaughton*
McNair
McNairn
McNakard, *Caird*
McNally
McNamara
McNamarra, *McNamara*
McNamarrow, *McNamara*
McNamee
McNarin, *McNairn*
McNarry, *McNally*
McNaryn, *McNairn*
McNauchtan, *McNaughton*
McNauchton, *McNaughton*
McNaught, *McNaughton*
McNaughtan, *McNaughton*
McNaughten, *McNaughton*
McNaughton
McNauton, *McNaughton*
McNay, *McNee*
McNayer, *McNair*
McNea, *McNee*
McNeal, *Neil*
McNeale, *Neil*
McNeall, *Neil*
McNecaird, *Caird*
McNee
McNeel, *Neil*
McNeelis, *McNelis*
McNeely, *McNeilly*
McNeese, *McNeice*
McNeice
McNeigh, *McNee*
McNeight, *McNaughton*
McNeil, *Neil*
McNeill, *Neil*
McNeille, *Neil*
McNeillie, *McNeilly*
McNeilly
McNeir, *McNair*
McNeiry, *McEnery*
McNeish, *McNeice*
McNelis
McNelly, *McNeilly*
McNerhenny, *McNairn*
McNerlan, *McErlean*
McNerlin, *McErlean*
McNern, *McNairn*
McNerny, *McNairn*
McNess, *McNeice*
McNevin, *Nevin*
McNey, *McNee*
McNia, *McNee*
McNichol, *Nicholas*
McNicholas, *Nicholas*
McNicholl, *Nicholas*
McNickle, *Nicholas*
McNicol, *Nicholas*
McNicoll, *Nicholas*
McNidder
McNider, *McNidder*
McNiel, *Neil*
McNillie, *McNeilly*
McNirney, *McNairn*
McNish, *McNeice*
McNisse, *McNeice*
McNitt, *McNaughton*
McNiven, *Nevin*
McNokerd, *Caird*
McNucator
McNuir, *McNair*
McNulty
McNutt, *McNaughton*
McNuyer, *McNair*
McOmie, *McComb*
McOmish
McOnachie, *McDonagh*
McOnechy, *McDonagh*
McOnochie, *McDonagh*
McPake, *McPeake*
McParlan, *McFarlane*
McParland, *McFarlane*
McParlane, *McFarlane*
McParlin, *McFarlane*
McPartlan, *McFarlane*
McPartland, *McFarlane*
McPeake
McPerson, *McPherson*
McPhade, *Pate*
McPhaden, *McFadden*
McPhaid, *Pate*
McPhaiden, *McFadden*
McPhail, *McFall*
McPharlain, *McFarlane*
McPharland, *McFarlane*
McPhate, *Pate*
McPhedric, *Patrick*
McPhee, *Duffy*
McPherson
McPhetrish, *McFetridge*
McPhial, *McFall*
McPhie, *Duffy*
McPhiel, *McFall*
McPhilip, *Philip*
McPhillips, *Philip*
McPhun, *McMunn*
McQuade, *McQuaid*
McQuaid
McQuarie, *McQuarry*
McQuarrey, *McQuarry*
McQuarrie, *McQuarry*
McQuarry
McQuaston, *McCutcheon*
McQueen
McQueenie, *Sweeney*
McQuenzie, *McKenzie*
McQueston, *McCutcheon*
McQueyn, *Sweeney*
McQuillan
McQuilliam, *McWilliam*
McQuilliams, *McWilliam*
McQuilly, *Quilly*
McQuine, *Sweeney*
McQuistan, *McCutcheon*
McQuisten, *McCutcheon*
McQuistin, *McCutcheon*
McQuiston, *McCutcheon*
McQuoid, *McQuaid*
McRaith, *McCrae*
McRanald, *Ronald*
McRannal, *Ronald*
McRaw, *McCrae*
McRay, *McCrae*
McRea, *McCrae*
McReadie, *McCready*
McReady, *McCready*
McReath, *McCrae*
McReavy, *Reavey*
McRedie, *McCready*
McRee, *McCrae*
McReilly, *Reilly*
McRie, *McCrae*
McRitchie, *Rich*
McRobb, *Robert*
McRobbie, *Roby*
McRobert, *Robert*
McRoberts, *Robert*
McRobin, *Robin*
McRoory, *Rory*
McRory, *Rory*
McRury, *Rory*
McSeveny, *Sweeney*
McShane, *Shane*
McShanley, *Shanley*
McShanly, *Shanley*
McSharry
McShee, *Sheehy*
McSheehy, *Sheehy*
McSherry, *McSharry*
McShiehie, *Sheehy*
McShihy, *Sheehy*
McSorley, *Sorley*
McSparran, *Sporran*
McSporran, *Sporran*
McStoker, *Stoker*
McSween, *Sweeney*
McSweeney, *Sweeney*
McSwine, *Sweeney*
McSwiney, *Sweeney*
McTaggart, *Taggart*
McTaggert, *Taggart*
McTague, *Montagu*
McTavish
McTeague, *Montagu*
McTear, *McIntyre*
McTeigue, *Montagu*
McTerrelly
McTerrens, *McTerrelly*
McTier, *McIntyre*
McTigue, *Montagu*
McTimney, *Timony*
McTirlay, *McTerrelly*
McTorrilogh, *McTerrelly*
McTurk
McTurlogh, *McTerrelly*
McUre, *Ure*
McVail, *McFall*
McVain, *Bean*
McVarish, *Morris*
McVarnock, *Warnock*
McVarry, *McAree*
McVay, *McBeth*
McVeagh, *McBeth*
McVeigh, *McBeth*
McVerry, *McAree*
McVey, *McBeth*
McVicar, *Vickar*
McVicker, *Vickar*
McVie, *McBeth*
McVitie
McVittie, *McVitie*
McVitty, *McVitie*
McVrehoune, *Brain*
McWalrick, *McGoldrick*
McWalter, *Walter*
McWard, *Bard*
McWatters, *Walter*
McWeeney, *McKenzie*
McWhan, *Sweeney*
McWhannell, *McConnell*
McWharrie, *McQuarry*
McWhin, *Sweeney*
McWhinney, *McKenzie*
McWhinnie, *McKenzie*
McWhirter
McWhiston, *McCutcheon*
McWiggan, *McGuigan*
McWilliam
McWilliams, *McWilliam*
McWinney, *McKenzie*
McWray, *McCrae*
Meacham, *Machin*
Meachem, *Machin*
Meachen, *Machin*
Meacher, *Maher*
Meachin, *Machin*
Meacock, *May*
Mead
Meade, *Mead*
Meadow
Meadows, *Meadow*
Meads, *Mead*
Meager, *Maigre*
Meagers, *Maigre*
Meagher, *Maigre*
Meaken, *Makin*
Meakin, *Makin*
Meakings, *Makin*
Meakins, *Makin*
Mealing
Mealley, *Mally*
Meally, *Mally*
Meaney
Meany, *Meaney*
Méar, *Mayer*
Mear
Meara, *O'Mara*
Meares, *Mear*
Mearns
Mears, *Mear*
Mease, *May*
Meath, *McNamee*
Meatyard
Meazzi, *Bartholomew*
Mebes, *Bartholomew*
Mebis, *Bartholomew*
Mebius, *Bartholomew*
Mebs, *Bartholomew*
Mebus, *Bartholomew*
Mecacci, *Dominique*
Mecchi, *Dominique*
Mecco, *Dominique*

Menchetti, *Dominique*
Menchetto, *Dominique*
Menchi, *Dominique*
Menchini, *Dominique*
Menchino, *Dominique*
Menci, *Dominique*
Mencini, *Dominique*
Menciotti, *Dominique*
Mencken, *Mayne*
Menco, *Dominique*
Menconi, *Dominique*
Mencotti, *Dominique*
Mencucci, *Dominique*
Mende, *Ende*
Mendel
Mendelevitch, *Mendel*
Mendelevitz, *Mendel*
Mendelevsky, *Mendel*
Mendelewicz, *Mendel*
Mendelovic, *Mendel*
Mendelovich, *Mendel*
Mendelovici, *Mendel*
Mendelovics, *Mendel*
Mendelovicz, *Mendel*
Mendelovitch, *Mendel*
Mendelovits, *Mendel*
Mendelovitz, *Mendel*
Mendelowicz, *Mendel*
Mendelowisz, *Mendel*
Mendelowitz, *Mendel*
Mendelsohn, *Mendel*
Mendelson, *Mendel*
Mendelssohn, *Mendel*
Mendelsson, *Mendel*
Mendelzon, *Mendel*
Mendes, *Menéndez*
Méndez, *Menéndez*
Mendham
Mendieta
Mendizabal
Mendlevich, *Mendel*
Mendlevitz, *Mendel*
Mendlewicz, *Mendel*
Mendlovic, *Mendel*
Mendonça, *Mendoza*
Mendoza
Meneely, *McNeilly*
Menegazzi, *Dominique*
Menegazzo, *Dominique*
Meneghelli, *Dominique*
Meneghello, *Dominique*
Meneghetti, *Dominique*
Meneghetto, *Dominique*
Meneghi, *Dominique*
Meneghini, *Dominique*
Meneghino, *Dominique*
Menego, *Dominique*
Menegone, *Dominique*
Menegucci, *Dominique*
Meneguzzi, *Dominique*
Menel, *Meynell*
Menéndez
Menescal, *Marshall*
Meneses
Mengard, *Ermgard*
Mengardi, *Dominique*
Mengardo, *Dominique*
Mengardon, *Ermgard*
Mengarduque, *Ermgard*
Mengazzi, *Dominique*
Menge, *Menger*
Mengel, *Menger*
Mengele, *Menger*
Mengeler, *Menger*
Menger
Menghelli, *Dominique*
Mengheni, *Dominique*
Menghetti, *Dominique*
Menghi, *Dominique*
Menghini, *Dominique*
Mengle, *Menger*
Mengler, *Menger*
Mengo, *Dominique*
Mengoni, *Dominique*
Mengossi, *Dominique*
Mengotti, *Dominique*
Mengozzi, *Dominique*
Mengucci, *Dominique*
Mengue, *Dominique*
Menguy, *Mingay*
Meni, *Dominique*
Menicacci, *Dominique*
Menichelli, *Dominique*
Menichetti, *Dominique*
Menichetto, *Dominique*
Menichi, *Dominique*
Menichiello, *Dominique*
Menichillo, *Dominique*
Menichini, *Dominique*
Menichino, *Dominique*
Menico, *Dominique*
Menicocci, *Dominique*
Meniconi, *Dominique*
Menicucci, *Dominique*
Meniguzzi, *Dominique*
Ménil, *Meynell*
Menini, *Dominique*
Menis, *Dominique*
Menjard, *Ermgard*
Menjaud, *Dominique*
Menjon, *Ermgard*
Menk, *Mayne*
Menke, *Mayne*
Menne, *Mayne*
Mennecke, *Mayne*
Menneke, *Mayne*
Menneking, *Mayne*
Mennell, *Meynell*
Mennenga, *Mayne*
Menning, *Mayne*
Menoghi, *Dominique*
Menoni, *Dominique*
Menotti, *Dominique*
Menozzi, *Dominique*
Mens, *Mayne*
Mensen, *Mayne*
Menshchikov, *Menshikov*
Menshikov
Menshov, *Menshikov*
Ment, *Maynard*
Mente, *Maynard*
Menteith, *Monteith*
Menth, *Maynard*
Menthe, *Maynard*
Mentler, *Mantell*
Mentz, *Maynard*
Mentzelmann, *Hermann*
Menuchin, *Menuhin*
Menuhin
Menukhin, *Menuhin*
Menz, *Maynard*
Menzelmann, *Hermann*
Menzen, *Maynard*
Menzies
Menzler, *Hermann*
Meo, *Bartholomew*
Mer, *Mayer*
Meraviglia, *Marvel*
Mercadante, *Marchant*
Mercadanti, *Marchant*
Mercadé, *Mercadier*
Mercader, *Mercadier*
Mercadié, *Mercadier*
Mercadier
Mercado
Mercante, *Marchant*
Mercanti, *Marchant*
Mercantini, *Marchant*
Mercanton, *Marchant*
Mercantone, *Marchant*
Mercatante, *Marchant*
Mercatanti, *Marchant*
Mercer
Mercereau, *Mercer*
Merceron, *Mercer*
Mercerot, *Mercer*
Merchadier, *Mercadier*
Merchán, *Marchant*
Merchant, *Marchant*
Merchier, *Mercer*
Merciai, *Mercer*
Mercier, *Mercer*
Merck, *Mark*
Merckx, *Mark*
Meredith
Méret, *Mayer*
Mereweather, *Merryweather*
Mérey, *Mayer*
Mergin, *Bergin*
Mergue, *Dominique*
Méric, *Henry*
Mériel, *Henry*
Mériet, *Henry*
Mérigeau, *Henry*
Mérigon, *Henry*
Mérigot, *Henry*
Mériguet, *Henry*
Mérimée
Merino
Mériot, *Henry*
Merit, *Merriot*
Meriton
Meritt, *Merriot*
Merkado, *Mercado*
Merkante, *Marchant*
Merkel, *Mark*
Merker, *Marker*
Merkle, *Mark*
Merlat, *Merle*
Merlaud, *Merle*
Merlault, *Merle*
Merle
Merleau, *Merle*
Merlet, *Merle*
Merletti, *Merle*
Merletto, *Merle*
Merli, *Merle*
Merlier, *Merle*
Merlin
Merlini, *Merle*
Merlino, *Merle*
Merlo, *Merle*
Merloni, *Merle*
Merlot, *Merle*
Merlotti, *Merle*
Merloz, *Merle*
Mérot, *Mayer*
Merrall, *Merrill*
Merralls, *Merrill*
Merre, *Mayer*
Merredy, *Meredith*
Merrel, *Merrill*
Merrells, *Merrill*
Merrett, *Merriot*
Merrick
Merriday, *Meredith*
Merridew, *Meredith*
Merrifield
Merrikin, *Marie*
Merril, *Merrill*
Merrill
Merrills, *Merrill*
Merriman, *Merry*
Merriment, *Merry*
Merrington, *Meriton*
Merriot
Merrit, *Merriot*
Merritt, *Merriot*
Merriweather, *Merryweather*
Merry
Merryett, *Merriot*
Merryweather
Merrywether, *Merryweather*
Mersand, *Meersand*
Mersch, *Marsh*
Merschmann, *Marsh*
Mersh, *Marsh*
Mersier, *Mercer*
Merson, *Mayer*
Merta, *Marthe*
Mertel, *Martin*
Merten, *Martin*
Mertens, *Martin*
Mertgen, *Martin*
Mertin, *Martin*
Merton
Mertsching, *Martin*
Mertz, *Martin*
Merula, *Merle*
Merveille, *Marvel*
Merwe, van der
Méry, *Amery*
Merzari, *Mercer*
Merzaro, *Mercer*
Mes, *Metz*
Mesa
Mesarov, *Myasnikov*
Mesclou, *Marshall*
Meser, *Messer*
Meserman, *Messer*
Mesman, *Metz*
Mesme, *Maxime*
Mesmer, *Mesner*
Mesmon, *Maxime*
Mesnard, *Maynard*
Mesner
Mesnil, *Meynell*
Mesquita
Message, *Messenger*
Messager, *Messenger*
Messana, *Messina*
Messanelli, *Messina*
Messaneo, *Messina*
Messeguer
Messenger
Messer
Messerer, *Messer*
Messerle, *Messer*
Messerman, *Messer*
Messerschmidt, *Messer*
Messerschmitt, *Messer*
Messina
Messineo, *Messina*
Messinese, *Messina*
Messinetti, *Messina*
Messing, *Messinger*

Messinger
Messiter, *Masheter*
Messmer, *Mesner*
Messner, *Mesner*
Mestadié, *Métayer*
Mestadier, *Métayer*
Mestayé, *Métayer*
Meste, *Metz*
Mestemacher, *Metz*
Mester, *Master*
Mestivier, *Métivier*
Mestre, *Master*
Mestrel, *Master*
Mestres, *Master*
Mestrier, *Master*
Mestwarb, *Metz*
Mestwerdt, *Metz*
Mészáros, *Myasnikov*
Métadier, *Métayer*
Métais, *Métayer*
Métayé, *Métayer*
Métayer
Metcalf
Metcalfe, *Metcalf*
Meteyard, *Meatyard*
Meth, *Mead*
Methuen, *Methven*
Methven
Métivier
Métoyer, *Métayer*
Métreau, *Master*
Metschke, *Matthew*
Mett, *Moult*
Mette, *Moult*
Metternich
Mettke, *Moult*
Metyard, *Meatyard*
Metz
Metze, *Moult*
Metzel, *Matthew*
Metzen, *Moult*
Metzer, *Metz*
Metzger
Metzig, *Matthew*
Metzing, *Matthew*
Metzke, *Matthew*
Meugnot, *Mignot*
Meulder, *Miller*
Meulders, *Miller*
Meulen, *Mill*
Meunié, *Miller*
Meunier, *Miller*
Meurer, *Maurer*
Meurice, *Morris*
Meuris, *Morris*
Meurisse, *Morris*
Meus, *Bartholomew*
Meusel, *Maus*
Meuser, *Maus*
Meusnier, *Miller*
Meuwissen, *Bartholomew*
Mew, *Maw*
Mewe, *Bartholomew, Maw*
Mewett, *Moët*
Mewhinney, *McKenzie*
Mewis, *Bartholomew*
Mexner, *Meisner*
Mey, *May*
Meye, *May, Mayne*
Meyer, *Mayer*
Meyerinck, *Mayer*
Meyering, *Mayer*
Meyerink, *Mayer*
Meyerovitch, *Mayer*
Meyerovitz, *Mayer*
Meyerowitz, *Mayer*
Meyers, *Mayer*
Meyersohn, *Mayer*
Meyerson, *Mayer*
Meyfarth, *Meiffert*
Meyffarth, *Meiffert*
Meyler, *Mailer*
Meyn, *Mayne*
Meynard, *Maynard*
Meyne, *Mayne*
Meynell
Meynen, *Mayne*
Meyns, *Mayne*
Meyr, *Mayer*
Meyrick, *Merrick*
Meys, *Bartholomew*
Meystre, *Master*
Meyz, *May*
Mezger, *Metzger*
Mezler, *Metzger*
Miall, *Myhill*
Miani, *Émilien*
Miano, *Émilien*
Miasnik, *Myasnikov*
Miatt, *Myatt*
Miazzi, *Bartholomew*
Micale, *Michael*
Micaletti, *Michael*
Micaletto, *Michael*
Micali, *Michael*
Micalini, *Michael*
Micalizio, *Michael*
Micalizzi, *Michael*
Micalli, *Michael*
Micallo, *Michael*
Mičan, *Mička*
Mićanović, *Michael*
Micco, *Dominique*
Miceli, *Michael*
Micelli, *Michael*
Micello, *Michael*
Micelon, *Michael*
Michael
Michaelides, *Michael*
Michaelis, *Michael*
Michaelov, *Michael*
Michaelovici, *Michael*
Michaelovitch, *Michael*
Michaelowici, *Michael*
Michaelowsky, *Michael*
Michaels, *Michael*
Michaelsen, *Michael*
Michaelson, *Michael*
Michal, *Michael*
Michalak, *Michael*
Michalczyk, *Michael*
Michalec, *Michael*
Michálek, *Michael*
Michalewicz, *Michael*
Michalewski, *Michael*
Michalik, *Michael*
Michalke, *Michael*
Michałkiewicz, *Michael*
Michallaud, *Michael*
Michallon, *Michael*
Michalon, *Michael*
Michałowicz, *Michael*
Michałowsky, *Michael*
Michalski, *Michael*
Michard, *Michael*
Michaut, *Michael*
Michaux, *Michael*
Miché, *Michael*
Micheau, *Michael*
Micheelsen, *Michael*
Michel, *Michael*
Michelacci, *Michael*
Michelassi, *Michael*
Michelato, *Michael*
Michelaud, *Michael*
Michelazzi, *Michael*
Michelazzo, *Michael*
Michele, *Michael*
Michelet, *Michael*
Micheletti, *Michael*
Micheletto, *Michael*
Michelevitz, *Michael*
Micheli, *Michael*
Michelin, *Michael*
Michelini, *Michael*
Michelino, *Michael*
Michelis, *Michael*
Michelk, *Michael*
Michell, *Mitchell*
Michelmore, *Mitchelmore*
Michelon, *Michael*
Michelone, *Michael*
Micheloni, *Michael*
Michelot, *Michael*
Michelotti, *Michael*
Michelotto, *Michael*
Michelozzi, *Michael*
Michelozzo, *Michael*
Michels, *Michael*
Michelsen, *Michael*
Michelski, *Michael*
Michelson, *Michael, Mitchell*
Michelucci, *Michael*
Michelutti, *Michael*
Micheluz, *Michael*
Micheluzzi, *Michael*
Michenet, *Michael*
Michenot, *Michael*
Micheson, *Michie*
Michet, *Michael*
Michetti, *Michael*
Micheu, *Michael*
Michey, *Michael*
Michez, *Michael*
Michi, *Michael*
Michie
Michiel, *Michael*
Michielazzo, *Michael*
Michieletti, *Michael*
Michieletto, *Michael*
Michieli, *Michael*
Michielin, *Michael*
Michiels, *Michael*
Michieson, *Michie*
Michiewicz, *Michael*
Michils, *Michael*
Michin, *Michael*
Michler, *Michael*
Michlik, *Michael*
Michlin, *Michael*
Michling, *Michael*
Michlis, *Michael*
Michniewicz, *Michael*
Michnik, *Michael*
Michon, *Michael*
Michot, *Michael*
Michou, *Michael*
Michoud, *Michael*
Michu, *Michael*
Michurin, *Dmitriev*
Mićić, *Michael*
Micieli, *Michael*
Micielon, *Michael*
Micillo, *Michael*
Mićka, *Dmitriev*
Micka, *Mička*
Mička
Mickeleit, *Nicholas*
Mickelsson, *Michael*
Mickiewicz, *Dmitriev*
Mickle, *Meikle*
Micklebride, *Kilbride*
Micklejohn, *Meiklejohn*
Micklethwaite
Micklewright
Mico, *Michael*
Micoli, *Michael*
Micone, *Dominique*
Micotti, *Dominique*
Micou, *Michael*
Micoud, *Michael*
Micoux, *Michael*
Mićović, *Michael*
Middleditch
Middlehurst
Middlemas, *Middlemass*
Middlemass
Middlemiss, *Middlemass*
Middlemist, *Middlemass*
Middlemost, *Middlemass*
Middler
Middleton
Midgley
Midhurst
Miebes, *Bartholomew*
Miel, *Myhill*
Mielczarek
Mielczarski, *Mielczarek*
Miell, *Myhill*
Miellet, *Myhill*
Mierosławski
Miers, *Mayer*
Mierula, *Merle*
Mierzejewski
Mies, *Moss*
Mieser, *Moss*
Miettinen, *Clement*
Migale, *Michael*
Migaleddu, *Michael*
Migali, *Michael*
Migalini, *Michael*
Migalizzi, *Michael*
Migalli, *Michael*
Miggles, *Michael*
Mighele, *Michael*
Migheli, *Michael*
Mighell, *Myhill*
Mighill, *Myhill*
Mignan, *Magnien*
Migne, *Mignot*
Mignon, *Mignot*
Mignonneau, *Mignot*
Mignot
Mignoton, *Mignot*
Migot, *Michael*
Migueis, *Michael*
Miguel, *Michael*
Miguet, *Michael*
Mihaileano, *Michael*
Mihaileanu, *Michael*
Mihăilescu, *Michael*
Mihailović, *Michael*
Mihajlović, *Michael*
Mihály, *Michael*
Mihályfi, *Michael*
Mihić, *Michael*

Mijalković, *Michael*
Mijatović, *Michael*
Mijović, *Michael*
Mijušković, *Michael*
Míka, *Nicholas*
Mika, *Nicholas*
Mikaelian, *Michael*
Mikailiv, *Michael*
Mikalaevich, *Michael*
Mikeš, *Nicholas*
Mikeshin, *Nikitin*
Mikhailichev, *Michael*
Mikhailin, *Michael*
Mikhailov, *Michael*
Mikhailychev, *Michael*
Mikhalchat, *Michael*
Mikhalchenko, *Michael*
Mikhalenya, *Michael*
Mikhalkov, *Michael*
Mikhantyev, *Michael*
Mikhnev, *Michael*
Mikhnevich, *Michael*
Mikhnov, *Michael*
Mikić, *Michael*
Mikisch, *Michael*
Mikitenko, *Nikitin*
Mikitin, *Nikitin*
Mikitka, *Nikitin*
Mikkelsen, *Michael*
Mikkola
Mikkonen, *Michael*
Mikladze, *Michael*
Miklós, *Nicholas*
Mikó, *Michael*
Mikołajczyk, *Nicholas*
Mikołajewicz, *Nicholas*
Mikoláš, *Nicholas*
Mikolášek, *Nicholas*
Mikolyunas, *Nicholas*
Mikota, *Nicholas*
Mikoyan, *Michael*
Miksa, *Nicholas*
Mikšovský, *Nicholas*
Mikuła, *Nicholas*
Mikula, *Nicholas*
Mikulanda, *Nicholas*
Mikuláš, *Nicholas*
Mikulášek, *Nicholas*
Mikulich, *Nicholas*
Mikulík, *Nicholas*
Mikulin, *Nicholas*
Mikulka, *Nicholas*
Mikulski, *Nicholas*
Míl
Milà
Miláček, *Míl*
Milačić, *Míl*
Milan, *Milano*
Milanese, *Milano*
Milanesi, *Milano*
Milani, *Milano*
Milano
Milau, *Milhaud*
Milbauer, *Mill*
Milberg, *Mill*
Milborne
Milbourne
Milburn
Milćević, *Míl*
Milczarek, *Mielczarek*
Milczarski, *Mielczarek*
Mildmay
Mile, *Miles*
Milec, *Míl*
Milekić, *Míl*
Miler, *Miller*
Milerad, *Mill*
Miles
Mileson, *Miles*
Milfirer, *Mill*
Milford
Milgram, *Milgrim*
Milgraum, *Milgrim*
Milgrim
Milgrom, *Milgrim*
Milgroom, *Milgrim*
Milgroum, *Milgrim*
Milgrum, *Milgrim*
Milhaud
Milhavés, *Milhaud*
Milián, *Émilien*
Milian, *Émilien*
Miliani, *Émilien*
Milić, *Míl*
Milien, *Émilien*
Milijanić, *Max*
Milijanović, *Max*
Milinaire, *Miller*
Milion, *Émilien*
Milisavljević, *Míl*
Miljanić, *Max*
Miljanović, *Max*
Miljević, *Míl*
Miljković, *Míl*
Mill
Millà, *Émilien*
Millán, *Émilien*
Millar, *Miller*
Millard, *Millward*
Millau, *Milhaud*
Millavois, *Milhaud*
Mille, *Miles, Mill*
Millen, *Mullen*
Millens, *Mullen*
Miller
Millership, *Millichamp*
Milles, *Mill*
Millet
Millett, *Millet*
Milliani, *Émilien*
Milliar, *Millier*
Millican, *Milligan*
Millichamp
Millichap, *Millichamp*
Millichip, *Millichamp*
Millichop, *Millichamp*
Millichope, *Millichamp*
Millien, *Émilien*
Millier
Milligan
Milligen, *Milligan*
Milligram, *Milgrim*
Milliken, *Milligan*
Millikin, *Milligan*
Millinaire, *Miller*
Milling, *Mullen*
Millington
Million, *Émilien*
Millis, *Mill*
Millman, *Mill*
Millmann, *Mill*
Millon, *Miles*
Millot, *Miles*
Millour, *Miller*
Mills, *Mill*
Millstein
Millward
Millwood, *Millward*
Milman, *Mill*
Milmann, *Mill*
Miln, *Mill*
Milne, *Mill*
Milner, *Miller*
Milnes, *Mill*
Milns, *Mill*
Milojević, *Míl*
Milojković, *Míl*
Milon, *Miles*
Milono, *Mill*
Milosavljević, *Míl*
Milošević, *Míl*
Miłosz, *Míl*
Milot, *Miles*
Milović, *Míl*
Milrad, *Mill*
Milshtein, *Millstein*
Milsom, *Miles*
Milson, *Miles*
Milstein, *Millstein*
Milsztejn, *Millstein*
Milton
Miltz, *Milz*
Milward, *Millward*
Milyear, *Millier*
Milz
Minář, *Miller*
Minardi, *Maynard*
Minardo, *Maynard*
Minařík, *Miller*
Minc, *Minter*
Minch, *McNeice*
Minchi, *Dominique*
Minck, *Mayne*
Mincke, *Mayne*
Mincotti, *Dominique*
Mincucci, *Dominique*
Mindel
Mindlin, *Mindel*
Minelli, *Dominique*
Miner
Miners, *Miner*
Mines, *Minn*
Miness, *Minn*
Mingardi, *Dominique*
Mingardo, *Dominique*
Mingay
Mingazzi, *Dominique*
Mingeon, *Ermgard*
Mingey, *Mingay*
Minghelli, *Dominique*
Minghetti, *Dominique*
Minghi, *Dominique*
Minghini, *Dominique*
Mingo, *Dominique*
Mingone, *Dominique*
Mingotti, *Dominique*
Mingozzi, *Dominique*
Mingucci, *Dominique*
Minguzzi, *Dominique*
Minichelli, *Dominique*
Minichi, *Dominique*
Minichiello, *Dominique*
Minichini, *Dominique*
Minichino, *Dominique*
Minico, *Dominique*
Miniconi, *Dominique*
Minicozzi, *Dominique*
Minicucci, *Dominique*
Minigo, *Dominique*
Minigucci, *Dominique*
Minihan, *Monaghan*
Minihane, *Monaghan*
Miniszewki, *Dominique*
Minjard, *Ermgard*
Mink, *Dominique, Mayne*
Minke, *Mayne*
Minkema, *Mayne*
Minn
Minnerk, *McNairn*
Minners, *Maynard*
Minnert, *Maynard*
Minnett, *Minn*
Minnich, *Monk*
Minning, *Mayne*
Minnish, *McNeice*
Minnitt, *Minn*
Minnock, *Minogue*
Minns, *Minn*
Minocchi, *Dominique*
Minogue
Minor, *Miner*
Minors, *Miner*
Minotti, *Dominique*
Minozzi, *Dominique*
Minshull
Mint, *Maynard*
Minten, *Maynard*
Minter
Minto
Minton
Mintor, *Minter*
Mintz, *Minter*
Mintzer, *Minter*
Minucci, *Dominique*
Minz, *Minter*
Minzer, *Minter*
Mion, *Simon*
Mioni, *Simon*
Miot, *Myatt*
Miquel, *Michael*
Miquelard, *Michael*
Miquelet, *Michael*
Miquelon, *Michael*
Mir, *Mirón*
Miralles
Miranda
Mirea, *Mironov*
Mirecki, *Mirski*
Miret, *Mirón*
Mirfield, *Merrifield*
Miró, *Mirón*
Mirón
Mironescu, *Mironov*
Mironichev, *Mironov*
Mironov
Miroshkin, *Mironov*
Mirowski, *Mirski*
Mirra, *Merle*
Mirralls, *Merrill*
Mirrington, *Meriton*
Mirski
Misch, *Michael*
Mischak, *Michael*
Mischan, *Michael*
Mischanek, *Michael*
Mische, *Michael*
Mischer, *Michael*
Mischke, *Michael*
Mischner, *Michael*
Mischnik, *Michael*
Mischok, *Michael*
Míšek, *Nicholas*
Mishanin, *Michael*
Mishatkin, *Michael*
Mishchenko, *Michael*
Mishechkin, *Michael*

Mishenev, *Michael*
Mishenin, *Michael*
Mishenkin, *Michael*
Mishkin
Mishkunas, *Michael*
Mishukov, *Michael*
Mishulin, *Michael*
Mishunov, *Michael*
Mishurenko, *Michael*
Mishurin, *Michael*
Mishurov, *Michael*
Mishutin, *Michael*
Mishutushkin, *Michael*
Misiak, *Michael*
Mišić, *Mishkin*
Miška, *Nicholas*
Miśkiewicz, *Michael*
Miskin
Mišković, *Mishkin*
Miśkovský, *Nicholas*
Misrachi, *Mizrachi*
Misrahi, *Mizrachi*
Mistre, *Master*
Miszczak, *Michael*
Miszkiewicz, *Michael*
Mitasov, *Dmitriev*
Mitcalfe, *Metcalf*
Mitchel, *Mitchell*
Mitchell
Mitchelmore
Mitchelson, *Mitchell*
Mitchieson, *Michie*
Mitchison, *Michie*
Mitelman, *Mittelman*
Mitelmann, *Mittelman*
Mitford
Mitić, *Dmitriev*
Mitin, *Dmitriev*
Mitkin, *Dmitriev*
Mitkov, *Dmitriev*
Mitrikhin, *Dmitriev*
Mitrikov, *Dmitriev*
Mitro, *Dmitriev*
Mitrofanov
Mitrofanyev, *Mitrofanov*
Mitroshin, *Dmitriev*
Mitroshinov, *Dmitriev*
Mitroshkin, *Dmitriev*
Mitrović, *Dmitriev*
Mitrukov, *Dmitriev*
Mitryaev, *Dmitriev*
Mitskevich, *Dmitriev*
Mitsnovich, *Michael*
Mittelman
Mittelmann, *Mittelman*
Mitter, *Mittmann*
Mitter
Mitterer, *Mitter, Mittmann*
Mitterhofer, *Mitter*
Mittermeier, *Mitter*
Mittermüller, *Mitter*
Mitterreiter, *Mitter*
Mitterreuter, *Mitter*
Mittleman, *Mittelman*
Mittmann
Mitton
Mitusov, *Dmitriev*
Mityaev, *Dmitriev*
Mityagin, *Dmitriev*
Mityakov, *Dmitriev*
Mityanin, *Dmitriev*
Mityashev, *Dmitriev*
Mityashin, *Dmitriev*
Mitykhin, *Dmitriev*
Mityukov, *Dmitriev*
Mityurev, *Dmitriev*
Mityushin, *Dmitriev*
Mityushkin, *Dmitriev*
Mixa, *Nicholas*
Mixhel, *Michael*
Mizen
Mizerski
Mizon, *Mizen*
Mizrachi
Mizrahi, *Mizrachi*
Mizrahy, *Mizrachi*
Mizzen, *Mizen*
Mizzi, *James*
Mlawer, *Malave*
Mlejnek, *Miller*
Mlinarski, *Miller*
Mlnařík, *Miller*
Mlotek, *Molotov*
Mlynář, *Miller*
Młynarczyk, *Miller*
Młynarski, *Miller*
Mlynarski, *Miller*
Młyński, *Miller*
Mnuchin, *Menuhin*
Mnukhin, *Menuhin*
Mnushkin, *Menuhin*
Mnuskin, *Menuhin*
Mo
Moan, *Mohan*
Moat
Mobbs, *Mabb*
Moberg, *Mo*
Moberly
Möbius, *Bartholomew*
Mobley, *Moberly*
Mockridge, *Muggeridge*
Moczkowski
Modén, *Moody*
Modig, *Moody*
Modigh, *Moody*
Modigliani, *Modigliano*
Modigliano
Modin, *Moody*
Modrzejewski
Modrzewski, *Modrzejewski*
Moe, *Mo*
Moen, *Mohan*
Moens, *Simon*
Moer, *Moore*
Moerinck, *Moore*
Moerman, *Moore*
Moët
Moffatt
Moffett, *Moffatt*
Moffitt, *Moffatt*
Mogenot, *Dominique*
Mogg, *Magg*
Moggridge, *Muggeridge*
Moghan, *Mohan*
Moghane, *Mohan*
Mogk, *Maw*
Mogren, *Mo*
Mogridge, *Muggeridge*
Mohan
Möhl, *Mill*
Möhlber, *Melber*
Möhlbert, *Melber*
Möhle, *Mill*
Mohlén, *Mo*
Möhler, *Mahler*
Mohlin, *Mo*
Mohr, *Moore*
Möhring, *Moore*
Möhrke, *Moore*
Mohrmann, *Moore*
Moinard, *Monk*
Moinat, *Monk*
Moinaud, *Monk*
Moinault, *Monk*
Moiné, *Monk*
Moine, *Monk*
Moineau, *Monk*
Moinel, *Monk*
Moinet, *Monk*
Moinot, *Monk*
Moir, *Moore*
Moïse, *Moses*
Moise, *Moses*
Moiseev, *Moses*
Moiseiev, *Moses*
Moisescu, *Moses*
Moisio, *Moses*
Moiso, *Moses*
Moisseef, *Moses*
Moita
Moizo, *Moses*
Mojsilović, *Moses*
Mojžíš, *Moses*
Mojžíšek, *Moses*
Mol, *Mole*
Molchanov
Molchanovsky, *Molchanov*
Molchansky, *Molchanov*
Mold, *Moult*
Moldenaer, *Miller*
Mole
Moleiro, *Miller*
Molén, *Mo*
Molenaar, *Miller*
Molenaer, *Miller*
Molenaers, *Miller*
Molero, *Muela*
Molesworth
Mølgaard, *Mølgård*
Mølgård
Molin, *Mill, Mo*
Molina, *Mill*
Molinuri, *Miller*
Molinaro, *Miller*
Molinaroli, *Miller*
Molinarolo, *Miller*
Molinas, *Mill*
Molineaux, *Molyneux*
Molinelli, *Mill*
Moliner, *Miller*
Molinero, *Miller*
Molinese, *Mill*
Molinetti, *Mill*
Molini, *Mill*
Molinier, *Miller*
Molino, *Mill*
Molins, *Mill, Mullen*
Molitor, *Miller*
Moll
Mollan, *Mullen*
Møller, *Miller*
Möller, *Miller*
Moller, *Miller*
Möllering, *Miller*
Molloy
Molnár, *Miller*
Molner, *Miller*
Molodozhnikov, *Mielczarek*
Molohan, *Milligan*
Moloney
Molony, *Moloney*
Molotkov, *Molotov*
Molotov
Molson, *Moult*
Mölter, *Malter*
Molter, *Malter*
Moltke
Moltmann, *Malter*
Molvin, *Melvin*
Molyneux
Mombrum, *Mombrun*
Mombrun
Momery, *Mowbray*
Momigliano
Mommen, *Mommsen*
Mommsen
Monaboe, *Abbott*
Monacelli, *Monk*
Monacello, *Monk*
Monachello, *Monk*
Monachino, *Monk*
Monaci, *Monk*
Monaco, *Monk*
Monaghan
Monahan, *Monaghan*
Monari, *Miller*
Monaro, *Miller*
Monash
Monasterio
Monastyrski, *Monasterio*
Monbrum, *Mombrun*
Monbrun, *Mombrun*
Moncey, *Mounsey*
Mönch, *Monk*
Monck, *Monk*
Monclús
Moncreiff, *Moncrieff*
Moncreiffe, *Moncrieff*
Moncrieff
Moncur
Moncuso, *Manco*
Mondadori
Monday
Mondy, *Monday*
Monedero, *Minter*
Monego, *Monk*
Monelli, *Simon*
Monet, *Hammond*
Monet
Moneta, *Minter*
Monetti, *Simon*
Money
Moneypenny
Monfort, *Montfort*
Monge, *Monk*
Mongeaud, *Dominique*
Mongenot, *Dominique*
Mongeot, *Dominique*
Monger, *Menger*
Monget, *Dominique*
Mongin, *Dominique*
Monico, *Monk*
Monier, *Minter*
Monini, *Simon*
Moniz, *Muño*
Monje, *Monk*
Mönk, *Monk*
Monk
Mönke, *Monk*
Monkhouse
Monkman, *Monk*
Monks, *Monk*
Monnereau, *Minter*
Monneret, *Minter*
Monnerot, *Minter*
Monnet, *Monet*

Mönnich, *Monk*
Monnick, *Monk*
Monnier, *Miller*
Monnier, *Minter*
Monosson, *Monash*
Monot, *Edmond*
Monque, *Monk*
Monreal
Monro, *Munro*
Monroe, *Munro*
Monsky, *Mann*
Monson, *Magnus*
Mont
Montacute, *Montagu*
Montag, *Monday*
Montagna, *Montagne*
Montagne
Montagni, *Montagne*
Montagnié, *Montagne*
Montagnier, *Montagne*
Montagnini, *Montagne*
Montagnino, *Montagne*
Montagnon, *Montagne*
Montagnoni, *Montagne*
Montagu
Montague, *Montagu*
Montagut, *Montagu*
Montaigne, *Montagne*
Montaigu, *Montagu*
Montalvo
Montan, *Montagne*
Montaña, *Montagne*
Montana, *Montagne*
Montané, *Montaner*
Montanelli, *Montagne*
Montaner
Montañés, *Montagne*
Montani, *Montagne*
Montanier, *Montagne*
Montano, *Montagne*
Montat, *Mont*
Monté, *Montero*
Monte, *Mont*
Monteagudo, *Montagu*
Monteath, *Monteith*
Monteau, *Mont*
Monteaux, *Mont*
Montefiore
Monteiro, *Montero*
Monteith
Montejo, *Mont*
Montel, *Mont*
Montelli, *Mont*
Montello, *Mont*
Montenegro
Montero
Montes, *Mont*
Montesano, *Mont*
Montesino, *Mont*
Montesinos, *Mont*
Montessori
Montet, *Mont*
Monteverde
Monteverdi, *Monteverde*
Montford, *Montfort*
Montfort
Montgolfier
Montgomerie, *Montgomery*
Montgomery
Montgomry, *Montgomery*
Monti, *Mont*
Monticelli, *Mont*
Montigiani, *Mont*
Montilla, *Mont*
Montilla
Montillon, *Mont*
Montin, *Mont*
Montini, *Mont*
Montmorency
Montolio, *Montoliu*
Montoliu
Montoro
Montserrat
Monypenny, *Moneypenny*
Monzón
Moodey, *Moody*
Moodie, *Moody*
Moody
Moog, *Maw*
Moogk, *Maw*
Moohan, *Mohan*
Moolenaar, *Miller*
Moon
Moone, *Moon*
Mooney, *Meaney*
Moor, *Moore, Morris*
Moorby
Moorcock, *Moore*
Moorcraft, *Moorcroft*
Moorcroft
Moore
Moores, *Moore*
Moorfield
Moorhead, *Muirhead*
Moorhouse
Mooring, *Moore*
Moorley, *Morley*
Moorman, *Moore*
Moormann, *Moore*
Moors, *Moore*
Moos, *Moss*
Mooser, *Moss*
Moosmann, *Moss*
Mór, *Morris*
Mor, *Moore*
Móra, *Mora, Morris*
Morà, *Morant*
Mora
Morais, *Mora*
Moral, *Mora*
Moraleda, *Mora*
Moralee, *Morley*
Morales, *Mora*
Morán, *Morant*
Moran
Morand, *Morant*
Morandat, *Morant*
Morandeau, *Morant*
Morandi, *Morant*
Morandin, *Morant*
Morandini, *Morant*
Morando, *Morant*
Moranduzzo, *Morant*
Morant
Morante, *Morant*
Morariu, *Miller*
Moraru, *Miller*
Moras, *Moore*
Morassi, *Moore*
Morasso, *Moore*
Morata
Moratilla, *Morata*
Morava, *Moravec*
Moravčík, *Moravec*
Moravec
Moravia, *Moravec*
Morawiec, *Moravec*
Morawski, *Moravec*
Morazzi, *Moore*
Morce, *Morris*
Mørch, *Mörk*
Morchan, *Morgan*
Morcillo
Mørck, *Mörk*
Morcom, *Morcombe*
Morcombe
Mordaunt
Moré, *Moore*
More, *Moore*
Moreau, *Morrell*
Morehead, *Muirhead*
Morehouse, *Moorhouse*
Moreira, *Mora*
Morel, *Morrell*
Moreland
Morelet, *Morrell*
Morell, *Morrell*
Morellet, *Morrell*
Morelli, *Morrell*
Morello, *Morrell*
Morellon, *Morrell*
Morelon, *Morrell*
Morelot, *Morrell*
Morely, *Morley*
Moreman, *Moore*
Morena, *Moreno*
Moreno
Morera, *Mora*
Mores, *Moore*
Moresby
Moret, *Moore*
Moreton, *Morton*
Moretti, *Moore*
Moretto, *Moore*
Morey, *Moore*
Morgado
Morgan
Morgenrot
Morgenroth, *Morgenrot*
Morgenstern
Mori, *Moore*
Moriarty
Morice, *Morris*
Moricet, *Morris*
Möricke, *Moore*
Móricz, *Morris*
Mörike, *Moore*
Morill, *Morrell*
Morilla, *Mora*
Morillas, *Mora*
Morillo, *Morrell*
Morin, *Moore*
Morineau, *Moore*
Morinet, *Moore*
Möring, *Moore*
Moring, *Moore*
Morini, *Moore*
Morino, *Moore*
Moriotti, *Moore*
Moriotto, *Moore*
Moris, *Morris*
Morison, *Morris*
Morisse, *Morris*
Morissen, *Morris*
Morisset, *Morris*
Morisson, *Morris*
Morissy, *Morrissey*
Moritz, *Morris*
Moritzen, *Morris*
Moritzer, *Morris*
Moriz, *Morris*
Morize, *Morris*
Morizet, *Morris*
Morizot, *Morris*
Mørk, *Mörk*
Mörk
Morkan, *Morgan*
Mörke, *Moore*
Morkin, *Morgan*
Morkúnas, *Mark*
Morland, *Moreland*
Mörle, *Moore*
Morlet, *Morrell*
Morley
Morlin, *Morling*
Morling
Morlot, *Morrell*
Morman, *Moore*
Mornet, *Moore*
Moro, *Moore*
Moron, *Moore*
Morón
Moroney
Moroni, *Moore*
Morooney, *Moroney*
Morot, *Moore*
Moroz, *Mróz*
Morozov, *Mróz*
Morozowski, *Mróz*
Morozzi, *Moore*
Morpat, *Morpeth*
Morpeth
Morphy, *Murphy*
Morpurgo
Morpuss, *Malpas*
Morrall, *Morrell*
Morrel, *Morrell*
Morrell
Morren, *Moore*
Morres, *Moorhouse*
Morrice, *Morris*
Morrill, *Morrell*
Morrin, *Moore*
Morrington, *Meriton*
Morris
Morrisey, *Morrissey*
Morrish, *Morris*
Morrison, *Morris*
Morriss, *Morris*
Morrissey
Morrissy, *Morrissey*
Morrough, *Morrow*
Morrow
Morrowson, *McMorrough*
Mörsch, *Marsh*
Mörschner, *Marsh*
Morse, *Morris*
Morss, *Morris*
Mort
Mortagh, *Murdoch*
Mörtel, *Martin*
Mortensen, *Martin*
Morthe, *Marthe*
Mortiboys
Mortimer
Mortimor, *Mortimer*
Mortimore, *Mortimer*
Mortlock
Morton
Morucchio, *Moore*
Morucci, *Moore*
Moruzzi, *Moore*
Mosaiov, *Moses*
Mosayov, *Moses*
Mosby
Mosca, *Mouche*

Moscardi, *Mouche*
Moscardó, *Mouche*
Moscardo, *Mouche*
Moschella, *Mouche*
Moschelli, *Mouche*
Moschetta, *Mouche*
Moschetti, *Mouche*
Moschetto, *Mouche*
Moschi, *Mouche*
Moschin, *Mouche*
Moschini, *Mouche*
Moschino, *Mouche*
Moschitta, *Mouche*
Moschowitsch, *Moses*
Moscolini, *Mouche*
Moscon, *Mouche*
Moscone, *Mouche*
Mosconi, *Mouche*
Moscovici, *Moses*
Moscovicz, *Moses*
Moscovitch, *Moses*
Moscovitz, *Moses*
Moscoviz, *Moses*
Moscowicz, *Moses*
Moscowitz, *Moses*
Mose, *Moses*
Moseev, *Moses*
Moseichev, *Moses*
Moseley
Moselli, *Moses*
Mosello, *Moses*
Moser, *Moss*
Moses
Mosesohn, *Moses*
Mosetti, *Moses*
Mosezon, *Moses*
Moshaiov, *Moses*
Moshaiow, *Moses*
Moshayof, *Moses*
Moshayov, *Moses*
Moshcovitch, *Moses*
Moshcovitz, *Moses*
Moshe, *Moses*
Moshes, *Moses*
Mosheshvili, *Moses*
Mosheshvily, *Moses*
Moshevitch, *Moses*
Moshevitz, *Moses*
Mosheyoff, *Moses*
Mosheyov, *Moses*
Moshkovich, *Moses*
Moshkovitch, *Moses*
Moshkovitz, *Moses*
Moshkoviz, *Moses*
Moshkowich, *Moses*
Moshkowitz, *Moses*
Mosichev, *Moses*
Mosienko, *Moses*
Moskovic, *Moses*
Moskovich, *Moses*
Moskovici, *Moses*
Moskovics, *Moses*
Moskovicz, *Moses*
Moskovitch, *Moses*
Moskovits, *Moses*
Moskovitz, *Moses*
Moskowich, *Moses*
Moskowics, *Moses*
Moskowicz, *Moses*
Moskowitch, *Moses*
Moskowits, *Moses*
Moskowitz, *Moses*
Moskowski
Moskowsky, *Moskowski*
Mösl, *Moss*
Mosley, *Moseley*
Moss
Mossberg, *Moss*
Mosse, *Moses, Moss*
Mossesohn, *Moses*
Mossman, *Moss*
Mössmer, *Mesner*
Mössner, *Mesner*
Mösst, *Most*
Möst, *Most*
Most
Mostert, *Most*
Mostinck, *Most*
Mosyagin, *Moses*
Moszkovicz, *Moses*
Moszkowicz, *Moses*
Mota, *Motte*
Mote, *Motte*
Motel
Motelsohn, *Motel*
Motet, *Motte*
Mothe, *Motte*
Mothersill, *Mothersole*
Mothersole
Motier, *Motte*
Motion
Mott, *Motte*
Motta, *Motte*
Motte
Mottershead
Mottet, *Motte*
Mottier, *Motte*
Mottinelli, *James*
Mottini, *James*
Mottishead, *Mottershead*
Motto, *James*
Motton, *Motte*
Motton, *Mutton*
Mottram
Mouat, *Mowat*
Mouatt, *Mowat*
Moubray, *Mowbray*
Moucha, *Mukhin*
Mouche
Mouchel, *Mouche*
Mouchelet, *Mouche*
Mouchet, *Mouche*
Mouchez, *Mouche*
Mouchot, *Mouche*
Mouchotte, *Mouche*
Moudrý, *Mędrzak*
Mouet, *Moët*
Mouez, *Moët*
Mougel, *Dominique*
Mougenel, *Dominique*
Mougeot, *Dominique*
Mouget, *Dominique*
Mough, *Maw*
Moughan, *Mohan*
Moughane, *Mohan*
Mougin, *Dominique*
Mould, *Moult*
Moulding, *Moult*
Moulds, *Moult*
Moule, *Moult, Mule*
Moulin, *Mill*
Moulineau, *Mill*
Mouliner, *Miller*
Moulinet, *Mill*
Moulinier, *Miller*
Moulinot, *Mill*
Moulins, *Mill*
Moull, *Moult*
Moullin, *Mill*
Moulson, *Moult*
Moult
Moulton
Mouncey, *Mounsey*
Mounic, *Hammond*
Mounié, *Miller*
Mounier, *Miller*
Mounsey
Mounsie, *Mounsey*
Mount, *Mont*
Mountain, *Montagne*
Mountbatten
Mounter, *Mont*
Mountford
Mountfort, *Montfort*
Mountney
Mouque, *Mouche*
Mouquet, *Mouche*
Mouré, *Moore*
Moureau, *Morrell*
Moureaux, *Morrell*
Mourek, *Morris*
Mourer, *Mora*
Mouret, *Moore*
Mourier, *Mora*
Mouriès, *Mora*
Mouriez, *Mora*
Mourin, *Moore*
Mouritsen, *Morris*
Mouritzen, *Morris*
Mourlot, *Morrell*
Mouro, *Moore*
Mourot, *Moore*
Mousley, *Moseley*
Moussaieff, *Moses*
Moustardier, *Mustard*
Moutard, *Mustard*
Moutardier, *Mustard*
Moutenet, *Mutton*
Mouthenet, *Mutton*
Mouthenot, *Mutton*
Mouthon, *Mutton*
Moutinho
Mouton, *Mutton*
Moutonneau, *Mutton*
Moutonnet, *Mutton*
Moutonnier, *Mutton*
Moutou, *Mutton*
Movesian, *Moses*
Mowat
Mowatt, *Mowat*
Mowbray
Mowbury, *Mowbray*
Mowe, *Maw*
Mowen, *Mohan*
Mower
Mowl, *Mule*
Mowle, *Mule*
Mowles, *Mule*
Moxham, *Magg*
Moxom, *Magg*
Moxon, *Magg*
Moxsom, *Magg*
Moxson, *Magg*
Moyà, *Moyano*
Moyano
Moyce, *Moses*
Moyes, *Moses*
Moylan, *Mullen*
Moylane, *Mullen*
Moyle
Moynan, *Moynihan*
Moynard, *Monk*
Moyne, *Monk*
Moynet, *Monk*
Moynihan
Moynot, *Monk*
Moyse, *Moses*
Moyses, *Moses*
Mozart
Moze, *Moses*
Mozes, *Moses*
Mozet, *Mozart*
Mozo
Mozzetti, *James*
Mozzi, *James*
Mozzini, *James*
Mráček
Mráz, *Mróz*
Mrázek, *Mróz*
Mrkić, *Marchewa*
Mrkvička, *Marchewa*
Mroczek, *Mráček*
Mroczkowski, *Mráček*
Mrówczyński, *Mrówka*
Mrowiński, *Mrówka*
Mrówka
Mróz
Mrozek, *Mróz*
Mrożewski, *Mróz*
Mroziński, *Mróz*
Mrozowicz, *Mróz*
Mrozowski, *Mróz*
Mucci, *James*
Muccino, *James*
Much, *Mutch*
Mucha, *Mukhin*
Mucillo, *James*
Muckle, *Meikle*
Mucklejohn, *Meiklejohn*
Mucklow
Mudd
Muddeman, *Moody*
Muddiman, *Moody*
Mudge, *Magg*
Mudr, *Mędrzak*
Mudra, *Mędrzak*
Muehl, *Mill*
Muehlbauer, *Mill*
Muehlrad, *Mill*
Muela
Muelas, *Muela*
Mueller, *Miller*
Muff, *Maw*
Muffatt, *Moffatt*
Muffett, *Moffatt*
Muggeridge
Muggridge, *Muggeridge*
Mugnai, *Miller*
Mugnaini, *Miller*
Mugnaro, *Miller*
Mugnerot, *Miller*
Mugnier, *Miller*
Mugniot, *Miller*
Mugnot, *Miller*
Mugridge, *Muggeridge*
Mühl, *Mill*
Muhl, *Maul, Mill*
Mühle, *Mill, Maul*
Muhlke, *Maul*
Muhr, *Moore*
Mührer, *Maurer*
Mührmann, *Maurer*
Muir
Muirhead
Muis, *Maus*
Mukhin

Mulà, *Muela*
Mulard, *Mule*
Mularski, *Maurer*
Mulatier, *Mule*
Mulberry, *Mowbray*
Mulbery, *Mowbray*
Mulbry, *Mowbray*
Mulcahy
Mulcaster, *Muncaster*
Mulcreevy
Mulder, *Miller*
Mulders, *Miller*
Muldon, *Muldoon*
Muldoon
Muldowney, *Moloney*
Mule
Mulero, *Mule*
Mulet, *Mule*
Mulfaul, *Lavelle*
Mulgan, *Milligan*
Mulgrew, *Mulcreevy*
Mulgroo, *Mulcreevy*
Mulgrue, *Mulcreevy*
Mulhall
Mulhane, *Mullen*
Mulhern
Mulholland
Mulier, *Mule*
Mulin, *Mule*
Mulinari, *Miller*
Mulini, *Mill*
Mulino, *Mill*
Mulkern, *Mulhern*
Mulkerns, *Mulhern*
Mulkerrin, *Mulhern*
Mullagan, *Milligan*
Mullaley, *Mullally*
Mullally
Mullaly, *Mullally*
Mullan, *Mullen*
Mullane, *Mullen*
Mullarkey
Mulldowney, *Moloney*
Mullen
Mullens, *Mullen*
Müller, *Miller*
Muller, *Miller*
Mullet, *Mule*
Mullett, *Mule*
Mulligan, *Milligan*
Mullikin, *Milligan*
Mullin, *Mullen*
Mullinacci, *Mill*
Mullinar, *Mullen*
Mullindar, *Mullen*
Mulliner, *Mullen*
Mullinger, *Mullen*
Mullings, *Mullen*
Mullins, *Mullen*
Mullis
Müllner, *Miller*
Mullon, *Mullen*
Mulloney, *Moloney*
Mullowney, *Moloney*
Mulloy, *Molloy*
Mullveen, *Melvin*
Mulqueen
Mulran, *Mulryan*
Mulrine, *Mulryan*
Mulroney, *Moroney*
Mulrooney, *Moroney*
Mulroy
Mulryan
Mulryne, *Mulryan*
Multer, *Malter*
Mulvaney
Mulvany, *Mulvaney*
Mulveen, *Melvin*
Mulvenna, *Mulvaney*
Mulvey
Mulvihil, *Melville*
Mulvihill, *Melville*
Mulvin, *Melvin*
Mulyar, *Maurer*
Mulzer, *Malter*
Mumbray, *Mowbray*
Mumby
Mumford, *Mountford*
Mummen, *Mommsen*
Mummery, *Mowbray*
Mummsen, *Mommsen*
Munaretti, *Miller*
Munaretto, *Miller*
Munari, *Miller*
Munarin, *Miller*
Munarini, *Miller*
Muncaster
Münch, *Monk*
Munch, *Monk*
Munchay, *Mounsey*
Muncie, *Mounsey*
Munck, *Monk*
Munday, *Monday*
Munden
Mundford, *Mountford*
Mundy, *Monday*
Muneron, *Miller*
Munerotto, *Miller*
Munford, *Mountford*
Municio
Munier, *Miller*
Muñiz, *Muño*
Münk, *Monk*
Munk, *Monk*
Munkki, *Monk*
Munkman, *Monk*
Munks, *Monk*
Munn, *Moon*
Munné, *Miller*
Munnelly
Münnich, *Monk*
Munns, *Moon*
Muño
Muñoz, *Muño*
Munro
Munroe, *Munro*
Munrow, *Munro*
Muns, *Mont*
Munsey, *Mounsey*
Munson, *Moon*
Munt, *Mont*
Muntané, *Montaner*
Munté, *Montero*
Munteanu, *Montagne*
Münter, *Minter*
Muntze, *Minter*
Munz, *Minter*
Munze, *Minter*
Münzer, *Minter*
Munzer, *Minter*
Mur, *Muro*
Mura, *Mora*
Murat
Muratet, *Murat*
Murchan, *Morgan*
Murchie, *McMorrough*
Murchison, *McMorrough*
Murcia
Murciano, *Murcia*
Murdoch
Murdock, *Murdoch*
Murdough, *Murdoch*
Murdow, *Murdoch*
Murdy, *Murdoch*
Mure, *Muir*
Murgatroyd
Muriel, *Muro*
Murillo, *Muro*
Murkin, *Morgan*
Murnane
Muro
Murphy
Murray
Murrell, *Merrill*
Murrells, *Merrill*
Murrey, *Murray*
Murrie, *Murray*
Murril, *Merrill*
Murrill, *Morrell*
Murroney, *Moroney*
Murrough, *Morrow*
Murrow, *Morrow*
Murry, *Murray*
Murta, *Murdoch*
Murtha, *Murdoch*
Murtimer, *Mortimer*
Murton
Musaev, *Moses*
Musaiov, *Moses*
Musayov, *Moses*
Musca, *Mouche*
Muscas, *Mouche*
Muselli, *James*
Muser, *Maus*
Musgrave
Musgrove, *Musgrave*
Musiał
Musiałek, *Musiał*
Musiałowicz, *Musiał*
Musiałowski, *Musiał*
Musil, *Musiał*
Musílek, *Musiał*
Musin, *Moses*
Musnier, *Miller*
Mussaioff, *Moses*
Musset
Mussetti, *James*
Mussettini, *James*
Mussilli, *James*
Mussillon, *Musset*
Musso, *James*
Mussolini
Musson
Mussot, *Musset*
Mussotti, *James*
Mustard
Mustart, *Mustard*
Mustert, *Most*
Musto, *Mustoe*
Mustoe
Mustonen
Mustow, *Mustoe*
Muszinsky, *Mukhin*
Muszyński, *Mukhin*
Mutch
Mutterperl, *Pearl*
Mutton
Muys, *Maus*
Muzaev, *Moses*
Mužík
Muzzi, *James*
Muzzillo, *James*
Muzzini, *James*
Muzzolo, *James*
Muzzullo, *James*
Myadzvedzki, *Medvedev*
Myall, *Myhill*
Myasnikov
Myatt
Myddleton, *Middleton*
Myers, *Mayer*
Myerscough
Myhill
Mykyta, *Nikitin*
Myles, *Miles*
Mynn, *Minn*
Myott, *Myatt*
Myslivec
Myslivećek, *Myslivec*
Myszka, *Maus*
Myszkorowski, *Maus*
Myszkowski, *Maus*
Myton
Mytton, *Myton*

N

Naatz, *Ignace*
Nabais
Nabarro, *Navarro*
Näbeling, *Nieblich*
Naber, *Neighbour*
Nabier, *Neape*
Nabokov
Nabuhr, *Neighbour*
Nabur, *Neighbour*
Nacci, *John*
Nacewicz, *Ignace*
Nachbar, *Neighbour*
Nachbauer, *Neighbour*
Nachbaur, *Neighbour*
Nachbur, *Neighbour*
Nachimovski, *Nahum*
Nachimson, *Nahum*
Nachimzon, *Nahum*
Nachman, *Nachmann*
Nachmani, *Nachmann*
Nachmann
Nachmanovici, *Nachmann*
Nachmanovitz, *Nachmann*
Nachmanowitz, *Nachmann*
Nachmanson, *Nachmann*
Nachmany, *Nachmann*
Nachminovici, *Nachmann*
Nachminovitch, *Nachmann*
Nachtergael, *Nightingale*
Nachtigal, *Nightingale*
Nachtigall, *Nightingale*
Nachumovsky, *Nahum*
Nadal, *Noel*
Nadali, *Noel*
Nadau, *Noel*
Nadaud, *Noel*
Nadel, *Nadler*
Nadelman, *Nadler*
Nadelstecher, *Nadler*
Nadelstern, *Nadler*
Nadelstock, *Nadler*
Näder, *Näher*
Nader, *Näher*
Nadin, *Noel*
Nadler
Nadot, *Noel*
Nádvorník
Naesmith, *Naysmith*

Näf, *Neve*
Naftali
Naftalin, *Naftali*
Naftalis, *Naftali*
Naftalison, *Naftali*
Naftalovici, *Naftali*
Naftaly, *Naftali*
Nafthalie, *Naftali*
Naftolin, *Naftali*
Naftulin, *Naftali*
Naftulis, *Naftali*
Nafz
Nafzer, *Nafz*
Nafzger, *Nafz*
Nagar
Nagari, *Nagar*
Nagarin, *Nagar*
Nägel, *Naylor*
Nagel, *Naylor*
Nagelberg, *Naylor*
Nägele, *Naylor*
Nagelmacher, *Naylor*
Nagelmaeker, *Naylor*
Nagelmaekers, *Naylor*
Nagelmaker, *Naylor*
Nagelmakers, *Naylor*
Nagelschmidt, *Naylor*
Nagelsmit, *Naylor*
Nagelstein, *Naylor*
Näger, *Näher*
Nager, *Nagar*
Naggar, *Nagar*
Naghten, *Naughton*
Nagle, *Nangle*
Nagler, *Naylor*
Nagtegaal, *Nightingale*
Nagy
Näher
Nahimson, *Nahum*
Nahl, *Naylor*
Nähler, *Naylor*
Nahman, *Nachmann*
Nahmani, *Nachmann*
Nahmany, *Nachmann*
Nahum
Nahumi, *Nahum*
Nahumovsky, *Nahum*
Nahumson, *Nahum*
Nain, *Neame*
Nairn
Nairne, *Nairn*
Naisbet, *Nisbit*
Naisbit, *Nisbit*
Naisbitt, *Nisbit*
Naish, *Nash*
Naismith, *Naysmith*
Najman, *Newman*
Nakhumovich, *Nahum*
Nalder
Naldi, *Naud*
Naldini, *Naud*
Naldone, *Naud*
Naldrett, *Nalder*
Nallini, *Naud*
Nally, *McNally*
Nanard, *Neame*
Nancarrow
Naneau, *Neame*
Naneix, *Neame*
Nanelli, *John*
Nanet, *Neame*
Nangle
Nani, *John*
Nanin, *Neame*
Nankervis
Nankivell
Nanne
Nanneke, *Nanne*
Nannen, *Nanne*
Nannetti, *John*
Nanni, *John*
Nanning, *Nanne*
Nanninga, *Nanne*
Nannini, *John*
Nannizzi, *John*
Nannoni, *John*
Nannuzzi, *John*
Nanot, *Neame*
Nansen, *Nanne*
Nanuccio, *John*
Naper, *Napier*
Napier
Napleton, *Appleton*
Napoleoni
Napoletano, *Napoli*
Napoli
Napolioni, *Napoleoni*
Napolitano, *Napoli*
Napper, *Napier*
Nápravník
Naquard, *Naquet*
Naquet
Naquin, *Naquet*
Narangi, *Naranjo*
Naranjo
Narciso
Nardeau, *Nardi*
Nardelli, *Nardi*
Nardello, *Nardi*
Nardet, *Nardi*
Nardi
Nardiello, *Nardi*
Nardin, *Nardi*
Nardini, *Nardi*
Nardo, *Nardi*
Nardon, *Nardi*
Nardone, *Nardi*
Nardoni, *Bernard, Nardi*
Nardonneau, *Nardi*
Nardou, *Nardi*
Nardoux, *Nardi*
Narducci, *Nardi*
Nardulli, *Nardi*
Narduzzi, *Nardi*
Nari, *January*
Narkis, *Narciso*
Narkiss, *Narciso*
Narracott, *Northcott*
Narrour, *Arcas*
Nascimento
Nash
Nasi, *John*
Naslednikov
Nasmith, *Naysmith*
Nasmyth, *Naysmith*
Nassau
Nassi, *John*
Nast
Nastagi, *Anstice*
Nastase, *Anstice*
Nastasi, *Anstice*
Nasti, *Anstice*
Nastić, *Anstice*
Natale, *Noel*
Natali, *Noel*
Natan, *Nathan*
Natanov, *Nathan*
Natans, *Nathan*
Natansohn, *Nathan*
Natanson, *Nathan*
Natanzon, *Nathan*
Natenzon, *Nathan*
Näter, *Näher*
Nathan
Nathans, *Nathan*
Nathansen, *Nathan*
Nathansohn, *Nathan*
Nathanson, *Nathan*
Nathanzon, *Nathan*
Näthbom, *Nutt*
Näther, *Näher*
Nather, *Näher*
Nation, *Nathan*
Natten, *Naughton*
Natton, *Naughton*
Natz, *Ignace*
Nauber, *Neubauer*
Nauck, *Novák*
Naucke, *Novák*
Naud
Naude, *Naud*
Naudet, *Naud*
Naudin, *Naud*
Naudon, *Naud*
Naudot, *Naud*
Naughtan, *Naughton*
Naughten, *Naughton*
Naughton
Naugolnikov
Naujock, *Novák*
Naukamm, *Newcombe*
Nault, *Naud*
Naum, *Nahum*
Nauman, *Newman*
Naumann, *Newman*
Naumchik, *Nahum*
Naumenko, *Nahum*
Naumov, *Nahum*
Naumović, *Nahum*
Naumshin, *Nahum*
Naumychev, *Nahum*
Nava
Navaro, *Navarro*
Navarre, *Navarro*
Navarrete
Navarro
Navas, *Nava*
Navàs
Navier, *Neape*
Navière, *Neape*
Naville, *Neville*
Navin, *Nevin*
Navrátil
Navumchik, *Nahum*
Navumenko, *Nahum*
Navumov, *Nahum*
Nawrocki
Nawrot, *Nawrocki*
Nay, *Nye*
Naybour, *Neighbour*
Naylar, *Naylor*
Nayldor, *Nadler*
Nayler, *Naylor*
Naylor
Naysmith
Nazaire
Nazari, *Nazaire*
Nazarian, *Nazaire*
Nazarov, *Nazaire*
Nazarski, *Nazaire*
Nazartsev, *Nazaire*
Nazaryev, *Nazaire*
Nazaryevykh, *Nazaire*
Nazzari, *Nazaire*
Nazzaro, *Nazaire*
Neachell, *Etchells*
Neagle, *Nangle*
Neal
Neale, *Neal*
Neall, *Neal*
Nealon, *Neil*
Neame
Neander, *Newman*
Neape
Neary
Neat
Neate, *Neat*
Neave, *Neve*
Neaves, *Neve*
Nebe, *Neve*
Nebeling, *Nieblich*
Nébodon, *Neveu*
Nebot, *Neveu*
Nebout, *Neveu*
Nebulone, *Napoleoni*
Nebuloni, *Napoleoni*
Nechells, *Etchells*
Neddermann, *Nieder*
Neder, *Näher*
Nedergaard, *Nedergård*
Nedergård
Nedham, *Needham*
Nedvěd, *Medvedev*
Nee
Neebe, *Neve*
Need
Needham
Needle, *Nadler*
Needler, *Nadler*
Neef, *Neve*
Neeff, *Neve*
Neefken, *Neve*
Neefs, *Neve*
Neegaard, *Nedergård*
Neegård, *Nedergård*
Neel, *Neil*
Neelan, *Neil*
Neeland, *Neil*
Neelands, *Neil*
Neeld, *Neil*
Neelder, *Nadler*
Neele, *Neil*
Neelis, *McNelis*
Neels, *Corneille, Neil*
Neely, *McNeilly*
Neenan, *Noonan*
Neep, *Neape*
Neerman, *Nieder*
Nees, *Annis*
Neese, *Annis*
Neesen, *Annis*
Neeson, *McNeice*
Neeve, *Neve*
Neeven, *Neve*
Neeves, *Neve*
Neff, *Neve*
Neffe, *Neve*
Nefgen, *Neve*
Nefimanov, *Yefimov*
Nefimonov, *Yefimov*
Nefzger, *Nafz*
Negel, *Naylor*
Neger, *Näher*
Negeris, *Näher*
Negrato, *Noir*
Nègre, *Noir*

Negrea, *Noir*
Negreanu, *Noir*
Negrel, *Noir*
Negrelli, *Noir*
Negrello, *Noir*
Negresco, *Noir*
Negri, *Noir*
Negrin, *Noir*
Negrini, *Noir*
Negrino, *Noir*
Negro, *Noir*
Negron, *Noir*
Negrone, *Noir*
Negroni, *Noir*
Negrotto, *Noir*
Negru, *Noir*
Negus
Negustor, *Negus*
Neher, *Näher*
Nehl, *Corneille*
Nehls, *Corneille*
Nehlsen, *Corneille*
Nehse, *Annis*
Neier, *Näher*
Neiger, *Näher*
Neighbour
Neijman, *Newman*
Neil
Neilan, *Neil*
Neiland, *Neil*
Neilane, *Neil*
Neild, *Neil*
Neilder, *Nadler*
Neill, *Neil*
Neilly, *McNeilly*
Neilson, *Neil*
Neising, *Dennis*
Neison, *McNeice*
Neissen, *Dennis*
Neisson, *McNeice*
Nejedlý
Nekhlyudov, *Nekludov*
Nekludov
Nekola, *Nekolný*
Nekolný
Nekrashevich, *Nekrasov*
Nekrasov
Nekula, *Nekolný*
Nel, *Nell*
Nelan, *Neil*
Nelane, *Neil*
Nelder, *Nadler*
Neldrett, *Nalder*
Neles, *Corneille*
Nelis, *Corneille*
Nelissen, *Corneille*
Nelius, *Corneille*
Neljes, *Corneille*
Nell, *Corneille*
Nell
Nelle, *Corneille*
Nellen, *Corneille*
Nellies, *Corneille*
Nelmes, *Elm*
Nelms, *Elm*
Nelsen, *Neil*
Nelson
Nemchinov
Němec, *Nemchinov*
Němeček, *Nemchinov*
Nemes
Német, *Nemchinov*
Németh, *Nemchinov*
Nemmock, *Nimmo*
Nemo, *Nimmo*
Nemtsev, *Nemchinov*
Nencetti, *Lawrence*
Nenci, *Lawrence*
Nencini, *Lawrence*
Nencioli, *Lawrence*
Nenciolini, *Lawrence*
Nencioni, *Lawrence*
Nenneke, *Nanne*
Nepveu, *Neveu*
Nérat, *Noir*
Néraud, *Noir*
Néré, *Noir*
Néreau, *Noir*
Néret, *Noir*
Neretti, *Noir*
Nerhenny, *McNairn*
Neri, *Noir*
Nerini, *Noir*
Nerisson, *Noir*
Nerny, *McNairn*
Nero, *Noir*
Néron, *Noir*
Nerone, *Noir*
Neroni, *Noir*
Nérot, *Noir*
Nerozzi, *Noir*
Nerucci, *Noir*
Nerud, *Neruda*
Neruda
Nesbit, *Nisbit*
Nesbitt, *Nisbit*
Nesen, *Annis*
Nešić, *Nesterov*
Nešković, *Nesterov*
Nešović, *Nesterov*
Ness
Nesterin, *Nesterov*
Nesterov
Nesti, *Ernst*
Nestle, *Nast*
Nestlé, *Nast*
Nestorović, *Nesterov*
Neter, *Näher*
Netheler, *Nadler*
Nether, *Näher*
Nethercott
Netherton
Netherwood
Nethler, *Nadler*
Neto, *Nieto*
Netter, *Näher*
Netterman, *Näher*
Netti, *John*
Nettlefield, *Nettlefold*
Nettlefold
Nettleton
Neu, *New*
Neubauer
Neuber, *Neubauer*
Neubert, *Neubauer*
Neufville, *Neville*
Neuhaus, *Newhouse*
Neuhauser, *Newhouse*
Neukamm, *Newcombe*
Neukomm, *Newcombe*
Neuman, *Newman*
Neumann, *Newman*
Neuper, *Neubauer*
Neupert, *Neubauer*
Neuville, *Neville*
Neužil
Nevado
Nevalainen
Neve
Neveling, *Nieblich*
Neven, *Neve, Nevin*
Neves, *Nieves*
Nevet, *Knight*
Neveu
Neveux, *Neveu*
Nevile, *Neville*
Nevill, *Neville*
Neville
Nevin
Nevins, *Nevin*
Nevinson, *Nevin*
Nevison, *Nevin*
Nevitt, *Knight*
Nevoux, *Neveu*
New
Newall
Neway, *Newey*
Newbald, *Newbold*
Newberry
Newbery, *Newberry*
Newbold
Newbolt, *Newbold*
Newborough, *Newberry*
Newbould, *Newbold*
Newboult, *Newbold*
Newbrough, *Newberry*
Newburgh, *Newberry*
Newbury, *Newberry*
Newby
Newcombe
Newcome, *Newcombe*
Newcomen, *Newcombe*
Newell, *Neville*
Newey
Newham
Newhouse
Newill, *Neville*
Newing, *New*
Newland
Newlands, *Newland*
Newman
Newnham, *Newham*
Newport
Newsam, *Newsome*
Newsham, *Newsome*
Newsholme, *Newsome*
Newsom, *Newsome*
Newsome
Newson, *New, Newsome*
Newstead
Newsum, *Newsome*
Newton
Ney, *New, Nye*
Neye, *New*
Neyge, *New*
Neylan, *Neil*
Neyland, *Neil*
Neylane, *Neil*
Neylon, *Neil*
Neyman, *Newman*
Neyrat, *Noir*
Neyraud, *Noir*
Neyret, *Noir*
Neyron, *Noir*
Neyroud, *Noir*
Niall, *Neil*
Niblett
Niccola, *Nicholas*
Niccolai, *Nicholas*
Niccoli, *Nicholas*
Niccolini, *Nicholas*
Niccolo, *Nicholas*
Niccols, *Nicholas*
Niccolucci, *Nicholas*
Nice
Nichol, *Nicholas*
Nicholas
Nicholds, *Nicholas*
Nicholes, *Nicholas*
Nicholetts, *Nicholas*
Nicholl, *Nicholas*
Nicholls, *Nicholas*
Nichols, *Nicholas*
Nicholson, *Nicholas*
Nick, *Nicholas*
Nickal, *Nicholas*
Nickalls, *Nicholas*
Nickel, *Nicholas*
Nickeleit, *Nicholas*
Nickell, *Nicholas*
Nickells, *Nicholas*
Nickels, *Nicholas*
Nickelsen, *Nicholas*
Nickerson, *Nicholas*
Nickes, *Nicholas*
Nickinson, *Nicholas*
Nickisch, *Nicholas*
Nickisson, *Nicholas*
Nickl, *Nicholas*
Nicklas, *Nicholas*
Nicklassen, *Nicholas*
Nicklaus, *Nicholas*
Nickle, *Nicholas*
Nickleson, *Nicholas*
Nickless, *Nicholas*
Nicklin, *Nicholas*
Nicklisch, *Nicholas*
Nickman, *Nicholas*
Nickol, *Nicholas*
Nickolaus, *Nicholas*
Nickolds, *Nicholas*
Nickoles, *Nicholas*
Nickolls, *Nicholas*
Nickols, *Nicholas*
Nicks, *Nicholas*
Nicksch, *Nicholas*
Nickson, *Nixon*
Nickusch, *Nicholas*
Niclas, *Nicholas*
Niclasen, *Nicholas*
Niclaus, *Nicholas*
Niclausse, *Nicholas*
Niclot, *Nicholas*
Nicloux, *Nicholas*
Nicogossian, *Nicholas*
Nicol, *Nicholas*
Nicola, *Nicholas*
Nicolae, *Nicholas*
Nicolaï, *Nicholas*
Nicolai, *Nicholas*
Nicolaides, *Nicholas*
Nicolaie, *Nicholas*
Nicolaisen, *Nicholas*
Nicolajsen, *Nicholas*
Nicolao, *Nicholas*
Nicolaou, *Nicholas*
Nicolás, *Nicholas*
Nicolas, *Nicholas*
Nicolassen, *Nicholas*
Nicolau, *Nicholas*
Nicoleit, *Nicholas*
Nicolescu, *Nicholas*
Nicolet, *Nicholas*
Nicoletti, *Nicholas*
Nicoli, *Nicholas*
Nicolin, *Nicholas*

Nicolini, *Nicholas*
Nicoll, *Nicholas*
Nicollet, *Nicholas*
Nicolli, *Nicholas*
Nicollic, *Nicholas*
Nicolls, *Nicholas*
Nicolo, *Nicholas*
Nicolou, *Nicholas*
Nicolovius, *Nicholas*
Nicolson, *Nicholas*
Nicolucci, *Nicholas*
Nicolussi, *Nicholas*
Nicora, *Nicholas*
Nicorelli, *Nicholas*
Nicorini, *Nicholas*
Nicou, *Nicholas*
Nicoud, *Nicholas*
Nicoux, *Nicholas*
Niculescu, *Nicholas*
Nie, *Nye*
Nieber, *Neubauer*
Nieblich
Nieblig, *Nieblich*
Niebling, *Nieblich*
Niebuhr, *Neubauer*
Niebur, *Neubauer*
Nieddu, *Noir*
Nieder
Niederer, *Nieder*
Niederman, *Nieder*
Niedermann, *Nieder*
Niederst, *Nieder*
Niedzielski
Niedźwiecki, *Medvedev*
Niedzwiecki, *Medvedev*
Niedzwiedz, *Medvedev*
Niedźwiedzki, *Medvedev*
Niel, *Neil*
Nield, *Neil*
Niell, *Neil*
Nielsen, *Neil*
Nielson, *Neil*
Nielsson, *Neil*
Nieman, *Newman*
Niemann, *Newman*
Niembsch, *Nemchinov*
Niemcewicz, *Nemchinov*
Niemchenok, *Nemchinov*
Niemczyk, *Nemchinov*
Niemetz, *Nemchinov*
Niemi, *Nieminen*
Niemic, *Nemchinov*
Niemiec, *Nemchinov*
Niemilä, *Nieminen*
Nieminen
Niemitz, *Nemchinov*
Niemocow, *Nemchinov*
Niemsch, *Nemchinov*
Niemtchik, *Nemchinov*
Niemtschke, *Nemchinov*
Nier, *Noir*
Nierenberg
Niermann, *Nieder*
Nies, *Dennis*
Niese, *Dennis*
Niesel, *Dennis*
Niesen, *Annis*
Niesewand, *Nieswand*
Niesewandt, *Nieswand*
Niesgen, *Dennis*
Niesing, *Dennis*
Niess, *Dennis*
Niessen, *Dennis*
Nieswand
Nieswandt, *Nieswand*
Nieto
Nietschmann, *Nicholas*
Nietzsche, *Nicholas*
Nietzschold, *Nicholas*
Nieves
Niewiadomski
Niewiarowski
Niezen, *Dennis*
Niezold, *Nicholas*
Nige, *New*
Nigel
Nigg, *Nicholas*
Niggl, *Nicholas*
Niggli, *Nicholas*
Nightingale
Nightingall, *Nightingale*
Nighton, *Knighton*
Nigrelli, *Noir*
Nigrello, *Noir*
Nigri, *Noir*
Nigriello, *Noir*
Nigris, *Noir*
Nigro, *Noir*
Nihell, *Neil*
Nihill, *Neil*
Nijman, *Newman*
Nijns, *John*
Nijs, *Dennis*
Nijssen, *Dennis*
Nikashin, *Nicholas*
Nikčević, *Nicholas*
Nikić, *Nicholas*
Nikiforov
Nikishov, *Nikitin*
Nikitaev, *Nikitin*
Nikitenko, *Nikitin*
Nikitin
Nikitnikov, *Nikitin*
Nikityuk, *Nikitin*
Niklasson, *Nicholas*
Niklaus, *Nicholas*
Nikodém
Nikolaev, *Nicholas*
Nikolaevski, *Nicholas*
Nikolaishvili, *Nicholas*
Nikolajević, *Nicholas*
Nikolajewski, *Nicholas*
Nikolajewsky, *Nicholas*
Nikolajsen, *Nicholas*
Nikolaus, *Nicholas*
Nikolayevski, *Nicholas*
Nikoleishivili, *Nicholas*
Nikoleishvili, *Nicholas*
Nikolić, *Nicholas*
Nikolodze, *Nicholas*
Nikolov, *Nicholas*
Nikolyukin, *Nicholas*
Nikšić, *Nicholas*
Nikulin, *Nicholas*
Nilan, *Neil*
Niland, *Neil*
Niles, *Neil*
Nilges, *Corneille*
Nillane, *Neil*
Nilles, *Corneille*
Nilon, *Neil*
Nilson, *Neil*
Nilsson, *Neil*
Nimchenko, *Nemchinov*
Nimchuk, *Nemchinov*
Nimitz, *Nemchinov*
Nimmo
Nimzowitz, *Nemchinov*
Ninio, *Niño*
Ninni, *John*
Ninnis, *Innes*
Ninnoli, *John*
Nino, *Niño*
Niño
Ninotti, *John*
Ninyo, *Niño*
Niper, *Neubauer*
Nipper, *Neubauer*
Nirenberg, *Nierenberg*
Nirnberg, *Nierenberg*
Nirney, *McNairn*
Nisan, *Nissen*
Nisanov, *Nissen*
Nisard, *Dennis*
Nisbaum, *Nutt*
Nisbet, *Nisbit*
Nisbit
Nisboim, *Nutt*
Nisel, *Nissen*
Niselevich, *Nissen*
Niselovitz, *Nissen*
Nisen, *Dennis*
Nisenbaum, *Nutt*
Nisenboim, *Nutt*
Nisenzon, *Nissen*
Niset, *Dennis*
Nish, *Angus*
Nisius, *Dennis*
Nislbaum, *Nutt*
Nisot, *Dennis*
Nissan, *Nissen*
Nissani, *Nissen*
Nissanov, *Nissen*
Nissany, *Nissen*
Nissbaum, *Nutt*
Nissel, *Nissen*
Nisselbaum, *Nutt*
Nissen
Nissenbaum, *Nutt*
Nissensohn, *Nissen*
Nissenson, *Nissen*
Nissle, *Dennis*
Nissnbaum, *Nutt*
Nitsche, *Nicholas*
Nitscher, *Nicholas*
Nitschke, *Nicholas*
Nitschker, *Nicholas*
Nitschmann, *Nicholas*
Nitschold, *Nicholas*
Nitti, *John*
Nitto, *Bennett*
Nitzsche, *Nicholas*
Nitzschke, *Nicholas*
Nitzschmann, *Nicholas*
Niuwemann, *Newman*
Niven, *Nevin*
Nix, *Nicholas*
Nixon
Nixson, *Nixon*
Nizard, *Dennis*
Nizet, *Dennis*
Nizot, *Dennis*
Noä, *Noy*
Noach, *Noy*
Noad, *Noade*
Noade
Noades, *Noade*
Noah, *Noy*
Noak, *Noake*
Noake
Noakes, *Noake*
Noaks, *Noake*
Nobb
Nobbs, *Nobb*
Nobel, *Nobelius*
Nobelius
Nobels, *Noble*
Nobes, *Nobb*
Nobile, *Noble*
Nobili, *Noble*
Noble
Nobles, *Noble*
Noblet, *Noblett*
Noblett
Noblini, *Noblett*
Noblot, *Noblett*
Nobre, *Noble*
Nocenti, *Innocenti*
Nocentini, *Innocenti*
Nocentino, *Innocenti*
Nochimowski, *Nahum*
Nochtin, *Naughton*
Nock, *Knox, Noake*
Nocke, *Knox*
Nöckl, *Knox*
Nocton, *Naughton*
Nodelman, *Nadler*
Nodes, *Noade*
Noe, *Noy*
Noel
Noellet, *Noel*
Nogal, *Noyer*
Nogales, *Noyer*
Noger, *Noyer*
Nogin
Nogué, *Noyer*
Nogueira, *Noyer*
Noguer, *Noyer*
Noguera, *Noyer*
Nogués, *Noyer*
Noguès, *Noyer*
Noguier, *Noyer*
Noha, *Nogin*
Noháč, *Nogin*
Nohatý, *Nogin*
Nøhr, *North*
Noice, *Noy*
Noir
Noiraud, *Noir*
Noiré, *Noir*
Noireau, *Noir*
Noireault, *Noir*
Noireaut, *Noir*
Noireaux, *Noir*
Noiret, *Noir*
Noirez, *Noir*
Noiron, *Noir*
Noirot, *Noir*
Noirtin, *Noir*
Noise, *Noy*
Noke, *Noake*
Nokes, *Noake*
Nolan
Noland, *Nolan*
Nolde, *Naud*
Nöldeke, *Naud*
Nolder, *Nadler*
Nöldner, *Nadler*
Noldner, *Nadler*
Noldt, *Naud*
Noli, *John*
Nolin, *Bernard*
Nölke, *Naud*
Nölken, *Naud*
Nölker, *Naud*
Noll, *Naud*

Nolleau, *Bernard*
Nollet, *Bernard*
Nolli, *John*
Nöllner, *Nadler*
Nolot, *Bernard*
Nolte, *Naud*
Nolten, *Naud*
Nölting, *Naud*
Nolting, *Naud*
Nonckel, *Uncle*
Noni, *John*
Noon
Noonan
Noone
Noor, *North*
Noorman, *North*
Nopkins, *Nobb*
Nopps, *Nobb*
Nops, *Nobb*
Norberg, *North*
Norbury
Norchard, *Orchard*
Norcott, *Northcott*
Norcross
Norcutt, *Northcott*
Nord, *North*
Nordahl, *North*
Nordberg, *North*
Nordell, *North*
Nordén, *North*
Nordgren, *North*
Nordh, *North*
Nordin, *North*
Nordling, *North*
Nordlöf, *North*
Nordlund, *North*
Nordman, *North*
Nordmann, *North*
Nordmark, *North*
Nordqvist, *North*
Nordström, *North*
Nordvall, *North*
Nordwall, *North*
Norelius, *North*
Norell, *North*
Norén, *North*
Norfolk
Norgaard, *Norgård*
Norgård
Norgren, *North*
Norgrove
Norie, *Norris*
Noriega
Norin, *North*
Norington, *Norrington*
Noriss, *Norris*
Norkett, *Northcott*
Norkutt, *Northcott*
Norlin, *North*
Norling, *North*
Norman
Normand, *Norman*
Normann, *North*
Normant, *Norman*
Noronha
Norrby, *North*
Norregaard, *Norgård*
Norregård, *Norgård*
Norreys, *Norris*
Norrie, *Norris*
Nørring, *North*
Norrington
Norris
Norrish, *Norris*
Norrman, *North*
Norström, *North*
North
Northall
Northcote, *Northcott*
Northcott
Northen, *North*
Northern, *North*
Northey
Northfield
Northington, *Norrington*
Northmore
Northwood, *Norwood*
Norton
Norwood
Nosák, *Nosek*
Nosek
Noskes, *Nathan*
Noskovitz, *Nathan*
Noskowitz, *Nathan*
Noszkes, *Nathan*
Notari, *Nutter*
Notario, *Nutter*
Notaro, *Nutter*
Notbohm, *Nutt*
Noteboom, *Nutt*
Notes, *Nathan*
Nothard, *Nutter*
Nothmann, *Notman*
Notier, *Nutter*
Notkin, *Nathan*
Notkovich, *Nathan*
Notley
Notman
Noto, *John*
Notowitz, *Nathan*
Nott
Nottage
Nottebohm, *Nutt*
Notti, *John*
Nottidge, *Nottage*
Nottier, *Nutter*
Notting, *Nott*
Nottman, *Notman*
Notton
Notts, *Nott*
Nouau, *Noel*
Nouaud, *Noel*
Nouger, *Noyer*
Nougier, *Noyer*
Nouguès, *Noyer*
Nouguier, *Noyer*
Nouhaud, *Noel*
Nourse, *Norris*
Nouveau, *Nuevo*
Nouvel, *Nuevo*
Nouvet, *Nuevo*
Nováček, *Novák*
Novais
Novak, *Novák*
Novák
Novaković, *Novák*
Novakovsky, *Novák*
Novčić, *Novák*
Noveck, *Novák*
Novel, *Nuevo*
Novelli, *Nuevo*
Novello, *Nuevo*
Novic, *Novák*
Novichenko, *Novák*
Novičić, *Novák*
Novick, *Novák*
Novicki, *Novák*
Noviello, *Nuevo*
Novik, *Novák*
Novikoff, *Novák*
Novikov, *Novák*
Novillo, *Nuevo*
Novitzki, *Novák*
Novo, *Nuevo*
Novotný, *Novák*
Nový, *Novák*
Nowack, *Novák*
Nowacki, *Novák*
Nowaczyk, *Novák*
Nowak, *Novák*
Nowakowski, *Novák*
Nowell, *Noel*
Nowers, *Over*
Nowicki, *Novák*
Nowik, *Novák*
Nowill, *Noel*
Nowiński, *Novák*
Nowlan, *Nolan*
Nowles, *Knowles*
Noy
Noyce, *Noy*
Noyer
Noyes, *Noy*
Noyret, *Noir*
Nozzoli, *John*
Nozzolini, *John*
Nucator, *McNucator*
Nuccii, *John*
Nuccitelli, *John*
Nuciotti, *John*
Nücklaus, *Nicholas*
Nudd
Nudel, *Nadler*
Nudelman, *Nadler*
Nudler, *Nadler*
Nuevo
Nugent
Nuhimovsky, *Nahum*
Nukhimovich, *Nahum*
Nulty, *McNulty*
Numan, *Newman*
Nunan, *Noonan*
Nuneham, *Newham*
Nunes, *Nuño*
Núñez, *Nuño*
Nunn
Nunns, *Nunn*
Nuno, *Nuño*
Nuño
Nureev, *Nuriev*
Nurenberg, *Nierenberg*
Nureyev, *Nuriev*
Nuriev
Nurmi
Nurminen, *Nurmi*
Nürnberg, *Nierenberg*
Nurnberg, *Nierenberg*
Nurrish, *Norris*
Nurse, *Norris*
Nusan, *Nathan*
Nusbaum, *Nutt*
Nusboim, *Nutt*
Nuscha, *John*
Nusche, *John*
Nuschke, *John*
Nusen, *Nathan*
Nusenbaum, *Nutt*
Nusilevitz, *Nissen*
Nusinov, *Nathan*
Nusinovitz, *Nathan*
Nusinowitz, *Nathan*
Nusinzon, *Nathan*
Nüss, *Dennis*
Nuss, *Nutt*
Nussbamer, *Nutt*
Nussbaum, *Nutt*
Nussbaumer, *Nutt*
Nussboim, *Nutt*
Nüssen, *Dennis*
Nussenbaum, *Nutt*
Nüssgen, *Dennis*
Nussi, *John*
Nussinov, *Nathan*
Nussinovitz, *Nathan*
Nusynowicz, *Nathan*
Nusynowitz, *Nathan*
Nuta, *Nathan*
Nuthall, *Nuttall*
Nuti, *Benvenuti*
Nutin, *Nathan*
Nutini, *Benvenuti*
Nutkevitch, *Nathan*
Nutkevitz, *Nathan*
Nutkewicz, *Nathan*
Nutkewitz, *Nathan*
Nutkiewicz, *Nathan*
Nutt
Nuttall
Nutter
Nutting, *Nutt*
Nuutinen, *Knott*
Nuvolone, *Napoleoni*
Nuvoloni, *Napoleoni*
Nuzzetti, *John*
Nuzzi, *John*
Nyberg, *New*
Nyblom, *New*
Nye
Nyegaard, *Nygård*
Nyegård, *Nygård*
Nygaard, *Nygård*
Nygård
Nygren, *New*
Nyhan
Nyhlén, *New*
Nyholm, *New*
Nykodým, *Nikodém*
Nylander, *New*
Nylén, *New*
Nylund, *New*
Nyman, *Newman*
Nyqvist, *New*
Nys, *Dennis*
Nyssen, *Dennis*
Nyssens, *Dennis*
Nystedt, *New*
Nyström, *New*

O

Oade
Oades, *Oade*
Oag, *Ogg*
Oak
Oakden, *Ogden*
Oake, *Oak*
Oakeley, *Oakley*
Oaker, *Oak*
Oakes, *Oak*
Oakland
Oakley
Oaks, *Oak*
Oastler, *Ostler*
Oaten, *Oade*
Oates, *Oade*

Oatley
Oats, *Oade*
Ó Balbháin, *Balfe*
O'Balivan, *Balfe*
O'Banane, *Bannan*
O'Bannan, *Bannan*
O'Bannion, *Bannan*
Ó Beagáin, *Begg*
O'Beirne, *Byrne*
Ober
Oberer, *Ober*
Oberg, *Åberg*
Öberg, *Öman*
Oberholster, *Oberholz*
Oberholtz, *Oberholz*
Oberholz
Oberlin, *Albert*
Oberman, *Ober*
Obermann, *Ober*
O'Berne, *Byrne*
Oberst, *Ober*
Obert, *Albert*
Obin, *Albin*
Obispo, *Bishop*
Oblomov
O'Boghan, *Bowen*
Obolensky
O'Bougan, *Bowen*
O'Boughan, *Bowen*
O'Boughelly, *Buckley*
O'Boyle, *Boyle*
O'Brackan, *Bracken*
Ó Bradacháin, *Brady*
O'Bradaghan, *Brady*
O'Bradane, *Braden*
O'Bradden, *Braden*
O'Braddigan, *Brady*
O'Brady, *Brady*
O'Branagan, *Brannigan*
O'Branigan, *Brannigan*
O'Brannigan, *Brannigan*
Obray, *Aubrey*
O'Brean, *Breen*
O'Breassell, *Brazil*
Obrecht, *Albert*
O'Breckan, *Bracken*
O'Breen, *Breen*
Ó Breisleáin, *Brazil*
Ó Breislein, *Brazil*
O'Brenane, *Brennan*
O'Brennan, *Brennan*
O'Breslane, *Brazil*
Ó Briain, *Bryan*
O'Brian, *Bryan*
O'Brien, *Bryan*
O'Brinan, *Brennan*
O'Brinane, *Brennan*
O'Brodigan, *Brady*
O'Broghan, *Banks*
O'Brognan, *Brogan*
O'Brognane, *Brogan*
O'Brohan, *Banks*
Ó Brolcháin, *Brolly*
O'Brollaghan, *Brolly*
O'Bruen, *Breen*
Ó Bruic, *Brock*
O'Bryan, *Bryan*
O'Buhilly, *Buckley*
O'Bynnan, *Bannan*
O'Byrne, *Byrne*
O'Caherny, *Carney*
O'Cahill, *Cahill*
O'Cahsedy, *Cassidy*
O'Callaghan, *Callaghan*
O'Callahan, *Callaghan*
Ocaña
O'Canavan, *Canavan*
O'Cannan, *Cannon*
O'Cannavan, *Canavan*
O'Cannon, *Cannon*
O'Cannovane, *Canavan*
Ó Caomháin, *Keefe*
O'Carney, *Carney*
O'Carran, *Curran*
O'Carroll, *Carroll*
O'Carrowill, *Carroll*
O'Carvill, *Carroll*
O'Carwell, *Carroll*
O'Casey, *Casey*
O'Cassidy, *Cassidy*
Occhi, *Ochila*
Occhillo, *Ochila*
Occhini, *Ochila*
Occhino, *Ochila*
Occhioni, *Ochila*
Occhiuti, *Ochila*
Occhiuto, *Ochila*
Ó Cearbhaill, *Carroll*
Ochiello, *Ochila*
Ochila
Ochiuzzi, *Ochila*
Ochoa
Ó Cionaodha, *Kenny*
Ocke, *Oade*
Ockenden
Ockens, *Oade*
Öcker, *Oade*
Ocker
Ockermann, *Ocker*
Öckl, *Eck*
O'Clearkane, *Cleary*
O'Cleary, *Cleary*
Ó Cléirchín, *Cleary*
Ó Cléireacháin, *Cleary*
Ó Cléirigh, *Cleary*
O'Clercan, *Cleary*
O'Clery, *Cleary*
O'Codihie, *Cody*
O'Coffey, *Coffey*
O'Coffie, *Coffey*
O'Coghlaine, *Coughlan*
O'Coghlane, *Coughlan*
O'Cogley, *Quickley*
O'Cohey, *Coffey*
O'Coigley, *Quickley*
Ó Coimín, *Cumming*
O'Coleman, *Coleman*
O'Collaine, *Cullen*
O'Collan, *Cullen*
Ó Colmáin, *Coleman*
Ó Comáin, *Cumming*
O'Comane, *Cumming*
O'Comman, *Cumming*
Ó Conaráin, *Conroy*
O'Conely, *Connolly*
O'Coneran, *Conroy*
O'Conlan, *Quinlan*
O'Connally, *Connolly*
O'Connell, *Connell*
O'Connellaine, *Quinlan*
O'Connolly, *Connolly*
O'Connor, *Connor*
O'Conoran, *Conroy*
O'Coonaghan, *Cooney*
O'Cooney, *Cooney*
Ó Corcain, *Corkery*
Ó Corcráin, *Corkery*
O'Corcrane, *Corkery*
O'Corhane, *Curran*
O'Corkan, *Corkery*
O'Corkerane, *Corkery*
O'Corkran, *Corkery*
Ó Corragáin, *Corr*
O'Corren, *Curran*
O'Corrie, *Cory*
O'Corrigane, *Corr*
O'Corrin, *Curran*
O'Corry, *Cory*
Ó Coscracháin, *Cosgrove*
O'Cosgra, *Cosgrove*
O'Cosker, *Cusker*
O'Coskerry, *Cosgrove*
O'Coskery, *Cosgrove*
O'Coskirr, *Cusker*
O'Cowmane, *Cumming*
O'Coyne, *Coyne*
Ó Craobháin, *Cray*
O'Crevan, *Cray*
O'Crevy, *Cray*
O'Criane, *Creggan*
O'Cridigan, *Creggan*
O'Crigan, *Creggan*
O'Crigane, *Creggan*
O'Croley, *Crowley*
O'Croly, *Crowley*
O'Crowley, *Crowley*
O'Crowly, *Crowley*
Ó Cuanacháin, *Cooney*
O'Cuayn, *Coyne*
O'Cuddie, *Cody*
O'Cuill, *Quill*
Ó Cuimín, *Cumming*
O'Cuirk, *Quirke*
O'Cumyn, *Cumming*
O'Curran, *Curran*
O'Currane, *Curran*
O'Currigan, *Corr*
O'Currine, *Curran*
O'Cwigley, *Quickley*
O'Daa, *Daw*
Ó Daimhín, *Devane*
O'Daly, *Daly*
Odam
Odams, *Odam*
O'Daniel, *Donald*
Odasi, *Oade*
O'Dasshowne, *Desmond*
Odasso, *Oade*
O'Dassuny, *Desmond*
O'Dawe, *Daw*
O'Daye, *Daw*
Odazio, *Oade*
Odazzi, *Oade*
Odd, *Oade*
Odde, *Oade*
Oddenino, *Oade*
Oddey, *Oade*
Oddi, *Oade*
Oddicini, *Oade*
Oddie, *Oade*
Oddini, *Oade*
Oddino, *Oade*
Oddo, *Oade*
Oddone, *Oade*
Oddoni, *Oade*
Oddono, *Oade*
Oddy, *Oade*
Ode, *Oade*
O'Dea, *Daw*
Ó Déaghain, *Dean*
O'Deane, *Dean*
O'Deason, *Desmond*
O'Deay, *Daw*
O'Deere, *Dwyer*
O'Deevey, *Devoy*
O'Deevy, *Devoy*
Odeke, *Oade*
Odelin, *Oade*
O'Dell, *Odell*
Odell
Odello, *Oade*
Odemann, *Oade*
O'Dempsey, *Dempsey*
Oden, *Oade*
Odens, *Oade*
O'Deoran, *Doran*
Öder, *Eder*
Oder
Oderberg, *Oder*
Öderer, *Eder*
O'Desmonde, *Desmond*
Odet, *Oade*
Odetti, *Oade*
O'Devlin, *Devlin*
Odgear, *Edgar*
Ödgen, *Oade*
Odger, *Edgar*
Odgers, *Edgar*
Odham, *Odam*
Odhams, *Odam*
Odi, *Oade*
Ó Diaghaidh, *Daw*
Ó Diarmada, *Dermott*
Odicini, *Oade*
Odicino, *Oade*
Odier, *Edgar*
Odin, *Oade*
Odinet, *Oade*
Odinga, *Oade*
Odini, *Oade*
Odinot, *Oade*
Odlin, *Oade*
Odling, *Oade*
O'Doane, *Devane*
O'Dogherty, *Doherty*
O'Doherty, *Doherty*
Ó Doibhlin, *Devlin*
Ó Doinn, *Dunn*
Ó Doirnín, *Dornan*
O'Dolane, *Dolan*
Odom, *Odam*
Ó Domhnaill, *Donald*
Ó Domhnalláin, *Donald*
Odon, *Oade*
O'Donaghie, *Donohue*
Odone, *Oade*
O'Donegaine, *Donegan*
O'Donegan, *Donegan*
O'Donelan, *Donald*
O'Donellan, *Donald*
Odoni, *Oade*
O'Donill, *Donald*
O'Donlan, *Donald*
O'Donleavy, *Dunleavy*
O'Donlon, *Donald*
O'Donnell, *Donald*
O'Donnellan, *Donald*
O'Donnelly, *Donnelly*
O'Donochowe, *Donohue*
O'Donoghue, *Donohue*
O'Donogue, *Donohue*
O'Donohoe, *Donohue*
O'Donohue, *Donohue*
O'Donovan, *Donovan*
O'Doogan, *Duggan*
O'Dooghaine, *Duggan*

O'Doolan, *Doolan*
O'Dooley, *Dooley*
O'Doran, *Doran*
O'Dorcey, *Darcy*
O'Dorchie, *Darcy*
O'Dorghie, *Darcy*
O'Doroghie, *Darcy*
O'Dougherty, *Doherty*
O'Douill, *Dougall*
O'Dowane, *Devane*
O'Dowd, *Duddy*
O'Dowey, *Duffy*
O'Dowgaine, *Duggan*
O'Dowilly, *Dougall*
O'Dowlane, *Dolan*
O'Dowlaney, *Delaney*
O'Dowley, *Dooley*
O'Downe, *Devane*
O'Downlay, *Dunleavy*
O'Doyane, *Devane*
O'Doyle, *Dougall*
O'Doyne, *Devane*
O'Driscole, *Driscoll*
O'Driscoll, *Driscoll*
O'Duan, *Devane*
O'Duane, *Devane*
Ó Dubhghaill, *Dougall*
O'Duffey, *Duffy*
O'Duffie, *Duffy*
O'Duffy, *Duffy*
O'Dugan, *Duggan*
O'Duggan, *Duggan*
O'Duhie, *Duffy*
O'Duhig, *Duffy*
Ó Duibhgeannáin, *Deegan*
O'Duigenain, *Deegan*
Ó Duinn, *Dunn*
O'Duire, *Dwyer*
O'Dulaney, *Delaney*
Ó Dulchonta, *Delahunty*
O'Dunaghy, *Donohue*
O'Dungan, *Donegan*
O'Dunleavy, *Dunleavy*
O'Dunn, *Dunn*
O'Dunne, *Dunn*
O'Dunneen, *Dineen*
O'Dunnion, *Dineen*
O'Duvire, *Dwyer*
O'Dwyer, *Dwyer*
Ody, *Oade*
O'Dyeane, *Dean*
Oest, *East*
Oetjen, *Oade*
Oetken, *Oade*
Oeuillet, *Ochila*
Oeuvrard, *Everard*
O'Faghy, *Fahy*
O'Fahy, *Fahy*
O'Falie, *Feely*
O'Fallon, *Fallon*
O'Fallone, *Fallon*
O'Fallowne, *Fallon*
O'Falvey, *Feely*
O'Falvie, *Feely*
O'Falvy, *Feely*
O'Fanane, *Finn*
O'Farrell, *Farrell*
O'Farrelly, *Farrell*
O'Farris, *Fergus*
O'Farrisa, *Fergus*
O'Faughy, *Fahy*
O'Fay, *Fee*
O'Faye, *Fahy*
Ó Fearghailaigh, *Farrell*
Ó Fearghaile, *Farrell*
Ó Fearghuis, *Fergus*
Ó Fearghusa, *Fergus*
O'Fearguise, *Fergus*
O'Fee, *Fee*
O'Feehan, *Fee*
O'Feeney, *Feeney*
Ofen, *Offen*
O'Fenane, *Finn*
O'Fenegane, *Finn*
Ofener, *Offen*
O'Feolane, *Whelan*
O'Fergus, *Fergus*
O'Ferrall, *Farrell*
O'Ferrally, *Farrell*
O'Ferris, *Fergus*
Offen
Offener, *Offen*
Offer
Offerman, *Oppermann*
Offermann, *Oppermann*
Offermanns, *Oppermann*
Office, *Officer*
Officer
Offield, *Oldfield*
Offman, *Hoffmann*
Offner, *Offen*
Offord
Ó Fhallamhain, *Fallon*
Ó Fhógartaigh, *Fogarty*
Ó Fiacháin, *Fee*
Ofield, *Oldfield*
O'Fielly, *Feely*
O'Fighane, *Fee*
O'Fihillie, *Feely*
O'Fihily, *Feely*
O'Finane, *Finn*
O'Finegane, *Finn*
O'Finn, *Finn*
Ó Finn, *Finn*
O'Finne, *Finn*
O'Fionn, *Finn*
Ó Fionnagáin, *Finn*
Ó Fionnáin, *Finn*
Ó Fionnghaile, *Fennell*
Ó Fionnghalaigh, *Fennell*
O'Flagherty, *Flaherty*
O'Flaherty, *Flaherty*
O'Flannelly, *Flannery*
O'Flannylla, *Flannery*
O'Flinn, *Flynn*
O'Floine, *Flynn*
O'Floinge, *Flynn*
O'Flynn, *Flynn*
Ofman, *Hoffmann*
O'Foedy, *Foody*
Ó Fógartaigh, *Fogarty*
O'Fogarty, *Fogarty*
O'Fogerty, *Fogarty*
O'Folane, *Whelan*
O'Foley, *Foley*
O'Folowe, *Foley*
O'Foodie, *Foody*
O'Foody, *Foody*
O'Foran, *Foran*
Ó Freaghaile, *Farrell*
O'Fylan, *Whelan*
O'Gaeney, *Gaffney*
Ó Gairbheith, *Garvey*
Ó Gairbhith, *Garvey*
O'Gallagher, *Gallagher*
O'Galleghure, *Gallagher*
Ó Gamhnáin, *Gaffney*
Oganesian, *John*
Oganian, *John*
O'Gara, *Geary*
O'Garey, *Geary*
O'Garry, *Geary*
O'Garven, *Garvin*
O'Garvey, *Garvey*
O'Garvie, *Garvey*
O'Garvin, *Garvin*
Ogborne
Ogden
Ogé, *Edgar*
O'Geary, *Geary*
O'Geiry, *Geary*
Oger, *Edgar*
Ogg
Oggeri, *Edgar*
Oggero, *Edgar*
Oggieri, *Edgar*
Ogier, *Edgar*
Ogilby, *Ogilvie*
Ogill, *Ogle*
Ogilvie
Ogilvy, *Ogilvie*
Ogilwy, *Ogilvie*
O'Glassane, *Gleesan*
Ogle
O'Gleasan, *Gleesan*
O'Glesaine, *Gleesan*
Oglethorpe
Ogley
O'Gooney, *Gaffney*
Ogórek, *Ogurtsov*
O'Gorman, *Gorman*
O'Gormeley, *Gormley*
O'Gormley, *Gormley*
O'Gorumley, *Gormley*
O'Gownain, *Gaffney*
O'Gownane, *Gaffney*
O'Gowney, *Gaffney*
Ograbek
O'Grada, *Grady*
O'Grady, *Grady*
O'Greefa, *Griffin*
Ögren, *Öman*
O'Griffy, *Griffin*
O'Grighie, *Griffin*
O'Grimley, *Gormley*
Ogrodowczyk, *Ogrodowski*
Ogrodowicz, *Ogrodowski*
Ogrodowski
Ogrodzki, *Ogrodowski*
O'Grogaine, *Grogan*
O'Growgane, *Grogan*
O'Guindelane, *Quinlan*
Ogurek, *Ogurtsov*
Ogurtsov
O'Hagan, *Hagan*
O'Hagerty, *Hegarty*
O'Hagher, *Hare*
O'Hagirtie, *Hegarty*
O'Hahir, *Hare*
Ó hAilín, *Allen*
Ó hAilpín, *Alpin*
O'Haire, *Hare*
O'Hallaghan, *Hallahan*
O'Hallaran, *Halloran*
O'Halleghane, *Hallahan*
O'Halleran, *Halloran*
O'Halleron, *Halloran*
O'Halloraine, *Halloran*
O'Halloran, *Halloran*
O'Hallyn, *Allen*
O'Halowrane, *Halloran*
O'Halpen, *Alpin*
O'Halpin, *Alpin*
O'Handlon, *Hanlon*
Ohanessian, *John*
O'Hanlee, *Handley*
O'Hanley, *Handley*
O'Hanlon, *Hanlon*
O'Hanlone, *Hanlon*
O'Hanlowne, *Hanlon*
O'Hanly, *Handley*
Ó hAnnagáin, *Hanna*
Ó hAnnáin, *Hanna*
O'Hannon, *Hanna*
O'Hanrahan, *Hanrahan*
O'Hara
O'Haraghtane, *Harrington*
O'Haran, *Heron*
O'Hare, *Hare*
O'Harn, *Heron*
O'Harragan, *Hanrahan*
O'Harran, *Heron*
O'Harrane, *Heron*
O'Harrighton, *Harrington*
O'Hart, *Hart*
Ó hArtagáin, *Hart*
O'Harte, *Hart*
O'Hartigan, *Hart*
Ohde, *Oade*
O'Headen, *Hayden*
O'Headyne, *Hayden*
O'Heagane, *Higgins*
O'Heagertie, *Hegarty*
O'Heaken, *Higgins*
O'Healie, *Healey*
O'Healihy, *Healey*
O'Healy, *Healey*
O'Heanesey, *Hennessy*
O'Heany, *Heaney*
O'Heare, *Hare*
O'Heden, *Hayden*
O'Hederscoll, *Driscoll*
O'Hedian, *Hayden*
O'Hedin, *Hayden*
O'Hegane, *Higgins*
O'Hegertie, *Hegarty*
O'Hehir, *Hare*
Oheim, *Eame*
Öheim, *Eame*
Öheimb, *Eame*
O'Hely, *Healey*
O'Henery, *Henry*
O'Henesey, *Hennessy*
O'Henessey, *Hennessy*
O'Henessy, *Hennessy*
O'Henesy, *Hennessy*
O'Heney, *Heaney*
O'Hennesey, *Hennessy*
O'Hennessey, *Hennessy*
O'Hennessy, *Hennessy*
O'Hennesy, *Hennessy*
O'Herlehy, *Herlihy*
O'Herlihy, *Herlihy*
O'Heron, *Heron*
O'Herraghton, *Harrington*
O'Heyden, *Hayden*
O'Heyne, *Hynes*
Öhgren, *Öman*
O'Hickee, *Hickey*
O'Hickey, *Hickey*
O'Hidirscoll, *Driscoll*
O'Hierlehy, *Herlihy*
O'Hifferan, *Heffernan*
O'Hifferane, *Heffernan*
O'Hiffernan, *Heffernan*
O'Higane, *Higgins*

O'Higgins, *Higgins*
O'Hirwen, *Irvine*
Ohlbaum
Ohle, *Old*
Öhlenschläger, *Ohlenschlager*
Öhlenschlager, *Ohlenschlager*
Ohlenschlager
Ohler, *Oyler*
Öhler, *Oyler*
Ohlerich, *Ulrich*
Öhlerking, *Ulrich*
Ohleyer, *Oyler*
Ohligschläger, *Ohlenschlager*
Ohligschlager, *Ohlenschlager*
Ohlmacher, *Oyler*
Ohlmann, *Old, Oyler*
Öhlrichs, *Ulrich*
Öhlschläger, *Ohlenschlager*
Öhlschlager, *Ohlenschlager*
Öhlschlegel, *Ohlenschlager*
Ohlsen, *Oliff*
Ohlsson, *Oliff*
Ohm, *Eame*
Öhm, *Eame*
Öhman, *Öman*
Ohme, *Eame*
Öhme, *Eame*
Öhmichen, *Eame*
Öhmke, *Eame*
Ohms, *Eame*
Öhms, *Eame*
Ohmsen, *Eame*
Ohnemus, *Jerome*
O'Hoasy, *Hussey*
O'Hogaine, *Hogan*
O'Hogan, *Hogan*
O'Hogane, *Hogan*
O'Hogertie, *Fogarty*
O'Hohy, *Howey*
O'Honeen, *Hooney*
O'Honie, *Hooney*
O'Hoonin, *Hooney*
O'Hora, *O'Hara*
O'Horgan, *Hanrahan*
O'Horigan, *Hanrahan*
O'Horogan, *Hanrahan*
O'Hosey, *Hussey*
O'Hossy, *Hussey*
O'Hourigan, *Hanrahan*
O'Hourihan, *Hanrahan*
O'Howney, *Hooney*
O'Hownyn, *Hooney*
O'Howrane, *Hanrahan*
Ohrbach, *Auerbach*
Ohrt, *Ort*
Ohrtmann, *Ort*
Ohst, *East*
Ó hUaithnín, *Hooney*
O'Huggin, *Higgins*
O'Huhy, *Howey*
O'Hunnyn, *Hooney*
Oiseau, *Uccello*
Oistrakh
Ojala
Ojeda
Oke, *Oak*
O'Kearney, *Kearney*
O'Keaty, *Keaty*
O'Keavane, *Keefe*
O'Keefe, *Keefe*
O'Keeve, *Keefe*
O'Kegley, *Quickley*
O'Kelaghan, *Callaghan*
Okeley, *Oakley*
O'Kelly, *Kelly*
Okely, *Oakley*
O'Kenaith, *Kenny*
O'Kenna, *Kenny*
O'Kennavain, *Canavan*
O'Kenneally, *Kenneally*
O'Kennedy, *Kennedy*
O'Kennellan, *Quinlan*
O'Kennelly, *Kenneally*
O'Kenney, *Kenny*
O'Kenny, *Kenny*
O'Kenolan, *Quinlan*
Okeover
O'Kerevan, *Kirwan*
O'Kerrigane, *Kerrigan*
O'Kerrywane, *Kirwan*
O'Kevane, *Keefe*
O'Kierrigain, *Kerrigan*
O'Kine, *Coyne*
O'Kineally, *Kenneally*
O'Kinedy, *Kennedy*
O'Kinna, *Kenny*
O'Kinneally, *Kenneally*
O'Kinney, *Kenny*
O'Kinny, *Kenny*
O'Kirwan, *Kirwan*
O'Knavin, *Nevin*
O'Knee, *Nee*
Okrainetz, *Ukraintsev*
Oksanen
O'Kuddyhy, *Cody*
O'Kynsillaghe, *Kinsella*
O'Lagan, *Logan*
O'Lagane, *Logan*
O'Laghlan, *Lachlan*
O'Laghnane, *Loughnane*
Oláh, *Vlach*
Olalla
O'Lalor, *Lawlor*
O'Lalour, *Lawlor*
O'Lane, *Lane*
O'Lanegane, *Lennon*
O'Langan, *Langan*
O'Langane, *Langan*
O'Lanigan, *Lennon*
O'Lannan, *Lennon*
O'Lannegan, *Lennon*
Olasz, *Vlach*
O'Laughlan, *Lachlan*
Olausson, *Oliff*
Olavsson, *Oliff*
O'Lawler, *Lawlor*
O'Lawry, *Lowry*
O'Layne, *Lane*
Olböter, *Altbüsser*
Olbrecht, *Albert*
Olbrechts, *Albert*
Olbricht, *Albert*
Olbrycht, *Albert*
Olbrychtowicz, *Albert*
Olbrysz, *Albert*
Olcha, *Olszewski*
Olchik, *Olszewski*
Olchovski, *Olszewski*
Olczak, *Alexis*
Olczyk, *Alexis*
Old
Oldcastle
Olde, *Old*
Oldemann, *Old*
Olden, *Alden, Old*
Oldenburg
Oldenschläger, *Ohlenschlager*
Older, *Old*
Oldershaw, *Ollerenshaw*
Oldfield
Oldham
Oldis, *Aldous*
Oldman, *Old*
Oldřich, *Ulrich*
Oldroyd
Olds, *Old*
Oldsen, *Old*
O'Leaghan, *Lehane*
O'Leane, *Lean*
O'Leary, *Leary*
Olech, *Alexis*
Olechnowicz, *Alexis*
Olechowicz, *Alexis*
O'Lee, *Lee*
O'Lehane, *Lehane*
Olejník, *Oyler*
Olek, *Alexis*
Olekhov, *Alexis*
Oleksiak, *Alexis*
Oleksiński, *Alexis*
O'Lenaghan, *Lenihan*
O'Lenan, *Lennon*
O'Lenane, *Lennon*
Olenchenko, *Alexander*
Olenchikov, *Alexander*
O'Leneghan, *Lenihan*
Olenichev, *Alexander*
Olenikov, *Alexander*
Olenin, *Alexander*
O'Lennan, *Lennon*
O'Lennane, *Lennon*
Olennikov, *Alexander*
Olenov, *Alexander*
O'Lensie, *Lynch*
Olerenshaw, *Ollerenshaw*
Oleś, *Alexis*
Olesen, *Oliff*
Oleshunin, *Alexis*
Oleszczak, *Alexis*
Oleszczuk, *Alexis*
Oleszkiewicz, *Alexis*
Olexa, *Alexander*
O'Leye, *Lee*
O'Leyne, *Lane*
Ölgeschlager, *Ohlenschlager*
Oliari, *Oyler*
O'Lie, *Lee*
Olie, *Oyler*
Oliemann, *Oyler*
Olier, *Oyler*
Olieslager, *Ohlenschlager*
Oliesleger, *Ohlenschlager*
Olifant, *Oliphant*
Oliff
Oliffe, *Oliff*
Olij, *Oyler*
Olijve, *Oliva*
Olimpiev
Oliphant
Oliva
Olivant, *Oliphant*
Olivar, *Oliva*
Olivares, *Oliva*
Olivari, *Oliva*
Olivas, *Oliva*
Olivato, *Oliva*
Olivazzi, *Oliva*
Olivé, *Oliver*
Olive, *Oliva*
Oliveira, *Oliva*
Olivella, *Oliva*
Olivelli, *Oliva*
Olivello, *Oliva*
Olivenbaum, *Oliva*
Olivenstein, *Oliva*
Oliver
Olivera, *Oliva*
Oliveri, *Oliver*
Oliverio, *Oliver*
Olivero, *Oliver*
Oliveros, *Oliver*
Olivestone, *Oliva*
Olivet, *Oliva*
Oliveti, *Oliva*
Oliveto, *Oliva*
Olivetta, *Oliva*
Olivetti, *Oliva*
Olivi, *Oliva*
Olivier, *Oliver*
Olivieri, *Oliver*
Oliviero, *Oliver*
Olivo, *Oliva*
Olivotti, *Oliva*
Olivreau, *Oliver*
Oljeschlager, *Ohlenschlager*
Olkhin, *Olszewski*
Olkowicz, *Alexis*
Ollarenshaw, *Ollerenshaw*
Ollé, *Oller*
Oller
Ollerearnshaw, *Ollerenshaw*
Ollerenshaw
Öllerich, *Ulrich*
Öllerking, *Ulrich*
Ollerton
Olley, *Doyley*
Ollie, *Doyley*
Ollier, *Oller*
Ollier, *Oyler*
Olliff, *Oliff*
Olliffe, *Oliff*
Ollive, *Oliva*
Ollivier, *Oliver*
Öllrich, *Ulrich*
Olm, *Elm*
Olman, *Old*
Olmeda, *Olmo*
Olmedo, *Olmo*
Olmi, *Olmo*
Olmo
Olmos, *Olmo*
Olney
O'Lochan, *Logan*
Ó Lochlainn, *Lachlan*
Olofsson, *Oliff*
O'Logan, *Logan*
O'Logher, *Loughrey*
O'Loghlan, *Lachlan*
O'Loghlen, *Lachlan*
O'Loghlin, *Lachlan*
O'Loghnane, *Loughnane*
O'Loghrane, *Loughrey*
Ó Loingseacháin, *Lynch*
Ó Lonagáin, *Lennon*
O'Lonagan, *Lennon*
O'Lonan, *Lennon*
O'Lonane, *Lennon*
O'Lonegan, *Lennon*
O'Longan, *Langan*
O'Longane, *Langan*
O'Lonnan, *Lennon*
O'Looney, *Looney*
O'Loran, *Loughrey*
Olorenshaw, *Ollerenshaw*
O'Loughane, *Logan*
O'Loughlan, *Lachlan*

O'Loughlen, *Lachlan*
O'Loughlin, *Lachlan*
O'Loughnan, *Loughnane*
O'Loughnane, *Loughnane*
O'Loughran, *Loughrey*
O'Lowry, *Lowry*
O'Loye, *Lee*
O'Loyne, *Lane*
Olsen, *Oliff*
Olshevski, *Olszewski*
Olshevsky, *Olszewski*
Olsson, *Oliff*
Olszacki, *Olszewski*
Olszak, *Olszewski*
Olszański, *Olszewski*
Olszewski
Olszycki, *Olszewski*
Olszyński, *Olszewski*
Oltukhov, *Yevtikhiev*
Ó Luchaireáin, *Loughrey*
O'Lucherin, *Loughrey*
O'Lucry, *Loughrey*
Olufsen, *Oliff*
Olver, *Oliver*
O'Lye, *Lee*
Olyff, *Oliva*
O'Lyhane, *Lehane*
O'Lynche, *Lynch*
O'Lynchy, *Lynch*
O'Lyneseghane, *Lynch*
Olyonov, *Alexander*
Olyoshin, *Alexis*
Olyoshkin, *Alexis*
Olyunin, *Alexis*
Om, *Elm*
Ó Madagáin, *Madden*
O'Madagane, *Madden*
O'Maddane, *Madden*
O'Madden, *Madden*
O'Madigane, *Madden*
O'Maely, *Mally*
O'Mahoney, *Mahon*
O'Mahony, *Mahon*
O'Mailie, *Mally*
O'Malley, *Mally*
O'Mallie, *Mally*
O'Mally, *Mally*
Oman, *Hammond*
Öman
O'Managhane, *Monaghan*
O'Manahan, *Monaghan*
O'Mara
Ó Marcacháin, *Markey*
O'Marcahan, *Markey*
O'Markaghaine, *Markey*
Ó Mathghamhna, *Mahon*
O'Meagher, *Maher*
O'Meally, *Mally*
O'Mealy, *Mally*
O'Meara, *O'Mara*
O'Meehan, *Meehan*
O'Melane, *Mullen*
O'Mellegan, *Milligan*
Ó Mhurcháin, *Morgan*
O'Milligane, *Milligan*
O'Mochaine, *Mohan*
O'Moeney, *Meaney*
O'Moghan, *Mohan*
O'Moghane, *Mohan*
O'Moleghan, *Milligan*
O'Mollane, *Mullen*
O'Mollegane, *Milligan*
O'Molleghan, *Milligan*
O'Monaghan, *Monaghan*
O'Monahan, *Monaghan*
Omond, *Hammond*
O'Money, *Meaney*
Omont, *Osmond*
O'Moon, *Mohan*
O'Mooney, *Meaney*
O'Moore, *Moore*
O'Mora, *Moore*
O'Moraghan, *Morgan*
O'Moraine, *Moran*
O'Moran, *Moran*
O'Morane, *Moran*
O'Morchoe, *Murphy*
O'Morey, *Moore*
O'Morghane, *Morgan*
O'Morierty, *Moriarty*
O'Morisa, *Morrissey*
O'Moronie, *Moroney*
O'Morphy, *Murphy*
O'Morrisane, *Morrissey*
O'Morrissey, *Morrissey*
O'Moughan, *Mohan*
O'Moughane, *Mohan*
O'Moylane, *Mullen*
O'Moylegane, *Milligan*
O'Moyney, *Meaney*
Oms, *Elm*
Ó Muircheartaigh, *Moriarty*
Ó Muirgheasáin, *Morrissey*
O'Mulcreevy, *Mulcreevy*
O'Muldoon, *Muldoon*
O'Mulghan, *Milligan*
O'Mullally, *Mullally*
O'Mullan, *Mullen*
O'Mullane, *Mullen*
O'Mullegan, *Milligan*
O'Mulleghan, *Milligan*
O'Mullwine, *Melvin*
O'Mulmichell, *Melville*
O'Mulrean, *Mulryan*
O'Mulrigan, *Mulryan*
O'Mulroyan, *Mulryan*
O'Mulryan, *Mulryan*
O'Multilly, *Tully*
O'Multully, *Tully*
O'Mulveill, *Melville*
O'Mulvihil, *Melville*
O'Mulvihill, *Melville*
Ó Murcháin, *Morgan*
O'Murchan, *Morgan*
O'Murghesan, *Morrissey*
O'Murphy, *Murphy*
O'Murrissa, *Morrissey*
O'Naghtan, *Naughton*
O'Naghten, *Naughton*
O'Naughton, *Naughton*
Onciulesco, *Uncle*
Onckelet, *Uncle*
Ondra, *Andrew*
Ondráček, *Andrew*
Ondrák, *Andrew*
Ondrášek, *Andrew*
Ondřiček, *Andrew*
Ondřich, *Andrew*
Ondróušek, *Andrew*
Ondruš, *Andrew*
Ondrúšek, *Andrew*
O'Nea, *Nee*
Ó Neachtain, *Naughton*
O'Neaghten, *Naughton*
O'Neal, *Neil*
O'Nee, *Nee*
O'Neil, *Neil*
O'Neilane, *Neil*
O'Neill, *Neil*
Ó Néill, *Neil*
O'Nelane, *Neil*
O'Ney, *Nee*
O'Neylane, *Neil*
Ongarelli, *Unger*
Ongari, *Unger*
Ongaro, *Unger*
Ó Nialláin, *Neil*
Onians, *Onion*
O'Nillane, *Neil*
Onimus, *Jerome*
Onion
Onions, *Onion*
O'Noland, *Nolan*
O'Nolane, *Nolan*
O'Noulane, *Nolan*
O'Nowan, *Noone*
O'Nowlan, *Nolan*
O'Nown, *Noone*
Onslow
Onyon, *Onion*
Oom, *Eame*
Oomen, *Eame*
Ooms, *Eame*
Oonin, *Hooney*
Oost, *East*
Opatovsky, *Apt*
Opatowski, *Apt*
Opatowsky, *Apt*
Opdam, *Dam*
Opdenort, *Ort*
Opdenorth, *Ort*
Opdyck, *Ditch*
Opel, *Albert*
Openhaime, *Oppenheim*
Openhajm, *Oppenheim*
Openheim, *Oppenheim*
Openheimer, *Oppenheim*
Openshaw
Opfermann, *Oppermann*
O'Phelane, *Whelan*
Ophüls, *Hilse*
Opie
Oppenhaim, *Oppenheim*
Oppenheim
Oppenheimer, *Oppenheim*
Oppermann
O'Prey
O'Quane, *Coyne*
O'Quigley, *Quickley*
O'Quigly, *Quickley*
O'Quill, *Quill*
O'Quin, *Quinn*
O'Quine, *Quinn*
O'Quinelane, *Quinlan*
O'Quirk, *Quirke*
O'Quirke, *Quirke*
O'Quyn, *Quinn*
Öqvist, *Oman*
Ó Raghailligh, *Reilly*
O'Raghtagan, *Rattigan*
O'Rahilly, *Reilly*
Ó Ráighne, *Rainey*
Ó Raighne, *Rainey*
Oram, *Orme*
Orange
Orbach, *Auerbach*
Orbahn, *Urban*
Orchard
Ord
Orde, *Ord*
Ordelt, *Ort*
Ordemann, *Ort*
Örder, *Ort*
Ordóñez
O'Reagan, *Regan*
O'Really, *Reilly*
O'Reallye, *Reilly*
O'Realy, *Reilly*
O'Reaney, *Rainey*
O'Reddie, *Ready*
O'Ree, *Reavey*
O'Reedan, *Riordan*
O'Reely, *Reilly*
O'Regan, *Regan*
O'Regane, *Regan*
O'Reilly, *Reilly*
O'Reily, *Reilly*
Orel, *Orlov*
Orellana
Orenstein, *Horn*
Orensztein, *Horn*
O'Reogh, *Reavey*
O'Revoay, *Reavey*
O'Reyley, *Reilly*
Orfaure, *Offer*
Orfeur, *Offer*
Orfèvre, *Offer*
Orff
Orford
Organ
Organer, *Organ*
O'Ria, *Reavey*
Ó Riabhaigh, *Reavey*
O'Riegaine, *Regan*
O'Riellie, *Reilly*
O'Rielly, *Reilly*
Orieux, *Oriol*
O'Rinne, *Wren*
Oriol
O'Riordan, *Riordan*
Oriot, *Oriol*
Oriou, *Oriol*
O'Riourdane, *Riordan*
Orive
O'Riverdan, *Riordan*
Orlandelli, *Rowland*
Orlandi, *Rowland*
Orlandini, *Rowland*
Orlando, *Rowland*
Orlandoni, *Rowland*
Orlanducci, *Rowland*
Orlicki, *Orlov*
Orlický, *Orlov*
Orlik, *Orlov*
Orlikowski, *Orlov*
Orliński, *Orlov*
Orlov
Orlovitch, *Orlov*
Orlovitz, *Orlov*
Orlovski, *Orlov*
Orlovsky, *Orlov*
Orlowitz, *Orlov*
Orłowski, *Orlov*
Orlowski, *Orlov*
Orlowsky, *Orlov*
Ormaeche, *Hormaeche*
Ormaechea, *Hormaeche*
Orman, *Ormond*
Orme
Ormeau, *Orme*
Ormerod
Ormes, *Orme*
Ormesher, *Ormshaw*
Ormesson, *Orme*
Ormiston
Ormond

Ormonde, *Ormond*
Ormrod, *Ormerod*
Ormsby
Ormshaw
Ormston, *Ormiston*
Ornstein, *Horn*
O'Roan, *Ruane*
Ó Rodacháin, *Ready*
O'Rodane, *Roden*
O'Roddy, *Ready*
O'Rodeghan, *Ready*
O'Ronane, *Ronan*
O'Ronayne, *Ronan*
O'Roney, *Rooney*
O'Rorke, *Rourke*
Orosz, *Rusakov*
O'Rourke, *Rourke*
O'Rowane, *Ruane*
O'Rowarke, *Rourke*
O'Rownoe, *Rooney*
O'Rowwarke, *Rourke*
Orozco
Orpen, *Orpin*
Orpin
Orr
Orrey, *Wooldridge*
Orrick
Orridge, *Orrick*
Orrum, *Orme*
Orry, *Wooldridge*
Ors, *Ort*
Orseau, *Orso*
Orsel, *Orso*
Orselli, *Orso*
Orsello, *Orso*
Orset, *Orso*
Orsetti, *Orso*
Orsi, *Orso*
Orsini, *Orso*
Orso
Orsolillo, *Orso*
Orsolini, *Orso*
Orsolino, *Orso*
Orsone, *Orso*
Orsoni, *Orso*
Orsucci, *Orso*
Országh
Ort
Orta, *Ort*
Ortas, *Ort*
Orteau, *Ort*
Orteaux, *Ort*
Ortega
Örtel, *Ort*
Ortells, *Ort*
Örtelt, *Ort*
Ortet, *Ort*
Orteu, *Ort*
Orth, *Ort*
Orthmann, *Ort*
Ortiz, *Fort*
Ortler, *Ort*
Ortman, *Ort*
Ortner, *Ort*
Orton
Orts, *Ort*
Ortsman, *Ort*
Ortuño
Ó Ruairc, *Rourke*
O'Ruane, *Ruane*
O'Ruddane, *Roden*
O'Rudden, *Roden*
O'Ruddy, *Ready*
Orum, *Orme*
Orwell
O'Ryan, *Ryan*
Orzechowski
Ös, *Oswald*
O'Sawra, *Summer*
O'Sawrie, *Summer*
Osbahr, *Osborn*
Osband, *Osborn*
Osbon, *Osborn*
Osborn
Osborne, *Osborn*
Osbourn, *Osborn*
Osbourne, *Osborn*
Osburn, *Osborn*
O'Scandall, *Scannell*
O'Scandlon, *Scannell*
O'Scanlaine, *Scannell*
O'Scanlan, *Scannell*
O'Scanlon, *Scannell*
O'Scannell, *Scannell*
O'Scannill, *Scannell*
Ó Scannláin, *Scannell*
Ösch, *Oswald*
Öschlin, *Oswald*
Oschwald, *Oswald*
Ó Scoláin, *Scully*
O'Scollee, *Scully*
Oscroft
O'Scully, *Scully*
Ó Seanacháin, *Shane*
Ó Seanáin, *Shane*
Oseletti, *Uccello*
Oselli, *Uccello*
O'Serie, *Seerey*
Oserovitch, *Osher*
Oserovitz, *Osher*
Oserow, *Osher*
O'Sesnane, *Sexton*
O'Seyry, *Seerey*
Osgood
O'Shanahan, *Shane*
O'Shanan, *Shane*
O'Shanesy, *Shaughnessy*
O'Shanley, *Shanley*
O'Shanna, *Shane*
O'Shannessy, *Shaughnessy*
O'Shanney, *Shane*
O'Shannon, *Shane*
O'Shanny, *Shane*
O'Shaughnessy, *Shaughnessy*
O'Shea, *Shea*
O'Sheahan, *Sheehan*
O'Sheal, *Shield*
O'Sheanaghaine, *Shane*
O'Shee, *Shea*
O'Sheehan, *Sheehan*
O'Shehane, *Sheehan*
O'Shenane, *Shane*
O'Shennan, *Shane*
O'Sheny, *Shane*
Osher
Osherenko, *Osher*
Osheri, *Osher*
O'Sheridane, *Sheridan*
Osheroff, *Osher*
Osherov, *Osher*
Osherovitch, *Osher*
Osherovitz, *Osher*
Osherovsky, *Osher*
Osherowich, *Osher*
Osherowicz, *Osher*
Osherowitz, *Osher*
O'Shesnan, *Sexton*
O'Shiegane, *Sheehan*
O'Shiel, *Shield*
O'Shiell, *Shield*
O'Shill, *Shield*
O'Shiridane, *Sheridan*
O'Shirie, *Seerey*
O'Shoughnessy, *Shaughnessy*
Oshrov, *Osher*
Oshrovitz, *Osher*
O'Shrue, *Seerey*
O'Shydie, *Sheedy*
O'Shyry, *Seerey*
Osichev, *Joseph*
Osiecki
O'Siegall, *Shield*
Osier, *Dozier*
Osinin
Osiński, *Osinin*
Osinski, *Osinin*
Osipenko, *Joseph*
Osipov, *Joseph*
O'Slattery, *Slattery*
O'Slattra, *Slattery*
Osler, *Ostler*
O'Slowey, *Slowey*
Osman, *Osmond*
Osmant, *Osmond*
Osment, *Osmond*
Osmint, *Osmond*
Osmon, *Osmond*
Osmond
Osmont, *Osmond*
Osmund, *Osmond*
Osório, *Osorio*
Osorio
O'Spallane, *Spillane*
O'Spillane, *Spillane*
O'Spollane, *Spillane*
Ossietzky, *Osiecki*
Ossipenko, *Joseph*
Ossowski
Ossterling, *Easter*
Ost, *East*
Öst, *East*
Ostafyev, *Ostapov*
Ostal, *Hostal*
Ostankin, *Ostapov*
Ostanov, *Ostapov*
Ostapets, *Ostapov*
Ostapishin, *Ostapov*
Ostapov
Ostashkin, *Ostapov*
Ostashko, *Ostapov*
Ostashkov, *Ostapov*
Ostaszewski, *Stace*
Ostau, *Hostal*
Ostberg, *East*
Östberg, *East*
Ostepenya, *Ostapov*
Oster, *Easter*
Öster, *Easter*
Österberg, *Easter*
Osterer, *Easter*
Österer, *Easter*
Østergaard, *Østergård*
Østergård
Östergren, *Easter*
Österholm, *Easter*
Österle, *Easter*
Österlein, *Easter*
Österlin, *Easter*
Osterling, *Easter*
Österlund, *Easter*
Osterman, *Easter*
Österman, *Easter*
Ostermann, *Easter*
Östermann, *Easter*
Ostern, *Easter*
Osterreicher, *Oistrakh*
Österreicher, *Oistrakh*
Ostersetzer, *Easter*
Osterweil, *Easter*
Ostfeld, *East*
Östh, *East*
Ostin, *Austin*
Östing, *East*
Ostler
Östlin, *East*
Östlind, *East*
Östling, *East*
Östlund, *East*
Östman, *Eastman*
Ostreich, *Oistrakh*
Ostreicher, *Oistrakh*
Öström, *Öman*
Ostrowski
Ostrý, *Vostrý*
Ostwald, *East, Oswald*
Ostwind, *East*
O'Sullivan, *Sullivan*
Osuna
Oswald
Oswell
O'Swerte, *Seward*
Oswin
O'Sworde, *Seward*
Oszerowski, *Osher*
Ó Tadhgán, *Tighe*
Otanelli, *Oade*
Otava, *Votava*
O'Tearney, *Tierney*
O'Ternane, *Tierney*
O'Terney, *Tierney*
Otero
Othon, *Oade*
O'Tiernan, *Tierney*
O'Tierney, *Tierney*
O'Tierny, *Tierney*
Ó Tíghearnáin, *Tierney*
Otino, *Oade*
Otis, *Oade*
Otke, *Oade*
Ötke, *Oade*
Ötker, *Oade*
O'Toole, *Toole*
O'Toomey, *Twomey*
O'Toughill, *Toole*
O'Touhill, *Toole*
O'Towie, *Tuohy*
O'Trasey, *Treacy*
O'Trassy, *Treacy*
O'Trehy, *Troy*
O'Tressy, *Treacy*
O'Trevir, *Trevor*
O'Trover, *Trevor*
Ott, *Oade*
Ottaway, *Ottoway*
Otte, *Oade*
Ottel, *Oade*
Öttel, *Oade*
Otten, *Oade*
Ottens, *Oade*
Otter
Otterway, *Ottoway*
Otterwell, *Ottoway*
Ottesen, *Oade*
Ottewell, *Ottoway*
Ottewill, *Ottoway*
Ottin, *Oade*

Ottini, *Oade*
Ottiwell, *Ottoway*
Öttle, *Oade*
Ottler, *Oade*
Otto, *Oade*
Ottolenghi
Ottoli, *Oade*
Ottolin, *Oade*
Ottolini, *Oade*
Ottolino, *Oade*
Otton, *Oade*
Ottone, *Oade*
Ottonelli, *Oade*
Ottonello, *Oade*
Ottoni, *Oade*
Ottosen, *Oade*
Ottosson, *Oade*
Ottoway
Ottsen, *Oade*
Ottway, *Ottoway*
O'Tuale, *Toole*
Ötvös, *Eötvös*
Otway, *Ottoway*
O'Twohill, *Toole*
O'Twohy, *Tuohy*
O'Twomey, *Twomey*
Otzen, *Oade*
Oud, *Old*
Oude, *Old*
Oudeman, *Old*
Oudet, *Oade*
Oudin, *Oade*
Oudineau, *Oade*
Oudinet, *Oade*
Oudinot, *Oade*
Oudon, *Oade*
Oudot, *Oade*
Oudt, *Old*
Ough
Oughtright, *Uttridge*
Ougier, *Edgar*
Ould, *Old*
Oulds, *Old*
Oulier, *Oller*
Ourry, *Wooldridge*
Ours, *Orso*
Oursel, *Orso*
Ourselin, *Orso*
Ourtic, *Ort*
Ouseley, *Ousley*
Ousley
Oustal, *Hostal*
Oustalet, *Hostal*
Oustalot, *Hostal*
Oustau, *Hostal*
Out, *Old*
Outin, *Austin*
Outridge, *Uttridge*
Outright, *Uttridge*
Outteridge, *Uttridge*
Outzen, *Oade*
Ovanesian, *John*
Óvári, *Óváry*
Óváry
Ovasapian, *Joseph*
Ovdkimov, *Yevdokimov*
Ovejero
Ovenden
Over
Overal, *Overall*
Overall
Overell, *Overall*
Overend
Overgaard, *Overgård*
Overgård
Overill, *Overall*
Overmann, *Ober*
Overton
Overy
Ovesen, *Oliff*
Oviedo
Ovseev, *Eusébio*
Ovsienko, *Eusébio*
Ovtukhov, *Yevtikhiev*
Owczarczyk, *Owczarz*
Owczarek, *Owczarz*
Owczarz
Owen
Ower, *Over*
Owers, *Over*
O'Whalen, *Whelan*
O'Whealane, *Whelan*
Owsiejczyk, *Eusébio*
Owsik, *Eusébio*
Owsley, *Ousley*
Oxenham
Oxlee, *Oxley*
Oxley
Oxnard
Oyler
Ozerov, *Jeziorski*
Ozintsev, *Joseph*
Ozyornikov, *Jeziorski*

P

Paal, *Paul*
Paapke, *Pope*
Paasch, *Pask*
Paasche, *Pask*
Paaske, *Pask*
Pabel, *Paul*
Pabelik, *Paul*
Pabian, *Fabian*
Pabiańczyk, *Fabian*
Pabiański, *Fabian*
Pabich, *Fabian*
Pabijańczyk, *Fabian*
Pabimak, *Fabian*
Pabin, *Fabian*
Pabisiak, *Fabian*
Pablo, *Paul*
Pablos, *Paul*
Pabon, *Peacock*
Pabst, *Pope*
Páč, *Pačes*
Pač, *Pačes*
Pacák
Pacan, *Pain*
Pacandet, *Pain*
Pacant, *Pain*
Pacard, *Packard*
Paccard, *Packard*
Pace
Pacelli, *Pace*
Pačes
Pacetti, *Pace*
Pacey
Pach, *Bach, Paul*
Pache, *Pace, Paul*
Pacheco
Pacher, *Bach*
Pachmann, *Bach*
Pacholczyk, *Pacholski*
Pacholek, *Pacholski*
Pacholke, *Pacholski*
Pacholl, *Pacholski*
Pacholski
Pachot, *Pace*
Pachoud, *Pace*
Pächt, *Peter*
Pachta, *Paul*
Paci, *Pace*
Paciello, *Pace*
Pacifici, *Pacifico*
Pacifico
Pacilli, *Pace*
Pacini, *Pace*
Pacino, *Pace*
Pacinotti, *Pace*
Paciotti, *Pace*
Pacitti, *Pace*
Paciullo, *Pace*
Pack
Packard
Packe, *Pack*
Packer
Packham
Packman
Packwood
Pacock, *Peacock*
Pacovský, *Pacák*
Pacquet, *Paquet*
Pacteau, *Paquet*
Pactot, *Paquet*
Pacy, *Pacey*
Pacześ, *Pakuła*
Paczesny, *Pakuła*
Padan, *Patrick*
Padarzewski, *Paderewski*
Padawer, *Padovano*
Paddock
Paddon
Paderewski
Padfield
Padgett, *Page*
Padgham, *Packham*
Padieu, *Pardoe*
Padilla
Padmore
Padoan, *Padovano*
Padoani, *Padovano*
Padova, *Padovano*
Padovan, *Padovano*
Padovani, *Padovano*
Padovano
Padover, *Padovano*
Padró, *Patrone*
Padrós, *Pedrosa*
Paduan, *Padovano*
Paduani, *Padovano*
Paduano, *Padovano*
Padyn, *Patrick*
Páez, *Pelayo*
Paff, *Pope*
Paffe, *Pope*
Paffen, *Pope*
Pagan, *Pain*
Pagan
Paganelli, *Pain*
Paganetti, *Pain*
Paganetto, *Pain*
Pagani, *Pain*
Paganin, *Pain*
Paganini, *Pain*
Paganino, *Pain*
Pagano, *Pain*
Paganoni, *Pain*
Paganotto, *Pain*
Paganucci, *Pain*
Paganuzzi, *Pain*
Page
Pageard, *Page*
Pageaud, *Page*
Pagel, *Paul*
Pagelon, *Peacock*
Pagels, *Paul*
Pagelsen, *Paul*
Pagelun, *Peacock*
Pagen, *Pagan*
Pagenet, *Page*
Pagenot, *Page*
Pageon, *Page*
Pageot, *Page*
Pagès, *Pays*
Paget, *Page*
Pagett, *Page*
Paggia, *Paille*
Paggiarin, *Paillier*
Paggiaro, *Paillier*
Paggio, *Page*
Pagin, *Pagan*
Pagli, *Paille*
Paglia, *Paille*
Pagliacci, *Paille*
Pagliai, *Paillier*
Pagliari, *Paillier*
Pagliaro, *Paillier*
Pagliaroli, *Paillier*
Pagliarolo, *Paillier*
Pagliarulo, *Paillier*
Pagliazzi, *Paille*
Paglicci, *Paille*
Paglieri, *Paillier*
Paglietta, *Paille*
Pagliocca, *Paille*
Paglione, *Paille*
Pagliucca, *Paille*
Pagnard, *Pagnol*
Pagni, *Compagnon*
Pagnier, *Pain*
Pagniez, *Pain*
Pagnin, *Compagnon*
Pagnini, *Compagnon*
Pagnol
Pagnon, *Pagnol*
Pagnone, *Pain*
Pagnoni, *Compagnon*
Pagnot, *Pagnol*
Pagnotti, *Compagnon*
Pagnotto, *Pain*
Pagnoul, *Pagnol*
Pagnoux, *Pagnol*
Pagnussi, *Compagnon*
Pagnut, *Compagnon*
Pagnutti, *Compagnon*
Pagon, *Pagan*
Pagram, *Pilgrim*
Pahl, *Paul, Peel*
Pahler, *Paul*
Pahlke, *Peel*
Pahlmann, *Peel*
Påhlsson, *Paul*
Pahnke, *Pank*
Paice, *Pace*
Paiero, *Paillier*
Paietta, *Paille*
Paige, *Page*
Paik, *Pack*
Pailhès, *Paillier*
Pailhié, *Paillier*
Pailin, *Hayling*
Paillard, *Paille*
Paille
Pailler, *Paillier*

Pailleret, *Paillier*
Paillier
Paim, *Böhm*
Pain
Paine, *Pain*
Paines, *Pain*
Painter
Painty, *Penty*
Paiola, *Paille*
Paiotta, *Paille*
Pairpoint, *Pierrepont*
Pais, *Pelayo*
Paisant, *Pays*
Paish, *Pask*
Paisley
Paiva
Paix, *Pace*
Paixão
Pająk, *Paukov*
Pajares, *Paillier*
Pajor
Pajot, *Page*
Pakenham, *Packham*
Pakentreger, *Packman*
Pakes, *Pask*
Pakuła
Pakulski, *Pakuła*
Pál, *Paul*
Pála, *Paul*
Palacci, *Palacio*
Palach, *Palacio*
Palache, *Palacio*
Palachi, *Palacio*
Palachy, *Palacio*
Palacín
Palacio
Palacios, *Palacio*
Palacky, *Palacio*
Palagi, *Palacio*
Palais, *Palacio*
Pałasz
Palatchi, *Palacio*
Palau, *Palacio*
Palazzetti, *Palacio*
Palazzi, *Palacio*
Palazzini, *Palacio*
Palazzo, *Palacio*
Palazzoli, *Palacio*
Palazzolo, *Palacio*
Palazzotto, *Palacio*
Palczewski
Pałczynski, *Pałka*
Paleček, *Paluch*
Pälegrimm, *Pilgrim*
Pálek, *Paul*
Palencia
Palensya, *Palencia*
Paler, *Payler*
Palermi
Palermo, *Palermi*
Palethorpe
Paley
Palfery, *Palfrey*
Pálffi, *Paul*
Pálffy, *Paul*
Pálfi, *Paul*
Palframan, *Palfrey*
Palfreeman, *Palfrey*
Palfreman, *Palfrey*
Palfrène, *Palfrey*
Palfrey
Palfreyman, *Palfrey*
Pálfy, *Paul*
Palgrave
Palhié, *Paillier*
Palhier, *Paillier*
Palin, *Hayling*
Paling, *Hayling*
Palister, *Palliser*
Paljić, *Paul*
Pałka
Pallarès, *Paillier*
Pallàs, *Paillier*
Pallas, *Paul*
Pallasch, *Paul*
Pallaske, *Paul*
Palle, *Paul*
Pallejà
Pallesen, *Paul*
Palleske, *Paul*
Pallet, *Peel*
Pallett
Pallez, *Peel*
Pallis, *Palliser*
Palliser
Pallister, *Palliser*
Pallu
Palluschek, *Paul*
Palm, *Palmer*
Palma, *Palmer*
Palma, *Palmer*
Palmar, *Palmer*
Palmberg, *Palmer*
Palme, *Palmer*
Palmeiro, *Palmer*
Palmen, *Palmer*
Palmenbaum, *Palmer*
Palmér, *Palmer*
Palmer
Palmeri, *Palmer*
Palmerin, *Palmer*
Palmerini, *Palmer*
Palmerio, *Palmer*
Palmero, *Palmer*
Palmerucci, *Palmer*
Palmés, *Palmer*
Palmes, *Palmer*
Palmgren, *Palmer*
Palmholz, *Palmer*
Palmieri, *Palmer*
Palmiero, *Palmer*
Palminteri, *Parmenter*
Palmov, *Palmer*
Palmucci, *Palmer*
Palomar
Palomares, *Palomar*
Palomba, *Palomo*
Palombella, *Palomo*
Palombi, *Palomo*
Palombini, *Palomo*
Palombino, *Palomo*
Palombo, *Palomo*
Palomer, *Palomo*
Palomero, *Palomo*
Palomino, *Palomo*
Palomo, *Palomo*
Palomo
Palotai, *Palacio*
Palou, *Palacio*
Palphreyman, *Palfrey*
Palser, *Palliser*
Pålsson, *Paul*
Palu, *Pallu*
Paluat, *Pallu*
Paluch
Palud, *Pallu*
Paluel, *Pallu*
Palumberi, *Palomo*
Palumbieri, *Palomo*
Palumbo, *Palomo*
Paluszewski, *Paluch*
Paluszkiewicz, *Paluch*
Palut, *Pallu*
Paly, *Palliser*
Palys, *Palliser*
Pamias, *Pamies*
Pàmies, *Pamies*
Pamies
Pammenter, *Parmenter*
Pan, *Pain*
Panadero, *Panther*
Panadés
Panas, *Panek*
Panasewicz, *Panek*
Panasik, *Afanasyev*
Panasov, *Afanasyev*
Panattieri, *Panther*
Panchenko, *Afanasyev*
Panchishin, *Pankridge*
Panҫi, *Pantaleone*
Panckridge, *Pankridge*
Pane, *Pain*
Pánek, *Panek*
Panek
Panelli, *Pain*
Panello, *Pain*
Panes, *Pain*
Panetier, *Panther*
Panetti, *Pain*
Pani, *Pain*
Paniagua
Panier, *Pain*
Panizo
Pank
Panke, *Pank*
Pankeev, *Pankridge*
Pankhurst
Pankiewicz, *Panek*
Pankowski, *Panek*
Pankratov, *Pankridge*
Pankratyev, *Pankridge*
Pankratz, *Pankridge*
Pankraz, *Pankridge*
Pankrazer, *Pankridge*
Pankridge
Pankrushin, *Pankridge*
Pannaman, *Penny*
Pannetier, *Panther*
Pannier, *Pain*
Panov, *Panek*
Panozzo, *Pain*
Panshi, *Pantaleone*
Pantaleo, *Pantaleone*
Pantaleone
Pantalone, *Pantaleone*
Pantaloni, *Pantaleone*
Pantchev, *Pantaleone*
Pantecôte, *Pentecost*
Pantel, *Pantaleone*
Pantele, *Pantaleone*
Pantelei, *Pantaleone*
Panteleoni, *Pantaleone*
Pantelić, *Pantaleone*
Pantelmann, *Pantaleone*
Panther
Pantić, *Pantaleone*
Pantl, *Pantaleone*
Pantleev, *Pantaleone*
Pantlen, *Pantaleone*
Pantleon, *Pantaleone*
Panton
Pantović, *Pantaleone*
Panzavuota, *Pauncefoot*
Panzer
Panzner, *Panzer*
Paolacci, *Paul*
Paolazzi, *Paul*
Paoletti, *Paul*
Paoletto, *Paul*
Paoli, *Paul*
Paolicchi, *Paul*
Paolillo, *Paul*
Paolinelli, *Paul*
Paolini, *Paul*
Paolino, *Paul*
Paolo, *Paul*
Paolon, *Paul*
Paolone, *Paul*
Paoloni, *Paul*
Paolotti, *Paul*
Paolotto, *Paul*
Paolozzi, *Paul*
Paolucci, *Paul*
Paone, *Peacock*
Pap, *Pope*
Papa
Papaccio, *Papa*
Papatov, *Popov*
Papazzo, *Papa*
Pape, *Papa*
Papen, *Pope*
Papež, *Pope*
Papić, *Pope*
Papierz, *Pope*
Papiewski, *Pope*
Papież, *Pope*
Papigai, *Pobgee*
Papigay, *Pobgee*
Papillard, *Papillon*
Papillaud, *Papillon*
Papillon
Papineau, *Papot*
Papinot, *Papot*
Papis, *Pope*
Päpke, *Pope*
Papke, *Pope*
Paponnot, *Papot*
Papot
Papotto, *Papa*
Papoušek, *Pobgee*
Papp, *Papot, Pope*
Pappa, *Papot*
Pappagallo, *Pobgee*
Pappi, *Pope*
Pappone, *Papot*
Papponeau, *Papot*
Paprocki
Paprotny, *Paprocki*
Papuziński, *Pobgee*
Papworth
Paquereau, *Paquier*
Paquet
Paqueteau, *Paquet*
Paquetot, *Paquet*
Paquette, *Paquet*
Paquier
Paquin, *Paquet*
Paquot, *Paquet*
Paradowski
Paragreen, *Pilgrim*
Paraire, *Parant*
Páramo
Paran, *Parant*
Parant
Paranteau, *Parant*
Pardal

Pardelli, *Bard*
Pardew, *Pardoe*
Pardey, *Pardoe*
Pardi, *Bard*
Pardieu, *Pardoe*
Pardini, *Bard*
Pardo
Pardoe
Parducci, *Bard*
Pardy, *Pardoe*
Paredes
Pareis, *Parish*
Parejo
Parell, *Peter*
Parellada
Parelli, *Kaspar*
Parent
Parentaud, *Parent*
Parente, *Parent*
Parenteau, *Parent*
Parenti, *Parent*
Parentin, *Parent*
Parer, *Pear*
Parera, *Pear*
Parés, *Pear*
Parès, *Pear*
Parésy, *Pear*
Pareti, *Paredes*
Pareto, *Paredes*
Parfait, *Parfitt*
Parfect, *Parfitt*
Parffrey, *Palfrey*
Parfit, *Parfitt*
Parfitt
Parfrement, *Palfrey*
Parfrey, *Palfrey*
Pargeter, *Pargetter*
Pargetter
Pargiter, *Pargetter*
Parham
Pariente, *Parent*
Parier, *Pear*
Paries, *Parish*
Parieser, *Parish*
Parigi, *Parish*
Parigini, *Parish*
Parigot, *Parish*
Parin, *Pear*
Parini, *Kaspar*
Parion, *Pear*
Pariot, *Pear*
París, *Aparicio*
Paris, *Parish*
Parisato, *Parish*
Parisatti, *Parish*
Parise, *Parish*
Parisel, *Parish*
Pariser, *Parish*
Pariset, *Parish*
Parish
Parisi, *Parish*
Parisiani, *Parish*
Parisini, *Parish*
Parisio, *Parish*
Parisius, *Parish*
Pariso, *Parish*
Parisot, *Parish*
Parisotti, *Parish*
Parisse, *Parish*
Parissi, *Parish*
Parisy, *Parish*
Pariz, *Parish*
Pařizek
Parizel, *Parish*
Parizer, *Parish*
Parizet, *Parish*
Parizot, *Parish*
Parizy, *Parish*
Park
Parke, *Park*
Parker
Parkes, *Park*
Parkhill
Parkhouse
Parkin
Parkins, *Parkin*
Parkinson, *Parkin*
Parkman, *Park*
Parks, *Park*
Parkyn, *Parkin*
Parler, *Pearl*
Parley
Parlie, *Parley*
Parly, *Parley*
Parmantier, *Parmenter*
Parmentel, *Parmenter*
Parmentelot, *Parmenter*
Parmenter
Parmentier, *Parmenter*
Parmet, *Permenter*
Parmeter, *Parmenter*
Parmieri, *Palmer*
Parmiero, *Palmer*
Parminter, *Parmenter*
Parmiter, *Parmenter*
Parnall, *Parnell*
Parnas, *Parnes*
Parnass, *Parnes*
Parnasz, *Parnes*
Parnell
Parnes
Parness, *Parnes*
Parnham
Parnwell, *Parnell*
Paron, *Patrone*
Paroni, *Patrone*
Parpaillon, *Papillon*
Parpalhol, *Papillon*
Parpillon, *Papillon*
Parquet, *Park*
Parquier, *Parker*
Parquin, *Park*
Parr
Parra
Parrack, *Park*
Parram, *Parham*
Parramon
Parrant, *Parent*
Parras, *Parra*
Parratt, *Parrott*
Parreira, *Parra*
Parren, *Perrin*
Parrent, *Parent*
Parret, *Parrott*
Parrett, *Parrott*
Parri, *Kaspar*
Parrilla, *Parra*
Parrini, *Kaspar*
Parris, *Parish*
Parrish, *Parish*
Parrisius, *Parish*
Parrock, *Park*
Parrot, *Parrott*
Parrott
Parrucci, *Kaspar*
Parruck, *Park*
Parry
Parseval, *Percival*
Parsley, *Parslow*
Parsloe, *Parslow*
Parslow
Parsonage
Parsons
Partanen
Partington
Parton
Partriche, *Partridge*
Partrick, *Partridge*
Partridge
Partzefall, *Percival*
Parviainen
Pasca, *Pask*
Pascal, *Pascall*
Pascale, *Pascall*
Pascaletto, *Pascall*
Pascali, *Pascall*
Pascalin, *Pascall*
Pascalino, *Pascall*
Pascalis, *Pascall*
Pascall
Pascarel, *Paquier*
Pascau, *Pascall*
Pascaud, *Pascall*
Pascault, *Pascall*
Pascaut, *Pascall*
Paschal, *Pascall*
Paschdag, *Pask*
Pasche, *Pask*
Paschek, *Paul*
Paschen, *Pask*
Paschetti, *Pask*
Paschetto, *Pask*
Paschi, *Pask*
Paschini, *Pask*
Paschke, *Paul*
Paschoud, *Pace*
Pasco, *Pask*
Páscoa, *Pask*
Pascoal, *Pascall*
Pascoe
Pascoletti, *Pask*
Pascoli, *Pask*
Pascolini, *Pask*
Pascolo, *Pask*
Pascolutti, *Pask*
Pascot, *Pascall*
Pascotti, *Pask*
Pascow, *Pascoe*
Pascual, *Pascall*
Pascucci, *Pask*
Pasculesco, *Pascall*
Pascullo, *Pask*
Pascutti, *Pask*
Pascutto, *Pask*
Pascuzzi, *Pask*
Pascuzzo, *Pask*
Pasdag, *Pask*
Pase, *Pace*
Pašek, *Paul*
Pasek, *Paul*
Paselli, *Pace*
Pasello, *Pace*
Pasetti, *Pace*
Pasetto, *Pace*
Pash, *Pask*
Pashaev, *Paul*
Pashanin, *Paul*
Pashe, *Pask*
Pashenkov, *Paul*
Pashetkin, *Paul*
Pashikhin, *Paul*
Pashin, *Paul*
Pashinin, *Paul*
Pashinkin, *Paul*
Pashinov, *Paul*
Pashintsev, *Paul*
Pashkeev, *Paul*
Pashkin, *Paul*
Pashkov, *Paul*
Pashley
Pashnev, *Paul*
Pashunin, *Paul*
Pashutin, *Paul*
Pasi, *Pace*
Pasikowski, *Paul*
Pasin, *Pace*
Pasinetti, *Pace*
Pasini, *Pace*
Pasino, *Pace*
Pasio, *Pace*
Pask
Paska, *Pask*
Paskal, *Pascall*
Paskalski, *Pascall*
Påske, *Pask*
Paske, *Pask*
Paskell, *Pascall*
Paskin, *Pask*
Pasley, *Parslow*
Paslow, *Parslow*
Pasman, *Parmenter*
Pasmanik, *Parmenter*
Pasmanter, *Parmenter*
Pasmantirer, *Parmenter*
Pasmore, *Passmore*
Pasoli, *Pace*
Pasolini, *Pace*
Pasolli, *Pace*
Pasotti, *Pace*
Pasotto, *Pace*
Pasqua, *Pask*
Pasqual, *Pascall*
Pasquale, *Pascall*
Pasqualetti, *Pascall*
Pasqualetto, *Pascall*
Pasquali, *Pascall*
Pasqualini, *Pascall*
Pasqualino, *Pascall*
Pasqualis, *Pascall*
Pasqualotto, *Pascall*
Pasquard, *Pascall*
Pasquati, *Pask*
Pasquato, *Pask*
Pasquazzo, *Pask*
Pasque, *Pask*
Pasquelin, *Pascall*
Pasquelli, *Pask*
Pasquer, *Paquier*
Pasques, *Pask*
Pasquet, *Pascall*
Pasquetti, *Pask*
Pasquez, *Pascall*
Pasqui, *Pask*
Pasquié, *Paquier*
Pasquier, *Paquier*
Pasquill, *Pascall*
Pasquinelli, *Pask*
Pasquini, *Pask*
Pasquino, *Pask*
Pasquinucci, *Pask*
Pasquinuzzi, *Pask*
Pasquotti, *Pask*
Pass, *Pascall*
Passalacqua, *Parslow*
Passe, *Pascall*
Passelègue, *Parslow*

Passelergue, *Parslow*
Passeligue, *Parslow*
Passenger
Passifull, *Percival*
Pässler, *Peter*
Passler, *Peter*
Passman, *Parmenter*
Passmanik, *Parmenter*
Passmore
Passos, *Palacio*
Passy
Paster, *Pastor*
Pasterfield, *Baskerville*
Pasternack, *Pasternak*
Pasternak
Pasteur, *Pastor*
Pastinack, *Pasternak*
Paston
Pastor
Pastore, *Pastor*
Pastorelli, *Pastor*
Pastorello, *Pastor*
Pastori, *Pastor*
Pastorini, *Pastor*
Pastorino, *Pastor*
Pastour, *Pastor*
Pastoureau, *Pastor*
Pastourel, *Pastor*
Pastre, *Pastor*
Pastrello, *Pastor*
Pastukhov
Pastushenko, *Pastukhov*
Pastushik, *Pastukhov*
Pastushonok, *Pastukhov*
Pastusiak, *Pastukhov*
Pastuszko, *Pastukhov*
Pasutti, *Pace*
Pasutto, *Pace*
Paszak, *Paul*
Paszek, *Paul*
Paszkiewicz, *Paul*
Paszkowski, *Paul*
Pásztor, *Pastor*
Pataki, *Potocki*
Pataky, *Potocki*
Patard, *Patte*
Patart, *Patte*
Patat, *Patte*
Pataud, *Patte*
Patch, *Pack*
Patchett, *Pask*
Patchin, *Pask*
Patching, *Pask*
Paté, *Patte*
Pate
Pátek, *Piątkowski*
Pateman, *Pate*
Patenostro, *Paternoster*
Patenôtre, *Paternoster*
Pater
Patera
Paternault, *Paternoster*
Paternoster
Paternostro, *Paternoster*
Paterson, *Pate*
Pates, *Pate*
Patey, *Pate*
Patey, *Patte*
Patez, *Patte*
Pathé, *Patte*
Patience
Patient, *Patience*
Patillo, *Patullo*
Patin, *Patten*
Patineau, *Patten*
Patinet, *Patten*
Patinier, *Patten*
Patison, *Pate*
Patman, *Pate*
Patmore
Patočka
Patoka, *Patočka*
Patón, *Patte*
Paton, *Pate, Patte*
Patora
Patou, *Patte*
Patoureau, *Pastor*
Patourel, *Pastor*
Patout, *Patte*
Patoux, *Patte*
Patric, *Patrick*
Patrice, *Patrick*
Patrício, *Patrick*
Patrick
Patricot, *Patrick*
Patrigeon, *Patrick*
Patrikeev, *Patrick*
Patrikeivin, *Patrick*
Patris, *Patrick*
Patrix, *Patrick*
Patron, *Patrone*
Patrone
Patroni, *Patrone*
Patrono, *Patrone*
Patruno, *Patrone*
Patrushev, *Patrick*
Patry, *Patrick*
Patt, *Pate*
Patte
Patten
Pattenden
Patterson, *Pate*
Patteson, *Pate*
Pattillo, *Patullo*
Pattin, *Patten*
Pattinson, *Pate*
Pattison, *Pate*
Pattman, *Pate*
Patton, *Pate*
Pattrick, *Patrick*
Pattullo, *Patullo*
Pattyson, *Pate*
Patu, *Patte*
Patullo
Patura, *Patora*
Patvine, *Potvin*
Patzelt, *Peter*
Pau, *Paul*
Paucker, *Pauker*
Pauel, *Paul*
Pauels, *Paul*
Pauer, *Bauer*
Paugels, *Paul*
Pauker
Paukov
Paul
Paula, *Paul*
Paulack, *Paul*
Paulat, *Paul*
Paulath, *Paul*
Paulazzi, *Paul*
Paule, *Paul*
Pauleau, *Paul*
Pauleit, *Paul*
Pauler, *Paul*
Paulet, *Paul, Pawlett*
Pauletti, *Paul*
Pauletto, *Paul*
Pauley, *Paul*
Pauli, *Paul*
Paulich, *Paul*
Paulig, *Paul*
Paulillo, *Paul*
Paulin, *Paul*
Pauling, *Paul*
Paulino, *Paul*
Paulisch, *Paul*
Paulitschke, *Paul*
Paull, *Paul*
Paulley, *Paul*
Paulling, *Paul*
Paulmann, *Paul*
Paulmier, *Palmer*
Paulo, *Paul*
Paulon, *Paul*
Paulot, *Paul*
Paulou, *Paul*
Pauls, *Paul*
Paulsen, *Paul*
Paulson, *Paul*
Paulsson, *Paul*
Paulucci, *Paul*
Paulus, *Paul*
Paulusch, *Paul*
Pauluweit, *Paul*
Pauluzzi, *Paul*
Pauly, *Paul*
Paumier, *Palmer*
Paun, *Peacock*
Pauncefoot
Pauncefort, *Pauncefoot*
Pauncefote, *Pauncefoot*
Paustian, *Sebastian*
Paustovski
Pauw, *Peacock*
Pauwel, *Paul*
Pauwels, *Paul*
Pavanelli, *Padovano*
Pavanello, *Padovano*
Pavanetti, *Padovano*
Pavanetto, *Padovano*
Pavanini, *Padovano*
Pávek, *Paul*
Pavel, *Paul*
Paveley, *Pawley*
Pavelić, *Paul*
Pavelka, *Paul*
Pavely, *Pawley*
Pavelyev, *Paul*
Paver, *Pavier*
Pavese, *Pavey*
Pavett, *Pavey*
Pavey
Pavić, *Paul*
Pavičević, *Paul*
Pavie, *Pavey*
Pavier
Pavior, *Pavier*
Paviour, *Pavier*
Pavitt, *Pavey*
Pavkin, *Paul*
Pavković, *Paul*
Pavlášek, *Paul*
Pavlata, *Paul*
Pavlenko, *Paul*
Pavlenkov, *Paul*
Pavlenov, *Paul*
Pavley, *Pawley*
Pavlić, *Paul*
Pavlíček, *Paul*
Pavličić, *Paul*
Pavlík, *Paul*
Pavlik, *Paul*
Pavlikhin, *Paul*
Pavlikov, *Paul*
Pavlishchev, *Paul*
Pavlishintsev, *Paul*
Pavlitschek, *Paul*
Pavlitsev, *Paul*
Pavlov, *Paul*
Pavlović, *Paul*
Pavlovský, *Paul*
Pavluk, *Paul*
Pavlukhin, *Paul*
Pavlushin, *Paul*
Pavlushkin, *Paul*
Pavly, *Pawley*
Pavlygin, *Paul*
Pavlyukhov, *Paul*
Pavlyukov, *Paul*
Pavna, *Padovano*
Pavnai, *Padovano*
Pavolillo, *Paul*
Pavolini, *Paul*
Pavón, *Peacock*
Pavone, *Peacock*
Pavoni, *Peacock*
Pavshin, *Paul*
Pavshukov, *Paul*
Pavsky, *Peacock*
Pavy, *Pavey*
Pavyer, *Pavier*
Pavyuchikov, *Paul*
Pavyushkov, *Paul*
Paw
Pawe, *Paw*
Paweł, *Paul*
Pawel, *Paul*
Pawełczak, *Paul*
Pawełczyk, *Paul*
Pawelec, *Paul*
Pawełek, *Paul*
Pawelke, *Paul*
Pawełkiewicz, *Paul*
Pawellek, *Paul*
Pawels, *Paul*
Pawelski, *Paul*
Pawlaczyk, *Paul*
Pawlata, *Paul*
Pawle, *Paul*
Pawlett
Pawley
Pawlick, *Paul*
Pawlicki, *Paul*
Pawlik, *Paul*
Pawlikiewicz, *Paul*
Pawlikowski, *Paul*
Pawling, *Paul*
Pawliński, *Paul*
Pawłowicz, *Paul*
Pawłowski, *Paul*
Pawlyn, *Paul*
Pawson, *Paw*
Paxmann, *Pask*
Paxton
Pay
Payan, *Pain*
Payen, *Pain*
Payer, *Payeur*
Payet, *Payeur*
Payeur
Payler
Paylor, *Payler*
Payman, *Pay*
Paymer, *Böhm*
Payn, *Pain*

Payne, *Pain*
Paynell, *Pain*
Paynes, *Pain*
Paynter, *Painter*
Payon, *Payeur*
Payot, *Payeur*
Pays
Paysan, *Pays*
Paysant, *Pays*
Payton
Payze, *Pace*
Paz
Pazdera
Pazdernik, *Pazdera*
Pazos, *Palacio*
Pea, *Peacock*
Peabody
Peace, *Pace*
Peach, *Peachey*
Peache, *Peachey*
Peachey
Peacock
Peacocke, *Peacock*
Peaddie, *Peter*
Peagram, *Pilgrim*
Peagrim, *Pilgrim*
Peak
Peake, *Peak*
Peaker, *Peak*
Peakman, *Peak*
Peale, *Peel*
Péan, *Pain*
Peaple, *Pepys*
Pear
Pearce
Pearcey, *Percy*
Pearcy, *Percy*
Pearl
Pearlin, *Pearl*
Pearlman, *Pearl*
Pearlstine, *Pearl*
Pearman, *Pear*
Pearmund, *Pear*
Pearpoint, *Pierrepont*
Pears, *Pearce*
Pearse, *Pearce*
Pearsey, *Percy*
Pearson, *Pearce*
Pearsy, *Percy*
Peart
Peartree, *Pear*
Pease
Peasey, *Pusey*
Peat, *Peter*
Peattie, *Peter*
Pebjoy, *Pobgee*
Pebre, *Pepper*
Peces, *Pesce*
Pech, *Peter, Puy*
Pecha, *Peter*
Pecháček, *Peter*
Pechan, *Peter*
Pechar, *Pecher*
Peche, *Peter*
Péchels
Pecher
Pêcheur
Pêcheux, *Pêcheur*
Pechey, *Peachey*
Pechhold, *Peter*
Péchin, *Pettit*
Pechner, *Pecher*
Pechold, *Peter*
Péchon, *Pettit*
Pechon, *Pettit*
Péchot, *Pettit*
Pechot, *Pettit*
Péchou, *Pettit*
Péchoux, *Pettit*
Pechstein, *Bechstein*
Pecht, *Peter*
Pechwasser, *Pecher*
Peck
Peckham
Pecora
Pecorai, *Pecora*
Pecorari, *Pecora*
Pecoraro, *Pecora*
Pecorella, *Pecora*
Pecorelli, *Pecora*
Pecori, *Pecora*
Pecorini, *Pecora*
Pecqueur, *Pêcheur*
Pecqueux, *Pêcheur*
Pedan, *Patrick*
Peddar, *Pedler*
Pedder, *Pedler*
Peddie, *Peter*
Pedeferro, *Pettifer*
Pedel, *Beadle*
Peden, *Patrick*
Peder, *Bader*
Pedersen, *Peter*
Pedilepore, *Pedler*
Pedlar, *Pedler*
Pedler
Pedley
Pedlow, *Pedley*
Pedoux, *Pou*
Pedraza, *Pierre*
Pedrazzi, *Peter*
Pedreira, *Pierre*
Pedrelli, *Peter*
Pedrera, *Pierre*
Pedretti, *Parrott*
Pedri, *Peter*
Pedrick, *Pethick*
Pedrielli, *Peter*
Pedrin, *Perrin*
Pedrinelli, *Perrin*
Pedrini, *Perrin*
Pedrioli, *Peter*
Pedrizzoli, *Peter*
Pedro, *Peter*
Pedró
Pedrocchi, *Peter*
Pedrocco, *Peter*
Pedroli, *Peter*
Pedrolini, *Peter*
Pedrollo, *Peter*
Pedron, *Peter, Pierre*
Pedroni, *Peter*
Pedrosa
Pedroso, *Pedrosa*
Pedrotini, *Parrott*
Pedrotto, *Parrott*
Pedrozzi, *Peter*
Pedrucci, *Peter*
Pędziwiatr
Pee, *Peacock, Peter*
Peear, *Pear*
Peebles
Peech, *Peachey*
Peeck, *Pike*
Peecock, *Peacock*
Peek, *Peak, Pike*
Peel
Peele, *Peel*
Peer, *Pear, Peter*
Peereboom, *Birnbaum*
Peers, *Pearce, Peter*
Peet, *Peter*
Peeter, *Peter*
Peetermann, *Peter*
Peeters, *Peter*
Peever, *Pepper*
Peffer, *Pepper*
Peffers, *Pepper*
Pegaire, *Pecher*
Pegeaud, *Pègue*
Pegeon, *Pègue*
Pegeot, *Pègue*
Pegg
Peggram, *Pilgrim*
Peghaire, *Pecher*
Pegler, *Pedler*
Pegorari, *Pecora*
Pegoraro, *Pecora*
Pegorer, *Pecora*
Pegoretti, *Pecora*
Pegorin, *Pecora*
Pegorini, *Pecora*
Pegram, *Pilgrim*
Pegrum, *Pilgrim*
Pègue
Peguet, *Pègue*
Peguri, *Pecora*
Pehlgrimm, *Pilgrim*
Pehrsson, *Peter*
Pei, *Peter*
Peickert, *Pauker*
Peidró, *Peter*
Peifer, *Piper*
Peile, *Peel*
Peimer, *Böhm*
Peinado
Peintre, *Painter*
Peiper, *Piper*
Peipers, *Piper*
Peircey, *Percy*
Peire, *Peter*
Peire, *Pierre*
Peiretti, *Parrott*
Peirier, *Perrier*
Peiró, *Peter*
Peiro, *Peter*
Peiroli, *Peter*
Peirone, *Peter*
Peisach
Peisachovitz, *Peisach*
Peisachowitch, *Peisach*
Peiser, *Peyzer*
Peiser
Peisson, *Pesce*
Peix, *Pesce*
Peixero, *Pêcheur*
Peixinho, *Pesce*
Peixoto, *Pesce*
Peixotto, *Pesce*
Peizer, *Peyzer*
Pękala
Pękalski, *Pękala*
Pekař, *Piekarski*
Pekárek, *Piekarski*
Pekić, *Piekarski*
Pěkný
Peković, *Piekarski*
Peláez, *Pelayo*
Pelard, *Pellé*
Pelat, *Pellé*
Pelayo
Pełczyński
Pelé, *Pellé*
Pelegrí, *Pilgrim*
Pelegri, *Pilgrim*
Pélégrin, *Pilgrim*
Pélegrin, *Pilgrim*
Pelegrín, *Pilgrim*
Pelegry, *Pilgrim*
Pélerin, *Pilgrim*
Pelerin, *Pilgrim*
Pelgram, *Pilgrim*
Pelgrim, *Pilgrim*
Pelgrin, *Pilgrim*
Pelham
Pélicier, *Pelisse*
Pelicier, *Pelisse*
Péligry, *Pilgrim*
Pelikán
Peliks, *Felix*
Pelisiak, *Felix*
Pelisier, *Pelisse*
Pelisse
Pelisseri, *Pelisse*
Pelissero, *Pelisse*
Pélissié, *Pelisse*
Pélissier, *Pelisse*
Pélisson, *Pelisse*
Pelizza, *Pelisse*
Pelizzari, *Pelisse*
Pelizzaro, *Pelisse*
Pelizzeri, *Pelisse*
Pelizzi, *Pelisse*
Pelizzon, *Pelisse*
Pelizzoni, *Pelisse*
Pełka
Pell
Pellat, *Pellé*
Pellé
Pellegrin, *Pilgrim*
Pellegrinelli, *Pilgrim*
Pellegrinetti, *Pilgrim*
Pellegrini, *Pilgrim*
Pellegrino, *Pilgrim*
Pellegrinotti, *Pilgrim*
Peller, *Pill*
Pellerini, *Pilgrim*
Pellerino, *Pilgrim*
Pelletier
Pellew, *Pedley*
Pellicaio, *Pelisse*
Pellicari, *Pelisse*
Pellicceri, *Pelisse*
Pellicchio, *Pelisse*
Pellicci, *Pelisse*
Pelliccia, *Pelisse*
Pellicciari, *Pelisse*
Pellicciaro, *Pelisse*
Pelliccioni, *Pelisse*
Pellicciotta, *Pelisse*
Pellicer, *Pelisse*
Pelling
Pellisé, *Pelisse*
Pelliser, *Pelisse*
Pellisier, *Pelisse*
Pellissero, *Pelisse*
Pellisson, *Pelisse*
Pellissone, *Pelisse*
Pellissoni, *Pelisse*
Pellitteri, *Pelletier*
Pellizza, *Pelisse*
Pellizzari, *Pelisse*
Pellizzaro, *Pelisse*
Pellizzeri, *Pelisse*
Pellizzi, *Pelisse*
Pellizzon, *Pelisse*

Pellizzoni, *Pelisse*
Pellman, *Pill*
Pellow
Pelly, *Pell*
Pelman, *Pill*
Pelser, *Pilcher*
Pelt, *Pelletier*
Pelter, *Pelletier*
Peltier, *Pelletier*
Peltola, *Peltonen*
Peltonen
Peltz, *Pilcher*
Peltzer, *Pilcher*
Pelz, *Pilcher*
Pelzer, *Pilcher*
Pelzman, *Pilcher*
Pelzmann, *Pilcher*
Pelzner, *Pilcher*
Pemberton
Pena, *Peña*
Peña
Peñas, *Peña*
Pendegast, *Prendergast*
Pendelton, *Pendleton*
Pender, *Pinder*
Pendergast, *Prendergast*
Pendergrast, *Prendergast*
Pendgrast, *Prendergast*
Pendlebury
Pendleton
Pendreigh
Pendrich, *Pendreigh*
Pendrigh, *Pendreigh*
Pendry, *Parry*
Pendy, *Parry*
Penev, *Stephen*
Penfold
Pengelley, *Pengelly*
Pengelly
Pengilley, *Pengelly*
Pengilly, *Pengelly*
Penhaligon
Pěnkava, *Pinch*
Penman
Penn
Penna
Pennacci, *Peña*
Pennall, *Parnell*
Pennazzi, *Peña*
Pennecuik, *Pennycuick*
Pennell, *Parnell*
Pennella, *Peña*
Pennelli, *Peña*
Penner, *Penn*
Pennetier, *Panther*
Pennetta, *Peña*
Pennetti, *Peña*
Penney, *Penny*
Penneycuik, *Pennycuick*
Penni, *Peña*
Pennie, *Penny*
Penniello, *Peña*
Penniman, *Penny*
Penninck, *Penny*
Penning, *Penny*
Pennings, *Penny*
Pennington
Pennini, *Peña*
Pennino, *Peña*
Pennone, *Peña*
Pennoni, *Peña*
Pennson, *Penn*
Penny
Pennycock, *Pennycuick*
Pennycook, *Pennycuick*
Pennycuick
Pennyman, *Penny*
Penrose
Penson, *Penn*
Penswick
Pentecost
Pentercost, *Pentecost*
Pentey, *Penty*
Penticost, *Pentecost*
Pentland
Pentreath
Penty
Pentycross, *Pentecost*
Penwarden, *Penwarne*
Penwarne
Penzer, *Peyzer*
Peopall, *Pepys*
People, *Pepys*
Peoples, *Pepys*
Pepall, *Pepys*
Peper, *Pepper*
Peperel, *Pepper*
Peperman, *Pepper*
Pepernick, *Pepper*
Pepernik, *Pepper*
Peperwell, *Pepper*
Pépi, *Pepys*
Pépin, *Pepys*
Pepin, *Pepys*
Pépineau, *Pepys*
Pépineaux, *Pepys*
Pepino, *Pepys*
Pépinot, *Pepys*
Peploe, *Peplow*
Peplow
Peppar, *Pepper*
Pepper
Pepperall, *Pepper*
Pepperell, *Pepper*
Peppett, *Pepys*
Peppiatt, *Pepys*
Peppiett, *Pepys*
Peppin, *Pepys*
Pepprell, *Pepper*
Pepy, *Pepys*
Pepys
Pequeño, *Piccini*
Pequeur, *Pêcheur*
Pequeux, *Pêcheur*
Pera, *Pear*
Peracco, *Peter*
Peral, *Pear*
Perales, *Pear*
Peralta
Pérard, *Pierre*
Perassi, *Peter*
Perasso, *Peter*
Pérault, *Pierre*
Péraut, *Pierre*
Perazzi, *Peter*
Perazzo, *Peter*
Perce, *Pearce*
Perceval, *Percival*
Percevau, *Percival*
Percevaut, *Percival*
Percevaux, *Percival*
Percey, *Percy*
Perciavalle, *Percival*
Perciavalli, *Percival*
Perciballi, *Percival*
Percifull, *Percival*
Percipalli, *Percival*
Percival
Percivale, *Percival*
Percivalle, *Percival*
Percivalli, *Percival*
Percy
Perdigão, *Partridge*
Perdiguès, *Partridge*
Perdrigeon, *Partridge*
Perdriget, *Partridge*
Perdrigon, *Partridge*
Perdriguier, *Partridge*
Perdrix, *Partridge*
Perdrizet, *Partridge*
Perdrizot, *Partridge*
Perdue, *Pardoe*
Péré, *Pear*
Pere, *Pear, Peter*
Péreau, *Pierre*
Pereda, *Pear*
Peregrín, *Pilgrim*
Peregrine, *Pilgrim*
Peregrino, *Pilgrim*
Pereira, *Pear*
Perek
Pérel, *Pierre*
Perel, *Pearl*
Perell, *Peter*
Perella, *Pear*
Perellas, *Pear*
Perelli, *Peter*
Perello, *Peter*
Perelló
Perelman, *Pearl*
Perelmann, *Pearl*
Perelmuter, *Pearl*
Perelmutter, *Pearl*
Perelsman, *Pearl*
Perelson, *Pearl*
Perelstein, *Pearl*
Perepelitsa, *Perepyolkin*
Perepelizky, *Perepyolkin*
Perepyolkin
Perera, *Pear*
Pérès, *Pear*
Peres, *Peter*
Péret, *Parrott*
Peret, *Parrott*
Perett, *Parrott*
Peretti, *Parrott*
Peretto, *Parrott*
Peretto, *Pear*
Perevodchikov
Pérez, *Peter*
Perfect, *Parfitt*
Perfett, *Parfitt*
Perfitt, *Parfitt*
Pergament, *Permenter*
Pergamenter, *Permenter*
Pergens, *Peter*
Perham
Peri, *Perry*
Peri, *Peter*
Perić, *Peter*
Périé, *Pear*
Periello, *Peter*
Périer, *Pear*
Perilli, *Peter*
Perillio, *Peter*
Perillo, *Peter*
Periman, *Perry*
Perin, *Perrin*
Peřina, *Perov*
Périnel, *Perrin*
Perinelli, *Perrin*
Perinello, *Perrin*
Périnet, *Perrin*
Perinetti, *Perrin*
Perini, *Perrin*
Perino, *Perrin*
Peris, *Peter*
Perišić, *Peter*
Periz, *Peter*
Perizzi, *Peter*
Perka, *Perek*
Perken, *Parkin*
Perkin, *Parkin*
Perkins, *Parkin*
Perkowski, *Perek*
Perks, *Park*
Perl, *Pearl*
Perla, *Pearl*
Perlberg, *Pearl*
Perlberger, *Pearl*
Perle, *Pearl*
Perler, *Pearl*
Perles, *Pearl*
Perlesman, *Pearl*
Perlgut, *Pearl*
Perli, *Pearl*
Perlin, *Pearl*
Perliński, *Pearl*
Perlinski, *Pearl*
Perlis, *Pearl*
Perlman, *Pearl*
Perlmann, *Pearl*
Perlmuter, *Pearl*
Perlmutter, *Pearl*
Perlov, *Pearl*
Perlow, *Pearl*
Perlowski, *Pearl*
Perlrot, *Pearl*
Perlroth, *Pearl*
Perlschein, *Pearl*
Perlstein, *Pearl*
Perlszweig, *Pearl*
Perlus, *Pearl*
Permann, *Bermann*
Permenter
Perna, *Pearl*
Pernelle, *Parnell*
Pernet, *Perrin*
Pernin, *Perrin*
Pernod, *Perrin*
Pernollet, *Perrin*
Pernot, *Perrin*
Pero, *Peter*
Perocci, *Peter*
Peroli, *Peter*
Perolo, *Peter*
Peron, *Peter, Pierre*
Perone, *Peter*
Péroneau, *Pierre*
Péronel, *Pierre*
Peroni, *Peter*
Perony, *Pierre*
Pérot, *Parrott*
Perot, *Parrott*
Perott, *Parrott*
Perotto, *Parrott*
Peroutka, *Perov*
Perov
Perović, *Peter*
Perowne, *Perrowne*
Perozzi, *Peter*
Perozzo, *Peter*
Perpillou, *Papillon*
Perrain, *Perrin*
Perram, *Perham*
Perrard, *Pierre*

Perrat, *Parrott, Pierre*
Perrault, *Pierre*
Perraut, *Pierre*
Perreau, *Pierre*
Perrein, *Perrin*
Perrelli, *Peter*
Perren, *Perrin*
Perrenet, *Perrin*
Perrennet, *Perrin*
Perrès, *Parrott*
Perret, *Parrott*
Perretti, *Parrott*
Perretto, *Parrott*
Perri, *Perry, Peter*
Perriault, *Pierre*
Perrie, *Perry*
Perrier
Perrillo, *Peter*
Perriman, *Perry*
Perriment, *Perry*
Perrin
Perrineau, *Perrin*
Perrinet, *Perrin*
Perring, *Perrin*
Perrino, *Perrin*
Perrins, *Perrin*
Perriot, *Parrott*
Perris, *Pearce*
Perris, *Peter*
Perron, *Perrowne, Pierre*
Perrone, *Peter*
Perroneau, *Pierre*
Perronel, *Pierre*
Perronelle, *Parnell*
Perronet, *Pierre*
Perroni, *Peter*
Perronin, *Pierre*
Perronneau, *Pierre*
Perronnelle, *Parnell*
Perronnin, *Pierre*
Perronot, *Pierre*
Perrot, *Parrott*
Perroteau, *Parrott*
Perrotin, *Parrott*
Perroton, *Parrott*
Perroux, *Pierre*
Perrowne
Perruc, *Pierre*
Perrucci, *Peter*
Perruccio, *Peter*
Perruli, *Peter*
Perrulo, *Peter*
Perry
Perrycost, *Pentecost*
Perryman, *Perry*
Perryn, *Perrin*
Persay, *Percy*
Perschke, *Peter*
Perscke, *Peter*
Perse, *Pearce*
Perseval, *Percival*
Pershing, *Pfirsich*
Persiado, *Precious*
Persian, *Peter*
Persich, *Peter*
Persicke, *Peter*
Persse, *Pearce*
Perssiado, *Precious*
Persson, *Peter*
Pertek
Perthold, *Berthold*
Perthuis, *Pertwee*
Perthuy, *Pertwee*
Pertini, *Bert*
Pertkiewicz, *Pertek*
Pertoldi, *Berthold*
Pertotti, *Bert*
Pertuce, *Pertwee*
Pertuis, *Pertwee*
Pertuiset, *Pertwee*
Pertuisot, *Pertwee*
Pertus, *Pertwee*
Pertwee
Perucci, *Peter*
Perulli, *Peter*
Perullo, *Peter*
Perut, *Peter*
Perutti, *Peter*
Perutto, *Peter*
Peruzzi, *Peter*
Peruzzo, *Peter*
Pery, *Perry*
Peryman, *Perry*
Peš, *Peter*
Pesach, *Peisach*
Pesachov, *Peisach*
Pesachovitz, *Peisach*
Pesah, *Peisach*
Pesahovitz, *Peisach*
Pesahson, *Peisach*
Pešák, *Peter*
Pesakhowich, *Peisach*
Pescador, *Pêcheur*
Pescadou, *Pêcheur*
Pescaire, *Pêcheur*
Pescatore, *Pêcheur*
Pescatori, *Pêcheur*
Pesce
Pescetto, *Pesce*
Peschel, *Peter*
Peschelt, *Peter*
Pescheur, *Pêcheur*
Pescheux, *Pêcheur*
Peschi, *Pesce*
Peschio, *Pesce*
Peschione, *Pesce*
Peschka, *Peter*
Peschke, *Peter*
Peschmann, *Peter*
Pescini, *Pesce*
Pesciolini, *Pesce*
Pešek, *Peter*
Peshes, *Peshin*
Peshin
Peshkin, *Peshin*
Peshkov
Pešić, *Peter*
Pešík, *Peter*
Peskin, *Peshin*
Peso
Pesolt, *Peter*
Pesquer, *Pêcheur*
Pesqueur, *Pêcheur*
Pesqueux, *Pêcheur*
Pesquier, *Pêcheur*
Pessach, *Peisach*
Pessah, *Peisach*
Pessahov, *Peisach*
Pessahovitz, *Peisach*
Pessel, *Peshin, Peter*
Pesselov, *Peshin*
Pessler, *Peter*
Pessoa
Pessold, *Peter*
Pessolt, *Peter*
Pest, *Sebastian*
Pestalozzi
Pestana
Pesteil, *Pistol*
Pestel, *Pistol*
Pestelard, *Pistol*
Pestell, *Pistol*
Pesterfield, *Baskerville*
Pesteur, *Pistol*
Pestlin, *Sebastian*
Pestour, *Pistol*
Pestre, *Pistol*
Pestureau, *Pistol*
Petaev, *Peter*
Pétain, *Petter*
Peták, *Peter*
Pétard, *Petter*
Petasch, *Peter*
Pétat, *Petter*
Pétaud, *Petter*
Pétavin, *Potvin*
Pétavy, *Potvin*
Petch, *Peachey*
Petche, *Peachey*
Petchey, *Peachey*
Petegree, *Pettigrew*
Pétel, *Pistol*
Pételat, *Pistol*
Pételaz, *Pistol*
Pétellat, *Pistol*
Péter, *Peter*
Peter
Petera, *Peter*
Péterffy, *Peter*
Péterfy, *Peter*
Péteri, *Peter*
Peterick, *Peter*
Petermann, *Peter*
Peternell, *Parnell*
Peternot, *Paternoster*
Peternotte, *Paternoster*
Peters, *Peter*
Peterse, *Peter*
Petersen, *Peter*
Peterson, *Peter*
Petetin, *Pettit*
Petetot, *Pettit*
Pethard, *Petter*
Pether, *Peter*
Petherick, *Pethick*
Pethers, *Peter*
Pethick
Pethybridge
Petichev, *Peter*
Petiet, *Pettit*
Pétin, *Petter*
Petin, *Peter*
Petinov, *Peter*
Petion, *Pettit*
Petiot, *Pettit*
Petipa
Petit, *Pettit*
Petiteau, *Pettit*
Petitet, *Pettit*
Petiton, *Pettit*
Petitot, *Pettit*
Petkó, *Peter*
Petkov, *Peter*
Petković, *Peter*
Petlyura, *Peter*
Petö, *Peter*
Petöfi, *Peter*
Péton, *Petter*
Pétot, *Petter*
Petour, *Petter*
Petr, *Peter*
Petracchi, *Peter*
Petracci, *Peter*
Petracco, *Peter*
Petráček, *Peter*
Petrachkov, *Peter*
Petraev, *Peter*
Petráitis, *Peter*
Petrák, *Peter*
Petrakov, *Peter*
Petráň, *Peter*
Petran, *Peter*
Petránek, *Peter*
Petrás, *Peter*
Petrasch, *Peter*
Petrášek, *Peter*
Petrásek, *Peter*
Petrashkevich, *Peter*
Petrashkov, *Peter*
Petrashov, *Peter*
Petrasso, *Peter*
Petráuskas, *Peter*
Petrazzi, *Peter*
Petré, *Peter*
Petre, *Peter, Pistol*
Pétrel, *Pistol*
Petrelli, *Peter*
Petrello, *Peter*
Petrelluzzi, *Peter*
Petrén, *Peter*
Petrenko, *Peter*
Petrescu, *Peter*
Petrettini, *Parrott*
Petri, *Peter*
Petrić, *Peter*
Petriccelli, *Peter*
Petriccini, *Peter*
Petricciolo, *Peter*
Petříček, *Peter*
Petrichat, *Peter*
Petrick, *Peter*
Petrie
Petriello, *Peter*
Petřík, *Peter*
Petrik, *Peter*
Petrilli, *Peter*
Petrillo, *Peter*
Petrin, *Perrin*
Petřína, *Peter*
Petrini, *Perrin*
Petris, *Peter*
Petrishchev, *Peter*
Petrizzelli, *Peter*
Petrizzi, *Peter*
Petroccello, *Peter*
Petrocchi, *Peter*
Petroccini, *Peter*
Petroff, *Peter*
Petroli, *Peter*
Petrolini, *Peter*
Petrolino, *Peter*
Petrolli, *Peter*
Petrolo, *Peter*
Pétron, *Pistol*
Petroni, *Peter*
Petronis, *Peter*
Petroselli, *Peter*
Petrosian, *Peter*
Petrotto, *Parrott*
Petrou, *Peter*
Petroulis, *Peter*
Petrov, *Peter*
Petrović, *Peter*
Petrovykh, *Peter*
Petrozzi, *Peter*
Petrozzini, *Peter*

Petrů, *Peter*
Petru, *Peter*
Petruccelli, *Peter*
Petrucchini, *Peter*
Petrucci, *Peter*
Petruccini, *Peter*
Petrucco, *Peter*
Petruichev, *Peter*
Petruk, *Peter*
Petrulis, *Peter*
Petrullo, *Peter*
Petrunin, *Peter*
Petrunkin, *Peter*
Petrus, *Peter*
Petrusch, *Peter*
Petrusevich, *Peter*
Petrushanko, *Peter*
Petrushevich, *Peter*
Petrushka, *Peter*
Petrushkevich, *Peter*
Petruska, *Peter*
Petruskevich, *Peter*
Petrussi, *Peter*
Petruszka, *Peter*
Petruzzelli, *Peter*
Petruzzi, *Peter*
Petruzziello, *Peter*
Petruzzio, *Peter*
Petruzzo, *Peter*
Petry, *Peter*
Petryashov, *Peter*
Petrykowski, *Peter*
Petsch, *Peter*
Petschel, *Peter*
Petschelt, *Peter*
Pett, *Pitt*
Pettafor, *Pettifer*
Pettefar, *Pettifer*
Pettefer, *Pettifer*
Pettegree, *Pettigrew*
Pettelat, *Pistol*
Pettendrich, *Pendreigh*
Pettengell, *Pettingell*
Pettengill, *Pettingell*
Petter
Petters, *Peter*
Pettersson, *Peter*
Pettet, *Pettit*
Petticrew, *Pettigrew*
Petticrow, *Pettigrew*
Pettie, *Pettit*
Pettifar, *Pettifer*
Pettifer
Pettiford, *Pettifer*
Pettigree, *Pettigrew*
Pettigrew
Pettingale, *Pettingell*
Pettingall, *Pettingell*
Pettingell
Pettingill, *Pettingell*
Pettipher, *Pettifer*
Pettit
Pettitt, *Pettit*
Pettiver, *Pettifer*
Pettkó, *Peter*
Pettman, *Pitt*
Pettour, *Petter*
Petts, *Pitt*
Petttersson, *Peter*
Petty, *Pettit*
Pettyfer, *Pettifer*
Pettyfor, *Pettifer*
Petuchowski, *Petukhov*
Petugin, *Peter*
Petukhov
Petuzzo, *Peter*
Petyakov, *Peter*
Petyanin, *Peter*
Petyankin, *Peter*
Petyt, *Pettit*
Petz, *Peter*
Petzold, *Peter*
Petzolt, *Peter*
Peu, *Puy*
Peuch, *Puy*
Peuchert, *Pauker*
Peugeot, *Pègue*
Peuker, *Pauker*
Peutherer
Peuvret, *Pepper*
Peux, *Puy*
Peverall, *Pepper*
Peverel, *Pepper*
Peverell, *Pepper*
Peverill, *Pepper*
Pevsner, *Pevzner*
Pevzner
Pew, *Pugh*
Pewsey
Pewterer, *Peutherer*
Pey, *Pay, Puy*
Peyman, *Pay*
Peyraud, *Pierre*
Peyre, *Pierre*
Peyro, *Peter*
Peyron, *Pierre*
Peyroneau, *Pierre*
Peyronet, *Pierre*
Peyronin, *Pierre*
Peyrony, *Pierre*
Peyrot, *Parrott*
Peyruc, *Pierre*
Peysson, *Pesce*
Peyssoneau, *Pesce*
Peytavi, *Potvin*
Peytavin, *Potvin*
Peytel, *Pistol*
Peytou, *Pistol*
Peytour, *Pistol*
Peyzer
Pezey, *Pusey*
Pezout, *Pou*
Pezron, *Pierre*
Pfab, *Peacock*
Pfabian, *Fabian*
Pfabigan, *Fabian*
Pfaffe, *Pope*
Pfäffle, *Pope*
Pfahl, *Peel*
Pfähler, *Peel*
Pfahler, *Peel*
Pfaitler, *Pfeidler*
Pfau, *Peacock*
Pfeffel, *Pope*
Pfeffelin, *Pope*
Pfeffer, *Pepper*
Pfefferbaum, *Pepper*
Pfefferbluth, *Pepper*
Pfefferkranz, *Pepper*
Pfefferle, *Pepper*
Pfefferlein, *Pepper*
Pfeffermann, *Pepper*
Pfeidler
Pfeifer, *Piper*
Pfeiffer, *Piper*
Pfeil
Pfeiler, *Pfeil*
Pfeilschmidt, *Pfeil*
Pfeitler, *Pfeidler*
Pfell, *Faille*
Pfennig, *Penny*
Pfenning, *Penny*
Pfersching, *Pfirsich*
Pfersich, *Pfirsich*
Pfertner, *Porter*
Pfeuffer, *Piper*
Pfiffer, *Piper*
Pfingst, *Pentecost*
Pfingsten, *Pentecost*
Pfingstmann, *Pentecost*
Pfingstner, *Pentecost*
Pfirsching, *Pfirsich*
Pfirsich
Pfister
Pfisterer, *Pfister*
Pfitzer, *Pfützer*
Pfitzmann, *Pfützer*
Pfitzner, *Pfützer*
Pflaum, *Plum*
Pflaumbaum, *Plum*
Pfläumer, *Plum*
Pfliegner, *Plowman*
Pflimlin, *Plum*
Pflöschner, *Flaschner*
Pflug, *Plowman*
Pflüger, *Plowman*
Pflugner, *Plowman*
Pföffer, *Pepper*
Pfoh, *Peacock*
Pforr, *Poireau*
Pförsching, *Pfirsich*
Pförtner, *Porter*
Pfost, *Post*
Pföstl, *Post*
Pfraumbaum, *Plum*
Pfräumer, *Plum*
Pfuhl, *Pool*
Pfuhler, *Pool*
Pfuhlmann, *Pool*
Pfützer
Pfützmann, *Pfützer*
Pfützner, *Pfützer*
Phair, *Fair*
Phaisey, *Vaisey*
Phalip, *Philip*
Phalp, *Philip*
Pharaoh, *Farrar*
Pharrow, *Farrar*
Phasey, *Vaisey*
Phayre, *Fair*
Phazey, *Vaisey*
Phear, *Fear*
Pheasey, *Vaisey*
Pheazey, *Vaisey*
Phelan, *Whelan*
Phélip, *Philip*
Phelip, *Philip*
Phélipeau, *Philip*
Phélipot, *Philpott*
Phelips, *Philip*
Phélit, *Philip*
Phelp, *Philip*
Phelps, *Philip*
Phemister, *Femister*
Phenix, *Fenwick*
Phethean, *Vivian*
Pheysey, *Vaisey*
Philan, *Whelan*
Philbert
Philbey, *Filby*
Philby, *Filby*
Philcock, *Philip*
Philcott, *Philip*
Philcox, *Philip*
Philibert, *Philbert*
Philip
Philipard, *Philip*
Philipart, *Philip*
Philipault, *Philip*
Philipeau, *Philip*
Philipeaux, *Philip*
Philipet, *Philip*
Philipon, *Philip*
Philipot, *Philpott*
Philipp, *Philip*
Philippard, *Philip*
Philippart, *Philip*
Philippault, *Philip*
Philippe, *Philip*
Philippeau, *Philip*
Philippeaux, *Philip*
Philippet, *Philip*
Philippi, *Philip*
Philippon, *Philip*
Philippot, *Philpott*
Philippou, *Philip*
Philipps, *Philip*
Philippsen, *Philip*
Philippsohn, *Philip*
Philippson, *Philip*
Philips, *Philip*
Philipsen, *Philip*
Philipsohn, *Philip*
Philipson, *Philip*
Philipsson, *Philip*
Phillcox, *Philip*
Phillimore
Phillins, *Philip*
Phillip, *Philip*
Phillippot, *Philpott*
Phillipps, *Philip*
Phillips, *Philip*
Phillipson, *Philip*
Phillis, *Philip*
Phillp, *Philip*
Phillpot, *Philpott*
Phillpots, *Philpott*
Phillpott, *Philpott*
Phillps, *Philip*
Philosoph
Philossoph, *Philosoph*
Philott, *Philip*
Philozof, *Philosoph*
Philp, *Philip*
Philpot, *Philpott*
Philpots, *Philpott*
Philpott
Philpotts, *Philpott*
Philps, *Philip*
Philson, *Philip*
Phimister, *Femister*
Phin, *Finn*
Phinn, *Finn*
Phippen, *Philip*
Phippin, *Philip*
Phipps, *Philip*
Phips, *Philip*
Phipson, *Philip*
Phizackerley, *Fazakerley*
Phizackerly, *Fazakerley*
Phlipon, *Philip*
Phlips, *Philip*
Phoenix, *Fenwick*
Phyffe, *Fyfe*
Phythian, *Vivian*
Phytian, *Vivian*

Pi, *Pine*
Piacentini, *Pleasance*
Piacentino, *Pleasance*
Piacenza, *Pleasance*
Piaget
Pian, *Plain*
Piana, *Plain*
Pianella, *Plain*
Pianelli, *Plain*
Pianese, *Plain*
Pianetti, *Plain*
Piangiani, *Plain*
Piani, *Plain*
Piano, *Plain*
Pianon, *Plain*
Pianone, *Plain*
Piasecki
Piaseczny, *Piasecki*
Piasentin, *Pleasance*
Piasentini, *Pleasance*
Piaskowiak, *Piasecki*
Piaskowski, *Piasecki*
Piasny, *Piasecki*
Piątek, *Piątkowski*
Piątkiewicz, *Piątkowski*
Piątkowski
Piaz, *Place*
Piazza, *Place*
Piazzese, *Place*
Piazzesi, *Place*
Piazzi, *Place*
Piazzini, *Place*
Piazzola, *Place*
Piazzoli, *Place*
Piazzolla, *Place*
Pic, *Pike*
Pica, *Pye*
Picard, *Pickard, Pike*
Picardi, *Pickard*
Picardino, *Pickard*
Picardo, *Pickard*
Piçarra, *Pizarro*
Picart, *Pickard*
Picassó, *Picazo*
Picaud, *Pike*
Picault, *Pike*
Picazo
Piccard, *Pickard*
Piccardi, *Pickard*
Piccardino, *Pickard*
Piccardo, *Pickard*
Picchetti, *Piggott*
Picchi, *Pike*
Picchio, *Pike*
Picchioni, *Pike*
Piccin, *Piccini*
Piccinelli, *Piccini*
Piccini
Piccinin, *Piccini*
Piccinini, *Piccini*
Piccinino, *Piccini*
Piccinni, *Piccini*
Piccinno, *Piccini*
Picciocchi, *Piccini*
Piccioli, *Piccini*
Picciolo, *Piccini*
Piccione, *Pidgeon*
Piccioni, *Pidgeon*
Picciotto, *Piccini*
Piccitto, *Piccini*
Picciulli, *Piccini*
Picciullo, *Piccini*
Picciuzzo, *Piccini*
Piccoli, *Piccini*
Piccolin, *Piccini*
Piccolini, *Piccini*
Piccolino, *Piccini*
Piccolo, *Piccini*
Piccolomini, *Piccolomo*
Piccolomo
Pichan, *Peter*
Pichard, *Pike*
Pichaud, *Pike*
Pichault, *Pike*
Piche, *Peter*
Picher, *Pike*
Pichert, *Pike*
Pichetti, *Piggott*
Pichl, *Bühler*
Pichler, *Bühler*
Pichmann, *Peter*
Pichon, *Pidgeon*
Pichon, *Pike*
Pichonneau, *Pike*
Pichot, *Piggott*
Pichou, *Pidgeon*
Pichounier, *Pidgeon*
Pick
Pickard
Picken, *Pick*
Pickerden
Pickerell
Pickerill, *Pickerell*
Pickerin, *Pickering*
Pickering
Pickersgil, *Pickersgill*
Pickersgill
Pickett, *Piggott*
Pickford
Pickholz
Pickin, *Pick*
Pickles
Pickless, *Pickles*
Pickrell, *Pickerell*
Pickrill, *Pickerell*
Pickton, *Picton*
Pickup
Picolotto, *Piccini*
Picon, *Pike*
Picot, *Piggott*
Picq, *Pike*
Picquet, *Piggott*
Picquot, *Piggott*
Picton
Pidal
Piddington
Pideon, *Pidgeon*
Pidgen, *Pidgeon*
Pidgeon
Pidler, *Pedler*
Pidon, *Pidgeon*
Pié, *Piera*
Pie, *Peter*
Piech, *Peter*
Piecha, *Peter*
Piechnik, *Peter*
Piechocki, *Piechota*
Piechota
Piechowiak, *Piechota*
Piedade
Piedra, *Pierre*
Piegrome, *Pilgrim*
Piehl, *Pfeil*
Piekarski
Piekarz, *Piekarski*
Pieksma, *Pike*
Piel, *Pfeil*
Piele, *Peel*
Pielk, *Pfeil*
Pielke, *Pfeil*
Pielmann, *Pfeil*
Pien, *Peter*
Pieńkowski
Piens, *Peter*
Pieper, *Piper*
Piepers, *Piper*
Piera
Pieracci, *Peter*
Piérard, *Pierre*
Piérat, *Pierre*
Pierazzi, *Peter*
Pierce, *Pearce*
Piercey, *Percy*
Piercy, *Percy*
Pieretti, *Parrott*
Pierettini, *Parrott*
Pieri, *Peter*
Pierini, *Perrin*
Pieroni, *Peter*
Pierotto, *Parrott*
Pierozzi, *Peter*
Pierpon, *Pierrepont*
Pierpont, *Pierrepont*
Pierrard, *Pierre*
Pierrat, *Pierre*
Pierre
Pierrepoint, *Pierrepont*
Pierrepont
Pierret, *Parrott*
Pierrey, *Parrott*
Pierrez, *Parrott*
Pierri, *Peter*
Pierrier, *Perrier*
Pierro, *Peter*
Pierron, *Pierre*
Pierrot, *Parrott*
Pierrou, *Pierre*
Piers, *Pearce*
Pierse, *Pearce*
Piersma, *Peter*
Pierson, *Pearce*
Pierucci, *Peter*
Pieruccio, *Peter*
Pieruzzi, *Peter*
Pierzchała
Pierzchalski, *Pierzchała*
Piesold, *Peter*
Piet, *Peter, Piggott*
Pieter, *Peter*
Pieters, *Peter*
Pieterse, *Peter*
Pietersen, *Peter*
Pietersma, *Peter*
Pietranek, *Peter*
Pietras, *Peter*
Pietrasiak, *Peter*
Pietrasik, *Peter*
Pietraszek, *Peter*
Pietri, *Peter*
Pietringa, *Peter*
Pietrini, *Perrin*
Pietrkiewicz, *Peter*
Pietroni, *Peter*
Pietrowicz, *Peter*
Pietrowski, *Peter*
Pietrucci, *Peter*
Pietruschka, *Peter*
Pietrusiak, *Peter*
Pietrusikiewicz, *Peter*
Pietruszewicz, *Peter*
Pietruszewski, *Peter*
Pietruszka, *Peter*
Pietrzak, *Peter*
Pietrzycki, *Peter*
Pietrzyk, *Peter*
Pietrzykowski, *Peter*
Pietsch, *Peter*
Pietucha, *Petukhov*
Pietuchowski, *Petukhov*
Pietz, *Peter*
Pietzke, *Peter*
Pietzker, *Peter*
Pietzner, *Peter*
Pieu, *Peel*
Pieuchot, *Peel*
Pieyre, *Pierre*
Pigault, *Pike*
Pigeon, *Pidgeon*
Pigg
Piggin, *Pidgeon*
Piggini, *Pidgeon*
Piggot, *Piggott*
Piggott
Piggrem, *Pilgrim*
Pighi, *Pike*
Pighills, *Pickles*
Pigler, *Bühler*
Pigoni, *Pike*
Pigot, *Piggott*
Pigott, *Piggott*
Pigotti, *Piggott*
Pigozzi, *Piggott*
Pigozzo, *Piggott*
Pigram, *Pilgrim*
Pigrome, *Pilgrim*
Pigue, *Pike*
Pihl, *Pfeil*
Pijlman, *Pfeil*
Pike
Pikett, *Piggott*
Pikhardt, *Pickard*
Pikhart, *Pickard*
Pikhno, *Philip*
Pikholz, *Pickholz*
Pilař, *Pilshchikov*
Pilar, *Pilshchikov*
Pilarczyk, *Pilshchikov*
Pilarek, *Pilshchikov*
Pilarski, *Pilshchikov*
Pilartz, *Pilshchikov*
Piłat, *Pilshchikov*
Pilát, *Pilshchikov*
Pilc, *Pilz*
Pilch, *Pilcher*
Pilcher
Pile
Pilet, *Pile*
Piletić, *Philip*
Pilger, *Pilcher*
Pilgram, *Pilgrim*
Pilgrim
Pilipets, *Philip*
Pilipović, *Philip*
Pilipyak, *Philip*
Pilkington
Pill
Pillay
Piller, *Bühler, Pill*
Pillet, *Pile*
Pilley, *Pillay*
Pilling, *Pill*
Pillitteri, *Pelletier*
Pillman, *Pill*
Pillmann, *Bühler*
Pillon, *Pile*
Pillot, *Pile*

Pilnik, *Pilshchikov*
Pilon, *Pile*
Pilosof, *Philosoph*
Pilossof, *Philosoph*
Pilot, *Pile*
Pils, *Pilz*
Pilshchikov
Pilter, *Pelletier*
Piltz, *Pilz*
Pilz
Pilzer, *Pilz*
Pim, *Pimm*
Pimblet, *Pimm*
Pimblett, *Pimm*
Pimblott, *Pimm*
Pimenta
Pimentel, *Pimenta*
Pimenthal, *Pimenta*
Pimlet, *Pimm*
Pimlett, *Pimm*
Pimlott, *Pimm*
Pimm
Pin, *Pine*
Piña, *Pine*
Pina, *Peña*
Pinar, *Pine*
Pinard
Pinardeau, *Pinard*
Pinardel, *Pinard*
Pinardon, *Pinard*
Pinart, *Pinard*
Pinas, *Pinchas*
Pinat, *Pine*
Pincas, *Pinchas*
Pinch
Pinchard, *Pincher*
Pinchart, *Pincher*
Pinchas
Pinchasi, *Pinchas*
Pinchasov, *Pinchas*
Pinchasow, *Pinchas*
Pinchaut, *Pincher*
Pinchback, *Pinchbeck*
Pinchbeck
Pinchen, *Pinson*
Pincheon, *Pinson*
Pincher
Pinches, *Pinchas*
Pinchin, *Pinson*
Pinching, *Pinson*
Pinchon, *Pinson*
Pinck, *Pinch*
Pinckney, *Pinkney*
Pincoffs, *Pinchas*
Pinçon, *Pinson*
Pincov, *Pinchas*
Pincovich, *Pinchas*
Pincovici, *Pinchas*
Pincowitz, *Pinchas*
Pincowski, *Pinchas*
Pincus, *Pinchas*
Pindar, *Pinder*
Pinder
Pindor, *Pinder*
Pine
Pineau, *Pine*
Pineaux, *Pine*
Pineda, *Pine*
Pinède, *Pine*
Pinedo, *Pine*
Piñeiro, *Pine*
Pinel, *Pine*
Pineles, *Pinchas*
Pinelli, *Pine*
Pinello, *Pine*
Piñero, *Pine*
Pinero, *Pine*
Pines, *Pinchas*
Pinet, *Pine*
Pinets, *Pine*
Pinetti, *Pine*
Pinfold, *Penfold*
Pinhal, *Pine*
Pinhas, *Pinchas*
Pinhasi, *Pinchas*
Pinhasov, *Pinchas*
Pinhasovich, *Pinchas*
Pinhasovitch, *Pinchas*
Pinhassi, *Pinchas*
Pinhassof, *Pinchas*
Pinhassovitch, *Pinchas*
Pinhassovitz, *Pinchas*
Pinhasy, *Pinchas*
Pinheiro, *Pine*
Pinho, *Pine*
Pini, *Pine*
Pinié, *Pine*
Pinier, *Pine*
Pinilla, *Peña*
Pinilla, *Pine*
Pink, *Pinch*
Pinkas, *Pinchas*
Pinkason, *Pinchas*
Pinkasovitz, *Pinchas*
Pinkerton
Pinkett, *Pinch*
Pinkney
Pinko, *Pinchas*
Pinkoffs, *Pinchas*
Pinkovitz, *Pinchas*
Pinkowitz, *Pinchas*
Pinks, *Pinch*
Pinkus, *Pinchas*
Pinnell, *Pine*
Pinner
Pinnes, *Pinchas*
Pino, *Pine*
Piñol, *Pine*
Pinon, *Pine*
Pinot, *Pine*
Pinoteau, *Pine*
Pinotti, *Pine*
Pinoy, *Pine*
Pinsard, *Pincher*
Pinsent, *Pinson*
Pinshon, *Pinson*
Pinson
Pinta, *Pinto*
Pintado, *Pinto*
Pinter, *Pinto*
Pintó, *Painter*
Pinto
Pintoricchio, *Painter*
Pintus, *Pinto*
Pinus, *Pinchas*
Pioch, *Peter*
Pioch, *Puy*
Piotr, *Peter*
Piotrkovski, *Peter*
Piotrkovsky, *Peter*
Piotrkowski, *Peter*
Piotrkowsky, *Peter*
Piotrowicz, *Peter*
Piotrowski, *Peter*
Pipe, *Piper*
Piper
Pipers, *Piper*
Pipes, *Piper*
Pipon, *Pepys*
Pippin, *Pepys*
Piquard, *Pickard*
Piquart, *Pickard*
Piqué, *Pike*
Pique, *Pike*
Piquer, *Pike*
Piquet, *Piggott*
Piqueton, *Piggott*
Piraro, *Pear*
Piras, *Pear*
Pirazzi, *Peter*
Pirch, *Birch*
Pircher, *Birch*
Pirchner, *Birch*
Pirelli, *Peter*
Pirello, *Peter*
Pires, *Peter*
Piretto, *Pear*
Pirie, *Perry*
Pirioli, *Peter*
Piris, *Peter*
Pirk, *Birch*
Pirker, *Birch*
Pirkis, *Purchase*
Pirkiss, *Purchase*
Pirkl, *Birch*
Pirkner, *Birch*
Pirner, *Pear*
Piro, *Peter*
Pirocchi, *Peter*
Piroddi, *Pear*
Pirolini, *Peter*
Pirotti, *Parrott*
Pirozzi, *Peter*
Pirozzolo, *Peter*
Pirpamer, *Birnbaum*
Pirri, *Peter*
Pirrie, *Perry*
Pirrone, *Peter*
Pirrotti, *Parrott*
Pisa, *Pisani*
Pisanelli, *Pisani*
Pisanello, *Pisani*
Pisani
Pisaniello, *Pisani*
Pisano, *Pisani*
Pisanu, *Pisani*
Písař, *Pisarski*
Pisarczyk, *Pisarski*
Pisareff, *Pisarski*
Pisarek, *Pisarski*
Pisarenko, *Pisarski*
Pisarev, *Pisarski*
Pisarevski, *Pisarski*
Písařík, *Pisarski*
Pisarkiewicz, *Pisarski*
Pisarski
Pisarz, *Pisarski*
Pischel, *Peter*
Pischof, *Bishop*
Pischoff, *Bishop*
Pisco, *Bishop*
Piscopello, *Bishop*
Piscopiello, *Bishop*
Piscopo, *Bishop*
Piscot, *Bishop*
Piscotti, *Bishop*
Pisculli, *Bishop*
Piser, *Peyzer*
Pisera, *Pisarski*
Piskač
Piskáček, *Piskač*
Pissarenko, *Pisarski*
Pissarra, *Pizarro*
Pištěk, *Piskač*
Pister, *Pfister*
Pisterman, *Pfister*
Pisteur, *Pfister*
Pistol
Pistor, *Pfister*
Pistore, *Pfister*
Pistorello, *Pfister*
Pistori, *Pfister*
Pistorini, *Pfister*
Pistorino, *Pfister*
Pistorio, *Pfister*
Pitarch
Pitard, *Python*
Pitault, *Python*
Pitavin, *Potvin*
Pitcher
Pitchers, *Pitcher*
Pitchford
Pitchforth, *Pitchford*
Pite
Pitel, *Python*
Piterman, *Butter*
Pitet, *Python*
Pithers, *Peter*
Pithon, *Python*
Pitiot, *Pettit*
Pitkänen
Pitman, *Pitt*
Piton, *Python*
Pitone, *Peter*
Pitou, *Python*
Pitrasso, *Peter*
Pitrelli, *Peter*
Pitrillo, *Peter*
Pitt
Pittaway
Pittendreigh, *Pendreigh*
Pittendrigh, *Pendreigh*
Pitter, *Pitt*
Pittet, *Pettit*
Pittiot, *Pettit*
Pittman, *Pitt*
Pittner, *Büttner*
Pittoli, *Peter*
Pitts, *Pitt*
Pivec, *Piwoński*
Pivko, *Piwoński*
Pivník, *Piwoński*
Pivoňka, *Piwoński*
Pivovař, *Piwowarski*
Piwoński
Piwowarski
Pizarro
Pizey, *Pusey*
Pizzey, *Pusey*
Pizzie, *Pusey*
Pizzin, *Piccini*
Pizzinelli, *Piccini*
Pizzini, *Piccini*
Pizzinini, *Piccini*
Pizzioli, *Piccini*
Pizziolo, *Piccini*
Pizzoli, *Piccini*
Pizzolo, *Piccini*
Pla, *Plain*
Plab, *Blau*
Plabst, *Blau*
Place
Plaček
Plachký, *Plachý*
Plachý
Plackett

Plaice, *Place*
Plain
Plaine, *Plain*
Plaisance, *Pleasance*
Plaistow, *Plaster*
Plaix, *Place*
Plan, *Plain*
Plana, *Plain*
Planas, *Plain*
Planaz, *Plain*
Planchard, *Planche*
Planche
Planchet, *Planche*
Planchette, *Planche*
Planchon, *Planche*
Planck, *Planche*
Plancke, *Planche*
Plançon, *Planche*
Plancon, *Planche*
Plane, *Plain*
Planeau, *Plain*
Planeix, *Plain*
Planel, *Plain*
Planella, *Plain*
Planelle, *Plain*
Planells, *Plain*
Planet, *Plain*
Plank, *Planche*
Plänker, *Planche*
Plankl, *Planche*
Plankmann, *Planche*
Planque, *Planche*
Planquette, *Planche*
Plant
Plante, *Plant*
Plaschke, *Blaise*
Plass, *Place*
Plasse, *Place*
Plaster
Plastow, *Plaster*
Plas, van den
Plat, *Platt*
Platard, *Platt*
Plateau, *Platt*
Platel, *Platt*
Plath, *Platt*
Platonikhin, *Platonov*
Platonikov, *Platonov*
Platonnikov, *Platonov*
Platonov
Platoshkin, *Platonov*
Platt
Plattard, *Platt*
Platte, *Platt*
Platten, *Platt*
Platts, *Platt*
Platygin, *Platonov*
Platz, *Place*
Platzer, *Place*
Platzmann, *Place*
Platzner, *Place*
Play, *Place*
Player
Playfair
Playfer, *Playfair*
Playford
Plaz, *Place*
Plaza, *Place*
Plazman, *Place*
Pleace, *Place*
Pleaden, *Blevin*
Pleasance
Pleasaunce, *Pleasance*
Pleass, *Place*
Pleavin, *Blevin*
Pleavins, *Blevin*
Plecháč, *Plechatý*
Plechatý
Plecitý
Pleece, *Place*
Pleix, *Place*
Plemyannikov
Plenderleath, *Plenderleith*
Plenderleith
Plenty
Plesse, *Place*
Plessier, *Place*
Plessing, *Blaise*
Plessis, *Place*
Plessix, *Place*
Plessy, *Place*
Pleuger, *Plowman*
Pleuman, *Plowman*
Pleven, *Blevin*
Plevin, *Blevin*
Plevins, *Blevin*
Plewright, *Plowright*
Plews, *Plowman*
Plez, *Place*
Plichet, *Pelisse*
Plichon, *Pelisse*
Plimmer, *Plummer*
Plisson, *Pelisse*
Plissoneau, *Pelisse*
Plissonier, *Pelisse*
Ploch, *Vlach*
Płóciennik, *Płuciennik*
Ploeg, *Plowman*
Ploeger, *Plowman*
Plog, *Plowman*
Plögemaker, *Plowright*
Plöger, *Plowman*
Ploix, *Place*
Plomaker, *Plowright*
Plomer, *Plummer*
Plomley, *Plumley*
Płoński
Ploog, *Plowman*
Płoszaj
Płoszajski, *Płoszaj*
Płoszyński, *Płoszaj*
Plot, *Plotnik*
Plotka
Plotke, *Plotka*
Plotkin, *Plotka*
Plotnick, *Plotnik*
Plotnicki, *Plotnik*
Plotnicov, *Plotnik*
Plotnik
Plotnikov, *Plotnik*
Plotnitzki, *Plotnik*
Plotnitzky, *Plotnik*
Plotnizki, *Plotnik*
Plotnizky, *Plotnik*
Plott, *Plotnik*
Ploug, *Plowman*
Plouvier
Plovier, *Plouvier*
Plowden
Plowman
Plowright
Plows, *Plowman*
Płuciennik
Pluciński, *Pluta*
Plucknett, *Plunkett*
Pluhař, *Plowman*
Pluincéid, *Plunkett*
Plum
Plümaker, *Plowright*
Plumb, *Plum*
Plumbe, *Plum*
Plumbley, *Plumley*
Plumbohm, *Plum*
Plume, *Plum*
Plümecke, *Plum*
Plumeke, *Plum*
Plümer, *Plum*
Plumer, *Plummer*
Plumke, *Plum*
Plumkett, *Plunkett*
Plumley
Plummer
Plumptre, *Plum*
Plumptree, *Plum*
Plumstead
Plumtre, *Plum*
Plumtree, *Plum*
Plunket, *Plunkett*
Plunkett
Pluntsch, *Bluntschli*
Plunz, *Bluntschli*
Pluta
Plutheroe, *Protheroe*
Pluymaker, *Plowright*
Plzák
Pobgee
Pobjoy, *Pobgee*
Poça, *Puits*
Poch
Poche, *Poke*
Pochet, *Poke*
Pochon, *Poke*
Pochot, *Poke*
Pocket, *Poke*
Pockett, *Poke*
Pocknee, *Pockney*
Pockney
Pocock, *Peacock*
Pococke, *Peacock*
Pocque, *Poke*
Pocquet, *Poke*
Podczaski
Podell, *Podolski*
Poder, *Potter*
Podeur, *Potter*
Podevin, *Potvin*
Podgor, *Podgórski*
Podgora, *Podgórski*
Podgorny, *Podgórski*
Podgórski
Podgur, *Podgórski*
Podhorský, *Podgórski*
Podkidyshev
Podlashuk, *Podlesiak*
Podlasiak, *Podlesiak*
Podlaski, *Podlesiak*
Podlešák, *Podlesiak*
Podlesiak
Podmore
Podoler, *Podolski*
Podolier, *Podolski*
Podoloff, *Podolski*
Podolov, *Podolski*
Podolski
Podolsky, *Podolski*
Podoly, *Podolski*
Podroužek
Podvin, *Potvin*
Poe, *Peacock*
Poelman, *Pool*
Poelstra, *Pool*
Poeuf, *Puy*
Pogány, *Pain*
Poggetti, *Puy*
Poggi, *Puy*
Poggini, *Puy*
Poggio, *Puy*
Poggioli, *Puy*
Poggiolini, *Puy*
Poggs
Pogner, *Bow*
Pogonowicz, *Pogoński*
Pogoński
Pogorzelski
Pogosian, *Paul*
Pogson, *Poggs*
Pohl, *Paul*
Pohl, *Pool*
Pöhler, *Pool*
Pöhling, *Paul*
Pohlmann, *Pool*
Pöhls, *Paul*
Pöhlsen, *Paul*
Pohořelý, *Pogorzelski*
Poidevin, *Potvin*
Poillon, *Pou*
Poincaré
Poincelet, *Poinçon*
Poincelin, *Poinçon*
Poincelot, *Poinçon*
Poincignon, *Poinçon*
Poinçon
Poinçot, *Poinçon*
Poinset, *Poinçon*
Poinsett, *Poinçon*
Poinsignon, *Poinçon*
Poinson, *Poinçon*
Poinsot, *Poinçon*
Point, *Points*
Pointel, *Points*
Pointer
Pointon
Points
Poiraux, *Poireau*
Poireau
Poirel, *Poireau*
Poirier, *Pear*
Poirot, *Pear*
Poirrier, *Pear*
Poirriez, *Pear*
Poissenot, *Pesce*
Poisson, *Pesce*
Poissonnet, *Pesce*
Poitevin, *Potvin*
Poittevin, *Potvin*
Poitvin, *Potvin*
Poivre, *Pepper*
Poke
Pokney, *Pockney*
Pokora, *Pokorný*
Pokorny, *Pokorný*
Pokorný
Pokorski, *Pokorný*
Pokrovski
Pol, *Paul, Polak*
Pol
Polacci, *Paul*
Poláček, *Polak*
Polacek, *Polak*
Polachek, *Polak*
Polack, *Polak*
Polaczek, *Polak*
Polák, *Polak*
Polak
Polakevitch, *Polak*
Polakiewicz, *Polak*

Polakowski, *Polak*
Polanecký, *Polański*
Polanowski, *Polański*
Polanski, *Polański*
Polański
Polanský, *Polański*
Polansky, *Polański*
Polášek, *Polak*
Polatchek, *Polak*
Polatsek, *Polak*
Polatshek, *Polak*
Polawski, *Polański*
Polazzi, *Paul*
Polczynski, *Polański*
Polenaer, *Polak*
Polet, *Paul*
Poletti, *Paul*
Poletto, *Paul*
Polgár, *Burger*
Polglase
Poli, *Paul*
Poli, *Polly*
Poliakov, *Polak*
Poliakove, *Polak*
Poliakow, *Polak*
Poliard, *Polly*
Poliet, *Polly*
Polin, *Paul*
Polini, *Paul*
Polino, *Paul*
Poliński, *Polański*
Poliot, *Polly*
Polit, *Hipólito*
Politelli, *Hipólito*
Politi, *Hipólito*
Polito, *Hipólito*
Politov, *Hipólito*
Polívka
Polk
Polka, *Polak*
Polka, *Polk*
Polke, *Polk*
Polkinghorne
Polkowski, *Polak*
Poll, *Pol*
Pollack, *Polak*
Pollag, *Polak*
Pollak, *Polak*
Pollard
Pollatsek, *Polak*
Polley, *Polly*
Polli, *Polly*
Polliak, *Polak*
Polliet, *Polly*
Pollini, *Poule*
Pollins, *Paul*
Polliot, *Polly*
Pollit, *Hipólito*
Pollitt, *Hipólito*
Pollo, *Poule*
Pollock
Pollok, *Pollock*
Polloni, *Poule*
Polly
Polman, *Pol*
Polman, *Pool*
Polo, *Paul*
Polon, *Paul*
Poloni, *Paul*
Polotti, *Paul*
Polotto, *Paul*
Pols, *Pol*
Polshin, *Hipólito*
Polski, *Polak*
Polsky, *Polak*
Polson, *Paul*
Polster
Pölsterl, *Polster*
Polstra, *Pool*
Pölt, *Hipólito*
Polte, *Hipólito*
Poltes, *Hipólito*
Pöltl, *Hipólito*
Polucci, *Paul*
Polunin, *Hipólito*
Polutov, *Hipólito*
Poluzzi, *Paul*
Poly, *Polly*
Polyakov, *Polak*
Polyanov, *Polański*
Polyanski, *Polański*
Polyblank
Polykhov, *Hipólito*
Polyukhin, *Hipólito*
Polyushkin, *Hipólito*
Polyusov, *Hipólito*
Pomarański, *Pomerantz*
Pomaranzik, *Pomerantz*
Pomarède, *Pomeroy*
Pombo, *Palomo*
Pomeranc, *Pomerantz*
Pomerancblum, *Pomerantz*
Pomerance, *Pomerantz*
Pomeranchik, *Pomerantz*
Pomerants, *Pomerantz*
Pomerantz
Pomeranz, *Pomerantz*
Pomeranzblum, *Pomerantz*
Pomeranzik, *Pomerantz*
Pomeroy
Pomery, *Pomeroy*
Pomfret
Pomfrett, *Pomfret*
Pomfrey, *Pomphrey*
Pommerais, *Pomeroy*
Pommeray, *Pomeroy*
Pommeraye, *Pomeroy*
Pommerehne, *Pomorski*
Pommerening, *Pomorski*
Pommerenke, *Pomorski*
Pommerschein, *Pomorski*
Pommery, *Pomeroy*
Pomorski
Pomphray, *Pomphrey*
Pomphrett, *Pomfret*
Pomphrey
Pomrince, *Pomerantz*
Pomrinse, *Pomerantz*
Pomroy, *Pomeroy*
Poms, *Points*
Ponce, *Points*
Poncet, *Points*
Ponci, *Points*
Poncin, *Points*
Poncy, *Points*
Pond
Ponder, *Pond*
Pongrác, *Pankridge*
Pongrácz, *Pankridge*
Ponkratz, *Pankridge*
Ponomarenko, *Ponomaryov*
Ponomaryov
Pons, *Points*
Ponsard, *Points*
Ponsford, *Pauncefoot*
Ponson, *Points*
Ponsonby
Pont
Ponte, *Pont*
Pontefract, *Pomfret*
Pontel, *Pont*
Pontelli, *Pont*
Pontello, *Pont*
Pontes, *Pont*
Pontet, *Pont*
Ponti, *Pont*
Ponticeli, *Pont*
Ponticiello, *Pont*
Pontillo, *Pont*
Pontillon, *Pont*
Pontin, *Pont*
Ponting, *Pont*
Pontini, *Pont*
Ponton, *Pont*
Pontoni, *Pont*
Ponzetti, *Points*
Ponzi, *Points*
Ponzio, *Points*
Ponzo, *Points*
Ponzone, *Points*
Ponzoni, *Points*
Pook
Pooke, *Pook*
Pool
Poole, *Pool*
Pooley
Poolman, *Pool*
Poolton, *Poulton*
Poor, *Power*
Poore, *Power*
Poort, *Port*
Pop, *Popov*
Popa, *Popov*
Pope
Popejoy, *Pobgee*
Popel, *Popp*
Popelka, *Popp*
Popenko, *Popov*
Popescu, *Popov*
Popescul, *Popov*
Popham
Popić, *Popov*
Popjoy, *Pobgee*
Popkema, *Popp*
Popken, *Popp*
Popkess, *Popkiss*
Popkiss
Popławski
Popov
Popović, *Popov*
Popp
Poppe, *Popp*
Pöppel, *Popp*
Poppen, *Popp*
Popper, *Popp*
Poppinga, *Popp*
Pöppl, *Popp*
Poppleton
Popplewell
Popugaev, *Pobgee*
Poque, *Poke*
Pór, *Bauer*
Porcari, *Porcher*
Porcaro, *Porcher*
Porcellazzi, *Purcell*
Porcelletti, *Purcell*
Porcelli, *Purcell*
Porcellini, *Purcell*
Porcellino, *Purcell*
Porcello, *Purcell*
Porcellotto, *Purcell*
Porché, *Porcher*
Porcher
Porcheron, *Porcher*
Porchez, *Porcher*
Porciello, *Purcell*
Poreau, *Poireau*
Porkiss, *Purchase*
Porosz, *Preuss*
Porquier, *Porcher*
Porr, *Poireau*
Porras
Porrmann, *Poireau*
Porsche, *Borisov*
Porschke, *Borisov*
Port
Porta, *Port*
Porta, *Port*
Portail
Portal, *Portail*
Portalier, *Portail*
Portch
Porte, *Port*
Porteiro, *Porter*
Portela, *Port*
Portell, *Port*
Portella, *Port*
Portelli, *Port*
Portenaer, *Porter*
Porteous
Porter
Porterat, *Porter*
Portereau, *Porter*
Porteret, *Porter*
Porteron, *Porter*
Porterot, *Porter*
Porteu, *Porter*
Porteur, *Porter*
Porti, *Port*
Portier, *Porter*
Portilla, *Port*
Portillo, *Port*
Portingale, *Pettingell*
Portman, *Port*
Portmann, *Port*
Pörtner, *Porter*
Portner, *Porter*
Portnoi, *Portnov*
Portnoj, *Portnov*
Portnov
Portnoy, *Portnov*
Portnyagin, *Portnov*
Portnyakov, *Portnov*
Porto, *Port*
Portogallo, *Pettingell*
Portoghese, *Pettingell*
Portoghesi, *Pettingell*
Portret, *Porter*
Portron, *Porter*
Portugaels, *Pettingell*
Portugais, *Pettingell*
Portugal, *Pettingell*
Portugali, *Pettingell*
Portugaly, *Pettingell*
Portugheis, *Pettingell*
Portugues, *Pettingell*
Portuguese, *Pettingell*
Portuguez, *Pettingell*
Portwin, *Potvin*
Portwine, *Potvin*
Poruchikov
Porumbe, *Palomo*
Porz, *Porter*
Porzier, *Porter*
Porzig, *Borisov*
Posada

Pöschel, *Peter*
Poser, *Peyzer*
Posgate, *Postgate*
Positero, *Posada*
Poskett, *Postgate*
Poskitt, *Postgate*
Posner, *Poznański*
Posnett, *Postlethwaite*
Posnette, *Postlethwaite*
Pośpiech, *Pospíšil*
Pośpieszyński, *Pospíšil*
Pospíšil
Poss, *Peter*
Possa, *Peter*
Posse, *Peter*
Possek, *Peter*
Possell, *Postle*
Posselt, *Peter*
Posselwhite, *Postlethwaite*
Post
Poste
Posteau, *Poste*
Postel, *Poste*
Postema, *Post*
Postgate
Posthill, *Postle*
Postigo
Postill, *Postle*
Postle
Postlethwaite
Postma, *Post*
Poteau, *Poste*
Potel, *Poste*
Potell, *Pott*
Poterot, *Potter*
Potgieter, *Potter*
Pothier, *Potter*
Potier, *Potter*
Potiez, *Potter*
Potiphar, *Pettifer*
Potisman, *Pott*
Potkin, *Pott*
Potkins, *Pott*
Potman, *Pott*
Potocki
Potocký, *Potocki*
Potočník, *Potocki*
Potok, *Potocki*
Pott
Pottage, *Pottinger*
Pottbecker, *Potter*
Pottebakker, *Potter*
Pötter, *Potter*
Potter
Potterall, *Putterill*
Potterill, *Putterill*
Pottgiesser, *Potter*
Pottgieter, *Potter*
Pottier, *Potter*
Pottinger
Pottiphar, *Pettifer*
Pottle, *Pott*
Pottock, *Puttock*
Potton
Pottrill, *Putterill*
Potts, *Pott*
Potůček, *Potocki*
Potvin
Potwin, *Potvin*
Potyomkin
Pötzold, *Peter*
Pou
Pouch, *Poke*
Poucher, *Poke*
Pouchet, *Poke*
Pouchin, *Poussin*
Pouchon, *Poke*
Pouck, *Pook*
Poueigh, *Puy*
Pouey, *Puy*
Pougher, *Poke*
Pouillard, *Pou*
Pouillaud, *Pou*
Pouillet, *Pou*
Pouilleux, *Pou*
Pouillot, *Pou*
Poujade, *Pujadas*
Poul, *Poule*
Poulain, *Pullen*
Poulan, *Pullen*
Poulard, *Poule*
Poulas, *Poule*
Poulastre, *Poule*
Poulat, *Poule*
Poule
Poulenc, *Pullen*
Poulet, *Poule*
Pouleteau, *Poule*
Poulin, *Poule*
Poullain, *Pullen*
Poulle, *Poule*
Poullet, *Poule*
Poullot, *Poule*
Poulney, *Pountney*
Poulot, *Poule*
Poulsen, *Paul*
Poulsom, *Paul*
Poulson, *Paul*
Poulsum, *Paul*
Poulteau, *Poule*
Poulter, *Poule*
Poultney, *Pountney*
Poulton
Pound
Pounder, *Pound*
Pounds, *Pound*
Pountney
Pourceau, *Purcell*
Pourcel, *Purcell*
Pourcheiroux, *Porcher*
Pourcher, *Porcher*
Pourdieu, *Purdy*
Poureau, *Poireau*
Pouriau, *Poireau*
Pouriel, *Poireau*
Pourquié, *Porcher*
Pourquier, *Porcher*
Pourrel, *Poireau*
Pourtier, *Porter*
Pous, *Pou, Puits*
Pousineau, *Poussin*
Poussin
Poussineau, *Poussin*
Poussinet, *Poussin*
Pouteau, *Poste*
Pouter, *Peutherer*
Pouthier, *Potter*
Poutier, *Potter*
Poutrel, *Putterill*
Pouts, *Puits*
Pouvereau, *Power*
Pouvreau, *Power*
Poux, *Pou, Puits*
Pouy, *Puy*
Pouzet, *Puits*
Pouzin, *Puits*
Pouzinot, *Poussin*
Pouzol, *Puits*
Povarov
Povarsky, *Povarov*
Poveda
Poverelli, *Power*
Povero, *Power*
Povey
Povlsen, *Paul*
Pow, *Powe*
Powderill, *Putterill*
Powdrell, *Putterill*
Powdrill, *Putterill*
Powe
Poweleit, *Paul*
Powell
Power
Powers, *Power*
Powles, *Powell*
Powley, *Paul*
Powling, *Paul*
Pownall
Powney, *Pownall*
Powter, *Peutherer*
Poxon, *Poggs*
Poy, *Puy*
Poynder, *Pound*
Poyner
Poynor, *Poyner*
Poynter, *Pointer*
Poynton, *Pointon*
Poyntz, *Points*
Poyser, *Peyzer*
Poyssenot, *Pesce*
Poyzer, *Peyzer*
Poza, *Puits*
Pozas, *Puits*
Pozetti, *Puits*
Pozetto, *Puits*
Poznański
Pozo, *Puits*
Pozuelo, *Puits*
Pozza, *Puits*
Pozzi, *Puits*
Pozzo, *Puits*
Pozzoli, *Puy, Puits*
Pozzolini, *Puy*
Pozzolo, *Puits, Puy*
Pra, *Pré*
Praast, *Provost*
Prachař, *Prochownik*
Prack, *Brack*
Präckl, *Brack*
Prada, *Pré*
Pradas, *Pré*
Prade, *Pré*
Pradeau, *Pré*
Pradeaux, *Pré*
Pradel, *Pré*
Pradella, *Pré*
Pradelle, *Pré*
Prades, *Pré*
Pradetto, *Pré*
Pradillo, *Pré*
Pradillon, *Pré*
Pradine, *Pré*
Prado, *Pré*
Pradolin, *Pré*
Pradon, *Pré*
Prados, *Pré*
Pradoux, *Pré*
Praetorius
Prager
Pragerman, *Prager*
Pragst, *Provost*
Prais, *Preuss*
Praiss, *Preuss*
Prakepyonok, *Prokop*
Prakst, *Provost*
Prandi, *Brand*
Prandin, *Brand*
Prandini, *Brand*
Prando, *Brand*
Prandoni, *Brand*
Prantl, *Brand*
Prantoni, *Brand*
Prášek
Prat, *Pré*
Prata
Pratas, *Prata*
Pratella, *Pré*
Pratelli, *Pré*
Prater, *Praetorius*
Prati, *Pré*
Pratlett, *Pratt*
Prato, *Pré*
Pratolini, *Pré*
Prats, *Pré*
Pratt
Pratten, *Pratt*
Pratx, *Pré*
Pratz, *Pré*
Praundl, *Brown*
Praundlin, *Brown*
Prax, *Pré*
Pray, *O'Prey*
Praz, *Pré*
Pražák, *Prager*
Pražanský, *Prager*
Prazeres
Pražský, *Prager*
Prchal
Prchlík, *Prchal*
Pré
Preater, *Praetorius*
Préau, *Pré*
Préaux, *Pré*
Prebble
Preble, *Prebble*
Preciado, *Precious*
Precious
Predda, *Pear*
Preddy, *Preedy*
Prée, *Pré*
Preece, *Price*
Preedy
Préel, *Pré*
Preis, *Preuss*
Preiser, *Preuss*
Preiserowicz, *Preuss*
Preiss, *Preuss*
Preissler, *Preuss*
Preissman, *Preuss*
Preissner, *Preuss*
Preist, *Priest*
Preister, *Priest*
Preite, *Priest*
Prel, *Pré*
Premack, *Primak*
Premak, *Primak*
Prencipe, *Prince*
Prendegast, *Prendergast*
Prendeguest, *Prendergast*
Prendergast
Prendergat, *Prendergast*
Prendergrass, *Prendergast*
Prendergrast, *Prendergast*
Prendgrast, *Prendergast*
Prentice
Prentis, *Prentice*

Prentiss, *Prentice*
Prescod, *Prescott*
Prescot, *Prescott*
Prescott
Preskett, *Prescott*
Presland
Presley, *Priestley*
Presman, *Priest*
Press, *Priest*
Presser, *Priest*
Pressland, *Presland*
Presslee, *Priestley*
Pressley, *Priestley*
Presslie, *Priestley*
Pressly, *Priestley*
Pressman, *Priest*
Prest, *Priest*
Prester, *Priest*
Presteri, *Priest*
Presti, *Priest*
Prestieri, *Priest*
Prestige, *Prestwich*
Prestino, *Priest*
Presto, *Priest*
Preston
Prestre, *Priest*
Prestt, *Priest*
Prestwich
Prete, *Priest*
Pretheroe, *Protheroe*
Preti, *Priest*
Pretious, *Precious*
Preto, *Peter, Prieto*
Pretor, *Praetorius*
Pretorius, *Praetorius*
Prêtre, *Priest*
Pretti, *Peter*
Prettre, *Priest*
Pretty
Prettyman, *Pretty*
Pretyman, *Pretty*
Preu, *Brewer*
Preudhomme, *Pridham*
Preuer, *Brewer*
Preuss
Preussler, *Preuss*
Preussner, *Preuss*
Preux
Preve, *Priest*
Prevedel, *Priest*
Prevedello, *Priest*
Prevel, *Pepper*
Prevete, *Priest*
Previ, *Priest*
Previte, *Priest*
Previtero, *Priest*
Previti, *Priest*
Previto, *Priest*
Prévost, *Prevost*
Prevost
Prévosteau, *Prevost*
Prévostel, *Prevost*
Prévôt, *Prevost*
Prévoteau, *Prevost*
Prévotet, *Prevost*
Prew, *Prowse*
Prewett, *Prowse*
Prewse, *Prowse*
Prey, *Brewer, O'Prey, Pré*
Preyer, *Brewer*
Prez, *Pré*
Přibáň, *Przybysz*
Přibík, *Przybysz*
Pribul, *Prebble*
Přibyl, *Przybysz*
Price
Prichard, *Pritchard*
Prickett, *Pryke*
Priday, *Prideaux*
Priddey, *Preedy*
Priddy, *Preedy*
Prideaux
Pridham
Prier, *Prior*
Priest
Priester, *Priest*
Priestland, *Presland*
Priestley
Priestly, *Priestley*
Priestman, *Priest*
Prieto
Prieu, *Prior*
Prieur, *Prior*
Prieux, *Prior*
Příhoda, *Przygoda*
Primack, *Primak*
Primak
Prime
Primerose, *Primrose*
Primrose
Prin, *Perrin, Prime*
Prince
Princigalli, *Percival*
Principalli, *Percival*
Principe, *Prince*
Principi, *Prince*
Princivalle, *Percival*
Princivalli, *Percival*
Prinet, *Perrin*
Prinetti, *Perrin*
Pring, *Prime*
Pringle
Prinn, *Prime*
Prinne, *Prime*
Prins, *Prince*
Prinsen, *Prince*
Printz, *Prince*
Prinz, *Prince*
Prinzen, *Prince*
Prinzivalle, *Percival*
Prinzivalli, *Percival*
Priol, *Prior*
Priolo, *Prior*
Prior
Priore, *Prior*
Priori, *Prior*
Priou, *Prior*
Prioul, *Prior*
Prioux, *Prior*
Priscott, *Prescott*
Prisley, *Priestley*
Pritchard
Pritchatt, *Pryke*
Pritchet, *Pryke*
Pritchett, *Pryke*
Pritty, *Pretty*
Priuli, *Prior*
Privat
Privé, *Privat*
Privett
Privey, *Privat*
Privez, *Privat*
Privitelli, *Priest*
Probert
Probin, *Robin*
Probst, *Provost*
Procházka
Prochownik
Prochowski, *Prochownik*
Prockter, *Proctor*
Procktor, *Proctor*
Procter, *Proctor*
Proctor
Prodda, *Pear*
Prodham, *Pridham*
Prodhomme, *Pridham*
Prodhon, *Pridham*
Proemen, *Plum*
Proença, *Province*
Profumo
Proger, *Prager*
Proietti, *Proietto*
Proietto
Prokeš, *Prokop*
Prokhnov, *Prokop*
Prokhorchik, *Prokhorov*
Prokhorikhin, *Prokhorov*
Prokhorov
Prokić, *Prokop*
Prokisch, *Prokop*
Prokofiev, *Prokop*
Prokofyev, *Prokop*
Prokonov, *Prokop*
Prokop
Prokopchik, *Prokop*
Prokopczyk, *Prokop*
Prokopec, *Prokop*
Prokopf, *Prokop*
Prokopovich, *Prokop*
Prokoš, *Prokop*
Prokoshev, *Prokop*
Prokoshkin, *Prokop*
Proksch, *Prokop*
Prokunin, *Prokop*
Prokůpek, *Prokop*
Pron, *Pierre*
Pronchishchev, *Prokop*
Pronet, *Pierre*
Pronichev, *Prokop*
Pronichkin, *Prokop*
Pronin, *Prokop*
Pronk
Pronkin, *Prokop*
Pronov, *Prokop*
Pronty, *Prunty*
Pronyaev, *Prokop*
Pronyakov, *Prokop*
Proom
Proome, *Proom*
Proost, *Provost*
Prosch, *Ambrose*
Proschek, *Ambrose*
Proschke, *Ambrose*
Prosek, *Ambrose*
Prošek, *Prokop*
Proshchin, *Prokop*
Proske, *Ambrose*
Prosser
Prost, *Provost*
Prot, *Provost*
Protais
Protas, *Protais*
Protat, *Protais*
Proteau, *Protais*
Proteaux, *Protais*
Protet, *Protais*
Prothais, *Protais*
Prothero, *Protheroe*
Protheroe
Protherough, *Protheroe*
Prothin, *Protais*
Prothon, *Protais*
Protopopov
Prou, *Preux*
Proud
Proude, *Proud*
Proudfoot
Proudhon, *Pridham*
Prouhère, *Priest*
Prouse, *Prowse*
Proust, *Provost*
Prout, *Proud*
Prouvaire, *Priest*
Prouvère, *Priest*
Prouvéze, *Priest*
Prouvost, *Provost*
Prouvot, *Provost*
Proux, *Preux*
Provan
Provand, *Provan*
Provazník
Proven, *Provan*
Provençal, *Province*
Provensal, *Province*
Provensau, *Province*
Provensaux, *Province*
Provenza, *Province*
Provenzal, *Province*
Provenzale, *Province*
Provenzali, *Province*
Provenzani, *Province*
Provenzano, *Province*
Provest, *Provost*
Province
Provinciali, *Province*
Provins, *Province*
Provis, *Provost*
Proviteri, *Priest*
Provost
Provot, *Provost*
Prow, *Prowse*
Prowse
Prox, *Prokop*
Prozillo, *Peter*
Prozzo, *Peter*
Prucci, *Peter*
Pruce, *Prowse*
Průcha, *Prokop*
Prückner, *Bridge*
Prudham, *Pridham*
Prudhoe
Prudhomme, *Pridham*
Prudhommeau, *Pridham*
Prudhon, *Pridham*
Prudon, *Pridham*
Prue, *Prowse*
Pruen
Pruett, *Prowse*
Pruijs, *Preuss*
Pruim, *Plum*
Pruimboom, *Plum*
Pruin, *Pruen*
Pruis, *Preuss*
Pruitt, *Prowse*
Prumbaum, *Plum*
Prumenbaum, *Plum*
Prune, *Plum*
Pruneau, *Plum*
Prunel, *Plum*
Prunet, *Plum*
Prunier, *Plum*
Prunner, *Bourne*
Prunty
Prus, *Preuss*
Průša, *Prokop*
Pruski, *Preuss*

Prüss, *Preuss*
Prüsse, *Preuss*
Prüssing, *Preuss*
Prüssmann, *Preuss*
Prusso, *Peter*
Prust, *Priest*
Pruszczyński, *Preuss*
Pruszyński, *Preuss*
Prutz, *Preuss*
Pruvost, *Provost*
Pruvot, *Provost*
Pruyn, *Pruen*
Pruys, *Preuss*
Pryce, *Price*
Prydderch, *Protheroe*
Pryde
Pryer, *Prior*
Pryke
Prynn, *Prime*
Prynne, *Prime*
Pryor, *Prior*
Prytherch, *Protheroe*
Prytherick, *Protheroe*
Przbył, *Przybysz*
Przbyła, *Przybysz*
Przybyłak, *Przybysz*
Przybyłek, *Przybysz*
Przybyłowski, *Przybysz*
Przybylski, *Przybysz*
Przybysz
Przybyszewski, *Przybysz*
Przygocki, *Przygoda*
Przygoda
Przygodzki, *Przygoda*
Przykowicz, *Kaspar*
Pschorn, *Pschorr*
Pschorr
Ptáček, *Pták*
Ptáčník
Pták
Ptasiński, *Ptaszyński*
Ptaszyński
Puccini
Puch, *Puy*
Puchner, *Buch*
Pudda, *Poule*
Puddefoot, *Puddephat*
Puddephat
Puddifant, *Potvin*
Puddifer, *Pettifer*
Puddifin, *Potvin*
Puddifoot, *Puddephat*
Puddinu, *Poule*
Puddu, *Poule*
Puddy
Pudephat, *Puddephat*
Pudge, *Pugh*
Pudifoot, *Puddephat*
Puebla
Puech, *Puy*
Puechon, *Puy*
Puente, *Pont*
Puentes, *Pont*
Puerta, *Port*
Puertas, *Port*
Puerto, *Port*
Puey
Pueyo, *Puy*
Pugach, *Pugachyov*
Pugachyov
Pugatch, *Pugachyov*
Pugatchov, *Pugachyov*
Pugatz, *Pugachyov*
Pugatzky, *Pugachyov*
Puget, *Puy*
Pugh
Pughe, *Pugh*
Pugin, *Puy*
Pugmire
Puhl, *Pool*
Puhlmann, *Pool*
Puig, *Puy*
Puis, *Puits*
Puits
Pujadas
Pujade, *Pujadas*
Pujol, *Puy*
Pulford
Pulham
Pulido, *Polly*
Puliti, *Polly*
Pulke, *Polk*
Pullan, *Pullen*
Pullein, *Pullen*
Pulleine, *Pullen*
Pullen
Puller, *Pill*
Pulleyblank, *Polyblank*
Pulleyn, *Pullen*
Pulliblank, *Polyblank*
Pullin, *Pullen*
Pullman, *Pill*
Pulman, *Pill*
Pulteney, *Pountney*
Pulver
Pulvermacher, *Pulver*
Pulvertaft
Pumfray, *Pomphrey*
Pumfrett, *Pomfret*
Pummell
Pummery, *Pomeroy*
Pumphery, *Pomphrey*
Pumphrey, *Pomphrey*
Pumphreys, *Pomphrey*
Punainen
Punanen, *Punainen*
Punch, *Points*
Punchard, *Points*
Punchet, *Points*
Punchon, *Points*
Pund, *Pound*
Punshon, *Poinçon*
Punton
Punyer, *Poyner*
Punzetti, *Points*
Punzetto, *Points*
Punzi, *Points*
Punzio, *Points*
Punzo, *Points*
Punzone, *Points*
Puorto, *Port*
Purcaro, *Porcher*
Purčel, *Purcell*
Purcell
Purcelli, *Purcell*
Purchas, *Purchase*
Purchase
Purches, *Purchase*
Purchese, *Purchase*
Purcifer, *Percival*
Purday, *Purdy*
Purdey, *Purdy*
Purdham, *Pridham*
Purdie, *Purdy*
Purdom, *Pridham*
Purdon, *Pridham*
Purdu, *Purdy*
Purdue, *Purdy*
Purdy
Purdye, *Purdy*
Purkess, *Purchase*
Purkins, *Parkin*
Purkis, *Purchase*
Purkiss, *Purchase*
Purnell, *Parnell*
Purry, *Perry*
Purse, *Purser*
Purser
Pursey, *Percy*
Purtill, *Putterill*
Purton
Purves
Purvess, *Purves*
Purvey, *Purves*
Purvis, *Purves*
Pury, *Perry*
Pusateri, *Posada*
Pusey
Pushkar
Pushkarchuk, *Pushkar*
Pushkarenko, *Pushkar*
Pushkarev, *Pushkar*
Pushkarevich, *Pushkar*
Pushkin
Puskás, *Pushkar*
Pussey, *Pusey*
Pussy, *Pusey*
Pustelnik
Put, *Pfützer*
Puter, *Butter*
Puterman, *Butter*
Putfarken, *Puttfarken*
Putman, *Pitt*
Putnam
Putt, *Pitt*
Puttack, *Puttock*
Puttenham, *Putnam*
Putter, *Butter, Pfützer, Pitt*
Puttergill, *Pettingell*
Putterill
Putterman, *Butter*
Puttfarken
Puttick, *Puttock*
Puttifent, *Potvin*
Puttifoot, *Puddephat*
Puttock
Puttrell, *Putterill*
Putts, *Pitt*
Puttuck, *Puttock*
Putwaine, *Potvin*
Puxbaum, *Buchs*
Puy
Puyol, *Puy*
Puzzolo, *Puits*
Puzzu, *Puits*
Puzzulu, *Puits*
Py, *Pine*
Pyatuch, *Petukhov*
Pye
Pygott, *Piggott*
Pyke, *Pike*
Pykett, *Piggott*
Pyl, *Pfeil*
Pyle, *Pile*
Pym, *Pimm*
Pymm, *Pimm*
Pyne, *Pine*
Pyper, *Piper*
Pyser, *Peyzer*
Pytel
Python
Pyzer, *Peyzer*

Q

Quackel, *Quail*
Quad, *McQuaid*
Quadling, *Codlin*
Quaggin, *Keogh*
Quaglia, *Quail*
Quaglieri, *Quail*
Quaglietta, *Quail*
Quaglino, *Quail*
Quagliotto, *Quail*
Quaid, *McQuaid*
Quail
Quaile, *Quail*
Quaine, *Coyne*
Quale, *Quail*
Qualter, *Qualtrough*
Qualterough, *Qualtrough*
Qualters, *Qualtrough*
Qualtrough
Quane, *Coyne*
Quant
Quantin, *Quinton*
Quantrell, *Quantrill*
Quantrill
Quarch, *Quark*
Quard, *Bard*
Quarello, *Pascall*
Quaresma
Quarg, *Quark*
Quark
Quarles
Quarmby, *Wharmby*
Quarrell
Quarrie, *Quarry*
Quarrier, *Carrier*
Quarry
Quartermain
Quartermaine, *Quartermain*
Quarterman, *Quartermain*
Quatermain, *Quartermain*
Quatermaine, *Quartermain*
Quay, *McKay*
Quaye, *McKay*
Quayle, *Quail*
Queally, *Keeley*
Quealy, *Keeley*
Queely, *Keeley*
Queille
Queirós, *Quirós*
Quémin, *Chemin*
Quemin, *Chemin*
Quêne
Queneau, *Jack*
Quéneau, *Quêne*
Queneaux, *Jack*
Quenel, *Jack*
Quénel, *Quêne*
Quenell, *Quennell*
Quénet, *Quêne*
Quennell
Quenot, *Jack*
Quentin, *Quinton*
Quenu, *Chenu*
Quer
Queralt
Quernel, *Corneille*
Queró, *Quer*
Querol, *Quer*
Quesada
Quesnay, *Quêne*
Quesne, *Quêne*
Quesneau, *Quêne*
Quesnel, *Quêne*

Quesnet, *Quêne*
Quesney, *Quêne*
Quesnot, *Quêne*
Quesnoy, *Quêne*
Quested
Queuille, *Queille*
Quéval, *Cavallo*
Queval, *Cavallo*
Quevreux, *Cheever*
Queyeiro, *Cheeseman*
Queyos, *Cheeseman*
Quick
Quicke, *Quick*
Quickley
Quiddihy, *Cody*
Quièvre, *Cheever*
Quiévreux, *Cheever*
Quigley, *Quickley*
Quigly, *Quickley*
Quijada
Quiles, *Quilici*
Quílez, *Quilici*
Quilichini, *Quilici*
Quilici
Quilico, *Quilici*
Quilis, *Quilici*
Quill
Quillan, *Quill*
Quilliam, *McWilliam*
Quilligan, *Quill*
Quilly
Quilter
Quin, *Quinn*
Quincey
Quincy, *Quincey*
Quinde, *Quant*
Quine, *Quinn*
Quineau, *Jack*
Quineaux, *Jack*
Quinel, *Jack*
Quinell, *Quennell*
Quinet, *Jack*
Quinlan
Quinlevan, *Quinlan*
Quinlivan, *Quinlan*
Quinn
Quiñones
Quinot, *Jack*
Quinsee, *Quincey*
Quinsey, *Quincey*
Quintana
Quintanilla, *Quintana*
Quintas, *Quintana*
Quintin, *Quinton*
Quintini, *Quinton*
Quintino, *Quinton*
Quinton
Quintrell, *Quantrill*
Quirico, *Quilici*
Quiriconi, *Quilici*
Quirk, *Quirke*
Quirke
Quiroga
Quirós
Quist, *Qvist*
Quodling, *Codlin*
Qvist

R

Raaf, *Raven*
Raap, *Rapa*
Rabadán
Rabaud
Rabault, *Rabaud*
Rabb, *Robert*
Rabbatts, *Rabbitt*
Rabbe, *Rabaud, Rabbitt*
Rabbeke, *Rabaud, Rabbitt*
Rabbino, *Rabin*
Rabbits, *Rabbitt*
Rabbitt
Rabbitte, *Rabbitt*
Rabbitts, *Rabbitt*
Rabbold, *Rabaud*
Rabe, *Raven*
Rabeau, *Ravel*
Rabel, *Ravel*
Rabenu, *Rabin*
Rabet, *Rabbitt*
Rabets, *Rabbitt*
Rabetts, *Rabbitt*
Rabey, *Roby*
Rabie, *Roby*
Rabier, *Rapa*
Rabin
Rabiner, *Rabin*
Rabinerson, *Rabin*
Rabino, *Rabin*
Rabinov, *Rabin*
Rabinovich, *Rabin*
Rabinovici, *Rabin*
Rabinovics, *Rabin*
Rabinovitch, *Rabin*
Rabinovits, *Rabin*
Rabinovitsh, *Rabin*
Rabinovitz, *Rabin*
Rabinow, *Rabin*
Rabinowicz, *Rabin*
Rabinowitch, *Rabin*
Rabinowitsch, *Rabin*
Rabinowitz, *Rabin*
Rabinski, *Rabin*
Rabinsky, *Rabin*
Rabinsohn, *Rabin*
Rabinson, *Rabin*
Rabl, *Raven*
Rablan, *Robert*
Rablin, *Robert*
Rabone, *Rathbone*
Rabson, *Robert*
Raby, *Roby*
Racamier, *Récamier*
Raccio, *Peter*
Rachet
Rachez, *Rachet*
Rachine, *Racine*
Rachinel, *Racine*
Rachlin, *Rochlin*
Rachwał, *Raphael*
Racine
Racinet, *Racine*
Racineux, *Racine*
Rackcliff, *Ratcliffe*
Rackcliffe, *Ratcliffe*
Rackel, *Rat*
Rackham
Rackl, *Rat*
Rackley
Rackliff, *Ratcliffe*
Rackliffe, *Ratcliffe*
Ractigan, *Rattigan*
Rácz
Raczek, *Rak*
Raczkowski, *Rak*
Raczyński
Rada, *Radecki*
Radaković, *Radecki*
Radbone, *Rathbone*
Radcliff, *Ratcliffe*
Radcliffe, *Ratcliffe*
Radclyffe, *Ratcliffe*
Raddie, *Ready*
Radecke, *Rat*
Radecki
Radecký
Radek, *Radecki*
Radeke, *Rat*
Rademacher, *Rademaker*
Rademächers, *Rademaker*
Rademaker
Rademann, *Rat*
Radenković, *Radecki*
Radet, *Rat*
Radetzky, *Radecký*
Radfirth, *Radford*
Radford
Radforth, *Radford*
Radić, *Radecki*
Radics, *Radecki*
Radigon, *Radigue*
Radigue
Radiguet, *Radigue*
Radišić, *Radecki*
Radjenović, *Radecki*
Radke, *Radecki*
Radkiewicz, *Radecki*
Radleigh, *Radley*
Radlesco, *Radecki*
Radley
Radloff, *Ralph*
Radmanović, *Radecki*
Radmore
Radnedge
Radó, *Radecki*
Radojčić, *Radecki*
Radojević, *Radecki*
Radojičić, *Radecki*
Radojković, *Radecki*
Radolf, *Ralph*
Radomanović, *Radecki*
Radomski
Radon, *Rat*
Radonjić, *Radecki*
Radošević, *Radecki*
Radot, *Rat*
Radou, *Ralph*
Radouan, *Redwin*
Radouin, *Redwin*
Radovanović, *Radecki*
Radović, *Radecki*
Radu, *Radecki*
Radulesco, *Radecki*
Rădulescu, *Radecki*
Radulović, *Radecki*
Radunović, *Radecki*
Radzicki, *Radziejewski*
Radziejewski
Radzik, *Radziejewski*
Radzikowski, *Radziejewski*
Radziński, *Radziejewski*
Radziwill, *Radziwiłł*
Radziwiłł
Radziwiłłowski, *Radziwiłł*
Radziwiłowski, *Radziwiłł*
Radziwilski, *Radziwiłł*
Raeburn
Raedemaeker, *Rademaker*
Raemaeker, *Rademaker*
Raemakers, *Rademaker*
Raes, *Erasmus*
Rafacz, *Raphael*
Rafael, *Raphael*
Rafaeli, *Raphael*
Rafaelof, *Raphael*
Rafaeloff, *Raphael*
Rafaelovich, *Raphael*
Rafaelovici, *Raphael*
Rafaelovitz, *Raphael*
Rafaely, *Raphael*
Rafajlović, *Raphael*
Rafalski, *Raphael*
Rafanel, *Ravano*
Rafe, *Ralph*
Rafeli, *Raphael*
Raff, *Rabin, Ralph*
Raffaele, *Raphael*
Raffaeli, *Raphael*
Raffaello, *Raphael*
Raffel, *Raphael*
Raffelli, *Raphael*
Raffeneau, *Ravano*
Raffenel, *Ravano*
Rafferty
Raffield, *Raphael*
Raffle, *Raphael*
Raffles, *Raphael*
Rafn, *Raven*
Ràfols, *Real*
Ragazzi, *Ragazzo*
Ragazzini, *Ragazzo*
Ragazzo
Ragazzone, *Ragazzo*
Ragazzoni, *Ragazzo*
Raggett
Ragnarsson, *Rayner*
Ragona, *Aragón*
Ragone, *Aragón*
Ragoneau, *Raine*
Ragoneaux, *Raine*
Ragonese, *Aragón*
Ragonot, *Raine*
Ragot, *Raine*
Ragueneau, *Raine*
Raguenet, *Raine*
Raguet, *Raine*
Raguin, *Raine*
Rahier, *Rayer*
Rahl, *Rollo*
Rahlf, *Ralph*
Rahlke, *Rollo*
Rahlmann, *Rollo*
Rahloff, *Ralph*
Rahls, *Rollo*
Rahmaker, *Rademaker*
Rahmakers, *Rademaker*
Rahn
Rahncke, *Rahn*
Rahnsch, *Rahn*
Raho, *Rollo*
Raiber, *Räuber*
Raible, *Räuber*
Raich, *Rich*
Raikes
Raikov, *Radecki*
Raimann, *Raine*
Raimbaud, *Rainbow*
Raimbault, *Rainbow*
Raimbert, *Rainbird*
Raiment, *Raymond*
Raimo, *Raymond*
Raimond, *Raymond*
Raimondi, *Raymond*
Raimondo, *Raymond*
Raimund, *Raymond*

Raimundo, *Raymond*
Rain, *Raine*
Rainalder, *Reynold*
Rainaldi, *Reynold*
Rainaldis, *Reynold*
Rainaldo, *Reynold*
Rainalducci, *Reynold*
Rainals, *Reynold*
Rainalter, *Reynold*
Rainard, *Reynard*
Rainaud, *Reynold*
Rainbird
Rainbow
Raincock, *Raine*
Raine
Raineau, *Raine*
Rainer, *Rayner*
Raineri, *Rayner*
Rainero, *Rayner*
Raines, *Raine*
Rainey
Rainford
Rainger, *Ranger, Ringer*
Rainie, *Rainey*
Rainieri, *Rayner*
Rainiero, *Rayner*
Rainin, *Raine*
Rainis, *Raine*
Rainmann, *Raine*
Rainnie, *Rainey*
Rainoldi, *Reynold*
Rainon, *Raine*
Rainsford, *Rainford*
Rainy, *Rainey*
Raison
Raisonnier, *Raison*
Raistrick
Raj, *Rajski*
Rajala
Rajch, *Rich*
Rajchbart, *Rich*
Rajcher, *Rich*
Rajchert, *Richard*
Rajchman, *Rich*
Rajewski, *Rajski*
Rajkowski, *Rajski*
Rajnerman, *Rayner*
Rajski
Rak
Rake, *Raikes*
Rakes, *Raikes*
Rakhmaninov
Rákos
Rákosník, *Rákos*
Rakowiecki, *Rak*
Rakowski, *Rak*
Rakušan
Ralegh, *Raleigh*
Raleigh
Rales, *Ralph*
Raley, *Raleigh*
Ralf, *Ralph*
Ralfe, *Ralph*
Ralfes, *Ralph*
Ralfs, *Ralph*
Ralley, *Raleigh*
Rallin, *Rawling*
Ralling, *Rawling*
Rallings, *Rawling*
Rallins, *Rawling*
Rallison, *Rawling*
Ralls, *Ralph*
Rally, *Raleigh*
Ralph
Ralphs, *Ralph*
Ralphson, *Ralph*
Ralwes, *Ralph*
Ram
Rama, *Ram*
Ramachers, *Rademaker*
Ramacker, *Rademaker*
Ramage
Ramaker, *Rademaker*
Ramakers, *Rademaker*
Ramalhete, *Ram*
Ramalho, *Ram*
Ramard, *Ram*
Ramart, *Rainbird*
Ramas, *Ram*
Rambaldi, *Rainbow*
Rambart, *Rainbird*
Rambaud, *Rainbow*
Rambaudi, *Rainbow*
Rambault, *Rainbow*
Rambaut, *Rainbow*
Ramberg, *Ram*
Rambert, *Rainbird*
Ramble, *Rainbow*
Rame, *Ram*
Rameau, *Ram*
Rameaux, *Ram*
Ramecker, *Rademaker*
Rameckers, *Rademaker*
Ramel, *Ram*
Ramelet, *Ram*
Ramelot, *Ram*
Rames, *Ram*
Ramet, *Ram*
Ramey, *Ram*
Ramírez, *Reinmar*
Ramiro, *Reinmar*
Ramlot, *Ram*
Ramm, *Ram*
Ramme, *Ram*
Rammell, *Rainbow*
Ramón, *Raymond*
Ramon, *Raymond*
Ramond, *Raymond*
Ramondelli, *Raymond*
Ramondenc, *Raymond*
Ramondi, *Raymond*
Ramondini, *Raymond*
Ramondino, *Raymond*
Ramondo, *Raymond*
Ramondou, *Raymond*
Ramonenc, *Raymond*
Ramonic, *Raymond*
Ramos, *Ram*
Ramplin, *Ram*
Rampling, *Ram*
Ramsay, *Ramsey*
Ramsbotham, *Ramsbottom*
Ramsbottom
Ramsdale
Ramsden
Ramsey
Ramshaw
Ramskill
Ramstedt, *Ram*
Ramström, *Ram*
Ramundi, *Raymond*
Ranald, *Ronald*
Ranalder, *Reynold*
Ranaldi, *Reynold*
Ranaldo, *Reynold*
Ranaldson, *Ronald*
Ranalli, *Reynold*
Ranaudo, *Reynold*
Ranaulo, *Reynold*
Ranauro, *Reynold*
Ranavolo, *Reynold*
Rance, *Rand*
Rand
Randall
Randell, *Randall*
Randerson, *Randall*
Randle, *Randall*
Randles, *Randall*
Randlesome, *Randall*
Randolph
Randon, *Rand*
Rands, *Rand*
Randt, *Rand*
Randy, *Rand*
Ranek, *Rahn*
Raner, *Rayner*
Raneri, *Rayner*
Raney, *Rainey*
Ranger
Ranieri, *Rayner*
Raniero, *Rayner*
Ranis, *Raine*
Ränisch, *Rahn*
Ranisch, *Rahn*
Rank
Ranke, *Rahn*
Ranken, *Rankin*
Rankin
Rankine, *Rankin*
Ranking, *Rankin*
Ranner, *Rayner*
Rannie, *Rainey*
Ranolff, *Randolph*
Ranshaw, *Renshaw*
Ransley, *Rawnsley*
Ransom, *Rand*
Ransome, *Rand*
Ranson, *Rand*
Rant, *Rand*
Ranta
Rantala, *Ranta*
Rantanen, *Ranta*
Rantke, *Rahn*
Ranucci, *Raine*
Ranusch, *Rahn*
Ranuzzi, *Raine*
Ranzetti, *Naranjo*
Ranzi, *Naranjo*
Rao, *Rollo*
Raoli, *Rollo*
Raoul, *Ralph*
Raoulin, *Rawling*
Raoult, *Ralph*
Raoux, *Ralph*
Rapa
Rapaport, *Rappaport*
Rapetti, *Rapa*
Rapetto, *Rapa*
Raphael
Raphaeli, *Raphael*
Raphaelly, *Raphael*
Raphaelof, *Raphael*
Raphaeloff, *Raphael*
Raphaelov, *Raphael*
Raphaely, *Raphael*
Raphanel, *Ravano*
Raphel, *Raphael*
Rapholdt, *Rabaud*
Rapi, *Rapa*
Rapini, *Rapa*
Rapino, *Rapa*
Rapkins, *Robert*
Rapoport, *Rappaport*
Raposo
Rapp, *Raven*
Rapp
Rappaport
Rappe, *Raven*
Rappelt, *Rabaud*
Rappeneau, *Ravano*
Rappl, *Raven*
Räppli, *Raven*
Rappold, *Rabaud*
Rappolder, *Rabaud*
Rappoport, *Rappaport*
Rappot, *Rabbitt*
Rappuzzi, *Rapa*
Rapson, *Robert*
Rapucci, *Rapa*
Raš, *Rasch*
Ras, *Rasch*
Rasch
Raschek, *Rasch*
Raschka, *Rasch*
Raschke, *Rasch*
Rašek, *Rasch*
Rasem, *Erasmus*
Rash
Rask, *Rasch*
Raška, *Rasch*
Raskin, *Erasmus*
Rasmus, *Erasmus*
Rasmussen, *Erasmus*
Rasp
Rasputin
Rassek, *Rasch*
Rassineux, *Racine*
Rassinier, *Racine*
Rassmann, *Erasmus*
Rastel, *Rateau*
Rastelli, *Rateau*
Rastello, *Rateau*
Rastiello, *Rateau*
Rastrelli, *Rateau*
Rastrick, *Raistrick*
Rat
Rataj, *Ratajski*
Ratajczyk, *Ratajski*
Ratajski
Ratchford, *Rochford*
Ratcliff, *Ratcliffe*
Ratcliffe
Rateau
Rateaud, *Rateau*
Rateaux, *Rateau*
Ratel, *Rateau*
Ratet, *Rat*
Ratford, *Radford*
Rath, *Rat*
Rathaus, *Rat*
Rathause, *Rat*
Rathbone
Rathborne, *Rathbone*
Rathbourn, *Rathbone*
Rathe, *Rat*
Ratheau, *Rateau*
Rathenau, *Ratner*
Rathgen, *Rat*
Rathié, *Rayer*
Rathier, *Rayer*
Rathje, *Rat*
Rathjen, *Rat*
Rathke, *Rat*
Rathmann, *Rothmann*
Rathouse, *Rat*
Ratican, *Rattigan*

Ratier, *Rayer*
Ratigan, *Rattigan*
Ratillon, *Rat*
Ratin, *Rat*
Ratineau, *Rat*
Ratliff, *Ratcliffe*
Ratliffe, *Ratcliffe*
Ratner
Rato, *Rat*
Raton, *Rat*
Rattcliff, *Ratcliffe*
Ratti, *Rat*
Rattigan
Rattner, *Ratner*
Ratto, *Rat*
Rattray
Raty, *Rat*
Ratzek, *Rasch*
Ratzka, *Rasch*
Ratzke, *Rasch*
Rau, *Rauch, Rollo*
Rauber, *Räuber*
Räuber
Raucci, *Rollo*
Rauccio, *Rollo*
Rauch
Rauh, *Rauch*
Raulet, *Ralph*
Raulic, *Ralph*
Raulin, *Rawling*
Raulins, *Rawling*
Rault, *Ralph*
Raun, *Ruane*
Rauprich, *Robert*
Rautainen
Rautenbach
Rauter, *Reuter*
Rauth, *Reuter*
Rauthmann, *Reuter*
Rautman, *Reuter*
Raux, *Ralph*
Rava, *Rapa*
Ravagni, *Ravano*
Ravaillac
Ravanelli, *Ravano*
Ravanello, *Ravano*
Ravani, *Ravano*
Ravano
Rave, *Raven*
Raveau, *Ravel*
Ravel
Ravella, *Rapa*
Ravelli, *Rapa*
Raven
Raveneau, *Ravano*
Ravenel, *Ravano*
Ravening, *Raven*
Ravens, *Raven*
Ravenscroft
Ravenshaw, *Renshaw*
Ravenshear, *Renshaw*
Raventós
Ravert, *Haber*
Raves, *Ralph*
Ravetta, *Rapa*
Ravetti, *Rapa*
Ravi, *Rapa*
Ravier, *Rapa*
Ravin, *Rabin*
Ravina, *Rapa*
Ravinovicz, *Rabin*
Ravinsky, *Rabin*
Ravinzki, *Rabin*
Ravn, *Raven*

Raw
Rawcliff, *Rawcliffe*
Rawcliffe
Rawe, *Raw*
Rawes, *Raw*
Rawlcliffe, *Rawcliffe*
Rawle, *Ralph*
Rawlence, *Rawling*
Rawles, *Ralph*
Rawley, *Raleigh*
Rawlin, *Rawling*
Rawling
Rawlings, *Rawling*
Rawlingson, *Rawling*
Rawlins, *Rawling*
Rawlinson, *Rawling*
Rawlison, *Rawling*
Rawll, *Ralph*
Rawlyns, *Rawling*
Rawnsley
Raws, *Raw*
Rawse, *Raw*
Rawson, *Raw*
Rawsthorn, *Rawsthorne*
Rawsthorne
Rawstorn, *Rawsthorne*
Rawstorne, *Rawsthorne*
Rawstron, *Rawsthorne*
Ray
Raybould, *Rainbow*
Raye, *Ray*
Rayer
Rayeur, *Rayer*
Rayleigh
Rayman, *Rye*
Rayment, *Raymond*
Raymond
Raymonenc, *Raymond*
Raymonencq, *Raymond*
Raymont, *Raymond*
Raymund, *Raymond*
Raynard, *Reynard*
Raynaud, *Reynold*
Raynbird, *Rainbird*
Rayne, *Raine*
Rayner
Raynor, *Rayner*
Raynouard, *Renouard*
Razgovorov
Razou, *Ralph*
Razoul, *Ralph*
Razouls, *Ralph*
Razous, *Ralph*
Razout, *Ralph*
Razoux, *Ralph*
Ré, *Ray*
Rea, *Rye*
Reacher, *Richer*
Read
Readdie, *Ready*
Readdy, *Ready*
Reade, *Read*
Reader
Readers, *Reader*
Readey, *Ready*
Readhead, *Redhead*
Reading
Readman, *Read, Reader*
Readwin, *Redwin*
Ready
Reagan, *Regan*
Réal, *Real*
Real
Reale, *Real*

Realff, *Relph*
Reali, *Real*
Really, *Reilly*
Realy, *Reilly*
Reaman, *Rye*
Reaney, *Rainey*
Reanney, *Rainey*
Reanny, *Rainey*
Reany, *Rainey*
Rearden, *Riordan*
Reardon, *Riordan*
Rease, *Rhys*
Reason, *Raison*
Réau, *Real*
Réault, *Real*
Réaumur
Reaux, *Real*
Reavell, *Revell*
Reaves, *Reeves*
Reavey
Reay, *Rye*
Rebaudi, *Ribaud*
Rebaudo, *Ribaud*
Rebelo
Rebert, *Robert*
Rebhahn, *Rebhun*
Rebhun
Rebichon, *Robert*
Rebmann
Rebollo
Rebour, *Rebours*
Rebours
Rebourseau, *Rebours*
Rebourseaux, *Rebours*
Rebourset, *Rebours*
Rebous, *Rebours*
Reboussin, *Rebours*
Rebout, *Rebours*
Récamier
Recasens
Recio
Reckitt, *Rich*
Record, *Rickwood*
Records, *Rickwood*
Red, *Read*
Redahan, *Ready*
Redcliffe, *Ratcliffe*
Redclift, *Ratcliffe*
Redd, *Read*
Reddan, *Roden*
Reddecliff, *Ratcliffe*
Reddich, *Rettig*
Reddick
Reddie, *Ready*
Reddiford, *Radford*
Reddig, *Rettig*
Reddin, *Roden*
Redding, *Reading*
Reddington
Reddish
Reddy, *Ready*
Redehan, *Ready*
Redeke, *Rat*
Redeker, *Rademaker*
Reder, *Reader*
Redfearn, *Redfern*
Redfern
Redford, *Radford*
Redgate
Redgewell, *Ridgewell*
Redgrave
Redgwell, *Ridgewell*
Redhead
Redicliffe, *Ratcliffe*

Reding, *Reading*
Redman, *Read, Roth*
Redmayne
Redmond, *Raymond*
Redmonds, *Raymond*
Redolfi, *Rolf*
Redon, *Round*
Redondet, *Round*
Redondin, *Round*
Redondo, *Round*
Redonet, *Round*
Redonnet, *Round*
Redouin, *Redwin*
Redouté
Redpath
Redshaw
Redsmith, *Smith*
Redwin
Redwood
Reece, *Rhys*
Reed, *Read*
Reeder, *Reader*
Reeders, *Reader*
Reedie, *Ready*
Reedman, *Reader*
Reef, *Roper*
Reekie
Reely, *Reilly*
Reeman, *Rye*
Reemt, *Rainbird*
Reendels, *Reynold*
Reenen, *Raine*
Reents, *Reynard*
Reep, *Roper*
Reeper, *Roper*
Reepmaeker, *Roper*
Rees, *Rhys*
Reese, *Rhys*
Reeve
Reeves
Refael, *Raphael*
Refaeli, *Raphael*
Refaelov, *Raphael*
Refaelove, *Raphael*
Refaely, *Raphael*
Refalovicz, *Raphael*
Refalovitch, *Raphael*
Refoy
Regan
Regazzi, *Ragazzo*
Regazzini, *Ragazzo*
Regazzo, *Ragazzo*
Regazzoni, *Ragazzo*
Rege, *Ray*
Regenhardt, *Reynard*
Regenold, *Reynold*
Regenprecht, *Rainbird*
Reger
Regerman, *Reger*
Regibus, *Ray*
Regidor
Regina, *Raine*
Regis, *Ray, Régis*
Régis
Regisser, *Régis*
Régissier, *Régis*
Regnard, *Reynard*
Regnaud, *Reynold*
Regnault, *Reynold*
Régnier, *Rayner*
Rego
Regorz, *Gregory*
Řeháček, *Rehák*
Řehák

Rehm, *Remy, Riemer*
Rehme, *Riemer*
Rehmer, *Riemer*
Rehn, *Raine*
Rehnen, *Raine*
Rehnert, *Reynard*
Rehor, *Gregory*
Řehoř, *Gregory*
Řehořek, *Gregory*
Rehorz, *Gregory*
Rei, *Ray*
Reiban, *Rybak*
Reiband, *Rybak*
Reibe, *Ryba*
Reibisch, *Ryba*
Reibke, *Ryba*
Reich, *Rich*
Reichardt, *Richard*
Reichartz, *Richard*
Reicharz, *Richard*
Reichbach, *Rich*
Reichbard, *Rich*
Reichbart, *Rich*
Reichberg, *Rich*
Reiche, *Rich*
Reichel, *Rich*
Reichelt, *Rich*
Reichenbach
Reichenbaum, *Rich*
Reichenberg, *Rich*
Reichenstein, *Rich*
Reichental, *Rich*
Reichenthal, *Rich*
Reicher, *Rich, Richer*
Reichert, *Richard*
Reicherz, *Richard*
Reichfeld, *Rich*
Reichgold, *Rich*
Reichgott, *Rich*
Reichhardt, *Richard*
Reichhold, *Rickwood*
Reichkind, *Rich*
Reichler, *Rich*
Reichlin, *Rich*
Reichman, *Rich*
Reichmann, *Rich*
Reichnadel, *Rich*
Reichnudel, *Rich*
Reichold, *Rickwood*
Reicholz, *Rickwood*
Reichstein, *Rich*
Reichtaler, *Rich*
Reichwald, *Rickwood*
Reick, *Rich*
Reicke, *Rich*
Reickl, *Rich*
Reid, *Read*
Reiddie, *Ready*
Reidy, *Ready*
Reielts, *Reynold*
Reig, *Ray*
Reignard, *Reynard*
Reignaud, *Reynold*
Reignier, *Rayner*
Reijmers, *Reinmar*
Reilly
Reily, *Reilly*
Reim, *Raymond*
Reimbaud, *Rainbow*
Reimbert, *Rainbird*
Reimbold, *Rainbow*
Reimelt, *Rainbow*
Reimer, *Reinmar*
Reimers, *Reinmar*
Reimert, *Rainbird*
Reimpert, *Rainbird*
Reimund, *Raymond*
Rein, *Raine*
Reina, *Raine*
Reinaert, *Reynard*
Reinard, *Reynard*
Reinartz, *Reynard*
Reinaud, *Reynold*
Reinbold, *Rainbow*
Reindel, *Reynard*
Reindl, *Raine*
Reine, *Raine*
Reinecke, *Raine*
Reinecken, *Raine*
Reinege, *Raine*
Reineke, *Raine*
Reineken, *Raine*
Reineking, *Raine*
Reinel, *Raine*
Reinelt, *Reynold*
Reinelts, *Reynold*
Reinen, *Raine*
Reiner, *Rayner*
Reinerding, *Reynard*
Reiners, *Rayner*
Reinert, *Reynard*
Reinerts, *Reynard*
Reines, *Raine*
Reineward, *Renouard*
Reinhard, *Reynard*
Reinhardt, *Reynard*
Reinhart, *Reynard*
Reinhold, *Reynold*
Reinholdt, *Reynold*
Reinholtz, *Reynold*
Reinholz, *Reynold*
Reinick, *Raine*
Reinicke, *Raine*
Reinicken, *Raine*
Reinié, *Rayner*
Reinier, *Rayner*
Reining, *Raine*
Reininga, *Raine*
Reinis, *Raine*
Reinisch, *Raine*
Reinke, *Raine*
Reinken, *Raine*
Reinkena, *Raine*
Reinkens, *Raine*
Reinking, *Raine*
Reinl, *Raine*
Reinle, *Raine*
Reinmann, *Raine*
Reinmar
Reinmund, *Raymond*
Reinold, *Reynold*
Reins, *Raine*
Reinsch, *Raine*
Reint, *Reynard*
Reintjes, *Reynard*
Reints, *Reynard*
Reintsch, *Raine*
Reintsema, *Reynard*
Reinuss, *Raine*
Reinwald, *Reynold*
Reinwaldt, *Reynold*
Reinwarth, *Renouard*
Reinwerth, *Renouard*
Reinwold, *Reynold*
Reipert, *Rainbird*
Reiprecht, *Rainbird*
Reiprich, *Rainbird*
Reis, *Ray*
Reis
Reisen
Reisenberg, *Rose*
Reisenstein, *Rose*
Reisman, *Reis*
Reismann, *Reis*
Reisner, *Reisen*
Reiss, *Reis*
Reitbard, *Roth*
Reitberg, *Rothenberg*
Reitberger, *Rothenberg*
Reitblatt, *Roth*
Reitbord, *Roth*
Reiten, *Reuter*
Reiter, *Reuter*
Reith
Reither, *Reuter*
Reithmann, *Reuter*
Reitman, *Roth*
Reix, *Ray*
Réjau, *Real*
Réjaud, *Real*
Reker, *Rademaker*
Relandeau, *Rowland*
Relf, *Relph*
Relfe, *Relph*
Relin, *Rollo*
Relph
Rembaud, *Rainbow*
Rembert, *Rainbird*
Rembold, *Rainbow*
Remedi, *Remy*
Remedio, *Remy*
Remeis, *Remy*
Remensnider, *Riemer*
Remer, *Reinmar, Riemer*
Remers, *Reinmar*
Remi, *Remy*
Remiens, *Remy*
Remigeau, *Remy*
Remigeon, *Remy*
Remillon, *Remy*
Remington, *Rimmington*
Remion, *Remy*
Remiot, *Remy*
Remmers, *Reinmar*
Remmert, *Rainbird*
Remmy, *Remy*
Rémon, *Raymond*
Rémond, *Raymond*
Remondeau, *Raymond*
Remondon, *Raymond*
Rémont, *Raymond*
Remy
Renad, *Reynard*
Renaldi, *Reynold*
Renaldini, *Reynold*
Renals, *Reynold*
Renan, *Ronan*
Renand, *Ronan*
Renard, *Reynard*
Renardeau, *Reynard*
Renardet, *Reynard*
Renardin, *Reynard*
Renardot, *Reynard*
Renat, *René*
Renaud, *Reynold*
Renaudeau, *Reynold*
Renaudel, *Reynold*
Renaudet, *Reynold*
Renaudin, *Reynold*
Renaudon, *Reynold*
Renaudot, *Reynold*
Renauleau, *Reynold*
Renault, *Reynold*
Renaut, *Reynold*
Renaux, *Reynold*
Renbold, *Rainbow*
Rendall, *Randall*
Rendell, *Randall*
Render
Rendle, *Randall*
Rendsburg, *Rensburg, van*
René
Reneaud, *Reynold*
Reneault, *Reynold*
Renelt, *Reynold*
Renet, *Reynard*
Renhard, *Reynard*
Renié, *Rayner*
Renier, *Rayner*
Renieri, *Rayner*
Renisch, *Raine*
Renison, *Rainey*
Renn, *Raine*
Rennard, *Reynard*
Renne, *Raine*
Renneke, *Raine*
Rennell, *Reynold*
Rennels, *Reynold*
Rennen, *Raine*
Renner
Rennert, *Reynard*
Renney, *Rainey*
Rennie, *Rainey*
Rennings, *Raine*
Rennold, *Reynold*
Rennolds, *Reynold*
Rennoll, *Reynold*
Rennsen, *Raine*
Renny, *Rainey*
Renoldi, *Reynold*
Renolleau, *Reynold*
Renon, *Raine*
Renouard
Rens, *Lawrence*
Rensburg, van
Rensen, *Lawrence*
Renshall, *Renshaw*
Renshaw
Renshell, *Renshaw*
Rensi, *Lawrence*
Rente, *Reynard*
Renting, *Reynard*
Renton
Rentoul, *Rintoul*
Rentsch, *Raine*
Rentschke, *Raine*
Rentz, *Lawrence*
Renus, *Raine*
Renward, *Renouard*
Renwick
Renyard, *Reynard*
Renz, *Lawrence*
Renzetti, *Lawrence*
Renzi, *Lawrence*
Renzini, *Lawrence*
Renzo, *Lawrence*
Renzoni, *Lawrence*
Renzulli, *Lawrence*
Renzullo, *Lawrence*
Reolfi, *Rolf*
Reolfo, *Rolf*
Rep, *Roper*
Řepa, *Repin*
Reper, *Roper*
Rephael, *Raphael*
Rephaeli, *Raphael*

Repin
Řepka, *Repin*
Repp, *Roper*
Repton
Requena
Reschke, *Gregory*
Resende
Resnais, *René*
Resnick, *Rzeźnik*
Restif, *Rétif*
Restifo, *Rétif*
Restivo, *Rétif*
Restorick
Reszka, *Ryzhakov*
Retallack
Retallick, *Retallack*
Retchford, *Rochford*
Retford, *Radford*
Rethel, *Roth*
Retief, *Rétif*
Rétif
Retig, *Rettig*
Retter
Rettich, *Rettig*
Rettier, *Retter*
Rettig
Réty, *Rétif*
Reubbens, *Reuben*
Reubel, *Robert*
Reuben
Reubens, *Reuben*
Reuble, *Robert*
Reuss
Reuter
Reuters, *Reuter*
Reuther, *Reuter*
Reuven, *Reuben*
Revan, *Raven*
Revans, *Raven*
Revel, *Ravel, Revell*
Revell
Revels, *Revell*
Revens, *Raven*
Rever, *Rouvre*
Revett, *Rivett*
Revill, *Revell*
Revilla
Reville, *Revell*
Revis, *Reeves*
Revuelta
Rew, *Rowe*
Rewan, *Ruane*
Rey, *Ray*
Reyes, *Ray*
Reyger, *Reger*
Reymers, *Reinmar*
Reymond, *Raymond*
Reynaert, *Reynard*
Reynal, *Reynold*
Reynalds, *Reynold*
Reynard
Reynaud, *Reynold*
Reynaudi, *Reynold*
Reyne, *Raine*
Reynell, *Reynold*
Reyner, *Rayner*
Reynier, *Rayner*
Reynold
Reynolds, *Reynold*
Reynoldson, *Reynold*
Reynouard, *Renouard*
Rež, *Rye*
Řezáč
Rezek, *Ryzhakov*
Rezik, *Ryzhakov*
Řezníček, *Rzeźnik*
Reznik, *Rzeźnik*
Řezník, *Rzeźnik*
Reznikoff, *Rzeźnik*
Reznikov, *Rzeźnik*
Režný, *Rye*
Rhategan, *Rattigan*
Rhatigan, *Rattigan*
Rhein
Rhind, *Rind*
Rhoades, *Rhodes*
Rhodes
Rhynd, *Rind*
Rhys
Rian, *Ryan*
Riba, *Rive, Ryba*
Ribach, *Rybak*
Riback, *Rybak*
Ribak, *Rybak*
Ribalta
Ribar, *Rybak*
Ribard, *Ribaud*
Ribas, *Rive*
Ribaud
Ribaudo, *Ribaud*
Ribault, *Ribaud*
Ribaut, *Ribaud*
Ribback, *Rybak*
Ribbe, *Rippert*
Ribbeck, *Rybak*
Ribbentrop
Ribbert, *Rippert*
Ribé, *Rivero*
Ribe, *Rive*
Ribeiro, *Rivero*
Ribera, *Rivers*
Ribereau, *Rivers*
Riberole, *Rivers*
Riberolles, *Rivers*
Ribert, *Rippert*
Ribes, *Rive*
Ribet, *Ribaud*
Ribeyras, *Rivers*
Ribeyre, *Rivers*
Ribeyrolles, *Rivers*
Ribière, *Rivers*
Ribó
Ribon, *Ribaud*
Ribot, *Ribaud*
Riboton, *Ribaud*
Riboud, *Ribaud*
Ribout, *Ribaud*
Ribra, *Rubbra*
Ric, *Rich*
Rica, *Rich*
Ricard, *Richard*
Ricarde, *Richard*
Ricardet, *Richard*
Ricardin, *Richard*
Ricardo, *Richard*
Ricardon, *Richard*
Ricardot, *Richard*
Ricardou, *Richard*
Ricards, *Richard*
Ricart, *Richard*
Ricaud, *Rickwood*
Ricaut, *Rickwood*
Ricaux, *Rickwood*
Riccard, *Richard*
Riccardelli, *Richard*
Riccardi, *Richard*
Riccardini, *Richard*
Riccardo, *Richard*
Riccelli, *Ricci*
Riccetti, *Ricci*
Ricchini, *Rich*
Ricchino, *Rich*
Ricci
Ricciardelli, *Richard*
Ricciardello, *Richard*
Ricciardi, *Richard*
Ricciardiello, *Richard*
Ricciardo, *Richard*
Riccini, *Ricci*
Riccio, *Ricci*
Ricciolino, *Ricci*
Riccioni, *Ricci*
Ricciotti, *Ricci*
Ricciulli, *Ricci*
Ricco, *Rich*
Riccone, *Rich*
Rice, *Rhys*
Rich
Richard
Richardeau, *Richard*
Richardes, *Richard*
Richardet, *Richard*
Richardin, *Richard*
Richardon, *Richard*
Richardot, *Richard*
Richards, *Richard*
Richardson, *Richard*
Richardsson, *Richard*
Richardt, *Richard*
Richartz, *Richard*
Richarz, *Richard*
Richaud, *Rickwood*
Riche, *Rich*
Richemond, *Richmond*
Richemont, *Richmond*
Richer
Riches, *Rich*
Richet, *Rich*
Richeton, *Rich*
Richez, *Rich*
Richi, *Rich*
Richier, *Richer*
Richies, *Rich*
Richman, *Rich*
Richman, *Richmond*
Richmond
Richmont, *Richmond*
Richold, *Rickwood*
Richon, *Rich*
Richou, *Rich*
Richt, *Richard*
Richten, *Richard*
Richter
Richtering, *Richter*
Richters, *Richter*
Ricioli, *Ricci*
Riciolini, *Ricci*
Rick, *Rich*
Rickaert, *Richard*
Rickard, *Richard*
Rickardes, *Richard*
Rickards, *Richard*
Rickardsson, *Richard*
Ricke, *Rich*
Rickelt, *Rickwood*
Rickelts, *Rickwood*
Ricken, *Rich*
Rickena, *Rich*
Rickens, *Rich*
Ricker, *Richard, Richer*
Rickerd, *Richard*
Rickers, *Richer*
Rickert, *Richard*
Rickertsen, *Richard*
Ricket, *Rich*
Rickett, *Rich*
Ricketts, *Rich*
Rickolts, *Rickwood*
Ricks, *Rich*
Rickson, *Rich*
Rickward, *Rickwood*
Rickwood
Rickword, *Rickwood*
Rico, *Rich*
Ricote, *Rich*
Ricq, *Rich*
Ricque, *Rich*
Ridal, *Riddell*
Riddall, *Riddell*
Riddel, *Riddell*
Riddell
Ridder, *Rider*
Riddering, *Rider*
Ridders, *Rider*
Riddick, *Reddick*
Ridding, *Reading*
Riddle, *Riddell*
Ride, *Read*
Rideal, *Riddell*
Rideout, *Ridout*
Rider
Ridge
Ridgeway, *Ridgway*
Ridgewell
Ridgway
Ridgwell, *Ridgewell*
Riding, *Reading*
Ridler
Ridley
Ridolfi, *Rolf*
Ridolfo, *Rolf*
Ridout
Ridoutt, *Ridout*
Ridpath, *Redpath*
Ridsdale
Ridulfo, *Rolf*
Rieban, *Rybak*
Rieband, *Rybak*
Riebe, *Ryba*
Riebisch, *Ryba*
Rieckmann, *Rich*
Riedel, *Rode*
Riediger, *Roger*
Rief, *Rolf*
Riefenstahl
Rieflin, *Rolf*
Riefstahl, *Riefenstahl*
Rieger, *Roger*
Riehm, *Riemer*
Rieke, *Rich*
Rielly, *Reilly*
Riem, *Riemer*
Riemann, *Rhein*
Rieme, *Riemer*
Riemenschneider, *Riemer*
Riemer
Riemersma, *Riemer*
Riemschneider, *Riemer*
Riemsnijder, *Riemer*
Rienholt, *Reynold*
Rienolt, *Reynold*
Riepe, *Rippert*
Riepel, *Robert*
Riepen, *Rippert*
Riepena, *Rippert*
Rieper, *Roper*

Riepl, *Robert*
Riera
Ries, *Riese*
Riesco
Riese
Riesgo
Rieti, *Rieu*
Rietsche, *Rich*
Rietschel, *Rich*
Rietti, *Rieu*
Rietveld
Rieu
Rieuf, *Rieu*
Rieux, *Rieu*
Rifkin
Rifkind, *Rifkin*
Rigal, *Rickwood*
Rigard, *Richard*
Rigardeau, *Richard*
Rigaudet, *Rickwood*
Rigaudin, *Rickwood*
Rigault, *Rickwood*
Rigaut, *Rickwood*
Rigaux, *Rickwood*
Rigby
Rigg, *Ridge*
Rigge, *Ridge*
Riggert, *Richard*
Rigglesford, *Wrigglesworth*
Riggs, *Ridge*
Riggulsford, *Wrigglesworth*
Rigley, *Wrigley*
Rignault, *Reynold*
Rigneault, *Reynold*
Rigter, *Richter*
Rigts, *Richard*
Riguard, *Richard*
Říha, *Gregory*
Říhánek, *Gregory*
Řihošek, *Gregory*
Rikin
Rikke, *Rich*
Riklin, *Rikin*
Riklis, *Rikin*
Riley
Rimbaud, *Rainbow*
Rimbault, *Rainbow*
Rimbert, *Rainbird*
Rimedi, *Remy*
Rimedio, *Remy*
Rimediotti, *Remy*
Rimer
Rimerman, *Riemer*
Rimmer, *Rimer*
Rimmington
Rimmon, *Rimon*
Rimon
Rimondi, *Raymond*
Rimondini, *Raymond*
Rimpler, *Rumbold*
Rinaldelli, *Reynold*
Rinaldeschi, *Reynold*
Rinaldi, *Reynold*
Rinaldin, *Reynold*
Rinaldini, *Reynold*
Rinaldis, *Reynold*
Rinaldo, *Reynold*
Rinalducci, *Reynold*
Rinalduzzi, *Reynold*
Rinallo, *Reynold*
Rinaudi, *Reynold*
Rinck, *Ring*
Rincke, *Ring*
Rincón
Rind
Rinelli, *Perrin*
Rinero, *Rayner*
Rinetti, *Perrin*
Ring
Ringel, *Ring*
Ringer
Ringger, *Ringer*
Ringle, *Ring*
Ringrose
Rings, *Ring*
Rini, *Perrin*
Rink, *Ring*
Rinke, *Ring*
Rinker, *Ringer*
Rinne, *Wren*
Rintoul
Rinucci, *Perrin*
Rinuccini, *Perrin*
Río, *Rieu*
Rio, *Rieu*
Rioja
Riol, *Rieu*
Riolfi, *Rolf*
Riolfo, *Rolf*
Riols, *Rieu*
Riordan
Ríos, *Rieu*
Rios, *Rieu*
Riou, *Rieu*
Riozzi, *Rieu*
Řípa, *Repin*
Ripert, *Rippert*
Ripke, *Rippert*
Ripley
Ripoche, *Rippe*
Ripoll
Ripollès, *Ripoll*
Ripon, *Rippe*
Ripot, *Rippe*
Ripoteau, *Rippe*
Rippe
Rippen, *Rippert*
Rippens, *Rippert*
Ripper
Rippert
Ripping, *Rippert*
Rippke, *Rippert*
Rippon
Riquet, *Henry*
Riquier, *Richer*
Riquiez, *Richer*
Risby
Risch, *Rush*
Rische, *Rush*
Rischer, *Rush*
Risco, *Riesco*
Riseborough
Risebrow, *Riseborough*
Risk, *Rusk*
Risley
Risse, *Morris*
Risso, *Ricci*
Rissolo, *Ricci*
Rissone, *Ricci*
Rita
Ritch, *Rich*
Ritchard, *Richard*
Ritchie, *Rich*
Ritschen, *Rich*
Ritscher, *Rich*
Ritson, *Richard*
Ritter, *Rider*
Ritterman, *Rider*
Ritters, *Rider*
Ritz, *Rich*
Ritze, *Rich*
Ritzen, *Rich*
Ritzer, *Rich*
Ritzke, *Rich*
Riu, *Rieu*
Rius, *Rieu*
Riva, *Rive*
Rival, *Reuben*
Rivani, *Rive*
Rivano, *Rive*
Rivas, *Rive*
Rive
Riveau, *Rive*
Rivel, *Reuben*
Riveles, *Reuben, Rifkin*
Rivelis, *Rifkin*
Rivelli, *Rieu*
Rivelon, *Rive*
Rivenzon, *Reuben*
Rivera, *Rivers*
Rivero
Rivers
Rives, *Rifkin, Rive*
Rivet, *Rive*
Rivett
Rivetti, *Rive*
Rivier, *Rivero*
Riviera, *Rivers*
Rivière, *Rivers*
Rivierre, *Rivers*
Rivilis, *Reuben*
Rivkes, *Rifkin*
Rivkin, *Rifkin*
Rivkind, *Rifkin*
Rivkovich, *Rifkin*
Rivlin, *Reuben, Rifkin*
Rivoire, *Rivers*
Rivolet, *Rieu*
Rivollet, *Rieu*
Rivolo, *Rieu*
Rix
Rix, *Rich*
Rixen, *Rich*
Rixon, *Rich*
Riz, *Riese*
Rizzardi, *Richard*
Rizzardini, *Richard*
Rizzardo, *Richard*
Rizzelli, *Ricci*
Rizzello, *Ricci*
Rizzetti, *Ricci*
Rizzetto, *Ricci*
Rizzi, *Ricci*
Rizziello, *Ricci*
Rizzillo, *Ricci*
Rizzini, *Ricci*
Rizzioli, *Ricci*
Rizzo, *Ricci*
Rizzoli, *Ricci*
Rizzolo, *Ricci*
Rizzon, *Ricci*
Rizzone, *Ricci*
Rizzoni, *Ricci*
Rizzotti, *Ricci*
Rizzotto, *Ricci*
Roa, *Rode*
Roach
Road, *Rhodes*
Roadknight
Roads, *Rhodes*
Roaf, *Rolf*
Roake, *Rock*
Roalfe, *Rolf*
Roan, *Ruane*
Roane, *Ruane*
Roata, *Rode*
Robaldo, *Ribaud*
Robalo
Robard, *Robert*
Robardet, *Robert*
Robardey, *Robert*
Robart, *Robert*
Robarts, *Robert*
Robatham, *Rowbottom*
Robathan, *Rowbottom*
Robaudo, *Ribaud*
Robb, *Robert*
Robbe, *Robert*
Röbbeke, *Robert*
Robbel, *Robert*
Robben, *Robert*
Robbens, *Robin*
Robberds, *Robert*
Robberecht, *Robert*
Robbert, *Robert*
Robberts, *Robert*
Robbie, *Roby*
Robbin, *Robin*
Robbins, *Robin*
Robbs, *Robert*
Robé, *Robert*
Robeçon, *Robert*
Robel, *Robert*
Robelet, *Robert*
Robelin, *Robert*
Robelot, *Robert*
Robens, *Robin*
Robers, *Robert*
Roberson, *Robert*
Róbert, *Robert*
Robert
Robertacci, *Robert*
Robertazzi, *Robert*
Robertelli, *Robert*
Robertet, *Robert*
Roberti, *Robert*
Robertis, *Robert*
Roberto, *Robert*
Robertot, *Robert*
Roberts, *Robert*
Robertsen, *Robert*
Robertshaw
Robertson, *Robert*
Robertsson, *Robert*
Robertucci, *Robert*
Robertz, *Robert*
Robeson, *Robert*
Robespierre
Robet, *Robert*
Robey, *Robert*
Robez, *Robert*
Robic, *Robert*
Robichon, *Robert*
Robie, *Roby*
Robin
Robineau, *Robin*
Robinet, *Robin*
Robinot, *Robin*
Robinov, *Rabin*
Robinovich, *Rabin*
Robinovitz, *Rabin*
Robinow, *Rabin*
Robins, *Robin*
Robinsohn, *Rabin*
Robinson, *Rabin*
Robinson, *Robin*

Robinzon, *Rabin*
Robion, *Robert*
Robiot, *Robert*
Robiou, *Robert*
Robison, *Robin*
Röbke, *Robert*
Röbken, *Robert*
Röbker, *Robert*
Robledo, *Rouvre*
Robles, *Rouvre*
Roblet, *Robert*
Roblett, *Robert*
Roblin, *Robert*
Roblot, *Robert*
Robot, *Robert*
Robottom, *Rowbottom*
Robredo, *Rouvre*
Robshaw, *Robertshaw*
Robson, *Robert*
Robuchon, *Robert*
Robusti
Roby
Robyn, *Robin*
Robyns, *Robin*
Roc, *Roach*
Roca, *Roach*
Rocca, *Roach*
Rocchelli, *Roch*
Rocchetti, *Roch*
Rocchi, *Roch*
Rocchini, *Roch*
Rocci, *Roch*
Roccon, *Roch*
Rocconi, *Roch*
Roch
Rocha, *Roach*
Roche, *Roach*
Rochel, *Roach*
Rochelle, *Roach*
Rochester
Rochet, *Roach*
Rochette, *Roach*
Rochford
Rochlin
Rochon, *Roach*
Rochs, *Roch*
Rochus, *Roch*
Rochussen, *Roch*
Rock
Rockall, *Roach*
Rocke, *Rock*
Rockefeller
Rockell, *Roach*
Rocker, *Rock*
Rockley
Rocks, *Rock*
Rockwell
Rocque, *Roach*
Rocques, *Roach*
Rocquet, *Roach*
Rocquette, *Roach*
Rocuzzo, *Roch*
Roda, *Rode*
Rodan, *Roden*
Rodaughan, *Ready*
Rodaway, *Rodway*
Rodd, *Rhodes*
Roddam
Roddan, *Roden*
Rodden, *Roden*
Rödding, *Rode*
Roddy, *Ready*
Rode
Rodel, *Rode*
Roden
Ródenas
Rodera
Roderas, *Rodera*
Roderick
Roderighi, *Roderick*
Roderigo, *Roderick*
Rodés
Rodet, *Rode*
Rodge, *Roger*
Rodgeman, *Roger*
Rodger, *Roger*
Rodgers, *Roger*
Rodgerson, *Roger*
Rodgett, *Roger*
Rodgier, *Roger*
Rodié, *Rode*
Rodier, *Rode*
Rödiger, *Roger*
Rodilon, *Rode*
Rodin, *Rode*
Röding, *Rode*
Rödinger, *Roger*
Rodknight, *Roadknight*
Rodney
Rodolf, *Rolf*
Rodolfi, *Rolf*
Rodolico, *Roderick*
Rodolphe, *Rolf*
Rodon, *Rode, Round*
Rodot, *Rode*
Rodrig, *Roderick*
Rodrigo, *Roderick*
Rodrigue, *Roderick*
Rodrigues, *Roderick*
Rodríguez, *Roderick*
Rodriguez, *Roderick*
Rodriques, *Roderick*
Rodway
Rodwell
Roe, *Ray*
Roebotham, *Rowbottom*
Roebuck, *Ray*
Roël, *Roach*
Roelands, *Rowland*
Roelandts, *Rowland*
Roele, *Rollo*
Roelofs, *Rolf*
Roelofsen, *Rolf*
Roelvink, *Rolf*
Rofe, *Rofé, Rolf*
Rofé
Rofeh, *Rofé*
Roff, *Rofé, Rolf*
Roffe, *Rofé, Rolf*
Roffey
Rogacki
Rogaczewski, *Rogacki*
Rogala, *Rogalski*
Rogalewicz, *Rogalski*
Rogaliński, *Rogalski*
Rogalski
Rogeon, *Roger*
Roger
Rogeron, *Roger*
Rogerot, *Roger*
Rogers, *Roger*
Rogerson, *Roger*
Roget, *Roger*
Rogez, *Roger*
Rogge, *Roger*
Roggeman, *Roger*
Rogger, *Roger*
Roggeri, *Roger*
Roggero, *Roger*
Roggerone, *Roger*
Roggers, *Roger*
Roggieri, *Roger*
Roggiero, *Roger*
Roghtigan, *Rattigan*
Rogier, *Roger*
Rogister, *Rochester*
Roglieri, *Roger*
Rogliero, *Roger*
Rogoff, *Rogov*
Rogov
Rogover, *Rogov*
Rogovsky, *Rogov*
Rogow, *Rogov*
Rogowski, *Rogacki, Rogov*
Rogowsky, *Rogov*
Rogoziński
Rogulski, *Rogalski*
Rohan
Rohde, *Rode*
Rohel, *Roach*
Rohfsen, *Rolf*
Röhl, *Rollo*
Rohlf, *Rolf*
Rohlfing, *Rolf*
Rohlfs, *Rolf*
Röhlig, *Rollo*
Rohlík, *Rogalski*
Röhling, *Rollo*
Rohling, *Rollo*
Röhlke, *Rollo*
Rohloff, *Rolf*
Rohls, *Rollo*
Rohlsen, *Rollo*
Röhmer, *Romero*
Rohmer, *Romero*
Röhr, *Rohr*
Rohr
Röhreke, *Rohr*
Rohrer, *Rohr*
Röhrich, *Rohr*
Röhricht, *Rohr*
Röhrle, *Rohr*
Rohrmann, *Rohr*
Roig, *Rudge*
Rois, *Rose*
Roisen, *Rose*
Roisman, *Roseman*
Roit, *Roth*
Roitblit, *Roth*
Roiter, *Roth*
Roitkof, *Roth*
Roitman, *Roth*
Roiz, *Rose*
Roizenbaum, *Rose*
Roizin, *Rose*
Roizman, *Roseman*
Roizn, *Rose*
Rojas
Rojek
Rojewski, *Rojek*
Rojo, *Rouse*
Rojter, *Roth*
Roke, *Rock*
Rokos, *Rákos*
Rol, *Rollo*
Rolance, *Rowland*
Roland, *Rowland*
Rolandeau, *Rowland*
Rolandi, *Rowland*
Rolandino, *Rowland*
Roldán, *Rowland*
Role, *Rollo*
Rolendi, *Rowland*
Roles, *Rollo*
Rolet, *Rollo*
Rolf
Rolfe, *Rolf*
Rolfi, *Rolf*
Rolfini, *Rolf*
Rolfo, *Rolf*
Rolfs, *Rolf*
Rolin, *Rollo*
Roling, *Rollo*
Rolinson, *Rollo*
Rolison, *Rollo*
Rölke, *Rollo*
Roll, *Rollo*
Rolland, *Rowland*
Rollang, *Rowland*
Rollant, *Rowland*
Rollason, *Rollo*
Rölle, *Rollo*
Rolle, *Rollo*
Rollerson, *Rollo*
Rolles, *Rollo*
Rolleston, *Rolston*
Rollet, *Rollo*
Rollett, *Rollo*
Rollin, *Rollo*
Rolling, *Rollo*
Rollings, *Rollo*
Rollingson, *Rollo*
Rollins, *Rollo*
Rollinson, *Rollo*
Rollison, *Rollo*
Rollit, *Rollo*
Rollitt, *Rollo*
Rollman, *Rollo*
Rollo
Rollon, *Rollo*
Rollons, *Rowland*
Rollot, *Rollo*
Rolls, *Rollo*
Rolo
Roloff, *Rolf*
Rolon, *Rollo*
Rolph, *Rolf*
Rolston
Rolstone, *Rolston*
Romà, *Roman*
Roma, *Roman*
Romagosa
Romahn, *Roman*
Romain, *Roman*
Romaine, *Roman*
Román, *Roman*
Roman
Romanazzi, *Roman*
Romanchat, *Roman*
Romanchuk, *Roman*
Romand, *Roman*
Romanelli, *Roman*
Romanello, *Roman*
Romanenya, *Roman*
Romanet, *Roman*
Romanets, *Roman*
Romanetti, *Roman*
Romani, *Roman*
Romaniello, *Roman*
Romanikhin, *Roman*
Romanin, *Roman*
Romanini, *Roman*
Romanino, *Roman*
Romanitsa, *Roman*
Romaniuk, *Roman*
Romano, *Roman*

Romanoff, *Roman*
Romanov, *Roman*
Romanovich, *Roman*
Romanowicz, *Roman*
Romanowski, *Roman*
Romans, *Roman*
Romański, *Roman*
Romanucci, *Roman*
Romanychev, *Roman*
Romão, *Roman*
Romashov, *Roman*
Romayn, *Roman*
Romayne, *Roman*
Rombaut, *Rumbold*
Rombeau, *Rumbold*
Römbold, *Rainbow*
Romboud, *Rumbold*
Rombouts, *Rumbold*
Rombulow, *Rumbelow*
Rome, *Roman*
Romei, *Romero*
Romeijn, *Roman*
Romeis, *Remy*
Romeo, *Romero*
Rømer, *Romero*
Römer, *Romero*
Romer, *Romero*
Romerio, *Romero*
Romero
Romeu, *Romero*
Romeuf, *Romero*
Romeyn, *Roman*
Romi, *Roman*
Romier, *Romero*
Romijn, *Roman*
Romilly
Romin, *Roman*
Rominov, *Roman*
Romme, *Roman*
Rommel
Römmele, *Rommel*
Römmler, *Rommel*
Romney
Romo
Romsay, *Rumsey*
Romsey, *Rumsey*
Ronald
Ronaldson, *Ronald*
Ronan
Ronane, *Ronan*
Ronayne, *Ronan*
Roncero
Roncin
Rond, *Round*
Ronde, *Round*
Rondeau, *Round*
Rondel, *Round*
Rondelet, *Round*
Rondello, *Arundel*
Rondet, *Round*
Rondot, *Round*
Rondou, *Round*
Roney, *Rooney*
Rongeron, *Rongier*
Ronget, *Rongier*
Rongier
Rönisch, *Raine*
Rønn, *Rønne*
Rönn, *Rowntree*
Rönnberg, *Rowntree*
Rönnbergh, *Rowntree*
Rønne
Rönnqvist, *Rowntree*
Ronsard, *Roncin*
Rönsch, *Raine*
Ronsin, *Roncin*
Ronson, *Rowland*
Röntsch, *Raine*
Ronymus, *Jerome*
Roobottam, *Rowbottom*
Rood, *Roth*
Roode, *Roth*
Roodman, *Rothmann*
Roof, *Räuber, Rolf*
Roofe, *Rolf*
Rook
Rooke, *Rook*
Rooker, *Rock*
Rookes, *Rook*
Rookledge, *Routledge*
Rooks, *Rook*
Room, *Roman*
Roome, *Roman*
Roomer, *Romero*
Rooms, *Jerome*
Roon, *Ruane*
Rooney
Roop, *Roper*
Roope, *Roper*
Rooper, *Roper*
Roos, *Rose*
Roos, *Ross*
Roose, *Rose*
Roose, *Ross*
Roosevelt
Root
Roote, *Root*
Rootes, *Root*
Rooth, *Root*
Rootham
Roots, *Root*
Rooze, *Rose*
Ropars, *Robert*
Ropartz, *Robert*
Röpcke, *Robert*
Röpe, *Robert*
Rope, *Roper*
Roper
Ropero
Ropert, *Robert*
Ropes, *Roper*
Rophe, *Rofé*
Röpke, *Robert*
Röpkes, *Robert*
Röpking, *Robert*
Ropkins, *Robert*
Ropp, *Robert*
Rops, *Robert*
Roque, *Roach, Roch*
Roques, *Roach*
Roquet, *Roach*
Roquette, *Roach*
Rorie, *Rory*
Rörig, *Rohr*
Röring, *Rohr*
Rorison, *Rory*
Rorke, *Rourke*
Rory
Ros, *Rose, Rouse*
Rosa, *Rose*
Rosa
Rosado
Rosák, *Rosa*
Rosal
Rosales, *Rosal*
Rosamond, *Roseman*
Rosander, *Rose*
Rosário
Rosas, *Rose, Roses*
Rosberg, *Rose*
Röschen, *Rush*
Röschmann, *Rush*
Roscoe
Rosé, *Rosado*
Rose
Rosefield, *Rose*
Rösel, *Rose*
Rosell, *Rose, Russell*
Roselli, *Rose*
Rosellini, *Rose*
Roselló
Roseman
Rosemann, *Roseman*
Rosén, *Rose*
Rosenbarg, *Rose*
Rosenbaum, *Rose*
Rosenberg, *Rose*
Rosenberger, *Rose*
Rosenblad, *Rose*
Rosenbladh, *Rose*
Rosenblat, *Rose*
Rosenblath, *Rose*
Rosenblatt, *Rose*
Rosenbloom, *Rose*
Rosenblum, *Rose*
Rosenboim, *Rose*
Rosenbojm, *Rose*
Rosenbusch, *Rose*
Rosenbush, *Rose*
Rosencrantz, *Rose*
Rosencranz, *Rose*
Rosencwaig, *Rose*
Rosendahl, *Rose*
Rosendorf, *Rose*
Rosenfarb, *Rose*
Rosenfeld, *Rose*
Rosenfelder, *Rose*
Rosenfield, *Rose*
Rosenfrucht, *Rose*
Rosengart, *Rose*
Rosengarten, *Rose*
Rosengren, *Rose*
Rosenhaupt, *Rose*
Rosenhaus, *Rose*
Rosenkranc, *Rose*
Rosenkrance, *Rose*
Rosenkrantz, *Rose*
Rosenkranz, *Rose*
Rosenman, *Roseman*
Rosenmann, *Roseman*
Rosenqvist, *Rose*
Rosensaft, *Rose*
Rosenschein, *Rose*
Rosenshine, *Rose*
Rosenshtein, *Rose*
Rosenshtock, *Rose*
Rosenshtok, *Rose*
Rosenshtrom, *Rose*
Rosenstein, *Rose*
Rosenstengel, *Rose*
Rosenstiel, *Rose*
Rosenstock, *Rose*
Rosenstok, *Rose*
Rosental, *Rose*
Rosenthal, *Rose*
Rosenthol, *Rose*
Rosentholer, *Rose*
Rosentol, *Rose*
Rosentoler, *Rose*
Rosenvasser, *Rose*
Rosenwald, *Rose*
Rosenwasser, *Rose*
Rosenzveig, *Rose*
Rosenzweig, *Rose*
Roses
Roset, *Rose*
Rosetti, *Rose*
Rosettini, *Rose*
Rosevear, *Roseveare*
Roseveare
Roseveer, *Roseveare*
Roseveor, *Roseveare*
Rosewall
Rosewell, *Rosewall*
Rösgen, *Rose*
Rosi, *Rose*
Rosiak, *Rosa*
Rosić, *Rusakov*
Rosicki, *Rosa*
Rosiello, *Rose*
Rosignuoli, *Rossignol*
Rosík, *Rosa*
Rosin, *Rose*
Rosina, *Rose*
Rosini, *Rose*
Rosiński, *Rosa*
Rosita, *Rose*
Roskelly, *Roskilly*
Roskilly
Rösle, *Rose*
Röslen, *Rose*
Rosman, *Ross*
Rosner, *Ross*
Rosoman, *Roseman*
Roson, *Rose*
Rosone, *Rose*
Rosoni, *Rose*
Rospars, *Robert*
Rosqvist, *Rose*
Ross
Rossall
Rossander, *Rose*
Rosseels, *Russell*
Rossell, *Russell*
Rosselli, *Russell*
Rossellini, *Russell*
Rosselló, *Roselló*
Rosser, *Roger*
Rosset, *Rouse*
Rossett, *Rouse*
Rossetti, *Rouse*
Rossettini, *Rouse*
Rossetto, *Rouse*
Rossey, *Rouse*
Rossi, *Rouse*
Rossiello, *Russell*
Rossigneux, *Rossignol*
Rossignol
Rossignon, *Rossignol*
Rossillo, *Russell*
Rossin, *Rouse*
Rossington
Rossini, *Rouse*
Rossino, *Rouse*
Rossiter, *Rochester*
Rossitti, *Rouse*
Rossitto, *Rouse*
Rossler, *Ross*
Rossman, *Ross*
Rossner, *Ross*
Rosso, *Rouse*
Rosson, *Rouse*
Rossone, *Rouse*
Rossoni, *Rouse*
Rossotti, *Rouse*
Rossotto, *Rouse*

Rosswald, *Ross*
Rostaing
Rostand, *Rostaing*
Rostang, *Rostaing*
Rostern, *Rawsthorne*
Rosterne, *Rawsthorne*
Rosthorne, *Rawsthorne*
Rostron, *Rawsthorne*
Rostropovich
Roszak, *Rosa*
Roszczyk, *Rosa*
Roszkowski, *Rosa*
Rot, *Roth*
Rotapel, *Roth*
Rotband, *Roth*
Rotbard, *Roth*
Rotbart, *Roth*
Rotbarth, *Roth*
Rotbaum, *Roth*
Rotblat, *Roth*
Rotblit, *Roth*
Rotblum, *Roth*
Rotchell, *Roach*
Rötchen, *Roth*
Rotellini, *Parrott*
Rotenberg, *Rothenberg*
Roter, *Roth*
Roterband, *Roth*
Roterman, *Roth*
Rotermund, *Roth*
Rotfarb, *Roth*
Rotfeld, *Roth*
Rotgé, *Roger*
Rotgerber
Rotgold, *Roth*
Rotgolz, *Roth*
Roth
Rothberg, *Rothenberg*
Rothchild, *Rothschild*
Rothe, *Roth*
Röthel, *Roth*
Rothenberg
Rothenberger, *Rothenberg*
Rother, *Roth*
Rotheram, *Rotherham*
Rotherforth, *Rutherford*
Rotherham
Rothert, *Roth*
Rothfeld, *Roth*
Rothkopf, *Roth*
Röthlein, *Roth*
Rothman, *Roth*
Rothmann, *Roth*
Rothmann
Rothmensch, *Roth*
Rotholz, *Roth*
Rothschild
Rothstein, *Roth*
Rothwell
Rotier, *Rutter*
Rotkirch, *Roth*
Rotkopf, *Roth*
Rotlauf, *Rolf*
Rotleder, *Roth*
Rotman, *Roth*
Rotmann, *Roth*
Rotmench, *Roth*
Rotmensh, *Roth*
Rotmensz, *Roth*
Rotrubin, *Roth*
Rotschild, *Rothschild*
Rotshtein, *Roth*
Rotstein, *Roth*
Rotsztein, *Roth*
Rotsztejn, *Roth*
Röttcher, *Roger*
Rottenberg, *Rothenberg*
Rotter, *Rutter*
Rotterman, *Roth*
Rottfeld, *Roth*
Röttger, *Roger*
Röttgers, *Roger*
Rotti, *Parrott*
Rottier, *Rutter*
Rottmann, *Roth*
Rotwald, *Roth*
Rouane, *Ruane*
Roubeix, *Robert*
Roubert, *Robert*
Roubíček
Roubin, *Robin*
Roubineau, *Robin*
Roubinet, *Robin*
Roubottom, *Rowbottom*
Rouby, *Robin*
Rouček
Rouché, *Roach*
Rouchès, *Roach*
Rouchet, *Roach*
Rouchon, *Roach*
Rouchousse, *Roach*
Rouchoux, *Roach*
Roudeix, *Rode*
Roudet, *Rode*
Roudié, *Rode*
Roudier, *Rode*
Roué, *Ray*
Rouf, *Rolf*
Rouff, *Rolf*
Rougé, *Roger*
Rouge, *Rudge*
Rougeau, *Rudge*
Rougeaux, *Rudge*
Rougeot, *Rudge*
Rouger, *Roger*
Rouget, *Rudge*
Rougetet, *Rudge*
Rough, *Rauch*
Roughley, *Rowley*
Rougier, *Roger*
Roujon, *Rudge*
Roujou, *Rudge*
Roul, *Rollo*
Rouland, *Rowland*
Roulet, *Rollo*
Roulland, *Rowland*
Roullet, *Rollo*
Roully, *Rollo*
Roulot, *Rollo*
Roulson, *Rollo*
Roulston, *Rolston*
Rouly, *Rollo*
Roume, *Roman*
Roumier, *Romero*
Roumieu, *Romero*
Roumieux, *Romero*
Rounce, *Round*
Round
Roundell, *Round*
Rounds, *Round*
Roundtree, *Rowntree*
Rountree, *Rowntree*
Roura, *Rouvre*
Roure, *Rouvre*
Rourke
Rous, *Rouse*
Rouse
Rousel, *Russell*
Rouselet, *Russell*
Rousell, *Russell*
Rousic, *Rouse*
Rousseau, *Russell*
Rousseaux, *Russell*
Roussel, *Russell*
Rousselin, *Russell*
Roussell, *Russell*
Rousselot, *Russell*
Rousset, *Rouse*
Roussignol, *Rossignol*
Roussin, *Rouse*
Roussineau, *Rouse*
Roussot, *Rouse*
Roussy, *Rouse*
Roustaing, *Rostaing*
Roustan, *Rostaing*
Roustang, *Rostaing*
Rout
Routenberg, *Rothenberg*
Routledge
Rouveix, *Rouvre*
Rouvet, *Rouvre*
Rouveyre, *Rouvre*
Rouvière, *Rouvre*
Rouvrais, *Rouvre*
Rouvray, *Rouvre*
Rouvre
Rouvreau, *Rouvre*
Rouvroy, *Rouvre*
Rouw, *Ruth*
Roux, *Rouse*
Rouxel, *Russell*
Rouy, *Rudge*
Rouyer, *Rode*
Rouz, *Rouse*
Rouzé, *Rosado*
Rouzet, *Rose*
Rouzic, *Rouse*
Rove, *Rolf*
Röver, *Räuber*
Rover
Rovere, *Rouvre*
Roveri, *Rouvre*
Rovira, *Rouvre*
Row, *Rowe*
Rowan, *Ruane*
Rowat, *Rowett*
Rowatt, *Rowett*
Rowberry, *Rubbra*
Rowbotham, *Rowbottom*
Rowbottam, *Rowbottom*
Rowbottom
Rowbry, *Rubbra*
Rowbury, *Rubbra*
Rowden
Rowe
Rowell
Rowen, *Rowntree*
Röwer, *Räuber*
Rowes, *Rowe*
Rowet, *Rowett*
Rowett
Rowland
Rowlands, *Rowland*
Rowlandson, *Rowland*
Rowlatt, *Rollo*
Rowlerson, *Rollo*
Rowles, *Rollo*
Rowleston, *Rolston*
Rowlestone, *Rolston*
Rowlett, *Rollo*
Rowley
Rowling, *Rollo*
Rowlings, *Rollo*
Rowlingson, *Rollo*
Rowlinson, *Rollo*
Rowlison, *Rollo*
Rowlson, *Rollo*
Rowney
Rownson, *Rowland*
Rowntree
Rowse, *Rouse*
Rowsell, *Russell*
Rowson, *Rowe*
Rowston, *Rolston*
Rowstone, *Rolston*
Roxburgh
Roy
Royal, *Royle*
Royall, *Royle*
Royan, *Ruane*
Royce, *Rose*
Roycraft, *Rycroft*
Roycroft, *Rycroft*
Royds, *Rhodes*
Royer, *Rode*
Royle
Royo, *Rudge*
Royse, *Rose*
Royston
Royter, *Roth*
Royzman, *Roseman*
Roz, *Roch, Rose*
Różalski, *Rose*
Różański, *Rose*
Rozas
Rozdestvenski
Rozé, *Rosado*
Roze, *Rose*
Rozec, *Rose*
Rozestvenski, *Rozdestvenski*
Rozet, *Rose*
Rózsa, *Rose*
Rozwadowski
Różycki, *Rose*
Rua, *Rouvre*
Ruane
Ruano
Rubanenko, *Reuben*
Rubartelli, *Robert*
Rubbens, *Reuben, Robert*
Rubbert, *Robert*
Rubberts, *Robert*
Rubbra
Rubel, *Reuben, Rublyov*
Rübel
Ruben, *Reuben*
Rubenchik, *Reuben*
Rubenczik, *Reuben*
Rubenczyk, *Reuben*
Rubenfeld, *Reuben*
Rubenov, *Reuben*
Rubenovic, *Reuben*
Rubens, *Reuben, Robert*
Ruberry, *Rubbra*
Rubert, *Robert*
Rubertelli, *Robert*
Ruberti, *Robert*
Rubertis, *Robert*
Ruberto, *Robert*
Rubery, *Rubbra*
Rubeš, *Reuben*
Rubia, *Rudge*
Rubik, *Reuben*
Rubin, *Reuben*
Rubinchik, *Reuben*
Rubinek, *Reuben*

Rubinfajn, *Reuben*
Rubinfeld, *Reuben*
Rubinivitz, *Reuben*
Rubinlicht, *Reuben*
Rubinov, *Reuben*
Rubinovici, *Reuben*
Rubinovisch, *Reuben*
Rubinovitsch, *Reuben*
Rubinow, *Reuben*
Rubinowich, *Reuben*
Rubinowicz, *Reuben*
Rubinowitch, *Reuben*
Rubinowitsch, *Reuben*
Rubinowitz, *Reuben*
Rubinsaft, *Reuben*
Rubinshtein, *Reuben*
Rubinsky, *Reuben*
Rubinsohn, *Reuben*
Rubinstein, *Reuben*
Rubinsztein, *Reuben*
Rubio, *Rudge*
Rübke, *Robert*
Rublyov
Rubnov, *Reuben*
Rubottom, *Rowbottom*
Ruciński, *Rutecki*
Ruck, *Rook*
Rucker, *Rock*
Rückert, *Roger*
Rückhard, *Roger*
Rucklidge, *Routledge*
Ruda, *Rudakov*
Rudakov
Rudd
Rudden, *Roden*
Ruddick, *Ruddock*
Ruddiforth, *Rutherford*
Ruddock
Ruddon, *Roden*
Ruddy, *Ready, Rudd*
Rudeforth, *Rutherford*
Rudeiko, *Rudakov*
Rüdel, *Rode*
Rudenko, *Rudakov*
Rudge
Rudican, *Ready*
Rüdiger, *Roger*
Rudihan, *Ready*
Rüdinger, *Roger*
Rudkin, *Rudd*
Rudledge, *Routledge*
Rudling, *Rudd*
Rudloff, *Rolf*
Rudman, *Rudd*
Rudmann, *Rothmann*
Rudniak, *Rudakov*
Rudnicki, *Rudakov*
Rudolf, *Rolf*
Rudolfer, *Rolf*
Rudy, *Rudakov*
Rudyonok, *Rudakov*
Rudzevich, *Rudakov*
Rudziński, *Rudakov*
Rudzki, *Rudakov*
Rudzko, *Rudakov*
Rue
Rueda, *Rode*
Ruf, *Rolf*
Ruff, *Rolf*
Ruffell, *Rolf*
Ruffer, *Rover*
Ruffi, *Ruffo*
Ruffin
Ruffinelli, *Ruffin*
Ruffini, *Ruffin*
Ruffino, *Ruffin*
Ruffinoni, *Ruffin*
Ruffle, *Rolf*
Ruffles, *Rolf*
Rüffli, *Rolf*
Ruffo
Ruffoli, *Ruffo*
Ruffolo, *Ruffo*
Rufin, *Ruffin*
Rufini, *Ruffin*
Rufino, *Ruffin*
Rufo, *Ruffo*
Rufolo, *Ruffo*
Ruge, *Rauch*
Rüger, *Roger*
Ruggeri, *Roger*
Ruggero, *Roger*
Ruggier, *Roger*
Ruggieri, *Roger*
Ruggiero, *Roger*
Ruggiu, *Rouse*
Ruggles, *Rudge*
Ruggs, *Ridge*
Rugieri, *Roger*
Rugiero, *Roger*
Rugman, *Ridge*
Ruhe, *Rauch*
Rühl, *Rollo*
Ruhland, *Rowland*
Rühle, *Rollo*
Rühlemann, *Rollo*
Rühlicke, *Rollo*
Ruhmann, *Roman*
Ruisdael, *Ruysdael*
Ruiu, *Rouse*
Ruivo, *Rudge*
Ruiz, *Roderick*
Ruju, *Rouse*
Ruland, *Rowland*
Rule
Rulf, *Rolf*
Rülke, *Rollo*
Rull, *Rolo*
Rullmann, *Rollo*
Rumball, *Rumbold*
Rumbell, *Rumbold*
Rumbellow, *Rumbelow*
Rumbelow
Rumble, *Rumbold*
Rumbles, *Rumbold*
Rumbol, *Rumbold*
Rumbold
Rumboll, *Rumbold*
Rumbolt, *Rumbold*
Rummel, *Rommel*
Rümmele, *Rommel*
Rummer, *Romero*
Rümmler, *Rommel*
Rumney, *Romney*
Rump
Rumpel, *Rumbold*
Rumpelt, *Rumbold*
Rümpler, *Rumbold*
Rumpler, *Rumbold*
Rumpold, *Rumbold*
Rumpole, *Rumbold*
Rumsay, *Rumsey*
Rumsey
Runacres
Runagle, *Runacres*
Runchman, *Roncin*
Runcie, *Roncin*
Runcieman, *Roncin*
Runciman, *Roncin*
Rundall, *Rundle*
Rundell, *Rundle*
Rundle
Runge
Runicles, *Runacres*
Runnacles, *Runacres*
Runnagall, *Runacres*
Ruocco, *Roch*
Ruoff, *Rolf*
Ruotsalainen
Rüpel, *Robert*
Rupert, *Robert*
Ruperti, *Robert*
Ruperto, *Robert*
Rüpke, *Robert*
Rupp, *Robert*
Ruppel, *Robert*
Rüppele, *Robert*
Rüppeli, *Robert*
Rüppelin, *Robert*
Ruppert, *Robert*
Ruppertz, *Robert*
Rüpprecht, *Robert*
Rupprecht, *Robert*
Ruprecht, *Robert*
Ruprechter, *Robert*
Ruprich, *Robert*
Rus, *Rusakov*
Rusak, *Rusakov*
Rusakov
Rusek, *Rusakov*
Rush
Rusher, *Rush*
Rushfirth, *Rushforth*
Rushforth
Rushmer
Rushmere, *Rushmer*
Rushton
Rushworth
Rusiecki, *Rusakov*
Rusin, *Rusakov*
Rusinkiewicz, *Rusakov*
Rusiñol, *Rossignol*
Rusinov, *Rusakov*
Rusk
Ruskin
Rusman, *Rusakov*
Russ, *Rouse*
Russak, *Rusakov*
Russel, *Russell*
Russell
Russello, *Russell*
Russesco, *Rusakov*
Russetti, *Rouse*
Russi, *Rouse*
Russill, *Russell*
Russino, *Rouse*
Russinyol, *Rossignol*
Russo, *Rouse*
Russotti, *Rouse*
Russotto, *Rouse*
Rust
Ruston
Rusu, *Rouse*
Ruszczak, *Rusakov*
Ruszczyk, *Rusakov*
Ruszczyński, *Rusakov*
Ruszkiewicz, *Rusakov*
Ruszkowski, *Rusakov*
Ruta, *Rutecki*
Rutberg, *Rothenberg*
Rutecki
Rutenberg, *Rothenberg*
Rüters, *Reuter*
Rutgers, *Roger*
Ruth
Rutherfoord, *Rutherford*
Rutherford
Rutherfurd, *Rutherford*
Ruthven
Rutkiewicz, *Rutkowski*
Rutkowski
Rutland
Rutledge, *Routledge*
Rutt, *Root*
Rutten, *Rode*
Ruttenberg, *Rothenberg*
Rutter
Rutterford, *Rutherford*
Ruttgers, *Roger*
Ruusa, *Rose*
Ruvel, *Reuben*
Ruys, *Rush*
Ruysdael
Růžek, *Rose*
Ružić, *Rose*
Růžička, *Rose*
Ryal, *Royle*
Ryall, *Royle*
Ryan
Ryb, *Ryba*
Ryba
Rybák, *Rybak*
Rybak
Rybakiewicz, *Rybak*
Rybakin, *Rybak*
Rybakov, *Rybak*
Rybalchenko, *Rybak*
Rybalka, *Rybak*
Rybalkin, *Rybak*
Rybalko, *Rybak*
Rybalow, *Rybak*
Rybář, *Rybak*
Rybarczyk, *Rybak*
Rybarkiewicz, *Rybak*
Rybarz, *Rybak*
Rybczyński, *Ryba*
Rybiałek, *Rybak*
Rybicki, *Ryba*
Rybín, *Ryba*
Rybin, *Ryba*
Rybiński, *Ryba*
Rybka, *Ryba*
Rybkin, *Ryba*
Rybniček
Rybowicz, *Ryba*
Rybushkin, *Ryba*
Rychtář, *Richter*
Rychtářík, *Richter*
Rychter, *Richter*
Rychtera, *Richter*
Rycraft, *Rycroft*
Rycroft
Ryde, *Read*
Ryder, *Rider*
Ryding, *Reading*
Rydings, *Reading*
Rye
Ryhill, *Royle*
Ryhorovich, *Gregory*
Rykena, *Rich*
Rykert, *Richard*
Rykowicz, *Rikin*
Rylance, *Ryland*
Ryland
Rylands, *Ryland*
Ryle, *Royle*

Ryley, *Riley*
Ryman, *Rye*
Rymer, *Riemer*
Rynn, *Wren*
Rynne, *Wren*
Rys, *Rysev*
Ryšánek, *Ryzhakov*
Ryšavý, *Ryzhakov*
Rysev
Rysin, *Rysev*
Rytíř, *Rider*
Rytter, *Rider*
Ryvkin, *Rifkin*
Ryvkind, *Rifkin*
Ryzhago, *Ryzhakov*
Ryzhakov
Ryzhikov, *Ryzhakov*
Ryzhkov, *Ryzhakov*
Ryzhochin, *Ryzhakov*
Ryzhov, *Ryzhakov*
Ržanek, *Rye*
Rzehor, *Gregory*
Rzehorz, *Gregory*
Rzepa, *Repin*
Rzepczyński, *Repin*
Rzepecki, *Repin*
Rzepka, *Repin*
Rzepkowski, *Repin*
Rzetelski
Rzeźnicki, *Rzeźnik*
Rzeźnik
Rzymski, *Roman*

S

Sá, *Sale*
Saari, *Saarinen*
Saarinen
Saavedra
Sabadie, *Abbey*
Sabadin, *Sabbato*
Sabadini, *Sabbato*
Saban, *Sabin*
Sabastida, *Bastide*
Sàbat, *Sabbato*
Sabat, *Sabbato*
Sabaté, *Savatier*
Sabatelli, *Sabbato*
Sabatello, *Sabbato*
Sabater, *Savatier*
Sabatés, *Savatier*
Sabath, *Sabbato*
Sabathé, *Savatier*
Sabathier, *Savatier*
Sabatié, *Savatier*
Sabatiello, *Sabbato*
Sabatier, *Savatier*
Sabatini, *Sabbato*
Sabatino, *Sabbato*
Sabato, *Sabbato*
Sabatov, *Sabbato*
Sabatovski, *Sabbato*
Sabatowski, *Sabbato*
Sabattier, *Savatier*
Sabatucci, *Sabbato*
Sabbadin, *Sabbato*
Sabbadini, *Sabbato*
Sabbatelli, *Sabbato*
Sabbatiello, *Sabbato*
Sabbatier, *Savatier*
Sabbatini, *Sabbato*
Sabbatino, *Sabbato*
Sabbato

Sabbatucci, *Sabbato*
Sabben, *Sabin*
Sabberton
Sabby, *Sabin*
Sabelli, *Savelyev*
Saben, *Sabin*
Sabháiste, *Savage*
Sabhaois, *Savage*
Sabi, *Sabin*
Sabin
Sabina, *Sabin*
Sabine, *Sabin*
Sabini, *Sabin*
Sabino, *Sabin*
Sablin, *Sabin*
Sabline, *Sabin*
Sabourand, *Savoureux*
Saboureau, *Savoureux*
Sabouret, *Savoureux*
Saboureux, *Savoureux*
Sabourin, *Savoureux*
Sabrié, *Sabrier*
Sabrier
Saburov
Saby, *Sabin*
Sacaze, *Casa*
Saccheri, *Sack*
Sacchet, *Sack*
Sacchetti, *Sack*
Sacchetto, *Sack*
Sacchi, *Sack*
Sacchieri, *Sack*
Sacchini, *Sack*
Sacco, *Sack*
Saccon, *Sack*
Saccone, *Sack*
Sacconi, *Sack*
Saccucci, *Sack*
Sacerdote
Sach, *Sack*
Šach, *Salomon*
Sachar, *Sacher*
Sachariasch, *Zachary*
Sacharov, *Sacher*
Sacharow, *Sacher*
Sacher
Sacherl, *Zachary*
Sachers, *Sacher*
Sachet, *Sack*
Sachot, *Sack*
Sachs
Sachsé, *Sachs*
Sachse, *Sachs*
Sack
Sacker, *Sack*
Sackett, *Sack*
Sackheim, *Sack*
Sacks, *Sachs*
Sackur, *Sack*
Sackville
Sackwild, *Sackville*
Saclosa, *Close*
Sacquépée, *Saxby*
Sacramento
Sacreste, *Sexton*
Sacristán, *Sexton*
Sacriste, *Sexton*
Sadd
Saddington
Saddler, *Sadler*
Sade
Sadelmacher, *Sadler*
Sadler
Sadlier, *Sadler*

Sadournin, *Saturnin*
Sadourny, *Saturnin*
Sadovnik, *Sadowski*
Sadovnikov, *Sadowski*
Sadovshchikov, *Sadowski*
Sadovski, *Sadowski*
Sadovsky, *Sadowski*
Sadownik, *Sadowski*
Sadowski
Sadowsky, *Sadowski*
Saegaert, *Sawyer*
Saeger, *Sawyer*
Saelemaeker, *Sadler*
Saelman, *Sadler*
Sáenz, *Sancho*
Saer, *Sayer*
Sáez, *Sancho*
Šafář, *Schaffer*
Šafařík, *Schaffer*
Saffer
Saffran, *Safran*
Saffré, *Savory*
Saffre, *Saffer*
Saffroy, *Savory*
Safont, *Font*
Sáfrán, *Safran*
Safran
Šafránek, *Safran*
Safranovitch, *Safran*
Sáfrány, *Safran*
Safré, *Savory*
Safre, *Saffer*
Sagal, *Segal*
Sagalov, *Segal*
Sagalovich, *Segal*
Sagan
Saganowski, *Sagan*
Sagański, *Sagan*
Sagar, *Seagar*
Sagarra, *Segarra*
Sagarriga, *Jarry*
Sage
Sägebrecht, *Siebert*
Sagel, *Sage*
Sageon, *Sage*
Sagcot, *Sage*
Säger, *Sawyer*
Sager, *Sawyer*
Sager, *Seagar*
Sägerbarth, *Siebert*
Saget, *Sage*
Saggers, *Seagar*
Saggio, *Sage*
Sagne
Sagnes, *Sagne*
Sagnier, *Sagne*
Sagrestain, *Sexton*
Sagristà, *Sexton*
Sahlberg, *Sale*
Sahlén, *Sale*
Sahlin, *Sale*
Sahlmann, *Salmon*
Sahlström, *Sale*
Sahuc, *Sureau*
Sahucquet, *Sureau*
Sahuquet, *Sureau*
Sahut, *Sureau*
Saiger, *Seagar*
Saigne, *Sagne*
Saignier, *Sagne*
Sailer, *Saylor*
Saillant, *Saylor*
Saillier, *Saylor*
Sainclair, *Sinclair*

Sainer, *Senior*
Sains, *Saint*
Sainsberry, *Sainsbury*
Sainsbury
Sainson, *Samson*
Saint
Saint-Clair, *Sinclair*
Saint-Clare, *Sinclair*
Sainteau, *Saint*
Sainte-Beuve
Sainte-Marie, *Santa María*
Saint-Exupéry
Saint-Georges
Saint-Hilaire, *Sandler*
Sainthill
Saint-Hillaire, *Sandler*
Saintignon, *Saint*
Saintin, *Saint*
Saint-Jean
Saint-Just
Saint-Lagar, *Salinger*
Saint-Laurent
Saint-Laux, *Sandler*
Saint-Léger, *Salinger*
Saint-Lo, *Sandler*
Saint-Martin, *San Martín*
Saint-Maur, *Seymour*
Saint-Mieux, *San Miguel*
Saint-Mihiel, *San Miguel*
Sainton, *Saint*
Saint-Paul, *Semple*
Saint-Pé, *Samper*
Saint-Père, *Samper*
Saint-Pierre, *Samper*
Saint-Pol, *Semple*
Saint-Romans, *San Román*
Saint-Saëns
Saintsbury, *Sainsbury*
Saint-Supéry, *Saint-Exupéry*
Sáinz, *Sancho*
Saisset, *Sachs*
Saisson, *Sachs*
Saive, *Sage*
Saivet, *Sage*
Sáiz, *Sancho*
Saker, *Sack*
Sakharov, *Zachary, Zuccheri*
Sakhnov, *Sashin*
Saks, *Sachs*
Saksi, *Sachs*
Sala, *Sale*
Saladdino, *Saladin*
Saladin
Saladini, *Saladin*
Saladino, *Saladin*
Salado, *Salé*
Salaman, *Salomon*
Salamanca
Salamans, *Salomon*
Salamo, *Salomon*
Salamon, *Salomon*
Salamone, *Salomon*
Salamoni, *Salomon*
Salamonovits, *Salomon*
Salamonovitz, *Salomon*
Šalamoun, *Salomon*
Salamovitz, *Salomon*
Salandini, *Saladin*
Salardino, *Saladin*
Salas, *Sale*
Salat, *Salé*
Salatino, *Saladin*
Salaün, *Salomon*
Salazar

Salc, *Salt*
Salce, *Sauce*
Salcedo, *Sauce*
Salch, *Sale*
Salcher, *Sale*
Salchner, *Sale*
Salci, *Sauce*
Šalda, *Salomon*
Salé
Sale
Šálek, *Salomon*
Saleman, *Salomon*
Salén, *Sale*
Sales
Salesbury, *Salisbury*
Salet, *Sale*
Saletti, *Sauce*
Salgado, *Salé*
Salge, *Sealey*
Salgueiro, *Salguero*
Salguero
Salice, *Sauce*
Saliceti, *Sauce*
Salicetti, *Sauce*
Salici, *Sauce*
Salicini, *Sauce*
Salido
Salieri, *Salter*
Salinas
Salinero, *Salinas*
Salingar, *Salinger*
Salinger
Salini, *Sauce*
Salinier, *Salter*
Salisberry, *Salisbury*
Salisbury
Salivonok, *Selwyn*
Salizzoli, *Sauce*
Salked
Säll, *Sealey*
Sall, *Sale*
Sallagar, *Salinger*
Sallaway, *Selway*
Sallé, *Salé*
Salle, *Sale*
Salles, *Sale*
Sallet, *Sale*
Sallez, *Sale*
Sallman, *Salmon*
Salloway, *Selway*
Salman, *Salmon*
Salmanov, *Salmon*
Salmansohn, *Salmon*
Salmanson, *Salmon*
Salmen, *Salmon*
Salmenson, *Salmon*
Salmi, *Salminen*
Salminen
Salmon
Salmond, *Salmon*
Salmone, *Salmon*
Salmoni, *Salmon*
Salmonov, *Salmon*
Salmons, *Salmon*
Salmonsson, *Salmon*
Salo, *Salonen*
Salomon
Salomonczyk, *Salomon*
Salomone, *Salomon*
Salomoni, *Salomon*
Salomonivitch, *Salomon*
Salomonof, *Salomon*
Salomonovitz, *Salomon*
Salomonowicz, *Salomon*
Salomonowitz, *Salomon*
Salomons, *Salomon*
Salomonsen, *Salomon*
Salomonson, *Salomon*
Salomonsson, *Salomon*
Salomowicz, *Salomon*
Salon, *Sale*
Salonen
Salot, *Sale*
Salou, *Sale*
Salsbury, *Salisbury*
Salski, *Sale*
Sälström, *Sealey*
Salt
Salter
Salters, *Salthouse*
Salthouse
Saltilo, *Sault*
Saltman, *Salt*
Salts, *Salt*
Saltsman, *Salt*
Saltykov
Saltz, *Salt*
Saltzman, *Salt*
Saltzmann, *Salt*
Salusbury, *Salisbury*
Salvà, *Selwyn*
Salvado, *Sauvé*
Salvador
Salvadore, *Salvador*
Salvadori, *Salvador*
Salvage, *Savage*
Salvaggi, *Savage*
Salvagneschi, *Selwyn*
Salvagni, *Selwyn*
Salvagnini, *Selwyn*
Salvagno, *Selwyn*
Salvagnoni, *Selwyn*
Salvani, *Selwyn*
Salvanini, *Selwyn*
Salvano, *Selwyn*
Salvat, *Sauvé*
Salvator, *Salvador*
Salvatore, *Salvador*
Salvatorelli, *Salvador*
Salvatorello, *Salvador*
Salvatori, *Salvador*
Salvetti, *Salvi*
Salvi
Salvidge, *Savage*
Salvin, *Selwyn*
Salvinelli, *Salvi*
Salvinello, *Salvi*
Salvini, *Salvi*
Salvio, *Salvi*
Salvioli, *Salvi*
Salvione, *Salvi*
Salvioni, *Salvi*
Salvo, *Salvi*
Salvucci, *Salvi*
Salvy, *Salvi*
Salway, *Selway*
Salwey, *Selway*
Salz, *Salt*
Salzberg, *Salt*
Salzer, *Salter*
Salzhandler, *Salter*
Salzhauer, *Salter*
Salzman, *Salt*
Salzmann, *Salt*
Salzstein, *Salt*
Sam, *Samson*
Šámal
Samardžić, *Semrád*
Sambell, *Semple*
Samber, *Samper*
Sambeth, *Samet*
Sambrook
Samek, *Samuel*
Samel, *Samuel*
Samelionis, *Samuel*
Samelsohn, *Samuel*
Samet
Sameth, *Samet*
Sametnik, *Samet*
Samman, *Sand*
Samme, *Samson*
Sammet, *Samet*
Sammonds, *Salmon*
Sammons, *Salmon*
Samms, *Samuel*
Sammt, *Samet*
Samoilov, *Samuel*
Samokhin, *Samuel*
Samonin, *Samuel*
Samoshkin, *Samuel*
Sampaio
Sampaolesi, *Semple*
Sampaoli, *Semple*
Sampaolo, *Semple*
Sampedro, *Samper*
Samper
Sampford, *Sandford*
Sampier, *Samper*
Sampieri, *Samper*
Sampiero, *Samper*
Sampietro, *Samper*
Sample, *Semple*
Sampo, *Semple*
Sampson, *Samson*
Sams, *Samuel*
Samsin, *Samson*
Samsó, *Samson*
Samson
Samsonov, *Samson*
Samsonovich, *Samson*
Samsonovitz, *Samson*
Samu, *Samuel*
Sámuel, *Samuel*
Samuel
Samueli, *Samuel*
Samuelli, *Samuel*
Samuels, *Samuel*
Samuelsen, *Samuel*
Samuelsohn, *Samuel*
Samuelson, *Samuel*
Samuelsson, *Samuel*
Samugin, *Samuel*
Samuilyonok, *Samuel*
Samukhin, *Samuel*
Samul, *Samuel*
Samulak, *Samuel*
Samulczyk, *Samuel*
Samulski, *Samuel*
Samunin, *Samuel*
Samus, *Samuel*
Samusev, *Samuel*
Samusyev, *Samuel*
Samways
Samwell, *Samuel*
Samylin, *Samuel*
Samylov, *Samuel*
Samyshkin, *Samuel*
Sanahuja
Sanches, *Sancho*
Sánchez, *Sancho*
Sanchís, *Sancho*
Sanchis, *Sancho*
Sánchiz, *Sancho*
Sanchiz, *Sancho*
Sancho
Sanctuary, *Sentry*
Sand
Sandak
Sandars, *Sander*
Sandbach
Sandberg, *Sand*
Sande, *Sand*
Sandeford, *Sandford*
Sandek, *Sandak*
Sandel, *Sandell*
Sandelin, *Sandell*
Sandelius, *Sandell*
Sandell
Sandeman, *Sander*
Sandemann, *Sand*
Sandén, *Sand*
Sander
Sandercock, *Sander*
Sandering, *Sander*
Sanderman, *Sander*
Sanders, *Sander*
Sandersen, *Sander*
Sanderson, *Sander*
Sandes, *Sand*
Sandeson, *Sander*
Sandever, *Sandford*
Sandeyron, *Sander*
Sandford
Sandgarten, *Sand*
Sandgren, *Sand*
Sandh, *Sand*
Sandham
Sandhaus, *Sand*
Sandhouse, *Sand*
Sandić, *Sander*
Sandieson, *Sander*
Sandifer, *Sandford*
Sandiford, *Sandford*
Sandik, *Sandak*
Sandilands
Sandin, *Sand*
Sandison, *Sander*
Sandlar, *Sandler*
Sandler
Sandlerman, *Sandler*
Sandlund, *Sand*
Sandman, *Sand*
Sandmann, *Sand*
Sandmark, *Sand*
Sandner, *Sand*
Sándor, *Sander*
Sandoval
Sandović, *Sander*
Sandow, *Sander*
Sandquist, *Sand*
Sandre, *Sander*
Sandrelli, *Sander*
Sandri, *Sander*
Sandrin, *Sander*
Sandrini, *Sander*
Sandrolini, *Sander*
Sandron, *Sander*
Sandroni, *Sander*
Sandrucci, *Sander*
Sands, *Sand*
Sandstein, *Sand*
Sandström, *Sand*
Sandt, *Sand*
Sandy
Sandyfirth, *Sandford*
Sandys, *Sand*

Sanford, *Sandford*
Sanftleben, *Senf*
Sänger, *Sanger*
Sanger
Sangers, *Sanger*
Sangnier, *Sagne*
Sangster, *Sanger*
Sanichkin, *Sashin*
Sanin, *Sashin*
San José
San Juan, *Saint-Jean*
Sanjuan, *Saint-Jean*
Sankey
Sankin, *Samson, Sashin*
Sankov, *Sashin*
Sanky, *Sankey*
Sanmann, *Sand*
Sanmartí, *San Martín*
San Martín
San Miguel
Sanne, *Samson*
Sannié, *Sagne*
Sannier, *Sagne*
Sannmann, *Sand*
Sanov, *Sashin*
San Pedro, *Samper*
San Román
Sans, *Saint, Sancho*
Sansam, *Samson*
San Segundo
Sansom, *Samson*
Sansome, *Samson*
Sanson, *Samson*
Sansone, *Samson*
Sansonetti, *Samson*
Sansoni, *Samson*
Sansonnet, *Samson*
Sansot, *Samson*
Sansuc, *Saint*
Sansum, *Samson*
Sant, *Saint*
Santamaria, *Santa María*
Santa María
Santana
Santel, *Saint*
Santelli, *Saint*
Santello, *Saint*
Santesson, *Saint*
Santi, *Saint*
Santiago
Santilli, *Saint*
Santillo, *Saint*
Santin, *Saint*
Santini, *Saint*
Santino, *Saint*
Santler, *Sandler*
Santo, *Saint*
Santon, *Saint*
Santoni, *Saint*
Santorelli, *Santoro*
Santori, *Santoro*
Santoriello, *Santoro*
Santorini, *Santoro*
Santorio, *Santoro*
Santoro
Santorum, *Santoro*
Santos, *Saint*
Santot, *Saint*
Santry, *Sentry*
Santucci, *Saint*
Santulli, *Saint*
Santullo, *Saint*
Santuzzo, *Saint*
Sanvoisin
Sanyutin, *Sashin*
Sanz, *Sancho*
Sanzio, *Sancho*
Sanzogno, *Samson*
Sanzone, *Samson*
Sanzonio, *Samson*
Saoner, *Soper*
Saoul, *Soul*
Sapena, *Peña*
Saperstein, *Sapir*
Sapeyre, *Pierre*
Saphir, *Sapir*
Saphire, *Sapir*
Saphyr, *Sapir*
Sapieha, *Sapiński*
Sapin
Sapiński
Sapio, *Sage*
Sapir
Sapochnikov, *Sapozhnikov*
Sapojnikoff, *Sapozhnikov*
Sapojnikov, *Sapozhnikov*
Saponari, *Soper*
Saponaro, *Soper*
Saponaru, *Soper*
Saponieri, *Soper*
Saporta, *Port*
Saportas, *Port*
Saposhnik, *Sapozhnikov*
Saposhnikov, *Sapozhnikov*
Sapozhnikov
Sapoznik, *Sapozhnikov*
Sapoznikov, *Sapozhnikov*
Sapoznikow, *Sapozhnikov*
Sapsford
Sapy, *Sapin*
Saquet, *Sack*
Saquetoux, *Sack*
Saqueville, *Sackville*
Saraceni, *Sarson*
Saraceno, *Sarson*
Saracini, *Sarson*
Saracino, *Sarson*
Saragosi, *Zaragoza*
Saragossi, *Zaragoza*
Saragosti, *Zaragoza*
Saragusti, *Zaragoza*
Sarain, *Sarson*
Saraino, *Sarson*
Saraiva
Sarasin, *Sarson*
Sarassin, *Sarson*
Sarazin, *Sarson*
Sarbesco, *Serbinov*
Sarch, *Surridge*
Sarci, *Sarson*
Sarcinelli, *Sarson*
Sarcino, *Sarson*
Sardet, *Sardou*
Sardi, *Sardou*
Sardin, *Sardou*
Sardinha
Sardo, *Sardou*
Sardou
Sare, *Sayer*
Saretti, *Balthasar*
Sarfati, *Sarfatti*
Sarfatti
Sarfatty, *Sarfatti*
Sarfaty, *Sarfatti*
Sargant, *Sergeant*
Sarge, *Surridge*
Sargeant, *Sergeant*
Sargeantson, *Sergeant*
Sargeaunt, *Sergeant*
Sargent, *Sergeant*
Sargentson, *Sergeant*
Sargeson, *Sergeant*
Sarginson, *Sergeant*
Sargint, *Sergeant*
Sargison, *Sergeant*
Sargisson, *Sergeant*
Sargossi, *Zaragoza*
Sarieu, *Rieu*
Sarjant, *Sergeant*
Sarjantson, *Sergeant*
Sarjent, *Sergeant*
Sark, *Surridge*
Sarkin, *Sorin*
Sarkisian, *Sergio*
Sarkissian, *Sergio*
Sarmento, *Sarmiento*
Sarmiento
Saro, *Balthasar*
Sarotti, *Balthasar*
Sarpot, *Serpe*
Sarrà, *Serre*
Sarracino, *Sarson*
Sarrail
Sarraille, *Sarrail*
Sarraillié, *Sarrail*
Sarraillier, *Sarrail*
Sarraino, *Sarson*
Sarralh, *Sarrail*
Sarralhié, *Sarrail*
Sarralhier, *Sarrail*
Sarran, *Serre*
Sarrasin, *Sarson*
Sarrat, *Serrat*
Sarrazin, *Sarson*
Sarre, *Serre*
Sarreau, *Serre*
Sarret, *Serre*
Sarrey, *Serre*
Sarri, *Balthasar*
Sarrin, *Serre*
Sarron, *Serre*
Sarrot, *Serre*
Sarry, *Serre*
Sarson
Sarsons, *Sarson*
Sarthon, *Sartre*
Sarthou, *Sartre*
Sarthre, *Sartre*
Sarti, *Sartre*
Sartini, *Sartre*
Sarto, *Sartre*
Sarton, *Sartre*
Sartoni, *Sartre*
Sartor, *Sartre*
Sartore, *Sartre*
Sartorelli, *Sartre*
Sartoret, *Sartre*
Sartoretto, *Sartre*
Sartori, *Sartre*
Sartorio, *Sartre*
Sartorius, *Sartre*
Sartou, *Sartre*
Sartre
Sartucci, *Sartre*
Sarvis, *Servis*
Sas, *Sachs*
Sasák, *Sachs*
Šašek
Sashenkov, *Sashin*
Sashin
Sashkin, *Sashin*
Sashkov, *Sashin*
Sasiak, *Sachs*
Sasin, *Sachs*
Saska, *Sachs*
Sason
Sasportas, *Port*
Sass, *Sachs*
Sasse, *Sachs*
Sasso, *Sachs*
Sassoli, *Sachs*
Sasson, *Sachs, Sason*
Sassone, *Sachs*
Sassoni, *Sachs, Sason*
Sassonov, *Sason*
Sassoon, *Sason*
Sassoun, *Sason*
Sastre, *Sartre*
Satch, *Sack*
Satchel, *Sack*
Satchell, *Sack*
Satelman, *Sadler*
Satler, *Sadler*
Satre, *Sartre*
Sattel, *Sadler*
Satterfitt, *Satterthwaite*
Satterthwaite
Sättler, *Sadler*
Sattler, *Sadler*
Saturnin
Satz
Sauber
Säuberlich, *Sauber*
Sauberman, *Sauber*
Saubert, *Sauber*
Saüc, *Sureau*
Sauce
Saucet, *Sauce*
Saucey, *Sauce*
Sauer
Sauerbrunn, *Sauer*
Säuerle, *Sauer*
Sauerman, *Sauer*
Sauermann, *Sauer*
Sauerquell, *Sauer*
Sauerstrom, *Sauer*
Sauerteig, *Sauer*
Saul
Saule, *Saul*
Sauli, *Saul*
Saulino, *Saul*
Saull, *Saul*
Saulle, *Saul*
Saulli, *Saul*
Saullo, *Saul*
Saulnier, *Salter*
Sault
Saulter, *Sauter*
Saulxures, *Sauce*
Saunder, *Sander*
Saunders, *Sander*
Saunderson, *Sander*
Saunier, *Salter*
Saunt, *Saint*
Saur, *Soar*
Saura, *Soar*
Saurat, *Soar*
Saurel, *Soar*
Sauret, *Soar*
Saurin, *Soar*
Saury, *Soar*
Sausse, *Sauce*
Sausset, *Sauce*
Saussure, *Sauce*
Saut, *Sauter*
Sauter

Sautereau, *Sautour*
Sauterel, *Sautour*
Sauteron, *Sautour*
Sautour
Sautreau, *Sautour*
Sautt, *Sauter*
Sautter, *Sauter*
Sauvage, *Savage*
Sauvageau, *Savage*
Sauvageon, *Savage*
Sauvageot, *Savage*
Sauvain, *Selwyn*
Sauvan, *Selwyn*
Sauvanet, *Selwyn*
Sauvanon, *Selwyn*
Sauvat, *Sauvé*
Sauvé
Sauven, *Selwyn*
Sauvent, *Selwyn*
Sauvignon, *Selwyn*
Sauvy, *Salvi*
Saux, *Sachs*
Sauze, *Sauce*
Sauzet, *Sauce*
Savage
Savaric, *Savory*
Savarit, *Savory*
Savary, *Savory*
Savasteev, *Sebastian*
Savatier
Save, *Sage*
Saveall, *Saville*
Savege, *Savage*
Savell, *Saville*
Savelli, *Savelyev*
Savellini, *Savelyev*
Savelyev
Savery, *Savory*
Savetier, *Savatier*
Savi, *Sage*
Savić, *Sawicki*
Savićević, *Sawicki*
Savidge, *Savage*
Savignac
Savignat, *Savignac*
Savignon, *Sabin*
Savigny, *Savignac*
Savil, *Saville*
Savile, *Saville*
Savill, *Saville*
Saville
Savin, *Sabin, Selwyn*
Savina, *Sabin*
Savine, *Sabin*
Savineau, *Sabin*
Savini, *Sabin*
Savinio, *Sabin*
Savino, *Sabin*
Savinov, *Sabin*
Savinykh, *Sabin*
Savio, *Sage*
Savioli, *Sage*
Saviotti, *Sage*
Saviozzi, *Sage*
Savković, *Sawicki*
Savlichev, *Savelyev*
Savoia, *Savoie*
Savoiardi, *Savoie*
Savoie
Savois, *Savoie*
Savon, *Soper*
Savonichev, *Sebastian*
Savory
Savoskin, *Sebastian*
Savourat, *Savoureux*
Savouré, *Savoureux*
Savouret, *Savoureux*
Savoureux
Savourez, *Savoureux*
Savoury, *Savory*
Savov, *Sabin*
Savoyant, *Savoie*
Savoye, *Savoie*
Savoyen, *Savoie*
Savoyer, *Savoie*
Savreux, *Savoureux*
Savyolov, *Savelyev*
Sawczyk, *Sawicki*
Sawell, *Sewell*
Sawer, *Sawyer*
Sawicki
Sawicz, *Sawicki*
Sawle, *Saul*
Sawyer
Sawyers, *Sawyer*
Sax, *Sachs*
Saxby
Saxon
Saxton
Say
Sayce, *Sachs*
Saycell, *Cecil*
Saye, *Say*
Sayer
Sayers, *Sayer*
Saylor
Sayman, *Seaman*
Sayre, *Sayer*
Saywell, *Sewell*
Saz, *Sauce*
Scafe, *Scaife*
Scaife
Scala, *Eschelle*
Scale, *Scholes*
Scalera, *Eschelle*
Scales, *Scholes*
Scali, *Eschelle*
Scalia, *Eschelle*
Scallan, *Scully*
Scally, *Scully*
Scalon, *Scully*
Scammell
Scandlon, *Scannell*
Scanlan, *Scannell*
Scanlon, *Scannell*
Scannell
Scantlebury
Scarborough
Scard, *Sieghard*
Scarf, *Scarfe*
Scarfe
Scarff, *Scarfe*
Scarffe, *Scarfe*
Scargill
Scarisbrick
Scarlata, *Scarlett*
Scarlati, *Scarlett*
Scarlato, *Scarlett*
Scarlatti, *Scarlett*
Scarlet, *Scarlett*
Scarlett
Scarselli, *Scarso*
Scarsello, *Scarso*
Scarsi, *Scarso*
Scarsini, *Scarso*
Scarso
Scarth
Scatchard
Scattergood
Šćepanović, *Stephen*
Schaaf, *Shipman*
Schaap, *Shipman*
Schaapherder, *Sheppard*
Schächter, *Schechter*
Schachter, *Schechter*
Schacter, *Schechter*
Schade, *Shade*
Schadow
Schaechter, *Schechter*
Schaepman, *Shipman*
Schaf, *Shipman*
Schafer, *Schäfer*
Schäfer
Schäffer, *Schaffer*
Schäffer, *Schäfer*
Schaffer
Schafferlin, *Schaffer*
Schaffler, *Schäffler*
Schäffler
Schaffner, *Schaffer*
Schaid, *Scheidt*
Schaidt, *Scheidt*
Schaier, *Scheuer*
Schainman, *Schön*
Schakespear, *Shakespeare*
Schalch, *Schalk*
Schalck, *Gottschalk*
Schalk
Schalkl, *Schalk*
Schälkle, *Schalk*
Schandel, *Chandler*
Schäpe, *Stephen*
Schäper, *Schäfer*
Schaper, *Schäfer*
Schäpers, *Schäfer*
Schapiro, *Shapiro*
Schäpke, *Stephen*
Schaposchnik, *Shapochnikov*
Scharf, *Sharp*
Scharfe, *Sharp*
Scharff, *Sharp*
Scharfherz, *Sharp*
Scharfman, *Sharp*
Scharfstein, *Sharp*
Scharlach, *Scarlett*
Scharnach, *Chernyakov*
Scharnhorst
Scharnke, *Chernyakov*
Scharp, *Sharp*
Schärping, *Sharp*
Scharping, *Sharp*
Scharrer
Schatt, *Schatz*
Schatz
Schatzberg, *Schatz*
Schätzer, *Schatz*
Schatzer, *Schatz*
Schätzl, *Schatz*
Schatzl, *Schatz*
Schätzler, *Schatz*
Schatzler, *Schatz*
Schatzman, *Schatz*
Schatzmann, *Schatz*
Schau, *Schuh*
Schauber, *Schauer*
Schauchet, *Shoikhet*
Schauer
Schauert, *Schauer*
Schaumaker, *Schuh*
Schaumann, *Schuh*
Schechner, *Schechter*
Schechter
Schechterman, *Schechter*
Schechtman, *Schechter*
Scheck, *Schecker*
Schecke, *Schecker*
Scheckenmacher, *Schecker*
Schecker
Schecter, *Schechter*
Scheef, *Schief*
Scheefe, *Schief*
Scheel, *Schiller*
Scheele, *Schiller*
Scheepers, *Schäfer*
Scheerer, *Shearer*
Scheewe, *Schief*
Schefer, *Schäfer*
Scheff, *Schief*
Scheffel, *Schäffler*
Scheffer, *Schäfer*
Scheffers, *Schaffer*
Scheffl, *Schäffler*
Scheffler, *Schäffler*
Scheffner, *Schaffer*
Schefler, *Schäffler*
Schegg, *Schecker*
Scheggenmacher, *Schecker*
Scheider, *Scheidt*
Scheidler, *Scheidt*
Scheidt
Scheier, *Scheuer*
Schein, *Schön*
Scheinbach, *Schön*
Scheinbaum, *Schön*
Scheinberg, *Schön*
Scheinberger, *Schön*
Scheinblatt, *Schön*
Scheinbrun, *Schön*
Scheindel, *Scheinis*
Scheiner, *Schön*
Scheinerman, *Schön*
Scheines, *Scheinis*
Scheineson, *Scheinis*
Scheinfein, *Schön*
Scheinfeld, *Schön*
Scheinfuchs, *Schön*
Scheingarten, *Schön*
Scheingut, *Schön*
Scheinherz, *Schön*
Scheinholz, *Schön*
Scheinhorn, *Schön*
Scheinin, *Scheinis*
Scheinis
Scheinker, *Schenke*
Scheinkin, *Scheinis*
Scheinkman, *Schenke*
Scheinman, *Schön*
Scheinmann, *Schön*
Scheinrok, *Schön*
Scheintuch, *Schön*
Scheinwald, *Schön*
Scheit, *Scheidt*
Schelb, *Schiller*
Schelber, *Schiller*
Schelbert, *Schiller*
Schelch, *Schiller*
Schelcher, *Schiller*
Schell
Schellach, *Schilling*
Schellack, *Schilling*
Schelle, *Schell*
Scheller, *Schell*
Schellig, *Schell*
Schellinck, *Schilling*
Schellinckx, *Schilling*
Schelling, *Schilling*

Schellini, *Francis*
Schelzel, *Schultz*
Schemel, *Schemmel*
Schemmel
Schempf, *Schimpf*
Schempp, *Schimpf*
Schen, *Schön*
Schenbein, *Schön*
Schenberg, *Schön*
Schenck, *Schenke*
Schencke, *Schenke*
Schendel, *Scheinis*
Schenfeld, *Schön*
Schenk, *Schenke*
Schenke
Schenker, *Schenke*
Schenkman, *Schenke*
Schenman, *Schön*
Schenthal, *Schön*
Schepan, *Stephen*
Schepang, *Stephen*
Schepe, *Stephen*
Scheper, *Schäfer*
Schepers, *Schäfer*
Schepke, *Stephen*
Scheppan, *Stephen*
Scheppang, *Stephen*
Scheppe, *Stephen*
Scherer, *Shearer*
Schermer, *Scrimgeour*
Schernig, *Chernyakov*
Scherning, *Chernyakov*
Scherp, *Sharp*
Scherping, *Sharp*
Scherrer, *Shearer*
Scherschewski, *Sierota*
Schertz, *Scherzer*
Schertzer, *Scherzer*
Scherz, *Scherzer*
Scherzer
Schetti, *Francis*
Schettini, *Francis*
Scheuer
Scheuerman, *Scheuer*
Scheuermann, *Scheuer*
Scheumann, *Scheuer*
Scheunemann, *Scheuer*
Scheurer, *Scheuer*
Scheve, *Schief*
Scheyn, *Schön*
Schiaparelli
Schichman, *Schuh*
Schichmann, *Schuh*
Schick
Schicke, *Schick*
Schickel, *Schick*
Schickele, *Schick*
Schicker, *Schick*
Schickert, *Schick*
Schickl, *Schick*
Schief
Schiegel, *Schuh*
Schiel, *Schiller*
Schiele, *Schiller*
Schiele, *Schuh*
Schieli, *Schuh*
Schiementz, *Simon*
Schiemenz, *Simon*
Schiepers, *Schäfer*
Schiersch, *George*
Schiestel, *Schuster*
Schiesterl, *Schuster*
Schiestl, *Schuster*
Schieve, *Sheriff*
Schiff, *Shipman*
Schiffer, *Shipman*
Schiffman, *Shipman*
Schiffmann, *Shipman*
Schigl, *Schuh*
Schilbert, *Gilbert*
Schilcher, *Schiller*
Schild
Schilder, *Schild*
Schildhaus, *Schild*
Schildt, *Schild*
Schilgen, *Schild*
Schillack, *Schilling*
Schillak, *Schilling*
Schiller
Schilling
Schilloga, *Schilling*
Schillok, *Schilling*
Schilter, *Schild*
Schimank, *Simon*
Schimann, *Simon*
Schimaschke, *Simon*
Schimek, *Simon*
Schimkat, *Simon*
Schimke, *Simon*
Schimkus, *Simon*
Schimmang, *Simon*
Schimmel
Schimon, *Simon*
Schimonek, *Simon*
Schimoni, *Simon*
Schimonowitz, *Simon*
Schimpf
Schimpfer, *Schimpf*
Schimpfle, *Schimpf*
Schimpke, *Simon*
Schimpp, *Schimpf*
Schinasi, *Ashkenazi*
Schindel, *Shingler*
Schindelman, *Shingler*
Schindl, *Shingler*
Schindler, *Shingler*
Schinetti, *Francis*
Schinle, *Schön*
Schip, *Shipman*
Schipek, *Stephen*
Schipke, *Stephen*
Schippan, *Stephen*
Schippang, *Stephen*
Schipper, *Shipman*
Schippig, *Stephen*
Schippke, *Stephen*
Schirach, *George*
Schirak, *George*
Schirm, *Scrimgeour*
Schirmer, *Scrimgeour*
Schirok, *George*
Schivani, *Stephen*
Schkolnik, *Schuler*
Schlächter, *Slaughter*
Schlachter, *Slaughter*
Schlayer, *Schleier*
Schlecht
Schlechter, *Slaughter*
Schlee, *Schliemann*
Schleemann, *Schliemann*
Schlegel
Schlegl, *Schlegel*
Schlei, *Schliemann*
Schleich, *Schleicher*
Schleicher
Schleier
Schleif, *Schleifer*
Schleifer
Schleifman, *Schleifer*
Schlein
Schleirmacher, *Schleier*
Schlensog, *Schlessinger*
Schlensok, *Schlessinger*
Schlesinger, *Schlessinger*
Schlessinger
Schleusser, *Schliesser*
Schleuter, *Schliesser*
Schley, *Schliemann*
Schleyer, *Schleier*
Schlich, *Schlick*
Schlicht, *Schlecht*
Schlichte, *Schlecht*
Schlichter, *Schlecht*
Schlichting, *Schlecht*
Schlichtmann, *Schlecht*
Schlick
Schlicke, *Schlick*
Schlickmann, *Schlick*
Schlie, *Schliemann*
Schlieker, *Schleicher*
Schliemann
Schliep, *Schleifer*
Schlieper, *Schleifer*
Schliesser
Schlögl, *Schlegel*
Schlomkowich, *Salomon*
Schlomovich, *Salomon*
Schlomovitz, *Salomon*
Schlomowich, *Salomon*
Schloss
Schlossberg
Schlösser, *Schloss*
Schlosshauer, *Schloss*
Schlossmacher, *Schloss*
Schlossmann, *Schloss*
Schluck, *Schlick*
Schlucker, *Schlick*
Schlunk
Schlüter, *Schliesser*
Schmädicke, *Smith*
Schmahl, *Small*
Schmal, *Small*
Schmall, *Small*
Schmalt, *Schmalz*
Schmaltz, *Schmalz*
Schmalz
Schmalzer, *Schmalz*
Schmalzl, *Schmalz*
Schmälzle, *Schmalz*
Schmedding, *Smith*
Schmedeke, *Smith*
Schmeder, *Smith*
Schmedtje, *Smith*
Schmeling, *Small*
Schmelkes, *Samuel*
Schmelkin, *Samuel*
Schmetten, *Smetana*
Schmid, *Smith*
Schmidt, *Smith*
Schmied, *Smythe*
Schmiedel, *Smith*
Schmieder, *Smith*
Schmieder, *Smythe*
Schmiedle, *Smith*
Schmitt, *Smith*
Schmitz, *Smith*
Schmoldt, *Schmalz*
Schmolt, *Schmalz*
Schmolz, *Schmalz*
Schmolzl, *Schmalz*
Schmoueli, *Samuel*
Schmuck
Schmuel, *Samuel*
Schmueli, *Samuel*
Schmuely, *Samuel*
Schmugge, *Schmuck*
Schnabel
Schneck
Schnee, *Snow*
Schneeberg, *Snow*
Schneele, *Snow*
Schneersohn, *Schneir*
Schneerson, *Schneir*
Schneeweiss, *Snow*
Schnegel, *Schneck*
Schnegg, *Schneck*
Schnegge, *Schneck*
Schneibaum, *Snow*
Schneider
Schneiderman, *Schneider*
Schneidermann, *Schneider*
Schneiders, *Schneider*
Schneidman, *Schneider*
Schneir
Schneirovitz, *Schneir*
Schnell, *Snell*
Schneller, *Snell*
Schnelli, *Snow*
Schnellmann, *Snell*
Schnetz, *Schnitzer*
Schnetzer, *Schnitzer*
Schnetzler, *Schnitzer*
Schneubaum, *Snow*
Schneuer, *Schneir*
Schneur, *Schneir*
Schneursohn, *Schneir*
Schneurson, *Schneir*
Schnicke, *Schneck*
Schnieder, *Schneider*
Schnieders, *Schneider*
Schnier, *Schneider*
Schnierer, *Schnur*
Schnierl, *Schnur*
Schniers, *Schneider*
Schnigge, *Schneck*
Schnirer, *Schnur*
Schnirman, *Schnur*
Schnirr, *Schnur*
Schnitz, *Schnitzer*
Schnitzer
Schnitzler, *Schnitzer*
Schnöll, *Snell*
Schnoor, *Schnur*
Schnorr, *Schnurrer*
Schnorrer, *Schnurrer*
Schnur
Schnürchen, *Schnur*
Schnürer, *Schnur*
Schnürle, *Schnur*
Schnurmacher, *Schnur*
Schnurman, *Schnur*
Schnurr, *Schnurrer*
Schnurre, *Schnurrer*
Schnurrer
Schoales, *Scholes*
Schochet, *Shoikhet*
Schöck, *Schecker*
Schoemaker, *Schuh*
Schoemann, *Schuh*
Schoen, *Schön, Schuh*
Schoenbach, *Schön*
Schoenbaum, *Schön*
Schoenberg, *Schön*
Schoenberger, *Schön*
Schoenfeld, *Schön*
Schoengut, *Schön*

Schoenherz, *Schön*
Schoenholz, *Schön*
Schoenhorn, *Schön*
Schoenlicht, *Schön*
Schoenmaker, *Schuh*
Schoenmann, *Schuh*
Schoenrock, *Schön*
Schoenwald, *Schön*
Schöfer, *Schaffer*
Schöffel, *Schäffler*
Schöffler, *Schäffler*
Schofield
Scholar
Schölch, *Schiller*
Scholefield, *Schofield*
Schöler, *Schuler*
Scholer, *Scholar*
Schölermann, *Schuler*
Scholes
Scholey
Scholfield, *Schofield*
Schölig, *Schell*
Schöll, *Schell*
Scholl
Schöller, *Schell*
Scholte, *Schultz*
Scholten, *Schultz*
Scholtens, *Schultz*
Scholtis, *Schultz*
Scholts, *Schultz*
Scholtz, *Schultz*
Scholz, *Schultz*
Schölzel, *Schultz*
Schomaker, *Schuh*
Schömann, *Schön*
Schomann, *Schuh*
Schon, *Schön*
Schön
Schonbach, *Schön*
Schonbaum, *Schön*
Schönberg, *Schön*
Schonberg, *Schön*
Schonberger, *Schön*
Schonblum, *Schön*
Schondorf, *Schön*
Schöne, *Schön*
Schöneke, *Schön*
Schönemann, *Schön*
Schöner, *Schön*
Schönert, *Schön*
Schonert, *Schön*
Schonfeld, *Schön*
Schöngauer
Schongut, *Schön*
Schönherr, *Schön*
Schonholz, *Schön*
Schöning, *Schön*
Schonkopf, *Schön*
Schönle, *Schön*
Schönlein, *Schön*
Schönmann, *Schön*
Schonshein, *Schön*
Schonstadt, *Schön*
Schonthal, *Schön*
Schoolnik, *Schuler*
Schoon, *Schön*
Schoop, *Chopin*
Schöpe, *Stephen*
Schopenhauer, *Chopin*
Schopp, *Chopin*
Schoppa, *Stephen*
Schoppan, *Stephen*
Schoppe, *Chopin*
Schoppe, *Stephen*
Schoppenhauer, *Chopin*
Schor, *Schauer*
Schorman, *Schauer*
Schormann, *Schauer*
Schörmer, *Scrimgeour*
Schornach, *Chernyakov*
Schornack, *Chernyakov*
Schörnich, *Chernyakov*
Schornich, *Chernyakov*
Schornig, *Chernyakov*
Schorr, *Schauer*
Schory, *Schauer*
Schot, *Scott*
Schöteldreyer, *Schüssel*
Schott, *Scott*
Schötte, *Schüssel*
Schotte, *Scott*
Schottlander, *Scotland*
Schöttle, *Scott*
Schöttler, *Schüssel*
Schou, *Shaw*
Schout, *Schultz*
Schoute, *Schultz*
Schouteden, *Schultz*
Schouten, *Schultz*
Schouthede, *Schultz*
Schpitz, *Spitz*
Schraawen, *Gray*
Schrader, *Schröder*
Schramke, *Schramm*
Schramm
Schramme, *Schramm*
Schrammel, *Schramm*
Schreber, *Schreiber*
Schrei, *Schreier*
Schreiber
Schreibman, *Schreiber*
Schreibmann, *Schreiber*
Schreier
Schreiert, *Schreier*
Schreinemaker, *Schreiner*
Schreiner
Schreinert, *Schreiner*
Schremmel, *Schramm*
Schrempf, *Schramm*
Schrempp, *Schramm*
Schreuder, *Schröder*
Schreuders, *Schröder*
Schreur, *Schröder*
Schreurs, *Schröder*
Schrevens, *Graf*
Schrieber, *Schreiber*
Schriefer, *Schreiber*
Schrieve, *Sheriff*
Schriever, *Schreiber*
Schrievers, *Schreiber*
Schrieves, *Sheriff*
Schriewer, *Schreiber*
Schrijnmaeker, *Schreiner*
Schrijnmaker, *Schreiner*
Schrijver, *Schreiber*
Schrimp, *Schramm*
Schrimpf, *Schramm*
Schrive, *Sheriff*
Schröder
Schroier, *Schröder*
Schrörs, *Schröder*
Schröter, *Schröder*
Schrötter, *Schröder*
Schubart, *Schubert*
Schübel
Schubert
Schübler, *Schübel*
Schubort, *Schubert*
Schuch, *Schuh*
Schüchel, *Schuh*
Schuchert, *Schubert*
Schuck, *Schuh*
Schuckert, *Schubert*
Schuckmann, *Schuh*
Schuerman, *Scheuer*
Schuffenhauer, *Chopin*
Schüffner, *Chopin*
Schug, *Schuh*
Schügl, *Schuh*
Schuh
Schuhardt, *Schubert*
Schühel, *Schuh*
Schuhhardt, *Schubert*
Schühle, *Schuh*
Schühlein, *Schuh*
Schuhmacher, *Schuh*
Schuhmann, *Schuh*
Schuhrke, *George*
Schüle, *Schuh*
Schüler, *Schuler*
Schuler
Schüller, *Schuler*
Schuller, *Schuler*
Schullerus, *Schuler*
Schulman, *Schuler*
Schulmeister
Schulsinger, *Schuler*
Schulte, *Schultz*
Schulten, *Schultz*
Schultheiss, *Schultz*
Schulthess, *Schultz*
Schülting, *Schultz*
Schultz
Schultze, *Schultz*
Schulz, *Schultz*
Schulze, *Schultz*
Schumacher, *Schuh*
Schümann, *Scheuer*
Schumann, *Schuh*
Schünemann, *Scheuer*
Schüppenhauer, *Chopin*
Schuppenhauer, *Chopin*
Schuricht, *George*
Schuricke, *George*
Schurig, *George*
Schürmer, *Scrimgeour*
Schüssel
Schüssler, *Schüssel*
Schuster
Schüsterl, *Schuster*
Schusterman, *Schuster*
Schüstl, *Schuster*
Schut, *Schutz*
Schütt, *Schütze*
Schütte, *Schütze*
Schütz, *Schütze*
Schutz
Schützbier
Schütze
Schutzer, *Schutz*
Schutzman, *Schutz*
Schuurman, *Scheuer*
Schuwart, *Schubert*
Schuyler, *Schuler*
Schwab
Schwabe, *Schwab*
Schwabel, *Schwab*
Schwäble, *Schwab*
Schwaf, *Schwab*
Schwahn, *Swan*
Schwalb, *Swallow*
Schwalbe, *Swallow*
Schwälble, *Swallow*
Schwan, *Swan*
Schwand
Schwander, *Schwand*
Schwandner, *Schwand*
Schwandt, *Schwand*
Schwaneke, *Swan*
Schwanenfeld, *Swan*
Schwank, *Swan*
Schwanke, *Swan*
Schward, *Schwarz*
Schwarde, *Schwarz*
Schwart, *Schwarz*
Schwarte, *Schwarz*
Schwartekopp, *Schwarzkopf*
Schwarten, *Schwarz*
Schwarting, *Schwarz*
Schwartz, *Schwarz*
Schwartze, *Schwarz*
Schwartzer, *Schwarz*
Schwartzkopf, *Schwarzkopf*
Schwartzmann, *Schwarz*
Schwarz
Schwarze, *Schwarz*
Schwärzel, *Schwarz*
Schwarzer, *Schwarz*
Schwarzkopf
Schwarzmann, *Schwarz*
Schwarzschild
Schwebel
Schwed, *Schweder*
Schweder
Schweiger
Schweitzer
Schweizer, *Schweitzer*
Schwemmer
Schwen, *Swain*
Schwende, *Schwand*
Schwendemann, *Schwand*
Schwender, *Schwand*
Schwendler, *Schwand*
Schwendner, *Schwand*
Schweneke, *Swan*
Schwenke, *Swan*
Schwenn, *Swain*
Schwennen, *Swain*
Schwennesen, *Swain*
Schwennsen, *Swain*
Schwepe
Schwepenhauer, *Schwepe*
Schweppe, *Schwepe*
Schwert, *Sword*
Schwertl, *Sword*
Schwibbe, *Schwippe*
Schwimer, *Schwimmer*
Schwimmer
Schwippe
Schwippke, *Schwippe*
Schwippl, *Schwippe*
Schwob, *Schwab*
Schwöpe, *Schwippe*
Sciacovelli, *Jacob*
Scibilia, *Sevilla*
Scibilla, *Sevilla*
Scimo, *Simon*
Scimone, *Simon*
Scimonelli, *Simon*
Scimoni, *Simon*
Scinelli, *Francis*
Scini, *Francis*
Sciuscietto, *Francis*
Slachter, *Slaughter*
Sclater, *Slater*
Scobie

Scoefield, *Schofield*
Scoffield, *Schofield*
Scofield, *Schofield*
Scolefield, *Schofield*
Scoles, *Scholes*
Scolfield, *Schofield*
Scollard, *Scholar*
Scolnic, *Schuler*
Scolnik, *Schuler*
Scolts, *Schultz*
Scopes
Scorah, *Scorer*
Scorcia, *Scorza*
Scorer
Scorrer, *Scorer*
Scorsone, *Scorza*
Scorthals, *Shortall*
Scorza
Scorzelli, *Scorza*
Scorzetti, *Scorza*
Scorziello, *Scorza*
Scorzon, *Scorza*
Scorzone, *Scorza*
Scothern
Scoti, *Scott*
Scotland
Scoto, *Scott*
Scotson, *Scott*
Scott
Scotti, *Francis*
Scottini, *Francis*
Scotts, *Scott*
Scougall
Scoular, *Scholar*
Scoyles, *Scholes*
Scrase
Screech
Scribe
Scribner, *Scriven*
Scribot, *Scribe*
Scrimgeour
Scrimgeoure, *Scrimgeour*
Scrimger, *Scrimgeour*
Scrimiger, *Scrimgeour*
Scriminger, *Scrimgeour*
Scrimshaw, *Scrimgeour*
Scrive, *Scribe*
Scriven
Scrivener, *Scriven*
Scrivenor, *Scriven*
Scrivens, *Scriven*
Scrivings, *Scriven*
Scrivins, *Scriven*
Scrope
Scruton
Scrutton, *Scruton*
Scrymgeor, *Scrimgeour*
Scrymgeour, *Scrimgeour*
Scuce, *Skuse*
Scudamore
Scudder, *Scutt*
Scuderi, *Squire*
Scudieri, *Squire*
Scudiero, *Squire*
Scull
Scullion, *Scully*
Scullon, *Scully*
Scully
Scuotto, *Scott*
Scurmer, *Scrimgeour*
Scurrell, *Squirrel*
Scuteri, *Squire*
Scutieri, *Squire*
Scutiro, *Squire*
Scutt
Seabra
Seabrook
Seach, *Sykes*
Seacombe
Seagar
Seagars, *Seagar*
Seager, *Seagar*
Seagers, *Seagar*
Seagrave
Seagrief, *Seagrave*
Seagrove, *Seagrave*
Seal
Seale, *Seal*
Sealer, *Seal*
Seales, *Seal*
Sealey
Seally, *Sealey*
Seals, *Seal*
Sealy, *Sealey*
Seaman
Seamenn, *Seaman*
Seamons, *Seaman*
Seanor, *Senior*
Sear, *Sayer*
Search, *Surridge*
Seares, *Sayer*
Seargeant, *Sergeant*
Searight, *Surridge*
Searjeant, *Sergeant*
Searl, *Searle*
Searle
Searles, *Searle*
Searls, *Searle*
Sears, *Sayer*
Searson, *Sayer*
Seartáin, *Shortall*
Seath, *Sheehy*
Seaton
Seawright, *Surridge*
Sebass, *Sebastian*
Sebastià, *Sebastian*
Sébastian, *Sebastian*
Sebastián, *Sebastian*
Sebastian
Sebastianelli, *Sebastian*
Sebastiani, *Sebastian*
Sebastianini, *Sebastian*
Sebastiano, *Sebastian*
Sebastianutti, *Sebastian*
Sebastianutto, *Sebastian*
Sebastião, *Sebastian*
Sébastien, *Sebastian*
Sébaud, *Sibbald*
Šebek, *Sebastian*
Šebesta, *Sebastian*
Sebestyén, *Sebastian*
Sébille, *Sibley*
Sébilleau, *Sibley*
Sébillon, *Sibley*
Sébillot, *Sibley*
Sébire, *Sibley*
Sebley, *Sibley*
Sébline, *Sibley*
Sebök, *Sebastian*
Sebrecht, *Siebert*
Sebrechts, *Siebert*
Sécard, *Sieghard*
Seccombe
Séchet, *Seco*
Sechet, *Seco*
Secker
Seckerson, *Sexton*
Seco
Secombe, *Seccombe*
Second, *Segond*
Secondat, *Segond*
Secrétain, *Sexton*
Secrétan, *Sexton*
Secretan, *Sexton*
Sęczkowski, *Suk*
Šeda, *Sedov*
Seddon
Sedge
Sedgeman, *Sedge*
Sedger, *Sedge*
Sedgewick, *Sedgwick*
Sedgewicke, *Sedgwick*
Sedgley
Sedgwick
Sędicki, *Sędzicki*
Šedivý, *Sedov*
Sędkiewicz, *Sędzicki*
Sędkowski, *Sędzicki*
Sedláček, *Sedlák*
Sedlák
Sedler, *Sadler*
Sedman, *Seed*
Sedoff, *Sedov*
Sedov
Sedow, *Sedov*
Sedwick, *Sedgwick*
Sędzicki
Sędziński, *Sędzicki*
See
Seear, *Sayer*
Seebarth, *Siebert*
Seeck, *Siegel*
Seed
Seedman, *Seed*
Seeds, *Seed*
Seef, *Sieff*
Seefried, *Siegfried*
Seegar, *Seagar*
Seeger, *Sayer, Seagar*
Seegers, *Sayer*
Seegert, *Sayer*
Seel, *Seal, Seiler*
Seeler, *Seiler*
Seeley, *Sealey*
Seelig, *Selig*
Seeliger, *Selig*
Seelly, *Sealey*
Seels, *Seal*
Seely, *Sealey*
Seeman, *Seaman, See*
Seemann, *See*
Seemund, *Siegmund*
Seener, *Senior*
Seeney, *Senior*
Seerey
Seers, *Sayer*
Seery, *Seerey*
Seevers, *Siegfried*
Seffers, *Siegfried*
Seffrin, *Séverin*
Seffring, *Séverin*
Sefke, *Siegfried*
Šefl, *Schäffler*
Sefton
Segafredo, *Siegfried*
Ségal, *Segal*
Segal
Segalczyk, *Segal*
Segalescu, *Segal*
Segall, *Segal*
Segalov, *Segal*
Segalovich, *Segal*
Segalovitch, *Segal*
Segalovitz, *Segal*
Segalowitsch, *Segal*
Segalowitz, *Segal*
Segals, *Segal*
Segalson, *Segal*
Seganfreddo, *Siegfried*
Segard, *Sieghard*
Segarra
Segbarth, *Siebert*
Segbers, *Siebert*
Segebarth, *Siebert*
Segebrecht, *Siebert*
Segel, *Segal*
Segelke, *Siebert*
Segelken, *Siegel*
Segelstein, *Segal*
Segemund, *Siegmund*
Séger, *Sayer*
Seger, *Sawyer, Sayer, Seagar*
Segers, *Sayer*
Segert, *Sayer*
Seggeling, *Siegel*
Segger, *Sayer, Seagar*
Segler, *Seal*
Segond
Segondin, *Segond*
Segondy, *Segond*
Segovia
Segoviano, *Segovia*
Segrave, *Seagrave*
Segrestan, *Sexton*
Segrétain, *Sexton*
Segrétan, *Sexton*
Segrétin, *Sexton*
Ségui, *Seguí*
Seguí
Séguier, *Sayer*
Séguin, *Seguí*
Séguineau, *Seguí*
Séguiniol, *Seguí*
Séguinot, *Seguí*
Séguis, *Seguí*
Ségur
Ségura, *Ségur*
Segura, *Ségur*
Séguret, *Ségur*
Séguy, *Seguí*
Sehorsch, *Gregory*
Seiber, *Siebert*
Seiberlich, *Sauber*
Seibers, *Siebert*
Seibert, *Siebert*
Seibertz, *Siebert*
Seibicke, *Siebert*
Seid, *Seide*
Seide
Seideman, *Seide*
Seidemann, *Seide*
Seiden, *Seide*
Seidenband, *Seide*
Seidenbaum, *Seide*
Seidenberg, *Seide*
Seidenfeld, *Seide*
Seidenman, *Seide*
Seidenschnir, *Seide*
Seidenwurm, *Seide*
Seidl, *Siegel*
Seidler, *Seide*
Seidman, *Seide*
Seidmann, *Seide*
Seidner, *Seide*
Seidweber, *Seide*
Seif, *Soper*

Seifart, *Siegfried*
Seifarth, *Siegfried*
Seifer, *Soper, Siegfried*
Seiferlin, *Siegfried*
Seifert, *Siegfried*
Seiff, *Soper*
Seiffert, *Siegfried*
Seifman, *Soper*
Seigel, *Segal*
Seigneur
Seigneuret, *Seigneur*
Seignior, *Senior*
Seignoret, *Seigneur*
Seignouret, *Seigneur*
Seiler
Seiller, *Seiler*
Seis, *Seuss*
Seiser, *Seuss*
Seisill, *Cecil*
Seiter, *Sauter*
Seiterle, *Sauter*
Seitterle, *Sauter*
Seixas
Sejersen, *Sayer*
Séjournant
Séjourné, *Séjournant*
Séjournet, *Séjournant*
Sęk, *Suk*
Sękowski, *Suk*
Selbey, *Selby*
Selbie, *Selby*
Selby
Selcraig, *Selkirk*
Seld
Selden
Seldes, *Zeldes*
Seldin, *Zeldes*
Seldis, *Zeldes*
Seldmann, *Seld*
Seldner, *Seld*
Seldom, *Selden*
Seldon, *Selden*
Seldt, *Seld*
Seldte, *Seld*
Self
Selfe, *Self*
Selfridge
Selge, *Sealey*
Selifanov, *Selwyn*
Selifonov, *Selwyn*
Selig
Seliger, *Salinger, Selig*
Seligman, *Selig*
Seligmann, *Selig*
Seligsohn, *Selig*
Seligson, *Selig*
Selikson, *Selig*
Selinger, *Salinger*
Selivanov, *Selwyn*
Seliverstov, *Silvester*
Selivonok, *Selwyn*
Selkirk
Sell
Sellaio, *Seller*
Sellar, *Seller*
Sellaro, *Seller*
Sellaroli, *Seller*
Sellars, *Seller*
Selle, *Sell*
Seller
Selleret, *Seller*
Sellers, *Seller*
Sellés, *Seller*
Selley
Sellick, *Sealey*
Sellier, *Seller*
Sellig, *Selig*
Sellinger, *Salinger*
Sellman, *Selman*
Sellner, *Seld*
Sellors, *Seller*
Sells, *Sell*
Sellwood, *Selwood*
Selly, *Selley*
Selman
Selmi, *Ansell*
Selmini, *Ansell*
Selous
Seltmann, *Seld*
Seltzer, *Salter*
Selva, *Silva*
Selvaggi, *Savage*
Selvaggini, *Savage*
Selvaggio, *Savage*
Selvatici, *Savage*
Selve, *Silva*
Selvester, *Silvester*
Selvi, *Silva*
Selway
Selwin, *Selwyn*
Selwine, *Selwyn*
Selwood
Selwyn
Selwyne, *Selwyn*
Selzer, *Salter*
Semakin, *Simon*
Seman, *Seaman*
Semanov, *Simon*
Sémard, *Siemer*
Sember, *Samper*
Semchikhin, *Simon*
Semchishchev, *Simon*
Semchishin, *Simon*
Semechik, *Simon*
Semel, *Semmel*
Semenas, *Simon*
Semendyaev, *Simon*
Semenikov, *Simon*
Semenischev, *Simon*
Semennikov, *Simon*
Semenovich, *Simon*
Semens, *Seaman*
Sementsov, *Simon*
Semenyutin, *Simon*
Semerád, *Semrád*
Semichev, *Simon*
Semirád, *Semrád*
Semischev, *Simon*
Semkin, *Simkin*
Semler, *Semmel*
Semmel
Semmelmann, *Semmel*
Semmelweis, *Semmel*
Semmence, *Seaman*
Semmens, *Seaman*
Semmler, *Semmel*
Semmola, *Semmel*
Semola, *Semmel*
Semolini, *Semmel*
Sémond, *Siegmund*
Sémonin, *Simon*
Semper, *Samper*
Sempf, *Senf*
Sempill, *Semple*
Sempkins, *Simkin*
Semple
Semplice, *Semple*
Semplici, *Semple*
Semplicini, *Semple*
Semrád
Semyanovich, *Simon*
Semyashkin, *Simon*
Semyonikhin, *Simon*
Semyonov, *Simon*
Semyonychev, *Simon*
Sena
Sénac
Senchell, *Seneschal*
Senchenko, *Simon*
Sendall
Sender, *Sander*
Senderoff, *Sander*
Senderov, *Sander*
Senderovicz, *Sander*
Senderovitch, *Sander*
Senderovits, *Sander*
Senderovitz, *Sander*
Senderovski, *Sander*
Senderowicz, *Sander*
Senderowitz, *Sander*
Senderowsky, *Sander*
Senders, *Sander*
Sendler, *Sandler*
Sendra
Sendrovitz, *Sander*
Sendrowicz, *Sander*
Sendrowitz, *Sander*
Sénécal, *Seneschal*
Senecal, *Seneschal*
Sénécaut, *Seneschal*
Sénécaux, *Seneschal*
Sénéchal, *Seneschal*
Sénéchault, *Seneschal*
Sénéchaut, *Seneschal*
Senescal, *Seneschal*
Seneschal
Seneschall, *Seneschal*
Senet, *Sinnott*
Senf
Senff, *Senf*
Senft, *Senf*
Senftleben, *Senf*
Senftleber, *Senf*
Senger, *Sanger*
Sengers, *Sanger*
Senier, *Senior*
Senior
Sennett, *Sinnott*
Sennitt, *Sinnott*
Sensicall, *Seneschal*
Sensicle, *Seneschal*
Senskell, *Seneschal*
Sentís
Sentry
Sentyurikhin, *Simon*
Sentyurin, *Simon*
Senyagin, *Simon*
Senyard, *Senior*
Senyavin, *Simon*
Sephton, *Sefton*
Seppälä
Seppänen
Seppings
Sepúlveda
Sequeira
Seracini, *Sarson*
Seracino, *Sarson*
Serafim
Serafin, *Serafim*
Serafiniuk, *Serafim*
Serafinowicz, *Serafim*
Serafiński, *Serafim*
Serasin, *Sarson*
Serasini, *Sarson*
Serbinov
Serck, *Surridge*
Seretti, *Balthasar*
Serettini, *Balthasar*
Serfati, *Sarfatti*
Serfaty, *Sarfatti*
Sergachyov, *Sergio*
Serganov, *Sergio*
Sergant, *Sergeant*
Sergean, *Sergeant*
Sergeant
Sergeaunt, *Sergeant*
Sergeev, *Sergio*
Sergenson, *Sergeant*
Sergent, *Sergeant*
Sergevin, *Sergio*
Sergi, *Sergio*
Sergievski, *Sergio*
Serginson, *Sergeant*
Sérgio, *Sergio*
Sergio
Sergiou, *Sergio*
Sergius, *Sergio*
Sergunchikov, *Sergio*
Sergunkov, *Sergio*
Sergunov, *Sergio*
Seri, *Seigneur*
Serier, *Cerisier*
Seriers, *Cerisier*
Seriés, *Cerisier*
Serieys, *Cerisier*
Serieyx, *Cerisier*
Serjeant, *Sergeant*
Serjeantson, *Sergeant*
Serjent, *Sergeant*
Serle, *Searle*
Serlin, *Sorin*
Serman, *Sermon*
Sermin, *Sermon*
Sermon
Serna
Sernin, *Saturnin*
Seroni, *Balthasar*
Serotti, *Balthasar*
Serpe
Serpeau, *Serpe*
Serpell, *Serpe*
Serpette, *Serpe*
Serpin, *Serpe*
Serpinet, *Serpe*
Serpot, *Serpe*
Serpy, *Serpe*
Serrà, *Serre*
Serra, *Serre*
Serracino, *Sarson*
Serraino, *Sarson*
Serrano, *Serre*
Serrão, *Serre*
Serras, *Serre*
Serrat
Serre
Serreau, *Serre*
Serrell, *Searle*
Serres, *Serre*
Serresi, *Serre*
Serret, *Serre*
Serretta, *Serre*
Serri, *Serre*
Serrick, *Surridge*
Serries, *Sergio*
Serrini, *Serre*
Serrone, *Serre*

Serrotti, *Serre*
Sertell, *Shortall*
Sertill, *Shortall*
Sertorio, *Sartre*
Servadio
Servais, *Servis*
Servent, *Sergeant*
Service, *Servis*
Servis
Servoise, *Servis*
Seryozhechkin, *Sergio*
Seryozhichev, *Sergio*
Sessions
Šesták
Sesti, *Six*
Sestini, *Six*
Sesto, *Six*
Seth, *Sheehy*
Seton, *Seaton*
Setterfield, *Satterthwaite*
Settle
Seuberlich, *Sauber*
Seuffert, *Siegfried*
Seurat, *Séverin*
Seuret, *Séverin*
Seurin, *Séverin*
Seurot, *Séverin*
Seuss
Seute, *Sweet*
Seutemann, *Sweet*
Seuter, *Sauter*
Seuterle, *Sauter*
Seuterlin, *Sauter*
Seutter, *Sauter*
Seuvan, *Selwyn*
Ševc, *Szewc*
Ševčík, *Szewc*
Seveke, *Siegfried*
Seven, *Sabin*
Sevène, *Sabin*
Sevenet, *Sabin*
Sevens, *Sabin*
Severa, *Severov*
Severin, *Séverin*
Séverin
Severing, *Séverin*
Severini, *Séverin*
Severino, *Séverin*
Severinsen, *Séverin*
Severn
Severne, *Severn*
Severov
Severt, *Siegfried*
Severy, *Savory*
Severyn, *Séverin*
Severyns, *Séverin*
Sevestre, *Silvester*
Seveter, *Silvester*
Sevi, *Sabin*
Sévigné
Sevilia, *Sevilla*
Sevilla
Sevillano, *Sevilla*
Seville, *Saville*
Sevillia, *Sevilla*
Sevilya, *Sevilla*
Sevin, *Sabin*
Sevrain, *Séverin*
Sévrin, *Séverin*
Sewall, *Sewell*
Seward
Sewell
Sewer
Sewerin, *Séverin*
Seweryn, *Séverin*
Seweryniak, *Séverin*
Seweryński, *Séverin*
Sewill, *Sewell*
Sewter, *Sauter*
Sexon, *Sexton*
Sexston, *Sexton*
Sexten, *Sexton*
Sexton
Seyerlin, *Sauer*
Seyers, *Sayer*
Seyfahrt, *Siegfried*
Seyffahrt, *Siegfried*
Seyler, *Seiler*
Seyman, *Seaman*
Seymard, *Siemer*
Seymer, *Seymour*
Seymore, *Seymour*
Seymour
Seymoure, *Seymour*
Seyner, *Senior*
Seynor, *Senior*
Seys, *Sachs*
Sforza, *Force*
Shabat, *Sabbato*
Shabath, *Sabbato*
Shabathoff, *Sabbato*
Shabato, *Sabbato*
Shabaton, *Sabbato*
Shabatov, *Sabbato*
Shabatt, *Sabbato*
Shabes, *Sabbato*
Shackel, *Shackell*
Shackell
Shacklady
Shackle, *Shackell*
Shackles, *Shackell*
Shackleton
Shacklock
Shaddick, *Chadwick*
Shaddock, *Chadwick*
Shade
Shadwell
Shadwick, *Chadwick*
Shafe, *Shaw*
Shafran, *Safran*
Shafranovitch, *Safran*
Shafranski, *Safran*
Shaftoe
Shagalov, *Segal*
Shain, *Schön*
Shainbach, *Schön*
Shainbaum, *Schön*
Shainberg, *Schön*
Shainfeld, *Schön*
Shainkind, *Schön*
Shairp, *Sharp*
Shakelady, *Shacklady*
Shakespeare
Shakspeare, *Shakespeare*
Shalcross, *Shallcross*
Shale
Shallcrass, *Shallcross*
Shallcross
Shalom, *Sholem*
Shalomoff, *Sholem*
Shanaghan, *Shane*
Shanahan, *Shane*
Shanan, *Shane*
Shand
Shane
Shanghan, *Shane*
Shanihan, *Shane*
Shank, *Shanks*
Shanks
Shanley
Shanly, *Shanley*
Shannagh, *Shane*
Shannessy, *Shaughnessy*
Shanney, *Shane*
Shannon, *Shane*
Shanny, *Shane*
Shapcott
Shaper
Shapero, *Shapiro*
Shapir, *Shapiro*
Shapira, *Shapiro*
Shapiro
Shápka, *Chape*
Shapley, *Shipley*
Shapochnikov
Shaposhnik, *Shapochnikov*
Shaposhnikov, *Shapochnikov*
Shapster, *Shaper*
Shard, *Sheard*
Shardlow
Sharer, *Shearer*
Sharkey
Sharman, *Sherman*
Sharp
Sharpe, *Sharp*
Sharpf, *Sharp*
Sharples
Sharpless, *Sharples*
Sharps, *Sharp*
Sharratt, *Sherratt*
Sharrock, *Shorrock*
Sharrocks, *Shorrock*
Shasnan, *Sexton*
Shatski, *Schatz*
Shatsky, *Schatz*
Shattock, *Chadwick*
Shatz, *Schatz*
Shatzberg, *Schatz*
Shatzkin, *Schatz*
Shatzman, *Schatz*
Shatzov, *Schatz*
Shaughnessy
Shaul, *Saul*
Shauli, *Saul*
Shaulick, *Saul*
Shauloff, *Saul*
Shaulov, *Saul*
Shaulsky, *Saul*
Shaulson, *Saul*
Shauly, *Saul*
Shave, *Shaw*
Shaves, *Shaw*
Shaw
Shawcross, *Shallcross*
Shawe, *Shaw*
Shay, *Shaw*
Shayes, *Shaw*
Shays, *Shaw*
Shcharbakov, *Shcherbakov*
Shcherbak, *Shcherbakov*
Shcherbakov
Shcherban, *Shcherbakov*
Shcherbatov, *Shcherbakov*
Shchukin
Shchupak, *Shchukin*
Shea
Sheach, *Sheehy*
Shead, *Sheedy*
Sheahan, *Sheehan*
Sheal, *Shield*
Sheals, *Shield*
Shean, *Sheehan*
Sheane, *Sheehan*
Shear
Sheara, *Shearer*
Sheard
Sheards, *Sheard*
Shearer
Sheares, *Shear*
Shearing, *Shear*
Shearman, *Sherman*
Shears, *Shear*
Shearwood, *Sherwood*
Shechter, *Schechter*
Shechterman, *Schechter*
Shechtman, *Schechter*
Sheddan, *Sheddon*
Shedden, *Sheddon*
Sheddon
Shee, *Shea*
Sheean, *Sheehan*
Sheedy
Sheehan
Sheehy
Sheekey, *Sheehy*
Sheen, *Sheehan*
Sheeny, *Shane*
Sheep, *Shipman*
Sheepshanks
Sheer, *Shear*
Sheere, *Shear*
Sheeres, *Shear*
Sheerman, *Sherman*
Sheers, *Shear*
Shefer, *Schäfer*
Sheferman, *Schäfer*
Sheffer, *Schäfer*
Sheffield
Shefler, *Schäffler*
Sheil, *Shield*
Sheilds, *Shield*
Sheils, *Shield*
Shein, *Schön*
Sheinbach, *Schön*
Sheinbaum, *Schön*
Sheinbein, *Schön*
Sheinberg, *Schön*
Sheinberger, *Schön*
Sheinenson, *Scheinis*
Sheiner, *Schön*
Sheinerberg, *Schön*
Sheinerman, *Schön*
Sheines, *Scheinis*
Sheinfein, *Schön*
Sheinfeld, *Schön*
Sheingarten, *Schön*
Sheinhaus, *Schön*
Sheinholz, *Schön*
Sheinhorn, *Schön*
Sheinin, *Scheinis*
Sheinis, *Scheinis*
Sheinkar, *Schenke*
Sheinker, *Schenke*
Sheinkerman, *Schenke*
Sheinkinder, *Schön*
Sheinman, *Schön*
Sheintal, *Schön*
Sheintuch, *Schön*
Shelby
Sheldon
Sheldrake
Sheldrick, *Sheldrake*
Shellcross, *Shallcross*
Shelley
Shelly, *Shelley*
Shelton

Shenk, *Schenke*
Shenkar, *Schenke*
Shenker, *Schenke*
Shenkerman, *Schenke*
Shenkman, *Schenke*
Shenton
Shepard, *Sheppard*
Shepeard, *Sheppard*
Sheperd, *Sheppard*
Sheperdson, *Sheppard*
Shephard, *Sheppard*
Shepheard, *Sheppard*
Shepherd, *Sheppard*
Shepherdson, *Sheppard*
Sheppard
Sheppardson, *Sheppard*
Shepperd, *Sheppard*
Shepperdson, *Sheppard*
Shepperson, *Sheppard*
Sher, *Shear*
Shera, *Shearer*
Sherard, *Sherratt*
Sheraton
Sherborn, *Sherborne*
Sherborne
Sherbourne, *Sherborne*
Sherburn, *Sherborne*
Shere, *Shear*
Sheremetev, *Sheremetyev*
Sheremetyev
Sherer, *Shearer*
Shereshevski, *Sierota*
Sheridan
Sheriff
Sheriffs, *Sheriff*
Sherington
Sherlock
Sherman
Shermann, *Sherman*
Shermeister, *Sherman*
Sherott, *Sherratt*
Sherr, *Shear*
Sherrad, *Sherratt*
Sherrard, *Sherratt*
Sherratt
Sherreard, *Sherratt*
Sherred, *Sherratt*
Sherrett, *Sherratt*
Sherridan, *Sheridan*
Sherriff, *Sheriff*
Sherriffs, *Sheriff*
Sherrington, *Sherington*
Shershevski, *Sierota*
Shershevsky, *Sierota*
Sherwen, *Sherwin*
Sherwin
Sherwood
Shettlesworth, *Shuttleworth*
Shevchenko, *Szewc*
Shevchik, *Szewc*
Shevchuk, *Szewc*
Shevtsov, *Szewc*
Sheynbaum, *Schön*
Shiach, *Sheehy*
Shick, *Schick*
Shiel, *Shield*
Shield
Shields, *Shield*
Shiells, *Shield*
Shielman, *Schuler*
Shiels, *Shield*
Shik, *Schick*
Shildrake, *Sheldrake*
Shildrick, *Sheldrake*
Shiler, *Schiller*
Shiling, *Schilling*
Shiller, *Schiller*
Shilling, *Schilling*
Shillingford
Shillito
Shilman, *Schuler*
Shilton
Shimkevich, *Simon*
Shimkevicz, *Simon*
Shimkevitz, *Simon*
Shimkewitz, *Simon*
Shimon, *Simon*
Shimoni, *Simon*
Shimonoff, *Simon*
Shimonov, *Simon*
Shimonovich, *Simon*
Shimonovitz, *Simon*
Shimonowitz, *Simon*
Shimony, *Simon*
Shimshon, *Samson*
Shimshovits, *Samson*
Shimsoni, *Samson*
Shimsony, *Samson*
Shimuk, *Simon*
Shinagh, *Tinney*
Shine, *Sheehan*
Shingler
Shingles, *Shingler*
Shinkar, *Schenke*
Shinn, *Skinner*
Shinnagh, *Tinney*
Shinnick, *Tinney*
Shinnock, *Tinney*
Shinwick, *Tinney*
Ship, *Shipman*
Shiplee, *Shipley*
Shipley
Shipman
Shipp, *Shipman*
Shippam
Shippard, *Sheppard*
Shippen
Shipperbottom, *Shufflebottom*
Shipside
Shipsides, *Shipside*
Shipster, *Shaper*
Shipstone
Shipton
Shipway
Shireff, *Sheriff*
Shirer, *Shearer*
Shires, *Shear*
Shiriff, *Sheriff*
Shirley
Shirra, *Sheriff*
Shirreff, *Sheriff*
Shirreffs, *Sheriff*
Shirrefs, *Sheriff*
Shkolnik, *Schuler*
Shlanski, *Schlessinger*
Shlansky, *Schlessinger*
Shlasky, *Schlessinger*
Shlechter, *Slaughter*
Shleicher, *Schleicher*
Shlemovich, *Salomon*
Shlesinger, *Schlessinger*
Shlomkovitz, *Salomon*
Shlomkowitz, *Salomon*
Shlomof, *Salomon*
Shlomov, *Salomon*
Shlomovich, *Salomon*
Shlomovici, *Salomon*
Shlomovics, *Salomon*
Shlomovitch, *Salomon*
Shlomovits, *Salomon*
Shlomovitz, *Salomon*
Shlomowitz, *Salomon*
Shlonsky, *Schlessinger*
Shmider, *Smith*
Shmidman, *Smith*
Shmidt, *Smith*
Shmil, *Samuel*
Shmilovitch, *Samuel*
Shmilovitz, *Samuel*
Shmouel, *Samuel*
Shmueli, *Samuel*
Shmuely, *Samuel*
Shmuilov, *Samuel*
Shmuilovich, *Samuel*
Shmulevich, *Samuel*
Shneebaum, *Snow*
Shneerson, *Schneir*
Shneiderov, *Schneider*
Shneor, *Schneir*
Shneur, *Schneir*
Shnur, *Schnur*
Shochet, *Shoikhet*
Shoebotham, *Shufflebottom*
Shoebottom, *Shufflebottom*
Shoemaker, *Schuh*
Shoen, *Schön*
Shoenberg, *Schön*
Shoenberger, *Schön*
Shoenbrot, *Schön*
Shoenfeld, *Schön*
Shoesmith
Shohet, *Shoikhet*
Shohetman, *Shoikhet*
Shoichet, *Shoikhet*
Shoikhet
Shol, *Scholl*
Sholem
Sholemoff, *Sholem*
Sholl
Sholokhov
Sholokov, *Sholokhov*
Shon, *Schön*
Shonberg, *Schön*
Shonberger, *Schön*
Shonbrot, *Schön*
Shondorf, *Schön*
Shongut, *Schön*
Shonnagh, *Tinney*
Shonshein, *Schön*
Shonstein, *Schön*
Shoosmith, *Shoesmith*
Shooter
Shor, *Schauer*
Shore
Shores, *Shore*
Shori, *Schauer*
Shorr, *Schauer*
Shorrock
Shorrocks, *Shorrock*
Short
Shortall
Shorten, *Shortall*
Shorter, *Short*
Shorters, *Shorthouse*
Shorthall, *Shortall*
Shorthose, *Shorthouse*
Shorthouse
Shortis, *Shorthouse*
Shortle, *Shortall*
Shortman, *Short*
Shortt, *Short*
Shory, *Schauer*
Shoshin
Shoshkes, *Shoshin*
Shoshkin, *Shoshin*
Shostack, *Shostakovich*
Shostag, *Shostakovich*
Shostak, *Shostakovich*
Shostakovich
Shotter, *Shooter*
Shottlender, *Scotland*
Shotton
Shouler, *Shovell*
Shovel, *Shovell*
Shovelbottom, *Shufflebottom*
Shovell
Shoveller, *Shovell*
Showell, *Shovell*
Showl, *Shovell*
Showler, *Shovell*
Shpitz, *Spitz*
Shpitzer, *Spitz*
Shpringer, *Springer*
Shrapnel, *Carbonell*
Shreeve, *Sheriff*
Shreeves, *Sheriff*
Shreier, *Schreier*
Shreve, *Sheriff*
Shrimpton, *Sherington*
Shrives, *Sheriff*
Shroff
Shtark, *Stark*
Shtarker, *Stark*
Shtarkman, *Stark*
Shtarkmann, *Stark*
Shterenglass, *Starr*
Shtern, *Starr*
Shternberg, *Starr*
Shterngartz, *Starr*
Shternshuss, *Starr*
Shtiglitz, *Szczygiel*
Shtil, *Still*
Shtiler, *Still*
Shtilerman, *Still*
Shtill, *Still*
Shtiller, *Still*
Shtivel, *Stiefel*
Shtolzer, *Stolz*
Shtrauss, *Strauss*
Shtroi, *Straw*
Shtrom, *Ström*
Shtroy, *Straw*
Shtul
Shtull, *Shtul*
Shtulman, *Shtul*
Shturm, *Storm*
Shubotham, *Shufflebottom*
Shuchmacher, *Schuh*
Shuchman, *Schuh*
Shufflebotam, *Shufflebottom*
Shufflebotham, *Shufflebottom*
Shufflebottom
Shugg
Shugrue, *Sugrue*
Shulem, *Sholem*
Shulimson, *Sholem*
Shunnagh, *Tinney*
Shunny, *Tinney*
Shupack, *Shchukin*
Shupak, *Shchukin*
Shurlock, *Sherlock*
Shurman, *Sherman*
Shurrock, *Shorrock*
Shustak, *Shostakovich*
Shustek, *Shostakovich*
Shuster, *Schuster*

Shusterman, *Schuster*
Shut, *Shutt*
Shute
Shuter, *Shooter*
Shutt
Shutte, *Shutt*
Shutter, *Shooter*
Shuttleworth
Shutts, *Shutt*
Shvanenfeld, *Swan*
Shvets, *Szewc*
Shvetsov, *Szewc*
Shwalb, *Swallow*
Shynn, *Skinner*
Sibaud, *Sibbald*
Sibault, *Sibbald*
Sibaux, *Sibbald*
Sibbald
Sibbe, *Siebert*
Sibbelt, *Sibbald*
Sibbers, *Siebert*
Sibbersen, *Siebert*
Sibbert, *Siebert*
Sibbett
Sibbit, *Sibbett*
Sibbitt, *Sibbett*
Sibble, *Sibley*
Sibbles, *Sibley*
Sibers, *Siebert*
Sibiglia, *Sevilla*
Sibilano, *Sevilla*
Sibilia, *Sevilla*
Sibilio, *Sevilla*
Sibilla, *Sevilla*
Sibillano, *Sevilla*
Sibillat, *Sibley*
Sibille, *Sibley*
Sibilleau, *Sibley*
Sibillo, *Sevilla*
Sibillot, *Sibley*
Sibilski, *Sibley*
Sibiński, *Sibley*
Sibley
Sibly, *Sibley*
Sibson, *Sibley*
Sica, *Siegel*
Sicard, *Sieghard*
Sicardi, *Sieghard*
Sicca, *Siegel*
Siccardi, *Sieghard*
Siccardo, *Sieghard*
Sicco, *Siegel*
Sicely, *Sisley*
Sich, *Sykes*
Ších, *Simon*
Šícha, *Simon*
Sichard, *Sieghard*
Sichardt, *Sieghard*
Sichert, *Sieghard*
Sicilia
Siciliani, *Sicilia*
Siciliano, *Sicilia*
Sick, *Siegel*
Sickama, *Siegel*
Sickel, *Siegel*
Sickert, *Sieghard*
Sicks, *Siegel*
Siddall
Siddenham, *Sydenham*
Siddle, *Siddall*
Sidebotham, *Sidebottom*
Sidebottom
Sidell, *Siddall*
Sidenham, *Sydenham*

Sidgewick, *Sedgwick*
Sidgwick, *Sedgwick*
Šidlo, *Szydłowski*
Sidney
Sidor, *Isidore*
Sidorchik, *Isidore*
Sidorczyk, *Isidore*
Sidorenko, *Isidore*
Sidorin, *Isidore*
Sidorkov, *Isidore*
Sidorov, *Isidore*
Sidorovnin, *Isidore*
Sidorowicz, *Isidore*
Sidorshin, *Isidore*
Sidorski, *Isidore*
Sidwell, *Sitwell*
Sieb, *Siebert*
Siebe, *Siebert*
Siebeck, *Siebert*
Siebecke, *Siebert*
Siebeke, *Siebert*
Siebel, *Sibbald*
Siebels, *Sibbald*
Sieben, *Siebert*
Siebens, *Siebert*
Siebers, *Siebert*
Siebert
Siebertz, *Siebert*
Siebke, *Siebert*
Siebken, *Siebert*
Siebrecht, *Siebert*
Siebs, *Siebert*
Sieczkowski
Siedl, *Siegel*
Siedlecki
Siefers, *Siegfried*
Sieff
Siefke, *Siegfried*
Siefken, *Siegfried*
Siegbert, *Siebert*
Siegel
Siegelman, *Siegel*
Siegemund, *Siegmund*
Sieger, *Sayer*
Siegeris, *Sexton*
Siegerist, *Sexton*
Siegers, *Sayer*
Siegert, *Sayer*
Siegfried
Sieghard
Sieghart, *Sieghard*
Siegl, *Siegel*
Siegler, *Seal*
Siegmann, *Siegel*
Siegmund
Siegrist, *Sexton*
Siegwein, *Seguí*
Sieh, *Siegel*
Siehard, *Sieghard*
Siekiera
Sielski
Siem, *Siemer*
Siemandl, *Simon*
Siemann, *Siemer*
Siemantel, *Simon*
Siemen, *Siemer*
Siemens, *Siemer*
Siemensen, *Siemer*
Siemer
Siemers, *Siemer*
Siemiński
Siemon, *Simon*
Siemons, *Simon*
Siems, *Siemer*

Siemsen, *Siemer*
Siemssen, *Siemer*
Siemund, *Siegmund*
Sienkiewicz, *Siemiński*
Sieradzki
Sierant, *Sierota*
Sierkierski, *Siekiera*
Sierociński, *Sierota*
Sierocki, *Sierota*
Sieroczewski, *Sierota*
Sieroń, *Sierota*
Sieroszewski, *Sierota*
Sieroszewski, *Sierota*
Sierota
Sierra, *Serre*
Siess, *Sweet*
Sieur, *Seigneur*
Sieveke, *Siegfried*
Sieveking, *Siegfried*
Sieverding, *Siegfried*
Sievering, *Siegfried*
Sievers, *Siegfried*
Sieversen, *Siegfried*
Sievert, *Siegfried*
Sieverts, *Siegfried*
Sievertsen, *Siegfried*
Siewers, *Siegfried*
Siewert, *Siegfried*
Siewertsen, *Siegfried*
Siewiera, *Severov*
Siewierski, *Severov*
Siffert, *Siegfried*
Siffredi, *Siegfried*
Siffrin, *Séverin*
Siffring, *Séverin*
Sifredi, *Siegfried*
Sigal, *Segal*
Sigert, *Sieghard*
Sighart, *Sieghard*
Sigier, *Sayer*
Sigismondi, *Siegmund*
Sigismondo, *Siegmund*
Sigismund, *Siegmund*
Sigle, *Siegel*
Sigliente, *Seal*
Signoraccio, *Seigneur*
Signore, *Seigneur*
Signorelli, *Seigneur*
Signorello, *Seigneur*
Signoretti, *Seigneur*
Signori, *Seigneur*
Signoriello, *Seigneur*
Signorini, *Seigneur*
Signorino, *Seigneur*
Signoroni, *Seigneur*
Sigrist, *Sexton*
Sigsworth
Siguier, *Sayer*
Siguret, *Ségur*
Sijmons, *Simon*
Sikes, *Sykes*
Sikora
Sikorski, *Sikora*
Silber, *Silver*
Silberbach, *Silver*
Silberbaum, *Silver*
Silberberg, *Silver*
Silberblatt, *Silver*
Silberbusch, *Silver*
Silberdick, *Silver*
Silberdik, *Silver*
Silberfaden, *Silver*
Silberfarb, *Silver*
Silberfeld, *Silver*

Silberfenig, *Silver*
Silberfreund, *Silver*
Silberhertz, *Silver*
Silberherz, *Silver*
Silberlicht, *Silver*
Silberman, *Silver*
Silbermann, *Silver*
Silbermintz, *Silver*
Silberminz, *Silver*
Silbernadel, *Silver*
Silberpfennig, *Silver*
Silberphenig, *Silver*
Silberschatz, *Silver*
Silberschlag, *Silver*
Silberschmidt, *Silver*
Silbershatz, *Silver*
Silbershein, *Silver*
Silbersohn, *Silver*
Silberson, *Silver*
Silberspitz, *Silver*
Silberstein, *Silver*
Silbert, *Silver*
Silberwasser, *Silver*
Silberzahn, *Silver*
Silberzweig, *Silver*
Silcock, *Sill*
Silcocks, *Sill*
Silcox, *Sill*
Šilhan, *Šilhavý*
Šilhánek, *Šilhavý*
Šilhavý
Silk
Silke, *Silk*
Silkin, *Sill*
Silkstone
Sill
Sillett, *Sill*
Silley, *Sealey*
Sillito, *Shillito*
Sillitoe, *Shillito*
Sillman, *Selman*
Sills, *Sill*
Silly, *Sealey*
Silman, *Selman*
Silva
Silvagni, *Selwyn*
Silvagno, *Selwyn*
Silvain, *Selwyn*
Silván, *Selwyn*
Silvan, *Selwyn*
Silvani, *Selwyn*
Silvano, *Selwyn*
Silvant, *Selwyn*
Silveira, *Silva*
Silver
Silverberg, *Silver*
Silvério
Silverman, *Silver*
Silvers, *Silver*
Silvershmid, *Silver*
Silverstein, *Silver*
Silverston, *Silverstone*
Silverstone
Silverstov, *Silvester*
Silverthorne
Silverton
Silverwood
Silvester
Silveston, *Silverstone*
Silvestre, *Silvester*
Silvestrelli, *Silvester*
Silvestrini, *Silvester*
Silvestris, *Silvester*
Silvestro, *Silvester*

Silvestroni, *Silvester*
Silvestrov, *Silvester*
Silvestrovich, *Silvester*
Sim
Šíma, *Simon*
Šimáček, *Simon*
Simagin, *Simon*
Šimák, *Simon*
Simakov, *Simon*
Šiman, *Simon*
Šimánek, *Simon*
Simanenko, *Simon*
Simans, *Simon*
Simão, *Simon*
Simar, *Siemer*
Simard, *Siemer*
Simarov, *Simon*
Simble, *Semple*
Simbola, *Semmel*
Simbula, *Semmel*
Simchenko, *Simon*
Simcock, *Sim*
Simcocks, *Sim*
Simcox, *Sim*
Sime, *Sim*
Šimeček, *Simon*
Šimek, *Simon*
Simel, *Semmel*
Simenel, *Simon*
Simenet, *Simon*
Simenon, *Simon*
Simenot, *Simon*
Simeoli, *Simon*
Simeon, *Simon*
Simeone, *Simon*
Simeoni, *Simon*
Simeonov, *Simon*
Simeons, *Simon*
Simes, *Simson*
Simić, *Simon*
Šimić, *Simon*
Simiński, *Siemiński*
Simioli, *Simon*
Simion, *Simon*
Simionato, *Simon*
Simione, *Simon*
Simionescu, *Simon*
Simioni, *Simon*
Simison, *Simon*
Simka, *Simon*
Simkievitz, *Simkin*
Simkin
Simkins, *Simkin*
Simkiss, *Simkin*
Simkó, *Simon*
Simko, *Simon*
Simkovic, *Simkin, Simon*
Simkovich, *Simkin, Simon*
Simkovits, *Simkin*
Simkovitz, *Simkin, Simon*
Simler, *Semmel*
Simm, *Sim*
Simmance, *Simon*
Simmank, *Simon*
Simmans, *Simon*
Simmel, *Semmel*
Simmen, *Simon*
Simmens, *Simon*
Simmer, *Summer*
Simmers, *Summer*
Simmgen, *Simon*
Simmie, *Sim*
Simmig, *Simon*
Simmins, *Simon*
Simmler, *Semmel*
Simmon, *Simon*
Simmond, *Siegmund*
Simmonds, *Simon*
Simmonite, *Simon*
Simmons, *Simon*
Simms, *Simson*
Simnel, *Simon*
Simnell, *Simon*
Simner, *Sumner*
Simnett, *Simon*
Simnor, *Sumner*
Simó, *Simon*
Simoens, *Simon*
Simões, *Simon*
Simón, *Simon*
Šimon, *Simon*
Simon
Simonaitis, *Simon*
Simonard, *Simon*
Simonassi, *Simon*
Simonato, *Simon*
Simonazzi, *Simon*
Simoncelli, *Simon*
Simoncello, *Simon*
Simoncini, *Simon*
Simond, *Siegmund*
Simondi, *Siegmund*
Simondini, *Siegmund*
Simonds, *Simon*
Simone, *Simon*
Simoneau, *Simon*
Simonel, *Simon*
Simonelli, *Simon*
Simoneschi, *Simon*
Simonet, *Simon*
Simoneton, *Simon*
Simonett, *Simon*
Simonetti, *Simon*
Simonetto, *Simon*
Simonffy, *Simon*
Simonfy, *Simon*
Simoni, *Simon*
Simonian, *Simon*
Simonich, *Simon*
Simonin, *Simon*
Simonini, *Simon*
Simonite, *Simon*
Simonitto, *Simon*
Simonitz, *Simon*
Simonnet, *Simon*
Simonnin, *Simon*
Simonnot, *Simon*
Simonof, *Simon*
Simonon, *Simon*
Šimononský, *Simon*
Simonot, *Simon*
Simonou, *Simon*
Simonov, *Simon*
Simonović, *Simon*
Simonovici, *Simon*
Simonovitch, *Simon*
Simonovitz, *Simon*
Simonow, *Simon*
Simonowicz, *Simon*
Simonowitz, *Simon*
Simons, *Simon*
Simonsen, *Simon*
Simonsohn, *Simon*
Simonson, *Simon*
Simonsson, *Simon*
Simonutti, *Simon*
Simony, *Simon*
Simonyi, *Simon*
Simoulin, *Semmel*
Simounet, *Simon*
Simov, *Simon*
Simović, *Simon*
Simper, *Samper*
Simpkin, *Simkin*
Simpkins, *Simkin*
Simpkinson, *Simkin*
Simpkiss, *Simkin*
Simple, *Semple*
Simplot, *Semple*
Simpole, *Semple*
Simpson, *Simson*
Sims, *Simson*
Simson
Simukov, *Simon*
Simula, *Semmel*
Simulev, *Samuel*
Simulin, *Semmel*
Simulin, *Simon*
Šimůnek, *Simon*
Simushin, *Simon*
Simyagin, *Simon*
Simyson, *Simon*
Sinatora, *Sinatra*
Sinatra
Sinclair
Sinclaire, *Sinclair*
Sincock, *Sim*
Sincoe, *Sim*
Šindelář, *Shingler*
Singer, *Sanger*
Singers, *Sanger*
Singleton
Singman, *Sanger*
Sinisbury, *Sainsbury*
Siniscalchi, *Seneschal*
Siniscalco, *Seneschal*
Sinkin, *Simkin*
Sinkings, *Simkin*
Sinkins, *Simkin*
Sinkinson, *Simkin*
Sinnatt, *Sinnott*
Sinnett, *Sinnott*
Sinnott
Sint, *Saint*
Sinton
Sinyard, *Senior*
Sinyer, *Senior*
Siosbrick, *Scarisbrick*
Šíp
Šípek, *Šíp*
Sipp, *Siebert*
Sippings, *Seppings*
Sircutt, *Circuit*
Sire, *Seigneur*
Sired, *Syrett*
Siret, *Seigneur*
Sirett, *Syrett*
Sirette, *Syrett*
Sirkes, *Sorin*
Sirkett, *Circuit*
Sirkin, *Sorin*
Sirman, *Sermon*
Sirmon, *Sermon*
Siron, *Seigneur*
Sirot, *Seigneur*
Sirota, *Sierota*
Siroteau, *Seigneur*
Sirotek, *Sierota*
Sirotenko, *Sierota*
Sirotin, *Sierota*
Sirotinin, *Sierota*
Sirotkin, *Sierota*
Sirotyuk, *Sierota*
Sirvent, *Sergeant*
Siskin, *Zisin*
Siskind, *Süsskind*
Sisley
Sislin, *Zisin*
Sismondi, *Siegmund*
Sismondo, *Siegmund*
Sissens, *Sisley*
Sissman, *Sweet*
Sissmilch, *Sweet*
Sisson, *Sisley*
Sissons, *Sisley*
Sist, *Six*
Sisterson, *Sisley*
Sisti, *Six*
Sisto, *Six*
Sitarek, *Sitarz*
Sitarski, *Sitarz*
Sitarz
Sitch, *Sykes*
Sittart, *van*
Sittich
Sitwell
Sivachyov, *Siwiec*
Sivertsen, *Siegfried*
Sivestre, *Silvester*
Sivestri, *Silvester*
Siviglia, *Sevilla*
Sivilia, *Sevilla*
Sivilla, *Sevilla*
Sivilli, *Sevilla*
Siviter, *Silvester*
Sivochin, *Siwiec*
Sivolobov, *Siwiec*
Sivtsov, *Siwiec*
Sivyakov, *Siwiec*
Siwek, *Siwiec*
Siwiec
Siwiński, *Siwiec*
Six
Sixl, *Six*
Sixsmith
Sixt, *Six*
Sixta, *Six*
Sixtus, *Six*
Sizebrick, *Scarisbrick*
Sjöberg, *See*
Sjöblom, *See*
Sjöborg, *See*
Sjödén, *See*
Sjödin, *See*
Sjögren, *See*
Sjöholm, *See*
Sjölin, *See*
Sjölund, *See*
Sjöman, *See*
Sjöqvist, *See*
Sjöstedt, *See*
Sjöstrand, *See*
Sjöström, *See*
Skaife, *Scaife*
Skakle, *Shackell*
Skála, *Skalski*
Skałecki, *Skalski*
Skalicky, *Skalski*
Skally, *Scully*
Skalník, *Skalski*
Skalski
Škarda
Skate, *Skeat*
Skates, *Skeat*
Skeat
Skeate, *Skeat*

Skeates, *Skeat*
Skeats, *Skeat*
Skeen, *Skene*
Skeene, *Skene*
Skeet, *Skeat*
Skeete, *Skeat*
Skeffington
Skegg
Skeggs, *Skegg*
Skelding
Skeldon
Skelly, *Scully*
Skelton
Skene
Skepper, *Skipper*
Skermer, *Scrimgeour*
Skett, *Skeat*
Skevington, *Skeffington*
Skewes, *Skuse*
Skewis, *Skuse*
Skews, *Skuse*
Skiba
Skibicki, *Skiba*
Skibiński, *Skiba*
Skidmore, *Scudamore*
Skierski, *Siekiera*
Skiffington, *Skeffington*
Skilton, *Skelton*
Skin, *Skinner*
Skinner
Skiöld, *Schild*
Skipp, *Skipper*
Skipper
Skipsey
Skipwith
Skipworth, *Skipwith*
Skirmer, *Scrimgeour*
Skitmore, *Scudamore*
Skitt, *Scutt*
Skivington, *Skeffington*
Skjöld, *Schild*
Sklář, *Szklar*
Sklenář, *Szklar*
Skoczylas
Škoda
Skog, *Shaw*
Skogh, *Shaw*
Sköld, *Schild*
Skoler, *Schuler*
Skolnick, *Schuler*
Skolnik, *Schuler*
Skolnikov, *Schuler*
Skoneczny, *Konieczny*
Skonieczka, *Konieczny*
Skonieczko, *Konieczny*
Skonieczny, *Konieczny*
Skoog, *Shaw*
Skoogh, *Shaw*
Skoolnik, *Schuler*
Skóra
Skórek, *Skóra*
Skorek
Skořepa, *Skorupa*
Skórka, *Skóra*
Skórnik, *Skóra*
Skorochod, *Skorokhodov*
Skorohod, *Skorokhodov*
Skorokhodov
Skórski, *Skóra*
Skorupa
Skorupski, *Skorupa*
Skórzewski, *Skóra*
Skotte, *Scott*
Skou, *Shaw*
Skov, *Shaw*
Skovgård
Skowron
Skowroński, *Skowron*
Skrimshire, *Scrimgeour*
Skripkin, *Skrzypek*
Skřivan, *Skowron*
Skřivánek, *Skowron*
Skriver, *Schreiber*
Skrypkin, *Skrzypek*
Skrzydlewski
Skrzynecki, *Schreiner*
Skrzypczak, *Skrzypek*
Skrzypczyński, *Skrzypek*
Skrzypek
Skrzypiński, *Skrzypek*
Skulnik, *Schuler*
Skupień
Skupiński, *Skupień*
Skurtul, *Court*
Skuse
Škvor, *Skorek*
Skvortsov
Skwara
Skwarnecki, *Skwara*
Skwarnek, *Skwara*
Skwarski, *Skwara*
Skyner, *Skinner*
Skynner, *Skinner*
Słabiak, *Słaby*
Słabicki, *Słaby*
Slabý, *Słaby*
Słaby
Slachter, *Slaughter*
Slack
Slacke, *Slack*
Sladden, *Sladen*
Slade
Sládek
Sladen
Slader, *Slade*
Sladký, *Słodski*
Sladovník, *Sládek*
Sladovský, *Sládek*
Slafter, *Slaughter*
Slagter, *Slaughter*
Sláma, *Słomski*
Śląski, *Schlessinger*
Slate, *Slater*
Slater
Slatin, *Zlatin*
Slatine, *Zlatin*
Slatkin, *Zlatin*
Slatkine, *Zlatin*
Slator, *Slater*
Slatter, *Slater*
Slattery
Slaughter
Slavíček, *Słowik*
Slavík, *Słowik*
Slavin
Slavković, *Sławiński*
Slawin, *Slavin*
Sławiński
Slay
Slaymaker, *Slay*
Slayter, *Slaughter*
Slaytor, *Slaughter*
Ślązak, *Schlessinger*
Slazenger, *Schlessinger*
Sleath, *Sly*
Sleator, *Slaughter*
Slechten, *Schlecht*
Slee, *Sly*
Sleeman, *Sly*
Slegt, *Schlecht*
Sleith, *Sly*
Slemming, *Sly*
Slemmings, *Sly*
Slemmonds, *Sly*
Slesinger, *Schlessinger*
Slessinger, *Schlessinger*
Slevin
Sleymovich, *Salomon*
Slezák, *Schlessinger*
Slezak, *Schlessinger*
Ślęzak, *Schlessinger*
Sligh, *Sly*
Slight
Slim
Sliman, *Sly*
Slimming, *Sly*
Slimmon, *Sly*
Slinger
Slingsby
Slipper, *Schleifer*
Sliva, *Śliwa*
Śliwa
Śliwiński, *Śliwa*
Sloan
Sloane, *Sloan*
Slocom, *Slocombe*
Slocombe
Slocum, *Slocombe*
Słodak, *Słodski*
Słodkiewicz, *Słodski*
Słodski
Sloey, *Slowey*
Sloman, *Slowman*
Słomczewski, *Słomski*
Słomczyński, *Słomski*
Słomiński, *Słomski*
Slomka, *Salomon*
Słomkowski
Slomovici, *Salomon*
Slomovits, *Salomon*
Slomovitz, *Salomon*
Słomski
Slone, *Sloan*
Slongo, *Long*
Sloper
Slot, *Schloss*
Sloth, *Schloss*
Slotmaeker, *Schloss*
Slotmaker, *Schloss*
Slotnick, *Zolotaryov*
Slotnik, *Zolotaryov*
Slough, *Slow*
Slováček, *Slovák*
Slovák
Slovin, *Slavin*
Slow
Slowan, *Sloan*
Slowe, *Slow*
Slowes, *Slavin*
Slowey
Słowik
Słowikowski, *Słowik*
Słowiński, *Słowik*
Slowman
Sloy, *Slowey*
Sloyan, *Sloan*
Sloyne, *Sloan*
Slucki, *Slutsky*
Slucky, *Slutsky*
Sluis
Sluman, *Slowman*
Ślusarczyk, *Ślusarski*
Ślusarek, *Ślusarski*
Ślusarski
Slutski, *Slutsky*
Slutsky
Slutzk, *Slutsky*
Slutzker, *Slutsky*
Slutzky, *Slutsky*
Sly
Slyman, *Sly*
Slyusar, *Ślusarski*
Smaele, *Small*
Smaile, *Small*
Smailes, *Small*
Smal, *Small*
Smale, *Small*
Smales, *Small*
Small
Smalle, *Small*
Smallen, *Spillane*
Smalles, *Small*
Smalley
Smallman
Smalls, *Small*
Smallshaw
Smallwood
Smally, *Smalley*
Smalman, *Smallman*
Smart
Smartman, *Smart*
Smead, *Smeeth*
Smeal, *Small*
Smeall, *Small*
Smeath, *Smeeth*
Smeathman, *Smeeth*
Smeaton
Smed, *Smith*
Smeder, *Smith*
Smedley
Smee, *Smeeth*
Smeed, *Smeeth*
Smeesters, *Master*
Smeeth
Smeeton, *Smeaton*
Šmejkal
Smeken, *Smith*
Smekens, *Smith*
Smellie, *Smillie*
Smělý, *Śmiałkowski*
Smerdon
Smet, *Smith*
Smetana
Smetanka, *Smetana*
Smethurst
Smets, *Smith*
Smeyers, *Mayer*
Smeysters, *Master*
Śmiałkowski
Smid, *Smith*
Šmíd, *Smith*
Šmídek, *Smith*
Smidman, *Smith*
Smidt, *Smith*
Smidth, *Smith*
Śmiech
Śmiechowicz, *Śmiech*
Śmiechowski, *Śmiech*
Śmietana, *Smetana*
Śmietanka, *Smetana*
Smieton, *Smeaton*
Śmigielski, *Szmigiel*
Smiles, *Small*
Smiley
Smillie
Smirnov, *Smirnyagin*

Smirnyagin
Smíšek, *Smiech*
Smisson, *Smith*
Smit, *Smith*
Smith
Smithe, *Smythe*
Smither, *Smith*
Smitherman, *Smith*
Smithers, *Smith*
Smithies, *Smythe*
Smithson, *Smith*
Smithyes, *Smythe*
Smits, *Smith*
Smola, *Smolarek*
Smolarek
Smolders, *Miller*
Smoleński
Smolík, *Smolarek*
Smollan, *Spillane*
Smollett
Smrček
Smrčka, *Smrček*
Smulczyk, *Samuel*
Smulders, *Miller*
Smulevich, *Samuel*
Smulian, *Samuel*
Smuliewicz, *Samuel*
Smullen, *Spillane*
Smulski, *Samuel*
Smut, *Smith*
Smutný
Smuts, *Smith*
Smylie, *Smiley*
Smyth, *Smith*
Smythe
Smythson, *Smith*
Smythyes, *Smythe*
Šnábl, *Schnabel*
Snadden, *Snowden*
Snaith
Šnajdr, *Schneider*
Snape
Snawdon, *Snowden*
Snead, *Snaith*
Sneath, *Snaith*
Snedden, *Snowden*
Sneddon, *Snowden*
Snee, *Snaith*
Sneed, *Snaith*
Sneider, *Schneider*
Snel, *Snell*
Snelgrove, *Snellgrove*
Snell
Snellgrave, *Snellgrove*
Snellgrove
Snelling, *Snell*
Snellman, *Snell*
Snelman, *Snell*
Snelson, *Snell*
Sneyd, *Snaith*
Sneyder, *Schneider*
Sneyders, *Schneider*
Śniady
Snider, *Schneider*
Sniderman, *Schneider*
Sniders, *Schneider*
Snieder, *Schneider*
Snieders, *Schneider*
Snijders, *Schneider*
Sniyder, *Schneider*
Snoad, *Snaith*
Šnobl, *Schnabel*
Snoddie, *Snoddy*
Snoddon, *Snowden*
Snoddy
Snode, *Snaith*
Snodgers, *Snodgrass*
Snodgrass
Snoek, *Snook*
Snook
Snooks, *Snook*
Snow
Snowball
Snowden
Snowdon, *Snowden*
Snowling, *Snow*
Snyder, *Schneider*
Snyders, *Schneider*
Soal, *Sole*
Soall, *Sole*
Soame
Soames, *Soame*
Soan, *Soane*
Soane
Soanes, *Soane*
Soans, *Soane*
Soaper, *Soper*
Soar
Soares, *Soar*
Soares, *Suero*
Soars, *Soar*
Soave, *Schwab*
Soavi, *Schwab*
Sobalski, *Sobota*
Sobański, *Sobota*
Sobczak, *Sobota*
Sobczyk, *Sobota*
Sobczyński, *Sobota*
Sobek, *Sobota*
Sobel
Sobelman, *Sobel*
Sobiech, *Sobota*
Sobieraj
Sobierajski, *Sobieraj*
Sobieski, *Sobota*
Sobieszczak, *Sobota*
Sobieszek, *Sobota*
Sobiński, *Sobota*
Sobkiewicz, *Sobota*
Sobol, *Sobel*
Sobolewitz, *Sobel*
Sobolewski, *Sobel*
Soboliev, *Sobel*
Sobota
Sobotka, *Sobota*
Sobral
Sobrero, *Soubeyre*
Sobrino
Sobusiak, *Sobota*
Socha
Sochacki, *Socha*
Sochala, *Socha*
Sochor
Sochůrek, *Sochor*
Socol, *Sokol*
Socolof, *Sokol*
Socoloff, *Sokol*
Socolov, *Sokol*
Socolow, *Sokol*
Socquet, *Such*
Socquin, *Such*
Soden, *Sowden*
Söder, *South*
Söderbäck, *South*
Söderberg, *South*
Söderblom, *South*
Södergren, *South*
Söderholm, *South*
Söderlind, *South*
Söderlindh, *South*
Söderling, *South*
Söderlund, *South*
Södermann, *South*
Söderqvist, *South*
Söderstöm, *South*
Søe, *See*
Søegaard, *Søgård*
Søegård, *Søgård*
Soeiro, *Suero*
Sofer
Soferman, *Sofer*
Soffer, *Sofer*
Söffing, *Siegfried*
Söffker, *Siegfried*
Söfker, *Siegfried*
Søgaard, *Søgård*
Søgård
Sohier, *Sayer*
Sohn, *Soane*
Söhnchen, *Soane*
Söhndl, *Soane*
Söhngen, *Soane*
Söhnke, *Soane*
Sohnker, *Soane*
Söhnlein, *Soane*
Söhns, *Soane*
Sohns, *Soane*
Söhren, *Séverin*
Soibelman, *Sobel*
Soiberman, *Sauber*
Soifer, *Sofer*
Soikin
Soissons, *Sessions*
Sojka, *Soikin*
Sokal, *Sokol*
Sokalski, *Sokol*
Sokić, *Sokol*
Sokół, *Sokol*
Sokol
Sokole, *Sokol*
Sokolik, *Sokol*
Sokoll, *Sokol*
Sokolof, *Sokol*
Sokoloff, *Sokol*
Sokolov, *Sokol*
Sokolović, *Sokol*
Sokolow, *Sokol*
Sokołowicz, *Sokol*
Sokołowski, *Sokol*
Sokółski, *Sokol*
Sokolski, *Sokol*
Sokolsky, *Sokol*
Sol
Solà, *Solano*
Solana, *Solano*
Solanas, *Solano*
Solanes, *Solano*
Solano
Solans, *Solano*
Solarek, *Salter*
Solari, *Soler*
Solarino, *Soler*
Solario, *Soler*
Solaro, *Soler*
Solaroli, *Soler*
Solarski, *Salter*
Solarz, *Salter*
Solass, *Solis*
Šolc, *Schultz*
Soldan, *Sowden*
Soldani, *Sowden*
Soldano, *Sowden*
Soldevila
Soldevilla, *Soldevila*
Soldi, *Izard*
Soldmann, *Salt*
Söldner, *Seld*
Solé, *Soler*
Sole
Solecki, *Salter*
Soler
Soleri, *Soler*
Solero, *Soler*
Soles, *Sole*
Solier, *Soler*
Solieri, *Soler*
Solignac
Solinhac, *Solignac*
Soliński, *Salter*
Solis
Soliss, *Solis*
Sollier, *Soler*
Söllner, *Seld*
Solmon, *Salmon*
Solomon, *Salomon*
Solovchik, *Solovey*
Solovei, *Solovey*
Soloveichik, *Solovey*
Soloveitshik, *Solovey*
Solovej, *Solovey*
Solovey
Solovieczyk, *Solovey*
Solovitzik, *Solovey*
Soloway, *Solovey*
Soloweiczyk, *Solovey*
Solowieczyk, *Solovey*
Solsona
Šolta, *Schultz*
Sölter, *Salter*
Solter, *Salter*
Soltmann, *Salt*
Sołtys, *Schultz*
Šoltys, *Schultz*
Sołtysiak, *Schultz*
Sołtysik, *Schultz*
Solvay, *Solovey*
Solzhenitsyn
Somer, *Summer*
Somerfreund, *Summer*
Somerlad, *Summerlad*
Somerman, *Summer*
Somers, *Summer*
Somerscale, *Somerscales*
Somerscales
Somerschein, *Summer*
Somerset
Somersett, *Somerset*
Somerstein, *Summer*
Somervail, *Somerville*
Somervaille, *Somerville*
Somervell, *Somerville*
Somerville
Somes, *Soame*
Sommer, *Summer*
Sommerfeld, *Summer*
Sommerfeldt, *Summer*
Sommerlad, *Summerlad*
Sommerlat, *Summerlad*
Sommerman, *Summer*
Sommers, *Summer*
Sommersett, *Somerset*
Sommerstein, *Summer*
Sommerville, *Somerville*
Somner, *Sumner*
Somoza
Son, *Soane*

Sønder, *South*
Søndergaard, *Søndergård*
Søndergård
Sondermann, *South*
Sønderup
Sone, *Soane*
Sones, *Soane*
Soneur, *Sonnier*
Songer, *Sanger*
Sönksen, *Soane*
Sonn, *Soane*
Sönnecken, *Soane*
Sonnenschein
Sonneur, *Sonnier*
Sonnier
Sönnischen, *Soane*
Sonntag
Sonschein, *Sonnenschein*
Sontag, *Sonntag*
Soolivan, *Sullivan*
Soonhouse, *Souness*
Soord, *Sword*
Sopena, *Sopeña*
Sopeña
Soper
Soponaru, *Soper*
Sopper, *Soper*
Soquet, *Such*
Sor, *Soar*
Sorba, *Sorbier*
Sorbet, *Sorbier*
Sorbie, *Sowerby*
Sorbier
Sorbon, *Sorbier*
Sorby, *Sowerby*
Sordet, *Sourd*
Sordi, *Sourd*
Sordini, *Sourd*
Sordo, *Sourd*
Sordon, *Sourd*
Sordoni, *Sourd*
Soreano, *Soria*
Soreau, *Soar*
Soref, *Zoref*
Soreff, *Zoref*
Sorel, *Soar*
Sören, *Séverin*
Sørens, *Séverin*
Sørensen, *Séverin*
Sorenson, *Sorin*
Sörensson, *Séverin*
Soret, *Soar*
Sorg, *Sorge*
Sorge
Sörgel, *Sorge*
Sorger, *Sorge*
Sorghe, *Sorge*
Soria
Soriano, *Soria*
Sorin
Soriyano, *Soria*
Sorkin, *Sorin*
Sorkis, *Sorin*
Sorley
Sorlie, *Sorley*
Sornin, *Saturnin*
Soroff
Soroka, *Sorokin*
Soroker, *Sorokin*
Sorokin
Soroko, *Sorokin*
Sorrel, *Soar*
Sorrell, *Soar*
Sorribas
Sorribes, *Sorribas*
Sorrie, *Sorley*
Sörries, *Sergio*
Sorrill, *Soar*
Sorsbie, *Sowerby*
Sorsby, *Sowerby*
Sosin, *Shoshin*
Sosis, *Shoshin*
Soskin, *Shoshin*
Sosna, *Sosnin*
Sosnak, *Sosnin*
Sosner, *Sosnin*
Sosnevits, *Sosnin*
Sosniak, *Sosnin*
Sosnick, *Sosnin*
Sosnicki, *Sosnin*
Sosnin
Sosnovitz, *Sosnin*
Sosnovsky, *Sosnin*
Sosnowiec, *Sosnin*
Sosnowski, *Sosnin*
Söte, *Sweet*
Sotelo, *Sault*
Söth, *Sweet*
Sotham, *Southam*
Sotheby
Sotheran, *South*
Sothern, *South*
Sotheron, *South*
Sotillo, *Sault*
Sotillos, *Sault*
Soto, *Sault*
Sotti, *Izard*
Soubayrol, *Soubeyre*
Soubeiran, *Soubeyre*
Soubeyran, *Soubeyre*
Soubeyre
Soubeyrol, *Soubeyre*
Soubiran, *Soubeyre*
Soubirou, *Soubeyre*
Soubirous, *Soubeyre*
Soubran, *Soubeyre*
Soubrier, *Soubeyre*
Souček, *Suk*
Souch, *Such*
Souche, *Such*
Souchet, *Such*
Souchon, *Such*
Soudan, *Sowden*
Soudant, *Sowden*
Soukup
Soul
Soula, *Solano*
Soulan, *Solano*
Soulanet, *Solano*
Soulard, *Soul*
Soulas, *Solis*
Soulé, *Soulier*
Soulié, *Soulier*
Soulier
Soullier, *Soulier*
Soulsby
Soult
Souness
Sounness, *Souness*
Souque, *Such*
Souquet, *Such*
Sourd
Sourdat, *Sourd*
Sourdeau, *Sourd*
Sourdet, *Sourd*
Sourdillon, *Sourd*
Sourdin, *Sourd*
Sourdou, *Sourd*
Sourkes, *Sorin*
Sousa
Souster
Soutar, *Sauter*
Souter, *Sauter*
South
Southall
Southam
Southan, *South*
Southcott
Southee, *Southey*
Southerin, *South*
Southerland, *Sutherland*
Southern, *South*
Southey
Southgate
Southon, *South*
Southorn, *South*
Southward, *Southworth*
Southwell
Southwood
Southworth
Souto, *Sault*
Souttar, *Sauter*
Soutter, *Sauter*
Souza, *Sousa*
Sova, *Sowa*
Sowa
Sowała, *Sowa*
Sowden
Sowerby
Sowersby, *Sowerby*
Sowiak, *Sowa*
Sowiński, *Sowa*
Sowman, *South*
Sowter, *Sauter*
Soyer, *Sayer*
Soyez, *Sayer*
Spaak
Spaans, *Pagnol*
Spaar, *Spark*
Špaček
Spackman, *Speakman*
Spada, *Espada*
Spadari, *Espada*
Spadaro, *Espada*
Spadazzi, *Espada*
Spadelli, *Espada*
Spadini, *Espada*
Spadolini, *Espada*
Spadon, *Espada*
Spadoni, *Espada*
Spadotto, *Espada*
Spaducci, *Espada*
Spaduzza, *Espada*
Spaduzzi, *Espada*
Spagnol, *Pagnol*
Spagnoleto, *Pagnol*
Spagnoletti, *Pagnol*
Spagnoli, *Pagnol*
Spagnolo, *Pagnol*
Spagnul, *Pagnol*
Spagnulo, *Pagnol*
Spagnuolo, *Pagnol*
Spahn, *Spooner*
Spahr, *Spark*
Spaight, *Speight*
Spain
Spalane, *Spillane*
Spalding
Spalton, *Spaughton*
Spanier, *Pagnol*
Spanierman, *Pagnol*
Spaniol, *Pagnol*
Spanjaard, *Pagnol*
Spanjer, *Pagnol*
Spanton
Spargo
Spark
Sparke, *Spark*
Sparkes, *Spark*
Sparks, *Spark*
Sparling, *Sparrow*
Sparmann, *Spohrer*
Sparrow
Sparrowe, *Sparrow*
Spasić, *Spasski*
Spasojević, *Spasski*
Spasski
Spata, *Espada*
Spatari, *Espada*
Spataro, *Espada*
Spătarul, *Espada*
Späth, *Spath*
Spath
Späthe, *Spath*
Späthmann, *Spath*
Spatoni, *Espada*
Spatuzza, *Espada*
Spaughton
Spaulding, *Spalding*
Spawforth, *Spofforth*
Spawton, *Spaughton*
Speaight, *Speight*
Speak
Speake, *Speak*
Speakman
Speaks, *Speak*
Spear
Speare, *Spear*
Speares, *Spear*
Spearing, *Spear*
Spearman
Spearon, *Sperrin*
Spears, *Spear*
Specht, *Speight*
Speciale, *Spicer*
Speciali, *Spicer*
Speck
Speckäter, *Speck*
Speckesser, *Speck*
Specketer, *Speck*
Speckle, *Speck*
Speckter, *Speck*
Spector
Spectorman, *Spector*
Spedding
Spedracci, *Peter*
Spedroni, *Peter*
Speed
Speedie, *Speed*
Speek, *Speak*
Speeks, *Speak*
Speer, *Spear*
Speer
Speers, *Spear*
Spegel, *Spiegler*
Spehr, *Spohrer*
Spehrer, *Spohrer*
Speight
Speir, *Spear*
Speirs, *Spear*
Speis, *Speiser*
Speiser
Speisman, *Speiser*
Speizman, *Speiser*
Speke, *Speak*
Spekman, *Speck*

Spektor, *Spector*
Spelar, *Speller*
Spellane, *Spillane*
Speller
Spellman, *Speller*
Spelman, *Speller*
Spelmann, *Spiller*
Spence
Spencer, *Spence*
Spender
Spendlove
Spendlow, *Spendlove*
Spener, *Spooner*
Spengel, *Spengler*
Spengler
Spenlow, *Spendlove*
Spens, *Spence*
Spenser, *Spence*
Sperber
Sperberg, *Sperber*
Sperck, *Sparrow*
Sperelli, *Kaspar*
Sperk, *Sparrow*
Sperl, *Sparrow*
Sperlich, *Sparrow*
Sperling, *Sparrow*
Sperner, *Spohrer*
Speroni, *Kaspar*
Sperotto, *Kaspar*
Sperrin
Sperring, *Sperrin*
Sperryn, *Sperrin*
Sperski, *Kaspar*
Spervogel, *Sparrow*
Speth, *Spath*
Spethmann, *Spath*
Speziale, *Spicer*
Speziali, *Spicer*
Spice, *Spicer*
Spicer
Spick, *Speak*
Spiegel, *Spiegler*
Spiegelman, *Spiegler*
Spiegelmann, *Spiegler*
Spiegheleer, *Spiegler*
Spieght, *Speight*
Spiegl, *Spiegler*
Spiegler
Spielberg
Spielberger, *Spielberg*
Spieler, *Spiller*
Spielman, *Spiller*
Spielmann, *Spiller*
Spier
Spierer, *Spier*
Spierling, *Sparrow*
Spiers, *Spear*
Spieser, *Speiser*
Spievak, *Spivak*
Spiewak, *Spivak*
Śpiewak, *Spivak*
Spigel, *Spiegler*
Spigelman, *Spiegler*
Spigler, *Spiegler*
Spillane
Spiller
Spilling
Spillings, *Spilling*
Spillman
Spillmann, *Spiller*
Spilman, *Spiller*
Spilsbury
Spina, *Épine*
Spinas, *Épine*
Spindel, *Spindler*
Spindler
Spinella, *Épine*
Spinelli, *Épine*
Spinello, *Épine*
Spinetti, *Épine*
Spini, *Épine*
Spiniello, *Épine*
Spink
Spinke, *Spink*
Spinks, *Spink*
Spino, *Épine*
Spínola, *Épine*
Spinozzi, *Épine*
Spira, *Spire*
Spire
Spirer, *Spire*
Spires, *Spire*
Spirett, *Spire*
Spiring, *Spire*
Spirit, *Spire*
Spiro, *Spire*
Spital, *Spittle*
Spitaleri, *Spittle*
Spitall, *Spittle*
Spitalnik, *Spittle*
Spiteri, *Spittle*
Spittel, *Spittle*
Spitteler, *Spittle*
Spittle
Spittler, *Spittle*
Spittles, *Spittle*
Spitz
Spitzer, *Spitz*
Spitzler, *Spitz*
Spitzman, *Spitz*
Spitzweg
Spivack, *Spivak*
Spivak
Spivakovsky, *Spivak*
Spiwak, *Spivak*
Spjut
Spjuth, *Spjut*
Splaine, *Spillane*
Splane, *Spillane*
Spock, *Spaak*
Spode
Spoffard, *Spofforth*
Spofford, *Spofforth*
Spofforth
Spohn, *Spooner*
Spohr, *Spohrer*
Spohrer
Spohrmann, *Spohrer*
Spollan, *Spillane*
Spollane, *Spillane*
Spollen, *Spillane*
Spolton, *Spaughton*
Spooner
Spoor, *Spohrer, Spurr*
Spoormaeker, *Spohrer*
Spoors, *Spurr*
Spore, *Spurr*
Spörer, *Spohrer*
Spörl, *Sparrow*
Spormann, *Spohrer*
Spörner, *Spohrer*
Sporran
Sporton, *Spaughton*
Sposito, *Esposito*
Spotswood, *Spottiswoode*
Spottiswood, *Spottiswoode*
Spottiswoode
Spotton, *Spaughton*
Spragg, *Spark*
Spragge, *Spark*
Sprague, *Spark*
Sprake, *Spark*
Spranger, *Springer*
Sprason, *Spray*
Spratt
Spray
Spreeuw, *Sparrow*
Sprenger, *Springer*
Sprigg
Spriggs, *Sprigg*
Spring
Springall
Springate, *Spring*
Springell, *Springall*
Springer
Springett, *Spring*
Springfield
Springhall, *Springall*
Springle, *Springall*
Sproat, *Sprott*
Sprott
Spruce
Spry
Spurling, *Sparrow*
Spurr
Spurren, *Sperrin*
Spurrier, *Spurr*
Spurring, *Sperrin*
Spurrs, *Spurr*
Spurway
Spychała, *Spychalski*
Spychalski
Squeers, *Squire*
Squibb
Squier, *Squire*
Squiers, *Squire*
Squire
Squires, *Squire*
Squirl, *Squirrel*
Squirrel
Squirrell, *Squirrel*
Šrámek, *Schramm*
Srb, *Serbinov*
Srba, *Serbinov*
Srbek, *Serbinov*
Srbík, *Serbinov*
Sroczyński, *Sroka*
Sroka
Srol, *Israel*
Sroloff, *Israel*
Srolov, *Israel*
Srolovitz, *Israel*
Srul, *Israel*
Srulevich, *Israel*
Srulewitch, *Israel*
Srulikov, *Israel*
Srulov, *Israel*
Srulovich, *Israel*
Srulovici, *Israel*
Srulovitz, *Israel*
Srulowitz, *Israel*
Staab, *Stabe*
Staal, *Steel*
Staap, *Stabe*
Staas, *Stace*
Staasen, *Stace*
Staat, *Stace*
Staats, *Stace*
Stabe
Stabeler, *Stables*
Stäble, *Stabe*
Stable, *Stables*
Stabler, *Stables*
Stables
Stace
Stacey, *Stace*
Stach, *Stace*
Stach
Stächelin, *Stace*
Stachl, *Stace*
Stachlewski, *Stach*
Stachowiak, *Stach*
Stachowicz, *Stach*
Stachowski, *Stach*
Stachura, *Stach*
Stachurski, *Stach*
Stachvanyonok, *Stephen*
Stack
Stackpole, *Stackpoole*
Stackpoole
Stacpoole, *Stackpoole*
Stad, *Stead*
Stadden, *Staddon*
Staddon
Stadel, *Stadler*
Stadelmann, *Stadler*
Stadler
Stadmann, *Stadler*
Städtler, *Stadler*
Stadtler, *Stadler*
Stadtmann, *Stadler*
Staes, *Stace*
Staesen, *Stace*
Staff, *Stabe*
Staffke, *Stephen*
Stafford
Staffurth, *Stafford*
Stagg
Stäheli, *Steel*
Stähelin, *Steel*
Ståhl, *Steel*
Stahl, *Steel*
Ståhlberg, *Steel*
Ståhle, *Steel*
Stähler, *Steel*
Stahler, *Steel*
Stählin, *Steel*
Stæhr, *Starling*
Staiger, *Steiger*
Stain, *Stein*
Stainburn
Stainer
Staines
Stainmetz, *Steinmetz*
Stainsby
Stainthorpe
Stainton, *Stanton*
Stait
Stak, *Stack*
Stake, *Stack*
Stakes
Stakhanov
Stakheev, *Stakhanov*
Stakhevich, *Stakhanov*
Stakhovich, *Stakhanov*
Stål, *Steel*
Stålberg, *Steel*
Stalder
Staley, *Stallard*
Stalker
Stallard
Stalley, *Stallard*
Stallmach, *Stellmacher*
Stallwood, *Stallard*
Stallworthy, *Stallard*
Stalworthy, *Stallard*

Stam, *Stamm*
Stamford, *Stanford*
Stamitz, *Steinmetz*
Stamm
Stammer
Stammers, *Stammer*
Stamp
Stamps, *Stamp*
Stanberry, *Stanbury*
Stanborough, *Stanbury*
Stanbra, *Stanbury*
Stanbridge
Stanbury
Stancliffe
Stańczak, *Stanisławski*
Stańczyk, *Stanisławski*
Stańczykowski, *Stanisławski*
Standage, *Standish*
Standen
Standeven
Standford, *Stanford*
Standidge, *Standish*
Standing, *Standen*
Standish
Standley, *Stanley*
Stanecki, *Stanisławski*
Staněk, *Stanisławski*
Stanek, *Stanisławski*
Stanford
Stanger
Stanhope
Staniak, *Stanisławski*
Staniaszczyk, *Stanisławski*
Staniaszek, *Stanisławski*
Stanić, *Stanisławski*
Staniecki, *Stanisławski*
Stanier
Staniford, *Stanford*
Staniforth, *Stanford*
Stanikowski, *Stanisławski*
Stanilewicz, *Stanisławski*
Stanisavljević, *Stanisławski*
Stanišić, *Stanisławski*
Stanislav, *Stanisławski*
Stanislavsky, *Stanisławski*
Stanisławski
Stanisz, *Stanisławski*
Staniszewski, *Stanisławski*
Stankiewicz, *Stanisławski*
Stanković, *Stanisławski*
Stankowski, *Stanisławski*
Stanleigh, *Stanley*
Stanley
Stanly, *Stanley*
Stanmore, *Stammer*
Stannard
Stannett, *Stannard*
Stansbie, *Stainsby*
Stansfeld, *Stansfield*
Stansfield
Stanton
Stanyer, *Stanier*
Stanyforth, *Stanford*
Stapanian, *Stephen*
Staple
Staples, *Staple*
Stapleton
Stapley
Stapylton, *Stapleton*
Starčević, *Starikov*
Stärck, *Stark*
Starck, *Stark*
Starcke, *Stark*
Starcks, *Stark*
Starczewski, *Starikov*
Starczyk, *Starikov*
Stárek, *Starikov*
Starek, *Starikov*
Staricoff, *Starikov*
Starik, *Starikov*
Starikov
Stark
Starke, *Stark*
Stärkel, *Stark*
Starker, *Stark*
Starkey, *Stark*
Starkie, *Stark*
Starkings, *Stark*
Stärkle, *Stark*
Starkman, *Stark*
Starkmann, *Stark*
Starling
Starman, *Starr*
Staroń, *Starikov*
Staroske, *Starikov*
Starosta
Starostecki, *Starosta*
Starov, *Starikov*
Starr
Starrett, *Start*
Starshenko, *Starikov*
Starski, *Starikov*
Start
Starte, *Start*
Startifant, *Sturtivant*
Startin
Starý, *Starikov*
Starzycki, *Starikov*
Starzyk, *Starikov*
Starzyński, *Starikov*
Stasewski, *Stanisławski*
Stasewsky, *Stanisławski*
Stashevski, *Stanisławski*
Stashevsky, *Stanisławski*
Stashewski, *Stanisławski*
Stashewsky, *Stanisławski*
Stashinin, *Stakhanov*
Stasi, *Anstice*
Stasiak, *Stanisławski*
Stasiński, *Stanisławski*
Stasio, *Anstice*
Staśkiewicz, *Stanisławski*
Stasov, *Stakhanov*
Stassen, *Anstice*
Stassi, *Anstice*
Stassino, *Anstice*
Št'astný
Staszak, *Stanisławski*
Staszczyk, *Stanisławski*
Staszewski, *Stanisławski*
Staszkiewicz, *Stanisławski*
Statham
Stauch, *Stauche*
Stauche
Staude
Stäuder, *Staude*
Stäudle, *Staude*
Staudt, *Staude*
Staufer, *Stauffer*
Staufert, *Stauffer*
Stauffer
Staunton, *Stanton*
Stawiak, *Stawski*
Stawicki, *Stawski*
Stawiński, *Stawski*
Stawiszyński, *Stawski*
Stawowski, *Stawski*
Stawski
Staziker, *Stirzaker*
Stead
Steadman, *Stead*
Stear, *Steer*
Stearman, *Steer*
Stearn, *Stern*
Stearne, *Stern*
Stearns, *Stern*
Stears, *Steer*
Stebbing
Stebbings, *Stebbing*
Štěch, *Stephen*
Steckel, *Styles*
Steckelmacher, *Steckler*
Steckelman, *Steckler*
Steckl, *Steckler*
Steckler
Stede, *Stead*
Stedman, *Stead*
Stedmont, *Stead*
Steed, *Stead*
Steede, *Stead*
Steedman, *Stead*
Steeds, *Stead*
Steeg, *Steiger*
Steel
Steele, *Steel*
Steels, *Steel*
Steeman, *Stead*
Steen, *Stein, Stone*
Steenke, *Stone*
Steenken, *Stone*
Steenman, *Stone*
Steenmann, *Stone*
Steenson, *Stein*
Steenstra, *Stone*
Steeples
Steer
Steere, *Steer*
Steers, *Steer*
Steert, *Start*
Stefan, *Stephen*
Štefan, *Stephen*
Stefanczyk, *Stephen*
Stefanek, *Stephen*
Stefanelli, *Stephen*
Stefanescu, *Stephen*
Stefani, *Stephen*
Stefaniak, *Stephen*
Stefanini, *Stephen*
Stefankiewicz, *Stephen*
Stefano, *Stephen*
Stefanoni, *Stephen*
Stefanov, *Stephen*
Stefanović, *Stephen*
Stefanowicz, *Stephen*
Stefanowski, *Stephen*
Stefansen, *Stephen*
Stefanski, *Stephen*
Stefanutti, *Stephen*
Stefanutto, *Stephen*
Štefek, *Stephen*
Steff, *Stephen*
Steffan, *Stephen*
Steffani, *Stephen*
Steffanini, *Stephen*
Steffek, *Stephen*
Steffen, *Stephen*
Steffens, *Stephen*
Steffensen, *Stephen*
Steffke, *Stephen*
Steffl, *Stephen*
Stefi, *Stephen*
Stefutti, *Stephen*
Steg, *Steiger*
Stegel, *Styles*
Stegell, *Styles*
Stegeman, *Steiger*
Stegemann, *Steiger*
Stegena, *Steiger*
Steger, *Steiger*
Steggall, *Styles*
Steggalls, *Styles*
Steggals, *Styles*
Steggle, *Styles*
Steggles, *Styles*
Stegman, *Steiger*
Stegmann, *Steiger*
Stegner, *Steiger*
Stehlík, *Szczygieł*
Stehmann, *Stone*
Stehn, *Stone*
Stehnke, *Stone*
Stehnmann, *Stone*
Steichen, *Stauche*
Steidle, *Staude*
Steig, *Steiger*
Steiger
Steigman, *Steiger*
Steimann, *Stone*
Stein
Steinbach, *Stone*
Steinbaum, *Stone*
Steinberg, *Stone*
Steinberger, *Stone*
Steinchen, *Stone*
Steindl, *Stone*
Steinecke, *Stone*
Steineke, *Stone*
Steinemann, *Stone*
Steiner, *Stainer, Stone*
Steinert, *Stone*
Steinfeld, *Stone*
Steingart, *Stone*
Steingarten, *Stone*
Steingold, *Stone*
Steinhard, *Stone*
Steinhardt, *Stone*
Steinhertz, *Stone*
Steinherz, *Stone*
Steinhorn, *Stone*
Steinhouse, *Stonehouse*
Steinicke, *Stone*
Steinig, *Stone*
Steiniger, *Stone*
Steinke, *Stone*
Steinl, *Stone*
Steinle, *Stone*
Steinman, *Stone*
Steinmann, *Stone*
Steinmassel, *Steinmetz*
Steinmeissel, *Steinmetz*
Steinmetz
Steinmetzel, *Steinmetz*
Steinor, *Stainer*
Steinreich, *Stone*
Steinway, *Steinweg*
Steinweg
Steinwercel, *Stone*
Steinwurzel, *Stone*
Stejskal
Stekel, *Styles*
Stekler, *Steckler*
Stekles, *Styles*
Stell, *Still*
Stella
Stellacci, *Stella*
Stelli, *Stella*

Stellin, *Stella*
Stellini, *Stella*
Stellino, *Stella*
Stellmach, *Stellmacher*
Stellmacher
Stellon, *Stella*
Stelloni, *Stella*
Stelmach, *Stellmacher*
Stelmashenko, *Stellmacher*
Stelmashonok, *Stellmacher*
Stelmasiak, *Stellmacher*
Stelmaszczyk, *Stellmacher*
Sten, *Stone*
Stenbäck, *Stone*
Stenberg, *Stone*
Stendahl, *Stendal*
Stendal
Stendel, *Stendal*
Stendhal, *Stendal*
Stenholm, *Stone*
Stenhouse
Stenius, *Stone*
Stenman, *Stone*
Stenmark, *Stone*
Stenner, *Stone*
Stenning
Steno, *Stephen*
Stenqvist, *Stone*
Stenson
Stenström, *Stone*
Stenton, *Stanton*
Stenton, *Stenson*
Štěpán, *Stephen*
Stepanaitis, *Stephen*
Stepanchikov, *Stephen*
Štěpánek, *Stephen*
Stepanenko, *Stephen*
Stepanets, *Stephen*
Stepanichev, *Stephen*
Stepanishchev, *Stephen*
Stepanov, *Stephen*
Stepanović, *Stephen*
Stepanychev, *Stephen*
Stępczyński, *Stępień*
Stephan, *Stephen*
Stéphane, *Stephen*
Stephanelli, *Stephen*
Stephanello, *Stephen*
Stephani, *Stephen*
Stephano, *Stephen*
Stephansen, *Stephen*
Stephen
Stephens, *Stephen*
Stephensen, *Stephen*
Stephenson, *Stephen*
Stephinson, *Stephen*
Stepichev, *Stephen*
Stępień
Stępiński, *Stępień*
Stepishchev, *Stephen*
Stepke, *Stephen*
Stępkowski, *Stępień*
Stęplewski, *Stępień*
Stępniak, *Stępień*
Štěpnička, *Stephen*
Stępniewski, *Stępień*
Stępnik, *Stępień*
Stepovich, *Stephen*
Stępowski, *Stępień*
Steppan, *Stephen*
Steppuhn, *Stephen*
Stepulev, *Stephen*
Stepunin, *Stephen*
Stepura, *Stephen*
Stepurin, *Stephen*
Stepykin, *Stephen*
Stepynin, *Stephen*
Stepyryov, *Stephen*
Stepyuk, *Stephen*
Štěrba
Stercken, *Stark*
Sterckens, *Stark*
Sterckmans, *Stark*
Sterckx, *Stark*
Sterdt, *Start*
Sterenberg, *Starr*
Sterental, *Starr*
Sterenzis, *Starr*
Sterk, *Stark*
Sterkmans, *Stark*
Sterling, *Stirling*
Sterman, *Steer*
Stern
Sternbach, *Starr*
Sternbaum, *Starr*
Sternberg, *Starr*
Sternberger, *Starr*
Sternblitz, *Starr*
Sternbuch, *Starr*
Sterne, *Stern*
Sternfeld, *Starr*
Sternfinkel, *Starr*
Sternfinkiel, *Starr*
Sternglanz, *Starr*
Sternglass, *Starr*
Sternheim, *Starr*
Sternhell, *Starr*
Sternhertz, *Starr*
Sternklar, *Starr*
Sternkuker, *Starr*
Sternlib, *Starr*
Sternlicht, *Starr*
Sternlieb, *Starr*
Sterns, *Stern*
Sternschein, *Starr*
Sternschuss, *Starr*
Sternshos, *Starr*
Sterntal, *Starr*
Sternthal, *Starr*
Sternzis, *Starr*
Sterritt, *Start*
Stersaker, *Stirzaker*
Stert, *Start*
Stertz, *Start*
Stertzel, *Start*
Steshenko, *Stephen*
Štětina
Stetskiv, *Stephen*
Stetsyuk, *Stephen*
Stetsyura, *Stephen*
Steuart, *Stewart*
Steuben, *Stubbe*
Steubesand, *Stuyvesant*
Steudle, *Staude*
Steur, *Sturgeon*
Stevaen, *Stephen*
Stevanelli, *Stephen*
Stevani, *Stephen*
Stevanini, *Stephen*
Stevano, *Stephen*
Stevanović, *Stephen*
Steven, *Stephen*
Stevenel, *Stephen*
Stevenet, *Stephen*
Stevenin, *Stephen*
Stevens, *Stephen*
Stevenson, *Stephen*
Steventon
Steverson, *Stephen*
Stević, *Stephen*
Stevinga, *Stephen*
Stevinson, *Stephen*
Stevović, *Stephen*
Steward, *Stewart*
Stewardson, *Stewart*
Stewart
Stewartson, *Stewart*
St George, *Saint-Georges*
Stibor
Stícha, *Stephen*
Stickel, *Styles*
Stickells, *Styles*
Stickels, *Styles*
Stickles, *Styles*
Stiddard, *Stoddart*
Stiddolph
Stidolph, *Stiddolph*
Stief, *Stephen*
Stiefel
Stiefke, *Stephen*
Stiefler, *Stiefel*
Stieger, *Steiger*
Stiegler, *Styles*
Stieglitz, *Szczygiel*
Stiehr, *Steer*
Stienen, *Austin*
Stienes, *Austin*
Stienfeld, *Stone*
Stienke, *Austin*
Stienmets, *Steinmetz*
Stienmetz, *Steinmetz*
Stier, *Steer*
Stierle, *Steer*
Stierman, *Steer*
Sties, *Stephen*
Stievano, *Stephen*
Stiévenard, *Stephen*
Stiévenart, *Stephen*
Stifanelli, *Stephen*
Stifani, *Stephen*
Stifano, *Stephen*
Stiff
Stiffelman, *Stiefel*
Stigand
Stigant, *Stigand*
Stiggants, *Stigand*
Stiggins, *Stigand*
Stiggles, *Styles*
Stigler, *Styles*
Stiglitz, *Szczygiel*
Stile, *Styles*
Stileman, *Styles*
Stiles, *Styles*
Still
Stille, *Still*
Stiller, *Still*
Stillert, *Still*
Stillingfleet
Stillman, *Still*
Stilman, *Still*
Stimpson, *Stenson*
Stimson, *Stenson*
Stinchcombe
Stinnes, *Austin*
Stinson, *Stenson*
Stirk
Stirland, *Strickland*
Stirling
Stirrup
Stirsacre, *Stirzaker*
Stirton, *Startin*
Stirzaker
Stitt, *Studd*
Stivanelli, *Stephen*
Stivani, *Stephen*
Stivanini, *Stephen*
Stivelman, *Stiefel*
Stiven, *Stephen*
Stjernqvist, *Starr*
Stjernström, *Starr*
St John, *Saint-Jean*
Stoak, *Stoke*
Stoaks, *Stoke*
Stobart, *Stobbart*
Stobbart
Stobbe, *Stubbe*
Stobbs, *Stubbe*
Stöbesand, *Stuyvesant*
Stobie
Stobo, *Stobie*
Stock
Stockdale
Stockdill, *Stockdale*
Stocke, *Stock*
Stöcken, *Stock*
Stocken, *Stock*
Stöcker, *Stock*
Stocker, *Stock*
Stöckle, *Stock*
Stockleigh, *Stockley*
Stockley
Stockman, *Stock*
Stöckmann, *Stock*
Stockmann, *Stock*
Stocks, *Stock*
Stockton
Stockwell
Stodart, *Stoddart*
Stoddard, *Stoddart*
Stoddart
Stodhart, *Stoddart*
Stöffel, *Christopher*
Stoffel, *Christopher*
Stoffels, *Christopher*
Stöffen, *Stephen*
Stoffer, *Christopher*
Stoffers, *Christopher*
Stoffersen, *Christopher*
Stoffler, *Christopher*
Stogdale, *Stockdale*
Stok, *Stock*
Stoke
Stökel, *Stock*
Stokeley, *Stockley*
Stokely, *Stockley*
Stoker
Stokes, *Stoke*
Stokoe
Stokowski
Stolar, *Stolarski*
Stolarczyk, *Stolarski*
Stolarek, *Stolarski*
Stolarski
Stolarz, *Stolarski*
Stoldt, *Stolz*
Stoler, *Stolarski*
Stolersky, *Stolarski*
Stoliar, *Stolarski*
Stollard, *Stallard*
Stoller, *Stolarski*
Stolt, *Stolz*
Stolte, *Stolz*
Stolten, *Stolz*
Stolter, *Stolz*
Stölting, *Stolz*
Stolting, *Stolz*

Stoltz, *Stolz*
Stoltze, *Stolz*
Stöltzel, *Stolz*
Stolworthy, *Stallard*
Stolyarov, *Stolarski*
Stolz
Stolze, *Stolz*
Stölzel, *Stolz*
Stonard, *Stannard*
Stone
Stoneham
Stonehouse
Stoneman, *Stone*
Stoner, *Stone*
Stones, *Stone*
Stonham, *Stoneham*
Stonhard, *Stannard*
Stonier, *Stanier*
Stonor
Stook, *Stoke*
Stookes, *Stoke*
Stopard, *Stopford*
Stopford
Stopforth, *Stopford*
Stopher, *Christopher*
Stoppard, *Stopford*
Stopper, *Stopford*
Storah, *Storer*
Storch, *Stork*
Störchel, *Stork*
Storck, *Stork*
Stordy, *Sturdy*
Storer
Stores, *Storer*
Storey
Storie, *Storey*
Stork
Störkel, *Stork*
Storm
Storme, *Storm*
Stormes, *Storm*
Storms, *Storm*
Storr, *Storey*
Storrar, *Storer*
Storrie, *Storey*
Storror, *Storer*
Storrow, *Storer*
Storti, *Tort*
Storto, *Tort*
Stortone, *Tort*
Story, *Storey*
Stothard, *Stoddart*
Stothart, *Stoddart*
Stothert, *Stoddart*
Stott
Stourton
Stout
Stoute, *Stout*
Stoutt, *Stout*
Stövesand, *Stuyvesant*
Stow
Stowe, *Stow*
Stöwesand, *Stuyvesant*
Straatman, *Street*
Strachan
Strack, *Astruc*
Strada, *Street*
Stradella, *Street*
Stradi, *Street*
Stradivari
Stradtmann, *Street*
Straeter, *Street*
Straetje, *Street*
Straetjes, *Street*
Strafford, *Stratford*
Stragio, *Strange*
Strahan, *Strachan*
Strahl
Strahler, *Strahl*
Strain, *Strachan*
Strainge, *Strange*
Strak, *Astruc*
Straka, *Sroka*
Straker, *Striker*
Strand
Strandberg, *Strand*
Strandh, *Strand*
Straneo, *Strange*
Strang, *Strong*
Strange
Stranger, *Strange*
Strangeway, *Strangeways*
Strangeways
Strangewick, *Strangeways*
Strangman, *Strong*
Strangways, *Strangeways*
Strani, *Strange*
Stranieri, *Strange*
Straniero, *Strange*
Stranio, *Strange*
Strano, *Strange*
Stránský
Strasman, *Street*
Strasser, *Street*
Strässler, *Street*
Strassler, *Street*
Strassmann, *Street*
Strässner, *Street*
Strassner, *Street*
Stratfield
Stratford
Strathmann, *Street*
Strating, *Street*
Stratmann, *Street*
Stratton
Straub
Strauber, *Straub*
Sträuble, *Straub*
Straughan, *Strachan*
Straus, *Strauss*
Strauss
Sträussle, *Strauss*
Straussman, *Strauss*
Straussmann, *Strauss*
Strausz, *Strauss*
Straw
Streake, *Streek*
Streat, *Street*
Streater, *Street*
Streatfield, *Stratfield*
Streatley
Streek
Streep
Street
Streete, *Street*
Streeter, *Street*
Streetley, *Streatley*
Streetly, *Streatley*
Streets, *Street*
Streicher, *Striker*
Streissle, *Strauss*
Strelchenko, *Streltsov*
Strelchuk, *Streltsov*
Strelec, *Streltsov*
Streletz, *Streltsov*
Střelka, *Streltsov*
Strelley, *Streatley*
Streltsov
Streng, *Strong*
Strete, *Street*
Stretfield, *Stratfield*
Strettell
Stretton, *Stratton*
Strickland
Stride
Strike, *Striker*
Striker
Strindberg, *Strand*
String, *Stringer*
Stringer
Stringfellow
Strnad
Strobel, *Straub*
Strode, *Stroud*
Stroev
Stroganoff, *Stroganov*
Stroganov
Strogonov, *Stroganov*
Stroh, *Straw*
Strohane
Ströhlein, *Straw*
Strohman, *Straw*
Strohmann, *Straw*
Stroic, *Astruc*
Stroich, *Astruc*
Strom, *Ström*
Ström
Strömbäck, *Ström*
Strömberg, *Ström*
Strömblad, *Ström*
Strömblom, *Ström*
Strömbom, *Ström*
Strömgren, *Ström*
Strömqvist, *Ström*
Strömvall, *Ström*
Strömwall, *Ström*
Stromwasser, *Ström*
Stronach
Strong
Stronge, *Strong*
Strongitharm, *Armstrong*
Stroock, *Astruc*
Strood, *Stroud*
Strook, *Astruc*
Stroud
Stroux, *Astruc*
Stróżyński
Strube, *Straub*
Strubel, *Straub*
Strübing, *Straub*
Strudwick
Strufe, *Straub*
Strüfing, *Straub*
Struijs, *Strauss*
Strumiłło
Strumiński, *Strumiłło*
Strusman, *Strauss*
Struss, *Strauss*
Strussgen, *Strauss*
Struthers
Strutt
Strutz, *Strauss*
Struwe, *Straub*
Strüwing, *Straub*
Struys, *Strauss*
Strzałkowski
Strzelczyk, *Streltsov*
Strzelecki, *Streltsov*
Stuart, *Stewart*
Stubbe
Stubber, *Stubbe*
Stubbert, *Stobbart*
Stubbings, *Stebbing*
Stubbins, *Stebbing*
Stubbs, *Stubbe*
Stübe, *Stubbe*
Stubley
Stucley, *Stukeley*
Studart, *Stoddart*
Studd
Studdard, *Stoddart*
Studdeard, *Stoddart*
Studdert, *Stoddart*
Stüde, *Staude*
Stüdemann, *Staude*
Stüder, *Staude*
Stüdle, *Staude*
Studley
Studman, *Studd*
Studniarek, *Studziński*
Studnicki, *Studziński*
Studzieński, *Studziński*
Studziński
Stühmann, *Staude*
Stukeley
Stukely, *Stukeley*
Stümbcke, *Stümbke*
Stümbke
Stümcke, *Stümbke*
Stümke, *Stümbke*
Stump
Stümpke, *Stümbke*
Sturdee, *Sturdy*
Sturdevant, *Sturtivant*
Sturdy
Sturdza, *Étourneau*
Sturge, *Sturgess*
Sturgeon
Sturges, *Sturgess*
Sturgess
Sturgis, *Sturgess*
Sturm, *Storm*
Sturman
Sturmi, *Storm*
Stürmle, *Storm*
Sturmli, *Storm*
Sturraker, *Stirzaker*
Sturrock
Sturrocks, *Sturrock*
Stursaker, *Stirzaker*
Sturt, *Start*
Sturtevant, *Sturtivant*
Sturtivant
Sturza, *Étourneau*
Sturzaker, *Stirzaker*
Stutt, *Stout*
Stuttard, *Stoddart*
Stüve, *Stubbe*
Stüven, *Stubbe*
Stüwe, *Stubbe*
Stuyvesant
Styan, *Stigand*
Styance, *Stigand*
Styants, *Stigand*
Styczyński
Stygal, *Styles*
Stygall, *Styles*
Style, *Styles*
Styles
Styokhin, *Stephen*
Styopushkin, *Stephen*
Suárez, *Suero*
Subileau, *Sibley*
Subirà, *Soubeyre*
Subirana, *Soubeyre*
Subirats, *Soubeyre*

Subrero, *Soubeyre*
Šubrt, *Schubert*
Suc
Such
Suchan, *Suchý*
Suchánek, *Suchý*
Suchat, *Suc*
Suchecki, *Suchý*
Suchet, *Suc*
Suchocki, *Suchý*
Suchý
Suckling
Suddaby, *Sotheby*
Sudell
Sudermann, *South*
Sudour, *Sauter*
Sudran, *South*
Sudre, *Sauter*
Sudron, *South*
Sudworth
Suero
Sueur, *Sauter*
Suffert, *Siegfried*
Süfke, *Siegfried*
Sugarman, *Zucker*
Sugden
Sugdon, *Sugden*
Suggate, *Southgate*
Suggett, *Southgate*
Suggitt, *Southgate*
Sugrue
Suhr, *Sauer*
Suhrmann, *Sauer*
Suiker, *Zucker*
Suikerman, *Zucker*
Suikermans, *Zucker*
Suire, *Sauter*
Suk
Šulc, *Schultz*
Suliman, *Salomon*
Sulimani, *Salomon*
Sulimanian, *Salomon*
Sulimanof, *Salomon*
Sulimanoff, *Salomon*
Sullevan, *Sullivan*
Sulley
Sullivan
Sully
Sultan, *Sowden*
Summer
Summerfield, *Somerville, Summer*
Summerhayes
Summerhill
Summerlad
Summerland, *Summerlad*
Summerly
Summers, *Summer*
Summerscale, *Somerscales*
Summerscales, *Somerscales*
Summersett, *Somerset*
Summersgill, *Somerscales*
Summerskill, *Somerscales*
Summerson, *Summer*
Summerville, *Somerville*
Sumner
Sumpner, *Sumner*
Sumpter
Sund
Sundberg, *Sund*
Sundblad, *Sund*
Sundelin, *Sund*
Sundelius, *Sund*
Sundell, *Sund*
Sundén, *Sund*
Sunderland
Sundgren, *Sund*
Sundh, *Sund*
Sundin, *Sund*
Sundman, *Sund*
Sundqvist, *Sund*
Sundstedt, *Sund*
Sundström, *Sund*
Sundvall, *Sund*
Sundwall, *Sund*
Suñé, *Sunyer*
Suñer, *Sunyer*
Sunshine, *Sonnenschein*
Sunter, *Sumpter*
Sunyé, *Sunyer*
Sunyer
Suominen
Suquet, *Suc*
Surby, *Sowerby*
Surcoate, *Circuit*
Surcot, *Circuit*
Surcutt, *Circuit*
Surdi, *Sourd*
Surdo, *Sourd*
Sureau
Surel, *Sureau*
Surgener, *Surgeon*
Surgenor, *Surgeon*
Surgeon
Surgeoner, *Surgeon*
Surgey, *Surgeon*
Surgison, *Sergeant*
Surin, *Séverin*
Surin, *Sorin*
Suris, *Sorin*
Surizon, *Sorin*
Surkes, *Sorin*
Surkin, *Sorin*
Surkis, *Sorin*
Surman, *Sermon*
Surmon, *Sermon*
Surowiec
Surowiecki, *Surowiec*
Surrage, *Surridge*
Surridge
Surtees
Surtill, *Shortall*
Susin, *Zisin*
Suskin, *Zisin*
Suskovitz, *Zisin*
Süss, *Sweet*
Suss, *Sweet*
Sussapfel, *Sweet*
Süsse, *Sweet*
Susser, *Sweet*
Sussholz, *Sweet*
Süsskin, *Zisin*
Susskind, *Süsskind*
Süsskind
Susskovitch, *Zisin*
Sussman, *Sweet*
Süssmann, *Sweet*
Sussmann, *Sweet*
Sussmanowitz, *Sweet*
Šusta, *Schuster*
Sutch, *Such*
Sutcliff, *Sutcliffe*
Sutcliffe
Suter, *Sauter*
Sutherby, *Sotheby*
Sutherin, *South*
Sutherlan, *Sutherland*
Sutherland
Suthern, *South*
Suthren, *South*
Sutor, *Sauter*
Sutter, *Sauter*
Sutterer, *Sauter*
Sütterle, *Sauter*
Sütterlin, *Sauter*
Sutton
Suwalski
Sváb, *Schwab*
Šváb, *Schwab*
Sváček, *Svatoš*
Svach, *Svatoš*
Svačina, *Svatoš*
Svahn, *Swan*
Svanberg, *Swan*
Švanda, *Svatoš*
Svane, *Swan*
Svanetti, *John*
Svanini, *John*
Svanström, *Swan*
Švarc, *Schwarz*
Svärd, *Sword*
Svärdh, *Sword*
Svášek, *Svatoš*
Svátek, *Svatoš*
Svatoň, *Svatoš*
Svatoš
Švec, *Szewc*
Svedberg, *Svedin*
Svedin
Švehelka, *Svehla*
Švehla
Švehlák, *Svehla*
Švehlík, *Svehla*
Švejcar, *Schweitzer*
Švejda, *Schweder*
Svendsen, *Swain*
Svenningsen, *Swain*
Svensson, *Swain*
Svoboda
Swaab, *Schwab*
Swaby
Swaelu, *Swallow*
Swaelus, *Swallow*
Swahn, *Swan*
Swain
Swaine, *Swain*
Swainson, *Swain*
Swalke, *Swallow*
Swallow
Swaluwe, *Swallow*
Swan
Swanie, *Swan*
Swann, *Swan*
Swannell
Swanney, *Swan*
Swansborough
Swansbury, *Swansborough*
Swanson, *Swan*
Swanston
Swanton
Swanwick
Swarbrick
Swart, *Schwarz*
Swarte, *Schwarz*
Swatkins, *Watt*
Swatman, *Sweet*
Swayn, *Swain*
Swayne, *Swain*
Sweatman, *Sweet*
Swedberg, *Svedin*
Swedenborg, *Svedin*
Swedlund, *Svedin*
Sweeney
Sweet
Sweeting
Sweetman, *Sweet*
Sweetsir
Sweetsur, *Sweetsir*
Sweetzer, *Sweetsir*
Swemmer, *Schwemmer*
Swenerton, *Swinnerton*
Swenson, *Swain*
Swerts, *Schwarz*
Swetman, *Sweet*
Swett, *Sweet*
Sweynson, *Swain*
Świątczak, *Świątek*
Świątek
Świątkowski, *Świątek*
Swibel, *Zwiebel*
Świderek, *Świderski*
Świderski
Święcicki, *Świątek*
Świercz
Świerczyński, *Świercz*
Swiers, *Squire*
Swift
Swinarton, *Swinnerton*
Swinbourn, *Swinburn*
Swinbourne, *Swinburn*
Swinburn
Swinburne, *Swinburn*
Swindell, *Swindells*
Swindells
Swindlehurst
Swinerton, *Swinnerton*
Swiney, *Sweeney*
Swinglehurst, *Swindlehurst*
Swingler
Swinley
Swinnerton
Swinnington, *Swinnerton*
Swinscoe
Swinton
Swire, *Squire*
Swires, *Squire*
Swithenbank
Switser, *Schweitzer*
Switsur, *Sweetsir*
Switzer, *Sweetsir*
Swonnell, *Swannell*
Sword
Sworde, *Sword*
Sworder, *Sword*
Swyer, *Squire*
Swynerton, *Swinnerton*
Swynnerton, *Swinnerton*
Sy, *Siegel*
Syarkeev, *Sergio*
Syddenham, *Sydenham*
Sydenham
Sydney, *Sidney*
Sye, *Siegel*
Sykes
Sýkora, *Sikora*
Sylburski, *Silver*
Sylvain, *Selwyn*
Sylvaine, *Selwyn*
Sylvest, *Silvester*
Sylvester, *Silvester*
Sylvestre, *Silvester*
Sylwester, *Silvester*
Sylwestrowicz, *Silvester*
Sylwestrowski, *Silvester*
Sylwestrzak, *Silvester*
Symber, *Samper*

Symbestyrek, *Silvester*
Symcox, *Sim*
Syme, *Sim*
Symers, *Summer*
Symes, *Simson*
Symington
Symmers, *Summer*
Symmons, *Simon*
Symms, *Simson*
Symon, *Simon*
Symonds, *Simon*
Symondson, *Simon*
Symons, *Simon*
Syms, *Simson*
Synnot, *Sinnott*
Synnott, *Sinnott*
Synot, *Sinnott*
Syomin, *Simon*
Sypniewski
Syrad, *Syrett*
Syratt, *Syrett*
Syred, *Syrett*
Syrett
Syrový, *Surowiec*
Syson, *Simon*
Szablewski
Szabliński, *Szablewski*
Szabłowski, *Szablewski*
Szabó
Szadkowski
Szafran, *Safran*
Szafrański, *Safran*
Szainfeld, *Schön*
Szajn, *Schön*
Szajner, *Schön*
Szántó
Szapira, *Shapiro*
Szapiro, *Shapiro*
Szaposznik, *Shapochnikov*
Szappanos, *Soper*
Szarf, *Sharp*
Szarfharc, *Sharp*
Szarfherc, *Sharp*
Szarfstein, *Sharp*
Szász, *Sachs*
Szászy, *Sachs*
Szatz, *Schatz*
Szczeciński
Szczepanek, *Stephen*
Szczepaniak, *Stephen*
Szczepanik, *Stephen*
Szczepankiewicz, *Stephen*
Szczepanowicz, *Stephen*
Szczepanowski, *Stephen*
Szczepański, *Stephen*
Szczerba, *Štěrba*
Szczerbiak, *Štěrba*
Szczęścikowicz, *Šťastný*
Szczęśniak, *Šťastný*
Szcześniak, *Šťastný*
Szczęśnowicz, *Šťastný*
Szczęsny, *Šťastný*
Szczupak, *Shchukin*
Szczupakiewicz, *Shchukin*
Szczygiel
Szczygielski, *Szczygiel*
Szechter, *Schechter*
Szefer, *Schäfer*
Szeinfeld, *Schön*
Szeinkman, *Schenke*
Szeinrok, *Schön*
Szejn, *Schön*
Szejnberg, *Schön*
Szejnbojm, *Schön*
Szeles, *Széll*
Széll
Szenbrot, *Schön*
Szenes, *Scheinis*
Szenfeld, *Schön*
Szenkier, *Schenke*
Szente, *Saint*
Szentgyörgyi, *Saint-Georges*
Szepe, *Joseph*
Szerb, *Serbinov*
Szerer, *Shearer*
Szereszewski, *Sierota*
Szerman, *Sherman*
Szewc
Szewczyk, *Szewc*
Szichman, *Schuh*
Szigeti
Szimon, *Simon*
Szimoni, *Simon*
Szimszewicz, *Samson*
Szklar
Szklarek, *Szklar*
Szklarski, *Szklar*
Szkoler, *Schuler*
Szkolerman, *Schuler*
Szkolnik, *Schuler*
Szkudlarek
Szlachter, *Slaughter*
Szlezynger, *Schlessinger*
Szlezyngier, *Schlessinger*
Szlomowicz, *Salomon*
Szlosberg, *Schlossberg*
Szmidman, *Smith*
Szmidt, *Smith*
Szmigiel
Szmigielski, *Szmigiel*
Szmit, *Smith*
Szmuel, *Samuel*
Szmul, *Samuel*
Szmulewicz, *Samuel*
Szmulewitz, *Samuel*
Szmyt, *Smith*
Sznajder, *Schneider*
Sznajderman, *Schneider*
Sznejberg, *Snow*
Sznejor, *Schneir*
Szochatowicz, *Shoikhet*
Szochet, *Shoikhet*
Szor, *Schauer*
Szostak, *Shostakovich*
Szostek, *Shostakovich*
Szotland, *Scotland*
Szpajzer, *Speiser*
Szpilberg, *Spielberg*
Szpilman, *Spiller*
Szrajner, *Schreiner*
Szram, *Schramm*
Szrayer, *Schreier*
Szreiber, *Schreiber*
Szrejner, *Schreiner*
Sztajn, *Stone*
Sztajnbaum, *Stone*
Sztajnberg, *Stone*
Sztein, *Stone*
Szteinberg, *Stone*
Sztejnbaum, *Stone*
Sztejnberg, *Stone*
Sztejnman, *Stone*
Szterenbojm, *Starr*
Sztern, *Starr*
Szternfinkel, *Starr*
Szternzys, *Starr*
Sztolc, *Stolz*
Sztrom, *Ström*
Szuba
Szubert, *Schubert*
Szubski, *Szuba*
Szulc, *Schultz*
Szulczewski, *Schultz*
Szulman, *Schuler*
Szulsinger, *Schuler*
Szurgot
Szürke
Szuster, *Schuster*
Szwajcer, *Schweitzer*
Szwalb, *Swallow*
Szwarc, *Schwarz*
Szwed, *Schweder*
Szwedziński, *Schweder*
Szweitzer, *Schweitzer*
Szydłowiecki, *Szydłowski*
Szydłowski
Szymanczyk, *Simon*
Szymanek, *Simon*
Szymaniak, *Simon*
Szymankiewicz, *Simon*
Szymanowicz, *Simon*
Szymanowski, *Simon*
Szymański, *Simon*
Szymczak, *Simon*
Szymczewski, *Simon*
Szymczyk, *Simon*
Szymczykiewicz, *Simon*
Szymczyński, *Simon*
Szymkiewicz, *Simon*
Szymon, *Simon*
Szymoni, *Simon*
Szymonowicz, *Simon*

T

Taaffe, *David*
Tabacznik, *Tabak*
Tabah, *Tabor*
Tabak
Tabakero, *Tabak*
Tabakman, *Tabak*
Tabard
Tabareau, *Tabard*
Tabarel, *Tabard*
Tabarin, *Tabard*
Tabart, *Tabard*
Tabary, *Tabard*
Tabashnikov, *Tabak*
Tabatchnik, *Tabak*
Tabatchnikov, *Tabak*
Tabatznik, *Tabak*
Tabberer, *Tabor*
Tabberner, *Tabor*
Tabbitt, *Tabard*
Tabborah, *Tabor*
Tabekman, *Tabak*
Taber, *Tabor*
Taberer, *Tabor*
Taberner, *Tabor, Taverner*
Tabernero, *Taverner*
Tabiner, *Tabor*
Tabner, *Tabor*
Taboada
Tabor
Tábori, *Taborski*
Tabori, *Tabor*
Taborski
Táborský, *Taborski*
Tabory, *Tabor*
Tabour, *Tabor*
Taboureaux, *Tabor*
Tabourel, *Tabor*
Tabouret, *Tabor*
Tabourin, *Tabor*
Tabournier, *Tabor*
Tabourot, *Tabor*
Tabrar, *Tabor*
Tabur, *Tabor*
Taburet, *Tabor*
Taché, *Tache*
Tache
Tacheau, *Tache*
Tachet, *Tache*
Tachon, *Tache*
Tachot, *Tache*
Taddei, *Tadié*
Taddeini, *Tadié*
Taddeo, *Tadié*
Taddeucci, *Tadié*
Taddia, *Tadié*
Taddio, *Tadié*
Taddye, *Tadié*
Tadei, *Tadié*
Tadeo, *Tadié*
Tadeusiak, *Tadié*
Tadeusiewicz, *Tadié*
Tadeusik, *Tadié*
Tadeusz, *Tadié*
Tadić, *Tadié*
Tadié
Tadini, *Tadié*
Tadolini, *Tadié*
Taes, *Stace*
Taferner, *Taverner*
Taffee, *David*
Taffie, *David*
Tafintsev, *Ostapov*
Taft, *Toft*
Tagart, *Taggart*
Tägeder, *Zehender*
Taggairt, *Taggart*
Taggard, *Taggart*
Taggart
Taggert, *Taggart*
Tagliaferro, *Telfer*
Tagliavini
Tague, *Tighe*
Taier, *Dear*
Taigman, *Teig*
Taillade, *Tallis*
Taillandier, *Taylor*
Taillant
Taillard, *Taillant*
Taillbois, *Talboys*
Taillé, *Tallis*
Taille, *Tallis*
Taillefer, *Telfer*
Tailleur, *Taylor*
Tailly, *Tallis*
Tailour, *Taylor*
Tainturier, *Teinturier*
Taisson, *Tasso*
Tait
Taitel, *Teitelbaum*
Taitelbaum, *Teitelbaum*
Taitelman, *Teitelbaum*
Taitz, *Deutsch*
Tajchman, *Teich*
Tajer, *Dear*
Tajtelbaum, *Teitelbaum*
Takács, *Tkach*
Taks, *Dachs*
Tal, *Dale*
Talabot, *Talbot*
Talavera

Talbot
Talbott, *Talbot*
Talboys
Talbut, *Talbot*
Talbutt, *Talbot*
Talfourd, *Telford*
Talhade, *Tallis*
Talifert, *Telfer*
Talis, *Tallis*
Talisman, *Tallis*
Talisnik, *Tallis*
Talit, *Tallis*
Talitman, *Tallis*
Tall
Tallamach, *Tollemache*
Tallant, *Taillant*
Tallard, *Taillant*
Tallboy, *Talboys*
Tallboys, *Talboys*
Tallemach, *Tollemache*
Tallendier, *Taylor*
Talleyrand
Tallis
Tallon
Tally, *Tully*
Talma
Talmachev, *Tolmachev*
Talmacio, *Tolmachev*
Talmaciu, *Tolmachev*
Talmadge, *Tollemache*
Talmage, *Tollemache*
Talon, *Tallon*
Talún, *Tallon*
Tamás, *Thomas*
Tamási, *Thomas*
Tamblin, *Tamblyn*
Tambling, *Tamblyn*
Tamblyn
Tamborino, *Tabor*
Tambour, *Tabor*
Tambourier, *Tabor*
Tambourin, *Tabor*
Tambur, *Tabor*
Tamburelli, *Tabor*
Tamburello, *Tabor*
Tamburi, *Tabor*
Tamburini, *Tabor*
Tamburino, *Tabor*
Tamburlini, *Tabor*
Tamburo, *Tabor*
Tamburri, *Tabor*
Tamcke, *Dankmar*
Tame
Tamlin, *Tamblyn*
Tamlyn, *Tamblyn*
Tamm, *Dankmar*
Tammage, *Tollemache*
Tammaro, *Dankmar*
Tamme, *Dankmar*
Tammen, *Dankmar*
Tamminen
Tamminga, *Dankmar*
Tamms, *Dankmar*
Tammurello, *Tabor*
Tamplin, *Tamblyn*
Tams, *Dankmar*
Tănase, *Afanasyev*
Tanase, *Afanasyev*
Tanăsescu, *Afanasyev*
Tanasi, *Afanasyev*
Tanasijević, *Afanasyev*
Tanasković, *Afanasyev*
Tanc, *Tanzer*
Tanck, *Dankmar*
Tancman, *Tanzer*
Tancock, *Andrew*
Tancred
Tancrède, *Tancred*
Tancredi, *Tancred*
Tandler, *Tendler*
Tandy, *Andrew*
Taneev, *Toney*
Tanenbaum, *Tanne*
Tanenboim, *Tanne*
Tanenholz, *Tanne*
Tanenwurzel, *Tanne*
Taney
Tang, *Tong*
Tange, *Tong*
Tangney, *Tanguy*
Tangredi, *Tancred*
Tanguy
Tangye, *Tanguy*
Tani, *Gaetano*
Tanini, *Gaetano*
Tank, *Dankmar*
Tankard
Tann
Tanne
Tanneguy, *Tanguy*
Tannenbaum, *Tanne*
Tannenwald, *Tanne*
Tanner
Tanneret, *Tanner*
Tanneur, *Tanner*
Tanret, *Tanner*
Tanron, *Tanner*
Tansey
Tansi, *Constant*
Tansini, *Constant*
Tansley
Tansorier, *Treasure*
Tantzer, *Tanzer*
Tantzman, *Tanzer*
Tanucci, *Gaetano*
Tänzer, *Tanzer*
Tanzer
Tanzi, *Constant*
Tanzilli, *Constant*
Tanzillo, *Constant*
Tanzini, *Constant*
Tänzler, *Tanzer*
Tanzoni, *Constant*
Tàpia, *Tapia*
Tapia
Tàpias, *Tapia*
Tapias, *Tapia*
Tapié, *Tapia*
Tapie, *Tapia*
Tàpies, *Tapia*
Tapin, *Tapp*
Taplin, *Tapp*
Tapp
Tappe, *Tapp*
Tappenden
Tapper, *Tapster*
Tappert, *Tabard*
Tapping, *Tapp*
Tapps, *Tapp*
Tappson, *Tapp*
Tapster
Taque, *Tache*
Taquet, *Tache*
Taragan, *Tarragó*
Taragano, *Tarragó*
Taranov, *Tarasov*
Taras, *Tarasov*
Tarasenya, *Tarasov*
Tarashkevich, *Tarasov*
Tarasikov, *Tarasov*
Tarasov
Tarasyev, *Tarasov*
Tarasyonok, *Tarasov*
Tarasyuk, *Tarasov*
Tarbin, *Thorburn*
Tarbock
Tarbox, *Tarbock*
Tarbuck, *Tarbock*
Tarbun, *Thorburn*
Tarczyński
Tarde
Tardew, *Tardif*
Tardieu, *Tardif*
Tardif
Tardiveau, *Tardif*
Tardivel, *Tardif*
Tardivon, *Tardif*
Tardon, *Tardif*
Tardy, *Tardif*
Target, *Taggart*
Targownik
Targowski, *Targownik*
Tarkowski
Tarleton
Tarling
Tarlton, *Tarleton*
Tarn
Tarnovski, *Tarnowski*
Tarnovsky, *Tarnowski*
Tarnowski
Tarpey
Tarr
Tarragó
Tarrant
Tarrés
Tarry, *Terry*
Tartaglia
Tartakowski
Tartarelli, *Tatarinov*
Tartari, *Tatarinov*
Tartarini, *Tatarinov*
Tartarino, *Tatarinov*
Tartaro, *Tatarinov*
Tartaroni, *Tatarinov*
Tarterat, *Tartier*
Tarterini, *Tatarinov*
Tartier
Tartière, *Tartier*
Tartrat, *Tartier*
Tasche, *Tash*
Tascher, *Tasker*
Taschereau, *Tasker*
Tash
Tasić, *Afanasyev*
Tasin, *Tasso*
Tasini, *Tasso*
Tasker
Tasman, *Tasse*
Tassard, *Tasse*
Tassaud, *Tasse*
Tasse
Tasselli, *Tasso*
Tasset, *Tasse*
Tassetto, *Tasso*
Tassi, *Tasso*
Tassié, *Tasse*
Tassier, *Tasse*
Tassin, *Tasse*
Tassino, *Tasso*
Tasso
Tasson, *Tasse*
Tassot, *Tasse*
Tassotto, *Tasso*
Tatam, *Tatham*
Tatar, *Tatarinov*
Tatárek, *Tatarinov*
Tatarewicz, *Tatarinov*
Tatarinov
Tatarintsev, *Tatarinov*
Tatarkiewicz, *Tatarinov*
Tatarowicz, *Tatarinov*
Tatarski, *Tatarinov*
Tate
Tatelbaum, *Teitelbaum*
Tatelman, *Teitelbaum*
Tatem, *Tatham*
Tatford, *Titford*
Tatham
Tatishchev
Tatlar, *Tatler*
Tatler
Tatlor, *Tatler*
Tattersall
Tattersfield
Tattershall, *Tattersall*
Tattershaw, *Tattersall*
Tattersill, *Tattersall*
Tattler, *Tatler*
Tatton
Tatum, *Tatham*
Taub, *Tauber*
Taube
Taubenblat, *Taube*
Taubenblatt, *Taube*
Taubenfeld, *Taube*
Taubenhaus, *Taube*
Taubenhouse, *Taube*
Taubenschlag, *Taube*
Täuber, *Taube*
Tauber
Tauberg, *Taube*
Täubert, *Taube*
Taubert, *Taube*
Taubes, *Taube*
Taubin, *Taube*
Taubkin, *Taube*
Taubman, *Taube, Tauber*
Taubmann, *Tauber*
Taubner, *Taube*
Täufer, *Taufer*
Taufer
Tauffer, *Taufer*
Taulbut, *Talbot*
Taupeau, *Taupin*
Taupeneau, *Taupin*
Taupenot, *Taupin*
Taupin
Taupinard, *Taupin*
Taureau, *Toro*
Taurel, *Toro*
Tavares
Tavender, *Taverner*
Tavener, *Taverner*
Tavenner, *Taverner*
Tavenor, *Taverner*
Tavergnier, *Taverner*
Taverna, *Taverner*
Tavernai, *Taverner*
Tavernari, *Taverner*
Taverne, *Taverner*
Taverner
Taverni, *Taverner*
Tavernier, *Taverner*
Tavernieri, *Taverner*
Tavernor, *Taverner*
Taviner, *Taverner*

Tavner, *Taverner*
Tavor, *Tabor*
Tavori, *Tabor*
Tavory, *Tabor*
Tawney, *Taney*
Tawyer
Tax, *Dachs*
Tayer, *Dear*
Tayler, *Taylor*
Taylerson, *Taylor*
Taylor
Taylorson, *Taylor*
Taylour, *Taylor*
Taytel, *Teitelbaum*
Taytelboim, *Teitelbaum*
Tchaikovsky, *Czajkowski*
Tcharni, *Chernyakov*
Tchernatzki, *Chernyakov*
Tchernichovsky, *Chernyakov*
Tchernovitz
Teacher
Teage, *Tighe*
Teague
Teahan, *Tighe*
Teal, *Teale*
Teale
Teall, *Teale*
Tear, *McIntyre*
Tearall, *Tyrrell*
Teare, *McIntyre*
Tearle
Tearney, *Tierney*
Teasdale
Tebaldeschi, *Theobald*
Tebaldi, *Theobald*
Tebaldini, *Theobald*
Tebb, *Theobald*
Tebbell, *Theobald*
Tebbet, *Theobald*
Tebbett, *Theobald*
Tebbit, *Theobald*
Tebbitt, *Theobald*
Tebble, *Theobald*
Tebbs, *Theobald*
Tebbut, *Theobald*
Tebbutt, *Theobald*
Teboth, *Theobald*
Tech, *Tess*
Techel, *Tess*
Techen, *Tess*
Teck, *Tess*
Teckel, *Tess*
Tedd
Tedeschi, *Tedesco*
Tedeschini, *Tedesco*
Tedesco
Tedoradze, *Théodore*
Tedorenko, *Théodore*
Teds, *Tedd*
Tedstone
Tee, *Tye*
Teehan, *Tighe*
Teek, *Tighe*
Teewen, *Thiess*
Tegart, *Teggart*
Tegeder, *Zehender*
Tegeler, *Tiler*
Tegg
Teggart
Tegler, *Tiler*
Tegtmann, *Zehender*
Teich
Teicher, *Teich*
Teichert, *Teich*
Teichler, *Teich*
Teichman, *Teich*
Teichmann, *Teich*
Teichner, *Teich*
Teifel, *Deville*
Teig
Teige, *Tighe*
Teigfeld, *Teig*
Teigman, *Teig*
Teigue, *Tighe*
Teil
Teilhard, *Teil*
Teillard, *Teil*
Teillaud, *Teil*
Teillet, *Teil*
Teillon, *Teil*
Teinturier
Teissaire, *Tissier*
Teissèdre, *Tissier*
Teisseire, *Tissier*
Teissier, *Tissier*
Teitel, *Teitelbaum*
Teitelbaum
Teitelboim, *Teitelbaum*
Teitelbom, *Teitelbaum*
Teitelman, *Teitelbaum*
Teitz, *Deutsch*
Teitzman, *Deutsch*
Teixeira, *Tasso*
Teixidó, *Tissier*
Teixidor, *Tissier*
Teixier, *Tissier*
Tejada, *Teil*
Tejeda, *Tasso*
Tejedor, *Tissier*
Tejero, *Tiler*
Tejtelbaum, *Teitelbaum*
Tekach, *Tkach*
Telegin
Telemann, *Terry*
Teler, *Teller*
Teles, *Tello*
Telezhkin, *Telegin*
Telfair, *Telfer*
Telfer
Telford
Telge, *Tell*
Telgmann, *Tell*
Telhard, *Teil*
Teliga, *Telegin*
Tell
Telle, *Tell*
Teller
Téllez, *Tello*
Tellmann, *Tell*
Tello
Tellow, *Tell*
Teml, *Thomas*
Temmerman, *Zimmermann*
Tempany, *Timpany*
Tempelaar, *Temple*
Tempelman, *Temple*
Tempeny, *Timpany*
Tempest
Tempesta, *Tempest*
Tempesti, *Tempest*
Tempestini, *Tempest*
Templar, *Temple*
Temple
Templeman, *Temple*
Templer, *Temple*
Templeton
Templier, *Temple*
Tena
Tenant, *Tennant*
Ten Berge, *Berg*
Ten Boom, *Baum*
Tenbosch, *Bush*
Tenbrinck, *Brink*
Ten Brink, *Brink*
Tenbrink, *Brink*
Ten Broek, *Brook*
Ten Broeke, *Brook*
Tenbrug, *Bridge*
Ten Cate, *Coates*
Tendahl, *Dale*
Tendam, *Dam*
Tendler
Tendyck, *Ditch*
Teneur, *Tennant*
Tengel, *Dengler*
Tengeler, *Dengler*
Tengelmann, *Dengler*
Tengler, *Dengler*
Tengue, *Tanguy*
Tenhaeff, *Hofer*
Teniente, *Tennant*
Ten Kate, *Coates*
Tennant
Tennent, *Tennant*
Tennents, *Tennant*
Tenner, *Tanner, Tennant*
Tenneson, *Tenney*
Tenney
Tenniel
Tennison, *Tenney*
Tennyson, *Tenney*
Tenon, *Stephen*
Tenot, *Stephen*
Tenpenny, *Timpany*
Tenpeny, *Timpany*
Tensorier, *Treasure*
Tentzer, *Tanzer*
Tenzer, *Tanzer*
Teobaldi, *Theobald*
Teodorczyk, *Théodore*
Teodorescu, *Théodore*
Teodori, *Théodore*
Teodoro, *Théodore*
Teodorović, *Théodore*
Teodorovich, *Théodore*
Teodorowicz, *Théodore*
Teodorski, *Théodore*
Teper, *Töpfer*
Teperman, *Töpfer*
Teperson, *Töpfer*
Tepfer, *Töpfer*
Teplý
Tepper, *Töpfer*
Tepperberg, *Töpfer*
Teppermann, *Töpfer*
Terbeck, *Bach*
Terbeek, *Bach*
Terbocke, *Tarbock*
Terbrugge, *Bridge*
Terbrüggen, *Bridge*
Tereshkov
Ter Haar, *Haar*
Terhardt, *Hardt*
Terheggen, *Hedge*
Terhorst, *Hurst*
Teri, *Walter*
Terkel, *Turk*
Terkelsen, *Thirkill*
Terkildsen, *Thirkill*
Terlinden, *Linde*
Termeer, *Meer*
Termeulen, *Mill*
Termöhlen, *Mill*
Ternan, *Tierney*
Ternedden, *Nieder*
Terney, *Tierney*
Ternoster, *Paternoster*
Terrall, *Tyrrell*
Terrance, *McTerrelly*
Terrell, *Tyrrell*
Terrey, *Terry*
Terrill, *Tyrrell*
Terrón
Terry
Terschüren, *Scheuer*
Tersmeden, *Smythe*
Teruel
Terveen, *Fenn*
Tervooren, *Ford*
Terweij, *Weide*
Terwey, *Weide*
Téry, *Terry*
Tesař, *Cieślak*
Tesárek, *Cieślak*
Tesařik, *Cieślak*
Tesator, *Tissier*
Tesauro, *Treasure*
Tesh, *Tash*
Teshe, *Tash*
Teske, *Tess*
Teslenko, *Cieślak*
Tesler, *Cieślak*
Tesler, *Tischler*
Teslyuk, *Cieślak*
Tess
Tessadro, *Tissier*
Tessarin, *Tissier*
Tessarini, *Tissier*
Tessaro, *Tissier*
Tessaroli, *Tissier*
Tessarolo, *Tissier*
Tessarotto, *Tissier*
Tessel, *Tasso*
Tessen, *Tess*
Tesserand, *Tissier*
Tessereau, *Tissier*
Tesserin, *Tissier*
Tesserini, *Tissier*
Tessier, *Tissier*
Tessieri, *Tissier*
Tessiore, *Tissier*
Tessitore, *Tissier*
Tessitori, *Tissier*
Tessler, *Tischler*
Tessmann, *Tess*
Tesson, *Tasso*
Tessore, *Tissier*
Testa, *Teste*
Testar, *Teste*
Testard, *Teste*
Testart, *Teste*
Testaud, *Teste*
Teste
Testeegen, *Steiger*
Tester, *Teste*
Testi, *Teste*
Testini, *Teste*
Testino, *Teste*
Teston, *Teste*
Testone, *Teste*
Testoni, *Teste*
Testore, *Tissier*
Testori, *Tissier*
Testot, *Teste*
Testu, *Teste*
Teszler, *Tischler*

Tétard, *Teste*
Tétart, *Teste*
Têtaud, *Teste*
Tête, *Teste*
Tetley
Tétot, *Teste*
Tetsall, *Tattersall*
Tettersell, *Tattersall*
Tétu, *Teste*
Tetze, *Terry*
Tetzel, *Tess*
Tetzke, *Tess*
Tetzmann, *Tess*
Teuber, *Taube*
Teubert, *Taube*
Teubner, *Taube*
Teuer, *Dear*
Teuerstein, *Dear*
Teufel, *Deville*
Teuffel, *Deville*
Teulié, *Tiler*
Teulier, *Tiler*
Teunisse, *Thon*
Teunissen, *Thon*
Teupel, *Theobald*
Tevelov, *David*
Tew
Tewelson, *David*
Tewes, *Thiess*
Tews, *Thiess*
Tewson, *Tuson*
Texandier, *Tissier*
Texereau, *Tissier*
Texier, *Tissier*
Tey, *Tye*
Teyerstein, *Dear*
Teysandier, *Tissier*
Teysédou, *Tissier*
Teyssaire, *Tissier*
Teyssèdre, *Tissier*
Teysseyre, *Tissier*
Teyssier, *Tissier*
Teyte, *Tait*
Thackara, *Thackeray*
Thacker
Thackeray
Thackerey, *Thackeray*
Thackery, *Thackeray*
Thackore, *Thacker*
Thackra, *Thackeray*
Thackrah, *Thackeray*
Thackray, *Thackeray*
Thackwray, *Thackeray*
Thaddée, *Tadié*
Thaddey, *Tadié*
Thade, *Terry*
Thain
Thaine, *Thain*
Thake
Thaker, *Thacker*
Thakkar, *Thacker*
Thakker, *Thacker*
Thal, *Dale*
Thaler, *Dale*
Thaller, *Dale*
Thalmann, *Dale*
Thälmann, *Terry*
Thämel, *Thomas*
Thämelt, *Thomas*
Thamm, *Dankmar*
Thams, *Dankmar*
Thamsen, *Dankmar*
Thanase, *Afanasyev*
Thanner, *Tanner*
Tharp, *Thorpe*
Thatcher
Thaxter, *Thacker*
Thayne, *Thain*
Thaysen, *Thiess*
Theaker
Thébaud, *Theobald*
Thébault, *Theobald*
Thede, *Terry*
Theden, *Terry*
Thedens, *Terry*
Theding, *Terry*
Thedinga, *Terry*
Thee, *Terry*
Theeck, *Terry*
Theeden, *Terry*
Theedens, *Terry*
Theeder, *Terry*
Theeding, *Terry*
Theel, *Terry*
Theele, *Terry*
Thees, *Thiess*
Theesinga, *Thiess*
Theil, *Teil, Terry*
Theile, *Terry*
Theilemann, *Terry*
Theilley, *Teil*
Theimann, *Terry*
Theinel, *Deinhard*
Theinelt, *Deinhard*
Theis, *Thiess*
Theisen, *Thiess*
Theismann, *Thiess*
Theiss, *Thiess*
Theissen, *Thiess*
Thele, *Terry*
Thelemann, *Terry*
Thelen, *Terry*
Thelens, *Terry*
Thelwall
Thelwell, *Thelwall*
Themann, *Thomas*
Theml, *Thomas*
Thénard, *Stephen*
Thénault, *Stephen*
Thénaut, *Stephen*
Thenet, *Stephen*
Theng, *Thon*
Thenner, *Tanner*
Thenon, *Stephen*
Thénot, *Stephen*
Theobald
Theobalds, *Theobald*
Theobold, *Theobald*
Theodbald, *Theobald*
Theodorakis, *Théodore*
Théodore
Theodoresco, *Théodore*
Theodoridis, *Théodore*
Théolier, *Tiler*
Theopold, *Theobald*
Thépaud, *Theobald*
Thériot, *Terry*
Therkelsen, *Thirkill*
Therkildsen, *Thirkill*
Théron
Thérond, *Théron*
Théroude, *Thorold*
Théry, *Terry*
Thesing, *Thiess*
Thessen, *Thiess*
Theun, *Thon*
Theunissen, *Thon*
Theuriet, *Terry*
Theuss, *Thiess*
Theussen, *Thiess*
Theuvenet, *Stephen*
Theuveney, *Stephen*
Theuveny, *Stephen*
Theuvissen, *Thiess*
Thevan, *Stephen*
Thevand, *Stephen*
Thévard, *Stephen*
Thévenard, *Stephen*
Théveneau, *Stephen*
Thévenet, *Stephen*
Thévenin, *Stephen*
Thevenon, *Stephen*
Thévenot, *Stephen*
Théveny, *Stephen*
Theveny, *Stephen*
Thevessen, *Thiess*
Thevet, *Stephen*
Thevin, *Stephen*
Thevissen, *Thiess*
Thevot, *Stephen*
Thevs, *Thiess*
Thewes, *Thiess*
Thewissen, *Thiess*
Thewles, *Thewlis*
Thewless, *Thewlis*
Thewlis
Thews, *Thiess*
Thewys, *Thiess*
Thibaud, *Theobald*
Thibaudat, *Theobald*
Thibaudeau, *Theobald*
Thibaudet, *Theobald*
Thibaudin, *Theobald*
Thibault, *Theobald*
Thibou, *Theobald*
Thibout, *Theobald*
Thick, *Dick*
Thicke, *Dick*
Thicks, *Dick*
Thiébaud, *Theobald*
Thièble, *Stephen*
Thieblin, *Stephen*
Thieblot, *Stephen*
Thiede, *Terry*
Thiedemann, *Terry*
Thiéfaine, *Tiffin*
Thieke, *Terry*
Thiel, *Terry*
Thiele, *Terry*
Thieleck, *Terry*
Thieleke, *Terry*
Thielen, *Terry*
Thielens, *Terry*
Thielking, *Terry*
Thielmann, *Terry*
Thielsch, *Terry*
Thielscher, *Terry*
Thiemann, *Terry*
Thieme, *Dietmar*
Thiemeke, *Timm*
Thiendl, *Deinhard*
Thienert, *Deinhard*
Thienot, *Stephen*
Thier, *Dear*
Thiérard, *Terry*
Thiérart, *Terry*
Thierrard, *Terry*
Thierrart, *Terry*
Thierry, *Terry*
Thiers, *Tiers*
Thiéry, *Terry*
Thies, *Thiess*
Thiese, *Thiess*
Thiesen, *Thiess*
Thiesing, *Thiess*
Thiess
Thiessen, *Thiess*
Thiévin, *Stephen*
Thijssen, *Thiess*
Thil, *Teil*
Thill, *Teil*
Thillard, *Teil*
Thillaye, *Teil*
Thillet, *Teil*
Thillier, *Teil*
Thimm, *Timm*
Thimmann, *Timm*
Thin
Thiolier, *Tiler*
Thioller, *Tiler*
Thireau, *Terry*
Thirieau, *Terry*
Thiriet, *Terry*
Thiriez, *Terry*
Thirion, *Terry*
Thiriot, *Terry*
Thirkell, *Thirkill*
Thirkettle, *Thirkill*
Thirkhill, *Thirkill*
Thirkill
Thirtle, *Thirkill*
Thirwell
Thiry, *Terry*
Thistlewaite
Thistlewood
Thivet, *Stephen*
Thoburn, *Thorburn*
Thode, *Terry*
Thoden, *Terry*
Thoin, *Toney*
Thoine, *Toney*
Thoinet, *Toney*
Thoinot, *Toney*
Thöl, *Terry*
Thöle, *Terry*
Thölen, *Terry*
Tholen, *Terry*
Thölke, *Terry*
Thölken, *Terry*
Thom, *Thomas*
Thoma, *Thomas*
Thomann, *Thomas*
Thomas
Thomasen, *Thomas*
Thomason, *Thomas*
Thomasseau, *Thomas*
Thomassen, *Thomas*
Thomasset, *Thomas*
Thomassin, *Thomas*
Thomasson, *Thomas*
Thomazeau, *Thomas*
Thomazet, *Thomas*
Thomazin, *Thomas*
Thomazon, *Thomas*
Thombleson, *Thomas*
Thomé, *Thomas*
Thome, *Thomas*
Thömel, *Thomas*
Thomelin, *Thomas*
Thömen, *Thomas*
Thomerson, *Thomas*
Thomesson, *Thomas*
Thomet, *Thomas*
Thöminga, *Thomas*
Thomke, *Thomas*
Thomlinson, *Thomas*

Thompsett, *Thomas*
Thompson, *Thomas*
Thoms, *Thomas*
Thomsen, *Thomas*
Thomsett, *Thomas*
Thomson, *Thomas*
Thomsson, *Thomas*
Thön, *Thon*
Thon
Thönes, *Thon*
Thönges, *Thon*
Thonjes, *Thon*
Thor
Thorbahn, *Urban*
Thorburn
Thoré, *Thorel*
Thoreau, *Thorel*
Thorel
Thoresson, *Thor*
Thoret, *Thorel*
Thorez, *Thorel*
Thorgood, *Thorogood*
Thorkell, *Thirkill*
Thörl, *Thor*
Thorley
Thorman, *Thurman*
Thormann, *Thor*
Thörmer, *Thurn*
Thormühlen, *Mill*
Thorn
Thornber
Thornberry, *Thornber*
Thornborough, *Thornber*
Thornborrow, *Thornber*
Thornburgh, *Thornber*
Thornbury, *Thornber*
Thorndick, *Thorndike*
Thorndike
Thorndyke, *Thorndike*
Thorne, *Thorn*
Thornell, *Thornhill*
Thörner, *Thorn*
Thornes, *Thorn*
Thornhill
Thornley, *Thorley*
Thorns, *Thorn*
Thornton
Thorogood
Thorold
Thoroughgood, *Thorogood*
Thorougood, *Thorogood*
Thorowgood, *Thorogood*
Thorp, *Thorpe*
Thorpe
Thorrold, *Thorold*
Thorrowgood, *Thorogood*
Thorsen, *Thor*
Thorsson, *Thor*
Thorstensson, *Thurston*
Thorvaldsen, *Thorold*
Thorwart, *Thor*
Thorwarth, *Thor*
Thorwest, *West*
Thorwesten, *West*
Thoumas, *Thomas*
Thoumasson, *Thomas*
Thourault, *Thorold*
Thouroude, *Thorold*
Thouvenel, *Stephen*
Thouvenet, *Stephen*
Thouvenin, *Stephen*
Thouvenot, *Stephen*
Thouvet, *Stephen*
Thouvignon, *Stephen*
Thowless, *Thewlis*
Thoytes, *Thwaite*
Thrane
Thrasher, *Drescher*
Threadgall, *Threadgold*
Threadgill, *Threadgold*
Threadgold
Threadgould, *Threadgold*
Threadkell, *Threadgold*
Threapleton
Threlfall
Thresher, *Drescher*
Thridgould, *Threadgold*
Thrift, *Firth*
Thripp, *Thorpe*
Thrippleton, *Threapleton*
Throp, *Thorpe*
Throssell, *Thrussell*
Throup, *Thorpe*
Thrower
Thrupp, *Thorpe*
Thrush, *Thrussell*
Thrussell
Thrustle, *Thrussell*
Thubron, *Thorburn*
Thuesen, *Thiess*
Thuilier, *Tiler*
Thuillier, *Tiler*
Thum, *Thumb*
Thumann, *Thomas*
Thumb
Thumm, *Thumb*
Thümnel, *Thomas*
Thunder, *Tondeur*
Thurbahn, *Urban*
Thurban, *Thorburn*
Thurbon, *Thorburn*
Thurburn, *Thorburn*
Thürch, *Turk*
Thureau, *Arthur*
Thurel, *Arthur*
Thuresson, *Thor*
Thuret, *Arthur*
Thurgate, *Thorogood*
Thurgell, *Thirkill*
Thurgood, *Thorogood*
Thurin, *Arthur*
Thurkell, *Thirkill*
Thurkettle, *Thirkill*
Thurkittle, *Thirkill*
Thurloe, *Thurlow*
Thurlow
Thurm, *Thurn*
Thurman
Thurmand, *Thurman*
Thurmer, *Thurn*
Thurn
Thurner, *Thurn*
Thuron, *Arthur*
Thurot, *Arthur*
Thursfield
Thurstan, *Thurston*
Thurstans, *Thurston*
Thursting, *Thurston*
Thurston
Thurtell, *Thirkill*
Thurtle, *Thirkill*
Thwaite
Thwaites, *Thwaite*
Thwaytes, *Thwaite*
Thygesen, *Thiess*
Thynn, *Thin*
Thynne, *Thin*
Thys, *Thiess*
Thyssen, *Thiess*
Thywissen, *Thiess*
Tiago, *Santiago*
Tiark, *Terry*
Tiarks, *Terry*
Tibald, *Theobald*
Tibaldi, *Theobald*
Tiball, *Theobald*
Tibault, *Theobald*
Tibb, *Theobald*
Tibballs, *Theobald*
Tibbats, *Theobald*
Tibbatts, *Theobald*
Tibbets, *Theobald*
Tibbett, *Theobald*
Tibbetts, *Theobald*
Tibbins, *Theobald*
Tibbits, *Theobald*
Tibbitt, *Theobald*
Tibbitts, *Theobald*
Tibble, *Theobald*
Tibbles, *Theobald*
Tibbott, *Theobald*
Tibbotts, *Theobald*
Tibbs, *Theobald*
Tibold, *Theobald*
Tiboldi, *Theobald*
Ticháček, *Cichy*
Tichband, *Tichborne*
Tichbon, *Tichborne*
Tichborne
Tichbourne, *Tichborne*
Tichelaar, *Tiler*
Tichner, *Titchener*
Tichý, *Cichy*
Tickel, *Tickle*
Tickell, *Tickle*
Tickle
Tickner, *Titchener*
Tidbald, *Theobald*
Tidball, *Theobald*
Tidbold, *Theobald*
Tiddeman, *Tidman*
Tidman
Tidmarsh
Tidy
Tiebe, *Matthew*
Tieck, *Terry*
Tiecke, *Terry*
Tiede, *Terry*
Tiedebohl, *Theobald*
Tiedmann, *Terry*
Tiegeler, *Tiler*
Tiel, *Terry*
Tielker, *Terry*
Tienke, *Austin, Martin*
Tienken, *Austin, Martin*
Tienot, *Stephen*
Tiepel, *Theobald*
Tier, *McIntyre*
Tieri, *Walter*
Tiernan, *Tierney*
Tierney
Tierny, *Tierney*
Tiero, *Walter*
Tiers
Tiessen, *Thiess*
Tietböhl, *Theobald*
Tietz, *Terry*
Tietze, *Terry*
Tietzel, *Terry*
Tietzmann, *Terry*
Tiévant, *Stephen*
Tifeneau, *Tiffin*
Tifenneau, *Tiffin*
Tiffany, *Tiffin*
Tiffen, *Tiffin*
Tiffeneau, *Tiffin*
Tiffenneau, *Tiffin*
Tiffin
Tiffney, *Tiffin*
Tifon, *Tiffin*
Tigg, *Tegg*
Tighe
Tigue, *Tighe*
Tijssen, *Thiess*
Tikhanov, *Tikhonov*
Tikhonov
Til, *Teil*
Tilas, *Tilson*
Tilbrook
Tilbury
Tilcock, *Till*
Tilden
Tildesley, *Tyldesley*
Tildsley, *Tyldesley*
Tiler
Tiles, *Tilson*
Tiley, *Tilley*
Tilford, *Telford*
Tilfourd, *Telford*
Tilke, *Terry*
Tilkin, *Tilson*
Till
Tillard, *Teil*
Tillcock, *Till*
Tille, *Till*
Tillequin, *Teil*
Tiller
Tilles, *Tilson*
Tilleson, *Tilson*
Tillet, *Teil, Till*
Tillett, *Till*
Tilleul, *Teil*
Tilley
Tillich, *Terry*
Tillie, *Tilley*
Tillier, *Teil, Tiller*
Tilling
Tillis, *Tilson*
Tillman, *Tiller*
Tillmann, *Till*
Tillmanns, *Terry*
Tillon, *Teil*
Tillot, *Till*
Tillotson, *Tilson*
Tillott, *Till*
Tillou, *Teil*
Tilloy, *Teil*
Tills, *Tilson*
Tillsley, *Tyldesley*
Tillson, *Tilson*
Tilly, *Tilley, Tully*
Tillyard, *Tiller*
Tillyer, *Tiller*
Tilquin, *Teil*
Tilsley, *Tyldesley*
Tilson
Tily, *Tilley*
Tilyer, *Tiller*
Tilzey, *Tyldesley*
Timachyov, *Timofeev*
Timakov, *Timofeev*
Timár
Timashaev, *Timofeev*
Timberlake
Timblick, *Timberlake*
Timblin, *Timm*

Timbrell
Timchenko, *Timofeev*
Timchishin, *Timofeev*
Timeshov, *Timofeev*
Timin, *Timofeev*
Timkin, *Timm*
Timkin, *Timofeev*
Timkiss, *Timm*
Timkó, *Timofeev*
Timm
Timme, *Timm*
Timmer, *Zimmermann*
Timmerman, *Zimmermann*
Timmermann, *Zimmermann*
Timmermans, *Zimmermann*
Timmes, *Timm*
Timmies, *Timm*
Timmins, *Timm*
Timmis, *Timm*
Timmons
Timms, *Timm*
Timney, *Timony*
Timochin, *Timofeev*
Timofeev
Timonin, *Timofeev*
Timony
Timoshchuk, *Timofeev*
Timoshenko, *Timofeev*
Timoshin, *Timofeev*
Timoshkin, *Timofeev*
Timoshkov, *Timofeev*
Timoteu, *Timofeev*
Timothy, *Tomelty*
Timotijević, *Timofeev*
Timpanaro, *Timpany*
Timpanelli, *Timpany*
Timpano, *Timpany*
Timpany
Timperley
Timpson, *Timm*
Tims, *Timm*
Timshin, *Timofeev*
Timson, *Timm*
Timuev, *Timofeev*
Timushev, *Timofeev*
Timyashaev, *Timofeev*
Tindal, *Tindale*
Tindale
Tindall, *Tindale*
Tindell, *Tindale*
Tindill, *Tindale*
Tindle, *Tindale*
Tingay, *Tanguy*
Tingey, *Tanguy*
Tingle
Tingler, *Tingle*
Tinguy, *Tanguy*
Tinkel, *Donker*
Tinkelmann, *Donker*
Tinker
Tinkler, *Tinker*
Tinney
Tinot, *Martin*
Tinsley
Tinter, *Teinturier*
Tintner, *Teinturier*
Tintore, *Teinturier*
Tintorello, *Teinturier*
Tintoretto, *Teinturier*
Tinu, *Constantine*
Tioli
Tiosso, *Tioli*
Tiozzi, *Tioli*
Tipaldi, *Theobald*
Tiphaigne, *Tiffin*
Tiphaine, *Tiffin*
Tipheneau, *Tiffin*
Tiphine, *Tiffin*
Tiphon, *Tiffin*
Tiplady
Tipp, *Theobald*
Tippell, *Theobald*
Tipper
Tippett, *Theobald*
Tippetts, *Theobald*
Tipping
Tippings, *Tipping*
Tippins, *Theobald*
Tipple, *Theobald*
Tipples, *Theobald*
Tippold, *Theobald*
Tipson, *Theobald*
Tipton
Tirado
Tirand, *Tyrrell*
Tirant, *Tyrrell*
Tirard, *Tyrrell*
Tirial, *Tyrrell*
Tirpitz
Tirrell, *Tyrrell*
Tischbein
Tischer, *Tischler*
Tischler
Tischman, *Tischler*
Tischmann, *Tischler*
Tischner, *Tischler*
Tisdall
Tishchenko, *Tikhonov*
Tisheev, *Tikhonov*
Tishler, *Tischler*
Tishman, *Tischler*
Tishmann, *Tischler*
Tishutkin, *Tikhonov*
Tison, *Tyson*
Tissandier, *Tissier*
Tisser, *Tissier*
Tisserand, *Tissier*
Tissier
Tissot, *Tissier*
Titaev, *Tito*
Titanov, *Tito*
Titchener
Titford
Titi, *Tito*
Titkin, *Tito*
Titkov, *Tito*
Titley
Titman, *Tidman*
Titmas, *Titmus*
Titmus
Titmuss, *Titmus*
Tito
Titolo, *Tito*
Titone, *Tito*
Titov, *Tito*
Tits, *Terry*
Titta, *Baptiste*
Titterington
Tittman, *Tidman*
Tittoni, *Baptiste*
Titushin, *Tito*
Titze, *Terry*
Tiussi, *Tioli*
Tivolier, *Tiler*
Tivollier, *Tiler*
Tixidre, *Tissier*
Tixier, *Tissier*
Tiziani, *Tiziano*
Tiziano
Tizzanini, *Tiziano*
Tizziani, *Tiziano*
Tizziano, *Tiziano*
Tjarcks, *Terry*
Tjark, *Terry*
Tjellander, *Käll*
Tjellberg, *Käll*
Tjellén, *Käll*
Tjellgren, *Käll*
Tjellström, *Käll*
Tkach
Tkachuk, *Tkach*
Tkacz, *Tkach*
Tkaczyk, *Tkach*
Tkatsh, *Tkach*
Tłustowski, *Tolstoy*
Tłusty, *Tolstoy*
Tlustý, *Tolstoy*
Toal, *Toole*
Toale, *Toole*
Tobel
Tobey, *Tobias*
Töbi, *Tobias*
Tobiański, *Tobias*
Tóbiás, *Tobias*
Tobías, *Tobias*
Tobias
Tobiasewicz, *Tobias*
Tobiasz, *Tobias*
Tobie, *Tobias*
Tobin
Tobis, *Taube, Tobias*
Tobisch, *Tobias*
Tobler, *Tobel*
Tobola, *Tobias*
Tobolewicz, *Tobias*
Tobsch, *Tobias*
Tobusch, *Tobias*
Toby, *Tobias*
Tocker, *Tokarz*
Tocqueville
Tocquoy, *Touche*
Tod, *Todd*
Todarello, *Théodore*
Todari, *Théodore*
Todarini, *Théodore*
Todaro, *Théodore*
Todd
Tode, *Terry*
Todeo, *Théodore*
Toderbrügge, *Bridge*
Toderi, *Théodore*
Toderini, *Théodore*
Todeschini, *Tedesco*
Todhunter
Tódor, *Théodore*
Todorov, *Théodore*
Todorović, *Théodore*
Todrick, *Terry*
Todsen, *Terry*
Todt, *Toth*
Tofanelli, *Christopher*
Tofanini, *Christopher*
Tofano, *Christopher*
Toffalo, *Christopher*
Toffaloni, *Christopher*
Toffanelli, *Christopher*
Toffanini, *Christopher*
Toffano, *Christopher*
Töffel, *Christopher*
Toffel, *Christopher*
Toffetto, *Christopher*
Toffler, *Christopher*
Toffoletto, *Christopher*
Toffolini, *Christopher*
Toffolo, *Christopher*
Toffoloni, *Christopher*
Tofful, *Christopher*
Toft
Tofte, *Toft*
Tofts, *Toft*
Toghill, *Thirkill*
Tognacci, *Toney*
Tognazzi, *Toney*
Tognello, *Toney*
Tognetti, *Toney*
Togni, *Toney*
Tognini, *Toney*
Tognoli, *Toney*
Tohall, *Toole*
Tohill, *Toole*
Toibin, *Taube*
Toifel, *Deville*
Toin, *Toney*
Toine, *Toney*
Toinet, *Toney*
Toinot, *Toney*
Toivonen
Tojbin, *Taube*
Tokarczyk, *Tokarz*
Tokarek, *Tokarz*
Tokarevich, *Tokarz*
Tokarski, *Tokarz*
Tokarz
Tokarzewicz, *Tokarz*
Toke, *Tooke*
Toker, *Tokarz*
Tolaldi, *Theobald*
Tolaldo, *Theobald*
Tolbert
Tolces, *Duce*
Tolciss, *Duce*
Tole, *Towle*
Toledano, *Toledo*
Toledo
Toley, *Towle*
Tölke, *Terry*
Tölken, *Terry*
Toll, *Towle*
Tollemache
Toller
Tolley, *Towle*
Töllner, *Toller*
Tolmachev
Tolmatcz, *Tolmachev*
Tolomei, *Bartholomew*
Tolomelli, *Bartholomew*
Tolomio, *Bartholomew*
Toloni, *Bartholomew*
Tolosa, *Toulouse*
Tolossi, *Bartholomew*
Tolotti, *Bartholomew*
Tolsma, *Toller*
Tolson, *Towle*
Tolstenev, *Tolstoy*
Tolstov, *Tolstoy*
Tolstoy
Tolstyakov, *Tolstoy*
Tolstykh, *Tolstoy*
Toltzis, *Duce*
Tolumello, *Bartholomew*
Tolussi, *Bartholomew*
Tolver, *Telfer*
Tolzis, *Duce*
Tom, *Thomas*
Toma, *Thomas*
Tomadini, *Thomas*

Tomadoni, *Thomas*
Tomaelli, *Thomas*
Tomaello, *Thomas*
Tomaini, *Thomas*
Tomaino, *Thomas*
Tomala, *Thomas*
Tomalczyk, *Thomas*
Tomalin, *Thomas*
Toman, *Thomas*
Tománek, *Thomas*
Tomanek, *Thomas*
Tomankiewicz, *Thomas*
Tomankowski, *Thomas*
Tomáš, *Thomas*
Tomás, *Thomas*
Tomàs, *Thomas*
Tomas, *Thomas*
Tomaschke, *Thomas*
Tomášek, *Thomas*
Tomasek, *Thomas*
Tomaselli, *Thomas*
Tomasello, *Thomas*
Tomasetti, *Thomas*
Tomašević, *Thomas*
Tomashevich, *Thomas*
Tomashkov, *Thomas*
Tomashov, *Thomas*
Tomasi, *Thomas*
Tomasian, *Thomas*
Tomasicchio, *Thomas*
Tomasiewicz, *Thomas*
Tomasik, *Thomas*
Tomasini, *Thomas*
Tomasino, *Thomas*
Tomaskaitis, *Thomas*
Tomaskunas, *Thomas*
Tomasoni, *Thomas*
Tomassetti, *Thomas*
Tomassini, *Thomas*
Tomassoni, *Thomas*
Tomasutti, *Thomas*
Tomasuzzi, *Thomas*
Tomasz, *Thomas*
Tomaszczyk, *Thomas*
Tomaszek, *Thomas*
Tomaszewicz, *Thomas*
Tomaszewski, *Thomas*
Tomaszkiewicz, *Thomas*
Tomaszyński, *Thomas*
Tomblin, *Thomas*
Tombling, *Thomas*
Tomblings, *Thomas*
Tomborg, *Burke*
Tombreul, *Brühl*
Tombrinck, *Brink*
Tombrink, *Brink*
Tombrock, *Brock*
Tombs, *Thomas*
Tomczak, *Thomas*
Tomczyk, *Thomas*
Tomczykiewicz, *Thomas*
Tomczykowski, *Thomas*
Tomczyński, *Thomas*
Tomdieck, *Ditch*
Tome, *Bartholomew, Thomas*
Tomé, *Thomas*
Tomeček, *Thomas*
Tomei, *Bartholomew, Thomas*
Tomek, *Thomas*
Tomelty
Tomeo, *Thomas*
Tomeš, *Thomas*
Tomes, *Thomas*
Tomfohr, *Ford*
Tomfor, *Ford*
Tomforde, *Ford*
Tomfort, *Ford*
Tomhaeve, *Hofer*
Tomić, *Thomas*
Tomich, *Thomas*
Tomicki, *Thomas*
Tomik, *Thomas*
Tomini, *Thomas*
Tomisch, *Thomas*
Tomkies, *Thomas*
Tomkin, *Thomas*
Tomkins, *Thomas*
Tomkinson, *Thomas*
Tomkiss, *Thomas*
Tomkowicz, *Thomas*
Tomkys, *Thomas*
Tomlin, *Thomas*
Tomlins, *Thomas*
Tomlinson, *Thomas*
Tommaselli, *Thomas*
Tommasello, *Thomas*
Tommaseo, *Thomas*
Tommasetti, *Thomas*
Tommasi, *Thomas*
Tommasini, *Thomas*
Tommasino, *Thomas*
Tommasoni, *Thomas*
Tommasuzzi, *Thomas*
Tomme, *Bartholomew*
Tommei, *Bartholomew, Thomas*
Tommen, *Thomas*
Tommeo, *Thomas*
Tommis, *Thomas*
Tomović, *Thomas*
Tomowicz, *Thomas*
Tompkin, *Thomas*
Tompkins, *Thomas*
Tompkinson, *Thomas*
Tompkiss, *Thomas*
Tompsett, *Thomas*
Tompson, *Thomas*
Toms, *Thomas*
Tomsa, *Thomas*
Tomsen, *Thomas*
Tomsett, *Thomas*
Tomson, *Thomas*
Tomšů, *Thomas*
Ton, *Toney*
Tonassi, *Toney*
Toncelli, *Toney*
Tondeur
Toneev, *Toney*
Tonei, *Toney*
Tonelier, *Tonnellier*
Tonelli, *Toney*
Tonellotto, *Toney*
Toner
Tonet, *Toney*
Tonetti, *Toney*
Toney
Tong
Tonge, *Tong*
Tongs, *Tong*
Tongue, *Tong*
Toni, *Thon, Toney*
Toniacci, *Toney*
Toniazzi, *Toney*
Tonicchi, *Toney*
Tonicelli, *Toney*
Tonietti, *Toney*
Tonin, *Toney*
Tonini, *Toney*
Toniolli, *Toney*
Toniolo, *Toney*
Tönissen, *Thon*
Tonissi, *Toney*
Tonitto, *Toney*
Toniutti, *Toney*
Tonizzi, *Toney*
Tonizzo, *Toney*
Tonjes, *Thon*
Tonkin, *Thomas*
Tonks, *Thomas*
Tonnellier
Tonolli, *Toney*
Tonolo, *Toney*
Tonotto, *Toney*
Tönsen, *Thon*
Tönsing, *Thon*
Tonso, *Tous*
Tonussi, *Toney*
Tonutti, *Toney*
Tony, *Toney*
Tooby, *Tobias*
Tooey, *Tuohy*
Toogood
Toohill, *Toole*
Toohy, *Tuohy*
Took, *Tooke*
Tooke
Tookey, *Tooke*
Toole
Tooley, *Towle*
Toombes, *Thomas*
Toombs, *Thomas*
Toomey, *Twomey*
Toon, *Toner*
Toone, *Toner*
Toop
Toope, *Toop*
Tootal, *Tootell*
Tootell
Tooth
Tootill, *Tootell*
Tootle, *Tootell*
Toovey, *Tovey*
Toper, *Töpfer*
Töpfer
Topham
Topiol, *Topol*
Toplady, *Tiplady*
Topley, *Tiplady*
Topol
Topolansky, *Topol*
Topoliansky, *Topol*
Topolski, *Topol*
Topolsky, *Topol*
Topp
Töpper, *Töpfer*
Topping, *Topp*
Töppler, *Doppler*
Topsch, *Tobias*
Toquoy, *Touche*
Torbeck, *Bach*
Torelli, *Toro*
Torello, *Toro*
Toresson, *Thor*
Toretta, *Tower*
Toretti, *Tower*
Toretto, *Toro*
Torgeman, *Tolmachev*
Tori, *Toro*
Toribio
Toriello, *Toro*
Toritto, *Toro*
Torjman, *Tolmachev*
Torkuhl, *Kuhl*
Torley, *McTerrelly*
Tormo
Tormühlen, *Mill*
Tornadou, *Turner*
Tornadour, *Turner*
Tornedden, *Nieder*
Tornier, *Turner*
Toro
Torode, *Thorold*
Török, *Turk*
Torosian, *Théodore*
Torp, *Thorpe*
Torpy, *Tarpey*
Torquemada
Torr
Torra, *Tower*
Torrado
Torralba
Torrance
Torras, *Tower*
Torre, *Tower*
Torrecilla, *Tower*
Torrecillas, *Tower*
Torrejón, *Tower*
Torrence, *Torrance*
Torrens, *Torrance, Torrente*
Torrent, *Torrente*
Torrente
Torrents, *Torrente*
Torrès, *Tower*
Torres, *Tower*
Torrese, *Tower*
Torresi, *Tower*
Torrey, *Terry*
Torri, *Tower*
Torricella, *Tower*
Torricina, *Tower*
Torrie, *Terry*
Torrijos, *Tower*
Torrini, *Tower*
Torris, *Terry*
Torrisi, *Tower*
Torritti, *Tower*
Torry, *Terry*
Torsson, *Thor*
Torstensen, *Thurston*
Torstensson, *Thurston*
Tort
Tortat, *Tort*
Torteau, *Tort*
Tortel, *Tourte*
Tortellier, *Tourte*
Torti, *Tort*
Tortora, *Turtle*
Tortorella, *Turtle*
Tortorelli, *Turtle*
Tortorello, *Turtle*
Tortosa
Torturiello, *Turtle*
Tosato, *Tous*
Tosatti, *Tous*
Tosatto, *Tous*
Toscan, *Toscano*
Toscanelli, *Toscano*
Toscanello, *Toscano*
Toscanese, *Toscano*
Toscanesi, *Toscano*
Toscani, *Toscano*
Toscanini, *Toscano*
Toscanino, *Toscano*
Toscano
Toschach, *McIntosh*
Toschi, *Toscano*
Tosco, *Toscano*

Toselli, *Tous*
Tosetti, *Tous*
Tosetto, *Tous*
Tosh, *McIntosh*
Toshach, *McIntosh*
Toshack, *McIntosh*
Toshak, *McIntosh*
Tosi, *Tous*
Tosini, *Tous*
Tositti, *Tous*
Toso, *Tous*
Tosolini, *Tous*
Tosoni, *Tous*
Tostain, *Thurston*
Tót, *Tóth*
Totain, *Thurston*
Totaro, *Théodore*
Tóth
Toth
Tothill, *Tootell*
Tott, *Toth*
Töttel, *Toth*
Tottle, *Tootell*
Touche
Touchet, *Touche*
Touchon, *Touche*
Toucquoy, *Touche*
Tough
Toughill, *Toole*
Touhill, *Toole*
Toulousain, *Toulouse*
Toulousan, *Toulouse*
Toulouse
Toulousy, *Toulouse*
Toulouze, *Toulouse*
Toulson, *Towle*
Toulza, *Toulouse*
Toulzan, *Toulouse*
Toulze, *Toulouse*
Touquoy, *Touche*
Tour, *Tower*
Touret, *Tower*
Tourette, *Tower*
Tourgeman, *Tolmachev*
Tourgis, *Sturgess*
Tourjeman, *Tolmachev*
Tournadre, *Turner*
Tournay, *Turney*
Tourneur, *Turner*
Tourneux, *Turner*
Tournier, *Turner*
Tournois, *Towers*
Tourot, *Tower*
Touroude, *Thorold*
Tourpin, *Turpin*
Tourry, *Tower*
Tourte
Tourteau, *Tourte*
Tourtel, *Tourte*
Tourtelier, *Tourte*
Tourtellier, *Tourte*
Tourtier, *Tourte*
Tous
Toussaint
Toustain, *Thurston*
Toutain, *Thurston*
Toutin, *Thurston*
Touvet, *Stephen*
Touzard, *Tous*
Touzé, *Tous*
Touzeau, *Tous*
Touzel, *Tous*
Touzelin, *Tous*
Touzet, *Tous*
Touzin, *Tous*
Tovar
Tovee, *Tovey*
Tovell
Tovey
Tovia, *Tobias*
Tovias, *Tobias*
Tow, *Tough*
Toward
Towe, *Tough*
Towell, *Towle*
Tower
Towers
Towes, *Tough*
Towey, *Tuohy*
Towgood, *Toogood*
Towlard, *Toller*
Towle
Towler, *Toller*
Towll, *Towle*
Towlson, *Towle*
Towmey, *Twomey*
Town, *Toner*
Towne, *Toner*
Towneley, *Townley*
Townen, *Townsend*
Townend, *Townsend*
Towner, *Toller*
Townes, *Toner*
Towning, *Toner*
Townley
Towns, *Toner*
Townsend
Townshend, *Townsend*
Townsley, *Townley*
Townson, *Thomas*
Toy
Toye, *Toy*
Tozer
Tozzetti, *Dodd*
Tozzi, *Dodd*
Tozzini, *Dodd*
Tozzoni, *Dodd*
Tracey
Trachtenberg
Tracy, *Tracey*
Tracz
Traczyk, *Tracz*
Tradescant
Tradewell, *Treadwell*
Tradwell, *Treadwell*
Trafford
Trage, *Trager*
Träger, *Trager*
Trager
Traherne, *Trehearne*
Trahms, *Bertram*
Trainer, *Trainor*
Trainor
Traister, *Trost*
Traistman, *Trost*
Trajković, *Trojan*
Trajstman, *Trost*
Trakhimovich, *Trofimov*
Trams, *Bertram*
Tranchaire, *Tranchant*
Tranchand, *Tranchant*
Tranchant
Tranchard, *Tranchant*
Tranchillon, *Tranchant*
Tranchon, *Tranchant*
Tranquard, *Tranchant*
Tranter
Trapero, *Draper*
Trapp, *Trappe*
Trappe
Trassy, *Treacy*
Tratsyakov, *Tretyakov*
Traub
Traube, *Traub*
Traubel, *Traub*
Träuble, *Traub*
Traubmann, *Traub*
Traubner, *Traub*
Traubnik, *Traub*
Traver, *Travers*
Travers
Traversa, *Travers*
Traverse, *Travers*
Traversi, *Travers*
Traversini, *Travers*
Traverso, *Travers*
Travert, *Travers*
Traves, *Travers*
Travieso, *Travers*
Travis, *Travers*
Traviss, *Travers*
Trávníček, *Trawiński*
Travor, *Trevor*
Travors, *Trevor*
Trawczyński, *Trawiński*
Trawiński
Traxler, *Drechsler*
Traynor, *Trainor*
Trazzi, *Peter*
Trčić, *Tretyakov*
Treacher
Treacy
Treadgold, *Threadgold*
Treadwell
Treanor, *Trainor*
Treasey, *Treacy*
Treasure
Trebilcock
Trečić, *Tretyakov*
Tredgold, *Threadgold*
Tredinnick
Tredwell, *Treadwell*
Tree, *Trow*
Treece, *Trow*
Treen
Trees, *Trow*
Trefus, *Dreyfuss*
Trefusis
Tregair, *Tregear*
Tregare, *Tregear*
Tregaskis, *Trevaskis*
Tregaskiss, *Trevaskis*
Tregear
Tregeare, *Tregear*
Tregears, *Tregear*
Tregenza
Treger, *Trager*
Tregerman, *Trager*
Tregona, *Tregunna*
Tregonan, *Tregoning*
Tregoning
Tregonna, *Tregunna*
Tregonnan, *Tregoning*
Tregonning, *Tregoning*
Tregonnowe, *Tregunna*
Tregunna
Tregunno, *Tregunna*
Trehearne
Treibel, *Traub*
Treiber, *Driver*
Treibman, *Driver*
Treille
Treilles, *Treille*
Treillet, *Treille*
Treiman, *Trow*
Treinen, *Catlin*
Treister, *Trost*
Treistman, *Trost*
Trejster, *Trost*
Trelawney
Trelawny, *Trelawney*
Treleaven
Treleven, *Treleaven*
Trelfall, *Threlfall*
Tremain, *Tremaine*
Tremaine
Tremayne, *Tremaine*
Trembath
Trembeth
Tremblay, *Tremble*
Tremble
Tremblet, *Tremble, Tremlett*
Tremblot, *Tremble*
Tremenheer, *Tremenheere*
Tremenheere
Tremenhere, *Tremenheere*
Tremlett
Trémoille, *Tremble*
Trémouille, *Tremble*
Trench
Trenchant, *Tranchant*
Trenchard, *Tranchant*
Trenerry
Trent
Trenter, *Tranter*
Trépard, *Tripp*
Trepat
Trépaud, *Tripp*
Trerice, *Trerise*
Trerise
Trescher, *Drescher*
Tresidder
Tresise, *Trezise*
Tresize, *Trezise*
Třešňák
Tressy, *Treacy*
Trethevy, *Trethewey*
Trethewey
Trethewy, *Trethewey*
Trethowan
Tretilov, *Tretyakov*
Tretnikov, *Tretyakov*
Tretwell, *Treadwell*
Tretyak, *Tretyakov*
Tretyakov
Tretyukhin, *Tretyakov*
Treu, *Trow*
Treue, *Trow*
Treuherz, *Trow*
Treumann, *Trow*
Treumann, *Trueman*
Trevail
Trevaldwyn
Trevarthen
Trevaskis
Trève, *Dreyfuss*
Trevellan, *Trevelyan*
Trevellion, *Trevelyan*
Trevellyan, *Trevelyan*
Trevelyan
Trevena
Trevener, *Trevena*
Trevenna, *Trevena*
Trevenner, *Trevena*
Treverrow
Trèves, *Dreyfuss*

Treves, *Dreyfuss*
Trevethan
Trevethick, *Trevithick*
Trevis, *Dreyfuss, Travers*
Trevithick
Trevor
Trevorrow
Trevors, *Trevor*
Trew, *Trow*
Trewheela, *Trewhella*
Trewhella
Trewin
Trewman, *Trueman*
Treyor, *Trevor*
Trezise
Trezize, *Trezise*
Trias, *Treille*
Tribot, *Trillo*
Tribouillard, *Trillo*
Triboul, *Trillo*
Triboulet, *Trillo*
Triboulot, *Trillo*
Tribout, *Trillo*
Tribus, *Dreyfuss*
Trick
Tricker, *Trick*
Trickett, *Trick*
Triene, *Catlin*
Trienen, *Catlin*
Trier, *Dreyfuss*
Triffault, *Truffault*
Trigg
Trigge, *Trigg*
Triggs, *Trigg*
Trigo
Triguero, *Trigo*
Trillat, *Treille*
Trille, *Treille*
Trillet, *Treille*
Trillo
Triltsche, *Trouillet*
Trim
Trimble, *Trumbull*
Trimlett, *Tremlett*
Trimmer
Trimouille, *Tremble*
Trincard, *Tranchant*
Trindade
Trinder
Trine, *Catlin*
Tripconey
Tripe, *Tripp*
Tripeau, *Tripp*
Tripet, *Tripp*
Tripette, *Tripp*
Tripié, *Tripp*
Tripier, *Tripp*
Tripon, *Tripp*
Tripp
Tripper, *Tripp*
Trishkin, *Trofimov*
Třiška, *Tříska*
Tříska
Trivas, *Dreyfuss*
Trives, *Dreyfuss*
Trivier, *Dreyfuss*
Trivis, *Dreyfuss*
Trivus, *Dreyfuss*
Trnka
Trobridge, *Trowbridge*
Trochimowicz, *Trofimov*
Trock
Trocker, *Trock*
Trocki, *Trock*
Trofimov
Troitski
Trojan
Trojančík, *Trojan*
Trojánek, *Trojan*
Trojanowski, *Trojan*
Trojášek, *Trojan*
Trojek, *Trojan*
Trokhinchik, *Trofimov*
Trollop, *Trollope*
Trollope
Tröltsch, *Trouillet*
Troman, *Trueman*
Tromans, *Trueman*
Tronchon, *Trunchion*
Troncin, *Trunchion*
Troni, *Peter*
Tronson, *Trunchion*
Tronyaev, *Trofimov*
Troop, *Troup*
Troost, *Trost*
Trösch, *Drescher*
Trösche, *Drescher*
Tröscher, *Drescher*
Troshchenko, *Trofimov*
Trossier
Trøst, *Trost*
Trost
Tröster, *Trost*
Trostman, *Trost*
Troth
Trotier, *Trotter*
Trotignon, *Trotter*
Trotin, *Trotter*
Trotman, *Trotter*
Trotmann, *Trotter*
Trotot, *Trotter*
Trotski, *Trock*
Trotsky, *Trock*
Trott, *Trotter*
Trotteleau, *Trotter*
Trotter
Trottereau, *Trotter*
Trottier, *Trotter*
Trottmann, *Trotter*
Troubat, *Trouvé*
Troubridge, *Trowbridge*
Troude, *Thorold*
Troughton
Trouillard, *Trouillet*
Trouillet
Trouillon, *Trouillet*
Trouillot, *Trouillet*
Trounson, *Trunchion*
Troup
Troupe, *Troup*
Troussié, *Trossier*
Trout
Trouton, *Troughton*
Trouvat, *Trouvé*
Trouvé
Trouvin, *Trouvé*
Trovatelli, *Trouvé*
Trovatello, *Trouvé*
Trovati, *Trouvé*
Trovato, *Trouvé*
Trow
Trowbridge
Trower, *Thrower, Trevor*
Trowman, *Trueman*
Trowmans, *Trueman*
Troy
Trübner, *Traub*
Trubridge, *Trowbridge*
Truc
Truchet, *Truc*
Truchetet, *Truc*
Truchon, *Truc*
Truchot, *Truc*
Truchy, *Truc*
Trudeau, *Thorold*
Trudgeon
Trudgian, *Trudgeon*
Trudgill
Trudon, *Thorold*
True, *Trow*
Trueman
Truett, *Tyrwhitt*
Truffaudier, *Truffault*
Truffault
Truffaut, *Truffault*
Truffot, *Truffault*
Truhlář
Trujillo
Trüll, *Trouillet*
Trull, *Trouillet*
Trüller, *Trouillet*
Trültsch, *Trouillet*
Truman, *Trueman*
Trumble, *Trumbull*
Trumbull
Trunchion
Trupin, *Turpin*
Trupp, *Thorpe*
Truquet, *Truc*
Truscott
Truss, *Trossier*
Trussel, *Trussell*
Trussell
Trussman, *Trossier*
Truswell, *Trussell*
Trygg, *Trigg*
Tryon
Tryoshnikov, *Tretyakov*
Trzcieński, *Trzciński*
Trzciński
Trzeciak, *Tretyakov*
Trzepałkowski
Trzepiński, *Trzepałkowski*
Tsaddik, *Zadik*
Tsadok
Tsaplin, *Chaplin*
Tschäche, *Čech*
Tschäpe, *Stephen*
Tscharnach, *Chernyakov*
Tscharnke, *Chernyakov*
Tschech, *Čech*
Tscheche, *Čech*
Tschepe, *Stephen*
Tschernack, *Chernyakov*
Tschernak, *Chernyakov*
Tscherne, *Chernyakov*
Tscherning, *Chernyakov*
Tschernke, *Chernyakov*
Tscherny, *Chernyakov*
Tschersich, *George*
Tschiersch, *George*
Tschierschke, *George*
Tschierse, *George*
Tschirsch, *George*
Tschirschke, *George*
Tschirschky, *George*
Tschöpe, *Stephen*
Tschöppe, *Stephen*
Tschorn, *Chernyakov*
Tschörner, *Chernyakov*
Tschornig, *Chernyakov*
Tschursch, *George*
Tseder, *Ceder*
Tsherniak, *Chernyakov*
Tshernichov, *Chernyakov*
Tshernichow, *Chernyakov*
Tshorni, *Chernyakov*
Tsibulya, *Zwiebel*
Tsigler, *Ziegler*
Tsimafeev, *Timofeev*
Tsin, *Zinn*
Tsitov, *Tito*
Tsitovich, *Tito*
Tsodek, *Tsadok*
Tsvetkov, *Kwiatek*
Tsvetkovski, *Kwiatek*
Tsybulkin, *Zwiebel*
Tsyganov
Tubb
Tubbs, *Tubb*
Tubby, *Tubb*
Tuc, *Truc*
Tuček
Tucher, *Tuchmann*
Tuchert, *Tuchmann*
Tuchler, *Tuchmann*
Tuchmacher, *Tuchmann*
Tuchman, *Tuchmann*
Tuchmann
Tuchschneider, *Tuchmann*
Tuchsznajder, *Tuchmann*
Tuck, *Tooke*
Tucker
Tuckey, *Tooke*
Tuckwell
Tudbald, *Theobald*
Tudball, *Theobald*
Tuddenham
Tudela
Tudisco, *Tedesco*
Tudman, *Tuddenham*
Tudor, *Théodore*
Tugnetti, *Toney*
Tugnoli, *Toney*
Tugwell, *Tuckwell*
Tugwood, *Toogood*
Tuháček
Tuhy, *Tuohy*
Tuijnman, *Toner*
Tuilier, *Tiler*
Tuillier, *Tiler*
Tuin, *Toner*
Tuinman, *Toner*
Tuite
Tuke, *Tooke*
Tull
Tullier, *Tiler*
Tulliez, *Tiler*
Tulliver, *Telfer*
Tulloch
Tullock, *Tulloch*
Tulloh, *Tulloch*
Tully
Tůma, *Thomas*
Tumanov
Tumasian, *Thomas*
Tumayan, *Thomas*
Tumelty, *Tomelty*
Tuminelli, *Thomas*
Tumini, *Thomas*
Tumiotto, *Thomas*
Tumpany, *Timpany*
Tundidor, *Tondeur*
Tune, *Toner*
Tungate
Tunick, *Tunik*

Tunik
Tunioli, *Toney*
Tunkel, *Donker*
Tunney
Tunnicliff, *Tunnicliffe*
Tunnicliffe
Tunstall
Tunstell, *Tunstall*
Tunstill, *Tunstall*
Tuohy
Tuominen
Tuomy, *Twomey*
Tupper
Tuquet, *Truc*
Tur, *Turov*
Tura, *Ventura*
Turajczyk, *Turov*
Turała, *Turov*
Turalski, *Turov*
Turban, *Urban*
Turbin, *Thorburn*
Turc, *Turk*
Turchelli, *Turk*
Turcheschi, *Turk*
Turchetti, *Turk*
Turchetto, *Turk*
Turchi, *Turk*
Turchini, *Turk*
Turchio, *Turk*
Turci, *Turk*
Turck, *Turk*
Turco, *Turk*
Turcq, *Turk*
Turcu, *Turk*
Turcul, *Turk*
Turczak, *Turk*
Tureau, *Arthur*
Tureček, *Turk*
Turek, *Turk*
Turel, *Arthur*
Turella, *Ventura*
Turelli, *Ventura*
Turello, *Ventura*
Turesson, *Thor*
Turet, *Arthur*
Turgell, *Thirkill*
Turgeman, *Tolmachev*
Turgenev
Turgill, *Thirkill*
Turgis, *Sturgess*
Turgman, *Tolmachev*
Turgoose, *Sturgess*
Turgot, *Thorogood*
Turiello, *Toro*
Turin, *Arthur*
Türk, *Turk*
Turk
Turkel, *Thirkill*
Turkheim, *Durkheim*
Turkheimer, *Durkheim*
Turkiewicz, *Turk*
Turkill, *Thirkill*
Turkington
Turkisher, *Turk*
Turkov, *Turk*
Turkow, *Turk*
Turkowski, *Turk*
Turley, *McTerrelly*
Turnbill, *Turnbull*
Turnbull
Turner
Turney
Turnham
Turnor, *Turner*
Turnour, *Turner*
Turock, *Turov*
Turok, *Turov*
Turon, *Arthur*
Turot, *Arthur*
Turov
Turovetz, *Turov*
Turowicz, *Turov*
Turowski, *Turov*
Turp, *Thorpe*
Turpie, *Turpin*
Turpin
Türpitz, *Tirpitz*
Turquet, *Turk*
Turquetil, *Thirkill*
Turquety, *Thirkill*
Turquin, *Turk*
Turrell, *Tyrrell*
Turri, *Tower*
Turrini, *Tower*
Turrisi, *Tower*
Turski, *Turov*
Turtill, *Thirkill*
Turtle
Turton
Turtura, *Turtle*
Turturiello, *Turtle*
Turturo, *Turtle*
Turuk, *Turov*
Turvey
Tuscano, *Toscano*
Tuson
Tussaud, *Truc*
Tusse, *Truc*
Tusseau, *Truc*
Tustain, *Thurston*
Tustian, *Thurston*
Tustin, *Thurston*
Tusting, *Thurston*
Tutchener, *Titchener*
Tutchings, *Titchener*
Tutin, *Thurston*
Tuting, *Thurston*
Tuton, *Thurston*
Tutt
Tuttle, *Thirkill*
Tutton, *Thurston*
Tutty
Tuvey, *Tovey*
Tuvia, *Tobias*
Tuvya, *Tobias*
Tuvyahu, *Tobias*
Tuyn, *Zauner*
Tuynman, *Toner*
Tuyns, *Zauner*
Tverdashov, *Tvrdík*
Tverdyukov, *Tvrdík*
Tvrdík
Tvyordyshev, *Tvrdík*
Twaddell, *Tweddle*
Twaddle, *Tweddle*
Twaite, *Thwaite*
Twaites, *Thwaite*
Twaits, *Thwaite*
Tward, *Tvrdík*
Twardogora, *Tvrdík*
Twardowski, *Tvrdík*
Twardy, *Tvrdík*
Twatt, *Thwaite*
Tweats, *Thwaite*
Tweddell, *Tweddle*
Tweddle
Tweed
Tweedale, *Tweddle*
Tweedie
Tweedle, *Tweddle*
Tweedy, *Tweedie*
Tweig, *Twigg*
Twell, *Attwell*
Twells, *Attwell*
Twigg
Twigge, *Twigg*
Twin
Twinn, *Twin*
Twiss, *Twist*
Twist
Twitchen, *Titchener*
Twitching, *Titchener*
Twitchings, *Titchener*
Twite, *Thwaite*
Twohill, *Toole*
Twohy, *Tuohy*
Twomey
Twoohy, *Tuohy*
Twoomy, *Twomey*
Twyford
Tyas
Tydeman, *Tidman*
Tydsley, *Tyldesley*
Tye
Tyers, *Tyas*
Tyldeslegh, *Tyldesley*
Tyldesley
Tyler, *Tiler*
Tyley, *Tilley*
Tylor, *Tiler*
Tym, *Timm*
Tyma, *Timofeev*
Tymański, *Timofeev*
Tymkiewicz, *Timofeev*
Tymm, *Timm*
Tymmany, *Timony*
Tymms, *Timm*
Tymowski, *Timofeev*
Tympany, *Timpany*
Tynan
Tyndale, *Tindale*
Tyndall, *Tindale*
Tyre, *McIntyre*
Tyrell, *Tyrrell*
Tyrer
Tyrie, *McIntyre*
Tyringham
Tyrrell
Tyrwhitt
Tyson
Tyssen, *Thiess*
Tytel, *Teitelbaum*
Tyzack
Tzadik, *Zadik*
Tzadikian, *Zadik*
Tzadok, *Tsadok*
Tzarkov, *Kaiser*
Tzaryov, *Kaiser*
Tzeitlin, *Zeitlin*
Tzin, *Zinn*
Tzinger, *Tong*
Tzudick, *Tsadok*
Tzuker, *Zucker*
Tzung, *Tong*

U

Ubach, *Bach*
Uc, *Hugh*
Uccelletti, *Uccello*
Uccelli, *Uccello*
Uccello
Ucciero, *Edgar*
Uceda
Uciński
Udall
Uddin
Ude, *Ulrich*
Udell, *Udall*
Udovchik, *Widdow*
Udovenko, *Widdow*
Udovichenko, *Widdow*
Ufer
Ufermann, *Ufer*
Ufert, *Ufer*
Ufford
Ugalde
Ugarte
Ugge, *Edgar*
Uggeri, *Edgar*
Uggieri, *Edgar*
Ughelli, *Hugh*
Ughetti, *Hugh*
Ughi, *Hugh*
Ughini, *Hugh*
Ugo, *Hugh*
Ugoletti, *Hugh*
Ugolini, *Hugh*
Ugolotti, *Hugh*
Ugon, *Hugh*
Ugoni, *Hugh*
Ugotti, *Hugh*
Uhde, *Ulrich*
Uher, *Unger*
Uhl, *Ulrich*
Uhle, *Ulrich*
Ühlein, *Ulrich*
Uhlemann, *Ulrich*
Uhlich, *Ulrich*
Uhlig, *Ulrich*
Uhlík, *Uhlíř*
Ühlin, *Ulrich*
Uhlíř
Uhlmann, *Ulrich*
Uhrig, *Ulrich*
Uijs, *Uys*
Uken, *Ulrich*
Ukena, *Ulrich*
Ukrainetz, *Ukraintsev*
Ukraïnko, *Ukraintsev*
Ukraintsev
Ulanov
Ulanowski, *Ulanov*
Ułański, *Ulanov*
Ulański, *Ulanov*
Ulatowski
Ulbricht, *Albert*
Ulbrig, *Albert*
Ulcelli, *Uccello*
Ulejski, *Ulrich*
Uli, *Ulrich*
Ulik, *Ulrich*
Uliot, *Wolfit*
Ulisch, *Ulrich*
Uliva, *Oliva*
Ulivelli, *Oliva*
Ulivi, *Oliva*
Ulivieri, *Oliver*
Ulke, *Ulrich*
Ulken, *Ulrich*
Ulkes, *Ulrich*
Ullerich, *Ulrich*
Ullett, *Wolfit*
Ullman, *Ulman*
Ullmann, *Ulrich*

Ullrich, *Ulrich*
Ullyat, *Wolfit*
Ullyate, *Wolfit*
Ullyatt, *Wolfit*
Ullyett, *Wolfit*
Ullyott, *Wolfit*
Ulman
Ulph, *Wolf*
Ulrich
Ulrici, *Ulrich*
Ulsch, *Ulrich*
Ultsch, *Ulrich*
Ulusch, *Ulrich*
Ulyachin, *Julian*
Ulyanchev, *Julian*
Ulyanichev, *Julian*
Ulyanishchev, *Julian*
Ulyankin, *Julian*
Ulyanov, *Julian*
Ulyashkov, *Julian*
Ulyashov, *Julian*
Ulyate, *Wolfit*
Ulyatt, *Wolfit*
Ulyet, *Wolfit*
Ulyett, *Wolfit*
Ulyot, *Wolfit*
Umfraville, *Umfreville*
Umfreville
Umphraville, *Umfreville*
Umpleby
Unbegaun, *Unbehauen*
Unbehauen
Unbehaun, *Unbehauen*
Uncle
Uncles, *Uncle*
Underhill
Underwood
Undrell, *Underhill*
Ungár, *Unger*
Ungar, *Unger*
Ungarelli, *Unger*
Ungaretti, *Unger*
Ungari, *Unger*
Ungaro, *Unger*
Unger
Ungerer, *Unger*
Ungerland, *Unger*
Ungerman, *Unger*
Ungermann, *Unger*
Ungerson, *Unger*
Ungherelli, *Unger*
Unghérese, *Unger*
Ungles, *Uncle*
Ungless, *Uncle*
Unrau, *Unruh*
Unruh
Unsworth
Unwin
Upjohn
Upton
Uran, *Uren*
Urane, *Uren*
Urbain, *Urban*
Urbán, *Urban*
Urban
Urbańczyk, *Urban*
Urbanec, *Urban*
Urbánek, *Urban*
Urbanek, *Urban*
Urbani, *Urban*
Urbaniak, *Urban*
Urbaniec, *Urban*
Urbaniello, *Urban*
Urbanke, *Urban*
Urbano, *Urban*
Urbanov, *Urban*
Urbanovich, *Urban*
Urbanovsky, *Urban*
Urbanowicz, *Urban*
Urbanowski, *Urban*
Urbański, *Urban*
Urbantsev, *Urban*
Urbantsov, *Urban*
Urbasch, *Urban*
Urben, *Urban*
Urbin, *Urban*
Urbisch, *Urban*
Ure
Urech, *Ulrich*
Uren
Ureña
Urene, *Uren*
Urevich, *Horowitz*
Urey, *Wooldridge*
Uría
Urian, *Uren*
Uriarte
Uribarri
Uribe
Urich, *Ulrich*
Urie, *Wooldridge*
Urien, *Uren*
Urig, *Ulrich*
Urin, *Uren*
Urine, *Uren*
Uring, *Uren*
Urion, *Uren*
Urlin, *Harling*
Urling, *Harling*
Urlwin, *Harling*
Urmantsev, *Urban*
Urmantsov, *Urban*
Urne, *Uren*
Uron, *Uren*
Urquhart
Urquijo
Urran, *Uren*
Urren, *Uren*
Urrin, *Uren*
Urron, *Uren*
Urrutia
Urry, *Wooldridge*
Urshalimi, *Yerushalmi*
Ursi, *Orso*
Ursillo, *Orso*
Ursini, *Orso*
Ursino, *Orso*
Urso, *Orso*
Ursul, *Orso*
Urvine, *Irvine*
Urwin, *Irvine*
Urwitz, *Horowitz*
Ury, *Wooldridge*
Uryn, *Uren*
Urzędowicz, *Urzędowski*
Urzędowski
Usatchov, *Wąsik*
Usatych, *Wąsik*
Usborne, *Osborn*
Ushakov
Usher
Usherov, *Usher*
Usherovitz, *Usher*
Usherowicz, *Usher*
Usherwood, *Isherwood*
Usignuolo, *Rossignol*
Ussell, *Uccello*
Ussher, *Usher*
Ustimenko, *Justin*
Ustimov, *Justin*
Ustimovich, *Justin*
Ustinikov, *Justin*
Ustinnikov, *Justin*
Ustinov, *Justin*
Ustyanov, *Justin*
Ustyukhin, *Justin*
Uszerowicz, *Usher*
Utley
Utridge, *Uttridge*
Utteridge, *Uttridge*
Uttin, *Utting*
Utting
Uttley, *Utley*
Uttridge
Utz, *Ulrich*
Ützle, *Ulrich*
Utzmann, *Ulrich*
Uvedale, *Udall*
Uys
Uzielli, *Uccello*
Uzzell, *Uccello*

V

Vaamonde, *Baamonde*
Vaandrager
Vaas, *Jarvis*
Vabre, *Vaur*
Vaca, *Vacca*
Vacar, *Vaccaro*
Vacas, *Vacca*
Vacca
Vaccai, *Vaccaro*
Vaccarelli, *Vaccaro*
Vaccarello, *Vaccaro*
Vaccari, *Vaccaro*
Vaccariello, *Vaccaro*
Vaccarini, *Vaccaro*
Vaccarino, *Vaccaro*
Vaccaro
Vaccaroni, *Vaccaro*
Vacchelli, *Vacca*
Vaccher, *Vaccaro*
Vacchi, *Vacca*
Vacek, *Václav*
Vacelet, *Vass*
Vácha, *Václav*
Vacha, *Vaccaro*
Váchal, *Václav*
Vaché, *Vaccaro*
Vachek, *Václav*
Vachel, *Václav*
Vacher, *Vaccaro*
Vacherat, *Vaccaro*
Vacheret, *Vaccaro*
Vacheron, *Vaccaro*
Vacherot, *Vaccaro*
Vachet, *Vacca*
Vachette, *Vacca*
Vachey, *Vacca*
Vacheyron, *Vaccaro*
Vachez, *Vacca*
Vachier, *Vaccaro*
Vachl, *Václav*
Vachon, *Vacca*
Vachot, *Vacca*
Vachoux, *Vacca*
Vachrameev, *Bartholomew*
Vacík, *Václav*
Vacks, *Wachsmann*
Václav
Václavek, *Václav*
Václavík, *Václav*
Václavovský, *Václav*
Václavů, *Václav*
Vacquerel, *Vaccaro*
Vacquez, *Vacca*
Vacquier, *Vaccaro*
Vacquin, *Vacca*
Vacuík, *Václav*
Vacula, *Václav*
Vad, *Wade*
Vadé, *Wade*
Vadel, *Wade*
Vadet, *Wade*
Vadez, *Wade*
Vadillo, *Wade*
Vadimov
Vado, *Wade*
Vadon, *Wade*
Vagd, *Vogt*
Vagedes, *Vogt*
Vagel, *Vogel*
Vageler, *Fowler*
Vagg, *Fagg*
Vaggs, *Fagg*
Vagman, *Wäger*
Vágner, *Wagner*
Vagt, *Vogt*
Vagts, *Vogt*
Vaguer, *Vaccaro*
Vaida, *Vajda*
Vail, *Veil*
Vaillant, *Valiant*
Vainberg, *Weinberg*
Vainberger, *Weinberg*
Vainer, *Wein*
Vainerman, *Wein*
Vaines, *Fane*
Vainio
Vainstein, *Wein*
Vaintal, *Wein*
Vair
Vairel, *Vair*
Vairet, *Vair*
Vairon, *Vair*
Vairow, *Farrar*
Vais, *White*
Vaisey
Vaisfeld, *White*
Vaisman, *White*
Vaissade, *Vaysse*
Vaissat, *Vaysse*
Vaisse, *Vaysse*
Vaisset, *Vaysse*
Vaissette, *Vaysse*
Vaissié, *Vaysse*
Vaissier, *Vaysse*
Vaissière, *Vaysse*
Vaith, *Vito*
Vaitl, *Vito*
Vaivre, *Vaur*
Vaizey, *Vaisey*
Vajda
Vajselfisz, *Weisselfisch*
Vajser, *White*
Vakhlov, *Bartholomew*
Vakhnin, *Bartholomew*
Vakhonin, *Bartholomew*
Vakhov, *Bartholomew*
Vakhrushev, *Bartholomew*
Vakhrushin, *Bartholomew*
Vakhrushkov, *Bartholomew*
Vaks, *Wachsmann*
Vaksman, *Wachsmann*

Val, *Vale*
Vála, *Valentine*
Valadéz, *Baud*
Valadier, *Vallat*
Valadon, *Vallat*
Valance, *Vallance*
Valantin, *Valentine*
Valášek, *Valentine*
Valat, *Vallat*
Valayer, *Vallat*
Valbuena
Valcarce, *Valcárcel*
Valcárcel
Vald, *Wald*
Valdberg, *Wald*
Valdboim, *Wald*
Valderrama
Valdes, *Baud*
Valdéz, *Baud*
Valdman, *Wald*
Valdovinos, *Baldwin*
Vale
Valeano, *Vale*
Válek, *Valentine*
València, *Valencia*
Valencia
Valenciano, *Valencia*
Valenta, *Valentine*
Valente
Valentí, *Valentine*
Valenti, *Valente*
Valentim, *Valentine*
Valentín, *Valentine*
Valentin, *Valentine*
Valentine
Valentinelli, *Valentine*
Valentinetti, *Valentine*
Valentini, *Valentine*
Valentino, *Valentine*
Valentinuzzi, *Valentine*
Valenza, *Valencia*
Valenzani, *Valencia*
Valenzano, *Valencia*
Valenzi, *Valencia*
Valenziano, *Valencia*
Valenzuela, *Valencia*
Valer, *Valerio*
Valera
Valère, *Valerio*
Valéri, *Valerio*
Valeri, *Valerio*
Valérian, *Valeriano*
Valeriani, *Valeriano*
Valeriano
Valerianov, *Valeriano*
Valerini, *Valerio*
Valério, *Valerio*
Valerio
Valerius, *Valerio*
Valero, *Valerio*
Valéry, *Valerio*
Valeš, *Valentine*
Valet, *Vallet*
Valeton, *Vallet*
Valett, *Vallet*
Valetta, *Vale*
Valette, *Vale*
Valiant
Valiente, *Valente*
Valier, *Valerio*
Valintine, *Valentine*
Valíš, *Valentine*
Valk, *Falcon*
Valkó, *Valerio*
Vall
Valla, *Vale*
Valladier, *Vallat*
Vallance
Vallans, *Vallance*
Vallantin, *Valentine*
Vallantine, *Valentine*
Vallarini, *Vale*
Vallarino, *Vale*
Vallario, *Vale*
Vallaro, *Vale*
Vallat
Vallayer, *Vallat*
Valle, *Vale*
Vallejo, *Vale*
Vallender
Vallentin, *Valentine*
Vallentine, *Valentine*
Valleri, *Valerio*
Valles, *Vale*
Vallès
Vallese, *Vale*
Vallesi, *Vale*
Vallet
Valleteau, *Vallet*
Vallette, *Vale*
Valletti, *Vale*
Valli, *Vale*
Vallier, *Valerio*
Vallillo, *Vale*
Vallintine, *Valentine*
Vallis, *Valois*
Vallon, *Vale*
Vallone, *Vale*
Valloni, *Vale*
Vallot, *Vallet*
Vallotto, *Vale*
Valls, *Vall*
Vallvé, *Beaver*
Vallverdú
Valois
Valot, *Vallet*
Valotto, *Vale*
Valperga, *Walburg*
Valteau, *Vallet*
Valter, *Walter*
Valtieri, *Walter*
Valtin, *Valentine, Vallet*
Valtl, *Valentine*
Valton, *Vallet*
Valtot, *Vallet*
Valvassori, *Vavasour*
Valverde
Vámbéry, *Bamberger*
Vaňa, *Václav*
Vaňáč, *Václav*
Van Akkeren, *Acker*
Van Ark, *Arkwright*
Vaňásek, *Václav*
Van Baaren, *Barr*
Van Baren, *Barr*
Van Beek, *Bach*
Van Beneden, *Nieder*
Van Berge, *Berg*
Van Bergen, *Berg*
Van Bosse, *Bush*
Van Boven, *Ober*
Van Brach, *Brach*
Van Breugel, *Brühl*
Van Breukelen, *Brühl*
Van Brug, *Bridge*
Van Bruggen, *Bridge*
Vanbrugh, *Bridge*
Van Buren, *Bower*
Van Buuren, *Bower*
Van Camp, *Champ*
Van Campen, *Champ*
Van Cassel, *Castle*
Van Castele, *Castle*
Vančata, *Václav*
Vance, *Fenn*
Vanchakov, *John*
Vanchikov, *John*
Vančura, *Václav*
Van Daal, *Dale*
Van Daalen, *Dale*
Van Dael, *Dale*
Van Dale, *Dale*
Van Dalen, *Dale*
Van Dam, *Dam*
Van Damme, *Dam*
Van Dantzig, *Danzig*
Van de Brinck, *Brink*
Van de Brink, *Brink*
Van de Capelle, *Chappell*
Van de Castele, *Castle*
Van de Kamp, *Champ*
Van de Keppel, *Chappell*
Van de Leest, *Last*
Van de Loo, *Loo*
Van de Meij, *May*
Van de Mey, *May*
Van den Berck, *Birch*
Van den Berg, *Berg*
Van den Berge, *Berg*
Van den Bergh, *Berg*
Van den Berk, *Birch*
Van den Beuken, *Buch*
Van den Bogaarde, *Baumgarten*
Van den Bogaert, *Baumgarten*
Van den Bogarde, *Baumgarten*
Van den Boom, *Baum*
Van den Borcht, *Burke*
Van den Borne, *Bourne*
Van den Borre, *Bourne*
Van den Bos, *Bush*
Van den Bosch, *Bush*
Van den Braak, *Brach*
Van den Brinck, *Brink*
Van den Brink, *Brink*
Van den Broek, *Brook*
Van den Broeke, *Brook*
Van den Bueren, *Bower*
Van den Burcht, *Burke*
Van den Burg, *Burke*
Van den Burgh, *Burke*
Van den Camp, *Champ*
Van den Dael, *Dale*
Van den Daele, *Dale*
Van den Doorne, *Thorn*
Van den Dorpe, *Thorpe*
Van den Driesch, *Driesch*
Van den Eynde, *Ende*
Van den Glas, *Glass*
Van den Hende, *Ende*
Van den Heuvel, *Hill*
Van den Heyden, *Heath*
Van den Hoed, *Huth*
Van den Hoek, *Hook*
Van den Hooft, *Head*
Van den Hoorn, *Horn*
Van den Horn, *Horn*
Van den Hout, *Holt*
Van den Houte, *Holt*
Van den Hove, *Hofer*
Van den Kamp, *Champ*
Van den Klooster, *Klostermann*
Van den Land, *Land*
Van den Noort, *North*
Van den Oever, *Over*
Van den Oord, *Ort*
Van den Peereboom, *Birnbaum*
Van den Pijl, *Pfeil*
Van den Pijll, *Pfeil*
Van den Pol, *Pol*
Van den Poll, *Pol*
Van den Put, *Pfützer*
Van den Putten, *Pfützer*
Van den Sande, *Sand*
Van den Steen, *Stone*
Van den Storm, *Storm*
Van den Swaan, *Swan*
Van den Tol, *Toller*
Van den Tuin, *Toner*
Van den Veen, *Fenn*
Van den Velde, *Field*
Van den Velden, *Field*
Van den Veldt, *Field*
Van den Ven, *Fenn*
Van den Vinne, *Fenn*
Van den Vorst, *Forrest*
Van den Wall, *Wall*
Van den Water, *Water*
Van den Weijden, *Weide*
Van den Weijer, *Weiher*
Van den Weyden, *Weide*
Van den Zande, *Sand*
Van den Zanden, *Sand*
Van den Zwaan, *Swan*
Van de Plaats, *Place*
Van de Poel, *Pool*
Van der Akkere, *Acker*
Van der Baaren, *Barr*
Van der Beek, *Bach*
Van der Beken, *Bach*
Van der Beld, *Bilt*
Van der Belt, *Bilt*
Van der Bij, *Bee*
Van der Bijl, *Bill*
Van der Bilt, *Bilt*
Vanderborn, *Bourne*
Vanderborne, *Bourne*
Van der Brug, *Bridge*
Van der Brugge, *Bridge*
Van der Brule, *Brühl*
Van der Cleie, *Clay*
Van der Daal, *Dale*
Van der Ende, *Ende*
Van der Essen, *Ash*
Van der Eycke, *Oak*
Van der Geest, *Geest*
Van der Geynst, *Genest*
Van der Gheynst, *Genest*
Van der Haar, *Haar*
Van der Haeghe, *Haig*
Van der Hall, *Hall*
Van der Hart, *Hardt*
Van der Heide, *Heath*
Van der Hejde, *Heath*
Van der Hengst, *Hengst*
Van der Hilst, *Hilse*
Van der Horst, *Hurst*
Van der Hulst, *Hilse*
Van der Klei, *Clay*
Van der Kooi, *Kooy*
Van der Kroon, *Corona*
Van der Kruijs, *Cross*
Van der Kruis, *Cross*
Van der Kruys, *Cross*
Van der Linde, *Linde*

Van der Linden, *Linde*
Van der Mark, *Mark*
Van der Meer, *Meer*
Van der Meersch, *Marsh*
Van der Meulen, *Mill*
Van der Moeren, *Moore*
Van der Molen, *Mill*
Van der Moolen, *Mill*
Van der Most, *Most*
Van der Osten, *East*
Van der Palme, *Palmer*
Van der Placke, *Place*
Van der Plaëtse, *Place*
Van der Plaetsen, *Place*
Van der Pluijm, *Plummer*
Van der Pluym, *Plummer*
Van der Poel, *Pool*
Van der Post, *Post*
Van der Rest, *Ash*
Van der Schueren, *Scheuer*
Van der Sluijs, *Sluis*
Van der Sluis, *Sluis*
Van der Sluys, *Sluis*
Van der Spek, *Speck*
Van der Steeg, *Steiger*
Van der Steegen, *Steiger*
Van der Ster, *Starr*
Van der Straeten, *Street*
Van der Struijs, *Strauss*
Van der Struys, *Strauss*
Van der Valk, *Falcon*
Van der Velde, *Field*
Van der Voet, *Foot*
Van der Voort, *Ford*
Van der Wegen, *Way*
Van der Weghe, *Way*
Van der Weide, *Weide*
Van der Wel, *Well*
Van der Wels, *Well*
Van der Werff, *Werf, Van der*
Van der Weyden, *Weide*
Van der Winkel, *Winckel*
Van der Zee, *See*
Van der Zyl, *Zyl, van*
Van de Star, *Starr*
Van de Veer, *Veerman*
Van de Velde, *Field*
Van de Ven, *Fenn*
Van Deventer, *Deventer*
Van de Vliet, *Fleet*
Van de Vorst, *Forrest*
Van de Weg, *Way*
Van de Wijngaerden, *Winyard*
Van de Winckel, *Winckel*
Van de Woude, *Wald*
Van Dijck, *Ditch*
Van Dijk, *Ditch*
Van Dijken, *Ditch*
Van Dongen, *Dung*
Van Donks, *Dung*
Van Doorn, *Thorn*
Van Dorp, *Thorpe*
Van Duijn, *Duin*
Van Duinen, *Duin*
Van Duyn, *Duin*
Van Dyck, *Ditch*
Van Dyk, *Ditch*
Van Dyken, *Ditch*
Vane, *Fane*
Vaněček, *Václav*
Van Ede, *Eder*
Van Eden, *Eder*
Van Eeden, *Eder*
Van Eekelen, *Oak*
Van Eeken, *Oak*
Vaneev, *John*
Van Eijk, *Oak*
Vaňek, *Václav*
Vanelli, *John*
Van Engeland, *English*
Van Es, *Ash*
Vanes, *Fane*
Van Esch, *Ash*
Vaneschi, *John*
Van Essen, *Ash*
Van Eyk, *Oak*
Vang, *Wang*
Van Geest, *Geest*
Van Gelder, *Geller*
Van Gelderen, *Geller*
Van Gent, *Gaunt*
Van Gheest, *Geest*
Van Ghent, *Gaunt*
Van Gog, *Gogh*
Van Gogh, *Gogh*
Van Hagendoren, *Hawthorn*
Van Hall, *Hall*
Van Harten, *Hardt*
Van Havre, *Haber*
Van Heden, *Heath*
Van Hee, *Heath*
Van Hees, *Hayes*
Van Heesen, *Hayes*
Van Heghe, *Hedge*
Van Hes, *Hayes*
Van Heuvel, *Hill*
Van Hille, *Hill*
Van Hilst, *Hilse*
Van Hoeck, *Hook*
Van Hoek, *Hook*
Van Hoorn, *Horn*
Van Hoppe, *Höpfner*
Van Horn, *Horn*
Van Houten, *Holt*
Van Houtte, *Holt*
Van Hove, *Hofer*
Van Huis, *House*
Van Huizen, *House*
Van Hulle, *Hill*
Van Hulst, *Hilse*
Vaníček, *Václav*
Vanichev, *John*
Vanichkin, *John*
Vanichkov, *John*
Vanier, *Vannier*
Vanin, *John*
Vanini, *John*
Vaniš, *Václav*
Van Kamp, *Champ*
Van Kampen, *Champ*
Vankeev, *John*
Van Keppel, *Chappell*
Van Kessel, *Kessel*
Van Keulen, *Cullen*
Vankin, *John*
Van Klaveren, *Klee*
Van Klooster, *Klostermann*
Van Kooi, *Kooy*
Vankov, *John*
Van Kruys, *Cross*
Van Lent, *Lenz*
Van Lint, *Linde*
Van Loo, *Loo*
Van Loon, *Loo*
Vann, *Fenn*
Vannacci, *John*
Vannar, *Fanner*
Vanne, *Fenn*
Vannelli, *John*
Vanner, *Fanner*
Vannereau, *Vannier*
Van Nes, *Ash*
Vannetti, *John*
Vanneur, *Vannier*
Vanni, *John*
Vannier
Vannikov, *John*
Vannini, *John*
Vannoni, *John*
Van Noord, *North*
Van Noorden, *North*
Vannozzi, *John*
Vannucci, *John*
Vannuccini, *John*
Van Oest, *East*
Van Oord, *Ort*
Van Oort, *Ort*
Van Oost, *East*
Van Oosten, *East*
Vaňous, *Václav*
Van Parijs, *Parish*
Van Pelt, *Pelletier*
Van Poorten, *Port*
Van Praag, *Prager*
Van Praagh, *Prager*
Van Putten, *Pfützer*
Van Rhyn, *Rhein*
Van Rijn, *Rhein*
Van Rode, *Rhodes*
Van Roij, *Rhodes*
Van Roijen, *Rhodes*
Van Rooij, *Rhodes*
Van Rooijen, *Rhodes*
Van Rooy, *Rhodes*
Van Rooyen, *Rhodes*
Van Roy, *Rhodes*
Van Ryn, *Rhein*
Vanshenkin, *John*
Vanshev, *John*
Vanshin, *John*
Van Sluijs, *Sluis*
Van Sluys, *Sluis*
Van Steen, *Stone*
Van Straaten, *Street*
Van Straten, *Street*
Vant, *Infante*
Van't Deurp, *Thorpe*
Van't Hoff, *Hofer*
Van Tol, *Toller*
Van Trier, *Dreyfuss*
Van Troost, *Trost*
Vantsov, *John*
Van't Woud, *Wald*
Vanucchi, *John*
Van Veen, *Fenn*
Van Velden, *Field*
Van Vlaanderen, *Fleming*
Van Vliet, *Fleet*
Van Voorst, *Forrest*
Van Wel, *Well*
Van Wels, *Well*
Van West, *West*
Van Westen, *West*
Van Wijk, *Wick*
Van Wijngaarden, *Winyard*
Van Winckel, *Winckel*
Van Wyck, *Wick*
Van Wynkel, *Winckel*
Vanyakin, *John*
Vanyarkin, *John*
Vanyashin, *John*
Vanyashkin, *John*
Vanyatin, *John*
Vanyukhin, *John*
Vanyukov, *John*
Vanyushin, *John*
Vanyushkin, *John*
Vanyutin, *John*
Van Zanden, *Sand*
Van Zee, *See*
Van Zijl, *Zyl, van*
Vaqué, *Vaccaro*
Vaqueiro, *Vaccaro*
Vaquer, *Vaccaro*
Vaquerizo, *Vaccaro*
Vaquero, *Vaccaro*
Vaquié, *Vaccaro*
Vaquier, *Vaccaro*
Vara
Varah, *Farrar*
Varanda, *Baranda*
Varandas, *Baranda*
Varas, *Vara*
Varden, *Vardon*
Varder, *Verdier*
Vardon
Varela, *Vara*
Varenne, *Warren*
Varey, *Farrar*
Varfalameev, *Bartholomew*
Varfolomeev, *Bartholomew*
Varga
Vargas
Varin, *Waring*
Varini, *Waring*
Varlet, *Vallet*
Varley
Varlot, *Vallet*
Varnerin, *Warner*
Varnerini, *Warner*
Varnes, *Fern*
Varney
Varnier, *Warner*
Varnieri, *Warner*
Varnon, *Vernon*
Varns, *Fern*
Varone, *Baron*
Varran, *Farren*
Varrone, *Baron*
Varrow, *Farrar*
Vartoli, *Bartholomew*
Varty, *Verity*
Varune, *Baron*
Varvara, *Barbary*
Varvarin, *Barbary*
Varvarinski, *Barbary*
Varvarkin, *Barbary*
Varveri, *Barbary*
Vary, *Farrar*
Varyushin, *Barbary*
Vas, *Jarvis*
Vása, *Václav*
Vašák, *Václav*
Vásári
Vasari
Vásáry, *Vásári*
Vaschetti, *Vasco*
Vaschini, *Vasco*
Vasco
Vasconcelos
Vasechkin, *Basil*
Vašek, *Václav*
Vasenin, *Basil*
Vasenkov, *Basil*
Vasentsov, *Basil*
Vasey, *Vaisey*

Vashchenko, *Basil*
Vasić, *Basil*
Vašíček, *Václav*
Vasichev, *Basil*
Vasiescu, *Basil*
Vasilchenko, *Basil*
Vasilchikov, *Basil*
Vasile, *Basil*
Vasilechko, *Basil*
Vasilenko, *Basil*
Vasilevich, *Basil*
Vasilić, *Basil*
Vasiliev, *Basil*
Vasilik, *Basil*
Vasilishchev, *Basil*
Vasiliu, *Basil*
Vasiljević, *Basil*
Vasilkov, *Basil*
Vasilmanov, *Basil*
Vasilov, *Basil*
Vasiltsov, *Basil*
Vasilyev, *Basil*
Vasilyevski, *Basil*
Vasilyonok, *Basil*
Vasin, *Basil*
Vasishchev, *Basil*
Vasius, *Jarvis*
Vaskin, *Basil*
Vaško, *Václav*
Vaskov, *Basil*
Vaslet, *Vallet*
Vaslin, *Jarvis*
Vaslot, *Vallet*
Vasnetsov, *Basil*
Vasnev, *Basil*
Vasoli, *Jarvis*
Vasolin, *Jarvis*
Vasolini, *Jarvis*
Vason, *Jarvis*
Vasović, *Basil*
Vasques, *Velasco*
Vass
Vassal, *Vassall*
Vassall
Vassalli, *Vassall*
Vassallo, *Vassall*
Vassard, *Vass*
Vassberg, *Wass*
Vasse, *Vass*
Vasselin, *Vass*
Vasselot, *Vass*
Vasserot, *Vavasour*
Vasseur, *Vavasour*
Vassilchenko, *Basil*
Vassilenko, *Basil*
Vassilian, *Basil*
Vassle, *Jarvis*
Vassor, *Vavasour*
Vaster, *Forrest*
Vasyaev, *Basil*
Vasyagin, *Basil*
Vasyanin, *Basil*
Vasyatkin, *Basil*
Vasyuchov, *Basil*
Vasyukhichev, *Basil*
Vasyukhin, *Basil*
Vasyukhnov, *Basil*
Vasyukov, *Basil*
Vasyunichev, *Basil*
Vasyunin, *Basil*
Vasyunkin, *Basil*
Vasyushkhin, *Basil*
Vasyutichev, *Basil*
Vasyutin, *Basil*
Vasyutkin, *Basil*
Vasyutochkin, *Basil*
Vászoly, *Basil*
Vatcher, *Vaccaro*
Vatel, *Wade*
Vatelot, *Wade*
Vatin, *Wade*
Vatini, *Abbé*
Vaton, *Wade*
Vattiato
Vattin, *Wade*
Vaubel, *Volpert*
Vaugham, *Vaughan*
Vaughan
Vaughn, *Vaughan*
Vaupel, *Volpert*
Vauquelin
Vaur
Vaure, *Vaur*
Vaurs, *Vaur*
Vaus, *Vause*
Vause
Vauss, *Vause*
Vauth, *Vogt*
Vauthier, *Walter*
Vauthrin, *Walter*
Vautier, *Walter*
Vautrin, *Walter*
Vautrinot, *Walter*
Vautrot, *Walter*
Vaux, *Vale, Vause*
Vavasour
Vavasseur, *Vavasour*
Vavilin, *Babel*
Vavilov, *Babel*
Vávra, *Lawrence*
Vavřička, *Lawrence*
Vavřík, *Lawrence*
Vavřín, *Lawrence*
Vavruš, *Lawrence*
Vavruška, *Lawrence*
Vax, *Wachsmann*
Vaxman, *Wachsmann*
Vaylet, *Vallet*
Vayne, *Fane*
Vaynzof, *Wein*
Vayset, *Vaysse*
Vaysette, *Vaysse*
Vayssade, *Vaysse*
Vaysse
Vayssié, *Vaysse*
Vayssier, *Vaysse*
Vayssière, *Vaysse*
Vaz, *Velasco*
Vázquez, *Velasco*
Vdovenko, *Widdow*
Vdovin, *Widdow*
Veail, *Veil*
Veal
Veall, *Veal*
Veare, *Ver*
Veasey, *Vaisey*
Veasy, *Vaisey*
Veau, *Veal*
Veaux, *Veal*
Veazey, *Vaisey*
Vécard, *Bishop*
Vecchi, *Veal*
Vecchietti, *Veal*
Vecchiettini, *Veal*
Vecchini, *Veal*
Vecchio, *Veal*
Vecchione, *Veal*
Vecchioni, *Veal*
Vecchiotti, *Veal*
Vecchiotto, *Veal*
Vecchiuzzo, *Veal*
Večeřek, *Wieczorek*
Večerka, *Wieczorek*
Veck, *Levick*
Vedder, *Feather*
Vedekhin, *Bennett*
Vedekhov, *Bennett*
Vedel, *Veal*
Vedeneev, *Bennett*
Vedenichev, *Bennett*
Vedeniktov, *Bennett*
Vedenisov, *Bennett*
Vedentyev, *Bennett*
Vedenyakin, *Bennett*
Vedenyapin, *Bennett*
Vedeshkin, *Bennett*
Vedikhov, *Bennett*
Vedin, *Wood*
Vedishchev, *Bennett*
Vedmidski, *Medvedev*
Vedoa, *Widdow*
Vedova, *Widdow*
Vedovati, *Widdow*
Vedovato, *Widdow*
Vedovelli, *Widdow*
Vedovetto, *Widdow*
Vedovotto, *Widdow*
Vedyaev, *Bennett*
Vedyashkin, *Bennett*
Vedyasov, *Bennett*
Veel, *Veal*
Veenman, *Fenn*
Veenstra, *Fenn*
Veerman
Vega
Vegas, *Vega*
Veggi, *Veal*
Végh
Vehster, *Silvester*
Veidt, *Vito*
Veiga, *Vega*
Veil
Veillet, *Veil*
Veilletet, *Veil*
Veillier, *Veil*
Veillon, *Veil*
Veillot, *Veil*
Veinbaum, *Wein*
Veinberg, *Weinberg*
Veiner, *Wein*
Veinman, *Wein*
Veinstein, *Wein*
Veis, *White*
Veisbein, *White*
Veisbuch, *White*
Veisman, *White*
Veisser, *White*
Veit, *Vito*
Veitch, *Vacca*
Veith, *Vito*
Veitle, *Vito*
Vejvoda
Vela
Velasco
Velázquez, *Velasco*
Veld, *Field*
Velden, *Field*
Veldman, *Field*
Veldstra, *Field*
Velek, *Velík*
Velekhov, *Benjamin*
Vélez, *Vela*
Velez, *Vela*
Veličković, *Velík*
Velík
Velikhov, *Benjamin*
Velikov
Velikovski, *Velikov*
Velimirović, *Velík*
Velíšek, *Velík*
Veljić, *Velík*
Veljković, *Velík*
Veljović, *Velík*
Velkel, *Volk*
Velkovics, *Velikov*
Vellacott
Vellet, *Veal*
Vélo, *Veal*
Veloso
Vélot, *Veal*
Velte, *Valentine*
Velten, *Valentine*
Veltjes, *Valentine*
Veltl, *Valentine*
Veltman, *Field*
Velyashev, *Benjamin*
Velyugin, *Benjamin*
Velyushin, *Benjamin*
Venables
Venâncio
Venc, *Wenzel*
Vencl, *Wenzel*
Venclík, *Wenzel*
Vender, *Deventer*
Venditti, *Bennett*
Vendrell
Vendricks, *Vaandrager*
Vendryes
Venediktov, *Bennett*
Venegas, *Viegas*
Venema, *Fenn*
Venes, *Venus*
Veness, *Venus*
Venezia
Venezian, *Venezia*
Veneziani, *Venezia*
Veneziano, *Venezia*
Venezkey, *Winnick*
Vengerov, *Unger*
Vengrov, *Unger*
Venis, *Venus*
Venise, *Venus*
Venn, *Fenn*
Vennekohl, *Fennell*
Vennekold, *Fennell*
Venneman, *Fenn*
Venner
Venning, *Fenn*
Venour, *Venner*
Venter, *Deventer*
Venters, *Ventris*
Venton, *Fenton*
Ventosa
Ventre
Ventress, *Ventris*
Ventrillon, *Ventre*
Ventris
Ventur, *Venture*
Ventura
Venture
Venturella, *Ventura*
Venturelli, *Ventura*
Venturi, *Ventura*
Venturin, *Ventura*
Venturini, *Ventura*
Venturino, *Ventura*

Venturoli, *Ventura*
Venturucci, *Ventura*
Venus
Venutelli, *Benvenuti*
Venuti, *Benvenuti*
Venutti, *Benvenuti*
Venzi, *Vincent*
Véquaud, *Bishop*
Vèque, *Bishop*
Ver
Vera
Verabei, *Vorobyov*
Veraldi, *Beraud*
Veralli, *Beraud*
Veras, *Vera*
Verba, *Vrba*
Verbeek, *Bach*
Verbeke, *Bach*
Verboom, *Baum*
Verbrugge, *Bridge*
Verbruggen, *Bridge*
Verbrugghen, *Bridge*
Verburg, *Burke*
Vercleyen, *Clay*
Vercruysse, *Cross*
Verd, *Verde*
Verdacci, *Verde*
Verdaguer
Verde
Verdeguer, *Verdaguer*
Verdel, *Verde*
Verdelet, *Verde*
Verdelli, *Verde*
Verden, *Vardon*
Verdet, *Verde*
Verdi, *Verde*
Verdicchio, *Verde*
Verdié, *Verdier*
Verdier
Verdin, *Vardon, Verde*
Verdini, *Verde*
Verdon, *Vardon, Verde*
Verdone, *Verde*
Verdonnet, *Verde*
Verdú, *Vardon*
Verdu, *Vardon*
Verdugo
Verduin, *Vardon*
Verdun, *Vardon*
Verduyn, *Vardon*
Vere, *Ver*
Vérel, *Vair*
Vérelet, *Vair*
Veres, *Vörös*
Veress, *Vörös*
Veresschen, *Ash*
Veresse, *Ash*
Veressen, *Ash*
Verest, *Ash*
Véret, *Vair*
Vereycke, *Oak*
Vergara
Verge, *Virgo*
Vergeer, *Gore*
Vergeest, *Geest*
Verger, *Verdier*
Vergés, *Verdier*
Vergès, *Verdier*
Vergier, *Verdier*
Vergin, *Virgo*
Vergine, *Virgo*
Vergna, *Ver*
Vergnas, *Ver*
Vergne, *Ver*
Vergnol, *Ver*
Vergnolle, *Ver*
Vergo, *Virgo*
Verhaar, *Haar*
Verhaaren, *Haar*
Verhaeghe, *Haig*
Verhagen, *Haig*
Verhavaert, *Haber*
Verhegge, *Hedge*
Verheij, *Heath*
Verheijen, *Heath*
Verhey, *Heath*
Verheyden, *Heath*
Verheyen, *Heath*
Verhoeven, *Hofer*
Verhulst, *Hilse*
Veríssimo
Verity
Verkerk, *Kirk*
Verlaan, *Lane*
Verlaeken, *Lake*
Verlaine
Verlet, *Vair*
Verley, *Varley*
Verlinde, *Linde*
Verlinden, *Linde*
Vermaas, *Maas*
Vermeer, *Meer*
Vermeeren, *Meer*
Vermeersch, *Marsh*
Vermette, *Moult*
Vermeulen, *Mill*
Vermolen, *Mill*
Vern, *Fern*
Vernay, *Varney*
Verne, *Fern, Ver*
Verner
Vernes, *Ver*
Vernet, *Ver*
Verney, *Varney*
Vernhe, *Ver*
Vernier
Vernière, *Ver*
Vernon
Vernou, *Vernon*
Vernum, *Vernon*
Verny, *Varney*
Verona
Veronese, *Verona*
Veronesi, *Verona*
Verpillat, *Goupil*
Verplaetse, *Place*
Verplaetsen, *Place*
Verpy, *Goupil*
Verran
Verrier
Verriour, *Verrier*
Verschoor, *Scheuer*
Verschuer, *Scheuer*
Verschuren, *Scheuer*
Vershinin
Versluijs, *Sluis*
Versluis, *Sluis*
Versluys, *Sluis*
Verspreeuwen, *Sparrow*
Versteeg, *Steiger*
Verster, *Starr*
Verstraete, *Street*
Vert, *Verde*
Verty, *Virtue*
Vervliet, *Fleet*
Vervoort, *Ford*
Verwaest, *Wüst*
Verweij, *Weide*
Verwey, *Weide*
Verweyden, *Weide*
Verwoerd, *Worth*
Verwohl, *Wald*
Verwoude, *Wald*
Very
Veschi, *Bishop*
Vesco, *Bishop*
Vescovini, *Bishop*
Vescovo, *Bishop*
Veselago, *Veselov*
Veselinović, *Veselov*
Veselov
Veselý, *Veselov*
Vesely, *Veselov*
Vesey, *Vaisey*
Vesić, *Veselov*
Vesović, *Veselov*
Vespucci
Vesque, *Bishop*
Vessely, *Veselov*
Vessey
Vessie, *Vessey*
Vest, *West*
Vester, *Silvester, West*
Vestri, *Silvester*
Vestrini, *Silvester*
Vestris, *Silvester*
Vestrucci, *Silvester*
Vetch, *Vacca*
Vetraio, *Verrier*
Vetranović, *Vetrov*
Vetrov
Větrovec, *Vetrov*
Větrovský, *Vetrov*
Vetter
Vetterle, *Vetter*
Vettor, *Victor*
Vettorel, *Victor*
Vettorelli, *Victor*
Vettorello, *Victor*
Vettoretti, *Victor*
Vettoretto, *Victor*
Vettori, *Victor*
Veughelen, *Vogel*
Veverka
Vexelbaum, *Wechsler*
Vexelman, *Wechsler*
Vexler, *Wechsler*
Veyradier, *Verrier*
Veyrier, *Verrier*
Veyron, *Vair*
Veyset, *Vaysse*
Veysette, *Vaysse*
Veysey, *Vaisey*
Veyssade, *Vaysse*
Veyssié, *Vaysse*
Veyssier, *Vaysse*
Veyssière, *Vaysse*
Vezey, *Vaisey*
Vezin, *Voisin*
Vial, *Vitale*
Viala, *Ville*
Viale, *Vitale*
Vialet, *Vitale*
Vialetto, *Vitale*
Viali, *Vitale*
Viall, *Vitale*
Vialle, *Ville*
Vialon, *Vitale*
Vialot, *Vitale*
Vials, *Vitale*
Vian, *Vivian*
Viana
Vianelli, *Vivian*
Vianello, *Vivian*
Vianey, *Vivian*
Viani, *Vivian*
Vianini, *Vivian*
Viano, *Vivian*
Viau, *Vitale*
Viaud, *Vitale*
Viault, *Vitale*
Viaux, *Vitale*
Vicaire, *Vicario*
Vicar, *Vickar*
Vicarey, *Vickar*
Vicari, *Vicario*
Vicario
Vicaro, *Vicario*
Vicars, *Vickers*
Vicary, *Vickar*
Viccars, *Vickers*
Viccary, *Vickar*
Viceconte, *Visconte*
Viceconti, *Visconte*
Vicedomini, *Visdomini*
Vicedomino, *Visdomini*
Vicens, *Vincent*
Vicent, *Vincent*
Vicente, *Vincent*
Vićentijević, *Vincent*
Vicenzi, *Vincent*
Vicenzo, *Vincent*
Vích, *Victor*
Vicidomini, *Visdomini*
Vicinelli, *Voisin*
Vicini, *Voisin*
Vicino, *Voisin*
Vick, *Frederick, Levick*
Vickar
Vickarman, *Vickers*
Vickars, *Vickers*
Vickary, *Vickar*
Vicker, *Vickar*
Vickers
Vickery, *Vickar*
Vickmann, *Wik*
Vickström, *Wik*
Vico
Victor
Victorsson, *Victor*
Victouron, *Victor*
Vida, *Guy, Vita*
Vidaković, *Vito*
Vidal, *Vitale*
Vidale, *Vitale*
Vidalet, *Vitale*
Vidali, *Vitale*
Vidalin, *Vitale*
Vidall, *Vitale*
Vidalon, *Vitale*
Vidalot, *Vitale*
Vidau, *Vitale*
Videan, *Vivian*
Videau, *Vitale*
Videira
Videll, *Weide*
Videneev, *Bennett*
Vidgen, *Vivian*
Vidgeon, *Vivian*
Vidi, *Vito*
Vidić, *Vito*
Vidineev, *Bennett*
Vidler
Vido, *Vito*
Vidollo, *Vito*
Vidon, *Vitale*

Vidoni, *Vito*
Vidos, *Vito*
Vidossi, *Vito*
Vidot, *Vitale*
Vidotti, *Vito*
Vidotto, *Vito*
Vidović, *Vito*
Vidus, *Vito*
Vidussi, *Vito*
Vidusso, *Vito*
Vidyapin, *Bennett*
Vié, *Vitale*
Viebig, *Fieback*
Viegas
Vieil, *Veal*
Vieillot, *Veal*
Vieira
Viejo, *Veal*
Viel, *Vitale, Vito*
Vielli, *Vito*
Vielmetti, *William*
Vielmi, *William*
Vielmini, *William*
Viénet, *Vivian*
Viennet, *Vivian*
Viennot, *Vivian*
Viénot, *Vivian*
Vier, *Oliver*
Vieri, *Oliver*
Vierin, *Oliver*
Vierini, *Oliver*
Viero, *Oliver*
Vierucci, *Oliver*
Viet, *Vito*
Vieten, *Vito*
Vieth, *Vito*
Vietjen, *Vito*
Vietken, *Vito*
Viets, *Vito*
Vietsen, *Vito*
Viett, *Vito*
Vietti, *Vito*
Vietto, *Vito*
Vietze, *Vincent*
Vieux, *Veal*
Viezenz, *Vincent*
Vigano, *Vico*
Vigário, *Vicario*
Vigars, *Viggars*
Vigato, *Vico*
Vigder, *Avigdor*
Vigderovitsch, *Avigdor*
Vigderson, *Avigdor*
Vigdor, *Avigdor*
Vigdorchik, *Avigdor*
Vigdorovitch, *Avigdor*
Vigdorowicz, *Avigdor*
Vigdorowitz, *Avigdor*
Vigeon, *Vivian*
Vigers, *Viggars*
Vigetti, *Vico*
Viggars
Viggers, *Viggars*
Vigghi, *Vico*
Vighi, *Vico*
Vigiani, *Vico*
Vigiano, *Vico*
Vigié, *Vicario*
Vigier, *Vicario*
Viglia, *William*
Viglietti, *William*
Viglietto, *William*
Viglini, *William*
Viglione, *William*
Vigliotti, *William*
Vigliotto, *William*
Vigna, *Vine*
Vigné, *Vine*
Vigne, *Vine*
Vigneau, *Vine*
Vigneri, *Vine*
Vignes, *Vine*
Vignié, *Vine*
Vignier, *Vine*
Vignini, *Vine*
Vignodolli, *Benvenuti*
Vignol, *Vine*
Vignola, *Vine*
Vignoli, *Vine*
Vignolini, *Vine*
Vignolle, *Vine*
Vignolo, *Vine*
Vignon, *Vine*
Vignone, *Vine*
Vignoni, *Vine*
Vignoto, *Vine*
Vignotto, *Vine*
Vignozzi, *Vine*
Vignudelli, *Benvenuti*
Vignudini, *Benvenuti*
Vigo, *Vico*
Vigodner, *Wygodarz*
Vigolo, *Vico*
Vigone, *Vico*
Vigoni, *Vico*
Vigors, *Viggars*
Vigotti, *Vico*
Vigoureux, *Viggars*
Vigouroux, *Viggars*
Vigours, *Viggars*
Vigrass, *Viggars*
Vigreux, *Viggars*
Vigroux, *Viggars*
Viguié, *Vicario*
Viguier, *Vicario*
Vigurs, *Viggars*
Vigus, *Viggars*
Vigutto, *Vico*
Viguzzi, *Vico*
Vijg, *Feige*
Vijgenboom, *Feige*
Vikár, *Vicario*
Vikmann, *Wik*
Vikström, *Wik*
Viktora, *Victor*
Viktorevich, *Victor*
Vilà, *Ville, Villiers*
Vila, *Ville*
Vilagrassa
Vilain, *Villain*
Vilalba, *Villalba*
Vilalta
Vilan, *Villain*
Vilanova, *Villanueva*
Vilaplana
Vilar, *Villiers*
Vilardell, *Villiers*
Vilares, *Villiers*
Vilaret, *Villiers*
Vilaró, *Villiers*
Vilas, *Ville*
Vilaseca
Vilder, *Filzer*
Vilela, *Ville*
Vilella, *Ville*
Vilette, *Ville*
Vilhelmsen, *William*
Vilhelmsson, *William*
Vilhena, *Villena*
Vilím, *William*
Vilímek, *William*
Vilímovský, *William*
Villa, *Ville*
Villagrasa, *Vilagrassa*
Villain
Villalba
Villalobos
Villan, *Villain*
Villaneau, *Villain*
Villanelli, *Villain*
Villanello, *Villain*
Villanetti, *Villain*
Villani, *Villain*
Villano, *Villain*
Villanova, *Villanueva*
Villanueva
Villar, *Villiers*
Villard, *Villiers*
Villarel, *Villiers*
Villaret, *Villiers*
Villaron, *Villiers*
Villarreal
Villarrubia
Villars, *Villiers*
Villas, *Ville*
Villate
Villaume, *William*
Villaverde
Ville
Villefranche
Villefranque, *Villefranche*
Villegas
Villena
Villenave, *Villanueva*
Villeneuve, *Villanueva*
Villerme, *William*
Villers, *Villiers*
Villette, *Ville*
Villetti, *Ville*
Villiers
Villin, *Villain*
Villino, *Ville*
Villis, *Villiers*
Villon, *Ville*
Villot, *Ville*
Villotta, *Ville*
Villotti, *Ville*
Villsson, *Will*
Villumsen, *William*
Vilnai, *Willner*
Vilner, *Willner*
Vilsson, *Will*
Viña, *Vine*
Vinagre
Viñals, *Vinyals*
Vinař, *Vine*
Viñas, *Vine*
Vinblad, *Wein*
Vinbladh, *Wein*
Vince, *Vincent*
Vincendeau, *Vincent*
Vincendet, *Vincent*
Vincendon, *Vincent*
Vincenot, *Vincent*
Vincens, *Vincent*
Vincent
Vincenti, *Vincent*
Vincenzi, *Vincent*
Vincenzot, *Vincent*
Vincenzotto, *Vincent*
Vincett, *Vincent*
Vinci, *Vincent*
Vinck, *Fink*
Vinckler, *Winckel*
Vinçon, *Vincent*
Vinçonneau, *Vincent*
Vincot, *Vincent*
Vincze, *Vincent*
Vindiš, *Wendt*
Vine
Vinecký, *Vine*
Viner, *Vine*
Vines, *Vine*
Viney
Vinický, *Vine*
Vinitzky, *Winnick*
Vink, *Fink*
Vinke, *Fink*
Vinklář, *Winckel*
Vinnick, *Fenwick*
Vinnik, *Winnick*
Vinogradov
Vinogradski, *Vinogradov*
Vinokur
Vinš, *Wendt*
Vinsen, *Vincent*
Vinson, *Vincent*
Vinsonneau, *Vincent*
Vinsun, *Vincent*
Vinter, *Winter*
Vinuesa
Vinya, *Vine*
Vinyals
Vinyas, *Vine*
Vinz, *Vincent*
Vinzel, *Vincent*
Vinzenz, *Vincent*
Vio, *Vito*
Viola
Viole, *Viola*
Violet, *Viola*
Violetta, *Viola*
Violetti, *Viola*
Violi, *Viola*
Violin, *Viola*
Violini, *Viola*
Violino, *Viola*
Violle, *Viola*
Violleau, *Viola*
Viollet, *Viola*
Viollot, *Viola*
Violot, *Viola*
Viotti, *Vito*
Viotto, *Vito*
Virde, *Verde*
Virdi, *Verde*
Virdis, *Verde*
Virgili
Virgin, *Virgo*
Virgo
Virgoe, *Virgo*
Virley, *Varley*
Virtanen
Virtue
Vis, *Fish*
Visbeen, *Fischbein*
Visch, *Fish*
Vischi, *Bishop*
Visco, *Bishop*
Visconte
Visconti, *Visconte*
Viscovi, *Bishop*
Visdomini
Víšek, *Vito*
Visin, *Voisin*
Visini, *Voisin*

Vispo, *Bishop*
Visscher, *Fisher*
Visser, *Fisher*
Vissers, *Fisher*
Vít, *Vito*
Vita
Vitáček, *Vito*
Vital, *Vitale*
Vitale
Vitaletti, *Vitale*
Vitali, *Vitale*
Vitalini, *Vitale*
Vitalis, *Vitale*
Vitalitti, *Vitale*
Vitall, *Vitale*
Vitalone, *Vitale*
Vitaloni, *Vitale*
Vitalzon, *Vita*
Vitard, *Guitart*
Vitas, *Vita*
Vitášek, *Vito*
Vitau, *Vitale*
Vítek, *Vito*
Vitel, *Veal*
Vitelleschi, *Vito*
Vitelli, *Veal, Vito*
Vitello, *Veal, Vito*
Vitelson, *Vita*
Vites, *Vita*
Vitet, *Guy*
Viti, *Vito*
Vitić, *Vito*
Vitillo, *Vito*
Vitin, *Vita*
Vitkes, *Vita*
Vitkin, *Vita*
Vitkind, *Vita*
Vitkovski, *Vito*
Vitkovsky, *Vito*
Vitlin, *Vita*
Vitlov, *Vita*
Vito
Vitolo, *Vito*
Vitone, *Vito*
Vitoni, *Vito*
Vítor, *Victor*
Vitorino, *Victor*
Vitorović, *Victor*
Vitouš, *Vito*
Vitoušek, *Vito*
Vítovec, *Vito*
Vitović, *Vito*
Vítovský, *Vito*
Vitrac, *Vitry*
Vitrat, *Vitry*
Vitrey, *Vitry*
Vitry
Vitte, *Guy*
Vittelli, *Veal*
Vittello, *Veal*
Vittet, *Guy*
Vitti, *Vito*
Vittlin, *Vita*
Vitton, *Guy*
Vittor, *Victor*
Vittore, *Victor*
Vittorelli, *Victor*
Vittori, *Victor*
Vittozzi, *Vito*
Vittozzo, *Vito*
Vittuozzo, *Vito*
Vítů, *Vito*
Vitucci, *Vito*
Vitulli, *Vito*
Vitullo, *Vito*
Vitussi, *Vito*
Vitzethum, *Visdomini*
Vius, *Vito*
Viussi, *Vito*
Vivaldi
Vivan, *Vivian*
Vivant, *Vivian*
Vivar, *Weiher*
Vivas
Viveiro, *Weiher*
Viver, *Weiher*
Vivers, *Weiher*
Vivès, *Weiher*
Vives, *Vivas*
Vivian
Viviand, *Vivian*
Viviani, *Vivian*
Viviano, *Vivian*
Vivians, *Vivian*
Vivie, *Vivian*
Vivien, *Vivian*
Vivier, *Weiher*
Vix, *Vito*
Vizard, *Wishart*
Vizcaíno
Vlaanderen, *Fleming*
Vlach
Vlachovský, *Vlach*
Vladescu, *Vladimirov*
Vladimirescо, *Vladimirov*
Vladimirescu, *Vladimirov*
Vladimirov
Vladimirski, *Vladimirov*
Vladimirsky, *Vladimirov*
Vladyka
Vlahović, *Vlach*
Vlajić, *Vlach*
Vlajković, *Vlach*
Vlaminck, *Fleming*
Vlaming, *Fleming*
Vlas, *Vlasák*
Vlasák
Vlašánek, *Vlach*
Vlášek, *Vlach*
Vlásek, *Vlasák*
Vlasenko, *Blaise*
Vlasenkov, *Blaise*
Vlašić, *Vlach*
Vlasin, *Blaise*
Vlašín, *Vlach*
Vlasman, *Flax*
Vlasov, *Blaise*
Vlasyev, *Blaise*
Vlasyuk, *Blaise*
Vlček, *Wilk*
Vleck, *Fleck*
Vleesauwer, *Flesher*
Vleeschauwer, *Flesher*
Vleeschouwer, *Flesher*
Vleesouwer, *Flesher*
Vlek, *Fleck*
Vleminck, *Fleming*
Vleminckx, *Fleming*
Vlesave, *Flesher*
Vlietman, *Fleet*
Vlietstra, *Fleet*
Vlk, *Wilk*
Vluchkov, *Wilk*
Vnouček, *Wnuk*
Voak, *Foulkes*
Vobora
Vobořil
Voborník, *Vobora*
Voborský, *Vobora*
Vodička
Vodopyanov
Voerman, *Führer*
Voet, *Foot*
Vogel
Vogelaar, *Fowler*
Vogelblat, *Vogel*
Vögele, *Vogel*
Vögelein, *Vogel*
Vögeler, *Fowler*
Vogeler, *Fowler*
Vogelfang, *Vogel*
Vögeli, *Vogel*
Vogelman, *Vogel*
Vogels, *Vogel*
Vogelsang, *Vogel*
Voghel, *Vogel*
Voghels, *Vogel*
Vögler, *Fowler*
Vogler, *Fowler*
Vognar, *Wagner*
Vögt, *Vogt*
Vogt
Vögting, *Vogt*
Vögtle, *Vogt*
Vogts, *Vogt*
Voicu, *Vojtěch*
Voiello, *Boeuf*
Voigh, *Vogt*
Voight, *Vogt*
Voigt, *Vogt*
Voisey, *Vaisey*
Voisin
Voisset, *Vaysse*
Voit, *Vogt*
Voitekh, *Vojtěch*
Voitekhov, *Vojtěch*
Voitl, *Vogt*
Voitsekhov, *Vojtěch*
Voivre, *Vaur*
Voizey, *Vaisey*
Vojka, *Vojtěch*
Vojnar, *Wagner*
Vojta, *Vojtěch*
Vojtárek, *Vojtěch*
Vojtaš, *Vojtěch*
Vojtas, *Vojtěch*
Vojtášek, *Vojtěch*
Vojtěch
Vojtěchovský, *Vojtěch*
Vojtěk, *Vojtěch*
Vojtek, *Vojtěch*
Vojtík, *Vojtěch*
Vojtíšek, *Vojtěch*
Vojvodić, *Vejvoda*
Vokes, *Foulkes*
Vokoun
Volach, *Vlach*
Volák
Volbarth, *Volpert*
Volber, *Volpert*
Volberding, *Volpert*
Volbering, *Volpert*
Volbers, *Volpert*
Volbert, *Volpert*
Volborth, *Volpert*
Volbracht, *Volpert*
Volbrecht, *Volpert*
Volbring, *Volpert*
Volbrod, *Volpert*
Volchik, *Wilk*
Volchonsky, *Olszewski*
Volder, *Fuller*
Voldřich, *Ulrich*
Volejník, *Oyler*
Volek, *Ulrich*
Volf, *Wolf*
Volfing, *Wolf*
Volfman, *Wolf*
Volfovich, *Wolf*
Volfovici, *Wolf*
Volfovski, *Wolf*
Volfovsky, *Wolf*
Völgyi
Volichman, *Vlach*
Volk, *Foulkes*
Volk
Volkamer, *Volmer*
Volke, *Foulkes, Volk*
Völke, *Volk*
Völkel, *Volk*
Völker, *Fulcher*
Volker, *Fulcher*
Völkering, *Fulcher*
Volkering, *Fulcher*
Völkers, *Fulcher*
Volkers, *Fulcher*
Volkert, *Folkard*
Volkerts, *Folkard*
Volkes, *Foulkes*
Volkhin, *Olszewski*
Volkman, *Volk*
Volkmann, *Volk*
Volkmar, *Volmer*
Volkmeier, *Volmer*
Völkmer, *Volmer*
Volkmer, *Volmer*
Volkov, *Wilk*
Volks, *Foulkes*
Voll, *Volk*
Vollbarth, *Volpert*
Vollborth, *Volpert*
Vollbracht, *Volpert*
Vollbrecht, *Volpert*
Volle, *Volk*
Voller, *Fuller*
Vollers, *Fuller*
Vollert, *Folkard*
Völlmar, *Volmer*
Vollmar, *Volmer*
Völlmeke, *Volmer*
Völlmer, *Volmer*
Vollmer, *Volmer*
Vollmert, *Volmer*
Volloch, *Vlach*
Völm, *Volmer*
Volmer
Volmert, *Volmer*
Völmle, *Volmer*
Völmy, *Volmer*
Volný, *Wolniak*
Volodich, *Vladimirov*
Volodichev, *Vladimirov*
Volodimerov, *Vladimirov*
Volodin, *Vladimirov*
Volodko, *Vladimirov*
Volodzhko, *Vladimirov*
Volokhov, *Vlach*
Volosheninov, *Vlach*
Voloshinov, *Vlach*
Volpe
Völpel, *Volpert*
Volpella, *Volpe*
Volpelli, *Volpe*
Volper, *Volpe*
Volpers, *Volpert*
Volpert

Volperts, *Volpert*
Volpi, *Volpe*
Volpicella, *Volpe*
Volpicelli, *Volpe*
Volpin, *Volpe*
Volpini, *Volpe*
Volpino, *Volpe*
Volpis, *Volpe*
Volpone, *Volpe*
Volponi, *Volpe*
Volprecht, *Volpert*
Volpt, *Volpert*
Völpts, *Volpert*
Völsch, *Volk*
Völser, *Volk*
Volta
Völtz, *Volk*
Voltz, *Volk*
Völz, *Volk*
Volz, *Volk*
Völzle, *Volk*
Vonášek, *Andrew*
Vonck, *Funke*
Von der Dunk, *Dung*
Vondra, *Andrew*
Vondráček, *Andrew*
Vondrach, *Andrew*
Vondrák, *Andrew*
Vondrášek, *Andrew*
Vondruška, *Andrew*
Vondrys, *Andrew*
von Lausitz, *Luzzatto*
Vons, *Wąsik*
Voogd, *Vogt*
Voogel, *Vogel*
Voogt, *Vogt*
Voortman, *Ford*
Voorzanger
Vooth, *Foot*
Vopel, *Volpert*
Vorchheimer, *Forchheimer*
Vorel, *Orlov*
Vorlíček, *Orlov*
Vorlický, *Orlov*
Vormann, *Führer*
Vorobei, *Vorobyov*
Vorobets, *Vorobyov*
Vorobyov
Vorona, *Voronin*
Voronevski, *Voronov*
Voronich, *Voronov*
Voronin
Voronov
Vörös
Vorotnikov
Vorst, *Forrest*
Vorster, *Forrest*
Vortman, *Wortman*
Vortsman, *Wortman*
Vortzman, *Wortman*
Vos, *Fosse*
Vosátka
Vöske, *Fox*
Voss, *Fosse, Fox*
Vossen, *Fox*
Vössgen, *Fox*
Vossing, *Fox*
Vostárek, *Vostrý*
Voster, *Forrest*
Vostřák, *Vostrý*
Vostrý
Votava
Voth, *Foot*
Votruba
Vötter, *Vetter*
Vötterl, *Vetter*
Vouls, *Fowle*
Vovchenko, *Wilk*
Vovk, *Wilk*
Vovkovich, *Wilk*
Vowell, *Fowle*
Vowells, *Fowle*
Vowels, *Fowle*
Vowler, *Fowler*
Vowles, *Fowle*
Voyer, *Vicario*
Voyeu, *Vicario*
Voyeur, *Vicario*
Voyeux, *Vicario*
Voysey, *Vaisey*
Voyzey, *Vaisey*
Vozka, *Woźniak*
Vözke, *Volk*
Vrabec, *Vorobyov*
Vrána, *Voronin*
Vraneš, *Voronin*
Vranić, *Voronin*
Vrátný, *Vorotnikov*
Vrba
Vrbenský, *Vrba*
Vrbík, *Vrba*
Vrbka, *Vrba*
Vrbský, *Vrba*
Vree, *Fried*
Vreede, *Firth*
Vreugde, *Freud*
Vreurich, *Frederick*
Vriend, *Friend*
Vriens, *Friend*
Vrieseman, *Fries*
Vrings, *Séverin*
Vrolijk, *Fröhlich*
Vronovitz, *Voronin*
Vronsky, *Voronin*
Vroom, *Fromm*
Vroome, *Fromm, Froome*
Vršecký
Vrydagh, *Freitag*
Vučenović, *Wilk*
Vučetić, *Wilk*
Vučić, *Wilk*
Vučićević, *Wilk*
Vučinić, *Wilk*
Vučković, *Wilk*
Vuillaume, *William*
Vuillaumet, *William*
Vuillaumin, *William*
Vuilleaume, *William*
Vuillemain, *William*
Vuillemenot, *William*
Vuillemet, *William*
Vuillemin, *William*
Vuilleminet, *William*
Vuilleminot, *William*
Vuillemot, *William*
Vuillerme, *William*
Vuillermet, *William*
Vuillermot, *William*
Vuillin, *Will*
Vuillod, *Will*
Vuillot, *Will*
Vuitte, *Guy*
Vuittet, *Guy*
Vuitton, *Guy*
Vukčević, *Wilk*
Vukčić, *Wilk*
Vukelić, *Wilk*
Vukić, *Wilk*
Vukičević, *Wilk*
Vukičić, *Wilk*
Vukotić, *Wilk*
Vuković, *Wilk*
Vulfov, *Wolf*
Vulfovich, *Wolf*
Vulkov, *Wilk*
Vulpi, *Volpe*
Vulpis, *Volpe*
Vuorinen
Výborný
Vydra, *Otter*
Vyghen, *Feige*
Vyner, *Vine*
Vyskočil
Vyvyan, *Vivian*

W

Waage, *Wäger*
Wabbel, *Walburg*
Waber, *Weaver*
Wabersich, *Lawrence*
Wabersinke, *Lawrence*
Wace
Wach, *Lawrence, Wenzel*
Wache, *Wenzel*
Wachman, *Wakeman*
Wachmann, *Wakeman*
Wachowiak, *Lawrence*
Wachowicz, *Lawrence*
Wachowiec, *Lawrence*
Wachowski, *Lawrence*
Wachs, *Wachsmann*
Wachsman, *Wachsmann*
Wachsmann
Wachtel
Wächter, *Wachter*
Wachter
Wachtman, *Wachter*
Wachtmann, *Wachter*
Wackley, *Wakeley*
Wacławski, *Václav*
Waddel, *Waddell*
Waddell
Waddingham
Waddington
Waddle, *Waddell*
Waddy, *Walthew*
Wade
Wademan, *Wader*
Wademann, *Wade*
Wader
Wadeson, *Wade*
Wadham
Wadington, *Waddington*
Wadley
Wadman, *Wader*
Wadsworth, *Wordsworth*
Wagemann, *Wäger*
Wagenaar, *Wagner*
Wagenaer, *Wagner*
Wagener, *Wagner*
Wagenmann, *Wain*
Wäger
Waggoner, *Wagner*
Waghorn
Waghorne, *Waghorn*
Wagman, *Wäger*
Wagmann, *Wäger*
Wagner
Wagoner, *Wagner*
Wągrowski
Wagstaff
Wagstaffe, *Wagstaff*
Wahl
Wahlberg, *Wall*
Wahlgren, *Wall*
Wahlquist, *Wall*
Wahlsted, *Wall*
Wahlström, *Wall*
Wahncke, *John*
Wähner, *Wagner*
Wahner, *Wagner*
Wähnert, *Wagner*
Wahnke, *John*
Waide, *Wade, Weide*
Waidenfeld, *Weide*
Waider, *Wader*
Waidson, *Wade*
Waigh, *Way*
Waight, *Waite*
Waighte, *Waite*
Wailer, *Wheeler*
Wailes, *Wale*
Wain
Wainapel, *Wein*
Wainbaum, *Wein*
Wainberg, *Weinberg*
Wainberger, *Weinberg*
Waine, *Wain*
Wainer, *Wagner, Wein*
Wainerman, *Wein*
Waines, *Wain*
Wainewright, *Wainwright*
Wainfeld, *Wein*
Waingart, *Wein*
Waingarten, *Wein*
Wainman, *Wain, Wein*
Wainrauch, *Weinreich*
Wainright, *Wainwright*
Wainrigt, *Wainwright*
Wainrober, *Wein*
Wainryb, *Wein*
Wainsaft, *Wein*
Wainshenker, *Wein*
Wainshtein, *Wein*
Wainshtok, *Wein*
Waintal, *Wein*
Waintraub, *Weintraub*
Waintrob, *Weintraub*
Wainwright
Waisblat, *White*
Waisbrot, *White*
Waisman, *White*
Waison, *Wace*
Waiss, *White*
Waissbaum, *White*
Waissman, *White*
Waissztein, *White*
Waistcoat, *Westcott*
Waistell, *Wastell*
Waistuch, *White*
Waiswohl, *White*
Wait, *Waite*
Waite
Waites, *Waite*
Waits, *Waite*
Wajdenbaum, *Weide*
Wajnbaum, *Wein*
Wajnberg, *Weinberg*
Wajner, *Wein*
Wajnerman, *Wein*
Wajngrod, *Vinogradov*
Wajnryb, *Wein*
Wajnszelbaum, *Weinschel*
Wajnsztajn, *Wein*

Wajnsztok, *Wein*
Wajntraub, *Weintraub*
Wajntrob, *Weintraub*
Wajs, *White*
Wajsbaum, *White*
Wajsbecker, *White*
Wajsberg, *White*
Wajsczyk, *White*
Wajsfeld, *White*
Wajsfogiel, *White*
Wajsglus, *White*
Wajsgras, *White*
Wajshof, *White*
Wajsman, *White*
Wajsmehl, *White*
Wajsowski, *White*
Wake
Wakefield
Wakeford
Wakeham
Wakelam, *Wakeling*
Wakeley
Wakelin, *Wakeling*
Wakeling
Wakely, *Wakeley*
Wakem, *Wakeham*
Wakeman
Wakenshaw, *Walkingshaw*
Wakley, *Wakeley*
Wakling, *Wakeling*
Waks, *Wachsmann*
Waksman, *Wachsmann*
Walach, *Vlach*
Walak, *Valentine*
Walas, *Valentine*
Walasik, *Valentine*
Walaszczyk, *Valentine*
Walbanck, *Wallbank*
Walbancke, *Wallbank*
Walbank, *Wallbank*
Walburg
Walch, *Vlach, Walsh*
Walcker, *Walker*
Walcot
Walcote, *Walcot*
Walcott, *Walcot*
Walczak, *Valentine*
Walczyński, *Valentine*
Wald
Walde, *Wald*
Waldeck
Waldegrave
Walden
Walder, *Wald*
Waldfogel, *Wald*
Waldherr, *Walter*
Waldhorn, *Wald*
Walding, *Wald*
Waldman, *Wald*
Waldmann, *Wald*
Waldner, *Wald*
Waldo, *Walthew*
Waldorf
Waldraff, *Waldron*
Waldram, *Waldron*
Waldren, *Waldron*
Waldron
Waldrum, *Waldron*
Waldstein, *Wald*
Waldy, *Walthew*
Wale
Walent, *Valentine*
Walenta, *Valentine*
Walentkiewicz, *Valentine*
Walentynowicz, *Valentine*
Wales, *Wale*
Walewicz, *Valentine*
Walewski, *Valentine*
Waley, *Whalley*
Walford
Walicki, *Valentine*
Walisiak, *Valentine*
Waliszek, *Valentine*
Waliszewski, *Valentine*
Walkden
Walker
Walkiewicz, *Valentine*
Walkingshaw
Walkinshaw, *Walkingshaw*
Walklin, *Wakeling*
Walkling, *Wakeling*
Walklyn, *Wakeling*
Walkowski, *Valentine*
Wall
Wallace
Wallach, *Vlach*
Wallakh, *Vlach*
Wallander, *Wall*
Wallas, *Wallace*
Wallbank
Wallbanks, *Wallbank*
Wallberg, *Wall*
Wallburg, *Walburg*
Walle, *Wall*
Wallén, *Wall*
Wallenberg, *Wall*
Wallenius, *Wall*
Wallentin, *Valentine*
Waller
Walles, *Wallace*
Walley, *Whalley*
Wallgren, *Wall*
Wallice, *Wallace*
Wallin, *Wall*
Wallington
Wallis, *Wallace*
Wallman, *Wall*
Wallmann, *Wall*
Wallner, *Wald, Wall*
Walloch, *Vlach*
Wallop
Wallrabe, *Waldron*
Wallraff, *Waldron*
Wallraven, *Waldron*
Walls, *Wall*
Wallström, *Wall*
Wallwork
Walmesley, *Walmsley*
Walmisley, *Walmsley*
Walmsley
Walpl, *Walburg*
Walpole
Walrafen, *Waldron*
Walrand, *Waldron*
Walraven, *Waldron*
Walrond, *Waldron*
Walsch, *Vlach*
Walsh
Walshaw
Walshe, *Walsh*
Walshman, *Walsh*
Walsingham
Walsman, *Walsh*
Walten, *Walton*
Walter
Walters, *Walter*
Walterson, *Walter*
Walther, *Walter*
Walthew
Waltho, *Walthew*
Wälti, *Walter*
Walton
Wältz, *Walter*
Waltz, *Walter*
Wälz, *Walter*
Walz, *Walter*
Walzel, *Walter*
Wamsley, *Walmsley*
Wancke, *John*
Wand, *Wander*
Wander
Wanderschek, *Andrew*
Wandrach, *Andrew*
Wandrack, *Andrew*
Wandrey, *Andrew*
Wandrich, *Andrew*
Wandt, *Wander*
Wandtke, *John*
Wane, *Wain*
Wanek, *John*
Wang
Wänger, *Wang*
Wanger, *Wang*
Wängler, *Wang*
Wangner, *Wang*
Wanjek, *John*
Wanka, *John*
Wanke, *John*
Wannamaker, *Wanner*
Wanner
Wanzel, *Wenzel*
Waple, *Walpole*
Waples, *Walpole*
Waplington
Warboy, *Warboys*
Warboys
Warburton
Warbutton, *Warburton*
Ward, *Bard*
Ward
Wardale, *Wardle*
Wardall, *Wardle*
Warde, *Ward*
Wardel, *Wardle*
Wardell, *Wardle*
Warden
Wardhaugh
Wardill, *Wardle*
Wardlaw
Wardle
Wardley
Wardman, *Ward*
Wardrobe, *Wardrop*
Wardrop
Wardrope, *Wardrop*
Wardroper, *Wardrop*
Wardropper, *Wardrop*
Wardrupp, *Wardrop*
Wards, *Ward*
Ware
Waredraper, *Wardrop*
Wareham
Wareing, *Waring*
Wares, *Ware*
Warfield
Warham, *Wareham*
Warin, *Waring*
Waring
Wark
Warke, *Wark*
Warman
Warmington
Warmoll, *Wormald*
Warmsley, *Walmsley*
Warn, *Warne*
Warncke, *Warner*
Warnders, *Warner*
Warne
Warnecke, *Warner*
Warneke, *Warner*
Warneking, *Warner*
Warner
Warners, *Warner*
Warnes
Warnherr, *Warner*
Warninck, *Warner*
Warning, *Warner*
Warnke, *Warner*
Warnken, *Warner*
Warnkes, *Warner*
Warnkönig, *Warner*
Warnoch, *Warnock*
Warnock
Warns, *Warner*
Warntje, *Warner*
Warntjen, *Warner*
Warr
Warran, *Warren*
Warrand, *Warren*
Warrant, *Warren*
Warre, *Warr*
Warremann, *Warner*
Warren
Warrender, *Warren*
Warrener, *Warren*
Warrenne, *Warren*
Warrentjes, *Warner*
Warrick, *Warwick*
Warrier, *Warr*
Warriner, *Warren*
Warring, *Waring*
Warrington
Warrior, *Warr*
Warschauer, *Warszawski*
Warschavski, *Warszawski*
Warschavsky, *Warszawski*
Warschaw, *Warszawski*
Warschawer, *Warszawski*
Warschawski, *Warszawski*
Warschawsky, *Warszawski*
Warscher, *Warszawski*
Warshaviak, *Warszawski*
Warshavski, *Warszawski*
Warshavsky, *Warszawski*
Warshaw, *Warszawski*
Warshawiak, *Warszawski*
Warshawski, *Warszawski*
Warshawsky, *Warszawski*
Warsop
Warszakowski, *Warszawski*
Warszavski, *Warszawski*
Warszawczyk, *Warszawski*
Warszawer, *Warszawski*
Warszawiak, *Warszawski*
Warszawski
Warters, *Water*
Warth
Warthe, *Warth*
Warther, *Warth*
Warwick
Wascher, *Washer*
Wase
Waser, *Wase*
Washbourn, *Washbourne*
Washbourne
Washbrook

Washburn
Washburne, *Washburn*
Washer
Washington
Washtell, *Wastell*
Wasiak, *Lawrence*
Wasiel, *Basil*
Wasiela, *Basil*
Wasielczyk, *Basil*
Wasielewicz, *Basil*
Wasielewski, *Basil*
Wąsiewicz, *Wąsik*
Wąsik
Wąsikiewicz, *Wąsik*
Wąsikowski, *Wąsik*
Wasilewicz, *Basil*
Wasilewski, *Basil*
Waslin, *Wace*
Wasmann, *Wachsmann*
Wasmer, *Wase*
Wasner, *Wase*
Wason, *Wace*
Wąsowicz, *Wąsik*
Wąsowski, *Wąsik*
Wass
Wassall, *Wastell*
Wassberg, *Wass*
Wasselin, *Wace*
Wassell, *Wastell*
Wassenaar, *Wachsmann*
Wasser, *Water*
Wassermann, *Waterman*
Wasserstrom, *Ström*
Wassmann, *Wachsmann*
Wasson, *Wace*
Wastall, *Wastell*
Wastell
Wastling, *Wace*
Wasylkiewicz, *Basil*
Waszak, *Lawrence*
Waszczyk, *John*
Waszczykowski, *John*
Waszkiewicz, *John*
Watel, *Wade*
Watelet, *Wade*
Watelot, *Wade*
Water
Waterdrinker, *Drinkwater*
Waterfield
Waterhouse
Waterman
Watermann, *Waterman*
Waters, *Water*
Waterson, *Water*
Waterton
Waterworth
Wates, *Waite*
Watford
Watin, *Wade*
Watkeys, *Watt*
Watkin, *Watt*
Watking, *Watt*
Watkins, *Watt*
Watkinson, *Watt*
Watkiss, *Watt*
Watley, *Wheatley*
Watlin, *Watt*
Watling, *Watt*
Watman
Watmaugh, *Watmough*
Watmoor, *Whatmore*
Watmore, *Whatmore*
Watmough
Watmuff, *Watmough*
Watson, *Watt*
Watt
Watteau, *Wade*
Wattel, *Wade*
Watters, *Water*
Watterson, *Water*
Wattin, *Wade*
Wattis, *Watt*
Watts, *Watt*
Wätzold, *Wenzel*
Waud, *Wald*
Waugh
Waumsley, *Walmsley*
Waus, *Vause*
Wauss, *Vause*
Wauter, *Walter*
Wauters, *Walter*
Wauton, *Walton*
Wavell
Wawer, *Lawrence*
Wawn, *Gavin*
Wawne, *Gavin*
Wawrzecki, *Lawrence*
Wawrzeńczyk, *Lawrence*
Wawrzkiewicz, *Lawrence*
Wawrzonek, *Lawrence*
Wawrzyk, *Lawrence*
Wawrzyńczak, *Lawrence*
Wawrzyniak, *Lawrence*
Wawrzyniec, *Lawrence*
Wawrzyński, *Lawrence*
Wax, *Wachsmann*
Waxman, *Wachsmann*
Way
Waye, *Way*
Wayler, *Wheeler*
Wayman, *Wyman*
Waymark, *Wymer*
Waymont, *Wyman*
Wayne, *Wain*
Waysberg, *White*
Waysbrot, *White*
Wayson, *Wace*
Wayt, *Waite*
Wayte, *Waite*
Waytes, *Waite*
Wąż, *Wężyk*
Wdowczak, *Widdow*
Wdowiak, *Widdow*
Weafer, *Weaver*
Weake
Weald, *Wald*
Wealthall, *Weatherall*
Wear
Wearden
Weare, *Wear*
Wearing, *Waring*
Wearne, *Warne*
Wearne
Wears, *Wear*
Weate, *Wheat*
Weather
Weatherall
Weatherburn, *Wedderburn*
Weatherby, *Weathersby*
Weatherell, *Weatherall*
Weatherhead
Weatherhill, *Weatherall*
Weatherill, *Weatherall*
Weatherilt, *Weatherall*
Weatheritt, *Weatherall*
Weatherley
Weatherly, *Weatherley*
Weathers, *Weather*
Weathersby
Weatherspoon, *Witherspoon*
Weathrall, *Weatherall*
Weaver
Weavers, *Weaver*
Weavill, *Wavell*
Web, *Webb*
Webb
Webbe, *Webb*
Webber, *Weaver, Webb*
Webberman, *Weaver*
Webbers, *Weaver*
Weber, *Weaver*
Weberman, *Weaver*
Webers, *Weaver*
Webley
Webman, *Weaver*
Websdale
Webster, *Webb*
Węcewicz, *Vincent*
Wechselberg, *Wechsler*
Wechselfisch, *Wechsler*
Wechselfish, *Wechsler*
Wechselman, *Wechsler*
Wechselmann, *Wechsler*
Wechsler
Weck, *Wedekind*
Wecke, *Wedekind*
Wecken, *Wedekind*
Weckes, *Wedekind*
Wecking, *Wedekind*
Wecklein, *Wedekind*
Wecklin, *Wedekind*
Węckowski, *Vincent*
Węczkowicz, *Vincent*
Wedberg, *Wood*
Weddel, *Waddell*
Weddell, *Waddell*
Wedderburn
Wedderspoon, *Witherspoon*
Weddle, *Waddell*
Wede, *Wood*
Wedekind
Wedemann, *Wood*
Wederell, *Weatherall*
Wedewer, *Widdow*
Wedge
Wedgewood
Wedgwood, *Wedgewood*
Wedin, *Wood*
Wedlock, *Woodlock*
Weech, *Wich*
Weeden, *Weedon*
Weedon
Week, *Weake*
Weekes, *Weake*
Weekley
Weekly, *Weekley*
Weeks, *Weake*
Weems, *Wemyss*
Weet, *Wheat*
Weetch, *Wich*
Weetman, *Watman*
Wefer, *Weaver*
Wefers, *Weaver*
Wegeler, *Wagner*
Wegener, *Wagner*
Weger, *Wäger*
Wegg, *Wedge*
Weggin, *Keogh*
Węgier, *Unger*
Węgierski, *Unger*
Wegler, *Wagner*
Wegman, *Wäger, Way*
Wegmann, *Way*
Wegner, *Wagner*
Węgrzyn, *Unger*
Wegsman, *Way*
Wegstra, *Way*
Weh, *Wood*
Wehber, *Weaver*
Wehde, *Wood*
Wehe, *Wood*
Wehkind, *Wedekind*
Wehmann, *Wood*
Wehner, *Wagner*
Wehnert, *Wagner*
Wehrle, *Warner*
Wehrli, *Warner*
Wehtag, *Vojtěch*
Weichard, *Guichard*
Weichert, *Guichard*
Weichhard, *Guichard*
Weicht, *Wiggin*
Weickert, *Guichard*
Weid, *Weide*
Weidberg, *Weide*
Weide
Weidel, *Weide*
Weiden, *Weide*
Weidenbaum, *Weide*
Weidenfeld, *Weide*
Weidenkopf, *Weide*
Weider, *Weide*
Weidhorn, *Weide*
Weidle, *Weide*
Weidler, *Weide*
Weidman, *Weide*
Weidmann, *Weide*
Weidner, *Weide*
Weidtler, *Weide*
Weidwasser, *Weide*
Weier, *Weiher*
Weifers, *Weaver*
Weigand, *Wiggin*
Weigang, *Wiggin*
Weigel, *Wiggin*
Weigelt, *Wiggin*
Weigert, *Guichard*
Weigh, *Way*
Weightman, *Wight*
Weigl, *Wiggin*
Weigt, *Wiggin*
Weiher
Weijde, *Weide*
Weijer, *Weiher*
Weijers, *Weiher*
Weil
Weiland, *Wieland*
Weild, *Wald*
Weile, *Weil*
Weiler, *Villiers, Weil*
Weilert, *Villiers*
Weill, *Weil*
Weiller, *Weil*
Weimann, *Wein*
Wein
Weinapel, *Wein*
Weinbach, *Wein*
Weinbaum, *Wein*
Weinberg
Weinberger, *Weinberg*
Weinblatt, *Wein*
Weinblot, *Wein*
Weinblum, *Wein*
Weinblut, *Wein*
Weinbren, *Wein*
Weinbrenn, *Wein*

Weindorf, *Wein*
Weiner, *Wein*
Weinerman, *Wein*
Weinfeld, *Wein*
Weingardt, *Winyard*
Weingart, *Winyard*
Weingarten, *Winyard*
Weingarter, *Winyard*
Weingärtner, *Winyard*
Weingartner, *Winyard*
Weingartz, *Winyard*
Weingold, *Wein*
Weingrod, *Vinogradov*
Weingrub, *Wein*
Weinhaus, *Wein*
Weinholtz, *Wein*
Weinholz, *Wein*
Weinisch, *Wein*
Weinish, *Wein*
Weinkeller, *Wein*
Weinlager, *Wein*
Weinman, *Wein*
Weinmann, *Wein*
Weinpres, *Wein*
Weinraub, *Wein*
Weinrauch, *Weinreich*
Weinreb, *Wein*
Weinrebe, *Wein*
Weinreich
Weinrib, *Wein*
Weinrich, *Weinreich*
Weinrieber, *Wein*
Weinrober, *Wein*
Weinrot, *Wein*
Weinsaft, *Wein*
Weinschal, *Weinschel*
Weinschall, *Weinschel*
Weinschel
Weinschelbaum, *Weinschel*
Weinschenk, *Wein*
Weinschenker, *Wein*
Weinshel, *Weinschel*
Weinshelbaum, *Weinschel*
Weinshnabel, *Wein*
Weinshtock, *Wein*
Weinstein, *Wein*
Weinsteiner, *Wein*
Weinstock, *Wein*
Weinstok, *Wein*
Weintal, *Wein*
Weinthal, *Wein*
Weintraub
Weintrob, *Weintraub*
Weinzweig, *Wein*
Weir
Weis, *White, Wise*
Weisbecker, *White*
Weisbein, *White*
Weisberg, *White*
Weisberger, *White*
Weisblat, *White*
Weisblum, *White*
Weisbom, *White*
Weisbrem, *White*
Weisbrod, *White*
Weisbrodt, *White*
Weisbuch, *White*
Weise, *Wise*
Weiser, *Wise*
Weisfeld, *White*
Weisfield, *White*
Weisfisch, *White*
Weisgarten, *White*
Weisglas, *White*
Weisglass, *White*
Weishaus, *White*
Weiskopf, *White*
Weisman, *White*
Weismann, *Wise*
Weisrosen, *White*
Weiss, *White*
Weissadler, *White*
Weissalz, *White*
Weissbaum, *White*
Weissbecher, *White*
Weissbecker, *White*
Weissbein, *White*
Weissberg, *White*
Weissberger, *White*
Weissblat, *White*
Weissblatt, *White*
Weissblech, *White*
Weissbloom, *White*
Weissblum, *White*
Weissbluth, *White*
Weissbrem, *White*
Weissbrod, *White*
Weissbrun, *White*
Weissbuch, *White*
Weissburg, *White*
Weisse, *White*
Weisselfisch
Weisser, *White*
Weissert, *White*
Weissfeld, *White*
Weissfisch, *White*
Weissgerber
Weissglas, *White*
Weisshaut, *White*
Weisshof, *White*
Weisskirch, *White*
Weisskopf, *White*
Weissman, *White*
Weissmann, *White*
Weissmel, *White*
Weistuch, *White*
Weiswasser, *White*
Weisz, *White*
Weiszberger, *White*
Weiszkopf, *White*
Weiter
Weitz, *Wheat*
Weitzberg, *Wheat*
Weitzfeld, *Wheat*
Weitzhändler, *Wheat*
Weitzhendler, *Wheat*
Weitzman, *Wheat*
Weitzmann, *Wheat*
Weitzner, *Wheat*
Weizman, *Wheat*
Weizmann, *Wheat*
Wekking, *Wedekind*
Wekselman, *Wechsler*
Weksler, *Wechsler*
Weland
Welbourne
Welburn, *Welbourne*
Welch, *Walsh*
Welcker, *Walker*
Welcome
Welcomme, *Welcome*
Weld, *Wald*
Welden, *Weldon*
Weldon
Welford
Welham
Welkovitch, *Velikov*
Welkovitz, *Velikov*
Well
Wellam, *Welham*
Welland, *Weland*
Wellcome, *Welcome*
Wellden, *Weldon*
Welldon, *Weldon*
Welle, *Well*
Weller, *Well*
Wellesley
Welliam, *William*
Welling, *Well*
Wellings, *Well*
Wellington
Wellisch, *Vlach*
Wellman, *Well*
Wellmann, *Well*
Wells, *Well*
Wellum, *Welham*
Welman, *Well*
Welscher, *Vlach*
Welsh, *Walsh*
Welter, *Walter*
Welters, *Walter*
Welti, *Walter*
Welton
Weltsch, *Vlach*
Weltscher, *Vlach*
Welz, *Walter*
Welzel, *Walter*
Wemes, *Wemyss*
Wemyss
Wend, *Wendt*
Wende, *Wendt*
Wendisch, *Wendt*
Wendland, *Wendt*
Wendländer, *Wendt*
Wendlandt, *Wendt*
Wendt
Wenger, *Unger*
Wengerik, *Unger*
Wengier, *Unger*
Wenham
Wenig
Weniger, *Wenig*
Wenman, *Wain*
Wennmaker, *Wanner*
Went
Wentscher, *Wendt*
Wentworth
Wentz, *Warner*
Wentzel, *Wenzel*
Wentzig, *Wenzel*
Wentzke, *Wenzel*
Wentzler, *Wenzel*
Wenz, *Warner, Wenzel*
Wenzel
Wenzig, *Wenzel*
Wenzke, *Wenzel*
Wenzler, *Wenzel*
Weöres, *Vörös*
Wepner
Weppler, *Wepner*
Weppner, *Wepner*
Werba, *Vrba*
Werder, *Werth*
Were, *Ware*
Werfel, *Würfel*
Werf, Van der
Werle, *Warner*
Werlein, *Warner*
Werndl, *Warner*
Wernecke, *Warner*
Werneke, *Warner*
Werneking, *Warner*
Werner, *Warner*
Wernher, *Warner*
Werning, *Warner*
Wernle, *Warner*
Wernlein, *Warner*
Werntjen, *Warner*
Werntjes, *Warner*
Werntz, *Warner*
Wernz, *Warner*
Werren, *Waring*
Werring, *Waring*
Werth
Werthaimer, *Wertheim*
Werthajm, *Wertheim*
Werthammer, *Wertheim*
Wertheim
Wertheimer, *Wertheim*
Wertz, *Warner*
Wescher, *Washer*
Wescot, *Westcott*
Wescott, *Westcott*
Wesker
Weskett, *Westcott*
Weslake, *Westlake*
Wesley
Wesołek, *Veselov*
Wesołowski, *Veselov*
Wessel, *Warner*
Wesseler, *Wechsler*
Wesseley, *Veselov*
Wesseling, *Warner*
Wesselmann, *Warner*
Wessels, *Warner*
Wesson, *Weston*
West
Westacott, *Westcott*
Westberg, *West*
Westbrock, *Westbrook*
Westbrook
Westbrooke, *Westbrook*
Westbury
Westby
Westcoate, *Westcott*
Westcot, *Westcott*
Westcote, *Westcott*
Westcott
Weste, *West*
Wester, *West*
Westerberg, *West*
Westerdahl, *West*
Westergren, *West*
Westerholm, *West*
Westerink, *West*
Westerlind, *West*
Westerling, *West*
Westerlund, *West*
Westerman, *West*
Westermann, *West*
Westermark, *West*
Western, *West*
Westgate
Westh, *West*
Westhead
Westholm, *West*
Westhuizen, van der
Westicott, *Westcott*
Westin, *West*
Westing, *West*
Westlake
Westley, *Wesley*
Westling, *West*
Westlund, *West*
Westly, *Wesley*
Westman, *West*

Westmoreland, *Westmorland*
Westmorland
Weston
Westra, *West*
Westray
Westren, *West*
Westron, *West*
Westrop
Westwood
Wetherald, *Weatherall*
Wetherall, *Weatherall*
Wetherbee, *Weathersby*
Wetherby, *Weathersby*
Wethered, *Weatherhead*
Wetherell, *Weatherall*
Wetherhead, *Weatherhead*
Wetheril, *Weatherall*
Wetherill, *Weatherall*
Wetherilt, *Weatherall*
Wetherspoon, *Witherspoon*
Wettin
Wetton
Wettwer, *Widdow*
Wetz, *Wenzel*
Wetzel, *Wenzel*
Wetzig, *Wenzel*
Weuste, *Wüst*
Wevell, *Wavell*
Wever, *Weaver*
Weverinck, *Weaver*
Wevers, *Weaver*
Wevill, *Wavell*
Wewers, *Weaver*
Wexelbaum, *Wechsler*
Wexler, *Wechsler*
Wey, *Way*
Weyer, *Weiher*
Weyman, *Wyman*
Weymont, *Wyman*
Wężyk
Whaites, *Waite*
Whaits, *Waite*
Whale
Whalen, *Whelan*
Whaler, *Wheeler*
Whales, *Whale*
Whaley, *Whalley*
Whall, *Whale*
Whalley
Whamond, *Wyman*
Whannell, *McConnell*
Wharin, *Waring*
Wharmby
Wharrick, *Warwick*
Wharrier, *Warr*
Whartmouth, *Watmough*
Wharton
Whate, *Wheat*
Whateley, *Wheatley*
Whately, *Wheatley*
Whatkins, *Watt*
Whatley, *Wheatley*
Whatling, *Watt*
Whatly, *Wheatley*
Whatman, *Watman*
Whatmaugh, *Watmough*
Whatmoor, *Whatmore*
Whatmore
Whatmough, *Watmough*
Whatmouth, *Watmough*
Whatmuff, *Watmough*
Whatrup, *Wardrop*
Whay, *Way*
Whayman, *Wyman*
Whaymand, *Wyman*
Whaymond, *Wyman*
Whaymont, *Wyman*
Wheal, *Wheel*
Wheale, *Wheel*
Whealler, *Wheeler*
Wheals, *Wheel*
Wheat
Wheatcroft
Wheate, *Wheat*
Wheatleigh, *Wheatley*
Wheatley
Wheatly, *Wheatley*
Wheatman, *Watman*
Wheaton
Wheeker, *Weake*
Wheel
Wheelan, *Whelan*
Wheelden, *Wheeldon*
Wheeldon
Wheele, *Wheel*
Wheeler
Wheelhouse
Wheeller, *Wheeler*
Wheels, *Wheel*
Wheelwright, *Wheeler*
Wheetman, *Watman*
Wheildon, *Wheeldon*
Whelan
Wheldon, *Wheeldon*
Whelehan, *Whelan*
Wheler, *Wheeler*
Whenman, *Wain*
Whent, *Went*
Where, *Ware*
Whewell, *Wheel*
Whick, *Wick*
Whicker, *Wick*
Whickman, *Wick*
Whieldon, *Wheeldon*
Whiffen, *Wiffen*
Whiffin, *Wiffen*
Whild, *Wild*
Whilde, *Wild*
While, *Wheel*
Whiler, *Wheeler*
Whilesmith, *Wheeler*
Whimster, *Femister*
Whin, *Sweeney*
Whineray, *Winrow*
Whinery, *Winrow*
Whinnerah, *Winrow*
Whinray, *Winrow*
Whinrow, *Winrow*
Whinwray, *Winrow*
Whipp
Whipple
Whiscard, *Wishart*
Whisker, *Wishart*
Whistler
Whiston
Whitaker, *Whittaker*
Whitamore, *Whitmore*
Whitbread
Whitby
Whitchurch
Whitcomb, *Whitcombe*
Whitcombe
Whitcroft, *Wheatcroft*
White
Whiteaker, *Whittaker*
Whitear, *Whittier*
Whitecross
Whitefield, *Whitfield*
Whiteford
Whitehair, *Whittier*
Whitehead
Whitehorn
Whitehorne, *Whitehorn*
Whitehouse
Whiteing, *White*
Whitelam, *Whitlam*
Whitelaw
Whiteley
Whitell, *Whitwell*
Whitelock, *Whitlock*
Whitelocke, *Whitlock*
Whitelum, *Whitlam*
Whitely, *Whiteley*
Whiteman, *Whitman*
Whitemore, *Whitmore*
Whiter
Whites, *White*
Whiteside
Whitesides, *Whiteside*
Whitesmith, *Smith*
Whiteson, *White*
Whitey, *Whitty*
Whitfield
Whitford
Whitgift
Whithair, *Whittier*
Whithear, *Whittier*
Whithorn, *Whitehorn*
Whithous, *Whitehouse*
Whitie, *Whitty*
Whiting, *White*
Whitington, *Whittington*
Whitla, *Whiteley*
Whitlam
Whitlaw, *Whitelaw*
Whitley, *Whiteley*
Whitlock
Whitlum, *Whitlam*
Whitman
Whitmarsh
Whitmer, *Whitmore*
Whitmore
Whitney
Whitson, *White*
Whitsun, *White*
Whitt, *White*
Whitta, *Whiter*
Whittaker
Whittamore, *Whitmore*
Whitte, *White*
Whittear, *Whittier*
Whittell, *Whitwell*
Whittemore, *Whitmore*
Whitter, *Whiter*
Whitters, *Whitehouse*
Whittey, *Whitty*
Whitticase, *Whittaker*
Whittier
Whittimore, *Whitmore*
Whitting, *White*
Whittingham
Whittington
Whittla, *Whiteley*
Whittle
Whittley, *Whiteley*
Whitton
Whitty
Whitwell
Whitworth
Whooley, *Hooley*
Whorall, *Worrall*
Whorisky, *Fourish*
Why, *Guy*
Whyard, *Wyatt*
Whyatt, *Wyatt*
Whybro, *Whybrow*
Whybrow
Whye, *Guy*
Whyman, *Wyman*
Whymant, *Wyman*
Whyte, *White*
Whytehead, *Whitehead*
Whytelaw, *Whitelaw*
Whytlaw, *Whitelaw*
Wiarda, *Guichard*
Wiards, *Guichard*
Wiart, *Guichard*
Wibroe, *Whybrow*
Wibrow, *Whybrow*
Wich
Wichan, *Wich*
Wicharz, *Guichard*
Wicher, *Guichard*
Wichers, *Guichard*
Wichert, *Guichard*
Wick
Wickberg, *Wik*
Wicke, *Wick*
Wicken, *Wick*
Wickens, *Wick*
Wicker, *Wick*
Wickert, *Guichard*
Wickerts, *Guichard*
Wickes, *Wick*
Wickham
Wickins, *Wick*
Wicklund, *Wik*
Wickman, *Wick*
Wickmann, *Wik*
Wicks, *Wick*
Wickström, *Wik*
Wiczkiewicz, *Vincent*
Widdas, *Widdow*
Widde, *Wood*
Widdecombe, *Withycombe*
Widdekind, *Wedekind*
Widders, *Widdow*
Widderson, *Widdow*
Widdeson, *Widdow*
Widdess, *Widdow*
Widdicombe, *Withycombe*
Widdison, *Widdow*
Widdow
Widdowes, *Widdow*
Widdows, *Widdow*
Widdowson, *Widdow*
Widdrington
Widegren, *Weide*
Widell, *Weide*
Widén, *Weide*
Widerberg, *Weide*
Widerström, *Weide*
Widgren, *Weide*
Widholm, *Weide*
Widlund, *Weide*
Widman, *Weide*
Widmann, *Weide*
Widmark, *Weide*
Widowson, *Widdow*
Więcek, *Vincent*
Wiech, *Wich*
Wiechers, *Guichard*
Wiechert, *Guichard*
Wieck, *Wick*
Więckowski, *Vincent*
Więclawicz, *Václav*

Więcławski, *Václav*
Więczkiewicz, *Vincent*
Wieczorek
Wieczorkiewicz, *Wieczorek*
Wieczorkowski, *Wieczorek*
Wiede, *Weide*
Wiedemann, *Weide*
Wiedmann, *Weide*
Wiegand, *Wiggin*
Wiegandt, *Wiggin*
Wiegank, *Wiggin*
Wiegard, *Guichard*
Wieger, *Guichard*
Wiegers, *Guichard*
Wiegert, *Guichard*
Wieghardt, *Guichard*
Wieland
Wieleman, *Wheel*
Wiemann, *Weide*
Wien
Wiener, *Wien*
Wientzek, *Vincent*
Wienzek, *Vincent*
Wiert, *Guichard*
Wierzbicki
Wierzbowski, *Wierzbicki*
Wiese
Wiesemann, *Wiese*
Wiesen, *Wiese*
Wiesenberg, *Wiese*
Wiesener, *Wiese*
Wiesenfeld, *Wiese*
Wiesengrund, *Wiese*
Wiesenstern, *Wiese*
Wiesenthal, *Wiese*
Wieser, *Wiese*
Wiesner, *Wiese*
Wiestner, *Wüst*
Wiffen
Wigan, *Wiggin*
Wigand, *Wiggin*
Wigandt, *Wiggin*
Wigder, *Avigdor*
Wigdor, *Avigdor*
Wigdorchik, *Avigdor*
Wigdorczik, *Avigdor*
Wigdorowicz, *Avigdor*
Wigens, *Wiggin*
Wigg
Wiggans, *Wiggin*
Wigger, *Guichard, Wigg*
Wiggers, *Guichard*
Wiggert, *Guichard*
Wiggin
Wiggins, *Wiggin*
Wigglesworth
Wiggs, *Wigg*
Wigham, *Wickham*
Wight
Wightman, *Wight*
Wigin, *Wiggin*
Wigley
Wigmore
Wignal
Wigoder, *Wygodarz*
Wigodman, *Wygodarz*
Wigodner, *Wygodarz*
Wiingaard, *Winyard*
Wiingård, *Winyard*
Wijk, *Wick*
Wijnberg, *Weinberg*
Wijnbergen, *Weinberg*
Wijnen, *Wein*
Wijngaard, *Winyard*
Wijnyaerd, *Winyard*
Wijsman, *Wise*
Wik
Wikander, *Wik*
Wikberg, *Wik*
Wike, *Wick*
Wiklund, *Wik*
Wikmann, *Wik*
Wikner, *Wik*
Wikström, *Wik*
Wiktor, *Victor*
Wiktorczyk, *Victor*
Wiktorowicz, *Victor*
Wiktorowski, *Victor*
Wiktorski, *Victor*
Wil, *Will*
Wilame, *William*
Wilbarth, *Wilbert*
Wilberding, *Wilbert*
Wilberforce, *Wilberfoss*
Wilberfoss
Wilbers, *Wilbert*
Wilbert
Wilbertz, *Wilbert*
Wilbrecht, *Wilbert*
Wilby
Wilcher, *Wiltshire*
Wilck, *Wilk*
Wilcock
Wilcocke, *Wilcock*
Wilcocks, *Wilcock*
Wilcockson, *Wilcock*
Wilcox, *Wilcock*
Wilcoxon, *Wilcock*
Wilcoxson, *Wilcock*
Wilczak, *Wilk*
Wilczek, *Wilk*
Wilczyński, *Wilk*
Wild
Wildash, *Wildish*
Wilde, *Wild*
Wildeman, *Wild*
Wildemann, *Wild*
Wilden, *Wilding*
Wilder, *Wild*
Wilderman, *Wild*
Wildig
Wildigg, *Wildig*
Wilding
Wildish
Wildman, *Wild*
Wildmann, *Wild*
Wildner, *Willner*
Wildon, *Wheeldon*
Wildt, *Wild*
Wildy
Wileman
Wiler, *Wheeler*
Wiles, *Wileman*
Wilesmith, *Wheeler*
Wilets, *Will*
Wilgrass, *Willgress*
Wilgress, *Willgress*
Wilhalm, *William*
Wilharm, *William*
Wilhelm, *William*
Wilhelmer, *William*
Wilhelmi, *William*
Wilhelms, *William*
Wilhelmsen, *William*
Wilhelmsson, *William*
Wiliems, *William*
Wilimowski, *William*
Wiliński, *William*
Wilk
Wilke, *Wilk, Will*
Wilken, *Wilkin, Will*
Wilkens, *Wilkin, Will*
Wilkenson, *Wilkin*
Wilkerson, *Wilkin*
Wilkes, *Wilk*
Wilkie, *Wilk*
Wilkieson, *Wilk*
Wilkin
Wilkins, *Wilkin*
Wilkinson, *Wilkin*
Wilkowicz, *Wilk*
Wilks, *Wilk*
Will
Willame, *William*
Willament, *William*
Willard
Willats, *Will*
Willaume, *William*
Willcock, *Wilcock*
Willcocks, *Wilcock*
Willcockson, *Wilcock*
Willcox, *Wilcock*
Willcoxon, *Wilcock*
Willcoxson, *Wilcock*
Willday, *Wildy*
Willdig, *Wildig*
Willdigg, *Wildig*
Wille, *Will*
Willeke, *Will*
Willekens, *Will*
Willem, *William*
Willème, *William*
Willemet, *William*
Willemin, *William*
Willemot, *William*
Willems, *William*
Willemse, *William*
Willemsen, *William*
Willer, *Willard*
Willerding, *Willard*
Willers, *Willard*
Willert, *Willard*
Willerton
Willes, *Will*
Willeson, *Will*
Willet, *Will*
Willett, *Will*
Willetts, *Will*
Willey
Willgress
Willgross, *Willgress*
William
Williams, *William*
Williamson, *William*
Williment, *William*
Willimont, *William*
Willimott, *William*
Willing, *Will*
Willings, *Will*
Williot, *Will*
Willis, *Will*
Willishire, *Wiltshire*
Willison, *Will*
Willitt, *Will*
Willm, *William*
Willmann, *Will*
Willmanns, *Will*
Willment, *William*
Willmett, *William*
Willmetts, *William*
Willmin, *William*
Willmore
Willmot, *William*
Willmott, *William*
Willmotts, *William*
Willms, *William*
Willmsen, *William*
Willmutt, *William*
Willner
Willock
Willocks, *Willock*
Willot, *Will*
Willott, *Will*
Willoughby
Willox, *Willock*
Wills, *Will*
Willshaw, *Wiltshire*
Willshear, *Wiltshire*
Willsher, *Wiltshire*
Willshere, *Wiltshire*
Willshire, *Wiltshire*
Willson, *Will*
Willsson, *Will*
Willumsen, *William*
Wilm, *William*
Wilman, *Will*
Wilmann, *Will*
Wilmanowski, *Will*
Wilmański, *Will*
Wilmin, *William*
Wilmore, *Willmore*
Wilmot, *William*
Wilmott, *William*
Wilms, *William*
Wilner, *Willner*
Wils, *Will*
Wilsens, *Will*
Wilshaw, *Wiltshire*
Wilsher, *Wiltshire*
Wilshere, *Wiltshire*
Wilshire, *Wiltshire*
Wilson, *Will*
Wilsson, *Will*
Wilton
Wiltshaw, *Wiltshire*
Wiltshear, *Wiltshire*
Wiltsher, *Wiltshire*
Wiltshier, *Wiltshire*
Wiltshire
Wimmers, *Wymer*
Wimpenny
Wimpey
Winberg, *Weinberg*
Winblad, *Wein*
Winbladh, *Wein*
Winceniuk, *Vincent*
Wincentowicz, *Vincent*
Winch
Winchester
Winckel
Winckelmann, *Winckel*
Winckler, *Winckel*
Wind
Winde, *Wind*
Winder
Winderlich, *Wunderlich*
Windham, *Wyndham*
Windisch, *Wendt*
Windischmann, *Wendt*
Windle
Windsor
Windt, *Wind*
Winekrantz, *Wein*
Winekranz, *Wein*
Winfield
Wing

Wingard, *Winyard*
Wingate
Wingert, *Winyard*
Wingett, *Wingate*
Wingfield, *Winfield*
Wingrove
Winiarski, *Wein*
Winick, *Winnick*
Winicki, *Winnick*
Winickman, *Winnick*
Winiecki, *Wein*
Winik, *Winnick*
Winikman, *Winnick*
Winikoff, *Winnick*
Winikov, *Winnick*
Winitzky, *Winnick*
Wink, *Winch*
Winkel, *Winckel*
Winkelaar, *Winckel*
Winkelman, *Winckel*
Winkelmann, *Winckel*
Winkelsberg, *Winckel*
Winkelstein, *Winckel*
Winkler, *Winckel*
Winn
Winnard, *Winyard*
Winnberg, *Weinberg*
Winnick
Winnik, *Winnick*
Winnikow, *Winnick*
Winocour, *Vinokur*
Winocur, *Vinokur*
Winograd, *Vinogradov*
Winogradow, *Vinogradov*
Winokur, *Vinokur*
Winpenny, *Wimpenny*
Winquist, *Wein*
Winrow
Winsch, *Wendt*
Winschmann, *Wendt*
Winser, *Windsor*
Winslow
Winsor, *Windsor*
Winstanley
Winston
Winstone, *Winston*
Winter
Winterberg, *Winter*
Winterborn, *Winterbourne*
Winterborne, *Winterbourne*
Winterbotham, *Winterbottom*
Winterbottom
Winterbourn, *Winterbourne*
Winterbourne
Winterburn, *Winterbourne*
Winterl, *Winter*
Winterle, *Winter*
Winterlein, *Winter*
Winters, *Winter*
Winterson, *Winter*
Winterstein, *Winter*
Winterton
Winthrop
Wintle, *Windle*
Winton
Wintour, *Winter*
Wintscher, *Wendt*
Winyard
Winzar, *Windsor*
Winzer, *Windsor*
Winzor, *Windsor*
Wirth
Wirthgen, *Wirth*
Wirths, *Wirth*
Wirtz, *Wirth*
Wisdom, *Wise*
Wise
Wiseman, *Wise*
Wishart
Wiskar, *Wishart*
Wisker, *Wishart*
Wiśniak
Wiśniewski
Wiśniowiecki, *Wiśniewski*
Wiśniowski, *Wiśniewski*
Wisser, *Fisher*
Wissler, *Wechsler*
Wissler, *Whistler*
Wiszniewski, *Wiśniewski*
Witasiak, *Vito*
Witaszek, *Vito*
Witcomb, *Whitcombe*
Witcombe, *Whitcombe*
Witczak, *Vito*
Witek, *Vito*
Witekind, *Wedekind*
Witelson, *Vita*
Witelzon, *Vita*
Wites, *Vita*
With, *Wythe*
Withacombe, *Withycombe*
Witham
Withams, *Witham*
Withe, *Wythe*
Withecombe, *Withycombe*
Wither
Witherby, *Weathersby*
Withers, *Wither*
Witherspoon
Withey
Withington
Withnell
Withy, *Withey*
Withycombe
Witkiewicz, *Vito*
Witkin, *Vita*
Witkind, *Vita*
Witkovitz, *Vito*
Witkovsky, *Vito*
Witkowitz, *Vito*
Witkowski, *Vito*
Witkowsky, *Vito*
Witley, *Whiteley*
Witney
Witt, *White*
Wittamore, *Whitmore*
Wittams, *Witham*
Wittber, *Widdow*
Witte, *White*
Wittels, *Vita*
Wittelsbach
Witten, *White*
Wittes, *Vita*
Wittey, *Witty*
Wittgen, *White*
Wittgens, *White*
Wittiber, *Widdow*
Witting, *White*
Wittje, *White*
Wittke, *White*
Wittkowski, *Vito*
Wittkowsky, *Vito*
Wittman, *Whitman*
Witts, *White*
Wittwer, *Widdow*
Witty
Witzel, *Wiggin*
Witzthum, *Visdomini*
Witztum, *Visdomini*
Wix, *Wick*
Włoch, *Vlach*
Wloch, *Vlach*
Włochowicz, *Vlach*
Włodarczyk, *Włodarski*
Włodarek, *Włodarski*
Włodarski
Wlodasch, *Vladimirov*
Włodek, *Vladimirov*
Włodkowicz, *Vladimirov*
Włodzimierski, *Vladimirov*
Włodzimirski, *Vladimirov*
Włoski, *Vlach*
Włoszek, *Vlach*
Wlotzka, *Vladimirov*
Wlotzke, *Vladimirov*
Wnuk
Wöbb, *Walburg*
Wobbe, *Walburg*
Wöbbeking, *Walburg*
Wobben, *Walburg*
Wöbcke, *Walburg*
Wöber, *Weaver*
Wober, *Weaver*
Wöbke, *Walburg*
Wöbken, *Walburg*
Woddell, *Waddell*
Wodehouse, *Woodhouse*
Wodeman, *Wader*
Wodhams, *Woodham*
Wodzyński
Woffenden, *Wolfenden*
Woffendon, *Wolfenden*
Woffindin, *Wolfenden*
Woffindon, *Wolfenden*
Woffit, *Wolfit*
Wogan
Wöhl, *Walter*
Wohl
Wohlberg, *Wohl*
Wohld, *Wald*
Wöhlder, *Walter*
Wöhldert, *Walter*
Wöhle, *Walter*
Wohler, *Walter*
Wohlers, *Walter*
Wohlert, *Walter*
Wohlfarth, *Wohl*
Wohlfeld, *Wohl*
Wohlfinger, *Wohl*
Wohlfromm, *Wolfram*
Wohlgemueth, *Wohl*
Wöhling, *Walter*
Wöhlk, *Walter*
Wöhlke, *Walter*
Wöhlken, *Walter*
Wöhlkens, *Walter*
Wöhlking, *Walter*
Wohlman, *Wohl*
Wohlmann, *Wohl*
Wohlrab, *Waldron*
Wohlspiegel, *Wohl*
Wohlstadter, *Wohl*
Wohlstaedter, *Wohl*
Wohlstein, *Wohl*
Wohlters, *Walter*
Wohltmann, *Wald*
Wöhrle, *Warner*
Wöhrlein, *Warner*
Woiner, *Wagner*
Woitek, *Vojtěch*
Woitke, *Vojtěch*
Woitschek, *Vojtěch*
Woitzik, *Vojtěch*
Wójcicki, *Wójcik*
Wojciech, *Vojtěch*
Wojciechowicz, *Vojtěch*
Wojciechowski, *Vojtěch*
Wojcieszek, *Vojtěch*
Wójcik
Wójcikiewicz, *Wójcik*
Wójcikowski, *Wójcik*
Wójciński, *Wójcik*
Wojewoda, *Vejvoda*
Wojewódzki, *Vejvoda*
Wojnar, *Wagner*
Wojnarowski, *Wagner*
Wójt, *Wójcik*
Wojtak, *Vojtěch*
Wojtala, *Vojtěch*
Wojtan, *Vojtěch*
Wojtanowicz, *Vojtěch*
Wojtanowski, *Vojtěch*
Wojtas, *Vojtěch*
Wojtasik, *Vojtěch*
Wojtaszewski, *Vojtěch*
Wojtczak, *Vojtěch*
Wojtczyk, *Vojtěch*
Wojtecki, *Vojtěch*
Wojtera, *Vojtěch*
Wojtkiewicz, *Vojtěch*
Wojtkowiak, *Vojtěch*
Wojtkowski, *Vojtěch*
Wójtowicz, *Wójcik*
Wojtowicz, *Vojtěch*
Wojtych, *Vojtěch*
Wojtyła, *Vojtěch*
Wojtylak, *Vojtěch*
Wojtyło, *Vojtěch*
Wojtysiak, *Vojtěch*
Wol, *Wool*
Wolach, *Vlach*
Wolburg, *Walburg*
Wolcott, *Woolcott*
Wold, *Wald*
Wolde, *Wald*
Wöldeke, *Walter*
Wolder, *Walter*
Woldering, *Walter*
Wolders, *Walter*
Wolds, *Wald*
Woldstra, *Wald*
Wolf
Wolfberg, *Wolf*
Wolfe, *Wolf*
Wölfel, *Wolf*
Wolfen, *Wolf*
Wolfenden
Wolfensohn, *Wolf*
Wolfenson, *Wolf*
Wolfes, *Wolf*
Wolff, *Wolf*
Wölfflin, *Wolf*
Wolffsohn, *Wolf*
Wolfgen, *Wolf*
Wolfgram, *Wolfram*
Wolfheim, *Wolf*
Wolfin, *Wolf*
Wolfit
Wölfle, *Wolf*
Wölflin, *Wolf*
Wolfman, *Wolf*
Wolfmann, *Wolf*
Wolfner, *Woolnough*
Wolford, *Woolford*
Wolfovitch, *Wolf*
Wolfovits, *Wolf*

Wolfovitz, *Wolf*
Wolfovsky, *Wolf*
Wolfowich, *Wolf*
Wolfowicz, *Wolf*
Wolfowitch, *Wolf*
Wolfowitz, *Wolf*
Wolfram
Wolfrom, *Wolfram*
Wolfrum, *Wolfram*
Wolfsen, *Wolf*
Wolfsohn, *Wolf*
Wolfson, *Wolf*
Wolfstein, *Wolf*
Wolichman, *Vlach*
Wöljen, *Walter*
Wolk, *Wilk*
Wölke, *Walter*
Wölken, *Walter*
Woll, *Wool*
Wollach, *Vlach*
Wollard, *Woolford*
Wollaston
Wolle, *Wool*
Woller, *Wool*
Wollett, *Wolfit*
Wolley, *Woolley*
Wollman, *Wool*
Wollmann, *Wool*
Wollner, *Wool*
Wolloch, *Vlach*
Wollrabe, *Waldron*
Wollring, *Walter*
Wollstonecraft, *Wolstonecraft*
Wolman, *Wool*
Wolmansky, *Wool*
Wolner, *Wool*
Wolnerman, *Wool*
Wolniak
Wolnicki, *Wolniak*
Wolniewicz, *Wolniak*
Wołodkiewicz, *Vladimirov*
Wołodko, *Vladimirov*
Wołosz, *Vlach*
Wołoszyn, *Vlach*
Wołowiec, *Volák*
Wołowski, *Volák*
Wolpe, *Volpe*
Wolper, *Volpe*
Wolpert, *Volpert*
Wolpole, *Walpole*
Wolrich, *Wooldridge*
Wolsey
Wolski, *Zwolski*
Wolstanholme, *Wolstenholme*
Wolstencroft, *Wolstonecraft*
Wolstenholme
Wolstenhulme, *Wolstenholme*
Wolston, *Woolston*
Wolstoncraft, *Wolstonecraft*
Wolstonecraft
Wolstonholm, *Wolstenholme*
Wolstonholme, *Wolstenholme*
Wolter, *Walter*
Wölterges, *Walter*
Woltering, *Walter*
Wolterke, *Walter*
Wolterkes, *Walter*
Wolters, *Walter*
Wöltjes, *Walter*
Wolveridge, *Wooldridge*
Wombell, *Wombwell*
Wombwell
Womersley
Womwell, *Wombwell*
Wondraschek, *Andrew*
Wońicko, *Woźniak*
Wons, *Wąsik*
Wood
Woodall, *Woodhall*
Woodard
Woodbridge
Woodburn
Woodburne, *Woodburn*
Woodcock
Woodcocks, *Woodcock*
Woodcott, *Woodcock*
Wooddin, *Wood*
Woode, *Wood*
Wooder, *Wood*
Wooders, *Woodhouse*
Woodfield
Woodford
Woodforde, *Woodford*
Woodfords, *Woodford*
Woodgate
Woodgates, *Woodgate*
Woodget, *Woodgate*
Woodgett, *Woodgate*
Woodhall
Woodham
Woodhams, *Woodham*
Woodhatch
Woodhead
Woodhouse
Woodin, *Wood*
Wooding, *Wood*
Woodings, *Wood*
Woodjetts, *Woodgate*
Woodlake, *Woodlock*
Woodland
Woodlands, *Woodland*
Woodleigh, *Woodley*
Woodley
Woodlock
Woodman
Woodroff, *Woodruff*
Woodroffe, *Woodruff*
Woodroof, *Woodruff*
Woodroofe, *Woodruff*
Woodrooffe, *Woodruff*
Woodrough, *Woodruff*
Woodrow
Woodruff
Woodruffe, *Woodruff*
Woodrup, *Woodruff*
Woods, *Wood*
Woodside
Woodus, *Woodhouse*
Woodward
Woodyatt, *Woodgate*
Woof, *Wolf*
Wooff, *Wolf*
Woofinden, *Wolfenden*
Wookey
Wool
Woolard, *Woolford*
Woolatt, *Wolfit*
Woolcock, *Woolcott*
Woolcot, *Woolcott*
Woolcott
Wooldridge
Wooler, *Wool*
Woolett, *Wolfit*
Wooley, *Woolley*
Woolf, *Wolf*
Woolfarth, *Woolford*
Woolfe, *Wolf*
Woolfenden, *Wolfenden*
Woolfit, *Wolfit*
Woolfitt, *Wolfit*
Woolfoot, *Woolford*
Woolford
Woolforde, *Woolford*
Woolforth, *Woolford*
Woolgar
Woolgard, *Woolgar*
Woolger, *Woolgar*
Wooll, *Wool*
Woollard, *Woolford*
Woollaston, *Wollaston*
Woollcott, *Woolcott*
Wooller, *Wool*
Woollett, *Wolfit*
Woolley
Woollin
Woollston, *Woolston*
Woolman, *Wool*
Woolner, *Woolnough*
Woolnoth, *Woolnough*
Woolnough
Woolrich, *Wooldridge*
Woolridge, *Wooldridge*
Woolright, *Wooldridge*
Woolsey, *Wolsey*
Woolstencroft, *Wolstonecraft*
Woolstenhulme, *Wolstenholme*
Woolston
Woolstone, *Woolston*
Woolveridge, *Wooldridge*
Woolvett, *Wolfit*
Woolward, *Woolford*
Woombell, *Wombwell*
Woombill, *Wombwell*
Woomble, *Wombwell*
Woosey, *Wolsey*
Woosnam, *Wolstenholme*
Wooster
Wooten, *Wootton*
Wooton, *Wootton*
Wootten, *Wootton*
Wootton
Worboys, *Warboys*
Worcester, *Wooster*
Worden
Wordman, *Ward*
Wordsworth
Worgan
Workman
Worley
Wörlin, *Warner*
Worm, *Orme*
Wormal, *Wormald*
Wormald
Wörmbke, *Orme*
Wormell, *Wormald*
Wormhall, *Wormald*
Wörmke, *Orme*
Wormull, *Wormald*
Wörn, *Warner*
Wörndle, *Warner*
Wörner, *Warner*
Wörnhör, *Warner*
Wörnle, *Warner*
Wörnz, *Warner*
Worona, *Voronin*
Wörpel, *Würfel*
Worral, *Worrall*
Worrall
Worrell, *Worrall*
Worril, *Worrall*
Worsencroft, *Wolstonecraft*
Worsfield, *Worsfold*
Worsfold
Worsick, *Worswick*
Worsley
Worsman, *Wolstenholme*
Worst, *Wurst*
Worstencroft, *Wolstonecraft*
Worstenholme, *Wolstenholme*
Worster, *Wooster*
Worsthorne
Worswick
Wort
Worters, *Water*
Worth
Worthalter, *Wortman*
Worthington
Worthy
Wortley
Wortman
Worton
Worts, *Wort*
Wortt, *Wort*
Woś, *Vojtěch*
Wosencroft, *Wolstonecraft*
Wosik, *Vojtěch*
Wöst, *Wüst*
Wöste, *Wüst*
Wostear, *Wooster*
Wostenholm, *Wolstenholme*
Wöstmann, *Wüst*
Woszczak, *Vojtěch*
Woszczyk, *Vojtěch*
Wotek, *Vojtěch*
Wotherspoon, *Witherspoon*
Wotton, *Wootton*
Wötzel, *Wenzel*
Wouda, *Wald*
Woudman, *Wald*
Woudstra, *Wald*
Would, *Wald*
Woulde, *Wald*
Woulds, *Wald*
Woulfe, *Wolf*
Wouter, *Walter*
Wouters, *Walter*
Woutersen, *Walter*
Wouts, *Walter*
Woyzek, *Vojtěch*
Wozencroft, *Wolstonecraft*
Woźniacki, *Woźniak*
Woźniak
Woźniakiewicz, *Woźniak*
Woźniakowski, *Woźniak*
Woźnicki, *Woźniak*
Woźny, *Woźniak*
Wozzek, *Vojtěch*
Wra, *Wray*
Wraight, *Wright*
Wraighte, *Wright*
Wraith
Wrate, *Wright*
Wray
Wrede, *Wraith*
Wree, *Wraith*
Wreight, *Wright*
Wren
Wrenn, *Wren*
Wreth, *Wraith*
Wrey, *Wray*
Wrigglesworth
Wright
Wrighte, *Wright*
Wrightson, *Wright*
Wriglesworth, *Wrigglesworth*
Wrigley

X

Y

Yefroimovich, *Yefremov*
Yeger, *Jäger*
Yegerlev, *Jäger*
Yegorchenkov, *George*
Yegorev, *George*
Yegorkin, *George*
Yegorkov, *George*
Yegorov, *George*
Yegorovnin, *George*
Yegorshin, *George*
Yegoshin, *George*
Yekaterinin, *Catlin*
Yekaterinski, *Catlin*
Yekel, *Jacob*
Yelen, *Jelen*
Yeliashev, *Ellis*
Yelin, *Jelen*
Yelinek, *Jelen*
Yelinovitz, *Jelen*
Yelinsohn, *Jelen*
Yelland
Yellen, *Jelen*
Yellin, *Jelen*
Yellinek, *Jelen*
Yellon, *Jelen*
Yelon, *Jelen*
Yelyashev, *Ellis*
Yeman, *Yeoman*
Yemelyan, *Émilien*
Yemelyanchikov, *Émilien*
Yemelyanov, *Émilien*
Yemyashev, *Émilien*
Yental, *Jentel*
Yeo
Yeoh, *Yeo*
Yeoman
Yeomans, *Yeoman*
Yeoward, *Ewart*
Yeowart, *Ewart*
Yeowell, *Yule*
Yepifanov
Yepifanyev, *Yepifanov*
Yepikhin, *Yepifanov*
Yepishchev, *Yepifanov*
Yepishev, *Yepifanov*
Yepishin, *Yepifanov*
Yepiskopov, *Bishop*
Yerasov, *Jeremy*
Yerburgh
Yeremeev, *Jeremy*
Yerin, *Jeremy*
Yerkhov, *Jeremy*
Yerkin, *Jeremy*
Yerkov, *Jeremy*
Yermiahu, *Jeremy*
Yermus, *Jeremy*
Yernmonger, *Ironmonger*
Yeroshalmi, *Yerushalmi*
Yeroushalmi, *Yerushalmi*
Yershin, *Jeremy*
Yerushalmi
Yerushalmy, *Yerushalmi*
Yerushamsky, *Yerushalmi*
Yerychov, *Jeremy*
Yeryomin, *Jeremy*
Yeryuchin, *Jeremy*
Yeryushev, *Jeremy*
Yesenev, *Joseph*
Yesenin, *Joseph*
Yesichev, *Joseph*
Yesinin, *Joseph*
Yesinov, *Joseph*
Yesipov, *Joseph*
Yeskin, *Joseph*
Yeskov, *Joseph*
Yestifeev, *Yevtikhiev*
Yetman, *Yate*
Yetts, *Yate*
Yeuell, *Yule*
Yevdokimov
Yevfimov, *Yefimov*
Yevseev, *Eusébio*
Yevsenov, *Eusébio*
Yevsikov, *Eusébio*
Yevstifeev, *Yevtikhiev*
Yevstikheev, *Yevtikhiev*
Yevsyunin, *Eusébio*
Yevsyutin, *Eusébio*
Yevteev, *Yevtikhiev*
Yevtifeev, *Yevtikhiev*
Yevtikheev, *Yevtikhiev*
Yevtikhiev
Yevtikhov, *Yevtikhiev*
Yevtushenko, *Yevtikhiev*
Yevtyugin, *Yevtikhiev*
Yevtyukhov, *Yevtikhiev*
Yewen, *Ewan*
Yezafovich, *Joseph*
Yezhov
Yirmiyahu, *Jeremy*
Yisrael, *Israel*
Yisraeli, *Israeler*
Yisraelit, *Israeler*
Yisraely, *Israeler*
Yitschaky, *Isaac*
Yitshak, *Isaac*
Yitshaki, *Isaac*
Yitzchaki, *Isaac*
Yitzhak, *Isaac*
Yitzhaki, *Isaac*
Yitzhakof, *Isaac*
Yitzhakov, *Isaac*
Yitzhaky, *Isaac*
Yitzhok, *Isaac*
Yitzkovicz, *Isaac*
Yitzkovitz, *Isaac*
Yitzkowitz, *Isaac*
Yizhak, *Isaac*
Yizhaki, *Isaac*
Yoachimsohn, *Joachim*
Yockelman, *Jacob*
Yodla, *Yolkin*
Yoel
Yoeli, *Yoel*
Yoell, *Yule*
Yoelson, *Yoel*
Yokel, *Jacob*
Yolkin
Yolleck, *Yoel*
Yolles, *Yoel*
Yona, *Jonas*
Yonah, *Jonas*
Yong, *Young*
Yonge, *Young*
Yonis, *Jonas*
Yonovitz, *Jonas*
York
Yorke, *York*
Yorkson, *Yorkston*
Yorkston
Yorston, *Yorkston*
Yorstoun, *Yorkston*
Yoselevitch, *Joseph*
Yoseloff, *Joseph*
Yoselson, *Joseph*
Yosevitz, *Joseph*
Yosifov, *Joseph*
Yosko, *Joseph*
Yoskowitz, *Joseph*
Yoslow, *Joseph*
Yoslowitz, *Joseph*
Yosselevitch, *Joseph*
Youat, *Ewart*
Youatt, *Ewart*
Youel, *Yule*
Youels, *Yule*
Youens, *Ewan*
Youhill, *Yule*
Youings, *Ewan*
Youle, *Yule*
Youles, *Yule*
Youll, *Yule*
Young
Younge, *Young*
Younger
Youngman, *Yeoman*
Youngs, *Young*
Younkman, *Yeoman*
Youren, *Uren*
Yourenson, *Uren*
Yourn, *Uren*
Yourne, *Uren*
Youron, *Uren*
Youronson, *Uren*
Yourston, *Yorkston*
Yrois, *Ireland*
Yubero
Yuda, *Jude*
Yudayov, *Jude*
Yudeikin, *Jude*
Yudelevitz, *Jude*
Yudelewitz, *Jude*
Yudelovitz, *Jude*
Yudevitz, *Jude*
Yudin, *Jude*
Yudiovitch, *Jude*
Yuditzki, *Jude*
Yudkevitz, *Jude*
Yudkin, *Jude*
Yudko, *Jude*
Yudkowski, *Jude*
Yudovitz, *Jude*
Yudowicz, *Jude*
Yudowitz, *Jude*
Yuell, *Yule*
Yuile, *Yule*
Yuill, *Yule*
Yuille, *Yule*
Yukhin, *George*
Yukhnev, *George*
Yukhnevich, *George*
Yukhnin, *George*
Yukhnov, *George*
Yukhov, *George*
Yukhtin, *George*
Yule
Yuranov, *George*
Yurasov, *George*
Yurchenko, *George*
Yurchishin, *George*
Yurenev, *George*
Yurenin, *George*
Yurevich, *George*
Yurikov, *George*
Yurin, *George*
Yurinov, *George*
Yurivtsev, *George*
Yurkevich, *George*
Yurkin, *George*
Yurkov, *George*
Yurlov, *George*
Yurmanov, *George*
Yurochkin, *George*
Yurov, *George*
Yurshev, *George*
Yurtsev, *George*
Yurukhin, *George*
Yuryaev, *George*
Yuryatin, *George*
Yuryev, *George*
Yurygin, *George*
Yuryichev, *George*
Yuryshev, *George*
Yushachkov, *George*
Yushankin, *George*
Yushin, *George*
Yushkin, *George*
Yushkov, *George*
Yushmanov, *George*
Yust, *Just*
Yuste, *Just*
Yuster, *Just*
Yustman, *Just*
Yusupov, *Joseph*
Yve, *Ive*
Yvelin, *Ive*
Yven, *Ive*
Yvenec, *Ive*
Yves, *Ive*
Yvon, *Ive*
Yvonnet, *Ive*
Yvonou, *Ive*
Ywersen, *Ivor*

Z

Zaal, *Sale*
Zabala
Zaballa, *Zabala*
Zabatino, *Sabbato*
Zaborovsky, *Zaborowski*
Zaborowski
Zaborski, *Zaborowski*
Zábrana, *Zábranský*
Zábranský
Zac, *Satz*
Zaccaria, *Zachary*
Zaccarielli, *Zachary*
Zaccariello, *Zachary*
Zaccarini, *Zachary*
Zaccarino, *Zachary*
Zaccherini, *Zachary*
Zaccheroni, *Zachary*
Zacchetti, *Jack*
Zacchi, *Jack*
Zacchini, *Jack*
Zacchiroli, *Zachary*
Zacco, *Jack*
Zaccone, *Jack*
Zacconi, *Jack*
Žáček, *Zak*
Zach, *Zachary*
Zachara, *Zachary*
Zacharia, *Zachary*
Zachariades, *Zachary*
Zachariáš, *Zachary*
Zacharias, *Zachary*
Zachariash, *Zachary*
Zachariasz, *Zachary*
Zachariessen, *Zachary*
Zacharin, *Zachary*
Zachariou, *Zachary*
Zacharis, *Zachary*
Zacharish, *Zachary*
Zacharovitch, *Zachary*

Zacharovits, *Zachary*
Zacharovitz, *Zachary*
Zacharowicz, *Zachary*
Zacharowitz, *Zachary*
Zacharski, *Zachary*
Zachary
Zachelli, *Jack*
Zacher, *Zachary*
Zacherl, *Zachary*
Zachert, *Zachary*
Zachetti, *Jack*
Zachreis, *Zachary*
Zachries, *Zachary*
Zachris, *Zachary*
Zachrisson, *Zachary*
Zackrisson, *Zachary*
Zadek, *Zadik*
Zadelaar, *Sadler*
Zadickoviz, *Zadik*
Zadik
Zadiki, *Zadik*
Zadikoff, *Zadik*
Zadikov, *Zadik*
Zadok, *Tsadok*
Zaffren, *Safran*
Zafra
Zafren, *Safran*
Zaghetti, *Deakin*
Zaghetto, *Deakin*
Zaghi, *Deakin*
Zaghini, *Deakin*
Zaghino, *Deakin*
Zago, *Deakin*
Zagone, *Jack*
Zagorac, *Zagórski*
Zagórny, *Zagórski*
Zagórowski, *Zagórski*
Zagórski
Zagorsky, *Zagórski*
Zagotti, *Deakin*
Zagotto, *Deakin*
Zagursky, *Zagórski*
Zahareanu, *Zachary*
Zaharia, *Zachary*
Zaharianu, *Zachary*
Zaharovich, *Zachary*
Zahn
Zähnle, *Zahn*
Záhoř, *Gregory*
Záhora, *Zagórski*
Záhorský, *Zagórski*
Zahrádka, *Zahradník*
Zahradníček, *Zahradník*
Zahradník
Zähringen
Zaicik, *Zaitsev*
Zaidman, *Seide*
Zaif, *Soper*
Zaifman, *Soper*
Zaiss, *Zeiss*
Zaissle, *Zeiss*
Zaitsev
Zaitsov, *Zaitsev*
Zaitz, *Zaitsev*
Zaitzov, *Zaitsev*
Zaizov, *Zaitsev*
Zając, *Zaitsev*
Zajac, *Zaitsev*
Zajacek, *Zaitsev*
Zajączek, *Zaitsev*
Zajączkowski, *Zaitsev*
Zajczyk, *Zaitsev*
Zajdel, *Siegel*
Zajdensznir, *Seide*
Zajdenvorm, *Seide*
Zajdler, *Seide*
Zajec, *Zaitsev*
Zajecek, *Zaitsev*
Zajf, *Soper*
Zajfert, *Siegfried*
Zajíc, *Zaitsev*
Zajíček, *Zaitsev*
Žák, *Żak*
Żak
Zakariás, *Zachary*
Zakhariev, *Zachary*
Zakharov, *Zachary*
Zakharyev, *Zachary*
Zakharyin, *Zachary*
Zakheim, *Sack*
Zakheym, *Sack*
Żakiewicz, *Żak*
Zákostelecký, *Kościelski*
Zákostelecký
Žákovec, *Zak*
Žákovský, *Zak*
Żakowski, *Żak*
Zakrisson, *Zachary*
Zakrzeski, *Zakrzewski*
Zakrzewski
Zaks, *Sachs*
Zalasa, *Zaleski*
Zalasik, *Zaleski*
Zalaznik, *Zaliznyak*
Zalc, *Salt*
Zalcberg, *Salt*
Zalcman, *Salt*
Zalcstein, *Salt*
Zalcwasser, *Salt*
Załęcki
Załęski, *Załęcki*
Zaleski
Záleský, *Zaleski*
Zalesky, *Zaleski*
Zalewski
Zalewsky, *Zalewski*
Zaliznyak
Zalman, *Salmon*
Zalmanoff, *Salmon*
Zalmanov, *Salmon*
Zalmanovich, *Salmon*
Zalmanovici, *Salmon*
Zalmanovics, *Salmon*
Zalmanovicz, *Salmon*
Zalmanovitch, *Salmon*
Zalmanovitz, *Salmon*
Zalmanowitz, *Salmon*
Zalmanson, *Salmon*
Zalmen, *Salmon*
Zalmenov, *Salmon*
Zalmenovitz, *Salmon*
Zalmon, *Salmon*
Zalmonovich, *Salmon*
Zals, *Salt*
Zalsberg, *Salt*
Zalsman, *Salt*
Zaltberg, *Salt*
Zaltz, *Salt*
Zaltzberg, *Salt*
Zaltzman, *Salt*
Zalz, *Salt*
Zalzman, *Salt*
Zámečník
Zámek, *Zámečník*
Zammit
Zamora
Zamorano, *Zamora*
Zanardi, *John*
Zanassi, *John*
Zand, *Sand*
Zandberg, *Sand*
Zandsztajn, *Sand*
Zandt, *Zahn*
Zanelli, *John*
Zanetello, *John*
Zanetti, *John*
Zanettini, *John*
Zanetto, *John*
Zänger, *Zenger*
Zanger, *Sanger, Zenger*
Zangerl, *Zenger*
Zängerle, *Zenger*
Zangers, *Sanger*
Zangvil, *Zangwill*
Zangwill
Zani, *John*
Zanicchi, *John*
Zanichelli, *John*
Zaninelli, *John*
Zanini, *John*
Zaniolo, *John*
Zanitti, *John*
Zannelli, *John*
Zannetti, *John*
Zanni, *John*
Zannichelli, *John*
Zannini, *John*
Zannoli, *John*
Zannolli, *John*
Zannoni, *John*
Zannotti, *John*
Zanobbi, *Zinovyev*
Zanobelli, *Zinovyev*
Zanobetti, *Zinovyev*
Zanobi, *Zinovyev*
Zanoletti, *John*
Zanoli, *John*
Zanolini, *John*
Zanolli, *John*
Zanoni, *John*
Zanotelli, *John*
Zanotti, *John*
Zanucioli, *John*
Zanussi, *John*
Zanutti, *John*
Zanutto, *John*
Zapater, *Savatier*
Zapatero, *Savatier*
Zappa
Zapparoli, *Zappa*
Zappelli, *Zappa*
Zappellini, *Zappa*
Zappetta, *Zappa*
Zappetti, *Zappa*
Zappettini, *Zappa*
Zappi, *Zappa*
Zappini, *Zappa*
Zappino, *Zappa*
Zappoli, *Zappa*
Zappulli, *Zappa*
Zapulla, *Zappa*
Zaragoza
Zárate
Zaręba, *Zaremba*
Zarębski, *Zaremba*
Zarecki, *Zarzecki*
Zarecky, *Zarzecki*
Zaremba
Zarembski, *Zaremba*
Zaretski, *Zarzecki*
Zaretzki, *Zarzecki*
Zarezki, *Zarzecki*
Zarfati, *Sarfatti*
Zarfatti, *Sarfatti*
Zarfaty, *Sarfatti*
Zarges, *Nazaire*
Zarncke, *Chernyakov*
Zarnke, *Chernyakov*
Zarraga
Záruba, *Zaremba*
Zarza
Zarzecki
Zarzycki, *Zarzecki*
Zasada
Zasadziński, *Zasada*
Zatelman, *Sadler*
Zatorski
Zatorsky, *Zatorski*
Zatz, *Satz*
Zäuner, *Zauner*
Zauner
Závada, *Zawadzki*
Zavadil, *Zawadzki*
Zavadzki, *Zawadzki*
Zavateri, *Savatier*
Zavatieri, *Savatier*
Zavattari, *Savatier*
Zavattaro, *Savatier*
Zavattiero, *Savatier*
Zavatzky, *Zawadzki*
Zavěta, *Zavetaev*
Zavetaev
Zavitteri, *Savatier*
Zawacki, *Zawadzki*
Zawada, *Zawadzki*
Zawader, *Zawadzki*
Zawadowski, *Zawadzki*
Zawadski, *Zawadzki*
Zawadzki
Zawierucha
Zawiślak
Zayas
Zazo
Zdan, *Zdeněk*
Zdanowicz, *Zdeněk*
Zdanowski, *Zdeněk*
Zděnek, *Zdeněk*
Zdeněk
Zděnovec, *Zdeněk*
Zdrojewski
Zduńczyk, *Zduniak*
Zdunek, *Zduniak*
Zduniak
Zdunkiewicz, *Zduniak*
Zeal, *Seal*
Zeale, *Seal*
Zealey, *Sealey*
Zealley, *Sealey*
Żebrak, *Żebrowski*
Żebrowski
Zec, *Zaitsev*
Zecchetti, *Francis*
Zecchi, *Francis*
Zecchin, *Francis*
Zecchini, *Francis*
Zečević, *Zaitsev*
Zechel, *Zachary*
Zecherle, *Zachary*
Zechinelli, *Francis*
Zeder, *Ceder*
Zederbaum, *Ceder*
Zedníček, *Zedník*
Zedník
Zeeck, *Siegel*
Zeeman, *See*
Zeggiato, *Lilly*

Zola
Zolese, *Zola*
Zolesi, *Zola*
Zoli, *Zola*
Zolini, *Francis*
Zolla, *Zola*
Zöller, *Toller*
Zoller, *Toller*
Zolli, *Zola*
Zollman, *Toller*
Zollmann, *Toller*
Zöllner, *Toller*
Zollner, *Toller*
Zolman, *Toller*
Zolotar, *Zolotaryov*
Zolotaref, *Zolotaryov*
Zolotarenko, *Zolotaryov*
Zolotariov, *Zolotaryov*
Zolotaryonok, *Zolotaryov*
Zolotaryov
Zoloter, *Zolotaryov*
Zoltán, *Sowden*
Zomer, *Summer*
Zomerman, *Summer*
Zommer, *Summer*
Zonari, *January*
Zondag, *Sonntag*
Zondagh, *Sonntag*
Zonenschein, *Sonnenschein*
Zonenshein, *Sonnenschein*
Zonenshine, *Sonnenschein*
Zopetti, *Zoppo*
Zoppetto, *Zoppo*
Zoppi, *Zoppo*
Zoppini, *Zoppo*
Zoppino, *Zoppo*
Zoppo
Zordan, *Jordan*
Zoref
Zoreff, *Zoref*
Zorn
Zörnchen, *Zorn*
Zorndt, *Zorn*
Zörneke, *Chernyakov*
Zörnle, *Zorn*
Zorrilla
Zorzenoni, *George*
Zorzet, *George*
Zorzetti, *George*
Zorzi, *George*
Zorzin, *George*
Zorzini, *George*
Zorzoni, *George*
Zorzutti, *George*
Zotti, *Francis*
Zottoli, *Francis*
Zoubek, *Zubakov*
Zouch, *Such*
Zoyer, *Sauer*
Zschäpe, *Stephen*
Zschepang, *Stephen*
Zsigmond, *Siegmund*
Zuan, *John*
Zuanazzi, *John*
Zuanelli, *John*
Zuann, *John*
Zuazo
Zub, *Zubakov*
Zubakov
Zuban, *Zubakov*
Zubarev, *Zubakov*
Zubashkevich, *Zubakov*
Zubavin, *Zubakov*
Zubek, *Zubakov*
Zubiaur
Zubin, *Zubakov*
Zubkin, *Zubakov*
Zubko, *Zubakov*
Zucaro, *Zuccheri*
Zucca, *Zucchi*
Zuccarelli, *Zuccheri*
Zuccarello, *Zuccheri*
Zuccari, *Zuccheri*
Zuccarini, *Zuccheri*
Zuccarino, *Zuccheri*
Zuccaro, *Zuccheri*
Zucchelli, *Zucchi*
Zucchello, *Zucchi*
Zuccheri
Zuccherini, *Zuccheri*
Zuccherino, *Zuccheri*
Zucchetta, *Zucchi*
Zucchetti, *Zucchi*
Zucchetto, *Zucchi*
Zucchi
Zucchini, *Zucchi*
Zucchino, *Zucchi*
Zucco, *Zucchi*
Zuccoli, *Zucchi*
Zuccolini, *Zucchi*
Zuccolo, *Zucchi*
Zucconi, *Zucchi*
Zuccotti, *Zucchi*
Zuccotto, *Zucchi*
Zucker
Zuckerbaum, *Zucker*
Zuckerberg, *Zucker*
Zuckerberger, *Zucker*
Zuckerblum, *Zucker*
Zuckerbrot, *Zucker*
Zuckerkandel, *Zucker*
Zuckerman, *Zucker*
Zuckermann, *Zucker*
Zuckerstein, *Zucker*
Zudkevitz, *Tsadok*
Zuenelli, *John*
Zuian, *Julian*
Zuiani, *Julian*
Żuidema, *South*
Żuk, *Zhukov*
Zuker, *Zucker*
Zukerberg, *Zucker*
Zukerfein, *Zucker*
Zukerkandel, *Zucker*
Zukerman, *Zucker*
Zukernik, *Zucker*
Zukerovitz, *Zucker*
Zukerwasser, *Zucker*
Żukierman, *Zucker*
Żukowski, *Zhukov*
Zuli, *Júlio*
Zulian, *Julian*
Zuliano, *Julian*
Zulin, *Júlio*
Zulueta
Zumbichl, *Bühler*
Zumbrink, *Brink*
Zumbühl, *Bühler*
Zumbusch, *Bush*
Zumdieck, *Ditch*
Zumer, *Summer*
Zumhoff, *Hofer*
Zumkleg, *Clay*
Zumloh, *Loo*
Zummer, *Summer*
Zumsteeg, *Steiger*
Zumtobel, *Tobel*
Zumwinkel, *Winckel*
Zündel, *Zunder*
Zundel, *Zunder*
Zunder
Zündler, *Zunder*
Zundler, *Zunder*
Zunser, *Zunz*
Zuntz, *Zunz*
Zunz
Żuraw
Żurawski, *Żuraw*
Zürcklert, *Zirkler*
Zurdo
Zurita
Zurkaulen, *Kuhl*
Zurmühlen, *Mill*
Zurnedden, *Nieder*
Zurwesten, *West*
Zuscovitch, *Zisin*
Zuserblum, *Sweet*
Zusman, *Sweet*
Zusmanovics, *Sweet*
Zusmanovitch, *Sweet*
Zusmanovitz, *Sweet*
Zusmans, *Sweet*
Zusskind, *Süsskind*
Zussman, *Sweet*
Zutler, *Sadler*
Zvezdochyotov
Zwaan, *Swan*
Zwart, *Schwarz*
Zwartjes, *Schwarz*
Zwarts, *Schwarz*
Zweig, *Twigg*
Zweigel, *Twigg*
Zweigenbaum, *Twigg*
Zweigenberg, *Twigg*
Zweigenhaft, *Twigg*
Zweighaft, *Twigg*
Zweigl, *Twigg*
Zweigle, *Twigg*
Zwibel, *Zwiebel*
Zwiebel
Zwiebelmann, *Zwiebel*
Zwiebler, *Zwiebel*
Zwiefel, *Zwiebel*
Zwiefler, *Zwiebel*
Zwierzchowski
Zwierzyński
Zwilling
Zwillinger, *Zwilling*
Zwingli, *Zwilling*
Zwoliński, *Zwolski*
Zwolski
Zyablikov
Zych, *Siegmund*
Zychoń, *Siegmund*
Zychowicz, *Siegmund*
Zychowski, *Siegmund*
Żydak, *Zhidovinov*
Zydowicz, *Zhidovinov*
Zygmański, *Siegmund*
Zygmuńczyk, *Siegmund*
Zygmunt, *Siegmund*
Zygmuntowicz, *Siegmund*
Zýka, *Siegmund*
Zykán, *Siegmund*
Zylber, *Silver*
Zylberbaum, *Silver*
Zylberberg, *Silver*
Zylberdik, *Silver*
Zylberfarb, *Silver*
Zylbering, *Silver*
Zylberman, *Silver*
Zylberspic, *Silver*
Zylberstein, *Silver*
Zylberstrom, *Silver*
Zylbersztajn, *Silver*
Zylbersztein, *Silver*
Zylbersztejn, *Silver*
Zylman, *Zyl, van*
Zylstra, *Zyl, van*
Zyl, van
Zymbalist, *Zimbalist*
Zymbalista, *Zimbalist*
Zyprecht, *Siebert*
Zyskin, *Zisin*
Zyskind, *Süsskind*